T4-APU-644

University Casebook Series

April, 1977

ACCOUNTING AND THE LAW, Third Edition (1964), with Problem Pamphlet

The late James L. Dohr, Director, Institute of Accounting, Columbia University.
Ellis L. Phillips, Jr., Professor of Law, Columbia University.
George C. Thompson, Professor, Columbia University Graduate School of Business, and
William C. Warren, Professor of Law, Columbia University.

ACCOUNTING, MATERIALS ON, (1959), with 1968 Supplement

Robert Amory, Jr., Esq.,
W. Covington Hardee, Esq., Third Edition by
David R. Herwitz, Professor of Law, Harvard University, and
Donald T. Trautman, Professor of Law, Harvard University.

ADMINISTRATIVE LAW, Sixth Edition (1974), with 1974 Problems Supplement

Walter Gellhorn, University Professor, Columbia University, and
Clark Byse, Professor of Law, Harvard University.

ADMIRALTY (1969) with 1972 Supplement

Jo Desha Lucas, Professor of Law, University of Chicago.

ADVOCACY, INTRODUCTION TO, Second Edition (1976) with 1970 Supplementary Cases Pamphlet

Board of Student Advisers, Harvard Law School.

AGENCY–ASSOCIATIONS–EMPLOYMENT–PARTNERSHIPS, Second Edition (1977)

Reprinted from Conard, Knauss & Siegel's Enterprise Organization

AGENCY, see also Enterprise Organization

ANTITRUST AND REGULATORY ALTERNATIVES (1977)

Louis B. Schwartz, Professor of Law, University of Pennsylvania.
John J. Flynn, Professor of Law, University of Utah.

ANTITRUST SUPPLEMENT—SELECTED STATUTES AND RELATED MATERIALS (1977)

John J. Flynn, Professor of Law, University of Utah.

ARBITRATION (1968)

The late Shelden D. Elliott, Professor of Law, New York University.

BANKRUPTCY ACT (Annotated) 1967 Edition

The late James Angell MacLachlan, Professor of Law Emeritus, Harvard University.

BIOGRAPHY OF A LEGAL DISPUTE, THE: An Introduction to American Civil Procedure (1968)

Marc A. Franklin, Professor of Law, Stanford University.

BUSINESS ORGANIZATION, see also Enterprise Organization

BUSINESS PLANNING (1966) with 1977 Problem Supplement
David R. Herwitz, Professor of Law, Harvard University.

BUSINESS TORTS (1972)
Milton Handler, Professor of Law Emeritus, Columbia University.

CIVIL PROCEDURE, see Procedure

COMMERCIAL AND CONSUMER TRANSACTIONS (1972) with 1973 Supplement
William E. Hogan, Professor of Law, Cornell University.
William D. Warren, Dean of the School of Law, University of California, Los Angeles.

COMMERCIAL AND INVESTMENT PAPER, Third Edition (1964) with Statutory Materials
Roscoe T. Steffen, Professor of Law, University of California, Hastings College of the Law.

COMMERCIAL LAW, CASES & MATERIALS ON, Third Edition (1976)
E. Allan Farnsworth, Professor of Law, Columbia University.
John Honnold, Professor of Law, University of Pennsylvania.

COMMERCIAL PAPER, Second Edition (1976)
E. Allan Farnsworth, Professor of Law, Columbia University.

COMMERCIAL PAPER AND BANK DEPOSITS AND COLLECTIONS (1967) with Statutory Supplement
William D. Hawkland, Professor of Law, University of Illinois.

COMMERCIAL TRANSACTIONS—Text, Cases and Problems, Fourth Edition (1968)
Robert Braucher, Professor of Law, Harvard University, and
The late Arthur E. Sutherland, Jr., Professor of Law, Harvard University.

COMPARATIVE LAW, Third Edition (1970)
Rudolf B. Schlesinger, Professor of Law, Hastings College of the Law.

COMPETITIVE PROCESS, LEGAL REGULATION OF THE (1972) with Statutory Supplement and 1975 Supplement
Edmund W. Kitch, Professor of Law, University of Chicago.
Harvey S. Perlman, Professor of Law, University of Nebraska.

CONFLICT OF LAWS, Sixth Edition (1971), with 1975 Supplement
Willis L. M. Reese, Professor of Law, Columbia University, and
Maurice Rosenberg, Professor of Law, Columbia University.

CONSTITUTIONAL LAW, Fifth Edition (1977), with 1977 Supplement
Edward L. Barrett, Jr., Professor of Law, University of California, Davis.

CONSTITUTIONAL LAW, Ninth Edition (1975), with 1977 Supplement
Gerald Gunther, Professor of Law, Stanford University.

CONSTITUTIONAL LAW, INDIVIDUAL RIGHTS IN, Second Edition (1976), with 1977 Supplement
Gerald Gunther, Professor of Law, Stanford University.

CONTRACT LAW AND ITS APPLICATION, Second Edition (1977)
Addison Mueller, Professor of Law Emeritus, University of California, Los Angeles.
Arthur I. Rosett, Professor of Law, University of California, Los Angeles.

CONTRACT LAW, STUDIES IN, Second Edition (1977)
Edward J. Murphy, Professor of Law, University of Notre Dame.
Richard E. Speidel, Professor of Law, University of Virginia.

CONTRACTS, Third Edition (1977)
John P. Dawson, Professor of Law Emeritus, Harvard University, and
William Burnett Harvey, Professor of Law and Political Science, Boston University.

CONTRACTS, Second Edition (1972) with Statutory Supplement
E. Allan Farnsworth, Professor of Law, Columbia University.
William F. Young, Jr., Professor of Law, Columbia University.
Harry W. Jones, Professor of Law, Columbia University.

CONTRACTS (1971) with Statutory and Administrative Law Supplement
Ian R. Macneil, Professor of Law, Cornell University.

COPYRIGHT, Unfair Competition, and Other Topics Bearing on the Protection of Literary, Musical, and Artistic Works, Second Edition (1974)
Benjamin Kaplan, Professor of Law Emeritus, Harvard University, and
Ralph S. Brown, Jr., Professor of Law, Yale University.

CORPORATE FINANCE (1972), with 1975 New Developments Supplement
Victor Brudney, Professor of Law, Harvard University.
Marvin A. Chirelstein, Professor of Law, Yale University.

CORPORATE READJUSTMENTS AND REORGANIZATIONS (1976)
Walter J. Blum, Professor of Law, University of Chicago.
Stanley A. Kaplan, Professor of Law, University of Chicago.

CORPORATION LAW, with Statutory Supplement (1973)
Detlev F. Vagts, Professor of Law, Harvard University.

CORPORATIONS, Fourth Edition—Unabridged (1969) with 1977 Supplement and 1976 Special Supplement
William L. Cary, Professor of Law, Columbia University.

CORPORATIONS, Fourth Edition—Abridged (1970) with 1977 Supplement and 1976 Special Supplement
William L. Cary, Professor of Law, Columbia University.

CORPORATIONS, THE LAW OF: WHAT CORPORATE LAWYERS DO (1976)
Jan G. Deutsch, Professor of Law, Yale University.
Joseph J. Bianco.

CORPORATIONS COURSE GAME PLAN (1975)
David R. Herwitz, Professor of Law, Harvard University.

CORPORATIONS, see also Enterprise Organization

CREDIT TRANSACTIONS AND CONSUMER PROTECTION (1976)
John Honnold, Professor of Law, University of Pennsylvania.

CREDITORS' RIGHTS, Fifth Edition (1957)
The late John Hanna, Professor of Law Emeritus, Columbia University, and
The late James Angell MacLachlan, Professor of Law Emeritus, Harvard University.

CREDITORS' RIGHTS AND CORPORATE REORGANIZATION, Fifth Edition (1957)
The late John Hanna, Professor of Law Emeritus, Columbia University, and
The late James Angell MacLachlan, Professor of Law Emeritus, Harvard University.

CREDITORS' RIGHTS, see also Debtor-Creditor Law

CRIMINAL LAW (1973)

Fred E. Inbau, Professor of Law, Northwestern University.
James R. Thompson, U. S. Attorney for the Northern District of Illinois.
Andre A. Moenssens, Professor of Law, University of Richmond.

CONSTITUTIONAL CRIMINAL PROCEDURE (1977)

James E. Scarboro, Professor of Law, University of Colorado.
James B. White, Professor of Law, University of Chicago.

CRIMINAL PROCEDURE (1974) with 1976 Supplement

Fred E. Inbau, Professor of Law, Northwestern University.
James R. Thompson, U. S. Attorney for the Northern District of Illinois.
James B. Haddad, First Assistant State's Attorney, Cook County, Illinois.
James B. Zagel, Chief, Criminal Justice Division, Office of Attorney General of Illinois.
Gary L. Starkman, Assistant U. S. Attorney, Northern District of Illinois.

CRIMINAL JUSTICE, THE ADMINISTRATION OF, CASES AND MATERIALS ON, Second Edition (1969)

Francis C. Sullivan, Professor of Law, Louisiana State University.
Paul Hardin III, Professor of Law, Duke University.
John Huston, Professor of Law, University of Washington.
Frank R. Lacy, Professor of Law, University of Oregon.
Daniel E. Murray, Professor of Law, University of Miami.
George W. Pugh, Professor of Law, Louisiana State University.

CRIMINAL JUSTICE ADMINISTRATION AND RELATED PROCESSES, Successor Edition (1976)

Frank W. Miller, Professor of Law, Washington University.
Robert O. Dawson, Professor of Law, University of Texas.
George E. Dix, Professor of Law, University of Texas.
Raymond I. Parnas, Professor of Law, University of California, Davis.

CRIMINAL LAW, Second Edition (1975)

Lloyd L. Weinreb, Professor of Law, Harvard University.

CRIMINAL LAW AND ITS ADMINISTRATION (1940), with 1956 Supplement

The late Jerome Michael, Professor of Law, Columbia University, and
Herbert Wechsler, Professor of Law, Columbia University.

CRIMINAL LAW AND PROCEDURE, Fifth Edition (1977)

Rollin M. Perkins, Professor of Law, University of California, Hastings College of the Law.
Ronald N. Boyce, Professor of Law, University of Utah.

CRIMINAL PROCESS, Second Edition (1974), with 1977 Supplement

Lloyd L. Weinreb, Professor of Law, Harvard University.

DAMAGES, Second Edition (1952)

The late Charles T. McCormick, Professor of Law, University of Texas, and
The late William F. Fritz, Professor of Law, University of Texas.

DEBTOR-CREDITOR LAW (1974) with 1975 Case-Statutory Supplement

William D. Warren, Dean of the School of Law, University of California, Los Angeles.
William E. Hogan, Professor of Law, Cornell University.

DECEDENTS' ESTATES (1971)

Max Rheinstein, Professor of Law Emeritus, University of Chicago.
Mary Ann Glendon, Professor of Law, Boston College Law School.

DECEDENTS' ESTATES AND TRUSTS, Fifth Edition (1977)

John Ritchie III, Professor of Law, University of Virginia,
Neill H. Alford, Jr., Professor of Law, University of Virginia.
Richard W. Effland, Professor of Law, Arizona State University.

DECEDENTS' ESTATES AND TRUSTS (1968)

Howard R. Williams, Professor of Law, Stanford University.

DOMESTIC RELATIONS, Second Edition (1974)

Monrad G. Paulsen, Dean of the Law School, Yeshiva University.
Walter Wadlington, Professor of Law, University of Virginia.
Julius Goebel, Jr., Professor of Law Emeritus, Columbia University.

DOMESTIC RELATIONS—Civil and Canon Law (1963)

Philip A. Ryan, Professor of Law, Georgetown University, and
Dom David Granfield, Associate Professor, Catholic University of America.

DYNAMICS OF AMERICAN LAW, THE: Courts, the Legal Process and Freedom of Expression (1968)

Marc A. Franklin, Professor of Law, Stanford University.

ELECTRONIC MASS MEDIA (1976) (paper back)

William K. Jones, Professor of Law, Columbia University.

ENTERPRISE ORGANIZATION, Second Edition (1977)

Alfred F. Conard, Professor of Law, University of Michigan.
Robert L. Knauss, Dean of the School of Law, Vanderbilt University.
Stanley Siegel, Professor of Law, University of California, Los Angeles.

ENVIRONMENTAL PROTECTION, SELECTED LEGAL AND ECONOMIC ASPECTS OF (1971)

Charles J. Meyers, Professor of Law, Stanford University.
A. Dan Tarlock, Professor of Law, Indiana University.

EQUITY AND EQUITABLE REMEDIES (1975)

Edward D. Re, Adjunct Professor of Law, St. John's University.

EQUITY, RESTITUTION AND DAMAGES, Second Edition (1974)

Robert Childres, Professor of Law, Northwestern University.
William F. Johnson, Jr., Adjunct Professor of Law, New York University.

ESTATE PLANNING PROBLEMS (1973) with 1977 Supplement

David Westfall, Professor of Law, Harvard University.

ETHICS, see Legal Profession

EVIDENCE, Third Edition (1976)

David W. Louisell, Professor of Law, University of California, Berkeley.
John Kaplan, Professor of Law, Stanford University.
Jon R. Waltz, Professor of Law, Northwestern University.

EVIDENCE, Sixth Edition (1973) with 1976 Supplement

John M. Maguire, Professor of Law Emeritus, Harvard University.
Jack B. Weinstein, Professor of Law, Columbia University.
James H. Chadbourn, Professor of Law, Harvard University.
John H. Mansfield, Professor of Law, Harvard University.

EVIDENCE (1968)

Francis C. Sullivan, Professor of Law, Louisiana State University.
Paul Hardin, III, Professor of Law, Duke University.

FAMILY LAW: STATUTORY MATERIALS, Second Edition

Monrad G. Paulsen, Dean of the Law School, Yeshiva University.
Walter Wadlington, Professor of Law, University of Virginia.

FEDERAL COURTS, Sixth Edition (1976)

The late Charles T. McCormick, Professor of Law, University of Texas.
James H. Chadbourn, Professor of Law, Harvard University, and
Charles Alan Wright, Professor of Law, University of Texas.

FEDERAL COURTS AND THE FEDERAL SYSTEM, Second Edition (1973) with 1977 Supplement

The late Henry M. Hart, Jr., Professor of Law, Harvard University.
Herbert Wechsler, Professor of Law, Columbia University.
Paul M. Bator, Professor of Law, Harvard University.
Paul J. Mishkin, Professor of Law, University of California, Berkeley.
David L. Shapiro, Professor of Law, Harvard University.

FEDERAL RULES OF CIVIL PROCEDURE, 1975 Edition

FEDERAL TAXATION, see Taxation

FREE ENTERPRISE AND ECONOMIC ORGANIZATION, Fourth Edition (1972)

Louis B. Schwartz, Professor of Law, University of Pennsylvania.

FUTURE INTERESTS AND ESTATE PLANNING (1961) with 1962 Supplement

The late W. Barton Leach, Professor of Law, Harvard University, and
James K. Logan, Dean of the Law School, University of Kansas.

FUTURE INTERESTS (1958)

The late Philip Mechem, Professor of Law Emeritus, University of Pennsylvania.

FUTURE INTERESTS (1970)

Howard R. Williams, Professor of Law, Stanford University.

GOVERNMENT CONTRACTS, FEDERAL (1975)

John W. Whelan, Professor of Law, Hastings College of the Law.
Robert S. Pasley, Professor of Law, Cornell University.

HOUSING (THE ILL-HOUSED) (1971)

Peter W. Martin, Professor of Law, Cornell University.

INJUNCTIONS (1972)

Owen M. Fiss, Professor of Law, Yale University.

INSURANCE (1971)

William F. Young, Professor of Law, Columbia University.

INTERNATIONAL LAW, See also Transnational Legal Problems and United Nations Law

INTERNATIONAL LEGAL SYSTEM (1973) with Documentary Supplement

Noyes E. Leech, Professor of Law, University of Pennsylvania.
Covey T. Oliver, Professor of Law, University of Pennsylvania.
Joseph Modeste Sweeney, Dean of the School of Law, Tulane University.

INTERNATIONAL TRADE AND INVESTMENT, REGULATION OF (1970)

Carl H. Fulda, Professor of Law, University of Texas.
Warren F. Schwartz, Professor of Law, University of Virginia.

INTERNATIONAL TRANSACTIONS AND RELATIONS (1960)

Milton Katz, Professor of Law, Harvard University, and
Kingman Brewster, Jr., President, Yale University.

INTRODUCTION TO THE STUDY OF LAW (1970)
E. Wayne Thode, Professor of Law, University of Utah.
J. Leon Lebowitz, Professor of Law, University of Texas.
Lester J. Mazor, Professor of Law, University of Utah.

INTRODUCTION TO LAW, see also Legal Method, also On Law in Courts, also Dynamics of American Law

JUDICIAL CODE: Rules of Procedure in the Federal Courts with Excerpts from the Criminal Code, 1976 Edition
The late Henry M. Hart, Jr., Professor of Law, Harvard University, and Herbert Wechsler, Professor of Law, Columbia University.

JURISPRUDENCE (Temporary Edition Hard Bound) (1949)
Lon L. Fuller, Professor of Law, Harvard University.

JUVENILE COURTS (1967)
Hon. Orman W. Ketcham, Juvenile Court of the District of Columbia.
Monrad G. Paulsen, Dean of the Law School, Yeshiva University.

JUVENILE JUSTICE PROCESS, Second Edition (1976)
Frank W. Miller, Professor of Law, Washington University.
Robert O. Dawson, Professor of Law, University of Texas.
George E. Dix, Professor of Law, University of Texas.
Raymond I. Parnas, Professor of Law, University of California, Davis.

LABOR LAW, Eighth Edition (1977) with Statutory Supplement
Archibald Cox, Professor of Law, Harvard University, and
Derek C. Bok, President, Harvard University.
Robert A. Gorman, Professor of Law, University of Pennsylvania.

LABOR LAW (1968) with Statutory Supplement
Clyde W. Summers, Professor of Law, University of Pennsylvania.
Harry H. Wellington, Dean of the Law School, Yale University.

LAND FINANCING, Second Edition (1977)
Norman Penney, Professor of Law, Cornell University.
Richard F. Broude, of the California Bar.

LAW, LANGUAGE AND ETHICS (1972)
William R. Bishin, Professor of Law, University of Southern California.
Christopher D. Stone, Professor of Law, University of Southern California.

LEGAL METHOD, Second Edition (1952)
Noel T. Dowling, late Professor of Law, Columbia University,
The late Edwin W. Patterson, Professor of Law, Columbia University, and
Richard R. B. Powell, Professor of Law, University of California, Hastings College of the Law.
Second Edition by Harry W. Jones, Professor of Law, Columbia University.

LEGAL METHODS (1969)
Robert N. Covington, Professor of Law, Vanderbilt University.
E. Blythe Stason, Professor of Law, Vanderbilt University.
John W. Wade, Professor of Law, Vanderbilt University.
The late Elliott E. Cheatham, Professor of Law, Vanderbilt University.
Theodore A. Smedley, Professor of Law, Vanderbilt University.

LEGAL PROFESSION (1970)
Samuel D. Thurman, Dean of the College of Law, University of Utah.
Ellis L. Phillips, Jr., Professor of Law, Columbia University.
The late Elliott E. Cheatham, Professor of Law, Vanderbilt University.

LEGISLATIVE AND ADMINISTRATIVE PROCESSES (1976)

Hans A. Linde, Professor of Law, University of Oregon.
George Bunn, Professor of Law, University of Wisconsin.

LEGISLATION, Third Edition (1973)

Horace E. Read, Vice President, Dalhousie University.
John W. MacDonald, Professor of Law, Cornell Law School.
Jefferson B. Fordham, Professor of Law, University of Utah, and
William J. Pierce, Professor of Law, University of Michigan.

LOCAL GOVERNMENT LAW, Revised Edition (1975)

Jefferson B. Fordham, Professor of Law, University of Utah.

MASS MEDIA LAW (1976)

Marc A. Franklin, Professor of Law, Stanford University.

MENTAL HEALTH PROCESS, Second Edition (1976)

Frank W. Miller, Professor of Law, Washington University.
Robert O. Dawson, Professor of Law, University of Texas.
George E. Dix, Professor of Law, University of Texas.
Raymond I. Parnas, Professor of Law, University of California, Davis.

MODERN REAL ESTATE TRANSACTIONS, Second Edition (1958)

Allison Dunham, Professor of Law, University of Chicago.

MUNICIPAL CORPORATIONS, see Local Government Law

NEGOTIABLE INSTRUMENTS, see Commercial Paper

NEW YORK PRACTICE, Third Edition (1973)

Herbert Peterfreund, Professor of Law, New York University.
Joseph M. McLaughlin, Dean of the Law School, Fordham University.

OIL AND GAS, Third Edition (1974)

Howard R. Williams, Professor of Law, Stanford University,
Richard C. Maxwell, Professor of Law, University of California, Los Angeles, and
Charles J. Meyers, Professor of Law, Stanford University.

ON LAW IN COURTS (1965)

Paul J. Mishkin, Professor of Law, University of California, Berkeley.
Clarence Morris, Professor of Law, University of Pennsylvania.

OWNERSHIP AND DEVELOPMENT OF LAND (1965)

Jan Krasnowiecki, Professor of Law, University of Pennsylvania.

PARTNERSHIP PLANNING (1970) (Pamphlet)

William L. Cary, Professor of Law, Columbia University.

PATENT, TRADEMARK AND COPYRIGHT LAW (1959)

E. Ernest Goldstein, Professor of Law, University of Texas.

PLEADING & PROCEDURE: STATE AND FEDERAL, Third Edition (1973)

David W. Louisell, Professor of Law, University of California, Berkeley, and
Geoffrey C. Hazard, Jr., Professor of Law, Yale University.

POLICE FUNCTION (1976) (Pamphlet)

Chapters 1–11 of Miller, Dawson, Dix & Parnas' Criminal Justice Administration, Second Edition.

PROCEDURE—Biography of a Legal Dispute (1968)

Marc A. Franklin, Professor of Law, Stanford University.

PROCEDURE—CIVIL PROCEDURE, Second Edition (1974)

James H. Chadbourn, Professor of Law, Harvard University, and
A. Leo Levin, Professor of Law, University of Pennsylvania.
Philip Shuchman, Professor of Law, University of Connecticut.

PROCEDURE—CIVIL PROCEDURE, Third Edition (1973)

Richard H. Field, Professor of Law, Harvard University, and
Benjamin Kaplan, Professor of Law, Harvard University.

PROCEDURE—CIVIL PROCEDURE, Third Edition (1976)

Maurice Rosenberg, Professor of Law, Columbia University.
Jack B. Weinstein, Professor, of Law, Columbia University.
Hans Smit, Professor of Law, Columbia University.
Harold L. Korn, Professor of Law, Columbia University.

PROCEDURE—FEDERAL RULES OF CIVIL PROCEDURE, 1975 Edition

PROCEDURE PORTFOLIO (1962)

James H. Chadbourn, Professor of Law, Harvard University, and
A. Leo Levin, Professor of Law, University of Pennsylvania.

PRODUCTS AND THE CONSUMER: DECEPTIVE PRACTICES (1972)

W. Page Keeton, Dean of the School of Law, University of Texas.
Marshall S. Shapo, Professor of Law, University of Virginia.

PRODUCTS AND THE CONSUMER: DEFECTIVE AND DANGEROUS PRODUCTS (1970)

W. Page Keeton, Dean of the School of Law, University of Texas.
Marshall S. Shapo, Professor of Law, University of Virginia.

PROFESSIONAL RESPONSIBILITY (1976) with Special California Supplement

Thomas D. Morgan, Professor of Law, University of Illinois.
Ronald D. Rotunda, Professor of Law, University of Illinois.

PROPERTY, Third Edition (1972)

John E. Cribbet, Dean of the Law School, University of Illinois,
The late William F. Fritz, Professor of Law, University of Texas, and
Corwin W. Johnson, Professor of Law, University of Texas.

PROPERTY—PERSONAL (1953)

The late S. Kenneth Skolfield, Professor of Law Emeritus, Boston University.

PROPERTY—PERSONAL, Third Edition (1954)

The late Everett Fraser, Dean of the Law School Emeritus, University of Minnesota—Third Edition by
Charles W. Taintor II, late Professor of Law, University of Pittsburgh.

PROPERTY—REAL—INTRODUCTION, Third Edition (1954)

The late Everett Fraser, Dean of the Law School Emeritus, University of Minnesota.

PROPERTY—REAL PROPERTY AND CONVEYANCING (1954)

Edward E. Bade, late Professor of Law, University of Minnesota.

PROPERTY, MODERN REAL, FUNDAMENTALS OF (1974)

Edward H. Rabin, Professor of Law, University of California, Davis.

PROPERTY, REAL, PROBLEMS IN (Pamphlet) (1969)

Edward H. Rabin, Professor of Law, University of California, Davis.

PROSECUTION AND ADJUDICATION (1976) (Pamphlet)

Chapters 12–16 of Miller, Dawson, Dix & Parnas' Criminal Justice Administration, Second Edition.

PUBLIC UTILITY LAW, see Free Enterprise, also Regulated Industries

REAL ESTATE PLANNING (1974) with 1976 Problems and Statutory Supplement

Norton L. Steuben, Professor of Law, University of Colorado.

RECEIVERSHIP AND CORPORATE REORGANIZATION, see Creditors' Rights

REGULATED INDUSTRIES, Second Edition, 1976

William K. Jones, Professor of Law, Columbia University.

RESTITUTION, Second Edition (1966)

John W. Wade, Professor of Law, Vanderbilt University.

SALES AND SECURITY, Fourth Edition (1962), with Statutory Supplement

George G. Bogert, James Parker Hall Professor of Law Emeritus, University of Chicago.
The late William E. Britton, Professor of Law, University of California, Hastings College of the Law, and
William D. Hawkland, Professor of Law, University of Illinois.

SALES AND SALES FINANCING, Fourth Edition (1976)

John Honnold, Professor of Law, University of Pennsylvania.

SECURITY, Third Edition (1959)

The late John Hanna, Professor of Law Emeritus, Columbia University.

SECURITIES REGULATION, Fourth Edition (1977) with Statutory Supplement

Richard W. Jennings, Professor of Law, University of California, Berkeley.
Harold Marsh, Jr., Professor of Law, University of California, Los Angeles.

SENTENCING AND THE CORRECTIONAL PROCESS, Second Edition (1976)

Frank W. Miller, Professor of Law, Washington University.
Robert O. Dawson, Professor of Law, University of Texas.
George E. Dix, Professor of Law, University of Texas.
Raymond I. Parnas, Professor of Law, University of California, Davis.

SOCIAL WELFARE AND THE INDIVIDUAL (1971)

Robert J. Levy, Professor of Law, University of Minnesota.
Thomas P. Lewis, Dean of the College of Law, University of Kentucky.
Peter W. Martin, Professor of Law, Cornell University.

TAX, POLICY ANALYSIS OF THE FEDERAL INCOME (1976)

William A. Klein, Professor of Law, University of California, Los Angeles.

TAXATION, FEDERAL INCOME (1976) with Supplement

Erwin N. Griswold, Dean Emeritus, Harvard Law School.
Michael J. Graetz, Professor of Law, University of Virginia.

TAXATION, FEDERAL INCOME, Second Edition (1977)

James J. Freeland, Professor of Law, University of Florida.
Stephen A. Lind, Professor of Law, University of Florida.
Richard B. Stephens, Professor of Law, University of Florida.

TAXATION, FEDERAL INCOME, Volume I, Personal Tax (1972) with 1977 Supplement; Volume II, Corporate and Partnership Taxation (1973)

Stanley S. Surrey, Professor of Law, Harvard University.
William C. Warren, Professor of Law, Columbia University.
Paul R. McDaniel, Professor of Law, Boston College Law School.
Hugh J. Ault, Professor of Law, Boston College Law School.

TAXATION, FEDERAL WEALTH TRANSFER (1977)

Stanley S. Surrey, Professor of Law, Harvard University.
William C. Warren, Professor of Law, Columbia University, and
Paul S. McDaniel, Professor of Law, Boston College Law School.
Harry L. Gutman, Instructor, Harvard Law School and Boston College Law School.

TAXES AND FINANCE—STATE AND LOCAL (1974)
Oliver Oldman, Professor of Law, Harvard University.
Ferdinand P. Schoettle, Professor of Law, University of Minnesota.

TORT LAW AND ALTERNATIVES: INJURIES AND REMEDIES (1971), with 1976 Supplement
Marc A. Franklin, Professor of Law, Stanford University.

TORTS, Third Edition (1976)
The late Harry Shulman, Dean of the Law School, Yale University.
Fleming James, Jr., Professor of Law Emeritus, Yale University.
Oscar S. Gray, Professor of Law, University of Maryland.

TORTS, Sixth Edition (1976)
The late William L. Prosser, Professor of Law, University of California, Hastings College of the Law.
John W. Wade, Professor of Law, Vanderbilt University.
Victor E. Schwartz, Professor of Law, University of Cincinnati.

TRADE REGULATION (1975) with 1977 Supplement
Milton Handler, Professor of Law Emeritus, Columbia University.
Harlan M. Blake, Professor of Law, Columbia University.
Robert Pitofsky, Professor of Law, Georgetown University.
Harvey J. Goldschmid, Professor of Law, Columbia University.

TRADE REGULATION, see Free Enterprise

TRANSNATIONAL LEGAL PROBLEMS, Second Edition (1976) with Documentary Supplement
Henry J. Steiner, Professor of Law, Harvard University.
Detlev F. Vagts, Professor of Law, Harvard University.

TRIAL ADVOCACY (1968)
A. Leo Levin, Professor of Law, University of Pennsylvania.
Harold Cramer, Esq., Member of the Philadelphia Bar, (Maurice Rosenberg, Professor of Law, Columbia University, as consultant).

TRUSTS, Fourth Edition (1967)
George G. Bogert, James Parker Hall Professor of Law Emeritus, University of Chicago.
Dallin H. Oaks, President, Brigham Young University.

TRUSTS AND SUCCESSION, Second Edition (1968)
George E. Palmer, Professor of Law, University of Michigan.

UNFAIR COMPETITION, see Competitive Process and Business Torts

UNITED NATIONS IN ACTION (1968)
Louis B. Sohn, Professor of Law, Harvard University.

UNITED NATIONS LAW, Second Edition (1967) with Documentary Supplement (1968)
Louis B. Sohn, Professor of Law, Harvard University.

WATER RESOURCE MANAGEMENT (1971) with 1973 Supplement
Charles J. Meyers, Professor of Law, Stanford University.
A. Dan Tarlock, Professor of Law, Indiana University.

WILLS AND ADMINISTRATION, 5th Edition (1961)
The late Philip Mechem, Professor of Law, University of Pennsylvania, and
The late Thomas E. Atkinson, Professor of Law, New York University.

WORLD LAW, see United Nations Law

University Casebook Series

TRANSNATIONAL LEGAL PROBLEMS

MATERIALS AND TEXT

By

2487924

HENRY J. STEINER
Professor of Law, Harvard University

and

DETLEV F. VAGTS
Professor of Law, Harvard University

SECOND EDITION

Mineola, New York
THE FOUNDATION PRESS, INC.
1976

Library of Congress Catalog Card Number: 75–35387

Steiner & Vagts Legal Prob. 2d Ed.–UCB
1st Reprint—1977

PREFACE

The preface to many coursebooks could better appear as a postscript, for an author's description of his purposes may say little to the student who has yet to cross the threshold of a course. Nonetheless, the statement that follows should serve the student as an introduction to the book's themes. It should also enable teachers who may be considering using the book to understand our purposes and methods.

Recent decades witnessed a number of innovations in introducing students to legal problems that have some international dimension. Much and often contentious writing developed new perspectives upon this field and raised searching questions about the traditional approaches. A growing number of teachers of courses in international or comparative law introduced novel kinds of class materials. Others uprooted topics from the traditionally defined subjects and sought to integrate them in courses that stressed their interrelationships.

This academic ferment led to several experiments at Harvard Law School. The most pertinent to the First Edition of our book in 1968 was a course developed in the 1950's by Professor Milton Katz and (then) Professor Kingman Brewster. Drawing upon topics from national and international law, that course introduced a broader perspective upon problems that had been confined to discrete parts of the curriculum. It led to the pioneer casebook of Professors Katz and Brewster, The Law of International Transactions and Relations (1960), an inventive work that departed from existing models. Our first "effort" found its inspiration in that book. In the course of preparing the several drafts of the materials that appeared in the First Edition, we struck other paths, to the point where our approach and methods and much of our subject matter differed markedly from the Katz and Brewster volume. Nonetheless, in retrospect our debt was clear. Other coursebooks departing from the traditional presentation of international-law materials were also helpful to us in encouraging thought in different directions. The Second Edition, to which the following remarks refer, represents an elaboration of ideas as well as an updating of information in the initial volume. It also enters some new paths to which we call attention below.

The word "transnational," which we have chosen to describe in a comprehensive way the varied topics in our book, is permanently associated with Judge Jessup's imaginative Storrs Lectures, Transnational Law (1956). The author defined that title (p. 2) "to include all law which regulates actions or events that transcend national frontiers. Both public and private international law are included, as are other rules which do not wholly fit into such standard categories." The term is more than congenial to us; it well expresses the boundaries that we have traced, boundaries so spacious that a highly selective choice of topics was necessary within them.

The topics which we have chosen to develop the themes of our book are drawn from subjects with such familiar titles as international law or institutions, the conflict of laws, comparative law, constitutional law, jurisprudence, economic regulation and international business transactions. Insofar as the problems that we explore involve the principles, processes or structure of international law and institutions, comparative law, or the conflict of laws, their transnational character is evident. The many aspects of national legal systems which the book considers deal with principles and with procedures for decision-making that have been specifically developed to regulate problems having some foreign element. Together with international law and institutions, such fields of national law form a complex of policies, rules and processes which help to order some of the relationships among nations or among their business entities and citizens.

A variety of topics could have served these purposes. To achieve some coherence among the thirteen chapters, we have given principal but not exclusive attention to problems that are relevant not only to governments but also to the private participants—individual or corporate—in transnational life. Thus our topics stress the movement, and related regulation and protection under national or foreign or regional or international law, of persons and investment and trade. They include domestic regulatory and constitutional problems involving foreign affairs; the defense of human rights; the expropriation and protection of foreign investments; cooperation among national judiciaries; relationships among national legal systems in fields of criminal and economic regulation with extraterritorial reach; and the role and activities of multinational enterprises and organizations (particularly the European Common Market).

Through such topics, the course seeks to develop a conceptual framework for understanding and analyzing problems involving more than one legal and political system. A domestic comparison may be helpful. The lawyer in the United States considers questions of domestic law against the developed background of his education and experience. He is aware not only of the doctrinal foundation of the fields of law in which he works, but also of this country's constitutional structure, of the relationships between federal and state governments, and of those political, economic and cultural institutions or forces which contribute to the development of our legal system. Moreover, the perceptive lawyer will understand the practical limitations upon what his legal system can achieve, and the values—political, economic and ethical—which that system will recognize and foster.

Through the materials in this book, we hope to alert the student to the different values, policies and processes which he should appreciate in order to grasp the nature of transnational problems. The book's subjects stress the new considerations which become relevant, and the characteristics of the legal-political environment within which solutions to those problems must be sought. They also emphasize the different perspectives from which transnational problems may be viewed. Sometimes the relevant perspective is defined in terms of political groupings: this country, a foreign country or related group of countries, or a larger international-community perspective. Sometimes it is defined in terms of the different participants in transnational activity: private individuals or firms, national courts or legislators or treaty-makers, governmental instrumentalities, international officials, or regional and international organizations.

In the light of our description, it should be clear that our book has no rigid compartments, no clear separation of one topic from the other. Rather it suggests that all the topics occupy different positions on a spectrum between the extremes of "national" and "international" law, or on one between "private" and "public" law. One topic flows into the other; the later chapters attempt to integrate and to apply to their problems the general themes which Parts One and Two of the book develop. Given our purpose of using different topics to illustrate characteristics of transnational problems, it should be apparent that we have not purported to be exhaustive in our treatment of any one.

We have not explored one transnational problem that arises on an intergovernmental plane, the vital problem of contemporary international law: peacekeeping and the control of violence. It did not appear to us that our coursebook could contain a useful exploration of such themes together with the other topics which we wished to develop. Choice was necessary, and we simply wish to make clear the choice which we made. We should also indicate that our treatment of international law departs from the classical coursebooks on that subject. Rather than presenting in detail its doctrinal content or development, we have stressed its distinctive characteristics and processes, frequently by way of contrast with familiar conceptions of law and legal systems in national settings.

Two further points should be noted. First, when considering problems of international law or institutions, we have repeatedly drawn analogies to domestic law and legal processes. The perils in comparisons between any one legal system and international law or institutions are evident, but so to us are the advantages. Our purpose was to provide a familiar starting point for students, and thereby to help them to perceive more vividly the contrast between domestic and transnational problems.

Second, to provide illustrations of a number of problems in national legal systems, we have stressed the federal and state law of this country. The United States offers a particularly helpful point of departure towards consideration of many transnational problems, for its federal structure offers illuminating comparisons with the horizontal or vertical dimensions of the international scene. Our choice also reflects our belief that a developed appreciation of a range of legal-political problems posed in any one nation, and of the solutions which that nation has reached, will prove more instructive than the limited familiarity with diverse solutions that brief glimpses of many foreign countries can provide. Through intelligent observation of and extrapolation from our own experiences with transnational problems, the student can envision the kinds of choices to which foreign legal systems will be put. Where appropriate, we have sketched the different perspectives—political, economic and historical—from which other nations will view transnational problems in their own legal systems, or problems of international law and politics. In some sections, principally Chapter VII, we have explored more thoroughly the approaches of foreign legal systems.

The Second Edition holds to the basic structure of the First. Many of its changes simply reflect developments between 1967 and 1975. But we should note four more significant departures from the First Edition. (*1*) We have expanded our textual treatment of jurisprudential issues about the nature of law and its relationship to economic and political order. These changes are most prominent in the introductory and concluding materials to Chapter III, and in the treatment of property protection in Chapter IV. (*2*) Chapter XII contains new materials. Part of it is given to an examination of the multinational corporation from political and economic perspectives, while the larger part consists of a series of case studies and practical problems in the structuring of international business arrangements. Together with the other, more conceptual, chapters developing a framework for understanding transnational problems, these materials should permit use of the book in a course attentive to the techniques of international transactions. (*3*) The text and materials on the European Common Market, in Chapter XIII, have been expanded. On the other hand, the materials on the General Agreement on Tariffs and Trade and on the International Monetary Fund have been shortened and now consist entirely of our own text. We do not believe it possible to present within a brief space source documents or case law for those two institutions which could give accurate or revealing views of their internal structures or substantive effects. Nor could we present those materials in such a way as to make them amenable to class discussion. Thus the text in Chapter XI is meant to serve as a background for the study either of the multinational corporation (Chapter XII) or of the European Common Market (Chapter XIII). (*4*) Developments since 1967 have led to emphases on several new topics. The domestic and international experiences of the Vietnam war produced new materials in Chapter II, treating domestic constitutional issues, and in Chapter VIII, treating the international law of crime. Chapter IV contains added information about public and private institutions protecting human rights. The materials in Chapter VI on sovereign immunity have been sharply cut in view of pending statutory proposals (which are included).

Pedagogical Comments: The book is intended for use in a course of 60 hours or 45 hours in the second or third year of law school. (1) Even for a full-year or one semester course of 60 hours, our experience in using the First Edition suggests that pruning is necessary. (2) A shorter one-semester course in the second or third year introducing students to transnational problems might stress the development of a conceptual framework for understanding such problems, or stress issues of international economic regulation, or stress problems of a more practice-oriented character attending activities of multinational firms. (3) Finally the book could, with or without supplementation, serve a shorter third-year course or seminar for students who had covered several of its topics through a prior course.

We have included much of our own text, in excess of that customary for coursebooks in law schools. Through these sections, we have attempted to provide students with sufficient background (historical, jurisprudential, doctrinal, political, economic) about the problems in the many different fields into which they are led, and thus to free class time for discussion of problems rather than communication of information.

The book also contains numerous questions and hypothetical problem cases. Our experience has frequently led us to bypass class discussion of particular cases, statutes, treaties, or accounts of international disputes, and rather to build class hours around the questions or problems requiring students to reflect upon or apply such materials. Other teachers may entertain different views. For this reason, we have separated the questions and problems from our text, so that others can make appropriate detours or substitute their own as they desire. Within each chapter the problem cases are confined as much as possible to the materials there under discussion.

Editorial Comments: A separate Documentary Supplement has been published by The Foundation Press for use in connection with this book. In deciding whether documentary materials would be included in this book or the Supplement, we have followed two general principles. If references appear in several parts of the book to any one document, it appears in the Supplement. And even if a document is relevant to only one section, it has been included in the Supplement if its length was such as to interfere unduly with the development of a topic. In most cases, it will be obvious to the reader when source materials that are referred to herein appear in the Supplement. In cases where this may be less than obvious, we have indicated that a particular statute or treaty can be found in the Supplement through an asterisk (i. e., 28 U.S.C. § 1332*). We have not given citations in the book to documents appearing in the Supplement.

PREFACE

Our source materials in the coursebook reflect amendments to federal statutes in this country through May 1975, and to state law through 1974. Every effort has been made to include amendments to bilateral or multilateral treaties through May 1975. To some extent, as indicated in the book, we have relied upon secondary sources published at earlier dates for a description of the provisions of some foreign laws. Unless otherwise noted, translations of foreign laws or cases are our own.

References to additional reading appear as we considered appropriate. Since the book is designed for teaching rather than research, it does not offer exhaustive bibliographical citations.

Most cases have been sharply edited, and we have indicated omissions through the conventional use of dots. Generally footnotes have been omitted from judicial decisions, other source materials and excerpts from the writings of other authors. Those which we retained have been renumbered, and those which we added are so designated.

HENRY J. STEINER
DETLEV F. VAGTS

Cambridge, Massachusetts
December, 1975

ACKNOWLEDGMENTS

A book which treats in varying detail some twenty distinct fields of legal doctrine as well as concepts common to these fields poses special problems for its authors. In the course of preparing the manuscript for the first edition, we drew heavily upon the time and help of colleagues and others, all of which is acknowledged in that edition. Since its publication we have had advice, criticism and assistance from users of the book, students and colleagues here and elsewhere, but in so many different forms and at such different times that it would be difficult to enumerate and do justice to our advisers and critics here.

We express our appreciation to Sheila Davidson and Troy Miller, who so competently assumed the burden of typing and retyping drafts of the revised and new material.

We gratefully acknowledge permission extended by the following authors, publishers, and organizations to reprint excerpts from the books, periodicals and other documents indicated in parentheses: American Bar Association Journal (excerpts); American Journal of Comparative Law (excerpts); American Law Institute (excerpts from the Restatement (Second) Conflicts of Law, and Restatement (Second) Foreign Relations Law); American Society of International Law (excerpts from the American Journal of International Law, the Proceedings of the Society, and International Legal Materials); Association of the Bar of the City of New York (excerpts from the Record of the Association of the Bar of the City of New York); Commerce Clearing House (translated cases and other excerpts from the Common Market Reporter); Common Market Law Reports Limited (translations from Common Market Law Reports); Denver Law Journal (excerpts); Foundation Press, Inc. (excerpts from Henkin, Foreign Affairs and the Constitution); Mr. K. Goldschmid (excerpts from International Licensing Contracts); Harvard Law Review (excerpts); Harvard University Press and W. E. Butler (excerpts from Tunkin, Theory of International Law, Butler trans.); Johns Hopkins Press (excerpts from Dunn, The Protection of Nationals); Little, Brown & Co. (excerpt from von Mehren and Trautman, The Law of Multistate Transactions, 1965); Manchester University Press (excerpts from Parry, Sources and Evidences of International Law); Matthew Bender & Co. (excerpt from Moore's Federal Practice); Michigan Law Review (excerpt); New York Times (excerpts); Oxford University Press (excerpts from Brierly, Law of Nations); Praeger Publishers Inc. (excerpt from Hartshorn, Politics and World Oil Economics, and Vernon, How Latin America Views the Foreign Investor); Princeton University Press (excerpts from Cohen and Chiu, People's China and International Law); Quadrangle Books (excerpts from Taylor, Nuremberg and Vietnam: An American

Tragedy); Simon & Schuster, Inc. (excerpt from Barnet and Mueller, Global Reach); South Dakota Law Review (excerpts); Syracuse Law Review (excerpts); John Wiley & Sons, Inc. (excerpts from Kaplan and Katzenbach, The Political Foundations of International Law); Yale Law Journal and Fred B. Rothman & Company (excerpts from the Yale Law Journal). To all such holders of copyrights © we are indebted.

HENRY J. STEINER
DETLEV F. VAGTS

SUMMARY OF CONTENTS

Chapter III. Distinctive Characteristics of the International Legal Process—Continued

PART THREE: THE ROLE OF NATIONAL JUDICIARIES IN BUILDING A TRANSNATIONAL LEGAL SYSTEM

PART FOUR: THE TRANSNATIONAL REACH OF NATIONAL LEGAL SYSTEMS

Chapter IX. The Transnational Reach of Economic Regulation —Continued

PART FIVE: TRADE AND INVESTMENT IN THE WORLD COMMUNITY: LEGAL STRUCTURES, POLICY CONTEXT AND CASE STUDIES

PART SIX: THE DEVELOPING PROCESSES OF INTERNATIONAL ORGANIZATIONS

*

TABLE OF CONTENTS[1]

PART ONE: TRANSNATIONAL PROBLEMS WITHIN NATIONAL LEGAL SYSTEMS

[1] Sections entitled "Comment," "Questions" and "Problem" have been omitted from the Table of Contents.

Chapter I. Some Responses of a National Legal System to Aliens and Their Activities—Continued

D. Access of Aliens to Economic Activities—Continued

Chapter II. Distribution of National Powers to Deal With Transnational Problems—Continued

PART TWO: INTERNATIONAL LAW AND ITS RELATIONSHIP TO NATIONAL LEGAL SYSTEMS

Chapter III. Distinctive Characteristics of the International Legal Process—Continued

Chapter IV. Development of an International Minimum Standard: The International Legal Process Illustrated —Continued

Chapter IV. Development of an International Minimum Standard: The International Legal Process Illustrated —Continued

C. Expropriation of Alien-Owned Property—Continued

PART FOUR: THE TRANSNATIONAL REACH OF NATIONAL LEGAL SYSTEMS

Chapter IX. The Transnational Reach of Economic Regulation —Continued

Chapter XI. The World Economic Environment: GATT and IMF—Continued

Chapter XIII. The European Economic Community (Common Market)—Continued

Chapter XIII. The European Economic Community (Common Market)—Continued

C. The Structural Framework and Processes for the Development of Community Law—Continued

*

TABLE OF CASES

Principal cases are in italic type. Cases discussed or cited are in roman type. References are to pages.

A. United States Cases

B. Decisions of International Tribunals

C. Decisions of Foreign National and Regional Tribunals

TRANSNATIONAL LEGAL PROBLEMS

Part One

TRANSNATIONAL PROBLEMS WITHIN NATIONAL LEGAL SYSTEMS

In a world composed of politically organized societies set off from each other by territorial boundaries, each nation inevitably pays some heed to phenomena that are foreign, that bear some relationship to the outside world. The most primitive reaction to such phenomena would be to attempt to insulate a nation and its population from things foreign: prohibition of commerce, of travel, of the flow of ideas across national boundaries and so on. But the inescapable decision in the contemporary world is to participate in the life of the international community. Defining the terms of that participation is a vastly complicated task, one involving political, economic and cultural considerations. It will require the creation of a more or less elaborate body of legal doctrine and some distinctive legal processes to make effective the national policies towards foreign matters. We are concerned in this Part One with some of the manifestations in a national legal system of such policies.

The problems that have some foreign dimension and require a special response within a legal system take many forms. Some of the participants in a nation's social or economic life may be alien (or alien-controlled) individuals or corporations. Their links with other countries and their relatively distant relationship to the traditions, political life and aspirations of the host country raise inevitable concerns. Rules must be developed which govern their right to enter or remain, and which determine their other rights, disabilities or duties within the host country. Trade across national boundaries and the distinctive problems which it entails call for further elaboration of policies and rules within a national legal system. A variety of other examples comes readily to mind.

In one sense every aspect of a legal system, however local in character, may affect non-citizens. The alien businessman temporarily in

Massachusetts is of course subject to state law. He may, for example, have to pay a sales tax or a fine for a traffic violation. But we are here concerned with processes, policies and rules that have been developed specifically in response to problems of some foreign character. The nature of such responses necessarily affects other countries and their nationals. Such expressions of a national legal system can thus be viewed as having a transnational character. Their significance, by definition, transcends a national frontier. Together with private and public international law and with international organizations or institutions, such phases of national law form a complex of legal processes, policies and rules which help to regulate some of the relationships among nations or among their citizens.

In Part One, we consider transnational aspects of domestic legal systems, particularly that of the United States. In these two chapters, we isolate from discussion and bypass the body of international law and the international organizations or institutions which in varying degrees will determine, confine or encourage solutions that national legal systems bring to transnational problems. Later chapters will develop these other components of transnational law and the relationships among them. We also postpone consideration of another factor that influences decisions on transnational matters. National officials are often influenced by what they anticipate the responses of foreign governments will be, even though there may be no principles or rules of international law on the question which they may understand to be relevant. Coursebooks can, however, defer consideration more readily than courts. You will note that several cases in Part One allude to these themes.

Chapter I

SOME RESPONSES OF A NATIONAL LEGAL SYSTEM TO ALIENS AND THEIR ACTIVITIES

A fundamental category of problems which all political societies must face stems from the recurring contact with those societies of natural or legal persons who are not members, who are in some sense alien. The critical fact that is common to the varied problems considered in this chapter is the alienage of an individual or corporation.

A. LINKS OF INDIVIDUALS TO POLITICAL COMMUNITIES

An individual may be linked to a country in a number of ways, including his nationality, domicile or residence. What relationships to the country do these terms imply, and in what respects are such relationships important?

UNITED STATES v. WONG KIM ARK

Supreme Court of the United States, 1898.
169 U.S. 649, 18 S.Ct. 456, 42 L.Ed. 890.

[Wong Kim Ark was born in 1873 in California. Upon his return in 1895 from a brief trip to China, he was denied permission to land in the United States on the ground that he was not a United States citizen and was not within any of the exceptions from classes of persons excluded from the United States under the Chinese Exclusion Acts which were then in effect. In these habeas corpus proceedings, the question posed was whether Wong Kim Ark was a citizen. The federal district court ordered that he be discharged and permitted to enter the country. Excerpts from the opinion upon appeal of the Supreme Court, by JUSTICE GRAY, appear below.]

The question presented by the record is whether a child born in the United States, of parents of Chinese descent, who at the time of his birth are subjects of the emperor of China, but have a permanent domicile and residence in the United States, and are there carrying on business, and are not employed in any diplomatic or official capacity under the emperor of China, become at the time of his birth a citizen of the United States, by virtue of the first clause of the fourteenth amendment of the constitution: "All persons born or naturalized in the United States, and subject to the jurisdiction thereof, are citizens of the United States and of the state wherein they reside." . . .

The constitution of the United States, as originally adopted, uses the words "citizen of the United States" and "natural-born citizen of the United States." By the original constitution, every representative in congress is required to have been "seven years a citizen of the United States," and every senator to have been "nine years a citizen of the United States"; and "no person except a natural-born citizen or a citizen of the United States at the time of the adoption of this constitution, shall be eligible to the office of president." Article 2, § 1. The fourteenth article of amendment, besides declaring that "all persons born or naturalized in the United States, and subject to the jurisdiction thereof, are citizens of the United States and of the state wherein they reside," also declares that "no state shall make or enforce any law which shall abridge the privileges or immunities of citizens of the United States; nor shall any state deprive any person of life, liberty, or property, without due process of law; nor deny to any person within its jurisdiction the equal protection of the laws." And the fifteenth article of amendment declares that "the right of citizens of the United States to vote shall not be denied or abridged by the United States, or by any state, on account of race, color, or previous condition of servitude."

The constitution nowhere defines the meaning of these words, either by way of inclusion or of exclusion, except in so far as this is done by the affirmative declaration that "all persons born or naturalized in the United States, and subject to the jurisdiction thereof, are citizens of the United States." Amend. art. 14. In this, as in other respects, it must be interpreted in the light of the common law, the principles and history of which were familiarly known to the framers of the constitution. . . .

The fundamental principle of the common law with regard to English nationality was birth within the allegiance—also called "ligealty," "obedience," "faith," or "power"—of the king. The principle embraced all persons born within the king's allegiance, and subject to his protection. Such allegiance and protection were mutual . . . and were not restricted to natural-born subjects and naturalized subjects, or to those who had taken an oath of allegiance; but were predicable of aliens in amity, so long as they were within the kingdom. Children, born in England, of such aliens, were therefore natural-born subjects. But the children, born within the realm, of foreign ambassadors, or the children of alien enemies, born during and within their hostile occupation of part of the king's dominions, were not natural-born subjects, because not born within the allegiance, the obedience, or the power, or, as would be said at this day, within the jurisdiction, of the king. . . .

The same rule was in force in all the English colonies upon this continent down to the time of the Declaration of Independence, and in the United States afterwards, and continued to prevail under the constitution as originally established. . . .

Passing by questions once earnestly controverted, but finally put at rest by the fourteenth amendment of the constitution, it is beyond doubt that, before the enactment of the civil rights act of 1866 or the adoption of the constitutional amendment, all white persons, at least, born within the sovereignty of the United States, whether children of citizens or of foreigners, excepting only children of ambassadors or public ministers of a foreign government, were native-born citizens of the United States.

In the forefront, both of the fourteenth amendment of the constitution, and of the civil rights act of 1866, the fundamental principle of citizenship by birth within the dominion was reaffirmed in the most explicit and comprehensive terms. . . .

. . . As appears upon the face of the amendment, as well as from the history of the times, this was not intended to impose any new restrictions upon citizenship, or to prevent any persons from becoming citizens by the fact of birth within the United States, who would thereby have become citizens according to the law existing before its adoption. It is declaratory in form, and enabling and extending in effect. Its main purpose doubtless was, as has been often recognized by this court, to establish the citizenship of free negroes, which had been denied in the opinion delivered by Chief Justice Taney in Scott v. Sanford (1857) 19 How. 393; and to put it beyond doubt that all blacks, as well as whites, born or naturalized within the jurisdiction of the United States, are citizens of the United States. Slaughter House Cases (1873) 16 Wall. 36, 73. . . .

The foregoing considerations and authorities irresistibly lead us to these conclusions: The fourteenth amendment affirms the ancient and fundamental rule of citizenship by birth within the territory, in the allegiance and under the protection of the country, including all children here born of resident aliens, with the exceptions or qualifications (as old as the rule itself) of children of foreign sovereigns or their ministers, or born on foreign public ships, or of enemies within and during a hostile occupation of part of our territory, and with the single additional exception of children of members of the Indian tribes owing direct allegiance to their several tribes. The amendment, in clear words and in manifest intent, includes the children born within the territory of the United States of all other persons, of whatever race or color, domiciled within the United States. Every citizen or subject of another country, while domiciled here, is within the allegiance and the protection, and consequently subject to the jurisdiction, of the United States. His allegiance to the United States is direct and immediate, and, although but local and temporary, continuing only so long as he remains within our territory, is yet, in the words of Lord Coke in Calvin's Case, 7 Coke, 6a, "strong enough to make a natural subject, for, if he hath issue here, that issue is a natural-born subject"; and his child, as said by Mr. Binney in his essay before quoted, "if born in the country, is as much a citizen as the natural-born child of a citizen, and by operation of the same principle." It can hardly be denied that an alien is completely subject to the political jurisdiction of the country in which he resides, seeing that, as said by Mr. Webster, when secretary of state, in his report to the president on Thrasher's case in 1851, and since repeated by this court: "Independently of a residence with intention to continue such residence; independently of any domiciliation; independently of the taking of any oath of allegiance, or of renouncing any former allegiance,—it is well known that by the public law an alien, or a stranger born, for so long a time as he continues within the dominions of a foreign government, owes obedience to the laws of that government, and may be punished for treason or other crimes as a native-born subject might be, unless his case is varied by some treaty stipulations." Executive Documents H.R. No. 10, 1st Sess. 32d Cong. p. 4; 6 Webster's Works, 526; U. S. v. Carlisle, 16 Wall. 147, 155. . . .

To hold that the fourteenth amendment of the constitution excludes from citizenship the children born in the United States of citizens or subjects of other countries, would be to deny citizenship to thousands of persons of English, Scotch, Irish, German, or other European parentage, who have always been considered and treated as citizens of the United States. . . .

The power of naturalization, vested in congress by the constitution, is a power to confer citizenship, not a power to take it away. . . . Congress having no power to abridge the rights conferred by the constitution upon those who have become naturalized citizens by virtue of acts of congress, a fortiori no act or omission of congress, as to providing for the naturalization of parents or children of a particular race, can affect citizenship acquired as a birthright, by virtue of the constitution itself, without any aid of legislation. The fourteenth amendment, while it leaves the power, where it was before, in congress, to regulate naturalization, has conferred no authority upon congress to restrict the effect of birth, declared by the constitution to constitute a sufficient and complete right to citizenship. . .

Upon the facts agreed in this case, the American citizenship which Wong Kim Ark acquired by birth within the United States has not been lost or taken away by anything happening since his birth. No doubt he might himself, after coming of age, renounce this citizenship, and become a citizen of the country of his parents, or of any other country; for by our law, as solemnly declared by congress, "the right of expatriation is a natural and inherent right of all people," and "any declaration, instruction, opinion, order or direction of any officer of the United States, which denies, restricts, impairs or questions the right of expatriation, is declared inconsistent with the fundamental principles of the republic." Rev.St. § 1999, reenacting Act July 27, 1868, c. 249, § 1 (15 Stat. 223, 224). . . .

Order affirmed.

[Dissenting opinion of CHIEF JUSTICE FULLER omitted.]

COMMENT

In Wong Kim Ark, citizenship was critical because of its effect upon an individual's right to enter the United States. This right to enter or return has been strongly protected by the courts. Consider

Worthy v. United States, 328 F.2d 386 (5th Cir. 1964). The United States imposed restrictions on passports to prevent its citizens from travelling in certain designated areas. Worthy, a newspaperman, violated past restrictions, refused to agree to abide by present restrictions and consequently was denied a passport. Nonetheless, he visited Cuba, which was then on the restricted list. After his return to the United States in 1961, he was charged by indictment with unlawfully entering the United States, under Section 215(b) of the Immigration and Nationality Act of 1952. That section made it unlawful for a citizen ". . . to depart from or enter . . . the United States unless he bears a valid passport." 66 Stat. 190 (1952), 8 U.S.C.A. § 1185 (b). Worthy was found guilty. The Court of Appeals reversed the conviction, holding the statute unconstitutional insofar as it made it unlawful for a citizen to *enter* the country without a valid passport. The opinion stated in part (at 394):

> We think it is inherent in the concept of citizenship that the citizen, when absent from the country to which he owes allegiance, has a right to return, again to set foot on its soil. . . .
>
> We do not think that a citizen, absent from his country, can have his fundamental right to have free ingress thereto subject to a criminal penalty if he does not have a passport. The citizen, culpable though he may have been in leaving his country without a passport which he could not obtain, and subject, as he probably was, to a criminal penalty for departing without a passport, cannot, we think, be required to choose between banishment or expatriation on the one hand or crossing the border on the other hand, being faced with criminal punishment and the loss of some of the rights and privileges of citizenship as a felon. Citizenship, the Supreme Court has recently said, is a most precious right. . . .[1]

Note some of the categories of persons who are United States citizens at birth under Section 301 of the Immigration and Nationality Acts of 1952 *. Subsection (a)(1) has a constitutional foundation, independent of implementing legislation, under the Fourteenth Amendment. The others derive from the general legislative powers of the Congress. The alternate route towards citizenship, naturalization, is twice referred to in the Constitution: Art. I, Sec. 8, and Section 1 of the Fourteenth Amendment.

The American nationality laws refer to the two traditional bases for acquiring nationality at birth: the place of birth (*jus soli*), and

1. [Eds.]—The precise issue in the Worthy case has not been decided by the Supreme Court. However, a statement in the opinion of the Court in United States v. Laub, 385 U.S. 475, 481, 87 S.Ct. 574, 578, 17 L.Ed.2d 526, 531 (1967), may cast some doubt upon the holding in Worthy. The issue before the Court was whether Section 215(b) would support a criminal prosecution of citizens bearing passports who had violated area restrictions attaching to all passports by travel to Cuba. In the course of a general discussion of the section, the Court stated: "Departure for Cuba or entry from Cuba without a passport would be a violation of § 215(b), exposing the traveler to the criminal penalties provided in that section."

the nationality of one or both of the parents (*jus sanguinis*). Note the varying influence of these two bases and the interplay between them in Articles 1 and 2 of the Costa Rican Aliens and Nationalization Act of 1950; Sections 1, 3, and 8 of the Danish Citizenship Act No. 252; and Articles 6 and 8 of the Polish Nationality Act of 1951 *.

For purposes of immigration and naturalization, many countries draw distinctions among the national origin (and hence indirectly among ethnic or racial categories) of applicants. Note, for example, Article 2 of the Costa Rican Law, or the "national origin" system, p. 19, infra, under earlier United States legislation. Ethnic and religious categories may become explicitly relevant, as in the Israeli Nationality Law of July 14, 1952 (5712–1951/52) Laws of the State of Israel 50, which provides that nationality is acquired not only by such traditional bases as birth or naturalization, but also by "return". That term refers to the Law of Return of July 5, 1950 (5710–49/50) Laws of the State of Israel 114, providing that "every Jew has the right to" emigrate to Israel. For the difficulties in determining such status for purposes of immigration, the population registry, and nationality, see Case Note, 10 Colum.J.Trans.L. 133 (1971).

Additional reading: Silving, Nationality in Comparative Law, 5 Am. J.Comp.L. 410 (1956).

QUESTIONS

(1) Each of the nationality laws noted above refers both to the *jus soli* and the *jus sanguinis* as a basis for acquiring a nationality at birth. Which principle is dominant in the United States, and what factors in American history have caused the laws governing nationality to stress that principle? What differences in the historical development or contemporary situation of countries such as Costa Rica or Denmark would have led them to formulate their nationality laws with a different stress?

(2) Consider any of the three foreign nationality laws together with the United States law. Would it be possible for a person to be born a citizen of two countries? To be born without any citizenship? To become stateless after birth?

(3) Suppose that the Fourteenth Amendment had been adopted without the first sentence in its Section 1. Should the Supreme Court have affirmed or reversed the order of the District Court in Wong Kim Ark?

NOTE ON DENATIONALIZATION

The last paragraph of the Wong Kim Ark opinion indicated that since 1868, legislation has assured United States citizens of their right to voluntary expatriation. But the notion that an individual should be free to leave his country and shed his nationality is not common to all legal systems. Note, for example, the provisions of Article 11 of the Polish Nationality Act of 1951 *. Recall also the debates in the early 1970's in the American press and Congress about Soviet restrictions on the emigration of Soviet Jews to Israel, ranging from quota restrictions to exit fees and denials of permission.[2]

Sections 349 and 352 * of the Immigration and Nationality Act state the grounds upon which a native born or naturalized citizen may, against his will, lose his nationality. A series of Supreme Court decisions starting with Perez v. Brownell, 356 U.S. 44, 78 S.Ct. 568, 2 L.Ed.2d 603 (1958), explored the legality of these provisions, held a number of them to be unconstitutional and raised serious doubts about the constitutionality of others. In the Perez case, the Court upheld the predecessor statute to Section 349(a)(5). But other decisions declared unconstitutional the predecessor to present Section 349(a)(8), Section 349(a)(10), and Section 352(a)(1).[3] In view of the number of separate opinions and the varied grounds upon which they were written, it did not appear possible to compose a rationale common to a majority of the Court on the constitutionality of denationalization provisions. But that effort became academic with Afroyim v. Rusk, 387 U.S. 253, 87 S.Ct. 1660, 18 L.Ed.2d 757 (1967), which overruled Perez v. Brownell. In a 5–4 decision, the Court held that a naturalized citizen could not be deprived of his citizenship because he voted in a foreign political election. The categorical denial of any power in the Congress to deprive a person of his citizenship without his consent is apparent in the following excerpts from the opinion delivered for the Court by Mr. Justice Black (387 U.S. at 257, 87 S.Ct. at 1662, 18 L.Ed. 2d at 761):

> First we reject the idea expressed in *Perez* that, aside from the Fourteenth Amendment, Congress has any general power, express or implied, to take away an American citizen's citizenship without his assent. This power cannot, as *Perez* indicated, be sustained as an implied attribute of sovereignty possessed by all nations. Other nations are governed by their own constitutions, if any, and we can draw no support from theirs. In our country the people are sovereign and the Government cannot sever its relationship to the people by taking away their citizenship. Our Constitution governs us and we must never forget that our Constitution limits the Government to those powers specifically granted or those that are necessary and proper to carry out the specifically granted ones. The Constitution of course, grants Congress no express power to strip people of their citizenship, whether in the exercise of the implied power to regulate foreign affairs or in the exercise of any specifically granted power. . . .

2. For an argument that the right of emigration has a foundation in international law, see Knisbacher, *Aliyah* of Soviet Jews: Protection of the Right of Emigration under International Law, 14 Harv.Int.L.J. 89 (1973). That article refers among other sources to Art. 13(2) of the U.N. Universal Delaration of Human Rights of 1948 (see p. 387, infra), providing that "Every person has the right to leave any country, including his own, and to return to his country."

3. Those decisions were Trop v. Dulles, 356 U.S. 86, 78 S.Ct. 590, 2 L.Ed.2d 630 (1958); Kennedy v. Mendoza-Martinez, 372 U.S. 144, 83 S.Ct. 554, 9 L.Ed.2d 644 (1963); and Schneider v. Rusk, 377 U.S. 163, 84 S.Ct. 1187, 12 L.Ed.2d 218 (1964).

> Because the legislative history of the Fourteenth Amendment and the expatriation proposals which preceded and followed it, like most other legislative history, contains many statements from which conflicting inferences can be drawn, our holding might be unwarranted if it rested entirely or principally upon that legislative history. But it does not. Our holding we think is the only one that can stand in view of the language and the purpose of the Fourteenth Amendment, and our construction of that Amendment, we believe, comports more nearly than *Perez* with the principles of liberty and equal justice to all that the entire Fourteenth Amendment was adopted to guarantee. Citizenship is no light trifle to be jeopardized any moment Congress decides to do so under the name of one of its general or implied grants of power. In some instances, loss of citizenship can mean that a man is left without the protection of citizenship in any country in the world—as a man without a country. Citizenship in this Nation is a part of a cooperative affair. Its citizenry is the country and the country is its citizenry. The very nature of our free government makes it completely incongruous to have a rule of law under which a group of citizens temporarily in office can deprive another group of citizens of their citizenship. We hold that the Fourteenth Amendment was designed to, and does, protect every citizen of this Nation against a congressional forcible destruction of his citizenship, whatever his creed, color, or race. Our holding does no more than to give to this citizen that which is his own, a constitutional right to remain a citizen in a free country unless he voluntarily relinquishes that citizenship.

The opinion in Afroyim introduced the difficult problem of determining when a citizen "voluntarily" relinquishes his citizenship. It cast doubt upon a number of other denationalization provisions of Section 349, such as subsection (a)(3) or (a)(4). Indeed, it became unclear whether nationality would be lost under subsection (a)(1) through naturalization in a foreign state when the application for that naturalization did not specifically require renunciation of prior nationality.

But a number of decisions interpreting the Afroyim opinion suggest that there are paths toward loss of nationality, described in Section 349(a)(6) and (7), that are consistent with Afroyim. The opinions have wrestled with the question whether, under Afroyim, there must be a specific subjective intention to relinquish nationality, an intention difficult to prove, or simply action that could be viewed as inconsistent with the intention to retain American citizenship.[4]

In its most recent decision on the denationalization laws, Rogers v. Bellei, 401 U.S. 815, 91 S.Ct. 1060, 28 L.Ed.2d 499 (1971), the Court found constitutional the predecessor statute to present Section 301(b). It reasoned that one deriving United States citizenship *jus sanguinis* was not within the provision of the Fourteenth Amendment referring

4. Compare Baker v. Rusk, 296 F.Supp. 1244 (C.D.Cal.1969), with King v. Rogers, 463 F.2d 1188 (9th Cir. 1972).

to native-born or naturalized citizens. Therefore, in granting citizenship to those born abroad to one American parent, Congress could impose a condition precedent of residence in this country. The opinion concluded that the imposition of a condition subsequent would likewise not violate the Due Process Clause of the Fifth Amendment.

VAN DER SCHELLING v. U. S. NEWS & WORLD REPORT, INC.

United States District Court, Eastern District of Pennsylvania, 1963.
213 F.Supp. 756, aff'd per curiam 324 F.2d 956 (3d Cir. 1963),
cert. denied 377 U.S. 906, 84 S.Ct. 1166, 12 L.Ed.2d 177 (1964).

[The plaintiff, a citizen of the United States, had been a permanent and continuous resident of Mexico since 1950. She had sold all her property in the United States, had not sought renewal of her passport since 1952, and had the status in Mexico of an "immigrado," which gave her the "right of definitive residence" but did not confer upon her Mexican citizenship. Plaintiff brought a libel action in the District Court against a Delaware corporation which had its principal place of business in the District of Columbia. Federal jurisdiction was invoked on the basis of diversity of citizenship under 28 U.S.C. § 1332.* Defendant moved to dismiss the complaint for want of jurisdiction. It argued that plaintiff, although a citizen of the United States, was not a citizen of any state therein because of her foreign domicile, and that consequently the suit was not between "citizens of different States" as required under Section 1332(a)(1). Plaintiff contended that the District Court nonetheless had jurisdiction under Section 1332(a)(2), which confers jurisdiction over certain civil actions between "citizens of a State, and foreign states or citizens or subjects thereof." She argued that she was a "subject" of a foreign state within the meaning of this statute. The District Court granted defendant's motion to dismiss and held that plaintiff was not a "subject" of Mexico within the meaning of Section 1332. Excerpts from the opinion of JUDGE LORD appear below.]

In Nagle v. Loi Hoa, 275 U.S. 475, 48 S.Ct. 160, 72 L.Ed. 381 (1928), speaking of the word "subject" as used in the Chinese Exclusion Act, the Court said, at page 477, 48 S.Ct. at pages 160, 161, 72 L.Ed. 381:

> "The sole question presented is whether the word 'subject' as used in § 6 is to be taken as including only those persons who by birth or naturalization owe permanent allegiance to the government issuing the certificate, or as embracing also those who, being domiciled within the territorial limits of that government, owe it for that reason obedience and temporary allegiance.
>
> "The word may be used in either sense. . . ."

> In 2 Kent's Commentaries (14th Ed.) at page 75, it is said: ". . . So, an American citizen may obtain a foreign domicile, which will impress upon him a national character for commercial purposes, in like manner as if he were a subject of the government under which he resided; and yet without losing on that account his original character, or ceasing to be bound by the allegiance due to the country of his birth. . ."

Thus, in The Pizzaro, 15 U.S. (2 Wheat.) 227, 4 L.Ed. 226 (1817), the claimant of a Spanish vessel seized as a prize had been born in Great Britain. However, he was a domiciliary of Spain and asserted certain favorable rights given to Spanish subjects under a Treaty of 1795 between Spain and the United States. No question of federal jurisdiction was involved. Justice Story said, at page 246, 4 L.Ed. 226:

> ". . . Indeed, in the language of the law of nations, which is always to be consulted in the interpretation of treaties, a person domiciled in a country, and enjoying the protection of its sovereign, is deemed a subject of that country. He owes allegiance to the country, while he resides in it; temporary, indeed, if he has not, by birth or naturalization, contracted a permanent allegiance; but so fixed that, as to all other nations, he follows the character of that country, in war as well as in peace. . . ."

Thus, it is undoubtedly true that domicile may impress one with the characteristics of a subject of the place of domicile for commercial purposes. Is this different from the sense of the word "subject" as used in Article III, Section 2 of the Constitution? I think it is.

That Article authorizes federal jurisdiction in controversies "between a State, or the Citizens thereof, and foreign States, Citizens or Subjects." The Judicial Code of 1789 and the present § 1332 are Congressional implements of this Article. Thus, to determine the meaning of § 1332 we must first determine the meaning of the Constitution. Some examination of the reason for making federal jurisdiction available to citizens or subjects of a foreign state will be helpful.

In "The Federalist", No. 80, it is said (pp. 588–589):

> ". . . The fourth point rests on this plain proposition, that the peace of the WHOLE, ought not to be left at the disposal of a PART. The union will undoubtedly be answerable to foreign powers for the conduct of its members. And the responsibility for an injury, ought ever to be accompanied with the faculty of preventing it. As the denial or perversion of justice by the sentences of courts, is with reason classed among the just causes of war, it will follow, that the federal judiciary ought to have cognizance of all causes in which *the citizens* of other countries are concerned. This is not less essential to the preservation of the public faith, than to the security of the public tranquillity. A distinction may perhaps be imagined, between cases arising upon treaties and the laws of nations, and those which may stand merely on the footing of the municipal law. The former kind may be supposed proper for the federal jurisdiction, the latter for that of the states. But it is at least problematical, whether an unjust sentence against a *foreigner*, where the subject of controversy was wholly relative to the *lex loci*, would not, if unredressed, be an aggression upon *his sovereign*, as well as one which violated the stipulations of a treaty, or the general law of nations. And a still greater objection to the distinction would result from the immense difficulty, if not impossibility, of a practical discrimination between the cases of one complexion and those of the other. So great a proportion of the controversies in which *foreigners* are parties, involve national questions, that it is by far most safe, and most expedient, to

refer all those in which they are concerned to the national tribunals. * * * " (Emphasis added.)

[Excerpts in the opinion from remarks of James Wilson in the debates in Pennsylvania concerning adoption of the Constitution have been omitted.]

Two things are immediately apparent. First, both Hamilton and Wilson, in discussing Article III, Section 2, refer to citizens, subjects and foreigners interchangeably. These references, it seems to me, are an equation, perhaps unconscious, in the minds of the framers that "citizen" and "subject" mean the same thing. Second, if the main purpose was to provide a national forum with the object of preserving the peace, it seems hardly likely that a foreign sovereign or government would become martially exorcised over a wrong to a citizen of the United States who can go into his native courts as a native.

The legislators of 1789 who enacted the Judiciary Act of 1789 apparently felt that Article III, Section 2, was not concerned with Americans abroad, for that first implementing Act provided federal access where the suit was between a citizen of the United States and *aliens,* a designation that persisted until the Act was amended in 1875. There is no reason to suppose that the first Congress deliberately failed to exercise a power given by the Constitution, and the inference is, I think, that those who stood close to the framing of the Constitution, both in point of time and association, intended to exhaust the grant of federal jurisdiction. The necessary concomitant is that by using "aliens", they embraced "citizens or subjects" as constitutionally used in Article III. The necessary conclusion is, then, that the Constitution did not cover American citizens domiciled abroad, for these are not aliens. . . .

Viewed against the background of history and the context of the times, it is not surprising that the men who drafted the Constitution equated "citizen" and "subject". Until the Colonies had successfully won their freedom from England, their inhabitants were *subjects* of the King. With the birth of the United States, the sovereignty that had previously been that of one man,—the King,— was transferred to the collective body of the people. Those who had been subjects of the King were now *citizens* of the State. . . .

In Minor v. Happersett, 88 U.S. (21 Wall.) 162, 22 L.Ed. 627 (1875), the Court pointed out that a citizen is a member of a political community. The Court then said, at page 166, 22 L.Ed. 627:

> ". . . For convenience it has been found necessary to give a name to this membership. The object is to designate by a title the person and the relation he bears to the nation. For this purpose the words 'subject,' 'inhabitant,' and 'citizen' have been used, and the choice between them is sometimes made to depend upon the form of the government. Citizen is now more commonly employed, however, and as it has been considered better suited to the description of one living under a republican government, it was adopted by nearly all of the States upon their separation from Great Britain, and was afterwards adopted in the Articles of Confederation and in the Constitution of the United States. When used in this sense it is understood as conveying the idea of membership of a nation, and nothing more. . . ."

In light of my conclusion, defendant's motion to dismiss for want of jurisdiction must be granted.

QUESTIONS

(1) In view of the cases that are described and the excerpts from them that are quoted in the Van der Schelling opinion, in what contexts and to which questions might the term "subject" be relevant?

(2) Before the adoption of the Fourteenth Amendment, on what ground could an alien, alleging that he was discriminated against in a civil action or criminal proceeding in a state court, seek direct or collateral review of the state decision in a federal court?

NOTE ON SOME RELATIONSHIPS BETWEEN AN INDIVIDUAL AND A POLITICAL COMMUNITY

Basic to the Van der Schelling decision is the doctrine developed at an early period by the federal courts that state citizenship, for purposes of the diversity jurisdiction, depends both upon United States citizenship and upon domicile (in the traditional sense of the term that is described below) in the state. Compare Section 1 of the Fourteenth Amendment.

The opinion in Van der Schelling suggests the different ways in which the relationship between an individual and a particular political community, whether state or nation, can be described. Recall the different terms that are used: citizen, subject, national (or their opposites, foreigner or alien), resident and domiciliary. Some of these terms require further explanation.

The distinction between nationality and citizenship in the United States is minimal and fading. Note the definitions in Section 101(a)(3), (21) and (22) of the Immigration and Nationality Act. Nationals at the present time are only those persons born in the areas noted in subsection (29) of Section 101(a). In some other countries, the distinction retains greater vitality. A citizen, as opposed to a national, may designate an individual who is entitled to enjoy such political rights as voting and holding elective office.

The term "subject" has a lingering but diminished vitality on the current international scene. Its primary significance is within the British Commonwealth. The British Nationality Act of 1948, 11 & 12 Geo. 6, Ch. 56, as amended by the British Nationality Act of 1958, 6 & 7 Eliz. 2, Ch. 10, provided in Section 1 that every person who was a citizen of the United Kingdom or colonies, or a citizen of designated Commonwealth countries, would "by virtue of that citizenship have the status of British subject. . . . Any person having the status aforesaid may be known either as a British subject or as a Commonwealth citizen . . . ." Various prerogatives attached to the status of British subject, including immigration or entry privileges and the right to participate in the political life of the United Kingdom. Subsequent events and legislation in the United Kingdom have diminished the significance of this status by restricting rights such as immigration, and certain members of the British Commonwealth have barred their citizens from enjoying the simultaneous status of British subject or Commonwealth citizen. For the significance of such status as of the early 1960's see Wilson and Clute, Commonwealth Citizenship and Common Status, 57 Am.J.Int.L. 566 (1963).

Domicile is a concept that has significance to many fields of law. As is true of most terms serving such varied purposes, it eludes a clear definition. Domicile is basically a legal description of the relationship between a person and a particular territorial unit for a particular legal purpose. It can generally be identified with that unit in which an individual has his "home." That is, domicile usually refers to the state or nation with which an individual has his most significant personal connection. Various rules serve to identify the so-called "domicile of origin", or domicile at birth, frequently by reference to the domicile of one's father. American courts generally identify two criteria which must be met before a person can acquire a new domicile (domicile of choice): physical presence of the person in the new state or nation, and a present intention of that person to make that place his home (or at least, the absence of any present intention to make any other place his home).

It is important to bear in mind that statutes or courts may use the term to connote different kinds of relationships between a person and a territorial unit, sometimes relationships less intimate than the description above. The meaning of the term may vary with the purpose for which it is relevant, perhaps choice of law or adjudicatory jurisdiction or diversity of citizenship or taxation. Given this plurality of purposes and meanings, it has come to be recognized that an individual may at any one time have more than one domicile, at least for different purposes. Compare the following two statements:

> "The very meaning of domicile is the technically preëminent headquarters that every person is compelled to have in order that certain rights and duties that have been attached to it by the law may be determined. . . . In its nature it is one; and if in any case two are recognized for different purposes, it is a doubtful anomaly." Mr. Justice Holmes in Williamson v. Osenton, 232 U.S. 619, 625, 34 S.Ct. 442, 443, 58 L.Ed. 758, 761 (1913).

> "The presupposition of jurisdiction in this case is the common law doctrine of a single domiciliary status. That for purposes of legal rights and liabilities a person must have one domicile, and can have only one, is an historic rule of the common law and justified by much good sense. Nevertheless, it often represents a fiction. . . . Even assuming that there is general agreement as to the elements which in combination constitute domicile, a slight shift of emphasis in applying the formula produces contradictory results. But, on the whole, the doctrine of domicile has adequately served as a practical working rule in the simpler societies out of which it arose. . . . In view of the enormous extent to which intangibles now constitute wealth, and the increasing mobility of men, particularly men of substance, the necessity of a single headquarters for all legal purposes, particularly for purposes of taxation, tends to be a less and

less useful fiction. In the setting of modern circumstances, the inflexible doctrine of domicile—one man, one home—is in danger of becoming a social anachronism." Mr. Justice Frankfurter, dissenting in State of Texas v. State of Florida, 306 U.S. 398, 428, 59 S.Ct. 563, 577, 83 L.Ed. 817, 836 (1939).

The case which follows, Roboz v. Kennedy, requires the court to interpret also another term, "residence," which can be as elusive in content as domicile. It may be used to signify the same relationship to a nation that is indicated by domicile. It may suggest a less permanent presence. Statutory definitions of residence are often tailored to meet the needs of a particular legislative scheme. See, for example, Section 101(a)(33) of the Immigration and Nationality Act of 1952, which is relevant to such provisions as Section 301(a)(3).

Additional reading: Restatement Second, Conflict of Laws §§ 11–23 (1971); Goodrich, Conflict of Laws 30–61 (4th ed., Scoles, 1964); Reese and Green, That Elusive Word, "Residence," 6 Vand.L.Rev. 561 (1953).

QUESTION

Consider the difficulties involved in identifying the domicile or residence of John Doe, a British subject with a rented apartment in London, who spends several months each year at his bachelor resort house in France and five consecutive months each year in a rented apartment in New York, where he manages his American business interests. For what purposes would you imagine that administrative officials or courts in several nations might conclude that Doe was a local domiciliary or resident?

ROBOZ v. KENNEDY

United States District Court for the District of Columbia, 1963.
219 F.Supp. 892.

YOUNGDAHL, DISTRICT JUDGE. This is a suit for the return of property vested in the Attorney General under the International Claims Settlement Act, as amended in 1955 to deal with Bulgaria, Hungary, and Rumania, 22 U.S.C.A. § 1631. The suit is brought pursuant to § 1631f(a), which provides that any person who has not pursued an administrative remedy for the return of vested funds "may institute a suit in equity" in the United States District Court for the District of Columbia "by the filing of a complaint which alleges—"

> "(1) that the claimant is a person other than Bulgaria, Hungary, or Rumania, or a national thereof as defined in Executive Order 8389 of April 10, 1940, as amended; and
>
> "(2) that the claimant was the owner of such property immediately prior to its vesting, or is the successor in interest of such owner by inheritance, devise, or bequest."

Plaintiff has made both these essential allegations. The defendant, however, has moved to dismiss the complaint for lack of jurisdiction on the ground that the plaintiffs are "nationals" of Hungary within the meaning of Executive Order 8389, mentioned in paragraph (1), supra, the so-called "freezing order" of April 10, 1940, set forth following 12 U.S.C.A. § 95a.

Executive Order 8389 defines the word "national" to include:

> "Any person who has been domiciled in, or a subject, citizen or resident of a foreign country at any time on or since the effective date of this Order . . . ."

The Order was applied to Hungary on March 13, 1941. 6 F.R. 2897. The issue, therefore, is whether the undisputed facts demonstrate that plaintiffs were "domiciled in, or a subject, citizen or resident of" Hungary after March 13, 1941. If the facts do so demonstrate, then defendant's motion must be granted and the case dismissed.

The following facts must be accepted as true for purposes of this motion. Plaintiffs are mother and son, the widow and sole child, respectively, of Erno Vincze, a Jew who was killed in the Dachau concentration camp on January 14, 1945, and who before the war was one of Hungary's leading leather manufacturers. In 1940, when Jews were being persecuted, Erno Vincze transferred funds to New York; it is the proceeds of these funds which plaintiffs seek in this action. On May 28, 1940, within several weeks after the transfer of these funds to New York, Erno Vincze was arrested without charge, was placed in the Margit-Korut military prison in Budapest, was "beaten inhumanly" for weeks, his factory was seized by the government, and he did not face charges for over two years. His wife, one of the plaintiffs herein, tried unsuccessfully to find a lawyer who would help her obtain her husband's release. She then wrote a letter to a government ministry pointing out that her husband had been imprisoned without any charges having been given. Shortly thereafter, she was arrested too, and was imprisoned without charge for nine months. While she was in prison, her husband was tried by a secret military tribunal, which found him guiilty of certain (unspecified) crimes, and sentenced him to eleven years in prison. He remained in the Margit-Korut prison until the Russian troops approached Budapest in December, 1944. He was then sent to Dachau, and was killed in a gas chamber on January 14, 1945.

In the meantime, all of the family's business property was confiscated. The two plaintiffs herein were forced to abandon their home and move to designated "Jewish houses" where ten strangers lived in one room and from which plaintiffs were allowed to leave for only two hours each day. Plaintiffs could not vote, they could not earn a living, they lacked police protection, and they had no access to the courts. Thousands of Jews were being sent to concentration camps, but plaintiffs escaped such fate by hiding in fields and cellars. They were in Budapest all during this period.

As far as plaintiffs' intent is concerned, the mother states as follows:

> "In view of the increasing Nazi orientation of the Hungarian Government, my husband and I had made plans since 1939 to leave Hungary permanently. . . . Both my son and I obtained United States visas in 1940 and were to leave Hungary in 1940 forever. The imprisonment of my husband made this impossible and was the only reason why we did not leave in 1940. I made every possible attempt to secure his release with a view to fleeing the country if I succeeded. We wanted to leave the country at whatever cost as soon as my husband had been released. Unable to obtain his release, we did not depart solely because of the dire consequences to my husband which could be expected to follow our departure."

Immediately after the war, the mother states that her intention continued to be to leave Hungary:

> "Continuing my resolve to leave the country which had subjected me to such unspeakable persecution and which immediately fell under a dictatorship of a different hue, I could hardly wait to leave the blood stained soil and made every effort to depart at the earliest possible moment. I finally succeeded . . . early in 1947, and arrived in the United States in May 1947 resolved never to return to Hungary under any circumstances."

The son became a United States citizen in 1952. The mother did so in 1954. Both have resided in the United States continually from their arrival in 1947. They arrived in 1947 on visitors' visas.

Given these facts, were plaintiffs "domiciled in, or a subject, citizen or resident of" Hungary within the meaning and purpose of the International Claims Settlement Act? All of the words in that definition imply some reciprocal duties and obligations between the person and the country. The facts as outlined above demonstrate conclusively that plaintiffs had a firm and continuing intent to leave Hungary forever before March 13, 1941, the date Executive Order 8389 was applied to Hungary. In addition, they lost their home, they had no rights in law, they could not vote. Clearly, they were involuntarily in Hungary. They therefore cannot be considered either domiciled in, or subjects, citizens or residents of Hungary for purposes of a suit under 22 U.S.C.A. § 1631f(a). Congress could not have intended so inequitable a result, and Congress has specified that, in proceedings under this section, this Court sits as a court "in equity." Ibid.

This is apparently a case of first impression under this statute, since the only other reported case was dismissed because the claimant failed to allege that she was not a "national" of her country of origin, Rumania. Schrager-Singer v. Attorney General of the United States, 106 U.S.App.D.C. 258, 271 F.2d 841 (1959). There are, however, cases under section 9(a) of the Trading with the Enemy Act, 50 U.S.C.A. App. § 9(a), which are analogous, and support the Court's conclusion. See McGrath v. Zander, 85 U.S.App.D.C. 334, 177 F.2d 649 (1949); Kaku Nagano v. McGrath, 187 F.2d 759 (7th Cir., 1951); Guessefeldt v. McGrath, 342 U.S. 308, 72 S.Ct. 338, 96 L.Ed. 342 (1952). "[O]ur concept of a citizen is one who has the right to exercise all the political and civil privileges extended by his government . . . . Citizenship conveys the idea of membership in a nation." Kaku Nagano, supra, 187 F.2d at 768. "'"[R]esident within the territory" . . . connotes something different from and more than living within the specified areas. It is rather indicative of a settled and permanent place of abode, volitionally acquired and voluntarily assumed. . . .'" McGrath v. Zander, 85 U.S. App.D.C. at 337, 177 F.2d at 652. "Such legislation strongly counsels against literalness of application. It favors a wise latitude of construction in enforcing its purposes." Guessefeldt, 342 U.S. at 319, 72 S.Ct. at 344, 96 L.Ed. 342.

The defendant's motion will therefore be denied.

COMMENT

Compare Stifel v. Hopkins, 477 F.2d 1116 (6th Cir. 1973), holding that for purposes of diversity jurisdiction, a federal prisoner would not be precluded from establishing domicile within the state of his incarceration by showing that he had developed the requisite intention to be domiciled there. It was not conclusive that his presence in that state was initially involuntary and resulted from circumstances beyond his control. The court noted by way of analogy that refugees forced to leave a country for fear of political persecution can establish a domicile in the jurisdiction in which they (are in some sense forced to) seek asylum.

QUESTIONS

(1) Suppose that before the plaintiffs became United States citizens, they acquired a domicile in New Jersey, and that either had brought a tort action in a federal district court in New York to recover damages of $15,000 against a United States citizen domiciled in that state. Would the district court have had jurisdiction under 28 U.S.C.A. § 1332?

(2) The court states that all four terms in the definition of "national" imply "some reciprocal duties and obligations between the person and the country." Do you agree? Which of these terms could most readily be construed to imply significant duties and obligations?

B. IMMIGRATION AND DEPORTATION

NOTE ON IMMIGRATION LAWS AND POLICIES

We here consider the legal framework for the historical and contemporary regulation of immigration, together with those changing policies which have determined from time to time the content of the immigration laws. You should read the provisions of the Immigration and Nationality Act of 1952 that are designated below by an asterisk.

The Historical Development

With relatively minor exceptions, governmental policy from 1789 to the early 20th Century favored unfettered immigration. Rapid westward expansion and the dynamic growth of the economy meant that important economic purposes were served through a growing population. Moreover, immigration proved attractive to many Europeans from both an economic perspective and that of realizing cherished ideals. Not only were there job opportunities but also the sense of a promised land, an escape from religious or ethnic persecution, a haven for the foundation of a new and better life.

But concern over economic competition from immigrants together with racial prejudices led to increasing pressure by the end of the 19th Century to restrict immigration. Laws excluding Orientals and aliens within certain categories (paupers, felons, certain contract laborers and so on) were enacted during those decades, which witnessed a marked change in the ethnic composition of immigrants. In the decade 1871–80, 74% of the immigrants came from Northern and Western Europe. From 1901 to 1910, approximately 22% of the immigrants came from these areas, while immigrants from Southern and Eastern Europe accounted for 71% of the arrivals.

A fear, acute within the nascent labor union movement, that immigration meant keener competition for jobs, combined with fears of "old stock" Americans of a dramatically changed ethnic complexion to produce the first comprehensive restrictive laws. Legislation between 1917 and 1921 added new restrictive categories, and the 1921 laws initiated the national quota system which survived until 1965. An act of 1924 based its quota provisions upon "national origin," excluded various Oriental groups, and incorporated a new formula for computing and distributing annual immigration quotas. The 1952 Act, enacted over President Truman's veto, continued many of these policies.

The "national-origin" system as defined under the 1924 and 1952 acts tended to preserve the "racial" or "national-origin" composition of the United States as of 1920, since the quotas for immigrants from any one nation were calculated in terms of 1/6 of 1% of persons of that national origin then in the United States. There was an absolute ceiling of 2,000 upon immigrants originating (even several generations removed) from the so-called "Asia-Pacific Triangle," embracing most Far Eastern countries. The 1952 Act provided for a total of some 150,000 quota immigrants per year. The quota system so divided this total that substantial allocations, ranging up to 65,000 immigrants from Great Britain, were available for many European countries, and minimal quotas of 100 immigrants attached to many other countries. The larger quotas in fact remained unused to a substantial extent, while applicants from countries with minimal quotas remained on long waiting lists. Immigrants born within any independent country in the Western Hemisphere, subject to certain exceptions, were not however held to the quota limitations.

The quota system exposed the contradictions within the prevailing ideology of an earlier period of our history, that of the "melting pot" within which all new immigrants were to be absorbed to compose one homogeneous American people. Rather, pluralistic groups that were defined in racial, religious and ethnic as well as economic terms had become rooted and dominant features of American culture and politics. Such groups, whether organized as a labor union or church or ethnic community, could then begin to perceive new arrivals as threats to an already precarious "balance."

The harsh consequences of the quota system were alleviated by special legislation after World War II, particularly to benefit displaced persons and refugees. Many domestic groups attacked the principle of national quotas as expressive of racist biases that should not be incorporated into law. Some of its aspects, such as the provisions governing the Asia-Pacific triangle, were unsuccessfully challenged in the courts as violating the Constitution and various international agreements. See Hitai v. Immigration and Naturalization Service,

343 F.2d 466 (2d Cir. 1965). The United States was frequently confronted by the protests of foreign governments and by tensions in its foreign relations caused by the inconsistency between its democratic, egalitarian protestations and restrictive, discriminatory practices. The forces for change finally led to a congressional review of the 1952 Act, pursuant to a Presidential recommendation, and the passage of the 1965 amendments.

The key features of the allocation of immigrant visas under the 1965 revision are: (1) the abolition of the national-origin system as of June 30, 1968, with transitional provisions for the pooling of unused quotas; (2) the establishment of a new system for admission of up to 170,000 immigrants per fiscal year, with preferences allocated under Section 203 * on the basis of a series of priorities such as family ties (which became more significant under the revision) and occupational skills; (3) the establishment of a limit of 20,000 per fiscal year (with several exceptions) on immigrants from any one country; and (4) the establishment of a category of "special immigrants," including those born in Western Hemisphere countries, who benefit from a separate quota of 120,000 per fiscal year, and of other categories (e. g., immediate relatives) outside the quota system. Note that the subjection of immigrants from Western Hemisphere countries to a quota was among several provisions of the 1965 revision which had a restrictive effect upon immigration.

Another critical provision tightening requirements for immigration is found in Section 212(a)(14)*, which grants the Secretary of Labor increased authority to protect the domestic labor market from the competition of nonimmigrant aliens and certain categories of immigrant aliens. Note the finding which must be made (by the Manpower Administration of the Department of Labor as delegee of the Secretary) that there are not sufficient workers in the United States who are "able, willing, qualified, and available" to perform the skilled or unskilled labor designated by the alien applicant. That finding must conclude that alien employment "will not adversely affect the wages and working conditions" of similarly employed resident workers. The recurring court decisions which have found an inadequate basis for denials by the Manpower Administration of requests for labor certification suggest the stringent criteria applied in the bureaucratic processing.[5]

In view of the blend of liberalizing and restrictive amendments, it was difficult to anticipate what effect the 1965 revisions would have upon the annual average over the preceding decade of about 295,000 admitted aliens. The early experience under the Act demonstrated that it dramatically changed immigration patterns.[6] Among immigrants, there was an increased percentage of professional and tech-

5. See, e. g., the holding of an abuse of discretion by the Manpower Administration in Acupuncture Center of Washington v. Brennan, 364 F.Supp. 1038 (D.D.C.1974).

6. The data in the text is taken from the New York Times, August 31, 1970, p. 1, and from Keely, Immigration Composition and Population Policy, 185 Science 587 (August 16, 1974).

nical workers, and a sharp decrease in clerical workers—30% and 10% professional and clerical from 1969–1972. Such changes, together with increased immigration of relatives of citizens and permanent residents, responded to the new preference priorities of Section 203 *. English, Irish, Dutch, and German immigrants were being replaced by increased numbers from such countries as the Philipines, China, Italy, Greece and several African countries. From 1961–1965, Europeans constituted 42% of immigrants; from 1969–1972, 28%. The revisions did intensify the problem of long waiting lists of applicants for immigrant visas, particularly in the Western Hemisphere countries whose residents now must compete under the 120,000 hemispheric total. For fiscal year 1970, a total of 358,000 immigrants were admitted to this country; while over 400,000 were admitted in fiscal year 1973.

The 1965 amendments left intact much of the structure of the 1952 Act. Aliens entering the United States are classified within two major categories: immigrants, as to whom the preceding rules apply, and nonimmigrants, those aliens desiring to spend a limited or unlimited period of time in the United States but not entitled to acquire citizenship. The classification of nonimmigrant aliens appears in Section 101(a)(15)*. All aliens entering the country must possess stated documents, including a passport or its equivalent issued by the alien's government and a visa of the appropriate category issued by the Department of State. In addition to qualifying for admission as an immigrant or nonimmigrant, all aliens must survive general exclusionary tests set forth in Section 212 *. Note the related definitions in Section 101(a)(37) and (40)*. After entry, both immigrants and nonimmigrants are subject to special statutory regulation, which includes requirements of registration and periodic reporting. Immigrant aliens desiring to become citizens through naturalization must meet detailed statutory requirements.

Mexican Immigrants and Agricultural Labor: An Illustration

By suggesting the degree to which fear of economic competition and a lower living standard explain restrictive immigration policies, the preceding description introduces a recurring issue in this book. To what extent does the historical or contemporary nation-state perceive itself as an autonomous framework for welfare maximization? To what extent does it view itself as part of a larger process and community, and thus responsive to policies of redistribution of welfare among nations? These questions are illustrated by the contrast between the immigration provisions described above and the developing policies and laws with respect to the free movement of workers within the European Economic Community, pp. 1326–1330, infra.

Within this country, the conflicting welfare considerations at work within the immigration laws are highlighted by the problem of Mexican agricultural laborers.[7] The so-called *bracero* program—Mexi-

7. Some information in this discussion is taken from Note, Alien in the Fields: The "Green-Card Commuter" Under the Immigration and Nationali-

can contract laborers working in the United States pursuant to provisions of our agricultural legislation—was initiated in 1943 to solve wartime labor shortages.[8] Congress terminated the program in 1964, thus raising issues of law and policy about the status of the seasonal Mexican commuters who spent several months each year in American fields, and of the daily commuters from the border areas with homes in Mexico and work in the United States. Since the Mexican "commuters" were willing to work at wages unacceptable to United States residents, severe wage competition resulted. The presence of these workers was viewed hostilely by labor unions seeking to organize domestic farm laborers, and thus to control or eliminate the supply of alien laborers to whom American farmers could turn for seasonal aid. Thus both wage competition and intensification of the organizational problems of unions in border areas resulted from the *bracero* program.

In 1968 there were about 45,000 daily commuters, upon whom perhaps 250,000 Mexican family members were dependent. Thus the Mexican government had an interest in the outcome of our domestic debate about what, if any, commitment we had made to present commuters, and about the degree to which border regions would be viewed as interdependently Mexican and American for economic viability.

Recall that the 1965 amendments added to the protection of United States labor from job competition and adverse working standards through Section 212(a)(14). But the INS has viewed the Mexican commuters whose work and migratory patterns had developed before termination of the *bracero* program in 1964 as "returning immigrants," since they were initially admitted to this country as immigrant aliens. Thus the INS took the administrative position that certification under Section 212(a)(14) was unnecessary, for that provision does not apply to returning immigrants.

That position has been attacked in several court actions brought by United States citizens and by organizing committees for labor unions. In Saxbe v. Bustos, 419 U.S. 65, 95 S.Ct. 272, 42 L.Ed.2d 231 (1974), the Court concluded that the long-standing administrative practice of the INS was valid, both for seasonal and daily commuters. Neither category should be classified as non-immigrant. It found that the administrative practice of not requiring certifications under Section 212(a)(14) was well known to the Congress which had never disavowed it. The Court stressed the "considerable" dimensions of the problem, and cited an estimate that if Mexican commuters were cut off, their annual losses would be about $50 million.

Additional reading: Jaffe, The Philosophy of Our Immigration Law, 21 Law & Contemp.Prob. 358 (1956); Scully, Is the Door Open

ty Laws, 21 Stan.L.Rev. 1750 (1969), and from the account in the opinion in Bustos v. Mitchell, 156 U.S.App.D.C. 304, 481 F.2d 479 (1973), aff'd in part and rev'd in part sub nom. Saxbe v. Bustos, 419 U.S. 65, 95 S.Ct. 272, 42 L.Ed.2d 231 (1974).

8. The *braceros* should be distinguished from the so-called "wetbacks", a term referring to Mexican agricultural laborers who illegally enter the United States by crossing the Rio Grande.

Again?—A Survey of Our New Immigration Law, 13 U.C.L.A. L.Rev. 227 (1966); Developments in the Law—Immigration and Nationality, 66 Harv. L.Rev. 643 (1953). Two comprehensive texts are Gordon and Rosenfield, Immigration Law and Procedure (rev. ed. 1969) and Wasserman, Immigration Law and Practice (1961).

QUESTION

"With few exceptions, there are no convincing economic arguments today for extensive immigration. Of course, if this country has shortages in specific areas—such as medical personnel or other qualified professionals—it should encourage competent foreigners in such fields to immigrate and remain. But there are no other persuasive arguments for permitting other than nominal, symbolic immigration. We are not a haven for the underprivileged of this world. Any attempt to absorb significant numbers of the needy, of political refugees, or of other categories of aliens would only serve to lower our welfare standards."

Do you agree with these observations? If not, what arguments would you advance today to support larger immigration quotas, and what distinctions would you draw (to establish immigration priorities) among categories of immigrants defined in terms of ethnic or national groups, job or professional competences, reasons for desiring immigration, or other terms? (Note in this connection not only aggregate and specific quotas, but also the preference priorities of Section 203.)

FONG YUE TING v. UNITED STATES

Supreme Court of the United States, 1893.
149 U.S. 698, 13 S.Ct. 1016, 37 L.Ed. 905.

[An act of 1892 required that Chinese laborers in the United States acquire certificates of residence, within a stated period, and that all Chinese laborers without such certificates would be deemed unlawfully within the United States and would be deported. The certificates were to be issued upon presentation of applications, which were to include satisfactory proof of the residence and lawful status of the applicant within the United States. These cases arose upon petitions for writs of habeas corpus of Chinese laborers who were held for deportation because of their failure to acquire the certificates of residence or inability to acquire them under the strict requirements of proof stated by the act. The writs were dismissed by a United States Circuit Court. Excerpts from the opinion upon appeal of the Supreme Court, delivered by JUSTICE GRAY and affirming dismissal of the writs, appear below.]

In the recent case of Nishimura Ekiu v. U. S., 142 U.S. 651, 659, 12 S.Ct. 336, the court, in sustaining the action of the executive department, putting in force an act of congress for the exclusion of aliens, said: "It is an accepted maxim of international law that every sovereign nation has the power, as inherent in sovereignty, and essential to self-preservation, to forbid the entrance of foreigners within its dominions, or to admit them only in such cases and upon such conditions as it may see fit to prescribe. In the United States this power is vested in the national government, to which the constitution has committed the entire control of international relations, in peace as well as in war. It belongs to the political department of the government, and may be exercised either through treaties made by the president and senate or through statutes enacted by congress."

The same views were more fully expounded in the earlier case of Chae Chan Ping v. U. S., 130 U.S. 581, 9 S.Ct. 623, in which the validity of a former act of congress, excluding Chinese laborers from the United States, under the circumstances therein stated, was affirmed.

In the elaborate opinion delivered by Mr. Justice Field in behalf of the court it was said: . . . "To preserve its independence, and give security against foreign aggression and encroachment, is the highest duty of every nation; and to attain these ends nearly all other considerations are to be subordinated. It matters not in what form such aggression and encroachment come, whether from the foreign nation acting in its national character, or from vast hordes of its people crowding in upon us. The government, possessing the powers which are to be exercised for protection and security, is clothed with authority to determine the occasion on which the powers shall be called forth; and its determination, so far as the subjects affected are concerned, is necessarily conclusive upon all its departments and officers. If, therefore, the government of the United States, through its legislative department, considers the presence of foreigners of a different race in this country, who will not assimilate with us, to be dangerous to its peace and security, their exclusion is not to be stayed because at the time there are no actual hostilities with the nation of which the foreigners are subjects. The existence of war would render the necessity of the proceeding only more obvious and pressing. The same necessity, in a less pressing degree, may arise when war does not exist, and the same authority which adjudges the necessity in one case must also determine it in the other. In both cases its determination is conclusive upon the judiciary. If the government of the country of which the foreigners excluded are subjects is dissatisfied with this action, it can make complaint to the executive head of our government, or resort to any other measure which, in its judgment, its interests or dignity may demand; and there lies its only remedy. The power of the government to exclude foreigners from the country, whenever, in its judgment, the public interests require such exclusion, has been asserted in repeated instances, and never denied by the executive or legislative departments." . . .

The right of a nation to expel or deport foreigners who have not been naturalized or taken any steps towards becoming citizens of the country, rests upon the same grounds, and is as absolute and unqualified, as the right to prohibit and prevent their entrance into the country. . . .

The statements of leading commentators on the law of nations are to the same effect.

Vattel says: "Every nation has the right to refuse to admit a foreigner into the country, when he cannot enter without putting the nation in evident danger, or doing it a manifest injury. What it owes to itself, the care of its own safety, gives it this right; and, in virtue of its natural liberty, it belongs to the nation to judge whether its circumstances will or will not justify the admission of the foreigner." "Thus, also, it has a right to send them elsewhere, if it has just cause to fear that they will corrupt the manners of the citizens; that they will create religious disturbances, or occasion any other disorder, contrary to the public safety. In a word, it has a right, and is even obliged, in this respect, to follow the rules which prudence dictates." Vatt.Law Nat. lib. 1, c. 19, §§ 230, 231. . . .

The right to exclude or to expel all aliens, or any class of aliens, absolutely or upon certain conditions, in war or in peace, being an inherent and inalienable right of every sovereign and independent nation, essential to its safety, its independence, and its welfare, the question now before the court is whether the manner in which congress has exercised this right in sections 6 and 7 of the act of 1892 is consistent with the constitution. . . .

In exercising the great power which the people of the United States, by establishing a written constitution as the supreme and paramount law, have vested in this court, of determining, whenever the question is properly brought before it, whether the acts of the legislature or of the executive are consistent with the constitution, it behooves the court to be careful that it does not undertake to pass upon political questions, the final decision of which has been committed by the constitution to the other departments of the government. . . .

Before examining in detail the provisions of the act of 1892, now in question, it will be convenient to refer to the previous statutes, treaties, and decisions upon the subject.

[The Court traced the history of the treaties and statutes relating to the exclusion of the Chinese.]

In the case of Chae Chan Ping, already often referred to, a Chinese laborer, who had resided in San Francisco from 1875 until June 2, 1887, when he left that port for China, having in his possession a certificate issued to him on that day by the collector of customs, according to the act of 1884, and in terms entitling him to return to the United States, returned to the same port on October 8, 1888, and was refused by the collector permission to land, because of the provisions of the act of October 1, 1888, above cited. It was strongly contended in his behalf that by his residence in the United States for 12 years preceding June 2, 1887, in accordance with the fifth article of the treaty of 1868, he had now a lawful right to be in the United States, and had a vested right to return to the United States, which could not be taken from him by any exercise of mere legislative power by congress. . . .

Yet the court unanimously held that the statute of 1888 was constitutional, and that the action of the collector in refusing him permission to land was lawful. . . .

It thus appears that in that case it was directly adjudged, upon full argument and consideration, that a Chinese laborer, who had been admitted into the United States while the treaty of 1868 was in force, by which the United States and China "cordially recognize the inherent and inalienable right of man to change his home and allegiance, and also the mutual advantage of the free migration and emigration of their citizens and subjects, respectively, from one country to the other," not only for the purpose of curiosity or of trade, but "as permanent residents," and who had continued to reside here for 12 years, and who had then gone back to China, after receiving a certificate, in the form provided by act of congress, entitling him to return to the United States, might be refused readmission into the United States, without judicial trial or hearing, and simply by reason of another act of congress, passed during his absence, and declaring all such certificates to be void, and prohibiting all Chinese laborers who had at any time been residents in the United States, and had departed therefrom and not returned before the passage of this act, from coming into the United States. . . .

Chinese laborers, therefore, like all other aliens residing in the United States for a shorter or longer time, are entitled, so long as they are permitted by the government of the United States to remain in the country, to the safeguards of the constitution, and to the protection of the laws, in regard to their rights of person and of property, and to their civil and criminal responsibility. But they continue to be aliens, having taken no steps towards becoming citizens, and incapable of becoming such under the naturalization laws; and therefore remain subject to the power of congress to expel them, or to order them to be removed and deported from the country, whenever, in its judgment, their removal is necessary or expedient for the public interest. . . .

Upon careful consideration of the subject, the only conclusion which appears to us to be consistent with the principles of international law, with the constitution and laws of the United States, and with the previous decisions of this court, is that in each of these cases the judgment of the circuit court dismissing the writ of habeas corpus is right, and must be affirmed.

[Dissenting opinions of JUSTICE BREWER, JUSTICE FIELD and CHIEF JUSTICE FULLER have been omitted. JUSTICE BREWER rested his dissent on several grounds, statutory and constitutional. His closing paragraph inquired: "In view of this enactment [that is, the 1892 Act] of the highest legislative body of the foremost Christian nation, may not the thoughtful Chinese disciple of Confucius fairly ask, 'Why do they send missionaries here?' "]

HARISIADES v. SHAUGHNESSY

Supreme Court of the United States, 1952.
342 U.S. 580, 72 S.Ct. 512, 96 L.Ed. 586.

[The Alien Registration Act of 1940 amended prior laws to authorize the deportation of a legally resident alien who had been a member of an organization advocating overthrow of the Government by force and violence, even though the alien's membership terminated before enactment of the Act.

Harisiades, a Greek national, came to the United States in 1916 when 13 years of age. He took a wife and sired two children, all citizens. In 1925, Harisiades joined the Communist Party (then known as the Workers Party), and acted as an organizer and editor of a paper. His membership was discontinued in 1939. Harisiades disclaimed personal belief in the use of force and violence but stated that he believed in the general philosophy of the Communist Party.

Mascitti, an Italian citizen, came to the United States in 1920, when 16 years old. He married and had an American-born child. He was a member of the Communist Party between 1923 and 1929. Mascitti stated that he was aware of the Party's advocacy of force and violence if necessary, and said that he did not personally believe in violence. He resigned from the Party in 1929, apparently because he lost sympathy with it.

Mrs. Coleman, a native of Russia, came to the United States in 1914, when 13 years old. She married and had three American-born children. She was a member of the Communist Party in 1919, from 1928 to 1930, and from 1936 to 1938, but she held no office and her activities were not significant. She disavowed much knowledge of party principles and claimed that she had joined on each occasion because of some injustice which the Party was then fighting.

Each of the three aliens was ordered deported because each, after entry into the United States, had been a member of an organization advocating overthrow of the Government by force and violence. Each sought relief from deportation in the federal courts, and each obtained review in the Supreme Court of denials of relief by the lower courts. The three aliens challenged the 1940 Act on grounds that it deprived them of liberty without due process of law in violation of the Fifth Amendment; that it abridged their freedoms of speech and assembly in violation of the First Amendment; and that it was an *ex post facto* law in violation of Article I, Section 9 of the Constitution.

Excerpts from the opinion of the Court, delivered by JUSTICE JACKSON, appear below.]

We have in each case a finding, approved by the court below, that the Communist Party during the period of the alien's membership taught and advocated overthrow of the Government of the United States by force and violence. Those findings are not questioned here.

These aliens ask us to forbid their expulsion by a departure from the long-accepted application to such cases of the Fifth Amendment provision that no person shall be deprived of life, liberty or property without due process of law. Their basic contention is that admission for permanent residence confers a "vested right" on the alien, equal to that of the citizen, to remain within the country, and that the alien is entitled to constitutional protection in that matter to the same extent as the citizen. Their second line of defense is that if any power to deport domiciled aliens exists it is so dispersed that the judiciary must concur in the grounds for its exercise to the extent of finding them reasonable. The argument goes on to the contention that the grounds prescribed by the Act of 1940 bear no reasonable relation to protection of legitimate interests of the United States and concludes that the Act should be declared invalid. Admittedly these propositions are not founded in precedents of this Court.

For over thirty years each of these aliens has enjoyed such advantages as accrue from residence here without renouncing his foreign allegiance or formally acknowledging adherence to the Constitution he now invokes. Each was admitted to the United States, upon passing formidable exclusionary hurdles, in the hope that, after what may be called a probationary period, he would desire and be found desirable for citizenship. Each has been offered naturalization, with all of the rights and privileges of citizenship, conditioned only upon open and honest assumption of undivided allegiance to our government. But acceptance was and is not compulsory. Each has been permitted to prolong his original nationality indefinitely.

So long as one thus perpetuates a dual status as an American inhabitant but foreign citizen, he may derive advantages from two sources of law—American and international. He may claim protection against our Government unavailable to the citizen. As an alien he retains a claim upon the state of his citizenship to diplomatic intervention on his behalf, a patronage often of considerable value. The state of origin of each of these aliens could presently enter diplomatic remonstrance against these deportations if they were inconsistent with international law, the prevailing custom among nations or their own practices.

The alien retains immunities from burdens which the citizen must shoulder. By withholding his allegiance from the United States, he leaves outstanding a foreign call on his loyalties which international law not only permits our Government to recognize but commands it to respect. In deference to it certain dispensations from conscription for any military service have been granted foreign nationals. They cannot, consistently with our international commitments, be compeled "to take part in the operations of war directed against their own country." In addition to such general immunities they may enjoy particular treaty privileges.

Under our law, the alien in several respects stands on an equal footing with citizens, but in others has never been conceded legal parity with the citizen. Most importantly, to protract this ambiguous status within the country is not his right but is a matter of permission and tolerance. The Government's power to terminate its hospitality has been asserted and sustained by this Court since the question first arose.

War, of course, is the most usual occasion for extensive resort to the power. Though the resident alien may be personally loyal to the United States, if his nation becomes our enemy his allegiance prevails over his personal preference and makes him also our enemy, liable to expulsion or internment, and his property becomes subject to seizure and perhaps confiscation. But it does not require war to bring the power of deportation into existence or to authorize its exercise. Congressional apprehension of foreign or internal dangers short of war may lead to its use. So long as the alien elects to continue the ambiguity of his allegiance his domicile here is held by a precarious tenure.

That aliens remain vulnerable to expulsion after long residence is a practice that bristles with severities. But it is a weapon of defense and reprisal confirmed by international law as a power inherent in every sovereign state. Such is the traditional power of the Nation over the alien and we leave the law on the subject as we find it.

This brings us to the alternative defense under the Due Process Clause—that, granting the power, it is so unreasonably and harshly exercised by this enactment that it should be held unconstitutional.

In historical context the Act before us stands out as an extreme application of the expulsion power. There is no denying that as world convulsions have driven us toward a closed society the expulsion power has been exercised with increasing severity, manifest in multiplication of grounds for deportation, in expanding the subject classes from illegal entrants to legal residents, and in greatly lengthening the period of residence after which one may be expelled.[9] This is said to have reached a point where it is the duty of this Court to call a halt upon the political branches of the Government.

It is pertinent to observe that any policy toward aliens is vitally and intricately interwoven with contemporaneous policies in regard

9. An open door to the immigrant was the early federal policy. It began to close in 1884 when Orientals were excluded. 23 Stat. 115. Thereafter, Congress has intermittently added to the excluded classes, and as rejections at the border multiplied illegal entries increased. To combat these, recourse was had to deportation in the Act of 1891, 26 Stat. 1086. . . .

From those early steps, the policy has been extended. In 1910, new classes of resident aliens were listed for deportation, including for the first time political offenders such as anarchists and those believing in or advocating the overthrow of the Government by force and violence. 36 Stat. 264. In 1917, aliens who were found after entry to be advocating anarchist doctrines or the overthrow of the Government by force and violence were made subject to deportation, a five-year time limit being retained. 39 Stat. 889. A year later, deportability because of membership in described subversive organizations was introduced. 40 Stat. 1012; 41 Stat. 1008. . . .

to the conduct of foreign relations, the war power, and the maintenance of a republican form of government. Such matters are so exclusively entrusted to the political branches of government as to be largely immune from judicial inquiry or interference.

These restraints upon the judiciary, occasioned by different events, do not control today's decision but they are pertinent. It is not necessary and probably not possible to delineate a fixed and precise line of separation in these matters between political and judicial power under the Constitution. Certainly, however, nothing in the structure of our Government or the text of our Constitution would warrant judicial review by standards which would require us to equate our political judgment with that of Congress.

Under the conditions which produced this Act, can we declare that congressional alarm about a coalition of Communist power without and Communist conspiracy within the United States is either a fantasy or a pretense? . . .

Congress received evidence that the Communist movement here has been heavily laden with aliens and that Soviet control of the American Communist Party has been largely through alien Communists. It would be easy for those of us who do not have security responsibility to say that those who do are taking Communism too seriously and overestimating its danger. But we have an Act of one Congress which, for a decade, subsequent Congresses have never repealed but have strengthened and extended. We, in our private opinions, need not concur in Congress' policies to hold its enactments constitutional. Judicially we must tolerate what personally we may regard as a legislative mistake.

We are urged, because the policy inflicts severe and undoubted hardship on affected individuals, to find a restraint in the Due Process Clause. But the Due Process Clause does not shield the citizen from conscription and the consequent calamity of being separated from family, friends, home and business while he is transported to foreign lands to stem the tide of Communism. If Communist aggression creates such hardships for loyal citizens, it is hard to find justification for holding that the Constitution requires that its hardships must be spared the Communist alien. . . .

We think that, in the present state of the world, it would be rash and irresponsible to reinterpret our fundamental law to deny or qualify the Government's power of deportation. However desirable worldwide amelioration of the lot of aliens, we think it is peculiarly a subject for international diplomacy. It should not be initiated by judicial decision which can only deprive our own Government of a power of defense and reprisal without obtaining for American citizens abroad any reciprocal privileges or immunities. Reform in this field must be entrusted to the branches of the Government in control of our international relations and treaty-making powers.

We hold that the Act is not invalid under the Due Process Clause. These aliens are not entitled to judicial relief unless some other constitutional limitation has been transgressed, to which inquiry we turn.

[The Court, citing Dennis v. United States, 341 U.S. 494, 71 S.Ct. 857, 95 L.Ed. 1137 (1951), held that the First Amendment did not protect the practice or incitement of violence and did not prevent the deportation of these aliens. With respect to the contention that the Act conflicted with the Ex Post Facto Clause (Art. I, Sec. 9 of the Constitution), the Court first stated that Congress had maintained since 1920 a "standing admonition to aliens, on pain of deportation, not to become members of any organization that advocates overthrow of the United States government by force and violence, a category repeatedly held to include the Communist Party." Thus the Court raised doubt whether the Act indeed was retroactive in application. Then, assuming that the Act were found to be retroactive, the Court observed that the Clause had always been considered to forbid penal legislation imposing or increasing criminal punishment for conduct which was lawful previous to its enactment. The Court stated:]

. . . Deportation, however severe its consequences, has been consistently classified as a civil rather than a criminal procedure. Both of these doctrines as original proposals might be debatable, but both have been considered closed for many years and a body of statute and decisional law has been built upon them. In Bugajewitz v. Adams, 228 U.S. 585, 591, 33 S.Ct. 607, 608, 57 L.Ed. 978, Mr. Justice Holmes, for the Court, said: "It is thoroughly established that Congress has power to order the deportation of aliens whose presence in the country it deems hurtful. The determination by facts that might constitute a crime under local law is not a conviction of crime, nor is the deportation a punishment; it is simply a refusal by the government to harbor persons whom it does not want. The coincidence of the local penal law with the policy of Congress is an accident. . . . The prohibition of *ex post facto* laws in article 1, § 9, has no application . . . and with regard to the petitioner, it is not necessary to construe the statute as having any retrospective effect."

. . .

When the Communist Party as a matter of party strategy formally expelled alien members en masse, it destroyed any significance that discontinued membership might otherwise have as indication of change of heart by the individual. Congress may have believed that the party tactics threw upon the Government an almost impossible burden if it attempted to separate those who sincerely renounced Communist principles of force and violence from those who left the party the better to serve it. Congress, exercising the wide discretion that it alone has in these matters, declined to accept that as the Government's burden.

We find none of the constitutional objections to the Act well founded. The judgments accordingly are affirmed.

MR. JUSTICE FRANKFURTER, concurring.

It is not for this Court to reshape a world order based on politically sovereign States. In such an international ordering of the world a national State implies a special relationship of one body of people, *i. e.*, citizens of that State, whereby the citizens of each State are aliens in relation to every other State. . . . Though as a matter of political outlook and economic need this country has traditionally welcomed aliens to come to its shores, it has done so exclusively as a matter of political outlook and national self-interest. This policy has been a political policy, belonging to the political branch of the Government wholly outside the concern and the competence of the Judiciary.

Accordingly, when this policy changed and the political and lawmaking branch of this Government, the Congress, decided to restrict the right of immigration about seventy years ago, this Court thereupon and ever since has recognized that the determination of a selective and exclusionary immigration policy was for the Congress and not for the Judiciary. The conditions for entry of every alien, the particular classes of aliens that shall be denied entry altogether, the basis for determining such classification, the right to terminate hospitality to aliens, the grounds on which such determination shall be based, have been recognized as matters solely for the responsibility of the Congress and wholly outside the power of this Court to control.

The Court's acknowledgment of the sole responsibility of Congress for these matters has been made possible by Justices whose cultural outlook, whose breadth of view and robust tolerance were not exceeded by those of Jefferson. In their personal views, libertarians like Mr. Justice Holmes and Mr. Justice Brandeis doubtless disapproved of some of these policies, departures as they were from the best traditions of this country and based as they have been in part on discredited racial theories or manipulation of figures in formulating what is known as the quota system. But whether immigration laws have been crude and cruel, whether they may have reflected xenophobia in general or anti-Semitism or anti-Catholicism, the responsibility belongs to Congress. . . .

MR. JUSTICE DOUGLAS, with whom MR. JUSTICE BLACK concurs, dissenting. . . .

The view that the power of Congress to deport aliens is absolute and may be exercised for any reason which Congress deems appropriate rests on Fong Yue Ting v. United States, 149 U.S. 698, 13 S. Ct. 1016, 37 L.Ed. 905, decided in 1893 by a six-to-three vote. That decision seems to me to be inconsistent with the philosophy of constitutional law which we have developed for the protection of resident aliens. We have long held that a resident alien is a "person" within the meaning of the Fifth and the Fourteenth Amendments. He therefore may not be deprived either by the National Government or by any state of life, liberty, or property without due process of law. Nor may he be denied the equal protection of the laws. . . .

The right to be immune from arbitrary decrees of banishment certainly may be more important to "liberty" than the civil rights which all aliens enjoy when they reside here. Unless they are free from arbitrary banishment, the "liberty" they enjoy while they live here is indeed illusory. Banishment is punishment in the practical sense. It may deprive a man and his family of all that makes life worth while. Those who have their roots here have an important stake in this country. Their plans for themselves and their hopes for their children all depend on their right to stay. If they are uprooted and sent to lands no longer known to them, no longer hospitable, they become displaced, homeless people condemned to bitterness and despair.

This drastic step may at times be necessary in order to protect the national interest. There may be occasions when the continued presence of an alien, no matter how long he may have been here, would be hostile to the safety or welfare of the Nation due to the nature of his conduct. But unless such condition is shown, I would stay the hand of the Government and let those to whom we have extended our hospitality and who have become members of our communities remain here and enjoy the life and liberty which the Constitution guarantees.

Congress has not proceeded by that standard. It has ordered these aliens deported not for what they are but for what they once were. Perhaps a hearing would show that they continue to be people dangerous and hostile to us. But the principle of forgiveness and the doctrine of redemption are too deep in our philosophy to admit that there is no return for those who have once erred.

COMMENT

The Alien Registration Act under which Harisiades was deported and the earlier laws which it amended were largely superseded in this respect by later legislation. Any effort today to deport individuals in the position of Harisiades would rely principally on the provisions of Section 241(a)(6)* of the Immigration and Nationality Act of 1952, pertaining to membership in Communist organizations. The decisions under that section and its predecessor statutes have become intertwined with decisions of the Supreme Court arising under statutes that have imposed criminal sanctions on members of organizations advocating the overthrow of the Government by force, decisions which have interpreted the term "membership" to require an "active" rather than nominal or passive identification with an organization. For a review of these cases, see Note, The Status of Anti-Communist Legislation, 1965 Duke L.J. 369. Section 241 was at issue in Gastelum-Quinones v. Kennedy, 374 U.S. 469, 83 S.Ct. 1819, 10 L.Ed.2d 1013 (1963). The Court there held that the Government had not sustained its burden in deportation proceedings of establishing that an alien was a "meaningful" member of the Communist party, as "contemplated" by Section 241(a)(6)(C). Using the language of a prior case, it stated that, based upon the testimony of the Government's witnesses, ". . . the dominating impulse to petitioner's 'affiliation' with the Communist Party may well have been wholly devoid of any 'political' implications." An order of deportation based on Section 241(a) was reversed in Berdo v. Immigration & Naturalization Service, 432 F.2d 824 (6th Cir. 1970). The court concluded that petitioner, a Hungarian, was "practically, after numerous procrastinating delays on his part, forced to accept membership in the Communist Party thereafter in order to avoid the grossest deprivation." His membership in Hungary, particularly in view of his earlier street fighting against Soviet forces during the 1956 revolution, was viewed as "devoid of political implications."

In other respects as well, the Supreme Court has tightened the requirements for deportation, either by restrictively interpreting the substantive basis for deportation proceedings or by imposing stringent requirements of proof upon the Government. In Woodby v. Immigration and Naturalization Service, 385 U.S. 276, 284, 87 S.Ct. 483, 487, 17 L.Ed.2d 362, 368 (1966), the Court stated:

> The petitioners urge that the appropriate burden of proof in deportation proceedings should be that which the law imposes in criminal cases—the duty of proving the essential facts beyond a reasonable doubt. The Government, on the other hand, points out that a deportation proceeding is not a criminal case, and that the appropriate burden of proof should consequently be the one generally imposed in civil cases and administrative proceedings—the duty of prevailing by a mere preponderance of the evidence.
>
> To be sure, a deportation proceeding is not a criminal prosecution. Harisiades v. Shaughnessy, 342 U.S. 580,

72 S.Ct. 512, 96 L.Ed. 586. But it does not syllogistically follow that a person may be banished from this country upon no higher degree of proof than applies in a negligence case. This Court has not closed its eyes to the drastic deprivations that may follow when a resident of this country is compelled by our Government to forsake all the bonds formed here and go to a foreign land where he often has no contemporary identification. In words apposite to the question before us, we have spoken of "the solidity of proof that is required for a judgment entailing the consequences of deportation, particularly in the case of an old man who has lived in this country for forty years . . . ." Rowoldt v. Perfetto, 355 U.S. 115, 120, 78 S.Ct. 180, 183, 2 L.Ed.2d 140.

In denaturalization cases the Court has required the Government to establish its allegations by clear, unequivocal, and convincing evidence. The same burden has been imposed in expatriation cases. That standard of proof is no stranger to the civil law.

No less a burden of proof is appropriate in deportation proceedings. The immediate hardship of deportation is often greater than that inflicted by denaturalization, which does not, immediately at least, result in expulsion from our shores. And many resident aliens have lived in this country longer and established stronger family, social, and economic ties here than some who have become naturalized citizens.

We hold that no deportation order may be entered unless it is found by clear, unequivocal, and convincing evidence that the facts alleged as grounds for deportation are true. . . .

NOTE ON PROCEDURES FOR EXCLUSION AND DEPORTATION

The first hurdle to be overcome by an alien seeking to enter the United States is obtaining a visa from the United States Consul in his country. A visa, the denial of which is not reviewable, is a necessary but not a sufficient condition for entry into the country. If the alien arrives in the United States but the Government deems him to be ineligible for admission (see Section 212 of the Immigration and Nationality Act), exclusion proceedings will be instituted. In such cases, Section 236 generally calls for a hearing by a special inquiry officer, followed by administrative appeal within the Department of Justice. Judicial review by habeas corpus is expressly provided for by Section 106(b). If the result of the exclusion proceedings is adverse to the alien, he is then deported to the country whence he came.

However, it is not clear that either a hearing or judicial review is constitutionally required in exclusion cases. Section 235(c) explicitly gives the Attorney General power to exclude aliens on grounds connected with subversion, on the basis of confidential information and without a hearing. Support for the constitutionality of that section is found in a case under an older statute which, like the present Section 215, in general terms authorized the President to exclude aliens or classes of aliens during times of national emergency. The Supreme Court, on review of habeas corpus proceedings brought by an alien detained at an entrance point to the United States, held that denial of a hearing and refusal to reveal such confidential information did not violate the Constitution. In that case, United States ex rel. Knauff v. Shaughnessy, 338 U.S. 537, 543, 70 S.Ct 309, 312, 94 L.Ed. 317, 324 (1950), the Court said: "Whatever the rule may be concerning deportation of persons who have gained entry into the United States, it is not within the province of any court, unless expressly authorized by law, to review the determination of the political branch of the Government to exclude a given alien. . . . Whatever the procedure authorized by Congress is, it is due process as far as an alien denied entry is concerned." Cf. Shaughnessy v. United States ex rel. Mezei, 345 U.S. 206, 73 S.Ct. 625, 97 L.Ed. 956 (1953).

Somewhat different considerations prevail in cases of deportation in the technical sense—that is, cases in which an alien has been admitted to the country in a regular manner.[10] If the authorities believe that such an alien is deportable on one of the grounds stated in Section 241, they must follow the procedures spelled out in the Act. Upon a warrant of the Attorney General, the alien may be arrested and held in custody or released on parole while his status is being determined. The Act, primarily in Section 242, defines the nature of the administrative proceedings to determine deportability and the nature of the hearing to which the alien is entitled. He has the right (at his own expense) to be represented by counsel, to examine evidence against him, and to cross examine government witnesses. He is entitled to judicial review, within limits provided in Section 106 of the Act. Certain categories of deportable aliens, primarily those falling within enumerated "hardship" cases, are eligible for suspension of deportation and may be granted permanent residence. Special problems arise under Section 243, which designates the countries to which aliens are to be deported, because of political upheavals abroad and, in some cases, the unwillingness of any country to accept the alien.

With respect to deportation, unlike exclusion, such safeguards appear to have a constitutional foundation. Consider the language of the Court in a deportation case, Yamataya v. Fisher (The Japanese Immigrant Case), 189 U.S. 86, 100, 23 S.Ct. 611, 614, 47 L.Ed. 721, 725 (1903):

> . . . But this court has never held, nor must we now be understood as holding, that administrative officers, when executing the provisions of a statute involving the liberty of persons, may disregard the fundamental principles that inhere in "due process of law" as understood at the time of the adoption of the Constitution. One of these principles is that no person shall be deprived of his liberty

10. The lines between exclusion and deportation proceedings are often difficult to draw. Aliens admitted on parole, crewmen on shore leave and other comparable categories suggest the kinds of distinctions which legislation and the courts have had to draw. See, e. g., United States ex rel. Stellas v. Esperdy, 366 F.2d 266 (2d Cir. 1966).

> without opportunity, at some time, to be heard, before such officers, in respect of the matters upon which that liberty depends . . . . No such arbitrary power can exist where the principles involved in due process of law are recognized.
>
> This is the reasonable construction of the acts of Congress here in question, and they need not be otherwise interpreted. . . . An act of Congress must be taken to be constitutional unless the contrary plainly and palpably appears. . . .

Referring to the Japanese Immigrant Case in Wong Yang Sung v. McGrath, 339 U.S. 33, 49, 70 S.Ct. 445, 454, 94 L.Ed. 616, 628 (1950), modified on rehearing, 339 U.S. 908, 70 S.Ct. 564, 94 L.Ed. 1336 (1950), the Court said:

> The Constitutional requirement of procedural due process of law derives from the same source as Congress' power to legislate and, where applicable, permeates every valid enactment of that body. It was under compulsion of the Constitution that this Court long ago held that an antecedent deportation statute must provide a hearing at least for aliens who had not entered clandestinely and who had been here some time even if illegally. . . .

KLEINDIENST v. MANDEL

Supreme Court of the United States, 1972.
408 U.S. 753, 92 S.Ct. 2576, 33 L.Ed.2d 683.

[Mandel, a Belgian journalist and Marxist theoretician who had described himself as "a revolutionary Marxist," was invited to the United States in 1969 for a brief stay to participate at a conference at Stanford University on Technology and the Third World, and to visit faculty members at several other universities from whom invitations had also been received. His assigned subject at one conference was "Revolutionary Strategy in Imperialist Countries."

Mandel was found ineligible for admission under Section 212(a)(28)(D) * of the Immigration and Nationality Act. The Department of State recommended to the Attorney General that Mandel's ineligibility be waived pursuant to a discretionary power of the Attorney General under Section 212(d) of the Act. The Attorney General declined to waive ineligibility, basing his decision on several factors including some unscheduled activities (appearances at conferences and meetings, one of which involved fund raising) by Mandel on a previous visit to the United States when a waiver was granted.

Joined by eight United States citizens who were university professors in the social sciences and who had invited him to speak, Mandel brought an action to compel the Attorney General to exercise his discretion under the Act to grant him a temporary visa. The American plaintiffs contended that these statutory provisions, as applied, prevented them from hearing Mandel in person, in contravention of the First Amendment. (Further allegations of an "arbitrary and capricious" application of Section 212(d) to Mandel are not considered in these excerpts.) The three-judge District Court concluded that citizens of this country had a First Amendment right to have Mandel enter so that they might hear him, and enjoined enforcement of Section 212 as to him. Excerpts from the opinion of the Supreme Court by JUSTICE BLACKMUN appear below.]

We thus have almost continuous attention on the part of Congress since 1875 to the problems of immigration and of excludability of certain defined classes of aliens. The pattern generally has been one of increasing control with particular attention, for almost 70 years now, first to anarchists and then to those with communist affiliation or views.

It is clear that Mandel personally, as an unadmitted and nonresident alien, had no constitutional right of entry to this country as a nonimmigrant or otherwise. [Citations omitted].

The appellees concede this. Brief for Appellees 33; Tr. of Oral Arg. 28. Indeed, the American appellees assert that "they sue to enforce their rights, individually and as members of the American public, and assert none on the part of the invited alien." Brief for Appellees at 14. "Dr. Mandel is in a sense made a plaintiff because he is symbolic of the problem," Tr. of Oral Arg. 22.

The case, therefore, comes down to the narrow issue whether the First Amendment confers upon the appellee professors, because they wish to hear, speak, and debate with Mandel in person, the ability to determine that Mandel should be permitted to enter the country or, in other words, to compel the Attorney General to allow Mandel's admission.

In a variety of contexts this Court has referred to a First Amendment right to "receive information and ideas":

. . . And in Lamont v. Postmaster General, 381 U.S. 301, 85 S.Ct. 1493, 14 L.Ed.2d 398 (1965), the Court held that a statute permitting the Government to hold "communist political propaganda" arriving in the mails from abroad unless the addressee affirmatively requested in writing that it be delivered to him placed an unjustifiable burden on the addressee's First Amendment right. This Court has recognized that this right is "nowhere more vital" than in our schools and universities. . . .

. . .

The Government also suggests that the First Amendment is inapplicable because appellees have free access to Mandel's ideas through his books and speeches, and because "technological developments," such as tapes or telephone hook-ups readily supplant his physical presence. This argument overlooks what may be particular qualities inherent in sustained, face-to-face debate, discussion and questioning. While alternative means of access to Mandel's ideas might be a relevant factor were we called upon to balance First Amendment rights against governmental regulatory interests—a balance we find unnecessary here in light of the discussion that follows in Part V—we are loath to hold on this record that existence of other alternatives extinguishes altogether any constitutional interest on the part of the appellees in this particular form of access.

Recognition that First Amendment rights are implicated, however, is not dispositive of our inquiry here. In accord with ancient principles of the international law of nation-states, the Court in The Chinese Exclusion Case, 130 U.S. 581, 609, 9 S.Ct. 623, 631, 32 L.Ed. 1068 (1889), and in Fong Yue Ting v. United States, 149 U.S. 698, 13 S.Ct. 1016, 37 L.Ed. 905 (1893), held broadly, as the Government describes, it, Brief for Appellants 20, that the power to exclude aliens is "inherent in sovereignty, necessary for maintaining normal international relations and defending the country against foreign encroachments and dangers—a power to be exercised exclusively by the political branches of government . . . ." Since that time the Court's general reaffirmations of this principle have been legion. The Court without exception has sustained Congress' "plenary power to make rules for the admission of aliens and to exclude those who possess those characteristics which Congress has forbidden." Boutilier v. Immigration and Naturalization Service, 387 U.S. 118, 123, 87 S.Ct. 1563, 1567, 18 L.Ed.2d 661 (1967). "[O]ver no conceivable subject is the legislative power of Congress more complete than it is over" the admission of aliens. . . .

. . . The appellees recognize the force of these many precedents. In seeking to sustain the decision below, they concede that Congress could enact a blanket prohibition against entry of all aliens falling into the class defined by §§ 212(a)(28)(D) and (G)(v), and that First Amendment rights could not override that decision. Brief for Appellees 16. But they contend that by providing a waiver procedure, Congress clearly intended that persons ineligible under the broad provision of the section would be temporarily admitted when appropriate "for humane reasons and for reasons of public interest." S.Rep.No. 1137, 82d Cong., 2d Sess., 12 (1952). They argue that the Executive's implementation of this congressional mandate through decision whether to grant a waiver in each individual case must be limited by the First Amendment rights of persons like appellees. Specifically, their position is that the First Amendment rights must prevail, at least where the Government advances no justification for failing to grant a waiver. They point to the fact that waivers have been granted in the vast majority of cases.

Appellees' First Amendment argument would prove too much. In almost every instance of an alien excludable under § 212(a)(28), there are probably those who would wish to meet and speak with him. The ideas of most such aliens might not be so influential as those of Mandel, nor his American audience so numerous, nor the planned discussion forums so impressive. But the First Amendment does not protect only the articulate, the well known, and the popular. Were we to endorse the proposition that governmental power to withhold a waiver must yield whenever a bona fide claim is made that American citizens wish to meet and talk with an alien excludable under § 212(a)(28), one of two unsatisfactory results would necessarily ensue. Either every claim would prevail, in which case the plenary discretionary authority Congress granted the Executive becomes a nullity, or courts in each case would be required to weigh the strength of the audience's interest against that of the Government in refusing a waiver to the particular alien applicant, according to some as yet undetermined standard. The dangers and the undesirability of making that determination on the basis of factors such as the size of the audience or the probity of the speaker's ideas are obvious. Indeed, it is for precisely this reason that the waiver decision has, properly, been placed in the hands of the Executive.

. . .

In summary, plenary congressional power to make policies and rules for exclusion of aliens has long been firmly established. In the case of an alien excludable under § 212(a)(28), Congress has delegated conditional exercise of this power to the Executive. We hold that when the Executive exercises this power negatively on the basis of a facially legitimate and bona fide reason, the courts will neither look behind the exercise of that discretion, nor test it by balancing its justification against the First Amendment interests of those who seek personal communication with the applicant. What First Amendment or other grounds may be available for attacking exercise of discretion for which no justification whatsoever is advanced is a question we neither address or decide in this case.

Reversed.

[A dissenting opinion by JUSTICE MARSHALL observed that none of the precedents for exclusion of aliens that were relied upon in the Court's opinion were concerned with rights of American citizens, but involved only rights of the excluded aliens themselves. "At least when the rights of Americans are involved, there is no basis for concluding that the power to exclude aliens is absolute. . . . [A]ll governmental power—even the war power, the power to maintain national security, or the power to conduct foreign affairs—is limited by the Bill of Rights." In the case of Mandel, the government has offered no "compelling governmental interest" that would justify a bar on even temporary admission, for "the Government's desire to keep certain ideas out of circulation in this country . . . is hardly a compelling governmental interest. Section (a)(28) may not be the basis for excluding an alien when Americans wish to hear him."]

QUESTIONS

(1) If the three aliens in the Harisiades case had become naturalized citizens, in what respects would their rights or obligations in the United States have changed?

(2) Do you think that the courts should draw a distinction between the substantive scope of judicial review of grounds for exclusion and grounds for deportation, at least with respect to long-resident immigrant aliens such as Harisiades? On what principles, or on what practical considerations relating to the remedies which a court could afford, could such a distinction be justified? Consider, for example, a statute providing that all resident aliens of a stated national origin, race or religion be deported. Consider (cf. Kleindienst v. Mandel) a statute providing that all aliens who have publicly criticized U. S. foreign policy be excluded.

(3) Suppose that deportation proceedings are instituted against an indigent alien. As a matter of policy, should he be afforded counsel? Could you develop an effective argument that he has a constitutional right to be provided with counsel? Compare Gideon v. Wainwright, 372 U.S. 335, 83 S.Ct. 792, 9 L.Ed.2d 799 (1963).

(4) Suppose that a case similar in all respects to Harisiades arose today. As counsel for the alien facing deportation, in what respects could you most effectively challenge Justice Jackson's opinion?

C. PROTECTION OF THE ALIEN UNDER NATIONAL LAW

A comprehensive discussion of the protection afforded an alien would require consideration not only of the internal law of the country in which the alien is present, but also of customary international law and any treaties which might be relevant. Indeed, discussion would necessarily go beyond such legal aspects of our topic to include a nation's political and cultural traditions as well as political considerations bearing upon its foreign policy. Maltreatment of aliens has been a prime source of friction between nations, and the occasion for the application of economic or other sanctions, or at times the use of armed force, by the alien's government.

We postpone such further considerations to Chapter IV and here examine the rights which an alien can assert and the protection to which he is entitled under national law. The materials below treat principally federal law in the United States. The legal situation in other countries varies markedly about the degree to which the alien is assured of the security of his person and property and is assimilated to a citizen in such respects. This variety will become evident from the materials in Chapter IV.

WONG WING v. UNITED STATES

Supreme Court of the United States, 1896.
163 U.S. 228, 16 S.Ct. 977, 41 L.Ed. 140.

[Appellants had been brought before a commissioner of a circuit court of the United States upon a charge of being Chinese persons unlawfully within the United States and not entitled to remain. The commissioner found the charge accurate, and ordered that the appellants be imprisoned at hard labor in the Detroit House of Correction for sixty days and thereafter be deported from the United States to China. Appellants sought a writ of habeas corpus in the Circuit Court, and this appeal was from a discharge by that court of the writ.

In its opinion, the Supreme Court traced briefly the history of the Chinese exclusion acts which were referred to in Fong Yue Ting v. United States, p. 23, supra. The Court summarized its precedents which had upheld the power of the Congress to exclude or to expel aliens, absolutely or upon certain conditions, as an inherent and inalienable right of every sovereign nation. The opinion, delivered by JUSTICE SHIRAS, continued:]

The present appeal presents a different question from those heretofore determined. It is claimed that even if it be competent for congress to prevent aliens from coming into the country, or to provide for the deportation of those unlawfully within its borders, and to submit the enforcement of the provisions of such laws to executive officers, yet the fourth section of the act of 1892, which provides that "any such Chinese person, or person of Chinese descent, convicted and adjudged to be not lawfully entitled to be or remain in the United States, shall be imprisoned at hard labor for a period not exceeding one year, and thereafter removed from the United States," inflicts an infamous punishment, and hence conflicts with the fifth and sixth amendments of the constitution, which declare that no person shall be held to answer for a capital or otherwise infamous crime, unless on a presentment or indictment of a grand jury, and that in all criminal prosecutions the accused shall enjoy the right to a speedy and public trial, by an impartial jury of the state and district wherein the crime shall have been committed. . . .

On the other hand, it is contended on behalf of the government that it has never been decided by this court that in all cases where the punishment may be confinement at hard labor the crime is infamous; and many cases are cited from the reports of the state supreme courts where the constitutionality of statutes providing for summary proceedings, without a jury trial, for the punishment by imprisonment at hard labor of vagrants and disorderly persons, has been upheld. . . .

We think it clear that detention or temporary confinement, as part of the means necessary to give effect to the provisions for the exclusion or expulsion of aliens, would be valid. Proceedings to exclude or expel would be vain if those accused could not be held in custody pending the inquiry into their true character, and while arrangements were being made for their deportation. Detention is a usual feature in every case of arrest on a criminal charge, even when an innocent person is wrongfully accused; but it is not imprisonment in a legal sense.

So, too, we think it would be plainly competent for congress to declare the act of an alien in remaining unlawfully within the United States to be an offense punishable by fine or imprisonment, if such offense were to be established by a judicial trial.

But the evident meaning of the section in question—and no other is claimed for it by the counsel for the government—is that the detention provided for is an imprisonment at hard labor, which is to be undergone before the sentence of deportation is to be carried into effect, and that such imprisonment is to be adjudged against the accused by a justice, judge, or commissioner, upon a summary hearing. . . .

Our views upon the question thus specifically pressed upon our attention may be briefly expressed thus: We regard it as settled by our previous decisions that the United States can, as a matter of public policy, by congressional enactment, forbid aliens or classes of aliens from coming within their borders, and expel aliens or classes of aliens from their territory, and can, in order to make effectual such decree of exclusion or expulsion, devolve the power and duty of identifying and arresting the persons included in such decree, and causing their deportation, upon executive or subordinate officials.

But when congress sees fit to further promote such a policy by subjecting the persons of such aliens to infamous punishment at hard labor, or by confiscating their property, we think such legislation, to be valid, must provide for a judicial trial to establish the guilt of the accused.

No limits can be put by the courts upon the power of congress to protect, by summary methods, the country from the advent of aliens whose race or habits render them undesirable as citizens, or to expel such if they have already found their way into our land, and unlawfully remain therein. But to declare unlawful residence within the country to be an infamous crime, punishable by deprivation of liberty and property, would be to pass out of the sphere of constitutional legislation, unless provision were made that the fact of guilt should first be established by a judicial trial. It is not consistent with the theory of our government that the legislature should, after having defined an offense as an infamous crime, find the fact of guilt, and adjudge the punishment by one of its own agents.

In Ex parte Wilson, 114 U.S. 428, 5 S.Ct. 935, this court declared that, for more than a century, imprisonment at hard labor in the state prison or penitentiary or other similar institution has been considered an infamous punishment in England and America. . . .

And in the case of Yick Wo v. Hopkins, 118 U.S. 369, 6 S.Ct. 1064, it was said: "The fourteenth amendment to the constitution is not confined to the protection of citizens. It says: 'Nor shall any state deprive any person of life, liberty or property without due process of law; nor deny to any person within its jurisdiction the equal protection of the law.' These provisions are universal in their application to all persons within the territorial jurisdiction, without regard to any differences of race, of color, or nationality; and the equal protection of the laws is a pledge of the protection of equal laws." Applying this reasoning to the fifth and sixth amendments, it must be concluded that all persons within the territory of the United States are entitled to the protection guarantied by those amendments, and that even aliens shall not be held to answer for a capital or other infamous crime, unless on a presentment or indictment of a grand jury, nor be deprived of life, liberty, or property without due process of law.

Our conclusion is that the commissioner, in sentencing the appellants to imprisonment at hard labor at and in the Detroit House of Correction, acted without jurisdiction, and that the circuit court erred in not discharging the prisoners from such imprisonment, without prejudice to their detention according to law for deportation. . . .

[An opinion of JUSTICE FIELD, concurring in part and dissenting in part, is omitted.]

QUESTIONS

(1) Since Congress clearly could have kept Wong Wing out of the country, why should it not be able to treat Wong Wing as it chooses once it has permitted him to enter? Is the argument for such power stronger if the provisions applied against the alien were on the books at the time of his entry?

(2) What arguments could you develop to justify distinct treatment of aliens with respect to criminal procedure? What of the right of an alien to cross examine? The right of an indigent alien defendant in state criminal proceedings to be provided with counsel?

(3) Are the considerations different in civil proceedings, perhaps tort or contract actions, in which an alien is plaintiff? Are there valid constitutional objections to the denial to an alien of access to the courts, or to the imposition of special conditions upon access such as the payment of special fees? See 28 U.S.C.A. § 2502 * and its requirement of reciprocity which may preclude an alien from suing the United States in the Court of Claims.

NOTE ON THE PROTECTION OF ALIENS UNDER DOMESTIC LAW

The Note at p. 33, supra, describes procedural safeguards for aliens in certain exclusion proceedings and in deportation proceedings. The Wong Wing case, although related to deportation proceedings, suggests the wide range of constitutional provisions which apply equally to aliens and citizens in this country. The comments below treat some special problems and special categories of aliens.

The consistent ruling of the United States courts has been that the property of alien friends, resident or nonresident, is entitled to the protection of the Fifth Amendment against takings without compensation. This view was forcefully reiterated in the following passage from Sardino v. Federal Reserve Bank of New York, 361 F.2d 106, 111 (2d Cir. 1966):

> The Government's second answer that "The Constitution of the United States confers no rights on non-resident aliens" is so patently erroneous in a case involving property in the United States that we are surprised it was made. Throughout our history the guarantees of the Constitution have been considered applicable to all actions of the Government within our borders—and even to some without. Cf. Reid v. Covert, 354 U.S. 1, 5, 8, 77 S.Ct. 1222, 1 L.Ed.2d 1148 (1957). This country's present economic position is due in no small part to European investors who placed their funds at risk in its development, rightly believing they were protected by constitutional guarantees; today, for other reasons, we are still eager to attract foreign funds. In Russian Volunteer Fleet v. United States, 282 U.S. 481, 489, 491–492, 51 S.Ct. 229, 75 L.Ed. 473 (1931), the Court squarely held that an alien friend is entitled to the protection of the Fifth Amendment's prohibition of taking without just compensation—even when his government was no longer recognized by this country. And the Court has declared unequivocally, with respect to non-resident aliens owning property within the United States, that they "as well as citizens are entitled to the protection of the Fifth Amendment." United States v. Pink, 315 U.S. 203, 228, 62 S.Ct. 552, 564, 86 L.Ed. 796 (1942). . . .

The holding in the Sardino case, p. 436, infra, indicates an important qualification to these statements. For present purposes, it is sufficient to note the reference by the court to an "alien friend" as one who is entitled to the protection of the Fifth Amendment. The property of enemy aliens has, in both World Wars, been "vested" under the Trading with the Enemy Act, 40 Stat. 411 (1917), as amended, 50 U.S.C.A.App. § 1 et seq. Vesting meant that title was absolutely transferred to the United States; the return of the property, or the payment of part or all of the proceeds of its sale, to persons defined in this legislation as "enemies" has been regarded as a matter of grace. See, e. g., United States v. Chemical Foundation, Inc., 272 U.S. 1, 11, 47 S.Ct. 1, 4, 71 L.Ed. 131, 141 (1926). The term "enemy" was defined in the 1917 Act to include persons resident or doing business in enemy or enemy-occupied territory. The World War II revisions, intended to prevent evasion, have been construed to include citizens or residents (including corporations) of neutral territory who were "tainted" with enemy relations. See Clark v. Uebersee Finanz-Korp., A. G., 332 U.S. 480, 68 S.Ct. 174, 92 L.Ed. 88 (1947). As so construed, the Trading with the Enemy Act was consistently found to be constitutional. See Silesian American Corp. v. Clark, 332 U.S. 469, 68 S.Ct. 179, 92 L.Ed. 81 (1947). This legislation gave rise to the Interhandel cases, pp. 244 and 844, infra.

Nonresident enemy aliens have been subject not only to such measures affecting property but also to varied disabilities, such as being unable to sue. See Ex parte Kawato, 317 U.S. 69, 63 S.Ct. 115, 87 L.Ed. 58 (1942). *Resident* aliens have been largely exempt from these disabilities, although they may be subject to internment during wartime. Indeed, during World War II restrictions upon location and movement reached past enemy aliens to one group of natural-born United States citizens, those of Japanese ancestry. Legislation in 1942, as implemented by executive and military orders and criminal sanctions, provided that all American citizens of Japanese descent should be excluded from certain areas, primarily on the West Coast. Such citizens were required to report to assembly points and, in large part, were to be detained during the war period in assembly or relocation centers. In Korematsu v. United States, 323 U.S. 214, 65 S.Ct. 193, 89 L.Ed. 194 (1944), the Court, over three vigorous dissents, upheld the constitutionality of a criminal conviction of a natural-born citizen of Japanese descent who had refused to leave the defined area. However, in Ex parte Endo, 323 U.S. 283, 65 S.Ct. 208, 89 L.Ed. 243 (1944), the Court held that the detention of such persons against their will in relocation centers was not authorized by the relevant legislation and executive order. Later legislation provided for compensation for certain categories of losses caused by the relocation. 62 Stat. 1231 (1948), as amended, 50 U.S.C.A.App. §§ 1981–1987. In a number of cases renunciations of American citizenship made in relocation centers were later set aside at the request of those detained as having been, under the circumstances, involuntary. See, e. g., Acheson v. Murakami, 176 F.2d 953 (9th Cir. 1949).

Some disabilities attach to various other aliens. There is scattered and inconclusive authority to the effect that aliens illegally in this country are deprived of certain rights. Compare Coules v. Pharris, 212 Wis. 558, 250 N.W. 404 (1933) (alien illegally in country cannot sue for wages), with Janusis v. Long, 284 Mass. 403, 188 N.E. 228 (1933) (alien illegally in country can sue for personal injury). A recent federal decision held in part that a Canadian corporation (which the Court treated as a nonresident alien) having no assets in the United States did not have "standing" to protest the inclusion of its name by the Securities and Exchange Commission on a "blacklist" of corporations whose securities were believed to have been illegally distributed in the United States. Kukatush Mining Corp. v. SEC, 309 F.2d 647 (D.C.Cir. 1962).

D. ACCESS OF ALIENS TO ECONOMIC ACTIVITIES

Nations have mixed feelings about granting to alien individuals or enterprises the right to participate in economic activity within their borders, whether directly through branches or subsidiaries or indirectly through equity or debt investments in local enterprises. One can start from the premise that few if any countries are so situated that they will not benefit from some foreign participation. Even an advanced industrial country finds that foreign enterprise brings special skills and capacities, together with useful capital resources. The creation of such economic links between countries through the commercial activities of their nationals may simultaneously serve other purposes such as fostering a sense of political interdependence.

Attitudes towards private foreign investment vary markedly among countries, shaped by and reflecting political as well as economic experience or aspirations: the historical experience with foreign investors, the relative stage of development of an economy, the extent to which foreign capital and technology are critical to developmental ambitions, the principles or ideology which characterize the domestic economy, the character of the political system, and so on. This section explores restrictions upon aliens and the attitudes from which they derive in some characteristic countries of the developed and underdeveloped worlds.

One can assume that the starting point for a firm contemplating a foreign venture is the question: will it be profitable? Reaching that business judgment involves considerable speculation; the uncertainities surrounding domestic investment may appear minor by comparison with those stemming from the novel conditions abroad. Dominantly the economic and political factors will influence decision. But large areas of the foreign legal system will be germane to the business judgment. The investor has an interest not only in the foreign country's economic regulation (tax, labor, antitrust legislation and so on) but also in areas of private law that may affect the proposed venture: security devices for sales, tort liability for defective products. The nature of the foreign country's legal institutions may influence judgment. For example, the quality and the status (independent or otherwise) of the foreign judiciary could prove to be significant, as in a dispute over compensation for expropriation.

This section considers a narrower range of laws and institutions: those specifically directed towards foreign investors which may bar the alien from working or establishing an enterprise or which may attach onerous conditions to any such activities. We first consider state and federal laws in this country. The materials examining these laws suggest the kinds of political attitudes, economic fears and legal restrictions which the United States investor is likely to encounter abroad. We then examine a critical question posed by legislation restricting economic activities of "aliens": what criteria are relevant to determining when a corporation should be characterized as "alien"? The final portion of the materials describes some laws and attitudes of foreign countries.

---

1. RESTRICTIONS IN THE UNITED STATES

At earlier periods in our history, foreign capital played a substantial, but not crucial, role in the development of the economy—for example, in railroad construction during the second half of the 19th

Century. On the other hand, direct foreign investment—ownership coupled with active control—has not been significant in this country since colonial times. It has been estimated that, from an early period in the 19th Century, foreign investment of all kinds never amounted to more than 5% of the national wealth. On the other hand, estimates of comparable figures for certain periods in a number of Latin American countries have ranged from 25% to 65%. Thus the United States has been able to adhere to a generally hospitable attitude towards the establishment of alien-owned business and the acquisition by aliens of such local assets as were necessary to conduct that business. Specific problems have led to the emergence of rather sporadic restrictions: concern about national security, a desire to wring reciprocal treatment from other countries, worries about excessive competition in a particular industry, concern about permitting foreigners to enjoy the advantages of subsidization, or alarm at absentee ownership. Indeed, within the last decade important changes have occurred in popular and legal incentives or disincentives to foreign investment—changes related to balance-of-payment problems, dollar devaluation, and fear of strong foreign economic penetration. See pp. 65–68, infra.

In American history, it is helpful to distinguish between state and federal law in examining restrictions upon economic activities of aliens. Those restrictions range from restraints on alien ownership of business interests (as through equity ownership by nonresident aliens in domestic corporations) to restraints on the employment or professional opportunities of aliens admitted to the United States for permanent residence. As we shall observe, the domestic "law" relevant to such participation by aliens in our economic life involves constitutional principles, statutory or administrative regulation, and treaty provisions.

NOTE ON STATE RESTRICTIONS

Recent decisions of the Supreme Court on the validity of state restrictions on the economic activity of aliens have resolved inconsistencies and contradictions in the earlier case law. A brief review of the pattern of state restrictions will reveal some trends in the earlier decisions. That review also facilitates comparisons between historical attitudes in this and foreign countries towards alien presence, or alien investment or ownership in domestic business.

The range of state statutes limiting aliens' access to trades or professions has been extraordinarily broad. A sampling of the confused pattern of such legislation appeared in a Note, Constitutionality of Restrictions on Aliens' Right to Work, 57 Colum.L.Rev. 1012 (1957). As of that date, aliens were barred in all states from the practice of law, and in most states from participation in the health professions (physicians, pharmacists and so on). Many states gave citizens exclusive or priority rights to all public employment, while others limited only particular jobs (such as teachers in public schools) to citizens. The prohibited categories then became more or less random, with one or more states excluding aliens from such diverse occupations as funeral directors, real estate brokers, billiard-room operators and accountants. Several decisions treating state restrictions are summarized below:

Truax v. Raich, 239 U.S. 33, 36 S.Ct. 7, 60 L.Ed. 131 (1915).

An Arizona statute provided that any employer of more than five workers, regardless of the kind of work, must employ not less than 80 percent qualified electors or native-born citizens. In litigation testing the application of this statute to Raich, a native of Austria and inhabitant of Arizona who was employed as a cook in an Arizona restaurant seven of whose nine employees were noncitizens, the Supreme Court found the statute to be unconstitutional.

The Court described the purpose of the act as the protection of citizens in their employment against noncitizens. Its opinion had two foundations. (*1*) The alien, lawfully admitted under federal law, benefits from the Equal Protection Clause of the Fourteenth Amendment. In this case, the "right to work for a living in the common occupations of the community is of the very essence of the personal freedom and opportunity that it was the purpose of the Amendment to secure." The opinion, using categories developed in earlier cases, noted that the Arizona statute did not relate to regulation or distribution "of the public domain, or of the common property or resources of the people of the state." It did not deal with "real property", and was "not limited to persons who are engaged on public work or receive the benefit of public moneys". (*2*) The Court also noted that the "legitimate interests of the state . . . cannot be so broadly conceived as to bring them into hostility to exclusive federal power." The authority to admit or exclude aliens is an exclusive federal power, and state denial to aliens of opportunity to earn a livelihood "would be tantamount to the assertion of the right to deny them entrance and abode."

State of Ohio ex. rel. Clark v. Deckebach, 274 U.S. 392, 47 S.Ct. 630, 71 L.Ed. 1115 (1927).

The Court upheld a Cincinnati ordinance prohibiting issuance to aliens of licenses to operate billiard rooms. The state argued that billiard rooms were "meeting places of idle and vicious persons" as well as scenes of numerous crimes; that noncitizens as a class were "less familiar with the law and customs of this country;" and that maintenance by them of billiard rooms would be a "menace to society". The Court found no violation of the Equal Protection Clause since there was no "plainly irrational discrimination" against aliens, and since it was "enough for present purposes that the ordinance, in the light of facts admitted or generally assumed, does not preclude the possibility of a rational basis for legislative judgment and . . . we have no such knowledge of local conditions as would enable us to say that it is clearly wrong." Cincinnati could exclude from the conduct of a "dubious business an entire class rather than its objectionable members selected by more empirical methods."

Terrace v. Thompson, 263 U.S. 197, 44 S.Ct. 15, 68 L.Ed. 255 (1923).

A statute of the state of Washington provided that aliens (other than those who in good faith declared their intention to become citizens) could not have any title or right to benefit of land. The Court upheld the statute as applied to bar Japanese subjects resident in Washington from leasing land from American citizens for a period of five years for agricultural purposes. Under federal legislation then in effect, aliens of Oriental descent were not eligible to become citizens.

The Court first stated that, despite Congress's exclusive jurisdiction over immigration, each state had (in the absence of a contrary treaty provision) the "power to deny to aliens the right to own land." It then concluded that the exercise of such power did not violate the Equal Protection Clause. It agreed with the District Court that "one who is not a citizen and cannot become one lacks an interest in . . . the welfare of the state," and thus may be denied the right to own or lease real property. Else, it was "within the realm of possibility that every foot of land within the state might pass to the ownership or possession of noncitizens." It distinguished Truax v. Raich on the ground that the earlier case involved "an opportunity to earn a living in common occupations," while the Washington statute involved the "privilege of owning or controlling agricultural land within the state. The quality and allegiance of those who own, occupy and use the farm lands within its borders are matters of highest importance and affect the safety and power of the state itself."

The restrictions on alien ownership of land that were debated in Terrace v. Thompson had substantial historical roots in this country. The states inherited common-law rules against landholding by aliens which went back to medieval England. Those restrictions were born largely of the conception that land and its ownership were central to the character of a society. However, this country presented markedly different conditions, as large numbers of immigrants became engaged in farming or other occupations based upon land ownership. Such conditions led to abolition or modification of the restrictive laws in many states. But after 1880 the agrarian or populist movement included among its objectives the prevention of absentee landlordism by foreigners. At about the same time, animosity towards Orientals began to develop along the Pacific coast, producing statutes such as that in Terrace v. Thompson. As of 1962—as described in Sullivan, The Alien Land Laws: A Re-evaluation, 36 Temple L.Q. 15 (1962)—state and territorial laws ranged from the restrictive common-law rules to more limited acreage or industrial restrictions, and to full national treatment with citizens.[11]

11. State reciprocity statutes and treaties affecting these matters are considered at pp. 166–172 and 631–635, infra.

Takahashi v. Fish and Game Commission, 334 U.S. 410, 68 S.Ct. 1138, 92 L.Ed. 1478 (1948)

The California Fish and Game Code banned issuance of fishing licenses to any "person ineligible to citizenship." At that time, federal law permitted Japanese to enter and reside in the country, but made them ineligible for United States citizenship. Because of this state provision, Takahashi, who met all other requirements, was denied a license to fish in ocean waters, apparently both within and without the three-mile coastal belt. Takahashi started proceedings to compel issuance of a license, but the state Supreme Court upheld the statute as applied. The United States Supreme Court reversed that judgment.

The Court observed that "the power of a state to apply its laws exclusively to its alien inhabitants as a class is confined within narrow limits." The Court was unable to find any "special public interest" as support for the state ban on Takahashi's commercial fishing. It observed that to whatever extent fish in the three-mile belt off California was capable of ownership by California, it thought that ownership "inadequate to justify California in excluding any or all aliens who are lawful residents of the State from making a living by fishing in the ocean off its shores while permitting all others to do so." It noted that putting the claim of the State upon title (to the fish) was to lean upon a "slender reed." The Court referred to the decisions upholding state laws barring aliens ineligible to citizenship from land ownership. "Assuming the continued validity of those cases, we think they could not in any event be controlling here." The power to control devolution and ownership of land had been long exercised by states and was "supported on reasons peculiar to real property."

Before reading the contemporary decisions which follow, you should have in mind two trends in constitutional litigation under the Equal Protection Clause which influenced them:

(*1*) Note the various standards under which the Supreme Court determined the validity of the state legislation in the preceding cases. It inquired, for example, whether distinctions between aliens and citizens were "arbitrary", "unsupported by reasonable considerations of public policy", "unjustly discriminatory", or "irrational". It asked whether the distinction was supported by "a rational basis for the legislative judgment", or whether it reflected a "reasonable classification . . . consistent with a legitimate interest in the state". Such terms or standards were not used in a consistent or clearly defined manner. For example, the statute in the Truax case could be viewed as a rational response to a state policy that could be considered rational, namely the preservation of employment opportunities for citizens. The problem posed was whether that policy could be pursued by a state consistently with the Constitution. To respond to that question, the

Court inquired whether the statute created a "reasonable classification" or served "legitimate" state interests. Recall the different inquiries, and different degree of deference to state determinations, in Clarke v. Deckebach, and note the different formulation of governing standards of review in the cases which follow.

(*2*) Discrimination against aliens must be viewed in a larger context of constitutional jurisprudence, particularly with respect to two trends in the Supreme Court decisions. In recent decades, the Court has shown great deference to legislative classifications in the field of economic legislation. It is now, for example, unlikely that one could successfully challenge under the Due Process or Equal Protection Clause state discriminations (perhaps amounting to licensing or other requirements) among different occupations or trades.

During these same decades, however, legislative discriminations based upon race have become almost *per se* indefensible. One of the central issues posed by the preceding and following cases is the determination of where limitation of economic opportunities for aliens belongs within these different doctrinal categories. Bear in mind that discrimination against aliens may take on a racial character, as in Terrace v. Thompson, by covering only identifiable categories of aliens such as Orientals. But the statutes at issue in the following cases reach all aliens and hence cannot be fit within conceptions of racial discrimination. Nonetheless, note the reach of the category of "inherently suspect classifications" in these decisions.

GRAHAM v. RICHARDSON

Supreme Court of the United States, 1971.
403 U.S. 365, 91 S.Ct. 1848, 29 L.Ed.2d 534.

[Welfare cases from two states were before the Court. Arizona's assistance program to disabled persons was supported in part by federal grants-in-aid and was administered by Arizona under federal guidelines. Under an Arizona statute, only United States citizens or persons resident in this country for 15 years were eligible for assistance. The appellee in this case was a lawfully admitted resident alien who had emigrated from Mexico in 1956 and had since resided in Arizona. She was 64, totally disabled and met all other eligibility requirements at the time that she instituted proceedings in 1969 for declaratory relief and assistance payments.

Pennsylvania's welfare program under challenge in the second case was not federally supported. In relevant part, that program restricted assistance to United States citizens. Appellee was a lawfully admitted resident alien who entered this country from Scotland in 1965 and has since been a Pennsylvania resident. She sought assistance after illness forced her to give up her employment. Appellee requested in the lower court declaratory relief and back payments. It was stipulated that denial of assistance to aliens (otherwise eligible) caused them "undue hardship" and discouraged "continued residence in Pennsylvania of indigent resident aliens."

The three-judge federal district courts in both cases upheld the aliens' challenges to these state statutes under the Equal Protection

Clause and gave appropriate relief. Excerpts from the Supreme Court's opinion upon appeal, by MR. JUSTICE BLACKMUN, follow:]

II

The appellants argue initially that the States, consistent with the Equal Protection Clause, may favor United States citizens over aliens in the distribution of welfare benefits. It is said that this distinction involves no "invidious discrimination" such as was condemned in King v. Smith, 392 U.S. 309, 88 S.Ct. 2128, 20 L.Ed.2d 1118 (1968), for the State is not discriminating with respect to race or nationality.

. . .

Under traditional equal protection principles, a State retains broad discretion to classify as long as its classification has a reasonable basis. . . . But the Court's decisions have established that classifications based on alienage, like those based on nationality or race, are inherently suspect and subject to close judicial scrutiny. Aliens as a class are a prime example of a "discrete and insular" minority (see United States v. Carolene Products Co., 304 U.S. 144, 152–153, n. 4, 58 S.Ct. 778, 783–784, 82 L.Ed. 1234 (1938)) for whom such heightened judicial solicitude is appropriate. . . .

Arizona and Pennsylvania seek to justify their restrictions on the eligibility of aliens for public assistance solely on the basis of a State's "special public interest" in favoring its own citizens over aliens in the distribution of limited resources such as welfare benefits. It is true that this Court on occasion has upheld state statutes that treat citizens and noncitizens differently, the ground for distinction having been that such laws were necessary to protect special interests of the State or its citizens. Thus, in Truax v. Raich, 239 U.S. 33, 36 S.Ct. 7, 60 L.Ed. 131 (1915), the Court, in striking down an Arizona statute restricting the employment of aliens, emphasized that "[t]he discrimination defined by the act does not pertain to the regulation or distribution of the public domain, or of the common property or resources of the people of the state, the enjoyment of which may be limited to its citizens as against both aliens and the citizens of other states." 239 U.S., at 39–40, 36 S.Ct., at 10. And in Crane v. New York, 239 U.S. 195, 36 S.Ct. 85, 60 L.Ed. 218 (1915), the Court affirmed the judgment in People v. Crane, 214 N.Y. 154, 108 N.E. 427 (1915), upholding a New York statute prohibiting the employment of aliens on public works projects. The New York court's opinion contained Mr. Justice Cardozo's well-known observation:

> "To disqualify aliens is discrimination indeed, but not arbitrary discrimination, for the principle of exclusion is the restriction of the resources of the state to the advancement and profit of the members of the state. Ungenerous and unwise such discrimination may be. It is not for that reason unlawful. . . . The state in determining what use shall be made of its own moneys, may legitimately consult the welfare of its own citizens, rather than that of aliens. Whatever is a privilege, rather than a right, may be made dependent upon citizenship. In its war against poverty, the state is not required to dedicate its own resources to citizens and aliens alike." 214 N.Y., at 161, 164, 108 N.E., at 429, 430.

See Heim v. McCall, 239 U.S. 175, 36 S.Ct. 78, 60 L.Ed. 206 (1915); Ohio ex rel. Clarke v. Deckebach, 274 U.S. 392, 47 S.Ct. 630, 71 L.Ed. 1115 (1927). On the same theory, the Court has upheld statutes that, in the absence of overriding treaties, limit the right of noncitizens to engage in exploitation of a State's natural resources, restrict the devolution of real property to aliens, or deny to aliens the right to acquire and own land.

Takahashi v. Fish & Game Comm'n, 334 U.S. 410, 68 S.Ct. 1138, 92 L.Ed. 1478 (1948), however, cast doubt on the continuing validity of the special public-interest doctrine in all contexts. . . .

Whatever may be the contemporary vitality of the special public-interest doctrine in other contexts after *Takahashi,* we conclude that a State's desire to preserve limited welfare benefits for its own citizens is inadequate to justify Pennsylvania's making noncitizens ineligible for public assistance, and Arizona's restricting benefits to citizens and longtime resident aliens. First, the special public interest doctrine was heavily grounded on the notion that "[w]hatever is a privilege, rather than a right, may be made dependent upon citizenship." People v. Crane, 214 N.Y., at 164, 108 N.E., at 430. But this Court now has rejected the concept that constitutional rights turn upon whether a governmental benefit is characterized as a "right" or as a "privilege." . . .

> Second, as the Court recognized in *Shapiro* [v. *Thompson*]: "[A] State has a valid interest in preserving the fiscal integrity of its programs. It may legitimately attempt to limit its expenditures, whether for public assistance, public education, or any other program. But a State may not accomplish such a purpose by invidious distinctions between classes of its citizens. . . . The saving of welfare costs cannot justify an otherwise invidious classification." 394 U.S., at 633, 89 S.Ct., at 1330.

Since an alien as well as a citizen is a "person" for equal protection purposes, a concern for fiscal integrity is no more compelling a justification for the questioned classification in these cases than it was in *Shapiro.*

. . .

We agree with the three-judge court in the Pennsylvania case that the "justification of limiting expenses is particularly inappropriate and unreasonable when the discriminated class consists of aliens. Aliens like citizens pay taxes and may be called into the armed forces. Unlike the short-term residents in *Shapiro,* aliens may live within a state for many years, work in the state and contribute to the economic growth of the state." 321 F.Supp., at 253. See also Purdy & Fitzpatrick v. California, 71 Cal.2d 566, 581–582, 79 Cal.Rptr. 77, 456 P.2d 645, 656 (1969). There can be no "special public interest" in tax revenues to which aliens have contributed on an equal basis with the residents of the State.

Accordingly, we hold that a state statute that denies welfare benefits to resident aliens and one that denies them to aliens who have not resided in the United States for a specified number of years violate the Equal Protection Clause.

III

An additional reason why the state statutes at issue in these cases do not withstand constitutional scrutiny emerges from the area of federal-state relations. The National Government has "broad constitutional powers in determining what aliens shall be admitted to the United States, the period they may remain, regulation of their conduct before naturalization, and the terms and conditions of their naturalization." Takahashi v. Fish & Game Comm'n, 334 U.S., at 419, 68 S.Ct., at 1142; Hines v. Davidowitz, 312 U.S. 52, 66, 61 S.Ct.

399, 403, 85 L.Ed. 581 (1941); . . . . Pursuant to that power, Congress has provided, as part of a comprehensive plan for the regulation of immigration and naturalization, that "[a]liens who are paupers, professional beggars, or vagrants" or aliens who "are likely at any time to become public charges" shall be excluded from admission into the United States, 8 U.S.C.A. §§ 1182(a)(8) and 1182(a)(15), and that any alien lawfully admitted shall be deported who "has within five years after entry become a public charge from causes not affirmatively shown to have arisen after entry. . . ." 8 U.S.C.A. § 1251(a)(8). Admission of aliens likely to become public charges may be conditioned upon the posting of a bond or cash deposit. 8 U.S.C.A. § 1138. But Congress has not seen fit to impose any burden or restriction on aliens who become indigent after their entry into the United States. Rather, it has broadly declared: "All persons within the jurisdiction of the United States shall have the same right in every State and Territory . . . to the full and equal benefit of all laws and proceedings for the security of persons and property as is enjoyed by white citizens. . . ." 42 U.S.C.A. § 1981. The protection of this statute has been held to extend to aliens as well as to citizens. *Takahashi,* 334 U.S., at 419 n. 7, 68 S.Ct., at 1142. Moreover, this Court has made it clear that, whatever may be the scope of the constitutional right of interstate travel, aliens lawfully within this country have a right to enter and abide in any State in the Union "on an equality of legal privileges with all citizens under nondiscriminatory laws." *Takahashi,* 334 U.S., at 420, 68 S.Ct., at 1143.

State laws that restrict the eligibility of aliens for welfare benefits merely because of their alienage conflict with these overriding national policies in an area constitutionally entrusted to the Federal Government. In Hines v. Davidowitz, 312 U.S., at 66–67, 61 S.Ct., at 403–404, where this Court struck down a Pennsylvania alien registration statute (enacted in 1939, as was the statute under challenge in No. 727) on grounds of federal pre-emption, it was observed that "where the federal government, in the exercise of its superior authority in this field, has enacted a complete scheme of regulation . . . states cannot, inconsistently with the purpose of Congress, conflict or interfere with, curtail or complement, the federal law, or enforce additional or auxiliary regulations." . . .

. . .

In *Truax* the Court considered the "reasonableness" of a state restriction on the employment of aliens in terms of its effect on the right of a lawfully admitted alien to live where he chooses:

. . . . The same is true here, for in the ordinary case an alien, becoming indigent and unable to work, will be unable to live where, because of discriminatory denial of public assistance, he cannot "secure the necessities of life, including food, clothing and shelter." State alien residency requirements that either deny welfare benefits to noncitizens or condition them on longtime residency, equate with the assertion of a right, inconsistent with federal policy, to deny entrance and abode. Since such laws encroach upon exclusive federal power, they are constitutionally impermissible.

IV

Arizona suggests, finally, that its 15-year durational residency requirement for aliens is actually authorized by federal law. Reliance is placed on § 1402(b) of the Social Security Act of 1935, added by the Act of Aug. 28, 1950, § 351, 64 Stat. 556, as amended, 42 U.S.C.A. § 1352(b). That section provides:

> "The Secretary shall approve any plan which fulfills the conditions specified in subsection (a) of this section, except that he shall not approve any plan which imposes, as a condition of eligibility for aid to the permanently and totally disabled under the plan—
>
> . . . .
>
> "(2) Any citizenship requirement which excludes any citizen of the United States."

The meaning of this provision is not entirely clear. On its face, the statute does not affirmatively authorize, much less command, the States to adopt durational residency requirements or other eligibility restrictions applicable to aliens; it merely directs the Secretary not to approve state-submitted plans that exclude citizens of the United States from eligibility. Cf. Shapiro v. Thompson, 394 U.S., at 638–641, 89 S.Ct., at 1333–1335.

We have been unable to find in the legislative history of the 1950 amendments any clear indication of congressional intent in enacting § 1402(b). The provision appears to have its roots in identical language of the old-age assistance and aid-to-the-blind sections of the Social Security Act of 1935 as originally enacted. 49 Stat. 620, 42 U.S.C.A. § 302(b); 49 Stat. 645, 42 U.S.C.A. § 1202(b). The House and Senate Committee Reports expressly state, with reference to old-age assistance, that:

> "A person shall not be denied assistance on the ground that he has not been a United States citizen for a number of years, if in fact, when he receives assistance, he is a United States citizen. This means that a State may, if it wishes, assist only those who are citizens, but must not insist on their having been born citizens or on their having been naturalized citizens for a specified period of time."

It is apparent from this that Congress' principal concern in 1935 was to prevent the States from distinguishing between native-born American citizens and naturalized citizens in the distribution of welfare benefits. It may be assumed that Congress was motivated by a similar concern in 1950 when it enacted § 1402(b). As for the indication in the 1935 Committee Reports that the States, in their discretion, could withhold benefits from noncitizens, certain members of Congress simply may have been expressing their understanding of the law only insofar as it had then developed, that is, before *Takahashi* was decided. But if § 1402(b), as well as the identical provisions for old-age assistance and aid to the blind, were to be read so as to authorize discriminatory treatment of aliens at the option of the States, *Takahashi* demonstrates that serious constitutional questions are presented. Although the Federal Government admittedly has broad constitutional power to determine what aliens shall be admitted to the United States, the period they may remain, and the terms and conditions of their naturalization, Congress does not have the power to authorize the individual States to violate the Equal Protection Clause. Shapiro v. Thompson, 394 U.S., at 641, 89 S.Ct. at 1335. Under Art. I, § 8, cl. 4, of the Constitution, Congress' power is to "establish an uniform Rule of Naturalization." A congressional enactment construed so as to permit state legislatures to adopt divergent laws on the subject of citizenship requirements for federally supported welfare programs would appear to contravene this explicit constitutional requirement of uniformity.[12] Since "statutes should be construed whenever possible so as to uphold their constitutionality," United States v. Vuitch, 402 U.S. 62, 70, 91 S.Ct. 1294, 1298, 28 L.Ed.2d 601 (1971), we conclude that § 1402(b) does not authorize the Arizona 15-year national residency requirement.

The judgments appealed from are affirmed.

It is so ordered.

Affirmed.

MR. JUSTICE HARLAN joins in Parts III and IV of the Court's opinion, and in the judgment of the Court.

IN RE GRIFFITHS

Supreme Court of the United States, 1973.
413 U.S. 717, 93 S.Ct. 2851, 37 L.Ed.2d 910.

MR. JUSTICE POWELL delivered the opinion of the Court.

This case presents a novel question as to the constraints imposed by the Equal Protection Clause of the Fourteenth Amendment on the qualifications which a State may require for admission to the bar. Appellant, Fre Le Poole Griffiths, is a citizen of the Netherlands who came to the United States in 1965, originally as a visitor. In 1967 she married a citizen of the United States and became a resident of Connecticut.[13] After her graduation from law school, she applied in 1970 for permission to take the Connecticut bar examination. The County Bar Association found her qualified in all respects save that she was not a citizen of the United States as required by Rule 8(1) of the Connecticut Practice Book (1963) and on that account refused to allow her to take the examination. She then sought judicial relief, asserting that the regulation was unconstitutional but her claim was rejected first by the Superior Court and ultimately by the Connecticut Supreme Court. 162 Conn. 249, 294 A.2d 281 (1972). We noted probable jurisdiction, 406 U.S. 966, 92 S.Ct. 2413, 32 L.Ed.2d 665 (1972), and now hold that the rule unconstitutionally discriminates against resident aliens.

I

We begin by sketching the background against which the State Bar Examining Committee attempts to justify the total exclusion of aliens from the practice of law. From its inception, our Nation welcomed and drew strength from the immigration of aliens. Their contributions to the social and economic life of the country were self-evident, especially during the periods when the demand for human resources greatly exceeded the native supply. This demand was

12. We have no occasion to decide whether Congress, in the exercise of the immigration and naturalization power, could itself enact a statute imposing on aliens a uniform nationwide residency requirement as a condition of federally funded welfare benefits.

13. Appellant is eligible for naturalization by reason of her marriage to a citizen of the United States and residence in the United States for more than three years, 8 U.S.C.A. § 1430(a). She has not filed a declaration of intention to become a citizen of the United States, 8 U.S.C.A. § 1445(f), and has no present intention of doing so. Appellant's Brief, p. 4. In order to become a citizen, appellant would be required to renounce her citizenship of the Netherlands. 8 U.S.C.A. § 1448(a).

by no means limited to the unskilled or the uneducated. In 1872, this Court, noted that admission to the practice of law in the courts of a State

> "in no sense depends on citizenship of the United States. It has not, as far as we know, ever been made in any State, or in any case, to depend on citizenship at all. Certainly many prominent and distinguished lawyers have been admitted to practice, both in the State and Federal courts, who were not citizens of the United States or of any State." Bradwell v. The State, 16 Wall. 130, 139, 21 L.Ed. 442 (1872).

But shortly thereafter, in 1879, Connecticut established the predecessor to its present rule totally excluding aliens from the practice of law. 162 Conn., at 253, 294 A.2d, at 283. In subsequent decades, wide-ranging restrictions for the first time began to impair significantly the efforts of aliens to earn a livelihood in their chosen occupations.

. . .

The Court has consistently emphasized that a State which adopts a suspect classification "bears a heavy burden of justification," McLaughlin v. Florida, 379 U.S. 184, 196, 85 S.Ct. 283, 290, 13 L.Ed.2d 222 (1964), a burden which, though variously formulated, requires the State to meet certain standards of proof. In order to justify the use of a suspect classification, a State must show that its purpose or interest is both constitutionally permissible and substantial, and that its use of the classification is "necessary to the accomplishment" of its purpose or the safeguarding of its interest.

Resident aliens, like citizens, pay taxes, support the economy, serve in the armed forces, and contribute in myriad other ways to our society. It is appropriate that a State bear a heavy burden when it deprives them of employment opportunities.

II

We hold that the Committee, acting on behalf of the State, has not carried its burden. The State's ultimate interest here implicated is to assure the requisite qualifications of persons licensed to practice law. It is undisputed that a State has a constitutionally permissible and substantial interest in determining whether an applicant possesses "the character and general fitness requisite for an attorney and counselor-at-law." . . . But no question is raised in this case as to appellant's character or general fitness. Rather, the sole basis for disqualification is her status as a resident alien.

The Committee defends Rule 8(1)'s requirement that applicants for admission to the bar be citizens of the United States on the ground that the special role of the lawyer justifies excluding aliens from the practice of law. In Connecticut, the Committee points out, the maxim that a lawyer is an "officer of the court" is given concrete meaning by a statute which makes every lawyer a "commissioner of the Superior Court." As such, a lawyer has authority to "sign writs and subpoenas, take recognizances, administer oaths and take depositions and acknowledgements of deeds." Conn.Gen.Stat. § 51–85. In the exercise of this authority, a Connecticut lawyer may command the assistance of a county sheriff or a town constable. Conn.Gen. Stat. § 52–90. Because of these and other powers, the Connecticut Supreme Court commented that:

> "the courts not only demand [lawyers'] loyalty, confidence and respect but also require them to function in a manner

which will foster public confidence in the profession and, consequently, the judicial system." 162 Conn., at 262–263, 294 A.2d, at 287.

In order to establish a link between citizenship and the powers and responsibilities of the lawyer in Connecticut, the Committee contrasts a citizen's undivided allegiance to this country with a resident alien's possible conflict of loyalties. From this, the Committee concludes that a resident alien lawyer might in the exercise of his functions ignore his responsibilities to the courts or even his clients in favor of the interest of a foreign power.

We find these arguments unconvincing. It in no way denigrates a lawyer's high responsibilities to observe that the powers "to sign writs and subpoenas, take recognizances, [and] administer oaths" hardly involve matters of state policy or acts of such unique responsibility as to entrust them only to citizens. Nor do we think that the practice of law offers meaningful opportunities adversely to affect the interest of the United States. Certainly the Committee has failed to show the relevance of citizenship to any likelihood that a lawyer will fail to protect faithfully the interest of his clients.

Nor would the possibility that some resident aliens are unsuited to the practice of law be a justification for a wholesale ban. . . .

Connecticut has wide freedom to gauge on a case-by-case basis the fitness of an applicant to practice law. Connecticut can, and does, require appropriate training and familiarity with Connecticut law. Apart from such tests of competence, it requires a new lawyer to take both an "attorney's oath" to perform his functions faithfully and honestly and a "commissioner's oath" to "support the Constitution of the United States, and the Constitution of Connecticut." Appellant has indicated her willingness and ability to subscribe to the substance of both oaths, and Connecticut may quite properly conduct a character investigation to insure in any given case "that an applicant is not one who 'swears to an oath *pro forma* while declaring or manifesting his disagreement with or indifference to the oath.' Bond v. Floyd, 385 U.S. 116, 132 [87 S.Ct. 339, 347, 17 L.Ed.2d 235]. Law Students Research Council v. Wadmond, supra, 401 U.S. at 164,[14] 91 S.Ct., at 727. Moreover, once admitted to the bar, lawyers are subject to continuing scrutiny by the organized bar and the courts. In addition to discipline for unprofessional conduct, the range of postadmission sanctions extends from judgments for contempt to criminal prosecutions and disbarment. In sum, the Committee simply has not established that it must exclude all aliens from the practice of law in order to vindicate its undoubted interest in high professional standards.

14. We find no merit in the contention that only citizens can in good conscience take an oath to support the Constitution. We note that all persons inducted into the armed services, including resident aliens, are required by 10 U.S.C.A. § 502 to take the following oath:

"I, ________, do solemnly swear (or affirm) that I will support and defend the Constitution of the United States against all enemies, foreign and domestic; that I will bear true faith and allegiance to the same; and that I will obey the orders of the President of the United States and the orders of the officers appointed over me, according to regulations and the Uniform Code of Military Justice. So help me God."

If aliens can take this oath when the Nation is making use of their services in the national defense, resident alien applicants for admission to the bar surely cannot be precluded, as a class, from taking an oath to support the Constitution on the theory that they are unable to take the oath in good faith.

III

In its brief, the Examining Committee makes another, somewhat different argument in support of Rule 8(1). Its thrust is not that resident aliens lack the attributes necessary to maintain high standards in the legal profession, but rather that lawyers must be citizens almost as a matter of definition. The implication of this analysis is that exclusion of aliens from the legal profession is not subject to any scrutiny under the Equal Protection Clause.

The argument builds upon the exclusion of aliens from the franchise in all 50 States and their disqualification under the Constitution from holding office as President, Art. 2, § 1, cl. 4, or as a member of the House of Representatives, Art. 1, § 2, cl. 2, or of the Senate, Art. 1, § 3, cl. 3. These and numerous other federal and statutory and constitutional provisions reflect, the Committee contends, a pervasive recognition that "participation in the government structure as voters and office holders" is inescapably an aspect of citizenship. Appellee's Brief, p. 11. Offered in support of the claim that the lawyer is an "office holder" in this sense is an enhanced version of the proposition, discussed above, that he is an "officer of the court." Specifically, the Committee states that the lawyer "is an officer of the court who acts by and with the authority of the state" and is entrusted with the "exercise of actual government power." Appellee's Brief, p. 5.

. . .

Lawyers do indeed occupy professional positions of responsibility and influence that impose on them duties correlative with their vital right of access to the courts. Moreover, by virtue of their professional aptitudes and natural interests, lawyers have been leaders in government throughout the history of our country. Yet, they are not officials of government by virtue of being lawyers. Nor does the status of holding a license to practice law place one so close to the core of the political process as to make him a formulator of government policy.

We hold that § 8(1) violates the Equal Protection Clause. The judgment of the Connecticut Supreme Court is reversed, and the case is remanded for further proceedings not inconsistent with this opinion.

Reversed and remanded.

[In his dissenting opinion, CHIEF JUSTICE BURGER stressed the "monopoly" powers granted a lawyer by the state—such as trying cases, or commanding the presence of persons or production of documents at trial. The concept of the lawyer "as an officer of the court" is deep in the common law, but has been subject to an unfortunate erosion in recent decades in the public mind. The lawyer owes his first duty to his client, but within basic legal constraints. There is "a reasonable, rational basis" for a state to conclude that citizens will better grasp such traditions of duty and constraint in the profession.

MR. JUSTICE REHNQUIST's dissent covered both this case and the companion case of Sugarman v. Dougall, 413 U.S. 634, 93 S.Ct. 2842, 37 L.Ed.2d 853 (1973). In *Sugarman,* the Court held unconstitutional a provision of New York's Civil Service Law to the effect that only citizens could hold permanent positions in the competitive class of the state civil service. The Court found that provision too indiscriminate and unrelated to substantial state interests to withstand challenge under the Equal Protection Clause. The opinion rejected the doctrine developed in earlier cases that public employment involved a "special public interest" justifying discrimination against aliens. The Court stressed, however, that the holding did not cover an "individualized determination" that alienage disqualified an applicant from a particular position in view of "legitimate state interests" relating to that position. Nor did the holding mean that a state could not, "in an appropriately defined class of positions", require citizenship. The state retained broad power to exclude aliens "from participation in its democratic political institutions," in view of aliens' special status within a "political community."

Justice Rehnquist took issue particularly with the Court's rejection of a standard of judicial review used in a number of earlier decisions involving aliens—that legislative classifications "were subject to the rational basis test of equal protection." Rather the Court in recent cases had adopted the view that "classifications based on alienage . . . . are inherently suspect." In Justice Rehnquist's view, the proper standard in the two cases was "whether any rational justification exists for prohibiting aliens from employment in the competitive civil service and from admission to a state bar." The Justice found such justification in both cases.]

NOTE ON FEDERAL CONTROL OVER ECONOMIC ACTIVITIES OF ALIENS

An inventory of restraints imposed by the federal government on aliens' entry into economic activity turns up a brief list of barriers to foreign participation in defined fields of industrial or commercial activity.[15]

(*1*) Since 1789 legislation has restricted ownership of vessels of United States registry entitled to fly the American flag to American nationals. Over the years the definition of American citizen has been refined so as to prevent alien domination through the device of foreign stockownership or managerial control. American registry in turn is a prerequisite to the right to engage in "cabotage", or the movement of goods or passengers from one American port to another. A series of exceptions, granted to protect the interests of particular ports or to ease the operations of foreign lumber and oil concerns dependent on the ownership of barges or tugs, has done something to undermine that rule. American registry is also a necessity if one wishes to claim the benefit of the subsidies for construction and operation which are conferred on vessels that continue to compete under the American flag in the international shipping business, despite the advantages that accrue to fleeing to other flags (see pp. 970–973, infra).

(*2*) Since the first federal legislation on civil aviation, foreign interests have been barred from participation in terms similar to those of the current shipping laws. Only planes of U. S. registry can carry

15. An up-to-date review of these statutes appears in Foreign Investment in the United States, Hearings before the Subcommittee on International Finance of the Senate Committee on Banking, Housing and Urban Affairs, pt. 1, 93rd Cong., 2d Sess., pp. 146–150, (1974). For their history see Vagts, The Corporate Alien, 74 Harv.L.Rev. 1489 (1961).

passengers from one point to another within the country. Foreign airlines, of course, fly from U. S. airports to foreign points but only pursuant to arrangements worked out between U. S. and foreign government authorities.

(*3*) Radio and television licenses for broadcasting and transmission can only be held by American individuals or corporations. The stated reason (see pp. 76–78, infra) has been the requirement of national security in case of hostilities.

(*4*) Defense contractors must satisfy a number of tests of reliability, including that of U. S. ownership and management. For parallel reasons, only citizens and domestic corporations can obtain licenses to use or produce radioactive materials under legislation relating to the Atomic Energy Commission.

(*5*) Land and mineral rights possessed by the federal government have generally been reserved for sale or lease to citizens. As the federal government's stock of saleable land has shrunk, particularly with the statehood of Hawaii and Alaska, those rules have diminished in importance. There is still some significance in the Mineral Leasing Act, but its permissiveness towards leasing by aliens whose governments grant reciprocal rights to American nationals has narrowed its practical application.

(*6*) Fishing rights of nonresident aliens in the territorial sea and a broader exclusive fisheries zone are now the subject of intense national and international debate, as described at pp. 270–274, infra.

(*7*) Federal law governing banking operations makes special provisions for certain types of participation by aliens.

The federal government has thus not been active in restricting access of individual aliens or alien-owned corporations to particular economic activities within the private sector. Indeed, as we have observed, the judiciary has applied the federal Constitution to limit state power in this field. Moreover, the federal civil-rights legislation of the post-Civil War and contemporary periods has been drawn upon as an additional constraint upon official and, to a limited extent, private discrimination against aliens.[16] Nonetheless, federal legislation does bar aliens from extensive fields of *federal* employment and provides for only limited exceptions to the exclusion of aliens from the competitive federal civil service.

16. The court in Guerra v. Manchester Terminal Corp., 350 F.Supp. 529 (S.D. Tex.1972) drew upon the 1870 Civil Rights Act, now amended and codified as 42 U.S.C.A. § 1981, in finding support for a registered alien's action charging his employer and union with private rather than state discrimination against him in employment opportunities. That opinion refers to a decision of the Supreme Court which drew upon related civil rights legislation as a supplemental basis for invalidating state restrictions on aliens. In Espinoza v. Farah Manufacturing Co., Inc., 414 U.S. 86, 94 S.Ct. 334, 38 L.Ed.2d 287 (1973), the Court concluded that the anti-discrimination provisions, applicable to private employers, of Title VII of the 1964 Civil Rights Act did not cover discrimination against aliens as such.

In comparing the scope of federal legislation in this field with state laws, and the constitutional considerations relevant to federal or state law, bear in mind the following considerations:

(*1*) The Equal Protection Clause of the Fourteenth Amendment governs of course only state action, and the Constitution contains no such clause which is binding on the federal government. Nonetheless, in Bolling v. Sharpe, 347 U.S. 497, 499, 74 S.Ct. 693, 694, 98 L.Ed. 884, 886 (1954), the Supreme Court noted that ". . . the concepts of equal protection and due process, both stemming from our American ideal of fairness, are not mutually exclusive. The 'equal protection of the laws' is a more explicit safeguard of prohibited unfairness than 'due process of law,' and, therefore, we do not imply that the two are always interchangeable phrases. But, as this Court has recognized, discrimination may be so unjustifiable as to be violative of [Fifth Amendment] due process." The Court held that racial segregation in public schools in the District of Columbia violated the Due Process Clause.

(*2*) The federal government is armed with a variety of powers affecting aliens and foreign relations that are denied to the states or exercisable by the states only as permitted by federal law. We have encountered such powers in several judicial decisions in this chapter. Moreover, recall that the finding of a conflict between state legislation discriminating against aliens and a paramount or exclusive federal power over the admission or residence of aliens appeared to stand as an independent ground for invalidating state legislation in Truax v. Raich, p. 46, supra, and Graham v. Richardson, p. 49, supra. Thus the question arises whether the current demanding standard for state justification of anti-alien discrimination should be applied to the federal government as well—and, if not, under what criteria the federal legislation would be tested. Would the judiciary, for example, consider federal policy about economic opportunities of aliens to be related to foreign affairs and thus within the category of "political questions" that were stressed by the Court in Harisiades v. Shaughnessy, p. 26, supra?

(*3*) The restrictive federal legislation described at the start of this Note must be supplemented by the single most comprehensive federal regulation over economic activities of individual aliens, namely the Immigration and Nationality Act of 1952. Recall that many provisions of that Act make admission of an alien dependent upon the domestic employment situation and determine the ability of nonimmigrant aliens to work while in this country on visas of limited duration: Section 101(a)(15)*, defining the status and permitted range of activities of nonimmigrant aliens; Section 203 * and the preferences that it establishes for immigrants; Section 212(a)(14)*, treating the relationship between the domestic labor market and exclusionary policies; and Section 241(a) (9)*, making the nonimmigrant alien deportable if he violates the restrictive conditions to his admission.

In view of the special considerations applicable to federal regulation of aliens, it appeared doubtful that a successful constitutional challenge could be mounted to federal legislation that limited economic opportunities or welfare benefits to citizens. But the force of the Supreme Court decisions invalidating state legislation has encouraged lower federal courts to subject federal legislation to probing inquiry and, thus far in a few cases, to find the legislation invalid. Two such decisions—both of which, it should be stressed, involve application of federal restrictions to resident aliens rather than to aliens present under short-term visas—are summarized below:

Diaz v. Weinberger, 361 F.Supp. 1 (S.D.Fla.1973), probable juris. noted, 416 U.S. 980, 94 S.Ct. 2381, 40 L.Ed.2d 757 (1974).

Cuban refugees, all aliens, challenged the constitutionality of provisions in the supplemental medical insurance plan, established as a part of the federal Medicare program, that disqualified from benefits all aliens except those who were lawfully admitted for permanent residence and who had resided in the United States continuously for five years prior to their application for enrollment. The insurance plan pays a substantial part of the cost of medical services. A three-judge district court found the alien eligibility requirement unconstitutional as a denial of the due process guaranteed by the Fifth Amendment.

The court noted the distinctions between federal and state power in this field, and observed that "we cannot say that Congress may never be held to a lesser constitutional standard than the states, but . . . neither can we accept the view that Congress may never be held to the same standard." The opinion stressed the susceptibility of aliens, not represented politically in state or federal legislatures, to "open discrimination at the hands of the political process." Thus, it observed, there could be instances "when application of a compelling interest standard is warranted in review of state and federal enactments to protect aliens from discrimination resulting from their lack of political representation."

The court concluded that, whether a "compelling interest standard" or a "rational basis test" were used, the legislation could not withstand scrutiny. It found inadequate the asserted justifications of the federal government's need to achieve fiscal integrity and of the need to bar aliens temporarily visiting or residing in the U. S. from medical-treatment benefits. Thus the five-year residency requirement violated "equal protection notions inherent in Fifth Amendment due process." The court ended its opinion by observing:

> America once held her arms open wide, beckoning other lands to "[g]ive me your tired, your poor, your huddled

> masses yearning to breathe free, the wretched refuse of your teeming shores . . . ." Although it may be, as some cynics have remarked, that this is exactly what she got, to the extent our nation continues to hold out a promise of refuge to victims of political and natural misfortune, the Constitution requires that we accept them to reside here on an equal basis with citizens.

Wong v. Hampton, 500 F.2d 1031 (9th Cir. 1974), cert. granted, 417 U.S. 944, 94 S.Ct. 3067, 41 L.Ed.2d 664 (1974).

The court concluded that the United States civil service regulations, 5 C.F.R. § 338.101 (1971), reserving employment in the federal competitive civil service to citizens, unreasonably discriminated against resident aliens and hence violated the Due Process Clause of the Fifth Amendment. The court relied upon Sugarman v. Dougall, p. —, supra, stressing that opinion's observation that state discrimination against employment of aliens must be based upon a legitimate state interest relating to necessary qualifications for a particular position or to the characteristics of a particular employee. "To state that Congress' plenary power over aliens enables the federal government to unreasonably discriminate against aliens, neglects to consider the fact that even congressional plenary power is subject to constitutional limits." Thus the rationales and holdings of Sugarman v. Dougall and Graham v. Richardson, p. 49, supra, were "instructive and significant" even though they dealt with state power under the Fourteenth Amendment. In finding the regulations violative of due process, the court nonetheless rejected the contention that "the protection provided by the Fifth Amendment is co-extensive with the equal protection clause of the Fourteenth Amendment."

The court observed that the federal regulations shared the vice of the regulations in Sugarman, namely their "broad sweep". The appellants named in this class action included a janitor, file clerk, typist and mail clerk—positions which, like "the majority of civil service positions do not actually participate either in the making or in the execution of national policy . . ." The court rejected the justifications for the regulations that were urged by the Government. Principal among them was the assertion of the government's "right to provide for the economic security of its citizens before its resident aliens." The court stressed that resident aliens assumed important obligations, including tax obligations and liability to military service, and contributed to the growth and welfare of this country. It found the argument of national-security considerations inapplicable to the present broad discrimination, but noted that such a governmental interest, on other facts, might be sufficient to justify discrimination. It viewed as irrelevant the fact that there was a "universal practice of other nations requiring civil servants to be citizens," for that fact did not prove the "compelling government interest" necessary to justify a broad discrimination under the United States Constitution.

QUESTIONS

(1) "Whatever the differences in subject matter, the state statutes in Truax v. Raich and Terrace v. Thompson involved identical state concerns." Do you agree? If so, how would you identify those concerns?

(2) "The holdings in Sugarman v. Dougall (p. 57, supra) and Wong v. Hampton are not extensions but simply reaffirmations of Truax v. Raich. 'Private' employment is as much a public resource of the country as is 'public' employment. If aliens cannot be excluded from the first, there is no greater reason to exclude them from the second." Do you agree?

PROBLEMS

I

The chapter of the codified Laws of the State of Ames entitled Restrictions on Aliens contains the following sections:

> 1. No alien shall be eligible for employment as a police officer within the Police Department of the state or of any political subdivision thereof.
>
> 2. No alien individual or alien corporation shall engage in the business of extracting minerals from deposits or own lands containing such deposits within this State. An alien corporation is a corporation (a) organized outside the United States, or (b) more than 50% of whose voting stock is owned beneficially by aliens, or (c) more than half of whose board of directors consists of aliens.

Several cities in Ames have substantial communities of resident aliens of Canadian and Cuban nationality. One Jorge Rodriguez, a Cuban national admitted to the United States on an immigrant visa six years ago, had his application to join the police force of a city in Ames denied because of his alien status.

Doe, a United States citizen, owned land in Ames which contained sulfur deposits. He entered into a contract for the sale of such land to International Ventures, Inc., an Ames corporation all of whose common stock was owned by aliens. International Ventures intends to exploit the sulfur deposits for sale in this country or abroad as the market dictates. Doe now refuses to consummate the contract on the ground that acquisition and exploitation by International Ventures would violate Ames law.

Rodriguez instituted a declaratory judgment action in the Ames court, seeking a judgment that Section 1 was invalid on its face or as applied. International Ventures brought an action in the Ames courts against Doe to compel specific performance. The lower courts found both laws valid and denied the relief requested. In each case, the Ames Supreme Court affirmed. Both decisions are now on appeal before the United States Supreme Court.

As the attorney general of Ames, you will argue these cases before the Supreme Court as counsel for the State or as *amicus curiae*. Your research indicates that the legislative history for these two enactments is sparse and uninformative. There is some indication that the restrictions on police officers were based upon considerations of loyalty and security, while the restrictions on mineral extraction had as one of several possible purposes the retention of scarce natural resources within this country.

State the lines of argument that you will stress before the Supreme Court, and the responses that you will make to the positions that you can expect Rodriguez and International Ventures to assert.

II.

You are legislative assistant to a United States senator who is wondering what position to take on proposed legislation that would authorize the Secretary of Labor to withdraw existing permissions and otherwise prohibit all aliens, resident or temporarily in this country, from employment, in the event that domestic unemployment exceeds a stated percentage of the working population. The senator has asked you to express your view of the legality and advisability of such legislation.

NOTE ON UNITED STATES ATTITUDES TOWARDS FOREIGN INVESTMENT IN THIS COUNTRY

Over most of its history the United States has been able to take a detached view of investment by foreigners in its economy, partly for the reasons stated at p. 45, supra. In his famous Report on Manufacturers, Alexander Hamilton praised foreign capital as a source of growth for the new country. Foreign funds financed the American agricultural export trade and provided the wherewithal for the construction of American canals, railroads and mines. Significantly, foreign investment in the 19th Century was overwhelmingly portfolio investment—that is, in bonds or in small blocks of stock not carrying with them the capacity for control. European investors were content to allow American entrepreneurs to manage for them; indeed, communications and managerial techniques then would not have allowed the Erie Railroad to be run from Frankfurt or London. Although some legislation, particularly that affecting land in the federal territories, reflected concern about foreign control, this theme was muted.

The great epoch of foreign investment in the United States came to an end in 1914–17. Britain and France had to require the sale of large portions of their citizens' holdings to raise dollars to buy food and munitions. German assets, on the other hand, were confiscated after our entry into the war under the Trading with the Enemy Act, p. 42, supra. Thus the United States entered the 1920's largely freed of indebtedness towards foreigners and under pressure to furnish funds for reconstruction and expansion abroad. Although some foreign funds returned to the United States securities markets in the inter-war period, this trend was less pronounced than the outward flow. World War II then caused another sharp decline in foreign investment.

It was only in the 1960's that increased prosperity in Europe and Japan, coupled with a weakening in the position of the dollar vis-a-vis other currencies, made it practical for foreign enterprises to think seriously about investing in the United States. Moved by a worsening balance of payments, the government caused studies of the foreign investment problem to be made. Pursuant to those studies' recommendations, the tax laws were reformed to ease the burden of foreigners on income from such investments (p. 1102, infra); the Securities and Exchange Commission relaxed its application of registration requirements to securities sold abroad; and so on. Foreign industry's stake in the United States economy grew as Japanese, British, Swiss and Dutch firms sought access to large United States markets, as well as to its relatively cheap real estate and other assets. American-style investment company promotion by mutual funds such as Investors Overseas Services (and others more solidly based) spread U. S. investments around Europe.

By the 1970's the pace started to pick up as foreign labor costs rose to meet American levels. Other costs were equalized by the devaluation of the dollar, which also had the effect of making foreign imports into this country more expensive. The 10% U. S. surtax in 1971 (see p. 116, infra) on imports further prejudiced foreign exporters to this country and encouraged operations within it. Moreover, our balance-of-payments deficits had built up large foreign liquid holdings; particularly the Arab oil-producing countries found themselves with enormous holdings of dollars which they could not immediately use.

Total foreign direct investment in the United States (here defined as foreign ownership interests of 25% or more in domestic enterprises) has become substantial. Estimates of the increase in foreign direct investment inflow in 1973 range from $2 to $3 billion, and those of the accumulated total of foreign direct investment run from $14.4 to $38 billion.[17] This may be compared with about $86 billion direct United States investment abroad. The leading countries of origin of the direct investment here are, in descending order, the United Kingdom, Canada, the Netherlands and Switzerland. Small and medium-sized foreign firms have established new business operations here, while such multinational giants as Unilever, Olivetti, British Petroleum and Lever Brothers have expanded their U. S. bases. Still, none of the studies has pointed to any branch of the American economy that is foreign-controlled to the point of 99.5% (like Canadian petroleum) or 45% (like the French radio and television equipment industry). And, in particular, none of the industries referred to as "commanding heights"—fast-moving technology areas such as computers—is under foreign control.

17. H.R.Rep.No.93–1183, 93rd Cong., 2nd Sess. (1974), p. 2. As witnesses before the various congressional hearings in 1974 and 1975 on foreign investment in this country made clear, statistical information was incomplete, and statistical methods (such as recording investments at book value) further qualified the significance of comparisons between direct foreign investment here and American direct investment abroad. The witnesses from the Executive Branch in several of the hearings used the figures (as of the end of 1972) of approximately $14 billion of direct foreign investment here, compared with about $96 billion of American direct investment abroad. Estimates of private groups of foreign direct investment here ranged up to the higher figure of $38 billion.

Gradually American reactions developed. Some industries felt threatened by foreign competition; U. S. securities dealers, for example, worried about competition from foreign banks which, unlike American firms, are not excluded from having affiliates that are broker-dealers. The targets of foreign take-over bids fought back with suits alleging such matters as the failure of tender offers to disclose significant facts to shareholders, the anti-competitive effects of the proposed acquisition, or violations of the margin limits on borrowing on the strength of securities. Texasgulf, a firm with substantial mining interests in Canada which it had, ironically, acquired without much disclosure, defended vigorously against a Canadian firm's attempt to buy a controlling block of its stock. The other party, Canadian Development Corporation (CDC), was founded by the Canadian government as a vehicle for building up Canadian equity investment in its own industry. The defense evoked the following judicial response in Texasgulf, Inc. v. Canadian Development Corp., 366 F.Supp. 374, 418–419 (S.D.Tex.1973):

> The Court is aware that the issue of a possible conflict of interest also must be considered in a larger and broader context of public policy and national interest. That is, what should our national policy be in protecting the national interest of the American people from a real or an imaginary threat of the multinational corporation, regardless if it is a private foreign corporation or one that is ostensibly a private corporation but nevertheless is an instrument, directly or indirectly, of a foreign nation-state, such as the Japanese corporations who are now buying tracts of timber land and cotton fields in this country, or one such as CDC (which will sell to the Canadian public all but 10% of its common stock in the near future) and British Petroleum which is almost 50% owned by the Government of Great Britain and has recently been reported to want to increase their ownership of Standard Oil of Ohio from a 25% interest to a 50% interest.
>
> It seems to this Court that if the threat is real, it makes little difference if the foreign multinational is government owed and controlled or not. If it is government controlled, at least we will know "our enemy" and to whom it owes this allegiance, and through diplomacy and treaties could balance their political influence and their economic power. But the private multinational corporation has no allegiance except to itself and its management who alone knows what it does. It has been accused of producing where labor is cheap, paying taxes where taxes are low and selling where the price is right. With their great quantities of liquid assets and resources, they are now able by transferring funds from one currency to another to frustrate government policies, and change the value of a currency. Because the U.S. multinationals can in effect export jobs and have been accused of doing so, there is little wonder that members of Congress are beginning to feel the pressure of organized labor.
>
> But this coin of international finance has another side and that is that many believe that these multinationals are the answer to some of the historical evils of nationalism. It

will probably be the multinational that will pierce the Iron Curtain and open China's door; not with force of arms but with the salesman, engineer and businessman. Perhaps these defenders of the multinationals are correct: that the entire world will benefit from an economic integration.

Be that as it may, we must realize that it is our multinationals who are the real giants—ITT, Xerox, Standard Oil, General Motors, Singer, Goodyear, IBM, Colgate-Palmolive, National Cash Register, Eastman Kodak, Minnesota Mining and Manufacturing, International Harvester, and many others.

Should we expect to operate freely around the world and exclude a foreign corporation such as CDC?

The answer of this Court *in this case* is no. This particular acquisition is not a threat to the U.S. In fact, it might be, that if their acquisition is thwarted, our long time friend, neighbor and ally, who we all know is now experiencing an an increasing feeling of economic nationalism, might look to other methods of expressing this growing sense of economic nationalism.

It is an issue of public policy and national interest as to the role multinationals will play in the future, but this Court cannot decide generally in the context of this case what this role may be. It belongs in the Legislature and Executive Branches of government. This broad issue is too fraught with economic subtleties and questions of delicate balances of trade, as well as problems of economic reciprocity. Remember, turn about is fair play.

Suffice to say this case is not the vehicle to wander into this bog of uncertainty.

Of course, what makes this problem so pertinent now is the constant and continuous devaluation of the U.S. dollar, the depressed stock prices of many U.S. companies and the long period of unfavorable balances of trade. These factors emphasize and multiply this whole issue.

There are many good buys today in the U.S. by foreign held American dollars as well as by foreign currencies. This acquisition, eventually successful or not, will not be the last one and especially from Canada where it is said that the U.S. controls 60% of their mining industry and 80% of their smelting and refining capacity. The CDC emphasizes that this acquisition would help our balance of trade to the extent of $290,000,000.

How can a court of law or equity even consider a problem so complex, hard and difficult? Only the Congress or the Executive Branch has the resources to determine what is in the best interest of this country in the increasing problems of multinationals.

As this opinion notes, the inflow of foreign capital has called forth legislative proposals that would reach much further than the very selective statutes that now exist (pp. 58–59, supra). One such proposal would provide that acquisition by foreigners of a small percentage of the stock of any major American firm would have to be reported; another would restrict investments in selected fields such as energy-related industries; a third would prohibit a foreigner from owning over 5% of the stock of any company registered under the Securities Exchange Act of 1934—having $1,000,000 of assets and 500 shareholders. Thus far, only the Foreign Investment Study Act of 1974, 88 Stat. 1450, has been enacted; when the Secretaries of the Treasury and of Commerce have completed the elaborate study called for by that Act further legislative action may follow.

In a series of Congressional hearings in 1974 and 1975, some of which are cited at the end of this Note, spokesmen for the Executive Branch opposed the pending bills that would restrict direct or portfolio investment by aliens. The arguments of such officials from the Department of State, the Department of Commerce, the Council on International Economic Policy and other Executive agencies stressed such factors as (1) the need for this country to continue to express its commitment to principles of free trade to achieve international efficiency in resource allocation; (2) the insubstantial amount of foreign investment present here; (3) the adequacy of present legislation to protect valid national concerns or interests; and (4) the fear of retaliation in the form of restrictive legislation by nations in which American corporations had substantial direct investments. The proponents of the restrictive measures expressed a variety of concerns and fears, some similar to those motivating earlier anti-alien state legislation, but most stressing the events of the early 1970's which had shifted vast amounts of capital to the Arab oil-producing countries. Estimates of the assumed surplus of funds in such countries that would be available for investment abroad were highly speculative, changing significantly even within a one-year period. But they continued to range into the hundreds of billions of dollars of accumulated investment capital by the early 1980's. Thus many congressmen perceived the circumstances of the mid-1970's to pose a novel problem—a possibility of large amounts of foreign investment, from capital concentrated in one interrelated group of countries, and from capital either directly managed or under the close supervision of foreign governments rather than privately owned foreign enterprises. Speculation was indeed the keynote of hearings such as those referred to below, as proponents of restrictive bills expressed their views of the ways in which the surplus funds of the oil producers would be applied, of likely monetary developments, and so on.

Additional reading: Hellmann, The Challenge to U. S. Dominance of the International Corporation ch. 6 (1970); Vagts, United States of America's Treatment of Foreign Investment, 17 Rutgers L.Rev. 374 (1963); Young, The Acquisition of United States Businesses by Foreign Investors, 30 Bus.Law 111 (1974). A number of congressional hearings collected considerable data about foreign investment in this country, and many opinions about the desirability of more stringent controls. See, e. g., Hearings on Foreign Investment in the United States before the Subcommittee on International Finance of the Committee on Banking, Housing, and Urban Affairs, U. S. Senate, 93rd Cong., 2nd Sess., Part I (1974); Hearings on Foreign Investment in the United States before the Subcommittee on Foreign Economic Policy of the Committee on Foreign Affairs, H.Rep., 93rd Cong., 2nd

Sess., (1974); Hearing before Subcommittee on Foreign Commerce and Tourism of the Committee on Commerce on S. 3955, U. S. Senate, 93rd Cong., 2nd Sess. (1974).

QUESTIONS

(1) What problems from the perspectives both of broad policies and of legal technique do you see in a legislative proposal that would limit any one foreign person or firm to 5% of the outstanding stock of a listed company?

(2) What comparisons would you make between the federal concern over foreign direct investment in the mid-1970's and the concerns that led to the state legislation restricting alien activities that figured in the cases at pp. 46–48, supra?

(3) Do you agree with the court in Texasgulf that it makes little difference, with respect to this country's concerns, whether direct investment is by "private" foreign multinational firms or by foreign governments? If not, what special problems do you see in governmental investment?

---

2. PROBLEMS IN IDENTIFYING AND CONTROLLING THE FOREIGN CORPORATION

All the preceding cases concern individuals, in their personal or business activities. But increasingly the scale and complexity of modern business life demand that it be conducted in corporate form. Over 90% of this country's industrial production, for example, is accounted for by corporations. On the international scene, business tends to be even more complex and to demand even larger aggregations of capital, equipment and skills. The parties involved in conducting international commerce thus include many corporations, ranging in size from small importing and exporting firms to sprawling giants such as Unilever, Royal Dutch Shell, International Business Machines, Exxon, Mitsubishi and General Motors. Some companies operating in different countries outdo their "host" governments in wealth, number of employees and international influence; the former position of United Fruit Company in Central America is an outstanding example. There is a growing body of political and scholarly opinion which sees such "international" or "multinational" corporations becoming independent actors in the international community, conducting their own foreign policies and exercising an economic influence which will exceed that of many nations. The bases for that opinion are examined in the Note at p. 1179, infra.

Thus any set of rules that purports to define the role of the alien in the domestic order, from economic or political or social perspectives, will have to find some way of handling corporations that are, in some sense, alien. Here the rulemakers encounter special problems. Many rules that affect an individual in a literal manner, such as those for exclusion or deportation, are relevant to corporations only in a metaphorical sense. They "enter" countries only in the sense that persons within the country, whether nationals or aliens, act for them, in their names. Other questions are however as critical and applicable to legal as to natural persons: capacity to sue, protection against arbitrary deprivation of rights, the right to own property or to engage in economic activity within the foreign country. Adapting rules developed with individuals in mind to corporations is a difficult process, as Mr. Justice Rutledge pointed out in United States v. Scophony Corp. of America, 333 U.S. 795, 803, 68 S.Ct. 855, 859, 92 L.Ed. 1091, 1098 (1948):

> The process of translating group or institutional relations in terms of individual ones, and so keeping them distinct from the nongroup relations of the people whose group rights are thus integrated, is perennial, not only because the law's norm is so much the individual man, but also because the continuing evolution of institutions more and more compels fitting them into individualistically conceived legal patterns. Perhaps in no other field have the vagaries of this process been exemplified more or more often than in the determination of matters of jurisdiction, venue and liability to service of process in our federal system. It has gone on from Bank of the United States v. Deveaux, 5 Cranch 61, 3 L.Ed. 38, and Baptist Association v. Hart's Executors, 4 Wheat. 1, 4 L.Ed. 499, to International Shoe Co. v. Washington, 326 U.S. 310, 66 S.Ct. 154, 90 L.Ed. 95, 161 A.L.R. 1057, and now this case.[18]

The analogy between the problems of domestic federalism that were suggested in the preceding footnote and the problems in the international community is evident.

NOTE ON A FOREIGN CORPORATION'S RIGHT TO SUE

The first set of questions that arises about an alien corporation frequently concerns its right to bring a civil action to protect its rights. Assume for the moment that an alien or foreign corporation is one which has been organized under the laws of another state or nation. One of the most fundamental attributes of a domestic corporation is that it can sue or be sued. Does a foreign corporation share this characteristic? Debates on this topic have frequently started from a conceptual point of view. One can begin with the proposition that a corporation is, in the famous words of Chief Justice Marshall in Dartmouth College v. Woodward, 17 U.S. (4 Wheat.) 518, 636, 4 L.Ed. 629, 659 (1819), "an artificial being, invisible, intangible and existing only in contemplation of law." Is it not then logical to accept the argument put forth in Bank of Augusta v. Earle, 38 U.S. (13 Pet.)

18. The very federalism of our structure magnifies the problem, by multiplying state and other governmental boundaries across which corporate activity runs with the greatest freedom. The problem arises on constitutional as well as statutory and common-law levels. Cf. International Shoe Co. v. Washington, 326 U.S. 310, 66 S.Ct. 154, 90 L.Ed. 95, 161 A.L.R. 1057; Puerto Rico v. Russell & Co., 288 U.S. 476, 53 S.Ct. 447, 77 L.Ed. 903.

519, 588, 10 L.Ed. 274, 308 (1839), that "as a corporation is a mere creature of a law of the state, it can have no existence beyond the limits in which that law operates?" On this assumption, a corporation cannot sue outside its home state or indeed "make" a contract or "own" property elsewhere. The Supreme Court in the Bank of Augusta case followed this line of reasoning so far as to say that Alabama was not constitutionally required to recognize a corporation organized in Georgia for purposes of bringing suit in Alabama on a contract that it regarded as having been made in Alabama. However it held for plaintiff, finding that there was no showing sufficient to rebut the presumption that Alabama law would as a matter of "comity," or out of a regard for "the deep and vital interests which bind [the states] so closely together," permit a suit under such circumstances.

Our constitutional doctrine subsequently developed so as to afford substantial protection to the foreign (other state) corporation. Whatever the present status of that doctrine, the general practice of the states has crystallized into a definite pattern. Each state will permit a foreign corporation to bring suit in its courts without complying with any special local requirements. However, in the event that the foreign corporation has been engaged in so many activities as to be regarded as "doing business" within the state but has not qualified to do business in accordance with the applicable statutes, it may forfeit the right to sue.

Foreign countries have had considerable difficulty with this problem. For example, France has adhered to the "restrictive theory" of foreign corporations partially followed in Bank of Augusta, to the extent that a foreign corporation may be "recognized" for purposes of bringing suit in France only if a decree has been issued which accords that right to corporations of the country of which it is a national or if a treaty confers that right. 1 Batiffol, Droit International Privé 250–58 (5th ed., Lagarde, 1970).

Note that the question of capacity to sue almost inevitably leads a court to define the foreignness of the corporation in terms of its having been organized under the laws of a foreign state. Whatever the inadequacies of this formal and conceptual approach to questions of court actions, more vexing problems arise in applying it to the other kinds of questions raised below. Those questions accent the tension between a legalistic view, stressing issues of "creation" and existence, and a realistic approach which sees the corporation as a convenient grouping of individual energies and assets, as a complex business instrumentality sprawling over different countries.

NOTE ON A FOREIGN CORPORATION'S RIGHT TO DO BUSINESS

If the question of recognizing a foreign corporation to the extent of allowing it to sue is resolved in its favor, the further question arises whether it should be permitted to do business. There is no vivid boundary between these questions. If a foreign corporation can sue, can it negotiate and "make" a contract in another nation? Can it purchase and own personal or real property? These activities, viewed as isolated acts or investments of the foreign corporation, could be thought of as comparable to the question of capacity to sue. That is, each raises the issue of recognizing "legal" existence outside the home country for a particular purpose. But at some stage the activities abroad will cease being sporadic. They will shade into the regular doing of business, the taking of an active part in some other nation's commercial or industrial life. Different questions of policy arise with respect to such conduct of a foreign corporation, in contrast with its appearance in court or the negotiation of an occasional contract.

Within our federal system, the states have resolved the question of general capacity to do business of foreign corporations in a fairly uniform way. Whatever may be their constitutional power today to exclude such corporations entirely from the transaction of local business, they have chosen to admit them on compliance with certain requirements. In most situations, these requirements are not of an onerous nature: providing certain information, submitting to the jurisdiction of local courts, and assuming certain fiscal obligations. Such requirements are felt to serve an essential protective purpose; they stop short of the comprehensive set of rules in the corporation laws applicable to domestic corporations. For certain kinds of corporations, particularly those operating in highly regulated industries such as insurance or banking, the requirements may become substantial and indeed approximate the full range of local regulation brought to bear upon domestic corporations transacting comparable businesses.[19] The following provisions of the New York Business Corporation Law typify "qualification" laws of general applicability.

§ 1301. AUTHORIZATION OF FOREIGN CORPORATIONS.—

(a) A foreign corporation shall not do business in this state until it has been authorized to do so as provided in this article. A foreign corporation may be authorized to do in this state any business which may be done lawfully in this state by a domestic corporation, to the extent that it is authorized to do such business in the jurisdiction of its incorporation, but no other business.

(b) Without excluding other activities which may not constitute doing business in this state, a foreign corporation shall not be considered to be doing business in this state, for the purposes of this chapter, by reason of carrying on in this state any one or more of the following activities:

(1) Maintaining or defending any action or proceeding, whether judicial, administrative, arbitrative or otherwise, or effecting settlement thereof or the settlement of claims or disputes.

19. That these requirements or "conditions" upon which the foreign corporation is admitted to business are subject to certain constitutional limitations has become clear through decisional law. See, e. g., Terrall v. Burke, p. 527, infra.

(2) Holding meetings of its directors or its stockholders.

(3) Maintaining bank accounts.

. . .

(c) The specification in paragraph (b) does not establish a standard for activities which may subject a foreign corporation to service of process under this chapter or any other statute of this state.

§ 1303. VIOLATIONS.—The attorney-general may bring an action to restrain a foreign corporation from doing in this state without authority any business for the doing of which it is required to be authorized in this state, or from doing in this state any business not set forth in its application for authority or certificate of amendment filed by the department of state. . . .

§ 1304. APPLICATION FOR AUTHORITY; CONTENTS.

(a) A foreign corporation may apply for authority to do business in this state. An application . . . . shall set forth:

(3) A statement of the business which it proposes to do in this state and a statement that it is authorized to do that business in the jurisdiction of its incorporation.

. . .

(5) A designation of the secretary of state as its agent upon whom process against it may be served and the post office address within or without this state to which the secretary of state shall mail a copy of any process against it served upon him.

. . .

(b) Attached to the application for authority shall be a certificate by an authorized officer of the jurisdiction of its incorporation that the foreign corporation is an existing corporation. If such certificate is in a foreign language, a translation thereof under oath of the translator shall be attached thereto.

§ 1305. APPLICATION FOR AUTHORITY; EFFECT. Upon filing by the department of state of the application for authority the foreign corporation shall be authorized to do in this state any business set forth in the application. Such authority shall continue so long as it retains its authority to do such business in the jurisdiction of its incorporation and its authority to do business in this state has not been surrendered, suspended or annulled in accordance with law.

Section 102(7) of this Law defines the term "foreign corporation" to mean one "formed under laws other than the statutes of this state."

Like this New York statute, most state laws do not distinguish between *other-state* and *other-country* corporations. There are, however, state statutes which separately define alien or foreign (other-country) corporations to which statutory prohibitions are made applicable. Such statutes may define the alien corporation, for example, by reference to such factors as a percentage of equity ownership or numbers of alien directors. Unlike the normal "qualification" laws, such statutes do not merely prohibit a corporation that is regarded as "foreign" from transacting business through a local branch before complying with certain requirements. They may go further and impose an absolute bar, not only to establishment of a local branch but also to the use of a subsidiary organized under local law for the designated purposes (i. e., ownership of certain land resources or engaging in specified activities.) Of course the constitutional decisions at pp. 47–57, supra, may invalidate or cast doubt upon some of this legislation.

In other countries the rules confronted by a foreign corporation vary widely, determined as they are by a complex of political attitudes, particularly in countries still in the throes of development. A country such as the Federal Republic of Germany may simply impose requirements of registration, similar to New York's, upon a foreign corporation that transacts business in it through a local branch. Another country may insist upon local incorporation of a subsidiary, or may impose special requirements such as the duty to obtain governmental authorization for each corporate venture, or may prohibit operations in certain or all fields that are conducted directly or indirectly by aliens. To a considerable degree these questions of the right of aliens to conduct local business through a local branch or subsidiary, questions referred to generally as pertaining to the "right of establishment," are regulated on the international scene by bilateral treaties of friendship, commerce and navigation or by multilateral treaties.[20]

Additional reading: Henderson, The Position of Foreign Corporations in American Constitutional Law (1918); Comment, 1961 Duke L.J. 274; Note, 47 Cornell L.Q. 273 (1962); Note, 63 Colum.L.Rev. 117 (1963).

NOTE ON DIFFERENT APPROACHES TO ATTRIBUTING A "NATIONALITY" TO A CORPORATION

The cases involving regulation of individual aliens suggest reasons why, in an international community composed of separate nations, it is necessary to link the individual with one among them. What factors are relevant to defining such a link for legal persons? Courts often use the same term that is applied to individuals, corporate "nationality," but it has an artificial ring. As one pushes the analogy further and asks whether a corporation could have citizenship by *jus soli* or *jus sanguinis,* the artificiality becomes the more apparent.

A realistic approach to the question requires a legislature or a court to ask which of the many aspects of a corporation are relevant to defining its national link. As the following cases indicate, it may be important to identify that link for a variety of purposes. Certain rights or privileges under national law, perhaps the right to benefit

20. Such treaties are considered at pp. 619–620, infra.

from a governmental subsidy or to engage in certain strategic businesses, may be reserved to nationals. Or certain risks, perhaps the risk of seizure of property of enemy aliens, may be incurred by the foreign investor. Among the factors considered to characterize a corporation as alien, foreign incorporation is of course significant and may be determinative. But in the statutes and judicial decisions, varying combinations of the following additional factors have been considered to be pertinent or conclusive:

(a) nationality of shareholders;

(b) nationality of directors;

(c) nationality of officers;

(d) nationality of employees;

(e) nationality of the holders of debt obligations;

(f) nationality of the owners of patents or trademarks which the corporation is licensed to use;

(g) the nation in which the general direction or day-by-day direction of the corporation is centered (the French term *siège social*, p. 97, infra, roughly corresponds to this criterion);

(h) the nation in which the industrial or commercial activities of the corporation are centered; and

(i) the nation with which, under some all-embracing standard, the corporation is most significantly identified.

In choosing among these factors, or a combination of them, a number of considerations must be borne in mind. The resulting standard should be administrable. That is, the authorities enforcing it should be able to ascertain the necessary facts without too much delay or doubt. The outcome of any official determination should be predictable. Otherwise foreign investors might be intimidated from participating in forms or areas of business activity that were not meant to be proscribed, or domestic investors might be discouraged from joint enterprises with some element of foreign capital or entrepreneurship. Finally, the test should be reasonably evasion-proof and should not lend itself to accommodating superficial disguises.

The problems of evasion are particularly acute with respect to restrictions on aliens relating to the holding of shares. In the United States, each corporation must keep a register showing the names and addresses of the shareholders for the purpose, *inter alia*, of mailing them dividends and notices of meetings. The value of the information given by that record is diminished by the fact that, for convenience or concealment, many shares are held in the names of brokers or banks on behalf of clients. Such technical problems are of course relevant to the proposals described at p. 67, supra, for new federal restraints on direct investment by aliens in this country. For a description of the problems in tracing share ownership to determine the percentage of aliens, see Westinghouse Radio Stations, Inc., 10 P & F

Radio Reg. 878 (1955). In other legal systems it is possible for a corporation to issue bearer shares, the holders of which obtain their dividends by cashing coupons attached to their share certificates and receive notice of meetings through publication. Enforcement of restraints on alien holdings is impossible under such circumstances and a law imposing restraints has to begin by requiring the registration of shares. See Schlesinger, Comparative Law 570–89 (3d ed. 1970).

The earlier federal statutes in this country usually gave the courts no more guidance than a general statement that particular rights were reserved for "citizens," or that particular disabilities were imposed upon "aliens." No effort was made to elaborate these terms with reference to corporations. But in recent decades, the statutory definitions and judicial approaches to this question have become more sophisticated and complex. As the following case suggests, this statutory complexity has by no means solved for the courts all the problems which they face.

Additional reading: Kronstein, The Nationality of International Enterprises, 52 Colum.L.Rev. 983 (1953); Vagts, The Corporate Alien: Definitional Questions in Federal Restraints on Foreign Enterprise, 74 Harv.L.Rev. 1489 (1961).

NOE v. FEDERAL COMMUNICATIONS COMMISSION

United States Court of Appeals, District of Columbia, 1958.
104 U.S.App.D.C. 221, 260 F.2d 739, cert. denied 359 U.S. 924.
79 S.Ct. 607, 3 L.Ed.2d 627 (1959).

WASHINGTON, CIRCUIT JUDGE.

This appeal arises from a comparative proceeding before the Federal Communications Commission to determine which of three applicants should be awarded authority to operate a commercial television station on VHF Channel 4 in New Orleans, Louisiana. The hearing examiner recommended a grant to the Times-Picayune Publishing Company, preferring it over appellant James A. Noe & Company and over intervenor Loyola University, a Jesuit educational institution in New Orleans. The Commission, after hearing argument en banc, awarded the license to Loyola University. Each of the disappointed applicants appealed, but the appeal now before this court is that of James A. Noe & Company.

The primary contention of appellant Noe is that Loyola, by reason of its connection with the Society of Jesus, is the "representative" of an "alien," and is a corporation whose stock is "voted" by "representatives" of aliens, within the meaning of Section 310(a) of the Communications Act of 1934, 48 Stat. 1086, 47 U.S.C.A. § 310(a), rendering it ineligible to hold a television license.[21]

21. The pertinent portion of the text of Section 310(a) recites:
"(a) The station license required hereby shall not be granted to or held by—
"(1) Any alien or the representative of any alien;
"(2) Any foreign government or the representative thereof;
"(3) Any corporation organized under the laws of any foreign government;
"(4) Any corporation of which any officer or director is an alien or of which more than one-fifth of the capital stock is owned of record or voted by aliens or their representatives or by a foreign government or representative

Briefly, the record shows that the Society of Jesus is an order of Roman Catholic priests, with a total membership of some 32,000, of whom about 7,500 reside in the United States. The record also shows that Loyola is an educational corporation chartered by the State of Louisiana in 1912. It is a nonprofit, non-stock corporation; it has no shares. Its property is its own, possessed in trust for educational purposes. It is legally and financially autonomous; it does not support or receive support from the Society of Jesus in a monetary way. Under the corporate charter, its directors must be priests of the Society of Jesus attached to Loyola University. All the directors are American citizens. The head of the Jesuit religious community at Loyola—the Rector—is ex officio the President of the University and corporation, and a member of the Board of Directors. He is appointed as head of the religious community by the Superior General of the order—presently a Belgian citizen residing in Rome—on the recommendation of the Provincial Superior, the head of the New Orleans Province of the Society. The Rector has the power to appoint one to three members of the Board of Directors and to submit a list of names to the Provincial Superior, from which list the latter appoints the other three leaders of the religious community, who ex officio become officers of the corporation and members of the Board. Transfers and assignments of priests belonging to the religious community at Loyola, with the exception of the Rector, are controlled by the Provincial Superior, who is an American citizen.

In support of appellant Noe's position language is cited from our opinion in WOKO, Inc., v. Federal Communications Commission, 1946, 80 U.S.App.D.C. 333, 338, 153 F.2d 623, 628, to the effect that Section 310(a) was directed against "corporations which have an alien tinge." Furthermore Noe contends that, on the basis of the Commission's opinion in Kansas City Broadcasting Co., 5 Pike & Fischer R.R. 1057 (1952), the purpose of the section is "to safeguard the United States from foreign influence in the field of radio. . . ." Id. at 1093. The emphasis that the appellant places on "alien tinge" and "foreign influence" is misplaced, however. In a letter of March 22, 1932, to the Chairman of the Senate Interstate Commerce Committee, the Secretary of the Navy stated that—

> "[T]he lessons that the United States had learned from the foreign dominance of the cables and the dangers from espionage and propaganda disseminated through foreign-owned radio stations in the United States prior to and during the war brought about the passage of the Radio Act of 1927 [superseded by the Communications Act of 1934], which was intended to preclude any foreign dominance in American radio. . . ."

Quoted in Hearings on H.R. 8301 Before the House Committee on Interstate and Foreign Commerce, 73d Cong., 2d Sess. 26 (1934). . . . From this legislative history we may conclude that although Section 310(a) was directed against alien control of our communica-

thereof, or by any corporation organized under the laws of a foreign country;

"(5) Any corporation directly or indirectly controlled by any other corporation of which any officer or more than one-fourth of the directors are aliens, or of which more than one-fourth of the capital stock is owned of record or voted, after June 1, 1935, by aliens, their representatives, or by a foreign government or representative thereof, or by any corporation organized under the laws of a foreign country, if the Commission finds that the public interest will be served by the refusal or the revocation of such license."

tions facilities, this limitation was primarily based "upon the idea of preventing alien activities against the Government during the time of war." 68 Cong.Rec. 3037 (1927). The relationship of Loyola to the Society of Jesus hardly seems to endanger our national security. Certainly the mere fact that the Rector is appointed by an ecclesiastical superior who is an alien is not enough to bring Loyola within the interdiction of the cited statute.

We recognize that the Society of Jesus is an hierarchical organization, and that within the organization some power and control is vested in persons who are not directly a part of the University or the corporation, and a few of whom reside abroad. But the record shows that this hierarchical chain of authority—which extends from the Superior General in Rome to the Provincial Superior and the Rector, and in some rare situations might include the Pope—has never been used in the past to impinge upon the independence of the University in the operation of its radio station. Under all the circumstances, even if Section 310(a) be thought to have a semblance of relevance to the present case, it nevertheless would be inapplicable since it was incorporated in the Communications Act to "guard against alien control and not the mere possibility of alien control." S.Rep.No. 781, 73d Cong., 2d Sess. 7 (1934). In sum, therefore, we find nothing in the legislative history of the statutory provisions, or in the record of the present case, which would require us to overrule the Commission's rejection of Noe's argument. Loyola seems to us to fall neither within the letter nor the spirit of the statute. . . .

The brief of amicus curiae also urges that Loyola is an "instrumentality of the Holy Roman Pontificate," and that the latter is a foreign sovereignty and "the true beneficiary of the proposed grant." The grant, it says, would be contrary to the public policy of the United States and adverse to its sovereignty. To the extent that these contentions duplicate the arguments considered above, we need not discuss them further. To the extent that they differ from those arguments, they are unsupported in the present record, were not presented to the Commission, and are not, strictly speaking, appropriate for our consideration. Nevertheless, we have considered them. We find nothing therein which would lead us to hold that the Commission's determination of the issues before it was clearly wrong or contrary to law. . . .

[The court, after considering certain other issues, affirmed the Commission's order.]

QUESTIONS

(1) Suppose that a business corporation had been involved in the Noe case. Note the tests that it would have to meet under the statute. Why did Congress select the stock ownership figure used in Section 310(a)(4)? Given the probable purpose of such a requirement, what would you consider to be the minimum safe percentage of domestic shareholding that such a statute should require? 67%? 51%? less? (Note that such percentage requirements can create difficult problems of proof of compliance for corporations which one would normally think of as strictly "American." Cf. Westinghouse Radio Stations, Inc., 10 P&F Radio Reg. 878 (1955).)

(2) To what extent does the statute invoke the criterion of "control"? What do you suppose the court means when it refers to control? In a large, publicly held corporation, which individuals or groups exercise control? Shareholders, directors, officers, important debt holders, licensors of critical patents? What additional facts might you wish to know before you answered this question about any one corporation?

(3) What independent significance do you attribute to the other requirements in Section 310(a)? For example, why should the statute disqualify corporations organized under the laws of foreign jurisdictions? Why should the fact that *any* officer or director is an alien (perhaps one of five directors, or one of ten executive officers) disqualify?

In the two following cases, consider (1) what reasons probably underlay the French and Polish enactments and (2) given those reasons, which of the criteria noted at p. 75, supra, would best serve to identify alien corporations.

SOCIÉTÉ REMINGTON TYPEWRITER v. KAHN

Cour de Cassation, France, May 12, 1931.
1936 Dalloz Jurisp.I. 121.

. . . Whereas the appeal criticizes the judgment appealed from . . . for having excluded the Société Remington Typewriter from the benefit of the law of 30 June 1926, on the ground that it is not a French corporation;

But whereas the judgment establishes that the Société was founded as to 16/18ths of its capital by the contributions of the great American company of the same name, that these contributions consisted of the commercial assets used in France by the American company for the sale of typewriters;

Whereas, furthermore, it establishes that the Société, although it has its *siège social* in Paris, is managed by a board composed exclusively of alien members, that it does not use its capital in France and that it limits itself to selling machines made in America by the parent corporation and bearing marks of that origin;

Whereas the judgment could deduce from the circumstances conclusively established that the company, although operating in France did not have its center of operations there and was not a French corporation within the meaning of the law of 30 June 1926, [the appeal is rejected.]

[The law of 30 June 1926 to which the opinion refers regulates commercial rentals, affording lease renewal rights to certain parties, and provides in part that its provisions cannot be invoked by "commercial or industrial [tenants] of foreign nationality."]

IN RE OIL INDUSTRY ASSOCIATION LIMITED, CRACOW

Poland, Supreme Court, Third Division (Full Meeting).
12 November, 1921.
[1919–1922] Ann.Dig. 245 (No. 172).[22]

THE FACTS.—Under a statute of 1920 (passed during the period of inflation in order to prevent large estates from passing into alien hands for sums which were comparatively trifling), aliens

22. The summary is that appearing in the Annual Digest.

can acquire real property in Poland only on obtaining the consent of the Council of Ministers. Two aliens formed a limited liability company for the purpose, *inter alia,* of acquiring (and selling) real estate. The law requires the registration of limited liability companies with the competent court. The District Court of Cracow (Commercial Division) rejected the request for registration, since such registration would make the company a Polish one and would thus enable the two partners to accomplish what individually they would be prevented by the law from doing. The Court of Appeal of Cracow allowed the appeal lodged against that decision, and held that the seat of the company is the sole criterion, under the law, of its national or foreign character; that the nationality of the corporators is of no consequence in this connection, such companies being rather a form of association of capital; that limitations of the right of aliens to purchase real estate do not apply to national companies; and that questions of extending prohibitions and restrictions aimed at aliens to alien capital lie in the field of legislative policy and transcend the field of the jurisdiction of courts. On appeal to the Supreme Court, the latter

Held, reversing the decision of the Court of Appeal: That since neither partner had the capacity to acquire real estate, they did not have such capacity jointly and they cannot confer it upon themselves by forming a company of which they are the sole shareholders. [Report: O.S.P., I, No. 589.]

QUESTION

Suppose that the Remington company was 70% beneficially owned by French nationals, but that effective control was lodged in one American corporation which held the remaining 30%. Should the case have been decided the same way?

---

3. REGULATION OF FOREIGN INVESTMENT IN SOME FOREIGN COUNTRIES

The decision to seek profits by direct participation in the economic life of another country—through establishment of a foreign branch or wholly-owned subsidiary, or through a company owned jointly with nationals of the foreign country—may stem from various considerations. Exports by the prospective investor from its plant in the United States may not be feasible, because of such factors as high transportation costs or severe import restrictions (tariffs, quotas, or exchange controls) of the foreign country. If a manufacturing enterprise is planned, production abroad may permit more intensive development of the market in the foreign country or its neighbors. Lower wages for labor-intensive industries may provide added inducement. The very affiliation with the country through local production may impart some local flavor to the firm and prove to be a significant business asset.[23] The motivation for such investment

23. For manufacturing operations, export and direct investment are not the sole choices. For a variety of considerations, a firm may prefer to license the patents or trade-marks that it owns in the foreign country to foreign

is most clear in extractive enterprises, for access to minerals or other raw materials in the foreign country may be critical to support home industries.

In addition to economic considerations, the prospective investor will be alert to the political climate, to signs of hostility towards foreign enterprise which may culminate in serious restrictions upon it or indeed in expropriation. Another threshold consideration is of course those foreign laws or administrative practices which regulate the alien firm's entrance into the country. Many such laws have clear counterparts in the United States—for example, prohibition of alien ownership in the telecommunications industry.[24] But in a large number of countries, the legislation directly applicable to alien enterprise far exceeds in scope and importance that in the United States. Such legislation may be designed to encourage rather than inhibit foreign investment; for example, tax or other incentives may be offered in certain fields. One particular class of legislation, so-called exchange-control laws whose key characteristics are described at pp. 1164–1168, infra, will figure significantly in the investor's calculations.

The text below refers to two groups of countries which have had widely different reactions to foreign investment. France is taken as representative of a group of nations which, by any test, have highly developed economies but at the same time are concerned about the impact of foreign, particularly American, investment.[25] But there are major differences within that group. For example, Canada and Japan have similarly developed economies. Their situations differ from France's in that, for example, Canada has extraordinarily high proportions of foreign capital in its industry as a whole and in certain branches in particular, while Japan's government has managed to keep foreign investment to an unusually low level without sacrificing economic or technological progress. Nonetheless, their reactions have roughly paralleled those of France.

The second group consists of the "developing", "underdeveloped" or "less developed" countries. Because of their number and political as well as economic diversity, it is harder to choose from among such countries any one to serve as an example.

NOTE ON FRENCH ATTITUDES TOWARDS FOREIGN INVESTMENT

Countries such as France have highly developed industries of their own backed by native entrepreneurial talent and domestic capi-

business firms, and to earn profits solely through the license fees that it charges.

24. The formal bars on establishment of alien-owned enterprises often cover such additional fields as banking, insurance, the press, extraction of certain minerals, and a varying group of industries that are considered strategic.

25. Direct United States investment in Europe grew from $1.7 billion to $19.4 billion from 1950 to 1968. During the same period, direct European investment in the United States grew from $2.2 billion to $7.8 billion, a trend later intensified for reasons developed at p. 65, supra.

tal sources. But particularly since 1960 and particularly from the United States, the inflow of foreign investment has caused them concern. Although the inflow of foreign investment into France in recent years has not amounted to more than 3.5% of new domestic investment (and that from the United States is less than half of this percentage), the accumulation of foreign capital in certain industries is much larger. What makes that capital seem particularly threatening is its tendency to weigh heavily in industries making substantial technological improvements which are regarded as "the commanding heights" of the economy, such as computers, aviation equipment, or petrochemicals.[26] The policy of a country such as France must, therefore, attempt to be highly selective, to preserve a role for national industry in endangered areas while not being, or seeming to be, hostile to foreign investment in general. This need, in the context of a sophisticated legal regime governing industrial and commercial activity in general, means that restrictive rules appear to the prospective investor as exceptions to a general assumption that the law relating to foreigners will be the same as that governing nationals.

Legal limitations on foreign economic activity in France fall into three principal categories. First, there are rules, rather like the federal and state rules in the United States described above, which bar certain trades and professions to alien individuals and to corporations defined in various ways to be alien. The areas affected include the hydroelectric, aircraft, shipping, publishing and armaments industries. For a listing of the rather disparate set of statutes and decrees as they existed several years ago, see Dairaines, Les Etrangers et les Sociétés Etrangères en France 151–183 (1957).

Second, there exists a requirement that a foreigner, before engaging in business in France, secure a *carte de commerçant* (merchant's card); aliens proposing either to engage in business for themselves or to become the heads of French branches of foreign corporations or of companies organized in France must comply with these rules. The requirement of a *carte de commerçant* is distinct from that of the *carte de travail,* which applies to alien employees. Both permits serve a function similar to a visa authorizing an alien to work in the United States. The *carte de commerçant* is issued, after an application which must be backed by extensive documentation and after consultation with the local chamber of commerce, by the prefect of the appropriate *département* upon the decision of the Minister of Industry and Commerce. The authorities have wide discretion to consider such factors as the local need for the alien's business talents. Their decision is virtually immune from review.

The *carte de commerçant* originated in 1938 and represented a response to the flow into France, then still gripped by the depression,

26. IBM has, for example, a near monopoly in Europe in data processing, and as of 1973 about 90% of computers installed in Europe were based on American technology. For reactions to such situations including proposals for technological cooperation or mergers among European firms within the European Economic Community (Common Market), see pp. 1400 and 1414, infra.

of a large number of refugees from central Europe and Spain. Although conditions have changed, the institution has been vigorously defended by the French authorities against all proposed limitations. It has not on the whole been used to ward off foreign (particularly American) investment and indeed, being a measure directed at personnel, is not well suited to controlling investment.[27]

Third, there is a set of rules designed to give the French administration explicit authority to approve or disapprove of proposed foreign investments. Formally, these have been classified as exchange controls, although with the passage of time it has become evident that France's foreign exchange problems are not the primary consideration in their administration. Although the predecessor rules enacted in 1939 clearly were needed to curb the flight of French capital to more secure countries, by the late 1960's France's holdings of gold and dollars were enough to pose serious problems for the United States. Indeed, at some points the French government has reversed its position so as to discourage inflows of the dollar and thereby prevent the franc from rising to the point where it would have to be drastically revalued upward. Most payments between residents and nonresidents were being authorized by the government in the mid 1970's despite a return to the earlier stringency during the crisis of 1968 and despite revisions in exchange rates and controls during the international crisis stemming from the oil embargo during 1973–74.

In fact, in 1966 a law (Law 66–1008 of December 28, 1966) abolished all previous legislation on the topic of exchange controls, providing in Article 1 that "financial relations between France and foreign countries are free". However, Article 3 provided that the government, in order "to assume the defense of national interests", could, by decree, "submit to declaration, prior authorization and control" all exchange operations and "the constitution and liquidation of foreign investments in France." The decree (No. 67–78), of January 27, 1967, as complemented and amended by other official acts, exercised this power and withdrew much that the law seemed to have granted. As modified in 1971, largely by way of apparent liberalization vis-a-vis fellow members of the European Community, these decrees remain in effect.

For present purposes, the most significant requirement of the new regulations is that foreign investments in France, and French investments abroad, must be declared to the Ministry of Finance before they are made. This requirement covers all direct investments in France by nonresidents. French companies under "foreign control" (a term not defined in the implementing decrees) are treated for this purpose as nonresidents. Direct investment consists of the creation or extension of any business, branch or enterprise, and of the acquisition or increase of control in an existing company or the

27. In particular France resisted the pressure of the member states of the European Community to end the requirement of a *carte de commerçant* for their nationals. See, p. 1333, infra.

expansion of a company already controlled. The regulations further provide that acquisition of 20% or less of the capital of a company quoted on an exchange is not a direct investment. In a few special situations, such as investments by nationals of other Common Market countries, only prior declaration is required. In other situations, prior authorization is necessary. The Ministry has broad discretion to agree, to refuse, to request postponement, and so on.

The information demanded in the declaration or request for authorization consists of formal data (name of firm, country of incorporation and so on), the identity and percentage holdings of the principal shareholders (indicating of course their nationality), the nature of the proposed investment, and its motives and likely effects (particularly expected benefits, such as increased exports and employment or new research techniques) upon the French economy. The Ministry can refer declarations or requests for authorizations to other interested ministries and to regional planning agencies for their comments. Final decision is, however, with the Ministry.

The criteria under which the Ministry decides have never been published. Nonetheless, observers have been able to infer certain patterns which show what considerations weigh heavily with the authorities, noting that some administrations have been much more liberal than others. Denials have typically come in cases where the foreign investor was a large multinational enterprise (see p. 1176, infra) that would dominate the sector of the economy it entered, especially if that sector were an object of special official solicitude (computers, for example). Favorable attention would be given upon a showing of positive effects upon the French balance of payments or upon a showing that entry would further the objects of the French national economic plan as either strengthening a sector of the economy or an underdeveloped region. A newly founded enterprise in a field presently dominated by inefficient establishments would have better prospects than a takeover of an existing domestic firm.

Additional reading: On the French rules, see Torem & Craig, Control of Foreign Investment in France, 66 Mich.L.Rev. 669 (1968), and Developments in the Control of Foreign Investment in France, 70 Mich. L.Rev. 285 (1971); Frank, La Carte de Commerçant, 5 Harv.Int.L.Club J. 1 (1963); and CCH Common Market Reporter ¶¶ 22,651–22,681. For comparison with Canada, see Foreign Direct Investment in Canada (1972) (generally known as "the Gray Report"); and for Japan see Henderson, Foreign Enterprise in Japan (1973).

NOTE ON ATTITUDES OF LESS DEVELOPED COUNTRIES TOWARDS FOREIGN INVESTMENT

Less developed countries of Latin American, the Middle East, Asia and Africa have more urgent needs for foreign capital and skills, but also have significant grounds for fearing the collateral consequences of their arrival. In many such countries, foreign investment dominates infrastructure industries and the manufacture of hard consumer goods. Thus alien-controlled enterprises inevitably affect vital aspects of economic and political life, in a way visible to the general public as well as to government officials. The magnitude and strategic location of foreign capital may cause a fushion in some countries between a general hostility to capitalism or free enterprise as such, and a specific resentment of foreign control. That is, the reactions against foreign investment may become characteristic not only of the political parties or sentiment of the left, but of nationalist sentiment that may permeate conservative political groups as well. A country in these circumstances is faced with difficult choices: to exclude foreign business and undertake to develop itself with its own or borrowed resources, to accept foreign business with all its risks, or to seek so to control and channel it as to realize the advantages it brings without experiencing its most serious drawbacks.

Before turning to specific examples of foreign restrictive legislation, this Note summarizes the principal critiques and defenses of private foreign investment, with stress upon the attitudes expressed in the writings of Latin American government officials, political thinkers, academics and businessmen. Some of these themes are restated and further developed with particular reference to the contemporary dispute over the role of the multinational enterprise, in the Note at pp. 1179–1189, infra, which could be read together with this Note.

Both advocates and opponents of a liberal regime for foreign investment in Latin America seek support for their positions in historical data, data which is often incomplete or from which a number of inferences might be drawn. Even when expressed in the language of statistics, these arguments often make evident their roots in political beliefs or conceptual frameworks, as well as in deeply felt emotions born of a particular country's experience with the industrialized world and economic imperialism. Our effort here is to expose such foreign attitudes which are germane not only to an understanding of foreign legislation restricting aliens but also to the controversies over expropriation which figure in Chapter IV.

The advantages to the host country of private foreign investment are fairly evident. A country with a short supply of foreign exchange, particularly of hard currencies, will benefit to the extent that the foreign investor brings dollars to be converted into local currency for local expenses, or capital goods that could otherwise be obtained only through drawing upon limited foreign-exchange resources. The extractive or public-service or manufacturing enterprises owned by aliens will provide employment for a portion of the labor force and may spur economic development in other sectors of the national economy. For example, the power utility or railroad built with foreign capital and designed to service alien-owned business may have the further (if unintended) consequence of stimulating local entrepreneurs to activity dependent upon such power or transportation. And with foreign capital comes foreign technology, the know-how of the industrialized world applied to local operations. Thus foreign-owned enterprises provide useful training in technical and managerial skills to portions of the local population. In these respects, private foreign investment is a useful and, in some circumstances, perhaps indispensable complement to grant funds or the funds borrowed by the host country from foreign governmental agencies (such as the Agency for International Development in the United States) or from international institutions (such as the International Bank for Reconstruction and Development).

Critics of foreign investment challenge some or all of these putative advantages. Or they may concede the validity of these arguments with respect to a particular country, but nonetheless assert that the attendant drawbacks of foreign investment are so severe as to suggest that its future role be strictly limited. Their arguments include the following:

(1) Foreign ownership and control of manufacturing enterprises, public-service industries, agricultural land or extractive enterprises are a lingering form of colonialism. They assure the continued *dependence* of the host country upon the investor's country—in present times, particularly the United States. This concern becomes the greater where the foreign firm has a monopoly or dominant position in the field in which it transacts business. Foreign ownership of certain assets—particularly infrastructural industry, public-service industries, agricultural land and extractive enterprises—directly conflicts with a basic and irrepressible national aspiration, the aspiration to control one's own essential services and natural resources. (That aspiration has of course found expression within the United States through the state and federal statutes restricting alien activities and evaluated in the constitutional decisions at pp. 46–62, supra, as well as in the proposals before the Congress in the mid-1970's (p. 67, supra) for limitations on foreign direct investment.)

(2) In planning its activities, the foreign firm is naturally attentive to maximization of its own profits (or related goals) rather than to the economic or political development which the host country may consider more important for its long-range plans. In particular, heavy foreign investment in extractive enterprise or primary agricultural commodities may lead to an unbalanced economy which perpetuates the *dependence* of the host country upon the industrialized world.

(3) Foreign firms have traditionally excluded participation by local capital and entrepreneurs in their activities, with the result that all profits derived from the local business eventually make their way into foreigners' hands. Further, in managing their local enterprises, such firms have traditionally drawn upon their own nationals to staff executive and technical posts of importance, thus stifling the growth of a competent and trained class of citizens. It should be noted that, although this argument has much historical validity, the trend in recent decades has been towards increased participation of local private or governmental capital and towards training programs which bring lo-

cal citizens into positions of importance within the firm. Recent legislation in a number of less developed countries makes such policies of foreign investors mandatory.

(4) Contrary to its asserted effect of alleviating balance-of-payments problems of the host country by introducing dollars and other hard currencies, foreign capital often intensifies such problems. Repatriation of dividends or interest or license fees—or eventually of the initial investment, in event of liquidation—to the investor's country imposes an excessive strain upon the sparse foreign-exchange resources of many countries. Even if profits are not repatriated and are reinvested to expand the local enterprises, that reinvestment inhibits the fresh importation of scarce foreign currency. Moreover, foreign owned enterprises often compete with nationals for scarce national capital available from the local banking system. Such adverse effects of private foreign investment are all the greater because of the unduly high profits which such firms are alleged to earn through their local activities. Much debate has raged about this position; it is difficult to make any generally valid statement about the impact of a particular foreign investment upon a particular country's balance of payments in the medium or long run. Note, for example, the following comments directed to Mexico, which would be equally valid as applied to a large number of Latin American countries. They appear in Vernon, "An Interpretation of the Mexican View," in Vernon (ed.), How Latin America Views the U. S. Investor 95, 110 (1966).

> The argument that foreign investment has been bad for the Mexican balance-of-payments has had a strong impact on Mexican thinking. Mexicans have noted that the flow of dividends, interest, and royalty payments to foreign investors in any year has usually outweighed the flow of fresh capital into Mexico. Accordingly, the foreign companies have been seen as "decapitalizing" the Mexican economy.
>
> The full balance-of-payments effects of these investments, of course, have been very much more complicated. Apart from affecting the flow of capital and service payments, investors have had other effects in Mexican payments. They have contributed to the great wave of import-replacement which has characterized Mexico during the past two decades, thereby presumably saving foreign exchange. They have been responsible in some measure for the increase in exports of manufactured products from Mexico during the same period. Just to complicate matters further, however, these enterprises also have been responsible for some of the increase in Mexico's demand for capital goods and industrial materials, thus throwing new strains on the Mexican balance of payments. And, finally, insofar as these foreign investments increased Mexico's real income, they also have increased the aggregate demand of Mexican consumers for foreign goods.
>
> Any efforts to balance out factors such as these are inevitably an exercise in conjecture. . . .

Note the recurrence of the word *dependence* in the preceding catalogue of criticisms. Indeed, the explicit theme of *dependencia* has become an important component of political and economic writings from Latin America that are hostile to foreign investment. We have observed that such a theme may figure both in socialist-oriented and nationalist-oriented thought, but it has in fact been particularly characteristic of the political left. In this sense, *dependencia* theory frequently becomes a concrete expression of the more general, Marxist-derived theory of imperialism as a framework for understanding and evaluating relationships between developed and underdeveloped countries.[28] The charges of denationalization of industry and decapitalization of the monetary economy figure heavily in such writings, as does the more general argument that the function of foreign investment in basic industries is to establish an economic and political dominance assuring that the economies of the underdeveloped countries fit within the schemes and aspirations of the developed.

At times, the *dependencia* literature works within this dichotomy of developed and underdeveloped countries. At times it uses a related image of the center and periphery, emphasizing the peripheral countries as they are worked into the production and marketing structures of the central countries so as to service the central countries' conceptions of a well functioning world economy.

We turn from such general considerations to the types of legislation that await the foreign investor. In contrast with its circumstances in a nation such as France, the United States corporation contemplating establishment of a branch or subsidiary in many less developed countries is apt to encounter a threshold difficulty in ascertaining with any degree of precision what its openings and constraints, or its rights and obligations, are. The corporation enters a political and legal culture that is foreign in the full sense of that word. The political structures and forces within which a "legal system" functions may be so radically different as to invalidate domestic conceptions of planning within a relatively coherent and comprehensible legal system. Statutory law may be fragmentary, and the gaps left by it may never have been filled by judicial decisions or by executive or ministerial decrees. Alternatively, those decrees may be so numerous, rapid in their issuance, and disorganized as to frustrate systematic research that would reveal the prevailing "state of law" on a given matter. In fact, the applicable "law" may in some instances be little other than a broad administrative discretion. The judicial system may lack independence from the frankly political branches, and corruption through bribery or other forms may achieve a different dimension and receive a tolerance beyond that experienced in the investor's home country. Moreover, the venture engaged in by the foreign investor may be so different from any attempted within the host country that not even past administrative practice or discre-

28. Two recent expressions from Latin American authors of such writings, which reflect a range of general political perspectives, are Cardoso and Faletto, Dependencia y Desarrollo en America Latina (Lima 1967), and Caputo and Pizarro, Desarrollismo y Capital Extranjero (Chile 1970).

tion or judicial decisions can serve as an authoritative starting point for prediction.

Even if the investor can identify present statutory or administrative or judicial rules or policies about a given point, there may be little assurance that such policies or rules will not be changed in the future to the investor's disadvantage. The demand for such changes, reflecting the ebb and flow of different political attitudes towards foreign investment, may indeed be strengthened by successful business operations. A popular call for retaining a larger share of the profits, through concession fees or taxes or other legal forms, may be irresistible, particularly if a discernible trend in other countries has shifted a higher percentage of earnings to the local treasury. The experiences of foreign-owned oil companies in recent decades are illustrative; the experience of American copper companies in Chile, recounted at p. 444, infra, offers another example.

In order to minimize this uncertainty and encourage the investor to incur the greater risks of a foreign venture, a number of countries have adopted codes or policies designed to afford assurance of defined treatment. Two recent examples are set forth in the Documentary Supplement: The Investment Incentive Code of 1966 of the Republic of Liberia, and a statement issued in 1972 by the Ministry of Planning and Employment of Sri Lanka (Ceylon), entitled Policy on Private Foreign Investment. These examples are characteristic of many others, although variations in detail, emphasis and liberality are numerous and significant. Typical themes in these laws include the following:

> **(1)** Various "incentives" are offered the foreign investor, a feature not characteristic of the laws of developed countries.[29] These include outright tax relief, special tax rates or depreciation provisions, exemptions from customs duties on raw materials or components which the enterprise must import, tariff protection against goods that compete with the investor's output, and special options or prices for the purchase or lease of land.
>
> **(2)** Through the authorizations that are required to make incentives or other provisions of these laws applicable, the government exercises choice as to the kinds of investments that it will admit. That choice will reflect in part the allocations between the public and private sectors of the economy made by its planning agencies. The investor is often asked to fit into a "planned" domestic pattern; private enterprise, whether domestic or foreign, will often be cate-

29. It should be noted that Congress has in recent years responded to this country's balance-of-payments problems by enacting laws which could fairly bear the description of "incentive" legislation. In particular, amendments to the Internal Revenue Code of 1954 have made certain kinds of foreign investment in the United States more attractive. See pp. 1102–1103, infra.

gorically excluded from certain fields. The Sri Lanka statement makes this explicit.

(3) Under these laws, the investor must often agree to contribute in certain ways to the development of the local economy and to the training of local personnel to staff responsible posts—technical and administrative—in the new enterprise.

(4) The laws often attempt to give the investor some assurance that he can bring home, in his own currency, dividends and interest on, and ultimately some portion of the principal of, his investment. Sometimes the assurances are quite explicit as to conversion rates, the availability of foreign exchange and so forth. Sometimes they are quite general, as in the section of the Sri Lanka statement entitled "Facilities granted to the Foreign Investor."

(5) The assurances frequently include a guaranty that the investor will receive nondiscriminatory treatment and that his assets will be expropriated only against a payment of adequate compensation. See the section of the Sri Lanka statement entitled "Security of Investment."

These investment incentive laws often provide for the negotiation of agreements between the investor and the government, known generally as "concession agreements." See section 8 of the Liberian law. In addition to incorporating some or all of the provisions of the investment incentive law, such agreements often provide additional benefits for the investor or impose additional obligations. For example, agreements relating to extractive enterprises frequently require the investor to provide the infrastructure necessary to support its operations, as by building housing for workers, wharves and piers for exporting its products, transportation facilities to the coast and so on. Concession agreements raise numerous legal questions of contemporary importance, to be considered in Part D of Chapter IV.

Additional reading: Bernstein (ed.), Foreign Investment in Latin America: Cases and Attitudes (1966); Friedmann and Pugh (eds.), Legal Aspects of Foreign Investment (1959); Vernon (ed.), How Latin America Views the U. S. Investor (1966); Vernon, Foreign-Owned Enterprise in the Developing Countries, XV Public Policy 361 (1966). See also the readings referred to in the Note on multinational enterprises, p. 1179, infra.

E. CHOICE OF LAW: THE ROLE OF A PERSONAL LAW FOR INDIVIDUALS OR CORPORATIONS

The preceding materials have examined problems in various fields of national law to which the foreign link of an individual or corporation was relevant, and sometimes critical. Here we consider the relevance of an individual's foreign nationality or domicile, and of a corporation's foreign place of organization or principal office, to problems of choice of law.

NOTE ON CHOICE OF LAW

This chapter has examined aspects of national legal systems, primarily that of the United States, which affect other countries or their nationals and which thus have a transnational character. Later chapters explore aspects of public international law. The body of law which this Note introduces, the conflict of laws, is intimately related to both these fields.[30]

The field known in the United States as the "conflict of laws" and known in most foreign countries as "private international law" traditionally includes three general subjects: the bases on which a court will assert jurisdiction to adjudicate, the effect to be given to judgments rendered by courts of another state or nation, and choice of law. These subjects share one basic characteristic: the situation before the court is not entirely "domestic." Not all parties or persons or property to be affected by the court's judgment are physically within or related in all respects to the forum state or nation. Or not all events or facts relevant to the litigation occurred within or are exclusively related to the forum state or nation. Within a federal country such as the United States, problems within the conflict of laws arise most frequently in an interstate setting. Our primary concern is with situations where the foreign aspect of a problem involves not another state but another nation.

Consider the following illustrations of problems raising issues of choice of law.

> (a) Plaintiff, in state or country X, enters into a contract with defendant obligating defendant to perform certain services in state or country Y, where defendant lives. Defendant fails to perform, contending that impossibility or force majeure excuses him from performance. In view of the facts relied upon by the defendant, he would prevail under the common or statutory law of Y. Plaintiff, however, would prevail under the different rules expressed by the common or statutory law of X. Plaintiff sues in X. The court, drawing upon principles of choice of law, must determine whether the contract law of X or Y governs this issue.
>
> (b) Defendant publishes through a radio broadcast in X a statement about plaintiff which plaintiff considers defamatory. Plaintiff lives in Y, into which the radio broadcast is transmitted. The statement is privileged under X

30. Later materials draw upon the principles of the conflict of laws in sections treating contracts between a government and an alien (pp. 502–508, infra), the act of state doctrine, (pp. 673–676, infra), adjudicatory jurisdiction and the enforcement of foreign-country judgments (pp. 729–809, infra), and the transnational reach of national laws (pp. 935–946, infra).

law. Under Y law, it would be considered actionable. Plaintiff might sue in the courts of X or Y. Either court, drawing upon principles of choice of law, would have to determine whether the tort law of X or Y governed this issue.

In brief, choice of law is that body of principles or rules to which the forum court looks to determine the state or nation whose law should govern. The necessity for a choice between the forum's law and foreign law arises because of some foreign element in the litigation: a party may be a national or domiciliary of another nation, conduct relevant to a contract or tort action may have taken place elsewhere, the property in dispute may be located elsewhere, and so on. The relevance of such "foreign" facts to the court's determination of the applicable law will depend upon the precise issue before the court and the principles of choice of law which the court invokes. For the moment, we can consider these principles to form part of the domestic law of the state or country in which the court sits.

In either of the cases sketched above, the plaintiff's choice of forum need not decide the question of choice of law. Both courts might reach the same decision as to which law was applicable. Both might, for example, conclude that the tort law of X should govern in illustration (b). Indeed, one of the principal policies in the field of choice of law (one that often conflicts with others) is to seek uniformity of result, whatever the forum in which an action might be brought. These problems of choice of law often permit no easy answer. We mean here simply to stress that choice is generally open to a court to apply *lex fori* or foreign law.

The direct concern of this Note is with situations where the relevant foreign fact pertains not to the place of conduct or the location of property, but to one or both of the parties. That is, a natural person may be a national or domiciliary of a foreign country, or a corporation may be organized or have its place of management in a foreign country. Generally, as in the two illustrations, such foreign facts would be relatively insignificant to the choice of law. However, for a number of issues that are frequently described as part of a "personal law," such facts may be critical in choosing the appropriate law.

We consider first the personal law for individuals. The importance of a person's nationality or domicile for choice of law varies among countries. In general, this personal law is relevant to questions of personal status, testamentary dispositions, and broad areas of family law. A frequent example of a question of status would be the determination whether a party had legal capacity to contract. Suppose, for example, that in illustration (a) above the defendant in the contract action was 17 years old and pleaded his minority (lack of capacity to contract) as a defense. If X law provided that a person had legal capacity at age 16 and Y law provided for age 21, a choice-of-law problem would arise. Under some circumstances, a court might refer to the personal law of the defendant to resolve this issue.

What that personal law should be is another disputed area of choice of law. In the Anglo-American countries, the reference is generally to a person's domicile. In many civil-law countries, the reference for many issues would be to the law of his nationality. The following case illustrates one of the difficulties which any rigid reference to a personal law can encounter.

Additional reading: Cavers, The Choice-of-Law Process 1–87 (1965); I Rabel, The Conflict of Laws: A Comparative Study 109–212 (2d ed., Drobnig, 1958); Nadelmann, Mancini's Nationality Rule and Non-Unified Legal Systems, 17 Am.J.Comp.L. 418 (1969).

LAURINE v. LAURINE

Supreme Court of Sweden, 1949.

16 Zeitschrift für Ausländisches und Internationales Privatrecht 145 (1951).[31]

[In 1940 Estonia was absorbed into the U.S.S.R. Four years later, the Laurines, who had been Estonian nationals, fled Estonia and came to Sweden where they maintained a permanent residence. An action seeking a judicial separation was instituted before a Swedish court. Under the facts of the case a separation was available if the domestic Swedish law were applied. Another Swedish law, the International Marriage Act (IÄL), governed certain questions relating to marriage and allied family problems that involved other countries or their nationals. Under its provisions, noted below, the separation decree could not be granted. The Supreme Court reversed the lower courts, which had applied the IÄL and had thus refused to grant the separation decree. Its opinion stated in part:]

Pursuant to § 2 of Chapter 3 of the IÄL a separation decree cannot be given unless, under the legislation of the state of which the man and wife are nationals, this kind of separation is permitted and a ground for separation exists both under the parties' national law and under Swedish law. There are no express statutory provisions regulating judicial separation in the case of persons who, with respect to legal relations involving their personality, are subject to the law of the country in which they have their permanent residence. If the permanent residence is in Sweden, Swedish law alone decides whether separation can be ordered. The facts do not give any grounds for assuming that Mr. and Mrs. Laurine, who now have their permanent residence in Sweden, are stateless. Nevertheless, it is clear from the fact that the Laurines came to Sweden in 1944 as political refugees that they do not now enjoy Soviet protection and do not intend to return to Russia. The Russian nationality, which the Laurines acquired as a consequence of Estonia's incorporation in the U.S.S.R., is entirely formal in its nature.

When the IÄL was enacted giving a foreign nationality legal effects with respect to personal status—including effects as to the requirements requisite for judicial separation, the legislator clearly had not reckoned with the kind of nationality with which we are concerned here. It would be incompatible with the policies underlying the provisions of law pursuant to which a person's nationality shall be

31. The English translation in von Mehren and Trautman, The Law of Multistate Problems 445–46 (1965), is from the German translation of the Swedish original in Nytt Juridiskt Arkiv 1949.I.82.

decisive for the legal effects in question to accord to nationality in cases such as the one presently before the court the decisive importance that it has in the normal situation. On the contrary, the policies that produced the rule subjecting stateless persons, so far as legal relations respecting their personality are concerned, to the laws of the country in which they have their permanent residence, also apply in substance to foreign nationals in the position of the Laurines, that is to say, to foreign nationals who no longer have a real tie with their homeland. . . . Consequently, the case is to be decided under the provisions of Swedish law respecting judicial separation.

COMMENT

The general problem before the court in the Laurine case is similar to that posed in the previous materials: what consequences flow from a given relationship between an individual and a political community. Here the inquiry is for purposes of choice of law, in an area where the "personal law" plays a key role.

Note that the Swedish court refers (a) to the substantive law of Sweden regulating separations and (b) to another body of Swedish law, here set forth in a statute that had adopted as internal law certain provisions of an international convention, to resolve the question of choice of law. In one sense, this statute was as firmly a part of the national legal system as the Swedish substantive law of separation. In another sense, it sought to resolve questions that would often involve the interests and policies of other nations. Like many principles or rules of the conflict of laws, this Swedish statute forms at once part of a national and a transnational legal order.

Among the most influential advocates of the nationality principle was Pasquale Stanislao Mancini, an Italian jurist. That principle has been widely adopted in continental Europe as a reference to resolve many issues pertaining to an individual's status, capacity and family relationships. Consider the brief excerpts below, treating questions of status, from a report of Mancini at a meeting in 1874 of the Institut de Droit International and published in 1 J. du Droit International Privé 221, 293 (1874).[32]

> . . . The national character and spirit reveals itself principally in the relations of the private law, for, the acts and customs which depend on free spontaneity of those who perform them, the laws of each people with their character of tacit pacts among the families that make up the society, these sometimes rest simply on morals, habits, and domestic tradition.
>
> The climate, the temperature, the geographic conditions, mountainous or maritime, the nature and the fertility of the soil, the diversity of needs and mores, these determine almost entirely each people's *system of legal relations*. They even determine, to a greater or lesser extent, the speed of physical and moral development, the organization of family relations, the preferred occupations, and the kinds of activities and

32. The English translation in von Mehren and Trautman, The Law of Multistate Problems 445–46 (1965), is from the German translation of the Swedish original in Nytt Juridiskt Arkiv 1949.I.82.

commercial relations that are most frequently encountered. For these reasons also, the status and capacity of individuals under the private law of different nations must differ according to the diversity of conditions. One cannot ignore this difference without doing violence to nature, and without reversing the effects of nature with great injustice. The age for majority can be cited as an example.

The rule, that a stranger arriving in our territory retains *his personal status and his juridical capacity of origin* cannot be considered as an arbitrary and generous concession by the legislator. What an unjust pretension it would be to require the contrary!

An individual coming from a cold country, where nature is lethargic and the development of physical and mental faculties slow, remains with reason, under the laws of his country, in a status of minority and incapacity for a larger time than he would under the laws of a hot country, warmed by a tropical sun. If, in traveling, such a person arrives in a country of southern Europe or in Africa and takes up residence there does he instantly, as a consequence of that fact, acquire the physical and moral qualities which he lacks, so that one applies to him the conditions of majority established by the laws of these countries? . . .

The status of persons and families constitutes a complex of attributes and qualities which do not belong to every human being, but to an individual having a particular nationality. If one attributes to a person Italian, French or German nationality, the effect is to raise up instantaneously the idea of all the personal rights and rights relating to the organization of the family which belong to all the individuals making up each of these nationalities. A man can change his nationality by accepting the nationality of another country, but he cannot retain his nationality and repudiate its conditions, for these conditions are like a mirror which reflects his own nationality. . . .

In the United States, the personal law has not been as significant for choice of law. Nonetheless, it has important application to a number of issues, including questions relating to the disposition of an individual's personal property upon death, many questions (often expressed in terms of a court's jurisdiction) of family law (marriage, divorce, separation, adoption), and questions of personal immunities and capacity. The personal law to which reference is made in such situations is almost invariably an individual's domicile.

QUESTIONS

(1) If the Laurines had been French nationals who were living in Sweden for a limited period, the court would probably have referred to French law to determine whether a separation should be granted. Why? What reasons additional to those stated in the excerpts from Mancini would support a reference to the national law? Would any interests or policies of France be relevant?

(2) Suppose that the Laurines were United States citizens who had sold their New York home in 1970, put their furniture into storage, and moved to Sweden where Mr. Laurine had then taken a job for three years.

The Laurines intended to move to the West Coast after their return. In 1972, a separation action was commenced in Sweden. What additional problems would the Swedish court face under these facts?

(3) Could a federation make extensive use of the nationality principle? Even in cases involving foreign nationals, can you identify historical and practical reasons why state law in the United States generally views a domicile in this country as the appropriate reference to a personal law?

NOTE ON CHOICE OF LAW FOR THE INTERNAL AFFAIRS OF CORPORATIONS

We consider here the analogue in corporate law to a personal law for individuals, in particular the kinds of questions which have been referred to that law for resolution, and the criteria by which that law has been identified.

In most situations, the fact that a corporation is a party to litigation would not disturb those principles of choice of law that would be applicable if only natural persons were involved. For example the defendants in illustrations (a) and (b) on pp. 91–92, supra, might have been individuals or corporations. However, there is a group of issues that is frequently referred to as involving the "internal affairs" of a corporation. These issues are primarily matters affecting the organization or dissolution of a corporation; organic changes (such as merger) in its structure; the internal organization and administration (composition of board of directors, declaration of dividends and so on); and certain aspects of relationships between the corporation (or its officers, directors or shareholders) and third parties—such matters as liability of shareholders for debts of the corporation, or liability of directors to creditors injured by corporate activities that involve the misconduct of directors.

In Anglo-American countries, questions pertaining to internal affairs are generally answered by reference to the law of the state of incorporation. The reference to such law, no matter where litigation arises or where events germane to the litigation occur, serves the need for certainty and predictability for corporations engaged in multistate or multinational activities—the need to be subject to one identifiable legal system with respect to internal affairs.

Consider the following illustrations:

(a) A corporation organized in State X transacts business in X, Y, and Z. It borrows funds from a bank in Z. The board of directors, which meets in the principal office of the corporation in Y, declares a dividend which is then paid to shareholders. The corporation thereafter becomes insolvent and cannot repay the bank. The bank sues the directors personally in a court in Y, alleging that the dividend was illegal and that the directors are therefore personally liable to unpaid creditors. Whether the dividend was illegal and, if so, whether the directors are personally liable are questions relating to the internal affairs of the corporation. The court in Y would normally look to X law to answer these questions.

(b) Suppose that the facts are the same, except that the bank is located in Y, where all the corporation's industrial activities are carried on and where all its shareholders, directors and principal creditors reside. In cases of this character, a few state courts have held that the law of the state with which the corporation is so significantly linked, rather than the state of incorporation with which it has nominal contacts, governs certain issues that are usually considered to be within a corporation's internal affairs. See Latty, Pseudo-Foreign Corporations, 65 Yale L.J. 137 (1955). In this respect such American courts have moved partly towards solutions similar to those arrived at by European courts using the concept of *siège social* described below.

As in Anglo-American jurisdictions, courts of civil law countries generally refer to the "personal law" of a corporation to resolve problems relating to its internal affairs. The personal law, however, is not that of the country in which the corporation is organized but that of the country in which it has what French law refers to as its *siège social*, or German law as its *Geschäftssitz* or *Sitz*.

Examination of the concept of *siège social* reveals that identification of a given corporation's *siège* is a good deal more complex than finding its place of incorporation. The extensive French case law on the subject, which is not wholly uniform or internally consistent, illustrates the difficulties. The French courts have drawn upon many factors to identify the *siège*, often translated as the "head office" or "business seat." Basically they appear to stress the nation in which the direction of the corporation is centered—the place of control and management, the headquarters, the "brain." This standard is more easily stated than applied, for shareholders, directors or managers may act in different countries. Other standards invoked by the French courts have included the place where a corporation's dominant activities are conducted, or the country of which most shareholders (or a controlling group) are nationals. A court may simply accept the *siège* designated in the constitutive documents of the corporation. It may go one step further and require that the corporation's designation not have been entirely divorced from the economic realities of its life, that the *siège* be "serious" or "real." This test would be satisfied if any one of a number of contacts were found to point to the designated *siège*—the place where shareholders or directors act, the place where the principal business of the firm is done or the place where its controlling shareholders reside. A court might go further and substitute its judgment for that of the corporation's promoters as to where the direction of the corporation is really centered.

Several approaches to this problem are reflected in a French decision, Weber v. Société Générale Anglaise et Française, Tribunal Commercial, Nancy, 18 Feb. 1907, 34 J. du Droit International Privé 765 (1907). This was one of a number of cases in which French promoters, fearful of the safeguards imposed under French law for the benefit of shareholders or other persons dealing with the corporation, selected a formal head office on the Isle of Jersey off the French coast in order to take advantage of its more lenient corporate and tax rules. Note the following language from the opinion (at 765):

> Whereas the nationality of a commercial association is determined by the country in which it has its *siège social*;—But the designation of this *siège social* must be serious and sincere, must correspond to the place where the management of the corporation is really carried on by its managers, where its activities are centralized, whence comes the impetus given to its different organs, and upon which there converge the results of their activity. If the *siège social* does not satisfy these conditions, if, aside from making the choice of a foreign country as a *siège social,* the corporation presents all the characteristics of a French corporation, if not only is the majority of the shareholders made up of Frenchmen resident in France and if almost all of the capital is furnished by these Frenchmen but if even the managers are all French; if nowhere and under no circumstances can one find any trace of any action of any kind being taken at the foreign *siège social;* if, finally, the operations of the corporation take place exclusively in France, one has the right to say that the designation of the *siège social* is only a fiction and has only been conceived in order to keep the requirements of French law from applying to the founding and functioning of the company, that the latter has nothing foreign about it but the name, and it is not able to take advantage of the immunities belonging to foreign corporations. . . .

It will be noted that this case is one in which the French courts were alert to prevent what they regarded as evasions of French law. It does not follow that they would, in comparable circumstances, relieve a corporation that had designated a *siège* in France of the consequences of that choice or that they would handle in the same way a case in which the issue was whether a corporation's *siège* was in the United States or in Germany.

The consequences of a finding that a corporation's *siège social* does not correspond with its place of organization or registered head office vary among European countries. At a minimum, the law of the *siège social* would be applicable to those issues that were considered within the corporation's internal affairs. At times, other protective legislation of the *siège social* intended, for example, to benefit shareholders or creditors, is considered applicable. And on occasion, the courts have refused to recognize the corporation and have treated it as "void," on the ground that it has been fraudulently created with the intent to avoid obligations imposed by the law of the *siège social.*

Of course the French courts, as illustrated by the Remington case, p. 79, supra, have been required to attribute a national character to corporations for purposes other than choice of law for internal affairs. When considering issues such as the applicability of local regulatory laws, some courts have directly invoked the concept of *siège social.* But in other settings, the courts have not referred to the *siège,* although they have developed criteria such as the place of management or place of control which are related to that concept.

Concepts such as the *siège social* have not played a significant role in American corporation law. Consider, however, 28 U.S.C.A. § 1332 *, which provides that, for purposes of diversity jurisdiction, a "corporation shall be deemed a citizen of any State by which it has been incorporated and of the State where it has its principal place of business." Note that the first part of the definition carries forward the traditional place-of-incorporation test which the courts developed in the early 19th Century, without legislative guidance. The second part represents a recent congressional move to limit the breadth of the diversity jurisdiction. In interpreting this amendment, some courts have drawn upon criteria which are closely allied to the *siège social.* Kelly v. United States Steel Corp., 284 F.2d 850 (3d Cir. 1960), illustrates this point. The court, to determine if it had diversity jurisdiction, had to designate the "principal place of business" of a corporation with 14 divisions, manufacturing in almost every state and many foreign countries. The choice was narrowed to New York and Pennsylvania. New York was the place where the board of directors made final decisions on corporate policy, particularly on financing. However the Operation Policy Committee, to which authority was delegated by the Board, directed the regular business of the corporation from Pennsylvania and appointed officers up to the level of vice-president. Most of the important executives had their offices and staffs in Pennsylvania. The court concluded that the business was "centered" in Pennsylvania. It also noted but gave less weight to the fact that many more workers and much more of the physical plant were located in Pennsylvania.

Additional reading: 1 Batiffol, Droit International Privé 233–257, 2 id. 19 (5th ed., Lagarde, 1970); Loussouarn, La Condition des Personnes Morales en Droit International Privé, 96 Academie de Droit International, Recueil des Cours 447 (1959); Note, 74 Harv.L.Rev. 1429 (1961); II Rabel, The Conflict of Laws: A Comparative Study 31–93 (2d ed., Drobnig, 1960); Reese and Kaufman, The Law Governing Corporate Affairs: Choice of Law and the Impact of Full Faith and Credit, 58 Colum.L.Rev. 1118 (1958).

QUESTIONS

(1) What advantages and disadvantages do you see in the use of the *siège social* rather than the place of incorporation as a choice-of-law reference?

(2) Newco, a New York corporation, intends to extend its manufacturing operations to Frantaly, a continental European country. It is con-

sidering three possible legal routes: (a) organization of a wholly-owned Frantalian subsidiary, (b) organization of a New York subsidiary which would own and control the Frantalian assets, and (c) establishment of a branch of Newco in Frantaly. If it uses route (a), Newco intends to elect company officials to the board of directors (or equivalent body under Frantalian law) and to make important decisions about the foreign operation in New York. Newco now has gross assets stated at $10,000,000 and intends to invest about $3,000,000 in its Frantalian operations. In addition, some funds will be borrowed in Frantaly, where most of the foreign production will be sold. Identify the problems of choice of law concerning internal affairs to which Newco should be alert with respect to each possibility.

Chapter II

DISTRIBUTION OF NATIONAL POWERS TO DEAL WITH TRANSNATIONAL PROBLEMS

In Chapter I we observed the kinds of solutions that national legal systems bring to transnational issues. Here we are concerned with the ways in which powers to deal with such issues are distributed between branches or levels of government within a nation. The question posed is the degree to which the transnational aspect of a problem may alter the usual processes of decision-making.

In any nation with constitutional principles of the separation of powers, problems arise of how to distribute powers to deal with foreign matters. The executive may claim primacy as the branch most capable of making those speedy and informed policy judgments that are involved in relations with foreign countries or their nationals. The legislature will often leave large scope to the executive, but will at other times assert its primary law-making role and attempt to impose its views on that branch. With respect to both executive and legislative acts, a judiciary with the competence to review action by another branch must determine whether it should defer absolutely to the judgment of those branches on some or all transnational matters, or whether it should exercise the same standard of review and the same law-making powers that it does in most domestic matters.

When a country is federal in structure, a new series of problems arises. Almost any federal system will deny to its component states a major participation in the making or conduct of foreign policy, even in the development of laws that are apt to raise difficult transnational problems. But the complex task remains of defining the borderline between those areas where a nation can afford to allocate competences between federal and state levels, and those areas where a uniform national policy is critical.

These matters raise fundamental political and constitutional issues. During the 20th century, and particularly since World War II, there has been a proliferation in the United States and many foreign countries of laws and executive or administrative practices which regulate the personal or commercial activities of participants in transnational life. The issues below range from the right of an individual to travel as tourist in a foreign country or devise property to a foreign national, to the right of a corporation to export or import a given commodity.

The individual or corporation may be significantly affected by the processes through which a regulatory scheme is developed and applied, and by the extent to which the courts will review any such scheme or will defer to the judgments or findings of the legislative or executive branches. But whatever the relevance of decision-making processes for the particular private participant in transnational activities, those processes have had a deep effect upon matters as vast as the waging of war in Vietnam.

We explore these problems only within the United States. The materials involve primarily common, statutory or constitutional law. But in this country, many problems of this type have arisen in the context of treaties or executive agreements with foreign countries, or of customary international law. We postpone to Chapter V consideration of the bearing of international agreements or custom upon these problems.

A. DISTRIBUTION OF POWERS WITHIN THE FEDERAL GOVERNMENT

---

1. POWERS OF THE EXECUTIVE, DELEGATED AND INHERENT, AND CONTROL BY CONGRESS AND THE COURTS

UNITED STATES v. CURTISS-WRIGHT EXPORT CORP.

Supreme Court of the United States, 1936.
299 U.S. 304, 57 S.Ct. 216, 81 L.Ed. 255.

MR. JUSTICE SUTHERLAND delivered the opinion of the Court.

On January 27, 1936, an indictment was returned in the court below, the first count of which charges that appellees, beginning with the 29th day of May, 1934, conspired to sell in the United States certain arms of war, namely, fifteen machine guns, to Boliva, a country then engaged in armed conflict in the Chaco, in violation of the Joint Resolution of Congress approved May 28, 1934, and the provisions of a proclamation issued on the same day by the President of the United States pursuant to authority conferred by section 1 of the resolution. In pursuance of the conspiracy, the commission of certain overt acts was alleged, details of which need not be stated. The Joint Resolution (chapter 365, 48 Stat. 811) follows:

> "*Resolved by the Senate and House of Representatives of the United States of America in Congress assembled,* That if the President finds that the prohibition of the sale of arms and munitions of war in the United States to those countries now engaged in armed conflict in the Chaco may contribute to the reestablishment of peace between those countries, and if after consultation with the governments of other American Republics and with their cooperation, as well as that of such other governments as he may deem necessary, he makes proclamation to that effect, it shall be

unlawful to sell, except under such limitations and exceptions as the President prescribes, any arms or munitions of war in any place in the United States to the countries now engaged in that armed conflict, or to any person, company, or association acting in the interest of either country, until otherwise ordered by the President or by Congress.

"Sec. 2. Whoever sells any arms or munitions of war in violation of section 1 shall, on conviction, be punished by a fine not exceeding $10,000 or by imprisonment not exceeding two years, or both."

The President's proclamation (48 Stat. 1744, No. 2087), after reciting the terms of the Joint Resolution, declares:

"Now, Therefore, I Franklin D. Roosevelt, President of the United States of America, acting under and by virtue of the authority conferred in me by the said joint resolution of Congress, do hereby declare and proclaim that I have found that the prohibition of the sale of arms and munitions of war in the United States to those countries now engaged in armed conflict in the Chaco may contribute to the reestablishment of peace between those countries, and that I have consulted with the governments of other American Republics and have been assured of the cooperation of such governments as I have deemed necessary as contemplated by the said joint resolution; and I do hereby admonish all citizens of the United States and every person to abstain from every violation of the provisions of the joint resolution above set forth, hereby made applicable to Bolivia and Paraguay, and I do hereby warn them that all violations of such provisions will be rigorously prosecuted. . . ."

On November 14, 1935, this proclamation was revoked. . . .

Appellees severally demurred to the first count of the indictment. . . . The points urged in support of the demurrers were, first, that the Joint Resolution effects an invalid delegation of legislative power to the executive; second, that the Joint Resolution never became effective because of the failure of the President to find essential jurisdictional facts; and, third, that the second proclamation operated to put an end to the alleged liability under the Joint Resolution.

The court below sustained the demurrers upon the first point, but overruled them on the second and third points. (D.C.) 14 F. Supp. 230. The government appealed to this court under the provisions of the Criminal Appeals Act of March 2, 1907, 34 Stat. 1246, as amended, U.S.C., title 18, § 682 (18 U.S.C.A. § 682). . . .

First. It is contended that by the Joint Resolution the going into effect and continued operation of the resolution was conditioned (a) upon the President's judgment as to its beneficial effect upon the reestablishment of peace between the countries engaged in armed conflict in the Chaco; (b) upon the making of a proclamation, which was left to his unfettered discretion, thus constituting an attempted substitution of the President's will for that of Congress; (c) upon the making of a proclamation putting an end to the operation of the resolution, which again was left to the President's unfettered discretion; and (d) further, that the extent of its operation in particular cases was subject to limitation and exception by the President, controlled by no standard. In each of these particulars, appellees urge that Congress abdicated its essential functions and delegated them to the Executive.

Whether, if the Joint Resolution had related solely to internal affairs, it would be open to the challenge that it constituted an unlawful delegation of legislative power to the Executive, we find it unnecessary to determine. The whole aim of the resolution is to affect a situation entirely external to the United States, and falling within the category of foreign affairs. The determination which we are called to make, therefore, is whether the Joint Resolution, as applied to that situation, is vulnerable to attack under the rule that forbids a delegation of the lawmaking power. In other words, assuming (but not deciding) that the challenged delegation, if it were confined to internal affairs, would be invalid, may it nevertheless be sustained on the ground that its exclusive aim is to afford a remedy for a hurtful condition within foreign territory?

It will contribute to the elucidation of the question if we first consider the differences between the powers of the federal government in respect of foreign or external affairs and those in respect of domestic or internal affairs. . . .

The two classes of powers are different, both in respect of their origin and their nature. The broad statement that the federal government can exercise no powers except those specifically enumerated in the Constitution, and such implied powers as are necessary and proper to carry into effect the enumerated powers, is categorically true only in respect of our internal affairs. In that field, the primary purpose of the Constitution was to carve from the general mass of legislative powers *then possessed by the states* such portions as it was thought desirable to vest in the federal government, leaving those not included in the enumeration still in the states. Carter v. Carter Coal Co., 298 U.S. 238, 294, 56 S.Ct. 855, 865, 80 L.Ed. 1160. That this doctrine applies only to powers which the states had is self-evident. And since the states severally never possessed international powers, such powers could not have been carved from the mass of state powers but obviously were transmitted to the United States from some other source. During the Colonial period, those powers were possessed exclusively by and were entirely under the control of the Crown. . . .

As a result of the separation from Great Britain by the colonies, acting as a unit, the powers of external sovereignty passed from the Crown not to the colonies severally, but to the colonies in their collective and corporate capacity as the United States of America. Even before the Declaration, the colonies were a unit in foreign affairs, acting through a common agency—namely, the Continental Congress, composed of delegates from the thirteen colonies. . . . A political society cannot endure without a supreme will somewhere. Sovereignty is never held in suspense. When, therefore, the external sovereignty of Great Britain in respect of the colonies ceased, it immediately passed to the Union. See Penhallow v. Doane, 3 Dall. 54, 80, 81, 1 L.Ed. 507, Fed.Cas.No.10925. That fact was given practical application almost at once. The treaty of peace, made on September 3, 1783, was concluded between his Brittanic Majesty and the "United States of America." 8 Stat., European Treaties, 80.

. . . The Framers' Convention was called and exerted its powers upon the irrefutable postulate that though the states were several their people in respect of foreign affairs were one. . . .

It results that the investment of the federal government with the powers of external sovereignty did not depend upon the affirmative grants of the Constitution. The powers to declare and wage war, to conclude peace, to make treaties, to maintain diplomatic relations with other sovereignties, if they had never been mentioned in the Constitution, would have vested in the federal government as necessary concomitants of nationality. . . . The power to acquire territory by discovery and occupation (Jones v. United States, 137 U.S. 202, 212, 11 S.Ct. 80, 34 L.Ed. 691), the power to expel undesirable aliens (Fong Yue Ting v. United States, 139 U.S. 698, 705 et seq., 13 S.Ct. 1016, 37 L.Ed. 905), the power to make such international agreements as do not constitute treaties in the constitutional sense (Altman & Co. v. United States, 224 U.S. 583, 600, 601, 32 S.Ct. 593, 56 L.Ed. 894; Crandall, Treaties, Their Making and Enforcement [2d Ed.] p. 102 and note 1), none of which is expressly affirmed by the Constitution, nevertheless exist as inherently inseparable from the conception of nationality. This the court recognized, and in each of the cases cited found the warrant for its conclusions not in the provisions of the Constitution, but in the law of nations. . . .

Not only, as we have shown, is the federal power over external affairs in origin and essential character different from that over internal affairs, but participation in the exercise of the power is significantly limited. In this vast external realm, with its important, complicated, delicate and manifold problems, the President alone has the power to speak or listen as a representative of the nation. He *makes* treaties with the advice and consent of the Senate; but he alone negotiates. Into the field of negotiation the Senate cannot intrude; and Congress itself is powerless to invade it. As Marshall said in his great argument of March 7, 1800, in the House of Representatives, "The President is the sole organ of the nation in its external relations, and its sole representative with foreign nations." Annals, 6th Cong., col. 613. The Senate Committee on Foreign Relations at a very early day in our history (February 15, 1816), reported to the Senate, among other things, as follows:

> "The President is the constitutional representative of the United States with regard to foreign nations. He manages our concerns with foreign nations and must necessarily be most competent to determine when, how, and upon what subjects negotiation may be urged with the greatest prospect of success. For his conduct he is responsible to the Constitution. The committee considers this responsibility the surest pledge for the faithful discharge of his duty. They think the interference of the Senate in the direction of foreign negotiations calculated to diminish that responsibility and thereby to impair the best security for the national safety. The nature of transactions with foreign nations, moreover, requires caution and unity of design, and their success frequently depends on secrecy and dispatch." 8 U.S.Sen. Reports Comm. on Foreign Relations, p. 24.

It is important to bear in mind that we are here dealing not alone with an authority vested in the President by an exertion of legislative power, but with such an authority plus the very delicate, plenary and exclusive power of the President as the sole organ of the federal government in the field of international relations—a power which does not require as a basis for its exercise an act of Congress, but which, of course, like every other governmental power, must be exercised in subordination to the applicable provisions of the Constitution. It is quite apparent that if, in the maintenance of our international relations, embarrassment—perhaps serious embarrassment —is to be avoided and success for our aims achieved, congressional legislation which is to be made effective through negotiation and inquiry within the international field must often accord to the President a degree of discretion and freedom from statutory restriction which would not be admissible were domestic affairs alone involved. Moreover, he, not Congress, has the better opportunity of knowing the conditions which prevail in foreign countries, and especially is this true in time of war. He has his confidential sources of information. He has his agents in the form of diplomatic, consular and other officials. Secrecy in respect of information gathered by them may be highly necessary, and the premature disclosure of it productive of harmful results. Indeed, so clearly is this true that the first President refused to accede to a request to lay before the House of Representatives the instructions, correspondence and documents relating to the negotiation of the Jay Treaty—a refusal the wisdom of which was recognized by the House itself and has never since been doubted. . . .

Practically every volume of the United States Statutes contains one or more acts or joint resolutions of Congress authorizing action by the President in respect of subjects affecting foreign relations, which either leave the exercise of the power to his unrestricted judgment, or provide a standard far more general than that which has always been considered requisite with regard to domestic affairs. Many, though not all, of these acts are designated in the footnote.[1]
. . .

We deem it unnecessary to consider, *seriatim,* the several clauses which are said to evidence the unconstitutionality of the Joint Resolution as involving an unlawful delegation of legislative power. It is enough to summarize by saying that, both upon principle and in accordance with precedent, we conclude there is sufficient warrant for the broad discretion vested in the President to determine whether the enforcement of the statute will have a beneficial effect upon the reestablishment of peace in the affected countries; whether he shall make proclamation to bring the resolution into operation; whether and when the resolution shall cease to operate and to make proclamation accordingly; and to prescribe limitations and exceptions to which the enforcement of the resolution shall be subject.

[The Court then considered two other challenges to the indictment. It concluded that the President had made the required findings before issuing the proclamation, and that the second proclamation of the President revoking the first proclamation did not abrogate the Joint Resolution or preclude its enforcement with respect to offenses committed during the life of the first proclamation. The Court reversed the judgment below and remanded the case for further proceedings. JUSTICE MCREYNOLDS dissented without opinion.]

1. Thus, the President has been broadly "authorized" to suspend embargo acts passed by Congress, "if in his judgment the public interest should require it" (Act of December 19, 1806, c. 1, § 3, 2 Stat. 411. . . .

Other acts, for retaliation against discriminations as to United States commerce, have placed broad powers in the hands of the President, "authorizing" even the total exclusion of vessels of any foreign country so offending (Act of June 19, 1886, c. 421, § 17, 24 Stat. 79, 82, 83 [46 U.S.C.A. § 142]), or the increase of duties on its goods or their total exclusion from the United States (Act of June 17, 1930, c. 497, § 388, 46 Stat. 590, 704 [19 U.S.C.A. § 1338]). . . .

Congress has also passed acts for the enforcement of treaties or conventions, to be effective only upon proclamation of the President. Some of them may be noted which "authorize" the President to make proclamation when he shall be "satisfied" or shall receive "satisfactory evidence" that the other nation has complied. . . .

Where appropriate, Congress has provided that violation of the President's proclamations authorized by the foregoing acts shall be penalized. . . .

COMMENT

The historical and constitutional (or extra-constitutional) interpretations developed by Justice Sutherland in this opinion have been targets of sharp criticism by later scholars.[2] That criticism rests on several grounds. The critics note numerous examples of the retention and exercise of powers of "external sovereignty" by the states prior to ratification of the Constitution, contrary to the Justice's contention that such powers moved without visible obstruction from the Crown to the federal government. Again, the opinion leaps from an assertion of paramount *federal* power to more particular assertions about *presidential* power. Moreover, scholars have pointed out misinterpretations by Justice Sutherland of remarks by late 18th Century statesmen or jurists which, in context, did not support the Justice's reference to the "delicate, plenary and exclusive" power of the President with respect to international relations—an inherent rather than delegated power, indeed a power not based upon the enumerated "foreign affairs" powers of the President, but rather derived from consideration of the nature of sovereignty and of international law or relations, as well as from a reading of history.

There is some irony in the criticism of Justice Sutherland's opinion, from a different perspective, by Senator Fulbright, in American Foreign Policy in the Twentieth Century under an Eighteenth Century Constitution, 47 Cornell L.Q. 1 (1961). The Senator concluded that the Justice's reference to "plenary" powers of the President in foreign relations was an overstatement and that indeed the Executive, excessively hampered by the Congress in the conduct of foreign relations, lacked sufficient power.

Nonetheless, whatever the doubts about the opinion's historical accuracy or constitutional wisdom, whatever the criticism that portions of the opinion treating the President's "plenary" and inherent powers were unnecessary and thus *dicta*, Curtiss-Wright has proved to be an influential precedent, a point of departure for debate about executive power on issues ranging from presidential powers to enter into executive agreements (see pp. 589–602, infra) to claims of executive privilege. References to the opinion were frequent in the extensive debates over Vietnam and war powers summarized at pp. 142–159, infra.

QUESTIONS

(1) Review Articles I and II of the Constitution. Note all powers related to foreign matters, and whether they are exclusive to one branch or shared in some manner with another. What basis does the Constitutional text afford for the views in the Curtiss-Wright case?

2. See, e. g., Levitan, The Foreign Relations Power: An Analysis of Mr. Justice Sutherland's Theory, 55 Yale L.J. 467 (1946); Lofgren, United States v. Curtiss-Wright Export Corporation: An Historical Assessment, 83 Yale L.J. 1 (1973); Berger, The Presidential Monopoly of Foreign Relations, 71 Mich.L.Rev. 1, 26–33 (1972); and Henkin, Foreign Affairs and the Constitution 19–26 (1972).

(2) As a Congressman, why would you have voted for the Joint Resolution, rather than support explicit and self-contained legislation that did not depend upon implementation by the Executive? Did the Joint Resolution in fact delegate broad powers to the President?

(3) Was it necessary for Justice Sutherland to look past the power delegated to the President and to develop in this case the argument of inherent power, of the "very delicate, plenary, and exclusive power of the President as the sole organ of the federal government in the field of international relations . . . . " ? (The Note following these questions suggests the uncertain state of the delegation doctrine at that time.)

(4) Does it appear from the opinion that, without a legislative foundation, an executive order could have made the sale of munitions to designated countries a crime? Would your answer differ if that order placed an embargo on munitions, instructing appropriate officials to bar their export, without imposing criminal penalties?

NOTE ON THE DELEGATION OF LAW-MAKING POWERS FOR ECONOMIC REGULATION

The Curtiss-Wright case arose during a period when the Supreme Court applied the doctrine of unconstitutional delegation of powers much more stringently than it would today. The great majority of the cases involving an allegation of excessive delegation of legislative power have been in the area of economic regulation. For the cases that raised only domestic issues, the high tide of the delegation doctrine is captured in two decisions that struck down portions of a key piece of the economic legislation of the New Deal, the National Industrial Recovery Act (NIRA). Panama Refining Co. v. Ryan, 293 U.S. 388, 55 S.Ct. 241, 79 L.Ed. 446 (1935), invalidated a section of that Act that authorized the President to prohibit the transportation in interstate commerce of petroleum produced in excess of the amount allowed by state regulations. Schechter Poultry Corp. v. United States, 295 U.S. 495, 55 S.Ct. 837, 79 L.Ed. 1570 (1935), invalidated a poultry code that had been promulgated under a section authorizing the President to approve industry-developed codes of "fair competition," a term not helpfully defined anywhere in the Act. Later cases involving New Deal legislation, wartime statutes on price controls and renegotiation, and postwar acts have found that the delegations to the executive branch were under the limitation of an "intelligible principle" and were thus valid. Probably, however, none of these cases has involved as unrestrained a discretion in the executive as that condemned in the NIRA cases. Thus it cannot be said that their doctrine is dead.

With respect to international trade, three regulatory schemes have been challenged on the ground of excessive delegation of authority. The first is the tariff system. Until 1930 Congress kept close control over customs duties and legislated in detail. The earliest delegations to the President of the power to adjust these statutory structures were hesitant and circumscribed with procedural safeguards. Two of them are referred to by Mr. Justice Cardozo in his dissenting opinion in Panama Refining Co. J. W. Hampton, Jr. & Co. v. United States, 276 U.S. 394, 48 S.Ct. 348, 72 L.Ed. 624 (1928), upheld portions of the Tariff Act of 1922 authorizing the President, after investigation by the Tariff Commission, to increase or decrease duties within stated limits to equalize differences between the American and foreign costs of producing the goods involved. Marshall Field & Co. v. Clark, 143 U.S. 649, 12 S.Ct. 495, 36 L.Ed. 294 (1892), had earlier approved a tariff provision of 1890 authorizing the President, when he was satisfied that other countries were imposing tariffs on United States agricultural commodities that were "reciprocally unequal and unreasonable," to suspend statutory provisions permitting the free introduction into this country of such commodities.

In the 1930's Congress began to give the President a broader scope of discretion. Substantial grants came in connection with the program under which President Roosevelt sought to lower tariff barriers, then at an unprecedentedly high level, by a series of bilateral agreements with other countries that led to reciprocal tariff reductions. These agreements received the force of domestic law by virtue of a series of Trade Agreements acts giving the President the authority to proclaim those changes in the statutory structure needed to carry out the United States' commitments. Since World War II these negotiations have been carried out within the framework of the General Agreement on Tariffs and Trade (see pp. 1149–1164, infra), which has converted them to a multilateral process.

Thus the present tariff legislation of the United States consists of a schedule of rates, now dating back to 1930, plus a series of wide, but not unlimited, grants of authority to lower or raise those rates if lower rates are negotiated or if it is found that foreign countries are failing to live up to their commitments or are subsidizing exports or if it is found that foreign firms are "dumping" goods at cut rates in this country. The constitutionality of this system was sustained in Star-Kist Foods, Inc. v. United States, 275 F.2d 472 (C.C.P.A.1959), in which an American producer challenged the legality of a reduction in duties on tuna. That reduction had been proclaimed under Section 350(a) of the Trade Agreements Act of 1934, as amended, which authorized the President to reduce rates of duty by not more than 50% if that reduction carried out commitments under a trade agreement with a foreign country, the President being at the same time authorized to enter into such agreements. The court sustained the reduction in an opinion which discussed the Curtiss-Wright, Field and Hampton cases and concluded (at p. 480):

> A constitutional delegation of powers requires that Congress enunciate a policy or objective or give reasons for seeking the aid of the President. In addition the act must specify when the powers conferred may be utilized by establishing a standard or "intelligible principle" which is suffi-

cient to make it clear when action is proper. And because Congress cannot abdicate its legislative function and confer carte blanche authority on the President, it must circumscribe that power in some manner. This means that Congress must tell the President what he can do by prescribing a standard which confines his discretion and which will guarantee that any authorized action he takes will tend to promote rather than flout the legislative purpose. It is not necessary that the guides be precise or mathematical formulae to be satisfactory in a constitutional sense.

In the act before us the Congressional policy is pronounced very clearly. The stated objectives are to expand foreign markets for the products of the United States "by regulating the admission of foreign goods into the United States in accordance with the characteristics and needs of various branches of American production so that foreign markets will be made available to those branches of American production which require and are capable of developing such outlets by affording corresponding market opportunities for foreign products in the United States . . . ." These objectives are in their nature no different than those of the Tariff Act of 1890 wherein the stated policy was to secure reciprocally equal trade with countries producing certain enumerated articles, and the Tariff Act of 1922 which was designed to enable domestic producers to compete on an equal basis with foreign producers in the marketplaces of the United States.

The court then compared the procedures to be followed in changing tariff rates under the acts of 1890, 1922 and 1934. It noted that the 1934 Act, unlike its predecessors, provided for foreign trade agreements which were to be followed by proclamations of the new duties. The court referred to the Supreme Court's "recognition of the necessity of flexibility in the laws affecting foreign relations," compared the discretion granted the President under the 1934 Act with that conferred under the various provisions of the 1890 and 1922 acts, and concluded "that the 1934 act does not grant an unconstitutional delegation of authority to the President."

The President in 1971 sought to exercise a different and even broader power in dealing with customs duties. His actions were reviewed by the Customs Court in the opinion which follows this Note.

A second regulatory scheme dealing with foreign commerce that has raised issues of delegation is the Trading with the Enemy Act. Section 5(b) of that Act, 40 Stat. 415 (1917), as amended, 50 U.S.C.A.App. § 5(b), reads as follows:

(b)(1) During the time of war or during any other period of national emergency declared by the President, the President may, through any agency that he may designate, or otherwise, and under such rules and regulations as he may prescribe, by means of instructions, licenses, or otherwise—

(A) investigate, regulate, or prohibit, any transactions in foreign exchange, transfers of credit or payments between, by, through, or to any banking institution, and the importing, exporting, hoarding, melting, or earmarking of gold or silver coin or bullion, currency or securities, and

(B) investigate, regulate, direct and compel, nullify, void, prevent or prohibit, any acquisition holding, withholding, use, transfer, withdrawal, transportation, importation or exportation of, or dealing in, or exercising any right, power, or privilege with respect to, or transactions involving, any property in which any foreign country or a national thereof has any interest,

by any person, or with respect to any property, subject to the jurisdiction of the United States; . . .

The power thus conferred has been used for purposes not connected with active, declared warfare. A "national emergency" within the meaning of Section 5(b) was declared to be in effect by President Truman on December 16, 1950, after the outbreak of the Korean War. That emergency has been referred to in and reiterated by several later orders, as described in fn. 6, p. 129, infra. Currently three sets of limitations on trade with foreign countries have been issued by the Treasury, to which the President has delegated his power. The Foreign Assets Control Regulations, 31 C.F.R. Part 500 (1973), continue to impose a general embargo on transactions with China, North Korea and North Viet-Nam or their residents. Note the breadth of these regulations, which even forbid unlicensed transactions in stated categories of goods from other countries if there is a significant danger that goods of that type might be of forbidden origin. The following excerpt from the regulations is illustrative.

§ 500.204 Importation of and dealings in certain merchandise.

(a) Except as specifically authorized by the Secretary of the Treasury (or any person, agency, or instrumentality designated by him) by means of regulations, or rulings, instructions, licenses, or otherwise, persons subject to the jurisdiction of the United States may not purchase, transport, import, or otherwise deal in or engage in any transaction with respect to any merchandise outside the United States specified in following subparagraph (1) of this paragraph, and they may not import into the United States merchandise specified in following subparagraphs (2), (3), or (4) of this paragraph:

(1) Merchandise the country of origin of which is China (except Formosa), North Korea, or North Viet-Nam. . . .

(2) Merchandise specified in this subparagraph, howsoever processed, unless such merchandise originated in a country named as excepted for that type of merchan-

dise and is imported into the United States directly from that country:

Type of merchandise	*Excepted countries*
(i) All merchandise, not elsewhere specified in this paragraph, if prior to December 17, 1950, imports thereof into the United States were chiefly of Chinese origin within the meaning of this chapter, and	None.
(ii) All of the following specified types of merchandise:	
Aniseed, star	None.
Aniseed oil	None.
. . .	
Bamboo, split	None.
Braids, straw	Italy, Japan

Note, however, that § 500.547, introduced as part of the policy of the Nixon administration to normalize relations with the People's Republic of China, has virtually cancelled the effectiveness of the above rules as respects China:

(a) Except as provided in paragraphs (b) and (c) of this section, all transactions prohibited by § 500.204 are licensed.

(b) This section does not authorize:

. . .

(2) Any transaction involving merchandise, the country of origin of which is North Korea or North Vietnam.

Other rules under this Act, probably more important as of 1975 than those relating to the Far East, impose economic quarantines on Cuba, 31 C.F.R. Part 515 (1973) and Southern Rhodesia, 31 C.F.R. Part 530 (1973). Indeed, note that each of these Treasury regulations purports to govern American nationals even when they conduct transactions outside this country's territorial limits, as through branches or wholly-owned subsidiaries in foreign countries. However, this extraterritorial feature of the Cuban regulations was ended by the United States, in August 1975, following a decision of the Organization of American States that relaxed restrictions on trade with Cuba. See pp. 1223–1224, infra. Note that violations of these rules can entail criminal sanctions.

The third important delegation of legislative power to regulate international trade lies in the Export Administration Act.[3] This Act is of limited duration, as was its predecessor, the Export Control Act of 1949. The renewed authority granted in 1974 terminates on September 30, 1976. The change in title is significant as it signalled a

3. The Export Administration Act, 83 Stat. 1553, as amended 50 U.S.C.A. App. §§ 2401–2413, was further amended in late 1974 by 88 Stat. 1553.

change in emphasis towards the liberalization of East-West trade. The following sections of the Act reveal the degree of delegation involved.

Sec. 3. Congressional declaration of policy

The Congress makes the following declarations:

(1) It is the policy of the United States both (A) to encourage trade with all countries with which we have diplomatic or trading relations, except those countries with which such trade has been determined by the President to be against the national interest, and (B) to restrict the export of goods and technology which would make a significant contribution to the military potential of any other nation or nations which would prove detrimental to the national security of the United States.

(2) It is the policy of the United States to use export controls (A) to the extent necessary to protect the domestic economy from the excessive drain of scarce materials and to reduce the serious inflationary impact of foreign demand, (B) to the extent necessary to further significantly the foreign policy of the United States and to fulfill its international responsibilities, and (C) to the extent necessary to exercise the necessary vigilance over exports from the standpoint of their significance to the national security of the United States.

(3) It is the policy of the United States (A) to formulate, reformulate, and apply any necessary controls to the maximum extent possible in cooperation with all nations, and (B) to formulate a unified trade control policy to be observed by all such nations.

(4) It is the policy of the United States to use its economic resources and trade potential to further the sound growth and stability of its economy as well as to further its national security and foreign policy objectives.

. . .

(7) It is the policy of the United States to use export controls, including license fees, to secure the removal by foreign countries of restrictions on access to supplies where such restrictions have or may have a serious domestic inflationary impact, have caused or may cause a serious domestic shortage, or have been imposed for purposes of influencing the foreign policy of the United States. . . .

Sec. 4. Authority to effectuate policy

[T]he Secretary [of Commerce] shall review any list of articles, materials, or supplies, including technical data or other information, the exportation of which from the United States, its territories and possessions, was heretofore prohibited or curtailed with a view to making promptly such changes and revisions in such list as may be necessary or desirable in furtherance of the policy, purposes, and provisions of this Act.

. . .

(b)(1) To effectuate the policies set forth in section 3 of this Act, the President may prohibit or curtail the exportation from the United States, its territories and possessions, of any articles, materials, or supplies, including technical data or any other information, except under such rules and regulations as he shall prescribe. To the extent necessary to achieve effective enforcement of this Act, these rules and regulations may apply to the financing, transporting, and other servicing of exports and the participation therein by any person. Rules and regulations may provide for denial of any request or application for authority to export articles, materials, or supplies, including technical data, or any other information, from the United States, its territories and possessions, to any nation or combination of nations threatening the national security of the United States if the President determines that their export would prove detrimental to the national security of the United States, regardless of their availability from nations other than any nation or combination of nations threatening the national security of the United States, but whenever export licenses are required on the ground that considerations of national security override considerations of foreign availability, the reasons for so doing shall be reported to the Congress in the quarterly report following the decision to require such licenses on that ground to the extent considerations of national security and foreign policy permit. The rules and regulations shall implement the provisions of section 3(5) of this Act and shall require that all domestic concerns receiving requests for the furnishing of information or the signing of agreements as specified in that section must report this fact to the Secretary of Commerce for such action as he may deem appropriate to carry out the purposes of that section. . . .

(2) The Secretary of Commerce, in cooperation with appropriate United States Government departments and agencies and the appropriate technical advisory committees established under section 5(c) shall undertake an investigation to determine which articles, materials, and supplies, including technical data and other information, should no longer be subject to export controls because of their significance to the national security of the United States. Notwithstanding the provisions of paragraph (1), the President shall remove unilateral export controls on the export from the United States of articles, materials, or supplies, including technical data or other information, which he determines are available without restriction from sources outside the United States in significant quantities and comparable in quality to those produced in the United States, except that any such control may remain in effect if the President determines that adequate evidence has been presented to him demonstrating that the absence of such a control would prove detrimental to the national security of the United States. The nature of such evidence shall be included in the special report required by paragraph (4).

Necessity of authorization or permission to export

(d) Nothing in this Act or the rules or regulations hereunder shall be construed to require authority or permission to export, except where required by the President to effect the policies set forth in section 3 of this Act.

Delegation of Presidential authority and power

> (e) The President may delegate the power, authority, and discretion conferred upon him by this Act to such departments, agencies, or officials of the Government as he may deem appropriate.

The authority given by the Act to the President and subdelegated to the Commerce Department has been used chiefly to curb exports of strategic goods and technical data to Communist countries, although exports of a few items found to be in short supply domestically (e. g., leather for the manufacture of shoes, or walnut logs) have been restrained as to all countries. An exporter desiring to ascertain the steps necessary to export a given item consults the Commodity Control List. After finding the applicable commodity classification, he notes what letters, symbolizing certain groups of countries, are placed opposite the classification. If the country to which he wishes to export is included in such a group, he must obtain specific permission, a "validated license," before he can export. If his country of destination is not so included, the exporter can proceed under a "general license," amounting to a general permission to export. For example, a firm desiring to export toluene to France and Poland would find next to the item "toluene" a "W", indicating the need for a validated license for Poland, but no "V" that would have indicated the need for a validated license for France.

The Export Administration Act provides for criminal penalties (fines or imprisonment) for violation of the Act or any regulation, order or license issued thereunder; it also allows the imposition of a civil penalty of up to $1,000 for each violation. The authorities, without express statutory basis, claim the power of denying "export privileges" to violators here or abroad. 15 C.F.R. parts 387, 388 (1973). If such a "denial order" is entered against a person and he is placed on the export "blacklist," no American party may enter into an export transaction with him. Thus a foreign person who has diverted goods to a buyer in Eastern Europe when they were licensed only for Western Europe may be placed on the "blacklist," and no American may export to him without himself violating the Act and regulations (§ 387.10).

The regulations provide for an administrative hearing before a Commissioner in all denial-order cases. The decision about denial is made by the Director of the Office of Export Control, subject to review by an Appeals Board within the Department. The regulations state that determinations by the Board are "final."

Note that the Act makes inapplicable the provisions established by the Administrative Procedure Act, 60 Stat. 237 (1946), 5 U.S.C.A. §§ 1001 et seq. (1970), for rule making (except as to their publication) and adjudication.

Additional reading: Berman and Garson, United States Export Controls—Past, Present, and Future, 67 Colum.L.Rev. 791 (1967); Haight,

United States Controls over Strategic Transactions, 1965 U.Ill.L.Forum 337; and Timberg, Wanted: Administrative Safeguards for the Protection of the Individual in International Economic Regulation, 17 Admin.L. Rev. 159 (1965).

YOSHIDA INTERNATIONAL, INC. v. UNITED STATES

United States Customs Court, 1974.
378 F.Supp. 1155.[4]

BOE, CHIEF JUDGE:

The plaintiff has filed a motion for summary judgment challenging the validity of Presidential Proclamation 4074 promulgated August 15, 1971, which imposed a surcharge in the form of a supplemental duty in the amount of 10 percent ad valorem upon most articles imported into the United States from and after August 16, 1971. The merchandise involved herein—consisting of zippers—was imported from Japan and entered at the port of New York on August 17, 25 and 26, 1971. In addition to being assessed with duty at the rate of 23.5 percent ad valorem pursuant to item 745.72, Tariff Schedules of the United States, the merchandise in question was assessed with an additional duty of 10 percent ad valorem pursuant to item 948.00 which was added to the tariff schedules by Presidential Proclamation 4074.

The defendant has filed a cross-motion for summary judgment contending that Presidential Proclamation 4074 was lawfully authorized by (1) the "termination" authority delegated to the President by the Congress in section 350(a)(6) of the Tariff Act of 1930, as amended (19 U.S.C.A. § 1351(a)(6)) and section 255(b) of the Trade Expansion Act of 1962 (19 U.S.C.A. § 1885(b)); and (2) the authority vested in the President by section 5(b) of the Trading with the Enemy Act, as amended (50 U.S.C.A. App. § 5(b)).

Presidential Proclamation 4074 provides in relevant part (F.R. Doc. 71–12120):

> *Whereas,* there has been a prolonged decline in the international monetary reserves of the United States, and our trade and international competitive position is seriously threatened and, as a result, our continued ability to assure our security could be impaired;
>
> *Whereas,* the balance of payments position of the United States requires the imposition of a surcharge on dutiable imports;
>
> *Whereas,* pursuant to the authority vested in him by the Constitution and the statutes, including, but not limited to, the Tariff Act of 1930, as amended (hereinafter referred to as "the Tariff Act"), and the Trade Expansion Act of 1962 (hereinafter referred to as "the TEA"), the President entered into, and proclaimed tariff rates under, trade agreements with foreign countries;
>
> *Whereas,* under the Tariff Act, the TEA, and other provisions of law, the President may, at any time, modify or terminate, in whole or in part, any proclamation made under his authority;

4. An appeal from this decision was filed in the Court of Customs and Patent Appeals later in 1974. 8 Customs Bull. & Decisions No. 41, p. 39.

Now, Therefore, I, Richard Nixon, President of the United States of America acting under the authority vested in me by the Constitution and the statutes, including, but not limited to, the Tariff Act, and the TEA, respectively, do proclaim as follows;

A. I hereby declare a national emergency during which I call upon the public and private sector to make the efforts necessary to strengthen the international economic position of the United States.

B. (1) I hereby terminate in part for such period as may be necessary and modify prior Presidential Proclamations which carry out trade agreements insofar as such proclamations are inconsistent with, or proclaim duties different from, those made effective pursuant to the terms of this Proclamation.

(2) Such proclamations are suspended only insofar as is required to assess a surcharge in the form of a supplemental duty amounting to 10 percent ad valorem. Such supplemental duty shall be imposed on all dutiable articles imported into the customs territory of the United States from outside thereof, which are entered, or withdrawn from warehouse, for consumption after 12:01 a. m., August 16, 1971, ...

. . .

I

The courts on frequent occasions have considered the question relating to the right of the legislative branch of government to delegate the powers vested in it by the Constitution to the executive branch. It would be only time-consuming to review these many decisions at length. Suffice it to say that the Congress cannot divest itself of the legislative powers with which it has been constitutionally invested.

[The court referred to the Field, Hampton, Schechter, and Curtiss-Wright decisions, pp. 102–109, supra.]

The Tariff Act of 1930, as amended, and the Trade Expansion Act of 1962 were enacted by the Congress in full appreciation of the inability of the legislative branch to singly supervise or administer that comprehensive power vested in it by article I, section 8 of the Constitution which provides that:

> The Congress shall have Power To lay and collect Taxes, Duties, Imposts and Excises . . . .

Congress has delegated by these Acts broad and general authority to the President to enter into negotiations with foreign nations to the end that bilateral trade agreements might be effected by the contracting parties. As a corollary power, the President has been further authorized to proclaim such modifications with respect to existing duties or other import restrictions as may be required to carry out the provisions of any particular negotiated trade agreement. Inasmuch as a trade agreeement is not self-executing the provisions or modifications contained therein must be proclaimed by the President in order that they have the effect of domestic law.

Thus, section 350 of the Tariff Act of 1930, as amended (19 U.S.C.A. § 1351), provides in part:

> (a)(1) For the purpose of expanding foreign markets for the products of the United States (as a means of assist-

> ing in establishing and maintaining a better relationship among various branches of American agriculture, industry, mining, and commerce) by regulating the admission of foreign goods into the United States in accordance with the characteristics and needs of various branches of American production so that foreign markets will be made available to those branches of American production which require and are capable of developing such outlets by affording corresponding market opportunities for foreign products in the United States, the President, whenever he finds as a fact that any existing duties or other import restrictions of the United States or any foreign country are unduly burdening and restricting the foreign trade of the United States and that the purpose above declared will be promoted by the means hereinafter specified, is authorized from time to time—
>
> (A) To enter into foreign trade agreements with foreign governments or instrumentalities thereof: . . . .
>
> (B) To proclaim such modifications of existing duties and other import restrictions, or such additional import restrictions, or such continuance, and for such minimum periods, of existing customs or excise treatment of any article covered by foreign trade agreements, as are required or appropriate to carry out any foreign trade agreement that the President has entered into hereunder.

Similar provisions were again included by the Congress in the enactment of the Trade Expansion Act of 1962 (19 U.S.C.A. § 1801 et seq.).
. . .

. . .

Finally, the President has been delegated authority to "terminate, in whole or in part," prior proclamations which have implemented the provisions of foreign trade agreements. And it is this power, defendant contends, which authorized the President to impose the additional 10 percent duty here in issue.

In this connection, it is to be noted that section (B)(1) of Presidential Proclamation 4074 provides:

> I hereby terminate in part for such period as may be necessary and modify prior Presidential Proclamations which carry out trade agreements insofar as such proclamations are inconsistent with, or proclaim duties different from, those made effective pursuant to the terms of this Proclamation.

There can be no doubt that this phraseology, viewed in its customary and ordinary usage, is intended as the exercise of the power of termination.

The statutes are brief and concise in delineating this prerogative. Section 350(a)(6) of the Tariff Act of 1930, as amended (19 U.S.C.A. § 1351(a)(6)) provides:

> The President may at any time terminate, in whole or in part, any proclamation made pursuant to this section.

Similarly, section 255(b) of the Trade Expansion Act of 1962 (19 U.S.C.A. § 1885(b)) provides:

> The President may at any time terminate, in whole or in part, any proclamation made under this subchapter.

. . .

We conclude that the authority granted by statute to "terminate, in whole or in part, any proclamation" does not include the power to determine and fix unilaterally a rate of duty which has not been previously legally established. On the contrary, the "termination" authority, as statutorily granted, merely provides the President with a mechanical procedure of supplanting or replacing existing rates with rates which have been established by prior proclamations or by statute. . . .

. . .

This court likewise is unable to accept the further argument propounded by the defendant—that the maxim of statutory construction providing that a broader authority includes the lesser—is applicable to the case at bar. In reference thereto, the defendant suggests that if the President has the power to terminate all prior proclamations, thus bringing into effect the statutory rate, *a fortiori*, he has the power to impose a new rate, higher than the terminated rate, yet lower than the statutory note. Such a conclusion is fallacious. The power granted to the President with respect to the adjustment of rates pursuant to his termination authority is limited to the use of termination proclamations (1) to increase rates to the highest level, i. e., the statutory rate, or (2) to raise or lower rates to conform to rates which have been established by a prior proclamation. In either of these instances, the rates, to which conformance may be sought, have been previously established either by the Congress (statutory rate) or by a bilateral negotiation embodied in a trade agreement pursuant to statutory authority. In short, the power to fix a new and independent rate requires a greater grant of power than that delegated to the President by the termination authority. Pursuant to the latter authority, the President is constrained, with the exception noted above, to follow a fixed order of reversion established by the Congress, "resting" only on those rates previously established. Indeed, should the establishment of new and independent rates be considered a lesser power included in the termination authority, all concession rates previously established through bilateral negotiation could be totally ignored thereby giving the President complete and broad discretion to impose any rate whatsoever up to the statutory rate. We fail to find wherein the statutes evidence an intention on the part of the Congress to grant the President such unrestrained unilateral authority.

. . .

[I]t is to be observed that the Senate adopted an amendment to H.R. 11970, the Trade Expansion bill, which would have added a new section 353, as follows (108 Cong.Rec. 19875 (1962)):

> Notwithstanding any other provision of law, the President may, when he finds it in the national interest, proclaim with respect to any article imported into the United States—
>
> (1) the increase of any existing duty on such article to such rate as he finds necessary,
>
> (2) the imposition of a duty on such article (if it is not otherwise subject to duty) at such rate as he finds necessary, and
>
> (3) the imposition of such other import restrictions as he finds necessary.

It is obvious that had this provision been enacted into law, it would have authorized a surcharge such as provided for in Presidential Proclamation 4074. However, the provision was deleted by the House-Senate Conference Committee. Conference Report No.

2518 (87th Cong., 2d Sess. (1962) (2 U.S.Code Cong. & Admin.News (1962), p. 3142)). Deletion of the provision not only demonstrates that Congress was unwilling to grant such expansive discretionary power to the President, but also indicates a probable recognition by Congress that such an unrestrained grant of authority to increase existing duties and impose nonexisting duties may well have been an invalid delegation of legislative power vested solely in the Congress by the Constitution.

. . .

II

With respect to defendant's contention that the Trading with the Enemy Act (50 U.S.C.A. App.) serves as further authority for the validity of Presidential Proclamation 4074, the plaintiff submits that no consideration should be given thereto inasmuch as the Proclamation does not specifically refer to this Act as a part of its statutory authority.

To sustain the plaintiff's contention would be to place an unwarranted limitation upon judicial review. Presidential Proclamation 4074 does not seek to designate the Tariff Act of 1930, as amended, and the Trade Expansion Act of 1962 as the sole sources of authority. On the contrary, the Proclamation refers to the President as "acting under the authority vested in me by the Constitution and the statutes, including, but not limited to, the Tariff Act, and the TEA [Trade Expansion Act] . . . ." This court, accordingly, has considered the argument presented by the defendant with respect to the authority that may have been delegated to the President by the provisions of the Trading with the Enemy Act. Toledo, P. & W. R. R. v. Stover, 60 F.Supp. 587 (S.D.Ill.1945).

It has been long recognized that war, itself, effects a suspension of commercial intercourse between belligerent nations. However, changes in economic conditions as well as changes in the evolving philosophy of man have dictated that legislative modifications be enacted in lieu of the inflexible rule of law terminating all commercial intercourse between warring nations existing at common law and in the law of nations. In so doing, controls have been provided through legislative enactment with respect to authorized foreign trade and intercourse which prior thereto would have been prohibited.

The present Trading with the Enemy Act may be said to have its roots in the Act of Congress of July 13, 1861, 12 Stat. 255, 257. Pursuant thereto the President through the Secretary of the Treasury, was authorized in his discretion to "license and permit commercial intercourse" with all or any part of the States in insurrection.

The system of licensing, thus first authorized during the Civil War, again became an integral part of the Trading with the Enemy Act of 1917. The provisions thereof prohibited any trade with the enemy "except with the license of the President." 40 Stat. 412, section 3(a).

It will be noted that in each of the foregoing legislative enactments the words "license" and "permit" were used to describe the form of regulation delegated to the President. From the congressional committee hearings, reports and debates on the Trading with the Enemy Act of 1917, as well as from the statement voiced by the Secretary of the Treasury, it appeared, however, that the statutory provisions afore referred to did not provide sufficient authority to the President to adequately control imports—a power considered essential during a time of war. Therefore, the Congress, in enacting the Trading with the

Enemy Act of 1917, added section 11 which gave broad and expansive powers to the President to control imports during World War I. 40 Stat. 422, section 11.

The significance of the afore-quoted section, insofar as it relates to the immediate question presented to us for determination, is found in the fact that the extremely broad power given to the President thereunder to regulate imports terminated at the end of World War I and was never reenacted in subsequent amendments.

In 1933 during the domestic crisis occasioned by the depression of that decade, the President's authority to act under section 5(b) was extended to "any other period of national emergency declared" by him, and he was given the power "by means of licenses or otherwise" to regulate "transfers of credit between or payments by banking institutions." 48 Stat. 1.

In 1941 the Act was amended in order to give the President more flexibility over alien property, 55 Stat. 839. Again, the mode of regulation authorized by the statute included a system of licenses.

In support of its contention the defendant places specific reliance on section 5(b) of the present Trading with the Enemy Act . . . .

. . .

Recognizing that a declaration of a national emergency is within the discretion of the President and that a determination as to the need or desirability of affirmatively exercising such authority is not a judicial function, this court will refrain from offering any gratuitous comment as to the existence or nonexistence of the national emergency declared in Presidential Proclamation 4074. Sardino v. Federal Reserve Bank of New York, 361 F.2d 106 (2d Cir. 1966); Werner v. United States, 119 F.Supp. 894 (S.D.Cal.1954, aff'd 233 F.2d 52 (9th Cir. 1956).

The plaintiff urges that the regulatory powers conferred upon the President by the Trading with the Enemy Act are directed against and applicable only to enemy countries and against property having an "enemy taint." Such a construction with respect to the purview of this Act is too restrictive. The statute relates to ". . . any property in which any foreign country or a national thereof has any interest, ..." The usage of the word "any" negates such a limited construction. The successive amendments to the Act likewise indicate the intent of the Congress to expand its scope rather than to narrow its application. United States v. Broverman, 180 F.Supp. 631 (S.D.N.Y.1959).

The gravamen of the defendant's contention appears to rest on the construction of the words contained in section 5(b)(1)(B), ". . . regulate . . . importation . . . of . . . any property in which any foreign country or a national thereof has any interest, ..." Pointing with particularity to this statutory language, the defendant further contends that Congress has, in effect, delegated to the President the regulatory power inherent in and originating from its constitutional authority to regulate foreign commerce. Citing McGoldrick v. Gulf Oil Corp., 309 U.S. 414, 60 S.Ct. 664, 84 L.Ed. 840 (1940) as authority, the defendant argues that it necessarily follows that the imposition of the surcharge in the form of a supplemental duty is thus within the authority delegated to the President by section 5(b)(1)(B). We do not agree that the *McGoldrick* case or the decisions referred to therein justify the application of this reasoning to the case at bar.

. . .

From the foregoing decisions, it is well established that the constitutional grants of power to lay and collect taxes and duties on imports and the power to regulate foreign commerce are separate and independent grants of authority distinct from each other. Although the primary purpose of the power to tax and impose duties may be to obtain revenue, it may also serve as a regulatory measure.

Similarly, the imposition of a duty on imports may constitute, *inter alia,* an exercise of the constitutional power to regulate foreign commerce. In connection with this latter power, however, it must be borne in mind that the extent and mode of any regulatory authority delegated by the Congress must be determined in each individual instance by the statutory language and an examination of all the surrounding circumstances. It cannot be said that the investiture of a power to "regulate" necessarily includes, *per se,* the power to levy duties. . . .

In determining whether section 5(b) of the Trading with the Enemy Act serves as authority for the imposition of an additional duty, we must accord the word "regulate" the sense in which the Congress intended it to be used. The meaning of a statute or of the words therein is not to be derived from any single section, but from all of the parts comprising the entirety and, in turn, from their relationship to the ultimate purpose sought to be attained. Nor can the Act be read intelligibly if the eye is closed to the purpose and objectives evidenced in complementary statutes or in the known temper of legislative intent or historical usage. For legislation delegating restrictive regulatory authority cannot operate, merely upon the declaration of an emergency, to the exclusion of other legislative acts providing procedures prescribed by the Congress for the accomplishment of the very purpose sought to be attained by Presidential Proclamation 4074. Youngstown Sheet & Tube Co. v. Sawyer, 343 U.S. 579, 72 S.Ct. 863, 96 L.Ed. 1153 (1952).

The words "instructions, licenses, or otherwise" contained in section 5(b)(1) define the nature and mode of the regulatory authority intended to be delegated to the President. These words conform to the phraseology used throughout the history of the Act in the establishment of a system of licenses and permits for the control of property during a time of war and crisis and which have come to be recognized as the hallmark and distinguishing feature of the Act. These words likewise serve to evidence a recognition on the part of the Congress that such delineating and restrictive phraseology, in fact, was employed in order to preclude the all-encompassing construction now urged by the defendant. If the words "regulate . . . importation" were given the construction contended by the defendant, the President by the declaration of a national emergency could determine and fix rates of duty at will, without regard to statutory rates prescribed by the Congress and without the benefit of standards or guidelines which must accompany any valid delegation of a constitutional power by the Congress. Hampton & Co. v. United States, supra, 276 U.S. p. 409, 48 S.Ct. 348, 72 L.Ed. 624. The delegation of such an unrestrained and unbridled authority to lay duties, indeed, might well be deemed an abdication by the Congress of its constitutional power to regulate foreign commerce.

In the case of Panama Refining Co. v. Ryan, 293 U.S. 388, 55 S.Ct. 241, 79 L.Ed. 446 (1935), the Supreme Court, speaking through Mr. Chief Justice Hughes reaffirmed the principle that the Congress cannot abdicate its legislative powers, vested by the Constitution. . . .

. . .

Accordingly, we take the position that section 5(b)(1) of the Trading with the Enemy Act conveys to the President an authority consisting only of a specific mode of regulation, as distinguished from the full and all-inclusive power to regulate foreign commerce. The delegation of the specific regulatory authority, "by means of instructions, licenses, or otherwise," manifestly is restrictive in scope and is but one branch of many attached to the trunk of the tree in which is lodged the all-inclusive substantive power to regulate foreign commerce, vested solely in the Congress.

We, therefore, conclude that section 5(b)(1) of the Act contains such restrictive standards and guidelines as to meet the test of constitutionality, but which, in turn, precludes the President from laying the supplemental duties provided by Presidential Proclamation 4074.

. . .

This court is not without appreciation of the burdensome problems encountered by the Executive as he represents these United States in the society of nations. Nor can the court fail to recognize the efforts of the President to achieve stability in the international trade position and monetary reserves of this country. But neither need nor national emergency will justify the exercise of a power by the Executive not inherent in his office nor delegated by the Congress. Expedience cannot justify the means by which a deserving and beneficial national result is accomplished. To indulge in judicial rationalization in order to sanction the exercise of a power where no power in fact exists is to strike the deadliest of blows to our Constitution.

The power to levy and collect taxes, duties, imposts and excises and to regulate foreign commerce has been vested solely in the Congress by the Constitution.

. . .

The motion of the plaintiff for summary judgment is granted and the cross-motion of the defendant is denied.

Let judgment be entered accordingly.

MALETZ, JUDGE (concurring).

I am in accord with the well-reasoned opinion of Chief Judge Boe. Withal, I believe it may be helpful to add some further comments with respect to the defendant's contention that when a national emergency is declared by the President—as was done in Proclamation 4074—he has unlimited discretion to impose supplemental duties on imports by virtue of the authority delegated to him by section 5(b) of the Trading with the Enemy Act . . ..

. . .

Section 5(b) was last amended on December 18, 1941, by section 301 of the First War Powers Act of 1941 (55 Stat. 839) in order to give the President more comprehensive control over the seizure, vesting and disposition of all property of any foreign country or national. To accomplish this purpose, the President was authorized, among other things, to regulate "by means of *instructions*, licenses, or otherwise . . . any acquisition holding, withholding, use, transfer, withdrawal, transportation, *importation* or exportation . . . involving, any property in which any foreign country or a national thereof has any interest . . .." As summed up by Representative Kefauver on the House floor (87 Cong.Rec. 9865 (1941)):

> It was explained to us by representatives of the Treasury that it was absolutely necessary for the present act—5(b)—to be reenacted in order to enable the Treasury to car-

ry out its policy of freezing certain credits and of handling certain financial interests during the war. The explanation made to us, and I think it is carried out in this bill, is that the only change the Treasury wanted in 5(b) of the Trading With the Enemy Act was to give the executive department power not only to passively freeze credits and to negatively handle the operation of some manufacturing plants by a system of licenses or controls that they have to work under at the present time, but also to give the President the power to actively put into operation those interests or those securities or plants that might be taken over and be seized under authority of 5(b) of the present act.

Thus it can be seen that the amendments to section 5(b) successively extended the President's licensing authority in the areas of foreign exchange, banking and currency transactions and transactions involving property in which foreign countries or nationals have an interest.[5] However, nowhere in the Congressional debates, committee hearings or reports on section 5(b) and the amendments thereto is there even a glimmer of a suggestion that Congress ever intended—or even considered—this section as a vehicle for delegating any of its tariff-making authority.

Furthermore, a finding that the President has the power under section 5(b) to impose whatever tariff rates he deems desirable simply by declaring a national emergency would not only render our trade agreements program nugatory, it would subvert the manifest Congressional intent to maintain control over its Constitutional powers to levy tariffs. The fact is that Congress has never lightly delegated its authority in this area and any delegation of such power has been—with the exception of section 11, the temporary wartime provision of the Trading with the Enemy Act—specific and restricted in its operation.

. . .

COMMENT

The decision of the Customs Court in the Yoshida International case was cited approvingly in a 2–1 decision of the Court of Appeals in Commonwealth of Massachusetts v. Simon (D.C.Cir., No. 75–1281, August 11, 1975). In a group of cases consolidated upon appeal, Massachusetts and seven other states, together with a group of utilities, sought to overturn the imposition of license fees for importation of oil and petroleum products. These fees were required under proclamations of Presidents Ford and Nixon, as implemented through regulations adopted by the Federal Energy Administration. The

5. For an example of regulations which license or authorize transactions subject to executive control under section 5(b) upon declaration of a national emergency, see the Foreign Assets Control Regulations, as amended, 31 C.F.R. Part 500 (1973) . . . .

. . .

Another example of the exercise under section 5(b) of Presidential authority to regulate international financial transactions is the Foreign Direct Investment Program established pursuant to Executive Order 11387 which was issued on January 1, 1968 (33 F. R. 47) on the basis of the continuing national emergency declared by President Truman in 1950. This program restricts transfers of capital to foreign countries by investors in the United States and requires repatriation to this country by such investors of portions of their foreign earnings and short-term financial assets held abroad. [Eds. This Program is noted at p. 1166, infra.]

relevant statute, 19 U.S.C. § 1862(b) (1970), authorized the President to "take such action, and for such time, as he deems necessary to adjust the imports of [an] article and its derivatives so that . . . imports [of such article] will not so threaten to impair the national security." That section had initially been drawn upon by President Eisenhower in 1959 to institute quotas under the so-called Mandatory Oil Import Program, which was based upon a determination that oil products were being imported in such quantities and at such low costs as to threaten to impair national security by inhibiting the development of domestic production and refinery capacity.

In 1973 President Nixon changed the existing quota system and imposed a schedule of license fees. After a 1975 amendment to Section 1862(b), in 88 Stat. 1978, imposing certain procedural requirements, President Ford signed Proclamation No. 4341, January 23, 1975, significantly increasing the license fees by imposing supplemental fees of up to $3 per barrel on imported crude oil and $1.20 per barrel on petroleum products in scheduled phases.

The Court of Appeals reversed a judgment of the District Court which had found that the President had authority to impose the license fees under Section 1862(b). Recognizing the gravity of the problem stemming from the country's increasing dependence on foreign petroleum products (spending on foreign oil having increased from $2.7 billion in 1972 to about $24 billion in 1974), the Court of Appeals nonetheless concluded from the legislative history that Section 1862(b) did not authorize the fees, and that the authority granted by Congress to limit imports was through "direct" methods, principally import quotas. It stressed that Congressional delegations within the field of trade provisions had been "narrow and explicit in order to effectuate well-defined goals," and it noted that "the number of articles potentially covered under the umbrella of 'national security' is great." As a regulatory measure, as an indirect control on imports, the acts of Presidents Ford and Nixon were "thus outside the scope of section 1862(b)." The challenged regulations were set aside, the judgment reversed and the case remanded with instructions to enter "appropriate relief" for appellants.

The Court of Appeals took pains to stress that "we do not say that Congress cannot constitutionally delegate, accompanied by an intelligible standard, such authority to the President; we merely find that they have not done so by this statute." It also observed:

> More fundamentally, this case raises a question about the way Government should operate when responding to crises. Neither the term "national security" nor "emergency" is a talisman, the thaumaturgic invocation of which should, *ipso facto*, suspend the normal checks and balances on each branch of Government. Our laws were not established merely to be followed only when times are tranquil. If our system is to survive, we must respond to even the most difficult of problems in a manner consistent with the lim-

> itations placed upon the Congress, the President, and the Courts by our Constitution and our laws. We believe we reaffirm that basic principle today.

Compare Youngstown Sheet and Tube Co. v. Sawyer, 343 U.S. 579, 72 S.Ct. 863, 96 L.Ed. 1153 (1952). The United Steelworkers of America gave notice of a nation-wide strike in 1951, during the Korean War. After settlement efforts involving governmental mediation had failed, the President issued an executive order, not expressly based upon any statutory authority, directing the Secretary of Commerce to take possession of and operate most steel mills. The order contained the finding that such action was necessary to avoid a national catastrophe, in view of the effect of a work stoppage upon the national defense during the Korean conflict. Steel companies immediately challenged the order. A district court issued a preliminary injunction restraining the Secretary from acting under authority of the executive order, and the Supreme Court affirmed, holding that the order was not within the constitutional powers of the President. JUSTICE BLACK, in his opinion for the Court, said in part (343 U.S. at 586, 72 S.Ct. at 866, 96 L.Ed. at 1167):

> Moreover, the use of the seizure technique to solve labor disputes in order to prevent work stoppages was not only unauthorized by any congressional enactment; prior to this controversy, Congress had refused to adopt that method of settling labor disputes. When the Taft-Hartley Act was under consideration in 1947, Congress rejected an amendment which would have authorized such governmental seizures in cases of emergency. Apparently it was thought that the technique of seizure, like that of compulsory arbitration, would interfere with the process of collective bargaining. Consequently, the plan Congress adopted in that Act did not provide for seizure under any circumstances. Instead, the plan sought to bring about settlements by use of the customary devices of mediation, conciliation, investigation by boards of inquiry, and public reports. . . .
>
> It is clear that if the President had authority to issue the order he did, it must be found in some provisions of the Constitution. And it is not claimed that express constitutional language grants this power to the President. The contention is that presidential power should be implied from the aggregate of his powers under the Constitution. Particular reliance is placed on provisions in Article II which say that "the executive Power shall be vested in a President . . ."; that "he shall take Care that the Laws be faithfully executed"; and that he "shall be Commander in Chief of the Army and Navy of the United States."
>
> The order cannot properly be sustained as an exercise of the President's military power as Commander in Chief of the Armed Forces. . . . [W]e cannot with faithfulness to our constitutional system hold that the Commander in Chief of the Armed Forces has the ultimate power as such to take possession of private property in order to keep labor disputes from stopping production. This is a job for the Nation's lawmakers, not for its military authorities.

Nor can the seizure order be sustained because of the several constitutional provisions that grant executive power to the President. In the framework of our Constitution, the President's power to see that the laws are faithfully executed refuses the idea that he is to be a lawmaker. The Constitution limits his functions in the lawmaking process to the recommending of laws he thinks wise and the vetoing of laws he thinks bad. And the Constitution is neither silent nor equivocal about who shall make laws which the President is to execute. . . .

The President's order does not direct that a congressional policy be executed in a manner prescribed by Congress—it directs that a presidential policy be executed in a manner prescribed by the President. The preamble of the order itself, like that of many statutes, sets out reasons why the President believes certain policies should be adopted, proclaims these policies as rules of conduct to be followed, and again, like a statute, authorizes a government official to promulgate additional rules and regulations consistent with the policy proclaimed and needed to carry that policy into execution. The power of Congress to adopt such public policies as those proclaimed by the order is beyond question. . . . The Constitution did not subject this law-making power of Congress to presidential or military supervision or control.

[There were three concurring and three dissenting opinions. In his concurring opinion, JUSTICE JACKSON observed:]

The actual art of governing under our Constitution does not and cannot conform to judicial definitions of the power of any of its branches based on isolated clauses or even single Articles torn from context. While the Constitution diffuses power the better to secure liberty, it also contemplates that practice will integrate the dispersed powers into a workable government. It enjoins upon its branches separateness but interdependence, autonomy but reciprocity. Presidential powers are not fixed but fluctuate, depending upon their disjunction or conjunction with those of Congress. We may well begin by a somewhat over-simplified grouping of practical situations in which a President may doubt, or others may challenge, his powers, and by distinguishing roughly the legal consequences of this factor of relativity.

1. When the President acts pursuant to an express or implied authorization of Congress, his authority is at its maximum, for it includes all that he possesses in his own right plus all that Congress can delegate. In these circumstances, and in these only, may he be said (for what it may be worth), to personify the federal sovereignty. If his act is held unconstitutional under these circumstances, it usually means that the Federal Government as an undivided whole lacks power. A seizure executed by the President pursuant to an Act of Congress would be supported by the strongest of presumptions and the widest latitude of judicial interpretation, and the burden of persuasion would rest heavily upon any who might attack it.

2. When the President acts in absence of either a congressional grant or denial of authority, he can only rely upon his own independent powers, but there is a zone of twilight

in which he and Congress may have concurrent authority, or in which its distribution is uncertain. Therefore, congressional inertia, indifference or quiescence may sometimes, at least as a practical matter, enable, if not invite, measures on independent presidential responsibility. In this area, any actual test of power is likely to depend on the imperatives of events and contemporary imponderables rather than on abstract theories of law.

3. When the President takes measures incompatible with the expressed or implied will of Congress, his power is at its lowest ebb, for then he can rely only upon his own constitutional powers minus any constitutional powers of Congress over the matter. Courts can sustain exclusive Presidential control in such a case only by disabling the Congress from acting upon the subject. Presidential claim to a power at once so conclusive and preclusive must be scrutinized with caution, for what is at stake is the equilibrium established by our constitutional system.

QUESTION

In view of the opinion in Yoshida International, how should the court decide if the President invokes the Trading with the Enemy Act to prohibit all imports of automobiles because of their competitive success in taking trade from American manufacturers in a period of surplus production and unemployment? Should it be relevant (a) whether other federal legislation explicitly permits such action by the President in accordance with specified procedures, or (b) whether no other federal legislation is in point?

PROBLEMS

I

You represent John Marchand, who has attempted to import some split bamboo without special license. The bamboo is being held at customs pending resolution of the controversy. It is evidently suspected that the bamboo is the product of North Vietnam. He convinces you (a) that he did not know of the prohibition and (b) that the bamboo was in fact the product of Burma. Evaluate the following arguments that you might make on his behalf, and decide which you will give priority to in any proceedings for release of the bamboo.

(1) The Trading with the Enemy Act involves an unconstitutional delegation of authority.

(2) The rules exceed the scope of the power Congress intended to grant because they embrace transactions such as Marchand's that are in fact totally innocent.

(3) Bamboo cannot be withheld on the basis of regulations issued under Section 5(b) of the Act, since that section authorizes issuance of rules and regulations only during a time of war or "any other period of national emergency declared by the President." The quoted phrase was added to the Act in 1933, 49 Stat. 1, during the economic crisis of the depression. The regulations here in issue depend upon Proclamation 2914, issued by President Truman on December 16, 1950 at the time that the Korean War broke out, 3 C.F.R. 99 (1949–1953 Comp.).[6]

II

Marchand would like to import and distribute some movies taken by the armed forces of North Vietnam, showing military action, refugees and other scenes from the struggle in South Vietnam; he intends to remit the proceeds for use in reconstruction and rehabilitation. He finds that the present regulations permit imports of films and literature only if a specific license is obtained and if they are received as gifts or if all payments are made into blocked accounts. Publications and films are licensed in any case for limited use by educational institutions. Marchand asks you whether he would be subject to criminal prosecution if he imported the films without obtaining a license and if he then forwarded the proceeds as he intends.

III

You again represent Marchand who states that, after an administrative hearing, the Director of the Office of Export Control has entered a denial order under the Export Administration Act depriving him of all rights to export for five years. The Director found that Marchand sold microcircuits under a general license to an English firm which then had assembled the microcircuits and other components made in England into computers and shipped the computers to destinations in the Soviet Union. Marchand convinces you that he did not know about the English firm's intentions or of its reputation in this respect. The Director, however, found that Marchand and his employees "should have known" those facts about the English firm and were therefore negligent in not taking special precautions to ensure that Marchand was not in effect exporting to a non-excepted country without a validated license. Thus, even though the English firm was not on the blacklist, the Director concluded that Marchand had violated the Act and regulations, as construed by the Department of Commerce. Marchand states that the order, if it becomes final, will ruin his flourishing export business. Consider the relative merits of the following arguments that you might make on his behalf before the Appeals Board or in an attempt to obtain judicial review:

(1) Arguments based on unconstitutional delegation and, in the alternative, on the ground that the regulations exceeded the authority un-

6. In evaluating this argument, you should be aware that the 1950 Proclamation has been referred to in a number of subsequent Presidential proclamations or executive orders. Proclamation 3004 of January 17, 1953, 3 C.F.R. 180 (1949–1953, Comp.) was issued by President Truman under Section 215 of the Immigration and Nationality Act of 1952, and it then stated specifically that the national emergency declared by the earlier proclamation "still exists." Later proclamations or executive orders issued by President Eisenhower and President Kennedy, used comparable language, as by referring to the "continuing emergency" proclaimed in 1950. See, e. g., Executive Order 11037 issued by President Kennedy on July 20, 1962, 3 C.F.R. 621 (1959–1963 Comp.). Two of the more extended judicial discussions of such proclamations or executive orders and their role in making effective certain federal legislation are found in MacEwan v. Rusk, 228 F.Supp. 306, 311–313 (E.D.Pa.1964), aff'd per curiam, 344 F.2d 963 (3d Cir. 1965), and Sardino v. Federal Reserve Bank of New York, 361 F.2d 106, 109–110 (2d Cir. 1966). Recall the proclamation of President Nixon set forth in the Yoshida International case, p. 116, supra.

der the statute. Are such arguments stronger or weaker, under the facts of and specific regulations applicable to this case, than the comparable arguments in a criminal prosecution?

(2) An argument based on the fact that the Commerce Department pursuant to 15 C.F.R. § 388.7 (1974), did not permit Marchand or his counsel below to examine the classified information on which the suspension was based while admitting into evidence an unclassified summary prepared by the staff. This practice has been justified as follows:

> "We regard our use of classified evidence in this limited way [a summary of unclassified portions is given respondent] as authorized by the Supreme Court [citing the Curtiss Wright case, p. 102, supra] and by our repeated disclosure and Congressional approval of the procedure in connection with renewals of the Act that have occurred every 2 or 3 years. In addition, the practice is embodied in one of our published rules." Thau, Control of Exports from the U.S.A., 19 Bus.Law. 845, 848 (1964).

Do you agree with Mr. Thau's use of authority? With his ultimate conclusion?

(3) An argument that the administrative action should be judicially reviewed. Recall that the Act is silent as to this question except for Section 7, which makes inapplicable various provisions of the APA including those providing for such review. If review were obtained, which of the various legal issues or factual determinations underlying the denial order might a court be most likely to reexamine?

NOTE ON DELEGATION PROBLEMS IN THE FIELD OF FOREIGN TRAVEL

The Passport Act of 1926, 44 Stat. 887, 22 U.S.C.A. § 211(a), provides in pertinent part: "The Secretary of State may grant and issue passports . . . under such rules as the President shall designate and prescribe for and on behalf of the United States . . . ." Section 215(b) of the Immigration and Nationality Act, 66 Stat. 190 (1952), 8 U.S.C.A. § 1185(b), renders it illegal for any citizen, during the existence of a national emergency proclaimed by the President, to enter or depart from this country "unless he bears a valid passport." See Worthy v. United States, p. 6, supra. The proclamation required by Section 215 was in effect at the time of the events that were relevant to the following cases.

In Kent v. Dulles, 357 U.S. 116, 78 S.Ct. 1113, 2 L.Ed.2d 1204 (1958), the Court concluded that those Acts did not delegate to the Secretary of State "unbridled discretion to grant or withhold a passport from a citizen for any substantive reason he may choose," and invalidated the practice of denying passports to members and sympathizers of the Communist Party. It did not reach the question whether Congress could have authorized the Secretary so to act.

In Aptheker v. Secretary of State, 378 U.S. 500, 84 S.Ct. 1659, 12 L.Ed.2d 992 (1964), the question before the Court was the constitutionality of Section 6 of the Subversive Activities Control Act of 1950, 64 Stat. 993, 50 U.S.C.A. § 785. That section made it a crime for members of Communist organizations, as defined, to apply for a passport or its renewal or to use a passport. The State Department, invoking this section, revoked the passports of certain leaders of the Communist Party. The Court held that Section 6 was unconstitutional on its face, since it "too broadly and indiscriminately restricts the right to travel and thereby abridges the liberty guaranteed by the Fifth Amendment." It drew upon the statement of the Court in Kent v. Dulles that the right to travel abroad was "an important aspect of the citizen's 'liberty' " guaranteed by the Due Process Clause of the Fifth Amendment, and noted that the prohibition of Section 6 "indiscriminately excludes plainly relevant considerations such as the individual's knowledge, activity, commitment, and purposes in and places for travel."

In Zemel v. Rusk, 381 U.S. 1, 85 S.Ct. 1271, 14 L.Ed.2d 179 (1965), the issue was whether the Passport Act of 1926 had authorized the Secretary to refuse to validate passports for travel to Cuba, a practice of the Secretary begun in 1961 after the termination of diplomatic relations with the Castro government. The Court held that the imposition by the Secretary of area restrictions on travel was authorized by that Act and was constitutional. In reaching this conclusion, it relied in part upon the legislative history of the Act, subsequent action or inaction by Congress and interpretation of the Act by the Executive. However, United States v. Laub, 385 U.S. 475, 87 S.Ct. 574, 17 L.Ed.2d 526 (1967), held that persons who violated such area restrictions but who had valid passports could not be criminally prosecuted under Section 215(b) of the Immigration and Nationality Act. It is uncertain whether the Laub decision would preclude the Government from prosecuting persons who bear valid passports but violate area restrictions under 18 U.S.C.A. § 1544, which forbids use of a passport "in violation of the conditions or restrictions therein contained, or of the rules prescribed pursuant to the laws regulating the issuance of passports . . . ."

Additional reading: Ehrlich, Passports, 19 Stan.L.Rev. 129 (1966).

QUESTIONS

(1) Although Zemel v. Rusk and the Yoshida International case both involve foreign relations, are the arguments for a broad interpretation of Congressional authorization equally persuasive in the two cases? Can one treat all "foreign-relations" problems as raising the same considerations of policy and benefitting from the liberal judicial attitude towards delegation that was expressed in the Curtiss-Wright case?

(2) Suppose that there were no Congressional legislation on passports. (Indeed, throughout most of American history, it was not necessary for a citizen to obtain a passport in order to leave or enter the United States.) Would the President have power to impose area restrictions on travel abroad by United States citizens?

NOTE ON THE JUDICIARY, POLITICAL QUESTIONS AND FOREIGN AFFAIRS

Few concepts concerning the jurisdiction and functions of the federal courts have proven to be as elastic in meaning as that of "political questions". This concept has been particularly germane to foreign affairs, to cases in which the relief requested would require a court to review congressional or executive acts pertaining to relations between this country and aliens or foreign countries. Before turning to such examples, this Note describes characteristics of the "political question" doctrine as it has recently developed in a domestic context.

The starting point for contemporary debate of these issues is the decision in Baker v. Carr, 369 U.S. 186, 82 S.Ct. 691, 7 L.Ed.2d 663 (1962), in which the Court held to be justiciable a complaint alleging that malapportionment of the state legislature denied plaintiffs the equal protection of the laws. That is, the Court concluded that the complaint did not raise issues that were beyond the judicial competence to decide, did not require the courts to remit plaintiffs to whatever remedies the political process would yield. The right which plaintiffs asserted was "within the reach of judicial protection." The opinion stated:

> We have said that "In determining whether a question falls within [the political question] category, the appropriateness under our system of government of attributing finality to the action of the political departments and also the lack of satisfactory criteria for a judicial determination are dominant considerations." Coleman v. Miller, 307 U.S. 433, 454–455, 59 S.Ct. 972, 982, 83 L.Ed. 1385. The nonjusticiability of a political question is primarily a function of the separation of powers. Much confusion results from the capacity of the "political question" label to obscure the need for case-by-case inquiry. Deciding whether a matter has in any measure been committed by the Constitution to another branch of government, or whether the action of that branch exceeds whatever authority has been committed, is itself a delicate exercise in constitutional interpretation, and is a responsibility of this Court as ultimate interpreter of the Constitution. To demonstrate this requires no less than to analyze representative cases and to infer from them the analytical threads that make up the political question doctrine. We shall then show that none of those threads catches this case.
>
> . . .
>
> It is apparent that several formulations which vary slightly according to the settings in which the questions arise may describe a political question, although each has one or more elements which identify it as essentially a function of the separation of powers. Prominent on the surface of any case held to involve a political question is found a textually demonstrable constitutional commitment of the issue to a coordinate political department; or a lack of judicially discoverable and manageable standards for resolving it; or the impossibility of deciding without an initial policy determina-

tion of a kind clearly for nonjudicial discretion; or the impossibility of a court's undertaking independent resolution without expressing lack of the respect due coordinate branches of government; or an unusual need for unquestioning adherence to a political decision already made; or the potentiality of embarrassment from multifarious pronouncements by various departments on one question.

Unless one of these formulations is inextricable from the case at bar, there should be no dismissal for non-justiciability on the ground of a political question's presence. The doctrine of which we treat is one of "political questions," not one of "political cases." The courts cannot reject as "no law suit" a bona fide controversy as to whether some action denominated "political" exceeds constitutional authority. The cases we have reviewed show the necessity for discriminating inquiry into the precise facts and posture of the particular case, and the impossibility of resolution by any semantic cataloguing.

Powell v. McCormack, 395 U.S. 486, 89 S.Ct. 1944, 23 L.Ed.2d 491 (1969), applied the criteria defined in Baker v. Carr. The Court held that plaintiff's claim of constitutional entitlement to take the seat to which he had been elected in the House of Representatives did not present a political question. The excerpts below note some of the arguments for non-justiciability that were rejected by the Court, including those based upon Art. I, Sec. 5 of the Constitution that "Each House shall be the judge of the . . . qualifications of its own Members . . . "

Had the intent of the Framers emerged from these materials with less clarity, we would nevertheless have been compelled to resolve any ambiguity in favor of a narrow construction of the scope of Congress' power to exclude members-elect. A fundamental principle of our representative democracy is, in Hamilton's words, "that the people should choose whom they please to govern them." . . .

Unquestionably, Congress has an interest in preserving its institutional integrity, but in most cases that interest can be sufficiently safeguarded by the exercise of its power to punish its members for disorderly behavior and, in extreme cases, to expel a member with the concurrence of two-thirds. In short, both the intention of the Framers, to the extent it can be determined, and an examination of the basic principles of our democratic system persuade us that the Constitution does not vest in the Congress a discretionary power to deny membership by a majority vote.

For these reasons, we have concluded that Art. I, § 5, is at most a "textually demonstrable commitment" to Congress to judge only the qualifications expressly set forth in the Constitution. Therefore, the "textual commitment" formulation of the political question doctrine does not bar federal courts from adjudicating petitioners' claims.

Respondents' alternate contention is that the case presents a political question because judicial resolution of petitioners' claim would produce a "potentially embarrassing confrontation between coordinate branches" of the Federal Government. But, as our interpretation of Art. I, § 5, discloses, a determination of petitioner Powell's right to sit would require no more than an interpretation of the Constitution. Such a determination falls within the traditional role accorded courts to interpret the law, and does not involve a "lack of the respect due [a] coordinate [branch] of government," nor does it involve an "initial policy determination of a kind clearly for nonjudicial discretion." Baker v. Carr, 369 U.S. 186, at 217, 82 S.Ct. 691, at 710. Our system of government requires that federal courts on occasion interpret the Constitution in a manner at variance with the construction given the document by another branch. The alleged conflict that such an adjudication may cause cannot justify the courts' avoiding their constitutional responsibility. See . . . Youngstown Sheet & Tube Co. v. Sawyer, 343 U.S. 579, 613–614, 72 S.Ct. 863, 898, 96 L.Ed. 1153 (1952) (Frankfurter, J., concurring); . . .

Nor are any of the other formulations of a political question "inextricable from the case at bar." Baker v. Carr, supra, at 217, 82 S.Ct. at 710. Petitioners seek a determination that the House was without power to exclude Powell from the 90th Congress, which, we have seen, requires an interpretation of the Constitution—a determination for which clearly there are "judicially . . . manageable standards." Finally, a judicial resolution of petitioners' claim will not result in "multifarious pronouncements by various departments on one question." For, as we noted in Baker v. Carr, supra, at 211, 82 S.Ct., at 706 it is the responsibility of this Court to act as the ultimate interpreter of the Constitution. Marbury v. Madison, 1 Cranch (5 U.S.) 137, 2 L.Ed. 60 (1803). Thus, we conclude that petitioners' claim is not barred by the political question doctrine, and having determined that the claim is otherwise generally justiciable, we hold that the case is justiciable.

It is difficult to piece out of such pronouncements a coherent theory of the "political question." The penultimate paragraph quoted above from Baker v. Carr notes six distinct criteria or tests, but with no indication of their relative significance or applicability to different settings. Those tests cover a spectrum of judicial attitudes, from "hands-off, nonjusticiable" to "justiciable, but . . . "—that is, the latter attitude representing the view that courts will defer to certain types of legislative or executive determinations that are relevant to the final judicial decision on the merits. Out of such opinions, scholars have sought to develop a more coherent framework for understanding political questions. One scholar [7] described three such theories:

(*1*) The *classical explanation* treats political questions as a matter of constitutional interpretation, and asks (in the language of Baker v. Carr) whether there is a "textually demonstrable constitutional commitment" of the issue to another branch of government. A court, for example, when it decides that it is bound by a presidential determination

7. Scharpf, Judicial Review and the Political Question: A Functional Analysis, 75 Yale L.J. 517 (1966).

that a certain government is to be recognized, is engaging in normal constitutional interpretation by concluding that such determinations are committed to the Executive. The excerpts above from the Powell case suggest the attraction of such an approach.

(*2*) A *prudential theory* stresses the discretionary element in the political question, and views conclusions of a court that certain matters are not within its province to review less as acts of constitutional interpretation than as the exercise of a discretion to withhold constitutional judgment for a variety of prudential reasons.[8]

(*3*) A *functional theory* of the political question seeks to develop principled grounds for refusal to decide, grounds derived from recognition of the limitations of the judicial process. Such a theory, for example, would take into account the limited ability of the court to gather facts (and hence to review the bases for a Presidential determination resting on national-security grounds); to fashion an appropriate remedy (as to end military operations); or indeed to develop legal standards for particular problems (as for recognition of a foreign government).

When one considers judicial attitudes towards review of congressional or executive action involving foreign affairs, a number of cases appearing above could be cited for the proposition that courts will show particular deference to such determinations. Recall, for example, the statements in Harisiades v. Shaughnessy, p. 26, supra:

> It is pertinent to observe that any policy toward aliens is vitally and intricately interwoven with contemporaneous policies in regard to the conduct of foreign relations, the war power, and the maintenance of a republican form of government. Such matters are so exclusively entrusted to the political branches of government as to be largely immune from judicial inquiry or interference.
>
> These restraints upon the judiciary, occasioned by different events, do not control today's decision but they are pertinent. It is not necessary and probably not possible to delineate a fixed and precise line of separation in these matters between political and judicial power under the Constitution. Certainly, however, nothing in the structure of our Government or the text of our Constitution would warrant judicial review by standards which would require us to equate our political judgment with that of Congress.

Such cases do not, of course, involve "political questions" in the strong sense that the issue presented by plaintiff would be viewed as nonjusticiable. The Court had competence to decide the issue, and indeed decided that the type of congressional determinations before it were within Congress' constitutional power.

8. Such views are associated primarily with Professor Bickel, as developed in The Least Dangerous Branch (1962).

In evaluating the contemporary significance of such attitudes, it should be borne in mind that cases such as Harisiades treat the rather special determinations whether aliens should be admitted to or expelled from this society. A number of recent cases demonstrate that the "political" character of many judgments involving foreign affairs is insufficient to forestall judicial review or to lead courts to accept without question the legislative judgment—at least where constitutionally based rights of individual plaintiffs are alleged to have been violated by the legislation under review. This point was forcefully made in Faruki v. Rogers, 349 F.Supp. 723 (D.D.C.1972). At the request of a naturalized citizen, a district court enjoined State Department officials from enforcing a statutory provision that no person would be eligible for appointment as a Foreign Service officer until he had been a citizen of the United States for at least ten years. In his opinion holding the relevant statutory section to violate due process, Judge J. Skelly Wright observed:

> We are unpersuaded by the Goverment's contention that Section 515, notwithstanding the distinction it draws between the naturalized and the native-born, should be granted special deference because it relates to the conduct of foreign affairs. Where constitutionally protected rights are at stake —here the interest in freedom from invidious discrimination on the basis of place of birth and parentage—notions of automatic deference disappear. The need for careful judicial scrutiny of assertions of diplomatic exigency was made clear in Schneider v. Rusk, [p. 8, supra] which dealt with a classification very similar to this one. And we believe the weakness of the automatic deference argument in the foreign relations area was made emphatically clear just a year ago in New York Times Co. v. United States, 403 U.S. 713, 91 S.Ct. 2140, 29 L.Ed.2d 822 (1971) [the *Pentagon Papers* case].

Indeed, such cases involving assertions by individuals of constitutional rights related to foreign relations constitute an important number of all the decisions during the last two decades in which the Supreme Court has found federal legislation to be unconstitutional.[9] Recall the expatriation cases described at p. 8, supra, and Aptheker v. Secretary of State, p. 130, supra. Other cases include Reid v. Covert, 354 U.S. 1, 77 S.Ct. 1222, 1 L.Ed.2d 1148 (1957), p. 564, infra (involving overseas courts-martial of dependents of servicemen), and Lamont v. Postmaster General, 381 U.S. 301, 85 S.Ct. 1493, 14 L.Ed.2d 398 (1965) (law imposing restrictions on distribution through mails of Communist propaganda from foreign countries). The presence of the Aptheker case in this list signals that no watertight compartment separates cases decided on the issue of the scope of a delegated power from cases decided on substantive constitutional grounds. Thus the Court may prefer to say that a given practice of the Executive raises so many constitutional doubts that it will be deemed not to have been authorized by Congress (as it did

9. Recall in this connection the decisions described at pp. 45–58 supra, in which state legislation restricting aliens' economic opportunities was found to be unconstitutional.

in Kent v. Dulles, p. 000, supra), rather than construe the statute as authorizing the practice and then find it unconstitutional (as it did in Aptheker).

The cases referred to above all involved challenges by plaintiff to *Congressional legislation.* Different but related considerations are present when plaintiffs request courts to invalidate *executive decisions* affecting foreign affairs, whether such decisions are within an asserted inherent power of the Executive or pursuant to legislation whose constitutionality is not at issue. The executive decisions treating foreign affairs could be divided among several categories such as:

(*1*) Determinations by an executive official which are presented to a court in the context of litigation between private parties and which strongly influence the outcome of the litigation. Such determinations would include recognition of foreign states or governments, as well as decisions whether to suggest that a foreign sovereign be treated as immune from the jurisdiction of United States courts.[10] A comparable issue of the deference to be accorded to executive determinations is raised by International Products Corp. v. Koons, p. 140, infra.

(*2*) Cases in which courts are asked to review determinations made by executive officials in the course of direct judicial review of executive or administrative action involving such determinations. In the field of deportation, for example, courts have traditionally shown great deference to executive determinations. A strong expression of judicial deference appears in Chicago and Southern Air Lines, Inc. v. Waterman S. S. Corp., 333 U.S. 103, 68 S.Ct. 431, 92 L.Ed. 568 (1948), in which judicial review of orders of the Civil Aeronautics Board was at issue. In accordance with his statutory authority, the President had advised the Board of changes which he required in an order involving certificates for air routes. The Court stated:

> In this case, submission of the Board's decision was made to the President, who disapproved certain portions of it and advised the Board of the changes which he required. The Board complied and submitted a revised order and opinion which the President approved. Only then were they made public, and that which was made public and which is before us is only the final order and opinion containing the President's amendments and bearing his approval. Only at that stage was review sought, and only then could it be pursued, for then only was the decision consummated, announced and available to the parties.

10. Questions of the effect to be given by courts to executive determinations about sovereign immunity are examined in Chapter VI.

> While the changes made at direction of the President may be identified, the reasons therefor are not disclosed beyond the statement that "because of certain factors relating to our broad national welfare and other matters for which the Chief Executive has special responsibility, he has reached conclusions which require" changes in the Board's opinion.
>
> The court below considered, and we think quite rightly, that it could not review such provisions of the order as resulted from Presidential direction. The President, both as Commander-in-Chief and as the Nation's organ for foreign affairs, has available intelligence services whose reports neither are nor ought to be published to the world. It would be intolerable that courts, without the relevant information, should review and perhaps nullify actions of the Executive taken on information properly held secret. Nor can courts sit in camera in order to be taken into executive confidences. But even if courts could require full disclosure, the very nature of executive decisions as to foreign policy is political, not judicial. Such decisions are wholly confided by our Constitution to the political departments of the government, Executive and Legislative. They are delicate, complex, and involve large elements of prophecy. They are and should be undertaken only by those directly responsible to the people whose welfare they advance or imperil. They are decisions of a kind for which the Judiciary has neither aptitude, facilities nor responsibility and have long been held to belong in the domain of political power not subject to judicial intrusion or inquiry. . . . We therefore agree that whatever of this order emanates from the President is not susceptible of review by the Judicial Department.

The Waterman decision has influenced the Court's development of doctrine affecting other areas of executive prerogative, such as the privileged character of presidential conversations.[11]

(*3*) Cases involving challenges to extensive executive courses of action which allegedly violate the constitutional

11. In United States v. Nixon, 418 U.S. 683, 94 S.Ct. 3090, 41 L.Ed.2d 1039 (1974), the Court upheld a district court's subpoena of tapes of presidential conversations allegedly bearing upon the Watergate cover-up, for use (after *in camera* inspection by the district court) in the prosecution of former White House aides and other government officials. Although rejecting defendant's claim of an absolute, unqualified presidential privilege of immunity of such conversations from judicial process, the Court did recognize a constitutionally based "presumptive privilege" that was overcome on the facts before it by the requirements of the criminal process. The Court commented on the absence of "a claim of need to protect military, diplomatic or sensitive national security secrets." It observed that "[a]s to these areas of Art. II duties the courts have traditionally shown the utmost deference to Presidential responsibilities," then quoting some of the excerpts from the Waterman opinion appearing above.

allocation of authority for such action to the legislative branch. Prominent within this category are cases raising "political questions" where the challenge was to the authority of the Executive to wage combat in Vietnam. Such issues are considered at p. 142, infra.

The opinion in Baker v. Carr applied its general views of political questions to different areas of congressional and executive action, including the field of "foreign relations". Its remarks about that field appear below:

> *Foreign relations:* There are sweeping statements to the effect that all questions touching foreign relations are political questions. Not only does resolution of such issues frequently turn on standards that defy judicial application, or involve the exercise of a discretion demonstrably committed to the executive or legislature; but many such questions uniquely demand single-voiced statement of the Government's views. Yet it is error to suppose that every case or controversy which touches foreign relations lies beyond judicial cognizance. Our cases in this field seem invariably to show a discriminating analysis of the particular question posed, in terms of the history of its management by the political branches, of its susceptibility to judicial handling in the light of its nature and posture in the specific case, and of the possible consequences of judicial action. For example, though a court will not ordinarily inquire whether a treaty has been terminated, since on that question "governmental action . . . must be regarded as of controlling importance," if there has been no conclusive "governmental action" then a court can construe a treaty and may find it provides the answer. Compare Terlinden v. Ames, 184 U.S. 270, 285, 22 S.Ct. 484, 490, 46 L.Ed. 534, with Society for the Propagation of the Gospel in Foreign Parts v. New Haven, 8 Wheat. 464, 492–495, 5 L.Ed. 662. Though a court will not undertake to construe a treaty in a manner inconsistent with a subsequent federal statute, no similar hesitancy obtains if the asserted clash is with state law. Compare Whitney v. Robertson, 124 U.S. 190, 8 S.Ct. 456, 31 L.Ed. 386, with Kolovrat v. Oregon, 366 U.S. 187, 81 S.Ct. 922, 6 L.Ed.2d 218.
>
> While recognition of foreign governments so strongly defies judicial treatment that without executive recognition a foreign state has been called "a republic of whose existence we know nothing," and the judiciary ordinarily follows the executive as to which nation has sovereignty over disputed territory, once sovereignty over an area is politically determined and declared, courts may examine the resulting status and decide independently whether a statute applies to that area. Similarly, recognition of belligerency abroad is an executive responsibility, but if the executive proclamations fall short of an explicit answer, a court may construe them seeking, for example, to determine whether the situation is such that statutes designed to assure American neutrality have become operative. The Three Friends, 166 U.S. 1, 63, 66, 17 S.Ct. 495, 502, 503, 41 L.Ed. 497. Still again, though it is the executive that determines a person's status as representative of a foreign government, Ex parte Hitz, 111 U.S. 766, 4 S.Ct. 698, 28 L.Ed. 592, the executive's statements will be

construed where necessary to determine the court's jurisdiction, In re Baiz, 135 U.S. 403, 10 S.Ct. 854, 34 L.Ed. 222. Similar judicial action in the absence of a recognizedly authoritative executive declaration occurs in cases involving the immunity from seizure of vessels owned by friendly foreign governments. Compare Ex parte Republic of Peru, 318 U.S. 578, 63 S.Ct. 793, 87 L.Ed. 1014, with Mexico v. Hoffman, 324 U.S. 30, 34–35, 65 S.Ct. 530, 532, 89 L.Ed. 729.

QUESTION

In Harisiades v. Shaughnessy, p. 26, supra, consider which of the following questions are "political," and for what reasons: (*a*) The legislative finding that the Communist Party, during the period of membership by the aliens, advocated overthrow of the Government of the United States by force and violence; (*b*) the legislative determination that it was undesirable for past members, even if they were not active, to remain in the United States; (*c*) more broadly phrased, Congressional decisions of whatever nature relating to the admission and deportation of aliens.

COMMENT

The preceding materials suggest reasons why courts may refrain from review on the merits of types of legislative or executive determinations treating foreign affairs. The Koons case below poses a different issue—the degree to which courts will follow executive suggestions about administration of justice when those suggestions raise foreign-affairs issues.

INTERNATIONAL PRODUCTS CORP. v. KOONS

United States Court of Appeals, Second Circuit, 1963.
325 F.2d 403.

[A district judge issued an order in a diversity action enjoining defendants and their counsel "from publishing or disclosing to any third party any of the testimony, documents or writing contained or referred to in any of the depositions in the action or documents or writings produced or submitted to this Court, concerning payments to officials of any South American Government. . . ." Plaintiff's affidavit had alleged that disclosure of these matters, which a deposition taken by defendants had explored, "could be extremely embarrassing and cause great inconvenience and hardship" to plaintiff and "would be contrary to the best interests of the foreign policy of the United States." The affidavit was supported by a Suggestion of Interest filed by the United States Attorney for the Southern District of New York on behalf of the Department of State, stating that disclosure of the alleged improper payments could "lead the Government of the aforesaid friendly country to react in a manner inimical to private American business interests in that country and contrary to the foreign policy objective [sic] of the United States." Accordingly, the Department requested that the court preclude disclosure to third parties.

Defendants appealed from the order. The Court of Appeals, after considering some procedural matters, referred to F.R.C.P. 30, which provides in part that a court can order a deposition to be sealed and opened only upon court order and can "make any other order which justice requires to protect the party or witness from annoyance, embarrassment, or oppression." The opinion, delivered by JUDGE FRIENDLY, continued:]

The portion of the order which seals the deposition of Seldes and limits defendants and others in their use of information obtained therefrom was plainly authorized by F.R.Civ.Proc. 30(b), and we entertain no doubt as to the constitutionality of a rule allowing a federal court to forbid the publicizing, in advance of trial, of information obtained by one party from another by use of the court's processes. Whether or not the Rule itself authorizes so much of the order as also seals all affidavits submitted by defendants on various motions, we have no question as to the court's jurisdiction to do this under the inherent "equitable powers of courts of law over their own process, to prevent abuses, oppression, and injustices," Gumbel v. Pitkin, 124 U.S. 131, 144, 8 S.Ct. 379, 31 L.Ed. 374 (1888). . . .

What causes concern here is that the order went further and curtailed disclosure of information and writings which defendants and their counsel possessed before they sought to take Seldes' deposition. We fail to see how the use of such documents or information in arguing motions can justify an order preventing defendants and their counsel from exercising their First Amendment rights to disclose such documents and information free of governmental restraint. . . . The issue that remains is whether any different conclusion is called for in this case because of the Suggestion of Interest of the United States.

Appellants claim in the first instance that the suggestion was unauthorized since the United States has no financial interest in the litigation. But the statute, 5 U.S.C.A. § 316, is not limited by its terms to cases of financial interest; it authorizes the Attorney General to send any officer of the Department of Justice "to attend to the interests of the United States in any suit pending in any of the courts of the United States, or in the courts of any State . . . ." Long before the present statute, which derives from the Act of June 22, 1870, c. 150, § 5, 16 Stat. 162, the Attorney General had submitted suggestions as to the immunity of the property of foreign sovereigns, The Schooner Exchange v. M'Faddon, 7 Cranch 116, 147, 11 U.S. 116, 147, 3 L.Ed. 287 (1812), as he has frequently done thereafter. Yet "the interests of the United States" in such cases are simply its interests in friendly intercourse with other nations and in avoiding reprisals by them—the same interests asserted here.

Whatever the case may be as to suggestions of sovereign immunity, . . . it is plain that the suggestion here did not bind the court and certainly did not relieve it of the necessity of considering whether the action proposed to be taken would violate the First Amendment. We know of no authority that a court may restrain a private citizen in peace time from giving vent to his views, or publicizing his own information, as to the conduct of officials of foreign governments—any more than it may exert prior restraint on his publication of views concerning officials of our own. Near v. Minnesota ex rel. Olson, 283 U.S. 697, 51 S.Ct. 625, 75 L.Ed. 1357 (1934). The facts here are far, indeed, from the "exceptional cases" of valid prior restraints recognized in Near—"No one would question but that a government might prevent actual obstruction to its recruiting service or the publication of the sailing dates of transports or the number and location of troops," 283 U.S. at 716, 83 S.Ct. 631, 75 L.Ed. 1357; we need not attempt to determine just where the line runs. The conduct of our country's international relations might indeed be somewhat easier if citizens could be prevented from publicly reflecting on officials of foreign governments even when their information had been privately obtained. But the price of any such facilitation is higher than we have chosen to pay; we rely instead on the responsibility of the press and on the ability of the foreign service to explain to other governments that our Constitution does not permit such suppression of private thought.[12]

We therefore suggest that the District Court modify its order so as to make it plain that no restrictions are imposed on the freedom of the persons named therein to make whatever use they wish of writings (other than papers filed in court) or information which have come into their possession otherwise than through the court's processes. . . .

---

2. WAR POWERS AND VIETNAM: CONTROVERSY OVER THE REACH AND CONTROL OF EXECUTIVE POWER

Never has this country experienced as widespread, intense and bitter criticism of the foreign policies pursued by its government as from the mid 1960's to 1973. The domestic opposition to our massive military operations in Indochina—North and South Vietnam, Cambodia and Laos—was expressed through all forms of the political process, from demonstrations or meetings to petitions and votes. In its extreme form, that opposition took the form of violations of law ranging from violent protest to refusals to comply with induction notices or military commands.

The dissent over the Vietnamese war had many dimensions—moral, strategic or utilitarian, and constitutional. It is primarily the constitutional issues which here concern us. Those issues raised afresh the problem of the inherent or delegated powers of the Executive, in the context of powers to wage combat without a congressional declaration of war. The constitutional struggle asserted itself pri-

12. Although we sustain the power of the Attorney General to submit the State Department's letter, the case raises a question, already mooted as to suggestions of sovereign immunity, see Cardozo, Sovereign Immunity: The Plaintiff Deserves a Day in Court, 67 Harv.L.Rev. 608, 617–18 (1954), whether the Department of State ought not adopt procedures—which could be quite informal—to assure a hearing of the other side before it moves into a case like this. Although a hearing is not required by statute, neither § 4 nor § 5 of the Administrative Procedure Act being applicable, the weight properly given by the courts to representations from the Department of State would appear to make it desirable that, before deciding to interpose its views in a private litigation, the Department normally should hear why it ought not as well as why it ought. It seems not unlikely that if appellants had been given an opportunity to present their views, the Department might have concluded that, in the light of considerations which it has regarded as generally militating against its intervention in private litigation, well described in Bilder, supra, 56 Am.J.Int'l Law at 678, the interests of the United States were not in such jeopardy as to warrant the action taken here, or, at least, that the Government should not indorse the full relief sought. However, the order to show cause should have alerted appellants to the likelihood of action by the Department of State, and there is nothing to indicate a request on their part for a conference with the Legal Adviser. . . .

marily between congressmen who were hostile to the war and sought its earliest possible termination, and the Johnson and Nixon administrations which either intensified our involvement or reduced it at a pace and with qualifications that further exacerbated the congressional-executive tensions. The judiciary, as we shall see, played a minor role in the unfolding and present resolution of the controversy over war powers.

The question of war powers and the Indochinese hostilities offer a contemporary illustration of themes developed in the earlier sections of this chapter. Moreover, it is at least plausible that this controversy and the suspicion or hostility towards the executive that it generated will have implications for other, less dramatic exercises of executive power in areas such as economic regulation. The selective description of events, legislation and a few court decisions which appear below seek to capture the basic themes in this complex skein of events.

NOTE ON THE CHARACTER OF THE STRUGGLE BETWEEN CONGRESS AND THE EXECUTIVE

The basic facts of the war in Indochina are familiar history to a generation of Americans. Our military involvement spanned three presidents. 1962 witnessed the first presence of United States military advisors. Within several years, over 500,000 Americans were committed to combat in Indochina, combat which as late as 1972 included major new operations against Cambodia and Laos. By the end of the American troop involvement in the war in 1973, there were over 50,000 American dead, over 300,000 wounded, bombing and spoliation of the areas involved without precedent in warfare, and over $100 billion of our war-related expenditures. The personal, psychological and material "costs" to the Vietnamese, military and civilian, are beyond meaningful calculation.

Framework for the Constitutional Controversy

The fact that Congress never "declared war" was the starting point for acrimonious debate during a period of at least eight years. The textual framework for that debate reveals the complexity of the matter, for the Constitution confers powers upon both the Congress and the President that are germane to foreign hostilities. Art. I, Sec. 8, states that Congress shall have the power to "provide for the common Defence"; "declare War . . . and make Rules concerning Captures on Land and Water"; "raise and support Armies"; "provide and maintain a Navy"; "make Rules for the Government and Regulation of the Land and Naval Forces"; and "make all Laws which shall be necessary and proper for carrying into Execution the foregoing Powers, and all other Powers vested by this Constitution in the Government of the United States, or in any Department of Officer thereof." Sec. 9 adds that no money shall be drawn from the Treasury "but in Consequence of Appropriations made by Law." On the other hand, Art. II, Sec. 2, provides that the "President shall be the Commander in Chief of the Army and Navy," while Sec. 3 states that the President shall "take care that the Laws be faithfully executed . . ."

Few of the challenges to our policies in Vietnam insisted upon a precise declaration of war as a condition to the legality of foreign combat. The State Department insisted that there was no such "rigid formalism" in the Constitution [13], while those challenging the war's constitutionality emphasized the purpose of the "declaration" clause to check executive prerogative. Nonetheless, most recognized the legal consequences (the effect upon the President's domestic powers, upon treaties, upon relations with other countries under international law, and so on) of a formal declaration, and hence the desirability of flexibility in the ways in which congressional assent to military operations could be expressed. Moreover, in many instances there would be a problem of defining when hostilities reached the status of a "war".

The Executive advanced four principal arguments. The first and most far-reaching stressed the Commander-in-Chief clause, and drew from it and Article II as a whole an inherent power in the presidency, confirmed by history, to commit forces without explicit congressional approval. Of 125 instances from 1789 to the present of commitment of United States military forces abroad, only five were preceded by formal "declarations". Although the record of the precise basis for presidential decision in each such case was somewhat clouded, some of these involvements were pursuant to other forms of congressional authorization, while in others the President acted on his inherent authority.

Dispute centered on the character and significance of this historical record. The critics of the war generally conceded an inherent power in the presidency, derived from the very nature of sovereignty and from the specific language of Article II, to respond to attack. Even this defensive war-making power, however, raised difficult issues as to the nature of the attack made or threatened, the measure of an appropriate response, and the further commitments to which the President's use of force could bind the country. The Executive argued that the inherent power of the presidency reached past such defensive situations to include a power to respond to any threat to the country's security. Since security interests were threatened by actions abroad as well as at home, the potentially vast scope of this power disturbed the critics. For a country intricately involved in world politics and mutual defense arrangements, the concession of so broadly defined a power was viewed as vitiating the "declaration" clause of any significance.

The historical record was interpreted more narrowly by the critics. They stressed that many foreign interventions had the purpose of protecting the lives or properties of United States citizens,

13. Department of State, Office of Legal Adviser, The Legality of United States Participation in the Defense of Viet Nam, 75 Yale L.J. 1085 (1966).

frequently in situations of local unrest in the foreign country. Moreover, the large majority of such interventions were minor and posed little risk of a major United States involvement like the Vietnamese war. Nonetheless, the country's military involvements after World War II could only with difficulty be embraced within such narrow categories. The use of force in Korea (President Truman), Lebanon (President Eisenhower), in the Cuban missile crisis (President Kennedy) and in the Dominican Republic (President Johnson) rested on varying justifications, involved in one instance a major conflict, and could not easily be limited to defense of United States lives or property or territorial integrity. None of these interventions was preceded by explicit congressional authorization.

The Executive also advanced three arguments (in addition to that of inherent power) to the effect that the President's policies in fact rested upon approval by part or all of the Congress. Those arguments were:

> (*1*) Although Congress had not declared war, for a number of years it had voted appropriations part of which were directed to the Indochinese military operations. Congress had voted Selective Service Acts for the purpose of maintaining an army of the size necessary to meet the Indochinese demands. The basis for these arguments and responses thereto are sketched in this Note and in the court decisions following it.

> (*2*) The Congress explicitly authorized military operations through the Gulf of Tonkin Resolution, 78 Stat. 384 (1964), which stated that Congress "approves and supports the determination of the President . . . to take all necessary measures to repel any armed attack against the forces of the United States and to prevent further aggression." This and equally strong language in other sections of the Resolution led the President to argue that it was a functional equivalent of a declaration of war. Those challenging this executive interpretation stressed the emergency circumstances under which the Resolution was debated, quarreled with the expansive interpretation of its terms, and alleged that the Congress had not been fully informed of all circumstances. The continuation of hostilities after the repeal of this Resolution in January 1971 is considered in the judicial opinions below.

> (*3*) The Executive also argued that its commitment of armed forces was authorized, indeed required, under various treaty engagements, including the United Nations Charter and the Southeast Asia Collective Defense Treaty (SEATO). Since treaties constitute "supreme law" under Article VI and the President is obligated faithfully to execute the laws, his commitment of forces was constitutional. Critics quarreled with the interpretations of these treaties, neither

of which authorized the President to bypass domestic constitutional requirements, as well as with the notion that a treaty consented to only by the Senate could displace a constitutional requirement of authorization of war by the entire Congress.

Congressional Action and the War Powers Resolution

Three formal actions within the Congress, one of continuing significance, reveal the evolution of sentiment and argument as the war slowly came to a close.

In 1967 Senator Fulbright, Chairman of the Foreign Relations Committee, submitted a resolution on national commitments (of armed forces abroad) which, as amended, was adopted as Senate Resolution 85, on June 25, 1969, by a vote of 70–16. This Resolution asserted that the Executive threatened both separation of powers and individual liberty through its Vietnamese policies. "It is the sense of the Senate that a national commitment by the United States results only from affirmative action taken by the executive and legislative branches . . . by means of a treaty, statute, or concurrent resolution of both Houses of Congress, specifically providing for such commitment." When reminded, during the debate on this Resolution, of his 1961 article referred to at p. 107, supra, Senator Fulbright stressed President Eisenhower's reluctance to use executive power, in contrast with the "very active period under President Johnson." There was "no doubt that I have changed my mind as to which is the more dangerous to the welfare of the country. The restraining influence of Congress upon an overactive and overambitious President is the much safer course for the country." [14]

After continuing rebuff by the President, the Congress enacted in 1973 Section 108 of the Continuing Appropriations Law for the Fiscal Year 1974, 87 Stat. 134, which provided:

> Notwithstanding any other provision of law, on or after August 15, 1973, no funds herein or heretofore appropriated may be obligated or expended to finance directly or indirectly combat activities by United States military forces in or over or from off the shores of North Vietnam, South Vietnam, Laos or Cambodia.

The last bombing operations by United States military forces in the designated areas were terminated within hours of the required deadline.

The war has left a specific congressional mark upon our legal-political system in the form of the War Powers Resolution of November 7, 1973, 87 Stat. 555, enacted after both houses overcame a presidential veto, accompanied by the President's assertion that the Resolution unconstitutionally encroached upon his inherent powers. The key sections of that Resolution provide:

> SEC. 2. (a) It is the purpose of this joint resolution to fulfill the intent of the framers of the Constitution of the United

14. 115 Cong.Rec. 16625, 91st Cong., 1st Sess. (1969).

States and insurer that the collective judgment of both the Congress and the President will apply to the introduction of United States Armed Forces into hostilities, or into situations where imminent involvement in hostilities is clearly indicated by the circumstances, and to the continued use of such forces in hostilities or in such situations.

(b) Under article I, section 8, of the Constitution, it is specifically provided that the Congress shall have the power to make all laws necessary and proper for carrying into execution, not only its own powers but also all other powers vested by the Constitution in the Government of the United States, or in any department or officer thereof.

(c) The constitutional powers of the President as Commander-in-Chief to introduce United States Armed Forces into hostilities, or into situations where imminent involvement in hostilities is clearly indicated by the circumstances, are exercised only pursuant to (1) a declaration of war, (2) specific statutory authorization, or (3) a national emergency created by attack upon the United States, its territories or possessions, or its armed forces.

SEC. 3. The President in every possible instance shall consult with Congress before introducing United States Armed Forces into hostilities or into situations where imminent involvement in hostilities is clearly indicated by the circumstances, and after every such introduction shall consult regularly with the Congress until United States Armed Forces are no longer engaged in hostilities or have been removed from such situations.

SEC. 4. (a) In the absence of a declaration of war, in any case in which United States Armed Forces are introduced—

(1) into hostilities or into situations where imminent involvement in hostilities is clearly indicated by the circumstances;

(2) into the territory, airspace or waters of a foreign nation, while equipped for combat, except for deployments which relate solely to supply, replacement, repair, or training of such forces; or

(3) in numbers which substantially enlarge United States Armed Forces equipped for combat already located in a foreign nation;

the President shall submit within 48 hours to the Speaker of the House of Representatives and to the President pro tempore of the Senate a report, in writing, setting forth—

(A) the circumstances necessitating the introduction of United States Armed Forces;

(B) the constitutional and legislative authority under which such introduction took place; and

(C) the estimated scope and duration of the hostilities or involvement.

. . .

SEC. 5(b) Within sixty calendar days after a report is submitted or is required to be submitted pursuant to section 4(a)(1), whichever is earlier, the President shall terminate any use of United States Armed Forces with respect to which such report was submitted (or required to be submitted), unless the Congress (1) has declared war or has enacted a specific authorization for such use of United States Armed Forces, (2) has extended by law such sixty-day period, or (3) is physically unable to meet as a result of an armed attack upon the United States. Such sixty-day period shall be extended for not more than an additional thirty days if the President determines and certifies to the Congress in writing that unavoidable military necessity respecting the safety of United States Armed Forces requires the continued use of such armed forces in the course of bringing about a prompt removal of such forces.

(c) Notwithstanding subsection (b), at any time that United States Armed Forces are engaged in hostilities outside the territory of the United States, its possessions and territories without a declaration of war or specific statutory authorization, such forces shall be removed by the President if the Congress so directs by concurrent resolution.

. . .

SEC. 8. (a) Authority to introduce United States Armed Forces into hostilities or into situations wherein involvement in hostilities is clearly indicated by the circumstances shall not be inferred—

(1) from any provision of law (whether or not in effect before the date of the enactment of this joint resolution), including any provision contained in any appropriation Act, unless such provision specifically authorizes the introduction of United States Armed Forces into hostilities or into such situations and states that it is intended to constitute specific statutory authorization within the meaning of this joint resolution; or

(2) from any treaty heretofore or hereafter ratified unless such treaty is implemented by legislation specifically authorizing the introduction of United States Armed Forces into hostilities or into such situations and stating that it is intended to constitute specific statutory authorization within the meaning of this joint resolution.

. . .

(d) Nothing in this joint resolution—

(1) is intended to alter the constitutional authority of the Congress or of the President, or the provisions of existing treaties; or

(2) shall be construed as granting any authority to the President with respect to the introduction of United States Armed Forces into hostilities or into situations wherein involvement in hostilities is clearly indicated by the circumstances which authority he would not have had in the absence of this joint resolution.

In its Report on an earlier version of the Resolution, a Senate committee [15] referred to the "sense of the Senate" Commitments Resolution of 1969, and expressed disappointment that the Executive has "chosen to ignore congressional expressions of constitutional principles which do not carry the force of law". Senator Fulbright noted in the Report (p. 27) that in his view "the war in which we are now engaged is unconstitutional as well as unwise."

In July 1974, the Judiciary Committee of the House of Representatives debated whether to recommend to the House the adoption of articles of impeachment against President Nixon. After voting for three articles of impeachment relating to the Watergate cover-up (by a vote of 27–11), abuse of power (28–10) and failure to comply with subpoenas issued by the Committee (21–17), the Committee defeated (26–12) a proposed Article IV charging that President Nixon, subsequent to March 1969, authorized and ratified the concealment from Congress of facts and the submission to Congress of misstatements concerning American bombing operations in Cambodia, "in derogation of the power of the Congress to declare war, to make appropriations and to raise and support armies . . ." The proponents of Article IV stressed that not until July 16, 1973 did the Secretary of Defense formally reveal to a Senate committee that bombing in Cambodia occurred prior to May 1970, the date of the American incursion into that country. Those who voted against the proposed Article stressed three grounds. In a general way, some Representatives supported the "national security" prerogatives of the President, a theme related to presidential assertions of inherent power. A larger number emphasized that the Congress was complicit with the President throughout this period and (in the words of one Representative) that "the usurpation of power by the President . . . has come about not through the bold power of the President but rather through sloth and default on the part of the Congress." Others who were opposed noted evidence that a small but importantly placed number of congressmen (such as chairmen of a few committees) had been advised of the bombing by the Executive, but had not passed this information on to the entire Congress.

Throughout these years, the issue of the legality of the war arose in several contexts in judicial proceedings—sometimes as defenses to criminal prosecutions for refusal to submit to the draft or to follow military orders to serve in Vietnam, sometimes in actions brought by members of Congress and others to enjoin military operations. For reasons that appear in the excerpts below from several opinions, the courts were not significant participants in the unfolding or contemporary resolution of this controversy over the manner of committing this country to major hostilities.

QUESTIONS

In the Hearings on War Powers Legislation before the Subcommittee on National Security Policy and Scientific Developments of the House Com-

15. S.Rep.No.92–606 of Committee on Foreign Relations, to accompany S. 2956, 92nd Cong., 2d Sess., January 9, 1972, p. 8.

mittee on Foreign Affairs, 92nd Cong., 1st Sess., several present or past government officials and scholars testified about the advisability of the War Powers Resolution (as then drafted, before revision to the form in which it was enacted). Taking the Resolution as enacted, how do you assess the following observations?

(*1*) John R. Stevenson, a former Legal Adviser to the State Department, considered the proposed Resolution of doubtful constitutionality. Those powers of the President which were constitutionally based could not be definitively defined through legislation, but had to be worked out through a process of accommodation involving the political interaction between the President and Congress. The asserted bases for the congressional enactment were insufficient to rework the constitutionally determined balance and separation of powers.

(*2*) Professor Arthur Schlesinger, Jr., viewed the proposed legislation as embracing an "expansive theory of defensive war". He urged that legislation simply leave the President with whatever his inherent powers to commit troops might be, rather than legitimate that power and implicitly invite its utilization.

(*3*) Several of those testifying took the position that even had the proposed legislation been in effect in 1965, Presidents Johnson and Nixon could have followed their historical courses of conduct in Vietnam consistently with the Resolution.

Additional reading: The information in the Note above was drawn from the following sources. Among them, the most helpful review of the relevant history and problems appears in a Note, Congress, the President, and the Power to Commit Forces to Combat, 81 Harv.L.Rev. 1771 (1968). Other useful references include van Alstyne, Congress, the President, and the Power to Declare War: A Requiem for Vietnam, 121 U.Pa.L.Rev. 1 (1972); Bickel, Congress, the President, and the Power to Wage War, 47–48 Chic.-Kent L.Rev. 131 (1971); Department of State, Office of Legal Adviser, The Legality of United States Participation in the Defense of Viet Nam, 75 Yale L.J. 1085 (1966); and Rostow, Great Cases Make Bad Law: The War Powers Act, 50 Tex.L.Rev. 833 (1972).

ORLANDO v. LAIRD

United States Court of Appeals, Second Circuit, 1971.
443 F.2d 1039, cert. denied 404 U.S. 869, 92 S.Ct. 94, 30 L.Ed.2d 113 (1971).

Before LUMBARD, CHIEF JUDGE, and KAUFMAN and ANDERSON, CIRCUIT JUDGES.

ANDERSON, CIRCUIT JUDGE:

Shortly after receiving orders to report for transfer to Vietnam, Pfc. Malcolm A. Berk and Sp. E5 Salvatore Orlando, enlistees in the United States Army, commenced separate actions in June 1970, seeking to enjoin the Secretary of Defense, the Secretary of the Army and the commanding officers, who signed their deployment orders, from enforcing them. The plaintiffs-appellants contended that these executive officers exceeded their constitutional authority by ordering them to participate in a war not properly authorized by Congress.

In Orlando's case the district court held in abeyance his motion for a preliminary injunction pending disposition in this court of Berk's expedited appeal from a denial of the same preliminary relief. On

June 19, 1970 we affirmed the denial of a preliminary injunction in Berk v. Laird, 429 F.2d 302 (2 Cir. 1970), but held that Berk's claim that orders to fight must be authorized by joint executive-legislative action was justiciable. The case was remanded for a hearing on his application for a permanent injunction. We held that the war declaring power of Congress, enumerated in Article I, section 8, of the Constitution, contains a "discoverable standard calling for *some* mutual participation by Congress," and directed that Berk be given an opportunity "to provide a method for resolving the question of when specified joint legislative-executive action is sufficient to authorize various levels of military activity," and thereby escape application of the political question doctrine to his claim that congressional participation has been in this instance, insufficient.

After a hearing on June 23, 1970, Judge Dooling in the district court denied Orlando's motion for a preliminary injunction on the ground that his deployment orders were constitutionally authorized, because Congress, by "appropriating the nation's treasure and conscripting its manpower," had "furnished forth the sinew of war" and because "the reality of the collaborative action of the executive and the legislative required by the Constitution has been present from the earliest stages." Orlando v. Laird, 317 F.Supp. 1013, 1019 (E.D. N.Y.1970).

On remand of Berk's action, Judge Judd of the district court granted the appellees' motion for summary judgment. Finding that there had been joint action by the President and Congress, he ruled that the method of congressional collaboration was a political question. Berk v. Laird, 317 F.Supp. 715, 728 (E.D.N.Y.1970).

The appellants contend that the respective rulings of the district court that congressional authorization could be expressed through appropriations and other supporting legislation misconstrue the war declaring clause, and alternatively, that congressional enactments relating to Vietnam were incorrectly interpreted.

It is the appellants' position that the sufficiency of congressional authorization is a matter within judicial competence because that question can be resolved by "judicially discoverable and manageable standards" dictated by the congressional power "to declare War." See Baker v. Carr, 369 U.S. 186, 217, 82 S.Ct. 691, 7 L.Ed.2d 663 (1962); Powell v. McCormack, 395 U.S. 486, 89 S.Ct. 1944, 23 L.Ed.2d 491 (1969). They interpret the constitutional provision to require an express and explicit congressional authorization of the Vietnam hostilities though not necessarily in the words, "We declare that the United States of America is at war with North Vietnam." In support of this construction they point out that the original intent of the clause was to place responsibility for the initiation of war upon the body most responsive to popular will and argue that historical developments have not altered the need for significant congressional participation in such commitments of national resources. They further assert that, without a requirement of express and explicit congressional authorization, developments committing the nation to war, as a *fait accompli,* became the inevitable adjuncts of presidential direction of foreign policy, and, because military appropriations and other war-implementing enactments lack an explicit authorization of particular hostilities, they cannot, as a matter of law, be considered sufficient.

Alternatively, appellants would have this court find that, because the President requested accelerating defense appropriations and extensions of the conscription laws after the war was well under way,

Congress was, in effect, placed in a strait jacket and could not freely decide whether or not to enact this legislation, but rather was compelled to do so. For this reason appellants claim that such enactments cannot, as a factual matter, be considered sufficient congressional approval or ratification.

The Government on the other hand takes the position that the suits concern a non-justiciable political question; that the military action in South Vietnam was authorized by Congress in the "Joint Resolution to Promote the Maintenance of Internal Peace and Security in Southeast Asia" (the Tonkin Gulf Resolution) considered in connection with the Seato Treaty; and that the military action was authorized and ratified by congressional appropriations expressly designated for use in support of the military operations in Vietnam.

We held in the first *Berk* opinion that the constitutional delegation of the war-declaring power to the Congress contains a discoverable and manageable standard imposing on the Congress a duty of mutual participation in the prosecution of war. Judicial scrutiny of that duty, therefore, is not foreclosed by the political question doctrine. Baker v. Carr, supra; Powell v. McCormack, supra. As we see it, the test is whether there is any action by the Congress sufficient to authorize or ratify the military activity in question. The evidentiary materials produced at the hearings in the district court clearly disclose that this test is satisfied.

The Congress and the Executive have taken mutual and joint action in the prosecution and support of military operations in Southeast Asia from the beginning of those operations. The Tonkin Gulf Resolution, enacted August 10, 1964 (repealed December 31, 1970) was passed at the request of President Johnson and, though occasioned by specific naval incidents in the Gulf of Tonkin, was expressed in broad language which clearly showed the state of mind of the Congress and its intention fully to implement and support the military and naval actions taken by and planned to be taken by the President at that time in Southeast Asia, and as might be required in the future "to prevent further aggression." Congress has ratified the executive's initiatives by appropriating billions of dollars to carry out military operations in Southeast Asia [16] and by extending the Military Selective Service Act with full knowledge that persons conscripted under that Act had been, and would continue to be, sent to Vietnam.

16. In response to the demands of the military operations the executive during the 1960s ordered more and more men and material into the war zone; and congressional appropriations have been commensurate with each new level of fighting. Until 1965, defense appropriations had not earmarked funds for Vietnam. In May of that year President Johnson asked Congress for an emergency supplemental appropriation "to provide our forces [then numbering 35,000] with the best and most modern supplies and equipment." 111 Cong.Rec. 9283 (May 4, 1965). Congress appropriated $700 million for use "upon determination by the President that such action is necessary in connection with military activities in Souteast Asia." Pub.L. 89–18, 79 Stat. 109 (1965). Appropriation acts in each subsequent year explicitly authorized expenditures for men and material sent to Vietnam. The 1967 appropriations act, for example, declared Congress' "firm intention to provide all necessary support for members of the Armed Forces of the United States fighting in Vietnam" and supported "the efforts being made by the President of the United States . . . to prevent an expansion of the war in Vietnam and to bring that conflict to an end through a negotiated settlement . . . ." Pub.L. 90–5, 81 Stat. 5 (1967).

The district court opinion in Berk v. Laird, 317 F.Supp. 715 (E.D.N.Y.1970), sets out relevant portions of each of these military appropriation acts and discusses their legislative history.

Moreover, it specifically conscripted manpower to fill "the substantial induction calls necessitated by the current Vietnam buildup." [17]

There is, therefore, no lack of clear evidence to support a conclusion that there was an abundance of continuing mutual participation in the prosecution of the war. Both branches collaborated in the endeavor, and neither could long maintain such a war without the concurrence and cooperation of the other.

Although appellants do not contend that Congress can exercise its war-declaring power only through a formal declaration, they argue that congressional authorization cannot, as a matter of law, be inferred from military appropriations or other war-implementing legislation that does not contain an express and explicit authorization for the making of war by the President. Putting aside for a moment the explicit authorization of the Tonkin Gulf Resolution, we disagree with appellants' interpretation of the declaration clause for neither the language nor the purpose underlying that provision prohibits an inference of the fact of authorization from such legislative action as we have in this instance. The framers' intent to vest the war power in Congress is in no way defeated by permitting an inference of authorization from legislative action furnishing the manpower and materials of war for the protracted military operation in Southeast Asia.

The choice, for example, between an explicit declaration on the one hand and a resolution and war-implementing legislation, on the other, as the medium for expression of congressional consent involves "the exercise of a discretion demonstrably committed to the . . . legislature," Baker v. Carr, supra 9 at 211, 82 S.Ct. at 707, and therefore, invokes the political question doctrine.

Such a choice involves an important area of decision making in which, through mutual influence and reciprocal action between the President and the Congress, policies governing the relationship between this country and other parts of the world are formulated in the best interests of the United States. If there can be nothing more than minor military operations conducted under any circumstances, short of an express and explicit declaration of war by Congress, then extended military operations could not be conducted even though both the Congress and the President were agreed that they were necessary and were also agreed that a formal declaration of war would place the nation in a posture in its international relations which would be against its best interests. For the judicial branch to enunciate and enforce such a standard would be not only extremely unwise but also would constitute a deep invasion of the political question domain. As the Government says, ". . . decisions regarding the form and substance of congressional enactments authorizing hostilities are determined by highly complex considerations of diplomacy, foreign

17. In H.Rep.No.267, 90th Cong., 1st Sess. 38 (1967), in addition to extending the conscription mechanism, Congress continued a suspension of the permanent ceiling on the active duty strength of the Armed Forces, fixed at 2 million men, and replaced it with a secondary ceiling of 5 million. The House Report recommending extension of the draft concluded that the permanent manpower limitations "are much lower than the currently required strength." The Report referred to President Johnson's selective service message which said, ". . . that without the draft we cannot realistically expect to meet our present commitments or the requirements we can now foresee and that volunteers alone could be expected to man a force of little more than 2.0 million. The present number of personnel on active duty is about 3.3 million and it is scheduled to reach almost 3.5 million by June, 1968 if the present conflict is not concluded by then." H.Rep.No. 267, 90th Cong., 1st Sess. 38, 41 (1967).

policy and military strategy inappropriate to judicial inquiry." It would, indeed, destroy the flexibility of action which the executive and legislative branches must have in dealing with other sovereigns. What has been said and done by both the President and the Congress in their collaborative conduct of the military operations in Vietnam implies a consensus on the advisability of *not* making a formal declaration of war because it would be contrary to the interests of the United States to do so. The making of a policy decision of that kind is clearly within the constitutional domain of those two branches and is just as clearly not within the competency or power of the judiciary.

Beyond determining that there has been *some* mutual participation between the Congress and the President, which unquestionably exists here, with action by the Congress sufficient to authorize or ratify the military activity at issue, it is clear that the constitutional propriety of the means by which Congress has chosen to ratify and approve the protracted military operations in Southeast Asia is a political question. The form which congressional authorization should take is one of policy, committed to the discretion of the Congress and outside the power and competency of the judiciary, because there are no intelligible and objectively manageable standards by which to judge such actions. Baker v. Carr, supra, 369 U.S. at 217, 82 S.Ct. 691; Powell v. McCormack, supra, 395 U.S. at 518, 89 S.Ct. 1944.

The judgments of the district court are affirmed.

IRVING R. KAUFMAN, CIRCUIT JUDGE (concurring):

In light of the adoption by Congress of the Tonkin Gulf Resolution, and the clear evidence of continuing and distinctly expressed participation by the legislative branch in the prosecution of the war, I agree that the judgments below must be affirmed.

COMMENT

Compare the opinion in United States v. Sisson, 294 F.Supp. 511 (D.Mass.1968), where defendant moved to dismiss an indictment that charged him with willful refusal to submit to the draft. Defendant argued that there was no constitutional authority to conscript him to serve in a war not declared by Congress. Chief Judge Wyzanski denied the motion on the ground that defendant sought "adjudication of what is a political question . . ." His opinion stated in part:

> Congress in 1967 extended the Selective Service Act, Pub.L. No. 90–40, 81 Stat. 100. Congress acted with full knowledge that persons called for duty under the Act had been, and are likely to be, sent to Vietnam. Indeed, in 1965 Congress had amended the same Act with the hardly concealed object of punishing persons who tore up their draft cards out of protest at the Vietnam war. See United States v. O'Brien, 391 U.S. 367, 88 S.Ct. 1673, 20 L.Ed.2d 672.
>
> Moreover, Congress has again and again appropriated money for the draft act, for the Vietnam war, and for cognate activities. Congress has also enacted what is called the Tonkin Gulf Resolution, which some have viewed as advance authorization for the expansion of the Vietnam war.
>
> What the court thus faces is a situation in which there has been joint action by the President and Congress, even if the joint action has not taken the form of a declaration of war.

The absence of the formal declaration of war is not to be regarded as a trivial omission. A declaration of war has more than ritualistic or symbolic significance. . . .

But the fact that a declaration of war is a far more important act than an appropriation act or than an extension of a Selective Service Act does not go the whole way to show that in every situation of foreign military action, a declaration of war is a necessary prerequisite to conscription for that military engagement.

We are reminded by McCulloch v. Maryland, 17 U.S. (4 Wheat.) 316, 4 L.Ed. 579, and its progeny, that the national government has powers beyond those clearly stipulated in the Constitution. That the Constitution expresses one way of achieving a result does not inevitably carry a negative pregnant. Other ways may be employed by Congress as necessary and proper. Indeed, the implied powers may be not only Congressional but sometimes Presidential. In re Debs, 158 U.S. 564, 15 S.Ct. 900, 39 L.Ed. 1092. And this implication may be most justifiable in foreign affairs. United States v. Curtiss-Wright Export Corp., 299 U.S. 304, 57 S.Ct. 216, 81 L.Ed. 255. What may be involved in the present case is a choice between a limited undeclared war approved by the President and Congress and an unlimited declaration of war through an Act of Congress. The two choices may find support in different, related, but not inconsistent Constitutional powers.

If the national government does have two or more choices there are readily imagined reasons not to elect to exercise the expressly granted power to declare war.

A declaration of war expresses in the most formidable and unlimited terms a belligerent posture against an enemy. In Vietnam it is at least plausibly contended by some in authority that our troops are not engaged in fighting any enemy of the United States but are participating in the defense of what is said to be one country from the aggression of what is said to be another country. It is inappropriate for this court in any way to intimate whether South Vietnam and North Vietnam are separate countries, or whether there is a civil war, or whether there is a failure on the part of the people in Vietnam and elsewhere to abide by agreements made in Geneva. It is sufficient to say that the present situation is one in which the State Department and the other branches of the executive treat our action in Vietnam as though it were different from an unlimited war against an enemy.

Moreover, in the Vietnam situation a declaration of war would produce consequences which no court can fully anticipate. A declaration of war affects treaties of the United States, obligations of the United States under international organizations, and many public and private arrangements. A determination not to declare war is more than an avoidance of a domestic constitutional procedure. It has international implications of vast dimensions. Indeed, it is said that since 1945 no country has declared war on any other country. Whether this is true or not, it shows that not only in the United States but generally, there is a reluctance to take a step which symbolically and practically entails multiple unforeseeable consequences.

From the foregoing this Court concludes that the distinction between a declaration of war and a cooperative action by the legislative and executive with respect to military activities in foreign countries is the very essence of what is meant by a political question. It involves just the sort of evidence, policy considerations, and constitutional principles which elude the normal processes of the judiciary and which are far more suitable for determination by coordinate branches of the government.

HOLTZMAN v. SCHLESINGER

United States Court of Appeals, Second Circuit, 1973.
484 F.2d 1307.

Before MULLIGAN, OAKES and TIMBERS, CIRCUIT JUDGES.

MULLIGAN, CIRCUIT JUDGE:

This is an appeal from a judgment of the United States District Court, Eastern District of New York, Hon. Orrin G. Judd, District Judge, dated July 25, 1973, 361 F.Supp. 553, granting plaintiffs' motion for summary judgment and providing both declaratory and injunctive relief. The judgment declared that "there is no existing Congressional authority to order military forces into combat in Cambodia or to release bombs over Cambodia, and that military activities in Cambodia by American armed forces are unauthorized and unlawful . . . ." The order further enjoined and restrained the named defendants and their officers, agents, servants, employees and attorneys "from participating in any way in military activities in or over Cambodia or releasing any bombs which may fall in Cambodia." The effective date of the injunction was postponed . . . .

. . .

I

At the outset, as the parties agreed below and on the argument on appeal, we should emphasize that we are not deciding the wisdom, the propriety or the morality of the war in Indo-China and particularly the on-going bombing in Cambodia. This is the responsibility of the Executive and the Legislative branches of the government. The role of the Judiciary is to determine the legality of the challenged action and the threshold question is whether under the "political question" doctrine we should decline even to do that. . . . It is significant that the court [in Orlando v. Laird, p. 150, supra] noted that the Tonkin Gulf Resolution of August 10, 1964 had since been repealed on December 31, 1970.

In Da Costa v. Laird, 448 F.2d 1368 (2d Cir. 1971), cert. denied 405 U.S. 979, 92 S.Ct. 1193, 31 L.Ed.2d 255 (1972), this court specifically rejected the contention that the repeal by Congress of the Tonkin Gulf Resolution removed the Congressional authorization previously found sufficient in *Orlando*. We noted:

> As the constitutional propriety of the means by which the Executive and the Legislative branches engaged in mutual participation in prosecuting the military operations in Southeast Asia, is, as we held in *Orlando*, a political question, so the constitutional propriety of the method and means by which they mutually participate in winding down the conflict and in disengaging the nation from it, is also a

political question and outside of the power and competency of the judiciary. Id. at 1370.

The most recent holding of this court now pertinent is Da Costa v. Laird, 471 F.2d 1146 (1973) where an inductee urged that the President's unilateral decision to mine the harbors of North Vietnam and to bomb targets in that country constituted an escalation of the war, which was illegal in the absence of additional Congressional authorization. Judge Kaufman found that this was a political question which was non-justiciable, recognizing that the court was incapable of assessing the facts. He stated in part:

> Judges, deficient in military knowledge, lacking vital information upon which to assess the nature of battlefield decisions, and sitting thousands of miles from the field of action, cannot reasonably or appropriately determine whether a specific military operation constitutes an "escalation" of the war or is merely a new tactical approach within a continuing strategic plan. What if, for example, the war "de-escalates" so that it is waged as it was prior to the mining of North Vietnam's harbors, and then "escalates" again? Are the courts required to oversee the conduct of the war on a daily basis, away from the scene of action? In this instance, it was the President's view that the mining of North Vietnam's harbors was necessary to preserve the lives of American soldiers in South Vietnam and to bring the war to a close. History will tell whether or not that assessment was correct, but without the benefit of such extended hindsight we are powerless to know.

We fail to see how the present challenge involving the bombing in Cambodia is in any significant manner distinguishable from the situation discussed by Judge Kaufman in Da Costa v. Laird. Judge Judd found that the continuing bombing of Cambodia, after the removal of American forces and prisoners of war from Vietnam, represents "a basic change in the situation: which must be considered in determining the duration of prior Congressional authorization." He further found such action a tactical decision not traditionally confided to the Commander-in-Chief. These are precisely the questions of fact involving military and diplomatic expertise not vested in the judiciary, which make the issue political and thus beyond the competence of that court or this court to determine. We are not privy to the information supplied to the Executive by his professional military and diplomatic advisers and even if we were, we are hardly competent to evaluate it. If we were incompetent to judge the significance of the mining and bombing of North Vietnam's harbors and territories, we fail to see our competence to determine that the bombing of Cambodia is a "basic change" in the situation and that it is not a "tactical decision" within the competence of the President. It is true that we have repatriated American troops and have returned American ground forces in Vietnam but we have also negotiated a cease fire and have entered into the Paris Accords which mandated a cease fire in Cambodia and Laos. The President has announced that the bombing of Cambodia will terminate on August 15, 1973 and Secretary of State Rogers has submitted an affidavit to this court providing the justification for our military presence and action until that time. The situation fluctuates daily and we cannot ascertain at any fixed time either the military or diplomatic status. We are in no position to determine whether the Cambodian insurgents are patriots or whether in fact they are inspired and manned by North Vietnam Communists. While we as men may well agonize and bewail the horror of this or any war, the sharing of Presidential and Congressional responsibility particularly at this juncture is a bluntly political and not a judicial question.

. . .

The court below and our dissenting Brother assume that since American ground forces and prisoners have been removed and accounted for, Congressional authorization has ceased as determined by virtue of the so-called Mansfield Amendment, P.L. 92–156, 85 Stat. 430, § 601. The fallacy of this position is that we have no way of knowing whether the Cambodian bombing furthers or hinders the goals of the Mansfield Amendment. That is precisely the holding of Da Costa v. Laird, supra, 471 F.2d at 1157. Moreover although § 601 (a)(1) of the Amendment urges the President to remove all military forces contingent upon release of American prisoners, it also in § 601 (a)(2) urges him to negotiate for an immediate cease fire by all parties in the hostilities in *Indo-China.* (Emphasis added). In our view, the return and repatriation of American troops only represents the beginning and not the end of the inquiry as to whether such a basic change has occurred that the Executive at this stage is suddenly bereft of power and authority. That inquiry involves diplomatic and military intelligence which is totally absent in the record before us, and its digestion in any event is beyond judicial management. The strictures of the political question doctrine cannot be avoided by resort to the law of agency as the court did below, finding the Congress the principal and the President an agent or servant. Judicial *ipse dixits* cannot provide any proper basis particularly for the injunctive relief granted here which is unprecedented in American Jurisprudence.[18]

II

Since the argument that continuing Congressional approval was necessary, was predicated upon a determination that the Cambodian bombing constituted a basic change in the war not within the tactical discretion of the President and since that is a determination we have found to be a political question, we have not found it necessary to dwell at length upon Congressional participation. We see no need to address ourselves to the Fulbright provisos discussed in Judge Oakes' opinion since they predate the Paris Accord which places the military stance in Cambodia in such focus that we cannot judge their present efficacy or applicability. In any event we agree with his conclusion that they do not affect American forces which is the issue here. We cannot resist however commenting that the most recent expression of Congressional approval by appropriation, the Joint Resolution Continuing Appropriations for Fiscal 1974 (P.L. 93–52), enacted into law July 1, 1973, contains the following provision:

> Sec. 108. Notwithstanding any other provision of law, on or after August 15, 1973, no funds herein or heretofore appropriated may be obligated or expended to finance directly

18. To date no other federal court has attempted to halt American involvement in hostilities in Southeast Asia. Our own court as well as the First Circuit has concluded that the war-implementing legislation passed by Congress was sufficient authorization. [Citations omitted] Numerous courts have dismissed suits challenging American involvement on the ground that a "political question" was involved. [Citations omitted] Other suits challenging the legality of the war have been dismissed on other grounds. [Eds. The omitted citations involve holdings based principally upon plaintiff's lack of standing.]

or indirectly combat activities by United States military forces in or over or from off the shores of North Vietnam, South Vietnam, Laos or Cambodia.

Assuming arguendo that the military and diplomatic issues were manageable and that we were obliged to find some participation by Congress, we cannot see how this provision does not support the proposition that the Congress has approved the Cambodian bombing. The statute is facially clear but its applicability is contested by plaintiffs on several grounds which were essentially adopted by the court below. The argument is made that the Congress didn't really mean what it said because it was coerced by the President who had vetoed Congressional Bills which would have immediately cut off Cambodian funds. Not being able to muster sufficient strength to overcome the veto, the argument runs, the Congress was forced willy nilly to enact the appropriation legislation. Resort is made to the floor debate which it is argued bolsters the view that individual legislators expressed personal disapproval of the bombing and did not interpret the appropriation as an approval to bomb but simply a recognition that it gave the President the power to bomb. It is further urged that since the Constitution entrusts the power to declare war to a majority of the Congress, the veto exercised makes it possible for the President to thwart the will of Congress by holding one-third plus one of the members of either House. We find none of these arguments persuasive.

. . .

The judgment is reversed. . . .

[A dissenting opinion of JUDGE OAKES is omitted.]

QUESTIONS

(1) Recall the Note treating political questions, p. 132, supra. Do you agree with the courts that this doctrine was properly applicable to the cases appearing above? If so, what aspects of the doctrine, what justifications for its invocation, would you have stressed? If not, what more specific standards would you as a judge have been able to develop to determine the legality of the war? And if you believed the war to be unconstitutionally waged, what type of relief (injunctive or other) would you have ordered?

(2) "The extended controversy over the Vietnamese war reveals how 'lawless' an environment we live in when courts refuse to decide and leave decision to the political branches. Our constitutional problems of the allocation and separation of powers become no different from political disputes between nations that cannot find resolution in any supranational judicial tribunal. There were no effective legal constraints upon the Executive, and the quarrel became one of brute will and power between Congress and the President. There was no Rule of Law, but only a process of political bargaining and threats." State what qualifications, if any, you would make to these assertions. If you disagree with them, how would you respond to their proponent?

B. FOREIGN AFFAIRS AND FEDERALISM

In his opinion in the Curtiss-Wright case, p. 102, supra, Justice Sutherland described the historical process by which the federal government rather than the states acquired powers over foreign affairs. Whatever the accuracy of this description, it is clear that the Constitution vests in the federal government powers to deal with an impressive array of transnational problems. Recall the observations about the role of the states and the federal government in the international community in the excerpts from The Federalist that were quoted in Van der Schelling v. U. S. News & World Report, at p. 11, supra, and similar comments in Fong Yue Ting v. United States, at p. 23, supra. To some extent, the federal power is expressed through the constitutional provisions relating to treaties which Chapter V examines.

There has been little and generally ineffective challenge of the federal power to lay down rules binding the states on matters bearing upon foreign relations. The following materials do not examine the bases for the exercise of federal legislative power in this field, but rather the degree to which state law-making power is deemed to be curtailed or preempted by federal rules in the field, or by the authorization in the Constitution of a federal power, even if unexerted, to make rules.

Read Section 10 of Article I of the Constitution. And in connection with the following case, recall the discussion in Graham v. Richardson, p. 49, supra.

HINES v. DAVIDOWITZ

Supreme Court of the United States, 1941.
312 U.S. 52, 61 S.Ct. 399, 85 L.Ed. 581.

[The Court held that the federal Alien Registration Act of 1940, together with the immigration and naturalization laws, formed a comprehensive and integrated scheme for regulation of aliens and thus foreclosed enforcement of a Pennsylvania statute which required registration of aliens under a distinct state administrative program involving registration, identification cards and related matters. Excerpts from the opinion of the Court, delivered by MR. JUSTICE BLACK, appear below.]

. . . That the supremacy of the national power in the general field of foreign affairs, including power over immigration, naturalization and deportation, is made clear by the Constitution was pointed out by the authors of The Federalist in 1787, and has since been given continuous recognition by this Court. When the national government by treaty or statute has established rules and regulations touching the rights, privileges, obligations or burdens of aliens as such, the treaty or statute is the supreme law of the land. No state can add to or take from the force and effect of such treaty or statute. . . . The Federal Government, representing as it does the collective interests of the forty-eight states, is entrusted with full and exclusive responsibility for the conduct of affairs with foreign sovereignties. . . . Our system of government is such that the interest of the cities, counties and states, no less than the interest of the people of the whole nation, imperatively requires that federal power in the field affecting foreign relations be left entirely free from local interference. . . .

One of the most important and delicate of all international relationships, recognized immemorially as a responsibility of government, has to do with the protection of the just rights of a country's own nationals when those nationals are in another country. Experience has shown that international controversies of the gravest moment, sometimes even leading to war, may arise from real or imagined wrongs to another's subjects inflicted, or permitted, by a government. This country, like other nations, has entered into numerous treaties of amity and commerce since its inception—treaties entered into under express constitutional authority, and binding upon the states as well as the nation. Among those treaties have been many which not only promised and guaranteed broad rights and privileges to aliens sojourning in our own territory, but secured reciprocal promises and guarantees for our own citizens while in other lands. And apart from treaty obligations, there has grown up in the field of international relations a body of customs defining with more or less certainty the duties owing by all nations to alien residents—duties which our State Department has often successfully insisted foreign nations must recognize as to our nationals abroad. In general, both treaties and international practices have been aimed at preventing injurious discriminations against aliens. . . .

Legal imposition of distinct, unusual and extraordinary burdens and obligations upon aliens—such as subjecting them alone, though perfectly law-abiding, to indiscriminate and repeated interception and interrogation by public officials—thus bears an inseparable relationship to the welfare and tranquillity of all the states, and not merely to the welfare and tranquillity of one. Laws imposing such burdens are not mere census requirements, and even though they may be immediately associated with the accomplishment of a local purpose, they provoke questions in the field of international affairs. And specialized regulation of the conduct of an alien before naturalization is a matter which Congress must consider in discharging its constitutional duty "To establish an uniform Rule of Naturalization . . . ." . . . And where the federal government, in the exercise of its superior authority in this field, has enacted a complete scheme of regulation and has therein provided a standard for the registration of aliens, states cannot, inconsistently with the purpose of Congress, conflict or interfere with, curtail or complement, the federal law, or enforce additional or auxiliary regulations. There is not—and from the very nature of the problem there cannot be—any rigid formula or rule which can be used as a universal pattern to determine the meaning and purpose of every act of Congress. This Court, in considering the validity of state laws in the light of treaties or federal laws touching the same subject, has made use of the following expressions: conflicting; contrary to; occupying the field; repugnance; difference, irreconcilability; inconsistency; violation; curtailment; and interference. But none of these expressions provides an infallible constitutional test or an exclusive constitutional yardstick. In the final analysis, there can be no one crystal clear distinctly marked formula. Our primary function is to determine whether, under the circumstances of this particular case, Pennsylvania's law stands as an obstacle to the accomplishment and execution of the full purposes and objectives of Congress. And in that determination, it is of importance that this legislation is in a field which affects international relations, the one aspect of our government that from the first has been most generally conceded imperatively to demand broad national authority. Any concurrent state power that may exist is restricted to the narrowest of limits; the state's power here is not bottomed on the same broad base as is its power to tax. And it is also of importance that this legislation deals with the rights, liberties, and personal freedoms of human beings, and is in an entirely different category from state tax statutes or state pure food laws regulating the labels on cans.

Our conclusion is that appellee is correct in his contention that the power to restrict, limit, regulate, and register aliens as a distinct group is not an equal and continuously existing concurrent power of state and nation, but that whatever power a state may have is subordinate to supreme national law. We proceed therefore to an examination of Congressional enactments to ascertain whether or not Congress has acted in such manner that its action should preclude enforcement of Pennsylvania's law. . . .

We have already adverted to the conditions which make the treatment of aliens, in whatever state they may be located, a matter of national moment. And whether or not registration of aliens is of such a nature that the Constitution permits only of one uniform national system, it cannot be denied that the Congress might validly conclude that such uniformity is desirable. The legislative history of the Act indicates that Congress was trying to steer a middle path, realizing that any registration requirement was a departure from our traditional policy of not treating aliens as a thing apart, but also feeling that the Nation was in need of the type of information to be secured. Having the constitutional authority so to do, it has provided a standard for alien registration in a single integrated and all-embracing system in order to obtain the information deemed to be desirable in connection with aliens. When it made this addition to its uniform naturalization and immigration laws, it plainly manifested a purpose to do so in such a way as to protect the personal liberties of law-abiding aliens through one uniform national registration system, and to leave them free from the possibility of inquisitorial practices and police surveillance that might not only affect our international relations but might also generate the very disloyalty which the law has intended guarding against. Under these circumstances, the Pennsylvania Act cannot be enforced. . . .

[Dissenting opinion of JUSTICE STONE omitted.]

NOTE ON STATE "IRON CURTAIN" ACTS

Laws in effect in nearly half the states restrict the inheritance of property by residents of certain foreign countries. Prominent among these are the so-called "iron curtain acts." These statutes affect primarily Communist countries. They frequently require a finding on the part of the court, before distribution from an estate to a designated foreign beneficiary (used herein to refer to an heir, a legatee or devisee) will be authorized, that the beneficiary will receive the "benefit, use and control" of the distribution. Such statutes generally provide either for withholding and safekeeping of the affected property, until it can be distributed, or for outright surrender of the property to the state by the potential takers.[19]

19. Another related group of laws, referred to as "reciprocity" statutes, restrict inheritance of property by a resident of a given foreign country if

Section 2218 of the New York Surrogate's Court Procedure Act is a typical "benefit" withholding statute. It provides:

> 1. (a) Where it shall appear that an alien legatee, distributee or beneficiary is domiciled or resident within a country to which checks or warrants drawn against funds of the United States may not be transmitted by reason of any executive order, regulation or similar determination of the United States government or any department or agency thereof, the court shall direct that the money or property to which such alien would otherwise be entitled shall be paid into court for the benefit of said alien or the person or persons who thereafter may appear to be entitled thereto. The money or property so paid into court shall be paid out only upon order of the surrogate or pursuant to the order or judgment of a court of competent jurisdiction.
>
> (b) Any assignment of a fund which is required to be deposited pursuant to the provisions of paragraph one (a) of this section shall not be effective to confer upon the assignee any greater right to the delivery of the fund than the assignor would otherwise enjoy.
>
> 2. Where it shall appear that a beneficiary would not have the benefit or use or control of the money or other property due him or where other special circumstances make it desirable that such payment should be withheld the decree may direct that such money or property be paid into court for the benefit of the beneficiary or the person or persons who may thereafter appear entitled thereto. The money or property so paid into court shall be paid out only upon order of the court or pursuant to the order or judgment of a court of competent jurisdiction.
>
> 3. In any such proceeding where it is uncertain that an alien beneficiary or fiduciary not residing within the United States, the District of Columbia, the Commonwealth of Puerto Rico or a territory or possession of the United States would have the benefit or use or control of the money or property due him the burden of proving that the alien beneficiary will receive the benefit or use or control of the money or property due him shall be upon him or the person claiming from, through or under him.

Section 103(8) of the Act defines "beneficiary" as "any person entitled to any part or all of the estate of a decedent under a will or in intestacy." The predecessor statute of Section 2218 was originally enacted in 1939 with the stated purpose of preventing inheritances to residents of Germany from being misappropriated by the Nazi authorities.

As the opinions in the state courts applying the "iron curtain" acts often reveal, these statutes have a political foundation which vividly distinguishes them from the usual state laws governing the disposition of a decedent's estate. And as the language with which some courts have embellished their opinions suggests, this field can

an American heir would not be able to receive the benefits of an inheritance from a resident of that nation. Reciprocity statutes raise further issues considered in Part D of Chapter V.

have troubling aspects from the point of view of this country's foreign relations. Note the following example from the opinion of a state court holding applicable an "iron curtain" statute, In re Belemecich's Estate, 411 Pa. 506, 192 A.2d 740 (1963), rev'd (on the ground that a treaty controlled), 375 U.S. 395, 84 S.Ct. 452, 11 L.Ed.2d 411 (1964):

> This Act carries the sobriquet of "Iron Curtain Act" because its purpose is to protect the moneys, physically in America, but belonging to people who fatefully find themselves behind the Iron Curtain of Communism. It is a commendable and salutary piece of legislation because it provides for the safekeeping of these funds even with accruing interest, in the steel-bound vaults of the Commonwealth of Pennsylvania until such time as the Iron Curtain lifts or sufficiently cracks to allow honest money to pass through and be honestly delivered to the persons entitled to them. Otherwise, wages and other monetary rewards faithfully earned under a free enterprise democratic system could be used by Communist forces which are committed to the very destruction of that free enterprising world of democracy.
>
> The Consul General of Yugo Slavia, Drago Novak, who appeared at the hearing before the Orphans' Court as an attorney-in-fact for the named heirs of Anton Belemecich, excepted to the findings of the Court. . . .
>
> . . . The Yugo Slavian consul appealed, contending that the Orphans' Court erred in concluding that the heirs of Anton Belemecich would not have the actual benefit, use, enjoyment and control of the money due them from the estate in question. . . .
>
> To argue that Yugo Slavia is not behind the Iron Curtain is to argue that it is not on the eastern side of the Atlantic Ocean. There are certain well-known, indisputable geographical and historical facts which require no substantive proof in Court, and one of those irrefutable, if unfortunate, realities, is that Yugo Slavia, as the Court below found, is a satellite state where the residents have no individualistic control over their destiny, fate or pocketbooks, and where their politico-economic horizon is raised or lowered according to the will, wish or whim of a self-made dictator.
>
> President Judge Roberts of the Orphans' Court of Erie County, now Justice Roberts, said in the case of Dopierala Estate, 7 Fid.Rep. 262, 263:
>
> "It is notorious and regrettable that the unfortunate people of Poland and other residents enslaved behind 'Iron Curtain' dictatorship are denied basic human and property rights. Common knowledge and experience indicate that funds transmitted to residents, subject to police state absolutism, rarely reach the intended individual. More frequently the funds are wholly or partially confiscated by unfair rates of exchange or by other direct or indirect police state pressures or devices exerted against the intended recipient or his family, either by the government itself or by its unscrupulous officials or functionaries. *Of these deplorable facts we take judicial notice,* and upon careful consideration of all the attending circumstances, as they now appear, we find that if distribution to this beneficiary were made, she would not

have 'the actual benefit, use, enjoyment or control' of her inheritance." . . .

All the known facts of a Sovietized state lead to the irresistible conclusion that sending American money to a person within the borders of an Iron Curtain country is like sending a basket of food to Little Red Ridinghood in care of her "grandmother." It could be that the greedy, gluttonous grasp of the government collector in Yugo Slavia does not clutch as rapaciously as his brother confiscators in Russia, but it is abundantly clear that there is no assurance upon which an American court can depend that a named Yugo Slavian individual beneficiary of American dollars will have anything left to shelter, clothe and feed himself once he has paid financial involuntary tribute to the tyranny of a totalitarian regime. . . .

Drago Novak, the Yugo Slavian Consul General already mentioned, asserted gravely in court that the flag of freedom had never been furled in Yugo Slavia and that there are no restrictions on private ownership or means of production in that country. . . .

The Judge, who heard and saw Drago Novak, obviously placed very little credence in what he said. . . .

These statutes have been challenged in the courts on a number of grounds. The following federal regulations indicate the principal federal controls that may have some bearing upon this problem.

(1) Foreign Assets Control Regulations, 31 C.F.R. Part 500 (1973), under the Trading with the Enemy Act, p. 42, supra, administered by the Treasury Department. These regulations prohibit most merchandise and financial transactions, except as permitted by more specific regulations or by general or specific licenses, with Communist China, North Vietnam, North Korea, and persons in those countries. Similar regulations, 31 C.F.R. Parts 515 and 530 (1973), are directed at Cuba and Southern Rhodesia.

(2) A Treasury Circular, 31 C.F.R. Part 211 (1973), issued under 54 Stat. 1086 (1940), 31 U.S.C.A. § 123. These provisions authorize the Secretary of the Treasury to withhold government checks destined to payees who, because of conditions in the countries where they reside, would not be likely to receive them or be able to "negotiate [them] for full value". They referred as of a recent date to Albania, Communist China, Cuba, East Germany, North Korea and North Vietnam, as areas where there was no reasonable likelihood that the payees would receive the checks or be able to negotiate them for full value.

ZSCHERNIG v. MILLER

Supreme Court of the United States, 1968.
389 U.S. 429, 88 S.Ct. 664, 19 L.Ed.2d 683.

MR. JUSTICE DOUGLAS delivered the opinion of the Court.

This case concerns the disposition of the estate of a resident of Oregon who died there intestate in 1962. Appellants are decedent's sole heirs and they are residents of East Germany. Appellees include members of the State Land Board that petitioned the Oregon probate court for the escheat of the net proceeds of the estate under the provisions of Ore.Rev.Stat. § 111.070 (1965), which provides for escheat in cases where a nonresident alien claims real or personal property unless three requirements are satisfied:

(1) the existence of a reciprocal right of a United States citizen to take property on the same terms as a citizen or inhabitant of the foreign county;

(2) the right of United States citizens to receive payment here of funds from estates in the foreign country; and

(3) the right of the foreign heirs to receive the "benefit, use or control of" the proceeds of Oregon estates "without confiscation."

The Oregon Supreme Court held that the appellants could take the Oregon realty involved in the present case by reason of Article IV of the 1923 Treaty with Germany (44 Stat. 2132, 2135) but that by reason of the same Article, as construed in Clark v. Allen, 331 U.S. 503, 67 S.Ct. 1431, 91 L.Ed. 1633, they could not take the personalty. 243 Or. 567, 412 P.2d 781; 243 Or. 592, 415 P.2d 15. We noted probable jurisdiction. 386 U.S. 1030 . . . .

. . . [W]e conclude that the history and operation of this Oregon statute make clear that § 111.070 is an intrusion by the State into the field of foreign affairs which the Constitution entrusts to the President and the Congress. See Hines v. Davidowitz, 312 U.S. 52, 63, 61 S.Ct. 399, 402, 85 L.Ed. 581.

As already noted one of the conditions of inheritance under the Oregon statute requires "proof that such foreign heirs, distributees, devisees or legatees may receive the benefit, use or control of money or property from estates of persons dying in this state without confiscation, in whole or in part, by the governments of such foreign countries," the burden being on the nonresident alien to establish that fact.

This provision came into Oregon's law in 1951. Prior to that time the rights of aliens under the Oregon statute were defined in general terms of reciprocity, similar to the California Act which we had before us in Clark v. Allen, 331 U.S., at 506, 67 S.Ct., at 1433 n. 1.

We held in Clark v. Allen that a general reciprocity clause did not on its face intrude on the federal domain.[20] 331 U.S. 516–517, 67 S. Ct. 1438–1439. We noted that the California statute, then a recent enactment, would have only "some incidental or indirect effect in foreign countries." Id., at 517, 67 S.Ct., at 1439.[21]

20. [Eds.] Reciprocity clauses and the decision in Clark v. Allen are considered at pp. 626 and 632, infra. Read now the brief excerpt at p. 632 from Justice Douglas' opinion for the Court in that case.

21. . . . [W]hen [Clark v. Allen] reached this Court, petitioner contended that the statute was invalid not because of the legislature's motive, but because on its face the statute constituted "an invasion of the ex-

Had that case appeared in the posture of the present one, a different result would have obtained. We were there concerned with the words of a statute on its face, not the manner of its application. State courts, of course, must frequently read, construe, and apply laws of foreign nations. It has never been seriously suggested that state courts are precluded from performing that function, although there is a possibility, albeit remote, that any holding may disturb a foreign nation—whether the matter involves commercial cases, tort cases, or some other type of controversy. At the time Clark v. Allen was decided, the case seemed to involve no more than a routine reading of foreign laws. It now appears that in this reciprocity area under inheritance statutes, the probate courts of various States have launched inquiries into the type of governments that obtain in a particular foreign nation—whether aliens under their law have enforceable rights, whether the so-called "rights" are merely dispensations turning upon the whim or caprice of government officials, whether the representation of consuls, ambassadors, and other representatives of foreign nations are credible or made in good faith, whether there is in the actual administration in the particular foreign system of law any element of confiscation. . . .

In its brief *amicus curiae*, the Department of Justice states that: "The government does not . . . contend that the application of the Oregon escheat statute in the circumstances of this case unduly interferes with the United States' conduct of foreign relations."

The Government's acquiescence in the ruling of Clark v. Allen certainly does not justify extending the principle of that case, as we would be required to do here to uphold the Oregon statute as applied; for it has more than "some incidental or indirect effect in foreign countries," and its great potential for disruption or embarrassment makes us hesitate to place it in the category of a diplomatic bagatelle.

As we read the decisions that followed in the wake of Clark v. Allen, we find that they radiate some of the attitudes of the "cold war," where the search is for the "democracy quotient" of a foreign regime as opposed to the Marxist theory. The Oregon statute introduces the concept of "confiscation," which is of course opposed to the Just Compensation Clause of the Fifth Amendment. And this has led into minute inquiries concerning the actual administration of foreign law, [and] into the credibility of foreign diplomatic statements . . . .

That kind of state involvement in foreign affairs and international developments—matters which the Constitution entrusts solely to the Federal Government—is not sanctioned by Clark v. Allen. Yet such forbidden state activity has infected each of the three provisions of § 111.070, as applied by Oregon.

[The Court's discussion of the Oregon cases construing the "benefit, use or control" provision of the statute, Subsection (1)(c), has been omitted. The Court noted that one such case had prompted the Government of Bulgaria to register a complaint with the State Department, described as follows in a letter from the Department to the

clusively Federal field of control over our foreign relations." In discussing how the statute was applied, petitioner noted that California courts had accepted as conclusive proof of reciprocity the statement of a foreign ambassador that reciprocal rights existed in his nation. Brief for petitioner in Clark v. Allen, No. 626, October Term 1946, pp. 73–74. Thus we had no reason to suspect that the California statute in Clark v. Allen was to be applied as anything other than a general reciprocity provision requiring just matching of laws. . . .

Oregon trial court: "The Government of Bulgaria has raised with this Government the matter of difficulties reportedly being encountered by Bulgarian citizens resident in Bulgaria in obtaining the transfer to them of property or funds from estates probated in this country, some under the jurisdiction of the State of Oregon . . . ."]

As one reads the Oregon decisions, it seems that foreign policy attitudes, the freezing or thawing of the "cold war" and the like are the real desiderata.[22] Yet they of course are matters for the Federal Government, not for local probate courts.

This is as true of (1)(a) of § 111.070 as it is of (1)(b) and (1)(c).

[Discussion of Oregon cases construing subsection 1(a) omitted.]

In short, it would seem that Oregon judges in construing § 111.070 seek to ascertain whether "rights" protected by foreign law are the same "rights" that citizens of Oregon enjoy. If . . . the alleged foreign "right" may be vindicated only through Communist-controlled state agencies, then there is no "right" of the type § 111.070 requires. The same seems to be true if enforcement may require approval of a Fascist dictator . . . . The statute as construed seems to make unavoidable judicial criticism of nations established on a more authoritarian basis than our own.

It seems inescapable that the type of probate law that Oregon enforces affects international relations in a persistent and subtle way. The practice of state courts in withholding remittances to legatees residing in Communist countries or in preventing them from assigning them is notorious. The several States, of course, have traditionally regulated the descent and distribution of estates. But those regulations must give way if they impair the effective exercise of the Nation's foreign policy. . . . Where those laws conflict with a treaty, they must bow to the superior federal policy. See Kolovrat v. Oregon, 366 U.S. 187, 81 S.Ct. 922. Yet, even in absence of a treaty, a State's policy may disturb foreign relations. As we stated in Hines v. Davidowitz, supra, 312 U.S., at 64, 61 S.Ct., at 402, "Experience has shown that international controversies of the gravest moment, sometimes even leading to war, may arise from real or imagined wrongs to another's subjects inflicted, or permitted, by a government." Certainly a State could not deny admission to a traveler from East Germany nor bar its citizens from going there. Passenger Cases, 7 How. 283, 12 L.Ed. 702; cf. Crandall v. State of Nevada, 6 Wall. 35, 18 L.Ed. 744; Kent v. Dulles, 357 U.S. 116, 78 S.Ct. 1113, 2 L.Ed.2d 1204. If there are to be such restraints, they must be provided by the Federal Government. The present Oregon law is not as gross an intrusion in the federal domain as those others might be. Yet, as we have said, it has a direct impact upon foreign relations and may well adversely affect the power of the central government to deal with those problems.

The Oregon law does, indeed, illustrate the dangers which are involved if each State, speaking through its probate courts, is permitted to establish its own foreign policy.

Reversed.

22. Such attitudes are not confined to the Oregon courts. [Eds.—The Court quoted from opinions of a number of state courts, including Belemecich's Estate, p. 164, supra.]

[JUSTICE STEWART, joined by JUSTICE BRENNAN, concurred. He found that "all three of the statutory requirements on their face are contrary to the Constitution." His opinion stated:]

The Solicitor General, as *amicus curiae*, says that the Government does not "contend that the application of the Oregon escheat statute in the circumstances of this case unduly interferes with the United States' conduct of foreign relations." But that is not the point. We deal here with the basic allocation of power between the States and the Nation. Resolution of so fundamental a constitutional issue cannot vary from day to day with the shifting winds at the State Department. Today, we are told, Oregon's statute does not conflict with the national interest. Tomorrow it may. But, however that may be, the fact remains that the conduct of our foreign affairs is entrusted under the Constitution to the National Government, not to the probate courts of the several States. To the extent that Clark v. Allen, 331 U.S. 503, 67 S.Ct. 1431, 91 L.Ed. 1633, is inconsistent with these views, I would overrule that decision.

[JUSTICE HARLAN concurred because he believed (1) that rather than resolve the major constitutional issue of preemption, the Court should have decided whether the 1923 treaty with Germany prevented application of the Oregon statute, (2) that "correctly construed" the treaty had such effect, and (3) that the constitutional ground relied upon by the majority was "untenable." As to the last he said:]

It seems to me impossible to distinguish the present case from Clark v. Allen in this respect in any convincing way. To say that the additional conditions imposed by the Oregon statute amount to such distinctions would be to suggest that while a State may legitimately place inheritance by aliens on a reciprocity basis, it may not take measures to assure that reciprocity exists in practice and that the inheritance will actually be enjoyed by the person whom the testator intended to benefit. The years since the *Clark* decision have revealed some instances in which state court judges have delivered intemperate or ill-advised remarks about foreign governments in the course of applying such statutes, but nothing has occurred which could not readily have been foreseen at the time Clark v. Allen was decided.

Nor do I believe that this aspect of the Clark v. Allen decision should be overruled, as my Brother STEWART would have it. Prior decisions have established that in the absence of a conflicting federal policy or violation of the express mandates of the Constitution the States may legislate in areas of their traditional competence even though their statutes may have an incidental effect on foreign relations.[23] Application of this rule to the case before us compels the conclusion that the Oregon statute is constitutional. Oregon has so legislated in the course of regulating the descent and distribution of estates of Oregon decedents, a matter traditionally within the power of a State. . . . Apart from the 1923 treaty, which the Court finds it unnecessary to consider, there is no specific interest of the Federal Government which might be interfered with by this statute. The appellants concede that Oregon might deny inheritance rights to all nonresident aliens.[24] Assuming that this is so, the statutory ex-

23. See, e. g., State of Ohio ex rel. Clarke v. Deckebach, 274 U.S. 392, 47 S.Ct. 630, 71 L.Ed. 1115; . . . Terrace v. Thompson, 263 U.S. 197, 44 S.Ct. 15, 68 L.Ed. 255; Heim v. McCall, 239 U.S. 175, 36 S.Ct. 78, 60 L.Ed. 206.

24. Brief for Appellants, p. 13. Thus, this case does not present the question whether a uniform denial of rights to nonresident aliens might be a denial of equal protection forbidden by the Fourteenth Amendment. Cf. Blake v. McClung, 172 U.S. 239, 260–261, 19 S.Ct. 165, 173, 43 L.Ed. 432.

ception permitting inheritance by aliens whose countries permit Americans to inherit would seem to be a measure wisely designed to avoid any offense to foreign governments and thus any conflict with general federal interests: a foreign government can hardly object to the denial of rights which it does not itself accord to the citizens of other countries.

The foregoing would seem to establish that the Oregon statute is not unconstitutional on its face. And in fact the Court seems to have found the statute unconstitutional only as applied. Its notion appears to be that application of the parts of the statute which require that reciprocity actually exist and that the alien heir actually be able to enjoy his inheritance will inevitably involve the state courts in evaluations of foreign laws and governmental policies, and that this is likely to result in offense to foreign governments. There are several defects in this rationale. The most glaring is that it is based almost entirely on speculation. My Brother DOUGLAS does cite a few unfortunate remarks made by state court judges in applying statutes resembling the one before us. However, the Court does not mention, nor does the record reveal, any instance in which such an occurrence has been the occasion for a diplomatic protest, or, indeed, has had any foreign relations consequence whatsoever. The United States says in its brief as *amicus curiae* that it

> does not . . . contend that the operation of the Oregon escheat statute in the circumstances of this case unduly interferes with the United States' conduct of foreign relations.

At an earlier stage in this case, the Solicitor General told this Court:

> The Department of State has advised us . . . that State reciprocity laws, including that of Oregon, have had little effect on the foreign relations and policy of this country . . .. Appellants' apprehension of a deterioration in international relations, unsubstantiated by experience, does not constitute the kind of 'changed conditions' which might call for a re-examination of Clark v. Allen.

Essentially, the Court's basis for decision appears to be that alien inheritance laws afford state court judges an opportunity to criticize in dictum the policies of foreign governments, and that these dicta may adversely affect our foreign relations. In addition to finding no evidence of adverse effect in the record, I believe this rationale to be untenable because logically it would apply to many other types of litigation which come before the state courts. It is true that, in addition to the many state court judges who have applied alien inheritance statutes with proper judicial decorum, some judges have seized the opportunity to make derogatory remarks about foreign governments. However, judges have been known to utter dicta critical of foreign governmental policies even in purely domestic cases, so that the mere possibility of offensive utterances can hardly be the test.

If the flaw in the statute is said to be that it requires state courts to inquire into the administration of foreign law, I would suggest that that characteristic is shared by other legal rules which I cannot believe the Court wishes to invalidate. For example, the Uniform Foreign Money-Judgments Recognition Act provides that a foreign-country money judgment shall not be recognized if "it was rendered under a system which does not provide impartial tribunals or procedures compatible with the requirements of due process of law." [25] When there is a dispute as to the content of foreign law, the court is required under the common law to treat the question as one of fact and to consider any evidence presented as to the actual administration of the foreign legal system. And in the field of choice of law there is a nonstatutory rule that the tort law of a foreign country will not be applied if that country is shown to be "uncivilized." Surely, all of these rules possess the same "defect" as the statute now before us. Yet I assume that the Court would not find them unconstitutional.

[Dissenting opinion of JUSTICE WHITE omitted.]

QUESTIONS

(1) "The upshot of Zschernig is that a state may enact an iron curtain statute but not an effective one. The reasoning of the opinion would appear to sustain a statute prohibiting inheritance by alien domiciliaries of countries whose laws *on their face* deny benefit, use and control or deny reciprocity." Comment.

(2) "Zschernig reaffirms Clark v. Allen while striking down 'benefit' statutes raising similar problems but far more justified from the perspective of state law's traditional functions. The opinion should have done just the reverse." Comment.

(3) From the perspective of a probate court judge in Orefornia, one of the 50 States, how would you resolve the following cases and what inquiries as to foreign laws or facts would you make? In each case assume that T dies domiciled in Orefornia and that B is a resident of Bukovina, a Communist country.

> (*a*) A will states that T's property shall go to his cousin B, but if B may not have full use or enjoyment of the property, it shall go to C, a citizen of the United States.
>
> (*b*) T dies intestate. Under Orefornia law T's property would normally go to his niece X and nephew B. However, a statute provides that any member of a class entitled to take by intestacy shall be excluded if it appears that he will not be able to have full use or enjoyment of such property.
>
> (*c*) T leaves his property in trust to X who is to pay the income thereon annually for the education and support of B "to the extent and in the amount which he deems useful," the rest to go to a specified charity. X, believing that no payments to B will effectively reach him, petitions for instructions.

(4) The Oregon statute provided for escheat, whereas most "iron curtain" statutes—such as the New York act quoted at p. 163, supra—require payment of the proceeds of the estate into a fund held until further order of the court. Should this distinction have been considered relevant to a decision on the constitutionality of "iron curtain" statutes?

(5) You are the legislative assistant to an influential Senator who is dismayed by the Zschernig decision. He asks you for a memorandum outlining what Congress can do to fill the gap in regulation created by the decision.

25. [Eds.—The Act is considered at p. 794, infra.]

(6) Could the federal regulations described at p. 165, supra, have been drawn upon to support a constitutional challenge? Would an argument based upon them have led to different conclusions (a) if the alien resided in East Germany *or* Poland, (b) if in the first case East Germany had been placed on the Treasury Circular List during the litigation, or (c) if in the second case Poland had been struck from that list at the same time?

COMMENT

A number of the federal and state post-Zschernig decisions attempting to puzzle out the implications of that case are collected in Comment, The Demise of the "Iron Curtain" Statute, 18 Vill.L.Rev. 49 (1972). Several of those decisions, in upholding state "iron curtain" statutes, have stressed the observation in Justice Harlan's concurrence that the Oregon statute was "not unconstitutional on its face" but was found to be "unconstitutional only as applied". In upholding, while limiting, several state statutes, the courts have thus required probate judges to be satisfied that the plaintiff has met his burden of proof to show reciprocity through a "routine reading" of foreign law, rather than to engage in analysis of the practical administration of that law. Such courts have stressed the absence of the types of remarks or conduct on the part of probate judges referred to in Zschernig, and some have distinguished Zschernig on grounds that the state statute in question did not involve escheat and did not demand a formal finding of reciprocity, but simply an affirmative finding as to "benefit and use". The statutes which have been found unconstitutional under the criteria set forth in Zschernig have been viewed, for example, as requiring the court's consideration of local circumstances in the operation of the foreign statute.

NOTE ON FOREIGN RELATIONS AND FEDERAL COMMON LAW

The "iron curtain" statutes and cases posed the question whether state law was compatible with a paramount and frequently exclusive federal control over foreign relations. The decision in Zschernig invalidating the state law (at least as applied) is the more significant in that no federal constitutional provision explicitly resolved the issue, and neither the federal legislative nor treaty power had been exercised with respect to the distribution of estates to nonresident aliens. At most, there were federal regulations serving different purposes by controlling the export of merchandise or funds.

This Note introduces a distinct but related question. Does the federal judiciary have the power to develop rules to resolve certain problems affecting foreign relations, rules which would be binding upon the states, in the absence of explicit constitutional grants to the judiciary of such a lawmaking power, and of relevant international agreements or federal legislation which the federal courts could "interpret"? Here too basic issues of federal-state regulations are raised, issues which recur in Chapter VII in the context of the enforcement by federal or state courts of foreign-country judicial judgments.

The holding in Erie R. Co. v. Tompkins, 304 U.S. 64, 58 S.Ct. 817, 82 L.Ed. 1188 (1938), that the federal court exercising diversity jurisdiction must follow state substantive law, was accompanied by the broad statement in the opinion that "there is no federal general common law". Nonetheless, in the succeeding decades the federal courts gave content and application to precisely such a law, in a number of relatively specialized fields.[26] Even preceding Erie, the federal courts had developed rules of decision, without statutory foundation, in maritime law and in the resolution of controversies between states. In both instances, the judicial power to develop such rules was derived from the jurisdictional grants under Article III relating to the two categories of cases. Since Erie, those categories expanded to include other instances of judicial lawmaking that could not be understood as simply another manifestation of the inevitable "lawmaking function" of the courts through their interrelated application and interpretation of the Constitution, of federal statutes or implementing regulations, or of international agreements. These new areas have principally involved the judicial development of rules in fields strongly affected by federal legislation or regulations, rules frequently involving the activities of federal agencies or the proprietary interests of the United States.

The question here posed is whether, in the field of foreign relations, there are as persuasive reasons for a federal common law, even if such law cannot be linked to specific constitutional provisions or to particular statutes, regulations or treaties. Consider from this perspective a decision of the Supreme Court to which we return in Chapter VI, Banco Nacional de Cuba v. Sabbatino, 376 U.S. 398, 84 S.Ct. 923, 11 L.Ed.2d 804 (1964). Property located in Cuba and indirectly owned by United States citizens was expropriated without compensation by the Cuban government, and the proceeds of the sale by a Cuban agency of that expropriated property were later brought into the United States. The former owners of the property obtained the proceeds and defended a conversion action brought by the Cuban agency on the ground that the expropriation was invalid under international law because of the absence of compensation and hence should be denied effect by United States courts. The case thus concerned what has come to be known as the "act of state doctrine," which traditionally precluded courts from inquiring into the validity of public acts of a foreign sovereign committed within its own territory. The Supreme Court decided that the act of state doctrine was applicable, and thus prevented federal courts from questioning the validity under international law of the Cuban taking, which should be treated as presumptively valid.

The action was brought by the Cuban agency in a federal district court in New York, whose jurisdiction was based on diversity of citizenship. The following excerpts from the opinion of the Su-

26. Illustrative cases are set forth in Hart and Wechsler's, The Federal Court and the Federal System (Bator, Mishkin, Shapiro, and Wechsler, 2d ed. 1973), pp. 756–832.

preme Court, delivered by JUSTICE HARLAN, consider whether the answer to the question posed above (whether the act of state doctrine, which would preclude judicial review of the validity of the expropriation, should apply) was to be governed by federal or state law (376 U.S. at 423, 84 S.Ct. at 938, 11 L.Ed.2d at 821).

> The act of state doctrine does, however, have "constitutional" underpinnings. It arises out of the basic relationships between branches of government in a system of separation of powers. It concerns the competency of dissimilar institutions to make and implement particular kinds of decisions in the area of international relations. The doctrine as formulated in past decisions expresses the strong sense of the Judicial Branch that its engagement in the task of passing on the validity of foreign acts of state may hinder rather than further this country's pursuit of goals both for itself and for the community of nations as a whole in the international sphere. Many commentators disagree with this view; they have striven by means of distinguishing and limiting past decisions and by advancing various considerations of policy to stimulate a narrowing of the apparent scope of the rule. Whatever considerations are thought to predominate, it is plain that the problems involved are uniquely federal in nature. If federal authority, in this instance this Court, orders the field of judicial competence in this area for the federal courts, and the state courts are left free to formulate their own rules, the purposes behind the doctrine could be as effectively undermined as if there had been no federal pronouncement on the subject.
>
> We could perhaps in this diversity action avoid the question of deciding whether federal or state law is applicable to this aspect of the litigation. New York has enunciated the act of state doctrine in terms that echo those of federal decisions decided during the reign of Swift v. Tyson, 16 Pet. 1, 10 L.Ed. 865. . . .
>
> However, we are constrained to make it clear that an issue concerned with a basic choice regarding the competence and function of the Judiciary and the National Executive in ordering our relationships with other members of the international community must be treated exclusively as an aspect of federal law.[27] It seems fair to assume that the Court did not have rules like the act of state doctrine in mind when it decided Erie R. Co. v. Tompkins. Soon thereafter, Professor Philip C. Jessup, now a judge of the International Court of Justice, recognized the potential dangers were Erie extended to legal problems affecting international relations. He cautioned that rules of international law should not be left to divergent and perhaps parochial state interpretations. His basic rationale is equally applicable to the act of state doctrine.
>
> The Court in the pre-Erie act of state cases, although not burdened by the problem of the source of applicable law, used language sufficiently strong and broad-sweeping to

27. At least this is true when the Court limits the scope of judicial inquiry. We need not now consider whether a state court might, in certain circumstances, adhere to a more restrictive view concerning the scope of examination of foreign acts than that required by this Court.

suggest that state courts were not left free to develop their own doctrines (as they would have been had this Court merely been interpreting common law under Swift v. Tyson, supra). . . . We are not without other precedent for a determination that federal law governs; there are enclaves of federal judge-made law which bind the States. A national body of federal-court-built law has been held to have been contemplated by § 301 of the Labor Management Relations Act, Textile Workers Union of America v. Lincoln Mills, 353 U.S. 448, 77 S.Ct. 912, 1 L.Ed.2d 972. Principles formulated by federal judicial law have been thought by this Court to be necessary to protect uniquely federal interests, D'Oench, Duhme & Co. v. Federal Deposit Ins. Corp., 315 U.S. 447, 62 S.Ct. 676, 86 L.Ed. 956; Clearfield Trust Co. v. United States, 318 U.S. 363, 63 S.Ct. 573, 87 L.Ed. 838. Of course the federal interest guarded in all these cases is one the ultimate statement of which is derived from a federal statute. Perhaps more directly in point are the bodies of law applied between States over boundaries and in regard to the apportionment of interstate waters.

In Hinderlider v. La Plata River Co., 304 U.S. 92, 110, 58 S.Ct. 803, 811, 82 L.Ed. 1202, in an opinion handed down the same day as Erie and by the same author, Mr. Justice Brandeis, the Court declared, "For whether the water of an interstate stream must be apportioned between the two States is a question of 'federal common law' upon which neither the statutes nor the decisions of either State can be conclusive." Although the suit was between two private litigants and the relevant States could not be made parties, the Court considered itself free to determine the effect of an interstate compact regulating water apportionment. The decision implies that no State can undermine the federal interest in equitably apportioned interstate waters even if it deals with private parties. This would not mean that, absent a compact, the apportionment scheme could not be changed judicially or by Congress, but only that apportionment is a matter of federal law. Cf. State of Arizona v. State of California, 373 U.S. 546, 597–598, 83 S.Ct. 1468, 1496, 10 L.Ed. 2d 542. The problems surrounding the act of state doctrine are, albeit for different reasons, as intrinsically federal as are those involved in water apportionment or boundary disputes. The considerations supporting exclusion of state authority here are much like those which led the Court in United States v. California, 332 U.S. 19, 67 S.Ct. 1658, 91 L. Ed. 1889, to hold that the Federal Government possessed paramount rights in submerged lands though within the three-mile limit of coastal States. We conclude that the scope of the act of state doctrine must be determined according to federal law.[28]

QUESTIONS

(1) Assume that the holding in Sabbatino that the act of state doctrine was applicable is not in any matter qualified by later federal leg-

28. Various constitutional and statutory provisions indirectly support this determination, see U.S.Const., Art. I, § 8, cls. 3, 10; Art. II, §§ 2, 3; Art. III, § 2; 28 U.S.C.A. §§ 1251(a)(2), (b)(1), (b)(3), 1332(a)(2), 1333, 1350, 1351, by reflecting a concern for uniformity in this country's dealings with foreign nations and indicating a desire to give matters of international significance to the jurisdiction of federal institutions. . . .

islation or treaties. A case arises in a state court in which a United States company seeks the value of property expropriated without compensation within a foreign country by a foreign government and sold by that government to the vendee-defendant in the United States. The question posed is whether the state court should apply the act of state doctrine. The court refuses to, and concludes that the foreign taking is in violation of international law and should be denied effect. The court further concludes that the vendee never received good title to the confiscated (stolen) goods and hence must pay their value to the former (and present) plaintiff-owner. The decision is affirmed by the state's highest court. As counsel for defendant, on what provision of 28 U.S.C.A. would you rely in seeking review in the United States Supreme Court, and if that Court reviewed the decision, how would you develop your argument that the state decision should be reversed?

(2) "The holding in Sabbatino is simply an application and working out, in a distinct but related setting, of those same principles which underlay the Court's decision in Hines v. Davidowitz." Comment.

Additional reading: Hart and Wechsler's, The Federal Court and the Federal System (Bator, Mishkin, Shapiro, and Wechsler, 2d Ed. 1973) pp. 756–832; Comment, Federal Common Law and Article III: A Jurisdictional Approach to Erie, 74 Yale L.J. 325 (1964); Note, The Federal Common Law, 82 Harv.L.Rev. 1512 (1969); and Maier, The Bases and Range of Federal Common Law in Private International Matters, 5 Vand. J.Transnational L. 133 (1971).

PROBLEM

The Public Works Agency (PWA) of the state of Ames seeks competitive bids for the supply of steel for a pending construction project, pursuant to an Ames law requiring that supply contracts in such situations be awarded to the lowest *bona fide* bidder. The bid submitted by X firm is the lowest; the steel that it will provide if it is awarded the contract will be of Japanese manufacture. The lowest bid involving steel manufactured in the United States was submitted by Y firm. The PWA announces that the contract will be awarded to Y, on the basis of another Ames statute, the Ames Buy American Act, requiring contracts related to the construction of public works to be awarded to firms agreeing to supply materials manufactured in the United States.

You are counsel to X, which consults you to determine if there are grounds for challenging the PWA's decision, and if so, what judicial remedies could be pursued. You may assume that there are no relevant international agreements, and that if an action is brought, it would be before an Ames court. What advice would you give?[29]

29. Cf. Bethlehem Steel Corp. v. Board of Commissioners of Department of Water and Power of the City of Los Angeles, 276 Cal.App.2d 221, 80 Cal. Rptr. 800 (1969).

Part Two

INTERNATIONAL LAW AND ITS RELATIONSHIP TO NATIONAL LAW LEGAL SYSTEMS

Chapter III

DISTINCTIVE CHARACTERISTICS OF THE INTERNATIONAL LEGAL PROCESS

In Part One we examined some ways in which domestic legal systems respond to aliens and transnational problems, without consideration of ways in which the international community and international law control or influence such responses. Part Two explores such questions. It does not attempt to present a developed and detailed understanding of the doctrinal body of public international law. Rather it stresses distinctive characteristics and processes of international law, as well as its substance in several fields that are relevant to the general themes of this book. The following materials will, however, be more instructive if the student has some familiarity with the historical development of international law. Students lacking that familiarity would profit from reading a concise text such as Brierly, The Law of Nations 1–56 (6th ed., Waldock, 1963).

Additional reading: General references which treat much of the subject matter in this chapter include the leading casebooks of Bishop, International Law (3d ed. 1971), and Briggs, The Law of Nations (2d ed. 1952). Two comprehensive treatises are Hyde, International Law, Chiefly as Interpreted and Applied by the United States (2d rev. ed. 1947), and Oppenheim, International Law (8th ed., H. Lauterpacht, Vol. I, 1955; 7th ed., H. Lauterpacht, Vol. II, 1952). Two digests are Hackworth, Digest of International Law (8 vols. 1940–1944), and Whiteman, Digest of International Law (15 vols. to present, 1963–1973). These works contain extensive citations to source and secondary materials. Further citations appear throughout this chapter; in particular, Part F refers to contemporary critiques of classical approaches to international law, and to several approaches towards an understanding of international law which those critics have developed.

A. COMPARISONS WITH CONCEPTIONS OF LAW AND LEGAL PROCESS IN NATIONAL SYSTEMS

The study of international law leads the student educated to an understanding of the common law and the contemporary American legal system to radically different forms, institutional expressions and jurisprudential conceptions of law. The experience is as much one in "comparative law" as would (literally) be the study of a European or Moslem or tribal legal system. It poses similar difficulties in achieving an understanding of different legal conceptions, and offers similar opportunities in opening new perspectives upon one's own, familiar legal system.

To ease the difficulties and heighten the opportunities, we briefly state in Part A some basic conceptions of law developed by theorists of the Western tradition and finding expression in the Western legal systems. We also sketch some salient characteristics of the contemporary legal process within the United States, as an introduction to the radically different phenomena on the international arena. The categories of thought about law that we describe below have been selected with a view towards their utility in deepening understanding of the distinctive character of international law—whether by way of comparisons or contrasts between these descriptions and the later international materials.

Although major thinkers about law, and excerpts from their writings, figure in our descriptions, it should be clear that our effort is solely to sketch some relevant conceptions of law rather than to offer a complete or even accurate view of the ideas of particular thinkers who contributed towards those conceptions. Moreover, these conceptions were formulated in the framework of national societies and of their legal orders, involving primarily the structuring of relationships among private parties in a society. But as we shall observe, much of international law treats relationships between states. Our closing comments in Part A suggest some domestic analogues to that radically different situation.

NOTE ON POSITIVISM AND THE COMMAND THEORY OF LAW

The fountainhead of modern legal positivism, of a will or command theory of law, is found in the mid-17th Century writings of Hobbes. It is the jurisprudential tradition which Hobbes spawned—one developed in different directions by thinkers such as Bentham or Holmes—that is least hospitable to endowing the rules of international life with the characterization of law. Our description of that tradition is based principally on Hobbes.[1]

Hobbes pictures a pre-state natural condition of mankind in which "men live without a common power to keep them all in awe; they are in that condition which is called war, and such a war as is of every man against every man." Indeed, absent a "common power," there is no security, indeed no industry, for the industrious would not be protected in the fruits of their labor. There are "no arts; no letters; no society; and, which is worst of all, continual fear and

1. The excerpts are from Chapters 13 and 14 of Hobbes, Leviathan (Schneider ed. 1958).

danger of violent death; and the life of man is solitary, poor, nasty, brutish, and short."

In this natural condition where all compete for power, there are maxims of prudence (one view of Hobbes' laws of nature) which it is in men's interests generally to obey.[2] But they cannot be counted upon to obey. "Notions of right and wrong, justice and injustice, have there no place. Where there is no common power, there is no law; where no law, no injustice." Consider the performance of covenants made in what we would term executory contracts. In "the condition of mere nature," such a covenant

> is void; but if there be a common power set over them both, with right and force sufficient to compel performance, it is not void. For he that performs first has no assurance the other will perform after, because the bonds of words are too weak to bridle men's ambition, avarice, anger, and other passions without the fear of some coercive power which in the condition of mere nature, where all men are equal and judges of the justness of their own fears, cannot possibly be supposed. And therefore he which performs first does but betray himself to his enemy. . . .

To gain security, men enter into society. There they purchase security at the price of the liberty—that is, the absence of authoritative external restraints—enjoyed by them in the state of nature. The state, or Leviathan, finds justification solely in terms of this utilitarian criterion, the security and order which it brings to its subjects. The Hobbesian sovereign is absolute, a powerful force keeping peace and enforcing sanctions. He is author rather than subject of law, unlimited by custom or natural law or social contract or by any conception close to the Western notion of the Rule of Law. The choice is one between drastic extremes: a natural condition of chaos, or a society of total order under an absolute sovereign (government) whose will is expressed through coercively enforced law.

Within this conception, law is the command of the sovereign about conduct, backed by sanctions. There is no place for notions of customary law or dictates of natural law, except insofar as the sovereign accepts such laws and wills them as the positive law of his realm. All law is consciously (man) made, and instrumental in character—fundamentally of course an instrument for order within Hobbes' universe. It is law which creates rights such as property, or which generates claims to justice. Duty, justice, and rights or entitlements (with few exceptions) follow rather than precede law, which in turn is a companion to or follows rather than precedes society organized under government.

2. Hobbes can be read to rest these laws of nature on "rights" derived from the nature of man's being or personality. In this sense, his political theory includes the conception of natural rights. But from a perspective more significant for our discussion, Hobbes stands opposed to any conception of natural right or natural law as a constraint upon the sovereign with respect to the content of positive law.

NOTE ON LAW AS A FACILITATIVE FRAMEWORK

We here describe a number of ideas characteristic of theorists within the Western liberal tradition of society and law from Locke to the contemporary period. Two interrelated themes figure in our description, both distinct from Hobbesian will theory, but as suggestive as the positivist tradition for an understanding of aspects of international law. Those themes are (1) that society, and forms of law, precede the state (government, the sovereign), which thus has the function of improving rather than creating the conditions for and character of fruitful social intercourse; and (2) that law is better understood not as a coercive system for maintaining order or imposing social control, but as a facilitative framework permitting those subject to it better to realize their private aims.

The first idea finds expression in theorists of the liberal tradition from Locke to contemporary authors such as von Hayek and Fuller.[3] Locke's state of nature, though troubled by insecurity, nonetheless possessed a character and commerce more stable and complex than that of Hobbes. People cultivated land, produced utensils or clothing, and traded. Conceptions of property and right, of natural right, were more developed than in Hobbes. When entering into society through the fictional social contract, men carried with them an already established social and economic order, a sense of right and wrong, a relative stability of expectations, which it was the function of society to protect and perfect.

In the writings of Hayek, there is the image of a spontaneous order, of a form of order (market ordering in his case) growing out of countless decentralized decisions and actions. Out of such decisions and actions, or interactions, there develop patterns of expectations, and some shared and abstract principles that form the framework within which spontaneous order forms and reforms over time. Fuller's writings talk of patterns of human interaction, whether in the context of economic or family life, that lead to "stabilized interactional expectancies".

All these conceptions treat or refine the notion of customary law, of law neither contractual nor enacted and imposed in nature, but growing out of human intercourse and attaining a broad consensus as to what is permitted, required or proscribed in social interactions. Relationships between such conceptions of customary law within domestic orders and among nations are suggested at pp. 250–253, infra. This conception of legal obligation as growing out of customary practice is of course antagonistic to the positivist assertion that only those commands issuing from the state that are backed by threats of force merit characterization as law. Fuller further qualifies the

3. The quotations below from Locke are taken from Chapters VII and IX of The Second Treatise of Civil Government (Gough ed. 1946). See also Hayek, Rules and Order (1973), and Fuller, "Human Interaction and the Law," in Wolff (ed.), The Rule of Law 171 (1971).

positivist position by arguing that enacted law itself will generally rest on interactional foundations, on the human interactions to which law responds.

Common to such conceptions is a resistance to the idea that law works from the top down as a form of social control. Rather law grows out of and supplements social arrangements of a natural origin. It is evident that theorists of this orientation will be more hospitable to conceptions of natural law and natural right which find their origin in God's law or in nature or in human nature. Such law or rights not only have their origin other than in the will of the state, but may be seen to transcend and qualify positive law, to contain it within previously established laws and rights.

Such ideas have been historically related to our second theme, the function of government and positive law. Here the difference between Hobbes and Locke is instructive. While the former stresses security, order, fear and coercion, the latter sees law less as imposition or limitation than as a framework for social intercourse and production. The state does provide the necessary security lacking in the state of nature, but its function is to permit harmonic interaction whereby individuals or groups will be able to maximize their welfare. In Locke's terms, this welfare consisted of men's "property, . . . their lives, liberties and estates." And the "chief end" of men's putting themselves under government "is the preservation of their property." Society and law exist to advance—and indeed their legitimate power does not extend beyond—"the common good." All powers of government are to be directed "to no end but the peace, safety, and public good of the people." In brief, law does not limit but enlarges freedom by assuring these framework conditions in which maximum self-realization can take place.

As liberal and market-oriented societies developed in the West, those essential legal conditions were thought to be the protection of property rights and a regime of freedom of contract, supported by necessary provisions of the law of tort and crime. That is, the basic understanding of state or government or law as a facilitative framework rests upon the same political, moral and psychological postulates that underlie the broad theory of the liberal state. The individual is to be subject to the minimum necessary restraint to assure conditions necessary for the welfare of society, and should be aided in the search for satisfaction of his desires or for self-realization by the legal norms and institutions which society has created.

It is this same tradition of thought which is dominantly associated with the Rule of Law. The essentials again are in Locke, best expressed through his oft-repeated image of law as fences. Those fences mark out autonomous spheres of individual action, through general, clear and certain rules (applied by "indifferent" courts) which determine rights and duties of individuals and the state (sovereign). The fences separate the property of individual subjects from each other, and also protect the individual from the sovereign, itself subject to law. Note that this classic conception of the Rule of Law assumes a relatively autonomous legal system, one relatively divorced from political and economic life and possessing its distinctive institutions and even logic (forms of legal reasoning, systematization of doctrine, and so on). Law, as it were, stands apart and above, a reference point for all in society, a neutral framework for harmonic interaction and accommodation. Again the relationship can be perceived between such an ideal of government under law, the stress upon government's "framework" function, and the psychological and moral premises to liberal-state theory. The root idea is expressed in numerous familiar maxims, such as *Non sub Homine sed sub Deo et Lege.*

A prominent contemporary theory of the American legal process, one familiar to many American law students, has its roots in the jurisprudential and political tradition of liberal-state theory growing out of Locke. We refer to Hart and Sacks, The Legal Process: Basic Problems in the Making and Application of Law (Tent. ed. 1958), in which the authors develop an analytic framework that offers useful comparisons with the international legal process. The views of Professors Hart and Sacks about the legal process and the functions of law draw upon and develop the conception of law as a facilitative framework, under which individuals are permitted and encouraged to advance their welfare as they may perceive it within political and legal structures that are designed to achieve the maximum possible welfare for society as a whole. Thus, as in much theory of the liberal state, the stress is upon process or path or framework rather than upon a final end or purpose—except of course for the general purpose of maximizing welfare as it may be differently perceived over time. The essential morality is one of process rather than of particular ends or a particular state of society.

Thus Professors Hart and Sacks stress the constitutive and procedural "understandings" which form the distinctive core of a legal system, the understandings which enable that legal system to reconcile the wants of individuals or groups which live in a state of interdependence within society. Their analysis emphasizes the processes within a legal system by which decisions are hammered out in an authoritative manner, and the institutions and procedures forming part of this process which serve to settle questions of group concern. The authors underscore the importance of general acceptance of the notion of *institutional settlement*, by which they mean the principle that decisions duly arrived at within a society should be accepted as binding until they are duly changed. That notion bears an evident similarity to—or better said, represents one possible elaboration of —the concept of the Rule of Law. "General acceptance" by the population of a number of such basic notions, and relative stability through time and consensus about basic social purposes and values, appear to be necessary premises to much of the authors' analysis.

NOTE ON MARXIST-ORIENTED CONCEPTIONS OF LAW IN LIBERAL SOCIETY

By referring to "Marxist-oriented" conceptions, we mean to describe those themes which characterize the analysis of law—particularly of law in liberal-capitalist (bourgeois) society—of many theorists within the Marxist tradition of social thought. Some of these themes of course figure heavily in the writings of non-Marxists; some have deeply influenced the social perceptions of reformist advocates of welfare statism whose intellectual and political roots are within Western liberal thought. On the other hand, it is impossible to identify an inclusive conceptual framework to which all "Marxists" would adhere. Marx's writings relate law to his total dialectical conception of human history and society, but his treatment of law is not exhaustive—even as supplemented by the writings of Engels. Later "Marxists" theorists have followed varied paths.[4]

For our purpose of (later) comparison between a Marxist theory of law and present conceptions of international law that are held by socialist countries and, to some extent, by non-socialist countries of the less developed world, it is sufficient to signal the following themes:

Independently of their will, as determined by the existing social structure and their place within it, men enter into relations forming the economic structure of society, the so-called infrastructure or "real foundation." This foundation consists of the forces of production (technology, factory organization and so on) and the relations of production (the ownership of and command over productive resources, hence also determining the distribution of a society's wealth). It is the tensions and contradictions between the forces and relations of production which constitute the engine or core of historical change.

Within this historical dialectical process, class conflict and polarity grow—in Marx's day, the conflicting classes (defined in terms of their place in the process of production and their legal status with respect to relations of production) being the bourgeoisie (capitalist) and the proletariat. The relationship between the two is one of exploitation and oppression, as capitalists appropriate to their benefit the surplus value created by the wage-labor proletariat. In Marx's philosophy of history and sociology, it was the proletariat that was the designated historical agent for change from capitalism to a higher form of society, communism. The proletariat's particular historical interests were simultaneously an expression of the universal, of final historical purpose.

4. Two useful commentaries are Schlesinger, Soviet Legal Theory (2d ed. 1951) and Kelsen, The Communist Theory of Law (1955), both of which are attentive to original Marxist theory. For a description of some divergences among theorists which have developed, see Fuller, Pashukanis and Vyschinsky: A Study in the Development of Marxist Legal Theory, 47 Mich.L.Rev. 1157 (1949). For a description of Soviet law, see Berman, Justice in the U.S.S.R. (1963).

The economic structure, or infrastructure, of a society to which we have referred constitutes, in Marx's words, the "real foundation on which rise legal and political superstructures . . ." These superstructural aspects of a society reach beyond legal and political institutions to ways of thinking, ideologies, moral beliefs, and so on. The critical conception is that such institutions, ideas or beliefs are derived from or depend upon economic infrastructural circumstances —i. e., the forces and relations of production and related class antagonisms.

But in the writings of Marx and Engels, as well as of later theorists within this tradition, it is clear that the relationship between infrastructure and superstructure cannot be reduced to a one-way causation or determination. To be sure, the core of Marxist analysis is the stress on the dominance of the economic infrastructure. Politics, law, systems of ideas are not independent of this economic influence; they are not autonomous. But political and legal institutions, ideas and beliefs are more than a faithful reflection of the forces and relations of production, or of the interests of the dominant bourgeoisie. They in turn influence and regulate the infrastructure. They order a system of class domination and create the institutional and ideological framework in which relations of production are maintained or slowly changed.

Like other parts of the superstructure, law cannot aspire to universalism or to the transcendence of particular class interests. Like politics and the state, it is the "organized power of one class for oppressing another." An emanation of the state, law institutionalizes and maintains through its coercive machinery the relations of production; property, for example is the mere legal expression for bourgeoisie-proletariat relations of production. Nonetheless, law is not entirely dependent upon the economic infrastructure. For example, the search for inner consistency and the effort at rationalization of doctrine influence the content of a legal system to the point where again it is not merely a reflection of but itself influences the "real foundation."

Part of law's function in society is ideological, in the sense that it serves to justify or legitimate existing relations of production by disguising them as abstract, universal and evenhanded principles. Thus bourgeois domination, translated into the legal norms of bourgeois society, assumes the character of even-handed rules of property or freedom of contract, or of even-handed principles such as the Rule of Law. In fact such rules or principles serve to institutionalize domination and to reserve the avenues of change to those possessing economic and thus political power. Law cannot escape its self-interest, in securing the interests of society's dominant classes. Thus all rhetoric of justice, equality, natural rights and so on—however deeply believed by those acting in the light of such principles—must ultimately be understood as ideological support for society's economic infrastructure.

NOTE ON SOME CHARACTERISTICS OF THE CONTEMPORARY AMERICAN LEGAL PROCESS

The three preceding Notes described, from jurisprudential and sociological perspectives, basic conceptions about the nature or function of law in society. Our purpose here is a different one. We are concerned not with normative or explanatory theory but simply with description. We describe some structural and institutional aspects of the contemporary American legal system and process, emphasizing the interplay between public and private processes and institutional relationships. Through this description, we mean to facilitate comparisons in the following sections with the structural and institutional characteristics of international law and the international legal process.

The utility of any such comparisons may be questioned at the outset, in view of the fact that the domestic legal process primarily treats relationships among individuals under the same government, whereas international law is concerned with arrangements or disputes between governments and private parties, or among governments themselves. Thus we start our description (generally bypassing the complications of our domestic federalism) with legal relationships and disputes between individuals, but then bring into the picture (federal and state) governments as well.

By way of contrast with a lawyer's approach to problems of international law involving foreign states, consider the response to the recurrent domestic problems which a lawyer confronts, perhaps a contract dispute or a possible tort action. A compromise or settlement might be possible, or litigation may be inevitable. Whichever route were followed, the lawyer would attempt to characterize the situation in legal terms under principles or rules that he considered to be relevant. He would ultimately define as best he could the duties or rights of the parties in the light of those principles or rules, of the remedial paths open to the disputing parties, and of the practical restraints upon pursuit of those remedies.

Note the basic assumption implicit in his reasoning of an authoritative body of principles or rules, authoritative because the institutions (dominantly legislatures and courts) formulating and applying them enjoy a broadly accepted legitimacy. To ascertain the relevant principles or rules, the lawyer would turn to the various familiar sources: perhaps an ultimate constitutional norm, statutes, administrative regulations, judicial interpretations of them, the common law. He and his adversary counsel would entertain a common understanding of the relative significance of those different expressions of a national legal system, and of the legal and extra-legal considerations which give direction to doctrinal or legislative change.

The parties and lawyers also share an awareness of those official agencies (administrative, judicial or other) through which a dispute can be authoritatively resolved. If the parties fail to resolve the problem and do not agree upon arbitration, either can resort to a court whose jurisdiction is compulsory, independent of the consent of the defendant. Both recognize that a judgment of that court resolving disputes as to "facts" and defining the parties' duties or rights will be binding—and if not voluntarily complied with, can generally be made effective through application of a coercive public power.

If litigation does occur, the adversary lawyers may differ about the facts and the controlling principles or rules as well as about how they should be interpreted and applied. Nonetheless, they share a general view of the framework of considerations within which a court would reach its decision, although the judgment and discretion inherent in the identification or application of controlling rules may well make impossible an accurate prediction of the outcome. (The problem of prediction becomes of course the more acute at the trial level before a jury, where the assertion of a common framework of considerations among parties, court and jury becomes more questionable.) Whatever the range of discretion, there remains a common sense of the limits within which the court functions, of the factors which control discretion even as they enable the parties to shape their own arguments towards and expectations about the legal result. Whatever their own social or economic status in society or their political commitments, the parties will have in most situations a common understanding of those purposes and interests, personal or moral or economic, which their legal system recognizes and advances. It will be the exceptional period or field of law in which those purposes and interests are so disputed or so much in flux that links of common perception among parties and court will be severed.

Suppose that a party discontented with prevailing doctrine doubts that decisional law will move in the desired direction, or is aware that the desired changes are beyond the competence of a court to make. What avenues are open to him? Again, and among most citizens whatever their socio-economic status or political affiliation, we find broadly shared assumptions about the role of the legislature and of the legitimacy of the political processes through which that institution is organized and pressures upon it are exerted. The representation of different interest groups through that process, the resulting pluralist character of the legislature, and compromise and accommodation within the legislative process help to sustain this sense of legitimacy.

The description in Hart and Sacks, supra p. 182, of the legal process stresses some of these characteristics. The American legal process is described as a complex interaction of public and private procedures and decisions, with important institutional differentiations. Officials legislate or prosecute or adjudicate; private parties, empowered to plan and create duties and resolve disputes through such legal modes as contracts or wills, often act as decentralized "lawmakers." The larger part of a legal system is self-applying, in the sense that private participants in social or economic life will generally comply with duties deriving from contract, criminal law, or other bodies of law. Thus little official coercion is necessary; much "compliance" will stem less from a fear of legal sanctions than from habit, shared ethical standards, or utilitarian self-interest of private parties. But the possibility of recourse to official institutions to resolve problems remains generally open.

The authors note the distinctions among the roles of the different institutions forming the structure within which the legal process unfolds. We have mentioned the "private lawmakers." The authors describe the dual function of courts in resolving disputes and making law through the generalizations resulting from decisions, and state (p. 185) that "[i]n the development of Anglo-American legal systems, courts have functioned characteristically as the place of initial resort for the settlement of problems which have failed of private solution." Notwithstanding the limited discretion available to a court in contrast with other institutions, they stress the role of courts in our society as a creative law-making force. They observe (p. 124) that any system involving the principle of institutional settlement "has necessarily to include one or more institutions authorized to reach additional general understandings for handling new problems or dealing more effectively with old ones." The legislature, with its broad continuing discretion, is not subject to "the restraint of the obligation of reasoned decision and hence of reasoned elaboration of a fabric of doctrine governing successive decisions." (p. 172). Its function is inherently discretionary, the discretion as broad as the infinite variety of changes (subject to constitutional limitations and to ultimate political constraints imposed through the electoral process) which can be made in existing arrangements.

Let us modify our discussion of the domestic legal process to carry it one step closer to the problems of international law. We do so by introducing arrangements or disputes between a private party and (state or federal) government. Distinct considerations emerge. For example, sovereign immunity may insulate the governmental party from the normal jurisdiction of the courts, although that immunity (see p. 638, infra) has been waived by the federal and state governments in a large number of situations. Other interrelated considerations which arise more rarely in private litigation—the problems of standing to challenge types of governmental action, of "political questions" or areas of governmental discretion that are considered immune from judicial scrutiny—will burden the claim of the private party. And when a court exercises jurisdiction and reaches the merits, different rules of law may become applicable, for even in tort and contract cases the same rules that bind private parties may not govern the actions of a public official or agency.

Suppose that the plaintiff prevails. Consider the distinctive problems that arise in a national legal system when a court judgment, even one for money damages, is entered against a governmental defendant rather than a private party. If a private party prevails in a suit against the United States in the Court of Claims or in a federal district court, he cannot have his judgment enforced by a levy upon the Government's property. Rather, he is dependent upon the Congress, for the judgment can only be satisfied by payment from the Treasury pursuant to a general appropriation act for amounts up to $100,000 per judgment, or pursuant to a special appropriation bill after the judgment for larger amounts.[5] A study in 1933 indicated that there had been about 15 cases during the preceding 70 years in which Congress had refused to appropriate funds to pay a judgment. "This historical record, surely more favorable to prevailing parties than that obtaining in private litigation, may well make us doubt whether the capacity to enforce a judgment is always indispensable for the exercise of judicial power." Glidden Co. v. Zdanok, 370 U.S. 530, 570, 82 S.Ct. 1459, 1483, 8 L.Ed.2d 671, 699 (1962). Indeed in H. Liebes & Co. v. Commissioner, 90 F.2d 932 (9th Cir. 1937), the court held that a private party which had recovered a final judgment against the United States in the Court of Claims was required to include its amount in taxable income for that year, despite the fact that Congress had not yet appropriated funds to satisfy it.

These observations—the legislative and judicial attrition of the immunity doctrine, and the record of compliance with money judgments—touch upon only one aspect of a much broader problem: the extent to which government officials will observe the standards of a legal system and comply with institutional decisions about limitations on their powers, and about the government's duties and liabilities. By and large, one can assume within our national legal system that the government has a shared interest in encouraging compliance with the principle of institutional settlement, or Rule of Law. That principle commands broad acceptance, assures when observed an important degree of political and social stability, and expresses moral and political values to which many if not all in government adhere. The governmental interest in compliance with this principle is perhaps given most vivid expression when the power to engage in conduct which government officials desire is denied them.

Consider in this connection the cases in Chapters I and II in which governmental action was ordered or enjoined: release of a prisoner on habeas corpus, issuance of a passport, return of steel mills seized by order of the Executive and so on. In no case did governmental compliance with a court decree rest upon the "power" of the court to enforce; the court possesses no such power. Nor did it follow upon any threat posed by an executive or military force extrinsic to the court. Had the government so desired, such force could likely have been utilized to resist rather than to enforce a court decree. Compliance rested upon the utilitarian and ethical considerations more basic to this society that we have sketched above.

Of course the "sharing" of such considerations is general, not absolute. Corruption continues in government as in the private sector, at times to the extremes of lawless behavior in the federal gov-

5. See 70 Stat. 678 (1956), as amended, 31 U.S.C.A. § 724a, and 28 U.S.C.A. §§ 2414, 2517(a) and 2518.

ernment exemplified in the early-to-mid 1970's by Watergate or the misconduct of intelligence agencies. But the conception of government under and answerable to law in its relationships with private parties is fundamental to the American tradition, surely as a prevailing ideology and aspiration if not always in fact.

A still closer comparison between the national and international communities is achieved if we eliminate the private party from a dispute and consider conflict within this country between branches of government (legislature and executive), levels of government (federal and state), or different states. It is significant that such disputes more rarely find their way into the courts or, if they do, more rarely lead to affirmative judicial resolution. The problem of political questions (p. 132, supra) will loom large and inhibit the judicial elaboration of limits to the power of another branch of government. Tensions between the legislative and executive branches of government as to the proper scope of the President's or the Congress's (war and other) powers (see p. 143, supra, and p. 603, infra) offer illustrations.

But in some contexts of entirely public litigation, the courts have been active and influential. For example, the volume of litigation between states or between the federal government and a state is not insignificant.[6] See generally Chapter III of Hart and Wechsler, The Federal Courts and the Federal System (2d ed., Bator, Mishkin, Shapiro and Wechsler, 1973). It has been pointed out that the subject matter of that litigation, chiefly disputes over boundaries, water rights in interstate streams and rights to tidelands, finds a significant parallel in litigation between nations before international tribunals. Chayes, A Common Lawyer Looks at International Law, 78 Harv.L. Rev. 1396, 1408 (1965).

Problems of enforcement of judgments of the Supreme Court in litigation between states can become acute. The opinion in Glidden Co. v. Zdanok, p. 188, supra, notes that in the litigation between Virginia and West Virginia over the shares of the public debt of the State of Virginia prior to separation, the Supreme Court was not able to impose a solution involving a money liability of the losing state, West Virginia. In Hart and Wechsler, The Federal Courts and the Federal System, 269 (2d ed., Bator, Mishkin, Shapiro and Wechsler, 1973), this litigation is described from the original bill to a "[l]ong opinion by Chief Justice White saying definitely and in strong language that the judgment was enforceable but not saying exactly how;" and to an act of the West Virginia legislature carrying out a compromise between the states. Nonetheless one can say that, despite the

6. If one takes into account the fact that issues germane to allocations of power between the states or between the federal and state governments may be raised in the context of litigation involving a private party, the kinds of disputes involving interests of different states which find their way into the courts are considerably broader. Litigation under the Interstate Commerce Clause or the Due Process Clause of the Fourteenth Amendment to determine the reach of a state's tax power affords an example.

absence of sheriffs levying upon state or federal treasuries, the system "works" because of the respect of appropriating authorities for the judicial system and its pronouncements.

In recent decades the prime examples of tensions which have threatened the normal working of our legal-political system and thus the principle of institutional settlement have been the civil rights problem and the Vietnamese war. The two episodes are instructive about the consequences within a national legal tradition of conflict over basic values; the erosion of consensus provides insight into the dilemma of the international legal system. Consider first the civil rights issues. Compliance with the federal Constitution and statutes as interpreted by federal courts has been sought by various means. Litigation and, occasionally, the application of federal military power have achieved acceptance of the developing legal norms only slowly and in the face of great opposition. The political and other considerations which inhibit a more pervasive application of federal force suggest the limitations of a federal legal system in resolving disputes between governmental units. Unlike other episodes of popular resistance to federal law—prohibition, for example—resistance to integration has been most intense, and has crystallized around organized political entities, at a state and local level. To that extent, the civil rights experience more closely resembles conflicts between territorially defined nations with different traditions and mores. The analogy to international protection of human rights is evident.

Conflict and dissent were more generalized during the war in Vietnam. Efforts of opponents to use the legal process to check the draft or military operations were by and large unsuccessful. See pp. 150–159, supra and 928–931, infra. The political process was slow in responding to popular pressures, and massive protests spilled over into sporadic violence and unprecedented numbers of refusals to submit to induction. Again in vital respects the principle of institutional settlement was threatened for lack of agreement over issues fundamental to the society.

Note that courts figured in our discussion even with respect to issues as politically divisive as civil rights or Vietnam, and with respect to disputes between state governments or the state and federal governments. It is indeed difficult not to assign a central position to courts, as settlers of disputes and lawmakers and expounders of the Constitution, for any discussion of the legal system or process within this country. Our notion of a legal system, our concept of law, is profoundly related to this phase of the principle of institutional settlement.

Nonetheless, as our discussion progressed from disputes between individuals to individuals and governments, and finally to disputes between branches or levels of government, resolution of problems became more detached from the workings of the formal legal process, particularly litigation. Apart from the issues of judicial jurisdiction and "political questions" that may arise, the question whether there is a "legal" answer to a problem itself tends to recede. All these observations are made in the setting of an American society which, as critics have pointed out ever since de Tocqueville, goes further than any other society in translating political issues into legal questions and expecting courts and lawyers to solve them.

By way of contrast, consider the attitudes of Chinese and Japanese societies which go to the other extreme: abhorrence of lawyers, laws and, above all, litigation. Professor Jerome Cohen begins his article, Chinese Mediation on the Eve of Modernization, 54 Calif.L. Rev. 120 (1966), by quoting a Chinese proverb: "It is better to be vexed to death than to bring a lawsuit." Such an attitude implies a preference for conciliation and mediation for the resolution of controversies. Its further implications are felt in many respects. For instance, in the drafting of a contract, it is thought to be insulting to provide for the settlement of differences that may arise under it since such provisions reflect a lack of confidence in the other party. See Kawashima, Dispute Resolution in Contemporary Japan, in von Mehren (ed.), Law in Japan 41 (1963). The reasons for this aversion include a dislike of the publicity attending litigation, lack of confidence in the impartiality of the available courts, a fear that legal rules are too abstract and rigid to accommodate the realities of particular cases, and an anxiety to avoid the disruptions of harmonious relationships attending a clear-cut victory and defeat in litigation. One is sometimes inclined to believe that the Oriental perspective furnishes an easier point of departure towards international law than does our own.

Comparisons with the jurisprudential traditions and the structure of our domestic legal system appear throughout Part Two, particularly in the concluding Part F of this chapter. They probe a number of obvious but critical questions. To what extent has the international community developed meaningful analogies to the private ordering, arbitrations, courts or other techniques for planning cooperative arrangements and resolving disputes on the domestic scene? Are there institutions for achieving change in principles or rules that play a role comparable to that of the domestic legislature or judiciary? To what extent can one find shared values, to which hostile and more immediate national interests will be subordinated, supporting a body of international law? Is it possible to achieve a consensus on the international scene comparable to that over purposes and values—political, economic, philosophical or moral—which prevails in a large part of our domestic life? How can any such consensus be imposed upon dissident members of the international community? More broadly stated, is the concept of law and the legal process that our domestic traditions of legal and political thought and our experience have led us to develop meaningful when applied to a transnational arena?

B. INTERNATIONAL TRIBUNALS

Arbitral or adjudicatory tribunals created by international agreements provide the closest analogy on the international scene to domestic institutions, here of course courts. Although their significance is pale compared with that of their domestic counterparts, such tribunals offer a convenient point of departure towards an understanding of international law and processes.

As one moves from domestic to transnational problems, many of the techniques for resolving disputes that are available to private parties remain significant. For example, disputes between an alien and a citizen or an alien and a government may work their way through the normal domestic judicial processes, as indeed happened in a number of cases in Chapters I and II. If, however, the conflict between alien and government is not satisfactorily resolved through regular processes, it may become elevated to a dispute between two governments, the host government and the alien's government. And of course many disputes between governments, generally those of a significant political character, will arise on an intergovernmental level without direct participation by private parties in the process of negotiation.

What institutional means are available to aid two or more nations to settle their differences? Compare with the techniques of a national legal system the following, in which the involvement and influence of "neutral" individuals, nations or international institutions grow as the list develops. If the two governments fail to reach agreement through diplomatic negotiations unaided by third parties, another nation can tender its "good offices" and attempt to induce the parties to negotiate further. This offer of "good offices" shades into mediation when a third country, or a person agreed upon by the disputants, assumes an active role in the negotiations. The parties may resort to commissions of inquiry, which are constituted to investigate the facts relevant to a dispute and to make findings as to them. Through the process known as "conciliation," a neutral government or commission studies the controversy and issues a report stating its recommendations, which are meant to be advisory and not to bind the parties. The remaining processes, arbitration or adjudication by international tribunals, have a significantly different character. Each involves an agreement by the disputants to be bound by the decision reached by the tribunal. All these methods of dispute-resolution are referred to in Article 33 * of the United Nations Charter.[7]

7. This list omits certain forms of interposition by third countries or international organizations which are beyond the scope of the subject matter of this book. Such action, which may or may not be based upon the consent of the disputing parties, has particular relevance to problems of peace-keeping and the control of violence. It may involve the application of force by the foreign nation or international organization. Articles 39–42 of the United Nations Charter today provide a legal basis for intervention by that organization.

NOTE ON INTERNATIONAL ARBITRAL TRIBUNALS

Development of international arbitration. The Jay Treaty of 1794 between Great Britain and the United States, which established an arbitral commission consisting of nationals of the two countries, introduced the modern era of international arbitration. Throughout the 19th century, there was a considerable volume of arbitration. Among the most significant was the Alabama Claims Arbitration of 1871–1872, which was organized to settle certain disputes between the United States and Great Britain stemming from acts of both countries during the Civil War. That tribunal consisted of a national of each country and three nationals of "neutral" countries appointed by three foreign powers. Most later arbitrations in the 19th century were by such "mixed commissions."

The Hague Peace Conferences of 1899 and 1907, and the Conventions for the Pacific Settlement of International Disputes to which they gave birth, sought to eliminate the need to create *ad hoc* tribunals whenever two countries wanted to arbitrate. The Conventions led to the formation of the Permanent Court of Arbitration—in fact, simply a panel of available arbitrators, nominated by member states, from which adversary states could select the number necessary to form a particular tribunal. These Conventions were of importance because of their statements of procedural rules which would govern arbitrations under them, absent other provision by the parties, and because of their aspiration towards greater use of arbitration as the prime means of settling disputes "of a legal nature" between states. Since they did not make compulsory the jurisdiction of tribunals over the parties to the Conventions, a separate agreement between disputants to submit to arbitration ("*compromis*") remained essential.

The first three decades of this century witnessed a large number of treaties containing clauses (so-called "compromissory clauses") which required the parties to submit to arbitration. Such compromissory clauses covered only disputes arising out of the provisions of a particular treaty—for example, a compromissory clause in a treaty fixing land boundaries requiring arbitration only for conflicts over those boundaries. Some treaties contained obligations to submit a broader category of disputes between the parties to arbitration. Efforts were made in such treaties to distinguish "justiciable" from "non-justiciable" (political) questions. Neither compromissory clauses nor general arbitration treaties usually contained operative provisions for an arbitral tribunal. Consequently their implementation required a later agreement in order to constitute a tribunal and define its powers.

The United States entered into a number of such general arbitration treaties. Characteristic provisions appear in the Arbitration Treaty between the United States and France, February 6, 1928, 46 Stat. 2269, T.S. No. 785. Its preamble recites the desire of the parties to adhere "to the policy of submitting to impartial decision all justiciable controversies that may arise between them . . . ." Under Article I, disputes "of whatever nature they may be" were to be submitted for investigation and report to a Permanent International Commission formed under a prior treaty, "when ordinary diplomatic proceedings have failed and the [parties] do not have recourse to adjudication by a competent tribunal. . . ." Article II provided that "[a]ll differences relating to international matters in which the [parties] are concerned by virtue of a claim of right made by one against the other under treaty or otherwise," which were not adjusted pursuant to the techniques stated in Article I, and "which are justiciable in their nature by reason of being susceptible of decision by the application of the principles of law or equity," were to be submitted to the Permanent Court of Arbitration, or to another tribunal as decided in each case by special agreement. That agreement was to "provide for the organization of such tribunal if necessary . . . ."[8] Article III excepted certain disputes from the provisions of the Treaty. Such treaties thus had the character of "agreements to agree," of statements of intention that the parties would consider arbitration of disputes as each might arise. The definition of disputes within the coverage of the Treaty illustrates the difficulties in distinguishing the "justiciable" from the "non-justiciable," difficulties to be resolved by the parties before the formation of a tribunal. In fact, treaties of this character did not prove to be significant incentives to arbitration.

Efforts were made in the League of Nations to codify the general principles governing arbitration in the Geneva General Act for the Settlement of International Disputes of 1928. In 1949, this Act was amended by the United Nations, but few states have acceded to it and its importance lies primarily in its influence upon provisions of bilateral arbitration treaties. The International Law Commission of the United Nations later prepared Model Rules on Arbitral Procedure which were intended to resolve some of the problems which this Note describes. In 1958, the U. N. General Assembly recommended the Model Rules for use by member states when appropriate.

Since World War II there has been scant use of general arbitration treaties. However, over 20 international arbitral tribunals have been constituted. Many were organized pursuant to peace treaties or special agreements to handle disputes between the victorious and defeated states, often disputes involving claims on behalf of nationals of the allied powers. Several tribunals were established to resolve differences over international boundaries and waterways and over international agreements involving aviation or postal matters. In addition, a growing number of treaties—such as treaties of friendship, commerce and navigation or the treaties relating to the investment guaranty program that are considered at p. 475, infra—have included provisions for arbitration of disputes arising under them.

8. The special agreement constituting the tribunal required the advice and consent of the Senate, and thus constituted a "treaty" under United States law. See p. 589, infra.

Few arbitration agreements have confronted the basic problem of peacekeeping and peaceful change, principally because of the inherent difficulties in subjecting many such issues to binding decision by a third person. One relatively distinctive form of arbitration has emerged since World War II, that between international organizations and their member countries.

To some degree, "national" claims commissions have displaced international tribunals in the post-war world with respect to disputes arising out of the alleged mistreatment of a claimant state's nationals by the respondent state. In such situations, the settlement arrived at through negotiations between the disputants has required the payment of a "lump sum" by the respondent to the claimant state, and the distribution of that sum by the recipient state to its injured nationals. The national commission determines the manner in which the "lump sum" is to be allocated among nationals with claims frequently far in excess of that sum.

Formation of tribunal. The characteristic form of the modern international arbitral tribunal is the "mixed commission." Members are appointed by a variety of techniques, and decision is generally by majority vote. A classic problem in international arbitration has been the formation of a tribunal when one of the parties to an agreement to arbitrate refuses to participate. The Convention for the Pacific Settlement of International Disputes of 1907 and the Geneva General Act for the Pacific Settlement of Disputes of 1928 attempted to resolve this problem but were not fully successful. The Model Rules proposed by the International Law Commission (see Articles 1 and 3 *) provide an effective procedure for establishing the tribunal, but it is questionable to what extent states today would agree in advance, through a general arbitration treaty, to follow them.

Jurisdiction and compromis. Jurisdiction rests upon consent of the parties. That consent may be given in a general arbitration treaty. More frequently, it is given in the context of a particular treaty and refers exclusively to disputes arising under it, or in a *compromis* treating a particular dispute. The *compromis* or treaty clause is in effect the charter of the tribunal, at once constituting it and defining its powers and procedure. Because it is a consensual arrangement tailored to meet the needs of particular parties and disputes, the powers which it grants a tribunal vary widely. One critical principle became established in the jurisprudence of 19th Century arbitration: a tribunal has the power to determine its own jurisdiction under a treaty or *compromis*. See Article 9 of the Model Rules.

The *compromis* may be quite explicit. For example, it may state procedural and evidentiary rules that govern the proceedings. On the other hand, it may leave much for development or implementation by the arbitrators. At a minimum, the *compromis* should provide for the constitution and powers of the tribunal and should define the dispute to be resolved. It may authorize a tribunal to award monetary damages, but not any form of injunctive or other equitable relief. Or it may provide that the tribunal should select among stated solutions to the problem before it. See Article 2 of the Model Rules. For an example of a *compromis* that led to a series of important arbitrations, see the excerpts from the Convention of 1923 between the United States and Mexico establishing a General Claims Commission.* Some of the opinions rendered by that Commission appear in Chapter IV.

Disputes over validity of arbitral awards. The rule that an arbitral award is final and binding on the parties is well established, and frequently the *compromis* so states. However, a variety of problems arise which, by comparison with the solution to comparable problems in a national legal system, suggest the relative anarchy in legal structure of the international community. What if a party to the arbitration asserts that the award is null and void, on the ground that the arbitrators exceeded the powers conferred upon them and therefore acted without jurisdiction? Or what if a party alleges that the arbitration failed to conform to basic procedural standards of fairness by denying the party a fair hearing? In a national legal system, statutes governing arbitration between private parties generally provide for appeal to the courts on stated grounds, and the courts will refuse to enforce awards which violate certain fundamental principles.[9] Within the international community, the problem of providing some form of "appellate review" over arbitral tribunals, or of resolving disputes between parties over the effect of an arbitral award, has not met a satisfactory solution. There have been various suggestions for conferring "appellate" powers on the international court described below. See Articles 33 through 36 of the Model Rules.

Additional reading: Carlston, The Process of International Arbitrations (1946); Ralston, The Law and Procedure of International Tribunals (Rev. ed. 1933, Supp.1936); Simpson and Fox, International Arbitration (1959); Sohn, The Function of International Arbitration Today, 108 Académie de Droit International, Recueil des Cours 1 (1963); Sohn, Report on International Arbitration to the Helsinki Conference of the International Law Association (1966); United Nations Secretariat, Survey of Treaty Provisions for the Pacific Settlement of International Disputes, 1949–1962 (1966).

NOTE ON THE FORMATION AND JURISDICTION OF THE INTERNATIONAL COURT

In 1921, *ad hoc* arbitral tribunals were first supplemented by an international court. The Assembly of the League of Nations then adopted a Statute for the Permanent Court of International Justice (P.C.I.J.), thereby implementing certain provisions in the Covenant of the League. Between 1922 and 1939, 66 cases were brought before the Court. Many arose out of the dislocations and problems stemming from World War I. Twelve were settled. There were 27

9. See the discussion at pp. 824–835, infra, about judicial enforcement or review in this country of arbitral awards involving private parties.

opinions under the Court's "advisory jurisdiction" and 32 judgments under its "contentious jurisdiction." Although the United States was neither a member of the League nor party to the Statute, several of its citizens were judges of the P.C.I.J.

The Court was dormant during World War II. After the organization of the United Nations, the P.C.I.J. was formally dissolved and replaced by the International Court of Justice (I.C.J.). Read Articles 7 and 92–96 of the United Nations Charter. Article 92 makes evident the significant continuity between the P.C.I.J. and the present Court.[10]

The I.C.J., operating within the framework of the Charter, exercises a judicial (non-political) function in contrast with the other U. N. organs. See Articles 33(1) and 36(3) of the Charter. The Statute of the I.C.J. annexed to the Charter states the rules under which the Court functions. Read the excerpts from the Statute which appear in the Documentary Supplement.

The composition of the Court is determined pursuant to Articles 2 and 3 of the Statute. Candidates are nominated by "national groups" within the member states, and their election requires an absolute majority of both the General Assembly and the Security Council. Since World War II there has been a decline in the number of European judges and a corresponding increase in the number from the "new" countries. See Article 9 of the Statute. Note also the provision for *ad hoc* judges in Article 31, a clause more reminiscent of arbitration than of adjudication. Questions persistently arise as to the capacity of judges to disassociate themselves from their nations' positions towards issues before the Court, whether or not their governments are parties to litigation. A survey indicated that in several cases a judge formed part of a majority against his own state, but in none did a judge dissent from a judgment in its favor. In no case had a regular judge been in solitary dissent in favor of his own country, although this occurred several times with *ad hoc* judges.[11]

The I.C.J. exercises two kinds of jurisdiction: the contentious (adversary litigation) jurisdiction (Articles 33, 36 and 94 of the Charter) and the advisory jurisdiction (Article 96). We are here concerned primarily with the contentious jurisdiction.

The Charter and Statute carry forward from the P.C.I.J. two basic principles of classical international law. First, only states (the sole "subjects" of international law under a classical view of the

10. This Note treats only the I.C.J. A number of other "international courts" have been created pursuant to regional treaties of economic or political cooperation. The most significant is the Court of Justice of the European Economic Community, considered in Chapter XIII, infra. Other treaties have constituted international courts with a more strictly defined function and jurisdiction. A contemporary example is the European Court of Human Rights, created pursuant to the European Convention for the Protection of Human Rights and Fundamental Freedoms, p. 386, infra.

11. Table 17 appearing in 2 Rosenne, The Law and Practice of the International Court 939 (1965); 1 id. at 204–5.

field) may be parties to litigation before the I.C.J. under its contentious jurisdiction, a rule expressed in Article 34 of the Statute. Second, jurisdiction rests upon a state's consent. At the San Francisco Conference in 1945 which gave birth to the Charter, several smaller nations advocated compulsory jurisdiction of the Court over U. N. members. The larger powers, including the United States and the Soviet Union, were hostile towards such suggestions.

Statements in several opinions of the P.C.I.J. stress this continuing theme of the International Court. In its Advisory Opinion Concerning the Status of Eastern Carelia, P.C.I.J., Ser. B, No. 5 (1923), that court observed (at p. 27):

> This rule, moreover, only accepts and applies a principle which is a fundamental principle of international law, namely, the principle of the independence of States. It is well established in international law that no State can, without its consent, be compelled to submit its disputes with other States either to mediation or to arbitration, or to any other kind of pacific settlement. Such consent can be given once and for all in the form of an obligation freely undertaken, but it can, on the contrary, also be given in a special case apart from any existing obligation.

Article 36 of the Statute is the focal point for consideration of the Court's jurisdiction. Distinct jurisdictional bases are stated in its first two paragraphs. Under paragraph (1), a dispute between two countries might come before the Court pursuant to a special reference by the parties, rather like an arbitral *compromis.* Or the Court's jurisdiction may rest upon a bilateral treaty providing for submission to the I.C.J. of any disputes arising under it. See, e. g., Article XVI of the Convention of Establishment between the United States and France.* Similar provisions appear in multilateral treaties such as the 1958 Geneva Conventions on the Law of the Sea, an optional protocol to which states that disputes arising under the Conventions are within the compulsory jurisdiction of the I.C.J. The United States ratified these Conventions, but not the protocol.

Under paragraph (2), a state may make a unilateral declaration of submission to the Court's compulsory jurisdiction, effective upon filing with the Secretary General of the U. N., without special agreement between that state and other parties to the Statute.

As of 1974, 45 countries had on deposit declarations of submission. These included none of the Communist countries of the world, from Cuba to North Korea. Missing also were major countries of other groupings: the Federal Republic of Germany and Italy in Europe and, in Latin America, Argentina, Chile and Venezuela. Nine countries had allowed their submissions to expire or terminated them: Bolivia, Brazil, China, France, Guatemala, Iran, South Africa, Thailand and Turkey.

Read the declarations of France, Norway and the United States, set forth in the Documentary Supplement. Note that the French declaration was revoked in January 1974 as part of the French defiance of the Court's proceedings in the Nuclear Test Cases, [1973] I.C.J.Rep. 99, [1974] I.C.J.Rep. 253.

Note that the United States and French declarations contain reservations. This practice of qualifying declarations under Article 36 (2) has become widespread, with unfortunate consequences for the significance and effectiveness of the I.C.J. The introductory paragraph of the United States Declaration contains a characteristic reservation *ratione temporis*, for it covers only "legal disputes hereafter arising." Other reservations appearing in the concluding clauses (a) to (c) include the so-called Connally Amendment in clause (b), considered at p. 326, infra.

Established practice has confirmed the right of states to attach in this manner important conditions to their jurisdictional submissions, although Article 36 expressly contemplates only a few conditions. Note two clauses in that article which magnify the importance of any reservation. Article 36(2) refers to submissions that recognize as compulsory the jurisdiction of the Court "in relation to any other state accepting the same obligation," and Article 36(3) states that declarations may be made "on condition of reciprocity on the part of several or certain states."

According to a long line of judicial authority dating from early decisions of the P.C.I.J., whose Statute contained similar provisions, these clauses are read to mean that the condition of reciprocity is imported into every declaration. A respondent state can thus draw upon a claimant state's reservations. The function of these provisions is to establish equality of the parties to any litigation with respect to their declarations, for jurisdiction is conferred on the Court only to the extent to which the two declarations coincide. In the Interhandel Case (Switzerland v. United States), [1959] I.C.J.Rep. 6, 23, the I.C.J. stated:

> Reciprocity in the case of Declarations accepting the compulsory jurisdiction of the Court enables a Party to invoke a reservation to that acceptance which it has not expressed in its own Declaration but which the other Party has expressed in its Declaration. For example, Switzerland, which has not expressed in its Declaration any reservation *ratione temporis*, while the United States has accepted the compulsory jurisdiction of the Court only in respect of disputes subsequent to August 26th, 1946, might, if in the position of Respondent, invoke by virtue of reciprocity against the United States the American reservation if the United States attempted to refer to the Court a dispute with Switzerland which had arisen before August 26th, 1946. This is the effect of reciprocity in this connection. Reciprocity enables the State which has made the wider acceptance of the jurisdiction of the Court to rely upon the reservations to the acceptance laid down by the other Party. . . .

Analysis of the 45 declarations listed in the Yearbook 1974–1975 of the International Court of Justice shows that only seven had no reservations or limitations of any kind. Eleven contained reservations *ratione temporis* as to disputes arising before their effective date. A number limited their effectiveness to a specified period of time, typically five years, or provided for denunciation to be effective after a stated notice period. Other reservations were more fundamental, ranging from reservations as to disputes with other Commonwealth countries, to reservations as to disputes arising during hostilities, to the Connally Reservation and its imitations.

Given the prevalence of such complex declarations, questions about the jurisdiction of the Court frequently arise. The first problem posed in such situations is whether the Court has the power to determine its own jurisdiction. The Court's answer to this question appears in a preliminary opinion in the Nottebohm Case (Liechtenstein v. Guatemala, [1953] I.C.J.Rep. 111, 119–120:

> Paragraph 6 of Article 36 merely adopted, in respect of the Court, a rule consistently accepted by general international law in the matter of international arbitration. Since the Alabama case, it has been generally recognized, following the earlier precedents, that, in the absence of any agreement to the contrary, an international tribunal has the right to decide as to its own jurisdiction and has the power to interpret for this purpose the instruments which govern that jurisdiction. . . .
>
> This principle . . . assumes particular force when the international tribunal is no longer an arbitral tribunal constituted by virtue of a special agreement between the parties for the purpose of adjudicating on a particular dispute, but is an institution which has been pre-established by an international instrument defining its jurisdiction and regulating its operation, and is, in the present case, the principal judicial organ of the United Nations. . . .

The I.C.J. and arbitral tribunals represent two possible paths towards dispute-settlement. Assuming the willingness to be bound by a tribunal's decision, which path should a nation follow? Sohn in his Report on International Arbitration to the Helsinki Conference of the International Law Association (1966), suggests a number of pertinent considerations. The Report notes that arbitration tends to be less expensive and time consuming, and has the further advantage of receiving less publicity. Indeed the parties to a *compromis* can stipulate that the proceedings be closed and that the record be kept confidential. The ability to shape the procedure of an arbitral tribunal to the precise demands of the parties may make that medium more convenient for the resolution of certain kinds of claims, particularly a large number of related but distinct claims of one government based upon conduct of the other towards the claimant's nationals.

The Report and a number of commentators suggest that arbitration may be a more appropriate path with respect to disputes that are frankly political in character and escape settlement through the development or application of legal principles—namely, disputes to be decided *ex aequo et bono*. The ability of the parties to stipulate for an arbitral tribunal those substantive rules which it should apply may help them to realize their goals. Although the I.C.J. can be empowered by the parties to decide *ex aequo et bono* pursuant to Article 38(2) of the Statute, commentators have suggested that its role is better confined to the development and application of "international law," and that its contribution to this field and influence in the international community might be impaired if it were called upon to exercise a distinct and more frankly political function. The willingness of parties to submit political disputes to arbitration may be affected by their ability to select the tribunal's members, whereas (with the minor exception of *ad hoc* judges noted above) the composition of the International Court is predetermined. Another factor that may be decisive is the restriction of the Court's jurisdiction to disputes between states. The *compromis* for an arbitral tribunal can authorize private parties to appear as claimants against a governmental respondent.

Additional reading: Briggs, Reservations to the Acceptance of Compulsory Jurisdiction of the International Court of Justice, 93 Académie de Droit International, Recueil des Cours 229 (1958); Henkin, Editorial Comment, 65 Am.J.Int.L. 374 (1971); Jenks, The Prospects of International Adjudication (1964); Lauterpacht, The Development of International Law by the International Court (1958); Rosenne, The World Court (3d Ed. 1973). A Symposium on the I.C.J. appears in 11 Va.J.Int.L. 291–373 (1971).

QUESTIONS

(1) In the Nottebohm Case, p. 212, infra, Liechtenstein filed its Application commencing an action against Guatemala before the I.C.J. on December 17, 1951. Guatemala had filed its declaration under Article 36(2), recognizing the Court's compulsory jurisdiction "for a period of five years," on January 27, 1947. Guatemala claimed that the Court ceased to have jurisdiction over the case after January 26, 1952. What decision?

(2) Suppose that Switzerland instituted proceedings against the United States in July 1948. Switzerland alleges that the United States violated international law in 1945 by governmental measures adversely affecting property of Swiss nationals in the United States. It states that actions in United States courts, brought by Swiss nationals to recover their property, continued until 1947, when the first Swiss diplomatic protest was made to and rejected by the United States. The United States asks the Court to dismiss the application because of its reservation *ratione temporis*. (a) What decision? (b) Would the answer be different or clearer under the French form of reservation *ratione temporis*? (c) Suppose that Switzerland had submitted to the jurisdiction of the I.C.J. with respect to "disputes arising after January 1, 1949." Should this affect the Court's decision?

(3) In both cases above, why shouldn't the respondent state prevail on the basis of the acknowledged principle that jurisdiction of the I.C.J. rests on the consent of the parties?

NOTE ON ENFORCEMENT OF AWARDS AND JUDGMENTS OF INTERNATIONAL TRIBUNALS

The jurisdictional problems that abound at the threshold of litigation may be succeeded by problems at the end of the process over enforcement of a judgment. In most cases, judgments of international tribunals involve simply a declaration whether international law was violated or an award of money damages. That is, international tribunals rarely enter what lawyers in the United States would refer to as "equity decrees," such as mandatory or prohibitory injunctions or orders for specific restitution. A *compromis* may empower a tribunal to enter such a decree, or indeed more unusual decrees such as those defining boundary lines between disputant nations or establishing rules to govern the parties' future conduct.

Article 60 of the Statute of the I.C.J. and Article 94 of the Charter make clear the duties imposed by a judgment. Note that Article 94 does not refer to decisions of other kinds of international tribunals. The principle that awards are binding runs deep in the history of international arbitration. See Article 30 of the Model Rules of the International Law Commission.

There have been only infrequent instances of failure to comply with arbitral awards or judgments of the International Court. One such case arose under a judgment of the P.C.I.J., and Albania did refuse to satisfy a judgment of the I.C.J. imposing money judgments against it in proceedings brought by the United Kingdom.[12] In proceedings brought by the United Kingdom against Iran, the I.C.J. ordered Iran to comply with certain preliminary measures. Iran refused, but in the following year the Court, before reaching the merits of the dispute, concluded that it did not have jurisdiction and withdrew its initial order.[13]

In recent years the Court has encountered several brusque refusals to comply with its orders that have shaken its prestige. In 1971, in the South-West Africa Case, [1971] I.C.J.Rep. 16, it held that the continued presence of South Africa in Namibia or South-West Africa, after its mandate had been cancelled by the United Nations, was illegal. Four years later, despite that ruling and various resolutions of the Security Council and the General Assembly, the South African presence is still manifest. In the Fisheries Jurisdiction Case, the interim orders issued by the Court, [1973] I.C.J.Rep. 3, 49, were stated by Iceland to be without validity. Iceland meanwhile refused to make an appearance in the case. Similarly, France conducted nuclear

12. The judgment in The Wimbledon Case, P.C.I.J., Ser. A, No. 1 (1923), was not carried out since the Reparations Court (of which France was a member) refused to order it paid. See Hudson, The Permanent Court of International Justice 596 (1943). The Albanian refusal, based on a claim of excess of jurisdiction, occurred in the Corfu Channel Case (United Kingdom v. Albania), [1949] I.C.J.Rep. 4, 36; [1949] I.C.J.Rep. 244, 250.

13. Anglo-Iranian Oil Co. Case (United Kingdom v. Iran), Request for the Indication of Interim Measures of Protection, [1951] I.C.J.Rep. 89, 93-94; Jurisdiction, [1952] I.C.J.Rep. 93, 114.

tests in the Pacific in defiance of interim orders in the Nuclear Test Case. See [1973] I.C.J.Rep. 99, 135.

The arbitral awards which have most frequently led to refusals to comply have been those affecting strongly felt national interests, such as territorial boundaries. In assessing the generally favorable record of states, a commentator has observed: [14]

> . . . . The fact that there has been statistically a good record of compliance must be assessed in the light of the relatively unimportant disputes that have been submitted to arbitration or judicial settlement. Should there be a wider acceptance of compulsory jurisdiction—as through compromissory clauses in treaties or declarations under Article 36, paragraph 2, of the Statute—the chances of non-performance would almost certainly increase; for it is evident that a state would not then be as prepared to accept an adverse decision as where it had agreed to the submission of a particular dispute. Obviously, any extension of international adjudication into the area of more "vital" questions would also increase the risk of non-compliance.

The United States has on occasion rejected arbitral awards, on grounds that the arbitrators exceeded their powers and rendered an improper award. The Chamizal boundary dispute with Mexico led to such a reaction after an adverse arbitral decision was rendered in 1911, and it was not until 1964 that the United States brought itself to cede the territory involved.[15] In other cases, this country promptly executed awards which it believed to have involved a serious misapplication of controlling principles. For example, in an arbitration of 1922 between the United States and Norway, the arbitrators rendered an award in Norway's favor. Norwegian Shipowners' Claims (1922), 1 U.N.R.I.A.A. 309. In 1923, Secretary of State Hughes wrote to the Norwegian Minister at Washington advising him that the Congress had appropriated funds to satisfy the award and that a draft in full payment of the award was enclosed. In his letter, appearing in 1 U.N.R.I.A.A. at 344, Secretary Hughes stated:

> By this action [the transmittal of the draft] the Government of the United States gives tangible proof of its desire to respect arbitral awards and it again acknowledges devotion to the principle of arbitral settlements even in the face of a decision proclaiming certain theories of law which it cannot accept. Faithful to its traditional policy, my Government is most desirous to promote the judicial determination of international disputes of a justiciable character and in this interest to give its due support to judicial determinations.
>
> It is because of this established policy that my Government especially regrets that it seems to be necessary to refer to statements contained in the present award, but with due

14. Schachter, The Enforcement of International Judicial and Arbitral Decisions, 54 Am.J.Int.L. 1, 5 (1960).

15. See 1 Hackworth, International Law 411–17 (1940); Convention of 1963, 15 U.S.T. & O.I.A. 21, T.I.A.S. No. 5515; 78 Stat. 184 (1964), 22 U.S.C.A. §§ 277d–17 to 277d–25.

regard for the maintenance of the principles of international law, my Government finds itself compelled to say that it cannot accept certain apparent bases of the award as being declaratory of that law or as hereafter binding upon this Government as a precedent.

When a respondent state fails to honor a judgment or award, the prevailing state confronts the problem of what enforcement action it can take. Experience here is meagre, particularly since the United Nations Charter (see Article 2) is generally viewed as prohibiting measures taken during the 19th century by creditor nations—recourse to armed force to collect a debt or enforce awards. Beyond diplomatic negotiations and the economic pressures which a state may be able to exert to secure compliance, various routes would be explored: attachment of property of the debtor state within the territory of the creditor state, or efforts to attach property of the debtor state in third countries through recourse to the political or judicial procedures of such countries.[16] Article 94(2) of the U. N. Charter treats the problem of enforcement only with respect to judgments of the I.C.J. Its ultimate effect will depend upon the answers given to a number of unresolved questions: To what extent are the powers granted the Security Council by Article 94 independent of those defined in other parts of the Charter; under what criteria should the Security Council review a judgment which has not been honored; what is the nature of the measures that it can include in its recommendations or decisions?

Additional reading: Schachter, The Enforcement of International Judicial and Arbitral Decisions, 54 Am.J.Int.L. 1 (1960).

QUESTION

Suppose that an arbitral award requires the United States to pay $50,000,000 to the claimant state. As a Congressman, you must decide whether to vote to appropriate funds to satisfy the award. Although strongly opposed to the principles of international law upon which the award rests, and believing that the tribunal erred in stating such principles to be part of international law you recognize that the proceedings were fair and that the arbitrators acted within the powers conferred upon them by the *compromis*. In what respects, if any, would your attitude differ in deciding whether to vote in favor of appropriating funds in this instance, or funds to satisfy a judgment of like amount in favor of United States citizens rendered by the Court of Claims and based upon an interpretation of a federal statute which you believe to be erroneous and contrary

16. Attachment of property raises a number of problems, principally the immunity of property of a foreign sovereign from attachment intended for execution of a judgment. Such problems are considered at pp. 637–671, infra. Further, an effort to base an action before a national court upon a judgment of an international tribunal raises the question of the status and effect of such a judgment under national law. A recent illustration of an effort to clarify this second question is found in the Convention on the Settlement of Investment Disputes between States and Nationals of Other States, and in United States legislation of 1966 implementing that Convention, at pp. 484–486, infra. See also "Socobel" v. Greek State, 1951 Int.L.Rep. 3 (Civ.Trib., Brussels, April 30, 1951).

to the national interest? [17] Do the different considerations in these two cases point towards a stronger or weaker argument for honoring the arbitral award?

C. PROTECTION BY STATES OF THEIR NATIONALS

The principle of Article 34 of the I.C.J. Statute permitting only states to be parties before that Court under its contentious jurisdiction, has been departed from in some *compromis* for arbitration and contemporary treaties creating other international tribunals. Nonetheless, that rule reflects ideas that have deep roots in classical international law. It rests in part upon the belief that the equality and dignity of sovereign states would be compromised if states were sued by private parties, and in part upon the classical view that international law imposes duties and confers rights only upon states, its sole "subjects."

That view raises no problems for diplomatic negotiations or litigation between states over certain kinds of disputes. Suppose that state X claims that state Z has violated international law by sending its troops into X's territory, or by laying mines in time of peace in waters where X's warships had a right of passage and thereby injuring one of them, or by seizing X's embassy in Z. These charges involve injuries felt "directly" by state X: direct interferences with its claims to territorial integrity, to freedom of navigation by its vessels, or to immunity of its diplomatic premises from seizure. The conflict arises on an intergovernmental level. Of course, to say that the state is "directly" injured should not blur the fact that the injury ultimately may be felt by some or all of X's citizens.

The materials in this book examine primarily those conflicts between governments which follow a different path, conflicts which originate in a dispute between a national of the claimant state and governmental authorities of the respondent state. Of course, this distinction says of itself nothing about the relative significance of disputes arising in one or the other way. Alien-state disputes ripening into state-state disputes may reach basic economic or political issues and of course may pose issues of fundamental human rights.

Suppose that Z, without hearing or trial imprisons Y, a citizen of X, or expropriates Y's property without compensation or breaks

17. Compare the Texas City Disaster litigation, which involved claims against the United States under the Federal Tort Claims Act for injuries suffered from an explosion and fire allegedly caused by negligence of the United States. Over 300 claims asserted damages exceeding $200,000,000. In a test case, a plaintiff was awarded damages in the district court, but the judgment was reversed by the court of appeals. The Supreme Court affirmed this reversal in 1953 in Dalehite v. United States, p. 640, infra, by interpreting the Act to insulate the United States from liability under the facts before it. In 1955, Congress passed a statute providing relief up to a stated amount per claimant. 69 Stat. 707.

a contract with him. Assume that such acts, under the circumstances, violate international law. Can Y himself successfully assert a right under international law to release or compensation? Can he vindicate those rights before the national courts of X or Z? If not, can X assert a claim based upon international law against Z? On what theory would such a claim be supported? The following case gives the classical answer to this last question.

---

1. PROTECTION OF INDIVIDUALS

MAVROMMATIS PALESTINE CONCESSIONS (JURISDICTION)

Permanent Court of International Justice, 1924.
P.C.I.J., Ser. A, No. 2.

[In 1924, the Greek Government commenced proceedings before the Court against Great Britain, the Mandatory Power for Palestine. Its claim arose out of the refusal of the Palestine Government to recognize certain rights acquired in Palestine by a Greek national, Mavrommatis, pursuant to certain concessions antedating the Mandate for Palestine between Mavrommatis and Ottoman authorities. The Greek Government alleged that this refusal violated Article 11 of the Palestine Mandate, which provided that the Palestine Government "subject to any international obligations accepted by the Mandatory, shall have full power to provide for public ownership or control of any of the natural resources of the country or of the public works, services and utilities established or to be established therein." The "international obligations" clause referred to provisions of the Peace Treaty with Turkey, subsequently entered into, which provided that pre-1914 concessions granted by Turkey were to be maintained by the new authorities in territories detached from Turkey.

The British Government protested the jurisdiction of the Court, which rested upon Article 26 of the Palestine Mandate. The Court ruled that it had jurisdiction. Excerpts from its opinion appear below.]

Article 26 of the Mandate contains the following clause:

> "The Mandatory agrees that, if any dispute whatever should arise between the Mandatory and another Member of the League of Nations relating to the interpretation or the application of the provisions of the Mandate, such dispute, if it cannot be settled by negotiation, shall be submitted to the Permanent Court of International Justice provided for by Article 14 of the Covenant of the League of Nations."

. . .

Before considering whether the case of the Mavrommatis concessions relates to the *interpretation* or *application* of the Mandate and whether consequently its nature and subject are such as to bring it within the jurisdiction of the Court as defined in the article quoted above, it is essential to ascertain whether the case fulfils all the other conditions laid down in this clause. Does the matter before the Court constitute a dispute between the Mandatory and another Member of the League of Nations? Is it a dispute which cannot be settled by negotiation?

A dispute is a disagreement on a point of law or fact, a conflict of legal views or of interests between two persons. The present suit between Great Britain and Greece certainly possesses these characteristics. The latter Power is asserting its own rights by claiming from His Britannic Majesty's Government an indemnity on the ground that M. Mavrommatis, one of its subjects, has been treated by the Palestine or British authorities in a manner incompatible with certain international obligations which they were bound to observe.

In the case of the Mavrommatis concessions it is true that the dispute was at first between a private person and a State—i. e. between M. Mavrommatis and Great Britain. Subsequently, the Greek Government took up the case. The dispute then entered upon a new phase; it entered the domain of international law, and became a dispute between two States. . . . .

. . . . It is an elementary principle of international law that a State is entitled to protect its subjects, when injured by acts contrary to international law committed by another State, from whom they have been unable to obtain satisfaction through the ordinary channels. By taking up the case of one of its subjects and by resorting to diplomatic action or international judicial proceedings on his behalf, a State is in reality asserting its own rights—its right to ensure, in the person of its subjects, respect for the rules of international law.

The question, therefore, whether the present dispute originates in an injury to a private interest, which in point of fact is the case in many international disputes, is irrelevant from this standpoint. Once a State has taken up a case on behalf of one of its subjects before an international tribunal, in the eyes of the latter the State is sole claimant. The fact that Great Britain and Greece are the opposing Parties to the dispute arising out of the Mavrommatis concessions is sufficient to make it a dispute between two States within the meaning of Article 26 of the Palestine Mandate. . . .

NOTE ON INTERNATIONAL CLAIMS

The Mavrommatis Case further develops a topic that was central to Chapter I, the significance of nationality. There the focus of discussion was national legal systems; here, international law.

It should be appreciated that claims brought by a state on behalf of an individual or corporation, allegedly injured by foreign governmental action violating international law, rarely come before international tribunals. At the start, the private claimant will generally seek relief through whatever paths—judicial, executive or legislative—are open to him in the foreign country. If he does not succeed, he might then formulate a request to the State Department that it take up his case against the foreign government.

Within the Department, responsibility for handling claims rests in the Office of the Legal Adviser.[18] Precise formulation of rules for

18. In addition to performing for the Department the advisory functions that are indicated by its title, this Office furnishes drafting and negotiating skills in connection with international agreements as well as domestic laws that bear upon foreign affairs. It also represents the United States before international tribunals. Although the Office does not represent the Department or the United States before domestic courts (a role normally filled by the Department of Justice), it may be called upon by judges or parties to submit its views about customary international law, treaty

the presentation of claims by private parties to the Office is hardly feasible, considering the diversity of circumstances from which international claims arise. Often a claim is informally presented and followed by discussions with Departmental officials which indicate the necessary documentation. General suggestions published by the Department request a formal claim in narrative form which must be sworn. Unlike the usual complaint before domestic courts, the claim must not only assert a basis for protection by the United States but must also be accompanied by affidavits and documents that establish the claimant's case.

In deciding whether to recommend that the Government take action on behalf of the claimant, the Legal Adviser will weigh various considerations: respect for the claimant's rights, adherence to principles of international law, the effect of any governmental action upon political relations with the foreign country, the influence that espousal of a claim may have as a precedent in future cases, and so on. In short, once a claim has been filed, its fate is largely out of its author's hands, particularly since the decision reached by the Legal Adviser or Department may not be open to judicial review. In many fields of decision-making, the Department has considered itself to be exempt from sections of the Administrative Procedure Act, 80 Stat. 381 (1966), 5 U.S.C.A. §§ 551–559—and in particular, from the provisions for judicial review of agency action in Section 10 of the Act. That section excepts agency action which "is by law committed to agency discretion." There have been few, and unsuccessful, efforts by private parties to obtain court orders directing the Secretary of State to enter into diplomatic negotiations with a foreign country to assist an American citizen.[19]

interpretation, United States foreign policy on a particular issue, and so on. See generally Bilder, The Office of the Legal Adviser: The State Department Lawyer and Foreign Affairs, 56 Am.J.Int.L. 633 (1962). The complex relationship between the Department of State and the courts in decision-making in cases involving questions of sovereign immunity is examined at pp. 637–672, infra.

19. In United States ex rel. Keefe v. Dulles, 222 F.2d 390 (D.C.Cir. 1954), the court stated that the Secretary "was not under a legal duty to attempt through diplomatic processes to obtain Keefe's release. Quite to the contrary, the commencement of diplomatic negotiations with a foreign power is completely in the discretion of the President and the head of the Department of State, who is his political agent. The Executive is not subject to judicial control or direction in such matters [citing United States v. Curtiss-Wright Export Corp., p. 102, supra]. Accordingly we hold the petition [which the court regarded as seeking affirmative injunctive relief against the Secretary of State] was properly dismissed . . . ." Compare the discussion of takings, treaties and the prosecution of international claims in Aris Gloves, Inc. v. United States, 190 Ct.Cl. 367, 420 F.2d 1386 (1970). But compare 15 Stat. 224 (1868), 22 U.S.C.A. § 1732 which provides that the President, if informed that any citizen has been "unjustly deprived of his liberty" by a foreign government, has the duty to make inquiry of the foreign government. If "it appears to be wrongful and in violation of the rights of American citizenship, the President shall forthwith demand the release of such citizen . . . ." If the demand is refused, the President "shall use" such means, not amounting to acts of war, as he thinks necessary and proper to obtain the release, and shall communicate all facts and proceedings to the Congress.

If the Department decides to proceed, copies of the claim are sent to the foreign government. The range of measures which the Department might itself initiate or recommend to other government branches is broad. The Government might espouse the claim through informal discussions with the foreign government, or through formal diplomatic protests. The Mavrommatis principle would of course support such diplomatic initiatives on behalf of the national. If a settlement is not forthcoming, the Government may be in a position to exert various economic and political pressures against the foreign state—perhaps quota limitations on imports from it, or suspension of foreign aid programs. In former times, military intervention was a distinct possibility. Examples of each of these reactions appear in subsequent chapters.

Recourse to international tribunals is thus often a matter of last resort. In many cases, that method of resolving disputes will be unavailable, since the "respondent" state will not have submitted to a tribunal's jurisdiction. Assuming that the jurisdictional hurdle can be cleared, the Mavrommatis principle that a state, by espousing its national's claim, makes the claim its own, has important consequences. Jurisdictional provisions of tribunals such as Article 34 of the I.C.J. Statute can thus be satisfied. It also follows that the state conducts the litigation and decides whether to compromise the claim or abandon the action. Any money judgment would be paid to the state, although in the usual case it will distribute such funds to the injured nationals. The United States has upon occasion refused to pay over an award to a claimant whom it regarded as not entitled to it. See, e. g., La Abra Silver Mining Co. v. United States, 175 U.S. 423, 20 S.Ct. 168, 44 L.Ed. 223 (1899). The procedure usually followed, 29 Stat. 32 (1896), 31 U.S.C. § 547 (1970), provides for the payment of funds into the Treasury, which disburses them upon certification by the Secretary of State.

It is less clear what the implications of the Mavrommatis principle are in the area of damages. Does one measure them by the injury to the national or to the nation? Customarily the damages asserted will bear a close relationship to the injury suffered by the national. One arbitral tribunal, however, in a case involving the illegal seizure of a British vessel by an American cruiser on the high seas, awarded damages of $25,000 to the Canadian Government for the insult to the flag, although it awarded nothing for the loss of the ship which was owned and controlled by a group of American rum-runners. The I'm Alone (Canada v. United States), 2 Hackworth, Digest of Internation Law 703–08 (1941).

The fact that states *can* espouse claims on behalf of nationals does not mean that private parties *cannot* prosecute their own claims before international tribunals. The compromis establishing an arbitral tribunal or treaty establishing an international court may authorize individuals or corporations to bring actions before them.[20]

20. In some instances, individuals have been defendants before international courts. A prominent example is the Nuremberg International Military Tri-

Frequently cited examples include the Mixed Arbitral Tribunals that were established to settle claims at the end of World War I, the tribunal set up by Poland and Germany in 1922 to handle controversies over the treatment of minorities in Upper Silesia, and the Central American Court of Justice. See Jessup, A Modern Law of Nations 18 (1952). The Permanent Court of Arbitration, p. 193, supra, adopted rules in 1962 which permit agreements between states and private parties to provide for arbitration under its auspices. See 57 Am.J. Int.L. 500 (1963). Similarly, the Convention on the Settlement of Investment Disputes between States and Nationals of Other States, p. 484, infra, establishes a framework for arbitration between the parties described in its title. The European Convention for the Protection of Human Rights and Fundamental Freedoms created two organs, the European Commission of Human Rights and the European Court of Human Rights. The Court came into being in 1958. An individual may file an application with the Commission alleging deprivation of a right guaranteed him by the Convention, and the Commission or an interested state may take his case to the Court under specified conditions. See p. 386, infra. The Court of Justice of the European Economic Community, considered in Chapter XIII, is also open to private parties in certain cases.

Additional reading: Bilder, The Office of the Legal Adviser: The State Department Lawyer and Foreign Affairs, 56 Am.J.Int.L. 633 (1962); Department of State Memorandum of March 1, 1961 (procedure for filing claims to be asserted against Cuba), reprinted in 56 Am.J.Int.L. 166 (1962); Lillich and Christenson, International Claims: Their Preparation and Presentation (1962); Note, The Nature and Extent of Executive Power to Espouse the International Claims of United States Nationals, 7 Vand.J. Trans.L. 95 (1973).

PROBLEM

In 1974 Guatador expropriated a plant worth $30,000,000 belonging to Overseas Investment, Inc. (OII), a Delaware corporation. It has paid no compensation and has stated that it intends to pay none. As a result of 1973 elections, Guatador is governed by a regime regarded by many in the United States as Communist-oriented. Relations between it and the United States are tense but there are prospects that the chief points of strain may be worked out by negotiations. OII has consulted eminent experts in this country, and is advised by them that Guatador's actions have violated international law. Guatador entertains the contrary view. OII has presented a claim to the State Department. (You may assume that it has exhausted local remedies in Guatador.)

(1) Consider the situation from the perspective of the Legal Adviser. What factors should influence his recommendations about the action, if any, to be taken? To which of them should he give priority?

(2) Suppose that the Department advises OII that it will send a note of protest to the Guatador Government but that it will not at this time

bunal, before which a number of leading Nazis were tried for crimes defined in the international agreements constituting that Tribunal. The principles upon which the Tribunal acted are considered at p. 904, infra.

press OII's case more aggressively. Do you suppose that OII has any means, judicial or other, of obtaining more favorable action?

(3) Consider the situation from the perspective of an attorney for OII engaged in drafting a prospectus for a new public issue of stock of OII. The plant was a material part of OII's total assets. Its expropriation and the ensuing claim have been widely noted in the press. You must meet the requirements of the Securities Act of 1933, which provides for civil and other relief against persons responsible for prospectuses which omit "to state a material fact . . . necessary to make the statements therein not misleading." What points about the situation would you include in the Prospectus in order to comply with that mandate?

THE CANEVARO CASE

Award of 1912, Tribunal of the Permanent Court of Arbitration, under a Compromis between Italy and Peru dated April 26, 1910.
Scott, The Hague Court Reports 284 (1916).

Whereas, by a *compromis* dated April 25, 1910, the Italian and Peruvian Governments agreed to submit the following questions to arbitration:

Should the Peruvian Government pay in cash, or in accordance with the provisions of the Peruvian law of June 12, 1889, on the domestic debt, the bills of exchange (*cambiali, libramientos*) now in the possession of the brothers Napoléon, Carlos, and Rafael Canevaro, which were drawn by the Peruvian Government to the order of the firm of José Canevaro & Sons for the sum of 43,140 pounds sterling, plus the legal interest on the said amount? . . .

Has Count Rafael Canevaro a right to be considered as an Italian claimant? . . .

Whereas, in order to simplify the following statement it is deemed best to pass first upon the third question contained in the *compromis*, that is, the question of the status of Rafael Canevaro;

Whereas, according to Peruvian legislation (Article 34 of the Constitution), Rafael Canevaro is a Peruvian by birth because born on Peruvian territory,

And, whereas, on the other hand, according to Italian legislation (Article 4 of the Civil Code) he is of Italian nationality because born of an Italian father;

Whereas, as a matter of fact, Rafael Canevaro has on several occasions acted as a Peruvian citizen, both by running as a candidate for the Senate, where none are admitted except Peruvian citizens and where he succeeded in defending his election, and, particularly, by accepting the office of Consul General for the Netherlands, after having secured the authorization of both the Peruvian Government and the Peruvian Congress;

Whereas, under these circumstances, whatever Rafael Canevaro's status as a national may be in Italy, the Government of Peru has a right to consider him a Peruvian citizen and to deny his status as an Italian claimant. . . .

[The tribunal proceeded to examine the claims of Rafael Canevaro's brothers.]

COMMENT

One of the recurrent questions before international tribunals has been the degree of conclusiveness to be attributed to national determinations of citizenship. The Flutie Cases before the American-Venezuelan Mixed Claims Commission pursuant to the Protocol of Feb. 17, 1903, Ralston (ed.), Venezuelan Arbitrations of 1903, at 38 (1904), 9 U.N.R.I.A.A. 148, involved a claimant who had received a citizenship certificate from a United States court. Venezuela asserted that he had not in fact spent five years in residence in the United States prior to naturalization, as required by the United States statute. The Commission sustained Venezuela's defense. See generally Briggs, The Law of Nations 471–73 (2d ed. 1952).

Another problem is that of the time at which the individual must be shown to have the nationality of the claimant state. The generally accepted rule requires that the individual possess continuous nationality in the claimant state from the time of injury to the time of the litigation. See, e. g., Panevezys-Saldutiskis Ry. Case (Estonia v. Lithuania), P.C.I.J., Ser. A/B, No. 76 (1939). General instructions for claimants, appearing in a Department of State publication of October 1, 1924, state that the Government "as a rule, declines to support claims that have not belonged to claimants [of American nationality] from the date the claim arose to the date of its settlement." Treaties and statutes have occasionally departed from this rule, by stipulating other categories of individuals on whose behalf claims can be brought or to whom sums received from another state will be distributed by a national claims commission. See the discussion in 53 Am.J.Int.L. 144–51 (1959).

QUESTIONS

(1) A respondent state asserts that the claimant state cannot represent the individual claimant, who is a citizen of both the claimant country and a third country. What decision? Is Canevaro helpful on this point?

(2) What effect would the Hague Convention on Certain Questions Relating to the Conflict of Nationality Laws * have today on these issues if a question arose between two countries that had adopted it? Note particularly Articles 4 and 5.

NOTTEBOHM CASE (LIECHTENSTEIN v. GUATEMALA)

International Court of Justice, 1955.
[1955] I.C.J.Rep. 4.

[Nottebohm was born a German national in 1881, at Hamburg. In 1905, he went to Guatemala to take up residence and establish headquarters for his business activities in commerce and plantations. In 1937, he became head of the Nottebohm firm in Guatemala. After 1905, he made occasional business and holiday visits to Germany and other countries, continued to have business connections in Germany, and occasionally visited a brother who had lived in the Principality of Liechtenstein since 1931. Some of his relatives and friends were in Germany, others in Guatemala. His fixed abode was in Guatemala until 1943.

In 1939, Nottebohm travelled to Hamburg and Liechtenstein. On October 9, 1939, shortly after Germany's attack on Poland, he applied for naturalization as a Liechtenstein citizen. The Liechtenstein Law of 1934 concerning naturalization required an applicant to prove his acceptance into the "Home Corporation" of a Liechtenstein commune in order to acquire nationality, and to prove loss of former nationality upon naturalization (this condition being subject to waiver). Naturalization was made conditional upon residence of at least three years in the Principality, but this requirement was also subject to waiver. Certain documents (including evidence of residence in the Principality, certificates of good conduct and proof of an agreement with Liechtenstein tax authorities) and payment of a naturalization fee were required. The 1934 Law provided that the government, after examining and approving the documents, should submit the application for naturalization to the Diet, and if approved by the Diet, to the Prince, who alone could confer nationality.

Nottebohm sought a waiver of the three-year residence requirement and submitted documents as to financial responsibility and a tax agreement with local authorities. Taxes were paid in October, and after obtaining all requisite approvals, Nottebohm took the oath of allegiance on October 20, 1939. Nottebohm obtained a Liechtenstein passport, had it visa-ed by the Guatemalan Consul General in Zurich in December 1939, and returned to Guatemala in early 1940 to resume his business activities.

In 1943, after Guatemala entered World War II against Germany, Guatemalan authorities took Nottebohm into custody, and arranged for his removal to the United States for internment during the war as a dangerous enemy alien. Internment continued until 1946, and upon his release Nottebohm went to Liechtenstein. Guatemalan decrees and legislation during the war relating to enemy aliens, and final legislative measures in the late 1940's, transferred ownership of most of Nottebohm's property in that country to the government.

In 1951, Liechtenstein commenced proceedings against Guatemala before the I. C. J. It filed a Memorial in which it alleged that the Government of Guatemala, by arresting and expelling Nottebohm and seizing his property without compensation, violated international law and thus was obliged to pay damages to Liechtenstein. In its replies, Guatemala contended that the Liechtenstein claim was inadmissible since Nottebohm's naturalization as a Liechtenstein citizen was not in accordance with generally recognized principles. It was fraudulently obtained by Nottebohm to acquire the status of a neutral, without any intention of establishing a "durable link" between himself and Liechtenstein. Guatemala further alleged, in the alternative, that Nottebohm had not pursued local remedies and that, in any event, the Guatemalan action against Nottebohm and his property was not in violation of international law.

The Court did not reach the merits of these further contentions but disposed of the case on the basis of Guatemala's first defense. It rejected Liechtenstein's argument that Guatemala was precluded from challenging Nottebohm's Liechtenstein nationality since it had admitted Nottebohm on a Liechtenstein passport. With respect to the questions of international law relating to nationality, the Court's opinion stated in part:]

Guatemala has referred to a well-established principle of international law, which it expressed in Counter-Memorial, where it is stated that "it is the bond of nationality between the State and the individual which alone confers upon the State the right of diplomatic protection". This sentence is taken from a Judgment of the Permanent Court of International Justice (Series A/B, No. 76, p. 16), which relates to the form of diplomatic protection constituted by international judicial proceedings.

Liechtenstein considers itself to be acting in conformity with this principle and contends that Nottebohm is its national by virtue of the naturalization conferred upon him. . . .

. . . . Counsel for Liechtenstein said: "the essential question is whether Mr. Nottebohm, having acquired the nationality of Liechtenstein, that acquisition of nationality is one which must be recognized by other States". This formulation is accurate, subject to the twofold reservation that, in the first place, what is involved is not recognition for all purposes but merely for the purposes of the admissibility of the Application, and, secondly, that what is involved is not recognition by all States but only by Guatemala.

The Court does not propose to go beyond the limited scope of the question which it has to decide, namely whether the nationality conferred on Nottebohm can be relied upon as against Guatemala in justification of the proceedings instituted before the Court. It must decide this question on the basis of international law; to do so is consistent with the nature of the question and with the nature of the Court's own function. . . .

. . . . The Court will deal with this question without considering that of the validity of Nottebohm's naturalization according to the law of Liechtenstein.

It is for Liechtenstein, as it is for every sovereign State, to settle by its own legislation the rules relating to the acquisition of its nationality, and to confer that nationality by naturalization granted by its own organs in accordance with that legislation. It is not necessary to determine whether international law imposes any limitations on its freedom of decision in this domain. Furthermore, nationality has its most immediate, its most far-reaching and, for most people, its only effects within the legal system of the State conferring it. Nationality serves above all to determine that the person upon whom it is conferred enjoys the rights and is bound by the obligations which the law of the State in question grants to or imposes on its nationals. This is implied in the wider concept that nationality is within the domestic jurisdiction of the State. . . .

The naturalization of Nottebohm was an act performed by Liechtenstein in the exercise of its domestic jurisdiction. The question to be decided is whether that act has the international effect here under consideration.

International practice provides many examples of acts performed by States in the exercise of their domestic jurisdiction which do not necessarily or automatically have international effect, which are not necessarily and automatically binding on other States or which are binding on them only subject to certain conditions: this is the case, for instance, of a judgment given by the competent court of a State which it is sought to invoke in another State. . . .

[The Court noted cases before national or international tribunals in which two States had conferred nationality upon the same individual.]

In most cases arbitrators have not strictly speaking had to decide a conflict of nationality as between States, but rather to determine whether the nationality invoked by the applicant State was one which could be relied upon as against the respondent State, that is to say, whether it entitled the applicant State to exercise protection. . . . In order to decide this question arbitrators have evolved certain principles for determining whether full international effect was to be attributed to the nationality invoked. The same issue is now before the Court: it must be resolved by applying the same principles . . . .

International arbitrators have . . . . given their preference to the real and effective nationality, that which accorded with the facts, that based on stronger factual ties between the person concerned and one of the States whose nationality is involved. Different factors are taken into consideration, and their importance will vary from one case to the next: the habitual residence of the individual concerned is an important factor, but there are other factors such as the centre of his interests, his family ties, his participation in public life, attachment shown by him for a given country and inculcated in his children, etc.

Similarly, the courts of third States, when they have before them an individual whom two other States hold to be their national, seek to resolve the conflict by having recourse to international criteria and their prevailing tendency is to prefer the real and effective nationality.

The same tendency prevails in the writings of publicists and in practice. This notion is inherent in the provisions of Article 3, paragraph 2, of the Statute of the Court. National laws reflect this tendency when, *inter alia,* they make naturalization dependent on conditions indicating the existence of a link, which may vary in their purpose or in their nature but which are essentially concerned with this idea. The Liechtenstein Law of January 4th, 1934, is a good example.

The practice of certain States which refrain from exercising protection in favour of a naturalized person when the latter has in fact, by his prolonged absence, severed his links with what is no longer for him anything but his nominal country, manifests the view of these States, that, in order to be capable of being invoked against another State, nationality must correspond with the factual situation. A similar view is manifested in the relevant provisions of the bilateral nationality treaties concluded between the United States of America and other States since 1868, such as those sometimes referred to as the Bancroft Treaties, and in the Pan-American Convention, signed at Rio de Janeiro on August 13th, 1906, on the status of naturalized citizens who resume residence in their country of origin.

The character thus recognized on the international level as pertaining to nationality is in no way inconsistent with the fact that international law leaves it to each State to lay down the rules governing the grant of its own nationality. The reason for this is that the diversity of demographic conditions has thus far made it impossible for any general agreement to be reached on the rules relating to nationality, although the latter by its very nature affects international relations. It has been considered that the best way of making such rules accord with the varying demographic conditions in different countries is to leave the fixing of such rules to the competence of each State. On the other hand, a State cannot claim that the rules it has thus laid down are entitled to recognition by another State unless it has acted in conformity with this general aim of making the legal bond of nationality accord with the individual's genuine connection with the State which assumes the defence of its citizens by means of protection as against other States.

The requirement that such a concordance must exist is to be found in the studies carried on in the course of the last thirty years upon the initiative and under the auspices of the League of Nations and the United Nations. It explains the provision which the Conference for the Codification of International Law, held at The Hague in 1930, inserted in Article I of the Convention relating to the Conflict of Nationality Laws, laying down that the law enacted by a State for the purpose of determining who are its nationals "shall be recognized by other States in so far as it is consistent with . . . international custom, and the principles of law generally recognized with regard to nationality". In the same spirit, Article 5 of the Convention refers to criteria of the individual's genuine connections for the purpose of resolving questions of dual nationality which arise in third States.

According to the practice of States, to arbitral and judicial decisions and to the opinions of writers, nationality is a legal bond having as its basis a social fact of attachment, a genuine connection of existence, interests and sentiments, together with the existence of reciprocal rights and duties. It may be said to constitute the juridical expression of the fact that the individual upon whom it is conferred, either directly by the law or as the result of an act of the authorities, is in fact more closely connected with the population of the State conferring nationality than with that of any other State. . . .

Diplomatic protection and protection by means of international judicial proceedings constitute measures for the defence of the rights of the State. . . .

Since this is the character which nationality must present when it is invoked to furnish the State which has granted it with a title to the exercise of protection and to the institution of international judicial proceedings, the Court must ascertain whether the nationality granted to Nottebohm by means of naturalization is of this character or, in other words, whether the factual connection between Nottebohm and Liechtenstein in the period preceding, contemporaneous with and following his naturalization appears to be sufficiently close, so preponderant in relation to any connection which may have existed between him and any other State, that it is possible to regard the nationality conferred upon him as real and effective, as the exact juridical expression of a social fact of a connection which existed previously or came into existence thereafter. . . .

At the time of his naturalization does Nottebohm appear to have been more closely attached by his tradition, his establishment, his interests, his activities, his family ties, his intentions for the near future to Liechtenstein than to any other State? . . .

[The Court then summarized Nottebohm's activities, stressing his relationships with Guatemala and indicating how minimal his connections with Liechtenstein were.]

These facts clearly establish, on the one hand, the absence of any bond of attachment between Nottebohm and Liechtenstein and, on the other hand, the existence of a long-standing and close connection between him and Guatemala, a link which his naturalization in no way weakened. That naturalization was not based on any real prior connection with Liechtenstein, nor did it in any way alter the manner of life of the person upon whom it was conferred in exceptional circumstances of speed and accommodation. In both respects, it was lacking in the genuineness requisite to an act of such importance, if it is to be entitled to be respected by a State in the position of

Guatemala. It was granted without regard to the concept of nationality adopted in international relations.

Naturalization was asked for not so much for the purpose of obtaining a legal recognition of Nottebohm's membership in fact in the population of Liechtenstein, as it was to enable him to substitute for his status as a national of a belligerent State that of a national of a neutral State, with the sole aim of thus coming within the protection of Liechtenstein but not of becoming wedded to its traditions, its interests, its way of life or of assuming the obligations—other than fiscal obligations—and exercising the rights pertaining to the status thus acquired.

Guatemala is under no obligation to recognize a nationality granted in such circumstances. Liechtenstein consequently is not entitled to extend its protection to Nottebohm vis-à-vis Guatemala and its claim must, for this reason, be held to be inadmissible. . . .

[The opinion of the Court, holding the claim by Liechtenstein to be inadmissible, was supported by eleven votes. There were three dissenting opinions. Each dissenting judge opposed final disposition of the case on the record then before the Court and would have joined the claim of Guatemala concerning nationality to a full hearing on the merits. Excerpts from the dissenting opinion of JUDGE READ follow.]

. . . . I cannot overlook the fact that the allowance of the plea in bar would ensure that justice would not be done on any plane, national or international. I do not think that a plea in bar, which would have such an effect, should be granted, unless the grounds on which it is based are beyond doubt. . . .

To begin with, I do not question the desirability of establishing some limitation on the wide discretionary power possessed by sovereign States: the right, under international law, to determine, under their own laws, who are their own nationals and to protect such nationals.

Nevertheless, I am bound, by Article 38 of the Statute, to apply international law as it is—positive law—and not international law as it might be if a Codification Conference succeeded in establishing new rules limiting the conferring of nationality by sovereign States. It is, therefore, necessary to consider whether there are any rules of positive international law requiring a substantial relationship between the individual and the State, in order that a valid grant of nationality may give rise to a right of diplomatic protection.

Both Parties rely on Article I of The Hague Draft Convention of 1930 as an accurate statement of the recognized rules of international law. . . .

> "It is for each State to determine under its own law who are its nationals. This law shall be recognized by other States in so far as it is consistent with international conventions, international custom, and the principles of law generally recognized with regard to nationality." . . .

No "international conventions" are involved and no "international custom" has been proved. There remain "the principles of law generally recognized with regard to nationality", and it is on this qualification of the generality of the rule in Article I that Guatemala has relied both in the Pleadings and in the Oral Proceedings. . . .

. . . . It has been conceded by Guatemala that "there is no system of customary rules", but the link theory is supported by the view that certain international conventions suggest the existence of a trend. . . .

[JUDGE READ referred to the bilateral and multinational conventions described by the Court at p. 215, supra.]

The fact that it was considered necessary to conclude the series of bilateral conventions and to establish the multilateral Convention referred to above indicates that the countries concerned were not content to rely on the possible existence of a rule of positive international law qualifying the right of protection. Further, even within that part of the Western hemisphere which is South of the 49th Parallel, the ratifications of the multilateral Convention were not sufficiently general to indicate consensus of the countries concerned. Taking them together, the Conventions are too few and far between to indicate a trend or to show the general consensus on the part of States which is essential to the establishment of a rule of positive international law.

It is suggested that the link theory can be justified by the application to this case of the principles adopted by arbitral tribunals in dealing with cases of double nationality.

There have been many instances of double nationality in which international tribunals have been compelled to decide between conflicting claims. In such cases, it has been necessary to choose; and the choice has been determined by the relative strength of the association between the individual concerned and his national State. There have been many instances in which a State has refused to recognize that the naturalization of one of its own citizens has given rise to a right of diplomatic protection, or in which it has refused to treat naturalization as exempting him from the obligations incident to his original citizenship, such as military service.

But the problems presented by conflicting claims to nationality and by double nationality do not arise in this case. There can be no doubt that Mr. Nottebohm lost his German nationality of origin upon his naturalization in Liechtenstein in October 1939. I do not think that it is permissible to transfer criteria designed for cases of double nationality to an essentially different type of relationship.

It is noteworthy that, apart from the cases of double nationality, no instance has been cited to the Court in which a State has successfully refused to recognize that nationality, lawfully conferred and maintained, did not give rise to a right of diplomatic protection . . . .

It is also suggested that the naturalization of Mr. Nottebohm was lacking in genuineness, and did not give rise to a right of protection . . . . Along the same lines, it is suggested that he did not incorporate himself in the body politic which constitutes the Liechtenstein State . . . .

I have difficulty in accepting the position taken with regard to the nature of the State and the incorporation of an individual in the State by naturalization. To my mind the State is a concept broad enough to include not merely the territory and its inhabitants but also those of its citizens who are resident abroad but linked to it by allegiance. Most States regard non-resident citizens as a part of the body politic. In the case of many countries such as China, France, the United Kingdom and the Netherlands, the non-resident citizens form an important part of the body politic and are numbered in their hundreds of thousands or millions. Many of these non-resident citizens have never been within the confines of the home State. I can see no reason why the pattern of the body politic of Liechtenstein should or must be different from that of other States. . . .

Nationality, and the relation between a citizen and the State to which he owes allegiance, are of such a character that they demand certainty. When one considers the occasions for invoking the relationship—emigration and immigration; travel; treason; exercise of political rights and functions; military service and the like—it becomes evident that certainty is essential. There must be objective tests, readily established, for the existence and recognition of the status. That is why the practice of States has steadfastly rejected vague and subjective tests for the right to confer nationality—sincerity, fidelity, durability, lack of substantial connection—and has clung to the rule of the almost unfettered discretionary power of the State, as embodied in Article I of The Hague Draft Convention of 1931.

Nationality and diplomatic protection are closely inter-related. The general rule of international law is that nationality gives rise to a right of diplomatic protection.

Fundamentally the obligation of a State to accord reasonable treatment to resident aliens and the correlative right of protection are based on the consent of the States concerned. When an alien comes to the frontier, seeking admission, either as a settler or on a visit, the State has an unfettered right to refuse admission. That does not mean that it can deny the alien's national status or refuse to recognize it. But by refusing admission, the State prevents the establishment of legal relationships involving rights and obligations, as regards the alien, between the two countries. On the other hand, by admitting the alien, the State, by its voluntary act, brings into being a series of legal relationships with the State of which he is a national. . . .

[JUDGE GUGGENHEIM (an *ad hoc* Judge) noted in his dissenting opinion, that there was no doubt as to the effectiveness of Nottebohm's naturalization under Liechtenstein law and agreed that the issue was whether such naturalization could be asserted against Guatemala. He distinguished some cases of dual nationality, cases in which a state had imposed its nationality without adequate basis and cases in which specific rules of international law had been violated, e. g., where a state conferred nationality on children born to foreign diplomats within its borders. His opinion continued:]

Are there other situations, apart from those which have been referred to, in which third States are entitled to regard the naturalization of a foreign national as inoperative when the foreign national has agreed to the grant of nationality and when his former nationality has not been retained? To be justified in saying so, it would be necessary to point to repeated and recurrent acts on the international level, which would establish that, in circumstances identical with or similar to those in which naturalization was granted to F. Nottebohm by Liechtenstein, third States have refused to recognize the naturalization so that it can be said that an established usage has developed displaying the characteristics of a general practice accepted as law (Article 38, paragraph 1(*b*), of the Statute of the Court and P.C.I.J., Series A, No. 10, p. 28; I.C.J. Asylum case, *Reports* 1950, pp. 276 et seq.). No evidence of such a custom, which would forbid the grant of nationality in the circumstances in which Liechtenstein granted her nationality to F. Nottebohm, has been given in these proceedings. It is not sufficient for this purpose merely to affirm—without any evidence—that there is no other State law permitting naturalization in the circumstances in which it was granted to F. Nottebohm.

Moreover, none of the attempts made to define the "bond of attachment" according to criteria other than those which have just been mentioned and which are in accordance with existing international law, has succeeded. This failure to arrive at such a definition is not fortuitous. It arises from the fact that in order to define the bond necessary to make naturalization binding, it is sought to supplement the objective criteria (absence of compulsion in relation to the applicant; dual nationality; the grant of nationality without withdrawal of nationality by the State to which the naturalized person formerly belonged) by subjective considerations such as the "genuineness of the application", "loyalty to the new State", "creation of a centre of economic interests in the new State", "the intention to become integrated in the national community"; or, again, rules are stated which are in no way in accordance with present international practice, or vague principles are formulated which would open the door to arbitrary decisions. International law does not, for example, in any way prohibit a State from claiming as its nationals, at the moment of their birth, the descendants of its nationals who have been resident abroad for centuries and whose only link with the State which grants its nationality is to be found in descent, without the requirement of any other element connecting them with that State, such as religion, language, social conceptions, traditions, manners, way of life, etc. . . .

Moreover, to dissociate the question of the validity of nationality from that of diplomatic protection leaves a further problem unsolved. Is the question one of the general non-validity of the naturalization on the international level, thus going beyond the limited right of third States to deny the claim to exercise diplomatic protection, or does such non-validity merely affect the right of Liechtenstein to exercise diplomatic protection as against Guatemala? . . .

Even if it be admitted that nationality can be dissociated from diplomatic protection in the present case, there remains the question as to what are the consequences of the total or partial invalidity under international law of a nationality validly acquired under municipal law. Is the invalidity confined to the sphere of diplomatic protection, or does it extend to the other effects of nationality on the international level, for example, treaty rights enjoyed by the nationals of a particular State in regard to monetary exchange, establishment and access to the municipal courts of a third State, etc.?

A refusal to recognize nationality and therefore the right to exercise diplomatic protection, would render the application of the latter—the only protection available to States under general international law enabling them to put forward the claims of individuals against third States—even more difficult than it already is.

If the right of protection is abolished, it becomes impossible to consider the merits of certain claims alleging a violation of the rules of international law. If no other State is in a position to exercise diplomatic protection, as in the present case, claims put forward on behalf of an individual, whose nationality is disputed or held to be inoperative on the international level and who enjoys no other nationality, would have to be abandoned. The protection of the individual which is so precarious under existing international law would be weakened even further and I consider that this would be contrary to the basic principle embodied in Article 15(1) of the Universal Declaration of Human Rights adopted by the General Assembly of the United Nations on December 8th, 1948, according to which everyone has the right to a nationality. Furthermore, refusal to exercise protection is not in accordance with the frequent attempts made at the present time to prevent the increase in the number of cases of stateless persons and to provide protection against acts violating the fundamental human rights recognized by international law as a minimum standard, without distinction as to nationality, religion or race. . . .

COMMENT

The principle of the Nottebohm Case has influenced a number of later treaty provisions and decisions of national courts. Illustrations in this book include certain provisions of the Geneva Conventions on the Law of the Sea and decisions of American courts involving so-called flag-of-convenience ships, pp. 969–985, infra. On the other hand, the theory of "effective nationality" was restrictively viewed by a later international tribunal, the Italian-United States Conciliation Commission. See United States ex rel. Flegenheimer v. Italy, September 20, 1958, 5 Collection of Decisions of Italian-United States Conciliation Commission, No. 182, at pp. 91–95.

QUESTIONS

(1) The Court states that "[d]iplomatic protection and protection by means of international judicial proceedings constitute measures for the defence of the rights of the State . . . ." Do you agree? What reasons and policies would you stress in support of this form of protection?

(2) If the Court had reached the merits of the dispute, to what issues would Nottebohm's nationality have been relevant? Does the Court's opinion indicate how those issues would have been decided?

(3) Nottebohm returned to Liechtenstein after he was released from his internment in the United States. It appears that he was resident in Liechtenstein from 1946 until 1951. Why were not these facts sufficient to support a claim at that time by Liechtenstein?

(4) Suppose that a German Jew, sensing the direction of the Nazi Government's policies in 1934, acquired Liechtenstein nationality in that year under the same circumstances as in the Nottebohm Case and immediately left for Guatemala. Suppose that in the 1940's, Guatemala expropriated his property without compensation, under general legislation and not under laws relating to enemy aliens. Based upon that action, Liechtenstein brings proceedings on his behalf before the I.C.J. in 1951. Should the same decision as in Nottebohm be reached? If not, why?

(5) Suppose that Nottebohm engaged in business in the United States after 1946, and brought a suit in 1956 in a federal court for a tax refund based upon provisions in a tax treaty of 1954 between Liechtenstein and the United States which exempted Liechtenstein "nationals" from certain domestic taxes. Assume that the treaty displaces any inconsistent provisions of the Internal Revenue Code. Should the Nottebohm Case have any effect upon the United States court's interpretation of the word "nationals" in the treaty?

(6) Suppose that an alien in the United States who has been domiciled here for many years is convicted of a crime in a foreign country which he briefly visits. He alleges that the procedures under which he was tried violate international law. Does the Nottebohm Case have any relevance to the right of the United States to extend protection?

Additional reading: Jones, The Nottebohm Case, 5 Int. & Comp.L.Q. 230 (1956); Paul de Visscher, L'Affaire Nottebohm, 60 Revue Générale de Droit International Public 238 (1956); Kunz, The Nottebohm Judgment (Second Phase), 54 Am.J.Int.L. 536 (1960); Leigh, Nationality and Diplomatic Protection, 20 Int. & Comp.L.Q. 453 (1971). See generally Van Panhuys, The Role of Nationality in International Law (1959).

---

2. PROTECTION OF CORPORATIONS

Particularly in matters of foreign investment, disputes between states characteristically involve a corporation. Chapter I noted some of the difficulties in fitting corporations into national legislation affecting aliens. We here examine a comparable problem—how to fit a corporation into the scheme of protection by a state of its nationals —from the perspective of the international community and international law.

The question whether a state can or should extend protection to a corporation or its shareholders may arise at several stages. At the start, a government must decide whether it will espouse a claim. The state to whom diplomatic protests may be directed must determine whether it will treat the relationship between the claimant state and the injured corporation or shareholders as sufficient to support the claim. If arbitration or adjudication occurs, a *compromis* or other agreement between the parties may spell out those corporate or shareholder interests which can be included within the claimant state's demand for damages. Absent such provisions, it will be under customary international law, as the Court in the Nottebohm Case indicated, that an international tribunal will determine whether there is an adequate nexus to support a claim.

CASE CONCERNING THE BARCELONA TRACTION, LIGHT AND POWER COMPANY, LIMITED (NEW APPLICATION: 1962) (BELGIUM v. SPAIN)

International Court of Justice, 1970.
[1970] I.C.J. Rep. 4.

[The Barcelona Traction, Light and Power Company, Limited was incorporated in 1911 in Toronto, Canada, the site of its head office, as a holding company to develop a system for the production and distribution of electric power in Catalonia, Spain. Barcelona Traction formed operating and other subsidiaries, three under Canadian law and about 12 under Spanish law with their registered offices in Spain. Sometime after World War I, its share capital (as alleged by Belgium) came to be held largely by Belgian natural persons and corporations, particularly by one powerful Belgian financial group.

Barcelona Traction issued series of bonds payable in sterling and pesetas, secured by charges on the bonds and shares of various subsidiaries and by mortgages on the property of a subsidiary. The bonds were serviced out of transfers to Barcelona Traction by the subsidiaries. The Spanish Civil War of 1936 led to suspension of payments, which were partially resumed for some of the bonds after 1940.

Continuing difficulties over foreign exchange authorizations arose with Spanish authorities, particularly with respect to service of the sterling bonds.

In February 1948, three Spanish holders of recently acquired sterling bonds of Barcelona Traction petitioned a Spanish court for a declaration of bankruptcy for Barcelona Traction for failure to pay interest on the bonds. A judgment of bankruptcy was entered several days later. The court ordered seizure of the assets of Barcelona Traction, and of the shares of various subsidiaries that were held outside Spain. The receiver appointed Spanish directors for the companies involved.

Under the Spanish declaration of bankruptcy and related aspects of Spanish law (as reported in F. A. Mann, *The Protection of Shareholders' Interests in the Light of the Barcelona Traction Case*, 67 Am. J.Int.L. 259 (1973)), Barcelona Traction lost capacity to administer any of its properties or to be party to any proceedings other than the bankruptcy proceedings. The administrators appointed pursuant to the bankruptcy judgment had plenary authority with respect to the property of the companies involved. In Canada, however, Barcelona Traction continued to have its own board of directors and later a receiver appointed by a Canadian court. Bankruptcy proceedings in Spain were expressly denied recognition by the Supreme Court of Ontario.

After proceedings in Spain in which challenges were made to the jurisdiction of a Spanish court to decree the bankruptcy of Barcelona Traction, a Spanish court in 1949 authorized the issuance of new shares for the subsidiaries, which were then sold in 1952 by public auction, and purchased by a newly formed Spanish corporation which thus obtained complete control of the electric utility undertaking in Spain.

Representations to the Spanish government about the bankruptcy proceedings were made by the United States, Great Britain, the Canadian government (in a series of diplomatic notes from 1948 to 1952) and the Belgian government. Eventually Belgium instituted proceedings against Spain in 1958 before the International Court of Justice, relying for compulsory jurisdiction upon a 1927 treaty between the two countries. The Belgian Memorial argued that the Spanish state organs, in declaring Barcelona Traction bankrupt and in seizing and liquidating its assets and those of its subsidiaries (including the Canadian subsidiaries), violated international law.

The Belgian submissions argued that Spain usurped bankruptcy jurisdiction, and had acted arbitrarily in ways amounting to denial of justice in the conduct of the bankruptcy proceeding. Belgium sought reparations in the neighborhood of $90 million (Canadian), or 88% thereof for the pro rata share of the asserted share interest of Belgian nationals. Spain's fundamental objection was based upon the lack of Belgian nationality of Barcelona Traction, and Spain denied the right of Belgium to protect its national shareholders because of alleged injury in violation of international law to a non-Belgian corporation.

The case was discontinued in 1961 with a view to settlement, but the attempt failed. Belgium filed a new Application in 1962, seeking reparation for damages to the Belgian national shareholders on account of the acts committed in respect of Barcelona Traction in violation of international law. It sought reparations in the amount of 88% of the net value of Barcelona Traction as of February 1948. A 1964 judgment of the ICJ decided that Spain's third Preliminary Objection, challenging the *jus standi* of Belgium, would be joined to the merits. [1964] I.C.J.Rep. 6.

Excerpts from the opinion of the Court and summaries of portions of two Separate Opinions follow:]

32. In these circumstances it is logical that the Court should first address itself to what was originally presented as the subject-matter of the third preliminary objection: namely the question of the right of Belgium to exercise diplomatic protection of Belgian shareholders in a company which is a juristic entity incorporated in Canada, the measures complained of having been taken in relation not to any Belgian national but to the company itself.

33. When a State admits into its territory foreign investments or foreign nationals, whether natural or juristic persons, it is bound to extend to them the protection of the law and assumes obligations concerning the treatment to be afforded them. These obligations, however, are neither absolute nor unqualified. In particular, an essential distinction should be drawn between the obligations of a State towards the international community as a whole, and those arising vis-à-vis another State in the field of diplomatic protection. By their very nature the former are the concern of all States. In view of the importance of the rights involved, all States can be held to have a legal interest in their protection; they are obligations *erga omnes*.

34. Such obligations derive, for example, in contemporary international law, from the outlawing of acts of aggression, and of genocide, as also from the principles and rules concerning the basic rights of the human person, including protection from slavery and racial discrimination. Some of the corresponding rights of protection have entered into the body of general international law (*Reservations to the Convention on the Prevention and Punishment of the Crime of Genocide, Advisory Opinion, I.C.J. Reports 1951*, p. 23); others are conferred by international instruments of a universal or quasi-universal character.

35. Obligations the performance of which is the subject of diplomatic protection are not of the same category. It cannot be held, when one such obligation in particular is in question, in a specific case, that all States have a legal interest in its observance. In order to bring a claim in respect of the breach of such an obligation, a State must first establish its right to do so, for the rules on the subject rest on two suppositions:

> "The first is that the defendant State has broken an obligation towards the national State in respect of its nationals. The second is that only the party to whom an international obligation is due can bring a claim in respect of its breach." (*Reparation for Injuries Suffered in the Service of the United Nations, Advisory Opinion, I.C.J. Reports 1949*, pp. 181–182.)

In the present case it is therefore essential to establish whether the losses allegedly suffered by Belgian shareholders in Barcelona Traction were the consequence of the violation of obligations of which they were the beneficiaries. In other words: has a right of Belgium been violated on account of its nationals' having suffered infringement of their rights as shareholders in a company not of Belgian nationality?

. . .

37. In seeking to determine the law applicable to this case, the Court has to bear in mind the continuous evolution of international

law. Diplomatic protection deals with a very sensitive area of international relations, since the interest of a foreign State in the protection of its nationals confronts the rights of the territorial sovereign, a fact of which the general law on the subject has had to take cognizance in order to prevent abuses and friction. From its origins closely linked with international commerce, diplomatic protection has sustained a particular impact from the growth of international economic relations, and at the same time from the profound transformations which have taken place in the economic life of nations. These latter changes have given birth to municipal institutions, which have transcended frontiers and have begun to exercise considerable influence on international relations. One of these phenomena which has a particular bearing on the present case is the corporate entity.

38. In this field international law is called upon to recognize institutions of municipal law that have an important and extensive role in the international field. This does not necessarily imply drawing any analogy between its own institutions and those of municipal law, nor does it amount to making rules of international law dependent upon categories of municipal law. All it means is that international law has had to recognize the corporate entity as an institution created by States in a domain essentially within their domestic jurisdiction. This in turn requires that, whenever legal issues arise concerning the rights of States with regard to the treatment of companies and shareholders, as to which rights international law has not established its own rules, it has to refer to the relevant rules of municipal law. . . .

. . .

41. Municipal law determines the legal situation not only of such limited liability companies but also of those persons who hold shares in them. Separated from the company by numerous barriers, the shareholder cannot be identified with it. The concept and structure of the company are founded on and determined by a firm distinction between the separate entity of the company and that of the shareholder, each with a distinct set of rights. The separation of property rights as between company and shareholder is an important manifestation of this distinction. So long as the company is in existence the shareholder has no right to the corporate assets.

42. It is a basic characteristic of the corporate structure that the company alone, through its directors or management acting in its name, can take action in respect of matters that are of a corporate character. The underlying justification for this is that, in seeking to serve its own best interests, the company will serve those of the shareholder too. Ordinarily, no individual shareholder can take legal steps, either in the name of the company or in his own name. If the shareholders disagree with the decisions taken on behalf of the company they may, in accordance with its articles or the relevant provisions of the law, change them or replace its officers, or take such action as is provided by law. Thus to protect the company against abuse by its management or the majority of shareholders, several municipal legal systems have vested in shareholders (sometimes a particular number is specified) the right to bring an action for the defence of the company, and conferred upon the minority of shareholders certain rights to guard against decisions affecting the rights of the company vis-à-vis its management or controlling shareholders. Nonetheless the shareholders' rights in relation to the company and its assets remain limited, this being, moreover, a corollary of the limited nature of their liability.

. . .

44. Notwithstanding the separate corporate personality, a wrong done to the company frequently causes prejudice to its shareholders. But the mere fact that damage is sustained by both company and shareholder does not imply that both are entitled to claim compensation. Thus no legal conclusion can be drawn from the fact that the same event caused damage simultaneously affecting several natural or juristic persons. Creditors do not have any right to claim compensation from a person who, by wronging their debtor, causes them loss. In such cases, no doubt, the interests of the aggrieved are affected, but not their rights. Thus whenever a shareholder's interests are harmed by an act done to the company, it is to the latter that he must look to institute appropriate action; for although two separate entities may have suffered from the same wrong, it is only one entity whose rights have been infringed.

45. However, it has been argued in the present case that a company represents purely a means of achieving the economic purpose of its members, namely the shareholders, while they themselves constitute in fact the reality behind it. It has furthermore been repeatedly emphasized that there exists between a company and its shareholders a relationship describable as a community of destiny. The alleged acts may have been directed at the company and not the shareholders, but only in a formal sense: in reality, company and shareholders are so closely interconnected that prejudicial acts committed against the former necessarily wrong the latter; hence any acts directed against a company can be conceived as directed against its shareholders, because both can be considered in substance, i. e., from the economic viewpoint, identical. Yet even if a company is no more than a means for its shareholders to achieve their economic purpose, so long as it is *in esse* it enjoys an independent existence. Therefore the interests of the shareholders are both separable and indeed separated from those of the company, so that the possibility of their diverging cannot be denied.

. . .

47. The situation is different if the act complained of is aimed at the direct rights of the shareholder as such. It is well known that there are rights which municipal law confers upon the latter distinct from those of the company, including the right to any declared dividend, the right to attend and vote at general meetings, the right to share in the residual assets of the company on liquidation. Whenever one of his direct rights is infringed, the shareholder has an independent right of action. On this there is no disagreement between the Parties. But a distinction must be drawn between a direct infringement of the shareholder's rights, and difficulties or financial losses to which he may be exposed as the result of the situation of the company.

. . .

51. On the international plane, the Belgian Government has advanced the proposition that it is inadmissible to deny the shareholders' national State a right of diplomatic protection merely on the ground that another State possesses a corresponding right in respect of the company itself. In strict logic and law this formulation of the Belgian claim to *jus standi* assumes the existence of the very right that requires demonstration. In fact the Belgian Government has repeatedly stressed that there exists no rule of international law which would deny the national State of the shareholders the right of diplomatic protection for the purpose of seeking redress pursuant to unlawful acts committed by another State against the company in which

they hold shares. This, by emphasizing the absence of any express denial of the right, conversely implies the admission that there is no rule of international law which expressly confers such a right on the shareholders' national State.

52. International law may not, in some fields, provide specific rules in particular cases. In the concrete situation, the company against which allegedly unlawful acts were directed is expressly vested with a right, whereas no such right is specifically provided for the shareholder in respect of those acts. Thus the position of the company rests on a positive rule of both municipal and international law. As to the shareholder, while he has certain rights expressly provided for him by municipal law as referred to in paragraph 42 above, appeal can, in the circumstances of the present case, only be made to the silence of international law. Such silence scarcely admits of interpretation in favour of the shareholder.

. . .

55. The Court will now examine other grounds on which it is conceivable that the submission by the Belgian Government of a claim on behalf of shareholders in Barcelona Traction may be justified.

56. For the same reasons as before, the Court must here refer to municipal law. Forms of incorporation and their legal personality have sometimes not been employed for the sole purposes they were originally intended to serve; sometimes the corporate entity has been unable to protect the rights of those who entrusted their financial resources to it; thus inevitably there have arisen dangers of abuse, as in the case of many other institutions of law. Here, then, as elsewhere, the law, confronted with economic realities, has had to provide protective measures and remedies in the interests of those within the corporate entity as well as of those outside who have dealings with it: the law has recognized that the independent existence of the legal entity cannot be treated as an absolute. It is in this context that the process of "lifting the corporate veil" or "disregarding the legal entity" has been found justified and equitable in certain circumstances or for certain purposes. The wealth of practice already accumulated on the subject in municipal law indicates that the veil is lifted, for instance, to prevent the misuse of the privileges of legal personality, as in certain cases of fraud or malfeasance, to protect third persons such as a creditor or purchaser, or to prevent the evasion of legal requirements or of obligations.

57. Hence the lifting of the veil is more frequently employed from without, in the interest of those dealing with the corporate entity. However, it has also been operated from within, in the interest of—among others—the shareholders, but only in exceptional circumstances.

58. In accordance with the principle expounded above, the process of lifting the veil, being an exceptional one admitted by municipal law in respect of an institution of its own making, is equally admissible to play a similar role in international law. It follows that on the international plane also there may be in principle special circumstances which justify the lifting of the veil in the interest of shareholders.

59. Before proceeding, however, to consider whether such circumstances exist in the present case, it will be advisable to refer to two specific cases involving encroachment upon the legal entity, instances of which have been cited by the Parties. These are: first, the treatment of enemy and allied property, during and after the First and Second World Wars, in peace treaties and other inter-

national instruments; secondly, the treatment of foreign property consequent upon the nationalizations carried out in recent years by many States.

60. With regard to the first, enemy-property legislation was an instrument of economic warfare, aimed at denying the enemy the advantages to be derived from the anonymity and separate personality of corporations. Hence the lifting of the veil was regarded as justified *ex necessitate* and was extended to all entities which were tainted with enemy character, even the nationals of the State enacting the legislation. The provisions of the peace treaties had a very specific function: to protect allied property, and to seize and pool enemy property with a view to covering reparation claims. Such provisions are basically different in their rationale from those normally applicable.

61. Also distinct are the various arrangements made in respect of compensation for the nationalization of foreign property. Their rationale too, derived as it is from structural changes in a State's economy, differs from that of any normally applicable provisions. Specific agreements have been reached to meet specific situations, and the terms have varied from case to case. Far from evidencing any norm as to the classes of beneficiaries of compensation, such arrangements are *sui generis* and provide no guide in the present case.

62. Nevertheless, during the course of the proceedings both Parties relied on international instruments and judgments of international tribunals concerning these two specific areas. It should be clear that the developments in question have to be viewed as distinctive processes, arising out of circumstances peculiar to the respective situations. To seek to draw from them analogies or conclusions held to be valid in other fields is to ignore their specific character as *lex specialis* and hence to court error.

63. The Parties have also relied on the general arbitral jurisprudence which has accumulated in the last half-century. However, in most cases the decisions cited rested upon the terms of instruments establishing the jurisdiction of the tribunal or claims commission and determining what rights might enjoy protection; they cannot therefore give rise to generalization going beyond the special circumstances of each case. Other decisions, allowing or disallowing claims by way of exception, are not, in view of the particular facts concerned, directly relevant to the present case.

64. The Court will now consider whether there might not be, in the present case, other special circumstances for which the general rule might not take effect. In this connection two particular situations must be studied: the case of the company having ceased to exist and the case of the company's national State lacking capacity to take action on its behalf.

65. As regards the first of these possibilities the Court observes that the Parties have put forward conflicting interpretations of the present situation of Barcelona Traction. There can, however, be no question but that Barcelona Traction has lost all its assets in Spain, and was placed in receivership in Canada, a receiver and manager having been appointed. It is common ground that from the economic viewpoint the company has been entirely paralyzed. It has been deprived of all its Spanish sources of income, and the Belgian Government has asserted that the company could no longer find the funds for its legal defence, so that these had to be supplied by the shareholders.

66. It cannot however, be contended that the corporate entity of the company has ceased to exist, or that it has lost its capacity to take corporate action. It was free to exercise such capacity in the Spanish courts and did in fact do so. It has not become incapable in law of defending its own rights and the interests of the shareholders. In particular, a precarious financial situation cannot be equated with the demise of the corporate entity, which is the hypothesis under consideration: the company's status in law is alone relevant, and not its economic condition, nor even the possibility of its being "practically defunct"—a description on which argument has been based but which lacks all legal precision. Only in the event of the legal demise of the company are the shareholders deprived of the possibility of a remedy available through the company; it is only if they became deprived of all such possibility that an independent right of action for them and their government could arise.

67. In the present case, Barcelona Traction is in receivership in the country of incorporation. Far from implying the demise of the entity or of its rights, this much rather denotes that those rights are preserved for so long as no liquidation has ensued. Though in receivership, the company continues to exist. Moreover, it is a matter of public record that the company's shares were quoted on the stockmarket at a recent date.

. . .

69. The Court will now turn to the second possibility, that of the lack of capacity of the company's national State to act on its behalf. The first question which must be asked here is whether Canada—the third apex of the triangular relationship—is, in law, the national State of Barcelona Traction.

70. In allocating corporate entities to States for purposes of diplomatic protection, international law is based, but only to a limited extent, on an analogy with the rules governing the nationality of individuals. The traditional rule attributes the right of diplomatic protection of a corporate entity to the State under the laws of which it is incorporated and in whose territory it has its registered office. These two criteria have been confirmed by long practice and by numerous international instruments. This notwithstanding, further or different links are at times said to be required in order that a right of diplomatic protection should exist. Indeed, it has been the practice of some States to give a company incorporated under their law diplomatic protection solely when it has its seat (*siège social*) or management or centre of control in their territory, or when a majority or a substantial proportion of the shares has been owned by nationals of the State concerned. Only then, it has been held, does there exist between the corporation and the State in question a genuine connection of the kind familiar from other branches of international law. However, in the particular field of the diplomatic protection of corporate entities, no absolute test of the "genuine connection" has found general acceptance. Such tests as have been applied are of a relative nature, and sometimes links with one State have had to be weighed against those with another. In this connection reference has been made to the *Nottebohm* case. In fact the Parties made frequent reference to it in the course of the proceedings. However, given both the legal and factual aspects of protection in the present case the Court is of the opinion that there can be no analogy with the issues raised or the decision given in that case.

71. In the present case, it is not disputed that the company was incorporated in Canada and has its registered office in that country. The incorporation of the company under the law of Canada was an

act of free choice. Not only did the founders of the company seek its incorporation under Canadian law but it has remained under that law for a period of over 50 years. It has maintained in Canada its registered office, its accounts and its share registers. Board meetings were held there for many years; it has been listed in the records of the Canadian tax authorities. Thus a close and permanent connection has been established, fortified by the passage of over half a century. This connection is in no way weakened by the fact that the company engaged from the very outset in commercial activities outside Canada, for that was its declared object. Barcelona Traction's links with Canada are thus manifold.

72. Furthermore, the Canadian nationality of the company has received general recognition. Prior to the institution of proceedings before the Court, three other governments apart from that of Canada (those of the United Kingdom, the United States and Belgium) made representations concerning the treatment accorded to Barcelona Traction by the Spanish authorities. The United Kingdom Government intervened on behalf of bondholders and of shareholders. Several representations were also made by the United States Government, but not on behalf of the Barcelona Traction company as such.

73. Both Governments acted at certain stages in close co-operation with the Canadian Government. An agreement was reached in 1950 on the setting-up of an independent committee of experts. While the Belgian and Canadian Governments contemplated a committee composed of Belgian, Canadian and Spanish members, the Spanish Government suggested a committee composed of British, Canadian and Spanish members. This was agreed to by the Canadian and United Kingdom Governments, and the task of the committee was, in particular, to establish the monies imported into Spain by Barcelona Traction or any of its subsidiaries, to determine and appraise the materials and services brought into the country, to determine and appraise the amounts withdrawn from Spain by Barcelona Traction or any of its subsidiaries, and to compute the profits earned in Spain by Barcelona Traction or any of its subsidiaries and the amounts susceptible of being withdrawn from the country at 31 December 1949.

74. As to the Belgian Government, its earlier action was also undertaken in close co-operation with the Canadian Government. The Belgian Government admitted the Canadian character of the company in the course of the present proceedings. It explicitly stated that Barcelona Traction was a company of neither Spanish nor Belgian nationality but a Canadian company incorporated in Canada. The Belgian Government has even conceded that it was not concerned with the injury suffered by Barcelona Traction itself, since that was Canada's affair.

75. The Canadian Government itself, which never appears to have doubted its right to intervene on the company's behalf, exercised the protection of Barcelona Traction by diplomatic representation for a number of years, in particular by its note of 27 March 1948, in which it alleged that a denial of justice had been committed in respect of the Barcelona Traction, Ebro and National Trust companies, and requested that the bankruptcy judgment be cancelled. It later invoked the Anglo-Spanish treaty of 1922 and the agreement of 1924, which applied to Canada. Further Canadian notes were addressed to the Spanish Government in 1950, 1951 and 1952. Further approaches were made in 1954, and in 1955 the Canadian Gov-

ernment renewed the expression of its deep interest in the affair of Barcelona Traction and its Canadian subsidiaries.

76. In sum, the record shows that from 1948 onwards the Canadian Government made to the Spanish Government numerous representations which cannot be viewed otherwise than as the exercise of diplomatic protection in respect of the Barcelona Traction company. Therefore this was not a case where diplomatic protection was refused or remained in the sphere of fiction. It is also clear that over the whole period of its diplomatic activity the Canadian Government proceeded in full knowledge of the Belgian attitude and activity.

77. It is true that at a certain point the Canadian Government ceased to act on behalf of Barcelona Traction, for reasons which have not been fully revealed, though a statement made in a letter of 19 July 1955 by the Canadian Secretary of State for External Affairs suggests that it felt the matter should be settled by means of private negotiations. The Canadian Government has nonetheless retained its capacity to exercise diplomatic protection; no legal impediment has prevented it from doing so: no fact has arisen to render this protection impossible. It has discontinued its action of its own free will.

78. The Court would here observe that, within the limits prescribed by international law, a State may exercise diplomatic protection by whatever means and to whatever extent it thinks fit, for it is its own right that the State is asserting. Should the natural or legal persons on whose behalf it is acting consider that their rights are not adequately protected, they have no remedy in international law. All they can do is to resort to municipal law, if means are available, with a view to furthering their cause or obtaining redress. The municipal legislator may lay upon the State an obligation to protect its citizens abroad, and may also confer upon the national a right to demand the performance of that obligation, and clothe the right with corresponding sanctions. However, all these questions remain within the province of municipal law and do not affect the position internationally.

79. The State must be viewed as the sole judge to decide whether its protection will be granted, to what extent it is granted, and when it will cease. It retains in this respect a discretionary power the exercise of which may be determined by considerations of a political or other nature, unrelated to the particular case. Since the claim of the State is not identical with that of the individual or corporate person whose cause is espoused, the State enjoys complete freedom of action. Whatever the reasons for any change of attitude, the fact cannot in itself constitute a justification for the exercise of diplomatic protection by another government, unless there is some independent and otherwise valid ground for that.

80. This cannot be regarded as amounting to a situation where a violation of law remains without remedy: in short, a legal vacuum. There is no obligation upon the possessors of rights to exercise them. Sometimes no remedy is sought, though rights are infringed. To equate this with the creation of a vacuum would be to equate a right with an obligation.

. . .

82. Nor can the Court agree with the view that the Canadian Government had of necessity to interrupt the protection it was giving to Barcelona Traction, and to refrain from pursuing it by means of other procedures, solely because there existed no link of compulsory

jurisdiction between Spain and Canada. International judicial proceedings are but one of the means available to States in pursuit of their right to exercise diplomatic protection (*Reparation for Injuries Suffered in the Service of the United Nations, Advisory Opinion, I.C.J. Reports 1949*, p. 178). The lack of a jurisdictional link cannot be regarded either in this or in other fields of international law as entailing the non-existence of a right.

. . .

85. The Court will now examine the Belgian claim from a different point of view, disregarding municipal law and relying on the rule that in inter-State relations, whether claims are made on behalf of a State's national or on behalf of the State itself, they are always the claims of the State. As the Permanent Court said,

> "The question, therefore, whether the . . . dispute originates in an injury to a private interest, which in point of fact is the case in many international disputes, is irrelevant from this standpoint." (*Mavrommatis Palestine Concessions, Judgment No. 2, 1924, P.C.I.J., Series A, No. 2*, p. 12. See also *Nottebohm, Second Phase, Judgment, I.C.J. Reports 1955*, p. 24.)

86. Hence the Belgian Government would be entitled to bring a claim if it could show that one of its rights had been infringed and that the acts complained of involved the breach of an international obligation arising out of a treaty or a general rule of law. The opinion has been expressed that a claim can accordingly be made when investments by a State's nationals abroad are thus prejudicially affected, and that since such investments are part of a State's national economic resources, any prejudice to them directly involves the economic interest of the State.

87. Governments have been known to intervene in such circumstances not only when their interests were affected, but also when they were threatened. However, it must be stressed that this type of action is quite different from and outside the field of diplomatic protection. When a State admits into its territory foreign investments or foreign nationals it is, as indicated in paragraph 33, bound to extend to them the protection of the law. However, it does not thereby become an insurer of that part of another State's wealth which these investments represent. Every investment of this kind carries certain risks. The real question is whether a right has been violated, which right could only be the right of the State to have its nationals enjoy a certain treatment guaranteed by general international law, in the absence of a treaty applicable to the particular case. On the other hand it has been stressed that it must be proved that the investment effectively belongs to a particular economy. This is, as it is admitted, sometimes very difficult, in particular where complex undertakings are involved. Thus the existing concrete test would be replaced by one which might lead to a situation in which no diplomatic protection could be exercised, with the consequence that an unlawful act by another State would remain without remedy.

88. It follows from what has already been stated above that, where it is a question of an unlawful act committed against a company representing foreign capital, the general rule of international law authorizes the national State of the company alone to make a claim.

89. Considering the important developments of the last half-century, the growth of foreign investments and the expansion of the

international activities of corporations, in particular of holding companies, which are often multinational, and considering the way in which the economic interests of States have proliferated, it may at first sight appear surprising that the evolution of law has not gone further and that no generally accepted rules in the matter have crystallized on the international plane. Nevertheless, a more thorough examination of the facts shows that the law on the subject has been formed in a period characterized by an intense conflict of systems and interests. It is essentially bilateral relations which have been concerned, relations in which the rights of both the State exercising diplomatic protection and the State in respect of which protection is sought have had to be safeguarded. Here as elsewhere, a body of rules could only have developed with the consent of those concerned. The difficulties encountered have been reflected in the evolution of the law on the subject.

90. Thus, in the present state of the law, the protection of shareholders requires that recourse be had to treaty stipulations or special agreements directly concluded between the private investor and the State in which the investment is placed. States ever more frequently provide for such protection, in both bilateral and multilateral relations, either by means of special instruments or within the framework of wider economic arrangements. Indeed, whether in the form of multilateral or bilateral treaties between States, or in that of agreements between States and companies, there has since the Second World War been considerable development in the protection of foreign investments. The instruments in question contain provisions as to jurisdiction and procedure in case of disputes concerning the treatment of investing companies by the States in which they invest capital. Sometimes companies are themselves vested with a direct right to defend their interests against States through prescribed procedures. No such instrument is in force between the Parties to the present case.

. . .

92. Since the general rule on the subject does not entitle the Belgian Government to put forward a claim in this case, the question remains to be considered whether nonetheless, as the Belgian Government has contended during the proceedings, considerations of equity do not require that it be held to possess a right of protection. It is quite true that it has been maintained that, for reasons of equity, a State should be able, in certain cases, to take up the protection of its nationals, shareholders in a company which has been the victim of a violation of international law. Thus a theory has been developed to the effect that the State of the shareholders has a right of diplomatic protection when the State whose responsibility is invoked is the national State of the company. Whatever the validity of this theory may be, it is certainly not applicable to the present case, since Spain is not the national State of Barcelona Traction.

93. On the other hand, the Court considers that, in the field of diplomatic protection as in all other fields of international law, it is necessary that the law be applied reasonably. It has been suggested that if in a given case it is not possible to apply the general rule that the right of diplomatic protection of a company belongs to its national State, considerations of equity might call for the possibility of protection of the shareholders in question by their own national State. This hypothesis does not correspond to the circumstances of the present case.

94. In view, however, of the discretionary nature of diplomatic protection, considerations of equity cannot require more than the

possibility for some protector State to intervene, whether it be the national State of the company, by virtue of the general rule mentioned above, or, in a secondary capacity, the national State of the shareholders who claim protection. In this connection, account should also be taken of the practical effects of deducing from considerations of equity any broader right of protection for the national State of the shareholders. It must first of all be observed that it would be difficult on an equitable basis to make distinctions according to any quantitative test: it would seem that the owner of 1 per cent. and the owner of 90 per cent. of the share-capital should have the same possibility of enjoying the benefit of diplomatic protection. The protector State may, of course, be disinclined to take up the case of the single small shareholder, but it could scarcely be denied the right to do so in the name of equitable considerations. In that field, protection by the national State of the shareholders can hardly be graduated according to the absolute or relative size of the shareholding involved.

95. The Belgian Government, it is true, has also contended that as high a proportion as 88 per cent. of the shares in Barcelona Traction belonged to natural or juristic persons of Belgian nationality, and it has used this as an argument for the purpose not only of determining the amount of the damages which it claims, but also of establishing its right of action on behalf of the Belgian shareholders. Nevertheless, this does not alter the Belgian Government's position, as expounded in the course of the proceedings, which implies, in the last analysis, that it might be sufficient for one single share to belong to a national of a given State for the latter to be entitled to exercise its diplomatic protection.

96. The Court considers that the adoption of the theory of diplomatic protection of shareholders as such, by opening the door to competing diplomatic claims, could create an atmosphere of confusion and insecurity in international economic relations. The danger would be all the greater inasmuch as the shares of companies whose activity is international are widely scattered and frequently change hands. It might perhaps be claimed that, if the right of protection belonging to the national States of the shareholders were considered as only secondary to that of the national State of the company, there would be less danger of difficulties of the kind contemplated. However, the Court must state that the essence of a secondary right is that it only comes into existence at the time when the original right ceases to exist. As the right of protection vested in the national State of the company cannot be regarded as extinguished because it is not exercised, it is not possible to accept the proposition that in case of its non-exercise the national States of the shareholders have a right of protection secondary to that of the national State of the company. Furthermore, study of factual situations in which this theory might possibly be applied gives rise to the following observations.

97. The situations in which foreign shareholders in a company wish to have recourse to diplomatic protection by their own national State may vary. It may happen that the national State of the company simply refuses to grant it its diplomatic protection, or that it begins to exercise it (as in the present case) but does not pursue its action to the end. It may also happen that the national State of the company and the State which has committed a violation of international law with regard to the company arrive at a settlement of the matter, by agreeing on compensation for the company, but that the foreign shareholders find the compensation insufficient. Now, as a matter of principle, it would be difficult to draw a distinc-

tion between these three cases so far as the protection of foreign shareholders by their national State is concerned, since in each case they may have suffered real damage. Furthermore, the national State of the company is perfectly free to decide how far it is appropriate for it to protect the company, and is not bound to make public the reasons for its decision. To reconcile this discretionary power of the company's national State with a right of protection falling to the shareholders' national State would be particularly difficult when the former State has concluded, with the State which has contravened international law with regard to the company, an agreement granting the company compensation which the foreign shareholders find inadequate. If, after such a settlement, the national State of the foreign shareholders could in its turn put forward a claim based on the same facts, this would be likely to introduce into the negotiation of this kind of agreement a lack of security which would be contrary to the stability which it is the object of international law to establish in international relations.

. . .

99. It should also be observed that the promoters of a company whose operations will be international must take into account the fact that States have, with regard to their nationals, a discretionary power to grant diplomatic protection or to refuse it. When establishing a company in a foreign country, its promoters are normally impelled by particular considerations; it is often a question of tax or other advantages offered by the host State. It does not seem to be in any way inequitable that the advantages thus obtained should be balanced by the risks arising from the fact that the protection of the company and hence of its shareholders is thus entrusted to a State other than the national State of the shareholders.

100. In the present case, it is clear from what has been said above that Barcelona Traction was never reduced to a position of impotence such that it could not have approached its national State, Canada, to ask for its diplomatic protection, and that, as far as appeared to the Court, there was nothing to prevent Canada from continuing to grant its diplomatic protection to Barcelona Traction if it had considered that it should do so.

101. For the above reasons, the Court is not of the opinion that, in the particular circumstances of the present case, *jus standi* is conferred on the Belgian Government by considerations of equity.

102. In the course of the proceedings, the Parties have submitted a great amount of documentary and other evidence intended to substantiate their respective submissions. Of this evidence the Court has taken cognizance. It has been argued on one side that unlawful acts had been committed by the Spanish judicial and administrative authorities, and that as a result of those acts Spain has incurred international responsibility. On the other side it has been argued that the activities of Barcelona Traction and its subsidiaries were conducted in violation of Spanish law and caused damage to the Spanish economy. If both contentions were substantiated, the truth of the latter would in no way provide justification in respect of the former. The Court fully appreciates the importance of the legal problems raised by the allegation, which is at the root of the Belgian claim for reparation, concerning the denials of justice allegedly committed by organs of the Spanish State. However, the possession by the Belgian Government of a right of protection is a prerequisite for the examination of these problems. Since no *jus standi* before the Court has been established, it is not for the Court in its Judgment to pronounce upon any other aspect of the case, on which it should take

a decision only if the Belgian Government had a right of protection in respect of its nationals, shareholders in Barcelona Traction.

103. Accordingly,

THE COURT

rejects the Belgian Government's claim by fifteen votes to one, twelve votes of the majority being based on the reasons set out in the present Judgment.

[Three judges, agreeing with the reasoning and conclusions of the Judgment, made Declarations adding brief observations of their own. Eight judges, concurring in the result but disagreeing with different aspects of the reasoning of the Judgment, appended Separate Opinions. Judge *ad hoc* RIPHAGEN rendered a Dissenting Opinion. Summaries of portions of two of the Separate Opinions follow:

In his Separate Opinion, SIR GERALD FITZMAURICE noted some distinctions between the domestic and international situations of companies and shareholders seeking reparations for injuries. He stressed the close domestic link in most cases between corporate and shareholder interests; shareholders could assume that corporate management would act (as by pressing legal claims) so as to maximize the shareholders' equity. Moreover, under domestic law, shareholders had a legal right to compel corporations to assert claims, or to bring actions themselves against third parties in circumstances involving matters such as fraud or improper behavior of management in failing to protect a corporation's interests. Internationally, however, there was no assurance that a government requested by a corporation to extend diplomatic protection might not decide on grounds distinct from those persuasive for the injured corporation.

The opinion then inquired whether the international law of diplomatic protection gave equivalent protection to shareholder interests to those afforded under municipal law. It noted the one established exception permitting representation of shareholder interests, namely where the corporation allegedly injured in violation of international law was incorporated within the respondent state. Had Barcelona Traction been a Spanish corporation, Belgium could have pressed its shareholders' claims.

Sir Gerald concluded that "in the present state of the law," the Canadian nationality of Barcelona Traction must "rule out the Belgian claim." It argued, however, that although this conclusion was "correct on the basis of extant law, this law itself, as it now stands, is in this respect unsatisfactory." International law showed itself to be "in this respect an under-developed system." "An enlightened rule, while recognizing that the national government of the company can never be *required* to intervene, and that its reasons for not doing so cannot be questioned even though they may have nothing to do with the merits of the claim, would simply provide that in such event the government of the shareholders may do so—particularly if, as is frequently the case, it is just because the shareholding is mainly foreign that the government of the company feels that no sufficient national interest exists to warrant intervention on its own part . . . .. Practical difficulties there might be; but this is not a serious objection where no inherent necessity of the law stands in the way."

The opinion then considered the *Nottebohm* case. It suggested that the fact that the parties did not contest Canada's right to press a claim on behalf of Barcelona Traction did not absolve the Court from inquiring into this "fundamental" issue. The opinion found the analogy to *Nottebohm* "clearly striking," and sketched an argument to the effect that Canada lacked a sufficient or genuine link with Barcelona Traction to qualify it to sustain a claim. Without pronouncing on the substance of the matter, the opinion speculated whether it would be "correct to say that a finding of Canadian *disqualification* (if such had been the outcome) should automatically have entailed a recognition of Belgian capacity to claim" on behalf of shareholders of Belgian nationality. Indeed, the broader question was raised whether "in all the circumstances, the very 'nationality' of the Barcelona Company itself should not be held to be Belgian rather than Canadian." It questioned whether, in circumstances comparable to this case, a test of nationality (for purposes of international law) other than the state of incorporation should be developed. "The Parties should have been requested to present a full argument on the subject."

The opinion also considered the complex issues of fact about determination of the nationality of shareholders in Barcelona Traction, given the involved patterns of individual and corporate shareholdings, and the fact that a substantial number of shares of Barcelona Traction, allegedly beneficially owned by Belgian corporate and natural shareholders, were held of record by nominees and trustees outside Belgium.

JUDGE JESSUP, in his Separate Opinion, complained that the Court had failed to "include in its Judgment a wider range of legal considerations" relevant to the different aspects of this litigation. Given the paucity of international litigation, the Court should not necessarily confine its reasoning to the narrowest possible ground for decision. As the principal judicial organ of the United Nations, it has a broader function to contribute to the development of international law.

Judge Jessup concluded that Canada did not have a right to claim on behalf of Barcelona Traction; that "as of matter of general international law, it is also my conclusion that a State, under certain circumstances, has a right to present a diplomatic claim on behalf of shareholders who are its nationals"; but that "Belgium did not succeed in proving the Belgian nationality, between the critical dates, of those natural and juristic persons on whose behalf it sought to claim. The Belgian claim must therefore be rejected."

The opinion reviewed the representations made to the Spanish government with respect to Barcelona Traction by Canada, Belgium, Great Britain and the United States. It concluded that only Belgium had a serious and continuing interest in the bankruptcy of Barcelona Traction, and in the diplomatic protection of the interests clustered around that company. It reviewed the various tests under national and international law for determining the "national character of a corporation," for a variety of purposes, and noted the degree to which commercial treaties and claims conventions contained their own definitions of corporate nationalities for purposes of the particular agreement.

With respect to general international law, Judge Jessup argued that the *Nottebohm* decision was relevant to diplomatic protection of corporations. If there were in fact no "genuine link" between a corporation and a claimant State, "the State to which diplomatic representations are made may, on that ground reject them." No rule of law or principle forbids another state whose nationals own all shares of the company and in which the "actual management and control of the company are carried on" to extend its diplomatic protection to those shareholder interests.

The opinion then noted that the important decisions and vital planning for Barcelona Traction were made or carried out by persons whose instructions issued from Great Britain, the United States, Belgium and Spain, "but rarely if ever from Canada." The Canadian corporation was advantageous for tax and related reasons, but such corporate events as shareholder meetings in Canada were generally "*pro forma* affairs."

The opinion cited examples from state practice indicating the degree to which states consider their own interests to have been affected when their own nationals compose a "substantial" or "significant" interest in the share capital of a corporation allegedly injured in violation of international law but organized under the laws of another state.

Judge Jessup then turned to examination of the nationality of shareholders in Barcelona Traction. He reasserted the traditional rule of international law that a claimant state must prove that the persons injured had its nationality on the date when the wrongful injury was inflicted—in this situation, the bankruptcy declaration of February 1948. Under the principle of continuity of nationality, Judge Jessup concluded that such Belgian nationality of the injured persons had to remain unchanged until the second Belgian Application to the ICJ was filed in 1962. Judge Jessup also observed (again by analogy to *Nottebohm*) that Belgium would not be legally competent to protect Belgian corporate shareholders in Barcelona Traction unless it established a genuine link with those corporations—in this case, a link to be tested by the shareholdings in those Belgian corporations.

Reviewing the complex events surrounding the relevant shareholdings—events further complicated by wartime measures to lessen the risk of German control during the occupation of Belgium—and noting the ambiguities left in the record and not sufficiently clarified by Belgium, Judge Jessup concluded that Belgium had not "established the Belgian character of any substantial number of shares throughout the critical period which the continuity rule defines." He also observed that Belgium had failed to prove any other basis for its state interest during the relevant period.]

COMMENT

The observations in Barcelona Traction about changes in economic and legal environments stemming from the operations of multinational enterprises capture some of the themes explored in the Note on such enterprises at p. 1179, infra.

NOTE ON PROTECTION OF CORPORATIONS AND SHAREHOLDERS

Unlike the Barcelona Traction case, many opinions of international tribunals treating these questions rest on the interpretation of a particular convention.[21] Although a convention or *compromis* can state whatever the parties agree upon with respect to corporations on

21. See, e. g., In re Mexico Plantagen G.m.b.H., German-Mexican Claims Commission, 1930, [1930–1932] Ann. Dig. 265 (No. 135).

whose behalf claims can be asserted, their provisions are often sufficiently vague to require interpretation by the tribunal. The variety of such provisions and the diversity in diplomatic practice concerning corporations accent the difficulty in formulating a generally accepted rule of international law.

The orthodox view referred to in Barcelona Traction, which dates from the period when corporations began to figure in transnational activities, stressed the tie between a company and the state where it was created. Foreign offices or international tribunals acknowledged the right of a state to represent its national *shareholders* in a *foreign corporation* only under limited circumstances.[22] But the trend noted in domestic law—the abandonment of a formal view of corporate nationality or presence and a more realistic appraisal of a corporation's affiliations with different jurisdictions—also affected international problems. The Barcelona Traction opinion suggests this trend among statesmen and international agreements and codifiers to give increased attention to the shareholder, to his nationality and to the injury which he suffers. Consider the following excerpt from Restatement (Second), Foreign Relations Law of the United States:

> § 172. **Alien Shareholder of Domestic Corporation.** When a domestic corporation, in which an alien is directly or indirectly a shareholder, is injured by action attributable to a state that would be wrongful under international law if the corporation were an alien corporation, the state is not responsible under international law for the injury to the corporation. The state is, however, responsible for the consequent injury to the alien to the extent of his interest in the corporation, if
>
> (a) a significant portion of the stock of the corporation is owned by the alien or other aliens of whatever nationality,
>
> (b) the state knows or has reason to know of such ownership at the time of the conduct causing the injury to the corporation,
>
> (c) the corporation fails to obtain reparation for the injury,
>
> (d) such failure is due to causes over which the alien or other alien shareholders cannot exercise control, and
>
> (e) a claim for the injury to the corporation has not been voluntarily waived or settled by the corporation.

The present practice of the United States may be summarized as follows: (a) The United States will generally consider a claim on behalf of corporations organized in the United States if 50% or more of their stock is owned by United States citizens. (b) The United

22. See, e. g., The Romano-Americana Claim, 5 Hackworth, Digest of International Law 840–43 (1943), for a statement of Great Britain's view. Cf. Agency of Canadian Car & Foundry Co., Ltd. (United States v. Germany), Mixed Claims Commission 1939, 5 Hackworth, Digest of International Law 833 (1943), 8 U.N.R.I.A.A. 460, and the Alsop Claim, United States-Chile Claims Commission (1901), Appendix to Case of the United States Relating to the Alsop Claim before his Majesty George V (1910), Vol. 2, p. 558, both of which involved interpretation of a *compromis*.

States will consider a claim on behalf of domestic shareholders under the circumstances described in Section 172 of the Restatement, the American stock ownership being usually regarded as significant if it is 25% or more.[23] This practice is evidenced to a large degree by post-war bilateral agreements between this country and other nations which have settled disputes relating to the expropriation of foreign investments. The practice is not uniform, and in addition some federal legislation has stated different standards in defining eligible stockholder claimants before national claims commissions disbursing funds that have been received under lump-sum settlement agreements or from other sources.

The settlement agreements have frequently spelled out whom the claimant state can represent, by identifying the percentage of shares in a corporation organized in the respondent state which must be owned by a claimant state's nationals. They tend to be more specific in their definitions than the standard of a "substantial and bona fide interest," which appears in Article 1 of the 1923 Convention between the United States and Mexico.* Consider now one such settlement between the United States and Poland, July 16, 1960, 11 U.S.T. & O.I.A. 1953, T.I.A.S. No. 4545. Under it, the United States agreed to accept $40,000,000 in satisfaction of its nationals' claims for the taking by Poland of their property and for debts owed them by enterprises nationalized by Poland. The United States was to distribute that sum, by means of a national claims commission organized under federal law, to the individual or corporate claimants. The following Annex to the agreement spells out those "nationals of the United States" who are entitled to present claims before the national commission. To the extent allowed by that commission, such claims would be satisfied *pro rata* out of the lump-sum payment.

ANNEX

A. For the purpose of distribution by the Government of the United States of the sum to be paid by the Government of Poland, "claims of nationals of the United States" are rights and interests in and with respect to property nationalized, appropriated or otherwise taken by Poland which, from the date of such nationalization, appropriation or other taking to the date of entry into force of this Agreement, have been continuously owned, subject to the provisions of paragraphs B and C of this Annex,

(a) directly by natural persons who were nationals of the United States;

(b) directly by juridical persons organized under the laws of the United States or of a constituent State or other political entity thereof, of which fifty per cent or more of the outstanding capital stock or proprietary interest was owned by nationals of the United States;

(c) directly by juridical persons organized under the laws of the United States or of a constituent State or other

23. See Reporter's Notes, No. 2 to Sections 171 and 172 of the Restatement and Lillich and Christenson, International Claims: Their Preparation and Presentation 15–20 (1962).

political entity thereof, of which fifty per cent or more of the outstanding capital stock or proprietary interest was owned by natural persons who were nationals of the United States, directly, or indirectly through interests in one or more juridical persons of any nationality;

. . .

(e) indirectly by persons within category (a), (b) or (c) above through ownership of capital stock or direct proprietary interests in juridical persons organized under the laws of Poland, any part of whose property has been taken by Poland, or in juridical persons organized under the laws of Germany, a major part of whose property has been taken by Poland;

. . .

(g) indirectly by persons within category (a), (b), (c) or (d) above through interests which collectively are substantial in amount, through any number of juridical persons organized under the laws of any country, a substantial part of whose property has been taken by Poland, excepting, however, interests which are compensable through any other international agreement to which Poland is a party.

QUESTIONS

(1) How do you evaluate the distinction drawn in Barcelona Traction between "obligations of a State towards the international community as a whole" and those "arising vis-à-vis another State in the field of diplomatic protection" (¶¶ 33–35)? Is the difference one of importance in the types of issues posed? One of the risk of retaliation presented by a failure to perform obligations? Simply one of history and state practice, without other justification?

(2) "Nottebohm and Barcelona Traction are of a piece jurisprudentially. Exhaustive surveys of state practice and analyses of the problem culminate in restrictive rules which further impede dispute-resolution through international law and tribunals. Both are from this perspective regressive decisions." (*a*) Do you agree that the two opinions are in a fundamental sense similar? (*b*) Do you agree that the holdings in these cases are "regressive"?

(3) "State practice is hardly a certain guide to the judicial articulation of a rule of customary law. Tribunals can make of state practice what they will, simply by characterizing it—for example—as expressive of an understood obligation, or as special and deviant, and so on. There is the greatest ambiguity in any record of practice relied upon to establish custom." Illustrate with references to the Barcelona Traction opinion.

(4) "This opinion means that another tribunal sharing this Court's approach can never articulate a rule of entitlement of one state vis-à-vis another in a situation where the interests of many states—or in particular of the complaining and respondent states—are in conflict. It stresses consent of states, and never seeks to develop a broader community perspective on these issues." Do you agree? To what rule would a community (international) perspective on the problem point?

(5) Do you see any answer to the Court's view that "adoption of the theory of diplomatic protection of shareholders as such" would create "confusion and insecurity in international economic relations"? Does Restatement § 172, supra, fall subject to this criticism, if it were followed by a large number of countries?

PROBLEM

Assume in the following cases that the states involved have submitted to the jurisdiction of an international tribunal, and that the compromis does not define the corporations or shareholders on whose behalf claims can be asserted. Consider whether the Nottebohm Case and Barcelona Traction are helpful in developing answers to the questions posed by these cases.

(1) 30% of the common stock of Foreign Enterprises Company (FEC), a Delaware corporation, is owned by United States nationals, and 70% by French nationals. FEC's principal assets consist of land, a factory, machinery, and goods in process in Guatador. These assets are valued at approximately $10,000,000 while FEC's total assets amount to $11,000,000. FEC owes $2,000,000 to banks in the United States. Guatador expropriates without compensation the local assets of FEC, and FEC is denied access to the Guatadorian courts to press a claim for compensation.

> (*a*) On whose behalf should or could the United States or France extend protection, in the form of diplomatic protests or other action vis-à-vis Guatador? Should it be relevant whether the French interest existed at the time of the organization of FEC or was acquired from United States shareholders at a later date?
>
> (*b*) What problems would arise in determining the amount of the claim to be made by the United States or by France? What complications if both countries pressed claims?
>
> (*c*) If the claim of the United States ripened into litigation before the I.C.J., how should the Court treat Guatador's argument that the United States lacks sufficient interest to extend protection?

(2) Assume that FEC was wholly U.S.-citizen owned and had organized a subsidiary corporation in Guatador which owned all the local assets and which had incurred the $2,000,000 of debt. After the expropriation the subsidiary brings an unsuccessful action in the Guatador courts for compensation. Would these facts affect your answers to the preceding questions? Would the answers differ if Guatador had taken the assets of the subsidiary, which retained its corporate existence, or had caused the dissolution of the subsidiary and the transfer of all its assets to the government?

(3) Assume the same facts as in paragraph (2) above, except that FEC is 70% Guatadorian-citizen owned and 30% U.S.-citizen owned. How do your answers change?

Additional reading: Paul de Visscher, La Protection Diplomatique des Personnes Morales, 102 Académie de Droit International, Recueil des Cours 394 (1961); Domke, Piercing the Corporate Veil in the Law of Economic Warfare, 1955 Wisc.L.Rev. 77 (1955); Jones, Claims on Behalf of Nationals Who Are Shareholders in Foreign Companies, 26 Brit.Ybk.

Int.L. 225 (1949); Lillich and Metzger, Two Perspectives on the Barcelona Traction Case, 65 Am.J.Int.L. 522 (1971).

---

3. EXHAUSTION OF LOCAL REMEDIES

Assuming no problems about jurisdictional submissions or the nationality of the private claimant, a number of obstacles nonetheless remain before a tribunal will reach the merits of the dispute. One of the most significant is the requirement of exhaustion of local remedies, although that requirement can be waived by agreement between states. See Article V of the Convention of 1923 between the United States and Mexico.*

When reading the following case, compare the policies that appear relevant on the international scene with those expressed by the two examples below of the notion of exhaustion of remedies on the domestic scene. The first concerns an aspect of the relationship between federal and state courts. Any comparison between, on the one hand, federal and state courts and, on the other hand, international and national tribunals must take account of the fact that the federal-court system has several levels, and that actions involving federal questions may in most instances be initiated in the federal judiciary without prior recourse to state courts. Nonetheless, the notion of exhaustion is relevant with respect to the appellate jurisdiction of the United States Supreme Court over decisions of state tribunals. 28 U.S.C.A. § 1257 * refers to review by the Supreme Court of "[f]inal judgments or decrees rendered by the highest court of a State in which a decision could be had . . . ." The effect of this provision is that a litigant in state proceedings must pursue state judicial remedies as far as possible to obtain a favorable resolution of the federal question before invoking the jurisdiction of the United States Supreme Court. See Wright, Handbook of the Law of Federal Courts §§ 49, 107 (2d ed. 1970).

The notion of exhaustion also affects the relationship between different branches of government within the same (federal or state) system. The courts have developed a rule that they will not entertain challenges to or review administrative action until they are satisfied that the litigant has exhausted his remedies within the administrative agency. The purposes of the rule may be said to be a desire to safeguard the integrity and reputation of the administrative agency and to protect the courts from excessive litigation, particularly on questions where they need the guidance of the specialized agency. The courts must weigh against these purposes the possibility that an individual may be denied justice for a long time, perhaps suffering great expense and injury which could not be remedied by a later judicil proceeding. Commentators have identified among the factors that affect a court's decision (1) the amount of specialized knowledge which the agency can bring to bear on the issues, (2) the importance of uninterrupted agency proceedings, (3) the injury to be suffered by the plaintiff from prolongation of the agency process, (4) the degree to which agency action is obviously invalid, (5) the adequacy of the administrative remedies that are available, and (6) the court's general confidence in the agency. See Chapter 20 of Davis, Administrative Law Text (3d ed. 1972).

INTERHANDEL CASE (SWITZERLAND v. UNITED STATES OF AMERICA) (PRELIMINARY OBJECTIONS)

International Court of Justice, 1959.
[1959] I.C.J. Rep. 6.

[This case arose out of the vesting by the United States under the Trading with the Enemy Act, p. 42, supra, of almost all the shares of General Aniline and Film Corporation, a Delaware corporation. These shares,, nominally at least, belonged to a corporation organized in Switzerland and referred to as Interhandel. The vesting depended upon the proposition that Interhandel either held the shares in trust for I. G. Farbenindustrie A. G. (a German, "enemy" corporation) or was itself so German-controlled that it was subject to treatment as if it were an "enemy". In 1945 Interhandel commenced administrative, and in 1948 judicial, proceedings in the United States to recover these assets, under provisions of the Trading with the Enemy Act that called for return of property of persons who were not enemies. Swiss legislation, however, prevented compliance by Interhandel with discovery orders under the Federal Rules of Civil Procedure that were designed to explore the relationship between German interests and Interhandel. The district court therefore ordered the suit dismissed. The court of appeals affirmed, although it allowed an additional six months for compliance with the orders, and the Supreme Court denied certiorari. After expiration of that period the district court entered a final order of dismissal, which was affirmed by the court of appeals. However, the Supreme Court then granted certiorari and in 1958 reversed the decision.[24]

In its submission to the I.C.J. in October 1957, Switzerland asserted that the United States had violated "the general rules of international law" and the Washington Accord of 1946. That Accord provided for the liquidation of German assets in Switzerland and their payment to the allied authorities, and for the freeing of Swiss accounts abroad. A special Swiss Authority of Review was established to determine whether assets in Switzerland were German or not. That Authority decided that Interhandel was not German in character and freed its assets. Switzerland asserted, and the United States denied, that this decision affected assets of Interhandel in the United States.

The relief Switzerland sought before the I.C.J. was, in part, that the United States be required to return to Interhandel its shares in General Aniline. The excerpts below from the opinion of the I.C.J. treat the question of exhaustion of local remedies, the subject of the Third Preliminary Objection of the United States to the jurisdiction of the I.C.J.]

The Third Preliminary Objection seeks a finding that "there is no jurisdiction in this Court to hear or determine the matters raised

24. The opinion of the Supreme Court appears at p. 844, infra.

by the Swiss Application and Memorial, for the reason that Interhandel, whose case Switzerland is espousing, has not exhausted the local remedies available to it in the United States courts".

Although framed as an objection to the jurisdiction of the Court, this Objection must be regarded as directed against the admissibility of the Application of the Swiss Government. Indeed, by its nature it is to be regarded as a plea which would become devoid of object if the requirement of the prior exhaustion of local remedies were fulfilled.

The Court has indicated in what conditions the Swiss Government, basing itself on the idea that Interhandel's suit had been finally rejected in the United States courts, considered itself entitled to institute proceedings by its Application of October 2nd, 1957. However, the decision given by the Supreme Court of the United States on October 14th, 1957, on the application of Interhandel made on August 6th, 1957, granted a writ of *certiorari* and readmitted Interhandel into the suit. The judgment of that Court on June 16th, 1958, reversed the judgment of the Court of Appeals dismissing Interhandel's suit and remanded the case to the District Court. It was thenceforth open to Interhandel to avail itself again of the remedies available to it under the Trading with the Enemy Act, and to seek the restitution of its shares by proceedings in the United States courts. Its suit is still pending in the United States courts. The Court must have regard to the situation thus created.

The rule that local remedies must be exhausted before international proceedings may be instituted is a well-established rule of customary international law; the rule has been generally observed in cases in which a State has adopted the cause of its national whose rights are claimed to have been disregarded in another State in violation of international law. Before resort may be had to an international court in such a situation, it has been considered necessary that the State where the violation occurred should have an opportunity to redress it by its own means, within the framework of its own domestic legal system. *A fortiori* the rule must be observed when domestic proceedings are pending, as in the case of Interhandel, and when the two actions, that of the Swiss company in the United States courts and that of the Swiss Government in this Court, in its principal Submission, are designed to obtain the same result: the restitution of the assets of Interhandel vested in the United States.

The Swiss Government does not challenge the rule which requires that international judicial proceedings may only be instituted following the exhaustion of local remedies, but contends that the present case is one in which an exception to this rule is authorized by the rule itself. . . .

In the first place, it is contended that the rule is not applicable for the reason that the measure taken against Interhandel and regarded as contrary to international law is a measure which was taken, not by a subordinate authority but by the Government of the United States. However, the Court must attach decisive importance to the fact that the laws of the United States make available to interested persons who consider that they have been deprived of their rights by measures taken in pursuance of the Trading with the Enemy Act, adequate remedies for the defence of their rights against the Executive.

It has also been contended on behalf of the Swiss Government that in the proceedings based upon the Trading with the Enemy Act, the United States courts are not in a position to adjudicate in accordance with the rules of international law and that the Supreme Court, in its decision of June 16th, 1958, made no reference to the many questions of international law which, in the opinion of the Swiss Government, constitute the subject of the present dispute. But the decisions of the United States courts bear witness to the fact that United States courts are competent to apply international law in their decisions when necessary. In the present case, when the dispute was brought to this Court, the proceedings in the United States courts had not reached the merits, in which considerations of international law could have been profitably relied upon. . . .

Finally, the Swiss Government laid special stress on the argument that the character of the principal Submission of Switzerland is that of a claim for the implementation of the decision given on January 5th, 1948, by the Swiss Authority of Review and based on the Washington Accord, a decision which the Swiss Government regards as an international judicial decision. "When an international decision has not been executed, there are no local remedies to exhaust, for the injury has been caused directly to the injured State." It has therefore contended that the failure by the United States to implement the decision constitutes a direct breach of international law, causing immediate injury to the rights of Switzerland as the Applicant State. The Court notes in the first place that to implement a decision is to apply its operative part. In the operative part of its decision, however, the Swiss Authority of Review "Decrees: (1) that the Appeal is sustained and the decision subjecting the appellant to the blocking of German property in Switzerland is annulled. . . ." The decision of the Swiss Authority of Review relates to the unblocking of the assets of Interhandel in Switzerland; the Swiss claim is designed to secure the restitution of the assets of Interhandel in the United States. Without prejudging the validity of any arguments which the Swiss Government seeks or may seek to base upon that decision, the Court would confine itself to observing that such arguments do not deprive the dispute which has been referred to it of the character of a dispute in which the Swiss Government appears as having adopted the cause of its national, Interhandel, for the purpose of securing the restitution to that company of assets vested by the Government of the United States. This is one of the very cases which give rise to the application of the rule of the exhaustion of local remedies. . . .

[By nine votes to six, the Court sustained the Third Preliminary Objection and held that the Swiss Application was inadmissible. The settlement of this dispute is noted at p. 848, infra.]

QUESTIONS

(1) What purposes does the rule that local remedies must be exhausted serve from the point of view of the claimant state, the respondent state, the injured national, and the international tribunal?

(2) Suppose that Switzerland's claim was that the United States had broken a treaty obligation with Switzerland to pay it a stated sum. Should the Swiss government be compelled to pursue remedies, if available in the United States courts, before commencing an international action?

(3) See Article XVI of the Convention of Establishment between the United States and France.* Must an American national who allegedly has been denied the right to establish a business in France that the Convention secures pursue local remedies before any proceedings could be instituted by the United States before the I.C.J.?

(4) Suppose that the local courts in which the alien ordinarily must "exhaust" his remedies have in previous decisions ruled firmly against

the position asserted by the alien. How should this consideration affect the requirement of exhaustion of local remedies?

NOTE ON LOCAL REMEDIES AND INTERNATIONAL TRIBUNALS

The requirement of exhaustion has importance outside the context of litigation before international tribunals. In deciding whether to espouse the claim of a national, government officials generally require evidence of his having pursued all meaningful local remedies. And in replying to a note of protest, a government may state that the alien who has allegedly been injured in violation of international law should have recourse to local remedies before a claim by his government will be entertained on the merits.

A memorandum of March 1, 1961 of the Department of State, reprinted in 56 Am.J.Int.L. 166 (1962), treated problems of nationalization of property of American nationals by the Cuban government. The memorandum noted that the State Department was ready to receive and consider for presentation any claims that were properly documented and were "valid from an international legal standpoint." It stated in part:

> [E]vidence should also be submitted showing that the American national exhausted such legal remedies as were available in Cuba and in the process sustained a denial of justice, as that term is understood in international law, or that the laws of Cuba do not provide a remedy or, if provided, that it would be futile to attempt to exhaust such remedy. The requirement for exhaustion of legal remedies . . . . does not mean that "legal remedies" must be exhausted if there are none to exhaust or if the procurement of justice would be impossible . . . . Generally, unsupported assertions to the effect that it would be useless to exhaust or attempt to exhaust legal remedies would, of course, have less evidentiary value than a court decree or other documentary evidence demonstrating the futility of exhausting or attempting to exhaust legal remedies.

Difficult issues may arise in deciding whether a private party has exhausted the available local remedies. How diligently must he act? If he brought and lost a court action but erred in deciding which substantive claim to pursue or which procedural paths to follow and thereby weakened his chance for success, will his government be barred from an international tribunal? In the Ambatielos Claim (Greece v. United Kingdom), Arbitration Commission, March 6, 1956, [1956] Int.L.Rep. 306, the United Kingdom Government and the Greek Government agreed to submit to arbitration the question whether the United Kingdom had maltreated a Greek national, Ambatielos. One of the questions put to the arbitrators was whether Ambatielos had exhausted his legal remedies. The United Kingdom contended that Ambatielos had not, because in his action before English courts, he had failed to call a certain witness whose testimony was later asserted by the Greek Government to be critical to his case. The arbitral commission agreed with this argument. Res judicata would bar Ambatielos from suing again in England.

Ambatielos and Interhandel suggest several questions about relationships between national and international courts or judicial systems, questions which have received little illumination from the few decisions of international tribunals that have explored them. Consider the review by federal courts in the United States of decisions of state courts or action of administrative agencies. All are embraced within one coherent legal structure. The record established in the state court or in administrative proceedings is certified to the federal court. Questions of fact are generally resolved within the state court or administrative agency. Deference may also be shown by the federal court to the manner in which the administrative agency has resolved certain legal issues, perhaps interpretation of a statutory provision. On the other hand, the state court or the administrative agency is bound by the federal court's decision.

Note the distinctions between such appeals to federal tribunals and litigation before an international tribunal after an effort by a national of the claimant state to secure satisfaction in the respondent state's courts or administrative agencies. Are the national and international proceedings related in any meaningful sense, or are the latter *de novo*? Are even the parties the same? What deference should the international tribunal show towards findings of fact, or conclusions of the national court about national or international law?

Additional reading: Texts cited at p. 177, supra: Amerasinghe, The Exhaustion of Procedural Remedies in the Same Court, 12 Int. & Comp. L.Q. 1285 (1963); Bagge, Intervention on the Ground of Damage Caused to Nationals, With Particular Reference to Exhaustion of Local Remedies and the Rights of Shareholders, 34 Brit.Ybk.Int.L. 162 (1958); Mummery, The Content of the Duty to Exhaust Local Judicial Remedies, 58 Am.J.Int.L. 389 (1964); Schwebel and Wetter, Arbitration and the Exhaustion of Local Remedies, 60 Am.J.Int.L. 484 (1966); Restatement (Second), Foreign Relations Law of the United States §§ 206–210.

D. THE PROCESSES BY WHICH INTERNATIONAL LAW DEVELOPS

As part of our inquiry into the character of international legal order and its relationship to the conceptions of law outlined at pp. 178–191, supra, we here examine the means of development of international law. We start with a threshold question: how does one ascertain principles or rules thought to constitute part of international law that may influence conduct or contribute towards the resolution of disputes.

Consider the variety of perspectives from which that question can be asked. The private party planning a transnational venture may be concerned with phases of international law which regulate or protect his investments. An alien injured by a government's acts has an evident interest in principles of international law which may offer him some chance of relief. National administrative officials or judiciaries may be competent to consider claims of a violation of, and thus be required to explore, international law. Executive officials and their legal adviser may wish to determine what international law has to "say" about a particular issue when planning conduct or responses to the conduct of other nations. They may seek recognition by other states that certain conduct of their government is permitted by or that certain conduct of other governments violates international law. Officials of international organizations or scholars preparing treatises face comparable questions for their different purposes. And of course an international tribunal may be required to adjudicate a controversy under principles of international law. Whatever the reason for the inquiry, whatever influence upon decision-making the result of the inquiry may have, all such parties must proceed under some understanding of the formal manifestations and channels of development of international law.

Article 38 of the Statute of the I.C.J. is a traditional and convenient point of departure for such an inquiry:

> 1. The Court, whose function is to decide in accordance with international law such disputes as are submitted to it, shall apply:
>
> a. international conventions, whether general or particular, establishing rules expressly recognized by the contesting states;
>
> b. international custom, as evidence of a general practice accepted as law;
>
> c. the general principles of law recognized by civilized nations;
>
> d. subject to the provisions of Article 59, judicial decisions and the teachings of the most highly qualified publicists of the various nations, as subsidiary means for the determination of rules of law.
>
> 2. This provision shall not prejudice the power of the Court to decide a case *ex aequo et bono*, if the parties agree thereto.

This list has significance not only for tribunals but also for officials or scholars pursuing the inquiries described above. We here consider the four clauses of Article 38(1) as suggestive of the processes by which international law develops. In this Part D we examine separately these clauses, as well as the role of international organizations, through illustrative problems drawn from a wide variety of fields. In Chapter IV, we illustrate the relationships among these elements of a complex international legal process through a more intensive exploration of one area of international law.

When reading the following materials, consider whether such a formal list significantly contributes to an understanding of an international legal process that is still at a rudimentary stage of development. One might prepare a comparable list even for a highly developed legal system such as that in the United States. It would include (a) the federal Constitution; (b) federal statutes, administrative regulations and treaties; (c) court decisions interpreting the foregoing; and (d) federal common law. If state law were relevant, the list would expand. Whatever its accuracy, could any such list fairly portray the role in this society of the legislature, executive or judiciary? Would it reveal the complex relationships among its parts or among branches of government, or express the many considerations and understandings which underlie our domestic legal process? Would it tell us anything about the social or economic roles or effects of the legal system? What other observations would be necessary to flesh out so skeletal a view?

---

1. THE ROLE OF CUSTOM

Custom has been referred to as "the oldest and the original source of international law." 1 Oppenheim, International Law 25–26 (8th ed., H. Lauterpacht, 1955). Clause (b) of Article 38(1) states that the I.C.J. shall apply "international custom, as evidence of a general practice accepted as law." Through the Nottebohm Case and two other leading decisions of the International Court, we here illustrate the different ways in which that clause has been interpreted and applied. Those decisions also serve as points of departure towards a broader discussion of the influence of customary international law upon the conduct of and relationships among nations.

NOTE ON CUSTOM IN ANGLO-AMERICAN LEGAL SYSTEMS

Authors and courts have viewed custom from different perspectives, attributed different meanings and functions to it, and consequently have accorded varying significance to its historical or present role.[25] By custom, we refer to conduct, or the conscious abstention from certain conduct, of members of a society which becomes in some measure a part of the legal order of that society. By virtue of a developing custom, particular conduct may be considered to be permitted or obligatory in legal terms, or abstention from particular conduct may come to be considered a legal duty.

The members of a society may regulate themselves in accordance with an established customary practice, so that no official intervention or declaration of custom is necessary. A commonplace example would be aspects of commercial practice engaged in by businessmen, reminiscent of the traditional law merchant. Or there may be some form of official declaration, as when a court relies upon customary practice to formulate or interpret a rule defining the duties or rights

25. See, e. g., Braybrooke, Custom as a Source of English Law, 50 Mich.L. Rev. 71 (1951); Hart and Sacks, The Legal Process: Basic Problems in the Making and Application of Law 427–457 (Tent. ed. 1958); and Plucknett, A Concise History of the Common Law 307–314 (5th ed. 1956).

of parties to a controversy. And of course a legislature, when codifying a particular field of law, may draw upon practices within the field to draft a statute.

Custom has played a larger role in rudimentary legal systems than in the developed legal orders which are characteristic of modern societies. At an early period, it appears that the English common law was largely a customary law. The communal courts before the Norman Conquest "declared" a customary law. That is, they drew upon local established practice to determine rights or duties in controversies. After the Conquest, feudal and manorial custom continued to play an important role, sometimes as general custom of the land and sometimes as a local practice. Examples of rules established by custom include the duty of neighboring villages to contribute specified shares of the expenses of maintaining a common church or the rights of tenants vis-à-vis their feudal lord, such as their right to graze cattle on certain of his lands. Braybrooke, fn. 25, supra, notes that in many of these customs there was a strong element of action or claim by one party matched by acquiescence in the action or claim by another, a process which is characteristic of customary international law.

As the King's courts expanded their jurisdiction and displaced a local customary law with a general national law, precise identification of local practice became less critical. The courts began to look to their own precedents, perhaps at the start as a means of finding the "custom" which those precedents evidenced, but increasingly as authority in and of themselves. Customary law gradually shaded into a common law based upon prior decisions. The "custom", it could be said, became that of the court in invoking prior decisions and developing habits of legal reasoning. When referring to the influential treatise of Bracton in the 13th Century, Maitland states: [26]

> Thus at a very early time English "common law" shows a tendency to become what it afterwards definitely became, namely, "case law." The term "common law" was being taken over from the canonists by English lawyers, who used it to distinguish the general law of the land from local customs, royal prerogatives, and in short from all that was exceptional or special.

As late as the 18th Century, Blackstone referred to the common law as in good part a customary law, and noted tests of custom which included immemorial usage without interruption, peaceful acquiescence in the usage, acceptance of the particular custom or practice as compulsory, and certainty. 1 Bl.Comm.* 67–79. Later writers have disputed these observations and contended that custom was a less rigid, a more flexible and dynamic force.

One important consequence of an emphasis upon prevailing custom rather than upon judicial precedents as a law-making process is that much "law" develops in the private sphere of activities through

26. Maitland, History of English Law, appearing in Cam (ed.), Selected Historical Essays of F. W. Maitland 105 (1957).

"private legislators" rather than through institutional decisions. Those forming the custom through practice help to establish the "rules" under which their conduct is to be regulated. Under a formal view, during the period when custom played a larger role the courts did no more than "declare" a custom to be established, rather than exercise a law-making competence. The analogies to the international scene, past and present, are significant.

Consider some of the ways in which custom, whether general or particular to a region or group, remains important within a developed legal system as a source of judicial lawmaking or background for legislation.

(1) Custom may serve to complete, to give content to, general standards such as "due care" or "seaworthy." In the T. J. Hooper, 60 F.2d 737 (2d Cir. 1932), an admiralty action, the court concluded that certain tugs were "unseaworthy" because they did not carry adequate radio receiving sets which would have given warning of a storm. The court stated:

> . . . . It is not fair to say that there was a general custom among coastwise carriers so to equip their tugs. One line alone did it; as for the rest, they relied upon their crews, so far as they can be said to have relied at all. An adequate receiving set suitable for a coastwise tug can now be got at small cost and is reasonably reliable if kept up; obviously it is a source of great protection to their tows. . . .
>
> Is it then a final answer that the business had not yet generally adopted receiving sets? There are, no doubt, cases where courts seem to make the general practice of the calling the standard of proper diligence; we have indeed given some currency to the notion ourselves. . . . Indeed in most cases reasonable prudence is in fact common prudence; but strictly it is never its measure; a whole calling may have unduly lagged in the adoption of new and available devices. It never may set its own tests, however persuasive be its usages. Courts must in the end say what is required; there are precautions so imperative that even their universal disregard will not excuse their omission. . . . But here there was no custom at all as to receiving sets; some had them, some did not; the most that can be urged is that they had not yet become general. Certainly in such a case we need not pause; when some have thought a device necessary, at least we may say that they were right, and the others too slack. . . . The injury was a direct consequence of this unseaworthiness.

Note that custom, by infusing new content into such standards as "due care," can act as an important agency for the development of legal norms. Community practice may help to determine community obligation.

(2) Custom may suggest the proper interpretation of commercial documents. The practice of businessmen in interpreting or fulfilling standard contracts in a particular fashion may be relevant or indeed decisive for a court that must determine the duties created by the contract. Cf. Dixon, Irmaos & Cia. Ltda. v. Chase National Bank, 144 F.2d 759 (2d Cir. 1944).

(3) Trends in constitutional law often reflect developing beliefs or aspirations in a society. It may be more confusing than helpful to refer to such community mores or attitudes as "custom." But at times recourse by courts to community practice to decide constitutional questions becomes explicit and approaches a more traditional notion of custom. The conduct observed may be that of private persons or of officials. Consider the opinion in Wolf v. Colorado, 338 U.S. 25, 69 S.Ct. 1359, 93 L.Ed. 1782 (1949), holding that the Fourteenth Amendment did not require the exclusion of illegally seized evidence from state-court proceedings. In writing for the Court, Justice Frankfurter reviewed the practice of various states and nations. He concluded that since "most of the English-speaking world does not regard as vital . . . the exclusion of evidence thus obtained, we must hesitate to treat this remedy as an essential ingredient of the right [to be free from illegal search and seizure.]" The Justice noted that 30 states in this country had rejected the federal exclusionary rule while 17 agreed with it.[27] Such "state counting" bears some resemblance to the "head counting" in the T. J. Hooper opinion. Compare the "nation counting" in the following case, which offers one of the more elaborate and influential opinions of an international tribunal on the nature and role of custom.

CASE OF THE S.S. "LOTUS"

Permanent Court of International Justice, 1927.
P.C.I.J., Ser. A, No. 10.

[In 1926, a collision occurred between a French steamer, the "Lotus," and a Turkish collier, about five nautical miles off the coast of Turkey, and consequently on the high seas rather than within Turkey's territorial waters. The Turkish collier sank and eight Turkish nationals were lost in the accident. The officer of the watch on the "Lotus" at the time of the accident was M. Demons, a French national. The "Lotus" continued to Constantinople, where Turkish authorities called upon M. Demons to give evidence about the accident. After testifying, he was arrested and charged with involuntary manslaughter under Turkish law. A conviction, fine and brief imprisonment followed. The French Government protested the action of the Turkish authorities in bringing a criminal action against Demons and contended that the Turkish prosecution violated principles of international law. By special agreement, France and Turkey submitted this dispute to the P.C.I.J., where France sought indemnity from Turkey for the injury resulting from the prosecution. The question before the Court was whether international law prohibited Turkey from asserting "jurisdiction" to prosecute Demons.

The decision of the Court referred to the Convention of Lausanne of 1923, to which France and Turkey were parties. Article 15 of the

27. The decision was subsequently overruled in Mapp v. Ohio, 367 U.S 643, 81 S.Ct. 1684, 6 L.Ed.2d 1081 (1961).

Convention stated that "all questions of jurisdiction shall, as between Turkey and other contracting Powers, be decided in accordance with the principles of international law." The Court concluded that "the wording ultimately adopted by common consent for Article 15 can only refer to the principles of general international law relating to jurisdiction."

The basic argument advanced by the French Government was that only that state whose flag was flown on a ship had "jurisdiction" under international law to attach legal consequences to acts occurring on board that ship on the high seas, and consequently to prosecute any person for his conduct on board. This argument, the contrary arguments advanced by the Turkish Government, and other arguments developed by the Court are of considerable importance, in that they consider what limits international law imposes upon a state's ability to prescribe and enforce rules regulating conduct outside its borders. The reasoning of the Court on these issues, and the implications of the holding for international law generally in fields far removed from the sea, are examined in Chapters VIII and IX, which consider the transnational reach of criminal and regulatory legislation. The excerpts below focus not on the merits of the dispute, but on the manner in which the Court found the applicable "principles of general international law."]

The Court, having to consider whether there are any rules of international law which may have been violated by the prosecution in pursuance of Turkish law of Lieutenant Demons, is confronted in the first place by a question of principle which, in the written and oral arguments of the two Parties, has proved to be a fundamental one. The French Government contends that the Turkish Courts, in order to have jurisdiction, should be able to point to some title to jurisdiction recognized by international law in favour of Turkey. On the other hand, the Turkish Government takes the view that Article 15 allows Turkey jurisdiction whenever such jurisdiction does not come into conflict with a principle of international law.

The latter view seems to be in conformity with the special agreement itself, No. 1 of which asks the Court to say whether Turkey has acted contrary to the principles of international law and, if so, what principles. According to the special agreement, therefore, it is not a question of stating principles which would permit Turkey to take criminal proceedings, but of formulating the principles, if any, which might have been violated by such proceedings.

This way of stating the question is also dictated by the very nature and existing conditions of international law.

International law governs relations between independent States. The rules of law binding upon States therefore emanate from their own free will as expressed in conventions or by usages generally accepted as expressing principles of law and established in order to regulate the relations between these co-existing independent communities or with a view to the achievement of common aims. Restrictions upon the independence of States cannot therefore be presumed.

. . .

It follows from the foregoing that the contention of the French Government to the effect that Turkey must in each case be able to cite a rule of international law authorizing her to exercise jurisdiction, is opposed to the generally accepted international law . . . .

[The Court developed the argument that the "guilty act" committed on the high seas should be viewed as having an effect on Turkish territory (that is, the Turkish collier), since a ship on the high seas is assimilated for various purposes to the territory of the state whose flag it flies. It then reached the "conclusion" that no rule of international law prohibited the state of the flag of the ship on which the effect of the act was felt from treating the offence (manslaughter) as having been committed on its territory and from prosecuting the wrongdoer. The Court continued:]

This conclusion could only be overcome if it were shown that there was a rule of customary international law which, going further than the principle stated above, established the exclusive jurisdiction of the State whose flag was flown. The French Government has endeavoured to prove the existence of such a rule, having recourse for this purpose to the teachings of publicists, to decisions of municipal and international tribunals, and especially to conventions which, whilst creating exceptions to the principle of the freedom of the seas by permitting the war and police vessels of a State to exercise a more or less extensive control over the merchant vessels of another State, reserve jurisdiction to the courts of the country whose flag is flown by the vessel proceeded against.

In the Court's opinion, the existence of such a rule has not been conclusively proved.

In the first place, as regards teachings of publicists, and apart from the question as to what their value may be from the point of view of establishing the existence of a rule of customary law, it is no doubt true that all or nearly all writers teach that ships on the high seas are subject exclusively to the jurisdiction of the State whose flag they fly. But the important point is the significance attached by them to this principle; now it does not appear that in general, writers bestow upon this principle a scope differing from or wider than that explained above and which is equivalent to saying that the jurisdiction of a State over vessels on the high seas is the same in extent as its jurisdiction in its own territory. On the other hand, there is no lack of writers who, upon a close study of the special question whether a State can prosecute for offences committed on board a foreign ship on the high seas, definitely come to the conclusion that such offences must be regarded as if they had been committed in the territory of the State whose flag the ship flies, and that consequently the general rules of each legal system in regard to offences committed abroad are applicable.

In regard to precedents, it should first be observed that, leaving aside the collision cases which will be alluded to later, none of them relates to offences affecting two ships flying the flags of two different countries, and that consequently they are not of much importance in the case before the Court . . . .

On the other hand, there is no lack of cases in which a State has claimed a right to prosecute for an offence, committed on board a foreign ship, which it regarded as punishable under its legislation. Thus Great Britain refused the request of the United States for the extradition of John Anderson, a British seaman who had committed homicide on board an American vessel, stating that she did not dispute the jurisdiction of the United States but that she was entitled to exercise hers concurrently. This case, to which others might be added, is relevant in spite of Anderson's British nationality, in order to show that the principle of the exclusive jurisdiction of the country whose flag the vessel flies is not universally accepted.

The cases in which the exclusive jurisdiction of the State whose flag was flown has been recognized would seem rather to have been cases in which the foreign State was interested only by reason of the nationality of the victim, and in which, according to the legislation of that State itself or the practice of its courts, that ground was not regarded as sufficient to authorize prosecution for an offence committed abroad by a foreigner.

Finally, as regards conventions expressly reserving jurisdiction exclusively to the State whose flag is flown, it is not absolutely certain that this stipulation is to be regarded as expressing a general principle of law rather than as corresponding to the extraordinary jurisdiction which these conventions confer on the state-owned ships of a particular county in respect of ships of another country on the high seas. Apart from that, it should be observed that these conventions relate to matters of a particular kind, closely connected with the policing of the seas, such as the slave trade, damage to submarine cables, fisheries, etc., and not to common-law offences. Above all it should be pointed out that the offences contemplated by the conventions in question only concern a single ship; it is impossible therefore to make any deduction from them in regard to matters which concern two ships and consequently the jurisdiction of two different States.

The Court therefore has arrived at the conclusion that the second argument put forward by the French Government does not, any more than the first, establish the existence of a rule of international law prohibiting Turkey from prosecuting Lieutenant Demons. . . .

[The Court then considered another argument (referred to below as the "third argument") advanced by the French Government—namely, that the principle of exclusive jurisdiction of the state whose flag is flown is specially applicable in collision cases. The Court stated:]

In the Court's opinion, this conclusion is not warranted. Even if the rarity of the judicial decisions to be found among the reported cases were sufficient to prove in point of fact the circumstance alleged by the Agent for the French Government, it would merely show that States had often, in practice, abstained from instituting criminal proceedings, and not that they recognized themselves as being obliged to do so; for only if such abstention were based on their being conscious of having a duty to abstain would it be possible to speak of an international custom. The alleged fact does not allow one to infer that States have been conscious of having such a duty; on the other hand, as will presently be seen, there are other circumstances calculated to show that the contrary is true.

So far as the Court is aware there are no decisions of international tribunals in this matter; but some decisions of municipal courts have been cited. Without pausing to consider the value to be attributed to the judgments of municipal courts in connection with the establishment of the existence of a rule of international law, it will suffice to observe that the decisions quoted sometimes support one view and sometimes the other. Whilst the French Government have been able to cite the *Ortigia—Oncle-Joseph* case before the Court of Aix and the *Franconia—Strathclyde* case before the British Court for Crown Cases Reserved, as being in favour of the exclusive jurisdiction of the State whose flag is flown, on the other hand the *Ortigia—Oncle-Joseph* case before the Italian Courts and the *Ekbatana—West-Hinder* case before the Belgian Courts have been cited in support of the opposing contention.

Lengthy discussions have taken place between the Parties as to the importance of each of these decisions as regards the details of which the Court confines itself to a reference to the Cases and Counter-Cases of the Parties. The Court does not think it necessary to stop to consider them. It will suffice to observe that, as municipal jurisprudence is thus divided, it is hardly possible to see in it an indication of the existence of the restrictive rule of international law which alone could serve as a basis for the contention of the French Government.

On the other hand, the Court feels called upon to lay stress upon the fact that it does not appear that the States concerned have objected to criminal proceedings in respect of collision cases before the courts of a country other than that the flag of which was flown, or that they have made protests: their conduct does not appear to have differed appreciably from that observed by them in all cases of concurrent jurisdiction. This fact is directly opposed to the existence of a tacit consent on the part of States to the exclusive jurisdiction of the State whose flag is flown, such as the Agent for the French Government has thought it possible to deduce from the infrequency of questions of jurisdiction before criminal courts. It seems hardly probable, and it would not be in accordance with international practice, that the French Government in the *Ortigia—Oncle-Joseph* case and the German Government in the *Ekbatana—West-Hinder* case would have omitted to protest against the exercise of criminal jurisdiction by the Italian and Belgian Courts, if they had really thought that this was a violation of international law. . . .

The conclusion at which the Court has therefore arrived is that there is no rule of international law in regard to collision cases to the effect that criminal proceedings are exclusively within the jurisdiction of the State whose flag is flown.

This conclusion moreover is easily explained if the manner in which the collision brings the jurisdiction of two different countries into play be considered.

The offence for which Lieutenant Demons appears to have been prosecuted was an act—of negligence or imprudence—having its origin on board the *Lotus*, whilst its effects made themselves felt on board the *Boz-Kourt*. These two elements are, legally, entirely inseparable, so much so that their separation renders the offence non-existent. Neither the exclusive jurisdiction of either State, nor the limitations of the jurisdiction of each to the occurrences which took place on the respective ships would appear calculated to satisfy the requirements of justice and effectively to protect the interests of the two States. It is only natural that each should be able to exercise jurisdiction and to do so in respect of the incident as a whole. It is therefore a case of concurrent jurisdiction.

The Court, having arrived at the conclusion that the arguments advanced by the French Government either are irrelevant to the issue or do not establish the existence of a principle of international law precluding Turkey from instituting the prosecution which was in fact brought against Lieutenant Demons, observes that in the fulfilment of its task of itself ascertaining what the international law is, it has not confined itself to a consideration of the arguments put forward, but has included in its researches all precedents, teachings and facts to which it had access and which might possibly have revealed the existence of one of the principles of international law contemplated in the special agreement. The result of these researches has not been to establish the existence of any such principle. . . .

[Dissenting opinions are omitted.]

NOTE ON SOME ASPECTS OF CUSTOM IN INTERNATIONAL LAW

Authorities on international law have identified several requirements for the development of principles or rules of customary law. These requirements are meant to shape one's judgment whether there exists among nations a recognition that certain conduct, or abstention from certain conduct, is obligatory under or consistent with international law. They have been stated to be: (*1*) "concordant practice" by a number of states relating to a particular situation; (*2*) continuation of that practice over "a considerable period of time"; (*3*) a conception that the practice is required by or consistent with international law; and (*4*) general acquiescence in that practice by other states.[28] Each raises troublesome issues. Some we explore here, others through the questions at p. 274, infra.

(1) What amount of proof as to the generality and duration of a practice will an executive official or court require before accepting past practice as evidence of present obligation? Note the cautious approach of the Court in Lotus, and its statement at p. 254, supra, that "rules of law binding upon States therefore emanate from their own free will as expressed in conventions or by usages generally accepted as expressing principles of law . . . . Restrictions upon the independence of States cannot therefore be presumed." The case can be read as imposing a heavy burden of proof upon the advocate of any rule that limits sovereign discretion.

Such aspects of the Lotus opinion have led commentators to describe it as illustrating an extreme "positivist" approach to international law. Whatever its legal and philosophical connotations in other contexts (see the discussion of the command theory of law at p. 178, supra), the term "positivism" has come to assume a specific meaning in an international setting. "[I]t teaches that international law is the sum of the rules by which states have *consented* to be bound, and that nothing can be law to which they have not consented. This consent may be given expressly, as in a treaty, or it may be implied by a state acquiescing in a customary rule." See Brierly, The Law of Nations 51 (6th ed., Waldock, 1963). Positivism thus implies a careful empirical inquiry into state practice and rigorous criteria as to the duration and generality of a practice.[29] By stressing consent, it attempts to reconcile international obligation with national sovereignty. Obligation derives not from superior power of others, natural law

28. See Hudson, Working Paper on Article 24 of the Statute of the International Law Commission, U.N.Doc. A/CN.4/16 March 3, 1950, p. 5, appearing in 1950 Yearbook of The International Law Commission, Vol. II, p. 26.

29. Compare the opinions of the dissenting Judges in the Nottebohm Case, at pp. 217 and 219, supra. Note particularly the view of Judge Guggenheim that Guatemala's position should be supported by proof of "repeated and recurrent acts on the international level" in order to show that an "established" usage had developed.

principles, or an evaluation by some authoritative official that a rule meets the needs of the international community, but from consent among coordinate states. Positivism thus stresses decentralized law-making by the participants in the international legal process, and casts an international tribunal in the role of declarer of a customary norm rather than of a creative law-maker.

(2) Consider the third requirement, that a practice be required by or consistent with international law, and note its relationship to the concluding words of Article 38(1)(b). Some courts and writers have stressed two aspects of custom: the "material" (that is, precise conduct or abstention from identifiable conduct), and the "psychological," the *opinio juris sive necessitatis* (that is, the sense that the conduct or abstention was under "compulsion" of law, responsive to some conception of legal duty). The Lotus Case offers an example of this second aspect, when the Court (p. 256) discounts the rarity of national criminal proceedings involving maritime collisions and foreign-flag ships as evidence of state practice because it was not shown that states abstained from prosecutions under consciousness of a "duty." International tribunals have only rarely referred to this aspect of custom.[30]

One can imagine the difficulty in marshalling evidence of the reasons why state officials reached a particular decision. Consider the following illustrations:

> (a) The courts of the large majority of nations have not asserted civil or criminal jurisdiction over foreign ambassadors, even prior to treaty regulation. Has this "abstention" (which may of course be the consequence of "affirmative" decisions of executive officials not to prosecute or of the executive's advice to the courts) ripened into a customary rule? In such a situation, which is close in character to the issue in the Lotus Case, the requirement that abstention be under the consciousness of a duty appears reasonable. Suppose, for example, that evidence could be summoned to show that most state officials believed that a prosecution would be consistent with international law. Abstention simply because they exercised their discretion not to prosecute, on grounds of convenience or expediency, would not easily

30. A prominent example is the Asylum Case (Colombia v. Peru), [1950] I.C.J.Rep. 266, 277. Colombia referred to many cases in which diplomatic asylum had been granted and respected. The Court commented: "But [Colombia] has not shown that the alleged rule . . . was, apart from conventional stipulations, exercised by the States granting asylum as a right appertaining to them and respected by the territorial States as a duty incumbent on them and not merely for reasons of political expediency. The facts brought to the knowledge of the Court disclose so much uncertainty and contradiction . . . and the practice has been so much influenced by considerations of political expediency in the various cases, that it is not possible to discern in all this any constant and uniform usage, accepted as law, with regard to the alleged rule . . . . The Court cannot therefore find that the Colombian Government has proved the existence of such a custom. . . ."

foster the growth of a rule supporting a claim against a state which prosecuted an ambassador. Note that, unlike the following illustration, state practice in the form of "abstention" would not of itself induce an immediate reaction on the part of other states. Compare the reference in the Nottebohm Case, p. 215, supra, to the practice of states that refrained from exercising protection in favor of naturalized citizens who had tenuous links to them.

(b) Suppose that a nation acts in a way that immediately affects interests of other nations, as by expropriating without compensation the property of aliens, making claims to a larger territorial sea, or sending military aircraft over those nations at high altitudes. In such situations, the nation makes a claim of freedom to act in a particular manner without violating rights of other nations under international law. Is it meaningful to talk here of a "psychological" element, when the question is later raised about the legality of such conduct under international law? The nation surely has not acted under a sense of "duty." It may, to be sure, act in a way that it considers to be reasonable and justified in the context of existing principles; such an expanded notion of *opinio juris* could then be satisfied by state affirmative conduct. And to some extent, the projection of its claim may involve a correlative duty, namely the duty to recognize as valid comparable claims made by other nations. But this is a different matter from the phenomenon referred to by the Court in Lotus. What does appear relevant to the acting nation's claim of right or privilege is the *reaction* of other states, in the form of active or tacit acquiescence or of protest. Action and reaction, claims and responses, are here the critical components of the growth of a customary rule. The Lotus Case illustrated such a situation when the Court (p. 257) noted the absence of protest by states over prosecutions brought in courts of other states for collisions caused by foreign-flag ships.

Consider the following comments in Parry, The Sources and Evidences of International Law (1965), at 63–4:

> . . . . If we say that people originating in one part of the world very often have gone to other parts we make a purely factual statement. If we translate this statement into the proposition that nationals of one State have habitually entered the territory of others, we are guilty of allowing at least one foot to stray from the straight path of fact on to the adjoining meadow of thought. This trespass into the category of theory is, however, permissible since we postulate the existence of the State or we would not be talking about the actions of States at all. If we now go further and say that States habitually admit foreign nationals we have gone a step further into the delectable fields. We may even have falsified the facts. For we know very well that, though

nowadays States erect barriers at which the passports of foreigners are examined, this was not always the case. The fact was that people simply arrived. They were at first merely people and only later classified as nationals of this or that State. Indeed they arrived at geographical points before these were characterized as the frontiers of States at all. And even when the theory of the State was conceived and put into practice the position was not necessarily that States affirmatively permitted the entry of each other's nationals. More often than not they merely abstained from interfering with an immemorial coming and going. Much water has gone under the bridge since that point in time was reached and much rationalization has taken place. Thus we are now accustomed to say that States habitually affirmatively permit the relatively free entry of foreign nationals to their territory. The fact cannot be gainsaid. Despite immigration restrictions and Berlin walls, by and large the ancient wanderings are still tolerated. The process of toleration can be expressed, if it is desired, in terms of the actions of States. It is not, however, to be deduced that it is a rule of international law that States are under a duty to admit foreign nationals. Such is strenuously denied. What are construed to be the actions of States in tolerating the traffic must therefore be construed also to be actions undertaken otherwise than in the conviction of obligation.

(3) Note that the creation of expectations, the inducement of reliance by others that past practice offers a fair clue to future conduct, may provide a strong policy foundation for the observance of customary law. Consider, for example, illustration (a) above of abstention from prosecuting foreign ambassadors, and its effect upon the methods by which diplomatic intercourse is conducted. But suppose that a nation were to announce that it intended to hold foreign ambassadors subject to the jurisdiction of its courts on the same terms as its citizens, that it withdrew its consent to diplomatic immunity. This example suggests that considerations other than reliance or "tacit consent" support the observance of customary rules, for in many circumstances it is doubtful that a state could escape from the compass of a customary rule by prospectively "changing" expectations. The rule may express and reflect continuing needs of the international community, or standards of conduct of governments towards individuals that have come to be thought of as basic and essential.

(4) How can one determine the "practice" of states with respect to a given problem? What avenues of research should be explored? Note the examples of state practice which were offered by the Guatemalan and French Governments in the Nottebohm and Lotus cases, and the varying relevance to the establishment of a customary rule which the Court attributed to them.

At the start, one is confronted with the problem that the state speaks with many voices. The executive, legislature and judiciary may each have occasion to consider and make decisions concerning international law and relations. Some parts of government, particularly the foreign office, will have more frequent occasions to express views about these questions. Do its pronouncements—opinions of its officials, advice to the courts, positions taken during diplomatic negotiations, protests directed towards other nations—merit greater weight in determining the "practice" of that state on a particular point? Other branches of the executive that handle international problems—a war department, commerce department and so on—may have treated the same questions. National legislation on international matters may enjoy priority on many issues within the domestic legal order and control the position taken by the executive in the conduct of international relations. Decisions of national courts without benefit of advice from the executive may be pertinent. These complexities are often submerged beneath an easy reference to "state practice."

In addition, as pointed out in Parry, The Sources and Evidences of International Law 67–82 (1965), the lawyer, executive official or judge examining state practice may face procedural obstacles, particularly as to nations foreign to the researcher. The enormous bulk of and the difficulty in achieving access to archives of foreign offices, as well as the fragmentary quality of printed materials or digests in many nations, further burden the task of determining the "practice" of many states.

Additional reading: Texts cited at p. 177, supra; MacGibbon, Some Observations on the Part of Protest in International Law, 30 Brit.Ybk. Int.L. 293 (1953); MacGibbon, Customary International Law and Acquiescence, 33 Brit.Ybk.Int.L. 115 (1957); Parry, The Sources and Evidences of International Law, Ch. III (1965); Sorenson, Les Sources de Droit International, Ch. IV (1946); D'Amato, The Concept of Custom in International Law (1971); Baxter, Treaties and Custom, 129 Academie de Droit International, Recueil des Cours, 27 (1970).

FISHERIES CASE (UNITED KINGDOM v. NORWAY)

International Court of Justice, 1951.
[1951] I.C.J. Rep. 116.

[The United Kingdom instituted proceedings against Norway in accordance with declarations filed by both countries which accepted the compulsory jurisdiction of the I.C.J. pursuant to Article 36(2) of its Statute. The litigation arose out of a dispute over fishing rights of Britain and British fishing vessels in Norwegian coastal waters. Norway had arrested and condemned a number of British trawlers in such waters. The central issue was the validity under international law of a Norwegian Royal Decree of 1935 which delimited Norway's exclusive fisheries zone (an area which both parties assumed to be equivalent to Norway's territorial seas) off her Northern coast. Under that Decree, the fishery limit was a line drawn four miles seaward of baselines which connected 48 base points. These base points were islands off the coast, prominent headlands and rocks, known collectively as the "Skjaergaard" (rock rampart). The baselines did not follow the low-water mark along the coast and often did not touch headlands of bays. The map below illustrates their course.

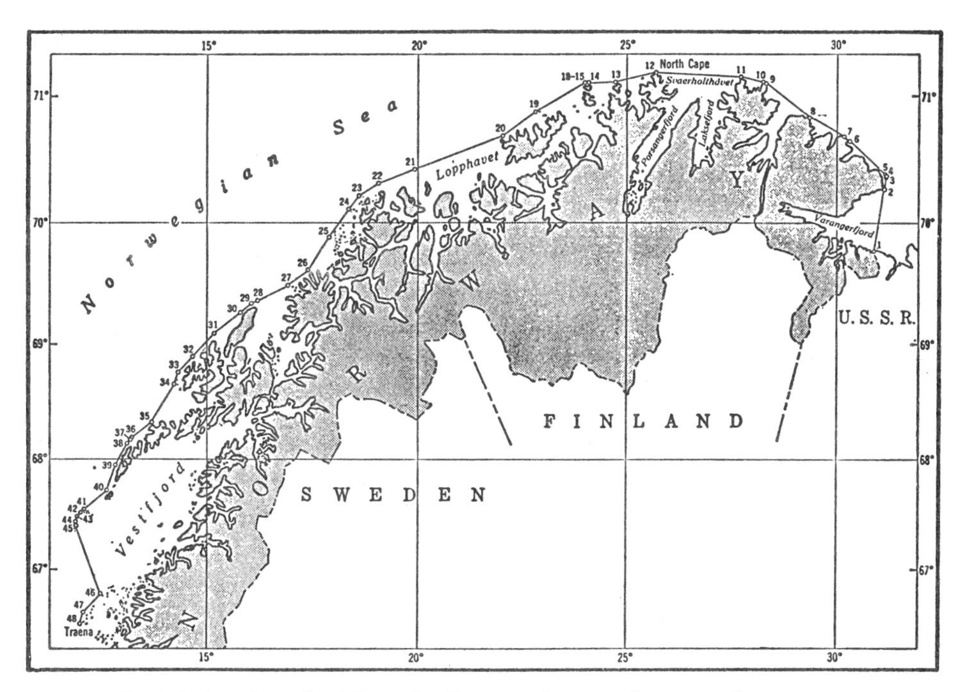

Straight baselines laid down by Norway along its skjaergaard coast under The Norwegian Royal Decree of 1935.[31]

[B1931]

The United Kingdom conceded that Norway had an "historic title" to four miles of territorial waters and to all internal waters of fjords and bays. It contended, however, that the Decree could not be enforced against it because the baselines conflicted with the customary rule of international law to the effect that baselines (subject to exceptions applying to bays and other internal waters) must follow the low-water mark along the actual coast. Norway supported the 1935 Decree by denying the existence of any customary rule requiring baselines to follow the low-water mark, by arguing that even if such a customary rule existed it had no application to the peculiar conditions of the broken Norwegian coast, and by claiming an historic title to the territorial waters delimited under the straight baseline system used in the 1935 Decree.

Excerpts from the opinion of the Court which treat some of the arguments of the parties appear below.]

The claim of the United Kingdom Government is founded on what it regards as the general international law applicable to the delimitation of the Norwegian fisheries zone.

The Norwegian Government does not deny that there exist rules of international law to which this delimitation must conform. It contends that the propositions formulated by the United Kingdom Government in its "Conclusions" do not possess the character attributed to them by that Government. It further relies on its own

31. The map appears as Figure 14 in Shalowitz, Shore and Sea Boundaries 69 (Vol. I, 1962).

system of delimitation which it asserts to be in every respect in conformity with the requirements of international law. . . .

The coastal zone concerned in the dispute is of considerable length. It lies north . . . of the Arctic Circle, and it includes the coast of the mainland of Norway and all the islands, islets, rocks and reefs, known by the name of the "skjaergaard" (literally, rock rampart), together with all Norwegian internal and territorial waters. The coast of the mainland, which, without taking any account of fjords, bays and minor indentations, is over 1,500 kilometres in length, is of a very distinctive configuration. Very broken along its whole length, it constantly opens out into indentations often penetrating for great distances inland . . . . The number of insular formations, large and small, which make up the "skjaergaard", is estimated by the Norwegian Government to be one hundred and twenty thousand. From the southern extremity of the disputed area to the North Cape, the "skjaergaard" lies along the whole of the coast of the mainland; east of the North Cape, the "skjaergaard" ends, but the coast line continues to be broken by large and deeply indented fjords.

Within the "skjaergaard", almost every island has its large and its small bays; countless arms of the sea, straits, channels and mere waterways serve as a means of communication for the local population which inhabits the islands as it does the mainland. The coast of the mainland does not constitute, as it does in practically all other countries, a clear dividing line between land and sea. What matters, what really constitutes the Norwegian coast line, is the outer line of the "skjaergaard". . . .

In these barren regions the inhabitants of the coastal zone derive their livelihood essentially from fishing.

Such are the realities which must be borne in mind in appraising the validity of the United Kingdom contention that the limits of the Norwegian fisheries zone laid down in the 1935 Decree are contrary to international law.

The Parties being in agreement on the figure of 4 miles for the breadth of the territorial sea, the problem which arises is from what base-line this breadth is to be reckoned. . . .

The Court has no difficulty in finding that, for the purpose of measuring the breadth of the territorial sea, it is the low-water mark as opposed to the high-water mark, or the mean between the two tides, which has generally been adopted in the practice of States. This criterion is the most favourable to the coastal State and clearly shows the character of territorial waters as appurtenant to the land territory. The Court notes that the Parties agree as to this criterion, but that they differ as to its application. . . .

The Court finds itself obliged to decide whether the relevant low-water mark is that of the mainland or of the "skjaergaard". Since the mainland is bordered in its western sector by the "skjaergaard", which constitutes a whole with the mainland, it is the outer line of the "skjaergaard" which must be taken into account in delimiting the belt of Norwegian territorial waters. This solution is dictated by geographic realities.

Three methods have been contemplated to effect the application of the low-water mark rule. The simplest would appear to be the method of the *tracé parallèle,* which consists of drawing the outer limit of the belt of territorial waters by following the coast in all its sinuosities. . . . Such a coast, viewed as a whole, calls for the application of a different method. Nor can one characterize as exceptions to the rule the very many derogations which would be necessitated by such a rugged coast. The rule would disappear under the exceptions. . . .

[A portion of the opinion rejecting the "arcs of circles" method is omitted.]

The principle that the belt of territorial waters must follow the general direction of the coast makes it possible to fix certain criteria valid for any delimitation of the territorial sea; these criteria will be elucidated later. The Court will confine itself at this stage to noting that, in order to apply this principle, several States have deemed it necessary to follow the straight base-lines method and that they have not encountered objections of principle by other States. This method consists of selecting appropriate points on the low-water mark and drawing straight lines between them. This has been done, not only in the case of well-defined bays, but also in cases of minor curvatures of the coast line where it was solely a question of giving a simpler form to the belt of territorial waters. . . .

By "historic waters" are usually meant waters which are treated as internal waters but which would not have that character were it not for the existence of an historic title. The United Kingdom Government refers to the notion of historic titles both in respect of territorial waters and internal waters, considering such titles, in both cases, as derogations from general international law. In its opinion Norway can justify the claim that these waters are territorial or internal on the ground that she has exercised the necessary jurisdiction over them for a long period without opposition from other States, a kind of *possessio longi temporis*, with the result that her jurisdiction over these waters must now be recognized although it constitutes a derogation from the rules in force. Norwegian sovereignty over these waters would constitute an exception, historic titles justifying situations which would otherwise be in conflict with international law.

As has been said, the United Kingdom Government concedes that Norway is entitled to claim as internal waters all the waters of fjords and sunds which fall within the conception of a bay as defined in international law whether the closing line of the indentation is more or less than ten sea miles long. But the United Kingdom Government concedes this only on the basis of historic title; it must therefore be taken that that Government has not abandoned its contention that the ten-mile rule is to be regarded as a rule of international law.[32]

In these circumstances the Court deems it necessary to point out that although the ten-mile rule has been adopted by certain States both in their national law and in their treaties and conventions, and although certain arbitral decisions have applied it as between these States, other States have adopted a different limit. Consequently, the ten-mile rule has not acquired the authority of a general rule of international law.

In any event the ten-mile rule would appear to be inapplicable as against Norway inasmuch as she has always opposed any attempt to apply it to the Norwegian coast.

The Court now comes to the question of the length of the baselines drawn across the waters lying between the various formations

32. [Eds.] This ten-mile rule referred to the maximum length of the closing line for internal waters.

of the "skjaergaard". Basing itself on the analogy with the alleged general rule of ten miles relating to bays, the United Kingdom Government still maintains on this point that the length of straight lines must not exceed ten miles.

In this connection, the practice of States does not justify the formulation of any general rule of law. The attempts that have been made to subject groups of islands or coastal archipelagoes to conditions analogous to the limitations concerning bays (distance between the islands not exceeding twice the breadth of the territorial waters, or ten or twelve sea miles), have not got beyond the stage of proposals. . . .

Consequently, the Court is unable to share the view of the United Kingdom Government, that "Norway, in the matter of base-lines, now claims recognition of an exceptional system". As will be shown later, all that the Court can see therein is the application of general international law to a specific case. . . .

It does not at all follow that, in the absence of rules having the technically precise character alleged by the United Kingdom Government, the delimitation undertaken by the Norwegian Government in 1935 is not subject to certain principles which make it possible to judge as to its validity under international law. The delimitation of sea areas has always an international aspect; it cannot be dependent merely upon the will of the coastal State as expressed in its municipal law. Although it is true that the act of delimitation is necessarily a unilateral act, because only the coastal State is competent to undertake it, the validity of the delimitation with regard to other States depends upon international law.

In this connection, certain basic considerations inherent in the nature of the territorial sea, bring to light certain criteria which, though not entirely precise, can provide courts with an adequate basis for their decisions, which can be adapted to the diverse facts in question.

Among these considerations, some reference must be made to the close dependence of the territory sea upon the land domain. It is the land which confers upon the coastal State a right to the waters off its coasts. It follows that while such a State must be allowed the latitude necessary in order to be able to adapt its delimitation to practical needs and local requirements, the drawing of base-lines must not depart to any appreciable extent from the general direction of the coast.

Another fundamental consideration, of particular importance in this case, is the more or less close relationship existing between certain sea areas and the land formations which divide or surround them. The real question raised in the choice of base-lines is in effect whether certain sea areas lying within these lines are sufficiently closely linked to the land domain to be subject to the regime of internal waters. This idea, which is at the basis of the determination of the rules relating to bays, should be liberally applied in the case of a coast, the geographical configuration of which is as unusual as that of Norway.

Finally, there is one consideration not to be overlooked, the scope of which extends beyond purely geographical factors: that of certain economic interests peculiar to a region, the reality and importance of which are clearly evidenced by a long usage.

Norway puts forward the 1935 Decree as the application of a traditional system of delimitation, a system which she claims to be in complete conformity with international law. The Norwegian

Government has referred in this connection to an historic title, the meaning of which was made clear by Counsel for Norway at the sitting on October 12th, 1951: "The Norwegian Government does not rely upon history to justify exceptional rights, to claim areas of sea which the general law would deny; it invokes history, together with other factors, to justify the way in which it applies the general law." This conception of an historic title is in consonance with the Norwegian Government's understanding of the general rules of international law. In its view, these rules of international law take into account the diversity of facts and, therefore, concede that the drawing of base-lines must be adapted to the special conditions obtaining in different regions. In its view, the system of delimitation applied in 1935, a system characterized by the use of straight lines, does not therefore infringe the general law; it is an adaptation rendered necessary by local conditions. . . .

[The Court then referred to earlier Norwegian decrees and diplomatic correspondence pertaining to delimitation of its territorial seas. It found an underlying consistency between methods asserted by Norway in the 1935 decree and those developed in earlier decrees of 1812, 1869 and 1889. It referred to diplomatic correspondence between Norway and France during 1869–1870 in which Norway contended that its system was consistent with international law and in which France, while maintaining its position as a matter of principle, indicated its willingness to accept the 1869 decree as resting upon the peculiar conditions of the Norwegian coast. The Court rejected contentions of the United Kingdom that diplomatic correspondence between the United Kingdom and Norway during 1906–1908 led to modifications of the Norwegian position. It continued:]

From the standpoint of international law, it is now necessary to consider whether the application of the Norwegian system encountered any opposition from foreign States.

Norway has been in a position to argue without any contradiction that neither the promulgation of her delimitation Decrees in 1869 and in 1889, nor their application, gave rise to any opposition on the part of foreign States. Since, moreover, these Decrees constitute, as has been shown above, the application of a well-defined and uniform system, it is indeed this system itself which would reap the benefit of general toleration, the basis of an historical consolidation which would make it enforceable as against all States.

The general toleration of foreign States with regard to the Norwegian practice is an unchallenged fact. For a period of more than sixty years the United Kingdom Government itself in no way contested it. . . . It would appear that it was only in its Memorandum of July 27, 1933, that the United Kingdom made a formal and definite protest on this point.

The United Kingdom Government has argued that the Norwegian system of delimitation was not known to it and that the system therefore lacked the notoriety essential to provide the basis of an historic title enforceable against it. The Court is unable to accept this view. As a coastal State on the North Sea, greatly interested in the fisheries in this area, as a maritime Power traditionally concerned with the law of the sea and concerned particularly to defend the freedom of the seas, the United Kingdom could not have been ignorant of the Decree of 1869 which had at once provoked a request for explanations by the French Government. Nor, knowing of it, could it have been under any misapprehension as to the significance of its terms, which clearly described it as constituting the application of a system. . . .

The notoriety of the facts, the general toleration of the international community, Great Britain's position in the North Sea, her own interest in the question, and her prolonged abstention would in any case warrant Norway's enforcement of her system against the United Kingdom.

The Court is thus led to conclude that the method of straight lines, established in the Norwegian system, was imposed by the peculiar geography of the Norwegian coast; that even before the dispute arose, this method had been consolidated by a constant and sufficiently long practice, in the face of which the attitude of governments bears witness to the fact that they did not consider it to be contrary to international law.

The question now arises whether the Decree of July 12th, 1935, which in its preamble is expressed to be an application of this method, conforms to it in its drawing of the base-lines, or whether, at certain points, it departs from this method to any considerable extent. . . .

[The Court concluded that the 1935 Decree in fact conformed to the method established in the preceding decrees. By 10 votes to 2, the Court found "that the method employed for the delimitation of the fisheries zone by the Royal Norwegian Decree of July 12th, 1935, is not contrary to international law . . .." By a vote of 8 to 4, the Court found "that the base-lines fixed by the said Decree in application of this method are not contrary to international law." Several dissenting opinions vigorously challenged the manner in which the Court read the historical record and disputed the Court's definition of the applicable principles of international law.

In a concurring opinion, JUDGE ALVAREZ stressed different principles. He stated in part:]

In accordance with uniformly accepted doctrine, international judicial tribunals must, in the absence of principles provided by conventions, or of customary principles on a given question, apply the *general principles of law.* This doctrine is expressly confirmed in Article 38 of the Statute of the Court.

It should be observed in this connection that international arbitration is now entering a new phase. It is not enough to stress the general principles of law recognized by civilized nations; regard must also be had, as I have said, to the modifications which these principles may have undergone as a result of the great changes which have occurred in international life, and the principles must be *adapted* to the new conditions of international life; indeed, if no principles exist covering a given question, principles must be *created* to conform to those conditions. . . .

What are the principles of international law which the Court must have recourse to and, if necessary, adapt? And what are the principles which it must in reality create?

It should, in the first place, be observed that frequent reference is made to the *principles* of the law of nations, in conventions and in certain of the Judgments of the Permanent Court of International Justice, but it is not said what those principles are nor where they may be found.

Some clarification is therefore necessary on this point.

In the first place, many of the principles, particularly the great principles, have their origin in the legal conscience of peoples (the psychological factor). This conscience results from social and international life; the requirements of this social and international life naturally give rise to certain norms considered necessary to govern the conduct of States *inter se.*

As a result of the present dynamic character of the life of peoples, the principles of the law of nations are continually being created, and they undergo more or less rapid modification as a result of the great changes occurring in that life.

For the principles of law resulting from the juridical conscience of peoples to have any value, they must have a tangible manifestation, that is to say, they must be expressed by authorized bodies.

Up to the present, this juridical conscience of peoples has been reflected in conventions, customs and the opinions of qualified jurists.

But profound changes have occurred in this connection. *Conventions* continue to be a very important form for the expression of the juridical conscience of peoples, but they generally lay down only new principles, as was the case with the Convention on genocide. On the other hand, *customs* tend to disappear as the result of the rapid changes of modern international life; and a new case strongly stated may be sufficient to render obsolete an ancient custom. Customary law, to which such frequent reference is made in the course of the arguments, should therefore be accepted only with prudence.

The further means by which the juridical conscience of peoples may be expressed at the present time are the resolutions of diplomatic assemblies, particularly those of the United Nations and especially the decisions of the International Court of Justice. Reference must also be made to the recent legislation of certain countries, the resolutions of the great associations devoted to the study of the law of nations, the works of the Codification Commission set up by the United Nations, and finally, the opinions of qualified jurists.

These are the new elements on which the new international law, still in the process of formation, will be founded. This law will, consequently, have a character entirely different from that of traditional or classical international law, which has prevailed to the present time.

Let us now consider the elements by means of which the general principles brought to light are to be adapted to the existing conditions of international life and by means of which new principles are, if necessary, to be created.

The starting point is the fact that, for the traditional *individualistic* régime on which social life has hitherto been founded, there is being substituted more and more a new régime, a régime of *interdependence,* and that, consequently, the *law of social interdependence* is taking the place of the old individualistic law.

The characteristics of this law, so far as international law is concerned, may be stated as follows:

(*a*) This law governs not merely a *community* of States, but an organized international *society.*

(*b*) It is not exclusively juridical; it has also aspects which are political, economic, social, psychological, etc. It follows that the traditional distinction between *legal* and *political* questions, and between the domain of law and the domain of politics is considerably modified at the present time.

(*c*) It is concerned not only with the delimitation of the rights of States but also with harmonizing them.

(*d*) It particularly takes into account the general interest.

(*e*) It also takes into account all possible aspects of every case. . . .

(*h*) It adapts itself to the needs of international life and develops side by side with it. . . .

NOTE ON DEVELOPMENTS SUBSEQUENT TO THE FISHERIES CASE

Those whose piscatorial interests are whetted by the Fisheries Case should consult Johnston, The International Law of Fisheries (1965). Some points noted in that book illuminate the Anglo-Norwegian conflict. Johnston refers (p. 40) to the fact that Norway derives 3% of its national income from fisheries, a percentage exceeded only by Iceland. Norway lands 48 tons of fish per 100 inhabitants per year. At the same time the quantity of fish taken by British vessels in the Norwegian fisheries area steadily increased as modern trawlers developed the capacity to operate further from home ports (pp. 179–81). By 1951, the British catch in certain areas previously exploited only by Norway was nearly three times the Norwegian (p. 179).

Britain and Norway entered into a Fishery Agreement, November 17, 1960, 398 U.N.T.S. 189, in order to "stabilize fishery relations" between them. The countries agreed (Articles II–IV) to an exclusive Norwegian fisheries zone "within the limit of 12 miles from the base line from which the territorial sea of Norway is measured," but with a proviso that until 1970 British-registered trawlers could operate within this zone between six and twelve miles from the baselines. Article VIII provided that nothing in the Agreement would be "deemed to prejudice the views held by either Contracting Party as to the delimitation and limitation in international law of territorial waters or of exclusive jurisdiction in fishery matters." Annexes to the Agreement spelled out in detail rules governing the operations of the fishing vessels of both parties and rules relating to the policing of the fisheries. A multilateral European convention on fisheries of 1964 expressed similar principles.[33]

The problems at issue between Britain and Norway have not been unique; similar questions have caused friction between Britain and Iceland. British long range trawlers have been active for many years in waters regarded by Iceland as within its own domain and, in the process, have been depleting a resource vital to Iceland's economy. In 1952 Iceland issued new regulations drawing a base line according to principles laid down in the Norwegian Fisheries case. Protracted negotiations between the two countries ensued, influenced by the then pending Geneva Conference on the Law of the Sea. An Exchange of Notes in 1961 set forth an agreement that accepted a 12 mile fishing limit, with provisions for a phased withdrawal of British vessels from that area. It contained a compromissory clause. In 1971 Iceland proclaimed a fisheries limit of 50 miles around its shores.

33. Articles 2–5 of the Fisheries Convention, March 9, 1964, [1963–1964] Great Britain Command Papers, No. 2355.

Negotiations ensued, punctuated by several British naval interventions to protect trawlers.

The United Kingdom then instituted proceedings in the International Court of Justice.[34] Iceland responded that the Court had no jurisdiction because Iceland had validly denounced the 1961 agreement on which its consent to jurisdiction rested. It further refused to obey an interim order of the Court after the Court decided that it did have jurisdiction. In its judgment on the merits, the Court concluded that Iceland could not oppose its 50 mile limits to the United Kingdom and could not exclude British vessels in the zone between a 12-mile limit (which the parties had accepted) and a 50-mile limit. The Court did decide, however, that both parties had an obligation to negotiate in good faith about arrangements in the 12-to-50-mile belt which would recognize both Iceland's "special dependence" on the fisheries and Britain's established rights in the area—and also the rights of third countries as well as the general problem of depletion of fishing resources in the Atlantic. It notes that the "former *laissez faire* treatment of the living resources of the sea" was no longer workable.

The Pacific, too, has seen controversy. Since 1947 Peru, with the backing of other Latin American states, particularly Ecuador and Chile, has claimed a 200 mile exclusive fishing zone. The United States has consistently refused to recognize these assertions and there has been a long series of episodes involving Peruvian seizures of American tuna boats, their release after the payment of fines, and protests by the United States government (which has often paid the fines).

There have been efforts to resolve the fisheries zone issue by world-wide agreement. In 1958 and 1960, conferences at Geneva sponsored by the United Nations developed four Conventions on the Law of the Sea. The United States is a party to each, although the Senate refused consent to the optional protocol bringing disputes under them within the compulsory jurisdiction of the I.C.J. The Convention on the Territorial Sea and the Contiguous Zone, April 29, 1958, 15 U.S.T. & O.I.A. 1606, T.I.A.S. No. 5639, 516 U.N.T.S. 205, treats problems debated in the Norwegian Fisheries Case. Article 3 states that the normal baseline for measuring the breadth of the territorial sea is the low-water coastal line. Article 4 sets forth a method of drawing straight baselines joining appropriate points from which the breadth of the territorial sea is measured "where the coast line is deeply indented and cut into, or if there is a fringe of islands along the coast . . . ." The baselines "must not depart to any appreciable extent from the general direction of the coast . . . ." In determining those lines, "account may be taken . .

34. See Fisheries Jurisdiction Case (United Kingdom v. Iceland), [1972] I.C.J.Rep. 12, 181; [1973] I.C.J.Rep. 3, 302; [1974] I.C.J.Rep. 3 (merits). Parallel proceedings brought by the Federal Republic of Germany are reported at [1972] I.C.J.Rep. 30, 188; [1973] I.C.J.Rep. 49, 96, 313; [1974] I.C.J.Rep. 175 (merits).

of economic interests peculiar to the region concerned, the reality and the importance of which are clearly evidenced by a long usage." The Convention authorizes states to exclude foreign fishing only in the territorial sea, which is more or less assimilated to land territory. Article 24 does provide for a "contiguous zone" in the high seas, not extending beyond 12 miles from the baseline for the territorial sea, within which the coastal state may exercise the control necessary to "[p]revent infringement of its customs, fiscal, immigration or sanitary regulations within its territory or territorial sea . . . ." [35]

The Geneva Conferences were, however, unable to achieve agreement over how many miles seaward from the low-water line or straight baselines the territorial seas should extend, or over the breadth of the exclusive fisheries zone. By one vote, the 1960 Conference failed to approve a compromise proposed by the United States and Canada for a six-mile territorial sea, plus a six-mile exclusive fisheries zone.

In 1970 preparations began for a new Conference on the Law of the Sea which first met at Caracas in 1974. It debated these issues along with others such as mineral rights on the ocean floor and continental shelves, the right to control maritime exploration and research, and the right of passage through straits. A 1975 session in Geneva produced a draft for further discussion which, among other things, provides for a 200-mile coastal fishing zone. As of mid-1975, it remained to be seen whether a third session, then scheduled to be held in New York, would achieve agreement on the fisheries zone.

Meanwhile, the United States has considered unilateral action with respect to its fishing limits and has adopted some legislation. Note that the interests of its domestic fishing industry are not entirely at one on this point. While New England fishermen support the extension of boundaries that would keep Soviet trawlers out of Atlantic coastal waters, tuna fishermen would be adversely affected by any action that by implication ratified Peru's enforcement of its wider claims.

In 1966, Congress considered proposals for legislation which would extend this country's exclusive fisheries zone to a line drawn nine nautical miles from the boundaries of the territorial sea. Since the United States traditionally claimed a territorial sea of three miles, the proposals amounted to a twelve-mile fishery zone. Data given the Congress by the Department of State indicated that 91 of 114 United Nations members were coastal nations.[36] Of these, 49 claimed a twelve-mile exclusive fishery jurisdiction, 10 claimed some distance between three and twelve miles, 15 claimed the traditional

35. Article 7 of the Convention resolves another of the disputed issues referred to in the Fisheries Case. With various qualifications, it authorizes a closing line delimiting internal waters of not exceeding 24 miles for bays. One qualification states that the Article does not apply in any case where a straight baseline system is authorized under Article 4.

36. Table, as of June 1, 1966, appearing in Sen.Rep.No.1280, 89th Cong., 2d Sess., June 15, 1966, p. 5.

three miles, and 17 more than twelve miles. The last group included a number of countries with claims up to 200 miles. A letter from an official of the Department of State to the Congressional committees considering the proposed legislation stated in part: [37]

> Since the 1960 Law of the Sea Conference there has been a trend toward the establishment of a 12-mile fisheries rule in international practice. Many states acting individually or in concert with other states have extended or are in the process of extending their fisheries limits to 12 miles. Such actions have no doubt been accelerated by the support for the proposals made at the Geneva Law of the Sea Conferences in 1958 and 1960, of a fisheries zone totaling 12 miles as part of a package designed to achieve international agreement on the territorial sea.
>
> In view of the recent developments in international practice, action by the United States at this time to establish an exclusive fisheries zone extending 9 miles beyond the territorial sea would not be contrary to international law. It should be emphasized that such action would not extend the territorial sea beyond our traditional 3-mile limit and would not affect such traditional freedoms of the sea as freedom of navigation or of overflight. With one or two possible exceptions, it is not likely that such action would be unfavorably received by other governments in view of the provision for recognition of traditional fishing, which the Department regards as a desirable provision.
>
> In the above circumstances, the Department has no objection from the standpoint of U. S. foreign relations to establishing a 12-mile exclusive fisheries zone subject to the continuation of such traditional fishing by foreign states as may be recognized by the U. S. Government.
>
> . . . . Inasmuch as U. S. establishment of a 12-mile exclusive fisheries zone would tend to support the trend already referred to, the passage of the proposed legislation would make it more difficult, from the standpoint of international law, to extend the zone beyond 12 miles in the future. . . .

The House Report stated that the need for the legislation arose from the fact that in recent years "there has been a tremendous increase in the taking of fishery resources by foreign vessels within 12 miles of U. S. shores. While our Nation's fishing resources are bountiful, they are not unlimited, and must be protected and intelligently conserved to meet future demands of our fishing industries and supply the needs of our citizens. Since 81 percent of the total U. S. fishery catch is taken within 12 miles of our shores, your committee deems it imperative that these highly productive areas be protected from ruthless exploitation by foreign fishing fleets."[38] The legislation was enacted the same year. 80 Stat. 908, 16 U.S.C.A. §§ 1091–94.

37. The letter appears in Sen.Rep.No. 1280, 89th Cong., 2d Sess., June 15, 1966, pp. 12–13.

38. H.Rep.No.2086, 89th Cong., 2d Sess., Sept. 26, 1966, p. 3.

In 1974–75 Congress again had before it proposals (H. 400, 94th Cong. 1st Sess.) for unilateral extension of the fisheries zone which drew support from the New England delegation but raised questions in the minds of other congressmen and parts of the federal government concerned with different aspects of the fisheries problems and with preservation of our bargaining position at future international conferences on the fisheries zone.

Additional Reading: Waldock, The Anglo-Norwegian Fisheries Case, 28 Brit.Ybk.Int.L. 114 (1951); Loring, The United States-Peruvian "Fisheries" Dispute, 23 Stan.L.Rev. 391 (1971); Bilder, The Anglo-Icelandic Fisheries Dispute, 1973 Wis.L.Rev. 37; Koers, Fishery Proposals in the United Nations Seabed Committee, 5 J.Mar.L. & Comm. 183 (1974); Dean, Second Geneva Conference on the Law of the Sea, 54 Am.J.Int.L. 751 (1960).

QUESTIONS

(1) Recall that Article 38(1)(b) refers to evidence of a "general" practice accepted as law. Consider in the context of the Fisheries Case how general the acquiescence in one state's practice must be. Would agreement of a majority of seafaring nations be required? Sufficient? Is it relevant whether (a) France and Denmark or (b) Burma and Ghana indicated their approval of Norway's system?

(2) Note the statement in the Norwegian Fisheries Case that the Court "has no difficulty in finding that, for the purpose of measuring the breadth of the territorial sea, it is the low-water mark as opposed to the high-water mark, or the mean between the two tides, which has generally been adopted in the practice of States." On the other hand the Court observed that "certain States" adopted a ten-mile rule with respect to the closing line of internal waters such as bays, but "other States have adopted a different limit. Consequently, the ten-mile rule has not acquired the authority of a general rule of international law." Do you think that the Court's different approaches to these two issues simply reflect the fact that it could "count" fewer states supporting the second rule?

(3) Suppose that Italian fishing vessels first infringed the Norwegian baseline system in 1952. Does the Fisheries Case suggest that Italy, which never before had reason to protest, is bound by that system? Or does the opinion bind only Great Britain to honor the Norwegian claims? Note that an affirmative answer to the last question would suggest a close relationship between a Norwegian practice ripening into a customary rule binding upon Great Britain, and a bilateral treaty between those two countries incorporating the baseline system.

(4) These questions raise the issue whether it is meaningful to talk in terms of bilateral or regional custom. Do some rules of international law, rather like treaty rules, govern relationships only between identifiable pairs of states or within coherent regional blocks? Must custom be universal before it can govern bilateral relationships?

(5) Suppose that Chile, which has a similar coastal configuration, follows Norway's example and establishes a baseline system in 1952. Can it exclude British trawlers? Argentinian trawlers? An answer may rest upon your judgment whether the Fisheries Case involved recognition of a general rule of international law or of a limited exception to such a rule.

(6) Does the Norwegian Fisheries Case require a particular period of time before practice shades into customary law? For example, would it have been sufficient if Norway had first asserted its position in 1945, and if no protests were heard until 1949? Under such circumstances, would it have been relevant if foreign trawlers had been arrested within the alleged territorial belt in 1946? Consider in this connection the following comments in Parry, The Sources and Evidences of International Law 59 (1965):

> In a community containing as few members as the international community, the difference between introducing a change into the law which is of universal application and merely asserting and establishing for oneself a claim to the benefit of an exception to the existing law, which nevertheless remains unchanged, is not enormous. As a result, there is some difficulty about pointing to an unmistakable example of the emergence of a new customary rule of general validity. One is tempted to put forward, as such an example, the recent growth of the doctrine of the continental shelf. Forty years ago a writer on international law could ask 'Whose is the bed of the sea?' and give the pretty certain general answer that it belonged to nobody. But, beginning with President Truman's proclamation of an intention on the part of the United States to assert an exclusive control over the bed and subsoil of the so-called continental shelf of the United States, we have had a wealth of similar proclamations and have reached the position that every State is without doubt entitled to assert a control similar to that which the United States claimed in a region bearing a similar relation to its own territory.[39] Is, however, this the example for which we seek?
>
> In the first place, the rapidity of the process is troublesome. The [International Court] speaks of 'constant and uniform' practice, epithets which somehow suggest practice over a substantial period of time. The same overtone is of course carried by the words custom and usage. The notion of a 'custom' arising in so short a space puts one in mind irresistibly of the story of the students of a brand-new university who exhibited a notice reciting that 'A new tradition will begin today'. At the same time, even an old tradition must have begun somewhere.

(7) Note the Court's approach to the problem of ascertaining whether there was acquiescence in Norway's claims. Need acquiescence be express, or can one imply it from silence? What conditions might you insist upon before silence of the foreign offices of other seafaring nations was held tantamount to acceptance?

COMMENT

In the Lotus and Fisheries cases, the Court stressed positions taken by nations—protests over or acquiescence in the conduct of

39. [Eds.] A footnote here referred to the Convention on the Continental Shelf, 15 U.S.T. & O.I.A. 471, T.I.A.S. No. 5578, 499 U.N.T.S. 311, drafted at the 1958 Geneva Conference on the Law of the Sea.

other nations—through their executive branches, although national legislation and judicial decisions were also considered to be relevant evidence of state practice. Compare the role of the executive in the field of foreign affairs from the perspective of a domestic legal system. Recall the decisions in Chapter II which gave the executive prominence in certain matters and generally showed greater deference in foreign than domestic problems to its acts or determinations.

Consider the following observations of Professor Myres McDougal. The author describes the process of decision-making in the international community, the variety of "decision-makers," and the double role which such persons or institutions play within the national and international legal processes. His observations, made in the context of a discussion of the law of the sea but with a more general relevance, appear in Editorial Comment: The Hydrogen Bomb Tests and the International Law of the Sea, 49 Am.J.Int.L. 356–59 (1955). In that comment, McDougal argues that hydrogen bomb tests conducted by the United States off Pacific islands held by it under a trusteeship agreement with the United Nations did not violate international law.

> From the perspective of realistic description, the international law of the sea is not a mere static body of rules but is rather a whole decision-making process, a public order which includes a structure of authorized decision-makers as well as a body of highly flexible, inherited prescriptions. It is in other words, a process of continuous interaction, of continuous demand and response, in which the decision-makers of particular nation states unilaterally put forward claims of the most diverse and conflicting character to the use of the world's seas, and in which other decision-makers, external to the demanding state and including both national and international officials, weigh and appraise these competing claims in terms of the interests of the world community and of the rival claimants, and ultimately accept or reject them. As such a process, it is a living, growing law, grounded in the practices and sanctioning expectations of nation-state officials, and changing as their demands and expectations are changed by the exigencies of new interests and technology and by other continually evolving conditions in the world arena.
>
> The factual claims asserted by nation state decision-makers to the use of the world's seas, the events to which the "regime of the high seas" is authoritative response, vary enormously in the comprehensiveness and particularity of the interests sought to be secured, in the location and size of the area affected, in the duration of claim, and in the degree of interference with others. Such claims range, in rough categorization, from the comprehensive and continuous claim to practically all competence in the "territorial sea," through the continuous but limited claims to navigation, fishing, and cable-laying upon the "high seas," to the relatively temporary and limited claims to exercise authority and control beyond territorial boundaries for a vast array of national purposes, such as security and self-defense, enforcement of health, neutrality and customs regulations, conservation or monopolization of fisheries, ex-

ploitation of the sedentary fisheries and mineral resources of the sea bed and continental shelf, the conducting of naval maneuvers and other military exercises, and so on. It may be observed, however, that, despite their variety in institutional nuance, all these claims share certain common characteristics: they are all unilateral assertions of demands by particular claimants to the individual use of a great common resource and all are affected in equal degree—navigation and fishing no more and no less than the others—with a community interest in fullest utilization and conservation and with specific national interest, which, though varying in particular instances with geographic propinquity, is in the sum of all instances common to all claimants.

The authoritative decision-makers put forward by the public order of the high seas to resolve all these competing claims include, of course, not merely judges of international courts and other international officials, but also those same nation-state officials who on other occasions are themselves claimants. This duality in function (*"dédoublement fonctionnel"*), or fact that the same nation-state officials are alternately, in a process of reciprocal interaction, both claimants and external decision-makers passing upon the claims of others, need not, however, cause confusion: it merely reflects the present lack of specialization and centralization of policy functions in international law generally. Similarly, it may be further observed, without deprecating the authority of international law, that these authoritative decision-makers projected by nation states for creating and applying a common public order, honor each other's unilateral claims to the use of the world's seas not merely by explicit agreements but also by mutual tolerances—expressed in countless decisions in foreign offices, national courts, and national legislatures—which create expectations that effective power will be restrained and exercised in certain uniformities of pattern. This process of reciprocal tolerance of unilateral claim is, too, but that by which in the present state of world organization most decisions about jurisdiction in public and private international law are, and must be, taken.[40] . . .

. . . . For all types of controversies the one test that decision-makers have in fact invoked and applied is that simple and ubiquitous, but indispensable, standard of what, considering all relevant policies and variables in context, is *reasonable* as between the parties; and for the clarification of detailed policies in ascribing meaning to particular prescriptions and terms, such decision-makers have habitually turned to all those sources authorized for the International Court of Justice, including not only "international conventions, whether general or particular" but also "international custom, as evidence of a general practice accepted as law," "the general principles of law rec-

40. It is not of course unilateral claims but rather the reciprocal tolerances of the external decision-makers which create the expectations of pattern and uniformity in decision, of practice in accord with rule, commonly regarded as law. The great bulk of claims to authority and control upon the high seas are honored and protected, it may be emphasized, not by explicit bilateral or multilateral agreement, but by this process of mutual tolerance. . . .

ognized by civilized nations," "judicial decisions and the teachings of the most qualified publicists," and considerations "*ex aequo et bono.*" [41]

QUESTIONS

Consider the reasoning of the Court in the Fisheries Case in relationship to the Lotus Case and the remarks of Professor McDougal, particularly those in fn. 41.

(1) Is the Lotus Case fairly described by many commentators as within the positivist tradition in international law? Consider the penultimate paragraph in the excerpts from the Court's opinion, at p. 257, supra.

(2) Do you agree that the Court in Fisheries was less constrained by the requirement of a formal, positive identification of practice and more responsive to economic and social "realities" or "needs"? For the Court in Fisheries, is the basis of customary law and the obligation to comply with it found in "consent" evidenced by the practice of states, or in the degree to which practice is responsive to state and community needs? (Recall similar Question (4), p. 241, supra, directed towards the Barcelona Traction Case.)

(3) Does the Fisheries opinion permit a clear choice between these two approaches? For example, if England and France had protested the Norwegian Decree immediately after it was promulgated and if ships registered in those countries had entered the Norwegian fisheries area, was it likely that the Court would nonetheless have ruled in Norway's favor?

(4) Do you view the provisions on baselines in the Geneva Conventions as codifying or "amending" the Fisheries opinion?

(5) How does custom change? Is the first party to act inconsistently with existing understandings at once a violator of the old norm and a builder of new normative order? What relevance to these questions have the justifications offered by the acting party or the reactions of others?

NOTE ON OTHER ASPECTS OF ARTICLE 38

Clause (c) of Article 38(1) states that the Court shall apply "the general principles of law recognized by civilized nations." Some decisions of international tribunals have invoked that clause, but in general treaties and custom have played the dominant role in international litigation.

41. Stat. I.C.J., Art. 38. A decision-maker is thus not confined, in determination of lawfulness, to explicit agreements or inferences from prior customary behavior, but may draw creatively upon a great variety of principles, precedents, analogies, and considerations of fairness. An excellent example of this process by which external decision-makers appraise unilateral claims is offered by the Anglo-Norwegian Fisheries Case, Judgment of Dec. 18, 1951, [1951] I.C.J. Rep. 116. In this case Norway asserted claims which could not be justified by reference to either explicit agreement or widely accepted custom, and which had been protested by other nation states, but by drawing upon all relevant sources of policy and a great variety of considerations in the context, the Court concluded that Norway's claims were lawful. . . .

What "general principles of law" implies has been the subject of much scholarly writing. At times, it appears to be used to signify a notion close to custom. More frequently, authorities on international law view the phrase as referring to principles of general significance in the legal systems of all or most "civilized" or developed countries. In this sense, the phrase invites recourse to comparative law, to an exploration of different legal systems in order to ascertain common themes upon which an international tribunal may draw to give more body to the less complete and coherent system of international law. It encourages reasoning by analogy to national laws. The level of abstraction at which these themes are identified may of course determine their significance for international law. And the nature of the search for common legal principles—that is, whether it embraces only one region or culture or whether it seeks to extrapolate principles from diverse regions and cultures—will affect the degree to which common themes can be found. Characteristic examples of general principles in the decisions of international tribunals include estoppel, laches and res judicata.

Clause (d) refers to "judicial decisions and the teachings of the most highly qualified publicists" as "subsidiary" means for determining rules of law. Its reference to Article 59 * has been variously interpreted. Viewed narrowly, it simply states the obvious, that a decision has binding force only upon the parties. Viewed broadly, it would impair the notion of stare decisis in international jurisprudence. In fact, a limited view of the relevance of judicial precedents would be consistent with a system of law that stressed custom, the practice of participants in the international community. Precedents would serve primarily as evidence of what custom was. Compare the comments about the early development of English common law, p. —, supra. But as scholars have observed, international tribunals and particularly the International Court have shown a tendency to cite precedents. This has been particularly marked in the post-war years and perhaps reflects the fact that decisions of the International Court have become sufficiently numerous to support case citations.

Additional reading: Bin Cheng, General Principles of Law as Applied by International Courts and Tribunals (1953); Lauterpacht, Private Law Sources and Analogies of International Law (1927); Lauterpacht, The Development of International Law by the International Court (1958).

NOTE ON APPLICABLE LAW FOR INTERNATIONAL ARBITRAL TRIBUNALS

Absent provision in a *compromis* to the contrary, the general doctrine appears to be that arbitral tribunals will apply the principles of "international law" to disputes before them. Those principles today would likely be ascertained by reference to Article 38 of the Statute of the I.C.J. See Article 10 of the Model Rules on Arbitral Procedure.*

A distinctive aspect of arbitration is that the *compromis* can define the principles to be applied by the arbitrators. In effect, it can constitute ad hoc "legislation" to be applied to the dispute, an observation which underscores the importance of reading arbitral awards in the light of the provisions of the compromis. For example, the Jay Treaty of 1794 between Great Britain and the United States provided that decision on one of the claims should be in accord with "justice, equity and the laws of nations." Malloy, Treaties between United States of America and other Foreign Powers, Vol. I, p. 596. A series of protocols in 1903 between several nations and Venezuela, which provided for submission of a large number of disputes to arbitration, stated that the arbitral commission "shall decide all claims upon a basis of absolute equity, without regard to objections of a technical nature, or of the provisions of local legislation." E. g., 9 U.N.R.I.A.A. 115, 321, 353. Note also the concluding clause to Article I * of the 1923 Convention between the United States and Mexico establishing a General Claims Commission.[42]

The problems are legion of giving content to general concepts in a *compromis* such as "equity and justice," particularly in an international legal climate which may embrace discordant values and legal traditions. Consider the following excerpts from an individual opinion of Judge Hudson in a case before the P.C.I.J., The Diversion of Water from the Meuse, Ser. A/B, No. 70, p. 76 (1937):

> What are widely known as principles of equity have long been considered to constitute a part of international law, and as such they have often been applied by international tribunals. . . . A sharp division between law and equity, such as prevails in the administration of justice in some States, should find no place in international jurisprudence; even in some national legal systems, there has been a strong tendency towards the fusion of law and equity. Some international tribunals are expressly directed by the *compromis* which control them to apply "law and equity". . . . Of such a provision, a special tribunal of the Permanent Court of Arbitration said in 1922 that "the majority of international lawyers seem to agree that these words are to be understood to mean general principles of justice as distinguished from any particular systems of jurisprudence." Proceedings of the United States—Norwegian Tribunal (1922), p. 141. . . .
>
> The Court has not been expressly authorized by its Statute to apply equity as distinguished from law. . . . Article 38 of the Statute expressly directs the application of "general principles of law recognized by civilized nations", and in more than one nation principles of equity have an established place in the legal system. The Court's recognition of equity as a part of international law is in no way restricted by the special power conferred upon it "to decide a

42. The *compromis* may be quite explicit. The Treaty of Washington of 1871, the foundation for the Alabama Claims Arbitration between the United States and the United Kingdom, directed that the arbitral commission should apply stated rules as to the duties of neutrals which the United Kingdom and the United States had accepted. 17 Stat. 863, T.S. No. 133.

> case *ex aequo et bono*, if the parties agree thereto". . . .
> It must be concluded, therefore, that under Article 38 of the Statute, if not independently of that Article, the Court has some freedom to consider principles of equity as part of the international law which it must apply.

See also Cayuga Indians (Great Britain v. United States), Nielsen's Rep. 203, 6 U.N.R.I.A.A. 173 (1926).

2. THE ROLE OF TREATIES

We here consider the role of treaties in imposing some order upon the international community. Our viewpoint is that of an international official, divorced from any one nation. Chapter V, which explores the relationship between treaties and national legal systems, views the treaty from the perspective of national executive and judicial officers.

NOTE ON TREATIES

The United Nations Treaty Series (U.N.T.S.), which reproduces treaties registered with the U. N. Secretariat, exceeds 800 volumes. The old League of Nations Treaties Series ran to 205 volumes. These compilations, together with the listings in the Index to Multilateral Treaties (Mostecky ed., Doyle asst. ed., 1965) and in the current edition of the State Department's publication "Treaties in Force," convey a sense of the volume and diversity of treaty law. Even the terminology varies. International agreements are referred to as pacts, protocols (generally supplementary to another agreement), conventions, charters, exchanges of notes and concordats (agreements between a nation and the Holy See), as well as treaties. These terms are more or less interchangeable in legal significance.[43]

Consider the different purposes which treaties serve. Some reaching critical national interests have a basic political character: alliances, peace settlements, atom bomb test ban. Others, while less politically charged, also involve relationships between governments or government agencies and affect private parties only indirectly: agreements on foreign aid, cooperation in the provision of governmental services such as weather forecasting and the mails. But treaties often have a direct and specific impact upon private parties. Tariff accords, income tax conventions, and treaties of friendship, commerce and navigation determine the conditions under which the nationals or residents of one signatory can export to, or engage in business activities within, the other signatory's territory.

Domestic analogies to the treaty help to portray its distinctive character. Some treaties settling particular disputes resemble a pri-

43. The term "treaty" has a particular significance in the internal law of the United States, because of the references to "treaties" in the Constitution. See p. 589, infra.

vate accord and satisfaction: an agreement over boundaries, an agreement to pay a stated sum as compensation for injury to the receiving nation or its nationals. Others are closer in character to private contracts of continuing significance or to domestic legislation, for they regulate recurrent problems by defining rights and obligations of the parties and their nationals: agreements over rules of navigation, income taxation, or the enforcement of foreign-country judgments. Their provisions may be stated in terms of constitutional breadth (expressed by the French term *traité cadre*) or may have the relative specificity of domestic legislation or indeed the precision of administrative regulations (*traité loi*). Indeed, the term "international legislation" has gained some currency,[44] particularly with respect to multilateral treaties that state rules regulating conduct.

Nonetheless, domestic legislation differs in several critical respects from the characteristic treaty. A statute is generally enacted by the majority of a legislature and binds all members of the relevant society. Even changes in a constitution, which usually require approval by the legislature and other institutions or groups, can be accomplished over substantial dissent. The ordinary treaty, on the other hand, is a consensual arrangement. With few exceptions, such as Article 2(6) of the U. N. Charter,* it purports to bind or benefit only parties. Alteration of its terms by one party generally requires the consent of all.

The other principal domestic analogy is the contract. Like the treaty, a contract can be said to make or create law between the parties—for within the constraints of governing law, courts recognize and enforce contract-created duties. The treaty shares a contract's consensual basis, but treaty law lacks the coherence and completeness of a national body of contract law. It has preserved a certain Roman law flavor ("*pacta sunt servanda*", "*rebus sic stantibus*") acquired during the long period from the Renaissance to the 19th century, when continental European scholars dominated the field. But it often reflects the diversity of approaches which lawyers bring to the topic from their domestic legal systems. While sharing some conceptions, the law of contracts prevailing in Great Britain, France, Saudi Arabia or the Soviet Union differs in salient respects from our own.

Duties Imposed by Treaty Law

Note that the first clause of Article 38(1) of the Statute of the I.C.J. refers to "international conventions." Whatever its purpose or character, the international agreement is generally recognized from the perspective of international law as an authoritative starting point for legal reasoning about any dispute to which it is relevant. The maxim *pacta sunt servanda* is at the core of treaty law. It embodies a widespread recognition that commitments publicly, formally and (more or less) voluntarily made by a nation should be honored. As

44. A basic compilation of treaty materials bears this title. Hudson, International Legislation, 1919-1945, 9 vols. (1931–1950).

stated in Article 26 of the Vienna Convention on the Law of Treaties, referred to below: "Every treaty in force is binding upon the parties to it and must be performed by them in good faith." Whatever the jurisprudential or philosophical bases for this norm, one can readily perceive the practical reasons for and the national interests served by adherence to the principle that *pacta sunt servanda.* The treaty represents one of the most effective means for bringing some order to relationships among states or their nationals, and for the systematic development of new principles responsive to the changing needs of the international community. It is the prime legal form through which that community can realize some degree of stability and predictability.

Acceptance of this basic principle does not, however, mean that a problem between two countries is adequately solved from the perspective of legal ordering simply by execution of a treaty with satisfactory provisions. A body of law has necessarily developed to deal with such questions as the formation of a treaty, its interpretation and performance, remedies for breach, and amendment or termination. But that body of law is often fragmentary and vague, reflecting the scarcity of decisions of international tribunals and the political tensions which some aspects of treaty law reflect.[45]

There have been attempts to remedy this situation through more or less creative codification of the law of treaties. An important older version is the Harvard Research in International Law, 29 Am.J. Int.L., Supp. 2, p. 686 (1935). In 1965 the American Law Institute completed and published a Restatement (Second) of the Foreign Relations Law of the United States, several chapters of which are devoted to the law of treaties. In 1966, the International Law Commission of the United Nations completed its five-year effort to codify treaty law and submitted to the General Assembly its Draft Articles on the Law of Treaties. The United Nations Conference on the Law of Treaties was convened at Vienna, at the General Assembly's direction, and adopted a Convention on May 22, 1969.[46] Although then opened for signature, the Convention on the Law of Treaties as of mid 1975 had not received sufficient ratifications to come into force.

President Nixon submitted the Vienna Convention to the Senate, for its advice and consent, under a letter of transmittal of November 22, 1971.[47] The letter stresses the "growing importance of treaties in the orderly conduct of international relations," which has made

45. National courts have often confronted issues of treaty law, but they have generally treated questions such as the relationship of the treaty to the domestic legal system or interpretation rather than the unresolved problems noted below. See, e. g., the cases at pp. 555–567 and 611–615, infra. Further, such national decisions, written from a particular country's perspective and perhaps reflecting doctrines peculiar to its legal system, are less significant than those of international tribunals in creating some consensus over treaty law.

46. The text is reproduced in 63 Am.J. Int.L. 875 (1969) and 8 Int.Leg.Mat. 679 (1969), and is officially cited as U.N. Doc. No. A/Conf. 39/27.

47. The letter is set forth in 11 Int. Leg.Mat. 234 (1972).

evident "the need for clear, well-defined, and readily ascertainable rules of international law applicable to treaties." Even more important than aspects of the Convention treating interpretation and application, asserts the letter, "are the orderly procedures of the Convention for dealing with needed adjustments and changes in treaties, along with its strong reaffirmation of the basic principle *pacta sunt servanda* . . ." Failure of the Senate to grant its consent is traceable to a number of causes, including continuing tensions between the Executive and the Congress over the boundary line between treaties and executive agreements, and efforts of several senators to secure an understanding that the Convention, if ratified by the United States and if it becomes effective, would be applicable to present categories of executive agreements. See pp. 603–610, infra.

Treaty Formation

A treaty is formed by the express consent of its parties. Although there are no precise requirements for execution or form, certain procedures have become standard. Ordinarily an international agreement is concluded after face-to-face negotiations by representatives of the parties. It may take the form of an exchange of notes. If more formal, each party will cause its accredited representative to sign the same instrument in one or more copies, sometimes in more than one language, and affix the seal of his government. By choice of the parties, or in order to comply with the internal rules of a signatory country that are considered in Chapter V, it may be necessary to postpone the effectiveness of the agreement until a national legislative body has approved it and national executive authorities have ratified it. Instruments of ratification for bilateral agreements are then exchanged. In the case of multilateral treaties, such instruments are deposited with the national government or international organization that has been designated as the custodian of the authentic text and of all other instruments relating to the treaty, including subsequent adhesions by nations that were not among the original signatories. Thereafter a treaty will generally be proclaimed or promulgated by the executive in each country. If the treaty is to become operative as domestic law,[48] national practice or constitutional provisions may require that it be incorporated into a domestic statute.[49] Under Article 102 * of the U. N. Charter, many agreements are deposited with the Secretary General of the United Nations, a prerequisite to invocation of the treaty before any U. N. organ.

Requirements under domestic law such as legislative approval or executive ratification may raise questions as to whether a treaty has been formed. A nation allegedly party to a treaty may contend that necessary procedures under its law were not followed. Here recourse to principles in different systems of national law may be a use-

48. Treaties of friendship, commerce and navigation are commonplace examples of international agreements that are applied by national courts in suits brought by private parties.

49. See pp. 580–588, infra, for a discussion of "self-executing" and other treaties.

ful way of developing an international norm. But the domestic-law analogies may point in different directions. German law, for example, protects third parties who deal with commercial agents, especially those of corporations, from all limitations set by the principal on their authority but not actually known by such parties. Particularly as applied to corporations, the law of agency and contract in the United States has generally required third parties to acquaint themselves with the internal structure of the organization with which they are dealing. English law has developed an "indoor management" rule that stands somewhere between the two. In which direction should an international tribunal go? Authority is sparse. Article 46 of the Vienna Convention provides that a state cannot rely on its failure to follow requirements under its domestic law for the conclusion of treaties "unless that violation was manifest and concerned a rule of its internal law of fundamental importance." In the Eastern Greenland Case (Denmark v. Norway), P.C.I.J., Ser. A/B, No. 53 (1938), the Court did state that it regarded a response by the Minister of Foreign Affairs of Norway in regard to a question within his province as binding on Norway.

Consent and Reservations

Given the established principle that treaties are consensual, what rules prevail as to the character of that consent? Do domestic-law principles about the effect of duress carry over to the international field? A leader came to power in Germany with a platform stressing the proposition that the Versailles Treaty was dictated by force and therefore was not binding. The newly emergent countries have made claims that treaties under which the colonial powers withdrew were imposed upon them by the threat of force or as a condition to withdrawal, and therefore are not valid.

In a domestic legal system, a party cannot enforce a contract which was signed by a defendant at gunpoint. One could argue that victorious nations cannot assert rights under a peace treaty obtained by a whole army. It is not surprising that the large powers are reluctant to recognize that such forms of duress can invalidate a treaty. If duress were a defense, it would be critical to define its contours, for many treaties result from various forms of military, political or economic pressure.

The paucity of and doubts about international institutions with authority to develop answers to such questions underscore the reluctance to open treaties to challenge on these grounds. Another cause for hesitation may be the realization that international law does not possess a set of rules that would fill the gap left by an invalidated treaty. Note, for example, the developed rules under which a municipal legal system would adjust rights of the parties to an invalidated contract.

The interests in stability and predictability that a treaty serves here conflict with a basic principle of fairness expressed in most national legal systems. It is helpful to view treaties laid down by victorious powers less as a consensual arrangement than as legislation by the victor for the defeated. Of course, any legal analysis of agreements such as peace treaties falls short of an adequate evaluation of what they can accomplish. The different approaches of the victorious Western powers towards the defeated nations in World War I and World War II reflect the growing awareness that treaties, whatever their "legal" character, will survive only insofar as they bring satisfactory solutions to developing political, economic and social problems. Even from a legal perspective, the advent of the U. N. Charter after World War II, with its explicit rejection of war as a permitted instrument of national policy, may herald some evolution of legal doctrine in this field. Article 52 of the Vienna Convention states: "A treaty is void if its conclusion has been procured by the threat or use of force in violation of the principles of international law embodied in the Charter of the United Nations."

Problems of consent abound in the area of reservations to treaties, which Article 2(1)(d) of the Vienna Convention defines as unilateral statements made by a state accepting a treaty "whereby it purports to exclude or to vary the legal effect of certain provisions of the treaty in their application to that State." Ratification of a treaty with reservations presumably amounts in contractual terms to a counter offer. If it makes no objection, the other party may be held to have agreed to the reservation, particularly if it proceeds to comply with the other terms of the treaty. Considerable scholarly disputation and the few international cases have failed to define with clarity the conditions under which reservations are permitted and effective vis-à-vis other parties. There is more consensus over the general criteria than over their application. Such criteria have included the "intention" of the signatories as to reservations (Restatement, Section 125), and the compatibility of a reservation with the object and purpose of the treaty (Vienna Convention, Article 19). These issues become extremely complex for multilateral treaties. For example, some states may accept a reservation, others may remain silent, and others may reject it. Multilateral treaties frequently make explicit what reservations, if any, are permitted or prohibited. Note, for example, Articles 12, 13, 15 and 20 of the Hague Convention on the Choice of Court, p. 821, infra.

Termination, Suspension and Modification of Treaties

A treaty may expire at the end of a stated period or continue in effect thereafter until one party gives notice in accordance with its terms. See Article XVIII(2)* of the Convention of Establishment between the United States and France. Parties to multilateral treaties are often given the right of withdrawal. On the other hand, certain agreements such as the Rome Treaty establishing the European Economic Community (Common Market), considered in Chapter XIII, neither have time limitations nor sanction withdrawal.

Parties can abrogate a treaty or enter into a new agreement that by implication supersedes it. Mutual consent may be inferred where one party denounces the treaty—in the technical sense of giving notice to the other of its intention to consider the treaty terminated—and the other party acquiesces therein by failing to protest or by acting inconsistently with the treaty. Termination may also occur when a treaty's purpose has been fulfilled, as when claims for past injuries have been settled. More doubt surrounds the effect of war on prior treaties. Some treaties, such as those governing treatment of prisoners or neutrals, clearly contemplate war (the older ones would add ". . . which God forbid"). Others such as treaties of alliance previously entered into by hostile countries clearly fall. There is an ambiguous category between these extremes, involving matters as diverse as rules of navigation or commercial rights of one party's nationals in the other's territory. Most such treaties would at least be considered suspended during war. Whether they survive the war is a question to which countries have brought divergent answers. Our State Department and courts have concluded that many such treaties did survive and were operative after restoration of peace; some continental countries have been more sweeping in their rejection of prewar treaty commitments.

Violation of a treaty may lead to diplomatic protests and a claim before an international tribunal. But primarily because of the limited and qualified consents of nations to the jurisdiction of international tribunals, the offended party will usually resort to other measures. In a national system of contract law, well developed rules govern such measures. They may distinguish between a minor breach not authorizing the injured party to terminate its own performance, and a material breach providing justification for such a move. Such rules governing minor breaches may be more appropriate in a national setting, where the injured party has ready access to the courts for damages, than in the international community. Article 60 of the Vienna Convention states in paragraph (1) that a "material breach of a bilateral treaty by one of the parties entitles the other to invoke the breach as a ground for terminating the treaty or suspending its operation in whole or in part." Paragraph (3) defines "material breach" to mean an unjustified repudiation of a treaty or the "violation of a provision essential to the accomplishment of the object or purpose of the treaty." Section 158 of the Restatement provides alternatively for suspension of performance if the suspension is "reasonably related to the violation," termination of a separable part of the agreement including the obligations violated, or termination of the entire agreement if the violation "has the effect of depriving the aggrieved party of an essential benefit of the agreement." Treaties occasionally contain provisions about the rights of the parties under these circumstances.[50]

Amendments raise additional problems. The treaty's contractual aspect suggests that the consent of all parties is necessary. Parties may however agree in advance to be bound by the vote of a specified

50. Some practices of the Executive in this country on these questions of termination are considered at pp. 559–561, infra.

number. Such provisions in a multilateral treaty bring it closer in character to national legislation. They may be limited to changes which do not impose new obligations upon a dissenting party (see Article 108 * of the U. N. Charter) although a state antagonistic to an amendment could of course withdraw. But compare Article 236 * of the Rome Treaty establishing the European Economic Community. Absent some such provisions, a treaty may aggravate rather than resolve a fundamental problem of international law, how to achieve in a peaceful manner the changes in existing arrangements that are needed to adapt them to developing political, social or economic conditions.

One of the most contentious issues in treaty law is whether the emergence of conditions that were unforeseeable or unforeseen at the time of the treaty's conclusion terminates or modifies a party's obligation to perform. This problem borders the subject of treaty interpretation, considered below, since it is often described as a question whether an implied condition or an escape clause, called the *clausula rebus sic stantibus,* should be read into a treaty. Mature municipal legal systems have developed rules for handling situations wherein the performance of one party is rendered impossible or useless by intervening conditions. "Impossibility," "frustration," "force majeure" and "implied conditions" are the concepts used in Anglo-American law. "*Imprévision*" (unforeseeability) and "*Wegfall der Geschäftsgrundlage*" (disappearance of the basis of the transaction) are the labels given to rules of French and German law which are similar to but not identical with those of common-law systems.

At the international level, possibilities of changes in conditions that upset assumptions underlying an agreement are enhanced by the long duration of many treaties, the difficulty in amending them and the rapid political, economic and social vicissitudes in the 20th Century. Consider, for example, what has happened since 1904 to the Panama Canal, the Canal Zone and the Republic of Panama that would have made the application of the basic treaty of that year intolerable in the 1960's. Thus nations, including the United States, have occasionally used *rebus sic stantibus* as the basis for declaring treaties no longer effective. International tribunals have shed no illumination on the field. One attempt to define an international rule, in a carefully restricted fashion, appears in Section 153 of the Restatement, "Rule of Rebus Sic Stantibus: Substantial Change of Circumstances":

> (1) An international agreement is subject to the implied condition that a substantial change of a temporary or permanent nature, in a state of facts existing at the time when the agreement became effective, suspends or terminates, as the case may be, the obligations of the parties under the agreement to the extent that the continuation of the state of facts was of such importance to the achievement of the objectives of the agreement that the parties would not have intended the obligations to be applicable under the changed circumstances.

> (2) A party may rely on an interpretation of the agreement as indicated in Subsection (1) as a basis for suspending or terminating performance of the obligations in question only if it did not cause the change in the state of facts by action inconsistent with the purpose of the agreement and has otherwise acted in good faith.

Article 62 of the Vienna Convention has a different emphasis. It states that a "fundamental change of circumstances" which was not foreseen by the parties may not be invoked as a ground for terminating a treaty unless "(a) the existence of those circumstances constituted an essential basis of the consent of the parties . . . and (b) the effect of the change is radically to transform the extent of obligations still to be performed under the treaty."

Treaty Interpretation

There is no shortcut to a reliable sense of how a given treaty will be construed. Even immersion in a mass of diplomatic correspondence and cases would not develop such a skill. In view of the variety of treaties and of approaches to their interpretation, such learning would more likely shed light on the possibilities than provide a certain answer to any given question.

One obstacle to helpful generalization about treaty interpretation is the variety of purposes which treaties serve. Different approaches are advisable for treaties that lay down rules for a long or indefinite period, in contrast with those settling past disputes. The long-term treaty must benefit from a certain flexibility and room for development if it is to survive changes in circumstances and relations between the parties. Changes in conditions like those that make *rebus sic stantibus* an attractive doctrine may lead a court or executive official to interpret a treaty liberally so as to give it a sensible application to new circumstances.

The very style of a treaty will influence the approach of an official charged with interpreting it. Certain categories, such as income tax conventions, lend themselves to the detailed draftsmanship which will often be impractical and undesirable in a constitutional document such as the United Nations Charter. Treaties of friendship, commerce and navigation are often specific about their effect upon the laws of the signatory countries, but the subject matter covered is so varied and complex that clauses may speak in such terms as "fair and equitable" or "equal" treatment. Other conventions, such as those relating to human rights, may be even more general and vague.

In a national legal system, lawyers and courts can often give specific content to general statutory standards by resort to a common-law background or to a constitutional tradition, indeed by reference to the entire legal system and society within which these standards become operative. Interpretation can reach towards generally understood practices, customs or purposes. The process of statutory interpretation may have much in common with the type of purposive legal thought that has, in this country, characterized much of the common law process. But it may be far more difficult to interpret treaty standards of comparable generality embracing an international community with diverse national traditions. The problem becomes acute in multilateral treaties among nations from different regions, for one method of securing agreement may be to conceal rather than resolve differences through resort to general standards. In addition, the difficulty in achieving agreement over amendments to long-continuing multilateral treaties may encourage their draftsmen to express a "consensus" through norms of a general character, which have a better chance of surviving and carrying their broad purposes through changed conditions among the signatories.[51]

Another consideration is that many institutions and officials play a role in treaty interpretation. A lawyer in his domestic practice is apt to focus his attention on how a court will construe a particular clause, even if he does not expect that the issue will ever be litigated. But in international disputes, executive officials of parties to a treaty are more likely than international tribunals to resolve problems of interpretation. Indeed the number of cases in which such tribunals have construed international agreements (other than *compromis* conferring jurisdiction upon them) is small. In addition to jurisdictional considerations, certain disputes, such as those concerning treaties of alliances, are so inherently political as to be beyond judicial grasp. Others tend to be heard by national courts, primarily those over treaties in such fields as taxation or establishment which confer rights upon private parties. The requirement of exhaustion of local remedies will generally obligate such parties to press their claims initially before national tribunals.

Despite these considerations, the temptation to generalize has proved irresistible. Maxims similar to those found in domestic fields exist for treaties as well. The Restatement suggests relevant principles in Section 146, which states that the "primary object of interpretation is to ascertain the meaning intended by the parties for the terms in which the agreement is expressed, having regard to the context in which they occur and the circumstances under which the agreement was made. This meaning is determined in the light of all relevant factors." Section 147 states that international law requires the interpretative process to "give effect to the purpose of the international agreement which, as appears from the terms used by the parties, it was intended to serve." It notes factors "to be taken into account by way of guidance in the interpretative process. . . ." These factors include resort by courts to statements of "purpose and

51. The distinction suggested between interpretation of certain kinds of international agreements and domestic instruments becomes less tenable when one considers domestic constitutional problems. Decisions of the Supreme Court under the Due Process Clause and Equal Protection Clause of the Fourteenth Amendment, or under the Interstate Commerce Clause, offer apt illustrations. Recall the observation of Chief Justice Marshall in McCulloch v. Maryland, 17 U.S. (4 Wheat.) 316, 407, 4 L.Ed. 579, 602 (1819), that "we must never forget that it is a *constitution* that we are expounding."

scope" included in the text, the "ordinary meaning of the words," the "official record of the deliberations during the course of the negotiation," "the circumstances attending the negotiation of the agreement," "unilateral statements of understanding made by a signatory" prior to the agreement's effective date if such statements were available to the other party, subsequent practice of one or both parties, comparison of the texts in the different definitive languages, and compatibility between possible interpretations and international law or general principles of law common to principal legal systems. Many of these suggestions recall approaches of domestic courts to problems of contract as well as statutory construction.

One way to build a framework for construing treaties is to consider the continuum which lies between "strict" interpretation according to the "plain meaning" of the treaty, and "liberal" interpretation according to the interpreter's view of the best means of implementing the purposes expressed by the treaty. Actually both extremes of the spectrum are untenanted. One cannot wholly ignore the treaty's words, nor can one always find an expressed and relevant purpose. Our domestic cases construing contracts or statutes reflect a trend to look to purposes and policies and not to rely solely upon a linguistic analysis. History seems to be on the side of those judges who do not "make a fortress out of the dictionary," and who remember that "a word is the skin of a living thought."

Often an international tribunal will be unable to find a "plain meaning." Part of the difficulty is that treaties may be drafted in several languages. If domestic courts deem it unwise to "make a fortress out of the dictionary," it would seem particularly unwise when dictionaries in several languages (and in different legal systems according different means to linguistically similar terms) must be resorted to. Sometimes corresponding words in the different versions may shed more light on the intended meaning; at other times, they are plainly inconsistent.

Reliance upon literal construction may however be attractive to an international tribunal that is sensitive to its weak political foundation. It may be tempted to take refuge in the position that its decision is the ineluctable outcome of the drafter's desires and not a choice arrived at on the basis of the tribunal's own view of policy considerations. Reliance on legislative history or *travaux préparatoires* can achieve the same result of placing responsibility on the drafters. A comparison can here be drawn to those judges who prefer to "find" a rule of customary international law emerging from the impersonal operations of the international process, rather than to develop a rule that is felt to be just on the basis of present needs. The charge of "judicial legislation" evokes strong reactions in the United States; it inevitably influences judges of international tribunals. The temptation to take refuge in the dictionary may be reinforced if the decision it yields does not limit the sovereign discretion of the respondent state.

The appropriateness of literal interpretation may depend upon the relationship between the interpreting tribunal and the "legislature" creating the document. In some areas, it would be appropriate for a court to say: "This is the way the law reads; if you meant something else you can fix it." The court may realize that a more elaborate or flexible solution is desirable but feel that it does not have the knowledge or political judgment to impose it by "interpretation." The feasibility of a reference back to the legislature will vary. It is familiar lore that our Supreme Court takes a different attitude towards reading the Constitution than it does to parsing the Internal Revenue Code which Congress is constantly engaged in revising. But if amendment of a treaty is not a realistic possibility, there may emerge also on the international scene what Judge Friendly has termed "The Gap in Lawmaking—Judges Who Can't and Legislators Who Won't," 63 Colum.L.Rev. 787 (1963).

The scale between the literal and the purposive approaches is related to another pair of opposing principles that are described in the title to Judge Lauterpacht's classic article, Restrictive Interpretation and the Principle of Effectiveness in the Interpretation of Treaties, 26 Brit.Ybk.Int.L. 48 (1949). An interpretation which is literal is also apt to be "restrictive," in that it imposes the minimum possible restraint upon a party's sovereign discretion. Construction in terms of making a treaty an "effective" working arrangement and teleological construction in terms of purpose are virtually indistinguishable.

Additional reading: In addition to (a) the efforts to codify the law of treaties referred to at p. 283, supra, and the comments which accompany them, and (b) the texts cited at p. 177, supra, the following will be useful. Lissitzyn, Efforts to Codify or Restate the Law of Treaties, 62 Colum.L.Rev. 1166 (1962); Lissitzyn, The Law of International Agreements in the Restatement, 41 N.Y.U.L.Rev. 96 (1966); McNair, Law of Treaties (1961); Charles de Visscher, Problèmes d'Interprétation Judiciaire en Droit International Public (1963); Kearney and Dalton, The Treaty on Treaties, 64 Am.J.Int.L. 495 (1970); Hogg, The International Court: Rules of Treaty Interpretation, 43 Minn.L.Rev. 369, 44 id. 5 (1959).

The Boll Case which follows illustrates a number of problems of interpretation. In that case, a multilateral convention treating choice of law was at issue, but the different opinions raise questions that are pertinent to treaties of a more political character.

The portions of the Convention of 1902 which the case examines attempt to answer the question of what law should govern the guardianship of a child. Absent treaty regulation, various references would be possible: the nationality of the child, the domicile or residence of the child, the law of the forum. Recall the Note on choice of law at p. 91, supra, which stressed the relevance of a "personal law" to certain issues. The Convention illustrates one application of the personal law by referring to the child's nationality. Note that through the medium of a treaty, a question that would normally be resolved under the forum's principles of private international law was transformed into a question of public international law.

CASE CONCERNING THE APPLICATION OF THE CONVENTION OF 1902 GOVERNING THE GUARDIANSHIP OF INFANTS (THE BOLL CASE) (NETHERLANDS v. SWEDEN)

International Court of Justice, 1958.
[1958] I.C.J. Rep. 55.

[Marie Elisabeth Boll was born in Sweden in 1945. She was the daughter of Johannes Boll, of Dutch nationality, and his wife, who had possessed Swedish nationality before her marriage. Under these circumstances, Marie Elisabeth had Dutch nationality at birth. Mrs. Boll died in 1953, and under the Dutch Civil Code, Johannes Boll automatically became the child's guardian. Proceedings relating to the custody of Marie Elisabeth, who had lived in Sweden since her birth, began in both Sweden and the Netherlands. The Swedish Child Welfare Board at the child's place of residence decided to place Marie Elisabeth in the safekeeping of her maternal grandfather. It proceeded on the basis of Article 22(a) of a Swedish Law of 1924, applicable to all infants resident in Sweden. That Law provided for the protective upbringing of a child who is, in the family home, exposed to dangers affecting physical or mental health. Mr. Boll was accused of having committed an "infamous crime against his little daughter, then eight years old." (p. 112).

In the meantime, a court in the Netherlands discharged Johannes Boll as guardian, appointed a Madame Postema as guardian and awarded custody of the child to her. Madame Postema sought custody, or the award of custody to another Swedish family selected by her, through proceedings in the Swedish courts, but the decision of the Child Welfare Board was finally confirmed by the Supreme Administrative Court of Sweden. In respects other than protective upbringing (such as administration of property of the child, or indeed recognition of the status of Madame Postema as guardian to challenge the Child Welfare Board's order), the Swedish courts recognized Madame Postema as the guardian appointed in the Netherlands.

When it became apparent that Swedish authorities would not grant Madame Postema's demand for custody, the Netherlands Government in July 1957 filed an application instituting proceedings against Sweden in the I.C.J., relying on the acceptance of the Court's compulsory jurisdiction by the two nations. Its claim was based on the Hague Convention of 1902 on Guardianship of Infants, which had been drafted at a multilateral conference at the Hague and to which both countries were parties. The following provisions of the Hague Convention were particularly relevant:

> *Article 1:* The guardianship of an infant shall be governed by the national law of the infant.
>
> *Article 6, paragraph 1:* The administration of a guardianship extends to the person and to all the property of the infant, wherever situated.
>
> *Article 7:* Pending the institution of a guardianship, and in all cases of urgency, measures required for the protection of the person and interests of a foreign infant may be taken by the local authorities.

By 12 votes to 4, the I.C.J. rejected the claim of the Netherlands that the measures for protective upbringing affirmed by Swedish courts impeded the exercise by the guardian of the right to custody of the child which was guaranteed to her by the 1902 Convention. There were a number of separate concurring and dissenting opinions.

The excerpts below from several of the opinions touch upon the three principal issues which they examined:

(1) Were the Swedish measures ordering protective upbringing justifiable under the provisions for "cases of urgency" in Article 7 of the Convention?

(2) Did the Swedish measures amount to a "guardianship" under the Convention, or did they simply involve application of distinct Swedish laws which left the guardianship of Madame Postema intact? Or, as several Judges phrased the issue, was the Convention intended to cover Swedish proceedings of this character, which were said to have the purpose of protecting the public interest in raising children in a healthy environment rather than of adjusting private rights through the institution of guardianship?

(3) Was the 1924 Law a measure of *ordre public* which, by necessary implication, was permitted by the Convention?

The first argument was not pressed by Sweden nor given weight by most of the judges. The opinion of the Court decided for Sweden on the second argument, by concluding that the Convention did not cover the question of the protection of children. Judge Lauterpacht's concurring opinion stressed the third argument. The excerpts which follow are meant to illustrate the variety of approaches towards the construction of treaties.]

Opinion of the Court:

. . . . In adopting the national law of the infant as the proper law to govern guardianship, including the guardian's right to custody, the 1902 Convention was not intended to decide upon anything other than guardianship, the true purpose of which is to make provision for the protection of the infant; it was not intended to regulate or to restrict the scope of laws designed to meet preoccupations of a general character.

The same must be true of the Swedish Law on the protection of children and young persons. Considered in its application to children of Swedish nationality, the Law is not a law on guardianship, it does not relate to the legal institution of guardianship. It is applicable whether the infant be within the *puissance paternelle* of the parents or under guardianship. Protective upbringing which constitutes an application of the Law is superimposed, when that is necessary, on either, without bringing either to an end but paralyzing their effects to the extent that they are in conflict with the requirements of protective upbringing.

Is the 1902 Convention to be construed as meaning—tacitly, for the reason that it provides that the guardianship of an infant shall be governed by his national law—that it was intended to prohibit the application of any legislative enactment on a different subject-matter the indirect effect of which would be to restrict, though not to abolish, the guardian's right to custody? So to interpret the Convention would be to go beyond its purpose. That purpose was to put an end, in questions of guardianship, to difficulties arising from the conflict of laws. That was its only purpose. It was sought to achieve it by laying down to this end common rules which the contracting States must respect. To understand the Convention as limiting the right of contracting States to apply laws on a different topic would be to go beyond that purpose. . . .

The 1902 Convention did not seek to define what it meant by guardianship, but there is no doubt that the legal systems, as between which it sought to establish some harmony by prescribing what was the proper law to govern that situation, understood and understand by guardianship an institution the object of which is the protection of the infant: the protection and guidance of his person, the safeguarding of his pecuniary interests and the fulfilling of the functions rendered necessary by his legal incapacity. Guardianship and protective upbringing have certain common purposes. The special feature of the regime of protective upbringing is that it is put into operation only in respect of children who, for reasons inherent in them or for causes external to them, are in an abnormal situation—a situation which, if allowed to continue, might give rise to danger going beyond the person of the child. Protective upbringing contributes to the protection of the child, but at the same time, and above all, it is designed to protect society against dangers resulting from improper upbringing, inadequate hygiene, or moral corruption of young people. The 1902 Convention recognizes the fact that guardianship, in order to achieve its aim of individual protection, needs to be governed by the national law of the infant; to achieve the aim of the social guarantee which it is the purpose of the Swedish Law on the protection of children and young persons to provide, it is necessary that it should apply to all young people living in Sweden. . . .

It is scarcely necessary to add that to arrive at a solution which would put an obstacle in the way of the application of the Swedish Law on the protection of children and young persons to a foreign infant living in Sweden would be to misconceive the social purpose of that law, a purpose of which the importance was felt in many countries particularly after the signature of the 1902 Convention. The social problem of delinquent or even of merely misdirected young people, and of children whose health, mental state or moral development is threatened, in short, of those ill-adapted to social life, has often arisen; laws such as the Swedish Law now in question were enacted in several countries to meet the problem. The Court could not readily subscribe to any construction which would make the 1902 Convention an obstacle on this point to social progress.

It thus seems to the Court that, in spite of their points of contact and in spite, indeed, of the encroachments revealed in practice, the 1902 Convention on the guardianship of infants does not include within its scope the matter of the protection of children and of young persons as understood by the Swedish Law of June 6th, 1924. The 1902 Convention cannot therefore have given rise to obligations binding upon the signatory States in a field outside the matter with which it was concerned, and accordingly the Court does not in the present case find any failure to observe that Convention on the part of Sweden. . . .

Concurring Opinion of Judge Lauterpacht:

What is the meaning of the expression: "The Convention of 1902 does not cover a system such as that set up in the Swedish Law on Protective Upbringing"? It is admitted that guardianship under the Convention covers the right to decide on the residence and education of the minor—a right claimed and exercised by a Swedish authority and, on its behalf, by the Swedish maternal grandfather acting in pursuance of the Law on Protective Upbringing. If that is so, then the Convention does cover, in one of its essential aspects, the same powers and functions which are now exercised by Swedish authorities in pursuance of the Law on Protective Upbringing. . .

. . . . The treaty prohibits interference with its operation unless there is a justification for it, express or implied in the treaty; that justification cannot be found in the mere fact that the Law pursues an object different from the object pursued by the treaty. It can be found only in the fact that that particular object is expressly permitted by the treaty or implicitly authorized by it by virtue of some principle of public or private international law—a principle such as stems from public policy or from a cognate, although more limited, principle, which is often no more than another formulation of public policy, namely, that certain categories of laws, such as criminal laws, police laws, fiscal laws, administrative laws, and so on, are binding upon all the inhabitants of the territory notwithstanding any general applicability of foreign law. . . .

A State is not entitled to cut down its treaty obligations in relation to one institution by enacting in the sphere of another institution provisions whose effect is such as to frustrate the operation of a crucial aspect of the treaty. There is a disadvantage in accepting a principle of interpretation, coined for the purposes of a particular case, which, if acted upon generally, is bound to have serious repercussions on the authority of treaties. . . .

The view has been put forward that there can be no conflict between a Convention on Guardianship and the Law on Protective Upbringing for the reason that the Convention of 1902 is a convention of private international law and that guardianship with which it is exclusively concerned is an institution of private law, in particular of family law, while the Law on Protective Upbringing and the various measures authorized therein are in the sphere of public law seeing that they are concerned with safeguarding the interests of society. . . .

. . . . It is a matter of legislative technique and drafting whether the provisions for the protection of children in relation to whom normal guardianship has proved insufficient are, as in Holland, made part of the legislation relating to guardianship or whether, as in the case of Sweden, they are embodied in a separate enactment. In both instances they are intended to protect both the child and the society.

For it is clear that the distinction between the protection of the child and the protection of society is artificial. Both the laws relating to guardianship and those relating to protective upbringing are laws intended primarily for the protection of children and their interests. At the same time, the protection of children—through guardianship or protective upbringing—is pre-eminently in the interests of society. They are part of it—the most vulnerable and most in need of protection. All social laws are, in the last resort, laws for the protection of individuals; all laws for the protection of individuals are, in a true sense, social laws. . . .

. . . . In my view, the more accurate approach to the question is not that the system of protective upbringing is outside the Convention or that it pursues a different object but, rather, that it is not inconsistent with the Convention. In other words, that it is both covered and permitted by the Convention by virtue of public policy—*ordre public*—or some similar reason based on the right, conceded by international law, of a State to apply a particular law impairing or preventing the operation of the Convention.

In fact, it is in that sense that I understand—and concur in—that part of the Court's Judgment which stresses the beneficent social objects, of an urgent character, of the Swedish Law in question. That is a consideration closely related to those underlying the notion of *ordre public*. . . .

. . . . For there is no question here of choosing between the Convention and *ordre public*. If that were the alternative, clearly the Court would have no option but to apply the Convention. The question is whether the Convention, viewed in its entirety and in the light of relevant principles of interpretation—and not merely by reference to its bare letter—permits the exception of *ordre public*. For these reasons no assistance can be derived from the various pronouncements of the Permanent Court of International Justice to the effect that national legislation cannot be validly invoked as a reason for non-compliance with an international obligation. The problem now for the Court is, exactly, what is the international obligation at issue.

. . . . Apart from criminal law, it is difficult to conceive of a more appropriate and more natural object of *ordre public*, as generally understood, than the protection by the State of infants, especially when they are helpless, ill, an actual or potential danger to themselves or to society, a legitimate object of its compassion and assistance, and an occasion for public resentment whenever the State fails to measure up to its responsibilities in this respect. There are, in that wide and highly controversial province of *ordre public*, matters which are the object of uncertainty and occasional exaggerations of national prejudice reluctant to apply foreign law. But there is a hard core within that field which is not open to reasonable challenge. The protection of children, in the sense indicated above, is an obvious particle of that hard core. . . .

The notion of *ordre public* is generally used in two meanings: It is either applied as referring to specific spheres of the law, such as territorial laws, criminal laws, police laws, laws relating to national welfare, health and security, and the like; from this point of view, protective upbringing clearly comes within the notion of *ordre public*. Secondly, it is resorted to as embracing, more generally, fundamental national conceptions of law, decency and morality. From this point of view, too, the protection of the interests of the minor through measures such as protective upbringing falls naturally within the notion of *ordre public*. (It may be stated in the present context that although in this Opinion the French term *ordre public* is mainly used, it is not used as implying a substantial difference between it and the notion of public policy in common law countries such as the United Kingdom or the United States of America—although probably the conception of *ordre public* is somewhat wider. It is used here for the reason that it is current in the law of two States which are parties to the dispute.) . . . .

[I]n the sphere of private international law the exception of *ordre public*, of public policy, as a reason for the exclusion of foreign law in a particular case is generally—or, rather, universally—recognized. It is recognized in various forms, with various degrees of emphasis, and, occasionally, with substantial differences in the manner of its application. . . . On the whole, the result is the same in most countries—so much so that the recognition of the part of *ordre public* must be regarded as a general principle of law in the field of private international law. If that is so, then it may not improperly be considered to be a general principle of law in the sense of Article 38 of the Statute of the Court. That circumstance also provides an answer to the question as to the nature and the content of the conception of public policy by reference to which there must be judged the propriety of the Swedish legislation in the matter. Clearly, it is not the Swedish notion of *ordre public* which can provide the exclusive standard in this connection. The answer is that, the notion of *ordre public*—of public policy—being a general legal conception, its content must be determined in the same way as that of any other general principle of law in the sense of Article 38 of the Statute, namely, by reference to the practice and experience of the municipal law of civilized nations in that field. . . .

. . . . The same result is reached by way of another, no less cogent, principle of interpretation: In a case concerned with the interpretation of a treaty relating to a particular matter with regard to which the law and practice of both parties recognize the applicability of certain principles, due weight must be given to those principles. To give an example: If the law and practice of Sweden and Holland were to recognize that the distance of twenty miles is the proper limit of territorial waters, and if these two States were to conclude a treaty laying down that their vessels shall be bound to submit to certain restrictions within their respective territorial waters, then the expression "territorial waters" would have to be interpreted in the sense attached to it by the law and practice of those two States, namely, as extending to twenty miles. By the same token, if the law of Sweden or Holland recognizes the exception of public order in the sphere of private international law, then that factor must be considered as relevant to the interpretation, as between them, of the treaty in question. It is well known, and it is admitted by both Parties, that both in Sweden and Holland *ordre public* constitutes a valid reason for the exclusion of foreign law. Accordingly, the fact that a particular subject of private international law is covered by a convention does not, in the absence of an express prohibition to the contrary, in itself exclude the operation of *ordre public*, even if the convention is otherwise silent in the matter—provided always that the State invoking *ordre public* is, if its decision to invoke it is challenged, willing to submit to an impartial judicial or arbitral determination of the issue. . . .

At the same time . . . the circumstance that the Parties are bound by treaty in relation to a particular subject of private international law sets a limit to the application of *ordre public*. . . .

In the first instance, the existence of the treaty imposes upon municipal courts an obligation of restraint in invoking *ordre public* —a restraint additional to that which they impose upon themselves in matters of private international law generally. . . .

Secondly, the existence of a treaty limits the discretion of national courts in determining whether a particular subject is within the domain of *ordre public*; it limits it in the sense that in case of a dispute, and provided that an international tribunal is endowed with the requisite jurisdiction, it is for that tribunal to determine the matter. . . .

Thirdly—a view contended for by Holland but denied by Sweden —in the case of a dispute as to the manner in which the national authority has applied the exception of *ordre public*, that question is subject to review and determination by an international tribunal, if otherwise competent in the matter. . . .

Admittedly, the notion of *ordre public*—like that of public policy—is variable, indefinite and occasionally productive of arbitrariness and abuse. It has been compared in this respect, not without some justification, with the vagueness of the law of nature. . . . Yet these objections, justified as they are, do not alter the fact that the principle permitting reliance on *ordre public* in the sphere of private international law has become—and that it is—a general principle of law of most, if not all, civilized States. . . . The purpose of private international law is to make possible the application, within the territory of the State, of the law of foreign States. This is an object dictated by considerations of justice, convenience, the necessities of international intercourse between individuals and indeed, as has occasionally been said, by an enlightened conception of public policy itself. But there is an obvious element of simplification in the view that the law of a State should be deemed to have consented or that it should reasonably be expected to consent in advance to the application of foreign law without any limitations, in any circumstances whatsoever, without a safety valve, without a residuum of contingencies in which, because of the very nature of its structure and the fundamental legal, moral and political conceptions which underlie it, it should be able to decline to apply foreign law.

. . . . History—modern history—has occasionally produced examples of legislation manifesting eruptions of malevolent injustice, or worse, to which courts of foreign countries may find it utterly impossible to give effect and with regard to which the right to denounce the treaty may not provide a timely or practicable remedy.

It is that residuum of discretion, it is that safety valve, which has made private international law possible at all, and which, if kept within proper limits, is one of the principal guarantees of its continued existence and development. . . .

However, apart from an express or clearly implied prohibition, the correct principle seems to be that a convention in the sphere of private international law does not exclude reliance on *ordre public*. Nothing short of an express prohibition can rule out reliance on a firmly established principle of private international law. This seems to me to be the fairly unanimous view of writers. [A brief review of scholarly writings is omitted.]

In this connection reference may also be made to the preparatory work of the Convention of 1902. The study of that preparatory work shows that there was opposition—effective opposition—to incorporating in the Hague Conventions any general clause permitting reliance on *ordre public* (though no discussion on the subject took place with regard to the Convention on Guardianship). Does that mean that there was an intention to exclude altogether recourse to *ordre public* unless in cases expressly authorized? It may be doubted whether that was so. The authors of the Conventions wished to avoid the complications of a general and express authorization, of a general blank cheque, with regard to a notion so elastic and so comprehensive as *ordre public*. It is natural that they did not wish to inject into the Conventions, in express terms, a potential source of controversy or abuse. But does that mean that, by mere silence, the authors of the Conventions excluded indirectly from the operation of the Convention a firmly-established principle of private international law? That is not probable. It is doubtful whether Governments would have signed and ratified these Conventions if they had expressly denied the right to invoke, in any circumstances, their *ordre public* as a reason for excluding foreign law. . . .

. . . . In all the circumstances, on such evidence as there is, I am bound to assume that the action of the Swedish authorities was not such as to constitute a misapplication of the Law on Protective Upbringing on which they were clearly entitled to rely as part of their *ordre public*. . . .

Concurring Opinion of Judge Moreno Quintana:

Any appraisal of *ordre public* in international relations is necessarily a matter for interpretation by a court, provided that such an interpretation does not—to use the words of the Permanent Court in its advisory opinion concerning Polish postal service in Danzig—"lead to something unreasonable or absurd" (see *Judgments*, etc., Series B, No. 11, p. 39). And would the Court's decision be unreasonable or absurd if the result of it was to obviate the transplantation and the suffering of a child who would otherwise be torn from the arms of her grandparents, carried away far from the country of her birth and obliged to live in a foreign atmosphere? The law is not a metaphysical creation, a consequence of cold and abstract reasoning of the human mind, which has no regard for social reality. And States like the Netherlands and Sweden, which have incorporated rules of private international law in their international law, surely do not contemplate the application of inhuman solutions. Our own Court stated in the Anglo-Iranian case that it could not base itself on a purely grammatical interpretation of the text and that it must seek the interpretation which is in harmony with a natural and reasonable way of reading the text (see *I.C.J. Reports 1952*, p. 104). . . .

Concurring Opinion of Judge Spender:

[This opinion concluded that the 1924 Law was aimed at certain social problems concerning the state and community as a whole and was not a law of, or in relation to, guardianship. Despite the fact that the Law produced "effects which bear on guardianship," it was "[i]n principle . . . outside the domain of the Convention." The opinion read narrowly the purpose of the 1902 Convention: to end conflicts in choice-of-law rules as to guardianship, rather than to define all rights of the guardian and his immunities from local laws. The opinion further concluded that there was "no incompatibility between the measure of protective upbringing and the Convention . . . ." It noted that there was no allegation that Sweden had acted in bad faith or had used the 1924 Law to interfere with and impede the guardianship, rather than to implement the Law's own distinct and socially beneficial purposes. The opinion then considered the arguments of the parties relating to *ordre public*.]

Public policy in every country is in a constant state of flux. It is always evolving. It is impossible to ascertain any absolute criterion. It cannot be determined within a formula. It is a conception. The varying legal approaches made by the different domestic or municipal courts of different countries in the cases on which they have been called to adjudicate, and the wide differences of views on various and important aspects of public policy (*ordre public*) expressed by learned authorities are fairly evident. . . .

Attempts have been made to discern some definable principle or principles to explain or harmonize the different cases so decided in different countries, and to elevate these principles to the level of rules of international law. For myself, I am bound to say that I do not find them convincing. This is at least understandable. In each country, however or in reliance upon what domestic laws or general principles it may call in aid *ordre public* or public policy, is determining for itself, by its legislation, by its administrative agencies, or through its courts, the extent to which, if at all, it will admit or exclude foreign laws, or foreign rights otherwise applicable. It is, in each case, no doubt for good and sufficient reasons in the view of the State concerned, an assertion of national sovereignty. . . .

I think the issue in this case would have been clearer had less attention been directed to "*ordre public*" (public policy) and "public law", and more to consideration of the subject-matter, purpose and scope and operation of the Convention having regard to the terms in which it was drafted and agreed to. . . .

It should be repeated that what the Court is here being asked to do is to read into, or in legal terms to imply, a reservation—in what precise terms has never been made clear—excepting from the operation of the Convention all laws of contracting States which fall within "public policy" or within "public laws". The strongest of cases would have to be made out to justify the Court in doing so, for to do so permits States to determine for themselves the extent of their obligations under the Convention. It would permit this to be done even in derogation of what otherwise are obligations the Convention imposes. This could reduce the Convention to a shell. . . .

Before the Court would be justified in implying a clause of reservation, it would need to be quite satisfied that this was essential to be done in order to preserve the intention of the Parties. For otherwise there would be imposed a new and different agreement upon the contracting States.

No evidence was forthcoming that this was the intention. Reliance, however, was placed upon a so-called principle that such a reservation or exclusion must be read into conventions dealing with private law. . . .

It was open to the Parties expressly to stipulate such a reservation. Indeed in Sweden's case it was urged that a reservation of public policy is expressly stipulated in almost all treaties and those that do not do so are the exceptions. The Parties to the present Convention did not so stipulate. It is not I think for the Court to speculate as to why they did not. The minds of the drafters were clearly directed during the preparatory work to the question whether some clause to that effect should or should not be included. They deliberately refrained from including one. It would in my opinion be going against all rules of construction as I understand them to imply such a reservation now.

It is, I think, proper at this point to offer some general observations on the exercise of having recourse to preparatory work in seeking the proper interpretation to be accorded to treaties and conventions. Recourse to preparatory work of treaties or conventions may, in certain cases, be necessary. But whenever it is permissible it should, I think, be done with caution and restraint. For there is always the danger that, instead of interpreting the relevant treaty or convention, one will find oneself tending to interpret the preparatory work and then transferring that interpretation across to the treaty or convention which is the sole subject of interpretation.

The case before us presents, in my view, an example of this possibility. Some find nothing in the preparatory work of any real value, one way or the other. Others claim that it clearly supports the view that "public policy" is excepted from the Convention. Others are equally satisfied that the preparatory work just as clearly supports the opposite view. For my part, I would think this somewhat unsafe ground upon which to base any reasoning.

. . . . It is suggested that a State invoking the reservation is under some kind of duty to show that its public policy has been applied reasonably—whatever this in the present context means—and in good faith. The State should be ready to submit its actions to examination. In cases of dispute it is further urged that the acts of the States are subject to review by this Court provided it has jurisdiction. But what if the Court in any given case has not jurisdiction? Moreover, if we are to determine, as we must, the meaning of the Convention at the time it was entered into—1902—any consideration that in event of dispute this Court would be available as a reviewing tribunal, to mitigate the consequences of, or control the unreasonable use by a contracting State of, the reservation, is irrelevant. And what is to be the test or standard of reasonableness that is to be applied? . . .

The views which I have earlier expressed on the proper interpretation of the Convention reject any reservation, exception or exclusion of "public policy" or "public law". . . .

Dissenting Opinion of Judge Winiarski:

2. Article 1 of the Convention should here be recalled:

> "The guardianship of an infant shall be governed by the national law of the infant",

as well as Article 6, paragraph 1:

> "The administration of a guardianship extends to the person and to all the property of the infant, wherever situated."

Paragraph 2 provides that this rule may admit of an exception in respect of a certain type of immovable property; no exception, however, is provided with regard to the person. No effort of interpretation could make these clear provisions say what they do not say. The Convention was open only to States represented at the Third Conference of Private International Law and the members of this little family of nations who are bound by this Convention have, with regard to guardianship, a very old common fund of ideas and principles which was formulated in Roman law: *Tutor non rebus dumtaxat, sed et moribus pupilli praeponitur.*[52] . . .

Dissenting Opinion of Judge Córdova:

. . . . It has also been argued that there is a well-known principle of interpretation of treaties dealing with conflicts of national laws, the so-called Convention of Private International Law, which gives to the parties to such treaties the right to disregard its provisions relying on their own public laws or on their laws relating to public order. I do not believe that there is such principle of Public International Law—the only law between nations; on the contrary, I have always known the time-honoured and basic principle of *pacta sunt servanda,* which makes it impossible for the States to be released by their own unilateral decision from their obligations according to a treaty which they have signed.

52. [Eds.] A guardian appointed not only as to the property but also as to the behavior of the ward.

The place to be given to the national laws of *ordre public* and to those with a different scope and aim, whatever their classification might be, depends upon the interpretation of the treaty; but when such interpretation clearly includes within its provisions a subject-matter otherwise normally regulated by those kinds of national laws, the provisions of the treaty should be considered as having priority over them. To decide differently would mean complete anarchy in the relations of States, would leave the binding force of treaties in the unilateral hands of the legislative, judicial and administrative authorities of the States parties to such treaties and, finally, would completely destroy the indispensable hierarchy of the laws of the States and that of the international legislation. . . .

. . . . The decision of the Court, although putting aside the theory of *ordre public,* and basing its reasoning on the theory of the aim and scope differing from that of the treaty, nevertheless tries to interpret the Convention of 1902, stating that it was only intended to regulate the conflicts of national legislations regarding guardianship, a subject-matter alien and completely different from the protection of children and young persons, which is the only aim and scope of the Swedish Law of June 6th, 1924. With this basic proposition, I cannot agree.

In my way of thinking, the 1924 Swedish Law—at least as far as its Article 22(*a*) is concerned—is far from having an aim and scope different from that of the Convention. . . .

In spite of the Netherlands' own admission and Sweden's allegation to the contrary, it is my understanding that Article 7 of the Convention clearly comprehends the protective measures included in Article 22(*a*) of the Swedish Law of 1924, when it refers to the possibility of the local authorities to take "in all cases of urgency" measures "required for the protection of the person" of the infant. . . Moreover, although the Dutch law introducing the system of protection of infants was enacted after the year 1902, such legislation was already contemplated and prepared since 1901, and Sweden enacted its own law regarding protective upbringing in the year 1902, which makes it evident that the Netherlands and Sweden had already in mind the application of protective measures. It seems to me that the framers of the 1902 Convention, seeking only the good of the infants, although mainly referring to guardianship, tried to organize the adequate application of the different protective methods of the signatory States, guardianship as well as any other protective measures. They tried to make compatible the institution of national guardianship with the local protective legislations and measures by giving priority to the former (Articles 1 and 6) over the latter (Article 7).

I hold the above view in spite of the position of both Parties to the litigation before the Court which, as I have pointed out, believe that Article 7 of the Convention is not applicable. If the 1902 Convention had been a bilateral treaty, their common interpretation with regard to one of its Articles—Article 7—would have been enough for me to consider such a construction as final; but the 1902 Convention being a multilateral treaty, it is possible, I believe, to hold a different opinion from that of the two Parties before the Court with reference to the applicability of its Articles. . . .

NOTE ON THE HAGUE CONFERENCE, CHOICE-OF-LAW CONVENTIONS AND ORDRE PUBLIC

(1) The parties to the Boll litigation ratified the Convention of 1902 after it had been drafted at a multilateral conference at the Hague. The Hague Conference of Private International Law, which first met in 1893, is the paramount international institution devoted to the unification of rules in this field (choice of law, judicial jurisdiction, and enforcement of foreign judgments). The Conference, which consists of delegates from the member governments, now meets periodically at four-year intervals, with occasional extraordinary sessions. It has developed one of the more advanced institutional structures for negotiating and drafting multilateral treaties, and has thus made some progress towards meeting the need for adequate legislative machinery in the international community. After the required percentage of delegates has approved a draft convention, it is then submitted to the member governments for consideration and, it is hoped, ratification.

For many decades, the organization of the Conference was loose, and its membership was exclusively within Western Europe. Under a charter drafted in 1951, the organization assumed a permanent basis and a formal structure. The 28 members now include countries outside the European community, including Japan and (as of 1963) the United States. Ten conferences from 1893 to 1964 produced a large number of conventions which treated principally choice of law; member countries ratified and made effective a relatively small percentage of them. As was true of the Convention of 1902, the conventions prior to World War I treated mainly issues of family law. A growing discontent with the adoption by most of these conventions of the nationality principle—a discontent reflected in the opinions in the Boll Case—contributed to their demise. Over the last decade there have been efforts to revise many of them. The conferences during the inter-war period were largely unsuccessful, but conferences after World War II have had more successful issue. Seven conventions on a variety of problems of private international law have thus far become effective by receiving the necessary number of ratifications.[53] See Nadelmann, The United States Joins the Hague Conference on Private International Law, 30 Law & Contemp. Prob. 291 (1965).

(2) Consider the relevance to the opinions in the Boll Case of the fact that a court is determining in 1958 the effect of a 1902 Convention upon a 1924 Swedish statute (a predecessor of which was, however, enacted before Sweden ratified the Convention in 1904). As

53. Later materials in this book consider some of these conventions, as well as several proposed conventions that have been approved by the delegates and are open to ratification. An Extraordinary Session of the Conference in 1966 produced a convention on enforcement of foreign judgments, considered at p. 808, infra. For a current listing see 13 Int.Leg.Mat. 474 (1974).

the Court's opinion observes, most national laws for the protective upbringing of children were enacted after 1902. The problems that result are characteristic of much "treaty legislation." Whatever may be the political or other obstacles to renegotiation of bilateral treaties, the difficulties are compounded for multilateral conventions. More frequently than in national settings, where an institutionalized legislative machinery is available, a significant lag may develop between treaty provisions and the social or economic conditions of the communities whose problems they purport to regulate. The strain which these circumstances impose upon a court is evident throughout the Boll opinions.

(3) Are many of the difficulties faced by the Court in Boll traceable to a more basic concern—namely, that the subject matter may not be amenable to regulation by treaty? The number of multilateral treaties which has treated questions of choice of law is relatively small. To a large degree, the problems of choice of law have escaped successful treaty regulation because of their complexity, the difficulty in deciding upon neat and generally acceptable solutions to problems that can arise in a wide variety of factual settings, and a growing tendency of courts to treat choice-of-law issues in a highly particularistic manner. That is, cases posing choice-of-law questions may often lead a court to a close examination of the facts and policies in the relevant field of law. The court may be wary of resort to rigid choice-of-law rules that offer seemingly easy, but ultimately uneasy, solutions. Problems of guardianship and custody well illustrate these concerns. The personal situation of a child, his links to the forum or the country of his or his parents' nationality, and the options open to a court vary from case to case. Taut treaty rules may point towards solutions that strike a court as doubtful, or even unreasonable. The same observations apply to rigid rules that are stated in national codes or developed through decisional law. The desire to retain administrative and judicial flexibility, particularly where advance expectations of the parties and reliance by them upon past acts (as in marriage or divorce) may not be important considerations, often encourages efforts such as those in the Boll Case to avoid what appear to be formalistic solutions. See Steiner, The Development of Private International Law by International Organizations, 1965 Proc. Am.Soc.Int.L. 38.

The history of the 1902 Convention lends support to these observations. There have been a number of denunciations of the Convention, including one by Sweden after the Boll decision. In 1960, the Ninth Hague Conference produced a Draft Convention Concerning the Powers of Authorities and the Law Applicable in Respect of the Protection of Infants, which was intended to replace the 1902 Convention.[54] It attempted a compromise between the claims of the country of nationality and the country of "habitual residence" of the child. To some extent (Article 8), its provisions reflect and adopt the views

54. The Convention is reproduced in 9 Am.J.Comp.L. 708 (1960).

of the Boll opinion. However, unlike other Hague Conventions of this period, this 1960 Convention has enjoyed only slight success, having only six adherents. See Lipstein, The Hague Conventions on Private International Law, Public Law and Public Policy, 8 Int. & Comp.L.Q. 506 (1959).

(4) The opinions in Boll stress one of the tensions which the concept of *ordre public* reflects and seeks to resolve: that between national sovereignty and international obligation. The concept suggests a compromise between the certainty afforded by treaty regulation of a problem and the flexibility which national authorities may consider necessary in order to develop more satisfactory solutions. Flexibly interpreted, the concept is obviously an invitation to legal anarchy, each nation pursuing its own policies without regard to any notion of community interests or the interests of other nations. Applied more restrictively, it constitutes a safety valve for treaties among countries pursuing different social policies.

The omission of an *ordre public* clause from the 1902 Convention is not characteristic of the Hague Conventions. Indeed, the 1960 Convention referred to above states in its Article 16 that application of its provisions "can only be refused in the contracting states if such application is manifestly contrary to public policy." Recent Hague Conventions treating issues that lend themselves more readily to treaty regulation contain similar qualifications. For example, Article 6 of the Convention on the Law Applicable to International Sales of Goods [55] qualifies that Convention's choice-of-law rules by stating that "the application of the law determined by the present Convention may be excluded on the ground of public policy." Compare Article II(3) * of the Convention of Establishment Between the United States and France, and the following clause of a treaty that reaches a basic national interest. Article IV of the Nuclear Test Ban Treaty, August 5, 1963, gives each party "in exercising its national sovereignty" a "right to withdraw from the treaty if it decides that extraordinary events, related to the subject matter of this treaty, have jeopardized the supreme interests of its country." 14 U.S.T. & O.I.A. 1313, T.I.A.S. No. 5433.

Our own legal system offers several analogies to the European concept of *ordre public*. Comparable notions of "public policy," expressed in terms of norms of fairness or other values in our society, are stated in the Constitution through such provisions as the Due Process and Equal Protection clauses. These and other constitutional provisions contribute towards formulation of a concept of "public policy" that our statutes and courts have explicitly invoked to resolve certain questions of foreign or international law. Banco Nacional de Cuba v. Sabbatino, p. 691, infra, and the domestic cases and statutes in Chapter VII on the enforcement of foreign-country judgments illustrate the uses to which this concept may be put. See

55. The Convention is reproduced in 1 Am.J.Comp.L. 275 (1952). It was prepared in 1951 and became effective in 1964.

Nadelmann and von Mehren, Equivalences in Treaties in the Conflicts Field, 15 Am.J.Comp.L. 195, 199–201 (1967).

QUESTIONS

(1) If the "plain meaning" approach of Judge Winiarsky, p. 302, supra, had prevailed, what action could signatories of the Convention who found that reading unacceptable have taken to "amend" the decision?

(2) Do you view the approach of the Court or of Judge Lauterpacht as preferable, assuming a decision in Sweden's favor?

(3) Compare the opinion of the Court and the separate concurring opinions with the approach of the Court in the Fisheries Case. In Boll, do the opinions explore the purposes of the Convention and the interests of the two nations that are at stake, or do they appear motivated by concern for the best solution for Marie Elizabeth, the subject of the litigation?

(4) Several opinions refer to the domestic laws and policies of the two parties to the litigation. What relevance should such data have? Should an international tribunal interpret provisions in view of the legislation or practice subsequent to the treaty of all or a majority of the signatories, rather than of the immediate parties? If you answer this last question in the negative, how do you assess the risk that courts will give different interpretations to a multilateral treaty, depending upon the particular parties before it?

PROBLEM

Suppose that the United States and a foreign country, Guatador, were parties to the 1902 Convention. Suppose further that the 50 states in this country are constitutionally obligated to apply the Convention as "supreme" law to any dispute to which it is relevant. A child, now five-years old, was born in Guatador of an American mother and a Guatadorian father. The mother had lived in Guatador since she was 17. Under these facts, the child had Guatadorian but not American nationality. See Section 301(a)(7) * of the Immigration and Nationality Act of 1952. Upon the death of the father's parents two years ago, the family moved to the United States, the father entering on an immigrant visa. Under the 1952 Act, the child would have acquired American citizenship if the father had become a naturalized citizen before the child was 16.

Both parents were killed in an automobile accident, and guardianship proceedings have been instituted before a New York court. Two guardians resident in New York have been proposed: the maternal grandfather, and a married friend of the father. The father's will requested that, if the need arose, his friend be appointed guardian. Under Guatadorian law, a "person who has ever been convicted of any crime" is disqualified from appointment as a guardian. The friend, when a graduate student with the father one year before the accident, was convicted of violating a trespass statute through his participation in a university "sit-in" to protest the firing of instructors who had joined a teachers' union. He was fined $100 and given a one-year suspended sentence. The judge believes that the friend is preferable as a guardian from the child's point of view and would generally follow a parent's request. What inquiries would you pursue and arguments would you develop to persuade the judge that the 1902 Convention does not preclude him from appointing the friend?

3. THE ROLE OF INTERNATIONAL ORGANIZATIONS

In addition to setting forth specific rules which are to govern the conduct of the parties, a treaty may establish machinery for the development of further norms. This applies particularly to multilateral agreements, which may be specialized or general in subject matter, regional or worldwide in scope. At its simplest, such a treaty may provide for periodic meetings at which the signatories' representatives will exchange views, at official sessions or in the corridors. From such discussions the representatives may go on to negotiate new agreements, for the presence of delegates from several countries makes possible the adjustment at one time of interlocking problems that affect each of them. At the next level, the treaty may authorize the parties' delegates to pass advisory or recommendatory resolutions. As in the Hague Conferences, such meetings can produce draft conventions which will be submitted to the members for consideration and ratification.

In more advanced arrangements the structure created by treaty will include organs or agencies exercising stated powers. Sometimes they are authorized to mediate or put pressure on disputants to arbitrate. Sometimes their authority extends to issuing binding interpretations of the treaty. Such powers can go further and include competence to issue regulations, directives or resolutions binding upon the parties (a limited legislative function) or to apply the treaty to specific situations in an authoritative way (a limited judicial function). Finally, the treaty may give a stated majority of the members the power to amend the agreement in a manner binding all parties.

At some point in this progression we find that the treaty has created an international "organization." The growth of a permanent staff maintaining a continuous interim activity and the acquisition of a budget and buildings signal the emergence of a distinct entity with some life of its own. The members may endow this entity with a juridical personality and empower it to make contracts or treaties with private parties or governments and be a party to lawsuits. They may also confer upon the organization and its officials various immunities. One organization, the United Nations, has been held not only to have legal personality, but also to be competent to bring an international claim for injuries to its agents performing peacekeeping services on its behalf. Reparations for Injuries Suffered in the Service of the United Nations, [1949] I.C.J.Rep. 174.

Since 1945 such international organizations have come to play an important role in coping with transnational problems that do not lend themselves to resolution through the development of customary international law, through a network of bilateral treaties, or through a barebone multilateral treaty with no institutional character. Some attempt the critical political task of controlling armed conflict between states; some administer and develop cooperative arrangements of an economic and political nature among regional groups; some regulate and facilitate commercial or economic activities among more widespread nations. Chapters XI and XIII examine three such organizations: the International Monetary Fund, the General Agreement on Tariffs and Trade and the European Economic Community (Common Market). This section surveys some aspects of the chief political organization seeking to control conflict, the United Nations, and preliminarily sketches some characteristics of international organizations which have significantly affected the processes by which international law develops.

NOTE ON THE UNITED NATIONS

Were this book to stress problems of peacekeeping and world order, the United Nations would occupy a prominent position. The headlines of the 1950's and 1960's about the U. N.'s accomplishments and shortcomings in Korea, the Congo, Cyprus, Kashmir and the Near East were sufficient reminders of its importance. During the conflicts from the mid 1960's on, its role has become more marginal, although the political effects of its resolutions or debates, and the occasional provision of troops as in the Middle East, remain important. In view of our emphasis upon transnational problems other than the control of violence, we here compress—and to that extent inevitably distort—our description of the United Nations.[56] We stress those aspects of its activities which, while less important or dramatic than its basic peacekeeping function, are relevant to such problems. Note that the materials in this chapter have drawn upon the work of one U. N. organ, the International Court of Justice. The problems considered in Chapter IV involve several General Assembly resolutions and conventions prepared within the United Nations.

The Security Council. Article 23 of the Charter indicates how the Security Council is constituted. Under Article 27, nonprocedural decisions of the Security Council are subject to a veto by its permanent members: China, France, the U.S.S.R., the United Kingdom and the United States. Article 24 confers on the Council "primary responsibility for the maintenance of international peace and security," and Article 25 obligates U. N. members "to accept and carry out the decisions of the Security Council in accordance with the present Charter."

The powers of the Council are set out in Articles 33 to 42. Note the range of possible action, extending from a recommendation to the parties to a dispute to settle it by peaceful means (Articles 33 and 36) to "action by air, sea, or land forces" (Article 42). Herein lies one of the most distinctive features of the Charter and a major innovation in the powers of an international organization. The existence of the veto has restricted the capacity of the Security Council to act in cases in which the interests of a permanent member are affected in an important way. This has not, however, prevented

56. Students not familiar with the U.N. Charter should read the excerpts from it appearing in the Documentary Supplement together with the text below.

it from taking an active role in settling conflicts which have not directly involved the major powers or their vital interests.

The General Assembly. The composition and powers of the General Assembly are set forth in Chapter IV of the Charter. Those powers are stated largely in terms such as "initiate studies," "recommend," "promote," "encourage," and "discuss" (Articles 10–14). However, the veto power and other developments which have impaired the functioning of the Security Council early led the General Assembly to assume a more active role than the terms of the Charter indicate. One step that appeared to be notable at the time was the Resolution on Uniting for Peace, Resolution 377A(V), November 3, 1950, after the invasion of South Korea. It asserted that the Assembly had power to take certain action, primarily consideration of a matter and the making of recommendations, with respect to threats to or breaches of the peace "if the Security Council, because of lack of unanimity . . . fails to exercise its primary responsibility . . . ." But that assertion of power did not prove to be as significant as was assumed, through the events of the following decades.

In the exercise of its powers, the General Assembly acts by a simple or a two-thirds majority vote, as provided in Article 18. Within the scope of these powers, the Assembly has passed resolutions and declarations as to matters of such pervasive concern as racial discrimination and human rights. Its resolutions at pp. 462–469, infra, treat the problem of expropriation of property of alien investors. Action of the Assembly pursuant to Article 13 is apt to be of direct concern to private parties engaged in transnational activities. Indeed, during the 1970's, the most striking political measures recommended by the Assembly had more to do with trade and investment and with the economic relationships between the developed and less developed worlds, than with peacekeeping issues.

One explanation of this phenomenon lies in the continuing expansion of U. N. membership to include an ever larger number of countries of the less developed world. Inevitably this trend affects the nature of the debates within the Assembly and the resolutions which it adopts. The stress in recent resolutions, adopted by strong majorities over the abstention or dissent of many countries of the non-Socialist developed world, has been upon the duties of the developed countries to aid the development of others. Despite the formal multilateral framework, those debates and resolutions take on a "bloc" character, sometimes of a frankly bilateral nature.[57]

The Secretariat. Chapter XV of the Charter provides for the creation of a Secretariat consisting of the Secretary General and a staff. Although Article 97 makes him the "chief administrative officer," the Secretary General has tended to expand his role and occasionally take the initiative in political and peacekeeping matters. The

57. The 1974 Resolutions of the General Assembly addressing such issues are referred to at pp. 467–468, infra.

intention of the founders of the U. N. as to the staff was to create an international civil service independent of national control or influence. This goal has not been easy to achieve. There have also been tensions between the desire to select personnel for efficiency alone and the pressures for broad geographical representation. Still the U. N. Secretariat has succeeded, in the tradition of the League of Nations, in gathering a large number of dedicated career civil servants.

U.N. Committees, Councils and Commissions. The U. N. has a number of ancillary organs, some of which may take action of direct concern to private parties. Article 7 establishes an Economic and Social Council (ECOSOC), which operates under the supervision of the General Assembly in pursuing certain of its goals in the economic and social field. Its powers are limited in the sense that its acts are not binding upon members. However, ECOSOC can make studies (or ask another body to make them for it), make recommendations to member states, prepare drafts of conventions, and call international conferences. It also administers various programs, including some which involve the expenditure of U. N. funds for the benefit of members. ECOSOC carries out some of its work through commissions such as the Commission on Human Rights and the Economic Commissions.

The General Assembly has delegated some of its work to its seven committees. One of significance for lawyers is the Sixth, or Legal, Committee, which is charged with carrying out the Assembly's responsibilities under Article 13(1)(a) for "encouraging the progressive development of international law and its codification." Much of the initial work is now in fact performed by a more permanent and professional body, the International Law Commission. As constituted under its statute enacted by General Assembly Resolution 174(II) of November 21, 1947, as amended, the I.L.C. has 25 members, "persons of recognized competence in international law."

Article 15 of the Statute of the I.L.C. distinguishes between "development" ("the preparation of draft conventions on subjects which have not yet been regulated by international law or in regard to which the law has not yet been sufficiently developed in the practice of States") and "codification" ("the more precise formulation and systematization of rules of international law in fields where there already has been extensive state practice, precedent and doctrine"). The General Assembly is to take the initiative in selecting and referring to the I.L.C. topics for development, while the Commission is to survey "the whole field of international law" to identify areas ripe for codification. This distinction is sometimes more easily stated than realized in practice.

The development of the first round of the Conventions on the Law of the Sea, p. 271, supra, illustrates this process. The I.L.C. selected the topic in 1949 as suitable for "codification." In 1956 it produced its final version of the Conventions, and late that year the

Sixth Committee debated its proposals. Upon the Committee's recommendation, the General Assembly requested the Secretary General to call a conference of member nations and to prepare other needed working documents. The Conference met at Geneva for nine weeks in 1958 and opened the Conventions which it approved for signature. A second conference met in 1960 but failed to reach agreement on some critical issues left open in the 1958 drafts. After signature, the Conventions were opened for ratification. The last of these conventions did not become effective for the United States until 1966. The process, in brief, was time consuming.

Note however that the I.L.C. may follow other procedures. The Model Rules on Arbitral Procedure * were prepared by it for use as a model by countries drafting a bilateral treaty or a *compromis*. Or the Commission may issue a report rather like a Restatement of the American Law Institute. Nor is the I.L.C. the only source of codification within the U. N. The Sixth Committee itself drafted the Genocide Convention of 1948, and various conventions dealing with human rights have originated in the Third Committee, which has responsibility for that area.

During the last decade, the role of the I.L.C. has receded in importance. The major conventions proposed by U. N. organs have come out of the General Assembly or special committees created by it, as in preparation for the conferences of the 1970's (p. 272, supra) on the law of the sea. This trend both reflects and intensifies the deeply political character of the issues which are sought to be resolved through conventions.

The United Nations and "Specialized Agencies". Through ECOSOC, the U. N. is connected by agreements with a number of international organizations. These bodies, referred to in Article 57 of the Charter as "specialized agencies," are created by separate conventions among their members. The agreements provide for the coordination of the work of the U. N. and the agencies, some of which—for example, the International Monetary Fund—have widespread importance.

Several of the agencies act in a visible way vis-à-vis private parties. The World Health Organization is a prominent example. WHO is not conspicuous in the United States, for most of its activity is in countries less fortunately situated where it trains medical specialists and technicians, conducts demonstration campaigns against parasites or communicable diseases and provides supplies of vaccines and other medicines. The International Labor Organization has fostered the drafting of numerous conventions adopted by many countries, and has thereby contributed to improvement in working conditions. Its impact on the worker in this country has been less significant. The United States has generally refrained from adhering to those conventions, partly out of concern for state prerogatives in enacting domestic law and partly from a belief that our standards were already adequate. The International Civil Aviation Organization affects air travel. It has established improved standards for customs formalities for airborne travellers, communications codes and practices for pilots, and charts and weather-reporting services for navigators.

U. N. and Economic Development. The United Nations, its specialized agencies and other affiliated institutions have come to play an important role in furthering the economic development of the organization's members. In pursuance of this goal, either the U. N. or such agencies or institutions have sponsored a number of international agreements, developed rules governing financial or technical assistance through regulations or other legal acts, and entered into contracts with recipient states. Under these varied arrangements, there has been some financial aid and much technical assistance from the United Nations to less developed countries. Another aspect of the U. N.'s work in this field has been the compilation, analysis and debate of much statistical data, and the creation of a number of institutes through which technical skills can be transmitted to less developed countries. The techniques for this flow of funds and information vary widely. For example, some agreements between the United Nations or specialized agencies and the recipient countries involve the provision by the U. N. or the agencies of funds, equipment or trained personnel, while the recipient government may cover local currency expenses and provide complementary local personnel. These arrangements have several advantages over the bilateral foreign aid programs of the United States or Western European countries, for the "internationalization" of the transfer of funds and skills tends to avoid the political overtones inherent in many bilateral agreements and to provide a more neutral framework for international cooperation.

Even this brief review of the United Nations and its affiliated institutions suggests the variety of legal processes which have been developed to serve the ends of the member nations. The range of possibilities extends from "binding" decisions to recommendatory resolutions, from promulgation of rules binding member states to the drafting of conventions which are recommended for adoption by them, from requirements of unanimity for change in the underlying constitutive document to provisions for amendment by less than unanimous vote, from unilateral action by the institutions to contract provisions which spell out relationships between the U. N. or its organs and the members.

Additional reading: On international organizations generally, see Bowett, The Law of International Institutions (2d ed. 1970). On the United Nations, see Sohn, Cases on United Nations Law (2d ed. 1967); L. Goodrich, The United Nations (1960). On the International Law Commission, see Briggs, The International Law Commission (1965). On the ICAO, see Buergenthal, Law-Making in the International Civil Aviation Organization (1969).

NOTE ON SOME RELATIONSHIPS AMONG TREATIES, CUSTOM AND INTERNATIONAL ORGANIZATIONS

Despite the advantages of the treaty as a means of resolving past disputes and regulating future conduct, despite the considerable volume of treaties that has emerged over past centuries and particularly since World War I, one can question the treaty's significance for many transnational problems. Some, of course, have a pervasive importance for contemporary life, both through the rules they express and the structures which they create. But many of the problems considered in this book—protection of human rights, expropriation of alien-owned property, breach of contracts between governments and aliens, various aspects of private international law, and allocation of competence among different nations to regulate transnational economic activities—have yet to benefit from effective treaty regulation.

The preceding Notes and the Boll Case have suggested some of the reasons which later chapters will develop for this limited contribution of treaty law in many fields. Whatever the reasons, the fact remains that treaties should be viewed only as one force among many in the contemporary international legal process. This Note suggests relationships among some of these forces.

Thus far we have considered custom and treaties in separate compartments, although the two are related in several ways. There is for one thing an argument, more theoretical than practical, that some principles of customary international law are so fundamental that they cannot be changed by treaty. The reasoning would be that, just as certain contract clauses may be found invalid as violative of public policy, there are some rules from which states cannot depart in their treaties, perhaps because of the impact of their treaty arrangements on other states. This theory of *jus cogens* is expressed in Article 53 of the Vienna Convention and Section 116 of the Restatement.

Second, the question may arise of the extent to which a treaty should be read in the light of preexisting custom. Even when treaties are relevant to a given problem, they may be cast in language of such generality that the treaty norm must be viewed together with developing state practice or policies before its meaning can be ascertained. In addition, it will frequently be difficult to determine whether a treaty rule is intended to be "declaratory" of customary law or to depart from it. An answer to this question may affect both the interpretation given the treaty and the question whether the principle that it expresses survives its termination. Recall the different views in the opinions in the Boll Case, p. 293, supra, about the relationship between state practice and a treaty rule.

Third, to what extent can treaties give birth to rules of customary law? Will a succession of bilateral treaties among States A, B, C and D, each containing a provision giving indigent aliens the right to counsel at the government's expense in a criminal prosecution, create a custom that would bind State E, not party to any such treaty? Here as elsewhere, the answer which one brings will depend upon whether one adopts a positivist or a more purposive and value-oriented approach towards international law.[58] A positivist might argue that State E cannot be bound by a treaty to which it has not assented. The treaty structure among other countries simply constitutes an exception to a body of customary law which has left State E's discretion unimpaired in this matter. Indeed, that structure accents the contrary principle that prevails under customary law. The positivist would concede that the network of treaties might become so dense that a country would be deemed to have accepted *sub silentio* the duties expressed therein.

An "activist" would take a different view. He might conclude, for example, that a solution worked out by the statesmen of important and interested nations and ratified by their governments is apt to be the most practical and satisfying one. That solution, he might argue, should be considered relevant or persuasive for the development of a customary rule setting standards for all countries. A counterpart on the domestic scene is found in the treatment of statutes. Under one view, a statute affects only the precise area which it covers, while the common-law rules are left intact, even fortified, outside that area. Under another view, a statute can be used by analogy to develop common-law rules in related areas. See Landis, Statutes and the Sources of Law, in Harvard Legal Essays 217 (1934).

Several opinions in this chapter examined the relationship between recurrent patterns in bilateral treaties or provisions of multilateral treaties of large membership and the growth of customary law. Recall the approach of the Court in the Lotus Case, at p. 256, supra, to the use of treaties as sources or evidences of a customary rule. Contrast the different ways in which the Court and Judge Read in the Nottebohm case, at pp. 215 and 218, supra, assessed the relevance of the Bancroft Treaties to the issue before the Court.

The power of a multilateral treaty to create customary international law was recently considered by the Court in the North Sea Continental Shelf Cases, [1969] I.C.J.Rep. 3, in which Denmark and the Netherlands sought to utilize the principle of "equidistance"[59] in drawing international boundaries in the North Sea, which at that time had already revealed great promise as a source of oil wealth. They confronted the problem that the Federal Republic of Germany had not become a party to the 1958 Geneva Convention on the Continental Shelf which in its Article 6 embodied that principle. The Court first examined Article 6 to see whether it was strictly a "conventional" principle or whether it embodied a preexisting customary rule. Having decided—in part because the Convention permitted parties to enter reservations against Article 6—that Article 6 "did not

58. Recall the observations about the role of positivism in international law in the Note at p. 258, supra.

59. "Equidistance" implies that boundary lines should be drawn so that each point is within the jurisdiction of the state nearest to it.

embody or crystallize any pre-existing or emergent rule of customary law," the Court went on to inquire whether a customary rule had subsequently formed around it by a state practice which "should have been extensive and virtually uniform." Upon examination it found that there were some fifteen cases of the use of the principle but that many of them were by states which were parties to the Convention and that even states which had used the principle did not seem to feel bound to do so. It concluded (11 to 6) that the Federal Republic was not bound by the equidistance principle.

In the post-war years, the "population explosion" of international organizations has influenced the traditional processes for the development of customary law. The comments about the General Assembly and the International Law Commission of Judge Alvarez in his opinion in the Fisheries case, at p. 269, supra, are here pertinent. The forum provided by the United Nations of itself effects important changes. Political, economic and legal issues are now characteristically debated in a multilateral setting: the General Assembly, the International Law Commission, another organ of the U. N., the General Agreement on Tariffs and Trade, the International Monetary Fund, and so on. The long periods involved in the traditional processes—acts or claims, separate responses by one or a number of nations—are increasingly displaced by a more rapid formulation of viewpoints of different nations. The internal processes of international organizations such as the European Economic Community become ever more significant.

That acts of U. N. organs such as resolutions or proposed conventions exercise some influence upon customary international law is evident. Defining with clarity the measure of that influence is a complicated task, one undertaken in the materials of Chapter IV treating human rights and expropriation of property. We here anticipate some questions to be examined. How, for example, can such acts or proposals be accommodated within the traditional framework of Article 38(1) of the I.C.J.'s Statute? Or is that Article no longer an adequate expression of an evolving international legal process? Should resolutions or declarations of the General Assembly, which have only a "recommendatory" character, constitute evidence of a consensus among nations over the issues which they address—human rights, expropriation and so on? Should they father customary rules binding only those nations whose representatives voted in their favor? How broad a supporting vote, both in terms of the number and importance of the nations involved, should be necessary to incorporate the substance of the resolution into general international law? Do unanimous or nearly unanimous resolutions have a special status?

Additional reading: Parry, The Sources and Evidences of International Law (1965).

QUESTIONS

(1) In deciding whether a provision common to many bilateral treaties should be considered binding upon non-signatories, what relevance should the following considerations have? (a) Whether the parties believed that they were expressing an existing rule through codification, or that they were defining rights and duties that could not have been asserted under customary law. How could such a determination be made? (b) Whether the provision appeared to be part of a complex of concessions granted by different signatories in exchange for points which they won during intense bargaining sessions. Could this determination be made?

(2) "It is no surprise that custom has lost its vitality as a force in the development of international law. Anyone familiar with the progressive displacement of common law by legislation in the Anglo-American world could have predicted and stated the reasons for this phenomenon several decades ago." Do you agree with the observation? With the domestic analogy?

NOTE ON ORGANIZATIONAL APPROACHES TO THE FISHERIES PROBLEM

We have observed in the Note at p. 270, supra, the frustrations encountered subsequent to the Fisheries Case in specifying exclusive fisheries zones and the scope of the territorial sea. In a period of dissolution of a once-prevailing consensus, it became ever more difficult to achieve a new consensus in state practice, and to determine controlling norms through customary international law. Hence the efforts towards regulation by treaty, leading to the Geneva Conference in 1958, then to Caracas and back to Geneva. As the earlier Note indicated, such efforts towards multilateral treaties were accompanied by national legislation and by international decisions, leading to a complex of treaty law and national practice in a continuing dialogue with the elaboration of customary law.

In certain respects, the problems of fisheries have always escaped regulation through customary law. They have necessitated the development of institutional frameworks in the context of bilateral or multilateral treaties that sought to do more than allocate exclusive fishing or other rights to coastal governments. Custom or treaties may draw precise lines, but uncooperative fish refuse to integrate those lines into their life cycle. Hence territorial allocations, even if achievable, cannot solve problems of conservation of fish migrating between exclusive and common waters.

Some fish, for example, complete their life cycle close to shore. Others which start their life in national streams (e. g., salmon) range widely. Others never come into territorial waters at all. Fishing vessels have become ever more capable of operating more remotely from home ports, of catching more fish per man hour employed, and of transporting the catch farther, usually in frozen form. A situation in which there prevailed an unrestricted freedom to catch fish on the high seas might soon lead to the total extinction of the species being pursued or at least to drastically reduced future catches. In the case of certain fish, affirmative action must be taken to assist in the spawning and distribution of the species. But the benefits of action by any one state either to limit catches by its citizens or to promote fish hatcheries would not be recaptured by its nationals and would thus not seem worthwhile. For in the absence of some form of exclusive right to the specie of fish involved (analogous to the property right under private law), the long-run time frame and abstention from taking the highest possible immediate catch by the regulating state would simply lead to a redistribution of welfare away from that state to others (or their nationals) not sharing the same objectives.

Hence cooperative action is essential. The result has been an endeavor to regulate oceanic fisheries through multilateral conventions. The Convention on Fishing and Conservation of the Living Resources of the High Seas done at the Geneva Conference in 1958 [60] pledges all parties "to adopt or co-operate with other States in adopting, such measures for their respective nationals as may be necessary for the conservation of the living resources of the high seas." It provides that where two or more states are engaged in fishing the same stock, they should negotiate about the necessary conservation measures and outline a method for resolving differences not negotiated. Coastal states are given priority as to initiation of conservation measures in high seas adjacent to their territorial seas.

More specific agreements, some of which antedate the Geneva convention by many years, exist in several regions or as to particular species. Such conventions regulate the North-West Atlantic, North-East Atlantic and Northern Pacific fisheries. There are special conventions as to tuna, seals and whales. In its typical format, such a convention will establish a Commission (of which there are some 20) which will administer the program and conduct research. The Commission determines the size of each year's catch, striving to maintain a level of exploitation that will not deplete stocks but rather permit a steady level of sustainable yield. The year's total permissible catch must then be rationed out among the member countries in some way that is acceptable to them. At the same time the Commission may develop regulations limiting the gear and the tactics fishermen may use in catching the fish in question and may prohibit the catching of fish below a certain size or during certain seasons.

Various strains develop within such a Commission even in one whose members are relatively homogeneous in that they employ rather similar fishing methods and devote roughly equal energy to fishing activities. There has been a sense that several of the major Commissions have been politically unable to reduce quotas to a level that will actually result in a sustainable yield. This is particularly

60. In the Icelandic Fisheries case, p. 271, supra, the Court referred to the Geneva Convention in urging the parties to work out their differences.

true of the International Whaling Commission, under whose aegis the catch of whales has declined steadily as expansionist countries with highly mechanized floating factories pushed to retain their allocations. The blue whale and the humpback whale have become virtually extinct. The pressures will be even greater if the arrangements seek to include countries without the equipment and organization to participate actively in the catching operations. Either they will be unable to use the quotas that should be allocated them or some other entity will have to be able to use the resources on their account. There is also a question whether what should be maximized is the total yield or the total net revenue—a question which makes much difference to poorer, labor-intensive exploiters of fisheries vis-à-vis modern mechanized industries.

The difficulties in effective regulation are well illustrated by 1975 measures taken by the International Whaling Commission (as reported in the New York Times, June 28, 1975, p. 1, col. 4). At its annual meeting in London, the Commission gave almost total protection to the finback whale, the biggest of the whales still hunted legally. The sharpest cuts ever made by the Commission reduced the coming season's total whale catch from 37,000 to 27,000. A ban was placed on hunting the finback in the North Pacific, and a limit of 585 finback whales was placed upon the 1975–76 season elsewhere. The last season's finback catch quota was 1,550.

The chief American delegate to the Commission described the reductions as "a major step forward in the international effort to protect all species of whales from endangerment in the future." An American delegate observed: "It's finally dawned on the conservationists that the whaling fleets can't be scrapped just like that, and on the whalers that some species really are in danger of extinction. That's made it easier for both sides to make accommodations and for the commission to get down to its business of rational management of whaling stocks."

Under the rules of the Commission, nations need only lodge objections to measures taken within 90 days in order not to be bound by them. The Soviet Union and Japan between them account for 80% of the total whale catch. Comment on the reductions from Japan and the Soviet Union was not immediately forthcoming. The Commission's Norwegian chairman speculated that, despite obstruction to conservation efforts by both nations in the past, neither would lodge objections to these measures.

The present negotiations to arrive at a new regimen for the law of the sea will have to grapple with these problems, and do so in the context of an increasing pressure on all maritime resources that, it is estimated, will bring forth by the year 2000 a demand equivalent to seven times the present catch.

Additional Reading: Johnston, The International Law of Fisheries (1965); Proceedings of the Annual Conferences of the Law of the Sea Institute, Univ. of Rhode Island (1968-——); Lay, Churchill, Nordquist, New Directions in the Law of the Sea (1973).

E. CONFLICT WITH NATIONAL LAW: THE CONCEPT OF DOMESTIC JURISDICTION

Article 2(7) of the United Nations Charter provides that "[n]othing contained in the present Charter shall authorize the United Nations to intervene in matters which are essentially within the domestic jurisdiction of any state or shall require the Members to submit such matters to settlement under the present Charter . . . ." The Declaration of the United States * under Article 36 (2) of the I.C.J.'s Statute recognizing as compulsory that Court's jurisdiction stipulates, in a clause that has become known as the Connally Reservation, that the Declaration does not apply to "[d]isputes with regard to matters which are essentially within the domestic jurisdiction of the United States of America as determined by the United States of America . . . ." Nations frequently reject diplomatic protests or demands from other nations on the ground that the subject matter of the dispute is within their "domestic jurisdiction." What is meant by this phrase? Does it bear the same meaning in all the contexts in which it may be invoked?

TUNIS—MOROCCO NATIONALITY DECREES

Permanent Court of International Justice, 1923.
P.C.I.J., Ser. B, No. 4.

[Article 13 of the Covenant of the League of Nations provided that, whenever a dispute arose between members of the League which they recognized to be suitable for submission to arbitration or judicial settlement, they would so submit it. Article 15, Paragraph 1 stated that if Article 13 was not followed, the members would submit the matter to the Council of the League. The Council could hear the facts and make recommendations. Article 15, Paragraph 8 provided: "If the dispute between the parties is claimed by one of them, and is found by the Council, to arise out of a matter which by international law is solely within the domestic jurisdiction of that party, the Council should so report, and shall make no recommendation as to its settlement."

In 1921, nationality decrees were promulgated in Tunis and in Morocco, both French Protectorates. They provided that persons born in Tunis or Morocco of parents at least one of whom was also born there had French (or Tunisian or Moroccan) nationality. This apparently implied a liability to military service. Concerned with enforcement of the nationality decrees against British subjects, the British Government proposed arbitration to the French Government, which however refused on grounds that the dispute was not justiciable. After Britain had referred the dispute to the Council of the League pursuant to Article 15, Paragraph 1, the French Government invoked Paragraph 8 of that Article. Pursuant to Article 14 of the Covenant, which provided that the P.C.I.J. could give an advisory opinion upon any dispute or question referred to it by the Council, the Council requested the Court for an opinion on the question "whether the dispute . . . is or is not by international law solely a matter of domestic jurisdiction . . . ." Excerpts from the opinion of the Court follow.]

From one point of view, it might well be said that the jurisdiction of a State is *exclusive* within the limits fixed by international law—using this expression in its wider sense, that is to say, embracing both customary law and general as well as particular treaty law. But a careful scrutiny of paragraph 8 of Article 15 shows that it is not in this sense that exclusive jurisdiction is referred to in that paragraph.

The words "solely within the domestic jurisdiction" seem rather to contemplate certain matters which, though they may very closely concern the interests of more than one State, are not, in principle, regulated by international law. As regards such matters, each State is sole judge.

The question whether a certain matter is or is not solely within the jurisdiction of a State is an essentially relative question; it depends upon the development of international relations. Thus, in the present state of international law, questions of nationality are, in the opinion of the Court, in principle within this reserved domain.

For the purpose of the present opinion, it is enough to observe that it may well happen that, in a matter which, like that of nationality, is not, in principle, regulated by international law, the right of a State to use its discretion is nevertheless restricted by obligations which it may have undertaken towards other States. In such a case, jurisdiction which, in principle, belongs solely to the State, is limited by rules of international law. Article 15, paragraph 8, then ceases to apply as regards those States which are entitled to invoke such rules, and the dispute as to the question whether a State has or has not the right to take certain measures becomes in these circumstances a dispute of an international character and falls outside the scope of the exception contained in this paragraph. To hold that a State has not exclusive jurisdiction does not in any way prejudice the final decision as to whether that State has a right to adopt such measures.

This interpretation follows from the actual terms of paragraph 8 of Article 15 of the Covenant, and, in the opinion of the Court, it is also in harmony with that Article taken as a whole.

Article 15, in effect, establishes the fundamental principle that any dispute likely to lead to a rupture which is not submitted to arbitration in accordance with Article 13 shall be laid before the Council. The reservations generally made in arbitration treaties are not to be found in this Article.

Having regard to this very wide competence possessed by the League of Nations, the Covenant contains an express reservation protecting the independence of States; this reservation is to be found in paragraph 8 of Article 15. Without this reservation, the internal affairs of a country might, directly they appeared to affect the interests of another country, be brought before the Council and form the subject of recommendations by the League of Nations. Under the terms of paragraph 8, the League's interest in being able to make such recommendations as are deemed just and proper in the circumstances with a view to the maintenance of peace must, at a given point, give way to the equally essential interest of the individual State to maintain intact its independence in matters which international law recognizes to be solely within its jurisdiction.

It must not, however, be forgotten that the provision contained in paragraph 8, in accordance with which the Council, in certain circumstances, is to confine itself to reporting that a question is, by international law, solely within the domestic jurisdiction of one Party, is an exception to the principles affirmed in the preceding paragraphs and does not therefore lend itself to an extensive interpretation.

This consideration assumes especial importance in the case of a matter which, by international law, is, in principle, solely within the domestic jurisdiction of one Party, but in regard to which the other Party invokes international engagements which, in the opinion of that Party, are of a nature to preclude in the particular case such exclusive jurisdiction. A difference of opinion exists between France and Great Britain as to how far it is necessary to proceed with an examination of these international engagements in order to reply to the question put to the Court.

It is certain . . . that the mere fact that a State brings a dispute before the League of Nations does not suffice to give this dispute an international character calculated to except it from the application of paragraph 8 of Article 15.

It is equally true that the mere fact that one of the parties appeals to engagements of an international character in order to contest the exclusive jurisdiction of the other is not enough to render paragraph 8 inapplicable. But when once it appears that the legal grounds (*titres*) relied on are such as to justify the provisional conclusion that they are of juridical importance for the dispute submitted to the Council, and that the question whether it is competent for one State to take certain measures is subordinated to the formation of an opinion with regard to the validity and construction of these legal grounds (*titres*), the provisions contained in paragraph 8 of Article 15 cease to apply and the matter, ceasing to be one solely within the domestic jurisdiction of the State, enters the domain governed by international law.

If, in order to reply to a question regarding exclusive jurisdiction, raised under paragraph 8, it were necessary to give an opinion upon the merits of the legal grounds (*titres*) invoked by the Parties in this respect, this would hardly be in conformity with the system established by the Covenant for the pacific settlement of international disputes.

For the foregoing reasons, the Court holds, contrary to the final conclusions of the French Government, that it is only called upon to consider the arguments and legal grounds (*titres*) advanced by the interested Governments in so far as is necessary in order to form an opinion upon the nature of the dispute. While it is obvious that these legal grounds (*titres*) and arguments cannot extend either the terms of the request submitted to the Court by the Council or the competence conferred upon the Court by the Council's resolution, it is equally clear that the Court must consider them in order to form an opinion as to the nature of the dispute referred to in the said resolution—with regard to which the Court's opinion has been requested.

[The Court noted that it was competent for a State to enact nationality legislation for its own national territory. The question here was whether the same competence existed with respect to protected territory. This depended, under the circumstances, upon a number of treaties involving France, its Protectorates, and third countries. Consequently, stated the Court, the question whether the exclusive jurisdiction on national territory extended to the territory of protected States depends upon "an examination of the whole situation as it appears from the standpoint of international law. The question therefore is no longer solely one of domestic jurisdiction as defined above."

The British Government also relied upon treaties between it and Tunis and Morocco which, it claimed, gave British subjects a measure of extraterritoriality incompatible with the imposition of another nationality. The French Government contended that these treaties had lapsed after those states became protectorates. The Court noted that it could not make any pronouncement on this question without consideration of international-law rules relating to the duration and validity of treaties. Consequently this question also was not solely within the jurisdiction of the French Government. The British Government further relied upon a most-favored-nation clause in treaties between Great Britain and France. The Court stated that this question of treaty interpretation was not within the domestic jurisdiction of the French Government. For these reasons, the Court replied to the question submitted to it by the Council in the negative.]

NOTE ON DIFFERENT MEANINGS OF DOMESTIC JURISDICTION

Officials of national and international institutions are required to identify for various purposes the critical boundary line between matters regulated to some degree by international law and matters recognized to be within the unfettered discretion of national governments. This second category is often referred to as "domestic jurisdiction." The definition, or indeed the very notion, of a boundary line raises a number of vexing problems.

The line could be described in one of two ways. One could attempt to state the sum of relevant rules of international law which impose restraints or affirmative duties upon states. All national rules or conduct not within that sum could be viewed as within "domestic jurisdiction." Alternatively, one could attempt to define affirmatively those matters that are recognized to be within a nation's discretion.

Note that a like problem has developed in American constitutional law. Does the Tenth Amendment * merely restate that the federal government must rely on powers granted by the Constitution, or does it impose limitations and define state prerogatives with a separate force of its own? During most of its history, it has been construed to be a restatement of the rest of the Constitution, taking away no powers that the Constitution explicitly or by implication grants to the federal government.[61]

Does the concept of domestic jurisdiction have more utility in international relations than the Tenth Amendment does domestically? Note that each of the situations below to which domestic jurisdiction is relevant involves an aspect of the fundamental tension in the international community between state sovereignty and external restraints upon that sovereignty. Articles 1 and 2 of the United Nations Charter reflect this tension, as one compares the "internationalist" spirit

61. See United States v. Manning, 215 F.Supp. 272, 276–83 (W.D.La.1963), for a scholarly review of this history.

of Articles 1(1) and 2(6) with the traditional themes of state sovereignty in Article 2(1), (4), and (7).

(1) The concept is relevant to determining the authority of political organs of the United Nations. Indeed the precise phrase "domestic jurisdiction" first appeared in a major international agreement in Article 15(8) of the Covenant of the League of Nations, although phrases in earlier treaties, such as "reserved rights," served a comparable purpose. Note the difference between the wording of Article 15(8) of the Covenant, set forth in the Tunis-Morocco Case, and Article 2(7) of the Charter.

Within the United Nations, allegations that matters are within a nation's domestic jurisdiction are frequently made to support charges that the General Assembly is acting beyond its powers by debating certain issues, whether the debate terminates without firm action or leads to recommendations or resolutions. Note the broad mandate "to discuss any questions" that Article 10 of the Charter gives the Assembly, in contrast with the more limited provisions of Chapters V–VII that govern action by the Security Council. The issues leading to tensions between the Assembly and a member have included some of the major irritants of the post-war world: colonialism, deprivation of human rights, and protection of property interests of aliens. Apartheid in South Africa and the conflict between the United Kingdom and Rhodesia are striking examples.

Note that nations challenging action of the General Assembly can base their protests upon the provision of Article 2(7) barring intervention in matters of domestic jurisdiction. The Assembly has interpreted that provision to permit debate and occasionally resolutions on problems which have an undeniable international impact, even if there is no consensus over the degree to which international law does or should regulate the matter. The I.C.J. has not yet been asked for an advisory opinion whether a given matter was within the domestic jurisdiction of a state. If and when that occasion arises, the Court will have to determine whether it is competent to render such an opinion, since Article 96(1) * of the Charter authorizes advisory opinions only on "legal" questions. It would further have to decide whether General Assembly debates could be viewed as an "intervention" within the meaning of Article 2(7). Meanwhile, the practice of the political organs of the United Nations may be creating new law on the question of what domestic jurisdiction encompasses, at least with respect to the meaning of that phrase in Article 2(7).

(2) At the time of the creation of the League and the U. N., the domestic-jurisdiction clause could be said to have been "framed for the purpose of quieting the excessive jealousies which had been excited," to use the phrase Chief Justice Marshall applied to the Tenth Amendment in McCulloch v. Maryland, 17 U.S. (4 Wheat.) 316, 406, 4 L.Ed. 579, 601 (1819). Like states-rights advocates using that Amendment, foreign offices resisting pressures or protests from international bodies or officials of foreign states instinctively resort to the rhetoric of domestic jurisdiction. In diplomatic correspondence and domestic political pronouncements, the phrase mobilizes national sentiment more effectively than would be possible if one had to assert in a more complex way the limited reach into domestic problems of international law or organizations.

(3) The concept of domestic jurisdiction also plays a prominent role in arguments over the adjudicatory jurisdiction of international tribunals. It has particular importance for the International Court of Justice, in view of its inclusion in a number of declarations under Article 36(2). In fact, the Connally Reservation encouraged similar moves by other nations.

Before considering the purport and effect of such reservations, note how the I.C.J.'s jurisdiction is determined without them. The phrase "domestic jurisdiction" does not appear in those provisions of the Charter (Articles 92–96) which treat the Court or in the Court's Statute. It is probable that Article 2(7) applies to the Court; the issue was raised but not decided in the Anglo-Iranian Oil Co. Case (United Kingdom v. Iran), [1952] I.C.J.Rep. 89. However, the same issue that Article 2(7) raises could be put to the Court under a reservation which excluded from its jurisdiction matters of "domestic jurisdiction," but which did not include the self-judging proviso of the Connally Reservation. The question before the Court would be whether such a reservation or Article 2(7) limits its jurisdiction in any manner that is not already inherent in the provisions of Articles 36 and 38 of the Statute, which define the Court's function to be deciding cases under "international law."

The varied ways in which the word "jurisdiction" is used within national legal systems complicate and obscure this issue. The word suggests that what is at stake is the competence of the Court, a question which should be disposed of before the Court reaches the merits of a dispute. Such a question could arise, for example, under Article 34 of the Statute. A respondent might allege that a claimant was not in fact a "state," and that the Court consequently lacked jurisdiction because of Article 34's limitation.

If however, as some suggest, domestic jurisdiction in a reservation simply restates the limitations implicit in Articles 36 and 38, the Court would have to examine whether international law was relevant to a dispute before ruling upon that defense. Compare the Tunis-Morocco Case. Similar problems arise under 28 U.S.C.A. § 1331(a), which grants federal courts jurisdiction over claims arising under the Constitution, laws or treaties of the United States. A domestic court may have to consider the merits before deciding whether to dismiss a complaint on the ground of absence of a federal question. Note that Section 1331 is similar to Article 36 in that it is an affirmative grant of jurisdiction to hear cases raising federal questions, rather than a negative restraint like the Tenth Amendment or Article 2(7) of the Charter.

Consider now the Connally Reservation. That form of reservation, together with the self-judging proviso, has come before the I.C.J. on several occasions. In the Interhandel Case, p. 244, supra, the United States pleaded domestic jurisdiction with respect to one aspect of the litigation, namely its discretion to sell the vested shares claimed by Interhandel and substitute the proceeds as the object of the litigation. Since the Court decided that the Swiss Application was inadmissible because of the failure to exhaust local remedies, it did not reach the question of the validity of the reservation. In the Case of Certain Norwegian Loans, [1957] I.C.J.Rep. 9, France filed an Application against Norway, alleging that Norway violated international law by refusing to pay in accordance with their terms certain Norwegian bonds issued to French bondholders. At that time, France's original declaration under Article 36(2), containing a clause similar to the Connally Reservation, was in effect. The Norwegian Government, invoking reciprocity (see p. 199, supra), pleaded that the matter was within its domestic jurisdiction. Neither France nor Norway challenged the validity of the French reservation. The Court upheld Norway's defense but, in view of the mutual concessions of the clause's validity, did not consider the ultimate issue. In both cases, the opinions of individual judges—in particular the separate opinions of Judge Lauterpacht—argued that the American and French reservations vitiated both declarations and therefore that neither case was properly before the Court.

The coupling of the notion of reciprocity with the Connally Reservation has caused difficulties for the United States similar to those encountered by France in the Norwegian Loans Case—for example in proceedings brought by the United States against Bulgaria because of the Aerial Incident of 27 July 1955, [1959] I.C.J. Pleadings. In preliminary pleadings, the State Department asserted that Bulgaria's invocation under reciprocity of the Connally Reservation could not be "arbitrary" and was reviewable by the Court. It subsequently changed its position and discontinued the case. *Id.* at 308, 322–25, 676–77.

Note that in some situations, the United States has submitted to the jurisdiction of the I.C.J. without the "benefit" of the Connally Reservation. See, for example, Article XVI(2) of the Convention of Establishment between the United States and France,* which gives the Court jurisdiction under Article 36(1). Other treaties, however, echo the Connally Reservation's language.[62]

QUESTIONS

(1) The Court in the Tunis-Morocco Case defines domestic jurisdiction to be matters that are not "in principle" regulated by international law. It notes that in the present state of international law, questions of nationality are "in principle" within that phrase. Recall the comments

62. For a review of the history of the inclusion or omission of Connally clauses, see Bishop and Myers, Unwarranted Extension of Connally-Amendment Thinking, 55 Am.J.Int.L. 135 (1961).

about nationality and domestic jurisdiction in the Nottebohm Case, at pp. 214–215, supra. What perils do those comments suggest in any effort to describe matters that are not "in principle" regulated by international law? What of tariffs or exchange controls, 50 years ago or today?

(2) Suppose that Britain had instituted proceedings against France before the P.C.I.J., claiming that the nationality decrees infringed rights of British subjects in Tunis and Morocco under international law. Suppose further that the Court overrode French objections to its "jurisdiction" and ruled on the merits that the French decrees, and action taken pursuant to them, did not violate international law. Should its decision be viewed as stating that France's action was consistent with international law or that nationality questions were within France's domestic jurisdiction? Consider in this connection whether the decision in Lotus Case, p. 253, supra, could be viewed as resting on the ground of domestic jurisdiction, even though the opinion did not invoke that phrase. Do your answers to these questions have any practical consequences?

(3) Consider the allied problems of immigration and deportation. Recall the language in Harisiades v. Shaughnessy, at p. 28, supra, to the effect that the power to deport an alien was "confirmed" by international law. Is this tantamount to stating that questions of deportation are within the domestic jurisdiction of the United States? Suppose that the Greek government had sent a note to the United States protesting the deportation of Harisiades. Should this country have replied by stating that deportation was a question within its domestic jurisdiction or that deportation of Harisiades was consistent with international law? Might different consequences have followed these two possible replies?

(4) You are the legal adviser to the foreign ministry of a country that is contemplating submission to the jurisdiction of the I.C.J. It has been suggested by a legislator that a clause be inserted excluding matters within the domestic jurisdiction of your country, but without a self-judging proviso. Would you advise that such a clause serves a purpose?

(5) (a) You are the Legal Adviser to the State Department. Proceedings have been instituted against the United States before the I.C.J. The claimant nation charges that the United States has broken an unambiguous international agreement requiring it to exempt that nation's citizens doing business in the United States from certain taxes. Would you advise entering the plea of domestic jurisdiction? Would you view the Connally Reservation as subject to any criterion of "reasonableness" or as a frank "political out" whenever the United States does not welcome litigation? If the former, how would you define that criterion? (b) Suppose that the United States enters a plea of domestic jurisdiction. Should the Court adopt the views of Judge Lauterpacht about the status of its Declaration? Consider Article 92 of the Charter and Article 36(6) of the Statute.

(6) Identification of the concerns which underlay the Connally Reservation would be critical if and when the Senate is called upon to repeal that reservation. (a) As a Senator favoring repeal, what alternative to the Connally Reservation would you suggest that would eliminate the self-judging proviso and still respond to the concerns felt by a number of your colleagues? (b) Suppose that you were a Senator who was undecided about his vote. Your legislative assistant shows you the opinions of the International Court in the Lotus Case and in the Fisheries Case, including the concurring opinion of Judge Alvarez. How would each of these opinions affect your vote?

(7) Apart from the effect of changes in its membership, why do you suppose that the Senate consented to the Convention of Establishment with France, including Article XVI(2) *, after it had voted the Connally Reservation?

Additional reading: Abi-Saab, The Newly Independent States and the Scope of Domestic Jurisdiction, 1960 Proc.Am.Soc.Int.L. 84; Sohn, International Tribunals: Past, Present and Future, 48 A.B.A.J. 23 (1960); Wright, Domestic Jurisdiction as a Limit on National and Supra-National Action, 56 Nw.L.Rev. 11 (1961); Note, Alternative Reservations to the Compulsory Jurisdiction of the International Court of Justice, 72 Harv. L.Rev. 749 (1959); Proceedings of the Fourth Summer Conference at Cornell Law School on International Law, The Status of Domestic Jurisdiction (1962).

F. CONTEMPORARY PERSPECTIVES ON INTERNATIONAL LAW

From early times the scholar, in particular the treatise writer, has played a larger role in the development of international law than of the Anglo-American legal world. His prominence has been a consequence of the weakness of law-making institutions at the international level, the tendency of the civil law to value scholarly analysis and restatements of doctrine more than judicial development of principles, and the unsettled, abstract and speculative nature of many international-law issues. Even when scholars become diplomats or members of an international tribunal, their scholarly writings may be as influential as their official pronouncements or opinions. The reference in Article 38(1)(d) to "the teachings of the most highly qualified publicists" as "subsidiary means" of determining international law scarcely does justice to their influence. Familiarity with the ideas in ferment among contemporary scholars and critics of international law is thus essential to an understanding of the current scene and to any prediction of its likely development.

Additional reading: Brierly, The Law of Nations 1–93 (6th ed., Waldock, 1963); Carr, the Twenty Years' Crisis, 1919–1939 (1939); Falk and Black (eds.), The Future of the International Legal Order (Vols. I–IV, 1969–1972); Falk and Mendlovitz (eds.), The Strategy of World Public Order: International Law (Vol. II, 1966); Friedmann, The Changing Structure of International Law (1964); Henkin, How Nations Behave (1968); Jessup, A Modern Law of Nations (1948); Jessup, Transnational Law (1956); Kaplan and Katzenbach, The Political Foundations of International Law (1961); Lissitzyn, International Law Today and Tomorrow (1965); McDougal and Associates, Studies in World Public Order (1960); Charles de Visscher, Theory and Reality in Public International Law (Corbett Trans.1957).

NOTE ON THE CLASSICAL SYSTEM AND ITS PRESENT INADEQUACY

One can fairly describe the evolution of international law from the 17th century to 1914 as the development of a classical synthesis. While there were both growth and change during this period, consistency was its striking characteristic.

First, classical international law was largely the contribution of a single part of the world; it was a *European* law. The first systematic statements of a "modern" international law (that is, from about the start of the 17th century) appeared in the works of such Europeans as Gentile, Grotius and Vattel. Their writings were heavily tinged with principles of Roman law and, particularly in the earlier periods, with Christian ideals. Imperialism and colonialism spread European concepts of international law to all parts of the globe.

Second, classical international law was associated with a particular set of political circumstances. The period of its growth witnessed the development of the nation-state in Western Europe and the disintegration of the notion of a universal Christian community transcending national units. The theoretical foundations for international law reflected this emphasis upon the nation and national (territorial) sovereignty. Indeed, until the time of Bentham this body of law was referred to as the "law of nations." Note the introductory sentence to Brierly, The Law of Nations 1 (6th ed., Waldock, 1963): "The Law of Nations, or International Law, may be defined as the body of rules and principles of action which are binding upon civilized states in their relations with one another."

Those rules expressed the duties and rights of states, not individuals. And the subject matter which they treated was directly relevant to the function which international law served: bringing minimum order to relations between states by imposing certain restraints upon them and allocating certain competences among them. Those subjects included the creation, termination and recognition of states; the demarcation of land and sea boundaries, together with related rules about acquisition of territory; the formalities and courtesies of diplomatic relations between states during peace; restraints upon the conduct of belligerents; responsibility of a state for injuries to aliens; and fundamental aspects of treaty law. The Note on the United Nations, p. 309, supra, indicates one of the most significant innovations in principle of contemporary international law: the effort to develop norms, and machinery to enforce them, regulating armed conflict among states. Before the League of Nations, international law generally went no further than defining some rules for the *conduct* of war. A decision whether to engage in war was recognized to be within a nation's discretion—a recognition that reflected the stress upon state sovereignty and the decentralized decision-making in a community that lacked significant international institutions.

Third, classical international law absorbed prevailing attitudes towards economics. The countries which generated and spread it regarded economic activity primarily as the responsibility of individuals, although within such frameworks as mercantilism, governments did subsidize, protect and encourage them in various ways. These countries were of course capital-exporting and trading nations, rather than recipients of foreign investment. Until the 20th century, international law proper—a law among states—dealt only marginally with most areas of business or commercial activity, a field of private activity regulated by national law. The striking exceptions to this generalization were in the area of state responsibility for the protection of foreign investment, for the observance of contracts entered into with aliens, and for the safety of foreign, largely business, persons. Those rules sought to improve (from the perspective of the European community) conditions for and thus to encourage private transnational economic activity. Thus during the 18th and 19th centuries, as Western Europe and the United States developed in relatively laissez-faire directions, international law complemented the stress upon protection of property and contract rights within these national forms of liberal society.

Finally, international law experienced a change in its theory of the basis of obligation of a state to comply with it. Beginning with a foundation in Christian theology or natural-law theory,[63] it developed in the direction of positivism and stress upon a nation's consent as the basis of legal obligation. A consequence of this evolution in theory was a growing concentration upon the gathering and analysis of evidence of state practice. This endeavor to find consent through practice ripening into custom (or of course through treaties) suppressed the assumption of a more creative role in the development of international law by international institutions, especially tribunals.

This brief description is sufficient to suggest why classical international law is often inadequate to the contemporary world's problems. By the mid-20th century, European countries and other developed countries which grew out of European colonialism formed a minority of members of the world community. The over 120 states in the United Nations represent many cultures or social and economic ideologies, and have sharply divergent interests. However one describes the various blocs which displaced the 19th century's balance-of-power system among European nations—the capitalist and socialist worlds, the status-quo and revolutionary worlds, the democratic and totalitarian worlds, the developed and underdeveloped and third worlds, the major powers and less significant countries—international law can realize its major purposes only by bringing some minimum order to and facilitating cooperation among countries in an area broader than the Atlantic Community. To be sure, such a regional body of law continues to serve an important function. But with a

63. The famous statement of Maine is here pertinent. "The grandest function of the Law of Nature was discharged in giving birth to modern International Law. . . ." Maine, Ancient Law 92 (5th ed. 1963).

global rather than regional distribution of power, a distribution accelerated by this century's technological revolution and by the dependence of the developed world upon energy resources in other countries; with eruptions that endanger world peace no longer a monopoly of any one area; with trade and investment penetrating all parts of the globe; such regional systems no longer meet the larger needs of the contemporary world.

Beyond these considerations, today's political, economic and technological interdependence of nations makes new demands upon international law. It is not simply that many rules of classical international law—such as aspects of the law of the sea that are described in the Note following the Fisheries Case, p. 270, supra—have lost a consensus earlier achieved within a smaller (in terms of effective power) world community. New fields have become pertinent as governments have expanded their regulation of and participation in national economic life. Tariff and monetary policies, antitrust and tax policies and so on may have a significant impact upon the growth of the domestic economy, the volume and channels of international trade and investment, and ultimately upon the stability and well-being of the entire international community. These are problems which are not met through rules which go no further than delimit the authority of different states and establish conditions for avoiding undue friction. They can be solved only through more pervasive international cooperation and regulation, to be achieved through new organizational and institutional arrangements and more flexible processes for the development of international law.[64]

From another perspective, the lessons of World War II, the principles of the United Nations Charter, and the attitudes of the newer nations have brought increased attention to the individual and his claim to basic human rights. The emphasis of classical international law upon relations between states or states and aliens is under challenge. That maltreatment of individuals as well as maltreatment of states can cause grave problems for the international community is now a commonplace. Hence the (still weak) efforts described in Chapter IV to define basic human rights and develop procedures or institutions to assure that those rights are honored.

Of course many principles of the classical system remain as viable and cogent today as they were in prior centuries. Aspects of the law of diplomatic immunities and of treaty law are illustrative. But in fields that have become contentious, the danger arises that a rigid insistence upon standards formulated before 1914 will reinforce the views of other nations that international law is simply a legal expression of or ideological disguise for the political and economic interests of the states which developed it. That is, the "haves," the nations relatively satisfied with the status quo, become the defenders of the classical system; the "have-nots," nations whose economic and

64. Some of these arrangements and processes are examined in Chapters XI and XIII, in the context of a discussion of three major international organizations.

political aspirations contemplate or indeed require significant changes in the present international structure, lose any sense of commitment or attraction to legal processes. As one observer has stated, "We are in the midst of a succession of revolutionary systems—not on the verge of a stable one—and the solidity of international law will continue to remain in doubt." [65] The problem, now broadly stated but to be explored in a more confined setting in Chapter IV, is whether and how classical rules and processes of international law can be reformulated to serve a contemporary world. Else the probability grows that international law will play an ever more marginal role in furthering change.

NOTE ON THE NEW AND COMMUNIST NATIONS AND INTERNATIONAL LAW

After independence, the United States fitted rather smoothly into the existing framework of international law. It inherited and found compatible the larger part of the body of customary rules. As this country developed through the 19th century into a major industrial power, a natural community of interests developed between it and Europe. To be sure, there was occasional abrasion and the assertion of a distinctive United States position, including the doctrine of voluntary expatriation and such major pronouncements as the Monroe Doctrine.

The development of new attitudes and doctrines in Latin America, particularly in the second half of the 19th century, was the first important challenge to the dominant European character of international law. The situation of the nations south of the Rio Grande was such as to call into being new perspectives upon international law. After independence, many of these states remained economically dependent upon Europe (later the United States) and were politically unstable. As capital importers rather than exporters, they reacted against much of the traditional law of diplomatic protection and state responsibility (as described in Chapter IV), and advocated doctrines which sharply curtailed the right of a country to intervene on behalf of a national's property or contractual interests. These doctrines gave rise to the Calbo Clause, discussed at p. 522, infra, and to the Drago Doctrine, asserting that forceful intervention to vindicate contractual rights of nationals was contrary to international law. And among South American nations, special problems gave rise to rather special rules, such as those treating boundary questions and the right of asylum.[66]

The experience of Latin America found a sequel after World War II, when numerous colonies in Asia and Africa gained independence. It was not only their radically different economic situa-

65. Hoffmann, International Systems and International Law, in Knorr and Verba (eds.), The International System 205, 237 (1961).

66. See the dissenting opinion of Judge Alvarez in the Asylum Case (Colombia v. Peru), [1950] I.C.J. Rep. 266, 290.

tion which produced different attitudes towards some phases of classical international law. Confronted by what they perceived to be neocolonial pressures, and anxious to avoid becoming enmeshed in the East-West struggle, these countries sought recognition of new concepts that would express their needs and aspirations. In some ways, their challenge to the old order has been more pervasive than Latin America's. Witness the criticism of traditional international law in the following excerpts from an article by a former Indian judge, Roy, entitled Is the Law of Responsibility of States for Injuries to Aliens a Part of Universal International Law?, 55 Am.J.Int.L. 863, 881–83 (1961):

> If one confines oneself to the law as it stood at the turn of the century or at the commencement of World War II, without looking backward into its origins and phases of growth, one may well be tempted to take the law in its present form as having always been a part of universal international law in the sense that, at that point of history, it had been accepted by all the members of the extremely narrow international community of the past, including the few non-Western states admitted into that community at later stages. From this it is but a short step to the conclusion that every new member on its entry into the community of nations automatically accepts international law in all its parts, except what may be limited either expressly or by necessary implication to some members only.
>
> The bulk of existing international law is an undoubted legacy from the international community of the past—a community limited both racially and geographically. Beyond the frontiers of this community there was a vaster world. The contacts of the members of that community with this vaster world outside were not regulated by any kind of law. There was thus a division here of mankind into two distinct parts. The so-called international community, the smaller but more powerful part, dominated the bigger but weaker part. The universality, therefore, of even that part of international law which governed all the members of that old international community was the universality of a very small slice of our world—a slice which ignored the other part except for its own ends. In other words, it was a mere semblance of universality. From this point of view, whatever in international law is based on universally valid humanitarian or other principles can alone claim to be truly universal.
>
> . . . . Today's international community is supposed . . . to be merely an expanded version of the old, just like a club which does not necessarily cease to be the same old club because of an enlargement of its membership. This, like most analogies, seems superficial and misleading. . . A club may change its identity when structural or other changes, including a change of objectives, dictate the necessity or desirability of a new start. . . .
>
> When, during a particular phase of its history, the international community enlarged itself by the admission of only one or two members, there was nothing like a structural change of the community and it might well be said that it

> was the same old international community as before, the old and the new members being governed alike by the existing rules of international law. . . .
>
> If there is truly a new beginning here, is it not pertinent to inquire how far the law governing the members of the old community can legally govern the members of the new, in the absence of specific agreements among them? . . . The new-born world community must have a new set of laws to govern the interrelations of its members as well as other matters. This new set of laws may, of course, be built round a nucleus of as much of the old law as may be found to be conducive to the larger interests, not only of some of the members of this new community, but of all.

During the last decade, the new nations of Asia and Africa, together with many Latin American countries, have sought more fundamental change in the nature of international law. Mostly through U. N. Resolutions (supported by the socialist countries), they have sought to establish a principled duty of the developed world to aid others in development—in effect, to redistribute some of the world's wealth so as to minimize the vast disparities in standards of living. Here too the effort is to invest international law with an ever more explicit political character, to have it express affirmative obligations rather than simply constraints upon conduct impinging upon interests of others.[67]

Although a Communist government first took power in a country which had been a supporter of the international-law status quo under tsarism, the Soviet Union's attack on that status has been as fundamental as that of the newer countries. The initial thrust of Communist thought was to reject the entire corpus of international law as the creation of capitalist institutions and to discount the possibility that principles could be developed to bridge the gulf between capitalist and socialist camps. Later developments caused officials of the Soviet Union to profess adherence at least to some norms of international law and to condemn action by others as violations of such norms. They have also persuaded such officials to enter into treaties with capitalist countries and to insist upon their performance under the doctrine *pacta sunt servanda.* Within the socialist bloc, a network of treaties has emerged to regulate economic intercourse, establish military cooperation, and even to create some international institutions. There are, of course, many Western writers who assert that Communist countries use international law solely as an instrument of politics rather than respect it as a body of binding norms; the compliment is returned in kind by Soviet theorists.

Something of the flavor of Soviet attitudes towards international law can be gathered from the following observations of a leading Soviet jurist, Grigory Tunkin.

67. See the 1974 General Assembly Resolutions referred to at pp. 467–468, infra, for expressions of duties of economic cooperation and aid.

TUNKIN, THEORY OF INTERNATIONAL LAW

W. E. Butler Trans., 1974, excerpts.

Part I: Development of International Law Since the Great October Socialist Revolution

Ch. 2. Peaceful Coexistence and General International Law

A. The Unfoundedness of the Theory that the Developmental Base of International Law is Contracting

. . .

. . . Two international legal positions corresponding to two trends in international politics have emerged: one position, a component part of the policy "from a position of strength," amounts to an actual denial of the possibility of the existence of general international law and to a justification of power politics in international relations; the second position, the position of the socialist and other peaceloving states, proceeds from the fact that general international law exists and the possibilities of its progressive development are not diminishing, but are growing.

The concept that during the past fifty years the developmental base of general international law has contracted in consequence of the existence of states of two opposed social systems and opposed ideologies, as well as the emergence of a large number of new states whose cultural heritage is substantially different from western civilization, is widely disseminated in the bourgeois doctrine of international law. Politically, this concept reflects first and foremost the influence of the policy of anticommunism, which rejects peaceful coexistence of states with opposed social systems and the possibility of agreement between them. Bourgeois legal doctrine is its theoretical base.

By virtue of its class nature, bourgeois legal science seeks not to reveal the true essence of law but, on the contrary, to lead inquiry away from it, to seek its essence in those phenomena which would conceal the exploitative nature of bourgeois law and would permit it to be characterized as an expression of the interests of all of society. The easiest path leading in this direction is to search for the bases of law in general, and consequently, of international law, in a particular community, including a common ideology. Among the devotees of this concept, exceedingly widespread in the bourgeois theory of international law, we find writers of very different political complexions, from blatant anticommunists to actual proponents of peaceful coexistence.

Proceeding from the aforementioned idealistic concept, according to which law, including international law, is a reflection of common ideology, and stipulating that there is no such common ideology now between the states of the two systems, some bourgeois international lawyers maintain that general international law is impossible in the presence of two opposed social systems and ideologies or they believe that it only is functioning temporarily, insofar as the heritage of the past has remained with us, and gradually is breaking up into separate regional systems. Other bourgeois jurists express apprehension for the fate of general international law or assert that the developmental base of general international law has contracted with the emergence of socialist states and the new states of Asia and Africa.

. . .

The concept that the basis of law is community, particularly a common ideology, is completely unfounded. Proponents of this concept frequently point out that in the absence of a specific community between people, the existence of law in general and of international law in particular is impossible. Of course, in the absence of a specific community between people, the existence of human society, and consequently of law, is inconceivable, but it still does not follow that this community is the reason for the formation of law or is reflected in law. The history of human society shows completely the opposite: in a pre-class society, where this community between people was more significant, there was no law: only with the emergence of class contradictions, with the destruction of the tribal community, does law emerge.

Law, including international law, emerged not as a result of an increase in community among people, but as a result of the division of society into classes and the formation of new class contradictions unknown to tribal society. International law, just as municipal law, is a phenomenon peculiar to a class society.

The theoretical unfoundedness of the concept of a common ideology as a necessary condition for the existence and development of international law does not make this concept less dangerous.

. . .

The danger of this concept consists in the fact that the practical conclusions which are derived therefrom correspond to the political credo of the most reactionary circles of the imperialist powers. In reality, even putting to one side the aspersions relating to the foreign policy of the Soviet Union disseminated by the most reactionary adherents of this concept, the conclusion itself of the impossibility of agreement between capitalist and socialist states by virtue of the ideological differences existing between them plays into the hands of advocates of the policy "from a position of strength." As is well-known, the champions of this policy attempt to justify their assertions that agreements among capitalist and socialist states are impossible, that such agreements are of little value, and that in relations with the socialist countries one supposedly can only rely upon force. The former United States Secretary of State, John Foster Dulles, declared, for example, at a news conference on October 16, 1957: "An agreement is a meeting of the minds, and so far I do not know of any agreement that the Soviet Union has made which has reflected a real meeting of the minds. We may have agreed on the same form of words, but there has not been a meeting of the minds."

The aforesaid by no means signifies that ideological differences have no importance for the development of international law. But everything depends upon how concretely the question of ideology is raised.

Many international lawyers approach the question formalistically of whether the emergence of socialist states, as well as of new states created in consequence of the liberation of the colonies, has led to a limitation of the developmental base of general international law. They frequently point out that the Soviet Union did not recognize all norms of general international law prevailing at the time it emerged. However, in this connection the most important fact is lost sight of—that the Soviet Union refused to accept only reactionary norms of international law.

The Soviet state collided with the international law existing at the time of its formation, which, together with democratic principles and norms aimed at ensuring friendly relations among states (the principle of respect for state sovereignty, the principle of equality, the principle of noninterference, and others), contained reactionary principles and norms that reflected and strengthened the system of national oppression, colonial plundering, and imperialist robbery (colonies, protectorates, unequal treaties, spheres of influence, consular jurisdiction, and so forth).

. . .

It is correct that with the emergence of the Soviet state certain norms of the then existing norms of general international law rejected by the Soviet state ceased to be norms of general international law. But it is very important to add in this connection that the contraction of general international law occurred at the expense of reactionary norms.

There is, however, another aspect to this problem, which bourgeois international lawyers usually lose sight of. The Soviet Union, and now the other socialist states as well, tirelessly struggle for the introduction of new progressive principles and norms into international law so that it becomes a more effective means of strengthening international peace and developing friendly relations among states on the basis of equality and self-determination of peoples.

Proceeding therefrom, the Soviet Union and the other socialist countries favor the progressive development of international law and its strict observance by all states. . . .

. . .

From the concept that the basis of law, including international law, is a common ideology, it follows that the emergence of a large number of new states in the international arena whose cultural heritage undoubtedly is distinct from "western civilization" leads to a contraction of the developmental base of contemporary general international law. This conclusion is rarely expressed openly and expressly, but it inevitably arises out of the said concept.

In this case, however, this conclusion is groundless. The attitude of new states toward international law is defined first and foremost by the fact that they did not participate directly in its creation and that the principles and norms of international law were in their time frequently a means of enslaving and exploiting peoples of these countries. Their position, which coincides a great deal with the position of the Soviet state and which consists in the fact that they do not consider themselves automatically bound by principles and norms of international law only because such principles have been accepted as generally binding by existing states, is, therefore, wholly justified and, as we have seen above, a lawful one.

As the Indian member of the International Law Commission, R. Pal, correctly stated: "International law is no longer the almost exclusive preserve of peoples of European blood, 'by whose consent it exists and for the settlement of whose differences it is applied or at least invoked.' Now that international law must be regarded as embracing other peoples, it clearly required their consent no less . . ."

The new states declare that they reject all provisions relating to colonial seizures, colonial domination, and racial inequality, the doctrine of acquired rights, unequal treaties, the western doctrine of succession to international treaties, provisions concerning responsibility for harm caused to aliens, protection of foreign citizens, and others.

. . .

Graphic evidence of this [expansion and growth of the developmental base of international law] is the immeasurably higher rate of the progressive development of international law in our day in comparison with that, for example, of the League of Nations period. Suffice it to point out that only one conference for the codification of international law (1930) was convened in the period between the First and Second World Wars, and that ended in failure. In the years following the Second World War, numerous broad international conferences, as well as international organizations, have adopted a number of international conventions which frequently embrace entire branches of international law (the 1958 Geneva Conventions on the Law of the Sea, the 1961 Vienna Convention on Diplomatic Relations, the 1963 Vienna Convention on Consular Relations, the 1967 Treaty on Principles of Activities of States in Outer Space, the 1969 Vienna Convention on the Law of Treaties, the Treaty on Non-Proliferation of Nuclear Weapons, the Treaty on the Prohibition of the Emplacement of Nuclear Weapons and Other Weapons of Mass Destruction on the Sea-Bed and the Ocean Floor and the Subsoil Thereof, the Convention on the Prohibition of the Development, Production, and Stockpiling of Bacteriological [Biological] and Toxin Weapons and Their Destruction, and others).

The Soviet doctrine of international law has proceeded and does proceed from the fact that general international law, whose norms regulate relations among all states irrespective of their social systems, exists and the possibilities of its further development are increasing with the growth of the forces of peace.

. . .

Part II: The Process of Forming Norms of Contemporary General International Law

Ch. 4. The Basic Processes of Forming Norms of International Law

B. International Custom

. . .

Customary norms of international law are being formed in international practice, as a rule, gradually. What are the basic elements of international practice which lead to the creation of customary norms of international law?

It should be pointed out that the process of forming a customary norm of international law, just as a treaty norm, is the process of the struggle and cooperation of states. The formulation of a customary rule occurs as a result of the intercourse of states, in which each state strives to consolidate as norms of conduct those rules which would correspond to its interests.

. . .

It has been pointed out repeatedly in international legal literature that not every repetition creates a customary norm of international law. Repetition of one and the same action also may not lead to the creation of a norm of conduct, and if such a norm of conduct emerges, it is not necessarily a legal norm: it may be a usage (a custom which is not legally binding), a norm of international morality, or a norm of international comity. In international relations, especially in the area of diplomatic relations and maritime navigation, there are many norms that have existed for a long period which, however, are not norms of international law. Thus, exempting diplomats' baggage from customs inspection and a number of diplomats' privileges on the territory of third states ordinarily are granted by all states. Before the entry into force of the 1961 Vienna Convention on Diplomatic Relations, the respective norms were not regarded as international legal norms, but were considered to be norms of international comity.

. . .

As we use it, the term "custom" has two meanings: in the sense of a customary rule which is not a legal norm, and in the sense of a customary norm of international law. To avoid confusing different concepts, it would be advisable in the first instance to speak of an international custom, and in the second, of an international legal custom or, better still, of a customary norm of international law.

Consequently, the statement that an international custom (or usage) exists is not the same as a statement that a customary norm of international law exists, for a custom, or a customary rule of conduct, is not necessarily a legal norm.

The establishment of a custom is a specific stage in the formative process of a customary norm of international law. This process is completed when states recognize a custom as legally binding; that is to say, recognize a customary rule of conduct as a norm of international law.

The process of forming a customary norm of international law is completed and an international custom (or usage) becomes an international legal custom or, that is to say, a customary norm of international law, only as a result of such recognition.

. . .

An American professor, O. Lissitzyn, also decisively rejects the second element of a customary norm of international law, calling this construction "artificial." The author, following McDougal, mixes the legal and other elements or, rather, simply casts the legal elements aside. In rejecting the need for a usage to be recognized as a norm of international law, the author inevitably comes to proclaim practice as a norm of international law. " . . . Custom, or 'general practice,'" Lissitzyn writes, "creates legally binding norms."

The writers who deny the second element of an international legal norm lose sight of the specific features of legal norms. "Universal practice" creates not merely legal, but also moral international norms and norms of international comity. But of the general mass of such international norms, only those become norms of international law which acquire the said second element—recognition by states as international legal norms.

. . .

There have been instances, however, when a dispute involved precisely whether a norm recognized by a majority of states was binding upon other states who had not recognized this norm. The question of the three-mile breadth of territorial waters may serve as an example. As is well-known, at the 1958 and 1960 Geneva Conferences on the Law of the Sea the western states, relying upon the bourgeois doctrine adduced above, attempted to maintain that the three-mile limit of territorial waters had existed for a long time, and had been recognized as a norm of international law by the majority of states, and therefore is a norm of general international law binding upon all states. These claims of the western powers, however, did not obtain even two-thirds of the votes at the said conferences, the socialist states and a significant number of Asian and African states opposing the assertions of the western powers. Two conclusions follow from this. First, the three-mile rule is not a norm of general international law. Second, and more generally, an international legal norm recognized by a majority of states is not recognized by states as being binding upon all other states.

The doctrine that customary norms of international law recognized as such by a significant number of states are binding upon all states not only has no basis in contemporary international law but also conceals a very great danger. This doctrine in essence justifies the attempts of a specific group of states to impose upon new states, socialist or newly emergent states of Asia and Africa, for example, certain customary norms which never have been accepted by the new states and which may be partially or wholly unacceptable to them. Of course, this tendency on the part of the large imperialist powers to dictate norms of international law to other states in contemporary conditions is doomed to failure, but at the same time such attempts undoubtedly may lead to serious international complications.

. . .

C. Treaty and Custom in Contemporary International Law

Taking these circumstances into account, the Soviet doctrine of international law, while by no means denying the important role of custom, regards the international treaty as the basic source of international law.

The predominant role of the international treaty in the development of contemporary international law also is emphasized in the international legal literature of other socialist countries.

. . .

Ch. 5. Subsidiary Processes of Forming Norms of International Law

C. Decisions of the International Court and of International Arbitration Tribunals

There are two opposing points of view in bourgeois legal literature on the significance of decisions of international courts and arbitral tribunals as sources of international law.

One viewpoint, expressed most frequently in "common law" countries, exaggerates the role of judgments of the International Court. . . .

. . .

This concept finds no support in the provisions of the Statute of the International Court. Article 38 of the Statute says that the Court shall be obliged to decide disputes submitted to it on the basis of international law. With regard to the specific sources to be applied by the Court, Article 38(1)(d) says that the Court shall apply "subject to the provisions of Article 59, judicial decisions and the teachings of the most highly qualified publicists of the various nations, as subsidiary means for the determination of rules of law." Article 59 of the Statute provides: "The decision of the Court has no binding force except between the parties and in respect of that particular case."

It by no means follows that decisions of the Court "are evidence of the existence of a rule of law." This concept, arising out of Anglo-American "common law" doctrine, is inapplicable to international law. To ascribe such a role to the International Court is to go beyond the provisions of its Statute.

. . .

If the Court regarded its decisions as an embodiment of international law and consequently as binding upon states, this would expressly contravene its Statute. But the International Court, as any other international organ, was created on the basis of agreement: the United Nations Charter and the Statute of the Court. The powers and functions of an international organ, particularly of the International Court, are defined by its Statute, and the Court can not pretend that greater significance is attached to its decisions than has been established by the Statute of the Court.

There is no basis for presupposing that the Statute of the International Court has been changed by customary means on the basis of the general agreement of United Nations members. . . .

What role do decisions of the International Court have on the broader plane of forming norms of international law? The International Court does not consist of representatives of states. It is composed of persons elected by representatives of states (respectively, in the Security Council and General Assembly of the United Nations), but who act as "independent judges" (Article 2 of the Statute). Decisions of the Court reflect the opinion of the members of the Court, who are specialists in international law. This brings decisions of the Court closer to doctrine, and not without reason does the Statute of the Court speak of judicial decisions and teachings of international law simultaneously.

. . .

. . . [W]hat has been said previously with regard to the formation and modification of norms of international law by way of custom is applicable to decisions of the International Court. As part of international practice, decisions of the International Court can lead to completion of the process of norm-formation by their being recognized by states and being consolidated in international law. Of course, only those decisions of the International Court for which judges representing the different social and legal systems have voted and which frequently are cited in the practice of relations among states actually have a chance of being consolidated.

. . .

Part III: The Legal Nature and Essence of Contemporary General International Law

Ch. 9: The Character and Essence of Contemporary General International Law

A. Bourgeois Science on the Social Nature of International Law.

Bourgeois legal science denies the class character of the law of capitalist society and conceals its exploitative essence. It seeks the social content of law in categories which it characterizes as common to all nations, to all mankind. The same picture is to be observed, naturally, in the bourgeois theory of international law.

The positivists, including proponents of the theory of agreement as the sole mode of creating a norm of international law (Triepel, Anzilotti, Perassi, and others), have refused to investigate the social nature of norms of international law, saying that this is not a matter for legal science.

During the period of imperialism, positivism in bourgeois legal science is degenerating into pure normativism. Thus, normativism in the form of Kelsen's "pure theory of law" is characterized by the complete separation of law from other social phenomena. According to Kelsen, as already has been pointed out, the sphere of law is exclusive, divorced from the true reality of the system. By this means, Kelsen avoids investigating the social content of law in the sphere of nonexistent, "pure" legal norms.

At the same time, there has been a definite digression from positivism in the bourgeois theory of law and a rebirth of natural law concepts during the period of imperialism, especially during the general crisis of capitalism after the Great October Socialist Revolution.

The representatives of contemporary natural law theories seek the social content of international law in the "idea of law," "justice," "reason," the "idea of order," "conscience," and so forth.

. . .

Bourgeois scholars usually explain the rebirth of natural law theories as a reaction to normativism, especially the normativism of the "Vienna school" carried to an extreme, which, they say, has proved to be completely inadequate for an explanation of international legal phenomena.

There is no doubt that the exposure of the defects of normativism and its scientific unfoundedness was one reason for the departure of bourgeois science from normativist positivism. But the principal reason, of course, is not this. There were serious social reasons which first and foremost also explain the digression of bourgeois jurists from positivism and the rebirth of natural law theories. Capitalism has turned into a stage of imperialism, which, as V. I. Lenin has pointed out, is characterized by an aspiration for domination, and not for freedom, a sharp aggravation of all the contradictions of capitalism. With the victory of the Great October Revolution there commenced the period of the general crisis of capitalism. The breaking away of a number of European and Asian states from the capitalism system, the creation of the mighty world system of socialism, is convincing evidence of the correctness of the conclusions of the Marxist-Leninist theory concerning the inevitable demise of capitalism and its replacement by a higher social system. After the October Revolution, the breakup of the colonial system of imperialism, now living out its last days, commenced.

Seeing the threat to its domination, the imperialistic bourgeoisie are striving to repudiate the legality which they have created, including also in the domain of international relations, are striving to grasp hold of any kind of desperate attempts to preserve their own dominance. The references to general, abstract categories of "natural law" are appearing under these conditions. As Professor G. Schwarzenberger correctly remarks, the primary role of the natural law theory is to "justify action that by positive law is illegal . . ." Is it not because, in particular, the natural law doctrine possesses, according to the apt expression of one of its proponents, Professor H. van Panhuys, an "obstinate vitality"?

If during the period of bourgeois revolutions natural law theories were part of the ideology of the bourgeoisie who fought against feudalism and played a progressive role, then under contemporary conditions the reactionary bourgeoisie refers to "natural law."

In proclaiming "natural law" to be the basis of "positive" law and part of international law in general, bourgeois jurists, willingly or not, give imperialism the opportunity to cite in justification of its aggressive actions abstract, admittedly different, interpretations of "natural law" principles derived from the "nature of man," from the idea of justice, and so forth. It is characteristic that in our time aggressive circles more often prefer to resort to references to "justice" which correspond to the interests of monopolies, and not to generally-recognized principles and norms of international law.

. . .

The inability of bourgeois legal science to expose the essence of law in general and of international law in particular is determined by its class character, by the limits of the world outlook of the ruling class. As we have seen, bourgeois legal science either refuses to investigate the social nature of law in general or does not seek it where it in fact exists. It is not in a position to escape from the vicious circle because of its class character. To expose the class nature of bourgeois law would mean that bourgeois science would oppose this law—that is, would cease to be bourgeois science.

. . . Marxist-Leninist theory, as a genuinely scientific theory, allows us to analyze the complex system of interconnections of social phenomena, to separate major links from minor, primary from secondary, to establish the dependence of the partial laws of development of individual social phenomena from the general laws of development of human society. . . .

Applied to international law, historical materialism makes it possible to ascertain its place in the system of social phenomena, to establish the dependence of its development on the basic laws of the development of human society, and to reveal the specific developmental laws of international law.

International law, just as law in general, is a category of the superstructure. Therefore, the general law of the development of human society having the closest relationship to international law is the law of the dependence of the social superstructure on the base; that is, the economic structure of society.

. . .

State and law, as part of the superstructure, change with a modification of the base, and the state and law correspond to each socio-economic formation. How does this law of the dependence of the superstructure on the base operate with regard to international law? In contemporary conditions there exist two fundamental bases: the capitalist and the new socialist base coming to replace it. And at the same time there exists a general international law common to the socialist and capitalist states.

The critics of Marxist-Leninist international legal theory attempt to assert in this connection that Marxism is in no position to explain the existence of contemporary general international law and that supposedly the application of Marxist theory to international law leads to the conclusion that two international laws exist.

Thus E. McWhinney, a Canadian professor, writes: "Since law is, in Marxist terms, a product of the market-place and each economic system thus gets the body of law appropriate to its state of economic development, how may two economic systems—capitalism and communism—yield identical bodies of international legal doctrine? Or, putting it in more traditional Marxist language, if international law, like national law, belongs to the superstructure and is determined uniquely by the base of production relationships, how can radically different (Capitalist and Communist) economic bases yield the same superstructure of international law?"

The trouble with these critics of the Marxist-Leninist theory of international law lies in the fact that, just as the many other critics of Marxism who existed before them, they attempt to represent Marxist-Leninist theory as a form of vulgar materialism. Their assertion that Marxist-Leninist theory supposedly considers any phenomenon of the superstructure as directly determined by the economic system of society, as representing a simple reflection of economic relations, is nothing other than the fruit of their own imagination.

What Engels said nearly eighty years ago on the subject of distortion of Marxism is wholly applicable to these critics. In a letter to J. Bloch of September 21–22, 1890, Engels wrote: " . . . According to the materialist conception of history, the *ultimately* determining element in history is the production and reproduction of real life. More than this neither Marx nor I have ever asserted. Hence if somebody twists this into saying that the economic element is the *only* determining one, he transforms that proposition into a meaningless, abstract, senseless phrase. The economic situation is the basis, but the various elements of the superstructure—political forms of the class struggle and its results, to wit: constitutions established by the victorious class after a successful battle, and so forth, juridical forms, and even the reflexes of all these actual struggles in the brains of the participants, political, juristic, and philosophical theories, religious views and their further development into systems of dogma—also exercise their influence upon the course of the historical struggles and in many cases preponderate in determining their *form*. There is an interaction of all these elements in which, amid all the endless host of accidents . . . the economic movement finally asserts itself as necessary. Otherwise the application of the theory to any period of history would be easier than the solution of a simple equation of the first degree."

The view has been expressed in Soviet international legal literature that two groups of international legal principles and norms exist which correspond to the two socioeconomic systems, but as we pointed out in 1956, this view was never shared by the majority of Soviet international lawyers.

In fact, only Marxist-Leninist theory allows us to explain scientifically both the existence of contemporary general international law and its social nature. The Marxist-Leninist theory of international law, in revealing the mechanism of its development on the basis of the general tenets of historical materialism, shows why, despite the existence of two diametrically opposed bases, general international law exists and why these bases influence it.

The emergence of a new social system and the existence of two opposed social systems does not mean that they are isolated from one another. The intensity of international economic as well as of other ties is increasing with the growth of the productive forces of human society and with the development on this basis of a world division of labor. The division of the world into two opposed social systems, the formation of two world markets, has not stopped this objective world process, although it has introduced much that is new into it.

This general societal law is the major objective premise of the peaceful coexistence of states with a diametrically opposed social system and of general international law. At the same time, it is necessary to emphasize that the very possibility of peaceful coexistence of the socialist and capitalist states immediately conditions the possibility of the existence of general international law, since the basic contradiction of contemporary international relations lies in the relations between states of the two systems.

In proving that at the basis of societal development lies the development of its productive forces, which at each stage of their development correspond to a specific economic structure of society, and in showing how in connection with the development of productive forces the international division of labor develops and international economic and other international ties expand, and that in contemporary society these ties acquire legal forms, Marxist-Leninist theory creates a firm basis for international legal theory.

The concept of the concordance of wills of states (or agreement) as a mode of creating norms of contemporary international law, widely accepted in the Soviet science of international law, helps to reveal on the basis of the general tenets of the Marxist-Leninist theory of law the specific mechanism of the influence of the economic structure of society upon the development of international law—that is, the mechanism of the influence of the two bases upon contemporary international law.

As already has been pointed out, norms of contemporary international law are created and changed on the basis of agreement between states. This agreement embraces the concordant wills of states relating to the content of a particular rule of conduct and to its being recognized as a norm of international law.

Marxist-Leninist theory reveals the class content of the will of a state, showing that this will in a society with antagonistic classes is the will of the economically and politically ruling class in the particular society, and under socialism the will of the entire people led by the working class.

The content of the will of a state—that is, its international legal position—is formed under the influence of the entire aggregate of the conditions of the existence of the ruling class in a state, and under socialism, of the entire people. The economic structure of society is the primary base which defines in the final analysis the international legal position of a state in its primary features.

In reality, the economic structure determines the class nature of a state, the fundamental principles of its internal and foreign policy, the major features of its national law, and all other parts of the superstructure. This general societal law is the main societal law. But this does not mean that it is possible to "directly infer" the international legal position of a particular state from the economic structure of society.

Forming an international legal position, that is, the content of the will of a state, is a complex process in which the economic structure of society and its societal laws exert a determinative influence. Various parts of the superstructure, however, also exert influence upon the formation of the international legal position of a state: ideology, national law, international legal doctrine, and so forth. One can not reduce to a basic societal law nor "infer" the will of a state or the will of its ruling class in each individual instance from the economic structure of society without taking other influences into account. At the same time, it is possible to gain an understanding of this process only by proceeding from the societal laws of the co-relation of base and superstructure.

The economic structure of human society in our days is characterized by the existence of two opposed world economic systems whose development occurs pursuant to directly opposed laws. Moreover, there are developing countries whose economic system is characterized by a complex intertwining of elements of different socio-economic entities. All these bases exert, ultimately through the wills of states, a determining influence on the development of international law.

At the same time, international economic relations, which are a basis category and whose influence on international law is a basis influence, exert influence on international law. The view has been repeatedly expressed in Soviet international legal literature that international economic relations are the basis of international law. According to this view, international economic relations, as a secondary (basis), are determined by the fundamental bases but are themselves the basis of international law. This construction implies that the influence of the fundamental bases is effectuated only through international economic relations. An analysis of practice shows, however, that despite the growing weight of international economic relations in the life of society and in international relations, the decisive basis influence in forming the international legal position of states is the direct influence of the fundamental bases and the categories of the superstructure resting on these bases. Nonetheless, the role of the influence of international economic relations is growing in the overall amount of basis influences on international law.

Thus, the influence of the economic structure of society and its societal laws affects the process of creating norms of international law through the will of a state, since the content of this will basically is determined by the economic conditions of the existence of the ruling class in a given state. The economic structure of society exerts a decisive influence in the process of creating norms of international law upon the wills of states not only through "direct action" but also through other categories of the superstructure, whose operation in general can not go beyond the limits determined by the economic structure of society.

. . .

NOTE ON REALIST AND RELATED PERSPECTIVES

Within the Western legal community, the intellectual premises of the classical system have been sharply challenged from various directions. For the American law student, it is useful to think of some of these critiques as an extension to the international scene of the movement in our domestic legal thought known as legal realism, a movement formed by an influential group of judges, lawyers and academicians during the 1920's and 1930's. The influence of legal realism (whose international expressions are as varied as its domestic) is particularly felt in the writings on international law of American authors. But a "realist" spirit permeates the writings of foreign scholars as well, such as Charles de Visscher in his Theory and Reality in Public International Law (Corbett Trans. 1957).

The following passage from Kaplan and Katzenbach, The Political Foundations of International Law 73–75 (1961), suggests the relationship between legal realism and some contemporary critiques of international law.

> Three related features of law-government are worth special mention for they have been transferred into the in-

ternational arena by a substantial number of writers. All are associated with the intellectual *potpourri* which is usually lumped together as "legal realism" and is predominantly an American view. First, the notion that law is always an expression of "public policy," and therefore doctrine can be evaluated in terms of its contributions to goal values. Although such evaluation is normally the job of legislatures, it is also appropriate for judges to make evaluations within the areas of choice left open to them. Both judges and legislators should, therefore, according to this view, supplement doctrine with data from outside the formal system to assist in an informed policy determination. . . .

Second, to analyze law institutions in terms of achievement, judges or legislators must posit preferences about the kind of social structure they feel obligated by their role in society to support, and must then make competing choices about values. . . .

Third, the new jurisprudence saw law as a process rather than a body of formal rules. The lawyers of [the] new school were quick to see and appreciate the limitations of doctrine (often overstating them) and the need for new institutional arrangements, conceived in less formal terms, to cope with new governmental responsibilities they posited as proper. . . . [I]t is no exaggeration to say that all lawyers, whatever their jurisprudential label (if any), have been affected by these developments; that all are more sceptical of doctrine and doctrinal solutions; that few feel so intensely the importance of doctrinal consistency when it seems to lead to undesirable results. The old adage of the late nineteenth century that "hard cases make good law" would be subscribed to by relatively few today. By losing its exclusive concern with legal logic and the problems of adjudication and by taking a broader view of the legal process, the legal process has moved much closer to policy and thus to politics, ethics, morals, and justice.

Realism is less a theory than an approach that insists that processes of law-government cannot accurately be described or analyzed except in their appropriate contextual framework. It has, therefore, the effect of broadening the focus of scholarly attention by seeking to clarify the goals sought, the methods whereby they can be achieved, and assumptions about human and institutional behavior. The major objection of realists to positivism as developed by Austin and his followers was simply that courts did not behave and could not behave in accordance with its theory, and that it was probably a good thing that they did not. It is this effort to re-examine assumptions against experience and knowledge about individual and group behaviour that makes realism "realistic." But realism does not yet offer a definitive theory to replace those it has questioned.

We emphasize realism not because it is an international movement (though an argument could be made for this proposition) but because it is symptomatic of a prevalent scepticism and anxiety. As a result of the rapid political and social change of the last two generations, both domestically and internationally, we are still in the process of reexamination and re-evaluation of our ideas about social and political institutions generally. . . .

Note that such an approach to international law, or indeed to law in general, tends to stress process rather than legal doctrine. That process will be broadly defined, to embrace not simply formal legal institutions such as courts but also the broader political processes within which legal principles are shaped. Thus a "realist" might conceive of international law not as a body of rules or set of formal institutions, but rather as a complex process, involving national and international decision-makers, for the formulation, application and revision of norms that are intended to respond to needs of the international community. (Recall the comments of McDougal at p. 276, supra.)

This conception is particularly helpful for the understanding of international law. Whatever the peril of stress upon the formal structures of rules and syllogistic reasoning ("rule formalism") as a perspective upon national legal systems, that peril becomes far greater within the more fragile and chaotic international environment. More fragmented on many issues than bound together in community, with weak institutional structures for the negotiation or "enactment" or other elaboration of norms, with widely disparate interests and cultures, international society yields a form of legal order less autonomous and coherent than that of developed national legal systems. Hence consideration of the rules of international law, divorced from consideration of their political environment and of the processes through which they are developed, runs a greater risk on the international scene of producing a seriously distorted view of the nature of law. Thus realism—in its sociological manifestations—usefully directed attention to the relationship between existing principles or rules and the political, economic or social conditions of the community to which they were relevant.

As a jurisprudential movement with both national and international expressions, realism led to several and to some extent inconsistent or even polar trends in legal thought. Some thinkers moved past the essentially negative function of exposing fallacies and exploding myths, to the study of legal problems and ordering in the light of the values and purposes to be realized by the legal system. Others moved towards a deep cynicism about law, stressing its character as mere technique and its susceptibility to manipulation to achieve any purpose. We turn now to the first trend noted.

Many among a generation of post-realists sought to infuse their concept of law with a sense of purpose. We have seen an illustration of such thought in the jurisprudence of Professors Hart and Sacks (pp. 182 and 186, supra), with its stress upon the function of law to facilitate welfare-maximization. The approach of the I.C.J. in the Fisheries Case, p. 262, supra, offers an international analogy. The stress upon law as a means of achieving social purposes, of maximizing whatever values may be deemed paramount or desirable, is often accompanied by a policy-oriented analysis of legal problems, which draws upon methodology and disciplines such as economics or decision-theory, and which is meant to suggest desirable changes. Of course it has proved more difficult for theorists (as for statesmen and judges) to identify shared purposes or values which the legal system should seek to maximize on the international rather than domestic scene.

One of the most ambitious and influential of contemporary efforts to overcome these problems is that undertaken by Professor Myres McDougal. In numerous writings on international law (many cooperatively with, and drawing upon the conceptual framework developed by, Professor Harold Lasswell), he has developed a "policy-oriented jurisprudence" incorporating a set of "values of a public order of human dignity." The McDougal-Lasswell writings view law essentially as a form of policy, or as an instrument to realize community policies. Law is seen in terms of value articulation and distribution. The effort of these theorists is to view law wholly and contextually, taking into account all factors bearing upon authoritative decision-making. Law is integrated into a more complex conception of power processes as one form of decision-making. Indeed, a substantial criticism made of the McDougal-Lasswell framework is that it blurs all lines between law, politics, policy, morals and so on—so that one is left with little sense of the distinctive character or influence of legal process or structure in relation to other social processes or structures.

The McDougal-Lasswell system amounts to a complex, formal and elaborate prescriptive framework to permit optimum decision-making—namely, decision-making which maximizes desired values. Those values are meant to represent community or inclusive values, rather than values perceived from any one nation's distinctive perspective. The values identified have been drawn upon by a large number of authors to elaborate similar conceptual frameworks for their own studies. But they have not found widespread assent, and many scholars find them too vague and abstract to be helpful or, when they are given specific content, to be too oriented towards American interests and preferences.[68]

Another outgrowth of legal realism to which we referred has been a deeply cynical view of international law as a tool used when convenient to mask naked power. In the view of such critics, international law enters into decision-making by national officials principally as post-hoc rationalization of conduct, as a rhetorical device to lend legitimacy to conduct, and so on. It is manipulated by rather than an influence upon decision-makers to maximize whatever outcomes

68. Excerpts from an article in which McDougal and a co-author, Bebr, describe and apply their value system appear at p. 402, infra. For evaluation of McDougal's contribution to international-law theory, see Falk, Adequacy of Contemporary Theories of International Law, 50 Va.L.Rev. 231 (1964), and Note, The Lasswell-McDougal Enterprise: Toward a World Public Order of Human Dignity, 14 Va.J.Int.L. 535 (1974).

they may seek.[69] Others assert that the effort to introduce "legal" analysis into diplomacy or the conduct of foreign relations has led to harmful rigidities and distortions of national interest.

A critical view of *some* of these "negative" trends of realist analysis of international law is taken in the following comments of a leading scholar of international relations: Hoffmann, The Study of International Law and the Theory of International Relations, 1963 Proc. Am.Soc.Int.L. 26, 32–34:

> . . . . One does not at all weaken respect for law or an appreciation of the distinctive features of law if one tries to clarify and to understand the social and political underpinnings of the legal order.
>
> However, international lawyers would have many reasons for complaining if social scientists came to believe that a sociology of law or a policy science of law takes care of everything. After one has explained the origins, political implications and effects of a rule, one has not yet disposed of the rule itself. If the social scientist can broaden the horizons of the lawyer, the lawyer's domain remains indispensable to the social scientist.
>
> 1. All legal norms are rules prescribed *for* social conduct; when they are obeyed or enforced they become part *of* social conduct. The task of social science consists at least of studying how people actually behave; it ought to consist also of studying how people think they should behave, and what they try to institute and legislate so as to carry out their views. A social science which, under the name of behaviorism or what not, would neglect *law as a form of social control* would be poor indeed.
>
> (a) This is not to say that the social scientist must be concerned with all aspects of law. The political scientist realizes that much in the legal system is of no political significance, either because of its subject matter or because, although the subject matter (say, a constitution) is highly relevant, political realities do not at all conform to the legal prescriptions. Conversely, much of political life has nothing to do with law, being concerned with "strategies" and "policies" that do not take the form of rules. However, a great deal of political activity has either lawmaking (or law-amending, or law-destroying) purposes, or legal consequences; and a great deal of legal activity has political significance. Hence the idea of a continuum: legal decision-making is *a* form of policy.
>
> (b) This is as true of international law as it is of domestic law. The specialist of international relations who is trying to make sense out of the chaos of data, variables, hypotheses, et cetera, that diplomatic history, international economics, cultural anthropology, et cetera, provide him with, and who uses the concept of system in order to do so, will realize that international law gives a kind of cast or shape to his inquiry. A study of the substance of the norms

69. For two recent studies bearing upon these arguments, see Henkin, How Nations Behave (1968), and Chayes, The Cuban Missile Crisis (1974).

that are both valid and efficient at a given time will tell him a great deal about the restraints on, and the scope of, the contest among states, about the nature and solidity of the zone of predictability or comity that lies outside the contest, in other words about the degree to which the system resembles or differs from the Hobbesian model of a war of all against all. Since every Power wants to turn its interests, ideas and gains into law, a study of the "legal strategies" of the various units, i. e., of what kinds of norms they try to promote, and through what techniques, may be as fruitful for the political scientist as a study of more purely diplomatic, military or economic strategies.

2. It is however essential for the social scientist to understand that law is not merely a policy among others in the hands of statesmen, and that it is a tool with very *special characteristics and rôles:* the social scientist who forgets this and advises the Prince accordingly will debase the instrument and mislead the Prince.

(a) Law is distinguished from other political instruments by certain formal features: there is a certain solemnity to its establishment, i. e., it has to be elaborated in a certain way.

(b) More significantly, the legal order, even in international affairs, has a life and logic of its own: there are courts and legal experts who apply standards of interpretation often thoroughly divorced from the underlying political and social factors. . . . Law may be an instrument of policy, but it is one which has an "artificial reason." Consequently, not every legal norm can be traced back to political or social realities: a fact which should, in turn, put a sense of perspective and modesty into the minds of political sociologists of law.

(c) Most important is the fact that law has a distinct solemnity of effects: it is a normative instrument that creates rights and duties. Consequently it has a function that is both symbolic and conservative; it enshrines, elevates, consecrates the interests or ideas it embodies. We understand, thus, why law is an important stake in the contests of nations. What makes international law so special a tool for states is this solemnity of effects, rather than the fact that its norms express common interests; for this is far too simple: some legal instruments such as peace treaties reflect merely the temporary, forced convergence of deeply antagonistic policies. A situation of dependence or of superiority that is just a fact of life can be reversed through political action, but once it is solemnly cast in legal form, the risks of action designed to change the situation are much higher: law is a form of policy that changes the stakes, and often "escalates" the intensity, of political contests; it is a constraint comparable to force in its effects. To the extent to which the study of international relations is a "strategy of conflict," it must therefore both include the strategy of law-making and law-changing, and recognize its distinctive features. A better understanding of the symbolic "tripwire" nature of law and of its constraining quality would make political scientists realize that in a revolutionary world, the advocacy of *informal* restraints on the use of force may be much wiser than the advocacy of explicit agreements. For the unstable conditions and intense political competition that prevail in the world would condemn such covenants to shakiness, but their very solemnity could lead to formidable crises in case of violations or evasions: the breakdown of an informal restraint carries fewer risks than that of a solemn treaty.

NOTE AND QUESTIONS ON CONCEPTS OF NATIONAL AND INTERNATIONAL LAW

Although later chapters should deepen the student's perceptions about these questions, we here consider some comparisons between national and international law (legal process, legal system). We do so through brief observations interspersed with questions, both observations and questions assuming a familiarity with the text at pp. 177–191, supra.

(1) One can ask—and many have—whether so-called "international law" constitutes "law" at all. The answer will depend upon the conception of law held. Surely a rigorous adherence to a command theory of law, growing out of Hobbesian positivism and conceptions of sovereignty, would be least conducive to an affirmative answer. After all, in the international community power is diffused horizontally among states. There are no global institutions with effective and accepted authority to develop, apply and enforce legal norms. In a literal sense, there is no command of a sovereign backed by the threat of sanctions against violators.

A different starting point leads to a different answer. If we conceive of law as a process for the articulation and maximization of values, and as an instrumental technique for realizing welfare aims of those "subject" to it, then its domestic and international manifestations are on the same continuum. Formal attributes of national and international legal systems will differ, but the two categories will share a basic character and function.

(*a*) "Whatever the concept of law invoked, it is pointless to ask abstractly whether there is an international law. One must explore particular fields of 'international law' and form a judgment as to each. Recognition of the authority or indeed existence of international norms and compliance with them will vary, depending upon whether one is talking of diplomatic immunity, expropriation, or regulation of the use of force." Do you agree? Are the asserted distinctions in state attitudes and compliance among these fields relevant to the conclusion whether there is an international "law"?

(*b*) "International law seeks to respond to the same problem as does national law and hence bears a fundamental similarity to it. It is the Hobbesian problem, the basic need for maintaining order and curbing violence. Most of international law doctrine can be understood as responding to this need, however different from national law that response may be." Comment.

(*c*) "The command theory of law is as irrelevant to an understanding of domestic law as it is to international. Only a small portion of our national legal system seeks to compel obedience to mandatory norms by threat of sanctions. Most law is facilitative, enabling parties to realize their desires by drawing upon it (as with contract law). And so with international law, which stresses customary and treaty law, two facilitative frameworks through which the subjects of international law (states) 'make' the norms by which they are to be bound." Do you agree?

(*d*) Based on the topics thus far covered in this book, would you agree with the assertion that international law—since it lacks the backing of the sheriff or policeman under national law—is without effective sanctions that enter into expectations of states and that tend to induce compliance? If you do not agree, what types of sanctions for violations of international norms would you identify within the international legal-political system? Are they administered centrally? Are they necessarily "legal" in character? Are the most significant sanctions against violations of national law always centrally and officially administered and "legal" in character?

(2) A threshold difficulty encountered by the student of Anglo-American law who examines international law is the less "autonomous" character of that latter body of law. Whatever the teachings of other disciplines and the contributions of legal realism and its progeny, our conception of domestic law remains dominated by courts. We perceive the decisions of courts as the essence of law. And courts, whatever the varied influences upon their decisions, possess the aura of independence. They draw dominantly upon the legal tradition that is of their own creation. Moreover, their jurisdiction is compulsory, their decisions are in the vast majority of cases honored, and their decrees can be coercively enforced.

We speak domestically of "legal" thought or reasoning, of the structure of "legal argument." Whatever the ambiguities in these concepts—and they are many—they imply again a certain autonomous character to "law," as distinct from "politics" or "economics" or any other phase of social life. Indeed, such attributes of law that possess some measure of autonomy from other forms of social ordering figure at the core of the concept of the Rule of Law, of "law" as "fences" that separate private parties from each other and all such parties from government (pp. 181–182, supra). Law stands symbolically apart from, even in some measure "above", the play of political forces and economic interests.

Thus, while aware of the difficult character of the distinction, we continue to draw one between "law" and "politics". Surely the final products of legislatures are "law", just as are the decisions of courts. But the process yielding legislation we think of as quintessentially "political"—group pluralism, elections, interest bargaining and accomodation, log-rolling and so on. We do not talk of the "legal reasoning" of legislatures, but of that of courts (or of other bodies that "apply" or "develop" law in non-legislative settings, such as administrative agencies). As we tend to fragment learning, the organization or processes of legislatures is for the political sociologist or theorist to examine. The academic lawyer enters the scene at the moment of enactment (although the academic and the courts will look into the legislative process for such matters as "legislative history" to divine "legislative purpose").

Similar observations could be made about contract. A vast amount of "law" is made through private-party contracts, in the sense that parties will be bound to comply with their undertakings (or make good in damages) within contract law's framework. But again the legal scholar is rarely concerned with the "process" of contract negotiation, with exploration of the economic or other interests and circumstances which influence the outcomes of contract bargains. Again (unless involved in drafting) his attention tends to fasten at the final product, at the document which then must be viewed in the light of contract-law norms.

Of course we have overstated these distinctions, the better to illustrate their continuing vitality. Since the writings of Holmes, sociological jurisprudence, legal realism and its progeny, and policy science, we have become sensitive to the blurring of these lines within a more inclusive and illuminating view of the legal process. We have moved far from conceptions of legal formality and autonomy to perceptions of the interpenetration of law and politics and economics and culture. We have moved some (small) way towards a contextual study of our domestic legal system, stressing the influences of history, of political and socio-economic organization, and of philosophical and psychological postulates that underlie the entire legal-political system.

Such trends in jurisprudence and legal thought are reinforced by changes in social and political context. The 20th Century movement towards a more regulated and managed economy, as well as towards minimum welfare provision in our developing version of welfare statism, has further blurred the boundaries between law and politics or economics. We see more clearly the policy and political foundations to law, the complex social processes out of which the legal system develops and which that system seeks to order or change.

(*a*) "The assertion that our domestic law is more autonomous of politics or economic interests than international law is misleading. Since our courts and legislatures develop doctrinal structures of some complexity and continuity, and since those structures are generally viewed as legitimate and as authoritative guides to conduct, we tend to fasten on doctrinal manipulation or legal reasoning and thus to lose sight of the basic philosophical, political and economic premises or values that inform the entire doctrinal structure. In the international arena, without comparable courts or legislatures, politics is simply closer to the surface. There is no complex doctrinal or institutional structure within which basic political values and choices can be submerged and concealed." Do you agree, in part or whole?

(*b*) "It is no wonder that many observers deny the existence of an international 'law'. They are dominated by domestic notions of legislative and judicial elaboration of law. They ignore the fact that a vast amount of domestic law is made in a decentralized manner by private parties through contract. But that is precisely the proper starting point towards an understanding of international law. Both treaty and custom (at least within a positivist conception) are within an explicit or implicit contract framework. These are the basic legal-political processes. Of course they direct our attention more forcefully than does national law to interests and values of the parties involved, for we are forced to consider the reasons why states moved (often in an ad hoc manner) towards customary or treaty rules of law." Comment.

(3) For utilitarian (teleological) conceptions of law, the "purpose" to be achieved through legal ordering may be stated as broadly as "welfare maximization", with all the ambiguity and variable content of that phrase. It may refer to the maximization of the value of production of goods and services (similar to the utilitarian justification for market ordering and efficiency) or to other values (as in the Lasswell-McDougal system, supra) such as dignity or respect.

Whatever the values to be maximized, consider the distinctions between developing a coherent framework for maximization, to which law should be instrumentally responsive, within a national and international environment. Within a country such as the United States, the values or interests to which legal ordering is responsive are shaped by the political (electoral), legislative and judicial processes, as well of course as by broader aspects of our culture. There is a sense shared by courts and legislatures of a national political tradition, and of a dominant national culture, however much they may be in transition or subjected to challenge by groups within the society. Part of that legal culture in the United States consists of what Hart and Sacks (p. 182, supra) referred to as the principle of institutional settlement.

Consider the markedly different problems posed for decisionmakers in an international environment. Vast disparities exist in cultural traditions, wealth, aspirations and potential. There is, to be sure, a basic interdependence, never more vividly perceived than during a period of potentially destructive war for all. But at less draconian levels, how does one define the relevant community or the content of the welfare to be maximized within that community? Common interests and values may be difficult to identify in a sufficiently concrete manner to permit the design of normative or institutional structures that serve ends of welfare-maximization. Recall, for example, Question (4), p. 241, supra, about the Barcelona Traction Case, and Question (2), p. 278, supra, about the Fisheries Case.

Moreover, problems of the distribution of welfare among nations —ultimate political problems in national societies as individuals or groups compete for larger shares of the social pie—become even more explicit in the law-making processes among nations. Some principles may be "neutral", in the sense that they serve equally well the interests of all nations. Many, however, will disproportionately benefit some nations, and perhaps prejudice others.

(4) It is instructive to see how Tunkin, as a representative of Soviet legal theory, views aspects of the Western liberal-state legal tradition and international law. He seeks to come to terms with these phenomena from two perspectives: those of the contemporary political situation between the socialist and capitalist worlds, and of Marxist legal-political theory. Consider the following questions:

(*a*) What underlying consistency, if any, do you find in Tunkin's view of the nature of custom, of the effect of decisions of international tribunals, and of the natural-law tradition in liberal societies?

(*b*) How convincing do you find Tunkin's theoretical justification for the existence of international law between socialist and capitalist countries, against the background of the Marxist-oriented conception of law that was sketched at pp. 183–184, supra?

Chapter IV

DEVELOPMENT OF AN INTERNATIONAL MINIMUM STANDARD: THE INTERNATIONAL LEGAL PROCESS ILLUSTRATED

A. INTRODUCTORY NOTIONS

The development of the law of state responsibility for injuries to aliens exemplifies historical trends described in Part F of the preceding chapter. At the same time, that field of international law captures most aspects of the international legal process which Chapter III portrayed through illustrations drawn from many fields. State practice, custom, general principles of law or justice, bilateral and multilateral treaties, draft conventions, resolutions of international organizations, hortatory and scholarly writings of lawyers or moral philosophers or statesmen—all figure among the complex and interacting forces which have given shape to the several branches of this field. We stress two such branches, the protection of human rights and property rights.

The growth of the law of state responsibility reflected the more intense identification of the individual (or later, the corporation) with his country that accompanied the nationalistic trends of the 18th to early 20th centuries. That growth would not have taken place but for Western colonialism and economic imperialism which reached their zenith during this period. Transnational business operations centered in Europe, and later in the United States as well, penetrated Asia, Africa and Latin America. Thus security of the person and property of a national inevitably became a concern of his government. That concern manifested itself in the vigorous assertion of diplomatic protection and in the enhanced activity of arbitral tribunals. Often the arbitrations occurred under the pressure of actual or threatened military force by the aggrieved nations, particularly in Latin America.

To be sure, alien individuals or corporations generally turned first, for vindication of the rights which they asserted to be part of international law, to the domestic law and legal-political processes of the nations in which they were living, investing or transacting business. But their rights and duties varied markedly under the legal and political cultures of such nations, and often fell below a minimum international standard for the treatment of aliens which the developed Western countries asserted to be enshrined within international law. The very diversity of national traditions and laws was at once the occasion for and the source of the difficulty in defining that minimum standard.

If the growth of the law of state responsibility for injuries to aliens and of the minimum standard initially reflected the economic and political development of Western Europe and the United States, its more recent development (or, in part disintegration) illustrates the erosion of a consensus earlier achieved and the vexing problems of reaching new common understandings. The different perspectives from which countries of the less developed and socialist worlds view these questions are one source of such problems.[1] Themes of substantive justice—to borrow the concept employed by Max Weber to describe changes within the liberal societies of the industrialized West—achieve ever greater prominence. These claims for equal dignity or respect among nations, and for redistribution of wealth and power to weaker and less developed nations, are prominent.

Thus recent trends in the law of state responsibility illustrate the workings of the international legal process in a particularly thorny field. The variety of materials in this chapter reveal not only the political and economic obstacles to resolution of these problems through customary or conventional international law, but also much about the diverse nature of the participants in the development of international norms.

In each of the topics explored below, one can observe the existence of a more or less general consensus as of the early 20th century, its breakdown under the pressure of subsequent events, and the effort since World War II to achieve a new one. A statement in an arbitral proceeding in 1924 by Max Huber, a Swiss national and a Judge of the Permanent Court of International Justice, expresses some basic principles of the earlier consensus.[2]

> . . . It is true that the large majority of writers have a marked tendency to limit the responsibility of the State. But their theories often have political inspiration and represent a natural reaction against unjustified interventions in the affairs of certain nations . . .. On the other hand, there is a very developed jurisprudence of numerous mixed arbitral commissions on the subject of responsibility of States for damage suffered by aliens. . . .
>
> It is recognized that all law has the purpose of assuring the coexistence of interests worthy of legal protection. That is also without doubt true of international law. The conflicting interests with respect to the problem of compensation of aliens are, on the one hand, the interest of a State in exercising its public power in its own territory without

1. In addition to Part F of Chapter III, the Notes at pp. 81 and 84, supra, and at p. 1179, infra, describe varying attitudes towards foreign presence, particularly foreign investment.

2. Judge Huber delivered these remarks in his role as a Reporter (in effect, arbitrator) under a *compromis* of May 29, 1923 between Great Britain and Spain submitting to arbitration certain disputes involving claims of British subjects against Spanish authorities for alleged mistreatment of their person or property in the Spanish zone of Morocco. The excerpts (translated from French) are from Huber's Report of October 3, 1924, on the Responsibilities of the State in the Situations Covered by the British Claims, British Claims in the Spanish Zone of Morocco, 2 U.N.R.I.A.A. 615, 639.

interference or control of any nature by foreign States and, on the other hand, the interest of the State in seeing the rights of its nationals established in foreign countries respected and well protected. . . . By examining the different situations described in the [arbitral *compromis* referred to in fn. 2] and by considering the relative importance of the conflicting interests in question, one should be able to find a ground on which just and equitable conclusions could be reached, conclusions which would be borne out by precedents from international jurisprudence. . .

Three principles are hardly debatable: . . .

(2) In general, a person established in a foreign country is subject to the territorial legislation for the protection of his person and his property, under the same conditions as nationals of that country.

(3) A State whose national established in another State is deprived of his rights has a right to intervene *if the injury constitutes a violation of international law.* . . .

. . . The territorial character of sovereignty is so essential a trait of contemporary public law that foreign intervention in relationships between a territorial State and individuals subject to its sovereignty can be allowed only in extraordinary cases. . . .

On the other hand, it is undeniable that at a certain point the interest of a State in being able to protect its nationals and their property takes precedence over respect for national sovereignty, and that even in the absence of treaty obligations. This right of intervention has been claimed by all States; only its limits are under discussion. By denying this right, one would arrive at intolerable results: international law would become helpless in the face of injustices tantamount to the negation of human personality, for that is the subject which every denial of justice touches.

. . . The fact that it is an alien who is the victim of a common-law offence, for example of a theft or of an act of pillage, does not make the event one of international concern; the same applies if penal proceedings which follow fail, or if an action in restitution or for damages and interest does not lead to a satisfactory result. No police or other administration of justice is perfect, and it is doubtless necessary to accept, even in the best administered countries, a considerable margin of tolerance. However, the restrictions thus placed on the right of a State to intervene to protect its nationals assume that the general security in the country of residence does not fall below a certain standard, and that legal protection does not become purely illusory.

. . .

Note how Judge Huber describes the conflicting interests of the host and protecting states: territorial sovereignty, and compliance by all states with certain principles about the treatment of aliens. A broader inquiry would examine the interests not only of the disputant states, but also of the alien and of the international community as a whole. Note also the reference in the last quoted sentence to a "certain standard" below which a state's treatment of an alien must not fall, even if its own citizens do not benefit from that standard. To what materials would diplomats or arbitrators turn for help in defining the content of such a standard? Is it the same for arbitrations between Great Britain and Spain, Great Britain and Venezuela, Venezuela and Pakistan? Such questions are at the core of the disputes described below.

B. PROTECTION OF THE PERSON

The following arbitration arose out of the protracted political unrest in Venezuela around 1900, a period which witnessed numerous and substantial injuries to the person and property of aliens. The political situation also caused default upon Venezuelan public debts to aliens. Under the leadership of Great Britain and Germany, the European countries whose nationals were involved took action against the regime of President Castro, including a naval blockade and bombardments. The pressure of an excited American public opinion and President Theodore Roosevelt's invocation of the Monroe Doctrine helped to persuade the European powers to consent to arbitration, although Roosevelt's assertion that he presented Germany with a 24-hour ultimatum is not now credited by historians. Perkins, A History of the Monroe Doctrine 214–27 (Rev. ed. 1955).

This arbitration was under a Protocol of February 13, 1903, between Italy and Venezuela, one of several similar contemporaneous agreements. It was supplemented by a Protocol of May 7, 1903, stating in part that the Arbitral Commission's decisions "shall be based upon absolute equity, without regard to objections of a technical nature or of the provisions of local legislation."

BOFFOLO CASE

Italian-Venezuelan Mixed Claims Commission, 1903.
Under Protocol of February 13, 1903, as supplemented by Protocol of May 7, 1903.
Ralston (ed.), Venezuelan Arbitrations of 1903, at 696; 10 U.N.R.I.A.A. 528.

RALSTON, *Umpire:*

The above case has been referred to the umpire on disagreement between the honorable Commissioners for Italy and Venezuela.

It appears that Gennaro Boffolo, an Italian subject, reached Venezuela in June, 1898, and in the spring of 1900 was a householder in Caracas and the publisher of an Italian weekly newspaper entitled "Il Commercio Italo-Venezuolano." In the issue of April 1, 1900, appeared an article somewhat critical of the local minor judiciary, and also referring, but in an unimportant manner, to the President. Another article recommended the reading of El Obrero, a socialistic paper. Three days later (April 4) the Gaceta Oficial contained a decree directing Boffolo's expulsion . . . .

Immediately thereafter, or perhaps simultaneously, Boffolo was, as it is said, "summarily" arrested, transported by third-class ticket to Curaçao, but, through the intervention of the royal Italian legation, allowed to return about a month later.

It is further said, but no proof is offered, that during his absence his house was invaded and plundered, and articles taken belonging to others, the value of which he was compelled to reimburse, and that the claimant was subjected to police persecution, threatened with another arrest, and finally left Venezuela.

That a general power to expel foreigners, at least for cause, exists in governments can not be doubted. (See Hollander case in U. S. Foreign Relations for 1895, p. 775, and also see p. 801, same volume, citations to be found in sec. 206, vol. 2, Wharton's International Law Digest, and other citations hereinafter given.)

But it will be borne in mind that there may be a broad difference between the right to exercise a power and the rightful exercise of that power. Let us illustrate. In the Hollander case (cited above) the Government of Guatemala contended:

> The Government was not under obligation to allow him more or less time to get out of the country, nor to accommodate him in any way. All the practices of jurisprudence, supposing them to be certain and indisputable, fall down before a law clear that comes immediately from the sovereignty of a nation.

To this Secretary Olney very forcibly replied:

> The logical result of that proposition is, that whatever a state by legal formula wills to do, it may do; and that international obligations are annulled, not infringed, by legalized administrative action in contravention of those obligations. . . . I construe the language used to mean that, as a rule of international law, the right of expulsion is absolute and inherent in the sovereignty of a State, and that no other State can question the exercise of this right nor the manner of exercising it. . . . The modern theory and the practice of Christian nations is believed to be founded on the principle that the expulsion of a foreigner is justifiable only when his presence is detrimental to the welfare of the State, and that when expulsion is resorted to as an extreme police measure, it is to be accomplished with due regard to the convenience and the personal and property interests of the person expelled.

We may cite Rolin-Jaequemyns, who reported on the subject to the Institute of International Law in 1888 (Revue de Droit International, Vol. XX, p. 498), and after admitting the right of expulsion said:

> [. . . In his character as a human being he has the right not to be the object of useless severity and not to have his interests unjustly injured. In his character as a citizen of another country he can resort, against this severity or these depredations, to his sovereign's protection. . . . (Translation from French)]

Calvo (Dictionnaire du Droit International), title, "Expulsion," says:

> But when a government expels a foreigner without cause and in a harsh, inconsiderate manner (avec des formes blessantes), the State of which the foreigner is a citizen has

> a right to base a claim upon this violation of international law and to demand adequate satisfaction. . . .

In the recent Ben Tillet affair between England and Belgium, the arbitrator, M. Arthur Desjardins, of France, in his sentence examined thoroughly the reasons for the expulsion of Tillet (as we shall do hereafter in this case), and also as to the treatment accorded him in connection therewith, and maintained the right of Belgium to expel under the circumstances, and, as well, justified the manner in which Tillet was treated by Belgium. (Journal du Droit International Privé, Vol. 26 (1899), p. 203.) . . . .

Woolsey says (International Law, sec. 63, p. 85):

> 6. No state in peace can exclude the properly documented subjects of another friendly state, or send them away after they have been once admitted, without definite reasons, which must be submitted to the foreign government concerned.

In the opinion of the umpire it may be fairly deduced from the foregoing that—

1. A state possesses the general right of expulsion; but

2. Expulsion should only be resorted to in extreme instances and must be accomplished in the manner least injurious to the person affected.

Must explanation of reasons and justification of conduct be made to an arbitral tribunal when the occasion arises? The question is answered in Moore's Digest.

Orazio de Attellis, a naturalized American citizen, entered Mexico in 1833, and on June 24, 1835, the President issued an order for his expulsion on the ground that he had—

> occupied himself again (he had been expelled before becoming an American citizen) in the publication of a periodical in which some productions appear which tend to ridicule the nation and to plunge it into anarchy.

What the productions were and what was their offensive feature was not disclosed. The claimant was so expelled under circumstances of especial hardship. The American Commissioners contended that the expulsion was causeless, inspired by enmity, in violation of rights secured to inhabitants of the Republic by the constitution and contrary to treaty relations.

The umpire (p. 3334) gave judgment in favor of the claimant.

In the case of Zerman v. Mexico, before the American and Mexican Commission of 1868, Sir Edward Thornton (p. 3348) said:

> The umpire is of opinion that, strictly speaking, the President of the Republic of Mexico had the right to expel a foreigner from its territory who might be considered dangerous, and that during war or disturbances it may be necessary to exercise this right even upon bare suspicion; but in the present instance there was no war, and reasons of safety could not be put forward as a ground for the expulsion of the claimant without charges preferred against him or trial; but if the Mexican Government had grounds for such expulsion it was at least *under the obligation of proving* charges before this Commission. Its mere assertion, however, or that of the United States consul, in a dis-

patch to his Government, that the claimant was employed by the imperialist authorities, does not appear to the umpire to be sufficient proof that he was so employed or sufficient ground for his expulsion.

The umpire awarded the claimant $1,000.

It appears, therefore, that the Commission may inquire into the reasons and circumstances of the expulsion.

Let us apply the principles above laid down to the case before us.

Boffolo was expelled, as the claimant Government contends (and nothing else is before the Commission), because he published a certain article supposed to reflect upon the local judiciary and referring in some purely incidental way to the President, and, as stated, recommended a socialistic paper. It is not the province of the umpire to pass upon Boffolo's taste or justice in so doing. He is, however, obliged to examine somewhat, first, as to whether in so doing he offended the laws of Venezuela, and second, whether under the laws the expulsion was permissible. . . .

[Quoted excerpts from an executive proclamation and the Constitution of 1893 have been omitted.]

. . . [T]he powers of the officers of Government were not autocratic, but Venezuela was a country of laws, governed even in April, 1900, by officials of limited powers; for if their powers were not limited the personal guarantees of the constitution would have been inefficacious—an impossible conclusion, as they were expressly recognized by the proclamation of General Castro.

Let us therefore see what law governed the matter of expulsion, for if none existed the power to expel was wanting. Another conclusion would make Venezuela's Government despotic—not republican or democratic. . . .

According . . . to the constitution of Venezuela, only as the nondomiciled foreigner might be shown to be prejudicial to public order would he be expelled. Let us pass over the fact that the Boffolo decree of expulsion declared that his presence was prejudicial to "national interests" and not to the "public order," as limited by the constitution, and see if such cause has been presented to this Commission as would justify the expulsion.

It is suggested that the expulsion may have taken place because of any one of three reasons:

1. That he spoke disrespectfully of the President.
2. That he criticized a subordinate member of the judiciary.
3. That he recommended the reading of "El Obrero," a socialistic paper.

The effective answer to all of these propositions is that freedom of speech and of the press are guaranteed by the constitution of Venezuela, and an expulsion for either one would have been an infringement of the constitution of Venezuela, and this is not to be presumed the President would have done. The umpire is more disposed to believe that for public reasons satisfactory to itself the Government has chosen not to offer the basis of its action, rather preferring to submit to such judgment as to this Commission might seem meet in the case.

The further suggestion is made that Boffolo, being a foreigner, did not possess the right to criticize the Government to the same extent as Venezuelans, while the Government possessed a larger power over him. To this may be replied that the constitution of Venezuela conferred upon foreigners the same rights as were assured to natives, and for the supposed offenses not the slightest punishment could have been inflicted upon Venezuelans.

Summing up the foregoing, we may (in part repeating) say:

1. A State possesses the general right of expulsion; but,

2. Expulsion should only be resorted to in extreme instances, and must be accomplished in the manner least injurious to the person affected.

3. The country exercising the power must, when occasion demands, state the reason of such expulsion before an international tribunal, and an inefficient reason or none being advanced, accepts the consequences.

4. In the present case the only reasons suggested to the Commission would be contrary to the Venezuelan constitution, and as this is a country not of despotic power, but of fixed laws, restraining, among other things, the acts of its officials, these reasons (whatever good ones may in point of fact have existed) can not be accepted by the umpire as sufficient.

In view of the foregoing it only remains to consider the amount of damages to be awarded. The honorable representative of Italy has indicated that he would be content to accept 5,000 bolivars, and considering the harshness of expulsion as a remedy, the fact that only great provocation will, in the eyes of international law, justify its exercise, and the further fact that expulsion of foreigners so readily leads the way to the gravest international difficulties, as it may be regarded as a national affront, the amount asked seems not intrinsically unreasonable. But bearing in mind the low character of the man in question (as developed before the Commission), and that his speedy return was permitted, the umpire believes his full duty will be discharged in allowing him 2,000 bolivars, and an award of this amount will be entered. . . .

QUESTIONS

(1) Which among the grounds stated in the opinion for holding a deportation to violate international law do you consider sound? [3]

(2) Is the value of Boffolo as authority for customary international law affected by the circumstances under which the arbitral protocol was signed? By the "absolute equity" phrase in the supplementary protocol?

(3) On what sources does Ralston, a United States citizen, rely? Can a charge be made that they represent solely the views of the United States and Europe? Of "Christian nations" only? Was such a view more likely in 1903 than today? Inevitable?

(4) Suppose that a writer were developing the theme that by the early 20th century, many doctrines of classical international law had become respectable legal cloaks for economic imperialism. Would Boffolo support his position?

3. Compare the views of the scope of the deportation power under international law in Fong Yue Ting v. United States and Harisiades v. Shaughnessy, pp. 23 and 26, supra. Recall particularly Justice Jackson's statement in Harisiades that "expulsion after long residence . . . is a weapon of defence and reprisal confirmed by international law as a power inherent in every sovereign state."

NOTE ON THE ARBITRATIONS BETWEEN THE UNITED STATES AND MEXICO

The two following arbitrations were under the Convention of 1923 between the United States and Mexico Establishing a General Claims Commission.* Note the definition in the final clause of the first paragraph of Article I of the substantive principles to be applied by the arbitrators. The decisions under this Convention had considerable influence upon the development of the law of state responsibility. Some background data is useful to place them in their historical context.

After the revolutionary period that began in 1912 in Mexico, the United States and certain other countries, chiefly Great Britain and Germany, entered into agreements with Mexico setting up three-man mixed claims commissions. The history of the American Commission exemplifies the problems which arbitration confronts, although in an extreme setting. The experience of the Commission has been characterized as "one of the most dilatory, inefficient and unfortunate in our history." Briggs, The Settlement of Mexican Claims Act of 1942, 37 Am.J.Int.L. 222 (1943). The causes for this dilatoriness have been attributed to delays of the American claimants' counsel and of the State Department, personal difficulties among the commissioners, and uncooperativeness by the Mexican regimes. These factors led to several extensions of the original three-year term of the Commission and to a 1932 convention extending its life to 1937. About 2,800 claims filed against Mexico totalled over $500,000,000. The Commission decided only a small percentage of them, disallowing 50 and allowing 89 with aggregate awards of $4,600,000. 836 claims were filed by Mexicans against the United States.

The claims adjudicated by the Commission included cases of maltreatment of Americans by Mexican government forces and insurgent bodies. They also involved allegations that Mexican courts and law enforcement agencies had denied rights to American citizens, and had failed to protect them from depredations by Mexican nationals or to apprehend and try such offenders. In addition to cases of death, bodily injury, and illegal, overly long or overly harsh imprisonment, claims alleged the taking or destruction of property and breaches of contract by government authorities. Many cases posed only issues of fact, but a few among them, such as the two following this Note and the North American Dredging Case, p. 523, infra, have become classics.

The failure of the Commission to complete its work led to further negotiations and a complex settlement. The Claims Convention of November 19, 1941, 56 Stat. 1347 (1942), T.S. No. 980, dealt with (1) claims filed under the 1923 Convention, (2) claims arising from agrarian expropriations, and (3) miscellaneous property claims arising between 1927 and 1940. It excluded claims based upon oil property expropriations, the subject of another agreement signed the same day. Under the Convention, Mexico agreed to pay $40,000,000 in installments in settlement of the three described categories of claims. Simultaneously with and as a part of the general negotiations leading to the Convention, the United States agreed (1) to set up a $40,000,000 fund to stabilize the peso, (2) to finance Mexican road construction through a $30,000,000 credit and (3) to buy large quantities of Mexican silver at artificially set prices. 5 Dept. State Bull. 3901–4036 (1941). A 1942 Settlement of Mexican Claims Act of the Congress, 56 Stat. 1058, set up a three-man American-Mexican Claims Commission, a national commission in origin and composition. Its function was to resolve various categories of claims, including those under the 1923 Convention, which were to be satisfied out of the $40,000,000 settlement to the extent allowed and possible.

UNITED MEXICAN STATES (GARCIA & GARZA) v. UNITED STATES OF AMERICA

United States-Mexican Claims Commission, 1926.
Opinions of Commissioners under the Convention Concluded September 8, 1923 between the United States and Mexico, 1926–1927, at 163; 4 U.N.R.I.A.A. 119.

[This claim was presented by Mexico on behalf of the parents of a girl who was killed in 1919 by a shot from a United States cavalry patrol while she was crossing on a raft from the American to the Mexican side of the Rio Grande to her father awaiting her on the Mexican bank. The laws of both countries forbade crossing at that point, as the girl's father knew. The officer commanding the patrol was sentenced by a court martial to dismissal from the service but the findings and sentence were set aside by the President. The opinion stated in part:]

3. The killing and its circumstances being established the Commission has to decide, whether the firing as a consequence of which the girl was mortally wounded constituted a wrongful act under international law. . . .

4. The Commission makes its conception of international law in this respect dependent upon the answer to the question, whether there exists among civilized nations any international standard concerning the taking of human life. The Commission not only holds that there exists one, but also that it is necessary to state and acknowledge its existence because of the fact that there are parts of the world and specific circumstances in which human practice apparently is inclined to fall below this standard. The Commission, in its opinion on the Swinney case (Docket No. 130), speaking of the Rio Grande, stated already: "Human life in these parts, on both sides, seems not to be appraised so highly as international standards prescribe." Nobody moreover, will deny that in time of active war the value of human life even outside of battlefields is underrated. Authoritative writers in the field of domestic penal law in different countries and authoritative awards have emphasized that human life may not be taken either for prevention or for repression, unless in cases of extreme necessity. To give just two quotations on the subject: the famous Italian jurist Carrera does not hesitate to qualify as an abuse of power excessive harshness employed by agents of the public force to realize an arrest, and adds that it is to such abuse that the sheriffs of Toscane owe their sad reputation (Programma del corso di diritto criminale,

8th edition, Vol. V, 1911, pp. 114–115; compare for an historic development Vol. I, 1906, pp. 56–60); and in State v. Cunningham, 51 L.R.A. (N.S.) 1179, an American court said: "The highest degree of care is exacted of a person handling firearms. They are extraordinarily dangerous, and in using them extraordinary care should be exercised to prevent injury to others. . . . We unqualifiedly condemn this practice of the reckless use of firearms. Officers should make all reasonable efforts to apprehend criminals; but this duty does not justify the use of firearms, except in the cases authorized by law. Officers, as well as other persons, should have a true appreciation of the value of a human life."

5. If this international standard of appraising human life exists, it is the duty not only of municipal authorities but of international tribunals as well to obviate any reckless use of firearms. On the part of American authorities this duty for the American-Mexican border was recognized in Bulletin No. 12, May 30, 1917 ("Particularly will be punished such offenses as unnecessary shooting across the border without authority"), by paragraph 7 of our Bulletin No. 4, February 11, 1919 ("but firing on unarmed persons supposed to be engaged in smuggling or crossing the river at unauthorized places, is not authorized"), and by paragraph 20 of General Order No. 3, March 21, 1919 ("Troop Commanders will be held responsible that the provisions of Bulletin No. 4 . . . , February 11, 1919, is carefully explained to all men"). In the field of international law the said principle has been recognized in the fourth Hague Convention of 1907, where article 46 of the "Regulations respecting the laws and customs of war on land" provides that in occupied territory "the lives of persons . . . must be respected," article 3 of the treaty itself adding that the belligerent party which violates the provisions of the said Regulations shall, if the case demands, be liable to pay compensation and shall be responsible for all acts committed by persons forming part of its armed forces. In order to consider shooting on the border by armed officials of either Government (soldiers, river guards, custom guards) justified, a combination of four requirements would seem to be necessary: (a) the act of firing, always dangerous in itself, should not be indulged in unless the delinquency is sufficiently well stated; (b) it should not be indulged in unless the importance of preventing or repressing the delinquency by firing is in reasonable proportion to the danger arising from it to the lives of the culprits and other persons in their neighborhood; (c) it should not be indulged in whenever other practicable ways of preventing or repressing the delinquency might be available; (d) it should be done with sufficient precaution not to create unnecessary danger, unless it be the official's intention to hit, wound, or kill. . . .

[The Commission concluded that these requirements had not been met in the present case. It awarded $2,000 to Mexico. The dissenting opinion of the United States Commissioner, NIELSEN, is omitted.]

UNITED STATES OF AMERICA (B. E. CHATTIN) v. UNITED MEXICAN STATES

United States-Mexican Claims Commission, 1927.
Opinions of Commissioners under the Convention Concluded September 8, 1923 between the United States and Mexico, 1926–27, at 422; 4 U.N.R.I.A.A. 282.

[Chattin, a United States citizen, was a conductor on a railroad in Mexico from 1908 to 1910, when he was arrested for embezzlement of fares. Chattin's trial was consolidated with those of several other

Americans and Mexicans who had been arrested on similar charges. In February 1911 he was convicted and sentenced to two years' imprisonment. His appeal was rejected in July 1911. In the meantime the inhabitants of Mazatlán, during a political uprising, threw open the doors of the jail and Chattin escaped to the United States. In asserting Chattin's claims, the United States argued that the arrest was illegal, that Chattin was mistreated while in prison, that his trial was unreasonably delayed, and that there were irregularities in the trial. There were a number of detailed complaints about the conduct of the trial. Several of these were not proved or were rejected as irrelevant and non-prejudicial. Three of the major allegations were described as follows in the opinion of VAN VOLLENHOVEN, the Presiding Commissioner:]

17. The allegation (e) that the accused has not been duly informed regarding the charge brought against him is proven by the record, and to a painful extent. The real complainant in this case was the railroad company, acting through its general manager; this manager, an American, not only was allowed to make full statements to the Court on August 2, 3, and 26, 1910, without ever being confronted with the accused and his colleagues, but he was even allowed to submit to the Court a series of anonymous written accusations, the anonymity of which reports could not be removed (for reasons which he explained); these documents created the real atmosphere of the trial. Were they made known to the conductors? Were the accused given an opportunity to controvert them? There is no trace of it in the record, nor was it ever alleged by Mexico. . . . The court record only shows that on January 13, and 16, 1911, the conductors and one of their lawyers were aware of the existence, not that they knew the contents, of these documents. . . . It is not shown that the confrontation between Chattin and his accusers amounted to anything like an effort on the Judge's part to find out the truth. Only after November 22, 1910, and only at the request of the Prosecuting Attorney, was Chattin confronted with some of the persons who, between July 13 and 21, inclusive, had testified of his being well acquainted with Ramírez. It is regrettable, on the other hand, that the accused misrepresents the wrong done him in this respect. He had not been left altogether in the dark. According to a letter signed by himself and two other conductors dated August 31, 1910, he was perfectly aware even of the details of the investigations made against him; so was the American vice-consul on July 26, 1910 . . . . Owing to the strict seclusion to which the conductors contend to have been submitted, it is impossible they could be so well-informed if the charges and the investigations were kept hidden from them. . . .

19. The allegation (h) that the witnesses were not sworn is irrelevant, as Mexican law does not require an "oath" (it is satisfied with a solemn promise, *protesta*, to tell the truth), nor do international standards of civilization. . . .

21. The allegation (j) that the hearings in open court lasted only some five minutes is proven by the record. This trial in open court was held on January 27, 1911. It was a pure formality, in which only confirmations were made of written documents, and in which not even the lawyer of the accused conductors took the trouble to say more than a word or two.

22. The whole of the proceedings discloses a most astonishing lack of seriousness on the part of the Court. There is no trace of an effort to have the two foremost pieces of evidence explained (paragraphs 14 and 17 above). There is no trace of an effort to find one Manuel Virgen, who, according to the investigations of July 21, 1910,

might have been mixed in Chattin's dealings, nor to examine one Carl or Carrol Collins, a dismissed clerk of the railroad company concerned, who was repeatedly mentioned as forging tickets and passes and as having been discharged for that very reason. One of the Mexican brakemen, Batriz, stated on August 8, 1910, in court that "it is true that the American conductors have among themselves schemes to defraud in that manner the company, the deponent not knowing it for sure"; but again no steps were taken to have this statement verified or this brakeman confronted with the accused Americans.

. . . No investigation was made as to why Delgado and Sarabia felt quite certain that June 29 was the date of their trip, a date upon the correctness of which the weight of their testimony wholly depended. No search of the houses of these conductors is mentioned. Nothing is revealed as to a search of their persons on the days of their arrest; when the lawyer of the other conductors, Haley and Englehart, insisted upon such an inquiry, a letter was sent to the Judge at Culiacán, but was allowed to remain unanswered. Neither during the investigations nor during the hearings in open court was any such thing as an oral examination or cross-examination of any importance attempted. It seems highly improbable that the accused have been given a real opportunity during the hearings in open court, freely to speak for themselves. It is not for the Commission to endeavor to reach from the record any conviction as to the innocence or guilt of Chattin and his colleagues; but even in case they were guilty, the Commission would render a bad service to the Government of Mexico if it failed to place the stamp of its disapproval and even indignation on a criminal procedure so far below international standards of civilization as the present one. If the wholesome rule of international law as to respect for the judiciary of another country . . . shall stand, it would seem of the utmost necessity that appellate tribunals when, in exceptional cases, discovering proceedings of this type should take against them the strongest measures possible under constitution and laws, in order to safeguard their country's reputation. . . .

24. In Mexican law, as in that of other countries, an accused can not be convicted unless the Judge is convinced of his guilt and has acquired this view from legal evidence. An international tribunal never can replace the important first element, that of the Judge's being convinced of the accused's guilt; it can only in extreme cases, and then with great reserve, look into the second element, the legality and sufficiency of the evidence. . . .

26. From the record there is not convincing evidence that the proof against Chattin, scanty and weak though it may have been, was not such as to warrant a conviction. Under the article deemed applicable the medium penalty fixed by law was imposed, and deduction made of the seven months Chattin had passed in detention from July, 1910, till February, 1911. It is difficult to understand the sentence unless it be assumed that the Court, for some reason or other, wished to punish him severely. . . . The allegation that the Court in this matter was biased against American citizens would seem to be contradicted by the fact that, together with the four Americans, five Mexicans were indicted as well, four of whom had been caught and have subsequently been convicted—that one of these Mexicans was punished as severely as the Americans were—and that the lower penalties imposed on the three others are explained by motives which, even if not shared, would seem reasonable. . . . If Chattin's guilt was sufficiently proven, the small amount of the embezzlement (four pesos) need not in itself have prevented the Court from imposing a severe penalty. . . .

29. Bringing the proceedings of Mexican authorities against Chattin to the test of international standards . . . there can be no doubt of their being highly insufficient. Inquiring whether there is convincing evidence of these unjust proceedings . . . the answer must be in the affirmative. Since this is a case of alleged responsibility of Mexico for injustice committed by its judiciary, it is necessary to inquire whether the treatment of Chattin amounts even to an outrage, to bad faith, to wilful neglect of duty, or to an insufficiency of governmental action recognizable by every unbiased man . . . and the answer here again can only be in the affirmative.

30. An illegal arrest of Chattin is not proven. Irregularity of court proceedings is proven with reference to absence of proper investigations, insufficiency of confrontations, withholding from the accused the opportunity to know all of the charges brought against him, undue delay of the proceedings, making the hearings in open court a mere formality, and a continued absence of seriousness on the part of the Court. Insufficiency of the evidence against Chattin is not convincingly proven; intentional severity of the punishment is proven, without its being shown that the explanation is to be found in unfairmindedness of the Judge. Mistreatment in prison is not proven. Taking into consideration, on the one hand, that this is a case of direct governmental responsibility, and, on the other hand, that Chattin, because of his escape, has stayed in jail for eleven months instead of for two years, it would seem proper to allow in behalf of this claimant damages in the sum of $5,000.00, without interest.

[NIELSEN, the United States Commissioner, concurred in a separate opinion in which he made the following comments on the Mexican criminal system:]

So far as concerns methods of procedure prescribed by Mexican law, conclusions with respect to their propriety or impropriety may be reached in the light of comparisons with legal systems of other countries. And comparisons pertinent and useful in the instant case must be made with the systems obtaining in countries which like Mexico are governed by the principles of the civil law, since the administration of criminal jurisprudence in those countries differs so very radically from the procedure in criminal cases in countries in which the principles of Anglo-Saxon law obtain. This point is important in considering the arguments of counsel for the United States regarding irrelevant evidence and hearsay evidence appearing in the record of proceedings against the accused. From the standpoint of the rules governing Mexican criminal procedure conclusions respecting objections relative to these matters must be grounded not on the fact that a judge received evidence of this kind but on the use he made of it.

Counsel for Mexico discussed in some detail two periods of the proceedings under Mexican law in a criminal case. The procedure under the Mexican code of criminal procedure apparently is somewhat similar to that employed in the early stages of the Roman law and similar in some respects to the procedure generally obtaining in European countries at the present time. Counsel for Mexico pointed out that during the period of investigation a Mexican judge is at liberty to receive and take cognizance of anything placed before him, even matters that have no relation to the offense with which the accused is tried. The nature of some of the things incorporated into the record, including anonymous accusations against the character of the accused, is shown in the Presiding Commissioner's opinion.

Undoubtedly in European countries a similar measure of latitude is permitted to a judge, but there seems to be an essential difference between procedure in those countries and that obtaining in the Mexican courts, in that after a preliminary examination before a judge of investigation, a case passes on to a judge who conducts a trial. The French system, which was described by counsel for Mexico as being more severe toward the accused than is Mexican procedure, may be mentioned for purposes of comparison. Apparently under French law the preliminary examination does not serve as a foundation for the verdict of the judge who decides as to the guilt of the accused. The examination allows the examining judge to determine whether there is ground for formal charge, and in case there is, to decide upon the jurisdiction. The accused is not immediately brought before the court which is to pass upon his guilt or innocence. His appearance in court is deferred until the accusation rests upon substantial grounds. This trial is before a judge whose functions are of a more judicial character than those of a judge of investigation employing inquisitorial methods in the nature of those used by a prosecutor. When the period of investigation was completed in the cases of Chattin and the others with whom his case was consolidated, the entire proceedings so far as the Government was concerned were substantially finished, and after a hearing lasting perhaps five minutes, the same judge who collected evidence against the accused sentenced them. . . .

[NIELSEN further stated that, although there was "color to a complaint" of irregularities in Chattin's trial, he concluded that the Commission should award damages only for mistreatment of Chattin during the period of investigation, having "in mind the peculiarly delicate character of an examination of judicial proceedings by an international tribunal."

A dissent was filed by G. FERNANDEZ MACGREGOR, the Mexican Commissioner. He rejected the assertion "that the accused was ignorant of a single one of the charges made against him, for the simple reason that the records formed in a criminal process are not secret, according to Mexican law, and are, from the time of their commencement, at the disposal of the defendants or their counsel . . . ." MacGregor continued:]

8. It has been alleged that the trial proper (meaning by trial that part of the proceedings in which the defendants and witnesses as well as the Prosecuting Attorney and counsel appear personally before the Judge for the purpose of discussing the circumstances of the case) lasted five minutes at the most, for which reason it was a mere formality, implying thereby that there was really no trial and that Chattin was convicted without being heard. I believe that this is an erroneous criticism which arises from the difference between Anglo-Saxon procedure and that of other countries. Counsel for Mexico explained during the hearing of this case that Mexican criminal procedure is composed of two parts: Preliminary proceedings (sumario) and plenary proceedings (plenario). In the former all the information and evidence on the case are adduced; the corpus delicti is established; visits are made to the residences of persons concerned; commissions are performed by experts appointed by the Court; testimony is received and the Judge can cross-examine the culprits, counsel for the defense having also the right of cross-examination; public or private documents are received, etc. When the Judge considers that he has sufficient facts on which to establish a case, he declares the instruction closed and places the record in the

hands of the parties (the defendant and his counsel on the one side evidence has been received are the parties in the cause requested to and the Prosecuting Attorney on the other), in order that they may state whether they desire any new evidence filed, and only when such file their respective final pleas. This being done, the public hearing is held, in which the parties very often do not have anything further to allege, because everything concerning their interests has already been done and stated. In such a case, the hearing is limited to the Prosecuting Attorney's ratification of his accusation, previously filed, and the defendants and their counsel also rely on the allegations previously made by them, these two facts being entered in the record, whereupon the Judge declares the case closed and it becomes ready to be decided. This is what happened in the criminal proceedings which have given rise to this claim, and they show, further, that the defendants, including Chattin, refused to speak at the hearing in question or to adduce any kind of argument or evidence. In view of the foregoing explanation, I believe that it becomes evident that the charge, that there was no trial proper, can not subsist, for, in Mexican procedure, it is not a question of a trial in the sense of Anglo-Saxon law, which requires that the case be always heard in plenary proceedings, before a jury, adducing all the circumstances and evidence of the cause, examining and cross-examining all the witnesses, and allowing the prosecuting attorney and counsel for the defense to make their respective allegations. International law insures that a defendant be judged openly and that he be permitted to defend himself, but in no manner does it oblige these things to be done in any fixed way, as they are matters of internal regulation and belong to the sovereignty of States. . . .

10. I admit that [other deficiencies] exist and that they show that the Judge could have carried out the investigation in a more efficient manner, but the fact that it was not done does not mean any violation of international law. . . .

19. I consider that this is one of the most delicate cases that has come before the Commission and that its nature is such that it puts to a test the application of principles of international law. It is hardly of any use to proclaim in theory respect for the judiciary of a nation, if, in practice, it is attempted to call the judiciary to account for its minor acts. It is true that sometimes it is difficult to determine when a judicial act is internationally improper and when it is so from a domestic standpoint only. In my opinion the test which consists in ascertaining if the act implies damage, wilful neglect, or palpable deviation from the established customs becomes clearer by having in mind the damage which the claimant could have suffered. There are certain defects in procedure that can never cause damage which may be estimated separately, and that are blotted out or disappear, to put it thus, if the final decision is just. There are other defects which make it impossible for such decision to be just. The former, as a rule, do not engender international liability; the latter do so, since such liability arises from the decision which is iniquitous because of such defects. To prevent an accused from defending himself, either by refusing to inform him as to the facts imputed to him or by denying him a hearing and the use of remedies; to sentence him without evidence, or to impose on him disproportionate or unusual penalties, to treat him with cruelty and discrimination; are all acts which per se cause damage due to their rendering a just decision impossible. But to delay the proceedings somewhat, to lay aside some evidence, there existing other clear proofs, to fail to comply with the adjective law in its secondary provisions and other

deficiencies of this kind, do not cause damage nor violate international law. Counsel for Mexico justly stated that to submit the decisions of a nation to revision in this respect was tantamount to submitting her to a régime of capitulations. All the criticism which has been made of these proceedings, I regret to say, appears to arise from lack of knowledge of the judicial system and practice of Mexico, and, what is more dangerous, from the application thereto of tests belonging to foreign systems of law. For example, in some of the latter the investigation of a crime is made only by the police magistrates and the trial proper is conducted by the Judge. Hence the reluctance in accepting that one same judge may have the two functions and that, therefore, he may have to receive in the preliminary investigation (instrucción) of the case all kinds of data, with the obligation, of course, of not taking them into account at the time of judgment, if they have no probative weight. It is certain that the secret report, so much discussed in this case, would have been received by the police of the countries which place the investigation exclusively in the hands of such branch. This same police would have been free to follow all the clues or to abandon them at its discretion; but the Judge is criticized here because he did not follow up completely the clue given by Ramirez with respect to Chattin. The same domestic test—to call it such—is used to understand what is a trial or open trial imagining at the same time that it must have the sacred forms of common-law and without remembering that the same goal is reached by many roads. And the same can be said when speaking of the manner of taking testimony of witnesses, of cross-examination, of holding confrontations, etc.

20. In view of the above considerations, I am of the opinion that this claim should be disallowed.

COMMENT

The Garcia & Garza case raises the question whether a state should be held responsible for unauthorized acts of its officials or of its private citizens. The issues become sharper if one varies its facts: shots were fired solely because of personal malice of the cavalrymen, or were fired not by a patrol but by a group of picknicking Texans. For all such questions, domestic principles of the law of agency and the extensive learning with respect to the scope of "state action" under the Fourteenth Amendment have indirect but suggestive implications.

The Draft Convention of Professors Sohn and Baxter (Reporters) on the International Responsibility of States for Injuries to Aliens treats these issues.[4] A wrongful act is attributable to a state if it is the act "of any organ, agency, official, or employee of the State acting within the scope of the function of such organ, agency, official, or employee." Article 15. State organs include executive, legislative, administrative and judicial agencies, as well as agencies of a state government in a federal country. Articles 16–17. Several of the Mexican-American arbitrations posed one of the more

4. Draft No. 12 of this Convention appears together with extensive explanatory notes in a multilith edition of 1961. The articles, together with some of the explanatory notes, also appear in 55 Am.J.Int.L. 548 (1961). All references hereafter to the Draft Convention are to the multilith edition.

difficult problems of attribution: the extent to which a government is responsible for wrongful acts of revolutionary or insurrectionist forces.

Attempts to define an international minimum standard are often expressed in terms of deciding what constitutes a "denial of justice," a phrase discussed at length in omitted portions of the Chattin opinion. Presiding Commissioner Van Vollenhoven pointed out that the numerous claims against Mexico before that Commission stemmed from acts of executive officials, legislative acts (property expropriations), refusal of the judiciary to entertain claims by aliens to vindicate rights, and—as in the Chattin case—defective administration of justice by the courts. Criticizing the indiscriminate use of the phrase "denial of justice" to characterize all such claims, Van Vollenhoven attempted a more useful definition to lend clarity to this field. His efforts have not met with widespread assent. The ambiguous content of the phrase is described by Professors Sohn and Baxter in their Draft Convention, supra, at p. 80:

> This term has in the past been used in at least three different senses. In its broadest sense, this term seems to embrace the whole field of State responsibility, and has been applied to all types of wrongful conduct on the part of the State toward aliens. In its narrowest sense, this term has been limited to refusal of a State to grant an alien access to its courts or a failure of a court to pronounce a judgment. In an intermediate sense, the expression "denial of justice" is employed in connection with the improper administration of civil and criminal justice as regards an alien, including denial of access to courts, inadequate procedures, and unjust decisions. The last appears to be the most apposite usage, since the term may thus be usefully employed to describe a particular type of international wrong for which no other adequate phrase exists in the language of the law.

The usage proposed by the Draft Convention would thus distinguish between an unlawful act by the troops of a state, as in Garcia & Garza, and an unlawful act by the courts of a state, as in Chattin, designating only the latter as a "denial of justice." Note that the failure of the judiciary to give appropriate compensation in a case in the first category may be relevant to a private claimant in a different way. It may be necessary for that claimant or his government to prove that he has exhausted local judicial remedies before an international claim can be brought. Note further that unlike Chattin, the wrongful act in such a case is deemed to have taken place at the time of the shooting and not at the time of denial of judicial relief.

NOTE ON PROBLEMS IN FORMULATING A MINIMUM INTERNATIONAL STANDARD OF CRIMINAL PROCEDURE

As the Chattin opinions indicate, fundamental differences exist between common-law and civil-law criminal procedure. Further there are important differences within each group—for example, between France and Mexico. Another complicating factor is the prevalent misinformation about practices in foreign countries; for example, many Americans are convinced that under any continental system the accused is deemed guilty until he proves himself innocent. To illustrate variations among the civil-law systems, we here offer a brief description of aspects of the French judicial process that appear applicable to a case such as Chattin.[5]

In view of the kind of conduct and the small sum involved, Chattin's acts would likely be regarded as a *délit* (misdemeanor). Official procedures following a police inquiry would usually commence with a preparatory investigation, which is mandatory in cases of a *crime* (felony) (Article 79 of the French Code of Criminal Procedure). The *juge d'instruction* (examining magistrate) "shall undertake . . . all acts of investigation that he deems useful to the manifestation of the truth" (Art. 81). Witnesses are heard under oath but out of the presence of the accused, and their statements are reduced to writing. The accused is to be advised of "the acts that are imputed to him," that "he is free to make no statement" and that he has the right to counsel (Art. 114). However, the magistrate may make "appropriate observations" in the *dossier* (official file of the proceedings) when the accused remains silent.[6] The *dossier* is to be placed at the disposition of the accused both during and after the pretrial proceedings (Arts. 118, 183, 184), but his counsel may speak "only in order to pose questions after having been authorized by the examining magistrate" (Art. 120). The magistrate customarily visits the scene of the crime (Art. 92), accompanied by witnesses and, if he so desires, by the accused. He has authority to conduct searches (Arts. 95, 96), including the domicile of the accused, and may on his motion call experts or issue rogatories. Arts. 151–169.

At the end of his investigation, the magistrate performs a treble role. He performs the task, analogous to that of the grand jury in Anglo-American systems, of determining if the evidence is sufficient to justify further proceedings. Art. 176. If so, he determines the court to which the case will be sent—in cases of misdemeanors, the *Tribunal Correctionnel.* Arts. 178, 179, 181. Finally, he advises the court to which the case is referred of the pretrial proceedings by transmitting to it the *dossier.* Arts 180, 181. The magistrate is then forbidden to take any further part in the case (Art. 49), which is handled by a three-judge court (Art. 398) since a jury

5. This description is based upon the translation of the French *Code de Procédure Pénale* and comments thereon in The American Series of Foreign Penal Codes, No. 7, The French Code of Criminal Procedure (Kock trans. 1964), which incorporates amendments to that Code through January 1963.

6. Towe, Criminal Pretrial Procedure in France, 38 Tulane L.R. 469, 487 (1964).

(which serves a different function from the Anglo-American jury) is provided for only in the case of a *crime*.[7]

Hearings are public. Before hearing witnesses, the court's president interrogates the accused and hears his unsworn statement (Art. 442). There are no formal rules of evidence in the common-law sense. ". . . [O]ffenses may be established by any manner of proof, and the judge shall decide according to his thorough conviction. The judge may found his decision only on the evidence that is brought to him in the course of the trial and discussed before him by both sides" (Art. 427). After testimony, the president poses to a witness "the questions he judges necessary and, if it is appropriate, those that have been proposed to him by the parties" (Art. 454). Counsel for the accused may submit his conclusions and "shall always have the last word" (Art. 460).

Among the several stark contrasts between the Mexican or French procedures and criminal trials in this country is of course our traditional and constitutional requirement of trial by jury. Another more pervasive difference is the foundation of our judicial administration of criminal justice in what has loosely been termed an accusatorial or prosecutorial rather than an inquisitorial approach.[8] The court in the Anglo-American world is relatively quiescent. Initiative lies generally with the parties, who develop facts and seek evidence through personal or police inquiry, summon witnesses whom they examine, and generally give direction to the legal or factual inquiries pursued during pre-trial proceedings or at trial. The court aids them through the issuance of its official process, as necessary.

A critical ingredient of this approach is the emphasis which Anglo-American legal systems place upon direct confrontation and cross-examination. Compare, for example, the decision in Pointer v. Texas, 380 U.S. 400, 85 S.Ct. 1065, 13 L.Ed.2d 923 (1965), with the Mexican and French procedures. The Supreme Court there held that the Due Process Clause of the Fourteenth Amendment forbade the prosecutor in a state criminal trial to use a transcript of the witness's testimony which was given at a preliminary hearing at which the defendant, present without counsel, did not cross-examine. The witness himself was absent from the trial. The Court stated that "the Sixth Amendment's right of an accused to confront the witnesses against him is . . . a fundamental right and is made obligatory on the States by the Fourteenth Amendment. . . . There are few subjects, perhaps, upon which this Court and other courts have been more nearly unanimous than in their expressions of belief that the right of confrontation and cross-examination is an essential and fundamental requirement for the kind of fair trial which

7. Towe, fn. 6, supra, at 496, notes that the delay before a trial begins normally runs from 12 to 18 months for serious offenses. Such offenses (*crimes*) involve additional procedures before trial that are not applicable to misdemeanor cases.

8. For an analysis of this asserted distinction, from historical and sociological perspectives, see Damaska, Structures of Authority and Comparative Criminal Procedure, 84 Yale L.J. 480 (1975).

is this country's constitutional goal." The transcript, concluded the Court, had not been taken under circumstances giving the defendant "through counsel an adequate opportunity to cross-examine . . . ."

The experience of the Supreme Court in developing a nation-wide minimum standard under the Due Process Clause of the Fourteenth Amendment sheds further light on the more intractable problems confronting arbitral tribunals or codifiers attempting to define an international minimum standard. The traditional domestic approach has been to read into the Fourteenth Amendment not all of the specific restrictions which the Bill of Rights imposes on the federal government, but only those requirements of or restraints upon state action that are deemed to be fundamental and indispensable. In various decisions, the Supreme Court has spoken of due process as embodying "those canons of decency and fairness which express the notions of justice of English-speaking peoples," or those principles which are "so rooted in the traditions and conscience of our people as to be ranked as fundamental" or are "implicit in the concept of ordered liberty." [9] It has stressed that due process "unlike some legal rules, is not a technical conception with a fixed content unrelated to time, place and circumstances"; that it is not a "mechanical instrument" but "a process." [10] To some extent this determination has been made by a process of surveying the practice of the 50 states and also of other common-law jurisdictions.[11] Compare the discussion of custom as a law-making force at p. 250, supra.

Ferguson v. Georgia, 365 U.S. 570, 81 S.Ct. 756, 5 L.Ed.2d 783 (1961), illustrates the operation of this process. That opinion recounts in detail how the ancient common law disqualification of accused persons to testify in their own behalf was changed by state after state until the Court could say that Georgia is "the only State —indeed, apparently the only jurisdiction in the common-law world —to retain the common-law rule that a person charged with a criminal offense is incompetent to testify under oath in his own behalf at his trial." It then concluded that the Georgia practice of allowing the accused to make only an unsworn statement without aid of counsel violated the Fourteenth Amendment. The difficulties inherent in extending this process to the international scene are sug-

9. See Rochin v. California, 342 U.S. 165, 169, 72 S.Ct. 205, 208, 96 L.Ed. 183, 188 (1952).

10. Joint Anti-Fascist Refugee Committee v. McGrath, 341 U.S. 123, 162, 71 S.Ct. 624, 643, 95 L.Ed. 817, 849 (1951).

11. To what extent are practices in other countries relevant to the formulation of standards under the Due Process Clause? Consider Rudolph v. Alabama, 375 U.S. 889, 84 S.Ct. 155, 11 L.Ed.2d 119 (1963). In dissent from a denial of certiorari, Justice Goldberg argued that the Court should consider whether the Eighth and Fourteenth Amendments permitted imposition of the death penalty on a convicted rapist who had neither taken nor endangered human life. His opinion notes trends "both in this country and throughout the world against punishing rape by death," refers to a recent United Nations survey on laws relating to capital punishment, and inquires whether imposition of the death penalty violated (quoting from an earlier case) "standards of decency more or less universally accepted."

gested by the following excerpt from a comparative survey of the rights of the accused as a witness, included as an appendix to Judge Jerome Frank's dissent in United States v. Gruenwald, 233 F.2d 556, 587 (2d Cir. 1956), *rev'd,* 353 U.S. 391, 77 S.Ct. 963, 1 L.Ed.2d 931 (1957):

> In Western Europe, the privilege against compulsory self-incrimination is embodied in a system which recognizes a middle ground between (a) complete disqualification totally precluding a person unable to take the oath from giving evidence . . . and (b) absolute qualification whereby all testimony must be given under oath subject to cross-examination, impeachment and the penalties of perjury. This system is partially analogous to that of the English courts in the 19th century and of present-day Georgia, in that the accused, though not permitted to take the stand, is allowed to make an unsworn statement. . . . A significant distinction exists, however, since at common law the unsworn statement permitted to an accused was usually not allowed to be considered as evidence, but merely an argument on "what he claimed to be the facts." " . . . no finding can be founded by the jury on the strength of such a statement;" . . . . In European practice generally the accused's unsworn statements do constitute evidence and may be given conclusive weight in his favor by the triers of fact . . . .

QUESTIONS

(1) How do the commissioners in the American-Mexican arbitrations approach the task of identifying a minimum international standard? Is the effort similar to that in the Lotus Case, namely an effort to find a strong consensus in state practice permitting or proscribing particular conduct? Or do the opinions attempt to identify what constitutes fair and just criminal procedure from other perspectives? What other perspectives?

(2) Chattin raises questions of the adequacy under international law of a judicial procedure foreign to two of the commissioners. Consider the attitudes of the three opinions towards aspects of Chattin's experience that are referred to in the opinion of Van Vollenhoven:

(a) The remark "that the hearings in open court lasted only some five minutes."

(b) The comment about the "lack of seriousness on the part of the Court," shown in part by its failure to trace some of the evidence and witnesses.

(c) The stress on the fact that at no time during the investigation or hearings in open court "was any such thing as an oral examination or cross-examination of any importance attempted."

(3) Does the decision reached by Van Vollenhoven rest upon the failure of Mexican procedures to comply with international law requirements, of, for example, significant open hearings or confrontation, or upon the failure of the Mexican judiciary to provide a fair trial for Chattin even under the Mexican premises?

(4) What effect did the statement that the "insufficiency of the evidence against Chattin is not convincingly proven" appear to have upon the judgment of the Commission? Suppose that, at the time of the arbitration, Chattin were still detained in a Mexican jail. Suppose further that the Commission were convinced (a) that Chattin had an unfair trial but was obviously guilty, or (b) that he had a fair trial but the finding of guilt was clearly erroneous. How might an American tribunal, in normal appellate proceedings, deal with these problems? What special problems does an international tribunal encounter?

(5) Chattin was tried together with several Mexicans, who apparently were accorded the same treatment. There was no "discrimination." Why should he benefit from a more rigorous set of procedural safeguards than nationals of the county in which he chose to live?

NOTE ON PROBLEMS IN CODIFICATION OF THE LAW OF STATE RESPONSIBILITY

The challenge of recent decades to an earlier consensus over protection of aliens has been particularly acute with respect to property rights, but has inevitably affected other phases of the law of state responsibility. A number of current efforts to "restate" or "codify" that law—such as Sections 164–214 of Restatement (Second), Foreign Relations Law of the United States—have thus encountered vexing problems. Such efforts have evidenced the frailty of any boundary line between codification and creative development. Note the following comment in the preface to the Restatement (at p. xi):

> The inclusion of the international legal aspects of foreign relations law in the Restatement of this Subject presents certain problems, particularly those of source material, that have not been present in the preparation of other Restatements. This results in large part from differences in the sources of international law and domestic law. In general, rules of domestic law tend to be based upon authoritative declarations by legislatures and courts. While many of the rules of international law have been authoritatively declared as by a "law-making" international agreement or by an international tribunal, others are based primarily upon opinions held by experts or positions taken by governments in diplomatic correspondence with other governments. In these latter situations the positions or outlooks of particular states, including the United States, should not be confused with what a consensus of states would accept or support. Thus the Restatement of this Subject, in stating rules of international law, represents the opinion of The American Law Institute as to the rules that an international tribunal would apply if charged with deciding a controversy in accordance with international law.

One can question whether such an approach is realistic, given the nebulous character of much "law" in this field. The professed goal of the Restatement appears to reflect our domestic, court-oriented view of how a legal system develops and to underestimate the degree of political judgment that is involved. Is the perspective of an "international tribunal . . . deciding a controversy in accordance with international law" the same for judges or arbitrators from Mexico and the United States? South Africa and Liberia? Compare the following comment in Brierly, The Law of Nations 79–80 (6th ed., Waldock, 1963).

> This type of codification is common enough in municipal systems of law. But the codification of international law would be a very different task. The international codifier . . . would have to choose between competing rules, to fill up gaps on which the law is uncertain or silent, and to give precision to abstract general principles of which the practical application is unsettled; in short the codification of international law is only possible to the extent that political decisions can be obtained as to the law which the code is to contain. In circumstances such as these codification ceases to be a technical task which can be entrusted to lawyers; it becomes a political matter, a task of law creation, and the contents of the code can be settled only if governments can agree upon them.

Professor Richard Baxter has commented on some of the complexities in this task in Reflections on Codification in Light of the International Law of State Responsibility for Injuries to Aliens, 16 Syracuse L.Rev. 745, 756–58 (1965).

> So much has been written about the differing views which nations presently entertain on the position of aliens and the responsibility of states for injuries to them that nothing can or should be added in this short paper. This diversity of views is both the cause and effect of a tremendous diminution in the number of adjudicated international cases in this area as well as in the number of peaceful settlements of claims on the diplomatic level in conformity with what is assumed to be the law. At one time, in the 1910's or early 1920's, no topic could have appeared more ripe for codification than the law of state responsibility. An impressive body of judicial precedent had been built up. The number of international adjudications of state responsibility for injuries to aliens probably exceeded several times over all of the other international cases dealing with other areas of international law. . . .
>
> But thirty lean years have cast doubt on all that went before. . . . The most outrageous and offensive conduct toward aliens goes unredressed. National practice with respect to remedies for injuries to the persons of aliens through state action or inaction and for denials of justice is sparse. One can look to negotiated lump-sum settlements in so far as the property of aliens is concerned and take some consolation from the fact that it was possible to secure some compensation, however inadequate it may be. The jurisprudence of national claims commissions, such as the Foreign Claims Settlement Commission of the United States, has sharpened our understanding of the issues and would be a valuable source of law for international tribunals—if they existed. It is not in any belittlement of the work of these commissions . . . to say that on the international plane the decisions of national commissions can never command the same weight as those of international tribunals.

> Provisions of treaties, such as treaties of establishment and of friendship, commerce, and navigation can be looked to as a source of law. Despite the undiscriminating use which has sometimes been made of bilateral treaties as evidence of the law, it would require much further analysis to determine to what extent, if any, such treaties are declaratory of the law or are a source of new customary law. Until such a study is made, treaty provisions can be employed only with much hesitancy.
>
> If it were solely a question of articulating a body of law which is in flux and may not be tomorrow what it was yesterday, there are devices whereby a premature freezing of the law might be avoided. A declaration can be employed to photograph, as it were, the state of the customary law as of a given moment, without committing the parties to comply with that changing body of law in the future. But the problem with the law of state responsibility for injuries to aliens is that its motion stopped several decades ago.
>
> These assertions are not intended as a denial of the law of state responsibility but as a reminder that the evidence upon which we rely is not as fresh as it might be and that there is far from universal agreement that the traditional law is still the law of today. In the codification of the law there is no alternative to picking up where the tribunals left off, even though the exercise has a slightly academic quality.

The post-war years have witnessed a number of efforts within or under the auspices of the United Nations to codify this field through the preparation of draft conventions for submission to, and possible ratification by, member states. We here consider several articles of the Draft Convention, p. 373, supra, prepared by Professors Sohn and Baxter, as Reporters, at the request of the Secretary of the International Law Commission. In an explanatory note (p. 44), the Reporters observed:

> No attempt has been made in the drafting of this Convention to maintain a rigid distinction between [codification and] progressive development. . . . In order to reconcile conflicting views of the law . . . it has been necessary in some instances to set down that rule or principle which ought to govern the matter in question for the future. . . . Moreover, if this Convention is to gain any acceptance, it must enlist the support of those States, which will be bound by its obligations. . . . Where national views are at opposite poles, it has been thought wise to attempt compromises, even to the extent of laying down new law. . . . The success of [the codifier's] endeavors is measured by the degree to which the codification is responsive to the needs of the day as well as adapted to the demands of the future.

The following articles treat questions that are relevant to a case such as Chattin.

Article 5

1. The arrest or detention of an alien is wrongful:

(a) if it is a clear and discriminatory violation of the law of the arresting or detaining State;

(b) if the cause or manner of the arrest or detention unreasonably departs from the principles recognized by the principal legal systems of the world; . . .

(d) if the arrest or detention otherwise involves a violation by the State of a treaty.

2. The detention of an alien becomes wrongful after the State has failed:

(a) to inform him promptly of the cause of his arrest or detention, or to inform him within a reasonable time after his arrest or detention of the specific charges against him;

(b) to grant him prompt access to a tribunal empowered both to determine whether his arrest or detention is lawful and to order his release if the arrest or detention is determined to be unlawful;

(c) to grant him a prompt trial; or

(d) to ensure that his trial and any appellate proceedings are not unduly prolonged.

. . .

Article 7

. . . In determining the fairness of any hearing, it is relevant to consider whether it was held before an independent tribunal and whether the alien was denied: . . .

(c) full opportunity to know the substance and source of any evidence against him and to contest its validity;

(d) full opportunity to have compulsory process for obtaining witnesses and evidence;

(e) full opportunity to have legal representation of his own choice;

(f) free or assisted legal representation on the same basis as nationals of the State concerned or on the basis recognized by the principal legal systems of the world, whichever standard is higher; . . .

(h) full opportunity to communicate with a representative of the government of the State entitled to extend its diplomatic protection to him;

(i) full opportunity to have such a representative present at any judicial or administrative proceeding in accordance with the rules of procedure of the tribunal or administrative agency;

(j) disposition of his case with reasonable dispatch at all stages of the proceedings; or

(k) any other procedural right conferred by a treaty or recognized by the principal legal systems of the world.

Article 8

A decision or judgment of a tribunal or an administrative authority rendered in a proceeding involving the determination of the civil rights or obligations of an alien or of any criminal charges against him, and either denying him recovery in whole or in part or granting recovery against him or imposing a penalty, whether civil or criminal, upon him is wrongful:

(a) if it is a clear and discriminatory violation of the law of the State concerned;

(b) if it unreasonably departs from the principles of justice recognized by the principal legal systems of the world; or

(c) if it otherwise involves a violation by the State of a treaty.

NOTE ON POST-WAR MOVEMENTS TO EXPAND THE PROTECTION OF THE INDIVIDUAL UNDER INTERNATIONAL LAW

The foregoing materials signal one critical limitation on protection of personal or property rights under classical international law. Individuals or companies benefited from a minimum international standard *only* in their status as aliens. Note that the Draft Convention, supra, remains within this traditional framework. An explanatory note states (pp. 44–45):

> Holding States to a certain standard of conduct in their treatment of aliens has long been the one really effective way in which international law has been able to protect human rights. . . . By the establishment of an international standard, the law has not only protected aliens but has also suggested a desideratum for States in their relationships with their own nationals.

To this limited extent, classical international law directly affected *individuals,* although the theory of diplomatic protection reconciled this phenomenon with traditional notions of a law *among nations* through its premise that the state suffered injury through injury to its national.

Supplementing customary international law, numerous treaties have directly benefited alien individuals or companies. Perhaps the most significant are those of Friendship, Commerce and Navigation (sometimes designated Conventions of Establishment), which commonly have provisions as to civil liberties and judicial treatment of aliens. See, for example, Articles I to III of the Franco-American Convention of Establishment.* Such treaty relationships, however, have been primarily among the developed countries of the Atlantic Community and Japan. Other treaties, such as those regulating taxation or trade-marks, also afford protection and rights to individuals. They declare substantive rights of aliens pertaining to their economic activities, and frequently provide for more effective enforcement of those rights. Despite the fact that individuals or companies only rarely have access to international tribunals, see p. 209, supra, they can bring actions before national courts which frequently have the competence to enforce private rights under such treaties.[12]

In 1948, Professor Philip Jessup (later a Judge of the I.C.J.) stressed in his A Modern Law of Nations (p. 2) that "international law, like national law, must be directly applicable to the individual. It must not continue to be remote from him . . . ." Several initiatives since that date have pointed international law slowly and tentatively away from its exclusive concern with states and aliens. The individual as such has come to be recognized as a fit, indeed necessary, subject of its concern. The reasons are apparent. As stated in the preamble to the European Convention for the Protection of Human Rights and Fundamental Freedom, infra, such rights and freedoms "are the foundation of justice and peace in the world."

A second characteristic of the classical international law relating to human rights was the sparse protection that it afforded an individual, even in his status as alien. Basically it proscribed obvious, ascertainable injuries to the physical security of the person or egregious lapses in the administration of justice. State practices giving rise to such cases frequently occurred during periods of unrest; consequently the cases involved largely practices which even the "delinquent" state would regard as deplorable during normal times. The classical system neither aimed at nor had the effect of raising significantly the standard of individual rights and liberties. At least the aspirations have changed in the post-war period.

The European Convention on Human Rights

The most prominent of the regional treaty arrangements to advance international law in the directions noted is the European Convention for the Protection of Human Rights and Fundamental Freedoms, Novmber 4, 1950.[13] The Convention had been adhered to by 16 of the 18 member countries of the Council of Europe, a political organization embracing most countries of Western and Southeastern Europe.[14] Smaller numbers have ratified the various protocols. The preamble to the Convention, after referring to the Universal Declaration of Human Rights, infra, notes that the Council of Europe attempts greater unity among its members and that one method of pursuing this aim is the further realization of human rights and fundamental freedoms. It stresses that the member countries, "which are

12. The materials at pp. 531–552 and 553–621, infra, examine problems in assertion of rights under customary or conventional international law before domestic courts.

13. 213 U.N.T.S. 221, Eur.T.S.No. 5 The Convention has been supplmented or amended by Protocol of March 20, 1952, Eur.T.S. No. 9; Protocol No. 2, May 6, 1963, Eur.T.S. No. 44; Protocol No. 3, May 6, 1963, Eur.T.S. No. 45; Protocol No. 4, September 16, 1963, Eur.T.S. No. 46; and Protocol No. 5, January 6, 1966, Eur.T.S. No. 55.

14. Greece, then the subject of human-rights investigations, denounced the Convention in 1969 and ceased to be a party to it in 1970. France and Switzerland never ratified the Convention.

like-minded and have a common heritage of political traditions, ideals, freedom and the rule of law," were resolved to take "the first steps for the collective enforcement of certain of the Rights stated in the Universal Declaration."

The Convention (including the Protocols) defines comprehensively the "rights and freedoms" which are to be assured to all individuals within the territory of its parties, not simply to aliens. The rights guaranteed by the Convention are not as extensive as those set forth in the Universal Declaration. The Convention was designed not to create new rights, but to place under international protection some basic rights already recognized by the domestic laws of many of the member states.

The drafters adopted an intermediate approach, avoiding both rigid codification (to which it would be difficult to obtain multinational adherence) and generalities so broad as to make judicial application infeasible. Broadly speaking, with inevitable differences in emphasis and in greater detail, the Convention treats procedural and substantive themes similar to those appearing in our Bill of Rights. Thus Articles 6 and 7 spell out safeguards throughout the entire criminal process, from investigation to judgment. Articles 9 to 11 provide that "everyone has the right to freedom of" thought, religion, expression, peaceful assembly and association—subject to limitations in the nature of *ordre public*. In one of its few references to aliens, the Convention provides that the declaration of such freedoms will not prevent the parties "from imposing restrictions on the political activity of aliens." Article 16.

The Convention establishes a complicated international machinery for the enforcement of these rights. The organ of first instance, a European Commission of Human Rights consisting of a national of each party, may hear complaints of alleged breaches of the Convention that are referred to it by any party. By ratifying the Convention, a state recognizes the Commission's jurisdiction to hear complaints brought by another party (Art. 24). More significant and innovative is the provision of Article 25 that the Commission may receive petitions leading to investigation and official action "from any person, non-governmental organization or group of individuals claiming to be the victim of a violation by one of the High Contracting Parties of the rights set forth in this Convention." However, the jurisdiction of the Commission under this article rests upon an optional declaration of the respondent state recognizing the competence of the Commission in this respect. As of 1973, twelve member states had filed such declarations, which subject them to proceedings before the Commission initiated by petitions even of their own nationals. The Commission may handle a petition only "after all domestic remedies have been exhausted, according to the generally recognized rules of international law." Article 26.

If, after investigation, its efforts at friendly settlement of the dispute fail, the Commission prepares a report stating its opinion as to the facts and as to a breach. If the question is not referred to the Court described below within a stated period, another body, the Committee of Ministers, decides by a two-thirds majority "whether there has been a violation of the Convention." If so, the Committee "shall prescribe a period during which the High Contracting Party concerned must take the measures required by the decision of the Committee of Ministers." The parties agree "to regard as binding on them any decision" of the Committee. Article 32.

The Convention also establishes a European Court of Human Rights. Under Articles 44 and 48, only the Commission or directly involved member states may bring a case before the Court. The Court's jurisdiction is dependent upon optional declarations (which may be on condition of reciprocity) by the member states submitting to the Court's compulsory jurisdiction; eleven nations have filed such declarations. If the Court concludes that an act of a member country is in conflict with the Convention and if the internal law of that country "allows only partial reparation to be made for the consequences of this decision," the Court's decision shall "afford just satisfaction to the injured party." Article 50.

At the end of 1973, 6,402 applications introduced by individuals or groups of individuals had been registered before the Commission. Of this total, decision has been taken in 5,553 cases: 5,432 rejections of applications, (including among important reasons the withdrawal of applications or the failure to pursue claims), and 121 declared admissible. Against states which had filed optional declaration under Article 25, both nationals and aliens had filed applications. In 1973, for example, 35 aliens and 139 nationals filed applications against Germany, 15 aliens and 38 nationals against Belgium. The Commission has registered ten cases brought by one member state against another. A total of 42 cases were brought before the Committee of Ministers (8 interstate, 34 individual applications). Fifteen cases had been brought before the Court.[15]

This rather unimpressive caseload should, however, be viewed in the light of the not inconsiderable influence which the Convention has had on the actions of national judiciaries,[16] and of the generally high level of recognition within the member countries of the rights which the Convention declares.

The cases before the Commission and Court have raised the broadest possible variety of issues: allegations of violations of freedom of expression, of illegal detention, of torture, of denial of proce-

15. These figures come from the summaries and charts in Council of Europe, Stock-Taking on the European Convention on Human Rights 62–69 (1974).

16. In several of the member countries, the Convention is self-executing and thus automatically supplements the domestic law applied by those countries' judiciaries. For a collection of some earlier decisions of national administrative or judicial organs, see Stein and Hay, Law and Institutions in the Atlantic Area 990–1020 (1967). Problems relating to the effect of an international agreement upon the internal law of a member country are examined at pp. 621–625, infra.

dural fairness. Some conflicts in Western Europe have figured importantly in the work of these institutions—for example, the violence and preventive measures in Northern Ireland. Ireland indeed lodged its own application against the United Kingdom in 1971.

Efforts within the United Nations

(*1*) *Declarations and Conventions*: The work of the United Nations, expressed through declarations or draft conventions, has addressed two tasks assumed by the newer international law—expanding the categories of protected individuals and uplifting the general standard of human rights. Recall that Article 1 of the Charter states one purpose of the United Nations to be international cooperation "in promoting and encouraging respect for human rights and for fundamental freedoms . . . ." Much of the effort in this field has been based upon the mandate in Articles 55 to 56 of the Charter.*

In 1948 the General Assembly unanimously approved the Universal Declaration of Human Rights,[17] a statement of principles that was not meant to be "binding" on member states but rather to provide the foundation for multilateral treaties. The Declaration sets forth a comprehensive catalogue of rights—including freedoms of the person, expression, religion, association and movement, equal access to public services, education and leisure, and an adequate standard of living. It has frequently been invoked by the General Assembly as a code of conduct and as a basis for appeals urging governments to respect human rights. The Declaration has also inspired several of the conventions referred to below.

A number of important conventions were born within the United Nations—and generally, after adoption by the General Assembly, submitted to the member states for ratification. The Genocide Convention of 1948, building upon the Nuremberg Judgment's condemnation of crimes by individuals against humanity in connection with aggressive war, proscribed the intentional destruction in whole or part of "a national, ethnical, racial or religious group as such" and made individuals, in public or private positions, criminally responsible therefor. Other conventions have dealt with refugees, stateless persons, slavery, freedom of information, and the status of women. In addition, the General Assembly has given much attention to the problems of racial discrimination and frequently debated apartheid in South Africa and its introduction into the territory under the South West African mandate. In 1963 it adopted a Declaration on the Elimination of All Forms of Racial Discrimination and in 1966 a convention of the same name. 60 Am.J.Int.L. 650 (1966).

A substantial number of countries have become parties to some of these conventions. As of December 1973, 77 countries (through ratification, accession, or notification of succession) were parties to the Genocide Convention; 75 countries to the Convention on the Elim-

17. General Assembly Resolution 217A (III), 10 December 1948.

ination of All Forms of Racial Discrimination; 72 countries to the Convention on Political Rights of Women; and 91 countries to the Convention Concerning the Abolition of Forced Labor.[18] But such accessions often include relatively few of the major powers. The record of the United States with respect to the human rights conventions adopted by the General Assembly and recommended to states for ratification is particularly bleak.[19]

Two proposed conventions prepared under U. N. auspices deal specifically with the problems considered in this Part B. One is the Draft Convention on the International Responsibility of States for Injuries to Aliens, excerpts from which appear at p. 373, supra. The other, an International Covenant on Civil and Political Rights, represents a fundamental departure from traditional international law. Prepared by the Human Rights Commission and the Third Committee of the General Assembly, it is supplemented by a companion International Covenant on Economic, Social and Cultural Rights. The two cover a broad spectrum of topics ranging from freedom of expression or from discrimination to rights to education, fair conditions of work, union membership and a protected family life. In December 1966 the General Assembly approved both drafts and recommended that member states ratify the Covenants.[20] As of June 1974, 26 states had ratified the first of these covenants, whereas 35 ratifications were necessary before the covenant was to become effective. The ratifying states included as varied cultures and political systems as those in Chile, Germany, Iraq, Kenya, Sweden and the U.S.S.R.

The following selections from the International Covenant on Civil and Political Rights bear upon issues raised by the cases in Part B.

Article 13

An alien lawfully in the territory of a State Party to the present Covenant may be expelled therefrom only in pursuance of a decision reached in accordance with law and shall, except where compelling reasons of national security otherwise require, be allowed to submit the reasons against his expulsion and to have his case reviewed by, and be represented for the purpose before, the competent authority or a person or persons especially designated by the competent authority.

Article 14

1. All persons shall be equal before the courts and tribunals. In the determination of any criminal charge against him, or of his rights and obligations in a suit at law, everyone shall be entitled to

18. The figures are taken from the U. N. Secretariat, Multilateral Treaties in respect of which the Secretary-General Performs Repository Functions, List of Signatures, Ratifications, Accessions etc. as at 31 Dec. 1973.

19. The reasons for this aloofness, as well as contemporary efforts to win the consent of the Senate to ratification of such conventions, are considered at pp. 570–577, infra.

20. Annex to General Assembly Res. 2200A (XXI), adopted December 16, 1966. The Covenants are reproduced in 61 Am.J.Int.L. 861, 870 (1967).

a fair and public hearing by a competent, independent and impartial tribunal established by law. . . .

2. Everyone charged with a criminal offense shall have the right to be presumed innocent until proved guilty according to law.

3. In the determination of any criminal charge against him, everyone shall be entitled to the following minimum guarantees, in full equality;

(a) To be informed promptly and in detail in a language which he understands of the nature and cause of the charge against him;

(b) To have adequate time and facilities for the preparation of his defence and to communicate with counsel of his own choosing;

(c) To be tried without undue delay;

(d) To be tried in his presence, and to defend himself in person or through legal assistance of his own choosing; to be informed, if he does not have legal assistance, of this right; and to have legal assistance assigned to him, in any case where the interests of justice so require, and without payment by him in any such case if he does not have sufficient means to pay for it;

(e) To examine, or have examined, the witnesses against him and to obtain the attendance and examination of witnesses on his behalf under the same conditions as witnesses against him;

(f) To have the free assistance of an interpreter if he cannot understand or speak the language used in court;

(g) Not to be compelled to testify against himself or to confess guilt.

4. In the case of juvenile persons, the procedure shall be such as will take account of their age and the desirability of promoting their rehabilitation.

5. Everyone convicted of a crime shall have the right to his conviction and sentence being reviewed by a higher tribunal according to law.

6. When a person has by a final decision been convicted of a criminal offense and when subsequently his conviction has been reversed or he has been pardoned on the ground that a new or newly discovered fact shows conclusively that there has been a miscarriage of justice, the person who has suffered punishment as a result of such conviction shall be compensated according to law, unless it is proved that the non-disclosure of the unknown fact in time is wholly or partly attributable to him.

7. No one shall be liable to be tried or punished again for an offense for which he has already been finally convicted or acquitted in accordance with the law and penal procedure of each country.

Article 17

1. No one shall be subjected to arbitrary or unlawful interference with his privacy, family, home or correspondence, nor to unlawful attacks on his honor and reputation.

2. Everyone has the right to the protection of the law against such interference or attacks.

This Covenant would establish a Human Rights Committee to which the parties are to submit periodic reports on measures which they adopt to give effect to the defined rights. A party can further declare, under Article 41, that it recognizes the Committee's competence to receive communications from another party to the effect that it is not fulfilling its obligations. Various procedures looking towards conciliation and amicable settlement are then to be pursued. The Committee or an *ad hoc* conciliation commission may prepare reports for the parties to any dispute, including findings of fact and views about amicable settlement. Under an optional protocol, states can further recognize the Committee's competence to consider communications from individuals "who claim to be victims of a violation . . . of any of the rights set forth in the Covenant." Before submitting a communication to the Committee, an individual must have "exhausted all available domestic remedies." Again the proceedings look towards conciliation or amicable settlement. The Committee would report annually to the General Assembly.

These terse descriptions of the remedial provisions in the Covenant and the European Convention for the Protection of Human Rights and Fundamental Freedoms underscore a major obstacle to all such contemporary efforts. When international law treated only state-alien relationships, the problems of developing effective remedies to secure rights that were asserted under the law of state responsibility were of course legion. Current proposals looking towards a truly universal law magnify them. By definition, the medium of diplomatic protection is unavailable to a national complaining of his own government's conduct. As the descriptions above suggest, alternative remedial paths are possible but agonizingly cautious, slow, and at the present time largely ineffectual. One of the more effective techniques for assuring compliance is the requirement imposed upon parties to furnish periodic reports, and the availability of such reports as well as those prepared by investigatory bodies to other treaty parties. Publicity serves as sanction, although the material below treating the Chilean situation of 1973–75 raises questions about the effectiveness of that sanction. More ambitious proposals have included one for establishment of an international system of habeas corpus.[21]

(*2*) *The U. N. Commission on Human Rights.* This Commission was established in 1946 as a subsidiary organ of the Economic and Social Council (ECOSOC). Its initial function was to assist ECOSOC to fulfill its Charter-imposed duty to promote respect for human rights. Its members are elected so as to achieve distribution among the capitalist, socialist and less developed worlds.

21. A number of recent covenants prepared within the U. N. and recent proposals for more effective international regulation include institutional arrangements which raise problems under the United States Constitution and thus further inhibit our participation in such agreements. Such issues are examined in the Problem at p. 609, infra.

The Commission early had occasion to observe that it had no power to take action with respect to private complaints alleging violations of human rights. Two decades later, ECOSOC decided that the Commission could make a thorough study of situations revealing a consistent pattern of such violations—for example, apartheid in South Africa. Formal rule changes during the 1970–71 period gave this new power an institutional base, by providing for matters such as the filing of petitions by victims and others, the general requirement of exhaustion of local remedies, and the requirements of specificity in petitions. These rules stress the necessity of showing a "consistent pattern of gross and reliably attested violations." [22] Activities of the Commission and any Sub-Commissions remain confidential until (and if) the Commission decides to make recommendations to ECOSOC.

Private Organizations

Prominent among the non-governmental organizations committed to the recognition and protection of human rights are the International Commission of Jurists and Amnesty International. We describe briefly the structure and purposes of the latter organization.[23]

Founded in 1961, Amnesty is a worldwide institution independent of any government, political faction or religious creed. With headquarters in London, it embraces over 1,100 Amnesty Groups, linked through national sections which existed as of 1973 in 33 countries —ranging from Bangladesh, Ghana, Korea and Lebanon to Australia, the Federal Republic of Germany, Switzerland and the United States. Amnesty has consultative status with international organizations such as the United Nations, the Council of Europe, and the Organization of American States, a status giving it the right of petition, the right to have its observers attend debates, and a direct path for communicating its views to such organizations.

Amnesty's purpose is to seek the release of persons imprisoned because of their political, religious or other conscientiously held beliefs, or because of their ethnic, racial, or linguistic status. Such persons it terms Prisoners of Conscience. It seeks "global impartiality" in its program of aid, maintaining a neutrality among countries, political or economic systems, religions or geographical regions. Amnesty Groups are encouraged to seek the release of prisoners of "contrasting ideological backgrounds or holding different political or religious beliefs. Thus, one may be from a Communist country, another from a Western industrialized society and the third from a non-aligned Third World nation." Amnesty imposes one basic qualification upon its aid. "No [prisoner] is adopted who is proved to have advocated or used violence or engaged in espionage." As a pruden-

22. See Committee Report, Private Petition on Human Rights at the United Nations, 29 Record of the Ass'n of the Bar of the City of New York 500 (1974). See generally Sohn and Buergenthal, International Protection of Human Rights 739–855 (1973).

23. The information about Amnesty International is taken primarily from Amnesty International, Handbook for Groups (Amnesty International Publications, March 1973, mimeographed publication).

tial matter, it also adopts no prisoner if its adoption "would in any way jeopardize his position."

The Amnesty Groups, to whom names of Prisoners of Conscience are provided by a central secretariat, proceed through a variety of methods. Where appropriate, and necessarily with governmental permission, Amnesty will itself send representatives to a country to investigate allegations that rights of Prisoners of Conscience have been violated. Such representatives will issue reports. Amnesty itself will then make representations to governments and international organizations. But most of the work is through the Groups, which correspond with the government involved, with the prisoner "assigned" to the Group, and with that prisoner's family to provide financial and legal assistance and to sustain morale.

"The effectiveness and success of Amnesty International rests in mobilizing public opinion everywhere . . . It demonstrates continuously to prisoners and government that no one is forgotten, that the world *cares*, that injustice, mass arrests, mock trials and torture will never become just another news item." Amnesty-inspired publicity campaigns about a particular prisoner or a group of prisoners have penetrated the local press and international organizations, and in its view, have in numerous cases "had an identifiable effect on a government's actions. International public indignation can force a repressive government to re-assess its policies, and publicity has in many countries contributed to individual or partial amnesties, to better prison conditions, to open trials, and to the suspension of the death penalty." Where publicity promises to be a less expedient path than direct and private negotiation with a government, Amnesty so advises its local Group.

Perhaps Amnesty's primary stress has been on the containment of torture. Such efforts recently culminated in its publication, Report on Torture (London 1973). The book provides a sobering documentation of the wide-spread and systematic use of torture by governmental authorities against prisoners in general, and Prisoners of Conscience in particular. The variety of techniques are now familiar knowledge to a world accustomed to reports of inhumane treatment officially practiced or tolerated by many governments: beatings, abuse of sexual organs, sexual assault, electric shocks, and other sophisticated forms of physical degradation, together with the more ambiguous category of "psychological torture". The survey reported in the book "indicates that many states in the world today deliberately use torture" with the complicity of police, the military, doctors, scientists, judges and politicians. The field has experienced the same improved technology as industrial products in general, as foreign experts travel among countries to conduct "schools of torture." In some situations, such torture "plays an integral role in the political system itself," inducing a regime of uncertainty and terror which tends to contain any effort towards free expression of opinion, let alone political opposition. The purpose frequently is "to set torture as the price of dissent."

In this Report, Amnesty distinguishes between a *utilitarian* justification or criticism of torture, and a criticism based upon *natural rights* and the postulate of universal human values. (The root distinctions between these two philosophical frameworks for arguments about "rights" are described at pp. 409–413, infra.) The Report argues that an attempt to condone or abolish torture on the basis of a cost-benefit efficiency calculus is "totally inadmissible . . . To place the debate on such grounds is to give the argument away; in effect it means that if it can be shown to be efficient, it is permissible . . . Nowhere is the argument that the means corrupt the end more true." Rather, the Report rests upon the postulate of the individual as a moral and social being entitled to the "dignity and integrity of each human being." It supports such a natural-right position through recourse to teachings of the world's religions, to writings of philosophers and moralists, and to the development over the last three centuries "of a concept of inalienable human rights." "The argument against torture rests essentially on moral grounds."

Noting the strong injunctions against torture in international documents such as the U. N. Declaration of Human Rights and the European Convention on Human Rights, the Report calls attention to the inadequacy of existing remedies for victims of torture, and the continuing tension between national sovereignty and international protection. It comments that the U. N. Commission on Human Rights "has neither the will nor the power" to defend the Universal Declaration of Human Rights and its prohibition of torture. It notes, as will indeed be suggested at p. 394, infra, the character of that Commission as a public forum, with states frequently sharing interests in non-interference. The Report finds the Inter-American Commission on Human Rights, p. 395, infra, a more effective organization, and gives highest praise to the administration of the European Convention on Human Rights, noting, however, that Western Europe is a part of the world where principles of human dignity and principles of civil liberties underlying the Rule of Law are most respected.

An Illustration: Chile 1973–75 and the Work of Private and Governmental Human Rights Organizations

The instances of widespread and ruthless violations of the basic rights defined in the U. N. Declaration and other instruments are many and well known in the post-war world. When such violations are alleged to occur in countries of different political "blocs" or cultures, the opportunities for pressures to alleviate the situation may be few and slight even for well-intending foreign governments. We here select as an illustrative study a country generally linked by tradition and economy to Western Europe and the United States, and hence in theory more susceptible to pressures from governments, international organizations or private groups within or including those countries.

One of the more publicized and documented instances of widespread violations of human rights in recent years occurred in Chile, following the 1973 overthrow by military coup of the Socialist-Communist coalition government, the Popular Unity led by then Chilean President Allende. The military junta which has ruled in Chile since 1973 inherited a situation of political and economic disintegration. Its approach to the many problems before it has included as a central component the repression of all political activity which the junta views as threatening to the type of political and economic order that it would develop in Chile and to the stability that it would maintain. This repression has involved widespread, and in some important respects systematic, abuse of human rights—ranging from secret arrests and the holding of prisoners incommunicado in unknown locations, to the use of torture.

The governmental conduct within Chile has received unusually wide attention in the world press, and in government circles in numbers of other countries, including congressional hearings treating these matters within the United States. Information about Chilean conditions has been obtained not only from political refugees who have left the country but from reporters, delegations of foreign governments within Chile, and visits of groups representing governmental and private human rights organizations. Hence the Chilean situation affords an unusually complete and compact study of the means available outside a country to persuade a national government to a change in policy.

The situation in Chile has several times come before the U. N. Human Rights Commission. That Commission has been subjected to sharp attacks by critics stressing its sterile debates and propagandistic speeches. As of 1974, such criticism emphasized the Commission's failure to inquire into allegations of inhumane practices in eight countries, ranging from Brazil and Chile to Iran, Tanzania and Northern Ireland. A fundamental reason for the Commission's ineffectiveness appeared to be "obstructionist tactics" of groups of members, particularly within the Soviet bloc, who in general oppose any move towards interference by the Commission with internal political ordering. (Compare the remarks of Tunkin, at p. 405, infra.)

The Commission's session ending in March 1974 devoted much attention to Chile. But the debate ended inconclusively, as the Soviet Union and Chile agreed to a "trade-off". While the Soviet Union dropped its call for a resolution denouncing the Chilean junta, Chile abandoned its proposal for a condemnation of the U.S.S.R.'s treatment of the author Solzhenitsyn. In a 1975 meeting, the U. N. Commission did resolve to send an *Ad Hoc* Working Group of five members to Chile to investigate and prepare a report, an innovative procedure for the Commission. But several months after granting permission to the Working Group to visit Chile, the Chilean Government reversed its decision and denied entry. In July 1975 (as reported in the New York Times, July 12, 1975, p. 7, col. 1), Deputy Secretary of State Ingersoll expressed to a Chilean minister the strong displeasure of the United States at this position—particularly because the United States had earlier supported measures at the Organization of American States to postpone a discussion of the Chilean human-rights issue on grounds that the U.N. Commission was soon to visit Chile.

The Chilean events also came before the Inter-American Commission on Human Rights of the Organization of American States. The Commission of seven members was created in 1960, and became in 1970 a principal organ of the O.A.S. charged with the task of promoting "the observance and protection of human rights," and serving "as a consultative organ" of the O.A.S. In 1965, the Commission acquired power to deal with individual complaints charging violations of certain categories of basic rights set forth in the American Declaration of the Rights and Duties of Man.

Numerous communications charging systematic violations of human rights came before the Commission after the overthrow of President Allende. It also received a letter from 33 United States Congressmen urging the Commission to undertake a full investigation. The Commission received permission from the Chilean government to visit Chile in July of 1974. On the basis of its investigations and visits, it issued a report entitled "Status of Human Rights in Chile."[24]

The Report stressed that it could not "make a comparative study of the political systems that have succeeded each other in Chile in recent years, or . . . make a political evaluation of those systems." The Commission was "not in a position to pass judgment on the degree to which basic human rights were protected" during the Allende government. "It is not for the Commission to decide whether the present political regime is more or less desirable than the previous regime." The Report states that "after rational analysis" of the evidence, the Commission concluded that, "under the regime instituted in Chile beginning September 11, 1973, extremely serious violations of human rights occurred." Taking account of "the exceptional circumstances which resulted in the advent of that regime, with the employment of force and bitter confrontation," it eliminated from consideration the loss of life during the brief period following the military coup. Nonetheless, it found continuing violations of human rights "by acts of commission or omission of the present Government." The rights which it found violated included the right to life, to personal safety and liberty, to habeas corpus, to freedom of expression, to freedom of association, and to political rights. With respect to personal safety, it observed that the right was "directly and seriously violated by the practice of psychological and physical abuse in the form of cruel and inhuman treatment." The Commission transmitted its report to the Chairman of the Permanent Council of the O.A.S.

Inquiry into the Chilean situation was also pursued by a number of private human-rights organizations, including Amnesty International, supra, and the International Commission of Jurists. That

24. Excerpts from the Report on the Status of Human Rights in Chile, October 25, 1974, are set forth in 14 Int. Leg.Mat. 115 (1975).

Commission sent a team to Chile in April 1974, with three members including a United States citizen who was formerly an Assistant Secretary of State for Inter-American affairs.[25]

The Commission, which has consultative status with UNESCO and with the Council of Europe, describes its function as one "to defend the Rule of Law throughout the world, and to work towards the full observance of the provisions in the Universal Declaration of Human Rights." It describes itself as "a strictly non-political organization . . . [of] complete independence . . . [and] is supported by jurists from all continents . . . ." The mission of three went to Chile in response to a request of the World Council of Churches and to a public invitation issued by the Chilean Foreign Minister to "respected organizations" to come to Chile to "find out for themselves the true situation."

The Final Report noted that "normal democratic processes of the Constitution" have been overthrown, leading to an absence of freedom from arbitrary arrests and detention and military trial procedures. It referred to illustrations of coerced confessions, ex post facto application of law, and erroneous sentences from which there was no appellate review. The broad categories arrested included those suspected of violence and of political and intellectual opposition. There were instances of summary executions. "From information we received from sources we consider wholly reliable . . .," there was use of physical and psychological coercion to obtain information and confessions, and in certain instances compulsory "attendance at the torture of others." This Final Report was attacked within the United States, through press releases and paid advertisements in the press, by the Chilean government and the Chilean Bar Association, on the ground that it was distorted, biased and in error as to basic facts.

As of early 1975, the work of these official and private organizations had achieved wide publicity in the press within the United States and Western European countries. A number of United States Congressmen had publicly expressed concern about the Chilean situation. The Executive Branch, whatever its private communications to the military junta might have been, remained discreet in its public pronouncements. Although the United States expressed support for the investigations in Chile of missions from the O.A.S. and the U. N. Commission on Human Rights, it did not appear to apply strong pressure upon the Chilean government. But the notoriety given the Chilean events appeared to impose some constraint (in part from concerned Congressmen) upon the volume of financial support given

25. Now and formerly Professor Covey Oliver of the University of Pennsylvania Law School. The other members were Mr. Niall MacDermot, Q.C., Secretary-General of the International Commission of Jurists, and Dr. Kurt Madlener, Specialist in Latin American Penal Law at the Max-Planck Institute of Comparative and International Penal Law in Germany. The information above is taken from the Final Report of Mission to Chile, April 1974, to Study the Legal System and the Protection of Human Rights, issued in mimeographed form by the International Commission of Jurists.

by the United States to Chile, support that was resumed after the 1973 coup as evidence of satisfaction at the overthrow of the Allende government and as one base for the development of a stable, anti-communist order. The situation was described as follows in the New York Times, May 12, 1975, p. 1, col. 5:

> After 20 months in power Chile's military junta shows few signs of dismantling the vast apparatus of political repression created to "extirpate the Marxist cancer."
>
> The military took over when the country was bitterly polarized between an anti-Marxist majority and a leftist minority, and rapidly drifting toward economic chaos and a possible civil war. But from its beginning the junta has chosen to treat the followers of the late President Salvador Allende Gossens as a vanquished enemy capable at any time of posing a strong terrorist threat.
>
> According to Government estimates more than 41,000 people—one of every 250 Chileans—have been detained at least temporarily for political reasons.
>
> Church sources who have concerned themselves with political prisoners believe that the figure is closer to 95,000, one of every 100. Both the Government and its domestic critics appear agreed that there are still 5,000 people in prison camps for political reasons.
>
> While vast numbers of people passed through detention in the aftermath of the coup that toppled President Allende in 1973, the arrests and charges of torture have declined in recent months. Nonetheless, virtually all international human-rights organizations, including the United Nations and the Organization of American States, have reported systematic and gross violations after repeated visits to Chile.
>
> Earlier this year, in an unprecedented move, the Western European nations that are among Chile's largest creditors refused to consider renegotiating payments on her foreign debt until progress had been achieved in human rights.
>
> The junta and its supporters have attributed their still-deteriorating image to a concerted Marxist campaign that has infiltrated the highest international organizations and the mass media, universities and governmental circles in Western countries.
>
> Last week President Augusto Pinochet Ugarte unveiled a new series of rules to prevent "abuses of power that the Government has never approved." They call for the punishment of torturers and require that new detainees be released within five days or turned over to the courts. Intelligence services must inform a detainee's nearest relatives within 48 hours of his arrest.
>
> The junta's domestic critics remain skeptical because scores are still arrested every week and allegations of torture continue to make their way into public records.
>
> . . .
>
> The secret police apparatus has grown to such a degree that it has become a parallel government in the view of human-rights lawyers and concerned clergymen.

There are five intelligence services, with one or two of them rapidly gaining more power than the rest. A network of informers has expanded throughout the shantytowns, factories, schools and universities. Applicants to public agencies are often screened by the intelligence services.

The agents are able to ignore standards of conduct set by the Government for other officials and ordinary citizens . . . .

. . .

QUESTIONS

(1) Suppose that the events of the Chattin case occurred in 1974 and the case came that year before an international tribunal. What effect, if any, should the International Covenant on Civil and Political Rights have upon the decision under the following circumstances: (a) The Covenant has become effective through the required number (35) of ratifications, and Mexico and the United States are parties to it. (b) The Covenant has become effective, but neither the United States nor Mexico are parties. (c) The Covenant has not become effective, and only three African and two European countries have ratified it. It appears doubtful that 35 ratifications will be deposited.

(2) Do you view Article 14 of the Covenant as a successful effort to approach the problems raised in Chattin from an international rather than a national perspective?

(3) In evaluating the enforcement measures of the International Covenant on Civil and Political Rights and allied conventions, consider the relevance of such national institutions as the ombudsman, state commissions against discrimination, the federal civil rights commission, or federal habeas corpus proceedings. What additional difficulties do their international counterparts confront?

(4) In view of your knowledge of the history of the last decade during which these covenants have been debated and drafted within the United Nations, what significance or utility do you think they have in the contemporary world?

(5) Apart from the utility which you think that conventions of this character may have in regulating state conduct, what effect have the developments sketched in the two preceding Notes upon the concept of domestic jurisdiction? Do you consider this trend desirable and as some independent justification for the approval by the General Assembly of such conventions?

(6) From the materials in the preceding Note and from your general knowledge of these matters, how effective a sanction do you take publicity to be as a means of persuading a government to refrain from violation of human rights? What other types of sanctions are apt to be most effective—and under what conditions?

Additional reading: The best collection of source materials on these matters, together with rich bibliographical data, appear in Sohn and Buergenthal, International Protection of Human Rights (1973).

Two of the following comments address the work under United Nations auspices to expand the protection of the individual. The first includes strands of thinking that have long been present in the writings of Latin American scholars of international law and reflects aspects of South American experience with diplomatic protection which some cases in Part B have illustrated. The second is an attempt to define a set of values which would serve as foundation and guide for international programs for the protection of human rights. The third comment expresses a Soviet perspective on the various human rights efforts of the post-war years.

F. V. GARCIA-AMADOR, REPORT ON INTERNATIONAL RESPONSIBILITY

International Law Commission, Eighth Session.
U.N.Doc.No. A/CN.4/96, January 20, 1956, pp. 71–83;
[1956] 2 Int.L.Comm'n YBK. 173, 199–203.

In traditional international law the "responsibility of States for damage done in their territory to the person or property of foreigners" frequently appears closely bound up with two great doctrines or principles: the so-called "international standard of justice", and the principle of the equality of nationals and aliens. The first of these principles has been invoked in the past as the basis for the exercise of the right of States to protect their nationals abroad, while the second has been relied on for the purpose of rebutting responsibility on the part of the State of residence when the aliens concerned received the same treatment and were granted the same legal or judicial protection as its own nationals. Although, therefore, both principles had the same basic purpose, namely, the protection of the person and of his property, they appeared both in traditional theory and in past practice as mutually conflicting and irreconcilable.

Yet, if the question is examined in the light of international law in its present stage of development, one obtains a very different impression. What was formerly the object of these two principles—the protection of the person and of his property—is now intended to be accomplished by the international recognition of the essential rights of man. Under this new legal doctrine, the distinction between nationals and aliens no longer has any *raison d'être,* so that both in theory and in practice these two traditional principles are henceforth inapplicable. In effect, both of these principles appear to have been outgrown by contemporary international law. . . .

The abuses which had occurred in the exercise of diplomatic protection by certain States led, understandably, to a reaction against the very principle which used to be invoked as the foundation of the responsibility of the State. The Argentine jurist, Carlos Calvo, referring to this state of affairs, proclaimed the doctrine which has since been pleaded in answer to international claims based on the violation of the "international standard of justice". In his opinion, "Aliens who establish themselves in a country are certainly entitled to the same rights of protection as nationals, but they cannot claim any greater measure of protection." [26]

26. [Eds.] Citation omitted. The so-called Calvo Clause is considered at pp. 522–530, infra.

The principle was reaffirmed in identical terms on several later occasions and incorporated into international agreements. Thus, the Convention on Rights and Duties of States, signed at the Seventh International Conference of American States (Montevideo, 1933), provides in its article 9:

> The jurisdiction of States within the limits of national territory applies to all the inhabitants.
>
> Nationals and foreigners are under the same protection of the law and the national authorities and the foreigners may not claim rights either other or more extensive than those of the nationals. [Citation omitted.]

. . . It is noteworthy that the constitutions and the legislation of the American countries, and the inter-American conventions which relate to the status of aliens, treat aliens as on a footing of equality with nationals for the purposes of the enjoyment of civil rights and individual guarantees. . . .

The institution of diplomatic protection, and the principle underlying it, do not appear to constitute the most efficient means of protecting the rights and interests of aliens. In the first place, although diplomatic protection, being one of the functions of the national State, should constitute a duty on its part, history and international practice show that it has never been treated as such. Except for a very few writers, the bulk of legal opinion has never considered diplomatic protection as a duty of the State of nationality. . . . It is purely and simply a right which the State may exercise, or choose not to exercise, in its absolute discretion. Conclusive evidence of this is provided by the fact that, on occasions, the State concerned has refused to grant protection although requested to do so by the interested party and although the claim was justified; . . .

For its part the principle of the "international standard of justice", whether it is taken on its own merits or as a complement of diplomatic protection, has always suffered from a fundamental defect: its obvious vagueness and imprecision. None of the international bodies which have accepted and applied the principle has been able to define it: either no attempt to do so has been made, or, in the few cases where it has been made, it has been with little success. They have usually merely referred to it as a ground for their decision, or applied it to particular cases on which they tried to build up a general rule by means of inductive reasoning. When invoked directly by the State, the international standard of justice presents even greater disadvantages. One of its most determined advocates admits that "powerful States have at times exacted from weak States a greater degree of responsibility than from States of their own strength". [Citation omitted.] The origin of the "standard" may be traced to the sort of reasoning which gave rise to the system of capitulations or extraterritoriality that was for long imposed upon the peoples of Asia and Africa. The consequent discrimination in favour of the foreign groups of the population, and the infringement of the principle of equality among nations, became repugnant to public opinion and to legal thinking in the countries concerned. . . .

The principle of equality between nationals and aliens is likewise inadmissible, if its interpretation, or its practical application, should conflict with international law. It is certainly inadmissible in its extreme form—as an absolute principle which is not subject to any limitations whatsoever. For the same reason it is inapplicable if the conduct of the organs of the State does not respect those rules and safeguards which in all countries protect the person and property of individuals. The fact that nationals suffer equally from such a situation cannot constitute a valid excuse for a State to evade its international responsibility. However, apart from these cases, it would appear difficult, both legally and politically, to accept treatment giving preference to and implying privileges in favour of aliens. Aliens cannot rationally expect a privileged status as compared with nationals, especially when no greater obligations and responsibilities are required of them; in fact, they have fewer obligations and responsibilities than nationals.

Now, both the "international standard of justice" and the principle of equality between nationals and aliens, hitherto considered as antagonistic and irreconcilable, can well be reformulated and integrated into a new legal rule incorporating the essential elements and serving the main purposes of both. The basis of this new principle would be the "universal respect for, and observance of, human rights and fundamental freedoms" referred to in the Charter of the United Nations and in other general, regional and bilateral instruments. The object of the "internationalization" (to coin a term) of these rights and freedoms is to ensure the protection of the legitimate interests of the human person, irrespective of his nationality. Whether the person concerned is a citizen or an alien is then immaterial: human beings, as such, are under the direct protection of international law.

It will be easily seen how, from a purely legal point of view, both of the two traditional principles have been rendered obsolete by the development of international law. The "international standard of justice" was evolved and obtained recognition at a time when ideas differed from those which prevail at present: international law recognized and protected the essential rights of man in his capacity as an alien, or, in other words, by virtue of his status as a national of a certain State. The principle of equality between nationals and aliens, in its turn, was formulated in order to counteract the consequences of the difference in status which the law attached to nationals and aliens. . . .

The fact, however, that these two traditional principles are no longer applicable does not necessarily imply that the new legal system must ignore their essential elements and their basic purposes. On the contrary, the "international recognition of human rights and fundamental freedoms" constitutes precisely a synthesis of the two principles. In fact, from a study of the instruments in which these rights and freedoms have received international recognition, and of the two great Declarations and other international instruments defining these rights and freedoms, it becomes evident that all of them accord a measure of protection which goes well beyond the *minimum* protection which the rule of the "international standard of justice" was meant to ensure to aliens. . . .

Accordingly, it would be illogical, in law as in practice, to endeavour to maintain either of the two traditional principles in a codification of the law of international responsibility. Both principles have become obsolete and to press the case for either of them would be tantamount to ignoring one of the political and legal realities which is most clearly apparent in the contemporary world situation.

McDOUGAL AND BEBR, HUMAN RIGHTS IN THE UNITED NATIONS

58 Am.J.Int.L. 603–608 (1964).

The human rights program of the United Nations represents a tremendous collective effort, by the formulation of accepted principle and the establishment of new procedures, to extend protection of basic individual liberties, most broadly conceived, to levels of effective authority higher than the nation state. . . .

For its goals the United Nations program is heir to all the great historic movements for man's freedom (including the English, American, and French revolutions and the events they set in train), to the enduring elements in the tradition of natural law and natural rights and in most of the world's great religions and philosophies, and to the findings of contemporary science about the interrelations of simple respect for human dignity and all other individual and community values. It is familiar history how rudimentary demands for freedom from despotic executive tyranny have gradually been transformed into demands for, and provision of, protection against not only the executive but all institutions or functions of government and even private oppression, and how early demands for the barest "civil liberties," embodied in the most primitive conception of rule by "law," have burgeoned into insistence upon comprehensive "human rights" —that is, into demands for effective participation in all community value processes upon which minimum civil liberties depend. This history can be traced in the changing relation of the individual to the state, from the absolutist state through the liberal or "laissez-faire" state to the emerging conception of political organization as an instrument of all values, with government of, by, and for all people. From demands for physical security and inviolability of the person, with freedom from cruel and inhuman punishment and arbitrary detention, may be noted a progression to demands for freedom of expression and opinion, of conscience and worship, and of meeting and association. With the impact of industrialization, large-scale concentration of economic power, and urbanization, and the attendant ills of exploitation, unemployment, and inadequate housing, medical care, education, and so on, came not unnaturally demands for improved working and health conditions, fair and adequate wages, access to education and skill acquisition, and protection against the hazards of sickness, unemployment, old age, and the like. Today the recognition is general, and demands are made accordingly, that "liberty" requires "the ordering of social and economic conditions by governmental authority." [Citation omitted.]

It is in response to the ever increasing demands of people everywhere for greater access to, and wider sharing of, basic values, of the kind so impressionistically indicated above, that the United Nations program for human rights is being framed and implemented. For more systematic exposition and appraisal of the specific content of the United Nations formulations, these growing, common demands of people may be conveniently categorized in terms of certain particular values, as follows:

> the wide sharing of *power,* both formal and effective, including participation in the processes of government and of parties and pressure groups and equality before the law;
>
> the fundamental *respect* for human dignity which both precludes discriminations based on race, sex, color, religion,

political opinion or other ground irrelevant to capacity and provides a positive recognition of common merit as a human being and special merit as an individual;

the *enlightenment* by which rational decisions and other choices can be made, including freedom of inquiry, opinion, and communication;

equal and adequate access to *wealth* processes, to opportunities for work and to the resources and technology necessary to the production of goods and services for maintaining rising standards of living and comfort;

the opportunity to achieve health and *well-being,* and the inviolability of the person, with freedom from cruel and inhuman punishments and positive opportunity for the development of talents and enrichment of personality;

opportunity for the acquisition of the *skill* necessary to express talent and to achieve individual and community values to the fullest;

opportunity for *affection,* fraternity, and congenial personal relationships in groups freely chosen;

freedom to choose standards of *rectitude* and responsibility, to explain life, the universe, and values, and to worship as may seem best;

and, in sum, a *security* which includes not merely freedom from violence and threats of violence, but also full opportunity to preserve and increase all values by peaceful, non-coercive procedures.

Though it is for these values that men have long framed constitutions, established and administered governments, and sought an appropriate formulation of principle and balancing of power, the United Nations program seeks to extend this effort to more people, in a vaster area, at higher levels of authority, and "with a grander vision and on a more comprehensive scale" than hitherto attempted. [Citation omitted.]

The conditions under which the United Nations seeks its human rights goals may be described most generally in terms of two trends of contradictory impact: the first and most comprehensive trend is that toward an ever tightening global interdependence of all peoples in securing their basic values, and it is the increasing recognition by peoples of this interdependence that is the dynamic and integrating stimulus behind the human rights program; the interfering trend is that toward the relative bipolarization—or perhaps, more recently, tripolarization—or the world's power structures, which, with its rising crisis in security and continuously more imminent portents of violence, increases the unwillingness of active decision-makers in nation states to loosen controls over individuals and, hence, threatens the whole human rights program, as well as most of man's values and institutions, with disaster.

The major outlines of peoples' contemporary interdependences are only too clear. More than 150 years ago Kant wrote:

> The intercourse, more or less close which has been steadily increasing between the nations of the earth, has now extended so enormously that a violation of the right in one of the parts of the world is felt all over it. [Citation omitted.]

Today accelerating changes in technology, in population growth, in the demands and identifications of peoples, and in techniques of organization multiply by many times the intensity of this interdependence. In an earth-space arena of ever increasing dimensions and of hydrogen and atomic bombs, as well, perhaps, as of other new instruments of unimaginable destructiveness, it needs little emphasis that no people can be secure—even in the minimal sense of freedom from violence and threats of violence—unless all peoples are secure. It is scarcely less obvious that security, even in this minimal sense, is dependent upon the abundant production and wide sharing of all other values: upon, in terms of the categorizations suggested above, a sharing of power which does not repress and accumulate hatreds but gives outlet to constructive energies; upon a respect for human dignity which does not breed psychopathic personalities, resentments, and predispositions to violence, but rather gives ample opportunity for the fullest development of personality and creative capacity; upon a flow of enlightenment which facilitates realistic orientation in contemporary world processes and the making of decisions which rationally promote major objectives; upon the production and distribution of the goods and services necessary to maintain continually rising standards of living and the provision of ample opportunities for employment on respected jobs; upon maintenance of standards of health and well-being and protection of the person which permit the fullest and freest participation in all value processes; upon continually widening positive identifications of peoples with peoples and intensifying loyalties to larger areal groupings; and, finally, upon sufficient consensus in conceptions of right and wrong to support appropriate institutions and a growing sense of common responsibility, whatever the details of justification, for preservation and enhancement of the values of all peoples. Conversely, whatever values we summarize as "human rights," however narrowly or broadly we may conceive them, are with equal obviousness dependent upon "security" and all other values. Most broadly and rationally conceived, the "human rights" and "security" of any people and all peoples may in fact be said to be not merely "interdependent" but *identical;* the different words are but alternative ways of describing the same aspirations and interrelations of people.

It is not, however, rational co-operation in the peaceful pursuit of interdependent values, but rather the trend toward bipolarization or tripolarization, and contending systems of public order with nation states organizing themselves into "garrisoned camps," that today most conspicuously dominate the world arena. The growth of great power blocs, with several of the dominant Powers insisting upon the inevitability of world dominion by totalitarian measures, the destructive potentialities of the newly developed weapons, and the continued incidence in many parts of the world of ignorance, disease, poverty, and exploitation, with their attendant political instabilities, all combine to create general expectations of rising insecurities and more comprehensive violence. These expectations of imminent violence both increase the ordinary difficulties in co-operation between nation states and facilitate processes within nation states deeply inimical to human rights. As lines between probable combatants are more and more sharply drawn, proposals for co-operation between nation states for the promotion of "human rights" or "security" or any other value are appraised in terms, not of possible long-range effects in an ever receding peaceful world, but rather of immediate impact on fighting effectiveness. Within nation states, measures considered indispensable to security in a bipolar world of impending atomic war, whether rationally calculated or not, tend to move even the freer societies toward practices resembling those of the totalitarianism they fight. The whole global transformation has been aptly described as a movement toward "garrison-police" states, in which demands for power are accentuated at the expense of every other value, with increasing militarization, governmentalization, centralization, concentration, and regimentation, and in which all values other than power are "politicized" in such practices as "the compulsion to work" and the gradation and stabilization of income, the "requisitioning of talent and skill," the "administration of hate" and "withdrawal of affection," the "requisitioning of loyalty," the "dogmatization and ritualization" of rectitude, and so on. [Citation omitted.] In this context it is small wonder that the United Nations' human rights program exhibits some of the symptoms of incipient paralysis.

A later and more detailed articulation of the Lasswell-McDougal value system and conceptual framework, as applied to human rights, appears in McDougal, Human Rights and World Public Order, 14 Va. J.Int.L. 387 (1974). Consider the following remarks from another article of McDougal, Perspectives for an International Law of Human Dignity, 1959 Proc.Am.Soc.Int.L. 107, 111–112:

> The values we recommend for postulation as the goal values of human dignity are . . . merely the traditional values of humanitarianism and enlightenment bequeathed to us by most of the great religions and secular philosophies prevailing in recent centuries. . . . The strength and frequency of these shared demands are demonstrated in many different formulations of authority and expressions of effective control, both international and national, official and unofficial, such as the United Nations Charter, the Universal Declaration of Human Rights, the proposed Covenants on Human Rights, regional arrangements and programs, . . . national constitutions (old and new), political party platforms, pressure group and private association programs, and so on. . . . Historically, the values of human dignity have been justified by derivations from premises originating in many different sources . . . such as religion, natural law, metaphysics, science, history, common sense, and so on, and there would appear little need for invidious choices between different types of justification. Peoples of many different faiths and creeds have long demonstrated that they can cooperate for the achievement of common values, irrespective of their different derivations of these values. . . . It is common values and not common ideologies which are the indispensable sanction of an international law of human dignity.

TUNKIN, THEORY OF INTERNATIONAL LAW

W. E. Butler Trans., 1974, pp. 79–83.

The principle of respect for human rights. The emergence in international law of principles and norms affecting human rights was part of the process of progressive change in international law. Here the influence of the ideas of the Great October Socialist Revolution and of socialist democracy as a new, higher type of democracy has had a very distinct effect. It is sufficient to point out that if the provisions of the Covenant on Civil and Political Rights basically reflect similar legislative norms of capitalist and socialist states, the provisions of the Covenant on Social, Economic, and Cultural Rights reflect norms of Soviet legislation concerning the right to work, the right to social security, the right to education, and so forth.

. . .

The bitter struggle between states of the two systems unfolded in the United Nations during the process of drafting the Universal Declaration of Human Rights in 1947–1948. The Soviet Union and the other socialist countries sought to work out a document which could be used in the struggle for the rights of the working people. They insisted upon including in the Declaration provisions concerning economic and social rights, provisions aimed against colonialism, social discrimination, fascist propaganda, social and religious enmity, and so forth. This struggle of the socialist states was not without result; it positively affected the content of the Universal Declaration of Human Rights adopted by the United Nations General Assembly on December 10, 1948. The western powers, however, taking advantage of the "mechanical majority" they then had in the United Nations General Assembly, rejected many proposals of the Soviet Union and the other socialist countries. Because of this, the socialist states abstained in the voting on the Declaration.

An even more bitter and prolonged struggle between the states of the different socioeconomic systems unfolded as the covenants on human rights were being worked out. The crux of this struggle remained generally the same as in working out the Universal Declaration of Human Rights. However, the negative attitude of the capitalist states toward including obligations with regard to socioeconomic rights in an international convention was manifested even more clearly. As a result, at the insistence of the western powers the single draft covenant on human rights was divided into two covenants, one for civil and political, and another for the social, economic, and cultural rights. The covenant on economic, social, and cultural rights was so formulated that it does not impose strict obligations on its parties to grant such rights to citizens.

. . .

The content of the principle of respect for human rights as a principle of general international law is defined above all by the provisions of the Charter of the United Nations. It also is necessary to take into account in this connection other international documents concerning human rights. This content comes down roughly to the following: (a) all states have a duty to respect the fundamental rights and freedoms of all persons within their territories; (b) states have a duty not to allow discrimination by reason of sex, race, language, or religion; (c) states have a duty to promote universal respect for human rights and fundamental freedoms and to cooperate with one another in achieving this objective.

Contemporary international law proceeds from the fact, and this is exceedingly important, that a close link exists between a state's ensuring basic human rights and freedoms and the maintenance of international peace and security. This link is stressed in many international conventions (particularly the Convention on the Elimination of All Forms of Racial Discrimination and the covenants on human rights) and in United Nations General Assembly resolutions.

International law had intruded into an area which was considered to relate to the domestic jurisdiction of states and in which specific features of the different social systems are manifested very prominently and strongly. However, this "intrusion" of the regulatory influence of international law into the domain of human rights does not mean that human rights are directly regulated by international law nor that they have ceased basically to be the domestic affair of a state.

At the same time, the emergence in international law of norms relating to human rights raises a number of theoretical problems, especially as regards the content of such norms.

The extent and character of human rights within a specific state (they do not exist outside a state) are defined in the final analysis by the nature of the state, and this nature is itself a product of the economic system of a given society. And both the extent of rights and their substance are different in states with different social systems.

. . .

Second, it is also of great importance that international norms concerning human rights are expected to be implemented through the municipal law of individual states, taking into account the special features of their socioeconomic system. Conventions on human rights do not grant rights directly to individuals, but establish mutual obligations of states to grant such rights to individuals.

That which exists in contemporary international law pertaining to human rights is far from perfected, but it also is not the end of an ongoing evolution. There are many untapped possibilities for the further development of international law in this field, especially with regard to social and economic rights, as well as the improvement of methods for international control over the implementation of conventions on human rights. The further development of the international protection of human rights depends upon many circumstances, primarily upon improving the international situation, terminating the aggressive activities of imperialist powers, the arms race they have engendered, and the aggravation of international relations.

One proposition of cardinal importance should not be forgotten: securing human rights remains and will remain basically the domestic affair of states. Therefore, the principal field of struggle for human rights is the internal system of a state, and especially its socioeconomic system. The international protection of human rights, effectuated primarily by international legal means, is, although important, merely an auxiliary means of securing such rights.

QUESTIONS

(1) Are the values that are stated in the McDougal and Bebr article at a sufficient level of generality to win assent to them of such thinkers as Roy, p. 333, supra, Garcia-Amador, p. 399, supra, and Tunkin? What relation do they have, for example, to the arguments in the Amnesty Report on Torture, p. 392, supra?

(2) Even if these writers could agree upon such a common set of values, would that consensus be likely to help in drafting rules governing the questions that are treated in the excerpts above from the International Covenant on Civil and Political Rights? In drafting the provisions treating freedom of expression, political rights and allied questions? Would a creative arbitrator be able to draw guidance from this statement of values in resolving such disputes as Boffolo and Chattin?

(3) What are the practical consequences of Tunkin's argument for enforcement of human rights? How would you restate the argument in more direct terms? (When reading the materials at pp. 573–578, infra, on United States attitudes towards international protection of human rights, consider in what respects they appear to differ from Tunkin's.)

C. EXPROPRIATION OF ALIEN-OWNED PROPERTY

Prior to World War I, there appeared to be a consensus among the principal nations of the world—those whose nationals were trading with and investing in the less developed countries or European colonies—that the taking of an alien's property required a state to pay prompt and adequate compensation. To be sure, so general a standard had room for considerable flexibility in its application, but the principle itself appeared secure. The consensus was evidenced by the positions taken by statesmen in diplomatic notes (often accompanied by political, economic or military pressures against the expropriating state), decisions of arbitral tribunals, scholarly writings, and to a lesser degree by treaties between developed countries.

The incidence of expropriations, compared with the 20th century, was slight. Apart from the small number, a majority of these takings affected individuals, relatively small firms or churches. And many occurred during the same periods of political unrest that gave rise to the kinds of cases appearing in Part B. The Russian revolution during World War I was followed by broad Soviet expropriatory decrees. Since that time, and particularly since World War II, cataclysmic historical events and metaporphoses in economic theory and systems have caused the partial disintegration of principles that appeared to prevail in 1914. During this period, the significant expropriations of alien-owned property had a more deliberative and pervasive character, reflecting less transitory passions than relatively long-range efforts to wrest local wealth from foreign hands and to develop economies which gave larger roles to the public sector.

To explore this phase of the law of state responsibility, we draw upon a variety of sources: diplomatic correspondence, bilateral agreements, decisions of international tribunals, proposed multi-lateral conventions, national legislation or constitutions, and resolutions of the U. N. General Assembly. One important source is absent. Decisions of national courts in this field raise special problems, particularly the so-called act of state doctrine, and we defer consideration of them until Chapter VI.

We start with a discussion of property rights within the liberal-state tradition of the West, as prelude to analysis of the international controversies.

Additional reading: Fatouros, Government Guarantees to Foreign Investors (1962); Friedman, Expropriation in International Law (1953); Lillich (ed.), The Valuation of Nationalized Property in International Law (2 Vols. 1972–73); Miller and Stanger (eds.), Essays on Expropriation (1967); White, Nationalization of Foreign Property (1961); and Wortley, Expropriation in Public International Law (1959).

NOTE ON CONCEPTIONS OF PROPERTY AND BASES FOR ITS PROTECTION

Claims of expropriated parties for compensation rest on the premise that most national laws as well as international law recognize and protect interests of private parties in productive tangible and intangible assets. Here as elsewhere, the doctrines or principles of international law supporting such claims for vindication of property rights reveal various influences—dominantly the reigning political and jurisprudential conceptions of the 17th–Century period of birth of modern international law, and the legal expressions of the market societies which have developed in the West during the past two centuries.

The studies in this chapter expose the arguments for extensive protection (full compensation for takings) of private property under international law of the Western capitalist, capital-exporting countries, as well as the counter arguments from less developed countries and the socialist world. It is revealing to compare such arguments with those principal justifications for or attacks upon private property rights among Western theorists and courts of the past few centuries. Hence we briefly describe two traditional perspectives upon private property rights, as well as aspects of the Marxist critique of those rights.

Perhaps the paramount strand in Anglo-American thought about property rights has been one or another variant of natural-right theory. We read, for example, in Locke that

> every man has a property in his own person; this nobody has any right to but himself. The labour of his body and the work of his hands we may say are properly his. Whatsoever, then, he removes out of the state that nature hath provided and left it in, he hath mixed his labour with, and joined to it something that is his own, and thereby makes it his property.[27]

The stress is upon the investment of one's labor in a product, almost the extension of the self to creations of the self. What results is a postulated property right, an entitlement that precedes society and law and which both must "preserve." These are principles that appear to be expressive of the nature or self-realization of man, and of justice. It is of interest that Locke uses the term property to embrace one's own person as well as objects.

Locke endowed this social scheme of private property rights with a divine origin. "God and his reason commanded [man] to subdue the earth," to "lay out something upon it that was his own, his labour." He who responded to this command by cultivating the earth "thereby annexed to it something that was his property, which another had no title to, nor could without injury take from him."

27. The quotations in this Note from Locke are from Chapter V of The Second Treatise of Civil Government (Gough ed. 1946).

Other theorists, and many judges, have asserted and relied upon similarly powerful postulates of (natural) right or entitlement to objects one has created or developed without resort to theological premises. Rather, for example, such theorists have relied on premises about the nature of liberty or freedom as requiring recognition of interests of individuals (or companies) in their acquisitions, developments or creations. Within our court-law jurisprudence, such natural-right thought reached its zenith about the end of the 19th Century, as courts read expansive protection of property rights and freedom of contract into the guarantees against governmental interference of the Due Process Clause.

The powerful companion tradition to natural rights or entitlement in Anglo-American legal thought and common law has been the utilitarian tradition—that framework for thought which tests an act or rule (a statutory rule, a judicial holding, a constitutional norm) by its consequences for social life, and which argues for that act or rule which will achieve the greatest possible happiness or welfare (actually, the greatest possible net of benefits over costs) for the affected community. We can use aspects of the argument for private property developed by Bentham to sketch the main lines of a utilitarian perspective.[28]

Government (through law) creates property rights, together with all other rights, to maximize societal happiness (welfare). It ought never to impose a burden on one (for example, the burden to refrain from interfering with the property of another) except to confer "a benefit of a clearly greater value." Private property rights do indeed confer (net) benefits of great value. Their critical purpose is to achieve a primary object of law, security. Without security, productivity will diminish. "But assure to the cultivator the fruits of his industry, and perhaps in that alone you will have done enough." Without that assurance, "there would be no longer any motives for industry." Thus communal property (the commons, for example, in Bentham's period) will not be efficiently developed, since there will be no assured relationship between the labor one invests in such property and the personal gain one achieves. Others may reap. Law (as through the English enclosure acts) must repair such situations by assuring exclusive possession and use. The legal recognition of property interests—dominantly through legally enforced exclusion of interfering others—complements and releases man's natural acquisitive and maximizing urges. Legally based security is the essential condition for the release of productive energies.

Within this and similar utilitarian arguments, one can view law and property as serving to arrest threatening change. The legal base for property permits stability of expectations, some assurance about what the future holds. "The idea of property consists in an

28. The quotations from Bentham are from Part First of the Principles of the Civil Code, in The Theory of Legislation (Ogden ed., Hildreth trans., 1931).

established expectation." Such security and expectation "can only be the work of law"—in contrast to much natural-right thought (as in Locke) which views government's and law's function to be the preservation of previously existing property rights. "Law alone is able to create a fixed and durable possession which merits the name of property." Rights (property or other) do not underlie or precede but emerge from calculations of social utility as the creation of the state.

Attacks upon property—governmental confiscation, for example—bring social pains in excess of pleasures. They diminish welfare by inducing among owners the pain and fear of losing. They deaden industry. "When I despair of making myself sure of the product of my labor, I only seek to exist from day to day . . . An attack upon the property of an individual excites alarm among other proprietors. This sentiment spreads from neighbor to neighbor, till at last the contagion possesses the entire body of the state."

These natural-right and utilitarian approaches to private property interests, radically distinguished in the preceding text, are in fact intertwined in a complex manner in many writings and judicial opinions. Even Locke develops utilitarian justifications for property, related to the encouragement of industry; even Bentham can be viewed as resting his calculations of utility upon basic premises about rights. For much of the 19th Century, the two traditions served to complement or reinforce each other; the rhetoric of natural right of entitlement often pointed towards the same broad definitions of property or contract rights as did calculations of utility. But the traditions have at critical points diverged—for example, when utilitarian argument of the early 20th Century was advanced to support social limitation of property rights and contract freedom, against the opposition of adherents to natural-right conceptions. Both traditions have experienced a significant evolution in content and methodology.[29] Their premises and orientations about the nature of law and rights remain however fundamentally different.

The essentials of a Marxist perspective upon property are set forth in the description of the Marxist critique of law in liberal society at p. 183, supra. We repeat a few themes here. The conception of law and property is within the positivist tradition, and in this respect closer to the utilitarians. All law represents the "organized power of one class for oppressing another." The infrastructural relations of production, the root of class conflict and the engine of historical change, are shown in their "legal expression, property relations," the legal provisions for the ownership and control of productive resources. Through property, law restates and legitimates class relationships (exploitation) at the level of normative order.

29. For a contemporary illustration of arguments about property derived from these traditions, see Michelman, Property, Utility, and Fairness: Comments on the Ethical Foundations of "Just Compensation" Law, 80 Harv.L.Rev. 1165 (1967).

The relevance of such views of property to the international law of state responsibility to aliens is readily perceived. The studies below of expropriations involve arguments of the disputants that capture the principal themes described above. But of course different issues are also raised, as debate over property rights extends from national settings to international law.

Consider some obvious distinctions in international settings. From the perspective of natural-right theory, the now global rather than national environment offers radically different viewpoints about political and socio-economic organization, and thus about private property and its social regulation. Whatever consensus over social purposes or values may have inhabited the societies (or in any event, the relatively influential portions of those societies) in which natural-right justifications for private property flourished, far less agreement over rights or entitlements exists internationally. Postulates that were assumed to be eternal and universal will be perceived by those who reject them as geographically or culturally specific.

From the perspective of utilitarian thought, the problem emerges of definition of the geographical or cultural context in which welfare is to be maximized, as by protection of property rights. By the same token, the difficulty grows in securing agreement about what social consequences constitute benefits or costs, about the conception of that welfare which is to be maximized. That is, the framework for maximization is no longer one nation or one culture with its relative coherence, but a global process with its great diversity in character and aspiration. The identification of common, global purposes which all should implement to advance welfare considerations that transcend any one nation state is a politically complex and frustrating chore. Unlike a distinct social *group or class* within a nation that may, or may not, possess a self-consciousness about its position in society as well as distinctive attitudes towards prevailing social policies, *nations* feel keenly the ways in which their situations or interests differ from those of other nations. And they are not hesitant to express those feelings.

When considering disputes under international law, it will be useful to bear in mind two further aspects of our domestic experience with private property. First, note that several of the studies which follow involve so-called "general expropriations," involving vast sectors of the economy such as agrarian land, or in any event critically important natural resources such as the copper properties in Chile. In several cases, those expropriations were accompanied by serious or radical (root) political change, generally towards the socialist left. Contrast the relatively limited takings of private property, for relatively limited welfare purposes, by this country's state or federal governments, with relatively modest amounts of compensation payable as required by the federal (and state) constitutions. That is, because of the relative political stability and interstitial character of socio-economic change within the United States, the compensation issue assumes a different dimension from that within a country experiencing basic change, taking vast and valuable properties into its public sector, and becoming subject to demands for compensation that may be beyond its financial means. It is interesting that some notions of an unsupportable public burden stemming from demands for compensation do figure in domestic constitutional decisions treating "indirect takings" of the type considered at pp. 487–490, infra.

Second, it is important to recall that the nature and reach of "property rights" have experienced substantial change even within liberal market-oriented societies such as the United States. These changes are reflected in all levels of the legal system, from common law principles of tort or property or contract, to regulatory schemes such as zoning or price controls or taxation. All such trends deeply affect the "values" (exchange and use values) of private property interests, and some have substantial redistributional effects. But the property values of those who lose out are not generally viewed as "taken" by government (for purposes of the requirement of compensation) in such situations. Note, for example, the constitutional decisions about "indirect takings" at pp. 487–490, supra.

Indeed, it has been largely through the utilitarian framework, which in Bentham's time appeared to justify broad definitions of property rights and contract freedom, that legislators and courts have come to qualify those rights, to limit them in the light of other social policies and considerations of welfare maximization. This trend towards limitation has been influenced by perceptions of the possibilities for abusive and socially harmful use of private property. Thus the character of the private-property right within the industrialized West has become less secure against governmental redefinition and restriction, even as massive confrontations of political systems and ideologies occur on the international arena.

It remains true, however, that at the core rather than periphery —that is, for direct takings (dispossessions) rather than regulatory constraints that lower values—the principle of compensation by government remains entrenched in most societies of the industrialized West. But even in such circumstances, serious problems arise under national laws about the application of that principle—that is, about the conception of value and the criteria for its measurement that will determine the amount of compensation. As we shall observe, such problems have also been at the heart of many international disputes.

1. THE CONSENSUS AND THE CHALLENGE

CHORZOW FACTORY CASE

Permanent Court of International Justice, 1926–29.
P.C.I.J., Ser. A, Nos. 7, 9, 17, 19.

[This complex case made several appearances before the Court. The description below is based upon statements of the Court in Nos. 9 and 17 of its Collection of Judgments. The Court's conclusions as to applicable legal principles which are partly summarized below appear in Nos. 7, 9, and 17.

In 1915, the German Reich entered into a contract with Bayerische Stickstoffwerke A. G. (Bayerische), a private German company, pursuant to which Bayerische agreed to establish for the Reich and manage a nitrate factory at Chorzow, in (then German) Upper Silesia. The Reich acquired and owned the land. In 1919, a new German company, Oberschlesische Stickstoffwerke A. G. (Oberschlesische) was formed, and the Reich sold the factory to it. Bayerische was still to manage and to provide patent information and other know-how. Also in 1919, another company, Stickstoff Treuhand G.m.b.H. (Treuhand) was formed. It assumed all obligations of Oberschlesische to the Reich for payment for the factory and became, in consideration thereof, the sole shareholder of Oberschlesische. The Reich had a lien on all such shares to protect its rights as a creditor in Oberschlesische and could exercise voting power, but the right to manage remained in Bayerische. In 1920, Oberschlesische was entered on the land register in Chorzow as owner of the factory property.

The Treaty of Versailles, signed in 1919, provided for the cession by Germany to Poland of various territories but left for subsequent determination by plebiscite the status of certain disputed portions of Upper Silesia, including Chorzow. Article 256 of the Treaty gave countries to which Germany ceded territory the right to take property of the German Government, the value thereof to be credited against Germany's reparation obligations. In 1922 Germany and Poland entered into the Geneva Convention, which was intended to carry out the terms of the Treaty of Versailles and the results of various plebiscites and international conferences. The Convention ceded Polish Upper Silesia (P.U.S.) to Poland. Its Article 23 referred disputes over the application of the Convention to the P.C.I.J.

The Convention provided for the protection of "vested rights" of private German individuals or companies in P.U.S. which were acquired before the transfer of sovereignty over P.U.S. to Poland. Head III (in particular, Article 7) of the Convention gave Poland the right to expropriate certain properties of German nationals in P.U.S., in accordance with stated procedures. The Convention further provided in Article 6 that property interests of German nationals or companies controlled by such nationals could not be "liquidated" other than in accordance with such provisions governing expropriation. In 1922 a Polish court, relying on Article 256 of the Versailles Treaty and upon Polish legislation of 1920, decreed that the land registration in Chorzow be changed to indicate ownership in the Polish Treasury. Litigation then commenced in the Polish courts, before an arbitral tribunal, and before the P.C.I.J.

The P.C.I.J. had to examine "a series of questions, which were controversial mainly owing to a lack of any clear coherence between a number of scattered and unpleasantly complicated and confused treaty provisions for the liquidation of World War I, and to a dubious terminology which gave rise to all kinds of juristic riddles." I Verzijl, The Jurisprudence of the World Court 153 (1965). Among them were the following: Was the property private Germany property or state-owned? Had Germany transferred the property with a fraudulent intent to impair Poland's rights under these treaties? What was meant by the "liquidation" language? Did it allow Poland to enact the 1920 legislation, which applied equally to Polish nationals and others?

The Court resolved these issues in favor of Germany. It decided that the property was owned by Oberschlesische, a private German company, and that contractual rights of Bayerische to manage the factory had also been expropriated. It further decided that the transfers by the German government had not violated Poland's rights under the treaties. Finally it concluded that the treaties when taken together rendered Poland's taking of the factory unlawful.

The following language from Ser. A, No. 7, p. 22, is relevant to determining whether the Court recognized in these decisions a general rule of international law on expropriation.

> Further, there can be no doubt that the expropriation allowed under Head III of the Convention is a derogation from the rules generally applied in regard to the treatment of foreigners and the principle of respect for vested rights. As this derogation itself is strictly in the nature of an exemption, it is permissible to conclude that no further derogation is allowed. . . .
>
> It follows from these same principles that the only measures prohibited are those which generally accepted international law does not sanction in respect of foreigners; expropriation for reasons of public utility, judicial liquidation and similar measures are not affected by the Convention.

In Ser. A, No. 17, pp. 27–28, 46–48, the Court addressed itself to the amount of compensation due to Germany and made the following statements:]

It is a principle of international law that the reparation of a wrong may consist in an indemnity corresponding to the damage which the nationals of the injured State have suffered as a result of the act which is contrary to international law. . . . Rights or interests of an individual the violation of which rights causes damage are always in a different plane to rights belonging to a State, which rights may also be infringed by the same act. The damage suffered by an individual is never therefore identical in kind with that which will be suffered by a State; it can only afford a convenient scale for the calculation of the reparation due to the State. . . .

The action of Poland which the Court has judged to be contrary to the Geneva Convention is not an expropriation—to render which lawful only the payment of fair compensation would have been wanting; it is a seizure of property, rights and interests which could not be expropriated even against compensation, save under the exceptional conditions fixed by Article 7 of the said Convention. . . .

It follows that the compensation due to the German Government is not necessarily limited to the value of the undertaking at the moment of dispossession, plus interest to the day of payment. This limitation would only be admissible if the Polish Government had had the right to expropriate, and if its wrongful act consisted merely in not having paid to the two Companies the just price of what was expropriated; in the present case, such a limitation might result in placing Germany and the interests protected by the Geneva Convention, on behalf of which interests the German Government is acting, in a situation more unfavourable than that in which Germany and these interests would have been if Poland had respected the said Convention. Such a consequence would not only be unjust, but also, and above all, incompatible with the aim of Article 6 and following articles of the Convention—that is to say, the prohibition, in principle, of the liquidation of the property, rights and interests of German nationals and of companies controlled by German nationals in Upper Silesia—since it would be tantamount to rendering lawful liquidation and unlawful dispossession indistinguishable in so far as their financial results are concerned.

The essential principle contained in the actual notion of an illegal act—a principle which seems to be established by international practice and in particular by the decisions of arbitral tribunals—is that reparation must, as far as possible, wipe out all the consequences of the illegal act and reestablish the situation which would, in all probability, have existed if that act had not been committed. Restitution in kind, or, if this is not possible, payment of a sum corresponding to the value which a restitution in kind would bear; the award, if need be, of damages for loss sustained which would not be covered by restitution in kind or payment in place of it—such are the principles which should serve to determine the amount of compensation due for an act contrary to international law.

This conclusion particularly applies as regards the Geneva Convention, the object of which is to provide for the maintenance of economic life in Upper Silesia on the basis of respect for the *status quo*. The dispossession of an industrial undertaking—the expropriation of which is prohibited by the Geneva Convention—then involves the obligation to restore the undertaking and, if this be not possible to pay its value at the time of the indemnification, which value is designed to take the place of restitution which has become impossible. To this obligation, in virtue of the general principles of international law, must be added that of compensating loss sustained as the result of the seizure. The impossibility, on which the Parties are agreed, of restoring the Chorzow factory could therefore have no other effect but that of substituting payment of the value of the undertaking for restitution; it would not be in conformity either with the principles of law or with the wish of the Parties to infer from that agreement that the question of compensation must henceforth be dealt with as though an expropriation properly so called was involved.

[The Court then determined that, since the Chorzow undertaking involved "interdependent and complementary" interests of Oberschlesische and Bayerische, a single valuation rather than attempts to estimate separately the two interests should be made. In attempting to determine that value, the Court considered inconclusive certain evidence as to the cost of construction and as to prices stipulated in the 1919 sale contract and a later offer to sell. To obtain further enlightenment, it ordered an inquiry by three experts who were to examine the following questions. (IA) What was the value in 1922 of the undertaking in the hands of Bayerische and Oberschlesische? (IB) What would have been the earnings (or losses) from 1922 to the date of judgment if it had remained in their hands? (II) What would the value at the judgment date have been if it had remained in the hands of those companies and had been developed as were comparable undertakings of Bayerische? The inquiry thus ordered was not completed, since Poland and Germany came to an agreement and the proceedings were terminated. P.C.I.J., Ser. A, No. 19. The issue of damages in the Chorzow case is discussed in 2 Whiteman, Damages in International Law 1529–46 (1937).]

COMMENT

The Chorzow Factory Case suggests a number of issues which we briefly note, but which do not figure in the materials below.

(1) In the large majority of episodes in this Part C, tangible property, generally real property, was expropriated. More complex issues arise with respect to other kinds of property interests, such as the claims of aliens who were parties to contracts with an expropriated company, trade-mark and patent rights, and so on. Note that Articles I and II of the lump-sum settlement Agreement between the United States and Poland, p. 434, infra, address this question and define those interests which come within the compensation provisions. See also (*a*) Article 1 of the 1923 General Claims Convention between the United States and Mexico *, which refers to claims for damage suffered by citizens of either country by reason of damage to any corporation "in which such citizens have . . . a substantial and bona fide interest"; and (*b*) Article IV of the Convention of Establishment between the United States and France *, which refers in paragraph (1) to "lawfully acquired rights and interests" of nationals, and in paragraph (3) to "property" of nationals.

(2) These questions often shade into a series of problems about the situs of assets that were included within expropriation decrees. The episodes in Part C do not raise such problems, for in all cases the expropriated assets were within the expropriating country. Difficult choice-of-law issues arise if they are located elsewhere. Suppose that a government purports to expropriate all assets, real and personal, of all its nationals, wherever such assets are located. Will foreign countries where the assets are found give effect to and enforce such decrees? [30]

(3) The measure of compensation is as thorny a problem under international as under national law. Standards such as "reasonable" or "fair" or "just" value raise vexing questions. An approach based on the investor's "reasonable" or "legitimate" expectations may draw one into circular argument. "Fair market value" may under the circumstances be a meaningless inquiry; the "market values" of utilities or vast extractive enterprises are illustrations. Capitalization of earnings may not provide a feasible or fair index value. The cost of the investment when initially made may be an unsatisfactory measure. The "value" to the government may be as difficult to determine. The problems are legion.

30. These choice-of-law problems are touched upon in United States v. Belmont, p. 598, infra, United States v. Pink, p. 600, infra and Republic of Iraq v. First National City Bank, p. 712, infra.

QUESTIONS

Commentators and codifiers—particularly those advocating an international-law standard of prompt, adequate and effective compensation—have built a vast jurisprudential edifice upon the Chorzow Factory Case. Together with related opinions of the P.C.I.J. during the same period interpreting post-war treaties, the case contains the statements of the World Court that are most directly related to expropriation.

(1) Does the case support an argument that international law requires a state expropriating alien property to pay the alien fair compensation? What was the basis for Germany's claim?

(2) Does the reasoning of the Court with respect to damages shed light on the Court's view of the rules about compensation under general international law? For example, could the opinion have been cited by the United States as support for its position in the diplomatic notes to Mexico that follow these questions?

(3) The Court refers to the action of Poland as the "seizure of property, rights and interests." How would you describe the "interests" of Oberschlesische and of Bayerische in the Chorzow factory?

(4) A factory in Guatador is owned by a Guatadorian corporation, which in turn is entirely owned by nationals of Guatador. The corporation owes substantial debts to banks in the United States, some of which are secured by mortgages on the factory. Guatador nationalizes all the property of the company, without compensation, and the corporation consequently has no funds with which to pay its debts. Has any alien-owned "property" been expropriated? [31]

NOTE ON THE MEXICAN EXPROPRIATIONS OF AGRARIAN AND OIL PROPERTIES

The Mexican expropriations between 1915 and 1940 of agrarian and oil properties owned, directly or indirectly, by United States citizens provoked sharp political reactions in this country. The controversy led to a series of diplomatic notes in which the two governments set forth their positions on the question of compensation. The following correspondence relates primarily to the expropriation of agrarian properties.[32]

A note dated July 21, 1938 from Secretary of State Hull to the Mexican Ambassador read in part:

> Agrarian expropriations began in Mexico in 1915. Up to August 30, 1927, 161 moderate sized properties of American citizens had been taken. The claims arising therefrom were after much discussion referred to the General Claims Commission established by agreement between the two Gov-

31. See the treaty definitions in paragraph (1) of the preceding Comment. See also Articles I(A) and II(c) of the Agreement between the United States and Poland, p. 434, infra.

32. The excerpts below from notes sent be Secretary of State Hull and by the Mexican Minister of Foreign Affairs appear in 3 Hackworth, Digest of International Law 655–61 (1942).

ernments. It is appropriate to point out, however, that, as yet, and for whatever the reasons may be, not a single claim has been adjusted and none has been paid. The owners of these properties notwithstanding the repeated requests of this Government for settlement, lost their property, its use and proceeds, from eleven years to more than twenty years ago, and are still seeking redress.

Subsequent to 1927, additional properties, chiefly farms of a moderate size, with a value claimed by their owners of $10,132,388, have been expropriated by the Mexican Government. This figure does not include the large land grants frequently mentioned in the press. It refers to the moderate sized holdings which rendered only a modest living. None of them as yet has been paid for. . . .

The taking of property without compensation is not expropriation. It is confiscation. It is no less confiscation because there may be an expressed intent to pay at some time in the future.

If it were permissible for a government to take the private property of the citizens of other countries and pay for it as and when, in the judgment of that government, its economic circumstances and its local legislation may perhaps permit, the safeguards which the constitutions of most countries and established international law have sought to provide would be illusory. Governments would be free to take property far beyond their ability or willingness to pay, and the owners thereof would be without recourse. We cannot question the right of a foreign government to treat its own nationals in this fashion if it so desires. This is a matter of domestic concern. But we cannot admit that a foreign government may take the property of American nationals in disregard of the rule of compensation under international law. Nor can we admit that any government unilaterally and through its municipal legislation can, as in this instant case, nullify this universally accepted principle of international law, based as it is on reason, equity and justice.

. . . We are entirely sympathetic to the desires of the Mexican Government for the social betterment of its people. We cannot accept the idea, however, that these plans can be carried forward at the expense of our citizens, any more than we would feel justified in carrying forward our plans for our own social betterment at the expense of citizens of Mexico.

The whole structure of friendly intercourse, of international trade and commerce, and many other vital and mutually desirable relations between nations indispensable to their progress rest upon the single and hitherto solid foundation of respect on the part of governments and of peoples for each other's rights under international justice. The right of prompt and just compensation for expropriated property is a part of this structure. It is a principle to which the Government of the United States and most governments of the world have emphatically subscribed and which they have practiced and which must be maintained. It is not a principle which freezes the status quo and denies changes in property rights but a principle that permits any country to expropriate private property within its borders in furtherance of public purposes. It enables orderly change without violating the legitimately acquired interests of citizens of other countries.

The Secretary proposed an international arbitration to determine whether Mexico had complied with "the rule of compensation as prescribed by international law." The Mexican Minister of Foreign Affairs, in a reply dated August 3, 1938, stated in part:

> My Government maintains . . . that there is in international law no rule universally accepted in theory nor carried out in practice, which makes obligatory the payment of immediate compensation nor even of deferred compensation, for expropriations of a general and impersonal character like those which Mexico has carried out for the purpose of redistribution of the land.
>
> The expropriations made in the course of our agrarian reform, do, in fact, have this double character, which ought to be taken very much into account in order to understand the position of Mexico and rightly appraise her apparent failure to meet her obligations.
>
> Without attempting to refute the point of view of the American Government, I wish to draw your attention very specially to the fact that the agrarian reform is not only one of the aspects of a program of social betterment attempted by a government or a political group for the purpose of trying out new doctrines, but also constitutes the fulfilling of the most important of the demands of the Mexican people, who, in the revolutionary struggle, for the purpose of obtaining it, sacrificed the very lives of their sons. The political, social, and economic stability and the peace of Mexico depend on the land being placed anew in the hands of the country people who work it; a transformation of the country, that is to say, the future of the nation, could not be halted by the impossibility of paying immediately the value of the properties belonging to a small number of foreigners who seek only a lucrative end.
>
> As has been stated above, there does not exist in international law any principle universally accepted by countries, nor by the writers of treatises on this subject, that would render obligatory the giving of adequate compensation for expropriations of a general and impersonal character. Nevertheless Mexico admits, in obedience to her own laws, that she is indeed under obligation to indemnify in an adequate manner; but the doctrine which she maintains on the subject, which is based on the most authoritative opinions of writers of treatises on international law, is that the time and manner of such payment must be determined by her own laws.

The Mexican Government rejected the American offer of arbitration but suggested a meeting of representatives to determine the value of the properties involved and the manner of payment. Secretary Hull replied in a note of August 22, 1938:

> The fundamental issues raised by this communication from the Mexican Government are therefore, first, whether or not universally recognized principles of the law of nations

require, in the exercise of the admitted right of all sovereign nations to expropriate private property, that such expropriation be accompanied by provision on the part of such government for adequate, effective, and prompt payment for the properties seized; second, whether any government may nullify principles of international law through contradictory municipal legislation of its own; or, third, whether such Government is relieved of its obligations under universally recognized principles of international law merely because its financial or economic situation makes compliance therewith difficult.

The Government of the United States merely adverts to a self-evident fact when it notes that the applicable precedents and recognized authorities on international law support its declaration that, under every rule of law and equity, no government is entitled to expropriate private property, for whatever purpose, without provision for prompt, adequate, and effective payment therefor. In addition, clauses appearing in the constitutions of almost all nations today, and in particular in the constitutions of the American republics, embody the principle of just compensation. These, in themselves, are declaratory of the like principle in the law of nations. . . .

The Mexican Government refers to the fact that, when it undertook suspension of the payment of its agrarian debt, the measure affected equally Mexicans and foreigners. It suggests that if Mexico had paid only the latter to the exclusion of its nationals, she would have violated a rule of equity. . . .

Your Excellency's Government intimates that a demand for unequal treatment is implicit in the note of the Government of the United States, since my Government is aware that Mexico is unable to pay indemnity immediately to all of those affected . . ..

. . . The Government of the United States requests no privileged treatment for its nationals residing in Mexico. The present Government of the United States has on repeated occasions made it clear that it would under no circumstances request special or privileged treatment for its nationals in the other American republics, nor support any claim of such nationals for treatment other than that which was just, reasonable, and strictly in harmony with the generally recognized principles of international law.

The doctrine of equality of treatment, like that of just compensation, is of ancient origin. It appears in many constitutions, bills of rights and documents of international validity. The word has invariably referred to equality in lawful rights of the person and to protection in exercising such lawful rights. There is now announced by your Government the astonishing theory that this treasured and cherished principle of equality, designed to protect both human and property rights, is to be invoked, not in the protection of personal rights and liberties, but as a chief ground of depriving and stripping individuals of their conceded rights. It is contended, in a word, that it is wholly justifiable to deprive an individual of his rights if all other persons are equally deprived, and if no victim is allowed to escape. . . .

> . . . The statement in your Government's note to the effect that the foreigners who voluntarily move to a country not their own assume, along with the advantages which they may seek to enjoy, the risks to which they may be exposed and are not entitled to better treatment than nationals of the country, presupposes the maintenance of law and order consistent with principles of international law; that is to say, when aliens are admitted into a country the country is obligated to accord them that degree of protection of life and property consistent with the standards of justice recognized by the law of nations. . . .

In a note of September 1, 1938, the Mexican Government further developed its position as to general expropriations:

> This attitude of Mexico is not, as Your Excellency's Government affirms, either unusual or subversive. Numerous nations, in reorganizing their economy, have been under the necessity of modifying their legislation in such manner that the expropriation of individual interests nevertheless does not call for immediate compensation and, in many cases, not even subsequent compensation; because such acts were inspired by legitimate causes and the aspirations of social justice, they have not been considered unusual or contrary to international law. As my Government stated to that of Your Excellency in my note of August 3, it is indispensable, in speaking of expropriations, to distinguish between those which are the result of a modification of the juridical organization and which affect equally all the inhabitants of the country, and those others decreed in specific cases and which affect interests known in advance and individually determined.

In November 1938, the two governments agreed upon a procedure to determine the compensation for agrarian properties expropriated after August 30, 1927. An international commission was to find the value of the properties. Mexico undertook to pay $1,000,000 by May 31, 1939 as a first installment, and to pay $1,000,000 annually thereafter until the agreed-upon value was reached. In a Claims Convention of November 19, 1941, Mexico agreed to pay to the United States $40,000,000 in installments to settle these agrarian claims together with other outstanding claims. See p. 366, supra, for a description of the three categories of claims covered by that Convention and of the various commitments of the United States which were made as part of this general settlement.

In 1938, a Mexican decree expropriated certain oil properties, including those of American owned companies. After several years of diplomatic correspondence, the two countries agreed in 1941 upon a method of determining the value of these properties. Experts appointed by the two governments concluded that approximately $24,000,000 would settle outstanding claims. In 1943, the governments agreed that this sum would be paid in installments, with 3% interest from 1938. Final payment was made in 1947. 17 Dept.State Bull. 747 (1947).

VERNON, AN INTERPRETATION OF THE MEXICAN VIEW

Vernon (ed.), How Latin America Views the U. S. Investor 95–117 (1966).

. . .

In most accounts of Mexican history, the foreign investor is cast in the role of villain. Out of the oversimplification that passion and patriotism demand, the foreign investor emerges—along with the landlord and the Church—as one of the enduring symbols of economic exploitation of the Mexican people.

But all things change. Mexico is now half a century from its revolution. Its early need for a few unambiguous villain-figures is now declining. As the country's visible accomplishments grow, the self-assurance of its people increases too. A growing sense of self-assurance and a growing capacity for self-examination, one hopes, go hand-in-hand. It may be that the Mexican view of the foreign investor will prove increasingly complex in the future, reflecting a parallel change in the investor's role in the extraordinary country. For the present, however, one still must turn to history in order to acquire the beginnings of an understanding of the Mexican view. . . .

The year 1876 [when Porfirio Diaz took power], however, marks an historical turning point of sorts. By that year, Mexico had endured half a century of unbelievable turmoil. . . . But it had seen almost no foreign investment, except perhaps in a few mines and plantations and in a pitiful 400 miles of railroad track between Vera Cruz and Mexico City. . . .

Foreigners responded to the opportunities of the Porfirian era in a number of different ways.

Some foreigners migrated to Mexico; though maintaining their original citizenship and their home sources of capital during the first generation or two, many British, French, German, and Spanish entrepreneurs came to Mexico to set up textile mills, tobacco plants and breweries; others developed cotton, sugar, coffee, and henequen plantations, sometimes with related processing plants.

A larger group of foreigners, however, participated more vicariously in Mexico's development. The mining and petroleum companies of Britain and the United States set up their subsidiaries wherever rich supplies of raw materials could be found. The investors of the United States and Europe bought extraordinary quantities of Mexican government debt and of Mexican railroad and public utility securities. By 1911, we are told, foreigners had investments in Mexico totalling $2 billion, a figure said to account for about two-thirds of aggregate Mexican investment outside of the agriculture and handicraft industries. By that year, therefore, when Mexico's decade of revolution begins, foreigners had come to control so high a proportion of Mexico's wealth that the proportion may have set all-time records for any country claiming political independence.

The Porfirian period contributed powerfully to the deep-seated hostility of Mexico toward the foreign investor. Ironically, however, it also generated many of the indispensable conditions for the sustained growth of the Mexican economy that was to follow. . . .

But man does not live by fact alone; certainly not by the narrow type of economic fact which describes the accomplishments of the Porfirian era. What was done had been achieved at a high price. In the process, the Indian population had been cruelly abused and neglected. The nation's resources had been placed in the control of foreigners. National pride had been deeply and painfully offended. It is not surprising that, as the years went on, the collective Mexican memory and the collective Mexican interpretation emphasized the negative aspects of the period.

Foreigners who had the poor judgment to lend money to the Porfirian government probably suffered considerable losses from the decade of the Revolution. But foreigners who invested in railroads, public utilities, mines and petroleum managed to avoid catastrophe. . . .

The result was that the infrastructure acquired under the somewhat unusual conditions of the Porfirian era survived to serve Mexico's post-Revolutionary governments. . . .

As Mexico was pacified, the foreign-owned enterprises once more were drawn into business. Metal producers moderately expanded their output in Mexico during the 1920's, responding to the world's increased demand for nonferrous metals. Oil producers pushed their output to an all-time peak of 193 million barrels in 1921, then allowed their production to decline throughout the rest of the decade.

It is to be noted that there was a certain subdued quality in the reaction of the raw material foreign investors in this period. And there was good reason for them to feel a trifle subdued. The new Constitution of the Mexican Revolution, conceived in open convention in 1917, carried overtones of trouble for the foreign investor, especially the investor who based his activities upon Mexico's unreplenishable subsoil resources. Title to the wealth of the subsoil, according to the new Constitution's provisions, resided in the state, and that title was inalienable; hence, concessionaires who mined the subsoil seemed to hold their title only on the sufferance of the state. On top of this, the right of foreigners to hold property in Mexico was circumscribed in a number of specific ways. . . .

There is probably nothing that is totally inexorable in the broad sweep of history. But there did seem to be a certain element of inexorability in the steps that followed the era of the 1920's, leading to the Mexican recapture of the ownership of the oil resources, the public utilities, and much of the land previously in foreign hands. . . .

Picture the situation of the oil companies. After 1911, they had been living by their wits, partly by politicking intensively with a stream of insecure provisional governments, partly by bribing the necessary authorities in accordance with accepted practice, partly by recruiting private armies to protect their properties from marauders, partly by appealing to the United States Government for intervention and protection. A decade of this sort of maneuvering, during which the oil companies fared spectacularly well, was hardly calculated to put them in a mood for easy bargaining with the Mexican Government.

For its part, the Mexican officials of the 1920's and 1930's could not take an overly conciliatory view to the oil companies even if they wished. As far as important segments of the Mexican people were concerned, the Revolution had conquered its three enemies: the landlords, the Church and the foreigners. Overt concessions to any of them represented a betrayal of Revolutionary aims. . . .

All the elements for the ultimate confrontation were now in place. As the Mexican Government saw it, foreigners controlling the subsoil of Mexico were not only refusing to make appropriate payments for the right to export Mexico's precious subsoil resources; they were also damaging the country's economic interests by their arbitrary decisions to shift their production to more convenient sources. As the foreign companies saw it, the Mexicans were making outrageous demands in violation of their legal obligations and their earlier commitments.

The Great Depression and the advent of Lazaro Cardenas gave the companies their final reasons for feeling that they might be on a slippery slide and that they had nothing to lose by hard bargaining tactics. The signs of this hardening attitude were evident in the continued decline of production and the increasing use of wasteful exploitation methods in the oil fields. . . .

. . . As for the public officials of the 1930's, they represented a near-revolutionary government in near-revolutionary times; and they represented that time and period faithfully. Diego Rivera's caricature mural in the staircase of the Mexican Presidential Palace, depicting the greedy and debauched millionaires of Wall Street, came close to reflecting the official mood of the times.

It does not matter any longer whether or not the nationalization of oil might have been avoided. My own view has always been that the nationalization was a not-wholly-unexpected nor wholly-unintended consequence of the uninhibited negotiating tactics of the oil companies. If the oil companies had weathered the crises of 1938, they would certainly have been badgered unmercifully in the years that followed; in order to raise their taxes from the 15 or 20 percent typical of the 1920's to the 60 percent or so typical of the 1960's, a great deal of badgering would obviously have been required. Perhaps it was just as well for the long-run position of other foreign investors in Mexico and for the growth of the Mexican economy as a whole that the issue was settled once and for all by the draconian expropriation of 1938.

. . . With the end of World War II, the flow of foreign direct investment into Mexico had developed a different emphasis. By that time, foreign investors had begun to show a strong interest in manufacturing facilities to serve the Mexican market.

This interest was not wholly new. The Ford Motor Company had set up an assembly plant in Mexico as early as 1925, and other American manufacturing enterprises had appeared even earlier. But the Great Depression and the 1938 oil expropriations had soured the investor's taste for investment in Mexico. Eventually, however, the long period of Mexico's growth from the end of the Great Depression to the close of World War II made it a much more interesting target for United States producers; and President Aleman's policies of high tariffs plus import licensing after World War II provided the necessary spur for many exporters to take the leap by setting up production facilities inside the country. By the latter 1950's, United States-owned subsidiaries had come to account for about one-sixth of Mexico's manufacturing output. Since these subsidiaries were on the whole among the larger firms in the country, they seemed to the casual observer to dominate Mexican industrial life. . . .

The foreign manufacturing firms in Mexico often exhibited a heavy-handedness in their relations with the Mexican public which was calculated to do them no good in the long run. There were times, for instance, when the foreign community seemed to be placing itself in the position of resisting Mexican tax reforms. At the same time, however, these firms tended to set high standards by Mexican norms in such important areas as the payment of taxes, the adherence to labor agreements, the institution of inservice training, and so on. This generally salutary line of conduct may have been stimulated by a sense of what was necessary for survival; but, whatever the motivations, the performance helped provide constructive norms for Mexico's industrial class as a whole.

Confronted with a great flow of industrial investment coming principally from the United States, the reaction of a succession of Mexican administrations has been understandingly ambivalent. On the one hand, no president of Mexico could afford to embrace the presence of the foreign investor, given the Revolutionary symbolism of Mexico; on the other hand, this particular breed of investor was obviously being helpful to the Mexican economy in a number of different ways: in helping to tide over the short-term pressures on the Mexican balance of payments; in helping to meet the challenge of the import replacement program which Mexico so badly wished to achieve; and, in bringing technology of an advanced kind into the Mexican economy.

The result of the official ambivalence has been to provide a succession of responses from the Mexican political institutions which could hardly be called consistent in their approach. . . .

By the mid-1960's, many differences among the various business groups still remained. But there was one view they tended to share. This was the view that in some circumstances—the circumstances were somewhat differently defined by the different groups—foreign investment could be harmful to the proper development of the Mexican economy. In those cases, it was clear, restraint upon foreigners was justified. In other situations, however, the foreigners' contribution to Mexican growth would be warmly welcomed.

From the United States side of the border most of the recent developments in Mexico have tended to be seen through rose-colored spectacles: indeed, the picture of Mexico in the mid-1960's as seen by prospective U. S. investors was one of nearly unbounded enthusiasm. After forty years of political stability and almost as many years of economic growth, United States investors had come to see Mexico as an exemplary neighbor, a splendid market, and an outstanding area for investment. The nationalization of oil had long since faded out of the United States memory; the Mexican nationalization of the utilities had been accepted by the United States public as a fair and amicable arrangement; the Mexican discrimination against foreign-owned mining companies had been taken in stride; and the *ad hoc* pressures on foreign companies to admit local partners, buy local materials, and hire local technicians, had been accepted as the proper price for admission to a large and lucrative market. . . .

If the remaining area of mutual interests between Mexico and its foreign investors were small or were shrinking fast, one would be inclined to see trouble ahead. The area, however, is still large. If there are grounds for uneasiness, they stem from the fact that some foreign investors seem unaware that the area of mutual interest has its limits and that the limits, in time, may shrink. When that happens, a foreign investor without a proper sense of history may feel somehow betrayed, while a Mexican steeped in his concept of history will wonder at the reaction. The awakening is always ruder when the dreams have been sweet.

COMMENT

The diplomatic correspondence with Mexico underscores some of the basic tensions in disputes over expropriations between the United States or European countries and less developed countries. Note the themes in the Mexican notes that private property rights may impede the implementation of a government's duty towards its citizens; that individual interests must here bow to the public good; and that concepts of the "right" of citizens to property or the "duty" of governments to compensate should be thought of as peculiar to different national traditions rather than as part of an international standard.

Compare the remarks of Garcia-Amador, p. 399, supra. Consider whether the developing (or of course the socialist) countries would distinguish between an international-law standard for the security and liberties of the person on the one hand, and for security of property interests on the other. When comparing the materials in Parts B and C, consider whether developing international norms express different attitudes towards these two fields.

QUESTIONS

(1) Identify the precise dispute in the diplomatic correspondence between the United States and Mexico. (*a*) Is there any common ground as to Mexico's obligations, or as to an international-law standard with respect to compensation? (*b*) Would you characterize Secretary Hull's arguments for property protection as within the natural-right or utilitarian tradition?

(2) The Mexican notes identify two kinds of expropriations. What arguments would you develop to justify this distinction and the different rules of compensation that the Mexican government draws from it? How might they be refuted?

(3) The Mexican notes stress that the expropriations affected equally nationals and aliens.

> (*a*) Do you find more justification for Mexico's position that national treatment is sufficient with respect to protection of property interests than, for example, with respect to protection of the person and procedural fairness?
>
> (*b*) How do you evaluate the following arguments against national treatment as a sufficient standard? (1) The alien has no voice in the political processes through which decisions about expropriation are taken. (2) The alien does not benefit, directly or indirectly, from the hoped for improvement in the economic or social structure of a country that will follow a nationalization —for example, a land reform.

(4) Assuming that discrimination between aliens and nationals is relevant in determining whether there is liability and, if so, what the measure of damages should be, what meaning does this concept have? Consider the following examples: (i) Guatador expropriates "all oil properties" pursuant to a law which states no exceptions. In fact, all oil properties are owned by aliens. (ii) Guatador expropriates "all industrial property." 90% in value of the industrial enterprises in Guatador—or 50%, or 2%—is owned by aliens.

(5) Could the author of the Mexican notes have strengthened his arguments, or derived additional ones, through some of the facts set forth in Professor Vernon's account of Mexican history? Recall also the Note on attitudes of less developed countries towards foreign investment at p. 84, supra. Do these materials, together with the history of the settlement of past disputes with Mexico, give you confidence in advising an American client now contemplating a Mexican investment of the risks that he would encounter?

(6) What function did the notes in the United States-Mexican controversy serve? As their draftsman in the Office of the Legal Adviser, would you view your role as that of "detached expert" on international law, writing a minor treatise to be communicated to another nation, or that of advocate, making the strongest possible case for your country? At a minimum, what factors would inhibit you as to the kinds of arguments based upon international law which you would make? How do your answers to these questions bear upon the significance of diplomatic notes as evidence of state practice supporting a rule of customary international law?

NOTE ON POST-WAR DEVELOPMENTS AND THE POSITION OF THE UNITED STATES

Socialism, nationalism, and a general rebellion against economic penetration by the developed countries have led to expropriations since World War II that are significant in number and in the value of the properties involved. Indeed, the risk of expropriation has become an important ingredient in the decision-making of business firms about investment in less developed countries.

Examples of takings that were, at least initially, uncompensated include the dispute in 1951 over the Iranian oil expropriations; the expropriations by Egypt of the Suez properties which gave rise to the military intervention of France, Great Britain and Israel; the Indonesian expropriations of principally Dutch-owned property; the takings of American property in Brazil, p. 440, infra, Chile, p. 444, infra, Peru, and Guatamala; the Cuban expropriations, pp. 691–728, infra; and the extensive nationalizations in the states of Eastern Europe, pp. 433–436, infra.[33]

The materials below raise the critical issue whether international law's processes and doctrines can respond effectively to the rapid change in social, economic and political conditions among the expanding "family of nations." Consider the relevance to these post-war developments of the remarks of Roy and Tunkin, pp. 333 and 335, supra. Consider also further comments of Roy in the same article, Is the Law of Responsibility of States for Injuries to Aliens a Part of Universal International Law, 55 Am.J.Int.L. 863, 882–83 (1961):

> As time has laid bare the processes of exploitation and its effect on the exploited, the exploited parts of the world have been naturally looking forward to their emancipation from external exploitation and the exploiting parts equally

33. A summary of most of the takings appears in a Committee Print, dated July 19, 1963, of the House Committee on Foreign Affairs, 88th Cong., 1st Sess., prepared at the request of the Chairman by the Legislative Reference Service, Library of Congress, reprinted in 2 Int.Leg.Mat. 1066 (1963). This summary was brought up to 1971 by Department of State, Bureau of Intelligence and Research, Research Study RECS–14 of Nov. 30, 1971, reprinted at 11 Int.Leg.Mat. 84 (1971).

naturally to their preservation of as much as possible, in the changed circumstances of the time, of the old rights and interests, still in existence. . . . The primary requirement, however, for setting these conflicts at rest is the growth among the nations of the world, and particularly among those that claim to lead them, of a profound understanding of each other's problems, so that the ancestry of the rights and interests in question, together with the whole history of their working may be exposed to the searchlight of that understanding, and the rights and interests dealt with on principles of fairness, justice and equity.

This is probably impossible as long as the old international law of responsibility continues to be weighted in favor of the stronger states, for that, as already stated, is the way to the perpetuation of existing injustices. . . . Unless two states have their nationals in each other's territory in appreciable numbers, the question of reciprocity hardly arises. This basis of reciprocity was available among the European states when their practices laid the foundation of this law. But the era of colonialism did not provide any such basis of reciprocity between the colonial Powers on the one hand and their victims on the other, the relations between them being principally those between the exploiter and the exploited.

Since the end of World War II, the nationals of most states have been carrying on business or following other pursuits in one another's territory more or less on equal terms, except where colonialism still goes on fighting its last-ditch battles. This would thus appear to be an auspicious moment for this branch of international law to make a new beginning. . . .

To treat the existing law of responsibility as extending automatically to a state previously outside the community of nations but newly admitted to it, on its very entry into this community, is to confer on all other members of this community a right against such state of diplomatic protection of their nationals. Of course, it will also have a similar right against each of the other members. In existing circumstances, there may well be a basis of mutuality for such relations among most states which are free from foreign domination. If, therefore, the existing law with suitable modifications could be applied only to rights and interests to be created now or after the adoption of a new law of responsibility, a good deal of the objectionable features of this law from the point of view of the victims of colonialism are likely to disappear.

Consider also the following comments of Li Hao-p'ei, "Nationalization and International Law," in Cohen and Chiu, People's China and International Law 720–727 (1973) (reprinted by permission of Princeton University Press):

Whether or not the nationalizing state must compensate original owners of foreign nationality is also a public international law question. Opinions with respect to this question are not unanimous; they can be classified into three types. The first theory maintains that the nationalizing state must make compensation to owners of foreign nationality and that the compensation must be adequate, effective, and prompt. The second theory maintains that the nationalizing state should make partial compensation to owners of foreign nationality. The third maintains that no compensation is required.

1. The first theory is obviously based upon the sanctity and inviolability of private property advocated by the bourgeoisie. This theory can be further classified into two views. The first maintains that the validity of nationalization is conditioned on the making of adequate, effective, and prompt compensation to owners of foreign nationality. The second maintains that, although the validity of nationalization is not conditioned upon such compensation, the nationalizing state still has an obligation to make compensation.

. . .

2. Although the second theory also starts out from the principle of protecting private property, it takes into consideration the nationalizing state's ability to make compensation. It thus leans towards compromise. . . . The alien compensation agreements concluded between various countries from the end of World War I to the present generally provide only partial compensation and are thus frequently cited as support for this theory.

3. The rationale of the third theory is: since the end of World War I, many states have nationalized property in order to carry out large-scale economic and social reform. To require the nationalizing state to make compensation to owners of foreign nationality may frustrate the exercise of the sovereign right of a state to carry out economic and social reform, because it may be unable or difficult for such state to assume an obligation to make compensation. Therefore, this theory maintains that the nationalizing state only has an obligation not to discriminate against foreigners; if it does not compensate nationals who are owners, then it has no obligation to compensate owners of foreign nationality. . . .

. . .

We believe that the third theory is correct. With respect to the question of compensation, public international law has only established the rule of equal treatment between nationals and foreigners; it has not established the rule that foreigners must be compensated. Therefore, if a state does not compensate its own nationals, it need not compensate foreigners. In practice, the nationalizing state sometimes pays more or less compensation to foreigners, but this is not because public international law has already established the rule that a state must compensate owners of foreign nationality. [A state may compensate foreign nationals] because it also pays some compensation to its own nationals who were owners; or because of certain practical considerations (such as a desire to resume normal international economic relations, to obtain the release of frozen properties, or to conclude credit agreements); or even because of the illegal exercise of compulsion by imperialist countries. We will try to prove the correctness of this view.

(A) We can reach this conclusion from studying several famous nationalization cases of the past hundred or more years.

. . .

5. The Case of Mexico's Nationalization of Land and Petroleum Enterprises. In the dispute between Mexico and the United States arising out of Mexican nationalization of land and petroleum enterprises, the legal points held by both parties have been described above. The result of the dispute was that the parties could not agree with each other's legal points. Although Mexico, under strong pressure from American imperialism, in practice had to yield to the United States' demand to a relatively large degree, it did not make one concession in principle. Article [18] of the November 19, 1941, exchange of notes between the United States and Mexico relating to the compensation of nationals of the United States expressly provides: "Nothing contained in this note shall be regarded as a precedent or be invoked by either of the two governments in the settlement between them of any future difficulty, conflict, controversy, or arbitration. The action herein provided for is considered as singular and exceptional, appropriate solely to this case. . . ." Consequently, this case only specifically exposes two opposing views; it does not have the value of a precedent.

. . .

The position of the United States as expressed by the Executive —that a taking of alien property requires the payment of prompt, adequate and effective compensation—has not markedly changed since the correspondence with Mexico in the 1930's.[34] Consider the following provisions of the Restatement (Second), Foreign Relations Law of the United States.

(1) Section 185 provides that the taking by a state of alien-owned property is wrongful under international law if, *inter alia*, "there is not reasonable provision for the determination and payment of just compensation . . . under the law and practice of the state in effect at the time of taking." "Reasonable provision" requires a state to afford an alien fair legal proceedings, including impartial judicial or administrative authorities. Section 186 states that a failure to pay just compensation is wrongful, whether or not the taking itself was wrongful.

(2) Just compensation, as defined in Section 187, must be "adequate in amount," "paid with reasonable promptness," and "paid in a form that is effectively realizable by the alien, to the fullest extent that the circumstances permit."

(3) As to adequacy, Section 188 provides that under ordinary conditions, "the amount must be equivalent to the

34. For an evaluation of this position by a domestic court, see Banco Nacional de Cuba v. Sabbatino, p. 691, infra. For a recent Presidential statement to this effect, directed to the Chilean copper expropriations, see p. 452, infra.

full value of the property taken, together with interest to the date of payment." An explanatory comment states that full value "means fair market value if ascertainable. If fair market value is not ascertainable, it means the fair value as reasonably determined in the light of the international standard of justice."

(4) Promptness, under Section 189, means payment "as soon as is reasonable under the circumstances in the light of the international standard of justice."

(5) As to effectiveness, Section 190 states that compensation "must be in the form of cash or property readily convertible into cash." If not in the national currency of the injured alien, the payment "must be convertible into such currency and withdrawable," although this "may be delayed to the minimum extent necessary to assure the availability of foreign exchange for goods and services essential to the health and welfare of the people of the taking state." [35]

(6) In addition, one should note the provisions of Section 166 that state conduct causing injury to an alien "that discriminates against aliens generally, against aliens of his nationality, or against him because he is an alien, departs from the international standard of justice." Discriminatory conduct involves treating aliens differently from nationals or from aliens of a different nationality "without a reasonable basis for the difference."

QUESTION

What do the remarks of Roy suggest with respect to a metamorphosis in the attitudes of less developed countries when they become exporters of capital and know-how? Consider, for example, the position on questions such as compensation that countries such as Brazil and Mexico are likely to assert as more of their capital becomes invested in other Latin American countries.

---

2. SETTLEMENT OF SOME POST-WAR DISPUTES: SUBSTANCE AND TECHNIQUES

The principles espoused by the United States have been put to the test in a number of recent expropriations. Settlement of the

35. Compare the following provision of the Draft Convention of Professors Sohn and Baxter, p. 373, supra. Article 10 states that the taking of alien property is "wrongful if it is not accompanied by prompt payment of compensation" under defined standards. Section 4 of that Article provides that, if property is taken "in furtherance of a general program of economic and social reform, the just compensation required by this Article may be paid over a reasonable period of years," provided that the payment does not discriminate against aliens, a reasonable portion is paid promptly, bonds equal in fair market value to the remainder and bearing reasonable interest are given to the alien, and that the taking is not in violation of an express undertaking by the state.

large majority of these disputes has followed the Mexican pattern: extended diplomatic correspondence leading to a lump-sum payment. This section describes the content of the settlements and the means by which they were reached, as well as a major contemporary controversy that was settled only after a military coup and change in government.

NOTE ON EXPROPRIATIONS BY THE SOVIET UNION AND EASTERN EUROPEAN COUNTRIES [36]

Decrees of the Soviet Government soon after the revolution abolished private ownership of natural resources and of most productive property. The Soviet Government refused to pay any compensation for alien-owned property and insisted upon a general settlement which would also satisfy Soviet claims against the Allies. This attitude contributed to the refusal of the United States to recognize the Soviet Union until 1933. That recognition was part and parcel of a complex agreement which included the so-called Litvinov Assignment, pursuant to which the Soviet Union released and assigned to the United States certain funds in this country out of which claims by United States nationals deriving from confiscation of their property in the U.S.S.R. could be met.[37] The Litvinov Assignment was intended to be preliminary to a general settlement. That, however, has never been achieved.

The United States has frequently employed a national commission to adjudicate claims of individuals or corporations and to disburse to the claimants whatever sums were available, generally on a pro rata basis. For example, some of the claims against the Soviet Union have been satisfied out of the Litvinov Assignment through proceedings before the International Claims Commission [38] and the Foreign Claims Settlement Commission (FCSC), established in 1954 as successor to the International Claims Commission.[39] The principal activity of the FCSC has been the adjudication of claims arising out of nationalizations since World War II by the Communist coun-

36. Much of the information in this Note is based upon (1) a Committee Print, dated July 19, 1963, of the House Committee on Foreign Affairs, 88th Cong., 1st Sess., prepared at the request of the Chairman by the Legislative Reference Service, Library of Congress, reprinted in 2 Int.Leg.Mat. 1066 (1963); (2) Hearings before the House Committee on Foreign Affairs, 89th Cong., 1st Sess., on the Foreign Assistance Act of 1965 (Part VIII), March 10, 1965; and (3) Lillich, The Protection of Foreign Investment 167–88 (1965).

37. United States v. Belmont, p. 598, infra, and United States v. Pink, p. 600, infra, treat some of the complex problems that arose under the Litvinov Assignment.

38. That Commission was established in the Department of State by the International Claims Settlement Act of 1949, 64 Stat. 13 (1950), as amended, 22 U.S.C. §§ 1621–27 (1970).

39. Other claims against the Soviet Union were resolved through the War Claims Commission, which had earlier handled claims arising from World War II. That Commission's functions were also transferred to the FCSC.

tries of Eastern Europe.[40] Settlements negotiated with five of these countries are summarized below.

Yugoslavia. By an agreement of 1948, 62 Stat. 2658, T.I.A.S. No. 1803, Yugoslavia agreed to the creation of a fund of $17,000,000 to settle claims for nationalizations to that date. At the same time the United States agreed to release Yugoslavian assets which it had blocked—including gold bullion on deposit with the Federal Reserve Bank in New York that was needed by Yugoslavia to service its foreign exchange needs. Claims based upon later nationalizations were settled by a 1964 agreement calling for the payment by Yugoslavia, in five annual installments, of a total of $3,500,000. 16 U.S.T. & O.I.A. 1, T.I.A.S. No. 5750.

Rumania. By an agreement of 1960, 11 U.S.T. & O.I.A. 317, T.I.A.S. No. 4451, Rumania undertook to pay in five annual installments a total of $2,500,000, in addition to a $22,000,000 fund established by the United States in 1954 out of Rumanian assets in this country which it had vested.

Bulgaria. A 1963 agreement, 14 U.S.T. & O.I.A. 969, T.I.A.S. No. 5387, provided for a settlement of $3,500,000, of which $400,000 was to be paid by Bulgaria. The remainder was taken from Bulgarian assets in this country that had been vested.

Hungary. A 1973 agreement, 24 U.S.T. & O.I.A. 522, T.I.A.S. No. 7569, provided for a settlement to be funded by $3,320,000 from vested Hungarian assets plus $18,900,000 to be paid by Hungary in 20 annual installments.

Poland. In 1958 Poland and the United States arrived at a settlement, the principal terms of which are set forth in the following portions of the agreement of July 16, 1960, 11 U.S.T. & O.I.A. 1953, T.I.A.S. No. 4545.[41]

> The Government of the United States of America and the Government of the Polish People's Republic desiring to effect a a settlement of claims of nationals of the United States against Poland and desiring to advance economic relations between the two countries,
>
> Have agreed as follows:
>
> **Article I**
>
> A. The Government of the Polish People's Republic, hereinafter referred to as the Government of Poland, agrees to pay, and the Government of the United States agrees to accept, the sum of

40. For a description of the jurisdiction and procedures of the FCSC, see Re, The Foreign Claims Settlement Commission and the Adjudication of International Claims, 56 Am.J.Int.L. 728 (1962); and Re, The Foreign Claims Settlement Commission: Its Functions and Jurisdiction, 60 Mich. L.Rev. 1079 (1962).

41. Excerpts from the Annex to this agreement, including definitions of those equity interests that were covered by the settlement, appear at p. 240, supra.

$40,000,000.00 United States currency in full settlement and discharge of all claims of nationals of the United States, whether natural or juridical persons, against the Government of Poland on account of the nationalization and other taking by Poland of property and of rights and interests in and with respect to property, which occurred on or before the entry into force of this Agreement.

B. Payment of the sum of $40,000,000.00 by the Government of Poland shall be made to the Secretary of State of the United States in twenty annual installments of $2,000,000.00 United States currency, each installment to be paid on the tenth day of January, commencing on the tenth day of January 1961.

Article II

Claims to which reference is made in Article I and which are settled and discharged by this Agreement are claims of nationals of the United States for

(a) the nationalization or other taking by Poland of property and of rights and interests in and with respect to property;

(b) the appropriation or the loss of use or enjoyment of property under Polish laws, decrees or other measures limiting or restricting rights and interests in and with respect to property, it being understood that, for the purpose of this clause, the date of appropriation or the loss of use or enjoyment is the date on which such Polish laws, decrees or other measures were first applied to the property; and

(c) debts owed by enterprises which have been nationalized or taken by Poland and debts which were a charge upon property which has been nationalized, appropriated or otherwise taken by Poland.

. . .

Article VI

Within thirty days after the entry into force of this Agreement, the Government of the United States will release its blocking controls over all Polish property in the United States.

The specific inducements to enter into this settlement included not only the provisions of Article VI above but also the availability in this country of surplus agricultural commodities for transactions with Poland and legislative authority to extend to Poland most-favored-nation treatment for imports if the compensation agreement were reached.[42]

The presence in this country of funds, either vested or blocked, belonging to the Communist nations or their citizens was a fact not unrelated to the percentages of adjudicated claims that have been paid. The figures range, in *rough* terms, from 90% (Yugoslavia—1948 Agreement) to 75% (Bulgaria) and 40% (Rumania), not in-

42. See Lillich, The Protection of Foreign Investment 169–72 (1965).

cluding interest on the principal amounts. The FCSC completed in 1966 the adjudication of $680,000,000 of claims against Poland.[43]

In three of these five episodes, the United States employed the device of preadjudication. That is, nationals filed claims with the FCSC against Bulgaria, Hungary and Rumania which were adjudicated by the Commission, and payments were made from vested assets before the settlements, which added only minor percentages to the total sums available. Preadjudication procedures have also been followed for claims against Czechoslovakia, but no agreement with that country has yet been reached. The same procedures were followed with respect to expropriations by Cuba (larger in total value of properties taken than all Eastern European countries combined) and Communist China, although no settlements are in prospect.[44] Preadjudication serves the purpose of achieving fairly prompt hearings on claims while evidence and testimony are still fresh, and of giving the Executive Branch a more informed view of total American claims if and when diplomatic negotiations looking towards a settlement begin.

In his book, International Claims: Postwar British Practice (1967), Professor Lillich sheds some comparative light on the American practice of lump-sum settlements. Great Britain has concluded similar agreements with six Eastern European countries and with Egypt. The author notes that Great Britain, anxious to maintain its position as an international banker, has been reluctant to block bank accounts of foreign governments as a bargaining lever (p. 134). Thus settlements have often been less generous than what the United States has managed to achieve—for example, 18% of claims in the case of Yugoslavia. In the 1959 settlement with Egypt, resolving claims from expropriations that followed the Suez taking and the military activity by Britain, France and Israel against Egypt, Parliament appropriated sums to better the outcome for the individual claimants. It was felt that the expropriations had been so directly caused by the military intervention of 1956 that the claimants could not fairly be asked to bear the entire burden.

SARDINO v. FEDERAL RESERVE BANK OF NEW YORK

United States Court of Appeals, Second Circuit, 1966.
361 F.2d 106, cert. denied 385 U.S. 898, 87 S.Ct. 203, 17 L.E.2d 130 (1966).

[This case is one of many arising from the tensions between the United States and Cuba that grew shortly after Castro took power in 1959. Steps in this process included the reduction by our government in 1960 of the quota on sugar imports from Cuba, followed shortly by the Cuban expropriations of properties owned, directly

43. Re, The Foreign Claims Settlement Commission and the Cuban Claims Program, 1 The Int. Lawyer 81, 83 fn. 8 (1966).

44. The Cuban Claims Act of 1964, 78 Stat. 1110, as amended, 22 U.S.C.A. § 1643.

or indirectly, by United States corporations.[45] Those expropriations were part of a continuing process of drawing large segments of the Cuban economy into the public sector. Diplomatic relations were severed in 1961. Some of the subsequent United States moves to isolate or overthrow the Castro Regime—the landing at the Bay of Pigs and the missile episode—are familiar history.

Sardino, a Cuban citizen and resident, had a savings account in a New York bank. The bank would not remit funds to him in Cuba because the Cuban Assets Control Regulations issued under the Trading with the Enemy Act, pp. 41 and 110, supra, prohibited transfer outside this country of property owned by Cuban nationals without specific authorization, which was not forthcoming. In this action, Sardino requested an order that the license be issued or a declaration that none was required. The district court dismissed the complaint for failure to state a claim. The Court of Appeals, in an opinion by JUDGE FRIENDLY, affirmed.

The court first held that the Regulations were authorized by the Trading with the Enemy Act, and that the Act was not an unconstitutional delegation of legislative power, citing United States v. Curtiss-Wright Export Co., p. 102, supra. The opinion then considered Sardino's argument that the Regulations, as applied, deprived him of his property without due process of law in violation of the Fifth Amendment.]

The contention that Sardino has not been deprived of his property stresses that the Government has not taken over the bank account but has merely placed a temporary barrier to its transfer outside the United States. Indeed, the barrier is said to be not merely temporary but partial. Without a license Sardino can use the account to pay customs duties, taxes or fees owing to the United States, a state, or any instrumentality of either, 31 C.F.R. § 515.510, or can have the sum belonging to him invested in securities listed on a national securities exchange or issued by the United States, a state, or an instrumentality of either, 31 C.F.R. § 515.513; the Regulations also permit remittance not in excess of $100 a month for necessary living expenses, but only through payment to a blocked account of a Cuban bank in the United States, 31 C.F.R. § 515.521. Sardino effectively replies that he owes no customs duties, taxes or fees; that securities purchased at his instruction would be blocked to the same extent as the savings account; and that there would be little incentive for a Cuban bank to make monthly payments to him in Havana when the corresponding payments to it in the United States were blocked. . . . The due process clause speaks in terms not of taking but of deprivation; we find it hard to say there is no deprivation when a man is prevented both from obtaining his property and from realizing any benefit from it for a period of indefinite duration which may outrun his life. . . .

[The court, in a portion of its opinion appearing at p. 42, supra, then rejected the Government's argument that the Constitution confers no rights on nonresident aliens owning property in the United States. The opinion continued:]

It does not follow, however, that in dealing with the property of an alien the United States must be blind to the acts of the country of which he is a national; the Constitution protects the alien from arbitrary action by our government but not from reasonable response

45. A more detailed description of the American legislation and of Cuban reactions thereto appears in Banco Nacional de Cuba v. Sabbantino, p. 691, infra.

to such action by his own. The world today is not the classical international law world of black squares and white squares, where everyone is either an enemy or a friend. We are not formally at war with Cuba but only in a technical sense are we at peace . . . . The founders could not have meant to tie one of the nation's hands behind its back by requiring it to treat as a friend a country which has launched a campaign of subversion throughout the Western Hemisphere. . . . Hard currency is a weapon in the struggle between the free and the communist worlds; it would be a strange reading of the Constitution to regard it as demanding depletion of dollar resources for the benefit of a government [46] seeking to create a base for activities inimical to our national welfare. The Supreme Court's approval of wartime seizure of assets of a non-enemy alien "as a means of avoiding the use of the property to draw earnings or wealth out of this country to territory where it may more likely be used to assist the enemy than if it remains in the hands of this government," Silesian-American Corp. v. Clark, [p. 42, supra], is broad enough to justify the refusal of a license to Sardino.

Still other considerations support the constitutionality of the freezing order. Cuba has adopted a program expropriating property within its territory owned by designated American nationals, with a system of compensation holding out only an "illusory" possibility of payment. See Banco Nacional de Cuba v. Sabbatino, [p. 691, infra]. . . . There is a long history of governmental action compensating our own citizens out of foreign assets in this country for wrongs done them by foreign governments abroad. A famous instance is the Litvinov Assignment . . . . The Treaty of Berlin, 42 Stat. 1939, 1940–1941 (1921), terminating World War I with Germany, confirmed the retention of vested enemy property in the control of the United States until the German government had satisfied all war claims of our citizens; the Supreme Court has said "it does not matter whether this action was taken simply to secure claims of American citizens against Germany or was regarded as the rightful withholding of spoils of war." Guessefeldt v. McGrath, 342 U.S. 308, 313–314, 72 S.Ct. 338, 96 L.Ed. 342 (1952). The treaties of peace with Bulgaria, Hungary and Roumania at the end of World War II provided that any property of their nationals, blocked long before we were at war, Exec.Order No. 8389 of April 10, 1940, should vest in an agency or officer designated by the President and, after payment of debts owed by the owner, should be used to pay claims of United States nationals against the three countries. 22 U.S.C.A. §§ 1631a, 1641a. While these had been enemy countries, it is not clear that this was crucial. See Guessefeldt v. McGrath, supra; 2 O'Connell, International Law 846–48 (1965). In any event Congress followed the same course to compensate United States citizens for Czechoslovakian expropriations occurring after the war, setting up a fund out of the proceeds of Czech-owned steel mill equipment ordered here in 1947 and blocked and sold in 1954 by the Secretary of the Treasury. 22 U.S.C.A. §§ 1642a, 1642c, and 1642*l*; see 1958 U.S. Code Cong. & Ad.News 3299, 3301.

Congress has already taken steps to determine the claims of our nationals against Cuba, 22 U.S.C.A. § 1643, although without as yet providing for their payment. In Propper v. Clark, 337 U.S. 472, 484,

46. Any dollar exchange received by Sardino would have to be exchanged for pesos at the National Bank of Cuba within ten days, Laws No. 30 of Feb. 23, 1961, Art. 23, 29 Leyes del Gobierno Provisional de la Revolución 25 (1961); 13 International Monetary Fund Annual Report on Exchange Restrictions 91 (1962).

69 S.Ct. 1333, 1340, 93 L.Ed. 1480 (1949), the Court noted that a pre-war freezing order served the salutary purpose of immobilizing the assets of foreign nationals until our Government could determine whether they were needed "to compensate our citizens or ourselves for the damages done by the governments of the nationals affected." This would seem a rather clear intimation that if Congress should ultimately choose to apply the blocked assets of Cuban nationals to that purpose, the Fifth Amendment would not stand in its way. The unquestioned right of a state to protect its nationals in their persons and property while in a foreign country, see 1 Oppenheim, International Law § 319, at 686–87 (8th ed. Lauterpacht 1955), must permit initial seizure and ultimate expropriation of assets of nationals of that country in its own territory if other methods of securing compensation for its nationals should fail. See Colbert, Retaliation in International Law 63–69 (1948). To be sure, Congress has not yet chosen to invoke the ultimate sanction, having indeed eliminated a provision for the sale of certain Cuban assets to pay the expenses of administering the claims program, see 79 Stat. 988 (1965), amending 78 Stat. 113 (1964), and 1965 U.S. Code Cong. & Ad.News 3581, 3583–3584. Such commendable forbearance should not be understood as connoting lack of power. . . .

QUESTIONS

(1) As a Congressman, would you vote for legislation vesting all property in this country of Cuban nationals and residents to satisfy claims of American companies for former Cuban properties?

(2) If such legislation were enacted, do you agree with the Court's statement that Congress's present "commendable forbearance should not be understood as connoting lack of power"? As counsel to Sardino, what arguments would you make to a court challenging the application of that legislation to his property?

(3) Would you as a Congressman, after being reminded of the British practice towards its national claimants after Suez, p. 436, supra, vote to appropriate sums from general funds to help satisfy claims of American nationals against Cuba?

(4) Suppose that Guatador expropriates property of American owners, and that the United States blocks assets of the Guatador Government in this country amounting to $70,000,000. There is risk that Guatador will move sharply to the left and establish important trade and political relationships with the Soviet Union. To blunt these possibilities, to reestablish trade relations, and to gain Guatador's consent to extension of a 20-year lease (about to expire) on a naval base in Guatador, this country agrees to a lump-sum settlement of $30,000,000 and releases the blocked assets. The claims of United States companies amounted to $100,000,000.

(*a*) As counsel for one such company, what arguments would you make to the Congress for the proposition that the United States should compensate the American owners in whole for their loss? What counter arguments would you expect to meet? Are they stronger or weaker than in question (3) above?

(*b*) Is your case substantially strengthened if Guatador and the United States conclude a treaty extending the lease of the naval base and waiving all claims of the United States relating to the expropriations?

NOTE ON BRAZILIAN UTILITY EPISODES

Among the post-war disputes involving takings by non-Communist nations, the expropriation in 1962 by the Brazilian state of Rio Grande do Sul of the properties of a local subsidiary of International Telephone and Telegraph Corp. (ITT), an American company, had particular significance. Its impact upon Congressional opinion was immediate and led to important federal legislation described at p. 482, infra.

The episode assumes particular importance in view of the fact that Brazil, occupying about half of the land area of South America, containing about half of its population, and liberally endowed with natural resources, is a key country in Latin America. Foreign capital has pervaded Brazilian industry, particularly the larger and more technically advanced companies. One analysis of 1800 Brazilian corporations about the time of these takings indicated that they were 28% foreign-owned. Of 650 leading corporations with a capital of at least $1,000,000, 35% were controlled by Brazilian private capital, 35% by Brazilian government capital, and 30% by foreign private capital. Of the total foreign investment of approximately $3.5 billion at the end of 1966, capital from the United States represented over 37%—a figure that might have approached 45% if one accounted for equity ownership in this country of Canadian or other corporations with substantial Brazilian investments. Motor vehicles, chemicals and machinery represented about half of the United States investment. Western European countries as a group had Brazilian investments about equal to that of the United States. Latin American investments in Brazil, amounting to $185,000,000, were almost entirely Argentine.[47]

This degree of foreign ownership was then far in excess of that in France which led to the attitudes and reactions described at p. 81, supra. It may be compared with that found in Mexico before its revolutionary period and described at p. 423, supra. Brazil has never had such a dramatic experience as Mexico's, nor does its history suggest that a comparable experience is likely. Nonetheless, there are elements which might combine to create serious difficulties for foreign investment: anxiety about the extensive political and economic influence of the United States; concern about policies of foreign management, such as those governing repatriation of profits; and general nationalistic feelings. One sector particularly prone to such difficulties was the public utility field. Utilities have an everyday impact on Brazilian citizens, and their foreign ownership long raised problems.

There was a background of tension between Rio Grande do Sul and ITT—particularly over the level of telephone utility rates that

47. These figures are taken from surveys conducted by a number of private and governmental organizations in Brazil and reported in the Christian Science Monitor, Dec. 7, 1967, p. 23.

were regulated by the state. After abortive efforts to form a joint telephone enterprise of the state and ITT, the state issued a 1962 decree of expropriation and deposited the equivalent of about $400,-000 as compensation. ITT valued the assets between $7,000,000 and $8,000,000. These events occurred at a time when Brazilian President Goulart had arranged a trip to the United States to secure additional financial assistance, and the federal government of Brazil promised that it would try to secure fair compensation. Difficult problems of federal-state relations arose under Brazil's constitution. Negotiations began between ITT and the Brazilian state, and ITT filed suit in the local courts.

Following conversations between Presidents Kennedy and Goulart, the Brazilian Government issued Decree No. 1106. A press release, presumably written by the Brazilian Embassy in Washington,[48] stated that the Decree was "based on a proposal submitted by the largest American investors in Brazil and in line with similar expropriation laws issued in the past by Mexico, Argentina and Colombia. The new decree is also a result of mutual understanding on the subject arrived at high levels during the visit of President Goulart to the United States last April." The Decree read: [49]

> WHEREAS, at the present stage of the country's development the national interests may be better served by direct operation of public services or utilities, except in regard to municipal services or to those having a limited regional scope, where private concessions are justified;
>
> WHEREAS in the nationalization of public utilities companies the constitutional principles of guarantee of private property, both domestic and foreign, must be observed;
>
> WHEREAS the Council of Ministers, in its Plan of Government submitted to the Congress, recognized the necessity for the participation of foreign investments in the country as a supplement in the formation of internal capital, so that the country may attain and maintain the levels of economic and social development demanded by population growth and by the Brazilian people's just aspirations to social well being;
>
> WHEREAS the nationalization of public utilities companies should not result in a reduction of foreign investments in the country, nor in the creation of a climate discouraging to new investments, nor constitute a source of substantial increase in the exchange burdens arising out of such investments;
>
> Art. 1—A Commission answering to the President of the Council of Ministers is hereby created, to be composed of three members appointed by the President of the Republic, such Commission to be charged with a) submittal, for approval by the Council of Ministers, of a list of the services to be taken over for direct operation, indicating order of priority; b) negotiation, with the representatives of the concessionary companies, of the conditions and procedure

48. The release appears in 108 Cong. Rec., 87th Cong., 2d Sess., June 7, 1962, p. 9941.

49. The Decree appears in translation in 1 Int.Leg.Mat. 124 (1962).

for refund or indemnization to the shareholders, and submittal to the Council of Ministers of the plan resulting from each such negotiation;

Art. 2—The conditions governing refund or indemnization agreed upon with the concessionaries shall be subject to the following principles: a) initial payment of a portion not to exceed ten percent of the agreed total; b) deferred payment of a portion in installments compatible whenever possible with resources accumulated by the selfsame utility and with a minimum of additional public resources; c) obligation assumed by the concessionaries to reinvest in the country, in sectors or activities defined by the National Planning Commission as enjoying priority for the social and economic development, of not less than seventy five percent of the net amounts received as reimbursement or indemnization, such reinvestment not to be applied to the financing of, or participation in, any Brazilian enterprise already in operation;

Art. 3—The assets and the amounts to be received by the concessionaries as payment or indemnization shall be estimated by mutual agreement and, when necessary, through expert evaluation and/or arbitration by a representative of the Government and a representative of the concessionary, and experts appointed by joint agreement, or, in case of disagreement, by the President of the Council of Ministers, with the approval of the Cabinet . . . .

Negotiations between ITT and Rio Grande do Sul continued into 1963, when an interim settlement was reached, pending an ultimate determination by the Brazilian courts. The following description of the settlement appears at p. 11 of a Prospectus of ITT, dated August 3, 1966 and relating to sales of its common stock:

> In 1962, telephone operations in the State of Rio Grande do Sul, Brazil, were taken over by that State, the net assets seized being carried on the consolidated balance sheet of ITT at December 31, 1961, at a U. S. dollar equivalent cost of approximately $6,500,000. In 1963 ITT reached an interim agreement on payment for this expropriated telephone operating subsidiary, which provided for interim advances to ITT of the cruzeiro equivalent of $7,300,000, which was repatriated to ITT in U. S. dollars and of which $3,650,000 has been reinvested in Standard Electrica, S. A., a Brazilian manufacturing subsidiary, for expansion of manufacturing capacity. The final amount which ITT will be entitled to receive for such expropriation will not be determined until the settlement of legal actions pending in the Brazilian courts, as a result of which a portion of such advances may be repayable.

An ITT news release of June 19, 1967, announced that a settlement of the litigation had resulted in a sale of all ITT telephone facilities in Brazil (including some in the state of Paraná) for about $12,000,000. ITT stated it would reinvest about half of this sum in its telecommunications manufacturing facilities in Brazil. The release described the settlement as "an equitable and fair arrangement."

Another utility enterprise was terminated when, after extended negotiations, the American & Foreign Power Company entered into an agreement in 1964 with the Brazilian Government and a corporate agency thereof providing for the sale to the Government of shares of its electric utility subsidiaries in Brazil.[50] $10,000,000 of the agreed price of $135,000,000 was promptly paid and the balance was represented by notes bearing interest at 6% or 6½%. Approximately $25,000,000 in principal amount of the notes were payable over a 25-year period, and $100,000,000 over a 45-year period. The agreement states that this long-term investment would be viewed as meeting an earlier obligation assumed by the American corporation "to reinvest in Brazil in enterprises of primary importance to the economic development of the country" an amount corresponding to approximately 75% of the total price.

In 1966, Brazilian Light & Power Company, a Canadian corporation largely owned by United States shareholders, sold a number of its telephone subsidiaries to the Brazilian Government, under the condition that 75% of the proceeds were to be reinvested in other economic activities of the Company in Brazil.

QUESTIONS

(1) What relevance have the negotiated settlements with Eastern European countries and Brazil to the development of a rule of customary international law? If they are viewed as evidence of developing state practice, what are the principles about compensation which they support?

(2) Which of the economic and political factors which underlay these agreements might act as inducements to settlements in the future to (a) socialist countries or (b) non-Communist, less developed countries? Are any factors common to both groups of countries? Do these factors, and the general motives for payment, come within natural-right or utilitarian thought?

(3) If you attempted to assess the risk of expropriation incurred by foreign investment in different sectors of the economies of less developed countries, where would public utility investments figure in your list? Why?

(4) How would you describe the different motives which may lead a country to expropriate alien-owned property, with or without compensation? Consider the range of illustrations in this Part C, and recall the Note on attitudes of less developed countries towards foreign investment at p. 84, supra. Does your assessment of these motives give you confidence as to the present security of foreign investment in such countries, assuming an "enlightened" attitude of the foreign investor on such key issues as profit sharing and training of local personnel to assume positions of responsibility?

(5) Suppose that foreign investment in the United States were to increase to the point where foreign interests controlled 20 of our leading 100 corporations and were particularly evident in certain key areas of capital machinery and durable customer goods. What kinds of popular or official attitudes would you anticipate? Recall the attitudes reflected in

50. The agreement appears in 4 Int. Leg.Mat. 72 (1965).

cases such as Terrace v. Thompson, p. 47, supra, and in the legislative proposals to contain foreign investment, (p. 67, supra) that were before the Congress in the early 1970's.

NOTE ON THE CHILEAN COPPER EXPROPRIATIONS AND EXCESS PROFITS

During the early decades of this century, American corporations acquired interests in what proved to be extraordinarily rich copper properties in Chile and started to develop them. By the early 1970's, two such companies had vast stakes in these properties, which yielded during recent decades from 11% to 23% of world copper production. In 1971, the mining assets of both companies—The Anaconda Company and Kennecott Copper Corporation—were expropriated by the Chilean government, an act that led to one of the major disputes of the post-war period between a government and foreign investors, and an act whose consequences were resolved by settlement only after the overthrow of a duly elected Chilean coalition government of Socialist-Communist parties by a military coup establishing a military junta.

These events have great economic and political complexity, reaching back for more than half a century into Chilean life and Chilean-American relationships. They involve not only political forces and ideological conflict, but also technical problems of accounting for the hundreds of millions of dollars of values that were at issue. Since the settlement that is described below did not examine or clarify these technical issues, the observer is left at certain points with conflicting versions of the relevant financial past. This Note describes the major themes of this controversy, indicating the financial aspects of the dispute but not stressing the technical questions which they posed. The two companies involved had significantly different histories within Chile; this Note will discuss only one of them, Kennecott.[51]

51. A third American company, The Cerro Corporation, had important but less weighty copper interests in Chile that were expropriated together with Anaconda's and Kennecott's. The statistical and other information about Kennecott has been taken from a variety of sources: published balance sheets or statistical charts, contentious writings in legal briefs and periodicals, books on foreign extractive industries, and newspaper reports and press releases by Chile and the companies. References will be made below as appropriate. Much information treating Kennecott appears in a series of "White Papers" published by Kennecott from an original booklet in 1971 through Supplement no. 5 in 1975, and variously entitled "Expropriation of the El Teniente Copper Mine" or "Confiscation of El Teniente". These booklets contain Kennecott's arguments and views of the historical record and financial data, as well as translations of source documents. Translations of the basic Chilean laws or decrees and official proceedings also appear in 10 Int.Leg. Mat. 1067 (1971), 11 Int.Leg.Mat. 1013 (1972), and 12 Int.Leg.Mat. 983 (1973). The basic arguments underlying the Chilean position are set forth in a book by an official of the Chilean government from 1971 to 1973, Eduardo Novoa M., La Batalla Por el Cobre, published in Chile in 1972.

The Background: Copper Resources and Foreign Investors

During the last fifty years, copper accounted for annual percentages of 30% to 80% of Chilean exports, and copper production by Anaconda and Kennecott ranged from 7% to 20% of Gross National Product. Annual tax revenues from the copper industry amounted to 10% to 40% of total governmental expenditures. The larger copper mines were grouped within a legal-political category known as the *Gran Mineria,* almost wholly owned by American corporations. An American scholar has stated: "All of *Fortune's* 500 largest U. S. corporations combined do not play nearly the role in the economy of the United States [that Anaconda and Kennecott played in Chile] or pay more than a fraction of the percentage of U. S. taxes that Anaconda and Kennecott alone supplied in Chile." [52]

In view of the country's economic development, copper assumed particular significance during the 1950's and 1960's. Chile sought to correct its traditional dependence upon export-led growth requiring the importation of necessary manufactures from abroad, by initiating an import-substitution industrial policy that made necessary internal structural change. To this program foreign exchange earnings became essential, to acquire such imports as infrastructural plant equipment and heavy machinery. Hence the copper industry, the principal source of such exchange, stood as a potential brake upon national economic development.

In these circumstances, it is not difficult to visualize the inherent sources of tension between the host government and the foreign investors. Consider the typical issues to be settled and resettled in significantly different political contexts over an evolving 50-year relationship. (*1*) Questions will arise about the manner of exploitation of the natural resources. For example, there may be conflicting tendencies towards short-run profit maximization or towards a longer time frame for exploitation that would make conservation relevant. Or the foreign investor may wish to extract only the high grade ore, thus rendering uneconomical the later exploitation of lower grade ores. After the mining stage, the problem arises of where refining should take place before selling copper on the world market. Control over the directions of export sales and over the levels of export prices (within relevant constraints of world supply and demand) is likely to become a critical issue. (*2*) Once revenues are realized, their division between the copper corporations and the Chilean government or economy must be decided upon. The level of wages and other benefits for workers may lead to disputes.

52. Moran, Multinational Corporations and the Politics of Dependence: Copper in Chile 7 (1974). The information and analysis of bargaining strength in this section of the Note are based upon Moran and upon Mikesell (ed.), Foreign Investment in the Petroleum and Mineral Industries (1971), particularly Chapters 1, 2 and 17 written by the editor-author. See also Chapters 1 and 2 of Grunwald and Musgrove, Natural Resources in Latin American Development (1970), and the essay of Reynolds (pp. 203–257) in Mamalakis and Reynolds, Essays on the Chilean Economy (1965). The background problems of the Chilean economy are analyzed in Anibal Pinto, Chile: Una Economia Dificil (1964).

Structural characteristics of such natural-resource investments complicate the resolution of these problems. The foreign investor (in our case, Kennecott), with its multinational network of American and foreign mining properties, marketing and sales corporations and so forth, will generally plan its business operations so as to maximize its earnings (or the yield on invested capital, or its percentage of world markets, or any other goal). The framework for maximization will be the multinational enterprise itself. Whether production or sales occur in one or another country is less significant than the results of all production and sales for the enterprise as a whole. It may be a rational business decision to cut down production—in times of recession, for example—in one country rather than another, to invest fresh capital in whatever country seems to offer the highest marginal return, or to seek vertical integration through refining operations located outside the country of production.

On the other hand, it is evident that the host government will be less concerned with the global profits or long-run interests of the foreign corporation than with its national welfare. The tension may become acute when that welfare is so deeply affected by a sector as is Chilean welfare by copper. Thus the different national and global-corporate frameworks for planning and maximization of (different) values threaten to become an acute irritant to relationships.[53]

It is not simply economic factors that complicate the relationship. The dominance of copper in the Chilean economy, and the dominance of American firms in copper, breed political tensions that, in Chile's case, took the expression in the political literature of the theory of *dependencia*. The Chilean dependence was upon concentrated foreign ownership, upon private firms whose fundamental allegiance lay towards their internal corporate interests and, in political terms, towards the United States government. "Dependence" theory fit well within the more traditional, Marxist-derived theory of imperialism, and gave the dispute between the copper companies and Chile an important ideological as well as economic character. Moreover, the reaction against dependence became characteristic not only of socialist political thought but also of nationalist thought of the more conservative Chilean parties.

How tensions between Chile and the copper companies were resolved over this fifty-year period depended upon the political and economic climate at the time of each crisis. The different resolutions can be understood within a model of game theory or bargaining theory, in which Chile and the copper companies found themselves in varying positions of strength or weakness.[54] At the start, the host country lacks skills, technology, capital, even knowledge about the extent of its wealth in natural resources. It is entirely dependent

53. These and related problems are explored in the Note on reactions to foreign investment at p. 84, supra, and in the discussion of multinational enterprises in the Note at p. 1179, infra.

54. The models are developed in the books of Moran and of Mikesell, fn. 52, supra, and in Vernon, Sovereignty at Bay (1971).

upon investments and skills from the industrialized world. The initial arrangements thus tend to be favorable to the investor, which must be persuaded to assume the risks of a new venture. As the resources prove to be profitable—in Chile's case, exceptionally profitable given the quantity and quality of the copper ore—and as the foreign corporation "sinks" its investment in fixed assets in the host country, the bargaining position changes. The investor both influences and shapes, and is shaped by, political forces within the host country. Those forces react to the investor's success. The initial investments may be recaptured by earnings. Then, continuing high profits produce demands for a higher national percentage of revenues —whether in the form of taxes, exchange-control regulations, equity ownership, or at its extreme, expropriation. The host country develops an industrial infrastructure, financial sophistication, technology and skills, and thus greater capability of assuming management and dealing for itself in world markets. Despite fluctuations, the long-run trend will thus be towards greater bargaining power of the host government relative to the investor. With appropriate modifications, including emphasis upon Chile's special political developments, this model affords a useful explanation of fifty years of American copper companies in Chile.

Kennecott's Investments and the Experiment with "Chileanization"

In 1915, Kennecott was formed to combine ownership of mines in the United States and interests in what proved to be the world's largest underground copper mine, the El Teniente mine in Chile. The mining interests and assets in Chile were owned by, and mining operations were under the direct supervision of, Braden Copper Company, a wholly-owned American subsidiary of Kennecott. From that time until the mid-1960's, El Teniente was developed to a capacity of 180,000 tons annually. Management and employment policies so developed that by the time of the expropriation in 1971, there were two American citizens among the 10,000 employees at the mine.

Relations between Kennecott (and the other mining companies, particularly Anaconda) and the Chilean government followed an up-and-down course during this period, under the play of economic and political influences. Taxation rates ranged from an effective high of about 20% to 80%. At times—as with the *Nuevo trato* legislation of 1955—Chile sought to attract further investment by the copper companies through traditional inducements: lowering of taxes, returning control over pricing and marketing to the companies and so on. At other times, Chile intensified its regulation and asserted more managerial power.

Throughout this period, tensions of the types described above surfaced. We here signal a few, beyond the obvious disputes over revenue sharing through taxation or other forms of regulation.

The problem of "returns" (*retornos parciales*) to Chile of the foreign exchange earned by the companies from the export sales of copper lingered. Dollar receipts from sales by the Kennecott subsidiaries were kept in the United States, with return to Chile of that amount of foreign exchange necessary (whether or not through the purchase of Chilean currency) to satisfy taxes, local purchases, wages and other local expenditures. The parties differed both as to the total amounts involved or "returned" to Chile in relation to copper revenues, and as to the significance for Chile's balance of payments of keeping unexpended dollar revenues of Braden (beyond dividends paid to Kennecott) in the United States.

Severe tensions developed over export pricing policies. During World War II and the Korean War, there was unilateral price setting by the United States and by the copper companies without prior consultation of Chile, at levels below those which could have been achieved under the prevailing (war-inflationary) conditions. Chile alleged that it had sacrificed hundreds of millions of tax revenues to service the distinct aims of the United States government; on one occasion, negotiations between Chile and the United States led to price revisions.

There were allegations that during periods of recession, as in 1949, Chilean production had been cut back by the copper companies in an amount disproportionately large when compared with continuing production from the United States mines.

By the mid-1960's the Christian Democratic government of President Frei, heavily supported by the United States under the AID program as a moderate-reformist government to serve as a model for Latin American development, sought large new investments in copper mining and greater Chilean control over pricing and production. Previous strategies of the Chilean government to encourage more investment by Kennecott to repair and develop El Teniente had not proved successful. At this time, the growing technical competence of Chileans with respect to the mining operations, as well as the loss by the copper companies of support which they had traditionally enjoyed from the conservative Chilean parties, placed the companies in a difficult position. Kennecott was unwilling to make major new commitments, given the political risks of a country in which a coalition of Socialist and Communist parties had barely been defeated six years previously and remained a powerful force.

Negotiations and preliminary plans from 1964–1967 led to arrangements that were partly incorporated into Ministerial Decrees of 1967 under which the El Teniente mine was to be "Chileanized," so as to achieve expansion and joint ownership. The mining assets and interests of Braden were transferred to El Teniente Mining Company, a Chilean corporation, in which Braden received a 49% interest. The majority interest of 51% was acquired by a government instrumentality, the Chilean Copper Corporation (Codelco). In 1965, prior to the transfer, Braden's book values were revalued from $72 million to $244 million, and the mining assets appeared on the books of El Teniente Mining Company at a somewhat higher figure after further investments.

In exchange for the 51% interest that it sold, Braden received $80 million which it promptly reinvested through a loan to El Teniente Mining Company, together with all interest due on this loan until 1971, for a total of $92.7 million. In addition, Kennecott arranged for the further financing necessary to achieve the expansion in capacity of El Teniente (realized by 1971) from 180,000 to 280,000 tons annually. As finally revised, that further financing amounted to $110 million of loans from the United States Export-Import Bank, $37 million from Codelco, and $45 million from European and Japanese banks. Various agreements about taxes (considerably reduced in relation to the previous tax structure), revaluation of assets and other matters were entered into, some made formal through Ministerial Decrees with 20-year guarantees. Under the new arrangement, the Chilean government received a 20% tax on the earnings of El Teniente Mining Company (a tax that was raised when copper prices exceeded a certain level), as well as a tax of 30% on dividends distributed by El Teniente to Braden. Kennecott secured a contract of guarantee against expropriation from the United States governmental agency now succeeded by the Overseas Private Investment Corporation (OPIC), pp. 471–478, infra, covering $80 million of the $92.7 million in notes owed to Braden by El Teniente Mining Company.

As with other matters in this long and complicated history, the Chileanization arrangements were later perceived in radically different ways by Kennecott and political factions in Chile. The late 1960's witnessed a sharp rise in the price of copper, leading to increased earnings from existing production as well as from the expanded production achieved during this period. Kennecott was accused of gaining higher profits (partly through lower taxes) without any investment of fresh capital, since its sole financial commitment to the expanded mine was the reinvestment of the sales price for its 51% interest. Kennecott's response was that the amounts required would have demanded of it major new financing, the sacrifice of other corporate opportunities, and an assumption of risk that seemed disproportionately high. Surely one consequence that Kennecott sought from the actual financing was the involvement in El Teniente Mining Company of both the United States government (through the Export-Import Bank) and creditors of several other nations, so that any default in payment of the debt obligations would provoke private-company and governmental responses from different countries.

The Expropriation

The six-year term of Frei's presidency and Christian Democratic government ended in 1970. In September of that year, Salvador Allende won a plurality of 1.4% (40,000) of the popular vote, running against candidates of the center-left and of the political right. Allende was the candidate of the Popular Unity (Unidad Popular), a coalition dominated by Allende's own Socialist Party and the Communist Party, with numerous splinter factions ranging from the relatively moderate to the extreme left radicals. In accordance with constitutional tradition where a candidate failed to receive a majority but nonetheless won a plurality, the Congress confirmed Allende as President in November. That vote had the support of the Christian Democrats.

The Popular Unity and its left-coalition predecessors had long campaigned on a platform of basic structural change, involving important redistribution of wealth to the poorer classes, incorporation into the public sector of the large and influential parts of the industrial and financial sectors, and extensive land reform and redistribution. An important plank in that platform was the nationalization of the copper resources.

Allende promptly announced plans to expropriate the copper properties and submitted a bill to the Congress to be enacted as a law and constitutional amendment. In July 1971, that amendment was unanimously adopted by the Chilean Congress—that is, with the concurrence of all parties from the Popular Unity to the Christian Democrats and the conservative groups.[55] The amendment provided that for purposes of nationalization, the Comptroller General would be responsible for determining the "suitable compensation" to be paid to the companies. It defined the standard for "suitable compensation" as "the book value on December 31, 1970, *less* any reevaluations made by those companies or their predecessors after December 31, 1964," and *less* any "assets that the State does not receive in good operating condition." The compensation right extended only to physical assets, and "no right to compensation shall be allowed for rights to mineral deposits."

In addition, the amendment empowered the President "to order the Comptroller General, in computing the compensation, to deduct all or part of the excess profits earned annually by the nationalized companies [from 1955 on], giving special consideration to the normal profitability that they have obtained in their international operations as a whole." The President was to report his decision to the Comptroller General about such a deduction within a 30-day period after request. After a decision by the Comptroller about compensation, any affected party could appeal to a specially formed Tribunal consisting of five designated justices and executive officials. The decision of this special Tribunal "may not be appealed."

Thus the constitutional procedures preceding this amendment, which provided for compensation for expropriations and which permitted appeal to the normal courts, were specially structured for the copper situation. Moreover, as later interpreted by the special Tribunal, the constitutional amendment deprived that Tribunal of competence to review the determination by the President of excess profits, which thus stood as a final determination to be taken into account by the Comptroller General.

55. The constitutional amendment, in the form of law No. 17,450 of July 16, 1971, appears in translation in 10 Int.Leg.Mat. 1067 (1971).

In the proceedings contemplated by the amendment, the Comptroller General determined the net book value of El Teniente Mining Company to be $319 million as of December 31, 1970 (contrary to Kennecott's assertion of a book value of $365 million). From this amount, the Comptroller deducted $197 million traceable to the revaluation of assets in connection with the Chileanization agreements, and $21 million because of deficient equipment. This left a balance of $100 million, from which a further deduction would of course be necessary to account either for Kennecott's partial 49% interest or, if Kennecott were treated as whole owner, to account for the $80 million previously paid for the 51% interest.

Such questions, however they would have been resolved by the Comptroller or by the special Tribunal upon appeal, became academic. President Allende determined the excess profits for Kennecott for the years 1955–1970 to be $410 million, a figure which Kennecott alleged was in excess of the net after-tax earnings of Braden during this period. This final deduction from the previous balance of $100 million left a deficit of $310 million. When the special Tribunal determined that it lacked competence to review the figure of $410 million, Kennecott withdrew from proceedings in Chile and started to pursue its remedies in other countries as described in the Note at p. 677, infra.

Kennecott's outspoken criticism of the Chilean laws, procedures and findings rested generally upon the argument that international-law principles required compensation, and in particular upon the position of its government that the requirement was of prompt, adequate and effective compensation. The asserted violations of international law included both lack of compensation and failure to comply with the Chileanization agreements and guarantees. Although Kennecott never made public a definitive statement of its claim, a legal memorandum written on its behalf argued that compensation should amount to at least $176 million, in addition to the previous $80 million of notes for sale of the 49% interest.[56] The disagreements with the Chilean government extended past international law principles to principles of accounting, to the accuracy of historical or present data, and to the criteria relevant to fixing the value of the expropriated properties.

One basic legal point of Chilean law that remained in contention was whether the taking of the mineral resources required compensation. Chile contended that such in-place mineral wealth had never been alienated from the national patrimony within traditional Latin American legal principles about interests in underground resources. Kennecott, in Chile's view, had enjoyed simply a right to extract, and need be compensated only for physical assets (plant and equipment).

56. See Memorandum of Governing International Law Principles, by Covington and Burling, published by Kennecott in a "White Paper" of 1971 (pp. 64–92) entitled "Expropriation of El Teniente."

The Issue of Excess Profits

Argument over the question of excess profits continued between the Chilean government and Kennecott, which contended that international law proscribed the retroactive application of so vague and novel a limit on compensation. The public statements of the United States government made traditional points and spoke particularly to the claim of excess profits. Secretary of State Rogers referred to the "serious departure from accepted standards of international law," while President Nixon termed the excess-profits deductions "the application ex post facto of unprecedented legal rules" to nullify compensation. In 1972, President Nixon reaffirmed that this country expected its citizens to receive "prompt, adequate and effective compensation" and, in a message to the Congress, stressed that both public and private sources of capital would observe whether Chile met international obligations.

Given the nature of the settlement described below, the legal arguments about excess profits were never joined within a framework of negotiations or before any tribunal. Nor, as we shall observe, was there any principled resolution of these Chilean claims and American responses. Our purpose here is to recite the basic facts advanced by Chile and Kennecott, and then to suggest issues that should have been explored had the legal aspects of this dispute been more deeply and systematically probed.

Let us turn to figures. Kennecott's statistical presentation in its White Papers, fn. 51, supra, indicates that from 1916–1971, Braden and El Teniente Mining Company sold $3.4 billion of copper, of which $2.5 billion remained in Chile as taxes or dividends to the Chilean government, or to meet local expenses such as wages or purchases. Of the balance, $430 million was expended for imported materials, freight charges and so on, so that 73% of the total sales value ended up in one form or another within Chile. Kennecott's total earnings during this entire period amounted to $509 million. From 1965 to 1970, Kennecott asserted that it had retained as earnings 28% of total profits, after payment of taxes and dividends to Chile.

In the charges and responses, the period 1965–1970 commanded particular contention, the government claiming that Kennecott had unduly profited by the marked rise in the world price of copper and had increased its percentage profits more so than had Chile. The comparisons between Chilean and global operations seemed to involve different figures and statistical computations from the two sides. The Chilean calculations, as indicated in the Decree, found disproportionately high profits from Chile, the comparative percentages representing net earnings as a percentage of book value. Thus the relevant percentages for (1) Kennecott (excluding Braden and El Teniente) and (2) for Braden and El Teniente, were 16% and 48% in 1955, 8% and 33% in 1960 and 12% and 14% in 1965. The post-1965 figures presented by Chile were affected by the revaluation of assets (book value) before Chileanization, noted at p. 448, supra.

The percentages based on revaluation appear in parentheses. The same comparative figures were 7% and 106% (27%) in 1967, 10% and 205% (50%) in 1969.[57] Kennecott contended that the Chilean figures distorted the historical record and rested upon inadequate conceptions of book value.

The Chilean position on excess profits was presented in a variety of sources, governmental and academic, but never appears to have been given a definitive and principled exposition by the government itself. Recall that the provisions in the constitutional amendment treating excess profits point towards comparison between Chilean and global earnings. That was the sole guidance given by Congress to Allende, who issued in September 1971 a Presidential Decree Concerning Excess Profits of Copper Companies.[58] It referred to "international economic relations, from which our people have suffered," that were "based on an essentially unjust system which imposes on dependent countries unilateral decisions adopted by the hegemonic countries." The "vital resources" of the poor countries had been "appropriated or confiscated by a very limited group of large enterprises pursuing their profits at the expense of the underdevelopment and backwardness of the masses in those countries in which they establish themselves." The Decree referred to "unilateral discrimination" against Chile stemming from the pricing policies during World War II and the Korean War. It also stated that the company accounts in official balance sheets concealed benefits derived by Kennecott from transfer pricing policies—charging high prices for materials and for technological assistance rendered in Chile, and paying lesser sums for copper production that was refined elsewhere. It claimed that in Chile, as elsewhere in Latin America, "revenues produced by foreign capital contributions are much inferior to the disbursements engendered by profits of already-invested capital," an evocation of the theme of decapitalization described at p. 87, supra. The Decree found that the profits derived by the copper companies from capital invested in Chile, compared with profits received from aggregate international operations, were "much higher."

Based upon these and related facts, the President "has resolved that the annual return (profits) for nationalized enterprises and their predecessors shall be fixed at the rate of 10% of their respective book values." Any excess over this percentage was to be deducted from compensation as excess profits. As noted above, the finding of excess profits for Kennecott from 1955–1970 was $410 million.

57. The charts from which these figures are taken were dated September 1971, listed their sources as Annual Reports of Kennecott and financial statements presented by Braden or El Teniente to the Chilean Government, and were obtained from the Legal Counsellor at the Chilean Embassy in Washington. A chart in Moran, fn. 52 supra, at 109, based on Chilean and Kennecott published figures, calculates Kennecott's relative return on assets in Chile and elsewhere as 37.-9% and 13.39% from 1955–1960, and 19% and 7.6% from 1960–1965.

58. A translation of the Decree appears in 12 Int.Leg.Mat. 983 (1973).

The writings of Chilean officials and academics [59] support the claims of excess profits with themes drawn principally from domestic-law conceptions of unjust enrichment and of unconscionability, but also from expressions of those themes in international law.[60] For example, the Decree asserted that the copper companies had taken unjust advantage of Chile, and thereby received profits beyond what was reasonable at the expense of the Chilean collectivity. The conception of what was a reasonable or just price was never fully articulated, although references were made to legal traditions incorporating notions of a just price, from Roman law to medieval canon law, as well as to aspects of contemporary American law, ranging from utility rate regulation aiming at a reasonable return on invested capital, to government renegotiation of contracts, to the common law of unconscionability in contract.

As for the retroactive application of the principle, the Chilean justification stressed the remedying in the collective interest of older injustices, and drew again by analogy upon aspects of regulatory United States law which adversely and retroactively affected earnings or values of holders of property or contract rights—tax laws applicable to previous earnings, to some extent government renegotiation of contracts, mortgage moratoria, and so on.

There are evident difficulties in relying upon principles such as unjust enrichment or unconscionability that are so broad, diffused and variously employed at national and international law. Surely one of the traditional bases of the argument for compensation itself is that the expropriating state would otherwise be unjustly enriched at the expense of the investor. The principle as so invoked, either in defense or derogation of the compensation requirement, may serve more as rhetorical justification for than as explanation of the position asserted.

Had this controversy been further developed in a legal context, perhaps before an arbitral tribunal, more precise issues might have been usefully examined. Consider the difficulties in arriving at a coherent conception of a fair or reasonable or just profit to be earned by a foreign investor. The risks, political as well as economic, encountered by the foreign investor are surely relevant to what is a reasonable profit. High risk ventures surely will not attract capital at the same economic returns as low risk ventures. But analysis of risk poses complex problems: the economic and political situation confronting the corporation at the time of the initial or later investments, prospects in local and world markets, prospects of inflation, problems of present or future taxes or wages, and so on. Moreover, the conception of a fair profit from an investment already proved successful

59. See particularly Novoa, supra fn. 51, at 208–222 and 275–285, and Echeverria, *Enriquecimiento Injusto y Nacionalizacion,* Mensaje No. 207, March-April 1972, p. 11.

60. For a review of illustrations of the principle of unjust enrichment in international arbitrations or treaties, see Schreuer, Unjustified Enrichment in International Law, 22 Am.J.Comp. L. 281 (1974).

could include consideration of those (ultimately) fruitless explorations or investments in which natural-resource corporations must necessarily engage, perhaps even those in other countries.

The particular problem confronted by companies extracting natural resources is that an investment, once proved to be successful, may be extraordinarily so. As the initial risk in exploration and development fades, as infrastructure is built and relationships in world markets are established, as accumulated earnings come to exceed total invested capital, the company will almost inevitably be viewed as earning unduly high rewards in view of its investments, as gaining high rents from its monopoly or oligopoly position in the local or world economy. Such problems are rendered more acute by the long-term character of the relationship between the investor and the host government. It is indeed a "relationship" more than a "contract bargain," even if in formal terms the relationship assumes contractual form.

Such considerations do not of themselves resolve the legal issues and the amount of compensation due. It is through their exploration that disputes over these questions may slowly find resolution under international-law principles. It may be that foreign enterprises vital to a nation's wealth will become subject to more explicit regulation of profits and prices. They would thereby be assimilated to the present category of regulated public utilities in capitalist countries. The Andean Foreign Investment Code, prepared within the Andean Group of five Latin American countries bound together by a 1969 agreement, makes regulation of financial operations of foreign investors explicit by providing that earnings to be remitted annually cannot exceed 14% of the invested capital.[61] Of course that Code is meant to be applied prospectively to future conduct. The Chilean argument points towards the notion (applied here retroactively) of a fair return to a foreign investor occupying a dominant position in the local economy, to be determined other than through the normal play of business factors. But in the end, the Chilean dispute made little contribution towards advancement of this argument and clarification of the issues before the international community. It did succeed in giving those issues a new and dramatic emphasis, indeed a prominence which suggests that they may figure in future disputes over compensation through explicit legal argument.

Avenues Towards Remedies

During the 1970–1973 period of the Allende government, relationships between Chile and the United States steadily worsened. Although the expropriations of the copper properties and other American-owned interests were an important factor, they were probably not the dominant cause. The Popular Unity continued with its pro-

61. For a discussion of these and other provisions under the Andean Pact, see Furnish, The Andean Market's Common Regime for Foreign Investments, 5 Vand.J.Trans.L. 313 (1972); and Oliver, The Andean Foreign Investment Code, 66 Am.J.Int.L. 763 (1972).

gram of socialist change. Cordial relations were struck up with Cuba and the Soviet Union. Chile became a refuge for expatriate or persecuted leftists from a large number of Latin American countries.

The concern of the United States government appeared to be that the Chilean example of the electoral path towards socialism would influence other Latin American countries, a possibility viewed as threatening to this country's national security. The revelations in 1974 of the involvement of the Central Intelligence Agency with anti-Allende political forces within Chile, primarily through financing of various Chilean activities, suggest that the relatively mild public statements made by our government officials during this period did not express their real sentiment. The sharp cutback in credit to Chile by United States governmental institutions, and by international agencies in which the United States and other creditor countries had important voices, had of course one basis in the poor credit rating of a country in a politically perilous situation and in increasing economic difficulties. But that cutback also suggests a relatively concerted effort among various government agencies to burden the Allende government and diminish chances for its survival.[62]

During this period, multilateral negotiations continued between Chile and European creditor nations, and bilateral negotiations took place between representatives of the Chilean and United States governments. These bilateral talks treated renegotiation of maturities on the extensive Chilean debt to the United States. But the compensation issue for copper became a continuing theme in these talks, after negotiations between the companies themselves and the Chilean government had terminated. Settlement of that issue was generally understood to be a necessary, if not necessarily sufficient, condition to resolution of the questions of public debt.

Thus the major effort to enforce the claims of the companies, and the major sanctions to bring about compliance with the asserted requirements of international law, were at a governmental level—in this country, among European creditor governments with which Chile was also seeking debt rescheduling, and among international lending agencies. In the private sector, there was an expected sharp reduction in short-term and medium-term credits from American banks to Chilean borrowers. Moreover, this country generally became closed as a source of spare parts and replacements necessary to keep the mines functioning. Finally, Kennecott effectively pursued remedies in European countries to which Chile sought to sell its copper, arguing to courts in those countries that the proceeds of such sales should be given to it as lawful owner of the copper. These matters, raising complicated issues of the public policy of the countries involved and of the act of state doctrine, are considered at p. 677, infra.

62. Compare Sigmund, The "Invisible Blockade" and the Overthrow of Allende, 52 Foreign Affairs 322 (1974), with Farnsworth, More than Admitted, 16 Foreign Policy 127 (1974).

Why the Chilean government did not come to a negotiated settlement with the copper companies during Allende's administration is not entirely clear. The final settlements, both in the amount and in the schedule for their payment, would not have posed impossible financial burdens had they been agreed to by Allende. A settlement might have proved politically advisable to permit Chile to receive credit, achieve debt rescheduling, obtain spare parts, and alleviate other matters which would have contributed to the government's internal stability. But among other reasons, the chaotic political situation leading to pressures upon Allende from the radical left of his coalition as well as from the center and right parties appeared to frustrate all attempts at compromise. Here as elsewhere the problems of ideology and internal political stability were never resolved to the point where pursuit of more promising economic policies became politically possible.

The Settlement

In September 1973, the Chilean government was overthrown by a military coup which brought about the death of President Allende. The successor government, a military junta, repressed all activities of the political left and imposed a rigid authoritarian control over the nation's political life. The Junta sought to improve its relationships with the nations of the industrialized West and, in particular, with the United States. A special committee was formed to negotiate with respect to the claims of the copper companies.

In 1974, Kennecott came to a settlement with the military government. It amounted to $68 million, of which $6.5 million was in cash and the remainder payable over a 10-year period according to notes bearing 10% interest. This sum applied, of course, to the 49% interest of Braden in El Teniente Mining Company, and thus was in addition to the $80 million paid at the time of the sale of the 51% interest. (In fact, Kennecott received in 1972 $64.9 million, plus $2 million of accrued interest, to settle its insurance claim against OPIC. That amount represented the then market value of the OPIC-guaranteed notes relating to the sale to Chile of 51% of Braden's interests.)

The settlement followed intensive negotiations and took into account a large variety of political factors, economic claims and counterclaims. It was, for example, net of tax obligations asserted by the Chilean government. In short, the settlement reflected trade-offs among many items. There was no effort to state determinative legal principles. Neither party sought to find vindication through the terms of the settlement of the principles it had asserted about compensation, excess profits, or other issues. Indeed, it remained unclear to what degree the Junta shared or rejected the position of the Allende government about compensation principles.

The Decree-Law authorizing the settlement provided that the government Junta considered it to be in the "national interest", because the compensation was established "in agreement with the basic principles set forth in the Political Constitution of the State and with due consideration at the same time of the financial possibilities of the country." The agreements of the parties included one by Kennecott to terminate the litigation which it had commenced in European countries.

The formal record provides only partial insight into the adequacy of the settlement from Kennecott's perspective. It was well below the claims earlier made by Kennecott, which (as with Chile's counterclaims) had never been subjected to appraisal by a third-party decision-maker. Moreover, as with respect to other American companies whose foreign assets were expropriated, it is necessary to consider the effect of provisions of the federal income tax permitting deductions for losses from expropriations. The financial statements of Kennecott contained in its Annual Reports for 1973 and 1974 indicate some of these tax consequences. The 1973 Report states that Kennecott wrote off the company's equity interest in El Teniente at its historical cost of $50,363,988. However, that extraordinary charge (made in the 1972 Consolidated Income Statement) amounted only to $26,189,274, after taking account of the related income tax "effect" (i. e. deduction) of $24,174,714. The 1974 Annual Report indicates the effect upon that year's Consolidated Income Statement of the 1974 settlement with Chile. The net amount of that settlement (after deduction of Chilean taxes) of $68 million led to a United States tax liability of $25,694,352, leaving a net recovery of $42,305,648 that was reported in 1974 as an extraordinary credit.

QUESTIONS

(1) If you were arguing for Kennecott before an international tribunal which was to decide "under general principles of international law," to which aspects of this dispute would you give priority to sustain your contention that Chile's action violated international law?

(2) If you were arguing for Chile before that tribunal, on what grounds could you best justify the retroactive application of the standard for excess profits?

(3) In this dispute, what comfort could either party derive from the 1962–1974 U. N. Resolutions described at pp. 464–469, infra?

(4) From Chile's perspective, what were the "costs" to be anticipated from an expropriation without—in effect—compensation, whatever the strength of the legal-political arguments about excess profits? From the broader perspective of less developed countries of the non-socialist world, were any costs involved?

(5) Does the Note on conceptions of property rights at p. 409, supra, offer any general theoretical framework within which Chile's position in this dispute can be better understood?

(6) In view of the experiences of foreign investors during the last few decades—particularly but not exclusively in natural resources and public utilities, and particularly in sectors of the local economy of key significance to national development—what advice would you give to an American investor now considering entrance into an extractive industry in a less de-

veloped country seeking foreign capital and technology to realize its natural wealth? What economic strategies is the investor likely to pursue? What legal or political security can it achieve through the way that it structures the enterprise and its relationship with the foreign government?

COMMENT

In a study drawing upon the conceptual framework developed by Lasswell and McDougal, p. 349, supra, Professor Weston sought to develop a systematic framework for inquiry into problems in expropriations.[63] Weston makes some observations particularly relevant to the issues examined in this chapter.

(1) The author notes that the deprivor's (expropriating state's) objectives vary a great deal and are frequently confused. He draws a distinction between "welfare values" which deprivors seek to maximize (national wealth, well-being, and enlightenment), and so-called "deference values" (national power, respect, rectitude and so on). He argues that many post-war nationalizations involved dominantly welfare values, although observers frequently tended to stress the political, nationalistic or ideological bases for the deprivor's conduct. Nonetheless, "deference values" remain significant. "Control" over one's own natural resources, for example, is viewed as a matter of prestige as much as a matter of more fruitful exploitation of national wealth. Status and recognition, domestically and abroad, may follow upon successful nationalizations. Indeed, maximization of these "deference values" will affect not only the expropriated aliens but relations between the deprivor-country and the world at large.

(2) Weston refers to the "deference value" of rectitude, the viewing of the expropriation in an ethical light. He notes the polar perspectives upon this issue of the deprivor and deprivee. The deprivor-country will stress the elimination of exploitation, the proper resumption of control over national resources, and the moral victory (at least with respect to socialist countries) of conquering remnants of imperialism and colonialism. On the other hand, the deprivees (alien owners) will tend to see the expropriation as an attack upon liberty, freedom and democracy, associating private property with traditional liberal values. Thus the controversy takes on dimensions not simply of a quarrel over distribution of wealth, but over moral principle as well.

(3) Weston describes the various strategies of the deprivees, including both the alien companies and their governments. He notes that their goals range from prevention and deterrence, to (after deprivation) restoration or rehabilitation. He notes the range of strategies available to achieve any of these goals.

63. Weston, "International Law and the Deprivation of Foreign Wealth: A Framework for Future Inquiry," in Falk and Black (eds.), The Future of the International Legal Order 36 (Vol. II, Wealth and Resources, 1970).

QUESTIONS

(1) Within Weston's terminology, what wealth or deference values appeared to count most heavily with the deprivors in the Mexican and Chilean expropriations?

(2) How would you state systematically the kinds of strategies employed by deprivee companies and countries to realize the goals that Weston describes, if you were to draw upon the collective learning from the Mexican, Eastern European, Brazilian and Chilean expropriations?

---

3. EFFORTS TO DEVELOP A NEW CONSENSUS

NOTE ON PROVISIONS OF NATIONAL LAW AND OF TREATIES AS EVIDENCE OF STATE PRACTICE

The government official drafting a diplomatic note or negotiating a treaty, delegates to international organizations voting on resolutions or draft conventions, scholars and—more rarely today—members of international tribunals will of course look to the provisions of national law and of existing treaties to aid their efforts to state relevant and acceptable principles for compensation. These materials are undeniably pertinent to their task, however difficult it may be to accommodate such a comparative-law inquiry into domestic constitutional principles within the formal terms of Article 38(1) of the Statute of the I.C.J.* (Most likely the results of such an inquiry could be brought within clause (c) of Article 38, as "general principles of law recognized by civilized nations.")

National Laws

The text at p. 41, supra, describes the extent to which alien-owned property in the United States benefits from the protection of the Fifth Amendment against uncompensated takings. The Amendment's requirement of "just" compensation is a broad and generalized one, leaving much room for argument between property owner and government over what is "just" in a particular case. The same can be said of provisions similar to the Fifth Amendment that are found not only in the constitutions or practices of the large majority of developed, non-Communist countries, but also (as of 1967) in at least 50 capital-importing states. See the Report on The Compensation Requirement in the Taking of Alien Property (the "Report").[64] Over 15 Latin American countries appear on this list (Appendix V to the Report), including Brazil and Mexico. Article 150 of the Brazilian Constitution of 1967—the same in relevant part as the constitutional

64. Report by The Committee on International Law of the Association of the Bar of the City of New York, The Compensation Requirement in the Taking of Alien Property, 22 Rec. of N.Y.C. Bar Ass'n 195 (1967).

provisions in effect in 1962 at the time of the utility expropriation, p. 440, supra—provides:

> The Constitution assures Brazilians and aliens residing in the country of the inviolability of their rights concerning life, liberty, security, and property, in the following terms: . . . § 22. The guaranty of the right of property, except in the case of expropriation for necessity or public utility or in the social interest, with previous and just compensation in money [subject to an exception for rural property for which payment in public bonds is provided].

In addition, 17 less developed countries have enacted laws encouraging foreign investment which specifically provide for compensation upon expropriation of approved investments (Appendix IV of the Report). Some spell out in detail the method of computing the value of the property taken (e. g., The Investment Code of Algeria of 1966), and a number provide for arbitration in the event of failure to agree upon the appropriate amount (e. g., The Indonesian Foreign Capital Investment Law of 1967). Compare the provisions of the Policy on Private Foreign Investment of the Sri Lanka Government * under the heading "Security of Investment."

Treaty Provisions

The peace treaties after World War I (including provisions such as those at issue in the Chorzow Factory Case, p. 414, supra), and various agreements after World War II for the application of enemy property to the settlement of claims treated issues of compensation in a special setting. Recent decades have witnessed other efforts to state principles for compensation in multilateral conventions. Apart from regional agreements in the developed world, e. g., a Protocol to the European Convention on Human Rights, p. 384, supra, these efforts have not been successful.

The United States has tried several times to gain acceptance in multilateral treaties of the position that it espouses. The experience of this campaign was set forth in the following remarks in 1957 of a State Department official.[65]

> The experience of the Department of State over many years has convinced us that the bilateral treaty of friendship, commerce, and navigation offers the most practical means of affording treaty protection to American investors abroad. Multilateral negotiations have been found to produce unsatisfactory results, and the reasons are not difficult to perceive. There are great variances among nations as to the degree to which they are prepared to bind themselves legally to accord fair treatment, even among those which in fact accord fair treatment in practice. Some countries with federal constitutions, including Australia, Canada, and the United States, have special problems which limit the commitments they can undertake. Efforts at general uni-

65. Statement of Thorsten Kalijarvi, Deputy Assistant Secretary of State for Economic Affairs, appearing in Protection of Private Investments Overseas, Hearings before the Ad Hoc Subcommittee of the House Committee on Foreign Affairs, 85th Cong., 1st Sess., on H.J.Res. 160 (1957), p. 14.

form arrangements tend to break down over the differences among individual countries and their varying legal systems and economies. Consequently, bilateral negotiations, during which adjustments can be made to take care of individual differences, may be expected to produce the best results as far as United States interests are concerned.

We have come to these conclusions after three major multilateral attempts to provide a uniform system of protection for international investment. Each resulted in failure. In 1929, an international conference met at Geneva under League of Nations auspices, to consider a carefully prepared draft convention on the treatment of foreigners and foreign enterprises. Because of the reservations each country felt obliged to attach, the effectiveness of the proposed convention was so reduced that the project was abandoned. A second attempt was the section on economic development in the abortive ITO Charter, which, in order to accommodate the varying views of participating countries, equivocated on certain fundamental principles, including the standard of compensation in case of the expropriation of property.

Differences between legal systems, between national policies, and differences as to economic interests created in each case insuperable obstacles to the establishment of uniform principles applicable to each of the many countries concerned. Experience over the past few years in the U. N. with resolutions designed to encourage private investment, which have stimulated strong reactions against any forthright declaration of principle further indicate the futility of multilateral efforts under present conditions.

Most of the treaties of Friendship, Commerce and Navigation to which the United States is a party contain provisions which protect property owners against uncompensated expropriation. Six of these treaties are with less developed countries. Note the characteristic provisions in the Convention of Establishment with France * that appear in Articles IV and X(3) and in paragraphs 5, 6 and 15 of the Protocol.[66]

The experience of other developed countries provides a useful supplement to that of the United States. The Report indicates that over 50 capital importing states have signed bilateral treaties since 1945 which require compensation in the case of expropriation (Appendix III). The provisions are similar to those in the Franco-American Convention of Establishment. The Report also notes a large number of countries with which the Eastern European states have entered into agreements for compensation for *past* takings.

NOTE ON RESOLUTIONS OF THE GENERAL ASSEMBLY OF THE UNITED NATIONS

The political disputes stemming from the post-war expropriations were inevitably drawn into the debates within the United Nations.

66. See generally Wilson, United States Commercial Treaties and International Law (1960).

Those debates, and the resolutions in which they culminated during the period 1952–1974, offer an extraordinary account of the different perceptions about the issue of compensation, and of the changes in those perceptions during a period of only two decades. Of course those changes bear a close relationship to the expanding membership of the U. N. during that period.

When reading the resolutions, bear in mind their uncertain status or relevance with respect to traditional conceptions of international law. It is difficult to accommodate General Assembly resolutions within the clauses of Article 38 of the Statute of the ICJ, an observation which suggests the dated character of those clauses. But here as elsewhere, a less formal or positive and more sociological view of international law would be attentive to the effect of resolutions upon the behavior and attitudes of states. To the extent that these resolutions influence the expectations and conduct of parties about issues such as compensation, they partake of the character of "law" within a broad conception of custom. They surely form an important part of the processes of norm formation. Although not formally binding upon states voting for or against them, the resolutions may then exercise a significant influence upon the evolution of international-law norms.

On December 21, 1952, the General Assembly adopted Resolution No. 626 (VII), entitled "Right to Exploit Freely Natural Wealth and Resources."

> *The General Assembly,*
>
> *Bearing in mind* the need for encouraging the underdeveloped countries in the proper use and exploitation of their natural wealth and resources,
>
> *Considering* that the economic development of the underdeveloped countries is one of the fundamental requisites for the strengthening of universal peace,
>
> *Remembering* that the right of peoples freely to use and exploit their natural wealth and resources is inherent in their sovereignty and is in accordance with the Purposes and Principles of the Charter of the United Nations,
>
> 1. *Recommends* all Member States, in the exercise of their right freely to use and exploit their natural wealth and resources wherever deemed desirable by them for their own progress and economic development, to have due regard, consistently with their sovereignty, to the need for maintaining the flow of capital in conditions of security, mutual confidence and economic co-operation among nations;
>
> 2. *Further recommends* all Member States to refrain from acts, direct or indirect, designed to impede the exercise of the sovereignty of any State over its natural resources.

The United States voted against the resolution because of its failure to indicate that states taking private property should recognize rights of private investors under international law.

On December 14, 1962, at its Seventeenth Session, the General Assembly adopted Resolution No. 1803 (XVII) on Permanent Sovereignty over Natural Resources, passed in the form of a declaration. The vote was 87 in favor to 2 opposed, with 12 abstentions (principally the Soviet Union and Eastern European countries). The United States voted with the majority. Some paragraphs from the preamble and the Resolution appear below.

The General Assembly,

Recalling its resolutions 523 (VI) of 12 January 1952 and 626 (VII) of 21 December 1952, . . .

Considering that it is desirable to promote international co-operation for the economic development of developing countries, and that economic and financial agreements between the developed and the developing countries must be based on the principles of equality and of the right of peoples and nations to self determination,

Considering that the provision of economic and technical assistance, loans and increased foreign investment must not be subject to conditions which conflict with the interests of the recipient State,

Considering the benefits to be derived from exchanges of technical and scientific information likely to promote the development and use of such resources and wealth, and the important part which the United Nations and other international organizations are called upon to play in that connexion,

Attaching particular importance to the question of promoting the economic development of developing countries and securing their economic independence,

Noting that the creation and strengthening of the inalienable sovereignty of States over their natural wealth and resources reinforces their economic independence, . . .

Declares that:

1. The right of peoples and nations to permanent sovereignty over their natural wealth and resources must be exercised in the interest of their national development and of the well-being of the people of the State concerned.

2. The exploration, development and disposition of such resources, as well as the import of the foreign capital required for these purposes, should be in conformity with the rules and conditions which the peoples and nations freely consider to be necessary or desirable with regard to the authorization, restriction or prohibition of such activities.

3. In cases where authorization is granted, the capital imported and the earnings on that capital shall be governed by the terms thereof, by the national legislation in force, and by international law. The profits derived must be shared in the proportions freely agreed upon, in each case, between the investors and the recipient State, due care being taken to ensure that there is no impairment, for any reason, of that State's sovereignty over its natural wealth and resources.

4. Nationalization, expropriation or requisitioning shall be based on grounds or reasons of public utility, security or the national interest which are recognized as overriding purely individual or private interests, both domestic and foreign. In such cases the owner shall be paid appropriate compensation, in accordance with the rules in force in the State taking such measures in the exercise of its sovereignty and in accordance with international law. In any case where the question of compensation gives rise to a controversy, the national jurisdiction of the State taking such measures shall be exhausted. However, upon agreement by sovereign States and other parties concerned, settlement of the dispute should be made through arbitration or international adjudication. . . .

8. Foreign investment agreements freely entered into by or between sovereign States shall be observed in good faith; States and international organizations shall strictly and conscientiously respect the sovereignty of peoples and nations over their natural wealth and resources in accordance with the Charter and the principles set forth in the present resolution. . . .

On November 25, 1966, at its Twenty-first Session, the General Assembly adopted Resolution No. 2158 (XXI), also entitled Permanent Sovereignty over Natural Resources. 104 countries voted in favor; the United States was among the six countries which abstained. Some paragraphs from the Preamble and the Resolution appear below.

The General Assembly

Taking into account the fact that foreign capital, whether public or private, forthcoming at the request of the developing countries, can play an important role inasmuch as it supplements the efforts undertaken by them in the exploitation and development of their natural resources, provided that there is government supervision over the activity of foreign capital to ensure that it is used in the interests of national development, . . .

5. *Recognizes* the right of all countries, and in particular of the developing countries, to secure and increase their share in the administration of enterprises which are fully or partly operated by foreign capital and to have a greater share in the advantages and profits derived therefrom on an equitable basis, with due regard to development needs and objectives of the peoples concerned and to mutually acceptable contractual practices, and calls upon the countries from which such capital originates to refrain from any action which would hinder exercise of that right;

6. *Considers* that, when natural resources of the developing countries are exploited by foreign investors, the latter should undertake proper and accelerated training of national personnel at all levels and in all fields connected with such exploitation; . . .

The Resolution further declares that the United Nations should undertake a "maximum concerted effort" to enable countries to exercise their "inalienable right" of permanent sovereignty over natural resources. For this purpose, it recommends that various U. N. agencies keep these problems under review, and requests the Secretary General to coordinate activities in this field. Compare Paragraph 6 of the Resolution with Section 6(1)(a) of the Investment Incentive Code of the Republic of Liberia.*

In a statement explaining the abstention, the United States spokesman said:[67]

> The United States abstained . . . although [the resolution] contains much with which we agree. We favor the resolution's recalling and reaffirming resolution 1803 (XVII) . . . . At the same time, there are elements of the resolution with which the United States does not wholly agree. National participation in the administration of foreign enterprises is desirable in principle and is generally desirable in practice. However, it would be a mistake to state that there is a right to secure and increase a share in the administration of an enterprise regardless of the practical considerations, the contractual obligations and the equities of the case. Similarly, it is impossible for us to agree that under all circumstances there is a right of countries to secure and increase their share in the advantages and profits derived from the exploitation of their natural resources when it is fully or partly carried out by foreign capital. . . . [Paragraph 5] does not state with sufficient clarity the fact that no country can escape the obligations arising out of international law and economic cooperation and out of contractual arrangements which have been mutually accepted. . . . In general . . . I am afraid this resolution may discourage the flow of international capital, public and private, to developing countries. . . . May I add just this. This resolution, which is primarily concerned with the economics of permanent sovereignty over natural resources, does not change applicable international law or contracts one iota. For our part, we regret that it did not prove possible to attain a full measure of agreement on the resolution.

On December 17, 1973, the General Assembly adopted Resolution No. 3171 (XXVIII), on Permanent Sovereignty over Natural Resources.[68] The Resolution carried by a vote of 108 to 1, with 16 abstentions (including ten Western European countries and the United States). It reaffirmed the provisions about "inalienable rights" of states in the 1962 and 1966 Resolutions, supported developing countries "in their struggle to regain effective control over their natural resources," and provided in Paragraph 3:

> that the application of the principle of nationalization carried out by States, as an expression of their sovereignty in order to safeguard their natural resources, implies that each State is entitled to determine the amount of possible compensation, and the mode of payment, and that any disputes which might arise should be

67. Statement by Ambassador James Roosevelt, Alternate United States Representative to the 21st Session of the General Assembly, appearing in Press Release No. 4987 of the United States Delegation, November 25, 1966.

68. The Resolution is set forth in 13 Int.Leg.Mat. 238 (1974).

settled in accordance with the national legislation of each State carrying out such measure . . . .

On May 1, 1974, the General Assembly adopted without vote Resolution 3201 (S–VI), Declaration on the Establishment of a New International Economic Order.[69] The Declaration (accompanied by a Programme) stressed the "widening gap" between developed and developing countries; 70% of the world's population accounted for 30% of world income. Interdependence of the two groups of countries was an acknowledged fact. Cooperation was thus essential to assure "political, economic and social well-being" of all groups. Paragraph 4(e) stressed the right to nationalize natural resources, "this right being an expression of the full permanent sovereignty of the State." No mention was made of compensation. By way of contrast, Paragraph 4(f) asserted the right of all states and peoples under colonial domination "to restitution and full compensation for the exploitation and depletion" of their natural resources. Paragraph 7 concludes the Declaration by observing that it shall constitute "one of the most important bases of economic relations" among nations.[70]

Reservations were entered by several countries to these Resolutions. This country's representative at the U.N., Ambassador Scali, challenged the effort of some countries to present the Declaration and Programme as representing a "consensus".[71] The United States refrained from objecting since doing so "would only have served to exacerbate the divisions that we have worked to the best of our ability to bridge . . . ." Ambassador Scali singled out some provisions "to which the United States Government cannot lend its support." Foremost among them were the provisions about permanent sovereignty over natural resources. It was to be regretted that the "widespread agreement" reflected in the 1962 Resolution No. 1803 no longer obtained. This Declaration's formulation was not "acceptable" because of its failure to require compensation. "The governing international law cannot be and is not prejudiced by the passage of this resolution."

On December 12, 1974, the General Assembly adopted Resolution No. 3281 (XXIX), Charter of Economic Rights and Duties of States.[72] The vote was 120 to 6, the dissenters including five Western European countries and (with respect to some parts of the Charter, including those reproduced below) the United States, with ten abstentions

69. The Resolution is set forth in 13 Int.Leg.Mat. 715 (1974).

70. Also on May 1, 1974, the General Assembly adopted without vote Resolution 3202 (S–VI), Programme of Action on the Establishment of a New International Economic Order, implementing the Declaration. It is set forth in 13 Int.Leg.Mat. 720 (1974).

71. The remarks of Ambassador Scali are reproduced at 13 Int.Leg.Mat. 744 (1974).

72. The Resolution is set forth in 14 Int.Leg.Mat. 251 (1975).

(from Western Europe, Canada, Israel and Japan). Article 2 provides:

> 1. Every State has and shall freely exercise full permanent sovereignty, including possession, use and disposal, over all its wealth, natural resources and economic activities.
>
> 2. Each State has the right:
>
> (*a*) To regulate and exercise authority over foreign investment within its national jurisdiction in accordance with its laws and regulations and in conformity with its national objectives and priorities. No State shall be compelled to grant preferential treatment to foreign investment;
>
> (*b*) To regulate and supervise the activities of transnational corporations within its national jurisdiction and take measures to ensure that such activities comply with its laws, rules and regulations and conform with its economic and social policies. Transnational corporations shall not intervene in the internal affairs of a host State. Every State should, with full regard for its sovereign rights, co-operate with other States in the exercise of the right set forth in this subparagraph;
>
> (*c*) To nationalize, expropriate or transfer ownership of foreign property in which case appropriate compensation should be paid by the State adopting such measures, taking into account its relevant laws and regulations and all circumstances that the State considers pertinent. In any case where the question of compensation gives rise to a controversy, it shall be settled under the domestic law of the nationalizing State and by its tribunals, unless it is freely and mutually agreed by all States concerned that other peaceful means be sought on the basis of the sovereign equality of States and in accordance with the principle of free choice of means.

The U. S. Representative to the General Assembly, Senator Percy, made a statement about the Charter: [73]

> It is with deep regret that my delegation could not support the proposed Charter of Economic Rights and Duties of States.
>
> . . . [T]o command general support—and to be implemented—the proposed rights and duties must be defined equitably and take into account the concerns of industrialized as well as of developing countries.
>
> In extensive negotiations in Mexico City, Geneva, and here in New York, the United States worked hard and sincerely with other countries in trying to formulate a charter that would achieve such a balance. . . . Indeed, agreement was reached on many important articles, and our support for those was shown in the vote we have just taken.
>
> On others, however, agreement has not been reached. Our views on these provisions are apparent in the amendments proposed by the United States and certain other countries, but these regrettably have been rejected by the

73. The excerpts below are taken from the full text appearing in Dept. of State Bull., Feb. 3, 1975, p. 146.

majority here. Many of the unagreed provisions, in the view of my government, are fundamental and are unacceptable in their present form. To cite a few: the treatment of foreign investment in terms which do not fully take into account respect for agreements and international obligations, and the endorsement of concepts of producer cartels and indexation of prices. As a result, Mr. Chairman, we have before us a draft charter which is unbalanced and which fails to achieve the purpose of encouraging harmonious economic relations and needed development. Moreover, the provisions of the charter would discourage rather than encourage the capital flow which is vital for development.

For all these reasons, Mr. Chairman, my delegation felt compelled to vote against the charter as a whole. We have not closed our minds, however, to the possibility of further reconsideration at some future date should others come to the conclusion that an agreed charter would still be far preferable to one that is meaningless without the agreement of countries whose numbers may be small but whose significance in international economic relations and development can hardly be ignored. We stand ready to resume negotiations on a charter which could command the support of all countries.

COMMENT

Compare Article 17 of the Universal Declaration of Human Rights of 1948, p. 387, supra: "1. Everyone has the right to own property alone as well as in association with others. 2. No one shall be arbitrarily deprived of his property."

Note that several provisions of the 1962 Resolution, and to a lesser extent of the later resolutions, appear to refer to transactions, such as contractual relationships, that may develop *in the future*. Consider the different problems in agreeing upon rules governing future conduct among states of such divergent interests, and agreeing upon rules governing the treatment of past or existing investments or contractual relationships. Recall in this connection the comments of Roy, pp. 333–334, supra.

QUESTIONS

(1) The 1962 Resolution expresses the conflicting interests relating to foreign investment in natural resources which statesmen, codifiers and tribunals have sought to resolve. Based on the Resolution, how would you identify those interests? Which are common to private investors and differently situated groups of nations, so as to offer some hope of providing the foundation for a generally acceptable principle of compensation?

(2) Does the 1962 Resolution provide textual support for the United States' position? Does it help to know (a) that a Soviet amendment to have the Resolution refer to "the inalienable right" to "unobstructed . . expropriation" was defeated, or (b) that the United States representative, after withdrawing an amendment that would have made explicit the "prompt, adequate and effective" principle, stated without encountering objection that Article 4 in its present form reaffirmed that principle? See Schwebel, The Story of the U. N.'s Declaration on Permanent Sovereignty over Natural Resources, 49 A.B.A.J. 463 (1963).

(3) In Schachter, The Relation of Law, Politics, and Action in the United Nations, 109 Académie de Droit International, Receuil des Cours 165, 181–184 (1963), the author refers to the 1952 and 1962 Resolutions as an effort by the U.N. to assume a "legislative" function. He views those resolutions as informed less by the "ideological language of socialism or capitalism" than by relatively objective "empirical data" bearing on the relationship between foreign investment and objectives of economic development and political independence. The resolutions make an effort to identify a "common normative element" and to achieve broad consensus over basic concepts of the Charter and international law. "Collective judgments are in fact being made as to what is legal and permissible, and new, more specific legal norms are being elaborated to meet felt necessities. Whatever may be its shortcomings, the process of examination and evaluation constitutes a centralized institutional means on the international level for performing functions that in the national sphere are normally the province of judicial and legislative institutions . . . ."

(*a*) Do you agree with the view suggested in Schachter's article that such resolutions of the General Assembly, at least those adopted by a very substantial majority, constitute the most appropriate evidence for determining a norm of international law in the absence of a governing treaty?

(*b*) How valid do you think the analogy that Schachter draws to national legislation?

(*c*) From your reading of these excerpts from resolutions (which went on to address much broader issues of economic relationships among states), would you agree with Schachter's (early) evaluation that the resolutions manage to "reduce the distinctive 'ideological' content" of these issues and to achieve consensus based upon common recognition of relatively objective factors and aims?

(4) Consider the description of property interests within the Anglo-American tradition at pp. 409–411, supra. With respect to the issue of compensation, and based upon these resolutions, what influence would you attribute either to "natural rights" or to "utilitarian" thought in the formulation of principles? Consider not only the relevance of each approach or methodology, but the types of assertions made or conclusions reached within each of them.

(5) Is it sensible to attempt to elaborate general rules governing compensation for all forms of expropriations, rather than to take into account a number of variables which could affect the decision whether compensation for a particular taking was consistent with international law? For example, if the question of compensation arose before an executive official or an international tribunal today, which if any of the following factors should they consider relevant?

(*a*) The foreign exchange reserves and needs of the expropriating country—as relevant to whether compensation should be in local currency or foreign exchange;

(*b*) If nationals of the foreign country owned at least 50% in value of the total property taken, the fact that the alien received the same compensation—as relevant to the amount of compensation;

(*c*) Whether the expropriations were broad in character or affected only a particular industry or small sector of the economy, and what the financial position of the taking country is—as relevant to the question of deferred compensation;

(*d*) The economic or social reasons for the action of the expropriating country, such as land reform programs or government plans to control all public utilities—as relevant to the amount and time of compensation; and

(*e*) Whether attractive investment opportunities are open to a foreigner in the expropriating country—as relevant to a requirement that the alien reinvest a high percentage of the compensation or that compensation be made in inconvertible local currency.

(6) Given the possible minimum consensus that has developed—that *some* compensation is owing the foreign investor—what would you view as fruitful paths to pursue in defining the measure? Consider the following possibilities (some of which may not be meaningful under certain circumstances): (*1*) the fair market value of the property; (*2*) the present capitalized value of projected future earnings; (*3*) the present net worth of the investment, as shown on a balance sheet; (*4*) the dollar investment by the American firm in the foreign enterprise, not including reinvested local earnings; (*5*) the cost to the foreign government of constructing facilities similar to those which it has expropriated, taking into account the age and wear of the expropriated facilities; and (*6*) the "value" to the foreign government of the enterprise.

---

4. EFFORTS TO DEVELOP NEW TECHNIQUES TO ENFORCE STANDARDS OR SETTLE DISPUTES

NOTE ON THE UNITED STATES INVESTMENT GUARANTY PROGRAM

From the days of Marshall Plan aid to Europe to the current, diminished programs of aid to the less developed countries, private investment abroad has been expected to play a role complementing governmental policies and actions. It was hoped that private funding would relieve strains on the national treasury, that private initiative would identify opportunities for development which centralized planning for aid would overlook, and that know-how and personal skills available within American enterprises could be readily transferred abroad. In general, it was believed that strong private, "free enterprise" sectors in foreign countries would make them more sympathetic towards the United States and less inclined towards Communism. That is, private investment as well as public aid would serve political together with economic-developmental purposes—both in terms of securing relationships between this and foreign countries, and in terms of inducing or fortifying tendencies towards some form of private-enterprise system.

To spur such investment the Government instituted various forms of aid to the American investor going abroad, principally that of guaranteeing him against types of risks which businesses may not be prepared to shoulder by themselves. Of the three "specific risks" involved in this guaranty program, we shall not concern ourselves with currency devaluation or with war and insurrection. We are interested here only in protection against the risk of expropriation.

The successive forms of the legislative authorization for the investment guaranty program suggest the evolving sense of Congress about economic development and the means by which it should be pursued. The legislation as of 1975 calls for the encouragement and support of "private investments in less developed friendly countries and areas which are sensitive and responsive to the special needs and requirements of their economies and which contribute to the social and economic development of their people".[74] Consideration shall be given to their "willingness and ability to maintain conditions which enable private enterprise to make its full contribution to the development process." (§ 231(g)) Monopolistic practices are to be discouraged. At the same time, balance-of-payments objectives of the United States are to be furthered (§ 231(i)) and the operations are to be conducted with due regard to principles of risk management (§ 231(d)).

The 1974 amendments to the program, reflecting new concerns, mandate that preference be given to projects in those friendly less developed countries which have annual per capita incomes of less than $450 in 1973 U. S. dollars (§ 231(*l*)). They also insist upon avoidance of projects that would reduce employment in the United States by setting up "runaway plants" abroad. (§ 231(m)). Thus the task of administering this program involves the accommodation of a number of very different objectives.

Until the Foreign Assistance Act of 1969 was implemented in 1971, administration of the investment guaranty program was entrusted to successive branches of the executive. During the period of continuing expansion of these programs in the 1960's, that branch was the Agency for International Development (AID), an agency within the Department of State which also handled grants, low-cost loans and other assistance programs. The 1969 statute transferred the guaranty program (as well as certain lending functions) to the Overseas Private Investment Corporation (OPIC). That Corporation is in effect a semi-independent arm of the Government. The United States owns all of its capital stock (§ 232). Its chief executive officers and six of its eleven directors are appointed by the President with the advice and consent of the Senate, and the remaining directors are government officials. One of the non-official directors shall be experienced in small business, one in organized labor, and one in cooperatives (§ 233).

The move to OPIC represented a desire to place some distance between the political branches of the Government and an activity which, it was hoped, could ultimately be handled entirely as a com-

74. All citations in this Note are to sections of the Foreign Assistance Act of 1969, 83 Stat. 809, 22 U.S.C.A. §§ 2191–2200a, as amended by 88 Stat. 763 (1974). This quotation is from § 231(f).

mercial insurance operation, making ends meet through the insurance premiums or fees which it charged. The 1974 amendments contemplate that OPIC, after an interim period of collaboration with private insurers, will be out of the business of managing expropriation risks by December 31, 1979 (§ 234). OPIC has already entered into arrangements with Lloyd's of London and an American insurance group to share some of its risk portfolio.

The statute sets certain limits on the making of guaranties. The recipient must be an "eligible investor," either a United States citizen, or a corporation created under American law and substantially beneficially owned by citizens, or a foreign corporation wholly owned by citizens (§ 238(c)). Guaranties cannot exceed 20 years in duration or cover more than the original investment plus interest or profits thereon (§ 237(e)) and (f)). Total guaranties outstanding under all coverages at any one time may not exceed $7.5 billion (§ 235(a)). The present exposure amounts to $3.3 billion. Claims, to the extent to which the reserves accumulated by OPIC out of fees are not adequate, constitute obligations binding the full faith and credit of the United States (§ 237(c)).

Two definitions of importance appear in § 238(a) of the statute:

> (a) the term "investment" includes any contribution of funds, commodities, services, patents, processes, or techniques, in the form of (1) a loan or loans to an approved project, (2) the purchase of a share of ownership in any such project, (3) participation in royalties, earnings, or profits of any such project, and (4) the furnishing of commodities or services pursuant to a lease or other contract;
>
> (b) the term "expropriation" includes but is not limited to any abrogation, repudiation, or impairment by a foreign government of its own contract with an investor, where such abrogation, repudiation, or impairment is not caused by the investor's own fault or misconduct, and materially adversely affects the continued operation of the project . . . .

Within the authority granted by Congress, OPIC issues contracts of guaranty upon application by an eligible investor. These contracts take the form of "specific terms and conditions," tailor-made for the particular transaction, superimposed upon printed "general terms and conditions" which represent OPIC's general policy. An Incentive Handbook—Investment Insurance (currently in an edition dated July 1971) spells out for interested parties the policies which OPIC is following in approving applications. The contracts indicate the situations in which an investor can recover sums (calculated pursuant to a contractual formula) from OPIC because of action of a foreign government which has adversely affected the investment. The definition of "Expropriatory Action" is critical, for no recovery is possible unless the foreign government's action comes within its terms. OPIC views the statutory definition of "expropriation," supra, as representing the outer limit of its power to insure and does not incorporate that definition into its contract, which rather uses a "result" test. The current form of General Terms and Conditions used by OPIC (234 KGT 12–70) defines "Expropriatory Action" for both equity and debt investments. Article 1.13 states in part: [75]

> 1.13. *Expropriatory Action.* The term "Expropriatory Action" means any action which is taken, authorized, ratified or condoned by the Government of the Project Country, commencing during the Insurance Period, with or without compensation therefor, and which for a period of one year directly results in preventing:
>
> (a) the Investor from receiving payment when due in the currency specified of amounts which the Foreign Enterprise owes the Investor on or in respect of the Securities; or
>
> (b) the Investor from effectively exercising its fundamental rights with respect to the Foreign Enterprise either as shareholder or as creditor, as the case may be, acquired as a result of the Investment; provided, however, that rights acquired solely as a result of any undertaking by or agreement with the Government of the Project Country shall not be considered fundamental rights merely because they are acquired from such undertaking or agreement; or
>
> (c) the Investor from disposing of the Securities or any rights accruing therefrom; or
>
> (d) the Foreign Enterprise from exercising effective control over the use or disposition of a substantial portion of its property or from constructing the Project or operating the same; . . . .
>
> provided, however, that any action which would be considered to be an Expropriatory Action if it were to continue to have any of the effects described above for one year may, at the option solely of OPIC, be considered to be an Expropriatory Action at an earlier time if OPIC shall determine that such action has caused or permitted a dissipation or destruction of assets of the Foreign Enterprise substantially impairing the value of the Foreign Enterprise as a going concern.
>
> Notwithstanding the foregoing, no such action shall be deemed an Expropriatory Action if it occurs or continues in effect, during the aforesaid period, as a result of:
>
> (1) any law, decree, regulation or administrative action of the Government of the Project Country which is not by its express terms for the purpose of nationalization, confiscation or expropriation (including but not limited to intervention, condemnation or other taking), is reasonably related to constitutionally sanctioned governmental objectives, is not arbitrary, is based upon a reasonable classification of entities to which it applies and does not violate generally accepted principles of international law; or
>
> (2) failure on the part of the Investor or the Foreign Enterprise (to the extent within the Investor's control) to take

75. The "Investor" in Article 1.13 is intended to refer to the entity, typically a United States corporation, which is making the guaranteed investment in a subsidiary organized abroad, which is termed the "Foreign Enterprise."

all reasonable measures, including proceeding under then available administrative and judicial procedures in the Project Country, to prevent or contest such action; or

(3) action in accordance with any agreement voluntarily made by the Investor or the Foreign Enterprise; or

(4) provocation or instigation by the Investor or the Foreign Enterprise, provided that provocation or instigation shall not be deemed to include (i) actions taken in compliance with a specific request of the Government of the United States of America or (ii) any reasonable measure taken in good faith by the Investor or the Foreign Enterprise, by way of a judicial, administrative or arbitral proceeding respecting any action in which the Government of the Project Country is involved; or

. . .

(6) bona fide exchange control actions by the Government of the Project Country; or

(7) any action which (i) is lawful under laws of the Project Country of the type described in item (1), and (ii) is taken by the Government of the Project Country in its capacity or through the exercise of its powers, as shareholder, director or manager of the Foreign Enterprise; or

(8) any abrogation, impairment, repudiation or breach by the Government of the Project Country of any obligation to furnish funds or other property of value to the Foreign Enterprise as an equity investor.

The abrogation, impairment, repudiation or breach by the Government of the Project Country of any undertaking, agreement or contract relating to the Project shall be considered an Expropriatory Action only if it constitutes Expropriatory Action in accordance with the criteria set forth in this section.

The legislation authorizes issuance of guaranties only for investments in countries with which the United States has entered into an agreement to institute the guaranty program; indeed, it discourages any assistance (grants, loans, technical aid, etc.) under the Foreign Assistance Act to countries which have failed to sign such agreements. 22 U.S.C.A. § 2370(*l*) *. The legislation has been interpreted to authorize institution of a guaranty program even when no bilateral agreement with a foreign country is in effect but where an agreement is expected, the municipal law of the foreign country adequately protects this Government's interest, and the record of treatment of foreign investors has been good. But the general technique has been to enter into bilateral agreements, traditionally executive agreements rather than treaties, with the country. Such agreements have been signed with over 70 countries, although some agreements cover only one or two of the several types of guarantied risks. They characteristically require that the American investor obtain the approval of the foreign government for its project before OPIC will issue a guaranty, and the OPIC Handbook itself states that the investor must secure such approval.

The bilateral agreements also provide that, if the United States makes payment to an investor under the Contract of Guaranty, the foreign government will recognize the transfer by the investor to the United States of any right, title or interest of the investor in the guaranteed project, and the subrogation of the United States to any claim or cause of action relating to the project, provided that the foreign government had previously approved the project. The Contract of Guaranty requires the investor to transfer such rights to the United States upon receipt of payment.

The trouble spot in many recent bilateral agreements has been the arbitration clause. Three questions are critical to such a clause: (1) under what circumstances arbitration takes place, (2) how the arbitral tribunal is to be constituted, and (3) what substantive law it is to apply. The agreement with Ecuador is typical of many, particularly earlier, agreements.[76] The Government of Ecuador agreed, with respect to projects that it had approved:

> That any claim against the Government of Ecuador to which the Government of the United States of America may be subrogated as a result of any payment under such a guaranty, shall be the subject of direct negotiations between the two Governments. If, within a reasonable period, they are unable to settle the claim by agreement, it shall be referred for final and binding determination to a sole arbitrator selected by mutual agreement. If the Governments are unable, within a period of three months, to agree upon such selection, the arbitrator shall be one who may be designated by the President of the International Court of Justice at the request of either Government.

In effect, this provision deals only with the first two questions and fails to settle issues of substantive law. The agreement with Indonesia of January 7, 1967[77] first defines the occasion for and the constitution of the arbitral tribunal, and then deals explicitly with this last point. Paragraph 6(b) states: "The arbitral tribunal shall base its decision exclusively on the applicable principles and rules of public international law."

Recent arrangements with Latin American countries have attempted more specific resolution of the substantive issue. One such agreement is with Brazil.[78]

> **Article V**
>
> Nothing in this Agreement shall grant to the Guaranteeing Government other rights than those available to the subrogating investor with respect to any petition or claim or right to which the Guaranteeing Government may be subrogated.

76. Agreement effective March 29, 1955, 6 U.S.T. & O.I.A. 843, T.I.A.S. No. 3230, as modified by exchange of notes, 14 U.S.T. & O.I.A. 1251, T.I.A.S. No. 5426.

77. 18 U.S.T. & O.I.A. 1850, T.I.A.S. 6330.

78. 18 U.S.T. & O.I.A. 1807, T.I.A.S. No. 6327.

Article VI

> 2. Any claim against either Government concerning an investment guaranteed in accordance with this Agreement, which may constitute a matter involving public international law, shall, at the request of the Government presenting the claim, be submitted to negotiations. If at the end of six months following the request for negotiations the two Governments have not resolved the claim by mutual agreement, the claim, including the question of whether it constitutes a matter involving public international law, shall be submitted to arbitration in accordance with . . . this Article.
>
> 3. There shall be excluded from the negotiations and the arbitral procedures herein contemplated matters which remain exclusively within the internal jurisdiction of a sovereign state. It is accordingly understood that claims arising out of the expropriation of property of private foreign investors do not present questions of public international law unless and until the judicial process of the Recipient Country has been exhausted, and there exists a denial of justice, as those terms are defined in public international law.
>
> . . .

The agreement is silent about some critical points relating to constitution of the arbitral tribunal, particularly what is to be done if one party refuses to appoint an arbitrator. Article VI(4) provides that the tribunal shall be guided by the principles of public international law recognized in the General Treaty of Inter-American Arbitration signed in Washington on January 5, 1929. That Treaty listed categories of claims subject to arbitration that are identical with those appearing in clauses (a) through (d) of Article 36(2) of the Statute of the I.C.J.* It excepted controversies "within the domestic jurisdiction of any of the Parties to the dispute and . . . not controlled by international law." 49 Stat. 3153, T.S. No. 886, 130 L.N.T.S. 135.

The differences between the two countries' views of the meaning of the agreement were highlighted by a subsequent exchange of notes [79] in which the Brazilian government advised that the Brazilian Congress, in approving the agreement, had attached a reservation defining "denial of justice," as applied to the arbitration provisions, to mean:

> the nonexistence of regular courts or of normal means of access to justice; the refusal to render judgment on the part of competent authority; unjustifiable delay in rendering judicial decision in violation of internal procedural law.

The United States replied that it accepted the reservation, but added:

> This acceptance is without prejudice to the position of the United States Government with respect to the interpretation of the term "denial of justice" as a principle of international law. . . . [T]he United States holds to

79. Notes signed at Rio de Janeiro on September 2, 16 and 17, 1965.

the position that this term has a broader scope than the definition set forth in the reservation made by the Brazilian Congress.

NOTE ON DISPUTES BETWEEN OPIC AND INVESTORS: THE ITT–OPIC ARBITRATION

Investors holding guaranties must submit claims to OPIC in accordance with the provisions of the Contract of Guaranty. Legislation authorizes submission of disputes between the two to binding arbitration, conducted under the rules of the American Arbitration Association. The arbitral award, or any sum which OPIC agrees is owing to the investor, is backed by the full faith and credit of the United States. Depending upon the amount owing the investor and OPIC's reserves, it may be necessary for OPIC to request an appropriation from the Congress.

Probably the most significant of the arbitrations to date has been that between International Telephone and Telegraph Corporation, Sud America (ITTSA), a domestic wholly-owned subsidiary of ITT, and OPIC.[80] ITTSA had taken out contracts of guaranty against expropriation to protect its investment in CT Co., a Chilean corporation that had long operated a major telephone system in Chile. By January 1, 1971, ITTSA owned 70% of the equity in CT, a Chilean government agency owned 24%, and the Chilean public owned the balance of 6%. CT operated under a 1930 concession, as several times amended by later agreements. The 1967 amendment provided for the progressive acquisition of CT stock by the Chilean government. On September 29, 1971, the Chilean government "intervened" CT, taking over its management and assets. ITTSA filed a claim against OPIC in 1971, and OPIC denied the claim in 1973 on grounds of breach of the contracts of guaranty. The claim was then submitted to arbitration.[81]

The contracts of guaranty contained definitions of Expropriatory Action similar in essential respects to that appearing at p. 474, supra. (One contract contained a special provision, not relevant to this arbitration, including within Expropriatory Action specified failures or refusals of the Chilean government to grant reasonable rate increases.) A clause in the contract definition, comparable to that appearing in clause (2), supra, stated that ITTSA "will take all

80. Three other arbitral opinions are reported: Valentine Petrol. & Chem. Corp. v. AID, 9 Int. Leg. Mat. 889, 1144 (1970); International Bank of Wash. v. OPIC, 11 Int. Leg. Mat. 1216 (1972); Anaconda Co. v. OPIC, 14 Int.Leg.Mat. 1210 (1975). See generally, Note, Settlement of Disputes in Overseas Investment Guaranty Contracts, 12 Colum.J.Trans.L. 557 (1973).

81. All quotations below are from the Arbitrators' Opinion on Liability of November 4, 1974, In the Matter of the Arbitration between International Telephone and Telegraph Corporation, Sud America, and Overseas Private Investment Corporation, Case No. 16 10 0038 73, American Arbitration Association, reproduced in 13 Int.Leg. Mat. 1307 (1974). The three arbitrators were retired judges of the highest courts of three states.

reasonable measures to pursue and preserve" administrative and judicial remedies. Primarily on the basis of this clause, OPIC asserted that ITTSA had violated the contract through action (and that of its parent, ITT) in the United States and in Chile.

Some historical background is necessary. In the 1970 Chilean elections, Dr. Salvador Allende was the (Socialist) candidate of the Popular Unity, basically a Socialist-Communist coalition. Allende won a plurality of 36.3% in the September election, barely edging out the conservative candidate in a three-way race. Consistently with the Chilean constitution and Chilean practice when a candidate fails to achieve a majority, the Congress on October 24, 1970, elected the winner of the plurality (Allende) President for the customary six-year term. The Popular Unity had campaigned on a platform of basic structural change involving significant redistribution of wealth to the lower middle and lower classes at the expense of traditional and business elites. The arbitrators described Allende's platform as one of "extensive land law changes, rapid nationalization of basic industries, banks, and communication systems, and other extreme and radical activity." A falling-out soon developed between the Allende government and the United States, intensified by but not traceable primarily to expropriations of American-owned interests, particularly with respect to copper.

Problems soon developed for ITTSA, whose officials learned from Allende in May 1971 that CT would be nationalized. Negotiations between ITTSA officials and Allende led to an expected tension over valuation. A large gap between claim and offer developed. At one stage, the government estimated ITTSA's equity at about $58 million, while ITTSA claimed a book value of about $153 million. These negotiations did not look promising at the time that Chile "intervened" (took over) CT in September 1971. Even before that time, tensions over rates, mandatory wage increases and increases in fringe benefits, and some governmental control over CT's bank accounts had further exacerbated relations between ITTSA and the Allende government.

Most of the facts relevant to OPIC's defense on the contract claims became known through the 1973 hearings of a subcommittee headed by Senator Church. Other facts became public in 1972 and 1973 through investigation by and publication of information in the New York *Times*, and through the columnist Anderson. These facts related to ITTSA's and ITT's action *(1)* in the United States in 1970–71, and *(2)* in Chile in 1970.

(1) McCone, a former CIA Director and then one of the directors of ITT, conferred with the then CIA Director in 1970, the two agreeing that contact should be established between ITT (ITTSA) and the CIA to exchange information. The ITT President advised McCone on September 9, 1970, that ITT would contribute $1,000,000 to support efforts of the United States government to aid a Chilean political coalition that would seek to block the election of Allende as president. This offer was communicated to government officials,

and other similar communications took place at several levels from high officials of ITT to the CIA Director and to Dr. Kissinger. The arbitrators observed that there was no evidence on the record that the United States had followed up on these ITT suggestions. (The covert activities of the CIA in Chile after Allende's election, revealed through the press and through Congressional hearings, that were intended to frustrate his policies and strengthen his opposition, did not figure in the arbitral opinion. Knowledge of such activities became public, after initial denials by government officials, only after the overthrow and death of Allende in the military coup of September 1973 that was succeeded by the rule of a military junta.)

The other conduct of ITT that was noted in the opinion was the sending of a letter from an ITT employee to the Assistant to the President for International Economic Affairs. This letter in October 1971, soon after the intervention of CT, recommended 18 steps, including the end of U. S. economic aid, to convince Allende that he would be "held responsible for action against U. S. private enterprise." It urged that "everything should be done quietly but effectively to see that Allende does not get through the crucial next six months" of "monetary strain."

(*2*) The activities in Chile of ITTSA that were noted in the arbitral opinion involved talks by company officials with some Chilean political opponents of Allende, including mention of some financial support. The arbitrators observed that there was no evidence that "political contributions" were in fact given, or that if they were given, that such contributions would have constituted "a violation of Chilean law."

The arbitrators concluded that there had been no breach of the contracts of guaranty. The amount of the claim was left for settlement or a second arbitral proceeding. Noting that they did not pass on whether "approaches to the U. S. government were or were not appropriate or sound or unsound . . . corporate policy," the arbitrators stressed that there was no explicit contractual term that would bar the guaranteed investor from seeking "U. S. Government action in or towards a host country in support of the Investor's interests," or from engaging "in any political activity designed to protect the Investor's property within the host country." Nor could the legislative history "lead us to imply any contract prohibition or regulation of ITTSA's approaches to the United States government or its very limited 1970 action in Chile." The arbitrators further cast doubt on any causal relationship between the activity of ITT or ITTSA and the termination of negotiations between the Allende government and ITTSA over the amount of compensation. The hearings of the Church subcommittee, and the publication of letters or papers in the New York *Times* and by the columnist Anderson, occurred only after the breakdown of negotiations that followed the intervention. Responding to OPIC's claim that these documents affronted the "national dignity" of Chile and led to discontinuance of negotiations, the arbitrators noted that the contracts "did not require ITTSA to remain supine in view of the threat of expropriation."

The opinion emphasized that it was long regarded "as a legitimate function of the United States . . . to assist its nationals in the protection of their . . . property abroad . . . . The necessity of such executive assistance is particularly acute in dealing with communist countries and underdeveloped countries which may not recognize or like the principles of international law usually applied by the United States in such circumstances."

QUESTIONS

(1) Suppose that the following events had occurred: Before Allende won his plurality, ITTSA financed opposition parties in an overt manner, and warned in press releases in Chile that a victory of the Popular Unity would mean chaos and disaster for Chile. After Allende's election as President, ITT publicly urged the United States government to act harshly towards Chile and to seek the collapse of the Allende government by using its influence to terminate financial aid from domestic and foreign public and private sources. ITTSA continued to support opposition parties and newspapers in Chile. Assume that none of these acts violated Chilean or United States law. The Chilean government takes over ITTSA's interests in CT without compensation, stating that the ITT–ITTSA conduct was viewed as hostile and offensive and could not be permitted to continue. Assume that the contracts of guaranty are the same as described (including the clauses at p. 474, supra). What decision should the arbitrators reach on ITTSA's claim against OPIC?

(2) As a matter of general policy, what position should OPIC take about guaranteeing against expropriation investments in public-utility enterprises in foreign countries?

(3) Does the guaranty program, in addition to spurring private investment, serve other useful purposes by routing a citizen to OPIC for compensation when a foreign goverment refuses to pay? Are different domestic political pressures apt to follow the foreign expropriation of a guarantied and a non-guarantied investment? Does the answer differ when the claim exceeds OPIC's own reserves?

(4) Would you think that a country which has accepted the guaranty program under an agreement similar to that with Indonesia would feel more or less inhibited with respect to taking without compensation property covered by a guaranty contract?

(5) Under the Ecuadorian, Indonesian or Brazilian agreements, are the events which might require OPIC to pay an investor under the Contract of Guaranty necessarily the same as those which might lead to an arbitral award imposing a monetary liability upon those countries to the United States?

(6) What has been gained through the arbitration clause with Brazil? Suppose, for example, that a factory is expropriated without compensation. The investor brings an action in a Brazilian court, which holds (under fair procedures) that the claim of the investor for compensation in the amount that it demands is not supported by local or international law. Can OPIC require arbitration under the agreement after it pays the investor a sum higher that that awarded by the Brazilian court?

PROBLEM

Foreign Enterprises Inc. (FEI), a Delaware corporation, has a wholly-owned subsidiary in Guatador. FEI has entered into an investment guaranty contract with OPIC covering expropriation. The subsidiary's assets are taken without compensation by Guatador. Pursuant to its obligation in the contract, FEI and the subsidiary have brought an action in the Guatador courts for compensation. Thirteen months after the date of the expropriation, the action is still pending in a court of first instance. At that time, the United States pays FEI in accordance with the contract provisions. It thus becomes subrogated to whatever rights FEI or the subsidiary had in Guatador. The investment guaranty agreement between the United States and Guatador is identical with the Brazilian agreement above.

What path should the United States follow? Is it required to pursue the local-court action, in its own name or that of FEI, or can it press a claim through diplomatic channels for payment by Guatador to it—and failing satisfactory resolution, require arbitration?

NOTE ON THE HICKENLOOPER AMENDMENT

The expropriation in 1962 by a Brazilian state of assets of a local subsidiary of ITT, described at p. 440, supra, provoked a sharp Congressional response. Congress' reaction was particularly intense since the expropriation occurred shortly before a contemplated visit by Brazil's President to the United States in search of further financial assistance. Statements were made in both Houses of Congress that the United States should not show generosity through foreign aid towards foreign countries which seized assets of United States firms without meaningful compensation. Senator Hickenlooper proposed an amendment to the Foreign Assistance Act of 1962. Over the stated opposition of the President and the Secretary of State, it became Section 620(e)(1) of the Foreign Assistance Act of 1961, as amended. Read the current version of the Hickenlooper Amendment, 76 Stat. 260 (1962), as amended, 22 U.S.C.A. § 2370(e)(1).*

Controversy has developed over the amendment's effectiveness. It has been applied to Ceylon, and its application was threatened to a number of other countries, including Argentina, Brazil, Indonesia and Peru. In The Protection of Foreign Investment 117–46 (1965), Professor Lillich reviews these episodes and states (p. 145) "that the amendment has played a marginal, and perhaps even negative, role . . . ." He concludes that other factors were dominant in arriving at negotiated settlements in several of these disputes—particularly changes in the political complexion of the expropriating countries, and the promise of additional financial aid which acted as an inducement to settle a pending dispute.[82] On the other hand, Congressional supporters contend that the amendment has been an important deterrent and an aid towards achieving settlements. Indeed,

82. See, however, Section 620(g) of the Foreign Assistance Act.*

the Executive Branch retreated by 1963 from its initial blanket opposition to the amendment.[83]

QUESTIONS

(1) Read carefully the amendment's clauses defining the measure of compensation. Do you interpret them to state that "international law" requires the "prompt, adequate and effective" standard which the State Department has long espoused? If so, how do you assess the amendment in view of the preceding materials in this Part C?

(2) Guatador expropriates property of an American firm and offers compensation that the firm considers inadequate. Guatador curtly rejects diplomatic protests of the United States, contending that its action is consistent with international law.

> (*a*) Five months after the taking, Guatador advises the American firm that it will create a tribunal within the next few months consisting of two Guatadorian nationals and one person nominated by the firm to determine the amount of compensation by majority vote. It requests that the firm agree to accept any decision rendered, and assures full hearings and fair procedures. The firm promptly rejects this proposal. As Legal Adviser to the State Department, would you advise the President one month later that foreign aid programs to Guatador *should* be suspended?
>
> (*b*) Suppose that Guatador made this proposal eight months after the taking, two months after foreign aid had been suspended. Would you advise the President that foreign aid *can* be resumed?

(3) Guatador expropriates property of an American firm, and offers compensation in the form of ten-year bonds, 50% in principal amount to be in local currency. The Guatadorian courts can entertain suits against the government for compensation for takings. Based upon past experience, one can anticipate a period of about two years before the litigation runs its course through the original and appellate courts. The firm requests the State Department to press claims. As an official in the Department, how would you respond, in view of its traditional position that it will not act on behalf of a national until local remedies have been exhausted?

(4) As a Congressman, would you have voted for or against the Hickenlooper Amendment? Assume an attitude in the executive branch hostile to a vigorous enforcement of the Hickenlooper Amendment. Given the ambiguities in the statute, what restraints operate upon the executive branch to prevent it from interpreting it in a manner that appears to many Congressmen to be overly restrictive—that is, unfavorable to its application? Are these questions apt to arise before the courts? If not, what other checks exist?

83. Later materials examine some of the complex questions that the Hickenlooper Amendment has raised. See pp. 500 and 709, infra.

NOTE ON CONVENTION ON THE SETTLEMENT OF INVESTMENT DISPUTES BETWEEN STATES AND NATIONALS OF OTHER STATES

In view of the disappointing results of attempts at a multilateral agreement on protection of foreign investment, the thoughts of many observers turned to a more procedural direction: establishing more effective institutions for resolving disputes of this character. These thoughts ripened into the Convention on the Settlement of Investment Disputes Between States and Nationals of Other States (the Convention),* which was formulated in 1965 by the International Bank for Reconstruction and Development.

The IBRD's interest in facilitating the international flow of private capital for economic development led it from time to time to participate in the arbitration or mediation of disputes, and ultimately to prepare this Convention. The draftsmen sought to write provisions that would be acceptable to the largest possible number of governments, and solicited views of all member countries on preliminary drafts before opening the Convention in 1965 to member governments of the IBRD for signature. The Convention became effective in 1966 after receiving the necessary number of ratifications. As of July 1974, there were 65 parties to the Convention, including the United States. The list includes many countries of Western Europe, Africa and Asia. However, no Latin American country had signed the Convention. Some of the reasons for this striking phenomenon emerge in the following excerpts from Wionczek, "A Latin American View," in Vernon (ed.), How Latin America Views the U. S. Investor 3, 14 (1966):

> Whatever their political allegiances may be, Latin Americans resent the mounting offensive of large foreign corporations—corporations mainly headquartered in the U. S.—for special privileges and treatment in the capital receiving countries. This offensive was visible in the recent development of a Convention on the Settlement of Investment Disputes to which all Latin American states objected. . . . It has been apparent in direct pressures put on Latin American countries to sign bilateral foreign investment guarantee agreements under AID auspices, and in similar actions aimed at giving foreign private investors a special status in the capital receiving country. Objection is raised not only to giving special status to foreign nationals and corporations in their disputes with sovereign states, but also to the basic implication that the interests of foreign owners should override the interests of a national state. On this point, an overwhelming majority of politically literate Latin Americans would subscribe to a statement made recently not by a Latin American radical but by a conservative African banker: " . . . [W]e, too, need certain guarantees from you. This business of guarantees and assurances is a two-way street. The peoples in Africa have had and are still having unholy experiences with members of the free enterprise system—with members of capitalism—and

therefore they are justified in being fearful and in requiring certain guarantees from you." [Citation omitted.]

The Convention establishes a structure within which arbitration of any legal dispute arising directly out of an investment, between a Contracting State and a national of another Contracting State, can take place. Read now the provisions appearing in the Documentary Supplement. Nationals of other Contracting States are defined in Article 25, but the term "nationality," used in that Article to refer also to juridical persons, is not.[84]

Any Contracting State or national of a Contracting State can commence proceedings under the Convention by filing a request which indicates the nature of the dispute and that jurisdictional requirements have been satisfied. Jurisdiction of the arbitral tribunal depends upon the consent of both parties. Ratification of the Convention by a Contracting State does not of itself constitute consent to arbitration under it. Such consent may however be expressed in advance—in legislation of a Contracting State, in a separate agreement between Contracting States, or in an agreement between a Contracting State and a national of another Contracting State that might, for example, be included in a concession agreement. Or consent may be given by an *ad hoc compromis* to settle a particular dispute.

The arbitral tribunal is composed of members who are in most cases drawn from a panel of arbitrators designated principally by the Contracting States. Unless otherwise provided by the disputants, the arbitration is held in accordance with rules relating to procedures, finality of an award, or interpretation or revision of an award that are set forth in the Convention.[85]

The Centre's 1974 Annual Report disclosed that three arbitrations were in progress under its auspices: one by Holiday Inns against Morocco, one by Adriano Gardella SpA against Ivory Coast and one by the Alcoa, Kaiser and Reynolds aluminum firms against Jamaica. It also infers that the inclusion of clauses calling for resort to its proceedings in development agreements is becoming increasingly common.

The Report of the Executive Directors of the IBRD on the Convention states that the term "international law," in Article 42, "should be understood in the sense given to it by Article 38(1) of the Statute of the International Court of Justice, allowance being made for the fact that Article 38 was designed to apply to inter-State disputes." In a statement in support of the Convention, the Legal Adviser to the State Department said:[86]

84. The failure of the Convention to define this term or in any event to provide some guidelines for an arbitrator, could lead to difficult issues. Recall the discussion of corporate "nationality" at pp. 222–243, supra.

85. In many of these respects, the arrangements under the Convention are similar to the recently revised rules of the Permanent Court of Arbitration at the Hague, described at p. 193, supra.

86. Testimony of Leonard Meeker, Sen.Exec.Rep. No. 2, 89th Cong., 2d Sess., Appendix pp. 28–29, 1966.

> The World Bank Convention does not lay down any substantive rules regarding investment, responsibility of states to alien property holders, due compensation for the taking, and the like. The Bank's judgment, in which we concur, is that any attempt to lay down such rules could not have won the substantial support this convention has found among the less-developed states. However, it is anticipated that decisions through the convention's mechanism will create a significant new body of international law. Thus international law in this area can be expected to grow as the result of this convention. That growth will be free from the restriction of the traditional principle that only states and not private parties are the subject of international law. It will not require agreement in advance on the legal principles involved.

In accordance with Article 69 of the Convention, the Congress enacted a statute to carry out this country's obligations under it. 80 Stat. 344 (1966), 22 U.S.C.A. §§ 1650, 1650a. The Act provides in Section 3 that the award of an arbitral tribunal under the Convention "shall create a right arising under a treaty of the United States. The pecuniary obligations imposed by such an award shall be enforced and shall be given the same full faith and credit as if the award were a final judgment of a court of general jurisdiction of one of the several States." The federal district courts are given exclusive jurisdiction over such proceedings.[87]

Additional reading: Broches, The Convention on the Settlement of Investment Disputes: Some Observations on Jurisdiction, 5 Colum.J.Trans. L. 263 (1966); Rodley, Some Aspects of the World Bank Convention on the Settlement of Investment Disputes, 1966 Can.Ybk.Int.L. 43; and Note, International Arbitration Between States and Foreign Investors: The World Bank Convention, 18 Stan.L.Rev. 1359 (1966).

QUESTIONS

(1) Do you consider the Convention to be a significant step towards more effective international adjudication or remedies? To contribute to any significant trends in contemporary international law?

(2) Suppose that a state and a foreign investor agreed to arbitrate a dispute, and that the state fails to proceed with the arbitration or to comply with the award of the tribunal. Is the foreign investor's situation different if the agreement were independent of or within the framework of the Convention? How does the Convention affect the traditional requirement that the possibilities of diplomatic settlement be exhausted prior to arbitration proceedings? Is this, in your view, an improvement?

(3) The excerpts from Wionczek score the "special privileges and treatment" which the Convention seeks for foreign investors. What are they? In view of the materials in Chapters III and IV, what aspects of the Convention do you think that Latin American governments would find most troublesome?

87. The relationships among Articles 54 and 55 of the Convention, this recent statute and the doctrine of sovereign immunity are examined at 666, infra.

PROBLEM

Turocco, an African state, has signed an agreement with the United States covering an investment guaranty program. The agreement contains the usual provisions described at p. 476, supra, and has an arbitration clause identical with that appearing in the agreement between the United States and Indonesia. Turocco is also a party to the Convention on the Settlement of Investment Disputes. Delco, a Delaware corporation, has entered into a concession agreement with the Turoccan Government to establish a Turoccan subsidiary manufacturing bicycles. In that agreement, Delco and Turocco consented to the jurisdiction of the Centre under the Convention to settle any disputes that might arise under it.

Before making the investment, Delco applied to OPIC for a guaranty against expropriation. The investment meets OPIC's general criteria for the issuance of guaranties. As a staff officer administering the guaranty program, what problems would you encounter—particularly with regard to Articles 25–27 of the Convention? Would you advise that OPIC enter into a guaranty contract with Delco and, if so, would you suggest that special provisions be included in that contract to safeguard OPIC's interests?

---

5. THE SCOPE OF PROTECTION: INDIRECT OR "CREEPING" EXPROPRIATION

NOTE ON INDIRECT TAKINGS

Even if there were a firm consensus that a "taking" required a government to pay prompt, adequate and effective compensation, there remains the problem of defining the kinds of governmental action that constitute a "taking." It should first be noted that not all "direct" takings require compensation. For example, many national legal systems authorize the seizure of assets held or used in violation of laws forbidding obscene literature or defective drugs. Assuming standards that are not arbitrary and fair procedures to adjudicate the questions of obscenity or adequacy of a drug, such takings would not easily support a claim for compensation under international law.

Few international arbitrations have considered such problems. One example is Parsons (Great Britain) v. United States, November 30, 1925, 6 U.N.R.I.A.A. 165 (1925), in which the arbitrator rejected the claim of the British Government for losses resulting from destruction of a stock of liquor by American military authorities during an insurrection in the Philippines. "We are satisfied that the destruction was a matter . . . entirely within the powers of the military government and quite justified by the circumstances." Compare United States v. Caltex (Philippines), Inc., 344 U.S. 149, 73 S.Ct. 200, 97 L.Ed. 157 (1952), in which the Supreme Court held that there had been no taking within the meaning of the Fifth Amendment when U. S. Army troops demolished plaintiff's facilities as Japanese troops entered Manila.

More difficult problems are posed when the foreign investor must deal with governmental regulation which stops shy of an outright destruction or transfer of assets to the government but nonetheless severely limits the investor's freedom of action or imposes new and substantial obligations. Under what circumstances should such regulation be held to require compensation under an international-law standard? Before exploring this problem, it is useful to examine comparable questions that have arisen in the United States in developing a constitutional standard of what constitutes a taking (Fifth Amendment) or the deprivation of property without due process of law (Fourteenth Amendment). Consider the following two decisions of the United States Supreme Court.

Pennsylvania Coal Co. v. Mahon [88]

The Pennsylvania Coal Co. sold land to various persons, including the plaintiffs, under deeds which conveyed the surface but reserved the right in the Company to remove subsurface coal. In 1921, the Pennsylvania legislature enacted a statute prohibiting mining in a way which might cause subsidence of any private house. Plaintiffs brought an action in a Pennsylvania court to prevent the Company from mining, alleging that such mining endangered the support for their private houses. The Company argued that the statute was unconstitutional because it destroyed its property rights without compensation. The state courts held for plaintiffs. The Supreme Court, on a writ of error, reversed in an opinion by MR. JUSTICE HOLMES. The Court stated in part:

> Government hardly could go on if to some extent values incident to property could not be diminished without paying for every such change in the general law. As long recognized some values are enjoyed under an implied limitation and must yield to the police power. But obviously the implied limitation must have its limits or the contract and due process clauses are gone. One fact for consideration in determining such limits is the extent of the diminution. When it reaches a certain magnitude, in most if not in all cases there must be an exercise of eminent domain and compensation to sustain the act. So the question depends upon the particular facts. The greatest weight is given to the judgment of the legislature but it always is open to interested parties to contend that the legislature has gone beyond its constitutional power. . . .
>
> It is our opinion that the act cannot be sustained as an exercise of the police power, so far as it affects the mining of coal under streets or cities in places where the right to mine such coal has been reserved. . . . What makes the right to mine coal valuable is that it can be exercised with profit. To make it commercially impracticable to mine certain coal has very nearly the same effect for constitutional purposes as appropriating or destroying it. . . .
>
> . . . . The protection of private property in the Fifth Amendment presupposes that it is wanted for public

88. 260 U.S. 393, 43 S.Ct. 158, 67 L.Ed. 322 (1922).

use, but provides that it shall not be taken for such use without compensation. A similar assumption is made in the decisions upon the Fourteenth Amendment. . . . When this seemingly absolute protection is found to be qualified by the police power, the natural tendency of human nature is to extend the qualification more and more until at last private property disappears. But that cannot be accomplished in this way under the Constitution of the United States.

The general rule at least is that while property may be regulated to a certain extent, if regulation goes too far it will be recognized as a taking. It may be doubted how far exceptional cases, like the blowing up of a house to stop a conflagration, go—and if they go beyond the general rule, whether they do not stand as much upon tradition as upon principle. . . . We are in danger of forgetting that a strong public desire to improve the public condition is not enough to warrant achieving the desire by a shorter cut than the constitutional way of paying for the change. As we already have said this is a question of degree—and therefore cannot be disposed of by general propositions. But we regard this as going beyond any of the cases decided by this Court. . . .

[MR. JUSTICE BRANDEIS, in dissent, stated:]

Every restriction upon the use of property imposed in the exercise of the police power deprives the owner of some right theretofore enjoyed, and is, in that sense, an abridgment by the state of rights in property without making compensation. But restriction imposed to protect the public health, safety or morals from dangers threatened is not a taking. The restriction here in question is merely the prohibition of a noxious use. The property so restricted remains in the possession of its owner. The state does not appropriate it or make any use of it. The state merely prevents the owner from making a use which interferes with paramount rights of the public. . . .

. . . Restriction upon use does not become inappropriate as a means, merely because it deprives the owner of the only use to which the property can then be profitably put. . . . Nor is a restriction imposed through exercise of the police power inappropriate as a means, merely because the same end might be effected through exercise of the power of eminent domain, or otherwise at public expense. . . .

United States v. Central Eureka Mining Co.[89]

In 1941 and 1942, critical shortages of mining machinery and of skilled labor in non-ferrous metal mines developed. The War Production Board issued an order in 1942 requiring non-essential gold mines, including those owned by the plaintiffs, to cease operations. The Government did not take possession of or use the gold mines or any of their equipment. The order was intended to conserve equipment for essential uses and to attract gold miners to the non-ferrous

89. 357 U.S. 155, 78 S.Ct. 1097, 2 L.Ed. 2d 1228 (1958).

mines. Plaintiffs ceased operations and later brought an action against the United States, alleging that the order amounted to a taking of the right to mine gold which should be compensated under the Fifth Amendment. The Court of Claims held that plaintiffs were entitled to just compensation. The Supreme Court reversed, in an opinion delivered by MR. JUSTICE BURTON. The opinion stated in part:

> . . . Traditionally, we have treated the issue as to whether a particular governmental restriction amounted to a constitutional taking as being a question properly turning upon the particular circumstances of each case. See Pennsylvania Coal Co. v. Mahon . . . . In doing so, we have recognized that action in the form of regulation can so diminish the value of property as to constitute a taking. . . . However, the mere fact that the regulation deprives the property owner of the most profitable use of his property is not necessarily enough to establish the owner's right to compensation. . . . In the context of war, we have been reluctant to find that degree of regulation which, without saying so, requires compensation to be paid for resulting losses of income. E. g., . . . United States v. Caltex (Philippines), Inc., [p. 487, supra]. The reasons are plain. War, particularly in modern times, demands the strict regulation of nearly all resources. It makes demands which otherwise would be insufferable. But wartime economic restrictions, temporary in character, are insignificant when compared to the widespread uncompensated loss of life and freedom of action which war traditionally demands.
>
> We do not find in the temporary restrictions here placed on the operation of gold mines a taking of private property that would justify a departure from the trend of the above decisions. . . .

For a discussion of these and related problems within the United States, see Michelman, Property, Utility, and Fairness: Comments on the Ethical Foundations of "Just Compensation" Law, 80 Harv.L. Rev. 1165 (1967).

Problems in an International Setting

The materials in Part C have had occasion to refer several times to indirect takings. Recall particularly the following:

(1) Article II(b) of the agreement between the United States and Poland, p. 435, supra, referred to "the appropriation or the loss of use or enjoyment of property under Polish laws, decrees, or other measures limiting or restricting rights and interests in and with respect to property . . . ."

(2) Note paragraphs (b), (d) and (1) of the definition of "Expropriatory Action" in the OPIC General Terms and Conditions, p. 474, supra. In its Specific Risk, Investment Guaranty Handbook (Rev. Oct. 1966), p. 19, AID (the predecessor agency administering the guaranty program) stated that "indirect actions of a foreign government will be considered expropriatory action so long as those actions directly result in the type of interference described [in the contract's

definition]. Regulatory or revenue producing activities of the foreign government are considered expropriatory if such actions are discriminatory against the investor or against foreigners, or if the taxation or regulation is not reasonably related to the constitutionally sanctioned objectives of the foreign government or violates generally accepted principles of international law." The Handbook offered several illustrations (p. 20) of the kinds of governmental action that are within the contract's definition. They included "substantial interference in an investor's right of participation in the affairs of the enterprise, e. g., the government decrees that the managerial control over the enterprise shall thereafter be in the hands of some person or body other than that duly chosen by the owners of the enterprise . . . ." More recent instructional handbooks issued by OPIC do not appear to contain comparable illustrations.

(3) Note Clause (C) of Section 620(e)(1) of the Foreign Assistance Act.* During the congressional debates on this section, a statement was introduced entitled "Some Recent Instances or Threats of Creeping Expropriation." 109 Cong.Rec. 21773, Nov. 13, 1963. It listed 12 examples, including one in Brazil where an American-owned public utility was denied rate increases that it viewed as essential. It was therefore forced to cancel plans for expansion and was unable to maintain its existing plant.

These provisions were relevant to the settlement of past disputes, contract definitions, or conditions imposed upon foreign aid. There have been relatively few efforts to define the concept of a taking in treaties which attempt to regulate *future* conduct of the parties. Note, for example, the generality of Article IV of the Convention of Establishment between the United States and France.* Thus the task of formulating general principles in this field has been largely that of codifiers. Among the most elaborate of the efforts is the Draft Convention of Professors Sohn and Baxter, p. 373, supra. Article 10 provides in part:

> 3. (a) A "taking of property" includes not only an outright taking of property but also any such unreasonable interference with the use, enjoyment, or disposal of property as to justify an inference that the owner thereof will not be able to use, enjoy, or dispose of the property within a reasonable period of time after the inception of such interference. . . .
>
> 5. An uncompensated taking of property of an alien . . . which results from the execution of the tax laws; from a general change in the value of currency; from the action of the competent authorities of the State in the maintenance of public order, health, or morality; or from the valid exercise of belligerent rights; or is otherwise incidental to the normal operation of the laws of the State shall not be considered wrongful, provided:
>
> (*a*) it is not a clear and discriminatory violation of the law of the State concerned;

(*b*) it is not the result of a violation of any provision of Articles 6 to 8 [relating to the fairness of legal proceedings] of this Convention;

(*c*) it is not an unreasonable departure from the principles of justice recognized by the principal legal systems of the world; and

(*d*) it is not an abuse of the powers specified in this paragraph for the purpose of depriving an alien of his property.

Consider the following decisions of an international and national tribunal.

KÜGELE v. POLISH STATE

Upper Silesian Arbitral Tribunal, 1932.
[1931–32] Ann.Dig. 69 (No. 34).[90]

[This was an arbitration under the Convention ceding Polish Upper Silesia to Poland that was described at p. 414, supra.]

Prior to 1923 the claimant owned a brewery in Polish Upper Silesia. As the result of a series of license fees successively imposed by the authorities, the business ceased to be remunerative, and he was eventually obliged to close it. He claimed compensation for the losses caused to him by the impositions prior to 1923, as well as by the resulting closing of the business.

Held: that the claim must be dismissed. The Tribunal said: "The increase of the license fee was not in itself capable of taking away or impairing the rights of the plaintiff. . . . The increase of the tax cannot be regarded as a taking away or impairment of the right to engage in trade, for such taxation presupposes the engaging in the trade. It is true that taxation may render the trade less remunerative, or altogether unremunerative. However, there is an essential difference between the maintenance of a certain rate of profit in an undertaking and the legal and factual possibility of continuing the undertaking. The trader may feel compelled to close his business because of the new tax. . . . But this does not mean that he has lost the right to engage in the trade. For had he paid the tax, he would be entitled to go on with his business."

CORN PRODUCTS REFINING COMPANY CLAIM

United States International Claims Commission, 1951–54.
[1955] Int.L.Rep. 333.

[This was a proceeding before the International Claims Commission and its successor, the FCSC, described at p. 433, supra. The claimant filed under the 1948 agreement with Yugoslavia, p. 434, supra, which provided for pro rata distribution of the lump sum settlement in accordance with awards made by the Commission.

The claimant owned property in Yugoslavia taken by the government and upon which the Yugoslavian Government had previously imposed "mortgages." The question posed was whether the amount of the mortgages should be deducted from the value of the property to determine the compensation to be received by the claimant. One

90. The translation is that appearing in the Annual Digest.

mortgage of 39,000,000 dinars was imposed in 1946 pursuant to a decision of an administrative tax board. Excerpts from the opinion of the Commission relating to this mortgage and valuation of the property appear below.]

. . . With respect to the mortgage of 39,000,000 dinars for taxes for war profits, this encumbrance clearly represents a confiscatory measure adopted by the Government of Yugoslavia prior to the nationalization of the enterprise, but after the enterprise was taken over for management purposes. It is not necessary to point out that the amount of 39,000,000 dinars is out of any proportion with respect to the alleged war profits, because the aforestated figures disclose that the plant had an average earning of not more than 3,000,000 dinars per year. However, should we assume that the profits were much higher during the war, we never would arrive at the amount of 39,000,000 dinars, because this amount represents approximately three times the prewar value of the plant and a taxation to such an extent is nothing else but a total confiscation of the entire property. This mortgage for war profits taxes must be, therefore, disregarded for the purposes of this valuation. . . .

Compare the views on the relationship between taxation and confiscation that were expressed by Scrutton, L. J., in Aksionairnoye Obschestvo A. M. Luther v. James Sagor & Co., [1921] 3 K.B. 532, 559:

> . . . British citizens who may contribute to the state more than half their income in income tax and super tax, and a large proportion of their capital in death duties, can hardly declare a foreign state immoral which considers (though we may think wrongly) that to vest individual property in the state as representing all the citizens is the best form of proprietary right.

QUESTIONS

(1) Consider how the following cases would be decided under (a) an OPIC Contract of Guaranty covering expropriation of assets of a wholly-owned subsidiary organized in the foreign country, and (b) Article 10 of the Draft Convention:

> (*a*) The subsidiary sells its entire production in the foreign country. The government imposes price controls which lead to a reduction in the selling price of the product. This reduction prevents the foreign enterprise from making any profit and threatens operating losses. (1) Suppose that the subsidiary was the only manufacturer of this product. (2) Suppose that there were many manufacturers, but price controls were imposed only upon the subsidiary's products.
>
> (*b*) The subsidiary requires imported raw materials for its production. The government raises import duties to a point where the subsidiary cannot profitably conduct business. What further facts might be relevant to determining whether this action provides a basis for a claim under the OPIC contract or for diplomatic protest?

(2) Under the OPIC contract, would the "Expropriatory Action" that might require OPIC to pay an investor necessarily lead an arbitral tribunal, under the Ecuadorian, Indonesian or Brazilian bilateral agreements, to impose a monetary liability on the foreign government? Should OPIC, as a matter of policy, try to make the liabilities identical?

(3) Apart from outright expropriation cases, do you consider the contract's definition satisfactory from the investor's point of view? From the government's, given the policy objectives behind the program? What alternative approaches would you suggest towards defining the risks against which American industrial investments abroad are covered?

PROBLEM

Guatador, a South American country, has experienced years of deep social unrest. The present government has stated that it opposes the spread of Communist influence in South America, and that it believes essential the pursuit of several programs of economic and social reform. As part of those programs, it has taken into the public sector, through expropriation of assets, a number of utility companies, and has announced that in the future all utilities will be government-owned. In addition, it has instituted a program of land reform in certain regions involving expropriation of large holdings and their redistribution to small landholders or to cooperative farms.

These actions affected property interests held by local subsidiaries of United States companies which are stated by such companies to have an aggregate value of approximately $50,000,000. Other assets taken were owned by other aliens and (approximately 50% of the value of the property taken) by Guatadorian nationals. Compensation will be paid to the Guatadorian nationals in local currency through 20-year government bonds, the principal amount to be determined by agreement between the government and its nationals or through court proceedings.

Guatador is receiving financial aid from the United States. Its foreign-exchange position is such that, in the view of its government, it cannot afford to pay in dollars or other convertible currency the value alleged by the United States companies. It has, however, offered to pay 20% of a total value to be determined through its national judicial procedures in dollars, the balance to be paid in local currency over a five-year period. The Guatadorian judiciary has a reputation of fairness and has long proved itself to be impervious to governmental pressure. The local currency received by the American companies is to be available for reinvestment in stated sectors of the Guatadorian economy. Dividends and interest stemming from such reinvestments will qualify for exchange into dollars, which can be repatriated.

The United States companies are reluctant to settle on these terms. They are not attracted by the financial prospects in the designated areas of possible reinvestment, and are not in any event confident about the prospective political stability of Guatador. The United States Goverment has advised Guatador that it considers its action to violate international law. It has threatened termination of foreign aid and exclusion of Guatador from various programs which are being developed for a number of South American countries, unless Guatador meets "its obligations under international law." Guatador replied that it has met those obligations.

(1) Assume that Guatador stated that it was willing to submit the question of compensation to an international tribunal, including the I.C.J. The State Department is considering this suggestion. As a lawyer in the Office of the Legal Adviser, you have been asked to prepare a memorandum indicating what advantages and risks there are in such a proposal, and to

include your recommendation. You are to consider not only the likelihood of an adverse ruling of the I.C.J. if the United States were to institute proceedings, but also the effect of such a ruling upon the United States' position on compensation.

(2) Would you find more attractive an alternative suggestion made by Guatador, namely that it is willing to submit to arbitration, under the Convention on the Settlement of Investment Disputes, the question of what compensation is owing to the American companies? The parties to such an arbitration would of course be Guatador and the companies.

(3) From the point of view of the United States, would you prefer to have the question of compensation considered in one or a few opinions of the I.C.J., or in a much larger number of arbitrations over the years pursuant to the Convention or the bilateral treaties (assuming that the investments expropriated were guarantied) relating to the OPIC guaranty contracts?

D. DISPUTES OVER CONCESSION AGREEMENTS

NOTE ON POLITICAL AND ECONOMIC ASPECTS OF CONCESSION AGREEMENTS

Part D examines that branch of the law of state responsibility which treats agreements between a government and an alien, including a local corporation that is alien-owned. The disputes that are apt to arise between the parties to that agreement may indeed involve the expropriation of "property interests" of the alien, tangible and intangible, and hence may involve the issues of international law considered in Part C. That is, the breach of an agreement by a government may be accompanied by the seizure of property of the alien investor that was owned and managed in accordance with the agreement. Nonetheless, distinct issues are posed, including legal issues that are still more clouded by uncertainty than were the principles of compensation of Part C.

We consider so-called concession agreements, as distinguished from such common contractual arrangements between governments and aliens as public bonds held by aliens or purchase or sale contracts. By a "concession" agreement, sometimes referred to as an economic development agreement, we refer to what is usually a detailed and complex agreement granting the alien investor the right to engage in stated activities in the host country, and imposing upon it and the government a series of related rights and obligations. The "investment incentive contracts" entered into under Section 8 of the Investment Incentive Code of the Republic of Liberia * offer an illustration.[91] In its characteristic form, the concession agreement involves an extractive or utility enterprise, although there are a growing number involving manufacturing enterprises. The provisions of the agree-

91. The text at pp. 89–90, supra, notes characteristic provisions of investment incentive laws authorizing government agencies to enter into concession agreements with foreign companies.

ments vary widely among countries and industries, often reflecting the relative bargaining positions of the government and the investor.

A characteristic concession in an extractive industry might grant exclusive rights to the concessionaire to exploit mineral resources in stated areas, impose duties upon the concessionaire to build housing or productive facilities, make special provisions as to import duties or other regulatory laws of the host country, and provide for the sharing of profits between the alien and government, whether in the form of royalties or taxation or other contractual arrangements. Such agreements often contemplate (but less frequently realize) a duration of many years, perhaps 20 to 40.

Unlike traditional examples of government-alien contracts such as debt instruments or purchase and sale contracts, the concession agreement is frequently a peculiarly governmental instrument. It often involves rights in mineral or other interests owned or controlled by the government, and arrangements on matters such as taxation which are within a legislature's competence. It is also apt to be a unique instrument, tailored to meet unique needs, with no other comparable arrangements between a particular government and a private party in effect. In certain industries such as oil extraction, however, patterns for these agreements have developed. Not only "boilerplate" provisions but also such critical terms as those defining the percentages for profit sharing tend to recur in a large number of agreements.[92]

In its legal and procedural origins, as in its terms, the concession agreement has characteristics distinguishing it from more usual government-private party contracts. It may be entered into with great solemnity, at the ministerial or presidential level. The signing of the agreement may be preceded by legislation authorizing the execution, or the agreement may be submitted to legislative bodies for their approval. Indeed, the concession agreement—or critical portions of it such as those assuring the concessionaire of defined tax treatment over a period of years—may be embodied in laws, ministerial decrees, or other forms of legislative or executive acts. Hence the agreement partakes ambivalently of the character of both legislation and contract, analogously to the treaty between two governments.

The concession contract plays a significant role in the process of economic development. The concessionaire is generally a corporation of a developed country (or its local subsidiary), or one formed pursuant to a consortium among corporate interests of several developed countries. Such multinational corporations sometimes command economic resources which rival or surpass those of the host government. Given their significant role in the contracting government's economy, these agreements provide, as it were, a comprehensive legislative framework within which the cooperative undertakings of the

92. See Cattan, The Evolution of Oil Concessions in the Middle East and North Africa (1967); Symposium, Mining the Resources of the Third World: From Concession Agreements to Service Contracts, 1973 Proc.Am. Soc.Int.L. 227–245.

parties unfold. Consider the following comments in Vernon, Long-Run Trends in Concession Contracts, 1967 Proc.Ann.Soc.Int.L. 81, 83:

> Another factor pushes underdeveloped areas in the direction of such [*ad hoc*] arrangements. Such governments sometimes have not had—because they have not needed—laws of general application which would be applicable to matters such as the taxation of corporate income, the pollution of streams, the reforestation of timberlands, and so on. Underdeveloped nations commonly begin to worry about such matters after the first few large investors appear on their doorstep, not before. So it is not surprising that these preoccupations should first be dealt with *ad hoc* in the arrangements worked out with the large investors.

Of particular historical importance in such extractive fields as oil, copper, bauxite and iron ore, concession agreements open channels for the flow of capital from developed to developing countries, and for the flow of essential mineral resources to the industrialized world. In addition to attracting foreign capital, the host country benefits from the growth of enterprise that can earn needed foreign exchange for the development of other sectors of its economy, and from the introduction of know-how and the related training of its citizens who are employed by the concessionaire. As stated in Vernon, supra, at p. 86: "Concessionaires typically have bred a small group of local entrepreneurs in the construction business, in local trucking, and in other supply and service industries. Eventually, with government support or without it, these ancillary services have developed a separate business life of their own."

Nonetheless, concession agreements are likely to generate disputes between the parties. The reasons are various, starting with the length of term, degree of impact and uniqueness of the typical concession. Under such conditions it is not surprising that problems will turn up which were not contemplated by the draftsmen and for which no solutions or analogies can be found in legislation or decisional law.[93] Furthermore, certain sources of tension inhere in these arrangements. The economic and legal development of the host country may lead to demands that the concessionaire be subject to a broader range of local laws—health measures, labor regulations, revenue measures—and contribute more extensively to the developmental process. Infrastructure facilities, such as railroads or power plants which the concessionaire has constructed, may prove attractive to the government or local enterprise for distinct commercial purposes, and pressure may be exerted upon the concessionaire to permit partial use of the facilities for such purposes. The government may urge the concessionaire to train more rapidly local personnel to assume positions of responsibility in the enterprise. Note Section 6(1)(a) of

93. For illustrations of the kinds of problems which can arise, see Powell, LAMCO: A Case Study of a Concession Contract, 1967 Proc.Am.Soc.Int.L. 89. The author describes some of the experiences under a 1960 concession agreement with the Liberian Government for the extraction of iron ore.

the Liberian Investment Incentive Code * and Paragraph 6 of the 1966 U.N. Resolution on Permanent Sovereignty Over Natural Resources, p. 465, supra. If the private sector of the host country's economy is developing, the government may become critical of initial arrangements pursuant to which the full equity interest in the venture was in foreign hands, and argue that the government itself or domestic shareholders should enter the picture. Note Paragraph 5 of the U.N. Resolution.

Beyond such considerations, one must account for domestic political trends. Over the years it is likely that the government will change; new regimes may be under natural pressures to seek to discredit or outdo their predecessors. A natural focus of governmental demands in such situations has been the revenue-sharing provisions of the concession agreement. Particularly in the extractive industries, concessions may prove to be exceptionally and unexpectedly lucrative. The unmistakable pattern of change through renegotiation of concession agreements over the past decades has been to shift a larger percentage of revenues to the government. The fact that other less developed countries, in new agreements, are bargaining larger shares for themselves may be a further stimulus for revision.

Many of these tensions are expressed through the account of the relationship between Kennecott Copper Corporation and the Chilean government over a period of fifty years, at pp. 444–458, supra. Recall that some negotiations between Kennecott and Chile, particularly the "Chileanization" arrangements in the 1960's, took the form of understandings, undertakings and agreements, several of which were stated in ministerial decrees. The events following the Chileanization arrangements offer a graphic illustration of the themes in the preceding paragraphs.

The evolution of financial provisions in oil concessions in the Middle East during this century affords the most significant illustration of these themes. In the early agreements, the government of the producing country benefited only from a modest royalty or other minor advantages; a few agreements contained provisions for profit sharing giving the government about 20% of annual net income. Dramatic change in these relationships was initiated by the 1950 agreement between Saudi Arabia and the Arabian American Oil Company. That agreement introduced the concept of equal profit sharing, although the 50–50 division of net profits in the many new concessions or amendments over the past 25 years have taken various legal forms: contractual provisions for profit sharing, royalties, income taxes with various credit provisions and so on.

Over the last two decades, the oil-exporting countries achieved a vast increase in bargaining power vis-à-vis the multinational oil corporations, and indeed vis-à-vis the countries of the industrialized West. The creation in 1960 of an eleven-country Organization of Petroleum Exporting Countries (OPEC), including at its core the important Arab oil-producers and Iran, led to concerted action in pricing and to the dramatic oil embargo of 1973–74, which proved to be politically and economically effective. A number of changes in arrangements between the multinationals and the oil countries have taken place. There has been continuing growth in effective tax rates, reaching 55 to 60% several years ago, while some contemporary arrangements achieve an effective allocation of close to 80% of net profits to the host country. A number of countries have taken equity participations, ranging from 25% to a majority ownership, in the local operations of the multinational. The changing aspirations and escalating economic power of the oil countries have suggested to a number of oil multinationals that their status will become one of long-term purchasers of crude oil, and that the older type of concession agreements giving exclusive rights to extract and sell may be succeeded by what amount to technical service contracts under which the multinationals receive stated compensation for services rendered to a government-owned oil industry.[94]

When problems of so basic a political and economic character arise, lawyers are confronted with situations to which there are few analogies in disputes over contracts between private parties. The formal legal considerations tend to recede into the background. Unless the contract contains a firm agreement to submit disputes to arbitration, the chances of a party's resorting to third-party decision making are slim.[95] Most of the serious disputes over concession agreements in recent decades have not found their way into arbitration. And even where arbitration, or legal argument between an alien and a government, takes place, there is a dearth of useful precedents to serve as reference points. The problems of breach of concession agreements, from all the legal-political perspectives sketched below, lack even that minimum clarity or consensus about the nature of the issues posed and the questions to be resolved that was present in the expropriation disputes of Part C.

As a consequence, immediate tactical considerations and relative bargaining power tend to dominate. Over a long period of time, bargaining power may tend to move from one side to the other, for reasons sketched in the Note dealing with the Chilean copper expropriations at pp. 444–458, supra. That shift in bargaining power will affect not only the concessionaire and government, but also governments of industrialized countries. The possible outcomes of such confrontations of power are indicated, at their extreme, by Hartshorn, Politics and World Oil Economics 363 (Rev.Ed.1967):

> Doing without Middle East oil . . . has been attempted only once by the West and the oil companies, with relative

94. See Cattan, op. cit. fn. 92, supra, at 6–11, 69–72, 78–80, and the Symposium, fn. 92, supra, as well as Symposium, The Changing Framework of Concession Agreements and the Oil Industry, 7 Vand.J.Trans.L. 279–380 (1974).

95. The local courts may not be open to suits against the government because of principles of sovereign immunity. Or if open, they may have no authority to review the legality of new legislation or other governmental conduct which adversely affects the concessionaire.

> success but in an expensive emergency operation. Doing without Middle East and Venezuelan oil at once never has. Doing without the oil companies, on the other hand, was attempted once by Iran; it was a failure. Abadan and Suez are ugly object lessons that neither the petroleum exporting countries, the Western consuming nations, nor the oil companies might care to contemplate as benchmarks setting the limits of successful bargaining; they are on record, rather, as the danger signs showing where good sense foundered in the past. . . .

Those observations, of course, would have to be modified in view of the oil embargo imposed by the Arab oil-producing countries in 1973–74. But again one could repeat Hartshorn's observation that such experiences are significant not only as indications of changing balances of power but also of the "danger signs" for both sides to the controversy.

Beyond fears of confrontation, retaliation, the spurring of research in competitive energy resources and so on, a number of considerations might curb a government's desire to achieve a better bargain. They include: (*1*) fear that it would be so costly as to cripple the concessionaire's ability to compete in his export markets (and thus to earn taxes and foreign exchange for the government); (*2*) fear that the concessionaire would shift the scene of its new investments (say, from Mexico to other countries, see p. 424); (*3*) fear that, if the concessionaire limited or abandoned its activities, the government would have difficulty operating or finding other parties to operate the enterprise or exploiting the foreign markets developed by the concessionaire; and (*4*) fear of repercussions of the bargaining on relations with other potential investors or with investors' home governments.

Note, however, that some of these considerations embody a legal element. (*1*) Whether the concessionaire's home government takes active interest in a dispute—whether it extends diplomatic protection—may depend on whether it deems that a violation of international law has taken place. (*2*) Recall that the Hickenlooper Amendment, p. 482, supra, specifically makes a finding of contract repudiation the occasion for termination of foreign assistance. Clause (B) of Section 620(e)(1) of the Foreign Assistance Act *, relating to breach of contracts, was in fact added in a 1963 revision occasioned by Argentina's cancellation of petroleum concessions which it had granted American oil companies.[96] (*3*) The concessionaire's investment may have been covered by an investment guaranty from OPIC, p. 471, supra. If so, the dispute again may become inter-governmental. Thus the attitudes of investors and governments will be affected not only by their view of the economic issues and equities but also of the legal aspects of the situation. Whether in the context of negotiations between the alien and government or in the context of diplomatic pro-

96. See Note, Argentina and the Hickenlooper Amendment, 54 Calif.L.Rev. 2078 (1966).

tection, arguments based upon international law tend to legitimate the investor's (or its government's) position and add bargaining strength.[97]

Whatever the strength of the legal arguments, the concessionaire must carefully appraise the risks in the alternative courses of conduct before it: insistence on its position, negotiation and compromise, resort (if possible) to arbitration, efforts to enlist his government's support and so on. Consider the following comments in Powell, fn. 93, supra, at 95:

> The negotiations and discussions . . . which I have used by way of illustration have all taken place under the umbrella of the basic Concession Agreement and are governed in the last analysis by the spirit in which that Agreement was negotiated. Actual textual reference to the Concession Agreement is, however, relatively rare. A great deal more depends on the working relationships between the foreign investors and representatives of the Government at all levels; on the ability of the foreign investors to remain in communication with those representatives, to understand and appreciate their needs and concerns; and on the maintenance at the same time of the integrity of the basic commercial enterprise without which the Concession becomes valueless to all parties. These goals cannot be achieved simply by pointing to the small print in the Concession Agreement or by resort to the provision for arbitration of disputes. Whatever differences of opinion may arise must be resolved between the parties before they ever reach the arbitration or litigation stage, even if it is necessary to do a fast fandango in the process.

Note the image of dance (with its connotation of ever-adjusting positions of the partners) and the reference to "process" at the end of these remarks. As with all long-term relationships, the formal rules of contract law which govern isolated transactions or short-term relationships achieve less prominence in arguments between the parties. Changing circumstances, changing needs, changing relationships of power, changing perceptions of equity all figure in a discussion that may embrace events over one, two or three decades.

The vast majority of disputes over concession agreements have been settled by direct negotiation between the parties, or through negotiations involving the investor's government as well. Recourse to arbitration may under some circumstances "escalate" the controversy and impair the continuing harmonious relationships which are of prime importance. Nonetheless, the security of a concession agreement may be enhanced if it includes a promise to submit disputes arising under it to arbitration. This is the technique encouraged by the Convention on the Settlement of Investment Disputes between States and Nationals of Other States, p. 484, supra.

97. Of course, political considerations will weigh heavily in any decision of the investor's government whether (and how) to enter the dispute. These may be controlling considerations, overriding respectable legal arguments that the foreign government has committed a breach of international law. Compare the variety of factors that affected resolution of disputes in Part C over expropriation.

Additional reading: Carlston, Law and Organization in World Society (1962); Fatouros, Governmental Guarantees to Foreign Investors (1962); Hartshorn, Politics and World Oil Economics (Rev. ed. 1967); Cattan, The Evolution of Oil Concessions in the Middle East and North Africa (1967); Cattan, The Law of Oil Concessions in the Middle East and North America (1967); Symposium, The Changing Framework of Concession Agreements and the Oil Industry, 7 Vand.J.Trans.L. 279–380 (1974); Symposium, Mining the Resources of the Third World: From Concession Agreements to Service Contracts, 1973 Proc.Am.Soc.Int.L. 227–245; Smith & Wells, Mineral Agreements in Developing Countries: Structures and Substance, 69 Am.J.Int.L. 560 (1975).

NOTE ON SOME LEGAL ASPECTS OF CONCESSION AGREEMENTS

We have thus far stressed the economic and political background against which the origin, evolution and occasional collapse of concessions are to be understood. But legal considerations, even if not paramount as they may be in types of contract disputes within a domestic legal system, remain significant for those drafting concession agreements. They may become significant for dispute resolution, depending upon the nature and context of the dispute.

We here consider two generic problems in most types of concession agreements between aliens and host governments: (1) choice of law, and (2) the distinctive issues posed by the dual role of the state as a contracting party and as a legislator. Such issues have figured in many major arbitrations, the opinions in some of which constitute almost a plenary review (sometimes in less than lucid terms) of the formal legal aspects of these disputes. A prime example is the Arbitration betwen Saudi Arabia and the Arabian American Oil Company (Aramco), Arbitral Award, August 23, 1958, 27 Int.L.Rep. 117 (1963), to which occasional references will be made below.

(1) Choice of Law

We here examine in greater detail questions introduced in the Note on choice of law, p. 91, supra. See particularly illustration (a) in that Note. Commentators have termed choice of law with respect to contracts—even private ones—one of the most confusing fields in the conflict of laws. In an interstate setting in this country, the courts have invoked such references in a rigid but nonetheless inconsistent manner. The initial Restatement of the Conflict of Laws of 1934 distinguished among various issues, such as creation of a contract or questions relating to its performance, and identified different references for each. For example, questions of the creation and validity of contracts were generally to be answered by the law of the place of contracting (*lex loci contractus*), as defined, which was also to govern questions of capacity. A number of issues relating to performance were referred to the law of the place of performance (*lex loci solutionis*).

The rules had a deceptive clarity. Partly because of their arbitrary and rigid nature, they never commanded broad assent among the courts. And even more significant for the development of choice-of-law theory, scholars were sharply critical. They demonstrated with irresistible arguments how doubtful the premises underlying the Restatement's rules were, the arbitrary results which these rules fostered, and the defects in any methodology which resolved diverse questions (grouped within such categories as "creation" or "performance") by blind references to a particular jurisdiction's law—so-called "jurisdiction-selecting" rules.[98] That is, the Restatement directed attention to jurisdictions rather than to laws, to identification of the state whose law is to govern rather than to initial consideration of the laws themselves—their content, purposes, apparent or real conflicts—of the concerned states.

The trend in the Restatement (Second) has been to depart from such jurisdiction-selecting rules and to expand the types of considerations that are relevant to an appropriate choice of law. One key aspect of this trend has been to accord greater effect to party autonomy.[99] Note, for example, Section 187, which provides that the law of the state chosen by the parties to "govern their contractual rights and duties, will be applied," even if the particular issue is one that the parties could not have resolved by an explicit provision directed to that issue, unless "the chosen state has no substantial relationship to the parties or the transaction and there is no other reasonable basis for the parties' choice," or unless the application of that law "would be contrary to a fundamental policy of a state which has a materially greater interest . . . in the determination of the particular issue" and which would be the state of applicable law absent an effective choice of law by the parties. Absent such a choice, Section 188 provides that a number of factors are to be considered in order to determine the local law of the state which, with respect to a given issue, "has the most significant relationship to the transaction and the parties." The relevant factors entering into that determination include the place of contracting, place of negotiation, place of performance, location of subject matter, and nationality or domicile or place of business of the parties. Such provisions suggest a comparison with the English concept of a "proper law" of a contract, to be ascertained in the light of all relevant considerations. Special rules obtain for certain kinds of contracts, such as those transferring interests in land (Section 196—generally the state where the contract requires the services or a major portion thereof to be rendered).

98. See, e. g., Cavers, A Critique of the Choice-of-Law Problem, 47 Harv.L. Rev. 173 (1933); Cavers: The Choice-of-Law Process 59–87 (1965); Cook, The Logical and Legal Bases of the Conflict of Laws, 33 Yale L.J. 457 (1924); and Currie, Married Women's Contracts: A Study in Conflict-of-Laws Methods, 25 U.Chi.L.Rev. 227 (1958).

99. For a recent illustration of considerable deference to party autonomy by the U. S. Supreme Court, in a field (international choice-of-forum clauses) in which courts have traditionally limited private contractual power, see M/S Bremen v. Zapata Off-Shore Company, p. 812, infra.

The Restatement (Second), while rejecting much of the basic methodology of the earlier Restatement, leaves much uncertainty about prediction of courts' decisions in a field of domestic law where certainty is generally to be desired. This observation underscores the significance of the Restatement's greater attention to the parties' choice of law.[1]

Similar questions arise in concession agreements between governments and aliens which do not specify an applicable law. As noted in the Aramco arbitration, p. 502, supra, courts or arbitral tribunals in such situations may indulge in a presumption that the government's local law controls. That presumption makes sense for many types of concession contracts, which by definition are to be performed primarily or entirely within the government's jurisdiction.

In any event, reference by a court or arbitrator to another nation's law to resolve questions of contract interpretation or performance would be unlikely, particularly when the corporate party is a locally organized subsidiary of the foreign investor.[2] Thus the alien investor is apt to be governed by local law (often as applied by local tribunals) in event of a dispute, subject to whatever protection it may derive from a minimum standard of protection under international law. Indeed, at least among oil concession agreements with choice-of-law clauses, it appears that partial or exclusive reference to the law of the governmental party remains most common. Nonetheless, to avoid subjection to a foreign legal system with characteristics not fully appreciated by it, the investor may seek to insert in the contract a provision that certain of its aspects—perhaps questions of interpretation, performance, or *force majeure*—will be governed by another body of law.

1. For a general review of choice of law for contracts, see 1 Rabel, The Conflict of Laws: A Comparative Study 356–591 (2d ed., Drobnig, 1960). For a survey of choice-of-law principles applied in different countries, see 2 Battifol, Droit International Privé 207–274 (5th ed., Lagarde, 1970) (France); Cheshire, Private International Law 201–254 (9th ed., North, 1974) (England); and Goodrich and Scoles, Conflict of Laws 198–225 (4th ed. 1964) (United States). For discussions of recent trends in the United States, see Cavers, Re-Restating the Conflict of Laws: The Chapter on Contracts, in Nadelmann, von Mehren and Hazard (eds.), XXth Century Comparative and Conflicts Law 349 (1961); Von Mehren and Trautman, The Law of Multistate Problems 183–193 (1965); and Weintraub, The Contracts Proposals of the Second Restatement of Conflict of Laws —A Critique, 46 Iowa L.Rev. 713 (1961).

2. That reference would present certain complications in the case of a federal nation such as the United States. Most issues germane to a contract's interpretation or performance would here be governed by state common or statutory law. Thus a reference might have to identify a particular state, unless it were to refer to principles of contract law generally prevailing in the United States—or today, possibly to the Uniform Commercial Code. As later materials indicate, it should however be borne in mind that the special issues posed by contracts between a corporation and a government are often not resolved within the normal framework of contract law. This would suggest at least the possibility of a reference to those principles governing contracts between the federal government and private parties in the United States.

What that other law should be has been the subject of much and contentious writing. Tribunals and writers have advanced the following possibilities:

(*1*) *The law of the contract.* Under this view, the concession agreement would constitute a self-contained system within which the concessionaire and government operate. That is, the contract itself provides the legal framework for resolution of disputes. Apart from the conceptual problems which this approach presents—problems stemming from the traditional premise that a "contract" is a binding instrument by virtue of some body of law which gives it legal significance and attaches duties and rights to the parties—most disputes would force the parties or arbitrators to develop principles extrinsic to the contract to resolve questions of interpretation, remedies for breach, *force majeure* and so on. Nonetheless, there are contemporary examples of contracts—particularly of international organizations, such as the International Bank for Reconstruction and Development—which seek insulation from the law of any state and thus an autonomous character.

(*2*) *International law.* In effect, those who urge that international law applies to the concession agreement analogize it to a treaty, even though one party is a corporation. The inherently international character of the agreement, and the quasi-governmental status which the concessionaire often assumes in its activities, are drawn upon to support such an analogy. The implications of acceptance of this position are significant. Various principles of international law—such as *pacta sunt servanda,* which allows few justifications for departure from a party's obligation—would govern the agreement, although other doctrines such as *rebus sic stantibus* do render uncertain many areas even of treaty law.[3] More content could be read into a reference to "international law" if it extended past treaty law to include "general principles of law," as in paragraph (3) below. The Aramco Tribunal several times invoked international law as a measure of the validity of Saudi Arabian decrees and conduct, and inquired into the protection which that law afforded an alien against provisions of municipal law. These issues we consider at p. 515, infra.

(*3*) *General principles of law.* The Note at p. 278, supra, described some of the difficulties in giving concrete meaning to this phrase, one that appears in Article 38(1) of the Statute of the I.C.J. The Aramco Tribunal frequently referred to such principles. At times, it viewed them as tantamount to principles of customary in-

3. A description of basic principles of treaty law—formation, interpretation, consequences of a breach and remedies—appears in the Note at p. 281, supra.

Note that Article 42 of the Convention on the Settlement of Investment Disputes between States and Nationals of Other States * provides that, if the parties have not agreed upon the rules of law to be applied by the tribunal, it is to "apply the law of the Contracting State party to the dispute (including its rules on the conflict of laws) and such rules of international law as may be applicable."

ternational law, presumably including treaty law. In other instances, it appeared to invoke this concept in a distinct sense, as an invitation to a comparative survey of the contract law of developed legal systems in order to ascertain common or general principles. When operating in countries with less developed or highly unfamiliar legal systems that cannot cope with the kinds of issues that are apt to arise under concession agreements, the investor may find such an effort attractive. Nonetheless, it may create as many problems as it solves. To the extent that such a reference is intended to reach past the traditional corpus of contract law to special problems involving contracts between governments and private parties, numerous questions sketched below arise. If, in addition, the reference is not only to contract law but to all regulatory statutes bearing upon the subject matter of the concession, the difficulties in finding common principles in areas characterized by detailed and highly individualized legislation become almost insurmountable.

Several other arbitrations have also referred to general principles of law. A prominent example is Petroleum Development Ltd. v. Sheikh of Abu Dhabi, September 1951, [1951] Int.L.Rep. 144, decided under an arbitration clause in a petroleum concession between the parties. In his award, Lord Asquith (the Umpire appointed by the two arbitrators selected by the parties) stated:

> What is the "Proper Law" applicable in construing this contract? This is a contract made in Abu Dhabi and wholly to be performed in that country. If any municipal system of law were applicable, it would *prima facie* be that of Abu Dhabi. But no such law can reasonably be said to exist. The Sheikh administers a purely discretionary justice with the assistance of the Koran; and it would be fanciful to suggest that in this very primitive region there is any settled body of legal principles applicable to the construction of modern commercial instruments. Nor can I see any basis on which the municipal Law of England could apply. On the contrary, Clause 17 of the Agreement, cited above, repels the notion that the municipal Law of any country, as such, could be appropriate.[4] The terms of that clause invite, indeed prescribe, the application of principles rooted in the good sense and common practice of the generality of civilized nations—a sort of "modern law of nature." I do not think that on this point there is any conflict between the parties.
>
> But, albeit English Municipal Law is inapplicable *as such*, some of its rules are in my view so firmly grounded in reason, as to form part of this broad body of jurisprudence—this "modern law of nature." . . .

In applying these principles, the Umpire invoked certain interpretative rules of English law which appeared to him to be "no mere

4. [Eds.] That clause stated: "The Ruler and the Company both declare that they base their work in this Agreement on goodwill and sincerity of belief and on the interpretation of this Agreement in a fashion consistent with reason. The Company undertakes to acknowledge the authority of the Ruler and his full rights as Ruler of Abu Dhabi and to respect it in all ways, and to fly the Ruler's flag over the Company's buildings."

idiosyncrasy of our system, but [principles] of ecumenical validity"—for example, attaching paramount importance to the words of a contract rather than to arguments during negotiations. On the other hand, the Umpire disregarded other "rigid English rules," such as that excluding evidence of negotiations as relevant to the interpretation of the contract, and certain "English maxims" which owe their origin "to incidents of our own feudal polity and royal prerogative which are now ancient history"—for example, the rule that grants by a sovereign are to be construed against the grantee.

A number of concession agreements have stipulated that they shall be governed by principles of law common to "civilized nations"—for example, one of September 19, 1954 between Iran and a consortium of oil companies of the United States and European countries. That Agreement displaced a 1933 arrangement between Iran and the Anglo-Iranian Oil Co. which fell in 1951 when Iran expropriated oil properties. Article 41 of the Iran-Consortium Agreement of 1954 states in part: [5]

> A. The parties undertake to carry out the terms and provisions of this Agreement in accordance with the principles of mutual good will and good faith and to respect the spirit as well as the letter of the said terms and provisions.
>
> B. No general or special legislative or administrative measures or any other act whatsoever of or emanating from Iran or any governmental authority in Iran (whether central or local) shall annul this Agreement, amend or modify its provisions or prevent or hinder the due and effective performance of its terms. Such annulment, amendment or modification shall not take place except by agreement of the parties to this Agreement.
>
> C. Unless the parties otherwise agree, this Agreement shall not be terminated or dissolved prior to the expiration of its term except by a decision, made by an Arbitration Board or sole arbitrator appointed in accordance with Article 44 of this Agreement, that it has been terminated by breach or dissolved by total impossibility of performance.

Article 44 provides in part that, subject to certain exceptions, arbitration under its provisions "shall be the sole method of determining any dispute between the parties to this Agreement arising out of, or relating to, the execution or interpretation of this Agreement, the determination of the rights and obligations of the parties hereunder, or the operation of this Article . . . ." Article 46 of the Agreement states:

> In view of the diverse nationalities of the parties to this Agreement, it shall be governed by and interpreted and applied in accordance with principles of law common to Iran and the several nations in which the other parties to this Agreement are incorporated, and

5. The Agreement appears in 2 Hurewitz, Diplomacy in the Near and Middle East 348 (1956).

> in the absence of such common principles, then by and in accordance with principles of law recognized by civilized nations in general, including such of those principles as may have been applied by international tribunals.

Note that the reference to "principles of law recognized by civilized nations" is secondary, to be invoked only if the primary reference proves inadequate.

(2) Distinctive Problems Posed by Contracts between Governments and Private Parties

Under many systems of municipal law, distinctive principles apply to contracts between a government and private party. They include different rules as to apparent authority, impossibility of performance, assignment of contracts, or remedies for breach of contract. And of course sovereign immunity may preclude suit by the aggrieved private party.[6] Problems of a more fundamental nature, however, arise. They stem from the fact that the government is not only a contracting party but also a lawmaker, through its legislative or executive branches. Thus it may enact rules of contract law while the concession agreement is in effect which govern such questions as interpretation, impossibility or remedies.

More generally, certain tensions inhere in such contracts. On the one hand, principles such as *pacta sunt servanda* and the general role of expectations and predictability in contract law argue for a stable legal framework throughout the life of the agreement. On the other hand, there remains an undeniable need for the governmental party to preserve sufficient flexibility to enact laws which it considers to be in the general interest, without incurring excessive liabilities. The government is not only a contracting party but also a sovereign acting in the public interest. Such considerations have led to the growth of special doctrines in many legal systems—for example, the French law of the *contrat administratif*.[7]

These issues become acute in the context of concession agreements. Addressing matters of prime economic and political importance, the concession agreement may constitute more significant planning for the development of a country than would most legislation. In addition to risks attaching to most private contracts—that the other party will be unable or unwilling to perform—the alien investor faces the risk that the government will enact legislation that impinges upon its rights or privileges under the concession contract. Tax or tariff legislation may displace contractual rates; new laws may admit other firms to a field in which the investor was promised a monopoly.

Such considerations are of course pertinent when the concession contract is subject to the national law of the governmental party.

6. For a review of such problems in the United States, see Developments in the Law, Remedies Against the United States and its Officials, 70 Harv.L.Rev. 827, 884–87 (1957).

7. See Waline, Droit Administratif 565–636 (9th ed. 1963).

They are also pertinent when, as in the Aramco arbitration, a tribunal engages in a comparative-law survey to determine general principles of law in developed legal systems that treat concession contracts. The difficult question posed is the degree to which international law has established or can establish standards or minimum protection for the investor which would insulate it against the risk that the governmental party will change the rules of the game.

Before turning to that question, we look briefly at some illustrative cases in the United States that suggest the difficulties in formulating an international standard. The opinions below consider the impact of subsequent legislation upon contracts entered into by a state or the federal government. Suits by private parties that involve state legislation have been based upon the Contract Clause (Art. I, Sec. 10: "No State shall . . . pass any . . . Law impairing the Obligation of Contracts . . . .") and the Due Process Clause of the Fourteenth Amendment.

Stone v. Mississippi [8]

This decision upheld a provision of the Mississippi constitution of 1869 and a subsequent act of 1870, prohibiting the legislature from authorizing any lotteries and prohibiting operation of any lotteries previously authorized. The constitution and act had the effect of terminating a charter granted by the Mississippi legislature in 1867 to a private company, authorizing it to operate a lottery for 25 years in consideration of a payment by the company to the state and a promise of further annual installments. The company relied upon the Contract Clause. The Supreme Court, in an opinion of CHIEF JUSTICE WAITE, stated in part:

> The question is therefore directly presented, whether, in view of these facts, the legislature of a State can, by the charter of a lottery company, defeat the will of the people, authoritatively expressed, in relation to the further continuance of such business in their midst. We think it cannot. No legislature can bargain away the public health or the public morals. The people themselves cannot do it, much less their servants. The supervision of both these subjects of governmental power is continuing in its nature, and they are to be dealt with as the special exigencies of the moment may require. . . .
>
> The contracts which the Constitution protects are those that relate to property rights, not governmental. It is not always easy to tell on which side of the line which separates governmental from property rights a particular case is to be put; but in respect to lotteries there can be no difficulty. They are not, in the legal acceptation of the term, *mala in se*, but, as we have just seen, may properly be made *mala prohibita*. . . . Any one, therefore, who accepts a lottery charter does so with the implied understanding that the people, in their sovereign capacity, and through their properly constituted agencies, may resume it at any time when the public good shall require, whether it be paid for or not. All

8. 101 U.S. 814, 25 L.Ed. 1079 (1879).

that one can get by such a charter is a suspension of certain governmental rights in his favor, subject to withdrawal at will. He has in legal effect nothing more than a license to enjoy the privilege on the terms named for the specified time, unless it be sooner abrogated by the sovereign power of the State. It is a permit, good as against existing laws, but subject to future legislative and constitutional control or withdrawal.

Contributors to the Pennsylvania Hospital v. Philadelphia [9]

Plaintiff built a hospital in Philadelphia in 1841. Fearing excessive disturbance and noise, it persuaded the state legislature to enact an 1854 law prohibiting the opening of any street through specified grounds near the hospital. That law was conditioned upon the hospital's making certain payments and upon certain other provisions, all of which were accepted and complied with by plaintiff. When the city took steps in 1913 to acquire land by eminent domain for opening a street through the specified grounds, plaintiff brought a suit to protect its right of property and alleged contract under the 1854 law. The state courts denied relief, and the Supreme Court affirmed. Its opinion, by CHIEF JUSTICE WHITE, stated: "There can be now . . . no room for challenging the general proposition that the States cannot by virtue of the contract clause be held to have divested themselves by contract of the right to exert their governmental authority in matters which from their very nature so concern that authority that to restrain its exercise by contract would be a renunciation of power to legislate for the preservation of society or to secure the performance of essential governmental duties."

Horowitz v. United States [10]

Horowitz contracted to purchase silk from the Ordnance Department, with delivery assured at a specified date. The silk arrived several weeks late. It had not been shipped earlier because a government agency, the United States Railroad Administration, had placed a temporary embargo on shipments of silk by freight. Horowitz sought damages resulting from the alleged breach of contract. The Court of Claims sustained a demurrer, and the Supreme Court affirmed. Its opinion, delivered by JUSTICE SANFORD, noted that the Court of Claims had long held "that the United States when sued as a contractor cannot be held liable for an obstruction to the performance of the particular contract resulting from its public and general acts as a sovereign." The Court referred approvingly to an earlier statement in a decision of the Court of Claims to the effect that the dual character of the government—as contractor and as sovereign—could not be "fused" in a suit against it, so as to make the government liable as contractor for its acts as sovereign.[11]

9. 245 U.S. 20, 38 S.Ct. 35, 62 L.Ed. 124 (1917).

10. 267 U.S. 458, 45 S.Ct. 344, 69 L.Ed. 736 (1925).

11. The result in Horowitz may have been affected by the emergency character of the times. The silk was evidently war surplus and the railroads were still subject to wartime federal

El Paso v. Simmons [12]

Texas statutes in 1910 authorized the Land Board to sell public land allocated to the School Fund on long term contracts. In cases of default on payment of interest on the contract, the property was to be forfeited to the state and resold. However, the purchaser could reinstate his claim by paying the arrears. In 1941 the statute was amended to provide that the reinstatement right could be exercised only within five years of forfeiture. The purpose of the amendment was to restore confidence in the integrity of land titles and to enable the state to administer its property in an efficient and profitable manner. In 1910 Simmons' assignors executed installment contracts to purchase public land. Because of non-payment of interest the land was forfeited in 1947. An application by Simmons for reinstatement was denied on the ground that five years had elapsed, and in 1955, the state sold the land to the City of El Paso. Simmons brought suit in the federal court to determine title. On appeal, the Supreme Court held the 1941 law not to be a violation of the Contract Clause. Excerpts from the opinion for the Court of JUSTICE WHITE follow.

> . . . For it is not every modification of a contractual promise that impairs the obligation of contract under federal law, any more than it is every alteration of existing remedies that violates the Contract Clause. . . . Assuming the provision for reinstatement after default to be part of the State's obligation, we do not think its modification by a five-year statute of repose contravenes the Contract Clause.
>
> The decisions "put it beyond question that the prohibition is not an absolute one and is not to be read with literal exactness like a mathematical formula," as Chief Justice Hughes said in Home Building & Loan Assn. v. Blaisdell, 290 U.S. 398, 428, 54 S.Ct. 231, 236. The Blaisdell opinion, which amounted to a comprehensive restatement of the principles underlying the application of the Contract Clause, makes it quite clear that "[n]ot only is the constitutional provision qualified by the measure of control which the state retains over remedial processes, but the state also continues to possess authority to safeguard the vital interests of its people. It does not matter that legislation appropriate to that end 'has the result of modifying or abrogating contracts already in effect.' Stephenson v. Binford, 287 U.S. 251, 276, 53 S.Ct. 181, 189, 77 L.Ed. 288. Not only are existing laws read into contracts in order to fix obligations as between the parties, but the reservation of essential attributes of sovereign power is also read into contracts as a postulate of the legal order. . . . This principle of harmonizing the constitutional prohibition with the necessary residuum of state power has had progressive recognition in the decisions of this Court." 290 U.S., at 434–435, 54 S.Ct., at 238–239. Moreover, the "economic interests of the state may justify the

controls amounting to virtual temporary nationalization. See Dixon, Railroads and Government: Their Relations in the United States 1910–1921, Ch. IX (1922).

12. 379 U.S. 497, 85 S.Ct. 577, 13 L.Ed. 2d 446 (1965).

exercise of its continuing and dominant protective power notwithstanding interference with contracts." Id., at 437, 54 S. Ct., at 239. The State has the "sovereign right . . . to protect the . . . general welfare of the people . . . Once we are in this domain of the reserve power of a State we must respect the 'wide discretion on the part of the legislature in determining what is and what is not necessary.'" East New York Savings Bank v. Hahn, 326 U.S. 230, 232–233, 66 S.Ct. 69, 71. As Mr. Justice Johnson said in Ogden v. Saunders, "[i]t is the motive, the policy, the object, that must characterize the legislative act, to affect it with the imputation of violating the obligation of contracts." 12 Wheat. 213, 291, 6 L.Ed. 606.

Of course, the power of a State to modify or affect the obligation of contract is not without limit. "[W]hatever is reserved of state power must be consistent with the fair intent of the constitutional limitation of that power. The reserved power cannot be construed so as to destroy the limitation, nor is the limitation to be construed to destroy the reserved power in its essential aspects. They must be construed in harmony with each other. This principle precludes a construction which would permit the state to adopt as its policy the repudiation of debts or the destruction of contracts or the denial of means to enforce them." Blaisdell, supra, at 439, 54 S.Ct. at 240. But we think the objects of the Texas statute make abundantly clear that it impairs no protected right under the Contract Clause. . . .

MR. JUSTICE BLACK dissented. In his opinion, he replied to the Court's arguments as follows:

The Court in its due process "reasonableness" formula, true to the principle of that indefinable standard, weighs what it considers to be the advantages and disadvantages to Texas of enforcing the contract provision, against the advantages and disadvantages to the purchasers. The Court then concludes that in its judgment the scales tip on the side of Texas and therefore refuses to give full faith to the constitutional provision. On the side of the purchasers the Court finds nothing that weighs much: the promise to reinstate was not "central" or "primary"; the contracts as viewed today seem to have been very generous to the buyers; buyers were probably not substantially induced to enter into these contracts by the "defeasible right to reinstatement." The Court tries to downgrade the importance of the reinstatement obligation in the contract by volunteering the opinion that this obligation "was not the central undertaking of the seller [Texas] nor the primary consideration for the buyer's undertaking." Why the Court guesses this we are not told. My guess is different. This particular provision was bound, I think, to have been a great inducement to prospective purchasers of lots and blocks of land that the State of Texas was understandably eager to sell for many reasons. . . .

The Court observes that it believes "[t]he Constitution is 'intended to preserve practical and substantial rights, not to maintain theories.'" Of course I agree with that. But while deprivation of Simmons' right to have Texas carry out its obligation to permit him to reinstate his claim and purchase the land may seem no more than a "theory" to the Court, it very likely seems more than that to Texas, which by repudiating its contract has undoubtedly gained millions of dollars, and to purchasers who have concededly, and I think unconstitutionally, lost those millions. . . .

. . . At most the Court's reasons boil down to the fact that Texas' contracts, perhaps very wisely made a long time ago, turned out when land soared in value, and particularly after oil was discovered, to be costly to the State. . . . In plainer language, the State decided it had made a bad deal and wanted out. . . . No plethora of words about state school funds can conceal the fact that to get money easily without having to tax the whole public Texas took the easy way out and violated the Contract Clause of the Constitution as written and as applied up to now. . . .

Additional reading: Cattan, The Law of Oil Concessions in the Middle East and North Africa 31–112 (1967); McNair, The General Principles of Law Recognized by Civilized Nations, 33 Brit.Ybk.Int.L. 1 (1957); Mitchell, The Contracts of Public Authorities: A Comparative Study of the Law of the United Kingdom, United States and France (1954).

THE EL TRIUNFO CASE (UNITED STATES v. SALVADOR)

Arbitration under Protocol of 1901, 1902.
1902 For.Rel.U.S. 859.

[This was an arbitration under a *compromis* referring to three arbitrators the claims against the Republic of Salvador of a corporation organized in the United States and of several United States citizens who were together the principal stockholders in El Triunfo Company, Limited (the Company), a Salvador corporation. In 1894 Salvador awarded to the promoters of the Company an exclusive 25-year concession, later acquired by the Company, to develop steam navigation at the port of El Triunfo and carry on coastal trade with nearby ports. The concession granted certain import privileges and exemptions from taxation. The Company was obligated to construct facilities, certain of which were to belong to the Government, at its own expense, and to provide steamers. Shipping tariffs were to be approved by the Government. The concession was ratified in 1895 by the legislature.

The Company, which was created pursuant to the concession, developed and equipped the port. According to the majority of the arbitrators, it fulfilled in all substantial respects its obligations under the concession. From 1898 on it produced a profit. In 1898 some Salvadorean members of the Company's management, by wholly illegal proceedings, took over the Company and filed a petition in bankruptcy. Attempts to undo this proceeding were frustrated by a civil war and were ultimately made useless by an 1899 decree of the President of the Republic cancelling the Company's concession and issuing a new one to a group of citizens of Salvador.

The majority awarded $523,000 to the United States, including $402,000 for the value of the concession, $40,000 for the loss of specific company property and $80,000 for expenses. The $523,000 was calculated on the basis of 536/1000ths of the total losses, representing that portion of the Company's losses which had been borne by the eligible American shareholders. Portions of the award follow:]

Again, this is not a case of the despoliation of an American citizen by a private citizen of Salvador, on which, on appeal to the courts of Salvador, justice has been denied the American national, nor is it a case where the rules applying to that class of reclamations, so numerous in international controversies, have to do. This is a case where the parties are the American nationals and the Government of Salvador itself as a party to the contract; and in this case, in dealing with the other party to the contract, the Government of Salvador is charged with having violated its promises and agreements by destroying what it agreed to give, what it did give, and what it was solemnly bound to protect. . . .

In any case, by the rule of natural justice obtaining universally throughout the world wherever a legal system exists, the obligation of parties to a contract to appeal for judicial relief is reciprocal. If the Republic of Salvador, a party to the contract which involved the franchise to El Triunfo Company, had just grounds for complaint that under its organic law the grantees had, by misuser or nonuser of the franchise granted, brought upon themselves the penalty of forfeiture of their rights under it, then the course of that Government should have been to have itself appealed to the courts against the company and thereby, the due process of judicial proceedings, involving notice, full opportunity to be heard, consideration, and solemn judgment, have invoked and secured the remedy sought.

It is abhorrent to the sense of justice to say that one party to a contract, whether such party be a private individual, a monarch, or a government of any kind, may arbitrarily, without hearing and without impartial procedure of any sort, arrogate the right to condemn the other party to the contract, to pass judgment upon him and his acts, and to impose upon him the extreme penalty of forfeiture of all his rights under it, including his property and his investment of capital made on the faith of that contract.

Before the arbitrament of natural justice all parties to a contract, as to their reciprocal rights and their reciprocal remedies, are of equal dignity and are equally entitled to invoke for their redress and for their defense the hearing and the judgment of an impartial and disinterested tribunal.

It follows that the Salvador Commercial Company and the other nationals of the United States who were shareholders in El Triunfo Company, as hereinbefore named, are entitled to compensation for the result of the destruction of the concession and for the appropriation of such property as belonged to that company, excepting such property as was accumulated and constructed under the terms of the concession, to be vested in and owned by the Republic, to the extent of the interests of such American citizens in said concession and such property.

Under the terms of the protocol and by the accepted rules of international courts in such cases, nothing can be allowed as damages which has for its basis the probable future profits of the undertaking thus summarily brought to an end. Notwithstanding the evidence of the computable rate of increase of earnings and profits from the beginning until the end of the first half of 1898, and although the concession by its terms still had twenty-one years to run, yet we are precluded by the rule mentioned from assuming that the rate of profits would increase during the remainder of the term in the same ratio, or at all, or even that it would continue to earn at the rate actually shown by the evidence of Salvador itself, heretofore cited.

If on the tangible evidence for the assessment of the valuation of the franchise we give its value, in our view we can give nothing even for the cost of the buildings and structures erected by the capital of the company which, by the terms of the franchise, were to become the property of the Republic. . . .

On the clear and certain evidence before us, without involving ourselves in speculation, but computable on the uncontradicted and direct evidence presented, we find the value of the franchise, computed without reference to future or speculative profits or any speculative or imaginary basis whatever, to be $750,000. We think also that damages should be awarded for the value of the steamer Celia, less the balance of her purchase price, which remained unpaid at the closing of the business of the company. We find also that the value of the property of the company taken and left in Salvador, which was not the property of the Government, as before stated, but which was exclusively the property of the company, to be $45,000.

We are of opinion that the claimants before this tribunal are entitled to recover costs and reasonable attorneys' fees. . . .

We have not discussed the question of the right of the United States under international law to make reclamation for these shareholders in El Triunfo Company, a domestic corporation of Salvador, for the reason that the question of such right is fully settled by the conclusions reached in the frequently cited and well-understood Delagoa Bay Railway Arbitration.

NOTE ON THE INTERNATIONAL MINIMUM STANDARD

The Aramco Arbitration Agreement provided in Article IV(b) that "matters beyond the jurisdiction of Saudi Arabia" were to be decided by "the law deemed by the arbitration tribunal to be applicable." If a concessionaire does not benefit from such a clause referring the controversy to legal principles differing from those of the local law, its only recourse before an international tribunal is to argue that the government has violated an international minimum standard, or as the arbitrators in El Triunfo stated, "natural justice." Here international law, although not the "basic law" of the contract, operates as a secondary restraint on the primary application of the local law. Its function is roughly comparable to that of the Contract Clause or Due Process Clause of the United States Constitution; although a contract between an individual and a state is governed by state law, the federal court may review and reverse state action that amounts to an unconstitutional impairment of contract. International law's role in this setting is comparable to its role in the disputes considered in Part C, where international-law rules as to property protection established some limits upon the local law of eminent domain and expropriation.

There is even less agreement on the existence or content of an international minimum standard in this area than in expropriation. One source of difficulty is the variety of ways in which disputes over concession contracts may arise: (*1*) The government may assert—as did Argentina in a recent dispute over petroleum concessions [13]—

13. See Note, Argentina and the Hickenlooper Amendment, 54 Calif.L.Rev. 2078 (1966).

that the predecessor government which entered into the agreement lacked constitutional or statutory power to grant the concession. It may thus contend that the agreement was defective and that it is relieved of any obligation thereunder. (*2*) The government may argue that the alien has violated its obligations under the contract, and that the government is therefore entitled to vary or terminate its own obligations. Such disputes may present only issues of fact (has the investor acted or failed to act in a specified manner?) or also interpretative issues (what was the investor's obligation?). (*3*) The government may refuse to perform its obligations on the ground that it is incapable, for example, of affording certain services or paying certain sums to the investor in view of its economic circumstances. (*4*) The government may repudiate the contract without any bona fide claim that conduct of the alien justifies its measures. It may also expropriate the alien's assets. (*5*) The government may enact legislation or promulgate decrees which change only the provisions of the concession agreement or which are generally applicable to nationals and aliens but nonetheless affect the agreement.

Another source of difficulty is that questions of an international minimum standard may be intimately related to those of choice of law.[14] Consider a concession agreement which provides that it is to be governed by "international law." A tribunal resolving a dispute under that contract would not be bound by the government's local law. Thus it might consider and might indeed give effect to, but would not be bound by, defenses to contract claims that were available to the government under its law—perhaps a defense similar to that in the Horowitz case, p. 510, supra. Rather it *could* make a primary, direct reference to international law to decide the controversy, drawing by analogy upon treaty law or upon "general principles of law" that were relevant to concession agreements or a government's duty to aliens. Through such an approach, it might not be required to define a minimum international standard operating as a restraint upon a government's conduct towards a concessionaire. When concession agreements are governed by principles of law common to the contracting parties—as in Article 46 of the Iran-Consortium Agreement at p. 507, supra—it is again clear that local law as such is not applicable, and that the case *can* be decided without definition by the tribunal of a minimum standard. It is when local law *is* applicable that a tribunal may be *required* to attempt such a definition.

In earlier decades, questions of a minimum standard were bound up with the forceful techniques for intervention employed by the developed countries when contracts between their nationals and foreign governments had been repudiated. Indeed repudiation of the public

14. The forum for the litigation also is relevant to choice of law. As noted at p. 91, supra, a court or tribunal will normally invoke the choice-of-law principles of its local law in order to determine, for example, whether that substantive law or foreign law governs. When no such "local law" exists for an international tribunal,—as in the Aramco arbitration—the tribunal may resort to general principles among nations about choice of law. Such in fact was the path of the Aramco Tribunal.

debt led to the naval action of various European counties that helped to produce the conventions of 1902 and 1903 for the Venezuelan arbitrations, p. 360, supra. Such conduct was the inspiration for the so-called Drago Doctrine, which originated with Luis Drago, once Foreign Secretary of Argentina. That doctrine denied the right of intervention to make a government pay its public debts. It was partially recognized in the Second Hague Peace Conference of 1907 which, upon the initiative of the United States, adopted a Convention Respecting the Limitation of the Employment of Force for the Recovery of Contract Debts. Under Article I of the Convention, however, this restriction was not applicable when the debtor country refused arbitration or refused to comply with an award. Since that Convention, and in particular since the League of Nations and the United Nations, forcible intervention has lost justification as a technique for pressing contract claims.

In the field of expropriation, state practice had a certain relevance to attempts to define an international standard of protection. At least the rules espoused by a number of leading countries—for example, the United States' insistence upon a "prompt, adequate and effective" standard of compensation—were clear, even if the settlements emerging from negotiations between such countries and expropriating governments rarely satisfied those rules. For questions of breach of contract, however, state practice is sparser and less helpful. The practice of the United States, for example, has been ambivalent and difficult to define. Consider the following statement in the Reporter's Note to Section 212 of Restatement (Second), Foreign Relations Law of the United States:

> The Department of State has often stated that it will not espouse cases of breach of contract except when the breach is of a "tortious nature" or when there has been a "denial of justice." See 2 Hyde, International Law 988–994 (2d rev. ed. 1945). However, both these expressions have been rather flexibly interpreted, and the only types of claims that seem to be generally deemed unqualified for espousal are those where the breach does not constitute a violation of international law or is for default in payment of public debt. The general unwillingness of the Department to serve as "a collection agency" also appears to be a factor in minor commercial transactions. Contract claims are included in lump-sum settlements negotiated by the United States.
>
> Although the Department does not formally espouse debt claims as such, it has encouraged the organization and work of the Foreign Bondholders' Protective Council, a non-governmental entity that seeks to work out refinancing and other settlements of defaulted debt obligations in connection with claims settlements, development loans, and other obligations. Also, the Department itself seeks in claims settlement and other economic agreements to get commitments from defaulting states to resume service on defaulted debts.

Note the difficulty in giving specific content to such general and often question-begging terms as breach of a "tortious" nature or "denial of justice." One of the more ambitious efforts to draw some general principles from diplomatic practice and international arbitrations was undertaken by Dunn, in The Protection of Nationals (1932). He states (p. 167):

> If one examines these cases carefully, one finds that, so far as they can be said to contain any common ground at all, it is the feature of the use of governmental power to defeat the obligations of the contract. The types of cases set forth are as follows: (1) failure to provide adequate remedies in the local courts against breaches by the state; (2) arbitrary annullment by the contracting government without recourse to a judicial determination of the terms of the contract or of the legality of the government's act; and (3) various other "arbitrary" acts by the contracting government resulting in loss to the private contractor. In all of these cases the distinguishing feature is an interjection of governmental power to alter the situation envisaged in the contract. To the extent that one party to a contract is able to do this without the consent of the other party, the expectations created by the contractual relation are defeated. Hence it would seem that the test suggested has in fact played an important part, consciously or unconsciously, in controlling the course of decisions in past cases.

The failure to provide adequate remedies in local courts has been an important theme in many international arbitrations. Recall the El Triunfo arbitration; its holding could be viewed as resting upon a denial of justice in a procedural sense.[15] But even that relatively precise concept raises difficult questions. For example, the principle of sovereign immunity is common to many legal systems of the world. If a foreign government invokes that principle, and if its courts therefore refuse to assert jurisdiction in an action brought by an alien for breach of contract, is there sufficient basis for a diplomatic protest alleging a denial of justice? Whatever the play of the immunity doctrine with respect to disputes between a government and *its own* nationals, there is strong argument that a government is obliged to afford some independent forum, operating under fair procedures, in which the investor can press his claim. That argument might rest upon notions of minimum fairness in the conduct of transnational activities. Or it may rest upon the observation that sovereign immunity has been waived to a considerable degree for contract claims in most civil-law countries and countries of the Anglo-American world, at least with respect to actions for damages.[16] That historical trend could be viewed as establishing a minimum standard for aliens.

15. See the discussion of the various meanings of "denial of justice" at p. 374, supra.

16. The text at p. 638, infra, describes the gradual attrition of this doctrine with respect to claims against the federal and state governments in this country.

Another theme in many cases appears as clause (2) in Dunn's classification—"arbitrary annulment," repudiation of a contract without claim of legal justification.[17]

A third category of contract claims that would command a fair consensus among foreign offices and writers as being within a minimum standard involves discriminatory conduct of the host government. That is, repudiation of all purchase contracts with or debt obligations to aliens, or aliens of a particular nationality, more easily supports a diplomatic protest than would cases where a government alleges that it is unable to pay domestic as well as foreign creditors, or where general legislation affecting a concession contract has an adverse effect upon nationals also. Note however, the difficulty suggested by question (4) at p. 427, supra, in applying the concept of discrimination.

The most difficult issues in formulating an international minimum standard often are posed by legislation of a general character that is enacted after execution of a concession agreement and that varies the parties' rights and obligations. An agreement might give the concessionaire the right to sell wherever he chooses; a later law might require that a certain percentage of the production in the entire industry be reserved to the national market. The few decisions of international tribunals do not permit identification of any general principles. The cases in the United States, pp. 509–513, supra, are surely relevant to the formulation of a minimum standard, but also troublesome. Views among writers vary markedly. Some urge strict liability for breach of contract resulting from later legislation. Contrast the views expressed by F. A. Mann, a leading writer in this field, in State Contracts and State Responsibility, 54 Am.J.Int.L. 572, 590–91 (1960);

> It may be that a workable solution of the problem can be found only by generalizing an established principle of international law and at the same time taking a leaf out of the American Constitution and out of the books of authority to which it has given life: without prejudice to its liability for any other tort (such as denial of justice, discrimination, expropriation), the state shall be responsible for the injuries caused to an alien by the non-performance of its obligations stipulated in a contract with that alien if and insofar as such non-performance results from the application of the state's law enacted after the date of the contract; this shall not apply where the law so enacted is required for the protection of public safety, health, morality or welfare in general.

Even bilateral treaties between developed countries fail to address these questions directly. See, e. g., paragraphs (1) and (3) of Article IV of the Convention of Establishment between the United States and France,* and note the ambiguous content of terms such as "rights and interests," "property," or indeed "expropriation".

17. See e. g., the Shufeldt Claim (United States v. Guatemala), July 24, 1930, 2 U.N.R.I.A.A. 1079.

Note also paragraphs (3) and (8) of the 1962 Resolution of the General Assembly on Permanent Sovereignty over Natural Resources, and paragraph (5) of the 1966 Resolution, pp. 464 and 465, supra. By definition, this Resolution specifically addresses concession agreements, whereas much of the diplomatic practice has treated contracts of a more traditional and commercial character, such as debt obligations or purchase and sale contracts of the defaulting government.

Consider also the following provisions in Article 12 of the Draft Convention of Professors Sohn and Baxter, p. 373, supra:

> 1. The violation through an arbitrary action of the State of a contract or concession to which the central government of that State and an alien are parties is wrongful. In determining whether the action of the State is arbitrary, it is relevant to consider whether the action constitutes:
>
> (*a*) a clear and discriminatory departure from the proper law of the contract or concession as that law existed at the time of the alleged violation;
>
> (*b*) a clear and discriminatory departure from the law of the State which is a party to the contract or concession as that law existed at the time of the making of the contract or concession, if that law is the proper law of the contract or concession;
>
> (*c*) an unreasonable departure from the principles recognized by the principal legal systems of the world as applicable to governmental contracts or concessions of the same nature or category; or
>
> (*d*) a violation by the State of a treaty.
>
> 2. If the violation by the State of a contract or concession to which the central government of a State and an alien are parties also involves the taking of property, the provisions of Article 10 [see p. 491, supra] shall apply to such taking.

Additional reading: Jennings, State Contracts in International Law, 37 Brit.Ybk.Int.L. 156 (1961); Mann, Reflections on a Commercial Law of Nations, 33 Brit.Ybk.Int.L. 20 (1957); Mann, The Proper Law of Contracts Concluded by International Persons, 35 Brit.Ybk.Int.L. 34 (1959); Mann, State Contracts and State Responsibility, 54 Am.J.Int.L. 572 (1960); Schwebel, International Protection of Contractual Arrangements, 1959 Proc. Am.Soc.Int.L. 266; McNair, The General Principles of Law Recognized by Civilized Nations, 33 Brit.Ybk.Int.L. 1 (1957); Verdross, The Status of Foreign Private Interests Stemming from Economic Development Agreements with Arbitration Clauses, in Southwest Legal Foundation, Selected Readings on Protection by Law of Foreign Investments 117 (1964); Wetter and Schwebel, Some Little-known Cases on Concessions, 40 Brit.Ybk.Int.L. 183 (1964); Restatement (Second), Foreign Relations Law of the United States, §§ 193–195.

QUESTIONS

(1) Suppose that you were appointed arbitrator to resolve a dispute between Guatador and other parties to a Consortium Agreement similar to that with Iran appearing at p. 507, supra. Assume that the dispute originated in Guatadorian legislation of 1970 whcih imposed quotas on the amount of oil which could be extracted daily, in the interest of conservation of natural resources. Would you read Article 46 of the Agreement as incorporating treaty law, or as a reference to principles of contract law in different legal systems that were relevant to government-private party contracts? If the latter, what effect would you give to Paragraph B of Article 41? What effect would a comparable clause have had in the four American cases at pp. 509–513, supra?

(2) See Articles 3 and 8 of the 1962 Resolution of the General Assembly on Permanent Sovereignty over Natural Resources, p. 464, supra. (*a*) Do they suggest that a government is liable to an alien concessionaire if, by legislation of a general character that was enacted "in the public interest," it varied the terms of the concession contract? What interpretative problem would be posed if, for example, an export control law prohibited sales by any person or firm to a country in which the concessionaire and others had traditionally sold a sizeable percentage of their production? (*b*) Do the provisions of the Draft Convention at p. 520, supra, provide a statesman or arbitrator with a more helpful conceptual framework within which to analyze the problem?

PROBLEM

Guatador, a South American country receiving financial aid from the United States, is anxious to attract foreign capital and know-how to develop certain sectors of its economy. It has enacted an Investment Incentive Code similar to the Liberian Code.* The government planning agency has given high priority to development of a domestic automobile industry, which would lessen the pressure upon slender foreign exchange reserves by reducing car imports. After negotiations and proper authorizations from official agencies, the government entered in 1970 into a 20-year investment incentive contract (the Contract) with Chord Motor Co., a Delaware corporation and leading car manufacturer in the United States.

The Contract provided that it was to be governed by Guatadorian law. It obligated Chord to construct and manage a factory for manufacturing cars, and provided that the government "would not expropriate any property, real or personal, of Chord S.A. (the local subsidiary) except against payment of prompt, adequate and effective compensation." The Contract further stipulated that certain automobile parts would be purchased on the local market, and that certain materials for construction and other automobile parts could be imported from whatever source Chord S.A. chose, at specially low tariff rates. Steel was included in this second category, with a tariff rate of 5% ad valorem. Chord was obligated to sell a stated percentage of its production in the Guatador market, to the extent that there was demand, and was free to export the balance of its production to neighboring countries.

Chord made substantial sales and satisfactory profits during its first years of operation. Approximately 50% of its production was exported to neighboring countries, whose markets were open to Chord because of its competitive advantage over distant car manufacturers. In 1975, the planning agency determined that it was in the national interest to develop the local steel industry so that it could service the requirements of local construction and manufacturing. Substantial subsidies and tax exemptions were therefore granted to local companies to encourage them to expand production facilities, and several laws were enacted. One such law provided that the tariff on *all* steel would be raised to 50% ad valorem, except that the tariff would remain at its present level if it were officially determined that the local steel industry was incapable of producing sufficient steel to satisfy the demands of a local firm.

Chord is among the substantial buyers of steel in Guatador, as are a number of other alien-owned firms that now together absorb about 60% of the sales of the local steel industry. The new laws have a significant impact upon costs of production and prices, since the locally produced steel is approximately 30% more expensive than the imported steel (including transportation). Chord estimated that, if it complied with the new legislation, it would make fewer sales in the domestic market and would lose much of the foreign markets which it has developed. These factors would sharply reduce its profit margin.

Preliminary negotiations with the government indicated that no exceptions to the new law would be granted. Chord S.A. then commenced an action in the local courts, seeking a judgment that the law violated rights assured it under the Contract and the Guatadorian constitution. Proceedings were fairly conducted. The lower court ruled in favor of the government, and the highest appellate court affirmed, delivering its decision five months after the law was enacted. The appellate court cited some of its earlier decisions in favor of the Guatadorian Government against Guatadorian nationals. Those decisions stated that private rights must occasionally bow to the public good, and that general legislative measures enacted in the public welfare displace inconsistent provisions of any earlier contracts between the government and private parties.

Chord is continuing production. It now buys some locally produced steel, and expects that within a year or two most of its steel needs will be met by the local firms. It has asked the State Department what steps it is willing to take, and contends that the Guatadorian action is a patent violation of international law. As a member of the Office of the Legal Adviser, you have been requested to draft a memorandum indicating what steps can or should be taken, and whether an effective argument based upon international law can be made.

E. THE CALVO CLAUSE

The unhappy experiences of South American countries during the 19th century with diplomatic and military intervention on behalf of foreign investors led to the development of special South American attitudes towards international law, particularly towards that part treating the protection of aliens. We have referred to the Drago Doctrine, p. 517, supra. But the most conspicuous figure in this development was an Argentine jurist, Carlos Calvo (1824–1906). His name is attached to the Calvo Doctrine, which asserts that a foreigner doing business in a country is entitled only to nondiscriminatory treatment, and that by entering the country he impliedly consents to be treated as are its nationals. It is also attached to the Calvo Clause, designed to make that implication explicit. Such a clause was involved in the North American Dredging case set forth below. This case, the leading arbitral decision on the Calvo Clause, is another of the arbitrations under the United States-Mexican Claims Conventions of 1923.* (See p. 365, supra).

UNITED STATES OF AMERICA (NORTH AMERICAN DREDGING CO. OF TEXAS) v. UNITED MEXICAN STATES

United States-Mexican Claims Commission, 1926.
Opinions of Commissioners under the Convention Concluded September 8, 1923 between the United States and Mexico, 1926–27, at 21, 4 U.N.R.I.A.A. 26.

[This was a claim on behalf of an American corporation for about $233,000 for breach of a contract between it and the Mexican Government for dredging at a port. The contract included the following clause in Article 18:

> The contractor and all persons, who, as employees or in any other capacity, may be engaged in the execution of the work under this contract either directly or indirectly, shall be considered as Mexicans in all matters, within the Republic of Mexico, concerning the execution of such work and the fulfillment of this contract. They shall not claim, nor shall they have, with regard to the interests and the business connected with this contract, any other rights or means to enforce the same than those granted by the laws of the Republic to Mexicans, nor shall they enjoy any other rights than those established in favor of Mexicans. They are consequently deprived of any rights as aliens, and under no conditions shall the intervention of foreign diplomatic agents be permitted, in any matter related to this contract.

The Commission, in an opinion by VAN VOLLENHOVEN, considered this Calvo Clause:]

3. The Commission is fully sensible of the importance of any judicial decision either sustaining in whole or in part, or rejecting in whole or in part, or construing the so-called "Calvo clause" in contracts between nations and aliens. It appreciates the legitimate desire on the part of nations to deal with persons and property within their respective jurisdictions according to their own laws and to apply remedies provided by their own authorities and tribunals, which laws and remedies in no wise restrict or limit their international obligations, or restrict or limit or in any wise impinge upon the correlative rights of other nations protected under rules of international law. . . .

4. The Commission does not feel impressed by arguments either in favor of or in opposition to the Calvo clause, in so far as these arguments go to extremes. The Calvo clause is neither upheld by all outstanding international authorities and by the soundest among international awards nor is it universally rejected. The Calvo clause in a specific contract is neither a clause which must be sustained to its full length because of its contractual nature nor can it be discretionarily separated from the rest of the contract as if it were just an accidental postscript. The problem is not solved by saying yes or no; the affirmative answer exposing the rights of foreigners to undeniable dangers, the negative answer leaving to the nations involved no alternative except that of exclusion of foreigners from business. The present stage of international law imposes upon every international tribunal the solemn duty of seeking for a proper and adequate balance between the sovereign right of national jurisdiction, on the one hand, and the sovereign right of national protection of citizens on the other. No international tribunal should or may evade the

task of finding such limitations of both rights as will render them compatible within the general rules and principles of international law. . . .

5. At the very outset the Commission rejects as unsound a presentation of the problem according to which if article 18 of the present contract were upheld Mexico or any other nation might lawfully bind all foreigners by contract to relinquish all rights of protection by their governments. It is quite possible to recognize as valid some forms of waiving the right of foreign protection without thereby recognizing as valid and lawful every form of doing so. . . .

7. . . . As civilization has progressed individualism has increased; and so has the right of the individual citizen to decide upon the ties between himself and his native country. There was a time when governments and not individuals decided if a man was allowed to change his nationality or his residence . . . . To acknowledge that under the existing laws of progressive, enlightened civilization a person may voluntarily expatriate himself but that short of expatriation he may not by contract, in what he conceives to be his own interest, to any extent loosen the ties which bind him to his country is neither consistent with the facts of modern international intercourse nor with corresponding developments in the field of international law and does not tend to promote good will among nations.

8. The contested provision, in this case, is part of a contract and must be upheld unless it be repugnant to a recognized rule of international law. What must be established is not that the Calvo clause is universally accepted or universally recognized, but that there exists a generally accepted rule of international law condemning the Calvo clause and denying to an individual the right to relinquish to any extent, large or small, and under any circumstances or conditions, the protection of the government to which he owes allegiance. Only in case a provision of this or any similar tendency were established could a parallel be drawn between the illegality of the Calvo clause in the present contract and the illegality of a similar clause in the Arkansas contract declared void in 1922 by the Supreme Court of the United States (257 U.S. 529) because of its repugnance to American statute provisions. . . .

9. The commission does not hesitate to declare that there exists no international rule prohibiting the sovereign right of a nation to protect its citizens abroad from being subject to any limitation whatsoever under any circumstances. The right of protection has been limited by treaties between nations in provisions related to the Calvo clause. While it is true that Latin-American countries—which are important members of the family of nations and which have played for many years an important and honorable part in the development of international law—are parties to most of these treaties, still such countries as France, Germany, Great Britain, Sweden, Norway, and Belgium, and in one case at least even the United States of America . . . have been parties to treaties containing such provisions.

10. What Mexico has asked of the North American Dredging Company of Texas as a condition for awarding it the contract which it sought is, "If all of the means of enforcing your rights under this contract afforded by Mexican law, even against the Mexican Government itself, are wide open to you, as they are wide open to our own citizens, will you promise not to ignore them and not to call directly upon your own Government to intervene in your behalf in connection with any controversy, small or large, but seek redress under the laws of Mexico through the authorities and tribunals furnished by

Mexico for your protection?" and the claimant, by subscribing to this contract and seeking the benefits which were to accrue to him thereunder, has answered, "I promise."

11. Under the rules of international law may an alien lawfully make such a promise? The Commission holds that he may, but at the same time holds that he can not deprive the government of his nation of its undoubted right of applying international remedies to violations of international law committed to his damage. Such government frequently has a larger interest in maintaining the principles of international law than in recovering damage for one of its citizens in a particular case, and manifestly such citizen can not by contract tie in this respect the hands of his government. But while any attempt to so bind his government is void, the Commission has not found any generally recognized rule of positive international law which would give to his government the right to intervene to strike down a lawful contract, in the terms set forth in the preceding paragraph 10, entered into by its citizen. The obvious purpose of such a contract is to prevent abuses of the right to protection, not to destroy the right itself—abuses which are intolerable to any self-respecting nation and are prolific breeders of international friction. The purpose of such a contract is to draw a reasonable and practical line between Mexico's sovereign right of jurisdiction within its own territory, on the one hand, and the sovereign right of protection of the government of an alien whose person or property is within such territory, on the other hand. . . .

12. It being impossible to prove the illegality of the said provision, under the limitations indicated, by adducing generally recognized rules of positive international law, it apparently can only be contested by invoking its incongruity to the law of nature (natural rights) and its inconsistency with inalienable, indestructible, unprescriptible, uncurtailable rights of nations. The law of nature may have been helpful, some three centuries ago, to build up a new law of nations, and the conception of inalienable rights of men and nations may have exercised a salutary influence, some one hundred and fifty years ago, on the development of modern democracy on both sides of the ocean; but they have failed as a durable foundation of either municipal or international law . . . .

14. Reading [Article 18] as a whole, it is evident that its purpose was to bind the claimant to be governed by the laws of Mexico and to use the remedies existing under such laws. . . . It did not take from him his undoubted right to apply to his own Government for protection if his resort to the Mexican tribunals or other authorities available to him resulted in a denial or delay of justice as that term is used in international law. In such a case the claimant's complaint would be not that his contract was violated but that he had been denied justice. . . .

16. It is quite true that this construction of article 18 of the contract does not effect complete equality between the foreigner subscribing the contract on the one hand and Mexicans on the other hand. Apart from the fact that equality of legal status between citizens and foreigners is by no means a requisite of international law—in some respects the citizen has greater rights and larger duties, in other respects the foreigner has—article 18 only purposes equality between the foreigner and Mexicans with respect to the execution, fulfillment, and interpretation of this contract and such limited equality is properly obtained. . . .

[The Commission concluded that the claim should be dismissed.]

20. Under article 18 of the contract declared upon the present claimant is precluded from presenting to its Government any claim relative to the interpretation or fulfillment of this contract. If it had a claim for denial of justice, for delay of justice or gross injustice, or for any other violation of international law committed by Mexico to its damage, it might have presented such a claim to its Government, which in turn could have espoused it and presented it here. Although the claim as presented falls within the first clause of Article I of the Treaty,[18] describing claims coming within this Commission's jurisdiction, it is not a claim that may be rightfully presented by the claimant to its Government for espousal and hence is not cognizable here, pursuant to the latter part of paragraph 1 of the same Article I.

21. It is urged that the claim may be presented by claimant to its Government for espousal in view of the provision of Article V of the Treaty, to the effect "that no claim shall be disallowed or rejected by the Commission by the application of the general principle of international law that the legal remedies must be exhausted as a condition precedent to the validity or allowance of any claim." This provision is limited to the application of a general principle of international law to claims that may be presented to the Commission falling within the terms of Article I of the Treaty, and if under the terms of Article I the private claimant can not rightfully present its claim to its Government and the claim therefore can not become cognizable here, Article V does not apply to it, nor can it render the claim cognizable, nor does it entitle either Government to set aside an express valid contract between one of its citizens and the other Government. . . .

[Concurring opinion of the United States Commissioner, PARKER, omitted].

NOTE ON THE CALVO CLAUSE

(1) The North American Dredging case was followed in Mexican Union Ry., 5 U.N.R.I.A.A. 115, a case decided by the British-Mexican Claims Commission in 1930. The Commission held that a Calvo Clause barred a company's claim for damages from pillaging and destruction by troops during the revolution because it had not resorted to the Mexican courts or the Mexican national commission. The British-Mexican *compromis* contained a waiver of the exhaustion requirement similar to Article V of the 1923 Convention. In El Oro Mining & Ry. Co., 5 U.N.R.I.A.A. 191 (1931), the same commission refused to dismiss a similar claim where the British claimant and signatory to a Calvo Clause had spent nine years in vain attempts to procure redress before the Mexican National Commission. The Mexican Commissioner dissented on the ground that the agency had such a backlog that the time lapse was not excessive. He noted that the Mexican-American international commission had disposed of only 200 cases in six years.

The North American Dredging case was re-examined by the American-Mexican Claims Commission, the domestic commission es-

18. [Eds.] The cited provisions of the Convention of 1923 appear in the Documentary Supplement.

tablished by Congress in 1942 to adjudicate claims after a lump-sum settlement with Mexico.[19] That commission disagreed with the reasoning of the international commission with respect to the Calvo Clause and rendered an award in favor of the Dredging Company. Bishop, International Law 817, fn. 83 (3d ed. 1971). It found Article V of the 1923 Convention controlling, and relied upon the dissent in another decision of the international commission by Nielsen, who had not been a Commissioner when the Dredging case was decided. Nielsen had stated that the Dredging case "contains nothing of any consequence with which I agree." [20]

Since the 1930's there have been no significant international arbitrations concerning the Calvo Clause. It is still apparently used in certain Latin American countries. See the survey reported in Shea, The Calvo Clause 269–81 (1955). However, its importance has been diminished by several trends. Since 1930, the United States and other creditor countries have been more cautious about intervention in investment disputes and have renounced military forms of intervention in this field.[21] Negotiations between foreign investors and Latin American governments have also assumed a different character. Instead of the Calvo Clause, they treat such questions as investment guaranties, and tax and other incentives.

(2) The Calvo Clause appears not only in contracts but also in statutes or constitutions. Note Article 27 of the Mexican Constitution of 1917: [22]

> Legal capacity to acquire ownership of lands and waters of the nation shall be governed by the following provisions:
>
> (1) Only Mexicans by birth or naturalization and Mexican corporations have the right to acquire ownership of lands, waters, and their appurtenances, or to obtain concessions for working mines or for the utilization of waters or mineral fuel in the Republic of Mexico. The nation may grant the same right to aliens, provided they agree before the ministry of foreign relations to consider themselves as Mexicans in respect to such property, and bind themselves not to invoke the protection of their governments in matters relating thereto; under penalty, in case of non-compliance, of forfeiture to the nation of property so acquired.

(3) The "similar clause" referred to by the Commission at p. 524, supra, in its discussion of Terral v. Burke Construction Co., 257 U.S. 529, 42 S.Ct. 188, 66 L.Ed. 352 (1922), appeared in an Arkansas stat-

19. See p. 366, supra, for a description of the settlement and of the work of the domestic commission.

20. International Fisheries Co. Case, Opinions of Commissioners 1930–31, 207, 226, 4 U.N.R.I.A.A. 691, 704 (1931).

21. However, as recently as 1966 the State Department advised a prospective investor that it would not regard a Calvo clause as barring it from making representations on its behalf. See Graham, The Calvo Clause: Its Current Status as a Contractual Renunciation of Diplomatic Protection, 6 Texas Int.L.F. 289, 295 (1971).

22. Translation appearing in 2 Peaslee, Constitutions of Nations 668–69 (2d ed. 1956).

ute. It provided that the Arkansas secretary of state should revoke the authority of a foreign corporation to do business in the state if the corporation brought an action in, or removed an action to, a federal court. Burke Construction Co., a Missouri corporation qualified to do business in Arkansas, brought an action in the federal court in Arkansas. It sought an injunction preventing the secretary of state from withdrawing its license to do business. The opinion of the Supreme Court on appeal contained the following language:

> The principle established by the more recent decisions of this court is that a state may not, in imposing conditions upon the privilege of a foreign corporation's doing business in the state, exact from it a waiver of the exercise of its constitutional right to resort to the federal courts, or thereafter withdraw the privilege of doing business because of its exercise of such right, whether waived in advance or not. The principle does not depend for its application on the character of the business the corporation does, whether state or interstate, although that has been suggested as a distinction in some cases. It rests on the ground that the federal Constitution confers upon citizens of one state the right to resort to federal courts in another, that state action, whether legislative or executive, necessarily calculated to curtail the free exercise of the right thus secured is void because the sovereign power of a state in excluding foreign corporations, as in the exercise of all others of its sovereign powers, is subject to the limitations of the supreme fundamental law. . . . The appellant in proposing to comply with the statute in question and revoke the license was about to violate the constitutional right of the appellee. In enjoining him the District Court was right, and its decree is affirmed.

(4) Two recent codifications of international law have accepted the Calvo Clause, but with significant limitations.

(*a*) Section 202 of the Restatement (Second), Foreign Relations Law of the United States would validate the Calvo Clause if (1) the interests affected are economic, (2) the investor in fact receives national treatment and (3) there is a bona fide remedy in the national courts that satisfies the requirements of procedural justice. The comments to those provisions add other important qualifications.

(*b*) Article 22(5) of the Draft Convention of Professors Sohn and Baxter, p. 373, supra, allows waivers of claims if the injuries are to economic interests acquired under the contract and if the state has complied with the agreement. Article 22(6) would sustain Calvo Clauses exacted of aliens proposing to enter "high risk" activities to the extent that the claim involves neglect by the State to protect the claimant—for example, an alien entering a state during a period of civil disturbance.

(5) Recent versions of the Calvo Clause appear in two documents considered elsewhere in these materials:

(*a*) See Article 27 of the Convention on the Settlement of Investment Disputes*, considered at pp. 484, supra.

(*b*) Decision No. 24 of the Andean Commission, the so-called Decision Concerning Treatment of Foreign Capital, seeks to create a common regime vis-à-vis foreign capital and technology among the member countries of the Andean Pact.[23] Article 51 of that Decision provides that no agreement concerning foreign investment shall contain provisions "which withdraw possible . . . controversies from the national jurisdiction of the recipient country, or which permit subrogation by the governments of the shares or rights of their national investors." [24]

QUESTIONS

(1) Consider the comments of the Commission on Terral v. Burke Construction Co. What differences in the relationship between state and federal law, on the one hand, and national and international law, on the other, may make the Terral case inapposite on the international level?

(2) Suppose that the provisions of Article V had not appeared in the Mexican Claims Convention. Would the Calvo clause, as construed by the Commission, have had any effect at all (a) if the Dredging Company had exhausted local remedies without obtaining relief, or (b) had not sought to exhaust local remedies? Do you concur in the Commission's solution of the problem of reconciling the Clause and the Convention?

(3) Note Paragraph 14 of the decision of the Commission. Suppose that a company enters into an agreement with the Mexican government granting it a monopoly position in a particular industry. The agreement contains a Calvo clause similar to Article 18. Later Mexican legislation abrogates or repeals all contracts or laws granting monopolies in the industrial sector. The company challenges the legislation in the Mexican courts and loses. Under the Commission's decision, what effect would the clause have upon an international claim? What effect do you think it should have?

(4) How do you react to the attempts made in the two codifications to distinguish between cases in which the clause will and will not be given effect? To another distinction that has been suggested: that the Clause bars the foreigner from seeking intervention by his government but does not bar that government from intervening on its own initiative?

(5) Compare with the classic form of Calvo Clause the following provisions which might appear in contracts between an alien and a government.

(*a*) An alien establishes a manufacturing business in Guatador, which then taxes income at a rate of 30%. Three years later the government raises the tax rate to 90% for alien-owned enterprises. Does such action of itself raise an issue under international law? Is the situation different if the alien, at the time of establishing its plant, had contracted with the government to receive permission to enter and if the contract had stated that the government could raise the tax rate to 90%?

23. Licensing aspects of Decision No. 24 are considered at pp. 1216–1217, infra.

24. The translation of Decision No. 24 from which this excerpt is taken appears in 10 Int.Leg.Mat. 152 (1971).

(b) At the time of establishing its factory, the alien signed a contract with the government permitting it to buy the alien's plant at a stated price, at the option of the government, within a ten-year period. The value markedly rises. The government exercises its option at the option price, then one-tenth of the value of the plant.

(c) At the time of establishing the factory, the alien, as a condition to entrance, is required to sign a contract with the government permitting it to expropriate industrial property without compensation at any time. The government later does so.

(6) Should it matter whether the Calvo Clause appears in a contract with the alien, in the country's constitution or in a statute that applies to all aliens in all situations? Suppose, for example, that a statute provided: "All property in this country shall be subject to expropriation without compensation when the public interest so requires." If an alien thereafter invests property, should the statute be a defense to a claim for compensation?

Chapter V

THE INTERPENETRATION OF NATIONAL AND INTERNATIONAL LAW

Chapters I and II, while suggesting that transnational problems affected domestic rules and allocations of competence in distinctive ways, bypassed most situations in which domestic institutions directly considered international law. To be sure, that formal observation can be given too much significance. Attentiveness to interests and reactions of other countries and to constraints upon domestic policies deriving from requirements of international ordering figured in the decisions reached. Similar considerations inhere in situations where international-law norms may be seen as explicitly applicable to our domestic situations.

This chapter turns to such situations and thus to formal and explicit analysis of the interaction of national and international law. It stresses the perspective of the national decision-maker—predominantly that of the United States, with some references to other countries—from which norms of international law are viewed and developed. And it emphasizes the official conduct within a nation—executive determinations or other action, adjudication, law-making and so on—that forms part of an international legal process. These materials should communicate a sense of the fuller constitutive and constitutional structures of international legal ordering, of the complex relationship between national and international law, officials and institutions and of their influence upon each other. Sometimes they work at cross purposes and sometimes contribute harmoniously towards the development of an international legal system.

A. CUSTOMARY INTERNATIONAL LAW BEFORE NATIONAL COURTS

PAQUETE HABANA

Supreme Court of the United States, 1900.
175 U.S. 677, 20 S.Ct. 290, 44 L.Ed. 320.

MR. JUSTICE GRAY delivered the opinion of the court:

These are two appeals from decrees of the district court of the United States for the southern district of Florida condemning two fishing vessels and their cargoes as prize of war.

Each vessel was a fishing smack, running in and out of Havana, and regularly engaged in fishing on the coast of Cuba; sailed under the Spanish flag; was owned by a Spanish subject of Cuban birth, living in the city of Havana; was commanded by a subject of Spain also residing in Havana; and her master and crew had no interest in the vessel, but were entitled to shares, amounting in all to two thirds, of her catch, the other third belonging to her owner. Her cargo consisted of fresh fish, caught by her crew from the sea, put on board as they were caught, and kept and sold alive. Until stopped by the blockading squadron she had no knowledge of the existence of the war or of any blockade. She had no arms or ammunition on board, and made no attempt to run the blockade after she knew of its existence, nor any resistance at the time of the capture. . . .

Both the fishing vessels were brought by their captors into Key West. A libel for the condemnation of each vessel and her cargo as prize of war was there filed on April 27, 1898; a claim was interposed by her master on behalf of himself and the other members of the crew, and of her owner; evidence was taken, showing the facts above stated; and on May 30, 1898, a final decree of condemnation and sale was entered, "the court not being satisfied that as a matter of law, without any ordinance, treaty, or proclamation, fishing vessels of this class are exempt from seizure."

Each vessel was thereupon sold by auction; the Paquete Habana for the sum of $490; and the Lola for the sum of $800. There was no other evidence in the record of the value of either vessel or of her cargo. . . .

We are then brought to the consideration of the question whether, upon the facts appearing in these records, the fishing smacks were subject to capture by the armed vessels of the United States during the recent war with Spain.

By an ancient usage among civilized nations, beginning centuries ago, and gradually ripening into a rule of international law, coast fishing vessels, pursuing their vocation of catching and bringing in fresh fish, have been recognized as exempt, with their cargoes and crews, from capture as prize of war.

This doctrine, however, has been earnestly contested at the bar; and no complete collection of the instances illustrating it is to be found, so far as we are aware, in a single published work, although many are referred to and discussed by the writers on international law, notable in 2 Ortolan, Règles Internationales et Diplomatie de la Mer (4th ed.) lib. 3, chap. 2, pp. 51–56; in 4 Calvo, Droit International (5th ed.) §§ 2367–2373; in De Boeck, Propriété Privée Ennemie sous Pavillon Ennemi, §§ 191–196; and in Hall, International Law (4th ed.) § 148. It is therefore worth the while to trace the history of the rule, from the earliest accessible sources, through the increasing recognition of it with occasional setbacks, to what we may now justly consider as its final establishment in our own country and generally throughout the civilized world.

The earliest acts of any government on the subject, mentioned in the books, either emanated from, or were approved by, a King of England.

In 1403 and 1406 Henry IV. issued orders to his admirals and other officers, entitled "Concerning Safety for Fishermen—*De Securitate pro Piscatoribus.*" By an order of October 26, 1403, reciting that it was made pursuant to a treaty between himself and the King of France; and for the greater safety of the fishermen of either country, and so that they could be, and carry on their industry, the more safely on the sea, and deal with each other in peace; and that the French King had consented that English fishermen should be treated likewise,—it was ordained that French fishermen might, during the then pending season for the herring fishery, safely fish for herrings and all other fish, from the harbor of Gravelines and the island of Thanet to the mouth of the Seine and the harbor of Hautoune. . . .

The same custom would seem to have prevailed in France until towards the end of the seventeenth century. For example, in 1675, Louis XIV. and the States General of Holland by mutual agreement granted to Dutch and French fishermen the liberty, undisturbed by their vessels of war, of fishing along the coasts of France, Holland, and England. . . .

The doctrine which exempts coast fishermen, with their vessels and cargoes, from capture as prize of war, has been familiar to the United States from the time of the War of Independence. . . .

In the treaty of 1785 between the United States and Prussia, article 23 . . . provided that, if war should arise between the contracting parties, "all women and children, scholars of every faculty, cultivators of the earth, artisans, manufacturers, and fishermen, unarmed and inhabiting unfortified towns, villages, or places, and in general all others whose occupations are for the common subsistence and benefit of mankind, shall be allowed to continue their respective employments, and shall not be molested in their persons, nor shall their houses or goods be burnt or otherwise destroyed, nor their fields wasted by the armed force of the enemy, into whose power, by the events of war, they may happen to fall; but if anything is necessary to be taken from them for the use of such armed force, the same shall be paid for at a reasonable price." . . .

Since the United States became a nation, the only serious interruptions, so far as we are informed, of the general recognition of the exemption of coast fishing vessels from hostile capture, arose out of the mutual suspicions and recriminations of England and France during the wars of the French Revolution. . . .

On January 24, 1798, the English government by express order instructed the commanders of its ships to seize French and Dutch fishermen with their boats. . . . After the promulgation of that order, Lord Stowell (then Sir William Scott) in the High Court of Admiralty of England condemned small Dutch fishing vessels as prize of war. In one case the capture was in April, 1798, and the decree was made November 13, 1798. *The Young Jacob and Johanna,* 1 C.Rob. 20. . . .

On March 16, 1801, the Addington Ministry, having come into power in England, revoked the orders of its predecessors against the French fishermen; maintaining, however, that "the freedom of fishing was nowise founded upon an agreement, but upon a simple concession;" that "this concession would be always subordinate to the convenience of the moment," and that "it was never extended to the great fishery, or to commerce in oysters or in fish." And the freedom of the coast fisheries was again allowed on both sides. . .

Lord Stowell's judgment in *The Young Jacob and Johanna,* 1 C. Rob. 20, above cited, was much relied on by the counsel for the United States, and deserves careful consideration.

The vessel there condemned is described in the report as "a small Dutch fishing vessel taken April, 1798, on her return from the Dogger bank to Holland;" and Lord Stowell, in delivering judgment, said: "In former wars it has not been usual to make captures of these small fishing vessels; but this rule was a rule of comity only, and not of legal decision; it has prevailed from views of mutual accommodation between neighboring countries, and from tenderness to a poor and industrious order of people. In the present war there has, I presume, been sufficient reason for changing this mode of treatment; and as they are brought before me for my judgment they must be referred to the general principles of this court; they fall under the character and description of the last class of cases; that is, of ships constantly and exclusively employed in the enemy's trade." And he added: "it is a further satisfaction to me, in giving this judgment, to observe that the facts also bear strong marks of a false and fraudulent transaction."

Both the capture and the condemnation were within a year after the order of the English government of January 24, 1798, instructing the commanders of its ships to seize French and Dutch fishing vessels, and before any revocation of that order. Lord Stowell's judgment shows that his decision was based upon the order of 1798, as well as upon strong evidence of fraud. Nothing more was adjudged in the case.

But some expressions in his opinion have been given so much weight by English writers that it may be well to examine them particularly. The opinion begins by admitting the known custom in former wars not to capture such vessels; adding, however, "but this was a rule of comity only, and not of legal decision." Assuming the phrase "legal decision" to have been there used, in the sense in which courts are accustomed to use it, as equivalent to "judicial decision," it is true that so far as appears, there had been no such decision on the point in England. The word "comity" was apparently used by Lord Stowell as synonymous with courtesy or goodwill. But the period of a hundred years which has since elapsed is amply sufficient to have enabled what originally may have rested in custom or comity, courtesy or concession, to grow, by the general assent of civilized nations, into a settled rule of international law. . . .

The French prize tribunals, both before and after Lord Stowell's decision, took a wholly different view of the general question. . .

The English government [by orders in council of 1806 and 1810] unqualifiedly prohibited the molestation of fishing vessels employed in catching and bringing to market fresh fish. . . .

Wheaton, in his Digest of the Law of Maritime Captures and Prizes, published in 1815, wrote: "It has been usual in maritime wars to exempt from capture fishing boats and their cargoes, both from views of mutual accommodation between neighboring countries, and from tenderness to a poor and industrious order of people. This custom, so honorable to the humanity of civilized nations, has fallen into disuse; and it is remarkable that both France and England mutually reproach each other with that breach of good faith which has finally abolished it." Wheaton, Captures, chap. 2, § 18.

This statement clearly exhibits Wheaton's opinion that the custom had been a general one, as well as that it ought to remain so. His assumption that it had been abolished by the differences between France and England at the close of the last century was hardly justified by the state of things when he wrote, and has not since been borne out. . . .

In the war with Mexico, in 1846, the United States recognized the exemption of coast fishing boats from capture. . . .

In the treaty of peace between the United States and Mexico, in 1848, were inserted the very words of the earlier treaties with Prussia, already quoted, forbidding the hostile molestation or seizure in time of war of the persons, occupations, houses, or goods of fishermen. 9 Stat. at L. 939, 940. . . .

France in the Crimean war in 1854, and in her wars with Italy in 1859 and with Germany in 1870, by general orders, forbade her cruisers to trouble the coast fisheries, or to seize any vessel or boat engaged therein, unless naval or military operations should make it necessary. . . .

Since the English orders in council of 1806 and 1810 . . . in favor of fishing vessels employed in catching and bringing to market fresh fish, no instance has been found in which the exemption from capture of private coast fishing vessels honestly pursuing their peaceful industry has been denied by England or by any other nation. And the Empire of Japan (the last state admitted into the rank of civilized nations), by an ordinance promulgated at the beginning of its war with China in August, 1894, established prize courts, and ordained that "the following enemy's vessels are exempt from detention," including in the exemption "boats engaged in coast fisheries," as well as "ships engaged exclusively on a voyage of scientific discovery, philanthrophy, or religious mission." Takahashi, International Law, 11, 178.

International law is part of our law, and must be ascertained and administered by the courts of justice of appropriate jurisdiction as often as questions of right depending upon it are duly presented for their determination. For this purpose, where there is no treaty and no controlling executive or legislative act or judicial decision, resort must be had to the customs and usages of civilized nations, and, as evidence of these, to the works of jurists and commentators who by years of labor, research, and experience have made themselves peculiarly well acquainted with the subjects of which they treat. Such works are resorted to by judicial tribunals, not for the speculations of their authors concerning what the law ought to be, but for trustworthy evidence of what the law really is. Hilton v. Guyot, 159 U.S. 113, 163, 164, 214, 215, 40 L.Ed. 95, 108, 125, 126, 16 Sup.Ct.Rep. 139. . . .

Chancellor Kent says: "In the absence of higher and more authoritative sanctions, the ordinances of foreign states, the opinions of eminent statesmen, and the writings of distinguished jurists, are regarded as of great consideration on questions not settled by conventional law. In cases where the principal jurists agree, the presumption will be very great in favor of the solidity of their maxims; and no civilized nation that does not arrogantly set all ordinary law and justice at defiance will venture to disregard the uniform sense of the established writers on international law." 1 Kent, Com. 18.

It will be convenient, in the first place, to refer to some leading French treatises on international law, which deal with the question now before us, not as one of the law of France only, but as one determined by the general consent of civilized nations. . . . [Discussion of French treatises omitted.]

No international jurist of the present day has a wider or more deserved reputation than Calvo, who, though writing in French, is a citizen of the Argentine Republic, employed in its diplomatic service abroad. In the fifth edition of his great work on international law, published in 1896, he observes, in § 2366, that the international authority of decisions in particular cases by the prize courts of France, of England, and of the United States is lessened by the fact that the principles on which they are based are largely derived from the internal legislation of each country; and yet the peculiar character of maritime wars, with other considerations, gives to prize jurisprudence a force and importance reaching beyond the limits of the country in which it has prevailed. He therefore proposes here to group together a number of particular cases proper to serve as precedents for the solution of grave questions of maritime law in regard to the capture of private property as prize of war. Immediately, in § 2367, he goes on to say: "Notwithstanding the hardships to which maritime wars subject private property, notwithstanding the extent of the recognized rights of belligerents, there are generally exempted, from seizure and capture, fishing vessels." . . .

The modern German books on international law, cited by the counsel for the appellants, treat the custom by which the vessels and implements of coast fishermen are exempt from seizure and capture as well established by the practice of nations. Heffter, § 137; 2 Kalterborn, § 237, p. 480; Bluntschli, § 667; Perels, § 37, p. 217. . . .

Two recent English text-writers cited at the bar (influenced by what Lord Stowell said a century since) hesitate to recognize that the exemption of coast fishing vessels from capture has now become a settled rule of international law. Yet they both admit that there is little real difference in the views, or in the practice, of England and of other maritime nations; and that no civilized nation at the present day would molest coast fishing vessels so long as they were peaceably pursuing their calling and there was no danger that they or their crews might be of military use to the enemy. . . .

But there are writers of various maritime countries, not yet cited, too important to be passed by without notice. . . .

[The opinion quotes from writing from the Netherlands, Spain, Austria, Portugal and Italy.]

This review of the precedents and authorities on the subject appears to us abundantly to demonstrate that at the present day, by the general consent of the civilized nations of the world, and independently of any express treaty or other public act, it is an established rule of international law, founded on considerations of humanity to a poor and industrious order of men, and of the mutual convenience of belligerent states, that coast fishing vessels, with their implements and supplies, cargoes and crews, unarmed and honestly pursuing their peaceful calling of catching and bringing in fresh fish, are exempt from capture as prize of war. . . .

This rule of international law is one which prize courts administering the law of nations are bound to take judicial notice of, and to give effect to, in the absence of any treaty or other public act of their own government in relation to the matter. . . .

To this subject in more than one aspect are singularly applicable the words uttered by Mr. Justice Strong, speaking for this court: "Undoubtedly no single nation can change the law of the sea. The law is of universal obligation and no statute of one or two nations can create obligations for the world. Like all the laws of nations, it rests upon the common consent of civilized communities. It is of force, not because it was prescribed by any superior power, but because it has been generally accepted as a rule of conduct. Whatever may have been its origin, whether in the usages of navigation, or in the ordinances of maritime states, or in both, it has become the law of the sea only by the concurrent sanction of those nations who may be said to constitute the commercial world. . . . [Of these facts] we may take judicial notice. Foreign municipal laws must indeed be proved as facts, but it is not so with the law of nations." The

Scotia, 14 Wall. 170, 187, 188, sub nom. Sears v. The Scotia, 20 L. Ed. 822, 825, 826.

The position taken by the United States during the recent war with Spain was quite in accord with the rule of international law, now generally recognized by civilized nations, in regard to coast fishing vessels.

On April 21, 1898, the Secretary of the Navy gave instructions to Admiral Sampson, commanding the North Atlantic Squadron, to "immediately institute a blockade of the north coast of Cuba, extending from Cardenas on the east to Bahia Honda on the west." Bureau of Navigation Report of 1898, appx. 175. The blockade was immediately instituted accordingly. On April 22 the President issued a proclamation declaring that the United States had instituted and would maintain that blockade, "in pursuance of the laws of the United States, and the law of nations applicable to such cases." 30 Stat. at L. 1769. And by the act of Congress of April 25, 1898, chap. 189, it was declared that the war between the United States and Spain existed on that day, and had existed since and including April 21. 30 Stat. at L. 364.

On April 26, 1898, the President issued another proclamation which, after reciting the existence of the war as declared by Congress, contained this further recital: "It being desirable that such war should be conducted upon principles in harmony with the present views of nations and sanctioned by their recent practice." This recital was followed by specific declarations of certain rules for the conduct of the war by sea, making no mention of fishing vessels. 30 Stat. at L. 1770. But the proclamation clearly manifests the general policy of the government to conduct the war in accordance with the principles of international law sanctioned by the recent practice of nations. . . .

Upon the facts proved in either case, it is the duty of this court, sitting as the highest prize court of the United States, and administering the law of nations, to declare and adjudge that the capture was unlawful and without probable cause; and it is therefore, in each case, —

Ordered, that the decree of the District Court be reversed, and the proceeds of the sale of the vessel, together with the proceeds of any sale of her cargo, be restored to the claimant, with damages and costs.

MR. CHIEF JUSTICE FULLER, with whom concurred MR. JUSTICE HARLAN and MR. JUSTICE MCKENNA, dissenting:

The district court held these vessels and their cargoes liable because not "satisfied that as a matter of law, without any ordinance, treaty, or proclamation, fishing vessels of this class are exempt from seizure."

This court holds otherwise, not because such exemption is to be found in any treaty, legislation, proclamation, or instruction granting it, but on the ground that the vessels were exempt by reason of an established rule of international law applicable to them, which it is the duty of the court to enforce.

I am unable to conclude that there is any such establishd international rule, or that this court can properly revise action which must be treated as having been taken in the ordinary exercise of discretion in the conduct of war. . . .

This case involves the capture of enemy's property on the sea, and executive action, and if the position that the alleged rule *proprio vigore* limits the sovereign power in war be rejected, then I understand the contention to be that, by reason of the existence of the rule, the proclamation of April 26 must be read as if it contained the exemption in terms, or the exemption must be allowed because the capture of fishing vessels of this class was not specifically authorized.

The preamble to the proclamation stated, it is true, that it was desirable that the war "should be conducted upon principles in harmony with the present views of nations and sanctioned by their recent practice," but the reference was to the intention of the government "not to resort to privateering, but to adhere to the rules of the Declaration of Paris;" and the proclamation spoke for itself. The language of the preamble did not carry the exemption in terms, and the real question is whether it must be allowed because not affirmatively withheld, or, in other words, because such captures were not in terms directed. . . .

It is impossible to concede that the Admiral ratified these captures in disregard of established international law and the proclamation, or that the President, if he had been of opinion that there was any infraction of law or proclamation, would not have intervened prior to condemnation. . . .

In truth, the exemption of fishing craft is essentially an act of grace, and not a matter of right, and it is extended or denied as the exigency is believed to demand.

It is, said Sir William Scott, "a rule of comity only, and not of legal decision." . . .

It is difficult to conceive of a law of the sea of universal obligation to which Great Britain has not acceded. And I am not aware of adequate foundation for imputing to this country the adoption of any other than the English rule. . . .

It is needless to review the speculations and repetitions of the writers on international law. Ortolan, De Boeck, and others admit that the custom relied on as consecrating the immunity is not so general as to create an absolute international rule; Heffter, Calvo, and others are to the contrary. Their lucubrations may be persuasive, but not authoritative.

In my judgment, the rule is that exemption from the rigors of war is in the control of the Executive. He is bound by no immutable rule on the subject. It is for him to apply, or to modify, or to deny altogether such immunity as may have been usually extended. . .

COMMENT

Viewed from the perspective of two World Wars and other savagely fought hostilities, the Paquete Habana seems to impose surprisingly humane restrictions on the conduct of military operations. Its generous mood was reflected in the various Hague Conventions regulating land and naval warfare that were adopted during the ensuing decade. Specifically, note Article 3 of the Hague Convention of 1907 on Certain Restrictions with Regard to the Exercise of the Right to Capture in Naval War, 36 Stat. 2396, T.S. No. 544, proclaimed in 1910: "Vessels used exclusively for fishing along the coast . . . are exempt from capture, as well as their appliances, rigging, tackle, and cargo." Another antiquarian aspect of the Paquete Habana is that the naval personnel who captured the fishing vessels participated in the proceedings, for at that time captors were entitled to share in the proceeds of the sale of lawful prizes. An act of March 3, 1899, 30 Stat. 1007, ended this practice, and proceeds are now paid into the Treasury. 70A Stat. 475 (1956), 10 U.S.C.A. §§ 7651–81.

Some special characteristics of this opinion should be borne in mind, particularly its sea flavor. (*1*) Note the emphasis on the fact that the Supreme Court sat as a *prize court* administering the law of nations, and its references to the international character of the law maritime. That is, the Court was here resolving a controversy of a kind which national tribunals traditionally have considered as peculiarly international in flavor. Indeed, they were here almost assuming the role of an international tribunal, a consideration stressed in the excerpts from Calvo. (*2*) Although the opinion rests on customary rather than conventional law, note the continuing interaction of treaties and state practice in the growth of that law. (*3*) The Court looked to a relatively small number of countries for evidence of state practice, dominantly in Western Europe. It referred significantly to Japan as "the last state admitted into the rank of civilized nations." Even at the start of the 20th century, the world community creating international law was a small one.

QUESTIONS

(1) Does this Court approach the case in a manner different from an international tribunal that might today draw upon Article 38 of the Statute of the I.C.J.?

(2) Is the approach of the Court consistent with that of the P.C.I.J. in the Lotus Case, p. 253, supra? Suppose that the historical record showed that all maritime powers except the United States had always followed the rule exempting fishing vessels from capture.

(3) Suppose that a number of European powers had captured fishing vessels during the Napoleonic Wars, and that the executive branch of three leading maritime powers had indicated that those countries would not subscribe to any restrictive rule about capture. What would be the status of the "old" rule? Would there be a "new" rule, or "no" rule? Does the answer depend upon whether a national court approaches the question in the spirit of the International Court in Lotus or in the Fisheries Case, pp. 253 and 262, supra?

(4) As the dissent notes, the admiral in command ratified the captures. Was not this evidence that the United States chose to ignore any rule of exemption? If so, is the opinion sound? Recall that the Court stated that international law was part of our law "where there is no . . controlling executive . . . act." Consider in this connection the following cases.

THE OVER THE TOP

United States District Court, District of Connecticut, 1925.
5 F.2d 838.

[In October 1924, the "Over the Top," a schooner under British flag and registry which carried a cargo of whiskey, was boarded by a special agent of the United States Internal Revenue Department, at a point 19 miles distant from the United States shore. The crew of the vessel was unaware of his identity. The agent purchased whiskey, which was transferred to his sea sled, and returned to shore. The transaction occurred within one hour's running distance of the sea sled to shore. The United States Coast Guard seized the "Over the Top" the following day, and towed the ship and cargo into the Port of New London. The United States then brought libels against the schooner and its cargo, seeking decrees of forfeiture. It based its claim upon alleged violations of certain sections of the Tariff Act of 1922, particularly Section 586. That section provided that a vessel whose master allowed merchandise to be unladen within four leagues (12 miles) of the United States coast without official permission was subject to seizure and forfeiture, together with its cargo.

The United States also relied upon certain provisions of the American-British Treaty, effective May 22, 1924, to the effect that Great Britain would not object to the search of a British flag vessel when there was reasonable ground for suspicion that those on board were endeavoring to import alcoholic beverages into the United States in violation of its laws, or to the seizure of that vessel when there was reasonable cause to believe that the vessel was committing or attempting to commit "an offense against the laws of the United States" prohibiting the importation of alcoholic beverages. The Treaty provided that the seized vessel could be taken into a United States port for adjudication in accordance with United States laws. It further provided that the search and seizure should not be exercised at a greater distance from the United States coast than could be traversed in one hour. Excerpts from the opinion of JUDGE THOMAS appear below.]

The proposition is advanced that, regardless of our municipal legislation, the acts complained of could not constitute offenses against the United States when committed by foreign nationals, on foreign bottoms, on the high seas at a point beyond the territorial jurisdiction of the country. Well-known principles of international practice are invoked in support of this contention accompanied with the citation of authority. Upon careful consideration, however, I am led to conclude that a misconception exists here as to the status, in a federal forum, of so-called international law when that law encounters a municipal enactment.

If we assume for the present that the national legislation has, by its terms, made the acts complained of a crime against the United States even when committed on the high seas by foreign nationals upon a ship of foreign registry, then there is no discretion vested in the federal court, once it obtains jurisdiction, to decline enforcement. International practice is law only in so far as we adopt it, and like all common or statute law it bends to the will of the Congress. It is not the function of courts to annul legislation; it is their duty to interpret and by their judicial decrees to enforce it—and even when an act of Congress is declared invalid, it is only because the basic law is being enforced in that declaration. There is one ground only upon which a federal court may refuse to enforce an act of Congress and that is when the act is held to be unconstitutional. The act may contravene recognized principles of international comity, but that affords no more basis for judicial disregard of it than it does for executive disregard of it. These libels, therefore, cannot be attacked upon the ground that the territorial jurisdiction of the United States cannot be extended beyond the three-mile sea zone under international law.

If, however, the court has no option to refuse the enforcement of legislation in contravention of principles of international law, it does not follow that in construing the terms and provisions of a statute it may not assume that such principles were on the national conscience and that the congressional act did not deliberately intend to infringe them. In other words, unless it unmistakably appears that a congressional act was intended to be in disregard of a principle of international comity, the presumption is that it was intended to be in conformity with it. It is with such a principle in mind that we now proceed to an examination of the legislation upon which the government relies. . . .

[An analysis of other sections of the Tariff Act of 1922 is omitted.]

. . . Of utmost significance, therefore, is the language of section 586 of the act . . . . This enactment has been part of our legislation for over a hundred years. Here we have a distinct extension of our sea jurisdiction to a point 12 miles from the coast—an assertion of authority which may perhaps clash with international practice, but which, whether challenged or not, is unmistakable, and which, therefore, it is the business of our courts to enforce. Had the master and super cargo of Over the Top been guilty of unlading the liquor at a point within this 12-mile zone, it may be that we would have had no difficulty in sustaining the libels. . . .

My conclusion, then, is that as no statute embracing the subject-matter of sections 447, 448, 450, 453, 585, 586, 593, and 594 of the Tariff Act of 1922 has extended our territorial jurisdiction to a point on the high seas distant 19 miles from our coast, conduct which would have been in violation of these sections if performed within our territory cannot constitute an offense against the United States when performed at such a distance by foreign nationals on ships of foreign registry. If, for the purpose of our treasury, we can extend our sea jurisdiction to a point four leagues from the coast, I see no reason why we cannot extend it four leagues more. I merely observe that we have not done so yet.

I now come to the provisions of the American-British Treaty, which was obviously contracted for the purpose of preventing hovering ships from supplying intoxicating liquor to carriers running between the ships and the shore. . . .

It must be noted that the treaty does not define the acts constituting an offense against the laws of the United States prohibiting the importation of alcoholic beverages. These acts are defined in the statute. If reasonable grounds exist for believing that a vessel under British registry is in fact guilty of contravening the Prohibition Law (Comp.St.Ann.Supp.1923, § 10138¼ et seq.), then our government may seize it if it is within the specified area, and when seized its fate may then be determined in accordance with our laws. If it is not within the specified area, it may not even be seized. But if it is within the specified area, it does not follow that it is for that reason violating our laws.

Now the grant by one sovereign to another of the right to seize its nationals upon the high seas without process and by force majeure for crimes committed by those nationals against the offended sovereign, by no means declares that those acts when committed on the high seas constitute such crimes. If, before this treaty was contracted, the unlading of merchandise by a ship of British registry at a point more than four leagues removed from the coast of the United States did not constitute a crime against the United States (and there appears to be no contention that it did), then the treaty could not and did not make it a crime.

. . . It is not the function of treaties to enact the fiscal or criminal law of a nation. For this purpose no treaty is self-executing. Congress may be under a duty to enact that which has been agreed upon by treaty, but duty and its performance are two separate and distinct things. Nor is there any doubt that the treaty making power has its limitations. What these are has never been defined, perhaps never need be defined. Certain it is that no part of the criminal law of this country has ever been enacted by treaty.

Illustrations of congressional effectuation of treaties are plentiful. All treaties requiring payments of money have been followed by acts of Congress appropriating the amount. The treaties were the supreme law of the land, but they were ineffective to draw a dollar from the treasury. . . .

[References of the court to penal statutes enforcing treaties are omitted.]

The instances just cited indicate the practice of congressional action in order to effectuate the penal provisions of a treaty, and I have no doubt that such practice is necessary in order to accomplish the purposes of the treaties. It happens that the American-British Treaty here under consideration does not declare it a crime for a British national on a ship of British registry to sell liquor for purposes of importation into this country within one hour's running distance of our shore. Nor does the treaty forbid such an act. But even if such conduct had been prohibited by the terms of the treaty, no indictment could lie for transgressing that prohibition. If an indictment could not lie for violating the direct command of the Eighteenth Amendment to the Constitution until the Congress had defined the offense and proclaimed the penalty, then the fiat of a treaty would be inadequate for such a purpose. No distinction exists here between the necessary basis of an indictment and that of a libel for forfeiture. If the facts do not warrant an indictment, they do not warrant a penalty. . . .

Whether therefore the Senate and the Executive may constitutionally enact criminal legislation by the device of a mere treaty is a question which fortunately we need not discuss. It is sufficient to conclude that the American-British Treaty did not in fact enact new criminal legislation. . . .

The considerations as above expressed therefore impel the conclusion that there is no legal basis for these libels, and it follows that they must be and the same are dismissed. . . .

COMMENT

Compare Tag v. Rogers, 267 F.2d 664 (D.C.Cir. 1959). Pursuant to the Trading with the Enemy Act, p. 42, supra, orders were issued in 1943 and 1949 which vested in the Attorney General property in the United States of Tag, a German national and resident. In 1958, Tag instituted suit in the United States District Court to recover the property. He challenged provisions of the Act under which the vesting orders were issued, claiming that they were null and void because in conflict with international law and with a Treaty of 1923 between the United States and Germany. The District Court dismissed the complaint, and the Court of Appeals affirmed. The portion of its opinion considering Tag's claim under customary international law stated in part:

> The Act as passed in 1917 authorized the President, in time of war, to seize and confiscate enemy property found within the territories of the United States. . . . It did not provide for the reimbursement of enemy owners for their property when thus confiscated. It made no distinction between property acquired before or after the beginning of the war.
>
> Appellant contends, however, that there is now a practice amounting to an authoritative declaration of international law forbidding the seizure or confiscation of the property of enemy nationals during time of war, at least in the case of property acquired by the enemy national before the war and in reliance upon international agreements between the nations concerned. Appellant further contends that any seizure or confiscation of the property of an enemy national made by the United States contrary to the above declaration of international law is as null and void as though it were made in violation of the Constitution of the United States.
>
> Whatever force appellant's argument might have in a situation where there is no applicable treaty, statute, or constitutional provision, it has long been settled in the United States that the federal courts are bound to recognize any one of these three sources of law as superior to canons of international law. . . . There is no power in this Court to declare null and void a statute adopted by Congress or a declaration included in a treaty merely on the ground that such provision violates a principle of international law.

The preceding cases indicate that United States courts may draw upon principles of customary international law to fashion a rule, or to aid in the construction of a domestic rule, that may decide the controversy before them. Extensive scholarly writing has examined the theories under which domestic courts are considered competent to "apply" international law. Those theories differ among legal systems. Is the international principle or rule "transformed" into a domestic rule; is the entire body of international law "adopted" by or "incorporated" into a national legal system; is there piecemeal "acceptance" of a particular rule of international law insofar as it is consistent with general domestic principles and does not contradict applicable domestic rules? The following excerpts describe some approaches to answering these questions.

McDOUGAL, THE IMPACT OF INTERNATIONAL LAW UPON NATIONAL LAW: A POLICY-ORIENTED PERSPECTIVE

4 S.Dak.L.Rev. 25, 27–31 (1959).

. . . Scholarly opinion for several decades has ranged from the view, at one extreme, that international law is not law at all but mere rules of international morality, through varying versions of dualism or pluralism, to a monistic conception, at the other extreme, that international law dictates the content of national law. Brief and impressionistic illustration of some of the more influential of these views may serve to suggest the need for a very different mode of clarification. . . .

The dualist or pluralist theories, still perhaps the most popular of all theories, while not explicitly denying that international law is law and commonly conceding a wide scope to inclusive decision, exhibit as their most distinctive characteristic, an attempt to rigidify the fluid processes of world power interactions into two absolutely distinct and separate systems or public orders, the one of international law and the other of national law. Each system is, thus, alleged to have its own distinguishable subjects, distinguishable structures and processes of authority, and distinguishable substantive content. The subjects of international law are said to be states only (with occasional reluctant, contingent admission of international governmental organizations), while those of national law embrace individuals and the whole host of private associations. The sources of international law are found only in the customary behavior of states and in agreements between them, while the sources of national law are located in the state's structure of centralized and specialized institutions. The substantive content of international law is said to be rules regulating relations between states, while that of national law is that of rules regulating the interrelations of individuals and private associations. Concise expression of this point of view is offered by the late, most authoritative Professor Lassa Oppenheim:

> Neither can International Law *per se* create or invalidate Municipal Law, nor can Municipal Law *per se* create or invalidate International Law. International Law and Municipal Law are in fact two totally and essentially different bodies of law which have nothing in common except that they are both branches—but separate branches—of the tree of law. Of course, it is possible for the Municipal Law of an individual State by custom or by statute to adopt rules of International Law as part of the law of the land, and then the respective rules of International Law become *ipso facto* rules of Municipal Law.[1]

With its allegedly clear distinction between international law and national law achieved, the next task of any particular dualist or pluralist theory is of course to re-establish some link or connection between the systems, in order both to account for the past effectiveness of international law and to ensure some measure of future effectiveness. The books abound with elaborate theories of "coordination," "auto-limitation," "subordination," "adoption," "incorpora-

1. Introduction to Picciotto, Relation of International Law to the Law of England and the United States 10 (1915).

tion," "transformation," and so on, and in derivational exercises designed to demonstrate some mysterious "basis of obligation" in "natural law" or in the "common will" or "common consent" of states. None of these exercises has been widely persuasive, and there is a certain accuracy in the observation of one commentator that "the whole dualistic position" in measure denies "the juridical nature of international law by treating it as a kind of morality governing the relations between states and grounded only in their consent." [Citation omitted.]

The monist theories, in sharp contrast with the dualist or pluralist, find in the world arena a unitary legal system or public order, with international and national law having comparable, equivalent, or identical subjects, sources, and substantive contents. Though differing as to their reasons, whether "legal" or "scientific" or "political," monists commonly maintain the primacy or supremacy of international law in relation to national, and thus accord a very wide scope to inclusive decision. The distinguishing feature in the syntax of a monistic system is that it begins with a verbalization chosen as the "basic norm" (*Grundnorm*), such as *pacta sunt servanda* or the proposition that states ought to continue to behave in the way that they have customarily behaved, and by derivation from this basic norm establishes something called the "validity" of all lesser norms in a pyramid-like series of levels or stratas or hierarchies from top abstraction to lowest abstraction. The clearest, brief exposition of this theory, stating the supremacy of international law, is perhaps that of Professor Kunz: . . .

> [*A*]*ll* the activity of the single States is regulated by the supraordinated law of Nations. The so-called "domestic affairs" of the single States are not the affairs which are *not* regulated by international law, but the affairs which a State, *under international law*, has the exclusive competence to regulate as it pleases.[2]

. . . Underlying the differing formal definitions and syntactical derivations are differing perspectives about the institutions and values operative in the world arena and, especially, about the role of law in the more comprehensive social processes. The point has been most emphatically made by the master monist, Professor Kelsen:

> The choice between the primacy of international law and the primacy of national law is, in the last analysis, the choice between two basic norms. . . . It may be that our choice, though not determined by the science of law, is guided by ethical or political preferences. A person whose political attitude is that of nationalism and imperialism may be inclined to accept as a hypothesis the basic norm of his own national law. A person whose sympathy is for internationalism and pacifism may be inclined to accept as a hypothesis the basic norm of international law and thus proceed from the primacy of international law. From the point of view of the science of law, it is irrelevant which hypothesis one chooses. But from the point of view of politics, the choice may be important since it is tied up with the ideology of sovereignty.[3]

2. Kunz, "The 'Vienna School' and International Law," 11 N.Y.U.L.Q.Rev. 370, 399 (1934).

3. Kelsen, Principles of International Law 446–47 (1952).

Additional reading: Lauterpacht, Is International Law a Part of the Law of England, 25 Transactions of the Grotius Society 51 (1940); Sprout, Theories as to the Applicability of International Law in the Federal Courts of the United States, 26 Am.J.Int.L. 280 (1932).

LOPES v. REEDEREI RICHARD SCHRODER

United States District Court, Eastern District of Pennsylvania, 1963.
225 F.Supp. 292.

VAN DUSEN, DISTRICT JUDGE. . . . Plaintiff, an alien employed as a longshoreman and domiciled in Pennsylvania, has brought this civil action against the defendant shipowner, also an alien. Plaintiff bases jurisdiction on 28 U.S.C.A. § 1350 (hereinafter referred to as "§ 1350"), claiming that that section will support his cause of action grounded upon the unseaworthiness of defendant's vessel and defendant's negligence.

28 U.S.C.A. § 1350 provides: "The district courts shall have original jurisdiction of any civil action by an alien for a tort only, committed in violation of the law of nations or a treaty of the United States." [4]

Defendant's application to dismiss for lack of jurisdiction must be granted unless this case is transferred to the admiralty docket, since both of these questions must be answered in the negative because the words [italicized] below are inapplicable to this action:

(I) Is unseaworthiness a tort only, *committed in violation of the law of nations or a treaty of the United States;* and

(II) is the negligence alleged a tort only, *committed in violation of the law of nations or a treaty of the United States?*

I. *The Doctrine of Unseaworthiness*

The authorities submitted by counsel on whether unseaworthiness is a "tort only" are not conclusive, since the doctrine has many characteristics usually associated with contracts, even though, historically, the action was brought as a tort action. For the purpose of deciding the questions presented in this application, the court will proceed on the assumption that unseaworthiness is a "tort only," which leads to the next question, i. e., whether the "tort only" was "committed in violation of the law of nations or a treaty of the United States."

Justice Stewart traced the history of unseaworthiness in Mitchell v. Trawler Racer, Inc., 362 U.S. 539, 80 S.Ct. 926, 4 L.Ed.2d 941 (1960). After discussing the ancient rules of the sea relating to the rights of seafaring men, such as the Laws of Oleron and the Laws of Wisbuy, and their interpretation by the American courts, he continued at pp. 544–546 of 362 U.S., at pp. 930–931 of 80 S.Ct., 4 L.Ed.2d 941:

> "The earliest mention of unseaworthiness in American judicial opinions appears in cases in which mariners were

4. This language had its origin in the Judiciary Act of 1789 and an examination of [the] authorities concerning the language now in § 1350 and concerning the Judiciary Act of 1789 has not been helpful in deciding the questions now before the court. . . .

suing for their wages. They were required to prove the unseaworthiness of the vessel to excuse their desertion or misconduct which otherwise would result in a forfeiture of their right to wages. . . . The other route through which the concept of unseaworthiness found its way into the maritime law was via the rules covering marine insurance and the carriage of goods by sea. . . .

"Not until the late nineteenth century did there develop in American admiralty courts the doctrine that seamen had a right to recover for personal injuries beyond maintenance and cure. During that period it became generally accepted that a shipowner was liable to a mariner injured in the service of a ship as a consequence of the owner's failure to exercise due diligence. . . .

"This was the historical background behind Mr. Justice Brown's much quoted second proposition in The Osceola, 189 U.S. 158, 175 [23 S.Ct. 483, 487, 47 L.Ed. 760]: 'That the vessel and her owner are, both by English and American law, liable to an indemnity for injuries received by seamen in consequence of the unseaworthiness of the ship, or a failure to supply and keep in order the proper appliances appurtenant to the ship.' In support of this proposition the Court's opinion noted that '[i]t will be observed in these cases that a departure has been made from the Continental codes in allowing an indemnity beyond the expense of maintenance and cure in cases arising from unseaworthiness. This departure originated in England in the Merchants' Shipping Act of 1876 . . . and in this country, in a general consensus of opinion among the Circuit and District Courts, that an exception should be made from the general principle before obtaining, in favor of seamen suffering injury through the unseaworthiness of the vessel. We are not disposed to disturb so wholesome a doctrine by any contrary decision of our own.' "

In light of this history of the doctrine of unseaworthiness, it is apparent that this doctrine was judicially created by American judges who were disposed to adopt principles employed in our common law and apply them to accidents and occurrences transpiring in places where, traditionally, only admiralty remedies were available. These decisions, influenced, perhaps, by the Merchants' Shipping Act of 1876 and by changing American social values, gave the injured seaman much more than the traditional maintenance and cure given by our early case law or the ancient codes employed on the Continent and in Great Britain.

From the above history of the doctrine of unseaworthiness, the court concludes that (a) the awarding of damages for injuries occasioned by unseaworthiness of a vessel arose in American courts as a doctrine unique to this country, and (b) the doctrine does not come from the law of nations nor from any treaty to which the United States is a party.

II. The negligence alleged is not a tort only, *committed in violation of the law of nations*

What the law of nations is "may be ascertained by consulting the works of jurists, writing professedly on public laws; or by the general usage and practice of nations; or by judicial decisions recognising and enforcing that law." The court's examination of the phrase "the law of nations" must consider the words used as part of an "organic growth." See Romero v. International Term. Operating Co., 358 U.S. 354, 360, 79 S.Ct. 468, 3 L.Ed.2d 368 (1959).

The judicial decisions recognizing and enforcing "the law of nations" under § 1350 do not fully explain or define that phrase. At best, the cases arising under this section show only the connotation of "in violation of the law of nations." This phrase has been held to include acts such as the unlawful seizure of a vessel and its disposition as a prize, the seizure of neutral property upon the ship of a belligerent, unjustified seizure of an alien's property in a foreign country by a United States officer, failure to accord comity to ships of foreign countries, and concealment of a child's true nationality coupled with the wrongful inclusion of that child on another's passport. [Citations omitted.] The other cases arising under this section do not elucidate the meaning of this phrase.

Article I, Section 8, Clause 10, of the Constitution also contains the phrase "Law of Nations." Cases discussing this phrase have held the following to be "Offences against the Law of Nations": violations of the laws of war, suppression of slave trade, acts tending to incriminate, coerce, harass or bring into public disrepute any diplomatic or consular representative of a foreign government, and counterfeiting notes of foreign countries. [Citations omitted.] . . .

Kent defined the "Law of Nations" as "that code of public instruction which defines the rights and prescribes the duties of nations in their intercourse with each other," and continued that it is "founded on the principle that different nations ought to do each other as much good in peace and as little harm in war as possible without injury to their true interest." . . .

Story traced the development of the law of nations, stating that: "It first assumed the modest form of commercial usage; it was next promulgated under the more imposing authority of royal ordinances; and finally became by silent adoption a generally connected system founded in the natural convenience and asserted by the commercial nations of Europe." [Citation omitted.]

Nothing has been found to indicate that negligence, such as is alleged in this action, was in 1789 and succeeding years, or is, customarily treated as a violation of the law of nations.

After consideration of the above authorities, the conclusion of this court is that the phrase "in violation of the law of nations," for the purpose of deciding this issue, means, *inter alia* at least a violation by one or more individuals of those standards, rules or customs (a) affecting the relationship between states or between an individual and a foreign state, and (b) used by those states for their common good and/or in dealings *inter se.* Nothing has been found to indicate that the acts or omissions described as the negligence in this Complaint would be considered as a violation of the law of nations.

Since the requirements of 28 U.S.C.A. § 1350 have not been met and since the requisite diversity required by 28 U.S.C.A. § 1332 is not present, the Complaint will be dismissed, unless plaintiff submits within two weeks an order to transfer this case to the admiralty docket.

COMMENT

Note the court's closing observation that the complaint would be dismissed unless plaintiff transferred the case to the admiralty docket. One aspect of admiralty law is critical to an understanding of the

Lopes case—namely, the absence of right to trial by jury. One can infer that it was a desire for a jury that led counsel for Lopes to develop his ingenious theory in support of a non-admiralty federal question.

BERGMAN v. DE SIEYES

United States Court of Appeals, Second Circuit, 1948.
170 F.2d 360.

L. HAND, CHIEF JUDGE. This cause originated in the state court and was removed by the defendant for diversity of citizenship. The complaint was upon a cause of action for deceit, and the defendant was personally served with process in New York, while on his way to the Republic of Bolivia, to which he had been accredited as minister by the Republic of France. Bolivia, although it had not yet accepted him as minister, did so in due course after his arrival at La Paz; and it is to be understood that, in order to reach his post, the most convenient way was for him to pass through the City of New York, and that he had not been loitering there at the time he was served. The defendant pleaded as a defense to the action that, as an accredited diplomat he was exempt from personal service; and the plaintiff moved to strike out the defense. Judge Caffey denied the motion; thereupon the defendant moved to dismiss the suit, and it is from the grant of that motion that the appeal has been taken. . . . Moreover, since the defendant was served while the cause was in the state court, the law of New York determines its validity, and, although the courts of that state look to international law as a source of New York law, their interpretation of international law is controlling upon us, and we are to follow them so far as they have declared themselves. Whether an avowed refusal to accept a well-established doctrine of international law, or a plain misapprehension of it, would present a federal question we need not consider, for neither is present here.

The point has arisen three times in New York courts. . . .

[The court then considered the New York cases, which were not consistent and left open the question whether the immunity of a diplomat in transit implied only immunity from arrest and detention or implied also immunity from service of process in a civil suit. After stating that "it must be owned that the result is not clear" under the New York decisions, the court considered "The Research in International Law," published in 1932, of the Harvard Law School, and the discussions at and results of the Sixth International Conference of American States in Havana in 1928. The court then stated:]

Even so, in the end on authority the matter is not free from doubt; and for that reason we feel free to consider it as res integra, assuming for that purpose that diplomats in situ do have immunity from service of process, though unaccompanied by arrest and limiting ourselves to whether there are tenable grounds for distinguishing the case of diplomats in transitu. . . .

[The court noted the arguments in favor of and against the immunity, and concluded:]

. . . Thus, whatever there may be said, in line with the suggestions of the Havana Conference, for allowing civil actions to be brought against diplomats in all cases, it would appear, both from the point of view of the citizens of the third state, and from that of interference with the diplomat's performance of his duties, that there are better reasons for favoring the immunity of a diplomat in transitu. . . .

In conclusion, therefore, we are disposed to believe that the courts of New York would today hold that a diplomat in transitu would be entitled to the same immunity as a diplomat in situ. It is scarcely necessary to add that that immunity would be altogether frustrated, in the case of all diplomats seeking their posts for the first time, if it were limited to those already accepted by the sovereign to whom they are accredited. If such a limitation should be thought to exist in § 252, Title 22, U.S.Code, it is not relevant to the situation at bar.

Judgment affirmed.

COMMENT

There is extensive federal legislation in the general area of the Bergman case. See 28 U.S.C.A. §§ 1251(a)(2) and 1351.* Consider also 1 Stat. 117 (1790), as amended, 22 U.S.C.A. § 252, which provides that whenever any process is sued out or prosecuted by any person in any court in the United States whereby "any ambassador or public minister" of any foreign state, "authorized and received as such by the President," is arrested or imprisoned, such process "shall be deemed void."

In 1965, the United States ratified the Convention on Diplomatic Relations, prepared at the United Nations Conference on Diplomatic Intercourse and Immunities at Vienna in 1961. The text of the Convention, 500 U.N.T.S. 95, appears at 55 Am.J.Int.L. 1064 (1961). Article 40(1) states that, "[i]f a diplomatic agent passes through . . . a third state . . . while proceeding to take up or to return to his post, or when returning to his own country, the third state shall accord him inviolability and such other immunities as may be required to ensure his transit or return." The Convention uses the term "immunity" in granting resident diplomatic agents exemption from criminal, administrative and civil jurisdiction (Art. 31), and the term "inviolable" in speaking of their freedom from arrest or detention (Art. 29).

NOTE ON THE ROLE OF CUSTOMARY INTERNATIONAL LAW IN THE UNITED STATES

When the Constitution was drafted, passages in Blackstone's Commentaries and in opinions of Lord Mansfield to the effect that the law of nations was part of the law of England (of the common law) were well known in this country. Writers and courts of the 18th century held a larger concept of international law than their successors. They did not distinguish as sharply a law of nations, regulating relations between states, from a common or universal law, a *jus gentium,* interpreted by courts in all civilized nations to have much the same content and often regulating the conduct of individuals. Note, for example, that Art. I, Sec. 8 of the Constitution empowers the Congress to define and punish "Offenses against the Law of Nations." Decisions of courts in this country during the colonial period and under the Confederation, in both civil and criminal cases, evidenced the extent to which the law of nations was thought to be a part of the common or general law administered by the courts and to be applicable to individuals as well as countries. See Respublica v. DeLongchamps, 1 Dall. 111, 1 L.Ed. 59 (Pa.1784).

The law merchant and the law maritime were among the principal subjects of this universal law or *jus gentium*. In England, the law merchant was gradually absorbed into the common law. And English courts, sitting as common law and admiralty courts, applied the law maritime as a part of the law of nations. What traces there were of an international flavor to the law merchant, to "general commercial law," faded more rapidly in this country. Such commercial law became partly state and partly federal law, later principally state law.[5]

A similar but slower and less inclusive process of "nationalizing" a field that had been thought of as a part of universal law or the law of nations developed with respect to the law maritime.[6] Its international flavor, however, remains significant today, despite the inroads of divergent national legislation and of decisional law in several countries, particularly in fields such as maritime torts. The pressure for some degree of international consensus over maritime matters remains great, and now is felt more through the treaty-making process than through the judicial process. A prominent contemporary example is the Geneva Conventions on the Law of the Sea, p. 271, supra.

In view of the lesser relevance today of customary international law to decisions of national courts, in what kinds of cases does that law remain pertinent in the United States? One could note the following possibilities:

> **(1)** In some situations, a norm of international law may be dispositive of a controversy before a domestic court. For example, principles of the law of state responsibility may decide disputes over expropriations before national tribunals. International-law principles may be relevant to various treaty problems, such as the effect of war upon a prior treaty. Questions of immunity of a diplomat (compare the Bergman case) or of sovereign immunity may also be resolved or affected by principles of international law.
>
> **(2)** Specific rules or principles may affect the interpretation of domestic legislation. Recall the observations of the

5. Swift v. Tyson, 41 U.S. (16 Pet.) 1, 10 L.Ed. 865 (1842); Erie R.R. Co. v. Tompkins, 304 U.S. 64, 58 S.Ct. 817, 82 L.Ed. 1188 (1938).

6. See Dickinson, The Law of Nations as Part of the National Law of the United States, 101 U.Pa.L.Rev. 26, 792 (1952); Erades and Gould, The Relation Between International Law and Municipal Law in the Netherlands and in the United States 232–52 (1961).

court in The Over the Top, p. 540, supra. Compare United States v. State of California, 381 U.S. 139, 85 S.Ct. 1401, 14 L.Ed.2d 296 (1965).

(3) Even when domestic courts do not draw upon a specific rule of international law, they may seek to identify a general international principle as an aid in determining the propriety of domestic legislation. Cases involving deportation or expatriation, the scope of the Executive's delegated or inherent powers in the field of foreign affairs, or the extraterritorial reach of criminal or economic legislation are apt examples.

(4) Even in entirely domestic litigation between states over land boundaries or rights to waters of interstate rivers, the Supreme Court has drawn analogies from general principles of international law.

The opinions in these cases reveal widely different conceptions of international law. In decisions such as Bergman, that law is perceived as a body of detailed rules regulating conduct. In other settings, courts invoke international law as expressive of principles or policies about international ordering and national power, about reciprocal tolerances among nations in a larger common interest, that may shed light on the immediate cases. The decisions in Part Four treating the extraterritorial reach of legislation will offer illustrations.

QUESTIONS

(1) Given the categories of cases to which the jurisdiction of the federal courts extends under Art. III, Sec. 2 of the Constitution, what arguments would you make in support of the constitutionality of 28 U.S.C.A. § 1350, at issue in the Lopes case? Are any clauses of Art. I, Sec. 8 relevant? What do your answers suggest about the concept of international law that prevailed at the time of the original enactment of Section 1350, and about the relationship between the "law of nations" and federal (common) law? [7]

(2) Can you think of realistic examples today of actions which might be based upon Section 1350?

(3) Do you agree with the statement of the court in Bergman that it should attempt to identify New York's view of the rules of international law? What cases in Chapters I and II would you cite to support an argument that the immunity should be determined solely by federal law, or by the federal court's view of international law?

7. These questions are examined in Note, Federal Common Law and Article III: A Jurisdictional Approach to Erie, 74 Yale L.J. 325 (1964).

B. INTERNATIONAL AGREEMENTS AND NATIONAL LAW

The materials in Part B treat the relationship between international agreements and a domestic legal system, only with respect to the United States. Nonetheless, the problems raised in this country find analogues in the legal systems of most other nations and consequently have a broader relevance. Part C will sketch comparable problems in a number of European countries.

When reading the following materials, bear in mind the Constitution's references to treaties in Art. I, Sec. 10; Art. II, Sec. 2; Art. III, Sec. 2; and Art. VI. The following remarks about the treaty-making process in the United States complement the observations about treaties, made from an international perspective, at pp. 281–307, supra.

We here speak of treaties in the constitutional sense as distinct from executive agreements, a distinction of little or no consequence internationally. The conclusion of a treaty binding upon the United States normally involves three stages. First, negotiation of the treaty is usually conducted by an agent of the Executive, although members of the Senate have from time to time been brought into the process at an early stage as observers and advisers. The San Francisco Conference of 1945 on the United Nations and the Nuclear Test Ban Treaty are recent examples of such participation. The United States issues a Full Power to the persons who are to sign the treaty on its behalf.

Second, the President submits the treaty to the Senate for the advice and consent required by Art. II, Sec. 2. Usually the Committee on Foreign Relations studies the treaty, which is then passed on by the Senate as a whole. If it fails to receive the required two-thirds vote of those present, no further action may be taken on it. If it receives that vote, the President may ratify the treaty, although he is not bound to do so. Note the following warning as to terminology. "Although the advice and consent of the Senate is frequently spoken of as 'ratification,' as a matter of fact the Senate does not *ratify* treaties but instead advises and consents to their ratification by the President." 5 Hackworth, International Law 48 (1943).

Finally, ratification takes place by an exchange of instruments or, in the case of multilateral agreements, by a deposit thereof with a designated depositary. The President then proclaims the treaty, making it a matter of public notice and often effective as of that time. The treaty may of course provide when it becomes effective internally or between the parties.

One problem of considerable complexity, the domestic aspect of reservations, should be briefly noted. Reservations, particularly in the case of multilateral treaties, may be formulated by the United States representative at the negotiating conference. But they may also originate in the Senate, which in this sense continues the process of negotiation. When before the Senate for its advice and consent, the treaty is subject to "amendment," namely the insertion of reservations which constitute a condition to the Senate's consent. By Senatorial practice, a motion to attach reservations requires only a majority vote to carry. Such reservations must be included by the President in his act of ratification of the treaty.[8]

A lawyer exploring a treaty problem must familiarize himself with special research tools and techniques for which experience with the national reporter system and domestic statutes will not be very helpful. First, he must ascertain whether any treaties that may affect his problem are in force. His normal starting point would be the State Department's annual pamphlet, Treaties in Force. For possible recent changes, he may check the CCH Congressional Index for the progress of a treaty through the Senate, as well as recent issues of the Department of State Bulletin. He may also consult the Department's Assistant Legal Adviser for Treaty Affairs.

Once the treaty is identified, the lawyer must find a reliable text. Treaties concluded through the end of 1949 (and executive agreements beginning in 47 Stat.) were authoritatively published in the Statutes at Large (Stat.). Subsequent treaties have been officially published, pursuant to 1 U.S.C.A. § 112a in annual volumes entitled United States Treaties and Other International Agreements (cited as U.S.T. & O.I.A. or U.S.T.).

The State Department also publishes separate "slip sheets" for the Treaties and Other International Acts Series (T.I.A.S.) that become available well before the U.S.T. & O.I.A. version. Before 1945 there were two separate series: the Treaty Series (T.S.) and Executive Agreements Series (E.A.S.). Most law libraries have bound their sets of these slip sheets. Agreements from 1776 to 1937 may be found in a four-volume Treaties, Conventions, International Acts, Protocols and Agreements between the United States of America and other Powers, printed as Senate documents but usually known as "Malloy" after the editor of the first two volumes. (Volumes 3 and 4 are sometimes referred to as "Redmond" and "Trenwith" respectively.) Another eight-volume set, Treaties and Other International Acts of the United States, contains treaties from 1776 to 1863. Although published as a series of State Department publications, it is usually known as "Miller."

For further information, see Hynning, Treaty Law for the Private Practitioner, 23 U.Chi.L.Rev. 36 (1955); and Bilder, The Office of the Legal Adviser, 56 Am.J.Int.L. 632, 658 n. 48 (1962).

8. There are difficult and elusive distinctions between "reservations" and "understandings" by the Senate, and difficult problems of the extent to which Senate reservations can become operative as domestic law. For a summary, see Restatement (Second), Foreign Relations Law of the United States §§ 133–137. See also Power Authority of New York v. FPC, p. 568, infra.

1. THE CONSTITUTIONAL STATUS OF THE TREATY

It is difficult to read the Supremacy Clause of the Constitution and escape the conclusion that a treaty supersedes inconsistent state law, whether the state law is prior or subsequent thereto. Nonetheless, the establishment of this proposition caused some difficulties in those years of our history when both federal supremacy and recognition of property rights of Englishmen were new and, to some, unpalatable principles. In Ware v. Hylton, 3 U.S. (3 Dall.) 199, 1 L.Ed. 568 (1796), the Supreme Court had to reverse a federal circuit court ruling that the Treaty of Peace of 1783 did not override the Virginia law providing that payment to a Virginia official of a debt owing to a British subject discharged that obligation. John Marshall conducted the litigation for the debtor; it is said that Thomas Jefferson had to pay a debt twice because of the ruling. In Fairfax's Devisee v. Hunter's Lessee, 11 U.S. (7 Cranch) 603, 3 L.Ed. 453 (1813), the Supreme Court reversed the Virginia Court of Appeals for not giving effect to the provisions of the Jay Treaty of 1794 confirming to British subjects the American lands they had held from the Crown, including those escheated by Virginia law. Resistance was such that a second appeal to the Supreme Court was necessary before Lord Fairfax's devisee in fact prevailed.

A more difficult problem arises when the relationship between a treaty and a federal statute is at issue. Note the precise wording of the Supremacy Clause, and consider the following case.

DIGGS v. SCHULTZ

United States Court of Appeals, District of Columbia, 1972.
470 F.2d 461, cert. denied 411 U.S. 931, 93 S.Ct. 1897, 36 L.Ed.2d 1390 (1972).

Before BAZELON, CHIEF JUDGE, WILBUR K. MILLER, SENIOR CIRCUIT JUDGE and MCGOWAN, CIRCUIT JUDGE.

MCGOWAN, CIRCUIT JUDGE:

This is an appeal from the dismissal by the District Court of a complaint seeking declaratory and injunctive relief in respect of the importation of metallurgical chromite from Southern Rhodesia. The gravamen of this action was an asserted conflict between (1) the official authorization of such importation by the United States, and (2) the treaty obligations of the United States under the United Nations Charter. Plaintiff-appellants sought summary judgment, as did defendant-appellees alternatively to a motion to dismiss for failure to state a claim upon which relief could be given.

The District Court's ruling for appellees was grounded primarily upon lack of standing, but it encompassed as well a concept of the nonjusticiability of the issues raised. Although we believe there was standing upon the part of at least some of the appellants to pursue their cause of action judicially, we think that cause is not one in respect of which relief can be granted. Accordingly, we affirm the judgment of dismissal.

I

In 1966 the Security Council of the United Nations, with the affirmative vote of the United States, adopted Resolution 232 directing that all member states impose an embargo on trade with Southern Rhodesia—a step which was reaffirmed and enlarged in 1968. In compliance with this resolution, the President of the United States issued Executive Orders 11322 and 11419, 22 U.S.C.A. § 287c, establishing criminal sanctions for violation of the embargo. In 1971, however, Congress adopted the so-called Byrd Amendment to the Strategic and Critical Materials Stock Piling Act, 50 U.S.C.A. § 98–98h, which provides in part:

> Sec. 10. Notwithstanding any other provision of law . . . the President may not prohibit or regulate the importation into the United States of any material determined to be strategic and critical pursuant to the provisions of this Act, if such material is the product of any foreign country or area not listed as a Communist-dominated country or area . . . for so long as the importation into the United States of material of that kind which is the product of such Communist-dominated countries or areas is not prohibited by any provision of law.

Since Southern Rhodesia is not a Communist-controlled country, and inasmuch as the United States imports from Communist countries substantial quantities of metallurgical chromite and other materials available from Rhodesia, the Byrd Amendment contemplated the resumption of trade by this country with Southern Rhodesia. By direction of the President, the Office of Foreign Assets Control issued to the corporate appellees in this case a General License authorizing the importation of various materials from Southern Rhodesia, and they began importation.

Alleging that the Byrd Amendment did not and could not authorize issuance of such a license contrary to this country's treaty obligations, appellants sought to enjoin further importation, to require official seizure, and to restrain use, of materials already imported under the General License, and to declare the General License null and void.

II

[Appellants included Black citizens of the United States, including Congressmen, who had been denied entry to Southern Rhodesia; Rhodesians unable to return to their homeland; and an author whose books had been banned in Rhodesia. The court, in concluding that appellants had standing to seek the relief requested, observed:]

Appellants, along with many other persons, have suffered, and continue to suffer, tangible injuries at the hands of Southern Rhodesia. In an attempt to terminate the policies giving rise to those wrongs, the United Nations, with the United States as an assenting member, established the embargo. The precise injury of which appellants complain in this law suit is allegedly illegal present action *by the United States* which tends to limit the effectiveness of the embargo and thereby to deprive appellants of its potential benefits. That quarrel is directly and immediately with this government, and not with Southern Rhodesia.

Appellees suggest that the prospects of significant relief by means of the embargo are so slight that this relationship of intended benefit is too tenuous to support standing. But this strikes us as tantamount to saying that because the performance of the United Nations is not always equal to its promise, the commitments of a member may be disregarded without having to respond in court to a charge of treaty violation. It may be that the particular economic sanctions invoked against Southern Rhodesia in this instance will fall short of their goal, and that appellants will ultimately reap no benefit from them. But, to persons situated as are appellants, United Nations action constitutes the only hope; and they are personally aggrieved and injured by the dereliction of any member state which weakens the capacity of the world organization to make its policies meaningful.

Of course it is true that appellants' plight stems initially from acts done by Southern Rhodesia, and that their primary quarrel is with it. But this does not foreclose the existence of a judicially cognizable dispute between appellants, on the one hand, and appellees, on the other, who are said to be acting in derogation of the solemn treaty obligation of the United States to adhere to the embargo for so long as it is in being.[9]

III

The District Court, in its comments to the effect that non-justiciability would necessitate dismissal of the complaint even if standing be found, reasoned as follows: It is settled constitutional doctrine that Congress may nullify, in whole or in part, a treaty commitment. Congress, by the Byrd Amendment in 1971, acted to abrogate one aspect of our treaty obligations under the U.N. Charter, that is to say, our continued participation in the economic sanctions taken against Southern Rhodesia. The considerations underlying that step by Congress present issues of political policy which courts do not inquire into. Thus, appellants' quarrel is with Congress, and it is a cause which can be pursued only at the polls and not in the courts.

In this court appellants do not seriously contest the first of these propositions, namely, the constitutional power of Congress to set treaty obligations at naught.[10] They seek, rather, to show that, in the Byrd Amendment, Congress did not really intend to compel the Executive to end United States observance of the Security Council's sanc-

9. The passage of the Byrd Amendment was the subject of widespread notice and comment within the United Nations, resulting in the reaffirmation by the Security Council on February 8, 1972 of the sanctions against Southern Rhodesia. The resolution to this end declared that any legislation passed by any member state "with a view to permitting, directly or indirectly, the importation from Southern Rhodesia of any commodity falling within the scope of the obligations imposed (by the 1968 resolution), including chrome ore, would undermine sanctions and would be contrary to the obligations of States."

10. Moser v. United States, 341 U.S. 41, 45, 71 S.Ct. 553, 95 L.Ed. 729 (1951); Clark v. Allen, 331 U.S. 503, 508–509, 67 S.Ct. 1431, 91 L.Ed. 1633 (1947); Pigeon River Improvement, Slide & Boom Co. v. Cox, 291 U.S. 138, 160, 54 S.Ct. 361, 78 L.Ed. 695 (1934); Edye v. Robertson, 112 U.S. 580, 597, 5 S.Ct. 247, 28 L.Ed. 798 (1884).

Although appellants concede that Congress has the power to override treaty obligations (Appellants' Br. at 23), they contend that our commitment to the U.N. has more force than an ordinary treaty. Appellants argue on the basis of their interpretation of the U.N. Charter that Congress could override Resolution 232 only by withdrawing from the U.N. entirely. There is, however, no evidence that this country's membership in that organization was intended to be on the all-or-nothing basis suggested by appellants.

tions, and that, therefore, it is the Executive which is, without the essential shield of Congressional dispensation, violating a treaty engagement of this country. Appellants point out in this regard that the Byrd Amendment does not in terms require importation from Southern Rhodesia, but leaves open two alternative courses of action. The statute says the President may not ban importation from Rhodesia of materials classified as critical and strategic unless importation from Communist countries is also prohibited. Instead of permitting resumption of trade with Rhodesia, the President, so it is said, could (1) have banned importation of these materials from Communist nations as well as from Rhodesia, or (2) have taken steps to have these materials declassified, thereby taking them in either case out of the scope of the Byrd Amendment.

Citing the canon of construction that a statute should, if possible, be construed in a manner consistent with treaty obligations, appellants argue that the Byrd Amendment, although discretionary on its face, should be construed to compel the President to take one or the other of these two steps as a means of escape from the necessity of breaching the U.N. Charter. But these alternatives raise questions of foreign policy and national defense as sensitive as those involved in the decision to honor or abrogate our treaty obligations. To attempt to decide whether the President chose properly among the three alternatives confronting him "would be, not to decide a judicial controversy, but to assume a position of authority over the governmental acts of another and coequal department, an authority which plainly we do not possess." Frothingham v. Mellon, 262 U.S. 447, 489, 43 S.Ct. 597, 601, 67 L.Ed. 1078 (1923).

We think that there can be no blinking the purpose and effect of the Byrd Amendment. It was to detach this country from the U.N. boycott of Southern Rhodesia in blatant disregard of our treaty undertakings. The legislative record shows that no member of Congress voting on the measure was under any doubt about what was involved then; and no amount of statutory interpretation now can make the Byrd Amendment other than what it was as presented to the Congress, namely, a measure which would make—and was intended to make—the United States a certain treaty violator. The so-called options given to the President are, in reality, not options at all. In any event, they are in neither case alternatives which are appropriately to be forced upon him by a court.

Under our constitutional scheme, Congress can denounce treaties if it sees fit to do so, and there is nothing the other branches of government can do about it. We consider that this is precisely what Congress has done in this case; and therefore the District Court was correct to the extent that it found the complaint to state no tenable claim in law.

Affirmed.

WILBUR K. MILLER, SENIOR CIRCUIT JUDGE, concurs in the result.

COMMENT

The immediate background to the Security Council Resolution was the declaration of independence in 1965 of a white minority regime in Southern Rhodesia from Great Britain. Since this government had made clear that the black majority would be excluded from political participation, the Security Council condemned the declaration and urged all states not to recognize this "illegal racist minority regime." The United States observed the embargo imposed by the Resolution until the Byrd Amendment in 1971. From both utilitarian and moral perspectives, this country's departure from the embargo had adverse international consequences. The Assistant Secretary of State for African Affairs observed in 1973: "In my four years as Assistant Secretary the exemption on Rhodesian Sanctions had been the most serious blow to the credibility of our African policy . . . The fact that we have in African eyes chosen to go counter to a mandatory Security Council resolution and for our own purposes weakened sanctions suggest to the Africans that we do not attach importance to the institutions and issues of significance to them." [11]

QUESTIONS

(1) How would you have developed the argument of the plaintiffs that the court should distinguish between bilateral or other multilateral treaties, as to which the supremacy of a later federal statute was clear, and the United Nations treaty?

(2) "The Court reaches broadly to find standing for the plaintiffs involved, and then is able to reach the merits. It appears to do so simply to have the opportunity to castigate the United States for its conduct, since it is clear that the doctrine of political questions requires the court to accept the congressional judgment as binding". Is this an adequate analysis of the problems in Diggs?

NOTE ON TREATIES, FEDERAL STATUTES, AND TREATY TERMINATION

In fn. 10, supra, the court cited Edye v. Robertson (The Head Money Cases), one of a group of nearly contemporaneous decisions towards the end of the 19th Century which asserted the supremacy of federal statutes over prior treaties. The Supreme Court there observed that the Constitution gave the treaty "no superiority over an act of congress," and that lacking any "superior sanctity," the treaty was "subject to such acts as congress may pass for its enforcement, modification, or repeal." The same principle appears in the cases on the Chinese Exclusion Act of 1892 (including Fong Yue ting v. United States, p. 23, supra) and in Whitney v. Robertson, 124 U.S. 190, 8 S.Ct. 456, 31 L.Ed. 386 (1888) (treaty between the United States and Santo Domingo providing for duty-free admission of sugar and a later statute imposing a duty).

Consider some of the arguments supporting a view contrary to the Supreme Court's, such as those which might be based on the following from The Federalist No. 64 by John Jay.

> They who make laws may, without doubt, amend or repeal them; and it will not be disputed that they who make treaties may alter or cancel them; but still let us not forget

11. Quoted in Polan, Irony in Chrome, The Byrd Amendment Two Years Later (Interim Report of the Special Rhodesian Project of the Carnegie Endowment for International Peace), at p. 14 (1973).

> that treaties are made, not by only one of the contracting parties, but by both; and consequently, that as the consent of both was essential to their formation at first, so must it ever afterwards be to alter or cancel them. The proposed Constitution, therefore, has not in the least extended the obligation of treaties. They are just as binding, and just as far beyond the lawful reach of legislative acts now, as they will be at any future period, or under any form of government.

Of course the enactment of a later statute does not dispose of the treaty from an international point of view. The discussion of treaties at pp. 286–289, supra, referred to certain situations in which a treaty could be terminated (other than in accordance with its terms) without violation of international law. These, however, are the exceptional cases, and several decisions of the P.C.I.J. have expressed the cardinal rule that provisions of municipal law cannot prevail over a treaty.[12]

The enactment of a subsequent inconsistent statute is one of several ways in which a treaty may cease to be "supreme law." Some of the grounds for termination that were noted at pp. 286–289, supra, may require determination by an executive authority that the treaty has ceased to be binding. The President has paramount authority to make that determination. If an agreement provides for termination after denunciation by either party, he can furnish the prescribed notice. If another party has violated the agreement in such a way as to terminate the obligations of the United States, the President would ordinarily make the determination to that effect. Of course, he may elect not to terminate, to take no action. Whatever course is followed, the situation involves political issues which a court will be reluctant to consider.[13] There is some evidence of an earlier understanding that the advice and consent of the Senate was necessary to the denunciation of an agreement which was a treaty in the constitutional sense, or at least to its termination or replacement by mutual consent of its parties.[14]

A recent, conspicuous example of the termination power involves the Warsaw Convention, 49 Stat. 3000 (1936), T.S. No. 876, 137 L.N. T.S. 11. This Convention, to which most airpowers are parties, was formulated in 1929 to regulate certain aspects of carriers' liabilities for injuries to passengers and baggage sustained during international flights. It established a limit, equivalent as late as the 1960's to

12. Greco-Bulgarian "Communities," P.C.I.J., Ser. B., No. 17, p. 32 (1930); Treatment of Polish Nationals in Danzig, P.C.I.J., Ser. A/B, No. 44, p. 24 (1932).

13. Thus Charlton v. Kelly, 229 U.S. 447, 33 S.Ct. 945, 57 L.Ed. 1274 (1913), held that a party resisting extradition under a treaty between the United States and Italy could not prevail on the argument that (1) Italy had violated the treaty by refusing to extradite Italian citizens to the United States and that (2) the United States' obligation thereunder had therefore terminated, at least where the Executive had indicated that it considered the Treaty to remain in effect.

14. See Lissitzyn, The Law of International Agreements in the Restatement, 41 N.Y.U.L.Rev. 96, 122–23 (1966); Restatement (Second), Foreign Relations Law of the United States § 163.

$8,300, on damages for personal injury claims, except in cases of wilful misconduct by the carrier. This limit, apparently acceptable everywhere in 1929 and probably still acceptable in many countries with lower standards of living, became increasingly intolerable in a country where the "adequate award" in other kinds of personal injury cases may run to hundreds of thousands of dollars. Following several cases involving Americans who were held to the Convention's limit despite serious injuries, there were Senatorial demands for denunciation.

After encountering opposition from other countries to a substantial increase in the liability limit, and refusing to accede to an earlier Protocol that only would have doubled the existing limit, the State Department served notice pursuant to the Convention on November 15, 1965 that it was denouncing the Convention as of May 15, 1966. However, six months later, on May 14, 1966, the Department withdrew the denunciation. It announced that it had obtained a commitment, in the form of a carriers' agreement known as the Montreal Interim Agreement, effective May 16, 1966, from American and foreign air carriers of passengers to and from the United States to accept a $75,000 limit for carrier liability for injuries sustained in international flights touching the United States. At the same time the Montreal Interim Agreement provided that principles of strict liability rather than negligence law would govern recovery in such situations. The Civil Aeronautics Board then issued an Order, directed to all such carriers, implementing the Interim Agreement. Note that in this exceptional situation, action by the Executive together with international air carriers led to significant revisions of treaty obligations affecting private rights, without official participation by the Senate or the Congress as a whole.[15]

The problems of federalism considered in Chapter II, at pp. 160–176, supra, bypassed questions of customary or conventional international law, while Bergman v. De Sieyes, p. 549, supra, involved only the former. The following case examines another aspect of foreign relations and federalism, in the setting of international agreements and state law-making prerogatives.

15. For discussions of these matters, see Lowenfeld and Mendelsohn, The United States and the Warsaw Convention, 80 Harv.L.Rev. 497 (1967); and Note, Presidential Amendment and Termination of Treaties: The Case of the Warsaw Convention, 34 U.Chi.L.Rev. 580 (1967). Under the Guatemala Protocol of 1971 to the Warsaw Convention, effective after the necessary number of ratifications are deposited, no-fault liability of international air carriers will displace negligence liability, and the liability limit will be $100,000, subject to annual increases. For a description, see Mankiewicz, Warsaw Convention: The 1971 Protocol of Guatemala City, 20 Am.J.Comp.L. 335 (1972).

MISSOURI v. HOLLAND

Supreme Court of the United States, 1920.
252 U.S. 416, 40 S.Ct. 382, 64 L.Ed. 641.

MR. JUSTICE HOLMES delivered the opinion of the Court.

This is a bill in equity brought by the State of Missouri to prevent a game warden of the United States from attempting to enforce the Migratory Bird Treaty Act of July 3, 1918, c. 128, 40 Stat. 755, and the regulations made by the Secretary of Agriculture in pursuance of the same. The ground of the bill is that the statute is an unconstitutional interference with the rights reserved to the States by the Tenth Amendment, and that the acts of the defendant done and threatened under that authority invade the sovereign right of the State and contravene its will manifested in statutes. The State also alleges a pecuniary interest, as owner of the wild birds within its borders and otherwise . . . .

On December 8, 1916, a treaty between the United States and Great Britain was proclaimed by the President. It recited that many species of birds in their annual migrations traversed many parts of the United States and of Canada, that they were of great value as a source of food and in destroying insects injurious to vegetation, but were in danger of extermination through lack of adequate protection. It therefore provided for specified closed seasons and protection in other forms, and agreed that the two powers would take or propose to their lawmaking bodies the necessary measures for carrying the treaty out. 39 Stat. 1702. The above mentioned act of July 3, 1918, entitled an act to give effect to the convention, prohibited the killing, capturing or selling any of the migratory birds included in the terms of the treaty except as permitted by regulations compatible with those terms, to be made by the Secretary of Agriculture. Regulations were proclaimed on July 31, and October 25, 1918. . . . [T]he question raised is the general one whether the treaty and statute are void as an interference with the rights reserved to the States.

To answer this question it is not enough to refer to the Tenth Amendment, reserving the powers not delegated to the United States, because by Article 2, Section 2, the power to make treaties is delegated expressly, and by Article 6 treaties made under the authority of the United States, along with the Constitution and laws of the United States made in pursuance thereof, are declared the supreme law of the land. If the treaty is valid there can be no dispute about the validity of the statute under Article 1, Section 8, as a necessary and proper means to execute the powers of the Government. The language of the Constitution as to the supremacy of treaties being general, the question before us is narrowed to an inquiry into the ground upon which the present supposed exception is placed.

It is said that a treaty cannot be valid if it infringes the Constitution, that there are limits, therefore, to the treaty-making power, and that one such limit is that what an act of Congress could not do unaided, in derogation of the powers reserved to the States, a treaty cannot do. An earlier act of Congress that attempted by itself and not in pursuance of a treaty to regulate the killing of migratory birds within the States had been held bad in the District Court. United States v. Shauver, 214 Fed. 154. United States v. McCullagh, 221 Fed. 288. Those decisions were supported by arguments that migratory birds were owned by the States in their sovereign capacity for the benefit of their people, and that under cases like Geer v. Connecticut, 161 U.S. 519, 16 S.Ct. 600, 40 L.Ed. 793, this control was one that Congress had no power to displace. The same argument is supposed to apply now with equal force.

Whether the two cases cited were decided rightly or not they cannot be accepted as a test of the treaty power. Acts of Congress are the supreme law of the land only when made in pursuance of the Constitution, while treaties are declared to be so when made under the authority of the United States. It is open to question whether the authority of the United States means more than the formal acts prescribed to make the convention. We do not mean to imply that there are no qualifications to the treaty-making power; but they must be ascertained in a different way. It is obvious that there may be matters of the sharpest exigency for the national well being that an act of Congress could not deal with but that a treaty followed by such an act could, and it is not lightly to be assumed that, in matters requiring national action, "a power which must belong to and somewhere reside in every civilized government" is not to be found. Andrews v. Andrews, 188 U.S. 14, 33, 23 S.Ct. 237, 47 L.Ed. 366. What was said in that case with regard to the powers of the States applies with equal force to the powers of the nation in cases where the States individually are incompetent to act. We are not yet discussing the particular case before us but only are considering the validity of the test proposed. With regard to that we may add that when we are dealing with words that also are a constituent act, like the Constitution of the United States, we must realize that they have called into life a being the development of which could not have been foreseen completely by the most gifted of its begetters. It was enough for them to realize or to hope that they had created an organism; it has taken a century and has cost their successors much sweat and blood to prove that they created a nation. The case before us must be considered in the light of our whole experience and not merely in that of what was said a hundred years ago. The treaty in question does not contravene any prohibitory words to be found in the Constitution. The only question is whether it is forbidden by some invisible radiation from the general terms of the Tenth Amendment. We must consider what this country has become in deciding what that amendment has reserved.

The State as we have intimated founds its claim of exclusive authority upon an assertion of title to migratory birds, an assertion that is embodied in statute. No doubt it is true that as between a State and its inhabitants the State may regulate the killing and sale of such birds, but it does not follow that its authority is exclusive of paramount powers. To put the claim of the State upon title is to lean upon a slender reed. Wild birds are not in the possession of anyone; and possession is the beginning of ownership. The whole foundation of the State's rights is the presence within their jurisdiction of birds that yesterday had not arrived, tomorrow may be in another State and in a week a thousand miles away. If we are to be accurate we cannot put the case of the State upon higher ground than that the treaty deals with creatures that for the moment are within the state borders, that it must be carried out by officers of the United States within the same territory, and that but for the treaty the State would be free to regulate this subject itself.

As most of the laws of the United States are carried out within the States and as many of them deal with matters which in the silence of such laws the State might regulate, such general grounds are not enough to support Missouri's claim. Valid treaties of course "are as binding within the territorial limits of the States as they are elsewhere throughout the dominion of the United States." Baldwin v.

Franks, 120 U.S. 678, 683, 7 S.Ct. 656, 657, 32 L.Ed. 766. No doubt the great body of private relations usually fall within the control of the State, but a treaty may override its power. . . .

Here a national interest of very nearly the first magnitude is involved. It can be protected only by national action in concert with that of another power. The subject matter is only transitorily within the State and has no permanent habitat therein. But for the treaty and the statute there soon might be no birds for any powers to deal with. We see nothing in the Constitution that compels the Government to sit by while a food supply is cut off and the protectors of our forests and our crops are destroyed. It is not sufficient to rely upon the States. The reliance is vain, and were it otherwise, the question is whether the United States is forbidden to act. We are of opinion that the treaty and statute must be upheld. . . .

Decree affirmed.

Missouri v. Holland remains the most significant judicial decision exploring the question whether there are areas reserved by the Constitution for the law-making power of the states on which a treaty cannot trespass. The following cases involve two different, and equally rare, constitutional challenges to an international agreement.

REID v. COVERT

Supreme Court of the United States, 1957.
354 U.S. 1, 77 S.Ct. 1222, 1 L.Ed.2d 1148.

[Mrs. Covert and Mrs. Smith killed their husbands, who were then performing military service in England and Japan, respectively. They were each tried by courts-martial convened under Article 2(11) of the Uniform Code of Military Justice, which provided:

> The following persons are subject to this code:
>
> (11) Subject to the provisions of any treaty or agreement to which the United States is or may be a party or to any accepted rule of international law, all persons serving with, employed by, or accompanying the armed forces without the continental limits of the United States . . . .

After conviction, each lady sought release on a writ of habeas corpus, which was granted in the case of Mrs. Covert and denied in the case of Mrs. Smith. On direct appeal the Court affirmed Mrs. Covert's case and reversed Mrs. Smith's. There were four opinions. Six members of the Court agreed that civilian dependents of members of the armed forces overseas could not constitutionally be tried by a court-martial in time of peace for capital offenses, even if committed abroad. Justice Black (in an opinion joined by the Chief Justice, Justice Douglas and Justice Brennan) concluded that military trial of civilians was inconsistent with the Constitution—particularly with those provisions of Article III, Section 2 and of the Fifth and Sixth Amendments which assure indictment by grand jury and trial by jury. Justice Frankfurter and Justice Harlan, in concurring opinions, limited their holdings to capital cases. There was a dissenting opinion.

The excerpts below from the opinion of JUSTICE BLACK refer to "executive agreements." We shall consider such agreements at p. 589, infra. For present purposes, you should (as indeed Justice Black does) consider them to be the equivalent of treaties.]

At the time of Mrs. Covert's alleged offense, an executive agreement was in effect between the United States and Great Britain which permitted United States' military courts to exercise exclusive jurisdiction over offenses committed in Great Britain by American servicemen or their dependents.[16] For its part, the United States agreed that these military courts would be willing and able to try and to punish all offenses against the laws of Great Britain by such persons. In all material respects, the same situation existed in Japan when Mrs. Smith killed her husband. Even though a court-martial does not give an accused trial by jury and other Bill of Rights protections, the Government contends that article 2(11) of UCMJ, insofar as it provides for the military trial of dependents accompanying the armed forces in Great Britain and Japan, can be sustained as legislation which is necessary and proper to carry out the United States' obligations under the international agreements made with those countries. The obvious and decisive answer to this, of course, is that no agreement with a foreign nation can confer power on the Congress, or on any other branch of Government, which is free from the restraints of the Constitution. . . .

. . . There is nothing in [the language of Article VI of the Constitution] which intimates that treaties and laws enacted pursuant to them do not have to comply with the provisions of the Constitution. Nor is there anything in the debates which accompanied the drafting and ratification of the Constitution which even suggests such a result. These debates as well as the history that surrounds the adoption of the treaty provision in Article VI make it clear that the reason treaties were not limited to those made in "pursuance" of the Constitution was so that agreements made by the United States under the Articles of Confederation, including the important peace treaties which concluded the Revolutionary War, would remain in effect. It would be manifestly contrary to the objectives of those who created the Constitution, as well as those who were responsible for the Bill of Rights—let alone alien to our entire constitutional history and tradition—to construe Article VI as permitting the United States to exercise power under an international agreement without observing constitutional prohibitions. In effect, such construction would permit amendment of that document in a manner not sanc-

16. Executive Agreement of July 27, 1942, 57 Stat. 1193. The arrangement now in effect in Great Britain and the other North Atlantic Treaty Organization nations, as well as in Japan, is the NATO Status of Forces Agreement, 4 U.S. Treaties and Other International Agreements 1792, T.I.A.S. 2846, which by its terms gives the foreign nation primary jurisdiction to try dependents accompanying American servicemen for offenses which are violations of the law of both the foreign nation and the United States. Art. VII, §§ 1(b), 3(a). The foreign nation has exclusive criminal jurisdiction over dependents for offenses which only violate its laws. Art. VII, § 2(b). However, the Agreement contains provisions which require that the foreign nations provide procedural safeguards for our nationals tried under the terms of the Agreement in their courts. Art. VII, § 9. Generally, see Note, 70 Harv.L.Rev. 1043.

Apart from those persons subject to the Status of Forces and comparable agreements and certain other restricted classes of Americans, a foreign nation has plenary criminal jurisdiction, of course, over all Americans—tourists, residents, businessmen, government employees and so forth—who commit offenses against its laws within its territory.

tioned by Article V. The prohibitions of the Constitution were designed to apply to all branches of the National Government and they cannot be nullified by the Executive or by the Executive and the Senate combined.

There is nothing new or unique about what we say here. This Court has regularly and uniformly recognized the supremacy of the Constitution over a treaty.[17] For example, in Geofroy v. Riggs, 133 U.S. 258, 267, 10 S.Ct. 295, 297, 33 L.Ed. 642, it declared:

> "The treaty power, as expressed in the constitution, is in terms unlimited except by those restraints which are found in that instrument against the action of the government or of its departments, and those arising from the nature of the government itself and of that of the States. It would not be contended that it extends so far as to authorize what the constitution forbids, or a change in the character of the government or in that of one of the States, or a session of any portion of the territory of the latter, without its consent."

This Court has also repeatedly taken the position that an Act of Congress, which must comply with the Constitution, is on a full parity with a treaty, and that when a statute which is subsequent in time is inconsistent with a treaty, the statute to the extent of conflict renders the treaty null. It would be completely anomalous to say that a treaty need not comply with the Constitution when such an agreement can be overridden by a statute that must conform to that instrument.

There is nothing in State of Missouri v. Holland, 252 U.S. 416, 40 S.Ct. 382, 64 L.Ed. 641, which is contrary to the position taken here. There the Court carefully noted that the treaty involved was not inconsistent with any specific provision of the Constitution. The Court was concerned with the Tenth Amendment which reserves to the States or the people all power not delegated to the National Government. To the extent that the United States can validly make treaties, the people and the States have delegated their power to the National Government and the Tenth Amendment is no barrier.

In summary, we conclude that the Constitution in its entirety applied to the trials of Mrs. Smith and Mrs. Covert. Since their court-martial did not meet the requirements of Art. III, § 2, or the Fifth and Sixth Amendments we are compelled to determine if there is anything *within* the Constitution which authorizes the military trial of dependents accompanying the armed forces overseas. . . .

[The opinion concluded that the Constitution did not authorize such trials.]

COMMENT

Although Reid v. Covert involved a capital case, later decisions such as Kinsella v. United States ex rel. Singleton, 361 U.S. 234, 80 S.Ct. 297, 4 L.Ed.2d 268 (1960), extended it to non-capital cases as well.

Compare the problems which the United States has encountered in recent years in deciding whether to support conventions drafted

17. . . . We recognize that executive agreements are involved here but it cannot be contended that such an agreement rises to greater stature than a treaty.

within the United Nations. Notwithstanding their noble aspirations, some among them raise constitutional issues analogous to those in Reid v. Covert. For example, the General Assembly unanimously adopted in 1965, and opened for signature one year later, a Convention on the Elimination of All Forms of Racial Discrimination. Article 4 of the Convention, reproduced in 60 Am.J.Int.L. 650 (1966), states:[18]

> States parties condemn all propaganda and all organizations which are based on ideas or theories of superiority of one race or group of persons of one colour or ethnic origin, or which attempt to justify or promote racial hatred and discrimination in any form, and undertake to adopt immediate and positive measures designed to eradicate all incitement to, or acts of, such discrimination and, to this end, with due regard to the principles embodied in the Universal Declaration of Human Rights and the rights expressly set forth in Article 5 of this Convention *inter alia:*
>
> (*a*) Shall declare an offence punishable by law all dissemination of ideas based on racial superiority or hatred, incitement to racial discrimination, as well as all acts of violence or incitement to such acts against any race or group of persons of another colour or ethnic origin, and also the provision of any assistance to racist activities, including the financing thereof;
>
> (*b*) Shall declare illegal and prohibit organizations, and also organized and all other propaganda activities, which promote and incite racial discrimination, and shall recognize participation in such organizations or activities as an offence punishable by law;
>
> (*c*) Shall not permit public authorities or public institutions, national or local, to promote or incite racial discrimination.

In explaining the vote of the United States in favor of the Convention, the United States representative stated in the General Assembly (54 Dept. of State Bull. 216 (1966)):

> For the record, however, here in this Assembly I wish to state that the United States understands article 4 of the convention as imposing no obligation on any party to take measures which are not fully consistent with its constitutional guarantees of freedom, including freedom of speech and association. This interpretation is entirely consistent with the opening paragraph of article 4 of the convention itself, which provides that in carrying out certain obligations of the convention, states parties shall have "due regard to the principles embodied in the Universal Declaration of Human Rights and the rights expressly set forth in article 5 of this Convention." Article 5 in turn lists among its rights to be guaranteed without distinction as to race, color, or national or ethnic origin the right of freedom of opinion and of expression.

18. Comparable provisions in another draft covenant adopted by the General Assembly and noted at p. 388, supra, are considered in Seeley, Article Twenty of the International Covenant on Civil and Political Rights: First Amendment Comments and Questions, 10 Va.J.Int.L. 328 (1970).

POWER AUTHORITY OF NEW YORK v. FEDERAL POWER COMMISSION

United States Court of Appeals, District of Columbia, 1957.
101 U.S.App.D.C. 132, 247 F.2d 538, vacated 355 U.S. 64, 78 S.Ct. 141, 2 L.Ed.2d 107.

BAZELON, CIRCUIT JUDGE. Petitioner, an agency of the State of New York, applied to the Federal Power Commission for a license to construct a power project to utilize all of the Niagara River water which, under the 1950 treaty between the United States and Canada, is available for American exploitation.

In consenting to the treaty, the Senate had attached the following "reservation":

> The United States on its part expressly reserves the right to provide by Act of Congress for redevelopment, for the public use and benefit, of the United States share of the waters of the Niagara River made available by the provisions of the treaty, and no project for redevelopment of the United States share of such waters shall be undertaken until it be specifically authorized by Act of Congress. [1 U.S.T. 694, 699.]

The Commission dismissed petitioner's application on November 30, 1956, in an opinion and order declaring:

> "In the absence of the treaty reservation we would act on the Power Authority's application in accordance with the provisions of the Federal Power Act [16 U.S.C.A. § 791a et seq.] But if we are to accept the injunction of the reservation as it stands, we would have no authority to consider the application of the Power Authority on its merits. . .
>
> "Since the reservation here was intended by the Senate as part of the treaty and was intended to prevent our jurisdiction attaching to the water made available by the treaty, it is entirely authoritative with us as the Supreme Law of the Land under Article VI of the Constitution." . . .

The parties agree that, if the reservation to the 1950 treaty is not "Law of the Land," the order should be set aside. Since the reservation did not have the concurrence of the House of Representatives, it is not "Law of the Land" by way of legislation. The question is whether it became "Law of the Land" as part of the treaty. . .

The treaty was signed on behalf of the United States and Canada on February 27, 1950. It defined the quantity of Niagara River water which was to be available for power purposes and provided that it "shall be divided equally between the United States of America and Canada." How each party was to exploit its share of the water was left for that party to decide.

In transmitting the treaty to the Senate on May 2, 1950, the President pointed out that the treaty did not determine how the United States was to exploit its share of the water. He said:

> " . . . It is a question which we in the United States must settle under our own procedures and laws. It would not be appropriate either for this country or for Canada to require that an international agreement between them contain the solution of what is entirely a domestic problem." [Citation omitted.]

The Foreign Relations Committee of the Senate agreed that the question was "domestic in nature" and "concerns the United States constitutional process alone." It recommended the reservation because, without it, "the redevelopment for power purposes would be governed by the Federal Power Act. The Committee intends by the reservation to retain that power in the hands of Congress." [Citation omitted.] The Senate accepted the Committee's recommendation and consented to the ratification of the treaty with the reservation on August 9, 1950.

Meanwhile, the Canadian Parliament had approved the treaty as signed, without the reservation. In a note on August 17, 1950, the Legal Advisor of the Department of State called the attention of the Canadian Government to the Senate action . . . . A week later, without waiting for Canadian reaction to the reservation, the President ratified the treaty subject to the reservation. On September 21, 1950, the Canadian Ambassador, replying to the State Department's note, advised that his government accepted the reservation . . . . The Canadian view that the reservation was of purely domestic concern to the United States and of no concern to Canada was shared, as we have shown, by the President, the Department of State and the Senate. . . .

A true reservation which becomes a part of a treaty is one which alters "the effect of the treaty in so far as it may apply in the relations of [the] State with the other State or States which may be parties to the treaty." Report of the Harvard Research in International Law, 29 Am.J.Int'l L.Supp. 843, 857 (1935). . . . The purported reservation to the 1950 treaty makes no change in the relationship between the United States and Canada under the treaty and has nothing at all to do with the rights or obligations of either party. To the extent here relevant, the treaty was wholly executed on its effective date. Each party became entitled to divert its half of the agreed quantum of water. Neither party had any interest in how the share of the other would be exploited, nor any obligation to the other as to how it would exploit its own share. . . .

A party to a treaty may presumably attach to it a matter of purely municipal application, neither affecting nor intended to affect the other party. *But such matter does not become part of the treaty.* . . .

The constitutionality of the reservation as a treaty provision was extensively argued by the parties. The respondent merely suggests that "there is no apparent limit" to what may be done under the treaty power, citing State of Missouri v. Holland, 1920, 252 U.S. 416, 40 S.Ct. 382, 64 L.Ed. 641. Intervenor Rochester Gas and Electric Corporation puts the proposition more baldly. It defends this reservation as an "exercise of the treaty-making power to legislate in the domestic field . . .," calling our attention to the fact that the Supreme Court has never held a treaty provision unconstitutional. But it has been pointed out that the Court has never had occasion to consider a treaty provision which "lacked an obvious connection with a matter of international concern." [Citation omitted] . . . .

In State of Missouri v. Holland, 252 U.S. at page 433, 40 S.Ct. at page 383, Mr. Justice Holmes questioned, but did not decide, whether there was any constitutional limitation on the treaty-making power other than the formal requirements prescribed for the making of treaties.[19] The treaty he sustained related to a "national interest of

19. The question raised by Mr. Justice Holmes was given an affirmative answer by Mr. Justice Black in Reid v. Covert, 77 S.Ct. 1222.

very nearly the first magnitude" which "can be protected only by national action in concert with that of another power." . . . No court has ever said, however, that the treaty power can be exercised without limit to affect matters which are of purely domestic concern and do not pertain to our relations with other nations.

Our present Secretary of State [Dulles] has said that the treaty power may be exercised with respect to a matter which "reasonably and directly affects other nations in such a way that it is properly a subject for treaties which become contracts between nations as to how they should act"; and not with respect to matters "which do not essentially affect the actions of nations in relation to international affairs, but are purely internal." [Citation omitted.] . . . .

Charles Evans Hughes, just before he became Chief Justice and after he had been Secretary of State, addressing himself to the question whether there is any constitutional limitation of the treaty power, said: . . .

[The 1929 remarks of Hughes, delivered before the American Society of International Law, are set forth in the following Note, at p. 571, infra.]

In the Dulles view this reservation, if part of the treaty, would be an invalid exercise of the treaty power. In the Hughes view, its constitutionality would be a matter of grave doubt. . . . We construe the reservation as an expression of the Senate's desires and not a part of the treaty. We do not decide the constitutional question. . . .

The order under review is set aside and the case remanded to the Federal Power Commission.

[Dissenting opinion of JUDGE BASTIAN omitted.]

After Congress had acted on this matter, the judgment of the Court of Appeals was vacated and the case remanded as moot. American Public Power Association v. Power Authority of New York, 355 U.S. 64, 78 S.Ct. 141, 2 L.Ed.2d 107 (1957). The problem faced by the Court of Appeals is considered in Henkin, The Treaty Makers and the Law Makers: The Niagara Reservation, 56 Colum.L.Rev. 1151 (1956).

NOTE ON ASSERTED LIMITS ON THE TREATY POWER AND THE HUMAN RIGHTS CONVENTIONS

Asserted Limits

The three preceding cases questioned the reach of the treaty power and suggested different constraints upon its exercise. Those constraints could be divided into three categories: limits upon the federal lawmaking power imposed by our system of constitutional federalism; limits upon the federal lawmaking power growing out of specific constitutional guarantees such as the Bill of Rights; and the prohibition implied in the Constitution against treaties dealing with matters of strictly domestic concern. The first two limitations are of course common to other forms of federal lawmaking, such as legislation or regulations. This Note considers the third category.

We have observed a comparable problem when considering the concept of "domestic jurisdiction" and the reliance by the United States upon that concept in international controversies. See pp. 320–326, supra. No less here (in a domestic constitutional context) than there (in the context of the competence of international tribunals), the idea that there are matters of strictly domestic "concern" or "jurisdiction" has been subject to great stress. One need simply refer to the observation in the Tunis-Morocco Nationality Decrees opinion, pp. 320, 321, supra: whether a matter is solely within a nation's domestic jurisdiction is "an essentially relative question; it depends upon the development of international relations." The rapidity with which the international community—through customary law, multilateral conventions and international organization—has been expanding its fields of interest and activity gives added strength to that observation. Compare the observations of Professor Henkin (and his quotation of remarks of Charles Evans Hughes) in his Foreign Affairs and the Constitution 151–155 (1972):

> In their doctrine, at least, those who sought limitations on treaties in the separation of powers were not restricting federal power, only the authority of the President-and-Senate alone to adhere to certain treaties. Limitations based on federalism, on the other hand, would deny federal power, but presumably their object, too, was not to avoid those international undertakings but to prevent federal aggrandizement and diminution of state authority. (In theory, the United States could adhere to those treaties with the consent of all the States.) Arguments from both Separation and federalism, however, probably carried strands of deeper objection, of resistance to too-much-government, including too-much-government by agreement with other nations. With some, moreover—perhaps with Jefferson as with Senator Bricker—limitations on the Treaty Power supported particular resistance to unnecessary, novel "entanglements" with other countries, reflecting a desire to maintain for the United States a sacrosanct zone of isolation, autonomy, "privacy," freedom from foreign scrutiny. And so, when it proved that neither federalism nor separation of powers provided any significant limitation on the Treaty Power, a different limitation was conceived: under the Constitution only matters of "international concern" are permissible subjects for treaties. That limitation has been widely accepted, and some have invoked it to oppose adherence by the United States to modern international undertakings, e. g., human rights covenants.
>
> The antecedents of the doctrine are not wholly clear but its modern underpinnings are remarks that sprang full-blown from the mouth and mind of Charles Evans Hughes [in remarks before the American Society of International Law] in 1929:
>
> . . .
>
>> What is the power to make a treaty? What is the object of the power? The normal scope of the power can be found in the appropriate object of the power. The power is to deal with foreign nations with regard to matters of international

concern. It is not a power intended to be exercised, it may be assumed, with respect to matters that have no relation to international concerns.

. . .

So I come back to the suggestion I made at the start, that this is a sovereign nation; from my point of view the nation has the power to make any agreement whatever in a constitutional manner that relates to the conduct of our international relations, unless there can be found some express prohibition in the Constitution, and I am not aware of any which would in any way detract from the power as I have defined it in connection with our relations with other governments. But if we attempted to use the treaty-making power to deal with matters which did not pertain to our external relations but to control matters which normally and appropriately were within the local jurisdictions of the States, then I again say there might be ground for implying a limitation upon the treaty-making power that it is intended for the purpose of having treaties made relating to foreign affairs and not to make laws for the people of the United States in their internal concerns through the exercise of the asserted treaty-making power.

. . .

It may be that Hughes was merely echoing Jefferson's requirement that a treaty be a *bona fide* agreement between the United States and another country: by hypothesis, a *bona fide* treaty deals with a foreign nation about matters "which pertain to our external relations," which are of mutual, "international concern." But Hughes has been interpreted to mean that some matters are not appropriate subjects for agreement with another country because they are our own affair and not the legitimate "concern," not the "business" of any other country. . . .

If there is any basis for the Hughes doctrine,[20] and if it bars some hypothetical agreement on some hypothetical subject, surely it is not relevant where it has been invoked—to prevent adherence by the United States to international human rights conventions. Human rights have long been of international concern and the subject of international agree-

20. At the least, the Hughes doctrine should have a change of name. "International concern" suggests an objective standard as to what matters do, or should, or properly may, concern nations generally. Especially since international law and practice know no such conception, . . . there is no basis for finding it in the use of the word "treaties" or in the grant of the Treaty Power, in the Constitution. While Hughes used the phrase "international concern" he used other, better phrases even more frequently. He spoke of the power to make an agreement "that relates to the conduct of our international relations," not to deal with matters "which did not pertain to our external relations." He proposed "a limitation upon the treaty-making power that it is intended for the purpose of having treaties made relating to foreign affairs." (Later, as Chief Justice, he also spoke of the treaty power as reaching "all subjects that properly pertain to our foreign relations." Santovincenzo v. Egan, 284 U.S. 30, 40 (1931).) To say that a treaty must have a foreign relations purpose is indeed implied in the word "treaties" and in the constitutional framework, though that might go without saying.

ments—in the treaties of hundreds of years ago guaranteeing religious freedom, in the minority treaties of the 19th Century and Post-World War I, in the human rights provisions of World War II treaties, in the UN Charter,[21] in human rights arrangements now in effect in several regions of the world, in the UN covenants on human rights, on the elimination of racial discrimination, and on other specific rights.

For the United States parallel human rights undertakings have obvious foreign relations purposes.

The Human Rights Conventions and the Congress

As the excerpts above suggest, problems about the reach of the treaty power have influenced this country's decision whether to participate in conventions aiming at the international protection of human rights. In 1967, the Johnson administration decided to press the Senate for its consent to ratification of the Convention on the Abolition of Forced Labour, The Supplementary Convention on the Abolition of Slavery and Convention on the Political Rights of Women.[22] It did so partly because of the embarrassment caused American foreign policy by this country's position as one of few leading nations which had refused to accede to the major human rights conventions sponsored by the United Nations. The United States was criticized as a nation unwilling to support its pious declarations favoring these conventions with ratification and implementation.

The Supplementary Slavery Convention bars such practices as debt bondage, the exploitation of children or their labor, the involuntary marriage of women pursuant to parental arrangements, and the transfer of widows to relatives as inherited property. The Forced Labour Convention obligates parties not to make use of any form of "compulsory labour" as a means of political coercion, as punishment for holding political views, "as a means of labour discipline," or "as a punishment for having participated in strikes." The Convention on the Political Rights of Women assures equality of treatment with men for voting and qualification for election.

The objections to our participation in these conventions ranged from general protest that they were beyond the constitutional scope of, or at least traditional limitations upon, the treaty power, to specific objections. For example, some argued that the provisions quoted above of the Forced Labour Convention might lead a domestic tribunal to hold that imprisonment for participation in an illegal strike or for violation of an injunction against striking would violate that Convention.

The flavor of the more general objections can be gathered from the Report opposing ratification of the conventions of a committee of the American Bar Association.[23] The committee urged the ABA

21. [Eds.] See, e. g., Arts. 1(3), 13(1)(b), 55(c), and 56 of the Charter *.

22. The text at p. 387, supra, indicates the number of countries which have ratified a number of the human rights conventions as of late 1973.

23. Report and Recommendations on Human Rights Conventions of the

(through its House of Delegates) to favor recommendations by the United Nations on human rights, but to oppose ratification of covenants on human rights "which lie essentially within the domestic jurisdiction of the United States." The Report cautioned that ratification would open the door "to intervention by the United Nations in the field of human rights generally . . ." The House of Delegates followed the committee with respect to the Conventions on Forced Labour and Political Rights of Women but voted in 1967 to support the Supplementary Slavery Convention.[24] In 1967, the Supplementary Slavery Convention was consented to and ratified, 18 U.S.T. 3201, T.I.A.S. No. 6418 (1967).

Perhaps the most disputed of the conventions has been the International Convention on the Prevention and Punishment of the Crime of Genocide, 78 U.N.T.S. 277. Against the background of the Nazi extermination of Jewish populations, the Genocide Convention was adopted in 1948 by the General Assembly by a vote of 55–0, including the United States. The Convention entered into force in 1951 after the necessary number of ratifications were deposited, and had 77 parties as of 1974. A brief description follows.

In Article I, the parties confirm that genocide "in time of peace or in time of war, is a crime under international law." Genocide is defined (Article II) as acts committed with the intention of destroying "in whole or in part, a national, ethnical, racial or religious group"; and Article III makes punishable conspiracy, public incitement or attempts to commit genocide as well as complicity in it. Article IV provides that persons guilty of genocide should be punished "whether they are constitutionally responsible rulers, public officials or private individuals". In Article V, the parties "undertake to enact, in accordance with their respective Constitutions, the necessary legislation . . . to provide effective penalties for persons guilty of genocide . . ." Under Article VI, the trial of such persons is to be by national tribunals of a party "in the territory of which the act was committed", or by any international penal tribunal which might have jurisdiction. In Article VII, the parties agree to grant extradition in accordance with their laws and treaties in force, and further agree that genocide is not to be considered a "political crime" for purposes of extradition treaties. Pursuant to Article VIII, any party can request competent UN organs to take appropriate action under the Charter to prevent acts of genocide.

Note the distinctive characteristics of this convention. It does not simply proscribe or require particular acts, but seeks to punish the individuals committing such acts. Although provisions such as Article VIII could lead to consideration of action against governments, the primary thrust of the Convention is individual criminal

Standing Committee on Peace and Law through the United Nations of the American Bar Association, May 1967, appearing in 1 The Int. Lawyer 600–629 (1967).

24. A summary of the debates preceding the votes appears in 53 A.B.A.J. 973–76 (1967).

responsibility. The influence of the Nuremberg Charter and Judgment, pp. 904–906, infra, was strong. Finally, the Convention seeks to assure punishment through obligations of parties to enact domestic legislation or extradite to the competent state, or through resort to an international penal tribunal, if ever created.

The Convention was submitted to the Senate by President Truman in 1949. No final committee action was taken. No further pressure was exerted upon the Senate until President Nixon urged it in 1970 to institute new hearings, looking towards consent to ratification which would demonstrate that the United States (in the President's words) "desires to participate in the building of international order based on law and justice." In his message, the President stated that in the judgment of his Attorney General and Secretary of State, "There are no constitutional obstacles to United States ratification."

Extensive hearings before Senate and House committees and further debates in groups such as the American Bar Association took place. In 1970, the ABA refused (by a vote of 130–126) to reverse its earlier opposition to ratification of the Convention. The character of the arguments developed by members of the ABA, and presented to congressional committees by its spokesman, can be gathered from the following article: [25]

> On September 8, 1949, the American Bar Association, through its House of Delegates, expressed the sense of the Association "that the conscience of America like that of the civilized world revolts against Genocide . . .:" . . .
>
> The House nevertheless placed the Association of record as opposing approval by the Senate of the United States of the Convention on the Prevention and Punishment of the Crime of Genocide "as submitted" to the Senate for its advice and consent by President Truman less than three months earlier—on June 16.
>
> At its Midyear Meeting in Atlanta on February 23 of this year, the House reaffirmed the position taken in 1949, voting down by a narrow margin a recommendation for reversal of that position and for unreserved approval of the convention.
>
> The authors of this article are in complete accord with both the declaration of and the conclusion reached by the Association. This article is written as a record of the background of that position, which, in the last analysis, is simply that wholehearted concurrence in the lofty ideals that engender promotion of moral issues should not be permitted to substitute the ephemeral tissue of those ideals for the enduring fiber of constitutional limitations.
>
> . . .
>
> But the conviction of the authors is equally firm that having joined in such a declaration as to a matter which lies ultimately within the domestic sphere of each of the world's nations, the United States has gone far enough. She should

25. Phillips and Deutsch, Pitfalls of the Genocide Convention, 56 A.B.A. J. 641 (1970).

not, in our opinion, join in a convention by which she would commit herself in advance to protect the people of other nations against their own governments. Nor should she agree that such other countries may determine what is to be deemed to be genocide within the borders of the United States and invite them in advance, in the words of Article VIII of the Genocide Convention, to take through "the competent organs of the United Nations, such action under the Charter of the United Nations as they consider appropriate" for the "suppression" thereof.

. . .

The authors of this article do not agree with the extravagant statement in the Section report that "in terms of a threat to international peace and security, the occurrence of genocide anywhere in the world is as much a matter of international concern as, for example, the spread of nuclear weapons"; or that "when some states—or, as in this case, 74 states—consider a matter to be of sufficient concern to make a treaty about it, then realistically it is of international concern".

This is the old bootstrap doctrine by which a domestic issue, not subject as such to regulation by treaty, can be transmuted, by the very prohibited act of making it the subject of a treaty, into the arena of international affairs subject to regulation by treaty. It is the same doctrine that gave rise to the 1950 dictum by the Department of State that "there is no longer any distinction between 'domestic' and 'foreign' affairs".

. . .

The type of problem with which the United States might be faced in this regard, if it became a party to the Genocide Convention, is illustrated graphically and startlingly by a recent news item in *Time* of December 12, 1969, which reported that a "San Francisco lawyer who represents the [Black] Panthers . . . revealed plans to go before the United Nations and charge the United States with 'genocide' against the Panthers".

. . .

Nor can it be said cavalierly that it is not contemplated by the United States that an international penal tribunal is to be established. The minutes of the 74th meeting of the Sixth (Legal) Committee of the General Assembly of the United Nations, held at Paris in October, 1948, contain a significant statement to the effect that the United States delegation stated that it "intended, at a later stage, to show the need for the establishment of an appropriate international tribunal" in connection with Article VI of the Genocide Convention.

. . .

How can it be said in good conscience, in the face of this wealth of background material to the contrary, that Americans may rest assured that ratification of the Genocide Convention by the United States at this time will not carry with it the ultimate establishment of an international penal tribunal for the trial of citizens of the United States charged with commission of offenses thereunder?

An American citizen or any other person residing in the United States who is tried by an international tribunal created for the trial of persons charged with the offense of genocide would be deprived of many of the rights provided in our Constitution for persons charged with offenses against the laws of United States in our national courts. Among these are the right to be charged for a capital or infamous crime only on a presentment or indictment of a grand jury and the right to a speedy and public trial by an impartial jury of the state and district wherein the crime is alleged to have been committed. The privilege against self-incrimination and the protection against unreasonable searches and seizures also might disappear.

Another reason militating against ratification of the Genocide Convention arises from the provision of Article III(c) making punishable "direct and public incitement to commit genocide" vis-à-vis the First Amendment's guarantees of free speech and press. Suffice it to say here that there is at least grave doubt under recent decisions of the Supreme Court as to the effect to be given, even by that Court, to such a treaty provision in the circumstances of different cases—certainly completely incomprehensible to judges of an international tribunal to whom our concepts of freedom of thought and expression might be chimeric mysteries at best.

. . .

In the final analysis, the prohibition of genocide by treaty must become an exercise in futility. Adolf Hitler would hardly have restrained the frightful acts of genocide that gave rise to the convention, even if it had been in existence and Germany had been a party to it during the Nazi reign of terror. The Soviet Union and her Communist-bloc allies were not deterred from the 1968 invasion of Czechoslovakia by the nonaggression provisions of the Charter of the United Nations.

The Genocide Convention places in the hands of nations whose peoples have never known the freedoms guaranteed under our Constitution the power to judge whether those freedoms are being protected properly within our domestic borders.

. . .

In 1971, the Committee on Foreign Relations recommended that the Senate consent to ratification, subject to relatively minor "understandings" that were meant to clarify some ambiguities referred to by the Convention's critics. In its Report,[26] the Committee observed that the commission of genocide "cannot help but be of concern to the community of nations". It further observed that "if the United States Government is conceded the power to make treaties governing the killing of seals, it is capable of acceding to a treaty on the killing of people." It stressed that the Convention reached only systematic and massive efforts to destroy or permanently impair a substantial part of a group and thus did not affect many types of activities emphasized by the Convention's critics. The Report noted that the State Depart-

26. Exec.Rep.No. 92–6 on the Genocide Convention of the Senate Committee on Foreign Relations, 92nd Cong. 1st Sess., 1971.

ment did not intend to deposit an instrument of ratification, after Senate consent were obtained, until the Congress had enacted the implementing legislation. Such legislation would be within the congressional power in Art. I, Sec. 8, to define and punish "Offenses against the Law of Nations," as well as within the Necessary and Proper Clause. "The rhetoric of the opponents . . . has obscured what a modest step the convention represents." However modest, as of mid-1974, the Committee on Foreign Relations had again reported favorably, but the Senate had not granted its consent.

QUESTIONS

(1) In the excerpts above from his book, Professor Henkin observed that human rights undertakings by the United States (applicable of course to its own citizens as well as aliens within its borders) "have obvious foreign relations purposes". The Senate Committee comes to the same conclusion. How would you describe those purposes?

(2) Upon what cases or materials in this chapter would critics of the Supplementary Slavery Convention or the Genocide Convention have best relied in developing arguments that such conventions, if ratified, would be unconstitutional?

(3) Assume that you are a senator in favor of ratification, and that you must persuade some critics to vote in favor of the Genocide Convention to achieve the necessary two-thirds support. How do you respond to the following positions?

> (*a*) Of course treaties have long dealt with the protection of individual rights. Treaties of Friendship, Commerce and Navigation are prime examples. But such treaties have governed the conduct of the contracting parties towards *aliens* within their borders. Neither on constitutional nor policy grounds can the United States put its treatment of its own citizens under the supervision of foreign countries.
>
> (*b*) The Dean of Howard Law School observed in 1968 that "there is considerable evidence . . . that resistance to human rights treaties in general arises from a fear that eventually such treaties would touch upon and deal with the condition of blacks in the United States. . . . The fear is clearly that of a treaty which relates to race." [27] Assuming this to be a sound observation about some if not all opponents of ratification, how would you deal with such attitudes?
>
> (*c*) Such treaties are academic exercises in rhetoric. They lack assurance of enforcement or indeed any real bite. They would hardly inhibit any government otherwise determined to pursue genocidal policies.

NOTE ON FEDERALISM AND ASSERTED LIMITS ON THE TREATY POWER

We have seen that the expansion of international concerns and of the competence of international organizations has led some to renewed stress upon the concept of fields of domestic concern beyond

27. Ferguson, The United Nations Human Rights Covenants: Problems of Ratification and Implementation, 1968 Proc.Am.Soc.Int.L. 83, at p. 91.

the reach of the treaty power. This same expansion has also disturbed traditional views about limits to that power imposed by our federal structure. These related issues frequently merge in challenges to proposed treaties. For example, a Report of a committee of the American Bar Association opposing our ratification of three human rights conventions stated: [28]

> It is submitted that the cause of human rights neither justifies nor requires participation in treaties which would prejudice the domestic jurisdiction of the United States and the federal/state structure. The federal Government, being a government of limited powers, is still precluded from regulating large areas of intrastate matters. It is unnecessary and unsound to cut down this area of intrastate jurisdiction over human rights through the medium of international agreements. If that area is to be cut down, the way to do it is through internal legislation, debated and concluded by representatives of the people concerned, and not by a heterogeneous international gathering of officials representing some 125 different countries, each with its own concept of internal social standards.

Even with respect to matters that are generally acknowledged to be within the treaty power, those jealously guarding state prerogatives have assailed United States representatives in the United Nations for not consistently supporting the inclusion in conventions drafted within the U. N. of "federal-state" clauses. Such clauses would obligate federal nations that were parties to a convention only to apply the convention to the extent of the central government's constitutional competence, and for the balance to recommend to the states within the federalism their enactment of appropriate legislation.[29]

Inhibitions about federalism also curb the exercise of the treaty power with respect to private-law matters. For example, note that the Franco-American Convention of Establishment,* although it regulates many questions normally reserved to the states, has some provisions (especially Article VII and Paragraph 10 of the Protocol) which reflect concern for preservation of state prerogatives. Participation in multilateral conventions affecting private-law matters has also been inhibited; treaties relating to international judicial procedure or commercial transactions have been cautiously viewed by the United States. By and large, it has urged that international conferences debating such subjects simply propose uniform laws for adoption by participating countries or (for the United States or other federalisms) by any states within the federalism which so desire. Alternatively, the United States might enter into a treaty only if it contained a "federal-state" clause, although the present scope of the federal legislative

28. Report and Recommendations on Human-Rights Conventions of the Standing Committee on Peace and Law Through the United Nations of the American Bar Association, May 1967, appearing in 1 The Int. Lawyer 600–629 (1967), at p. 616.

29. See pp. 623–24 of the Report and Recommendations on Human-Rights Conventions of the Standing Committee on Peace and Law Through the United Nations of the American Bar Association, May 1967, appearing in 1 The Int. Lawyer 600 (1967).

and treaty power over matters relevant to foreign relations or transactions might not leave much play for such a clause.

One indication of a gradual change in attitude is this country's developing relationship with the Hague Conference on Private International Law. As noted, at p. 304, supra, the Hague Conference has for years been the principal institution devoted to preparing conventions on conflict-of-laws rules. Only in 1963 did the United States become a member. It took a further step in 1967 by ratifying a product of the Hague Conference, the Convention on the Service Abroad of Judicial and Extra-Judicial Documents in Civil or Commercial Matters.[30]

QUESTIONS

(1) Note that the Report of a committee of and the comments of delegates to the American Bar Association opposing ratification of the human rights conventions invoked principally the concept of "domestic jurisdiction," and made only passing references to federal-state problems within this country. That is, their arguments were directed only in small part towards the issues debated in Missouri v. Holland. Would such issues have been more pertinent if the human rights conventions had been debated in this country in the early 1950's? How have those issues been affected by subsequent internal developments in this country, including the Civil Rights Act of 1964, and the constitutional base for civil rights legislation found in the Commerce Clause and the Thirteenth as well as Fourteenth Amendment?

(2) Suppose that, absent any treaty, Congress enacts a statute providing that all aliens shall be entitled to own land on equal terms with citizens or shall be exempt from certain state taxes. What constitutional provisions and what cases in the preceding materials would support such legislation today? Would there be additional constitutional support if the legislation was enacted, as in Missouri v. Holland, pursuant to a treaty obligation?

Additional reading: Bitker, The Constitutionality of International Agreements on Human Rights, 12 Santa Clara Lawyer 279 (1972); Henkin, The Treaty Makers and the Law Makers: The Law of the Land and Foreign Relations, 107 U.Pa.L.Rev. 903 (1959).

---

2. SELF-EXECUTING TREATIES

SEI FUJII v. STATE

Supreme Court of California, 1952.
38 Cal.2d 718, 242 P.2d 617.

[In this litigation, Fujii, a Japanese who was ineligible for citizenship under the United States naturalization laws then in effect, brought an action to determine whether an escheat of certain land that he had purchased had occurred under provisions of the Califor-

30. This Convention, excerpts from which appear at p. 756, infra, makes some allowance for federal-state problems.

nia Alien Land Law. That Law (1 Deering's Gen.Laws, Act 261, as amended in 1945) provided in part:

> § 1. All aliens eligible to citizenship under the laws of the United States may acquire, possess, enjoy, use, cultivate, occupy, transfer, transmit and inherit real property, or any interest therein, in this state, and have in whole or in part the beneficial use thereof, in the same manner and to the same extent as citizens of the United States, except as otherwise provided by the laws of this state.
>
> § 2. All aliens other than those mentioned in section one of this act may acquire, possess, enjoy, use, cultivate, occupy and transfer real property, or any interest therein, in this state, and have in whole or in part the beneficial use thereof, in the manner and to the extent, and for the purposes prescribed by any treaty now existing between the government of the United States and the nation or country of which such alien is a citizen or subject, and not otherwise.
>
> § 7. Any real property hereafter acquired in fee in violation of the provisions of this act by any alien mentioned in section 2 of this act, . . . shall escheat as of the date of such acquiring, to, and become and remain the property of the state of California. . . .

The Superior Court of Los Angeles County concluded that the property purchased by Fujii had escheated to the State. This decision was reversed by the District Court of Appeals, Second District. That court held that the Alien Land Law was unenforceable because contrary to the letter and spirit of the Charter of the United Nations,* which as treaty was superior to state law. That decision was reviewed by the California Supreme Court. Excerpts from its opinion by CHIEF JUSTICE GIBSON appear below.]

It is first contended that the land law has been invalidated and superseded by the provisions of the United Nations Charter pledging the member nations to promote the observance of human rights and fundamental freedoms without distinction as to race. Plaintiff relies on statements in the preamble and in Articles 1, 55 and 56 of the Charter, 59 Stat. 1035.

It is not disputed that the charter is a treaty, and our federal Constitution provides that treaties made under the authority of the United States are part of the supreme law of the land and that the judges in every state are bound thereby. U.S.Const., art. VI. A treaty, however, does not automatically supersede local laws which are inconsistent with it unless the treaty provisions are self-executing. In the words of Chief Justice Marshall: A treaty is "to be regarded in courts of justice as equivalent to an act of the Legislature, whenever it operates of itself, without the aid of any legislative provision. But when the terms of the stipulation import a contract—when either of the parties engages to perform a particular act, the treaty addresses itself to the political, not the judicial department; and the Legislature must execute the contract, before it can become a rule for the court." Foster v. Neilson, 1829, 2 Pet. 253, 314, 7 L.Ed. 415.

In determining whether a treaty is self-executing courts look to the intent of the signatory parties as manifested by the language of the instrument, and, if the instrument is uncertain, recourse may be had to the circumstances surrounding its execution. . . . In order for a treaty provision to be operative without the aid of implementing legislation and to have the force and effect of a statute, it must appear that the framers of the treaty intended to prescribe a rule that, standing alone, would be enforceable in the courts. . . .

It is clear that the provisions of the preamble and of Article 1 of the charter which are claimed to be in conflict with the alien land law are not self-executing. They state general purposes and objectives of the United Nations Organization and do not purport to impose legal obligations on the individual member nations or to create rights in private persons. It is equally clear that none of the other provisions relied on by plaintiff is self-executing. . . . Although the member nations have obligated themselves to cooperate with the international organization in promoting respect for, and observance of, human rights, it is plain that it was contemplated that future legislative action by the several nations would be required to accomplish the declared objectives, and there is nothing to indicate that these provisions were intended to become rules of law for the courts of this country upon the ratification of the charter.

The language used in Articles 55 and 56 is not the type customarily employed in treaties which have been held to be self-executing and to create rights and duties in individuals. For example, the treaty involved in Clark v. Allen, 331 U.S. 503, 507–508, 67 S.Ct. 1431, 1434, 91 L.Ed. 1633, relating to the rights of a national of one country to inherit real property located in another country, specifically provided that "such national shall be allowed a term of three years in which to sell the [property] . . . and withdraw the proceeds . . ." free from any discriminatory taxation. See, also, Hauenstein v. Lynham, 100 U.S. 483, 488–490, 25 L.Ed. 628. In Nielsen v. Johnson, 279 U.S. 47, 50, 49 S.Ct. 223, 73 L.Ed. 607, the provision treated as being self-executing was equally definite. There each of the signatory parties agreed that "no higher or other duties, charges, or taxes of any kind, shall be levied" by one country on removal of property therefrom by citizens of the other country "that are or shall be payable in each state, upon the same, when removed by a citizen or subject of such state respectively." In other instances treaty provisions were enforced without implementing legislation where they prescribed in detail the rules governing rights and obligations of individuals or specifically provided that citizens of one nation shall have the same rights while in the other country as are enjoyed by that country's own citizens. . . .

It is significant to note that when the framers of the charter intended to make certain provisions effective without the aid of implementing legislation they employed language which is clear and definite and manifests that intention. [Quotations of Articles 104 * and 105 * have been omitted.] In Curran v. City of New York, 191 Misc. 229, 77 N.Y.S.2d 206, 212, these articles were treated as being self-executory. . . .

The provisions in the charter pledging cooperation in promoting observance of fundamental freedoms lack the mandatory quality and definiteness which would indicate an intent to create justiciable rights in private persons immediately upon ratification. Instead, they are framed as a promise of future action by the member nations. Secretary of State Stettinius, Chairman of the United States delegation at the San Francisco Conference where the charter was drafted, stated in his report to President Truman that Article 56 "pledges the various countries to cooperate with the organization by joint and separate action in the achievement of the economic and social objectives of the organization without infringing upon their right to order their national affairs according to their own best ability, in their own way, and in accordance with their own political and economic institutions and processes." [Citation omitted.] The same view was repeatedly expressed by delegates of other nations in the debates attending the drafting of article 56. [Citation omitted.]

The humane and enlightened objectives of the United Nations Charter are, of course, entitled to respectful consideration by the courts and Legislatures of every member nation, since that document expresses the universal desire of thinking men for peace and for equality of rights and opportunities. The charter represents a moral commitment of foremost importance, and we must not permit the spirit of our pledge to be compromised or disparaged in either our domestic or foreign affairs. We are satisfied, however, that the charter provisions relied on by plaintiff were not intended to supersede existing domestic legislation, and we cannot hold that they operate to invalidate the alien land law. . . .

[The Court then upheld plaintiff's alternative allegation that the Alien Land Law was invalid since violative of the Equal Protection Clause of the Fourteenth Amendment. See p. 48, supra. The concurring opinion of JUSTICE CARTER and dissenting opinion of JUSTICE SCHAUER are omitted.]

COMMENT

To understand the route followed by the District Court of Appeal in Sei Fujii, one must bear in mind the status as of 1950–51 of constitutional doctrine relevant to the alternative path for invalidating the California statute—namely, holding that it violated the Fourteenth Amendment. The materials at pp. 45–48, supra, indicate what that status was.

Later cases in which individuals unsuccessfully urged that Articles 55 and 56 or other provisions of the United Nations Charter were self-executing include Pauling v. McElroy, 164 F.Supp. 390 (D.C. 1958), aff'd, 278 F.2d 252 (D.C.Cir. 1960) (action based in part upon the Charter to enjoin Atomic Energy Commission and Secretary of Defense from detonating nuclear weapons in the Marshall Islands for test purposes); Camacho v. Rogers, 199 F.Supp. 155 (S.D.N.Y.1961) (action based in part on Articles 55 and 56 to enjoin enforcement of New York laws requiring literacy in English as a prerequisite for eligibility to vote); and Vlissidis v. Anadell, 262 F.2d 398 (7th Cir. 1959) (attempt to resist deportation on ground that Charter superseded "racist" provisions of immigration laws).

NOTE ON SELF-EXECUTING TREATIES

(1) A self-executing treaty has been defined as one "which prescribes by its own terms a rule for the Executive or for the courts or which creates obligations for individuals enforceable without legislative implementation." Evans, Self-Executing Treaties in the United States of America, 30 Br.Ybk.Int.L. 178, 185 (1953). Compare Section 141 of Restatement (Second), Foreign Relations Law of the United States, which states that a treaty "that manifests an intention that it shall become effective as domestic law of the United States at the time it becomes binding on the United States (a) is self-executing in that it is effective as domestic law of the United States . . . ."[31] Note the relationship between the concept of a self-executing treaty and the status of "supreme law" that is accorded the treaty under the Supremacy Clause.

When inquiring into the "intention" of the treaty's drafters, a court will of course look carefully at the text of the agreement. It will consider the verbs used—"does hereby" versus "shall undertake" —as well as other textual indications. Having exhausted such data, it may examine the broader context of the agreement, including the feasibility of construing a treaty to be self-executing in the light of the administrative and political problems inherent in creating operative rules without implementing or reinforcing legislation.

(2) On the borderline of the question of *intent* that a treaty be self-executing is the question whether there are limits to the *power* to make a treaty self-executing. The Over the Top, p. 540, supra, suggests that a treaty can make neither revenue nor criminal rules that are binding as domestic law.

Note that Art. I, Sec. 7 of the Constitution provides that revenue measures must originate in the House of Representatives. The conclusion is sometimes drawn that a treaty may not of its own power increase a tax burden. However, the mere fact that a treaty, if self-executing, will in some degree bypass the usual procedures for enacting domestic legislation expressing similar rules is not an insurmountable obstacle. Indeed, the number of treaties that, though treated as self-executing, in some manner affect government revenues is legion. But whatever the court's views as to whether a given treaty *can* constitutionally be self-executing, the fact that doubt exists is sure to add an element of caution before the court construes the treaty to be self-executing.

(3) The question of a plaintiff's standing to assert rights under a treaty is often linked to that of the treaty's self-executing character. For example, in Pauling v. McElroy, p. 583, supra, the court rebuffed a suit, based in part on the U. N. Charter, to enjoin the Atomic Energy Commission and the Secretary of Defense from detonating nuclear devices in the Marshall Islands for test purposes. Both grounds for seeking dismissal of the complaint were available to defendants. Indeed, the opinions in the district and circuit courts considered a third, related, problem—whether plaintiff's claim was "justiciable" or within the realm of political questions and thus immune from judicial consideration on the merits.

31. One could point towards a number of legislative or constitutional analogies in the United States. Section 1 of the Fourteenth Amendment, for example, is "self-executing" in the sense that courts apply the Due Process Clause or the Equal Protection Clause without legislative implementation. But note, on the other hand, that Section 5 of that amendment gives Congress the power to enforce it "by appropriate legislation." That is, the same text at once constitutes applicable "law" upon which private parties may rely in litigation, and provides a basis for federal legislation.

Problems of standing and of a treaty's self-executing quality interact in a variety of ways. For example, the Nuclear Test Ban Treaty with the Soviet Union could be considered self-executing, in the sense that it imposes an obligation on the Executive to cease certain tests. But the question of standing of a private plaintiff to prevent a violation of the Treaty raises distinct and decisive issues. Of course, many self-executing treaties are intended to confer rights upon individuals, particularly treaties defining rights or duties of aliens in the territory of a signatory. For example, many clauses in treaties of Friendship, Commerce and Navigation have long been considered self-executing.

(4) Whether the purpose of the treaty is to regulate conduct of or towards private persons may not be decisive in determining whether the treaty is self-executing. Treaties that are not principally directed at activities of private persons may be found to be self-executing and may thus be invoked by private parties. For example, an agreement between two countries settling a boundary dispute might be relevant to later litigation in either affecting real property in the disputed area. On the other hand, drafters of a treaty may primarily intend to benefit private parties but at the same time make clear that Congressional implementation is required. Thus a treaty with Guatador might state that the United States "undertakes to enact legislation enabling nationals of Guatador to own land for agricultural purposes."

(5) Whether a treaty is self-executing can concern not only private parties asserting rights or immunities under it and courts charged with making this determination, but also the legislative branch. For example, the Senate plays a critical role in the conclusion of a treaty by giving its advice and consent. But it—or more accurately, the Congress as a whole—may not be willing to relinquish power to supervise the implementation of the treaty, in order to make it effective as domestic law. The Congress may wish to exercise choice over the content and timing of implementing measures in the form of later legislation, rather than to leave the executive branch with full discretion to proceed if and as necessary by regulations, proclamations or orders which would fulfill this country's obligations under a "self-executing" treaty.

A prominent contemporary example is the International Coffee Agreement, 14 U.S.T. & O.I.A. 1911, T.I.A.S. No. 5505, 469 U.N.T.S. 169, formulated at the United Nations Coffee Conference in 1962. One year later, the Senate gave its advice and consent to the Agreement, and it was ratified by the President several months thereafter. The Agreement, to which all important coffee-exporting and coffee-importing countries are parties, attempts to regulate short-term market fluctuations in the price of coffee (a critical export commodity for a number of less developed countries), and to lend stability to coffee production and coffee prices through a quota system allocated among exporting countries on the basis of their past production. It seeks to make these principles effective through various requirements—the furnishing of statistics by different countries, certificates of origin on all coffee shipments to ascertain that the quota system has been complied with, and so on.

The United States, as the world's principal coffee-importing country, was of course a key participant in the Agreement. Tensions between the Congress and the executive branch led to the initial decision to submit the Agreement to the Senate as a treaty rather than to treat it as an executive agreement. There was, however, substantial opposition within the Senate, because of concern that the Agreement would raise coffee prices for the American consumer, would not prove effective in realizing its major goals, and might establish an unfortunate precedent for other international commodity agreements. A further concern was that advice and consent, followed by executive ratification, would strip the Congress of power to review the administration of the Agreement or exercise any control over it. To calm these Senatorial doubts, the executive branch made various commitments to the Congress. These assurances appeared to turn the tide. A committee report on the Agreement stated: [32]

> The agreement will require implementing legislation for U. S. participation. The main provision of such legislation, which will presumably come within the jurisdiction of the Committee on Finance, will be authority for the President to meet the obligations of the United States under the agreement with respect to requiring certificates of origin for coffee imports and limiting imports from non-participating countries.

Advice from the Executive Branch confirmed this view: [33]

> The Department of State agrees with the Committee on Foreign Relations that this treaty, if approved by the Senate, will not be self-executing. Since the United States cannot meet its obligations under the treaty without implementing legislation, the passage of such legislation is a prerequisite to active participation by the United States. . . . It is the intention of the executive branch to submit a request for enabling legislation to the Congress immediately after favorable consideration of the treaty by the Senate. The executive branch will not attempt to make its participation in the agreement effective until implementing legislation is approved by the Congress.

In the final statements before the vote was taken, Senator Aiken stated: [34]

> [I]n view of the understanding reached with the State Department that the treaty will not be self-executing; [and] the further understanding that the executive branch will not attempt to make U. S. participation in the agreement effective until implementing legislation is approved by Congress . . . I believe it to be in the interest of the United States to approve the agreement today.

32. Report of the Senate Foreign Relations Committee on the Agreement, Exec.Rep. No. 1, 88th Cong., 1st Sess., May 13, 1963, p. 5.

33. Letter from Acting Secretary Ball to Senator Humphrey, 109 Cong.Rec. (Daily Ed.), Senate, May 21, 1963, p. 8619.

34. 109 Cong.Rec. (Daily Ed.), Senate, May 21, 1963, p. 8623.

A diplomatic note from the Secretary of State to the Secretary General of the United Nations, dated June 24, 1963, gave notification of the intention of the United States to seek ratification. That note stated:

> However, under the Constitution of the United States, it will be necessary to secure domestic legislation in order to enable the United States to carry out certain of the obligations under the Agreement. In particular, it will be necessary for the United States Government to receive specific authorization from the Congress to require certificates of origin for all coffee imported into the United States, and to prohibit or limit imports of coffee from non-member countries.

The United States submitted a final ratification in December 1963, but implementing legislation was not enacted until 1965. 79 Stat. 112, 19 U.S.C.A. § 1356a et seq.[35]

(6) Comparable problems arise under the constitutional law or practice of foreign countries of determining the effect of a treaty as internal law, the extent to which it creates rights or duties enforceable by or against individuals without implementation by domestic statutes. Such problems are apt to be particularly acute in the case of multilateral treaties which are intended to create similar or identical legal situations within each of the contracting parties. One prominent example is the European Convention on Human Rights, p. 384, supra. The question has been posed before courts of several parties whether individuals can directly invoke the Convention to challenge governmental action which allegedly violates it.[36] Similar issues have arisen under the Rome Treaty creating the European Common Market, and of course under numerous bilateral treaties to which European countries were parties.[37]

(7) Generally it is not relevant to an international tribunal whether a treaty is self-executing, since a state is obligated under international law to do whatever may be required under its internal law to fulfill its treaty commitments. Sometimes, however, such a tribunal must pass upon the question whether a treaty became binding at once without further action by a party. Note the following comments from Jurisdiction of the Courts of Danzig, P.C.I.J., Ser. B, No. 15 (1928), pp. 17–18:

> It may be readily admitted that . . . the *Beamtenabkommen*, being an international agreement, cannot, as such, create direct rights and obligations for private individuals. But it cannot be disputed that the very object of an international agreement, according to the intention of the contracting Parties, may be the adoption by the Parties of

35. For detailed background and analysis of the Agreement, see Bilder, The International Coffee Agreement: A Case History in Negotiation, 28 Law & Contemp.Prob. 328 (1963).

36. For a review of the case law in several European countries under the Convention, see Stein and Hay, Law and Institutions in the Atlantic Area 955–58, 990–1020 (1967).

37. Such issues are examined in Part B of Chapter XIII.

some definite rules creating individual rights and obligations and enforceable by the national courts.

QUESTIONS

(1) Consider the following hypothetical clauses in treaties between the United States and Guatador. Some might never be effectively invoked before a court. For example, no litigant might have standing to base an action on the treaty, or sovereign immunity might bar suit. Consider how each clause might be pertinent to litigation, and whether it should be construed to be self-executing.

(a) A clause provides that the United States "shall pay" $5,000,000 to Guatador in settlement of Guatadorian citizens' claims (under international law) against the United States.

(b) A clause provides that the United States "shall receive" $5,000,000 from Guatador in satisfaction of United States citizens' claims (under international law) against Guatador.

(c) A clause provides that the United States "shall reimburse" Guatadorian citizens for taxes for the preceding year paid by such citizens on certain categories of income hereafter made exempt from tax.

(d) A clause defines (so as to decrease) the taxes to be paid in future years by Guatadorian citizens to the United States (and vice versa) on certain categories of income.

(e) A clause provides that a theft in Guatador by any Guatadorian citizen of property owned by the United States shall constitute a crime (with defined sanctions) under United States law. The clause provides for venue in the District of Columbia. A Guatadorian citizen accused of such theft is later found in this country.

(f) A clause provides that the United States "shall accord equitable treatment to nationals and companies" of Guatador in the United States "both as to their persons and as to their property, enterprises and other interests."

(2) Compare Article I of the Franco-American Convention of Establishment * with illustration (f). Is that Article self-executing? What other problems might a court encounter if a French national founded a claim (perhaps the right to receive unemployment insurance on "national treatment" terms) upon Article I?

(3) Suppose that the United States ratified the International Covenant on Civil and Political Rights, p. 388, supra. Would a provision such as Article 17 be treated as self-executing?

(4) The treaty in Missouri v. Holland contemplated implementing legislation by the parties. If the administrative or other structure necessary to make the treaty effective had not required Congressional action, the treaty might have been considered self-executing. Should the fact that Congress would not have participated in the creation of a regulatory scheme have affected the Court's holding?

3. EXECUTIVE AGREEMENTS

Alongside the treaty with its distinct constitutional status, the executive agreement, a type of international accord which the Constitution does not in terms authorize, has come to play a significant role in this country's foreign relations.[38] An executive agreement may be a formal document looking very much like a treaty; it may however consist of a short and informal exchange of notes with another government. The critical distinction between it and a treaty, a distinction underscored by the procedures that are constitutionally required for a treaty, is that the executive agreement is entered into without the advice and consent of the Senate.

Because it is simpler and speedier, the executive agreement has won increasing favor. The following table indicates its rate of growth relative to the treaty.[39]

	Treaties	Executive Agreements
1789–1839	60	27
1839–1889	215	238
1889–1939	524	917
1940–1945	30	432
1946–1972	368	5,590

In addition, as of 1972 there appear to have been over 400 secret agreements whose substance had not been made public by the State Department. Some executive agreements, relating for example to postal union matters, may be routine in character, but others are of vast significance. The destroyers-for-bases agreement with Great Britain in 1940, the Yalta Agreement of 1945 and the General Agreement on Tariffs and Trade are leading examples.

The excerpts below from Star-Kist Foods, Inc. v. United States, 275 F.2d 472 (C.C.P.A.1959), suggest some major questions about executive agreements. An American producer of canned tuna fish protested the reduction of the tariff on certain imported tuna that had been effected pursuant to a trade agreement with Iceland. That executive agreement had been entered into pursuant to Section 350(a) of the Trade Agreements Act of 1934, as amended.[40] When considering the plaintiff's argument that the agreement was void because it

38. The Constitution does use the term "Agreement" when it prohibits the states in Art. I, Sec. 10 from engaging in certain conduct with foreign countries.

39. The table is derived through 1945 from Sutherland, Restricting the Treaty Power, 65 Harv.L.Rev. 1305, 1327–28 (1952), and McClure, International Executive Agreements 4 (1941). The 1946–1972 figures appear in Hearings on S. 3475 before the Subcommittee on Separation of Powers of the Senate Committee of the Judiciary, 92nd Cong., 2d Sess., 1972, p. 416.

40. Section 350(a), and the portion of the opinion which treated plaintiff's contention that the Trade Agreements Act involved an unconstitutional delegation of legislative power to the President, appear at pp. 109, 117, supra.

had not received the advice and consent of the Senate, the court stated in part:

> We now come to the other contention of appellants, that the trade agreement with Iceland executed by the President pursuant to the Trade Agreements Act is null and void because it is, in fact, a treaty and lacks the concurrence of the Senate, required by Article II, § 2 of the Constitution and, further, that since the agreement is illegal the proclamation which effectuated the agreement is also without legal effect.
>
> This procedure was established by Congress so that its policy and the basic philosophy which motivated the passage of the Trade Agreements Act could be realized. From reading the act, it is apparent that Congress concluded that the promotion of foreign trade required that the tariff barriers in this and other countries be modified on a negotiated basis. Since the President has the responsibility of conducting the foreign affairs of this country generally, it gave to him the added responsibility of negotiating the agreements in pursuance of the spirit of the act. Such a procedure is not without precedent nor judicial approval. The Supreme Court in Altman & Co. v. United States, 224 U.S. 583, 601, 32 S.Ct. 593, 597, 56 L.Ed. 894, recognized that not all commercial compacts are treaties, saying:
>
> ". . . While it may be true that this commercial agreement, made under authority of the Tariff Act of 1897, § 3, was not a treaty possessing the dignity of one requiring ratification by the Senate of the United States, it was an international compact, negotiated between the representatives of two sovereign nations, and made in the name and on behalf of the contracting countries, and dealing with important commercial relations between the two countries, and was proclaimed by the President. If not technically a treaty requiring ratification, nevertheless it was a compact authorized by the Congress of the United States, negotiated and proclaimed under the authority of its President."
>
> In United States v. Curtiss-Wright Export Corp. [p. 102, supra], the Court observed that "the power to make such international agreements as do not constitute treaties in the constitutional sense, . . . [although not] expressly affirmed by the Constitution, nevertheless exist[s] as inherently inseparable from the conception of nationality."

The court then relied upon the opinions of the Supreme Court in United States v. Belmont and United States v. Pink, pp. 598–602, infra, and held that "the trade agreement with Iceland and the accompanying proclamation are valid."

NOTE ON EXECUTIVE AGREEMENTS

(1) Are areas reserved to the treaty on which the executive agreement cannot trespass? Some writers have asserted that the two are interchangeable instruments, that all arrangements appropriate for a treaty can be accomplished via executive agreements.[41] Others

41. See, e. g., McDougal and Lans, Treaties and Congressional-Executive or Presidential Agreements: Interchangeable Instruments of National Policy, 54 Yale L.J. 181, 534 (1945).

have forcefully challenged that position. They point to the procedural safeguards which the Constitution establishes for the treaty, and to the many instances in the debates over the Constitution or in writings such as The Federalist of an intention to control executive powers in foreign affairs. They ask whether the framers could have intended that such safeguards be by-passed simply by a decision to employ the executive agreement.[42]

(2) Where the President and Congress work towards the same end, as in Star-Kist, the executive agreement has a solid basis. That is, legislation has explicitly authorized it. But an executive agreement may be the product of only Presidential action, without legislative support at the time that it is entered into, and without executive intention of seeking legislative approval or implementation thereafter. In such cases, the President must rely upon his independent and inherent powers under the Constitution. Their scope has never been clearly defined but would evidently cover such executive agreements as those treating deployment and supply of troops, to the extent that such deployment came within the President's power as commander-in-chief, and agreements recognizing foreign governments and settling claims of United States nationals against a foreign country.[43]

(3) Difficulties arise where Congress and the President appear to work at cross-purposes. In United States v. Rathjen Bros., 137 F.2d 103 (C.C.P.A.1943), the President, acting under Section 350 of the Trade Agreements Act, had reduced the duty on imports of rum from Cuba to $2 in 1934. Congress passed a Revenue Act in 1938 raising the duty on distilled liquors to $2.25. With respect to certain imports not including rum, the Act stated that increases in duty should not take effect if "in conflict with any international obligation of the United States." The court held that the Act and agreement were "absolutely irreconcilable" and that consequently the (later) Act superseded the agreement.

The statute came first and the agreement later in United States v. Guy W. Capps, Inc., 204 F.2d 655 (4th Cir. 1953). The Agricultural Act of 1948 authorized the President to limit imports of commodities that interfered with agricultural price support programs, after and

42. See e. g., Borchard, Treaties and Executive Agreements—A Reply, 54 Yale L.J. 616 (1945); Berger, The Presidential Monopoly of Foreign Relations, 71 Mich.L.Rev. 1 (1972).

43. Cf. Avramova v. United States, 354 F.Supp. 420 (S.D.N.Y.1973), an action in which plaintiffs alleged that an executive agreement of 1963 with Bulgaria settling claims of United States citizens against that country for an additional $400,000 was unconstitutional. The Court observed that "the agreement was constitutionally valid without the consent of the Senate, for the settling of claims of United States citizens against foreign countries is within the implied powers given to the Executive by the Constitution." In support of this broad statement, the Court cited United States v. Belmont and United States v. Pink, pp. 598 and 600, infra. Both cases involved executive agreements of broader reach which combined financial settlements with the recognition of a foreign government and the establishment of diplomatic relations. Of course, an executive agreement settling claims of foreign citizens against the United States would require congressional appropriations for its implementation.

based upon the Tariff Commission's investigations, findings and recommmendations. Instead of following these procedures, the President entered into an executive agreement with Canada which curtailed imports of potatoes (other than seed potatoes) into this country. The agreement provided in part that Canadian exporters would include in their contracts with United States importers a clause in which the importer gave assurance that the potatoes would not be used for table stock purposes. The Government brought an action to recover damages against a firm that was aware of the agreement, imported potatoes from Canada, allegedly stated that the potatoes were being imported for planting, and sold them for food rather than for seed purposes. The court quoted the language from Youngstown Sheet & Tube Co. v. Sawyer appearing at pp. 126–128, supra. Its opinion by JUDGE PARKER stated in part:

> It is argued, however, that the validity of the executive agreement was not dependent upon the Act of Congress but was made pursuant to the inherent powers of the President under the Constitution. The answer is that while the President has certain inherent powers under the Constitution such as the power pertaining to his position as Commander in Chief of Army and Navy and the power necessary to see that the laws are faithfully executed, the power to regulate interstate and foreign commerce is not among the powers incident to the Presidential office, but is expressly vested by the Constitution in the Congress. It cannot be upheld as an exercise of the power to see that the laws are faithfully executed, for, as said by Mr. Justice Holmes in his dissenting opinion in Myers v. United States, 272 U.S. 52, 177, 47 S.Ct. 21, 85, 71 L.Ed. 160, "The duty of the President to see that the laws be executed is a duty that does not go beyond the laws or require him to achieve more than Congress sees fit, to leave within his power". . . .
>
> We think that whatever the power of the executive with respect to making executive trade agreements regulating foreign commerce in the absence of action by Congress, it is clear that the executive may not through entering into such an agreement avoid complying with a regulation prescribed by Congress. Imports from a foreign country are foreign commerce subject to regulation, so far as this country is concerned, by Congress alone. The executive may not bypass congressional limitations regulating such commerce by entering into an agreement with the foreign country that the regulation be exercised by that country through its control over exports. Even though the regulation prescribed by the executive agreement be more desirable than that prescribed by Congressional action, it is the latter which must be accepted as the expression of national policy.

The court found the executive agreement invalid, and held on that and an independent ground for the importer. The Supreme Court affirmed on other grounds. 348 U.S. 296, 75 S.Ct. 326, 99 L.Ed. 329 (1955). Consider the following comments on the opinion in Henkin, Foreign Affairs and the Constitution 181–182 (1972):

> Judge Parker's suggestion [in the first quoted paragraph above], it should be clear, would not only deny to

many executive agreements effect as domestic law in the United States; it denies the President's power to make them at all. His argument is unpersuasive. It takes the narrowest view of the President's power, not even mentioning his foreign affairs powers. Judge Parker finds the President has no power because Congress does. If the President cannot make agreements on any matter on which Congress could legislate, there could be no executive agreements with domestic legal consequences, since, we have seen, the legislative power of Congress has few and far limits. If Judge Parker denied the President the power to make executive agreements only as to matters on which Congress has "express" powers to legislate, he was drawing a line between express and implied powers of Congress that makes little sense for any purpose. In either event it is difficult to see why the powers of Congress to legislate are any more relevant to determine the scope of Presidential power to commit the United States by executive agreement than by treaty.

Judge Parker's dictum does not accord with the practice either before or since he wrote: Presidents have made executive agreements on matters as to which Congress could legislate, notably international trade. Others have suggested other limitations: a sole executive agreement can be only "temporary" or of short duration; or, it can be effective only for the term of the President who makes it. None of these or similar suggestions has any apparent basis relevant to the scope of Presidential power generally, or to the Treaty Power, where any limitations on the power to make executive agreements should lie. One might suggest that the President must go to the Senate with "important" agreements, but even that "definition" would have at least one major qualification: executive agreements have been used for some very important agreements where either or both parties desired that the agreement remain confidential.

(4) Recall that Reid v. Covert, p. 564, supra, considered whether an executive agreement was valid in the light of certain constitutional provisions. Similarly, Seery v. United States, 127 F.Supp. 601 (Ct.Cl. 1955), involved the Fifth Amendment and a 1947 agreement (signed by the United States High Commissioner in Austria) between the United States and Austria under which Austria, upon payment of a sum to it by the United States, assumed all obligations incurred by United States forces to Austrians and to other persons owning property in Austria. The singer Maria Jeritza Seery, a naturalized United States citizen, brought an action in the Court of Claims for damages caused by the looting of her estate in Austria by American occupation forces between 1945 and 1947. She asserted that these acts constituted a "taking" under the Fifth Amendment. The Court of Claims held that the agreement could neither impair plaintiff's rights under the Fifth Amendment nor supersede the United States statute conferring jurisdiction upon it over claims for takings based upon the Amendment.

(5) The nebulous boundary line, if indeed such a line exists as a matter of constitutional law and not simply of executive policy, between subjects appropriate for treaties and executive agreements is another example of the vague demarcation in the Constitution between executive and congressional powers over foreign affairs. The development of the executive agreement as a vital instrument of foreign policy is a prime illustration of long-sanctioned practice which ripens into contemporary constitutional doctrine. The analogy to state practice which ripens into customary international law is evident.

Ultimately the courts may play a role in marking the limits of the executive agreement, although many such agreements (military accords, arbitral *compromis*) are not likely to enter domestic litigation. In practice, it appears more likely that political factors and compromises will play a major role in determining the extent to which the agreement displaces the treaty. State Department Circular No. 175, and contemporary legislation and legislative proposals to regulate executive agreements, pp. 604–606, infra, are illustrative. The bargaining and tacit accords between the Executive and the Congress over this issue resemble the resolution of questions of international law among nations through accommodation and restraint rather than through binding third-party decisions.

(6) When one considers that the executive agreement may be self-executing, congressional concern over its use becomes more understandable. Through executive action alone, the agreement may have significant consequences within both the domestic and international legal orders. On the other hand, an executive agreement which requires implementing legislation before it can realize its purposes secures a role to the legislative branch, although its participation then requires a majority vote of both houses of the Congress rather than a two-thirds vote of the Senate alone.

These considerations were prominent in "bargaining" between the Congress and the Executive over the 1965 Automotive Products Agreement between the United States and Canada.[44] This Agreement was intended to resolve difficulties that arose in the 1960's from Canadian tariff measures designed to encourage automobile production in Canada at the expense of imports and to spur Canadian exports in this field.

Article I of the Agreement provided that both governments would "seek the early achievement" of objectives which included liberalization of automotive trade "in respect of tariff barriers and other factors tending to impede it, with a view to enabling the industries of both countries to participate on a fair and equitable basis in the expanding total market of the two countries." The United States undertook in Article II to "seek enactment of legislation authorizing duty-free treatment of imports of the products of Canada" described in an Annex. "Promptly after the entry into force of such legislation, the Government of the United States shall accord duty-free treatment" to

44. Agreement Concerning Automotive Products between the Government of the United States of America and the Government of Canada, January 16, 1965, 17 U.S.T. & O.I.A. 1372, T.I.A.S. No. 6093.

such products. Under Article VI, the Agreement was to "enter into force provisionally on the date of signature and definitively on the date upon which notes are exchanged between the two Governments giving notice that appropriate action in their respective legislatures has been completed."

The circumstances under which the Agreement had been concluded raised serious questions in the Congress, both political and legal in character. These can here be stated summarily, without regard to the complexities of tariff matters explored in Chapter XI. The tariff legislation then in effect [45] authorized the President to enter into international agreements reducing tariffs up to stated limits and under stated conditions. The Agreement was not within that legislation's terms. Further, the Agreement violated our commitment, as a party to the General Agreement on Tariffs and Trade, to extend a tariff concession granted to any one country to all parties to the General Agreement.[46]

A letter of January 28, 1965 from Senator Fulbright, Chairman of the Foreign Relations Committee, to the Secretary of State requested an explanation for the administration's reasons for believing that the executive branch was competent to "bring into effect [the Agreement] without approval as a treaty." [47] The response, by letter dated February 9, 1965 from the Acting Assistant Secretary for Congressional Relations, stated in part:

> As you know article I, section 7, of the Constitution requires that "All bills for raising revenue shall originate in the House of Representatives." It has been generally recognized that when international agreements relating to revenue matters are entered into by treaty, this constitutional provision requires that implementing legislation also be obtained. In other words, treaties relating to the raising of revenue are not considered "self-executing" but require separate legislation. . . . In the case of agreements relating to tariffs, in order to avoid presenting the Senate with the necessity to act twice upon the same matter, it has been customary to enter into such arrangements in the form of Executive agreements implemented under legislative authority. . . .
>
> The need for reaching an agreement with Canada which would make it possible for Canada to end its remission plan at the earliest possible time made it impractical to seek authorizing legislation prior to entering into the agreement. However, the agreement itself recognizes the need to obtain

45. The Trade Expansion Act of 1962 was a successor to the Trade Agreements Act of 1934, a key part of which (Section 350) appears at p. 117, supra.

46. See Article I of the General Agreement.* By a decision of December 20, 1965, the contracting parties of the General Agreement granted a limited waiver to the United States—enabling it to eliminate customs duties with respect to automotive products of Canada only—pursuant to Article XXV (5) of the General Agreement.* B.I.S.D., 14th Supp. (1966), p. 37. The waiver provisions of the General Agreement are noted at pp. 1154–1159, infra.

47. All letters referred to on this issue appear in 111 Cong Rec. 9063–65, Senate, April 30, 1965.

> such legislation. . . . Proposed legislation to permit the United States to remove its duties will be submitted shortly.
> . . .

In a second letter of February 15, 1965 to the Secretary of State, Senator Fulbright wrote that the reply "does not, in my opinion, meet the issue. The issue is constitutional and the Department's position should rest on constitutional grounds, not on the procedural convenience of the Senate; i. e., to avoid presenting the Senate with the necessity to act twice upon the same matter." The letter requested "such legal opinion as may underlie the Department's decision in this case." The reply of February 24, 1965, of the Acting Legal Adviser to the State Department said in part:

> It is well settled that the President, by virtue of his constitutional power to conduct foreign relations, may enter into many types of international agreements without resort to the treaty-making process. . . . Some of these executive agreements require implementing legislation, some do not, but the power to enter into such agreements is quite broad. . . .
>
> The next question with regard to an executive agreement is whether it is self-executing or whether congressional action is necessary to implement it. While the line of demarcation is not always wholly clear, legislation is necessary where the United States is required under the agreement to take actions not consistent with existing statutes. Because the primary purpose of the automotive agreement is to remove existing duties on automotive products, and because this step is not permitted by existing trade legislation, implementing legislation is necessary. Accordingly, we have made sure in the agreement that we undertake no obligations requiring changes in statutory provisions until such implementing legislation is secured.
>
> It is, of course, open to the President to enter into a trade agreement through the treatymaking process. In most instances, ratification by the President after advice and consent by the Senate will bring a treaty into force as law. However, in some cases, treaties are not self-executing but require implementing legislation. This is true of a treaty which deals with revenue matters, where it has been thought that legislation is required to satisfy the provisions of article I, section 7, of the Constitution . . . . Since the automotive agreement contemplates the elimination of customs duties, under this view legislation would have been required even if the agreement were in the form of a treaty.
>
> . . . The question of whether a trade agreement should be entered into as a treaty or executive agreement rests in the judgment of the President. His choice is not dictated by the Constitution but by his own appraisal of the merits of either choice. . . .
>
> The President's choice between the treaty and executive agreement procedures will be based on many factors, including foreign policy considerations. For example, with regard to several recent multilateral commodity agreements, it was the judgment of the President that the participation in the agreement by the United States should be made through the

> treaty process. As you know, these agreements are of great importance to the less developed member countries, and it was believed that the status of these agreements would be enhanced if the United States and the other member countries followed the formal treaty process in ratifying them. This procedure has usually been followed in multilateral agreements dealing with commodities, but in some cases . . . the President considered the executive agreement with legislation procedure appropriate.
>
> The United States-Canadian automotive agreement is bilateral and deals with the elimination of duties. It has been the regular practice for over 30 years to use the executive agreement-legislative authority procedure for agreements of this type. In the usual case, the legislative authority has been provided first and the executive agreement made later—as under the reciprocal trade legislation of 1934 and the Trade Expansion Act of 1962. However, it is equally within the constitutional powers of the President to make an executive agreement first, subject to the enactment of legislation and have the legislation follow. . . .

The legislation required to implement the Agreement—the Automotive Products Trade Act of 1965—was enacted soon after this correspondence. 79 Stat. 1021, 19 U.S.C.A. §§ 2001–2033.

QUESTIONS

(1) Do you agree with the court in Rathjen, p. 591, supra, in view of the quoted language? Should a court in such a situation presume that Congress did not intend to override international agreements—a presumption that could be overcome only by explicit statements to the contrary? Compare the observations in The Over The Top, at p. 540, supra.

(2) Do you agree with the Court of Appeals in Capps, p. 591, supra? Suppose that federal legislation provided that no American serviceman was to be surrendered to foreign officials for a criminal trial based on acts allegedly committed in that country, and that a later executive agreement provided that in some criminal cases, servicemen would be surrendered for trial by the host country's courts. Would the Capps opinion suggest that the agreement was invalid?

COMMENT

The preceding cases in which a party challenged an executive agreement involved arguments that the agreement was invalid (1) because it was not a "treaty," the only instrument authorized by the Constitution for making international agreement, (2) because it violated legislative commands, and (3) because it violated constitutional provisions which secured to an individual certain procedural or substantive rights. Like the treaty, the executive agreement has also been challenged on the ground that it invaded state prerogatives, areas reserved by the Constitution to the law-making power of the states.

The two following cases raise this last issue. They arose in a fairly complicated setting. By decrees of 1918 and 1919, the Soviet Government nationalized the business and assets of all Russian companies, wherever they or their assets were situated. In November

1933, the United States recognized the Soviet Government as the *de jure* government of the U.S.S.R. As an incident to that recognition, the United States accepted an assignment, known as the Litvinov Assignment, of certain claims. The Assignment, in the form of a letter to the President of the United States from Litvinov, the Soviet Commissar for Foreign Affairs, referred to pending claims by the United States, on behalf of its nationals, for property expropriated by the Soviet Union. The letter stated that, preparatory to a final settlement of such claims, the Soviet Union would not attempt to collect any amounts "admitted to be due or that may be found to be due it" from United States nationals and that the Soviet Union did "hereby release and assign all such amounts to the Government of the United States," which was to notify the Soviet Government of any amounts realized by it from the release and assignment. President Roosevelt, in a letter to Litvinov, stated: ". . . I shall be pleased to notify your Government . . . of any amount realized by . . . the United States from the release and assignment to it of the amounts admitted to be due, or that may be found to be due [the Soviet Government]." [48]

The decisions below concern assets of Russian companies in New York State. They raise a number of difficult issues concerning the Litvinov Assignment and its effect upon New York law. The excerpts treat principally the relationship between executive agreements and state law, and treat briefly, or omit mention of, the issues pertaining to New York principles of conflict of laws, recognition of the extraterritorial effect of Soviet decrees upon assets in New York, and the act of state doctrine.

UNITED STATES v. BELMONT

Supreme Court of the United States, 1937.
301 U.S. 324, 57 S.Ct. 758, 81 L.Ed. 1134.

[The Supreme Court, in an opinion by JUSTICE SUTHERLAND, reversed a decision of a federal court of appeals and held that a complaint by the United States seeking the recovery of sums deposited by a Russian corporation prior to 1918 with a New York private banker (Belmont) stated a cause of action.

The Court treated briefly the argument that recognition of the Soviet nationalization decrees of 1918 as having an effect upon deposits of Russian corporations in banks in New York State would violate the "controlling public policy" of that state. "We do not pause to inquire whether in fact there was any policy of the State of New York to be infringed, since we are of opinion that no state policy can prevail against the international compact here involved." The Court then referred to the Litvinov Assignment, upon which the United States based its claim.]

We take judicial notice of the fact that coincident with the assignment set forth in the complaint, the President recognized the Soviet government, and normal diplomatic relations were established

48. The use of funds derived through the Litvinov Assignment to satisfy claims of United States citizens against the Soviet Union is described at p. 433, supra.

between that government and the government of the United States, followed by an exchange of ambassadors. The effect of this was to validate, so far as this country is concerned, all acts of the Soviet government here involved from the commencement of its existence. The recognition, establishment of diplomatic relations, the assignment, and agreements with respect thereto, were all parts of one transaction, resulting in an international compact between the two governments. That the negotiations, acceptance of the assignment and agreements and understandings in respect thereof were within the competence of the President may not be doubted. Governmental power over internal affairs is distributed between the national government and the several states. Governmental power over external affairs is not distributed, but is vested exclusively in the national government. And in respect of what was done here, the Executive had authority to speak as the sole organ of that government. The assignment and the agreements in connection therewith did not, as in the case of treaties, as that term is used in the treaty making clause of the Constitution (article 2, § 2), require the advice and consent of the Senate.

A treaty signifies "a compact made between two or more independent nations, with a view to the public welfare." B. Altman & Co. v. United States, 224 U.S. 583, 600, 32 S.Ct. 593, 596, 56 L.Ed. 894. But an international compact, as this was, is not always a treaty which requires the participation of the Senate. There are many such compacts, of which a protocol, a modus vivendi, a postal convention, and agreements like that now under consideration are illustrations. . . .

Plainly, the external powers of the United States are to be exercised without regard to state laws or policies. The supremacy of a treaty in this respect has been recognized from the beginning. Mr. Madison, in the Virginia Convention, said that if a treaty does not supersede existing state laws, as far as they contravene its operation, the treaty would be ineffective. "To counteract it by the supremacy of the state laws, would bring on the Union the just charge of national perfidy, and involve us in war." 3 Elliot's Debates 515. And see Ware v. Hylton, 3 Dall. 199, 236, 237, 1 L.Ed. 568. And while this rule in respect of treaties is established by the express language of clause 2, article 6, of the Constitution, the same rule would result in the case of all international compacts and agreements from the very fact that complete power over international affairs is in the national government and is not and cannot be subject to any curtailment or interference on the part of the several states. Compare United States v. Curtiss-Wright Export Corporation, 299 U.S. 304, 316 et seq., 57 S.Ct. 216, 219, 81 L.Ed. 255. In respect of all international negotiations and compacts, and in respect of our foreign relations generally, state lines disappear. As to such purposes the state of New York does not exist. Within the field of its powers, whatever the United States rightfully undertakes, it necessarily has warrant to consummate. And when judicial authority is invoked in aid of such consummation, State Constitutions, state laws, and state policies are irrelevant to the inquiry and decision. It is inconceivable that any of them can be interposed as an obstacle to the effective operation of a federal constitutional power. Cf. Missouri v. Holland, 252 U.S. 416, 40 S.Ct. 382, 64 L.Ed. 641, 11 A.L.R. 984; Asakura v. Seattle, 265 U.S. 332, 341, 44 S.Ct. 515, 516, 68 L.Ed. 1041.

[The Court then rejected the argument that the enforcement of claims under the Litvinov Assignment would violate the provision of the Fifth Amendment that property not be taken without just compensation. It noted that the sole interest of the respondent banker was that of custodian for the funds, and that the record did not indicate any competing claims by United States citizens against the deposited funds.]

UNITED STATES v. PINK

Supreme Court of the United States, 1942.
315 U.S. 203, 62 S.Ct. 552, 86 L.Ed. 796.

[The First Russian Insurance Co. had opened a branch in New York State in 1907. The branch discontinued operations in 1925, and Pink (Superintendent of Insurance of New York State) took possession of its assets pursuant to state court orders. After having settled claims of domestic creditors arising from the business of the New York branch, Pink retained the balance of the assets for distribution, pursuant to state court orders, to foreign creditors and thereafter to the directors of the Russian company.

The United States brought suit under the Litvinov Assignment in the New York courts to recover these remaining assets. The New York Court of Appeals affirmed a dismissal of the complaint, relying upon its prior decision in Moscow Fire Insurance Co. v. Bank of New York & Trust Co., 280 N.Y. 286, 20 N.E.2d 758 (1939) to the effect that Soviet nationalization decrees had no extraterritorial effect with respect to assets in New York State and that, as a consequence, the United States acquired no rights with respect to such assets under the Litvinov Assignment. That decision had been affirmed by an equally divided Supreme Court, 309 U.S. 624, 50 S.Ct. 725, 84 L.Ed. 986 (1940).

The Supreme Court granted a writ of certiorari in the Pink case. Portions of the opinion, delivered by JUSTICE DOUGLAS, reversing the judgment of the New York Court of Appeals, appear below. The first part held that the affirmance by an equally divided Court in Moscow Fire Insurance Co. was not an authoritative determination of the issue posed.]

Second: The New York Court of Appeals held in the Moscow case that the Russian decrees in question had no extraterritorial effect. If that is true, it is decisive of the present controversy. For the United States acquired under the Litvinov Assignment only such rights as Russia had. Guaranty Trust Co. v. United States, 304 U.S. 126, 143, 58 S.Ct. 785, 793, 82 L.Ed. 1224. If the Russian decrees left the New York assets of the Russian insurance companies unaffected, then Russia had nothing here to assign. But that question of foreign law is not to be determined exclusively by the state court. The claim of the United States based on the Litvinov Assignment raises a federal question. United States v. Belmont, 301 U.S. 324, 57 S.Ct. 758, 81 L.Ed. 1134. . . .

We hold that so far as its intended effect is concerned the Russian decree embraced the New York assets of the First Russian Insurance Co.

Third: The question of whether the decree should be given extraterritorial effect is of course a distinct matter. One primary issue raised in that connection is whether under our constitutional system New York law can be allowed to stand in the way. . . .

. . . But, as we have seen, the Russian decree in question was intended to have an extraterritorial effect and to embrace funds of the kind which are here involved. Nor can there be any serious doubt that claims of the kind here in question were included in the Litvinov Assignment. It is broad and inclusive. It should be interpreted consonantly with the purpose of the compact to eliminate all possible sources of friction between these two great nations. . . .

The holding in the Belmont case is therefore determinative of the present controversy unless the stake of the foreign creditors in this liquidation proceeding and the provision which New York has provided for their protection call for a different result.

[The Court held (Part "Fourth") that neither New York policy nor the Fifth Amendment barred the United States from recovering assets in this contest between it and foreign creditors of the Russian Insurance Company whose claims did not arise out of transactions with the New York branch. It stressed the purpose of the Litvinov Assignment, "part and parcel" of the policy of recognition, to resolve tensions between the two countries by settling claims of United States nationals against the Soviet Union, and it concluded that the United States could secure for itself, on behalf of its nationals, priority over foreign creditors against the Russian Company's assets in New York. The Court continued:]

If the priority had been accorded American claims by treaty with Russia, there would be no doubt as to its validity. . . . The same result obtains here. The powers of the President in the conduct of foreign relations included the power, without consent of the Senate, to determine the public policy of the United States with respect to the Russian nationalization decrees. "What government is to be regarded here as representative of a foreign sovereign state is a political rather than a judicial question, and is to be determined by the political department of the government." Guaranty Trust Co. v. United States, supra, 304 U.S. page 137, 58 S.Ct. page 791, 82 L.Ed. 1224. That authority is not limited to a determination of the government to be recognized. It includes the power to determine the policy which is to govern the question of recognition. Objections to the underlying policy as well as objections to recognition are to be addressed to the political department and not to the courts. . . . Recognition is not always absolute; it is sometimes conditional. 1 Moore, International Law Digest (1906), pp. 73–74; 1 Hackworth, Digest of International Law (1940), pp. 192–195. Power to remove such obstacles to full recognition as settlement of claims of our nationals (Levitan, Executive Agreements, 35 Ill.L.Rev. 365, 382–385) certainly is a modest implied power of the President who is the "sole organ of the federal government in the field of international relations." United States v. Curtiss-Wright Corp., supra, 299 U.S. page 320, 57 S.Ct. page 221, 81 L.Ed. 225. Effectiveness in handling the delicate problems of foreign relations requires no less. Unless such a power exists, the power of recognition might be thwarted or seriously diluted. No such obstacle can be placed in the way of rehabilitation of relations between this country and another nation, unless the historic conception of the powers and responsibilities of the President in the conduct of foreign affairs (see Moore, Treaties and Executive Agreements, 20 Pol.Sc.Q. 385, 403–417) is to be drastically revised. It was the judgment of the political department that full recognition of the Soviet Government required the settlement of all outstanding problems including the claims of our nationals. Recognition and the Litvinov Assignment were interdependent. We would usurp the executive function if we held that that decision was not final and conclusive in the courts. . . .

It is of course true that even treaties with foreign nations will be carefully construed so as not to derogate from the authority and jurisdiction of the States of this nation unless clearly necessary to effectuate the national policy. . . . But state law must yield when it is inconsistent with or impairs the policy or provisions of a treaty or of an international compact or agreement. . . . Enforcement of New York's policy as formulated by the Moscow case would collide with and subtract from the Federal policy, whether it was premised on the absence of extraterritorial effect of the Russian decrees, the conception of the New York branch as a distinct juristic personality, or disapproval by New York of the Russian program of nationalization. For the Moscow case refuses to give effect or recognition in New York to acts of the Soviet Government which the United States by its policy of recognition agreed no longer to question. Enforcement of such state policies would indeed tend to restore some of the precise impediments to friendly relations which the President intended to remove on inauguration of the policy of recognition of the Soviet Government. In the first place, such action by New York, no matter what gloss be given it, amounts to official disapproval or non-recognition of the nationalization program of the Soviet Government. That disapproval or non-recognition is in the face of a disavowal by the United States of any official concern with that program. It is in the face of the underlying policy adopted by the United States when it recognized the Soviet Government. In the second place, to the extent that the action of the State in refusing enforcement of the Litvinov Assignment results in reduction or nonpayment of claims of our nationals, it helps keep alive one source of friction which the policy of recognition intended to remove. Thus the action of New York tends to restore some of the precise irritants which had long affected the relations between these two great nations and which the policy of recognition was designed to eliminate. . . .

We repeat that there are limitations on the sovereignty of the States. No State can rewrite our foreign policy to conform to its own domestic policies. Power over external affairs is not shared by the States; it is vested in the national government exclusively. It need not be so exercised as to conform to state laws or state policies whether they be expressed in constitutions, statutes, or judicial decrees. And the policies of the States become wholly irrelevant to judicial inquiry, when the United States, acting within its constitutional sphere, seeks enforcement of its foreign policy in the courts. . .

We hold that the right to the funds or property in question became vested in the Soviet Government as the successor to the First Russian Insurance Co.; that this right has passed to the United States under the Litvinov Assignment; and that the United States is entitled to the property as against the corporation and the foreign creditors. . . .

[JUSTICE FRANKFURTER concurred in a separate opinion. CHIEF JUSTICE STONE dissented in an opinion joined by JUSTICE ROBERTS.]

QUESTION

An executive agreement states that nationals of Guatador can practice medicine in the United States upon meeting certain qualifications. Do the opinions in Belmont and Pink support an argument that the agreement supersedes a state law barring aliens from the practice of medicine?

Additional reading: Borchard, Extraterritorial Confiscations, 36 Am. J.Int.L. 275 (1942); Cardozo, The Authority in Internal Law of International Treaties: The Pink Case, 13 Syracuse L.Rev. 544 (1962); Jessup, The Litvinov Assignment and the Pink Case, 36 Am.J.Int.L. 282 (1942).

4. CONTEMPORARY CONGRESSIONAL–EXECUTIVE TENSIONS OVER INTERNATIONAL AGREEMENTS

The heightened interdependence among nations since World War II, with its economic, political and legal implications, led to optimism among some within the United States about the developing world order, but to suspicion and distrust for others. The implosion of international concerns into the national legal-political order troubled many citizens anxious to preserve the country's "sovereignty" and autonomy. The fear that new principles derived from international politics, law or organizations would displace rules created within our own institutional structures found early expression in the insistence by the Senate upon the Connally Reservation, p. 320, supra.

Another reaction took the form of a group of proposals for constitutional amendments, collectively known as the Bricker Amendment, which provoked intense debate as they were introduced in the Senate during the period 1952–1954.[49] The proposals, a few among which failed only narrowly to gain the requisite two-thirds support in the Senate, sought to limit the use of the treaty power, particularly with respect to its effect upon state law; to control the use of self-executing treaties rather than treaties followed by legislation; and to determine the boundary between the treaty power and executive agreements. The political issues of that period which provoked these proposals are not difficult to envision. Many concerned the draft conventions which emerged from various bodies within the United Nations: the Genocide Convention, p. 387, supra, and the proposals bearing upon human rights which subsequently took form in documents such as the International Covenant on Civil and Political Rights and the Convention on Elimination of all Forms of Racial Discrimination, pp. 387–390, supra.

Although the proposals failed to achieve the necessary congressional and popular support, the prominence and the passion of the debate over them exerted a restraining influence on our foreign policy which has not wholly vanished today. Any prospect of our current participation in the human rights conventions appears stifled. Partly in response to the fears expressed by the proposals, the State Department issued in 1955 its Circular No. 175 (reprinted in 50 Am.J.Int.L. 784 (1956)) on the scope of the treaty power. That Circular reflected the concerns of the period in a provision in its Section 2 that treaties were "not to be used as a device for the purpose of effecting internal social changes or to try to circumvent the constitutional procedures established in relation to what are essentially matters of domestic concern."

49. See Buergenthal, International Human Rights: U. S. Policy and Priorities, 14 Va.J.Int.L. 611, 612–614 (1973), for a brief review of the Bricker Amendment and for references to source materials.

The State Department revised Circular No. 175 in 1969, and again in 1974.[50] As of early 1975, relevant portions of that Circular provided:

> 710 *Purpose*
>
> a. The purpose of this chapter is to facilitate the application of orderly and uniform measures and procedures in the negotiation, signature, publication, and registration of treaties and other international agreements of the United States. . . .
>
> . . .
>
> 720.2 *General Objectives*
>
> The objectives are:
>
> *a.* That the making of treaties and other international agreements for the United States is carried out within constitutional and other appropriate limits;
>
> . . .
>
> *c.* That timely and appropriate consultation is had with congressional leaders and committees on treaties and other international agreements;
>
> . . .
>
> 721 *Exercise of the International Agreement Power*
>
> 721.1 *Determination of Type of Agreement*
>
> The following considerations will be taken into account along with other relevant factors in determining whether an international agreement shall be dealt with by the United States as a treaty to be brought into force with the advice and consent of the Senate, or as an agreement to be brought into force on some other constitutional basis.
>
> 721.2 *Constitutional Requirements*
>
> There are two procedures under the Constitution through which the United States becomes a party to international agreements. Those procedures and the constitutional parameters of each are:
>
> *a. Treaties*
>
> International agreements (regardless of their title, designation, or form) whose entry into force with respect to the United States takes place only after the Senate has given its advice and consent are "treaties." The President, with the advice and consent of two-thirds of the Senators present, may enter into an international agreement on any subject genuinely of concern in foreign relations, so long as the agreement does not contravene the United States Constitution; and
>
> *b. International Agreements Other Than Treaties*
>
> International agreements brought into force with respect to the United States on a constitutional basis other than with the advice and consent of the Senate are "international agreements

50. Department of State, Foreign Affairs Manual, June 6, 1969—Chapter 700, Treaties and other International Agreements; Department of State, Foreign Affairs Manual, October 25, 1974—Chapter 700, Treaties and other International Agreements.

other than treaties." (The term "executive agreement" is appropriately reserved for agreements made solely on the basis of the constitutional authority of the President.) There are three constitutional bases for international agreements other than treaties as set forth below. An international agreement may be concluded pursuant to one or more of these constitutional bases:

(*1*) *Agreements Pursuant to Treaty*

The President may conclude an international agreement pursuant to a treaty brought into force with the advice and consent of the Senate, whose provisions constitute authorization for the agreement by the Executive without subsequent action by the Congress;

(*2*) *Agreements Pursuant to Legislation*

The President may conclude an international agreement on the basis of existing legislation or subject to legislation to be enacted by the Congress; and

(*3*) *Agreements Pursuant to the Constitutional Authority of the President*

The President may conclude an international agreement on any subject within his constitutional authority so long as the agreement is not inconsistent with legislation enacted by the Congress in the exercise of its constitutional authority. The constitutional sources of authority for the President to conclude international agreements include:

(*a*) The President's authority as Chief Executive to represent the nation in foreign affairs;

(*b*) The President's authority to receive ambassadors and other public ministers;

(*c*) The President's authority as "Commander-in-Chief"; and

(*d*) The President's authority to "take care that the laws be faithfully executed."

721.3 *Considerations for Selecting Among Constitutionally Authorized Procedures*

In determining a question as to the procedure which should be followed for any particular international agreement, due consideration is given to the following factors along with those in section 721.2:

a. The extent to which the agreement involves commitments or risks affecting the nation as a whole;

b. Whether the agreement is intended to affect State laws;

c. Whether the agreement can be given effect without the enactment of subsequent legislation by the Congress;

d. Past United States practice with respect to similar agreements;

e. The preference of the Congress with respect to a particular type of agreement;

f. The degree of formality desired for an agreement;

g. The proposed duration of the agreement, the need for prompt conclusion of an agreement, and the desirability of concluding a routine or short-term agreement; and

h. The general international practice with respect to similar agreements.

In determining whether any international agreement should be brought into force as a treaty or as an international agreement other than a treaty, the utmost care is to be exercised to avoid any invasion or compromise of the constitutional powers of the Senate, the Congress as a whole, or the President.

721.4 *Questions as to Type of Agreement To Be Used; Consultation With Congress*

a. All legal memorandums accompanying Circular 175 requests will discuss thoroughly the bases for the type of agreement recommended.

b. When there is any question whether an international agreement should be concluded as a treaty or as an international agreement other than a treaty, the matter is brought to the attention of the Legal Adviser of the Department. If the Legal Adviser considers the question to be a serious one that may warrant congressional consultation, a memorandum will be transmitted to the Assistant Secretary for Congressional Relations and other officers concerned. Upon receiving their views on the subject, the Legal Adviser shall, if the matter has not been resolved, transmit a memorandum thereon to the Secretary for his decision. Every practicable effort will be made to identify such questions at the earliest possible date so that consultations may be completed in sufficient time to avoid last-minute consideration.

c. Consultations on such questions will be held with congressional leaders and committees as may be appropriate. . . .

. . .

The 1974 revision of Circular No. 175 reflects the tensions described below that developed between the Congress and the Executive during the late 1960's and early 1970's, as well as the legislation cited below that was enacted or proposed during that period. Note, for example, the continuing attention to consultation with the Congress, and the considerations emphasized in § 721.3. Compare with the preceding materials the definition of the scope of the treaty power in § 721.2(a).

By the late 1960's different tensions over international agreements had developed. Although the human rights conventions continued to figure in congressional debates over these matters, it was the Vietnamese war which directed Congress and the nation to new concerns over executive prerogative. We have examined these issues with respect to the war powers of the Congress and the President, pp. 142–159, supra. But the controversy between the two branches spilled over into the field of international agreements. It has taken acute form with respect to the demarcation of a boundary line between treaties and executive agreements.

Some concern about excessive use of the executive agreement has always been present. But the prospect of defense and military commitments being made through bilateral agreements about bases and troop deployment, without participation by the Senate, stimulated several legislative proposals. Some addressed particularly those types of agreements which bear upon defense or military undertakings. Other proposals, no doubt inspired by the experience of the Vietnamese War, have sought to control executive prerogative more generally in the use of international agreements.

As of 1974, the most significant legislation that had been enacted was the Transmittal Act of 1972, 86 Stat. 619, 1 U.S.C.A. § 112b. This Act requires the Secretary of State to transmit to the Congress the text of "any international agreement, other than a treaty," as soon as practicable after it has entered into force with respect to the United States, within a maximum period of 60 days. In its report on this legislation, a House committee [51] noted that the Congress had "not always been adequately informed" about agreements, numbers of which remain secret. This situation tended to "create tensions and irritations" between the two branches and impede the prosecution of an effective foreign policy. The committee stressed that the "right of the President to *conclude* executive agreements is not in question here . . . [and] the bill in no way transgresses on the independent authority of the Executive in the area of foreign affairs."

In 1972, several senators introduced a bill on Congressional Review of Executive Agreements.[52] The bill noted that the powers of Congress "have been substantially eroded by the use of so-called executive agreements, and the Senate is hereby prevented from performing its duties under section 2, article II, of the Constitution . . ." Section 1 provides for the prompt transmittal to the Congress (subject to provisions for consideration in secrecy by members of Congress where national security so suggests) of all subsequent executive agreements. Such agreements would come into force for the United States not earlier than the end of 60 days of continuous session of the Congress after transmittal of the agreements, unless "both Houses pass concurrent resolutions stating in substance that both Houses do not approve the executive agreement." Section 2 defines an executive agreement as any international agreement or commitment other than a treaty "binding upon the United States" and made by an officer of the executive branch.

Senator Ervin, a sponsor, expressed the view that executive agreements had reached beyond "routine technical matters" and had begun "to deal with problems formerly dealt with only by treaty," thus circumventing the constitution. He viewed (the similar provi-

51. H.Rep. 92–1301 of the House Foreign Affairs Committee to Accompany S. 596, August 3, 1974.

52. The description of and quotations from the bill and the views of various persons about it are taken from Hearings on S. 3475 (Congressional Review of Executive Agreements) before the Subcommittee on Separation of Powers of the Senate Committee on the Judiciary, 92nd Cong. 2d Sess., April-May 1972.

sions of the 1969 version of) Circular No. 175, supra, as "a masterpiece of circularity" in its attempt to spell out the boundaries of the executive agreement. He cautioned that the "doctrine of inherent powers seems to have become the most important rationale used by the executive branch in recent years in its effort to usurp legislative power both in the domestic and foreign affairs arenas." [53]

In his testimony opposing enactment of the bill, John R. Stevenson, Legal Adviser to the State Department, stated that about 97% of executive agreements rested upon previous or subsequent statutory authority, with only 3% depending solely upon the President's inherent authority. (Such percentages did not include many technical cooperation agreements between individual government agencies and their foreign counterparts.) He thus disagreed with the view that executive agreements were displacing treaties and noted that in implementing Circular No. 175, the Legal Adviser's office had developed more specific criteria. Treaties should be used where (1) the subject matter traditionally had been dealt with by treaties; (2) the subject matter was not wholly within powers delegated by Congress or within the independent constitutional authority of the President; (3) the agreement was to have force of law without legislation and such action was not within the President's independent authority; (4) "the agreement involves important commitments affecting the nation as a whole, such as our defense commitments"; and (5) the agreement was thought to require the "utmost formality". These criteria, in his view, could not be made more precise. (Note that several of them appear in the 1974 revision of Circular No. 175, supra.) The best answer lay in following the consultation procedures of Circular No. 175.[54]

After hearings on the bill, no further action was taken by the 92nd Congress. The bill was reintroduced as S. 1472 in the 93rd Congress, but no action was taken on it. Another and similar bill, S. 3830, travelled as far—but only as far—as passage by the Senate.

QUESTIONS

(1) Would you support the bill (Congressional Review of Executive Agreements) in its present form? If not, with which of the following objections to it do you agree?

> (*a*) Mr. Stevenson stressed a traditional justification for the executive agreement, its speed and flexibility at a time when many technical arrangements had to be worked out and revised in the context of trade pacts, foreign-aid arrangements, surplus-food distributions and such matters. He viewed the bill as an expression of a deeper concern affecting basically defense and military matters. Such matters raised special problems in view of the President's constitutional role of commander-in-chief. Thus the legislation reached unnecessarily broadly to handle one complex and divisive set of issues.

53. Id. at 1–5.

54. Id. at 250.

(*b*) Mr. Stevenson observed that there are "some agreements—though probably an extremely small number—which it is solely within the President's authority to conclude and with which the Congress may not constitutionally interfere." He noted that the bill made no exceptions for such agreements.[55]

(*c*) Some favoring the policy underlying the bill found the bill insufficiently strict with the executive. One proposal was that the bill require the affirmative vote of the Senate and House before an executive agreement could become effective.

(2) Professor McDougal wrote to the Chairman of the Subcommittee holding the hearings[56] in opposition to the bill. "I don't believe any one branch of the government presently has the constitutional competence to regulate how another branch exercises its independent competence to make agreements . . . Hence, any new and clearer definition, if one is desirable and possible, would have to be made by constitutional amendment." Do you believe it advisable to seek such an amendment, and of what character?

PROBLEM

Our prior discussions of human-rights issues have addressed the substantive rather than remedial aspects of the conventions. Consider now the problems posed by methods of enforcing such conventions.[57]

(1) Suppose the Senate were debating consent to ratification of the International Covenant on Civil and Political Rights, pp. 388–390, supra. Debate extends to the declaration under Article 41, as well as to the optional protocol treating communications to the Human Rights Committee from individuals. How would you as a Senator resolve the following questions that are put to you?

(*a*) Suppose that a federal prisoner alleges that his trial was unduly delayed in violation of Article 14(3)(c) and seeks to file a complaint with the Human Rights Committee after denial of his claim in the domestic courts. Would there be constitutional or other objections to such a procedure? Could federal legislation make the work of the Committee more effective by giving Committee members the right to visit the prisoner, to hold informal hearings, or indeed to benefit from official process (such as the issuance of a subpoena at their request by the Attorney General acting on behalf of the Committee)?

(*b*) Suppose the facts were the same, but the prisoner had been convicted in a state court and was held in a state prison after exhaustion of local remedies.

55. Mr. Stevenson also developed a constitutional problem stemming from the use of concurrent resolutions by both Houses. Mr. Stevenson noted that the proposed procedure for use of a concurrent resolution not having the force of law might be in violation of the provisions of Article I, sec. 7, contemplating presidential approval or veto.

56. Letter of April 12, 1972, appearing in the Hearings, fn. 52, supra, at p. 627.

57. Some of these matters are considered in Nathanson, Constitutional Problems Involved in Adherence by the United States to a Convention for the Protection of Human Rights and Fundamental Freedoms, 50 Cornell L.Q. 235 (1965), and in Kutner, World Habeas Corpus, 24 U.Miami L.Rev. 352 (1970).

(2) Suppose the Senate were considering consent to ratification of a convention on the model of the European Convention on Human Rights, pp. 384–387, supra, including optional declarations relating to the jurisdiction of the Commission of Human Rights and the Court of Human Rights.

(*a*) Would you object—and if so, on what grounds—to the provisions relating to petitions from individuals (perhaps a prisoner in the circumstances described in question (1)(a) above), and to decisions possibly adverse to the United States on the part of the Commission and the Committee of Ministers, whose decision the parties agree "to regard as binding on them"?

(*b*) Would you object to the provisions relating to the Court, before whom the Commission might bring a case against the United States on behalf of a federal or state prisoner who had submitted a petition to it?

(3) Suppose that the United States ratifies the Genocide Convention, pp. 574–578, supra, and at a later stage considers whether to accede to a supplementary treaty providing for the international penal tribunal contemplated in Article VI of the Convention. Such a tribunal would find few international precedents, and those dominantly in the trial of German and Japanese war criminals after World War II. (See pp. 904–912, infra.)

(*a*) Assume that such a tribunal consisted of judges chosen so as to achieve varying representation from contracting parties, as in the case of the ICJ, and that the tribunal sat outside the United States. Assume that provisions for the payment of criminal fines or imprisonment would not require assistance from this country. If the acts (including conspiracy and attempts) constituting the crime of genocide were committed by a United States citizen within this country, would you object to a treaty obligation to surrender that person to the international penal tribunal for trial? If so, would you also object to the provisions in question (2) above requiring the United States to appear as defendant before an international Commission or Court which might afford relief to an individual plaintiff before it?

(*b*) Suppose the acts allegedly constituting genocide were committed by a United States citizen outside the United States, but the citizen had later returned here. Would your objections, if any, be the same?

(4) Suppose that a human rights convention provided for the right of direct appeal from the highest national tribunal to an international court, whenever a defendant in a criminal proceeding raised a claim under the Convention. Should the United States agree to such a provision?

---

5. TREATY INTERPRETATION BY NATIONAL COURTS

Chapter III considered some problems that confront international tribunals in construing treaties. We here view treaty construction from a national court's perspective. Significant differences emerge.

First, the type of treaty dealt with by domestic courts is more likely than treaties interpreted by international tribunals to affect rights of private parties and to be relatively detailed and specific.

Tax, tariff and extradition treaties are illustrative. Nonetheless, many of them—Friendship, Commerce and Navigation treaties, for example—resort occasionally to terms of constitutional breadth: "fair and equitable treatment," "national treatment," "free access."

Second, a national court may be reluctant to construe, indeed be precluded from construing, a treaty in a way inconsistent with national interests and desires, as expressed through the nation's executive or legislative branches. We consider below, for example, the degree to which a court may be bound to follow the views of the Executive in treaty interpretation. Even when the Executive is silent, it may be difficult for a court to suppress its nationalistic leanings and domestic biases. It may be more tempted than an international tribunal to construe a treaty as not significantly limiting the "sovereignty" of its country. Or the court may be subject in a subtle but pervasive way to a tendency to interpret treaty language in the sense suggested by its own domestic-law framework, and thus be less capable of composing conflicting national views. The national court is particularly sensitive to the fact that a treaty has a dual nature. At the same time, it (or legislation enacting the treaty as domestic law) is a part of the "law of the land" and an international obligation of a contractual nature. This sensitivity is evident in the two cases which follow.

Note that the relationship between a national court and an international tribunal has little similarity to a domestic appellate system. Even where a treaty provides for arbitration of disputes arising under it, national tribunals are often *de facto* the courts of last resort on questions of interpretation. They are particularly apt to be the courts of initial resort—as indeed would normally be required by the doctrine of exhaustion of local remedies—and of final resort for treaties that affect rights or duties of private parties: tax conventions, Friendship, Commerce and Navigation treaties, and so on. And if a treaty does come before an international tribunal after it has been interpreted by the national court, the international tribunal is of course not bound by that interpretation.[58]

LISI v. ALITALIA–LINEE AEREE ITALIANE, S.p.A.

United States Court of Appeals, Second Circuit, 1966.
370 F.2d 508.
Aff'd by an equally divided Court, 390 U.S. 455, 88 S.Ct. 1193, 20 L.Ed.2d 27 (1968).

[The text at p. 560, supra, describes the limited liability provisions of the Warsaw Convention, and the negotiations in 1965 and 1966 which led to the Montreal Interim Agreement among air carriers raising those limits. A 1960 crash of an Alitalia airplane en

58. See, e. g., The David J. Adams (United States–Great Britain Claims Arbitration, 1921), Neilsen's Reports 526, 6 U.N.R.I.A.A. 85. The text at p. 248, supra, describes some of the many unresolved questions of how an international tribunal would treat findings of fact or legal interpretations by national courts before which relief was initially sought by a national of the claimant state.

route from Rome to New York led to suits by American citizens, commenced before the 1966 Interim Agreement, against the Italian corporation for wrongful death and personal injuries. Alitalia pleaded as affirmative defenses those articles of the Convention which limited liability. Under Article 3(2) of the Convention, a carrier cannot take advantage of the provisions limiting liability if it "accepts a passenger without a passenger ticket having been delivered . . . ." The Convention further provides that the ticket must contain certain information, including a "statement that the transportation is subject to the rules relating to liability established by the convention." Plaintiffs alleged that the passenger tickets had not met these requirements, and moved for partial summary judgment to dismiss the affirmative defenses. The district judge granted their motion and stayed the trial pending an appeal on the question whether the challenged affirmative defenses were available to Alitalia.

The Court of Appeals, in an opinion by JUDGE KAUFMAN, affirmed the grant of partial summary judgment. Its opinion described two earlier cases under the Convention which had held that the Convention's liability limits were not available to defendants. In Mertens v. Flying Tiger Line, Inc., 341 F.2d 851 (2d Cir. 1965), the court held that presentation of the ticket to a passenger after he boarded the plane did not constitute a "delivery" within the meaning of Article 3(2). In Warren v. Flying Tiger Line, Inc., 352 F.2d 494 (9th Cir. 1965), the court held that "delivery" was insufficient when the passenger was given a boarding ticket at the foot of the ramp leading to the aircraft. In both cases, the courts had reasoned that tickets must be delivered to passengers sufficiently in advance of the flight to enable them to take measures to protect themselves against the limitation of liability, as by purchasing additional insurance. The Court of Appeals continued:]

We believe that the reasoning of the *Mertens* and *Warren* decisions is apposite to the case now before us. The Convention's arbitrary limitations on liability—which have been severely and repeatedly criticized [59]—are advantageous to the carrier. But the *quid pro quo* for this one-sided advantage is delivery to the passenger of a ticket and baggage check which give him notice that on the air trip he is about to take, the amount of recovery to him or his family in the event of a crash, is limited very substantially. Thus the passenger is given the opportunity to purchase additional flight insurance or to take such other steps for his self-protection as he sees fit.

This notice to passengers is especially important in this country where the overwhelming number of people who travel by air do so on domestic flights, for which the Convention's restrictions on liability are inapplicable. It is too much to expect these passengers to be sufficiently sophisticated to realize that although they are traveling the same number of miles on an international flight that they have frequently traveled domestically, the amount they may recover in the event of an accident is drastically reduced. In short, it is clear from the *ratio decidendi* of the *Mertens* and *Warren* cases, that the inquiry that must be made if the Convention's Articles are to be given meaning, is "[w]hether the ticket was delivered to the passenger in such a manner as to afford him a reasonable opportunity to take

59. [Eds.] A footnote of the court here referred to the criticism in this country of the Convention's limits on liability and to the events described at p. 561, supra, leading to the 1966 Interim Agreement.

self-protective measures . . . ." Mertens v. Flying Tiger Line, Inc., supra, 341 F.2d at 857.

We proceed to determine, therefore, whether the particular tickets and baggage checks involved in the present case gave the appellees adequate notice.[60] On the front of the ticket and baggage check, in exceedingly small print, was the following message: "Each passenger should carefully examine this ticket, particularly the Conditions on page 4." And, at this point, we note that one of our reasons in Mertens v. Flying Tiger Line, Inc., supra, for precluding the carrier from limiting its liability under the Convention was that the required statement on the ticket "was printed in such a manner as to virtually be unnoticeable and unreadable . . . ." Id., at 857.

Judge MacMahon appropriately characterized the "notice" to the passengers in his pithy conclusion as "camouflaged in Lilliputian print in a thicket of 'Conditions of Contract' . . . . Indeed the exculpatory statements on which defendant relies are virtually invisible. They are ineffectively positioned, diminutively sized, and unemphasized by bold face type, contrasting color, or anything else. The simple truth is that they are so artfully camouflaged that their presence is concealed." [61] 253 F.Supp. at 243. . . .

We agree that a jury could not reasonably have found that the tickets and baggage checks gave the passengers the required notice. . . .

MOORE, CIRCUIT JUDGE (dissenting):

The majority in their opinion indulge in judicial treaty-making. The language of the treaty (referred to as the Warsaw Convention) is clear. Its provisions are not difficult to comprehend. Its mandates are simply stated. Ascertainment of compliance should, therefore, present no real problem.

Passenger tickets were delivered to plaintiffs and their decedents on various dates between January 20, 1960 and February 20, 1960. The flight on which they travelled pursuant to their tickets did not depart until February 25, 1960. The ticket contained the particulars specified in Article 3(1) of the Convention, albeit the reference to the provisions of the Convention with respect to death or injury was in exceedingly small type.

The majority do not approve of the terms of the treaty and, therefore, by judicial fiat they rewrite it. They think a "one-sided advantage" is being taken of the passenger which must be offset by a judicial requirement that the passenger have notice of the limitation of liability. To support their argument they refer, quite illogically in my opinion, to cases in which the courts have held that there was no real delivery of a ticket to the passenger as contemplated by the treaty. Cases based upon facts tantamount to no effective

60. The parties have agreed that this is a question of law for the court to resolve. . . .

61. Moreover, even if a passenger were able to read the printing on the ticket and baggage check, it is highly questionable whether he would be able to understand the meaning of the language contained thereon. For example, the passenger is referred to the carrier's tariffs in order to determine whether his flight is considered "international carriage"; and the carrier's liability is expressed in terms of "French gold francs (consisting of 65½ milligrams of gold with a fineness of nine hundred thousandths)." [Eds.]—The court's footnote continued by quoting regulations of the Civil Aeronautics Board indicating that all carriers availing themselves of the liability limitations must provide tickets advising passengers of these limitations in the precise language appearing in the regulations.

pre-flight ticket delivery, are scarcely relevant to this case where the passengers had their tickets from 3 to 36 days before departure. Were actual notice to be the requirement, every airline would have to have its agents explain to every passenger the legal effect of the treaty and, in all probability, insist that each passenger be represented by counsel who would certify that he had explained the import of the Convention to his client who, in turn, both understood and agreed to the limitation.

The original limitations in the Convention may well be outmoded by now. Substantial revisions upward have been made but they have been made, as they should be, by treaty and not by the courts. Judicial predilection for their own views as to limitation of liability should not prevail over the limitations fixed by the legislative and executive branches of Government even though this result is obtained by ostensibly adding to the treaty a requirement of actual understanding notice. . . .

ASAKURA v. CITY OF SEATTLE

Supreme Court of the United States, 1924.
265 U.S. 332, 44 S.Ct. 515, 68 L.Ed. 1041.

[Plaintiff, a Japanese subject, was engaged in business since 1915 in Seattle as a pawnbroker. A Seattle ordinance of 1921 made it unlawful for a person to engage in such business without a license, which would be granted only to a citizen of the United States. Plaintiff brought an action to restrain enforcement of the ordinance. He contended that it violated a Treaty of 1911 between the United States and Japan, which provided in part that citizens or subjects of each country would have liberty to reside in the other and "to carry on trade, wholesale and retail . . . and generally to do anything incident to or necessary for trade upon the same terms as native citizens or subjects, submitting themselves to the laws and regulations there established . . . ." The case came to the Supreme Court on writ of error after a judgment of the Washington Supreme Court that the ordinance was valid. Excerpts from the opinion of the Supreme Court, by JUSTICE BUTLER, appear below.]

. . . The treaty was made to strengthen friendly relations between the two nations. As to the things covered by it, the provision quoted establishes the rule of equality between Japanese subjects while in this country and native citizens. Treaties for the protection of citizens of one country residing in the territory of another are numerous, and make for good understanding between nations. . . .

. . . It need not be considered whether the state, if it sees fit, may forbid and destroy the business generally. Such a law would apply equally to aliens and citizens, and no question of conflict with the treaty would arise. The grievance here alleged is that plaintiff in error, in violation of the treaty, is denied equal opportunity.

It remains to be considered whether the business of pawnbroker is "trade" within the meaning of the treaty. Treaties are to be construed in a broad and liberal spirit, and, when two constructions are possible, one restrictive of rights that may be claimed under it and the other favorable to them, the latter is to be preferred. . . . The ordinance defines "pawnbroker" to "mean and include every person whose business or occupation it is to take and receive by way of pledge, pawn or exchange, goods, wares or merchandise, or any kind of personal property whatever, for the repayment or security of any money loaned thereon, or to loan money on deposit or personal property," and defines "pawnshop" to "mean and include every place at which the business of pawnbroker is carried on." The language of the treaty is comprehensive. The phrase "to carry on trade" is broad. That it is not to be given a restricted meaning is plain. The clauses, "to . . . own or lease . . . shops, . . . to lease land . . . for . . . commercial purposes, and generally to do anything incident to or necessary for trade," and "shall receive . . . the most constant protection and security of their . . . property, . . ." all go to show the intention of the parties that the citizens or subjects of either shall have liberty in the territory of the other to engage in all kinds and classes of business that are or reasonably may be embraced within the meaning of the word "trade" as used in the treaty.

By definition contained in the ordinance, pawnbrokers are regarded as carrying on a "business." . . . We have found no state legislation abolishing or forbidding the business. Most, if not all, of the states provide for licensing pawnbrokers and authorize regulation by municipalities. While regulation has been found necessary in the public interest, the business is not on that account to be excluded from the trade and commerce referred to in the treaty. Many worthy occupations and lines of legitimate business are regulated by state and federal laws for the protection of the public against fraudulent and dishonest practices. There is nothing in the character of the business of pawnbroker which requires it to be excluded from the field covered by the above-quoted provision, and it must be held that such business is "trade" within the meaning of the treaty. The ordinance violates the treaty. . . .

Decree reversed.

QUESTIONS

(1) Are you persuaded by the court's opinion in the Alitalia case? Suppose that the crash had involved citizens of Guatador, a less developed country where tort damages for wrongful death rarely reach the equivalent of $5,000. If suit had been brought in Guatador, would the court have been as likely to read the Convention to require sufficient advance notice and fully comprehensible, legible prose before Alitalia's liability would be limited? Can you even guess what perspective upon these questions an international tribunal—composed of nationals of Europe, the United States and the less developed world—would have?

(2) Consider the Court's statement in Asakura that treaties are to be construed in a broad and liberal manner, one that has appeared in several Supreme Court decisions. Note, however, that repetition of this principle has not prevented our courts from reading narrowly treaty provisions which, linguistically, would have permitted the interpretation urged by an alien plaintiff. Can one explain the construction of the treaty provision in Asakura solely by reference to maxims of interpretation, or were judicial notions of policy as important?

NOTE ON RELATIONSHIPS BETWEEN THE EXECUTIVE AND THE COURTS IN THE INTERPRETATION OF TREATIES

Section 150 of the Restatement (Second), Foreign Relations Law of the United States asserts that, for purposes of applying an international agreement in litigation as the domestic law of the United States, the courts have "exclusive authority" to interpret it. Section 149 gives the Executive the authority "to determine the interpretation of an international agreement to be asserted by the United States in the conduct of its foreign relations." Section 152 states that courts applying agreements as domestic law give "great weight" to interpretations made by the Executive. The evident tension is between the concepts of a treaty as "supreme law" and as an act pursuing foreign-relations goals.

Acts and statements of the Executive and Senate prior to the ratification of a treaty are of course relevant to its interpretation by the judiciary. They constitute its domestic "legislative history," comparable in a sense to that of a statute. But a treaty has at least one foreign party. The question posed is whether it is fair to concentrate on the legislative history on one side of the process while ignoring the other.

Post-ratification acts of the Executive raise different questions. If a treaty is supreme law, it seems unsound to allow its content to vary with the current view of the Executive. At a minimum, however, the Executive may often make proper claim to expertness about the meaning of particular treaty terms and may be more likely to take into account the foreign country's views. Furthermore, problems of interpretation may occasionally shade into "political questions" on which a court will accept the Executive's determination—for example, such questions as whether a given entity is the recognized governmental successor of the entity executing the treaty or whether a treaty provision has survived a war between the parties.[62]

The Executive's interpretation of a treaty may be relevant not only to litigation involving a federal official or agency, as in tax or extradition treaties, but also to litigation between private parties (perhaps Warsaw Convention cases) or between a private party and a state official or agency, as in Friendship, Commerce and Navigation treaties. However, in many such cases it may be impossible to obtain information from the State Department about its views on a particular treaty provision. The case below is in this sense exceptional, for it involves an executive opinion on the precise issue relevant to litigation.

Kolovrat v. Oregon [63]

Two domiciliaries of Oregon died in 1953 without having made wills to dispose of their personal property in that state. Their heirs

62. See Reporter's Note to Section 152 of the Restatement, Second, Foreign Relations Law of the United States.

63. 366 U.S. 187, 81 S.Ct. 922, 6 L.Ed.2d 218 (1961).

were residents and nationals of Yugoslavia. Section 111.070 of the Oregon Revised Statutes made the right of non-resident aliens to "take" real or personal property or its proceeds by "succession or testamentary disposition" dependent upon certain conditions, including (*a*) the existence of a "reciprocal right" of United States citizens to take property and the proceeds thereof on the same conditions as citizens of the country of the alien, and (*b*) the right of United States citizens to receive payment within the United States of money derived from the estates of persons dying within that foreign country. If there were no next of kin except ineligible aliens, property of the deceased was to be taken by the state as escheated property. Oregon commenced proceedings to take the personal property. The Yugoslavian relatives and a Consul General of Yugoslavia (the "petitioners") contested.

Petitioners' principal argument rested upon a clause in a Treaty of 1881 between the United States and Serbia, now a part of Yugoslavia. Article II of that Treaty provided that

> [i]n all that concerns the right of acquiring . . . property, real or personal, citizens of the United States in Serbia and Serbian subjects in the United States, shall enjoy the rights which the respective laws grant or shall grant in each of these states to the subjects of the most favored nation. . . . [U]nder the same conditions as the subjects of the most favored nation, they shall be at liberty to acquire and dispose of such property, whether by . . . testament, inheritance, or in any other manner whatever. . . . They shall likewise be at liberty to export freely the proceeds of the sale of their property . . . without being subjected to pay any other or higher duties than those payable under similar circumstances by . . . subjects of the most favored state.

Petitioners called to the attention of the court a Friendship, Commerce and Navigation Treaty of 1853 between the United States and Argentina, Article IX of which provided that "the citizens of the two contracting parties shall reciprocally enjoy the same privileges, liberties, and rights, as native citizens . . ." in all matters relating to acquisition or disposition of property by sale or testament.

The Oregon Supreme Court held for the State. It stated that Article II of the 1881 Treaty was not applicable to petitioners since they were not resident within the United States, and it then held that condition (b) of Section 111.070 of the Oregon Revised Statutes was not satisfied. 220 Or. 448, 349 P.2d 255 (1960).

The Supreme Court reversed. With respect to the interpretation of the 1881 Treaty, the Court held that petitioners had "the same right to inherit their relatives' personal property as they would if they were American citizens living in Oregon . . . ." The fact that they were

Yugoslavian residents was not relevant under Article II of the Treaty. In reaching this conclusion, the Court stated in part:

> While courts interpret treaties for themselves, the meaning given them by the departments of government particularly charged with their negotiation and enforcement is given great weight. We have before us statements, in the form of diplomatic notes exchanged between the responsible agencies of the United States and of Yugoslavia, to the effect that the 1881 Treaty, now and always, has been construed as providing for inheritance by both countries' nationals without regard to the location of the property to be passed or the domiciles of the nationals. And relevant diplomatic correspondence and instructions issued by our State Department show that the 1881 Treaty was one of a series of commercial agreements which were negotiated and concluded on the basis of the most expansive principles of reciprocity. The Government's purpose in entering into that series of treaties was in general to put the citizens of the United States and citizens of other treaty countries on a par with regard to trading, commerce and property rights.

Appendix D to petitioners' brief before the Supreme Court contained some of the diplomatic correspondence to which the Supreme Court referred.

In a note of April 18, 1958 to the Secretary of State, the Yugoslavian Ambassador referred to several cases in the state courts (not naming Oregon) in which Article II of the 1881 Treaty had been interpreted to include only Yugoslavian citizens residing within the United States. The note stated that such an interpretation was "directly contrary to the past and present interpretation of the Yugoslav courts and authorities, who always have been applying the provisions of Article II . . . so that . . . American citizens are entitled to acquire property by inheritance . . . regardless of whether they are permanently residing in the United States of America, or anywhere else . . . . This can be clearly deduced from many a decision of the Yugoslav courts . . . ." The note stated that, by virtue of a treaty between Yugoslavia, and Poland relating to inheritance rights (which was read into the most-favored-nation clause in Article II of the 1881 Treaty), United States citizens enjoyed the same right of inheritance of property located in Yugoslavia as did Yugoslav nationals. The note affirmed that "Yugoslavia has always meticulously performed and carried out the obligations which, under its construction of the [Treaty], are due American citizens . . . ." The Ambassador requested the Government of the United States to advise whether it concurred in this construction of the Treaty.

In a note of April 24, 1958, the Secretary of State referred to the various Yugoslavian treaties and accords and to Article IX of the 1853 Treaty between the United States and Argentina. The Secretary stated: "It is well to bear in mind a general principle applied in the United States, namely, that although an expression of opinion by the Department of State with respect to the interpretation of a treaty provision will normally be given considerable weight by the courts, such an expression of opinion is not binding on the courts." The Secretary then stated that the Department of State concurred in the Yugoslavian interpretation of Article II, noting that "a liberal interpretation of the ambiguous portion [of Article II] produces a reasonable construction consonant with the spirit of the Treaty as a whole." It stated that the negotiating history for the 1881 Treaty, as well as the "consistent policy" of the United States reflected in other treaties concluded by it between 1850 and 1890, argued for this interpretation. The reply concluded: "This note, of course, is not to be considered as having the character of an international agreement or as effecting any modification of the treaty."

QUESTION

Spell out each link in the petitioners' argument that their claims under the 1881 Treaty prevailed over the Oregon statute. Do you agree with the Supreme Court's acceptance of that argument?

COMMENT

Kolovrat continues to be a significant authority as to such matters as the interpretation of the most-favored-nation clause, even though the end result—the non-application of the Oregon statute—can now be more simply arrived at by the route followed in Zschernig v. Miller, p. 166, supra. The decision in Clark v. Allen, p. 632, infra, would also be relevant.

Asakura, Kolovrat and indeed a majority of the domestic cases in these materials raising treaty issues involve bilateral treaties of Friendship, Commerce and Navigation. The primary purpose of these agreements is to declare rights of nationals of one of the signatories to trade, invest or establish and operate a business in the other country. The United States has entered into over 130 such treaties, tracing back to the 18th century. Twelve were concluded between the world wars, and more than 20 since 1945. The signatories include all the European Common Market countries, many other European countries and Japan, and a small selection of less developed countries.

The treaties have changed in form and content over the years. Now characteristically more specialized than they once were, they tend to leave consular, tariff and income-taxation problems to other agreements. Their emphasis is increasingly upon investment and establishment. Although the contemporary treaties bear a strong resemblance towards each other, they do occasionally vary in form and in certain substantive provisions. For example, the treaty with France is entitled a Convention of Establishment * and its form represents a concession to the model set by the French network of conventions.

Treaties such as the Franco-American contain some clauses of a very specific nature—for example, Article III. On the other hand, some provisions merely state that the parties will take such measures as they "deem appropriate", or "will make every effort" to grant a stated right (Article XI; Section 3 of Article X). The standard of "national treatment" (e. g., Section 4 of Article IV, Section 1 of Article VII) is characteristic of all such treaties. In the Franco-American Convention, the term is defined in Sections 1 and 2 of Article XIV. It is frequently confused with the most-favored-nation clause (e. g., Section 2 of Article IX), which was of decisive importance in the Kolovrat case. Note that the "national treatment" and "most-favored-nation" standards are often used in conjunction, as in Section 1 of Articles V and X. The following questions examine some of the difficulties in applying these two standards, as well as other provisions of the Convention.

Additional reading: Walker Modern Treaties of Friendship, Commerce and Navigation, 42 Minn.L.Rev. 805 (1958); Wilson, United States Commercial Treaties and International Law (1960).

QUESTIONS

(1) What policies do the national-treatment and most-favored-nation clauses express, and what domestic constitutional analogies can be drawn to each of them? Consider the following interpretative problems:

(a) Suppose that a French national, relying upon Section 1 of Article V of the Franco-American Convention, attempts to establish with fellow nationals a manufacturing corporation in the state of Ames (in the United States). The Ames corporation law provides that all directors of Ames corporations must be citizens of the United States. Can the French nationals organize a corporation with only French directors?

(b) Suppose that the Ames statute provided that at least one director must be a citizen of Ames, or that the principal executive officer must be a citizen of the United States.[64]

(c) Suppose that (in the context of the Kolovrat litigation) the Argentine treaty had lapsed in 1870, or in 1900. Or suppose that it was first entered into in 1900. Should the Supreme Court have reached the same result under each of these hypotheses?

(d) Note the relationship between the most-favored-nation clause in Kolovrat and the concept of "reciprocity," which is referred to in the Argentine treaty and in the Oregon statute. Was it relevant under the 1881 Treaty with Serbia whether or not Yugoslavia, at the time of the litigation, granted corresponding rights to American citizens with respect to estates in Yugoslavia? Recall the references to contemporary treatment in the note of the Yugoslavian Ambassador. Why did he regard this as relevant?

(2) Does the Franco-American Convention enable a Frenchman to enter the United States to carry on a business? Compare Article II and Paragraph 2(b) and (c) of the Protocol with Section 101(15)(e) of the Immigration and Nationality Act.*

(3) Does the Convention assure an indigent French defendant in a state criminal prosecution of counsel, at the state's expense? See Articles I and III(1), and Paragraph 1 of the Protocol.

64. Cf. Pearl Assurance Co. Limited v. Harrington, 38 F.Supp. 411 (D.Mass.), aff'd per curiam 313 U.S. 549, 61 S.Ct. 1120, 85 L.Ed. 1514 (1941).

(4) What effect does the Convention have upon the right of a French individual to engage in a business or profession in the United States contrary to existing laws restricting access by aliens? Could he establish a branch of his French business of selling perfumes or acting as a pawnbroker? Could he acquire a majority stock interest in a small broadcasting company subject to the Federal Communications Act? Could he purchase some shares (less than 1% of those outstanding) in an industrial corporation? See Articles V and VII, and Paragraphs 2 and 7 of the Protocol.

(5) Suppose that a corporation, organized and with its *siège social* in France and wholly-owned by French nationals, seeks to organize a subsidiary in the United States. Would it have the same rights under the Convention as a French individual? See Articles V and XIV. Suppose that 70% of the shares of the French corporation were owned by Belgian nationals, and that 30% of the shares were held by another French corporation. See Article XIII.

(6) Recall the description at pp. 83–84, supra, of the exchange-control system which became effective in France in 1967 and its impact upon foreign investment. Amco, a Delaware corporation, wishes to establish and finance a French subsidiary, with its *siège social* in France, to manufacture transistor radios. It submits the required information to the French authorities, but its application is denied. Amco understands that the government authorities are wary of excessive American investment in this field. Assume that it is unable to obtain relief permitting the investment from the French judiciary. It advises the State Department of the situation. Should the Department protest to the French Government that the Convention has been violated?

C. SOME FOREIGN COMPARISONS

Parts A and B have examined relationships in the United States between international norms or agreements and national law. An examination of comparable problems in a foreign country would reveal as many complex issues and require one to explore as thoroughly that country's traditions and contemporary political and legal system. We have not attempted such an examination. In its place, Part C illustrates different responses of foreign countries to the major questions considered in this chapter. Most illustrations are drawn from the constitutions or practice of countries that are members of the European Common Market. They at once suggest the variety of perspectives from which these problems may be viewed and provide the background necessary for the study of the "constitutional law" of the Common Market in Chapter XIII.[65] The reader should regard the excerpts from constitutional or other texts and the comments below with some caution, for a deeper study of any of the countries involved would inevitably suggest shadings and qualifications. Indeed, some of the

65. See in particular Part B, Sections 1 and 3, of Chapter XIII.

texts quoted below raise questions of as basic a character as has our Supremacy Clause.

(1) Customary international law and national law:

The United States attitude with respect to the adoption of customary international law as part of our domestic law has diverged somewhat from that developed in Great Britain, even though in the 18th century the views of Mansfield and Blackstone were influential in molding the original American understanding on this topic. Typical of more recent British judicial attitudes are the following extracts from West Rand Central Gold Mining Co., Ltd. v. The King, [1905] 2 K.B. 391, 406–08:

> The second proposition urged by Lord Robert Cecil, that international law forms part of the law of England, requires a word of explanation and comment. It is quite true that whatever has received the common consent of civilized nations must have received the assent of our country, and that to which we have assented along with other nations in general may properly be called international law, and as such will be acknowledged and applied by our municipal tribunals when legitimate occasion arises for those tribunals to decide questions to which doctrines of international law may be relevant. But any doctrine so invoked must be one really accepted as binding between nations, and the international law sought to be applied must, like anything else, be proved by satisfactory evidence, which must shew either that the particular proposition put forward has been recognised and acted upon by our own country, or that it is of such a nature, and has been so widely and generally accepted, that it can hardly be supposed that any civilized State would repudiate it. . . . The authorities which [Lord Robert Cecil] cited in support of the proposition are entirely in accord with and, indeed, well illustrate our judgment upon this branch of the arguments advanced on behalf of the suppliants. . . . But the expressions used by Lord Mansfield when dealing with the particular and recognised rule of international law on this subject, that the law of nations forms part of the law of England, ought not to be construed so as to include as part of the law of England opinions of text-writers upon a question as to which there is no evidence that Great Britain has ever assented, and a fortiori if they are contrary to the principles of her laws as declared by her Courts. . . .

Note also the statements in Chung Chi Cheung v. The King, [1939] A.C. 160 (P.C.1938), at 167–68:

> . . . It must be always remembered that, so far, at any rate, as the Courts of this country are concerned, international law has no validity save in so far as its principles are accepted and adopted by our own domestic law. There is no external power that imposes its rules upon our own code of substantive law or procedure. The Courts acknowledge the existence of a body of rules which nations accept amongst themselves. On any judicial issue they seek to ascertain what the relevant rule is, and, having found it, they will treat it as incorporated into the domestic law, so far as it is

not inconsistent with rules enacted by statutes or finally declared by their tribunals. . . .

The extent to which national legislation (or other forms of domestic law-making, such as executive decrees) will supersede rules of customary international law is less clear in some countries than in the United States. Note, for example, the following provisions of the *Grundgesetz* (Basic Law, or Constitution) of the Federal Republic of Germany:

> *Article 24:* (1) The Federation may by legislation transfer sovereign powers to international institutions.
>
> (2) For the preservation of peace, the Federation may enter a system of mutual collective security; in doing so it will consent to such limitations upon its rights of sovereignty as will bring about and secure a peaceful and enduring order in Europe and among the nations of the world.
>
> (3) For the settlement of disputes between nations, the Federation will enter into agreements concerning international arbitration of a general, comprehensive and compulsory character.
>
> *Article 25:* The general rules of international law form part of federal law. They take precedence over domestic law and create rights and duties directly for the inhabitants of the federal territory.
>
> *Article 100(2):* If in litigation it is doubtful whether a rule of international law forms part of federal law and whether it creates direct rights and duties for the individual (Article 25), the court is to obtain the decision of the Federal Constitutional Court.

Much scholarly writing in Germany has explored the meaning of these provisions, and decisions of tribunals have left unanswered some basic questions. For example, is the principle of *pacta sunt servanda* one of the "general rules of international law" incorporated into German law through Article 25, with the consequence that a treaty would thereby take precedence over a later inconsistent statute? The provisions of Article 100(2) suggest a more complex relationship between constitutional and international norms in the German system.[66]

(2) Legislative action before effectiveness of a treaty:

Not all countries require partial or full participation by the legislative branch before a "treaty" becomes a binding international obligation. (Of course, even in the United States special rules have been developed for executive agreements.) Thus, under Great Britain's "unwritten constitution," Her Majesty with the advice of Her Ministers (i. e., the executive branch) could in theory conclude any type of international agreement. McNair, Law of Treaties 67–69 (1961).

(3) Self-executing treaties:

Some of these countries, however, do not view treaties as part of the law of the land without further legislative action, even though they

66. For general comment, see 1 von Mangoldt-Klein, Das Bonner Grundgesetz 672–83 (2d ed. 1957).

have become internationally binding. That is, no treaty is self-executing, and questions posed in cases such as Sei Fujii v. State, p. 580, supra, do not arise. With very limited exceptions, such is the law in Great Britain. Because of this principle, treaties are usually ratified only after Parliament has enacted the necessary implementing legislation. Note that the principles of treaty law in Great Britain do, cumulatively, assure the legislative participation which our Constitution requires, if not more. McNair, Law of Treaties, 69, 81–110 (1961).

(4) Relation between treaties and statutes:

In some nations, the constitution gives a treaty precedence over domestic legislation, whether earlier or subsequent in time. For example, Article 66 of the Netherlands Constitution of 1953, as amended in 1956, reads:

> Legislation which is in force within the Kingdom shall not be applied if its application would be incompatible with provisions of agreements which are binding upon everyone whether such agreements have been entered into before or after the enactment of the legislation.

The "binding upon everyone" clause apparently was added to limit the article's effect to self-executing agreements. A full appreciation of the effect of Article 66 would require an understanding of the extent to which Dutch courts are empowered to exercise judicial review over the constitutionality of legislation.[67]

Another departure from American constitutional doctrine is found in the French Constitution of 1958, which provides in Article 55:

> Treaties or agreements duly ratified or approved have, as soon as they are published, an authority superior to that of laws, provided, for each treaty and agreement, that it shall be applied by the other party thereto.

This provision applies to treaties concluded prior to or after the enactment of inconsistent legislation. Its effect in the French courts, however, is different from that which one accustomed to American practice would expect. The function of determining a law's constitutionality is conferred by Articles 61 and 62 upon the Constitutional Council, which passes on this issue when draft legislation is submitted to it prior to enactment. French authorities reason that the role of that Council extends to reviewing compatibility of a new law with existing treaties and also to determining whether the other signatory is applying the treaty. It is thus questionable whether French courts would have the power to review the constitutionality of a later law. Their role in this area is further confined by their general deference

67. For further discussion, see Erades and Gould, The Relation Between International Law and Municipal Law in the Netherlands and the United States 393–419 (1961); van Panhuys, The Netherlands Constitution and International Law, 58 Am.J.Int.L. 88 (1964).

to the executive in matters of treaty interpretation (see section (6) below).[68]

(5) Relation between treaties and constitution:

In some countries, a treaty may disregard constitutional norms which would invalidate a statute to the same effect. See, for example, Article 63 of the Netherlands Constitution:

> If the development of the international legal order so requires, it shall be permissible for an agreement to depart from the provisions of the Constitution. In any such case approval can only be given expressly. The Chambers of the States-General can adopt such a Bill only by a two-thirds majority of the votes cast.

Note that the procedure required for adoption of such a bill is considerably less complex than that required for a constitutional amendment, although more demanding than for ordinary legislation or treaties.[69]

(6) Treaty interpretation:

The relationship between the executive and the judiciary in the interpretation of treaties varies widely among countries. In France, for example, the courts have not regarded themselves as competent to interpret treaties except within a limited area. The area reserved for official executive determination (usually by the Ministry of Foreign Affairs, upon its own initiatives or upon request by the Court) is variously defined as that involving "international public law" (*droit public international*) or "international public policy" (*ordre public international*). A commentator finds "uncertainty, not to say confusion" in the cases, resulting in part from lack of harmony between the judicial and administrative courts and even between different chambers of the Cour de Cassation.[70]

(7) Problems of federalism:

In other countries with federal constitutions, solutions of the problems associated with Missouri v. Holland, p. 562, supra, often diverge from ours. Take, for example, Canada. The validity of Canadian legislation enacted to implement the migratory bird treaty at issue in Missouri v. Holland was sustained in Rex v. Stuart, [1925] 1 D.L.R. 12 (Man.1924), as coming within Section 132 of the British

68. See Duverger, Institutions Politiques et Droit Constitutionnel 656 (9th ed. 1966); Vedel, Cours de Droit Constitutionnel et d'Institutions Politiques 1038–1041 (1961).

69. See Erades and Gould, op. cit. fn. 67, supra, pp. 65, 466–68; and van Panhuys, op. cit. fn. 67, supra.

70. Goldman, Note, 90 J. du Droit International 1044 (1963). In Banque Nationale pour le Commerce et l'Industrie Afrique v. Narbonne, Court of Appeals, Aix-en-Provence, Dec. 2, 1965, 5 Int.Leg.Mat. 473, the court, while finding that an Algerian nationalization law "seems theoretically contrary to the Evian Agreements" calling for just compensation for takings of property, went on to say that "the Court does not have the competence to interpret an international treaty when such interpretation would raise, as in the present case, a question of public international law."

North America Act of 1867 (Canada's constitution), which authorizes the Dominion legislature to pass laws necessary and proper for performing the obligations of Canada "arising under Treaties between the Empire and . . . Foreign Countries." Where the treaty is made by Canada under its own authority, the Dominion legislation necessary to carry it into effect cannot entrench upon matters reserved to the provinces. Thus in the Labour Convention Case (Atty. Gen. for Canada v. Atty. Gen. for Ontario), [1937] A.C. 326 (P.C.) (Can.), it was held that the Dominion could not, in order to enforce the wages and hours provisions of the Convention, pass statutes which invaded the prerogatives of the provinces. See Laskin, Canadian Constitutional Law, Ch. III (4th ed., Abel, 1973).

See also the comment by McWhinney, 35 Can.B.Rev. 842 (1957), discussing the German "Concordat Case," in which that country's Constitutional Court held that a treaty between the Federal Republic and the Vatican could not supersede contrary provisions of the law of one of the states (*Länder*) in the field of education, one specially reserved by the *Grundgesetz* to the states.

QUESTIONS

(1) Which of the foreign examples would have given comfort to the proponents of the Bricker Amendment—and as to what aspects of those proposals?

(2) What developments in European history and institutional differences between many European countries and the United States might have contributed to the willingness of some continental countries to give treaties and customary international law such a high place in their formal hierarchy of norms?

Additional reading: Paul de Visscher, Les Tendances Internationales des Constitutions Modernes, 80 Academie de Droit International, Recueil des Cours 515 (1952); Stein and Hay, Law and Institutions in the Atlantic Area 11–74 (1967); Schrever, The Interpretation of Treaties by Domestic Courts, 45 B.Y.I.L. 255 (1971).

D. NATIONAL LEGISLATION BASED ON RECIPROCITY

This chapter has examined various ways in which domestic institutions interact with principles of international law and "internalize" them—that is, apply them to relationships between private parties and government officials or agencies. Part D has a different focus. It examines an important technique of national law-making by which legislators attempt to create certain legal relationships in the international community and thus contribute towards the building of harmonious international relationships. We consider so-called "reciprocity" legislation—primarily statutes providing that nationals of foreign countries can assert certain rights in this country only if the foreign country accords the same rights or privileges to United States citizens. Although such legislation usually has its immediate effect upon foreign nationals, its ultimate aim is frequently to persuade foreign governments to change their policies towards nationals of the country enacting the reciprocity legislation. There were indications in Chapters I and IV that national law-makers were influenced by the consideration that legislation would evoke certain responses abroad. Reciprocity legislation makes that consideration explicit and paramount.

Reciprocity and retaliation are here as elsewhere allied concepts. Legislation may offer certain rights, conditioned upon reciprocal treatment by a foreign country. Or it may threaten certain conduct in the event of stated action by a foreign country. Note the relationships between legislation of either type and international law. It is possible for a statute to say: if you violate a stated international-law norm and thereby injure our citizens, we will do thus and so. The legislator thus asserts the validity and binding character of the international norm and attempts to reinforce it. A prime example is the Hickenlooper Amendment, p. 482, supra, given the Congressional understanding of the international-law norm. In other cases, the statute does not consider relevant any norm of international law, but rather offers rights, on the condition of reciprocity, beyond those required under international law. For example, the Mineral Leasing Act, 41 Stat. 437 (1920), as amended, 30 U.S.C.A. § 181, provides that citizens of another country "the laws, customs, or regulations of which deny similar or like privileges" to Americans shall not own any interest in a federal mineral lease. If a foreign country responds by allowing Americans to have like mineral rights in its domain, there arises a situation somewhat like a bilateral treaty in which the parties agree to confer ownership rights upon each other's nationals.

That we here consider the theme of reciprocity in the special and detailed context of legislation should not blur its pervasive relevance to the materials in this book—indeed, to international law and relations. At the very core of the processes by which customary international law develops are reciprocal claims and tolerances among nations. Reciprocal promises underlie many of the most significant treaty relationships in the contemporary world—whether the Nuclear Test Ban Treaty, a fisheries convention, or a Friendship, Commerce and Navigation treaty. And apart from the formal body of international law, domestic courts as well as executive officials and legislators will be attentive to the effect of their decision-making upon attitudes and laws of foreign countries. For many contemporary theorists of international law and relations, including allied fields such as the conflict of laws, reciprocity and the related concepts of accommodation and comity form the very cornerstone of the subject matter. Forbearance by a nation from exertion of its full power in an effort to encourage others to a comparable attitude of restraint, the principle that one should do to others as one would have done to oneself, are fundamental considerations in many areas of political and legal action.

NIPPON HODO COMPANY LTD. v. UNITED STATES

United States Court of Claims, 1961.
285 F.2d 766.

JONES, CHIEF JUDGE. Plaintiffs are Japanese corporations suing the United States on contract claims. In both cases, the defendant sought and was granted a separate trial on the issue of jurisdiction of this court; namely, whether such jurisdiction extends to suits against the United States by citizens of Japan. . . .

The plaintiffs proved that American citizens, in suits against the Government of Japan, are treated before the courts of Japan no less favorably than Japanese nationals. It is the defendant's main contention, however, that the plaintiffs have failed to prove that an American citizen in Japan could maintain against the Japanese Government the *precise suit* which plaintiffs bring here against the United States, and absent such proof this court is without jurisdiction under section 2502 of Title 28 United States Code.[71] . . .

The defendant continues to urge upon us its concept of reciprocity, a concept which demands that we do unto others precisely as they do unto us—*and no more.* Such a position, if accepted, would add no luster to the golden rule of conduct that long has guided our country in its international affairs. Furthermore, we doubt that it is in harmony with the attitude of Americans everywhere that their country is strong, generous, and willing to lead and act first. The Congress has provided that this court shall be open to any aliens whose government "accords to citizens of the United States the right to prosecute *claims* against their government in its courts." [Emphasis supplied.] We do not read "claims" to mean "claims of the precise nature brought before this court." The section contemplates only that American citizens enjoy an equal standing with foreigners in actions against the foreign State and does not require that the scope of actions for which the respective countries render themselves liable to suit shall be coextensively identical and *in pari materia.*

Perhaps there is some minimum amount of sovereign-liability in his own country which must be proved by an alien wishing to sue our Government in this court. We would carefully measure the scope of our jurisdiction in a situation where a rule in a foreign law book permits Americans free access to the courts but where it appears in practice that Americans are barred from the courts. The case before us does not present these difficulties. The plaintiffs have adequately proved that the Japanese open their courts to Americans in a multitude of causes against the Japanese Government, including, according to most authorities, suits for breach of contract.

The plaintiffs produced a deposition from a Japanese attorney, an experienced member of the Tokyo Bar Association, stating in unequivocal language that an American shared equally with a Japanese citizen "the right to sue the Japanese State for breach of Contract." This statement was affirmed by the Director of Litigation of the Japanese Ministry of Justice. Furthermore, in three separate inquiries our State Department sought to ascertain the status of Amer-

71. [Eds.] The section is set forth in the Documentary Supplement.

ican citizens before the courts of Japan. The replies from the Japanese Ministers of Foreign Affairs were as follows:

> "Citizens of the United States are given the right equally with the Japanese subjects to institute actions in Japanese courts against the Japanese Government in regard to claims arising from such legal relations between the citizens of the United States and the Japanese Government as belong to the domain of private law.
>
> "[T]he separateness of the courts of administrative law results in fact in few and unimportant suits against the Japanese Government whatever may be the statements in the codes with regard to the liability of the government to suits.
>
> "In civil cases the Japanese Government occupies a coordinate position before legal courts with Japanese subjects . . .. However, except in special instances which belong to the jurisdiction of the ordinary courts, legal matters concerning public law become questions for administrative litigation.
>
> "Contractual actions against the Japanese Government may be brought by both alien and Japanese nationals pursuant to general provisions of the Japanese civil and commercial codes."

The plaintiffs did fail to submit translations of any Japanese cases in which the State was sued for breach of contract. Little weight can be given to this omission when it is considered that we are dealing here not only with a different legal system but a different culture as well. Formal legal standards play a far less pervasive role in Japan in the creation and adjusting of principles regulating conduct than they play in the West. American scholars have repeatedly noted the amazing lack of litigation in Japan and the striking persistence in Japanese society of forms of dispute-resolution other than law. Those disputes involving public law which do arise are usually settled in administrative tribunals other than courts. The few court decisions available have only in recent years included a full statement of the facts in the published accounts.

The defendant has further emphasized that while the Japanese codes and statutes provide in some ways for suits against the Government, they fail to provide specifically for suits for breach of contract. We think the defendant has assumed too much, and has again overlooked the fact that the Japanese have accepted a system of jurisprudence whose tenets and history are different from those of our own. English common law started with the historic maxim that the "King can do no wrong," and the further proposition that the sovereign was immune from suit. "The King," reads a famous passage from Blackstone, "is not only incapable of doing wrong, but even of thinking wrong; he can never mean to do an improper thing; in him is no folly or weakness." [Citation omitted.] This theory of state infallibility and immunity was incorporated into the jurisprudence of American democracy even though we had no King; the Chief of State was never sovereign. From the beginning sovereign power resided in the people, and the rights of individuals against the State were fundamental among our earliest legal principles.

While no one would question that for many years our law restrained suits against the Government, the responsibility of this position never went without challenge. "It is not too much to say," wrote an English observer, "that the whole Constitution has been erected upon the assumption that the King not only is capable of doing wrong, but is more likely to do wrong than other men if he is given a chance." [Citation omitted.] Mr. Justice Frankfurter has asserted that whatever the ancient bases for the rule of immunity, "it undoubtedly runs counter to modern democratic notions of the moral responsibility of the State." Great Northern Life Ins. Co. v. Read, 322 U.S. 47, 59, 64 S.Ct. 873, 879, 88 L.Ed. 1121 (dissenting opinion).

Today we know that our Government may be sued on a multitude of causes. Nevertheless, the doctrine of severeign immunity has never been expressly repudiated by an American court. In our country the creation of State responsibility has been solely the result of legislation.

Civil law countries, on the other hand, particularly France, early in the development of their law, rejected both the concept that the King can do no wrong and the accompanying doctrine of sovereign immunity. These countries took the position instead that "the State is an honest man" and as such it will seek to repair damages caused by its wrongful acts. History shows that from this basic civil law premise the full development of state liability in these countries has been the handiwork of the judges and the courts.

Japanese law today is not the product of centuries of slow, organic growth; it did not develop along with, and as a part of, the whole society and culture. Less than a century ago the Japanese took their law bodily from the systems of continental Europe. The Japanese Civil Code is truthfully called the "fruit of comparative jurisprudence." [Citation omitted.] The drafters surveyed the French, Swiss, and particularly the German civil codes and adopted from them broad teachings but no specific rules as to state responsibility. The multitude of European cases was examined but discarded. The result is a paradox: state liability in Japan is a commonly accepted fact but its proof by statutes and cases is difficult.

With this brief background, it is easier to understand and accept the statement of plaintiffs' deponent—"I have never known of any question being raised whether the citizen can sue the State. . . . Since it is the general opinion of the Japanese Bar that a citizen may bring an action against the State, equally for breach of contract, for payment of salary or damages of other kinds".

Both parties have briefed and argued the application and effect of the 1953 Treaty of Friendship, Commerce and Navigation between the United States of America and Japan, 4 U.S. Treaties 2063. We believe the proper disposition of this case does not require us to reach the issues thereby presented.

The court concludes as a matter of law that the plaintiffs are entitled to maintain their suits in this court pursuant to 28 U.S.C. § 2502 . . . .

LARAMORE, JUDGE (dissenting).

I cannot agree with the majority for these reasons: The Treaty of Friendship entered into between the United States and Japan puts access to the courts on a reciprocal basis. Section 1 of Article IV of the Treaty provides that "nationals . . . of either party shall be accorded national treatment . . . with respect to access to the courts . . .."

National treatment is defined in section 1 of Article XXII of the Treaty as follows:

> "The term 'national treatment' means treatment accorded within the territories of a party upon terms no less favorable than the treatment accorded therein, in like situations, to nationals [or] companies, . . ., as the case may be, of such party."

This, it seems to me, must mean that each government shall give equal treatment to the other with respect to access to the respective courts. As a matter of fact, this would appear to be in complete harmony with the primary purpose of the statute which permits a foreign citizen or corporation to sue the United States in cases wherein a foreign government accords to citizens of the United States the right to prosecute claims against their government in its courts. In other words, "equal treatment" would seem to be the controlling factor in both the Treaty and the statute.

Under these circumstances, the burden would be on the plaintiffs to prove that a citizen of the United States could prosecute a claim for breach of contract against the Japanese Government. This, in my opinion, the plaintiffs have failed to do. No statute or article of the constitution of Japan has been put in evidence from which this court could conclusively find a provision for suits in breach of contract. On the contrary, the constitution of Japan quite clearly shows that only suits in tort are cognizable by the courts of Japan.

Consequently, I would hold that section 2502 requires that United States citizens have the right to sue the Japanese Government in contract in its courts as a condition to maintenance of plaintiffs' suits in contract in this court. Otherwise, a Japanese citizen would have greater rights in the United States courts than those accorded them in their own country. . . .

NOTE ON RECIPROCITY

(1) Other federal statutes make aliens' rights dependent upon reciprocity or authorize retaliation. Among these are a law recognizing steamship inspection certificates if issued by countries recognizing our certificates and having inspection laws "approximating those of the United States" (16 Stat. 453 (1871), as amended, 46 U.S.C.A. § 362); provisions for the reciprocal elimination of discriminatory tonnage duties (4 Stat. 308 (1828), as amended, 46 U.S.C.A. § 141); a provision of the Internal Revenue Code (§ 883) reciprocally excluding from gross income the earnings of foreign aircraft and vessels; other provisions (§§ 891 and 896) authorizing the increase of taxes on citizens of countries that impose "burdensome" or discriminatory taxes on our nationals; and a provision (61 Stat. 652 (1947), as amended, 17 U.S.C.A. § 9) that a foreign author shall benefit from our copyright rules only if the nation of which he is a citizen grants benefits "on substantially the same basis as to its own citizens," a state of affairs which is to be determined by Presidential proclamation.[72]

72. See also the references to retaliatory legislation in United States v. Curtiss-Wright Export Corp., fn. 1, p. 106, supra.

(2) Much state legislation embodies the idea of reciprocity in an interstate rather than international context. These laws characteristically treat such questions as admission of citizens of other states to professions such as law or accounting, permission for such citizens to engage in the banking or insurance businesses, and enforcement against them of support orders or extradition demands.[73] Note that the use of agreements between states instead of such legislation is restricted by the Compact Clause (Art. I, Sec. 10) of the Constitution.

Some state legislation is clearly aimed at activity of *aliens*—for example, the New York statute allowing branches of foreign banks to operate in the state on a reciprocal basis. N.Y.Banking Law § 202–a. Such provisions raise constitutional issues, in view of the many restrictions upon state action affecting this country's foreign relations that were considered in Part B of Chapter II.

In Clark v. Allen, 331 U.S. 503, 67 S.Ct. 1431, 91 L.Ed. 1633 (1947), the Supreme Court considered a California statute which provided in part that nonresident aliens could inherit personal property upon national-treatment terms, "dependent . . . upon the existence of a reciprocal right upon the part of citizens of the United States to take real and personal property . . . upon the same terms and conditions as residents and citizens of the respective countries of which such aliens are inhabitants and citizens. . . ." With respect to the application of the reciprocity requirement of the statute, the Court stated (331 U.S. at 516, 67 S.Ct. at 1439, 91 L.Ed. at 1645):

> The argument is that by this method California seeks to promote the right of American citizens to inherit abroad by offering to aliens reciprocal rights of inheritance in California. Such an offer of reciprocal arrangements is said to be a matter for settlement by the Federal Government on a nation-wide basis. . . . [H]ere there is no treaty governing the rights of succession to the personal property. Nor has California entered the forbidden domain of negotiating with a foreign country . . . or making a compact with it contrary to the prohibition of Article 1, § 10 of the Constitution. What California has done will have some incidental or indirect effect in foreign countries. But that is true of many state laws which none would claim cross the forbidden line.

In his opinion for the Court in Zschernig v. Miller, p. 166, supra, Justice Douglas found unconstitutional an Oregon inheritance statute which in part required reciprocity before a nonresident alien could inherit real or personal property. He attempted to distinguish, and refused to overrule, Clark v. Allen, in which he had written the opinion. Justice Stewart, in his concurring opinion, stated that he would have overruled the earlier case.

(3) Drafting reciprocity rules is an exacting task. One problem is how to define the required response by the foreign country. Con-

73. A full, if now obsolescent, discussion appears in Starr, Reciprocal and Retaliation Legislation in the American States, 21 Minn.L.Rev. 371 (1937).

sider the following example. A French Law of 1943 regulating commercial rentals gave tenants the right under stated conditions to remain in occupancy notwithstanding a landlord's desire to terminate the leasehold. It extended its advantages to nationals of foreign countries which offered Frenchmen the advantages of "analogous legislation." In a case under that Law involving a German national who sought to remain as a tenant, the court ruled adversely to him. The fact that German law did not discriminate against French nationals was, in the court's view, insufficient to meet the Law's requirements. Since German law established quite different conditions (for Germans or aliens) under which a tenant could renew a lease, the court found that reciprocity did not exist. Baringer v. Manuel, Court of Appeal, Paris, March 2, 1955, [1955] Revue des Loyers 349.

Contrast the extremely broad use of the concept of reciprocity in a former Constitution of Poland, which provided that "aliens enjoy, on condition of reciprocity, equality of rights with citizens of the Polish state . . . ."[74]

The usual approach, suggested by the Nippon Hodo Case, is to say "we shall do X to you if you do X to us." But where there is no symmetry of position between the countries involved, as in Baringer v. Manuel, such legislation misses the mark. Imagine, for example, the reaction of Saudi Arabia to the threat that, if it did not grant mineral privileges to Americans, the provisions of the Mineral Leasing Act set forth at p. 627, supra, would be applied against it. Direct reciprocity or retaliation would be of equally little avail in many tariff situations; Brazil would achieve little by threatening to raise its tariffs on foreign coffee if other countries raised theirs.

(4) Even if effectively drafted, the reciprocity or retaliation statute can lead to numerous problems in its application. Recall that the Hickenlooper Amendment requires the President to take steps upon the occurrence of certain events; other statutes are permissive and simply authorize retaliation. The question also arises whether the administration of such a statute should be left to the courts and, in particular, whether courts are able to make the necessary determinations of what a foreign state has in fact done or what its laws say. If the task is the court's, how is foreign law to be proved in judicial proceedings? Note the sources used by the courts in Nippon Hodo and Belemecich's Estate, pp. 628 and 164, supra, and compare their approaches with that of Surrogate Moss in Tybus' Estate, 28 Misc.2d 278, 217 N.Y.S.2d 913 (1961), a case requiring examination of certain Polish laws for purposes of a predecessor of the New York "iron curtain" statute set forth at p. 163, supra:

> As a result of representations made to this Court by the Consul General at Washington of the Polish People's Republic, that the situation in Poland was different from that generally believed, this court in an effort to do full justice to the many individuals residing in Poland who have been left

74. See Sazonow v. District Land (Reform) Board of Bialystok, Supreme Court of Poland, October 2, 1922, [1919–1922] Ann.Dig. 7, 247, No. 174.

> bequests by relatives and friends here, on its own initiative and at its own expense visited Poland for an on the spot investigation of the situation. In connection therewith, the Surrogate conferred with the Ambassador of the United States to Poland at Warsaw, the Secretary to the Embassy and the American Consul; with members of the Association des Juristes Polonais; members of the Bar Association of Warsaw, the Director-General of the Ministry of Finance, members of the staff of the Ministry of Finance and their Counsel; chiefs of divisions of the Ministry of Foreign Affairs; Chairman, officers and members of the Board of Directors of Bank Polska Kasa Opieki and their General Counsel, and others. The Surrogate also spent considerable time at the principal office of Bank Polska Kasa Opieki during the banking hours.

Explicit answers for federal courts to many of the procedural problems involved in determining an issue of foreign law are contained in F.R.C.P. 44.1.*

QUESTIONS

(1) Would the problem in Nippon Hodo have been better handled by treaty than by a reciprocity statute? In fact, the treaty referred to in the case appeared on its face to be relevant. Do you agree with the way in which the dissenting judge disposed of it?

(2) Assume that a federal statute provides that domestic courts shall be closed to aliens suing United States citizens, unless the courts of the alien's country are open to private suits brought by our citizens. To what challenges would such a statute be open under federal or international law? Would the statute be more or less apt than that in Nippon Hodo to achieve its purpose?

(3) A law of Guatador states that foreign accountants may be admitted to practice upon proof of their qualification under their national law, provided that such law does not restrict the right of Guatadorian accountants to practice. What result under the statute with respect to an accountant from Frantaly, a country which has no restrictive laws? The Frantalian Institute of Accountancy, a private society, does, however, impose various requirements, and in fact it is impossible to be an accountant in Frantaly unless one is a member of the Institute. Assume that the Institute requires all aspirant accountants to take an examination which, not unfairly, emphasizes matters of Frantalian law and practice that are difficult for Guatadorian accountants to master.

(4) Recall the Baringer case summarized at p. 633, supra. Does the construction of the statute seem appropriate? What would the result be if Germany had no rent control legislation of any kind? Suppose that the tenant were a United States national, and that New York City was the only part of the United States then subject to rent control. The tenant comes from (a) Georgia, (b) New York City.

Additional reading: Lenhoff, Reciprocity: The Legal Aspect of a Perennial Idea, 49 Nw.U.L.Rev. 619, 752 (1955).

E. A SNAPSHOT VIEW OF CHAPTERS I TO V

These five chapters portray the range of transnational laws and problems: from an "iron curtain" statute to a fisheries convention, from conflict between branches of government over control of foreign relations to conflicts between individuals of different nationality or different governments. Throughout these chapters, the profound and pervasive relationships between national and international law and policies have illustrated the difficulty in drawing any satisfactory line between domestic and international law. This is, to be sure, not a startling observation in an international community whose principal members and legislators, executive officials and adjudicators are generally nation states or their officials.

The eight remaining chapters examine particular problems in greater detail, to illustrate in various settings the general themes thus far developed and their interrelationships. The comments below offer a useful summary and review of those themes. They should help to create a synthesis among the varied subjects which we have considered, for all those subjects can be accommodated within the international-national spectrum which Professor McDougal describes in the concluding five paragraphs.

McDOUGAL, THE IMPACT OF INTERNATIONAL LAW UPON NATIONAL LAW: A POLICY-ORIENTED PERSPECTIVE

4 S.Dak.L.Rev. 25, 86–88 (1959).

From our inquiry above, it has become apparent that the interrelation of international law and national law is most realistically viewed, not in terms of the relative supremacy, other interrelation, or reception of rules, but rather in terms of the interpenetration of multiple processes of authoritative decision of varying territorial compass. The rules commonly referred to as international law and national law are but perspectives of authority—perspectives about who should decide what, with respect to whom, for the promotion of what policies, by what methods—which are constantly being created, terminated, and recreated by established decision-makers located at many different positions in the structures of authority of both states and international governmental organizations. No elaborate theories of supremacy, coordination, subordination, adoption, incorporation, or transformation are needed to account for the impact of processes of authority external to particular states upon the processes internal to such states. Each particular state of the world, whatever the fundamental goals of its elites, is inescapably enmeshed in an effective global power process, constituted by patterns both of authority and of control, which encompasses and affects, and is in turn affected by, not merely the processes of the various particular states but also hemispheric, continental, and oceanic processes, and even, in further emphasis of the porousness of state boundaries, the processes of the province, of the city, and of the humble village or township. The traditional focus upon inherited "rules" takes too little account of the factors which affect decision in the different power processes, of the consequences of decision for the different territorial communities and their component participants, and, hence, of the immense complexity of the continuous interactions by which the different power processes affect each other in variegated patterns of authority and control, crossing and recrossing state lines.

The principal point which we have sought to establish in the brief and impressionistic discussion above is that in this global process of authoritative and controlling decision, particular states are most substantially affected by inclusive policies prescribed in arenas external to any particular state and applied in consequential conformity both in such external arenas and in the internal arenas of particular states. The major outlines of this impact of inclusive policies upon the external strategies and internal policies of particular states have been traced through a number of different patterns of authority and control, including:

(1) the establishment by decision-makers external to any particular state, through inclusive policies, of a broad and flexible "constitutional" allocation of competence—reflected in the polar concepts of "international concern" and "domestic jurisdiction," their equivalents, and a multitude of detailed prescriptions on specific issues—for inclusive decision by the general community of states and exclusive decision by particular states;

(2) the exercise, in varying organized and unorganized structures of authority and through varying policy functions, by the general community of states of its competence so established for the prescription and application of inclusive policies which importantly affect particular states in all their power and other value interactions;

(3) the practice of particular states, through varying constitutional principles and procedures and by varying officials, of applying within internal arenas and with a consequential degree of uniformity, the inclusive policies so prescribed by the general community for the regulation of participants in internal value processes; and

(4) the practice by particular states of honoring appeals for alleged misapplications of inclusive policies in their internal arenas to the external arenas of the general community.

More extended inquiry might have revealed, further, that particular states in exercise of the exclusive competence allocated to them by inclusive constitutional policies are influenced in high degree in their exclusive prescription and application of policies, for the regulation of their internal affairs, by the general limits sought to be imposed by externally prescribed inclusive policies, constitutional and otherwise.

Part Three

THE ROLE OF NATIONAL JUDICIARIES IN BUILDING A TRANSNATIONAL LEGAL SYSTEM

CHAPTER VI

LOCAL COURTS AND FOREIGN SOVEREIGNTY: JURISDICTIONAL IMMUNITIES AND THE ACT OF STATE DOCTRINE

This chapter explores two facets of a general problem: the extent to which national courts can participate in the development of a transnational legal system by applying national or international law to the conduct of foreign governments. In view of the jurisdictional and political weaknesses of international tribunals, are national courts the more promising avenue in certain fields for the growth of a body of law regulating state conduct?

A. IMMUNITY OF FOREIGN SOVEREIGNS FROM THE JURISDICTION OF LOCAL COURTS

We here treat those immunities from judicial jurisdiction which are often accorded to foreign states and their instrumentalities. Sovereign immunity evokes many problems previously introduced: consideration of the nature of sovereignty and the consequences of a sovereign's acts; of the pervasive interplay between national and international legal systems; and of the appropriate relationship between the judicial and executive branches in the field of foreign affairs. This presentation of the historical development of sovereign immunity doctrine will stress the principal themes and sharply abridge a number of important but secondary issues. Our approach is strongly influenced by a pending legislative proposal, p. 668, infra, which, if enacted, will render those issues obsolete.

The following materials invite comparison between the policies underlying jurisdictional immunities in a domestic and a transnational setting. The "restrictive" theory of sovereign immunity expressed in the Tate Letter, p. 647, infra, and in the proposed legislation finds analogies in our domestic case law, as does the contemporary problem of determining when a government corporation should be accorded the same immunity as the foreign sovereign that organized it. And problems of execution of judgments rendered against foreign sovereigns are often similar to those present in an entirely domestic setting. To facilitate these comparisons, the following Note offers a synoptic view of some aspects of sovereign immunity relevant to suits against the United States.

NOTE ON THE JURISDICTIONAL IMMUNITY OF THE UNITED STATES

When considering the breadth of sovereign immunity for the United States, it is well to keep in mind the kinds of situations to which immunities of foreign government are relevant. In characteristic cases, a private party (the plaintiff or libellant or counterclaiming defendant) asserts a claim for money damages against a foreign state. The action may be at law or in admiralty; the jurisdictional basis may be civil attachment, a libel in rem, or the alleged consent of the foreign state to an in personam action; but the judgment sought is one for money damages. These actions involve principally contract claims but also tort claims for negligently or intentionally caused injury. They may rest upon domestic law (an alleged breach of a contract made and to be performed in this country), a foreign law (a contract made and to be performed abroad), or international law (a claim for compensation following expropriation of the private party's property in the foreign state's territory).

By stressing claims for *money damages* against *foreign states,* we wish to emphasize what the private parties in the following cases are *not* seeking. *(1)* They are not seeking *direct* judicial review by an American court to modify or annul executive or administrative action of the foreign government. *(2)* Nor do they seek non-monetary relief, such as replevin or specific performance or a mandatory or prohibitory injunction directed towards executive or diplomatic officials of the foreign state.[1] Such relief would increase the risk of interference with important policies of the foreign state and of political tensions; often it would also be beyond the power of domestic courts to enforce. *(3)* Finally, the defendant is the foreign state or its branch or corporate instrumentality, rather than a foreign official from whom the plaintiff seeks money damages.[2] Most of the actions (breach of contract) suggest the liability to be that of the state rather than its official; officials against whom a personal liability might be asserted are not apt to be within the United States; and diplomatic immunities here merge with sovereign immunities (see p. ——, infra) to complicate further the jurisdictional issues.

We pass lightly over certain characteristics of the domestic law of immunity which have no significant analogues in the international

1. One possible exception is The Schooner Exchange, p. 641, infra.

2. The one exception is Underhill v. Hernandez, p. 683, infra.

cases. *(1)* Private parties can often challenge an act or order of the United States or one of its agencies or officials by defending a criminal prosecution or enforcement action brought against them. *(2)* Many statutes specify the procedure and grounds for obtaining judicial review of government (agency) action. *(3)* Particularly in former times, absence of a remedy against the United States was partially compensated for by the right to sue the particular government officials involved, particularly in tort actions. In cases where the officials have a right to indemnity against the government, such suits serve as indirect routes to government liability. It may be noted that there is a tendency in such suits to grant government officials "privileges" to act in decision-making involving a high degree of discretion. Thus questions of the jurisdictional immunity of such officials tend to merge with substantive defences.[3] *(4)* Suits can sometimes be brought for specific performance of contracts by, or the recovery of particular property from, officials of the United States.[4]

The more useful comparisons in the domestic system are to cases involving the alleged breach by the government of a duty owing to a private party, and a claim for money damages against the government. By the mid-19th century, Supreme Court decisions had established the immunity of the United States from suits by private parties seeking compensation for harm. Legislative consent, express or implied, was thus a condition to suit. The explanations which later decisions and scholars have offered for the entrenchment of sovereign immunity in this country have been less than consistent. To a considerable extent, the immunity doctrines derived from a reading (or misreading) of those which had developed in England. To some extent, immunity was inferred from relatively abstract concepts of the nature of "sovereignty" or the "sovereign." The statement of Justice Holmes in Kawananakoa v. Polyblank, 205 U.S. 349, 27 S.Ct. 526, 51 L.Ed. 834 (1907), that "there can be no legal right as against the authority that makes the law on which the right depends" illustrates this strand of thought. Immunity was also thought to be required by quite practical considerations, such as the fear that allowance of suits would impair the efficiency of government and lead to extravagant, unmanageable liabilities.

The first legislative inroads upon the immunity doctrines occurred in the contract field. An Act of 1855 created the Court of Claims and conferred upon it jurisdiction over certain kinds of actions for money damages against the United States. The Tucker Act of 1887 broadened this jurisdiction. That Act, now codified in 28 U.S.C.A. §§ 1346(a) and 1491, confers jurisdiction upon the Court of Claims (or in certain cases upon the district courts) to render judgment

3. See, e. g., Gregoire v. Biddle, 177 F. 2d 579 (2d Cir. 1949), and Barr v. Matteo, 355 U.S. 171, 78 S.Ct. 204, 2 L.Ed.2d 179 (1957). Compare the "discretionary function" exception to the Federal Tort Claims Act, quoted at p. 640, infra.

4. See, e. g., Larson v. Domestic & Foreign Commerce Corp., 337 U.S. 682, 69 S.Ct. 1457, 93 L.Ed. 1628 (1949), and the cases to which that opinion refers.

upon claims against the United States "founded either upon the Constitution, or any Act of Congress, or any regulation of an executive department, or upon any express or implied contract with the United States, or for liquidated or unliquidated damages in cases not sounding in tort." The provisions on contract claims contain the widest and most unequivocal waivers. It is, however, true that special doctrines (a federal common law) have developed with respect to government contracts which distinguish actions on them in some important respects from private-party litigation. It is also true that many disputes over governmental contracts, particularly those relating to defense procurement, are handled at least initially through administrative processes.[5]

The Federal Tort Claims Act (FTCA), enacted in 1946 and now codified principally in 28 U.S.C.A. §§ 1346(b), 2671–2680, was the first statute of comprehensive scope allowing suit against the United States for common law torts of government employees. Section 1346(b) confers jurisdiction on the district courts over claims against the United States for money damages "for injury or loss of property, or personal injury or death caused by the negligent or wrongful act or omission of any employee of the Government while acting within the scope of his office or employment, under circumstances where the United States, if a private person, would be liable to the claimant in accordance with the law of the place where the act or omission occurred." Section 2674 provides that the United States shall be liable for such tort claims "in the same manner and to the same extent as a private individual under like circumstances. . . ." Various exceptions, stated in Section 2680, strongly qualify the waiver of immunity. The most troublesome relates to claims based upon "the exercise or performance or the failure to exercise or perform a discretionary function or duty on the part of a federal agency or an employee of the Government, whether or not the discretion involved be abused." Other exceptions refer to intentional torts (battery, false arrest, defamation and so on, but not including trespass) and to any "claim arising in a foreign country."

The leading case interpreting the exception for "discretionary" functions or duties gave it a broad interpretation. In Dalehite v. United States, 346 U.S. 15, 73 S.Ct. 956, 97 L.Ed. 1427 (1953), the Supreme Court held that the acts of the United States in preparing for export shipment a fertilizer which exploded, causing the Texas City disaster, were on a "planning" rather than "operational" level. Consequently the exception was applicable. On the other hand, since Dalehite the Court has read the provision of Section 2674, quoted above, in a restrictive manner.[6] It refused to import into that section

5. For a summary treatment of this area, see Goodman, Judicial and Non-Judicial Remedies of a Government Contractor, 18 Mil.L.Rev. 3 (1962). For more detail, see Symposium, Government Contracts, 29 Law & Contemp.Prob. 1 (1964).

6. See, e. g., Rayonier, Inc. v. United States, 352 U.S. 315, 77 S.Ct. 374, 1 L.Ed.2d 354 (1957) (action will lie for property damage resulting from alleged negligence of government employees in failure to prevent and fight forest fire).

the distinction between "governmental" and "non-governmental" or "proprietary" acts. That distinction had figured importantly in the law of municipal corporations, where characterization of a corporation's conduct in the latter category became the touchstone to liability. The Court discounted the argument that the governmental conduct involved in these cases was not that for which a "private individual" (Section 2674) could be held liable since private parties do not perform such activities. This domestic distinction between "governmental" and "proprietary" conduct [7] bears some relationship to that between acts *jure imperii* and acts *jure gestionis* which the Tate Letter, p. 647, infra, stresses as a means of determining the scope of a foreign sovereign's immunities.

Suits against states and municipalities raise problems similar to those against the United States. Whether through legislation or decisional law, immunities in this area appear to be on the wane. Special considerations of an historical and political nature control suits against states in the federal courts. See the Eleventh Amendment to the Constitution.*

If a court asserts jurisdiction over the United States or a state and renders a money judgment, questions about its enforceability arise. Recall the discussion at pp. 187–190, supra, of the special problems of enforcing judgments of our domestic courts against such defendants. That discussion was intended to underscore the even greater difficulties in enforcing judgments rendered by international tribunals. It is also relevant, however, to problems in this chapter of enforcing judgments rendered by national courts against foreign sovereigns.

Additional reading: Hart & Wechsler, The Federal Courts and the Federal System 1326–1423 (2d ed., Bator, Mishkin, Shapiro & Wechsler, 1973); Jaffe, Judicial Control of Administrative Action 197–260 (1965); Developments in the Law—Remedies Against the United States and Its Officials, 70 Harv.L.Rev. 829–911 (1957).

THE SCHOONER EXCHANGE v. McFADDON

Supreme Court of the United States, 1812.
11 U.S. (7 Cranch) 116, 3 L.Ed. 287.

This being a cause in which the sovereign right claimed by Napoleon, the reigning emperor of the French, and the political relations between the United States and France, were involved, it was, upon the suggestion of the Attorney General, ordered to a hearing in preference to other causes which stood before it on the docket. . . .

MARSHALL, CH. J., delivered the opinion of the Court as follows:

This case involves the very delicate and important inquiry, whether an American citizen can assert, in an American court, a

7. The distinction appears to be increasingly discounted in the state courts. See Muskopf v. Corning Hospital District, 55 Cal.2d 211, 359 P.2d 457 (1961) (result affected by legislation); Corning Hospital District v. Superior Court, 57 Cal.2d 488, 370 P.2d 325 (1962).

title to an armed national vessel, found within the waters of the United States.

The question has been considered with an earnest solicitude, that the decision may conform to those principles of national and municipal law by which it ought to be regulated.

In exploring an unbeaten path, with few, if any, aids from precedents or written law, the court has found it necessary to rely much on general principles, and on a train of reasoning, founded on cases in some degree analogous to this.

The jurisdiction of *courts* is a branch of that which is possessed by the nation as an independent sovereign power.

The jurisdiction of the nation within its own territory is necessarily exclusive and absolute. It is susceptible of no limitation not imposed by itself. Any restriction upon it, deriving validity from an external source, would imply a diminution of its sovereignty to the extent of the restriction, and an investment of that sovereignty to the same extent in that power which could impose such restriction.

All exceptions, therefore, to the full and complete power of a nation within its own territories, must be traced up to the consent of the nation itself. They can flow from no other legitimate source.

This consent may be either express or implied. In the latter case, it is less determinate, exposed more to the uncertainties of construction; but, if understood, not less obligatory.

The world being composed of distinct sovereignties, possessing equal rights and equal independence, whose mutual benefit is promoted by intercourse with each other, and by an interchange of those good offices which humanity dictates and its wants require, all sovereigns have consented to a relaxation in practice, in cases under certain peculiar circumstances, of that absolute and complete jurisdiction within their respective territories which sovereignty confers.

This consent may, in some instances, be tested by common usage, and by common opinion, growing out of that usage.

A nation would justly be considered as violating its faith, although that faith might not be expressly plighted, which should suddenly and without previous notice, exercise its territorial powers in a manner not consonant to the usages and received obligations of the civilized world.

This full and absolute territorial jurisdiction being alike the attribute of every sovereign, and being incapable of conferring extra-territorial power, would not seem to contemplate foreign sovereigns nor their sovereign rights as its objects. One sovereign being in no respect amenable to another; and being bound by obligations of the highest character not to degrade the dignity of his nation, by placing himself or its sovereign rights within the jurisdiction of another, can be supposed to enter a foreign territory only under an express license, or in the confidence that the immunities belonging to his independent sovereign station, though not expressly stipulated, are reserved by implication, and will be extended to him.

This perfect equality and absolute independence of sovereigns, and this common interest impelling them to mutual intercourse, and an interchange of good offices with each other, have given rise to a class of cases in which every sovereign is understood to waive the exercise of a part of that complete exclusive territorial jurisdiction, which has been stated to be the attribute of every nation.

[The opinion discussed three such cases: (1) the exemption of the person of a foreign sovereign from arrest or detention; (2) the immunity of foreign ministers; and (3) waiver of jurisdiction over troops of a foreign prince which have been allowed to pass through the territory.]

But the rule which is applicable to armies, does not appear to be equally applicable to ships of war entering the ports of a friendly power. The injury inseparable from the march of an army through an inhabited country, and the dangers often, indeed generally, attending it, do not ensue from admitting a ship of war, without special license, into a friendly port. A different rule therefore with respect to this species of military force has been generally adopted. If, for reasons of state, the ports of a nation generally, or any particular ports be closed against vessels of war generally, or the vessels of any particular nation, notice is usually given of such determination. If there be no prohibition, the ports of a friendly nation are considered as open to the public ships of all powers with whom it is at peace, and they are supposed to enter such ports and to remain in them while allowed to remain, under the protection of the government of the place.

In almost every instance, the treaties between civilized nations contain a stipulation to this effect in favor of vessels driven in by stress of weather or other urgent necessity. In such cases the sovereign is bound by compact to authorize foreign vessels to enter his ports. The treaty binds him to allow vessels in distress to find refuge and asylum in his ports, and this is a license which he is not at liberty to retract. It would be difficult to assign a reason for withholding from a license thus granted, any immunity from local jurisdiction which would be implied in a special license. . . .

To the Court, it appears, that where, without treaty, the ports of a nation are open to the private and public ships of a friendly power, whose subjects have also liberty without special license, to enter the country for business or amusement, a clear distinction is to be drawn between the rights accorded to private individuals or private trading vessels, and those accorded to public armed ships which constitute a part of the military force of the nation.

The preceding reasoning has maintained the propositions that all exemptions from territorial jurisdiction must be derived from the consent of the sovereign of the territory; that this consent may be implied or expressed; and that when implied, its extent must be regulated by the nature of the case, and the views under which the parties requiring and conceding it must be supposed to act.

When private individuals of one nation spread themselves through another as business or caprice may direct, mingling indiscriminately with the inhabitants of that other, or when merchant vessels enter for the purposes of trade, it would be obviously inconvenient and dangerous to society, and would subject the laws to continual infraction, and the government to degradation, if such individuals or merchants did not owe temporary and local allegiance, and were not amenable to the jurisdiction of the country. Nor can the foreign sovereign have any motive for wishing such exemption. His subjects thus passing into foreign countries, are not employed by him, nor are they engaged in national pursuits. Consequently there are powerful motives for not exempting persons of this description from the jurisdiction of the country in which they are found, and no one motive for requiring it. The implied license, therefore, under which they enter can never be construed to grant such exemption.

But in all respects different is the situation of a public armed ship. She constitutes a part of the military force of her nation; acts under the immediate and direct command of the sovereign; is employed by him in national objects. He has many and powerful motives for preventing those objects from being defeated by the interference of a foreign state. Such interference cannot take place without affecting his power and his dignity. The implied license therefore under which such vessel enters a friendly port, may reasonably be construed, and it seems to the Court, ought to be construed, as containing an exemption from the jurisdiction of the sovereign, within whose territory she claims the rights of hospitality.

Upon these principles, by the unanimous consent of nations, a foreigner is amenable to the laws of the place; but certainly in practice, nations have not yet asserted their jurisdiction over the public armed ships of a foreign sovereign entering a port open for their reception. . . .

It seems then to the Court, to be a principle of public law, that national ships of war, entering the port of a friendly power open for their reception, are to be considered as exempted by the consent of that power from its jurisdiction.

Without doubt, the sovereign of the place is capable of destroying this implication. He may claim and exercise jurisdiction either by employing force, or by subjecting such vessels to the ordinary tribunals. But until such power be exerted in a manner not to be misunderstood, the sovereign cannot be considered as having imparted to the ordinary tribunals a jurisdiction, which it would be a breach of faith to exercise. Those general statutory provisions therefore which are descriptive of the ordinary jurisdiction of the judicial tribunals, which give an individual whose property has been wrested from him, a right to claim that property in the courts of the country, in which it is found, ought not, in the opinion of this Court, to be so construed as to give them jurisdiction in a case, in which the sovereign power has impliedly consented to waive its jurisdiction.

The arguments in favor of this opinion which have been drawn from the general inability of the judicial power to enforce its decisions in cases of this description, from the consideration, that the sovereign power of the nation is alone competent to avenge wrongs committed by a sovereign, that the questions to which such wrongs give birth are rather questions of policy than of law, that they are for diplomatic, rather than legal discussion, are of great weight, and merit serious attention. But the argument has already been drawn to a length, which forbids a particular examination of these points.

The principles which have been stated, will now be applied to the case at bar.

In the present state of the evidence and proceedings, the Exchange must be considered as a vessel, which was the property of the Libellants, whose claim is repelled by the fact, that she is now a national armed vessel, commissioned by, and in the service of the emperor of France. The evidence of this fact is not controverted. But it is contended, that it constitutes no bar to an enquiry into the validity of the title, by which the emperor holds this vessel. Every person, it is alleged, who is entitled to property brought within the jurisdiction of our Courts, has a right to assert his title in those Courts, unless there be some law taking his case out of the general rule. It is therefore said to be the right, and if it be the right, it is the duty of the Court, to enquire whether this title has been extinguished by an act, the validity of which is recognized by national or municipal law.

If the preceding reasoning be correct, the Exchange, being a public armed ship, in the service of a foreign sovereign, with whom the government of the United States is at peace, and having entered an American port open for her reception, on the terms on which ships of war are generally permitted to enter the ports of a friendly power, must be considered as having come into the American territory, under an implied promise, that while necessarily within it, and demeaning herself in a friendly manner, she should be exempt from the jurisdiction of the country.

If this opinion be correct, there seems to be a necessity for admitting that the fact might be disclosed to the Court by the suggestion of the Attorney for the United States.

I am directed to deliver it, as the opinion of the Court, that the sentence of the Circuit Court, reversing the sentence of the District Court, in the case of the Exchange be reversed, and that of the District Court, dismissing the libel, be affirmed.

COMMENT

Under a treaty of 1831 between the United States and France, settling various claims under international law, the heirs of the two owners of the Schooner Exchange ultimately received a payment of $19,500 each, representing about 60% of her value. See Reeves, A Note on Exchange v. M'Fadden, 18 Am.J.Int.L. 320 (1924).

NOTE ON THE SUPREME COURT AND THE IMMUNITY OF FOREIGN SOVEREIGNS TO 1952

The Supreme Court dealt with the immunity of foreign sovereigns only occasionally after the Schooner Exchange, which has remained the authoritative text. In Berizzi Bros. Co. v. S. S. Pesaro, 271 U.S. 562, 46 S.Ct. 611, 70 L.Ed. 1088 (1926), the Court for the first time allowed immunity to a merchant vessel owned by and in the service of a foreign government, although the State Department had declined to recognize the immunity. Thus the United States refused to take part in the developing international movement towards the restrictive theory of immunity—that is, towards limiting immunity to sovereign, as opposed to commercial, acts. This movement had gained impetus from the increasing tendency of nations to assume economic functions outside of the traditional framework of administration and management—operating fleets of merchant vessels, for example. It received further impetus from the spread of state trading organizations, most conspicuously in socialist states, but in others as well. For further historical data, see The Tate Letter, p. 647, infra.

In Ex Parte Republic of Peru, 318 U.S. 578, 63 S.Ct. 793, 87 L.Ed. 1014 (1943), the Court held that the State Department's "certification and the request that the vessel [owned by Peru and libeled for an alleged failure to carry out a charter party] be declared immune must be accepted by the courts as a conclusive determination by the political arm of the government that the continued retention of the vessel interferes with the proper conduct of our foreign relations." The reigning principle was that "courts may not so exercise their jurisdiction, by seizure and detention of the property of a friendly sovereign, as to embarrass the executive arm of the government in conducting foreign relations."

In Republic of Mexico v. Hoffman, 324 U.S. 30, 65 S.Ct. 530, 89 L.Ed. 729 (1945), the vessel involved belonged to the government of Mexico but was in "the possession, operation and control" of a privately owned and operated Mexican corporation engaged in commercial carriage of cargoes for hire. A libel in rem was filed against the vessel for damage resulting from a collision. The State Department advised the lower court that it took no position with respect to the asserted immunity of the vessel from suit. It did cite two prior cases, which seemed to say that immunity extended only to vessels in the possession and service of the foreign government. The court denied immunity, and the Supreme Court affirmed. It noted that in the absence of recognition of immunity by the State Department, "courts may decide for themselves whether all the requisites of immunity exist," such requisites to be determined "in conformity to the principles accepted" by the State Department.

> We can only conclude that it is the national policy not to extend the immunity in the manner now suggested, and that it is the duty of the courts, in a matter so intimately associated with our foreign policy and which may profoundly affect it, not to enlarge an immunity to an extent which the government, although often asked, has not seen fit to recognize.

QUESTIONS

(1) As developed by Chief Justice Marshall, is the immunity doctrine (a) part of national law regulating the jurisdiction of the courts, or (b) part of customary international law applied in a manner comparable to the Paquete Habana, p. 531, supra? What practical consequences does your answer have? What policy considerations seem persuasive to the Court?

(2) Note how the issue of sovereign immunity was presented to the Court in the Schooner Exchange. Do you infer from that opinion that the Chief Justice would have considered the court free to disregard an executive suggestion?

(3) The cases after the Schooner Exchange state the "duty" of the court to follow an executive suggestion. Are they saying that sovereign immunity is within the realm of "political questions", i. e., like recognition of a foreign government? In other areas, e. g., passport and deportation cases, pp. 130 and 137 supra, courts have critically reviewed executive action. Why should sovereign immunity decisions enjoy greater deference?

(4) Courts have stated that compliance with executive requests avoids embarrassment to the conduct of our foreign relations. Would you prefer to defend the polar proposition—namely, that reliance by courts upon judicially developed doctrines, without executive intervention, is less apt to irritate foreign sovereigns?

THE "TATE LETTER"

26 Dept. State Bull. 984 (1952).

Following is the text of a letter addressed to Acting Attorney General Philip B. Perlman by the Department's Acting Legal Adviser, Jack B. Tate:

May 19, 1952.

My Dear MR. ATTORNEY GENERAL:

The Department of State has for some time had under consideration the question whether the practice of the Government in granting immunity from suit to foreign governments made parties defendant in the courts of the United States without their consent should not be changed. The Department has now reached the conclusion that such immunity should no longer be granted in certain types of cases. In view of the obvious interest of your Department in this matter I should like to point out briefly some of the facts which influenced the Department's decision.

A study of the law of sovereign immunity reveals the existence of two conflicting concepts of sovereign immunity, each widely held and firmly established. According to the classical or absolute theory of sovereign immunity, a sovereign cannot, without his consent, be made a respondent in the courts of another sovereign. According to the newer or restrictive theory of sovereign immunity, the immunity of the sovereign is recognized with regard to sovereign or public acts (*jure imperii*) of a state, but not with respect to private acts (*jure gestionis*). There is agreement by proponents of both theories, supported by practice, that sovereign immunity should not be claimed or granted in actions with respect to real property (diplomatic and perhaps consular property excepted) or with respect to the disposition of the property of a deceased person even though a foreign sovereign is the beneficiary.

The classical or virtually absolute theory of sovereign immunity has generally been followed by the courts of the United States, the British Commonwealth, Czechoslovakia, Estonia, and probably Poland.

The decisions of the courts of Brazil, Chile, China, Hungary, Japan, Luxembourg, Norway, and Portugal may be deemed to support the classical theory of immunity if one or at most two old decisions anterior to the development of the restrictive theory may be considered sufficient on which to base a conclusion.

The position of the Netherlands, Sweden, and Argentina is less clear since although immunity has been granted in recent cases coming before the courts of those countries, the facts were such that immunity would have been granted under either the absolute or restrictive theory. However, constant references by the courts of these three countries to the distinction between public and private acts of the state, even though the distinction was not involved in the result of the case, may indicate an intention to leave the way open for a possible application of the restrictive theory of immunity if and when the occasion presents itself.

A trend to the restrictive theory is already evident in the Netherlands where the lower courts have started to apply that theory following a Supreme Court decision to the effect that immunity would have been applicable in the case under consideration under either theory.

The German courts, after a period of hesitation at the end of the nineteenth century have held to the classical theory, but it should be noted that the refusal of the Supreme Court in 1921 to yield to pressure by the lower courts for the newer theory was based on the view that that theory had not yet developed sufficiently to justify a change. In view of the growth of the restrictive theory since that time the German courts might take a different view today.

The newer or restrictive theory of sovereign immunity has always been supported by the courts of Belgium and Italy. It was adopted in turn by the courts of Egypt and of Switzerland. In addition, the courts of France, Austria, and Greece, which were traditionally supporters of the classical theory, reversed their position in the 20's to embrace the restrictive theory. Rumania, Peru, and possibly Denmark also appear to follow this theory.

Furthermore, it should be observed that in most of the countries still following the classical theory there is a school of influential writers favoring the restrictive theory and the views of writers, at least in civil law countries, are a major factor in the development of the law. Moreover, the leanings of the lower courts in civil law countries are more significant in shaping the law than they are in common law countries where the rule of precedent prevails and the trend in these lower courts is to the restrictive theory.

Of related interest to this question is the fact that ten of the thirteen countries which have been classified above as supporters of the classical theory have ratified the Brussels Convention of 1926 under which immunity for government owned merchant vessels is waived. In addition the United States, which is not a party to the Convention, some years ago announced and has since followed, a policy of not claiming immunity for its public owned or operated merchant vessels. Keeping in mind the importance played by cases involving public vessels in the field of sovereign immunity, it is thus noteworthy that these ten countries (Brazil, Chile, Estonia, Germany, Hungary, Netherlands, Norway, Poland, Portugal, Sweden) and the United States have already relinquished by treaty or in practice an important part of the immunity which they claim under the classical theory.

It is thus evident that with the possible exception of the United Kingdom little support has been found except on the part of the Soviet Union and its satellites for continued full acceptance of the absolute theory of sovereign immunity. There are evidences that British authorities are aware of its deficiencies and ready for a change. The reasons which obviously motivate state trading countries in adhering to the theory with perhaps increasing rigidity are most persuasive that the United States should change its policy. Furthermore, the granting of sovereign immunity to foreign governments in the courts of the United States is most inconsistent with the action of the Government of the United States in subjecting itself to suit in these same courts in both contract and tort and with its long established policy of not claiming immunity in foreign jurisdictions for its merchant vessels. Finally, the Department feels that the widespread and increasing practice on the part of governments of engaging in commercial activities makes necessary a practice which will enable persons doing business with them to have their rights determined in the courts. For these reasons it will hereafter be the Department's policy to follow the restrictive theory of sovereign immunity in the consideration of requests of foreign governments for a grant of sovereign immunity.

It is realized that a shift in policy by the executive cannot control the courts but it is felt that the courts are less likely to allow a plea of sovereign immunity where the executive has declined to do so. There have been indications that at least some Justices of the Supreme Court feel that in this matter courts should follow the branch of the Government charged with responsibility for the conduct of foreign relations.

In order that your Department, which is charged with representing the interests of the Government before the courts, may be adequately informed it will be the Department's practice to advise you of all requests by foreign governments for the grant of immunity from suit and of the Department's action thereon.

Sincerely yours,

For the Secretary of State:

JACK B. TATE
Acting Legal Adviser

QUESTIONS

(1) Would you describe the Tate Letter as (a) "legislation" by the executive branch on a question of domestic law, (b) "advice" to the courts about how they should develop a field of domestic law, or (c) "advice" to the courts about how the executive branch interprets important trends in customary international law? What does the Tate Letter suggest about the general relationship in the field of sovereign immunity between domestic, comparative and international law?

(2) In view of the preceding cases, how do you assess the penultimate paragraph? Accurate? Strategic and self-effacing?

VICTORY TRANSPORT INC. v. COMISARIA GENERAL

United States Court of Appeals, Second Circuit, 1964.
336 F.2d 354, cert. denied 381 U.S. 934, 85 S.Ct. 1763, 14 L.Ed.2d 698 (1965).

SMITH, J.

. . .

The appellant, a branch of the Spanish Ministry of Commerce, voyage-chartered the S.S. Hudson from its owner, the appellee, to transport a cargo of surplus wheat, purchased pursuant to the Agricultural Trade Development and Assistance Act, 7 U.S.C.A. § 1691 et seq., from Mobile, Alabama to one or two safe Spanish ports. The charter agreement contained the New York Produce Arbitration Clause, providing for the arbitration of disputes before three commercial men in New York.[8] The ship was delayed and sustained hull damage in discharging its cargo in Spanish ports that were allegedly unsafe for a ship of the Hudson's size. When the appellant failed to pay for the damages or submit the dispute to arbitration, the appellee instituted this proceeding under Section 4 of the United States Ar-

8. "Should any dispute arise between Owners and the Charterers, the matter in dispute shall be referred to three persons at New York, one to be appointed by each of the parties hereto, and the third by the two so chosen; their decision or that of any two of them shall be final, and for the purpose of enforcing any award, this agreement may be made a rule of the Court. The Arbitrators shall be commercial men."

bitration Act, 9 U.S.C.A. § 4,[9] to compel arbitration. On March 22, 1963, appellee secured an ex parte order from the district court permitting service of its petition by registered mail at appellant's Madrid office. Service pursuant to this order was effected on April 1, 1963.

On October 15, 1963 the appellant moved to vacate the extraterritorial service as unauthorized by statute. Appearing specially and supported by an affidavit of the Spanish Consul, who stated that the appellant was a branch of the Spanish Government and immune from suit, counsel for the appellant also moved to dismiss the petition to compel arbitration because of a lack of jurisdiction and sovereign immunity. Rejecting these cross-motions, Judge Murphy held that the court had *in personam* jurisdiction and granted the appellee's motion to compel arbitration.

Sovereign Immunity

Appellant's primary contention is that as an arm of the sovereign Government of Spain, it cannot be sued in the courts of the United States without its consent, which it declines to accord in this case. There is certainly a great deal of impressive precedent to support this contention . . . . The doctrine originated in an era of personal sovereignty, when kings could theoretically do no wrong and when the exercise of authority by one sovereign over another indicated hostility or superiority. With the passing of that era, sovereign immunity has been retained by the courts chiefly to avoid possible embarrassment to those responsible for the conduct of the nation's foreign relations. . . . However, because of the dramatic changes in the nature and functioning of sovereigns, particularly in the last half century, the wisdom of retaining the doctrine has been cogently questioned. See, e. g., Lauterpacht, The Problem of Jurisdictional Immunities of Foreign States, 28 Brit.Y.B.Int'l L. 220 (1951). Growing concern for individual rights and public morality, coupled with the increasing entry of governments into what had previously been regarded as private pursuits, has led a substantial number of nations to abandon the absolute theory of sovereign immunity in favor of a restrictive theory. . . .

Meeting in Brussels in 1926, representatives of twenty nations, including all the major powers except the United States and Russia, signed a convention limiting sovereign immunity in the area of maritime commerce to ships and cargoes employed exclusively for public and non-commercial purposes.[10] After World War II the United

9. 9 U.S.C.A. § 4. "A party aggrieved by the alleged failure, neglect, or refusal of another to arbitrate under a written agreement for arbitration may petition any court of the United States which, save for such agreement, would have jurisdiction under the judicial code at law, in equity, or in admiralty of the subject matter of a suit arising out of the controversy between the parties, for an order directing that such arbitrarion proceed in the manner provided for in such agreement. Five days' notice in writing of such application shall be served upon the party in default. Service thereof shall be made in the manner provided by law for the service of summons in the jurisdiction in which the proceeding is brought. The court shall hear the parties, and upon being satisfied that the making of the agreement for arbitration or the failure to comply therewith is not in issue, the court shall make an order directing the parties to proceed to arbitration in accordance with the terms of the agreement. . . ."

10. International Convention for the Unification of Certain Rules Concerning the Immunities of State Ships. . . . Article I of the Convention provided: "Seagoing vessels owned or operated by States, cargoes owned by them, and cargoes and passengers carried on Government vessels, and the States owning or operat-

States began to restrict immunity by negotiating treaties obligating each contracting party to waive its sovereign immunity for state-controlled enterprises engaged in business activities within the territory of the other party. Fourteen such treaties were negotiated by our State Department in the decade 1948 to 1958. . . . And in 1952 our State Department, in a widely publicized letter from Acting Legal Adviser Jack B. Tate to the Acting Attorney General Philip B. Perlman, announced that the Department would generally adhere to the restrictive theory of sovereign immunity . . . .

In delineating the scope of a doctrine designed to avert possible embarrassment to the conduct of our foreign relations, the courts have quite naturally deferred to the policy pronouncements of the State Department. National City Bank of New York v. Republic of China, 348 U.S. 356, 360–361, 75 S.Ct. 423, 99 L.Ed. 389 (1955). . . . The Supreme Court's dictum in Republic of Mexico v. Hoffman, 324 U.S. 30, 35, 65 S.Ct. 530, 533, 89 L.Ed. 729 (1945)—"It is therefore not for the courts to deny an immunity which our government has seen fit to allow, or to allow an immunity on new grounds which the government has not seen fit to recognize"—has been variously construed, but we think it means at least that the courts should deny immunity where the State Department has indicated, either directly or indirectly, that immunity need not be accorded. It makes no sense for the courts to deny a litigant his day in court and to permit the disregard of legal obligations to avoid embarrassing the State Department if that agency indicates it will not be embarrassed. Cf. National City Bank v. Republic of China, supra, 348 U.S. at 360–361, 75 S.Ct. 423 (1955). Moreover, "recognition by the courts of an immunity upon principles which the political department of government has not sanctioned may be equally embarrassing to it in securing the protection of our national interests and their recognition by other nations." Republic of Mexico v. Hoffman, supra, 324 U.S. at 36, 65 S.Ct. at 533.

This is not to say that the courts will never grant immunity unless the State Department specifically requests it. A claim of sovereign immunity may be presented to the court by either of two procedures. The foreign sovereign may request its claim of immunity be recognized by the State Department, which will normally present its suggestion to the court through the Attorney General or some law officer acting under his direction. Alternatively, the accredited and recognized representative of the foreign sovereign may present the claim of sovereign immunity directly to the court. Ex parte Muir, 254 U.S. 522, 41 S.Ct. 185, 65 L.Ed. 383 (1921). In some situations the State Department may find it expedient to make no response to a request for immunity. Where, as here,[11] the court has received no

ing such vessels, or owning such cargoes, are subject in respect of claims relating to the operation of such vessels or the carriage of such cargoes, to the same rules of liability and to the same obligations as those applicable to private vessels, cargoes, and equipments."

Article II provided that these liabilities and obligations may be enforced by the same rules and procedure applied to private ships and cargoes, while Article III excepted from the application of the first articles "ships of war, Government yachts, patrol vessels, hospital ships, auxiliary vessels, supply ships, and other craft owned or operated by a State and used at the time a cause of action arises exclusively on Governmental and noncommercial service . . ." However, Article III did provide for certain remedies before the courts of the sovereign owning or operating a vessel as a public activity.

11. The plea of sovereign immunity for the Comisaria General in the district court was supported only by a conclusionary affidavit of the Spanish Con-

communication from the State Department concerning the immunity of the Comisaria General, the court must decide for itself whether it is the established policy of the State Department to recognize claims of immunity of this type. Republic of Mexico v. Hoffman, supra, 324 U.S. at 36, 65 S.Ct. 530.

Through the "Tate letter" the State Department has made it clear that its policy is to decline immunity to friendly foreign sovereigns in suits arising from private or commercial activity. But the "Tate letter" offers no guide-lines or criteria for differentiating between a sovereign's private and public acts. Nor have the courts or commentators suggested any satisfactory test. Some have looked to the nature of the transaction, categorizing as sovereign acts only activity which could not be performed by individuals. While this criterion is relatively easy to apply, it ofttimes produces rather astonishing results, such as the holdings of some European courts that purchases of bullets or shoes for the army, the erection of fortifications for defense, or the rental of a house for an embassy, are private acts. . . . Furthermore, this test merely postpones the difficulty, for particular contracts in some instances may be made only by states.[12] Others have looked to the purpose of the transaction, categorizing as *jure imperii* all activities in which the object of performance is public in character. But this test is even more unsatisfactory, for conceptually the modern sovereign always acts for a public purpose. Lauterpacht, supra, 28 Brit.Y.B.Int'l L. at 224. Functionally the criterion is purely arbitrary and necessarily involves the court in projecting personal notions about the proper realm of state functioning. . . .

The conceptual difficulties involved in formulating a satisfactory method of differentiating between acts *jure imperii* and acts *jure gestionis* have led many commentators to declare that the distinction is unworkable. However, the Supreme Court has made it plain that when the State Department has been silent on the question of immunity in a particular case, it is the court's duty to determine for itself whether the foreign sovereign is entitled to immunity "in conformity to the principles accepted by the department of the government charged with the conduct of foreign relations." Republic of Mexico v. Hoffman, supra, 324 U.S. at 35, 65 S.Ct. at 532. And since the State Department has publicly pronounced its adherence to the distinction, we must apply it to the facts of this case.

sul in New York. A consul is supposedly clothed with authority to act for his government only in commercial matters. Since nothing in the record indicates that the Spanish Consul was specially authorized to interpose a claim of sovereign immunity, the affidavit was plainly insufficient. . . .

On appeal the Spanish Ambassador to the United States has written a letter directly to this court claiming immunity for the Comisaria General and has moved for permission to appear specially in the proceeding. We find it unnecessary to decide whether this procedure is sufficient to raise the claim of sovereign immunity or whether the defense has been waived through a failure to present it properly. Under the view we take of sovereign immunity, permitting the Spanish Ambassador to intervene at this stage in the proceedings will not materially prejudice the appellee, who does not dispute appellant's sovereign status. We therefore grant the motion of the Spanish Ambassador and treat the claim of sovereign immunity as properly presented to the court.

12. Lauterpacht, supra, 28 Brit.Y.B. Int'l L., at 225; Lalive, *L' immunité de jurisdiction des États et des Organisations Internationales*, 3 Recueil des Cours, 205, 259–260 (Hague Academy of Int'l Law 1953). For example, any individual may be able to purchase a boat, but only a sovereign may be able to purchase a battleship. Should the purchase of a yacht be equated with the purchase of a battleship?

The purpose of the restrictive theory of sovereign immunity is to try to accommodate the interest of individuals doing business with foreign governments in having their legal rights determined by the courts, with the interest of foreign governments in being free to perform certain political acts without undergoing the embarrassment or hindrance of defending the propriety of such acts before foreign courts. Sovereign immunity is a derogation from the normal exercise of jurisdiction by the courts and should be accorded only in clear cases. Since the State Department's failure or refusal to suggest immunity is significant, we are disposed to deny a claim of sovereign immunity that has not been "recognized and allowed" by the State Department unless it is plain that the activity in question falls within one of the categories of strictly political or public acts about which sovereigns have traditionally been quite sensitive. Such acts are generally limited to the following categories:

(1) internal administrative acts, such as expulsion of an alien.

(2) legislative acts, such as nationalization.

(3) acts concerning the armed forces.

(4) acts concerning diplomatic activity.

(5) public loans.[13]

We do not think that the restrictive theory adopted by the State Department requires sacrificing the interests of private litigants to international comity in other than these limited categories. Should diplomacy require enlargement of these categories, the State Department can file a suggestion of immunity with the court. Should diplomacy require contraction of the categories, the State Department can issue a new or clarifying policy pronouncement.

The Comisaria General's chartering of the appellee's ship to transport a purchase of wheat is not a strictly public or political act. Indeed, it partakes far more of the character of a private commercial act than a public or political act.

The charter party has all the earmarks of a typical commercial transaction. It was executed for the Comisaria General by "El Jefe del Servicio Commercial," the head of its commercial division. The wheat was consigned to and shipped by a private commercial concern. And one of the most significant indicators of the private commercial nature of this charter is the inclusion of the arbitration clause. . . .

Maritime transport has been included among the commercial or business activities specifically mentioned in recent United States treaties restricting sovereign immunity.[14] And the 1926 Brussels Convention, the first major international attempt to restrict sovereign immunity, which Spain signed but never ratified, denied immunity to all maritime governmental activities except vessels operated ex-

13. Lalive, supra, 3 Recueil des Cours at 285–286.

14. A typical provision is contained in Article XVIII (Par. 3) of the FCN Treaty with Israel, signed August 23, 1951:

"No enterprise of either Party, including corporations, associations, and government agencies and instrumentalities, which is publicly owned or controlled shall, if it engages in commercial, manufacturing, processing, shipping or other business activities within the territories of the other Party, claim or enjoy, either for itself or for its property, immunity therein from taxation, suit, execution of judgment or other liability to which privately owned and controlled enterprises are subject therein." . . .

clusively on non-commercial service, such as warships, patrol vessels, or hospital ships.

Even if we take a broader view of the transaction to encompass the purchase of wheat pursuant to the Surplus Agricultural Commodities Agreement to help feed the people of Spain, the activity of the Comisaria General remains more in the commercial than political realm. Appellant does not claim that the wheat will be used for the public services of Spain; presumptively the wheat will be resold to Spanish nationals. Whether the Comisaria General loses money or makes a profit on the sale, this purchasing activity has been conducted through private channels of trade. Except for United States financing, permitting payment in pesetas, the Comisaria General acted much like any private purchaser of wheat.

Our conclusion that the Comisaria General's activity is more properly labelled an act *jure gestionis* than *jure imperii* is supported by the practice of those countries which have adopted the restrictive theory of sovereign immunity. . . . Though there are a few inconsistencies,[15] the courts in those countries which have adopted the restrictive theory have generally considered purchasing activity by a state instrumentality, particularly for resale to nationals, as commercial or private activity.[16]

Finally, our conclusion that the Comisaria General's claim of sovereign immunity should be denied finds support in the State Department's communication to the court in New York and Cuba Mail S.S. Co. v. Republic of Korea, 132 F.Supp. 684, 685 (S.D.N.Y.1955). There the Republic of Korea was allegedly responsible for damaging a ship while assisting in the unloading of a cargo of rice for distribution without charge to its civilian and military personnel during the Korean War. Though suggesting that Korea's property was immune from attachment, the State Department refused to suggest immunity "inasmuch as the particular acts out of which the cause of action arose are not shown to be of a purely governmental character." If the wartime transportation of rice to civilian and military personnel is not an act *jure imperii, a fortiori* the peacetime transportation of wheat for presumptive resale is not an act *jure imperii*.[17]

15. Takhowsky v. Gouvernement federal suisse et Regnier, 48 Journal du droit international 179 (Clunet) (Court of Appeal, Paris 1921) (holding that Switzerland was entitled to immunity in a suit arising from its charter of ships to transport cocoa for the Swiss chocolate industry during World War I because the venture was not exclusively commercial); Etienne v. Gouvernement neerlandais, Dalloz 84 (1948), Annual Digest, Case No. 30 (Tribunal Commercial de la Rochelle 1947) (holding that a ship requisitioned and operated by the Dutch Government to transport wheat for the reprovisioning of the Netherlands was a political rather than a commercial act). But these are decisions of courts of France where it is difficult to tell to what extent the restrictive theory of sovereign immunity has been adopted. The French decisions are uncertain and often contradictory. . . .

16. E. g., Monnoyer et Bernard v. Etat Francaise, 3 Pasicrisie Belge 129 (1927); Etat roumain v. Pascalet et Cie., Dalloz 260 (1924); Stato di Romania c. Trutta, I Monitore dei Tribunali 288 (1926), Annual Digest 179 (1925–26); Societe pour la fabrication des cartouches c. Col M., Ministre de la Guerre de Bulgarie, Belgique Judiciare 383 (1889) . . . .

17. Since in our view sovereign immunity does not apply, we find it unnecessary to consider whether the agreement to arbitrate constituted an implied waiver of sovereign immunity. . . .

JURISDICTION

Though in most cases jurisdiction over a foreign sovereign is obtained in an *in rem* proceeding, there is no bar to the assertion of *in personam* jurisdiction. See Kunglig Jarnvagsstyrelsen v. Dexter & Carpenter, 300 F. 891 (S.D.N.Y.1924) (L. Hand, J.), aff'd 32 F. 2d 195 (2 Cir. 1929). . . .

We hold that the district court had *in personam* jurisdiction to enter the order compelling arbitration. By agreeing to arbitrate in New York, where the United States Arbitration Act makes such agreements specifically enforceable, the Comisaria General must be deemed to have consented to the jurisdiction of the court that could compel the arbitration proceeding in New York. To hold otherwise would be to render the arbitration clause a nullity. In Farr & Co. v. Cia. Intercontinental De Navegacion, 243 F.2d 342 (2 Cir. 1957) and Orion Shipping & Trading Co. v. Eastern States Petro. Corp. of Panama, 284 F.2d 419 (2 Cir. 1960), this court held that § 4 of the United States Arbitration Act provides sufficient jurisdictional basis for the district court to order a foreign corporation which had agreed to arbitration in New York to submit to arbitration. . . . [I]t is clear that the court has *in personam* jurisdiction, for we see no reason to treat a commercial branch of a foreign sovereign differently from a foreign corporation. . . . Implicit in the agreement to arbitrate is consent to enforcement of that agreement.

The suggestion by the appellant that the subject matter of the controversy is without the admiralty jurisdiction of the United States courts is utterly devoid of merit. It has long been settled that a charter-party is a maritime contract and that disputes arising therefrom are within the admiralty jurisdiction of the United States courts. . . .

SERVICE OF PROCESS

The appellant has also challenged the propriety of the extraterritorial service employed here. But since the appellant has consented beforehand to the jurisdiction of the district court, the sole function of process in this case was, as Judge Murphy correctly noted below, to notify the appellant that proceedings had commenced. This function was certainly performed. Moreover, similar service of process on nongovernmental foreign corporations was held sufficient in the Farr and Orion cases, supra. No rule of international law requires special treatment for serving branches of foreign sovereigns. . . .

Section 4 of the Arbitration Act provides that service of the petition to compel arbitration shall be made in the manner provided by the Federal Rules of Civil Procedure. The language of Rule 4(d)(3), incorporated by reference into Rule 4(d)(7), which permits service in the manner employed in the state courts, provides for service on "a domestic or foreign corporation or upon a partnership or other unincorporated association which is subject to suit under a common name" and would seem broad enough to cover the Comisaria General. Moreover, Rule 4(e) provided, as of March 22, 1963, that:

> *"Whenever a statute of the United States or an order of court provides for service of a summons, or of a notice, or of an order in lieu of a summons upon a party not an inhabitant of or found within the state, service shall be made under the circumstances and in the manner prescribed by the statute, rule, or order."*

Since the appellant had consented to the jurisdiction of the court, Judge Dawson's order authorizing service by registered mail did not violate due process. And since service was effected pursuant to Judge Dawson's order, such service complied with the terms of Rule 4(e).

The order of the district court is affirmed.

RICH v. NAVIERA VACUBA, S.A.

United States Court of Appeals, Fourth Circuit, 1961.
295 F.2d 24.

PER CURIAM.

The vessel Bahia de Nipe sailed on August 8, 1961, from Cuba with a cargo of 5,000 bags of sugar destined for a Russian port. When on August 17 the ship was about 300 miles east of Bermuda the master and ten of his crewmen put the rest of the crew under restraint, turned the vessel towards Hampton Roads, Virginia, and notified the Coast Guard of their intention to seek asylum in the United States. As they crossed the three-mile limit and neared the entrance to the Chesapeake Bay the vessel was met by the Coast Guard and taken to anchorage off Lynnhaven, Virginia.

These proceedings were begun on August 18 by the filing of a libel against the vessel on behalf of two longshoremen who had earlier recovered judgments against the Republic of Cuba and Naviera Vacuba, S. A. The latter owned the vessel before she was taken over by the revolutionary government of Cuba. Shortly thereafter another libel was filed against the ship and cargo by Mayan Lines, S. A. which had previously recovered judgment by consent in a state court of Louisiana in the sum of $500,000 against the Republic of Cuba. A third libel was filed against the cargo only by the United Fruit Sugar Company which claimed that the sugar belonged to it, having been unlawfully confiscated in Cuba by the revolutionary government. Libels for wages were also filed by the defecting master and the ten crew members.

Upon the institution of these suits in the United States District Court for the Eastern District of Virginia at Norfolk, the Clerk, pursuant to law and the practice of the court, issued the customary in rem process and delivered the same to the United States Deputy Marshal to be served upon the ship. Service, however, was prevented by the Coast Guard, which purported to act "pursuant to orders" and in reliance upon the authority of 50 U.S.C.A. § 191. On being advised of his interference with the Marshal in the performance of his duties, the District Judge issued an order directed to the Captain of the Port and the Commander of the Coast Guard, requiring them to appear and to show cause why an order should not be entered permitting the Marshal to board the vessel to execute the writs.

A number of communications from and on behalf of the Secretary of State addressed to the Attorney General were presented to the court by the United States Attorney. While infelicitously expressed, we think these sufficiently set forth the requisites of a valid suggestion for the allowance of sovereign immunity.

Arguments extending over several days were heard by the District Court which then held that the Coast Guard and those who had directed it acted in excess of their authority in preventing the service of the court's process. We likewise do not condone the Coast

Guard's refusal to permit the Marshal to serve the process and find no authority therefor in section 191.

We turn to a consideration of the other questions raised. The chief defense, indeed the only one argued by the Government, is that the Republic of Cuba is a sovereign power immune from the jurisdiction of the courts of the United States, and that when the Department of State accepted Cuba's claim of ownership, possession and public operation of the ship, and ownership of the cargo, and so certified to the court and suggested that sovereign immunity be accorded, the court was bound to respect the determination and suggestion of the State Department.

The libellants argue that before sovereign immunity may be granted they should be heard by the court on whether the foreign government is in fact the owner and possessor of the property in question and, as to the ship, whether she was operated by that government not commercially but in a public capacity.

Mayan Lines, S. A. showed in addition that in the state court action wherein its $500,000 judgment was obtained against the Republic of Cuba, the defendant specifically waived its sovereign immunity in respect both to the adjudication of liability and the enforcement of the judgment by execution. It argued that it is both illegal and unconscionable for Cuba to attempt in the present proceedings to repudiate its unlimited waiver, solemnly made in the course of the Louisiana litigation.

For the libellant, United Fruit Sugar Company, evidence was adduced to prove that the very bags of sugar constituting the cargo were its property, expropriated from the company's plants in Cuba. Accordingly, this libellant asserted that release of the cargo under the doctrine of sovereign immunity, upon the mere certificate of the State Department without opportunity for further inquiry, would deprive it of its property without due process of law in violation of the Fifth Amendment. Similar contentions under the Fifth Amendment were advanced by the other libellants.

Despite these contentions, we conclude that the certificate and grant of immunity issued by the Department of State should be accepted by the court without further inquiry. Ex parte Republic of Peru, 318 U.S. 578, 63 S.Ct. 793, 87 L.Ed. 1014. See also Republic of Mexico v. Hoffman, 324 U.S. 30, 65 S.Ct. 530, 89 L.Ed. 729; . . . We think that the doctrine of the separation of powers under our Constitution requires us to assume that all pertinent considerations have been taken into account by the Secretary of State in reaching his conclusion.

The fact that the Mayan Lines' judgment was rendered in the Louisiana court after a specific waiver of immunity by the Cuban Government, both with respect to liability and enforcement of the judgment, does not significantly distinguish its position from that of the other libellants, in view of the controlling effect that must be given the State Department's action. We do not mean to suggest that the contention raised by this libellant as to the effect to be given the waiver would not be a suitable subject of inquiry in the absence of State Department action. In that case the question would be a proper one for the court to consider. The certification and suggestion of immunity, however, which has been made by the State Department in this matter affecting our foreign relations, withdraws it from the sphere of litigation. Especially is this so when the presence of the ship within the territorial jurisdiction of the court is made possible only by the barratry of the shipmaster. Refusal of the State Department in these circumstances to enforce Cuba's earlier waiver over its present assertion of immunity is within the Department's authority, and constitutes no violation of the libellant's rights under the Fifth Amendment . . . .

The order of the District Court is

Affirmed.

COMMENT

The background to the Rich case [18] is one of high drama. Following a series of "hijacking" episodes involving American and Cuban airplanes and vessels, arrangements for their return were made pursuant to diplomatic correspondence. The diplomatic notes gave particular attention to an Electra airplane owned by Eastern Airlines which had been flown to Havana under duress on July 24, 1961, and to a Cuban patrol vessel that had been brought to Key West. A United States Note of August 10 stated that this country was "prepared to release the Cuban patrol vessel SV8 as requested by the Cuban government" and assumed that "the Cuban Government is prepared to release the Eastern Air Lines Electra." A reply of August 11 stated that the "Revolutionary Government of Cuba accepts the concrete proposal of the Government of the United States to release the patrol boat . . . . Similarly, the Government of Cuba agrees to place at the disposal of Eastern Airlines the Electra airplane . . . . The Government of Cuba desires formally to reiterate the viewpoint expressed in [an earlier note] regarding the advisability of both governments adopting the most effective measures to avoid in the future the repetition of acts of piracy and seizure of ships and airplanes . . . ." This correspondence took place a few days before the arrival of the Bahia de Nipe in Norfolk.[19]

With respect to the Rich litigation, the Secretary of State had sent a letter of August 19 to the Attorney General, stating that it had been "determined that the release of this vessel would avoid further disturbance to our international relations in the premises." Another letter of August 20 from the Secretary noted that "assurances were given by the United States that the vessel would be released" upon certain conditions which Cuba had fulfilled, and concluded that "the prompt release of the vessel is necessary to secure the observance of the rights and obligations of the United States." [20]

NOTE ON THE DEVELOPMENT OF THE RESTRICTIVE THEORY SINCE THE TATE LETTER

(1) The Victory Transport and Rich cases illustrate the tension between the development through case law of criteria of distinction between sovereign and commercial acts more precise than those con-

18. Described in Cardozo, Judicial Deference to State Department Suggestions: Recognition of Prerogative or Abdication to Usurper?, 48 Cornell L.Q. 461, 464–67 (1963).

19. The correspondence appears in 45 Dept.State Bull. 407–408 (1961).

20. Both letters are set forth in the opinion of the District Court, 197 F. Supp. 710 (E.D.Va.1961).

tained in the Tate Letter, and the use of sovereign immunity determinations to achieve frankly political, diplomatic purposes. This is of course the same tension—between relatively principled laws developed and applied by courts, and *ad hoc* political decisions issuing from the Executive Branch—that characterizes other areas of the country's foreign relations law, including the act-of-state doctrine in Part B of this chapter.

The Supreme Court has written only once on this topic since 1952, in a case which did not involve a suggestion of immunity by the State Department. National City Bank v. Republic of China, 348 U.S. 356, 75 S.Ct. 423, 99 L.Ed. 389 (1955), does not in fact explore or apply the sovereign-commercial distinction. However, it appears that the Tate Letter and its negative attitude towards immunity, to which Mr. Jusice Frankfurter referred, helped the Justice towards the conclusion that when the Republic of China sued in a federal court to recover a deposit in a bank, it rendered itself liable to a counterclaim (amounting to a setoff since the bank dropped its demand for affirmative relief), even though the counterclaim arose from an entirely different transaction (the default of Treasury Notes of China held by the bank). "[T]he ultimate thrust of the consideration of fair dealing which allows a setoff or counterclaim based on the same subject matter reaches the present situation"—even though the Court appeared to agree that the Treasury Notes were *jure imperii* within the Tate Letter distinction. The Court observed that, since the United States could be sued here on a comparable claim and since China could be sued in its own courts on such a claim, there was no reason to believe that China would be affronted by this assertion of jurisdiction. The Court also observed that sovereign immunity "is not an explicit command of the Constitution. It rests on considerations of policy given legal sanction by this Court."

A few cases are indicative of problems in judicial elucidation of the Tate Letter. In Petrol Shipping Corp. v. Kingdom of Greece, 360 F.2d 103 (2d Cir. 1966), on its facts similar to Victory Transport, the State Department wrote to the Greek Government rejecting the request for sovereign immunity and citing the Tate Letter. The court followed that conclusion.

In Chemical Natural Resources, Inc. v. Republic of Venezuela, 420 Pa. 134, 215 A.2d 864 (1966), the controversy arose out of the Venezuelan government's cancellation of a contract to erect an electric power plant and its confiscation of the property of plaintiffs (a Delaware corporation and its Venezuelan subsidiary) connected with the project. Plaintiffs began an action by attaching a vessel in Philadelphia harbor allegedly owned by Venezuela. Venezuela obtained a State Department letter, after a hearing before the Legal Adviser, stating that "it recognizes and allows the sovereign immunity of the Republic of Venezuela."

The Pennsylvania Supreme Court ordered dismissal of the complaint. The majority affirmed that the State Department's determination, once properly presented to the courts, was still "conclusive." The Tate Letter, said the court, "certainly implies" that the State Department could no longer "control" the courts, "which are free to make their own determination." However, despite this "clear meaning, it appears that the State Department has silently abandoned" the new restrictive policy and substituted for it a "case by case" policy responsive to "foreign and diplomatic relations . . . at the particular time [and] . . . the best interests of our country at that particular time." The majority cited the Rich case as support for the view that Ex Parte Peru, p. 645, supra, still governed. A forceful dissent by Justice Musmanno asserted that the executive did not have primacy as to legal issues, upon which the State Department expressly rested its determination, and that sovereign immunity was an unhealthy "excrescence" that encouraged irresponsibility to world order and repudiated "international moral principles."

In Isbrandtsen Tankers v. President of India, 446 F.2d 1198 (2d Cir. 1971), the Court of Appeals had before it another case involving a contract for the use of plaintiff's vessels for the shipment of grain. Plaintiff's complaint contained three causes of action: (1) demurrage, or a contractual provision for damages in the event of delay in unloading; (2) detention, also based upon delay in unloading but an action in the nature of a tort requiring proof of wrongful conduct, and (3) unpaid freight. All of these claims arose out of the delays the vessels suffered because crowded conditions in the port of Calcutta prevented prompt unloading. The Court of Appeals stated that if it were required to apply the Tate Letter, "we might well find" the Indian government actions to be "purely private commercial decisions." Nonetheless, it accepted the State Department's advice that an explicit waiver of immunity in the contract did not apply to the second cause of action, in detention, which was apparently viewed as not arising under the charter party and hence as not covered by the waiver, and which "draws into issue acts of Indian government officials which were governmental rather than commercial in nature." The court said that it had no alternative but to accept the recommendation of the State Department.[21] It affirmed dismissal of the second cause of action.

Spacil v. Crowe, 489 F.2d 614 (5th Cir. 1974), involved a Cuban ship which was in Chilean waters unloading sugar when the 1973 coup by the Chilean military overthrew the Allende government. Fearing seizure by the new military regime, it left in such haste that several Chilean cranes were still on board. When the vessel touched on the Canal Zone, two Chilean corporations began an action for breach of the contract to deliver sugar and for the cranes. Cuba obtained a State Department letter that "recognizes and allows" Cuba's claim of immunity. The court rejected claims that the Department's determination was arbitrary and based on undisclosed information so that it should be subjected to at least limited judicial review under

21. The distinctions between the three causes of action are drawn more clearly in Note, Sovereign Immunity, 13 Harv.Int.L.J. 527 (1972).

the Administrative Procedure Act. "For more than 160 years American courts have consistently applied the doctrine of sovereign immunity when requested to do so . . . with no further review of the executive's determination." The court stressed separation-of-power principles and (citing the Curtiss-Wright case, p. 102, supra) the greater institutional competence to reach decisions of the executive "in the chess game that is diplomacy." The court would not require even a statement of reasons from the executive. "In the narrow band of government action where foreign policy interests are direct and substantial we must eschew even limited 'reasonableness review.' " Executive "preemption" obtained.

(2) Developments outside the United States are worthy of attention in connection with the evolution of the restrictive theory. Some work is in progress on the treaty front. Victory Transport refers to the 1926 Brussels Convention on the immunities of state ships (to which the United States is not a party) and to 14 treaties of friendship, commerce and navigation with clauses waiving immunity as to business activities of state-owned enterprises. A European Convention on State Immunity of May 16, 1972 would sharply restrict sovereign immunity by the technique of enumerating situations in which a signatory state is not entitled to claim immunity.[22] One of the most far-reaching of the thirteen categories is Article 4(1), which provides that a state may not claim immunity as to a contractual obligation to be discharged in the forum state. This applies even to public loans, an activity elsewhere listed as sovereign and hence immune.

There is also a continuously growing body of case law developing distinctions between sovereign and commercial acts, especially in European courts. From the conflicting case law developing the restrictive theory, it is still apparent that continental courts act principally or entirely on their own, without legislation or executive mandate. They do not feel bound to accept the answers of the Executive as conclusive—even in countries such as France where the courts have felt bound by executive interpretations of treaties to a greater extent than United States courts.

This case law lacks uniformity, to a large degree because each country's courts tend to look to their own national courts for precedent. That is, they tend to hold a foreign government liable to suit under circumstances in which their own government can be sued, or in which it can be sued in the ordinary or commercial courts as distinguished from a special tribunal such as the French *Conseil d'État*. Consider, for example, a 1963 decision of the German Constitutional Court, acting under Article 100(2) of the Basic Law, p. 623, supra:[23]

22. The text of the Convention appears at 66 Am.J.Int.L. 923 (1972); for comments, see Mann, New Developments in the Law of Sovereign Immunity, 36 Modern L.Rev. 18 (1973).

23. Decision of April 30, 1963, 16 Entscheidungen des Bundesverfassungsgerichts 27, 62–63.

> The classification of state activity as sovereign or non-sovereign must basically be undertaken as a matter of national law since international law . . . contains no criteria for this distinction. . . . It cannot be given decisive weight that the reference to national law theoretically gives the national law-giver the possibility, by an appropriate change of national law, of influencing the scope of the international law rule. The distinction between sovereign and non-sovereign state activities under national law primarily serves purposes other than the fixing of the scope of immunity of foreign countries.

Note that the court's last sentence could support arguments for or against using domestic categories for issues of international sovereign immunity. The court concluded that the contract, one for the repair of an embassy, was an act *jure gestionis,* and specifically rejected the opinion of the Federal Ministry of Justice that it was a sovereign act "regardless of the fact that such a contract elsewhere in German law would be regarded as subject to private law."

Note that the United States may be a defendant in such foreign litigation. The Departments of State and Justice have sometimes disagreed about how such cases should be handled. After consulting with the local American embassy and considering the status of the case under the restrictive theory of immunity, the State Department will advise the Department of Justice whether it should plead sovereign immunity. The Justice Department may not always follow this advice. Note extracts from a colloquy: [24]

> *Mr. Yingling* (Assistant Legal Adviser, Department of State): "We don't feel that the government should claim immunity in the type of case where it wouldn't grant it if the situation were reversed. Let's say some Italian national is suing, for example, the Post Exchange. The State Department will not claim immunity, because in a reverse situation, we would not allow it if Italy was being sued in a court of the United States by an American national, while Italy was engaged in a similar activity and the Italian embassy claimed immunity. We would not recognize the claim."
>
> *Mr. Wilkey* (Assistant Attorney General, Department of Justice): "When we are entrusted with the defense of a lawsuit, we feel that if the claim is not meritorious, we have a right to resort to the remedies or the defenses the law gives us in the particular jurisdiction in which we are in court. Therefore, under local law, from time to time, the Department pleads sovereign immunity, the same way you would plead the statute of limitations, in order to defeat a nonmeritorious claim."

Special legislation treats claims arising from noncombat activities of our armed forces. 70A Stat. 154 (1956), 10 U.S.C.A. § 2734, provides that "to promote and maintain friendly relations through the prompt settlement of meritorious claims," officers of the armed

24. Cornell Law School Summer Conference on International Law in National Courts 20–21 (1960).

services may pay claims up to $25,000 and certify larger ones to Congress. Section 2734a provides that the Secretary of Defense may pay claims where the United States is party to an international agreement under which the foreign country may adjudicate the question.[25]

(3) A major factor in the determination whether to grant sovereign immunity may be the institutional form which the foreign government has given to the transaction. The responsible body may be clearly designated as part of the country's political system, i. e., a ministry, or it may be a separately organized trading agency run along commercial lines, or it may be a corporation established under the country's commercial laws with all its stock owned by the government.

Consider the state trading systems of Communist countries, among which that of the Soviet Union is the most extensive. The overseas operations of the Soviet Union are under the control of the Minister of Foreign Trade, who plans them within the limits of the national economic plan and directs the work of subordinate agencies. In many countries the Ministry acts through trade delegations, considered as part of the Soviet diplomatic corps. The United States has, for fear of complications in the area of diplomatic immunity, refused to receive such a delegation. Other Soviet trade activities are carried out by some 28 foreign trade combines, each of which deals with the export or import of a specified class of commodity. They are juridical persons, created by a charter under Soviet law (activities outside the charter are *ultra vires*). Under Soviet law each can sue and be sued and hold property rights in its own name. The Soviet government is not responsible for its debts although the government receives the combine's net profits and can dissolve it at any time. The Ministry of Foreign Trade can issue orders to the head of a combine and can remove him.[26]

Note that two questions have to be kept separate: (*a*) is the defendant entity immune from suit because of its affiliation with the government creating it?; and (*b*) is the government responsible for the liabilities arising out of the activities of that entity?

25. The chief treaty provision implemented by that section is Article VIII(5) of the NATO Status of Forces Agreement of 1951, 4 U.S.T. & O.I.A. 1792, T.I.A.S. No. 2846, which provides that private claims for damage caused by members of the armed forces of one state, while in the performance of official duties in another state, shall be determined according to the procedures applicable to claims against the armed forces of the latter ("receiving") state. The receiving state pays a part, usually 25%, of the cost of the settlement. It may be inferred that this provision minimizes any tendency to be liberal at the expense of the United States treasury. It is reported that in France alone nearly 18,000 claims totalling over $5,000,000 were paid by the United States from 1953 to 1965. Mullins, The International Responsibility of a State for Torts of its Military Forces, 34 Mil.L.Rev. 59, 60 fn. 5 (1966).

26. Berman, The Legal Framework of Trade between Planned and Market Economies: The Soviet-American Example, 24 Law & Contemp.Prob. 482 (1959).

(4) One of the issues raised in Rich v. Naviera Vacuba was the effectiveness of Cuba's waiver of its sovereign immunity. The court observed: "Cuba has breached its contractual agreement not to plead immunity in the enforcement of the judgment, but the law suggests that this may be done." The Court in Victory Transport elected not to confront the issue whether the arbitration clause constituted a waiver of immunity (p. 654, fn. 17). A waiver can be asserted by the plaintiff either on the basis of a contractual clause antedating the controversy, as in Matter of United States of Mexico v. Schmuck, 293 N.Y. 264, 56 N.E.2d 577 (1944), or because defendant failed to raise the issue while making a general appearance in the litigation, as in Flota Maritima Browning de Cuba, S.A. v. Motor Vessel Ciudad de La Habana, 335 F.2d 619 (4th Cir. 1964), 363 F.2d 733 (4th Cir. 1966). On this issue, as on others, the reaction of the State Department has generally been accorded decisive weight. Of course, distinct issues are posed when the foreign government's agreement not to plead immunity has a treaty rather than contractual base.

QUESTIONS

(1) After the Tate Letter, on what principle can a court accept as binding a State Department determination that defendant is entitled to sovereign immunity, especially in a clearly commercial case? Was the Rich litigation really such a case? Do you consider the State Department's intervention there more or less justified than in Ex parte Peru or the Republic of Venezuela?

(2) How do you evaluate the claim of Mayan Lines in the Rich Case that release of the vessel in accordance with the State Department's suggestion violated its rights under the Fifth Amendment?

(3) Consider the problems involved in working out the commercial versus non-commercial distinction. How would the Lalive classification, set forth by the court in Victory Transport at p. 653, supra, resolve cases arising from the following transactions: (*a*) a contract to purchase army uniforms from a large manufacturer of clothing, (*b*) a contract to purchase tanks from a firm specializing in military equipment, (*c*) misuse of premises leased for diplomatic purposes, and (*d*) collection of matured amounts of a government loan, the proceeds of which were used for developing government-owned petroleum resources?

(4) Assume that a court asserted jurisdiction in each of the cases in Question (3), and rendered a money judgment for plaintiff. Are the problems that plaintiff would then confront identical in the four cases?

(5) Consider the provisions of the FCN treaty in fn. 14, p. 653, supra. What significance has the use of the word "enterprise"? Does the phrase "other business activities" appear to modify the preceding term "commercial"? If so, is such an interpretation of the term "commercial" different from the Tate Letter's? Note that the provision draws no distinction between immunity from suit and immunity of property from execution of a judgment.

NOTE ON SOME PROBLEMS OF ACQUIRING JURISDICTION AND ENFORCING JUDGMENTS

The substantive law of sovereign immunity has become enmeshed with various procedural problems. As made evident by the preceding materials, many of the cases arise within the admiralty jurisdiction of the United States and use the rather special procedures and terminology (i. e., libellant and respondent, rather than plaintiff and defendant) of admiralty courts. In particular one notes that land-based distinctions between *in rem, quasi in rem* and *in personam* claims do not apply in admiralty, where there is great emphasis upon a court's control over a vessel as a basis for adjudicating all claims, whether in tort or in contract, arising out of its operations. Absence of jury trial and absence of ordinary venue rules are other features of admiralty practice. Extension of the Federal Rules of Civil Procedure in 1966 to include admiralty and maritime matters have eliminated or blurred some of the traditional distinctions in procedure and terminology.

Effecting service of process has been a difficult preliminary hurdle for parties seeking to sue foreign governments. The F.R.C.P. do not expressly cover foreign governments, although governmental instrumentalities in corporate form may be directly covered by Rule 4(d)(3). Meanwhile, counsel for plaintiffs have discovered that service upon a foreign ambassador is likely to be quashed as unduly offensive to diplomatic sensitivities, Hellenic Lines, Ltd. v. Moore, 345 F.2d 978 (D.C.Cir.1965); that service upon a consul is treated as ineffective because not within the scope of a consul's limited functions, Purdy Co. v. Argentina, 333 F.2d 95 (7th Cir. 1964); and that attachment of a foreign government's property within the jurisdiction for use as the basis of *quasi in rem* jurisdiction (or comparable admiralty jurisdiction) is the only available alternative.

That last path, however, has its own difficulties, especially if the State Department raises objections to the attachment—as it did (with respect to attachment of the government's funds in New York banks) in New York and Cuba Mail S. S. Co. v. Republic of Korea, 132 F.Supp. 684 (S.D.N.Y.1955). That case was an admiralty suit in which libellant had sought damages for injuries to its vessel allegedly caused by respondent's ship during unloading operations of rice in a Korean port. The courts and State Department have not here followed a straight line of doctrine. Jurisdiction has been asserted, in the absence of the Department's intervention, on the basis of attachment of chattels and the garnishment of debts owed by a government which were not shown to be "directly related" to activities *jure imperii*,[27] and the Department has been interpreted by a court to take the position that it will not suggest that "property of a

27. Harris and Company Advertising, Inc. v. Republic of Cuba, 127 So.2d 687 (D.Ct.App.Fla.1961).

foreign state [presumably related to activities *jure gestionis*] is immune from attachment in aid of jurisdiction, but will continue to suggest that the same property is immune from execution.[28]

This last observation suggests the serious problem which a successful plaintiff encounters in collecting upon his judgment at the end of the litigation process. Execution against property of a sovereign is the ultimate denial of immunity. Problems of interference with the foreign government's performance of its functions can become acute. The sovereign can of course obtain release of any attached property which it considers necessary to performance of its governmental functions by posting a bond.

Property subject to execution would not in any event include certain critical categories, comparable to acts *jure imperii.* For example, under clearly established principles of international law, an embassy and related property would be immune.

Practice as to property not within these categories varies among countries. In a research study for the State Department, The International Law of Sovereign Immunity (1963), Professor Joseph Sweeney found in many European tribunals "no rule of absolute immunity for the property of foreign states. The common core of the absolute and restrictive concepts of immunity of property is immunity of property connected with public acts of the state. As to property connected with commercial and other private acts of the state, immunity is not required." In some countries, execution appears to depend upon authorization of the executive.[29] But in the United States, a judgment creditor must generally rely upon the moral (and political) effect of his judgment.

This problem of execution was earlier raised in these materials by Articles 54 and 55 of the Convention on the Settlement of Investment Disputes between States and Nationals of other States,* and the description at p. 486, supra, of the 1966 statute enacted to carry out this country's obligations under the Convention. Note that Article 55 refers only to immunity "from execution." Presumably a state against which an award had been rendered would be subject to the jurisdiction of courts of other parties to the Convention in an action looking towards execution. That state, however, could invoke the law of the forum and Article 55 to oppose a court order for execution against its property. The private party in whose favor an award had been rendered appears free to "forum shop" to select a country (party to the Convention) in which the defendant state had property and which entertained a restrictive view of immunity from execution. If that country had taken such measures as were necessary (Article 69) to carry out its obligations under Article 54, notions of forum non conveniens would presumably not apply.

28. Flota Maritima Browning de Cuba, S.A. v. Motor Vessel Ciudad de La Habana, 335 F.2d 619, 626 (4th Cir. 1964).

29. See Schmitthoff, The Claim of Sovereign Immunity in the Law of International Trade, 7 Int. & Comp.L.Q. 452, 461 (1958).

PROBLEM

Power Plants, Inc. (PPI) has been invited by National Power of Guatador (NPG), a government-owned corporation, to submit bids on three hydroelectric generators and associated equipment for a dam under construction near Guatador's capital. PPI would provide the equipment and supervise its installation at the site. The policy of NPG calls for its making part payment upon completion and the rest after a six-month testing period. PPI's management would like to bid on this project and feels confident of being able to undercut competitors. It is, however, concerned about the risk involved. NPG's engineers have a reputation for being ready to find flaws in the work of foreign technicians, and Guatador has at times been a bit slow in making payments, although there is no reason to doubt its political stability or fiscal responsibility.

PPI's management asks you for a memorandum indicating what contractual arrangements minimize its exposure to loss resulting from arbitrary action by NPG. Your memorandum should indicate as to each arrangement suggested the remaining area of risk and uncertainty. PPI does not wish to insist on conditions that might "unduly irritate" the somewhat susceptible feelings of NPG's personnel and thus impair its chances of winning the contract. If any facts unstated are needed to reach your conclusions, you should indicate what they are.

NOTE ON CODIFICATION OF THE LAW OF SOVEREIGN IMMUNITY

The promise of codification is an appealing one to the modern legal mind. It promises relative certainty and uniformity in place of a reigning dispute over legal principles. It suggests the ultimate "legalization" or "depoliticization" of a field that is hereafter to be governed by the law's paradigmatic positive expression, a statute. Of course the promise may prove to be illusory, either beyond realization or, if formally realized, unsuccessful in imposing order because of problems of interpretation and application of what may be general and ambiguous clauses. The fields of international law and our domestic foreign relations law offer recurring illustrations of both the allure and failure of the promise—the efforts to codify state responsibility for takings or for violations of human rights, the law of the sea and so on. Those illustrations underscore the obstacles to codification where political consensus is lacking.

It is then not surprising that the field of sovereign immunity has been the subject of various codification attempts, some restricted and successful, some broad and more problematic. Recall the references to bilateral treaties which seek to regulate this problem, at fn. 14, p. 653, supra, and p. 661, supra. Recall the Brussels Convention of 1926 referred to in the Tate Letter, at p. 648, supra, and the European Convention on State Immunities, p. 661, supra.

Against this background, the State Department has for a number of years expressed the belief that a multilateral treaty regulating sovereign immunity would be the desirable solution. After all, whatever its difficulties the field seems less politically charged, less given to divisive views, than the others noted above. But that large goal is still to be successfully pursued. In the meantime, the Department put its mind to codification of our internal law of sovereign immunity, whatever that law's blend of domestic and international law and policy. It and the Department of Justice co-sponsored a bill that was introduced to the Senate and House (S. 566, H.R. 3493) in the 93rd Cong., 1st Sess., and that was before the Congress in 1974. As of 1975 the two Departments indicated their intention to have a new bill introduced that would further refine the codification proposal. It seems likely that whatever legislation ultimately emerges from the process will bear at least a family resemblance to S. 566.

PROPOSED BILL ON SOVEREIGN IMMUNITY

S. 566, H.R. 3493, 93rd Cong., 1st Sess., 1973

[The bill would introduce a new Chapter 97 into 28 U.S.C.A., to which the section numbers below refer.]

§ 1602. Findings and declaration of purpose

The Congress finds that the determination by United States courts of the claims of foreign states to immunity from the jurisdiction of such courts would serve the interests of justice and would protect the rights of both foreign states and litigants in United States courts. Under international law, states are not immune from the jurisdiction of foreign courts insofar as their commercial activities are concerned, and their commercial property may be levied upon for the satisfaction of judgments rendered against them in connection with their commercial activities. Claims of foreign states to immunity should henceforth be decided by United States courts in conformity with these principles as set forth in this chapter and other principles of international law.

§ 1603. Definitions

(*a*) For the purposes of this chapter, other than sections 1608 and 1610, a "foreign state" includes a political subdivision of that foreign state, or an agency or instrumentality of such a state or subdivision.

(*b*) For the purposes of this chapter, a "commercial activity" means either a regular course of commercial conduct or a particular commercial transaction or act. The commercial character of an activity shall be determined by reference to the nature of the course of conduct or particular transaction or act, rather than by reference to its purpose.

§ 1604. Immunity of foreign states from jurisdiction

Subject to existing and future international agreements to which the United States is a party, a foreign state shall be immune from the jurisdiction of the courts of the United States and of the States except as provided in this chapter.

§ 1605. General exceptions to the jurisdictional immunity of foreign states

A foreign state shall not be immune from the jurisdiction of courts of the United States or of the States in any case—

(*1*) in which the foreign state has waived its immunity either explicitly or by implication, notwithstanding any withdrawal of the waiver which the foreign state may purport to effect after the claim arose;

(*2*) in which the action is based upon a commercial activity carried on in the United States by the foreign state; or upon an act performed in the United States in connection with a commercial activity of the foreign state elsewhere; or upon an act outside the territory of the United States in connection with a commercial activity of the foreign state elsewhere and that act has a direct effect within the territory of the United States;

(*3*) in which rights in property taken in violation of international law are in issue and that property or any property exchanged for such property is present in the United States in connection with a commercial activity carried on in the United States by the foreign state or that property or any property exchanged for such property is owned or operated by an agency or instrumentality of the foreign state or of a political subdivision of the foreign state and agency or instrumentality is engaged in a commercial activity in the United States;

(*4*) in which rights in property in the United States, acquired by succession or gift, or rights in immovable property situated in the United States are in issue; or

(*5*) in which money damages are sought against a foreign state for personal injury or death, or damage to or loss of property, caused by the negligent or wrongful act or omission in the United States of that foreign state or of any official or employee thereof.

. . .

§ 1606. Immunity in cases relating to the public debt of a foreign state

(*a*) A foreign state shall be immune from the jurisdiction of the courts of the United States and of the States in any case relating to its public debt, except if—

(*1*) the foreign state has waived its immunity explicitly, notwithstanding any withdrawal of the waiver which the foreign state may purport to effect after the claim arose; or

(*2*) the case, whether or not falling within the scope of section 1605, relates to the public debt of a political subdivision of a foreign state, or of an agency or instrumentality of such a state or subdivision.

. . .

§ 1607. Counterclaims

In any action brought by a foreign state in a court of the United States or of any State, the foreign state shall not be accorded immunity with respect to—

(*1*) any counterclaim arising out of the transaction or occurrence that is the subject matter of the claim of the foreign state; or

(*2*) any other counterclaim that does not claim relief exceeding in amount or differing in kind from that sought by the foreign state.

§ 1608. Service of process in United States district courts

Service in the district courts shall be made upon a foreign state or a political subdivision of a foreign state and may be made upon an agency or instrumentality of such a state or subdivision which agency or instrumentality is not a citizen of the United States as defined in [28 U.S.C.A. § 1332(c) and (d)] by delivering a copy of the summons and complaint by registered or certified mail, to be addressed and dispatched by the clerk of the court, to the ambassador or chief of mission of the foreign state accredited to the Government of the United States, to the ambassador or chief of mission of another state then acting as protecting power for such foreign state, or in the case of service upon an agency or instrumentality of a foreign state or political subdivision to such other officer or agent as is authorized under the law of the foreign state or of the United States to receive service of process in the particular case, and, in each case, by also sending two copies of the summons and of the complaint by registered or certified mail to the Secretary of State at Washington, District of Columbia, who in turn shall transmit one of those copies by a diplomatic note to the department of the government of the foreign state charged with the conduct of the foreign relations of that state.

§ 1609. Immunity from execution and attachment of assets of foreign states

The assets in the United States of a foreign state shall be immune from attachment and from execution, except as provided in section 1610 of this chapter.

§ 1610. Exceptions to the immunity from execution of assets of foreign states

(*a*) The assets in the United States of a foreign state or political subdivision of a foreign state, to the extent that they are used for a particular commercial activity in the United States, shall not be immune from attachment for purposes of execution or from execution of a judgment rendered against that foreign state or political subdivision if—

(*1*) such attachment or execution relates to a claim which is based on that commercial activity or on rights in property taken in violation of international law and present in the United States in connection with that activity, or

(*2*) the foreign state or political subdivision has waived its immunity from attachment for purposes of execution or from execution of a judgment either explicitly or by implication, notwithstanding any purported withdrawal of the waiver after the claim arose.

(*b*) The assets in the United States of an agency or instrumentality of a foreign state or of an agency or instrumentality of a political subdivision of a foreign state, which is engaged in a commercial activity in the United States, or does an act in the United States in connection with such a commercial activity elsewhere, or does an act outside the territory of the United States in connection with a commercial activity elsewhere and the act has a direct effect within the territory of the United States, shall not be immune from attachment for purposes of execution or from execution of a judgment rendered against that agency or instrumentality if—

(*1*) such attachment or execution relates to a claim which is based on a commercial activity in the United States or such an act, or on rights in property taken in violation of international law and present in the United States in connection with such a commercial activity in the United States, or on rights in property taken in violation of international law and owned or operated by an agency or instrumentality which is engaged in a commercial activity in the United States; or

(*2*) the agency or instrumentality or the foreign state or political subdivision has waived its immunity from attachment for purposes of execution or from execution of a judgment either explicitly or by implication, notwithstanding any purported withdrawal of the waiver after the claim arose.

§ 1611. Certain types of assets immune from execution

Notwithstanding the provisions of section 1610 of this chapter, assets of a foreign state shall be immune from attachment and from execution, if—

(*1*) the assets are those of a foreign central bank or monetary authority held for its own account; or

(*2*) the assets are, or are intended to be, used in connection with a military activity and (*a*) are of a military character, or (*b*) are under the control of a military authority or defense agency

. . . .

. . .

[Remaining provisions of the bill would amend existing provisions of Title 28 to provide for jurisdiction and venue in federal district courts for the actions covered by the bill, removal from state courts, and related matters.]

QUESTIONS

(1) Note how the bill shifts the function of making determinations about sovereign immunity from the State Department to the courts—without any explicit exception. Suppose facts similar to those in Rich v. Naviera Vacuba, p. 656, supra, were to recur. If the bill were enacted, should a court follow a State Department determination in that new case in the foreign sovereign's favor for political reasons, even though judicial precedents plainly say that the activity involved in the new case was "commercial" within the meaning of § 1605(2)?

(2) Victory Transport, p. 649, supra, expressed sympathy with the idea that the line between sovereign and commercial acts was an impossible one to draw. Does the bill succeed? How does it correspond with the Lalive list of categories at p. 653, supra?

(3) If the bill draws a clear line, is it always the right one? How does it deal with the case of a British destroyer running down a tug in New York harbor? Twenty miles offshore? What of a controversy stemming from an air accident arising out of an airline ticket sold by a government-owned airline in New York but covering passage between two foreign points? How does the bill deal with the question of a suit to enforce a provision of a public loan agreement made, for example, by the Kingdom of Norway? With an action under Rule 10b–5 charging deception in the sale of bonds of a foreign government?

(4) Note the treatment of the waiver issue touched upon in various cases above (pp. 657, 660 and 664, supra) and relevant to the Problem at p. 667, supra. If the bill were enacted, would you revise your answer to that Problem? Would you advise a client that his legal remedies against a foreign sovereign were as effective as those against a foreign private party, if a contract, say, to supply computers for use in the foreign government's tax bureau contained a waiver of immunity? Would your answer have to be made dependent on any factual questions?

(5) Why would the Department of State co-sponsor a bill which, if enacted, would cut so deeply into the flexibility and power which it has so long claimed to be vital to its conduct of foreign relations? Do you agree with its decision?

(6) The Department has suggested that if such a bill were enacted, the United States should submit to the jurisdiction of the ICJ, on condition of reciprocity, as to any sovereign immunity question. Presumably the Connally Amendment, p. 320, supra, would not cover this submission. (Recall that it does not reach jurisdictional submissions in some other areas, as in FCN treaties.) If the bill were enacted, which if any of its provisions would you view as raising serious issues under international law which might come before the ICJ?

Additional Reading: See, in general, under the heading "sovereign immunity," the treatises and digests referred to at p. 177, supra. See also Sucharitkul, State Immunities and State Trading Activities in International Law (1959); Giuttari, The American Law of Sovereign Immunity (1970); Restatement (Second), Foreign Relations Law of the United States §§ 62–82 (1965); Cardozo, Judicial Deference to State Department Suggestions: Recognition of Prerogative or Abdication to Usurper, 48 Cornell L.Q. 461 (1963); Note, Sovereign Immunity, 15 Harv.J.Int.L. 157 (1974); Lowenfeld, Claims against Foreign States—A Proposal for Reform of United States Law, 44 N.Y.U.L.Rev. 901 (1969).

B. THE ACT OF STATE DOCTRINE

Another principle of judicial restraint, the act of state doctrine, complements and often interacts with the doctrine of sovereign immunity. At least one of its purposes is similar: preventing courts from becoming involved in disputes which might lead to friction between a foreign nation and their own. Other aspects of the act of state doctrine, however, distinguish it from the problems of sovereign immunity.

It is true that both doctrines are attentive to the nature of the action taken (activity engaged in) by a foreign state. But sovereign immunity applies only where a foreign state or its instrumentality is sought to be made a *party* to litigation or where its property is involved. On the other hand, the act of state doctrine focuses entirely on the *action* taken by that state, and may be applicable to litigation between two private parties to which that action is relevant. It determines not whether a court can assert (or must relinquish) *jurisdiction* over a party but whether it can fully examine and decide certain claims *on the merits,* even when such claims rest on the asserted illegality of foreign governmental conduct. The doctrine protects parties, even private ones, who rest their complaints or defenses upon certain action of foreign states by preventing courts from finding that action to be invalid.

Note that in the contract or tort actions in Part A, national courts "apply law" to foreign states whose plea of sovereign immunity is denied. In most cases, that law would be either *lex fori* or the law of a foreign country.[30] But most litigation in which an "act of state" is in issue involves the expropriation of alien-owned property within a foreign state, and consequently principles of international law. The expropriatory act and its executive implementation (the foreign act of state) are frequently followed by efforts by the alien to recover (from the foreign government or its vendee) the property or its value in his own or in a third country. Sometimes, as in the Sabbatino litigation, p. 691, infra, the foreign government or its instrumentality will be a party to the court proceedings. More frequently, as in the litigation in European courts over Chilean copper, pp. 677–682, infra, the "defendant" will be a private party who has purchased the expropriated property from the foreign state. In either situation, the problem posed is whether the national court should examine the legality—under national, foreign or international law—of the expropriation and, if so, what consequences should flow from a conclusion that it was illegal.

Thus the act of state doctrine is principally applied to situations that bear a close relationship to the other aspects of expropriation explored in Chapter IV. The materials at pp. 414–487, supra, revealed that international tribunals had little opportunity in recent decades to apply and develop an international law on expropriation. A major question in this Part B is whether national courts can start to fill this vacuum by developing norms of transnational applicability in this controversial field.

NOTE ON RELATIONSHIPS AMONG PRINCIPLES OF CHOICE OF LAW, INTERNATIONAL LAW AND THE ACT OF STATE DOCTRINE

In order to appreciate one important component of the act of state doctrine, it is important to understand its interaction with traditional choice-of-law principles. The illustrations in the Note on choice of law at p. 91, supra, treated contract and tort cases of a multistate or multinational character. In the following illustrations, P represents plaintiff; D represents defendant; S represents the situs

30. See the Note on choice of law, p. 91, supra. Such actions in Part A may however raise choice-of-law issues, described below, that are related to the act of state doctrine. For example, the contract on which a domestic corporation sues a foreign state may be governed to some degree not by a national body of law but by international law or by general principles of law. See Part D of Chapter IV.

of the property at the time of the relevant acts; GS represents the government of the situs country; and F represents the forum for the litigation. Suppose, as in our first illustration, that a case raises questions of the ownership of or other rights in tangible personal property.

> (*a*) P, in country F, instructs his employee to transport personal property to a destination in country S. While in S, the employee sells the property, in violation of his instructions, to D, a bona fide purchaser. D thereafter carries the property into F, where P sues to recover it. Under the law of F, the employee could not pass title and P could recover. Under the law of S, D would acquire good title against P. The court, drawing upon F's principles of choice of law, must determine whether the law of F or S governs this issue.

In this situation, generally accepted principles of choice of law would point to the law of S. Traditionally, and often uncritically, courts have made this reference on grounds that S alone had "jurisdiction" to determine the effect of a transfer of personal property within its territory. This reference to situs law and stress upon "territorial jurisdiction" to legislate are particularly strong when real rather than personal property is involved, and questions of interests in the real property are litigated in a foreign forum.

In illustration (*a*), the reference to S law serves important purposes. It assures security of title to all, for if courts of all countries refer to the situs, commercial transactions may take place more freely within it and prospective vendees will not be inhibited from purchasing property.

Note that in other contexts, such considerations do not necessarily point towards situs law.

> (*b*) P and D, domiciled in F, contract in that country. P agrees to sell to D personal property located in S. The contract is to be executed by delivery in S in one week. A fire destroys the property two days later. P sues for the purchase price. Under F law, D bore the risk of such loss after the contract was signed; under S law, P bore the risk of loss until delivery. The court, drawing upon F's principles of choice of law, must determine whether the law of F or S governs this issue.

The questions in this litigation could be characterized as "property" and "contract". Note that interests of third parties who may have dealt in some manner with the property are not involved. Under these facts, a reference to S law on the ground that the situs must control is more doubtful.

The following illustration comes closer to the typical case involving the act of state doctrine.

> (*c*) GS expropriates without compensation personal property in S belonging to P, a citizen of S. GS then sells

the property to D, another citizen of S. P finds the property and D in country F, and sues D in that country for its return or value.

If the courts of F simply look to the situs, P clearly loses because—at least in the large majority of cases—the conduct of GS in expropriating property of P (a citizen of S) would be legal under S law. And in such a case, there is little doubt that S law governs. P might however ask the courts of F to declare the expropriation contrary to F's "public policy"—in this setting, a policy against giving effect to confiscatory laws.[31] If F's courts accept P's arguments, note that at least in this respect they will be applying F law to an essentially foreign transaction whose only link to F is from D's transfer to F. In such circumstances, the application of F's internal law may appear arbitrary. Note also that invocation of domestic concepts of "public policy" involves a certain element of insult to the foreign state whose law is being slighted. Of course the precise path followed by a court of F sympathetic to P's claim will indicate how much of F law is being applied and how extensive is the interference with S's policies. At an extreme, F would invoke the public policy of the forum to deny recognition to the expropriation, and then apply F's substantive property law to order return of the property to P.

Finally, we come to the variant case which involves the act of state question in acute form.

(*d*) GS expropriates without compensation personal property in S belonging to P, a citizen of F. GS then sells the property to D, a citizen of F, who imports the property into F. P sues D in F for the return or value of the property.

In view of P's nationality, there is now a claim that GS's taking violated international law. Thus the court in F will be faced with more complex choice-of-law issues. It might apply S law, holding for D; it might feel freer in this situation to apply F's concepts of "public policy" and F's property law to upset the taking; it might invoke principles of international law. Note some of the problems put before the court by this last alternative:

(*1*) What are the international-law rules relating to expropriation, compensation and connected issues?

(*2*) If the court concludes that international law has been violated, does the violation upset the taking itself (and thus the related transfer of title to GS), or merely create an obligation on the part of GS to pay for the property? Is this question to be answered under international or national law —and if the latter, whose?

31. The Boll case and the note following it, at pp. 293 and 306, supra, examine the concept of "public policy" or "*ordre public*."

(3) Even if the violation invalidates the taking itself, what effect upon title has the purchase of the property from GS, or from its vendee, by a "bona fide purchaser?"

(4) If GS seizes P's orange plantation in violation of international law, does P's claim of title extend to (a) the oranges in P's warehouse in S, (b) the oranges on the trees on the plantation, (c) next season's crop of oranges? Are the problems different if we substitute a mine, an oil well or a factory for the plantation?

Comparable problems arise if the litigation involves a concession agreement between P and GS. Does the breach of such an agreement, rather like the breach of a treaty clause, violate international law? If the agreement relates to extractive industries, does P or GS have title to the mineral deposit which is the subject of the concession?

It is possible to approach these problems without resort to the act of state doctrine. That doctrine was developed primarily in the United States for treating problems such as illustrations (*c*) and (*d*), and is generally invoked by a party to urge the court not to examine the validity of the expropriation under the "public policy" of the forum or under international law.

"Act of state" is not of itself a very illuminating phrase. Any domestic litigation which requires some reference to foreign law or a foreign legal system might be said to involve a foreign act of state, whether legislative (a law under which a party claims or defends) or judicial (a foreign judgment which a plaintiff seeks to enforce) or executive (registration of a trade-mark) in its origin.

When relied upon in the American cases below, the act of state doctrine generally has a more restricted application. In the context of the Sabbatino decision, p. 691, infra, it involves the validity of the public acts a recognized foreign sovereign power commits within its own territory. Act of state refers to "public acts" which have been completely "executed" within the foreign territory, as distinct from executory court judgments or penal or revenue laws whose enforcement is sought abroad.

Consider the definition in Section 41 of Restatement (Second), Foreign Relations Law of the United States: "an act of a foreign state by which that state has exercised its jurisdiction to give effect to its public interests." Comments to this section note that an act of state

> involves the public interests of a state as a state, as distinct from its interests in providing the means of adjudicating disputes or claims that arise within its territory. . . .
> A judgment of a court may be an act of state. Usually it is not because it involves the interests of private litigants or because court adjudication is not the usual way in which the state exercises its jurisdiction to give effect to its public interests. . . . A typical state action treated as an "act of state" is the taking by a state of property within its own territory.

Additional reading: Katzenbach, Conflicts on an Unruly Horse: Reciprocal Claims and Tolerances in Interstate and International Law, 65 Yale L.J. 1087 (1956).

NOTE ON EUROPEAN LITIGATION INVOLVING THE CHILEAN COPPER EXPROPRIATIONS

The Note at p. 444, supra, states the background to the European judicial proceedings described below. Recall that the Presidential Decree of 1972 determined the excess profits of Kennecott Copper Corporation to be $410 million, thus eliminating any compensation that might otherwise have been paid by Chile to Kennecott on account of the nationalization of its mining property. Recall also that the special Tribunal created by the 1972 constitutional amendment interpreted that amendment to deny it competence to review the Presidential determination. At that stage, Kennecott announced that it was "withdrawing from further legal proceedings in Chile and will pursue in other nations its remedies for the confiscated assets . . . Kennecott [is] informing all persons who may be concerned with copper from the El Teniente mine in Chile of [its] continued rights to the El Teniente copper and of [its] intention to take such action as may be considered necessary to protect [its] rights in the copper or its proceeds."

Kennecott then sent a letter to all customers of El Teniente copper, reaffirming its rights of ownership. "We draw your attention to the fact that any purchase . . . without our express permission would be contrary to governing principles of law, and inform you that we will take all such action as may be considered necessary in order to protect our rights, including rights with regard to such copper [and its] proceeds." [32]

The Chilean government responded through public pronouncements, denying Kennecott's allegations of continued ownership, and referring to Kennecott's "absurd threat" to potential buyers as constituting "an open act of aggression, designed to create uncertainty among Chile's regular customers, [and] to put the nation's economic interests in immediate jeopardy . . . The [Chilean government instrumentality in charge of copper] will initiate appropriate legal action" against Kennecott to obtain "total redress for whatever damage the campaign begun by Kennecott may occasion." [33]

In fact, Kennecott's strategy of initiating legal proceedings against vendees of Chile to obtain the price for the copper sold by Chile to those vendees proved to be a source of continuing harassment and economic distress to the Allende government. It created uncertainty in markets at a time when Chile's foreign exchange re-

32. These documents, as well as the translations of the judicial proceedings referred to below, appear in Supplements Nos. 3 and 4, dated respectively December 1972 and May 1973, of the "White Papers" published by Kennecott and referred to in fn. 51, p. 444, supra.

33. Chile Economic News, No. 5, October 1, 1972, issued by CORFO, p. 3.

serves were perilously low and when Chile was in default on a large volume of intergovernmental debt. For example, after Kennecott initiated the proceedings in France noted below, an official in the Chilean embassy in France observed that Kennecott "had chosen a critical moment, one when such an embargo is particularly able to arouse anxiety and a sense of insecurity in Chile's regular copper consumers in Europe . . . Possibly it wished to make trouble for Chile's important and thriving trade with France. Time and place, therefore, have been specially calculated to do great damage to Chile's trade." [34]

In all, court proceedings were initiated in five European countries. This Note describes the principal themes in two of those litigations, in France and Germany, that are relevant to the act-of-state doctrine.

The first proceedings were in France and were brought by Braden Copper Company, the wholly-owned subsidiary of Kennecott which had owned the Chilean assets.[35] Braden's petition to the Court of Extended Jurisdiction of Paris alleged that a designated French corporation owed the Chilean governmental corporation administering copper sales a stated sum as the purchase price of a cargo of copper extracted from the El Teniente mine and then bound by ship for France. The petition further alleged that Braden had acquired "true property rights under Chilean law" in that copper, "which constitutes the object of private appropriation." Since the assets of The El Teniente Mining Company, p. 448, supra, had been expropriated and the company had been effectively dissolved, Braden alleged that under French law relevant to such situations, it (as a 49% stockholder in El Teniente Mining Company) became the undivided co-owner of its assets and particularly of ore extracted from the El Teniente mine. Since the Chilean nationalization "was effected without a fair indemnification" in a manner "contrary to French public policy", the petition concluded that any rights acquired by Chile by virtue of the nationalization "are without any legal validity in French territory," and that French courts under these conditions "cannot recognize the validity of the alleged transfer of title effected by the Chilean state." Thus Braden sought a third-party attachment on the French purchaser, ordering it to pay amounts owing the Chilean government corporation to it instead.

In a decision of November 20, 1972, the French court determined that the Chilean governmental corporation could not plead sovereign immunity from jurisdiction or execution. It then stated that "no legal effect is recognized in France to a dispossession made by a foreign state without an equitable indemnity." Given the complex issues and facts in this case, the court concluded that "the dispute between the

34. Chile Economic News, No. 7/20, November 1, 1972, issued by CORFO, p. 2.

35. Translations of the various petitions to and decisions of the French court appear in Supplement No. 3, fn. 32, supra, and in 12 Int.Leg.Mat. 187 (1973).

parties over the reality in this case of such an indemnity makes recourse to a measure of investigation necessary." While admitting "the principle of a claim in favor of Braden," in view of the public order rule in France, the Court postponed a final decision and appointed a master to receive from all parties useful documents and to proceed to investigation of "the conflicting affirmations of the parties as to the existence of an equitable indemnity for the benefit of Braden," and "to gather all elements that could permit the global settlement of the dispute by the opposing parties."

This litigation never came to a definitive resolution. The settlement described at p. 457, supra, between Chile and the copper companies involved an agreement on the part of Kennecott to terminate all pending European litigation.

In the German litigation before the Hamburg District Court,[36] Kennecott sought to attach a copper shipment en route to and received by a German refinery. The copper had issued from the El Teniente mine. The petition of Kennecott argued that if Germany recognized "acts of foreign states which are in violation of international law, it thereby makes itself guilty of a violation of international law . . ." The petition relied upon Article 25 of the German Basic Law, p. 623, supra, granting primacy to international law over domestic law. In an effort to distinguish adverse German precedents, the petition argued that even if international law did not *command* the non-recognition and nullity of acts of expropriation in violation of international law, it did not *prohibit* non-recognition. That is, the German court could go beyond ordering compensation and treat the copper itself as still the property of Kennecott. The petition also argued that recognition of the expropriation would violate "national public policy." Whether one relied upon international law or German public policy, "the previous owner continues to be the owner vested with a right of action for replevin" in accordance with German procedural law.

After further proceedings, the district court lifted an attachment against the copper in the German refinery in its decision of January 22, 1973. The decision turned on a number of interrelated doctrines of German law. It first observed that under German private international law (conflict of laws), the reference to determine title would be to the place where mining, processing and initial transfer of the copper occurred—namely Chile, the *lex rei sitae*. The court then observed that the remaining question was whether it must recognize the expropriation itself. Excerpts from the decision follow:

> . . . Here the court adopts the opinion now prevailing in the Federal Republic of Germany that an expropriation which has been effected abroad must in principle be recognized as being formally valid, since in accordance with the internationally recognized principle of ter-

36. Petitions and other matters relating to the German proceedings, as well as a translation of the decision of the District Court set forth in part in text, appear in Supplement No. 4, fn. 32, supra. A translation of the decision also appears in 12 Int.Leg. Mat. 251 (1973).

ritoriality, measures of expropriation cover without limitation the property which was subject to the sovereignty of the expropriating state at the time of the expropriation. This means that an expropriation effected in the course of nationalization or socialization measures remains an internal matter of the foreign state as long as it does not cover property located outside of its boundaries . . . .

In modern *international law* there is no generally recognized principle that the foreign court is obligated under international law to consider as null and void from the very start a foreign act of sovereignty which is in violation of international law, or that the recognition of foreign acts which are in violation of international law, or, on the other hand, the recognition of a claim for surrender alleged by an earlier owner itself would again violate international law . . . . Even if an appropriation was effected under circumstances of discrimination or was pronounced without indemnification, it remains valid if an item of property which was in the expropriating country at the time of the expropriation has subsequently come into a foreign country . . . .

. . . Any other position would lead to impossible complications of a political and economic nature and interfere with international order . . . .

Nor is the principle of territoriality thereby violated, since said principle is intended to prevent expropriation extending to property which is abroad at the time of the act of expropriation. However, we are not confronted by such a case here.

(2) Nevertheless, an expropriation would not be recognized in the Federal Republic of Germany if the recognition of the foreign act were to violate basic principles of *German public policy.*

(a) The German court must, therefore, ask itself whether in our view the foreign procedure violates public policy or the purpose of a German law at the time of the rendering of the decision, and it is necessary further to determine whether there exists sufficient relationship to the country to justify the application of the exception contained in Art. 30 of the Introductory Law to the German Civil Code.

In the opinion of this Court, the consideration of the foreign law can here in fact lead to finding a *violation of public policy within the meaning of Art. 30 of the Introductory Law to the German Civil Code.* In any event, this viewpoint is defendable within the scope of summary proceedings in which exhaustive examination of the problem is not possible if merely for reasons of time available. In this connection, in the opinion of this Court, the events which lead to the expropriation are to be considered not in their individual acts, but as a whole; the expropriation was effected namely for all practical purposes without indemnification, it was effected under discriminatory conditions, and legal channels have been closed to the parties concerned.

There is a principle of international law which is confirmed in particular by United Nations Resolution No. 1,803 [p. 464, supra] that every expropriation or nationalization must provide for a reasonable indemnification . . . . Violation of international law would be material through Art. 25 of the Constitution within the scope of Art. 30 of the Introductory Law to the German Civil Code.

A reasonable indemnification was, in fact, not granted the petitioner. To be sure, the Chilean Expropriation Law of 1971 provides for indemnification for the expropriation of the mining equipment proper, but the law, with one stroke and at the same time as granting indemnification, creates a new and peculiar provision for the nonpayment of the indemnification; this leads—in combination with the profit adjustment tax stipulated in the same law—in effect, by way of a negative indemnification, to a taxing of the expropriated party.

However, even if this form of "equalization" were considered a "reasonable" indemnification, there would be still other considerations which establish a violation against German principles of law.

Furthermore, as has not been denied by the defendant or the intervening party, the expropriation was intended primarily for nationalization. A nationalization which is directed specifically against foreigners is to be considered, however, discriminatory and thus an act which is not to be approved in accordance with the principles of public policy . . . .

Even though it may be understandable for a State to wish to free itself of the position of economic power of foreign companies which control particularly important portions of its economy, on the other hand the principle of contractual loyalty which governs every legal system should not be violated.

As the petitioner has credibly shown, the [Chileanization arrangements of 1965–67, p. 448, supra] with the cooperation and approval of the former President of Chile, Mr. Frei, was effected specifically in view of the special economic conditions of Chile. Under these circumstances, the petitioner had to be able to rely on the fact that a few years later it would not be expropriated at short notice by the Chilean Government, since a majority participation had already been granted to the State of Chile. Here it was to have been expected that Chile would either grant the petitioner an effective indemnification reasonable with respect to the consequences of the sudden loss of property, or else grant the company a reasonable period of transition, as has recently become customary in the case of investment contracts with developing countries by a promise not to expropriate investment goods before the expiration of a stipulated period of time . . . .

. . .

The Court in this connection imparts particular weight to the following:

The petitioner has credibly shown that the continuation of the profit adjustment tax which is in an insoluble relationship to the expropriation proceedings, is effected by the President of the country at his own free discretion. This act of discretion which is not subject to any restriction is not subject to review by the courts, as the Copper Court itself stated in the grounds of its Decision. This means that legal channels are closed and the party concerned is denied a *legal hearing*. In this way, however, a fundamental principle of German law is violated, which—even though in this case a German citizen is not involved—is so severe that it must be found to be a violation of German public policy.

In any event, this conglomeration of acts of violation appears so serious as to be entirely unbearable under our view of legality and morality. . . . .

. . .

(b) This by itself, however, is not sufficient for the application of Art. 30 of the Introductory Law to the German Civil Code, since every clause providing for a reservation is a disturbing factor in international legal life. Only if the German legal system is substantially affected by the violation of public policy, and thus a close relationship between what has been done and German interests is created, is Art. 30 of the Introductory Law to the German Civil Code applicable . . . .

A close relationship to German interests could possibly be found to exist if—as the Court assumed in its Decision of January 5, 1973—the defendant had been the purchaser of the lot of copper and on basis of the petitioner's circular of September 7, 1972, had to run the risk of having to pay the purchase price again to the petitioner because of acquisition from the non-justified party.

A relationship to German interests which is material from a legal standpoint in this sense, however, does not exist when the copper is supplied to the German defendant merely for the carrying out of a processing contract. There is no question whatsoever in this connection of any ownership relationship on the part of the defendant.

The fact that the mere bringing of articles which have been expropriated without indemnification to Germany (Federal Republic of Germany) does not represent any essential relationship to German interests has been repeatedly confirmed by the decided cases . . . .

. . .

The court concluded that "neither international law nor German public policy in the given situation compels the German courts to deny recognition to the expropriation." Thus petitioner did not succeed in showing its right of ownership. The German proceedings continued further, and became subject to the same agreement of Kennecott, at the time of the final settlement, to terminate proceedings.

QUESTIONS

(1) Suppose that you had been appointed the master in the French judicial proceedings. What issues would you have thought it necessary to examine to pass upon the claims of the parties and determine if French "public order" was offended? What facts would have been necessary to the resolution of these issues? How effective a forum was the French court for examination and resolution of these questions of fact and legal issues?

(2) Consider with respect to both the French and German court proceedings the issue of the ownership of the underground copper ore. Recall Chile's position, p. 451, supra, that under Chilean law as under general Latin American law, in-place mineral wealth cannot be alienated from the national patrimony. One can have only a right to extract, and can become "owner" of the mineral only upon extraction.

(*a*) Would it be necessary for the French or German court, or court of any other country, to resolve this issue if it determined to explore the merits of the question of compensation under domestic conceptions of public policy or under international law?

(*b*) If the Chilean position were upheld, would Kennecott (or Braden) still be able to obtain an attachment or to maintain a claim for proceeds of the sale of the copper under shipment? If so, upon what legal basis?

(3) Compare the views of the French and the German courts about review of the validity of the expropriation with those expressed by American courts in the following Note and the Sabbatino litigation, p. 691, infra. Which attitude strikes you as more appropriate in the contemporary world context? Do you detect any substantial distinction between resting a decision to explore the validity of an expropriation upon conceptions of international law or conceptions of domestic policy or public order? What relationship between the two does the opinion of the Hamburg court suggest?

NOTE ON THE ACT OF STATE DOCTRINE IN FEDERAL COURTS BEFORE SABBATINO

We turn here to the federal-court precedents in the United States which form the background to the Supreme Court's influential opinion in Banco Nacional de Cuba v. Sabbatino.

Underhill v. Hernandez [37]

A revolution broke out in 1892 in Venezuela. General Hernandez commanded certain revolutionary forces. In August 1892, Hernandez entered and assumed command of the city of Bolivar. In October 1892, the United States recognized the revolutionary party as the legitimate government of Venezuela.

Underhill, a United States citizen, had constructed a water works system for Bolivar under a government contract and operated the system. Hernandez, by denying Underhill the requisite document to leave, coerced him into operating his water works until October 1892, when he received a passport and left the country.

Underhill later brought an action against Hernandez in a federal court in New York to recover damages for unlawful detention. The lower courts gave judgment for the defendant, and the Supreme

37. 168 U.S. 250, 18 S.Ct. 83, 42 L.Ed. 456 (1897).

Court granted a writ of certiorari. It affirmed in an opinion by CHIEF JUSTICE FULLER, excerpts from which appear below:

> Every sovereign state is bound to respect the independence of every other sovereign state, and the courts of one country will not sit in judgment on the acts of the government of another, done within its own territory. Redress of grievances by reason of such acts must be obtained through the means open to be availed of by sovereign powers as between themselves.
>
> Nor can the principle be confined to lawful or recognized governments, or to cases where redress can manifestly be had through public channels. The immunity of individuals from suits brought in foreign tribunals for acts done within their own states, in the exercise of governmental authority, whether as civil officers or as military commanders, must necessarily extend to the agents of governments ruling by paramount force as matter of fact. Where a civil war prevails (that is, where the people of a country are divided into two hostile parties, who take up arms and oppose one another by military force), generally speaking, foreign nations do not assume to judge of the merits of the quarrel. If the party seeking to dislodge the existing government succeeds, and the independence of the government it has set up is recognized, then the acts of such government, from the commencement of its existence, are regarded as those of an independent nation. . . .
>
> . . . The acts complained of were the acts of a military commander representing the authority of the revolutionary party as a government, which afterwards succeeded, and was recognized by the United States. We think the circuit court of appeals was justified in concluding "that the acts of the defendant were the acts of the government of Venezuela, and as such are not properly the subject of adjudication in the courts of another government." . . .

Oetjen v. Central Leather Co.[38]

Mexico in 1913 was in the grip of revolution. General Carranza, leader of one faction, commissioned General Villa as commander of part of his forces. General Villa captured the city of Torreon in October 1913 and required a contribution by its inhabitants to support his army. The citizens of Torreon negotiated with General Villa as to the amount to be paid and assessed the men of property of the city. Martinez, a Mexican citizen, fled and failed to pay the assessment imposed upon him. To satisfy the assessment, General Villa ordered that hides belonging to Martinez be seized. These hides were then sold in Mexico in 1914 to the Finnegan-Brown Company, a Texas corporation, and were shipped into the United States where Finnegan-Brown sold them to the defendant. The United States recognized the government of Carranza as the *de facto* government of Mexico in 1915, and as the *de jure* government in 1917.

38. 246 U.S. 297, 38 S.Ct. 309, 62 L.Ed. 726 (1918).

Plaintiff commenced this action in replevin in a state court of New Jersey to recover the hides, which plaintiff claimed to own as assignee of Martinez. Plaintiff contended that the "confiscation" by General Villa was contrary to the Hague Convention of 1907 respecting the laws and customs of war, and that consequently any title derived thereby was invalid. The state courts held for defendant. In an opinion by JUSTICE CLARKE, the Supreme Court affirmed.

The Court first raised questions about the applicability of the Hague Convention to a civil war, or to the conduct here involved. It stated that it preferred to rest its decision on certain "clearly settled principles of law", and referred to the Hernandez case. Its opinion continued:

> Applying these principles of law to the case at bar, we have a duly commissioned military commander of what must be accepted as the legitimate government of Mexico, in the progress of a revolution, and when conducting active independent operations, seizing and selling in Mexico, as a military contribution, the property in controversy, at the time owned and in the possession of a citizen of Mexico, the assignor of the plaintiff in error. Plainly this was the action, in Mexico, of the legitimate Mexican government when dealing with a Mexican citizen, and, as we have seen, for the soundest reasons, and upon repeated decisions of this court such action is not subject to re-examination and modification by the courts of this country.
>
> The principle that the conduct of one independent government cannot be successfully questioned in the courts of another is as applicable to a case involving the title to property brought within the custody of a court, such as we have here, as it was held to be to the cases cited, in which claims for damages were based upon acts done in a foreign country, for it rests at last upon the highest considerations of international comity and expediency. To permit the validity of the acts of one sovereign state to be re-examined and perhaps condemned by the courts of another would very certainly "imperil the amicable relations between governments and vex the peace of nations."
>
> It is not necessary to consider, as the New Jersey court did, the validity of the levy of the contribution made by the Mexican commanding general, under rules of international law applicable to the situation, since the subject is not open to reexamination by this or any other American court.
>
> The remedy of the former owner, or of the purchaser from him, of the property in controversy, if either has any remedy, must be found in the courts of Mexico or through the diplomatic agencies of the political department of our government. . . .

Ricaud v. American Metal Company, Ltd.[39]

This litigation arose out of the same Mexican revolution. General Pereyra commanded a brigade of the army led by General Car-

39. 246 U.S. 304, 38 S.Ct. 312, 62 L.Ed. 733 (1918).

ranza. The plaintiff, American Metal Co., claimed to have purchased in June 1913 a quantity of lead bullion in Mexico from the Penoles Mining Company, a Mexican company. In September 1913, General Pereyra demanded this bullion from Penoles, and gave a receipt to Penoles containing a promise to pay for the lead bullion "on the triumph of the revolution". Pereyra sold the bullion to defendant Ricaud, who sold it to another defendant, and Pereyra used the proceeds of sale to equip his army.

The lead bullion was held in bond by the customs collector at El Paso, Texas, when plaintiff brought this action in equity to recover it. The United States District Court in Texas held for plaintiff. Defendant appealed to the Circuit Court of Appeals, which certified certain questions to the Supreme Court. Excerpts from its opinion, delivered by JUSTICE CLARKE, appear below:

> It is settled that the courts will take judicial notice of such recognition, as we have here, of the Carranza government by the political department of our government . . . and that the courts of one independent government will not sit in judgment on the validity of the acts of another done within its own territory . . . . This last rule, however, does not deprive the courts of jurisdiction once acquired over a case. It requires only that when it is made to appear that the foreign government has acted in a given way on the subject-matter of the litigation, the details of such action or the merit of the result cannot be questioned but must be accepted by our courts as a rule for their decision. To accept a ruling authority and to decide accordingly is not a surrender or abandonment of jurisdiction but is an exercise of it. It results that the title to the property in this case must be determined by the result of the action taken by the military authorities of Mexico . . . .
>
> . . . The fact that the title to the property in controversy may have been in an American citizen, who was not in or a resident of Mexico at the time it was seized for military purposes by the legitimate government of Mexico, does not affect the rule of law that the act within its own boundaries of one sovereign state cannot become the subject of reexamination and modification in the courts of another. Such action when shown to have been taken, becomes, as we have said, a rule of decision for the courts of this country. Whatever rights such an American citizen may have can be asserted only through the courts of Mexico or through the political departments of our government. . . .

The Bernstein Litigation

The plaintiff in this action alleged that in 1937, when a German citizen and resident, he was imprisoned by Nazi officials because he was Jewish. Under threat of bodily harm, indefinite imprisonment and danger to his family, they forced him to execute documents transferring all the stock of a German corporation, the Arnold Bernstein Line, to a Nazi agent, one Boeger. Boeger took possession of all assets of the Line and transferred the ship "Gandia" to the defendant, a Belgian corporation. Plaintiff alleged that defendant, before taking possession, knew that plaintiff was a Jew and that the transfer to Boeger had been coerced. The ship was sunk during the war, while under British control. In 1939 plaintiff, after paying ransom, was allowed to leave Germany.

In 1946, when a resident of New York, he brought an action against defendant in a New York state court. He based jurisdiction on a writ of attachment of the proceeds of the insurance on the "Gandia," held on defendant's behalf in New York. Plaintiff demanded damages for detention of the vessel and the proceeds.

The defendant removed the case to the federal district court. That court quashed the attachment and dismissed the complaint on grounds that the claim was for a wrong done by "the German Government under the Nazi regime" and that, since the confiscation had occurred in German territory, it was "not subject to review in our courts."

Plaintiff appealed this order to the Court of Appeals, which affirmed in Bernstein v. Van Heyghen Freres Societe Anonyme, 163 F. 2d 246 (2d Cir. 1947). The opinion, delivered by JUDGE LEARNED HAND, first stated that the court could not pass upon the validity of the transfer under German law. It continued:

> . . . We have repeatedly declared, for over a period of at least thirty years, that a court of the forum will not undertake to pass upon the validity under the municipal law of another state of the acts of officials of that state, purporting to act as such. We have held that this was a necessary corollary of decisions of the Supreme Court, and if we have been mistaken, the Supreme Court must correct it.
>
> Thus the case is cleared for the second question: whether since the cessation of hostilities with Germany our own Executive, which is the authority to which we must look for the final word in such matters has declared that the commonly accepted doctrine which we have just mentioned, does not apply. Before examining the evidence put forward in support of this position, it will clarify our discussion, if we say what we understand to be the general law on the subject. . . . [I]t is a well-settled exception to the usual doctrine that a court of the forum will take as its model the rights and liabilities which have arisen where the transactions took place, that the foreign rights and liabilities must not be abhorrent to the moral notions of its own state. We may assume that the same is true of a defence to an obligation which under the law of the foreign state would otherwise have been there enforceable. If so, it would be possible in the case at bar for a court of New York to treat as a nullity the transfer of the plaintiff's shares upon the ground that its legal effect—depriving the plaintiff of property otherwise recognized in Germany itself—was utterly odious to the accepted standards of justice of that state. Hence, if in 1937 it had been the law of the Third Reich that any private person might seize a Jew and by threats of imprisonment or by torture force him to transfer his property, by hypothesis no court of New York would recognize such a transfer as

> affecting the victim's title, and, if the spoliator came to New York with the property in his possession, the victim could reclaim it. We will moreover assume for argument that anyone who knew how the spoliator had acquired the property would be in like case. The case at bar is indeed a variant of this, because the property of which the plaintiff has been despoiled, never came to New York; nor has the spoliator or his transferee; but we shall treat this difference as irrelevant. Therefore, the plaintiff's difficulty lies, not in any defect in the law of New York as to conflict of laws; but because of that other doctrine which we have mentioned: i. e. that no court will exercise its jurisdiction to adjudicate the validity of the official acts of another state. This the plaintiff acknowledges as generally true, but he says that it presupposes that the state of the forum has not acted to relieve its courts of restraint upon the exercise of their jurisdiction; and that our own government has already so acted. This is the remaining and the critical issue in the case; and we have to examine what those actions have been.

The opinion then considered the situation in Germany in 1945 and the Declaration of the four victorious powers by which the "supreme authority" in Germany was vested in the four commanders-in-chief, each in his own zone of occupation. It noted that the place where transfer to Boeger had occurred was in the then British zone. The court concluded that the legislation enacted in several of the zones proscribing any application of discriminatory legislation was essentially prospective in application and did not purport retroactively to invalidate earlier German laws. It further concluded that provisions in such legislation for restoration of seized property and reparations did not permit domestic courts to pass on these questions of validity at the time of the transfer. The opinion concluded:

> There remains only the plaintiff's argument drawn from the "Charter" and "Judgment" in the Nuremburg Trial,[40] which is based upon the fact that both recognized as crimes "inhumane acts, committed against any civilian population, before or during, the war, or persecutions on political, racial or religious grounds in execution of or in connection with any crime within the jurisdiction of the Tribunal, whether or not in violation of the domestic law of the country where perpetrated"—Article 6(c). The argument runs that, since we were a party to the prosecution, we recognized that a criminal liability would exist for a wrong such as the plaintiff has suffered; and it would be unreasonable to hold that a civil wrong did not exist as well. This we may accept arguendo; but it misses the point. In our discussion we have already assumed that, if the plaintiff had been despoiled by a private person in Germany in the way he was in fact despoiled, a New York court would not feel bound to concede the validity of the transfer, even though under the law of Germany it was valid. True, as we said, that is an extension of the usual doctrine that a court of the forum will not enforce a liability arising under a suf-

40. [Eds.] The principles on which the Nuremberg Trial was based are described at p. 904, infra.

ficiently repellant foreign law; nevertheless, we are assuming that it is a proper extension. Thus, it would not be necessary for a New York court to have recourse to the "Charter" or the "Judgment" in the Nuremburg Trial to ignore the transfer and to treat the plaintiff as the owner of the ship. Both the "Charter" and the "Judgment" are indeed necessary to support a criminal conviction before the "Tribunal," which was set up ad hoc; but by hypothesis they add nothing to the force of the plaintiff's position in the case at bar, for the transfer was invalid anyway.

On the other hand neither the "Charter" nor the "Judgment" aids the plaintiff in overcoming the real obstacle in his path; which is, not the absence of any substantive law—the law of New York—making the transfer invalid, but that no court of that, or any other state, is permitted to apply that law, since the claim is reserved for adjudication along with all other such claims as part of the final settlement with Germany. The fact that we acted as one of the prosecutors of the rulers of the Reich and in doing so asserted the existence of a criminal liability not to be found in any of its laws, has nothing whatever to do with the propriety of the district court's entertaining the action. . . .

Related proceedings, involving other ships owned by Bernstein and transferred, via Boeger, to a different defendant, led to the opinion of the Court of Appeals in Bernstein v. N. V. Nederlandsche-Amerikaansche Stoomvaart-Maatschappij, 173 F.2d 71 (1949). Excerpts from a per curiam decision of the Court of Appeals in the latter case, 210 F.2d 375 (1954), appear below:

In the prior appeal in this case, 173 F.2d 71, 75–76, because of the lack of a definitive expression of Executive Policy, we felt constrained to follow the decision of this court in Bernstein v. Van Heyghen Freres Societe Anonyme . . . by ordering the plaintiff to refrain from alleging matters which would cause the court to pass on the validity of acts of officials of the German government. Following our decision, however, the State Department issued Press Release No. 296 on April 27, 1949, entitled: "Jurisdiction of United States Courts Re Suits for Identifiable Property Involved in Nazi Forced Transfers." The substance of this Release follows:

"As a matter of general interest, the Department publishes herewith a copy of a letter of April 13, 1949 from Jack B. Tate, Acting Legal Advisor, Department of State, to the Attorneys for the plaintiff in Civil Action No. 31–555 in the United States District Court for the Southern District of New York.

"The letter repeats this Government's opposition to forcible acts of dispossession of a discriminatory and confiscatory nature practiced by the Germans on the countries or peoples subject to their controls; states that it is this Government's policy to undo the forced transfers and restitute identifiable property to the victims of Nazi persecution wrongfully deprived of such property; and sets forth that the policy of the Executive, with respect to claims asserted in the United States for restitution of such property, is to relieve American courts from any restraint upon the exer-

> cise of their jurisdiction to pass upon the validity of the acts of Nazi officials." . . .
>
> In view of this supervening expression of Executive Policy, we amend our mandate in this case by striking out all restraints based on the inability of the court to pass on acts of officials in Germany during the period in question. . . . This will permit the district court to . . . conduct the trial of this case without regard to the restraint we previously placed upon it.

[Bernstein thereafter settled his claim against the Holland-America Line. He later filed a claim before the Foreign Claims Settlement Commission under the War Claims Act of 1948, as amended. That Act provided for the payment, from funds derived from the vesting of German-owned assets during the war, of compensation to American nationals for property destroyed or taken during the war. He received a substantial further award. See 61 Am.J.Int.L. 1069 (1967).]

QUESTIONS

(1) Consider the Underhill case. On what law did plaintiff base his claim? What defense, other than act of state, might defendant have asserted?

(2) Which, if any, of the first three cases are authority for the proposition that the act of state doctrine bars an American court, in an expropriation case, from considering a claim based on international law? In which cases could such a claim plausibly have been made? In which was it explicitly made and disposed of by the court? Does the rationale for the rules of self-restraint in these decisions extend to such claims?

(3) Could the plaintiff in either Oetjen or Ricaud have later filed a claim within the terms of Article I of the General Claims Convention between the United States and Mexico*?

(4) "There remains a basic contradiction in the act of state doctrine as understood by Ricaud. The Court appears to draw on basic principles of international law or comity to conclude that a government "will not sit in judgment on the validity of the acts of another done within its own territory." But observance of that principle conflicts with the equally fundamental idea that international law limits a state's powers even within its own territory. The cult of territorial sovereignty, if made absolute, could undermine the entire international law of state responsibility." Comment.

(5) The opinion by Judge Hand in the Bernstein case illustrates, through the hypothetical case posed in it, the "public policy" exception to normal choice-of-law rules. Why did the court refuse to apply its concept of public policy to the facts before it?

(6) Under what principles could the events in Germany in the Bernstein litigation be challenged? Does the State Department letter mean that courts should apply domestic notions of "public policy" to upset transactions with which this country had no original connection?

BANCO NACIONAL DE CUBA v. SABBATINO

Supreme Court of the United States, 1964.
376 U.S. 398, 84 S.Ct. 923, 11 L.Ed.2d 804.

[In February and July of 1960, Farr, Whitlock & Co., an American commodity broker, contracted to purchase Cuban sugar from a wholly-owned Cuban subsidiary of Compania Azucarera Vertientes-Camaguey de Cuba (C.A.V.), a corporation organized under Cuban law whose capital stock was owned principally by United States residents. The sugar was to be purchased at specified prices free alongside the steamer shipping it from Cuba, and Farr, Whitlock agreed to pay for it in New York upon presentation of shipping documents and a sight draft.

On July 6, 1960, the Congress of the United States amended legislation relating to the import of sugar in order to authorize a presidentially directed reduction of the sugar quota for Cuba. On the same day, President Eisenhower exercised this power. On July 6, the Cuban Council of Ministers adopted Law No. 851, which provided in part as follows:

> WHEREAS, the attitude assumed by the government and the Legislative Power of the United States of North America, which constitutes an aggression, for political purposes, against the basic interests of the Cuban economy, as recently evidenced by the Amendment to the Sugar Act just enacted by the United States Congress at the request of the Chief Executive of that country, whereby exceptional powers are conferred upon the President of the United States to reduce American sugar market as a threat of the participation of Cuban sugars in the political action against Cuba, forces the Revolutionary Government to adopt, without hesitation, all and whatever measures it may deem appropriate or desirable for the due defense of the national sovereignty and protection of our economic development process. . . .
>
> NOW, THEREFORE: In pursuance of the powers vested in it, the Council of Ministers has resolved to enact and promulgate the following.
>
> LAW NO. 851
>
> ARTICLE 1. Full authority is hereby conferred upon the President and the Prime Minister of the Republic in order that, acting jointly through appropriate resolutions whenever they shall deem it advisable or desirable for the protection of the national interests, they may proceed to nationalize, through forced expropriations, the properties or enterprises owned by physical and corporate persons who are nationals of the United States of North America, or of the enterprises in which such physical and corporate persons have an interest, even though they be organized under the Cuban laws.

Other articles of Law No. 851 established a system for compensation, which provided that payment for expropriated property would consist of bonds bearing 2% annual interest, with maturities of at least 30 years. The interest was to be paid only out of 25% of the annual foreign exchange received from sales of Cuban sugar to the United States in excess of 3,000,000 Spanish long tons at a minimum price of 5.75 cents per English pound. In the preceding 10 years, the annual average price had never reached the 5.75 figure, and in only one such year had as many as 3,000,000 Spanish long tons been sold. The bonds were to be amortized only upon official authorization, possibly only out of this fund. The Cuban President and Prime Minister were to select appraisers who would value the expropriated property for purposes of this compensation.

The Department of State, in a note of July 16, 1960 to the Cuban Ministry of Foreign Relations, described Law No. 851 as "manifestly in violation of those principles of international law which have been accepted by the free countries of the West. It is in its essence discriminatory, arbitrary, and confiscatory."

Pursuant to the contracts with Farr, Whitlock, sugar destined for Morocco was loaded between August 6 and August 9 on the German vessel S.S. Hornfels standing offshore at a Cuban port, within Cuban territorial waters. On August 6, the Cuban President and Prime Minister, acting pursuant to Law No. 851, issued Executive Power Resolution No. 1. This Resolution stated in part:

> WHEREAS, the Chief Executive of the Government of the United States of North America, making use of said exceptional powers, and assuming an obvious attitude of economic and political aggression against our country, has reduced the participation of Cuban sugars in the North American market with the unquestionable design to attack Cuba and its revolutionary process.
>
> WHEREAS, this action constitutes a reiteration of the continued conduct of the government of the United States of North America, intended to prevent the exercise of its sovereignty and its integral development by our people thereby serving the base interests of the North American trusts, which have hindered the growth of our economy and the consolidation of our political freedom.
>
> WHEREAS, in the face of such developments the undersigned, being fully conscious of their great historical responsibility and in legitimate defense of the national economy are duty bound to adopt the measures deemed necessary to counteract the harm done by the aggression inflicted upon our nation. . . .
>
> WHEREAS, it is the duty of the peoples of Latin America to strive for the recovery of their native wealth by wrestling it from the hands of the foreign monopolies and interests which prevent their development, promote political interference, and impair the sovereignty of the underdeveloped countries of America.
>
> WHEREAS, the Cuban Revolution will not stop until it shall have totally and definitely liberated its fatherland.
>
> WHEREAS, Cuba must be a luminous and stimulating example for the sister nations of America and all the underdeveloped countries of the world to follow in their struggle to free themselves from the brutal claws of Imperialism.
>
> NOW, THEREFORE: In pursuance of the powers vested in us, in accordance with the provisions of Law No. 851, of July 6, 1960, we hereby,
>
> RESOLVE:
>
> FIRST. To order the nationalization, through compulsory expropriation, and, therefore, the adjudication in fee simple to the Cuban State, of all the property and enterprises located in the na-

tional territory, and the rights and interests resulting from the exploitation of such property and enterprises, owned by the juridical persons who are nationals of the United States of North America, or operators of enterprises in which nationals of said country have a predominating interest, as listed below, to wit: . . .

22. Compañá Azucarera Vertientes Camagüey de Cuba.

SECOND. Consequently, the Cuban State is hereby subrogated in the place and stead of the juridical persons listed in the preceding section, in respect of the property, rights and interests aforesaid, and of the assets and liabilities constituting the capital of said enterprises.

As a consequence of the Resolution, the consent of the Cuban Government was required before the ship could leave Cuban waters. To obtain this consent, Farr, Whitlock entered on August 11 into contracts with a Cuban bank, as representative of the Cuban Government. These contracts were identical with its earlier contracts with the subsidiary of C.A.V. The ship sailed for Morocco on August 12. The bank assigned the contracts to the plaintiff in these proceedings, Banco Nacional de Cuba, also an instrumentality of the Cuban Government. Banco Nacional instructed its commercial agent in New York, Société Générale, to deliver the shipping documents and a sight draft in the amount of $175,250.69 to Farr, Whitlock, in exchange for payment of the draft.

In August 1960, in an action brought by a shareholder of C.A.V. under a New York statute authorizing appointment of receivers of assets in New York of a foreign corporation which had been nationalized, a New York court appointed Sabbatino as receiver of C.A.V.'s assets in that state. Officers of C.A.V. advised Farr, Whitlock that C.A.V., not the Cuban Government, owned the sugar covered by the shipping documents then held by Société Générale. In return for a promise of C.A.V. to indemnify it against any loss, Farr, Whitlock agreed not to turn over the funds to Société Générale or Banco Nacional upon receipt of the shipping documents. Farr, Whitlock then obtained these documents, negotiated the bills of lading to its customers and received payment from them of the purchase price. Pursuant to an order of a New York court, Farr, Whitlock transferred the funds, less its commission, to the receiver Sabbatino, to await judicial determination as to their ownership.

Banco Nacional then commenced an action in the federal district court, alleging *inter alia,* diversity jurisdiction. Its complaint stated that Farr, Whitlock's refusal to return the shipping documents or pay the proceeds of sale to it constituted a conversion under New York tort law. Banco Nacional sought judgment in the amount of $175,250.69, and an injunction against Sabbatino's exercising jurisdiction over sums paid to him. The defendants argued that the sugar involved was the property of C.A.V. and not of the Cuban Government.

The District Court, 193 F.Supp. 375 (S.D.N.Y.1961), held for defendants. JUDGE DIMOCK stated that United States courts would not enforce foreign expropriatory decrees which are in violation of international law. The recognition and respect accorded foreign acts of state are not required when such acts defy international law rather than merely the public policy of the forum. United States courts, the opinion stated, have the obligation to respect and enforce international law because of this country's membership in the community of nations, because international law is a part of domestic law, and because the poverty of international remedies leaves the burden for enforcing standards on municipal courts. The opinion continued:]

Expropriation of C.A.V.'s property was not reasonably related to a public purpose involving the use of such property. The taking of the property was not justified by Cuba on the ground that the state required the property for some legitimate purpose or that transfer of ownership of the property was necessary for the security, defense or social good of the state. The taking was avowedly in retaliation for acts by the Government of the United States,[41] and was totally unconnected with the subsequent use of the property being nationalized. This fact alone is sufficient to render the taking violative of international law.

In addition the present nationalization measure is contrary to the standards of international law because of its discriminatory nature. The act classifies United States nationals separately from all other nationals, and provides no reasonable basis for such a classification. The decree does not justify the classification on the basis of the conduct of the owners in managing and exploiting their properties or on the basis of the importance to the security of the state where ownership of the property resides. The justification is simply reprisal against another government. . . .

Moreover the nationalization measure in the present action violates international law because it does not provide adequate compensation for the taking of the properties. . . . The condition placed on the payment of interest on the bonds, as well as the uncertainty of payment at maturity, render the bonds unmarketable and valueless. Further, the value of the expropriated property is to be determined solely by appraisers appointed by the Cuban Government, an obviously adverse party to the interests of the persons whose property has been seized. Clearly, this is not adequate compensation within the requirements of international law.

Since the Cuban expropriation measure is a patent violation of international law, this court will not enforce it. It follows that C.A.V. owned the sugar which was sold in the present case. . . .

[While plaintiff's appeal to the Court of Appeals was pending, two letters were submitted to that court. The first, dated October 18, 1961 and sent by the Legal Adviser to the State Department to an attorney for *amici* in the case, stated in part:

> The Department of State has not, in the Bahia de Nipe case or elsewhere, done anything inconsistent with the position taken on the Cuban nationalization by Secretary Herter. Whether or not these nationalizations will in the future be given effect in the United States is, of course, for the courts to determine. Since the Sabbatino case and other similar cases are at present before the courts, any comments on this question by the Department of State would be out of place at this time. As you yourself point out, statements by the executive branch are highly susceptible of misconstruction.

41. Whatever the provocation to Cuba of these acts by the United States Government, the acts were not in violation of international law. To assure an orderly and adequate supply of sugar to this country, the Government had since 1934 restricted the inflow of foreign sugar. . . .

In a letter dated November 14, 1961, responding to an inquiry from the same attorney, the Under Secretary of State for Economic Affairs stated:

> I have carefully considered your letter and have discussed it with the Legal Adviser. Our conclusion, in which the Secretary concurs, is that the Department should not comment on matters pending before the courts.

The Court of Appeals, 307 F.2d 845 (2d Cir. 1962), affirmed. It stated that under ordinary rules of the conflict of laws, title to the sugar would be determined by reference to Cuban law, namely the decree of expropriation in August, 1960. It concluded that the act of state doctrine, which holds that United States courts will not pass on the validity of acts of foreign governments performed in their capacities as sovereigns within their own territories, did not prevent such courts from examining the validity of the Cuban decree. The doctrine rests on various policies: the desire of the judiciary to avoid conflict with or embarrassment to the executive and legislative branches of government in the field of foreign relations; a positivistic concept of territorial sovereignty; and a fear of hampering international trade by rendering titles insecure. Past cases, observed the court, have recognized an exception to the doctrine when the executive branch announces that it does not oppose inquiry by the courts into the legality of foreign acts. It found this exception applicable, in view of the two letters from State Department officials. Nonetheless, the court said, it would not question the validity of the Cuban decree on the ground that it was not formally in compliance with rules of Cuban law or on the ground that it violated the public policy of the forum. The opinion by JUDGE WATERMAN continued:]

Thus we turn to a consideration of the appellees' third contention, that the appellant's title is invalid under international law. Although the law of nations is a hazy concept, its rules are more limited in scope than are the public policy concepts of a particular nation within the family of nations. Moreover, if we apply international law to the present case, we find that the reasons put forward in support of the act of state doctrine are either inapplicable or insufficient to preclude us from inquiring into the validity of the Cuban decree on the limited basis of an inquiry as to the decree's consistency with international rules of law. First, as pointed out earlier in the opinion, the State Department has no desire to interfere here with independent decision by the judiciary. Second, the very proposition that something known as international law exists carries with it the implication that national sovereignty is not absolute but is limited, where the international law impinges, by the dictates of this international law. . . . Third, when an agency of the expropriating country instead of some third party is the litigant relying upon the expropriation for its title, the problem of preserving the security of the titles to property that is the subject of international trade is not presented. . . . Finally, although it can be argued that nationalistic prejudice could affect decision in cases of this sort, it is also often claimed that other biases in various obnoxious forms are present in the minds of judges in other types of cases. Judges are properly admonished when reminded that judicial duty requires that controversies be decided fairly and without passion, but we also have a duty not to excuse ourselves from exercising the duty of decision when parties and subject matter are properly before us. . . .

. . . International law is derived indeed from the customs and usages of civilized nations, but its concepts are subject to generally accepted principles of morality whether most men live by these principles or not. . . . Judges of municipal courts, the bulk of whose decisions involve questions under a domestic law derived from a long-established and increasingly elaborate national legal system, will often find themselves unfamiliar with the ratiocination necessary for decision in this area, where recognized precedent and accepted authority are scant. Anyone who undertakes a search for the principles of international law cannot help but be aware of the nebulous nature of the substance we call international law. . . . But until the day of capable international adjudication among countries, the municipal courts must be the custodians of the concepts of international law, and they must expound, apply and develop that law whenever they are called upon to do so. . . .

One pitfall into which we could stumble would be the identification as a fundamental principle of international law of some principle which in truth is only an aspect of the public policy of our own nation and not a principle so cherished by other civilized peoples. In avoiding such an identification we must take a more cosmopolitan view of things and recognize that the rule of law which we municipally announce must be a rule applicable to sovereignties with social and economic patterns very different from our own. . . .

The first aspect of the nationalization of C.A.V.'s property which the appellees ask us to consider is the fact that the decree authorizing the seizure did not provide for the payment of adequate compensation [42] . . . .

But is the failure to provide adequate compensation for the compulsory taking of the property of a domestically chartered corporation owned by alien stockholders a violation of international law? The constitutions of most of the states in the Western Hemisphere contain language which appears to uphold the right of the owner to receive just compensation upon a governmental taking of private property. . . . The United States Department of State has asserted this proposition to foreign countries on numerous occasions. . . . A number of decisions by international tribunals have upheld the principle that just compensation should be provided.[43] And it appears that most of the writers on the subject have asserted that just compensation for governmental taking is a requirement of international law.

But some writers have asserted that the payment of adequate compensation is not required by international law. . . . Tremendous social and cultural changes are occurring in many parts of the world today. Many countries have acted upon the principle that, in order to carry out desired economic and social reforms of vast magnitude, they must have the right to seize private property without providing compensation for the taking. They argue that because of the paucity of funds in their governmental coffers it would be impossible to carry out large-scale measures in the name of social welfare if they had to provide immediate, or even delayed, compensation. The Reporter of the Restatement, Foreign Relations Law of the United States frankly admits that some states including ones in Latin Amer-

42. If there had been adequate compensation for the seizure, regardless of the other circumstances surrounding the expropriations, it would be very difficult to find any violation of international law.

43. E. g., Chorzow Factory Case (Indemnity), P.C.I.J. Judgment No. 13, September 13, 1928, ser. A. No. 17, 1 Hudson, World Court Reports 646, 677; . . . Arabian-American Oil Company v. Saudi Arabia, Award of Arbitral Tribunal, Geneva, 1956, at 61, 101–02, 109, 127 . . . .

ica other than Cuba, do not recognize any requirement to pay compensation. It is commonplace in many parts of the world for a country not to pay for what it takes. . . . Since it is unnecessary for this court in the present case to decide whether a government's failure, in and of itself, to pay adequate compensation for the property it takes is a breach of international responsibility, we decline at this time to attempt a resolution of that difficult question.

Instead, we narrow the question for decision to the following: Is it a violation of international law for a country to fail to pay adequate compensation for the property it seizes from *a particular class of aliens, when the purpose for the seizure of the property is to retaliate against the homeland of those aliens and when the result of such seizure is to discriminate against them only.* To answer this more limited question we must now consider the retaliatory purpose and the discriminatory operation of the nationalization decree here involved. It should appear obvious that these two features of the decree are closely related to one another. . . .

[Discussion of the sugar legislation of 1960 is omitted.]

. . . [O]n August 6, 1960, pursuant to Law No. 851, Executive Power Resolution No. 1 was issued, expropriating the Cuban assets of C.A.V., along with the assets of twenty-five other corporations owned by United States nationals. The preamble of the executive resolution included language almost identical with that in Law No. 851. . . . Thus we have no doubt that one of the basic reasons for the seizure here involved was to retaliate against the reduction by the United States in the sugar quota it had allotted to Cuba.

. . . Unlike the situation presented by a failure to pay adequate compensation for expropriated property when the expropriation is part of a scheme of general social improvement, confiscation without compensation when the expropriation is an act of reprisal does not have significant support among disinterested international law commentators from any country. And despite our best efforts to deal fairly with political and social doctrines vastly different from our own, we also cannot find any reasonable justification for such procedure. Peacetime seizure of the property of nationals of a particular country, as an act of reprisal against that country, appears to this court to be contrary to generally accepted principles of morality throughout the world.

The appellant seeks to justify retaliatory confiscation by the Cuban government by asserting that the United States was the first offender. . . . But, whether she was wise or unwise, fair or unfair, in what she did, the United States did not breach a rule of international law in deciding, for whatever reason she deemed sufficient, the sources from which she would buy her sugar. We cannot find any established principle of international jurisprudence that requires a nation to continue buying commodities from an unfriendly source. Accordingly it follows that the amendment to the Sugar Act of 1948 did not excuse Cuba's prima facie breach of international law.

We come now to the issue of whether this retaliation involved a discrimination against United States nationals of such a nature as to render the expropriation invalid under international law. By referring only to United States nationals, Law No. 851 and the decree of expropriation issued thereunder would appear to be discriminatory, since retaliation against a person's homeland is not a reasonable basis for a distinction in treatment. But the appellant points out that under the Agrarian Reform Law and the Urban Reform Law, the Castro government confiscated the property of persons who were not

United States nationals; and that the sugar enterprises owned by Cubans were expropriated on October 13, 1960, under yet another law, Law No. 890. Under the Agrarian Reform Law and the Urban Reform Law all large land holdings and multi-family dwellings were nationalized. These latter two pieces of legislation are of little relevance to the present case because of the substantial differences, in both policy and effect, between the nationalization of real estate as such and the nationalization of the means of production as such. But the seizure of Cuban-owned sugar enterprises on October 13, 1960, does bear directly upon whether the Cuban government discriminated against American-owned corporations, for it is obvious, of course, that the confiscation of Cuban-owned enterprises was not part of an effort by the Cuban government to retaliate against the United States. If the ultimate effect of all the expropriations by the Castro Cuban government was to treat Cuban-owned enterprises and American-owned enterprises exactly alike, it would be difficult for this court to find discrimination against American nationals. And, perhaps, international law is not violated when equal treatment is accorded aliens and natives, regardless of the quality of the treatment or the motives behind that treatment. . . .

But there was a difference between the treatment of American-owned sugar enterprises and Cuban-owned sugar enterprises. American-owned sugar enterprises were expropriated on August 6, 1960; Cuban-owned sugar enterprises were not seized until October 13, 1960. A short lapse of time between similar provisions in the same program, standing alone, would not create discrimination. But the difference in time here is quite significant, because the shipment of sugar involved in this case left Cuba and was sold abroad between August 6 and October 13. And this difference of ten weeks' time stems directly from the efforts of the Cuban government to retaliate against the United States and its sugar-buying policy. Since we have held above that seizure of the assets of nationals of an unfriendly sovereign as part of a scheme of reprisal against that country is illegal under international law, it follows that a difference in the treatment accorded those nationals based upon reprisal is discriminatory. Therefore, at least with respect to the shipment of sugar here in question, the Cuban government discriminated against United States nationals.

When a state treats aliens of a particular country, discriminatorily to their detriment, that state violates international law. . . . Certain circumstances may exist which would permit a state to treat all aliens differently from its own citizens, but those circumstances are not present in this case. . . .

Since the Cuban decree of expropriation not only failed to provide adequate compensation but also involved a retaliatory purpose and a discrimination against United States nationals, we hold that the decree was in violation of international law.

But that is not the end of the matter. We must consider whether the one whose property has been thus expropriated has no recourse except against the expropriator to obtain the just compensation not paid to him, or whether he may attack in the courts of the United States the validity of the expropriator's title. . . . If the appellant's title was not rendered void, Farr, Whitlock was guilty of conversion of the bills of lading and the proceeds of the sale even though C.A.V. has not been compensated for the taking. It has been argued that the wrong under international standards is not in the taking but in the failure to pay compensation for the taking. It has been pointed out, moreover, that international tribunals have never granted restitution of the property taken. Therefore, the argument runs, the expropriator possesses good title to the property seized subject to a duty to pay damages for the injury caused. But international tribunals are not the sole custodians of international law. As we stated earlier in this opinion, municipal courts also play a part in the development of that body of law. . . . Furthermore, municipal courts are competent to give a restitutory remedy. In fact, the New York court which holds the proceeds from the sale of sugar involved in the present case is in such a position. We need not at present go into the question whether the granting of this type of remedy is a feature of international law or of domestic law. But we do suggest that the failure of an international tribunal to give a remedy of this type results from the inability of that kind of court to enforce its awards and is not a result of the dictates of substantive international law principles.

Refusal by municipal courts of one sovereignty to sanction the action of a foreign state done contrary to the law of nations will often be the only deterrent to such violations. More important, the only relief open to persons injured by a confiscation will often be the invalidation of the confiscating country's title to the confiscated goods by decree of a court of another country. . . . This is particularly true in the present case because Art. 6 of Law No. 851 explicitly precludes review of the confiscation by the Cuban courts. And no aid appears to be available through diplomatic channels to the injured parties. Therefore, we conclude that, since the Cuban decree violated international law, the appellant's title is invalid and the district court was correct in dismissing the complaint.

Judgment affirmed.

[The Supreme Court granted a writ of certiorari "because the issues involved bear importantly on the conduct of the country's foreign relations and more particularly on the role of the Judicial Branch in this sensitive area." In an opinion delivered by JUSTICE HARLAN, the Court reversed the judgment below.

The Court first held that Banco Nacional, an instrumentality of the Cuban Government, was properly granted access to United States courts as a plaintiff despite the fact that diplomatic relations between Cuba and the United States had been severed. The privilege of resorting to such courts was available to a recognized sovereign power not at war with the United States; its exercise was not dependent upon proof of reciprocal treatment in the foreign sovereign's courts. The opinion continued:]

Respondents further contend that if the expropriation was of the sugar itself, this suit then becomes one to enforce the public law of a foreign state and as such is not cognizable in the courts of this country. They rely on the principle enunciated in federal and state cases that a court need not give effect to the penal or revenue laws of foreign countries or sister states. See, e. g., The Antelope, 10 Wheat. 66, 123, 6 L.Ed. 268; Wisconsin v. Pelican Ins. Co., 127 U.S. 265, 8 S.Ct. 1370, 32 L.Ed. 239; Huntington v. Attrill, 146 U.S. 657, 13 S.Ct. 224, 36 L.Ed. 1123 (all relating to penal laws); . . . City of Philadelphia v. Cohen, 11 N.Y.2d 401, 230 N.Y.S.2d 188, 184 N.E.2d 167 (all relating to revenue laws).

The extent to which this doctrine may apply to other kinds of public laws, though perhaps still an open question, need not be decided in this case. For we have been referred to no authority which suggests that the doctrine reaches a public law which, as here, has been fully executed within the foreign state. Cuba's restraint of the S.S. Hornfels must be regarded for these purposes to have constituted an effective taking of the sugar, vesting in Cuba C.A.V.'s property right in it.

In these circumstances the question whether the rights acquired by Cuba are enforceable in our courts depends not upon the doctrine here invoked but upon the act of state doctrine discussed in the succeeding sections of this opinion.

The classic American statement of the act of state doctrine . . . is found in Underhill v. Hernandez, 168 U.S. 250, p. 252, 18 S.Ct. 83, at p. 84, 42 L.Ed. 456, where Chief Justice Fuller said for a unanimous Court:

> Every sovereign state is bound to respect the independence of every other sovereign state, and the courts of one country will not sit in judgment on the acts of the government of another, done within its own territory. Redress of grievances by reason of such acts must be obtained through the means open to be availed of by sovereign powers as between themselves. . . .

None of this Court's subsequent cases in which the act of state doctrine was directly or peripherally involved manifest any retreat from Underhill. See American Banana Co. v. United Fruit Co., 213 U.S. 347, 29 S.Ct. 511, 53 L.Ed. 826; Oetjen v. Central Leather Co., 246 U.S. 297, 38 S.Ct. 309, 62 L.Ed. 726; Ricaud v. American Metal Co., 246 U.S. 304, 38 S.Ct. 312, 62 L.Ed. 733; Shapleigh v. Mier, 299 U.S. 468, 57 S.Ct. 261, 81 L.Ed. 355; United States v. Belmont, 301 U.S. 324, 57 S.Ct. 758, 81 L.Ed. 1134; United States v. Pink, 315 U.S. 203, 62 S.Ct. 552, 86 L.Ed. 796. . . .

In deciding the present case the Court of Appeals relied in part upon an exception to the unqualified teachings of Underhill, Oetjen, and Ricaud which that court had earlier indicated. [The Court here described the Bernstein litigation, pp. 686–689, supra.

This Court has never had occasion to pass upon the so-called Bernstein exception, nor need it do so now. For whatever ambiguity may be thought to exist in the two letters from State Department officials on which the Court of Appeals relied . . . is now removed by the position which the Executive has taken in this Court on the act of state claim; respondents do not indeed contest the view that these letters were intended to reflect no more than the Department's then wish not to make any statement bearing on this litigation.[44]

The outcome of this case, therefore, turns upon whether any of the contentions urged by respondents against the application of the act of state doctrine in the premises is acceptable: (1) that the doctrine does not apply to acts of state which violate international law, as is claimed to be the case here; (2) that the doctrine is inapplicable unless the Executive specifically interposes it in a particular case;

44. [Eds. In this paragraph of his opinion, Justice Harlan is referring to the fact that after certiorari was granted but before oral argument, the United States filed a brief as *amicus curiae*. The brief recognized that freedom of American courts to apply customary international law had "some appeal as a potential step toward the development of recognized international rules of conduct. We nonetheless believe that the balance of considerations strongly favors the retention of the traditional doctrine." The brief challenged the interpretation of the Court of Appeals of the earlier letters and asserted that they were "nothing more than a refusal to express an opinion." Unlike the communication in the Bernstein case, stated the brief, neither letter was meant to express a policy of the executive to permit courts to pass on the validity of foreign acts.]

and (3) that, in any event, the doctrine may not be invoked by a foreign government plaintiff in our courts.

Preliminarily, we discuss the foundations on which we deem the act of state doctrine to rest, and more particularly the question of whether state or federal law governs its application in a federal diversity case.[45]

We do not believe that this doctrine is compelled either by the inherent nature of sovereign authority, as some of the earlier decisions seem to imply . . . or by some principle of international law. If a transaction takes place in one jurisdiction and the forum is in another, the forum does not by dismissing an action or by applying its own law purport to divest the first jurisdiction of its territorial sovereignty; it merely declines to adjudicate or makes applicable its own law to parties or property before it. The refusal of one country to enforce the penal laws of another . . . is a typical example of an instance when a court will not entertain a cause of action arising in another jurisdiction. While historic notions of sovereign authority do bear upon the wisdom of employing the act of state doctrine, they do not dictate its existence.

That international law does not require application of the doctrine is evidenced by the practice of nations. Most of the countries rendering decisions on the subject fail to follow the rule rigidly.[46] No international arbitral or judicial decision discovered suggests that international law prescribes recognition of sovereign acts of foreign governments, see 1 Oppenheim's International Law, § 115aa (Lauterpacht, 8th ed. 1955), and apparently no claim has ever been raised before an international tribunal that failure to apply the act of state doctrine constitutes a breach of international obligation. If international law does not prescribe use of the doctrine, neither does it forbid application of the rule even if it is claimed that the act of state in question violated international law. The traditional view of international law is that it establishes substantive principles for determining whether one country has wronged another. Because of its peculiar nation-to-nation character the usual method for an individual to seek relief is to exhaust local remedies and then repair to the executive authorities of his own state to persuade them to champion his claim in diplomacy or before an international tribunal. . . . Although it is, of course, true that United States courts apply international law as a part of our own in appropriate circumstances, . . . The Paquete Habana, 175 U.S. 677, 700, 20 S.Ct. 290, 299, 44 L.Ed. 320, the public law of nations can hardly dictate to a country which is in theory wronged how to treat that wrong within its domestic borders.

45. Although the complaint in this case alleged both diversity and federal question jurisdiction, the Court of Appeals reached jurisdiction only on the former ground, 307 F.2d at 852. We need not decide, for reasons appearing hereafter, whether federal question jurisdiction also existed.

46. In English jurisprudence, in the classic case of Luther v. James Sagor & Co., [1921] 3 K.B. 532, the act of state doctrine is articulated in terms not unlike those of the United States cases. See Princess Paley Olga v. Weisz, [1929] 1 K.B. 718. But see Anglo-Iranian Oil Co. v. Jaffrate, [1953] 1 Weekly L.R. 246, [1953] Int'l L.Rep. 316 (Aden Sup.Ct.) (exception to doctrine if foreign act violates international law). Civil law countries, however, which apply the rule make exceptions for acts contrary to their sense of public order. See, e. g., Ropoit case, Cour de Cassation (France), [1929] Recueil Général Des Lois et Des Arrets (Sirey) Part I, 217; . . . Anglo-Iranian Oil Co. v. S. U. P. O. R. Co., [1955] Int'l L.Rev. 19, (Ct. of Venice) . . . . See also Anglo-Iranian Oil Co. v. Idemitsu Kosan Kabushiki Kaisha, [1953] Int'l L.Rep. 312 (High Ct. of Tokyo).

Despite the broad statement in Oetjen that "The conduct of the foreign relations of our government is committed by the Constitution to the executive and legislative . . . departments," 246 U.S. at 302, 38 S.Ct. at 311, 62 L.Ed. 726, it cannot of course be thought that "every case or controversy which touches foreign relations lies beyond judicial cognizance." Baker v. Carr, 369 U.S. 186, 211, 82 S.Ct. 691, 707, 7 L.Ed.2d 663. The text of the Constitution does not require the act of state doctrine; it does not irrevocably remove from the judiciary the capacity to review the validity of foreign acts of state.

[The Court then held that the scope of the act of state doctrine must be determined, even in diversity jurisdiction litigation, by federal rather than state law. For this portion of the opinion, see pp. 174–175, supra.]

If the act of state doctrine is a principle of decision binding on federal and state courts alike but compelled by neither international law nor the Constitution, its continuing vitality depends on its capacity to reflect the proper distribution of functions between the judicial and political branches of the Government on matters bearing upon foreign affairs. It should be apparent that the greater the degree of codification or consensus concerning a particular area of international law, the more appropriate it is for the judiciary to render decisions regarding it, since the courts can then focus on the application of an agreed principle to circumstances of fact rather than on the sensitive task of establishing a principle not inconsistent with the national interest or with international justice. It is also evident that some aspects of international law touch much more sharply on national nerves than do others; the less important the implications of an issue are for our foreign relations, the weaker the justification for exclusivity in the political branches. The balance of relevant considerations may also be shifted if the government which perpetrated the challenged act of state is no longer in existence, as in the Bernstein case, for the political interest of this country may, as a result, be measurably altered. Therefore, rather than laying down or reaffirming an inflexible and all-encompassing rule in this case, we decide only that the Judicial Branch will not examine the validity of a taking of property within its own territory by a foreign sovereign government, extant and recognized by this country at the time of suit, in the absence of a treaty or other unambiguous agreement regarding controlling legal principles, even if the complaint alleges that the taking violates customary international law.

There are few if any issues in international law today on which opinion seems to be so divided as the limitations on a state's power to expropriate the property of aliens.[47]

There is, of course, authority, in international judicial[48] and arbitral decisions, in the expressions of national governments, and among commentators for the view that a taking is improper under international law if it is not for a public purpose, is discriminatory, or is without provision for prompt, adequate, and effective compensation. However, Communist countries, although they have in fact provided a degree of compensation after diplomatic efforts, commonly

47. . . . We do not, of course, mean to say that there is no international standard in this area; we conclude only that the matter is not meet for adjudication by domestic tribunals.

48. . . . Chorzow Factory Case, P.C.I.J., ser. A., No. 17, at 46, 47 (1928).

recognize no obligation on the part of the taking country. Certain representatives of the newly independent and underdeveloped countries have questioned whether rules of state responsibility toward aliens can bind nations that have not consented to them [49] and it is argued that the traditionally articulated standards governing expropriation of property reflect "imperialist" interests and are inappropriate to the circumstances of emergent states.

The disagreement as to relevant international law standards reflects an even more basic divergence between the national interests of capital importing and capital exporting nations and between the social ideologies of those countries that favor state control of a considerable portion of the means of production and those that adhere to a free enterprise system. It is difficult to imagine the courts of this country embarking on adjudication in an area which touches more sensitively the practical and ideological goals of the various members of the community of nations.[50]

When we consider the prospect of the courts characterizing foreign expropriations, however justifiably, as invalid under international law and ineffective to pass title, the wisdom of the precedents is confirmed. While each of the leading cases in this Court may be argued to be distinguishable on its facts from this one—Underhill because sovereign immunity provided an independent ground and Oetjen, Ricaud, and Shapleigh because there was actually no violation of international law—the plain implication of all these opinions . . . is that the act of state doctrine is applicable even if international law has been violated. In Ricaud, the one case of the three most plausibly involving an international law violation, the possibility of an exception to the act of state doctrine was not discussed. . . .

The possible adverse consequences of a conclusion to the contrary of that implicit in these cases is highlighted by contrasting the practices of the political branch with the limitations of the judicial process in matters of this kind. Following an expropriation of any significance, the Executive engages in diplomacy aimed to assure that United States citizens who are harmed are compensated fairly. Representing all claimants of this country, it will often be able, either by bilateral or multilateral talks, by submission to the United Nations, or by the employment of economic and political sanctions, to achieve some degree of general redress. Judicial determinations of invalidity of title can, on the other hand, have only an occasional impact, since they depend on the fortuitous circumstance of the property in question being brought into this country.[51] Such decisions would, if the acts involved were declared invalid, often be likely to give offense to the expropriating country; since the concept of territorial sovereignty is so deep seated, any state may resent the refusal of the courts of another sovereign to accord validity to acts within its territorial borders. Piecemeal dispositions of this sort involving the probability of affront to another state could seriously interfere with negotiations

49. . . . Roy, Is the Law of Responsibility of States for Injuries to Aliens a Part of Universal International Law? 55 Am.J.Int'l L. 863 (1961).

50. There are, of course, areas of international law in which consensus as to standards is greater and which do not represent a battleground for conflicting ideologies. This decision in no way intimates that the courts of this country are broadly foreclosed from considering questions of international law.

51. It is, of course, true that such determinations might influence others not to bring expropriated property into the country . . . so their indirect impact might extend beyond the actual invalidations of title.

being carried on by the Executive Branch and might prevent or render less favorable the terms of an agreement that could otherwise be reached. Relations with third countries which have engaged in similar expropriations would not be immune from effect.

The dangers of such adjudication are present regardless of whether the State Department has, as it did in this case, asserted that the relevant act violated international law. If the Executive Branch has undertaken negotiations with an expropriating country, but has refrained from claims of violation of the law of nations, a determination to that effect by a court might be regarded as a serious insult, while a finding of compliance with international law would greatly strengthen the bargaining hand of the other state with consequent detriment to American interests.

Even if the State Department has proclaimed the impropriety of the expropriation, the stamp of approval of its view by a judicial tribunal, however impartial, might increase any affront and the judicial decision might occur at a time, almost always well after the taking, when such an impact would be contrary to our national interest. Considerably more serious and far-reaching consequences would flow from a judicial finding that international law standards had been met if that determination flew in the face of a State Department proclamation to the contrary. When articulating principles of international law in its relations with other states, the Executive Branch speaks not only as an interpreter of generally accepted and traditional rules, as would the courts, but also as an advocate of standards it believes desirable for the community of nations and protective of national concerns. In short, whatever way the matter is cut, the possibility of conflict between the Judicial and Executive Branches could hardly be avoided.

Respondents contend that, even if there is not agreement regarding general standards for determining the validity of expropriations, the alleged combination of retaliation, discrimination, and inadequate compensation makes it patently clear that this particular expropriation was in violation of international law. If this view is accurate, it would still be unwise for the courts so to determine. Such a decision now would require the drawing of more difficult lines in subsequent cases and these would involve the possibility of conflict with the Executive view. Even if the courts avoided this course, either by presuming the validity of an act of state whenever the international law standard was thought unclear or by following the State Department declaration in such a situation, the very expression of judicial uncertainty might provide embarrassment to the Executive Branch.

Another serious consequence of the exception pressed by respondents would be to render uncertain titles in foreign commerce, with the possible consequence of altering the flow of international trade.[52] If the attitude of the United States courts were unclear, one buying expropriated goods would not know if he could safely import them into this country. Even were takings known to be invalid, one would have difficulty determining after goods had changed hands several times whether the particular articles in question were the product of an ineffective state act.[53]

52. This possibility is consistent with the view that the deterrent effect of court invalidations would not ordinarily be great. If the expropriating country could find other buyers for its products at roughly the same price, the deterrent effect might be minimal although pattern of trade would be significantly changed.

53. Were respondents' position adopted, the courts might be engaged in the

Against the force of such considerations, we find respondents' countervailing arguments quite unpersuasive. Their basic contention is that United States courts could make a significant contribution to the growth of international law, a contribution whose importance, it is said, would be magnified by the relative paucity of decisional law by international bodies. But given the fluidity of present world conditions, the effectiveness of such a patchwork approach toward the formulation of an acceptable body of law concerning state responsibility for expropriations is, to say the least, highly conjectural. Moreover, it rests upon the sanguine presupposition that the decisions of the courts of the world's major capital exporting country and principal exponent of the free enterprise system would be accepted as disinterested expressions of sound legal principle by those adhering to widely different ideologies.

It is contended that regardless of the fortuitous circumstances necessary for United States jurisdiction over a case involving a foreign act of state and the resultant isolated application to any expropriation program taken as a whole, it is the function of the courts to justly decide individual disputes before them. Perhaps the most typical act of state case involves the original owner or his assignee suing one not in association with the expropriating state who has had "title" transferred to him. But it is difficult to regard the claim of the original owner, who otherwise may be recompensed through diplomatic channels, as more demanding of judicial cognizance than the claim of title by the innocent third party purchaser, who, if the property is taken from him, is without any remedy.

Respondents claim that the economic pressure resulting from the proposed exception to the act of state doctrine will materially add to the protection of United States investors. We are not convinced, even assuming the relevance of this contention. Expropriations take place for a variety of reasons, political and ideological as well as economic. When one considers the variety of means possessed by this country to make secure foreign investment, the persuasive or coercive effect of judicial invalidation of acts of expropriation dwindles in comparison. The newly independent states are in need of continuing foreign investment; the creation of a climate unfavorable to such investment by wholesale confiscations may well work to their long-run economic disadvantage. Foreign aid given to many of these countries provides a powerful lever in the hands of the political branches to ensure fair treatment of United States nationals. Ultimately the sanctions of economic embargo and the freezing of assets in this country may be employed. Any country willing to brave any or all of these consequences is unlikely to be deterred by sporadic judicial decisions directly affecting only property brought to our shores. If the political branches are unwilling to exercise their ample powers to effect compensation, this reflects a judgment of the national interest which the judiciary would be ill-advised to undermine indirectly.

It is suggested that if the act of state doctrine is applicable to violations of international law, it should only be so when the Executive Branch expressly stipulates that it does not wish the courts to pass on the question of validity. . . . We should be slow to reject the representations of the Government that such a reversal of the Bernstein principle would work serious inroads on the maximum

difficult tasks of ascertaining the origin of fungible goods, of considering the effect of improvements made in a third country on expropriated raw materials, and of determining the title to commodities subsequently grown on expropriated land or produced with expropriated machinery. . . .

effectiveness of United States diplomacy. Often the State Department will wish to refrain from taking an offical position, particularly at a moment that would be dictated by the development of private litigation but might be inopportune diplomatically. Adverse domestic consequences might flow from an official stand which could be assuaged, if at all, only by revealing matters best kept secret. Of course, a relevant consideration for the State Department would be the position contemplated in the court to hear the case. It is highly questionable whether the examination of validity by the judiciary should depend on an educated guess by the Executive as to probable result and, at any rate, should a prediction be wrong, the Executive might be embarrassed in its dealings with other countries. We do not now pass on the Bernstein exception, but even if it were deemed valid, its suggested extension is unwarranted.

However offensive to the public policy of this country and its constituent States an expropriation of this kind may be, we conclude that both the national interest and progress toward the goal of establishing the rule of law among nations are best served by maintaining intact the act of state doctrine in this realm of its application.

Finally, we must determine whether Cuba's status as a plaintiff in this case dictates a result at variance with the conclusions reached above. If the Court were to distinguish between suits brought by sovereign states and those of assignees, the rule would have little effect unless a careful examination were made in each case to determine if the private party suing had taken property in good faith. Such an inquiry would be exceptionally difficult, since the relevant transaction would almost invariably have occurred outside our borders. If such an investigation were deemed irrelevant, a state could always assign its claim.

It is true that the problem of security of title is not directly presented in the instance of a sovereign plaintiff, although were such a plaintiff denied relief, it would ship its goods elsewhere, thereby creating an alteration in the flow of trade. The sensitivity in regard to foreign relations and the possibility of embarrassment of the Executive are, of course, heightened by the presence of a sovereign plaintiff. The rebuke to a recognized power would be more pointed were it a suitor in our courts. . . .

Certainly the distinction proposed would sanction self-help remedies, something hardly conducive to a peaceful international order. Had Farr, Whitlock not converted the bills of lading, or alternatively breached its contract, Cuba could have relied on the act of state doctrine in defense of a claim brought by C.A.V. for the proceeds. It would be anomalous to preclude reliance on the act of state doctrine because of Farr, Whitlock's unilateral action, however justified such action may have been under the circumstances. . . .

Since the act of state doctrine proscribes a challenge to the validity of the Cuban expropriation decree in this case, any counterclaim based on asserted invalidity must fail. Whether a theory of conversion or breach of contract is the proper cause of action under New York law, the presumed validity of the expropriation is unaffected. Although, we discern no remaining litigable issues of fact in this case, the District Court may hear and decide them if they develop.

The judgment of the Court of Appeals is reversed and the case is remanded to the District Court for proceedings consistent with this opinion. It is so ordered.

[The dissenting opinion of MR. JUSTICE WHITE is omitted.]

COMMENT

The opinion traces the exchange of retaliatory measures back no further than the United States legislation of 1960 affecting the Cuban sugar import quota. There is evidence that some members of Congress supporting that statute viewed it as a partial response to the Cuban confiscation of an American-owned oil refinery because its management had refused to refine oil supplied by the Soviet Union. 106 Cong.Rec., Senate, June 30, 1960, pp. 15231–32.

Recall that, as further described in Sardino v. Federal Reserve Bank of New York, p. 436, supra, all Cuban assets in the United States were frozen as of 1963. Consequently any recovery by Banco Nacional would have been held subject to those restrictions. A possible ultimate outcome might have been their application towards a lump sum settlement of claims against Cuba. See the provisions for settlement of Cuban claims at p. 436, supra.

QUESTIONS

(1) The Sabbatino opinions reflect divergent views of the "rules" of international law relating to expropriation.

(*a*) The District Court offered three independent grounds for its conclusion that the expropriation was a "patent violation" of international law. What support for its holding do you find in Part C of Chapter IV or in this chapter?

(*b*) In Sardino v. Federal Reserve Bank of New York, p. 436, supra, a decision two years after the Sabbatino opinion, Judge Friendly observed that the "unquestioned right" of a state to protect its nationals' property in a foreign country "must permit initial seizure and ultimate expropriation of assets of nationals of that country in its own territory if other methods of securing compensation for its nationals should fail." Are these views consistent with Judge Waterman's, as to the status under international law of the taking of foreign nationals' property as reprisal or retaliation?

(*c*) Suppose that Cuba, pursuant to a general program of nationalization, had simultaneously taken American-owned and other sugar plantations, had not acted in response to "hostile" foreign measures, and had offered compensation on the terms present in this case. In view of the excerpts from its opinion, how do you think the Court of Appeals would have decided such a case? Do you find the distinctions between the hypothetical case and that before the court significant?

(2) "The views of the Supreme Court in Sabbatino about international law are about as promising for its development as the views of the Permanent Court in the Lotus Case [p. 253, supra]. The Court finds itself unable to 'focus on the application of an *agreed principle*' and therefore in effect concludes that there is *no law* on the subject which a court can develop and apply."

(*a*) Do you agree? If not, what distinctions would you draw between the Sabbatino and Lotus opinions with respect to their views about international law and the role of courts in developing it?

(*b*) Do the considerations on which the Supreme Court relied in refusing to examine the expropriation under customary international law apply with equal force to an international tribunal? To a national court in a legal system reflecting an allocation of competences among branches of government different from our own?

(3) Note how broadly the Supreme Court defined the problem before it. Rather than address the *general* question of expropriation and compensation, could it have more effectively approached the problem by limiting its opinion to the particular facts of this case? By taking into account variable factors such as those noted in question (5) at p. 470, supra? Are you persuaded by the reasons for which it refused to undertake so particularistic an inquiry?

(4) In view of the materials in Part C of Chapter IV, what additional evidence of international law principles requiring *some* meaningful compensation could or should the Court have included in its opinion? Should the Hickenlooper Amendment, Section 620(e)(1) to the Foreign Assistance Act,* discussed at p. 482, supra, have been *considered* by the Court? Considered *persuasive* by the Court?

(5) Does the act of state doctrine after Sabbatino simply rest upon the broad statement in the Oetjen case, p. 684, supra, that the "conduct of the foreign relations of our government is committed by the Constitution to the executive and the legislative—the political—departments of the government . . . ."? Or have more complex considerations become relevant, in view of the limited holding of the Supreme Court (at p. 702, supra) and of the various exceptions to the doctrine which it states?

(*a*) Suppose that the United States and Cuba had been parties to a treaty prohibiting expropriation without prompt and adequate compensation, and that the treaty was clearly violated by the Cuban action. Under the Sabbatino opinion, should a court determine the validity of such a taking? What arguments could be made against doing so?

(*b*) In such a case, should a court honor a request from the State Department that it not question the act of state since the United States was pursuing other avenues towards compensation?

(6) In view of the freezing of Cuban assets in this country, could the Supreme Court have reached the same result without reliance on the act of state doctrine and without discussion of the cloudy character of international law in this field? What narrower grounds appear possible? Compare United States v. Pink, p. 600, supra.

NOTE ON DEVELOPMENTS AFTER SABBATINO

The Sabbatino Amendment

The reaction to the Sabbatino decision of many businessmen and lawyers involved with foreign investment was intense and vocal. The campaign for "repeal" of Sabbatino made its way rapidly to the committees of the Congress. Acting with unusual speed, Congress enacted provisions as part of the Foreign Assistance Act of 1964, which, in effect, reverse important parts of the Sabbatino holding. Read those provisions in Section 620(e)(2) of the Foreign Assistance Act.* [54]

The reference in that Section (referred to in the text below as the Sabbatino Amendment) to "the principles of international law, including the principles of compensation and the other standards set out in this subsection . . ." is to the Hickenlooper Amendment, Section 620(e)(1) of the Foreign Assistance Act,* discussed at p. 482, supra, which should thus be read together with the Sabbatino Amendment.

The executive branch submitted a memorandum to the Congressional committees in opposition to the proposed Sabbatino Amendment. That memorandum stated in part: [55]

> Most American-owned property expropriated abroad is never brought to the United States and does not come within the jurisdiction of our courts. Most often, land or fixed installations are the object of expropriation. Where oil, sugar, or other commodities have been expropriated, it is very difficult to trace them in international commerce. Any recoveries that might be made by American claimants against expropriated property coming into the United States would be small, and haphazard. The amounts recovered would be trivial in comparison to the value of U. S. property abroad that has been expropriated. Thus, the "Sabbatino" amendment would not do American claimants very much good.
>
> In fact, the amendment would have an unintended effect adverse to the interest of American claimants. Over the years, the State Department has pressed in claims settlements for adherence to a standard of prompt, adequate, and effective compensation. We have had a fair measure of success in obtaining satisfactory settlements. If United States courts were to pass on the legality under the international law of foreign expropriations, and were to pass on the standards of compensation adhered to by a foreign government, we believe the negotiating position of the Executive would be undermined rather than strengthened. A review of U. S. court decisions, including the opinions of the District Court, the Court of Appeals, and the Supreme Court in the Sabbatino case, discloses that American judicial standards in regard to compensation are considerably lower than those pressed for by the Department of State in international claims negotiations. The end result, if the "Sabbatino" amendment were to become law, would probably be to decrease the over-all recovery by expropriated American property owners. Their loss would far outbalance such recoveries as might be made by the very small number of American claimants who could trace their property or locate foreign-government property to the United States.
>
> Finally, continuance in force of the "act of state" doctrine can give no aid or comfort to the Castro regime in Cuba. All Cuban assets in this country are frozen under Treasury Department regulations.

54. 78 Stat. 1013, 22 U.S.C.A. § 2370(e)(2) (1970).

55. Executive Branch Views in Opposition to "Sabbatino Amendment to Foreign Aid Legislation," July 28, 1964, submitted to Senate Foreign Relations Committee.

The Sabbatino Litigation Continued

At the time that the Amendment became effective, proceedings in the Sabbatino litigation were pending in the District Court, on remand from the Supreme Court. Note the instructions of the Supreme Court in the two final paragraphs of its opinion, at p. 706, supra. In Banco Nacional de Cuba v. Farr, 243 F.Supp. 957 (S.D.N.Y.1965) (subsequent proceedings having removed the receiver Sabbatino from the litigation), the District Court held that the Amendment applied to cases pending at the time of its effectiveness, and that it constituted supervening law binding the court under the Supremacy Clause. It rejected plaintiff's argument that "retroactive" application of the Amendment to this very case would violate the Constitution, particularly the Fifth Amendment. The court then considered proviso (2) of the Sabbatino Amendment. It stated in part:

> The provision in the Amendment giving the President the power to invoke the act of state doctrine in cases where national foreign policy interests so require does not oust the court of jurisdiction. Nor is it an unwarranted or unconstitutional interference with the judicial function.
>
> It is not unusual for Congress to enact statutes giving to the Executive Branch the power to determine finally, litigable questions in the foreign affairs field. . . . And it is quite clear that the Executive may tell the courts when it is in the national interest to grant sovereign immunity to a foreign state, and that suggestion by the Executive is conclusive. Ex parte Republic of Peru, 318 U.S. 578, 63 S.Ct. 793, 87 L.Ed. 1014 (1943); Rich v. Naviera Vacuba, S .A., 295 F. 2d 24 (4th Cir. 1961) (per curiam). The primacy that the Constitution delegates to the political branches in the field of foreign affairs dictates such a result. . . .
>
> Under the Amendment, as in the sovereign immunity situation, the President is not sitting as a court of review over decisions of the judiciary. He does not attempt to decide the merits of the controversy between the parties. He is merely given the power to determine whether the courts should abstain from deciding one aspect of the merits. The effect of what he does may not be determinative of the final outcome of the litigation. But its effect upon the foreign policy interests of the United States may well be vital.

The court reserved judgment to allow the executive branch to determine whether it wished to issue the suggestion contemplated by proviso (2). In a memorandum opinion, 272 F.Supp. 836 (1965), the court quoted a letter from the United States Attorney to the effect that no determination had been made or was contemplated. It concluded that the opinion of the Court of Appeals, deciding the international law issues in favor of the defendant, was binding upon it, since the Supreme Court did not reach the question of violation of international law. Consequently, it granted a motion to dismiss the complaint.

The Court of Appeals affirmed in an opinion by Judge Waterman, 383 F.2d 166 (2d Cir. 1967). In rejecting the argument that the Sabbatino Amendment was "legislative interference with the judicial power, and therefore violative of the constitutional doctrine of the separation of powers," the court stated:

> Appellant notes . . . that an important characteristic of [a political question] is "lack of judicially discoverable and manageable standards for resolving it." It compares this to the Supreme Court's express statement that, among the nations, there is disagreement as to relevant international law standards that should be applied when the property of aliens is expropriated, because of the divergent interests and different social ideologies of different nations. . . . But the Supreme Court here does not state that it could not resolve the international law issue if it felt itself called upon to do so. See The Paquete Habana, 175 U.S. 677, 700, 20 S.Ct. 290, 44 L.Ed. 320 (1900). Indeed, our Court of Appeals was able to resolve it on the original appeal. . . . [The Supreme] Court specifically stated that its result was not constitutionally required, and indicated the result was reached through the utilization of an abstention policy grounded upon the exercise of judicial discretion. Thus the application of the act of state doctrine in this case was not constitutionally compelled on the ground that the underlying issue was a political question which the Court was foreclosed from determining.

The Court rejected appellant's contention that the Amendment represented legislative interference with the exclusive power of the executive branch in the conduct of foreign affairs. It quoted from Oetjen v. Central Leather Co., p. 684, supra, to the effect that the conduct of foreign relations was "committed by the Constitution to the Executive *and Legislative* . . . Departments of the Government . . . ." Finally, the Court applied the Sabbatino Amendment and stated that "we will not extensively discuss the international law issue but reaffirm the discussion that is contained in our opinion on the first appeal." It noted that the "principles of compensation and other standards" in the Sabbatino Amendment, referring to the Hickenlooper Amendment, were if anything "more exacting upon the expropriating nations" than the "international law standards that we applied . . . ."

Effects Upon Sovereign Immunity

Litigation in this field has raised numerous questions about the scope and effect of the Sabbatino Amendment, such as its effect upon pleas of sovereign immunity. One such case was Chemical Natural Resources, Inc. v. Republic of Venezuela, p. 659, supra. The majority regarded the Amendment as irrelevant to that action, commenced by attachment to obtain damages for confiscation of property and cancellation of a concession agreement. Judge Musmanno, dissenting from the court's conclusion that the plea of sovereign immunity should be granted, regarded the Amendment as decisive (420 Pa. at 180–82, 215 A.2d at 886):

> Although the Majority Opinion would assign to the Executive Department of the government a constitutional infallibility which finds no justification in the law books, it

> refuses to recognize in the Legislative Department, another coordinate branch of the government, the authority which is conferred upon it by the United States Constitution. In 1964, the United States Congress enacted [the Sabbatino Amendment]. . . . The Majority Opinion gives but scant attention to this vital Act of Congress. . . . There was reason for the Congress of the United States to enact the [Amendment]. . . . Standing up to the neck in the flood of [foreign countries'] affronts, insults and outrages, the American Congress finally struck back and said that any government which, in violation of international law, confiscated American-owned property, would not be allowed, in United States courts, to plead the sovereign immunity doctrine. That is the purpose, practically the language of the [Amendment], which the Majority of this Court treats as if it had no more authority than a municipal ordinance.

In American Hawaiian Ventures, Inc. v. M. V. J. Latuharhary, 257 F.Supp. 622 (D.N.J.1966), an American firm sought damages for the confiscation of its property in Indonesia by a libel against an Indonesian-owned vessel, "in no way involved" in the acts complained of. The court disposed of the Sabbatino Amendment as follows:

> Both the [Sabbatino] case and the Amendment dealt only with the scope of inquiry permissible once the suit was heard. . . . Thus, the Amendment does not bear on the threshold question whether this Court's jurisdiction over Indonesia would be defeated by its right to sovereign immunity for acts *jure imperii.*

Recall that the proposed statute on sovereign immunity submitted as a bill to the Congress, p. 668, supra, gives particular attention to this problem. Section 1605 would provide that there is no jurisdictional immunity if "rights in property taken in violation of international law are in issue", and if that property or property exchanged for it is present in the United States in relation to commercial activities of the foreign state, or if that property is owned by an agency or instrumentality of that state engaged in the United States in commercial activity. Section 1610 complements this provision by denying to such property immunity from attachment and execution.

Situs of Expropriated Property

Two other post-Sabbatino decisions in the lower federal courts—involving not the Amendment but the case itself—should be noted. Both raise the important issue of the situs of the expropriated property and thus the extra-territorial reach of the foreign government's expropriatory act. Recall that in Sabbatino, the expropriated property was within the foreign state. Indeed the Court's holding, at p. 702, supra, was carefully restricted to a "taking of property within its own territory by a foreign sovereign government . . . ." Compare Republic of Iraq v. First National City Bank, 353 F.2d 47 (2d Cir. 1965). King Faisal II of Iraq was killed in a 1958 revolution. At his death, he had liquid funds and shares in a Canadian investment trust held in deposit and custody accounts of a New York bank. The bank transferred these assets to a court-appointed administrator. The new Iraqi government issued an ordinance confiscating all property of the dynasty, and the Republic of Iraq brought a diversity action against the administrator, based upon the confiscatory decree, to recover the assets. The Court of Appeals affirmed dismissal of the complaint.

In his opinion for the court, Judge Friendly characterized the confiscation decree as "the very archetype of an act of state." Noting the difficulties in identifying a situs for intangibles such as bank accounts and share interests, the court stated that in all significant respects the property at issue was within the United States. In view of the Supreme Court's holding in Sabbatino that act of state issues were to be resolved under federal law, the court concluded that such law governed despite the difference in situs between Sabbatino and the present case. "It would be baffling if a foreign act of state intended to affect property in the United States were ignored on one side of the Hudson but respected on the other; any such diversity between states would needlessly complicate the handling of the foreign relations of the United States."

The court held that the confiscatory decree would not be given effect, since it was inconsistent "with our policy and laws." "Our Constitution sets itself against confiscations such as that decreed by [Iraq] not only by the general guarantees of due process in the Fifth and Fourteenth Amendments, but by the specific prohibitions of bills of attainder in Article I. . . . Foreigners entrusting their property to custodians in this country are entitled to expect this historic policy to be followed save when the weightiest reasons call for a departure." The court distinguished United States v. Pink, p. 600, supra, on the ground that the Litvinov Assignment and the President's action "was considered to make the Soviet confiscation decrees consistent with the law and policy of the United States from that time forward, . . . In this case, by contrast, nothing remotely resembling the Litvinov agreement is present; on the contrary, the Department of State has disclaimed any interest of the executive department in the outcome of the litigation."

Similar questions arose in Maltina Corporation v. Cawy Bottling Company, 462 F.2d 1021 (5th Cir. 1972), cert. denied 409 U.S. 1060 (1972). The assets of a Cuban brewery corporation, Nueva Fabrica, were confiscated by a Cuban law of 1960. Nueva Fabrica had registered the trademark "Cerveza Cristal" in the United States Patent Office in 1957. The individual Cuban owners of Nueva Fabrica fled to the United States, and there sought to maintain the trademark registration, despite the fact that Neuva Fabrica had been dissolved pursuant to the 1960 law. The owners assigned the mark to a newly formed corporation, Maltina, intended as a successor in interest to Nueva Fabrica. Efforts were made to achieve production in the United States under this mark. The defendant sought to register the mark "Cristal", and brought proceedings to cancel plaintiffs' registration. In this action, Maltina and its owners sought injunctive and other relief from the defendant's alleged infringement.

The court held that expropriation of Neuva Fabrica and its resulting dissolution under Cuban law "neither deprived the acknowledged former owners and fiduciaries of the corporation of the right to make an effective assignment of the dissolved corporation's United States trademark nor cancelled that trademark." It distinguished Sabbatino and its conception of the act of state doctrine partly on the ground that the confiscation in that case had taken place within Cuban territory, whereas the trademark here involved would be deemed to have a local identity and situs distinct from its former foreign owner. Moreover, it was settled that courts would not give "extraterritorial effect" to foreign confiscatory decrees, even where directed against the foreign state's own nationals. If the Cuban law were treated as a decree purporting to expropriate property located within the United States without compensation, "such a deprivation without compensation would violate bedrock principles of this forum, embodied in the Fifth Amendment to the Constitution." To achieve equity, the court would treat the former owners of the dissolved corporation as continuing owners over property with an American situs.

In its discussion of Sabbatino, the court stressed that the political considerations developed in that decision to justify the act of state doctrine were consistent with the view that acts of state applied only when expropriatory acts were consummated within the foreign territory. The court noted, for example, that an extraterritorial decree of a foreign state conflicted with those very concepts of territorial sovereignty which underlay the act of state doctrine itself; hence, there was less chance of violated expectations of or offence to the foreign state. Here there was also less possibility of an embarrassing interference by the judiciary with executive control over foreign relations. The court referred to the criteria of Baker v. Carr, p. 132, supra, to support its conclusion that a judicial decision in favor of plaintiffs in this case would not involve undue interference with the executive. It noted that the judiciary had long exercised jurisdiction over property with an American situs which foreign states sought to expropriate. It stressed that the instant decision had no bearing upon the propriety or effectiveness of Cuban actions against the dissolved corporation within Cuba. Finally, it noted that the Cuban government had not demonstrated any interest in the outcome of the litigation. "Any offence to the Cuban state is purely hypothetical."

QUESTIONS

(1) "If the Hickenlooper Amendment represented a glancing blow at international law, if the Sabbatino opinion was a sorry reflection on its status, the Sabbatino Amendment is its ultimate parochial negation." Comment.

(2) A New York corporation (plaintiff) wholly owned by United States citizens owned a cigar manufacturing plant in Guatador which was expropriated by the Guatadorian government. Assume that the expropriation clearly violates the "principles of international law" referred to in the Sabbatino Amendment.

(*a*) The Guatadorian government has full diplomatic representation in the United States. In addition, Guatador keeps on deposit with a New York bank substantial sums of its official tourist agency, derived from advance payments by Americans for hotel and travel expenses in Guatador. Plaintiff wishes to sue the Guatadorian government to recover the fair value of its properties. What alternative courses would you recommend, and what problems do you see in each?

(*b*) The Guatador State Trading Agency, a governmental branch, ships a quantity of cigars to New York for storage and later sale there to American distributors. The cigars are identifiable as having been in plaintiff's warehouse in Guatador at the time of expropriation. Plaintiff wishes to recover these cigars. What advice?

(*c*) The Agency sells the cigars to an American importer (defendant), to whom title passes f. o. b. at a Guatadorian port. Upon the arrival of the cigars in New York, plaintiff wishes to bring an action against defendant to recover the cigars or their fair value. What advice? Is it relevant whether defendant had reason to know that the particular cigars which it purchased were in plaintiff's warehouse at the time of expropriation?

(3) The Guatadorian government expropriated late in 1974 a plantation owned by the plaintiff. It offers to pay plaintiff the full value over a ten-year period, half in local currency and half in dollars. In 1975, an American distributor (defendant) imported (a) coffee beans harvested in 1974 and 1975 on the plantation, (b) a quantity of instant coffee made from such beans, and (c) some chocolates flavored with extracts from such beans. Plaintiff wishes to bring an action against defendant.

(*a*) What problems and what advice?

(*b*) Would it help to show that Guatador, in a concession agreement with plaintiff, had promised not to confiscate the plantation except against "prompt and adequate compensation in dollars."?

(4) "The Sabbatino Amendment was basically an exercise in emotional catharsis on the part of the Congress. It may have been very useful for that purpose, but not for many others. For all its sound and fury, the Amendment signifies little." Comment.

(5) The Republic of Iraq case considers the Sabbatino opinion, the Pink case, and "the policy and laws of the United States." It does not invoke the Sabbatino Amendment. Why?

FIRST NATIONAL CITY BANK v. BANCO NACIONAL DE CUBA

Supreme Court of the United States, 1972.
406 U.S. 759, 92 S.Ct. 1808, 32 L.Ed.2d 466.

[In July 1958, First National City Bank loaned to the predecessor of Banco Nacional $15 million secured by a pledge of United States Government bonds. On September 16, 1960, after Castro's coming to power, the Cuban government seized all of petitioner's Cuban branches. A week later the bank retaliated by selling the collateral securing the unpaid balance of the loan. At least $1.8 million was left over after the proceeds were applied to the principal and interest. Banco Nacional sued petitioner to recover that excess and petitioner asserted, by way of set-off and counterclaim, its right to recover its expropriation losses out of that fund.

The District Court gave summary judgment in favor of petitioner except as to the amount of excess proceeds. After the parties had conceded that petitioner's expropriation losses exceeded $1.8 million, the court dismissed Banco Nacional's complaint. The Court of Appeals reversed. A petition for certiorari was filed and while it was pending the Department of State furnished its views in a letter, as follows:

> "Recent events in our view, make appropriate a determination by the Department of State that the act of state doctrine need not be applied when it is raised to bar adjudication of a counterclaim or setoff when (a) the foreign state's claim arises from a relationship between the parties existing when the act of state occurred; (b) the amount of the relief to be granted is limited to the amount of the foreign state's claim; and (c) the foreign policy interests of the United States do not require application of the doctrine.
>
> . . .
>
> In this case, the Cuban government's claim arose from a banking relationship with the defendant existing at the time the act of state—expropriation of defendant's Cuban property—occurred, and defendant's counterclaim is limited to the amount of the Cuban government's claim. We find, moreover, that the foreign policy interests of the United States do not require the application of the act of state doctrine to bar adjudication of the validity of a defendant's counterclaim or set-off against the Government of Cuba in these circumstances.
>
> The Department of State believes that the act of state doctrine should not be applied to bar consideration of a defendant's counterclaim or set-off against the Government of Cuba in this or like cases."

The Supreme Court granted certiorari and vacated the Court of Appeals judgment so that it could consider the views of the Department of State. The Court of Appeals adhered to its original position and the Supreme Court again granted certiorari.

The opinion of MR. JUSTICE REHNQUIST, excerpts from which follow, was joined by CHIEF JUSTICE BURGER and MR. JUSTICE WHITE:]

We must here decide whether, in view of the substantial difference between the position taken in this case by the Executive Branch and that which it took in [Banco Nacional de Cuba v. Sabbatino, 376 U.S. 398, 84 S.Ct. 923, 11 L.Ed. 804 (1964)], the act of state doctrine prevents petitioner from litigating its counterclaim on the merits. We hold that it does not.

. . .

The question which we must now decide is whether the so-called *Bernstein* exception to the act of state doctrine should be recognized in the context of the facts before the Court. In *Sabbatino,* the Court said: "This Court has never had occasion to pass upon the so-called *Bernstein* exception, nor need it do so now." 276 U.S., at 420, 84 S.Ct., at 936.

The act of state doctrine, like the doctrine of immunity for foreign sovereigns, has its roots not in the Constitution, but in the notion of comity between independent sovereigns. . . . It is also buttressed by judicial deference to the exclusive power of the Executive over conduct of relations with other sovereign power and the power of the Senate to advise and consent on the making of treaties. . . .

The line of cases from this Court establishing the act of state doctrine justify its existence primarily on the basis that juridical review of acts of state of a foreign power could embarrass the conduct of foreign relations by the political branches of the government. . . .

. . .

The act of state doctrine is grounded on judicial concern that application of customary principles of law to judge the acts of a foreign sovereign might frustrate the conduct of foreign relations by the political branches of the government. We conclude that where the Executive Branch, charged as it is with primary responsibility for the conduct of foreign affairs, expressly represents to the Court that the act of state doctrine would not advance the interests of American foreign policy, that doctrine should not be applied by the courts. In so doing, we of course adopt and approve the so-called *Bernstein* exception to the act of state doctrine. We believe this to be no more than an application of the classical common-law maxim that "the reason of the law ceasing, the law itself also ceases" (Black's Law Dictionary, p. 288).

Our holding is in no sense an abdication of the judicial function to the Executive Branch. The judicial power of the United States extends to this case, and the jurisdictional standards established by Congress for adjudication by the federal courts have been met by the parties. The only reason for not deciding the case by use of otherwise applicable legal principles would be the fear that legal interpretation by the judiciary of the act of a foreign sovereign within its own territory might frustrate the conduct of this country's foreign relations. But the branch of the government responsible for the conduct of those foreign relations has advised us that such a consequence need not be feared in this case. The judiciary is therefore free to decide the case free from the limitations that would otherwise be imposed upon it by the judicially created act of state doctrine.

It bears noting that the result we reach is consonant with the principles of equity set forth by the Court in National City Bank of New York v. Republic of China, 348 U.S. 356, 75 S.Ct. 423, 99 L.Ed. 389 [at p. 659, supra]. Here respondent, claimed by petitioner to be an instrument of the government of Cuba, has sought to come into our courts and secure an adjudication in its favor, without submitting to decision on the merits of the counterclaim which respondent asserts against it. Speaking of a closely analogous situation in *Republic of China*, supra, the Court said:

> "We have a foreign government invoking our law but resisting a claim against it which fairly would curtail its recovery. It wants our law, like any other litigant, but it wants our law free from the claims of justice. It becomes vital, therefore, to examine the extent to which the considerations which led this Court to bar a suit against a sovereign in *The Schooner Exchange* are applicable here to foreclose a court from determining, according to prevailing

law, whether the Republic of China's claim against the National City Bank would be unjustly enforced by disregarding legitimate claims against the Republic of China. As expounded in *The Schooner Exchange*, the doctrine is one of implied consent by the territorial sovereign to exempt the foreign sovereign from its 'exclusive and absolute' jurisdiction, the implication deriving from standards of public morality, fair dealing, reciprocal self-interest, and respect for the 'power and dignity' of the foreign sovereign."

The act of state doctrine, as reflected in the cases culminating in *Sabbatino*, is a judicially accepted limitation on the normal adjudicative processes of the courts, springing from the thoroughly sound principle that on occasion individual litigants may have to forego decision on the merits of their claims because the involvement of the courts in such a decision might frustrate the conduct of the Nation's foreign policy. It would be wholly illogical to insist that such a rule, fashioned because of fear that adjudication would infere with the conduct of foreign relations, be applied in the face of an assurance from that branch of the Federal Government which conducts foreign relations that such a result would not obtain. Our holding confines the courts to adjudication of the case before them, and leaves to the Executive Branch the conduct of foreign relations. In so doing, it is both faithful to the principle of separation of powers and consistent with earlier cases applying the act of state doctrine where we lacked the sort or representation from the Executive Branch which we have in this case.

We therefore reverse the judgment of the Court of Appeals, and remand the case to it for consideration of respondent's alternative bases of attack on the judgment of the District Court.

Reversed.

[MR. JUSTICE DOUGLAS, concurring, relied upon the *Republic of China* case, at p. 659, supra, arguing that it would "offend our sensibilities if Cuba could collect the amount owed on liquidation of the collateral for the loan and not be required to account for any setoff." The case raised *Sabbatino* issues of separation of powers and political questions only "if and to the extent that the setoff asserted exceeds the amount of Cuba's claim." As to any such excess, "I would disallow the judicial resolution of that dispute for the reasons stated in *Sabbatino*. . . ." Thus it is not the *Bernstein* exception but the principle of "fair dealing" in *Republic of China* that properly determines this case, and the district court should "allow the setoff up to the amount of respondent's claim."]

MR. JUSTICE POWELL, concurring in the judgment.

Although I concur in the judgment of reversal and remand, my reasons differ from those expressed by MR. JUSTICE REHNQUIST and MR. JUSTICE DOUGLAS. While Banco Nacional de Cuba v. Sabbatino, 376 U.S. 398, 419–420, 84 S.Ct. 923, 935–936, 11 L.Ed.2d 804 (1964), technically reserves the question of the validity of the *Bernstein* exception as MR. JUSTICE BRENNAN notes in his dissenting opinion, the reasoning of *Sabbatino* implicitly rejects that exception. Moreover, I would be uncomfortable with a doctrine which would require the judiciary to receive the executive's permission before invoking its jurisdiction. Such a notion, in the name of the doctrine of separation of powers, seems to me to conflict with that very doctrine.

Nor do I find National City Bank v. Republic of China, 348 U.S. 356, 75 S.Ct. 423, 99 L.Ed. 389 (1955), to be dispositive. The Court there dealt with the question of jurisdiction over the parties to hear a counterclaim asserted against a foreign State seeking redress in our courts. Jurisdiction does not necessarily imply that a court may hear a counterclaim which would otherwise be nonjusticiable. Jurisdiction and justiciability are, in other words, different concepts. One concerns the court's power over the parties; the other concerns the appropriateness of the subject matter for judicial resolution. Although attracted by the justness of the result he reaches, I find little support for MR. JUSTICE DOUGLAS' theory that the counterclaim is justiciable up to, but no further than, the point of setoff.

I nevertheless concur in the judgment of the Court because I believe that the broad holding of *Sabbatino* was not compelled by the principles, as expressed therein, which underlie the act of state doctrine. . . .

I do not disagree with these principles, only with the broad way in which *Sabbatino* applied them. Had I been a member of the *Sabbatino* Court, I probably would have joined the dissenting opinion of Mr. Justice White. The balancing of interests, recognized as appropriate by *Sabbatino*, requires a careful examination of the facts in each case and of the position, if any, taken by the political branches of government. I do not agree, however, that balancing the functions of the judiciary and those of the political branches compels the judiciary to eschew acting in all cases in which the underlying issue is the validity of expropriation under customary international law. Such a result would be an abdication of the judiciary's responsibility to persons who seek to resolve their grievances by the judicial process.

Nor do I think the doctrine of separation of powers dictates such an abdication. To so argue is to assume that there is no such thing as international law but only international political disputes that can be resolved only by the exercise of power. Admittedly, international legal disputes are not as separable from politics as are domestic legal disputes, but I am not prepared to say that international law may never be determined and applied by the judiciary where there has been an "act of state." Until international tribunals command a wider constituency, the courts of various countries afford the best means for the development of a respected body of international law. There is less hope for progress in this long neglected area if the resolution of all disputes involving "an act of state" is relegated to political rather than judicial processes.

Unless it appears that an exercise of jurisdiction would interfere with delicate foreign relations conducted by the political branches, I conclude that federal courts have an obligation to hear cases such as this. This view is not inconsistent with the basic notion of the act of state doctrine which requires a balancing of the roles of the judiciary and the political branches. When it is shown that a conflict in those roles exists, I believe that the judiciary should defer because, as the Court suggested in *Sabbatino*, the resolution of one dispute by the judiciary may be outweighed by the potential resolution of multiple disputes by the political branches.

In this case where no such conflict has been shown, I think the courts have a duty to determine and apply the applicable international law. I therefore join in the Court's decision to remand the case for further proceedings.

MR. JUSTICE BRENNAN, with whom MR. JUSTICE STEWART, MR. JUSTICE MARSHALL, and MR. JUSTICE BLACKMUN join, dissenting.

The Court today reverses the judgment of the Court of Appeals for the Second Circuit that declined to engraft the so-called "*Bern-*

stein" exception upon the act of state doctrine as expounded in Banco Nacional de Cuba v. Sabbatino, 376 U.S. 398, 84 S.Ct. 923, 11 L.Ed. 2d 804 (1964). The Court, nevertheless, affirms the Court of Appeals rejection of the "*Bernstein*" exception. Four of us in this opinion unequivocally take that step, as do MR. JUSTICE DOUGLAS and MR. JUSTICE POWELL in their separate concurring opinions.

I

On September 16 and 17, 1960, the Government of Cuba nationalized the branch offices of petitioner in Cuba. Petitioner promptly responded by selling collateral that had previously been pledged in security for a loan it had made to a Cuban instrumentality. Respondent—alleged by petitioner to be an agent of the Cuban Government—in turn, instituted this action to recover the excess of the proceeds of the sale over the accrued interest and principal of the loan. Petitioner then counterclaimed for the value of its Cuban properties, alleging that they had been expropriated in violation of international law.[56] . . . The Court of Appeals for the Second Circuit reversed on the ground that the act of state doctrine, as applied in *Sabbatino*, forecloses judicial review of the nationalization of petitioner's branch offices. 431 F.2d 394 (1970).[57]

56. Petitioner actually asserts two counterclaims—first, that the Cuban expropriation was invalid, giving rise to damages, and, second, that Cuba became indebted to petitioner, regardless of the validity of the expropriation decree. Moreover, petitioner invokes Cuban and United States as well as international law in support of both claims. These refinements are of no avail to petitioner. If applicable, the act of state doctrine, of course, bars consideration of both international law claims; although the Court in *Sabbatino* stated its holding in terms that "the Judicial Branch will not examine the *validity* of a taking of property within its own territory by a foreign sovereign government . . . ," 376 U.S., at 428, 84 S.Ct., at 940 (emphasis added), the holding clearly embraced judicial review not only of the taking but of the obligation to make "prompt, adequate, and effective compensation." Id., at 429, 84 S.Ct., at 940. See also id., at 433, 84 S.Ct., at 942.

Similarly, petitioner's allegations do not state cognizable claims under Cuban law. . . .

Finally, United States law becomes relevant only if the public-policy-of-the-forum exception to the *lex loci* conflicts-of-law rule is recognized—that is, if the American forum is free, because of its public policy, to deny recognition to Cuban law otherwise applicable as the law of the situs of the property seized. But the very purpose of the act of state doctrine is to forbid application of that exception. . . .

57. In arriving at this conclusion, the court found inapplicable the Hickenlooper Amendment to the Foreign Assistance Act of 1964, 78 Stat. 1013, as amended, 22 U.S.C.A. § 2370(e)(2). I agree with my colleagues in leaving that determination undisturbed. [Eds. Justice Brennan's reference is to what the coursebook text has referred to as the Sabbatino Amendment. In the Court of Appeals decision noted by Justice Brennan, that court explored the legislative history behind the Sabbatino Amendment and concluded that its purpose was to prevent the United States from becoming a "thieves' market for expropriated property." That is, the Amendment applied to expropriated property found in the United States, or perhaps more broadly when there was an attempt to market expropriated property in this country "and some aspect of such a transaction took place" here. "We cannot believe that . . . Congress intended to create a self-help seizure remedy for those few American firms fortunate enough to hold or have access to some assets of a foreign state at the time that the state nationalizes American property." 431 F.2d at 399–402. Moreover, the court concluded that a broader interpretation of the Sabbatino Amendment, or other refusal to apply the act of state doctrine, would allow First National City Bank a preferred position on its expropriation claims vis-a-vis other

II

The opinion of MR. JUSTICE REHNQUIST, joined by THE CHIEF JUSTICE and MR. JUSTICE WHITE, states that "[t]he only reason for not deciding the case by use of otherwise applicable legal principles would be the fear that legal interpretation by the judiciary of the act of a foreign sovereign within its own territory might frustrate the conduct of this country's foreign relations." Even if this were a correct description of the rationale for the act of state doctrine, the conclusion that the reason for the rule ceases when the Executive, as here, requests that the doctrine not be applied plainly does not follow. In *Sabbatino* this Court reviewed at length the risks of judicial review of a foreign expropriation in terms of the possible prejudice to the conduct of our external affairs. . . .

. . .

This reasoning may not apply where the Executive expressly stipulates that domestic foreign policy interests will not be impaired however the court decides the validity of the foreign expropriation. But by definition those cases can only arise where the political branch is indifferent to the result reached, and that surely is not the case before us. The United States has protested the nationalization by Cuba of property belonging to American citizens as a violation of international law. The United States has also severed diplomatic relations with that government. The very terms of the Legal Adviser's communication to this Court, moreover, anticipate a favorable ruling that the Cuban expropriation of petitioner's properties was invalid.[58]

Sabbatino itself explained why in these circumstances the representations of the Executive in favor of removing the act of state bar cannot be followed: "It is highly questionable whether the examination of validity by the judiciary should depend on an educated guess by the Executive as to probable result and, at any rate, should a pre-

claimants, in view of the federal provisions for claims settlement through the Foreign Claims Settlement Commission, p. 433, supra, and for blocking Cuban assets, p. 436, supra.]

58. The Legal Adviser states:

"Recent events, in our view, make appropriate a determination by the Department of State that the act of state doctrine need not be applied [in cases of this kind] . . . .

"The 1960's have seen a great increase in expropriations by foreign governments of property belonging to United States citizens. Many corporations whose properties are expropriated, financial institutions for example, are vulnerable to suits in our courts by foreign governments as plaintiff, for the purpose of recovering deposits or sums owed them in the United States without taking into account the institution's counterclaims for their assets expropriated in the foreign country."

The implication is clear that the Legal Adviser believes that such corporations are entitled to offsetting redress for the value of their nationalized property. Note, 12 Harv.Int'l L. J. 557, 576–577 (1971). It is also significant that the Government in the past has acknowledged "that a '*Bernstein* letter,' should one be issued in special circumstances where it might be appropriate, plainly does not seek to decide the case in question, but merely removes the act of state bar to judicial consideration of the foreign act." Brief for the United States as Amicus Curiae, in Banco Nacional de Cuba v. Sabbatino, No. 16, October Term 1963, at 38. The Government makes no such representation in this case. Note, supra, at 571 and n. 74. To the contrary, the Government now argues: "By disregarding [the] statement of Executive policy involving foreign investment by American firms, the court below has seriously restricted the capacity of the government to assist American investors in securing prompt, adequate and effective compensation for expropriation of American property abroad." Memorandum for the United States as Amicus Curiae, at 3.

diction be wrong, the Executive might be embarrassed in its dealings with other countries." Id., at 436, 84 S.Ct. at 944. Should the Court of Appeals on remand uphold the Cuban expropriation in this case, the Government would not only be embarrassed but find its extensive efforts to secure the property of United States citizens abroad seriously compromised.

Nor can it be argued that this risk is insubstantial because the substantive law controlling petitioner's claims is clear. The Court in *Sabbatino* observed that "[t]here are few if any issues in international law today on which opinion seems to be so divided as the limitations on a state's power to expropriate the property of aliens." Id., at 428, 84 S.Ct., at 940. And this observation, if anything, has more force in this case than in *Sabbatino,* since respondent argues with some substance that the Cuban nationalization of petitioner's properties, unlike the expropriation at issue in *Sabbatino,* was not discriminatory against United States citizens.

Thus, the assumption that the Legal Adviser's letter removes the possibility of interference with the Executive in the conduct of foreign affairs is plainly mistaken.

III

That, however, is not the crux of my disagreement with my colleagues who would uphold the "*Bernstein*" exception. My Brother REHNQUIST's opinion asserts that the act of state doctrine is designed primarily, and perhaps even entirely, to avoid embarrassment to the political branch. Even a cursory reading of *Sabbatino,* this Court's most recent and most exhaustive treatment of the act of state doctrine, belies this contention. . . .

. . .

Applying these principles to the expropriation before the Court, Mr. Justice Harlan noted the lack of consensus among the nations of the world on the power of a state to take alien property, and stated further that "[i]t is difficult to imagine the courts of this country embarking on adjudication in an area which touches more sensitively the practical and ideological goals of the various members of the community of nations." Id., at 430, 84 S.Ct., at 941. He reviewed as well the possible adverse effects from judicial review of foreign expropriations on the conduct of our external affairs, discussed above, and emphasized the powers of the Executive "to ensure fair treatment of United States nationals," id., at 435, 84 S.Ct., at 944, in comparison to the "[p]iecemeal dispositions," id., at 432, 84 S.Ct., at 942, that courts could make:

. . .

. . .

In short, *Sabbatino* held that the validity of a foreign act of state in certain circumstances is a "political question" not cognizable in our courts. Only one—and not necessarily the most important—of those circumstances concerned the possible impairment of the Executive's conduct of foreign affairs. Even if this factor were absent in this case because of the Legal Adviser's statement of position, it would hardly follow that the act of state doctrine should not foreclose judicial review of the expropriation of petitioner's properties. To the contrary, the absence of consensus on the applicable international rules, the unavailability of standards from a treaty or other agreement, the existence and recognition of the Cuban Government, the sensitivity of the issues to national concerns, and the power of the Executive alone to effect a fair remedy for all United States citizens who have been harmed all point toward the existence of a "political question." The Legal Adviser's letter does not purport to affect these considerations at all. In any event, when coupled with the possible consequences to the conduct of our foreign relations explored above, these considerations compel application of the act of state doctrine, notwithstanding the Legal Adviser's suggestion to the contrary.[59] The Executive Branch, however, extensive its powers in the area of foreign affairs, cannot by simple stipulation change a political question into a cognizable claim.[60]

Sabbatino, as my Brother REHNQUIST's opinion notes, formally left open the validity of the *"Bernstein"* exception to the act of state doctrine. But that was only because the issue was not presented there. As six members of this Court recognize today, the reasoning of that case is clear that the representations of the Department of State are entitled to weight for the light they shed on the permutation and combination of factors underlying the act of state doctrine. But they cannot be determinative.

59. A comparison of the facts in the *Bernstein* case . . . with the circumstances of this case reinforces this conclusion. As the Government itself has acknowledged, Brief for the United States as Amicus Curiae, . . . at 37–38:

"The circumstances leading to the State Department's letter in the *Bernstein* case were of course most unusual. The governmental acts there were part of a monstrous program of crimes against humanity; the acts had been condemned by an international tribunal after a cataclysmic world war which was caused, at least in part, by acts such as those involved in the litigation, and the German State no longer existed at the time of [the] State Department's letter. Moreover, the principle of payment of reparations by the successor German government had already been imposed, at the time of the '*Bernstein* letter,' upon the successor government, so that there was no chance that a suspension of the act of state doctrine would affect the negotiation of a reparations settlement." On these facts the result, though not the rationale, in *Bernstein* may be defensible. . . .

60. My Brother REHNQUIST's opinion attempts to bolster its result by drawing an analogy between the act of state doctrine and the rule of deference to the Executive in the areas of sovereign immunity and recognition of foreign powers. That rule has itself been the subject of much debate and criticism. The analogy, in any case, is not persuasive. When the Judicial Branch in the past has followed an Executive suggestion of immunity in behalf of a foreign government or accorded significant weight to the failure of the Executive to make such a suggestion, the result has been simply either to foreclose judicial consideration of the claim against that government or to allow the suit to proceed on the merits of the claim and any other defenses the government may have. See, e. g., Mexico v. Hoffman, 324 U.S. 30, 65 S. Ct. 530, 89 L.Ed. 729 (1945); Ex parte Peru, 318 U.S. 578, 63 S.Ct. 793, 87 L. Ed. 1014 (1943). Similarly, when the Judicial Branch has abided by an Executive determination of foreign sovereignty, the consequence has been merely to require or deny the application of various principles governing the attributes of sovereignty. See, e. g., United States v. Belmont, 301 U.S. 324, 57 S. Ct. 758, 81 L.Ed. 1134 (1937); Russian Socialist Federated Soviet Republic v. Cibrario, 235 N.Y. 255, 139 N.E. 259 (1923). In no event has the Judiciary necessarily been called upon to assess a claim under international law. The effect of following a "*Bernstein* letter," of course, is exactly the opposite—the Judicial Branch must reach a judgment despite the possible absence of consensus on the applicable rules, the risk of irritation to sensitive concerns of other countries, and the danger of impairment to the conduct of our foreign policy. E. g., Note, n. 7, supra, at 575–577. See also *Sabbatino,* supra, 376 U.S., at 438, 84 S.Ct., at 945.

. . .

IV

To find room for the *"Bernstein"* exception in *Sabbatino* does more than disservice to precedent. Mr. Justice REHNQUIST's opinion states: "Our holding is no sense an abdication of the judicial function to the Executive Branch." With all respect, it seems patent that the contrary is true. The task of defining the contours of a political question such as the act of state doctrine is exclusively the function of this Court. Baker v. Carr, 369 U.S. 186, 82 S.Ct. 691, 7 L.Ed.2d 663 (1962), and cases cited therein; see R. Falk, The Status of Law in International Society 413 (1970). The *"Bernstein"* exception relinquishes the function to the Executive by requiring blind adherence to its requests that foreign acts of state be reviewed. Conversely, its politicizes the Judiciary. For the Executive's invitation to lift the act of state bar can only be accepted at the expense of supplanting the political branch in its role as a constituent of the international law-making community. As *Sabbatino*, 376 U.S., at 422–433, 84 S.Ct. at 942, indicated, it is the function of the Executive to act "not only as an interpreter of generally accepted and traditional rules, as [do] the courts, but also as an advocate of standards it believes desirable for the community of nations and protective of national concerns." The *"Bernstein"* exception, nevertheless, assigns the task of advocacy to the Judiciary by calling for a judgment where consensus on controlling legal principles is absent. Note, 40 Ford.L.Rev. 409, 417 (1971). Thus, it countenances an exchange of roles between the Judiciary and the Executive, contrary to the firm insistence in *Sabbatino* on the separation of powers.

The consequence of adopting the *"Bernstein"* approach would only be to bring the rule of law both here at home and in the relations of nations into disrespect. Indeed, the fate of the individual claimant would be subject to the political considerations of the Executive Branch. Since those considerations change as surely as administrations change, similarly situated litigants would not be likely to obtain even-handed treatment. . . .

. . .

V

MR. JUSTICE REHNQUIST's opinion finds support for the result it reaches in National City Bank v. Republic of China, 348 U.S. 356, 75 S.Ct. 423, 99 L.Ed. 389 (1955), and MR. JUSTICE DOUGLAS bases his decision on that case alone. *National City Bank* held that, by bringing suit in our courts, a foreign sovereign waives immunity on offsetting counterclaims, whether or not related to the sovereign's cause of action. Nothing in that decision spoke to the applicability of the act of state doctrine. My Brother REHNQUIST's opinion, nevertheless, seizes on language there that a sovereign suing in our courts "wants our law" and so should be held bound by it as a matter of equity. In a similar vein, my Brother DOUGLAS states that "[i]t would . . . offend our sensibilities if Cuba could collect the amount owed on . . . [her claim] and not be required to account for any setoff." Yet, on the assumption that equitable principles are relevant to respondent's cause of action, see Note, 75 Harv. L.Rev. 1607, 1619 (1962), it is by no means clear that the balance of equity tips in petitioner's favor. It cannot be argued that by seeking relief in our courts on a claim that does not involve any act of state, respondent has waived the protection of the act of state doctrine in defense to petitioner's counterclaims. See ibid. Furthermore, as the Court of Appeals pointed out below, 442 F.2d, at 535, petitioner "is seeking a windfall at the expense of other" claimants whose property Cuba has nationalized. Our Government has blocked Cuban assets in this country for possible use by the Foreign Claims Settlement Commission to compensate fairly all American nationals who have been harmed by Cuban expropriations. Although those assets are not now vested in the United States or authorized to be distributed to claimants, it is reasonable to assume that they will be if other efforts at settling claims with Cuba are unavailing. In that event, if petitioner prevails here, it will, in effect, have secured a preference over other claimants who were not so fortunate to have had Cuban assets within their reach and whose only relief is before the Claims Commission. Conversely, if respondent prevails, its recovery will become a vested asset for fair and ratable distribution to all claimants, including petitioner. See 431 F.2d, at 403–404.

. . .

In *Sabbatino* itself . . . the Court went on to determine whether there were any remaining litigable issues for determination on remand and held that "any counterclaim [against Cuba] based on asserted invalidity [of her expropriation] must fail." Id., at 439, 84 S.Ct., at 946. *Sabbatino* thus answered the very point on which some of my brethren now rely—and, furthermore, did so in the face of *National City Bank,* as the Court's discussion of that decision in *Sabbatino,* id., at 438, 84 S.Ct., at 945, shows.

COMMENT

On remand, 478 F.2d 191 (2d Cir. 1973), the Court of Appeals affirmed the district court's original grant of summary judgment for First National City Bank. It agreed with the district court that the Government of Cuba and Banco Nacional "are one and the same for the purposes of this litigation." With respect to the legality of the expropriation, the court stated: "We see no reason to re-open the question whether the Cuban expropriation violated international law." It tersely concluded that the prior decisions of this same Court of Appeals in the Sabbatino litigation—307 F.2d 845 (p. 695, supra) and 383 F.2d 166 (p. 710, supra)—"establish that the actions of the government of Cuba and the Banco Nacional in the instant case were violations of international law."

An unusual situation results from the sequence of decisions in these two major litigations. In Sabbatino, Justice Harlan explored the ambiguous and politically contentious character of international law doctrine treating compensation for expropriation. Such considerations contributed to the Court's decision to apply the act of state doctrine. The only dissenting opinion (Justice White) did not reach the merits of the international-law issue. None of the opinions in the Supreme Court's decision in First National City Bank sought to resolve that issue, the critical issue in the two litigations. Thus the governing "law" about the international standard for compensation, at least for purposes of judicial decisions where the Sabbatino Amendment is inapplicable, would appear to be the first decision, 307 F.2d 845, p. 695, supra, of the Second Circuit Court of Appeals in Sabbatino, a decision on which that circuit has twice relied to terminate the Sabbatino and First National City Bank litigations.

In 1973, the Court of Appeals for the Second Circuit decided Menendez v. Saks & Co., a case raising issues of act of state under both the Sabbatino and First National City Bank decisions. The Supreme Court granted certiorari, *sub nom.* Alfred Dunhill of London, Inc. v. Republic of Cuba, 416 U.S. 981 (1974). The case was argued in December of that year, but later restored to the calendar for reargument during the 1975 Term. In its brief order to this effect, the Court noted: "In addition to other questions presented by this case, counsel are requested to brief and discuss during oral argument: Should this Court's holding in Banco Nacional de Cuba v. Sabbatino, 376 U.S. 398, be reconsidered?" 33 U.S.L.W. 3659 (U.S. June 16, 1975)

QUESTIONS

(1) Suppose that a lower federal court hears a case to which the Sabbatino Amendment is not applicable, and in which a plaintiff seeks recovery of the value of its assets expropriated by Guatador in an action against the Guatadorian state trading agency in this country and its commercial assets. The district court reviews the decision in First National City Bank. What guidance does he receive? Within that decision, what conditions must be met before the act of state doctrine is inapplicable?

(2) In his opinion, Justice Rehnquist observes (p. 718) that where the act of state doctrine applies, "individual litigants may have to forego decision on the merits of their claims . . ." Is this a fair description of the consequence of the Supreme Court's decision in the Sabbatino case itself? Is it a fair description of the more usual situation where an American plaintiff sues a foreign governmental entity for the value of its expropriated property?

(3) Based on the preceding decisions, how would you assess the relative significance of each of the following factors as a justification for the act of state doctrine? (*i*) The doctrine is an aspect of choice-of-law rules, within federal common law (rather than state rules of choice of law) because of its international consequences. The choice-of-law rule that it embodies stresses the control by foreign sovereigns over matters within their own territory, and hence is related to the public international law principle of territorial sovereignty. (*ii*) The doctrine stems from a reluctance of the judiciary to reach the full merits of a case when its holdings might embarrass the executive in its conduct of foreign relations. (*iii*) The doctrine is a variant of the (constitutional) principle of the nonjusticiability of political questions, and comports with the criteria established for the definition of political questions (see pp. 132–140, supra) in decisions such as Baker v. Carr, p. 132, supra.

(*a*) Is the willingness of a court to accept the "Bernstein letter exception" to the act of state doctrine dependent upon the theory about the doctrine (among the three sketched above) to which it gives prominence? For example, should a letter from the State Department urging a court to adjudicate under international law be given effect if the doctrine rests on the theory of political questions?

(*b*) How would you develop the argument for the "political question" base, particularly in light of the opinions of Justice Harlan in Sabbatino and of Justice Brennan in First National City Bank? Note also the reasoning of the court in Maltina Corporation v. Cawy Bottling Company, p. 713, supra. (It may be important to determine which of the several strands to the "political question" are here present, before answering question (a) above.)

(4) "Whatever theory may be viewed as underlying the act of state doctrine, unfortunate consequences follow acceptance of the Bernstein exception. No persuasive analogy can be drawn between letters from the State Department in these cases and letters treating sovereign immunity. At least letters in the latter category purport to develop principles that were stated in the Tate Letter (p. 647, supra), whereas advice from the Department in act-of-state cases promises to be a matter of ad hoc political intervention into the judicial process. Moreover, advice in sovereign immunity cases that the Department has no objection to a court's assuming jurisdiction over a defendant does not purport to influence the substantive outcome of that litigation. In act-of-state cases, when relying on a letter from the Department to bypass act of state and adjudicate on the merits of the international law issue, the court will be under great pressure to follow the executive view about the content of the international law norms. The end result is that the judicial process becomes compromised at every level, a parochial, politicized and subservient arm of the executive." In what respects do you agree or disagree with these remarks?

(5) "In view of the Sabbatino opinion of the Supreme Court, the State Department seems to be running some risk when it sends Bernstein letters. If and when the Supreme Court decides what are the relevant norms of international law about expropriation and compensation, it is difficult to believe that those norms will faithfully echo the Department's own position of prompt, adequate and effective compensation."

(*a*) What weight should the Court give to the Department's long-established views when it eventually confronts the merits of the international law issue?

(*b*) Do you agree with the prediction in the above quotation? If there were such a holding, what effect should the Court's more restrictive view of obligations under international law have upon the Department's internationally espoused position?

(*c*) Could the Congress then expand the coverage of the Sabbatino Amendment to provide that it covers all cases in which a plaintiff seeks compensation for assets expropriated by a foreign government in violation of the standards set forth in the Hickenlooper Amendment?

(*d*) Suppose that the Court reached the international-law issue and accepted the State Department's view of the applicable international standard. What contribution do you think such a holding would make towards the development of an international consensus over that standard? How would the opinion be perceived by foreign offices or by an international tribunal which might ultimately consider the same question?

Additional reading: Delson, The Act of State Doctrine—Judicial Deference or Abstention, 66 Am.J.Int.L. 82 (1972); Falk, Toward a Theory of the Participation of Domestic Courts in the International Legal Order: A Critique of Banco Nacional de Cuba v. Sabbatino, 16 Rutgers L.Rev. 1

(1961); Henkin, The Foreign Affairs Power of the Federal Courts: Sabbatino, 64 Colum.L.Rev. 805 (1964); Jennings, The Sabbatino Controversy, 20 Record of N.Y.C.B.A. 81 (1965); Lowenfeld, The Sabbatino Amendment—International Law Meets Civil Procedure, 59 Am.J.Int.L. 899 (1965); Lowenfeld, Act of State and Department of State: First National City Bank, 66 Am.J.Int.L. 795 (1972); Zander, The Act of State Doctrine, 53 Am.J.Int.L. 826 (1959); Report by the Committee on International Law of the Association of the Bar of the City of New York, The Effect to be Given in the United States to Foreign Nationalization Decrees, 19 Record of N.Y. C.B.A. Supp. 5 (1964); Restatement (Second), Foreign Relations Law of the United States §§ 41–43.

Chapter VII

CIVIL ACTIONS IN A TRANSNATIONAL SETTING: COOPERATION AND CONFLICT AMONG NATIONAL JUDICIARIES

The problems considered in Chapter Six had a transnational character because of one critical fact: litigation before national courts involved a foreign sovereign or its acts. The transnational elements in the civil litigation described in this chapter differ. Consider first comparable questions of interaction between courts that arise in an entirely domestic setting. In a unitary (nonfederal) nation, one central authority may determine the jurisdiction of courts, the procedures for gathering relevant information before or during a trial, and the means for enforcement of judgments. In a federal country, principles must be articulated, by constitution or statute or decisional law, to determine which among the different state or federal judicial systems hears and resolves a particular controversy. Even if a particular state (or any of several states) has "jurisdiction" to entertain an action, the court or parties may have need to draw upon the assistance of other judicial systems within the federalism to gather evidence—for example, to subpoena witnesses from other states. Finally, when a judgment is rendered by a state court, a victorious plaintiff may find it necessary to invoke the aid of a court of another state to enforce the judgment by execution against property located within it.

Such are the problems, transferred from a federal to a transnational context, which we here examine. We view them principally through civil suits between private parties in which the plaintiff seeks a money judgment, but to some extent through suits in which a governmental plaintiff seeks either a money judgment (as in a tax suit) or a decree (as in antitrust actions) requiring the defendant to perform or refrain from certain acts. The foreign element varies. With respect to jurisdictional issues, it may concern (a) the nationality, domicile or other affiliation of the defendant, or (b) the foreign location of property or foreign locus of certain events critical to the litigation. Information relevant to the litigation may be known by persons or found in records in foreign countries. Any judgment which the court renders may require a party to seek the assistance of a foreign judicial system for enforcement. Such foreign elements make evident the need for cooperation among different judiciaries, which can thereby contribute to the forging of closer political and legal bonds among countries.

A. JURISDICTION TO ADJUDICATE

In each country, rules have developed indicating when courts will decide cases that are not entirely "local" in character. One or more of the parties are present in or otherwise related to a foreign country; property relevant to the litigation is abroad; or events relevant to the litigation occurred in whole or part abroad. Perhaps it is best to start by indicating what we are *not* concerned with as we consider jurisdictional issues. Courts use the term "jurisdiction" to refer to several related but distinct problems, including:

(*1*) *Subject matter jurisdiction.* The courts hearing the cases below have such "jurisdiction," in the sense that they are competent to adjudicate and resolve the particular kind of claim before them. That is, they are empowered under relevant law to resolve questions of tort or contract or property, and to render money judgments in the amount requested.

(*2*) *Venue.* Once it is determined that courts of a given political unit (nation or state) have jurisdiction to adjudicate, venue rules determine in what subdivision within the political unit (department or district of a nation or state) the action should be brought. For example, 28 U.S.C. § 1391 specifies the federal judicial districts in which actions based upon diversity of citizenship or a federal question can be brought; it does not of itself confer jurisdiction to adjudicate upon any district court.

(*3*) *Notice.* By notice, we refer simply to the advice given all parties that a law suit has been commenced so that they may have an opportunity to respond and participate.

By the terms "jurisdiction," "jurisdiction to adjudicate," or "adjudicatory jurisdiction," we refer in this chapter not to such questions but to the question whether a court is empowered to entertain an action that is not entirely local in character.[1] We examine principally those jurisdictional bases which, in the United States, support so-called "in personam" actions. By these, we mean actions in which the plaintiff seeks a judicial determination of rights or duties between him and the defendant, and characteristically seeks as a remedy the award of money damages. Unlike actions in rem or quasi in rem, the court in these cases is generally requested to render a judgment that is not limited to a statement of rights in particular property, and not limited in amount to the value of that property.[2] The "jurisdictional" issue to which we are attentive is whether the relationship of the plaintiff or defendant or the cause of action to a particular state or nation justifies its courts in entering such a judgment against the defendant.

1. For a more elaborate explanation of these distinctions see the introduction to Chapter 3 on Judicial Jurisdiction, Restatement (Second), Conflict of Laws 100–102.

2. Certain of the cases below, such as those arising under the antitrust laws at p. 748, infra, are actions not for money damages but for injunctive relief. They raise special problems, both with respect to adjudicatory jurisdiction and enforcement.

Additional reading: von Mehren and Trautman, The Law of Multistate Problems Chs. V–VII (1965); von Mehren and Trautman, Jurisdiction to Adjudicate: A Suggested Analysis, 79 Harv.L.Rev. 1121 (1960); Note, Developments in the Law: State-Court Jurisdiction, 73 Harv.L.Rev. 909 (1960).

---

1. ADJUDICATORY JURISDICTION IN THE UNITED STATES

A study of jurisdictional principles for courts in this federal country offers useful insights into transnational problems. The question posed is the extent to which principles developed in an interstate setting, with 50 systems of state courts and a system of federal courts, are valid for litigation that has transnational elements.

NOTE ON ADJUDICATORY JURISDICTION FOR STATE-CREATED CAUSES OF ACTION

Historical Development

The principal common law bases for adjudicatory jurisdiction over individuals were consent (voluntary submission to the court's jurisdiction) and presence of the defendant within a given political unit. Consent seems obvious enough, although it may raise some doubts when extracted by the overwhelming bargaining power of one party or when the consenting party is ignorant of the meaning of a standard consent clause buried in masses of verbiage.[3] The case for presence as a basis was classically stated by Justice Holmes in McDonald v. Mabee, 243 U.S. 90, 91, 37 S.Ct. 343, 61 L.Ed. 608, 609 (1917): "The foundation of jurisdiction is physical power . . . ." When presence is the sole jurisdictional basis, note that service of a summons and complaint upon the defendant within a state is the very means of conferring jurisdiction upon the court; such service has the incidental if critical function of giving notice to the defendant. The recent trend has been to disassociate the bases for adjudicatory jurisdiction from notice. For example, Milliken v. Meyer, 311 U.S. 457, 61 S.Ct. 339, 85 L.Ed. 278 (1940), stated the traditional principle that domicile alone was sufficient to bring an absent defendant within a court's jurisdiction, provided that the substituted service was reasonably calculated to give adequate notice of the proceedings to the defendant. As is true of presence as a jurisdictional basis, domicile permits a court to adjudicate any personal action against the defendant, whether or not related to the forum.

With the expanding role played by corporations in interstate commerce, the subjection of corporations to a court's jurisdiction became an increasingly important constitutional issue. For such pur-

3. See the dissenting opinions in National Equipment Rental, Ltd. v. Szukhent, 375 U.S. 311, 84 S.Ct. 411, 11 L.Ed.2d 354 (1964). The topic of consent and jurisdiction is explored in the context of choice-of-forum clauses in Part C of this Chapter.

poses "domicile" has been generally associated with the state of incorporation. Corporations whose activities expand into other states have been held subject to jurisdiction if they are "doing business," an idea originally conceptually paired with "presence" on the part of an individual. Voluminous case law has accumulated around the question of what is enough activity to constitute doing business.

Another persistent issue has been the quantum of activity of a corporation in a state that is constitutionally required before causes of action unrelated to those activities can be asserted against the corporation. In International Shoe Co. v. State of Washington, 326 U.S. 310, 66 S.Ct. 154, 90 L.Ed. 95 (1945), a Washington court took jurisdiction over a suit brought by that State against a foreign corporation, employing 13 salesmen in the state, to enforce the corporation's liability for contributions to a state unemployment compensation fund. On review, the Supreme Court stated some general principles which have become the fountainhead for the subsequent development of jurisdictional bases (326 U.S. at 319–320, 66 S.Ct. at 160, 90 L.Ed. at 104):

> Whether due process is satisfied must depend rather upon the quality and nature of the activity in relation to the fair and orderly administration of the laws which it was the purpose of the due process clause to insure. . . . The obligation which is here sued upon arose out of [defendant corporation's activities within the state]. It is evident that these operations establish sufficient contacts or ties with the state of the forum to make it reasonable and just, according to our traditional conception of fair play and substantial justice, to permit the state to enforce the obligations which [the foreign corporation] has incurred there.

A third recurrent corporate question has been the amenability of a parent to suit in a state where a subsidiary does business, although it does not. The historic case is Cannon Manufacturing Co. v. Cudahy Packing Co., 267 U.S. 333, 45 S.Ct. 250, 69 L.Ed. 634 (1925). Cannon, a North Carolina corporation, brought an action against Cudahy, a Maine corporation, in a North Carolina federal court. Service upon Cudahy had been made by delivery of the summons and complaint to an agent of its wholly owned subsidiary, an Alabama corporation doing business in North Carolina. The district court concluded that the defendant was not "present" in North Carolina for purposes of adjudicatory jurisdiction; the Supreme Court affirmed. Despite plaintiff's evidence that defendant completely dominated its subsidiary, the Court rejected the argument that Cannon should be treated as identical with the subsidiary for jurisdictional purposes. It stressed that the corporate existence was kept distinct in all formal aspects, and that the distinct subsidiary could not be ignored in resolving the jurisdictional issue. The Court noted that the case did not involve an effort to hold the defendant liable for an act of its subsidiary, but solely a question of jurisdiction over the parent for its own conduct. The decision, which antedates the Federal Rules of Civil Procedure of 1938, appears to have been based upon "general law", and the Court expressly disclaimed resolution of any "question of the constitutional powers of the state, or of the federal government . . . ."

With respect to both individuals and corporations, recent cases have developed new grounds for jurisdiction, even as increasing criticism has been leveled at the use of jurisdictional bases such as transient personal presence or business activity unrelated to the cause of action. These cases have frequently arisen in a constitutional setting, the critical question being whether the assumption of jurisdiction by a state court over the defendant was consistent with the Due Process Clause of the Fourteenth Amendment. Such landmark decisions as Hess v. Pawloski, 274 U.S. 352, 47 S.Ct. 632, 71 L.Ed. 1091 (1927), and McGee v. International Life Insurance Co., 355 U.S. 220, 78 S.Ct. 199, 2 L.Ed.2d 223 (1957), have established that a court, consistently with the Due Process Clause of the Fourteenth Amendment, can found jurisdiction over the defendant upon events or transactions in which the defendant was involved and which had certain relationships to the state. In McGee, a California court asserted jurisdiction over a Texas insurance company, which had no office or agent in California and whose only relationship to the state was one life insurance contract, the subject of the suit, entered into by mail with a California domiciliary. The Court stated (355 U.S. at 222–223, 78 S.Ct. at 200–201, 2 L.Ed.2d at 225–226):

> In a continuing process of evolution this Court accepted and then abandoned "consent," "doing business" and "presence" as the standard for measuring the extent of state judicial power over [foreign] corporations. . . . Looking back over this long history of litigation a trend is clearly discernible toward expanding the permissible scope of state jurisdiction over foreign corporations and other nonresidents. In part this is attributable to the fundamental transformation of our national economy over the years. Today many commercial transactions touch two or more States and may involve parties separated by the full continent. With this increasing nationalization of commerce has come a great increase in the amount of business conducted by mail across state lines. At the same time modern transportation and communication have made it much less burdensome for a party sued to defend himself in a State where he engages in economic activity.

The Wisconsin Statutes—A Modern Example

We here set forth as illustrative of recent trends some jurisdictional provisions of Wisconsin law. The excerpts below from Section 262.05 Wisc.Stat.Ann., refer to "personal" or in personam jurisdiction. Note that only paragraph (1) covers causes of action unrelated to the State. Section 262.08(4) refers to another characteristic basis for adjudicatory jurisdiction of American courts—so-called "jurisdiction quasi in rem."

262.05 Personal jurisdiction, grounds for generally

A court of this state having jurisdiction of the subject matter has jurisdiction over a person served in an action pursuant to s. 262.06 under any of the following circumstances:

(*1*) *Local presence or status.* In any action whether arising within or without this state, against a defendant who when the action is commenced:

(a) Is a natural person present within this state when served; or

(b) Is a natural person domiciled within this state; or

(c) Is a domestic corporation; or

(d) Is engaged in substantial and not isolated activities within this state, whether such activities are wholly interstate, intrastate, or otherwise.

. . .

(*3*) *Local act or omission.* In any action claiming injury to person or property within or without this state arising out of an act or omission within this state by the defendant.

(*4*) *Local injury: foreign act.* In any action claiming injury to person or property within this state arising out of an act or omission outside this state by the defendant, provided in addition that at the time of the injury either:

(a) Solicitation or service activities were carried on within this state by or on behalf of the defendant; or

(b) Products, materials or things processed, serviced or manufactured by the defendant were used or consumed within this state in the ordinary course of trade.

(*5*) *Local services, goods or contracts.* In any action which:

(a) Arises out of a promise, made anywhere to the plaintiff or to some third party for the plaintiff's benefit, by the defendant to perform services within this state or to pay for services to be performed in this state by the plaintiff; or

(b) Arises out of services actually performed for the plaintiff by the defendant within this state, or services actually performed for the defendant by the plaintiff within this state if such performance within this state was authorized or ratified by the defendant; or

(c) Arises out of a promise, made anywhere to the plaintiff or to some third party for the plaintiff's benefit, by the defendant to deliver or receive within this state or to ship from this state goods, documents of title, or other things of value . . . .

. . .

262.08 Jurisdiction in rem or quasi in rem, grounds for generally

A court of this state having jurisdiction of the subject matter may exercise jurisdiction in rem or quasi in rem on the grounds stated in this section. A judgment in rem or quasi in rem may affect the interests of a defendant in the status, property or thing acted upon only if a summons has been served upon the defendant pursuant to s. 262.09. Jurisdiction in rem or quasi in rem may be invoked in any of the following cases:

(1) When the subject of the action is real or personal property in this state and the defendant has or claims a lien or interest, actual or contingent, therein, or the relief demanded consists wholly or partially in excluding the defendant from any interest or lien therein. This subsection shall apply when any such defendant is unknown.

(2) When the action is to foreclose, redeem from or satisfy a mortgage, claim or lien upon real estate within this state.

. . .

(4) When the defendant has property within this state which has been attached or has a debtor within the state who has been garnished. Jurisdiction under this subsection may be independent of or supplementary to jurisdiction acquired under subs. (1) and (2).

Other sections spell out the means for notifying out-of-state defendants that an action has been commenced. Despite the built-in relationships to the forum state which characterize these long arm statutes, the danger exists that such broad jurisdictional bases may permit an inappropriate state court to adjudicate. The Wisconsin statutes make provision for such possibilities.

262.19 Stay of proceeding to permit trial in a foreign forum

(1) Stay on initiative of parties. If a court of this state, on motion of any party, finds that trial of an action pending before it should as a matter of substantial justice be tried in a forum outside this state, the court may in conformity with sub. (3) enter an order to stay further proceedings on the action in this state. A moving party under this subsection must stipulate his consent to suit in the alternative forum . . . .

. . .

(3) Scope of trial court discretion on motion to stay proceedings. The decision on any timely motion to stay proceedings pursuant to sub. (1) is within the discretion of the court in which the action is pending. In the exercise of that discretion the court may appropriately consider such factors as:

(a) Amenability to personal jurisdiction in this state and in any alternative forum of the parties to the action;

(b) Convenience to the parties and witnesses of trial in this state and in any alternative forum;

(c) Differences in conflict of law rules applicable in this state and in any alternative forum; or

(d) Any other factors having substantial bearing upon the selection of a convenient, reasonable and fair place of trial.

. . .

State Causes of Action in the Federal Courts

Under the diversity jurisdiction, causes of action arising under state law may be brought in, or removed to, the federal courts. As the second of the following cases indicates, it is not clearly settled whether the court's jurisdiction to adjudicate is to be determined by state law under Erie R. Co. v. Tompkins or by federal law. The prevailing view is that, in the absence of federal legislation, the federal courts are limited to applicable state standards in cases arising under state laws. See Arrowsmith v. United Press International, 320 F.2d 219 (2d Cir. 1963), which rejected the view expressed in Jaftex Corp. v. Randolph Mills, Inc., 282 F.2d 508 (2d Cir. 1960), that whether a foreign corporation was "present" in a district was a question of federal law.

In any case Federal Rule of Civil Procedure 4 * sets forth explicitly the ways in which service upon a defendant is to be made. Note particularly the references in 4(d)(7), 4(e) and 4(f) to state law for authority to serve process upon defendants outside the state in which the district court sits. Few of these state laws are helpful on the question of service outside the United States. The National Conference of Commissioners on Uniform State Laws produced in 1962 a Uniform Interstate and International Procedure Act, which appears in 11 Am.J.Comp.L. 415 (1962), 13 U.L.Ann. 279 (Master ed. 1975). Article II has provisions comparable to Rule 4(i) which, when adopted, would make it clear that service may be made outside the United States in actions commenced in the state courts.

Given (1) the power of a federal court sitting in a diversity case to draw upon the provisions of state long-arm statutes and (2) the provisions of federal and state rules or statutes for effecting out-of-state service, the possibility arises that the particular federal district may be as inappropriate as a state court.[4] Compare Section 262.19 of the Wisconsin statutes, p. 735, supra, with 28 U.S.C.A. § 1404(a).* Note the limitations inherent in the federal statute when a more appropriate forum would be that of a foreign country, as opposed to another federal district. These limitations should be kept in mind as you read the cases below.

REGIE NATIONALE DES USINES RENAULT v. SUPERIOR COURT

California District Court of Appeal, 1962.
208 Cal.App.2d 702, 25 Cal.Rptr. 530.

[The California statutes that appear to be relevant to this litigation are (*a*) Section 411(2) of the Code of Civil Procedure, which provides that summons may be served in a civil action against a foreign corporation "doing business in this state" in the manner provided by certain sections of the corporation law, and (*b*) Sections 6501 and 6502 of the General Corporation Law, which provide that service may be made upon a foreign corporation which has not desig-

4. The federal rules as to venue do not significantly limit the capacity of a federal court to entertain actions against aliens. Under 28 U.S.C.A. § 1391(d), "[a]n alien may be sued in any district." This provision has been held to apply to alien corporations as well. State of Maryland v. Capital Airlines, Inc., 199 F.Supp. 335 (S.D.N.Y.1961).

nated an agent to receive service of process by personal delivery to the California Secretary of State, who shall give notice of such service to the corporation by registered mail.

The appellate court in this case, by a per curiam order, denied a petition seeking an order to the lower court to quash service to summons and complaint on petitioner. It adopted and quoted the opinion of the lower court, which read as follows:]

"The court has concluded that defendant Regie Nationale des Usines Renault, Billancourt (Seine), France (hereinafter referred to elliptically as 'Regie') has had adequate contacts with California and California residents so that the maintenance of the suit against it does not offend our notions of fair play and substantial justice (International Shoe Company v. Washington, 326 U.S. 310, 66 S.Ct. 154, 90 L.Ed. 95). It is, in other words, 'doing business' in California and is amenable to substituted service of process on the Secretary of State in the manner provided by Section 6501–6502 of the Corporations Code.

Defendant Regie is a business entity owned by the French government. As an automobile manufacturer, it inaugurates a flow of its products to the California market. It sells its products to defendant Renault, Inc., a wholly-owned subsidiary incorporated in the State of New York. Renault, in turn, sells to various American distributors, who in turn sell to retail dealers. There is a chain of sales leading from defendant Regie to California consumers. The product is such that negligence in manufacture and inspection might well cause injury to California citizens, as is alleged by the plaintiff and by the cross-complainant here.

Regie might choose to arrange its marketing process through a hierarchy of its own agents and employees. Then, by establishing agents in California to sell its products, it would undoubtedly be amenable to suit in this state. For reasons of its own it chooses to market its products through a wholly-owned American subsidiary and a network of independently-owned distributorships and dealerships. These choices on its part effect little, if any, alteration in the jurisdictional situation. The 'contacts' exist one way or the other and for precisely the same purposes. The differences are differences only in form and description.

Apparently, where the tort occurs within the state, extensive sales and promotional contacts with California consumers through nonexclusive, independent sales representatives may constitute 'doing business' (Cosper v. Smith & Wesson Arms Co., 53 Cal.2d 77, 346 P.2d 409). Here there are additional circumstances which, in composite, impel subjection to jurisdiction. These are: (a) the interest of this State in providing a forum for its residents; (b) the relative availability of evidence; (c) the relative burden of defense and prosecution in California rather than at some other place; (d) the ease of access to some alternative forum; (e) the extent to which the cause of action arises out of Regie's local activities. Fisher Governor Co. v. Superior Court, 53 Cal.2d 222, 225–226, 1 Cal.Rptr. 1.

As regards 'fair play' it is obvious that if California rejects jurisdiction, Regie may successfully bar plaintiff and cross-complainant from access to the courts of all states of the Union, including New York. Cannon Manufacturing Co. v. Cudahy Co., 267 U.S. 333, 45 S.Ct. 250, 69 L.Ed. 634; see also Fisher Governor Co. v. Superior Court, supra. Regie's argument would, in effect, confine the claimants to the courts of the Republic of France. Fairness to Regie does not entail this disadvantage to the claimants.

Renault, Inc., whether regarded as an individual corporate entity or as alter ego of Regie, is simply a medium through which the latter establishes its business contacts with the California public. As to the mechanics of process serving, Regie has received process via the California Secretary of State without reference to the 'presence' of Renault as its purported agent in California. Thus there is no point in deciding whether to respect the separate status of Renault or to regard it as merely the alter ego of Regie."

The order to show cause is discharged and the petition is denied.

VELANDRA v. REGIE NATIONALE DES USINES RENAULT

United States Court of Appeals, Sixth Circuit, 1964.
336 F.2d 292.

[Plaintiffs brought a diversity action in a district court in Michigan, based upon allegations of negligence and breach of warranty by the two corporations involved in Regie Nationale des Usines Renault v. Superior Court, p. 736, supra. The injury resulted from faulty brakes in a Renault automobile which plaintiffs had purchased in Ohio. Service of process was made upon the Michigan Secretary of State, who in turn notified the defendants. The District Court dismissed the complaints after finding that it lacked jurisdiction over the defendants. The Court of Appeals affirmed in this opinion by JUDGE WILSON, excerpts from which follow:]

Some argument has been devoted to the question whether, under the principle of Erie R. Co. v. Tompkins, state law rather than federal law governs the personal jurisdiction of a federal court over foreign corporations in diversity cases. This vexing question remains a source of controversy in other jurisdictions, but was recently resolved in favor of state law by this Court. In determining the personal jurisdiction of a federal court located in Michigan over these foreign corporations, this Court must therefore look to the law of Michigan.[5]

5. The Court may observe, incidentally, that some question might have been raised as to whether Regie, as the corporation of a foreign nation rather than a foreign state, should be treated differently than Renault. In a recent article Professor Elliott E. Cheatham has observed as follows:

"In this country, the principles of conflict of laws developed primarily in interstate matters. . . . When international cases came up, the principles developed in the *intra*national cases were transferred almost unquestionably to the *inter*national matters." [Cheatham, Some Developments in Conflict of Laws, 17 Vand.L.Rev. 193, 200 (1963).]

Professor Cheatham goes on to approve this practice, however. After having noted that the case of McGee v. International Life Ins. Co., 355 U.S. 220, 222–223, 78 S.Ct. 199, 2 L.Ed.2d 223 (1957) had explained recent expansions in state court jurisdiction in terms of "the fundamental transformation for our national economy over the years," "increasing nationalization of commerce," and "modern transportation and communication," which make it "less burdensome for a party sued to defend himself in a State where he engages in economic activity," [Cheatham, Some Developments in Conflict of Laws, 17 Vand.L.Rev. 193, 195 (1963).] Professor Cheatham declares that the practice of applying interstate principles to international problems "is fortunate in these days of expanding international relations." Ibid., 200.

On another point, Professor Cheatham refers to "the question whether international conflict of laws is governed by state law or by federal law," and states as follows:

"It has been widely assumed that except for treaties and federal statutes it is governed by state law, thus varying from state to state. . . . The question cannot be answered yet." [Ibid., 200–201.]

The law of Michigan in this regard may be found in the case of Jennings v. WSM, Inc., where the Supreme Court of Michigan confirmed its adherence to the rule of the landmark case of International Shoe Company v. Washington. . . .

. . . The existence or nonexistence of the necessary "minimum contacts" to justify the upholding of personal jurisdiction over foreign corporations under the Fourteenth Amendment as interpreted in the International Shoe Company case must obviously be worked out with reference to the facts of a particular case rather than in a statement of dogmatic rules of all-inclusive principles. . . .

Regie is a French corporate manufacturer of Renault automobiles.[6] Regie exports its automobiles into the United States through Renault, a New York corporation which is a wholly owned subsidiary of Regie and the exclusive American importer of Renault automobiles. Renault in turn distributes these automobiles to dealers throughout the United States by means of regional distributors, one of which at the time of the commencement of these suits was Renault Great Lakes, Inc. (Great Lakes), an Illinois corporation which is wholly owned by Renault, and which is the Renault distributor for the midwestern region of the United States, including the State of Michigan. Great Lakes carries on substantial economic activities in Michigan, among other things locating and granting franchises to Michigan dealers, and delivering to those dealers the automobiles it has purchased from Renault. The only evidence put into the record with regard to the volume of sales of Renault automobiles in Michigan is that there are three dealers in Detroit, one of whom sells a "substantial" number of Renaults, resulting in gross sales "upward" of $100,000.00. There is also evidence that at the time of a dealer retail sale to an individual in Michigan, an express written warranty in Regie's name is delivered to the purchaser.

Do the above facts establish such "minimum contacts" with the State of Michigan as to satisfy "traditional notions of fair play" so as to properly subject the defendant foreign corporation to the personal jurisdiction of the courts of Michigan?

Considering first the chain of corporate ownership, Regie owns 100% of the stock of Renault, and Renault in turn owns 100% of the stock of Great Lakes, which, as indicated, carries on substantial economic activities within the State of Michigan. However, the mere ownership by a corporation of all of the stock of a subsidiary ame-

Because the parties have raised no question as to the foregoing matters, and in view of the Professor Cheatham's comments thereon, the Court mentions these matters only in passing, and will proceed to apply the law of Michigan to Regie as well as to Renault.

6. The defendants have emphasized that Regie is not a private corporation, but rather is

"An instrumentality of the Government of the Republic of France under the direction of a President General Manager appointed by the French Government, and controlled by a board of directors some of whom are appointed by the Executive Department of the French Government and some of whom represent the financial and business community of France and the users of Renault's products."

The defendants have advanced no argument, however, that Regie should be treated differently than a private corporation for purposes of passing upon its amenability to the jurisdiction of the District Court.

Compare Restatement, Foreign Relations Law of the United States, sec. 72 (1962), with Cheatham, Some Developments in Conflict of Laws, 17 Vand.L.Rev. 193, 200 (1963):

"[T]he great increase of commercial activities by foreign nations and national agencies requires modification of the old principle that a foreign nation is immune from judicial jurisdiction."

nable to the jurisdiction of the courts of a state may not *alone* be sufficient to justify holding the parent corporation likewise amenable. In the early case of Cannon Mfg. Co. v. Cudahy Packing Co., the Supreme Court held that the activities of a subsidiary did not subject its parent corporation to the personal jurisdiction of local courts.

It should be noted that the ruling of the Cannon case, if not qualified by the subsequent ruling in the International Shoe Company case, has been at least qualified in later cases holding foreign corporations amenable to the personal jurisdiction of local courts because of the local activities of subsidiary corporations upon the theory that the corporate separation is fictitious,[7] or that the parent has held the subsidiary out as its agent, or, more vaguely, that the parent has exercised an undue degree of control over the subsidiary.

Unfortunately, such reasoning in these and similar cases, fails to explain the decisions of the courts adequately. Thus the law relating to the fictions of agency and of separate corporate entity was developed for purposes other than determining amenability to personal jurisdiction, and the law of such amenability is merely confused by reference to these inapposite matters.

The International Shoe decision represented an effort by the Supreme Court to clarify earlier concepts in the area of amenability of foreign corporations to the personal jurisdiction of state courts by sweeping aside any lingering notions that the earlier shibboleths of "consent," "presence," and "doing business" were self-defining abstractions, and by redefining those tests in terms of "minimum contacts." Following this decision it would seem appropriate, for the purpose of determining the amenability to jurisdiction of a foreign corporation which happens to own a subsidiary corporation carrying on local activities, to inquire whether the parent has the requisite minimum contacts with the State of the forum. Thus the ownership of the subsidiary carrying on local activities in Michigan represents merely one contact or factor to be considered in assessing the existence or non-existence of the requisite minimum contacts with the State of Michigan,[8] but is not sufficient of itself to hold the present foreign corporations amenable to personal jurisdiction.

Another contact alleged to exist between the defendant and the State of Michigan is the sale of the defendant's product, Renault automobiles, within the State of Michigan and the delivery within the State of a warranty thereon, to which warranty the defendant Regie is a party. It is proper to note that it has come to be increasingly recognized that activities—in particular sales of products—outside a

7. See, e. g., Intermountain Ford Tractor Sales Co. v. Massey-Ferguson Limited (C.D.Utah, 1962), 210 F.Supp. 930. The plaintiffs in the present case allege a fictitious corporate separation between Renault and Regie, but the record contains no evidence whatever that would justify the piercing of corporate veils, or the disregarding of corporate entities, under the principles traditionally associated with these matters.

8. The degree or extent of the ownership of such a subsidiary may also be important in assessing the nature and quality of the requisite minimum contacts of a parent corporation with a state in which its subsidiary is carrying on local activities. The parent might, for example, own only 99% or 51% or a minority but nevertheless controlling interest in the subsidiary, or the ownership might be divided in various proportions between two or more related or unrelated corporations, or between one or more corporations and one or more individuals, and so on. The point is, of course, that an analytical rather than a mechanical or formalistic approach is appropriate upon the issue of personal jurisdiction based upon ownership of the stock of a corporation carrying on local activities.

state resulting in consequences within the state may subject the actors to the personal jurisdiction of the courts within the state. In this regard the plaintiff relies strongly upon the case of Regie Nationale des Usines Renault v. The Superior Court of the State of California, 208 Cal.App.2d 702, 25 Cal.Rptr. 530, wherein the Court held these same defendants to be subject to the personal jurisdiction of a court in California under somewhat analogous circumstances. While the legal principles there enunciated as distinguished from the factual situation there before the Court, may be relevant to a resolution of the legal issues of "minimum contact" and "fair play" in this case, under the facts as they appear in the record of this case we are of the opinion that no sufficient showing has been made with reference to sales of the defendant's products within Michigan to establish such minimum contacts within the State, as to warrant subjecting the defendants to the personal jurisdiction of a court in Michigan. In determining whether minimum contacts exist on the basis of the presence or sale of a product within a state, the extent of the contact is related to a number of factors, including the number and value of sales within the state, their ratio to the total market for like or similar products within the state, the quantity or value of the defendant's production, the percentage of the total output sold within the state, as well as the nature of the product, particularly with reference to whether it is inherently dangerous or not. Obviously the manufacturer of a product that has a significant market within a state has more contact with that state than one whose product only has a minimal market. Likewise, a manufacturer whose total product or a large percentage of whose product is sold within a state has a more significant contact with that state than would be the case where only casual sales were made within the state or only a small portion of the manufacturer's production was sold within the state. Finally, the nature of the product may well have a bearing upon the issue of minimum contact, with a lesser volume of inherently dangerous products constituting a more significant contact with the state than would a larger volume of products offering little or no hazard to the inhabitants of the state. A careful and discriminating analysis of the nature and quality of the defendants' contacts with the foreign state must be made in each case.

All that appears in the record in this case is that three dealers for the sale of Renault automobiles exist in the City of Detroit and that one of these sells a "substantial" number of Renault automobiles, having gross sales of "upwards" of $100,000. This record of dealerships and sales, even when considered together with the existence of a subsidiary corporation doing business within the State and the distribution of warranties with automobiles sold, does not in our opinion establish a sufficient showing of contacts between the defendants and the State of Michigan so as to constitute the minimum contacts essential to permit the exercise of personal jurisdiction in that State over these foreign corporations under the International Shoe Company case.

The judgment of the Trial Court is therefore affirmed.

COMMENT

Although the opinion is not clear, it appears that the test applied by the court was whether defendant was "doing business" in Michigan. Apparently certain amendments to the Michigan statutes became effective on January 1, 1963, after commencement of these proceedings. Thus Mich.C.L.A. 600.715, now makes clear that certain "relationships between a corporation or its agent and the state shall constitute a sufficient basis of jurisdiction to enable the courts . . . to exercise limited personal jurisdiction over such corporation and to enable such courts to render personal judgments against such corporation arising out of the act or acts which create any of the following relationships: (1) The transaction of any business within the state (2) The doing or causing any act to be done, or consequences to occur, in the state resulting in an action for tort. . . ."

Note fn. 5 in the opinion. The question whether federal or state standards should govern adjudicatory jurisdiction over alien defendants can be equally pertinent to actions in the state courts. Compare Bergman v. De Sièyes, p. 549, supra.

TACA INTERNATIONAL AIRLINES, S.A. v. ROLLS–ROYCE OF ENGLAND, LTD.

New York Court of Appeals, 1965.
15 N.Y.2d 97, 204 N.E.2d 329, 256 N.Y.S.2d 129.

[Taca, an El Salvador corporation, sued Rolls-Royce of England Ltd. ("Ltd."), an English company, for damage resulting from a crash of its airplane in Nicaragua that was allegedly caused by Ltd.'s negligence in the manufacture of airplane engines. Ltd. owned all the stock of Rolls-Royce of Canada, Ltd., which in turn owned all the stock of Rolls-Royce, Inc. ("Inc."), a Delaware corporation authorized to do business in and with an office in New York. Ltd. had no officers in New York and was not authorized to do business there. Service of summons upon Ltd. was made by delivering the summons in New York to Inc. and to one Thomson. The trial court granted Ltd.'s motion to set aside the service of summons on ground that there was no basis for the court to assert in personam jurisdiction over it. The Appellate Division reversed and the Court of Appeals in an opinon by CHIEF JUDGE DESMOND affirmed the Appellate Division. The opinion stated in part:]

The Appellate Division's majority opinion contains this accurate summary of the undisputed facts:

". . . The business of Rolls-Royce, Inc., is solely in the sale of products manufactured by Rolls-Royce, Ltd., and the servicing of the purchasers of these products. The three mentioned companies have some directors in common and key executive personnel in Rolls-Royce, Inc., were former executives of either the English or Canadian company and were assigned to their positions by the parent English company. There are frequent conferences among executives of the three companies at which the policies of Rolls-Royce, Inc., are determined. Rolls-Royce, Inc., employees who require technical training are given it by Rolls-Royce, Ltd., in England. All sales literature used by Rolls-Royce, Inc., is written and published by Rolls-Royce, Ltd.

"Rolls-Royce, Inc., gets its income in several ways. It owns no automobiles, and when a sale is made to a customer it buys a car from Rolls-Royce, Ltd., in England and imports it. The sale is at a fixed price which is lower than the price to the ultimate purchaser. Rolls-Royce, Ltd., gives a warranty directly to the purchaser which Rolls-Royce, Inc., delivers with the car. Rolls-Royce, Ltd., pays Rolls-Royce, Inc., a fixed annual fee for services rendered to customers in connection with these warranties. As to airplane engines, the compensation for service is paid by Rolls-Royce of Canada and this payment is measured by the price of the spare parts sold by Rolls-Royce, Inc.

"All of the net income of Rolls-Royce, Inc., goes to Rolls-Royce of Canada and appears in that company's balance sheet. As affected by the other operations of the Canadian company it then appears in the balance sheet of Rolls-Royce, Ltd."

To that statement we add a few other items of fact. Rolls-Royce's manufacturing in England, plus the distribution, sales and servicing of its famous automobiles and aero engines throughout the world, is carried out by the English parent company and 16 subsidiaries, including those in Canada and the United States. These scattered subsidiary companies are all wholly owned by the English corporation, all are set up like the English company in auto and aero divisions, all are controlled from England, all are in major part staffed from England and important policies are arrived at in frequent conferences in England, New York and elsewhere attended by various officials of the various corporations. One of the active American administrators is Thomson who was here served with this summons. Inc. sells some aero engines but such transactions are usually handled from England or Canada. Inc. does sell autos and does perform on aero engines the operations required by Rolls-Royce warranties. The latter services are paid for to Inc. by Ltd. and Canada, Ltd. Inc. sells in the United States about $6,000,000 worth a year of Rolls-Royce autos and auto parts. The principal personnel of Inc. or most of them are former Ltd. employees and key employees are exchanged both ways between New York and England and considered part of the Rolls-Royce employee "group". All operations of Inc. are reported to Ltd. and Canada, Ltd., and all American business appears in the consolidated earnings statements and profit and loss statements of Ltd. Personnel of Inc. are trained by Ltd. in England. As against all this appellant Ltd. points to these facts only: that Thomson, who was actually served, was not an employee or officer of Ltd.; that Ltd. has no office, officer, bank account or telephone or directory listing in New York; that Ltd. and Inc. have entered into contracts whereby the latter gets a fixed percentage on its sales of cars and parts and is compensated for other services to Rolls-Royce customers.

Decision of this appeal does not require us to decide whether, under modern Federal and New York law, Ltd., treated as a corporation separate from Inc. has substantial enough contacts with our State to allow our State to subject Ltd. to a judgment in personam . . . . Our question is more nearly a factual one: was Inc. a really independent entity or a mere department of Ltd.? If the latter, then obviously Ltd. was doing extensive business in our State through its local department separately incorporated as Inc. The affirmative answer is compelled by our 1951 case of Rabinowitz v. Kaiser-Frazer Corp., 302 N.Y. 892, 100 N.E.2d 177, supra, decided on facts remarkably similar to those before us in the present case. . . .

NOTE ON SOME NEW YORK CASES ON JURISDICTION OVER ALIEN CORPORATIONS

Out of the large and growing body of case law involving assertions of jurisdiction over aliens, we here select some from New York, the prime overseas trading center. From within that body of law we consider a strand of cases that deal with a subject related to the TACA case: issues posed by actions against alien corporations either having affiliates in New York or selling through distributors (who may or may not be affiliated) in New York.[9] These cases, several of which are based upon events occurring outside New York, must be read in the light of the New York Civil Practice Law and Rules (CPLR), effective on September 1, 1963, which has two relevant sections. Section 301 provides that a court may continue to "exercise such jurisdiction . . . as might have been exercised heretofore." Section 302 is a "long arm" provision stating that a court may exercise in personam jurisdiction, as to a cause of action arising from one or several enumerated acts, over a person who (*1*) transacts any business in New York; (*2*) commits a tortious act there; (*3*) commits a tortious act without New York causing injury within the state, if he (i) regularly does business or derives substantial revenue in the state or (ii) "should reasonably expect" the act to have consequences in the state and derives substantial revenue from interstate or international commerce; or (*4*) owns real property in New York. Note that (*3*) was added by a provision effective September 1, 1966. Section 301 carries forward the result in the TACA case. Like results can be achieved under several of the subdivisions of 302.[10]

In 1967 the Court of Appeals decided two cases construing the CPLR provisions. Frummer v. Hilton Hotels International, 19 N.Y. 2d 533, 281 N.Y.S.2d 41, 227 N.E.2d 851, remittitur amended 20 N.Y. 2d 737, 283 N.Y.S.2d 99, 229 N.E.2d 696, held that Hilton Hotels (U.K.) Ltd., a British subsidiary of Hilton Hotels Corporation (a Delaware corporation), was subject to suit in New York in an action based upon injury sustained in a fall in the London Hilton. The court concluded that, no matter where the events occurred giving rise to the action, jurisdiction was properly asserted over Hilton (U.K.) because it was " 'doing business' here in the traditional sense". It cited CPLR § 301. The court stressed that "this appeal deals with the jurisdiction of our courts over a foreign corporation rather than the liability of a parent company for acts of a wholly owned subsidiary." Hilton (U.K.) owned the London Hilton, but it benefited from the services of the Hilton Reservation Service, which had a New York office and generated business for all Hilton hotels, performed public relations work and accepted and confirmed reservations (as for the London Hilton). The court observed that this Service, which was also owned by Hilton Hotels Corporation, "does all the business which Hilton (U.K.) could do were it here by its own officials."

9. These New York cases are discussed in Wellborn, Subsidiary Corporations in New York: When is Mere Ownership Enough to Establish Jurisdiction over the Parent, 22 Buffalo L.Rev. 681 (1973).

10. The number of cases involving foreign defendants arising under similar "long-arm" statutes grows apace. See, e. g., Duple Motor Bodies, Ltd. v. Hollingsworth, 417 F.2d 231 (9th Cir. 1968); Blum v. Kawaguchi, Ltd., 331 F.Supp. 216 (D.Neb.1971); Reilly v. P. J. Wolff & Sohne, 374 F.Supp. 775 (D.N.J.1974); Products Promotions v. Cousteau, 495 F.2d 483 (5th Cir. 1974).

Public Administrator v. Royal Bank of Canada, 19 N.Y.2d 127, 278 N.Y.S.2d 378, 224 N.E.2d 877 (1967), involved an action by the Public Administrator of the county of New York against the Royal Bank of Canada, which concededly did business in New York through its branch there. But the action was also against the Royal Bank of Canada (France), a separately incorporated French entity wholly owned by the Royal Bank of Canada. Royal Bank of Canada was found to treat the French corporation (the only one of its 1,145 branches in 22 countries to be separately incorporated) not as a separate entity, but as a fully integrated arm of its operations. The French corporation's assets and liabilities were treated as the parent's; its advertising, legal forms and personnel were all centrally controlled. The court concluded that, no matter where relevant events occurred, the Royal Bank of Canada (France) and its parent "are one and the same corporation" and held both liable to suit in New York.

By 1972, in Beja v. Jahangiri, 453 F.2d 959, 962, the Court of Appeals of the Second Circuit noted that "the New York Court of Appeals has sustained *in personam* jurisdiction . . . over foreign corporations each time it has considered the issue in the past decade." New York has "gone very far" in the direction of extending its jurisdiction over foreign corporations "to the fullest constitutional reach."

Within a fortnight Delagi v. Volkswagenwerk A.G., 29 N.Y.2d 426, 328 N.Y.S.2d 653, 278 N.E.2d 895 (1972), broke the sequence of cases. Plaintiff, in an action for negligence and breach of warranty, alleged that he purchased a Volkswagen from an authorized dealer in Germany and suffered injury from a defect-caused accident while driving the car in Germany. The German corporation, defendant, exported vehicles to a wholly owned subsidiary, Volkswagen of America, Inc., a New Jersey corporation, which in turn resold cars to fourteen wholesale distributors franchised but not owned by Volkswagen. The distributors took title to the cars on delivery here, and reshipped them to local independent franchised dealers in New York and elsewhere. The independent franchised dealer in New York was World-Wide Volkswagen Corp., wholly owned by U. S. investors. The court found that since there was no parent-subsidiary relation between either the German or the New Jersey corporations *and* World-Wide, the German parent (Volkswagen A.G.) was not subject to jurisdiction. It had no place of business in New York. The court limited cases in which the corporate parents were to be found present in New York to those in which the relationship gave rise to a valid inference of "an agency relationship," or in which control by the parent was "so complete that the subsidiary is, in fact, merely a department of the parent." Advertising in New York by Volkswagen of America, Inc., even if imputed to its German parent, was "mere solicitation" that did not produce a different result.

In Sunrise Toyota, Ltd. v. Toyota Motor Co., 55 F.R.D. 519 (S.D. N.Y.1972), an action under the antitrust laws and in state contract and tort claims, the judge combined these cases to hold a Japanese manufacturer subject to process under Section 301 because it wholly owned a New York distributor corporation, which it also controlled closely and held out as being part of its "network". The American distributor was found to operate as an agent of the Japanese parent, which was thus "doing business" in New York through its agent.

QUESTIONS

(1) Are different considerations presented when the Wisconsin statute is used in a tort action to assert jurisdiction over a manufacturer whose products have been distributed in Wisconsin but which conducts its business exclusively in (a) Florida, (b) Quebec, or (c) Milan?

(2) Whether or not the reasoning of the Cannon decision, p. 732, supra, is persuasive today in an interstate setting, are there stronger arguments on the international plane for holding that an adequately financed and independently managed subsidiary does not confer jurisdiction in an action against its alien parent? Distinguish between (a) an action related to the state (cf. Velandra), and (b) an unrelated action (cf. Taca).

(3) Assume that Renault, Inc. had branches in California and Michigan which maintained service departments for Renault cars. Inc. has a modest capitalization, with the minimum assets necessary to finance its selling and repairing activities. Plaintiff, a Michigan resident, had his Renault car repaired at a branch. He alleges that a later car accident in Michigan resulted from negligent repair, and he brings an action against Regie seeking sizeable damages, in excess of Inc.'s total assets.

> (*a*) What arguments would plaintiff make in support of the state or federal court's jurisdiction?
>
> (*b*) Assuming that the court will take jurisdiction and that the repairs were indeed negligently made, are additional facts relevant in deciding whether Regie should be liable for Inc.'s torts?
>
> (*c*) Assuming that the court renders a judgment against Regie, what legal principles should plaintiff examine in order to ascertain how useful the judgment will be to him?

(4) Futuria, an Italian partnership specializing in problems of industrial efficiency, sends an employee to Wisconsin at the request of plaintiff, a Wisconsin manufacturing corporation. One year later, Futuria and plaintiff conclude by mail a contract under which Futuria is to prepare plans for modifications of plaintiff's operations. Futuria fails to perform. Plaintiff brings an action for breach of contract in a federal district court in Wisconsin, with notice served upon an Italian partner in Rome under F.R.C.P. 4(i). What result? What additional facts might be relevant to the decision?

(5) If the contract related to proposed operations of plaintiff in Italy, would your answer be different? Why?

(6) To what extent do you think the considerations suggested by these problems affect the way in which a foreign corporation plans the structure for its transnational activities involving the United States? Consider, for example, the considerations put to such a corporation by the New York decisions in the preceding Note.

NOTE ON ADJUDICATORY JURISDICTION IN FEDERAL CAUSES OF ACTION

Different questions are posed when federal courts entertain *federal* causes of action brought by private parties or the United States. This Note examines the jurisdictional bases for such actions.

For present purposes, one can divide the actions into two broad groups: suits under federal statutes which contain no special "jurisdictional" or "venue" provisions, and suits under statutes with such provisions. With respect to the first group, there is some controversy whether a federal court can develop independent federal bases for jurisdiction, analogous to the long-arm provisions in state statutes, or whether it is held to statutory provisions of the state in which the district court sits. A related question is whether the political unit to which defendant's conduct should be related is the United States or the state in which the federal court sits. If the relevant test is "doing business," should inquiry be directed to the defendant's activities in that state, or generally in the United States?

A typical, fairly simple, case in the first group is Lone Star Package Car Co., Inc. v. Baltimore & O. R. Co., 212 F.2d 147 (5th Cir. 1954). A party sued under the Interstate Commerce Act, and the court held that it would apply a federal jurisdictional test rather than the Texas standard. Comparable but more complex problems arise in suits to enforce liabilities for taxes.[11] They can even occur in admiralty actions.[12] Whatever the outcome may be as to the power of a federal court to develop independent federal tests of jurisdiction, it is clear that a federal court may go as far as state law, including any relevant long arm statute, will permit. Note that F.R.C.P. 4 applies to such actions as well as to diversity cases.

The second group includes a number of federal statutes which state the judicial district in which an action can be brought *and* the means for service of process. The courts have generally read such statutes to establish independent "jurisdictional" bases which make unnecessary any recourse to state law. For example, Section 22(a) of the Securities Act of 1933, 48 Stat. 86, as amended, 15 U.S.C.A. § 77v(a), confers jurisdiction on federal district courts over suits to enforce any liability or duty under the act. "Any such suit . . . may be brought in the district wherein the defendant is found or is an inhabitant or transacts business, or in the district where the offer or sale took place, if the defendant participated therein, and process in such cases may be served in any other district of which the defendant is an inhabitant or wherever the defendant may be found." Note that this statute has its built-in "long arm" provisions, permitting the

11. See, e. g. United States v. Montreal Trust Co., 358 F.2d 239 (2d Cir. 1966); United States v. First National City Bank, 379 U.S. 378, 85 S.Ct. 528, 13 L.Ed.2d 365 (1965).

12. Scott v. Middle East Airlines Co., S.A., 240 F.Supp. 1 (S.D.N.Y.1965).

court to assert jurisdiction even when an alien defendant is not in any sense "present" within the United States. Under F.R.C.P. 4(i), a federal court with jurisdiction under this section could effect service outside the United States.[13]

The most important federal cases have involved Section 12 of the Clayton Act, 38 Stat. 736 (1914), 15 U.S.C.A. § 22. It provides that any suit under the antitrust laws against a corporation "may be brought not only in the judicial district whereof it is an inhabitant, but also in any district wherein it may be found or transacts business; and all process in such cases may be served in the district of which it is an inhabitant, or wherever it may be found." The decisions have expansively interpreted the words "found" and "transacts business." Thus courts have asserted jurisdiction over alien parents or subsidiaries of domestic corporation by, in effect, cutting through the distinct corporate structures and treating the alien company as transacting business or otherwise present in this country. To be sure, the cases described at pp. 742–746, supra, indicate that the principle of the Cannon case is no longer sacrosanct in private-party litigation under state law. But the distinctive aspect of the antitrust cases, which were earlier in time, is their stress upon the relevance of antitrust policy, of the substantive claims asserted by the government, to resolution of the jurisdictional issues. The courts read the statutory terms broadly to vindicate the underlying purposes of the antitrust laws. Whether proceeding upon an agency or other rationale for finding the alien defendant present in the United States, they viewed companies affiliated by stock holdings, or perhaps by extensive contractual arrangements, as part of one general business enterprise. They thereby drew the alien parent, subsidiary or perhaps contracting party into the United States for jurisdictional purposes.[14]

---

2. ADJUDICATORY JURISDICTION IN SOME EUROPEAN COUNTRIES

There appear below brief and selective summaries of jurisdictional principles in England, France and Germany. They treat almost exclusively those kinds of actions which, in the United States, would be considered *in personam*. We include them for three purposes: (a) to view within a comparative framework the jurisdictional bases employed in the United States; (b) to illustrate the sensitivity to reciprocal treatment which American courts will evidence in deter-

13. See SEC v. VTR, Inc., 39 F.R.D. 19 (S.D.N.Y.1966). Cf. Kane v. Central American Mining & Oil, Inc., 235 F. Supp. 559 (S.D.N.Y.1964).

14. The leading case is United States v. Scophony Corp. of America, 333 U.S. 795, 68 S.Ct. 855, 92 L.Ed. 1091 (1948). For excerpts from and discussion of Scophony and other important decisions, see Ebb, Regulation and Protection of International Business 218–246 (1964). See also Brewster, Antitrust and American Business Abroad 54–61 (1958). The authorities are reviewed in Hoffman Motors Corp. v. Alfa Romeo S.p.A., 244 F. Supp. 70 (S.D.N.Y.1965).

mining the jurisdictional reach they will assert; and (c) to provide background for those cases in Part B which deal with enforcement in one country of judgments rendered in another on a jurisdictional basis different from any recognized by the court in which enforcement is sought.

It is to be expected that more American courts will make comparative surveys of the type undertaken by Judge Breitel, dissenting in Frummer v. Hilton Hotels International, Inc., p. 744, supra:

> Nor in private international law can there be found in this or other countries a jurisdictional reach as extensive as this.
>
> It is well established in this country that a foreign parent corporation will not be subjected to the judicial jurisdiction of a State merely because of its ownership of a subsidiary corporation doing business within the State, if the parent diligently maintains the formal separateness of the subsidiary entity . . . .
>
> Similarly, courts in the United Kingdom evidently will not assert jurisdiction over a foreign corporation merely because it maintains a subsidiary in Britain (see The World Harmony [Konstantinidis v. World Tankers Corp.], [1965] 2 All E.R. 139, 147, 149). Liberal Canadian jurisdictional statutes likewise do not recognize such a basis of jurisdiction (Ontario Rules of Practice, rule 25[1]; Quebec Code of Civ.Pro., art. 94). The same is probably true in Australia (see Cowen, American-Australian Private International Law [1957], p. 38).
>
> In Civil Law and other code countries the recognized bases of personal jurisdiction over foreign corporations admits of the assertion of such jurisdiction only on the existence of a specially designated office, situs of headquarters, or what is described as "domicile" in a special sense (see Seidl-Hohenveldern, American-Austrian Private International Law [1963], p. 99; Garland, American-Brazilian Private International Law [1959], pp. 85–86; Philip, American-Danish Private International Law [1957], p. 20; Delaume, American-French Private International Law [2d ed., 1961], pp. 142–143; Kollewijn, American-Dutch Private International Law [1955], pp. 59–60; Lombard, American-Venezuelan Private International Law [1965], pp. 71–72). In some countries it has been held that a foreign corporation is not subject to personal jurisdiction even if it maintains branches in the country, through which it actually does business (see Cappelletti & Perillo, Civil Procedure in Italy [1965], pp. 92–93; cf. Etcheberry O., American-Chilean Private International Law [1960], pp. 29–30 [jurisdiction to tax]).
>
> These are striking limitations in the code countries. They suggest very strongly that the extension of personal jurisdiction projected in this case would hardly be tolerated. The influence in the code countries of domiciliary jurisdiction (in the Anglo-American sense) is much too great, and the equivalent "presence" doctrine much more restrictive than here. There is not the slightest suggestion in these materials that a formally separate foreign corporation

could be brought before a foreign forum because of some intercorporate relationship, however intimate, with a local corporation.

These limitations elsewhere, and in the past, bespeak caution for the future, and especially when one considers the salutary purposes served by permitting enterprises to limit and segregate their activities as they are extended into other and frequently less developed parts of the world. Of great significance, of course, is what was also mentioned earlier, that harmful extensions of doctrine in this area will easily lend themselves to reciprocal manipulation against American enterprises operating through subsidiaries or affiliates in other countries.

(a) England [15]

In England, as in the United States, the general principle obtained at common law that a court could entertain an in personam action only if the defendant were personally served within the jurisdiction. Even domicile appeared insufficient at common law to found jurisdiction over an absent defendant. Doctrines did develop as to corporate "presence." Such presence could be established through local agents of the corporation. The "presence" requirement has become increasingly identified with the local "transaction of business" by the corporation.

Service of a writ of summons can be made abroad only as permitted by statute. Order 11 of the Rules of the Supreme Court of Judicature, [1962] 3 Stat.Instr. 2529, 2552 (No. 2145), empowers courts to permit service of the writ of summons on an absent defendant under stated conditions. Order 11 is permissive and discretionary. Unlike United States long-arm statutes, it requires plaintiffs to obtain authorization from a court before they can use these special rules. Excerpts from Order 11, as amended in minor respects in 1962, appear below:

Principal cases in which service of writ out of jurisdiction is permissible

1. —(1) Subject to [certain other provisions], service of a writ, or notice of a writ, out of the jurisdiction is permissible with the leave of the Court in the following cases, that is to say— . . .

(*c*) if in the action begun by the writ relief is sought against a person domiciled or ordinarily resident within the jurisdiction;

. . .

(*f*) if the action begun by the writ is brought against a defendant not domiciled or ordinarily resident in Scotland to enforce, rescind, dissolve, annul or otherwise affect a contract, or to recover damages or obtain other relief in respect of the breach of a contract, being (in either case) a contract which—

(i) was made within the jurisdiction, or

15. The following summary is based upon Cheshire, Private International Law, 77–97 (9th ed. 1974).

(ii) was made by or through an agent trading or residing within the jurisdiction on behalf of a principal trading or residing out of the jurisdiction, or

(iii) is by its terms, or by implication, governed by English law;

(*g*) if the action begun by the writ is brought against a defendant not domiciled or ordinarily resident in Scotland or Northern Ireland, in respect of a breach committed within the jurisdiction of a contract made within or out of the jurisdiction, and irrespective of the fact, if such be the case, that the breach was preceded or accompanied by a breach committed out of the jurisdiction that rendered impossible the performance of so much of the contract as ought to have been performed within the jurisdiction;

(*h*) if the action begun by the writ is founded on a tort committed within the jurisdiction . . . . .

. . .

Application for, and grant of, leave to serve writ out of jurisdiction

4. —(*1*) An application for the grant of leave under rule 1 or 2 must be supported by an affidavit stating the grounds on which the application is made and that, in the deponent's belief, the plaintiff has a good cause of action, and showing in what place or country the defendant is, or probably may be found.

(*2*) No such leave shall be granted unless it shall be made sufficiently to appear to the Court that the case is a proper one for service out of the jurisdiction under this Order.

A judgment based on Rule 11 was at issue in Somportex Ltd. v. Philadelphia Chewing Gum Corp., p. 783, infra.

(b) France [16]

Radically different principles obtain in France. The only Code provisions specifically treating the international jurisdiction of French courts are Articles 14 and 15 of the Civil Code.

Article 14 states that an "alien, even one not residing in France, may be summoned *(cité)* before the French courts for the fulfillment of obligations contracted by him in France with a French person; he may be brought *(traduit)* before the French courts for obligations contracted by him in a foreign country towards French persons."

Article 15 states that a "Frenchman may be called before a French court for obligations contracted by him in a foreign country even towards an alien."

French courts have given an expansive interpretation to these sections. The term "obligation" has been construed to refer not only to contractual situations but also to torts, matrimonial matters, and other legal duties. Jurisdiction under Article 14 depends exclusively

16. The following summary is based upon 2 Batiffol, Droit International Privé (5th ed., Lagarde, 1970).

upon the French nationality of the plaintiff. The defendant need not be domiciled, resident or present in France; indeed, as indicated by the second clause of Article 14, there need not be *any* relationship between the "obligations" sued upon and France. All relevant events might have occurred in a foreign country. There are some exceptions to the coverage of Article 14, such as actions relating to real property located in a foreign country. A French national can invoke Article 14 before a French court even if he is not domiciled or resident in France. Indeed the French plaintiff need not have been a party to the instrument on which suit is brought, if (for example) a promissory note made by a foreigner (defendant) had been negotiated to a Frenchman by the initial foreign payee.

Article 14 covers legal as well as natural persons. French nationality is generally attributed to corporations with their principal office (*siège social*) in France, although recent cases have raised questions of the "nationality" of such corporations if they are controlled from abroad.[17]

Many and sharp criticisms have been directed towards Article 14.[18] French commentators and courts justifying Article 14 stressed the high quality of justice which France affords its nationals, the importance of the availability of French courts to French plaintiffs to assure such treatment, and the difficulty in concluding that all other legal systems afford as high a quality of fairness. More recently, they have emphasized its need because of the absence from French law of an equivalent to quasi-in-rem jurisdiction. Note that both such jurisdictional bases empower a court to try a totally unrelated cause of action involving a foreign and absent defendant.

The effect of Article 15 is to enable a foreigner to sue an absent French national without domicile or residence in France before a French court—even if (1) the foreigner is neither domiciled nor resident in France, and (2) the cause of action sued upon is unrelated to France.[19]

In some situations, French courts refuse to exercise jurisdiction on the basis of Articles 14 or 15. They will give effect to waivers of the French forum provided by these Articles, but under important qualifications. (1) Under Article 14, the choice of forum is, and consequently the waiver must be, the plaintiff's. (2) Under Article 15, waiver by both parties may be necessary. Explicit contractual waivers have been given effect, although the complex case law has drawn subtle distinctions. Waiver by defendant of "rights" under Article 15 is crucial when French courts are asked to enforce a foreign judgment against the defendant.

17. Recall the data at p. 97, supra on the concept of *siège social* under French law.

18. See, e. g., Nadelmann, "Jurisdictionally Improper Fora" in Nadelmann, von Mehren and Hazard (eds.), XXth Century Comparative and Conflicts Law 321 (1961).

19. The force of Article 15 is particularly felt with respect to enforcement in France of judgments against French nationals rendered by foreign courts, a problem considered at p. 802, infra.

Some treaties have restricted the right of the French courts to invoke Article 14 when nationals of the other contracting party are involved.

Internal "venue" rules determine in which political subdivision of France actions based on these articles can be brought. French courts have used these rules to provide bases for adjudicatory jurisdiction when Articles 14 and 15 are inapplicable—that is, when neither plaintiff nor defendant is of French nationality. As do most civil law countries, France follows the general principle *actor sequitur forum rei*—plaintiff must sue at defendant's domicile. Thus domicile of a defendant in France always affords a jurisdictional basis, even if plaintiff and defendant are aliens. Residence also may be sufficient, but bare presence ("transient jurisdiction" in the United States or England) will not suffice. For corporations, the principal office (*siège social*) serves as the equivalent of domicile. It appears that corporations with offices (but not principal offices) in France can be sued there on causes of action related to their French activities.

Other domestic venue rules relating to the place of the activity out of which the litigation arises have also become rules of adjudicatory jurisdiction in transnational cases, thus supplementing Articles 14 and 15. Article 20 provides that in a tort action the complaint may also be filed in the tribunal where the "act causing the injury took place". Article 420, referring to various commercial acts, affords plaintiff an option to sue either in the court at defendant's domicile, or "in that of the district in which the promise was made and the merchandise delivered" or "in that of the district in which payment was to be made." These enable one alien to sue another alien, not domiciled in France, where French activity was involved.

(c) Germany [20]

The German rules give primacy to the domicile of the defendant, a principle laid down by Sections 12 and 13 of the Zivilprozessordnung. Correspondingly, corporations may be sued where they have their seat or *Sitz* (Section 17), a concept similar to the *siège social* under French law. Certain alternative provisions are made. For example, actions involving the "existence or non-existence" or the "fulfillment or cancellation" of a contract may be brought where "the obligation in question is to be fulfilled" (Section 29), and actions for wrongful conduct (torts, roughly speaking) can be brought where the conduct took place (Section 32). Under Section 20, persons can be sued, but only on "pecuniary claims" *(Vermögensrechtliche Ansprüche)*,[21] during a protracted stay at a place where they are not resi-

20. The description is based upon 1 Stein and Jonas, Kommentar zur Zivilprozessordnung §§ 12–37 (19th ed., Pohle, 1964). For a description in English, see Lorenzen, The Conflict of Laws of Germany, 39 Yale L.J. 804, 816–27 (1930); deVries and Lowenfeld, Jurisdiction in Personal Actions—A Comparison of Civil Law Views, 44 Iowa L.Rev. 306 (1959).

21. "Pecuniary claims" has been construed to cover a wide variety of causes of action based on injuries to economic interests, regardless of the type of relief sought.

dent; the law refers to students and employees as example. Section 21(1) provides that persons (including legal persons) who have a branch for manufacturing, trade or other business in a given judicial district may be sued there on claims related to the local business.

These rules, primarily conceived in terms of allocating "jurisdiction" (compare our venue provisions) among German courts, are also used as bases for adjudicatory jurisdiction in cases with foreign elements. The foreignness of a plaintiff is irrelevant but the foreignness of defendant—his failure to possess a German domicile—can be fatal to plaintiff's action when such provisions as Sections 29 and 32 are inapplicable, particularly since his mere (transient) presence affords no jurisdictional basis.

In practice, Section 23 has been most used to confer jurisdiction on German courts over foreigners. It has also been subject to the sharpest criticism as being exceptional or "exorbitant". It reads:

> For complaints asserting pecuniary claims against a person who has no domicile within the country, the court of the district within which this person has property, or within which is found the object claimed by the complaint, has jurisdiction. . . .

As interpreted, the section permits a plaintiff to recover judgment for any amount, regardless of the value of the defendant's property within Germany. It has not been interpreted as equivalent to "quasi in rem" jurisdiction, as generally understood in the United States, under which a court's judgment is limited to the value of the property which was attached or garnished. German courts have applied Section 23 to situations where property of trivial value (such as a commercial account book of defendant) was within the jurisdiction.

PROBLEMS

Will the courts designated in the questions below exercise jurisdiction? If the preceding materials appear inadequate to resolve this question, indicate those principles of foreign law which require exploration before you can answer.

(1) (*a*) A German architect (plaintiff) and an American (defendant) negotiate and sign a contract in New York obligating the plaintiff to design a house. Plaintiff completes the plans in New York. The contract stipulates payment within six months, but defendant does not pay. Defendant travels to Munich for a business trip of one week. Plaintiff wishes to commence an action by serving notice of the contract claim upon defendant while in Munich. (*b*) Assume that the contract contemplates the design by plaintiff in Munich of a building for a German branch of defendant's business. Would the German courts now assert jurisdiction? (*c*) The facts are as stated in example (*a*), except that plaintiff is a French national. Notice of an action is served upon defendant while he is spending a week's vacation in Paris.

(2) (*a*) A French national (plaintiff) domiciled for many years in New York is injured in an automobile accident with an American citizen (defendant). Plaintiff returns to Paris intending to remain for several years and wishes to commence a negligence action. (*b*) The American citizen is the plaintiff and desires to commence an action against the French national, domiciled and present in New York, while the American is in Paris for several years.

(3) (*a*) A New York corporation (defendant) manufacturing widgets in New York exports them to its wholly owned French subsidiary, which has its *siège social* in Paris. The subsidiary sells the widgets to retail shops for resale. A widget explodes in the hands of a French consumer, who desires to bring a negligence action in France against defendant. (*b*) The facts are the same, except that the injured plaintiff is a British subject spending a summer vacation in France. (*c*) Assume that the subsidiary was established in Germany, where the injury occurs, and that the injured plaintiff is a German national. (*d*) Assume that the subsidiary is established in Germany, and that a German national attempts to bring an action against defendant based upon the alleged breach of an employment contract unrelated to the subsidiary's operations. (*e*) Would your answer to question (d) differ if the defendant had set up a branch rather than established a subsidiary in Germany?

---

3. SERVICE OF SUMMONS IN FOREIGN COUNTRIES

Each of the national laws to which Part A has referred permits actions to be commenced against absent alien defendants. In the United States, state long-arm statutes and certain federal statutes authorize such actions; some state provisions and F.R.C.P. 4(i) authorize service abroad. How is service of summons and notice accomplished in a foreign country?

Consider first an action commenced in a foreign country against a defendant within the United States. Service by registered mail, or possibly by consular officials of the foreign country, might be possible if permitted by the foreign law. A federal statute enacted in 1964, 28 U.S.C.A. § 1696,* first provided for cooperation by governmental authorities in this country.

Such a statute by itself provides more assurance of notice to defendant than do the laws and practice of some foreign countries. Former French procedure for service on an absent defendant was poorly calculated to assure that notice would reach the defendant. A summons and notice of the action was served by the plaintiff upon the Ministère Public of the French court having jurisdiction. He forwarded the document to the Ministry of Foreign Affairs for transmission, via diplomatic channels, to the foreign country and eventually the defendant. In fact, French courts consistently held such service valid even if defendant never received the summons. In 1965 a decree called for service by registered mail by a court official and provided for further delays and safeguards in case no receipt was obtained from defendant. See Normand, La Déliverance des Actes à l'Etranger et les Délais de Distance, 55 Rev.Crit. de Droit Int. Privé 386 (1966).

Efforts to solve these problems through domestic legislation are obviously more haphazard than resolution by treaty. At the Tenth

Session of the Hague Conference of Private International Law in 1964, a conference at which all 23 members (including the United States) were present, a draft convention pertaining to these matters was unanimously adopted. The United States was the first country to ratify, and the Convention became effective.[22] Certain of its provisions follow:

CONVENTION ON THE SERVICE ABROAD OF JUDICIAL AND EXTRAJUDICIAL DOCUMENTS IN CIVIL OR COMMERCIAL MATTERS

Article 2

Each contracting State shall designate a Central Authority which will undertake to receive requests for service coming from other contracting States and to proceed in conformity with the provisions of articles 3 to 6. . . .

Article 3

The authority or judicial officer competent under the law of the State in which the documents originate shall forward to the Central Authority of the State addressed a request conforming to the model annexed to the present Convention . . .

The document to be served or a copy thereof shall be annexed to the application. . . .

. . .

Article 5

The Central Authority of the State addressed shall itself serve the document or shall arrange to have it served by an appropriate agency, either:

(a) by a method prescribed by its internal law for the service of documents in domestic actions upon persons who are within its territory, or

(b) by a particular method requested by the applicant, unless such a method is incompatible with the law of the State addressed. . . .

Article 6

The Central Authority of the State addressed or any authority which it may have designated for that purpose, shall complete a certificate in the form of the model annexed to the present Convention.

The certificate shall state that the document has been served and shall include the method, the place and the date of service and the person to whom the document was delivered. If the document has not been served, the certificate shall set out the reasons which have prevented service. . . .

The certificate shall be forwarded directly to the applicant. . . .

22. 20 U.S.T. 361, T.I.A.S. No. 6638, 658 U.N.T.S. 163.

Article 8

Each contracting State shall be free to effect service of judicial documents upon persons abroad, without application of any compulsion, directly through its diplomatic or consular agents.

Any State may declare that it is opposed to such service within its territory, unless the document is to be served upon a national of the State in which the documents originate.

. . .

Article 10

Provided the State of destination does not object, the present Convention shall not interfere with—

(a) the freedom to send judicial documents, by postal channels, directly to persons abroad.

(b) the freedom of judicial officers, officials or other competent persons of the State of origin to effect service of judicial documents directly through the judicial officers, officials or other competent persons of the State of destination.

(c) the freedom of any person interested in a judicial proceeding to effect service of judicial documents directly through the judicial officers, officials or other competent persons of the State of destination.

. . .

Article 13

Where a request for service complies with the terms of the present Convention, the State addressed may refuse to comply therewith only if it deems that compliance would infringe its sovereignty or security.

It may not refuse to comply solely on the ground that, under its internal law, it claims exclusive jurisdiction over the subject-matter of the action or that its internal law would not permit the action upon which the application is based. . . .

Article 14

Difficulties which may arise in connection with the transmission of judicial documents for service shall be settled through diplomatic channels.

Article 15

Where a writ of summons or an equivalent document had to be transmitted abroad for the purpose of service, under the provisions of the present Convention, and the defendant has not appeared judgment shall not be given until it is established that—

(a) the document was served by a method prescribed by the internal law of the State addressed for the service of documents in domestic actions upon persons who are within its territory, or

(b) the document was actually delivered to the defendant or to his residence by another method provided for by this Convention,

and that in either of these cases the service or the delivery was effected in sufficient time to enable the defendant to defend.

Each contracting State shall be free to declare that the judge, notwithstanding the provisions of the first paragraph of this article, may give judgment even if no certificate of service or delivery has been received, if all the following conditions are fulfilled—

(a) the document was transmitted by one of the methods provided for in this Convention,

(b) a period of time not less than six months, considered adequate by the judge in the particular case, has elapsed since the date of the transmission of the document,

(c) no certificate of any kind has been received, even though every reasonable effort has been made to obtain it through the competent authorities of the State addressed.

Notwithstanding the provisions of the preceding paragraphs the judge may order, in case of urgency, any provisional or protective measures.

. . .

Article 18

. . . Federal States shall be free to designate more than one Central Authority.

. . .

PROBLEM

A Swiss corporation (defendant), an important supplier of widgets to the American market, sells a large quantity to a retailer in Wisconsin, who in turn sells a widget to plaintiff, a Wisconsin domiciliary. The widget collapses, to the injury of plaintiff. He invokes the diversity jurisdiction of the federal district court in Wisconsin to commence a negligence action against defendant. Service of the summons and complaint is made pursuant to clause (D) of F.R.C.P. 4(i)(1), by registered mail sent to the managing director of the defendant in Switzerland. The Swiss Ambassador sends a note to the Department of State recounting these facts and asserting that service of judicial documents is, under Swiss law, a governmental function to be exercised exclusively by Swiss authorities. The note states that service by mail infringes Swiss sovereignty and is incompatible with international law. It concludes that the documents should have been transmitted by the United States Embassy in Switzerland to the appropriate Swiss authorities for transmission.

(*1*) What should the State Department reply? If service by registered mail was in fact inconsistent with Swiss law, should the district court nonetheless proceed with the action?

(*2*) Do you think the Swiss claim more substantial if service upon the Swiss managing director had been made personally by a United States Consul in Switzerland, pursuant to clause (C) of Rule 4(i)(1)?

(*3*) How do the provisions of the Convention affect this problem?

Additional reading: For an example of such a diplomatic protest, see 56 Am.J.Int.L. 794 (1962). See generally Miller, International Cooperation in Litigation between the United States and Switzerland: Unilateral Procedural Accommodation in a Test Tube, 49 Minn.L.Rev. 1069, 1075–86 (1965). Compare SEC v. Briggs, 234 F.Supp. 618, 620–21 (N.D.Ohio 1964); Blackmer v. United States, p. 862, infra.

B. ENFORCEMENT OF FOREIGN-COUNTRY MONEY JUDGMENTS

Unless a defendant has assets within a state or nation, a judgment creditor may be required to invoke the aid of another judicial system to *enforce* his judgment. The cases in Part B involve such efforts, or efforts of a defendant to secure *recognition* of a judgment in its favor rendered by courts of another nation. We consider only judgments in actions for money damages. Recognition or enforcement of equity decrees raises special considerations both within the United States, in an interstate setting, and in a transnational setting.[23]

Note the difference, sometimes a significant one, between "enforcement" and "recognition." For enforcement, a plaintiff invokes the court processes of the forum to vindicate his foreign judgment. Recognition, where money judgments are involved, simply requires a dismissal of plaintiff's action. Where other judicial actions, such as a divorce decree, are involved, the consequences of recognition may be more complex.

Enforcement and recognition are examples of the effect accorded by one governmental authority to acts of another. From this perspective, our present inquiry bears some relationship to the act of state doctrine considered in Part B of Chapter VI.

---

1. ENFORCEMENT OF SISTER-STATE JUDGMENTS IN THE UNITED STATES

This section assumes familiarity with the principles underlying enforcement of sister-state judgments in the United States and with the gloss of judicial interpretation on the Full Faith and Credit Clause.[24]

The following materials illustrate the further reaches of that clause, and the policies which it expresses within a federal structure. The relevant constitutional and statutory provisions are Article IV, Section 1 of the Constitution and 28 U.S.C.A. § 1738.*

The method of enforcing money judgments varies among the states. In general, an action in debt or implied contract must be brought by the judgment creditor on his judgment, and a new judgment must be rendered in the forum in which enforcement is sought before execution is available against property of the defendant. Summary judgment procedures may of course expedite this action. In-

23. Problems of enforcement of equity decrees entered under regulatory statutes are considered at pp. 1038–1040, infra.

24. For a critical discussion of the historical and potential application of that clause, see Jackson, Full Faith and Credit—The Lawyer's Clause of the Constitution, 45 Colum.L.Rev. 1 (1945).

evitably, these procedures involve expenditure of time and effort. And they may have important consequences—such as affecting the priority of the initial judgment vis-à-vis claims of other creditors of the defendant in the state of enforcement. A number of states have adopted the Uniform Enforcement of Foreign Judgments Act either in its 1948 version, 9A U.L.Ann. 475, or its further simplified 1964 revision, 9A U.L.Ann. 488. Under the latter's provisions all that is necessary is the filing of the foreign judgment and issuance of notice thereof to the judgment debtor. After a specified period enforcement procedures are available as for a locally rendered judgment. In 1948, Congress provided for registration in any federal district court of a judgment rendered in any other district. "A judgment so registered shall have the same effect as a judgment of the district court of the district where registered and may be enforced in like manner." 28 U.S.C.A. § 1963.

NOTE ON SOME DOMESTIC CASES

(1) Fauntleroy v. Lum [25]

Mississippi statutes made dealing in futures a misdemeanor and prohibited courts from giving effect to any contract of that nature. Two Mississippi residents engaged in a cotton future transaction in Mississippi which violated these statutes. The parties submitted a dispute over the contract to arbitration in Mississppi, and an award was rendered against defendant. Plaintiff commenced an action on the award in a Missouri court, serving personally the defendant who was temporarily in Missouri. The Missouri court, rejecting defendant's evidence showing that the transactions were illegal under Mississippi law, submitted the case to a jury with instructions to find for the plaintiff if the jury believed that the award had been made. The verdict and subsequent judgment were in favor of plaintiff. Plaintiff then brought an action in a Mississippi court to enforce the Missouri judgment. The Supreme Court of Mississippi entered judgment for defendant. Upon review, the Supreme Court of the United States reversed. In deciding that the alleged illegality in Mississippi of the underlying contract could not be relied on as a basis for denying enforcement of a sister-state judgment, the court (per JUSTICE HOLMES) stated in part:

> . . . Whether the award would or would not have been conclusive, and whether the ruling of the Missouri court upon that matter was right or wrong, there can be no question that the judgment was conclusive in Missouri on the validity of the cause of action. . . . A judgment is conclusive as to all the *media concludendi* . . .; and it needs no authority to show that it cannot be impeached either in or out of the state by showing that it was based upon a mistake of law. Of course, a want of jurisdiction over either the person or the subject-matter might be shown.

25. 210 US. 230, 28 S.Ct. 641, 52 L.Ed. 1039 (1908).

> . . . But, as the jurisdiction of the Missouri court is not open to dispute, the judgment cannot be impeached in Mississippi even if it went upon a misapprehension of the Mississippi law. See Godard v. Gray, L.R. 6 Q.B. 139 . . . .
>
> We feel no apprehensions that painful or humiliating consequences will follow upon our decision. No court would give judgment for a plaintiff unless it believed that the facts were a cause of action by the law determining their effect. Mistakes will be rare. In this case the Missouri court no doubt supposed that the award was binding by the law of Mississippi. If it was mistaken, it made a natural mistake. The validity of its judgment, even in Mississippi, is, as we believe, the result of the Constitution as it always has been understood, and is not a matter to arouse the susceptibilities of the states, all of which are equally concerned in the question and equally on both sides.

In his dissenting opinion for four members of the Court JUSTICE WHITE stated in part:

> . . . The due faith and credit clause it is now decided means that residents of a state may, within such state, do acts which are violative of public policy, and yet that a judgment may be rendered in another state giving effect to such transactions, which judgment it becomes the duty of the state whose laws have been set at defiance to enforce. It must follow, if one state, by the mere form of a judgment, has this power, that no state has in effect the authority to make police regulations; or, what is tantamount to the same thing, is without power to enforce them. If this be true the doctrine now upheld comes to this,—that no state, generally speaking, possesses police power concerning acts done within its borders if any of the results of such acts may be the subject of civil actions, since the enforcement by the state of its police regulations as to such acts may be nullified by an exertion of the judicial power of another state. Indeed, the principle, as understood by me, goes further than this, since it not only gives to each of the states in the cases suggested the power to render possible an evasion of the police laws of all the other states, but it gives to each state the authority to compel the other states, through their courts, to give effect to illegal transactions done within their borders. It may not be denied that a state which has lawfully prohibited the enforcement of a particular character of transaction, and made the same criminal, has an interest in seeing that its laws are enforced and will be subjected to the gravest humiliation if it be compelled to give effect to acts done within its borders which are in violation of its valid police or criminal laws. . . .
>
> When the Constitution was adopted the principles of comity by which the decrees of the courts of one state were entitled to be enforced in another were generally known; but the enforcement of those principles by the several states had no absolute sanction, since they rested but in comity. Now, it cannot be denied that, under the rules of comity recognized at the time of the adoption of the Constitution, and which, at this time, universally prevail, no sovereignty was or is under the slightest moral obligation to give effect to

a judgment of another sovereignty, when to do so would compel the state in which the judgment was sought to be executed to enforce an illegal and prohibited contract, when both the contract and all the acts done in connection with its performance had taken place in the latter state. This seems to me conclusive of this case, since, both in treatises of authoritative writers (Story, Confl.L. § 609), and by repeated adjudications of this court, it has been settled that the purpose of the due faith and credit clause was not to confer any new power, but simply to make obligatory that duty which, when the Constitution was adopted, rested, as has been said, in comity alone. . . .

(2) Milwaukee County v. M. E. White Co.[26]

A county of Wisconsin brought suit in a federal district court in Illinois against an Illinois corporation on a judgment which the county had recovered in a Wisconsin state court for taxes assessed against defendant because of income received by it from business transacted in Wisconsin. The district court dismissed the action. The Supreme Court answered in the affirmative a certified question whether the district court should have entertained the action. The opinion delivered by MR. JUSTICE STONE stated in part:

> Even if the judgment is deemed to be colored by the nature of the obligation whose validity it establishes, and we are free to re-examine it, and, if we find it to be based on an obligation penal in character, to refuse to enforce it outside the state where rendered, see Wisconsin v. Pelican Insurance Co., 127 U.S. 265, 292 et seq., 8 S.Ct. 1370, 32 L.Ed. 239, compare Fauntleroy v. Lum, 210 U.S. 230, 28 S.Ct. 641, 52 L.Ed. 1039, still the obligation to pay taxes is not penal. It is a statutory liability, quasi contractual in nature, enforceable, if there is no exclusive statutory remedy, in the civil courts by the common-law action of debt or indebitatus assumpsit. . . .
>
> The faith and credit required to be given to judgments does not depend on the Constitution alone. . . . [The court here referred to the predecessor to 28 U.S.C.A. § 1738.*]
>
> Such exception as there may be to this all-inclusive command is one which is implied from the nature of our dual system of government, and recognizes that consistently with the full-faith and credit clause there may be limits to the extent to which the policy of one state, in many respects sovereign, may be subordinated to the policy of another. That there are exceptions has often been pointed out. . . . Without attempting to say what their limits may be, we assume for present purposes that the command of the Constitution and of the statute is not all-embracing, and direct our inquiry to the question whether a state to which a judgment for taxes is taken may have a policy against its enforcement meriting recognition as a permissible limitation upon the full-faith and credit clause. Of that question this court is the final arbiter. . . . Other obligations to pay

26. 296 U.S. 268, 56 S.Ct. 229, 80 L.Ed. 220 (1935).

money arising under the statutes of one state must be given recognition in courts of another. . . . But it is insisted that to this rule taxing statutes constitute an exception, analogous to that relating to penal laws, because the courts of one state should not be called upon to scrutinize the relations of a foreign state with its own citizens, such as are involved in its revenue laws, and thus commit the state of the forum to positions which might be seriously embarrassing to itself or its neighbors. . . .

A cause of action on a judgment is different from that upon which the judgment was entered. In a suit upon a money judgment for a civil cause of action, the validity of the claim upon which it was founded is not open to inquiry, whatever its genesis. Regardless of the nature of the right which gave rise to it, the judgment is an obligation to pay money in the nature of a debt upon a specialty. Recovery upon it can be resisted only on the grounds that the court which rendered it was without jurisdiction. . . .

Trial of these issues, even though the judgment be for taxes incurred under the laws of another state, requires no scrutiny of its revenue laws or of relations established by those laws with its citizens, and calls for no pronouncement upon the policy of a sister state. . . .

We can perceive no greater possibility of embarrassment in litigating the validity of a judgment for taxes and enforcing it than any other for the payment of money. The very purpose of the full-faith and credit clause was to alter the status of the several states as independent foreign sovereignties, each free to ignore obligations created under the laws or by the judicial proceedings of the others, and to make them integral parts of a single nation throughout which a remedy upon a just obligation might be demanded as of right, irrespective of the state of its origin. That purpose ought not lightly to be set aside out of deference to a local policy which, if it exists, would seem to be too trivial to merit serious consideration when weighed against the policy of the constitutional provision and the interest of the state whose judgment is challenged. In the circumstances here disclosed, no state can be said to have a legitimate policy against payment of its neighbor's taxes, the obligation of which has been judicially established by courts to whose judgments in practically every other instance it must give full faith and credit. Compare Fauntleroy v. Lum, supra. . . .

We conclude that a judgment is not to be denied full faith and credit in state and federal courts merely because it is for taxes.

We intimate no opinion whether a suit upon a judgment for an obligation created by a penal law, in the international sense, see Huntington v. Attrill, supra, 146 U.S. 657, 677, 13 S.Ct. 224, 36 L.Ed. 1123, is within the jurisdiction of the federal District Courts, or whether full faith and credit must be given to such a judgment even though a suit for the penalty before reduced to judgment could not be maintained outside of the state where imposed. . . .

The opinion in Milwaukee County leaves open the question whether a "suit upon a judgment for an obligation created by a penal law" benefits from the Full Faith and Credit clause. The case referred to, Huntington v. Attrill, 146 U.S. 657, 13 S.Ct. 224, 36 L.Ed. 1123 (1892), held that the Maryland courts were required to give full faith and credit to a New York judgment against defendant, the director of a New York corporation, based upon a New York statute making directors liable for all debts of a corporation if they signed and recorded false certificates as to the amount of its capital stock. The judgment creditor had lent money to the corporation. The Court held that the New York statute was not a "penal law in the international sense," largely on grounds that the action was not on behalf of a New York governmental authority for punishment of an offense against New York law. The test, stated the Court, was whether the statute "appears to the tribunal which is called upon to enforce it to be, in its essential character and effect, a punishment of an offense against the public, or a grant of a civil right to a private person." The "penal law" exception to the Full Faith and Credit Clause has today a narrow scope. The test stated in the Huntington case appears to include within the exception any action brought by a state to recover fines assessed in criminal proceedings. It is unclear whether the exception reaches money judgments, including penalty assessments relating to taxes, treble damages recovered by plaintiff in an antitrust action, and so on.

(3) Baldwin v. Iowa State Travelling Men's Ass'n [27]

An action in a federal district court led to a judgment for plaintiff. In that proceeding, defendant had argued that the district court lacked jurisdiction over it. Plaintiff brought a suit to enforce the judgment in another federal district court, and defendant raised the same objection. The court accepted the findings of fact made by the initial district court but held as a matter of law that, based upon such facts, the initial court had no basis for asserting jurisdiction over defendant. Consequently, it entered judgment for defendant on the enforcement suit. The court of appeals affirmed. The Supreme Court, noting that the Full Faith and Credit Clause was not applicable because neither court was a state court and that the question was rather one of res judicata, reversed. It stated in part:

> The substantial matter for determination is whether the judgment amounts to *res judicata* on the question of the jurisdiction of the court which rendered it over the person of the [defendant]. . . . Public policy dictates that there be an end of litigation; that those who have contested an issue shall be bound by the result of the contest; and that matters once tried shall be considered forever settled as between the parties. We see no reason why this doctrine should not apply in every case where one voluntarily appears, presents his case and is fully heard, and why he should not, in the absence of fraud, be thereafter concluded by the judgment of the tribunal to which he has submitted his cause.

27. 283 U.S. 522, 51 S.Ct. 517, 75 L.Ed. 1244 (1931).

Compare the statement of the Court in Durfee v. Duke, 375 U.S. 106, 111, 84 S.Ct. 242, 245, 11 L.Ed.2d 186, 191 (1963):

> From these decisions there emerges the general rule that a judgment is entitled to full faith and credit—even as to questions of jurisdiction—when the second court's inquiry discloses that those questions have been fully and fairly litigated and finally decided in the court which rendered the original judgment.

(4) Magnolia Petroleum Co. v. Hunt [28]

Consider the following excerpt from the opinion of the Court, delivered by CHIEF JUSTICE STONE:

> These consequences [the requirement that states enforce tax judgments or judgments based on actions violative of the public policy of the state of enforcement] flow from the clear purpose of the full faith and credit clause to establish throughout the federal system the salutary principle of the common law that a litigation once pursued to judgment shall be as conclusive of the rights of the parties in every other court as in that where the judgment was rendered, so that a cause of action merged in a judgment in one state is likewise merged in every other. The full faith and credit clause like the commerce clause thus became a nationally unifying force. It altered the status of the several states as independent foreign sovereignties, each free to ignore rights and obligations created under the laws or established by the judicial proceedings of the others, by making each an integral part of a single nation, in which rights judicially established in any part are given nationwide application. Milwaukee County v. M. E. White Co., [supra,] 276, 277 . . . . Because there is a full faith and credit clause a defendant may not a second time challenge the validity of the plaintiff's right which has ripened into a judgment and a plaintiff may not for his single cause of action secure a second or a greater recovery.

COMMENT

The Fauntleroy opinion suggests some of the relationships between questions of jurisdiction, enforcement of judgments, and choice of law. Recall the introductory note on p. 91, supra, on choice of law. On the facts of Fauntleroy, there appears little doubt that Mississippi law should have been applied to litigation on the gambling contract or on the award in any other state. Whether Missouri misinterpreted Mississippi law, or frankly applied its own law to the controversy, the Fauntleroy opinion appears to require that another state court give full faith and credit to the Missouri judgment.

In several decisions the Supreme Court has held that the Constitution, particularly the Full Faith and Credit Clause and the Due Process Clause of the Fourteenth Amendment, controls to some degree choice-of-law principles. That is, these constitutional provisions may (a) require a state court which either decides or is constitutionally ob-

28. 320 U.S. 430, 64 S.Ct. 208, 88 L.Ed. 149 (1943).

ligated to hear a particular controversy to apply the law of a given foreign state to its resolution, or (b) at a minimum, prohibit the court from applying to the controversy the law of a state (whether the forum or another) which is unrelated to the controversy and thus "arbitrary." [29]

QUESTIONS

(1) Assume that defendant in Fauntleroy v. Lum had some basis for arguing that the failure of the Missouri court to apply Mississippi law deprived him of property without the due process required by the Fourteenth Amendment. If the Missouri court rejected his argument, what path was open to him? Does that path suggest additional arguments in favor of the Supreme Court's opinion? Would such arguments have equal validity if, for example, the action on the award had been brought in a Mexican court (which, you can assume, had a proper basis for asserting jurisdiction over the defendant), and if the Mexican judgment were then sued upon in the Mississippi court?

(2) Do the excerpts from the opinions in Milwaukee County and Magnolia Petroleum Co. lend further support to the Fauntleroy opinion? To what extent are the considerations in support of enforcement of judgments that are developed in these three opinions—considerations developed in the light of the political, economic and legal relationships among states in our federalism—relevant to problems of enforcement of foreign-country judgments in our state or federal courts?

(*a*) From the perspective of the individual plaintiff who has obtained a judgment in Forum–1, what are the arguments for enforcement of that judgment in Forum–2? What traditional legal doctrine, operative in a unitary legal system, is also relevant when the courts of two states (or of two nations) are involved through enforcement proceedings?

(*b*) From the perspective of the state (or nation) rendering the initial judgment, what interests or policies are present that argue for enforcement of a judgment of its courts in another state (or nation)?

(*c*) From a national (or international) perspective what interests or policies are present that argue for enforcement of a judgment rendered in one state (or nation) in another state (or nation)? Note the references in the opinion in Milwaukee County to the interests or policies of the nation as a whole and of each of the states involved.

PROBLEMS

(1) Politnews, Inc., a Massachusetts corporation which mails to subscribers throughout the country a weekly newsletter published in its home state, includes in an issue critical comments about Upright, a Wisconsin domiciliary and a member of the state legislature. Upright brings a tort action against Politnews in a Wisconsin court, alleging that Politnews has defamed him. Jurisdiction is based upon Wisc.Stat.Ann. § 262.05, p. 734,

29. See generally Cheatham, Federal Control of Conflict of Laws, 6 Vand. L.Rev. 581 (1953).

supra, and Politnews receives timely notice of the action by registered letter in Massachusetts. It does not participate in the proceedings, which lead to a default judgment for Upright in the amount of $75,000. Upright brings suit upon the judgment in Massachusetts. Politnews alleges (a) that the Wisconsin court lacked jurisdiction over it, (b) that the Wisconsin judgment violates, under relevant decisions of the Supreme Court, its constitutionally protected right to free speech, and (c) that the judgment includes $25,000 of compensatory damages and $50,000 of punitive damages. It argues that any one of these allegations should prevent enforcement of the judgment. Which of these defenses can the Massachusetts court examine on the merits in the enforcement proceedings?

(2) Assume that Politnews defended the Wisconsin action, which led to an adverse judgment after a jury trial. It took no further action. In the Massachusetts enforcement proceeding, Politnews alleges that it was denied the right to cross examine certain witnesses. Can the Massachusetts court examine this allegation?

(3) Consider this question before and after reading the following cases in Section 2. Suppose that the facts were the same as in problem (1), except that Upright was a domiciliary and official of Ontario, where he brought his action, and that Politnews distributed its newsletter in the United States and Canada. Which of the defenses noted in problem (1) could, or should, the Massachusetts court explore?

---

2. ENFORCEMENT OF FOREIGN-COUNTRY JUDGMENTS IN THE UNITED STATES

HILTON v. GUYOT

Supreme Court of the United States, 1895.
159 U.S. 113, 16 S.Ct. 139, 40 L.Ed. 95.

[An action was brought in the Circuit Court for the Southern District of New York by the liquidator and the surviving members of a French firm against two United States citizens who had been trading as partners. The plaintiffs had recovered a judgment in the French courts upon which nearly $200,000 remained unpaid. Defendants' answer denied that they were indebted to plaintiffs and asserted that the French judgment was procured by fraud. Defendants also filed a bill in equity to enjoin the prosecution of the action. The plaintiffs prevailed in both cases and defendants, by writ of error and appeal, brought the cases to the Supreme Court.]

MR. JUSTICE GRAY, after stating the case, delivered the opinion of the court . . . .

International law, in its widest and most comprehensive sense,—including not only questions of right between nations, governed by what has been appropriately called the "law of nations," but also questions arising under what is usually called "private international law," or the "conflict of laws," and concerning the rights of persons within the territory and dominion of one nation, by reason of acts, private or public, done within the dominions of another nation,—is part of our law, and must be ascertained and administered by the courts of justice as often as such questions are presented in litigation between man and man, duly submitted to their determination.

The most certain guide, no doubt, for the decision of such questions is a treaty or a statute of this country. But when, as is the case here, there is no written law upon the subject, the duty still rests upon the judicial tribunals of ascertaining and declaring what the law is, whenever it becomes necessary to do so, in order to determine the rights of parties to suits regularly brought before them. In doing this, the courts must obtain such aid as they can from judicial decisions, from the works of jurists and commentators, and from the acts and usages of civilized nations . . . .

No law has any effect, of its own force, beyond the limits of the sovereignty from which its authority is derived. The extent to which the law of one nation, as put in force within its territory, whether by executive order, by legislative act, or by judicial decree, shall be allowed to operate within the dominion of another nation, depends upon what our greatest jurists have been content to call "the comity of nations." Although the phrase has been often criticised, no satisfactory substitute has been suggested.

"Comity," in the legal sense, is neither a matter of absolute obligation, on the one hand, nor of mere courtesy and good will, upon the other. But it is the recognition which one nation allows within its territory to the legislative, executive, or judicial acts of another nation, having due regard both to international duty and convenience, and to the rights of its own citizens, or of other persons who are under the protection of its laws . . . .

Chief Justice Taney, . . . speaking for this court, while Mr. Justice Story was a member of it, and largely adopting his words, said: . . . . "The comity thus extended to other nations is no impeachment of sovereignty. It is the voluntary act of the nation by which it is offered, and is inadmissible when contrary to its policy, or prejudicial to its interests. But it contributes so largely to promote justice between individuals, and to produce a friendly intercourse between the sovereignties to which they belong, that courts of justice have continually acted upon it as a part of the voluntary law of nations." "It is not the comity of the courts, but the comity of the nation, which is administered and ascertained in the same way, and guided by the same reasoning, by which all other principles of municipal law are ascertained and guided." Bank v. Earle (1839) 13 Pet. 519, 589; Story, Confl.Laws, § 38 . . . .

In order to appreciate the weight of the various authorities cited at the bar, it is important to distinguish different kinds of judgments. Every foreign judgment, of whatever nature, in order to be entitled to any effect, must have been rendered by a court having jurisdiction of the cause, and upon regular proceedings, and due notice. In alluding to different kinds of judgments, therefore, such jurisdiction, proceedings, and notice will be assumed. It will also be assumed that they are untainted by fraud, the effect of which will be considered later.

A judgment in rem, adjudicating the title to a ship or other movable property within the custody of the court, is treated as valid everywhere . . . .

Other judgments, not strictly in rem, under which a person has been compelled to pay money, are so far conclusive that the justice of the payment cannot be impeached in another country, so as to compel him to pay it again. For instance, a judgment in foreign attachment is conclusive, as between the parties, of the right to the property or money attached. Story, Confl.Laws (2d Ed.) § 592a . . .

Other foreign judgments which have been held conclusive of the matter adjudged were judgments discharging obligations contracted in the foreign country between citizens or residents thereof. Story, Confl.Laws, §§ 330–341 . . . .

The extraterritorial effect of judgments in personam, at law, or in equity may differ, according to the parties to the cause. A judgment of that kind between two citizens or residents of the country, and thereby subject to the jurisdiction in which it is rendered, may be held conclusive as between them everywhere. So, if a foreigner invokes the jurisdiction by bringing an action against a citizen, both may be held bound by a judgment in favor of either; and if a citizen sues a foreigner, and judgment is rendered in favor of the latter, both may be held equally bound . . . .

The effect to which a judgment, purely executory, rendered in favor of a citizen or resident of the country, in a suit there brought by him against a foreigner, may be entitled in an action thereon against the latter in his own country, as is the case now before us, presents a more difficult question, upon which there has been some diversity of opinion . . . .

The English cases [discussed in the omitted portion] have been stated with the more particularity and detail, because they directly bear upon the question, what was the English law, being then our own law, before the Declaration of Independence? They demonstrate that by that law, as generally understood, and as declared by Hardwicke, Mansfield, Buller, Camden, Eyre, and Ellenborough, and doubted by Kenyon only, a judgment recovered in a foreign country for a sum of money, when sued upon in England, was only prima facie evidence of the demand, and subject to be examined and impeached . . . .

The law upon this subject as understood in the United States at the time of their separation from the mother country was clearly set forth by Chief Justice Parsons, speaking for the supreme judicial court of Massachusetts, in 1813, and by Mr. Justice Story in his Commentaries on the Constitution of the United States, published in 1833. Both those eminent jurists declared that by the law of England the general rule was that foreign judgments were only prima facie evidence of the matter which they purported to decide; and that by the common law, before the American Revolution, all the courts of the several colonies and states were deemed foreign to each other, and consequently judgments rendered by any one of them were considered as foreign judgments, and their merits re-examinable in another colony, not only as to the jurisdiction of the court which pronounced them, but also as to the merits of the controversy, to the extent to which they were understood to be re-examinable in England . . .

It was because of that condition of the law, as between the American colonies and states, that the United States, at the very beginning of their existence as a nation, ordained that full faith and credit should be given to the judgments of one of the states of the Union in the courts of another of those states . . . .

From this review of the authorities, it clearly appears that, at the time of the separation of this country from England, the general rule was fully established that foreign judgments in personam were prima facie evidence only, and not conclusive of the merits of the controversy between the parties. But the extent and limits of the application of that rule do not appear to have been much discussed, or defined with any approach to exactness, in England or America, until the matter was taken up by Chancellor Kent and by Mr. Justice Story . . . .

Mr. Justice Story, in his Commentaries on the Conflict of Laws, first published in 1834, after reviewing many English authorities, said: "The present inclination of the English courts seems to be to sustain the conclusiveness of foreign judgments,"—to which, in the second edition, in 1841, he added: "Although, certainly, there yet remains no inconsiderable diversity of opinion among the learned judges of the different tribunals." Section 606.

He then proceeded to state his own view of the subject, on principle, saying: "It is, indeed, very difficult to perceive what could be done if a different doctrine were maintainable to the full extent of opening all the evidence and merits of the cause anew on a suit upon the foreign judgment. Some of the witnesses may be since dead; some of the vouchers may be lost or destroyed. The merits of the cause, as formerly before the court upon the whole evidence, may have been decidedly in favor of the judgment; upon a partial possession of the original evidence, they may now appear otherwise. Suppose a case purely sounding in damages, such as an action for an assault, for slander, for conversion of property, for a malicious prosecution, or for a criminal conversation; is the defendant to be at liberty to retry the whole merits, and to make out, if he can, a new case upon new evidence? Or is the court to review the former decision, like a court of appeal, upon the old evidence? In a case of covenant, or of debt, or of a breach of contract, are all the circumstances to be reexamined anew? If they are, by what laws and rules of evidence and principles of justice is the validity of the original judgment to be tried? Is the court to open the judgment, and to proceed ex aequo et bona? Or is it to administer strict law, and stand to the doctrines of the local administration of justice? Is it to act upon the rules of evidence acknowledged in its own jurisprudence, or upon those of the foreign jurisprudence? These and many more questions might be put to show the intrinsic difficulties of the subject. Indeed, the rule that the judgment is to be prima facie evidence for the plaintiff would be a mere delusion if the defendant might still question it by opening all or any of the original merits on his side; for, under such circumstances, it would be equivalent to granting a new trial. It is easy to understand that the defendant may be at liberty to impeach the original justice of the judgment by showing that the court had no jurisdiction, or that he never had any notice of the suit, or that it was procured by fraud, or that upon its face it is founded in mistake, or that it is irregular and bad by the local law, fori rei judicatae. To such an extent the doctrine is intelligible and practicable. Beyond this, the right to impugn the judgment is in legal effect the right to retry the merits of the original cause at large, and to put the defendant upon proving those merits." Section 607 . . . .

In view of all the authorities upon the subject, and of the trend of judicial opinion in this country and in England, following the lead of Kent and Story, we are satisfied that where there has been opportunity for a full and fair trial abroad before a court of competent jurisdiction, conducting the trial upon regular proceedings, after due citation or voluntary appearance of the defendant, and under a system of jurisprudence likely to secure an impartial administration of justice between the citizens of its own country and those of other countries, and there is nothing to show either prejudice in the court, or in the system of laws under which it was sitting, or fraud in procuring the judgment, or any other special reason why the comity of this nation should not allow it full effect, the merits of the case should not, in an action brought in this country upon the judgment, be tried afresh, as on a new trial or an appeal, upon the mere assertion of the party that the judgment was erroneous in law or in fact. The defendants, therefore, cannot be permitted, upon that general ground, to contest the validity or the effect of the judgment sued on.

But they have sought to impeach that judgment upon several other grounds, which require separate consideration.

It is objected that the appearance and litigation of the defendants in the French tribunals were not voluntary, but by legal compulsion, and, therefore, that the French courts never acquired such jurisdiction over the defendants that they should be held bound by the judgment . . . .

The present case is not one of a person traveling through or casually found in a foreign country. The defendants, although they were not citizens or residents of France, but were citizens and residents of the state of New York, and their principal place of business was in the city of New York, yet had a storehouse and an agent in Paris, and were accustomed to purchase large quantities of goods there, although they did not make sales in France. Under such circumstances, evidence that their sole object in appearing and carrying on the litigation in the French courts was to prevent property in their storehouse at Paris, belonging to them, and within the jurisdiction, but not in the custody, of those courts, from being taken in satisfaction of any judgment that might be recovered against them, would not, according to our law, show that those courts did not acquire jurisdiction of the persons of the defendants.

It is next objected that in those courts one of the plaintiffs was permitted to testify not under oath, and was not subjected to cross-examination by the opposite party, and that the defendants were therefore deprived of safeguards which are by our law considered essential to secure honesty and to detect fraud in a witness; and also that documents and papers were admitted in evidence, with which the defendants had no connection, and which would not be admissible under our own system of jurisprudence. But it having been shown by the plaintiffs, and hardly denied by the defendants, that the practice followed and the method of examining witnesses were according to the laws of France, we are not prepared to hold that the fact that the procedure in these respects differed from that of our own courts is, of itself, a sufficient ground for impeaching the foreign judgment . . . .

There is no doubt that both in this country, as appears by the authorities already cited, and in England, a foreign judgment may be impeached for fraud . . . .

It has often, indeed, been declared by this court that the fraud which entitles a party to impeach the judgment of one of our own tribunals must be fraud extrinsic to the matter tried in the cause, and not merely consist in false and fraudulent documents or testimony submitted to that tribunal, and the truth of which was contested before it and passed upon by it . . . .

But it is now established in England, by well-considered, and strongly-reasoned decisions of the court of appeal, that foreign judgments may be impeached, if procured by false and fraudulent representations and testimony of the plaintiff, even if the same question of fraud was presented to and decided by the foreign court . . . .

But whether those decisions can be followed in regard to foreign judgments, consistently with our own decisions as to impeaching domestic judgments for fraud, it is unnecessary in this case to determine, because there is a distinct and independent ground upon which we are satisfied that the comity of our nation does not require us to give conclusive effect to the judgments of the courts of France; and that ground is the want of reciprocity, on the part of France, as to the effect to be given to the judgments of this and other foreign countries . . . .

[References to various French statutes, discussed at p. 751, supra, omitted.]

The defendants, in their answer, cited the above provisions of the statutes of France, and alleged, and at the trial offered to prove, that by the construction given to these statutes by the judicial tribunals of France, when the judgments of tribunals of foreign countries against the citizens of France are sued upon in the courts of France, the merits of the controversies upon which those judgments are based are examined anew, unless a treaty to the contrary effect exists between the republic of France and the country in which such judgment is obtained (which is not the case between the republic of France and the United States), and that the tribunals of the republic of France give no force and effect, within the jurisdiction of that country, to the judgments duly rendered by courts of competent jurisdiction of the United States against citizens of France after proper personal service of the process of those courts has been made thereon in this country. We are of opinion that this evidence should have been admitted . . . .

By the law of France, settled by a series of uniform decisions of the court of cassation, the highest judicial tribunal, for more than half a century, no foreign judgment can be rendered executory in France without a review of the judgment au fond (to the bottom), including the whole merits of the cause of action on which the judgment rests . . . .

[An extensive discussion of Holker v. Parker, noted at p. 800, infra, and of other French authorities and authorities of other civil law countries omitted.]

It appears, therefore, that there is hardly a civilized nation on either continent which, by its general law, allows conclusive effect to an executory foreign judgment for the recovery of money. In France and in a few smaller states—Norway, Portugal, Greece, Monaco, and Hayti—the merits of the controversy are reviewed, as of course, allowing to the foreign judgment, at the most, no more effect than of being prima facie evidence of the justice of the claim. In the great majority of the countries on the continent of Europe,—in Belgium, Holland, Denmark, Sweden, Germany, in many cantons of Switzerland, in Russia and Poland, in Roumania, in Austria and Hungary (perhaps in Italy), and in Spain,—as well as in Egypt, in Mexico, and in a great part of South America, the judgment rendered in a foreign country is allowed the same effect only as the courts of that country allow to the judgments of the country in which the judgment in question is sought to be executed.

The prediction of Mr. Justice Story in section 618 of his Commentaries on the Conflict of Laws, already cited, has thus been fulfilled, and the rule of reciprocity has worked itself firmly into the structure of international jurisprudence.

The reasonable, if not the necessary, conclusion appears to us to be that judgments rendered in France, or in any other foreign country, by the laws of which our own judgments are reviewable upon the merits, are not entitled to full credit and conclusive effect when sued upon in this country, but are prima facie evidence only of the justice of the plaintiffs' claim.

In holding such a judgment, for want of reciprocity, not to be conclusive evidence of the merits of the claim, we do not proceed upon any theory of retaliation upon one person by reason of injustice done to another, but upon the broad ground that international law is founded upon mutuality and reciprocity, and that by the principles of international law recognized in most civilized nations, and by the comity of our own country, which it is our judicial duty to know and to declare, the judgment is not entitled to be considered conclusive.

By our law, at the time of the adoption of the constitution, a foreign judgment was considered as prima facie evidence, and not conclusive. There is no statute of the United States, and no treaty of the United States with France, or with any other nation, which has changed that law, or has made any provision upon the subject. It is not to be supposed that, if any statute or treaty had been or should be made, it would recognize as conclusive the judgments of any country, which did not give like effect to our own judgments. In the absence of statute or treaty, it appears to us equally unwarrantable to assume that the comity of the United States requires anything more.

If we should hold this judgment to be conclusive, we should allow it an effect to which, supposing the defendants' offers to be sustained by actual proof, it would, in the absence of a special treaty, be entitled in hardly any other country in Christendom, except the country in which it was rendered . . . .

[Both cases were reversed and the cause remanded for a new trial.]

MR. CHIEF JUSTICE FULLER, dissenting.

Plaintiffs brought their action on a judgment recovered by them against the defendants in the courts of France, which courts had jurisdiction over person and subject-matter, and in respect of which judgment no fraud was alleged, except in particulars contested in and considered by the French courts. The question is whether under these circumstances, and in the absence of a treaty or act of congress, the judgment is re-examinable upon the merits. This question I regard as one to be determined by the ordinary and settled rule in respect of allowing a party who has had an opportunity to prove his case in a competent court to retry it on the merits; and it seems to me that the doctrine of res judicata applicable to domestic judgments should be applied to foreign judgments as well, and rests on the same general ground of public policy, that there should be an end of litigation.

This application of the doctrine is in accordance with our own jurisprudence, and it is not necessary that we should hold it to be required by some rule of international law. The fundamental principle concerning judgments is that disputes are finally determined by them, and I am unable to perceive why a judgment in personam, which is not open to question on the ground of want of jurisdiction, either intrinsically or over the parties, or of fraud, or on any other recognized ground of impeachment, should not be held, inter partes, though recovered abroad, conclusive on the merits . . . .

The subjects of the suit were commercial transactions, having their origin, and partly performed, in France, under a contract there made, and alleged to be modified by the dealings of the parties there, and one of the claims against them was for goods sold to them there. They appeared generally in the case, without protest, and by counterclaims relating to the same general course of business, a part of them only connected with the claims against them, became actors in the suit, and submitted to the courts their own claims for affirmative relief, as well as the claims against them. The courts were competent, and they took the chances of a decision in their favor. As traders in France they were under the protection of its laws, and were bound by its laws, its commercial usages, and its rules of procedure. The fact that they were Americans and the opposite parties were citizens of France is immaterial, and there is no suggestion on the record that those courts proceeded on any other ground than that all litigants, whatever their nationality, were entitled to equal justice therein . . . . We are dealing with the judgment of a court of a civilized country, whose laws and system of justice recognize the general rules in respect to property and rights between man and man prevailing among all civilized peoples. Obviously, the last persons who should be heard to complain are those who identified themselves with the business of that country, knowing that all their transactions there would be subject to the local laws and modes of doing business. The French courts appear to have acted "judicially, honestly, and with the intention to arrive at the right conclusion," and a result thus reached ought not to be disturbed . . . .

I cannot yield my assent to the proposition that, because by legislation and judicial decision in France that effect is not there given to judgments recovered in this country which, according to our jurisprudence, we think should be given to judgments wherever recovered (subject, of course, to the recognized exceptions), therefore we should pursue the same line of conduct as respects the judgments of French tribunals. The application of the doctrine of res judicata does not rest in discretion; and it is for the government, and not for its courts, to adopt the principle of retorsion, if deemed under any circumstances desirable or necessary.

As the court expressly abstains from deciding whether the judgment is impeachable on the ground of fraud, I refrain from any observations on that branch of the case.

MR. JUSTICE HARLAN, MR. JUSTICE BREWER, and MR. JUSTICE JACKSON concur in this dissent.

NOTE ON SOME RELATIONSHIPS BETWEEN PRIVATE AND PUBLIC INTERNATIONAL LAW

Justice Gray's opinion in Hilton v. Guyot opens and concludes with observations about "international law," despite the fact that the enforcement of foreign judgments is now generally considered part of the field of domestic law known as the conflict of laws, or private international law. The Note at p. 91, supra, indicates that this field traditionally includes bases for adjudicatory jurisdiction, the effect to be given to foreign judgments, and choice of law. Hilton v. Guyot provides occasion for reflection about the relationships between private and public international law.

We earlier observed that, before the 20th and particularly before the 19th century, courts and scholars held a more catholic conception of international law, or the law of nations. The Note at p. 550, supra, sketched some of the relationships between the law of nations, thought of basically as ordering relations among states, and a common or universal law, a *jus gentium* similarly viewed in all civilized nations, which would often affect relations between individuals. It cited as examples the law merchant and the law maritime. The "international" flavor of both of these fields has faded, and in different degrees both became absorbed into systems of national law.

Similar observations can be made about private international law —particularly choice of law but also questions of jurisdiction and enforcement of judgments. Before the 19th century, authors often attempted no rigid separation between these fields. The subjects in the works of Grotius and Huber would today fall into both fields. If not explicitly thought of as governed by rules of international law, many problems of private international law were thought about and seen against the background of public international law and the purposes that it sought to achieve. Important writers on private international law in the 19th century built their theories of jurisdiction or choice of law upon fundamental concepts of public international law: sovereignty, nationality, and so on. To be sure, theories of jurisdiction or choice of law which these writers elaborated often had little in common, despite the common recourse to principles believed to be expressed by the law of nations.

The Court in Hilton v. Guyot quotes extensively from Justice Story, whose Commentaries on the Conflict of Laws of 1834 was a landmark treatise on choice of law and enforcement of judgments.[30] The opinion, and the quotations from Justice Story's writings, draw heavily upon the notion of "comity"—a concept to be sure, of dim contours but of pervasive significance to private and public international law. Justice Story based his writings on choice of law upon the concept of the "comity of nations," as

> the most appropriate phrase to express the true foundation and extent of the obligation of the laws of one nation within the territories of another. It is derived altogether from the voluntary consent of the latter; and is inadmissible, when it is contrary to its known policy, or prejudicial to its interests. . . . It is not the comity of the courts, but the comity of the nation, which is administered . . . .[31]

Justice Story here depended to a considerable degree upon the writings of Huber.

Another early American scholar, Livermore, writing on questions of choice of law, criticized the concept of comity and suggested what he took to be more accurate reasons why a nation would apply principles of foreign law to litigation with foreign elements.

> The people of an independent nation may, if they please, surround their territory with an impassable wall, and totally exclude all intercourse with other nations. But if a desire to

30. For an assessment of Justice Story's work in this field, see Nadelmann, Joseph Story's Contribution to American Conflicts Law: A Comment, 5 Am.J.Legal Hist. 230 (1961). On the earlier history of comity see Yntema, The Comity Doctrine, 65 Mich.L.Rev. 1 (1966) (with introduction by Nadelmann).

31. Commentaries on the Conflict of Laws 36–37 (2d ed. 1841).

> promote their own interest induces them to cultivate an intercourse with other people, they must necessarily adopt such principles, as a sense of common utility and of justice will inspire. . . . It has not been from comity, but from a sense of mutual utility, that nations have admitted the extension of personal statutes [that is, certain statutes of foreign countries relevant to the litigation]. It has arisen from a sort of necessity, and from a sense of the inconveniences which would result from a contrary doctrine. . . . [32]

Despite Story's stress upon comity, he and later Anglo-American writers did not attempt to blend private and public international law, as did many continental authors. Over the last century the rift between these bodies of law has broadened. The same "nationalization" of doctrine has occurred as with the law merchant and the law maritime. Most courts and authors today would view the enforcement of judgments or choice of law as within the domain of national law or private law, formally independent of international law except to the extent that they are brought within treaty arrangements.[33]

In more significant ways, thinking about private international law has departed radically from the premises of Story. Courts and scholars have stressed the inadequacy of a generic principle such as comity, or of general principles of customary international law, to resolve complex questions of jurisdiction, judgments or choice of law.

But viewed from a different perspective, the writings of Story or the continental authors remain as significant as do the relationships between these fields of law. The notion of unconnected bodies of national law on private international law, each following a quite separate path, is not one conducive to the growth of a transnational community encouraging travel and commerce among its members. There is a contemporary resurgence of writing stressing the identity or similarity of the values that systems of public and private international law seek to further—a community interest in common, or at least reasonable, rules on these matters in national legal systems. And such generic principles as reciprocity play an important role in both fields.

Additional reading: Nussbaum, The Rise and Decline of the Law of Nations Doctrine in the Conflict of Laws, 42 Colum.L.Rev. 189 (1942); Riphagen, The Relationship Between Public and Private Law and the Rules of Conflict of Laws, 102 Académie de Droit International Recueil des Cours 215 (1961); Stevenson, The Relationship of Private International Law to Public International Law, 52 Colum.L.Rev. 561 (1952); and Wortley, The Interaction of Public and Private International Law Today, 85 Académie de Droit International, Recueil des Cours 237 (1954). For a description and analysis of trends over the last decades in thinking about choice of law in the United States, see Cavers, The Choice-of-Law Process (1965).

32. S. Livermore, Dissertations on the Questions which Arise from the Contrariety of the Positive Laws of Different States and Nations 27–28 (1828).

33. For a treaty illustration, see The Boll Case, p. 293, supra.

NOTE ON RECIPROCITY AND ENFORCEMENT OF FOREIGN-COUNTRY JUDGMENTS

Hilton v. Guyot raises the fundamental question: why *should* an American court enforce another country's judgment? The Full Faith and Credit Clause is by its terms inapplicable. Still, some or all of the policies or values served by the Clause may be applicable on a transnational plane. If one were to decide that each of them had relevance transnationally, one might conclude that each doctrine developed under that Clause should be carried over to foreign-country judgments. On the other hand, to the extent that those policies or values are not applicable in transnational cases, one might conclude that more limited notions of enforcement would be appropriate. One way of testing such a proposition would be to reconsider the problem case at p. 766, supra, and to ask whether the arguments of policy in favor of recognizing the Ontario judgment are different from those in favor of recognizing that from Wisconsin.

The Court in Hilton v. Guyot relies heavily upon the concept of comity to lay some foundation in principle for enforcing foreign-country judgments. Some of the background of that concept, as well as some of the uncertainties in its application, are explored in the preceding note.

Justice Gray in his opinion shifts from concepts of comity to reciprocity. For example, towards the end of his opinion, he states that "international law is founded upon mutuality and reciprocity. . . ." We have encountered reciprocity before, particularly in Part D of Chapter V, as well as the idea of retaliation to which it is closely related. Arguments have been made from Hilton v. Guyot for a widespread resort to the reciprocity concept. These arguments raise the basic question whether there is a particular affinity between reciprocity and foreign judgments or whether reciprocity has significance for other areas of the conflict of laws. This issue was raised in Direction der Disconto-Gesellschaft v. United States Steel Corp., 300 Fed. 741 (S.D.N.Y.1924), aff'd, 267 U.S. 22, 45 S.Ct. 207, 69 L.Ed. 495 (1925). The question there posed was whether an English official or a German corporation was entitled to shares that had been issued by the defendant. The German corporation had originally bought the shares, and certificates representing them, endorsed in blank, were held by brokers in England. During the first World War, the shares were vested pursuant to English legislation in an English official. The district court held that the defendant should register the English official on its books as the shareholder. In the course of an opinion treating the many complex issues in this litigation, Judge Learned Hand stated:

> Finally, the plaintiffs argue that we should not recognize captures made in the United Kingdom until it appears that that nation extends a like recognition to captures made here. The point depends upon a misunderstanding of the effect of the case of Hilton v. Guyot, supra, 159 U.S. 113, 16

S.Ct. 139, 40 L.Ed. 95. Whatever may be thought of that decision the court certainly did not mean to hold that an American court was to recognize no obligations or duties arising elsewhere until it appeared that the sovereign of the locus reciprocally recognized similar obligations existing here. That doctrine I am happy to say is not a part of American jurisprudence. It is true that a judgment creates a debt, and is indeed an instance of the general principle. But it is a most especial instance, and no generalizations may properly be drawn from it. A judgment involves the direct action of a court against individuals, and offers more excuse for national jealousy than when the obligation arises from laws of general application. So far as I know, the doctrine of reciprocity has been confined to foreign judgments alone, and has no application to situations of this sort. Moreover, it is a doctrine in supposed protection of the nationals of the forum. On what theory citizens of a foreign state may invoke it I cannot understand. These plaintiffs are German citizens, and it would scarcely lie in their mouth to complain, even had it affirmatively appeared that the courts of England would not recognize similar captures made of shares under our own statutes. Much less must it be shown that they would so recognize them.

Additional reading: Lorenzen, The Enforcement of American Judgments Abroad, 29 Yale L.J. 188 (1919), and Nadelmann, Non-Recognition of American Money Judgments Abroad and What to Do About It, 42 Iowa L.Rev. 236 (1957).

QUESTIONS

(1) Does the Court in Hilton v. Guyot regard comity as comparable to the Full Faith and Credit Clause, as expressing the same policies? Does it, to the same extent as that Clause, stress not only relationships between nations (or states) but also the interests of the private parties involved?

(2) If you find the strategic arguments noted above in favor of a reciprocity requirement not persuasive, what practical arguments could you advance on its behalf? What strategic purpose could it be meant to serve? What appears to be the likelihood that it would realize such a purpose? Whether or not the purpose is ultimately realized, who suffers immediate injury? The foreign country?

(3) When in fact would a reciprocity requirement be satisfied? To entitle the plaintiff in Hilton to enforcement of his judgment, would it be necessary to show that French courts entertain challenges to a foreign judgment only and precisely on those grounds articulated in Hilton? Would *any* variation from such grounds lead to the conclusion that the reciprocity condition was not met? Suppose, for example, that French conditions for enforcement of foreign judgments were identical with those stated in Hilton, except that French courts refuse to enforce a judgment of a court which based jurisdiction solely on the transient presence of the defendant.

(4) Does the reciprocity requirement in Hilton apply to all enforcement actions? Suppose that both parties to the case had been United States citizens or French citizens.

(5) Does Judge Hand in the Disconto case succeed in showing that judgment cases are "most especial" and that principles such as reciprocity expressed in them are not to be applied in other situations?

NOTE ON DEFENSES TO ENFORCEMENT OF FOREIGN-COUNTRY JUDGMENTS

Whatever one concludes about the appropriate conceptual basis upon which a court should enforce foreign-nation judgments, *some* such judgments will be excluded. Recall the reasons discussed in the note at pp. 760–766, supra, why one American state need not enforce a sister-state's judgment. Compare such reasons with those suggested in Hilton v. Guyot as appropriate for impeaching a foreign country's judgment.

The Restatement, Second, Conflict of Laws states in Section 98 that "a valid judgment rendered in a foreign nation after a fair trial in a contested proceeding will be recognized in the United States. . . ." On its face that Section suggests various possible defences. The term "valid" brings into play requirements of other sections, applicable to sister state judgments as well, that a valid judgment must be based on proper judicial jurisdiction, follow after notice and opportunity to be heard, and be rendered by a competent court. Comment (g) to Section 98 indicates that some defences not available against sister-state judgments can be interposed to those from foreign countries: that the judgment is based on a governmental claim or that its enforcement would violate public policy. Note that although Section 98 refers only to *recognition* of foreign judgments, it appears to apply to *enforcement* as well. See Comment (d) to Section 100.

Case law exists with respect to some of these defences. For example, the question of denial of procedural due process in the foreign country was raised in Banco Minero v. Ross, 106 Tex. 522, 172 S.W. 711 (1915) in which a Texas court refused to enforce a money judgment rendered by a Mexican court. The opinion stated in part:

> As to Masterson, the Mexican court had jurisdiction, since he entered his appearance in the case. We are convinced, however, that upon another ground the judgment as to him is deserving of no recognition at the hands of the courts of this state. . . .
>
> But, jurisdiction being granted, the chief requisite for the recognition of a foreign judgment necessarily is that an opportunity for a full and fair trial was afforded. This means, not a summary proceeding, though sanctioned by the law of the forum, but an opportunity to be heard upon the proof where it is apparent that the cause involves questions of fact, and to have it considered by an unprejudiced court. The proceedings shown in relation to this judgment make it manifest that the trial of the case in the Mexican court was wanting in these essential elements. They reveal that the action was one unquestionably resting in questions of fact, and that Masterson pleaded what would have constituted a good defense, yet that he was denied the right to present it, it not appearing that his offer to support it was unseasonably made. If it be urged that this was warranted by the Mexican procedure, we are unwilling to give conclusiveness to a judgment which such a procedure sanctions. The judg-

> ment and the recitals which accompany it are a maze of words; but, as we interpret their vague and confused statements, it appears to have been rendered upon no proof whatever. It furthermore appears that Masterson was denied an appeal from the judgment upon what seems to us to have been a frivolous ground; namely, the omission to affix a stamp to the document of appeal. The entire proceeding appears to have been arbitrary in its nature and summary in its execution; and the court, in our opinion, properly declined to give the judgment effect.

A number of the decisions in this country treating enforcement of foreign judgments have turned on a critical condition to enforcement stated in Hilton v. Guyot: that the initial trial have been before a competent court conducting proceedings after "due citation or voluntary appearance of the defendant." The question raised is what standard should be applied by a court in the United States to determine whether the foreign court rendering the judgment met these conditions. Is the standard that expressed in the statutes or decisional law of the particular state in which the American court sits? Or is it expressed within the jurisdictional principles developed under the Due Process Clause of the Fourteenth Amendment? Or are there "international" standards which courts in this country should apply to determine when a particular foreign court had jurisdiction over a defendant?

Such questions suggest that "jurisdiction" cannot usefully be thought of solely in terms of the principles of the forum in which the initial action is brought, but must also take into account those of the forum for enforcement. It is evident that the tendency of any nation to expand the bases upon which it will assert jurisdiction is restrained by its anticipation of the negative reactions from courts of other countries in which enforcement of its judgments will sometimes be sought. The two cases described in this note and the decisions following it illustrate these difficulties.

Fisher v. Fielding [34]

In an action to enforce a judgment of an English court, defendant pleaded in part that the English court lacked jurisdiction over him. He was served with process while transiently stopping at a hotel in Birmingham. The opinion does not state where the cause of action involved arose. The Connecticut Supreme Court affirmed judgment for the plaintiff.

> An alien friend, however transient his presence may be, is entitled to a temporary protection, and owes in return a temporary allegiance. Story, Confl.Laws, §§ 18, 22, 541; Carlisle v. U. S., 16 Wall. 147, 154. The fact that the defendant was a foreigner, making but a brief stay in the country, and on the point of leaving it for his own, did not deprive the courts of England of all jurisdiction over him. . . .
>
> The courts of this state have never before had occasion to pass directly upon the defenses which may be open here to

34. 67 Conn. 91, 34 A. 714 (1895).

an action upon a judgment of a court of a foreign country, but they have often been called to consider the effect of legal proceedings instituted in one of the United States against a citizen of another; and the right to secure jurisdiction over a nonresident, who is served with process while transiently in the state, has been uniformly upheld. . . . These decisions are based on what has been deemed an accepted principle of international law, applicable between the states, on no other ground than that they are, as to such a question, in the position of foreign nations to each other. . . .

The English court having, then, jurisdiction of the parties, and presumably of the action and the subject-matter, as to which no question has been made, there is nothing in the defense now pleaded, that the suit was brought, as it was and when it was, "for the purpose of embarrassing and impeding the defendant, and to prevent his having a fair opportunity to defend said suit unless he prolonged his stay indefinitely at said Birmingham, and thereby said plaintiff sought to obtain an unjust and unfair advantage over said defendant." Where there is a legal right to do a certain act, the motive which induces the exercise of the right is of no importance. . . .

. . . The effect to be given to a foreign judgment in personam, for a money demand, must be determined either by the comity of nations, the rule of absolute reciprocity, or the personal obligation resting upon the defendant. Hilton v. Guyot, 159 U.S. 113, 16 S.Ct. 139. Whichever test may be adopted, the result would be the same where the question arises between the courts of England and those of an American state which was once an English colony. They are engaged in administering the same system of jurisprudence, and are bound together by common institutions and modes of thought, no less than by sharing the same language and the same history. The close and extensive commercial intercourse, also, between the United States and England, and across the long Canadian frontier, makes it especially important that the many controversies to which it must give rise should be promptly brought to a final settlement. When an American voluntarily places himself on English soil, he comes under a local and temporary allegiance to its sovereign, which makes it his duty to respect any summons with which he may there be served, to appear before the courts of the country. . . .

[A dissenting opinion noted that the defendant alleged that the cause of action involved did not arise in England and did not concern any activity of defendant in England. It went on to say:]

. . . When our court, in the exercise of its assumed power, is asked to grant execution of a judgment based on the right of such compulsion, its decision on the question of policy is controlled by no rule of international law. And certainly there can be no doubt but that public policy demands the refusal of execution in such case. It can hardly be claimed that the interests of our own citizens, or friendly intercourse with other nations, will be served by encouraging the establishment of a sort of international syndicate for promoting the collection of home debts through foreign courts, so that each traveler shall be compelled to run the gauntlet of such litigation under threat of snap judgments, upon which his own government must issue execution on his return. Such a policy would offer premiums to scavengers of sham and stale claims at every center of travel, breeding a class of process firers to lie in wait for their game at docks and railway stations. . . .

Grubel v. Nassauer [35]

Defendant in an enforcement action based upon a judgment of a German court argued that the German court lacked jurisdiction. Defendant, a German subject, had left Germany in 1901 and resided thereafter in New York, where he applied in 1906 for naturalization as a United States citizen. In 1907 the plaintiff, a German subject and resident, served notice upon defendant by publication of an action in a Bavarian court based upon an obligation allegedly incurred before defendant's departure from Germany. The New York court in this opinion affirmed judgment for defendant. It stated in part:

> . . . The whole argument of the appellant is based on the proposition that at the time of the recovery of the judgment the defendant was still a subject or citizen of Germany or Bavaria, and therefore, bound by its laws. In one sense this is doubtless true, and it may be assumed that the judgment is conclusive against the defendant in the country where it was recovered, and there would be enforced against him or his property. But the judgments of the courts of no country have necessarily any extraterritorial effect. When they are enforced in a foreign country, which as a rule they are to a certain extent, it is solely by virtue of comity. . . .
>
> The question, then, is how far comity should induce us to respect a foreign judgment obtained without personal service of process against a citizen of a foreign country domiciled here at the time of the recovery of the judgment. There is some confusion in the dicta of text-writers on the subject (Story's Conflict of Laws, § 599 et seq.; Black on Judgments, § 836 et seq.), and there has been fluctuation in the decisions of the courts. . . . By the requirement of the federal Constitution each state is required to give full faith and credit to the judgments of the other states. It is not a matter of comity between the states, but of obligation imposed by the paramount law. Yet it is settled that a judgment for money recovered in one state without personal service of process on the defendant in that state cannot be enforced without the state. In Pennoyer v. Neff, 95 U.S. 714, 727 (24 L.Ed. 565), it was held: "Process from the tribunals of one state cannot run into another state and summon parties there domiciled to leave its territory and respond to the proceedings against them. Publication of process or notice within the state where the tribunal sits cannot create any greater obligation upon the nonresident to appear. Process sent to him out of the state, and process published within it, are equally unavailing in proceedings to establish his personal liability." It seems to us unreasonable that we should give greater respect to judgments recovered in a foreign country than to a judgment recovered in one of our sister states.

35. 210 N.Y. 149, 103 N.E. 1113 (1913).

SOMPORTEX LIMITED v. PHILADELPHIA CHEWING GUM CORP.

United States Court of Appeals, Third Circuit, 1971.
453 F.2d 435, cert. denied 405 U.S. 1017, 92 S.Ct. 1294, 31 L.Ed.2d 479 (1972).

ALDISERT, CIRCUIT JUDGE. Several interesting questions are presented in this appeal from the district court's order, 318 F.Supp. 161, granting summary judgment to enforce a default judgment entered by an English court. To resolve them, a complete recitation of the procedural history of this case is necessary.

This case has its genesis in a transaction between appellant, Philadelphia Chewing Gum Corporation, and Somportex Limited, a British corporation, which was to merchandise appellant's wares in Great Britain under the trade name "Tarzan Bubble Gum." According to the facts as alleged by appellant, there was a proposal which involved the participation of Brewster Leeds and Co., Inc., and M. S. International, Inc., third-party defendants in the court below. Brewster made certain arrangements with Somportex to furnish gum manufactured by Philadelphia; M. S. International, as agent for the licensor of the trade name "Tarzan," was to furnish the African name to the American gum to be sold in England. For reasons not relevant to our limited inquiry, the transaction never reached fruition.

Somportex filed an action against Philadelphia for breach of contract in the Queen's Bench Division of the High Court of England. Notice of the issuance of a Writ of Summons was served, in accordance with the rules and with the leave of the High Court, upon Philadelphia at its registered address in Havertown, Pennsylvania, on May 15, 1967. The extraterritorial service was based on the English version of long-arm statutes utilized by many American states.[36] Philadelphia then consulted a firm of English solicitors, who, by letter of July 14, 1967, advised its Pennsylvania lawyers:

> I have arranged with the Solicitors for Somportex Limited that they will let me have a copy of their Affidavit and exhibits to that Affidavit which supported their application to serve out of the Jurisdiction. Subject to the contents of the Affidavit, and any further information that can be provided by Philadelphia Chewing Gum Corporation after we have had the opportunity of seeing the Affidavit, it may be possible to make an application to the Court for an Order setting the Writ aside. But for such an application to be successful we will have to show that on the facts the matter does not fall within the provision of (f) and (g) [of the long-arm statute, note 1, supra] referred to above.

36. [Eds.] [Here the court quotes from Order 11, p. 750, supra.]

Cf., the Pennsylvania Statute authorizing service on a foreign corporation, which provides:

> For the purpose of determining jurisdiction of courts within this Commonwealth, the doing by any corporation in this Commonwealth of a series of similar acts for the purpose of thereby realizing pecuniary benefit or otherwise accomplishing an object, or doing a single act in this Commonwealth for such purpose, with the intention of thereby initiating a series of such acts, shall constitute "doing business". For the purposes of this subsection the shipping of merchandise directly or indirectly into or through this Commonwealth shall be considered the doing of such an act in this Commonwealth. 15 Pa.Stat.Ann. § 2011, subd. C.

Pennsylvania decisional law has generously interpreted its long-arm statute. See state cases summarized in Siders v. Upper Mississippi Towing Corp., 423 F.2d 535 (3rd Cir. 1970).

> In the meantime we will enter a conditional Appearance to the Writ in behalf of Philadelphia Chewing Gum Corporation in order to preserve the status quo.

On August 9, 1967, the English solicitors entered a "conditional appearance to the Writ" and filed a motion to set aside the Writ of Summons.[37] At a hearing before a Master on November 13, 1967, the solicitors appeared and disclosed that Philadelphia had elected not to proceed with the summons or to contest the jurisdiction of the English Court, but instead intended to obtain leave of court to withdraw appearance of counsel. The Master then dismissed Philadelphia's summons to set aside plaintiff's Writ of Summons. Four days later, the solicitors sought to withdraw their appearance as counsel for Philadelphia, contending that it was a conditional appearance only. On November 27, 1967, after a Master granted the motion, Somportex appealed. The appeal was denied after hearing before a single judge, but the Court of Appeal, reversing the decision of the Master, held that the appearance was unconditional and that the submission to the jurisdiction by Philadelphia was, therefore, effective.[38] But the court let stand "the original order which was

37. The memorandum of conditional appearance was stamped with this formula: "This appearance is to stand as unconditional unless the defendant applies within fourteen days to set aside the writ and service thereof and obtains an order to that effect."

The motion alleged:

(1) that there was no agreement made between the Plaintiffs and Defendants on or about 17th December 1966;

(2) alternatively that if there was such an agreement:—

(a) it was not made within the jurisdiction of this honourable Court; or

(b) it was not made by or through an agent trading or residing within the jurisdiction on behalf of the Defendants a principal trading or residing out of the jurisdiction; or

(c) it was not by its terms or by implication to be governed by English law;

(3) in the further alternative that if there was such an agreement there has been no breach of the said agreement committed within the jurisdiction of this honourable court; . . .

38. Somportex v. Philadelphia Chewing Gum [1968], 3 All.E.R. 26, 29, Lord Denning:

In order to decide the point, I think that one has to put oneself in the position of the American company and their advisers when faced with this notice of the writ. They could have not entered an appearance at all, in which case by the law of Pennsylvania they would not be bound by any judgment. Instead of doing that, however, after consultation with a distinguished firm of lawyers in the city of London they decided to enter a conditional appearance. That was a very important step for them to take (especially if they had assets in England or were likely to bring assets into England) because it was an essential way of defending their own position. After all, if they did not enter an appearance at all, and in consequence the English courts gave judgment against them in default of appearance, that judgment could be executed against them in England in respect of assets in England. In order to guard against that eventuality, they had first to enter a conditional appearance here, then argue whether it was within the jurisdiction of the court or not. If it was outside the jurisdiction, all well and good. The writ would be set aside. They would go away free. If it was within the jurisdiction, however, their appearance became unconditional and they could fight out the case on the merits. In these circumstances it seems to me that they were very wise to enter a conditional appearance. It was a step which would be advised by any competent lawyer if there was a likelihood that assets would then or afterwards come into England.

We have, therefore, a wise course of action deliberately decided on by eminent firms in England and the United States after consultation, and I do not think that they should

made by the master on Nov. 13 dismissing the application to set aside. The writ therefore will stand. On the other hand, if the American company would wish to appeal from the order of Nov. 13, I see no reason why the time should not be extended and they can argue that matter out at a later stage if they should so wish."

Thereafter, Philadelphia made a calculated decision: it decided to do nothing. It neither asked for an extension of time nor attempted in any way to proceed with an appeal from the Master's order dismissing its application to set aside the Writ. Instead, it directed its English solicitors to withdraw from the case. There being no appeal, the Master's order became final.

Somportex then filed a Statement of Claim which was duly served in accordance with English Court rules. In addition, by separate letter, it informed Philadelphia of the significance and effect of the pleading, the procedural posture of the case, and its intended course of action.

Philadelphia persisted in its course of inaction; it failed to file a defense. Somportex obtained a default judgment against it in the Queen's Bench Division of the High Court of Justice in England for the sum of £39,562.10.10 (approximately $94,000.00). The award reflected some $45,000.00 for loss of profit; $46,000.00 for loss of good will and $2,500.00 for costs, including attorneys' fees.

Thereafter, Somportex filed a diversity action in the court below, seeking to enforce the foreign judgment, and attached to the complaint a certified transcript of the English proceeding. The district court granted two motions which gave rise to this appeal: it dismissed the third-party complaints for failure to state a proper claim under F.R.C.P. 14; and it granted plaintiff's motion for summary judgment, F.R.C.P. 56(a). . . .

Appellant presents a cluster of contentions supporting its major thesis that we should not extend hospitality to the English judgment. First, it contends, and we agree, that because our jurisdiction is based solely on diversity, "the law to be applied . . . is the law of the state," in this case, Pennsylvania law. Erie R. Co. v. Tompkins, 304 U.S. 64, 58 S.Ct. 817, 82 L.Ed. 1188 (1938); Svenska Handelsbanken v. Carlson, 258 F.Supp. 448 (D.Mass.1966).

Pennsylvania distinguishes between judgments obtained in the courts of her sister states, which are entitled to full faith and credit, and those of foreign courts, which are subject to principles of comity. In re Christoff's Estate, 411 Pa. 419, 192 A.2d 737, cert. denied, 375 U.S. 965, 84 S.Ct. 483, 11 L.Ed.2d 414 (1964).

Comity is a recognition which one nation extends within its own territory to the legislative, executive, or judicial acts of another. It is not a rule of law, but one of practice, convenience, and expediency. Although more than mere courtesy and accommodation, comity does not achieve the force of an imperative or obligation. Rather, it is a nation's expression of understanding which demonstrates due regard both to international duty and convenience and to the rights of per-

be allowed now to go back on it. It must be remembered that, on the faith of this entry of appearance, the English company have altered their position. They have not gone to the United States, as they might have done, and taken steps there against the American company. They have remained in this country and pursued the action here—on the faith that there was a conditional appearance entered which would become unconditional unless it was duly set aside. In the circumstances, I do not think that we should give leave to withdraw the appearance.

sons protected by its own laws. Comity should be withheld only when its acceptance would be contrary or prejudicial to the interest of the nation called upon to give it effect.[39] See Orfield and Re, International Law, Note, "Recognition and Enforcement of Foreign Judgments and Awards," pp. 736–737.

Thus, the court in *Christoff,* supra, 192 A.2d at 739, acknowledged the governing standard enunciated in Hilton v. Guyot, supra, 159 U.S. at 205, 16 S.Ct. at 159:

> When an action is brought in a court of this country by a citizen of a foreign country against one of our own citizens . . . and the foreign judgment appears to have been rendered by a competent court, having jurisdiction of the cause and of the parties and upon due allegations and proofs, and opportunity to defend against them, and its proceedings are according to the course of a civilized jurisprudence, and are stated in a clear and formal record, the judgment is prima facie evidence, at least, of the truth of the matter adjudged; and it should be held conclusive upon the merits tried in the foreign court, unless some special ground is shown for impeaching the judgment, as by showing that it was affected by fraud or prejudice, or that by the principles of international law, and by the comity of our own country, it should not be given full credit and effect.

It is by this standard, therefore, that appellant's arguments must be measured.

Appellant's contention that the district court failed to make an independent examination of the factual and legal basis of the jurisdiction of the English Court at once argues too much and says too little. The reality is that the court did examine the legal basis of asserted jurisdiction and decided the issue adversely to appellant.

Indeed, we do not believe it was necessary for the court below to reach the question of whether the factual complex of the contractual dispute permitted extraterritorial service under the English long-arm statute. In its opinion denying leave of defense counsel to withdraw, the Court of Appeal specifically gave Philadelphia the opportunity to have the factual issue tested before the courts; moreover, Philadelphia was allocated additional time to do just that. Lord Denning said: ". . . They can argue that matter out at a later stage if they should so wish." Three months went by with no activity forthcoming and then, as described by the district court, "[d]ur-

39. In Hilton v. Guyot, 159 U.S. 113, 16 S.Ct. 139, 40 L.Ed. 95 (1895), the Supreme Court spoke of the likelihood of reciprocity as a condition precedent to the recognition of comity. The doctrine has received no more than desultory acknowledgement. Direction der Disconto-Gesellschaft v. United States Steel Corp., 300 F. 741, 747 (S.D.N.Y. 1921); see also, Banco Nacional de Cuba v. Sabbatino, 376 U.S. 398, 411, 84 S.Ct. 923, 11 L.Ed.2d 804 (1963) (dictum). It has been rejected by the courts of New York, Johnston v. Compagnie Generale Transatlantique, 242 N.Y. 381, 152 N.E. 121 (N.Y.1926), and by statute in California. See Reese, "The Status in this Country of Judgments Rendered Abroad," 50 Col.L. Rev. 783, 790–93 (1950).

> We agree with the district court that this issue of the enforceability of foreign judgments has not frequently been litigated in Pennsylvania, and the Court has not been cited to, nor has independent examination revealed any Pennsylvania cases which even intimate that a finding of reciprocity is an essential precondition to their enforcing a foreign judgment.

Somportex Limited v. Philadelphia Chewing Gum Corp., 318 F.Supp. 161, 168 (E.D.Pa.1970).

ing this three month period, defendant changed its strategy and, not wishing to do anything which might result in its submitting to the English Court's jurisdiction, decided to withdraw its appearance altogether." Under these circumstances, we hold that defendant cannot choose its forum to test the factual basis of jurisdiction. It was given, and it waived, the opportunity of making the adequate presentation in the English Court.[40]

Additionally, appellant attacks the English practice wherein a conditional appearance attacking jurisdiction may, by court decision, be converted into an unconditional one. It cannot effectively argue that this practice constitutes "some special ground . . . for impeaching the judgment," as to render the English judgment unwelcome in Pennsylvania under principles of international law and comity because it was obtained by procedures contrary or prejudicial to the host state. The English practice in this respect is identical to that set forth in both the Federal and Pennsylvania rules of civil procedure.[41] F.R.C.P. 12(b)(2) provides the vehicle for attacking jurisdiction over the person, and, in Orange Theatre Corp. v. Rayherstz Amusement Corp., 139 F.2d 871, 874 (3d Cir. 1944), we said that Rule 12 "has abolished for the federal courts the age-old distinction between general and special appearances."[42] Similarly, a conditional or *"de bene esse"* appearance no longer exists in Pennsylvania.[43] Monaco v. Montgomery Cab Co., 417 Pa. 135, 208 A.2d 252 (1965), Pa.R.C.P. 1451(a)(7). A challenge to jurisdiction must

40. [Eds.] Here the court referred to Baldwin v. Iowa State Traveling Men's Ass'n, p. 764, supra.

41. "The time-honored recital of a 'special appearance' has no place under the rules." Wright, Federal Courts, § 66 at 279.

42. The Supreme Court has upheld the constitutionality of Texas statutes providing that a special appearance for a nonresident defendant for the purpose of pleading to the jurisdiction is a voluntary appearance which brings the defendant into court for all purposes. York v. Texas, 137 U.S. 15, 11 S.Ct. 9, 34 L.Ed. 604 (1890). . . .

43. Appellant attaches much significance to the July 14, 1967, letter of its English solicitors, supra, wherein its American counsel were told: "we will enter a conditional Appearance to the Writ in behalf of Philadelphia Chewing Gum Corporation in order to preserve the status quo." From that it builds the argument that it cannot be said to have ever consented to have entered an appearance which would have subjected it to the court's jurisdiction. In support thereof it contends that it and its American counsel took the phrase "conditional appearance" to mean *de bene esse.* The argument is totally without merit. We can perceive of no principle of law which removes one from the reach of a court's jurisdiction because of misunderstanding or misimpression by one counsel of advice from privately retained co-counsel. Moreover, as heretofore observed, the conditional appearance was described by Lord Denning in Somportex v. Philadelphia Chewing Gum, 3 All.E.R. 26, 27:

> "the memorandum of conditional appearance was stamped with the usual formula: 'This appearance is to stand as unconditional unless the defendant applies within fourteen days to set aside the writ and service thereof and obtains an order to that effect.'"

It can also be said that appellant may be estopped from advancing this argument before this court. Scarano v. Central R. Co. of New Jersey, 203 F.2d 510 (3rd Cir. 1953). In the district court, its counsel stated:

> "The English Court decided that a conditional appearance was a general appearance. We are not asking this court to redetermine that issue. We are saying that even assuming the English Court was correct, that judgment is not entitled to comity; no cases support it. Thank you."
> THE COURT: Now do you agree that the issue as to mistake in the law was litigated in the English Courts?
> COUNSEL: Yes, sir.

be asserted there by a preliminary objection raising a question of jurisdiction. Pa.R.C.P. 1017(b)(1).

Thus, we will not disturb the English Court's adjudication. That the English judgment was obtained by appellant's default instead of through an adversary proceeding does not dilute its efficacy. In the absence of fraud or collusion, a default judgment is as conclusive an adjudication between the parties as when rendered after answer and complete contest in the open courtroom. . . . The polestar is whether a reasonable method of notification is employed and reasonable opportunity to be heard is afforded to the person affected. Restatement (Second) Conflict of Laws, § 92 (Proposed Final Draft), 1967.

English law permits recovery, as compensatory damages in breach of contract, of items reflecting loss of good will and costs, including attorneys' fees. These two items formed substantial portions of the English judgment. Because they are not recoverable under Pennsylvania law, appellant would have the foreign judgment declared unenforceable because it constitutes an " . . . action on the foreign claim [which] could not have been maintained because contrary to the public policy of the forum," citing Restatement, Conflict of Laws, § 445. We are satisfied with the district court's disposition of this argument:

> The Court finds that . . . while Pennsylvania may not agree that these elements should be included in damages for breach of contract, the variance with Pennsylvania law is not such that the enforcement "tends clearly to injure the public health, the public morals, the public confidence in the purity of the administration of the law, or to undermine that sense of security for individual rights, whether of personal liberty or of private property, which any citizen ought to feel, is against public policy." Goodyear v. Brown, 155 Pa. 514, 518, 26 A. 665, 666 (1893).

Somportex Limited v. Philadelphia Chewing Gum Corp., 318 F.Supp. 161, 169 (E.D.Pa.1970).

Finally, appellant contends that since "it maintains no office or employee in England and transacts no business within the country" there were no insufficient contacts there to meet the due process tests of International Shoe Co. v. Washington, 326 U.S. 310, 66 S.Ct. 154, 90 L.Ed. 95 (1965). It argues that, at best, "the only contact Philadelphia had with England was the negotiations allegedly conducted by an independent New York exporter by letter, telephone and telegram to sell Philadelphia's products in England." In Hanson v. Denckla, 357 U.S. 235, 253, 78 S.Ct. 1228, 1240, 2 L.Ed.2d 1283 (1958), Chief Justice Warren said: "The application of [the requirement of contact] rule will vary with the quality and nature of the defendant's activity, but it is essential in each case that there be some act by which the defendant purposely avails itself of the privilege of conducting business within the forum State, thus invoking the benefits and protection of its laws." We have concluded that whether the New York exporter was an independent contractor or Philadelphia's agent was a matter to be resolved by the English Court. For the purpose of the constitutional argument, we must assume the proper agency relationship. So construed, we find his activity would constitute the "quality and nature of the defendant's activity" similar to that of the defendant in McGee v. International Life Ins. Co., 355 U.S. 220, 78 S.Ct. 199, 2 L.Ed.2d 223 (1957), there held to satisfy due process requirements.

For the reasons heretofore rehearsed we will not disturb the English Court's adjudication of jurisdiction; we have deemed as irrelevant the default nature of the judgment; we have concluded that the English compensatory damage items do not offend Pennsylvania public policy; and hold that the English procedure comports with our standards of due process.

In sum, we find that the English proceedings met all the tests enunciated in *Christoff,* supra. We are not persuaded that appellant met its burden of showing that the British "decree is so palpably tainted by fraud or prejudice as to outrage our sense of justice, or [that] the process of the foreign tribunal was invoked to achieve a result contrary to our laws of public policy or to circumvent our laws or public policy." *Christoff,* supra, 192 A.2d at 739.

The judgment of the district court will be affirmed.

COMMENT

Somportex was followed in British Midland Airways Ltd. v. International Travel, Inc., 497 F.2d 869 (9th Cir. 1974), a case in which a British airline (BMA) sued an American travel agency in England on a contract for charter flights. International's British attorneys appeared and defended the case, but BMA prevailed on a motion (in effect) for summary judgment. International failed to pursue its appeal rights. BMA sued on the judgment in United States District Court in the State of Washington. International claimed a denial of due process in that the British courts refused to allow further proceedings unless International made a deposit of the amount sought, and in that no record of the proceedings was kept. The Court of Appeals found the summary judgment proceeding fully adequate by American standards, observing that "United States courts . . . are hardly in a position to call the Queen's Bench a kangaroo court."

Compare Cherun v. Frishman, 236 F.Supp. 292 (D.D.C.1964), where the court enforced a default judgment of an Ontario court for money damages growing out of a land transaction between the American (citizen and resident) defendant and the Canadian plaintiff. Defendant had been personally served in the District of Columbia with a writ pursuant to Ontario law providing for service outside Ontario where any "contract . . . affecting land . . . situated within Ontario is sought to be . . . enforced." The court found that the reciprocity condition of Hilton v. Guyot was met, and also found that opinion's other conditions to be satisfied. It stated that the issue whether the foreign court had jurisdiction over the American citizen "should be determined by our own standards of judicial power as promulgated by the Supreme Court under the due process clause of the Fourteenth Amendment." Thus it concluded that the principles established by cases such as International Shoe and McGee "apply equally as well to the question of jurisdiction in its present international context . . ." It stressed that "Ontario has a very definite and substantial interest in providing its citizens with an effective remedy in situations such as this. . . ."

Compare the observation of a New York court, concluding that an English default money judgment against a New York corporation served in New York pursuant to Order 11, was conclusive.[44] "If the facts were the reverse, this court would have taken jurisdiction of the English defendant by extraterritorial service under our statutes. We can do no less now in affording the English court reciprocal acquisition of jurisdiction over the defendant here."

QUESTIONS

(1) Suppose that the defendant in Grubel v. Nassauer had retained counsel in Germany to appear for him to argue that the German court lacked jurisdiction and, if necessary, to defend on the merits of the controversy. Should the result in the New York case have been different? Compare Baldwin v. Iowa State Travelling Men's Ass'n, p. 764, supra.

(2) Do you agree with Fisher v. Fielding? Is it necessarily conclusive that the jurisdictional basis for the foreign court had a precise parallel in Connecticut law? How would you have developed an argument before the Connecticut court that it should have applied a different standard? How would you have described that standard?

(3) Consider the relationship between Grubel v. Nassauer and the later cases:

(*a*) Did the court in Grubel correctly identify the jurisdictional basis which the German court most likely used, in view of the description of German law at p. 753, supra?

(*b*) Does the opinion in Grubel suggest a distinct ground on which enforcement of the judgment could properly have been denied?

(*c*) In view of developments since 1913, including the enactment in 1963 of § 302 of the New York Civil Practice Law and Rules, p. 744, supra, should a New York lower court now follow Grubel v. Nassauer? Suppose that the foreign default judgment, like that in Somportex, was based on English Order 11. Would departure from prior precedent have been unfair to a defendant who had made a decision not to appear abroad, such as that taken by Philadelphia Chewing Gum Corporation and its counsel?

(4) What tactical alternatives were open to counsel for Philadelphia Chewing Gum when the English litigation was commenced? What would the consequence of each alternative have been for the attitude of the American court towards the British court's determinations?

(5) Note the standard of "public policy" employed by the court in that case. Would it include a British judgment based on a gambling contract as in Fauntleroy v. Lum, p. 760, supra?

(6) In view of the jurisdictional principles under French law, described at p. 751, supra, what was the probable jurisdictional basis for the French judgment that was sued upon in Hilton v. Guyot? Assume that the Court in Hilton concluded that lack of reciprocity did of itself bar enforcement. Should the jurisdictional basis for the foreign judgment have provided an independent basis for refusal to enforce? What arguments

44. Plugmay Ltd. v. National Dynamics Corp., 48 Misc.2d 913, 266 N.Y.S.2d 240 (Civ.Ct.N.Y.C.1966), rev'd (on grounds that issues of fact were presented which required full disclosure of the foreign court's jurisdiction), 53 Misc. 2d 451, 278 N.Y.S.2d 896 (App.Term, 1st Dept. 1967).

could you develop for and against such a refusal, in view of the facts underlying the litigation that are stated in the dissenting opinion at p. 773, supra?

NOTE ON ENFORCEMENT OF FOREIGN REVENUE AND PENAL JUDGMENTS

Recall that Milwaukee County v. M. E. White Co., p. 762, supra, held that a state was required to give full faith and credit to a tax judgment of a sister state. Absent the compulsion of the Full Faith and Credit Clause, should the same principle apply when the judgment creditor is a foreign governmental body?

In Government of India v. Taylor, [1955] A.C. 491, the plaintiff sought to prove before English courts an Indian tax claim in the course of liquidation of an English company. Lord Somervell of Harrow stated in his opinion, [1955] A.C. at 514–15:

> Tax gathering is an administrative act, though in settling the quantum as well as in the final act of collection judicial process may be involved. Our courts will apply foreign law if it is the proper law of a contract, the subject of a suit. Tax gathering is not a matter of contract but of authority and administration as between the State and those within its jurisdiction. If one considers the initial stages of the process, which may . . . be intricate and prolonged, it would be remarkable comity if State B allowed the time of its courts to be expended in assisting in this regard the tax gatherers of State A. Once a judgment has been obtained and it is a question only of its enforcement the factor of time and expense will normally have disappeared. The principle remains. The claim is one for a tax.
>
> That fact, I think, itself justifies what has been clearly the practice of States. . . . The position in the United States of America has been referred to, and I agree that the position as between member States of a federation, wherever the reserve of sovereignty may be, does not help,

Enforcement of revenue claims was denied. A more recent Canadian case, United States v. Harden, [1963] Can.Sup.Ct. 366, 41 D.L. R.2d 721, denied enforcement to a consent judgment of a United States district court rendered on a claim for taxes. The Supreme Court of Canada held that the foreign cause of action did not merge into the foreign judgment and that a foreign revenue claim would not be enforced directly or indirectly.[45]

QUESTIONS

(1) Do you agree with these holdings? What problems can you envision if a foreign government were allowed to bring an action in a United States court based on a tax judgment rendered in its courts, upon

45. For a discussion of an article of the tax convention between the United States and the Netherlands that seemed to modify the principle of non-enforcement of foreign tax claims, see United States v. van der Horst, 270 F.Supp. 365 (D.Del.1967).

proper jurisdiction, against a United States citizen? Against its own national?

(2) How should a court in the United States entertaining an action on a foreign-country judgment respond to defendant's allegation that it rested upon a penal law? Recall the quite narrow scope given to the "penal law" exception in an interstate setting in Huntington v. Attrill, p. 764, supra. Whatever the scope of this exception in an interstate setting, are different problems posed when the judgment issues from a foreign country?

(3) Part of the extensive litigation between Huntington and Attrill involved an action by Huntington in Ontario to enforce his New York judgment against local assets of Attrill. The basic question raised in that litigation was whether the action was penal "in the sense of international law." How should the Ontario court have ruled? See Huntington v. Attrill, [1893] A.C. 150 (P.C.1892).

(4) In some civil law countries a criminal court may, at the same time that it sentences the accused to a fine or imprisonment, also award a judgment for damages against him in favor of an injured party who may appear in the criminal proceedings. Is such an injured party barred by the United States doctrine of penal judgments from having his award enforced here?

NOTE ON FEDERAL-STATE RELATIONS IN THE ENFORCEMENT OF FOREIGN-COUNTRY JUDGMENTS

As early as the 1920's, the New York courts in Johnston v. Compagnie Général Transatlantique, 242 N.Y. 381, 152 N.E. 121 (1926), and Cowans v. Ticonderoga Pulp & Paper Co., 219 App.Div. 120, 219 N.Y.S. 284, aff'd, 246 N.Y. 603, 159 N.E. 669 (1927), held that they were not bound to follow Hilton v. Guyot and to require reciprocity. In Johnston a French judgment for defendant was *recognized as a bar* to plaintiff's second action on the *same* cause of action. In Cowans, a Quebec money judgment was *enforced*. Note the following observations in Johnston:

> To what extent is this court bound by Hilton v. Guyot? It is argued with some force that questions of international relations and the comity of nations are to be determined by the Supreme Court of the United States; that there is no such thing as comity of nations between the state of New York and the republic of France; and that the decision in Hilton v. Guyot is controlling as a statement of the law. But the question is one of private rather than public international law, of private right rather than public relations, and our courts will recognize private rights acquired under foreign laws and the sufficiency of the evidence establishing such rights. A right acquired under a foreign judgment may be established in this state without reference to the rules of evidence laid down by the courts of the United States. Comity is not a rule of law, but it is a rule of "practice, convenience and expediency. It is something more than mere courtesy, which implies only deference to the opinion of others, since it has a substantial value in securing uniformity of deci-

> sion, and discouraging repeated litigation of the same question." Brown, J., in Mast, Foos & Co. v. Stover Mfg. Co., 177 U.S. 485, 488, 20 S.Ct. 708, 710 (44 L.Ed. 865). It therefore rests, not on the basis of reciprocity, but rather upon the persuasiveness of the foreign judgment. Loucks v. Standard Oil Co., 224 N.Y. 99, 111, 120 N.E. 198. When the whole of the facts appear to have been inquired into by the French courts, judicially, honestly, and with full jurisdiction and with the intention to arrive at the right conclusion, and when they have heard the facts and come to a conclusion, it should no longer be open to the party invoking the foreign court against a resident of France to ask the American court to sit as a court of appeal from that which gave the judgment.
>
> I reach the conclusion that this court is not bound to follow the Hilton Case and reverse its previous rulings.

The more recent case law, as indicated in Somportex Ltd. v. Philadelphia Chewing Gum Corp., p. 783, supra, leans towards regarding the *enforcement or recognition* of foreign judgments as a matter to be determined by state law. The developments since 1938 that bear on this question are set forth at greater length in Svenska Handelsbanken v. Carlson, 258 F.Supp. 448, 450 (D.Mass.1966), a diversity action by a Swedish bank against a Massachusetts resident to enforce a Swedish money judgment:

> . . . It appears that the judgment of the Swedish court is a valid one under Swedish law, entered after actual notice and opportunity to defend was given to defendant, by a court which had jurisdiction under Swedish law. It is not clear, however, that it is entitled to conclusive effect in this court. In Hilton v. Guyot, 159 U.S. 113, 16 S.Ct. 139, 40 L.Ed. 95 the United States Supreme Court held that a judgment of a court of a foreign country would be given conclusive effect only if the courts of that nation would give similar effect to judgments rendered in the United States. Where such reciprocity does not exist the foreign judgment is only prima facie evidence of the correctness of the underlying claim. While the court in Banco Nacional de Cuba v. Sabbatino, 376 U.S. 398, 84 S.Ct. 923, 11 L.Ed.2d 804, did not accept the broad language of the Hilton opinion, it did not disturb the specific ruling of that case as to the effect to be given to foreign judgments. However, Massachusetts rather than federal law seems to be properly applicable here. Erie Railroad Co. v. Tompkins, 304 U.S. 64, 58 S.Ct. 817, 82 L.Ed. 1188. Although the Massachusetts cases are very old, the Massachusetts rule appears to be that a judgment of a court of a foreign country is only prima facie evidence of the underlying claim, and that defendant is entitled to all the defenses he might have made to the original action. . . .

The Restatement, Second, Conflict of Laws § 98, Comment (e), states that federal courts "may" be bound to follow the rule prevailing in the courts of the state where they sit. By omitting a reciprocity requirement, it follows Johnston rather than Hilton.

Several states have enacted statutes dealing with foreign country judgments. Two examples follow (the first of which, the California statute, was repealed in 1974 as no longer serving a useful purpose):

(*a*) *Cal.Code Civ.Proc.* § *1915*: "Except as provided in [California's enactment of the Uniform Foreign Money Judgments Recognition Act], a final judgment of any other tribunal of a foreign country having jurisdiction, according to the laws of such country, to pronounce the judgment, shall have the same effect as in the country where rendered, and also the same effect as final judgments rendered in this state." [46]

(*b*) *N.H.Rev.Stat.* § *524:11*: "In suits on judgments rendered in the courts of the Dominion of Canada or any province thereof, said judgments shall be given such faith and credit as is given in the courts of the Dominion of Canada or any province thereof to the judgments rendered in the courts of New Hampshire."

The New Hampshire statute obviously reflects practices in the Canadian provinces, particularly in Quebec which has denied conclusive effect to foreign judgments. See Nadelmann, Enforcement of Foreign Judgments in Canada, 38 Can.B.Rev. 68 (1960). A more elaborate statute is the Uniform Foreign Money Judgments Recognition Act approved in 1962 by the National Conference of Commissioners on Uniform State Laws and adopted by at least eight states. 13 U.L. Ann. 269 (Master ed. 1975). A statute patterned after the Act was passed in Massachusetts after Svenska Handelsbanken. Mass.Gen.L. Ch. 235 § 23A. In addition to stating that foreign countries' judgments are to be recognized—without mention of reciprocity—the Uniform Act sets forth specific grounds of non-recognition in Section 4 and in Section 5 deals extensively with one ground, want of jurisdiction. Critical sections of the Act follow:

§ 3. **[Recognition and Enforcement]**.—Except as provided in section 4, a foreign judgment meeting the requirements of section 2 is conclusive between the parties to the extent that it grants or denies recovery of a sum of money. The foreign judgment is enforceable in the same manner as the judgment of a sister state which is entitled to full faith and credit.

§ 4. **[Grounds for Non-recognition]**.—(a) A foreign judgment is not conclusive if

(1) the judgment was rendered under a system which does not provide impartial tribunals or procedures compatible with the requirements of due process of law;

(2) the foreign court did not have personal jurisdiction over the defendant; or

(3) the foreign court did not have jurisdiction over the subject matter.

46. Section 1915 as set forth was enacted in 1907 except for the introductory clause added in 1967 on California's adoption of the Uniform Act.

(b) A foreign judgment need not be recognized if

(1) the defendant in the proceedings in the foreign court did not receive notice of the proceedings in sufficient time to enable him to defend;

(2) the judgment was obtained by fraud;

(3) the [cause of action] [claim for relief] on which the judgment is based is repugnant to the public policy of this state;

(4) the judgment conflicts with another final and conclusive judgment;

(5) the proceeding in the foreign court was contrary to an agreement between the parties under which the dispute in question was to be settled otherwise than by proceedings in that court; or

(6) in the case of jurisdiction based only on personal service, the foreign court was a seriously inconvenient forum for the trial of the action.

§ 5. **[Personal Jurisdiction].**—(a) The foreign judgment shall not be refused recognition for lack of personal jurisdiction if

(1) the defendant was served personally in the foreign state;

(2) the defendant voluntarily appeared in the proceedings, other than for the purpose of protecting property seized or threatened with seizure in the proceedings or of contesting the jurisdiction of the court over him;

(3) the defendant prior to the commencement of the proceedings had agreed to submit to the jurisdiction of the foreign court with respect to the subject matter involved;

(4) the defendant was domiciled in the foreign state when the proceedings were instituted, or, being a body corporate had its principal place of business, was incorporated, or had otherwise acquired corporate status, in the foreign state;

(5) the defendant had a business office in the foreign state and the proceedings in the foreign court involved a [cause of action] [claim for relief] arising out of business done by the defendant through that office in the foreign state; or

(6) the defendant operated a motor vehicle or airplane in the foreign state and the proceedings involved a [cause of action] [claim for relief] arising out of such operation.

(b) The courts of this state may recognize other bases of jurisdiction.

QUESTIONS

(1) Do you find persuasive the reasoning in Svenska Handelsbanken that federal courts should, under the Erie doctrine, follow state rules as to foreign country judgments? Or would you find more convincing the argument it rejects, that federal common law should govern? What precedents would you regard as most strongly supporting those arguments?

(2) An argument that "federal" law should control must take account of the statements of the New York court in the Johnston case that "questions of international relations and the comity of nations are to be determined by the Supreme Court of the United States. . . ." But with respect to the action before it, that court stated that "the question is one of private rights rather than public relations. . . ." Is this distinction between "private rights" and "public relations" sound or meaningful, as applied to the question whether federal or state law should govern? [47]

(3) Consider the pre-1974 California statute. Suppose a Frenchman and a California domiciliary enter a contract made and to be entirely performed in California; the Frenchman, alleging breach of the contract, obtains a judgment in France based on Article 14 of the Civil Code, p. 751, supra. Does the statute make that judgment enforceable against the California domiciliary? Could it, consistently with the Due Process Clause of the Fourteenth Amendment? Compare Shelley v. Kramer, 334 U.S. 1, 68 S.Ct. 836, 92 L.Ed. 1161 (1948). Does it, literally construed, give greater effect to judgments rendered in foreign countries than is given to sister-state judgments? How much did California's adoption of the Uniform Act affect your answers?

(4) Could one make an effective argument that the New Hampshire statute would pose constitutional problems if Congress or the Supreme Court were to abolish the reciprocity requirement, set forth in Hilton, as a federal matter? Compare the excerpts from Zschernig v. Miller and Clark v. Allen, p. 632, supra.

PROBLEM

Guatador gives effect, subject to the basic conditions stated in Hilton v. Guyot, to foreign judgments. A national of Guatador obtains a money judgment in that country against a United States citizen, based on a tort committed in Guatador. The defendant participated in the court proceedings. The plaintiff seeks to enforce the judgment against assets of the defendant and therefor brings an action in a state court. Judgment is for defendant, on the ground that foreign judgments will be treated only as prima facie evidence of the liability and that plaintiff has the right to a new trial on the merits. The highest state court affirms.

What recourse has the plaintiff? What problems will he encounter in seeking review of the state court's judgment? If he obtains review, what arguments on the merits should he make and in what order of priority?

Additional reading: In addition to the leading articles noted earlier, other important articles include: Yntema, The Enforcement of Foreign Judgments in Anglo-American Law, 33 Mich.L.Rev. 1129 (1935); Reese, The Status in this Country of Judgments Rendered Abroad, 50 Colum.L.Rev. 783 (1950); Smit, International Res Judicata and Collateral Estoppel in the United States, 9 U.C.L.A. L.Rev. 44 (1962); and Peterson, Res Judicata and Foreign Country Judgments, 24 Ohio State L.J. 291 (1963); Kulzer, Recognition of Foreign Country Judgments in New York: The Uniform Foreign Money Judgments Recognition Act, 24 Ohio St.L.J. 291 (1963); R. von Mehren, ed., Enforcement of Foreign Country Judgments (Prac.L. Inst. 1974); A. von Mehren and Trautman, Recognition of Foreign Adjudications: A Survey and a Suggested Approach, 81 Harv.L.Rev. 1601 (1968).

47. Compare the holding in Republic of Iraq v. First National City Bank, p. 712, supra.

3. ENFORCEMENT OF FOREIGN-COUNTRY JUDGMENTS IN FRANCE [48]

In France, as in other countries, a foreign judgment as such has no "executory force." The procedure by which a plaintiff in France enforces a foreign-country judgment differs sharply from that in England and the United States.

The starting point is Article 2123 of the Civil Code, which provides that judgment liens can result only from such foreign-country judgments as have been declared subject to execution (*exécutoire*) by a French court. Article 546 of the Code of Civil Procedure generalizes this principle of Article 2123 to embrace all acts of execution of foreign judgments. The plaintiff must first seek issuance of an "exequatur", a writ rendering the foreign judgment executory in France. The theory is that the foreign judgment as such then becomes executory, whereas in an Anglo-American forum a new judgment must be rendered in an action based upon the foreign judgment. We shall have occasion to question whether these significant procedural distinctions have in fact, in and of themselves, important substantive consequences.

The proceeding for an exequatur is brought in a court of first instance. It is an adversary proceeding, in which the plaintiff must present proper proof of the foreign judgment. If exequatur is granted, it first gives the foreign judgment the force of res judicata (*chose jugée*) in France and executory force. If exequatur is refused, plaintiff can bring an action based upon the same facts and legal contentions relevant to the prior foreign action. This Section 3 concerns the grounds on which a French court may refuse to issue an exequatur.

These materials introduce two doctrines which have competed in the French case law. Neither lends itself to easy translation and we have thus throughout this section generally left them in the original French: "révision au fond" (implying roughly "review de novo") and "contrôle" (implying something less thorough than the English word "control", rather like "check").

CHARR v. HAZIM ULUSAHIM

Court of Appeal of Paris (1st Chamber), 1955.
1956 Dalloz Jurisp. I. 61, 83 Journal du Droit International 164 (1956).

THE COURT;—Deciding on the appeal of Georges Charr, of Turkish origin, naturalized French by decree of August 2, 1947, from a judgment of the Tribunal de la Seine dated June 22, 1953 which, upon request of Hazim Ulusahim, acting as liquidator of La Banque turque du commerce de Konya, ordered the enforcement

48. The information in this section is based largely upon 2 Batiffol, Droit International Privé 413–72 (5th ed., Lagarde, 1970).

of two judgments, dated respectively January 9 (and not 2), 1942 and March 5, 1943, in which the commercial section of the principal tribunal of the Turkish Republic of Istanbul ordered Charr to pay Hazim Ulusahim, in his official capacity, 6219 Turkish pounds and 37 piastres plus 5% interest and all costs (including 150 Turkish pounds as lawyer's fees);—Considering that appellant requests that the action for enforcement be dismissed while appellee requests that the decision be upheld;—Considering that it is hardly contested that, under the French rules of private international law governing jurisdiction, the Turkish tribunals had jurisdiction, in this particular case, to hear a personal transitory action brought against a defendant who, at the time, was not French and was domiciled in Istanbul (the Tribunal of Commerce of this city, it is almost superfluous to add, having, moreover, territorial jurisdiction internally by virtue of this very domicile under the Turkish lex fori);—Considering that the commercial transactions in dispute, taking place between Turkish nationals, in Turkey, which is where all the legal relations under consideration were exclusively localized, without the intervention of any foreign element, could only, under French rules of conflict of laws, be governed by Turkish law which has actually been applied; that the Turkish rules of procedure have been strictly complied with; particularly as regards the introduction of evidence and especially the administration of the oath and the examinations; that the decisions in dispute are executory in Turkey (and this under the rules of res judicata);—Considering that nothing in the proceedings where, as it appears from the records, the rights of the defendants have been fully respected, nor in the reasons given for decisions, nor in the final decision of the case and the terms of the judgments is of a nature likely to offend, in any way, the principles of French international public policy; and finally that there has been no proof of fraud;—Considering under these circumstances, that the question arises whether, apart from the *contrôle* bearing on the enumerated questions the outcome of which is entirely in favor of the two decisions in dispute, it is appropriate, in this instance, as appellant so requests, for the judge in this procedure to proceed to a *révision au fond* of the judgments which are submitted to him, in order that, finally, the granting or refusal of the enforcement order would depend on the opinion which might have been his, after the suit had been entirely tried de novo before him, with regard to the rightness or wrongness of those judgments, in fact or in law;—But considering that, despite the numerous and erratic precedents, such an apparent authority of *révision,* unanimously criticized by the authors and which no statutory text gives to the French judge—who would be, moreover, as it is worth emphasizing alone, along with the Belgian tribunals among the courts of civilized states, in pretending to such authority—cannot be considered as rightfully belonging to him;—Considering that such a privilege which leads to denying and to reducing to nought, at least provisionally, the value and the international authority of even the most regular and the best decided foreign judgments and which has the effect of compelling the person who secured them to undergo again in France the hazards of new litigation, is, in the first place, contrary to the principle of sound international judicial cooperation which cannot be reconciled with the systematic distrust of foreign jurisdictions implied by the authority of *révision*;—Considering that, on the other hand, nowadays the theory of *révision* has become a legal anachronism which cannot be justified today; that, indeed, it goes back to an era already long past where the ideas prevailing on the possible means of exercising the *contrôle* (legitimate if kept within reasonable bounds) of foreign judgments whose enforcement and perhaps execution are requested in France, were still singularly chaotic;—But considering that in the present state of French private international law, the conditions of this *contrôle* implying the examination of the various aspects hereabove considered of the foreign decisions, in this instance with regard to the two judgments in dispute, have been gradually clarified and defined precisely and offer in all respects amply sufficient guarantees which render completely unnecessary a *révision au fond*;—Considering that, in fact, this review has been progressively discarded, with good reason, as regards executory or declaratory judgments on the subject of the status of persons . . . . ; that in addition such *révision* is, henceforth, eliminated in all matters, by an increasing number of international conventions and that, finally, it has been absolutely excluded in imitation of recent foreign legislations, by the legal texts, inspired by France, which govern private international law in Morocco;—Considering moreover that, in addition to these abstract considerations, very practical ones require the exclusion of the authority of *révision au fond* which run the risk of confronting the French judge with tasks which would not normally devolve upon him and which he might find impossible to accomplish satisfactorily;—Considering that, in this respect, it could even seem surprising that in some cases a French tribunal, because of this theory of *révision*, might be led, in a sense, to sit as an appellate court over foreign judges, so as to control in law their interpretation of their own legislation in the cases where it happens to be applicable to the litigation;—But considering that the most serious problem resides in the practical difficulty (sometimes almost insuperable) which, with respect to the facts, the French judge might find and in fact often does find, in judging relevant circumstances related to remote societies of whose atmosphere he knows little, while the data, often incomplete, which are submitted to him, may be practically impossible to complete and, even more so, to interpret soundly; that the hazards that are intrinsically attached to the prerogative of *révision* to which he would so pretend, are increased even further in an unpredictable way to the prejudice of the parties;—Considering that consequently there is no reason, in this instance, for a *révision au fond* of the two decisions in dispute; that the enforcement must be granted on the basis only of the *côntrole* hereabove exercised;—Considering, though, that the judges of first instance having found it necessary to undertake the examination of the legal and factual aspects of the case, it can be ascertained in any case, although it is entirely superfluous, that from the reasons of the judgment to which one can refer in this respect, as well as from the elements and documents introduced in evidence in first instance and on appeal, it results that the limited partnership Imman Zedé Abdullah et Cie, in which Charr was a limited partner, was clearly debtor in respect to endorsed drafts without any fraud (evidence of which is not shown) and of promissory notes to the Banque de Konya for the amounts claimed and that appellant, having recovered in its entirety its prior contributions as a limited partner, remains personally liable to the said bank for those amounts which are clearly smaller than its repaid contributions;—Considering that, as was rightly admitted by the judges of first instance, it is obviously for dilatory purposes that Charr has opposed the enforcement and taken the present appeal;

On those grounds and on those of the judges of first instance which are not to the contrary, as to form, grants the appeal of Charr; on the merits, finds the appeal without grounds and dismisses it; confirms in all its dispositions the judgment below.

NOTE ON FRENCH STANDARDS FOR ENFORCEMENT OF FOREIGN JUDGMENTS

The opinion in Charr provides a terse review of principles controlling the grant of an exequatur as of 1956. This Note begins with a discussion of the power *révision au fond* which the 1st Chamber of the Court of Appeal in Paris refused to exercise in Charr. It then describes the general standards for enforcement developed by French courts.

Révision

The power of *révision*—the power to engage in a plenary review of the merits of the judgment for which exequatur is sought—was not given to French courts by statute. An early case, Holker v. Parker, Cour de Cass. (Ch. civ.) April 19, 1819, [1819] Sirey Jurisp. I. 288, decided by the highest of France's "civil" courts (the Cour de Cassation), held that French courts may proceed to a *révision au fond* of questions of fact or law which had been adjudicated in foreign proceedings.

The doctrine had broad scope. The French court could deny an exequatur if it considered the foreign judgment erroneous on any point of fact or law—including interpretation of contract provisions, assessment of the gravity of injury in a tort suit, the weight to be given to certain evidence, and so on. Indeed, the court could consider facts arising after the foreign judgment had been rendered which reflected upon its soundness. There were several qualifications to this power of revision: the judgment creditor could not add new demands in the exequatur proceedings, the burden of proof was on the defendant to show that the foreign judgment was erroneous, and the French court (with some exceptions) could not modify the judgment but simply enforce in accordance with its terms or deny enforcement. Treaties occasionally limited this power of French courts, and courts did not review in this manner foreign arbitral decrees or foreign consent judgments. Further, courts did not exercise this power when recognition of foreign judgments was sought (particularly in matters of status or capacity), rather than enforcement.

The doctrine was under heavy and constant challenge, domestically and in foreign countries. Note the reasons given by the Court of Appeal in finding *révision au fond* anachronistic in the contemporary world. After Charr, the status of this doctrine was somewhat uncertain, with different chambers of the Court of Appeal in Paris taking different positions. The 1st Chamber returned to the problem in Lestrade de Kyvon v. Roussel, Court of Appeal of Paris (1st Chamber), February 2, 1961, 50 Revue Critique de Droit International Privé 566 (1961). It held to the position taken in Charr and stressed that *révision au fond* was not required by the Code, was difficult to apply, was contrary to the requirements of international judicial cooperation, cast unnecessary doubt on the international authority of foreign decisions otherwise "regular", and was rendered unnecessary by the other standards invoked by French courts in exequatur proceedings.

In 1964, in Munzer v. Jacoby-Munzer,[49] the Cour de Cassation considered an American judgment granting a separation order to American spouses and ordering the husband to pay stated support. The husband disappeared. The wife found him many years later in France and sought a judgment in the French courts for arrears in support. The case came to the Cour de Cassation, which rejected an appeal by the husband from an adverse decision and said, with respect to *révision au fond:*

> "Whereas the appellate judgment under attack submits correctly that, in order to grant an exequatur, the French judge must make sure that five conditions are fulfilled, namely, jurisdiction of the foreign court which rendered the decision, regularity of the procedure adopted in that jurisdiction, the application of the law which governs according to the French conflicts rules, conformity with international public policy, and absence of evasion of the law; as this verification which suffices to protect the legal order and the interests of France, the very object of the exequatur proceeding, constitutes for all matters both the expression and the limit of the power of control of the judge charged with authorizing the enforcement in France of a foreign decision, without asking the judge to proceed to a revision of the substance of the decision."
>
> Whereas in the instant case the Court of Appeals finds that the decisions submitted to its control fulfil the conditions set for the grant of an exequatur, . . .
>
> For these reasons; Rejects . . . [the appeal]."

Although formally lower courts are not bound by decisions of the Cour de Cassation, it appears that as a practical matter a precedent which it establishes will be followed.

We now consider the traditional grounds for "contrôle" noted in Charr and Munzer. In general four such grounds are available.

Jurisdiction of the Foreign Tribunal

The French courts inquire whether the foreign tribunal had jurisdiction over the defendant under the standards of the foreign law governing that tribunal and under French jurisdictional principles. Compare the approach of the court in Somportex Ltd. v. Philadelphia Chewing Gum Corp., p. 783, supra. That is, in the absence of any international consensus about the proper bases for judicial jurisdiction, the French courts consider their own principles "proper" and review foreign judgments against them.

These French principles, in general, fall into two categories: mandatory and permissive. French courts view Articles 14 and 15 of

49. This translation is taken from Nadelmann, French Courts Recognize Foreign Money-Judgments, One Down and More to Go, 13 Am.J.Comp.L. 72, 76 (1964). The original citation is: Cour de Cass., Ch.Civ. (1st Sect.), Jan. 7, 1964, [1964] Bull. des Arrêts de la Cour de Cass., Ch.Civ., I. No. 15, p. 11. See also 53 Rev. crit. de droit int. privé 344 (1964).

the Civil Code (see p. 751, supra), even though cast in "permissive" language, as compulsory jurisdictional bases. If, as an example, a French defendant is sued before a foreign court, a judgment rendered against him will not entitle the judgment creditor to an exequatur in France—on the theory that Article 15 confers an *exclusive* jurisdiction upon French courts in such situations. The same principle obtains with respect to Article 14. The severity of this doctrine (note that it is irrelevant what connection the French defendant or plaintiff, or the facts relevant to the litigation, had to the foreign country) is somewhat relaxed by the principle that parties may renounce the protection of Articles 14 and 15. Recall the discussion of such waivers at p. 752, supra. A complex case law has developed as to when such a waiver is effective, particularly if the waiver is not explicit and must be implied from the French defendant's conduct. For example, a French defendant who appeared before a court in a foreign country to protect property there subject to attachment and execution will not be deemed to have waived the protection of Article 15. Nor will a French plaintiff, who lost a foreign action, be considered to have waived the protection of Article 14 and be precluded from suing again in France, if he was "required" to sue in the foreign country because, at that time, the only property of the defendant against which a judgment could be executed was located in that country.

Other French jurisdictional principles are considered only "permissive." That is, the fact that there existed possible bases for adjudicatory jurisdiction in France does not preclude foreign courts, from the French point of view, from exercising jurisdiction and entertaining the same cause of action. Such "permissive" principles are primarily those derived from domestic "venue" provisions. See p. 753, supra. For example, if a foreign defendant could be sued by a foreign plaintiff in France because of his French domicile, or because a contract to which he was a party was to be performed in France, the French courts will nonetheless consider valid a foreign judgment if the defendant was a resident or national of that country or if the contract was negotiated, made and perhaps partly performed there. Some jurisdictional bases other than Articles 14 and 15 are, however, exclusive, such as those pertaining to real property in France.

If there were no possible basis for jurisdiction of French courts on the underlying cause of action, such courts, when exequatur is sought, will nonetheless review adjudicatory jurisdiction of the foreign court—again largely by projecting French concepts of jurisdiction to the foreign country to determine if any such concepts would have supported litigation there.

Regularity of Procedure Followed in the Foreign Proceedings

The French courts will determine whether the foreign litigation was conducted in a manner consistent with foreign procedural rules. In addition, some notions of French *ordre public* are relevant. That is, the French courts will not give effect to a foreign judgment if the foreign proceedings did not give fair notice to the defendant or the opportunity to present his defense or proof, or if the proceedings discriminated against French nationals.

Choice of Law by the Foreign Court

After the apparent end of the doctrine of *révision au fond,* the most controversial of the French standards is that which leads a French court to determine if the foreign tribunal applied the appropriate law, under French concepts of choice of law. Contrast the holding of the Supreme Court in Fauntleroy v. Lum, p. 760, supra. The severity of this doctrine is somewhat tempered by the willingness of French courts to inquire whether, if the foreign court applied a law (perhaps its own) not applicable under French choice-of-law standards, the same result would have been reached under French law. This doctrine is also under extensive criticism, which may foreshadow its relaxation or abandonment.

Respect for Public Order

This principle of *contrôle,* involving general notions of public policy, provides an extensive protection which, as noted in Charr, makes the protection of *révision au fond* unnecessary. The foreign judgment may rest on principles offensive to French law. The concept is broad and indeterminate in scope, and perhaps invokes notions similar to those debated in Huntington v. Attrill, p. 764, supra.

Recognition

Foreign judgments can have effect in France without benefiting from an exequatur in some situations involving recognition as opposed to enforcement. That is, despite lack of exequatur, the foreign judgment may constitute a fact capable of producing legal consequences. The most obvious examples are those relating to recognition of status, as recognition of a foreign divorce decree which would permit the divorced party to remarry in France without there obtaining a divorce. The principle has however been expanded to embrace judgments declaring other kinds of rights between parties, as rights in property—often involving actions which would be traditionally characterized as "in rem" in the United States.

Of course, even when recognition is sought, it will generally be necessary to invoke the authority of the foreign judgment in French court proceedings, as when a "wife" sues for support and the "husband" pleads as defense a foreign divorce decree. In deciding whether to recognize, the French courts appear generally to apply the same standards that are relevant to enforcement and issuance of an exequatur.

QUESTION

Compare the French standards for enforcement with those developed in Hilton v. Guyot. (*a*) What are the principal legal hurdles that a judgment creditor has to surmount when he carries his judgment to France rather than the United States? (*b*) Are the French courts in any respect more receptive to foreign judgments than those in the United States? (c) Does it appear from the description above that the procedural distinctions between exequatur and obtaining a new judgment in the forum of enforcement help to explain the differing standards?

---

4. ENFORCEMENT OF FOREIGN-COUNTRY JUDGMENTS IN GERMANY [50]

When enforcement of a foreign judgment in Germany is desired, a special proceeding is required to validate that judgment. No such proceeding is necessary if only "recognition" is sought. Otherwise, similar standards apply to recognition and enforcement. Section 328 of the Code of Civil Procedure, apparently assuming that foreign judgments will generally be recognized or enforced, states the grounds upon which they may be rejected.

> Recognition of a judgment of a foreign court is excluded:
>
> 1. If the courts of a state, to which the foreign court belongs, do not have jurisdiction under German law;
>
> 2. If the unsuccessful defendant is a German and he did not appear in the proceeding, in so far as the summons or order initiating the proceedings was not served upon him personally in the state of the trial court or through German judicial assistance;
>
> . . .
>
> 4. If recognition of the judgment would be contrary to good morals or the purpose of a German law;
>
> 5. If reciprocity is not accorded.
>
> The provision of item 5 does not prevent recognition of a judgment if a judgment concerns a non-pecuniary claim and under German law domestic jurisdiction did not exist.

Note the similarities with and the distinctions from the standards for enforcement in France. As in France, in deciding whether the foreign court had judicial jurisdiction under paragraph (1), the German court "projects" German concepts of jurisdiction upon the foreign tribunal. Most bases of jurisdiction of German courts, including those discussed at p. 753, supra, are not exclusive, and judgments of foreign courts defensible upon an alternative basis of jurisdiction acceptable to German law will be recognized even if the underlying cause of action could also have been sued upon in Germany. In certain kinds of actions, particularly those affecting rights to property within Germany, the attribution of jurisdiction to German courts is considered exclusive (compare Article 15 of the French Civil Code),

50. The following description is based upon von Mehren and Trautman, The Law of Multistate Problems 859–863 (1965); Nadelmann, Non-Recognition of American Money Judgments Abroad and What to Do About It, 42 Iowa L.Rev. 236, 249–257 (1957); 2 Stein and Jonas, Kommentar zur Zivilprozessordnung, § 328 (18th ed., Schonke and Pohle, 1953); Baumbach, Lauterbach, Albers & Hartmann, Zivilprozessordnung § 328 (32d ed. 1974).

and foreign judgments relating to such property will be ignored. Apparently the facts underlying the foreign litigation, rather than the formal jurisdictional bases relied upon by the foreign court, are decisive. Unlike French courts, the German court will not verify the "internal" jurisdiction of the foreign court under foreign law. The omitted paragraph (3) of Section 328 provides that in certain areas, particularly family law, German courts will examine the choice of law made by the foreign tribunal and will not give effect to foreign judgments based upon foreign law when, under German standards, German law should have been applied. Under paragraph (4), recognition may be denied a judgment either because of a serious clash with German substantive law (one author refers to a judgment on a gambling contract as such a case) or because of a serious deficiency in procedural fairness.

The condition of reciprocity in paragraph (5) appears frequently in the codes of European and Latin American countries. Determination whether reciprocity exists involves different procedures in these countries. In some, the appropriate executive arm of the government must advise a court of a foreign country's practices. In others, such as Germany, the courts themselves determine whether reciprocity exists.

The extreme interpretation frequently given to reciprocity requirements, one that in effect seems to preclude recognition or enforcement of foreign judgments in most cases, is illustrated by an early German case. After the San Francisco fire in 1906, policy holders in California sued there a German fire insurance company which had been qualified to do business in California, and recovered a judgment. The judgment creditors sought enforcement in German courts, and the defendant company argued that reciprocity did not exist. The German Supreme Court agreed. Reichsgericht (7th Ch.), March 26, 1909, 70 Entscheidungen des Reichsgerichts in Zivilsachen 434. The German court so held despite the fact that Section 1915 of the California Code of Civil Procedure, p. 794 supra, had become effective as of March 11, 1907. The German court reasoned that under Section 1915, a California court ascertaining whether the foreign court had jurisdiction could reexamine various issues; that California law permitted a defense of fraud which reached further than the comparable defense under German law; and that certain procedures for impeaching judgments existed in California and not in Germany.

A recent decision refusing to recognize a South African judgment because South African courts would not apply reciprocity—measured by an exacting standard—indicates that there is still vitality in this restrictive reading of Section 328. See Bundesgerichtshof, July 9, 1969, 52 Entscheidungen des Bundesgerichtshofes in Zivilsachen 251. On the other hand, in a decision involving litigation over the delivery of 950,000 francs worth of gravestones by a French party to a German buyer, the German courts interpreted the recent French decisions abandoning *révision au fond* in a liberal way so as to find parallelism between French practice and Section 328. Decision of May 8, 1968, 50 Entscheidungen des Bundesgerichtshofes in Zivilsachen 100.

Note the special problems which obtain when a foreign court must ascertain whether reciprocity exists in the "United States." Is the reference to the state in which the judgment was rendered, to all states in the United States, or to the principles developed in the federal courts? Note the complications resulting from Hilton v. Guyot, Erie R. Co. v. Tompkins and questions present today as to whether state or federal law should govern questions of enforcement of foreign judgments.

PROBLEM

Widge S.A., a French corporation, is among the world's most efficient producers of widgets. Its headquarters and manufacturing plant are in France. Over the years, German nationals have acquired about 75% of its outstanding capital stock, and five of Widge's nine members of its supervisory council are now Germans who travel to Paris for meetings four times each year. Widge exports primarily to the Common Market countries, particularly Germany and England. It keeps substantial stocks of widgets in each of these countries to complete sales made by its British and German branch offices. Sporadic export sales are made to United States customers.

After extensive mail negotiations, Widge entered into a contract with Dynamo, Inc., a Delaware corporation with its principal place of business and manufacturing plant in Wisconsin. Under the contract, Widge was to manufacture to specifications 200 special widgets to fit the needs of Dynamo's plant operations. It shipped a first installment of 10 widgets to Dynamo which notified Widge that the products changed shape under high heat, contrary to the specifications, and were useless to it. Dynamo demanded replacement of the 10 widgets and proper quality on the remaining 190. Widge advised Dynamo by letter that it considered the rejection unjustified and the contract terminated. It requested return of the 10 widgets.

Dynamo's response was an action in the federal district court in Wisconsin for damages for breach of contract. Jurisdiction was based upon Wisc. Stat.Ann. § 262.05, p. 734, supra, and notice of the action was sent to Widge by registered mail pursuant to F.R.C.P. 4(i). Widge appeared by counsel to protest the court's jurisdiction. After a ruling adverse to it, it withdrew from the proceedings. The court, finding that the widgets were defective and determining the amount of damages under principles of Wisconsin law, entered a default judgment of $125,000.

You are counsel to Dynamo, which wonders what path to follow. The widgets in its possession have at best a market value of $5,000, and Widge has no other assets in the United States. (*a*) Indicate the various paths open to Dynamo, and the path that you would advise it to follow. (*b*) If 75% of the shares of Widge were owned by French rather than German nationals, would your recommendations change?

5. COOPERATIVE ARRANGEMENTS THROUGH TREATIES

In view of the diversity among legal systems over the bases for adjudicatory jurisdiction and conditions for enforcement of foreign judgments, treaties would appear to be the best means for establishing an effective international legal order responsive to the contemporary needs of the international community. Treaties regulating these matters could at once accommodate the interests of the different countries and satisfy the desires of private parties engaged in transnational activities for more consistent and stable rules.

The most significant present treaty is the Convention Relating to the Jurisdiction of Courts and the Enforcement of Judgments in Civil and Commercial Matters, signed in 1968 and effective in 1973 among some member states of the European Economic Community. This Convention had been foreshadowed in Article 220* of the Rome Treaty giving birth to the Community. It called for the negotiation of an agreement for "the simplification of the formalities governing the reciprocal recognition and enforcement of judgments of courts or tribunals and of arbitration awards". The Convention appears in an English translation in the CCH Common Market Reporter, ¶ 6003.

Under the Convention the signatory countries agree not to use, in cases involving a domiciliary of another signatory, specified bases of jurisdiction, including *inter alia* Section 23 of the German civil procedure rules and Articles 14 and 15 of the French Civil Code. Judgments of the courts in one country will be enforced in the others, subject to only limited exceptions including the public policy of the enforcing country. However, judgments resting on the "excessive" jurisdictional bases designated above will not be enforced in other signatory countries' courts if the defendant is a domiciliary of another signatory country. If, however, the defendant is not a domiciliary of such a country, the courts of all signatories are bound to enforce such judgments. Thus an American citizen sued in Paris under Article 14 on the basis of the French plaintiff's nationality might find that a British court was obligated to enforce the French judgment against the American defendant's property in London. The Convention contemplates future arrangements to give the Court of Justice of the European Community jurisdiction over questions arising under it. The Convention permits the member countries to negotiate agreements with countries outside the Community, under which member countries can stipulate that they will not enforce judgments in such circumstances against the other signatory's residents.

Negotiations were underway in 1975 between the United States and the United Kingdom, looking toward the conclusion of such an agreement. If it were signed, it would be the first convention relating to the enforcement of foreign judicial judgments to which the United States has become a party. In the past, concerns about encroaching upon the prerogatives of the States, as well as other constitutional and political issues, have inhibited action on this front.

One other multilateral initiative has potential importance. In 1966 the Hague Conference on International Law, p. 304, supra, prepared a broad Convention on the Recognition and Enforcement of Foreign Judgments in Civil and Commercial Matters, excerpts from which are reproduced in the Documentary Supplement. Although it has not received the ratifications needed to have it take effect, it is of substantial importance as representing current scholarly thought on the topic.

Examine that Convention with attention to its impact on the existing national practices described in this chapter. Compare Articles 4 and 5 with the grounds that national courts have used in refusing to enforce foreign judgments. Article 6 deals with service of process in foreign countries (see p. 755, supra), and Article 7 with disagreements over choice of law (p. 803, supra). Article 8 recalls the French practice of *révision au fond.* Article 10 raises jurisdictional questions pervading this entire chapter; it should be read in connection with the Supplementary Protocol.* Article 21 plays a crucial role. It contemplates the conclusion by parties to the Convention of supplementary agreements. Without such an agreement the Convention has no effect even if both countries involved in litigation over the enforcement of foreign judgments are parties to it.

Additional reading: Carl, The Common Market Judgments Convention—Its Threat and Challenge to Americans, 8 Int.Law. 446 (1974); Nadelmann, The Common Market Judgments Convention and a Hague Conference Recommendation—What Steps Next?, 82 Harv.L.Rev. 1282 (1969).

QUESTIONS

(1) How many of the grounds for refusal to enforce a foreign judgment that are stated in the Hague Convention would be available to a court in the United States? In your view, are such differences as may appear substantial?

(2) A French national and domiciliary enters into a contract in France, at the Paris branch office of the other party, a New York corporation. The contract is for personal services to be performed by the Frenchman entirely in New York. The French national fails to perform and, while briefly in New York on an unrelated business trip, is served with a summons in an action alleging breach of contract. A default judgment is rendered, and exequatur is sought in France. (a) What result? (b) What result if the Hague Convention were in effect between the two countries?

(3) Note paragraphs (2) and (4) of the Supplementary Protocol to the Hague Convention. What American jurisdictional practices described in the foregoing sections of this Chapter are in effect designated as exorbitant by (4)? What French practices? British practices? German practices?

C. THE UTILITY OF CHOICE-OF-FORUM CLAUSES

In disputes between sovereign states, we have seen, no international tribunal has jurisdiction unless the parties have given their consent. In a dispute between a private party and a state, the doctrine of sovereign immunity often means that the consent of the governmental party is required if a suit is to continue in its own courts or abroad. There is indeed doubt whether such a consent is effective unless made in the course of the litigation. See p. 664, supra. But the cases in this Chapter involving litigation between private parties have evidenced little concern with consent. Courts take jurisdiction over parties, consenting or not, on the basis of relevant principles of the legal system which they apply. It is true, however, that in some countries consent by a defendant is a separate, additional basis of jurisdiction.

In this Part C we turn to the question whether private parties can by advance agreement select the forum in which disputes between them will be litigated. This question is but part of the broader problem of how much autonomy will be granted to private parties to shape their transnational relationships by agreement, both as to the substance of their transactions and the means of resolving disputes that arise from them.

The breadth of and variety among bases for adjudicatory jurisdiction in national legal systems that were reviewed in Part A often give a plaintiff a choice among fora. That choice may, however, be more apparent than real. The principle of *forum non conveniens* may lead the court before which the plaintiff institutes proceedings to refuse to hear the action. If this obstacle is cleared, the plaintiff must consider whether any judgment which he wins may be denied enforcement in the foreign jurisdiction where defendant or his assets are located.

For such reasons potential parties to litigation, particularly the potential defendant, are left in considerable uncertainty as to the forum. For most tort actions, this uncertainty is inevitable; an agreement about a judicial forum could be made only after the potential plaintiff was injured. Contract relations, however, permit advance planning. Particularly in transnational contracts, there are evident advantages in avoiding later jurisdictional disputes. Transnational commercial activities would thereby be facilitated.

Such are the problems of this section. What role has private planning in these matters? Will agreements by contracting parties to litigate in a stipulated forum—to the exclusion of all other fora which, absent that stipulation, might have exercised jurisdiction over the parties—be honored by courts of different nations? [51]

51. Related questions that arise when parties seek, through an arbitration clause, to remove their controversies from the regular courts altogether are considered at pp. 824–835, infra.

NOTE ON SOME ASPECTS OF THE CHOICE-OF-FORUM CLAUSE

The characteristic choice-of-forum clause between, for example, Newco (a New York corporation) and Bonnco (a German corporation) might read: "The parties agree that all disputes relating to this contract shall be tried before the courts of Hamburg, to the exclusion of all other courts which might have had jurisdiction apart from this provision." Sometimes such stipulations are accompanied by choice of an applicable substantive law to govern the contract. The questions that can arise under choice-of-forum clauses include:

(1) Bonnco might commence an action in Hamburg based upon the clause. If Newco has no other links with Germany, and if, absent the clause, a German court would not be authorized to assert jurisdiction under the principles stated at p. 753, supra, will the clause constitute a legally sufficient consent and submission to jurisdiction? This aspect of choice-of-forum clauses, the conferral of jurisdiction upon a court, is often referred to as *prorogation.*

(2) Newco might bring an action in New York, assuming that the German corporation were present or that a "long arm" statute applied. Bonnco would plead the clause as a bar to the exercise of jurisdiction by the state or federal court. Will that court honor the clause and grant a motion to dismiss? These matters are frequently referred to as questions of *derogation.*

(3) In reaching its decision, under what law will the New York court determine the validity and effect of the clause? Will it invariably apply the standards of *lex fori,* or will it look to the law that it finds applicable to the substantive issues in the suit?

(4) Suppose that in paragraph (1) above, the German court entertained the suit and Bonnco seeks to enforce a judgment in New York. Assuming that all other conditions to enforcement are met, will the fact that jurisdiction rested on a choice-of-forum clause affect the decision whether to enforce?

(5) Suppose that the New York court in paragraph (2) exercises jurisdiction despite the clause. If an enforcement action is brought in Germany, how will these facts influence the German court?

To some extent, the issues raised in paragraphs (1) and (4) have been examined in the preceding sections, insofar as the description of bases for adjudicatory jurisdiction in Section A includes advance consent by a party. And recall Article 10(5) of the 1966 Hague Convention on the Recognition and Enforcement of Foreign Judgments.*

Consider another critical question raised by these clauses: the extent to which their "exclusivity" provisions will be honored by courts in other fora, the problem of paragraph (2) above. That question cannot be answered solely by reference to principles of jurisdiction. Like other provisions in a contract, the choice-of-forum clause may be rendered invalid by contract law, whether of the forum or of another country indicated under choice-of-law principles. The clause may be held to violate the public policy of the forum, to reflect the exercise of unfair bargaining power by one party, or otherwise to exceed the scope of party autonomy in contract matters. Such contract principles often become decisive in so called adhesion contracts, generally contracts prepared (often in a standard printed form) by a party of superior bargaining power rather than through active negotiations. Common examples include insurance contracts, standard lease provisions, and many contracts for the transportation of persons or goods.

The history of choice-of-forum clauses in our courts commenced with early cases expressing extreme suspicion if not outright hostility. They reiterated that private parties could not "oust" courts of jurisdiction, and that such clauses "violated public policy." Although such attitudes persisted in some recent opinions,[52] other decisions reflected a more liberal approach. It was difficult to summarize "the state of the law". For example, it was often unclear whether an opinion adverse to the clause was to be explained solely by abuse of power by one party to the contract; by some special statute applicable to the case that might be interpreted to outlaw a choice-of-forum clause; or by the unpalatable results feared to follow upon remission of the case to the particular foreign tribunal (and foreign law) involved. The uncertain status of the cases was reflected in successive drafts of the Restatement (Second), Conflict of Laws. In 1957,[53] it said:

> The parties' agreement as to the place of suit cannot prevent the exercise of judicial jurisdiction by a State. A provision to this effect will, however, be given effect by a court if it is deemed fair and reasonable.

The 1967 draft and the final version say: [54]

> The parties' agreement as to the place of the action cannot oust a state of judicial jurisdiction, but such an agreement will be given effect unless it is unfair or unreasonable.

The following Supreme Court decision brings some clarity to the field.

52. Kylar v. United States Trotting Ass'n, 12 A.D.2d 748, 210 N.Y.S.2d 25 (4th Dept. 1961); Huntley v. Alejandre, 139 So.2d 911 (D.Ct.App.Fla.1962); Arsenis v. Atlantic Tankers, Ltd., 39 Misc.2d 124, 240 N.Y.S.2d 69 (Civil Ct. N.Y.1963).

53. Tentative Draft No. 4, April 5, 1957 as amended at a meeting of the American Law Institute, 34 Ann. Meetings Proc. 395 (1957).

54. Proposed Official Draft, Part I, § 80 (May 2, 1967). Restatement (Second) Conflict of Laws § 80.

M/S BREMEN v. ZAPATA OFF-SHORE COMPANY

Supreme Court of the United States, 1972.
407 U.S. 1, 92 S.Ct. 1907, 32 L.Ed.2d 513.

MR. CHIEF JUSTICE BURGER delivered the opinion of the Court.

We granted certiorari to review a judgment of the United States Court of Appeals for the Fifth Circuit declining to enforce a forum selection clause governing disputes arising under an international towage contract between petitioner and respondent. The Circuits have differed in their approach to such clauses. For the reasons stated hereafter, we vacate the judgment of the Court of Appeals.

In November 1967, respondent Zapata, a Houston-based American corporation, contracted with petitioner Unterweser, a German corporation, to tow Zapata's ocean-going, self-elevating drilling rig Chaparral from Louisiana to a point off Ravenna, Italy, in the Adriatic Sea where Zapata had agreed to drill certain wells.

Zapata had solicited bids for the towage, and several companies including Unterweser had responded. Unterweser was the low bidder and Zapata requested it to submit a contract, which it did. The contract submitted by Unterweser contained the following provision which is at issue in this case:

> "Any dispute arising must be treated before the London Court of Justice."

In addition the contract contained two clauses purporting to exculpate Unterweser from liability for damages to the towed barge.

After reviewing the contract and making several changes, but without any alteration in the forum-selection or exculpatory clauses, a Zapata vice president executed the contract and forwarded it to Unterweser in Germany, where Unterweser accepted the changes and the contract became effective.

On January 5, 1968, Unterweser's deep sea tug *Bremen* departed Venice, Louisiana, with the Chaparral in tow bound for Italy. On January 9, while the flotilla was in international waters in the middle of the Gulf of Mexico, a severe storm arose. The sharp roll of the Chaparral in Gulf waters caused its elevator legs, which had been raised for the voyage, to break off and fall into the sea, seriously damaging the Chaparral. In this emergency situation Zapata instructed the *Bremen* to tow its damaged rig to Tampa, Florida, the nearest port of refuge.

On January 12, Zapata, ignoring its contract promise to litigate "any dispute arising" in the English courts commenced a suit in admiralty in the United States District Court at Tampa, seeking $3,500,000 damages against Unterweser *in personam* and the *Bremen in rem* alleging negligent towage and breach of contract. Unterweser responded by invoking the forum clause of the towage contract, and moved to dismiss for lack of jurisdiction or on *forum non conveniens* grounds, or in the alternative to stay the action pending submission of the dispute to the London Court of Justice. Shortly thereafter, in February, before the District Court had ruled on its motion to stay or dismiss the United States action, Unterweser commenced an action against Zapata seeking damages for breach of the towage contract in the High Court of Justice in London, as the contract provided. Zapata appeared in that court to contest jurisdiction, but its challenge was rejected, the English courts holding that the contractual forum provision conferred jurisdiction.[55]

In the meantime, Unterweser was faced with a dilemma in the pending action in the United States court at Tampa. The six-month period for filing action to limit its liability to Zapata and other potential claimants was about to expire, but the United States District Court in Tampa had not yet ruled on Unterweser's motion to dismiss or stay Zapata's action. On July 2, 1968, confronted with difficult alternatives, Unterweser filed an action to limit its liability in the District Court in Tampa. That court entered the customary injunction against proceedings outside the limitation court, and Zapata refiled its initial claim in the limitation action.[56]

It was only at this juncture, on July 29, after the six-month period for filing the limitation action had run, that the District Court denied Unterweser's January motion to dismiss or stay Zapata's initial action. In denying the motion, that court relied on the prior decision of the Court of Appeals in Carbon Black Export, Inc. v. The Monrosa, 254 F.2d 297 (C.A.5 1958), certiorari dismissed, 359 U.S. 180, 79 S.Ct. 710, 3 L.Ed.2d 723 (1959). In that case the Court of Appeals had held a forum selection clause unenforceable, reiterating the traditional view of many American courts that "agreements in advance of controversy whose object is to oust the jurisdiction of the courts are contrary to public policy and will not be enforced." 254 F.2d, at 300–301. Apparently concluding that it was bound by the *Carbon Black* case, the District Court gave the forum selection clause little, if any, weight. Instead, the court treated the motion to dismiss under normal *forum non conveniens* doctrine applicable in the absence of such a clause, citing Gulf Oil Corp. v. Gilbert, 330 U.S. 501, 67 S.Ct. 839, 91 L.Ed. 1055 (1947). Under that doctrine "unless the balance is strongly in favor of the defendant, the plaintiff's choice of forum should rarely be disturbed." The District Court concluded "the balance of convenience here is not strongly in favor of [Unterweser] and [Zapata's] choice of forum should not be disturbed."

Thereafter, on January 21, 1969, the District Court denied another motion by Unterweser to stay the limitation action pending determination of the controversy in the High Court of Justice in London and granted Zapata's motion to restrain Unterweser from litigating further in the London court. . . .

55. Zapata appeared specially and moved to set aside service of process outside the country. Justice Karminski of the High Court of Justice denied the motion on the ground the contractual choice of forum provision conferred jurisdiction and would be enforced absent a factual showing it would not be "fair and right" to do so. He did not believe Zapata had made such a showing, and held that it should be required to "stick to [its] bargain." The Court of Appeal dismissed an appeal on the ground that Justice Karminski had properly applied the English rule. . . .

56. In its limitation complaint, Unterweser stated it "reserve[d] all rights" under its previous motion to dismiss or stay Zapata's action, and reasserted that the High Court of Justice was the proper forum for determining the entire controversy, including its own right to limited liability, in accord with the contractual forum clause. Unterweser later counterclaimed, setting forth the same contractual cause of action as in its English action and a further cause of action for salvage arising out of the *Bremen's* services following the casualty. In its counterclaim, Unterweser again asserted that the High Court of Justice in London was the proper forum for determining all aspects of the controversy, including its counterclaim.

On appeal, a divided panel of the Court of Appeals affirmed, and on rehearing *en banc* the panel opinion was adopted, with six of the 14 *en banc* judges dissenting. As had the District Court, the majority holding rested on the *Carbon Black* decision, concluding that "at the very least" that case stood for the proposition that a forum selection clause "will not be enforced unless the selected state would provide a more convenient forum than the state in which suit is brought." From that premise the Court of Appeals proceeded to conclude that, apart from the forum selection clause, the District Court did not abuse its discretion in refusing to decline jurisdiction on the basis of *forum non conveniens*. It noted that (1) the flotilla never "escaped the Fifth Circuit's mare nostrum, and the casualty occurred in close proximity to the district court"; (2) a considerable number of potential witnesses, including Zapata crewmen resided in the Gulf Coast area; (3) preparation for the voyage and inspection and repair work had been performed in the Gulf area; (4) the testimony of the *Bremen* crew was available by way of deposition; (5) England had no interest in or contact with the controversy other than the forum selection clause. The Court of Appeals majority further noted that Zapata was a United States citizen and "the discretion of the district court to remand the case to a foreign forum was consequently limited"—especially since it appeared likely that the English courts would enforce the exculpatory clauses.[57] In the Court of Appeals' view, enforcement of such clauses would be contrary to public policy in American courts under Bisso v. Inland Waterways Corp., 349 U.S. 85, 75 S.Ct. 629, 99 L.Ed. 911 (1955), and Dixilyn Drilling Corp. v. Crescent Towing & Salvage Co., 372 U.S. 697, 83 S.Ct. 967, 10 L.Ed.2d 78 (1963). Therefore, "the district court was entitled to consider that remanding Zapata to a foreign forum, with little or no practical contact with the controversy, could raise a bar to recovery by a United States citizen which its own convenient courts would not countenance."

We hold, with the six dissenting members of the Court of Appeals, that far too little weight and effect was given to the forum clause in resolving this controversy. For at least two decades we have witnessed an expansion of overseas commercial activities by business enterprises based in the United States. The barrier of distance that once tended to confine a business concern to a modest territory no longer does so. Here we see an American company with special expertise contracting with a foreign company to tow a complex machine thousands of miles across seas and oceans. The expansion of American business and industry will hardly be encouraged if, notwithstanding solemn contracts, we insist on a parochial concept that all disputes must be resolved under our laws and in our courts. Absent a contract forum, the considerations relied on by the Court of Appeals would be persuasive reasons for holding an American forum convenient in the traditional sense, but in an era of expanding world trade and commerce, the absolute aspects of the doctrine of the *Carbon Black* case have little place and would be a heavy hand indeed on the future development of international commercial dealings by

57. The record contains an undisputed affidavit of a British solicitor stating an opinion that the exculpatory clauses of the contract would be held "prima facie valid and enforceable" against Zapata in any action maintained in England in which Zapata alleged that defaults or errors in Unterweser's tow caused the casualty and damage to Chaparral.

In addition, it is not disputed that while the limitation fund in the District Court in Tampa amounts to $1,390,000, the limitation fund in England would be only slightly in excess of $80,000 under English law.

Americans. We cannot have trade and commerce in world markets and international waters exclusively on our terms, governed by our laws and resolved in our courts.

Forum selection clauses have historically not been favored by American courts. Many courts, federal and state, have declined to enforce such clauses on the ground that they were "contrary to public policy," or that their effect was to "oust the jurisdiction" of the court. Although this view apparently still has considerable acceptance, other courts are tending to adopt a more hospitable attitude toward forum-selection clauses. This view, advanced in the well-reasoned dissenting opinion in the instant case, is that such clauses are prima facie valid and should be enforced unless enforcement is shown by the resisting party to be "unreasonable" under the circumstances. We believe this is the correct doctrine to be followed by federal district courts sitting in admiralty. It is merely the other side of the proposition recognized by this Court in National Equipment Rental, Ltd. v. Szukhent, 375 U.S. 311, 84 S.Ct. 411, 11 L.Ed. 2d 354 (1964), holding that in federal courts a party may validly consent to be sued in a jurisdiction where he cannot be found for service of process through contractual designation of an "agent" for receipt of process in that jurisdiction.

. . . This approach is substantially that followed in other common-law countries including England. It is the view advanced by noted scholars and that adopted by the Restatement of the Conflict of Laws. It accords with ancient concepts of freedom of contract and reflects an appreciation of the expanding horizons of American contractors who seek business in all parts of the world. Not surprisingly foreign businessmen prefer, as do we, to have disputes resolved in their own courts, but if that choice is not available, then a neutral forum with expertise in the subject matter. Plainly the courts of England meet the standards of neutrality and long experience in admiralty litigation. The choice of that forum was made in an arms-length negotiation by experienced and sophisticated businessmen and absent some compelling and countervailing reason it should be honored by the parties and enforced by the courts.

The argument that such clauses are improper because they tend to "oust" a court of jurisdiction is hardly more than a vestigial legal fiction. It appears to rest at core on historical judicial resistance to any attempt to reduce the power and business of a particular court and has little place in an era when all courts are overloaded and when businesses once essentially local now operate in world markets. It reflects something of a provincial attitude regarding the fairness of other tribunals. No one seriously contends in this case that the forum-selection clause "ousted" the District Court of jurisdiction over Zapata's action. The threshold question is whether that court should have exercised its jurisdiction to do more than give effect to the legitimate expectations of the parties manifested in their freely negotiated agreement, by specifically enforcing the forum clause.

There are compelling reasons why a freely negotiated private international agreement, unaffected by fraud, undue influence, or overweening bargaining power,[58] such as that involved here, should

58. The record here refutes any notion of overweening bargaining power. Judge Wisdom in the Court of Appeals noted:

"Zapata has neither presented evidence of nor alleged fraud or undue bargaining power in the agreement. Unterweser was only one of several companies bidding on the project. No evidence contradicts its Managing Director's affidavit that it specified English courts 'in an effort to meet

be given full effect. In this case, for example, we are concerned with a far from routine transaction between companies of two different nations contemplating the tow of an extremely costly piece of equipment from Louisiana across the Gulf of Mexico, and the Atlantic Ocean, through the Mediterranean Sea to its final destination in the Adriatic Sea. In the course of its voyage, it was to traverse the waters of many jurisdictions. The Chaparral could have been damaged at any point along the route, and there were countless possible ports of refuge. That the accident occurred in the Gulf of Mexico and the barge was towed to Tampa in an emergency were mere fortuities. It cannot be doubted for a moment that the parties sought to provide for a neutral forum for the resolution of any disputes arising during the tow. Manifestly much uncertainty and possibly great inconvenience to both parties could arise if a suit could be maintained in any jurisdiction in which an accident might occur or if jurisdiction were left to any place where the *Bremen* or Unterweser might happen to be found.[59] . . .

Thus, in the light of present day commercial realities and expanding international trade we conclude that the forum clause should control absent a strong showing that it should be set aside. Although their opinions are not altogether explicit, it seems reasonably clear that the District Court and the Court of Appeals placed the burden on Unterweser to show that London would be a more convenient forum than Tampa, although the contract expressly resolved that issue. The correct approach would have been to enforce the forum clause specifically unless Zapata could clearly show that enforcement would be unreasonable and unjust, or that the clause was invalid for such reasons as fraud or overreaching. Accordingly, the case must be remanded for reconsideration.

We note, however, that there is nothing in the record presently before us that would support a refusal to enforce the forum clause. The Court of Appeals suggested that enforcement would be contrary to the public policy of the forum under Bisso v. Inland Waterways Corp., 349 U.S. 85, 75 S.Ct. 629, 99 L.Ed. 911 (1955), because of the prospect that the English courts would enforce the clauses of the towage contract purporting to exculpate Unterweser from liability for damages to the Chaparral. A contractual choice of forum clause should be held unenforceable if enforcement would contravene a strong public policy of the forum in which suit is brought, whether declared by statute or by judicial decision. See, e. g., Boyd v. Grand Trunk W. R. R., 338 U.S. 263, 70 S.Ct. 26, 94 L.Ed. 55 (1949). It is clear, however, that whatever the proper reach of the policy expressed in *Bisso*, it does not reach this case. *Bisso* rested

Zapata Off-Shore Company half way.' Zapata's Vice President has declared by affidavit that no specific negotiations concerning the forum clause took place. But this was not simply a form contract with boilerplate language that Zapata had no power to alter. The towing of an oil rig across the Atlantic was a new business. Zapata did make alterations to the contract submitted by Unterweser. The forum clause could hardly be ignored. . . .

59. At the very least, the clause was an effort to eliminate all uncertainty as to the nature, location, and outlook of the forum in which these companies of differing nationalities might find themselves. Moreover, while the contract here did not specifically provide that the substantive law of England should be applied, it is the general rule in English courts that the parties are assumed, absent contrary indication, to have designated the forum with the view that it should apply its own law. . . . It is therefore reasonable to conclude that the forum clause was also an effort to obtain certainty as to the applicable substantive law.

on considerations with respect to the towage business strictly in American waters, and those considerations are not controlling in an international commercial agreement. . . .

. . .

Courts have also suggested that a forum clause, even though it is freely bargained for and contravenes no important public policy of the forum, may nevertheless be "unreasonable" and unenforceable if the chosen forum is *seriously* inconvenient for the trial of the action. Of course, where it can be said with reasonable assurance that at the time they entered the contract, the parties to a freely negotiated private international commercial agreement contemplated the claimed inconvenience, it is difficult to see why any such claim of inconvenience should be heard to render the forum clause unenforceable. We are not here dealing with an agreement between two Americans to resolve their essentially local disputes in a remote alien forum. In such a case, the serious inconvenience of the contractual forum to one or both of the parties might carry greater weight in determining the reasonableness of the forum clause. The remoteness of the forum might suggest that the agreement was an adhesive one, or that the parties did not have the particular controversy in mind when they made their agreement, yet even there the party claiming should bear a heavy burden of proof. Similarly, selection of a remote forum to apply differing foreign law to an essentially American controversy might contravene an important public policy of the forum. For example, so long as *Bisso* governs American courts with respect to the towage business in American waters, it would quite arguably be improper to permit an American tower to avoid that policy by providing a foreign forum for resolution of his disputes with an American towee.

This case, however, involves a freely negotiated international commercial transaction between a German and an American corporation for towage of a vessel from the Gulf of Mexico to the Adriatic Sea. As noted, selection of a London forum was clearly a reasonable effort to bring vital certainty to this international transaction and to provide a neutral forum experienced and capable in the resolution of admiralty litigation. Whatever "inconvenience" Zapata would suffer by being forced to litigate in the contractual forum as it agreed to do was clearly foreseeable at the time of contracting. In such circumstances it should be incumbent on the party seeking to escape his contract to show that trial in the contractual forum will be so gravely difficult and inconvenient that he will for all practical purposes be deprived of his day in court. Absent that there is no basis for concluding that it would be unfair, unjust, or unreasonable to hold that party to his bargain.

In the course of his ruling on Unterweser's second motion to stay the proceedings in Tampa, the District Court did make a conclusionary finding that the balance of convenience was "strongly" in favor of litigation in Tampa. However, as previously noted, in making that finding the court erroneously placed the burden of proof on Unterweser to show that the balance of convenience was strongly in its favor. Moreover, the finding falls far short of a conclusion that Zapata would be effectively deprived of its day in court should it be forced to litigate in London. Indeed, it cannot even be assumed that it would be placed to the expense of transporting its witnesses to London. It is not unusual for important issues in international admiralty cases to be dealt with by deposition. Both the District Court and the Court of Appeals majority appeared satisfied that Unterweser could receive a fair hearing in Tampa by using deposition testimony of its witnesses from distant places, and there is no reason to conclude that Zapata could not use deposition testimony to equal advantage if forced to litigate in London as it bound itself to do. Nevertheless, to allow Zapata opportunity to carry its heavy burden of showing not only that the balance of convenience is strongly in favor of trial in Tampa (that is, that it will be far more inconvenient for Zapata to litigate in London than it will be for Unterweser to litigate in Tampa), but also that a London trial will be so manifestly and gravely inconvenient to Zapata that it will be effectively deprived of a meaningful day in court, we remand for further proceedings.

. . .

[MR. JUSTICE DOUGLAS, dissenting, stressed that the "substantive rights" of respondent, an American citizen, would be adversely affected if respondent were remitted to the English court. The exculpatory clauses would not be enforceable in the United States but, according to evidence in the record, are enforceable in England.]

QUESTIONS

(1) Which Restatement formulation comes closer to summarizing the outcome in Zapata? Which do you prefer? Does Zapata provide a comprehensive list of the factors that you would regard as relevant to determining whether a clause is [un]fair or [un]reasonable?

(2) What relevance has Zapata to determining the validity of forum selection clauses in actions arising under the following federal statutes: (*a*) The Carriage of Goods by Sea Act, 49 Stat. 1207 (1936), 46 U.S.C.A. § 1300, which forbids "[a]ny clause, covenant or agreement . . . lessening" the carrier's liability for negligence, fault or dereliction of statutory duties; (*b*) the Automobile Dealers Franchise Act, 70 Stat. 1125 (1956), 15 U.S.C.A. §§ 1221–25, which is designed to equalize the bargaining position of dealers against manufacturers and to compel manufacturers to "act in good faith" in performing or terminating franchises, and which provides that a dealer may bring suit in any district in which the "manufacturer resides, or is found or has an agent"; (*c*) the Jones Act, 38 Stat. 1185, 46 U.S.C.A. § 688, which grants injured seamen a right of recovery against their employers?

(3) What impact should Zapata have on state courts (or federal courts in diversity cases) that consider international choice-of-forum clauses in ordinary contract cases?

NOTE ON FOREIGN ATTITUDES TOWARDS THE CHOICE-OF-FORUM CLAUSE [60]

Clauses which explicitly or by implication exclude the forum selected by plaintiff are usually an effective bar to an action in a number of European countries: Austria, Belgium, France, Germany and Switzerland. However, in each country exceptions are made, based on varying notions of local public policy. The clause is generally upheld only with respect to civil or commercial contracts and not, for

60. Lenhoff, The Parties' Choice of Forum: "Prorogation Agreements," 15 Rutgers L.Rev. 414 (1961); Hay, The United States and International Unification of Law: The Tenth Session of the Hague Conference, 1965 U.Ill.L. Forum 820, 845–847.

example, in contracts involving family matters. In some instances, a stipulation in an insurance contract that the insurer can be sued only in a particular jurisdiction will not be honored in a suit brought by a domiciliary or national of the forum. In Italy the clause appears to be effective only between aliens or between nonresident citizens and aliens. In addition, Italian law generally requires that choice-of-forum clauses be signed separately when they appear in adhesion contracts. In certain countries such as Spain the clause appears to be without effect.

Special problems arise under French law in view of the interpretation given to Article 15 of the Civil Code, pp. 751–753, supra. Recall that in the normal case, a foreign judgment rendered against a French national will not be enforced in France, on the ground that Article 15 confers an exclusive jurisdiction over such an action in the French courts. However, as indicated at the pages referred to, French courts will honor certain waivers by parties of their rights under this article. As stated in 2 Batiffol, Droit International Privé 365–72 (5th ed., Lagarde, 1970), French plaintiffs and defendants (individual or corporate) can waive the benefits of Article 15 by contract, and this frequently occurs through clauses conferring jurisdiction upon foreign courts.

The British courts have had a number of occasions to consider the effect of choice-of-forum clauses—among others in The Chapparal, [1968] 2 Lloyd's Rep. 158 (C.A.), in which they accepted the jurisdiction offered them by the very clause at stake in M/S Bremen v. Zapata Off-Shore Co. In the converse case, British courts have tended to accept jurisdiction where the clause pointed to another forum, as in The Fehmarn, [1958] 1 Weekly L.R. 159 (C.A.1957). A Russian company loaded turpentine at a Baltic port on a German ship. The bill of lading stated that the turpentine was shipped in good condition and was to be delivered, subject to stated conditions, including a requirement that the German shipowners make the ship seaworthy for the voyage. The bill of lading also provided that all "claims and disputes arising under and in connection with this bill of lading shall be judged in the U.S.S.R.," and that "all questions and disputes not mentioned in this bill of lading shall be determined according to the Merchant Shipping Code of the U.S.S.R." The Russian shippers sold the turpentine to English buyers, who became holders of the bill of lading. After the turpentine was unloaded in England, the importers complained of short delivery and contamination of the turpentine because the shipowner had not properly cleaned the ship tanks before loading. They brought an action in England against the shipowners, who moved to set aside the writ because of the quoted provisions in the bill of lading. The lower court allowed the action to proceed, although it stated: [61]

> . . . [I]t is well established that, where there is a provision in a contract providing that disputes are to be re-

61. [1957] 1 Weekly L.R. 815, 819–20.

ferred to a foreign tribunal, then, prima facie, this court will stay proceedings instituted in this country in breach of such agreement, and will only allow them to proceed when satisfied that it is just and proper to do so. . . . Where there is an express agreement to a foreign tribunal, clearly it requires a strong case to satisfy this court that that agreement should be overridden and that proceedings in this country should be allowed to continue. But in the end it is, and must necessarily be, a matter for the discretion of the court, having regard to all the circumstances of the particular case. . . .

An appeal to the Court of Appeals was dismissed. In his opinion, Lord Denning stated:

> Then the next question is whether the action ought to be stayed because of the provision in the bill of lading that all disputes are to be judged by the Russian courts. I do not regard this provision as equal to an arbitration clause, but I do say that the English courts are in charge of their own proceedings: and one of the rules they apply is that a stipulation that all disputes should be judged by the tribunals of a particular country is not absolutely binding. It is a matter to which the courts of this country will pay much regard and to which they will normally give effect, but it is subject to the overriding principle that no one by his private stipulation can oust these courts of their jurisdiction in a matter that properly belongs to them.
>
> I would ask myself therefore: Is this dispute a matter which properly belongs to the courts of this country? Here are English importers who, when they take delivery of the goods in England, find them contaminated. The goods are surveyed by surveyors on both sides, with the result that the English importers make a claim against the German shipowners. The vessel is a frequent visitor to this country. In order to be sure that their claim, if substantiated, is paid by the shipowners, the English importers are entitled by the procedure of our courts of Admiralty to arrest the ship whenever she comes here in order to have security for their claim. There seems to me to be no doubt that such a dispute is one that properly belongs for its determination to the courts of this country. But still the question remains: Ought these courts in their discretion to stay this action?
>
> It has been said by Mr. Roche that this contract is governed by Russian law and should be judged by the Russian courts, who know that law. And the dispute may involve evidence from witnesses in Russia about the condition of the goods on shipment. Then why, says Mr. Roche, should not it be judged in Russia as the condition says?
>
> I do not regard the choice of law in the contract as decisive. I prefer to look to see with what country is the dispute most closely concerned. Here the Russian element in the dispute seems to me to be comparatively small. The dispute is between the German owners of the ship and the English importers. It depends on evidence here as to the condition of the goods when they arrived here in London and on evidence of the ship, which is a frequent visitor to London. . . .

I think the dispute is more closely connected with England than Russia, and I agree with the judge that sufficient reason has been shown why the proceedings should continue in these courts and should not be stayed. I would therefore dismiss the appeal.

NOTE ON THE HAGUE CONVENTION ON THE CHOICE OF COURT

At the Tenth Session of the Hague Conference on Private International Law in 1964, the participating nations adopted a Convention on the Choice of Court, which is now open to ratification.[62] Certain provisions appear below:

Article 1

. . . [P]arties may by an agreement on the choice of court designate, for the purpose of deciding disputes which have arisen or may arise between them in connection with a specific legal relationship, either:

1. the courts of one of the contracting States, the particular competent court being then determined (if at all) by the internal legal system or systems of that State, or

2. a court expressly named of one of the contracting States, provided always that this court is competent according to the internal legal system or systems of that State.

Article 2

This Convention shall apply to agreements on the choice of court concluded in civil or commercial matters in situations having an international character.

It shall not apply to agreements on the choice of court concluded in the following matters:

1. the status or capacity of persons or questions of family law . . . .

. . .

3. questions of succession,

4. questions of bankruptcy . . . .

5. rights in immovable property.

Article 3

This Convention shall apply whatever the nationality of the parties.

Article 4

For the purpose of this Convention the agreement on the choice of court shall have been validly made if it is the result of the acceptance by one party of a written proposal by the other party expressly designating the chosen court or courts.

. . .

62. The full text is set forth in 13 Am.J.Comp.L. 629 (1964).

The agreement on the choice of court shall be void or voidable if it has been obtained by an abuse of economic power or other unfair means.

Article 5

Unless the parties have otherwise agreed only the chosen court or courts shall have jurisdiction.

. . .

Article 6

Every court other than the chosen court or courts shall decline jurisdiction except:

1. where the choice of court made by the parties is not exclusive,

2. where under the internal law of the State of the excluded court, the parties were unable, because of the subject-matter, to agree to exclude the jurisdiction of the courts of that State,

3. where the agreement on the choice of court is void or voidable in the sense of article 4,

4. for the purpose of provisional or protective measures.

Article 8.[63]

Decisions given by a chosen court in the sense of this Convention in one of the contracting States shall be recognised and enforced in the other contracting States in accordance with the rules for the recognition and enforcement of foreign judgments in force in those States.

Article 12

Any contracting State may reserve the right not to recognise agreements on the choice of court concluded between persons who, at the time of the conclusion of such agreements, were its nationals and had their habitual residence in its territory.

Article 13

Any contracting State may make a reservation according to the terms of which it will treat as an internal matter the juridical relations established in its territory between, on the one hand, physical or juridical persons who are there and, on the other hand, establishments registered on local registers, even if such establishments are branches, agencies or other representatives of foreign firms in the territory in question.

Article 15

Any contracting State may reserve the right not to recognise agreements on the choice of court if the dispute has no connection with the chosen court, or if, in the circumstances, it would be seriously inconvenient for the matter to be dealt with by the chosen court.

63. [Eds.] The permissive provisions of Article 8 reflect the unwillingness of the member nations to lay down rules with respect to foreign judgments before the Convention on the Recognition and Enforcement of Foreign Judgments * was drafted in 1966.

Article 20

Any State may, not later than the moment of its ratification or accession, make one or more of the reservations mentioned in articles 12, 13, 14 and 15 of the present Convention. No other reservation shall be permitted.

. . .

The United States delegation abstained in the vote taken on the Convention.[64] In its Report, the delegation, after observing that the Convention "has many good points," stressed three objections. (*1*) The Convention does not authorize refusal to uphold a choice-of-forum provision where the chosen court would be an inconvenient forum for the particular issue, although Article 15 does permit a reservation to this effect. (*2*) Article 5 states the "wrong" presumption. It should have provided that the chosen court would have an exclusive jurisdiction only if the parties expressly so agreed. (*3*) Article 6(2) leaves an unnecessarily broad avenue of escape from the Convention. The Report concluded "the United States should not ratify the Convention because of the defects mentioned above, and, more importantly, because (1) the effect to be given choice of forum provisions is a matter that traditionally lies within the control of the States and there is no compelling reason why the national government should enter the area, and (2) the Convention in so far as it requires that effect be given to a choice of forum provision may be contrary to prevailing American opinion."[65] Recall the discussion at p. 578, supra, of federal-state problems that are posed by international agreements.

QUESTIONS

(1) Suppose that the United States ratified the Convention with the reservations permitted by Articles 12, 13 and 15. Would the result in the Zapata case be required? What changes would have to be made in the Restatement formulation?

(2) If England ratified the Convention with the same reservations should a case with facts comparable to The Fehmarn come to a different conclusion?

(3) Assuming that a large number of nations ratifies the Convention, with all permitted reservations, how significant would the advance be towards predictability and certainty in commercial relations?

PROBLEM

You are a local counsel in the State of Ames for Beauté, S.A., a French cosmetics firm. It has just developed a new lipstick, Femme Fatale, to introduce to the American market. Beauté entered into negotiations with Highpressure, Inc., a corporation organized and with its principal office in Ames which distributes and advertises products in this field throughout the United States. The proposed contract gives Highpressure exclusive rights in the United States to import Femme Fatale. Title to the product

64. See 52 Dept.State Bull. 265, 270–271 (1965).

65. However, the Commissioners on Uniform State Laws have recommended a Model Choice of Forum Act that is designed after the Hague Convention. See 17 Am.J.Comp.L. 292 (1969).

will pass f. o. b. Le Havre. The contract requires Highpressure to follow certain procedures in promoting and distributing the product. In addition to its profits on resale, Highpressure will receive from Beauté an additional amount based on the quantity of Femme Fatale that is sold. Beauté anticipates that sales in the United States should soon reach an annual level of about $100,000. The contract terminates at the option of Beauté if sales fall below a stated annual amount. Beauté makes warranties in the contract as to the quality and safety of Femme Fatale.

Apart from this proposed venture, Beauté is not involved in any activities relating to the United States market. It informs you that litigation could arise over a number of provisions in the contract, and states that it is very anxious to confine all such litigation to the French courts. Ames has adopted a statute similar to Wisc.Stat.Ann. § 262.05, p. 734, supra. The Ames cases construing choice-of-forum clauses suggest an attitude similar to that of the Restatement (Second).

Advise Beauté of what problems it faces in attempting to restrict all litigation to France, and of what provisions could be inserted in the contract to attempt to realize its aims. Draft the contract clauses which you would counsel Beauté to submit to Highpressure during the negotiations, and consider what provisions could be included that might persuade a court to honor the clause.

Additional reading: Cowen and da Costa, The Contractual Forum: A Comparative Study, 43 Can.Bar Rev. 453 (1965); Lenhoff, The Parties' Choice of a Forum: "Prorogation Agreements," 15 Rutgers L.Rev. 414 (1961); Proceedings of the 1964 Annual Meeting of the American Foreign Law Association, The Validity of Forum Selecting Clauses, 13 Am.J. Comp.L. 157 (1964) (collected papers); Farquharson, Choice of Forum Clauses—A Brief Survey of Anglo-American Law, 8 Int.Law. 83 (1974).

D. INTERNATIONAL COMMERCIAL ARBITRATION

Often parties to an international commercial arrangement such as a license agreement, sales contract, or distributorship contract wish to include a clause providing for the settlement of disagreements by arbitration.[66] Even in domestic transactions, businessmen often prefer arbitration (a) as a quicker, cheaper and more informal process and (b) as a means of securing as arbitrators experts in the particular field of commerce involved. In an international transaction the question of neutrality of the arbitrator(s) may become paramount. Neither party may be willing to subject itself to the hazards of litigating on the other party's home ground under unfamiliar procedures and before judges belonging to the other party's social, economic and political system. Through arbitration they can select an intermediate ground—politically, linguistically and geographically. In this way an arbitration clause can accomplish what the parties hoped to achieve through the choice-of-forum clause examined in the preceding section.

In fact, an arbitration clause can be more finely attuned to the preferences of the parties, who often can specify what types of arbi-

66. Such clauses figure in some of the illustrative studies of international business transactions in Part B of Chapter XII.

trators or procedures and what range of outcomes they desire. The two parties may, of course, have quite different preferences about the nature of the arbitration. One party may possess sufficient bargaining power to coerce the other into accepting a solution both distasteful and inconvenient to it.

Usually the parties will not wish to specify all the incidents of a prospective arbitration. They can incorporate by reference elaborate procedures for arbitration that have been developed by such organizations as the International Chamber of Commerce. Such procedures thus somewhat resemble the procedures for incorporating rules intended for arbitrations between two governments or between a government and a foreign investor.[67] The arbitration clause may be accompanied by a reference to the substantive rules established for the business in question by some international or national trade association, commodity exchange or the like.

The issue of the validity of the clause (or an award based on it) can arise in three different ways. (1) A party may bring a suit in a court based on a cause of action which, under the relevant contract clause, should have been referred to an arbitrator; the defendant may rely on the clause as a bar to the action. (2) One party may initiate arbitration proceedings and the other may refuse to appear or participate in the arbitration. A court's aid may be invoked to order the party to participate. (3) After an award is entered, one party may refuse to comply and thereby require the prevailing party to seek enforcement in the courts.

The path towards international arbitration has been marked by serious obstacles. Courts in the common law systems suspected domestic arbitration of attempting to "oust" them of jurisdiction, and were even more skeptical towards out-of-state or international arbitration. Gradually the states in this country enacted statutes departing from the earlier rules, in some cases adopting the Uniform Arbitration Act with its provisions for recognition and enforcement of arbitration clauses and awards. Civil law countries, particularly in Latin America, have shown much skepticism. However, as of the 1970's the prospects for international arbitration stood much improved as a result of treaty developments.

The following case represents the first endeavor by the United States Supreme Court in this area:

SCHERK v. ALBERTO-CULVER COMPANY

Supreme Court of the United States, 1974.
417 U.S. 506, 94 S.Ct. 2449, 41 L.Ed.2d 270.

[Alberto-Culver Co., a corporation organized in Delaware and headquartered in Illinois, manufactures toiletries and hair products.

67. Compare the Model Rules on Arbitral Procedure,* designed for arbitrations between countries, and the procedures described at p. 484, supra, developed by the International Center for the Settlement of Investment Disputes for arbitrations between countries and foreign investors.

In an attempt to expand its overseas operations it entered into negotiations with Fritz Scherk, a German citizen residing in Switzerland who owned three business entities in that field, two in Germany and one in Liechtenstein. Starting in 1967 negotiations were carried on in both Europe and the United States for the acquisition by Alberto-Culver of the ownership of those entities along with all their rights to trade-marks in cosmetics. The contract was signed in Vienna, Austria, on February 1969 and the transaction was closed in Geneva, Switzerland, in June 1969. Scherk expressly warranted sole and unencumbered ownership of the trade-marks. Alberto-Culver paid Scherk with promissory notes. The contract contained arbitration clauses relating to each entity, each of which was similar to the following one:

> The parties agree that if any controversy or claim shall arise out of the agreement or the breach thereof and either party shall request that the matter shall be settled by arbitration, the matter shall be settled exclusively by arbitration in accordance with the rules then obtaining of the International Chamber of Commerce, Paris, France, by a single arbitrator, if the parties shall agree upon one, or by one arbitrator appointed by each party and a third arbitrator appointed by the other arbitrators. In case of any failure of a party to make an appointment referred to above within four weeks after notice of the controversy, such appointment shall be made by said Chamber. All arbitration proceedings shall be held in Paris, France, and each party agrees to comply in all respects with any award made in any such proceeding and to the entry of a judgment in any jurisdiction upon any award rendered in such proceeding. The laws of the State of Illinois, U.S.A. shall apply to and govern this agreement, its interpretation and performance.

Discovering in 1970, or so it alleged, that Scherk's trade-marks were subject to significant encumbrances, Alberto-Culver attempted to rescind the contract by tendering the assets back to him. Upon Scherk's refusal, it brought an action in the Illinois federal district court alleging that Scherk's misrepresentations about the trade-marks constituted a violation of Section 10(b) of the Securities Exchange Act of 1934 and of Rule 10b–5 promulgated thereunder. Scherk moved to dismiss or, alternatively, to stay the action pending arbitration. Alberto-Culver sought a preliminary injunction against arbitration which Scherk began, five months after the complaint was filed. Alberto-Culver prevailed in the District Court, which denied the motion to dismiss and granted an injunction, and the Court of Appeals (2–1) affirmed. The Supreme Court granted certiorari and reversed in an opinion by JUSTICE STEWART.]

The Arbitration Act of 1925, 9 U.S.C. § 1 et seq., reversing centuries of judicial hostility to arbitration agreements,[68] was designed to allow parties to avoid "the costliness and delays of litigation," and to place arbitration agreements "upon the same footing as other contracts . . . ." H.R.Rep.No.96, 68th Cong., 1st

68. English courts traditionally considered irrevocable arbitration agreements as "ousting" the courts of jurisdiction, and refused to enforce such agreements for this reason. This view was adopted by American courts as part of the common law up to the time of the adoption of the Arbitration Act. See H.R.Rep.No. 96, 68th Cong., 1st Sess., 1, 2 (1924); Sturges & Murphy, Some Confusing Matters Relating to Arbitration under the United States Arbitration Act, 17 Law & Contemp.Prob. 580.

Sess., 1 (1924); see also S.Rep.No.556, 68th Cong., 1st Sess. (1924). Accordingly the Act provides that an arbitration agreement such as is here involved "shall be valid, irrevocable, and enforceable, save upon such grounds as exist at law or in equity for the revocation of any contract." 9 U.S.C. § 2.[69] The Act also provides in § 3 for a stay of proceedings in a case where a court is satisfied that the issue before it is arbitrable under the agreement, and § 4 of the Act directs a federal court to order parties to proceed to arbitration if there has been a "failure, neglect, or refusal" of any party to honor an agreement to arbitrate.

In Wilko v. Swan, 346 U.S. 427, 74 S.Ct. 182, 98 L.Ed. 168, this Court acknowledged that the Act reflects a legislative recognition of the "desirability of arbitration as an alternative to the complications of litigation," id., at 431, 74 S.Ct., at 185, but nonetheless declined to apply the Act's provisions. That case involved an agreement between Anthony Wilko and Hayden, Stone & Co., a large brokerage firm, under which Wilko agreed to purchase on margin a number of shares of a corporation's common stock. Wilko alleged that his purchase of the stock was induced by false representations on the part of the defendant concerning the value of the shares, and he brought suit for damages under § 12(2) of the Securities Act of 1933, 15 U.S.C. § 77*l*. The defendant responded that Wilko had agreed to submit all controversies arising out of the purchase to arbitration, and that this agreement, contained in a written margin contract between the parties, should be given full effect under the Arbitration Act.

The Court found that "[t]wo policies, not easily reconcilable, [are] involved in this case." 346 U.S., at 438, 74 S.Ct., at 188. On the one hand, the Arbitration Act stressed "the need for avoiding the delay and expense of litigation," id., at 431, 74 S.Ct., at 185, and directed that such agreements be "valid, irrevocable, and enforceable" in federal courts. On the other hand, the Securities Act of 1933 was "[d]esigned to protect investors" and to require "issuers, underwriters, and dealers to make full and fair disclosure of the character of securities sold in interstate and foreign commerce and to prevent fraud in their sale," by creating "a special right to recover for misrepresentation . . . . " Id., at 431, 74 S.Ct., at 184 (footnote omitted). In particular, the Court noted that § 14 of the Securities Act, 15 U.S.C. § 77n, provides:

> "Any condition, stipulation, or provision binding any person acquiring any security to waive compliance with any provision of this subchapter or of the rules and regulations of the Commission shall be void."

The Court ruled that an agreement to arbitrate "is a 'stipulation,' and [that] the right to select the judicial forum is the kind of 'provision' that cannot be waived under § 14 of the Securities Act." Thus, Wilko's advance agreement to arbitrate any disputes subsequently arising out of his contract to purchase the securities was unenforceable under the terms of § 14 of the Securities Act of 1933.

69. Section 2 of the Arbitration Act renders "valid, irrevocable, and enforceable" written arbitration provisions "in any maritime transaction or a contract evidencing a transaction involving commerce . . . ," as those terms are defined in § 1. In Bernhardt v. Polygraphic Co., 350 U.S. 198, 76 S.Ct. 273, 100 L.Ed. 199, this Court held that the stay provisions of § 3 apply only to the two kinds of contracts specified in §§ 1 and 2. Since the transaction in this case constituted "commerce . . . with foreign nations," 9 U.S.C. § 1, the Act clearly covers this agreement.

Alberto-Culver, relying on this precedent, contends that the District Court and Court of Appeals were correct in holding that its agreement to arbitrate disputes arising under the contract with Scherk is similarly unenforceable in view of its contentions that Scherk's conduct constituted violations of the Securities Exchange Act of 1934 and rules promulgated thereunder. For the reasons that follow, we reject this contention and hold that the provisions of the Arbitration Act cannot be ignored in this case.

At the outset, a colorable argument could be made that even the semantic reasoning of the *Wilko* opinion does not control the case before us. *Wilko* concerned a suit brought under § 12(2) of the Securities Act of 1933, which provides a defrauded purchaser with the "special right" of a private remedy for civil liability, 346 U.S., at 431, 74 S.Ct., at 184. There is no statutory counterpart of § 12(2) in the Securities Exchange Act of 1934, and neither § 10(b) of that Act nor Rule 10b–5 speaks of a private remedy to redress violations of the kind alleged here. While federal case law has established that § 10(b) and Rule 10b–5 create an implied private cause of action, . . .

[T]he Act itself does not establish the "special right" that the Court in Wilko found significant. Furthermore, while both the Securities Act of 1933 and the Securities Exchange Act of 1934 contain sections barring waiver of compliance with any "provision" of the respective acts, certain of the "provisions" of the 1933 Act that the Court held could not be waived by Wilko's agreement to arbitrate find no counterpart in the 1934 Act. . . .

Accepting the premise, however, that the operative portions of the language of the 1933 Act relied upon in *Wilko* are contained in the Securities Exchange Act of 1934, the respondent's reliance on *Wilko* in this case ignores the significant and, we find, crucial differences between the agreement involved in *Wilko* and the one signed by the parties here. Alberto-Culver's contract to purchase the business entities belonging to Scherk was a truly international agreement. Alberto-Culver is an American corporation with its principal place of business and the vast bulk of its activity in this country, while Scherk is a citizen of Germany, whose companies were organized under the laws of Germany and Liechtenstein. The negotiations leading to the signing of the contract in Austria and to the closing in Switzerland took place in the United States, England, and Germany, and involved consultations with legal and trade-mark experts from each of those countries and from Liechtenstein. Finally, and most significantly, the subject matter of the contract concerned the sale of business enterprises organized under the laws of and primarily situated in European countries, and whose activities were largely, if not entirely, directed to European markets.

Such a contract involves considerations and policies significantly different from those found controlling in *Wilko*. In *Wilko*, quite apart from the arbitration provision, there was no question but that the laws of the United States generally, and the federal securities laws in particular, would govern disputes arising out of the stock purchase agreement. The parties, the negotiations, and the subject matter of the contract were all situated in this country, and no credible claim could have been entertained that any international conflict of laws problems would arise. In this case, by contrast, in the absence of the arbitration provision considerable uncertainty existed at the time of the agreement, and still exists, concerning the law applicable to the resolution of disputes arising out of the contract.

Such uncertainty will almost inevitably exist with respect to any contract touching two or more countries, each with its own substantive laws and conflict of law rules. A contractual provision specifying in advance the forum in which disputes shall be litigated and the law to be applied is, therefore, an almost indispensable precondition to achievement of the orderliness and predictability essential to any international business transaction. Furthermore, such a provision obviates the danger that a dispute under the agreement might be submitted to a forum hostile to the interests of one of the parties or unfamiliar with the problem area involved.[70]

A parochial refusal by the courts of one country to enforce an international arbitration agreement would not only frustrate these purposes, but would invite unseemly and mutually destructive jockeying by the parties to secure tactical litigation advantages. In the present case, for example, it is not inconceivable that if Scherk had anticipated that Alberto-Culver would be able in this country to enjoin resort to arbitration he might have sought an order in France or some other country enjoining Alberto-Culver from proceeding with its litigation in the United States. Whatever recognition the courts of this country might ultimately have granted to the order of the foreign court, the dicey atmosphere of such a legal no-man's-land would surely damage the fabric of international commerce and trade, and imperil the willingness and ability of businessmen to enter into international commercial agreements.[71]

The exception to the clear provisions of the Arbitration Act carved out by *Wilko* is simply inapposite to a case such as the one before us. In *Wilko* the Court reasoned that "[w]hen the security buyer, prior to any violation of the Securities Act, waives his right to sue in courts, he gives up more than would a participant in other business transactions. The security buyer has a wider choice of courts and venue. He thus surrenders one of the advantages the Act gives him . . . ." 346 U.S., at 435, 74 S.Ct., at 187. In the context of an international contract, however, these advantages

70. See Quigley, Accession by the United States to the United Nations Convention on the Recognition and Enforcement of Foreign Arbitral Awards, 70 Yale L.J. 1049, 1051 (1961). For example, while the arbitration agreement involved here provided that the controversies arising out of the agreement be resolved under "[t]he laws of the State of Illinois," . . . a determination of the existence and extent of fraud concerning the trademarks would necessarily involve an understanding of foreign law on that subject.

71. The dissenting opinion argues that our conclusion that *Wilko* is inapplicable to the situation presented in this case will vitiate the force of that decision because parties to transactions with many more direct contacts with this country than in the present case will nonetheless be able to invoke the "talisman" of having an "international contract." Concededly, situations may arise where the contacts with foreign countries are so insignificant or attenuated that the holding in *Wilko* would meaningfully apply. Judicial response to such situations can and should await future litigation in concrete cases. This case, however, provides no basis for a judgment that only United States laws and United States courts should determine this controversy in the face of a solemn agreement between the parties that such controversies be resolved elsewhere. The only contacts between the United States and the transaction involved here is the fact that Alberto-Culver is an American corporation and the occurrence of some—but by no means the greater part—of the pre-contract negotiations in this country. To determine that "American standards of fairness" must nonetheless govern the controversy demeans the standards of justice elsewhere in the world, and unnecessarily exalts the primacy of United States law over the laws of other countries.

become chimerical since, as indicated above, an opposing party may by speedy resort to a foreign court block or hinder access to the American court of the purchaser's choice.[72]

[The court then referred to M/S Bremen v. Zapata Off-Shore Co., p. 812, supra.]

An agreement to arbitrate before a specified tribunal is, in effect, a specialized kind of forum-selection clause that posits not only the situs of suit but also the procedure to be used in resolving the dispute. The invalidation of such an agreement in the case before us would not only allow the respondent to repudiate his solemn promise but would, as well, reflect a "parochial concept that all disputes must be resolved under our laws and in our courts . . . . We cannot have trade and commerce in world markets and international waters exclusively on our terms, governed by our laws, and resolved in our courts." Id., at 9, 92 S.Ct., at 1912.

For all these reasons we hold that the agreement of the parties in this case to arbitrate any dispute arising out of their international commercial transaction is to be respected and enforced by the federal courts in accord with the explicit provisions of the Arbitration Act.[73]

72. The dissenting opinion raises the specter that our holding today will leave American investors at the mercy of multinational corporations with "vast operations around the world . . . ." Our decision, of course, has no bearing on the scope of the substantive provisions of the federal securities laws for the simple reason that the question is not presented in this case.

73. Our conclusion today is confirmed by international developments and domestic legislation in the area of commercial arbitration subsequent to the *Wilko* decision. On June 10, 1958, a special conference of the United Nations Economic and Social Council adopted the Convention on the Recognition and Enforcement of Foreign Arbitral Awards. In 1970 the United States acceded to the treaty, [1970] 3 U.S.T. 2517, T.I.A.S. No. 6997, and Congress passed Chapter 2 of the United States Arbitration Act, 9 U.S.C. § 201 ff., in order to implement the Convention. Section 1 of the new chapter provides unequivocally that the Convention "shall be enforced in United States courts in accordance with this chapter."

The goal of the Convention, and the principal purpose underlying American adoption and implementation of it, was to encourage the recognition and enforcement of commercial arbitration agreements in international contracts and to unify the standards by which agreements to arbitrate are observed and arbitral awards are enforced in the signatory countries. See Convention on the Recognition and Enforcement of Foreign Arbitral Awards, S.Exec.E. 90th Cong., 2d Sess. (1968); Quigley, Accession by the United States to the United Nations Convention on the Recognition and Enforcement of Foreign Arbitral Awards, 70 Yale L.J. 1049 (1961). Article II(1) of the Convention provides:

"Each Contracting State shall recognize an agreement in writing under which the parties undertake to submit to arbitration all or any differences which have arisen or which may arise between them in respect of a defined legal relationship, whether contractual or not, concerning a subject matter capable of settlement by arbitration."

In their discussion of this Article, the delegates to the Convention voiced frequent concern that courts of signatory countries in which an agreement to arbitrate is sought to be enforced should not be permitted to decline enforcement of such agreements on the basis of parochial views of their desirability or in a manner that would diminish the mutually binding nature of the agreements. See Haight, Convention on the Recognition and Enforcement of Foreign Arbitral Awards, Summary Analysis of Record of United Nations Conference 24–28 (1958).

Without reaching the issue of whether the Convention, apart from the considerations expressed in this opinion, would require of its own force that the agreement to arbitrate be enforced in the present case, we think that

Accordingly, the judgment of the Court of Appeals is reversed and the case is remanded to that court with directions to remand to the District Court for further proceedings consistent with this opinion.

It is so ordered.

Reversed and remanded.

MR. JUSTICE DOUGLAS, with whom MR. JUSTICE BRENNAN, MR. JUSTICE WHITE, and MR. JUSTICE MARSHALL concur, dissenting.

. . .

There has been much support for arbitration of disputes; and it may be the superior way of settling some disagreements. If A and B were quarreling over a trade-mark and there was an arbitration clause in the contract, the policy of Congress in implementing the United Nations Convention on the Recognition and Enforcement of Arbitral Awards as it did in 9 U.S.C. § 201 et seq., would prevail. But the Act does not substitute an arbiter for the settlement of disputes under the 1933 and 1934 Acts. Art. II(3) of the Convention says:

> "The court of a Contracting State, when seized of an action in a matter in respect of which the parties have made an agreement within the meaning of this article, shall, at the request of one of the parties, refer the parties to arbitration, unless it finds that the said agreement is null and void, inoperative or incapable of being performed." [74] [1970] 3 U.S.T. 2519, T.I.A.S. No. 6997.

But § 29(a) of the 1934 Act makes agreements to arbitrate liabilities under § 10 of the 1934 Act "void" and "inoperative." Congress has specified a precise way whereby big and small investors will be protected and the rules under which the Alberto-Culver Co.'s of this Nation shall operate. They or their lawyers cannot waive those statutory conditions, for our corporate giants are not principalities of power but guardians of a host of wards unable to care for themselves. It is these wards that the 1934 Act tries to protect. . . .

This invocation of the "international contract" talisman might be applied to a situation where, for example, an interest in a foreign company or mutual fund was sold to an utterly unsophisticated American citizen, with material fraudulent misrepresentations made in this country. The arbitration clause could appear in the fine print of a form contract, and still be sufficient to preclude recourse to our courts, forcing the defrauded citizen to arbitration in Paris to vindicate his rights.

It has been recognized that the 1934 Act, including the protections of Rule 10b–5, applies when foreign defendants have defrauded

this country's adoption and ratification of the Convention and the passage of Chapter 2 of the United States Arbitration Act provide strongly persuasive evidence of congressional policy consistent with the decision we reach today.

74. The Convention also permits that arbitral awards not be recognized and enforced when a court in the country where enforcement is sought finds that "the recognition and enforcement of the award would be contrary to the public policy of that country." Article V(2)(b). [1970] 3 U.S.T. 2520, T.I.A.S. No. 6997. It also provides that recognition of an award may be refused when the arbitration agreement "is not valid under the law to which the parties have subjected it," in this case the laws of Illinois. . . . Article V(1)(a). Ibid.

American investors, particularly when, as alleged here, they have profited by virtue of proscribed conduct within our boundaries. This is true even when the defendant is organized under the laws of a foreign country, is conducting much of its activity outside the United States, and is therefore governed largely by foreign law.[75] The language of § 29 of the 1934 Act does not immunize such international transactions, and the United Nations Convention provides that a forum court in which a suit is brought need not enforce an agreement to arbitrate which is "void" and "inoperative" as contrary to its public policy. . . .[76]

Moreover, the international aura which the Court gives this case is ominous. We now have many multi-national corporations in vast operations around the world—Europe, Latin America, the Middle East, and Asia. The investments of many American investors turn on dealings by these companies. Up to this day, it has been assumed by reason of *Wilko* that they were all protected by our various federal securities Acts. If these guarantees are to be removed, it should take a legislative enactment. I would enforce our laws as they stand, unless Congress makes an exception.

The virtue of certainty in international agreements may be important, but Congress has dictated that when there are sufficient contacts for our securities laws to apply, the policies expressed in those laws take precedence. Section 29, which renders arbitration clauses void and inoperative, recognizes no exception for fraudulent dealings which incidentally have some international factors. The Convention makes provision for such national public policy in Art. II(3). Federal jurisdiction under the 1934 Act will attach only to some international transactions, but when it does, the protections afforded investors such as Alberto can only be full-fledged.

75. See, e. g., Leasco Data Processing Equip. Corp. v. Maxwell, 468 F.2d 1326, 1334–1339 (C.A.2 1972); Travis v. Anthes Imperial Ltd., 473 F.2d 515, 523–528 (C.A.8 1973); SEC v. United Financial Group, Inc., 474 F.2d 354 (C.A.9, 1973); Schoenbaum v. Firstbrook, 405 F.2d 200 (C.A.2 1968); Roth v. Fund of Funds, D.C., 279 F. Supp. 935, aff'd, 405 F.2d 421 (C.A.2 1968).

76. A summary of the conference proceedings which led to the adoption of the United Nations Convention was prepared by G. W. Haight, who served as a member of the International Chamber of Commerce delegation to the conference. G. Haight, Convention on the Recognition and Enforcement of Foreign Arbitral Awards: Summary Analysis of Record of United Nations Conference, May/June 1958 (1958).

When Art. II(3) was being discussed, the Israeli delegate pointed out that while a court could, under the draft Convention as it then stood, refuse enforcement of an *award* which was incompatible with public policy, " 'the court had to refer parties to arbitration whether or not such reference was lawful or incompatible with public policy.' " Id., at 27. The German delegate observed that this difficulty arose from the omission in Art. II(3) " 'of any words which would relate the arbitral agreement to an arbitral award capable of enforcement under the convention.' " Ibid.

Haight continues:

"When the German proposal was put to a vote, it failed to obtain a two-thirds majority (13 to 9) and the Article was thus adopted without any words linking agreements to the awards enforceable under the Convention. Nor was this omission corrected in the Report of the Drafting Committee (L. 61), *although the obligation to refer parties to arbitration was (and still is) qualified by the clause 'unless it finds that the agreement is null and void, inoperative or incapable of being performed.'*

NOTE ON THE TREATY STRUCTURE OF INTERNATIONAL ARBITRATION

As the preceding case indicates, the treatment of international arbitration in United States courts will be determined largely by the multilateral United Nations Convention on the Recognition and Enforcement of Foreign Arbitral Awards (referred to in footnotes 73 and 74 of the opinions) to which 41 other nations, including most leading commercial countries, are parties. That Convention imposes on signatories the obligations (1) to recognize an agreement to arbitrate and refer litigants in its courts to arbitration unless the agreement is found to be void, and (2) to recognize awards under such agreements and enforce them by proceedings not substantially more burdensome than those applicable to domestic awards.

The list of exceptions in Article V(1) to the latter duty is narrowly drawn: (a) incapacity or invalidity "of the contract under the law to which the parties have subjected it", (b) failure to give notice to a party of the proceedings so as to deprive him of the ability to defend, (c) entering an award outside the scope of the agreement, and (d) nonconformity of the proceedings with the agreement. Article V(2), quoted in footnote 74 to the dissent, also permits exceptions based on the nonarbitrability of the subject matter and public policy.

To come within the scope of the Convention, an arbitral award must be made outside the territory of the enforcing state and must not be considered as "domestic" by the law of that state. The Convention permits a signatory to limit its application to awards rendered in other signatory countries, a reservation the United States has made. The Convention also contains a "federalism clause", obligating a signatory's national government to put the treaty into effect as far as is within its own powers and for the balance, to recommend action to its constituent states.

As noted in footnote 73, Congress passed Chapter 2 of the Federal Arbitration Act to implement the Convention. Just as the Convention supersedes provisions about arbitration clauses in treaties of friendship, commerce and navigation with states also parties to the Convention,[77] Chapter 2 largely supersedes for international transactions Chapter 1 of that Act. Section 201 provides generally for the enforcement of the Convention. Section 202 limits the Act's applicability to awards arising out of "commercial relationships" and, in the case of dealings between citizens of the United States, to those

77. Many such treaties contain provisions as to arbitration, some with important qualifications or of limited affirmative content. See, e. g., Article III(2) of the Franco-American Convention of Establishment.* A more affirmative clause, one moving close to assurance of national treatment, appears in Article VI(2) of the FCN treaty with the Federal Republic of Germany, signed October 29, 1954, 7 U.S.T. & O.I.A. 1839, T.I.A.S. No. 3593. These provisions are particularly noteworthy in view of the silence of all FCN treaties of the United States on enforcement of foreign judicial judgment. See p. 807, supra.

arising out of a relationship that "involves property located abroad, envisages performance or enforcement abroad, or has some other reasonable relation with one or more foreign states." Section 203 vests jurisdiction over Convention cases in the federal courts without regard to the independent basis for federal jurisdiction that was required under the old law. Under the Act, federal courts can order arbitration as specified in the agreement even if the place agreed upon is outside the United States—something not possible under the old Act.[78]

QUESTIONS

(1) Does the court in Scherk v. Alberto-Culver hold that securities litigation is not within the exceptions for non-arbitrable and public policy issues made in Article V of the Convention? Is it saying that United States courts are obligated to enforce the agreement or that, being free to ignore it, the Court chooses to enforce? Would enforcement of this arbitration contract in fact be likely to do much harm to the United States scheme of securities regulation? (Compare pp. 1047–1073, infra).

(2) Suppose that the transactions in Scherk had involved, instead of Scherk, the foreign subsidiary of a New York corporation that owned the same trade-marks. Would an action to enforce the clause come within (a) the Convention, (b) the enforcing statute? Suppose that the two corporations were both organized in Delaware—would that pose an additional problem?

(3) What was the law to which the parties "subjected" the Alberto-Culver-Scherk transaction, within the meaning of the Convention? Suppose that the basic contract were void under the laws of the United States, Germany and Switzerland, but the parties had designated Liechtenstein. Would United States courts be obliged to enforce arbitration?

(4) If a court concluded that the party insisting on the arbitration clause was a vastly more powerful multinational enterprise and that the particular arbitral proceedings chosen prejudiced the other side's chances of obtaining a fair hearing, must it enforce arbitration?

(5) Compare the list of "excuses" for not recognizing foreign judicial judgments under the Hague Convention * with that applicable to foreign awards under Article V of the U.N. Convention on Arbitration. What accounts for the differences that you observe? Compare the current attitude of courts towards choice-of-forum clauses with the dictates of the Convention on Arbitration. Should the gap be narrowed further?

(6) Timeweek, an American weekly, also publishes a foreign language edition in Guatador, a country which is a party to the Convention on Arbitration. An article appearing both in the American and Guatadorian editions, based on apparently reliable information that was checked as carefully as possible, stated that a Guatadorian Senator Libella had taken a bribe in connection with his official duties. Libella demanded $300,000 (equivalent) in damages. Timeweek, which has about $100,000 in assets in Guatador and has little confidence in the local judiciary, agreed to arbitration in Guatador. Proceedings were fair and an award was rendered in the

78. The early case law under the Convention includes Island Territory of Curacao v. Solitron Devices, Inc., 489 F.2d 1313 (2d Cir. 1973); In re Fotochrome, Inc., 377 F.Supp. 26 (E.D.N.Y.1974).

sum requested. Libella brings a diversity action to enforce the award in the federal district court in New York. As counsel for Timeweek, what arguments do you make?

Additional reading: Quigley, The Convention on Foreign Arbitral Awards, 53 A.B.A.J. 821 (1972); Quigley, Accession by the United States to the United Nations Convention or the Recognition and Enforcement of Foreign Arbitral Awards, 70 Yale L.J. 1049 (1961); Domke, The Enforcement of Arbitration Awards, in R. von Mehren (ed.), Enforcement of Foreign Country Judgments (1974); Evans and Ellis, International Commercial Arbitration: A Comparison of Legal Regimes, 8 Tex.Int.L.J. 17 (1973).

E. OBTAINING EVIDENCE ABROAD FOR USE IN DOMESTIC CIVIL LITIGATION

We have seen that a court in one country must often rely on courts or other agencies of foreign countries to effectuate service of process to initiate an action or to enforce a judgment. Between those stages, during the course of the litigation, the same court (or more directly, the parties) may need to procure evidence, documentary or testimonial, available only in other countries and may have to ask courts in those countries for assistance in obtaining it. Collaboration among judiciaries here requires considerable mutual understanding between jurists whose conceptions not only of the rules of evidence, narrowly considered, but also of judicial procedure as a whole, may differ widely.

Some systems emphasize the oral presentation of evidence by direct witnesses, often accompanied by stress on cross examination as a key to the ascertainment of the truth. In such systems, other testimony is frowned upon as hearsay and is admissible only as a secondary, non-preferred, means of proof. Other systems tend to give primary weight to written evidence and regard it as the best guarantee of accuracy. No modern system, of course, can afford to disregard either type of evidence, but strong differences in emphasis are apparent. In the United States, the trial itself is a single more or less continuous session, quite distinct from the pre-trial processes of discovery. In other countries, this separation may be less rigid; the whole process may take place before the court and may be divided into quite a few sessions, held from time to time as the convenience of the judge, the parties and the witnesses indicates. In some countries, the judge is conceived basically as an arbiter to keep the contending counsel from violating the rules of fair play as they develop the case. In others, the judge is regarded as having the basic responsibility for developing the relevant facts and ferreting out the truth from the witnesses.[79] Much depends on whether the judge sits with a jury of laymen or whether he decides questions of fact as well as law.

79. In a criminal context, compare the Chattin case, p. 367, supra.

Problems may also arise from rules responding to values quite outside the law of procedure. The laws of all countries protect some types of records and some witnesses against disclosure even in litigation, thus putting other interests above that of the search for truth. The interests recognized as being so significant vary from country to country; they may affect official secrets, professional (e. g., lawyers', doctors', accountants' or journalists') and clerical confidences, and may even protect private commercial and economic interests, such as customers' interests in secrecy of bank records. These variations can produce acute international conflicts.

Under these circumstances it is not surprising that the United States experienced considerable difficulty in establishing satisfactory relationships with other countries in this field. In an earlier period, sheer geographic isolation diminished our courts' exposure to foreign practices and foreign needs. More recently, problems of federalism have proved to be a hindrance, particularly with respect to international conventions. On the other hand, various developments enhanced our preparedness to cope with such international problems. As more cases involving foreign judicial assistance arose, our courts acquired more sophistication. Increasing scholarly attention was paid to the topic. It became politically possible to appoint, under statutory authority, a Commission and Advisory Committee on International Rules of Judicial Procedure. That body, utilizing the work of the Columbia Project on International Procedure, developed proposals for changes in the Judicial Code and in the Federal Rules of Civil Procedure. Through the appropriate judicial and legislative processes, these changes became effective in 1964 and 1963 respectively. Congress in 1963 finally authorized this country's participation in the Hague Conference on Private International Law, which in 1964 treated selected issues of international judicial assistance as well as questions of foreign judgments.

The first fruit of this participation in the procedure field was the Convention on the Service Abroad of Judicial or Extrajudicial Documents in Civil or Commercial Matters, pp. 756–758, supra. A Convention on the Taking of Evidence Abroad in Civil or Commercial Matters was signed in 1970 and entered into force for the United States in 1972, 23 U.S.T. & O.I.A. 2555, T.I.A.S. No. 7444. However, as of 1974 Denmark and Norway were the only other parties. Where applicable, it pledges a government to cooperate in enforcing Letters of Request transmitted through specified channels from other signatory countries—unless cooperation is "incompatible" with its own internal law or is "impossible of performance" because of procedural or practical problems.

This Part E describes the basic approach of federal courts in the United States to the problems of procuring oral testimony and documentary evidence abroad in civil cases. State courts have comparable problems, complicated by the fact that they may have less well developed pre-trial procedures.

Additional Reading: For comparisons of foreign procedural systems with our own, see Kaplan, von Mehren and Schaefer, Phases of German Civil Procedure, 71 Harv.L.Rev. 1193, 1443 (1958); Cappelletti and Perillo, Civil Procedure in Italy (1965). On international legal assistance, see Jones, International Judicial Assistance: Procedural Chaos and a Program for Reform, 62 Yale L.J. 515 (1953); Smit, International Aspects of Federal Civil Procedure, 61 Colum.L.Rev. 1031 (1961); Smit, International Litigation under the U.S.Code, 65 Colum.L.Rev. 1015 (1965). On the Hague Conference, see Nadelmann, The United States Joins the Hague Conference on Private International Law, 30 Law & Contemp.Prob. 291 (1965).

NOTE ON CERTAIN TECHNIQUES FOR OBTAINING EVIDENCE ABROAD

Non-documentary Evidence. Although it is possible to present "live" witnesses from abroad at a trial, this path is frequently expensive and, if the witnesses are uncooperative, may be impossible. Thus it is more realistic under domestic practices to think in terms of depositions, since mere affidavits by foreign affiants will ordinarily be excluded under the hearsay rule. F.R.C.P. 6(d)(3) permits the use at trial of a deposition of a witness who "is out of the United States." The following paragraphs of this Note concentrate on the problems of taking depositions abroad; they assume a knowledge of the reader of discovery processes in this country.[80]

Recall that, domestically, the deposition is primarily a private affair. The witness is examined by counsel for one party and cross-examined by counsel for the other. His testimony is recorded verbatim by a court reporter, who is a private person paid by the parties for his work. This reporter can administer an oath to the witness because he is usually also a notary. This title in the United States (outside of Louisiana) does not imply a significantly public office—contrary to what it implies in a typical civil law country.

Official intervention may occur in any of several ways. A witness may refuse to answer a question; in such a case the parties may resort for a ruling to the court in which the action is pending. Note that under Rule 26(b), it is not a proper ground for refusal to answer that the testimony will be inadmissible at the trial—a point to recall in connection with the RCA case, p. 840, infra. Thus rulings are sought primarily when questions of privilege arise or if a party claims that the examination is being conducted so as to burden or harass him. If it is thought that many such instances may arise, and at points remote from that court, it may become convenient to ask the court to appoint (under Rule 28) a master to travel with the parties, make appropriate rulings and otherwise supervise the depositions. This has occurred in several complex (and expensive) patent and antitrust

80. See, e. g., Chadbourn, Levin and Schuchman, Civil Procedure ch. III (2d ed. 1974); or Field and Kaplan, Civil Procedure 390–424 (Temp.2d ed. 1968).

actions. If the witness refuses to answer after being ordered to do so, or will not appear at all, other official powers become relevant. Within the United States, the district court in whose district the witness is then present will come to the assistance of its fellow district court by issuing a subpoena commanding attendance. The court where the action is pending can under Rule 37 exert pressure on any *party* to the litigation from whom information is sought, including its officers or managing agents.

Depositions may be taken abroad in the accustomed domestic manner and without further ado, if (*a*) the witness is willing and (*b*) the foreign state does not regard the proceedings as the performance of a foreign official function on its soil. On the latter point, it is important to note that a foreign country may assume a deposition proceeding to be more "official" than, according to the foregoing description, it seems to Americans. If that country has a litigation system in which all activities analogous to "discovery" are part of the trial and are actively supervised or even conducted by the court, it is apt to remold American practices in that image. This may account for the Swiss view that taking depositions violates Section 271 of the Swiss Penal Code, penalizing any person who "without being authorized . . . takes on behalf of a foreign government any action which is solely within the province" of the Swiss authorities. Rule 28(b), as recently revised, attempts to leave litigants with the maximum flexibility in obtaining foreign depositions.

The Federal Rules exhibit a number of approaches to the problem of the unwilling witness. As noted above, the trial court has some power over *parties* to the litigation by virtue of Rule 37. If the non-party witness abroad is an American citizen, the court may issue a subpoena under the powers given it by 28 U.S.C.A. § 1783 * and Rule 45,* although its ability to assure compliance with the subpoena through the contempt power may depend upon whether the American has assets in this country or later reappears here.[81] With a foreign *non-party* witness, resort must be had to a foreign governmental agency with power to coerce. Sometimes a foreign authority will issue a subpoena not expressly provided for under foreign law to assist a deposition being conducted by counsel alone or being taken before a master or commissioner appointed by the trial court or a United States consul. Where such informal collaboration is not forthcoming or where the foreign state takes a negative view of depositions as foreign official intrusion on its territory, resort must be had to letters rogatory. The United States basis for such action is laid by Rule 28 (b)(3)* and by 28 U.S.C.A. § 1781.*

Note that Section 1781 also empowers courts in the United States to respond to foreign letters rogatory. In addition to its importance for foreign litigants, Section 1781 has significance for American parties in that it can be used to assure a foreign court that the United

81. See Blackmer v. United States, p. 862, infra.

States offers reciprocity in corresponding cases. (So can 28 U.S.C.A. § 1782.) Essentially, letters rogatory seek the aid of a foreign court, requesting it to add its official power to the American court's. This purpose is apparent in the following suggested form for use by federal courts.[82]

[Caption]

The President of the United States of America to the Appropriate Judicial Authority in ______, Greeting:

Whereas, a certain action is pending in our District Court for the ______ District of ______, in which ______ is plaintiff and ______ is defendant, and it has been suggested to us that justice cannot be completely done between said parties without the testimony of ______, who resides at ______, within your jurisdiction.

We, therefore, request that in the interest of justice you cause by your proper and usual process, said ______ to appear before you or some competent officer by you for that purpose authorized, at a time and place by you to be determined, then and there to make answer on his oath (or solemn affirmation) to the interrogatories and cross-interrogatories hereto annexed, and that you will cause his deposition to be reduced to writing, and such books, papers, or other articles that said witness may produce or identify be marked as Plaintiff's Exhibits or Defendant's Exhibits in the manner indicated in the interrogatories or cross-interrogatories, and to cause these to be returned to us under cover duly sealed and addressed to the Clerk of the United States District Court for the ______ District of ______, United States of America, and we shall be ready and willing to do the same for you in a similar case when required.

WITNESS, Hon. ______, Judge of the District Court of the United States for the ______ District of ______, the ______ day of ______, 19__.

______________________,
Clerk.

[Seal of the U. S. District Court]

[Certification by Judge of Clerk's office, signature and seal]

[Certification by Clerk of Judge's signature and office]

In honoring letters rogatory, the foreign court may merely issue an order requiring the witness to appear before counsel for the parties or the commissioner appointed by the United States court.[83] It may take a more active role and preside over the examination itself, or even conduct it to the more or less complete exclusion of counsel. It may impose its own conceptions of the rules of evidence. As the last sentence of Rule 28(b) indicates, if a deposition is obtained from

82. This was originally published in Moore's Federal Practice, 2nd edition, 1963 (vol. 4 ¶ 28.05) and is reprinted through the permission of the copyright owner Matthew Bender & Co., Inc., Copyright © 1963.

83. This was done, for example, in Radio Corp. of America v. Rauland Corp., p. 840, infra.

a foreign court it may deviate widely from the standard American product.

Documentary Evidence. Domestically, documentary evidence can usually be obtained from a non-party by a subpoena under Rule 45 (d) in conjunction with the taking of his deposition. Evidence of this type is usually procured from a party by a discovery order pursuant to Rule 34, compliance therewith being sanctioned by Rule 37. Abroad, evidence can be sought under Rules 34 and 37, subject to the risk that the foreign legal system may contain rules which make it impossible for the party to comply. This indeed was the critical problem in some of the cases that follow. With recalcitrant *non-party* witnesses abroad, resort must usually be had to letters rogatory. Frequently requests for testimony and for evidence are paired.

Even after the difficulties of obtaining foreign documents have been surmounted, a party faces the problem of introducing them into the court proceedings in this country over technical requirements and objections based on domestic rules of evidence. One aspect of this problem deserves brief mention, that of foreign official records. Official records have traditionally enjoyed certain special benefits in terms of authenticity and even of hearsay restrictions. Rule 44(a), as recently revised, attempts to extend these benefits to foreign official records.

The following cases illustrate how problems may arise in the execution of the various procedures for obtaining evidence for use in domestic litigation.

RADIO CORP. OF AMERICA v. RAULAND CORP.

Queen's Bench Division, 1956.
[1956] 1 Q.B. 618.

[Radio Corporation of America (RCA) brought an action in the United States District Court for the Northern District of Illinois against Rauland Corporation and Zenith Radio Corporation for patent infringement. Defendants alleged as defense and counterclaim a conspiracy since 1919 between RCA and others to violate the antitrust laws through licensing agreements, etc. Judge Igoe in the federal court granted defendants letters rogatory addressed to the judicial authorities in England and three other countries, requesting that certain witnesses, members of the boards of directors of three British companies not parties to the litigation, be called to appear before the United States consul for oral interrogation and be required to produce all relevant and material documentary evidence in their custody. MASTER GRUNDY made an order to that effect, relying on provisions of the Foreign Tribunals Evidence Act excerpted below. MASTER BURNAND, upon application by the British companies and their directors, made orders discharging them from compliance. Rauland and Zenith (the applicants) appealed and furnished a revised request asking (A) for more specifically identified documents and (B) for the oral testimony of specified persons. BARRY, J., of the Queen's Bench Division allowed the appeal in part, ordering that three directors be examined before a master, according to English court procedure, as to matters specified in B above and that these persons should, if given due notice, produce documents specified by the applicants. The two companies and the directors appealed. The Divisional Court reinstated MASTER BURNAND's order. Portions of the Court's orders follow:]

DEVLIN, J. This case concerns the proper construction of section 1 of the Foreign Tribunals Evidence Act, 1856, which provides:

> Where, upon an application for this purpose, it is made to appear to any court or judge having authority under this Act that any court or tribunal of competent jurisdiction in a foreign country, before which any civil or commercial matter is pending, is desirous of obtaining the testimony in relation to such matter of any witness or witnesses within the jurisdiction of such first-mentioned court, or of the court to which such judge belongs, or of such judge, it shall be lawful for such court or judge to order the examination upon oath, upon interrogatories or otherwise, before any person or persons named in such order, of such witness or witnesses accordingly.

That is the first limb of the first section, and the second limb goes on to say:

> it shall be lawful for the said court or judge, by the same order, or for such court or judge or any other judge having authority under this Act, by any subsequent order, to command the attendance of any person to be named in such order, for the purpose of being examined, or the production of any writings or other documents to be mentioned in such order.

That section has been invoked by the applicants in this case, the defendants in an action which has been proceeding in the District Court of Illinois for some very considerable time, who desire to obtain from certain witnesses in this country information, and originally they desired to obtain documents, in order to assist the proceedings in the District Court of Illinois.

It is necessary to indicate generally, the present stage of those proceedings; they are concerned with discovery. We have not had any evidence of American law and practice in relation to discovery, but what we need for the purposes of this case can be sufficiently ascertained from the documents that have been put in front of us. The essential principles of discovery in the United States do not seem to be very different from the principles in this country; that is to say, discovery is not merely limited to the obtaining, by means of disclosure, of such material as may be strictly relevant to the issues in the action such as might be admissible on the hearing of the action, but it covers also the obtaining of material which might lead to a line of inquiry which would itself disclose relevant material. It might be convenient for the purposes of this judgment if I refer to the first as "direct" material, that is, material which might be put in evidence in the action, and to the second as "indirect" material.

Recent cases in this country . . . have shown that discovery of documents may sometimes be obtained not only because they are relevant in the case itself but because they may fairly lead to a line of inquiry which would disclose relevant material, but it is plain that that principle has been carried very much further in the United States of America than it has been carried in this country. In the United States of America it is not restricted merely to obtaining a disclosure of documents from the other party to the suit, but there is a procedure, which might be called a pre-trial procedure, in the courts of the United States which allows interrogation not merely of the parties to the suit but also of persons who may be witnesses in the suit, or whom it may be thought may be witnesses in the suit, and which requires them to answer questions and produce documents. The questions would not necessarily be restricted to matters which were relevant in the suit, nor would the production be necessarily restricted to admissible evidence, but they might be such as would lead to a train of inquiry which might itself lead to relevant material.

It is that pre-trial procedure, the obtaining of depositions from witnesses with a view to discovery, which the District Court at Illinois is at present engaged upon, and accordingly the defendant corporations, the present applicants, applied to that court for process which under English law they could not possibly get in order to obtain what is in effect discovery from witnesses in this country. In accordance with the ordinary American procedure they were allowed to obtain that process and the application before the court, therefore, is not an application to examine witnesses for the purpose of their evidence being used directly in the suit but to examine witnesses in connection with the discovery proceedings.

Before the court has any jurisdiction to grant this application it must be made to appear that the foreign court is desirous of obtaining "testimony in relation to such matter" within the meaning of section 1 of the Foreign Tribunals Evidence Act, 1856, and the question that we have to determine is whether this testimony which it is sought to obtain is "testimony" within the meaning of the statute. Some authority is available upon the meaning of the Act, and authorities, which Sir Frank Soskice, who appears for the applicants, does not in this court challenge, show that he could not ask for discovery of documents. . . .

. . . [T]he distinction is made plain between discovery or "indirect" material on the one hand and proof or "direct" material on the other hand, and that is the true distinction with which one must approach the word "testimony" in this Act. Testimony which is in the nature of proof for the purpose of the trial is permissible. Testimony, if it can be called "testimony," which consists of mere answers to questions on the discovery proceeding designed to lead to a train of inquiry, is not permissible. Into which category does the present fall? It is perhaps enough to say that it is plain from what I have said of the nature of the proceedings in the court of Illinois that they fall into the latter category; they are pre-trial proceedings, proceedings by way of discovery. But if there be any doubt about that I do not think that one need do more than to look at the reasons which Judge Igoe, in the District Court of Illinois, gave when he granted the letters rogatory in this case. One passage is sufficient for my purpose. He said:

> I can find no authority, and none has been cited, for the proposition that a party must show what relevant and material evidence proposed witnesses have in their possession as a condition precedent to taking of depositions of alleged co-conspirators in an anti-trust case. It seems obvious that examination of the officers and agents of alleged co-conspirators may lead to the discovery of relevant evidence, and that is all that is required.

That shows, I think, plainly enough what the object of this procedure is. . . .

So far as the rules of evidence are concerned, whether the evidence is relevant or not would depend upon the rules of evidence that are appropriate in the foreign court. Sir Hartley Shawcross has not sought to argue otherwise; but whether it is relevant testimony within the meaning of the section depends upon whether it is testimony that is relevant to an issue in the matter and not whether it is testimony—if, as I say, "testimony" can be used in this sense at all—which is merely material which might lead to a line of inquiry which would in fact disclose the testimony. The judge, I think, was distinguishing perhaps between oral material and written material; but the difficulties to which such a distinction lead are manifest when one considers the order that has been made and the way in which Sir Frank Soskice has sought to justify it. Let me take as an example the agreement of 1902 which we heard discussed in the course of the case. The judge, having refused to order that the company, through its proper officer, should disclose that document, the order that he has made is one which empowers the applicants to put one of the directors of the company in the box and to give him notice to produce the document, which the company has not been ordered to produce. In other words, instead of producing it through its proper officer, it is to be required to produce it through a director. Of course, the company can pass a resolution quite properly—and Sir Frank Soskice does not argue otherwise—saying that its director, Sir George Nelson, is not to have any authority to produce the document. The company itself has been told that it need not produce it by its proper officer and it can deprive Sir George Nelson of any power or authority to produce it. What could Sir Frank in that event do? The answer is that he would ask Sir George Nelson questions about the document. In other words, the effect of the order is that although the company may not be ordered to produce the document itself its servants may be compelled to go into the witness-box and answer questions about it. The primary evidence not being allowed, secondary evidence would be brought in instead. That cannot, in my judgment, be the right distinction. There is in fact no distinction as far as principle is concerned between the two Parts of the request, A and B, and the judge, I think with respect, ought to have applied the same principle to both.

The consequence, in my judgment, is that the appeal ought to be allowed and the order of Master Burnand restored.

LORD GODDARD C. J. I agree. I would only add that I base my judgment upon two short points. First, whichever way one looks at this case it seems to me that it is in effect an application that the English companies should give discovery of their documents. It is agreed now that the order could not be made upon the companies because they are not parties to the action, and the device, if I may use that expression without offence to anybody, of saying that a direction is to be called and may be examined with regard to these documents seems to me only to be trying in another way to get discovery which cannot be ordered under the Act. Secondly, it seems to me perfectly clear from the passage in the judgment of Judge Igoe to which Devlin J. has referred, that this is merely an attempt to get evidence in the course of discovery proceedings which are known to the American courts—and are also known to the Canadian courts—which are a sort of pre-trial before the main trial. It is an endeavour to get in evidence by examining people who may be able to put the parties in the way of getting evidence. That is mainly what we should call a "fishing" proceeding which is never allowed in the English courts, and I think that that of itself would be a complete objection and ought to justify this court in refusing to make the order. For the rest, I have nothing to add to the judgment which my brother has given.

COMMENT

In re RCA v. Rauland, 5 D.L.R.2d 424 (1956), Gale, J. of the Ontario High Court set aside in part an ex parte order issued by another justice in response to letters rogatory issued by Judge Igoe in the same litigation. A Canadian statute largely paralleled the Foreign Tribunals Evidence Act. While ordering the attendance of designated witnesses, Justice Gale found that the order's "description of the documents is far too wide, too vague and too general." He stated that defendants could apply again for a production order if they could better identify the documents.[84]

SOCIÉTÉ INTERNATIONALE POUR PARTICIPATIONS INDUSTRIELLES ET COMMERCIALES, S.A. v. ROGERS

Supreme Court of the United States, 1958.
357 U.S. 197, 78 S.Ct. 1087, 2 L.Ed.2d 1255.

[Section 5(b) of the Trading with the Enemy Act, 40 Stat. 415, as amended, 50 U.S.C.A.App. § 5(b) authorizes the United States to seize during a period of war " . . . any property or interest of any foreign country or national." Section 9(a) of that Act, 40 Stat. 419, as amended, 50 U.S.C.A.App. § 9(a), authorizes recovery of the seized assets by any person " . . . not an enemy or ally of enemy" to the extent of that person's interest in the assets.

In this litigation, which began in 1948, Société Internationale, a Swiss corporate holding company also referred to as Interhandel, sought recovery under Section 9(a) of assets held in its name which had been vested in 1941 in the Alien Property Custodian (succeeded in interest by the time of the litigation by the Attorney General). These assets, valued at over $100,000,000, consisted of approximately 90% of the capital stock of General Aniline & Film Corporation, a Delaware corporation, and certain bank accounts. The vesting order was based upon an executive determination that the assets were "owned by or held for the benefit of" I. G. Farbenindustrie, a German corporation.

The litigation raised many complex issues under the Trading with the Enemy Act. In opposing the action, the Government argued basically that Interhandel was an "enemy" within the meaning of the Act since it was intimately connected with I. G. Farben and hence was affected with "enemy taint" despite its incorporation in Switzerland. The Government alleged that Interhandel had conspired with I. G. Farben, a Swiss banking firm (H. Sturzenegger & Cie.) and others to conceal the true ownership of Interhandel (directly) and General Aniline (indirectly through Interhandel), in order to avoid wartime confiscation.

One of the critical issues to the litigation thus became the nationality of the owners of Interhandel. In an effort to substantiate its allegations as to the character of Interhandel the Government filed a motion in 1949 under F.R.C.P. 26 and 34 requiring the pro-

84. Cf Re Raychem Corp. v. Canusa Coating Systems, Inc., 14 D.L.R.3d 684 (Ont.Ct.App.1970).

duction of a large number of the banking records of Sturzenegger. It alleged that Interhandel and Sturzenegger were "substantially identical". The district court found that Sturzenegger's papers were in Interhandel's "control" within the meaning of F.R.C.P. 34 and granted the motion.

Thereafter the Swiss Federal Attorney "confiscated" the Sturzenegger records; this "confiscation" left the papers in Sturzenegger's hands but amounted to an interdiction on their production. The Federal Attorney acted on the authority of the following provisions of Swiss law:

Article 273, Swiss Penal Code

> "Economic intelligence service in the interest of foreign countries: Whoever elicits a manufacturing or business secret in order to make it accessible to a foreign official, agency or to a foreign organization or private enterprise or to any agents of same,
>
> "Whoever makes accessible a manufacturing or business secret to a foreign official, agency, or to a foreign organization or private enterprise or to any agents of the same, shall be punished by imprisonment and in serious cases by penitentiary. In addition to that penalty, a fine may be imposed."

Article 47, Swiss Banking Law of 1934

> "Any person who wilfully . . . (b) in his capacity as organ, officer or employee of a bank, as auditor or assistant auditor, as member of the Banking Commission, officer or employee of its secretarial office, violates his duty to observe silence or the professional secrecy, or whoever induces or attempts to induce a person to commit such an offense, shall be fined not more than twenty thousand francs, and/or shall be imprisoned for not longer than six months.
>
> "If the offender acted negligently, the penalty is a fine of not more than ten thousand francs." [85]

There followed protracted maneuvers involving repeated motions for relief by Interhandel, repeated extensions of the deadline for compliance, the obtaining of waivers from many of Sturzenegger's clients and the production by July 1956 of a total of 190,000 documents. Some documents, in particular the books of account of the bank, were never submitted. Interhandel presented a plan, approved by the Swiss Government, whereby a neutral expert would examine the files and identify documents he deemed to be relevant, which Interhandel would then seek to produce. The district court rejected the plan and directed dismissal of the action. The Court of Appeals affirmed and certiorari was granted.

In its opinion, delivered by JUSTICE HARLAN, the Court first affirmed the propriety of the original order to produce under Rule 34. It next considered the propriety of the dismissal under Rule 37(b).* The Court discussed the variations in the use of the terms "refusal" or "refuses" (in the caption of Rule 37 and the text of 37(b)) and "failure to comply" (in the caption of 37(b)). It concluded that Interhandel's noncompliance constituted a refusal to obey within the meaning of Rule 37(b)(2), even though Interhandel had not will-

85. This translation is taken from the Master's Report at pp. 2817, 2822 of the Record.

fully refused but had been prevented by intervening authority despite its "good faith" efforts (as found by a master appointed by the district court) to comply. It then considered whether the sanction of dismissal, though within the terms of Rule 37, was excessive:]

We must discard at the outset the strongly urged contention of the Government that dismissal of this action was justified because petitioner conspired with I. G. Farben, Sturzenegger & Cie, and others to transfer ownership of General Aniline to it prior to 1941 so that seizure would be avoided and advantage taken of Swiss secrecy laws . . . . The findings below reach no such conclusions; indeed, it is not even apparent from them whether this particular charge was ever passed upon below. Although we do not mean to preclude the Government from seeking to establish such facts before the District Court upon remand, or any other facts relevant to justification for dismissal of the complaint, we must dispose of this case on the basis of the findings of good faith made by the Special Master, adopted by the District Court, and approved by the Court of Appeals.

The provisions of Rule 37 which are here involved must be read in light of the provisions of the Fifth Amendment that no person shall be deprived of property without due process of law, and more particularly against the opinions of this Court in Hovey v. Elliott, 167 U.S. 409, 17 S.Ct. 841, 42 L.Ed. 215, and Hammond Packing Co. v. State of Arkansas, 212 U.S. 322, 29 S.Ct. 370, 53 L.Ed. 530. These decisions establish that there are constitutional limitations upon the power of courts, even in aid of their own valid processes, to dismiss an action without affording a party the opportunity for a hearing on the merits of his cause . . . .

These two decisions leave open the question whether Fifth Amendment due process is violated by the striking of a complaint because of a plaintiff's inability, despite good-faith efforts, to comply with a pretrial production order . . . . Certainly substantial constitutional questions are provoked by such action. Their gravity is accented in the present case where petitioner, though cast in the role of *plaintiff,* cannot be deemed to be in the customary role of a party invoking the aid of a court to vindicate rights asserted against another. Rather petitioner's position is more analogous to that of a *defendant,* for it belatedly challenges the Government's action by now protesting against a seizure and seeking the recovery of assets which were summarily possessed by the Alien Property Custodian without the opportunity for protest by any party claiming that seizure was unjustified under the Trading with the Enemy Act. Past decisions of this Court emphasize that this summary power to seize property which is believed to be enemy-owned is rescued from constitutional invalidity under the Due Process and Just Compensation Clauses of the Fifth Amendment only by those provisions of the Act which afford a non-enemy claimant a later judicial hearing as to the propriety of the seizure . . . .

The findings below, and what has been shown as to petitioner's extensive efforts at compliance, compel the conclusion on this record that petitioner's failure to satisfy fully the requirements of this production order was due to inability fostered neither by its own conduct nor by circumstances within its control. It is hardly debatable that fear of criminal prosecution constitutes a weighty excuse for nonproduction, and this excuse is not weakened because the laws preventing compliance are those of a foreign sovereign. Of course this situation should be distinguished from one where a party claims that compliance with a court's order will reveal facts which may provide the basis for criminal prosecution of that party under the penal laws of a foreign sovereign thereby shown to have been violated. Cf. United States v. Murdock, 284 U.S. 141, 149, 52 S.Ct. 63, 76 L.Ed. 210. Here the findings below establish that the very fact of compliance by disclosure of banking records will itself constitute the initial violation of Swiss laws. In our view, petitioner stands in the position of an American plaintiff subject to criminal sanctions in Switzerland because production of documents in Switzerland pursuant to the order of a United States court might violate Swiss laws. Petitioner has sought no privileges because of its foreign citizenship which are not accorded domestic litigants in United States courts. Cf. Guaranty Trust Co. of New York v. United States, 304 U.S. 126, 133–135, 58 S.Ct. 785, 82 L.Ed. 1224. It does not claim that Swiss laws protecting banking records should here be enforced. It explicitly recognizes that it is subject to procedural rules of United States courts in this litigation and has made full efforts to follow these rules. It asserts no immunity from them. It asserts only its *inability* to comply because of foreign law.

In view of the findings in this case, the position in which petitioner stands in this litigation and the serious constitutional questions we have noted, we think that Rule 37 should not be construed to authorize dismissal of this complaint because of petitioner's noncompliance with a pretrial production order when it has been established that failure to comply has been due to inability, and not to willfulness, bad faith, or any fault of petitioner.

This is not to say that petitioner will profit through its inability to tender the records called for. In seeking recovery of the General Aniline stock and other assets, petitioner recognizes that it carries the ultimate burden of proof of showing itself not to be an "enemy" within the meaning of the Trading with the Enemy Act. The Government already has disputed its right to recovery by relying on information obtained through seized records of I. G. Farben, documents obtained through petitioner, and depositions taken of persons affiliated with petitioner. It may be that in a trial on the merits, petitioner's inability to produce specific information will prove a serious handicap in dispelling doubt the Government might be able to inject into the case. It may be that in the absence of complete disclosure by petitioner, the District Court would be justified in drawing inferences unfavorable to petitioner as to particular events. So much indeed petitioner concedes. But these problems go to the adequacy of petitioner's proof and should not on this record preclude petitioner from being able to contest on the merits.

On remand, the District Court possesses wide discretion to proceed in whatever manner it deems most effective. It may desire to afford the Government additional opportunity to challenge petitioner's good faith. It may wish to explore plans looking towards fuller compliance. Or it may decide to commence at once trial on the merits. We decide only that on this record dismissal of the complaint with prejudice was not justified.

The judgment of the Court of Appeals is reversed and the case is remanded to the District Court for further proceedings in conformity with this opinion.

COMMENT

This is the Supreme Court decision referred to in the Interhandel case before the International Court of Justice, p. 244 supra, as the basis for the conclusion that Interhandel had not exhausted local remedies. The litigation was subsequently settled by the parties on the basis of a sale to the American public of the General Aniline shares and a division of the proceeds.

INGS v. FERGUSON

United States Court of Appeals, Second Circuit, 1960.
282 F.2d 149, 82 A.L.R.2d 1397.

[The trustee of a corporation subject to reorganization under Chapter X of the bankruptcy act in a federal court in California brought an ancillary proceeding in the Southern District of New York to obtain data he needed to appraise the fairness of a proposed settlement of litigation involving the corporation. Subpoenas duces tecum were served on two Canadian banks with New York branches. The banks moved to quash the subpoenas as far as concerned records physically located in Canada. The district judge denied the motion and the banks appealed. Part of the opinion, by JUDGE MOORE, follows:]

Opinions (in affidavit form) from Canadian counsel for The Bank of Montreal, The Bank of Nova Scotia, The Toronto-Dominion Bank and The Royal Bank of Canada all came to the conclusion that Chapter 42 of the Statutes of Quebec, 6–7 Elizabeth II, 1957–1958 respecting records of business concerns in the Province of Quebec prohibit the banks and their employees from sending outside the Province any of the documents demanded by the subpoenas. A letter from other Canadian counsel submitted by the Trustee indicates a different interpretation of the statute. It is not necessary to attempt an interpretation of Canadian law. The fact that a conflict of theories exists between Canadian counsel only demonstrates the problem inherent in the issuance of subpoenas having extra-territorial effect upon Canadian subjects and parties to the litigation and points to the desirability of having the impact of Canadian statutes passed upon by Canadian courts.

An elementary principle of jurisdiction is that the processes of the courts of any sovereign state cannot cross international boundary lines and be enforced in a foreign country. Thus service of a United States District Court subpoena by a United States Marshal upon a Montreal branch of a Canadian bank would not be enforceable. However, amongst civilized nations, between which international comity exists, procedures have long been established whereby the requests of litigants in other countries seeking testimony and records are honored. Such reciprocity is evidenced by the laws which each of the sovereign states has enacted to enable this purpose to be achieved. Each state nevertheless by the very definition of sovereignty is entitled to declare its own national policy with respect to such limitations upon the production of records as its lawmakers may choose to enact.

For many years the time honored custom of seeking evidence in foreign countries, particularly in cases in which the aid of foreign courts may be necessary to secure the production of records, has been by letters rogatory. As the term implies this is a request made to the foreign court to give its aid, backed by its power, to secure the desired information. The Federal courts (and the New York State courts as well) have recognized this procedure in their provisions for letters rogatory. . . .

Provision for compliance with such requests is found in the Special Procedure Act of the Province of Quebec Chapter 342 (1941), section 16 which reads:

> "When, upon petition to that effect, it is shown to the Superior Court or to one of the judges thereof, charged with the administration of justice in the district, that a court of any other Province of Canada, or of any other British possession, or of a foreign country, before which any civil or commercial case is pending, desires to have the evidence of any party or witness in the district, such court or judge may order that such party or witness may be examined under oath, either by means of questions in writing or otherwise, before any person mentioned in the said order, and may summon, by the same or by a subsequent order, such party or witness to appear for examination, and may order him to produce any writing or document mentioned in the order, or any other writing or document relating to the matter, and which may be in his possession. R.S.1925, c. 277, s. 16."

Under this statute it would appear possible to secure both the testimony of witnesses and the production of the desired documents. Thus under the laws of both the United States and Canada procedures are available for securing evidence within the confines of the other's territory.

Subpoena power is not absolute. Even if exercised within proper territorial limits, the subpoena may be scrutinized by the courts. Every reason exists for careful scrutiny here. No claim is being made against either bank by any litigant. At most the bank is being called as a witness. The transactions did not originate in the New York Agencies. And the records sought are in the custody of branches in Canada. Under these circumstances it seems highly undesirable that the courts of the United States should countenance service of a subpoena upon a New York agency of a foreign bank which is not a party to the litigation and whose country has provided procedures for securing information, the production of which is consistent with its laws.

The Trustee advances the recent decision of this court in First National City Bank of New York v. Internal Revenue Service, 2 Cir., 271 F.2d 616, 618, certiorari denied 361 U.S. 948, 80 S.Ct. 402, 4 L. Ed.2d 381, as supporting the enforcement of the subpoena. In National City the subpoena was served at the main office in New York and required the production of records of a national bank located in its Panama branch. Sustaining the subpoena, the court said, "Any officer or agent of the corporation who has power to cause the branch records to be sent from a branch to the home office for any corporate purpose, surely has sufficient control to cause them to be sent on when desired for a governmental purpose properly implemented by a subpoena under 26 U.S.C.A. § 7602." There may be a serious question as to whether the manager of a New York Agency would have the power to direct the officers of a Canadian bank to send Canadian branch bank records out of the country in violation of a prohibitory statute and an opinion of counsel to that effect. However, it is unnecessary to resolve this question at this time because of other factors present. Even though the head office had control of its branches, enforcement of the subpoena was qualified in the event that compliance would violate the laws of Panama, the court saying, "If such were the fact we should agree that production of the Panama records should not be ordered" (271 F.2d at page 619).

A similar result was reached by the district court in this case with respect to the records of the Havana branch of The Royal Bank of Canada. The court, relying on National City, granted the motion to quash on the ground "that disclosure of information with regard to deposits and transactions in this situation would violate Cuban law, and might subject the officers and employees of the Cuban branch to criminal penalties."

Upon fundamental principles of international comity, our courts dedicated to the enforcement of our laws should not take such action as may cause a violation of the laws of a friendly neighbor or, at the least, an unnecessary circumvention of its procedures. Whether removal of records from Canada is prohibited is a question of Canadian law and is best resolved by Canadian courts. Cf. Gulf Oil Corp. v. Gilbert, 1947, 330 U.S. 501, 509, 67 S.Ct. 839, 91 L.Ed. 1055; Vanity Fair Mills, Inc. v. T. Eaton Co., 2 Cir., 1956, 234 F.2d 633, 645–647. Full opportunity to obtain such a decision is afforded to the Trustee by the procedural laws of this country and Canada. If upon such proceedings, i. e., letters rogatory, the records are produced the Trustee has by authorized means achieved this desire. If on the other hand production were declared illegal, the motion to quash should be granted as indicated in National City and in the decision below because the exception of illegality under foreign law would have been met. Only if, despite a ruling that production of the records or sending them outside the country would not be illegal, were there a refusal to make such records available, would it become necessary to consider whether a subpoena should issue.

The banks argue that important policy questions as to branch banking throughout the world are presented; that a subpoena served on a branch in New York might necessitate a search for, and the production of, records in hundreds of branches of foreign banks, and that were the subpoenas here attempted to be enforced, retaliatory laws might be enacted to the detriment of American business interests. Without minimizing the force of these arguments the decision here need not rest upon them except as they bear upon the exercise of the court's discretionary power.

Nor should the desire for haste because of the pendency of the New York stockholders' action justify a departure from authorized procedures. Were temporary expediency in every situation to create its own rules, well established principles of jurisdiction and due process would surely suffer. The zeal of the Trustee in endeavoring to benefit the many persons who may have been victimized by the indicted fugitive from justice is commendable but it should not be the basis for permitting him to avoid following the prescribed process for seeking information in a foreign country.

The order below should be modified by restricting it to records and other documents specified in the subpoenas which may be in the possession of the New York Agencies of The Bank of Nova Scotia and The Toronto-Dominion Bank, respectively, without costs.

COMMENT

Other cases have raised problems like those of the Interhandel case and Ings v. Ferguson. In von der Heydt v. Kennedy, 299 F.2d 459 (D.C.Cir. 1962), the court distinguished Interhandel, emphasizing that von der Heydt had been shown not to have complied in good faith with the court's production order, and affirmed the district court's dismissal of the action under F.R.C.P. 37(b) and other authority. In

Application of Chase Manhattan Bank, 297 F.2d 611 (2d Cir. 1962), the court, citing Ings, modified a grand jury subpoena calling on the Chase Manhattan Bank to produce documents in its Panama branch when Chase presented proof of a non-disclosure statute enacted by the Panamanian legislature on the day before the bank moved to show cause why the subpoena should not be modified. It left the subpoena outstanding so that the government could be assured of the bank's cooperation in its efforts to obtain authorization from the Panamanian authorities. Another grand jury subpoena was involved in United States v. First National City Bank, 396 F.2d 897 (2d Cir. 1968), in which it was held that the bank could not rely on the German bank secrecy rules to refuse data in its Frankfurt branch where German law created only a civil liability that seemed unlikely to result in serious damages being assessed against the bank.

PROBLEMS

I

Suppose that you are assigned to help develop the position which the United States delegation will take at a conference on multilateral arrangements for judicial assistance. The following points are put to you at a preliminary meeting:

(*a*) Are there constitutional difficulties about a treaty or federal legislation that would regulate the conduct of state courts in this area, particularly by requiring such courts to honor letters rogatory issued by foreign officials? Is such a treaty or legislation in any event likely to encounter strong political inhibitions? Would use of any other means of achieving the desired result, such as draft uniform state legislation, be likely to mitigate such difficulties? Would it create significant new problems?

(*b*) The negotiations may well involve arrangements for evidence for criminal as well as civil proceedings. If foreign officials ask domestic courts to assist them in procuring depositions or documents within the United States for use in criminal prosecutions abroad, can the courts consistently with the Sixth and Fourteenth amendments, collaborate in such endeavours? With respect to problems under the Fifth Amendment, refer to 28 U.S.C.A. § 1782(a).

II

Suppose that you are counsel for a person who has brought in a federal court an action alleging that she was injured in an automobile accident in Etruria because of the negligent conduct of defendant Kamikaze Motors (an Etrurian corporation served through its United States sales agency) which leased to her in Etruria a car that proved to have defective brakes. It becomes important for you to procure at the trial: (*a*) the contents of the rental agreement with Kamikaze Motors, which has the only signed copy in its Etrurian office; (*b*) the substance of the statements made to Inspector Maigret of the Etrurian police by eyewitnesses to the accident; (*c*) evidence as to what repairs, if any, had been made to the car before and after the accident either by a local Etrurian dealer in Kamikaze cars or by B. Cellini, an independent service station operator; and (*d*) records of the Merchants Bank of Etruria about payments made for the rental (which Kamikaze denies having received), the Bank having an American branch but all records of the transaction being at its Etrurian headquarters.

As to each of these items (*a*) through (*d*), consider (1) what evidence on the point would be relevant and admissible in an American court once obtained, (2) which of the various modes provided for by the federal rules and discussed in the Note, p. 837, supra, could be used to obtain the evidence in question, (3) what obstacles under foreign law each such approach is likely to encounter, and (4) the likely consequences for the outcome of the litigation of a failure to obtain the information sought by plaintiff. In the light of these considerations, how would you answer the following questions?

(a) Suppose that B. Cellini, the repairman, refuses to answer certain questions on the basis of an Etrurian law which says: "No person shall be compelled to testify concerning alterations made to any means of transportation after any accident for the purpose of preventing a recurrence thereof." Ought that to be a valid response? Suppose that the Etrurian authorities uphold Cellini's claim. How should that development affect the outcome of the litigation in the United States? Would the case be different if Cellini is an employee or a vice president of Kamikaze?

(b) Suppose that the Bank refuses to furnish the records, citing Etrurian statutes modelled on the Swiss statutes, quoted on p. 845, supra. How should that affect the litigation? Would the case be different if the New York branch possessed a copy of the records?

(c) Suppose that you needed to have Cellini's correspondence with Kamikaze and his files on the repairs made after the accident. Could you obtain such documentation without running afoul of the limits set in the RCA litigation, assuming that Etruria follows British law in this general field?

Part Four

THE TRANSNATIONAL REACH OF NATIONAL LEGAL SYSTEMS

Since a nation's concerns are not coterminous with its borders, efforts are inevitably made to regulate foreign-based conduct that may have important consequences within the domestic economic or political order. Or a nation may desire to attach certain consequences, such as tax liabilities, to conduct of its citizens wherever it may be engaged in. Thus several nations may have reason to regulate the same conduct, creating the risks of conflict among them and of imposing cumulative or conflicting duties upon the individual or corporate actors in transnational affairs.

Part Four treats such problems and thereby develops another aspect of the pervasive themes of conflict and accommodation among national legal systems. It examines the ways in which nations have attempted to regulate conduct occurring in whole or part outside their territory, or to visit sanctions upon persons outside that territory. That is, it examines the extraterritorial reach of criminal laws, economic regulation and fiscal legislation, as well as efforts to contain that reach through principles of national and international law.

The use of the word "extraterritorial" is traditional but troublesome. Courts and advocates sometimes suggest through it that the asserted reach of a statute is inappropriate, perhaps in violation of established legal principles. We mean no such connotation and use the term purely descriptively. Indeed, characterizing legislation as "intra-or-extra-territorial" is often dispensable to the kind of reasoning that should suggest whether a nation is asserting an exorbitant legislative power.

Chapter VIII introduces these problems of extraterritorial reach in the relatively simple setting of criminal legislation. Its cases illustrate the general principles relevant to this entire field. In Chapter IX, we apply those principles to the more complex problems of economic regulation in selected fields: welfare legislation for seamen, maritime labor, antitrust, and securities regulation. Chapter X examines one subject, transnational aspects of taxation, to illustrate an area in which unilateral and bilateral solutions to these problems have been relatively well developed.

Chapter VIII

THE TRANSNATIONAL REACH OF CRIMINAL LEGISLATION

Certain characteristics of criminal legislation and the adjudication of criminal cases assume particular significance for transnational problems. Consider the following distinctions between criminal laws or trials and the problems examined in Chapter VII.

(1) In civil litigation, numerous bases for adjudicatory jurisdiction complement the traditional Anglo-American stress upon the presence, transitory or substantial, of the defendant. Should the defendant fail to appear, a court may render a default judgment which will often be entitled to enforcement by a sister state and will frequently be enforced in a transnational setting. In criminal cases, custody of the person of the defendant is ordinarily essential.[1] One dramatic exception is the practice of certain countries—such as France, Italy or Turkey—of conducting some criminal trials *in absentia,* or *per incontumacium* as they put it. In these countries the accused, if subsequently arrested, is usually entitled to a trial *de novo*.[2]

(2) Previous chapters have stressed the significance of choice-of-law principles for resolving the merits of a dispute, for the enforcement of foreign-country judgments, and for the act of state doctrine.[3] But choice of law generally does not figure in criminal litigation. The court applies only the law of the state or nation from which it derives its authority, almost invariably the one in which it sits.[4] Courts refuse to act as enforcement organs for the criminal legislation of other jurisdictions.[5]

1. Blackmer v. United States, p. 862, infra, can be viewed as representing a partial exception to this rule.

2. See the description of this practice in Snee and Pye, Status of Forces Agreements and Criminal Legislation 137–42 (1957).

3. See in particular pp. 91, 502, 673, 760, supra.

4. This statement is subject to two exceptions. First, a military tribunal sitting in a foreign country may conduct a trial of a serviceman of the nationality of the tribunal under its national law or international agreement. Its authority to act in this manner may derive from national law or international agreements. Recall Reid v. Covert, p. 564, supra, and see the Note at p. 897, infra. Second, national courts or military tribunals may conduct trials of aliens under international criminal law, whether customary or conventional in character. See, pp. 903–931, infra. A prominent historical exception, no longer significant, was that of extraterritorial courts under the "capitulatory regimes" that were once a feature of the dominant role of the Western European countries and the United States in the Middle and Far East. See Ebb, Regulation and Protection of International Business 1–19 (1964).

5. It is not inconceivable that courts should so act. Somewhat remote analogies may be found in our federal system. For example, federal officers may remove to federal courts cases in which they are being prosecuted under state law for alleged crimes committed during their performance of federal duties. See 28 U.S.C.A. §§ 1442, 1442a. And compare the Federal Assimilative Crimes Act of 1948, 18 U.

The reasons are rarely stated. To some extent, they stem from basic notions of a court's function and authority. These notions inhibit officials of one country from giving effect to the public policies of another country as expressed in its criminal laws. Executive officials and judges hold office to vindicate their own criminal legislation, not to enforce or permit foreign officials to enforce a foreign country's criminal law. A familiar illustration of this attitude is the reluctance to enforce foreign-country judgments that have a penal character.[6] The traditional form of cooperation among states or nations in this field is extradition of the accused person to the foreign country for trial before its courts.[7]

To some extent, practical considerations explain this deeply rooted attitude: problems of applying sanctions such as imprisonment or fines that are imposed under the foreign law, or of trying criminal offenses defined by one legal system under the procedural code of another. Whatever the reasons, it is important to note in the criminal cases below that jurisdiction of the court over the defendant and application of *lex fori* go hand in hand—subject of course to the possibility of a court's concluding that *lex fori* is not applicable and that the action should be dismissed or some other form of judgment entered for defendant.

In determining whether forum law should be applied or whether judgment should be entered for the defendant because forum law is construed not to reach defendant's conduct, courts resort to various techniques of statutory interpretation. They may look to legislative history, may attempt in other ways to identify the purpose of the legislation, or may consider whether application of forum law is consistent with principles of domestic constitutional law, the conflict of laws, or international law.

(3) Despite the fact that foreign enforcement of criminal judgments such as fines is not to be expected, a conviction in one nation may have consequences in others.[8] Suppose that a defendant is convicted of a crime in nation X, and fined or imprisoned for a limited period. His conduct involved nation Y as well and constituted a crime under its laws—perhaps the fraudulent solicitation of funds by letters sent from X to persons in Y. Under such circumstances, domestic principles of Y such as double jeopardy may bar its authorities from later prosecuting the defendant for the same offense. On the other hand, Y may take no account of the prior foreign conviction.

S.C.A. § 13. That statute provides that persons on federal enclaves (such as military bases) guilty of acts which, although not made punishable by any law of Congress, would be punishable if committed within the jurisdiction of the state containing the enclave, "shall be guilty of a like offense and subject to a like punishment."

6. See Huntington v. Attrill, pp. 764 and 792, supra.

7. Some problems of extradition treaties are noted at pp. 901–903, infra.

8. See Pye, The Effect of Foreign Criminal Judgments within the United States, 32 U.Mo. at K.C.L.Rev. 114 (1964).

If a conviction abroad is for an offense separate from that later committed by the defendant in Y, that nation may indeed consider it relevant to the imposition of more severe sanctions under its own laws or to attaching other disabilities to that person. Y may regard a prior conviction as reason to impose upon the defendant, when later convicted of a separate offense, the higher penalties set forth in its multiple-offender statute. Or the prior conviction in X may disqualify the defendant from benefiting from various provisions under the laws of Y. One example is section 212 of the Immigration and Nationality Act of 1952*, which provides for the exclusion of aliens convicted of certain crimes.

Additional reading: Mueller and Wise, International Criminal Law (1965); Bassiouni and Nanda, A Treatise on International Criminal Law (1973).

A. THE GENERAL PRINCIPLES AND SOME ILLUSTRATIONS

HARVARD RESEARCH ON INTERNATIONAL LAW: JURISDICTION WITH RESPECT TO CRIME

29 Am.J.Int.L., Supp. 1, 435, 445 (1935).

. . .

An analysis of modern national codes of penal law and penal procedure, checked against the conclusions of reliable writers and the resolutions of international conferences or learned societies, and supplemented by some exploration of the jurisprudence of national courts, discloses five general principles on which a more or less extensive penal jurisdiction is claimed by States at the present time. These five general principles are: first, the territorial principle, determining jurisdiction by reference to the place where the offence is committed; second, the nationality principle, determining jurisdiction by reference to the nationality or national character of the person committing the offence; third, the protective principle, determining jurisdiction by reference to the national interest injured by the offence; fourth, the universality principle, determining jurisdiction by reference to the custody of the person committing the offence; and fifth, the passive personality principle, determining jurisdiction by reference to the nationality or national character of the person injured by the offence. Of these five principles, the first is everywhere regarded as of primary importance and of fundamental character. The second is universally accepted, though there are striking differences in the extent to which it is used in the different national systems. The third is claimed by most States, regarded with misgivings in a few, and generally ranked as the basis of an auxiliary competence. The fourth is widely though by no means universally accepted as the basis of an auxiliary competence, except for the offence of piracy, with respect to which it is the generally recognized principle of jurisdiction. The fifth, asserted in some form by a considerable number of States and contested by others, is admittedly auxiliary in character and is probably not essential for any State if the ends served are adequately provided for on other principles.

. . .

WILDENHUS'S CASE (MALI v. KEEPER OF THE COMMON JAIL)

Supreme Court of the United States, 1887.
120 U.S. 1, 7 S.Ct. 385, 30 L.Ed. 565.

WAITE, C. J. This appeal brings up an application made to the circuit court of the United States for the district of New Jersey, by Charles Mali, the "consul of his majesty the king of the Belgians, for the states of New York and New Jersey, in the United States," for himself, as such consul, "and in behalf of one Joseph Wildenhus, one Gionviennie Gobnbosich, and John J. Ostenmeyer," for the release, upon a writ of *habeas corpus,* of Wildenhus, Gobnbosich, and Ostenmeyer from the custody of the keeper of the common jail of Hudson county, New Jersey, and their delivery to the consul, "to be dealt with according to the law of Belgium." The facts on which the application rests are thus stated in the petition for the writ:

"*Second.* That on or about the sixth day of October, 1886, on board the Belgian steam-ship Noordland, there occurred an affray between the said Joseph Wildenhus and one Fijens, wherein and whereby it is charged that the said Wildenhus stabbed with a knife and inflicted upon the said Fijens a mortal wound, of which he afterwards died.

"*Third.* That the said Wildenhus is a subject of the kingdom of Belgium, and has his domicile therein, and is one of the crew of the said steam-ship Noordland, and was such when the said affray occurred.

"*Fourth.* That the said Fijens was also a subject of Belgium, and had his domicile and residence therein, and at the time of the said affray, as well as at the time of his subsequent death, was one of the crew of the said steam-ship.

"*Fifth.* That, at the time said affray occurred, the said steamship Noordland was lying moored at the dock of the port of Jersey City, in said state of New Jersey.

"*Sixth.* That the said affray occurred and ended wholly below the deck of the said steam-ship, and that the tranquillity of the said port of Jersey City was in nowise disturbed or endangered thereby.

"*Seventh.* That said affray occurred in the presence of several witnesses, all of whom were and still are of the crew of the said vessel, and that no other person or persons except those of the crew of said vessel were present or near by.

"*Eighth.* Your petitioner therefore respectfully shows unto this honorable court that the said affray occurred outside of the jurisdiction of the said state of New Jersey.

"*Ninth.* But, notwithstanding the foregoing facts, your petitioner respectfully further shows that the police authorities of Jersey City, in said state of New Jersey, have arrested the said Joseph Wildenhus, and also the said Gionviennie Gobnbosich and John J. Ostenmeyer, of the crew of the said vessel, (one of whom is a quarter-master thereof,) and that said Joseph Wildenhus has been committed by a police magistrate, acting under the authority of the said state, to the common jail of the county of Hudson, on a charge of an indictable offense under the laws of the said state of New Jersey, and is now held in confinement by the keeper of the said jail, and that the others of the said crew, arrested as aforesaid, are also detained in custody and confinement as witnesses to testify in such proceedings as may hereafter be had against the said Wildenhus."

Articles 8, 9, and 10 of a royal decree of the king of the Belgians, made on the eleventh of March, 1857, relating to consuls and consular jurisdiction, are as follows:

"Art. 8. Our consuls have the right of discipline on Belgian merchant vessels in all the ports and harbors of their district. In matters of offenses or crimes they are to make the examination conformably to the instructions of the disciplinary and penal code of the merchant service. They are to claim, according to the terms of the conventions and laws in force, the assistance of the local authorities for the arrest and taking on board of deserting seamen.

"Art. 9. Except in the case where the peace of the port shall have been compromised by the occurrence, the consul shall protest against every attempt that the local authority may make to take cognizance of crimes or offenses committed on board of a Belgian vessel by one of the ship's company towards one, either of the same company, or of the company of another Belgian vessel. He shall take the proper steps to have the cognizance of the case turned over to him, in order that it be ultimately tried according to Belgian laws.

"Art. 10. When men belonging to the company of a Belgian vessel shall be guilty of offenses or crimes out of the ship, or even on board the ship, but against persons not of the company, the consul shall, if the local authority arrests or prosecutes them, take the necessary steps to have the Belgians so arrested treated with humanity, defended, and tried impartially."

The application in this case was made under the authority of these articles.

Article 11 of a convention between the United States and Belgium "concerning the rights, privileges, and immunities of consular officers," concluded March 9, 1880, and proclaimed by the president of the United States, March 1, 1881, (21 St. 123,) is as follows: "The respective consuls general, consuls, vice-consuls, and consular agents shall have exclusive charge of the internal order of the merchant vessels of their nation, and shall alone take cognizance of all differences which may arise, either at sea or in port, between the captains, officers, and crews, without exception, particularly with reference to the adjustment of wages and the execution of contracts. The local authorities shall not interfere, except when the disorder that has arisen is of such a nature as to disturb tranquillity and public order on shore or in the port, or when a person of the country, or not belonging to the crew, shall be concerned therein. In all other cases, the aforesaid authorities shall confine themselves to lending aid to the consuls and vice-consuls or consular agents, if they are requested by them to do so, in causing the arrest and imprisonment of any person whose name is inscribed on the crew list, whenever, for any cause, the said officers shall think proper."

The claim of the consul is that, by the law of nations and the provisions of this treaty, the offense with which Wildenhus has been charged is "solely cognizable by the authority of the laws of the kingdom of Belgium," and that the state of New Jersey is without jurisdiction in the premises. The circuit court refused to deliver the prisoners to the consul, and remanded them to the custody of the jailer. 28 Fed.Rep. 924. To reverse that decision this appeal was taken.

. . .

It is part of the law of civilized nations that, when a merchant vessel of one country enters the ports of another for the purposes of trade, it subjects itself to the law of the place to which it goes, unless, by treaty or otherwise, the two countries have come to some different understanding or agreement; for, as was said by CHIEF JUSTICE MARSHALL in The Exchange, 7 Cranch, 144: "It would be obviously inconvenient and dangerous to society, and would subject the laws to continual infraction, and the government to degradation, if such . . . merchants did not owe temporary and local allegiance, and were not amenable to the jurisdiction of the country." United States v. Diekelman, 92 U.S. 520; 1 Phillim.Int.Law, (3rd Ed.) 483, § CCCLI. . . . As the owner has voluntarily taken his vessel, for his own private purposes, to a place within the dominion of a government other than his own, and from which he seeks protection during his stay, he owes that government such allegiance, for the time being, as is due for the protection to which he becomes entitled.

From experience, however, it was found long ago that it would be beneficial to commerce if the local government would abstain from interfering with the internal discipline of the ship, and the general regulation of the rights and duties of the officers and crew towards the vessel, or among themselves. And so by comity it came to be generally understood among civilized nations that all matters of discipline, and all things done on board, which affected only the vessel, or those belonging to her, and did not involve the peace or dignity of the country, or the tranquillity of the port, should be left by the local government to be dealt with by the authorities of the nation to which the vessel belonged as the laws of that nation, or the interests of its commerce should require. But, if crimes are committed on board of a character to disturb the peace and tranquillity of the country to which the vessel has been brought, the offenders have never, by comity or usage, been entitled to any exemption from the operation of the local laws for their punishment, if the local tribunals see fit to assert their authority. Such being the general public law on this subject, treaties and conventions have been entered into by nations having commercial intercourse, the purpose of which was to settle and define the rights and duties of the contracting parties with respect to each other in these particulars, and thus prevent the inconvenience that might arise from attempts to exercise conflicting jurisdictions. . . .

[The opinion traced the development of conventions dealing with crimes on vessels in foreign ports.]

Next came a form of convention which in terms gave the consuls authority to cause proper order to be maintained on board, and to decide disputes between the officers and crew, but allowed the local authorities to interfere if the disorders taking place on board were of such a nature as to disturb the public tranquillity, and that is substantially all there is in the convention with Belgium which we have now to consider. This treaty is the law which now governs the conduct of the United States and Belgium towards each other in this particular. Each nation has granted to the other such local jurisdiction within its own dominion as may be necessary to maintain order on board a merchant vessel, but has reserved to itself the right to interfere if the disorder on board is of a nature to disturb the public tranquillity.

The treaty is part of the supreme law of the United States, and has the same force and effect in New Jersey that it is entitled to elsewhere. If it gives the consul of Belgium exclusive jurisdiction over the offense which it is alleged has been committed within the territory of New Jersey, we see no reason why he may not enforce his rights under the treaty by writ of *habeas corpus* in any proper court of the United States. This being the case, the only important question left for our determination is whether the thing which has been done—the disorder that has arisen—on board this vessel is of a nature to disturb the public peace, or, as some writers term it, the "public repose," of the people who look to the state of New Jersey for their protection. If the thing done—"the disorder," as it is called in the treaty—is of a character to affect those on shore or in the port when it becomes known, the fact that only those on the ship saw it when it was done, is a matter of no moment. Those who are not on the vessel pay no special attention to the mere disputes or quarrels of the seamen while on board, whether they occur under deck or above. Neither do they, as a rule, care for anything done on board which relates only to the discipline of the ship, or to the preservation of order and authority. Not so, however, with crimes which from their gravity awaken a public interest as soon as they become known, and especially those of a character which every civilized nation considers itself bound to provide a severe punishment for when committed within its own jurisdiction. In such cases inquiry is certain to be instituted at once to ascertain how or why the thing was done, and the popular excitement rises or falls as the news spreads, and the facts become known. It is not alone the publicity of the act, or the noise and clamor which attends it, that fixes the nature of the crime, but the act itself. If that is of a character to awaken public interest when it becomes known, it is a "disorder," the nature of which is to affect the community at large, and consequently to invoke the power of the local government whose people have been disturbed by what was done. . . . It may not be easy at all times to determine to which of the two jurisdictions a particular act of disorder belongs. Much will undoubtedly depend on the attending circumstances of the particular case, but all must concede that felonious homicide is a subject for the local jurisdiction; and that, if the proper authorities are proceeding with the case in a regular way, the consul has no right to interfere to prevent it. That, according to the petition for the *habeas corpus*, is this case. . . .

The judgment of the circuit court is affirmed.

COMMENT

Had the position of the United States and Belgium in Wildenhus's Case been reversed, the United States might well have sought to prosecute. Consider United States v. Flores, 289 U.S. 137, 53 S.Ct. 580, 77 L.Ed. 1086 (1933). This prosecution was based on one of the sections of the Criminal Code (then Section 273, defining murder) applicable only to conduct falling within what is now called the "special maritime and territorial jurisdiction of the United States." Within that jurisdiction, federal criminal law has not only the function of punishing acts detrimental to federal interests but also of generally maintaining law and order—the traditional role of state law.

18 U.S.C.A. § 7 now defines the "special maritime and territorial jurisdiction of the United States" to include the high seas, certain other waters out of the jurisdiction of any particular state, vessels belonging to the United States or its citizens or domestic corporations when such vessels are within the defined waters, federal lands, and aircraft belonging to the United States or its citizens or domestic corporations when in defined airspace. At the time of the Flores

decision, Section 272 of the Criminal Code defined this special jurisdiction to include acts "committed within the admiralty and maritime jurisdiction of the United States . . . on board any vessel belonging in whole or in part to the United States or any citizen thereof, or to any corporation created by or under the laws of the United States, or of any state . . . thereof . . . ." Defendant, a United States citizen, was indicted for murdering another United States citizen upon an American flag vessel at anchor in a port (in what was then the Belgian Congo) remote from the sea—a place subject to Belgian sovereignty.

The Court, in an opinion by Justice Stone, held that the extension of the judicial power of the federal government "to all cases of admiralty and maritime jurisdiction" by Art. III, Sec. 2 of the Constitution conferred on the Congress the power to define and punish offences by a United States citizen on board an American vessel lying in navigable waters within the territorial limits of another country.

> It is true that the criminal jurisdiction of the United States is in general based on the territorial principle, and criminal statutes of the United States are not by implication given an extra-territorial effect. . . . But that principle has never been thought to be applicable to a merchant vessel, which, for purposes of the jurisdiction of the courts of the sovereignty whose flag it flies to punish crimes committed upon it, is deemed to be a part of the territory of that sovereignty, and not to lose that character when in navigable waters within the territorial limits of another sovereignty.

The Court, referring to Wildenhus's Case, noted that the sovereign in whose waters the foreign vessel lay might also assert jurisdiction, which could be regarded as concurrent.

> There is not entire agreement among nations or the writers on international law as to which sovereignty should yield to the other when the jurisdiction is asserted by both. . . . In the absence of any controlling treaty provision, and any assertion of jurisdiction by the territorial sovereign, it is the duty of the courts of the United States to apply to offenses committed by its citizens on vessels flying its flag, its own statutes, interpreted in the light of recognized principles of international law.

Recent cases have had to determine whether the "special maritime and territorial jurisdiction" extends to homicides committed (a) on an ice floe in the Arctic Ocean, United States v. Escamilla, 467 F.2d 341 (4th Cir. 1972); (b) on the grounds of a United States embassy in the Republic of Equatorial Guinea, United States v. Erdos, 474 F.2d 157 (4th Cir. 1973).

QUESTIONS

(1) Test the concept of the territorial character of a ship against the following events: (*a*) A United States public health inspector seeks to board a Belgian merchant vessel. (*b*) A United States marshal seeks to board it to serve a civil summons or to attach the ship by a libel in rem.

(*c*) The marshal seeks to arrest an American citizen who has taken refuge there.

(2) If you are not persuaded by the territorial premise, what arguments would you develop to support the positions of Belgium in Wildenhus and the United States in Flores? For example:

> (*a*) Which country's courts could try the case with the least inconvenience to Wildenhus and the owner and crew of the "Noordland"?
>
> (*b*) Which legal system is circumstanced to give a trial best calculated to evoke the truth about the episode?
>
> (*c*) Assuming that Wildenhus will be convicted and sentenced to a term of imprisonment less than life, which country's penal system should undertake the task of confining him and the effort to rehabilitate him?

(3) Should the following variations influence a decision whether to prosecute? (*a*) The "Noordland" is a merchant ship owned by an agency of the Belgian government. (*b*) The "Noordland" is a cruiser commanded by a captain having jurisdiction under Belgian law to convene an appropriate court martial. (*c*) The "Noordland", although flying the Belgian flag, is owned by a Belgian corporation in turn owned by five Americans.

(4) Assume that Belgian law made Wildenhus's act criminal. Should this influence a decision of New Jersey whether to prosecute? Would it matter if the penalties prescribed in the two laws were very different?

(5) Suppose that, on the other hand, the laws of two nations regulating certain conduct differed. For example, in the 1920's a federal statute made criminal the transportation of alcoholic beverages in "the United States and all territory subject to the jurisdiction thereof," but the law of the flag of certain vessels touching at United States ports made it criminal to operate a vessel not provided with an adequate store of "medicinal" liquors. Should the United States have attempted to enforce the statute against such vessels while within territorial waters? [9]

(6) What roles in deciding which authority should prosecute were played by the state prosecutor, the state and federal courts, the State Department, or Belgian authorities? Do you think that the allocation of responsibility thus revealed is the most desirable one?

BLACKMER v. UNITED STATES

Supreme Court of the United States, 1932.
284 U.S. 421, 52 S.Ct. 252, 76 L.Ed. 375.

MR. CHIEF JUSTICE HUGHES delivered the opinion of the Court.

The petitioner, Harry M. Blackmer, a citizen of the United States resident in Paris, France, was adjudged guilty of contempt of the Supreme Court of the District of Columbia for failure to respond to subpoenas served upon him in France and requiring him to appear

9. Cf. Cunard S. S. Co. v. Mellon, 262 U.S. 100, 43 S.Ct. 504, 67 L.Ed. 894 (1923).

as a witness on behalf of the United States at a criminal trial in that court. Two subpoenas were issued, for appearances at different times, and there was a separate proceeding with respect to each. The two cases were heard together, and a fine of $30,000 with costs was imposed in each case, to be satisfied out of the property of the petitioner which had been seized by order of the court. The decrees were affirmed by the Court of Appeals of the District [49 F.2d 523], and this Court granted writs of certiorari . . . .

The subpoenas were issued and served, and the proceedings to punish for contempt were taken under the provisions of the Act of July 3, 1926 . . . . The statute provides that whenever the attendance at the trial of a criminal action of a witness abroad, who is "a citizen of the United States or domiciled therein," is desired by the Attorney General, or any assistant or district attorney acting under him, the judge of the court in which the action is pending may order a subpoena to issue, to be addressed to a consul of the United States and to be served by him personally upon the witness with a tender of traveling expenses. Sections 2, 3 of the act (28 U.S.C.A. §§ 712, 713). Upon proof of such service and of the failure of the witness to appear, the court may make an order requiring the witness to show cause why he should not be punished for contempt, and, upon the issue of such an order, the court may direct that property belonging to the witness and within the United States may be seized and held to satisfy any judgment which may be rendered against him in the proceeding. Sections 4, 5 (28 U.S.C.A. §§ 714, 715). Provision is made for personal service of the order upon the witness and also for its publication in a newspaper of general circulation in the district where the court is sitting. Section 6 (28 U.S.C.A. § 716). If, upon the hearing, the charge is sustained, the court may adjudge the witness guilty of contempt and impose upon him a fine not exceeding $100,000, to be satisfied by a sale of the property seized. Section 7 (28 U.S.C.A. § 717). This statute and the proceedings against the petitioner are assailed as being repugnant to the Constitution of the United States.

First. The principal objections to the statute are that it violates the due process clause of the Fifth Amendment. These contentions are: (1) That the "Congress has no power to authorize United States consuls to serve process except as permitted by treaty"; (2) that the act does not provide "a valid method of acquiring judicial jurisdiction to render personal judgment against defendant and judgment against his property"; (3) that the act "does not require actual or any other notice to defendant of the offense or of the Government's claim against his property"; (4) that the provisions "for hearing and judgment in the entire absence of the accused and without his consent" are invalid; and (5) that the act is "arbitrary, capricious and unreasonable."

While it appears that the petitioner removed his residence to France in the year 1924, it is undisputed that he was, and continued to be, a citizen of the United States. He continued to owe allegiance to the United States. By virtue of the obligations of citizenship, the United States retained its authority over him, and he was bound by its laws made applicable to him in a foreign country. Thus, although resident abroad, the petitioner remained subject to the taxing power of the United States. Cook v. Tait, 265 U.S. 47, 54, 56, 44 S.Ct. 444, 68 L.Ed. 895. For disobedience to its laws through conduct abroad, he was subject to punishment in the courts of the United States. United States v. Bowman, 260 U.S. 94, 102, 43 S.Ct. 39, 67 L.Ed. 149. With respect to such an exercise of authority, there is no question of international law,[10] but solely of the purport of the municipal law which establishes the duties of the citizen in relation to his own government. While the legislation of the Congress, unless the contrary intent appears, is construed to apply only within the territorial jurisdiction of the United States, the question of its application, so far as citizens of the United States in foreign countries are concerned, is one of construction, not of legislative power. American Banana Co. v. United Fruit Co., 213 U.S. 347, 357, 29 S.Ct. 511, 53 L.Ed. 826, 16 Ann.Cas. 1047; United States v. Bowman, supra . . .. Nor can it be doubted that the United States possesses the power inherent in sovereignty to require the return to this country of a citizen, resident elsewhere, whenever the public interest requires it, and to penalize him in case of refusal. . . . What in England was the prerogative of the sovereign in this respect pertains under our constitutional system to the national authority which may be exercised by the Congress by virtue of the legislative power to prescribe the duties of the citizens of the United States. It is also beyond controversy that one of the duties which the citizen owes to his government is to support the administration of justice by attending its courts and giving his testimony whenever he is properly summoned. . . . And the Congress may provide for the performance of this duty and prescribe penalties for disobedience.

In the present instance, the question concerns only the method of enforcing the obligation. The jurisdiction of the United States over its absent citizen, so far as the binding effect of its legislation is concerned, is a jurisdiction in personam, as he is personally bound to take notice of the laws that are applicable to him and to obey them. United States v. Bowman, supra. But for the exercise of judicial jurisdiction in personam, there must be due process, which requires appropriate notice of the judicial action and an opportunity to be heard. For this notice and opportunity the statute provides. The authority to require the absent citizen to return and testify necessarily implies the authority to give him notice of the requirement. As his attendance is needed in court, it is appropriate that the Congress should authorize the court to direct the notice to be given, and that it should be in the customary form of a subpoena. Obviously, the requirement would be nugatory, if provision could not be made for its communication to the witness in the foreign country. The efficacy of an attempt to provide constructive service in this country would rest upon the presumption that the notice would be given in a manner calculated to reach the witness abroad. McDonald v. Mabee, 243 U.S. 90, 92, 37 S.Ct. 343, 61 L.Ed. 608, L.R.A.1917F, 458. The question of the validity of the provision for actual service of the subpoena in a foreign country is one that arises solely between the government of the United States and the citizen. The mere giving of such a notice to the citizen in the foreign country of the requirement of his government that he shall return is in no sense an invasion of any right of the foreign government and the citizen has no standing to invoke any such supposed right. While consular privileges in foreign countries are the appropriate subjects of treaties, it does not follow that every act of a consul, as, e. g., in communicating with citizens of his own country, must be predicated upon a specific provision of a treaty. . . . The point raised by the petitioner with re-

10. "The law of Nations does not prevent a State from exercising jurisdiction over its subjects travelling or residing abroad, since they remain under its personal supremacy." Oppenheim, International Law (4th Ed.) vol. 1, § 145, p. 281 . . . .

spect to the provision for the service of the subpoena abroad is without merit.

As the Congress could define the obligation, it could prescribe a penalty to enforce it. And, as the default lay in disobedience to an authorized direction of the court, it constituted a contempt of court, and the Congress could provide for procedure appropriate in contempt cases. The provision of the statute for punishment for contempt is applicable only "upon proof being made of the service and default." Section 4 (28 U.S.C.A. § 714). That proof affords a proper basis for the proceeding, and provision is made for personal service upon the witness of the order to show cause why he should not be adjudged guilty. For the same reasons as those which sustain the service of the subpoena abroad, it was competent to provide for the service of the order in like manner. It is only after a hearing pursuant to the order to show cause, and upon proof sustaining the charge, that the court can impose the penalty. The petitioner urges that the statute does not require notice of the offense, but the order to show cause is to be issued after the witness has failed to obey the subpoena demanding his attendance and the order is to be made by the court before which he was required to appear. This is sufficient to apprise the witness of the nature of the proceeding and he has full opportunity to be heard. The further contention is made that, as the offense is a criminal one, it is a violation of due process to hold the hearing, and to proceed to judgment, in the absence of the defendant. The argument misconstrues the nature of the proceeding. "While contempt may be an offense against the law and subject to appropriate punishment, certain it is that since the foundation of our government proceedings to punish such offenses have been regarded as sui generis and not 'criminal prosecutions' within the Sixth Amendment or common understanding." Myers v. United States, 264 U.S. 95, 104, 105, 44 S.Ct. 272, 273, 68 L.Ed. 577. . . . The requirement of due process in such a case is satisfied by suitable notice and adequate opportunity to appear and to be heard. . . .

The authorization of the seizure of the property belonging to the defaulting witness and within the United States, upon the issue of the order to show cause why he should not be punished for contempt . . . affords a provisional remedy, the propriety of which rests upon the validity of the contempt proceeding. As a witness is liable to punishment by fine if, upon the hearing, he is found guilty of contempt, no reason appears why his property may not be seized to provide security for the payment of the penalty. The proceeding conforms to familiar practice where absence or other circumstance makes a provisional remedy appropriate. . . . The order that is to be served upon the witness contains the direction for the seizure. The property is to be held pending the hearing, and is to be applied to the satisfaction of the fine imposed and unless it is paid. Given the obligation of the witness to respond to the subpoena, the showing of his default after service, and the validity of the provision for a fine in case default is not excused, there is no basis for objection to the seizure upon constitutional grounds. The argument that the statute creates an unreasonable classification is untenable. The disobedience of the defaulting witness to a lawful requirement of the court, and not the fact that he owns property, is the ground of his liability. He is not the subject of unconstitutional discrimination simply because he has property which may be appropriated to the satisfaction of a lawful claim. . . .

Third. The statute being valid, the question remains as to the procedure in its application against the petitioner. He insists that the showing for the issue of the subpoenas requiring him to attend was inadequate. But the "proper showing" required was for the purpose of satisfying the court that the subpoenas should issue. The petitions, in the instant cases, were presented to the judge of the court by the official representatives of the government, and their statement as to the materiality and importance of the testimony expected from the witness was unquestionably sufficient to give the court jurisdiction to issue the subpoenas, and, unless they were vacated upon proper application, the petitioner was bound to obey. . . .

Decrees affirmed.

GILLARS v. UNITED STATES

United States Court of Appeals, District of Columbia Circuit, 1950.
87 U.S.App.D.C. 16, 182 F.2d 962.

FAHY, CIRCUIT JUDGE. Appellant was convicted of treason in a jury trial in the United States District Court for the District of Columbia. Treason alone of crimes is defined in the Constitution, as follows:

> "Treason against the United States, shall consist only in levying War against them, or in adhering to their Enemies, giving them Aid and Comfort. . . . " U.S.Const. Art. III, § 3.

The First Congress, in 1790, provided by statute,

> " . . . That if any person or persons, owing allegiance to the United States of America, shall levy war against them, or shall adhere to their enemies, giving them aid and comfort within the United States or elsewhere, and shall be thereof convicted, on confession in open court, or on the testimony of two witnesses to the same overt act the treason whereof he or they shall stand indicted, such person or persons shall be adjudged guilty of treason against the United States, ..." 1 Stat. 112 (1790).[11]

The indictment alleges that appellant was born in Maine, was a citizen of and owed allegiance to the United States, that within the German Reich, after December 11, 1941, to and including May 8, 1945, in violation of her duty of allegiance she knowingly and intentionally adhered to the enemies of the United States, to wit, the Government of the German Reich, its agents, instrumentalities, representatives and subjects with which the United States was at war, and gave to said enemies aid and comfort within the United States and elsewhere, by participating in the psychological warfare of the German Government against the United States. This participation is alleged to have consisted of radio broadcasts and the making of phonographic recordings with the intent that they would be used in broadcasts to the United States and to American Expeditionary Forces in French North Africa, Italy, France and England. The indictment charges the commission of ten overt acts, each of which is

11. [Eds.] The present section of the Criminal Code, 18 U.S.C.A. § 2381 (1970), states: "Whoever, owing allegiance to the United States, levies war against them or adheres to their enemies, giving them aid and comfort within the United States or elsewhere, is guilty of treason and shall suffer death, or shall be imprisoned not less than five years and fined not less than $10,000; and shall be incapable of holding any office under the United States."

described, and, finally, that following commission of the offense the District of Columbia was the first Federal Judicial District into which appellant was brought. . . .

. . . [Appellant contends] that treason may not be committed by words, that all vocal utterances are, by reason of their nature and regardless of all else, an exercise of freedom of thought, which may not be prohibited by condemning the expression of thought by words. Expression of thought or opinion about the Government or criticism of it is not treason. The oppressive use of the power of government to destroy political enemies by accusing them of crime underlay the determination of the framers of our Constitution to limit treason to acts, and to such acts only as come within the definition which is embedded in the Constitution itself. In addition, the First Amendment bars enlarging treason to include the mere expression of views, opinion or criticism. There is more to the crime than this.

In Cramer v. United States, supra, 325 U.S. at page 29, 65 S.Ct. at page 932, the Supreme Court has said:

> " . . . the crime of treason consists of two elements: adherence to the enemy; and rendering him aid and comfort. A citizen intellectually or emotionally may favor the enemy and harbor sympathies or convictions disloyal to this country's policy or interest, but so long as he commits no act of aid and comfort to the enemy, there is no treason. On the other hand, a citizen may take actions which do aid and comfort the enemy—making a speech critical of the government or opposing its measures, profiteering, striking in defense plants or essential work, and the hundred other things which impair our cohesion and diminish our strength—but if there is no adherence to the enemy in this, if there is no intent to betray, there is no treason."

. . . While the crime is not committed by mere expressions of opinion or criticism, words spoken as part of a program of propaganda warfare, in the course of employment by the enemy in its conduct of war against the United States, to which the accused owes allegiance, may be an integral part of the crime. There is evidence in this case of a course of conduct on behalf of the enemy in the prosecution of its war against the United States. The use of speech to this end, as the evidence permitted the jury to believe, made acts of words. The First Amendment does not protect one from accountability for words as such. It depends upon their use. It protects the free expression of thought and belief as a part of the liberty of the individual as a human personality. But words which reasonably viewed constitute acts in furtherance of a program of an enemy to which the speaker adheres and to which he gives aid with intent to betray his own country, are not rid of criminal character merely because they are words. . . .

Appellant contends that she was erroneously precluded from proving that she was under threat, compulsion and in fear of her life in participating in the recordings. This argument rests upon the exclusion of certain testimony of witnesses Beckmann and Schafer regarding the fear under which they performed similar work. The court ruled that testimony of threats to persons other than the accused was immaterial and irrelevant but that testimony of conditions under which appellant herself worked would not be excluded. . . . The witness Beckmann was employed in the German Overseas Service as a news editor and was engaged in broadcasting. He testified that Horst Cleinow was the managing editor of the German

Overseas Service. From the testimony which we have set forth it seems clear that this witness could not say that the appellant herself was threatened. In the one instance in the record where he testified that the appellant told him she was threatened, by Cleinow, the evidence was not excluded.

. . . The witnesses did not testify that appellant was threatened or was under compulsion or acted in fear of her life, and appellant herself did not so testify. She did say that active opposition would have meant death. But she was not charged with having refused to engage in active opposition. . . .

Appellant urges that the crime of treason under the law of the United States does not have extra-territorial scope. It is said that this follows from the general presumption against giving extra-territorial application to criminal statutes, and also because, it is said, treason is not committed by a citizen who resides in enemy country and therefore must engage in some trafficking with the enemy. As to the first branch of the argument, the Supreme Court has decided that the Constitution does not forbid the application of the criminal laws of the United States to acts committed by its citizens abroad. It is a question in each case of the intent of the lawmakers. . . .

The treason statute, enacted by the first Congress in 1790, supra, condemns the giving to the enemy of "aid and comfort within the United States or elsewhere". This rebuts any presumption against extra-territorial application of our treason law which might have existed under the general rule. By the statute itself the overt act may be committed outside the United States. Adherence to the enemy and the treasonable intent, when they exist, attach to the act and to its perpetrator wherever he is. These factors too, therefore, may be outside the United States, and so, accordingly, may the whole of the crime. Aside from the intention of Congress expressed in the statute we are of the opinion that the usual presumption against extra-territorial application of the criminal law does not apply to treason. The purpose of a criminal statute ordinarily is to protect the domestic order, not to reach across national boundaries to take hold of persons within the jurisdiction of another nation. But treason is directed against the existence of the nation and by its nature consists of conduct which might ordinarily be exerted from without in aid of the enemy which is, usually, without. The act of adhering to the enemy, giving it aid and comfort, not unnaturally attaches to the enemy wherever it is. While the Constitution is silent on the question the statutory definition which quickly followed the Constitution was the handiwork of many of those who framed the greater instrument. The use in the statute therefore of the words, "within the United States or elsewhere," is strongly indicative of the territorial range of the constitutional provision. While treason shall consist only of that which is made so by the Constitution; while its nature is limited, Cramer v. United States, supra, the reasons which led the founders to circumscribe the conduct which would constitute the crime do not restrict its territorial reach. . . .

As a second branch of the present argument appellant states that a citizen of the United States residing in enemy country is under the obligation of local allegiance and one so situated is not guilty of treason by reason of some trafficking with the enemy. Therefore, it is said, doubt should be resolved against extra-territorial application. A kindred point grows out of appellant's objection to the court's instruction to the jury:

> " . . . she has stipulated that she was and is now an American citizen. During the period set forth in the indict-

> ment the defendant, being a citizen of the United States, owed allegiance to her native country and no obligation of local allegiance required or compelled the defendant to assist Germany in the conduct of its war against the United States."

As the court instructed, obedience to the law of the country of domicile or residence—local allegiance—is permissible but this kind of allegiance does not call for adherence to the enemy and the giving of aid and comfort to it with disloyal intent. . . . It would not be reasonable to say that treason can be committed only within the territory of the United States because the framers of the Constitution and the members of the First Congress must have known that some local allegiance was required of American citizens living in enemy territory. It is not disputed in this case that a citizen in enemy country owes temporary allegiance to the alien government, must obey its laws and may not plot or act against it. . . . The court adequately covered the particular point by instructing the jury, in addition to the instruction complained of by appellant, as follows:

> "This defendant, while residing in the German Reich, owed qualified allegiance to it. She was obliged to obey its laws, and she was equally amenable to punishment with citizens of that country if she did not do so. At the same time, the defendant, while residing in Germany during the period stated in the indictment, owed to her Government, that is, the United States Government, full, complete and true allegiance." . . .

[Affirmed.]

COMMENT

(1) The statute applied against Blackmer was enacted rather hastily to meet the needs of the so-called "Teapot Dome scandal" in which Blackmer was involved. Following improprieties in the leasing of federal oil lands, a Senate committee began investigations in late 1923 which had wide-spread repercussions, including the sentencing of a cabinet member to a prison term for accepting bribes. Blackmer's testimony was desired in various connections, but in February 1924, he proceeded to France and remained there despite subpoenas. In the course of the skirmishing, the United States assessed him $8,500,000 for income taxes and penalties, and unsuccessfully sought to extradite him for filing fraudulent tax returns. The statute has been revised and now appears in 28 U.S.C.A. § 1783.* Note also the related provisions of F.R.C.P. 4(i)* on service of subpoenas and of 28 U.S.C.A. § 1784 * on contempt.

In assessing the present vitality of the Blackmer decision, it should be borne in mind that recent decisions have gone far to impose upon criminal contempt proceedings safeguards parallel to those in regular criminal proceedings. In particular these cases have ended the power of judges, acting without juries, to impose penalties of six months' imprisonment or more—that being the borderline between "petty" crimes triable without a jury and serious offences; they have also imposed due process requirements upon contempts designed to narrow the gap between contempt and criminal proceedings. The most recent of these cases is Taylor v. Hayes, 418 U.S. 488, 94 S.Ct. 2697, 41 L.Ed.2d 897 (1974).

(2) Miss Gillars was tried in the District of Columbia under a statute which included only the first clause of the current venue provision, 18 U.S.C.A. § 3238:

> The trial of all offenses begun or committed upon the high seas, or elsewhere out of the jurisdiction of any particular State or district, shall be in the district in which the offender, or any one of two or more joint offenders, is arrested or is first brought; but if such offender or offenders are not so arrested or brought into any district, an indictment or information may be filed in the district of the last known residence of the offender or of any one of two or more joint offenders, or if no such residence is known the indictment or information may be filed in the District of Columbia.

Another treason case was tried in Boston because the aircraft bringing the accused was forced down there. Best v. United States, 184 F.2d 131 (1st Cir. 1950). Note the limitations as to the venue of criminal trials imposed by Art. III, Sec. 2 and the Sixth Amendment of the Constitution.*

(3) The treason statute in Gillars was predicated upon allegiance or nationality. Another example of such legislation is the "Logan Act", enacted in 1799 after a Quaker physician named Logan, a friend of Jefferson, visited France in an attempt to restore relations with the French government that had deteriorated under the Federalist regime.[12] As revised, the act (18 U.S.C.A. § 953) now reads:

> Any citizen of the United States, wherever he may be, who, without authority of the United States, directly or indirectly commences or carries on any correspondence or intercourse with any foreign government or any officer or agent thereof, with intent to influence the measures or conduct of any foreign government or of any officer or agent thereof, in relation to any disputes or controversies with the United States, or to defeat the measures of the United States, shall be fined not more than $5,000 or imprisoned not more than three years, or both.
>
> This section shall not abridge the right of a citizen to apply, himself or his agent, to any foreign government or the agents thereof for redress of any injury which he may have sustained from such government or any of its agents or subjects.

American citizens negotiated with the government of North Vietnam during the fighting in Indochina, but no prosecutions were brought under the Act. Some of the activities, aimed immediately at the release of prisoners and ultimately at the termination of hostilities, were strikingly similar to those of Dr. Logan himself. It is possible that American prosecutors regarded statements of President Johnson, to the effect that all possible avenues towards peace with

12. See Vagts, The Logan Act: Paper Tiger or Sleeping Giant?, 60 Am.J. Int.L. 268 (1966).

Hanoi should be pursued, as conferring "the authority of the United States" on these endeavors.

(4) Recall Van der Schelling v. U. S. News and World Report, Inc., p. 10, supra, and the relationship between domicile and citizenship in a particular state for such purposes as diversity jurisdiction. Can state statutes regulating conduct through the imposition of civil or criminal sanctions be predicated upon the "citizenship" of the defendant in the particular state?

Consider Skiriotes v. Florida, 313 U.S. 69, 61 S.Ct. 924, 85 L.Ed. 1193 (1941). The question before the Court was the validity of a Florida statute making it "unlawful for any person, persons, firm or corporation to maintain and use for the purpose of catching or taking commercial sponges from the Gulf of Mexico, or the Straits of Florida or other waters within the territorial limits of the State of Florida, diving suits, helmets or other apparatus used by deep sea divers." Defendant was convicted of using diving equipment to take sponges from the Gulf of Mexico at a point approximately two marine leagues (about 6 miles) from the Florida shoreline. The Court upheld the statute as applied. It noted that defendant was a United States citizen who had long been resident in Florida and had not claimed any other domicile. The Court reasoned that it was "just in assuming that [defendant] is a citizen of the United States and of Florida", and concluded that:

> If the United States may control the conduct of its citizens upon the high seas, we see no reason why the State of Florida may not likewise govern the conduct of its citizens upon the high seas with respect to matters in which the State has a legitimate interest and where there is no conflict with acts of Congress. Save for the powers committed by the Constitution to the Union, the State of Florida has retained the status of a sovereign. . . .

Later federal legislation and a decision of the Supreme Court [13] have developed new principles of ownership by coastal states of submerged lands in the Gulf of Mexico. Thus today, on the facts of Skiriotes, the Court might find unnecessary a discussion of Florida's control of conduct outside its territorial waters.

QUESTIONS

(1) Suppose that Congress were considering a bill that would impose criminal sanctions for intentional homicide by a United States citizen anywhere in the world. Would you support or oppose the bill and for what reasons?

(2) Miss Gillars used as a defense her obligation to obey the laws of Germany. Should the case have been decided differently if she had been able to show that her actions were caused by threats of imminent injury? Cf. United States v. Fleming, 7 U.S.C.M.A. 543, 23 C.M.R. 7 (1957) (army lieutenant colonel collaborating with enemy while incarcerated in Korean prisoner of war camp).

13. United States v. Florida, 363 U.S. 121, 80 S.Ct. 961, 4 L.Ed.2d 1096 (1960), final decree at 364 U.S. 502, 81 S.Ct. 258, 5 L.Ed.2d 247 (1960).

(3) Does Blackmer stand for the proposition that a United States national summoned from abroad to stand trial for a crime may be tried in absentia if he refuses to return, with any fine collected out of domestic assets? Compare in a civil setting Article 15 of the French Civil Code, p. 751, supra.

UNITED STATES v. BOWMAN

Supreme Court of the United States, 1922.
260 U.S. 94, 43 S.Ct. 39, 67 L.Ed. 149.

MR. CHIEF JUSTICE TAFT delivered the opinion of the Court.

This is a writ of error . . . to review the ruling of the District Court sustaining a demurrer of one of the defendants to an indictment for a conspiracy to defraud a corporation in which the United States was and is a stockholder, under section 35 of the Criminal Code . . . .

During the period covered by the indictment, i. e., between October, 1919, and January, 1920, the steamship Dio belonged to the United States. The United States owned all the stock in the United States Shipping Board Emergency Fleet Corporation. The National Shipping Corporation agreed to operate and manage the Dio for the Fleet Corporation, which under the contract was to pay for fuel, oil, labor, and material used in the operation. The Dio was on a voyage to Rio Janeiro under this management. Wry was her master, Bowman was her engineer, Hawkinson was the agent of the Standard Oil Company at Rio Janerio, and Millar was a merchant and ship repairer and engineer in Rio. Of these four, who were the defendants in the indictment, the first three were American citizens, and Millar was a British subject. Johnston & Co. were the agents of the National Shipping Corporation at Rio. The indictment charged that the plot was hatched by Wry and Bowman on board the Dio before she reached Rio. Their plan was to order, through Johnston & Co., and receipt for, 1,000 tons of fuel oil from the Standard Oil Company, but to take only 600 tons aboard, and to collect cash for a delivery of 1,000 tons through Johnston & Co., from the Fleet Corporation, and then divide the money paid for the undelivered 400 tons among the four defendants. This plan was to be, and was, made possible through the guilty connivance of the Standard Oil agent, Hawkinson, and Millar, the Rio merchant, who was to, and did, collect the money. Overt acts charged included a wireless telegram to the agents, Johnston & Co., from the Dio while on the high seas ordering the 1,000 tons of oil. The Southern District of New York was the district into which the American defendants were first brought and were found, but Millar, the British defendant, has not been found.

The first count charged a conspiracy by the defendants to defraud the Fleet Corporation, in which the United States was a stockholder, by obtaining and aiding to obtain the payment and allowance of a false and fraudulent claim against the Fleet Corporation. It laid the offense on the high seas, out of the jurisdiction of any particular state, and out of the jurisdiction of any district of the United States, but within the admiralty and maritime jurisdiction of the United States. The second count laid the conspiracy on the Dio on the high seas and at the port of Rio Janeiro, as well as in the city. The third count laid it in the city of Rio Janeiro. The fourth count was for making and causing to be made in the name of the Standard

Oil Company, for payment and approval, a false and fraudulent claim against the Fleet Corporation in the form of an invoice for 1,000 tons of fuel oil, of which 400 tons were not delivered. This count laid the same crime on board the Dio in the harbor of Rio Janeiro. The fifth count laid it in the city, and the sixth at the port and in the city.

. . . The sole objection was that the crime was committed without the jurisdiction of the United States or of any state thereof and on the high seas or within the jurisdiction of Brazil. The District Court considered only the first count, which charged the conspiracy to have been committed on the Dio on the high seas, and, having held that bad for lack of jurisdiction, a fortiori it sustained the demurrer as the others.

The court in its opinion conceded that under many authorities the United States as a sovereign may regulate the ships under its flag and the conduct of its citizens while on those ships . . . . The court said, however, that while private and public ships of the United States on the high seas were constructively a part of the territory of the United States—indeed, peculiarly so, as distinguished from that of the States—Congress had always expressly indicated it when it intended that its laws should be operative on the high seas. The court concluded that, because jurisdiction of criminal offenses must be conferred upon United States courts and could not be inferred, and because section 35, like all the other sections of chapter 4 (Comp. St. §§ 10191–10252), contains no reference to the high seas as a part of the locus of the offenses defined by it, as the sections in chapters 11 and 12 of the Criminal Code (Comp.St. §§ 10445–10483a) do, section 35 must be construed not to extend to acts committed on the high seas. It confirmed its conclusion by the statement that section 35 had never been invoked to punish offenses denounced, if committed on the high seas or in a foreign country.

We have in this case a question of statutory construction. The necessary locus, when not specially defined, depends upon the purpose of Congress as evinced by the description and nature of the crime and upon the territorial limitations upon the power and jurisdiction of a government to punish crime under the law of nations. Crimes against private individuals or their property, like assaults, murder, burglary, larceny, robbery, arson, embezzlement, and frauds of all kinds, which affect the peace and good order of the community must, of course, be committed within the territorial jurisdiction of the government where it may properly exercise it. If punishment of them is to be extended to include those committed outside of the strict territorial jurisdiction, it is natural for Congress to say so in the statute, and failure to do so will negative the purpose of Congress in this regard. We have an example of this in the attempted application of the prohibitions of the anti-trust law to acts done by citizens of the United States against other such citizens in a foreign country. American Banana Co. v. United Fruit Co., 213 U.S. 347, 29 S.Ct. 511, 53 L.Ed. 826, 16 Ann.Cas. 1047. That was a civil case, but as the statute is criminal as well as civil, it presents an analogy.

But the same rule of interpretation should not be applied to criminal statutes which are, as a class, not logically dependent on their locality for the government's jurisdiction, but are enacted because of the right of the government to defend itself against obstruction, or fraud wherever perpetrated, especially if committed by its own citizens, officers, or agents. Some such offenses can only be committed within the territorial jurisdiction of the government because of the local acts required to constitute them. Others are such that to limit their locus to the strictly territorial jurisdiction would be greatly to curtail the scope and usefulness of the statute and leave open a large immunity for frauds as easily committed by citizens on the high seas and in foreign countries as at home. In such cases, Congress has not thought it necessary to make specific provision in the law that the locus shall include the high seas and foreign countries, but allows it to be inferred from the nature of the offense. Many of these occur in chapter 4, which bears the title "Offenses against the Operation of the Government." Section 70 of that chapter (Comp.St. § 10238) punishes whoever as consul knowingly certifies a false invoice. Clearly the locus of this crime as intended by Congress is in a foreign country, and certainly the foreign country in which he discharges his official duty could not object to the trial in a United States court of a United States consul for crime of this sort committed within its borders. Forging or altering ship's papers is made a crime by section 72 of chapter 4 (Comp.St. § 10240). It would be going too far to say that because Congress does not fix any locus it intended to exclude the high seas in respect of this crime. The natural inference from the character of the offense is that the sea would be a probable place for its commission. . . . Section 39 (Comp.St. § 10203) punishes bribing a United States officer of the civil, military, or naval service to violate his duty or to aid in committing a fraud on the United States. It is hardly reasonable to construe this not to include such offenses when the bribe is offered to a consul, ambassador, and army or a naval officer in a foreign country or on the high seas, whose duties are being performed there, and when his connivance at such fraud must occur there. . . . Again, in section 36 of chapter 4 (Comp.St. § 10200), it is made a crime to steal, embezzle or knowingly apply to his own use ordinance, arms, ammunition, clothing, subsistence stores, money or other property of the United States furnished or to be used for military or naval service. . . .

What is true of these sections in this regard is true of section 35, under which this indictment was drawn. . . .

It is directed generally against whoever presents a false claim against the United States, knowing it to be such, to any officer of the civil, military or naval service or to any department thereof, or any corporation in which the United States is a stockholder, or whoever connives at the same by the use of any cheating device, or whoever enters a conspiracy to do these things. The section was amended in 1918 to include a corporation in which the United States owns stock. This was evidently intended to protect the Emergency Fleet Corporation in which the United States was the sole stockholder, from fraud of this character. That corporation was expected to engage in, and did engage in, a most extensive ocean transportation business, and its ships were seen in every great port of the world open during the war. The same section of the statute protects the arms, ammunition, stores, and property of the army and navy from fraudulent devices of a similar character. We cannot suppose that when Congress enacted the statute or amended it, it did not have in mind that a wide field for such frauds upon the government was in private and public vessels of the United States on the high seas and in foreign ports and beyond the land jurisdiction of the United States, and therefore intended to include them in the section.

Nor can the much-quoted rule that criminal statutes are to be strictly construed avail. . . .

They are not to be strained either way. It needs no forced construction to interpret section 35 as we have done. . . .

The three defendants who were found in New York were citizens of the United States, and were certainly subject to such laws as it might pass to protect itself and its property. Clearly it is no offense to the dignity or right of sovereignty of Brazil to hold them for this crime against the government to which they owe allegiance. The other defendant is a subject of Great Britain. He has never been apprehended, and it will be time enough to consider what, if any, jurisdiction the District Court below has to punish him when he is brought to trial.

The judgment of the District Court is reversed, with directions to overrule the demurrer and for further proceedings.

COMMENT

(1) Unlike the statute in United States v. Flores, p. 860 supra. Section 35 of the Criminal Code did not indicate its field of application. That is, it was not specifically made applicable to acts "committed within the admiralty and maritime jurisdiction of the United States." Thus the Court was required to resort to general principles of statutory interpretation, including relevant principles of international law, to determine whether a charge of conspiracy to violate the section could be applied to defendants' conduct.

(2) Compare Rocha v. United States, 288 F.2d 545 (9th Cir. 1961). Defendant aliens married United States citizens in order to enter the United States in a preferred (non-quota) status. After they entered the United States, they were indicted under a charge that the marriages were "sham", since it was intended that after entry the parties would take necessary legal steps to sever the marital ties. Each defendant had appeared before a United States consular officer in a foreign country to apply for an immigrant visa and had stated in his sworn application that he was married to a United States citizen and entitled to non-quota status. One of the counts in the indictment was based upon 18 U.S.C.A. § 1546, which provided for fine or imprisonment of "whoever" obtains or accepts any document required for entry into the United States knowing it to be procured by means of any false claim or statement, or of "whoever" knowingly makes under oath any false statement in any document required by the immigration laws or regulations.[14] Defendants contended that the criminal legislation of the United States was limited to acts committed within its territory and that Section 1546 was therefore inapplicable. The Court of Appeals affirmed that part of the opinion of the District Court denying the motion to dismiss the portion of the indictment resting on Section 1546. Its opinion stated in part:

> . . . The court below, in a careful and able analysis of what Congress intended . . . comes to the conclusion that Congress intended to give to § 1546 extraterritorial jurisdiction. We agree that such was the congressional intent. We are then faced with the question of whether such a purpose can be lawfully accomplished, i. e., is constitutional. . . .

14. Compare 18 U.S.C. § 1621, a perjury statute referring to testimony under oath before any competent person in any case where federal law authorizes an oath to be administered. Its final sentence reads: "This section is applicable whether the statement or subscription is made within or without the United States." 22 U.S.C.A. § 1203 has comparable provisions.

. . . Obviously the decision below herein rested not only on the act abroad, but also on the effect it produced within the boundaries of the United States, namely, the aliens' subsequent successful entrance at the border based on a document allegedly procured by fraud. This must have so occurred because the aliens were subsequently found and arrested within the United States, says the government. But suppose the act done abroad was the making of a false affidavit by "X" which enabled "Y" to enter the United States, and suppose further, "Y" never came into the United States, or entered on his own valid passport. Could "X" then be indicted? We see no reason why an alien coming within the territorial limits of a United States court should be placed in a more favorable position with respect to his actions taken against the sovereignty of the United States while he was abroad, than a United States citizen would be. We believe the principles enunciated by the Supreme Court in Strassheim v. Daily, 1911, 221 U.S. 280, 285, 31 S.Ct. 558, 55 L.Ed. 735, are here applicable. There Mr. Justice Holmes ruled: "Acts done outside a jurisdiction, but intended to produce and producing detrimental effects within it, justify a state in punishing the cause of the harm as if he had been present at the effect, if the state should succeed in getting him within its power." Id., 221 U.S. at page 285, 31 S.Ct. at page 560, citing cases, including American Banana Co. v. United Fruit Co., 1909, 213 U.S. 347, 356, 29 S.Ct. 511, 53 L.Ed. 826. . . .

The same rule logically should apply to national states, or nations. The acts done to violate § 1546 of Title 18 were all done outside the state, but they were intended (at least at the point of time when the fraudulent document was used to gain entry) to produce, and they did so produce, a detrimental effect on the sovereignty of the United States. Thus under "the protective principle," less well known than "the territorial principle," yet "claimed by most states," there is, and should be, jurisdiction. A sovereign state must be able to protect itself from those who attack its sovereignty. . . .

We agree with the court below that there are no constitutional provisions which prohibit the exercise of jurisdiction over an alien found within the sovereign's territory, under the protective principle theory. We do not think it necessary to search the Constitution to find specific authorization for such a jurisdiction.[15] "The powers of the government and the Congress in regard to *sovereignty* are broader than the powers possessed in relation to internal matters." United States v. Rodriguez, S.D.Cal.1960, 182 F.Supp. 479, 490, citing United States v. Curtiss-Wright Export Corp., 1936, 299 U.S. 304, 315, 57 S.Ct. 216, 81 L.Ed. 255.

15. The court below relied on Art. I, Sec. 8, Clause 10, which provides:

"The Congress shall have Power . . . To define and punish Piracies and Felonies committed on the high Seas, and Offences against the Law of Nations."

It has been suggested in an interesting note in 13 Stanford Law Review 155 (December, 1960) entitled: Federal Jurisdiction Over Crimes Committed Abroad by Aliens, at pp. 157–58, that there exists a specific grant of power under the "necessary and proper clause" (Art. I, Sec. 8, Clause 18) to establish "an Uniform Rule of Naturalization." (Art. I, Sec. 8, Clause 4.) But see Garcia-Mora article 19, U. Pitt.L.Rev. 567 (1958).

In United States v. Pizzarusso, 388 F.2d 8 (2d Cir. 1968), the court had before it a conviction for perjury abroad under the same section and sustained the conviction. However, Judge Medina differed from the court in Rocha as to the appropriate jurisdictional base:

> However, the objective territorial principle is quite distinct from the protective theory. Under the latter, all the elements of the crime occur in the foreign country and jurisdiction exists because these actions have a "potentially adverse effect" upon security or governmental functions, . . . and there need not be any actual effect in the country as would be required under the objective territorial principle. Courts have often failed to perceive this distinction. Thus, the Ninth Circuit [in Rocha], in upholding a conviction under a factual situation similar to the one in the instant case, relied on the protective theory, but still felt constrained to say that jurisdiction rested partially on the adverse effect produced as a result of the alien's entry into the United States. The Ninth Circuit also cited *Strassheim* and *Aluminum Company of America* as support for its decision. With all due deference to our brothers of the Ninth Circuit, however, we think this reliance is unwarranted. A violation of 18 U.S.C.A. § 1546 is complete at the time the alien perjures himself in the foreign country.

(3) The approach followed in Rocha was extended in Rivard v. United States, 375 F.2d 882 (5th Cir. 1967), to a conspiracy charge. Four Canadians were indicted and convicted of conspiracy to smuggle heroin into the United States, and Rivard also for the substantive offence of smuggling. A Canadian national named Caron was arrested in Laredo, Texas, pleaded guilty to smuggling, and testified against the defendants. A portion of the opinion follows:

> The first question we are called upon to decide is whether the District Court had jurisdiction to try an alien for a conspiracy to commit a crime against the United States, formed without the United States, several of the overt acts having been committed in furtherance of the conspiracy within the United States by a co-conspirator. . . .
>
> . . . Rivard twice sent co-conspirator Caron across the Canadian border to deliver caches of heroin brought back from Europe by Massey and Jones to another co-conspirator, Miller, in Connecticut. Caron also travelled by automobile from Quebec to Mexico through the United States and was on his way back through the United States with yet another load of heroin to be delivered in Connecticut when he was apprehended in Texas. There is thus no doubt that the object of the conspiracy was to violate the narcotics laws of the United States; that the conspiracy was carried on partly in and partly out of this country; and that overt acts were committed within the United States by co-conspirators. In the words of Mr. Chief Justice Taft: " . . . The conspiring was directed to violation of the United States law within the United States, by men within and without it, and everything done was at the procuration and by the agency of each for the other in pursuance of the conspiracy and the intended illegal importation. In such a case all are guilty of the offense of conspiring to violate the United States

law whether they are in or out of the country." Ford v. United States, 273 U.S. 593, 620, 47 S.Ct. 540. . . .

Such prosecutions of foreign-based drug activities were given a far-reaching statutory basis by the Controlled Substances Import and Export Act of 1970, 84 Stat. 1285, 21 U.S.C.A. § 951 et seq.[16] 21 U.S.C.A. § 959 makes it a crime to manufacture or distribute a "controlled substance", intending or knowing that it "will be unlawfully imported into the United States." The section states that "it is intended to reach acts of manufacture or distribution outside the territorial jurisdiction of the United States."

QUESTIONS

(1) To what extent could the various counts of the Bowman indictment (all of which were sustained by the Court's opinion) be considered "territorial" in principle—that is, within the admiralty and maritime jurisdiction of the United States? For example, should the case have been decided differently if the Dio were a foreign flag ship chartered to the United States by alien owners?

(2) Does the opinion support the view that the conspiracy charge rests upon the nationality principle? Consider particularly its references to defendant Millar. If Millar were before the trial court, should the Supreme Court have sustained his demurrer?

(3) The Court in Bowman defines the question as one of "statutory construction." As an aid to construction, it refers to "the territorial limitations upon the power and jurisdiction of a government to punish crime under the law of nations." Is the Court referring to developed principles or rules of customary international law? Does it identify the sources of these principles, or indeed the principles themselves?

(4) Do you find helpful one of the distinctions which the Court seems to draw, between crimes against individuals or their property and crimes against the government or direct governmental interests?

(5) Can Rocha v. United States be understood in terms of either the territorial or nationality principles? Without resort to any such principle, what reasons would you advance to support the court's interpretation of the statute? To challenge that interpretation?

(6) Does the 1970 Controlled Substances Act significantly extend the reach of American law beyond that achieved in cases such as Rivard? On what basis might it be defended to other nations? Suppose that a Turkish opium farmer comes within the grasp of the United States authorities who prosecute him for selling opium to an intermediary whom he knows to be engaged in exporting, via a processor in Marseilles, France, to the United States. What arguments can be made in behalf of that defendant?

NOTE ON CRIMINAL LAWS OF STATE WHERE CONDUCT RATHER THAN EFFECT OCCURS

The preceding cases involved situations where an act and its effect took place within the territory of the prosecuting nation, or

16. This statute is discussed in Collins, Traffic in the Traffickers: Extradition and the Controlled Substances Import and Export Act of 1970, 83 Yale L.J. 706 (1974).

where extraterritorial conduct produced effects within or threatened interests of that nation. But nations may also have an interest in proscribing conduct within their territory which threatens to have extraterritorial effects. Consider the following provisions in Title 18, U.S.C.A., imposing criminal sanctions for:

> *Section 43:* knowingly shipping bodies of animals or wild birds taken, transported or sold in a manner contrary to the laws of a foreign state;
>
> *Sections 481, 488:* possession of plates or dies designed for counterfeiting the obligations or currency of a foreign country;
>
> *Section 546:* smuggling goods by use of a United States flag vessel into a foreign country in violation of the laws thereof if, under the laws of that country, a penalty is provided for violating the United States customs laws;
>
> *Section 956:* conspiracy in the United States to injure specified property of a foreign government located abroad; and
>
> *Section 960:* outfitting a military expedition against a foreign government with which the United States is at peace.

Foreign policies or laws become particularly relevant when all that takes place in the prosecuting country is a conspiracy to violate foreign laws. A statute such as 18 U.S.C.A. § 956 above may point to a clear answer, but frequently that answer will have to be derived from reasoning of a general character.

Consider Board of Trade v. Owen, [1957] A.C. 602.[17] Defendants were charged in part with the common law crime of conspiracy. The object of their alleged agreement in England was to procure by fraud licenses from the German government which would have permitted them to export strategic metals from Germany to Eastern European countries, contrary to German law. Convictions on the conspiracy counts were reversed by the Court of Criminal Appeal, and the House of Lords affirmed. The opinion of Lord Tucker in the House of Lords stated in part:

> I have reached the conclusion that the decision of the Court of Criminal Appeal that a conspiracy to commit a crime abroad is not indictable in this country unless the contemplated crime is one for which an indictment would lie here is correct, and . . . it necessarily follows that a conspiracy of the nature of that charged . . . is not triable in this country, since the unlawful means and the ultimate object were both outside the jurisdiction. In so deciding I would, however, reserve for future consideration the question whether a conspiracy in this country which is wholly to be carried out abroad may not be indictable here on proof that its performance would produce a public mis-

17. Compare Treacy v. Director of Public Prosecutions, [1971] A.C. 537, sustaining a conviction for blackmail committed by mailing a menacing letter from the United Kingdom to the victim in Germany.

chief in this country or injure a person here by causing him damage abroad.

Similar questions have arisen under state law in this country.[18] Consider the following California cases.

California statutes at the time made criminal the procuring of an abortion and conspiracy to commit a crime. In addition, Section 184 of the California Penal Code required that some act, other than the making of an agreement, must be done within the state to give effect to a conspiracy before a conspiracy prosecution was possible. In People v. Buffum, 40 Cal.2d 709, 256 P.2d 317 (1953), the court reversed convictions of two Americans for conspiracy to produce abortions. The evidence showed that the defendants had made preliminary arrangements with women in California to drive them to and from Mexico, where the abortions were to take place. The court held that reversible error had been committed by admitting evidence that the abortions were illegal under Mexican law. It stated that, under proper instructions, there might have been sufficient evidence to sustain a conviction of conspiracy to perform abortions in California, on a theory that defendants first so conspired but later shifted the place of operations to Mexico because "the heat was on."

Buffum was distinguished in People v. Burt, 45 Cal.2d 311, 288 P.2d 503 (1955), a prosecution for soliciting to commit the crime of extortion. Defendant sought to persuade the prosecutrix in California to assist him in his scheme of luring men from Los Angeles to Tijuana, Mexico, where defendant and his associates, catching them *in flagrante,* could extort money from them. Noting that the statute making solicitations criminal singled out "twelve of the most serious crimes, all of which . . . are crimes under the law of all civilized nations," the court held that the statute had been violated. It reasoned that the statute was designed to protect the morals of California against such criminal influences.

QUESTIONS

(1) What were the probable motivations behind enactment of the different provisions of 18 U.S.C.A. at p. 879, supra?

(2) Do you agree with the holding in People v. Buffum? Absent Section 184, would you have reached the same conclusion?

NOTE ON PRINCIPLES USED TO JUSTIFY THE TRANSNATIONAL REACH OF STATUTES

Recall the five general principles stated in the Harvard Research at p. 856, supra. The preceding cases suggest some ambiguities in the first three. To the extent that such principles permit clearer analysis and comprehension of problems of legislative reach, they serve a useful purpose. To the extent that they divert attention from un-

18. See Scoles and Weintraub, Cases and Materials on Conflict of Laws 837–864 (1967).

derlying considerations to the mere (mechanical or conclusory) classification of particular legislation as expressing one or another principle, they do not. This risk of formal and arid classification is unfortunately a real one. It must be borne in mind that a classification may serve more a descriptive than a normative function. That is, the fact that the transnational reach of a statute can be brought within an existing "principle" does not *of itself* argue for or justify that reach.

Three general problems will often arise in connection with questions of extraterritorial reach. Indeed, all have appeared in the preceding cases. (*1*) Does the statute *purport* to reach the particular conduct? Sometimes it provides a clear answer, as in 18 U.S.C.A. § 1621, fn. 14, p. 875, supra. More frequently, as in United States v. Bowman, the statute is silent or ambiguous on this issue. Thus the court must engage in interpretation. To this task a variety of considerations are relevant, starting but not ending with an effort to identify the purpose of the statute and the degree to which vindication of that purpose points towards, or requires, giving it a transnational reach. (*2*) Interpretation will often take into account the following considerations: (*a*) Will the extraterritorial application of the statute raise serious issues about its constitutionality? United States v. Rocha considered this question in a relatively easy setting. (*b*) Will it raise issues of a violation of customary or conventional international law? (*3*) Apart from such traditional "legal" considerations, the court would often inquire whether expansive interpretation of the statute's reach would pose a risk of serious conflict with other countries.

To resolve these questions, resort to one or another "jurisdictional principle" that appears relevant will often be inadequate. A more particular and searching inquiry into statutory purposes, private expectations, and the policies or interests of concerned governments may be called for. Those interests will vary, depending upon the conduct involved, the strength of the arguments for deterring, permitting or encouraging it, and the nature and substantiality of the consequences that it entails. Indeed the general interests of the international community as a whole, or of identifiable political or commercial blocs within it, may be relevant when one considers the risks of overreach, of conflicting regulation. In such situations one must identify the various national policies or interests at issue in a given case and face the problem of resolving any conflicts among them. (Compare the discussion of developing choice-of-law methodology in civil cases at pp. 943–946, infra.)

Whatever the danger of too facile a resort to "jurisdictional principles" (what we refer to as principles of the transnational reach of national laws), certain among them are well established and frequently invoked by courts and commentators. The Restatement (Second), Foreign Relations Law of the United States, states accepted principles that are applicable in both criminal and civil settings. It refers to "jurisdiction to prescribe," and includes:

> *Section 17.* This section refers to jurisdiction of a state to prescribe rules of law attaching legal consequences to *conduct occurring within its territory,* whether or not the effect of that conduct is felt within the territory.
>
> *Section 18.* This section refers to jurisdiction to prescribe rules of law attaching legal consequences to extraterritorial conduct causing *an effect within the territory,* if (*a*) the conduct and effect are generally recognized as constituent elements of a crime or tort, or (*b*) the effect is substantial and a direct and foreseeable result of the conduct, and if (*c*) prescribing a law regulating such effect is not inconsistent with generally recognized principles of justice.
>
> *Section 30.* This section refers to jurisdiction to prescribe rules of law attaching legal consequences to *conduct of nationals,* wherever that conduct occurs.
>
> *Section 33.* This section (entitled "*Protective Principle*") refers to jurisdiction of a state to prescribe rules of law attaching legal consequences to extraterritorial conduct threatening "its security as a state", provided that the conduct is generally recognized as a crime. It uses as illustrations the counterfeiting of currency and false statements made to diplomatic officials at their foreign posts.

The Restatement here attempts in part to separate the permissible from the impermissible reach of national legislation under principles of international law. Whatever may be their relevance to indicating whether a prosecution would violate international law, these "jurisdictional" principles are less helpful in interpreting a statute that does not indicate its spatial application. They may however serve as convenient descriptive categories.

QUESTIONS

(1) Consider how you would classify within the Restatement's sections the following cases, involving contiguous nations X and Y (the prosecuting country), defendant D (a national of X), and victim V:

> (*a*) D, standing in X, shoots V in Y.
>
> (*b*) D negligently leaves his car on a hill in X without adequate brakes. It rolls into Y and injures V.
>
> (*c*) D sends from X a fraudulent prospectus, soliciting the purchase of securities, to V in Y.
>
> (*d*) D broadcasts incitements to mutiny from X into Y.
>
> (*e*) D conspires with its competitors in X to increase the price of goods exported to other countries, including Y.
>
> (*f*) D conspires with business associates in X to violate export restrictions of Y affecting merchandise to be shipped from Y.

(2) In each case, (*a*) what public interests does Y serve by prosecuting, (*b*) what substantial arguments, if any, can be made on behalf of D, and (*c*) what legitimate interests, if any, of X might be threatened by a prosecution and thus lead X to a diplomatic protest?

NOTE ON COMPARABLE PROBLEMS AMONG STATES WITHIN THE UNITED STATES

The United States federalism has given rise to analogous problems. Statutes in a number of states define the spatial reach of the criminal law. For example, Wis.Stat.Ann. § 939.03, entitled "Jurisdiction of state over crime," provides in part that a person is subject to prosecution under Wisconsin law if:

> (a) He commits a crime, any of the constituent elements of which takes place in this state; or (b) While out of this state, he aids and abets, conspires with, or advises, incites, commands, or solicits another to commit a crime in this state; or (c) While out of this state, he does an act with intent that it cause in this state a consequence set forth in a section defining a crime . . . .

A leading case on such problems is Strassheim v. Daily, 221 U.S. 280, 31 S.Ct. 558, 55 L.Ed. 735 (1911), relied upon in Rocha v. United States, p. 875, supra. In a habeas corpus proceeding, Daily sought discharge from custody under a warrant of the governor of Illinois directing his extradition to Michigan as a fugitive from justice from that state. He had been indicted in Michigan for bribery and for obtaining money from Michigan by false pretenses. The indictment was based upon the sale to Michigan of machinery which, under the sale contract, was to be new but which, because of the alleged fraud of Daily and others, was in fact second-hand. Daily was in Michigan at the time that certain transactions with the state took place, and was in Illinois at other times when arrangements were made with his friends (including one Armstrong) to perpetrate the alleged fraud. The Supreme Court, in an opinion by Justice Holmes, reversed an order of discharge by the district court and ordered the prisoner remanded to custody. One of the questions before it was whether Daily was a "fugitive from justice" for purposes of the extradition provisions. The opinion stated in part:

> If a jury should believe the evidence, and find that Daily did the acts that led Armstrong to betray his trust, deceived the board of control, and induced by fraud the payment by the state, the usage of the civilized world would warrant Michigan in punishing him, although he never had set foot in the state until after the fraud was complete. Acts done outside a jurisdiction, but intended to produce and producing detrimental effects within it, justify a state in punishing the cause of the harm as if he had been present at the effect, if the state should succeed in getting him within its power. . . . American Banana Co. v. United Fruit Co., 213 U.S. 347, 356, 53 L.Ed. 826, 832, 29 S.Ct.Rep. 511 . . . . We may assume, therefore, that Daily is a criminal under the laws of Michigan.

> Of course, we must admit that it does not follow that Daily is a fugitive from justice. . . . On the other hand, however, we think it plain that the criminal need not do within the state every act necessary to complete the crime. If he does there an overt act which is and is intended to be a material step toward accomplishing the crime, and then absents himself from the state and does the rest elsewhere, he becomes a fugitive from justice when the crime is complete, if not before. . . . For all that is necessary to convert a criminal under the laws of a state into a fugitive from justice is that he should have left the state after having incurred guilt there . . . and his overt act becomes retrospectively guilty when the contemplated result ensues. . . .

The materials at pp. 759–796, supra, develop distinctions between enforcement of money judgments in an interstate and international setting. They grow in part out of different constitutional requirements, in part out of different policies relevant to the federal and international contexts. Similar considerations should be kept in mind with respect to the reach of criminal legislation within the federalism. Constitutional provisions, particularly the Commerce Clause and the Due Process Clause of the Fourteenth Amendment, may check overreaching by a state. And the problem of a second prosecution by another state affected by the conduct leading to the first prosecution is controlled to some degree by the Double Jeopardy Clause and the Due Process Clause of the Fourteenth Amendment. Further, despite the differences among state policies in certain areas of the criminal law, one can point towards a relatively common tradition within the federalism, in contrast with the more significant differences among nations.

State criminal law may raise international as well as interstate questions. The two California cases described at p. 880, supra, are illustrative. In such situations, the constitutional clauses noted above limit the power of a state to prosecute. However, in event of a prosecution, the risk of a later prosecution in a foreign country based upon the same conduct remains. And an additional range of problems might arise in such settings. If the defendants were aliens, and if their conduct significantly involved a foreign country, international tensions might follow. In some circumstances, a question of the proper allocation of responsibility between federal and state governments in deciding whether to prosecute might arise.[19]

Additional reading: George, Extraterritorial Application of Penal Legislation, 64 Mich.L.Rev. 609 (1966).

19. Compare Wildenhus's Case, p. 857, supra. And compare similar tensions between state and federal law that arise in civil litigation involving aliens, such as the administration of iron curtain statutes described at pp. 162–172, supra.

CASE OF THE S.S. "LOTUS"

Permanent Court of International Justice, 1927.
P.C.I.J., Ser. A, No. 10.

[In 1926, a collision occurred between a French steamer, the "Lotus", and a Turkish collier, about five nautical miles off the coast of Turkey, and consequently on the high seas rather than within Turkey's territorial waters. The Turkish collier sank and eight Turkish nationals were lost in the accident. The officer of the watch on the "Lotus" at the time of the accident was M. Demons, a French national. The "Lotus" continued to Constantinople, where Turkish authorities called upon M. Demons to give evidence as to the accident. After testifying, he was arrested and charged with involuntary manslaughter under Turkish law. A conviction, fine and brief imprisonment followed. The French Government protested the action of the Turkish authorities in bringing a criminal action against M. Demons and contended that the Turkish prosecution was in violation of the principles of international law. By special agreement, the Governments of France and Turkey submitted this dispute to the P. C. I. J. where France sought indemnity from Turkey for the injury resulting from the prosecution. The question before the Court was whether international law prevented Turkey from asserting "jurisdiction" to attach legal consequences to acts occurring on board the "Lotus" on the high seas, and consequently to prosecute any person for his conduct on board.

The decision of the Court rested in part upon the Convention of Lausanne of 1923, to which France and Turkey were parties. Article 15 of the Convention stated that "all questions of jurisdiction shall, as between Turkey and the other contracting Powers, be decided in accordance with the principles of international law." The Court concluded that "the wording ultimately adopted by common consent for Article 15 can only refer to the principles of general international law relating to jurisdiction."

Excerpts from the opinion appeared in Chapter III, at p. 253, supra. They were intended to indicate the sources to which the Court looked in order to formulate the "principles of general international law." The excerpts below treat the merits of the "jurisdictional" issue. Their purpose is to suggest the implications of the decision for the transnational reach of national legislation.]

The prosecution was instituted in pursuance of Turkish legislation. The special agreement does not indicate what clause or clauses of that legislation apply. No document has been submitted to the Court indicating on what article of the Turkish Penal Code the prosecution was based; the French Government however declares that the Criminal Court claimed jurisdiction under Article 6 of the Turkish Penal Code, and far from denying this statement, Turkey, in the submissions of her Counter-Case, contends that that article is in conformity with the principles of international law. It does not appear from the proceedings whether the prosecution was instituted solely on the basis of that article.

Article 6 of the Turkish Penal Code, Law No. 765 of March 1st, 1926 (Official Gazette No. 320 of March 13th, 1926), runs as follows:

> "Any foreigner who, apart from the cases contemplated by Article 4, commits an offence abroad to the prejudice of Turkey or of a Turkish subject, for which offence Turkish law prescribes a penalty involving loss of freedom for a

> minimum period of not less than one year, shall be punished in accordance with the Turkish Penal Code provided that he is arrested in Turkey. The penalty shall however be reduced by one third and instead of the death penalty, twenty years of penal servitude shall be awarded.
>
> "Nevertheless, in such cases, the prosecution will only be instituted at the request of the Minister of Justice or on the complaint of the injured Party." . . .

Even if the Court must hold that the Turkish authorities had seen fit to base the prosecution of Lieutenant Demons upon the above-mentioned Article 6, the question submitted to the Court is not whether that article is compatible with the principles of international law; it is more general. The Court is asked to state whether or not the principles of international law prevent Turkey from instituting criminal proceedings against Lieutenant Demons under Turkish law. Neither the conformity of Article 6 in itself with the principles of international law nor the application of that article by the Turkish authorities constitutes the point at issue; it is the very fact of the institution of proceedings which is held by France to be contrary to those principles. Thus the French Government at once protested against his arrest, quite independently of the question as to what clause of her legislation was relied upon by Turkey to justify it. The arguments put forward by the French Government in the course of the proceedings and based on the principles which, in its contention, should govern navigation on the high seas, show that it would dispute Turkey's jurisdiction to prosecute Lieutenant Demons, even if that prosecution were based on a clause of the Turkish Penal Code other than Article 6, assuming for instance, that the offence in question should be regarded, by reason of its consequences, to have been actually committed on Turkish territory. . . .

International law governs relations between independent States. The rules of law binding upon States therefore emanate from their own free will as expressed in conventions or by usages generally accepted as expressing principles of law and established in order to regulate the relations between these co-existing independent communities or with a view to the achievement of common aims. Restrictions upon the independence of States cannot therefore be presumed.

Now the first and foremost restriction imposed by international law upon a State is that—failing the existence of a permissive rule to the contrary—it may not exercise its power in any form in the territory of another State. In this sense jurisdiction is certainly territorial; it cannot be exercised by a State outside its territory except by virtue of a permissive rule derived from international custom or from a convention.

It does not, however, follow that international law prohibits a State from exercising jurisdiction in its own territory, in respect of any case which relates to acts which have taken place abroad, and in which it cannot rely on some permissive rule of international law. Such a view would only be tenable if international law contained a general prohibition to States to extend the application of their laws and the jurisdiction of their courts to persons, property and acts outside their territory, and if, as an exception to this general prohibition, it allowed States to do so in certain specific cases. But this is certainly not the case under international law as it stands at present. Far from laying down a general prohibition to the effect that States may not extend the application of their laws and the jurisdiction of their courts to persons, property and acts outside their territory, it leaves them in this respect a wide measure of discretion which is only limited in certain cases by prohibitive rules; as regards other cases, every State remains free to adopt the principles which it regards as best and most suitable.

This discretion left to States by international law explains the great variety of rules which they have been able to adopt without objections or complaints on the part of other States; it is in order to remedy the difficulties resulting from such variety that efforts have been made for many years past, both in Europe and America, to prepare conventions the effect of which would be precisely to limit the discretion at present left to States in this respect by international law, thus making good the existing lacunae in respect of jurisdiction or removing the conflicting jurisdictions arising from the diversity of the principles adopted by the various States. . . .

It follows from the foregoing that the contention of the French Government to the effect that Turkey must in each case be able to cite a rule of international law authorizing her to exercise jurisdiction, is opposed to the generally accepted international law to which Article 15 of the Convention of Lausanne refers. . . .

Nevertheless, it has to be seen whether the foregoing considerations really apply as regards criminal jurisdiction, or whether this jurisdiction is governed by a different principle: this might be the outcome of the close connection which for a long time existed between the conception of supreme criminal jurisdiction and that of a State, and also by the especial importance of criminal jurisdiction from the point of view of the individual.

Though it is true that in all systems of law the principle of the territorial character of criminal law is fundamental, it is equally true that all or nearly all these systems of law extend their action to offences committed outside the territory of the State which adopts them, and they do so in ways which vary from State to State. The territoriality of criminal law, therefore, is not an absolute principle of international law and by no means coincides with territorial sovereignty.

This situation may be considered from two different standpoints corresponding to the points of view respectively taken up by the Parties. According to one of these standpoints, the principle of freedom, in virtue of which each State may regulate its legislation at its discretion, provided that in so doing it does not come in conflict with a restriction imposed by international law, would also apply as regards law governing the scope of jurisdiction in criminal cases. According to the other standpoint, the exclusively territorial character of law relating to this domain constitutes a principle which, except as otherwise expressly provided, would *ipso facto*, prevent States from extending the criminal jurisdiction of their courts beyond their frontiers; the exceptions in question, which include for instance extraterritorial jurisdiction over nationals and over crimes directed against public safety, would therefore rest on special permissive rules forming part of international law.

Adopting, for the purposes of the argument, the standpoint of the latter of these two systems, it must be recognized that, in the absence of a treaty provision, its correctness depends upon whether there is a custom having the force of law establishing it. The same is true as regards the applicability of this system—assuming it to have been recognized as sound—in the particular case. It follows that, even from this point of view, before ascertaining whether there may be a rule of international law expressly allowing Turkey to prosecute a foreigner for an offence committed by him outside Turkey, it is necessary to begin by establishing both that the system is well-founded and that it is applicable in the particular case. Now, in order to establish the first of these points, one must, as has just been seen, prove the existence of a principle of international law restricting the discretion of States as regards criminal legislation.

Consequently, whichever of the two systems described above be adopted, the same result will be arrived at in this particular case: the necessity of ascertaining whether or not under international law there is a principle which would have prohibited Turkey, in the circumstances of the case before the Court, from prosecuting Lieutenant Demons. . . .

The arguments advanced by the French Government, other than those considered above, are, in substance, the three following:

> (1) International law does not allow a State to take proceedings with regard to offences committed by foreigners abroad, simply by reason of the nationality of the victim; and such is the situation in the present case because the offence must be regarded as having been committed on board the French vessel.
>
> (2) International law recognizes the exclusive jurisdiction of the State whose flag is flown as regards everything which occurs on board a ship on the high seas.
>
> (3) Lastly, this principle is especially applicable in a collision case.

As regards the first argument, the Court feels obliged in the first place to recall that its examination is strictly confined to the specific situation in the present case, for it is only in regard to this situation that its decision is asked for.

As has already been observed, the characteristic features of the situation of fact are as follows: there has been a collision on the high seas between two vessels flying different flags, on one of which was one of the persons alleged to be guilty of the offence, whilst the victims were on board the other.

This being so, the Court does not think it necessary to consider the contention that a State cannot punish offences committed abroad by a foreigner simply by reason of the nationality of the victim. For this contention only relates to the case where the nationality of the victim is the only criterion on which the criminal jurisdiction of the State is based. Even if that argument were correct generally speaking—and in regard to this the Court reserves its opinion—it could only be used in the present case if international law forbade Turkey to take into consideration the fact that the offence produced its effects on the Turkish vessel and consequently in a place assimilated to Turkish territory in which the application of Turkish criminal law cannot be challenged, even in regard to offences committed there by foreigners. But no such rule of international law exists. No argument has come to the knowledge of the Court from which it could be deduced that States recognize themselves to be under an obligation towards each other only to have regard to the place where the author of the offence happens to be at the time of the offence. On the contrary, it is certain that the courts of many countries, even of countries which have given their criminal legislation a strictly territorial character, interpret criminal law in the sense that offences, the authors of which at the moment of commission are in the territory of another State, are nevertheless to be regarded as having been committed in the national territory, if one of the constituent elements of the offence, and more especially its effects, have taken place there. French courts have, in regard to a variety of situations, given decisions sanctioning this way of interpreting the territorial principle. Again, the Court does not know of any cases in which governments have protested against the fact that the criminal law of some country contained a rule to this effect or that the courts of a country construed their criminal law in this sense. Consequently, once it is admitted that the effects of the offence were produced on the Turkish vessel, it becomes impossible to hold that there is a rule of international law which prohibits Turkey from prosecuting Lieutenant Demons because of the fact that the author of the offence was on board the French ship. Since, as has already been observed, the special agreement does not deal with the provision of Turkish law under which the prosecution was instituted, but only with the question whether the prosecution should be regarded as contrary to the principles of international law, there is no reason preventing the Court from confining itself to observing that, in this case, a prosecution may also be justified from the point of view of the so-called territorial principle.

Nevertheless, even if the Court had to consider whether Article 6 of the Turkish Penal Code was compatible with international law, and if it held that the nationality of the victim did not in all circumstances constitute a sufficient basis for the exercise of criminal jurisdiction by the State of which the victim was a national, the Court would arrive at the same conclusion for the reasons just set out. For even were Article 6 to be held incompatible with the principles of international law, since the prosecution might have been based on another provision of Turkish law which would not have been contrary to any principle of international law, it follows that it would be impossible to deduce from the mere fact that Article 6 was not in conformity with those principles, that the prosecution itself was contrary to them. The fact that the judicial authorities may have committed an error in their choice of the legal provision applicable to the particular case and compatible with international law only concerns municipal law and can only affect international law in so far as a treaty provision enters into account, or the possibility of a denial of justice arises.

It has been sought to argue that the offence of manslaughter cannot be localized at the spot where the mortal effect is felt; for the effect is not intentional and it cannot be said that there is, in the mind of the delinquent, any culpable intent directed towards the territory where the mortal effect is produced. In reply to this argument it might be observed that the effect is a factor of outstanding importance in offences such as manslaughter, which are punished precisely in consideration of their effects rather than of the subjective intention of the delinquent. But the Court does not feel called upon to consider this question, which is one of interpretation of Turkish criminal law. It will suffice to observe that no argument has been put forward and nothing has been found from which it would follow that international law has established a rule imposing on States this reading of the conception of the offence of manslaughter.

The second argument put forward by the French Government is the principle that the State whose flag is flown has exclusive jurisdiction over everything which occurs on board a merchant ship on the high seas.

It is certainly true that—apart from certain special cases which are defined by international law—vessels on the high seas are subject to no authority except that of the State whose flag they fly. In virtue of the principle of the freedom of the seas, that is to say, the absence of any territorial sovereignty upon the high seas, no State may exercise any kind of jurisdiction over foreign vessels upon them. Thus, if a war vessel, happening to be at the spot where a collision occurs between a vessel flying its flag and a foreign vessel, were to send on board the latter an officer to make investigations or to take evidence, such an act would undoubtedly be contrary to international law.

But it by no means follows that a State can never in its own territory exercise jurisdiction over acts which have occurred on board a foreign ship on the high seas. A corollary of the principle of the freedom of the seas is that a ship on the high seas is assimilated to the territory of the State the flag of which it flies, for, just as in its own territory, that State exercises its authority upon it, and no other State may do so. All that can be said is that by virtue of the principle of the freedom of the seas, a ship is placed in the same position as national territory; but there is nothing to support the claim according to which the rights of the State under whose flag the vessel sails may go farther than the rights which it exercises within its territory properly so called. It follows that what occurs on board a vessel on the high seas must be regarded as if it occurred on the territory of the State whose flag the ship flies. If, therefore, a guilty act committed on the high seas produces its effects on a vessel flying another flag or in foreign territory, the same principles must be applied as if the territories of two different States were concerned, and the conclusion must therefore be drawn that there is no rule of international law prohibiting the State to which the ship on which the effects of the offence have taken place belongs, from regarding the offence as having been committed in its territory and prosecuting, accordingly, the delinquent.

This conclusion could only be overcome if it were shown that there was a rule of customary international law which, going further than the principle stated above, established the exclusive jurisdiction of the State whose flag was flown. The French Government has endeavoured to prove the existence of such a rule, having recourse for this purpose to the teachings of publicists, to decisions of municipal and international tribunals, and especially to conventions which, whilst creating exceptions to the principle of the freedom of the seas by permitting the war and police vessels of a State to exercise a more or less extensive control over the merchant vessels of another State, reserve jurisdiction to the courts of the country whose flag is flown by the vessel proceeded against.

In the Court's opinion, the existence of such a rule has not been conclusively proved. . . .

The cases in which the exclusive jurisdiction of the State whose flag was flown has been recognized would seem rather to have been cases in which the foreign State was interested only by reason of the nationality of the victim, and in which, according to the legislation of that State itself or the practice of its courts, that ground was not regarded as sufficient to authorize prosecution for an offence committed abroad by a foreigner. . . .

The Court therefore has arrived at the conclusion that the second argument put forward by the French Government does not, any more than the first, establish the existence of a rule of international law prohibiting Turkey from prosecuting Lieutenant Demons.

It only remains to examine the third argument advanced by the French Government and to ascertain whether a rule specially applying to collision cases has grown up, according to which criminal proceedings regarding such cases come exclusively within the jurisdiction of the State whose flag is flown.

[A portion of the opinion is set forth at p. 256, supra, discussing decisions of municipal courts as evidence of a rule of international law, is here omitted.]

In support of the theory in accordance with which criminal jurisdiction in collision cases would exclusively belong to the State of the flag flown by the ship, it has been contended that it is a question of the observance of the national regulations of each merchant marine and that effective punishment does not consist so much in the infliction of some months' imprisonment upon the captain as in the cancellation of his certificate as master, that is to say, in depriving him of the command of his ship.

In regard to this, the Court must observe that in the present case a prosecution was instituted for an offence at criminal law and not for a breach of discipline. Neither the necessity of taking administrative regulations into account (even ignoring the circumstance that it is a question of uniform regulations adopted by States as a result of an international conference) nor the impossibility of applying certain disciplinary penalties can prevent the application of criminal law and of penal measures of repression.

The conclusion at which the Court has therefore arrived is that there is no rule of international law in regard to collision cases to the effect that criminal proceedings are exclusively within the jurisdiction of the State whose flag is flown.

This conclusion moreover is easily explained if the manner in which the collision brings the jurisdiction of two different countries into play be considered.

The offence for which Lieutenant Demons appears to have been prosecuted was an act—of negligence or imprudence—having its origin on board the *Lotus*, whilst its effects made themselves felt on board the *Boz-Kourt*. These two elements are, legally, entirely inseparable, so much so that their separation renders the offence non-existent. Neither the exclusive jurisdiction of either State, nor the limitations of the jurisdiction of each to the occurrences which took place on the respective ships would appear calculated to satisfy the requirements of justice and effectively to protect the interests of the two States. It is only natural that each should be able to exercise jurisdiction and to do so in respect of the incident as a whole. It is therefore a case of concurrent jurisdiction.

The Court, having arrived at the conclusion that the arguments advanced by the French Government either are irrelevant to the issue or do not establish the existence of a principle of international law precluding Turkey from instituting the prosecution which was in fact brought against Lieutenant Demons, observes that in the fulfillment of its task of itself asertaining what the international law is, it has not confined itself to a consideration of the arguments put forward, but has included in its researches all precedents, teachings and facts to which it had access and which might possibly have revealed the existence of one of the principles of international law contemplated in the special agreement. The result of these researches has not been to establish the existence of any such principle. It must therefore be held that there is no principle of international law, within the meaning of Article 15 of the Convention of Lausanne of July 24th,

1923, which precludes the institution of the criminal proceedings under consideration. Consequently, Turkey, by instituting, in virtue of the discretion which international law leaves to every sovereign State, the criminal proceedings in question, has not, in the absence of such principles, acted in a manner contrary to the principles of international law within the meaning of the special agreement. . . .

[There were several dissenting opinions. The final vote for judgment for Turkey was 7–5.]

COMMENT

The specific holding of Lotus was in effect "reversed" by Article 11(1) of the Geneva Convention on the High Seas of 1958, 13 U.S.T. & O.I.A. 2312, T.I.A.S. No. 5200, 450 U.N.T.S. 82. That Article provides that in the event of a collision on the high seas involving the responsibility of any person in the service of the ship, no penal proceedings may be instituted against such person "except before the . . . authorities either of the flag State or of the State of which such person is a national."

The opinion in Lotus indicates the many ways in which the term "jurisdiction" is used. In Chapter VII, we considered questions of adjudicatory or judicial jurisdiction. The Turkish court before which Lieutenant Demons was present clearly had such jurisdiction, but clearly this did not resolve the controversy. The issue was whether Turkey could prosecute under its own criminal law. The Court states this most clearly, without resort to the language of "jurisdiction," when it asks "whether or not the principles of international law prevent Turkey from instituting criminal proceedings against Lieutenant Demons under Turkish law."

Recall that the Harvard Research at p. 856, supra, as well as the excerpts from Restatement (Second) at p. 882, supra, use the term "jurisdiction" to refer to the reach of legislative power. One frequently encounters the phrase "legislative jurisdiction" to describe these problems of spatial reach. The term has its difficulties, partially because it suggests the drawing of precise lines and a precise allocation of legislative competence among states. These materials generally avoid the word "jurisdiction" to describe such legislative problems.

The Lotus opinion also uses "jurisdiction" in a third sense when it describes (p. 886, supra) the "foremost restriction" in this field imposed by international law. A nation "may not exercise its power in any form in the territory of another state. In this sense jurisdiction is certainly territorial." The apparent reference is to such blunt forms of interference with the territorial sovereignty of another state as military incursions or, on a more subtle level, the service of process of United States courts in Switzerland which the Swiss government protested as an unauthorized intrusion on its authority. See p. 758, supra. Here again the terminology of "jurisdiction" is often invoked, sometimes in the phrase "executive jurisdiction."

QUESTIONS

(1) Are the principles on reach of legislative power that are stated in Restatement (Second) and in the Lotus case consistent? Do the two appear to entertain the same view of the borderline between the territorial and protective principles?

(2) Refer to the six hypothetical cases at p. 882, supra;

(*a*) Which provides the closest analogy to Lotus?

(*b*) Which prosecutions by Y would the Court in Lotus have regarded as resting upon a "territorial" principle? Which as violating international law?

(*c*) Does Lotus or the Restatement help to resolve a further question raised by those cases: at what point do the effects within a nation of extraterritorial conduct become so attenuated that they no longer justify a prosecution?

(3) Assume a prosecution in Turkey of a United States citizen for murdering a private Turkish citizen in the United States. What reasons would you stress in arguing to the Turkish court that Article 6 violated customary international law?

PROBLEM

In Gallagher v. United States, 423 F.2d 1371 (Ct. Cl. 1970), a soldier brought a suit for back pay that was lost by reason of a court-martial conviction for a crime committed against a German civilian while he was on leave in Germany. Plaintiff argued that the court-martial lacked jurisdiction over him, basing his argument on O'Callahan v. Parker, 395 U.S. 258, 89 S.Ct. 1683, 23 L.Ed.2d 291 (1969), which held that courts-martial could not try a soldier for a crime not service-connected committed in the United States. The court observed that the NATO Status of Forces Agreement, p. 898, infra, gave concurrent jurisdiction over soldiers in such circumstances to the sending state (the United States) and to the receiving state (Germany), which had "primary" jurisdiction that could be waived if requested. Germany did here waive its primary jurisdiction. In concluding that the court-martial had jurisdiction, the court noted that the consequence of a contrary holding would be that servicemen could be tried only by the foreign country involved. The court further observed:

> Thus it appears that plaintiff is asking us to exhibit our zeal for the Bill of Rights by holding that the protection of our Bill of Rights must be utterly withdrawn from servicemen stationed in foreign countries, whenever they are charged with offenses in the concurrent class. We say this, of course, not meaning to raise any hobgoblins about Germany, which has a highly developed system of jurisprudence, with its own system of safeguarding the accused. But we may notice judicially that our servicemen are stationed also in other countries, some of which have a reputation for harsh laws and savagely operated penal institutions. We are supposed to do this to defend the jury system, but counsel are unable to advise that jury trials are accorded to persons tried even under Germany's enlightened criminal statutes.
>
> It may be suggested that the Congress could legislate for domestic jury trials in Article III courts, for servicemen accused of

> crimes of violence against civilians in friendly foreign countries. We note that the Court of Military Appeals challenges this supposition and raises a doubt whether it is true in its *Keaton* opinion.
>
> On the hypothesis that the "service connection" of the offense had been rejected, it would appear that a statutory attempt to confer on Article III Federal courts, (or state courts), jurisdiction over the trial of crimes of violence committed against foreign nationals on the streets of foreign cities would encounter very serious problems of constitutional law and international law. . . . Supposing the legislative draftsmen found answers to all of these, there would still be no assurance that foreign police would surrender custody of offenders actually in their hands on the expectation that they would be tried thousands of miles away, under a statute that would appear as a gross invasion of their national sovereignty, and possibly ineffective too. . . .

What are the "very serious problems of constitutional law and international law" that would be posed? Would you oppose or support such legislation, taking into account constitutional and other considerations?

B. INTERNATIONAL COOPERATION IN CONTROLLING CRIMINAL CONDUCT

NOTE ON NATIONAL AND INTERNATIONAL RESPONSES TO AIRCRAFT HIJACKING

Prior to 1968 episodes of aircraft hijacking had occurred for several years at an average rate, world-wide, of about four or five per year. In 1968 the number suddenly jumped to 35, then to 88 in 1969 and 83 in 1970, with a moderate decline thereafter. A substantial number of these episodes involved the United States, and about a third of the American episodes were international in character, usually involving a diversion of the aircraft to a Cuban destination.

While some episodes involved escapes by nonpolitical convicts or simple financial extortion, others represented political gestures. The Popular Front for the Liberation of Palestine began a spectacular series of aircraft hijackings in support of its campaign against Israel; one episode extracted $5,000,000 from Lufthansa and another involved the destruction of four passenger aircraft (of United States, Swiss and United Kingdom registration) in order to obtain the release of prisoners and to gain world-wide impact. The publicity accruing to these exploits brought imitators into the field. The Eritrean Liberation Front, the Japan Red Army, the Kashmiri National Liberation Front, the Croatian Ustasha, Thai Black September, Iranian Communists, Philippine Maoists, the Organization of Unity of South Yemen and other groups became active in such exploits.

National governments made attempts to cope with this new terror. Some reactions were preventive. Airport searches of passengers and baggage, of varying degrees of thoroughness, became routine. "Profiles" were developed to aid in the identification of likely hijackers. "Sky marshals" or armed guards became participants in many air flights. Useful though this activity was, it was expensive, inconvenient and violative of the personal rights of ordinary passengers. At best it provided only partial protection.

When they could, countries whose aircraft or citizens were victimized prosecuted captured hijackers. Legislation was enacted to perfect the definition of the crime and to make penalties more severe. From 1961 to 1973 the United States was able to secure custody of 75 hijackers and convicted 48 of them, some others successfully pleading insanity or diminished responsibility. While no death sentences were either sought or imposed, sentences of imprisonment for life or for ten years or more have been common. In other countries punishments have ranged from severe (death in three cases, life imprisonment often) to light (eight or nine months). The self-styled "romantic pirate" Rafael Minichiello, who hijacked a plane from Los Angeles to Rome, was sentenced to seven and a half years but was released after serving only 18 months.

These enforcement efforts encountered major obstacles in the form of an unwillingness on the part of some countries to return accused hijackers for trial. Cuba, Algeria and Libya became particularly known as "havens" for such persons, but other countries also were moved to deny their cooperation in individual cases because of political sympathy for the hijacker or because of strong domestic pressures not to act.

Obviously an effort had to be made at the international level to assure at least that minimum cooperation among nations which would make criminal laws more effective. There are in fact three conventions; the Toyko Convention on Offences and Certain Other Acts Committed on Board Aircraft, 1963, 20 U.S.T. & O.I.A. 2941, T.I.A.S. No. 6768, The Hague Convention for the Suppression of Unlawful Seizure of Aircraft, 1970, 22 U.S.T. & O.I.A. 1641, T.I.A.S. No. 7192, and The Montreal Convention for the Suppression of Unlawful Acts against the Safety of Civil Aviation, 1971, T.I.A.S. No 7570.

These agreements overlap extensively in their coverage and exhibit parallel patterns, with increasing levels of detail and stringency. The Conventions, taken together, define the acts constituting "the offence" and bind each party to make the offence severely punishable. They provide that each state shall "take such measures as may be necessary to establish its jurisdiction" over cases in which the offence is committed in an aircraft registered in that state and over cases where that aircraft lands in its territory with the alleged offender still on board. A state in which an alleged offender appears shall take him into custody, notify other affected states and either subject the alleged offender to trial in its own courts or extradite him according to its established procedures. States are to cooperate with each other in restoring control of hijacked aircraft to their lawful commanders, bringing criminal proceedings, and notifying international authorities. Disputes may be arbitrated by the International Court of Justice.

Unfortunately not all affected states are parties to these conventions, none of which has more than about 60 signatories. While the United States is a party to each of these conventions and has responded to them in its criminal laws (see 49 U.S.C.A. § 1472), several countries have continued to show hospitality to aircraft hijackers. Some nations, seeking ways of bringing more pressure to bear upon uncooperative governments, have proposed an arrangement whereby an aggrieved nation can appeal to the International Civil Aeronautics Organization which, after hearings and negotiations, could impose sanctions, primarily suspension of the offending country's rights under the basic 1944 Chicago Convention on International Civil Aviation and International Air Services Transit Agreement. That suspension would amount to a virtual suspension of international civil air traffic. In June 1972, a 24-hour boycott on flights to certain countries designated as having refused to implement the conventions was called by the International Federation of Airline Pilots Associations; although unofficial, it proved impressively effective. The decline in the frequency of hijacking episodes in 1973–74 has apparently caused some slackening of the campaign of countermeasures, but the problem is still with us.

QUESTIONS

(1) Suppose that Peter Partisano, an adherent of the Baluchistan separatist movement, boards a Swedish airplane at Fiumicino airport in Rome and, while it is over French territory, forces the pilot by threat of violence to fly via Spain and Morocco to a landing in Algeria. Under orthodox principles of legislative reach, which countries can try Partisano under their separate national criminal law? Can you establish a system of priorities among them?

(2) Ivan Wilamowitz is a writer whose works have been suppressed in Volhynia, a Communist people's republic. After his latest, and highly critical, series of essays were "published" on a multilith edition, the authorities moved to arrest him and send him to a retraining camp for "antisocial elements". Forewarned, he boarded a local air flight and, by threatening the crew, compelled them to fly him to Burgundy, a country of Western Europe. Burgundy is anxious to curb hijacking but is disturbed at returning Wilamowitz. How would you draft a note explaining why Wilamowitz is not being returned even while Burgundy demands the delivery by Libya of four "revolutionaries" who compelled a Burgundian airliner to fly them to Libya after extracting a ransom of $2,000,000? Could you suggest language for a treaty that would separate such cases?

(3) Do you regard trial before an international tribunal as feasible? Could it solve problems such as those posed in question (2)?

Additional reading: Evans, Aircraft Hijacking: What is Being Done?, 67 Am.J.Int.L. 641 (1973); Aerial Piracy and International Law (McWhinney ed. 1971).

NOTE ON INTERNATIONAL COOPERATION IN CRIMINAL LAW

The preceding cases focus attention on areas of overlap and potential conflict between systems of criminal law. One should, however, be aware of the extensive cooperation between the police and prosecutors of different countries. After all, these officials often have common objectives, interests, and attitudes—and a common enemy.

In some cases cooperation is based on international agreements. These characteristically have dealt with crimes regarded with particular abhorrence by all civilized countries and involve international traffic that would tend to escape the regulatory efforts of any one country. The conventions on narcotics, slavery, and "white slavery" fall into this category. A broader cooperation is pledged by the European Convention on Mutual Assistance in Criminal Matters.[20] In other cases cooperation is highly informal. Indeed, it appears at times that police relationships may go further than some of the governments concerned would like. The French government, for example, reacted vigorously at the discovery that its secret police organizations had in October 1965 helped Moroccan forces cause the disappearance from France of a political enemy of the Moroccan regime. Some aspects of intergovernmental cooperation are described in the succeeding paragraphs.

Status of Forces Agreements.

In terms of volume of activity, the most important example of close cooperation is that involved in the Status of Forces Agreements concluded by the United States and various foreign countries linked by military alliances. These arrangements include 15 countries that are parties to the North Atlantic Treaty Organization, Japan, the Philippines and other countries.[21] The country (receiving state) in which troops of another (sending state) are stationed concedes to the sending state the right to try by court-martial within its borders members of its armed forces for violations of its military law. However, the receiving state has the right to try such persons for violations of its law in its ordinary courts.

Conflicts of jurisdiction in cases of acts illegal under both laws are provided for in the following way. The authorities of the sending state have primary authority over offences arising out of any act or omission done in the performance of an official duty, or offences solely against the property or security of the sending state or of another national of that state. In other cases the authorities of the receiving state have primary jurisdiction. Each country may waive its primary jurisdiction.[22]

20. See generally Chapters 2 and 4 of Mueller and Wise, International Criminal Law (1965).

21. One such arrangement was involved in Reid v. Covert, p. 564, supra.

22. In Wilson v. Girard, 354 U.S. 524, 77 S.Ct. 1409, 1 L.Ed.2d 1544 (1957), an American soldier had allegedly killed a Japanese woman while trying to frighten her away from a firing range area. After a determination by

The receiving state is characteristically obligated by these agreements to guarantee the accused certain rights. Note Article VII(9) of the NATO Status of Forces Agreement, 4 U.S.T. & O.I.A. 1792, T.I.A.S. No. 2846, 199 U.N.T.S. 67:

> Whenever a member of a force or civilian component or a dependent is prosecuted under the jurisdiction of a receiving State he shall be entitled—
>
> (a) to a prompt and speedy trial;
>
> (b) to be informed, in advance of trial, of the specific charge or charges made against him;
>
> (c) to be confronted with the witnesses against him;
>
> (d) to have compulsory process for obtaining witnesses in his favour, if they are within the jurisdiction of the receiving State;
>
> (e) to have legal representation of his own choice for his defence or to have free or assisted legal representation under the conditions prevailing for the time being in the receiving State;
>
> (f) if he considers it necessary, to have the services of a competent interpreter; and
>
> (g) to communicate with a representative of the Government of the sending State and, when the rules of the court permit, to have such a representative present at his trial.

Compare the attempts to define trial safeguards in the draft conventions appearing at pp. 382–383, 388–390, supra.

Despite this provision, the Senate expressed grave concern at the prospect of American personnel being subject to foreign criminal justice. This concern was expressed in the following resolution, expressing "the sense of the Senate" and accompanying its advice and consent to the NATO Status of Forces Agreement: [23]

> . . .
>
> 2. Where a person subject to the military jurisdiction of the United States is to be tried by the authorities of a receiving state, under the treaty the Commanding Officer of the Armed forces of the United States in such state shall examine the laws of such state with particular reference to the procedural safeguards contained in the Constitution of the United States;
>
> 3. If, in the opinion of such commanding officer, under all the circumstances of the case, there is danger that the accused will not be protected because of the absence or denial of constitutional rights he would enjoy in the United States, the commanding officer shall request the authorities of the receiving state to waive jurisdiction in accordance with the provisions of paragraph 3(c) of Article VII . . . and if such authorities refuse to waive jurisdiction, the commanding officer shall request the De-

the Army that the action was in the performance of Girard's duties, he was surrendered for trial by the Japanese authorities. The Supreme Court could "find no constitutional or statutory barrier" to the waiver.

23. 4 U.S.T. & O.I.A. 1828, T.I.A.S. No. 2846, p. 36.

partment of State to press such request through diplomatic channels and notification shall be given by the Executive Branch to the Armed Services Committees of the Senate and House of Representatives;

4. A representative of the United States . . . will attend the trial of any such person by the authorities of a receiving state under the agreement, and any failure to comply with the provisions of paragraph 9 of Article VII of the agreement shall be reported to the commanding officer of the armed forces of the United States in such state who shall then request the Department of State to take appropriate action to protect the rights of the accused, and notification shall be given by the Executive Branch to the Armed Services Committees of the Senate and House of Representatives.

These are not rare situations. For example, from 1953 to 1967, some 60,000 U. S. personnel were tried before the courts of 41 foreign countries, according to reports made by the military to the Senate Armed Services Committee, which has kept a watchful eye on the administration of the agreements. At the same time the receiving states had waived jurisdiction in some 70% of the cases. In the course of this experience American observers have attended a great many trials and have built up a formidable file of experience on comparative criminal law.

Problems have been occasioned for these observers because of the different standards expressed in the resolution—an accused may be deprived of a constitutional right (trial by jury) and still receive a trial complying with Article VII(9). As a result the military has frequently sought waivers on the theory that constitutional rights were being denied. Still, many observers express themselves as did the following observer in France: [24]

> . . . [W]hile the procedures in the trial court may be, and are, open to criticism, I am convinced that the system of pretrial hearings conducted by the Juge d'Instruction in the presence of the accused and counsel, plus the care exercised by the court at trial, provides a measure of protection of the accused at least equal to that of the safeguards enforced in American courts.

Evidentiary Problems

In the course of investigating a possible violation of its criminal law or of preparing a case for trial, the authorities of one country may encounter evidentiary problems similar to those that arise in civil litigation, p. 835, supra. At an informal level there must be a vast amount of interchange of data between police forces. When newspapers report that an airline hostess has been arrested on arrival in the United States and found to have concealed a quantity of narcotics

24. See Williams, An American's Trial in a Foreign Court: The Role of the Military's Trial Observer, 34 Mil.L. Rev. 1 (1966). Somewhat similar arrangements in Eastern Europe are described in Prugh, The Soviet Status of Forces Agreements, 20 Mil.L.Rev. 1 (1963).

upon her person, the likelihood is great that information furnished by the police in the country of origin made the arrest possible. A permanent structure for such interchanges is provided by the International Criminal Police Organization (Interpol), of which a large number of countries, including the United States, are members. It maintains files, publishes a Review and sponsors international conferences.

However, informal cooperation is sometimes not forthcoming or does not produce usable evidence. The problem may lie in the law of the state that proposes to use the evidence. Suppose that an American is arrested by foreign policemen who, unencumbered by the privilege against self-incrimination, interrogate him with an intensity and for a duration forbidden in the United States. If he is then turned over to a United States court of military authorities for trial, should the resulting confession be admitted? Or suppose that foreign authorities make a warrantless search of an American's home, turning up incriminating evidence. If it is turned over to United States authorities, are they free to use it? Does it matter that the American authorities either requested the interrogation or the search or were present as observers?[25] The reverse situation is illustrated by the so-called "wiretapping affair" in which West German police not authorized to listen to telephone conversations themselves enlisted the cooperation of Allied intelligence agencies which had that authority under various treaty arrangements concluded after World War II. The revelation of this affair elicited protests in the German press.

On the other hand, the problem may rest with the institutions of the state in which the evidence is located. Resistance to the intrusion of foreign evidence-gathering agencies, described in regard to civil cases at p. 835, supra, may be particularly acute where the foreign agency involved is one engaged in criminal law enforcement, an acutely sovereign activity. For example, to have an Italian criminal judge hear evidence at the Italian consulate in New York City involved an unusual degree of acquiescence by the United States in foreign governmental acts. Sorge v. City of New York, 56 Misc.2d 414, 288 N.Y.S.2d 787 (Sup.Ct.1968).

A unique example of cooperation in this field is represented by the Treaty between the United States and the Swiss Confederation on Mutual Assistance in Criminal Matters, signed in 1973 but not yet ratified.[26] This treaty is designed to deal with irritations arising from the use, actual or suspected, by American criminals of Swiss banks and other facilities as part of their criminal schemes. The Swiss bank secrecy law and practices described at p. 845, supra, were thought to be a powerful attraction, in particular for organized crime. Congress had attempted to deal with this problem through the Bank Secrecy Act of 1970, 84 Stat. 1114, 12 U.S.C.A. § 1829b, 31 U.S.C.A.

25. See, e. g., Stonehill v. United States, 405 F.2d 738 (9th Cir. 1968); Brulay v. United States, 383 F.2d 345 (9th Cir. 1967); United States v. Gresham, 4 U.S.C.M.A. 694, 16 C.M.R. 268 (1954).

26. 12 Int'l Leg.Mats. 916 (1973). See Note, 15 Harv.Int.L.J. 349 (1974).

§§ 1051–1122, which required (a) reports on various transactions by United States banks, (b) reports on the export or import of money in excess of $5000 and (c) reports on transactions between American citizens and foreign banks. The Treaty would obligate each party, subject to various safeguards in the interest of its sovereignty or security, to assist the other in obtaining evidence needed for criminal prosecutions in a wide variety of situations. It even would enable American authorities to penetrate Swiss bank secrecy in the case of serious offences where the evidence is shown to be important and where other efforts at obtaining it have failed. If the Treaty proves to be successful in operation, it will mark a major advance in international criminal cooperation and may prove to be a model for other arrangements.

Extradition Treaties

The physical presence of the accused is essential to a criminal prosecution, absent very special circumstances. International cooperation is frequently important in obtaining that custody. Sometimes this has been done non-judicially and without legal sanction. Note, for example, that Eichmann's presence at his trial in Israel (p. 912, infra) was obtained through his abduction from Argentina by a more or less private group of Israelis. The United States has also been involved in episodes of this type.[27] It is generally held that a person may not raise the irregularity of his capture as an objection to the trial, although the same facts may give rise to an international claim by the affronted state (i. e. Argentina in the Eichmann case).[28] The older American case law, e. g., Ker v. Illinois, 119 U.S. 436, 7 S.Ct. 225, 30 L.Ed. 421 (1888), and Frisbie v. Collins, 342 U.S. 519, 72 S.Ct. 509, 96 L.Ed. 541 (1952), held that the accused could not raise the issue of an unlawful arrest abroad. However, a recent decision, United States v. Toscanino, 500 F.2d 267 (2d Cir. 1974), held that a claim of unlawful seizure by American agents in Uruguay, in violation of treaty as well as of American principles, should be inquired into on remand. It noted the presence of a "constitutional revolution" in parallel matters affecting the treatment of criminal defendants by government agents.

The regular and formal manner of procuring the accused's presence from abroad is by extradition. Under United States practice this may be done only pursuant to treaty. The United States is a party to nearly 60 general extradition treaties, several of which bind some 20 former dominions or dependencies of European signatory

27. One Soblen, convicted of espionage in the United States, fled to Israel when the Supreme Court denied review. Israel placed Soblen on a plane destined for the United States; a fellow passenger was a United States marshal. On arrival in England, Soblen attempted to commit suicide and was removed to a hospital. When he had recovered, the British authorities ordered him deported to the United States, extradition not being available by treaty for that crime.

28. See O'Higgins, Disguised Extradition: The Soblen Case, 27 Mod.L.Rev. 521 (1964); Cardozo, When Extradition Fails, Is Abduction the Solution?, 55 Am.J.Int.L. 127 (1961).

states. It is also a party to the 1933 Montevideo Convention on Extradition, together with a number of Latin American states. 49 Stat. 3111, T.S. No. 882. These treaties range in time from 1856 to date; some have been supplemented once or several times.

Extradition procedure is governed by the terms of the particular treaty and, as to extradition from the United States, by statutory provisions, which have disposed of the early controversy whether an extradition treaty could be self-executing. They provide for the issue of a warrant for the wanted person, for his arrest and commitment, for a public hearing as to the sufficiency of the evidence that his case comes within the terms of the relevant treaty, and for his surrender to agents of the foreign government.

It is difficult to summarize the terms of so many treaties dating from such different times. They are less standardized and more affected by the details of national practice than are FCN treaties. All that is attempted here is to alert the reader to recurrent questions.

(*a*) For extradition to take place the fugitive must be accused of a crime designated in the treaty. The treaty lists of offenses vary widely and have a tendency to become obsolete as new forms of malfeasance are discovered. Treaties generally stipulate that the accused is not to be tried for an offense other than that designated in the request for his extradition.

(*b*) There is a general concept of "double criminality", i. e., that one can be extradited only if the acts alleged constituted a crime in both countries. Some treaties make this rule generally applicable; others apply it only to specific crimes, in which event the principle of *expressio unius* has been held to take effect. Factor v. Laubenheimer, 290 U.S. 276, 54 S.Ct. 191, 78 L.Ed. 315 (1933). The requirement of double criminality sometimes poses problems when the foreign law is a strange one. Thus the Canadian courts have had difficulty in finding a Canadian equivalent of federal crimes such as using the mails to defraud, in which the use of the mails has been made an element to satisfy American constitutional requirements. See 3 Loss, Securities Regulation 1995–2004 (2d ed. 1961).

(*c*) There is a well-established principle that political crimes are not subject to extradition. Application of that principle presents difficulties in such cases as a murder or a theft asserted by the fugitive to have been committed in order to further the goals of the revolutionary party to which he belonged.

(*d*) Some countries adhere to the position—sometimes embodied in their constitutions—that they will not extradite their own nationals. This results in variations among American treaties. To illustrate from three recent treaties: one relieves Brazil of any duty to extradite nationals; one with

Sweden leaves it to executive discretion whether to extradite nationals; and one with Israel provides that extradition may not be refused on the basis that the fugitive is a national.

(*e*) The traditional approach has allowed extradition only for crimes committed within the territory of the requesting state. What then of one who commits perjury or counterfeiting outside the requesting country in circumstances where the country would seek to apply its laws? Compare Rocha v. United States, p. 875, supra. Strassheim v. Daily, p. 883, supra, involved comparable problems in an interstate setting. Some recent treaties have sanctioned extradition in such cases if the laws of both countries authorize the application of criminal sanctions despite the degree of extraterritoriality involved.

Additional reading: Evans, The New Extradition Treaties of the United States, 59 Am.J.Int.L. 351 (1965). For current listings of the treaties, see 18 U.S.C.A., note following § 3181, and the State Department publication, Treaties in Force.

C. AN INTERNATIONAL LAW OF CRIMES: FROM NUREMBERG TO VIETNAM

As customary international law developed from the time of Grotius, certain conduct came to be considered a violation of the law of nations. It was in effect viewed as constituting a universal crime. Earliest among this limited category of crimes was piracy on the high seas, a reflection of the common interest of all nations in protecting commerce and navigation. Thus it was considered appropriate for any nation apprehending a pirate to prosecute in its own courts. Since the criminal acts had by definition occurred outside the territory of any nation, prosecution in an "unrelated" national court was often the only means of enforcement. But to the extent that the national courts sought to apply customary international law, either directly or as absorbed into national legislation, choice of forum became less significant. Here was a field where, to a certain degree, choice of law could be said to have played a role in national criminal proceedings. Nonetheless, the concept of a crime against the law of nations was an important exception to the maxim, stressed in the Lotus case, that criminal legislation was territorial in character.

It is the law or war—those rules which at once legitimate violence among nations and seek to contain its unnecessarily inhumane use—which has become the most significant branch of the international law of crimes. The contemporary principles have deep historical antecedents, expressed in earlier times primarily through uncodified practices and understandings among nations about belligerent conduct. This century has seen a number of conventions that have attempted to develop and codify the rules in this field—particularly the Fourth Hague Convention of 1907, the Geneva Conventions of 1929 and 1949 (regulating such matters as protection of civilians or war prisoners), and draft proposals issuing from contemporary conferences. Two World Wars of increasing barbarity and destructiveness led to extensive violations of the principles then in effect, and in turn acted as spurs towards the formulation of more comprehensive and humane principles. This Part C examines some trends after World War II in the law of war and related matters, trends bringing significant innovations in the concept of international criminal responsibility.

NOTE ON NUREMBERG AND OTHER TRIALS OF WAR CRIMINALS

As World War II came to an end, the Allied powers held several conferences to determine what policies they should follow towards the Germans responsible for the war and the barbarous excesses of the period. These conferences culminated in the (U. S., U.S.S.R., Britain, France) London Agreement of August 8, 1945, 59 Stat. 1544, E.A.S. No. 472, in which the parties determined to constitute "an International Military Tribunal for the trial of war criminals." The Charter annexed to the Agreement provided for the composition and basic procedures of the Tribunal and stated in its three critical articles:

Article 6.

The Tribunal established by the Agreement referred to in Article 1 hereof for the trial and punishment of the major war criminals of the European Axis countries shall have the power to try and punish persons who, acting in the interests of the European Axis countries, whether as individuals or as members of organizations, committed any of the following crimes.

The following acts, or any of them, are crimes coming within the jurisdiction of the Tribunal for which there shall be individual responsibility:

(a) CRIMES AGAINST PEACE: namely, planning, preparation, initiation or waging of a war of aggression, or a war in violation of international treaties, agreements or assurances, or participation in a common plan or conspiracy for the accomplishment of any of the foregoing;

(b) WAR CRIMES: namely, violations of the laws or customs of war. Such violations shall include, but not be limited to, murder, ill-treatment or deportation to slave labor or for any other purpose of civilian population of or in occupied territory, murder or ill-treatment of prisoners of war or persons on the seas, killing of hostages, plunder of public or private property, wanton destruction of cities, towns or villages, or devastation not justified by military necessity;

(c) CRIMES AGAINST HUMANITY: namely, murder, extermination, enslavement, deportation, and other inhumane acts committed against any civilian population, before or during the war, or persecutions on political, racial or religious grounds in execution of or in connection with any crime within the jurisdiction of the Tribunal, whether or not in violation of the domestic law of the country where perpetrated.

Leaders, organizers, instigators and accomplices participating in the formulation or execution of a common plan or conspiracy to commit any of the foregoing crimes are responsible for all acts performed by any persons in execution of such plan.

Article 7.

The official position of defendants, whether as Heads of State or responsible officials in Government Departments, shall not be considered as freeing them from responsibility or mitigating punishment.

Article 8.

The fact that the Defendant acted pursuant to order of his Government or of a superior shall not free him from responsibility, but may be considered in mitigation of punishment if the Tribunal determines that justice so requires.

Note the innovative character of these provisions. The Tribunal was international in formation and character, radically different from the national military courts before which the laws of war had previously been enforced. Moreover, at the core of the Charter lay the concept of crimes for which there would be "individual responsbility," a sharp change in direction from the then-existing customary law or conventions which stressed the *duties* of *nations* and which were generally quiet with respect to *sanctions* against *nations or individuals* for violations of those duties. Moreover, in defining the crimes within the Tribunal's jurisdiction, the Charter went beyond the traditional "war crimes" (paragraph (b) of Article 6) in two ways.

First, the Charter included the war-related "crimes against peace". International Law had long been innocent of such a concept. After a slow departure during the post-Reformation period from earlier distinctions of philosophers, theologians, and writers on international law between "just" and "unjust" wars, the European nations moved towards a conception of war as an instrument of national policy, much like any other, to be legally regulated only as to the manner of its conduct. The Covenant of the League of Nations did not frontally challenge this principle, although it attempted to control aggression through collective decisions of the League. The interwar period witnessed some fortification of the principles later articulated in the Nuremberg Charter, primarily through the Kellogg-Briand pact of 1927 in which this country, France and 42 other signatories renounced war as an instrument of national policy. Of course, today the United Nations Charter (signed in 1945) requires members (Article 2(4)) to "refrain in their international relations from the threat or use of force" against other states, while providing (Article 51) that nothing shall impair "the inherent right of individual or collective self-defense if an armed attack occurs against a Member . . ." When viewed in conjunction with the Nuremberg Charter, those provisions suggest the contemporary effort to distinguish not between "just" and "unjust" wars but between "self-defense" and "aggression"—the word used in defining "crimes against peace" in Article 6(a) of that Charter.

Second, Article 6(c) goes beyond any conduct necessarily connected with the instigation or implementation of war. That provision, for example, included the program of the Nazi government to exterminate Jews and other civilian groups "before or during" the war. Nonetheless, the Charter and the Nuremberg Judgment were concerned with war-related crimes. It remained for later agreements such as the Genocide Convention, p. 574, supra, to make such acts criminal in any circumstances.

In defining the charges against the major Nazi leaders tried at Nuremberg and its successor tribunals, the Allied powers took care to exclude those types of conduct which had not been understood to violate existing custom or conventions and in which they themselves had engaged—for example, the massive bombing of cities with necessarily high tolls of civilians.

The Judgment of the Nuremberg Tribunal of September 30, 1946 [29] held the major leaders guilty of the crimes defined in the Charter and laid down important principles in such areas as the defense of "superior orders". The Judgment declared, for example, that those committing acts which the Charter condemned as criminal under international law could not justify their conduct through their official positions or their duty to obey superiors. The true test, stated the Tribunal, was not whether one had acted under orders of a superior, but whether "moral choice was in fact possble". With respect to the charge of "crimes against peace" (planning and waging agressive war), Nuremberg and related tribunals produced a total of 15 convictions and 59 acquittals. The convictions were dominantly of those in high policy positions.

After the Nuremberg Judgment, the principles enunciated by the Tribunal and in its Charter were affirmed by a unanimous resolution of the General Assembly of the United Nations of December 11, 1946 (G.A.Res. 95(I), U.N.Doc. A/64/Add. 1). The principles particularly of Section 6(c) were reaffirmed and extended by the Convention for the Prevention and Punishment of Genocide, p. 574, supra. In 1949, four conventions drafted in Geneva revised and recodified the rules governing land and naval warfare.[30] Contemporary efforts at revision are underway.

29. The judgment is reprinted in 41 Am.J.Int.L. 172 (1947). It appeared officially in I Trial of the Major War Criminals before the International Military Tribunal 171 (1947).

30. The Conventions appear at 6 U.S.T. & O.I.A. 3114, 3217, 3316, 3516, T.I.A.S. Nos. 3362–65, 75 U.N.T.S. 31, 85, 135, 287.

In the Far East, Japanese military and civilian leaders were tried both before a military court and before a tribunal similar to Nuremberg that was established at Toyko to punish "crimes against peace," "conventional war crimes", and "crimes against humanity".[31] One of the trials before the United States military commission gave rise to a decision which, we shall see, became significant for issues relating to war crimes in the American involvement in Vietnam.

APPLICATION OF YAMASHITA

Supreme Court of the United States, 1946.
327 U.S. 1, 66 S.Ct. 340, 90 L.Ed. 499.

[General Yamashita, commander of the Japanese forces in the Philippines at the time of the re-invasion by the Allies, was convicted by a United States military commission and sentenced to hang. The charge is described in the opinion as follows:

> Neither Congressional action nor the military orders constituting the commission authorized it to place petitioner on trial unless the charge preferred against him is of a violation of the law of war. The charge, so far as now relevant, is that petitioner, between October 9, 1944 and September 2, 1945, in the Philippine Islands, "while commander of armed forces of Japan at war with the United States of America and its allies, unlawfully disregarded and failed to discharge his duty as commander to control the operations of the members of his command, permitting them to commit brutal atrocities and other high crimes against people of the United States and of its allies and dependencies, particularly the Philippines; and he . . . thereby violated the laws of war."
>
> Bills of particulars, filed by the prosecution by order of the commission, allege a series of acts, one hundred and twenty-three in number, committed by members of the forces under petitioner's command, during the period mentioned. The first item specifies the execution of "a deliberate plan and purpose to massacre and exterminate a large part of the civilian population of Batangas Province, and to devastate and destroy public, private and religious property therein, as a result of which more than 25,000 men, women and children, all unarmed noncombatant civilians, were brutally mistreated and killed, without cause or trial, and entire settlements were devastated and destroyed wantonly and without military necessity." Other items specify acts of violence, cruelty and homicide inflicted upon the civilian population and prisoners of war, acts of wholesale pillage and the wanton destruction of religious monuments.

The only Congressional action relied upon by the court, article 15 of the Articles of War, simply stated:

> The provisions of these articles conferring jurisdiction upon courts-martial shall not be construed as depriving military commissions . . . or other military tribunals of con-

31. The Tokyo Tribunal was established, T.I.A.S. No. 1589, by General MacArthur under authority of the Potsdam Agreement.

current jurisdiction in respect of offenders or offenses that by statute or by the law of war may be triable by such military commissions . . . or other military tribunals.

Petitioner applied to the United States Supreme Court for an original writ of habeas corpus and for a writ of certiorari to the Supreme Court of the Philippines. The majority opinion by CHIEF JUSTICE STONE and a dissenting opinion by JUSTICE RUTLEDGE, joined in by JUSTICE MURPHY, differed as to the procedures followed by the commission—whether adequate time to prepare had been given Yamashita's counsel, whether the use of depositions against the accused was proper. The dissenters, in a separate opinion, differed as to the merits—whether the prosecution had adequately pleaded and proved that Yamashita was personally responsible for the atrocities which troops under his command had unquestionably committed. Excerpts from the opinion of the Court follow:]

It is not denied that such acts directed against the civilian population of an occupied country and against prisoners of war are recognized in international law as violations of the law of war. Articles 4, 28, 46, and 47, Annex to Fourth Hague Convention, 1907, 36 Stat. 2277, 2296, 2303, 2306, 2307.[32] But it is urged that the charge does not allege that petitioner has either committed or directed the commission of such acts, and consequently that no violation is charged as against him. But this overlooks the fact that the gist of the charge is an unlawful breach of duty by petitioner as an army commander to control the operations of the members of his command by "permitting them to commit" the extensive and widespread atrocities specified. The question then is whether the law of war imposes on an army commander a duty to take such appropriate measures as are within his power to control the troops under his command for the prevention of the specified acts which are violations of the law of war and which are likely to attend the occupation of hostile territory by an uncontrolled soldiery, and whether he may be charged with personal responsibility for his failure to take such measures when violations result. That this was the precise issue to be tried was made clear by the statement of the prosecution at the opening of the trial.

It is evident that the conduct of military operations by troops whose excesses are unrestrained by the orders or efforts of their commander would almost certainly result in violations which it is the purpose of the law of war to prevent. Its purpose to protect civilian populations and prisoners of war from brutality would largely be defeated if the commander of an invading army could with impunity neglect to take reasonable measures for their protection. Hence the law of war presupposes that its violation is to be avoided through the control of the operations of war by commanders who are to some extent responsible for their subordinates.

This is recognized by the Annex to Fourth Hague Convention of 1907, respecting the laws and customs of war on land. Article I lays down as a condition which an armed force must fulfill in order to be accorded the rights of lawful belligerents, that it must be "commanded by a person responsible for his subordinates." 36 Stat. 2295. . . . And, finally, Article 43 of the Annex of the Fourth Hague Convention, 36 Stat. 2306, requires that the commander of a force occupying enemy territory, as was petitioner, "shall take all the measures in his power to restore, and ensure, as far as possible, public

32. [Eds.] Both Japan and the United States were parties to the Hague Convention Respecting the Law and Customs of War on Land, 36 Stat. 2277, T.S. No. 539.

order and safety, while respecting, unless absolutely prevented, the laws in force in the country."

These provisions plainly imposed on petitioner, who at the time specified was military governor of the Philippines, as well as commander of the Japanese forces, an affirmative duty to take such measures as were within his power and appropriate in the circumstances to protect prisoners of war and the civilian population. This duty of a commanding officer has heretofore been recognized, and its breach penalized by our own military tribunals. A like principle has been applied so as to impose liability on the United States in international arbitrations. Case of Jenaud, 3 Moore, International Arbitrations, 3000; Case of "The Zafiro," 5 Hackworth, Digest of International Law, 707.

We do not make the laws of war but we respect them so far as they do not conflict with the commands of Congress or the Constitution. There is no contention that the present charge, thus read, is without the support of evidence, or that the commission held petitioner responsible for failing to take measures which were beyond his control or inappropriate for a commanding officer to take in the circumstances. . . .

Obviously charges of violations of the law of war triable before a military tribunal need not be stated with the precision of a common law indictment. Cf. Collins v. McDonald, supra, 258 U.S. 420, 42 S. Ct. 328, 66 L.Ed. 692. But we conclude that the allegations of the charge, tested by any reasonable standard, adequately allege a violation of the law of war and that the commission had authority to try and decide the issue which it raised. . . .

[A dissenting opinion of JUSTICE MURPHY, joined in by JUSTICE RUTLEDGE, said in part:]

. . . He was not charged with personally participating in the acts of atrocity or with ordering or condoning their commission. Not even knowledge of these crimes was attributed to him. It was simply alleged that he unlawfully disregarded and failed to discharge his duty as commander to control the operations of the members of his command, permitting them to commit the acts of atrocity. The recorded annals of warfare and the established principles of international law afford not the slightest precedent for such a charge. This indictment in effect permitted the military commission to make the crime whatever it willed, dependent upon its biased view as to petitioner's duties and his disregard thereof, a practice reminiscent of that pursued in certain less respected nations in recent years.

In my opinion, such a procedure is unworthy of the traditions of our people or of the immense sacrifices that they have made to advance the common ideals of mankind. The high feelings of the moment doubtless will be satisfied. But in the sober afterglow will come the realization of the boundless and dangerous implications of the procedure sanctioned today. No one in a position of command in an army, from sergeant to general, can escape those implications. Indeed, the fate of some future President of the United States and his chiefs of staff and military advisers may well have been sealed by this decision. But even more significant will be the hatred and ill-will growing out of the application of this unprecedented procedure. That has been the inevitable effect of every method of punishment disregarding the element of personal culpability. The effect in this instance, unfortunately, will be magnified infinitely for here we are dealing with the rights of man on an international level. To subject an enemy belligerent to an unfair trial, to charge him with an unrecognized crime, or to vent on him our retributive emotions only antagonizes the enemy nation and hinders the reconciliation necessary to a peaceful world. . . .

If we are ever to develop an orderly international community based upon a recognition of human dignity it is of the utmost importance that the necessary punishment of those guilty of atrocities be as free as possible from the ugly stigma of revenge and vindictiveness. Justice must be tempered by compassion rather than by vengeance. In this, the first case involving this momentous problem ever to reach this Court, our responsibility is both lofty and difficult. We must insist, within the confines of our proper jurisdiction, that the highest standards of justice be applied in this trial of an enemy commander conducted under the authority of the United States. Otherwise stark retribution will be free to masquerade in a cloak of false legalism. And the hatred and cynicism engendered by that retribution will supplant the great ideals to which this nation is dedicated. . . .

International law makes no attempt to define the duties of a commander of an army under constant and overwhelming assault; nor does it impose liability under such circumstances for failure to meet the ordinary responsibilities of command. The omission is understandable. Duties, as well as ability to control troops, vary according to the nature and intensity of the particular battle. To find an unlawful deviation from duty under battle conditions requires difficult and speculative calculations. Such calculations become highly untrustworthy when they are made by the victor in relation to the actions of a vanquished commander. Objective and realistic norms of conduct are then extremely unlikely to be used in forming a judgment as to deviations from duty. The probability that vengeance will form the major part of the victor's judgment is an unfortunate but inescapable fact. So great is that probability that international law refuses to recognize such a judgment as a basis for a war crime, however fair the judgment may be in a particular instance. It is this consideration that undermines the charge against the petitioner in this case. The indictment permits, indeed compels, the military commission of a victorious nation to sit in judgment upon the military strategy and actions of the defeated enemy and to use its conclusions to determine the criminal liability of an enemy commander. Life and liberty are made to depend upon the biased will of the victor rather than upon objective standards of conduct.

The Court's reliance upon vague and indefinite references in certain of the Hague Conventions and the Geneva Red Cross Convention is misplaced. Thus the statement in Article 1 of the Annex to Hague Convention No. IV of October 18, 1907, 36 Stat. 2277, 2295, to the effect that the laws, rights and duties of war apply to military and volunteer corps only if they are "commanded by a person responsible for his subordinates," has no bearing upon the problem in this case. Even if it has, the clause "responsible for his subordinates" fails to state to whom the responsibility is owed or to indicate the type of responsibility contemplated. The phrase has received differing interpretations by authorities on international law. In Oppenheim, International Law (6th ed., rev. by Lauterpacht, 1940, vol. 2, p. 204, fn. 3) it is stated that "The meaning of the word 'responsible' . . . is not clear. It probably means 'responsible to some higher authority,' whether the person is appointed from above or elected from below; . . .." Another authority has stated that the word "responsible" in this particular context means "presumably to a higher authority," or "possibly it merely means one who controls his subordinates and who therefore can be called to account for their acts." Wheaton, International Law (14th ed., by Keith, 1944, p. 172, fn. 30). . . .

The Government claims that the principle that commanders in the field are bound to control their troops has been applied so as to impose liability on the United States in international arbitrations. Case of Jeannaud, 1880, 3 Moore, International Arbitrations (1898) 3000; Case of The Zafiro, 1910, 5 Hackworth, Digest of International Law (1943) 707. The difference between arbitrating property rights and charging an individual with a crime against the laws of war is too obvious to require elaboration. But even more significant is the fact that even these arbitration cases fail to establish any principle of liability where troops are under constant assault and demoralizing influences by attacking forces. The same observation applies to the common law and statutory doctrine, referred to by the Government, that one who is under a legal duty to take protective or preventive action is guilty of criminal homicide if he willfully or negligently omits to act and death is proximately caused. . . . [I]t must be remembered that we are not dealing here with an ordinary tort or criminal action; precedents in those fields are of little if any value. Rather we are concerned with a proceeding involving an international crime, the treatment of which may have untold effects upon the future peace of the world. That fact must be kept uppermost in our search for precedent.

The only conclusion I can draw is that the charge made against the petitioner is clearly without precedent in international law or in the annals of recorded military history. This is not to say that enemy commanders may escape punishment for clear and unlawful failures to prevent atrocities. But that punishment should be based upon charges fairly drawn in light of established rules of international law and recognized concepts of justice. . . .

COMMENT

Consider the following remarks on the Yamashita case in Note, Command Responsibility for War Crimes, 82 Yale L.J. 1274, 1283–4 (1973).

> . . . Thus, in a prominent conviction affirmed by the United States Supreme Court, the Japanese General Yamashita was found responsible for literally hundreds of crimes and criminal policies committed or engaged in by his subordinates in the Philippines. Because Yamashita maintained almost no communication with his subordinates, and there was no evidence he actually knew about these crimes, the case is commonly cited for the proposition that command responsibility incorporates "constructive knowledge." This is a confused reading of the case. Yamashita apparently was aware of no particular facts which might raise a duty to infer or investigate specific crimes or criminal policies. Rather, the military commission and the Supreme Court held that his total ignorance, and the complete delegation of authority associated with it, themselves raised unacceptable general risks of *future* subordinate criminality, those crimes becoming chargeable to him as soon as they occurred. By imposing duties of supervision and control, even where a commander is aware of no particular facts indicating that his subordinates are engaging in crimes, *Yamashita* accomplishes a greater expansion of command responsibility

than would a mere recognition of "constructive knowledge." Going even further, the Tokyo Tribunal found that unacceptable risks were raised by general supervisory defaults well short of Yamashita's nearly total abdication of command authority.[33]

QUESTION

(1) "Justice Murphy warned in his opinion in the Yamashita Case of the need to be free from the 'ugly stigma of revenge and vindictiveness. . . . Otherwise stark retribution will be free to masquerade in a cloak of false legalism.' He found the charges made against Yamashita 'clearly without precedent in international law . . . .' The same charge of *ex post facto* lawmaking by the victorious for the defeated can properly be made of the proceedings at Nuremberg. Retroactive criminal punishment may respond to political necessity, but can hardly be viewed as either a legal or moral proceeding. It denigrates rather than advances the cause of the Rule of Law in international life." Comment.

NOTE ON THE EICHMANN TRIAL

Adolf Eichmann, operationally in charge of the mass murder of Jews in Germany and German-occupied countries, fled Germany after the war. He was abducted from Argentina by Israelis, and brought to trial in Israel under the Nazi and Nazi Collaborators (Punishment) Law, enacted after Israel became a state. Section 1(a) of the Law provided:

> A person who has committed one of the following offences—(1) did, during the period of the Nazi regime, in a hostile country, an act constituting a crime against the Jewish people; (2) did, during the period of the Nazi regime, in a hostile country, an act constituting a crime against humanity; (3) did, during the period of the Second World War, in a hostile country, an act constituting a war crime; is liable to the death penalty.

The Law defined "crimes against the Jewish people" to consist principally of acts intended to bring about physical destruction. The other two crimes were defined similarly to the like charges at Nuremberg. The 15 counts against Eichmann involved all three crimes. The charges stressed Eichmann's active and significant participation in the "final solution to the Jewish problem" developed and administered by Nazi officials. Eichmann was convicted in 1961 and later executed. There appear below summaries of portions of the opinions of the trial and appellate courts.

33. The *Tokyo Judgment* stated that cabinet members, military commanders, civilian administrators "concerned with the well being of POW's," and officials having "direct and immediate control" over POW's, have duties in establishing and securing the continuous and efficient working of a system appropriate . . . to secure proper treatment of prisoners and to prevent their ill-treatment . . . . [The Commander] has a duty to ascertain that the system is working and if he neglects to do so, he is responsible. He does not discharge his duty merely by instituting an appropriate system and thereafter neglecting to learn of its application. . . .

The Attorney-General of the Government of Israel v. Eichmann [34]

Eichmann argued that the prosecution violated international law by inflicting punishment (1) upon persons who were not Israeli citizens (2) for acts done by them outside Israel and before its establishment, (3) in the course of duty, and (4) on behalf of a foreign country. In reply, the Court noted that, in event of a conflict between an Israeli statute and principles of international law, it would be bound to apply the statute. However, it then concluded that "the law in question conforms to the best traditions of the law of nations. The power of the State of Israel to enact the law in question or Israel's 'right to punish' is based . . . from the point of view of international law, on a dual foundation: The universal character of the crimes in question and their specific character as being designed to exterminate the Jewish people."

Thus the Court relied primarily on the universality and protective principles to justify its assertion of jurisdiction to try the crimes defined in the Law. It held such crimes to be offenses against the Law of Nations, much as was the traditional crime of piracy. It compared the conduct made criminal under the Israeli statute (particularly the "crime against the Jewish people") and the crime of genocide, as defined in Article 1 of the Convention for the Prevention and Punishment of Genocide.[35]

> The Contracting Parties confirm that genocide, whether committed in time of peace or in time of war, is a crime under international law which they undertake to prevent and to punish.[36]

The Court also stressed the relationship between the Law's definition of "war crime" and the pattern of crimes defined in the Nuremberg Charter. It rejected arguments of Eichmann based upon the retroactive application of the legislation, and stated that "all the reasons justifying the Nuremberg judgments justify *eo ipse* the retroactive legislation of the Israeli legislator."

The Court then discussed another "foundation" for the prosecution—the offence specifically aimed at the Jewish people.

> [This foundation] of penal jurisdiction conforms, according to [the] acknowledged terminology, to the protective principle . . . . The "crime against the Jewish people," as defined in the Law, constitutes in effect an attempt to exterminate the Jewish people . . . . If there is an ef-

34. District Court of Jerusalem, Judgment of December 11, 1961. This summary and the selective quotations are drawn from 56 Am.J.Int.L. 805 (1962) (unofficial translation).

35. The Convention, 78 U.N.T.S. 277, became effective in 1951. It has been ratified by more than fifty nations, including Israel but not including the United States, see pp. 387, 574, supra.

36. [Eds.] Article 6 of the Convention, the meaning and implications of which were viewed differently by the parties, states: "Persons charged with genocide or any of the other acts enumerated in Article III shall be tried by a competent tribunal of the State in the territory of which the act was committed, or by such international penal tribunal as may have jurisdiction with respect to those Contracting Parties which shall have accepted its jurisdiction."

> fective link (and not necessarily an identity) between the State of Israel and the Jewish people, then a crime intended to exterminate the Jewish people has a very striking connection with the State of Israel. . . . The connection between the State of Israel and the Jewish people needs no explanation.

The Court also rejected Eichmann's contention that international law barred a criminal prosecution, since Eichmann had been abducted from Argentina and forcibly brought into Israel.[37]

> It is an established rule of law that a person standing trial for an offence against the laws of the land may not oppose his being tried by reason of the illegality of his arrest or of the means whereby he was brought to the area of jurisdiction of the country. . . . [T]he contention of the accused against the jurisdiction of the Court by reason of his abduction from Argentina is in essence nothing but a plea for immunity by a fugitive offender on the strength of the refuge given him by a sovereign State.

Eichmann v. The Attorney-General of the Government of Israel [38]

After stating that it fully concurred in the holding and reasoning of the district court, the Supreme Court proceeded to develop arguments in different directions. It stressed that Eichmann could not claim to have been unaware at the time of his conduct that he was violating deeply rooted and universal moral principles. Particularly in its relatively underdeveloped criminal side, international law could be analogized to the early common law, which would be similarly open to charges of retroactive law making. Because the international legal system lacked adjudicatory or executive institutions, it authorized for the time being national officials to punish individuals for violations of its principles, either directly under international law or by virtue of municipal legislation adopting those principles.

The Court discounted Eichmann's argument that the Lotus decision, p. 885, supra, proscribed this extraterritorial application of the Israeli law. It read Lotus simply to require that a state, pursuant to the principle of territorial sovereignty, exercise its power to punish within its own borders. Subject to this restriction, Lotus authorized nations to exercise a wide discretion in applying their laws to acts committed outside their territory. Under Lotus, a state was prevented from applying its laws to certain conduct only if it were possi-

37. United Nations Security Council Resolution of June 23, 1960, Doc. S/4349 (1960), considered Argentina's complaint that the transfer of Eichmann to Israel had violated its sovereignty. In its preamble, the Security Council noted that it was "mindful . . . of the concern of people in all countries that Eichmann should be brought to appropriate justice for the crimes of which he is accused." The Council then declared that such acts may, "if repeated . . . endanger international peace and security," and requested Israel to make appropriate reparation to restore the friendly relations between the two countries. Apologies were in fact made.

38. Supreme Court sitting as Court of Criminal Appeals, May 29, 1962. This summary is based upon an English translation of the decision appearing in 36 Int'l.L.Rep. 14–17, 277 (1968).

ble to point to a specific rule of international law prohibiting the exercise of this discretion. Moreover, in this case Israel was the most appropriate jurisdiction for trial, a *forum conveniens* where witnesses were readily available. It was relevant that there had been no requests for extradition of Eichmann to other states for trial, or indeed protests by other states against a trial in Israel.

The Court affirmed the holding of the district court that each charge could be sustained. It noted, however, much overlap among the charges, and that all could be grouped within the inclusive category of "crimes against humanity."

QUESTIONS

(1) What were the alternatives to trial of Eichmann by the Israeli court? Would any international tribunal (the Nuremberg Tribunal having long since been dissolved) have been competent? Did the United Nations or any of its organs have competence to try Eichmann? Was it realistic to assume that another *ad hoc* international court such as the Nuremberg Tribunal could be organized? Would any other national court system have been preferable?

(2) Which if any of the Israeli charges against Eichmann raise troublesome issues with respect to their possible use as precedents for prosecutions in different contexts in other states?

(3) Do you agree with the interpretation given the Lotus case?

Additional reading: There is a vast literature on Nuremberg, the Eichmann case, and related problems. A good starting point is Taylor, Nuremberg and Vietnam: An American Tragedy (1970). Some basic references include U. S. Department of Defense, The Law of Land Warfare (FM 27–10) (1956); Silving, In re Eichmann, a Dilemma of Law and Morality, 55 Am.J.Int.L. 307 (1961); Woetzel, The Nuremberg Trials in International Law (with a postlude on the Eichmann Case) (1962).

PROBLEM

A Note, Extraterritorial Jurisdiction and Jurisdiction Following Forcible Abductions, 72 Mich.L.Rev. 1087 (1974), describes a recent Israeli military conviction:

> An Israeli military court recently convicted Faik Bulut, a twenty-three-year-old Turkish citizen, of the offense of belonging to Al-Fatah in Lebanon and Syria and sentenced him to seven years in prison. Bulut was captured in February 1972 during an Israeli raid 100 miles into Lebanon. Ten fedayeen, who were captured in Lebanon later in 1972, were scheduled to follow Bulut into court to be tried for the same offense. These are the first cases to be tried under a 1972 amendment to the Israeli Penal Law (Offenses Committed Abroad), which states in part: "The courts in Israel are competent to try under Israeli law a person who has committed abroad an act which would be an offense if it had been committed in Israel and which harmed or was intended to harm the State of Israel, its security, property or economy or its transport or communications links with other countries."
>
> The trials raise two important issues in international law. First, is there a substantive basis under international law for

the exercise of jurisdiction by the state of Israel despite the fact that the offenses were committed by nonnationals outside Israel? Second, is that exercise of jurisdiction consistent with international law despite the fact that the defendants were brought to Israel in a manner not condoned by international law? While these two issues will be analyzed separately, they are related: Both involve the relative freedom of an individual from the control of foreign legal systems.[39]

Consider the following questions:

(1) Assuming that membership in a Palestinian organization is not a crime under Lebanese law or under the laws of states with developed legal systems, is an Israeli conviction for the defined offenses consistent with the principles in the Harvard Research, p. 856, supra, or the Restatement?

(2) Would you view as sufficient an Israeli argument that the facts justified assertion of jurisdiction on the "universality" principle, by analogy to the offenses defined at Nuremberg, p. 904, supra.

NOTE ON VIETNAM, MY LAI AND THE CALLEY COURT MARTIAL

The extraordinary destructiveness of the Vietnamese war—a war involving the military forces of North and South Vietnam, the Viet Cong, and the United States—was the occasion for increasingly vocal charges that the participants, including the United States, violated the principles of Nuremberg which had become part of a customary and partly codified international law of war crimes. There were further charges of "crimes against peace" (in the Nuremberg sense), charges involving such issues as the justification for the American intervention, the character and meaning of earlier international accords, the relationship between North Vietnam and the Viet Cong, and the use of North Vietnamese troops in the South. Such charges had important consequences within this country, not only with respect to domestic political controversy and the resolution of American troop participation in the war, but also with respect to the military and civilian legal systems. This Note examines the charges of war crimes and the resulting courts-martial, concentrating upon the Calley case.

39. The domestic constitutionality of the Israeli statute and the validity of the convictions under the terms of the statute itself will be assumed; no attempt will be made to discuss those issues. The possibility that Bulut was a prisoner of war will also be left for other discussions. The Israeli military court found that Bulut was not a prisoner of war under article 4 of the Geneva Convention Relative to the Treatment of Prisoners of War, *opened for signature* August 12, 1949, [1956] 6 U.S.T. 3316, T.I.A.S. No. 3364, 75 U.N.T.S. 135, and that therefore the provisions of chapter III of that Convention (Penal and Disciplinary Sanctions) did not apply. In introducing the amendment under which Bulut was convicted to the Knesset and stressing its accordance with international law, the Israeli Minister of Justice noted that there was no intention to give competence to Israeli courts to try, for instance, Egyptian soldiers brought to Israel or representatives of weapons factories that sell weapons to Egypt or Jordan, exercises of jurisdiction that would be contrary to international law. *Diverey-Ha-Knesset* 2522 (Debates of the Knesset, in Hebrew), May 25, 1971.

We are here concerned with individual criminal responsibility. The cardinal fact in any such discussion is the absence of an international tribunal comparable to those at Nuremberg or Toyko. Hence the fora for trial of individuals were necessarily national—whether of the nationality of the soldier-defendant or of an enemy country which had captured the defendant. This national character of the tribunals had important consequences for the substance of the charges made, particularly those relating to "crimes against peace" and "aggressive war". With minor exceptions, such as certain proposals in the Genocide Convention, p. 574, supra, there had been no significant extensions since the Nuremberg and Toyko trials of concepts of personal criminal responsibility for violation of the laws of war.

The charges of war crimes asserted against the United States as a nation and against members of its armed forces included such varied aspects of our military operations as definitions of "free fire" and "free strike" zones that involved general risk to all persons within the designated areas; systematic spoliation of large portions of the countryside; and instances of military operations that involved the deliberate destruction of civilians as well as military forces. The most publicized of these episodes was that involving My Lai. The events at My Lai have been described as follows in Taylor, Nuremberg and Vietnam: An American Tragedy 126–129 (1970):

> What actually happened at Son My (better but inaccurately known as My Lai) in March of 1968 is and may well remain obscured by the fog of war, the passage of time, and the self-interest of surviving participants and observers. Especially in view of the criminal charges pending against a number of those involved, it is no part of the purpose of this book to point the finger of guilt at any individual. Whether the killings constituted a war crime is the question first to be examined and, for this purpose, it can be taken as undisputed that on March 16, 1968, American troops at Son My killed a large number of the village residents of both sexes and all ages. According to President Nixon, who presumably was well briefed: "What appears was certainly a massacre, under no circumstances was it justified. . . . We cannot ever condone or use atrocities against civilians . . . ."
>
> . . .
>
> The Son My killings took place in the course of a standard type of American military operation in Quang Ngai, the nature of which was a sudden lift of troops by helicopter, in and on all sides of a reported enemy unit, in an attempt to close a trap on it and destroy it. . . .
>
> . . .
>
> Consequently, when C Company of Task Force Barker went into Xom Lang that morning, expecting heavy opposition, it encountered none. The company had had little combat experience, and had recently suffered casualties from mines and boobytraps that had enraged and frightened the men; apparently there had been brutal and inexcusable killings of Vietnamese before the assault on Xom Lang.

What happened when the soldiers reached the dwellings is too well-known from newspaper and magazine photographs, and the accounts of numerous participants to warrant repetition. It appears certain that the troops had been told to destroy all the structures and render the place uninhabitable; what they had been told to do with the residents is not so clear. However that may be, the accounts indicate that C Company killed virtually every inhabitant on whom they could lay hands, regardless of age or sex, and despite the fact that no opposition or hostile behavior was encountered. There were few survivors, and based on the prior population of the area, the deaths attributable to C Company in Xom Lang and Binh Dong, together with other killings said to have been perpetrated a few hours later by a platoon of B Company a few miles to the east in the subhamlet My Hoi, amounted to about 500.

There was certainly nothing clandestine about the killings. About 80 officers and men went into the Xom Lang area on the ground. Above them, at various altitudes, were gunship, observation and command helicopters. There was constant radio communication between the various units and their superiors, and these were monitored at brigade headquarters. A reporter and a photographer from an Army Public Information Detachment went in with the troops and witnessed and recorded the course of events virtually from start to finish. The pilot of an observation helicopter, shocked by what he saw, reported the killings to brigade headquarters and repeatedly put his helicopter down to rescue wounded women and children. Command helicopters for the divisional, brigade and task force commanders were assigned air space over the field of action, and were there at least part of the time.

The massacre at My Lai produced demands for the punishment of those guilty. The earlier words of Justice Jackson, who had temporarily left his work at the Supreme Court to serve as United States Prosecutor at Nuremberg, were recalled: "If certain acts in violation of treaties are crimes, they are crimes whether the United States does them or whether Germany does them, and we are not prepared to lay down a rule of criminal conduct against others which we would not be willing to have invoked against us." [40]

Several soldier-participants in the My Lai operation were tried before courts-martial; one, Lieutenant Calley, was found guilty. The basis for those proceedings was found in the then operative Department of the Army Field Manual, The Law of Land Warfare, FM 27–10 (1956) and in the Uniform Code of Military Justice, 10 U.S.C.A. §§ 1–940. Relevant sections of the Field Manual provided:

40. International Conference on Military Trials, Dept. State Pub. No. 3880, p. 330. The legal framework for the debate over My Lai was complex and disputed. There were questions of what treaties or principles of customary law were applicable to the fighting in Indochina, since not all participants were parties to the relevant treaties. There were disputes over such factors as the civil or international character of the conflict, or distinctions between civilian or guerilla and military forces. Nonetheless, as pointed out by Taylor, p. 917, supra, the United States never denied that it was responsible for compliance with the inherited body of rules of the law of war.

498. Crimes Under International Law

Any person, whether a member of the armed forces or a civilian, who commits an act which constitutes a crime under international law is responsible therefor and liable to punishment. Such offenses in connection with war comprise:

a. Crimes against peace.

b. Crimes against humanity.

c. War crimes.

Although this manual recognizes the criminal responsibility of individuals for those offenses which may comprise any of the foregoing types of crimes, members of the armed forces will normally be concerned only with those offenses constituting "war crimes."

499. War Crimes

The term "war crime" is the technical expression for a violation of the law of war by any person or persons, military or civilian. Every violation of the law of war is a war crime.

505. Trials

. . .

d. How Jurisdiction Exercised. War crimes are within the jurisdiction of general courts-martial (UCMJ, Art. 18), military commissions, provost courts, military government courts, and other military tribunals (UCMJ, Art. 21) of the United States, as well as of international tribunals.

e. Law Applied. As the international law of war is part of the law of the land in the United States, enemy personnel charged with war crimes are tried directly under international law without recourse to the statutes of the United States. However, directives declaratory of international law may be promulgated to assist such tribunals in the performance of their function. (See pars. 506 and 507.)

507. Universality of Jurisdiction

a. Victims of War Crimes. The jurisdiction of United States military tribunals in connection with war crimes is not limited to offenses committed against nationals of the United States but extends also to all offenses of this nature committed against nationals of allies and of cobelligerents and stateless persons.

b. Persons Charged With War Crimes. The United States normally punishes war crimes as such only if they are committed by enemy nationals or by persons serving the interests of the enemy State. Violations of the law of war committed by persons subject to the military law of the United States will usually constitute violations of the Uniform Code of Military Justice and, if so, will be prosecuted under that Code. Violations of the law of war committed within the United States by other persons will usually constitute violations of federal or state criminal law and preferably will be prosecuted under such law (see pars. 505 and 506). Commanding officers of United States troops must insure that war crimes committed by members of their forces against enemy personnel are promptly and adequately punished.

509. Defense of Superior Orders

a. The fact that the law of war has been violated pursuant to an order of a superior authority, whether military or civil, does not deprive the act in question of its character of a war crime, nor does it constitute a defense in the trial of an accused individual, unless he did not know and could not reasonably have been expected to know that the act ordered was unlawful. In all cases where the order is held not to constitute a defense to an allegation of war crime, the fact that the individual was acting pursuant to orders may be considered in mitigation of punishment.

b. In considering the question whether a superior order constitutes a valid defense, the court shall take into consideration the fact that obedience to lawful military orders is the duty of every member of the armed forces; that the latter cannot be expected, in conditions of war discipline, to weigh scrupulously the legal merits of the orders received; that certain rules of warfare may be controversial; or that an act otherwise amounting to a war crime may be done in obedience to orders conceived as a measure of reprisal. At the same time it must be borne in mind that members of the armed forces are bound to obey only lawful orders (e. g., UCMJ, Art. 92).

The Field Manual (Sec. 506) noted that its provisions about war crimes were responsive to undertakings of the signatories to the Geneva Conventions of 1949 to enact legislation necessary to provide effective penal sanctions for persons committing "grave breaches" of those Conventions. Section 506 continued:

b. Declaratory Character of Above Principles. The principles quoted in *a,* above, are declaratory of the obligations of belligerents under customary international law to take measures for the punishment of war crimes committed by all persons, including members of a belligerent's own armed forces.

c. Grave Breaches. "Graves breaches" of the Geneva Conventions of 1949 and other war crimes which are committed by enemy personnel or persons associated with the enemy are tried and punished by United States tribunals as violations of international law.

If committed by persons subject to United States military law, these "grave breaches" constitute acts punishable under the Uniform Code of Military Justice. Moreover, most of the acts designated as "grave breaches" are, if committed within the United States, violations of domestic law over which the civil courts can exercise jurisdiction.

The UCMJ provides in Article 18 (10 U.S.C.A. § 818) that general courts-martial "have jurisdiction to try any person who by the law of war is subject to trial by a military tribunal and may adjudge any punishment permitted by the law of war." [41] Another relevant

41. Compare Ex Parte Quirin, 317 U.S. 1, 63 S.Ct. 1, 87 L.Ed. 3 (1942). Seven German saboteurs, with instructions to destroy war facilities, were landed in the United States in 1942 from a submarine and were soon apprehended in civilian dress. The President by proclamation ordered their trial by military commission for violation of the law of war, a charge subject to

section was Article 90 (10 U.S.C.A. § 890), providing for punishment of any person who "willfully disobeys a lawful command of his superior commissioned officer." The Calley court martial described below was in fact based upon Article 118 (10 U.S.C.A. § 918), stating that any person who "without justification or excuse, unlawfully kills a human being" intentionally, is guilty of murder.

At the court martial, there was evidence to support the charges that Lieutenant Calley had instructed those under his command to round up and kill with automatic fire a large group of unarmed, unresisting villagers of all ages, and had participated in the killing. He was convicted of murder and related charges and sentenced to dismissal and confinement at hard labor for life, a sentence soon reduced to confinement for twenty years. That conviction and sentence were approved by the Court of Military Review in the first appellate proceeding in United States v. Calley, 46 Court-Martial Rep. 1131 (1973). The court concluded that numerous statements about My Lai made by the President and such high-ranking officials as the Secretary of State, Secretary of the Army and Chief of Staff "had no influence on the Court members" and were not "generative of unlawful command influence." General Westmoreland, Chief of Staff, had declared that the killing of unarmed and non-combatant civilians was "strictly contrary to regulations and contrary to the instructions that were issued to the troops," and that an unlawful order from a superior "does not excuse or justify one of the soldiers in killing an innocent" civilian. The portions of the opinion treating the defense of "superior orders" and the amended sentence stated in part:

> Of the several bases for his argument that he committed no murder at My Lai because he was void of *mens rea*, appellant emphasized most of all that he acted in obedience to orders.
>
> Whether appellant was ever ordered to kill unresisting, unarmed villagers was a contested question of fact. The findings of a court-martial being in the nature of a general verdict, we do not know whether the court found that no such orders were given or, alternatively, concluded that the orders were given but were not exculpatory under the standards given to them in instructions.
>
> . . .
>
> If the members found that appellant fabricated his claim of obedience to orders, their finding was abundant support in the record. If they found his claim of acting in obedience to orders to be credible, he would nevertheless not

the death penalty. The Supreme Court upheld the President's order and found the military commission to be lawfully constituted. In its opinion, the Court held the charges against the seven to state violations of the law of war since the defendants were "unlawful combatants" (i. e., spies) rather than lawful and uniformed enemy soldiers entitled to be treated as prisoners of war. The Court also concluded that congressional legislation (the then Articles of War) granting to military commissions jurisdiction to try offenses "by the law of war" was constitutionally sufficient without congressional codification or precise specification of all such offenses.

automatically be entitled to acquittal. Not every order is exonerating.

The trial judge's instructions under which he submitted the issues raised by evidence of obedience to orders were entirely correct. After fairly summarizing the evidence bearing on the question, he correctly informed the members as a matter of law that any order received by appellant directing him to kill unresisting Vietnamese within his control or within the control of his troops would have been illegal; that summary execution of detainees is forbidden by law. A determination of this sort, being a question of law only, is within the trial judge's province. Article 51(b), UCMJ, 10 USC § 851(b); paragraph 57b, *Manual*, supra.

The instructions continued:

"The question does not rest there, however. A determination that an order is illegal does not, of itself, assign criminal responsibility to the person following the order for acts done in compliance with it. Soldiers are taught to follow orders, and special attention is given to obedience of orders on the battlefield. Military effectiveness depends upon obedience to orders. On the other hand, the obedience of a soldier is not the obedience of an automaton. A soldier is a reasoning agent, obliged to respond, not as a machine, but as a person. The law takes these factors into account in assessing criminal responsibility for acts done in compliance with illegal orders.

"The acts of a subordinate done in compliance with an unlawful order given him by his superior are excused and impose no criminal liability upon him unless the superior's order is one which a man of ordinary sense and understanding would, under the circumstances, know to be unlawful, or if the order in question is actually known to the accused to be unlawful."

Judge Kennedy amplified these principles by specifying the burden of proof and the logical sequence for consideration of the questions to be resolved. The members were told that if they found beyond reasonable doubt that appellant actually knew the orders under which he asserted he operated were illegal, the giving of the orders would be no defense; that the final aspect of the obedience question was more objective in nature, namely, that if orders to kill unresisting detainees were given, and if appellant acted in response thereto being unaware that the orders were illegal, he must be acquitted unless the members were satisfied beyond reasonable doubt that a man of ordinary sense and understanding would have known the orders to be unlawful.

. . .

Judge Kennedy's instructions were sound and the members' findings correct. An order of the type appellant says he received is illegal. Its illegality is apparent upon even cursory evaluation by a man of ordinary sense and understanding. A finding that it is not exonerating should not be disturbed. [citations omitted] Appellant's attempts to distinguish these cases fail. More candidly, he argues that they are all wrongly decided insofar as they import the objective standard of an order's illegality as would have been known by a man of ordinary sense and understanding. The argument is essentially that obedience to orders is a defense which strikes at *mens rea;* therefore in logic an obedient subordinate should be acquitted so long as he did not personally know of the order's illegality. Precedent aside, we would not agree with the argument. Heed must be given not only to subjective innocence-through-ignorance in the soldier, but to the consequences for his victims. Also, barbarism tends to invite reprisal to the detriment of our own force or disrepute which interferes with the achievement of war aims, even though the barbaric acts were preceded by orders for their commission. Casting the defense of obedience to orders solely in subjective terms of *mens rea* would operate practically to abrogate those objective restraints which are essential to functioning rules of war. The court members, after being given correct standards, properly rejected any defense of obedience to orders.

We find no impediment to the findings that appellant acted with murderous *mens rea*, including premeditation. The aggregate of all his contentions against the existence of murderous *mens rea* is no more absolving than a bare claim that he did not suspect he did any wrong act until after the operation, and indeed is not convinced of it yet. This is no excuse in law.

VIII—SENTENCE

In the report of the House Armed Services Investigating Subcommittee many of the extenuating circumstances affecting Lieutenant Calley are identified:

> "In a war such as that in Vietnam, our forces in the field must live for extended periods of time in the shadow of violent death and in constant fear of being crippled or maimed by booby traps and mines. And added to this is the fact that this is not war in the conventional sense. The enemy is often not in uniform. A farmer or a housewife or a child by day may well be the enemy by night, fashioning or setting mines and booby traps, or giving aid, comfort and assistance to the uniformed enemy troops. Under such circumstances, one can understand how it might become increasingly difficult for our troops to accept the idea that many of those who kill them by night somehow become 'innocent civilians' by day. Understandably such conditions can warp attitudes and mental processes causing temporary deviation from normality of action, reason or sense of values. And the degree of deviation may vary with each individual."

These general circumstances, and mitigating factors personal to Lieutenant Calley, were specifically considered by the convening authority who substantially reduced the confinement portion of the sentence to twenty years.

That decision was affirmed by the Court of Military Appeals, 22 U.S.C.M.A. 534, 48 C.M.R. 19 (1973) but the sentence was later reduced by the Secretary of the Army to 10 years. In its affirmance, the court found the trial judge's charge on superior orders to be adequate. It refused to accept as the governing test whether the order was so manifestly illegal that a person of "the commonest understanding" would be aware of the illegality. Even if Calley's captain had ordered him to kill, stated the court, there could be "no disagreement as to the illegality of the order to kill in this case . . . Whether Lieutenant Calley was the most ignorant person in the United States Army in Vietnam, or the most intelligent, he must be presumed to know that he could not kill the people involved here."

Calley then brought a petition in federal court seeking habeas corpus, and that court ordered that he be released from his confinement in United States Disciplinary Barracks. Calley v. Callaway, 382 F.Supp. 650 (M.D.Ga.1974). The district court concluded that Calley had been denied due process of law and hence that his conviction was constitutionally invalid. The opinion stressed the "massive and prejudicial publicity" preceding his military trials, which has cast a "pall of injustice" over the proceedings. Numbers of witnesses had communicated the essence of their testimony before military proceedings in advance to a range of communications media—press, periodicals, television and so on. Even some of the officers who sat in judgment on his case were exposed to "prejudicial pretrial publicity." It was as if the army itself were on trial. The court also concluded that Calley had been deprived of his constitutional right to confrontation with and subpoena of certain high-level witnesses whose testimony he had sought in his favor. The court concluded its opinion with the following observations:

> In World War II Churchill ordered the RAF nighttime saturation bombing of German cities, and Eisenhower had his bomber armada carry on the slaughter by day. Approximately a half million Germans were killed and a large percentage of this number were women and children. Yet Churchill was acclaimed as the great man of the Twentieth century and Eisenhower was twice elected President. Then Truman bombed Hiroshima, leaving 80,000 dead, most of whom were women and children, but he was later elected President. The airmen who dropped the bombs got medals and honorable discharges.
>
> . . .
>
> . . . [W]hen we take a young man into the Army and train him to kill and train him to take orders and send him into a strange foreign land to follow the flag and he then in the wild confusion of combat commits an act which, long after the event, is made the basis of a capital criminal charge, simple justice demands that he be treated fairly by the press, by his government and by the branch of the service in which he served. Sadly, it must be admitted that Calley was not accorded such consideration. Quite the contrary.
>
> He was pummelled and pilloried by the press.
>
> . . .
>
> His commander in chief publicly aligned himself with the prosecution.
>
> His government denied him access to evidence.
>
> His pleas to the Department of Justice went unanswered.
>
> His conviction was to be a cathartic to cleanse the national conscience and the impellent to improve the Army's image.

The decision of the district court to grant a writ of habeas corpus was reversed by the Fifth Circuit Court of Appeals, in an en banc decision (Calley v. Callaway, No. 74–3471) of Sept. 10, 1975. The circuit court restricted its review to the issues debated by the district court, and thus did not reach the substantive issues about war crimes that figured in the decisions of the appellate military tribunals. It concluded that Calley had received a fair trial and had not been deprived of "constitutional or fundamental rights."

PROBLEM

The 1956 Army Field Manual, supra, provides:

501. Responsibility for Acts of Subordinates

> In some cases, military commanders may be responsible for war crimes committed by subordinate members of the armed forces, or other persons subject to their control. Thus, for instance, when troops commit massacres and atrocities against the civilian population of occupied territory or against prisoners of war, the responsibility may rest not only with the actual perpetrators but also with the commander. Such a responsibility arises directly when the acts in question have been committed in pursuance of an order of the commander concerned. The commander is also responsible if he has actual knowledge, or should have knowledge, through reports received by him or through other means, that troops or other persons subject to his control are about to commit or have committed a war crime and he fails to take the necessary and reasonable steps to insure compliance with the law of war or to punish violators thereof.

In his book on Nuremberg and Vietnam, p. 917, supra, Telford Taylor, former United States prosecutor at Nuremberg. a retired brigadier general in the Army Reserve, and a professor at Columbia Law School, noted that "it should be emphasized that the consequence of allowing superior orders as a defense is not to eliminate criminal responsibility for what happened, but to shift its locus upwards." After referring to the sections of the Army Field Manual cited above, he recalled the Yamashita case and its principles, which were "of great importance in establishing the reach of criminal responsibility" for episodes such as those at My Lai. (pp. 52–53) In a television discussion program (as reported in the New York Times, Jan. 9, 1971, p. 3, col. 1), Professor Taylor noted that (commanding) General Westmoreland might be convicted of war crimes if the same standards established during World War II were applied to the General's administration of the Vietnam war:

> Professor Taylor implied, although he later declined to state so specifically, that similar verdict might ensue if some leading civilian officials of the Johnson Administration were tried, under other war crimes criteria established at Nuremberg, for war policies they had approved in Vietnam.
>
> In a book published last fall by Quadrangle Books, Professor Taylor had said the actions of the United States in Vietnam should be examined under the criteria established at Nuremberg and by the Yamashita precedent.

Mr. Cavett asked him if he had meant to suggest in the book that such men as the former Secretary of State, Dean Rusk; the former Defense Secretary, Robert S. McNamara, and the former Special Assistants to the President, McGeorge Bundy and Walt W. Rostow, should be brought to trial for war crimes.

"Well, I certainly suggest very strongly in the book and would be quite prepared to say it a little more explicitly that if you apply to the people you've mentioned, or to the high commanders at Nuremberg, like General Westmoreland, if you were to apply to them the same standards that were applied in the trial of General Yamashita, there would be very strong possibility that they would come to the same end as he did," Professor Taylor replied.

"Then you imply they would be found guilty?" Mr. Cavett asked.

"Could be found guilty," Professor Taylor replied.

. . .

Stanley Resor, the Secretary of the Army, had considered the Yamashita precedent "very closely" during the investigation of the Mylai case, in which more than 100 Vietnamese civilians were allegedly murdered, and had absolved General Westmoreland of responsibility under it. Mr. Resor had also later rejected a formal charge of war crimes under the Yamashita standard made against General Westmoreland by one of the Mylai defendants, Sgt. Esequiel Torres, the spokesman said.

Professor Taylor said in the telephone interview, however, that in his opinion what responsibility General Westmoreland could have for war crimes under the Yamashita precedent was not confined to the Mylai situation.

He said he considered "far more serious" than Mylai the civilian deaths caused by widespread bombing and shelling of Vietnamese hamlets in so-called free-fire zones, the forced evacuation of peasants from their hamlets and what he termed a failure to care adequately for the civilian casualties that resulted from this deliberate conduct of the war.

. . .

The only civilian leader to whom the Yamashita precedent might conceivably be applied, he said, would be Lyndon B. Johnson as Commander in Chief. Asked if he thought it ought to be applied to the former President, he said: "I don't think I want to answer that directly at this time."

. . .

In citing the Yamashita precedent as a standard that ought now to be applied, Professor Taylor said he was not specifically asserting that General Yamashita had been fairly tried and convicted. The Japanese general had presented considerable evidence that he lacked the communications to adequate control of his troops, but the American army commission said this failed to absolve him of responsibility. Yamashita's conviction was upheld by the United States Supreme Court.

"I do agree with the basic proposition that a general is responsible for controlling the conduct of his troops." Professor

Taylor said. "And I agree with the basic principle that a commander is liable for the conduct of his troops."

But he added: "All of these things that Yamashita did not have, like helicopters and radios and all that, Westmoreland and his commanders in Vietnam did have. They didn't have the problem of control that Yamashita had."

Consider the following questions:

(a) In view of the preceeding materials on the Vietnamese war, would you agree with the assertion that the Nuremberg principles were in fact "victor's law" without the necessary institutional or political base for consistent and objective enforcement in other settings?

(b) Professor Taylor mentioned a number of civilian officials to whom the principles of the post World War II trials might be applicable. What political or institutional possibilities were there for the trial of any such persons?

(c) What lessons do you draw from the *entire* Calley episode?

NOTE ON LITIGATION IN THE FEDERAL COURTS AND ALLEGED VIOLATIONS OF THE LAWS OF WAR

Unlike the courts-martial and the suggestions of trials of other military and civilian leaders for war-related crimes, the cases below do not involve personal criminal liability. Rather they involve efforts of defendants to resist induction orders during the Vietnam War or criminal prosecutions related to their anti-war activities. The defenses to the induction cases do not rest upon conscientious objection, but rather upon the assertion that the United States was committing war crimes or crimes against peace through the Vietnamese war and that individuals subject to induction might be forced into the personal commission of such crimes (with potential personal liability). The cases thus involve the types of constitutional-political issues discussed in Chapter V, particularly the absorption and incorporation of principles of international law into the domestic legal order.

The cases in this area raise general issues affecting the jurisdiction and competence of the federal courts.

(1) Standing: Courts have questioned whether defendants resisting induction had standing to rest on the defense that they would likely be implicated in war crimes if inducted and sent to Vietnam. The standing issue becomes more complicated for the defense related to aggressive war—given the precedents in the post World War II trials of restricting that criminal charge to the highest of policy makers.

(2) Ripeness: The defense of possible implication in war crimes also raised the issue of the ripeness of the claim, an issue no longer present when a soldier refuses to follow a combat order. On the other hand, a defense in a criminal prosecution that the war was illegal under international law, and hence that an induction order was without legal effect, would not present this legal obstacle.

(3) Political Questions. Recall the Note and the cases at pp. 132–141, supra, discussing aspects of political questions, particularly in the context of foreign relations. Those issues again become relevant to the cases below.

UNITED STATES v. SISSON

United States District Court, District of Massachusetts, 1968.
294 F.Supp. 515.

[There were several reported opinions of the District Court in this prosecution based on defendant's refusal to submit to induction into the armed forces, in violation of the Military Selective Service Act. In this opinion, defendant's motion to dismiss the indictment is at issue. Excerpts follow:]

WYZANSKI, CHIEF JUDGE. Defendant construes his motion to dismiss the indictment as including a contention that he is entitled to have the indictment dismissed on the ground that he is being ordered to fight in a genocidal war.

The issue of defendant's standing to raise the genocidal question and the issue whether the question is a question not within this Court's jurisdiction resemble the issues already considered by this Court in denying defendant's motion to dismiss the indictment on the ground that defendant has been ordered to fight in a conflict as to which Congress has not declared war. However, there are differences between the problems which the earlier motion presented and the ones now raised.

For argument's sake one may assume that a conscript has a standing to object to induction in a war declared contrary to a binding international obligation in the form of a treaty, in the form of membership in an international organization, or otherwise. One may even assume that a conscript may similarly object to being inducted to fight in a war the openly declared purpose of which is to wipe out a nation and drive its people into the sea. Conceivably, in the two situations just described, the conscript would have a standing to raise the issue and the court would be faced with a problem which was not purely a political question, but indeed fell within judicial competence.

The issue now tendered by this defendant is unlike either of the two cases just mentioned. At its strongest, the defendant's case is that a survey of the military operations in Vietnam would lead a disinterested tribunal to conclude that the laws of war have been violated and that, contrary to international obligations, express and implied, in treaty and in custom, the United States has resorted to barbaric methods of war, including genocide.

If the situation were as defendant contends, the facts would surely be difficult to ascertain so long as the conflict continues, so long as the United States government has reasons not to disclose all its military operations, and so long as a court was primarily dependent upon compliance by American military and civilian officials with its judicial orders. It should be remembered that the tribunal at Nuremberg, probably because it had a Russian judge, was unable to face up to the problems tendered by the Katyn massacres. Moreover, neither at Nuremberg nor at Tokyo, tribunals upon which an American judge sat, was there any attempt to resolve the problems raised by the nuclear bombing of Hiroshima and Nagasaki. It is inherent in a tribunal composed partly of judges drawn from the alleged offending nation that a wholly disinterested judgment is most unlikely to be achieved. With effort, self-discipline, and judicial training, men may transcend their personal bias, but few there are who in international disputes of magnitude are capable of entirely disregarding their political allegiance and acting solely with respect to legal considerations and ethical imperatives. If during hostilities a trustworthy, credible international judgment is to be rendered with respect to alleged national misconduct in war, representatives of the supposed offender must not sit in judgment upon the nation. An analogous path of reasoning must lead one to conclude that a domestic tribunal is entirely unfit to adjudicate the question whether there has been a violation of international law during a war by the very nation which created, manned, and compensated the tribunal seized of the case.

Because a domestic tribunal is incapable of eliciting the facts during a war, and because it is probably incapable of exercising a disinterested judgment which would command the confidence of sound judicial opinion, this Court holds that the defendant has tendered an issue which involves a so-called political question not within the jurisdiction of this Court. Cf. United States v. Mitchell, 369 F.2d 323 (2d Cir.).

The motion to dismiss the indictment is again denied.

. . .

UNITED STATES v. BERRIGAN

United States District Court, District of Maryland, 1968.
283 F.Supp. 336, aff'd 417 F.2d 1009 (4th Cir. 1969), cert. denied 397 U.S. 909, 90 S.Ct. 907, 25 L.Ed.2d 90 (1970).

NORTHROP, DISTRICT JUDGE. The defendants before this court are charged in three counts that they did willfully

1. injure property of the United States;
2. mutilate records filed in a public office of the United States; and
3. hinder the administration of the Military Selective Service Act.

Defendants wish to proffer an opening statement to the jury as to what they would present for their defense. Specifically, they contend that, by virtue of what they have read, heard, and seen, the war in Vietnam is immoral and illegal; and that the United States, in carrying on the war in Vietnam, is violating certain precepts of international law, constitutional law, and judgments which were handed down at Nurnberg.

To serve as a foundation and a basis for their beliefs, defendants wish to produce in court, among other evidence, "the outstanding experts" on international law who would testify that the acts of the United States government in Vietnam are illegal. Their conduct, they say, was prompted by their belief that the United States is acting illegally and was intended to prevent criminal acts from being committed. Because this belief prompted their acts, they argue that the necessary *mens rea* is lacking.

Initially, it must be pointed out that in law once the commission of a crime is established—the doing of a prohibited act with the necessary intent—proof of a good motive will not save the accused from conviction. . . .

. . .

That there is no legal precedent for defendants' proposition is not surprising. No civilized nation can endure where a citizen can select what law he would obey because of his moral or religious belief. It matters not how worthy his motives may be. It is axiomatic that chaos would exist if an individual were permitted to impose his beliefs upon others and invoke justification in a court to excuse his transgression of a duly-enacted law. . . .

. . .

The reasonableness of the belief of these defendants that the government is acting illegally in Vietnam is irrelevant to the present case; for, even if it were demonstrable that the United States is committing violations of international law, this violation by itself would afford the defendants no justifiable basis for their acts.

. . .

Finally, counsel contends that these defendants should be allowed to present to the jury what is popularly known as the "Nurnberg Defense." The trial of the Nazi war criminals at Nurnberg was premised on the generally accepted view that there are, as a part of international law, certain crimes against peace and humanity which are punishable. The Nurnberg Trial, 6 F.R.D. 69 (1946). It is urged here that the belief of these defendants that the United States was waging a war of aggression, and thus committing a crime against peace, justified the acts charged.

It is not clear what standing these defendants have to raise the legality of this country's involvement in Vietnam when they have not been called to serve in the armed forces, are not directly affected by our government's actions in that country, and are not even directly affected by the Selective Service apparatus. As pointed out by Judge Charles E. Wyzanski in an article in the February 1968 issue of the Atlantic Monthly:

> "As the Nuremberg verdicts show, merely to fight in an aggressive war is no crime. What is a crime is *personally* to fight by foul means." [Emphasis supplied.]

The important element in this defense, assuming its applicability in an American court, is the individual responsibility which is necessary before it can be raised. These defendants do not have standing to raise the validity of governmental actions, either under international law or constitutional law, on the grounds that the rights of parties not before this court are violated. . . .

. . .

But irrespective of the lack of standing of these defendants to raise the issue of the legality of the government's actions as they relate to the Vietnam situation, the proffered defense suffers from a more fundamental bar. It is clear that there are certain questions of substantive law, that is, "political questions", which are not cognizable in our courts because of the nature of our governmental system which is based upon a separation of functions among different branches of the government. . . . One such area in foreign relations. Baker v. Carr, supra, at 211, 82 S.Ct. at 691.

It is true that not every case which touches the foreign-relations power of the country is necessarily a "political question." Courts have usually decided the constitutional questions concerning international agreements, Reid v. Covert, 354 U.S. 1, 77 S.Ct. 1222, 1 L.Ed. 2d 1148 (1957), but the corresponding question of international law has been treated as a "political question."

The activities of these defendants were directed towards the Selective Service System, which system counsel has admitted is not criminal or illegal in and of itself. What is called into question here is the utilization of the armed forces by the executive and legislative branches. It cannot be disputed that the recognition of belligerency abroad, and the measures necessary to meet a crisis to preserve the peace and safety of this country, is uniquely an executive and a legislative responsibility. Whether the actions by the executive and the legislative branches in utilizing our armed forces are in accord with international law is a question which necessarily must be left to the elected representatives of the people and not to the judiciary. This is so even if the government's actions are contrary to valid treaties to which the government is a signatory. And the Supreme Court has held that Congress may constitutionally override treaties by later enactment of an inconsistent statute, even though the subsequent statute is in violation of international law.

The categorization of this defense as a "political question" is not an abdication of responsibility by the judiciary. Rather, it is a recognition that the responsibility is assumed by that level of government which under the Constitution and international law is authorized to commit the nation.

The "Nurnberg Defense" is premised on a finding that the government is acting in violation of international law in waging an aggressive war, and, as such, cannot be raised here because the question of violations of international law by the government is uniquely a "political" question.

Counsel will govern themselves accordingly, and the court's instructions to the jury will reflect this decision if any transgression makes it necessary.

QUESTIONS

(1) In his article cited below, Professor Falk notes the impossibility of convening an international tribunal to resolve any of the international-law issues raised by Vietnam. Hence, he argues, domestic courts must judge on the merits, in whatever context the cases may arise, issues such as war crimes and crimes against peace. Else, without judicial fora, the Nuremburg principles will become historical rhetoric, repudiated and forgotten. How do you react to this argument?

(2) Specifically, as counsel to defendant in a prosecution for failure to submit to the draft, what different lines of argument would you have developed, and what objections could you have anticipated to each of your defenses? Distinguish, for example, between assertions of potential personal criminal liability of the defendant and assertions of the illegality of the war under domestic and international law. Distinguish as well between defenses relating to war crimes and to aggressive war. Consider the distinct evidentiary and related issues, stemming in part from the doctrine of political questions, that are posed by each of these avenues of argument.

Additional reading: Taylor, Nuremberg and Vietnam: An American Tragedy (1970); Boudin, War Crimes and Vietnam: The Mote in Whose Eye, 84 Harv.L.Rev. 1940 (1971); D'Amato, Gould, and Woods, War Crimes and Vietnam: The "Nuremberg Defense" and the Military Service Resister, 57 Calif.L.Rev. 1055 (1969); Falk, Nuremberg: Past, Present, and Future, 80 Yale L.J. 1501 (1971); and Note, Command Responsibility for War Crimes, 82 Yale L.J. 1274 (1973).

Chapter IX

THE TRANSNATIONAL REACH OF ECONOMIC REGULATION

The problems posed when a nation's regulatory legislation in economic fields crosses national frontiers resemble those of Chapter VIII:

> **(1)** Most regulatory legislation gives courts or administrative agencies slight guidance as to when it should be applied to persons or events linked with other countries as well as the United States. Should Congress attempt to make these judgments? If so, under what standards?
>
> **(2)** Are these problems—often problems of conflicting efforts by several concerned nations to regulate—more amenable to solution by treaty than by national legislation?
>
> **(3)** Absent legislative or treaty specification, what considerations should shape the judgments of courts or administrative agencies whether to apply a regulatory statute to disputes of a transnational character?
>
> **(4)** Are there generally accepted principles of international law or the conflict of laws (so-called private as opposed to public international law) which help to delimit the reach of such legislation?

In the criminal cases, application of a statute to persons whose activities also involved another nation was unlikely to impinge upon important interests of that nation. In most of the situations that we considered, the two governments were apt to share in a general consensus among nations that criminal sanctions should be imposed upon persons committing homicide, theft, fraud and so on. Even in the Lotus situation, p. 885, supra, French and Turkish laws did not express significantly different policies, assuming that Lieutenant Demons had acted recklessly. Nor did the prosecutions in Wildenhus's case, p. 857, supra, or United States v. Bowman, p. 872, supra, threaten legitimate policies of other countries on criminal sanctions. The problem was not the "punishable" character of the conduct, but who should be competent to decide whether to punish.

In many fields of economic regulation, the problems become more complex: not only who should regulate, but what that regulation should be. Significant contrasts emerge between policies of different countries. Even nations with market-oriented economies reflect divergent approaches. The forms and substance of that regulation influence not only the development of the domestic economy but also a country's competitive position in the international community. Thus conflicting assertions of an exclusive right to regulate the same transnational activity are more likely to occur. Correspondingly the paths toward accommodation are harder to identify.

One further distinction should be noted. Modern regulatory statutes frequently involve complex administrative arrangements and a complex of interrelated substantive rules. They are not easily fragmented. Thus a court, in deciding whether a statute reaches particular persons or events, frequently must view the relevant provision in the setting of the entire statutory scheme. The question may become not whether a particular rule but whether the entire scheme should apply. The problems of maritime labor regulation, pp. 970–986, infra, are illustrative.[1]

Let us compare the problems of criminal and economic regulation from another perspective. Choice of law played a limited role in the criminal cases in Chapter VIII. The problem before the national court was to determine whether forum law (*lex fori*) reached a defendant's conduct, in view of the transnational character of the case. If not, judgment was entered for defendant, without recourse to a foreign law which had a sounder claim to govern.[2]

Although the civil cases in this chapter require modification of these observations, they remain in large part pertinent. Recall the hypothetical contract and tort actions set forth in the introductory Note on choice of law at p. 91, supra. In those illustrations, it was open to the courts of X or Y to apply either their own law or the law of the other jurisdiction. Both courts might have reached the same decision, to apply X or Y law, in which event a plaintiff's choice of forum would have been less significant. On the other hand, each might have decided to apply *lex fori*, so that different holdings would have followed from the plaintiff's choice of forum.[3] Their decision would have depended upon choice-of-law principles which each court followed and the manner in which those principles were applied. We briefly examine in Part A what those principles might be, and now stress only that choice is generally open to a court in such situations to draw upon *lex fori* or foreign law.

The cases in Parts B through F of this chapter, brought before either a court or an administrative agency, pose somewhat different problems. First, they involve statutes rather than common law. Second, those statutes are often complex schemes which regulate more than the particular conduct of a defendant at issue in the litigation. Third, the plaintiff in many cases was not a private party but the

1. In certain respects, the distinction stressed above between "criminal" and "economic" legislation may be blurred. Criminal sanctions may attach to violation of rules regulating economic conduct; "economic" crimes have become commonplace in such fields as antitrust law. It may often be difficult to determine whether criminal or civil sanctions pose the greater threat to a defendant.

2. See paragraph (2) at p. 854, supra.

3. For an extreme example of such a possibility, recall Fauntleroy v. Lum, p. 760, supra.

United States or an administrative agency, such as the National Labor Relations Board. Frequently the relief sought was a decree ordering the defendant to perform, or refrain from, certain acts. In such circumstances, choice of law in its full dimension is rarely operative. The governmental plaintiff seeks the enforcement of a regulatory statute of the forum, not of another nation. If a court or administrative agency concludes that the statute is not applicable, in view of the relationships of the parties or relevant events to the United States and other countries, it will dismiss the suit.

It is not inconceivable that a governmental authority would bring an action before a foreign court seeking money damages for, or requesting a court order to restrain violation of, a regulatory statute of its own country. But under prevailing doctrines, such a suit is not likely to succeed. Recall the comments at pp. 791–792, supra, indicating that courts will not generally entertain actions based on foreign legislation of a penal or fiscal character. Some of the regulatory statutes in this chapter express basic public policies and have punitive or fiscal aspects which offer some analogy to these other fields. In addition, the regulatory statutes considered below are often complex in substance and create complex administrative structures to realize their purposes. In such circumstances, drawing upon foreign law to resolve a controversy in the manner which that law contemplates may become too complicated a task for a court to handle. Such problems may indeed be insurmountable. Finally, notions of *forum non conveniens* may bar adjudication of such foreign-based claims. Even when the plaintiff is a private party, seeking monetary damages or equitable relief, the court may be unwilling to apply foreign law.[4]

The precise problem before the courts in the cases in Parts B to F of this Chapter was often the interpretation of a statute's spatial reach. That is, should a labor or antitrust or securities statute be construed to reach an alien defendant or to regulate acts which, in whole or part, occurred or produced significant effects outside this country? To this judgment, choice-of-law principles are undeniably relevant, even if choice of law in its traditional sense is not. Suppose, for example, that illustration (b) at p. 91, supra, involved statutes of X and Y defining the elements of a defamation action, rather than common law. Suppose—as is true of most statutes—that no legislative indication was given of their spatial reach. The same choice-of-law issue must be decided by the court in which plaintiff brought his action, now in a statutory context. In the cases below, it is as if the court in X or Y had only the option of determining whether or not its law applied.

A number of the opinions in regulatory cases explicitly invoke choice-of-law rules or principles. Others approach the question of statutory interpretation in a way reminiscent of choice-of-law think-

4. A number of cases below illustrate these comments, e. g., Lauritzen v. Larsen, p. 954, infra.

ing. To be sure, additional principles suggested by the criminal cases in Chapter VIII also become relevant: principles of international law and comity, ideas about reciprocity and retaliation, foreign-policy and other national concerns, and so on. But our effort in Part A below is to sketch some background against which the choice-of-law component in these cases can be recognized and critically dealt with.

A. INTRODUCTORY NOTIONS: THE UTILITY OF CHOICE-OF-LAW PRINCIPLES AND METHODOLOGY

The domestic field which we have chosen to illustrate a traditional and a developing choice-of-law methodology within the United States is that of tort. First, many of the statutory actions in this chapter are outgrowths of common-law torts, or their analogues in admiralty: seamen's remedies, fraud actions relating to the sale of securities, even antitrust actions. Thus the problems which they pose in determinations of their spatial reach suggest comparisons with tort more readily than other fields. Second, the developing methodology in choice of law has been particularly marked in tort cases which thus most vividly suggest the ways in which that methodology may be applied to the transnational cases below.

Like its rules in the field of contract [5], the Restatement of the Conflict of Laws of 1934 identified the choice of law in tort cases through certain facts which pointed toward the law of certain jurisdictions. The cardinal rule was *lex loci delicti.* Under Section 378, "The law of the place of wrong determines whether a person has sustained a legal injury." That place, under Section 377, was "the state where the last event necessary to make an actor liable for an alleged tort takes place." Most related issues—negligence or strict liability, causation, contributory negligence, vicarious liability and so on—were also referred to the *lex loci delicti.*

Unlike the contract rules, the *lex loci delicti* principle did command broad assent among the courts. One of its most powerful expressions was that of Justice Holmes, in Slater v. Mexican National R. R. Co., 194 U.S. 120, 126, 24 S.Ct. 581, 582, 48 L.Ed. 900, 902 (1904):

> . . . But when . . . a liability is enforced in a jurisdiction foreign to the place of the wrongful act, obviously that does not mean that the act in any degree is subject to the *lex fori,* with regard to either its quality or its consequences. On the other hand, it equally little means that the law of the place of the act is operative outside its own territory. The theory of the foreign suit is that although

5. See the discussion at pp. 502–504, supra.

the act complained of was subject to no law having force in the forum, it gave rise to an obligation, an *obligatio*, which, like other obligations, follows the person, and may be enforced wherever the person may be found. . . . But as the only source of this obligation is the law of the place of the act, it follows that that law determines not merely the existence of the obligation . . . but equally determines its extent. . . . [6]

Over the last decades, broad disaffection from the rule has developed, traceable in part to the often arbitrary results of its application. Again scholars were sharply critical of a methodology which resolved a variety of tort issues by blind reference to a particular jurisdiction's law—so-called "jurisdiction-selecting" rules.[7]

Those in the judicial, academic and practicing worlds who advocated change often shared little more than a rejection of the first Restatement and the decisional law on which it rested. Attempts to work out a new approach have made significant headway, but have yet to achieve any consensus among courts or writers. Consider the following effort to establish a new consensus, or at least to give some expression to the principal themes of the critics, in Restatement, Second, Conflict of Laws (1971):

§ 6. Choice-of-Law Principles

(1) A court, subject to constitutional restrictions, will follow a statutory directive of its own state on choice of law.

(2) When there is no such directive, the factors relevant to the choice of the applicable rule of law include (a) the needs of the interstate and international systems, (b) the relevant policies of the forum, (c) the relevant policies of other interested states and the relative interests of those states in the determination of the particular issue, (d) the protection of justified expectations, (e) the basic policies underlying the particular field of law, (f) certainty, predictability and uniformity of result, and (g) ease in the determination and application of the law to be applied.

§ 145. The General Principle

(1) The rights and liabilities of the parties with respect to an issue in tort are determined by the local law of the state which, with respect to that issue, has the most significant relationship to the occurrence and the parties under the principles stated in § 6.

(2) Contacts to be taken into account in applying the principles of § 6 to determine the law applicable to an issue include: (a) the place where the injury occurred, (b) the place where the conduct causing the injury occurred, (c) the domicil, residence,

6. [Eds.] Similar views are expressed in the opinion of Justice Holmes in American Banana Co. v. United Fruit Co., p. 1002, infra.

7. See, e. g., Cavers, A Critique of the Choice-of-Law Problem, 47 Harv.L. Rev. 173 (1933); Cavers, The Choice-of-Law Process 59–87 (1965); B. Currie, Survival of Actions: Adjudication versus Automation in the Conflict of Laws, 10 Stan.L.Rev. 205 (1958); von Mehren and Trautman, The Law of Multistate Problems 24–59, 102–148 (1965).

nationality, place of incorporation and place of business of the parties, and (d) the place where the relationship, if any, between the parties is centered.

These contacts are to be evaluated according to their relative importance with respect to the particular issue.

§ 146. Personal Injuries

In an action for a personal injury, the local law of the state where the injury occurred determines the rights and liabilities of the parties, unless, with respect to the particular issue, some other state has a more significant relationship under the principles stated in § 6 to the occurrence and the parties, in which event the local law of the other state will be applied.

Compare with the Restatement the following two decisions, leading examples of a new approach.

BABCOCK v. JACKSON

Court of Appeals of New York, 1963.
12 N.Y.2d 473, 191 N.E.2d 279, 240 N.Y.S.2d 743.

FULD, JUDGE. On Friday, September 16, 1960, Miss Georgia Babcock and her friends, Mr. and Mrs. William Jackson, all residents of Rochester, left that city in Mr. Jackson's automobile, Miss Babcock as guest, for a week-end trip to Canada. Some hours later, as Mr. Jackson was driving in the Province of Ontario, he apparently lost control of the car; it went off the highway into an adjacent stone wall, and Miss Babcock was seriously injured. Upon her return to this State, she brought the present action against William Jackson, alleging negligence on his part in operating his automobile.

At the time of the accident, there was in force in Ontario a statute providing that "the owner or driver of a motor vehicle, other than a vehicle operated in the business of carrying passengers for compensation, is not liable for any loss or damage resulting from bodily injury to, or the death of any person being carried in . . . the motor vehicle" (Highway Traffic Act of Province of Ontario [Ontario Rev.Stat. (1960), ch. 172], § 105, subd. [2]). Even though no such bar is recognized under this State's substantive law of torts . . . the defendant moved to dismiss the complaint on the ground that the law of the place where the accident occurred governs and that Ontario's guest statute bars recovery. The court at Special Term, agreeing with the defendant, granted the motion and the Appellate Division, over a strong dissent by JUSTICE HALPERN affirmed the judgment of dismissal without opinion.

The question presented is simply drawn. Shall the law of the place of the tort[8] *invariably* govern the availability of relief for the tort or shall the applicable choice of law rule also reflect a consideration of other factors which are relevant to the purposes served by the enforcement or denial of the remedy?

The traditional choice of law rule, embodied in the original Restatement of Conflict of Laws (§ 384), and until recently unquestion-

8. In this case, as in nearly all such cases, the conduct causing injury and the injury itself occurred in the same jurisdiction. The phrase "place of the tort," as distinguished from "place of wrong" and "place of injury," is used herein to designate the place where both the wrong and the injury took place.

ingly followed in this court . . . has been that the substantive rights and liabilities arising out of a tortious occurrence are determinable by the law of the place of the tort. . . . It had its conceptual foundation in the vested rights doctrine, namely, that a right to recover for a foreign tort owes its creation to the law of the jurisdiction where the injury occurred and depends for its existence and extent solely on such law. . . . Although espoused by such great figures as JUSTICE HOLMES (see Slater v. Mexican Nat. R. Co., 194 U.S. 120, 24 S.Ct. 581, 48 L.Ed. 900) and Professor Beale (2 Conflict of Laws [1935], pp. 1286–1292), the vested rights doctrine has long since been discredited because it fails to take account of underlying policy considerations in evaluating the significance to be ascribed to the circumstance that an act had a foreign situs in determining the rights and liabilities which arise out of that act. "The vice of the vested rights theory", it has been aptly stated, "is that it affects to decide concrete cases upon generalities which do not state the practical considerations involved". (Yntema, The Hornbook Method and the Conflict of Laws, 37 Yale L.J. 468, 482–483.) More particularly, as applied to torts, the theory ignores the interest which jurisdictions other than that where the tort occurred may have in the resolution of particular issues. It is for this very reason that, despite the advantages of certainty, ease of application and predictability which it affords . . . there has in recent years been increasing criticism of the traditional rule by commentators and a judicial trend towards its abandonment or modification. . . .

Realization of the unjust and anomalous results which may ensue from application of the traditional rule in tort cases has also prompted judicial search for a more satisfactory alternative in that area. In the much discussed case of Kilberg v. Northeast Airlines, Inc., 9 N.Y. 2d 34, 211 N.Y.S.2d 133, 172 N.E.2d 526, this court declined to apply the law of the place of the tort as respects the issue of the quantum of the recovery in a death action arising out of an airplane crash where the decedent had been a New York resident and his relationship with the defendant airline had originated in this State. In his opinion for the court, CHIEF JUDGE DESMOND described, with force and logic the shortcomings of the traditional rule . . . :

> "Modern conditions make it unjust and anomalous to subject the traveling citizen of this State to the varying laws of other States through and over which they move. . . . An air traveler from New York may in a flight of a few hours' duration pass through . . . commonwealths [limiting death damage awards]. His plane may meet with disaster in a State he never intended to cross but into which the plane has flown because of bad weather or other unexpected developments, or an airplane's catastrophic descent may begin in one State and end in another. The place of injury becomes entirely fortuitous. Our courts should if possible provide protection for our own State's people against unfair and anachronistic treatment of the lawsuits which result from these disasters."

The emphasis in Kilberg was plainly that the merely fortuitous circumstance that the wrong and injury occurred in Massachusetts did not give that State a controlling concern or interest in the amount of the tort recovery as against the competing interest of New York in providing its residents or users of transportation facilities there originating with full compensation for wrongful death. . . .

The "center of gravity" or "grouping of contacts" doctrine adopted by this court in conflicts cases involving contracts impresses us as likewise affording the appropriate approach for accommodating the competing interests in tort cases with multi-State contacts. Justice, fairness and "the best practical result" (Swift & Co. v. Bankers Trust Co., 280 N.Y. 135, 141, 19 N.E.2d 992, 995, supra) may best be achieved by giving controlling effect to the law of the jurisdiction which, because of its relationship or contact with the occurrence or the parties, has the greatest concern with the specific issue raised in the litigation. The merit of such a rule is that "it gives to the place 'having the most interest in the problem' paramount control over the legal issues arising out of a particular factual context" and thereby allows the forum to apply "the policy of the jurisdiction 'most intimately concerned with the outcome of [the] particular litigation'." (Auten v. Auten, 308 N.Y. 155, 161, 124 N.E.2d 99, 102 . . . .)

Such, indeed, is the approach adopted in the most recent revision of the Conflict of Laws Restatement in the field of torts.

Comparison of the relative "contacts" and "interests" of New York and Ontario in this litigation, vis-a-vis the issue here presented, makes it clear that the concern of New York is unquestionably the greater and more direct and that the interest of Ontario is at best minimal. The present action involves injuries sustained by a New York guest as the result of the negligence of a New York host in the operation of an automobile, garaged, licensed and undoubtedly insured in New York, in the course of a week-end journey which began and was to end there. In sharp contrast, Ontario's sole relationship with the occurrence is the purely adventitious circumstance that the accident occurred there.

New York's policy of requiring a tort-feasor to compensate his guest for injuries caused by his negligence cannot be doubted—as attested by the fact that the Legislature of this State has repeatedly refused to enact a statute denying or limiting recovery in such cases . . . and our courts have neither reason nor warrant for departing from that policy simply because the accident, solely affecting New York residents and arising out of the operation of a New York based automobile, happened beyond its borders. Per contra, Ontario has no conceivable interest in denying a remedy to a New York guest against his New York host for injuries suffered in Ontario by reason of conduct which was tortious under Ontario law. The object of Ontario's guest statute, it has been said, is "to prevent the fraudulent assertion of claims by passengers, in collusion with the drivers, against insurance companies" (Survey of Canadian Legislation, 1 U.Toronto L.J. 358, 366) and, quite obviously, the fraudulent claims intended to be prevented by the statute are those asserted against Ontario defendants and their insurance carriers, not New York defendants and their insurance carriers. Whether New York defendants are imposed upon or their insurers defrauded by a New York plaintiff is scarcely a valid legislative concern of Ontario simply because the accident occurred there, any more so than if the accident had happened in some other jurisdiction.

It is hardly necessary to say that Ontario's interest is quite different from what it would have been had the issue related to the manner in which the defendant had been driving his car at the time of the accident. Where the defendant's exercise of due care in the operation of his automobile is in issue, the jurisdiction in which the allegedly wrongful conduct occurred will usually have a predominant, if not exclusive, concern. In such a case, it is appropriate to look to the law of the place of the tort so as to give effect to that jurisdiction's interest in regulating conduct within its borders, and it would be almost unthinkable to seek the applicable rule in the law of some other place.

. . . Although the rightness or wrongness of defendant's conduct may depend upon the law of the particular jurisdiction through which the automobile passes, the rights and liabilities of the parties which stem from their guest-host relationship should remain constant and not vary and shift as the automobile proceeds from place to place. . . .

In conclusion, then, there is no reason why all issues arising out of a tort claim must be resolved by reference to the law of the same jurisdiction. Where the issue involves standards of conduct, it is more than likely that it is the law of the place of the tort which will be controlling but the disposition of other issues must turn, as does the issue of the standard of conduct itself, on the law of the jurisdiction which has the strongest interest in the resolution of the particular issue presented.

The judgment appealed from should be reversed, with costs, and the motion to dismiss the complaint denied.

VAN VOORHIS, JUDGE (dissenting).

. . .

Any idea is without foundation that cases such as the present render more uniform the laws of torts in the several States of the United States. Attempts to make the law or public policy of New York State prevail over the laws and policies of other States where citizens of New York State are concerned are simply a form of extraterritoriality which can be turned against us wherever actions are brought in the courts of New York which involve citizens of other States. This is no substitute for uniform State laws or for obtaining uniformity by covering the subject by Federal law. Undoubtedly ease of travel and communication, and the increase in interstate business have rendered more awkward discrepancies between the laws of the States in many respects. But this is not a condition to be cured by introducing or extending principles of extraterritoriality, as though we were living in the days of the Roman or British Empire, when the concepts were informed that the rights of a Roman or an Englishman were so significant that they must be enforced throughout the world even where they were otherwise unlikely to be honored by "lesser breeds without the law." Importing the principles of extraterritoriality into the conflicts of laws between the States of the United States can only make confusion worse confounded. If extraterritoriality is to be the criterion, what would happen, for example, in case of an automobile accident where some of the passengers came from or were picked up in States or countries where causes of action against the driver were prohibited, others where gross negligence needed to be shown, some, perhaps, from States where contributory negligence and others where comparative negligence prevailed? . . .

In my view there is no overriding consideration of public policy which justifies or directs this change in the established rule or renders necessary or advisable the confusion which such a change will introduce. . . .

NEUMEIER v. KUEHNER

Court of Appeals of New York, 1972.
31 N.Y.2d 121, 286 N.E.2d 454, 335 N.Y.S.2d 64.

CHIEF JUDGE FULD. A domiciliary of Ontario, Canada, was killed when the automobile in which he was riding, owned and driven by a New York resident, collided with a train in Ontario. That jurisdiction has a guest statute, and the primary question posed by this appeal is whether in this action brought by the Ontario passenger's estate, Ontario law should be applied and the New York defendant permitted to rely on its guest statute as a defense.

The facts are quickly told. On May 7, 1969, Arthur Kuehner, the defendant's intestate, a resident of Buffalo, drove his automobile from that city to Fort Erie in the Province of Ontario, Canada, where he picked up Amie Neumeier, who lived in that town with his wife and their children. Their trip was to take them to Long Beach, also in Ontario, and back again to Neumeier's home in Fort Erie. However, at a railroad crossing in the Town of Sherkston—on the way to Long Beach—the auto was struck by a train of the defendant Canadian National Railway Company. Both Kuehner and his guest-passenger were instantly killed.

Neumeier's wife and administratrix, a citizen of Canada and a domiciliary of Ontario, thereupon commenced this wrongful death action in New York against both Kuehner's estate and the Canadian National Railway Company. The defendant estate pleaded, as an affirmative defense, the Ontario guest statute and the defendant railway also interposed defenses in reliance upon it. In substance, the statute provides that the owner or driver of a motor vehicle is not liable for damages resulting from injury to, or the death of, a guest-passenger unless he was guilty of gross negligence. . . . It is worth noting, at this point, that, although our court originally considered that the sole purpose of the Ontario statute was to protect Ontario defendants and their insurers against collusive claims (see Babcock v. Jackson, 12 N.Y.2d 473, 482–483), "Further research . . . has revealed the distinct possibility that one purpose, and perhaps the only purpose, of the statute was to protect owners and drivers against suits by ungrateful guests." (Reese, Choice of Law, 71 Col.L.Rev. 548, 558; see Trautman, Two Views on Kell v. Henderson: A Comment, 67 Col.L.Rev. 465, 469.)

The plaintiff, asserting that the Ontario statute "is not available . . . in the present action", moved, pursuant to CPLR 3211 (subd. [b]), to dismiss the affirmative defenses pleaded. The court at Special Term, holding the guest statute applicable, denied the motions (63 Misc.2d 766) but, on appeal, a closely divided Appellate Division reversed and directed dismissal of the defenses (37 A.D.2d 70). It was the court's belief that this result was dictated by Tooker v. Lopez (24 N.Y.2d 569).

In reaching that conclusion, the Appellate Division misread our decision in the Tooker case—a not unnatural result in light of the variant views expressed in the three separate opinions written on behalf of the majority. It is important to bear in mind that in Tooker, the guest-passenger and the host-driver were both domiciled in New York, and our decision—that New York law was controlling—was based upon, and limited to, that fact situation. . . .

What significantly and effectively differentiates the present case is the fact that, although the host was a domiciliary of New York, the guest, for whose death recovery is sought, was domiciled in Ontario, the place of accident and the very jurisdiction which had enacted the statute designed to protect the host from liability for ordinary negligence. It is clear that, although New York has a deep interest in protecting its own residents, injured in a foreign state, against unfair or anachronistic statutes of that state, it has no legitimate interest in ignoring the public policy of a foreign jurisdiction—such as Ontario—and in protecting the plaintiff guest domiciled and injured there from legislation obviously addressed, at the very least, to a resident riding in a vehicle traveling within its borders.

To distinguish Tooker on such a basis is not improperly discriminatory. It is quite true that, in applying the Ontario guest statute to the Ontario-domiciled passenger, we, in a sense, extend a right less generous than New York extends to a New York passenger in a New York vehicle with New York insurance. That, though, is not a consequence of invidious discrimination; it is, rather, the result of the existence of disparate rules of law in jurisdictions that have diverse and important connections with the litigants and the litigated issue.

The fact that insurance policies issued in this State on New York-based vehicles cover liability, regardless of the place of the accident (Vehicle and Traffic Law, § 311, subd. 4), certainly does not call for the application of internal New York law in this case. The compulsory insurance requirement is designed to *cover* a car-owner's liability, not *create* it; in other words, the applicable statute was not intended to impose liability where none would otherwise exist. This being so, we may not properly look to the New York insurance requirement to dictate a choice-of-law rule which would invariably impose liability.

. . . In consequence of the change effected [in Babcock v. Jackson]—and this was to be anticipated—our decisions in multistate highway accident cases, particularly in those involving guest-host controversies, have, it must be acknowledged, lacked consistency. This stemmed, in part, from the circumstance that it is frequently difficult to discover the purposes or policies underlying the relevant local law rules of the respective jurisdictions involved. It is even more difficult, assuming that these purposes or policies are found to conflict, to determine on some principled basis which should be given effect at the expense of the others.

The single all-encompassing rule which called, inexorably, for selection of the law of the place of injury was discarded, and wisely, because it was too broad to prove satisfactory in application. There is, however, no reason why choice-of-law rules, more narrow than those previously devised, should not be successfully developed, in order to assure a greater degree of predictability and uniformity, on the basis of our present knowledge and experience. . . . Babcock and its progeny enable us to formulate a set of basic principles that may be profitably utilized, for they have helped us uncover the underlying values and policies which are operative in this area of the law. To quote again from the concurring opinion in Tooker (p. 584), "Now that these values and policies have been revealed, we may proceed to the next stage in the evolution of the law—the formulation of a few rules of general applicability, promising a fair level of predictability." Although it was recognized that no rule may be formulated to guarantee a satisfactory result in every case, the following principles were proposed as sound for situations involving guest statutes in conflicts settings (24 N.Y.2d, at p. 585):

"1. When the guest-passenger and the host-driver are domiciled in the same state, and the car is there registered, the law of that state should control and determine the standard of care which the host owes to his guest.

"2. When the driver's conduct occurred in the state of his domicile and that state does not cast him in liability for that conduct, he should not be held liable by reason of the fact that liability would be imposed upon him under the tort law of the state of the victim's domicile. Conversely, when the guest was injured in the state of his own domicile and its law permits recovery, the driver who has come into that state should not—in the absence of special circumstances—be permitted to interpose the law of his state as a defense.

"3. In other situations, when the passenger and the driver are domiciled in different states, the rule is necessarily less categorical. Normally, the applicable rule of decision will be that of the state where the accident occurred but not if it can be shown that displacing that normally applicable rule will advance the relevant substantive law purposes without impairing the smooth working of the multistate system or producing great uncertainty for litigants. (Cf. Restatement, 2d, Conflict of Laws, P.O.D., pt. II, §§ 146, 159 [later adopted and promulgated May 23, 1969].)"

The variant views expressed not only in Tooker but by Special Term and the divided Appellate Division in this litigation underscore and confirm the need for these rules. Since the passenger was domiciled in Ontario and the driver in New York, the present case is covered by the third stated principle. The law to be applied is that of the jurisdiction where the accident happened unless it appears that "displacing [the] normally applicable rule will advance the relevant substantive law purposes" of the jurisdictions involved. Certainly, ignoring Ontario's policy requiring proof of gross negligence in a case which involves an Ontario-domiciled guest at the expense of a New Yorker does not further the substantive law purposes of New York. In point of fact, application of New York law would result in the exposure of this State's domiciliaries to a greater liability than that imposed upon resident users of Ontario's highways. Conversely, the failure to apply Ontario's law would "impair"—to cull from the rule set out above—"the smooth working of the multi-state system [and] produce great uncertainty for litigants" by sanctioning forum shopping and thereby allowing a party to select a forum which could give him a larger recovery than the court of his own domicile. In short, the plaintiff has failed to show that this State's connection with the controversy was sufficient to justify displacing the rule of *lex loci delictus*.

. . .

In each action, the Appellate Division's order should be reversed, that of Special Term reinstated, without costs, and the questions certified answered in the negative.

NOTE ON THE DEVELOPING METHODOLOGY

Contemporary approaches to choice of law in cases such as Babcock and Neumeier develop a significantly different intellectual framework within which the issue before a court is to be thought about and resolved. It is not a matter of finding a "connecting fact," such as the place of contract or tort, which in turn invokes a "jurisdiction-selecting" rule. Rather the court looks to the "interests," "purposes," "policies," and "concerns" of the states to which the transaction or parties are related. Thus the Babcock opinion states that justice and the best practical result "may best be achieved by giving controlling effect to the law of the jurisdiction which, because of its relationship or contact with the occurrence or the parties, has the greatest concern with the specific issue raised in the litigation." The opinion compares the contacts and interests of New York and Ontario and attempts to state the purposes of guest statutes.

Some of these terms contain significant ambiguities. The word "interest," for example, is used by courts and writers to express a variety of meanings. Sometimes it appears synonymous with the policies or purposes reflected in a rule. Sometimes it appears to mean the specific reason for which a state may desire its rule to govern a particular interstate or transnational situation. Generally the term is used to signify "governmental interests." That is, it reflects a public rather than a private perspective upon a problem, the judicial or legislative reasons for developing a rule. Sometimes a court may be attentive both to governmental *and* private interests—perhaps the interest of a participant in interstate or transnational activity in being able to act with a reasonable ability to foresee the consequences of his action, or in being permitted to conduct interstate or transnational activities without undue interference by each concerned jurisdiction. Note however that these cases, characteristic in this respect of the recent decisions, do not attempt to define a community perspective or interest relevant to the litigation—perhaps a national or federal interest in a well-functioning federalism which permits individuals or companies to conduct their affairs without becoming arbitrarily subject to a particular state's laws. Some of the decisions below—particularly Lauritzen v. Larsen, p. 954, infra—do make the effort in an international setting to determine broader community policies which may help to indicate the applicable law.

One theme common to the recent decisions, Restatement, Second, and scholarly writing is a stress upon purpose. The court, before determining which law to apply, must consider what the competing laws seek to accomplish. Choice of law becomes, in brief, a teleological process. Its methods strive to relate solutions in a purposive manner to particular controversies. Its principles often draw inspiration from, and in turn advance the policies of, underlying substantive laws. Inevitably, viewing choice of law as a purposive process will breed skepticism about taut rules that produce seemingly easy, ultimately uneasy, solutions.

But purposes may not be easily identifiable, whether with respect to common law rules of considerable antiquity or new legislative enactments. Note, for example, the changing views of the purpose of the Ontario Statute in Babcock and Neumeier. Moreover, purposes are often plural, expressing a series of related or perhaps unrelated concerns which, within a particular jurisdiction, may combine to suggest development of the common law rule or legislation. Consider, for example, the difficulty in articulating one clear "purpose" for a statute of frauds or a statute of limitations. When choice of law is the issue, it may be necessary to select among these plural or ambiguous purposes that which appears most relevant to the particular litigation.

Assuming a court's ability to identify with some clarity the relevant interests and purposes, the difficult decision remains. Babcock was in a sense an "easy" decision. On the facts before it, the court was able to point convincingly to one jurisdiction's law. But under other facts, suggested in the questions below and indeed present in Neumeier, judgment would have been more complex. Some considerations would have pointed towards one jurisdiction's law, some to another's. Most important, genuine conflicts may appear between the laws of two or more concerned states. In view of the purposes expressed by their different rules and their interest in applying those rules to an interstate or transnational situation, each state may have a legitimate claim to govern. The final task—inescapable in many cases in this chapter—becomes the accommodation of these conflicting interests. Some of the dimensions of that task are suggested by the opinion in Neumeier. Consider from this perspective the following comments, which foreshadow the later parts of this chapter.[9]

> If human society were so organized that all aspects of life moved within economic, social, legal, and political spheres that were unitary and coextensive, the problems dealt with through choice of law would never arise. In primitive societies, economic, political, and social activity is often so confined: the tribe, family, or village furnish the basic—and almost exclusively relevant—unit for all aspects of human activity. In such an organizational framework, the motivations and principles affecting human conduct will be viewed largely from a single perspective. In the contemporary world, however, individuals and enterprises often participate in the affairs of several communities; a single course of conduct may be viewed in differing economic, social, and political terms by each of the communities to which the activity is in some sense related. The discipline of choice of law is concerned with the identification and systematic handling of situations in which the persons concerned and the interests and policies at stake have significant connections with more than one community.
>
> Even when the justice and wisdom of the various possible regulations of any particular situation are to be tested solely from the perspective of a single politically organized society, perplexing and difficult problems are often encountered. These problems are also present where situations or transactions are significantly connected with more than one society; but here a broader range of policies, as well as a greater variety of policy combinations, must frequently be taken into account. Consequently, even if a

9. von Mehren, Special Substantive Rules for Multistate Problems: Their Role and Significance in Contemporary Choice of Law Methodology, 88 Harv.L.Rev. 347, 349–50 (1974).

single, overarching political authority were charged with regulating multistate transactions, great difficulty would frequently be encountered in achieving a wise and just accommodation of the interests of the various concerned communities and in appropriately taking into account the legitimate expectations of the persons involved. Shared perceptions of justice depend upon a sharing of relevant values; as the standards with which individual communities evaluate a given issue diverge, agreement upon what constitutes a substantively just resolution becomes increasingly unlikely. And since the expectations and perceptions of justice of the individuals involved in such situations are shaped by their experience in communities with differing practices and values, at least some of those expectations and perceptions will necessarily be disappointed. Accordingly, even if multistate problems were litigated before international tribunals, the concerned societies and the involved individuals would frequently consider the results less just and less wise than those reached for problems set within a single state.

The problem of achieving just and wise results is further complicated by the fact that, with very few exceptions, multistate problems are handled in courts that exercise jurisdiction for only a single legal system. . . .

Situations of conflict can arise—as the questions below suggest—even when all the events occur within one jurisdiction. That is, in cases such as Babcock and Neumeier, the defendants committed their allegedly tortious acts and plaintiffs suffered their injuries within the same province or state. Conflict in national policies or interests, in claims to an exclusive right to govern, becomes the more likely as these incidents of a common-law tort or of a statutory action are divided among the concerned jurisdictions: blasting in one state which injures property in another; price-fixing in one nation which affects imports of the relevant product in another. Most of the cases in this chapter fall partly or wholly within this second category.

QUESTIONS

(1) In Babcock v. Jackson, should an Ontario court have reached the same result as the New York court?

(2) Reverse the pattern of laws of New York and Ontario. What problems? What decision of a New York or Ontario court?

(3) Suppose that Jackson had left Rochester on a summer trip to California. He stopped in the State of Ames, which has a guest statute similar to Ontario's, to pick up his friend Smith at his home. An accident injuring Smith occurs in the State of Langdell, whose laws provide that a guest can recover only on a showing of "gross negligence." No such showing can be made in this case.

(*a*) Smith sues Jackson in New York. What problems and what decision?

(*b*) Smith sues Jackson in Ames. What problems and what decision?

(4) What arguments stemming from the problems in Neumeier and the cases to which it refers would you make for adhering to the rules of the 1934 Restatement? Do they convince you?

B. WELFARE LEGISLATION FOR SEAMEN

STRATHEARN STEAMSHIP CO., LTD. v. DILLON

Supreme Court of the United States, 1920.
252 U.S. 348, 40 S.Ct. 350, 64 L.Ed. 607.

MR. JUSTICE DAY delivered the opinion of the Court.

This case presents questions arising under the Seamen's Act of March 4, 1915, 38 Stat. 1164. It appears that Dillon, the respondent, was a British subject, and shipped at Liverpool on the eighth of May, 1916, on a British vessel. The shipping articles provided for a voyage of not exceeding three years, commencing at Liverpool and ending at such port in the United Kingdom as might be required by the master, the voyage including ports of the United States. The wages which were fixed by the articles were made payable at the end of the voyage. At the time of the demand for one-half wages, and at the time of the beginning of the action, the period of the voyage had not been reached. The articles provided that no cash should be advanced abroad or liberty granted other than at the pleasure of the master. This, it is admitted, was a valid contract for the payment of wages under the laws of Great Britain. The ship arrived at the Port of Pensacola, Florida, on July 31, 1916, and while she was in that port, Dillon, still in the employ of the ship, demanded from her master one-half part of the wages theretofore earned, and payment was refused. Dillon had received nothing for about two months, and after the refusal of the master to comply with his demand for one-half wages, he filed in the District Court of the United States a libel against the ship, claiming $125.00, the amount of wages earned at the time of demand and refusal.

The District Court found against Dillon upon the ground that his demand was premature. The Circuit Court of Appeals reversed this decision, and held that Dillon was entitled to recover. 256 Fed. 631, 168 C.C.A. 25. A writ of certiorari brings before us for review the decree of the Circuit Court of Appeals.

In Sandberg v. McDonald, 248 U.S. 185, 39 S.Ct. 84, 63 L.Ed. 200, and Neilson v. Rhine Shipping Co., 248 U.S. 205, 39 S.Ct. 89, 63 L.Ed. 208, we had occasion to deal with section 11 of the Seamen's Act (Comp.St. § 8323), and held that it did not invalidate advancement of seamen's wages in foreign countries when legal where made. The instant case requires us to consider now section 4 of the same act. That section amends section 4530, U. S. Revised Statutes, and so far as pertinent provides:

> "Section 4530. Every seaman on a vessel of the United States shall be entitled to receive on demand from the master of the vessel to which he belongs one-half part of the wages which he shall have then earned at every port where such vessel, after the voyage has been commenced, shall load or deliver cargo before the voyage is ended and all stipulations in the contract to the contrary shall be void: Provided, such a demand shall not be made before the expiration of, nor oftener than once in five days. Any failure on the part of the master to comply with this demand shall release the seaman from his contract and he shall be entitled to full payment of wages earned. . . . And provided further, that this section shall apply to seamen on foreign vessels

> while in harbors of the United States, and the courts of the United States shall be open to such seamen for its enforcement." Comp.St. § 8322. . . .

The section, of which the statute now under consideration is an amendment, expressly excepted from the right to recover one-half of the wages those cases in which the contract otherwise provided. In the amended section all such contract provisions are expressly rendered void, and the right to recover is given the seamen notwithstanding contractual obligations to the contrary. The language applies to all seamen on vessels of the United States, and the second proviso of the section as it now reads makes it applicable to seamen on foreign vessels while in harbors of the United States. The proviso does not stop there, for it contains the express provision that the courts of the United States shall be open to seamen on foreign vessels for its enforcement. The latter provision is of the utmost importance in determining the proper construction of this section of the act. It manifests the purpose of Congress to give the benefit of the act to seamen on foreign vessels, and to open the doors of the federal courts to foreign seamen. . . .

It is said that it is the purpose to limit the benefit of the act to American seamen, notwithstanding this provision giving access to seamen on foreign vessels to the courts of the United States, because of the title of the act in which its purpose is expressed "to promote the welfare of American seamen in the merchant marine of the United States." . . . But the title of an act cannot limit the plain meaning of its text, although it may be looked to to aid in construction in cases of doubt. Cornell v. Coyne, 192 U.S. 418, 530, 24 S.Ct. 383, 48 L.Ed. 504, and cases cited. Apart from the text, which we think plain, it is by no means clear that if the act were given a construction to limit its application to American seamen only, the purposes of Congress would be subserved, for such limited construction would have a tendency to prevent the employment of American seamen, and to promote the engagement of those who were not entitled to sue for one-half wages under the provisions of the law. But, taking the provisions of the act as the same are written, we think it plain that it manifests the purpose of Congress to place American and foreign seamen on an equality of right in so far as the privileges of this section are concerned, with equal opportunity to resort to the courts of the United States for the enforcement of the act. Before the amendment, as we have already pointed out, the right to recover one-half the wages could not be enforced in face of a contractual obligation to the contrary. Congress, for reasons which it deemed sufficient, amended the act so as to permit the recovery upon the conditions named in the statute. In the case of Sandberg v. McDonald, 248 U.S. 185, 39 S.Ct. 84, 63 L.Ed. 200, supra, we found no purpose manifested by Congress in section 11 to interfere with wages advanced in foreign ports under contracts legal where made. That section dealt with advancements, and contained no provision such as we find in section 4. Under section 4 all contracts are avoided which run counter to the purposes of the statute. Whether consideration for contractual rights under engagements legally made in foreign countries would suggest a different course is not our province to inquire. It is sufficient to say that Congress has otherwise declared by the positive terms of this enactment, and if it had authority to do so, the law is enforceable in the courts.

We come then to consider the contention that this construction renders the statute unconstitutional as being destructive of contract rights. But . . . . we have no doubt as to the authority of

Congress to pass a statute of this sort, applicable to foreign vessels in our ports and controlling the employment and payment of seamen as a condition of the right of such foreign vessels to enter and use the ports of the United States. . . .

We find no error in the decree of the Circuit Court of Appeals and the same is

Affirmed.

NOTE ON THE SEAMEN'S ACT

(1) Compare with Justice Day's opinion a memorandum (draft opinion) written by Justice Brandeis and circulated among the Justices, but ultimately not handed down as the opinion of the Court.[10] Justice Brandeis notes at the outset the protest of the foreign vessel owner and the British Embassy over application of Section 4 of the Seamen's Act. "It will aid in determining the validity of these contentions to consider first the nature, the occasion, and the purpose of the provision in question." Justice Brandeis found that the Seamen's Act was "designed to complete the emancipation of American seamen and to make possible the participation of the United States in the foreign carrying trade."

His opinion drew upon reports of Congressional committees to the effect that the American merchant marine had declined because of foreign competition resulting from lower costs in building, equipping and operating foreign vessels, and "that the lower cost of operation was due mainly to their lower wage scale and the inferior living conditions of their crews; and that equalization of operating costs in this respect would be an indispensable factor in reestablishing our merchant marine." The committees reasoned that if seamen on foreign vessels were empowered to demand payment of a substantial part of wages previously earned but unpaid, foreign vessels engaged in American trade would be compelled to raise wages and working conditions or risk loss of seamen who would desert in American ports after recovering part back wages. "The purpose to effect such equalization of costs was clearly set forth in reporting the measure to Congress as will be hereafter shown. Such is the nature of the measure in question; such the evils against which it was aimed and the means by which it was proposed to overcome them."

The draft opinion disposed tersely of the contention that the Act as applied violated international law.

> It is urged that, by general consent of the nations, the regulation of the rights and duties of officers and crew are, like matters of internal discipline, to be determined by the law of the country to which the vessel belongs—and not by the law of the place where she may, from time to time, happen to be. This undoubtedly is the general rule. But it is such only because of the consent of each nation affected and

10. The memorandum appears in Bickel, The Unpublished Opinions of Mr. Justice Brandeis 35 (1957).

> to the extent to which such consent has been given either by implication from prevailing custom or expressly by treaty or legislation. . . . In the absence of such consent, express or implied, every foreign vessel owes temporary and local allegiance to the country whose port she enters and becomes amenable to the jurisdiction and laws of that country.

Justice Brandeis concluded that application of Section 4 would further the purpose of the Act to promote the welfare of American seamen and the American merchant marine, by equalizing conditions and operating costs and thereby increasing opportunities for employment.

(2) The history of another portion of the Seamen's Act, Section 11, as recited in Benz v. Compania Naviera Hidalgo, S. A., 353 U.S. 138, 144, 77 S.Ct. 699, 703, 1 L.Ed.2d 709, 714 (1957), furnishes an illustrative contrast to the fate of Section 4:

> . . . In the Seamen's Act of March 4, 1915, 38 Stat. 1164, the Congress declared it unlawful to pay a seaman wages in advance and specifically declared the prohibition applicable to foreign vessels "while in waters of the United States." . . . In Sandberg v. McDonald, 1918, 248 U.S. 185, 39 S.Ct. 84, 63 L.Ed. 200, this Court construed the Act as not covering advancements "when the contract and payment were made in a foreign country where the law sanctioned such contract and payment . . .. Had Congress intended to make void such contracts and payments a few words would have stated that intention, not leaving such an important regulation to be gathered from implication." . . . In 1928, Jackson v. S. S. Archimedes, 275 U.S. 463, 48 S.Ct. 164, 72 L.Ed. 374, was decided by this Court. It involved advance payments made by a British vessel to foreign seamen before leaving Manchester on her voyage to New York and return. It was contended that the advances made in Manchester were illegal and void. That there was "no intention to extend the provisions of the statute," the Court said, "to advance payments made by foreign vessels while in foreign ports, is plain. This Court had pointed out in the Sandberg case, supra, that such a sweeping provision was not specifically made in the statute . . .." . . . Soon thereafter several proposals were made in Congress designed to extend the coverage of the Seamen's Act so as to prohibit advancements made by foreign vessels in foreign ports. A storm of diplomatic protest resulted. Great Britain, Italy, Sweden, Norway, Denmark, the Netherlands, Germany, and Canada all joined in vigorously denouncing the proposals. In each instance the bills died in Congress.

(3) Unlike the criminal cases in Chapter VIII or most cases in this chapter, Strathearn could be viewed as presenting a characteristic choice-of-law issue. It was here open to a court to decide whether United States or foreign (English) law should apply, and then to decide on the merits under the applicable law. If, for example, the American and English law were reversed, so that English law gave the right to seamen on British vessels to demand part wages, the American court could have looked to that law and allowed plaintiff to recover.

Consider a domestic analogy. Suppose that a company hires an employee in New York for work in that state, under a contract containing a dismissal clause that was valid under New York law. The employee occasionally drives a truck to Massachusetts. He is fired in circumstances covered by the dismissal clause and is able to serve the employer in Massachusetts, where he brings an action for breach of contract. If the clause is invalid under Massachusetts law, would it be appropriate for Massachusetts to award the employee damages? [11]

Under generally accepted choice-of-law principles, the argument that English law should govern in Strathearn was strong, even compelling. The place of contract, the origin and termination of the voyage and the flag of the ship all pointed to it. Other factors that would normally be extraneous to choice-of-law thinking, such as the nationality of the plaintiff, buttress this conclusion. Absent the legislative considerations stressed in Justice Brandeis' draft opinion, the choice-of-law methodology developed in cases such as Babcock v. Jackson, p. 937, supra, points in the same direction. But Strathearn is an atypical choice-of-law case, in that the domestic statute (as construed) explicitly defined the field of its application.

QUESTIONS

(1) The Court in Strathearn alludes to certain purposes of the Congress which would be "subserved" by its construction of the statute. How does it support the view that the statute grew from such purposes? How do you evaluate the likelihood that the statute would effectuate those purposes?

(2) Would the wording of the statute have permitted a court to reach a contrary holding? On what basis?

(3) Is the different fate of Section 11 to be attributed to different language governing its coverage or to a difference in subject matter? Does the interpretation of Section 11 enable foreign shipowners substantially to undercut the intended effect of Section 4 as construed in Strathearn?

NOTE ON WELFARE LEGISLATION FOR MERCHANT SEAMEN

From early times it has been recognized that merchant seamen deserve special protection because of the special risks to which they are exposed: working under dangerous conditions, subject to strict discipline, at a disadvantage vis-à-vis the shipowner, often poorly paid and fed and not well educated. Thus the courts referred to them as "wards of admiralty" and developed rules to compensate them for injuries sustained in the course of their employment. In view of the distinctive aspects of admiralty procedure and of the special circumstances of maritime employment, it is not surprising that remedies developed along lines quite different from those that prevailed on land.

11. Such a choice of law in an interstate setting could raise substantial constitutional issues. See p. 765, supra.

A few rudimentary comments, based upon Gilmore and Black, Law of Admiralty Ch. VI (1957), are useful to put the following cases into their historical context.

Admiralty developed two principal alternative avenues of relief for seamen against their employers (usually but not invariably the shipowners). *First,* the ancient customary action for "maintenance and cure" is independent of any fault on the part of the owner. Only wilful misconduct by the claimant can render it inapplicable. The award recoverable represents the cost of curing the seaman of his injury, plus a continuation of his wages for a time. Note that the cost of cure may be limited by the availability, at little or no charge to the seaman, of hospital facilities of the United States Public Health Service.[12]

Second, there also gradually evolved a cause of action for "unseaworthiness," based on the theory that the shipowner owed his seamen the duty of furnishing them a vessel that was safe to go to sea.[13] This action, though to a lesser extent than maintenance and cure, has become increasingly independent of the fault notions that generally pervade tort law. In its traditional form it was limited to injuries resulting from the condition of the vessel at the time it left port; if the condition subsequently developed from an intervening cause, even through the negligence of other crew members, the unseaworthiness doctrine did not apply. In recent years the scope of unseaworthiness has expanded. For example, Mitchell v. Trawler Racer, Inc., 362 U.S. 539, 80 S.Ct. 926, 4 L.Ed.2d 941 (1960), held that a member of a fishing vessel's crew who, on return to port, slipped on a rail that had been made slippery by slime from fish, could recover on an unseaworthiness theory, even though the rail was clean when the vessel left port and there was no showing of negligence in failing to remove the slime as it was deposited during the unloading process.[14] As a result of these developments unseaworthiness is often the most attractive remedy for a sailor. In contrast to maintenance and cure, the remedy is damages measured by standards of loss comparable to those in general tort law.

Towards the end of the 19th century Congress began to enter the field on behalf of seamen. By this time the American merchant marine was past its zenith. Many factors contributed to this decline, including a reluctance of Americans to choose such a career, particularly at wage rates influenced by foreign competition. Congress' concern with protecting seamen on American ships was tempered by a fear that such measures might further weaken the competitive posi-

12. Further details of the American concept of maintenance and cure are given in Lauritzen v. Larsen, p. 954, infra.

13. See the outline of the history of unseaworthiness in Lopes v. Reederei Richard Schroder, p. 546, supra.

14. But compare Morales v. City of Galveston, 370 U.S. 165, 82 S.Ct. 1226, 8 L.Ed.2d 412 (1962), which found no liability for failure to furnish a forced ventilating system.

tion of a merchant marine that it desired to preserve for economic and military reasons.

This dual concern is evidenced in the legislation on seamen's wages described in the preceding Note. The following cases, dealing with the international aspects of remedies awarded seamen for injuries under the Jones Act, invade a more complex substantive area of law. That Act, 41 Stat. 1007 (1920), 46 U.S.C.A. § 688, provides:

> Any seaman who shall suffer personal injury in the course of his employment may, at his election, maintain an action for damages at law, with the right of trial by jury, and in such action all statutes of the United States modifying or extending the common-law right or remedy in cases of personal injury to railway employees shall apply . . . . Jurisdiction in such actions shall be under the court of the district in which the defendant employer resides or in which his principal office is located.[15]

The Jones Act has raised many questions, most of which have only marginal relevance to the questions considered below. They include (1) whether a seaman can join a suit under the Act with other causes of action (chiefly the maritime remedies of maintenance and cure and unseaworthiness); (2) whether pursuit of one remedy will affect the other claims; (3) the effect of such a joinder upon the right to trial by jury, which is provided for in the Jones Act but is not available in admiralty; (4) the effect to be given the reference in the Jones Act to rights under the Federal Employers' Liability Act (applicable to railway employees); and (5) whether questions not answered by the Jones Act or the FELA should be resolved under other bodies of law, including state law. In several of the following cases, actions under the Jones Act were joined with unseaworthiness or maintenance and cure claims. The excerpts from them treat only the Jones Act; the other claims present additional and complex issues of maritime law and choice of law.

"Congress, when it passed the Jones Act, apparently did not want to waste any time on thinking about the special problems of maritime workers", say Gilmore and Black, Law of Admiralty 296 (1957), speaking of its relation to the FELA. Apparently it did not wish to waste any time on its international implications either. Unlike the statute in the Strathearn case, the Jones Act does not benefit from congressional attention to this problem.

15. [Eds.] The apparent restrictiveness of the last sentence is affected by two judicial rulings: (1) that Jones Act allegations may be incorporated in a libel in admiralty and thereby subjected to the more liberal admiralty venue rules, Brown v. C. D. Mallory & Co., 122 F.2d 98 (3d Cir. 1941), and (2) that "resides" refers to any state in which a corporate defendant is licensed to do business, Pure Oil Co. v. Suarez, 384 U.S. 202, 86 S.Ct. 1394, 16 L.Ed.2d 474 (1966).

LAURITZEN v. LARSEN

Supreme Court of the United States, 1953.
345 U.S. 571, 73 S.Ct. 921, 97 L.Ed. 1254.

MR. JUSTICE JACKSON delivered the opinion of the Court.

The key issue in this case is whether statutes of the United States should be applied to this claim of maritime tort. Larsen, a Danish seaman, while temporarily in New York joined the crew of the Randa, a ship of Danish flag and registry, owned by petitioner, a Danish citizen. Larsen signed ship's articles, written in Danish, providing that the rights of crew members would be governed by Danish law and by the employer's contract with the Danish Seamen's Union, of which Larsen was a member. He was negligently injured aboard the Randa in the course of employment, while in Havana harbor.

Respondent brought suit under the Jones Act on the law side of the District Court for the Southern District of New York and demanded a jury. Petitioner contended that Danish law was applicable and that, under it, respondent had received all of the compensation to which he was entitled. He also contested the court's jurisdiction. Entertaining the cause, the court ruled that American rather than Danish law applied, and the jury rendered a verdict of $4,267.50. The Court of Appeals, Second Circuit, affirmed. Its decision, at least superficially, is at variance with its own earlier ones and conflicts with one by the New York Court of Appeals. We granted certiorari.

The question of jurisdiction is shortly answered. A suit to recover damages under the Jones Act is *in personam* against the ship's owner and not one *in rem* against the ship itself. The defendant appeared generally, answered and tendered no objection to jurisdiction of his person. As frequently happens, a contention that there is some barrier to granting plaintiff's claim is cast in terms of an exception to jurisdiction of subject matter. A cause of action under our law was asserted here, and the court had power to determine whether it was or was not well founded in law and in fact. . . .

Denmark has enacted a comprehensive code to govern the relations of her shipowners to her seagoing labor which by its terms and intentions controls this claim. Though it is not for us to decide, it is plausibly contended that all obligations of the owner growing out of Danish law have been performed or tendered to this seaman. The shipowner, supported here by the Danish Government, asserts that the Danish law supplies the full measure of his obligation and that maritime usage and international law as accepted by the United States exclude the application of our incompatible statute.

That allowance of an additional remedy under our Jones Act would sharply conflict with the policy and letter of Danish law is plain from a general comparison of the two systems of dealing with shipboard accidents. Both assure the ill or injured seafaring worker the conventional maintenance and cure at the shipowner's cost, regardless of fault or negligence on the part of anyone. But, while we limit this to the period within which maximum possible cure can be effected, Farrell v. United States, 336 U.S. 511, 69 S.Ct. 707, 93 L.Ed. 850, the Danish law limits it to a fixed period of twelve weeks, and the monetary measurement is different. The two systems are in sharpest conflict as to treatment of claims for disability, partial or complete, which are permanent, or which outlast the liability for maintenance and cure, to which class this claim belongs. Such injuries Danish law relieves under a state-operated plan similar to our workmen's compensation systems. Claims for such disability are not made against the owner but against the state's Directorate of Insurance Against the Consequences of Accidents. They may be presented directly or through any Danish Consulate. They are allowed by administrative action, not by litigation, and depend not upon fault or negligence but only on the fact of injury and the extent of disability. Our own law, apart from indemnity for injury caused by the ship's unseaworthiness, makes no such compensation for such disability in the absence of fault or negligence. But, when such fault or negligence is established by litigation, it allows recovery for elements such as pain and suffering not compensated under Danish law and lets the damages be fixed by jury. In this case, since negligence was found, United States law permits a larger recovery than Danish law. If the same injury were sustained but negligence was absent or not provable, the Danish law would appear to provide compensation where ours would not.

Respondent does not deny that Danish law is applicable to his case. The contention as stated in his brief is rather that "A claimant may select whatever forum he desires and receive the benefits resulting from such choice" and "A ship owner is liable under the laws of the forum where he does business as well as in his own country." This contention that the Jones Act provides an optional cumulative remedy is not based on any explicit terms of the Act, which makes no provision for cases in which remedies have been obtained or are obtainable under foreign law. Rather he relies upon the literal catholicity of its terminology. If read literally, Congress has conferred an American right of action which requires nothing more than that plaintiff be "any seaman who shall suffer personal injury in the course of his employment". It makes no explicit requirement that either the seaman, the employment or the injury have the slightest connection with the United States. Unless some relationship of one or more of these to our national interest is implied, Congress has extended our law and opened our courts to all alien seafaring men injured anywhere in the world in service of watercraft of every foreign nation—a hand on a Chinese junk, never outside Chinese waters, would not be beyond its literal wording.

But Congress in 1920 wrote these all-comprehending words, not on a clean slate, but as a postscript to a long series of enactments governing shipping. All were enacted with regard to a seasoned body of maritime law developed by the experience of American courts long accustomed to dealing with admiralty problems in reconciling our own with foreign interests and in accommodating the reach of our own laws to those of other maritime nations.

The shipping laws of the United States, set forth in Title 46 of the United States Code, 46 U.S.C.A., comprise a patchwork of separate enactments, some tracing far back in our history and many designed for particular emergencies. While some have been specific in application to foreign shipping and others in being confined to American shipping, many give no evidence that Congress addressed itself to their foreign application and are in general terms which leave their application to be judicially determined from context and circumstance. By usage as old as the Nation, such statutes have been construed to apply only to areas and transactions in which American law would be considered operative under prevalent doctrines of international law. . . .

This doctrine of construction is in accord with the long-heeded admonition of Mr. Chief Justice Marshall that "an Act of Congress ought never to be construed to violate the law of nations if any other possible construction remains . . . ." The Charming Betsey, 2

Cranch 64, 118, 2 L.Ed. 208. . . . And it has long been accepted in maritime jurisprudence that " . . . if any construction otherwise be possible, an Act will not be construed as applying to foreigners in respect to acts done by them outside the dominions of the sovereign power enacting. That is a rule based on international law, by which one sovereign power is bound to respect the subjects and the rights of all other sovereign powers outside its own territory." Lord Russell of Killowen in The Queen v. Jameson [1896], 2 Q.B. 425, 430. This is not, as sometimes is implied, any impairment of our own sovereignty, or limitation of the power of Congress. "The law of the sea", we have had occasion to observe, "is in a peculiar sense an international law, but application of its specific rules depends upon acceptance by the United States." Farrell v. United States, 336 U.S. 511, 517, 69 S.Ct. 707, 710, 93 L.Ed. 850. On the contrary, we are simply dealing with a problem of statutory construction rather commonplace in a federal system by which courts often have to decide whether "any" or "every" reaches to the limits of the enacting authority's usual scope or is to be applied to foreign events or transactions.

The history of the statute before us begins with the 1915 enactment of the comprehensive LaFollette Act, entitled, "An Act To promote the welfare of American seamen in the merchant marine of the United States; to abolish arrest and imprisonment as a penalty for desertion and to secure the abrogation of treaty provisions in relation thereto; and to promote safety at sea." 38 Stat. 1164. Many sections of this Act were in terms or by obvious implication restricted to American ships. Three sections were made specifically applicable to foreign vessels,[16] and these provoked considerable doubt and debate. Others were phrased in terms which on their face might apply to the world or to anything less. In this category fell § 20, a cryptic paragraph dealing with the fellow-servant doctrine, to which this Court ascribed little, if any, of its intended effect. Chelentis v. Luckenbach S. S. Co., 247 U.S. 372, 38 S.Ct. 501, 62 L.Ed. 1171. In 1920, Congress, under the title "An Act To provide for the promotion and maintenance of the American merchant marine . . ." and other subjects not relevant, provided a plan to aid our mercantile fleet and included the revised provision for injured seamen now before us for construction. 41 Stat. 988, 1007. It did so by reference to the Federal Employers' Liability Act, 45 U.S.C.A. § 51 et seq., which we have held not applicable to an American citizen's injury sustained in Canada while in service of an American employer. New York Central R. Co. v. Chisholm, 268 U.S. 29, 45 S.Ct. 402, 69 L.Ed. 828. And it did not give the seaman the one really effective security for a claim against a foreign owner, a maritime lien.

Congress could not have been unaware of the necessity of construction imposed upon courts by such generality of language and was well warned that in the absence of more definite directions than are contained in the Jones Act it would be applied by the courts to foreign events, foreign ships and foreign seamen only in accordance with the usual doctrine and practices of maritime law.

Respondent places great stress upon the assertion that petitioner's commerce and contacts with the ports of the United States are frequent and regular, as the basis for applying our statutes to incidents aboard his ships. But the virtue and utility of sea-borne com-

16. [Eds.] In a footnote, the Court here set forth Sections 4 and 11 involved in Strathearn Steamship Co. v. Dillon, p. 947, supra, and also Section 14, directing that certain requirements as to lifeboats should also apply to foreign vessels leaving United States ports.

merce lies in its frequent and important contacts with more than one country. If, to serve some immediate interest, the courts of each were to exploit every such contact to the limit of its power, it is not difficult to see that a multiplicity of conflicting and overlapping burdens would blight international carriage by sea. Hence, courts of this and other commercial nations have generally deferred to a non-national or international maritime law of impressive maturity and universality. It has the force of law, not from extraterritorial reach of national laws, nor from abdication of its sovereign powers by any nation, but from acceptance by common consent of civilized communities of rules designed to foster amicable and workable commercial relations.

International or maritime law in such matters as this does not seek uniformity and does not purport to restrict any nation from making and altering its laws to govern its own shipping and territory. However, it aims at stability and order through usages which considerations of comity, reciprocity and long-range interest have developed to define the domain which each nation will claim as its own. Maritime law, like our municipal law, has attempted to avoid or resolve conflicts between competing laws by ascertaining and valuing points of contact between the transaction and the states or governments whose competing laws are involved. The criteria, in general, appear to be arrived at from weighing of the significance of one or more connecting factors between the shipping transaction regulated and the national interest served by the assertion of authority. It would not be candid to claim that our courts have arrived at satisfactory standards or apply those that they profess with perfect consistency. But in dealing with international commerce we cannot be unmindful of the necessity for mutual forbearance if retaliations are to be avoided; nor should we forget that any contact which we hold sufficient to warrant application of our law to a foreign transaction will logically be as strong a warrant for a foreign country to apply its law to an American transaction.

In the case before us, two foreign nations can claim some connecting factor with this tort—Denmark, because, among other reasons, the ship and the seaman were Danish nationals; Cuba, because the tortious conduct occurred and caused injury in Cuban waters. The United States may also claim contacts because the seaman had been hired in and was returned to the United States, which also is the state of the forum. We therefore review the several factors which, alone or in combination, are generally conceded to influence choice of law to govern a tort claim, particularly a maritime tort claim, and the weight and significance accorded them.

1. *Place of the Wrongful Act.*—The solution most commonly accepted as to torts in our municipal and in international law is to apply the law of the place where the acts giving rise to the liability occurred, the *lex loci delicti commissi.* This rule of locality, often applied to maritime torts, would indicate application of the law of Cuba, in whose domain the actionable wrong took place. The test of location of the wrongful act or omission, however sufficient for torts ashore, is of limited application to shipboard torts, because of the varieties of legal authority over waters she may navigate. These range from ports, harbors, roadsteads, straits, rivers and canals which form part of the domain of various states, through bays and gulfs, and that band of the littoral sea known as territorial waters, over which control in a large, but not unlimited, degree is conceded to the adjacent state. It includes, of course, the high seas as to which the law was probably settled and old when Grotius wrote that it can-

not be anyone's property and cannot be monopolized by virtue of discovery, occupation, papal grant, prescription or custom.

We have sometimes uncompromisingly asserted territorial rights, as when we held that foreign ships voluntarily entering our waters become subject to our prohibition laws and other laws as well, except as we may in pursuance of our own policy forego or limit exertion of our power. Cunard Steamship Co. v. Mellon, 262 U.S. 100, 124, 43 S.Ct. 504, 507, 67 L.Ed. 894. This doctrine would seem to indicate Cuban law for this case. But the territorial standard is so unfitted to an enterprise conducted under many territorial rules and under none that it usually is modified by the more constant law of the flag. This would appear to be consistent with the practice of Cuba, which applies a workmen's compensation system in principle not unlike that of Denmark to all accidents occurring aboard ships of Cuban registry. The locality test, for what it is worth, affords no support for the application of American law in this case and probably refers us to Danish in preference to Cuban law, though this point we need not decide, for neither party urges Cuban law as controlling.

2. *Law of the Flag.*—Perhaps the most venerable and universal rule of maritime law relevant to our problem is that which gives cardinal importance to the law of the flag. Each state under international law may determine for itself the conditions on which it will grant its nationality to a merchant ship, thereby accepting responsibility for it and acquiring authority over it. Nationality is evidenced to the world by the ship's papers and its flag. The United States has firmly and successfully maintained that the regularity and validity of a registration can be questioned only by the registering state.

This Court has said that the law of the flag supersedes the territorial principle, even for purposes of criminal jurisdiction of personnel of a merchant ship, because it "is deemed to be a part of the territory of that sovereignty [whose flag it flies], and not to lose that character when in navigable waters within the territorial limits of another sovereignty." On this principle, we concede a territorial government involved only concurrent jurisdiction of offenses aboard our ships. United States v. Flores, 289 U.S. 137, 155–159, 53 S.Ct. 580, 584–586, 77 L.Ed. 1086, and cases cited. Some authorities reject, as a rather mischievous fiction, the doctrine that a ship is constructively a floating part of the flag-state,[17] but apply the law of the flag on the pragmatic basis that there must be some law on shipboard, that it cannot change at every change of waters, and no experience shows a better rule than that of the state that owns her.

It is significant to us here that the weight given to the ensign overbears most other connecting events in determining applicable law. As this Court held in United States v. Flores, supra, 289 U.S. at page 158, 53 S.Ct. at page 586, and iterated in Cunard S.S. Co. v. Mellon, supra, 262 U.S. at page 123, 43 S.Ct. at page 507:

> "And so by comity it came to be generally understood among civilized nations that all matters of discipline, and all things done on board, which affected only the vessel, or those belonging to her, and did not involve the peace or dignity of the country, or the tranquility of the port, should be

17. The theoretical basis used by this Court apparently prevailed in 1928 with the Permanent Court of International Justice in the case of The Lotus, P.C.I.J., Series A, No. 10. For criticism of it see Higgins and Colombos, International Law of the Sea (2d ed.), 193–195. We leave the controversy where we find it, for either basis leads to the same result in this case, though this might not be so with some other problems of shipping.

left by the local government to be dealt with by the authorities of the nation to which the vessel belonged as the laws of that nation, or the interests of its commerce should require. . . ."

This was but a repetition of settled American doctrine.

These considerations are of such weight in favor of Danish and against American law in this case that it must prevail unless some heavy counterweight appears.

3. *Allegiance or Domicile of the Injured.*—Until recent times there was little occasion for conflict between the law of the flag and the law of the state of which the seafarer was a subject, for the long-standing rule, as pronounced by this Court after exhaustive review of authority, was that the nationality of the vessel for jurisdictional purposes was attributed to all her crew. In re Ross, 140 U.S. 453, 472, 11 S.Ct. 897, 902, 35 L.Ed. 581. Surely during service under a foreign flag some duty of allegiance is due. But, also, each nation has a legitimate interest that its nationals and permanent inhabitants be not maimed or disabled from self-support. In some later American cases, courts have been prompted to apply the Jones Act by the fact that the wrongful act or omission alleged caused injury to an American citizen or domiciliary. We need not, however, weigh the seaman's nationality against that of the ship, for here the two coincide without resort to fiction. Admittedly, respondent is neither citizen nor resident of the United States. While on direct examination he answered leading questions that he was living in New York when he joined the Randa, the articles which he signed recited, and on cross-examination he admitted, that his home was Silkeburg, Denmark. His presence in New York was transitory and created no such national interest in, or duty toward, him as to justify intervention of the law of one state on the shipboard of another.

4. *Allegiance of the Defendant Shipowner.*—A state "is not debarred by any rule of international law from governing the conduct of its own citizens upon the high seas or even in foreign countries when the rights of other nations or their nationals are not infringed." Skiriotes v. State of Florida, 313 U.S. 69, 73, 61 S.Ct. 924, 927, 85 L.Ed. 1193. Steele v. Bulova Watch Co., 344 U.S. 280, 282, 73 S.Ct. 252, 253. Until recent times this factor was not a frequent occasion of conflict, for the nationality of the ship was that of its owners. But it is common knowledge that in recent years a practice has grown, particularly among American shipowners, to avoid stringent shipping laws by seeking foreign registration eagerly offered by some countries. Confronted with such operations, our courts on occasion have pressed beyond the formalities of more or less nominal foreign registration to enforce against American shipowners the obligations which our law places upon them. But here again the utmost liberality in disregard of formality does not support the application of American law in this case, for it appears beyond doubt that this owner is a Dane by nationality and domicile.

5. *Place of Contract.*—Place of contract, which was New York, is the factor on which respondent chiefly relies to invoke American law. It is one which often has significance in choice of law in a contract action. But a Jones Act suit is for tort, in which respect it differs from one to enforce liability for maintenance and cure. As we have said of the latter, "In the United States this obligation has been recognized consistently as an implied provision in contracts of marine employment. Created thus with the contract of employment, the liability, unlike that for indemnity or that later created by the

Jones Act, in no sense is predicated on the fault or negligence of the shipowner." Aguilar v. Standard Oil Co., 318 U.S. 724, 730, 63 S.Ct. 930, 933, 87 L.Ed. 1107. . . . But this action does not seek to recover anything due under the contract or damages for its breach.

The place of contracting in this instance, as is usual to such contracts, was fortuitous. A seaman takes his employment, like his fun, where he finds it; a ship takes on crew in any port where it needs them. The practical effect of making the *lex loci contractus* govern all tort claims during the service would be to subject a ship to a multitude of systems of law, to put some of the crew in a more advantageous position than others, and not unlikely in the long run to diminish hirings in ports of countries that take best care of their seamen.

But if contract law is nonetheless to be considered, we face the fact that this contract was explicit that the Danish law and the contract with the Danish union were to control. Except as forbidden by some public policy, the tendency of the law is to apply in contract matters the law which the parties intended to apply. We are aware of no public policy that would prevent the parties to this contract, which contemplates performance in a multitude of territorial jurisdictions and on the high seas, from so settling upon the law of the flag-state as their governing code. This arrangement is so natural and compatible with the policy of the law that even in the absence of an express provision it would probably have been implied. . . . We think a quite different result would follow if the contract attempted to avoid applicable law, for example, so as to apply foreign law to an American ship. . . .

We do not think the place of contract is a substantial influence in the choice between competing laws to govern a maritime tort.

6. *Inaccessibility of Foreign Forum.*—It is argued, and particularly stressed by an *amicus* brief, that justice requires adjudication under American law to save seamen expense and loss of time in returning to a foreign forum. This might be a persuasive argument for exercising a discretionary jurisdiction to adjudge a controversy; but it is not persuasive as to the law by which it shall be judged. . . .

Confining ourselves to the case in hand, we do not find this seaman disadvantaged in obtaining his remedy under Danish law from being in New York instead of Denmark. The Danish compensation system does not necessitate delayed, prolonged, expensive and uncertain litigation. It is stipulated in this case that claims may be made through the Danish Consulate. There is not the slightest showing that to obtain any relief to which he is entitled under Danish law would require his presence in Denmark or necessitate his leaving New York. And, even if it were so, the record indicates that he was offered and declined free transportation to Denmark by petitioner.

7. *The Law of the Forum.*—It is urged that, since an American forum has perfected its jurisdiction over the parties and defendant does more or less frequent and regular business within the forum state, it should apply its own law to the controversy between them. The "doing business" which is enough to warrant service of process may fall quite short of the considerations necessary to bring extraterritorial torts to judgment under our law. Under respondent's contention, all that is necessary to bring a foreign transaction between foreigners in foreign ports under American law is to be able to serve American process on the defendant. We have held it a denial of due process of law when a state of the Union attempts to draw into control of its law otherwise foreign controversies, on slight

connections, because it is a forum state. Hartford Accident & Indemnity Co. v. Delta & Pine Land Co., 292 U.S. 143, 54 S.Ct. 634, 78 L.Ed. 1178; Home Insurance Co. v. Dick, 281 U.S. 397, 50 S.Ct. 338, 74 L.Ed. 926. The purpose of a conflict-of-laws doctrine is to assure that a case will be treated in the same way under the appropriate law regardless of the fortuitous circumstances which often determine the forum. Jurisdiction of maritime cases in all countries is so wide and the nature of its subject matter so far-flung that there would be no justification for altering the law of a controversy just because local jurisdiction of the parties is obtainable. . . .

This review of the connecting factors which either maritime law or our municipal law of conflicts regards as significant in determining the law applicable to a claim of actionable wrong shows an overwhelming preponderance in favor of Danish law. The parties are both Danish subjects, the events took place on a Danish ship, not within our territorial waters. Against these considerations is only the fact that the defendant was served here with process and that the plaintiff signed on in New York, where the defendant was engaged in our foreign commerce. The latter event is offset by provision of his contract that the law of Denmark should govern. We do not question the power of Congress to condition access to our ports by foreign-owned vessels upon submission to any liabilities it may consider good American policy to exact. But we can find no justification for interpreting the Jones Act to intervene between foreigners and their own law because of acts on a foreign ship not in our waters.

In apparent recognition of the weakness of the legal argument, a candid and brash appeal is made by respondent and by *amicus* briefs to extend the law to this situation as a means of benefiting seamen and enhancing the costs of foreign ship operation for the competitive advantage of our own. We are not sure that the interest of this foreign seaman, who is able to prove negligence, is the interest of all seamen or that his interest is that of the United States. Nor do we stop to inquire which law does whom the greater or the lesser good. The argument is misaddressed. It would be within the proprieties if addressed to Congress. Counsel familiar with the traditional attitude of this Court in maritime matters could not have intended it for us.

The judgment below is reversed and the cause remanded to District Court for proceedings consistent herewith.

Reversed and remanded.

MR. JUSTICE BLACK agrees with the Court of Appeals and would affirm its judgment.

ROMERO v. INTERNATIONAL TERMINAL OPERATING CO.

Supreme Court of the United States, 1959.
358 U.S. 354, 79 S.Ct. 468, 3 L.Ed.2d 368.

[Plaintiff, a Spanish subject, was employed as a crew member on a ship of Spanish flag and registry, owned by a Spanish corporation, for a voyage beginning and ending in Spain. While the ship was within United States territorial waters, in the port of New York, plaintiff was seriously injured when struck by a cable on the deck of the ship. He filed suit on the law side of the federal district court in New York. The court dismissed the complaint, and the court of appeals affirmed. The excerpts below from the opinion of the Supreme Court, delivered by MR. JUSTICE FRANKFURTER, treat principally the claim against the Spanish employer (Compania Trasatlantica) under the Jones Act, although the opinion applies the same reasoning to dispose of the claims against the employer based on the general maritime law, particularly unseaworthiness and maintenance and cure. Claims against parties other than the employer—a New York agent of the employer and the stevedore and carpentry companies working on board at the time—were considered in omitted portions of the opinion.]

II. The Claims Against Compania Trasatlantica— The Choice-of-Law Problem.

. . . While Lauritzen v. Larsen [p. 954, supra] involved claims asserted under the Jones Act, the principles on which it was decided did not derive from the terms of that statute. We pointed out that the Jones Act had been written "not on a clean slate, but as a postscript to a long series of enactments governing shipping. All were enacted with regard to a seasoned body of maritime law developed by the experience of American courts long accustomed to dealing with admiralty problems in reconciling our own with foreign interests and in accommodating the reach of our own laws to those of other maritime nations." 345 U.S. at page 577, 73 S.Ct. at page 925. Thus the Jones Act was applied "to foreign events, foreign ships and foreign seamen only in accordance with the usual doctrine and practices of maritime law." 345 U.S. at page 581, 73 S.Ct. at page 927. The broad principles of choice of law and the applicable criteria of selection set forth in Lauritzen were intended to guide courts in the application of maritime law generally. Of course, due regard must be had for the differing interests advanced by varied aspects of maritime law. But the similarity in purpose and function of the Jones Act and the general maritime principles of compensation for personal injury, admit of no rational differentiation of treatment for choice of law purposes. Thus the reasoning of Lauritzen v. Larsen governs all claims here.

We are not here dealing with the sovereign power of the United States to apply its law to situations involving one or more foreign contacts. But in the absence of a contrary congressional direction, we must apply those principles of choice of law that are consonant with the needs of a general federal maritime law and with due recognition of our self-regarding respect for the relevant interests of foreign nations in the regulation of maritime commerce as part of the legitimate concern of the international community. These principles do not depend upon a mechanical application of a doctrine like that of *lex loci delicti commissi*. The controlling considerations are the interacting interests of the United States and of foreign countries, and in assessing them we must move with the circumspection appropriate when this Court is adjudicating issues inevitably entangled in the conduct of our international relations. We need not repeat the exposition of the problem which we gave in Lauritzen v. Larsen. Due regard for the relevant factors we there enumerated, and the weight we indicated to be given to each, preclude application of American law to the claims here asserted.

In this case, as in Lauritzen v. Larsen, the ship is of foreign registry and sails under a foreign flag. Both the injured seaman and the owner of the ship have a Spanish status: Romero is a Spanish subject and Compania Trasatlantica a Spanish corporation. Unlike the contract in Lauritzen, Romero's agreement of hire was entered into in Spain. By noting this fact, we do not mean to qualify our earlier view that the place of contracting is largely fortuitous and of little importance in determining the applicable law in an action of marine tort. Here, as in Lauritzen, the foreign law provides a remedy for the injury, and claims under that law may be conveniently asserted before the Spanish consul in New York.

In Lauritzen v. Larsen the injury occurred in the port of Havana and the action was brought in New York. Romero was injured while temporarily in American territorial waters. This difference does not call for a difference in result. Discussing the significance of the place of the wrongful act, we pointed out in Lauritzen that "[t]he test of location of the wrongful act or omission, however sufficient for torts ashore, is of limited application to shipboard torts, because of the varieties of legal authority over waters she may navigate. . . . the territorial standard is so unfitted to an enterprise conducted under many territorial rules and under none that it usually is modified by the more constant law of the flag." 345 U.S. at pages 583–584, 73 S.Ct. at page 929. Although the place of injury has often been deemed determinative of the choice of law in municipal conflict of laws, such a rule does not fit the accommodations that become relevant in fair and prudent regard for the interests of foreign nations in the regulation of their own ships and their own nationals, and the effect upon our interests of our treatment of the legitimate interests of foreign nations. To impose on ships the duty of shifting from one standard of compensation to another as the vessel passes the boundaries of territorial waters would be not only an onerous but also an unduly speculative burden, disruptive of international commerce and without basis in the expressed policies of this country. The amount and type of recovery which a foreign seaman may receive from his foreign employer while sailing on a foreign ship should not depend on the wholly fortuitous circumstance of the place of injury.

Thus we hold that the considerations found in Lauritzen v. Larsen to preclude the assertion of a claim under the Jones Act apply equally here, and affirm the dismissal of petitioner's claims against Compania Trasatlantica. . . .

MR. JUSTICE BLACK, dissenting.

. . . By its terms the Jones Act applies to "*any seaman* who shall suffer personal injury in the course of his employment." 41 Stat. 1007, 46 U.S.C. § 688, 46 U.S.C.A. § 688. (Italics added.) This Court in Lauritzen v. Larsen, 345 U.S. 571, 73 S.Ct. 921, 97 L.Ed. 1254, held that the words "any seaman" did not include foreign seamen sailing foreign ships and injured in foreign waters. I dissented from that holding. It was based, I thought, on the Court's concepts of what would be good or bad for the country internationally rather than on an actual interpretation of the language of the Jones Act. Thus, it seemed to me that the Lauritzen holding rested on notions of what Congress should have said, not on what it did say. Such notions, weak enough in Lauritzen, seem much weaker still in this case where the tort involved occurred in our own waters. I cannot but feel that, at least as to torts occurring within the United States, Congress knew what it was doing when it said "any seaman" and I must dissent from today's further and, I believe, unjustifiable reduction in the scope of the Jones Act. . . .

MR. JUSTICE DOUGLAS . . . . believes that Lauritzen v. Larsen, 345 U.S. 571, 73 S.Ct. 921, 97 L.Ed. 1254, is inapposite to the present case, because of the numerous incidents connecting this transaction with the United States. He therefore agrees with Mr. Justice Black that the District Court should take jurisdiction over petitioner's claim against Compania Trasatlantica.

[An opinion of MR. JUSTICE BRENNAN, dissenting in part and concurring in part, concurred in the Court's holding as to the applicability of the Jones Act.]

COMMENT

Although arising under a statute, in an international setting, and in the distinctive field of maritime law, Lauritzen has significantly influenced choice-of-law thinking in an interstate setting in the United States. Commentators, and to some extent courts, have drawn upon the case to illustrate the developing methodology in choice of law reflected in cases such as Babcock v. Jackson, p. 937, supra.[18] The similarities are striking. Note the opinion's critical view of rigid "jurisdiction-selecting" rules, such as the *lex loci delicti* principle, and its reference to the purposes of the domestic and foreign legislation. It seeks to relate the facts underlying the dispute to such purposes in order to determine which law should be applied. The opinion best illustrates this methodology when it attempts to determine the "significance of one or more connecting factors between the shipping transaction regulated and the national interest served by the assertion of authority."

QUESTIONS

(1) Is the opinion in Lauritzen faithful to the nature of the inquiry which it promises to undertake? How successful is the Court in identifying "national interests"? What purposes are attributed to Congress in enacting the Jones Act? For example, whom is the Act intended to regulate or benefit?

(2) Seven factors are explored by the Court to answer these questions, and an effort made to determine their weight and significance. Does the "overwhelming preponderance" in favor of Danish law depend simply upon the *number* of factors pointing to Denmark, or upon their *relevance* to Danish and American statutory purposes? Is the inquiry quantitative or qualitative?

(*a*) Why is the *lex loci delicti* rule rejected by Lauritzen—and by Romero?

(*b*) Does the court develop any relationship between the nationality of a plaintiff and a "national interest" or "purpose" served by the Act?

(*c*) Is it shown what relevance a defendant's allegiance may have to these inquiries?

(*d*) Even absent United States nationality or domicile of the plaintiff or defendant, could you identify a United States "interest" in affording relief under the Jones Act? Under what facts?

(3) Compare Justice Jackson's rejection of the argument that the statute should be interpreted so as to give American shipping a competitive advantage with the treatment of a like argument in Justice Bran-

18. See, e. g., Currie, The Silver Oar and All That: A Study of the Romero Case, 27 U.Chi.L.Rev. 1 (1959).

deis' draft opinion in Strathearn, p. 949, supra. Do the two situations warrant such different approaches?

(4) Do the Lauritzen and Romero opinions recognize a limiting rule of customary international law, based upon common consent and acceptance? Does either appear to view such a rule as did the opinion in the Paquete Habana, p. 531, supra? In what other sense might the Court be referring to "international law"?

(5) How would you identify the Danish government's interest in this litigation, as compared with the obvious interest of the shipowner in resisting recovery?

(6) Suppose that no Danish law had provided for recovery by the plaintiff under the facts in Lauritzen. Does the opinion suggest that such circumstances would have affected the decision?

(7) After finding the Jones Act inapplicable, would it have been open to the Court to entertain a claim based upon Danish law, and to afford whatever relief was appropriate under that law?

HELLENIC LINES LTD. v. RHODITIS

Supreme Court of the United States, 1970.
398 U.S. 306, 90 S.Ct. 1731, 26 L.Ed.2d 252.

MR. JUSTICE DOUGLAS delivered the opinion of the Court.

This is a suit under the Jones Act by a seaman who was injured aboard the ship *Hellenic Hero* in the Port of New Orleans. The District Court, sitting without a jury, rendered judgment for the seaman, 273 F.Supp. 248. The Court of Appeals affirmed, 412 F.2d 919. . . .

Petitioner Hellenic Lines Ltd. is a Greek corporation that has its largest office in New York and another office in New Orleans. More than 95% of its stock is owned by a United States domiciliary who is a Greek citizen—Pericles G. Callimanopoulos (whom we call Pericles). He lives in Connecticut and manages the corporation out of New York. He has lived in this country since 1945. The ship *Hellenic Hero* is engaged in regularly scheduled runs between various ports of the United States and the Middle East, Pakistan, and India. The District Court found that its entire income is from cargo either originating or terminating in the United States.

Respondent, the seaman, signed on in Greece, and he is a Greek citizen. His contract of employment provides that Greek law and a Greek collective-bargaining agreement apply between the employer and the seaman and that all claims arising out of the employment contract are to be adjudicated by a Greek court. And it seems to be conceded that respondent could obtain relief through Greek courts, if he desired.

The Jones Act speaks only of "the defendant employer" without any qualifications. In Lauritzen v. Larsen, 345 U.S. 571, 73 S.Ct. 921, 97 L.Ed. 1254, however, we listed seven factors to be considered in determining whether a particular shipowner should be held to be an "employer" for Jones Act purposes:

> (1) the place of the wrongful act; (2) the law of the flag; (3) the allegiance or domicile of the injured seaman; (4) allegiance of the defendant shipowner; (5) the place

where the contract of employment was made; (6) the inaccessibility of a foreign forum; and (7) the law of the forum.

Of these seven factors it is urged that four are in favor of the shipowner and against jurisdiction: the ship's flag is Greek; the injured seaman is Greek; the employment contract is Greek; and there is a foreign forum available to the injured seaman.

The *Lauritzen* test, however, is not a mechanical one. 345 U.S., at 582, 73 S.Ct. 921. We indicated that the flag that a ship flies may, at times, alone be sufficient. Id., at 585–586, 73 S.Ct. 929–930. The significance of one or more factors must be considered in light of the national interest served by the assertion of Jones Act jurisdiction. Moreover, the list of seven factors in *Lauritzen* was not intended as exhaustive. As held in Pavlou v. Ocean Traders Marine Corp., 211 F.Supp. 320, 325, and approved by the Court of Appeals in the present case, 412 F.2d, at 923 n. 7, the shipowner's *base of operations* is another factor of importance in determining whether the Jones Act is applicable; and there well may be others.

In *Lauritzen* the injured seaman had been hired in and was returned to the United States, and the shipowner was served here. Those were the only contacts of that shipping operation with this country.

The present case is quite different.

Pericles became a lawful permanent resident alien in 1952. We extend to such an alien the same constitutional protections of due process that we accord citizens. Kwong Hai Chew v. Colding, 344 U.S. 590, 596, 73 S.Ct. 472, 477, 97 L.Ed. 576. The injury occurred here. The forum is a United States court. Pericles' base of operations is New York. The *Hellenic Hero* was not a casual visitor; rather, it and many of its sister ships were earning income from cargo originating or terminating here. We see no reason whatsoever to give the Jones Act a strained construction so that this alien owner, engaged in an extensive business operation in this country, may have an advantage over citizens engaged in the same business by allowing him to escape the obligations and responsibility of a Jones Act "employer." The flag, the nationality of the seaman, the fact that his employment contract was Greek, and that he might be compensated there are in the totality of the circumstances of this case minor weights in the scales compared with the substantial and continuing contacts that this alien owner has with this country. If, as stated in Bartholomew v. Universe Tankships Inc., 263 F.2d 437, the liberal purposes of the Jones Act are to be effectuated, the facade of the operation must be considered as minor, compared with the real nature of the operation and a cold objective look at the actual operational contacts that this ship and this owner have with the United States. By that test the Court of Appeals was clearly right in holding that petitioner Hellenic Lines was an "employer" under the Jones Act.

Affirmed.

MR. JUSTICE HARLAN, with whom THE CHIEF JUSTICE and MR. JUSTICE STEWART join, dissenting.

. . .

. . . Yet despite the sweeping language it can hardly be doubted that congressional concern stopped short of the lengths to which the literal terms of the statute carry the Jones Act. This was emphasized in *Lauritzen* which pointed out that Congress wrote against a backdrop of "usage as old as the Nation," that "such statutes have been construed to apply only to areas and transactions in which American law would be considered operative under prevalent doctrines of international law." . . .

This Court only recently applied this principle in McCulloch v. Sociedad Nacional, 372 U.S. 10, 83 S.Ct. 671, 9 L.Ed.2d 547 (1963), ...

The *McCulloch* case followed a course marked early in our jurisprudence, and, in fact, built upon *Lauritzen* which had announced that the law of the flag, "the most venerable and universal rule of maritime law," would in Jones Act cases "overbear most other connecting events in determining applicable law . . . unless some heavy counterweight appears." 345 U.S., at 584, 585–586, 73 S.Ct. at 929–930.

Such a counterweight would exist only in circumstances where the application of the American rule of law would further the purpose of Congress. While some legislation in its purpose obviously requires extension beyond our borders to achieve national policy, this is not so, in my opinion, with an Act concerned with prescribing particular remedies, rather than one regulating commerce or creating a standard for conduct.

The only justification that I can see for extending extraterritorially a remedial-type provision like § 688 is that the injured seaman is an individual whose well-being is a concern of this country. It was for this reason that *Lauritzen* recognized the residence of the plaintiff as a factor that should properly be considered in deciding who is a "seaman" as Congress employed that term in § 688. . . .

In the early decisions involving citizen and resident alien seamen serving on foreign vessels, some additional factor, such as the vessel's presence in American waters or beneficial American ownership, was considered to be an element justifying recovery. . . . *Lauritzen* in enumerating these factors ("contacts") as independent considerations, was attempting to focus analysis on those factors that are the necessary ingredients for a statutory cause of action: first, as a matter of statutory construction, is plaintiff within that class of seamen that Congress intended to cover by the statute? and, second, is there a sufficient nexus between the defendant and this country so as to justify the assertion of legislative jurisdiction? In other words the Court must define "seaman" and "employer" as those words are used in § 688. In this regard the *situs* of the accident or the vessel's contacts with this country by virtue of its beneficial ownership or the frequency of calls at our ports simply serves as an adequate nexus between this country and defendant to assert jurisdiction in a case where congressional policy is otherwise furthered. But no matter how qualitatively substantial or numerous these kinds of contacts may be, they have no bearing in themselves on whether Jones Act recovery is appropriate in a given instance. For transactions occurring aboard foreign-flag vessels that question should be answered by reference to the plaintiff's relationship to this country. See Note, Admiralty and the Choice of Law: Lauritzen v. Larsen Applied, 47 Va.L.Rev. 1400 (1961).

Viewed in this perspective, today's decision and decisions of several lower courts that have taken the phenomenon of "convenient" foreign registry as a wedge for displacing the law of the flag, . . . have, I believe, misconstrued these basic premises on which *Lauritzen* was founded. . . .

This underlies today's decision which relies on the fact that Hellenic Lines is an American-based operation and its vessels would be accorded a competitive advantage over American-flag vessels were we to permit petitioners to avoid responsibility under the Jones Act. Liability is only one factor that contributes to the higher cost of operating an American-flag vessel. Indeed, recognizing the insurance factor, it is doubtful that this factor is a significant contribution to the competitive advantage of foreign-flag ships, especially given the higher crew wages (see 46 U.S.C.A. § 1132 requiring American crews) and construction costs for American-flag ships, which must be built in American yards if they are to participate in the congressional programs specifically designed to offset the higher costs that the Court today takes as justification for displacing settled international principles of choice of law. . . .

Even were Jones Act liability a significant uncompensated cost in the operation of an American ship, I could not regard this as a reason for extending Jones Act recovery to foreign seamen when the underlying concern of the legislation before us is the adjustment of the risk of loss between individuals and not the regulation of commerce or competition.

. . .

Where, as in the case before us, the injured plaintiff has no American ties, the inquiry should be directed toward determining what jurisdiction is primarily concerned with plaintiff's welfare and whether that jurisdiction's rule may, consistent with those notions of due process that determine the presence of legislative jurisdiction, govern recovery. In the case before us, there is no reason to disregard either the law of the flag or plaintiff's contractual undertaking to accept Greek law as controlling, thereby in effect, assuming that he signed articles under conditions that would justify disregarding the contractual choice of law. Rhoditis is a Greek national who resides in Greece. Under these circumstances Greek law provides the appropriate rule.

. . .

COMMENT

Various purposes of the shipowner are served through a corporate and business structure involving use of foreign subsidiaries and foreign registry for ships—purposes explored in the maritime labor cases in Part C of this chapter. At the time that Lauritzen was decided, the practice was incipient. By 1959 it had become widespread.

Both Lauritzen and Romero were in a sense "easy cases." Whatever the significance given each of the seven factors noted in Lauritzen, the facts in both cases argued strongly against application of the Jones Act. Rhoditis introduced complexities in the facts, and corresponding complexities in applying Lauritzen's methodology. Compare the comments after Babcock and Neumeier, p. 943, supra, and questions (3) and (4) at p. 946, supra.

Lower court cases between Lauritzen and Rhoditis have illustrated permutations of the seven factors referred to in Lauritzen and introduced new ones. Consider, for example, the following: (*1*) Bartholomew v. Universe Tankships, Inc., 263 F.2d 437 (2d Cir. 1959) (plaintiff, a British West Indies seaman resident in the United States, signing articles in the United States for a voyage between U. S. ports, held eligible to sue defendant shipowner, a Liberian Corporation owned by a Panama corporation in turn owned by American citizens, for an assault in United States waters aboard a Liberian-flag vessel); (*2*) Tsakonites v. Transpacific Carriers Corp., 368 F.2d 426 (2d Cir. 1966) (2–1 decision) (Greek seaman employed on Greek-flag vessel owned (indirectly) by Greek corporation and making frequent stops in Greece held ineligible to sue under Jones Act for accident in American port for which hospitalized here, although ship controlled from New York office and 96% shareholder of corporate owner was Greek national permanently resident in United States); (*3*) Pavlou v. Ocean Traders Marine Corp., 211 F.Supp. 320 (S.D.N.Y.1962) (Greek seaman employed on Greek-flag vessel held eligible to sue under Jones Act for injury occurring in Canada where vessel controlled from New York office and owned by Liberian corporation 48% owned by United States citizens).

The varying methodological approaches of these decisions are well illustrated by comparing Lauritzen with the following observations of the court in Bartholomew, supra:

> A study of the numerous adjudicated Jones Act cases reveals not only the vagueness inherent in the general and undefined direction in [Lauritzen v. Larsen] for the "valuing" and "weighing" of the various facts or groups of facts that are said to be "points of contact" between the transaction and the states whose competing laws are involved, but also a lack of any common principle of decision or method of approach to the problem. Sometimes the courts seem to be employing choice of law techniques, and not infrequently the result arrived at seems to be based on mere dialectic manipulation or guesswork. All this, however, is to be expected as new law develops in a new field. This substantial background of judicial consideration of a great variety of combinations of relevant factors in cases where application of the Jones Act is asserted on the one hand and denied on the other makes it possible for us to undertake a restatement of the method of approach and the principles to be applied.
>
> . . .
>
> Hence it must be said that in a particular case something between minimal and preponderant contacts is necessary if the Jones Act is to be applied. Thus we conclude that the test is that "substantial" contacts are necessary. And while as indicated supra one contact such as the fact that the vessel flies the American flag may alone be sufficient, this is no more than to say that in such a case the contact is so obviously substantial as to render unnecessary a further probing into the facts.
>
> Some of the advantages of this simple formula are that it states a rational method of ascertaining the congressional intent, and that in its application there is no occasion to consider and "weigh" the contacts that do not exist, nor to go through any process of balancing one set of facts that are present against another set of facts that are absent, without any sure guide as to how the balancing is to be done. Accordingly, the decisional process of arriving at a conclusion on the subject of the application of the Jones Act involves the ascertainment of the facts or groups of facts

which constitute contacts between the transaction involved in the case and the United States, and then deciding whether or not they are substantial. Thus each factor is to be "weighed" and "evaluated" only to the end that, after each factor has been given consideration, a rational and satisfactory conclusion may be arrived at on the question of whether all the factors present add up to the necessary substantiality. Moreover, each factor, or contact, or group of facts must be tested in the light of the underlying objective, which is to effectuate the liberal purposes of the Jones Act. We shall now proceed to apply these principles to the case before us. . . .

. . .

That the factors or contacts just discussed are in the aggregate substantial is clear beyond peradventure of doubt. No other conclusion is rationally admissible in the light of the decided cases. . . .

. . .

QUESTIONS

(1) Do Bartholomew and Rhoditis "develop" or rather reject the methodology suggested by Lauritzen? To the extent that either decision rejects it, what advantages do you see in the methodology that it pursues?

(2) Is the Rhoditis case really "quite different" from Lauritzen? If so, because of which factor or factors? For example, how critical is Pericles' residence in the United States? What of the Court's perception of the American shipping industry's tendency to flee to other flags? Is the latter a legitimate consideration for the interpretation and enforcement of the Jones Act?

(3) The court in Bartholomew observed that an American flag would always be sufficient to support application of the Jones Act. Why—as in a case where plaintiff is a non-resident alien injured on a trip between foreign ports, and temporarily in the United States to bring suit?

(4) If the controversy in Rhoditis or Bartholomew had come before a court in Erewhon, a forum without connection with the accident except that plaintiff was hospitalized there, should that court apply the Jones Act? Is the answer to that question at all relevant to American courts' decision whether to apply the Act?

(5) Given the problems experienced in applying the methodology of Lauritzen, would you favor amending the Jones Act to spell out when a plaintiff may invoke it? What factors should such an amendment take into consideration and what direction might be given to the courts as to how to deal with each one or combinations thereof?

C. MARITIME LABOR REGULATION

NOTE ON LABOR REGULATION AND FLAGS OF CONVENIENCE

The following case, McCulloch v. Sociedad Nacional de Marineros de Honduras, considers whether the National Labor Relations Act

(NLRA) applies to alien crews on foreign-flag vessels which are beneficially owned by United States citizens and engaged in the foreign commerce of the United States. That litigation arose out of disputes between American labor unions, seeking to organize and represent alien crews, and shipowners—disputes stemming from international conflicts of an economic, political and legal nature. This Note sketches the background against which McCulloch should be read.[19]

In the 1950's competition among the merchant shipping of different countries intensified, as construction led to surplus capacity. One consequence was a downward pressure upon shipping rates. United States shipowners, frequently operating under higher costs than foreign competitors, were disadvantaged. Some shipowners benefited from subsidies available under domestic legislation, particularly for liners plying essential routes. However other categories of ships, primarily tankers and "tramp" dry-cargo ships, did not qualify under the United States subsidy programs.

The higher rates which American flag ships charged traced in considerable part from the higher wages paid to their unionized crews. Federal legislation generally requires that crews of American-flag vessels be composed of at least 75% United States citizens, and the NLRA had in any event long been considered applicable to crews on these ships. Domestic tax rates were an important contributing factor to the high American freight charges.

These considerations prompted United States companies to secure foreign nationality for their ships by registering them in other countries, in search of the benefits of those countries' flags. Frequently, the ships were first transferred to a foreign subsidiary of the United States company, and then registered by such subsidiary under foreign law. Two principal advantages were thereby sought. The foreign subsidiary offered protection from high taxation in the United States, primarily deferral of United States taxation of earnings of the subsidiary until their remission (dividend payments) to the parent.[20] Countries in which the ships were registered generally imposed mild taxes. The other advantage was thought to be avoidance of high domestic wage costs. The foreign-flag ships employed alien crews under wage rates and working conditions far less demanding for the shipowners than those obtaining under unionized conditions in the United States.

The flags particularly prized were those of Panama, Liberia and Honduras, the so-called Panlibhon countries. Under these "flags of convenience" tax and wage costs were at a minimum. In a brief

19. The information in the Note is drawn principally from Boczek, Flags of Convenience (1962). Other basic reading in this field includes McDougal and Burke, The Public Order of the Oceans Ch. 8 (1962), and Note, Panlibhon Registration of American-owned Merchant Ships; Governmental Policy and the Problem of the Courts, 60 Colum.L.Rev. 711 (1960). See also OECD Study on Flags of Convenience, 4 J. Marit.L. & Comm. 231 (1973).

20. See p. 1115, infra, for a description of present tax provisions in this field.

period, the Panlibhon countries achieved an impressive stature in maritime commerce measured by their registered tonnage, about 40% of which was beneficially owned by American interests. In 1948, American-flag ships carried 53% of this country's foreign trade; by 1960, the figure was under 12%.

Flight from the American flag held bleak implications for domestic seamen. The fall in employment provoked a vigorous response from labor unions, which in the 1950's engaged in boycotts, picketing and a variety of efforts to organize alien crews on Panlibhon vessels. The assumption was that if unions were successful in organizing alien crews and in requiring American shipowners to bargain with them within the framework of the NLRA, resort to flags of convenience would become pointless, since alien and American crews would receive the same wages. The McCulloch litigation had its origin in such organizational efforts.[21]

American labor was not alone in its hostility to flags of convenience. Governments of European countries with maritime interests felt keenly the competition of Panlibhon fleets. These governments and American and international labor unions advocated provisions in multilateral conventions which would impose strict conditions upon ship registration and thus assure a "genuine link" between a ship and the country whose flag it carried. The effort was to provide a legal basis for ignoring the "foreign nationality" of flag-of-convenience ships, beneficially owned by nationals of other countries and often carrying cargo exclusively between ports of other countries.

Conferences in the 1950's sought to articulate this notion of a "genuine link" with precision sufficient to make it a feasible rule of international law. Practice among countries varied as to requirements for attribution of nationality to a ship. Some, as the United States, had extensive requirements including that of beneficial ownership within the flag country. Others, such as Panlibhon countries, imposed minimal conditions.

The Geneva Conference of 1958 on the Law of the Sea adopted a Convention on the High Seas, 13 U.S.T. & O.I.A. 2312, T.I.A.S. No. 5200, 450 U.N.T.S. 82, which entered into force for the United States in 1962. The Convention includes a controversial Article 5, incorporating the notion of "genuine link":

> Each State shall fix the conditions for the grant of its nationality to ships, for the registration of ships in its territory, and for the right to fly its flag. Ships have the nationality of the State whose flag they are entitled to fly. There must exist a genuine link between the State and the ship; in particular, the State must effectively exercise its jurisdiction and control in administrative, technical and social matters over ships flying its flag.

The Article is marked by significant ambiguities. It does not indicate what the essential "jurisdiction and control" requires. It does

21. The assumption seems questionable. Why should the alien crews have elected American union representatives in view of the ultimate consequence to them?

not suggest whether resort should be had to such criteria as beneficial ownership to determine if a genuine link exists. It does not state the consequences flowing from the failure to establish a genuine link, or what alternative nationality might envelop a ship, and for what purposes.

The United States representatives at the Geneva Conference generally sympathized with the opposition of the Panlibhon countries to any "genuine link" requirement. They did so because flags of convenience offered certain conveniences from the point of view of our national policy as well. United States shipowners had frequently argued to the Congress and the Executive that they would be forced to sell their fleets if required to operate under domestic tax and wage burdens. The executive branch in fact viewed these flags approvingly, and argued that a fleet of bulk carriers owned beneficially by domestic interests but operating under a foreign flag was preferable to no fleet at all. The inconveniences of the foreign flag, particularly the possibility that the state of the flag might interfere with requisition by the United States of ships during a national emergency, had been eased in two ways. Regulations of the United States Maritime Administration under the Shipping Act of 1916 required that American shipowners, as a condition to obtaining the required consent of the Maritime Administration to the transfer of a ship from American to foreign registry, agree to maintain United States ownership of the stock controlling the ship and to place the ship under governmental control during periods of emergency. American owners voluntarily entered into such agreements with respect to newly built ships initially placed under foreign flags; this path to the foreign flag had become more frequent after the surplus fleet resulting from World War II was exhausted. The Panlibhon countries, apparently through letter understandings with the United States government that have not been made formal through treaty arrangements, undertook not to dispute such American control in the event of requisition orders.

The provisions of the National Labor Relations Act, 49 Stat. 449 (1935), as amended, 29 U.S.C.A. §§ 151 et seq., that were relevant to McCulloch and related litigation follow:

Section 1:

> . . .
>
> The inequality of bargaining power between employees who do not possess full freedom of association or actual liberty of contract, and employers who are organized in the corporate or other forms of ownership association substantially burdens and affects the flow of commerce, and tends to aggravate recurrent business depressions, by depressing wage rates and the purchasing power of wage earners in industry and by preventing the stabilization of competitive wage rates and working conditions within and between industries.
>
> Experience has proved that protection by law of the right of employees to organize and bargain collectively safeguards commerce from injury, impairment, or interruption, and promotes

the flow of commerce by removing certain recognized sources of industrial strife, and unrest, by encouraging practices fundamental to the friendly adjustment of industrial disputes arising out of differences as to wages, hours, or other working conditions, and by restoring equality of bargaining power between employers and employees. . . .

It is declared to be the policy of the United States to eliminate the causes of certain substantial obstructions to the free flow of commerce and to mitigate and eliminate these obstructions when they have occurred by encouraging the practice and procedure of collective bargaining and by protecting the exercise by workers of full freedom of association, self-organization, and designation of representatives of their own choosing, for the purpose of negotiating the terms and conditions of their employment or other mutual aid or protection.

Section 9:

(*a*) Representatives designated or selected for the purposes of collective bargaining by the majority of the employees in a unit appropriate for such purposes, shall be the exclusive representatives of all the employees in such unit for the purposes of collective bargaining in respect to rates of pay, wages, hours of employment, or other conditions of employment . . . .

(c)(1) Whenever a petition shall have been filed, in accordance with such regulations as may be prescribed by the Board—

(*A*) by an employee or group of employees or any individual or labor organization acting in their behalf alleging that a substantial number of employees (i) wish to be represented for collective bargaining and that their employer declines to recognize their representative as the representative defined in subsection (a) of this section . . . .

the Board shall investigate such petition and if it has reasonable cause to believe that a question of representation affecting commerce exists shall provide for an appropriate hearing upon due notice. . . . If the Board finds upon the record of such hearing that such a question of representation exists, it shall direct an election by secret ballot and shall certify the results thereof. . . .

Section 10:

(*a*) The Board is empowered . . . to prevent any person from engaging in any unfair labor practice [as defined] affecting commerce. . . .

Section 2:

(*6*) The term "commerce" means trade, traffic, commerce, transportation, or communication among the several States . . . or between any foreign country and any State . . . .

(*7*) The term "affecting commerce" means in commerce, or burdening or obstructing commerce or the free flow of commerce, or having led or tending to lead to a labor dispute burdening or obstructing commerce. . . .

McCULLOCH v. SOCIEDAD NACIONAL DE MARINEROS DE HONDURAS

Supreme Court of the United States, 1963.
372 U.S. 10, 83 S.Ct. 671, 9 L.Ed.2d 547.

[The United Fruit Company (United Fruit), a New Jersey corporation doing business in the United States and Central and South America, owned all the stock of Empresa Hondurena de Vapores, S. A. (Empresa), a Honduran corporation, whose directors and officers (none of whom were common to United Fruit) were residents of Honduras. Empresa owned a fleet of vessels which sailed between United States and Latin American ports, carrying chiefly United Fruit products and supplies. The vessels involved in this litigation were registered under Honduran law, flew the Honduran flag and called regularly at Honduran ports. They were time chartered (with crews) by Empresa to United Fruit, which determined their sailing schedules and ports of call. Their crews consisted almost entirely of Hondurans recruited by Empresa in Honduras, who signed Honduran shipping articles, renewed periodically in Honduran ports. Their wages and other terms of employment were controlled by a bargaining agreement between Empresa and a Honduran union, Sociedad Nacional. Under the Honduran Labor Code, only a union whose "juridic personality" is recognized by Honduras and which is composed of at least 90% Honduran nationals can represent seamen on Honduran-registered ships. Under Honduran law, recognition by Empresa of Sociedad Nacional as bargaining agent requires it to deal exclusively with Sociedad Nacional on all matters covered by the contract.

The National Maritime Union of America, AFL–CIO (N.M.U.), a union which does not meet the requirements of Honduran law, petitioned the National Labor Relations Board under the National Labor Relations Act, 49 Stat. 449 (1935), as amended, 29 U.S.C.A. § 151, for certification as the bargaining representative of the alien seamen employed upon Empresa's vessels. The Board, after a hearing, ordered an election to determine whether such seamen desired to be represented for purposes of collective bargaining by N.M.U., by a Honduran union (Sindicato Maritimo Nacional de Honduras) which had intervened in the proceeding, or by no union at all. Sociedad Nacional did not appear in the proceedings, and its name was not to be included in the election ballot. The Board in effect concluded that United Fruit owned and operated an integrated operation; that it was a joint employer of the alien seamen covered by the N.M.U. petition; and that the many contacts with the United States outweighed those with Honduras and justified application of the Act.

The order of the Board gave rise to two independent but companion suits based on the same facts. Empresa initiated suit, *sub nom.* Empresa Hondurena de Vapores S. A. v. McLeod, in the District Court for the Southern District of New York, seeking to enjoin the Regional Director of the Board from taking steps to conduct an election. Sociedad Nacional initiated suit, *sub nom.* Sociedad Nacional de Marineros de Honduras v. McCulloch, in the District Court for the District of Columbia, seeking to enjoin the Chairman and other members of the Board from holding an election. Sociedad Nacional and Empresa contended that the Act did not cover representation elections for alien seamen employed upon Empresa's vessels in the circumstances presented by this case. They relied primarily on the sections of the Act appearing at pp. 973–974, supra.

Sociedad Nacional and Empresa further contended that the Board's order for a representation election was in contravention of the Treaty of Friendship, Commerce, and Consular Rights of 1927 between the United States and Honduras, December 7, 1927, 45 Stat. 2618, T.S. No. 764, 87 L.N.T.S. 421. Article X of the Treaty provides:

> Merchant vessels and other privately owned vessels under the flags of either of the High Contracting Parties . . . shall, both within the territorial waters of the other High Contracting Party and on the high seas, be deemed to be the vessels of the Party whose flag is flown.

Article XXII of the Treaty provides:

> A consular officer shall have exclusive jurisdiction over controversies arising out of the internal order of private vessels of his country . . . . [and] shall also have jurisdiction over issues concerning the adjustment of wages and the execution of contracts relating thereto provided the local laws so permit.

The plaintiffs in each action moved for a preliminary injunction and other relief. In Empresa Hondurena de Vapores, S. A. v. McLeod, the District Court for the Southern District of New York denied the motion for a preliminary injunction on grounds that so drastic a threshold remedy should not be granted. 200 F.Supp. 484 (1961). The Court of Appeals for the Second Circuit, 300 F.2d 222 (1962), in an opinion by JUDGE FRIENDLY, reversed. Excerpts from this opinion appear below.]

The defendant's position proceeds from the basis that § 9(c) of the Act authorizes direction of an election if the Board has determined that "a question of representation affecting commerce exists"; that "affecting commerce" is defined by § 2(7), 29 U.S.C.A. § 152(7), to mean "in commerce, or burdening or obstructing commerce, or the free flow of commerce, or having led or tending to lead to a labor dispute burdening or obstructing commerce or the free flow of commerce"; and that § 2(6) defines commerce to include "trade, traffic, commerce, transportation or communication . . . between any foreign country and any State, Territory, or the District of Columbia." Literally the words cover the case. Yet the Board would hardly insist that the words apply to everything within their literal reach; we have not heard it suggested that the Board considers its power to extend to the stevedores who load Empresa's ships in Honduras although they are engaged in "commerce" quite as much as the seamen who man them. Neither do we suppose the Board would think it could direct an election among miners employed by a wholly owned subsidiary of an American company abroad, even though the ore was shipped to the United States and American employees of the parent were objecting to what they regarded as unfair wage competition arising from lack of effective organization among the foreign miners, although again the words literally apply. Words are not thus stretched to their literal bounds because statutes relating to international matters are construed in accordance with international usage, Lauritzen v. Larsen, 345 U.S. 571, 577–579, 581–582, 73 S.Ct. 921, 97 L.Ed. 1254 (1953) . . . .

The problem of workers directly engaged in transportation is more difficult; the stevedores stay on the piers, the miners remain in the mines, but the seamen come to the United States and return.

. . .

The case made by plaintiff's complaint goes far beyond the flying of the Honduran flag, important as Lauritzen teaches that to be. In this case there are also the Honduran citizenship of the crews, the employment of the crews in Honduras under Honduran articles, the vessels' regular visits to Honduras, the Honduran corporate identity —admittedly not fictitious—of the owner, the long recognition of and contract with a Honduran union, and the provisions of Honduran law regulating labor matters. Though the vessels are engaged in the foreign commerce of the United States, they are also engaged in the foreign commerce of Honduras. The only United States contacts not matched by Honduran ones are United Fruit's stock ownership and its direction and use of the voyages; these are substantially outweighed, for the purpose here at issue, by Honduras' interests.

Although the application of the Jones Act to accidents on foreign registered vessels involves the probability of rules of liability and amounts of recovery different from the law of the flag, as the discussions in Lauritzen, 345 U.S. at 575–576, 73 S.Ct. 97 and in Romero, 358 U.S. at 358, 79 S.Ct. 468 show, imposition of United States law on the rights of a seaman to recover against a ship owner or operator for personal injury is not likely to involve either party in a breach of contract with a third person or in the violation of a foreign governmental requirement. The occasional application of the antitrust laws to activities abroad has not been without its problems, see British Nylon Spinners, Ltd. v. Imperial Chemical Industries, Ltd., [1952] 2 All.E.R. 780, 782, 784; United States v. Holophane Co., 352 U.S. 903, 77 S.Ct. 144, 1 L.Ed.2d 114 (1956), even though the activity is usually of relatively small significance to the total economy of the foreign land. Here, on the allegations of the complaint, the conflict between United States and Honduran law would be constant; far from dealing only with incidents while the ships were in American waters, the Board would be regularly applying the shifting standards of its own decisions, and those of American courts and American legislators, to conduct in Honduras, where the bargaining between Empresa and its employees has always taken place; it would be endeavoring to enforce its will on matters that Honduras, with a better claim, regards as for itself to decide. Compare Vanity Fair Mills v. T. Eaton Co., Ltd., 234 F.2d 633, 646–647 (2 Cir.), cert. denied, 352 U.S. 871, 77 S.Ct. 96, 1 L.Ed.2d 76 (1956). The situation here differs sharply from the United States' informing itself as to contracts relating to the movement of traffic between the United States and a foreign country, Kerr S. S. Co. v. United States, 284 F.2d 61 (2 Cir. 1960); Montship Lines, Ltd. v. Federal Maritime Board, 295 F.2d 147, 153 (D.C.Cir. 1961), or even taking action with respect thereto, Thomsen v. Cayser, 243 U.S. 66, 37 S.Ct. 353, 61 L.Ed. 597 (1917). The case is appropriate for application of Mr. Justice Jackson's warning that "in dealing with international commerce we cannot be unmindful of the necessity for mutual forbearance if retaliations are to be avoided; nor should we forget that any contact which we hold sufficient to warrant application of our laws to a foreign transaction will logically be as strong a warrant for a foreign country to apply its law to an American transaction," 345 U.S. at 582, 73 S.Ct. at 928. We realize that if the Labor Act is inapplicable, owners of foreign flag ships such as Empresa will be deprived of the protection against certain unfair labor practices by the Federal courts accorded employers subject to the Act by such provisions as § 10(*l*) and § 303; but the practical consequences of this are less serious than those of a contrary holding. At least so the owners think, with the apparent concurrence of the Supreme Court in Benz.

Our belief that the Labor Act should not be held applicable in a case such as this is reinforced by the Geneva Convention on the High Seas, ratified by the United States on March 24, 1961, but not yet effective for lack of required ratification by 22 nations. [The Court then quoted Article 5, Section 1, set forth at p. 972, supra.]

Discussion seems to have been centered on what happens if the "genuine link" does not exist; [22] neither the text nor such explanatory materials as we have found say specifically what happens if the conditions of the final sentence are met. Yet, since it was deemed so important to insist upon the existence of a "genuine link" and the flag state's effective exercise of "jurisdiction and control in administrative, technical and social matters over ships flying its flag," it would be unreasonable to conclude that when all this had been done other states do not owe some obligations of respect.

Three other matters ought be mentioned before we conclude:

(1) We have not discussed the conflicting contentions as to the effect of Article 22 of the Treaty with Honduras . . . .—plaintiff arguing that application of the Labor Act would violate the first clause, . . . and defendant contending that the matter is one of "the execution of contracts" as to which the final sentence permits the application of "local laws." The problem is not an easy one; the view we take of the instant case makes it unnecessary for us to decide it.

(2) We realize that American unions understandably desire to organize vessels which they conceive to be in substance a part of this country's merchant marine, and that attempts to implement that desire can lead to a breach of the industrial peace which the Board is bound to promote, particularly when, as here, the stockholder of the foreign flag ships operates American flag vessels as well. Last summer's strike of the American merchant marine, with which we have some familiarity, . . . sufficiently demonstrates this. Therefore, we recognize that a controversy between an American union and Empresa could lead or tend to lead "to a labor dispute burdening or obstructing commerce or the free flow of commerce" carried on by American flag ships, as well as directly obstructing commerce carried on by foreign ones. However, that scarcely is decisive—the question still is how far Congress intended to permit the Board to intervene in what would normally be the affairs of a foreign government in order to prevent this. Even if we were to make the unrealistic assumption that Congress was so far-seeing as not only to have contemplated the growth of flags of convenience when it adopted the Labor Act in 1935, but also to have anticipated cases where an American company would operate some ships under our own flag and others through foreign subsidiaries flying the flags of other countries,

22. The "genuine link" requirement as adopted was less stringent than proposals made by such governments as the United Kingdom and the Netherlands and by the International Labor Conference, "which would have enabled states other than the flag state to withhold recognition of the national character of a ship if they considered that there was no 'genuine link' between the state and the ship." Report of the Committee on Foreign Relations to the Senate, 106 Cong.Rec. 10382 (1960). The Senate was told that the effect of the language as adopted in Geneva is that "no state can claim the right to determine unilaterally that no genuine link exists between a ship and the flag state," but "Nevertheless, there is a possibility that a state, with respect to a particular ship, may assert before an agreed tribunal, such as the International Court of Justice, that no genuine link exists. In such event, it would be for the Court to decide whether or not a genuine link existed." Id.

we see no basis for believing Congress would have chosen to solve the problem by an exercise of jurisdiction which would create such a conflict with a foreign government as would seem inevitable here.
. . .

(3) In order to avoid any possible misunderstanding in this controversial area, we emphasize that we are deciding only the case before us; what the result should be when the contacts of the country of the flag are weaker relative to those of the United States than here, we do not say.

The order denying a temporary injunction is reversed.

[In Sociedad Nacional de Marineros de Honduras v. McCulloch, the District Court for the District of Columbia granted the preliminary injunction. 201 F.Supp. 82 (1962). The court held that the Act should not be construed to confer authority on the Board to conduct elections for collective bargaining purposes under the facts of this case. Among other grounds, the court noted that assertion of jurisdiction would appear to conflict with the provisions of the Treaty of Friendship, Commerce, and Consular Rights. If possible, stated the court, an act of Congress should be construed so as not to violate the law of nations or repeal by implication a prior treaty with which there would be an apparent inconsistency. The alien seamen, foreign flag and foreign employment contracts under foreign law were additional factors pointing towards a limiting interpretation of the Act.

Appeal of this decision was perfected to the Court of Appeals for the District of Columbia Circuit, and the Supreme Court granted certiorari before judgment in the Court of Appeals. The Supreme Court also granted certiorari to the decision of the Court of Appeals for the Second Circuit. Its decision for both cases was handed down in an opinion, delivered by JUSTICE CLARK. Excerpts appear below.]

Since the parties all agree that the Congress has constitutional power to apply the National Labor Relations Act to the crews working foreign-flag ships, at least while they are in American waters, The Exchange, 7 Cranch 116, 143, 3 L.Ed. 287 (1812); Wildenhus's Case, 120 U.S. 1, 11, 7 S.Ct. 385, 30 L.Ed. 565 (1887); Benz v. Compania Naviera Hidalgo, 353 U.S. 138, 142, 77 S.Ct. 699, 1 L.Ed.2d 709 (1957), we go directly to the question whether Congress exercised that power. Our decision on this point being dispositive of the case, we do not reach the other questions raised by the parties and the *amici curiae.*

The question of application of the laws of the United States to foreign-flag ships and their crews has arisen often and in various contexts. As to the application of the National Labor Relations Act and its amendments, the Board has evolved a test relying on the relative weight of a ship's foreign as compared with its American contacts. That test led the Board to conclude here, as in West India Fruit & Steamship Co., supra, that the foreign-flag ships' activities affected "commerce" and brought them within the coverage of the Act. Where the balancing of the vessel's contacts has resulted in a contrary finding, the Board has concluded that the Act does not apply.

Six years ago this Court considered the question of the application of the Taft-Hartley amendments to the Act in a suit for damages "resulting from the picketing of a foreign ship operated entirely by foreign seamen under foreign articles while the vessel [was] temporarily in an American port." Benz v. Compania Naviera Hidalgo, supra, 353 U.S., at 139, 77 S.Ct., at 700, 1 L.Ed.2d 709. We held that the Act did not apply, searching the language and the legislative history and concluding that the latter "inescapably describes the boundaries of the Act as including only the workingmen of our own country and its possessions." Id., at 144, 77 S.Ct., at 702, 703, 1 L.Ed.2d 709, . . .

It is contended that this case is nonetheless distinguishable from Benz in two respects. First, here there is a fleet of vessels not temporarily in United States waters but operating in a regular course of trade between foreign ports and those of the United States; and, second, the foreign owner of the ships is in turn owned by an American corporation. We note that both of these points rely on additional American contacts and therefore necessarily presume the validity of the "balancing of contacts" theory of the Board. But to follow such a suggested procedure to the ultimate might require that the Board inquire into the internal discipline and order of all foreign vessels calling at American ports. Such activity would raise considerable disturbance not only in the field of maritime law but in our international relations as well. In addition, enforcement of Board orders would project the courts into application of the sanctions of the Act to foreign-flag ships on a purely *ad hoc* weighing of contacts basis.[23] This would inevitably lead to embarrassment in foreign affairs and be entirely infeasible in actual practice. The question, therefore, appears to us more basic; namely, whether the Act as written was intended to have any application to foreign registered vessels employing alien seamen.

Petitioners say that the language of the Act may be read literally as including foreign-flag vessels within its coverage. But, as in Benz, they have been unable to point to any specific language in the Act itself or in its extensive legislative history that reflects such a congressional intent. Indeed, the opposite is true as we found in Benz, where we pointed to the language of Chairman Hartley characterizing the Act as "a bill of rights both for *American* workingmen and for their employers." 353 U.S., at 144, 77 S.Ct., at 702, 703, 1 L.Ed.2d 709. We continue to believe that if the sponsors of the original Act or of its amendments conceived of the application now sought by the Board they failed to translate such thoughts into describing the boundaries of the Act as including foreign-flag vessels manned by alien crews. Therefore, we find no basis for a construction which would exert United States jurisdiction over and apply its laws to the internal management and affairs of the vessels here flying the Honduran flag, contrary to the recognition long afforded them not only by our State Department[24] but also by the Congress.[25] In addition, our attention

23. Our conclusion does not foreclose such a procedure in different contexts, such as the Jones Act, 46 U.S.C.A. § 688, where the pervasive regulation of the internal order of a ship may not be present. As regards application of the Jones Act to maritime torts on foreign ships, however, the Court has stated that "[p]erhaps the most venerable and universal rule of maritime law relevant to our problem is that which gives cardinal importance to the law of the flag." Lauritzen v. Larsen, 345 U.S. 571, 584, 73 S.Ct. 921, 929, 97 L.Ed. 1254 (1953) . . . .

24. State Department regulations provide that a foreign vessel includes "any vessel regardless of ownership, which is documented under the laws of a foreign country." 22 CFR § 81.-1(f).

25. Article X of the Treaty of Friendship, Commerce and Consular Rights between Honduras and the United States, 45 Stat. 2618 (1927), provides that merchant vessels flying the flags and having the papers of either country "shall, both within the territorial waters of the other High Contracting Party and on the high seas, be deemed to be the vessels of the Party whose flag is flown."

is called to the well-established rule of international law that the law of the flag state ordinarily governs the internal affairs of a ship. See Wildenhus's Case, supra, 120 U.S., at 12, 7 S.Ct., at 387, 30 L.Ed. 565; Colombos, The International Law of the Sea (3d rev. ed. 1954), 222–223. The possibility of international discord cannot therefore be gainsaid. Especially is this true on account of the concurrent application of the Act and the Honduran Labor Code that would result with our approval of jurisdiction. Sociedad, currently the exclusive bargaining agent of Empresa under Honduran law, would have a head-on collision with N.M.U. should it become the exclusive bargaining agent under the Act. This would be aggravated by the fact that under Honduran law N.M.U. is prohibited from representing the seamen on Honduran-flag ships even in the absence of a recognized bargaining agent. Thus even though Sociedad withdrew from such an intramural labor fight—a highly unlikely circumstance—questions of such international import would remain as to invite retaliatory action from other nations as well as Honduras.

The presence of such highly charged international circumstances brings to mind the admonition of Mr. Chief Justice Marshall in The Charming Betsy, 2 Cranch 64, 118, 2 L.Ed. 208 (1804), that "an act of Congress ought never to be construed to violate the law of nations if any other possible construction remains . . . ." We therefore conclude, as we did in Benz, that for us to sanction the exercise of local sovereignty under such conditions in this "delicate field of international relations there must be present the affirmative intention of the Congress clearly expressed." 353 U.S., at 147, 77 S.Ct., at 704, 1 L.Ed.2d 709. Since neither we nor the parties are able to find any such clear expression, we hold that the Board was without jurisdiction to order the election. This is not to imply, however, "any impairment of our own sovereignty, or limitation of the power of Congress" in this field. Lauritzen v. Larsen, 345 U.S. 571, 578, 73 S.Ct. 921, 926, 97 L.Ed. 1254 (1953). In fact, just as we directed the parties in Benz to the Congress, which "alone has the facilities necessary to make fairly such an important policy decision," 353 U.S., at 147, 77 S. Ct., at 704, 1 L.Ed.2d 709, we conclude here that the arguments should be directed to the Congress rather than to us. Cf. Lauritzen v. Larsen, supra, 345 U.S., at 593, 73 S.Ct., at 933, 934, 97 L.Ed. 1254.

[The Court affirmed the judgment of the District Court of the District of Columbia and vacated the judgment of the Court of Appeals for the Second Circuit, directing that the complaint be dismissed.]

MR. JUSTICE DOUGLAS, concurring.

I had supposed that the activities of American labor organizations whether related to domestic vessels or to foreign ones were covered by the National Labor Relations Act, at least absent a treaty which evinces a different policy.[26] Cf. Cook v. United States, 288 U.S. 102, 118–120, 53 S.Ct. 305, 77 L.Ed. 641. But my views were rejected in Benz v. Compania Naviera Hidalgo, 353 U.S. 138, 77 S.Ct. 699, 1 L.Ed.2d 709; and, having lost that cause in Benz, I bow to the inexorable result of its extension here, though not without some misgivings. The practical effect of our decision is to shift from all the taxpayers to seamen alone the main burden of financing an executive

26. It is agreed that Article XXII of the Treaty of Friendship, Commerce, and Consular Rights between the United States and Honduras, 45 Stat. 2618 (1927), and Article X of the Convention with Liberia of October 7, 1938, 54 Stat. 1751, 1756, grant those nations exclusive jurisdiction over the matters here involved.

policy of assuring the availability of an adequate American-owned merchant fleet for federal use during national emergencies. . . .

COMMENT

(1) In Benz v. Compania Naviera Hidalgo, S. A., 353 U.S. 138, 77 S.Ct. 699, 1 L.Ed.2d 709 (1957), to which Justices Clark and Douglas refer in McCulloch, the question was whether the NLRA barred an action for damages brought by a foreign shipowner, a Panamian corporation, against American unions. These unions had cooperated with striking seamen from the owner's ship, then docked in Portland, Oregon, by establishing picket lines to compel the shipowner to reemploy at more favorable wage rates striking crew members whom the owner had discharged. Damages were sought under Oregon common law, which allowed damages when picketing was for an unlawful purpose. The unions contended that the trial court could not award damages because the NLRA had preempted the field.

The ship flew the Liberian flag. Evidence indicated that no American owned interests in it or the plaintiff company. The ship's crew was made up entirely of aliens, principally German and British sailors. The voyage had originated in Germany for a two-year period and was to terminate at a European port. British forms of articles of agreement, entered into with the crew in Germany, stated all wage conditions. The ship was to load wheat for delivery to India.

The Supreme Court concluded that the NLRA did not apply and that the Oregon courts were competent to award damages under state law. Excerpts from the opinion delivered by JUSTICE CLARK follow:

> It should be noted at the outset that the dispute from which these actions sprang arose on a foreign vessel. It was between a foreign employer and a foreign crew operating under an agreement made abroad under the laws of another nation. The only American connection was that the controversy erupted while the ship was transiently in a United States port and American labor unions participated in its picketing.
>
> It is beyond question that a ship voluntarily entering the territorial limits of another country subjects itself to the laws and jurisdiction of that country. Wildenhus' Case, 1887, 120 U.S. 1, 7 S.Ct. 385, 30 L.Ed. 565. The exercise of that jurisdiction is not mandatory but discretionary. Often, because of public policy or for other reasons, the local sovereign may exert only limited jurisdiction and sometimes none at all. Cunard S.S. Co. v. Mellon, 1923, 262 U.S. 100, 43 S.Ct. 504, 67 L.Ed. 894. It follows that if Congress had so chosen it could have made the Act applicable to wage disputes arising on foreign vessels between nationals of other countries when the vessel comes within our territorial waters. The question here therefore narrows to one of intent of the Congress as to the coverage of the Act. . . .
>
> Our study of the Act leaves us convinced that Congress did not fashion it to resolve labor disputes between nationals of other countries operating ships under foreign laws.

The whole background of the Act is concerned with industrial strife between American employers and employees. In fact, no discussion in either House of Congress has been called to our attention from the thousands of pages of legislative history that indicates in the least that Congress intended the coverage of the Act to extend to circumstances such as those posed here. It appears not to have even occurred to those sponsoring the bill. The Report made to the House by its Committee on Education and Labor and presented by the co-author of the bill, Chairman Hartley, stated that "the bill herewith reported has been formulated as a bill of rights both for *American* workingmen and for their employers." The report declares further that because of the inadequacies of legislation "the *American* workingman has been deprived of his dignity as an individual," and that it is the purpose of the bill to correct these inadequacies. (Emphasis added.) H.R.Rep. No. 245, 80th Cong., 1st Sess. 4. What was said inescapably describes the boundaries of the Act as including only the workingmen of our own country and its possessions. . . .

. . . The seamen agreed in Germany to work on the foreign ship under British articles. We cannot read into the Labor Management Relations Act an intent to change the contractual provisions made by these parties. For us to run interference in such a delicate field of international relations there must be present the affirmative intention of the Congress clearly expressed. It alone has the facilities necessary to make fairly such an important policy decision where the possibilities of international discord are so evident and retaliative action so certain. We, therefore, conclude that any such appeal should be directed to the Congress rather than the courts. . . .

MR. JUSTICE DOUGLAS, dissenting.

The case involves a contest between American unions and a foreign ship. The foreign ship came to Portland, Oregon, to load a cargo of wheat for carriage to India. The crew members were paid about one-third the amount of cash wages that are paid to American seamen on American vessels carrying grain to the Orient. This foreign ship is in competition with those American vessels.

American unions, therefore, have a vital interest in the working conditions and wages of the seamen aboard this foreign vessel. Their interest is in the re-employment of the foreign crew at better wages and working conditions. And they peacefully picketed the foreign vessel to further that interest.

The judgment we sustain today is one in damages against members of the American union who engaged in that peaceful picketing. It is for conduct precisely regulated by the Taft-Hartley Act. . . .

(2) The Supreme Court has had several further encounters with the problems of the NLRA and foreign shipping. International Longshoremen's Local 1416 AFL–CIO v. Ariadne Shipping Co., 397 U.S. 195, 90 S.Ct. 872, 25 L.Ed.2d 218 (1970), held the NLRA did apply and did preempt state law, so that American longshoremen could lawfully picket a foreign-flag vessel in an American port to protest the fact that the work of loading the vessel was being done by non-unionized American longshoremen at wages which they regarded as sub-standard.

In Windward Shipping, Ltd. v. American Radio Ass'n, 415 U.S. 104, 94 S.Ct. 959, 39 L.Ed.2d 195 (1974), six American maritime unions picketed foreign-flag vessels with foreign crews in order to protest the fact that the foreign crews were being paid wages well below American standards. The purpose of the picketing was to arrest a movement away from American flag vessels that had gone so far that 95% of American exports travelled in foreign bottoms. It was hoped that longshoremen and other workers would refuse to cross the picket lines. It had that effect, and the shipowners brought an injunction action in the Texas courts, alleging that the purpose of the picketing was the unlawful inducement of breach of pre-existing contracts by owners and crews. The Texas courts held that the NLRB had jurisdiction that preempted state action. The Supreme Court reversed. It noted that the picketing did "not involve the inescapable intrusion into the affairs of foreign ships that was present" in McCulloch and Benz. It observed, however, that these cases did not exhaust all the types of interference with the maritime operations of foreign vessels that would render the LMRA inapplicable. It stated:

> In this situation, the foreign vessels' lot is not a happy one. A decision by the foreign owners to raise foreign seamen's wages to a level mollifying the American pickets would have the most significant and far-reaching effect on the maritime operations of these ships throughout the world. A decision to boycott American ports in order to avoid the difficulties induced by the picketing would be detrimental not only to the private balance sheets of the foreign shipowners but to the citizenry of a country as dependent on goods carried in foreign bottoms as is ours. Retaliatory action against American vessels in foreign ports might likewise be considered, but the employment of such tactics would probably exacerbate and broaden the present dispute. Virtually none of the predictable responses of a foreign shipowner to picketing of this type, therefore, would be limited to the sort of wage-cost decision benefitting American workingmen which the LMRA was designed to regulate. This case therefore, falls under *Benz* rather than under *Ariadne.*

The Court therefore held that the picketing was not "in commerce" as defined by the Act and that the Texas courts were not preempted from entertaining the injunction action. A dissent written by Justice Brennan pointed to the critical decline of America as a competitor on the high seas and to the numerous items of legislation showing Congressional determination to support a healthy merchant marine. The decision in Windward was followed in a closely similar fact situation in American Radio Ass'n v. Mobile SS Ass'n, 419 U.S. 215, 95 S.Ct. 409, 42 L.Ed.2d 399 (1974), where the state injunction action was brought by the association of American stevedoring companies rather than the foreign owners.

(3) The Note at p. 973, supra, reports the favorable attitude of the executive branch to flags of convenience, and the policy of the Maritime Administration of permitting transfers from American to foreign flags. The United States filed an *amicus* brief [27] before the Supreme Court in a case related to McCulloch "to express the considered position of the Executive Branch." It argued that representation elections would embarrass the Government in its conduct of foreign relations by offending and conflicting with laws of foreign sovereigns. It contended that assertion of jurisdiction would likely prompt the sale of ships by American owners to foreign interests or transfers to other registries. These were possibilities which, in the considered judgment of the Secretary of Defense, raised "grave problems affecting national defense." Thus the United States argued for a restrictive interpretation of the NLRA but stopped short of requesting the Court to hold that the Board could never assert jurisdiction over foreign-flag vessels with alien crews.

The Board argued that there was "no substantial basis for the Department of Defense's assumption that defense policies would be subverted by . . . assertion of jurisdiction . . . [or] for the fear, voiced by the Department of State, that application of the Act . . . would unsettle international relations." [28]

(4) Prior to the McCulloch litigation, the Board decided two cases presenting facts more favorable to assertion of jurisdiction than McCulloch.

Peninsular and Occidental Steamship Co., 132 N.L.R.B. 10 (1961). An American union petitioned the Board to enjoin unfair labor practices upon a vessel registered under Liberian law and owned by the wholly-owned Liberian subsidiary of a corporation organized in the United States. The vessel operated between United States and Caribbean ports and had never entered Liberian waters. It was time chartered (with crew) to the American parent of the Liberian subsidiary, and the parent was the employer of its crew of nonresident aliens. The Board held that it had jurisdiction to enjoin unfair labor practices arising out of operations of the vessel.

Hamilton Bros. Inc., 133 N.L.R.B. 868 (1961). A Honduran labor union petitioned the Board for a representation election covering vessels owned and controlled by a corporation organized in the United States. The vessels were registered in Honduras and Nicaragua and flew the flags of those countries. They were manned by alien seamen recruited in Florida and various foreign ports, and they engaged in trade with a number of nations, including the nations of their registry.

27. Brief for the United States as *amicus curiae*, pp. 7, 11, in Incres Steamship Co., Ltd. v. International Maritime Workers Union, 372 U.S. 24, 83 S.Ct. 611, 9 L.Ed.2d 557 (1963), a related case before the Supreme Court.

28. Brief for the Regional Director and Members of the National Labor Relations Board, p. 17, in the McCulloch case.

The Board, finding that the maritime operations were an integral part of a domestically owned, located and operated business, held that it had jurisdiction to order an election.

QUESTIONS

(1) Note Justice Clark's reference to the legislative history of the NLRA (compare the excerpts from Section 1 on p. 973 (supra) and his stress upon protection of the "American workingman." Does his opinion advance that protective purpose, or permit American shipowners to insulate themselves at will from domestic labor regulations?

(2) Compare the approaches of Judge Friendly and Justice Clark to interpretation of the NLRA.

> (*a*) Which is more reminiscent of Lauritzen v. Larsen, p. 954, supra? Which do you consider preferable in the context of the NLRA?
>
> (*b*) How would the two cases described in paragraph (4) of the preceding comment probably have been decided under Judge Friendly's and Justice Clark's opinions?

(3) Is the Court vigorously affirming, in this different setting, the "cardinal importance [of] the law of the flag" which was stressed in Lauritzen? Are two separate questions posed in these foreign-flag cases: What "nationality" has the ship, as evidenced by its registration, documentation and flag? What significance should that nationality have in deciding what law is to be applied to aspects of the ship's operations or administration?

(4) Would critical premises to the opinion have been undermined if Honduras had no labor legislation, or is simply the *risk* of conflict with a foreign regulatory scheme a sufficient reason for restrictive interpretation of domestic legislation? Should the question be: which of two competing regulatory schemes should prevail? If so, on what criteria should a court make this determination?

(5) Do the references in the opinion to established rules of international law and the "law of nations" appear to influence significantly the outcome? Is the Court here referring to "rules" as identifiable and coherent as those relating to diplomatic immunities, or to generally relevant admonitions and policies in construing domestic statutes?

(6) Do the treaty provisions between the United States and Honduras appear determinative? Persuasive?

(7) What effect, if any, should have been given to the policies extrinsic to the NLRA referred to in the Note at p. 973, supra and stressed in the arguments of the Department of Defense described in paragraph (3) of the preceding comment?

D. ANTITRUST REGULATION

Antitrust laws are often regarded as a particularly American phenomenon. To be sure, other countries have developed comparable policies, particularly those in Western Europe which have been more attentive to antitrust problems since World War II and the growth of the Common Market.[29] But no other country gives such policies as central a role domestically or has sought as vigorously to export them. These tendencies have led to sporadic friction between the United States and foreign countries, and at times to episodes of head-on confrontation.

A study of transnational aspects of antitrust regulation entails special problems. Unlike the traditional criminal legislation considered in Chapter VIII, antitrust laws and policies do not lend themselves to an easy identification of legislative purpose. They often involve a subtle and complex network of domestic policies and rules which may at times be inconsistent or in conflict. This uncertain and plural character of antitrust policies distinguishes our present inquiry even from the earlier subject in this chapter of seamen's remedies, where legislative purpose and economic effects were more readily ascertainable. Whatever the difficulties, inquiry into domestic policies supporting antitrust legislation is inescapable for purposes of analysis of the transnational reach of our antitrust laws, for it is almost impossible to disentangle the considerations relevant to an entirely domestic setting from those relevant to foreign activities affecting foreign commerce. Injection of a foreign element into an antitrust problem adds new dimensions. But the underlying antitrust principles that may determine litigation of an entirely domestic complexion are also relevant in transnational settings. To complicate the matter further, the statutes are not helpful in resolving the transnational problems. Unlike certain fields, such as transnational aspects of taxation that are considered in Chapter X, the wording of the antitrust laws does not usefully delimit their spatial application.

---

1. PROBLEMS IN DETERMINING THE REACH OF THE ANTITRUST LAWS

NOTE ON ANTITRUST POLICIES

Domestic Antitrust Policies

No compact summary can begin to do justice to the Sherman Act, its reinforcing statutes, and the interpretations given this legislation by courts and administrative officials. What follows is designed to provide a general understanding of the terms and purposes of these laws.

Despite the difficulty in separating the economic from the political aspects of any society, it is possible to view antitrust legislation as aiming primarily at goals of an economic character. In a society in which the goal and ideology of market ordering continue to exercise a powerful influence upon social organization, the antitrust laws are thought to represent a critical means for approaching that goal as

29. The developing antitrust law of the Common Market is examined at pp. 1342–1420, infra.

closely as may be possible. They seek to assure that the market will remain competitive and thus achieve the objectives noted below.

The logic of the behavioral and legal premises underlying market ordering itself suggests the need for some regulation of the market to curb anti-competitive practices. It is axiomatic to market theory that individuals or firms seek to maximize their welfare, and that such efforts at maximization by countless individuals and firms combine to produce the highest aggregate social welfare. For economic life, welfare maximization generally involves profit maximization. But this behavioral postulate suggests that actors in society may seek to maximize within the competitive market, *or* in ways destructive of market ordering—coercive and dominant market power, collusion with others and so on.

Consider also a basic legal postulate underlying market theory, that of maximum possible freedom of contract. Actors can thereby work out their own welfare as they best perceive it. But that freedom can be abused through agreements which destroy basic aspects of market ordering—exclusive arrangements, price fixing, and so on.

That is, the final commitment of the individual actor will not be to the market as such but to personal maximization, whether within the economic and legal principles underlying the market or in violation of them. Hence, a societal commitment to maintain as competitive an economy as possible so as to realize the allocational and welfare aims of the market requires governmental vigilance in protection of market structures.

Thus the antitrust laws are justified as attempts to control anticompetitive practices among firms, and to regulate the growth and application of private economic power. That is, the governmental infrastructure of laws and institutions necessary for the functioning of the market not only provides a facilitative legal framework involving rules of contract, property, tort, and so on, but also defines the boundaries within which the private ordering taking advantage of that facilitative framework must proceed.

Antitrust regulation thus may be viewed as reinforcing the market-oriented aspects of our economy which stand as an alternative to pervasive governmental control and planning that would sharply curtail the domain of private decision-making, and of course as an alternative to government ownership of vital segments of the economy. It seeks to preserve, to as large a degree as possible, the "price" or "market" system under which the play of market forces within a regulatory framework determines the prices at which goods are produced or sold, hence the allocation of resources and nature of the goods produced, and hence the directions which the economy takes. A principal goal or premise underlying this system is that of efficiency, or the maximization of the value of production. That is, the premise of market theory is that an economy consisting of a large number of competitive producers, distributors and sellers, each dependent upon rather than controlling the forces of supply and demand, will direct resources to their most highly valued uses and thus maximize production through allocational efficiency.

Beyond such dominantly economic and material considerations, market theory and the antitrust statutes built upon it represent important political preferences. Perhaps the dominant value that has been expounded in the development of market theory—and in the allied development of liberal political theory—is that of decentralized decision-making by individuals or firms expressing their desires and seeking to maximize their welfare as they perceive it. Market and liberal theory thereby expresses a preference for a relatively pluralistic and decentralized form of society, one in which economic decision-making is dispersed to the largest possible degree. A truly competitive system achieves, by definition, that dispersal and decentralization. It also helps to realize an allied value—namely, that consumers signaling their preferences through the price and market system will have the maximum possible choice as to what goods are produced and offered to them, and that they will receive the lowest possible price for such goods. Moreover, antitrust enforcement curbing anticompetitive practices and the accumulation of monopoly power will tend to assure that fields of economic activity remain relatively open to newcomers, another aspect of choice.

Of course these premises are open to, and have been subjected to, recurrent and penetrating challenge. Our purpose here is not to explore that challenge or to analyze the achievements of market and price theory against its aspirations or against alternative forms of ordering, but to examine the asserted purposes—and to some extent the achievements—of antitrust regulation within the market framework. To permit that examination, a clearer conception of what we mean by the "market system" in contemporary America is helpful. Clearly today's industrial society goes well beyond any conception of a market within a sparse framework of contract and property law, complemented by elements of tort and criminal law. Competition and market allocation of resources occur within a complex regulatory framework, ranging from income or excise taxation to labor laws, zoning regulations, anti-pollution measures, minimum wage or tariff laws, agricultural price supports, and a host of other regulatory policies—at times reaching the extreme of the price and wage controls under the Economic Stabilization Program of the early 1970's. Moreover government welfare programs of a redistributional character, as well as government activities such as the maintenance of a military establishment and vast contract purchasing, structure the economy within which market choice can occur. Thus it is within a complicated and ambivalent society, from both economic and political perspectives, that antitrust policy must pursue its goals.

At the outset, it is well to bear in mind the arguments of critics who have vigorously challenged the possibility of maintaining conditions of "free competition" necessary to market theory within an economy which grows ever more complex, more managed, and more concentrated. Such critics speak from both sides of the political spectrum. Some, stressing the historical and present departures from the theory whose broad outlines we have sketched, urge intensification of the trend towards management of the economy and the assurance of minimum welfare through government intervention and redistributional policies. Others hold to the traditional premise that maximization of the value of production remains the primary goal and that whatever distribution emerges from the play of economic forces should be considered just. But they may deny that the market now constitutes the effective means towards that goal, and argue that the efficiency of a few giant firms and their capacity to plan comprehensively and for the long term are better safeguards for the performance of the economy. Nonetheless, such ideas have not displaced a primary and continuing emphasis in the rhetoric of American politics upon the goal of the market. Nor have they supplanted the emphasis on competition and the relative dispersal of economic power within a regime of maximum possible decentralized choice, as the reason for strengthening and enforcing the antitrust laws.

The economic, social and philosophical aspects of the antitrust laws were succinctly described by Judge Learned Hand in United States v. Aluminum Co. of America, 148 F.2d 416, 427 (2d Cir. 1945). In considering the Government's charge that the defendant had monopolized the domestic market in aluminum ingot in violation of the Sherman Act, Judge Hand stated:

> . . . [I]t is no excuse for "monopolizing" a market that the monopoly has not been used to extract from the consumer more than a "fair" profit. The Act has wider purposes. Indeed, even though we disregarded all but economic considerations, it would by no means follow that such concentration of producing power is to be desired, when it has not been used extortionately. Many people believe that possession of unchallenged economic power deadens initiative, discourages thrift and depresses energy; that immunity from competition is a narcotic, and rivalry is a stimulant, to industrial progress; that the spur of constant stress is necessary to counteract an inevitable disposition to let well enough alone. Such people believe that competitors, versed in the craft as no consumer can be, will be quick to detect opportunities for saving and new shifts in production, and be eager to profit by them. . . . [Congress] did not condone "good trusts" and condemn "bad" ones; it forbad all. Moreover, in so doing it was not necessarily actuated by economic motives alone. It is possible, because of its indirect social or moral effect, to prefer a system of small producers, each dependent for his success upon his own skill and character, to one in which the great mass of those engaged must accept the direction of a few. These considerations, which we have suggested only as possible purposes of the Act, we think the decisions prove to have been in fact its purposes.

In pursuit of these goals, Congress has developed a network of statutes. The basic provisions—Sections 1 and 2 of the Sherman Act, 26 Stat. 209 (1890), as amended, 15 U.S.C.A. §§ 1 and 2—are drafted in terms of almost constitution-like breadth and indefiniteness. In critical part, they read as follows:

> *Section 1:* Every contract, combination in the form of trust or otherwise, or conspiracy, in restraint of trade or commerce among the several States, or with foreign nations, is declared to be illegal . . . . Every person who shall make any contract or engage in any combination or conspiracy declared by this [Act] to be illegal shall be deemed guilty of a misdemeanor . . . .
>
> *Section 2:* Every person who shall monopolize, or attempt to to monopolize, or combine or conspire with any other person or persons, to monopolize any part of the trade or commerce among the several States, or with foreign nations, shall be deemed guilty of a misdemeanor . . . .

The sparse, legislative guidance as to how these provisions are to be interpreted, and the fact that they have been applied to a society of a dramatically changing economic complexion since their enactment in 1890, have required the courts to assume responsibility for developing antitrust policy. In effect, the basic antitrust statutes, those speaking in broadest terms to the widest segments of the economy, have amounted to a delegation of power to the courts to work out appropriate principles on a case-by-case basis, all within the formal framework of the interpretation of legislative policy. As judicially interpreted, Section 1 of the Sherman Act proscribes agreements between competing firms (horizontal agreements) or firms in a production and distribution chain (vertical agreements) that have anticompetitive effects. The courts have considered certain agreements—such as horizontal arrangements fixing prices or allocating marketing territories, which are not parts of arrangements that are viewed as having socially constructive purposes—to lack any social benefits which can offset or "justify" their anticompetitive effects. "[B]ecause of their pernicious effect on competition and lack of any redeeming virtue," such agreements "are conclusively presumed to be unreasonable and therefore illegal without elaborate inquiry as to the precise harm they have caused or the business excuse for their use." [30] They are often referred to as "*per se*" violations of the antitrust laws.

Note the broad language of Section 1 in proscribing "[e]very contract . . . in restraint of trade". Of course such a proscription cannot be taken literally. Every contract by definition restrains trade; the dealer who agrees to deliver a car to a purchaser can be said to restrain other dealers from making that sale. Hence qualification was essential. In fact, the Supreme Court early read into the Sherman Act the so-called "rule of reason".[31] Where that "rule" applies, courts must engage in a more detailed analysis of the adverse and meritorious effect of agreements potentially within the ban of

30. Northern Pacific R. Co. v. United States, 356 U.S. 1, 5, 78 S.Ct. 514, 518, 2 L.Ed.2d 545, 549 (1958).

31. Two early cases which originated and developed the "rule of reason" were Standard Oil Co. v. United States, 221 U.S. 1, 31 S.Ct. 502, 55 L. Ed. 619 (1911), and Chicago Board of Trade v. United States, 246 U.S. 231, 38 S.Ct. 242, 62 L.Ed. 683 (1918).

Section 1 before reaching a conclusion as to their legality. Many factors may become relevant to that conclusion: the motives behind a particular restraint; the past and present market position and the prospects of the parties to the agreement; the nature and severity of the restraint; its actual or probable effect upon the market, and so on. Characteristic agreements which are tested by the "rule of reason" include those through which a manufacturer makes a particular merchant its agent and exclusive distributor in a given territory, or two firms form a joint venture to achieve a goal that neither could easily achieve alone.

Section 2 deals with the single-firm monopolist which gains an excessive degree of economic power and is thus freed from the constraints of competition in setting its price and other policies. Judicial decisions have given different answers to the difficult questions posed by that section: how large a proportion of the defined market need a firm occupy to be a monopolist? need it be shown that such a firm used unlawful means to attain that monopoly? is it necessary that the firm actively sought to obtain and maintain its market position? or is it sufficient to show that the monopoly was not "thrust upon it" by circumstances? The answers to these questions depend partly upon whether one regards Section 2 as dealing with the "evil" behavior of creating a monopoly or with monopoly as an undesirable economic condition.

Ancillary to these fundamental statutes is a set of restrictions—most of them introduced by the Clayton Act of 1914, 38 Stat. 730, as amended, 15 U.S.C.A. §§ 12–27—that aim principally at business arrangements that are not yet far enough advanced to be subject to the Sherman Act. The most relevant to the following materials is Section 7, known as the "anti-merger" section of the Clayton Act. It prohibits the acquisition by a corporation of the stock or assets of another corporation engaged in commerce if the following condition, more severe to defendants than the Sherman Act's test, is met: "where in any line of commerce in any section of the country, the effect of such acquisition may be substantially to lessen competition or to tend to create a monopoly."

One additional statutory provision should be noted. Section 5 of the Federal Trade Commission Act, 38 Stat. 719 (1914), as amended, 15 U.S.C.A. § 45, proscribes "[u]nfair methods of competion in commerce, and unfair or deceptive acts or practices in commerce . . . ." Although the main thrust of Section 5 might appear directed at deceptive practices such as false advertising, that section has also been used to proceed against practices proscribed by the Sherman and Clayton Acts and some allied anticompetitive practices not covered by those statutes. In a sense, Section 5 serves as a reserve to fill gaps in the rest of the antitrust scheme.

These provisions may be enforced through proceedings brought by the Government or by private parties.

(*1*) The Department of Justice may bring a civil action under Section 4 of the Sherman Act and Section 15 of the Clayton Act to prevent and restrain violations. The relief granted may include not only a simple prohibitory injunction but also a complex decree ordering the divestiture of corporate assets or the modification or termination of contracts, or compelling a corporation to endeavor to compete in a market which it has heretofore refrained from entering.

(*2*) The Department of Justice may also prosecute criminally violators of the Sherman Act. This route has been followed only in cases of deliberate violations of rules, such as those against price fixing, which were well known to the business world. The penalties for violations of the Sherman Act have recently been increased to fines of $1,000,000 for corporations and $100,000 for individuals, with up to three years imprisonment. One should also note the provisions of Section 14 of the Clayton Act, to the effect that violations by a corporation of any penal provisions of the antitrust laws shall also be deemed to be violations by individual directors or officers who have "authorized, ordered, or done, any of the acts constituting in whole or in part such violation . . . ." Such individuals are subject to fines not exceeding $5,000 and to imprisonment for not exceeding one year.

(*3*) The Federal Trade Commission may, through administrative proceedings, order a party to cease and desist from practices that violate either the Clayton Act or Section 5 of the Federal Trade Commission Act. Because of the broad scope of Section 5, the Commission is indirectly authorized to enforce the Sherman Act as well. Such orders are of course subject to judicial review.

(*4*) In many cases, the sanction most feared by a potential defendant will be the treble-damage action brought by some private party—a customer, a supplier, or a competitor—who can prove that, in the words of Section 4 of the Clayton Act, he has been "injured in his business or property by reason of anything forbidden in the antitrust laws . . . ." In addition to allowing the victorious plaintiff three times his damages, Section 4 awards him a reasonable attorney's fee. Section 5 gives a plaintiff the right to use a relevant decree (except a consent decree) in an action brought by the Government in which the defendant was found to have violated the antitrust laws as prima facie evidence against the defendant in the private suit.

(*5*) A private party may also sue under Section 16 of the Clayton Act for an injunction against "threatened loss or damage by a violation of the antitrust laws."

Apart from the regulatory and interventionist policies of government that influence market choice, the specific pro-competition philosophy of the antitrust laws has been checked by other considerations which have at times weighed more heavily with the Congress. It is relevant to note here several of those considerations.

There are some classical situations in which the view has prevailed that competition is impractical because of considerations of efficiency relating to economies of scale, infrastructure investment and declining marginal costs per unit of production. Thus only one firm may be able to operate in a given market. For example, only one supplier of electricity can economically maintain a network of transmission lines in a given territory. Where such a "natural monopoly" obtains, the monopolist will at once be granted an exclusive franchise to operate and become subject as a public utility to regulation of its activities, including of course rates. Thus regulation designed to permit a "reasonable" return on investment is relied upon to keep rates at a fair level and to control entry of newcomers into the field.

In other situations, Congress has been persuaded by arguments that markets of large numbers of competing individuals or firms will be "ruinous". Such markets may force prices below the level at which producers can survive, lead to price fluctuations that will render planning impossible for consumers, and ultimately permit survival of only a few competitors who can then behave like monopolists. This argument has combined with that of "natural monopoly" to play a role in substituting regulation for free competition in numbers of fields. The different branches of the transportation industry are here illustrative. Railroads may well have been thought of as natural monopolies as they grew in the last century, but other reasons must be sought to explain the regulation of the newer transportation industries such as trucking and aviation. Among the reasons advanced to protect the older industries from new and possibly devastating competition has been the asserted public interest in the orderly development of infrastructure transportation.

Particularly where the buyers of a commodity, such as labor, are fewer and larger than the sellers, the basis is laid for the claim that sellers (laborers) have the right to act cooperatively so as to obtain a "countervailing power" in economic and political terms. In such situations, the shift in political forces and the changing political and social complexion of the society have of course been a major force in the legislative recognition of these claims. The antitrust exemptions for labor unions and for agricultural cooperatives are illustrations of permission being granted to parties to pool their economic resources to achieve economic aims.

Special rules of conduct have also been developed for certain areas of this country's foreign commerce. For example, the Webb-Pomerene Act permits some joint activity among American exporters that might otherwise constitute an unlawful conspiracy under Sections 1 and 2 of the Sherman Act or a violation of Section 7 of the

Clayton Act, p. 992, supra. The key provisions of Section 2 of the Act, 40 Stat. 517 (1918), 15 U.S.C.A. § 62, read:

> Nothing contained in sections [1–7 of Title 15, which include Sections 1 and 2 of the Sherman Act] shall be construed as declaring to be illegal an association entered into for the sole purpose of engaging in export trade and actually engaged solely in such export trade, or an agreement made or act done in the course of export trade by such association, provided such association, agreement, or act is not in restraint of trade within the United States, and is not in restraint of the export trade of any domestic competitor of such association: *Provided,* That such association does not, either in the United States or elsewhere, enter into any agreement, understanding, or conspiracy, or do any act which artificially or intentionally enhances or depresses prices within the United States of commodities of the class exported by such association, or which substantially lessens competition within the United States, or otherwise restrains trade therein.

Firms entering into such associations must file certain information with the Federal Trade Commission, which exercises a general supervisory power over the associations and refers recommendations, in the event that it concludes that an association violates the law, to the Attorney General for such action as he may deem proper. One of the important motivations for the Act was to enable American exporters, particularly smaller businesses which were not able to penetrate independently foreign markets, to combat foreign competition and in particular foreign cartels. The associations formed under the Act have performed varied functions, ranging from the fixing of export prices and allocations of sales to purely administrative or exploratory functions in the development of foreign markets. For a variety of reasons, the Act has not given birth to widespread and effective export operations among American firms. About 30 associations were operative in 1964, and in that year such associations accounted for less than 5% of the United States' total value in exports. The ambiguity of various provisions in the Act [32], its uncertain and complicated relationship to the antitrust laws, and the strict interpretation given the Act by officials in charge of antitrust enforcement are contributing reasons.

Proposals for changes in the Act recur sporadically. Some seek to expand it, particularly so that its protection would be available to construction firms bidding jointly on overseas projects involving services rather than exports of commodities. Others assert that such joint ventures are not illegal under the present law, that rulings (known as

32. The phrase "export trade" has been held not to cover the purchase of goods by the United States for its foreign aid program, with the result that no Webb Pomerene Act exemption applied. United States v. Concentrated Phosphate Export Ass'n, 393 U.S. 199, 89 S.Ct. 361, 21 L.Ed.2d 344 (1968). By way of contrast, note that the shipping of goods between Japan and Vietnam in support of U.S. military operations has been held to be part of "foreign commerce" so as to fall within the scope of the Sherman Act. Pacific Seafarers v. Pacific Far East Line, 131 U.S.App.D.C. 226, 404 F.2d 804 (1968).

business review letters) can be obtained from the Department of Justice that will protect the members from prosecution, and even that the Act is not useful and should be narrowed or even repealed.[33]

It should also be noted that the limited monopolies inherent in patents, copyrights and trade-marks derogate from the principle of unrestrained competition. Motivated in some measure by the belief that the grant of exclusive rights will stimulate competition and progress by encouraging inventors and writers, such grants nonetheless fence off portions of the economy and make them private preserves.

Additional reading: Areeda, Antitrust Analysis (2d ed. 1974) (leading cases, comments, questions); Kaysen and Turner, Antitrust Policy (1959); Neale, The Antitrust Laws of the U.S.A. (1960); Report of the Attorney General's National Committee to Study the Antitrust Laws (1955). An excellent discussion of transnational aspects of antitrust regulation is Brewster, Antitrust and American Business Abroad (1958). See also Fugate, Foreign Commerce and the Antitrust Laws (2d ed. 1973). For a collection of comments and articles on that topic, see International Law Association, Report of the Fifty-First Conference held at Tokyo 304–592 (1965). For a collection of statements on that topic, see Hearings Before the Subcommittee on Antitrust and Monopoly of the Senate Committee on the Judiciary, 89th Cong., 2d Sess., pt. 1 (1966).

Foreign Laws—Antitrust and Related Problems

Foreign antitrust laws offer a variety of parallels and contrasts. Several years before the Sherman Act Canada enacted a Combines Act. In Great Britain, the common-law tradition outlawing certain agreements in restraint of trade was allowed to perish through grudging interpretation, but in 1948 legislation reactivated the field. Since that time there has been continuing attention to problems of restoring competition, leading to the more potent 1956 Restrictive Trade Practices Act, and 1965 legislation relating to monopolies and mergers. On the Continent, antitrust legislation was enacted in most of the major Western countries after World War II. The German Law of 1957, which drew heavily on American experience and was influenced by the de-cartelization efforts of the American occupation authorities, is one of the more elaborate. These national antitrust laws have more recently been supplemented by Articles 85 to 90 of the Rome Treaty creating the European Common Market (European Economic Community, or EEC), and by the regulations and decisions which, in pursuance of those articles, have issued from the EEC's Commission and Court. See pp. 1342–1420, infra. Japan, also under American stimulus, has enacted antitrust legislation, the only significant example in Asia.

The variety of foreign antitrust laws is such that generalization is difficult. For purposes of this discussion, a few statements about typical features of foreign systems may be risked. First, most foreign laws permit more justifications for agreements among competi-

33. On the Webb Pomerene Act, see generally Fugate, Foreign Commerce and the Antitrust Laws 227–28 (2d ed. 1973).

tors than does the Sherman Act. For example, it may be shown under many statutes or administratively developed rules that the agreement restricting competition made possible more research, prevented undue price fluctuation, lowered production costs to the ultimate benefit of the consumer, and so on. Second, it is common for an administrative agency—the EEC Commission or the British Registrar and Restrictive Practices Court—to be given the task of reviewing agreements which are of a restrictive character (which, under different laws, are either required or permitted to be filed with a designated agency) and of granting dispensations to those agreements which are judged to be, on balance, beneficial. Thus foreign legal systems tend to rely less on traditional legal procedures and civil litigation than does the United States.

Third, it is rare for any foreign system to place such strong emphasis on discouraging monopoly or oligopoly as is found in Section 2 of the Sherman Act or Section 7 of the Clayton Act. Most countries do not have many giant enterprises comparable to General Motors or duPont; they are inclined to resort to other means of controlling those which they do have. Indeed, some foreign countries have tended to the view that it was important to build up large enterprises that would have the countervailing power to match "the American challenge." There are, however, signs that this attitude is shifting and that foreign authorities are becoming more sensitive to potential abuses of concentration.

Each of these foreign antitrust laws can be evaluated only in the broader context of a nation's economic system and philosophy. There are here many points of similarity. Almost all non-socialist countries have patent, trade-mark and copyright rules that circumscribe competition. Most have express or implied exemptions from the normal antitrust rules for certain industries. Thus laws may tolerate, or even provide for, the organization of firms in a given industry into a trade association or cartel which has the power to fix prices for domestic sales or exports, production quotas, quality standards and so on. Many carry much further the approach that regulation, even self regulation, is preferable to competition. In countries which emphasize national planning of industrial growth, cooperation between industrial leaders and the government planning agency is a prerequisite; this tends to imply cooperation between companies as well. For example, several firms may determine the extent to which each will expand its facilities in order to meet the government's target. In countries where the government has nationalized a particular sector of industry and, of course, in countries where all industry has been socialized, competition in our domestic sense ceases to be a significant factor. But in different forms and for different incentives, competition among business units may survive, together with prophylactic legislation. For example, Yugoslavia has instituted legislation penalizing managers of state-owned enterprises that set prices collusively.

In pursuing some or all of these policies, a foreign country is expressing a philosophy that protection or governmental regulation or planning or ownership serves the society better than would competitive forces in a relatively unregulated market, or that orderly industrial self-organization is preferable to cutthroat competition, particularly in industries plagued by over-capacity or in industries where a reputation for high quality is threatened by cost-cutting competitors. These are beliefs that we have selectively absorbed, but in general rejected.

Additional reading: The Organization for Economic Cooperation and Development maintains a loose-leaf Guide to Legislation on Restrictive Trade Practices, with texts, explanatory notes and bibliography. The CCH Common Market Reporter contains references to numerous source materials on Common Market antitrust law, vol. 2, ¶ 9901, sub par. 2000, and descriptions of national antitrust legislation in the Common Market countries in its volume "Doing Business in Europe" at ¶¶ 21,501, 23,001, 23,501, 24,001, 25,501 and 27,001. For reviews of foreign antitrust laws, see Edwards, Trade Regulations Overseas (1966); International Law Association, Report of the Fifty-First Conference held at Tokyo 418–510 (1965); and Surrey and Shaw (eds.), A Lawyer's Guide to International Business 639–92 (1963).

Antitrust Laws and the International Economy

The large variation in perspectives upon socio-economic organization and competition within national boundaries carries over to perspectives upon the organization of international commerce. Consider by way of contrast the notion of a world economy subject to definitive regulation by a single authoritative international agency. That agency might decide that unrestricted free trade and competition should be permitted to set the pattern of international commercial transactions. Analogously to market and price theory within national settings, the most efficient use of world resources could thereby be achieved. But the premises and consequences of such a policy would run contrary to the economic, social, military, or political aims of national governments.

No other coherent vision of the organization of international economic life could promise to yield a greater consensus. To a limited degree, matters relevant to international commerce are regulated by international agreement; the discussions in Chapter XI of tariff regulation through the General Agreement on Tariffs and Trade, and of monetary regulation through the International Monetary Fund, are examples. But in most respects relevant to the matters in this chapter, national policies remain supreme, and often in conflict. Most relevant to our discussion, nations either themselves restrict competition in international commerce or permit restrictions by private agreement.

From the United States' perspective, one might suppose that competition should be given full freedom, so that foreign markets would be open to American firms who can produce more efficiently than foreign industries, and foreign producers of goods sought by American consumers would be motivated to cut prices and improve quality on their exports to this country. American firms would also be free to make investments in foreign countries where their calculations indicated that profits will follow. Nonetheless, our tariff rules, import quotas on agricultural and other products and related legislation sharply restrict imports into this country, and, incidentally, sometimes protect domestic monopolies or oligopolies against foreign competition.[34] Moreover, both the federal and the state governments have pursued policies restricting or regulating investment in defined types of economic activities by aliens, and as of 1974 legislation before the Congress would impose serious constraints on aliens investing in a broad range of enterprises. See pp. 67–68, supra. Even with respect to exports, federal laws prevent United States manufacturers from trading in certain foreign markets, for reasons examined at pp. 110–115, supra. Concern about the balance of payments led during a recent period to imposition of restriction on foreign investments by American corporations.[35] Thus, whether for reasons of protection of domestic industry, domestic regulatory programs, national security or monetary stability, important policies and rules in this country sharply limit competition in an international setting.

The pattern varies markedly among foreign countries. Particularly in less developed countries, arguments in favor of protection of domestic producers against foreign competition may be strong. They are not dissimilar from those used in the United States since Alexander Hamilton's time to justify protecting "infant industries." Such countries emphasize that unrestricted competition will lead to domination of their markets by large producers, typically the multinational American corporation. The domestic market in a small or less prosperous country may not be large enough to support more than one local producer; the first firm to establish itself may acquire a local monopoly and be able to wring monopoly profits from local consumers. A country with an industrial pattern characterized by a large number of small producers may encourage them to cooperate with each other and perhaps to merge, in the hope that they can thus match the capacity of American firms and achieve the economies of scale available only to industrial giants, as in research and marketing. A country may particularly encourage cooperation among exporters, since breaking into foreign markets calls for skills and expenditures beyond the reach of small growers or manufacturers. A country or countries producing a vital commodity such as oil may decide to share in the monopoly profits extracted from vendees by a highly concentrated privately-owned distribution system. They may decide to raise prices, as in the case of the Organization of Petroleum Exporting Countries, by the concerted action in production controls and pricing policies of several countries. Thus different economic circumstances and political beliefs may lead to different policies towards competition domestically and in the international arena.

34. Chapter XI, pp. 1146–1164, infra, examines such restrictions and international regulation intended to reduce them.

35. See p. 1166, infra.

On balance, the United States may find that its national interest is served by encouraging or cooperating with some arrangements by other countries that restrain trade. For example, when international obligations inhibited the United States from raising tariff barriers on foreign textiles, this country found it convenient that Japanese producers combined to ration among themselves the import quota allotted to them.[36] More broadly, the United States may have an interest in increasing the prosperity of other countries; our foreign aid policy is sufficient testimony. One way in which to assist is to help a country manage its exports so as to maximize the income derived from them. In the coffee agreement described at p. 585, supra, the United States agreed to help to restrict world production by participating in the enforcement of a system allocating production quotas to the various producing countries and import quotas to the consumers. Such restraints, not fundamentally dissimilar from legislation affecting domestic agriculture, run counter to the theory of free competition.

NOTE ON TRANSNATIONAL ASPECTS OF UNITED STATES ANTITRUST LEGISLATION

In determining the application of the antitrust laws to transnational situations, courts find meagre assistance in the statutes. Their terms generally embrace foreign commerce but rarely indicate the intensity of that embrace.

Sections 1 and 2 of the Sherman Act apply to "trade or commerce . . . with foreign nations." Although the definition of "commerce" in Section 1 of the Clayton Act refers to "trade or commerce . . . with foreign nations," the provisions barring price discrimination and tied sales in Sections 2 and 3 of the Clayton Act apply only to sales "for use, consumption, or resale within the United States." On the other hand, Section 5 of the Federal Trade Commission Act is given explicit transnational application by Section 4 of the Export Trade Act (or Webb-Pomerene Act), 40 Stat. 516 (1918), 15 U.S.C.A. § 64, which extends the prohibition against "unfair methods of competition" to practices in export trade [defined as "trade or commerce in goods, wares, or merchandise exported . . . from the United States . . . to any foreign nation . . . ."] against competitors engaged in export trade, even though the acts constituting such unfair methods "are done without the territorial jurisdiction of the United States."

Section 73 of the Wilson Tariff Act, 28 Stat. 570 (1894), as amended, 15 U.S.C.A. § 8, makes unlawful agreements among im-

36. The basic agreement between the United States and Japan setting an overall quota on textile exports was negotiated under authority given the President by Congress. Antitrust problems were raised, but not resolved, with respect to the steel quota where no such legislative authority applied in Consumers Union of U. S., Inc., v. Kissinger, 506 F.2d 136 (D.C. Cir. 1974).

porters which restrain competition or increase the market price of goods imported into this country. Section 76 of that Act authorizes the forfeiture of property "owned under any contract or by any combination, or pursuant to any conspiracy, and being the subject thereof . . . imported into and being within the United States . . . ." [37]

The courts have thus had to work out the transnational reach of the antitrust laws for themselves. To this task they have brought learning not only from precedents in the antitrust field but from criminal and other regulatory fields as well.

Consider first the criminal statutes involved in Chapter VIII. One notes the obvious relationship: the Sherman Act *is* a criminal statute in one of its facets, although relatively few proceedings to enforce it are brought on the criminal side. Nonetheless, the Sherman Act is different from the usual criminal law in several important respects. (1) It attempts to establish in a comprehensive fashion a basic pattern for economic activity rather than merely to inhibit specific types of conduct. (2) That pattern is one that has fewer and less precise counterparts abroad than the usual type of criminal statute, reflecting as it does profound themes in the political and economic history or philosophy of this country. (3) Offenses against the Sherman Act normally have a more emphatic impact on society than does a simple larceny, and offenders are correspondingly more powerful and important.

One case under the Federal Trade Commission Act, Branch v. FTC, 141 F.2d 31 (7th Cir. 1944), provides a convenient bridge to the opinions which follow on the reach of antitrust legislation. The court there denied a petition to set aside a cease and desist order of the FTC prohibiting a firm organized and operating in the United States from engaging in certain practices that had been found to constitute false and deceptive advertising. The firm advertised its correspondence courses in newspapers in Latin America and also sent advertising materials to solicit customers in that area. The petitioner argued that the provisions of Section 5 did not reach such foreign business activity. The court replied in part:

> It is true that much of the objectionable activity occurred in Latin America; however, it was conceived, initiated, concocted, and launched on its way in the United States.

37. Other miscellaneous statutes have a tangential bearing on transnational aspects of antitrust regulation. Thus a provision of the Panama Canal Act, 37 Stat. 567 (1912), 15 U.S.C.A. § 31, bars the Canal to vessels owned or chartered by any person or company "doing business in violation of" the Sherman Act or Wilson Tariff Act. Other laws confer exemptions which may have an effect on international transactions only or on both domestic and foreign ones. An act "to assist in safeguarding the balance of payments position of the United States," 79 Stat. 672 (1965), 31 U.S.C.A. §§ 931–37, permits, on a temporary basis, voluntary agreements, subject to approval by the Attorney General, to restrict private flows of dollars abroad. Section 15 of the Shipping Act of 1916, 39 Stat. 733, as amended, 46 U.S.C.A. § 814, allows the Maritime Commission to exempt certain agreements between common carriers by water. The Civil Aeronautics Board has similar authority under Section 414 of the Federal Aviation Act of 1958, 72 Stat. 770, 49 U.S.C.A. § 1384.

> . . . The Federal Trade Commission does not assume to protect the petitioner's customers in Latin America. . . . It seeks to protect foreign commerce. If that commerce was being defiled by a resident citizen of the United States to the disadvantage of other competing citizens of the United States, the United States had a right to protect such commerce from defilement. . . . For protection of the competitors within the United States, the United States is the sovereign to look to. The right of the United States to control the conduct of its citizens in foreign countries in respect to matters which a sovereign ordinarily governs within its own territorial jurisdiction has been recognized repeatedly. Blackmer v. United States [p. 862, supra]. . . .

The following three cases, each under the Sherman Act, pose relatively simple antitrust problems. The earliest, American Banana Co. v. United Fruit Co., represents one of the first major attempts by the Supreme Court to cope with the problem of defining the reach of domestic legislation and adjusting it to a foreign government's activities. It involved allegations of a classic monopoly achieved by predatory practices. The second, United States v. Aluminum Co. of America, represents in its international aspect a fairly simple agreement by competitors to limit output. The third case, Continental Ore Co. v. Union Carbide & Carbon Corp., allegedly involved a fairly straight-forward boycott or agreement to exclude a competitor, as part of an attempt to achieve a monopoly position. Note that each of the defendants involved were major corporations with extensive market power. This has been a fairly characteristic situation in the leading antitrust cases posing questions of transnational reach. Most cases applying the antitrust laws in transnational settings have involved allegations of significant restraints on competition affecting American commerce, brought about by defendants of considerable size and power.

These three cases do not illustrate a number of substantive problems which concern firms engaged in contemporary transnational business. Some are noted later, but many are too complex for treatment within the boundaries of this section. They include questions arising from the establishment by domestic firms of exclusive distributorships abroad, mergers or acquisitions involving American and foreign firms, and various restrictions inserted in agreements that license the use of trade-marks, patents or unpatented confidential data.

AMERICAN BANANA CO. v. UNITED FRUIT CO.

Supreme Court of the United States, 1909.
213 U.S. 347, 29 S.Ct. 511, 53 L.Ed. 826.

MR. JUSTICE HOLMES delivered the opinion of the court:

This is an action brought to recover threefold damages under the act to protect trade against monopolies. July 2, 1890, chap. 647, § 7, 26 Stat. at L. 209, 210, U.S.Comp.Stat.1901, pp. 3200, 3202. The circuit court dismissed the complaint upon motion, as not setting forth a cause of action. 160 Fed. 184. This judgment was affirmed by the circuit court of appeals, 166 Fed. 261, and the case then was brought to this court by writ of error.

The allegations of the complaint may be summed up as follows: The plaintiff is an Alabama corporation, organized in 1904. The defendant is a New Jersey corporation, organized in 1899. Long before the plaintiff was formed, the defendant, with intent to prevent competition and to control and monopolize the banana trade, bought the property and business of several of its previous competitors, with provision against their resuming the trade, made contracts with others, including a majority of the most important, regulating the quantity to be purchased and the price to be paid, and acquired a controlling amount of stock in still others. For the same purpose it organized a selling company, of which it held the stock, that by agreement sold at fixed prices all the bananas of the combining parties. By this and other means it did monopolize and restrain the trade and maintained unreasonable prices. The defendant being in this ominous attitude, one McConnell, in 1903, started a banana plantation in Panama, then part of the United States of Colombia, and began to build a railway (which would afford his only means of export), both in accordance with the laws of the United States of Colombia. He was notified by the defendant that he must either combine or stop. Two months later, it is believed at the defendant's instigation, the governor of Panama recommended to his national government that Costa Rica be allowed to administer the territory through which the railroad was to run, and this although that territory had been awarded to Colombia under an arbitration agreed to by treaty. The defendant, and afterwards, in September, the government of Costa Rica, it is believed by the inducement of the defendant, interfered with McConnell. In November, 1903, Panama revolted and became an independent republic, declaring its boundary to be that settled by the award. In June, 1904, the plaintiff bought out McConnell and went on with the work, as it had a right to do under the laws of Panama. But in July, Costa Rican soldiers and officials, instigated by the defendant, seized a part of the plantation and a cargo of supplies and have held them ever since, and stopped the construction and operation of the plantation and railway. In August one Astua, by *ex parte* proceedings, got a judgment from a Costa Rican court, declaring the plantation to be his, although, it is alleged, the proceedings were not within the jurisdiction of Costa Rica, and were contrary to its laws and void. Agents of the defendant then bought the lands from Astua. The plaintiff has tried to induce the government of Costa Rica to withdraw its soldiers, and also has tried to persuade the United States to interfere, but has been thwarted in both by the defendant and has failed. The government of Costa Rica remained in possession down to the bringing of the suit.

As a result of the defendant's acts the plaintiff has been deprived of the use of the plantation, and the railway, the plantation, and supplies have been injured. The defendant also, by outbidding, has driven purchasers out of the market and has compelled producers to come to its terms, and it has prevented the plaintiff from buying for export and sale. This is the substantial damage alleged. . . . It is contended, however, that even if the main argument fails and the defendant is held not to be answerable for acts depending on the co-operation of the government of Costa Rica for their effect, a wrongful conspiracy resulting in driving the plaintiff out of business is to be gathered from the complaint, and that it was entitled to go to trial upon that.

It is obvious that, however stated, the plaintiff's case depends on several rather startling propositions. In the first place, the acts causing the damage were done, so far as appears, outside the jurisdiction of the United States, and within that of other states. It is surprising to hear it argued that they were governed by the act of Congress.

No doubt in regions subject to no sovereign, like the high seas, or to no law that civilized countries would recognize as adequate, such countries may treat some relations between their citizens as governed by their own law, and keep, to some extent, the old notion of personal sovereignty alive. . . . They go further, at times, and declare that they will punish anyone, subject or not, who shall do certain things, if they can catch him, as in the case of pirates on the high seas. In cases immediately affecting national interests they may go further still and may make, and, if they get the chance, execute, similar threats as to acts done within another recognized jurisdiction. An illustration from our statutes is found with regard to criminal correspondence with foreign governments. Rev.Stat. § 5335, U.S.Comp.Stat.1901, p. 3624. . . . But the general and almost universal rule is that the character of an act as lawful or unlawful must be determined wholly by the law of the country where the act is done. Slater v. Mexican Nat. R. Co., 194 U.S. 120, 126, 24 S.Ct. 581, 48 L.Ed. 900, 902. This principle was carried to an extreme in Milliken v. Pratt, 125 Mass. 374, 28 Am.Rep. 241. For another jurisdiction, if it should happen to lay hold of the actor, to treat him according to its own notions rather than those of the place where he did the acts, not only would be unjust, but would be an interference with the authority of another sovereign, contrary to the comity of nations, which the other state concerned justly might resent. . . .

Law is a statement of the circumstances, in which the public force will be brought to bear upon men through the courts. But the word commonly is confined to such prophecies or threats when addressed to persons living within the power of the courts. A threat that depends upon the choice of the party affected to bring himself within that power hardly would be called law in the ordinary sense. We do not speak of blockade running by neutrals as unlawful. And the usages of speech correspond to the limit of the attempts of the lawmaker, except in extraordinary cases. It is true that domestic corporations remain always within the power of the domestic law; but, in the present case, at least, there is no ground for distinguishing between corporations and men.

The foregoing considerations would lead, in case of doubt, to a construction of any statute as intended to be confined in its operation and effect to the territorial limits over which the lawmaker has general and legitimate power. "All legislation is prima facie territorial." Ex parte Blain, L.R. 12 Ch.Div. 522, 528; State v. Carter, 27 N.J.L. 499; People v. Merrill, 2 Park.Crim.Rep. 590, 596. Words having universal scope, such as "every contract in restraint of trade," "every person who shall monopolize," etc., will be taken, as a matter of course, to mean only everyone subject to such legislation, not all that the legislator subsequently may be able to catch. In the case of the present statute, the improbability of the United States attempting to make acts done in Panama or Costa Rica criminal is obvious, yet the law begins by making criminal the acts for which it gives a right to sue. We think it entirely plain that what the defendant did in Panama or Costa Rica is not within the scope of the statute so far as the present suit is concerned. Other objections of a serious nature are urged, but need not be discussed.

For again, not only were the acts of the defendant in Panama or Costa Rica not within the Sherman act, but they were not torts by the law of the place, and therefore were not torts at all, however contrary to the ethical and economic postulates of that statute. The substance of the complaint is that, the plantation being within the *de facto* jurisdiction of Costa Rica, that state took and keeps possession of it by virtue of its sovereign power. But a seizure by a state is not a thing that can be complained of elsewhere in the courts. Underhill v. Hernandez, 168 U.S. 250, 42 L.Ed. 456, 18 S.Ct. 83. The fact, if it be one, that *de jure* the estate is in Panama, does not matter in the least; sovereignty is pure fact. The fact has been recognized by the United States, and, by the implications of the bill, is assented to by Panama.

The fundamental reason why persuading a sovereign power to do this or that cannot be a tort is not that the sovereign cannot be joined as a defendant or because it must be assumed to be acting lawfully. The intervention of parties who had a right knowingly to produce the harmful result between the defendant and the harm has been thought to be a nonconductor and to bar responsibility (Allen v. Flood [1898] A.C. 1, 121, 151, etc.), but it is not clear that this is always true; for instance, in the case of the privileged repetition of a slander (Elmer v. Fessenden, 151 Mass. 359, 362, 363, 22 N.E. 635, 24 N.E. 208, 5 L.R.A. 724), or the malicious and unjustified persuasion to discharge from employment (Moran v. Dunphy, 177 Mass. 485, 487, 59 N.E. 125, 52 L.R.A. 115, 83 Am.St.Rep. 289). The fundamental reason is that it is a contradiction in terms to say that, within its jurisdiction, it is unlawful to persuade a sovereign power to bring about a result that it declares by its conduct to be desirable and proper. It does not, and foreign courts cannot, admit that the influences were improper or the results bad. It makes the persuasion lawful by its own act. The very meaning of sovereignty is that the decree of the sovereign makes law. . . .

The acts of the soldiers and officials of Costa Rica are not alleged to have been without the consent of the government, and must be taken to have been done by its order. It ratified them, at all events, and adopted and keeps the possession taken by them. . . . The injuries to the plantation and supplies seem to have been the direct effect of the acts of the Costa Rican government, which is holding them under an adverse claim of right. The claim for them must fall with the claim for being deprived of the use and profits of the place. As to the buying at a high price, etc., it is enough to say that we have no ground for supposing that it was unlawful in the countries where the purchases were made. Giving to this complaint every reasonable latitude of interpretation we are of opinion that it alleges no case under the act of Congress, and discloses nothing that we can suppose to have been a tort where it was done. A conspiracy in this country to do acts in another jurisdiction does not draw to itself those acts and make them unlawful, if they are permitted by the local law.

Further reasons might be given why this complaint should not be upheld, but we have said enough to dispose of it and to indicate our general point of view.

Judgment affirmed.

UNITED STATES v. ALUMINUM CO. OF AMERICA

United States Court of Appeals, Second Circuit, 1945.
148 F.2d 416.

[In this action, the United States sought a judgment (1) that Aluminum Co. of America ("Alcoa"), a Pennsylvania corporation, had monopolized interstate and foreign commerce in the manufacture and sale of virgin aluminum ingot in violation of Section 2 of the Sherman Act, p. 991, supra, and (2) that Alcoa and Aluminum Limited ("Limited"), a Canadian corporation, had entered into a conspiracy in restraint of foreign commerce in violation of Section 1 of the Sherman Act, p. 991, supra. The United States requested a decree of dissolution and other equitable relief. The district court held for the defendants, and the United States appealed. The excerpts below from the opinion of the Court of Appeals (to which the appeal was referred by the Supreme Court because it lacked a quorum of Justices qualified to hear it) by JUDGE LEARNED HAND omit the parts of the opinion considering the issue of monopoly. They treat primarily the relationship between Alcoa and Limited and the conduct of Limited to which Section 1 of the Sherman Act was alleged to be applicable.

Limited was incorporated in Canada in 1928 to take over properties of Alcoa outside the United States. In exchange for the properties conveyed to it, Limited issued all its common shares pro rata to Alcoa's common shareholders. By 1931, no officers were common to both companies and the formal separation was complete. At the time relevant to this litigation, two American families, Davis and Mellon, and the officers and directors of Alcoa (11 individuals in all) owned 48.9% of Alcoa's shares and 48.5% of Limited's shares.

The portion of the opinion below refers to "Alliance," a foreign cartel. Alliance was in form a Swiss corporation, created pursuant to a 1931 agreement among Limited and Swiss, German, French and British corporations. Its purpose was to limit production of aluminum by allocating production quotas to its different members in proportion to each member's share ownership in Alliance. An amendment in 1936 to this agreement provided that each participating company (shareholder) in Alliance was to have a stated production quota and was to pay a royalty to Alliance on any production in excess of the quota. The royalties were to be divided pro rata among Alliance's shareholders. The shareholders agreed that exports from them to the United States should be included in the production quotas. The agreement continued unchanged until March 1938, at which time it became apparent that it no longer served any purpose in view of Europe's developing political and military picture. Alliance in form survived the war and never was dissolved.

Judge Hand, reviewing the decision of the district court, found sufficient evidence to support the findings below that Alcoa itself had not participated in the formation of Alliance and was not privy to its purpose of limiting foreign production—even though that limitation might have had the effect of restricting imports to the United States that would be competitive with Alcoa's own production. A portion of the opinion dealing with the relationship between Alcoa and Limited follows.]

Even so, the question remains whether "Alcoa" should be charged with the "Alliance" because a majority of its shareholders were also a majority of "Limited's" shareholders; or whether that would be true, even though there were a group, common to both, less than a majority, but large enough for practical purposes to control each. It is quite true that in proportion as courts disregard the fictitious persona of a corporation—as perhaps they are increasingly disposed to do—they must substitute the concept of a group of persons acting in concert. Nevertheless, the group must not be committed legally except in so far as they have assented as a body, and that assent should be imputed to them only in harmony with the ordinary notions of delegated power. The plaintiff did not prove that in 1931, to say nothing of 1936, there was not a substantial minority in each company made up of those who held no shares in the other; and the existence of the same majority in the two corporations was not enough by itself to identify the two. "Alcoa" would not be bound, unless those who held the majority of its shares had been authorized by the group as a whole to enter into the "Alliance"; and considering the fact that, as we shall show, it was an illegal arrangement, such an authority ought convincingly to appear. It does not appear at all. For support of this proposition we need look no further than to the decisions of the Supreme Court under the "Commodity Clause." [Citations omitted.] There was in all these cases strong reason to hold that the railroads had an "indirect" interest in the coal moved, yet the decisions uniformly assumed that the ownership, not of a majority of the shares, but even of all the shares, did not make the corporations coalesce. Except when there was evidence that those in nominal control of one of the two corporations, exercised no independent decision, but followed the directions of the other, they were treated as juridically separate. Indeed, were it not so, a minority of shareholders would always be compelled to see to it that a majority —perhaps even a controlling fraction—of the shares did not pass to a confederated group who had a similar control over another corporation. For these reasons we conclude that "Alcoa" was not a party to the "Alliance," and did not join in any violation of § 1 of the Act, so far as concerned foreign commerce.

[The remaining question was whether Limited itself had violated Section 1. Limited had an important administrative office, perhaps its effective headquarters, in New York, so that the district court had jurisdiction over it.]

Did either the agreement of 1931 or that of 1936 violate § 1 of the Act? The answer does not depend upon whether we shall recognize as a source of liability a liability imposed by another state. On the contrary we are concerned only with whether Congress chose to attach liability to the conduct outside the United States of persons not in allegiance to it. That being so, the only question open is whether Congress intended to impose the liability, and whether our own Constitution permitted it to do so; as a court of the United States, we cannot look beyond our own law. Nevertheless, it is quite true that we are not to read general words, such as those in this Act, without regard to the limitations customarily observed by nations upon the exercise of their powers; limitations which generally correspond to those fixed by the "Conflict of Laws." We should not impute to Congress an intent to punish all whom its courts can catch, for conduct which has no consequences within the United States. American Banana Co. v. United Fruit Co., 213 U.S. 347, 357, 29 S. Ct. 511, 53 L.Ed. 826, 16 Ann.Cas. 1047; United States v. Bowman, 260 U.S. 94, 98, 43 S.Ct. 39, 67 L.Ed. 149; Blackmer v. United States, 284 U.S. 421, 437, 52 S.Ct. 252, 76 L.Ed. 375. On the other hand, it is settled law—as "Limited" itself agrees—that any state may impose liabilities, even upon persons not within its allegiance, for conduct outside its borders that has consequences within its borders which the state reprehends; and these liabilities other states will ordinarily recognize. Strassheim v. Daily, 221 U.S. 280, 284, 285, 31 S.Ct. 558, 55 L.Ed. 735 . . . . It may be argued that this Act extends further. Two situations are possible. There may be agreements made beyond our borders not intended to affect imports, which do affect them, or which affect exports. Almost any limitation of the supply of goods in Europe, for example, or in South America, may have repercussions in the United States if there is trade between the two. Yet when one considers the international complications likely to arise from an effort in this country to treat such agreements as unlawful, it is safe to assume that Congress certainly did not intend the Act to cover them. Such agreements may on the other hand intend to include imports into the United States, and yet it may appear that they have had no effect upon them. That situation might be thought to fall within the doctrine that intent may be a substitute for performance in the case of a contract made within the United States; or it might be thought to fall within the doctrine that a statute should not be interpreted to cover acts abroad which have no consequence here. We shall not choose between these alternatives; but for argument we shall assume that the Act does not cover agreements, even though intended to affect imports or exports, unless its performance is shown actually to have had some effect upon them. Where both conditions are satisfied, the situation certainly falls within such decisions as . . . United States v. Sisal Sales Corporation, 274 U.S. 268, 47 S.Ct. 592, 71 L.Ed. 1042 . . . . It is true that in those cases the persons held liable had sent agents into the United States to perform part of the agreement; but an agent is merely an animate means of executing his principal's purposes, and, for the purposes of this case, he does not differ from an inanimate means; besides, only human agents can import and sell ingot.

Both agreements would clearly have been unlawful had they been made within the United States; and it follows from what we have just said that both were unlawful, though made abroad, if they were intended to affect imports and did affect them. Since the shareholders almost at once agreed that the agreement of 1931 should not cover imports, we may ignore it and confine our discussion to that of 1936: indeed that we should have to do anyway, since it superseded the earlier agreement. The judge found that it was not the purpose of the agreement to suppress or restrain the exportation of aluminum to the United States for sale in competition with "Alcoa." By that we understand that he meant that the agreement was not specifically directed to "Alcoa," because it only applied generally to the production of the shareholders. If he meant that it was not expected that the general restriction upon production would have an effect upon imports, we cannot agree, for the change made in 1936 was deliberate and was expressly made to accomplish just that. It would have been an idle gesture, unless the shareholders had supposed that it would, or at least might, have that effect. The first of the conditions which we mentioned was therefore satisfied; the intent was to set up a quota system for imports.

The judge also found that the 1936 agreement did not "materially affect the . . . foreign trade or commerce of the United States"; apparently because the imported ingot was greater in 1936 and 1937 than in earlier years. We cannot accept this finding, based as it was upon the fact that, in 1936, 1937 and the first quarter of 1938, the gross imports of ingot increased. It by no means follows from such an increase that the agreement did not restrict imports; and incidentally it so happens that in those years such inference as is possible at all, leads to the opposite conclusion. . . . We shall dispose of the matter therefore upon the assumption that, although the shareholders intended to restrict imports, it does not appear whether in fact they did so. Upon our hypothesis the plaintiff would therefore fail, if it carried the burden of proof upon this issue as upon others. We think, however, that, after the intent to affect imports was proved, the burden of proof shifted to "Limited." In the first place a depressant upon production which applies generally may be assumed, ceteris paribus, to distribute its effect evenly upon all markets. Again, when the parties took the trouble specifically to make the depressant apply to a given market, there is reason to suppose that they expected that it would have some effect, which it could have only by lessening what would otherwise have been imported. If the motive they introduced was over-balanced in all instances by motives which induced the shareholders to import, if the United States market became so attractive that the royalties did not count at all and their expectations were in fact defeated, they to whom the facts were more accessible than to the plaintiff ought to prove it, for a prima facie case had been made. Moreover, there is an especial propriety in demanding this of "Limited," because it was "Limited" which procured the inclusion in the agreement of 1936 of imports in the quotas.

There remains only the question whether this assumed restriction had any influence upon prices. Apex Hosiery Co. v. Leader, supra, 310 U.S. 469, 60 S.Ct. 982, 84 L.Ed. 1311, 128 A.L.R. 1044. To that Socony-Vacuum Oil Co. v. United States, supra, 310 U.S. 150, 60 S.Ct. 811, 84 L.Ed. 1129, is an entire answer. It will be remembered that, when the defendants in that case protested that the prosecution had not proved that the "distress" gasoline had affected prices, the court answered that that was not necessary, because an agreement to withdraw any substantial part of the supply from a market would, if carried out, have some effect upon prices, and was as unlawful as an agreement expressly to fix prices. The underlying doctrine was that all factors which contribute to determine prices, must be kept free to operate unhampered by agreements. For these reasons we think that the agreement of 1936 violated § 1 of the Act.

[The court then considered what remedies would be appropriate. With respect to the Alliance cartel, the opinion stated in part:]

Unless the issue has become moot, "Limited" also must be enjoined from entering into any "cartel," or agreement like that of 1936, covering imports into the United States . . . . We think, however, that the issue has not become moot . . . .

The agreement of 1936 . . . was to last for 99 years, though it could be terminated on six months' notice by any shareholder who held 200 shares, and all held as many as 200. As we have seen, the two German smelters had been exempted from royalties; and it is not altogether clear what future part remained for them in the enterprise, although some past obligations were compromised. It is true that some eighteen months before war was declared the other shareholders ceased to perform the agreement, but no one ever gave the prescribed notice of dissolution and, formally at least, the agreement continued and still continues. Indeed, it is possible that all but the German shareholders can start up the system again without renewal, if they please. . . . "Alliance" itself, as a corporation, still persists, and all the original shareholders presumably remain such. The mere cessation of an unlawful activity before suit does not deprive the court of jurisdiction to provide against its resumption; a "case or controversy" may remain to be disposed of. . . . To disarm the court it must appear that there is no reasonable expectation that the wrong will be repeated. That is not true in the case at bar. Unless we are to grant an injunction, we ought not pass upon the issue; if we do not pass upon the issue, we are by no means persuaded that "Limited," when peace comes, will not enter into another "cartel" which again attempts to restrict imports. It has insistently argued that the Act does not cover such an agreement; and it alleges that it was forced into the "cartel," if it was to do a European business at all. It may be forced to do so again, unless a judgment forbids. . . .

. . . The injunctions granted will embrace the officers of those corporate defendants against which they run.

Judgment reversed, and cause remanded for further proceedings not inconsistent with the foregoing.

[In 1950 the district court considered the remedy to be applied in order to carry out the mandate of the foregoing opinion relating to Alcoa's monopolization of the domestic market in violation of Section 2 of the Sherman Act. 91 F.Supp. 333 (S.D.N.Y.). In view of the entry into the aluminum business of new producers and other considerations, the court determined that dissolution of Alcoa was not required. It did, however, order the link between Alcoa and Limited to be dissolved by sale by Alcoa's shareholders of their interest in Alcoa or Limited. It noted that changed circumstances had made it possible for Limited, now the largest producer of aluminum, to export in quantity to the United States and that it might use that power to restrain the growth of the new producers. Its description of the effects of the relationship between Limited and Alcoa (91 F. Supp. at 398) may color one's views of that relationship as described, in the context of the Alliance issue and Section 1 of the Sherman Act, in the opinion of the Court of Appeals.]

Nevertheless, since Limited is now a competitive factor in the domestic market, Alcoa's relationship to Limited jeopardizes the public interest to a degree not present when this case was tried before Judge Caffey. I think it too much to expect that the competition between Alcoa and Limited, now that they both participate in the same market, will be as keen and comprehensive as the Sherman Act demands. While there may be active rivalry between them for customers, since the controlling shareholders of these corporations may not prefer one of these companies over the other as the source of their dividends, it is doubtful that the stimulants to price competition and efficiency, from which the public benefits, can exist to the same degree as would be the case if these firms were wholly disassociated. . . .

Now that Limited is a vital competitive factor in the domestic market, some cognizance of these family ties must be taken into account. Among normal individuals, blood is usually thicker than water. By this, I do not mean to impugn the integrity of any of the above named persons. Much less do I suggest that any officer of these corporations will act in the interest of only a part of the shareholders whom he serves. Experience, nevertheless, demonstrates that, while possible impediments to competition between corporations, that are controlled by common interests, may benefit all their shareholders, such impediments may prove to be a distinct disservice to competitor companies, and the public as well. The Sherman Act is designed to prevent any such eventuality. . . .

Together, Limited and Alcoa are in position, at any time, to restrain effectively the growth of Reynolds and Kaiser. Accordingly, inasmuch as irreparable harm can result from a delay in remedies, it is unwise for this Court to relinquish jurisdiction of this action until it is assured that the aluminum industry has been oriented in a lawful direction.

One must indulge the conviction that the control which may be exercised over Aluminum Limited by the controlling stockholders of Alcoa, is a resource of enormous importance. No matter how lawful the relations with Limited may have been in the past, were I now to ignore the potential power which resides in the nexus above described, my duties in this proceeding, as I understand them, would not be adequately discharged.

CONTINENTAL ORE CO. v. UNION CARBIDE & CARBON CORP.

Supreme Court of the United States, 1962.
370 U.S. 690, 82 S.Ct. 1404, 8 L.Ed.2d 777.

[Continental brought an action under Section 4 of the Clayton Act, p. 993, supra, seeking treble damages for injuries resulting from asserted violations by defendants of Sections 1 and 2 of the Sherman Act. The defendants named in the complaint were two domestic corporations, Vanadium Corporation of America (VCA) and Union Carbide & Carbon Corp. (Carbide), and four wholly-owned subsidiaries of Carbide. One such subsidiary, Electro Metallurgical Company of Canada, Ltd. (Electro Met of Canada), was foreign, and no service was made upon it.

According to the complaint and other allegations of plaintiff, defendants acted in concert to exclude plaintiff from the vanadium business. Vanadium, a metal obtained from ores which are found in this country, is processed into vanadium oxide, which in turn is converted into ferrovanadium for use chiefly as an alloy in hardening steels. Defendants allegedly obtained control over substantially all the available ore deposits and vanadium oxide produced by others in this country, refused to sell vanadium oxide to other producers (including plaintiff) of ferrovanadium, and fixed prices and allocated sales of vanadium oxide and ferrovanadium. As a consequence, the complaint stated, plaintiff and other independent distributors and producers were eliminated from the business.

One of plaintiff's charges concerned its alleged elimination from sales in the Canadian market. Canadian laws during World War II vested in the Office of Metals Controller the right to regulate the procurement of strategic metals and their allocation to industrial users. The Controller delegated to Electro Met of Canada the sole right to purchase vanadium products for allocation within its discretion to Canadian industry. According to plaintiff, Electro Met of Canada used this power to divide Continental's former share of the Canadian market among the defendants.

Defendants prevailed after a jury trial; the court of appeals sustained the judgment. The Supreme Court, in an opinion delivered by MR. JUSTICE WHITE, vacated the judgment because of various errors below and remanded the case for a new trial. The following excerpts from the opinion treat only plaintiff's alleged elimination from the Canadian market.]

The Court of Appeals agreed with the trial court and concluded that Continental was not legally entitled to recover from respondents for the destruction of its Canadian business. The court said that no vanadium oxide could be imported into Canada by anyone other than the Canadian Government's agent, Electro Met of Canada, which refused to purchase from the petitioners. Thus, according to the court, "even if we assume that Electro Metallurgical Company of Canada, Ltd., acted for the purpose of entrenching the monopoly position of the defendants in the United States, it was acting as an arm of the Canadian Government, and we do not see how such efforts as appellants claim defendants took to persuade and influence the Canadian Government through its agent are within the purview of the Sherman Act." 289 F.2d, at 94. This ruling was erroneous and we hold that Continental's offer of proof was relevant evidence of a violation of the Sherman Act as charged in the complaint and was not inadmissible on the grounds stated by the courts below.

Respondents say that American Banana Co. v. United Fruit Co., 213 U.S. 347, 29 S.Ct. 511, 53 L.Ed. 826, shields them from liability. This Court there held that an antitrust plaintiff could not collect damages from a defendant who had allegedly influenced a foreign government to seize plaintiff's properties. But in the light of later cases in this Court respondents' reliance upon American Banana is misplaced. A conspiracy to monopolize or restrain the domestic or foreign commerce of the United States is not outside the reach of the Sherman Act just because part of the conduct complained of occurs in foreign countries. . . . United States v. Sisal Sales Corp., 274 U.S. 268, 47 S.Ct. 592, 71 L.Ed. 1042. Cf. Steele v. Bulova Watch Co., 344 U.S. 280, 73 S.Ct. 252, 97 L.Ed. 252; Branch v. Federal Trade Comm'n, 141 F.2d 31 (C.A. 7th Cir.). See United States v. Aluminum Co. of America, 148 F.2d 416 (C.A. 2d Cir.) . . .

Furthermore, in the Sisal case, supra, a combination entered into within the United States to monopolize an article of commerce produced abroad was held to violate the Sherman Act even though the defendants' control of that production was aided by discriminatory legislation of the foreign country which established an official agency as the sole buyer of the product from the producers and even though one of the defendants became the exclusive selling agent of that governmental authority. Since the activities of the defendants had an impact within the United States and upon its foreign trade, American Banana was expressly held not to be controlling.[38]

Olsen v. Smith, 195 U.S. 332, 25 S.Ct. 52, 49 L.Ed. 224; United States v. Rock Royal Co-op, 307 U.S. 533, 59 S.Ct. 993, 83 L.Ed. 1446; and Parker v. Brown, 317 U.S. 341, 63 S.Ct. 307, 87 L.Ed. 315, do not help respondents. These decisions, each of which sustained the validity of mandatory state or federal governmental regulations against a claim of antitrust illegality, are wide of the mark. In the present case petitioners do not question the validity of any action taken by the Canadian Government or by its Metals Controller. Nor

38. "The circumstances of the present controversy are radically different from those presented in American Banana Co. v. United Fruit Co., supra, and the doctrine there approved is not controlling here. . . .

"Here we have a contract, combination and conspiracy entered into by parties within the United States and made effective by acts done therein. The fundamental object was control of both importation and sales of sisal and complete monopoly of both internal and external trade and commerce therein. The United States complain of a violation of their laws within their own territory by parties subject to their jurisdiction, not merely of something done by another government at the instigation of private parties. True, the conspirators were aided by discriminating legislation, but by their own deliberate acts, here and elsewhere, they brought about forbidden results within the United States. They are within the jurisdiction of our courts and may be punished for offenses against our laws." 274 U.S., at 275–276, 47 S.Ct., at 593.

is there left in the case any question of the liability of the Canadian Government's agent, for Electro Met of Canada was not served. What the petitioners here contend is that the respondents are liable for actions which they themselves jointly took, as part of their unlawful conspiracy, to influence or to direct the elimination of Continental from the Canadian market. As in Sisal, the conspiracy was laid in the United States, was effectuated both here and abroad, and respondents are not insulated by the fact that their conspiracy involved some acts by the agent of a foreign government.

From the evidence which petitioners offered it appears that Continental complained to the Canadian Metals Controller that Continental had lost its Canadian business. The Controller referred Continental to one of the respondents. But there is no indication that the Controller or any other official within the structure of the Canadian Government approved or would have approved of joint efforts to monopolize the production and sale of vanadium or directed that purchases from Continental be stopped. The exclusion, Continental claims, resulted from the action of Electro Met of Canada, taken within the area of its discretionary powers granted by the Metals Controller and in concert with or under the direction of the respondents. The offer of proof at least presented an issue for the jury's resolution as to whether the loss of Continental's Canadian business was occasioned by respondents' activities. Respondents are afforded no defense from the fact that Electro Met of Canada, in carrying out the bare act of purchasing vanadium from respondents rather than Continental, was acting in a manner permitted by Canadian law. There is nothing to indicate that such law in any way compelled discriminatory purchasing, and it is well settled that acts which are in themselves legal lose that character when they become constituent elements of an unlawful scheme. . . .

The case of Eastern Railroad Presidents Conf. v. Noerr Motor Freight, Inc., 365 U.S. 127, 81 S.Ct. 523, 5 L.Ed.2d 464, cited by the court below and much relied upon by respondents here, is plainly inapposite. The Court there held not cognizable under the Sherman Act a complaint charging, in essence, that the defendants had engaged in a concerted publicity campaign to foster the adoption of laws and law enforcement practices inimical to plaintiffs' business. Finding no basis for imputing to the Sherman Act a purpose to regulate political activity, a purpose which would have encountered serious constitutional barriers, the Court ruled the defendants' activities to be outside the ban of the Act "at least insofar as those activities comprised mere solicitation of governmental action with respect to the passage and enforcement of laws." 365 U.S., at 138, 81 S.Ct., at 530. In this case, respondents' conduct is wholly dissimilar to that of the defendants in Noerr. Respondents were engaged in private commercial activity, no element of which involved seeking to procure the passage or enforcement of laws. To subject them to liability under the Sherman Act for eliminating a competitor from the Canadian market by exercise of the discretionary power conferred upon Electro Met of Canada by the Canadian Government would effectuate the purposes of the Sherman Act and would not remotely infringe upon any of the constitutionally protected freedoms spoken of in Noerr.

Since our decision concerning the alleged loss of Continental's Canadian business will in any event require a new trial of the entire case in view of the close interconnection between the Canadian and domestic issues, we shall remand the case to the District Court for further proceedings. . . .

NOTE ON INTERACTION BETWEEN AMERICAN AND FOREIGN ANTITRUST LAWS

Problems of the reach of United States antitrust laws to activities or persons outside this country's borders or allegiance find parallels in the laws of other countries. Such questions have been the subject of few judicial or administrative decisions in foreign countries and remain largely academic. But as antitrust legislation is fortified, particularly in the countries of Western Europe, one can anticipate that they will become more acute.

Several foreign laws enacted since World War II explicitly address transnational questions, either by limiting or extending the reach of national legislation. The British Restrictive Trade Practices Act of 1956 and the German Law of 1957 against Restraints on Competition offer examples. Thus, Section 98II of the German law states: "This law is applicable to all restraints of trade effective within the area of applicability of the law [i. e., the Federal Republic of Germany and West Berlin] even where such restraints result from acts committed outside such area." The developing antitrust law of the European Common Market raises numerous questions of this character.[39]

Situations in which American firms incur the risk of violating foreign antitrust laws, through plans formulated and pursued in whole or large part in this country, are not difficult to visualize. For example, one could simply reverse the fact patterns in some of the preceding cases; such business activities might indeed violate both domestic and foreign antitrust legislation. Or American producers might enter into an agreement, valid under the Webb-Pomerene Act, p. 1000, supra, in which they agree to export to a given area through a jointly organized association, at common prices and pursuant to quota allocations.

The Webb Pomerene Act has in fact been relied upon in litigation before foreign courts not involving American parties, as justification for practices of companies that were challenged under their own national legislation. A prominent example is In re National Sulphuric Acid Association's Agreement, 4 Restrict.Prac.L.Rep. 169, a 1963 decision of the British Restrictive Practices Court under the 1956 Act. An agreement among members of that Association included all manufacturers of sulphuric acid in the United Kingdom. The Association established a buying pool to purchase all imported elemental sulphur required by its members to produce sulphuric acid. Members paid a common delivered price for sulphur bought from the pool and agreed not to acquire imported acid sulphur in any other manner. The dominant suppliers of sulphur were in the United States. American min-

39. See pp. 1417–1420, infra. See generally Kronstein, Conflicts Resulting from the Extraterritorial Effects of the Antitrust Legislation of Different Countries, appearing in Nadelmann, von Mehren and Hazard (eds.), Legal Essays in Honor of Hessel Yntema, XXth Century Comparative and Conflicts Law 432 (1961), and the books or compilations referred to at p. 996, supra.

ing companies controlling all exports of certain sulphur had formed Sulexco, an export association under the Webb-Pomerene Act. Prices paid by foreign importers were negotiated with Sulexco rather than with the individual American firms.

The British Association sought to justify its practices under Section 21(1) of the Restrictive Trade Practices Act. That section provided in part that restrictive agreements would be deemed "contrary to the public interest unless the court is satisfied of any one or more of the following circumstances . . . (*d*) that the restriction is reasonably necessary to enable the persons party to the agreement to negotiate fair terms for . . . the acquisition of goods from, any one person not party thereto who controls a preponderant part of the trade or business of . . . supplying such goods . . . ." The court held that the restrictions in the Association's agreement would be declared not contrary to the public interest. It concluded that Sulexco had exercised its power of control over a preponderant part of the United Kingdom market to try to obtain more favorable ("and unreasonably favourable") terms than would have been possible without such power. The court found it probable that Sulexco would successfully impose price increases, likely to be followed by exporters in other countries, "if there were no common buying agreement among the United Kingdom manufacturers of acid who are thus able to oppose a buying monopoly against a selling monopoly of United States sulphur for export."

The case illustrates a characteristic way in which American and foreign antitrust laws can interact in litigation. Given the fact that many foreign policies run counter to our antitrust laws, the question can—and does—arise of what effect they should have upon agreements or practices that are challenged under our legislation. Can conflicts between American and foreign policies be adjusted by achieving a consensus as to which country has the dominant "interest" in regulating an agreement or transaction, or principally feels its effects? An effort to achieve resolution of these differences through identification of "interests" would recall the contemporary effort in the United States to develop a new methodology for (principally domestic) choice-of-law problems. It would also encounter, in a more diverse geographical setting and in a more complicated substantive context, the problems suggested by Babcock v. Jackson, p. 937, supra. Can one identify with clarity the interests or policies of different jurisdictions? If so, and if they appear to be in conflict, under what national or community principles should the conflict be resolved?

The question also arises whether—as foreign governments have asserted in diplomatic correspondence relating to American antitrust investigations or litigation—it should be sufficient to insulate practices from our laws to demonstrate that the challenged agreement or practice was planned or pursued in the foreign country, among nationals of that country, and with the consent or indeed encouragement of the government of that country.[40] Consider the following comment in an address of Professor Myres McDougal: [41]

> When Switzerland or Canada or any other country employs its governmental processes to protect business entrepreneurs in activities which impair the healthy functioning of community process within the United States, it is interfering with the internal domestic affairs of the United States fully as much as the United States may be interfering with the internal affairs of such other country in applying its Anti-trust laws to the injury-causing activities. Agreements made by private entrepreneurs in Switzerland and Canada, and ostensibly protected by the laws of those countries, may affect or determine the prices which I must pay within the United States for aluminum and watches. In an interdependent world interference by States in each other's community processes, including economic affairs, is inescapable. The question is by what principles and procedures such interference can be moderated and made reciprocally tolerable in the maintenance and expansion of an international economy.

Note that grounds advanced by defendants for giving conclusive effect to policies of foreign governments (whether permissive or mandatory in character) that validate a challenged agreement or practice could include (a) the "act of state" doctrine, p. 672, supra, (b) the argument that the defendants were obligated to comply with their governments' rules and should not be penalized for acting under duress, (c) the argument that the foreign governments' protective legislation such as tariffs had in fact eliminated all export "commerce" from the United States, so that none was left to be restrained by private parties, or (d) the argument that the governments were so implicated with the private parties as to confer upon the defendants the shelter of their sovereign immunity.[42]

Such issues involving the conduct of foreign governments in antitrust contexts have arisen in several recent cases.[43] Interamerican Refining Corp. v. Texaco Maracaibo, Inc., 307 F.Supp. 1291 (D.Del. 1970), affords an example. Plaintiff brought a treble-damage action against its suppliers and traders, some among which were Venezuelan subsidiaries of American companies, for allegedly entering into a concerted boycott to deny it crude oil from Venezuela. Defendants denied neither the refusal to deal with plaintiff, which was to refine the oil in New York Harbor, nor the damages sustained. They pleaded, how-

40. Compare the Swiss Watchmakers litigation, p. 1041, infra.

41. International Law Association, Report of the Fifty-first Conference Held at Tokyo 304, 331 (1965).

42. Problems of reaching a modus vivendi with foreign governments on restraints of competition occur not only in the context of substantive defenses to actions under the antitrust laws but also during the preliminary investigatory process when documents needed to prove antitrust violations are sought through the aid of a foreign government. See the cases and text at pp. 835–851, supra.

43. In addition to the case noted in text, see Occidental Petroleum v. Buttes Gas and Oil Co., 331 F.Supp. 92 (C.D.Calif.1971), aff'd 461 F.2d 1261 (9th Cir. 1972).

ever, that their refusal was under compulsion by the Venezuelan Government. "Nothing in the materials," observed the court, "indicates that defendants either procured the Venezuelan order or that they acted voluntarily pursuant to a delegation of authority to control the oil industry" in Venezuela. Rather it found "genuine compulsion," for reasons of oil pricing policy that were persuasive to the Venezuelan Government. "When a nation compels a trade practice, firms there have no choice but to obey. Acts of business become effectively acts of the sovereign . . . . Anticompetitive practices compelled by foreign nations are not restraints of commerce . . . because refusal to comply would put an end to commerce." The court refused to consider plaintiff's claim that the Venezuelan Minister involved had no authority to bar sales, and that therefore the orders were not legal or compelling. Citing the Sabbatino decision, p. 691, supra, the court stated: "For our courts to look behind the acts of a foreign government would impinge upon and perhaps impede the executive in that function. Whether or not Venezuelan officials acted within their authority and by legitimate procedures is therefore not relevant to the instant case."

QUESTIONS

(1) What, if any, of the learning of the American Banana case survives the two later antitrust cases, or such cases in the criminal field as United States v. Bowman, p. 872, supra? Consider the later views of Justice Holmes himself in Strassheim v. Daily, p. 883, supra.

(2) "Alcoa is an extravagant, a dangerous decision, particularly in Judge Hand's statement that it is 'settled law' that a country can impose liability upon aliens for conduct abroad that has 'consequences within its borders which the state reprehends.' That statement, and the holding of Judge Hand which rests upon it, is hardly consistent with generally recognized principles of international law. It is, to put it mildly, inappropriate to transfer to the antitrust field principles about 'consequences' or 'effects' that were developed in criminal cases involving such tangible acts as gunshots across a border, or developed in collision cases such as Lotus [p. 885, supra]. The principle would know no limits in so vague a field, where effects are often intangible and speculative. It simply provides a convenient pretext for exorbitant national claims to govern conduct that is rooted in foreign countries." Is this statement an accurate description of the Alcoa case? If so, do you agree with its criticism?

(3) Section 18 of Restatement, Second, Foreign Relations Law of the United States, p. 882, supra represents an effort to capture Alcoa's principles. Does it succeed? If not, in what respects is the section more restrictive or liberal as to extraterritorial application than Alcoa?

(4) In deciding whether the antitrust laws apply to a given transnational situation, should it be relevant to a court whether an action is brought by a private party (American Banana or Continental Ore) or by the Government (Alcoa)? Why?

PROBLEMS

The issues raised in the preceding cases can conveniently be divided into two categories: (1) Each of the cases poses the general question of the appropriate reach of American antitrust regulation. (2) The American Banana and Continental Ore cases, in attempting to respond to this question, also consider the effect to be given to foreign legislation or other governmental action that may aid a defendant in achieving its goals.

A. The Reach of the Antitrust Laws

In the following sequence of problems, consider (1) whether the United States antitrust laws should apply to the agreements or practices described in them, and (2) if so, whether it is likely that jurisdiction could be obtained in the United States over the parties to such agreements.[44] You can assume that all such agreements or practices would be illegal if they were planned and to be fully performed within the United States.

(1) Widgets are popular household appliances, with sales in the United States of about $200 million annually. Approximately 80% of the widgets sold are imported. Because of high wages for skilled labor and dependence upon essential raw materials not available in this country, it would be difficult to expand American production—at least in the face of foreign competition. The principal exporter to the United States is Austrasia. The widget industry is Austrasia's third largest category of manufactured exports and an important source of foreign exchange. About half these exports are to the United States.

An agreement, made and valid in Austrasia, restricts sales of widgets to the United States by allocating an export quota to and setting a common export price for each contracting party. Export contracts between American importers and individual Austrasian firms (which refer orders above their quota to other firms) are made by correspondence, title passing to the importer at the time and place of shipment. Consider whether the arguments for application of United States law are fortified or weakened if one varies the status of the parties to the agreement so that they are:

(*a*) two domestic (American) corporations with branches in Austrasia;

(*b*) two wholly owned subsidiaries of two American corporations, each organized and engaged in business in Austrasia;

(*c*) the two subsidiaries referred to in (b), together with three Austrasian corporations owned by Austrasian nationals;

(*d*) three such Austrasian corporations, two of which have branches in New York that act as sales agencies; or

(*e*) three such Austrasian corporations, with no American branches or subsidiaries.

(2) Assume that each of the following agreements is valid under Austrasian law. How would you state the argument in each case for application of United States law? How would you evaluate such arguments, in advice that you were giving to the companies involved? (Note generally the jurisdictional and remedial problems involved in these cases if United States law were applied.)

(*a*) An agreement among Austrasian companies owned by Austrasian nationals limits the quantity and determines the price of

44. The cases and text at pp. 747–748, supra, consider such problems of adjudicatory jurisdiction in antitrust and other settings. Whether a judgment for money damages or an equity decree of an American court could be enforced against foreign defendants raises distinct issues that are examined at pp. 1029–1040, infra.

exports of widget parts from Austrasia to Guatador. The parts will be used in Guatador to assemble completed widgets, some of which (about $40 million in value) will be exported to the United States.

(*b*) An agreement among such companies fixes the prices at which widgets are sold by manufacturers in Austrasia. None of the manufacturers sells to purchasers in the United States, but a substantial amount of their production (about $80 million in value) is purchased by Austrasian distributors and resold to importers in the United States.

(*c*) An agreement allocates to various manufacturing firms in Austrasia quotas for production of widgets. One of the parties is an Austrasian subsidiary of an American corporation. It has customarily purchased important components used in manufacturing widgets from the United States (about $20 million in value annually).

(*d*) An agreement provides for the merger of four Austrasian firms into one large corporation which will absorb all operations of the four, including their substantial sales of widgets to the United States. One such firm is owned by an American company. These firms together account for 95% of Austrasian widget production.

(*e*) In question (d), the one firm is equally owned by an American and English company.

B. Reconciliation with Foreign Governmental Action

Consider in the light of the American Banana and Continental Ore cases the kinds of defenses which might prevail in the sequence of problems below. Assume that (1) absent consideration of the foreign government's policies, United States antitrust laws would likely apply; (2) the described agreements or practices would be illegal if developed and pursued entirely within the United States; (3) unless otherwise indicated, at least one (but fewer than half) of the defendants is an Austrasian subsidiary of an American corporation; and (4) jurisdiction over the defendants is obtained before a federal court.

(1) Austrasia has no law prohibiting agreements in restraint of competition. Defendants enter into a price-fixing agreement for widgets, which controls exports to the United States.

(2) The law of Austrasia generally prohibits price-fixing agreements. However, it authorizes them for agricultural commodities and permits a majority of agricultural producers to fix prices binding upon all. Defendants, after voting against the price, adhere to it in their export sales of cheese to the United States.

(3) The law of Austrasia provides that an administrative board may fix the price of widgets, two of the members being industry representatives and three being government officials. Defendants adhere to the price so fixed in their export sales.

(4) Austrasian legislation sets the level of import quotas. Defendants are local manufacturers of dingbats, which are also imported into Austrasia from the United States. Defendants participated in lobbying the act through the Austrasian legislature which limits dingbat imports, and they adhere to the quota arrangement.

(5) Under Austrasian law a government-owned corporation has the sole right to import dingbats. It enters into an agreement with two American suppliers (the defendants) that it will buy from them only.

(6) The law of Austrasia has no provisions on restraints of competition. The five Austrasian firms that produce and sell dingbats in Austrasia advise the two American firms exporting to that country that, if they sell more than 10,000 dingbats each in 1964, the Austrasian firms will combine to drive them out of business. The two American firms (the defendants) accede to the ultimatum and sign the quota agreement.

---

2. PROBLEMS IN THE ENFORCEMENT ABROAD OF ANTITRUST DECREES OF AMERICAN COURTS

NOTE ON TRADE-MARKS, PATENTS AND RELATED TRANSNATIONAL ANTITRUST PROBLEMS

The litigation below involving Imperial Chemical Industries, Ltd. raises problems about the interaction between the antitrust and patent laws. A later discussion of antitrust policy in the European Common Market at pp. 1365–1378, supra, raises issues about the role of trade-mark protection. To place those discussions in context, this Note describes some aspects of trade-mark and patent law and some relationships between those bodies of law and antitrust laws in a transnational setting. Both historically and at the present time, a substantial percentage of transnational antitrust problems is linked to agreements involving trade-marks or patents.

Trade-Marks

Trade-marks initially served the purpose of identifying the source of the products to which they were affixed. In a complex society such as the United States, their present function is generally to assure consumers that products bearing the same trade-mark issue from a common source, rather than to identify the particular manufacturer of a product. To the extent that a trade-mark and a manufacturer have a common name (Kodak), the mark accomplishes both purposes. In addition to identifying source, a trade-mark may assume connotations of quality, efficiency, dependability and so on. The mark becomes a symbol with multiple references. In protecting its owner against infringement, the courts stress the role of the mark in identifying source, or common source, and indirectly protect its other attributes.

Protection of a trade-mark at common law or under a statutory scheme confers a limited monopoly of a word upon its owner, who alone can employ it to designate a particular product (True cigarettes, Ivory soap). Thus the law of trade-marks tends to run at cross-purposes with the law of antitrust in that it restrains competition and bars access to markets to new entrants. A mark legally prevents others from competing in the sale of like goods bearing that mark. It may also effectively restrict competition in the sale of like goods under other marks, for by solid performance or lavish advertising an owner may endow a mark with a reputation of quality and thereby capture a large market. The mark may then foreclose competitors. The justification for such a restriction is that it protects the owner of the mark in his investment in building up a favorable reputation among customers, and thereby serves a public interest by encouraging owners to undertake such investments. Moreover, protection of the mark protects the public against being deceived as to the source of what they are buying.

Trade-mark protection first developed at common law. Infringement of a mark established by use constituted a tort referred to as unfair competition or "passing off". Such infringement might take the form of imitating the originator's mark or of copying the shape or manner of packing of the product. However, common law has long been supplemented by federal legislation, chiefly the Trade-Mark Act of 1905 and now the Lanham Act of 1946, 60 Stat. 427, as amended, 15 U.S.C.A. §§ 1051–1127. This Act provides for a register of trade-marks to be maintained by the Patent Office. Proceedings can be initiated in the Patent Office to determine who has the right to obtain registration in the light of prior use of the same or similar marks. A trade-mark duly registered confers on its owner substantive rights under the Lanham Act against infringements upon the mark. The holder of a mark can enforce these rights through litigation in the federal courts, which can order changes in the register as well as grant injunctions or monetary relief either in the amount of the damages suffered by the trade-mark holder or of the profits made from the infringing activity.

Increasingly trade-marks have acquired international meaning as firms which have developed a trade-marked product in one country seek to exploit it abroad—Coca Cola, Kleenex, etc. While foreign countries have the same general interest in protecting their citizens against deception, they may be less interested in protecting the investment of foreign firms in the trade-marks, if, for example, that means seriously handicapping local bottlers who wish to compete with Coca Cola and if it means large drains on the country's foreign exchange by way of royalties payable under the trade-mark license. Basically trade-marks are territorial in nature. Each country's legal system specifies who can obtain a trade-mark valid within its territory and what rights accrue to such a mark. These provisions vary widely, especially with respect to such requirements as registration or use within the territory.

However, international anarchy in respect of these matters would be highly inconvenient where trade is as integrated as it now is. A series of treaties has mitigated the diversity that would otherwise exist. First, the typical bilateral Treaty of Friendship, Commerce and Navigation assures nationals and companies of one contracting party national treatment with respect to trade-mark in the other party's territory. See, e. g., Article VIII of the Convention of Establishment between the United States and France.*

Second, the United States is a party to the International Convention for the Protection of Industrial Property of Paris of 1883, now in the form of the Lisbon Revision of 1958.[45] More than 50 countries, including most industrialized nations, are parties to this. The Lanham Act reflects the Paris convention in various respects. In Section 44, for example, it guarantees national treatment for owners from treaty countries. It also protects foreign registrations of trade-marks by allowing the U. S. application—if filed within six months—to be dated back to the foreign date. Some provisions of the Lanham Act track the Convention even as to purely internal matters. Thus Section 14, in allowing cancellation at any time of a fraudulently obtained mark, follows Article 6 *bis* of the Convention.

Third, the United States is a party, with several Latin American countries, to the General Inter-American Convention of 1920, 46 Stat. 2907, T.S. No. 833, generally duplicating the Paris Convention. The United States does not, however, participate in the so-called Madrid Arrangement of 1891. Under the Arrangement, which is related to the Paris Convention, a trade-mark registered in any signatory country may, through the International Office for the Protection of Industrial Property Rights at Berne, Switzerland, also be registered in the offices of all other signatory countries.

Trade-marks raise similar transnational issues to those earlier discussed in this chapter. For example, should United States courts enjoin trade-mark infringements where all or some of the activity takes place abroad? This question has not been addressed by the Lanham Act but a few cases have been forced to explore it. Of these Steele v. Bulova Watch Co.,[46] is the most important. Defendant, an American citizen resident in San Antonio, Texas, was conducting a large scale operation within Mexico assembling watches from Swiss and American components and marketing them as "Bulova" watches. An attempted registration of the "Bulova" mark by Steele had been cancelled by the Mexican authorities. Some of defendant's "Bulova" watches found their way into the United States. The Supreme Court reversed a dismissal of the complaint, saying in part:

> . . . In the light of the broad jurisdictional grant in the Lanham Act, we deem its scope to encompass petitioner's activities here. His operations and their effects were not confined within the territorial limits of a foreign nation. He bought component parts of his wares in the United States, and spurious "Bulovas" filtered through the Mexican border into this country; his competing goods could well reflect adversely on Bulova Watch Company's trade reputation in markets cultivated by advertising here as well as abroad. Under similar factual circumstances, courts of the United States have awarded relief to registered trade-mark owners, even prior to the advent of the broadened commerce provisions of the Lanham Act. George W. Luft Co. v. Zande Cosmetic Co., 2 Cir., 1944, 142 F.2d

45. 13 U.S.T. & O.I.A. 1, T.I.A.S. No. 4931.

46. 344 U.S. 280, 73 S.Ct. 252, 97 L.Ed. 319 (1952).

> 536 . . . . Even when most jealously read, that Act's sweeping reach into "all commerce which may lawfully be regulated by Congress" does not constrict prior law or deprive courts of jurisdiction previously exercised. We do not deem material that petitioner affixed the mark "Bulova" in Mexico City rather than here, or that his purchases in the United States when viewed in isolation do not violate any of our laws. They were essential steps in the course of business consummated abroad; acts in themselves legal lose that character when they become part of an unlawful scheme. United States v. Bausch & Lomb Optical Co., 1944, 321 U.S. 707, 720, 64 S.Ct. 805, 812, 88 L.Ed. 1024 . . . . In sum, we do not think that petitioner by so simple a device can evade the thrust of the laws of the United States in a privileged sanctuary beyond our borders.

The Steele case has, however, apparently been limited by an important opinion of the Second Circuit in Vanity Fair Mills, Inc. v. T. Eaton Co.[47], which held that the Lanham Act did not extend to a case where the party committing acts of alleged infringement in Canada was not an American citizen and where the Canadian registration of the mark was still in litigation. It said the following by way of distinguishing Bulova:

> In the Bulova case, supra, the . . . . Supreme Court noted that the question of the effect of a valid registration in the foreign country was not before it. The Court affirmed the Fifth Circuit, holding that the federal district court had jurisdiction to prevent unfair use of the plaintiff's mark in Mexico. In doing so the Court stressed three factors: (1) the defendant's conduct had a substantial effect on United States commerce; (2) the defendant was a United States citizen and the United States has a broad power to regulate the conduct of its citizens in foreign countries; and (3) there was no conflict with trade-mark rights established under the foreign law, since the defendant's Mexican registration had been canceled by proceedings in Mexico. Only the first factor is present in this case.
>
> We do not think that the Bulova case lends support to plaintiff; to the contrary, we think that the rationale of the Court was so thoroughly based on the power of the United States to govern "the conduct of *its own citizens* upon the high seas or even in foreign countries *when the rights of other nations or their nationals are not infringed*", that the absence of one of the above factors might well be determinative and that the absence of both is certainly fatal. Plaintiff makes some argument that many American citizens are employed in defendant's New York office, but it is abundantly clear that these employees do not direct the affairs of the company or in any way control its actions. The officers and directors of defendant who manage its affairs are Canadian citizens. Moreover, the action has only been brought against Canadian citizens. We conclude that the remedies provided by the Lanham Act, other than in § 44, should not be given an extraterritorial application against

47. 234 F.2d 633 (2d Cir. 1956).

foreign citizens acting under presumably valid trade-marks in a foreign country.

The general anticompetitive effects of trade-marks to which we referred at the start of this section can be multiplied in international commerce. Section 42 of the Lanham Act and Section 526 of the Tariff Act of 1930, 19 U.S.C.A. § 526, allow the domestic owner of an American trade-mark to bar the importation of goods made abroad which bear that mark. The Tariff Act provision makes unlawful the importation of merchandise bearing a registered trade-mark "owned by a citizen of, or by a corporation . . . organized within the United States." The merchandise is subject to seizure.

These statutes do more than prohibit the sale of falsely labelled goods or of "passing off" by independent foreign producers exporting to this country who use an American mark. They may be applied to prevent importation by third parties of genuine goods manufactured by the same foreign firm which exports to this country through sales to the holder of the rights under the American trade-mark. Comparable provisions for the exclusion of imports are found in the laws of a number of foreign countries. Consider the following illustrations:

> (*1*) An American firm licenses the mark which it owns in country X to foreign firm A and its mark in country Y to foreign firm B, while retaining the same mark in this country for its exclusive use. Each firm may be able to bar importation into its respective country of like goods bearing that mark. This characteristic business arrangement may thus create three separate markets, each of them without competition in the sale of the trade-marked product. Subject to antitrust problems that may arise in view of stock or other affiliations among these parties, the American firm could exclude from this market goods made abroad by its licensees under the relevant trade-mark and sold, perhaps at significantly lower prices, to third persons who desired to export them to the United States.
>
> (*2*) Competing firms in this country and in country X, selling under different trade-marks, engage in cross-licensing. That is, the American firm licenses its mark in X to its competitor, and receives from the competitor a license for its mark in the United States. An effective division of territories and elimination of competition between the two firms might follow. The same situation might obtain if competing companies in two countries agreed to produce their products under the same trade-mark and each registered the mark in its own country.

In most of the judicial decisions, trade-mark arrangements were linked to more inclusive plans to restrain competition that colored, and often led to restrictions upon the use of, the trade-mark rights. Two cases indicate the range of possibilities.

In United States v. Guerlain, Inc., 155 F.Supp. 77 (S.D.N.Y. 1957), the Government brought a civil action charging three American corporations with a violation of Section 2 of the Sherman Act through their marketing of trade-marked toilet goods. Each defendant was affiliated by contract or stockholdings with a French firm that had originated the trade-mark. That firm supplied the products (or their essential ingredients) sold in this country by the American company under the same mark used by the French firm for its foreign sales. The French firms had transferred their trade-mark rights in the United States to the American companies, which registered the marks in the Patent Office. Each defendant, pursuant to Section 526 of the Tariff Act of 1930, had filed a certificate of registration to prevent the import of authentic products bearing the same trade-mark and sold by its French counterpart to third persons who sought to export to the United States. In each case, in view of the stock or contract relationships, the court concluded that one of the affiliated companies effectively controlled the other, and stated that each American defendant and its French counterpart "constitute a single international enterprise." It held that under these circumstances, the trade-mark laws and Section 526 did not permit the defendants to secure a monopoly in this country over the sale of the trade-marked products, or provide a shield against the Sherman Act. The court concluded that the Government was entitled to relief "in the form of an order enjoining the continuation of the conduct constituting the violation." While the case was on appeal, the Supreme Court, on motion of the Government, vacated the judgment below and remanded to the District Court, 358 U.S. 915, 79 S.Ct. 285, 3 L.Ed.2d 236 (1958), and the District Court dismissed the complaint with prejudice, upon the Government's motion. 172 F.Supp. 107 (S.D.N.Y.1959). Thus the effect was to give primacy to the trade-mark right rather than to the competing antitrust policies.[48]

In Timken Roller Bearing Co. v. United States, 341 U.S. 593, 71 S.Ct. 971, 95 L.Ed. 1199 (1951), the Government charged that affiliated American and foreign firms entered into agreements to divide world markets in the manufacture and sale of anti-friction bearings. These agreements provided in part for the licensing of trade-marks among and the use of common trade-marks by these firms. However, they went beyond such licensing and also restricted sales of items that were not trade-marked. The Supreme Court upheld the finding of the trial court that the agreements had "the central purpose of allocating trade territories," and thus concluded that they violated the Sherman Act. The American defendant failed to persuade the Court

48. The Solicitor General's motion in the Supreme Court, set forth in part in Ebb, Regulation and Protection of International Business 474 (1964), acknowledged the difficulty in interpreting Section 526 and the different views of that section that appeared to be held by the Justice Department and customs officials. In view of these considerations, the motion stated that the Executive Branch had decided to submit the problem to the Congress for legislative resolution. Despite efforts in Congress to clarify this issue, it remains unresolved.

that any trade restraints stemming from the agreements were only incidental to a permitted use of trade-mark rights. The Court, while stressing that the agreements before it used many techniques other than trade-mark licensing to accomplish their purposes, stated that a "trade-mark cannot be legally used as a device for a Sherman Act violation." [49]

Patents

The basic function of a patent is to protect an invention for a specified period of time against all subsequent finders of the same idea, regardless of whether they are imitators or independent discoverers. Unlike trade-mark law, the federal patent law is based on a specific constitutional grant of power to the federal government that has been used since the early days of the Republic. Although the requirements to be met to obtain a patent and the protection obtained vary widely from country to country (patents, like trade-marks, are territorially based and thus confer a monopoly only in the political sovereignty where they are created), the rules of the United States patent laws (codified in 35 U.S.C.A.) are illustrative.

35 U.S.C.A. § 101 authorizes the grant of a patent to the inventor or discoverer of "any new and useful process, machine, manufacture, or composition of matter . . .". Before the Patent Office will grant a patent there must be an application meeting complex requirements; a search will be made of the "prior art" or existing evidence as to what is known. The validity of an invention can be tested by interference proceedings in the Patent Office, followed perhaps by an appeal to the Court of Customs and Patent Appeals. However, many patents that have survived the tests of the Patent Office have been stricken by the courts when tested in infringement or other litigation. A patent might be held invalid because it was not workable, because it did not advance significantly beyond the prior art or for other reasons.

A valid patent gives the patentee the right for 17 years to exclude others from "making, using or selling the invention throughout the United States." 35 U.S.C.A. § 154. Another section (§ 271) complements this by providing that "whoever without authority makes, uses or sells any patented invention, within the United States . . . infringes the patent." An infringer can be enjoined from continuing the infringing acts and can be held liable in damages. Moreover, these rights have an important transnational reach. Foreign goods that come within a United States product patent or that have been produced abroad by a process subject to a United States process patent can be barred from importation by provisions similar to those ap-

49. The Court referred to Section 33(b) of the Lanham Act. That section provides that if the right to use a registered mark has become incontestable, registration is conclusive evidence of the registrant's exclusive right to use the mark, subject to certain exceptions. Subsection (7) notes one such exception: "That the mark has been or is being used to violate the antitrust laws of the United States."

plicable to trade-marks. Section 337 of the Tariff Act of 1930, 46 Stat. 703, as amended, and 54 Stat. 724 (1940), 19 U.S.C.A. §§ 1337, 1337a.[50] Comparable exclusionary provisions are found in the patent laws of a number of foreign countries.

The rights held by the inventor-patentee can be transferred to another en bloc by an assignment or they can be conveyed in parcels by licenses that may be either exclusive or non-exclusive. Assignees or licensees can, in general, bring actions against infringers.

As with trade-marks, there is an inherent tension between the goals of patent law and antitrust law. The patent grant is justified on the theory (a) that a grant for a limited term accompanied by full disclosure will lead to at least as much competition in inventing as a system in which firms try to keep inventions to themselves indefinitely through secrecy measures and (b) that a "head-start" such as that represented by a patent is necessary to justify risking substantial investments on new and untried inventions. In the United States a rather extensive case law has arisen to delimit the borderline between the valid exercise of patent rights and their misuse so as to cause antitrust violations. To touch on only a few salient points: (1) The accumulation by a firm of a large mass of patents, especially by purchase rather than development in its own laboratories, may be found to be part of the crime of monopolization. (2) American law has been applied strictly so as to prevent a patentee from conditioning the use of its patented item upon the use of unpatented supplies, components, etc. (3) Progressively, the case law has eliminated the patentee's right to fix the price at which the patented goods it sells are resold or at which others sell goods which they make under a license from the patentee.

Other countries' patent systems differ widely in detail, in the requirements for patentability, the closeness of the scrutiny they give applications and the duration and scope of the monopoly they grant. Some laws declare medicines or foodstuffs not to be subject to patent protection. Many of them make more intensive efforts to compel the patentee to exploit the patent than does United States law—as by subjecting it to compulsory licensing or forfeiture after nonuse for a stated period. Others exert pressure by increasing the amount of the current fees required to keep the patent in full force.

It is quite generally understood that a patent has a strictly territorial effect limited by the borders of the sovereign granting it. The same idea, therefore, will have to be protected by a series of different, though parallel, patents in each of the countries where the inventor

50. These provisions are comparable to the rules about importation of trade-marked products in Section 42 of the Lanham Act and Section 526 of the Tariff Act of 1930, p. 1024, supra. The reader of 19 U.S.C.A. §§ 1337 and 1337a may find a certain gap between the language of those sections and the description above of their effect. The liberal administrative and judicial interpretations of these sections close this gap. For a collection of some of the decisions, see Ebb, Regulation and Protection of International Business 499–523 (1964).

seeks protection and is willing to pay the not inconsiderable price. A device successfully patented in one country might turn out to be unpatentable elsewhere. Meanwhile, a United States court will regard itself as not competent to enjoin alleged infringements abroad, even if stated as violations of the foreign patent, and would ordinarily regard it as not appropriate to pass on the validity of foreign patents, even if the issue is raised in ordinary contract litigation.[51]

The separate national patent laws are loosely coordinated by the Paris Convention on the Protection of Industrial Property, which has been referred to at p. 1022, in connection with the protection it gives trade-marks. Salient features of that Convention are the guarantee of national treatment to inventors and the limitations placed on national government's rights to forfeit or license patents for non-use.

International patent licenses and other agreements raise a number of challenging difficulties. A number of them are discussed in Chapter XII. For the moment it is sufficient to note that international license agreements are common and useful arrangements. Foreign patent law may strongly favor the local manufacture of the foreign article, as does the British law described at p. 1031, infra,[52] and it may render difficult the foreign investment that would have to be made if the American party were to manufacture abroad. Even though license agreements may thus be virtually necessary, they raise serious antitrust issues. Consider the following illustrative examples.

> (*1*) A foreign patentee owning patents in the United States, in his own country X and in country Y, grants exclusive licenses of his United States patent to company A and his patent in Y to company B. Neither goods made in X nor Y can be sold in the United States because the American licensee can exclude all goods within the terms of the United States patent.
>
> (*2*) An American firm and a competing firm in country X may engage in cross-licensing, pursuant to which each licenses the other to produce exclusively under the patent which it owns in the other's country. This arrangement may be coupled with an agreement, to some degree implicit in the territorial character of the patents, that neither will export products within the licensing agreement to the other's country. Note that such an arrangement may serve constructive purposes by freeing each firm from the risk of infringing the other's patent, and allowing each to exploit all patents relevant to the manufacture of a particular product.

Thus patents as well as trade-marks can be used to divide markets among competitive firms. As with trade-marks, the mere fact that a patent is involved does not confer immunity on such arrange-

51. Cf. Ortman v. Stanray Corp., 371 F.2d 154, 156–58 (7th Cir. 1967).

52. See the discussion of English law in the Imperial Chemical Industries litigation, at p. 1029, infra.

ments. After a highly particularistic assessment of the facts, including all related business arrangements, a court may conclude that the underlying purpose was to divide markets in a manner forbidden by the antitrust laws. The case which follows involves such a situation.[53]

Additional reading: Areeda, Antitrust Analysis 423–429 (2d ed. 1974) (on the patent system generally); Callman, The Law of Unfair Competition and Trade-Marks, vol. 4, pp. 2196–2244 (2d ed. 1950, supp. 1965); Ebb, Regulation and Protection of International Business 353–678 (1964); Eckstrom, Licensing in Foreign Countries (3d. ed. 1974); Offner, International Trademark Protection (1965).

THE LITIGATION OVER THE ENFORCEMENT OF THE IMPERIAL CHEMICAL INDUSTRIES DECREE

[The litigation in United States and English courts in the 1950's involving Imperial Chemical Industries, Ltd. (ICI) commenced in this country with an action brought by the Government under the antitrust laws. In the first reported court proceeding, United States v. Imperial Chemical Industries, Ltd., 100 F.Supp. 504 (S.D.N.Y.1951), the principal defendants were ICI, which was organized under the laws of the United Kingdom and had its offices and principal place of business in London, and E. I. duPont deNemours and Company, Inc. (duPont), a Delaware corporation. Each company was a major producer of chemicals in its own country and an important force in world markets. The United States alleged that the defendants had violated Section 1 of the Sherman Act through various agreements that were designed to divide world territories and allocate customers and markets for chemical products. These agreements involved primarily the exchange and licensing of patents and processes for various chemical products, and the establishment of joint-venture companies in various countries. The District Court found that defendants, through such agreements, had violated the Sherman Act because of their unlawful purposes in entering into the agreements and the adverse effect of their conduct upon the import and export trade of the United States. It said in part (100 F.Supp. at 592):]

> We have found that the various patents and processes agreements were made in furtherance of the conspiracy alleged. These agreements, irrespective of their *per se* legality, were instruments designed and intended to accomplish the world-wide allocation of markets; their object was to achieve an unlawful purpose—an illegal restraint of trade prohibited by Section 1 of the Sherman Act. The agreements are unlawful because they provided a means for the accomplishment of this purpose and objective. We have also found that these agreements did, in operation, result in restraints of United States trade.

[DISTRICT JUDGE RYAN stated that the Government was entitled to relief "by appropriate decree of this Court," and invited the submis-

53. Other significant cases in which patent agreements were invalidated in view of their purpose and effect of restraining trade are United States v. National Lead Co., 63 F.Supp. 513 (S.D.N.Y.1945), aff'd 332 U.S. 319, 67 S.Ct. 1634, 91 L.Ed. 2077 (1947); Zenith Radio Corp. v. Hazeltine Research, Inc., 395 U.S. 100, 89 S.Ct. 1562, 23 L.Ed.2d 129 (1969). Further illustrations of antitrust problems are offered in connection with a patent licensing problem at pp. 1209–1222, infra.

sion of proposed decrees. In United States v. Imperial Chemical Industries, Ltd., 105 F.Supp. 215, 220 (S.D.N.Y.1952), Judge Ryan introduced his opinion by stating:]

> We now approach the task of formulating a final decree designed to prevent and restrain the violations of law which we have found. . . . Our objective is to fashion, in the terms of a decree, means by which the agreement found to exist is terminated, its revival prevented and its effects destroyed by the reestablishment of competitive conditions insofar as they pertain to United States exports and imports. . . .

[The portion of the opinion below deals with patents of ICI and duPont which had been found to serve as instruments by which the defendants achieved their unlawful purpose of dividing markets. The court noted that such misuse of patents "renders the future use of those rights subject to and amenable to judicial control to prevent a continued or new abuse." It decreed compulsory licensing of many United States patents owned by the defendants, on a "reasonable royalty basis." The following excerpts from the opinion consider the British patents owned by ICI.]

The Government does not seek a decree directing ICI to grant compulsory licenses of its British patents. The Government requests that ICI be required to grant immunity under its foreign patents which correspond to the United States patents which we have made subject to compulsory licensing. Such a provision was included in paragraph "7" of the final decree in National Lead, 63 F.Supp. 495, 534, and left undisturbed by the Supreme Court. We have had testimony offered on behalf of ICI by an expert in British law that a provision for granting immunities is contrary to British public policy and that a British court will not enforce such a provision in the judgment of a court of a foreign jurisdiction. As to this, we observe that, acting on the basis of our jurisdiction in personam, we are merely directing ICI to refrain from asserting rights which it may have in Britain, since the enforcement of those rights will serve to continue the effects of wrongful acts it has committed within the United States affecting the foreign trade of the United States.

We are not unmindful that under British law there are restrictions upon exports from the United States by reason of the existence of the British patents owned by ICI. The exclusion of unlicensed imports and the prohibition of unlicensed sales is enforceable because of the legal rights which attach to a British patent.

We accept as correct the statements in the brief of ICI that: "Under United States law if a product is patented, sale into the United States of that product constitutes clear infringement of the rights of the American patentee. Such sale will therefore subject the vendor to a suit for infringement even though his acquisition of the patented article abroad (and his use and sale of it there) may be wholly lawful. . . . This is true even though the vendor may hold the foreign patent on the article in question. . . .

"In the British Empire the law is even more stringent. The owner of a British patent may bar the importation of any product patented in Great Britain and also any product made by any process where the process is patented under British law. It is clear that a patent on a process essential to the production of a product is infringed by sale of an imported product made abroad by that process. . . .

"There is no requirement under American law which required duPont to license ICI under its United States patents or ICI to license duPont under its British patents. To the extent that each retained the right under the laws of its respective country to assert patents against imports, this resulted in no limitation upon such imports which in any way exceeded the limitation that would have existed had there been no agreement at all." But as we have heretofore observed these lawful rights were employed as means to accomplish the unlawful purpose of their underlying agreement.

While it is true that these rights exist independent of any provision in the patents and processes agreements, they were granted to ICI by the disclosure or assignment of inventions by duPont pursuant to the terms of these agreements. Inventions were also licensed by ICI to duPont for its exclusive use and exploitation in the United States in accordance with the agreements. In the first instance the patents were employed to restrain duPont's exports to Great Britain, in plain violation of American anti-trust laws; in the second instance, the patents were used as a means to prevent ICI exports to the United States and placed a restraint upon the foreign trade of Great Britain, in violation of her declared policy, if not her laws. It does not seem presumptuous for this court to make a direction to a foreign defendant corporation over which it has jurisdiction to take steps to remedy and correct a situation, which is unlawful both here and in the foreign jurisdiction in which it is domiciled. Two evils have resulted from the one understanding of ICI and duPont—restraints upon the foreign trade and commerce of the United States as well as on that of Great Britain. It is not an intrusion on the authority of a foreign sovereign for this court to direct that steps be taken to remove the harmful effects on the trade of the United States.

We recognize that substantial legal questions may be raised with respect to our power to decree as to duPont's foreign patents as well as those issued to ICI. Here we deal with the regulation of the exercise of rights granted by a foreign sovereign to a domestic corporate defendant and to a foreign corporate defendant. Our power so to regulate is limited and depends upon jurisdiction in personam; the effectiveness of the exercise of that power depends upon the recognition which will be given to our judgment as a matter of comity by the courts of the foreign sovereign which has granted the patents in question.

Where we have required ICI to grant immunity under British patents which are the counterpart of duPont's United States patents, the payment of reasonable royalty upon imports of articles manufactured under them into Great Britain shall be paid to ICI.

Full recognition is hereby given to the inherent property rights granted by the British patent to exclude from Great Britain merchandise covered by the patent. . . .

We are advised that the present policy of the British patent law is to foster manufacture in the United Kingdom rather than to permit importation from abroad . . . . The Patent Act of 1949, carried this public policy further in Sec. 37, to the extent that the comptroller of patents may order a "license of right" when, although the patented invention is capable of being worked in the United Kingdom, it is not being commercially worked "to the fullest extent that is reasonably practicable", or demand is "not being met on reasonable terms, or is being met to a substantial extent by importation," or "commercial working of the invention in the United Kingdom is being prevented or hindered by the importation of the patented article" (20th Century

Statutes, 1949, vol. 46, p. 1013). The grant of immunity under the British patents would be subject, of course, to the operation of these statutes and proscribed by such action as the comptroller of patents might take. This should not deter us from making directions we feel are required, even though the application of them be limited in operation by the possible action of an official of a foreign sovereign. . . .

We have found that nylon was wholly a duPont development to which ICI made no contribution (Op. p. 107). The basic patents covering nylon have not expired.

The history of the basic British nylon patents reveals a studied and continued purpose on the part of ICI and duPont to remove these patents from within the scope of any decree which might ultimately be made by this court (Op. pp. 115, 116, 197, 198). These British patents were issued to duPont. By the agreement of March 30, 1939, ICI received an exclusive license under them; in January, 1940, ICI granted irrevocable and exclusive rights to make nylon yarn from nylon polymer (which is manufactured by ICI) to British Nylon Spinners, Ltd. (BNS). ICI has a stock interest of 50% in BNS, the remaining 50% is held by Courtaulds, Inc. BNS is in the business of manufacturing and distributing nylon yarn. Not content with this arrangement and with the deliberate purpose to "materially reduce the risk of any loss of rights" as a result of this suit (Ex. 708, p. 2705), duPont pursuant to the nylon agreement of 1946 assigned the basic British nylon patents to ICI. It is now urged that we may not decree with reference to these British patents so as to direct ICI to remove restrictions on imports into Great Britain of nylon polymer or nylon yarn from the United States. It is argued that the sum total of all these agreements is not to create by itself any restrictions against American imports, and that those which exist arise from the right to be free from competition which is inherent in the British patents and cannot possibly be repugnant to the American anti-trust laws.

BNS is not before this court; although they were knowing participants in acts designed to thwart the granting of full relief, we may not direct our decree to them. The lack of majority stock ownership in ICI likewise prevents control of the future acts of BNS by this means; however, we are not without some remedy still available.

Objection is raised by ICI that we are without power to decree that the British nylon patents may not be asserted to prevent the importation of nylon polymer and nylon yarn into Great Britain because BNS has rights which exist independent of those possessed by ICI. This overlooks the circumstances under which BNS acquired its rights to these patents by licenses from ICI. . . .

The nylon agreement between duPont and ICI of December 31, 1946, provides in paragraph III (Ex.D. 1163, p. 7869) for the assignment of patents and patent applications listed in Schedule "A" of the agreement in the nylon field. By this writing, ICI became the owner of the British patents, in which its interest up to that time had been that of a licensee. Throughout all these negotiations it appears that BNS was advised of the dealings between ICI and duPont concerning the British nylon patents. Both ICI and duPont are parties to the instant suit; they were advised in fact and realized that the further use and control of the rights pertaining to the British nylon patents were subject to a decree of this court to be entered in this suit. We find that in fact Courtaulds and BNS were also fully advised of this situation. The first, or "manufacturing sub-license" which BNS received granted to it no greater rights than had been acquired by ICI; it was subject to the same infirmities as existed against ICI. The second license granted after the assignment of the patents to ICI did not come to BNS as an innocent party. BNS, again, knew exactly what it was receiving; its rights are wholly subject to the inherent vices of the agreements through which they were acquired. We have found them to be tainted with the illegality of the unlawful conspiracy; of this probability BNS was informed. . . .

We do not hesitate therefore to decree that the British nylon patents may not be asserted by ICI to prevent the importation of nylon polymer and of nylon yarn into Great Britain. What credit may be given to such an injunctive provision by the courts of Great Britain in a suit brought by BNS to restrain such importations we do not venture to predict. We feel that the possibility that the English courts in an equity suit will not give effect to such a provision in our decree should not deter us from including it.

In any event it appears that BNS would have the right under Section 63 of the Patents Act of 1949, as the exclusive licensee to bring suit for infringement against an importer of yarn and staple fiber. There would then be a speedy determination of the effectiveness of the immunity provision of the decree with reference to these products. If the British courts were not to give credit to this provision, no injury would have been done; if the holding of the British courts were to the contrary, a remedy available would not have been needlessly abandoned.

[The court then stated that the 1946 agreement between duPont and ICI on the British nylon patents should be cancelled. It required ICI to reconvey to duPont certain assigned patent rights. Before the decree was made final in the district court, BNS brought an action in England again ICI. It sought specific performance of its contract of 1947 with ICI, granting it exclusive licenses of certain nylon patents assigned to ICI, and an injunction restraining ICI from complying with the order of the United States district court relating to reconveyance. An injunction pending a full trial was granted by Upjohn, J., in the Chancery Division of the High Court, and an interlocutory appeal to the Court of Appeal was dismissed. The excerpts below are from the opinion of the Court of Appeal, British Nylon Spinners, Ltd. v. Imperial Chemical Industries, Ltd., [1953] Ch. 19 (1952), [1952] 2 All E.R. 780.[54]]

SIR RAYMOND EVERSHED, M. R.: The agreement of December 31, 1946, was an agreement whereby the defendant company acquired outright from du Pont de Nemours the patents (among others) which are specified in the schedule to the order, and one of the terms of the final judgment of the district judge, was that this agreement was thereby cancelled and terminated. That, however, was not all, for in a later part of the same judgment, Imperial Chemical Industries, Ltd. (the defendant company) was forbidden to make, among other things, "any disposition of foreign patents" (i. e., patents foreign to the United States of America and including the patents now in suit) unless it required, as a condition of the grant, that the grantee agreed in writing to hold its license subject to certain rights of immunity, viz., the rights of American manufacturers of these nylon products freely to import and vend in the United Kingdom articles manufactured in accordance with the patents or with comparable patents. The effect of any such condition, if insisted on, would, obviously, be to derogate in a most serious way from the value of the exclusive licences which the defendant company was under contract to grant to the plaintiff company.

54. The quoted excerpts are taken from the All England Law Reports.

Further, if the defendant company were to re-assign these various patents to du Pont de Nemours, as directed by the judgment of the district judge, it would, in fact, disable itself altogether thenceforward from granting licences in the terms which it had contracted to grant. . . .

This is an interlocutory matter, and, therefore, it is inappropriate for the court to say more about the case or its merits than is necessary to make clear the grounds of the conclusion which it reaches. It is plain from what I have said that there is here a question of what is sometimes called the comity which subsists between civilised nations. In other words, it involves the extent to which the courts of one country will pay regard and give effect to the decisions and orders of another country. I certainly should be the last to indicate any lack of respect for any decision of the district courts of the United States, but I think that in this case there is raised a somewhat serious question whether the order, in the form that it takes, does not assert an extraterritorial jurisdiction which the courts of this country cannot recognise, notwithstanding any such comity. Applied conversely, I conceive that the American courts would likewise be slow (to say the least) to recognise an assertion on the part of the British courts of jurisdiction extending, in effect, to the business affairs of persons and corporations in the United States. In a judgment which the district judge delivered in May, 1952 (the second of his opinions in the proceedings to which I have referred), it is plain that the learned judge carefully considered this matter, and, indeed, as UPJOHN, J., pointed out, expressed his own doubts whether, in giving effect, as he felt it his duty to do, to the implications of the Sherman Act, he might not be going beyond the normally recognised limits of territorial jurisdiction. But he said:

> "It is not an intrusion on the authority of a foreign sovereign for this court to direct that steps be taken to remove the harmful effects on the trade of the United States."

If by that passage the learned judge intended to say (as it seems to me that he did) that it was not an intrusion on the authority of a foreign sovereign to make directions addressed to that foreign sovereign, or to its courts, or to nationals of that foreign power, effective to remove (as he says) "harmful effects on the trade of the United States", I am bound to say that, as at present advised, I find myself unable to agree with it. Questions affecting the trade of one country may well be matters proper to be considered by the government of another country. Tariffs are sometimes imposed by one country which obviously affect the trade of another country, and the imposition of such tariffs, as it seems to me, is a matter for the government of the particular country which imposes them. And if that observation of the learned judge were conversely applied to directions designed to remove harmful effects on the trade, say, of Great Britain or British nationals in America, I should be surprised to find that it was accepted as not being an intrusion on the rights and sovereign authority of the United States. On the other hand, there is no doubt that it is competent for courts of a particular country, in a suit between persons who are either nationals or subjects of that country or are otherwise subject to its jurisdiction, to make orders in personam against one such party, directing it, for example, to do something or to refrain from doing something in another country affecting the other party to the action. As a general proposition, that would not be open to doubt, but the plaintiff in this case is neither a subject nor a national of the United States, nor (unlike the defendant company) was it a party to the proceedings before the district judge, nor is it otherwise subject to his jurisdiction.

What the precise relationship, commercially or otherwise, is between the plaintiff company and the defendant company we have not at this stage of the proceedings considered, and I proceed on the assumption (and I am not to be taken as hinting that the contrary is the fact) that the plaintiff is an independent trade corporation and entitled to be treated as independent of the defendant company. Being so independent, it has beyond question, according to the laws of England, certain rights, certain choses in action, by virtue of the contract of 1947, which the courts of this country, in exercise of the laws which they claim to be entitled to administer, will in this country protect and enforce. Broadly speaking, the contract of March, 1947, being an English contract, made between English nationals and to be performed in England, the right which the plaintiff company has may be described as its right, under the contract, to have it performed and, if necessary, to have an order made by the courts of this country, for its specific performance. That is a right, or, in other words, a species of property (seeing, particularly, that it is related to patents) which is English in character and is subject to the jurisdiction of the English courts, and it seems to me that the plaintiff company has, at least, established a prima facie case for saying that it is not competent for the courts of the United States, or of any other country, to interfere with those rights or to make orders, the observance of which by our courts would require that our courts should not exercise the jurisdiction which they have and which it is their duty to exercise in regard to those rights.

I think, however, that the matter goes somewhat further. I have said that the subject-matter of the contract of December, 1946, is a number of English and Commonwealth patents. An English patent is a species of English property of the nature of a chose in action and peculiar in character. By English law it confers on its proprietor certain monopoly rights, exercisable in England. A person who has an enforceable right to a licence under an English patent appears, therefore, to me to have, at least, some kind of proprietary interest which it is the duty of our courts to protect. And, certainly, so far as the English patents are concerned, it seems to me, with all deference to the judgment of the district judge, to be an assertion of an extraterritorial jurisdiction which we do not recognise for the American courts to make orders which would destroy or qualify those statutory rights belonging to an English national who is not subject to the jurisdiction of the American courts. . . .

DENNING, L. J.: I agree. It would be a serious matter if there was a conflict between the orders of the courts of the United States and the orders of the courts of this country. The writ of the United States does not run in this country, and, if due regard is had to the comity of nations, it will not seek to run here. But, as I read this judgment of the United States court, there is a saving clause which prevents any conflict, because, although the defendant company has been ordered to do certain acts by the United States court, nevertheless there is a provision which says that nothing in the judgment shall operate against the company for action taken in complying with the law of any foreign government or instrumentality thereof to which the defendant company is for the time being subject. In view of that saving clause I hope that there will be no conflict between the orders. I agree that the appeal should be dismissed.

Appeal dismissed.

ROMER, L. J.: I also agree.

[In a later proceeding in the Chancery Division involving a trial on the merits, British Nylon Spinners, Ltd. v. Imperial Chemical Industries, Ltd., [1955] Ch. 37 (1954), [1954] 3 All E.R. 88, the court held that ICI was required to perform its contract with BNS and granted BNS specific performance. Excerpts from the opinion of DANCKWERTS, J., appear below.[55]]

. . . The question, therefore, is whether the judgment of the United States Federal Court provides a defence for the defendant company, Imperial Chemical Industries, Ltd., in the present action for specific performance, and whether by reason of that judgment I should refuse to grant specific performance of the contract which has admittedly been made between the plaintiff company and the defendant company. . . .

It was argued on behalf of the defendant company that this court would not enforce a contract which involved the deliberate violation of the laws of a friendly country . . . . There is no evidence before me that the object of the contract of Mar. 5, 1947, was to do anything contrary to the law of the United States of America and no evidence that the plaintiff company was party to or had knowledge of any conspiracy contrary to the law of the United States when that contract was entered into. It is impossible for me to accept the conclusions of the United States court as findings of fact binding in this action against the plaintiff company which was not a party to the American proceedings. . . .

There are, however, further considerations which also lead to the same result. I had the advantage of the evidence of Mr. Marshall Konopak Skadden, a member of the Bar of the State of New York, practising in the relevant United States courts. His evidence was that the British court would be accepted under the law of the United States as an appropriate court having jurisdiction for the enforcement of the contract under consideration in the present case. Further, his evidence was that, if the defendant company, though prohibited from doing so by a judgment of a court in the United States, complied with an order of a British court and executed a licence, this would not be treated by an American court as a contempt of court. Mr. Skadden referred to a number of decisions of American courts in support of those propositions. This evidence indicates to me that the American courts would not regard a judgment of this court in the present circumstances enforcing against the defendant company the contract of Mar. 5, 1947, as in any way inappropriate, and there does not appear, therefore, to be any difficulty in regard to comity between the courts of the two countries in this case.

Furthermore, it would appear that the judgments of His Honour JUDGE SYLVESTER RYAN recognised this principle and were intended to provide for and limit his own judgment in this very respect. This appears to be in the intention of art. IV, para. 3, of the judgment of July 30, 1952:

> "No provision of this judgment shall operate against [the defendant company] for action taken in compliance with any law of the United States Government, or of any foreign government or instrumentality thereof, to which [the defendant company] is at the time being subject, and concerning matters over which, under the law of the United States, such foreign government or instrumentality thereof has jurisdiction."

55. The quoted excerpts are taken from the All England Law Reports.

"Instrumentality" of a government is an inaccurate, and, indeed, repellent, description of an English court; but it appears, none the less, that the learned judge was using the word in this manner from his observations on the occasions of further applications which were made to him. . . .

These passages indicate to me that His Honour JUDGE SYLVESTER RYAN has been careful so to limit his judgment that neither his judgment, nor any judgment of mine which the law of England requires me to give, will disturb the comity which the courts of the United States and the courts of England are so anxious and careful to observe. . . .

In the result, my conclusion is that, notwithstanding the judgment of the United States court of July 30, 1952, the defendant company is bound by English law to carry out the agreement of Mar. 5, 1947, and I ought to make the declaration which is asked by the amended statement of claim, and grant specific performance of the contract.

Judgment for the plaintiffs.

[DuPont's reaction to the outcome of the British litigation was to refuse to grant ICI a royalty-free immunity to import certain nylon products into the United States. The decree had required such a grant but duPont asserted that ICI's inability, perhaps a permanent one, to grant reciprocal immunities as to imports into Great Britain relieved it of that duty. When ICI applied for an order requiring duPont to grant the immunity, Judge Ryan denied the motion without prejudice to a renewal if ICI could grant reciprocal rights, 1954 Trade Cases ¶ 67,739 (S.D.N.Y.1954). He noted that "this regrettable situation . . . was not entirely unforeseen at the time of the drafting of these provisions of the judgment."]

COMMENT

The ICI litigation has similarities with another conflict between the United States and Great Britain over economic regulation, stemming from orders of the Federal Maritime Commission under Section 21 of the Shipping Act of 1916 (p. 1076, infra) and described at pp. 1076–1084, infra. One immediate source of that conflict was the possibility that sanctions would be visited upon British subjects or companies refusing to comply with orders of the Commission to file evidence. That is, United States courts or agencies did not there seek the aid of English courts to enforce their production orders but threatened themselves to act upon the British parties before them. The British response was measured to the threat: legislation designed to frustrate American efforts to compel production of evidence. Doubts were expressed in the debates in the House of Commons (pp. 1081–1084, *infra*) whether that legislation would prove effective. The answer depended in part upon what American demands would (in the words of the legislation) "constitute an infringement of the jurisdiction which, under international law, belongs to the United Kingdom . . . ."

NOTE ON THE ICI LITIGATION AND RECOGNITION OF FOREIGN EQUITY DECREES

The opinions of the district court and the English courts add a further dimension to certain problems introduced in Part B of Chapter VII; they consider what effect should be given in one country to an equity decree rather than money judgment entered in another. Frequently a court entering an equity decree requiring a defendant to perform certain acts in a foreign country [56] will lack the power to make that decree effective. There may be jurisdictional obstacles, inadequate statutory authority or indeed a substantive constitutional objection to applying sanctions, including those of civil or criminal contempt, against the party to whom an order has been directed. The party benefiting from the decree may thus consider invoking the aid of foreign courts, much as he would seek enforcement abroad of a money judgment. But consider whether characteristics inherent in equity decrees suggest that their foreign recognition and enforcement are less likely than was true of money judgments.

(1) An equity decree generally involves the exercise of a greater discretion by the court issuing it (F–1) than a money judgment. Broader considerations have traditionally been considered relevant, both in ruling upon the merits of a plaintiff's case and in shaping the relief to be granted. Comparable discretionary factors may affect the willingness of a foreign court (F–2) to act as an enforcement arm. Its own view of the merits or of the appropriateness of the relief granted may differ from that of F–1. The risk of divergence becomes acute when the decree of F–1 enjoins or requires conduct in F–2 (by which we refer as well to the foreign country in which the foreign court sits). More than a money judgment, such a decree may be viewed as unduly impinging upon F–2's interests. Such a reaction will often be expressed as an alleged intrusion of the decree into F–2's "territorial sovereignty."

(2) However different the procedures in different nations may be for enforcing a foreign money judgment [57] in no country do they impose particularly vexing burdens upon the court. The foreign judgment is translated into some form of domestic court order which requires payment of the amount stated in the initial judgment (or its equivalent in local currency). In the case of equity decrees, a cooperative F–2 would enter a decree of its own. However, the view of F–2 as to the propriety of the relief granted by F–1, and perhaps limitations under F–2's law upon the kinds of decrees that it can enter, may

56. This Note uses the term "equity decree" in an Anglo-American sense, to refer to court decrees requiring a defendant to perform or to refrain from certain acts, other than the payment of money damages to the plaintiff. It should be recalled that courts of most other nations have never known the distinction between law and equity. Nonetheless they will, of course, enter decrees comparable to the Anglo-American equity decree, whether under comparable or different conditions.

57. See pp. 759, 797 and 803, supra.

be relevant. That is, the F–2 decree would rarely parrot that of F–1, particularly with respect to the complex decrees entered in antitrust litigation. It should be noted that it may not be necessary in all cases for F–2 to enter its own decree even if it is willing to honor the decision of F–1. In the ICI case, for example, the English court hearing the BNS litigation could have supported the federal court's decree by refusing to grant specific performance of the contract between ICI and BNS, by "recognizing" rather than actively "enforcing" the decree.

(3) The characteristic sanction for violation of an equity decree in Anglo-American countries is civil or criminal contempt proceedings. But that sanction is not exclusive. For example, refusal by a party to comply with a decree ordering the transfer of land may be remedied by a court order directing the appropriate official (assuming that he is subject to the court's jurisdiction) to record the transfer on the land register. But such situations are atypical, and in general the court would act upon the defendant to coerce compliance with its decree. Whatever the sanctions in other countries may be, F–2 has a more onerous enforcement burden than in the case of money judgments. First, there may be difficulty in determining whether the foreign decree, or more precisely the F–2 decree modelled upon it, has been violated. Second, if this finding is made the F–2 court may be obliged to apply the contempt power against the defendant. There is an understandable reluctance to apply that power in aid of a decree originating in a foreign court's decision.

For these and related reasons, the status of equity decrees even within a federal nation may be less secure than that of a money judgment. The cases described at pp. 759–766, supra, indicated the extensive protection which the Full Faith and Credit Clause accorded to money judgments within the United States. An unsettled case law does make clear that equity decrees are not assured of extra-state recognition and enforcement to anywhere near the same degree.[58]

(4) Equity decrees that reach into other jurisdictions are also apt to raise choice-of-law problems in an acute form. The court in F–2 may conclude that the F–1 court applied F–1's law to a controversy which was as much or perhaps more the concern of F–2. The question whether to enforce the F–1 decree merges with the question whether, from F–2's perspective, F–1 has overreached. The ICI case illustrates this kind of reaction, in a setting where the courts of each nation believed that forum law had a primary claim to govern a particular aspect of the controversy before them.[59]

58. See Reese, Full Faith and Credit to Foreign Equity Decrees, 42 Iowa L. Rev. 183 (1957), and Developments in the Law—Injunctions, 78 Harv.L.Rev. 994, 1031–45 (1965).

59. Such reactions were critical to decisions in several cases appearing in Part E of Chapter VII and in Part F of this Chapter, cases in which a private party or the Government enlisted the aid of a United States court to obtain evidence from a foreign party that was located in foreign countries. Compare with the ICI problem the Interhandel case, p. 844, supra, and Mitsui Steamship Co., Ltd., 1077, infra. In those decisions, as in ICI, the reluc-

To be sure, conflicts over which nation's law should govern the underlying controversy can also arise in actions to enforce money judgments. Suppose, for example, that a private party recovered treble damages in an antitrust action against ICI in the United States, an action based in part upon ICI's conduct in England that allegedly had adverse effects upon the United States' foreign commerce and the plaintiff. The question arises whether an English court would be likely to enforce such a judgment, if for some reason the judgment creditor could not realize upon it in the United States.[60]

NOTE ON FOREIGN REACTIONS TO AMERICAN ANTITRUST PROCEEDINGS: THE SWISS WATCHMAKERS CASE

American antitrust proceedings involving foreign parties, whether or not leading to equity decrees, have provoked numerous foreign protests. The principal episodes include (1) a protest by the Netherlands Government against certain provisions of the proposed decree under the decision in United States v. General Electric Co., 82 F.Supp. 753 (D.N.J.1949), which found violations of the Sherman Act by a number of defendants including N. V. Philips' Gloeilampenfabrieken (Philips), a Dutch company; (2) a protest by the British Government against the investigation of an international oil cartel in 1952; and (3) a protest by the French Government in the 1920's directed towards a proceeding against a potash-producing group.[61]

American courts have made some efforts to alleviate the tensions in this field by entering decrees which take account of the special problems of foreign defendants who act consistently with their own governments' policies. We here note two such instances.

After the decision in the General Electric case above, the Government and a number of defendants, including Philips, submitted proposed forms of judgments to implement that decision. The court then entered a judgment, 115 F.Supp. 835 (D.N.J.1953), which contained special exemptions for Philips. For example, Section X of the judgment stated that the Department of Justice, subject to legally recognized privileges, should be permitted "reasonable access" to

tance of foreign courts to aid our government in the vindication of its regulatory policies was intensified because of a clash over which nation's regulatory policies should prevail and because of hostility to our government's basic policies.

60. Even in an interstate setting, recall the reaction of the Mississippi court in Fauntleroy v. Lunn, p. 760, supra, to the Missouri money judgment which it was ultimately required to enforce. An award of treble damages in the hypothetical problem in text would raise additional questions in any enforcement action. Compare Huntington v. Attrill, p. 764, supra, and the Note at p. 791, supra.

61. These and other episodes are listed in Becker, The Antitrust Laws and Relations with Foreign Nations, 1959 N.Y. State Bar Ass'n, Section on Antitrust Law, Proceedings 51, 58. A comprehensive list of protests in antitrust and related actions, compiled by G. W. Haight, appears in International Law Association, Report of the Fifty-First Conference Held at Tokyo 565–592 (1965); and later developments may be found in later Reports.

all books and other records of defendants for the purpose of securing compliance with the judgment. This provision, however, governed Philips only with respect to its records located in the United States, in view of the "international complications posed by the provision for investigation of Philips in the Netherlands . . . ." Section XI stated that "Philips shall not be in contempt of this Judgment for doing anything outside of the United States which is required or for not doing anything outside of the United States which is unlawful" under Dutch law or the law of any territory in which Philips might be doing business.[62]

Litigation involving, among others, Swiss associations in the watch industry and Swiss and American manufacturers of watches and watch machinery offers a more developed illustration. In United States v. The Watchmakers of Switzerland Information Center, Inc., 1963 Trade Cases ¶ 70,600 (S.D.N.Y.1962), the court examined the government's charge that a complex network of agreements and practices among these parties violated Section 1 of the Sherman Act and Section 73 of the Wilson Tariff Act, p. 1000, supra. Several defendants were affiliated firms, either American subsidiaries of Swiss companies or the reverse. The Swiss watch industry, the largest producer of watches in the world, exported approximately 95% of its production, principally to the United States. It also exported watch parts and watchmaking machinery. During a period of years relevant to the litigation, 95% of jeweled watches imported into the United States came from Switzerland, and our watch industry produced approximately 20% of all the watches sold in this country.

Most of the Swiss firms—both Swiss owned and subsidiaries of American firms—were members of the Federation Suisse des Associations de Fabricants d'Horlogerie ("FH"), an association organized pursuant to Swiss law to protect the general interests of Swiss manufacturers and assemblers. Among other things, FH coordinated economic policies of the numerous small watch producers and established general terms and conditions for the manufacture, sale and export of watches and movements. Another Swiss association, also organized in accordance with Swiss law, was principally concerned with problems of foreign competition and acted as the link between the watch industry and Swiss federal authorities. Together with an executive branch of the Swiss Government, that association exercised a certain power to grant or refuse applications for permits to export watches and watchmaking machinery. Swiss legislation of 1951 reaffirmed the principle that export permits would be issued "only for shipments which do not violate the common interests of the watch industry."

A series of agreements among various elements of the industry, known as the Collective Convention, bound the many participating

62. Compare the approach of the district court which ordered an American defendant to "use reasonable efforts" to make export sales in foreign markets previously allocated by licensing and other agreements to foreign companies. Article XI of the decree in United States v. Holophane Co., 1954 Trade Cases ¶ 67,679 (S.D.Ohio 1954), affirmed as to this clause by an equally divided Court, 352 U.S. 903, 77 S.Ct. 144, 1 L.Ed.2d 114 (1956).

firms to limit their exports of watches, watch parts and watchmaking machinery. Some American firms or their Swiss subsidiaries were parties to the Collective Convention, membership in which was not obligatory under Swiss law. The District Court found that the Collective Convention and allied agreements or practices, through the export and other limitations which they expressed, were intended to affect competition in the manufacture of watches and watch parts in the United States and the import and export to and from this country of such products and watchmaking machinery.

Counsel for the Swiss Confederation appeared as *amicus curiae* in the court proceedings, and the brief on the merits for the Confederation stated in part: [63]

> This case is of utmost concern to the Swiss Confederation. The attempt is here being made to apply the anti-trust laws of the United States to hold illegal action taken (a) in Switzerland, (b) at the behest and with the encouragement of the Swiss Confederation and in conformity with Swiss law, (c) by the Swiss watch industry, (d) which is both government regulated and affected with a public interest. This action of the Swiss watch industry does not discriminate in any way against the United States and is not aimed only at the United States; rather this action affects the world at large. . . .
>
> Nothing in the language of the anti-trust laws requires that these laws should be applied to this action and to these contracts of the Swiss watch industry, and the anti-trust laws should not be so applied. Such application, among other things, would infringe Swiss sovereignty, would violate international law and would be harmful to the international relations of the United States.
>
> . . . Not only does the present action constitute a direct attack upon the legislation and policy of the Swiss Confederation; it further seeks to regulate conditions in Switzerland and to limit the control which the Swiss Confederation may exercise over its own watch industry. . . . It has always been held that the anti-trust laws do not apply to acts done in the territory of a foreign sovereign in furtherance of that sovereign's law and policy. . . .
>
> The present action involves the Collective Conventions which were negotiated and executed in Switzerland by Swiss nationals and which were to be performed exclusively in Switzerland. All of the important contacts involving these Conventions were located in Switzerland, and Switzerland has the greatest interest in them. There is considerable doubt, to be sure, as to what law governs the validity of a contract in a case where the relevant contacts are divided among two or more States. But with respect to the Conventions, every contact of importance is located in Switzerland and obviously the parties expected and intended to have Swiss law applied. The law of every civilized nation and of every known Conflict of Laws authority would agree that the validity and effect of these Conventions are governed by Swiss law. . . .

63. These excerpts appear in International Law Association, Report of the Fifty-First Conference Held at Tokyo 575–76 (1965).

Nonetheless, in view of the effect of the Collective Convention and allied practices upon this country's commerce, the court concluded that the agreements violated our antitrust laws. It stated that the practices offending our laws "were not required by any Swiss law," and were illegal "notwithstanding that some of the conspirators are foreign nationals, that some of the agreements were entered into in a foreign country or that the acts of defendants were lawful in such foreign country [citing Continental Ore Co. v. Union Carbide & Carbon Corp., p. 1011, supra, and United States v. Aluminum Co. of America, p. 1006, supra]." In response to the arguments of the defendants and the Swiss Confederation, the court said:

> If, of course, the defendants' activities had been required by Swiss law, this court could indeed do nothing. An American court would have under such circumstances no right to condemn the governmental activity of another sovereign nation. In the present case, however, the defendants' activities were not required by the laws of Switzerland. They were agreements formulated privately without compulsion on the part of the Swiss Government. It is clear that these private agreements were then recognized as facts of economic and industrial life by that nation's government. Nonetheless, the fact that the Swiss Government may, as a practical matter, approve of the effects of this private activity cannot convert what is essentially a vulnerable private conspiracy into an unassailable system resulting from foreign governmental mandate. In the absence of direct foreign governmental action compelling the defendants' activities, a United States court may exercise its jurisdiction as to acts and contracts abroad, if, as in the case at bar, such acts and contracts have a substantial and material effect upon our foreign and domestic commerce. . . . The arguments of business necessity and foreign trade conditions asserted by the defendants cannot immunize the restraints imposed by them upon United States commerce. . . .

The court entered a final judgment in January 1964.[64] It found unlawful numerous provisions in the Collective Convention and contracts between the defendants (FH and the American and Swiss watch firms), which limited exports to or from or manufacture in this country of watches, movements, parts, and machinery. It ordered the defendants to terminate or stop enforcement of such provisions. In addition, each defendant was enjoined from maintaining or entering into any program or agreement which restrained production in, import into or export from the United States of these items. FH and a Swiss firm were ordered to amend the Collective Convention to end discrimination between sales of watch parts to the United States and sales to other countries or in Switzerland. FH was further enjoined from imposing a penalty on any FH member because of activity required or permitted by the court's judgment. Article XI of the judgment provided that nothing in it should be deemed to prohibit cer-

64. Unpublished. Civil Action No. 96–170, District Court for the Southern District of New York, Judge Cashin.

tain conduct, including conduct in Switzerland required of a defendant under Swiss law.

Notices of appeal were filed by some defendants. The Swiss Confederation, through the State Department, advised that it would support the appeal and ultimately endeavor to secure review by the International Court of Justice unless certain modifications were made in the judgment. A memorandum on behalf of the Swiss Ambassador urging modification noted that "[t]hese threats to Swiss sovereignty have created widespread anxiety within Switzerland." Further discussions between attorneys for Switzerland, for the defendants and the Department of Justice led to withdrawal of the notices of appeal and a motion to the court by the defendants seeking modification of the judgment. The United States filed a memorandum in support of the motion.

The chief points dealt with in the proposals for revision were as follows:

> (*1*) The judgment was modified so that sections and members of FH who had not been parties to the suit were not subject to it. Other provisions made clear that FH could be held responsible if its sections violated the decree. FH was no longer required to prohibit its members from violating the decree or to include portions of the decree in its bylaws. These provisions arguably had made FH an extraterritorial American law enforcement agency.
>
> (*2*) A provision which had enjoined certain types of agreements between defendants and other firms in third countries was rewritten so that it covered only arrangements specifically affecting imports to or exports from the United States or transactions by United States companies operating abroad. The prior clause seemed to cover a hypothetical agreement between a Swiss and a German firm limiting the German firm's purchases which might incidentally cut sales to it by American suppliers.
>
> (*3*) The Swiss Government promulgated an order whereby it took charge of controls on exports of watch parts, previously a matter of private agreement. The judgment was revised to acknowledge the legitimacy of the order and of steps taken pursuant to it.
>
> (*4*) A clause was added to make clear that production of documents to show compliance with the judgment would not be required if Swiss law would thereby be violated.

The court accepted the modifications in an opinion reported at 1965 Trade Cases ¶ 71,352 (S.D.N.Y.1965). It stated that it believed that "in the main the modifications relate to peripheral areas of the judgment." It noted that the Department of State had indicated that "a resolution of this litigation on a basis consistent with United States antitrust laws and the basic objectives of the judgment would be advantageous from the standpoint of American foreign policy." It further observed that the "modifications will prevent any situation from arising such as has occurred in other litigation in the past when there was believed to be a possible conflict between a decree of a United States court and the sovereignty of a foreign nation [citing the Imperial Chemical Industries litigation, p. 1029, supra.]." Section XI (E) of the amended judgment treated this problem by providing that nothing contained in the Final Judgment should be deemed to prohibit any defendant or other person from:

> (1) Performing any act in Switzerland which is required of it under the law of Switzerland;
>
> (2) Refraining from any act in Switzerland which is illegal under the law of Switzerland;
>
> (3) Taking any joint or individual action, consistent with the applicable law of the nation where the party taking such action is domiciled, to comply with conditions for the export of watch parts from Switzerland established by valid ordinances, or rules and regulations promulgated thereunder, of the Swiss Government;
>
> (4) Taking any joint or individual action required by the scheme of regulation of the Swiss watch industry based on Article 31 bis of the Swiss Constitution, with respect to imports of watch parts into Switzerland other than from U. S. companies;
>
> (5) Advocating the enactment of laws, decrees or regulations or urging upon any Swiss governmental body, department, agency or official the taking of any official action;
>
> (6) Furnishing to the Swiss Government or any body, department, agency or official thereof, its independent advice or opinion when requested to do so.

The participation in litigation before an American court of a foreign government, here as *amicus curiae*, and the communication to that court of views of the Department of State illustrate one of the procedures through which governments with antagonistic policies can seek to reach an accommodation. A more direct and less *ad hoc* method of mediating differences would of course be the conclusion of international agreements among the government involved. Despite the fact that a number of drafts have been proposed, little headway has been made towards treaty resolution of these issues.[65] Given the va-

65. The antitrust division of the Department of Justice reported that it maintains an informal "Antitrust Notification and Consultation Procedure" with Canada under which each antitrust office notifies the other prior to instituting antitrust actions affecting the other country's interests or nationals. On a less specific basis the division consults with officials of many other countries. Testimony of Mr. Zimmerman in International Aspects of Antitrust, Hearings before the Subcommittee on Antitrust and Monopoly of the Senate Judiciary Committee, 89th Congress, 2d Sess., pt. I, pp. 494–95 (1966). For a Canadian perspective, see Foreign Direct Investment in Canada (the "Gray Report") 270–79 (1970).

riety of governmental attitudes towards regulation, private enterprise and the most advantageous conditions under which a national economy should function, and given the radically different positions of countries in the world economy, many observers doubt that there is now a sufficient consensus on basic antitrust issues to provide the foundation for meaningful international agreements.[66] Certain regional arrangements, among countries with shared interests and, relatively speaking, shared traditions and approaches to these problems, have been developed and have proved effective. The most significant, the antitrust provisions of the Rome Treaty creating the European Economic Community, is considered in Chapter XIII. A number of treaties of friendship, commerce or navigation to which the United States is a party contain clauses comparable to Article XI of the Convention of Establishment between the United States and France.* [67] The Organization for Economic Cooperation and Development sponsors annual conferences in which antitrust officials of different countries participate. It also commissions publications on antitrust problems and has recently sought international agreement on procedures for consultation prior to the initiation by a member nation of specific antitrust procedures in a case with international implications.[68] To date, the contribution of these arrangements to international antitrust harmony has not been obvious, but it does appear that there is a rising awareness among national governmental agencies of the desirability of coordinated and cooperative action on competition.

QUESTIONS

(1) Note the extreme circumstances under which the ICI decree was issued. Defendant was an alien doing business dominantly in its own country. The patents were issued in England, under English law, and covered the sale of products or use of processes only in Great Britain. The exercise by defendant of its patent rights in England was consistent with English law.

> (*a*) Should the effect of defendant's conduct upon the foreign commerce of the United States be viewed as sufficient justification for a decree that so sharply conflicted with another country's policies?
>
> (*b*) Does the Alcoa case point towards issuance of such a decree? Does the complex contractual relationship between ICI and duPont?

66. Compare Becker, The Antitrust Laws and Relations with Foreign Nations, 1959 N.Y. State Bar Ass'n, Section on Antitrust Law, Proceedings 51, 58, with Brewster, Remarks on the Extraterritorial Application of Federal Antitrust Laws, id. at 63, 66–67.

67. Such a clause in a treaty with Japan was held to be no barrier to the civil antitrust proceeding in United States v. R. P. Oldham Co., 152 F. Supp. 818 (N.D.Calif.1957). See Haight, The Restrictive Business Practices Clause in United States Treaties: An Antitrust Tranquilizer for International Trade, 70 Yale L. J. 240 (1960).

68. The recommendations of the OECD are reprinted in 19 Antitrust Bull. 283 (1974). See also, Zisler, The Work of the OECD Committee of Experts on Restrictive Trade Practices, id. at 289. With respect to the OECD generally, see p. 1245, infra.

(2) Assuming that the district court could not count upon cooperation from English courts in policing the conduct of ICI, would it nonetheless have power to make its decree effective? By what techniques? Under the circumstances, would such enforcement techniques be likely or advisable? Might the effort to apply them raise serious issues under United States law? Recall the Interhandel case, p. 844, supra.

(3) Does the decree of Judge Ryan appear in any event advisable, on the assumption that compliance with it would have eliminated anticompetitive effects on United States foreign commerce which our antitrust laws were interpreted to make illegal? Was the court's attitude simply: "We'll try. If we succeed, so much the better. If we fail, nothing is lost." ? Was anything "lost" through these proceedings?

(4) How do you evaluate the argument of the Swiss Government, in its *amicus* brief in the Watchmakers case, that application of the antitrust laws to the conduct of Swiss firms and associations in Switzerland would "infringe Swiss sovereignty [and] violate international law?" What materials in this book would you draw upon to support such an argument?

(5) Suppose that the Swiss Government enacted legislation requiring all domestic manufacturers of watches, parts and watchmaking machinery to join a quasi-governmental organization with power to determine quality standards and prices for all exported goods and to limit exports. American firms with Swiss subsidiaries inquire whether they are violating United States law if their subsidiaries enter into these arrangements. How would you advise them?

(6) Suppose that the defendants in the Watchmakers case were only FH and Swiss firms, served through their sales agencies or other offices in this country. None had stock affiliations with American watch companies, and the only relationships to American companies were through sales contracts. Nonetheless, the Collective Convention and other agreements and practices affected exports of watches, parts and machinery to this country. Should the same decree have been issued?

(7) Can cases such as ICI or Swiss Watchmakers be resolved by deciding which of two countries has the dominant "interest" in regulating a given situation or practice? For example, in Watchmakers, is Switzerland's interest as the country of manufacture and of exports superior to that of the United States as a major importing country? Should the answer depend upon how important the watch industry is to Switzerland and to the United States? Upon comparing the volume of Swiss exports to all countries with the volume of exports to the United States? Upon other factors?

E. SECURITIES REGULATION

In recent years, differences in attitude and approach between the United States and other countries in the field of securities regulation have begun to cause international tensions, similar to but generally less acute than those affecting labor or antitrust matters. The United States is committed to maintain through regulation a securities market in which relatively large segments of the public, including investors whose individual stake is small, can participate with some degree of protection against abusive practices. Such a market cannot operate successfully without a system that provides the corporate or individual investor with the data needed to make informed decisions as to investment, more or less on an equal footing with "insiders"—those persons who might have access to special data because of their connections with corporations issuing securities ("issuers").

Hence the United States, through the Securities Act of 1933 and the Securities Exchange Act of 1934,[69] committed itself to a policy requiring each firm that makes an appeal to the public market for funds to disclose its affairs, at that time and periodically thereafter. Unlike some state laws, these federal statutes have not taken the further step of giving an administrative agency the power to determine what securities cannot be sold to the public, based on an evaluation of the merit of the underlying business venture and the securities.[70]

The principal function in this context of the Securities and Exchange Commission, the agency administering these acts, has been defining and enforcing the requirement of disclosure. In pursuit of that objective the SEC, in collaboration with the accounting profession, has been developing a set of standards for the presentation of the financial data that form the heart of the disclosure process.

In other parts of the capitalist world, regulation of the securities markets has developed on different premises. Investing and trading in securities, particularly in common stocks, have been regarded more than in this country as an economic function of a limited group—the rather small group of firms or individuals who can exercise an independent, informed judgment and who can suffer occasional losses with relative equanimity. The business communities of most European countries are more tightly knit and restricted than in the United States. Data can be transmitted informally, often orally, in a way not possible in the vast anonymity of the American commercial world. Foreign business firms inherit a longer and more pervasive tradition of "secrecy"—a tradition hostile to the notion that a privately-owned company's affairs are properly the public's concern.

More concretely, businessmen in other countries fear that the disclosure of data will assist their competitors. Americans expressed similar anxieties during the debates over the passage of the disclosure legislation of the 1930's but have since become reconciled to their operation. In any event, since the federal securities laws cover all major concerns in the entire United States, an American firm knows that its competitors are bound to equal disclosure requirements. The less integrated European markets raise different problems. A corporation

69. 48 Stat. 74 (1933), as amended, 15 U.S.C.A. §§ 77a–77aa; 48 Stat. 881 (1934), as amended, 15 U.S.C.A. §§ 78a–78hh.

70. For example, California has conditioned the right to sell securities in the state upon findings as to the proposed transaction's characterization as "fair, just, or equitable" and as to the issuer's intention "to transact its business fairly and honestly." The current version appears in West's Ann.Cal.Corp.Code § 25140 (Supp.1975). On state laws regulating securities, see generally 1 Loss, Securities Regulation ch. IB (2d ed. 1961) (hereafter referred to as Loss).

in, say, Germany may be reluctant to reveal information that its competitors in Italy can conceal.

Thus because of history and present circumstance there emerge definite differences of attitudes regarding the proper approach to and techniques of securities regulation. One should however note that marked differences appear among foreign countries, some of which are striving to establish disclosure standards comparable to those of the United States. A growing trend of opinion recognizes that capitalism in modern industrial society requires the support of an active securities market capable of tapping the savings of large numbers of people. It also stresses that a country wishing to remain economically competitive with the United States needs to establish a capital market that can provide for its enterprises what our markets do for the great American corporations. Recent years have therefore seen changes in the corporation and securities laws of most of the major European countries, all of which tend to narrow the gap between American practices and their own.[71]

We here examine three among the many aspects of American securities law that may have transnational consequence. One is that part of the Securities Act of 1933 which concerns the requirements of disclosure by an issuer offering securities to the public. The other two are regulations issued under the Securities Exchange Act of 1934. The first deals with the requirement that corporations which have made a public offering of securities or whose securities are fairly widely held supply periodic "follow-up" data to keep the trading public currently informed about their affairs. The second involves a rule requiring disclosure in sales by one holder of securities to another.

NOTE ON DISCLOSURE UNDER THE SECURITIES ACT OF 1933

Subject to various exemptions, any issuer must comply with two basic requirements when selling securities to the public, whether directly or through "underwriters" (firms which act as intermediaries in the process of distribution). It must (*1*) file a registration statement with the SEC in which it sets forth the extensive and detailed information called for by the statute and implementing regulations, and (*2*) furnish to each purchaser (after the registration statement has been declared effective by the SEC) a part of the statement known as the prospectus which, in somewhat less detail, contains the data which the purchaser supposedly needs to appraise the value of the securities. The information required in the prospectus includes (*a*) financial statements certified by independent public accountants, (*b*) a detailed description of the terms of the equity or debt securities offered for sale, (*c*) a statement of the intended use of the proceeds

71. This trend is particularly striking in Great Britain and other members of the European Common Market. Within the Common Market, proposals are now pending to harmonize national legislation affecting these problems. See p. 1336, infra.

of the financing, (*d*) a description of the issuer's business with particular reference to competitive conditions in its various markets, and (*e*) the issuer's relationships with affiliated concerns and its management—including the compensation received and stock or stock options held by its officers and directors.

It is plain from the face of the statute that Congress intended it to apply to foreign issuers who resorted to the United States capital market; the point is underlined by special provisions on issues by foreign governments. Indeed, part of the history which lay behind the enactment of the Act had to do with disappointments experienced by American investors in foreign issues—failure of firms in which they held equity interest, postponed payments or outright default on debt obligations. Since 1945, many foreign firms and governments have persistently resorted to the American market for funds, finding that market larger, cheaper and more efficient than their own.[72] In so acting, these foreign issuers have of course complied with the Act, filing registration statements declared effective by the SEC. Registration has raised particularly vexing problems in connection with financial statements. With the help of American accountants, foreign companies have often been required to revise over a period of years their published financial statements in order to make them closer in form and substance to American financial statements. Needless to say, the SEC's insistence upon disclosure of such information as salaries and stockholdings of officers and directors has proved particularly irritating to the foreign firms.

The converse situation, that of an American firm issuing securities only to foreign nationals on foreign markets, has been less common and is not explicitly contemplated by the statute. It is the generally understood position of the SEC that such an offering is not "a public offering" within the meaning of the Act because it is not one to the American public.[73] If, however, an American firm sells unregistered securities to a European purchaser knowing, or having reason to suspect, that the European will resell to parties in the United States, the Act has been violated. See Matter of Schwebel, 40 S.E.C. 347 (1960).

72. The balance-of-payments problems which the United States has experienced in the last decade have led to government policies and legislation inhibiting recourse to our capital market by foreign issuers, in order to reduce the amount of dollars flowing from this to foreign countries through securities purchases. The Interest Equalization Tax of 1964, described at p. 1166, infra, significantly curbed domestic sales of foreign securities. One consequence of this legislation and companion government policies was to spur development of foreign capital markets, particularly in Western Europe and Japan. Indeed, subsidiaries of American firms operating in foreign nations have been encouraged to obtain funds on those markets rather than domestically to finance their foreign operations. Nonetheless, sales by foreign governmental and private issuers on the American market continue.

73. See Securities Act Release No. 4708, July 9, 1964, 29 Fed.Reg. 9828. This release was published in the wake of an investigation of means of alleviating balance-of-payments problems by facilitating offerings to foreigners.

Enforcement of the Act against foreign violators has caused difficulties that should be fairly predictable from a reading of Chapters VII and VIII. The SEC has been particularly troubled by the operations of sellers of securities based in Canada and appealing to the American market by use of the telephone and mails. Despite a generally sympathetic attitude by the Canadian authorities, it has not proved easy to curb such activities. One weapon the SEC has used has been the maintenance of a restricted list on which appear the names of foreign firms, chiefly Canadian, whose securities are believed to be illegally traded in this country. This list serves as a warning to American brokers and dealers that trading in such securities may subject them to liability for participation in an unlawful distribution to the public.[74]

Section 24 makes a wilful violation by any person of the Act and the regulations thereunder a crime. The sweeping provisions of the mail fraud laws, 18 U.S.C.A. §§ 1341, 1343 are also available.

The more frequently used and more meaningful remedies are civil. Under Section 8(d) the SEC can issue a stop order suspending the "effectiveness" of a registration statement which appears to it to violate the Act's standards. In addition, Section 20 provides for injunctive actions brought by the SEC to restrain violations. But the private causes of action created by Sections 11 and 12 are potentially most troublesome to an issuer. These sections permit actions for rescission or money damages by purchasers of a security offered, sold or delivered in violation of the prospectus or registration requirements or sold by means of misrepresentations in the prospectus, registration statement or other document. Under Section 11, a purchaser may bring an action if any part of the registration statement, when it became effective, "contained an untrue statement of a material fact . . . required to be stated therein or necessary to make the statements therein not misleading . . . ." In such circumstances, the purchaser can sue among others every person who signed the registration statement (including the issuer and its principal executive officer or officers), and every director of the issuer at the time the registration statement was filed.

Sections 11 and 12 dispense with a number of common law doctrines which had been found to hamper recovery by injured investors. Thus persons responsible for inaccuracies in registration statements have the burden of showing they exercised due care, and they can no longer rely on concepts of "privity." Federal courts have jurisdiction over these actions, concurrently with state courts. Under Section 22, actions may be brought where the defendant is found or transacts business, or where the offer of sale took place, and process may be served wherever the defendant may be found, even outside the United States.

74. The legality of the SEC's use of the list was sustained in Kukatush Mining Corp. v. SEC, 309 F.2d 647 (D.C.Cir. 1962).

One further fact should be noted. All the provisions regarding registration are applicable only if the mails or some means of "interstate commerce" are used to sell the securities. Section 2(7) defines "interstate commerce" to refer to commerce in securities among the states and "between any foreign country" and the United States.

Additional Reading: Cohen and Throop, Investment of Private Capital in Foreign Securities, in Surrey and Shaw (eds.), A Lawyer's Guide to International Business Transactions 519 (1963); 1 Loss, Securities Regulation, Chs. 2E, 2F, 2 id. 1852–61, 1995–2005 (2d ed. 1961); Stevenson, Legal Aspects of the Public Offering of Foreign Securities in the United States Market, 28 Geo.Wash.L.Rev. 194 (1959); Note, Enforcing United States Securities Regulation against Canadians: Conflict of Laws Problems, 66 Harv.L.Rev. 1081 (1953).

PROBLEM

Krull Enterprises Ltd. manufactures and sells widgets exclusively in its home country, Canaguana, contiguous to the United States. The principal directors and officers are Krull himself, a German citizen; Villa, a citizen of Canaguana; and Sly, a United States citizen. All are domiciled in Canaguana. For the past year, Krull Enterprises has been selling its securities to American customers by mail and telephone from its home office. The sales, principally to customers in New York City, have been made with the knowledge and participation of the three named individuals. The common stock of Krull Enterprises is traded by dealers in Canaguana, but not in the United States.

The SEC believes that these communications not only constitute violations of the Securities Act by virtue of the unregistered character of the securities but also that they amount to fraud. In the past few months, adverse conditions in the widget industry have generated bleak prospects for its future, and the price of the common stock has fallen by 50%.

As a staff attorney at the SEC, you are asked:

(1) Will the district court for the Southern District of New York take jurisdiction over an injunction action against Krull Enterprises by the SEC?

(2) If it does, what problems are likely to be presented if enforcement of an injunction is sought in Canaguana?

(3) Suppose that the SEC decides to press for a criminal prosecution against Krull, Villa and Sly. Assuming that a typical extradition treaty is in force between the United States and Canaguana (see pp. 901–903, supra), what problems do you foresee in procuring their surrender for trial?

(4) If any of the foregoing are brought to trial in the United States, would they be able to make a plausible argument that the statute as applied represented an exorbitant legislative reach on the part of the United States?

Suppose that Krull Enterprises had registered the securities with the SEC. You are private counsel to disgruntled purchasers of Krull shares. Your clients allege that the registration statement contained false and misleading statements giving rise to liability under Section 11. Since Krull Enterprises now appears to be in doubtful financial shape, they prefer to sue Villa, a reputed millionaire, for money damages. What courses of action under Section 11 appear open to the purchasers, and what problems do you see in each?

NOTE ON SECTION 12(g) OF THE SECURITIES EXCHANGE ACT

The primary concern of the Securities Exchange Act of 1934 is with the post-distribution life of securities—the subsequent (secondary) trading in them. Certain of its provisions require the filing of periodic reports by issuers on their affairs in order to keep the investing public directly informed. Prior to 1964 those requirements applied only (*a*) to issuers whose securities were listed on a national securities exchange, which were required by Section 12 to file a registration statement under the 1934 Act at the time of listing and by Section 13 to make periodic reports thereafter, and (*b*) to most issuers which had initially registered securities under the Securities Act of 1933 (Section 15(d)). Companies required to register under Section 12 were also subject to the rules governing the solicitation of proxies (established by Section 14 and the regulations thereunder) and to those on trading in stock by "insiders" (defined in Section 16).

Finding that many important corporations in which there was widespread public interest were not subject to the 1934 Act, Congress amended it in 1964. A new subsection 12(g)(1) in effect subjects to the reporting requirements every issuer (*1*) which is engaged in interstate commerce (defined in Section 3 to include commerce between any foreign country and any state) or in a business affecting interstate commerce, or whose securities are traded by the mails or in interstate commerce, and (*2*) which has total assets exceeding $1,000,000 and a class of equity security held of record by 500 or more persons.

Section 12(g)(3) gives the SEC power to exempt from the reporting requirements any security of a foreign issuer if it finds such exemption to be "in the public interest and . . . consistent with the protection of investors." This provision reverses the originally proposed version, which would have exempted foreign issuers unless the SEC found that a substantial public market for the issuer's securities existed in the United States and that a continued exemption was not in the public interest. In short, Congress provided that, unless and until the SEC acts, any foreign issuer with $1,000,000 in assets, 500 shareholders anywhere in the world and a business that involves or affects commerce with the United States must comply with the disclosure rules of the 1934 Act. The disclosure so compelled includes directors' and officers' salaries, stock options, profit-sharing plans, material contracts and, of course, certified financial statements.

After granting an initial sweeping interim exemption, the SEC published proposed rules on November 16, 1965 in Exchange Act Release No. 7746 [75] and asked for comments. Among other things, the proposed rules (*1*) would have exempted from Section 12(g) foreign issuers which had less than 300 American shareholders, and (*2*) would have required of other foreign issuers not the detailed information and certified financial statements which domestic corporations file but only that information already disclosed by them abroad. The SEC referred to the recent general tightening of disclosure standards abroad.

A report on the proposed rules, excerpts from which appear below, was issued by the Committee on International Law of the Association of the Bar of the City of New York.

REPORT ON PROPOSED SEC RULES

Committee on International Law of the Association of the Bar of the City of New York.[76]

The basic principle established by the Permanent Court of International Justice in the Lotus case [p. 885, supra] is that legislative assertion of jurisdiction over conduct outside the territory of a state is lawful unless it violates a prohibitive rule of international law. However, it is implicit in the case that international law does impose limits on the extra-territorial assertion of jurisdiction by states—and, if jurisdiction is to be based on the fact that "one of the constituent elements of the offense, and more especially its effects," have taken place within the state asserting jurisdiction, that such effects must be, in the language of *Lotus,* "legally and entirely inseparable" from the conduct outside the territory, "so much so that their separation renders the offense nonexistent".

The principles of the Lotus case have been generally accepted by the municipal courts of most countries as applied to traditional crimes such as libel, fraud, homicide, etc. There is general recognition of the right of a state to assert jurisdiction over a crime committed in part outside the state where one or more of the essential constituent elements of the crime take place within the state and there is a sharply defined effect within the state asserting jurisdiction. . . . However, it has been stated that the territorial principle extends even further than this—that jurisdiction exists even if no essential constituent element of a crime takes place within the state asserting jurisdiction so long as the foreign conduct has a substantial effect within such state.

Obviously, in the case of many crimes, and in fact in most of the cases which have arisen in municipal courts where the question has been presented, the conduct complained of has not only had a direct and substantial effect within the state asserting jurisdiction but an essential constituent element has taken place there. The case . . . of a shot killing a person across the border is a clear example. However, cases can arise where all constituent elements of a crime are consummated outside the territory but where the crime

75. Reprinted in CCH Fed.Sec.L.Rep. (1964–1966 Transfer Binder) ¶ 77,301 and 5 Int.Leg.Mat. 251.

76. 21 Record of the N.Y.C. Bar Ass'n 240 (1966). It should be noted that, in making some of its general remarks, the Committee had in mind the extended reach to North American issuers which the amendments and the rules gave the proxy and insider-trading provisions.

has a substantial direct effect within the territory. Whether the territorial principle extends this far is not clear.

The most important support for this extension of the territorial principle is found in the recent *Restatement (Second), Foreign Relations Law of the United States.* [The Report here quoted Section 18 of the Restatement, which appears at p. 882, supra.]

Section 18(b) of the *Restatement* goes beyond the territorial principle as it is recognized by international practice. The main criticism is that an extension of the territorial principle to cover alien activity outside the territory on the ground that it produces an "effect" within the territory represents a departure from, even a negation of, the territorial principle. While such an assertion of jurisdiction purports to be "territorial", in fact it is not, as nothing has been done in the territory, no act has been committed there, not even a part of the activity commenced outside the territory can be found there. To assert jurisdiction over an alien for activity that takes place wholly abroad is to claim a jurisdiction based not on territory but on a unilateral decision of the prosecuting state. Such an assertion would not be confined to the few situations in which jurisdiction is claimed under the protective principle for crimes such as counterfeiting and forgery of state seals, but to any activity that a state might deem to have a harmful effect within its territory.

From the wording of Section 18, from the comments thereon, and from the Reporter's Note thereunder, it is clear that Section 18(b) was largely based upon the case of United States v. Aluminum Company of America [p. 1006, supra]. . . .

It is clear, however, that [this case] was intended to state a rule of municipal law of the United States, not international law. The court stated that it was concerned only with the question whether Congress had chosen to attach liability to conduct outside the United States by persons not in allegiance to the United States, and concluded that the only question was one of Congressional intention and that "as a court of the United States, we cannot look beyond [United States] law." Nevertheless, the view of jurisdiction expressed in the Alcoa case has been adopted by the Restatement as the basis for Section 18(b).

Whether 18(b) of the *Restatement* does or does not represent an accurate statement of international law with respect to jurisdiction, it is clear that it requires both a *substantial* effect within the state asserting jurisdiction and a direct causal relationship.

In the light of the analysis of international law set forth above, do the [Securities and Exchange] Act and Rules thereunder constitute a valid exercise of legislative jurisdiction by the United States? The Committee submits that the Act and Rules violate international law insofar as they impose criminal or civil sanctions for failure to register . . . on foreign corporations over which jurisdiction is asserted solely because of the presence in the United States of 300 shareholders and the use of the mails. . . .

. . . The only affirmative conduct involved here is having sufficient assets and issuing shares to the public abroad—but surely it cannot be said that the results—i. e., having 300 United States shareholders and the consequent illegality of a failure to register—are the "direct and foreseeable" consequence of such conduct.

Perhaps the most important objection to the Act and Rules is that they attempt to impose regulation on a shot-gun basis, with no attempt to draw distinctions which may be crucial in a determination of whether assertion of United States jurisdiction is reasonable or not. In any such determination it would seem essential to weigh the various interests involved, including of course not only the interests of the United States but of the international community as a whole and of the "home" state of the foreign corporation. Whether an action abroad has a "substantial effect" within the United States should be measured in terms of the effect abroad and the competing interests asserted outside the United States, and not by examining it from the standpoint of the United States alone. Thus, an effect in the United States which may be deemed "substantial" when looked at purely internally may become totally insubstantial when measured on a broader scale. The basic—and objectionable—thrust of the Act and Rules is that any company which has 300 United States shareholders and $1,000,000 in assets anywhere must register and thereby subject itself to the almost plenary regulation of the Commission.

Thus the Committee submits that the exercise of jurisdiction over foreign companies as proposed under the provisions of the Act and the Rules discussed above extends beyond anything hitherto recognized by international or municipal courts or by authorities in the field. They contravene the concept of territoriality, which is recognized both in the United States and abroad as the basic and primary element limiting the exercise of municipal power. . . .

It is relevant to examine the consequences which would result if the exercise by the United States of jurisdiction under the Act and the Rules thereunder were held to be valid under international law. It would mean that a state, residents of which held securities of a foreign corporation, could validly assert plenary jurisdiction to regulate the affairs of such corporation, by forcing such corporation to register, by forcing distribution of reports in the form required by such state, etc., all under the penalties of a criminal statute. If the United States had such jurisdiction, so also would any other state, residents of which held shares in a foreign corporation. The result would be that a corporation, the shares of which were internationally owned, would be subject to the valid assertion of plenary jurisdiction to regulate its internal affairs by each state in which it happened to have shareholders. The whole concept of territoriality in the assertion of such power, as recognized by international law, is based exactly on the necessity of avoiding such a result. . . .

. . . [E]ven if the United States did have jurisdiction, the Committee submits that compliance by the foreign corporation (having an "inadvertent" contact with the United States) with the laws of the country of its incorporation comports more closely with the standards of comity which are the basis of international law than the assertion of jurisdiction by each country in which such corporation has shareholders. . . .

. . . The Governments of Canada and Great Britain have, we understand, filed with the State Department objections to the proposed Rules on the ground that they are in violation of international law and the Governments of other countries may also file objections. . . .

. . . Surely, with increasing internationalization of commercial and financial affairs, the United States should not be a party to the gratuitous adoption of regulatory and penal measures which are in violation of international law.

In light of the above, the Committee recommends first that the proposed Rules issued by the Securities and Exchange Commission be re-examined and limited to the fullest extent possible, consistent with the legislative intent, in order to minimize if not eliminate the inconsistencies with accepted standards of international law. . . . Nor is it by any means clear in the legislative history that the registration requirements of Section 12(g) of the Act have to be extended to foreign companies which voluntarily furnish to the Securities and Exchange Commission the information which the proposed Rules would require them to furnish as part of the registration process. A Rule which would exempt from the Act companies which voluntarily furnish substantially the information required would certainly diminish the seriousness of the violation of international law, even though the fundamental problem of the extent of United States jurisdiction would remain. . . .

COMMENT

The SEC withdrew its proposed rules, granting a further temporary exemption in Exchange Act Release No. 7867. On April 28, 1967 it promulgated its new rules in Release No. 8066. Relevant portions of Rule 12g3–2, 17 C.F.R. § 240.12g3–2, state:

> (*a*)(*1*) Securities of any class issued by any foreign issuer shall be exempt from Section 12(g) of the Act if the class has fewer than 300 holders resident in the United States. . . .
>
> (*a*)(*2*)(*b*)(*1*) Securities of any foreign private issuer shall be exempt from Section 12(g) of the Act if the issuer, or a government official or agency of the country of the issuer's domicile or in which it is incorporated or organized,
>
> (A) shall furnish to the Commission whatever information in each of the following categories the issuer during its last fiscal year (i) has made public pursuant to the law of the country of its domicile or in which it is incorporated or organized, (ii) has filed with a stock exchange on which its securities are traded and which was made public by such exchange, or (iii) has distributed to its security holders;
>
> (B) shall furnish to the Commission a list identifying the information referred to in subparagraph (A) above . . .;
>
> (C) shall furnish to the Commission, during each subsequent fiscal year, whatever information is made public as described in . . . subparagraph (A) above promptly after such information is made public as described therein; and
>
> (D) shall, promptly after the end of any fiscal year in which any changes shall occur in the kind of information required to be published . . . furnish to the Commission a revised list reflecting such changes.

The SEC also stated in the release [77] its views as to dealings in foreign securities:

> The Commission has decided not to adopt at the present time special rules applicable to brokers and dealers who deal in foreign securities. The Commission does wish, however, to call to the attention of brokers, dealers and investors the fact that information concerning certain foreign issuers may not be available in the United States. Accord-

77. Reprinted in CCH Fed.Sec.L.Rep. (1966–1967 Transfer Binder) ¶ 77,443.

ingly, the Commission will issue lists from time to time showing which foreign issuers have registered securities under Section 12(g), which issuers have obtained exemptions by the provision of information in the manner noted, and those which have done neither—that is, failed to furnish any information to the Commission for public inspection. . . . While no sanction will attach to any broker or dealer by reason of its transactions in the securities of an issuer solely because it is listed as neither registered nor exempt, the Commission expects that brokers and dealers will consider this fact in deciding whether they have a reasonable basis for recommending these securities to customers.

A comparison of the rules promulgated in 1967 with those originally proposed reveals among other things (1) that the supplying of information in compliance with paragraph (a)(2)(b)(1) of the new rule no longer constitutes compliance with Section 12(g) but rather gives rise to an exemption from it (and from associated provisions of the Act), and (2) that the SEC explicitly states in paragraph (5) of the Rule that furnishing such information does not constitute an admission that the issuer is subject to the Act.[78]

QUESTIONS

(1) If you were a member of the Committee on International Law, would you have favored or opposed its approach to this problem of advocacy—namely, stressing the status of the proposed rules under the identified rules of international law? If the latter, what lines of argument would you have thought more persuasive to convince the SEC to amend its proposals? Is Babcock v. Jackson, p. 937, supra, helpful in suggesting these lines?

(2) Do you agree with the Committee's interpretation of the Lotus case? With its general conclusions as to the relevant rules of international law? With its pragmatic objections to the proposed rules on the basis of their unfairness to particular corporations or their tendency to cause international friction?

(3) Did Rule 12g3–2, as promulgated, meet the Committee's objections?

Additional Reading: Phillips and Shipman, An Analysis of the Securities Acts Amendments of 1964, 1964 Duke L.J. 706; Stevenson, The Effect of the New SEC Registration Requirements on Foreign Issuers, Address at Meeting of Banking, Corporation and Business Law Section, New York State Bar Association (Feb. 3, 1966); Buxbaum, Securities Regulation and the Foreign Issuer Exemption, A Study in the Process of Accomodating Foreign Interests, 54 Cornell L.Rev. 358 (1969).

78. The provisions extending the proxy and insider trading rules to North American issuers were also omitted from the final rules.

NOTE ON SECURITIES EXCHANGE ACT RULE 10b–5

Rule 10b–5, 17 C.F.R. § 240.10b–5, was promulgated by the SEC under the authority of Section 10 of the 1934 Act. It reads as follows:

> It shall be unlawful for any person, directly or indirectly, by the use of any means or instrumentality of interstate commerce, or of the mails or of any facility of any national securities exchange,
>
> (a) To employ any device, scheme, or artifice to defraud,
>
> (b) To make any untrue statement of a material fact or to omit to state a material fact necessary in order to make the statements made, in the light of the circumstances under which they were made, not misleading, or
>
> (c) To engage in any act, practice, or course of business which operates or would operate as a fraud or deceit upon any person,
>
> in connection with the purchase or sale of any security.[79]

Although Section 10(b) and Rule 10b–5 are silent as to private causes of action, the courts have implied such actions from their provisions. These suits come under Section 27 of the 1934 Act, which gives exclusive jurisdiction to the federal courts and permits a suit to be brought wherever any act or transaction constituting the violation occurs or wherever defendant may be found. Process may be served wherever defendant may be found, even outside the United States.

Most cases applying this rule involve allegations of a plaintiff that he has been the victim of fraud of a defendant to whom he sold or from whom he bought securities. Resort to the rule is favored by plaintiffs because it is not only more expansive in substance than state-law rules of fraud—in particular, its coverage of fraud committed by failure to disclose material facts—but is also more liberal in its procedural incidents.

Recent cases extending the rule to situations in which the plaintiff was neither a purchaser nor a seller involve more complex issues, both as to its substantive interpretation and transnational application. For example, a plaintiff asserts that X corporation, in which he is a shareholder, was induced by fraud to issue shares of its stock to defendants who occupied positions of trust in X. In effect he is asserting that X was the victim of fraud in a "sale" and that, as shareholder, he is entitled to vindicate the corporation's rights through a derivative action that will reimburse the corporation's treasury and indirectly benefit plaintiff and his fellow shareholders. Application of Rule 10b–5 to such a case means that federal law applied by federal courts is invading an area that has traditionally been governed by the state law of fiduciary duties. That law would characteristically have

79. [Eds.] Recall that Section 3 of the 1934 Act defines "interstate commerce" to include commerce between any foreign country and any state.

been the state of incorporation's, which generally governs the "internal affairs" of a corporation. See p. 96, supra.

When a plaintiff seeks application of Rule 10b–5 in this manner to the affairs of a foreign corporation, the risk of clash between the claims of American and foreign law becomes acute. Consider the following two cases, the first of which raises the problem of an invasion of a foreign corporation's internal affairs and the second of which is a more obvious fraud case.

SCHOENBAUM v. FIRSTBROOK

United States Court of Appeals, Second Circuit, 1968.
405 F.2d 200, on rehearing C.A., 405 F.2d 215.

[Plaintiff, an American shareholder of Banff Oil Ltd., a Canadian corporation, brought a derivative action to recover on Banff's behalf damages under Rule 10b–5 for sales in Canada of Banff treasury stock (stock belonging to the corporation itself) to defendants Aquitaine of Canada, Ltd., and Paribas Corporation. The theory of plaintiff's suit was that Banff was defrauded into making sales at the then market price of the stock although defendants knew that this was too low a price because of successful oil drilling operations by Banff. Aquitaine had acquired control of Banff in 1964 by a tender offer. Banff's directors were assumed to have known all of these facts.

A district court entered summary judgment for defendants, finding (a) that the Securities and Exchange Act did not apply extraterritorially, and (b) that the plaintiff failed to state a cause of action under Rule 10b–5. The first opinion of the Court of Appeals, by JUDGE LUMBARD, disagreed as to subject matter jurisdiction, point (a), but affirmed on point (b). On rehearing en banc it was held that a cause of action was stated against all defendants save Paribas and the case was reversed and remanded for trial. JUDGE HAYS, who had dissented in part from the first opinion, wrote the second.

The court en banc did not review but let stand as the holding of the court those portions of the first opinion by Judge Lumbard which deal with the issues of extraterritorial application and interstate commerce. Such portions of the first opinion follow:]

We disagree with the district court's conclusion. We believe that Congress intended the Exchange Act to have extraterritorial application in order to protect domestic investors who have purchased foreign securities on American exchanges and to protect the domestic securities market from the effects of improper foreign transactions in American securities. In our view, neither the usual presumption against extraterritorial application of legislation nor the specific language of Section 30(b) show Congressional intent to preclude application of the Exchange Act to transactions regarding stocks traded in the United States which are effected outside the United States, when extraterritorial application of the Act is necessary to protect American investors.

Section 2 of the Exchange Act, 15 U.S.C.A. § 78b, states that because transactions in securities are affected with "a national public interest" it is "necessary to provide for regulation and control of such transactions and of practices and matters related thereto, . . . necessary to make such regulation and control reasonably . . . complete state commerce and to insure the maintenance of fair and honest markets in such transactions."

The Act seeks to regulate the stock exchanges and the relationships of the investing public to corporations which invite public investment by listing on such exchanges. . . .

Banff common stock is registered and traded on the American Stock Exchange. To protect United States shareholders of Banff common stock, Banff is required to comply with the provisions of the Securities Exchange Act concerning financial reports to the SEC, § 13, 15 U.S.C.A. § 78m; proxy solicitation, § 14, 15 U.S.C.A. § 78n, and reports of insider holdings, § 16, 15 U.S.C.A. § 78p. Similarly, the anti-fraud provision of § 10(b), which enables the Commission to prescribe rules "necessary or appropriate in the public interest or for the protection of investors" reaches beyond the territorial limits of the United States and applies when a violation of the Rules is injurious to United States investors. "Acts done outside a jurisdiction, but intended to produce and producing detrimental effects within it, justify a state in punishing the cause of the harm as if [the actor] had been present at the [time of the detrimental] effect, if the state should succeed in getting him within its power." Strassheim v. Daily, 221 U.S. 280, 285, 31 S.Ct. 558, 560, 55 L.Ed. 735 (1911).

The Commission has recognized the broad extraterritorial applicability of the Act and has specifically exempted certain foreign issuers from the operation of Sections 14 and 16 of the Act, when enforcement would be impractical. Rule 3a12–3, 17 CFR 240, 3a12–3 (1967). The Commission has applied Section 15(a), 15 U.S.C.A. § 78*o*, to foreign broker-dealers who transact business through use of the mails. See Rule 17a–7, 17 CFR § 240.17a (1967); 2 Loss, Securities Regulation, 1292 n. 15 (2d ed. 1961). Although it has the power to grant exemptions from rules under § 10(b), see Rules 10b–6(d), 10b–7(n), 1 Loss, Securities Regulation, 799 n. 48 (2d ed. 1961), the Commission has not promulgated a rule exempting foreign transactions from Rule 10b–5.

The provision contained in Section 30(b) does not alter our conclusion that the Exchange Act has extraterritorial application. In our view, while Section 30(b) was intended to exempt persons conducting a business in securities through foreign securities markets from the provisions of the Act, it does not preclude extraterritorial application of the Exchange Act to persons who engage in isolated foreign transactions.

Section 30, entitled "Foreign Securities Exchanges," [80] deals

80. "Section 30. (a) It shall be unlawful for any broker or dealer, directly or indirectly, to make use of the mails or of any means or instrumentality of interstate commerce for the purpose of effecting on an exchange not within or subject to the jurisdiction of the United States, any transaction in any security the issuer of which is a resident of or is organized under the laws of, or has its principal place of business in, a place within or subject to the jurisdiction of the United States, in contravention of such rules and regulations as the Commission may prescribe as necessary or appropriate in the public interest or for the protection of investors or to prevent the evasion of this title.

(b) The provisions of this title or of any rule or regulation thereunder shall not apply to any person insofar as he transacts a business in securities without the jurisdiction of the United States, unless he transacts such business in contravention of such rules and regulations as the Commission may prescribe as necessary or appropriate to prevent the evasion of this title."

with the extent to which the Act applies to persons effecting securities transactions through foreign exchanges. Section 30(a) empowers the SEC to regulate all brokers and dealers who use the mails or interstate commerce, for the purpose of effecting a transaction in American securities on exchanges outside the United States. 2 Loss, Securities Regulation, 1170 n. 2 (2d ed. 1961). It was intended to prevent evasion of the Act through transactions on foreign exchanges. See Hearings on S.Res. 89 (72d Cong.), and S.Res. 56 and S.Res. 97 (73d Cong.) before the Committee on Banking and Currency, 73d Cong., 2d Sess. part 15, pp. 6569, 6578–79 (1934).

Section 30(b) states that the Act does not apply in the absence of SEC rule to prevent evasion of the Act to "any person insofar as he transacts a business in securities without the jurisdiction of the United States." The language of § 30(b) must be construed in light of the purpose of the subsection, and the definitions of terms contained in § 3(a) of the Act.

The purpose of this subsection is to permit persons in the securities business to conduct transactions in securities outside of the United States without complying with the burdensome reporting requirement of the Act and without being subject to its regulatory provisions, except insofar as the Commission finds it necessary and appropriate to regulate such transactions to prevent evasion of the Act. It is also designed to take the Commission out of the business of regulating foreign security exchanges unless the Commission deems regulation necessary to prevent evasion of the domestic regulatory scheme.[81] The exemption relieves the Commission of the impossible task of enforcing American securities law upon persons whom it could not subject to the sanctions of the Act for actions upon which it could not bring its investigatory powers to bear.

If § 30(b) had been meant to exempt every transaction by any person outside of the United States it would have been drafted to state that the Act does not apply to "any transaction in any security outside the jurisdiction of the United States," a phrase used in § 30 (a). The drafters used the phrase "any person insofar as he transacts a business in securities without the jurisdiction of the United States" in § 30(b) because it is a term which would exempt the business transactions not only of brokers and dealers but also of banks. The term "brokers and dealers," used in § 30(a), could not be used because the definitions of "broker" and "dealer" in §§ 3(a)(4) and 3(a)(5), 15 U.S.C.A. § 78c(a)(4) and (5), specifically exclude "banks" as defined in § 3(a)(6), 15 U.S.C.A. § 78c(a)(6). It is precisely the terminology that appears in § 30(b), when construed in light of § 3(a)(4) and (5) that exempts brokers and dealers and banks otherwise subject to the Act insofar as they conduct transactions not subject to § 30(a) outside the United States, even though their United States transactions are subject to the Act.

In Kook v. Crang, 182 F.Supp. 388 (S.D.N.Y.1960) the Court properly held that § 30(b) exempted from the margin requirements of Section 7(c) of the Act, 15 U.S.C.A. § 78g(c), sales to a United States citizen of Canadian stock in Canada by a Canadian broker, since the transactions were outside of the United States and part of the Canadian firm's business in securities. 2 Loss, Sec.Reg. 1292 n. 15 (2d ed. 1961). The Court found in § 30(b) a Congressional intent to exempt from application of the Act transaction of a business in securities outside the United States.

81. The SEC has not promulgated any rules or regulations under § 30.

This holding was extended in Ferraioli v. Cantor, CCH Fed.Sec. L.Rep. ¶ 91, 615 (S.D.N.Y.1965) to exempt an isolated transaction, not part of a business in securities, the private sale in Canada of controlling shares of a New York corporation in which plaintiff was a minority shareholder, on the ground that the Exchange Act does not have extraterritorial application. The Court reasoned that if Congress specifically exempted foreign business in securities it intended to exempt isolated transactions as well. We disagree with this reasoning.

We find that the language and purpose of § 30(b) show that it was not meant to exempt transactions that are conducted outside the jurisdiction of the United States unless they are part of a "business in securities." Indeed, since Congress found it necessary to draft an exemptive provision for certain foreign transactions and gave the Commission power to make rules that would limit this exemption, the presumption must be that the Act was meant to apply to those foreign transactions not specifically exempted.

We hold that the district court has subject matter jurisdiction over violations of the Securities Exchange Act although the transactions which are alleged to violate the Act take place outside the United States, at least when the transactions involve stock registered and listed on a national securities exchange, and are detrimental to the interests of American investors. See Ford v. United States, 273 U.S. 593, 619–624, 47 S.Ct. 531, 71 L.Ed. 793 (1927); United States v. Pizzarusso, 388 F.2d 8 (2d Cir. Jan. 9, 1968); United States v. Aluminum Company of America, 148 F.2d 416, 443–444 (2d Cir. 1945).

However, the district court found that the only harm alleged was to the foreign corporation on whose behalf plaintiff brought the action. We do not agree. A fraud upon a corporation which has the effect of depriving it of fair compensation for the issuance of its stock would necessarily have the effect of reducing the equity of the corporation's shareholders and this reduction in equity would be reflected in lower prices bid for the shares on the domestic stock market. This impairment of the value of American investments by sales by the issuer in a foreign country, allegedly in violation of the Act, has in our view, a sufficiently serious effect upon United States commerce to warrant assertion of jurisdiction for the protection of American investors and consideration of the merits of plaintiff's claim.[82] . . .

Use of Interstate Commerce

There can be no violation under Section 10 unless a rule of the Commission is contravened "directly or indirectly," by the use of any means or instrumentality of interstate commerce or of the mails, or of any facility of any national securities exchange. See generally 3 Loss, Sec.Reg. 1519–1524 (2d ed. 1961). The trial court found that the transactions in question were essentially Canadian, with insufficient contacts with the United States to fall within § 10(b) of the Act. We are uncertain whether the Court's finding was directed at the issues of extraterritorial application of the Exchange Act or at the jurisdictional requirements of § 10. In either case we dis-

82. However, if the wrong alleged also constitutes the basis for a cause of action under foreign law a district court might decline to exercise its jurisdiction under the doctrine of *forum non conveniens*. See Vanity Fair Mills, Inc. v. T. Eaton Co., 234 F.2d 633 (2d Cir.), cert. denied 352 U.S. 871, 77 S.Ct. 96, 1 L.Ed.2d 76 (1956).

agree with its conclusion. We have already discussed the reasons why a foreign purchase or sale of treasury shares by a corporation has sufficient effect upon interstate commerce to warrant extraterritorial application of the Exchange Act.

The present question is not whether this limited use of the mails and the facilities of interstate commerce would be a sufficient basis for subject matter jurisdiction over a foreign transaction which would otherwise be exempt from the Act, see Kook v. Crang, supra, but whether, once it has been determined that the Act applies to a particular foreign transaction, there is a use of the mails or interstate commerce sufficient to meet the requirement of § 10(b). We find that defendant's affidavits show a use of interstate commerce or the mails sufficient to bring both transactions within the scope of Section 10(b).

Since defendants admit that the Aquitaine purchase was delayed pending the successful conclusion of negotiations with the Treasury Department regarding tax rulings and negotiations with the American Stock Exchange regarding the listing of the additional shares, we find, on this record, that these negotiations were a part of the scheme for the sale of treasury stock to Aquitaine. And since it appears that, as plaintiff alleges, these negotiations with United States government and stock exchange officials must have made some use of the mails or other facilities of interstate commerce, there was at the very least use of interstate commerce [83] or the mails sufficient to bring the sales transactions within the scope of Section 10(b). . . .

The Paribas transaction likewise involved negotiations which must have taken place in part in the United States or made some use of the mails or interstate commerce. Furthermore, the purchase agreement was mailed from Paribas in New York to Banff in Canada; this in itself would establish a use of the mails sufficient to meet the requirement of Section 10.

LEASCO DATA PROCESSING EQUIPMENT CORP. v. MAXWELL

United States Court of Appeals, Second Circuit, 1972.
468 F.2d 1326.

[An American corporation and its wholly owned subsidiary, a Netherlands Antilles corporation (collectively called Leasco), brought an action under Section 10(b) of the Securities Exchange Act and Rule 10b–5 against various British defendants, alleging that they caused Leasco to buy stock of Pergamon Press Limited at prices in excess of its true value. One Kerman, a London solicitor, obtained a judgment by the District Court dismissing the complaint as to him for lack of jurisdiction over the person. Leasco appealed that judgment. This caused the Court of Appeals to express doubt that jurisdiction over the subject matter was present. The District Court certified these issues to the Court of Appeals under 28 U.S.C. § 1292 (b) and leave to appeal was granted.

The Court of Appeals assumed that Leasco at this stage of the proceedings was entitled to have every inference drawn in its favor.

83. The term "interstate commerce," as used in the Exchange Act, encompasses commerce "between any foreign country and any State." § 3(a)(17), 15 U.S.C. § 78c(a)(17).

According to Leasco, in early 1969 one Maxwell, a British subject who controlled Pergamon, opened negotiations with Leasco in Great Neck, N. Y. Maxwell and his assistants (in particular one Majhtenyi, an official of Pergamon's American subsidiary) met with officials of Leasco (in particular its president, Steinberg) at various times in New York and London. Maxwell also sent letters to Leasco enclosing financial reports. There were also transatlantic telephone conversations. Allegedly there were false statements in the reports and in the conversations.

On June 17, 1969 an agreement was signed in New York under which Leasco agreed that it would offer to acquire each outstanding share of Pergamon, in a tender offer subject to the "take over" code of the City of London and the London Stock Exchange regulations. Maxwell agreed to accept the offer as to his shares and to try to persuade other shareholders to do likewise. Leasco could cause the offer to be made by its Netherlands Antilles subsidiary (Leasco N.V.). After $22,000,000 of Pergamon stock had been acquired by Leasco on the London Stock Exchange, Leasco obtained information indicating that it had been defrauded. It then declined to go forward with the tender offer and brought this action.

After stating the facts the opinion by JUDGE FRIENDLY continues:]

II. *Subject Matter Jurisdiction*

One of the few points on which all parties are in accord is that subject matter jurisdiction depends on the applicability of the Securities Exchange Act. Leasco's principal place of business is in New York. Defendants Isthmus Enterprises, Inc., Maxwell Scientific International, Inc., and MSI Publishers, Inc. appear to have their principal offices in New York, and this is stated to be true of defendant Robert Fleming, Inc. Plaintiff Leasco World Trade Company (U.K.) Limited, the reason for whose joinder is not apparent, is a British corporation, and most of the defendants are British citizens or corporations. There is thus no jurisdiction under 28 U.S.C.A. § 1332(a). However, § 27 of the Securities Exchange Act vests the district court with jurisdiction over an action "to enforce any liability created by this title or the rules and regulations thereunder . . . ." Section 10(b) makes it unlawful, *inter alia*, for any person

> by the use of any means or instrumentality of interstate commerce or of the mails . . .
>
> . . . .
>
> To use or employ, in connection with the purchase or sale of any security registered on a national securities exchange or any security not so registered, any manipulative or deceptive device or contrivance in contravention of such rules and regulations as the Commission may prescribe as necessary or appropriate in the public interest or for the protection of investors.

We see no need for quoting Rule 10b-5, since this does not affect the question of subject matter jurisdiction; Leasco plainly alleged enough to show a violation of the Rule if the statute is applicable.[84]

It will be useful at the outset to differentiate the problem here presented from the point decided in Schoenbaum v. Firstbrook, 405

84. Section 3(a)(17) defines "interstate commerce" to include transportation or communication "between any foreign country and any State."

F.2d 200 (2 Cir.), modified with respect to the issue of liability of one set of defendants, 405 F.2d 215 (2 Cir. 1968), cert. denied, 395 U.S. 906, 89 S.Ct. 1747, 23 L.Ed.2d 219 (1969). *Schoenbaum* held § 10(b) to be applicable, *even when the fraudulent acts were all committed outside the United States* and the security was that of a foreign company doing no business in the United States, in a case where "the transactions involve stock registered and listed on a national securities exchange, and are detrimental to the interests of American investors." 405 F.2d at 208. If we treat the matter in terms of the distinctions drawn in the Restatement (Second) of Foreign Relations Law of the United States (1965), *Schoenbaum* raised the problem, considered in § 18, of the circumstances in which "[a] state has jurisdiction to prescribe a rule of law attaching legal consequences to conduct that occurs outside its territory and causes an effect within its territory . . . " and consequently may be thought to have meant to do so. If all the misrepresentations here alleged had occurred in England, we would entertain most serious doubt whether, despite United States v. Aluminum Co. of America, 148 F.2d 416, 443–444 (2 Cir. 1954), and *Schoenbaum,* § 10(b) would be applicable simply because of the adverse effect of the fraudulently induced purchases in England of securities of an English corporation, not traded in an organized American securities market, upon an American corporation whose stock is listed on the New York Stock Exchange and its shareholders. Cf. Vanity Fair Mills, Inc. v. T. Eaton & Co., 234 F.2d 633 (2 Cir.), cert. denied 352 U.S. 871, 77 S.Ct. 96, 1 L.Ed.2d 76 (1956). It is true, as Judge L. Hand pointed out in the Aluminum case, supra, 148 F.2d at 443, that if Congress has expressly prescribed a rule with respect to conduct outside the United States, even one going beyond the scope recognized by foreign relations law, a United States court would be bound to follow the Congressional direction unless this would violate the due process clause of the Fifth Amendment. However, the language of § 10(b) of the Securities Exchange Act is much too inconclusive to lead us to believe that Congress meant to impose rules governing conduct throughout the world in every instance where an American company bought or sold a security. When no fraud has been practiced in this country and the purchase or sale has not been made here, we would be hard pressed to find justification for going beyond *Schoenbaum.*

On plaintiffs' version of the facts, that issue does not here arise. The instant case deals rather with the problem considered in the Restatement's § 17, "Jurisdiction to Prescribe with Respect to Conduct, Thing, Status, or other Interest within Territory." While the black letter seems to require that, in a case like this, not only there should be conduct within the territory but also the conduct relate "to a thing located, or a status or other interest localized, in its territory," Comment A and Illustrations 1 and 2, the latter of which [85] is quite pertinent here, appear to be satisfied if there has been conduct within the territory. Conduct within the territory alone would seem sufficient from the standpoint of *jurisdiction* to prescribe a rule. It follows that when, as here, there has been significant conduct within the territory, a statute cannot properly be held inapplicable simply on the ground that, absent the clearest language, Congress will not be assumed to have meant to go beyond the limits recognized by foreign relations law.

85. X and Y are in State A. X makes a misrepresentation to Y. X and Y go to State B. Solely because of the prior misrepresentations, Y delivers money to X. A has jurisdiction to prescribe a criminal penalty for obtaining money by false pretenses.

Restatement, Second, Foreign Relations Law of the United States 45.

Defendants' reliance on the principle stated in Foley Bros. v. Filardo, 336 U.S. 281, 69 S.Ct. 575, 93 L.Ed. 680 (1949), that regulatory statutes will generally not be construed as applying to conduct wholly outside the United States, is thus misplaced. However, it would be equally errroneous to assume that the legislature always means to go to the full extent permitted. This is a question of the interpretation of the particular statute, which we will consider below with specific reference to § 10(b).

We would not wish defendants to think that in thus defining the issue we have failed to consider their argument that the critical misrepresentations, if such they were, were made in England during the four days of meetings in early June and in the interval between the signing of the agreement in New York and the beginning and continuation of the purchases on the London Stock Exchange. Even limiting ourselves to plaintiff's answers to defendants' interrogatories, as defendant Maxwell suggests, there were abundant misrepresentations in the United States. Maxwell's initial misrepresentations were made here, although then in a context of seeking to interest Steinberg in a joint venture. Further misrepresentations were made by Majhtenyi in late April or early May. These were elaborated by Maxwell and Majhtenyi at the hotel meeting in early May. . . . Finally, there were the meetings preceding the signature of the June 17 contract. Beyond this we see no reason why, for purposes of jurisdiction to impose a rule, making telephone calls and sending mail to the United States should not be deemed to constitute conduct within it. On what is now before us it is impossible to say that conduct in the United States was not "an essential link," Mills v. Electric Auto-Lite Co., 396 U.S. 375, 385, 90 S.Ct. 616, 24 L.Ed.2d 593 (1970), in leading Leasco into the contract of June 17, 1969. And that contract, signed in the United States, was "an essential link" in inducing Leasco to make the open-market purchases, whether these were triggered by a call from London to New York, as Leasco contends, or by a conversation in England, as defendants assert. Putting the matter in another way, if defendants' fraudulent acts in the United States significantly whetted Leasco's interest in acquiring Pergamon shares, it would be immaterial, from the standpoint of foreign relations law, that the damage resulted, not from the contract whose execution Maxwell procured in this country, but from interrelated action which he induced in England or, for that matter, which Leasco took there on its own. As said in a leading English case, "In order to establish a coherent chain of causation it is not necessary that the precise details leading up to the accident [here the loss] should have been reasonably foreseeable," Hughes v. Lord Advocate, [1963] A.C. 837, 852. We have approved this with the qualification, doubtless intended, that the damage was within the area where the defendant had unlawfully created a risk of loss. In re Kinsman Transit Co., 338 F.2d 708, 721–726 (2 Cir. 1964), cert. denied, 380 U.S. 944, 85 S.Ct. 1026, 13 L.Ed.2d 963 (1968). See also Hart and Honoré, Causation in the Law 234–48 (1959).

Up to this point we have established only that, because of the extensive acts alleged to have been performed in the United States, considerations of foreign relations law do not preclude our reading § 10 (b) as applicable here. The question remains whether we should. Appellants have three lines of defense: they claim (1) that § 10(b) has no application to transactions in foreign securities not on an organized American market; (2) that if it does, it has no application when such transactions occur outside the United States; and (3) that in any event it can have no application when the purchaser is not a citizen of the United States. Before considering these arguments, it will be well to review the relationship of the anti-fraud sections to other provisions of the federal securities laws.

[A discussion of § 17 of the Securities Act and its relation to § 10(b) is omitted.]

Since Congress thus meant § 10(b) to protect against fraud in the sale or purchase of securities whether or not these were traded on organized United States markets, we cannot perceive any reason why it should have wished to limit the protection to securities of American issuers. The New Yorker who is the object of fraudulent misrepresentations in New York is as much injured if the securities are of a mine in Saskatchewan as in Nevada. Defendants have pointed to nothing in the legislative history which would indicate an intention that the language of § 10(b) should be narrowed so as not to protect him.[86]

We likewise cannot see any sound reason for believing that, in a case like that just put, Congress would have wished protection to be withdrawn merely because the fraudulent promoter of the Saskatchewan mining security took the buyer's check back to Canada and mail-

86. The briefs discuss at length two matters of legislative history which seem to us to be of little relevance and may as well be dealt with at this point.

Section 30(a) of the Securities Exchange Act makes it unlawful for any broker or dealer to use the mails or an instrumentality of commerce to effect a transaction in securities of American issuers on a foreign securities exchange "in contravention of such rules and regulations as the Commissioner may prescribe as necessary or appropriate in the public interest or for the protection of investors or to prevent the evasion of this title." Section 30(b) says that, "[T]he provisions of this title or of any rule or regulation thereunder shall not apply to any person insofar as he transacts a business in securities" outside the United States unless he does so in contravention of rules and regulations promulgated by the Commissioner.

Defendants argue that this marked the limit of how far Congress wished to go with respect to transactions having a foreign aspect. The purpose of § 30(a) [then § 28], as explained by Thomas G. Corcoran, principal draftsman of the bill requiring registration and reporting by companies whose securities were listed on American stock exchanges, was to give the SEC a weapon with which to counter the threat, made by opponents of the bill, that its enactment would drive American securities to foreign exchanges. See Hearings on S.Res. 84, 56 and 97 before the Senate Committee on Banking and Currency, 73d Cong. 2d Sess., Part 15, 6569, 6578–79 (1934). It cannot fairly be read as restricting the scope of the anti-fraud provision, as that was broadened by the conference report. Section 30(b) clearly has no application here. See, as to all this, Schoenbaum v. Firstbrook, supra, 405 F.2d at 207–208; Roth v. Fund of Funds, Inc., 405 F.2d 421 (2 Cir. 1968), cert. denied 394 U.S. 975, 89 S.Ct. 1469, 22 L.Ed.2d 754 (1965).

In 1964, on the urging of the SEC, Congress amended § 12 of the Securities Exchange Act to include certain issuers whose securities were not listed on American securities exchanges. As originally drafted, the amendment exempted foreign issuers who would otherwise be subject to the new requirements, subject to termination of the exemption by the Commission. S. Rep.No.379, 68th Cong. 1st Sess. 29–31 (1963). As a result of the House hearings, Hearings on H.R. 6789, 6793, S. 1642 Before a Subcommittee of the House Committee on Interstate and Foreign Commerce, 88th Cong. 1st and 2d Sess., pp. 1286–87 (1964), this was reversed, see § 12(g)(13), so that the statute applies unless the Commission exempts. Plaintiffs consider this piece of history to work in their favor. Apart from question as to the propriety of interpreting the intention of the 1934 Congress from legislation passed 30 years later, a legislative decision on the ambit of the registration and reporting requirements of the Securities Exchange Act casts little light on the desired scope of the anti-fraud provision.

ed the certificate from there. In the somewhat different yet closely related context of choice of law, the mechanical test that, in determining the *locus delicti,* "The place of wrong is in the state where the last event necessary to make an actor liable for an alleged tort takes place," Restatement of the Conflict of Laws § 377 (1934), has given way, in the case of fraud and misrepresentation, to a more extensive and sophisticated analysis. See Restatement, (Second) Conflict of Laws § 148 (1971).

Our case, however, is not the simple one thus hypothesized. In that instance not only the fraudulent misrepresentation but the issuance of the check and the receipt of the securities occurred in the United States, although the check was deposited and the security mailed in Canada. Here it was understood from the outset that all the transactions would be executed in England. Still we must ask ourselves whether, if Congress had thought about the point, it would not have wished to protect an American investor if a foreigner comes to the United States and fraudulently induces him to purchase foreign securities abroad—a purpose which its words can fairly be held to embrace. While, as earlier stated, we doubt that impact on an American company and its shareholders would suffice to make the statute applicable if the misconduct had occurred solely in England, we think it tips the scales in favor of applicability when substantial misrepresentations were made in the United States.

This brings us to appellants' third line of defense, namely, that the purchaser was not an American but a Netherlands Antilles corporation.

Before proceeding to the main thrust of this argument, two other points should be considered. Defendants contend that Leasco N.V. is a necessary party; they fear that unless it is joined as plaintiff, they might be exposed to a subsequent action, particularly if losses resulting from the purchase of the Pergamon shares should render Leasco N.V. insolvent. They also contend that, absent Leasco N.V., the complaint does not allege a fraud "in connection with the purchase or sale" of a security, within the familiar principle of Birnbaum v. Newport Steel Corp., 193 F.2d 461 (2 Cir.), cert. denied, 343 U.S. 956, 72 S.Ct. 1051, 96 L.Ed. 1356 (1952), and that plaintiffs thus lack standing. These points are sufficiently answered by the agreement of plaintiffs' counsel in open court that Leasco N.V. will be joined as a plaintiff. We proceed on the basis of that stipulation.

Although we have already stated the principal facts relating to the involvement of Leasco N.V., a few more details may be pertinent. The instructions to Rothschild to proceed with the open-market purchases came from Leasco, and Rothschild began its purchases, on June 20, 1969, for that company's account. The permission granted by the Bank of England to make open-market purchases of Pergamon shares also ran to Leasco. Just who decided that the cash should be supplied by Leasco N.V., and when this was decided, are not clear. The shares are held in the names of nominees who have voted them in accordance with the instructions of Leasco. Finally, a letter from Leasco's Vice President-Finance to the Secretary of Pergamon states:

> Leasco Data has an interest in 5,206,210 Ordinary Shares purchased through N. M. Rothschild & Sons. These shares are held on behalf of Leasco International N.V., a wholly owned subsidiary of Leasco Data Processing Equipment Corporation in the following nominee names . . . .

It seems quite arguable from all this that Leasco N.V. is holding the shares merely as trustee for Leasco, which has the beneficial interest and is bound to reimburse Leasco N.V. for the latter's expenditures. If that were so, defendants' contention that the true purchaser was a foreigner would be drained of force. But even if Leasco N.V. is the beneficial owner, it would be elevating form over substance to hold that this entails a conclusion that the purchases did not have a sufficient effect in the United States to make § 10(b) apply. Whether Leasco N.V. is merely a financial conduit, as plaintiffs assert, or was planned to conduct an active business, as some of the SEC filings indicate, it was wholly-owned and its debt securities were guaranteed by Leasco and were convertible with Leasco common stock. We see no need to enter into the debate whether, as defendants contend and plaintiffs deny, Leasco obtained substantial tax and other advantages through the incorporation of Leasco N.V. and the use of the latter to acquire the Pergamon shares. Whatever may be the rule where the defrauded American investor chooses, deliberately and unilaterally, to have the purchase consummated abroad by a foreigner, here the situation was quite different. The Maxwell group expressly agreed in its written contract that Leasco could "at its election" have the offer made "by a wholly-owned subsidiary of Leasco or a wholly-owned subsidiary of such subsidiary," "providing Leasco shall remain responsible for the due performance" of the obligation to acquire the shares. This clause specifically covered Leasco N.V., which was part and parcel of Leasco in every realistic sense. In acceding to this provision the defendants themselves recognized that Leasco, the United States company, remained at all times intimately involved in the transaction; the foreign entity was accepted by both sides as the *alter ego* of the American. The case is quite different from another hypothetical we posed at argument, namely, where a German and a Japanese businessman met in New York for convenience, and the latter fraudulently induced the former to make purchases of Japanese securities on the Tokyo Stock Exchange.

Before leaving subject-matter jurisdiction, we should say a word in answer to the defendants' argument that since choice of law principles would select the law of England as the rule governing liability, application of § 10(b) of the Securities Exchange Act would violate international law. Cf. Lauritzen v. Larsen, 345 U.S. 571, 73 S.Ct. 921, 97 L.Ed. 1254 (1955). At first blush the contention that the courts of the forum transgress their jurisdiction if they apply the forum's own law when correct choice of law doctrines would require them to apply the law of another state as the normative principle would scarcely seem to warrant discussion, particularly in a case like this where the full faith and credit clause of the Constitution can have no application. However, the argument is more subtle. Defendants concede that a New York court or a federal court if diversity jurisdiction existed, seized of an action by plaintiffs for common law fraud, would not transgress international law if, after due consideration, it erroneously chose New York rather than English law; the difficulty alleged to exist here is that a federal court will feel constrained to apply § 10(b) of the Securities Exchange Act rather than the law of England. We are not as certain as the defendants that under the principles stated in § 148 of the Restatement of Conflicts Second, English law would necessarily govern an action in New York for common law fraud.[87] But if it would, the conclusion asserted by defend-

87. Professor Ehrenzweig contends that "no 'conflicts' case [of fraud] can be found in which the court would have decided differently had all elements of the case been entirely domestic" and that the rule "is this simple: the court in a fraud case involving foreign elements will apply its own law." Conflict of Laws 558–59 (1962).

ants would not follow. For, as we have already demonstrated, in the circumstances described in § 17 of the Restatement of Foreign Relations Law, under which this case fits, the nation where the conduct has occurred has jurisdiction to displace foreign law and to direct its courts to apply its own.

We therefore hold that the motions to dismiss for lack of subject matter jurisdiction were properly denied.

[Portions of the opinion on personal jurisdiction over individual defendants and *forum non conveniens* are omitted.]

. . .

The orders of Judge Ryan denying the motions to dismiss for lack of subject matter jurisdiction and for lack of personal jurisdiction over Fleming Ltd. are affirmed. His order denying the motion of Chalmers to dismiss for lack of personal jurisdiction is reversed, with instructions to enter an order of dismissal. The order of Judge Lasker dismissing the complaint against Kerman is vacated and the cause remanded for further proceedings consistent with this opinion. The suggestion for the issuance of mandamus directing the district court to dismiss the complaint on the ground of *forum non conveniens* is declined. The stay of discovery with respect to Fleming Ltd. is vacated. Discovery with respect to Chalmers must now proceed as against a non-party.

Plaintiffs may recover costs against all defendants except Chalmers, which may recover its costs against plaintiffs.

COMMENT

In 1975, two decisions of the Second Circuit Court of Appeals further developed principles of extraterritorial application of the antifraud provisions of the Securities Acts. Bersch v. Drexel Firestone, Inc., 519 F.2d 974; and IIT v. Vencap, Ltd. and Blackman, 519 F.2d 1001. In both cases Judge Friendly wrestled with the tangled affairs of Investors Overseas Services, a mutual fund captained by Bernard Cornfeld, whose international financial exploits met an early success but ultimately crashed ignominiously.

In these decisions, Judge Friendly reviewed basic principles of extraterritorial reach, before reaching judgment about the applicability of the antifraud provisions to the complicated situations before him. We here isolate some of his general observations that are particularly relevant to the decisions in Schoenbaum and Leasco, supra. In the Bersch decision, for example, Judge Friendly noted:

> (*1*) The principle of Section 18 of Restatement (Second), Foreign Relations Law, p. 882, supra, although justifying application of the antifraud provisions in a case such as Schoenbaum, would not support that application "if there was no intention that the securities should be offered to anyone in the United States, simply because in the long run there was an adverse effect on this country's general economic interests or on American security prices. Moderation is all." Thus antifraud provisions applied to acts committed abroad "only when these result in injury to purchasers or

sellers of those securities in whom the United States has an interest, not where acts simply have an adverse effect on the American economy or American investors generally."

(*2*) Such provisions would not apply simply because there were significant purchases by Americans resident abroad of securities allegedly fraudulently sold, at least where none of the defendants engaged in significant activities within the United States. "Congress surely did not mean the securities laws to protect the many thousands of Americans residing in foreign countries against securities frauds by foreigners acting there . . . ."

After resolving the issues of extraterritorial reach before him, Judge Friendly observed:

> We freely acknowledge that if we were asked to point to language in the statutes, or even in the legislative history, that compelled these conclusions, we would be unable to respond. The Congresses that passed these extraordinary pieces of legislation in the midst of the depression could hardly have been expected to foresee the development of offshore frauds thirty years later. We recognize also that reasonable men might conclude that the coverage was greater, or less, than has been outlined in this opinion and in *IIT v. Vencap, Ltd.*, this day decided. Our conclusions rest on case law and commentary concerning the application of the securities laws and other statutes to situations with foreign elements and on our best judgment as to what Congress would have wished if these problems had occurred to it.

In the Vencap decision, Judge Friendly commented upon some principles of legislative reach considered earlier in this chapter. For example:

(*1*) The fact that one defendant owning and controlling another defendant was a United States citizen would not alone make the antifraud provisions applicable. Although this country "has power to prescribe the conduct of its nationals everywhere in the world, . . . Congress does not often do so and courts are forced to interpret the statute at issue in the particular case." Judge Friendly distinguished the Steele decision, p. 1022, supra, as resting not simply on the American citizenship of the defendant but on effects of his acts in this country. "It is simply unimaginable that Congress would have wished the antifraud provisions of the securities laws to apply if, for example, [an American defendant] while in London had done all the acts here charged and had defrauded only European investors."

(*2*) The opinion again stressed that the effects within this country of allegedly fraudulent sales abroad must be "substantial", if such effects are alone relied upon (that is, without a companion basis for application of United States law, such as some conduct within this country) to justify regulation of acts principally occurring abroad.

In evaluating the past and predicting the future of Rule 10b–5 in its international dimension, it is well to recall that its status domestically is subject to some uncertainty. In Blue Chip Stamps v. Manor Drug Stores, —— U.S. ——, 95 S.Ct. 1917, 44 L.Ed.2d 539 (1975), the Supreme Court disapproved of a number of lower court opinions giving the Rule an expansive construction. It noted that there was no indication that either Congress, in enacting Section 10, or the SEC, in adopting the Rule, considered the question of private civil remedies, but that despite such silence (to be contrasted with "numerous carefully drawn express civil remedies" in both the 1933 and 1934 Acts) the courts had implied such relief. It also noted that "litigation under Rule 10b–5 presents a danger of vexatiousness different in degree and kind from that which accompanies litigation in general," and that a 10b–5 complaint had "a settlement value . . . out of any proportion to its prospect of success at trial."

As of early 1975 the American Law Institute was considering a tentative draft of a Federal Securities Code. § 1604 is entitled "Relation to Other Countries." It provides in subsection (a) that the Code applies (1) to sales, offers, proxy solicitations or tender offers from outside the United States into the country, (2) to attempts or conspiracies outside the United States to commit a Code violation within it, (3) to conduct whose constituent elements occur to a substantial extent within the United States or occur without the United States "but cause a substantial effect within it . . . as a direct and foreseeable result. . . ." In subsection (b) it provides that the Code does not apply to sales or offers initiated in this country but aimed abroad. Finally, it gives the SEC power "within the limits of international law" to make rules providing that the Code does not apply despite subsection (a) or that it does apply despite subsection (b).

QUESTIONS

(1) How would the Code formulation affect the Schoenbaum and Leasco cases? Would it make prediction of the outcome of subsequent cases easier or more difficult? Is the Code's rule as to conspiracies consistent with the criminal law principles developed at pp. 877–880, supra? Is the reference to international law helpful (in that it refers to a usable body of material) or is it an empty invocation?

(2) Suppose that a foreign owner of a foreign corporation, aware of the dangers of the American securities laws, remains outside the United States and causes all negotiations with and representations to American purchasers to take place either abroad or by correspondence. Does that strategy take him out of the reach of Rule 10b–5?

(3) If the foreign vendor presents financial statements prepared under the law of his home country and consistent with practices there, should an American court find him in violation of Rule 10b–5 if those statements fail to meet American standards?

(4) Recall (p. 96, supra) the emphasis placed by rules on conflicts of law on the law of the place of incorporation (*or siège social*) to resolve questions about the internal affairs of a corporation. Does the Schoenbaum ruling do violence to that conception? Is it apt on that account to give rise to adverse reactions abroad?

Additional reading: Goldman & Magrino, Some Foreign Aspects of Securities Regulation: 55 Va.L.Rev. 1015 (1969); Becker, Extraterritorial Dimensions of the Securities Exchange Act, 2 N.Y.U.J.Int.L. & Pol. 233 (1969).

F. OBTAINING EVIDENCE ABROAD TO ENFORCE REGULATORY LEGISLATION OF A TRANSNATIONAL REACH

Each of the evidentiary problems discussed at pp. 835–852, supra, in connection with private civil litigation and at pp. 899–901, supra, in relation to criminal proceedings, can emerge in the setting of civil actions by a government to enforce its regulatory statutes or policies. Indeed, such problems often become exacerbated by the sharpness with which the regulatory policy sought to be enforced offends the policies of the foreign state involved. Hence we examine this problem separately, in the context of a chapter treating conflicts among nations in regulatory schemes.

No clear line, of course, divides proceedings instituted by a government agency to enforce regulatory policies such as antitrust laws from ordinary civil litigation. Although it was an action between private parties, the RCA v. Rauland case, p. 840 supra, arose under the antitrust laws. The Interhandel case, p. 844, supra, was one to which the government, through the Attorney General, was a party and involved a policy, the vesting of enemy aliens' assets, not viewed with sympathy in other quarters.

Another link between evidentiary problems in civil litigation and those in agency proceedings is the fact that at some point a court is generally drawn into the agency action. Either the agency is required by its governing statute to obtain a subpoena or other order from a court or it must ask a court to take steps to enforce compliance with an order that it has itself issued. The respondent may itself resort to a court for an order quashing the agency subpoena or limiting its scope.

Many regulatory statutes can be enforced through alternative procedures. Thus the antitrust laws may be enforced by a Federal Trade Commission proceeding. They may also be enforced by civil actions brought by the government or a private party. The government may choose to proceed by a criminal action, the information for which would normally be developed by a grand jury which may resort to subpoenas. One such grand jury encountered considerable problems in Canada: [88]

> In 1947, subpoenas were issued out of this Court to some fifty Canadian pulp and paper companies, in the course of a Sherman Act investigation, requiring them to produce records before a grand jury in New York. The Ontario Parliament believed that this was an infringement upon the sovereignty of the Province and as a result, there was passed "The Business Records Protection Act", Revised Statutes of Ontario, 1950, Chap. 44, which prohibits any person in that Province from sending from Ontario to a point outside of Ontario any books, records, or other papers in response to any "order, direction or subpoena of any legislative, administrative, or judicial authority in any jurisdiction outside of Ontario". The statement in the Ontario Parliament by the Premier of Ontario on October 27, 1947 reflected the resentment against what the Premier called an attempt by the judicial authorities of the United States "to invade the territorial integrity of Canada" by the issuance of these subpoenas requiring the production of records from Canadian companies relating to business done in Canada. He stated at the conclusion of his remarks to the legislature: "I recognize that in population Ontario is a very small jurisdiction compared with that of the United States. Nevertheless, I trust no citizen of the United States will forget that Canadians are just as proud of their own nationality and just as jealous of their own sovereignty as is any citizen of their own country."

Other antitrust subpoena cases with international implications include In re Electric and Musical Industries, Ltd., 155 F.Supp. 892 (S.D.N.Y.1957), and In re Siemens & Halske, A.G., 155 F.Supp. 897 (S.D.N.Y.1957). In these parallel cases the court was asked to quash subpoenas served on foreign corporations at the offices of their American subsidiaries and declined to do so. In other cases parties served with such subpoenas have raised the defense of sovereign immunity with some success. In re Investigation of World Arrangements, 13 F.R.D. 280, 288 (D.D.C.1952); In re Grand Jury Investigation of the Shipping Industry, 186 F.Supp. 298 (D.D.C.1960).

Similarly, the federal statutes governing transactions in securities may be enforced through private or government civil actions, criminal indictments or proceedings before the Securities and Exchange Commission. One of the classic cases on administrative subpoenas is SEC v. Minas de Artemisa S.A., 150 F.2d 215 (9th Cir. 1945), which ordered a Mexican company "found" in Arizona to apply to the Mexican authorities for permission to produce for the SEC in Arizona books and records which it kept in Mexico or to have them inspected and copied there.[89] The following excerpts show, inter alia,

88. This statement of the episode appears in Vanity Fair Mills v. T. Eaton Co., 133 F.Supp. 522, 529 (S.D.N.Y.1955), which was affirmed by the decision of the court of appeals noted at p. 1023, supra.

89. Accord: Mines & Metals Corp. v. SEC, 200 F.2d 317 (9th Cir. 1952) (records in Panama ordered opened for inspection). 3 Loss, Securities Regulation 1961–62 (2d ed. 1961).

the similarity between the problems raised by orders to produce evidence that is located abroad before a court in this country and equity decrees, considered at pp. 1038, 1040, supra, requiring the performance of acts in a foreign country:

> . . . The Restatement of Conflict of Laws (§ 94) summarizes the applicable general rule thus: "A state can exercise jurisdiction through its courts to make a decree directing a party subject to the jurisdiction of the court to do an act in another state, provided such act is not contrary to the law of the state in which it is to be performed." The proposition thus stated has ample support in the authorities. Courts have frequently required persons within their jurisdiction to produce books and papers which were beyond the territorial limits of the court, even in cases where the documents were located in a foreign country. . . . In requiring the performance of acts in other jurisdictions the courts have gone much further than merely to direct the production or to permit the inspection of documents. In the Salton Sea Cases, 9 Cir., 172 F. 792, this court held that a court of equity may enjoin a continuing injury to real property within its jurisdiction as the result of flooding caused by works improperly maintained by the defendant in Mexico, notwithstanding compliance with the decree would require the performance of acts in Mexico. . . .
>
> Assuming the absence of conflict with Mexican law, the Commission is thus entitled to an order enforcing its subpena . . . .

To illustrate the evidentiary problems that are apt to arise in administrative proceedings to enforce a regulatory statute offensive to foreign countries, we present cases that involve the Federal Maritime Commission's actions and the reactions of foreign governments thereto. That Commission is empowered by § 21 of the Shipping Act of 1916 to "require any common carrier by water . . . to file with it . . . any account, record, rate, or charge . . . appertaining to the business of such carrier . . . subject to this Act." The Act also provides that whoever fails to file as ordered "shall forfeit to the United States the sum of $100 for each day of such default." These cases arose from investigations undertaken by the Commission starting in the early 1960's, to gain information about the operations of conferences of steamship operators. Such conferences involve agreements about rates and other items which, under certain conditions, are exempt from the antitrust laws. It has been asserted that the result of conference practices is that rates are charged which are too high or unjustly discriminatory or both. We do not explore the merits of these contentions except to note that foreign countries with differing interests in the shipping industry have taken a sharply different view about the advantage of conferences.[90]

90. For analysis of these conflicts see Note, Rate Regulation in Ocean Shipping, 78 Harv.L.Rev. 635 (1965); Lowenfeld, "To Have One's Cake . . ." The Federal Maritime Commission and the Conferences, 1 J.Mar. L. & Comm. 21 (1969).

The first decision in this sequence of cases was Kerr S. S. Co. v. United States, 284 F.2d 61 (2d Cir. 1960), which rejected various objections raised by American carriers: (1) the orders required production of documents outside the country, (2) the orders were unreasonably burdensome in scope and quantity and (3) secret agreements with persons not subject to the Act were called for. Other litigation followed:

MITSUI STEAMSHIP CO. LTD.—ALLEGED REBATES TO A. GRAF & CO.

Federal Maritime Commission, 1962.
7 F.M.C. 248.

[The Federal Maritime Board, predecessor of the Commission, instituted a proceeding to investigate possible illegal rebates or preferences given by Mitsui to Graf on exports from the United States to European ports. At a conference before the Hearing Examiner, the Examiner directed Mitsui to produce certain information. After Mitsui had complied only in part, the Commission issued an order under Section 21. Mitsui moved to vacate it. Portions of the Commission's opinion follow:]

. . . [T]he refusal of Mitsui's London office to submit the documents in their files was based upon the views of the Government of Japan as expressed in two aide memoire transmitted to the Department of State by the Japanese Embassy. The first aide memoire, dated August 23, 1960, was a protest lodged against a section 21 order of the Federal Maritime Board then under review by the Court of Appeals for the District of Columbia Circuit in the case of Montship Lines, Ltd. v. Federal Maritime Board, 295 F.2d 147 (D.C. Cir. 1961). Insofar as here relevant the aide memoire provided:

"The Ambassador of Japan . . . wishes to draw attention to the Order issued by the Federal Maritime Board on April 11, 1960 . . . which purports to require production of a wide range of documents . . . both within and without the United States and to state the views of the Government of Japan as follows:

"(1) The Government of Japan wishes to remind the Department of State of the memorandum of March 7, 1960, in which it stated that the subpoenas *duces tecum* issued in connection with the Grand Jury investigation of the shipping industry initiated by the United States and the Department of Justice purporting to require Japanese shipping companies to produce documents located in Japan are not in conformity with established principles of international law and that the authority of the said subpoenas does not extend to any documents which might be found within the territorial jurisdiction of Japan. The Government of Japan now reasserts its view as stated therein in connection with the proceedings instituted by the Federal Maritime Board under said order.

"(2) While the Government of Japan considers that the Japanese shipping companies involved will continue to cooperate with reasonable requests of the Federal Maritime Board which are deemed properly within the jurisdiction of the United States, it is felt that the instant Order, apparently involving a claim of jurisdiction over and beyond any such limitation, may give rise to conflicts of jurisdiction and maritime policies."

The second aide memoire dated March 20, 1961 expressed the views of the Japanese Government with respect to a bill (H.R. 4299) then before Congress to amend the Shipping Act. . . .

It appeared to the Commission from the evidence before it that there must be some misapprehension on the part of Mitsui or the Japanese Government or both as to the precise nature of the inquiry being conducted and the request for information made pursuant thereto. We therefore enlisted the aid of the Department of State in an attempt through diplomatic channels to clarify our position and dispel any misunderstandings. On February 28, 1962 we received the advice of the State Department based on its contacts with the Japanese Government. State informed us that the Government of Japan pointed out that the documents called for were not located within its territorial jurisdiction but were in the United Kingdom, and that Japan did not consider it appropriate even to suggest to Mitsui that it supply documents which were located in a third country.

Our efforts to secure cooperation having failed, we entered the section 21 order here under review on March 1, 1962. On March 30, 1962 Mitsui filed a motion to vacate this order. Accompanying the motion is a letter dated March 20, 1962 from the Japanese Minister of Transportation to Mitsui's president reading as follows:

"With reference to the section 21 order issued by the Federal Maritime Commission on March 5, 1962, in Docket No. 918, I order you not to comply with the order of the Commission insofar as it relates to the production of documents located outside the United States which might be in the possession of your company, for the following reasons:

"The above mentioned Order requests your Company to produce documents held by your Company outside the United States. It is well established international custom and practice that the U. S. Government if it desires to obtain documents located outside the United States, must obtain them through the judicial authorities of the foreign country wherein such documents are located. The attempt of the U. S. Government compelling you to produce documents located outside the United States would therefore constitute an act in disregard of this well established international practice. . . ."

The amount of discretion the Commission can exercise in a case such as this, is, in our opinion, limited. Our first duty is of course to Congress, for it is to the Commission that Congress looks for the effectuation of the regulatory program embodied in the shipping statutes. We have, it seems clear, the duty to expend every effort compatible with sound regulation, to obtain the information necessary to the determination that all who engage in our commerce do so in compliance with the law. We are asked now by Mitsui to cease all efforts to obtain information necessary to determine whether there exist in an export trade of the United States practices violative of the Shipping Act. In effect, we are asked to abandon our statutory duty to investigate alleged malpractices in the trade. Such a request exceeds the bounds of our discretion and cannot be granted.

Mitsui is a Japanese flag carrier with its principal office located in Japan, and is admittedly obligated to obey the laws of Japan. But as a common carrier by water which chooses to engage in the commerce of the United States, Mitsui is equally obligated to meet the terms and conditions imposed by Congress upon all who participate in our commerce. These terms and conditions prescribed in the regulatory shipping statutes enacted by Congress apply with equal force to all water carriers engaged in U. S. commerce, and they must be administered impartially. Obviously, they cannot be so administered if their application is to turn upon the incidental, or accidental, circumstance that needed information is not physically located within the United States. This would make a shambles of the law.

The Shipping Act, 1916, under which the present investigation was instituted, establishes the basic pattern of United States regulation of its ocean foreign commerce. The underlying philosophy of the Act was that certain practices then prevalent in such commerce constituted unjust, unfair and unreasonable methods of competition which should be prohibited or in some cases placed under government control and regulation. The practices outlawed included those of the type which the Commission is here seeking to investigate, and there can be no question that the traffic involved, namely, canned goods produced in this country and moving out of its ports, is properly a matter of concern to the United States. . . .

We cannot emphasize too strongly that, as respects regulation of the competitive practices of water carriers, all carriers regardless of flag or nationality are placed on an equal footing under our laws. It is a prime concern of these laws to insure that competition among carriers for cargo moving in United States foreign commerce should be open and above board, with no curtain of secrecy preventing the disclosure of pertinent data to the Commission. Foreign flag carriers, although charged with the responsibilities imposed by our laws, are also the recipients of the benefits they confer. Indeed, the respondent here, Mitsui, has availed itself of these benefits on occasion past. Before this Commission and its predecessors, Mitsui has found a forum in which to air its grievances and seek relief in connection with the competitive practices of other carriers. It would now appear, however, that the Government of Japan, by its directive ostensibly precluding Mitsui from producing information bearing upon the lawfulness of its practices in an export trade of the United States, is seeking to insulate Mitsui from the responsibilities imposed by our laws.

We are aware of no international custom or practice that would require the United States Government to resort to the courts of another country to obtain information needed in the exercise of its sovereign jurisdiction and functions. Moreover, the Japanese Government's aide memoire refers to such documents as might be found within the territorial jurisdiction of Japan, whereas the information here in question appears to be located in the United Kingdom. Other representations of the Japanese Government indicate that cooperation will be extended in those cases which do not prejudice the interests of Japan, but it is not indicated or shown how the interests of Japan are or can be prejudiced by the Commission's order for Mitsui's production of the information in question and certainly such prejudice is not self-evident. Even if the documents were located in Japan, the trade involved is not an import or export trade of Japan but is the United States export trade from Pacific Coast Ports to European ports in the Antwerp/Hamburg Range.

Japan has a natural and proper interest in the well-being of one of its citizens and is anxious to protect it from unjust or discriminatory treatment at the hands of a foreign government. But there is not the slightest basis here for any suggestion of such discrimination. On the contrary, as we have already noted, the sole purpose of the present inquiry is to insure that Mitsui as a participant in United States commerce is observing requirements of United States law which all other carriers operating in our foreign commerce are required to observe. It would be discriminatory in favor of Mitsui and against all other carriers if the inquiry were not carried out. We cannot believe that the purpose of the Japanese Government is to secure for its citizens either undue preference or unwarranted immunity under the laws of those countries in which they conduct their business.

Our responsibility as we have said, is to insure the effective and impartial administration of the shipping statutes within our jurisdiction. Mitsui's motion to vacate the order must therefore be denied.

COMMENT

The Mitsui opinion refers to Montship Lines, Ltd. v. Federal Maritime Board, 295 F.2d 147 (D.C.Cir. 1961). There the Board had entered an order under Section 21 requiring alien corporations engaged in the carriage of cargo and passengers between the United States and foreign countries to file copies of certain contracts involving the water-borne commerce of the United States. In reviewing this order the Court of Appeals—for reasons not here relevant—vacated the order and remanded the case to the Board. The following excerpts reject contentions of the petitioners that they should not be required to produce documents located abroad and, in any case, should not have to do so if foreign law were violated.

> In any event, in light of the coverage and the purposes of the Shipping Act, we can see no reason to restrict § 21 to cover only information within the United States. In enacting the Shipping Act, which deals with foreign as well as interstate commerce, Congress was clearly mindful of the fact that foreign flag as well as United States carriers were subject to regulation thereunder. See H.R.Rep. No. 659, 64th Cong., 1st Sess. (1916). If the Board's investigatory powers were limited to the territorial confines of the United States, regulation of foreign flag carriers would be hampered to a substantial degree. Consequently, we will not read into § 21 a territorial limitation which appears to be contrary to the purposes of the Shipping Act.
>
> We must reject petitioners' contentions regarding protests of foreign governments and extra-territorial enforcement of the Board's order. As the Second Circuit pointed out in Kerr, the protests of foreign governments are matters for consideration by the Executive and not the courts. And the question as to whether the order can be enforced by extra-territorial means is not presently before us. All that is here involved is whether the order was properly and validly issued. . . .
>
> Several petitioners, foreign steamship lines of Yugoslavia and Netherlands nationality assert that the production by them of documents required by the Board's § 21 order would be violative of their local national law. They point to provisions of the Yugoslav Criminal Code and the Netherlands Economic Competition Law which they contend preclude compliance with the Board's order.
>
> Prior to determining whether these foreign laws do in fact forbid the production of documents such as those required by the Board's order and, if so, what effect this should have upon compliance, the appropriate procedure is to require

these petitioners to make a good faith attempt to obtain a waiver of such restrictions from their respective governments. . . .

Consequently, these petitioners should upon the remand bring any arguments that their local law prohibits compliance before the Board so that it can then initially determine whether petitioners have made a good faith effort to secure waivers and, if so, whether compliance is to be required.

. . .

DEBATES IN THE HOUSE OF COMMONS ON THE SHIPPING CONTRACTS AND COMMERCIAL DOCUMENTS ACT, 1964

698 Parl.Deb. (Hansard) (5th Series) 1215–83 (1964).

[The reaction of certain foreign countries to the Commission's actions, partially depicted in the opinions above, was intense. We excerpt below some debates in the British House of Commons relating to the enactment of the Shipping Contracts and Commercial Documents Act, 1964, 12 & 13 Eliz. 2, c. 87. That act authorized various Ministers, including the Minister of Transport, to direct persons in the United Kingdom not to comply with any order from a court or authority of a foreign country to produce a commercial document not within the latter's territory if the Minister finds that such requirement "constitutes or would constitute an infringement of the jurisdiction which, under international law, belongs to the United Kingdom, . . . " Violations of ministerial directions are punishable by fines of up to £1000. These speeches, which were interspersed with comments on the merits of the American shipping policies, illustrate concerns and arguments prevalent in other countries. They develop the themes introduced in the ICI litigation, as suggested in the Comment at p. 1037, supra.]

Mr. Fletcher-Cooke:

This is a brave Bill, but, as the right hon. Member for Easington (Mr. Shinwell) reminded us, it is also a penal Bill. It must be unique in that the potential victims are rather welcoming the chains, but it is none the less, a Bill which imposes penalties and, therefore, it ought, under our rules, to be absolutely clear. I have some questions to put which suggest that it is not absolutely crystal clear.

The crux of the matter comes in Clauses 1 and 2, under which the Minister may make orders forbidding individuals or companies to obey orders of a foreign Power which

> "constitute an infringement of the jurisdiction which, under international law, belongs to the United Kingdom."

Those are brave words, but it is the first time, to my knowledge, that our Statute Book has appealed to the standards of international law, by which, presumably, is meant public international law.

The first difficulty is that public international law is so notoriously ambiguous that to appeal to it as a standard in a penal statute is to ask for trouble. Anyone on trial under it can always appeal, if that be the standard, to a textbook which almost invariably will conflict with previous textbooks or decision. However, that is the way the Bill has been drafted. It seems to me to make it open to anyone prosecuted under it to plead that the order made was *ultra vires* because either the jurisdiction does not belong to the United Kingdom, or, if it does, it belongs also to the other country, that is to say, there is a concurrent jurisdiction.

Do the words

> "constitute an infringement of the jurisdiction which, under international law, belongs to the United Kingdom"

mean belonging exclusively to the United Kingdom or do they mean belonging to the United Kingdom among others? Hon. Members will know that there are many cases in international law where there is concurrent jurisdiction, where one can sue in more than one court or more than one country. For instance, unless there are special conventions or specific exceptions, seamen can sue for their wages in a foreign court. Even though they are sailing under the British flag, if they put into a foreign port and have not been paid their wages, they can sue for them in the courts of the foreign country, although there would equally be concurrent jurisdiction in the courts here. This does not often happen nowadays because there are special conventions limiting it, but it is the basic rule. . . .

In this country we have always held the view that under public international law the law of the port is given very full power. We had a long battle with the French on this very point throughout the nineteenth century. The French always emphasized the law of the flag of the ship, saying that in many cases the law of the port should give way to the law of the flag. We held the contrary view, that the law of the port, however vexatious or however silly it might seem to the visiting ship,, prevailed. . . .

It is idle to say that these are documents made abroad, made here, that is to say between British shippers and shipowners, foreigners to America. Of course they are. But if they go to America, or copies of them go to America, or if secondary evidence must be given by oral examination of witnesses or however it may be, the Americans take the attitude: "If you want to come to our ports, you must observe our rules. We are entitled to compel you to disclose your evidence, oral or documentary, to make sure that you are obeying our rules."

I am not acting as devil's advocate. All that I am saying is that since we have to make our penal statutes clear beyond a peradventure there is an argument which any defendant could make. This is an ambiguous phrase—"which, according to international law, belongs to the British". It may belong to us in the sense that our courts can also demand to see these documents. But it is very arguable that it also belongs to the Americans and that we have always hitherto held that view of international law. It makes no difference in those circumstances whether the contracts are made outside the United States because the Americans say, "You foreign shippers and shipowners, in your Conference system, are indulging in restrictive trade practices".

The Maritime Commission is saying—and it is important to get this clear because we must come to an agreement with the Americans about this and therefore we had better understand their view, even if we oppose it—"We will allow you to use our ports only if you observe what we regard as correct methods of competitive trading". We do not regard them as correct methods of competitive trading, but they do. . . .

The deadlock is complete. I think that it is unwise for the United States Congress to adopt this attitude, although, as I say, I think it arguable under international law that it is entitled to do so. If the American Congress is entitled to do so, this Bill is a *brutum fulmen,* because any defendant can show that this jurisdiction does not belong exclusively to the British Government.

But, as we know, this Bill is only a shot across the bows. It is designed to give our shipowners and shippers the opportunity to plead in the American courts, quite rightly, that they may be subjected, albeit perhaps unfairly, to pains and penalties at home if they observe the requirements of the American Federal Maritime Commission. It is right to give them that protection.

The ultimate solution must surely be an agreement, and I hope that the Bill will make an agreement more rather than less likely. . . .

Mr. Irvine:

If as things are without the Bill a British ship is required to do something, and the requirement is an encroachment of the United Kingdom jurisdiction, and the ship's captain refuses to comply with the requirement, I would have thought that in that event the British Government would come to the aid of the ship's captain, or the shipping company, and would adopt his noncompliance with such an Order or requirement as an act of State making the matter thereby justiciable, if so much were needed by the International Court.

Is it really necessary to have the Bill and the machinery proposed by it to make certain issues justificiable before the International Court which are not at present justiciable? I would have doubted it and I would be interested to have that matter dealt with and the Government's view expressed.

Mr. Soskice:

. . . My right hon. Friend asked: what happens if a British ship sails the Atlantic and docks in New York Harbour, or any other American dock; it goes inside American territorial waters; it ties up alongside the quayside; the gangway is put down; the master of the vessel, and others, land on American soil? What is there to prevent an American Court saying, "You, the British Government, have no more right to legislate inside United States territorial waters, or on American soil, than you say we have to legislate on yours"?

Suppose the master is called on to produce documents, or suppose the vessel is sailing under the terms of a conference contract which, in point of fact, infringes what is provided for and prohibited by these two American Acts—when the vessel enters United States territorial waters, when those in charge of it embark on to the quayside in New York, or anywhere else on American soil, are they not directly subject to United States jurisdiction?

Suppose the master is prosecuted in an American court for refusing to disclose documents that he carries with him off his vessel, or suppose that he has them in a portfolio or briefcase on going ashore to visit shipping agents on behalf of his employers—what conceivable defence would he have in the American court? . . .

The Attorney-General:

Another point raised is whether the Order applying the Bill to particular foreign measures will have sufficient clarity to make shipowners in this country aware of the particular circumstances which they have to report to the Minister. The hon. and learned Gentleman was good enough to point out that shipowners have no anxieties on this head. I think that that is right. In any event, the Order made by the Minister applying the Bill to those foreign measures will be prayable against in the House and will be subject to the control of the House. If it is thought to be insufficiently clear, or if there are fears that it may create difficulties, the House will have it within their power by negative Resolution to rescind the Order. . . .

. . . The effect of the Bill, in the Government's view, does not derogate at all from the present law, and the shipowner or other person affected against whom an Order is made by the foreign authority will be no worse off by reason of the passing of the Bill. It will still be competent for him to argue, and for this country to argue as against the foreign country, that it is a matter entirely within the jurisdiction of this country and not of that foreign country, and that, therefore, the legislation of that foreign country ought not to have dealt with it.

A different view on the question has been put forward, particularly by some American lawyers. They have taken the view that if the law of either country could have dealt with a particular problem, and if British law does not deal with it, then American law is entitled to do so. The advantage which will be given by the Bill is that both in the American court and in the International Court no one will be able to say, once the Minister has made a direction, that there is, as it were, a vacuum in British law and therefore American law is entitled to operate.

The view of the British Government is that there could be three possible situations, as for instance where freight is payable in the United Kingdom under the terms of a contract which is partly to be carried out in America: it may be exclusively a matter for British law, it may be exclusively a matter for American law or it may be a matter of concurrent jurisdiction. Our view is that where it is a matter for concurrent jurisdiction the ordinary rules of international law will look at the substance of the matter and will see which of the two laws ought to be paramount. Then, applying the rules of international law, one can see that it is a matter which our courts or the American courts ought to deal with.

But lest it be argued anywhere that in the absence of British law the American law can operate in the circumstances in which directions have been made under the Bill, we feel that there should be no doubts left in anybody's mind that there is a direct conflict of jurisdiction, and then the International Court or the international body discussing the matter will have to resolve that conflict, and one will not be left in a position in which it may be said that there is no conflict at all because British law does not deal with the matter. . . .

Finally, the right hon. and learned Member for Newport said that he thought that perhaps these matters could best be settled by the International Court of Justice at The Hague. I hope that it will never be necessary for any such reference to be made. Despite the fact that I am a lawyer, I have never believed in litigation. It is a disaster for those who get involved, though not perhaps for the lawyers, and I hope that our two countries which have a very ancient alliance will be able sensibly to settle these difficult questions without any resort to litigation of an international nature.

QUESTIONS

(1) Is there strength in the argument by Japan that an order for the production of documents located in Japan violates international law? What if they belonged to an American company? Would the British take the same view? Would the posture of the United States in international law be improved if legislation said that every carrier proposing to send its ships into United States ports were obligated to sign a consent to future production orders and noncomplying carriers were excluded from American waters?

(2) Recall the Interhandel and Ings cases at pp. 844, 848, supra, on consequences of foreign prohibitions on the production of evidence. In treating a case where a foreign party has failed to comply and deciding whether to impose a penalty such as that under Section 21, should a court or agency consider any of the following as to the foreign prohibitory rule:

(*a*) whether the penalties set for producing doucuments in accordance with the subpoena are civil or criminal;

(*b*) whether the non-complying person had some share in inducing the enactment of the foreign rule prohibiting compliance;

(*c*) whether the policy justifying the foreign rule is based upon considerations to which American courts and legislatures also give weight; and

(*d*) whether the foreign rule antedated the American proceeding or was a response to it.

(3) In view of the materials in Chapters VIII and IX, how do you react to the statement of the Attorney General in the debates in the House of Commons that "the ordinary rules of international law" can be explored by an international court to determine which of the conflicting national laws "ought to be paramount"?

Chapter X

TRANSNATIONAL ASPECTS OF INCOME TAXATION

In exploring the reach of and accommodation among national income tax systems, this chapter differs in an important respect from the materials treating comparable problems in Chapters VIII and IX. Statutes and, to a lesser degree, treaties here dominate the scene. Particularly in the United States, the legislature has stated in detail the governing rules. Courts have played primarily an interstitial role, through their interpretation of some of the more troublesome statutory provisions. They have not been called upon to assume the larger task of developing basic policies or principles to aid in interpreting the relatively barebone provisions on transnational reach which were characteristic of criminal legislation and much economic regulation.

As you read the following materials, consider why legislation occupies so prominent a position. Are the needs and expectations of the business community such that some, even significant, ambiguities may be tolerated in fields such as trade-mark regulation and antitrust, but cannot be lived with in so everyday a field as taxation, with its immediate and recurrent impact upon profits and planning? Is the need for certainty so great that it must be met even at the cost of rules that at times assume a quite arbitrary character? Do the problems of taxation inherently lend themselves to more detailed treatment by the legislature? Is the legislature simply more accustomed to giving tax problems such treatment? And if the legislature had drafted in broad terms, reminiscent of the statutes in Chapter IX that speak of "foreign commerce," rules about the transnational reach of tax systems, would the courts have been competent to develop principles of interpretation and to draw the relatively crisp lines that tax litigation frequently requires? [1]

The rules set forth in the Internal Revenue Code of 1954 [2] reach a high degree of complexity and detail. Some of the implementing regulations under the Code reinforce this observation. This chapter

1. An analogy to these transnational problems is afforded by the history of the Supreme Court's attempts to delimit the powers of the states to tax net income resulting from activities in interstate commerce. In 1959, Congress tried to cope with the problem and overruled a number of decisions with a relatively limited statute. 73 Stat. 555, 15 U.S.C.A. §§ 381–384. Extensive study by Congressional committees subsequent to that statute may be a harbinger of more legislation in this field.

2. Unless otherwise noted, all section references are to the Internal Revenue Code of 1954, as amended. Excerpts from the Code appear in the Documentary Supplement and should be read together with the relevant portions of the text. These selective excerpts are adequate for an understanding of the text and the specific problems in this chapter. The student should, however, be aware that resort to the full text of the Code, and to the Regulations, is essential for the solution of many other problems suggested by the following materials.

is not intended to provide an exhaustive view of the statutory provisions. Its purpose is to illustrate basic principles of the reach of income tax systems, areas of conflict among nations, and means for resolving such conflicts. Further, its almost exclusive emphasis is on the income tax, which by its nature gives rise to the most frequent and difficult transnational problems. You should, however, be aware that in many countries the bulk of the tax paid by an enterprise may consist of other forms of taxes. In France, for example, 70% of tax revenues come from other levies, while in Germany the turnover (sales) tax has secured more revenues than any other single tax.

Additional reading: For a comprehensive survey of this field, see the description by Owens in Chapter 11, "International Aspects of Income Taxation," of the World Tax Series, Taxation in the United States (1963), and the supplement thereto. For subsequent developments through the 1966 Foreign Investors Tax Act, see Roberts and Warren, U. S. Income Taxation of Foreign Corporations and Nonresident Aliens (1966, Supp. 1967); and Ross, United States Taxation of Aliens and Foreign Corporations: The Foreign Investors Tax Act of 1966 and Related Developments, 22 Tax L.Rev. 279 (1967); Rhodes, Income Taxation of Foreign Related Transactions (1973), is a more recent and detailed survey of the field. An International Tax Journal began publication in 1974.

A. BASES FOR INCOME TAXATION

---

1. THE BASIC PRINCIPLES: STATUS AND SOURCE

The provisions of the Internal Revenue Code on transnational aspects of income taxation reflect in varying combinations the two basic principles upon which nations assert the power to tax: status of the taxpayer, and source of the income. It is important to keep both principles in mind before ascertaining the tax consequences of a transaction. Determination of the taxpayer's status may provide a prompt answer; it may follow that all income wherever earned is taxable, or that no income is taxable. On the other hand, it may follow that only certain income is taxable. Such categories of income are frequently defined in terms of their domestic or foreign or "mixed" source.

The criteria under which an individual's or corporation's status is ascertained vary among tax systems. Statutes may refer to the citizenship, domicile, residence or country of principal earnings of a natural person; they may refer to the country of incorporation, of principal beneficial ownership, of control or of the *siège social* of a legal person. The rules in different countries governing source of income also reflect important differences in approach. They tend to be quite specific and to define separately the source of different kinds of income: dividends, interest, sales profits and so on.

Almost all tax systems contain elements of the status and source principles. To some extent, the principle which a nation stresses in taxing income of a transnational character depends upon which of two basic categories of tax systems it falls within. These categories are frequently described as the "global" (or "unitary") and the "schedular." [3] Global systems draw relatively few distinctions among different kinds of income (dividends, rents, business operations, mining) and tend to subject them to taxation at the same rate. The United States, the United Kingdom and Germany are classified as the principal global systems, even though their tax codes do distinguish between some kinds of income, such as ordinary income and capital gains. Schedular systems draw many such distinctions (dividends, sale of goods, professional services and so on). Some European countries (principally Italy) and a large number of Latin American countries are classified among the schedular jurisdictions.

Global systems often stress the status of the taxpayer as the key to income taxation. Once linked to the taxing country by citizenship, residence or some other test, the taxpayer must generally pay a tax on his global income. Schedular systems are more apt to differentiate between foreign and domestic income and to require a "domestic" taxpayer to pay a tax only on his domestic source income. Many global jurisdictions are industrialized, capital-exporting countries; many schedular jurisdictions are less developed, capital-importing countries.

With some exceptions, one can describe the basic structure of the Internal Revenue Code by reference to the guiding principles of status and source. (1) United States citizens, resident aliens and domestic corporations (organized within the United States) are subject to taxation on their global income. (2) Non-resident aliens and foreign corporations (not organized within the United States) are subject to taxation only on their domestic source income. The Code achieves this result through a series of provisions which curtail an initial sweeping assertion of the tax power. Note Sections 1, 11, 61 and 63. To draw upon the illustration of Justice Jackson in Lauritzen v. Larsen, p. 954, supra, these provisions would subject to United States taxation the income earned by the owner of a Chinese junk carrying freight in Chinese territorial waters.

QUESTIONS

(1) What considerations would cause a government to withdraw from as bold an assertion of the power to tax as Sections 1, 11, 61 and 63 of the Code express? Are they comparable to those which led the Court in Lauritzen to pare down the scope of the Jones Act?

(2) What difficulties does the division of the world into developed and less developed segments, capital exporters and capital importers, present

3. See generally Norr, Jurisdiction to Tax and International Income, 17 Tax L.Rev. 431, 432–435 (1962).

for a mutually satisfactory solution of such problems as the taxation of dividends or interest on foreign investment?

(3) Recall the comparison between schedular and global systems of taxation. Does the tendency of the less developed countries to use a schedular system make good sense in terms of the revenue needs of such countries? In terms of the administration of their tax laws?

NOTE ON CRITERIA FOR ASCERTAINING THE STATUS OF A TAXPAYER AND ON SOME CONSEQUENCES OF STATUS

This Note and the cases following it examine some of the ways of ascertaining the tax status of natural and legal persons, and the various consequences which flow from a taxpayer's classification within a particular status.

(1) Natural Persons

It follows from Sections 1, 61 and 63 of the Code that United States citizens are subject to taxation on their global income. Consider the statements of the Supreme Court in Cook v. Tait, 265 U.S. 47, 44 S.Ct. 444, 68 L.Ed. 895 (1924), sustaining such a basis for taxation. The 1921 Revenue Act imposed a tax upon the net income of citizens and residents of the United States. An implementing regulation provided that citizens "wherever resident, are liable to the tax. It makes no difference that they may own no assets within the United States and may receive no income from sources within the United States." In this action to recover taxes paid, the plaintiff was a citizen who became domiciled in Mexico and earned income from real and personal property in that country. In affirming a judgment for defendant collector, the Court, by JUSTICE MCKENNA, stated in part:

> The question in the case, and which was presented by the demurrer to the declaration is, as expressed by plaintiff, whether Congress has power to impose a tax upon income received by a native citizen of the United States who, at the time the income was received, was permanently resident and domiciled in the city of Mexico, the income being from real and personal property located in Mexico.
>
> Plaintiff assigns against the power, not only his rights under the Constitution of the United States, but under international law, and in support of the assignments cites many cases. It will be observed that the foundation of the assignments is the fact that the citizen receiving the income and the property of which it is the product are outside of the territorial limits of the United States. These two facts, the contention is, exclude the existence of the power to tax. Or to put the contention another way, to the existence of the power and its exercise, the person receiving the income and the property from which he receives it must both be within the territorial limits of the United States to be within the taxing power of the United States. The contention is not justified, and that it is not justified is the necessary deduction of recent cases. In United States v. Bennett, 232 U.S.

299, 34 S.Ct. 433, 58 L.Ed. 612, the power of the United States to tax a foreign-built yacht owned and used during the taxing period outside of the United States by a citizen domiciled in the United States was sustained. The tax passed on was imposed by a tariff act, but necessarily the power does not depend upon the form by which it is exerted.

It will be observed that the case contained only one of the conditions of the present case, the *property* taxed was outside of the United States. . . .

We may make further exposition of the national power as the case depends upon it. It was illustrated at once in United States v. Bennett by a contrast with the power of a state. It was pointed out that there were limitations upon the latter that were not on the national power. The taxing power of a state, it was decided, encountered at its borders the taxing power of other states and was limited by them. There was no such limitation, it was pointed out, upon the national power, and that the limitation upon the states affords, it was said, no ground for constructing a barrier around the United States, "shutting that government off from the exertion of powers which inherently belong to it by virtue of its sovereignty."

The contention was rejected that a citizen's property without the limits of the United States derives no benefit from the United States. The contention, it was said, came from the confusion of thought in "mistaking the scope and extent of the sovereign power of the United States as a nation and its relations to its citizens and their relation to it." And that power in its scope and extent, it was decided, is based on the presumption that government by its very nature benefits the citizen and his property wherever found, and that opposition to it holds on to citizenship while it "belittles and destroys its advantages and blessings by denying the possession by government of an essential power required to make citizenship completely beneficial." In other words, the principle was declared that the government, by its very nature, benefits the citizen and his property wherever found and therefore has the power to make the benefit complete. Or, to express it another way, the basis of the power to tax was not and cannot be made dependent upon the situs of the property in all cases, it being in or out of the United States, nor was not and cannot be made dependent upon the domicile of the citizen, that being in or out of the United States, but upon his relation as citizen to the United States and the relation of the latter to him as citizen. . . .

The United States has placed so great an emphasis upon citizenship as a basis for taxation that the amendments to the Code made by the Foreign Investors Tax Act of 1966 (FITA) went so far (Section 877) as to impose special burdens for ten years on "expatriates", i. e. persons who abandon their American citizenship, if their expatriation has "for one of its principal purposes the avoidance of taxes." The chief thrust of that section is to make certain that expatriates do not pay less taxes on their U. S. source income than do citizens. On the other hand, the United States has occasionally, as in Section 911, relented to the point of abstaining from fully taxing the foreign income of its citizens.

Residence in the United States is also a basis for the imposition of taxes.[4] Thus resident aliens are subject to taxation on their global income in the same manner as citizens. A few relatively limited differentiations between the two classes are stated in Sections 891, 893 and 901(b)(3). In the practice of foreign countries, one finds residence used more frequently than citizenship as a link justifying taxation of foreign source income. Indeed, reliance upon citizenship alone is relatively rare.

For nonresident aliens, the source rules become critical, since such aliens are taxed only on their United States source income. Prior to the FITA, nonresident aliens were divided into three categories: (1) those "engaged in trade or business" in the United States, who were taxed on their United States source income in much the same way as resident taxpayers; (2) those not "engaged in trade or business," who were taxed only on their "fixed or determinable annual or periodical gains, profits and income" and on their "capital gains" and who paid a tax at a flat 30% of such income without deductions so long as their United States source income did not exceed a certain amount ($21,400 immediately before the FITA); (3) those not engaged in trade or business whose United States source income exceeded the cut-off figure and who were taxed only on their fixed or determinable income from United States sources as were taxpayers in category (2), but at graduated rates and with ordinary deductions comparable to those of category (1) nonresidents. The FITA substituted for such categories, which seemed to involve different statuses of taxpayers, a division into different categories of income, discussed at p. 1102, infra.

(2) Corporations

Like citizens and residents, domestic corporations are taxed on their worldwide income. Section 7701(a)(4) defines a corporation to be domestic if it is "created or organized in the United States or under the law of the United States or of any State or Territory". Section 7701(a)(5) defines other corporations to be "foreign".

In general the Code treats the foreign source income of domestic corporations in the same manner as domestic source income, subject to such basic relief provisions as the foreign tax credit, p. 1121, infra. There are, however, a number of special rules. For example, Sections 921 and 922 accord preferential treatment to the income of so-called "Western Hemisphere Trade Corporations." Although these provisions were initially intended to promote investment in Latin America, it appears that most corporations qualifying under Section 921 have been domestic subsidiaries purchasing goods from their domestic

4. The term "residence" has been defined as related to, but less substantial than, the common law concept of domicile. Treas.Reg. § 1.871–2(b). See the discussion of domicile and residence at pp. 14–18, supra.

parents for resale to foreign customers.[5] Corporations engaged in mineral extractive industries have also found the Western Hemisphere Trade Corporation an attractive way of doing business.

Before the FITA the Code divided foreign corporations into categories much as it did nonresident alien individuals: (1) corporations "engaged in trade or business" in this country and (2) those not so engaged. Class (1) corporations were taxed at regular corporate rates on all their United States source income. Class (2) corporations paid a flat 30% tax only on their fixed or determinable income. The FITA substituted for this "status of taxpayer" scheme one stressing categories of United States source income parallel to those established for individual nonresident aliens. The effects of that change are discussed at p. 1102, infra.

The criterion of place of incorporation, like that of citizenship for natural persons, is not employed by most other countries as a basis for taxation of a corporation's worldwide income. Compare with the American approach those of the English and German tax cases which follow. Note that foreign systems frequently categorize as domestic corporations those which meet any one of several tests, such as having a "seat" or "place of management" within the country. For example, Italy taxes the global income of a corporation formed in Italy, or having its head office there, or carrying on the principal activities of its enterprise there. World Tax Series, Taxation in Italy 5/2.2 (1964).

QUESTIONS

(1) Do you find the imposition of taxes on the income of a citizen domiciled and earning income abroad more or less difficult to justify than the obligations of citizenship that were considered in Blackmer v. United States, p. 862, supra and Gillars v. United States, p. 866, supra?

(2) Are you persuaded by the emphasis in Cook v. Tait upon the "benefits" that the taxpayer derived by virtue of his citizenship as a justification for the tax? If one were to accept this "benefit" theory as the sole justification for the tax, should not the Congress or the courts engage in a more rigorous analysis to determine precisely what benefits a nonresident citizen, earning income abroad, receives? How would you identify them, compared with the "benefits" of Americans domiciled and earning income in the United States?

(3) Do you find the imposition of the tax on a resident alien's global income more or less easy to justify than the tax of like scope upon nonresident citizens?

(4) Ames, an American citizen, is an actor who spent the years 1970 and 1971 working on movies in Spain, Italy and Greece. His earned income in each of those years was $50,000. In 1970 he earned $5,000 from dividends on stock issued by domestic and foreign corporations, and in 1971 he earned $20,000 as royalties based upon a 1965 movie made in Hollywood that he had participated in. To what extent is this income subject to United States taxation?

5. One example is the business of plaintiff corporation in A. P. Green Export Co. v. United States, p. 1097, infra.

(5) What considerations do you infer motivated the partial exemption of foreign-source income stated in Section 911, and the limitations on that exemption?

DE BEERS CONSOLIDATED MINES, LTD. v. HOWE

House of Lords, 1906.
[1906] A.C. 455.

LORD LOREBURN, L. C. My Lords, the question in this appeal is whether the De Beers Consolidated Mines, Limited, ought to be assessed to income tax on the footing that it is a company resident in the United Kingdom. . . .

Under the 2nd section of the Income Tax Act, 1853, Sched. D, any person residing in the United Kingdom must pay [tax] on his annual profits or gains arising or accruing to him "from any kind of property whatever, whether situate in the United Kingdom or elsewhere," and also "from any profession, trade, employment, or vocation, whether the same shall be respectively carried on in the United Kingdom or elsewhere." Now it is easy to ascertain where an individual resides, but when the inquiry relates to a company, which in a natural sense does not reside anywhere, some artificial test must be applied.

Mr. Cohen propounded a test which had the merits of simplicity and certitude. He maintained that a company resides where it is registered, and nowhere else. If that be so, the appellant company must succeed, for it is registered in South Africa.

I cannot adopt Mr. Cohen's contention. In applying the conception of residence to a company, we ought, I think, to proceed as nearly as we can upon the analogy of an individual. A company cannot eat or sleep, but it can keep house and do business. We ought, therefore, to see where it really keeps house and does business. An individual may be of foreign nationality, and yet reside in the United Kingdom. So may a company. Otherwise it might have its chief seat of management and its centre of trading in England under the protection of English law, and yet escape the appropriate taxation by the simple expedient of being registered abroad and distributing its dividends abroad. The decision of Kelly C.B. and Huddleston B. in the Calcutta Jute Mills v. Nichols and the Cesena Sulphur Co. v. Nicholson [citation omitted], now thirty years ago, involved the principle that a company resides for purposes of income tax where its real business is carried on. Those decisions have been acted upon ever since. I regard that as the true rule, and the real business is carried on where the central management and control actually abides. . . .

The case stated by the Commissioners gives an elaborate explanation of the way in which this company carried on its business. The head office is formally at Kimberley, and the general meetings have always been held there. Also the profits have been made out of diamonds raised in South Africa and sold under annual contracts to a syndicate for delivery in South Africa upon terms of division of profits realised on resale between the company and the syndicate. And the annual contracts contain provisions for regulating the market in order to realise the best profits on resale. Further, some of the directors and life governors live in South Africa, and there are directors' meetings at Kimberley as well as in London. But it is clearly established that the majority of directors and life governors live in England, that the directors' meetings in London are the meetings where the real control is always exercised in practically all the important business of the company except the mining operations. London has always controlled the negotiation of the contracts with the diamond syndicates, has determined policy in the disposal of diamonds and other assets, the working and development of mines, the application of profits, and the appointment of directors. London has also always controlled matters that require to be determined by the majority of all the directors, which include all questions of expenditure except wages, materials, and such-like at the mines, and a limited sum which may be spent by the directors at Kimberley.

The Commissioners, after sifting the evidence, arrived at the two following conclusions, viz.:—(1.) That the trade or business of the appellant company constituted one trade or business, and was carried on and exercised by the appellant company within the United Kingdom at their London office. (2.) That the head and seat and directing power of the affairs of the appellant company were at the office in London, from whence the chief operations of the company, both in the United Kingdom and elsewhere, were, in fact controlled, managed, and directed.

These conclusions of fact cannot be impugned, and it follows that this company was resident within the United Kingdom for purposes of income-tax, and must be assessed on that footing. I think, therefore, that this appeal fails. . . .

DECISION OF DECEMBER 18, 1963

Federal Finance Court (Federal Republic of Germany), 1963.
79 Entscheidungen des Bundesfinanzhofs 57.

[The taxpayer was a Japanese corporation with its seat and place of business management in Tokyo. Its stock was 99% owned by a German corporation, and German citizens resident in Japan managed it. Under the then German tax law a corporation was resident if either its seat or place of management was in Germany; if a corporation was resident it was taxable (subject to various exceptions) on its world-wide income. See World Tax Series, Taxation in Germany 711, 2208 (2d Ed. 1969).[6]

A provision (§ 15, par. 2 of the Law for the Adaptation of Taxes) stated that a legal entity, although separate according to civil law rules, may be treated as having its seat or place of management for tax purposes at the place in Germany where its parent is located if "from an economic point of view it represents a separately administered operation within the framework of an enterprise." German officials thus treated the corporation as subject to tax on all its income. The taxpayer appealed to the Federal Finance Court, asserting (1) that the law authorizing such taxation violated an international law rule within the meaning of Article 25 of the Basic Law, p. 623, supra, and (2) that the law, issued in 1934, represented National Socialist "arrogance" and thus was not applicable after 1945.

The Finance Court rejected these contentions, deciding that it was not even called upon to obtain an opinion of the Constitutional

6. Note that in 1972 West Germany enacted a new International Tax Reform Law, [1972] BGB1 1713, which abolished the system referred to in this case and substituted for it a system like that of the United States in which subsidiaries incorporated abroad pay no German tax. See Landwehrmann, International Corporate Taxation in Germany, 15 Harv. Int.L.J. 238 (1974).

Court under Article 100 of the Basic Law, p. 623, supra, since it regarded the international law question as not seriously debatable. Excerpts from its opinion follow:]

Article 25, Basic Law concedes to "general principles of international law" the character of internal law and priority over statutes. . . . If there exists a general rule of international law which is irreconcilable with § 15 par. 2 of the Law for the Adaptation of Taxes, then the former has priority under Art. 25 Basic Law. Thus there must exist a discernible principle under international law that a corporation with its place of management and seat abroad and with legal separateness cannot represent a business separately managed within the framework of a domestic enterprise. Such a general rule of international law is, however, not recognizable.

On the question whether international law limits the effective scope of the state's jurisdiction at all, especially in relation to taxation, Hensel (Tax Law 2d ed. Berlin 1927, p. 14) says: "The tax laws of the individual states coexisting under international law are basically unrestricted; accordingly there exists for them no legal restraint on extending their tax consequences as far as they wish. Of course each state will, in its own interest, accept certain limitations. . . ." Isay (International Tax Law, Stuttgart-Berlin 1934) argues for a strict international law application of the equivalence theory and believes that public duties may only be imposed upon the alien in relation to his enjoyment of benefits from the state. The state violates its limits if it imposes duties on the alien which exceed the quantum of an equivalent of the state benefits conferred on it. Taxes which exceed this limit are illegal. . . . For a global taxation of a legal person that state has jurisdiction in which the place of administration of the legal person is located. . . . This view of the law is to be respected as an academic opinion without its being regarded as representing predominant practice or the international law. . . . One must assume . . . that there exists as yet no general law, that is no law recognized by all of the states belonging to the international law community, in the area of taxation affecting international affairs. . . .

It must also be admitted that in the application of the statute in the context of German taxation difficulties may arise. For the present question whether a prescription of national tax law is superseded by a rule of international law, the question of enforceability is not decisive. . . . There is at least no international law rule which stands in the way of the issuance of a rule that is hard to enforce.

It may also be conceded that the "organ theory" [that a subsidiary is an organic part of the parent] has made no headway in tax law outside Germany. [The court then discussed various resolutions of international conferences on taxation and various double-taxation treaties].

It is also true that, contrary to the views of the Federal Finance Minister, the American Revenue Act 1962[7] and the English Finance Act 1957 avoid imposing duties upon the foreign corporations that are dominated by domestic corporations . . . and only tax the domestic companies. But even this fact is not proof that there exists a principle of international law that forbids the subjection of the foreign subsidiary to German corporation tax.

7. [Eds.] For an exposition of the provisions of the 1962 Act to which the court refers, see pp. 1112–1116, infra.

QUESTIONS

(1) The De Beers opinion notes that the test used is not as simple or clear as the American test. Should simplicity and clarity here be dominant considerations?

(2) How evasion-proof is the English or German test? How could a corporation organize its administration and operations so as to avoid the thrust of the opinions in the preceding cases?

COMMENT

Given the fact that the American and many other tax systems distinguish between domestic and foreign source income, particularly with reference to nonresident aliens and foreign corporations, the definition of "source" becomes critical. Not surprisingly, working out such a definition is not an easy matter. It is doubly difficult to develop an internationally acceptable set of definitions that might serve to curb exorbitant national claims. The problem is comparable to that of determining whether a country is entitled to regulate transnational conduct because it has its origin or impact or effect within it, an issue raised by such cases as United States v. Aluminum Co. of America, p. 1006, supra. Which countries are sufficiently involved to levy taxes on the income of an enterprise which pays dividends to an investor in Country A out of its activity of buying goods in B, processing them in C and selling them in D? Note how much more likely it is that there will be several overlapping assertions of a taxing power than of a regulatory power in fields such as antitrust.

We start our study of the application of source concepts with the American rules. These are stated in Sections 861 to 864. The detail and precision of those provisions are such as to leave relatively little room for judicial interpretation. Under earlier versions there was more. Thus in De Ganay v. Lederer, 250 U.S. 376, 39 S.Ct. 524, 63 L.Ed. 1042 (1919), the Court had to construe a tax imposed upon net income "from all property owned . . . in the United States by persons residing elsewhere." De Ganay, a French citizen and resident, owned securities of domestic corporations and bonds and mortgages secured by property in the United States. An agent of De Ganay in the United States held these securities under a power of attorney permitting it to reinvest the property, and remitted net income to De Ganay. The Court held that a tax was due. It rejected the argument that the maxim *mobilia sequuntur personam* applied, and that the situs of the "property" (securities) should therefore be considered to be the domicile of De Ganay in France. There were even constitutional challenges directed to the "extraterritorial" consequences of some source rules. See, e. g., United States v. Erie Ry., 106 U.S. 327, 1 S.Ct. 223, 27 L.Ed. 151 (1882), an opinion holding constitutional the imposition of a withholding tax on interest paid by a domestic transportation corporation to nonresident aliens purchasing and holding the corporation's bonds abroad and receiving interest payments there. The dissenting opinion of Justice Field concluded that the Congress lacked power to impose such a tax.

The following case suggests some of the problems posed by a relatively "simple" sales transaction, where the vendor is not simultaneously a producer. It arises in the context of one of the provisions of the Code according preferential treatment to certain foreign source income of domestic corporations—the provisions concerning the Western Hemisphere trade corporation. The court's approach is, however, characteristic of judicial interpretation of the source rules in other settings of the Code as well.

A. P. GREEN EXPORT CO. v. UNITED STATES

Court of Claims, 1960.
284 F.2d 383.

[This was a suit for refund of income taxes. Plaintiff was formed to operate as a Western Hemisphere trade corporation, the current definition of which appears in Section 921. It bought brick from its parent company which it sold to customers in Canada and Central and South America. Plaintiff maintained no sales force or business establishment abroad. It received orders at and sent offers from its headquarters in Missouri, to which acceptances were sent by customers. Goods were priced c. i. f. at the port of entry, or occasionally f. o. b. factory. Transportation costs were included in the quoted prices and were usually prepaid by plaintiff. Insurance policies were purchased by plaintiff for its benefit but were negotiable and covered the goods for some days after arrival abroad. Documents were surrendered on acceptance by the buyer. Payments were by 30-day sight drafts, frequently discounted by plaintiff's bank before acceptance.

The government took the position that plaintiff did not qualify as a Western Hemisphere trade corporation because (1) it was only exporting abroad and had no investment there, and (2) it did not meet the requirements now found in Section 921 of the Code as to the foreign source of its gross income. To this second point, the source rules of the 1939 Code, particularly those in Section 119, were relevant. The equivalent rules of the 1954 Code appear in Section 862.

The court rejected both positions. The part of its opinion, by CHIEF JUDGE JONES, relating to the second point is set forth below:]

II. Place of Sale

The place of sale is a conclusion which follows the application of the proper test to a series of commercial transactions. The choice of the proper test becomes very difficult when the effects of the determination sought go beyond the traditional area of the law of sales.

The title-passage test as determinative of where a sale has occurred, and, by reference to section 119, where plaintiff's income was derived, is open to serious criticism, for it causes the incidence of the United States tax to depend upon the vagaries of the law of sales. The time and place of passage of title to ascertained goods is subject to the consensual arrangements of the parties. Williston on Sales, sec. 259, 2d ed.; cf. Uniform Sales Act, sec. 18. This all-important consent is most frequently expressed by the parties, but if not it is determined at the time of controversy by a number of presumptions set up by the law of sales. These fairly complex rules regarding passage of title are extremely important in determining such questions as the risk of loss of goods in transit, or the rights of successive creditors, but have little or no bearing on the question of where income is earned and how it should be apportioned among the various countries in which business is conducted. . . . The title-passage test has been further criticized as imposing inequitable tax burdens on taxpayers engaged in substantially similar transactions, such as upon exporters, some of whose customers require that property in the goods passes in the United States. . . .

Whatever its weaknesses, however, the title-passage test as determinative of place of sale and source of income has been overwhelmingly adopted by the courts in recent decisions. . . . We believe no other suitable test providing an adequate degree of certainty for the taxpayer has been proposed. The use of vague "contacts" or "substance of the transaction" criteria would make it more difficult for corporations engaged in Western Hemisphere trade to plan their operations so as to receive the deductions granted them only if they derive their income from sources outside the United States. Tests based upon the destination of the property sold or on the locus of the selling activity are equally vulnerable to the charge of unfair discrimination. See United States v. Balanovski, 236 F.2d 298, at page 305.

If then the passage of title does control the place of sale and the source of income, logic demands that we specify the place where title to the goods passed. It is a black letter rule of the law of sales that title to specific goods passes from the seller to the buyer in any manner and on any condition explicitly agreed on by the parties. Amtorg Trading Corp. v. Higgins, 2 Cir., 150 F.2d 536; United States v. Balanovski, supra; Williston on Sales, sec. 259, rev. ed. (1948); cf. Uniform Commercial Code, sec. 2–401. Examination of the sales contracts before us shows that the parties expressed their intentions as follows:

> "Title to these goods and the responsibility for their shipment and safe carriage shall be in the A. P. Green Export Company until their delivery to the customer at destination."

Such a clear statement, undoubtedly binding upon the parties in an ordinary sales or contract dispute, would seem to end our inquiry into the intention of the parties. But the Government urges that the terms of shipment raise presumptions that the parties intended to pass title in the United States contrary to their stated intentions, and that we must acknowledge the effect of these presumptions. We find no merit in this contention. It is true that in some instances the shipping terms, particularly the c. i. f. (cost, insurance, and freight) transactions, indicate presumptively that title passed at the place of shipment. . . . But the authorities are agreed that these presumptions are useful in ascertaining intention only if no *express* intention of the parties appears. See Williston on Sales, supra, sec. 261, et seq., and cases cited. The Government does not suggest the expressions in the contract were fraudulent. It does maintain that we must disregard the *stated* intentions of the parties in determining where title passed because the ultimate motive for these statements was the plaintiff's desire to avoid a tax.

We believe the Government has erred in failing to distinguish two separate legal consequences flowing from the same act of expression by the parties, the consequences being the passage of title and the avoidance of a tax. Title passes in a sales transaction as a result of the mutual arrangement of the buyer and the seller, whatever the reason or motivation for the consent. It would be an unjustified distortion of this law for us to disregard the parties' stated intention to pass title outside the United States because they were principally motivated by a desire to avoid a tax. This is *not* to say that under the tax law, in an atmosphere of tax avoidance, we may not find that the passage of title no longer governs the place of sale and the source of income. The next section of our opinion covers this problem. It is perfectly clear, however, that the parties intended to pass title to the goods outside the United States; this being determinative, we find that title to the goods did pass outside the United States.

III. Tax Avoidance

We now come to the problem of tax avoidance to which we have just referred. The Government urges that we examine the transactions here in the penetrating light of Gregory v. Helvering, 293 U.S. 465, 55 S.Ct. 266, 79 L.Ed. 596, for it claims that plaintiff's principal purpose in organizing and operating the export corporation was tax avoidance.

Organizing a Western Hemisphere trade corporation does not constitute tax avoidance and the Commissioner of Internal Revenue has so ruled. . . . Neither the motives, occasion for, nor the time of the *organization* of the plaintiff corporation affects its eligibility for tax relief. The Code provisions themselves have created this new business norm, a norm motivated entirely by a tax result.

The questions concerning the methods of operating the export corporation are not so easily answered. The facts show that the plaintiff delayed the passage of title with at least one eye on the Revenue Code. See finding 25. May we, therefore, depart from the title-passage test in determining the place of sale and source of plaintiff's income? The defendant says we must and submits in support a ruling by the Commissioner which states:

> "Where the sales transaction is arranged for the primary purpose of tax avoidance, the foregoing rules [passage of title test] will not be applied. In such case, all factors of the transaction such as negotiations, execution of the agreement, location of the property and place of payment will be considered, and the sale will be treated as having been consummated at the place where the substance of the sale occurred." [G.C.M. 25131, 1947–2 Cum.Bull. 85.]

The defendant also relies on United States v. Balanovski, D.C., 131 F.Supp. 898, reversed in part, 2 Cir., 236 F.2d 298, 306, certiorari denied, 352 U.S. 968, 77 S.Ct. 357, 1 L.Ed.2d 322. At first glance the Balanovski case seems to give little support to the defendant's position. There, the facts showed that goods were purchased in the United States and sold to the Argentine Government. In determining the source of income of the Argentine broker, Balanovski, the district court applied a "substance of the transaction" test and determined that Balanovski had not earned income in the United States. The Court of Appeals for the Second Circuit reversed the district court on the exact point of where the sales had taken place. It rejected the "substance of the transaction" test and rested its decision on the traditional ground of looking to the point of passage of title.

But the final passage of Judge Clark's opinion in Balanovski, supra, is notable:

> "Of course this test [title-passage] may present problems, as where passage of title is formally delayed to avoid taxes. Hence it is not necessary, nor is it desirable, to require rigid adherence to this test under all circumstances."

The Government concludes from this that in instances where passage of title is formally delayed to avoid taxes the court would feel free to look beyond the question of where title passed. Furthermore, it is suggested that the court tacitly accepted a "substance of the transaction" criterion as only by examining the indicia of substance would it be possible to decide whether passage of title was delayed merely to avoid taxes.

Along with this we must consider the statement of Judge Learned Hand in the Gregory case that "a transaction, otherwise within an exception of the tax law, does not lose its immunity, because it is actuated by a desire to avoid, or, if one choose, to evade, taxation. Any one may so arrange his affairs that his taxes shall be as low as possible; he is not bound to choose that pattern which will best pay the Treasury; there is not even a patriotic duty to increase one's taxes." 69 F.2d 809, at page 810. . . . It is undeniable that this is a doctrine essential to industry and commerce in a society like our own in which as far as possible business is always shaped to the form best suited to keep down taxes. . . . The question always is whether the transaction under scrutiny is in fact what it appears to be in form. A corporate reorganization may be illusory; a contract of sale may be intended only to deceive others. In such cases the transaction as a whole is different from its appearance. It is the intent that controls, but the intent which counts is one which contradicts the apparent transaction, not the intent to escape taxation. Chisholm v. Commissioner, 2 Cir., 79 F.2d 14.

Why the parties in the present case wished to make the sales as they did is one thing, but that is irrelevant under the Gregory case so long as the consummated agreements were no different than they purported to be, and provided the retention of title was not a sham but had a commercial purpose apart from the expected tax consequences. . . . Plaintiff's operations meet these tests. The facts show that the parties did intend title to pass outside the United States. There was no sham. Retaining title until delivery served a legitimate business purpose apart from the expected tax consequences. A moment's contemplation of the current headline disputes among countries all over the world underscores the prudence of exporters who retain title to goods until delivery. A sudden trade embargo, a seizure or a nationalization of an industry, a paralyzing nationwide strike—under these circumstances the exporter who retains title diverts his shipments with little difficulty to friendlier ports and markets. Of additional significance is the fact that retaining title permits the shipper to insure his goods in the United States. If loss occurs he can recover directly and in dollars with the obvious benefits of avoiding circuitous litigation and the fluctuations of foreign currency. . . .

Our conclusion from all of the above is that the sales were made outside the United States. However, our conclusion would be no different if we followed the defendant's suggestion and went beyond the passage of title to the other elements "of substance" in the transactions. Orders were solicited outside the United States. In every case, the contract of sale was made outside the United States; the destinations of the goods and the competitive markets for the goods were outside the United States. In most cases, the place of payment was outside the United States.

Accordingly, the plaintiff is entitled to recover its back taxes for the years 1952 and 1953, together with interest as provided by law. Judgment will be entered to that effect.

COMMENT

The American way of identifying the source of income derived from a transnational sales transaction does not meet universal acceptance. For example, compare Sections 861(a)(6) and 862(a)(7) with Chas. J. Webb Sons & Co. v. Commissioner of Income Tax, 18 Inc.Tax Rep. 33 (East Punjab High Ct.1949). The problem in that case arose under Section 42 of the Indian Income-tax Act, which provided in part that "[a]ll income . . . arising . . . from any business connection in British India . . . shall be deemed to be income accruing or arising within British India . . . . In the case of a business of which all the operations are not carried out in British India, the profits . . . deemed . . . to accrue or arise in British India shall be only such . . . as are reasonably attributable to that part of the operations carried out in British India." [8] The court held that the purchase by a foreign company of wool as raw material for use in manufacturing carpets outside India was an "operation" under the statute which gave rise to profits in India. It stressed that the "wise purchase" of raw materials would be largely responsible for the extent of the profits, and noted the fallacy in regarding profits as arising solely at the place of sale.

QUESTIONS

(1) Does the rule in the Green case seem too rigid and mechanical from the point of view of the American interest in capturing a fair share of the revenue? Do you agree with the court's conclusion that the retention of title "served a legitimate business purpose"?

(2) What seems to account for the different emphasis of Indian and United States law?

(3) Under generally accepted accounting principles, income is not realized until goods are sold and title passes. Is that principle helpful in finding an appropriate solution to this problem?

(4) From an economic point of view, how different is the situation if the foreign firm made the wool into carpets in India and then sold the carpets abroad? Compare Section 863(b)(2).

8. Subsequent legislation has changed this rule. Income-tax Act, 1961, § 9(1) (Act No. 43 of 1961). For extracts of cases and the relevant background, see Ebb, Regulation and Protection of International Business 95–96 (1964); Bittker and Ebb, Taxation of Foreign Income 148–150 (2d ed. 1968).

NOTE ON SOME CONSEQUENCES OF THE STATUS AND SOURCE PRINCIPLES FOR OPERATIONS IN THE UNITED STATES OF FOREIGN BUSINESSES

To understand the tax liability of a nonresident alien or a foreign corporation, one must consider the relationship between the status and source rules. They indicate that a nonresident alien is taxed only if his income is classified as from United States sources, and that the same is true of the foreign corporation.

Since the FITA of 1966, one must divide that income into two categories in order to determine the tax payable by a foreign business on its United States source revenue. Income "effectively connected with the conduct of a trade or business within the United States" is taxed at the normal individual rate under Section 871(b) or at the normal corporate rate under Section 882. Income not so connected with a trade or business and falling within certain categories listed in Section 871(a)(1), as well as certain capital gains described in Section 871(a)(2), are taxed at a 30% rate for an individual. Section 881 has like provisions for corporations. Under Sections 1441 and 1442 the latter type of income is subject to withholding on the part of the United States payors.

Under this system an alien or foreign corporation may have two kinds of income, taxable at two different rates. Note that in shifting from a system in which the status of being engaged in trade or business was determinative of the tax owing on *all* an alien taxpayer's income, we abandoned what was called the "force of attraction" principle. This principle frequently had caused an alien to pay a higher tax on his investment income because he happened also to be engaged in business. The FITA change was designed in part to encourage foreign investment in this country by eliminating particularly burdensome aspects of the Code. It was also designed to bring us more into harmony with the practice of foreign countries and with the pattern that seemed to be emerging from treaty arrangements which we and other countries were negotiating. Consider the following remarks of Assistant Secretary of the Treasury Stanley Surrey, made when the proposals that ripened into the FITA were before the Congress: [9]

> This approach in turn leads us to two important questions. The first is that of ascertaining what are the criteria of rationality when we are seeking to frame a tax structure applicable to foreigners. Clearly we must keep in mind that we are here dealing with international tax relationships. This means we should see that any new rules are in conformity with acceptable international norms. The United States, with its large flows of capital and goods in and out of our country, has a responsibility to take a major role in developing a proper international tax framework against which the tax rules of any particular country can be considered. One basic factor in this respect is a fair and sensible allocation

9. 22 J. of Taxation 34, 37 (1965).

among the various countries of income from activities that reach across international borders. Another factor is a proper balance between the tax paid by our citizens on their U. S. income and that paid by foreigners on the same income. Still another factor is the desirability of maintaining as far as possible the free movement of capital and goods, with taxes in any country as neutral a factor as possible consistent with the domestic policies to be served by a tax system.

In distinguishing between income that is effectively connected with a trade or business and that which is not, one must be attentive to two questions. The first is whether the taxpayer is engaged in a trade or business. In general, the term implies that a corporation conducts regular and sustained activities in this country looking towards business profits. It is now defined in Section 864(b) with respect to two business situations: performing personal services for a foreign employer, and trading in securities. However, many other issues are left to resolution through case law. Several cases have concerned purchase or sale transactions, when the foreign corporation or individual is linked contractually with some person in the United States. Characterization of that person as an independent broker, agent, employee or independent vendee may be difficult but relevant to the determination whether that person's activities bring the corporation's income within Section 882 or the individual's within Section 871(b). For example, a foreign corporation is clearly engaged in trade or business if it ships goods to a warehouse in New York, where its employees negotiate sales contracts with consumers and arrange for delivery. It is not so engaged if it sells its goods to an independent New York distributor, which takes title at the foreign port of shipment and sells in this country for its own account. The variations between these extremes pose the difficult questions. These kinds of problems are related to and often affected by provisions in bilateral tax treaties which prevent one party from imposing a tax on profits of a corporation linked with the other, except on profits derived from a "permanent" establishment of that corporation within the taxing country.[10]

The second question is whether the income is effectively connected with such trade or business, a question which Section 864(c) attempts to answer. Note that under this section, the "effectively connected" concept seems to subject to taxation certain revenues which are not categorized as "United States source" income. It has been argued that this departure is more apparent than real; what happened has in effect been partial redefinition of the source rules to include income from certain transactions that, by virtue of the passage of title test, had escaped United States taxation even though the transactions were actively conducted from an American office or fixed place of business.

10. The problems at p. 1132, infra, consider simultaneously questions under Section 882 and questions of interpretation of this treaty term.

QUESTIONS

(1) Wurst, an alien residing in his home country, received $10,000 during 1974 from dividends on shares of a Delaware corporation. In addition, Wurst had a net gain of $15,000 in 1974 from purchases and sales of stock on the New York Stock Exchange. Wurst made several trips to New York in 1974, aggregating 105 days, in order to perform services as a consultant to an American advertising firm, for which he received $5,000. (Assume the $30,000 referred to above to be U. S. source income). Finally, Wurst had $20,000 of income from sources within his home country. (*a*) How much of Wurst's income is subject to United States taxation and at what rate(s)? (*b*) If Wurst had never worked in the United States, would your answer differ (and if so, how)? (*c*) Would your answer to question (*b*) be different if these events had all taken place in 1964?

(2) During 1974, Forco, a foreign corporation, maintained an office in New York from which it sold to Americans $200,000 worth of goods made by it in Europe. Its expenses related to those sales were $160,000. It also earned $5,000 from temporarily investing cash acquired by such sales in United States short term securities until the funds were needed. In addition, it obtained $30,000 from licensing to American users its American patent on a machine used by Forco in manufacturing the goods sold in the United States and elsewhere. (Assume all the above items are U. S. source income.) On how much income is Forco taxable by the United States, and at what rates?

NOTE ON SOME CONSEQUENCES OF THE STATUS AND SOURCE PRINCIPLES FOR THE FOREIGN OPERATIONS OF UNITED STATES BUSINESSES

The combination of the definitions of domestic and foreign corporations, the rules about taxation of their income and the Code's source rules has exerted a considerable influence upon the legal forms used by American businesses to conduct their foreign operations. The effect of these rules upon the taxpayer can be perceived through the following problem:

> Amco, a Delaware corporation, wishes to establish a plant in Guatador to manufacture widgets to be sold in that country. It organizes a corporation, Guatar, S.A., under Guatadorian law. Guatar builds and runs the plant. It earns a net income of $100,000 in each of the years 1969 to 1971 and a net income of $350,000 in each of the years 1972 and 1973. This income is taxed each year by Guatador at a rate of 20% and the larger portion of Guatar's after-tax earnings is reinvested in its business operations. In 1974, Guatar declares and pays a dividend of $100,000 to Amco. (*1*) Is Guatar subject to United States taxation on any of its 1969–1973 income? (*2*) Is Amco subject to United States taxation on any such income? (*3*) What are the tax consequences of the dividend payment in 1974? (The relevance of the foreign tax credit to the dividend payment is considered at p. 1121, infra.)

This example illustrates why the system of foreign operations through subsidiaries often proves advantageous. Commentators frequently describe the relevant Code provisions as permitting "tax deferral" of income earned from foreign operations. It does not follow that resort to the tax deferral method is always indicated. Note that an American corporation with a foreign subsidiary doing business abroad cannot, with a few exceptions, include that subsidiary in a consolidated return (Section 1504(b)(3)) or claim as to dividends received from that subsidiary the deduction provided by Section 243. And the income tax payable to the foreign country may be high enough to vitiate much of the benefit of deferring the United States tax, even though it is ultimately creditable against the latter tax (see p. 1121, infra). The advantages or limitations of deferral are clearly illustrated when one compares deferral with the provisions of Sections 921–922 on Western Hemisphere trade corporations which tax the income of such corporations immediately but at a reduced rate—effectively 14 percentage points less than income within the United States.

American corporations engaged in exports were given still another option in 1972 with the adoption of Sections 991–997 on the Domestic International Sales Corporation (DISC). These provisions, candidly designed to spur exports from the United States, permit the deferral of half the income from export sales so long as the earnings are invested in property used to generate further exports. The unique aspect of the DISC provisions is that they afford deferral to income that by any criterion is U. S. source and belongs to a U. S. corporation; in addition it is income that is apt to escape foreign taxation, unlike other income subject to deferral.

Given the advantages of tax deferral, what tax consequences attach to the sale by a United States shareholder of its stock in a foreign corporation or to the liquidation of that corporation? Prior to the Revenue Act of 1962, any gain resulting from a sale or a liquidation was, with few exceptions, subject to taxation at a capital gain rate, provided that the stock had been held for more than six months. Indeed it was sometimes possible for a United States parent to effect a liquidation of its foreign subsidiary under Section 332 so that no taxable gain was recognized at that point. However, Section 367 required a prior favorable ruling by the Treasury that the transaction did not have "as one of its principal purposes the avoidance of federal income taxes." The 1962 Act led to present Section 1248, p. 1116, infra, which severely curtails possibilities for reduction of taxes through foreign operations that the prior rules created.

QUESTIONS

(1) Under what circumstances would it be advantageous for a United States firm to conduct its manufacturing operations in Europe through a branch rather than a foreign subsidiary?

(2) Under what circumstances would corporate planners prefer to use a Western Hemisphere trade corporation rather than a foreign subsidiary to conduct a given type of business in a South American country?

2. SOME ABUSES OF THE STATUS AND SOURCE PRINCIPLES AND LEGISLATIVE REACTIONS TO THEM

The preceding materials suggest two techniques by which American businesses with foreign operations could lighten their domestic tax burdens. First, a domestic corporation that was involved with its foreign subsidiaries in an integrated international venture could attempt to shift as much of the income derived from that venture as possible to its foreign subsidiaries, thereby insulating that income from immediate domestic taxation. For example, a New York firm manufacturing widgets for sale abroad might establish foreign sales subsidiaries which would act as wholesalers abroad, and thereby realize smaller profits on sales to its subsidiaries than it would on higher priced sales direct to the foreign purchasers. Second, individual shareholders or a domestic corporation with interests in foreign manufacturing operations or in foreign investment securities could establish a foreign corporation to conduct the manufacturing and selling operations or to own and manage the foreign securities, thereby eliminating all United States taxation of the foreign earnings until dividend payments or liquidation.

Over the last few decades, several of these techniques have come to be viewed as inequitable, as abuses of the Code's provisions. A series of legislative and administrative measures have qualified in important ways the tax advantages previously stemming from foreign investments. The text below explores four such responses: the provisions of Section 482 relating to allocation of income and deductions; the provisions relating to foreign personal holding companies; the provisions relating to controlled foreign corporations; and the provisions dealing with foreign source income "effectively connected with" a United States office.

NOTE ON SECTION 482: ALLOCATION OF INCOME AND DEDUCTIONS

A domestic corporation involved in international trade has somewhat more leeway than a corporation acting entirely in a domestic setting in developing a business structure that will minimize its current taxes. Consider the various techniques which such a corporation (Amco) can use to sell abroad goods which it manufactures.

First, Amco could take advantage of the source rules by selling goods to its foreign subsidiary (Subco), which Subco would resell to retailers. To avoid domestic taxation, Subco's resales must be so arranged that they will be held to have taken place abroad; that is, Amco cannot simply pass title in New York to Subco, which would resell f. o. b. New York. Compare the Green Export Co. case, p. 1097, supra. Assuming that the tax rate imposed by Subco's country of incorporation or operations is lower than that of the United States,

Amco will benefit from tax deferral to the extent that it can shift abroad the income from the integrated sales operations.

To maximize foreign source and minimize domestic source revenues, Amco could also adjust prices. Suppose that Amco sells widgets to American wholesalers at $75 each, realizing income taxable in the United States of $25 on each sale. It also sells widgets to Subco at a price of $55 for resale by Subco. Thus the immediately taxable income of Amco would be $5 per widget. Subco resells at $100, realizing $45 of income not then taxable by the United States.

Such arrangements, as well as various domestic manipulations of corporate structures to minimize taxes, led to the enactment of Section 482. As inspection of its provisions shows, it is so elastic as to provide little guidance to the tax authorities or taxpayer. Attempts to clarify the matter in the Revenue Act of 1962 ended in failure and an expression of Congressional hope that the Treasury Department would use its powers to promulgate regulations under Section 482. These regulations were finally issued in 1968. For several categories of transactions, they attempt to set guidelines for determining what is an arm's length price or charge.

With respect to sales of goods, for example, these regulations have set up a hierarchy of standards by which to measure a transfer price [11]. First preference goes to a comparable arm's length transaction. However, the goods involved may be so specialized or the markets so different that no fair comparison is possible. The second choice is a method of computation which takes that margin of profit made by the purchasing corporation on goods which it resells after buying them in an arm's length transaction, and applies the same margin to the non-arm's length sale being tested. For example,[12] if X company's foreign subsidiary resells a drug bought from an unrelated German pharmaceutical firm at a 20% mark-up, a like 20% figure can be subtracted from the resale price of the drugs it obtains from its parent. Third priority goes to the "cost plus" method in which the selling corporation's costs of producing the item are computed, and an amount is then added which is equal to the margin of gross profit which the firm is achieving on arm's length sales of other products. Only if all of these approaches fail may other methods be resorted to. Surveys of practice in the area reveal wide discrepancies between the approaches of different Internal Revenue Service agents in proposing adjustments and in working out differences with the taxpayer's representatives.[13]

11. For recent decisions examining such problems, see Lufkin Foundry and Machine Co. v. Commissioner, 468 F.2d 805 (5th Cir. 1972); U. S. Gypsum Co. v. United States, 452 F.2d 445 (7th Cir. 1971); Eli Lilly & Co. v. United States, 178 Ct.Cl. 666, 372 F.2d 990 (1967).

12. These examples assume that the special provisions governing foreign base company sales income of controlled foreign corporations, p. 1113, infra, as well as the "effectively connected" provisions of the FITA, p. 1102, supra, are not applicable.

13. O'Connor and Russo, A Study of Corporate Experience with Sec. 482, The Tax Adviser, Sept. 1972, p. 526; United States Treasury, Summary of International Cases Involving Section 482 of the Internal Revenue Code (Jan. 1973).

The following problems illustrate the continuing difficulties in this field.

(1) Consider the widget sales. It may seem obvious that something is wrong about the $55–$75 discrepancy, but closer examination may justify at least part of it. The lower price for foreign sales may reflect the greater costs of Subco's selling effort in entering a new market or the lower manufacturing costs and higher wholesale mark-up of foreign competitors. Even if some $75 sales are made abroad to other wholesalers, Amco might argue that its credit experience with Subco is better than with non-affiliated wholesalers, or that it can rely on Subco to concentrate on selling only its goods whereas independent wholesalers disperse their efforts and achieve poorer results.

(2) Suppose that Amco owns ten domestic motels and Subco owns five foreign motels. Amco procures advertisements in American media with the theme, "Stop at Milton Motels." Each advertisement lists all 15 motels. Should Amco's income be charged with only a portion of the advertising expenditure? If so, is 10:5 fair? Or should one allocate those deductions according to the ratio of tourists who use the motels? The ratio of American tourists? Is it relevant that Amco's motels are well-established and fully occupied whereas Subco's are newer and under-used? The regulations say that such allocations "shall be consistent with the relative benefits intended from the services." They also provide that the district director "may make appropriate allocations to reflect an arm's length charge," allocating some of Amco's domestic advertising against the foreign subsidiary's income. Reg. § 1.482–2(b). Helpful?

(3) Subco is expanding its operations and needs funds for a one-year period. It finds that such a loan would cost 9% in the relevant foreign capital market and 6% at United States banks. Amco lends Subco $100,000, without interest, to be repaid in one year. Should interest income be imputed to Amco and interest expense deducted from Subco's income? [14] Does Section 482 give the authority to make such a change? If so, at what rate of interest? The regulations (Reg. § 1.482–2(a)) speak of a presumptive 5%.

(4) Amco has patents on a process which it uses in the United States. It informally permits Subco to use the process in its foreign operations. Should one add to Amco's in-

14. Note that any such allocation of income and deductions by United States tax authorities would not bind the authorities of Subco's country, absent treaty provisions on this point. However, allowance of deductions for Subco would become relevant when Subco is liquidated, see p. 1115, infra. Allocations of this kind also raise difficult questions under the foreign tax credit, p. 1121, infra.

come a fair royalty? Should one subtract such a royalty from Subco's income? How would one fix such a royalty? Would royalties charged to domestic licensees be a fair standard?

In addition to causing Amco to pay more tax, Section 482, if successfully applied, can upset tax planning in other ways. By changing the amount and character of income, it may cause a foreign company lending funds to its shareholders at nominal interest to have so much interest income as to become a foreign personal holding company (see below).

Further complexities arise because the foreign tax authorities involved may take a different view of what an arm's length price should be. They are inclined to suspect that the taxpayer's system is arbitrarily shifting income away from *their* jurisdictions. In particular, a taxpayer may find itself in difficulties if the United States recalculates the arm's length price (so as to allocate more income to the U. S. parent of the foreign subsidiary) for an earlier taxable year. The taxpayer must then go to the foreign taxing authorities and seek retroactive relief, which they may be quite unwilling to grant. The regulations attempt to deal with this problem, as do various tax treaties. See, for example, Article XVII(1) of the Tax Convention between the United States and the Federal Republic of Germany.* But such provisions are far from adequate. As Assistant Secretary of the Treasury Surrey, has noted, what is needed is "an internationally acceptable set of rational rules to govern the allocation of international income arising through these transactions." 24 J. of Taxation 54 (1966).

Additional reading: Miller, Proposals for Amelioration of Section 482 Allocations Affecting U. S. Taxpayers with Foreign Affiliates, 44 Taxes 209 (1966); Tillinghast, The Application of Section 482 to International Operations: Inter-Company Pricing Problems, 24 N.Y.U.Ann.Inst. on Fed. Tax. 1433 (1966).

NOTE ON FOREIGN PERSONAL HOLDING COMPANIES

Consider the following example of a form of an international business operation which would once have recommended itself under the Code's status and source rules:

> Three individual United States citizens own 75% of the shares of a Swiss corporation, Swissco, the balance being held by Swiss nationals. Swissco's assets consist entirely of shares and bonds issued by corporations of other European countries. Assuming that the withholding taxes of such other European countries on dividends or interest paid to Swissco and that the Swiss taxation of the dividend and interest income of Swissco were relatively light, what advantages to United States shareholders would flow from such an arrangement? How could such shareholders ultimately benefit from Swissco's earnings without becoming subject to United States taxation at normal progressive rates?

In the 1930's rules were developed (now appearing in Sections 551–558 [15] of the Code) to meet this particular problem. The legislative solution to some extent blurred the previously crisp distinction between domestic and foreign corporations. The new rules directly affected United States shareholders of a foreign corporation comparable in its operations to Swissco—a corporation termed under the Code a "foreign personal holding company" (FPHC). These rules extended to the foreign arena certain principles that had been developed to regulate domestic personal holding companies. When the conditions set forth below are met, United States shareholders are required to include in their gross income the "undistributed foreign personal holding company income" of the FPHC. Such income refers to the corporation's taxable income less certain deductions and adjustments. In effect, the rules treat this income as if it had been distributed as dividends to such shareholders. A foreign corporation is a FPHC if:

(1) a stated percentage (60% or 50% under varying circumstances) of its gross income constitutes "FPHC income," defined to include specified types of so-called "passive" income—principally dividends, interest, royalties and (under certain circumstances) rental income; and

(2) more than 50% in value of its outstanding stock is owned, directly or indirectly, by not more than five individuals who are citizens or residents of the United States. Certain attribution rules apply in determining whether this requirement is satisfied, so that, for example, the interposition of a closely held United States corporation in the chain of ownership would not shield an individual American taxpayer.

The FPHC provisions did open the door to taxation by the United States of domestic shareholders of foreign corporations, and produced litigation, Eder v. Commissioner, 138 F.2d 27 (2d Cir. 1943), indicating that such a step was constitutional. Nonetheless, these provisions left basically unaffected the mode of foreign operations leading to tax deferral. In particular, tax deferral continued to apply where the foreign subsidiary in question was owned not by individual Americans but by a publicly-owned American corporation, and of course when the subsidiary was not a recipient of "passive" income.

NOTE ON THE REVENUE ACT OF 1962 AND CONTROLLED FOREIGN CORPORATIONS

Background

The rules insulating foreign source income of foreign subsidiaries owned by United States corporations and citizens from United States taxation until repatriation were the subject of extensive debate in

15. These sections are not reproduced in the Documentary Supplement. The text below is intended to be self-sufficient.

the early 1960's. In part, this debate was prompted by the adverse balance of payments position of the United States. Advocates for revision of the Code urged the enactment of provisions that would subject the income of foreign corporations owned by United States nationals or residents to taxation as it was earned. They reasoned that such provisions would inhibit foreign investment at the same time that they increased governmental tax receipts. Such considerations raised difficult issues of policy, particularly whether amendments to a complex tax system were an appropriate method for dealing with balance of payments problems that had many sources and that might have a short or long duration. For one viewpoint, consider the following remarks of Assistant Secretary of the Treasury Surrey, made in reference to then pending proposals for revision of the rules of the Code governing taxation of the domestic source income of nonresident aliens: [16]

> Our balance of payments position is such that it is desirable for us at this time to obtain a higher level of foreign investment in the United States. . . . [H]ere also we can say that a change at this time is appropriate since change now is in harmony with our balance of payments program. In other words, balance of payments objectives can prompt the study of tax provisions and can properly affect the timing of desirable basic changes in tax concepts. But as far as possible, excepting measures specifically linked to a temporary period—such as the Interest Equalization Tax [17]—the basic changes should be of such a nature that it would be proper to retain the new provisions even if our balance of payments posture were to alter.

Arguments for revision of the tax laws were related to two broad themes. Both figured heavily in the extensive hearings before the Congressional committees that eventually culminated in the Internal Revenue Act of 1962.

(1) *Neutrality.* Advocates of change argued that the existing "deferral" rules departed from an asserted norm of neutrality between the tax treatment of domestic and foreign investment by United States shareholders. In view of the coupling of this deferral with relief against double taxation through the foreign tax credit under Section 902 of the Code (see p. 1121, infra), these advocates argued that shareholders investing abroad were in a more favorable position.

The business corporations and other interests supporting the existing rules sharply challenged these arguments. They stressed the additional risk incurred by foreign investment, the fact that domestic investment "benefited" to a considerably greater degree than foreign investment from domestic governmental services and the desirability of encouraging foreign investment in view of broader objectives of the foreign economic policy of the United States. They further argued that the relevant consideration was neutrality in the *foreign* country between foreign corporations operating there owned by United States

16. 22 J. of Taxation 35 (1965).

17. [Eds.] See p. 1166, infra.

citizens or corporations, or by shareholders of other countries. That is, if income of foreign corporations owned by United States shareholders were subjected to United States taxation as it was earned, even with the benefit of the tax credit such firms might not be able to compete with lower-taxed business entities (domestic to the foreign country, or owned by nationals of other foreign countries) operating in the foreign country.

(2) *Equity.* Arguments based upon tax equity were closely related to the theme of neutrality. Those urging new rules broadly asserted that it was unfair to provide more advantageous rules for Americans investing abroad. For a description and analysis of these various arguments, see the study published by the Brookings Institution: Krause and Dam, Federal Tax Treatment of Foreign Income 1–84 (1964).

The compromise between these positions that was reflected in the Internal Revenue Act of 1962 significantly changed the rules. The new rules apply directly to certain United States shareholders of certain foreign corporations, rather than to such corporations themselves. They draw important distinctions among foreign corporations with respect to the kind of business operations in which they engage and, to a lesser degree, with respect to the geographical location (developed or less developed countries) of such operations. In their most significant departure from the previous scheme, these rules treat all or part of the undistributed income of certain corporations as if it had in fact been distributed to the shareholders, and impose a tax, payable by the *shareholders,* on this attributable income. Nonetheless, the rules in essence constitute a redefinition of *corporations* which will be treated as "foreign" for purposes of the United States tax code.

The provisions of the 1962 Act reach a degree of complexity that has rarely if ever been matched in tax legislation. A comprehensive description is beyond our purpose. The text which follows is highly selective, treating only aspects of the 1962 Act that are most relevant to the related materials in this chapter and to the broad principles that the Act develops.[18] For an inclusive description, see the section written by Elizabeth Owens in World Tax Series, Taxation in the United States 1042–1080 (1963), and the supplements thereto.

The Basic Scheme: Foreign Base Company Income

The Act requires certain United States shareholders of a "controlled foreign corporation" (CFC) to include in their gross income their pro rata shares of certain income of the CFC. The basic scheme, set forth in Sections 951–972 of the Code, is described below.

A CFC is a foreign corporation in which United States shareholders own more than 50% of the voting power. Such shareholders

18. Only a few sections of the 1962 Act have been reproduced in the Documentary Supplement. Except where reference is made to such sections, the following text is intended to be self-sufficient.

are referred to as "United States persons," a category which includes citizens and residents of the United States and domestic corporations. However, in determining whether the required percentage of voting power is United States owned, only those United States persons owning (directly, indirectly or constructively) 10% or more of the voting power are counted. Thus, a foreign corporation wholly owned by United States persons would not constitute a CFC if, for example, a domestic corporation owned 50% of the voting stock, and 10 other individuals or corporations each owned 5% of the voting stock.

The only United States persons who are subject to a tax under these provisions are those owning stock representing 10% or more of the voting power. Such persons are subject to taxation on their share of certain categories of the undistributed income of the CFC. The most important category of such income is "foreign base company" (FBC) income. Expenses and deductions attributable to the FBC income are allowed, so that United States persons are in effect taxed with respect to undistributed net income. FBC income consists of:

(*a*) *Foreign personal holding company income,* which refers to "passive income" such as dividends, interest, license fees, and rents. It does not, however, include income of these types which is derived from the active conduct of a business and which is not received from "related persons" (essentially individuals or corporations affiliated with the CFC through some control relationship). Nor does it include such income as dividends or rents that is derived from a related person located in the same country, because such a transaction does not involve the business conduct that was a basic target of the CFC provisions—namely, using a "base" or "haven" country to minimize income taxes both of the United States and of the country of operations.[19]

(*b*) *FBC sales income,* which refers principally to income earned by the CFC from buying personal property from a related person (in most cases, its United States parent) and selling it to any person, *if* such property is produced *and* sold for use outside the country where the CFC is organized.

(*c*) *FBC service income,* which refers to income earned by the CFC from rendering services (managerial, engineering, commercial and so on) for or on behalf of a related person that are performed outside the country where the CFC is organized.

19. This paragraph indicates the existence of a family resemblance between the FPHC provisions and the CFC sections. Note, however, that there are important differences including (a) the different types of American shareholding required to make a corporation a CFC as opposed to a FPHC, (b) the somewhat different definitions of "tainted" income, and (c) the different consequences as to the treatment of "untainted" income which follow from the "10%–70%" (originally "30%–70%") provisions of the 1962 Act described at p. 1115, infra and from the "50%–60%" rules applicable to the FPHC, as noted at p. 1110, supra.

To fit these provisions within the general scheme of the Code, a series of technical adjustments were required. For example, any undistributed FBC income on which a United States person is subject to taxation increases the basis for his stock, while any later distributions of the CFC of amounts previously subject to tax reduce the basis of the stock and are received tax-free. Further adjustments were required with respect to the effect of the foreign tax credit, p. 1121, infra, on the undistributed FBC income that was made taxable.

These rules should make clear the kinds of foreign operations towards which the 1962 Act was directed. Unlike the broad proposals initially put to the Congress by President Kennedy, which with few exceptions would have imposed a tax on substantial United States shareholders on *all* undistributed income of a controlled foreign corporation, these rules affect primarily a limited form of business structure that had become significant—the so-called "tax haven" or "base company" structure. Consider the characteristic examples which follow and the arguments for or against permitting such kinds of foreign operations to benefit from tax deferral.

(1) Amco, a domestic corporation, owned certain patents in Europia, a European country. It transferred them to a wholly owned subsidiary, Panam, which it organized in Panama. Panam entered into a license contract with a Europian manufacturing company (Eurco), under which Eurco utilized the patents in its manufacturing operations. It paid royalties to Panam. Pursuant to a tax treaty between Europia and Panama, Europia did not impose any withholding taxes on the royalty payments. Panama did not tax its domestic corporations on foreign source income.

(2) Amco exported its manufactured products to European countries. It established a Swiss subsidiary (Swissco) to which it sold all its export production. Swissco entered into contracts with purchasers in different European countries, under which Amco's products (which would never enter Switzerland) would be shipped from a European port to such purchasers, title passing outside the United States. The profit on such resales by Swissco would be subject to relatively low taxation by Switzerland, as foreign source income.

Consider the tax advantages to Amco in setting up either of these business structures, and the ways in which Amco might ultimately utilize the income earned by Panam or Swissco. Compare the tax consequences of these arrangements before and after the 1962 Act with an arrangement under which Amco would have directly licensed its patents to Eurco or would directly have sold its production to the ultimate European purchasers.[20]

20. Another provision of the 1962 Act, now Section 1249 of the Code, further affects the first example above by providing that a United States person transferring a patent or similar property to a foreign corporation in which it owns more than 50% of the voting power is subject to taxation on any gain resulting from the transfer at ordinary income rates rather than capital gain rates. The second example above is affected by provisions of the 1962 Act appearing in Sections 970–72 of the Code. They exclude from FBC

The rules described above are subject to important qualifications simplifying or limiting the situations under which United States shareholders are taxed on their pro rata share of FBC income. Certain among them follow:

(*a*) If FBC income is less than 10% (originally 30%) of the CFC's gross income, no income of the CFC is treated as FBC income. If, however, FBC income is over 70% of the CFC's gross income, all the CFC's income is so treated.

(*b*) As the Note on p. 971, supra, indicates, tax considerations played a role in encouraging domestic firms to participate in international maritime activity by transferring ownership of their vessels to foreign subsidiaries which would register the vessels in flag-of-convenience countries. The 1962 Act contained special provisions designed to preserve the tax advantages of such international shipping arrangements, but the 1975 statute, p. 1119, infra, limited those benefits.

(*c*) Income otherwise constituting FBC income is not includible in that category if it is established to the Treasury's satisfaction that the creation of the CFC in the country which was chosen for it "does not have the effect of substantial reduction of income . . . or similar taxes." (Section 954(b)(4)).

As should be apparent, the operation of the 1962 Act involves information returns and accounting problems of a highly complex, technical and burdensome character. The Treasury Department has promulgated regulations (Treas.Reg. § 1.964) intended to make the administration of these difficult provisions as manageable as possible. The regulations, *inter alia*, attempt to develop some generally acceptable rules of international accounting with respect to the Code's references to earnings and profits, and to refine the concept of minimum distributions.[21]

Sale of Stock or Liquidation of CFC

Another provision of the 1962 Act affects a basic change in tax aspects of foreign operations. Recall that prior to that Act, a United States corporation could allow profits to accumulate in its foreign subsidiary, for reinvestment or other purposes, and could eventually sell its stock in the subsidiary or liquidate it with any gain taxed at capi-

income that income which is realized by exporting from the United States. The exclusion is limited by various safeguards designed to assure that the exemption's purpose, furthering the United States' export trade and improving its balance of payments, is realized. The most important of these safeguards is the requirement that such income be reinvested in assets needed in the export sales operation.

21. See generally the comments of Surrey in 21 J. of Taxation 358 (1964), and, in more detail Weiss, Application of American Accounting Methods to Foreign Operations, 23 N.Y.U.Ann. Inst. on Fed.Tax. 981 (1965).

tal gain rates. Section 1248, added by the 1962 Act, eliminates in many instances this advantage. It affects primarily sales by certain "United States persons" of their stock in "controlled foreign corporations," and the liquidation by a United States person of the controlled foreign corporation. The section provides that United States persons must treat any gain realized by their sale of the foreign corporation's stock or their liquidation of the corporation as a dividend, to the extent of the earnings and profits of the foreign corporation attributable to such stock that were accumulated after 1962 and during the period when the United States person held such stock. However, these provisions eliminating the favorable capital gain treatment apply only if, at any time during the five-year period ending on the date of the sale or liquidation, the corporation was a "controlled foreign corporation" and the United States person then owned 10% or more of its voting power. The section applies even though, at the time of the sale or liquidation, the United States person no longer has 10% ownership and the corporation no longer constitutes a controlled foreign corporation. The provisions of Section 1248 include a large number of adjustments made necessary by the foreign tax credit and by the other sections of the 1962 Act treating controlled foreign corporations.

After this panoramic survey of the 1962 Act, it is well to consider whether the tests used in it to "Americanize" foreign corporations are indeed radical innovations in tax legislation. One would wish to compare the criteria of management and control in such cases as De Beers, p. 1093, supra, and the tests identified in the decision of the German tax court at p. 1094, supra. One should also review illustrations in other chapters of emphasis upon the country (or upon persons within it) to which the beneficial ownership or control of a corporation can be principally attributed.[22] Note the varying pertinence of ownership or control to these statutes or principles. Sometimes the purpose of resort to these criteria is to characterize the corporation as "domestic" to entitle it to certain privileges or to subject it to special duties. Sometimes the purpose is to characterize the corporation as "alien" to deny it certain privileges or subject it or its shareholders to special duties.

22. For example, compare with CFC provisions of the Code the following statutes, decisions and general principles: (*a*) Section 310(a)(4) of the Communications Act of 1934, fn. 21, p. 76, supra; (b) Société Remington Typewriter v. Kahn, p. 79, supra; (*c*) In re Oil Industry Association, Ltd., Cracow, p. 79, supra; (*d*) Section 172, Restatement (Second), Foreign Relations Law of the United States, p. 239, supra; (*e*) the relevance of the *siège social* to choice of law, pp. 96–99, supra; (*f*) the relevance of the *siège social* to Articles 14 and 15 of the French Civil Code, p. 752, supra; (*g*) Sections 5(b) and 9(a) of the Trading with the Enemy Act as applied in Société Internationale v. Rogers, p. 844, supra; (*h*) the criminal statute applied in United States v. Flores, p. 860, supra; (*i*) United States v. Aluminum Co. of America, p. 1006, supra; and (*j*) SEC rule 12g–3, p. 1057, supra.

QUESTION

A CFC operates in Europia, a European country. Under the provisions of the 1962 Act, the United States imposes a tax on the earnings of the CFC by attributing them to its United States shareholders. (1) Would Europia have any practical motivations to protest to the United States that the 1962 Act has an exorbitant extraterritorial character and violates European sovereignty? (2) Would such a claim appear to be substantial?

COMMENT

The Foreign Investors Tax Act of 1966, like the 1962 Act, reached out to tax a class of persons who were establishing corporations or branches in a tax haven to minimize their international tax burden. However, in the case of the FITA, the haven in question was the United States. Typical of the transactions aimed at was a situation in which a European corporation maintained an American branch from which it made sales to South America. No United States tax was payable, under the prevailing status and source rules. In many cases the taxes of the European and South American countries were also avoided in whole or in part. Provisions introduced into the Code by the FITA (Sections 864(c), 872(a) and 882(a)) cause such sales to be subject to United States tax to the extent that they are "effectively connected with the conduct of a trade or business within the United States" involving "an office or other fixed place of business within the United States," and otherwise come within the terms of Section 864(c). Also, some sales to customers within the United States that previously would have been exempt from United States tax because title passed abroad (the converse of the situation in A. P. Green Export Co. v. United States, p. 1097, supra) are now taxed if the sales were through such offices. Some royalty or investment income is also reached by these provisions. Thus the concept of "effectively connected," introduced by the FITA to determine whether United States source income should be taxed as investment income or business income, is also used to reach some income of foreigners or foreign corporations which was previously exempt since classified as having a foreign source.

One final problem that is relevant to many provisions of the Code treating foreign income should be noted. Foreign income will of course generally be earned in foreign currency. But to determine the tax bill payable to the United States, the taxpayer must convert earnings in rupees, pounds or pesos into dollars. These problems of conversion can raise vexing questions: the date at which the conversion should be deemed to have taken place, the rate of conversion to use if there are both official and unofficial exchange rates of the foreign currency, and so on. Additional problems arise when foreign earnings are "blocked"—that is, when they are not convertible into dollars at all, because of exchange controls imposed by the foreign country. Under such circumstances, provisions of the Code permit a taxpayer to defer his domestic tax liability until the foreign income becomes readily convertible. These problems of multiple exchange rates or blocked currencies can become particularly troublesome in connection with the provisions of the Code treating controlled foreign corporations or the foreign tax credit.[23]

NOTE ON PROPOSED CHANGES

As of 1975, there were undercurrents in motion which threatened to bring about some basic changes in United States taxation of foreign income. Arguments and proposals rather like those of 1962 were being expounded with new vigor. Basically what was involved was the sense, most strongly held by American labor unions, that investment abroad by American business, profitable though it may be for the investor, was not in the best interest of the United States as a whole.

That argument breaks down into the following categories: (*1*) Investment abroad in manufacturing facilities substitutes foreign production for exports from United States plants—and may even result in imports into this country. One consequence is harm to the United States balance of payments. (*2*) The movement of plants abroad costs United States workers jobs which are given to foreigners. Many of the American workers involved are unskilled and live in depressed areas so that it is difficult to find substitute work for them. (*3*) The United States Treasury, after account is taken of the foreign tax credit, receives little from taxes on foreign operations by United States firms. Although there are counterarguments, vigorously presented by American industry, many have come to hold these positions.

This thinking came to the surface most conspicuously in the Hartke-Burke bill, S. 151 and H.R. 62, 93rd Cong. 1st Sess. 1973.[24] That bill attacked the foreign investment problem on several fronts, including import restrictions and restraints on technology outflow. One part of the bill drastically changes the tax position of foreign investments by eliminating deferral and the foreign tax credit. The first elimination thus would return to the theme of the original 1962 proposal that led to the controlled foreign corporation rules. The second is more significant to the companies concerned, since it would leave them with a mere deduction for foreign taxes. Largely as a reaction to the Hartke-Burke proposals, a bill was introduced that would withdraw deferral treatment from certain investments. Corporations making investments in plants constructed abroad, in order to take advantage of foreign countries' tax incentives or low labor costs, would be taxed on those earnings immediately.

If enacted, these provisions would repeat the 1962 pattern—retention of the general deferral concept at the expense of rapidly in-

23. These problems are exhaustively treated in Ravenscroft, Taxation and Foreign Currency (1973).

24. See Stone, United States Tax Policy toward Foreign Earnings of Multinational Corporations, 42 Geo.Wash. L.Rev. 557 (1974); Fisher, The Multinationals and the Crisis in United States Trade and Investment Policy, 53 B.U.L.Rev. 308 (1973).

creasing complexity in growing "exceptions". Note that at the same time the escalating price of oil has drawn attention to the petroleum industry and to its special, allegedly overprotected, tax situation. The Tax Reduction Act of 1975 changed special features of the taxes levied on foreign oil production and transportation and made other changes, the effect of which was to diminish the profitability of investment abroad.

B. ACCOMMODATION AMONG NATIONAL TAX SYSTEMS: UNILATERAL AND BILATERAL TECHNIQUES

The application of the tax laws of one nation to persons or transactions linked with other nations as well often leads to problems of overlapping or so-called "double" taxation. Indeed, the same interplay among different tax systems may occasionally result in the escape of certain income from all the tax systems involved, a phenomenon exploited by the base company operations of American firms that were briefly described at p. 1114, supra. These problems of "overlap" or "underlap" may arise because nations use explicitly different principles as bases for income taxation. One may refer principally to the geographical source of income, a second to the state of incorporation of the taxpayer, a third to the *siège social* of the corporate taxpayer. Or they may arise because two countries, although using what appears to be the same approach to income taxation, may read different meanings into the same label. For example, two countries following a source principle limiting the national tax power to domestic source income may follow different rules in determining the source of income from an international sales transaction. Even if all these legal differences can be adjusted through uniform national rules, inconsistent accounting concepts can allocate items of income or expense to different periods or to different parts of an international corporate family so as to produce inconsistent tax results.

Whatever the reasons, these relationships among the several tax systems which may be involved in a given business operation may well affect the volume or channels of international business. Part B examines the principal techniques used by nations to regulate these problems, and treats primarily the questions posed by double taxation.

Consider the possible meanings, rarely kept distinct by the courts or commentators, which that phrase can bear. (*1*) Is there double taxation simply because two countries impose taxes relating to income from the same transaction, perhaps an international sale or dividend payment? Does, in other words, the "double" mean only that two tax authorities are involved, without consideration of the aggregate tax burden? (*2*) If one stressed the actual tax burden, is there double taxation when nation X imposes a 15% withholding tax on dividends paid by a corporation in X to a corporation in nation Y, and Y imposes a tax at a rate of 15% on foreign dividend income—if the same dividend income paid entirely within either country would have been subject to a tax on the recipient at a rate of 40%? (*3*) Before one can protest against double taxation, should the total tax burden under X and Y law involve a tax liability greater than that which would have been incurred under X *or* Y law, if all relevant events and persons had been located in either X or Y?

Apart from these questions, there remains the problem of how broadly one defines the single transaction which allegedly gives rise to double taxation. An international dividend payment or international sales transaction or the business operations of a foreign branch are fairly clear examples of situations where two tax systems may assert claims against a unified transaction or business operation. Suppose however, that a foreign subsidiary is subject to an income tax in its country of incorporation, and that its dividend payments out of retained earnings to the parent are then subject to tax on the parent in its country. Can one still talk meaningfully of double taxation?

Whatever the difficulty in giving a satisfactory definition to this phrase, the cumulative tax burden frequently appears to be oppressive under any test. For this reason, nations have been able to make up their minds to take steps to mitigate the burden.

Some of these steps, perhaps the most important, have been unilateral. Appendix B (by Mills and Gumpel) to Federal Tax Treatment of Foreign Income, a booklet published in 1964 by the Brookings Institution, indicates the variety of techniques which nations here follow. The more significant among them are:

> **(1)** Countries which follow a relatively pure schedular system (see p. 1088, supra), today primarily Latin American countries, distinguish among different categories of income both with respect to the nature of the income (from an active business, from dividends) and with respect to the geographical source of the income. Such systems frequently exempt foreign source income, both of residents and nonresidents. When two such systems are involved their schedular principles may eliminate the possibility of double taxation in its simplest meaning.
>
> **(2)** A large number of countries, including leading European countries, have special provisions for the foreign source income of resident individuals or corporations. These systems frequently provide for a complete exemption from local income taxation of defined categories of such foreign income. Sometimes they afford partial relief by applying lower tax rates to such income. The rules vary a great deal. For example, the exemption in some countries of certain categories of foreign business income applies only if the income is generated by a "permanent establishment" in the foreign

country. Some of the rules of the United States Internal Revenue Code that were discussed in Part A reflect this approach. The distinctions drawn by the source rules (Sections 861–863) affect primarily foreign corporations and nonresident aliens, but to some extent they also affect United States citizens and domestic corporations (Sections 911, 921 and 922).

(3) A number of countries which impose a tax on global income earned by residents or domestic corporation or other persons—particularly the United States, the United Kingdom, Japan and West Germany—approach the problem by providing for a deduction from taxable income of foreign income taxes or for a credit for taxes (primarily on income) paid to a foreign country to be applied against the domestic tax bill. The conditions under which the credit may be taken vary considerably. Further, certain countries which have a foreign tax credit also rely upon alternative or cumulative provisions exempting certain foreign income of residents from local taxation.

In addition to these unilateral solutions, the tax treaty represents an increasingly important technique for limiting the national tax power through bilateral arrangements. Some 200 treaties, it is estimated, attack the problems of double or overlapping taxation by providing for the surrender, generally by the source country, of the right to tax certain income or by creating or confirming through the treaty the right to a foreign tax credit against taxes imposed by the country of origin of the taxpayer. Part B of this chapter considers the unilateral tax credit and the bilateral tax treaty as the basic techniques for adjustment.

---

1. THE FOREIGN TAX CREDIT

Since 1918, the United States tax laws have allowed a credit against the federal income tax of income and certain closely related taxes paid to foreign countries. This foreign tax credit gives rise to problems both at a general level of theory or policy and at a very practical and mechanical level. Before considering the questions of policy, one should achieve a working understanding of the operation of the credit.

PROBLEMS

The following series of problems is accompanied by references to the relevant sections of the Internal Revenue Code and by a series of computations showing how the result was reached. The problems assume a federal income tax rate of 50% and that Amcorp, the American corporation, has taxable income from its domestic as well as foreign operations.

Some of the computations with respect to Problems Four and Five require a close reading of Section 902(a) and (c) and more. These provisions are not distinguished by their clarity and require some familiarity with the legislative and judicial history of those complex and specialized provisions.

Problem One: Suppose that Amcorp receives $1,000 in dividends from a Guatadorian corporation. Guatador imposes a tax of 30% on such dividend income which it enforces by requiring the paying corporation to withhold from the dividend payment. What will the total tax burden be if Amcorp (a) deducts or (b) credits the tax? (References: Sections 164, 275, 901(a) and (b).)

	Deduction	Credit
Foreign income	1000	1000
Foreign Tax Paid	300	300
U. S. Taxable Income	700	1000
U. S. Tax before Credit		500
Credit		300
U. S. Tax (after credit, if any)	350	200
Total taxes paid	650	500

As this illustration indicates, the credit will generally be more advantageous to the taxpayer than the deduction. Under what circumstances might the deduction be preferable?

Problem Two: Suppose that Amcorp does business through branches in Hitax and Lotax. Hitax has a 60% tax rate and Lotax a 30% rate. Amcorp's total income earned in Hitax, Lotax and the United States is $3000, with $1000 being attributable to sources in each country. The American tax before a credit would therefore be $1500. What is the maximum credit that Amcorp can get? (Reference: Section 904).

Using per-country limitation:

	Hitax	Lotax
Tax paid	600	300
Limitation formula	1500 x 1000	1500 x 1000
	3000	3000
Limitation	500	500
Credit allowed	500	300
Total credit allowed	800	

Using over-all limitation:

Foreign taxes paid	900
Limitation formula	1500 x 2000
	3000
Limitation	1000
Credit allowed	900

pare the total taxes paid by Amcorp under each approach with yable if all Amcorp's income had been domestic.

blem Three: Suppose the same facts as in Problem Two t Amcorp loses $500 in Lotax and thus has a total income nd an American tax before credit of $750. What is credit that Amcorp can get?

Using per-country limitation:

	Hitax	Lotax
Tax paid	600	0
Limitation formula	$\frac{750 \times 1000}{1500}$	0
Limitation	500	0
Credit allowed	500	

Using over-all limitation:

Foreign taxes paid	600
Limitation formula	$750 \times \frac{500}{1500}$
Limitation	250
Credit allowed	250

Problem Four: Amcorp has a wholly-owned subsidiary, Guatacorp, which does business in Guatador, a less developed country, and is qualified as a "less developed country corporation".[25]

In 1974 Guatacorp has taxable income of $2,000 on which it pays an $800 tax to Guatador. In January 1975 it pays a $1,200 dividend to Amcorp, no further Guatador tax being payable. What is the amount of the tax credit to which Amcorp is entitled? Note that the limitations of Section 904 still apply. (References: Sections 902(a)(2), 902(c)(1)(B)).

Taxable dividend	$1200
U. S. tax before credit	600
Tax credit formula	$800 \times \frac{1200}{2000} \times \frac{1200}{1200}$
Tax credit	480
U. S. tax after credit	120
Total taxes paid	920

Problem Five: Assume the same facts as in Problem Four but substitute Eurocorp, a corporation operating in Europia, a developed country, for Guatacorp and Europia for Guatador. What is the amount of the tax credit to which Amcorp is entitled? (References: Sections 78, 902(a)(1), 902(c)(1)(A)).

Taxable dividend	1200
Tax credit formula	$800 \times \frac{1200}{1200}$
Tax credit	800
Dividend "grossed up" (§ 78), creating total U. S. taxable income	2000
U. S. tax before credit	1000
U. S. tax after credit	200
Total taxes paid	1000

25. The term "less developed country corporation" is elaborately defined in the Code, as of 1975 in Section 902(d), as a corporation deriving 80% or more of its gross income from sources within less developed countries and having more than 80% of its assets there. A less developed country is defined as one so designated by the President, who cannot, however, designate a country "within the Sino-Soviet bloc" or any country on a statutor list of industrialized countries.

The different definition of "accumulated profits" in Section 902(c)(1)(A) for use in Section 902(a)(1), together with the requirement of Section 78, lead to a different result in Problem Five. The tax of $800 is there related to the figure of $2,000, representing "accumulated profits", as defined.

The difficulties with the calculation of the indirect tax credit in connection with Problems Four and Five above derive from a decision, American Chicle Co. v. United States, 316 U.S. 450, 62 S.Ct. 1144, 86 L.Ed. 159 (1942), interpreting a former version of the foreign tax credit. Prior to 1962, the credit did not distinguish between developed and other countries. In American Chicle, the Supreme Court held that the taxpayer (assuming for this illustration the same facts as in Problem Four) was not entitled to a credit for the entire foreign tax paid, but only for that portion of it which related to the accumulated (i. e., the "after tax") profits (i. e., $1,200). Only such portion was to be considered "paid . . . on or with respect to the accumulated profits . . . ," a phrase retained in the 1962 amendments. The fractional computation resulting from the American Chicle rule has been described as follows by Owens, The Foreign Tax Credit 105 (1961):

$$\text{Foreign tax} \times \frac{\text{dividend}}{\text{accumulated profits}} \times \frac{\text{accumulated profits}}{\text{total profits}}$$

This fraction reduces to:

$$\text{foreign tax} \times \frac{\text{dividend}}{\text{total profits}}$$

Section 902(a)(2) preserves for less developed countries the rule of American Chicle and must be read in the light of that case. It is advantageous to the taxpayer because there is no need to "gross up" dividends under Section 78, a requirement that obtains in Problem Five. Thus results the first of the two fractions (1200/2000) in the formula in Problem Four. The second fraction (1200/1200) results from a reading of "accumulated profits" as defined in Section 902(c)(1)(B).

Suppose that the facts are the same as in Problems Four and Five except that the foreign country imposes a withholding tax at a rate of 5% (i. e., $60) on the dividend distribution to Amcorp. Compute the total tax credit available to Amcorp.

Suppose that the facts are the same as in Problems Four and Five except that the foreign subsidiary distributes only $600 to Amcorp as a dividend. Compute the total tax credit available to Amcorp.[26]

NOTE ON POLICY ISSUES UNDER THE FOREIGN TAX CREDIT

(1) Note that the general effect of the foreign tax credit (in- the limitations of Section 904) is that the American taxpayer t to a total income tax burden at the higher of the United he foreign rate. Through the credit, the United States

above examples have, sake, assumed 100% orp of its subsidi- is, proportionate- he ownership is 10%. Section 902(a). Further complexities arise from the permission, given by Section 902(b), to take into account taxes paid by a 50% (or more) owned subsidiary of a subsidiary.

absorbs the burden of the foreign tax. Note also that the foreign tax credit is not in any meaningful sense a departure from the global principle underlying United States taxation of the income of its citizens and domestic corporations. Rather it represents an effort to mitigate the consequences of that principle within carefully defined limits. It is often said that the purpose of the foreign tax credit is to achieve "neutrality" between taxpayers with domestic and foreign investments. Compare the following statement from Commissioner v. American Metal Co., 221 F.2d 134, 137 (2d Cir. 1955): "The primary objective of [the foreign tax credit] is to prevent double taxation and a secondary objective is to encourage American foreign trade."

(2) The foreign tax credit has special implications for the United States' policy of assisting less developed countries through its effect upon the flow of American private investment to such countries. The 1962 Act, by creating the difference between less developed and developed countries that was critical to Problems Four and Five, attempted to use the credit as an incentive. However, the credit can impede or negate certain efforts of less developed countries to attract foreign investments. Suppose that a less developed country wishes to attract foreign investment by cutting its usual 40% income tax to 10% of the income of a given project for the first few years of its operation. Note the effect upon such a policy of the United States tax credit when the parent wishes to repatriate its subsidiary's earnings by a dividend payment. The issue has arisen whether the United States should adjust its system to make effective such foreign tax incentives. A few years ago, so-called "tax sparing" clauses were proposed for treaties with Pakistan, India and the United Arab Republic but never became effective. These clauses would have allowed a foreign tax credit for taxes normally due to the less developed country but forgiven under its incentive program. Other developed countries, most significantly the Federal Republic of Germany, have made that concession.

(3) Given the diverse approaches to taxation in different countries, and the lesser weight given to an "income tax" comparable in character to the United States income tax in many countries, one can question the theory behind the limitation of the foreign tax credit to foreign "income" and closely allied taxes. The general test—the test exemplified in cases such as Commissioner v. American Metal Co., 221 F.2d 134 (2d Cir. 1955)—used to determine whether a foreign tax qualifies for the credit has been its similarity to the United States income tax. Given the ambiguity inherent even on our domestic tax scene in separating "income" taxes from other forms of taxes (with possible distinctions as to the manner in which the amount of the tax is measured, or in the title given the tax: franchise, gross receipts, privilege, etc.), it is not surprising that the cases have failed to develop a satisfactory set of criteria for characterizing the foreign tax. The consequence has been that numbers of foreign taxes which

may amount to a substantial or principal part of the American corporation's (or its foreign subsidiary's) tax burden, may not qualify for the credit, as in the American Metal Co. case.

(4) Even when the foreign tax is clearly an income tax, differences in the way in which it is applied may add complications to the application of the United States tax credit and significantly curtail its advantages for an American taxpayer. For example, a foreign country may impose a tax on income which the United States regards as having its source elsewhere. Or it may impose a tax the burden of which falls on X, an American, but which American tax classification regards as a tax on Y, a foreigner, with the consequence that no person can claim a credit. Differences in accounting practices between two systems can introduce additional complexities. For example, differences in accrual techniques or in the distinctions drawn between "expenses" and "capital improvements" would have an evident impact upon the amount of taxable income in a given year. Particularly if a year or more elapses between the earnings by a subsidiary and the dividend payment to a parent, questions of accumulated earnings and profits that are relevant to the application of Section 902 can become baffling.

(5) In general, the benefits of the foreign tax credit are intended for Americans. However, with some limitations, foreigners resident in the United States are entitled to a credit with respect to foreign source income (Section 901). The provisions of the FITA taxing foreigners on foreign source income effectively connected with a United States office have required the extension to such persons of an opportunity to credit foreign taxes (Section 906).

(6) Controversy has long surrounded the grant of a credit for amounts paid to a foreign government in connection with the production of oil. If such amounts are classified as a royalty or other compensation payable because the oil reservoir, which under local law belongs to the government, is being depleted, a mere deduction arises. If the same payment to the same government can be reclassified as an income tax and credited, a large tax saving can be generated. After a long period of favorable treatment for oil income, the 1975 Tax Reduction Act severely curtailed the credit available in such cases.

Additional reading: For a careful study of the many problems in this field, see Owens, The Foreign Tax Credit (1961). See also Surrey, Current Issues in the Taxation of Foreign Corporate Investment, 56 Colum.L.Rev. 815, 819–822 (1956); Owens and Ball, The Indirect Credit (1975).

QUESTIONS

(1) Do the 1962 Act's tax-credit provisions for less developed countries seem to be an effective way of stimulating investment? What is your evaluation of other tax provisions with a similar purpose, such as the "tax sparing" proposals referred to in paragraph (2) above? What would be the attitude towards such proposals of other underdeveloped countries which, in order to encourage investment, had always employed very low

income tax rates? How might "tax sparing" affect the decision of a United States parent whether to have its foreign subsidiary reinvest its earnings or repatriate them as dividends?

(2) Consider whether the taxes described in the following illustrations would qualify for the credit.

(*a*) Note first the various taxes imposed by West Germany that are described at p. 1129, infra. (Questions with respect to West Germany's taxes are now regulated by Articles I and XV of the Tax Convention between the United States and West Germany.)

(*b*) A country requires that 2% of the net earnings of a corporation owning a factory be paid to the plant workers' council to be used in establishing health, recreation and other welfare activities for the workers in the factory and their dependents.

(*c*) A country with a pronounced bias against the use of alcoholic beverages levies a special tax of 25% on the net earnings of all liquor sellers.

(*d*) A country imposes a 2% tax (labelled an "income tax") on the gross income derived by a mining company from the sale of its production.

(3) Amcorp is solely in the business of buying leather in India to sell in the United States. India, at one time, regarded the purchase of raw materials in India for purposes of manufacture or sale outside India as giving rise to profits which were subject to the Indian income tax.[27] Under this Indian rule, would Amcorp be able to credit the Indian income tax thus paid against its United States income tax? Cf. Burk Bros., 20 B.T.A. 657 (1930).

(4) Doe, a resident American, was entitled to a $10,000 dividend from Anglo, a British corporation doing business in Great Britain only. Under British law, Anglo withheld $3,800 and paid it into the British treasury. If Doe had been a British citizen, the consequence of the withholding would have been that Doe would not be obligated to pay the normal British income tax on this dividend income; he would, however, have had to pay a surtax depending on his particular tax bracket. All remedies for nonpayment of the $3,800 standard tax ran against the corporation. If for some reason a British taxpayer's income were not subject to standard tax—if, for example, his income were below the minimum—he might have procured a refund of the tax paid on his dividend. It was held in Biddle v. Commissioner, 302 U.S. 573, 58 S.Ct. 379, 82 L.Ed. 431 (1938), that Doe could not credit this British tax. Why?[28]

27. See the comment at p. 1101, supra.

28. The 1946 Convention between the United States and the United Kingdom, 60 Stat. 1377, T.I.A.S. No. 1546, Art. XV, overruled Biddle. The issue has become obsolete due to changes in the British corporate tax system. See the 1966 protocol to the Convention, T.I.A.S. No. 6089.

2. TAX TREATIES

The United States is a party to income tax treaties with some 24 other nations, most of which are industrially developed.[29] The countries involved account for about 60% of our foreign trade and foreign investment. About 80% of the United States source income of aliens (principally interest and dividends) that is subject to our withholding rules is destined for residents of those countries. Nevertheless, a careful student of these treaties has concluded that they "play a very marginal role in relieving double taxation" and suggests that "an appropriate time has arrived to reconsider whether treaties are necessary." [30] Other experts in this field view international tax conventions as considerably more important for our fiscal and foreign economic policies.[31] When reading the materials in this section, evaluate these different points of view (which, as explained, are less far apart than they appear), and compare the present and potential role of treaty regulation of income taxation with the potential role of treaties in accommodating different national points of view in the fields of economic regulation that were considered in Chapter IX.

A tax treaty does not form a logical, self-contained structure. It attempts to regulate a number of rather separate problems that have arisen under the tax laws of the two countries. Although these problems tend to recur in similar form in many bilateral relationships, the tax treaty is still apt to be somewhat more individualized than a friendship, commerce and navigation treaty.

To illustrate the principal characteristics of tax treaties, the following materials draw upon the Convention between the United States of America and the Federal Republic of Germany for the Avoidance of Double Taxation with Respect to Taxes on Income of July 22, 1954, as amended by a protocol signed September 17, 1965.* Through the 1965 amendments, this Convention reflects at various points the solutions reached in the Draft Convention for the Avoidance of Double Taxation with Respect to Taxes on Income and Capital, published in 1963 by the Organization for Economic Cooperation and Development (OECD) after having been prepared by its Fiscal Committee.[32] The OECD was established in 1960 by the member states (primarily West European) of the Organization for European Economic Co-Operation and by the United States and Canada, and the Draft Convention re-

29. The United States has also entered into a number of treaties regulating estate taxes.

30. Owens, United States Income Tax Treaties: Their Role in Relieving Double Taxation, 17 Rutgers L.Rev. 428, 430–31 (1963).

31. E. g., Surrey, International Tax Conventions: How They Operate and What They Accomplish, 23 J. of Taxation 364 (1965).

32. Excerpts from the Convention with Germany and from the Draft Convention appear in the Documentary Supplement. For a comprehensive review of problems of control by treaty of double taxation, see the Committee's Report, including commentary, on the Draft Convention. Report of the O.E.C.D. Fiscal Committee, Draft Double Taxation Convention on Income and Capital (1963).

flects the consensus achieved and compromises reached by the fiscal experts of a large number of developed countries.

The Convention with Germany thus departs in various respects from the pattern of prior United States tax treaties and can be said to represent the current approach of the United States to bilateral accommodation. In particular, it abandons the "force of attraction" principle (p. 1102, supra)—that is, it ceases to tax all a foreign party's income as business income because some of the income is business income. The Convention, as amended, also reflects the terminology of the OECD draft in the definition of a "permanent establishment" and in other points.

The OECD draft has had similar effects on other United States treaties entered into or amended since 1963 and has influenced movements towards harmonization of taxes among members of the EEC.[33] It is possible that with the multiplication of such arrangements between the major industrial nations a consensus may emerge that could serve as a basis for an international minimum standard in the field of taxation in the absence of treaty. That possibility would be enhanced if the OECD draft were extensively relied upon as a model. Such treaties may however be inappropriate in some ways for conclusion with less developed countries; several recent conventions (see p. 1134, infra) signed with such countries by the United States have contained special provisions to take account of their special needs.

Additional reading: Tillinghast, The Revision of the Income Tax Convention between the United States and the Federal Republic of Germany, 21 Tax L.Rev. 399 (1966); Gumpel, Revision of the Tax Convention between the United States and the Federal Republic of Germany, 44 Taxes 383 (1966).

NOTE ON THE GERMAN TAX SYSTEM AND ITS RELATION TO THE TREATY

The problems posed by a tax treaty are best understood if one can examine its effect upon parties linked with both of the countries involved: the nonresident alien and foreign corporation doing business in the United States, and United States citizens, residents or corporations doing business in the foreign country. This two-way analysis requires some knowledge of the foreign tax system involved. To facilitate such an analysis, this Note offers a summary statement of the principal elements of the German statutory tax scheme to complement the study of the Convention between the United States and Germany.[34] It presents only a skeletal outline of that scheme, emphasizing those rules which are relevant to American individuals and

33. Pearson, The OECD Draft Double Taxation Convention and Recent United States Treaties, 48 Taxes 426 (1970).

34. The information in this Note is, in general, based upon a summary of German taxes appearing in World Tax Series, Taxation in the Federal Republic of Germany (2d ed. 1969).

corporations doing business in Germany. Those taxes noted in Article I of the Convention are also referred to by their German names.

(a) An income tax (*Einkommensteuer*) on resident individuals on their income from domestic and foreign sources, at graduated rates from 19% to 53%. Nonresidents are taxed on their German-source income only, partly on an assessed basis with graduated rates, and partly by a withholding tax at a general rate of 25%. In rough terms, dividends, interest, wages and royalties are covered by withholding as to nonresidents, whereas only dividends and wages are withheld as to residents. Business income of nonresidents is taxed only if realized through a permanent establishment or permanent representative in Germany. Note that the German rules indicating the source of a given item of income may differ from those of the Internal Revenue Code; thus, the source of dividend or interest payments is identified with the seat (*Sitz*) or place of management of the payor.

(b) A corporation income tax (*Körperschaftsteuer*) on corporations resident in Germany in the sense of having a seat (*Sitz*) or place of management there. The tax rate is 51% on earnings retained in the enterprise and 15% on earnings distributed to the shareholders. This "split" rate is designed, *inter alia*, to cause income to flow as dividends from major established companies via shareholders into the general capital market. This, it was thought, would make it easier for new firms to obtain financing. Nonresident corporations are subject to a general 25% withholding tax on the categories of income noted in paragraph (a) above and are taxed at a flat 49% rate on other categories of income. Thus a branch of a foreign corporation in Germany is taxed at the 49% rate on its German-source income, whether distributed or not, and the income of a branch does not receive the benefits of the special relief accorded to a subsidiary on income it pays over as dividends to its parent. As in the case of individuals, business income of a nonresident corporation is not taxed unless realized through a permanent branch or a permanent representative.

(c) In years prior to 1968, a turnover tax on sales and services performed. It was, from the point of view of revenue collection, the most important single German tax. As of January 1, 1968, there was substituted a value-added tax. This tax, modeled after a French tax of the same name, has the merit of avoiding the effect known as "cascading," i. e., the building up of additional taxes with each transfer. Cascading tends to give an advantage to large integrated firms that do not have to "sell" products from one division to another. The value-added tax in effect gives credit for the tax paid by each previous transferor. Thus, even though levied at a 10%, and then an 11% rate, it did not produce substantially more than the turnover rate at 4%.

(d) Excise taxes on certain specified commodities and import duties.

(e) A municipal trade tax (*Gewerbesteuer*) on commercial enterprises. This is computed in part on the basis of the corporation income tax, in part on the net worth tax (below), and sometimes on the business payroll. The rate varies according to the fiscal needs of the municipality which collects the tax.

(f) A real property tax collected by municipalities.

(g) A net worth or capital tax (*Vermögensteuer*) based on the net worth (after important exemptions) of resident individuals and entities and on the German-situs property, whether real or personal (again with important exemptions), of nonresidents.

(h) Taxes on transfers of real property and of corporate securities.

(i) An inheritance and gift tax.

It is important to note that, although the German tax pattern is not too dissimilar from that of the United States, this general description conceals many differences. For example, note the description in World Tax Series, Taxation in the Federal Republic of Germany 507 (2d ed. 1969), of the German concept of "residence":

> A resident individual is one whose domicile or customary place of abode is in the Federal Republic or West Berlin. . . . "Customary place of abode" . . . is tantamount to mere physical presence for a somewhat extended period of time; with certain exceptions, it is always deemed to exist if the individual's stay in Germany exceeds a period of six months.

More significant, the rules followed by Germany and the United States to determine source of income differ in some respects, with an evident impact upon provisions of German and United States law which purport to tax only domestic source income.

In addition to possible ambiguities in legal terminology, one should be on the watch for concealed differences in accounting practices. One company's taxable "income" may be quite different when measured according to German or American practices.

With this background in mind, you should now make a general survey of the Convention. You will see that Article II has some very important definitions, particularly of "permanent establishment." There follow a series of Articles (III–X) each of which deals with a different type of income, chiefly in the sense of limiting or eliminating the tax placed on it by the source country. Article XV makes a treaty matter of the tax credit provisions of the two countries' laws. Articles XVI, XVII and XIX provide for cooperation by the tax authorities in the prevention of overlapping taxation, and tax evasion. Scattered throughout the treaty are clauses which attempt to achieve a uniform solution of the differences in concepts which have emerged in the two systems. As to "source," note Articles III(1), III(4), XIV and XVII(3)(c), comparing them with Sections 861–863 of the Code. As to "residence" observe Article II(2), comparing it with the observations as to the German definition above, and the American at p. 1091, supra. As to allocations of income or deductions between related enterprises, observe Articles III(2), IV, VII(4), VIII(5), XVII(3)(a) and (b) and compare them with Section 482.

Tax treaties raise problems of a kind generally treated in Chapter V, of the relation between treaty and statute, in this case the Code. Special Code provisions (Sections 894 and 7852(d)) deal with the impact of treaty provisions. On the other hand, Articles XV(1)(a) and XVIII(2) permit Code provisions to operate so as to allow the United States to continue to include all income of Americans taxable under the Code without regard to the Convention and so as to continue all deductions or exemptions otherwise in effect. There would be some question under Article I, Section 7 of the Constitution about a treaty which purported to increase rather than decrease a revenue burden.

The gap between the taxes which the Code imposes on foreigners in the United States and the taxes payable after application of the Treaty has been narrowed by the FITA of 1966 which in effect conceded unilaterally items that might otherwise have been held in reserve as a *quid pro quo* to induce like concessions by Germany. Thus in a sense the FITA reduced the executive's bargaining power in dealing with other countries. In Section 896 Congress sought to undo this effect by granting to the executive power to reverse these concessions with respect to a country refusing to reciprocate. Note the other retaliatory provisions found in Sections 883, 891 and 901(c).

PROBLEMS

After examining the Convention to gain a general knowledge of its structure, consider the following problems. The first set explores the impact of the Convention on United States taxation of German residents or companies with business activities in the United States; the second deals with the Convention's effect on taxation of American citizens, residents or companies in Germany.

Problem One: Bonnco, a German corporation, has a manufacturing subsidiary (Amco) organized in the United States. Amco generates $500,000 of net income from its American sales in 1974. $100,000 of this income is declared as a dividend to Bonnco in December 1974 for payment at the end of that month. What taxes are due under the Code, and by which taxpayers, on the $500,000 and $100,000? See Sections 11, 61, 861, 881 and 882. What is the effect of the Convention? See Articles II and VI.

Problem Two: Bonnco, in addition to the dividend income in 1974 that was referred to in Problem One, has $50,000 of gross income from German sources. In each of the years 1965 and 1966, it received $100,000 in dividends from Amco and earned $50,000 from its domestic operations. In January 1975, Bonnco pays a dividend of $75,000 to its shareholders, all German citizens resident in Germany. Is this dividend subject under the Code to United States taxation? If so, at what rate, and how would this tax be collected? See Sections 861 and 871. Suppose that, instead of receiving dividend income from Amco in the indicated amounts, Bonnco had done the manufacturing in the United States through a branch which had gross sales of $120,000 per year while its German gross income amounted to $100,000 a year. Is the operation of the Code sections in either case affected by the Convention? See Article XIV.

Problem Three: (*a*) Bonnco, instead of acting through a subsidiary, earns in 1967 $500,000 of net income from sales of goods in the United States that it manufactures in Germany. Such sales are solicited by various American agents, each of whom receives a 5% commission and each of whom does some business for other sellers. Each sales contract is made subject to confirmation by Bonnco at its home office. The goods are delivered from a stock kept at a warehouse leased by Bonnco in New Jersey and maintained and operated by ten of its employees. In addition, Bonnco holds as an unrelated investment bonds issued by a Delaware corporation, and an interest payment of $5,000 is due and to be paid in December 1974. Is the business income or interest income subject to United States tax and if so at what rate(s)? See Sections 861, 863, 881 and 882. Is the operation of these sections affected by Articles II, III and VII of the Convention? If so, why should the United States be willing to surrender such tax revenue? (*b*) Would the result under the Convention differ if the ten employees processed the goods to some degree to meet the particular specifications of customers? How? (*c*) Under the facts stated in (b), is the business or interest income received by Bonnco subject to taxation by Germany? If so, under what limitation? See Article XV.

Note that the relevant provisions of the German Convention represented a departure from the prior American treaty pattern, which left the former Code force-of-attraction rule intact.

Problem Four: Amco has a wholly-owned subsidiary, Subco, organized in Germany. Subco has net earnings in 1974 of $200,000 before taxes and transmits a $100,000 dividend to Amco. What German taxes are payable under the German law as described at p. 1130, supra? To what degree does Article VI(2) of the Convention reduce that burden? How does that compare with the sacrifice of revenue made by the United States under Article VI(1)? What tactic that might be engaged in by a company such as Amco does Article VI(3) try to prevent? Was the concern evidenced by that section a realistic one in the light of the consequences of such a tactic to Amco's total tax load?

Problem Five: Amco makes fairly regular sales of its American manufactured products in Germany through local commission merchants. These are not permanent representatives of Amco and do not constitute a permanent establishment. Does Article III involve more sacrifice of revenues by Germany than of the United States in the first set of facts in Problem Three?

Problem Six: Eurco, a corporation organized under the laws of Europia, a West European country, and having its formal seat there, transacts negligible business in Europia and has opened a manufacturing branch in Germany. 40% of its stock is owned by German nationals, the managing director and other principal officers are German residents, and meetings of the Eurco directors generally take place in Germany at the plant. The branch sells most of its production in Germany but also exports to the United States, where it has a leased advertising office and several salesmen who forward offers to the plant for acceptance. Can Eurco assert rights under the Convention? If a Canadian corporation maintained a similar branch in the United States and exported from it to Germany, could that corporation assert rights under the Convention? See Article II.

QUESTIONS

(1) Suppose that a German hotel corporation establishes a branch operation, namely a hotel, in New York. It advertises in Germany urging German tourists to stop at that hotel when in the United States. What is the status of these advertising expenses under Section 882(c) of the Code? Under Article III(3) of the Treaty? Do Articles XVII and XIX seem to be an effective avenue for resolving differences between the tax authorities on this point?

(2) Do the grants of retaliatory authority, particularly in Section 896 of the Code, pose problems as a matter of domestic executive-legislative relations or as a matter of international practice?

(3) What substantive effect does a non-discrimination clause, such as Article XVIII(3) of the Convention, have? (See also Article IX of the Franco-American Establishment Convention). For example, does the Article have any bearing upon the fact that both Germany and the United States in some cases tax income of nonresident aliens at flat rates without deductions, with the consequence that their tax burden may be higher than that of citizens?

(4) On the basis of your answers to the problems, do you find that the Convention significantly helps taxpayers? How many of the provisions simply shift taxes from one treasury to the other? Does your answer depend on the relationship of German tax rates to American? Does the taxpayer gain anything by way of convenience?

NOTE ON TAX TREATIES AND LESS DEVELOPED COUNTRIES

It has been doubted that a treaty of the type developed from negotiations between developed countries is suited to the needs of less developed countries. These doubts derive from the fact that such countries occupy a distinctive trade relationship with the United States. Although the flow of raw materials and commodities is towards the United States, the flow of manufactured goods is dominantly towards them. The net flow of income (as distinct from initial capital investment) is dominantly towards the United States. Consider, for example, the surrenders of revenue involved in Articles III(4), VI(2), VII(2), VIII(2) of the Convention, and the treatment by these articles of such income flows.

Various proposals to provide by treaty active incentives to American investment in less developed countries have reached different stages of realization. Recall that there are certain benefits to such investments in such countries included in our domestic tax legislation. Some feel that more should be done. The concept of "tax sparing", noted on p. 1125, supra has been largely abandoned. Both of the following proposals appear in each of the recently signed (but not yet ratified) treaties with Israel and Thailand.

(*a*) Under the Revenue Act of 1962 (Code Sections 38 and 46), the United States has, except for two periods of suspension, allowed credit against the income tax of 7% of the amount spent for machinery and equipment for use in this country. The first proposal was that this credit be allowed with respect to investments made in less developed countries, indeed expanded in its coverage so as not to be limited to machinery and equipment.

(*b*) Persons who contribute money or property to a domestic corporation in exchange for its stock in such a way that, after the exchange, they control the corporation generally recognize no gain or loss on that transaction by virtue of Section 351. "Control", as defined in Section 368(c), requires that the transferor own 80% of the stock of the corporation. However, under Section 367, such a transfer to a foreign corporation is, in effect, made taxable "unless, before such exchange, it has been established to the satisfaction of the [Treasury] that such an exchange is not in pursuance of a plan having as one of its principal purposes the avoidance of Federal income taxes." The second proposal was that such transfers, particularly of patents and associated rights, to companies in less developed countries should be nontaxable transactions, even if only a small portion of the stock of the new corporation in the underdeveloped country is owned by the American transferor.

Additional reading: Hellawell, United States Income Taxation and Less Developed Countries: A Critical Appraisal, 66 Colum.L.Rev. 1393 (1966).

QUESTIONS

(1) Do the current Code rules add up to a comprehensive, coherent and adequate program of tax assistance to investment in less developed countries?

(2) Would a finance minister of an underdeveloped country be willing to accept a treaty in the form of the Convention with Germany? Consider particularly Articles III(4), VI(2), VII(2) and VIII(2). What benefit might that country derive from them? Does Article III(3) tend to work to the disadvantage of such a country, for example in the context of the local activities of a multinational corporation?

(3) Do you find the proposals in paragraphs (a) and (b) above preferable to "tax sparing"? If they appear promising would you recommend simply enacting them into the Code? Are there reasons—relating to possible abuses by taxpayers, to possible reactions by the foreign countries or to the United States' negotiating position on related points—for preferring the treaty route? If you were negotiating a treaty containing such clauses, what commitments by the less developed country would you require?

JOHANSSON v. UNITED STATES

United States Court of Appeals, Fifth Circuit, 1964.
336 F.2d 809.

[Johansson, a Swedish citizen, fought Floyd Patterson three times for the heavyweight championship of the world, each time in the United States. The Government assessed taxes of approximately $1,000,000 on the resulting income and brought suit against Johansson to collect them. It also sought to foreclose tax liens on funds allegedly held by certain American fight promoters for his benefit; portions of the opinion by JUDGE RIVES relating to that issue have been omitted. The district court found for the Government. The court of appeals affirmed that part of the judgment holding Johansson liable for the taxes. It found that under Code Section 871, the taxes were authorized and that nothing in the United States tax convention with Sweden barred their levy. It then discussed the convention between the United States and Switzerland.]

. . . However, Johansson claims an exemption under the Income Tax Convention with Switzerland, May 24, 1951 [1951], 2 U.S.T. & O.I.A. 1751, T.I.A.S. No. 2316 (effective Sept. 27, 1951). Particular reliance is placed upon article X(1), which provides:

> "An individual resident of Switzerland shall be exempt from United States Tax upon compensation for labor or personal services performed in the United States . . . if he is temporarily present in the United States for a period or periods not exceeding a total of 183 days during the taxable year and . . .
>
> "(a) his compensation is received for such labor or personal services performed as an employee of, or under contract with, a resident or corporation or other entity of Switzerland . . .."

It is undisputed that Johansson was not present in the United States for more than 183 days in either of the tax years in question. But to bring himself within the purview of the treaty, Johansson had to establish (1) that he was a resident of Switzerland and (2) that he received the income in question as an employee of, or under contract with, a Swiss entity.

The term "resident" is nowhere defined in the Swiss treaty, but under article II(2) each country is authorized to apply its own definition to terms not expressly defined "unless the context otherwise requires." Johansson contends that, because of its position within the phrase "an individual resident of Switzerland," the term "resident" must be defined according to Swiss law. As conclusive proof that he comes within the Swiss definition of "resident" for tax purposes, he relies upon a determination by the Swiss tax authorities that he became a resident of Switzerland on December 1, 1959. Although the evidence on this point is ambiguous, the determination by the Swiss tax authorities may well have been based primarily upon Johansson's own declaration as to his residence in that country. . . . Be this as it may, we are not bound by the determination of the Swiss tax authorities. Article II(2) does no more than to provide the standard for defining the terms used in the rest of the treaty; the application of that standard to particular facts remains, in this case, the job of the courts. There is no reason to decide whether the applicable standard for defining "resident" as used in the Swiss treaty is to be found in Swiss or American law, for under both laws the criteria are the same. Compare Locher, statement of Dec. 29, 1962, in C.C.H. 1963 Stand.Fed.Tax Rep. Paragraph 6407, p. 71286 ("sojourn . . . with the intention to remain"), *with* Treas.Reg. § 1.871–2(b) ("intentions with regard to the length and nature of his stay").

Applying this standard to the facts of the present case, the district court concluded that Johansson was not a resident of Switzerland during the period in question. This conclusion is fully supported by the evidence. In the year and a half between the date Johansson claims to have moved to Switzerland and March 13, 1961, the record shows that he spent only 79 days in that country as compared with 120 days in Sweden and 218 days in the United States. Except for his activities in the United States during this period, his social and economic ties remained predominantly with Sweden. Indeed, the summary of Johansson's ties with Switzerland presented in his brief to this Court cites only his maintenance of an apartment and bank account there, his self-declaration of residence, and two acts by the Swiss government that may well have been predicated entirely upon his self-declaration of residence. . . .

Even if we were to find that the district court erred in determining that Johansson was not a resident of Switzerland, the tax exemption in the Swiss treaty does not apply unless Johansson received the income in question as an employee of or under contract with a Swiss entity. A contract of employment was entered into by Johansson in December 1959 with Scanart, S.A., a Swiss corporation formed that very month. Scanart's sole employee and sole source of revenue is Johansson, who is entitled under the terms of the contract to seventy per cent of Scanart's gross income, plus a pension fund. All expenses are to be paid by Scanart. During the period in question, Johansson conducted his affairs largely independent of Scanart's sole director or its stockholders. The circumstances surrounding the formation of Scanart, the terms of the contract, and the conduct of the parties under the contract led the district court to find that:

> "Scanart, S.A., had no legitimate business purpose, but was a device which was used by Ingemar Johansson as a controlled depositary and conduit by which he attempted to divert temporarily, his personal income, earned in the United States, so as to escape taxation thereon by the United States." (R., pp. 197–98.)

As with the question of Johansson's residence, the record amply supports this finding.

Of course, the fact that Johansson was motivated in his actions by the desire to minimize his tax burden can in no way be taken to deprive him of an exemption to which an applicable treaty entitles him. See Gregory v. Helvering, 293 U.S. 465, 469, 55 S.Ct. 266, 79 L.Ed. 596 (1935). And in determining the applicability of a treaty, we recognize the necessity for liberal construction. Jordan v. K. Tashiro, 278 U.S. 123, 127, 49 S.Ct. 47, 73 L.Ed. 214 (1928). But "To say that we should give a broad and efficacious scope to a treaty does not mean that we must sweep within the Convention what are legally and traditionally recognized to be . . . taxpayers not clearly within its protections; . . .". Maximov v. United States, 373 U.S. 49, 56, 83 S.Ct. 1054, 10 L.Ed.2d 184 (1963). In determining whether the taxpayer in a given case is protected by the terms of a treaty, abstract and desultory definitions of such terms as "resident" and "legitimate business purposes" are of limited, if any, assistance. "[T]o give the specific words of a treaty a meaning consistent with the genuine shared expectations of the contracting parties, it is necessary to examine not only the language, but the entire context of agreement." Maximov v. United States, 2 Cir., 1962, 299 F.2d 565, 568, aff'd, 373 U.S. 49, 83 S.Ct. 1054, 10 L.Ed.2d 184 (1963).

The primary objective of our treaty with Switzerland, as well as of those with more than twenty other countries, is the elimination of impediments to international commerce resulting from the double taxation of international transactions. The basic mechanism of these treaty arrangements is the establishment of standards for determining the single most appropriate locus for the taxation of any given transaction. Although some treaty provisions are inevitably the results of political compromise, the dominant criterion for determining the appropriate taxing locus is economic impact. Thus, as a general rule, the income from services is taxable where the services are rendered. See Smith, The Functions of Tax Treaties, 12 Nat'l Tax J. 317, 320 (1959). Where, as here, services are performed in the United States and the compensation for them is drawn from the wealth of the United States, this is the country of primary economic impact and, consequently, the appropriate taxing locus.

There are, however, a number of prudential exceptions to the general "economic impact" rule. Among these is the view that a business enterprise engaged in international commerce ought not to be subject to taxation in every country in which it may transact some business. Although such an enterprise does draw upon the wealth of all the various countries with which it comes into contact, the over-all objective of encouraging international commerce, as well as the practical necessities of business planning, are better satisfied by a centralized regime of taxation at the enterprise's "business seat" or "permanent establishment." The "business seat" exception is found in article III of the Swiss treaty.

Elements of this exception are also found in article X. Typical of what have become known as "commercial traveler provisions" in international tax conventions, the article is designed to assure business establishments in each of the contracting states that they may freely send their agents and employees into the other contracting state without thereby subjecting those employees to the latter's taxes. Like article III, it is an exception to the "economic impact" rule carved out in the interest of facilitating international trade. Where the practical reasons for the exception do not obtain, however, the general rule must apply. Thus, while Johansson may have brought himself within the words of the Swiss treaty by his "residence" in Switzerland and his "employment" by a "Swiss corporation," he has failed to establish any substantial reasons for deviating from the treaty's basic rule that income from services is taxable where the services were rendered. International trade will not be seriously encumbered by our refusal to grant special tax treatment to one only marginally, if at all, a Swiss resident and only technically, if at all, employed by a paper Swiss corporation. Therefore we affirm the district court's judgment that Johansson is liable for the taxes assessed against him in 1960 and 1961. . . .

COMMENT

Switzerland has been sensitive to charges that its legislation and tax treaties have been used by foreigners to obtain tax advantages that were not intended for their benefit. Not long after the passage of the Internal Revenue Act of 1962, the Swiss Government issued a decree that was intended to deny the benefits of Swiss tax rules (including treaty provisions) to corporations when the application of such rules would confer benefits upon parties not entitled thereto. For a discussion of the background to and application of this decree, see Note, Swiss Tax Decree Limits Advantages of Base Companies in Switzerland, 16 Stan.L.Rev. 416 (1964).

QUESTIONS

(1) Suppose that Johansson sought to bring himself under the tax treaty with Germany rather than Switzerland. What would he have had to do to qualify for the protection of the German Convention with the United States? Consider the provisions of Article X of the Convention, which corresponds to Article X of the Swiss treaty, and certain related definitions in Article II. The Swiss and German treaties here differ in some respects. The Swiss treaty has no provision like the second sentence in Article II(2); and instead of the definition in Article II(1)(f), the Swiss treaty simply defines a "Swiss corporation" to be one "created or organized under Swiss laws."

(2) Does the court pay sufficient heed to the actions of the Swiss Government in Johansson's case? Might the opinion impose unnecessary strain upon the relations between the American and Swiss fiscal authorities? Do the provisions of Articles XVI, XVII and XIX of the German Convention suggest a more helpful approach of American authorities to this problem if Johansson had resorted to Germany?

(3) Suppose that a problem of interpretation, involving the definition of "permanent establishment," arose under the German Convention in the context of a claim by the United States that a German corporation (Bonnco) was liable for taxes on its American source income. Suppose further that the United States tax authorities need information as to Bonnco's pricing and related policies to determine the amount of profits which were allocable to the alleged permanent establishment. Consider the following questions, based on Articles XVI, XVII and XIX of the Convention:

(*a*) What assistance can the United States expect from German authorities to uncover the relevant facts?

(*b*) What action might Bonnco take in an effort to persuade United States tax authorities not to press the claim to litigation?

(*c*) Assuming a proper jurisdictional basis for a tax suit, how should the United States court approach the problem of treaty interpretation? Should a statement of the Treasury Department be conclusive on this issue? What procedures should the Department follow in reaching its view of the proper interpretation of "permanent establishment?" What weight should the court give to judicial or executive interpretations of the same phrase in other tax treaties?

(*d*) Assume that a judgment is rendered in favor of the Government, but that Bonnco has insufficient assets in the United States to satisfy it. If Bonnco refuses to pay the judgment in full, can the United States invoke the assistance of German authorities under the Convention? What effect would the Convention have upon an action by the United States in German courts to enforce the judgment?

In the light of your answers to these questions, how effective do you think the provisions of the Convention on cooperation are? Would you consider it advisable for a tax treaty to attempt more?

Part Five

TRADE AND INVESTMENT IN THE WORLD COMMUNITY: LEGAL STRUCTURES, POLICY CONTEXT AND CASE STUDIES

Previous portions of this book have treated issues relevant to individuals, firms or government-related organizations conducting business transactions across national boundaries. Recall, for example, the materials on the security afforded foreign investments, pp. 408–522, supra, and on the international reach of labor and antitrust rules, pp. 970–1046, supra. We here stress problems of the world economy germane to international trade or investment and problems of those who seek either to regulate such activities or to engage in them.

In Chapter XI we examine the world economy in its two major aspects, trade and currency flows, from the perspective of one seeking to look at the system—if it can be called that—as a whole. We examine it both as a system resulting from the operation of decentralized forces generated by a multiplicity of independent private and governmental traders, and as a set of national and, ultimately, supra-national rules on trading and monetary organization that seek to regulate those forces and to impose collectively determined objectives upon them.

Chapter XII first describes a developing force on the international economic scene, the multinational enterprise, with respect to its size, its internal structure and its impact upon national governments and their efforts to realize national economic goals. It then undertakes a series of case studies illustrating, with reference to specific types of transactions, the complexities that confront firms and lawyers attempting to cope with different sets of national and international regulations in achieving business objectives.

Chapter XI

THE WORLD ECONOMIC ENVIRONMENT: GATT AND IMF

A. INTRODUCTION: MODELS FOR TRADE REGULATION

It is possible to conceive of the world economy as being organized according to one of three models, none of which has ever existed in its pure form. In the laissez faire model, there would be no governmental control or regulation of world trade, apart from the legal and economic infrastructure for a world market that was developed by government to facilitate trade by private parties. Merchants would do business with each other across national frontiers on whatever basis their economic advantage dictated within an open competitive framework. The model would necessarily assume relative dispersal of economic power and the presence of enough trading partners to permit uninhibited competition to take place, as well as the absence of collusive private agreements.

Under these conditions the location of production would be determined by relative costs, producers in each country tending to make those commodities in which they had the greatest advantage and to export them whenever and wherever transportation or other transaction costs permitted them to deliver goods abroad below effective prices prevailing at the point of delivery. At the same time each country's merchants would purchase abroad whenever they could do so at a price below that demanded by local sources. The workings of the law of comparative advantage,[1] as it is called, would tend to push the price of all commodities down to the lowest possible point, enabling consumers to have the cheapest goods that could be produced anywhere. By the same token, resources in each country would move to where they were most highly valued for productive purposes, and thus the global economic value of goods produced would be maximized.

A necessary concomitant of such free trade in goods would be some system whereby businessmen of different nations could conduct transactions safely and profitably even though the two trading partners came from countries with different currencies. Some method of exchanging currencies would be needed so that the system could rise above a primitive barter technique. One method would be simply to have a free market in currencies, rather like a stock exchange. Then

1. Economists speak of the law of comparative advantage because it applies even in the following situation: Country X can produce more economically than country Y both commodities A and B but its advantage is greater as to A. It will be more efficient for X to specialize in A and leave B to country Y. That "law" is described with reference to principles underlying the European Economic Community at p. 1250, infra.

if A, an American food wholesaler, wanted to buy some coffee, he need not offer B, the Brazilian planter, some bags of American fertilizer. Instead he could go to the exchange and with his dollars buy cruzeiros from some American exporter who had just sold fertilizer.

Such a market would register weaknesses and strengths in each country's balance of payments. Thus when a country's exports were in decline relative to imports, its currency would depreciate since fewer people would have occasion to buy it. Eventually the decline in value of its currency relative to other currencies would cheapen the prices of its exports in terms of those other currencies, and make it profitable for foreign merchants to buy there again. Thus a free currency market with floating rates would tend to develop a self-correcting mechanism that would facilitate a global efficient market in goods.

Another method of regulating currency aspects of international trade was represented by the gold standard, which committed a nation to allow each holder of a unit of its currency to exchange it for a stated amount of gold. Thus the amount of currency of each such country had a fixed relationship to its gold supply. Any foreign trader then would be able to demand from the central banking facility of the country with which he was trading the stipulated amount of gold for his holdings of local currency. He could take that gold home and present it to his own bank in order to obtain a corresponding quantity of its currency. But the vast majority of transactions would be carried out without resort to this expedient, which simply stood as a guaranty that foreign traders would obtain "their money's worth".

The free trade-gold standard system has obvious advantages if one accords the highest priority to an economically efficient world market that is intended to maximize the value of global production through unhindered trade. However, it also has serious disadvantages that have encouraged increasing resort to a second model, national regulation. (The analogy to the domestic equivalents of a "free market" or a "regulated" or "managed" economy should be evident.) A country that opens its frontiers to goods made abroad runs the risk that important domestic industries will be quickly wiped out by a shift to demand for those foreign goods and thus towards production abroad. This trend may lead to politically unacceptable amounts of unemployment.

Alternatively, it may lead to politically unacceptable dependence upon foreign sources of production. That dependence may—and in the case of less developed countries frequently will—find expression not simply in imports but also in dominant positions in sectors of the local economy that are occupied by subsidiaries of powerful foreign-based multinational companies. But excluding the multinational company and requiring it to sell to the local market only by exports may provide no satisfactory solution. It may be difficult to find local entrepreneurs willing to run the risk of challenging established foreign, large-scale production, even though the government is convinced that given some time, the new "infant industry" can achieve a sturdy, profitable position. For these and other reasons, the adverse welfare or distributional implications of the pure market model in trade (or establishment) may impel governments towards intensive regulation.

Free trade in currency can produce other awkward consequences. A currency may be driven into decline by rumours and political pressures. More pervasively, a nation's capacity to pursue an independent domestic economic policy is impaired. If it lowers its interest rates to encourage domestic borrowers in a period of recession, investors are apt to move their money to other countries. Thus investment funds will be less available to entrepreneurs in that country, cancelling out the benefits of low interest. A country seeking to throttle an inflationary boom by imposing high interest rates will have to fend off foreign investors seeking such attractive returns. Attempts to change the shares of different classes or groups in the national income may be frustrated by their transfers of currency abroad and out of reach of national regulation.

Such problems lead nations to seek goals other than efficient global maximization of production, by establishing controls on trade and currency movements. As to trade, these may take the form of *tariffs* which place a price disadvantage on imported goods and thus should enable domestic producers to compete effectively. Note that some tariffs have been used simply as revenue raising devices, particularly in places and at times when income taxes and similar levies posed great administrative problems. *Quantitative restrictions*, on the other hand, put a flat limit on the amounts of foreign goods that may be imported. Unlike tariffs, such quotas present serious questions as to who is to be entitled to what share of the imports that are permitted —with a chance that windfalls will come to those favored by being given a portion of the import quota. Exports, on the other hand, can be encouraged by cash bounties (such as tax forgiveness or direct subsidies to exporting industries) or other assistance. On the currency side, countries may impose exchange controls, of a greater or lesser degree of pervasiveness. They may also attempt to "manage" exchange rates by buying or selling foreign exchange from their reserves.

All these tactics, the instruments or means by which a country seeks to realize goals that depart from pure market efficiency, have problems of their own. Country X, by raising tariff barriers to imports of wheat, may benefit X's wheat growers by enabling them to charge higher prices. By the same token, however, these policies adversely affect the consumers of wheat in X and producers of wheat in Y. In effect, the tariff transfers or redistributes wealth between groups within a country and in different countries. Two redistributional problems arise. One is internal to X—in our example, producers and consumers of wheat. The other raises the question whether X will seek to maximize whatever values (whatever conception of social welfare) it advances through tariff or other regulation within the national setting of X, within the larger community of X and Y, or in a global framework.

As a consequence of X's decision, Y is pressed to react. If Y then raises barriers to imports of X's textiles or subsidizes lower prices for wheat exports, a new set of readjustments takes place. It is likely that when the readjustments have all been made, not only will the volume of trade have been diminished but the overall welfare of the parties, in terms of the gross amount of wheat and textiles produced, will have diminished. In terms of a more complex conception of welfare—one involving, for example, notions of distribution or increased national autonomy for developmental or military reasons—X or Y may prefer the new situation despite its international costs.

Similarly, attempts to better one country's currency position may provoke responses. Competitive devaluations of national currencies intended to attract foreign purchasers of exports may cancel each other out, leaving confusion in their wake. Exchange controls may diminish or expand the volume of foreign transactions, depending upon the implicit tax or subsidy to importers or exporters of the system of governmental controls. Of course such controls change the direction of trade from a free-market situation. Countries with exchange controls attempt to shift their purchases to countries with which they are in a strong exchange situation. In the extreme case, trade may then develop under bilateral arrangements, approaching a barter level, which is inherently less efficient in stimulating production than multilateral choice. But again the institution of exchange controls may be justified in national terms by a conception of welfare that departs from pure efficiency maximization—the rationing of scarce "hard" currencies for priority imports, the subsidization of a needed export industry, and so on. Nonetheless the instability, uncertainty and bureaucratic administrative apparatus of exchange control systems impose transaction costs which further discourage trade.

Thus one might well turn from a "system" composed of nations' efforts to maximize their separate welfares or security to a third model of a genuinely international system. Resistance to interference with a nation's sovereign power to regulate its economy and pursue its own conception of social welfare has thus far ensured that no plenary power be conferred on an international agency. What has fundamentally developed has been the creation of international bodies wherein countries can negotiate with, bargain with, cajole and persuade each other. The world monetary system does, however, have some financial power to back its persuasiveness. These international institutions have formed a useful function in enabling countries to work their way back, by mutually responsive steps, from the brink to which their self-protective measures have brought them.

The world has never conformed to any of the three models, although from time to time it has swung more towards one than another. Before the 19th Century, leading countries were strongly under the influence of the doctrine of "mercantilism", which involved close governmental supervision of and cooperation with private entrepreneurs and which set as a national goal the achievement of a favorable balance of trade and the accumulation of gold in the national treasury. To this end, countries raised customs duties, encouraged national manufactures (the Sevres porcelain and Gobelin tapestry factories were among the consequences) and sought to obtain wealthy colonies (to be developed partly by entrepreneurs under royal charters) and the exclusive right to trade with them.

In the 19th Century a liberal (laissez-faire, market oriented) economic philosophy gained ground. Under its impact England went far in the direction of de-controlling its foreign trade by abolishing import duties, which had protected chiefly English farmers at the expense of English manufacturers and workers; it also championed the gold standard. Other countries never went so far. The United States, out of concern for its "infant industries," adopted a policy of protecting manufacturers, a policy that grew stronger after the industrial North had prevailed in the Civil War over the cotton-producing, manufactures-importing South. Other countries, such as Germany, resorted to protectionism in their efforts to narrow the industrial lead which England possessed. Meanwhile the gold standard prevailed, with London as the center of its operations.

The trials and tribulations of 1914 to 1933 produced a strong swing towards national interference with international commerce. The United States' Smoot-Hawley Tariff of 1930 pushed rates up to an unprecedented level. Germany, in economic difficulties before 1933, followed a policy of self-sufficiency, bolstered by exchange controls and bilateral trading agreements, called *Autarky*. Other countries more or less reluctantly followed suit, with the strategy of defensive retaliation. International trade declined drastically.

Additional factors entered into the demise of that special version of a free system of international currency trade, the gold standard. It was found that it frequently did not work as planned. Prices did not respond to losses or gains in gold reserves (sometimes because governments resorted to countervailing policies, such as counter-inflationary measures that kept the money supply from expanding and prices from rising). When prices did respond, the inelasticity of demand for either imports or exports might prevent trade patterns from responding. Furthermore, the output of gold was proceeding at a rate totally inadequate to meet the growing needs of international trade.

That decline of the gold standard was both a cause and a result of the great depression. As the battered nations emerged from World War II, they shared a general revulsion against the extreme nationalist, "beggar-my-neighbor" policies of the recent past. This mood made possible the organization of the International Monetary Fund (IMF) and the General Agreement on Tariffs and Trade (GATT), as well as an atmosphere for international trade less encumbered by restrictive national laws.

As of early 1975 there are both ominous and hopeful signs. In many countries troubled by a mixture of inflation at disturbingly high rates and unemployment, both intensified by the rise in the cost of energy, there is an observable tendency to seek independent solutions involving the raising of barriers to imports and currency devaluations —perhaps most conspicuously the "Nixon shock" of 1971, analyzed in the Yoshida International case at p. 116, supra. As of early 1975, attempts were being made to breathe new life into both the GATT and the IMF so that flexibility and strength could be added to the international system.

We discuss first the United States system with respect to foreign trade, and then the international attempt to bring order into that field through the GATT. We then follow the same sequence for monetary policy—first national rules, and then the IMF.

B. UNITED STATES LEGISLATION ON TRADE BARRIERS

The United States laws on tariffs and other trade barriers constitute a large mass of rules, the domain of a specialized bar and a special customs court system. A look at Title 19, United States Code, reveals page after page of classifications of goods and the tariff rates applicable to them. A difference in the classification of a major import can result in a difference in duties payable amounting to large sums of money.[2] However, our concern here is only with the basic structure of these tariff laws.

As we saw in Chapter II, at pp. 109–110, supra, the core of the tariff system is the 1930 table of rates plus the powers delegated to the President to adjust rates. Most importantly, those powers include the right to modify duties so as to carry out trade agreements entered into under the same congressional authority. These authorizations originated in the 1934 Act, p. 110, supra, as amended by Extension Acts in 1949, 1951, 1953, 1954, 1955 and 1958 and then superseded by the Trade Expansion Act of 1962, 76 Stat. 872, 19 U.S.C.A. § 1801 et seq. Since the powers conferred by the 1962 Act had largely expired in 1967, this type of authority was for some time in limbo.

The Trade Act of 1974, 88 Stat. 1978, again provides the President with broad discretion (for the next five years) to negotiate agreements and to modify duties as well as non-tariff restrictions, although Section 102 requires congressional implementation of agreements reducing United States tariff barriers. Presidential authority covers not only tariff negotiations and agreements under the aegis of the General Agreement on Tariffs and Trade, but also (in Title IV) bargaining with "countries not currently receiving nondiscriminatory treatment," i. e., the Soviet Union and other Communist countries.[3]

2. For example, the issue in Mattel, Inc. v. United States, 287 F.Supp. 999 (Cust.Ct.1968)—whether interchangeable wigs for "Barbie" dolls were "parts of toys" at 35% ad valorem or "wigs" at 14%—was said to involve hundreds of thousands of dollars.

3. The East-West trade provisions became embroiled with efforts to link

While these provisions look to the reduction of tariffs, there have long been authorizations to *increase* tariff rates, to restore rates to levels existing before reductions or to impose other restraints on imports. Such authorizations are independent of the grant of bargaining authority and survived the lapse of the 1962 powers. The Trade Act of 1974 revised, reshuffled and expanded these provisions. Section 125 confers on the President sweeping authority to terminate international trade agreements. Section 301 carries forward Presidential power to respond to "unjustifiable or unreasonable" tariffs or import restrictions, or to discriminatory policies burdening U. S. exports, or to unjustifiable restrictions on access to resources and supplies. The authority given by Section 232 of the 1962 Act to curtail imports found "to threaten to impair the national security" continues. Section 351 of the 1962 Act, as amended in 1974, continues the "escape clause", long characteristic of trade legislation, which authorizes restrictions on imports "causing or threatening to cause serious injury" to domestic industry.

However, the 1962 Act introduced (and the 1974 Act expanded) provisions giving the government the power, as an alternative to granting such protection, to provide adjustment assistance to the domestic industry affected. That assistance might, for example, include loans or tax relief for the firms involved or retraining, relocation or readjustment allowances to displaced workers. It may also involve adjustment assistance for a community officially classified as a "trade impacted area." Section 122 of the 1974 Act adds a further power, that of ordering temporary increases in duties to meet balance of payments emergencies—the power that the Yoshida International case, p. 116, supra, found that the President did not have.

Outside of the 1962 Act, older legislation authorizes upward adjustments. The Anti-Dumping Act [4] allows the imposition of a special dumping duty when it has been determined that foreign merchandise is being or is likely to be sold in the United States, to the injury of American producers, at prices below those at which it is being sold in the principal markets of the country of export. Section 303 of the Tariff Act of 1930 provides for a "countervailing duty" whenever the exporting country pays or bestows a "bounty or grant" upon merchandise exported to this country.[5]

trade with the Soviet Union with an increase in the protection afforded Soviet citizens (particularly Jews) in that country seeking to emigrate. These efforts delayed passage of the Act until provisions responsive to them were included, and subsequent difficulties with the USSR may prevent implementation of that part of the law (Sections 402, 409).

4. The Anti-Dumping Act, 42 Stat. 11 (1921), as amended, 19 U.S.C.A. § 160 et seq., was further amended by § 321 of the Trade Act of 1974.

5. The countervailing duty provision was amended by § 331 of the Trade Act of 1974.

A full description of United States trade barriers also calls for a survey of direct curbs on entry, as distinguished from tariffs:

(1) The barriers under the Trading with the Enemy Act to trade with Communist China, North Korea, North Viet-Nam and Cuba, described at pp. 110–112, supra, apply to imports as well as exports.

(2) Certain statutes regulate or prohibit imports that are regarded as peculiarly dangerous: pornographic matter, insecticides, drugs, poisons, munitions. See, e. g., Section 305 of the Tariff Act of 1930, 46 Stat. 688, as amended, 19 U.S.C.A. § 1305.

(3) Some legislation authorizes the imposition of quantitative limitations on imports (a stated number of barrels of oil, bushels or tons of an agricultural commodity, and so on) in order to protect domestic producers of competitive products. These quotas or quantitative restrictions have an effect similar to tariffs in discouraging imports. But unlike a tariff, a quantitative restraint cannot be surmounted simply by paying a duty. It is more rigid, less responsive to changes in the demand for or supply of a product. It may further require definition of how the quota is to be allocated among various importers competing for the product or among various countries which export it. A tariff settles such questions by providing that whoever is willing to pay the exporter's price plus duty may import.

The chief examples of quantitative restrictions have been (a) the limitations established under the Agricultural Adjustment Act, 49 Stat. 773 (1935), as amended, 7 U.S.C.A. § 624, to protect American farmers and to prevent foreign production from interfering with the administration of price support programs, and (b) restrictions under the authority of the "national security" clause of the Trade Expansion Act of 1962, 76 Stat. 877, 19 U.S.C.A. § 1862, or predecessor statutes, pursuant to which the executive branch set quotas on the importation of crude and refined petroleum.

In some cases the task of limiting the quantity of imports is thrust upon the exporting countries in the form of "voluntary agreements." In the textile field there exists a special multilateral agreement under which the exporting countries, fearful that the importing countries left to themselves might take more drastic action, have agreed to limit the quantity of textiles they export. A comparable program involving an agreement among producers shipping steel to this country, one not given formal sanction by United States law though approved by the executive branch, has been subjected to court challenge as violating the antitrust laws.[6]

(4) The "Buy American Act," 47 Stat. 1520 (1933), as amended, 41 U.S.C.A. §§ 10a–10d, and related executive rules prohibit the purchase by federal agencies of foreign goods when domestic equivalents are available at comparable prices or when national security interests

6. See Consumers Union of U. S., Inc. v. Rogers, 352 F.Supp. 1319 (D.D.C. 1973); aff'd, 506 F.2d 136 (D.C. Cir. 1974). The voluntary restraints were immunized by the Trade Act of 1974.

are involved. The margin of preference given to domestic suppliers has varied from time to time. Some state statutes have comparable provisions.

(5) The holder of a valid American trade-mark can, under Section 526 of the Tariff Act of 1930, p. 1024, supra, keep out goods the importation of which would violate his exclusive right to use the mark in the United States. A similar power is given to the holder of a valid American patent by Sections 337 and 337a of the Tariff Act.

(6) Section 304 of the Tariff Act of 1930 requires the conspicuous and permanent marking of goods of foreign origin so as to indicate the country of origin. This rule has been criticized by importers as supporting domestic prejudices against foreign goods and putting foreign producers to unnecessary inconvenience and expense.

C. THE GENERAL AGREEMENT ON TARIFFS AND TRADE

The General Agreement on Tariffs and Trade (the GATT) is the product of a post war revulsion against the excesses of national separatism. In 1947–48 the representatives of 53 nations drafted the so-called Havana Charter, which in addition to reducing numerous tariff rates would have set up a rather elaborate International Trade Organization (ITO) to administer and enforce its substantive provisions. Although the United States had been a prime initiator of the Havana Charter, it became apparent that the United States Senate would not give its consent.

During the negotiation of the Havana Charter, a smaller group of countries, including the United States, put together a temporary or stop gap agreement intended to put into immediate operation many of the Charter's terms. Under the name of the General Agreement on Tariffs and Trade * this agreement became effective on January 1, 1948, after the required number of initial members had signed the Protocol of Provisional Application of October 30, 1947, 61 Stat. A2051, T.I.A.S. No. 1700, 55 U.N.T.S. 308. The Protocol was signed on that date on behalf of the United States, but neither it nor the General Agreement has ever been submitted to the Senate for its advice and consent. In fact, the General Agreement is still applied only through this Protocol, drafted when hopes for a permanent organization were directed towards the ITO. Its paragraph 1 states that the members undertake to apply Parts I and III of the General Agreement without qualification, and to apply Part II "to the fullest extent not inconsistent with existing legislation." Countries which later became parties to the GATT signed protocols substantially to the same effect. The text below summarizes the provisions of Parts I, II and III.

Congress, which never in so many words authorized accession to the GATT, has maintained a wary attitude towards it. A clause in the Trade Agreements Extension Act of 1951 stated: "The enactment of this Act shall not be construed to determine or indicate the approval or disapproval by the Congress of the Executive Agreement known as the General Agreement on Tariffs and Trade." 65 Stat. 75. Similar clauses were inserted in the Trade Agreement Extension Acts of 1953, 1954, 1955 and 1958.[7] Significantly, no such clause appeared in the Trade Expansion Act of 1962. Section 121 of the 1974 Act goes much further, urging the President to take specified action to revise decision-making procedures and substantive rules of GATT. It ends with the statement, "This authorization does not imply approval or disapproval by the Congress of all articles of The General Agreement on Tariffs and Trade."

The text below leads the reader on a swift and selective tour through the intricate provisions of the GATT. Those articles designated by an asterisk should be read together with the text.

The Preamble states the Agreement's cardinal objectives, particularly the "substantial reduction of tariffs and other barriers to trade" and the "elimination of discriminatory treatment." The GATT aims not at totally free trade, but at freer trade. In several instances, it states potent principles, followed by potent exceptions. These couplings of rules and qualifications reflect necessary compromises between the objective of a more open trading climate permitting each nation to compete with its neighbors with fewer artificial trade barriers, and the varied domestic policies which point towards some degree of protection of domestic industry and agriculture.

The Agreement seeks to realize its objectives through provisions that can be classified among (a) rules for tariff negotiations, which culminate in tariff schedules that become part of the Agreement, (b) rules governing the conduct of international trade and aiming at the liberalization of restrictive policies, and (c) provisions for consultations among and meetings of members, to provide a forum for discussion of prospective policies and for settlement of disputes. Although tariffs were initially thought to be the GATT's dominant concern and continue to draw most public attention because of the major conferences in which they are negotiated, the day-by-day work within the GATT treats largely other forms of trade barriers and attempts to develop general programs to increase world trade.

As initially drafted, the GATT was divided into three parts; a fourth part, which became effective in 1966, is described at p. 1162, infra. Part I (Articles I and II) deals solely with tariffs. Part II (Articles III to XXIII) treats principally restrictions other than tariffs, defines a number of exceptions which apply to all forms of trade barriers, and states some of the methods for resolving disputes. Part III (Articles XXIV to XXXV) contains procedural and administrative provisions, as well as some exceptions of general applicability and some rules for tariff negotiations. As this brief résumé suggests, the

7. 67 Stat. 472, 68 Stat. 360, 69 Stat. 162, and 72 Stat. 673. The 1955 clause is the one that has been codified in the form of Section 350(a).

Agreement does not strive to create a tightly defined set of rules or a carefully worked out set of procedures. Much of it reflects an assumption that it would be transitory in character.

NOTE ON TARIFFS AND OTHER RESTRICTIONS

Tariffs

Article I * states one of the GATT's basic principles, non-discrimination. That principle is expressed through a general and unconditional most-favored-nation clause, initially thought to be the GATT's principal objective and accomplishment. It has its most important application to tariff rates, where it displaces bilateral reciprocal trade agreements with an assurance of non-discrimination among all Contracting Parties. Other provisions of Article I state carefully qualified exceptions to most-favored-nation treatment for countries grouped in preferential tariff arrangements, such as the British Commonwealth.

Article II * imposes the obligation upon each party to accord to the commerce of other parties treatment (that is, exaction of duties) no less favorable than that provided for in schedules annexed to the Agreement. In this manner, Article II implements and makes concrete the obligations flowing from Article I. The schedules in fact occupy several volumes. Some 65,000 items (tariff classifications) that are included within them cover over half of the world's international trade. The schedules incorporate the results of original bilateral negotiations between member countries and of periodic renegotiations under the aegis of the GATT. The initial negotiation process within the GATT bore resemblance to a complex and interlocking group of bilateral tariff agreements. Tariff concessions which had been granted by any country to any other country in the course of the negotiations were combined into a single schedule, and such concessions represented a unitary commitment of that country to all other Contracting Parties. Concessions can take the form of "reductions" or of "bindings," commitments to bind existing duties at their present rate. Bindings become particularly relevant for low-tariff countries, which by definition have little to offer in the way of further reductions.

There are various procedures for modifying the rates included in the schedules under Article II. The most significant and dramatic are the periodic rounds of negotiations among member countries. In addition, Article XXVIII *, as amended in 1955, permits a party (the "applicant party") at three-year intervals to modify or withdraw tariff concessions. Such action may be taken after "negotiation and agreement" with the country with which the concessions were initially negotiated and with any other country determined by the Contracting Parties [8] to have a "principal supplying interest" in the product in-

8. The term "CONTRACTING PARTIES," when it appears in such type in the text of the GATT refers to the Contracting Parties acting jointly. See Article XXV(1). The text above does not make that distinction.

volved. However, the applicant party has the right to take such action even if agreement cannot be reached. Note that the other parties have the right, without duty of consultation with the Contracting Parties, to withdraw "substantially equivalent concessions" initially negotiated with the applicant party. Note also the significant change in bargaining techniques which the GATT here brings about. Cancelling a concession is no longer a bilateral matter. It involves negotiation with a number of countries in a public conference, raises more acute political considerations, and runs the risk of a proliferation of counter measures by the other parties involved.

Unless a member exercises its right to modify or withdraw a concession under these procedures, the schedules remain in effect for another three-year period. However, paragraph (4) of Article XXVIII introduces a necessary flexibility by permitting modification or withdrawal even during the three-year period. In such circumstances, consultation with the Contracting Parties is called for if agreement cannot be reached among the primarily concerned countries. If the applicant party carries through its plans, retaliatory measures—or, alternatively viewed, "compensation"—can again be taken by the designated countries.

Articles VI and XIX permit departures under limited circumstances from these tariff rules. The first treats anti-dumping and countervailing duties. As noted at p. 1147, supra, the United States has long had comparable legislation in effect. Under the GATT, the country to which a product is exported can impose an anti-dumping duty to offset the foreign country's practice if material injury to its domestic industry is threatened. It can also impose countervailing duties which are designed to counteract the foreign subsidization of exports.

Article XIX * states the same principle found in the "escape" clause which has long been characteristic of tariff legislation in the United States. This privilege to withdraw concessions if, because of "unforeseen developments," they have spurred imports to the point where they cause or threaten "serious injury to domestic producers," is limited in extent and time to the injury feared. Except in emergency circumstances, consultation with the countries adversely affected by the withdrawal must first take place. If the talks do not gain acquiescence by such countries in the action taken under Article XIX, they are authorized to withdraw "substantially equivalent concessions." In fact, the United States has invoked Article XIX several times, and retaliatory measures have in a few instances followed its action. The domestic version of the escape clause, as it appears in Section 351 of the Trade Expansion Act of 1962 (as amended in 1974), differs from the GATT version chiefly in not requiring that the "serious injury" to domestic producers be shown to have been caused by "unforeseen developments."

Restrictions other than Tariffs

The bulk of Part II of the Agreement states rules for the liberalization of trade restrictions other than tariffs. Generally the Agreement attempts to make tariffs as much as possible the sole authorized protective device.

Articles III to XI bar a variety of national measures which serve, directly or indirectly, to curb importation. For example, Article III proscribes the use of internal taxes or other regulatory measures in such a way as to afford protection to domestic production. It generally requires for imports "treatment no less favorable than that accorded to like products of national origin in respect of all laws, regulations and requirements affecting their internal sale, offering for sale, purchase, transportation, distribution or use." Here a national-treatment standard serves the same general purpose as the most-favored-nation clause: eliminating discrimination. Articles VII and VIII lay down general principles for the valuation of imported goods, the limitation of service fees other than duties and the simplification of customs formalities. Article IX imposes restraints upon national requirements of marks of origin of imported goods, in order to prevent unreasonably burdensome marking requirements on the one hand and fraudulent marking on the other.

The single most important prohibition in the Agreement appears in Article XI(1)*, which bars import restrictions other than duties, whether in the form of quotas limiting imports of a product or of licensing schemes involving discretion on the part of those administering them whether to permit particular imports. Administration of this clause and its varied exceptions has played a major role in the meetings of the Contracting Parties or other groups formed under the GATT to resolve disputes among members. The prohibition is softened by several exceptions in Article XI.

But the most broadly phrased exception, one that could vitiate much of the force of Article XI if liberally interpreted and applied, appears in Article XII *: quota restrictions which are designed to safeguard a country's balance of payments by restricting imports that drain the importing country of essential hard currency reserves. Note the various limitations upon the right to impose import restrictions for these purposes, and the complex procedures which must be followed by a country desiring to invoke that article. The GATT here implicitly recognizes the right of a member to pursue its own domestic policies even if they give rise to balance-of-payment problems, and to impose quotas in such a way as to establish priorities for the importation of essential products. But countries acting under Article XII make certain undertakings and become obligated to consult with the Contracting Parties as long as they impose quotas.

Amendments

Among the miscellaneous provisions of Part III, Article XXX provides that amendments to Part I of the GATT require acceptance by all Contracting Parties, while amendments to other parts of the GATT become effective, "in respect of those contracting parties which accept them," upon acceptance by two thirds of the Contracting Parties. These provisions bear a complex and uncertain relationship to Article XXV(5)*, for on occasion a waiver—particularly one of unlimited duration or of general application to a number of members—will share characteristics of an amendment.

NOTE ON TECHNIQUES FOR TARIFF NEGOTIATIONS

Obviously a major function of the GATT is to decrease further the tariffs set forth in the schedules to Article II. The Agreement itself says little about the rules under which such negotiations are to be conducted, and Article XXVIII *bis* * has had to be supplemented by a new set of rules for each of the conferences.

The five conferences preceding the Kennedy Round were conducted through "product-by-product" negotiations. Before negotiations began each participant sent "request lists" to countries from which concessions were sought. Such lists were distributed to all participants. Thus each country was aware at an early stage of the direction that negotiations would take and could anticipate the effect of tariff reductions requested by other countries upon its own trade. The responses to the "request lists" were stated in "lists of offers," which were distributed simultaneously to all participants which had made offers. The negotiations that then took place were basically bilateral, although small groups of countries could simultaneously debate interrelated requests and offers. As two countries reached agreement, their lists of concessions were filed with the Secretariat. However, such lists did not become final until all participants had filed their concessions, and revisions could take place as the results of all bilateral negotiations came in. At the end of the conference, all concessions were combined into the schedules.

Note that much of the bilateral character of the pre-war techniques for reciprocal trade agreements was preserved in these GATT negotiations. Further, countries generally continued to follow a *de facto* "principal supplier" rule, in order to minimize the effect of the most-favored-nation principle. A concession on product X would be granted by a country in the course of negotiations with a principal supplier of X; in exchange, that country would simultaneously bargain for concessions on products of which it was a principal supplier. One striking advantage over the bilateral trade agreement was the speed with which many countries were able to arrive at a common understanding. And negotiations had of course from the start an important multilateral aspect. Each participant was aware of what others were seeking or offering, and concessions became final only after all results were in. Thus, the first five conferences have been described as "bilateral-multilateral" negotiations on a product-by-product basis. The fact that bargaining took place over particular products enabled each participant, to the extent that it could withstand pressures exerted by other countries or win concessions without the sacrifice of important national interests, to seek to confine its concessions to imports which would not lead to excessive disruption in its domestic economy.

The first five conferences yielded substantial results, but the trend was towards smaller reductions and rates. Thus the Dillon Round of 1960–62 achieved only modest reductions. To some extent, this development was inevitable. As tariffs decreased in each round, nations tended to view more cautiously any further reductions and to seek to preserve some bargaining strength for future rounds. Moreover, in the case of the United States, negotiating authority was hedged by substantial restrictions, such as escape clauses and national security clauses.

The Kennedy Round faced new problems and attempted new solutions. It assumed that the Round would be centered on negotiations between the United States and the European Economic Community, pp. 1259–1260, infra. The Community posed a special threat to United States exports and hence to its troubled balance of payments, for it presented a single tariff wall rather than six varying national structures. This problem was intensified by the developing plans of the Community for the protection of its own agriculture, involving support of prices paid to European farmers and a variable levy on imports from outside Europe that was designed to protect the price support scheme. The internal political system of the Community made it difficult for it to bargain on a commodity-by-commodity basis without constant references back to the national governments. The rules for the Kennedy Round accommodated these needs. They assumed a basically bilateral character and an emphasis on general across-the-board reductions of tariffs—so called linear reductions.

After long delays in starting, due largely to internal problems of the Community, the Kennedy Round took place in 1967. In his review of the Round, the head of the American mission, Ambassador Roth, expressed his view that substantial progress had been made.[9] There were extensive tariff cuts, in the 35–50% range; the United States tariff concessions affected $7 to $8 billion of imports, and this country received equivalent benefits. Further cuts in tariffs were contingent upon modification by the United States Congress of the American Selling Price System affecting imports of chemical products. The A.S.P. System bases tariffs on certain important chemicals not on their foreign value but on the price at which domestic American producers sell them. This system would violate the GATT but for the fact that it antedates 1947. The failure of Congress to act on this matter prevented the corresponding concessions by other countries from coming into effect. There were also efforts to diminish non-tariff barriers, especially in certain industries. The gains in freedom of trade for agricultural commodities were real but modest.

9. 57 Dep't State Bull. 123, 173 (1967).

As of early 1975 it was unclear what direction the new round of negotiations for which preparations were being made would take. Preceding rounds brought tariff barriers to a low level, and economists doubt whether further cuts in rates of 10% or so have much effect on the volume of trade. There will necessarily be more stress on non-tariff barriers, such as quotas and exchange controls. It will be difficult to approach such barriers by traditional methods of negotiations at large and formal conferences on a most-favored-nation basis. Thought will also have to be given to barriers to exports as well as imports. The actions of the petroleum exporting countries (OPEC), and of the United States with respect to soybeans and then to wheat, demonstrate that access to sources can be as vital as access to markets, especially when exporters' actions to "protect" themselves are sudden and drastic. At a time when voices calling for additional protective barriers to protect their interests from economic change are heard more loudly and frequently, a new round of negotiations will pose complex political and procedural issues. The declaration of the Foreign Ministers of member countries of GATT in Toyko calling for the new round speaks only in general terms of the problems to be faced. B.I.S.D., 20th Supplement, 1974, p. 20.

NOTE ON TECHNIQUES FOR ADJUSTMENT OF DISPUTES

In addition to establishing general rules about the conduct of national trade policies and serving as a forum for multilateral tariff negotiations, the GATT serves a third function. This can be most broadly described as the resolution of differences between its members over the interpretation and application of its rules to particular situations. One is tempted to refer to this function partly as adjudication and partly as rule-making through decisions on particular disputes. But, as we shall see, this would be misleading in various ways. In particular it would suggest a more formal, more coercive process than in fact obtains.

The Agreement contains a wide variety of provisions determining the course which a party desiring to take certain action or protesting another's action should follow. Some require a formal decision of the Contracting Parties. For example, a country may seek a waiver of a provision in the Agreement which bars action that it deems necessary. See Article XXV(5). In other instances, a country may be free to take certain action but nonetheless be obligated to negotiate first with certain other parties or with the Contracting Parties. Other countries may then be free to take compensatory action. See, for example, the provisions in Article XIX for emergency action on imports. If a member considers that another member is violating a provision of, or nullifying or impairing a benefit of, the Agreement, it can set in motion the procedures under Articles XXII* and XXIII*. The latter is the key provision of the GATT under which the Contracting Parties may authorize withdrawal of concessions. Note the large discretion given the Contracting Parties to determine the degree to which an injured party may suspend application of "concessions or other obligations under this Agreement."

These procedures emphasize three factors that distinguish them from formal domestic adjudication:

> **(1)** Primary stress is upon consultation and negotiation. At the start, the immediate parties to a dispute attempt to resolve their differences. The next step is often referral of the dispute to a "panel," a small group whose members act in an individual capacity and which seeks to achieve conciliation. It is noteworthy that the General Agreement makes no reference to such panels, or indeed to dispute resolution through any group other than the Contracting Parties. This institutional evolution serviced the need for informal procedures conducive to an atmosphere of relative privacy. Finally, a dispute can come before the Contracting Parties as a whole. Read Article XXIII, noting the particular steps which it requires.
>
> **(2)** An effort is generally made to avoid formal "judgment," particularly specific condemnation of a practice as violative of the Agreement. Article XXIII(1) illustrates the parallel tendency to blur the treatment of conduct that merely "impairs benefits" under the Agreement with that given to unlawful conduct. Note that impairment within the meaning of that Article might be the consequence of action of a member that is consistent with the GATT—perhaps action under the "escape clause" of Article XIX.
>
> **(3)** Even when matters come to official decision by the Contracting Parties, as under Article XXIII, there is a tendency to avoid wherever possible the authorization of sanctions. Indeed, they are generally referred to as "compensatory" measures, and have only once been authorized.

This "soft" character of the mechanism for dispute-resolution within the GATT makes the Agreement in one sense less effective in keeping members in line with its rules. On the other hand, this character may have been essential to the survival of the GATT in times of stress. As one commentator has said, "the present procedures seem most effective when viewed as a conciliation process, and least effective if viewed as a sanction or compensation process." [10] Whatever the explanations, these procedures provide a striking contrast with the judicial method of dispute resolution for numerous (but not the most political) issues within the nine-country European Economic Community examined in Chapter XIII.

Consider three episodes illustrative of the adjustment process. In a dramatic move described at p. 116, supra, President Nixon imposed in August 1971 a temporary 10% surcharge on all imports in

10. Jackson, The Puzzle of GATT, 1 J. of World Trade 131, 160 (1967).

defense of a deteriorating balance of payments. A GATT working party met promptly and in September 1971 issued a report. It found the United States action "inappropriate", "not compatible with" Article II, and not justified by foreign exchange problems under Article XXIV. It does not, however, appear that this report did anything to accelerate United States termination of the surcharge. B.I.S.D., 18th Supplement, 1972, pp. 212–23.

The United States was also the focus of efforts by a working party over many years to modify the restrictive effects of actions under the Agricultural Adjustment Act of 1935, 49 Stat. 773, as amended, 7 U.S.C.A. § 624. Under that Act the government imposed quotas on imports of a number of products which benefited from the price support programs authorized by the same Act—including grain, cheese and other dairy products. In 1952 the Working Party authorized the Netherlands to take compensatory action by suspending GATT benefits as to 60,000 tons of wheat flour from the United States but, after thus finding that the United States had "nullified or impaired" its own concessions and thereby had infringed Article XI of the Agreement, it reluctantly granted a waiver in 1955. That waiver has continued to be in effect. Since that time, the Working Party received successive reports from the United States on "progress" towards the goal of ending these restrictions, most recently in 1970. B.I.S.D., 18th Supplement, p. 223. It can be expected that the developing perception of a world shortage of agricultural commodities will cause this particular problem to fade in importance.

Another notorious episode was the so-called "Chicken War". From 1958 to 1961 exports of chickens from the United States to Germany soared due to improvements in American poultry-raising techniques and to Germany's relaxation of import restrictions (the latter being due in part to pressures generated by GATT). In 1962, however, the German tariff was replaced by the higher import fees applicable under the European Economic Community's new agricultural program and its external tariff. The decline in the export of chickens from the United States was dramatic and the United States' reaction was acute.

In terms of the GATT, several issues were involved. One was the character of the EEC as a customs union. Article XXIV permits the formation of customs unions under specified conditions, although on its face a customs union violates the most-favored-nation principle of GATT. The GATT calls for negotiation to realize the necessary adjustments. Many issues were settled by negotiations between the United States and the EEC, but not the level of tariffs on poultry and other food products. It was also questionable whether the United States was "the principal supplying interest" entitled to invoke Article XXVIII, since the concession by which Germany was bound under GATT had been negotiated with Denmark.

The United States announced that it would act under Article XXVIII. This decision led to consultations between the United States and the EEC, which jointly asked the GATT Council of Representatives to appoint a panel. The panel was not to pass on any legal issues under the GATT but solely to render an advisory opinion on the value of United States exports of poultry to Germany as of September 1, 1960. A five member panel, including the Executive Secretary of GATT, rendered a report on November 21, 1963 concluding that "a figure of $26 million would reasonably represent the value" of those exports. Thereupon the United States, acting under the 1934 and 1962 Acts, raised bound rates to the older statutory rates on the agreed amount of imports from Community countries. The result was a substantial decline in trade in those commodities as well as in chicken exports. At least one observer, however, credits the panel's factual report with having averted ill feeling and excessive retaliation by the United States, which would likely have been followed by a round of retaliation by the Community.[11]

NOTE ON THE GATT AND LESS DEVELOPED COUNTRIES

From its inception, GATT has in varying forms given some expression to the special needs of less developed countries. Thus Article XVIII [12] recognized that "it may be necessary for [less developed countries], in order to implement programmes and policies of economic development designed to raise the general standard of living of their people, to take protective or other measures affecting imports, and that such measures are justified insofar as they facilitate the attainment of the objectives of this Agreement." That article gave additional authority to such countries to deviate from the GATT's general rules, particularly with respect to tariff protection required for the establishment of a particular industry and to quantitative restrictions for balance-of-payments purposes.

But such provisions, even liberally applied, have proved to be painfully inadequate. The large, and growing, gap between the standards of living in the developed and less developed countries has produced deep concern and discontent in the latter group and caused it to seek relief through new trade policies and measures. To some extent, these pressures are a consequence of the larger voice in the international community which such countries today command. The expansion in membership of the United Nations has been dominantly through underdeveloped countries freed of colonial or another dependent status. GATT itself, which started as a group of 23 principally developed countries, now numbers over 50 countries which could be characterized as less developed among its nearly 100 members.

Particularly since October 1973, a difference of interests has become evident between those less developed countries which possess

11. Walker, Dispute Settlement: The Chicken War, 58 Am.J.Int.L. 670 (1964).

12. Added by a Protocol signed in 1955, entered into force in 1957, 8 U.S.T. & O.I.A. 1767, 1778, T.I.A.S. No. 3930, 278 U.N.T.S. 168. The original Article XVIII appears at 61 Stat. A 53, T.I.A.S. No. 1700, at p. 49, 55 U.N. T.S. 187, 253.

large amounts of desired natural resources such as petroleum, bauxite or copper, and those which do not. Less developed countries in one category are increasingly able—depending on the market for their commodity—to extract large sums of foreign exchange from the world economic system to help them develop, whereas less fortunate nations are, in addition to their other problems, saddled with increasing obligations for outlays to obtain at escalating prices needed energy, fertilizer, and other products.

To many less developed countries, GATT has often appeared to be a "rich man's club." Its goals of reciprocal, nondiscriminatory tariff reductions and lower non-tariff barriers are thought to service principally the needs of the developed world—indeed, at times to frustrate the desires of the "other" world to achieve greater relative equality. To be sure, the underdeveloped countries have benefited from the generalizing effect of the most-favored-nation clause, often without being required to grant equivalent concessions. But that benefit, from their point of view, is marginal, for they are generally in no position to compete for export markets in the manufactures or semi-finished products which have figured so heavily in the GATT negotiations. Rather, such countries often view the GATT—whether by design or simply by operation—as a means of preserving their traditional dependence upon the developed world for manufactures.

The most-favored-nation principle now under challenge is one expression of the economists' conception of a world-wide market permitting the most efficient producing country to prevail. The departure from that principle permitted by Article XVIII of the GATT, to create tariff shelters in which infant industries could grow, finds many historical precedents among developing countries—including the United States in its earlier history. Such protection was thought to be vital, even though it meant that a country's consumers would have to pay higher prices for goods produced by an industry that, at least for the time being, was relatively inefficient. But the current thinking of developing countries goes one step further. Recognizing that their internal markets may be too small to support given manufacturing industries, they seek protected or preferential markets for them outside their borders. One route is to form a free trade area or common market and thereby "pool" the markets of several less developed countries within a preferential tariff scheme; the Latin American Free Trade Area is an example of such thinking which, however, proved of little consequence. Another route is to seek preferences in the markets of the developed countries, thus giving stimulus to their exports by advantaging them *vis-à-vis* competitive goods from developed countries.[13]

This last proposal raises numerous issues which have become the subject of dispute among economists and statesmen. Even assuming

13. The idea of such preferences is not wholly new. It has been common for colonial countries to include their colonies within their tariff walls—thus giving, for example, preference in Great Britain to cocoa from Ghana over cocoa from French West Africa. Some of these preferences, as within the Common Market, have survived the end of the colonial period.

that preferences will enable their proponents to realize their goals—more diversified economies with industrial sectors that will be able to compete in export markets with industry of the developed world—what scheme should be adopted? Some suggest a highly particularistic analysis. Their effort would be to select the most promising manufactures in each country for preferential treatment, making distinctions among industries and countries with respect to the degree and duration of the preference. Critics of such proposals stress the risk of fostering jealousies among underdeveloped countries because of the resulting discriminations, the difficulty of forecasting with any accuracy which industries can become economically viable within a given period, and the chaotic patterns of world trade which would result. Others urge the granting of preferences on a multilateral and nondiscriminatory basis, to all "less developed countries." Such proposals, however, might perpetuate the very inequities which these countries now find within the existing system of GATT, by treating equally a large and amorphous group of such countries which are in markedly different stages of development. They might also cause greater disorganization of markets than a system of selective preferences. One possible compromise might be to limit the preferences granted on a multilateral basis to those industries which appear most likely to be able to gain self-sufficiency, without preferences, in a relatively brief period of time.

The search for preferences is only one aspect of the endeavors of underdeveloped countries to improve their position. Another is the negotiation of commodity agreements that would improve (or at least preserve) the relative price levels (or terms of trade) for the commodities which (together with mineral resources) form about 85% of the export value—and the chief source of needed foreign exchange—for many such countries. Still another is the attempt to induce developed countries to reduce—even on a nonpreferential basis—the disparity between their tariffs on raw materials and those on semi-processed or processed goods. If developed countries levy little or no tariff on the import of iron ore but up to a 20% tariff on steel beams, less developed countries find it difficult to move from the status of a mere supplier of raw material (ore) to a supplier of manufactured steel.

The attitude of the developed countries towards these demands for changes in the organization of world trade has been mixed. There has been some sympathy, as might be expected from a group of countries that contribute billions of dollars each year in aid. On the other hand, there is much skepticism about the potential efficiency of the proposed new methods, in particular about trade preferences. There is also considerable commercial and economic self-interest at stake. This has been perhaps most evident in the textile field. Here it is possible for less developed countries, particularly in Asia, to export to Europe and the United States at prices below those of domestic output. This has caused anxieties about the ruin of established textile industries and complaints about "underpaid" foreign labor. It has also caused some restrictive action, chiefly by means of international agreements providing for quantitative restrictions largely administered by the exporting countries. It was possible to take the view that the United States had been particularly unhelpful in this whole area, "a lone voice of negation confronting a chorus of hopeful positive suggestions." H. Johnson, Economic Policies Towards Less Developed Countries 7 (1967). See, however, the more affirmative views stated in Solomon, United States Foreign Trade Policy and the Developing Countries, 57 Dep't State Bull. 180 (1967).

One upshot of these pressures has been the development of new organizations for the debate—and perhaps in the future the resolution—of these issues. In 1964, the first United Nations Conference on Trade and Development (UNCTAD) was convened in Geneva. About 90 of the 120 some participants could be characterized as less developed countries. The Conference has been termed a "forum for expression of discontent." Wielding a clear majority of voting power and then (as well as in subsequent meetings within the framework of UNCTAD) showing considerable solidarity and voting as a group, the underdeveloped countries assured adoption of a large number of resolutions favorable to their position. These were expressed in UNCTAD's Final Act [14], which included recommendations to spur exports from the less developed world of both primary commodities and industrial goods through commodity agreements, temporary tariff preferences, and preferential groupings among such countries. What effect such recommendations will have is of course problematic.

Despite the fact that it was "long on philosophy and doctrine, short on procedures," [15] UNCTAD gave birth to an organization with a continuing administrative machinery. More universal in membership than the GATT through inclusion of socialist countries, UNCTAD promises to become a continuing format for the discussion not only of specific trade issues but of larger questions of economic development. Its relationship to the GATT is uncertain, in process of evolution. But its effect upon the GATT has been fairly dramatic. In response to the growth of this organization, the GATT members accelerated plans for amendment of the Agreement. A new Part IV (Articles XXXVI to XXXVIII *) was added shortly after the first UNCTAD conference, introducing a new range of considerations and activities (committees and centers) to the GATT. Read now Part IV, which entered into force in 1966, less as a statement of specific commitments than as a resume of needs, goals and guidelines for future formulation of rules. Note carefully the degree to which it responds to the different requests of the underdeveloped countries sketched above.

The initial substantive move on the part of GATT was the waiver under Article XXV(5) given by the Contracting Parties to Australia

14. U.N.Doc. No. TD/B/AC. 1/1 (1965).

15. Greenwald, UNCTAD and GATT as Instruments for the Development of Trade Policy, 1967 Proc.Am.Soc.Int.L. 155, 156.

in 1966. B.I.S.D., 14th Supp. (1966), p. 23. Australia applied "for authority to grant preferential tariff treatment to certain goods of less-developed countries . . . when such goods are the products of industries that have not reached a stage of development that enables them to compete in the Australian market with like goods produced in the more industrialized countries." Australia's action was not dependent on reciprocal concessions by such countries. An annex attached to the application specified the goods that might be involved and the degree of tariff or quota preference that might be granted for each. The waiver gave Australia authority to vary the list of goods, duties and quotas and to terminate preferences. However, it required Australia, prior to taking any action, to notify the Contracting Parties and to consult with members of GATT that felt threatened with substantial injury, because of the preferences, to their trade with Australia. The Contracting Parties were to review the waiver annually.

At the Second UNCTAD Conference in 1968 two sweeping and potentially important proposals that related to the tariff preference problem were presented. One by the United States called for duty-free entry of goods, except shoes, textiles and petroleum products, subject to "escape clause" action to restore duties on imports causing substantial injury to American industry. The other, by the European Economic Community, proposed a tariff-free quota on each product, amounting to all imports of that item from the less developed countries in a base year plus 5% of all imports from developed countries in the preceding year.[16]

No agreement was reached so that both the United States and Europe were left free, by means of a general waiver granted by GATT, to put their proposals into effect. Europe did so in 1971 and the United States included in the Trade Act of 1974 provisions authorizing the President to grant such preferences but hedging that permission with many qualifications. One of these conditions, barring countries that belong to the Organization of Petroleum Exporting Countries or other commodity cartels, has awakened strenuous protests in Latin America. Other provisions disqualifying countries that are (in effect) in defiance of the Hickenlooper Amendment (p. 482, supra) or that refuse to recognize arbitral awards against them are also likely to cause problems.

The trade problems of the less developed countries have been increasing rather than diminishing in recent years, especially those of countries without their own supplies of petroleum. Accordingly, the declaration of the Ministers in Tokyo in 1973 calling for a new round of GATT negotiations puts considerable emphasis on action

16. See Cooper, Third World Tariff Tangle 123, 127–28, in A Reordered World: Emerging International Economic Problems (Cooper ed. 1973). The author was skeptical of the practical values of these offers. See Note, Trade Preferences for Developing Countries, 20 Stan.L.Rev. 1150 (1968); Comment, The United States Response to Common Market Trade Preferences and the Legality of the Import Surcharge, 39 U.Chi.L.Rev. 177 (1971).

to assist those countries. It is, however, vague as to what can or should in fact be done on their behalf.

Additional Reading: The two leading works on the GATT are Dam, The GATT—Law and Economic Organization (1970); and Jackson, World Trade and the Law of GATT (1969). A compact study is Catudal, The General Agreement on Tariffs and Trade: An Article-by-Article Analysis in Layman's Language (1961). See also Curzon, Multilateral Commercial Diplomacy (1965). For a collection of articles dealing with United States tariff problems, see Metzger, Law and International Trade (1966). Basic theory as to world trade can be found in any text on international economics, e. g., Kindleberger, International Economics (5th ed. 1973).

D. NATIONAL EXCHANGE CONTROLS

It would be misleading to designate the United States as a major illustration of a national system of exchange controls. This country has never had a comprehensive system of such controls, although from time to time controls have been imposed on some types of private activities. Thus, while briefly describing the recent development of United States rules bearing on foreign exchange, we will also present a sketch of a full fledged exchange control system.

NOTE ON UNITED STATES POLICY

Before March 1933 the United States was a straightforward adherent to the gold standard system, being committed to pay out gold to holders of its paper currency at a rate of one ounce to $21. At that time the new administration was faced by challenges eloquently described by the Attorney General in his argument in Norman v. Baltimore & Ohio R.R., appearing at 294 U.S. 240, 253 (1935):

> . . . [A]n emergency of the highest importance confronted the Nation. Banks, sound and unsound, were failing or closing upon every hand; gold coin, gold certificates, and, indeed, all other forms of currency, were being hoarded by millions of dollars, and, perhaps, by millions of people. Gold was taking flight either into foreign currencies or into foreign lands; and foreign trade had been brought to a standstill. International finance was completely disorganized. The whole situation was one of extreme peril. Price levels were falling. Industries were closing. Millions of people were out of work. Failures and bankruptcies were reaching enormous and, indeed, unparalleled proportions; and, with constant acceleration, our people confessedly, were slipping toward a lower level of civilization. I undertake to say that no man of imagination could have witnessed that distressing spectacle of painful retrogression without acute apprehension and profound sorrow.
>
> Now, in addition to that, we had the experiences of other nations; we had their example. There was not a nation on the face of the earth that was not in distress.

> At that time—and the time I refer to was the 6th day of March 1933—the Swiss franc, the Dutch guilder, and the United States dollar were the only coins that had not been devalued or depreciated. Country after country was going off the gold standard, and thirty countries had passed drastic legislation with regard to finance, foreign commerce, and the regulation of money. Embargoes, trade restrictions, and quotas were characteristic of the day and of the time.

The first official action to meet the crisis (on March 6) involved a presidential declaration of a "bank holiday" to prevent withdrawals of gold from banks, and presidential instructions to the Treasury not to make payments in gold. These were issued under Section 5 of the Trading with the Enemy Act of October 6, 1917. Three days later Congress in the Emergency Banking Act amended that provision; with subsequent amendments it has been codified as 50 U.S.C.A.App. § 5, p. 110, supra, and also as 12 U.S.C.A. § 95a. Congress also confirmed the President's prior actions. Other statutes, joint resolutions and orders forbade unlicensed exports of gold, required the surrender of all gold held in the country, fixed a new weight for the gold dollar (changed from $21 to $35 equals one ounce), and outlawed contractual clauses calling for payments in gold or in money measured by gold.[17] These actions survived challenges on constitutional grounds.[18]

The system as thus modified remained in effect until the 1960's. During the post-1945 period the financial position of the United States was strong, particularly in relation to the war-battered systems of Europe and Japan. A large surplus of exports over imports enabled the United States to finance civilian and military aid programs and to maintain a strong military force overseas. Gradually the situation changed. The United States' excess of exports dwindled and grew inadequate to support other drains on our reserves. Gold holdings fell from $24 billion in 1949 to $12 billion in 1967. More and more foreign parties found themselves holding supplies of dollars. They were willing to do so rather than demand conversion into gold because the dollar was a "reserve currency", generally accepted as a medium for international payments because people had confidence in it. The large "overhang" of dollar claims, most of them short term, began to trouble the United States government, since a loss of confidence in the dollar could come suddenly and lead to a disastrous run of demands of foreign agencies to exchange their dollar holdings for gold.

Beginning in the early 1960's, steps were taken to improve the balance of payments. They included the following actions: (1) The

17. The prohibition against gold clauses was extended by construction to clauses making debts payable in currencies other than the United States dollar. Guaranty Trust Co. v. Henwood, 307 U.S. 247, 59 S.Ct. 847, 83 L. Ed. 1266 (1939). The prohibitions on American holding of gold were terminated pursuant to 87 Stat. 352 (1973).

18. See, e. g., Norman v. Baltimore & Ohio R. R., 294 U.S. 240, 55 S.Ct. 407, 79 L.Ed. 885 (1935); Pike v. United States, 340 F.2d 487 (9th Cir. 1965).

government sought to stimulate exports through tax policies and other means, to increase the "balance-of-trade" surplus. (2) The foreign economic aid programs generally required that their beneficiaries make their purchases out of the loans in the United States. (3) The government sought to offset expenditures abroad by requiring foreign governments to purchase equipment from the United States to counterbalance our military expenditures there. (4) Amendments of the Internal Revenue Code in 1962 (p. 1110, supra) had the effect of making certain investments in developed foreign countries less attractive—and of encouraging repatriation of funds held abroad. (5) The Foreign Investors Tax Act of 1966 (p. 1102, supra) had as one goal the encouragement of foreign investments in the United States. (6) Monetary policies such as those controlling (generally raising) interest rates also had the effect of encouraging foreigners to invest here. Less directly, by dampening inflationary trends, they sought to make American exports more attractive in price and to reduce the propensity of Americans to import.

In 1964 the government instituted the Interest Equalization Tax (IET), Int.Rev.Code §§ 4911–4931, which was renewed several times but reduced to 0% in 1974. This tax was designed to discourage foreign issuers of securities from resorting to the United States capital market by imposing taxes of up to 15% of the value of the bonds or stock. It was expected that such burdens would offset the lower interest rates and higher stock prices prevailing in this country. There were exclusions designed to benefit less developed countries and others peculiarly dependent on the United States capital market. While portfolio investments of United States citizens in foreign securities were restrained in this way, different programs applied to direct investments (i. e., those carrying with them some share in control of the issuing enterprise.)

From 1965 to 1967 a "voluntary" program of restraints on investments abroad was imposed on a group of leading corporations. When the results of this guideline program proved insufficient, mandatory controls were issued, relying for their effectiveness on powers granted by Section 5 of the Trading with the Enemy Act, p. 110 supra. Under these regulations the amount an American investor could send abroad was limited according to standards that related to (a) the prior history of the firm's foreign investment in the 1965–66 base period and (b) the amount of earnings abroad. Again there were relaxations for less developed countries and others. In 1974 these controls were terminated. A program restricting bank loans abroad paralleled these rules.

In 1971 pressures on the dollar reached the point where President Nixon, concurrently with his announcement of a 10% surcharge on imports, p. 1157 supra, directed the Secretary of the Treasury to cease paying out gold for dollars. There followed a meeting of the major commercial nations at the Smithsonian Institute in Washington which resulted in the Smithsonian Agreement of December 1971. Pursuant to that agreement, Congress enacted the Par Value Modification Act of 1972, 86 Stat. 116, as amended, 31 U.S.C.A. § 449, authorizing a reduction in the par value of the dollar and changing its relationship to gold. In 1973 a further devaluation of 10% was approved by Congress. The devaluation of the dollar pursuant to these steps did much to relieve the balance-of-payments problems of the United States, although it caused considerable disarray and uncertainty in the international monetary system, much of which will persist until the International Monetary Fund's articles can finally be revised.

NOTE ON EXCHANGE CONTROL SYSTEMS

Contrast such particular laws and policies with a full exchange control system such as those maintained by many less developed countries and, during the critical post-war period, by European countries and Japan. Such a system may prohibit all unlicensed transactions in or possession of foreign exchange by residents. It characteristically appoints a limited number of banks or other instrumentalities as the only authorized agents for transactions in exchange. Thus an exporter is required to turn over to the bank any foreign exchange he receives (in exchange for the local currency at stipulated rates of exchange), along with documents showing that the amount surrendered is the amount actually received. Goods would not be cleared for transit through the port or across the border without the resulting authorization. The foreign exchange that enters the pool through this process is then, in effect, rationed out by the government. Top priority will be given to imports by government agencies or of goods regarded as vital necessities. Private importers must show their licenses to obtain foreign exchange as well as proof of actual importation. Other imports, in particular goods regarded as "luxuries", must make do with what is left. Sometimes an auction is held at which importers of non-vital goods compete for the supply of hard currency. Similar effects can be achieved by setting different rates of exchange (a multiple-rate system) for favored and disfavored categories, with respect to both import and export transactions.

Foreign investors also encounter exchange controls. Governments fear that, although the initial importation of capital has positive effects on the balance of payments, dividends or interest and repayment of principal will have a "decapitalizing" effect, i. e., will drain more foreign exchange from the country than the total originally imported plus that amount generated by the enterprise. See p. 87, supra. Thus a government will ask for assurances that the enterprise will have positive effects on foreign exchange by displacing imports or by generating exports. It will also set conditions in the license granted as to the amount of dividends that can be repatriated in any year, usually as a percentage of the original investments. Parallel controls apply to license fees for patents, trademarks and other intellectual property. Thus, a full foreign exchange control system reaches people in all walks of life, importers and their customers, travellers, exporters and their suppliers, and so on. One of the common features of such a system is the existence of a black market since the rewards available to those willing to do business at rates other than the official, legal one are apt to be substantial.

Note that it is common for governments to resort to less pervasive systems that produce less bureaucratic activity and less corruption. A government may lift controls on trade and other current transactions, retaining only controls on investment—controls which may as (in the case of France, p. 83, supra) serve purposes not directly related to foreign exchange. Or a system may be inoperative most of the time, being revived only for critical occasions.

Note the interrelationship between exchange controls and direct import restrictions. If only X million pesos are made available to buy widgets abroad, the amount of widget imports is limited just as much as if a quota expressed in terms of numbers of widgets were applied. Trade barriers and exchange controls simply treat different components of the circular flow of goods and funds that constitutes trade.

Descriptions of exchange-control systems in effect in different countries appear in an IMF publication, Annual Report on Exchange Restrictions.

E. THE INTERNATIONAL MONETARY FUND

The same negative experience with protectionist national measures in the 1930's that led to the GATT led to the Bretton Woods Conference in 1944. Years of exchange controls had throttled international trade. Endeavors to spur exports and stifle imports through devaluation of currency had led to cycles of competitive devaluation that wreaked havoc. There emerged from that Conference the Articles of Agreement of the International Monetary Fund, to which the United States adhered in 1945.[19] Practically all members of the U.N. except for the Soviet Union and other Communist states are among the Fund's 83 members.

The following description applies specifically to the IMF as it functioned from 1945 to 1971; the present uncertain and transitional state of affairs is treated thereafter.

The IMF has had two basic regulatory functions. First, it sought to curb nations' impulses to resort to currency devaluation

19. 60 Stat. 1401 (1945), T.I.A.S. No. 1501, 2 U.N.T.S. 39. Membership by the United States was authorized by the Bretton Woods Agreement Act of 1945, 59 Stat. 512, as amended, 22 U.S.C.A. § 286.

as a solution to transient difficulties with their balance of payments, primarily through its provisions about par value. A member of the IMF was required to establish a "par value" for its currency, expressed either in terms of gold content or of a U.S. dollar of a specified gold content. Thus the Agreement created a set of official exchange rates among the currencies of its parties. If the par value of the Guatadorian peso were 140 pesos equals one ounce of gold at a time when the U.S. dollar was at $35 equals one ounce, the exchange rate between peso and dollar was 4:1.

The agreement in Article IV obligated the members in general to keep their currencies' actual exchange rates within 1% of the agreed par values. A government could intervene in the free market by buying or selling foreign exchange or it could impose controls. It was recognized that at times greater flexibility would be necessary, and the Agreement has provided for greater changes in order to cope with "fundamental disequilibrium." Consultation with the Fund must precede such changes. But if the proposed changes, together with all prior changes, did not exceed 10% of the initial par value, it was provided that the Fund "shall raise no objection." If the proposal exceeded 10%, the Fund "may either concur or object." The Fund was expected to concur if "satisfied that the change was necessary to correct a fundamental disequilibrium."

A change in par value over objection by the Fund made the member "ineligible to use the resources of the Fund unless the Fund otherwise determines." Consultation was designed to enable the Fund not only to make its judgment felt but also to enable it to suggest other measures, perhaps involving assistance from the Fund, to help the member through its difficulties. These provisions did not always prove satisfactory. The secrecy necessary to prevent speculative pressures on the currency in question was incompatible with extensive negotiations. The Fund's interference with a member's economic policies was apt to infringe upon national pride. Thus there were a number of cases in which the Fund favored devaluation for countries which have been unwilling to propose it. On the other hand, countries have—sometimes in dramatic cases—drastically devalued without engaging in prior consultations with the Fund.

Second, the IMF sought to place restrictions on national resort to exchange controls. The limitations on the use of such controls are expressed in Article VIII, Section 2(a), and in the important definition of the term "current transactions" in Article XIX:

Article VIII, Section 2(a)

(a) Subject to the provisions of Article VII, Section 3(b), and Article XIV, Section 2, no member shall, without the approval of the Fund, impose restrictions on the making of payments and transfers for current international transactions.

Article XIX

. . .

(i) Payments for current transactions means payments which are not for the purpose of transferring capital, and includes, without limitation:

(1) All payments due in connection with foreign trade, other current business, including services, and normal short-term banking and credit facilities;

(2) Payments due as interest on loans and as net income from other investments;

(3) Payments of moderate amount for amortization of loans or for depreciation of direct investments;

(4) Moderate remittances for family living expenses.

The Fund may, after consultation with the members concerned determine whether certain specific transactions are to be considered current transactions or capital transactions.

The intended sweep of this provision even as to current transactions has never been achieved, largely because of the generous exemption appearing in Article XIV:

Article XIV

Section 1.

The Fund is not intended to provide facilities for relief or reconstruction or to deal with international indebtedness arising out of the war.

Section 2.

In the post-war transitional period members may, notwithstanding the provisions of any other articles of this Agreement, maintain and adapt to changing circumstances . . . restrictions on payments and transfers for current international transactions. Members shall, however, have continuous regard in their foreign exchange policies to the purposes of the fund; and, as soon as conditions permit, they shall take all possible measures to develop such commercial and financial arrangements with other members as will facilitate international payments and the maintenance of exchange stability. In particular, members shall withdraw restrictions maintained or imposed under this Section as soon as they are satisfied that they will be able, in the absence of such restrictions, to settle their balance of payments in a manner which will not unduly encumber their access to the resources of the Fund.

Section 3.

Each member shall notify the Fund before it becomes eligible . . . to buy currency from the Fund, whether it intends to avail itself of the transitional arrangements in Section 2 of this Article, or whether it is prepared to accept the obligations of Article VIII, Sections 2, 3, and 4. A member availing itself of the transitional arrangements shall notify the Fund as soon thereafter as it is prepared to accept the above-mentioned obligations.

Section 4.

. . . Five years after the date on which the Fund begins operations, and in each year thereafter, any member still retaining any restrictions inconsistent with Article VIII, Sections 2, 3, or 4, shall consult the Fund as to their further retention. The Fund may, if it deems such action necessary in exceptional circumstances, make representations to any member that conditions are favorable for the withdrawal of any particular restriction, or for the general abandonment of restrictions, inconsistent with the provisions of any other articles of this Agreement. The member shall be given a suitable time to reply to such representations. If the Fund finds that the member persists in maintaining restrictions which are inconsistent with the purposes of the Fund, the member shall be subject to Article XV, Section 2(a).

Section 5.

In its relations with members, the Fund shall recognize that the post-war transitional period will be one of change and adjustment and in making decisions on requests occasioned thereby which are presented by any member it shall give the member the benefit of any reasonable doubt.

Thus there have been in fact two classes of IMF members: "Article XIV countries" and "Article VIII countries". At the start only ten countries (the United States and nine other Western Hemisphere nations) fell in the Article VIII category. Only much later could the war-damaged European countries, and then Japan, accept the Article VIII obligations. Gradually the list has lengthened. In 1973 Qatar, South Africa, Bahamas and the United Arab Emirates followed suit, bringing the total to 41 countries. Note that Article XIV countries do not have unlimited freedom: the permission is given for use of controls only for balance-of-payments reasons and extends only to the right to "maintain and adapt" existing controls and not to devise wholly new ones. Art. VIII, § 2, provides that other countries shall not enforce contracts violating exchange controls maintained by members consistently with the Agreement.

The function of the IMF as a regulator of national monetary actions is backed by its prowess as a source of funds, as a "banker" in effect. A country which violates its obligations under the Agreement may be declared ineligible to use the resources of the Fund (Art. XV, § 2). Thus a nation in balance-of-payments difficulties is under great pressure to comply with the Fund's guidelines, which may include changes in its own internal fiscal policy—its money supply, interest rates, and so on. In fact, there has been some resentment among the "beneficiaries" of the Fund's assistance at the loss of national autonomy experienced in the course of the consultations and in the resulting understandings accompanying the loan agreements that followed.

The resources of the Fund are derived from the member nations. The contributions of the members fall into several categories. First, there are the members' subscriptions, established by quotas set in a schedule to the Agreement or separately fixed for countries that joined later. These subscriptions are paid partly in gold and partly in the member's national currency. As of late 1974 the members' quotas stood at the equivalent of $29.2 billion (the United States' portion being $6.7 billion).[20]

Second, there are "special drawing rights" (SDRs) established by an amendment that went into effect in 1970. Each member is allocated SDRs in proportion to its IMF quota, the total allocations being $9.3 billion SDRs. The SDR is currently valued by taking the equivalent of a "basket" of 16 currencies weighted according to their shares of international transactions. Each member may use its SDRs to obtain hard currency from other members; it may also incur an obligation to provide such currency upon designation by the IMF. Limits are spelled out as to the conditions under which SDRs may be drawn upon and as to the terms upon which repayment is to be made. The SDR arrangement not only expands the supply of currency available to solve balance-of-payments problems but also provides for greater speed and flexibility. It grants further discretionary power to the Fund. Note that a country with financial problems may resort to other external sources as well: private securities markets, other countries' governments, or other international agencies such as the World Bank and related institutions.

The powers conferred upon the Fund are, then, substantial—more than those exercisable by the GATT. The Agreement recognizes this by conferring on the Fund "full juridical capacity", and extensive immunities. The Fund functions through two central organs. Each member appoints one Governor to the Board of Governors. As contemplated by Article XII, the Board has delegated extensive powers to handle "general operations" to the Executive Directors. Of the 20 Executive Directors, five are appointed by the members having the largest quotas—in order, the United States, the United Kingdom, the Federal Republic of Germany, France and Japan. The rest are elected for two-year terms by other members pursuant to a complex voting formula.

Voting in the IMF is not on a per capita but a weighted basis, depending on national quotas and SDRs. Each appointed or elected director casts the number of votes pertaining to the country that appointed or elected him. In general "all decisions of the Fund shall be made by a majority of the votes cast." However, special voting procedures apply to certain actions of the Fund such as waivers under Article V and some decisions involving SDRs. In practice, observers find that Fund actions have been taken more on the basis of a sense of the meeting than as a result of formal votes.

20. IMF, Annual Report for 1974, p. 64.

The Executive Directors select a Managing Director as chief of the Fund's operating staff. Section 4(c) of Article XII states that in the discharge of their duties the Managing Director and the staff "shall owe their duty entirely to the Fund and to no other authority." Members of the Fund are enjoined to respect the "international character" of this duty and to refrain from attempts at influence. There are no comparable provisions for the Governors or Executive Directors.

The prospects for significant changes in the IMF and the world monetary system were difficult to assess as of early 1975. The critical moment was the "Smithsonian meeting" after President Nixon's actions of August 1971, at which conference various informal amendments of IMF arrangements were made. On July 26, 1972 the Board of Governors of the IMF established a Committee of the Board of Governors on Reform of the International Monetary System and Related Issues (the Committee of Twenty). That Committee issued its final report on June 14, 1974. It recognized that matters were changing at such a rate that it would not be feasible to work out details for all questions within the scope of its studies. There is good reason to believe that implementation of the Committee's proposal is not near at hand, and that a reconstruction of the IMF may take a very different form when it comes. The Report does, however, serve to set the problems of the present time in perspective.

(1) The emphasis placed on fixed exchange rates with a minimum of permissible deviation was discarded during the convulsions that followed the "Nixon shock." Although different par values were successively established for the dollar, the circumstances and the procedures were clearly not what the Agreement intended. Most major countries have permitted their currencies to "float"—that is, simply to find their own market level. That picture is complicated, however, by the fact that many countries intervene in the market from time to time in order to prevent or slow movements that they regard as erratic or speculative. At times the term "dirty float" is applied to a situation where interventions are unsystematic and surreptitious. A group of eight European countries have agreed to maintain the exchange rate of their currency vis-a-vis each others currency within a band—called "the snake" of 2.25% Many other currencies, particularly those of less developed countries, are maintained in a fixed relation to some important reserve currency, i. e., the dollar or pound sterling.

The Report of the Committee of Twenty would return to a par value system to avoid "competitive depreciation or undervaluation." Changes in exchange rates would still be a matter for international concern and consultation. However, although par values would be "stable", they would also be adjustable more than in the past. The Fund would also permit countries to "adopt floating rates in particular situations, subject to Fund authorization, surveillance and review." In the special terminology of this field, this approach would be termed "a crawling peg". It is not clear how much political support exists for the approach which the Report suggests.

(2) Closely related to the question of rates is the issue of the degree of flexibility to be given governments about when and how they make adjustments and settlements. Moreover, there is continuing debate over the standards under which the IMF shall judge that an adjustment is required, and over the means used to persuade the government in question to take the steps which the Fund regards as appropriate. Note that this issue arises even with respect to nations in a persistent surplus situation.

(3) The IMF was traditionally concerned with a shortage of liquidity in the international monetary system. In particular, the institution of SDRs was designed to respond to a "collective judgment that there is a global need to supplement reserves." In the later 1970's the critical problem may prove to be world-wide rampant inflation. The provision of an expansible supply of reserves may contribute to that inflationary process.

(4) The IMF has always been concerned with national imbalances of payment. The cure of the protracted deficits of most of the European nations and Japan in the 1945–60 period was one of the great achievements of that period, to which the IMF made a major contribution. Now a new set of imbalances is appearing. These are largely due to changes in the prices of oil and other primary commodities. These imbalances affect or threaten most of the major industrial countries, especially (and critically) Great Britain, Italy and Japan. On the other hand, some oil exporting countries find themselves accumulating enormous quantities of claims on other nations, a supply of money which they have no rational means of using currently. The "recycling" of these billions of dollars worth of claims into purchases of goods or investments is a major challenge to the world system.

Most troublesome of all is the plight of those countries which are less developed but have to import oil. Already in deep balance of payments difficulties due to the need to import machinery for industrialization and, sometimes, even food, these countries find their slender reserves of foreign exchange wiped out by the need to pay much higher prices for oil and for such derivatives from oil as artificial fertilizers. Those imbalances threaten to be persistent and difficult to deal with. The Fund has established an "oil facility" through which countries that satisfy the Fund that they need assistance because of increases in the cost of oil imports may draw on resources derived through borrowing from oil producing countries, currently about SDR 3 billion.

(5) Another new aspect of the international financial scene with which a renewed IMF must cope is the size and speed of international monetary movements. There are now in the hands of multinational enterprises and of oil producing countries' governments quantities of liquid assets far in excess of the reserves held by the central banks

of those industrialized countries which have borne the primary burden of maintaining an orderly international financial market. The growth of the holdings of these other entities has been accompanied by an increasing sophistication about foreign exchange and an increasing willingness to move large sums into one currency and out of another. These factors can exaggerate fluctuations in exchange rates and intensify crises affecting any significant national currency.

Additional reading: Primary sources are the publication of the IMF itself—its Annual Reports, its Staff Papers, its monthly International Financial Statistics. Useful overall reviews of the current status of affairs are Meier, The Bretton Woods Agreement—25 Years After, 23 Stan.L.Rev. 235 (1971); Kafka, The International Monetary System in Transition, 13 Va.J.Int.L. 135, 539 (1972). Basic theory as to the international monetary system can be found in any text on international economics, e. g., Kindleberger, International Economics, pt. IV (5th ed. 1973). Current problems are reviewed in several articles in 53 Foreign Affairs 201–263 (1975). The Staff Papers referred to above contain numerous articles, some also published elsewhere, by Joseph Gold, the Fund's General Counsel.

Chapter XII

THE MULTINATIONAL ENTERPRISE AND INTERNATIONAL BUSINESS TRANSACTIONS

We here consider first the general characteristics of the multinational enterprise (MNE) together with political perceptions of its role and effects. The chapter then turns to studies of characteristic types of international business transactions in which corporations—often MNEs—engage.

A. PERSPECTIVES UPON THE MULTINATIONAL ENTERPRISE

That the multinational enterprise is an actor of major significance on the world economic stage is a fact that has become widely recognized among decision-makers and the general public only within the last decade. It has figured heavily in this book's materials —in cases like Barcelona Traction, p. 222, supra; in the expropriation controversies examined in Chapter IV; in the antitrust problems of Chapter IX.

Taken individually, the economic power of the largest among the multinational enterprises can be compared with that of some medium-sized countries. Taken collectively, their power can be compared with that of such international institutions as the International Monetary Fund, or all national central banks together. Clearly any picture of the international economic scene must give prominence to multinational enterprises, and any scheme for the regulation of transnational economic activities must take account of them.

NOTE ON GENERAL CHARACTERISTICS AND ORGANIZATION OF THE MNE

General Characteristics: Legal and Statistical

We start with significant legal aspects of the MNE. First, it is a creature of national and not international law. Although there are proposals for internationalizing the MNE, there is no basis in present law for such a status. Second, the MNE is a creature of private corporate law—that is, a privately (shareholder) owned profit-seeking company.[1] Thus no simple analogy can be drawn between the MNE and a "government" or "political system". Its goals are dominantly economic rather than political in the broader sense, even though its economic interests inevitably give the MNE an interest in political as well as economic strategies towards its own government as well as towards foreign governments.

Third, an MNE is not a single entity, but rather a structure made up of many corporations each incorporated under the laws of some nation and tied together by links of stock ownership and other contractual arrangements. Less formalistically and more significantly, all the units do tend to respond to a common maximizing strategy directed from a single "nerve center".

These general characteristics leave room for considerable variation within the world of MNEs—from goliaths such as General Motors, IBM, British Petroleum or Philips Lamp to smaller corporations with branches or subsidiaries in a few foreign countries. Until now, there has been no necessity of defining a "multinational enterprise" in legally sufficient terms, precisely because there is no set of rules applicable to, and only to, such concerns. If and when such a definition is developed for some legal regulatory purpose, it would presumably include only those enterprises whose activities extended to more than two countries, and would likely include only those relatively large and financially powerful firms which pose the policy issues that we here sketch.

In the public mind, size is surely an outstanding feature of the MNE. Consider, for example, General Motors. As of 1973, it had assets of over $20 billion, annual sales of $35 billion, and net income of $2.3 billion. It employed a total of 700,000 people in the United States, in the 21 countries in which it had assembly and manufacturing operations, and elsewhere. Observers, particularly critics, of the MNE stress comparative statistics—namely, that the sales of General Motors are greater than the gross national product of Switzerland—although it is debatable just what such comparisons alone show.

But collectively, there is no doubt that the role of the MNEs is enormous. Some two-thirds of the industrial output of the non-socialist countries is in the hands of the 400 largest corporate conglomerations. It has been predicted that by the 1980's only 300 firms will have 75% of the non-socialist world's industrial power in their hands. The total liquid assets of the hundred largest U. S.-based MNEs have been

1. A caveat: When we speak of the goal of the MNE as being "profit-maximizing", we do so while aware that this may not be a technically accurate term. There is conflict in the specialized literature as to whether managements whose interests may diverge from those of their stockholders in fact seek to maximize profits or some other value such as total sales, market shares, or asset size. One should also recognize that an MNE cannot in any event approach each of the myriad decisions it must make in terms of direct profit-maximizing calculations but must employ rules of thumb that are intended in the average to produce profit-maximizing results. See Vagts, The Multinational Enterprise: A New Challenge for Transnational Law, 83 Harv.L.Rev. 739, 755–56 (1970).

estimated at $75 billion (including $25 billion in cash and marketable securities), a figure which greatly exceeds the currency reserves available to those national agencies charged with functions of stabilizing foreign exchange relations.[2]

Coupled with size in these absolute terms is size in terms of market position. There is a strong empirical correlation between MNE status within the definition suggested above, and possession of an oligopolistic market position. Indeed, what frequently makes it feasible for an MNE to enter a remote foreign market with the extra costs of long-range operations in a new and unfamiliar environment is its powerful market position, based on such factors as advanced technology, economies of scale, managerial skills, access to internal or borrowed funds, and so on—factors which frequently enable the large MNEs to dominate local competition in the foreign countries in which they operate. Such market positions, once acquired, may or may not be static. The ability of new competitors to enter will depend upon whether technology is diffused or captured in trade secrets or patents, and so on. Whatever the variations in circumstances, there is no doubt that MNEs are frequently possessed of strong competitive positions and long purses. There is less agreement over the implications of this power for the national or international community.

Internal Organization of the MNE

Before turning to political evaluations of the MNE, we here review some characteristics of its internal organization. That review should be helpful, among other things, to a clearer understanding of the ways in which an MNE may be capable of applying one common and coherent global strategy.

In these days of computer and communications technology, it is sometimes assumed that an MNE can be managed down to its smallest details by a small executive group which will allocate money, men, machines and merchandise all over the world so as to maximize net revenues. In fact, most such organizations are too large and complex to be managed in this manner. Simply in interests of efficiency, it is essential to delegate much authority to lower levels, either at home or abroad. The amount of delegation obviously varies among firms, among countries, and with the particular field involved. It is, for example, easier to centralize financial functions such as handling of liquid assets than it is to manage labor relations from 5,000 miles away. Moreover, there are variable factors such as the degree to which the reins of central management are tightened or relaxed.

Not only do considerations of efficiency argue against tight centralization of all decisions of any significance, but the presence of outside equity holdings in some affiliated corporations may also qualify the MNE's ability to manage exclusively from the center. Indeed, the

2. For general comparisons of MNE scale with that of nations, see Vernon, Sovereignty at Bay, Ch. 1 (1971). The statistics on liquid assets come from Robbins and Stobaugh, Money in the Multinational Enterprise 182 (1973).

foreign (local) corporation laws under which subsidiaries are organized may impose serious constraints on the ability of the parent to determine policy from an outside perspective. Of course, all these qualifications may be more significant at relatively everyday levels of management decisions than at the highest level of policy decisions which may remain within the exclusive competence of central management: where to allocate important new investment capital, when to innovate and expand production, and so on.

The internal organization necessary to carry out the global operations of the MNE varies, but certain common patterns have emerged. Multinational enterprises are frequently involved in a number of different lines of business. Characteristically, they are divided by product lines; a firm such as General Electric will have separate divisions for, among other products, hydroelectric turbines and household appliances. Division managers are given considerable operational autonomy; a division's performance is judged by figures on its own periodic income statement. The division is a "profit center". When such firms start foreign operations, those operations are generally placed in an international division which is also a profit center. This organization has raised difficult problems—for example, requiring a foreign manager to deal with too many products which he cannot fully understand. It may also tend to institutionalize conflicts of interest between the domestic product divisions and the overseas operations. Thus some firms have fragmented the international division and divided its functions among relevant product divisions which bear responsibility for both domestic and overseas operations for that product. The variations are numerous.

The efficiency of the overarching corporate structure may be reinforced by means such as a training program, conveying to executives from different societies a sense of the X Company "way of doing things". Incentive programs will reinforce the tendency to pursue the general goals which central headquarters sets. For all of that, there is inevitably some variation and great gaps in the "efficiency" structures, when markedly different people from markedly different countries may share in common only a remote parent. The MNE is not a huge calculating machine.

NOTE ON THE MNE AS HERO OR VILLAIN: POLITICAL PERSPECTIVES

It is not surprising that the MNE, particularly within the foreign countries entered by its branches or subsidiaries, has become the center of keen political controversy. It stands as a visible symbol of power. Of course the MNE, in its expansion in numbers and size in recent decades, is not itself the root of such controversy. The roots are deeper, in longer-run historical forces, in broader political or economic controversies within which the MNE figures, and in fundamental ideological conflict within which the MNE can be accommodated. Note, indeed, that analyzing an issue in terms of MNEs rather than within a more abstract framework such as international trade or global efficiency maximization tends both to reflect and affect one's approach to and politics about the international system. MNEs are more specific and vulnerable targets for criticism than abstract laws of economics, or more remote theories about capitalism. Criticism of the MNE draws adherents from broader groups than those committed to analysis of trade or investment within the theoretical frameworks of socialism and imperialism. Traditional criticism of the trade and investment policies of the industrialized west, within Marxist-derived conceptions of imperialism and domination, here are rendered concrete by reference to this striking corporate development of the post-war years.

The principal arguments of the antagonists in this conflict waged on the political and ideological level are fairly evident. The proponents of the MNE as a medium for international trade and investment stress those same considerations which underlie the policy and theoretical justifications for relatively free world trade and investment. The cardinal justification and goal remain the same as those for the relatively "unregulated" laissez-faire market within a national economy—namely, maximization of efficiency, or maximizing the value of the world's production through profit-oriented investment and production decisions of private (that is, non-governmental) actors on the world scene. This goal embraces varied business activities: the world's mineral resources would be most efficiently exploited, manufacturing industry would be located wherever marginal returns upon investment (in view of varying labor costs, markets, transportation factors and so on) were highest, and so on.

The arguments for hospitable attitudes towards foreign investment through the MNEs rest upon the asserted contributions which they make to the process of economic development. Of course investment means the infusion of scarce "hard" currencies for the investor to meet local expenditures, as well as the implantation in the local economy of factories and machinery which require in part foreign manufacture. Accompanying this investment in funds or equipment is the necessary fund of technology—whether protected in the form of patents or in the form of trade secrets—possessed by the MNE, as well as the organizational and managerial skills that are brought to bear upon the new enterprise. In many cases, a high proportion of the managerial or technical employees of the subsidiaries are nationals of the foreign country involved. Hence the MNE amounts to an important training center for the introduction of modern industrial technology and managerial skills.

In the view of corporate management, it is precisely the large MNEs which can best realize these goals because of their vast accumulated technology, capital, skills and resulting ability to operate efficiently in varied national environments. Some of these views, and some of the irritation felt by MNE management at developing criticisms, are reflected in the following remarks of the chairman of the board of Union Carbide Corporation: [3]

> . . . Despite—or perhaps as a result of—their economic success, they have become a focal point of criticism that is based on misconceptions, myths, and misinformation.
>
> These corporations exist because they fill a need that requires world-wide coordination in an era of international interdependence and mutual cooperation. Coordination operates within national and international legal frameworks that include regulatory policies and financial-reporting requirements. . . .
>
> Within this monitoring framework, they are not likely to pile up exorbitant profits at the expense of a host nation or to run roughshod over its national interests without incurring several long-term penalties. Nevertheless, there are those who maintain that the sovereignty of nation-states is jeopardized by the power of multinationals. Yet, recent history is replete with examples of nations that expropriated with impunity the assets of foreign companies whose annual sales exceeded the nations' gross national products.
>
> There are three other myths about American multinational corporations that persist despite a preponderance of data to the contrary. The myths are that they avoid taxes, export jobs and increase imports. In recent years, however, the Tariff Commission, Department of Commerce and others have found that American companies have increased exports by $3 billion and, in the process, *created* between 500,000 and 600,000 domestic jobs between 1966 and 1970.
>
> . . .
>
> The socio-economic benefits of Union Carbide's investment in a host country are equally important aspects of its multinational operations. The company's foreign investments have a "push effect" on the economics of host countries. The infusion of capital and technology, the introduction of training programs, the addition of jobs and payroll dollars and the creation of thousands of management opportunities for local nationals cannot but help developing nations.
>
> Multinationals have been extraordinarily successful in meeting the needs of the consumers of the world but, in the process, have failed to articulate their contributions to nation-state economies. Into this communications void rush those with ideological messages and global metaphors: Big is bad, small is good, and spaceship earth is now a wholly-owned subsidiary—and as always government intervention is their answer. But clever metaphors are no substitute for thorough understanding, sound empirical data and objective analyses.
>
> "Nothing fails like success." The success of multinationals has attracted a good deal of attention; their failure has been in articulation.

Of course the investments which these remarks evaluate require certain conditions within and assumptions about the foreign country's

3. Wilson, "Multinationals' Value," N. Y. Times, March 11, 1975, p. 35, col. 2.

political system and economic organization. The MNE assumes that the path to development is to be through the private sector in a non-collectivized economy. Its presence in a foreign country at once reflects and reinforces those premises about the route towards economic growth. Needless to say, the model of a "free, competitive" market innocent of public regulation or public intervention is at least as unrealistic in most developing countries as in the United States. More realistically, the MNE will find itself in societies whose economies involve heavy degrees of state regulation and state investment —economies approaching the description of "state capitalism". In the principal developing countries such as Brazil, for example, infrastructure or basic manufacturing investment may be almost evenly divided among the government, the national private sector, and foreign investors. Of course the MNE may function in societies with minimal private sectors—particularly in the case of extractive enterprises such as the oil multinationals in their Middle East operations, but even in the case of such companies as Fiat in the Soviet Union.

The arguments favoring the MNE reach further. It may be viewed as the destined historical agent for overcoming the archaic and provincial organization of the world into nation states, each with its own political and regulatory systems. In this sense, the MNE is perceived as the finest and purest incarnation of a global institution pursuing the maximization of the value of production—a maximizer which, if uninhibited by hostile or regulatory policies, could best realize the goals of market theory on a global level. Consider the following remarks: [4]

> "The political boundaries of nation-states," says William I. Spencer, president of the 90-nation First National City Corp., "are too narrow and constricted to define the scope and sweep of modern business."
>
> As Spencer and most of his executive-suite colleagues see it, that's all to the good; the "new globalists," in their own view, are the prime agents for economic development, international prosperity and even world peace. "They seek profitable opportunity in addressing themselves not to the demands of the privileged few," Spencer proclaims, "but to the urgent needs of the overwhelming many."

One of the rare statements from the highest levels of our government about the role and problems of the multinational enterprise was made in the context of an address in 1975 by Secretary of State Kissinger to the U. N. General Assembly (as reported in the N. Y. Times, Sept. 2, 1975, p. 20):

> Access to capital markets and special programs to transfer new technology are but two factors of accelerated growth. There is a third, which may well be one of the most effective engines of development—the transnational enterprise.

4. "Global Companies: Too Big to Handle?" *Newsweek* (November 20, 1972), p. 96.

> Transnational enterprises have been powerful instruments of modernization both in the industrial nations—where they conduct most of their operations—and in the developing countries, where there is often no substitute for their ability to marshal capital, management, skills, technology and initiative. Thus the controversy over their role and conduct is itself an obstacle to economic development.
>
> It is time for the world community to deal with the problems, real and perceived, that have arisen. If the nations assembled here cannot reach consensus on the proper role of these enterprises, the developing countries could lose an invaluable asset. Let us make this issue a test of our capacity to accommodate mutual concerns in practical agreement.
>
> Specifically, the United States believes that:
>
> Transnational enterprises are obliged to obey local law and refrain from unlawful intervention in the domestic affairs of host countries. Their activities should take account of public policy and national development priorities. They should respect local customs. They should employ qualified local personnel or qualify local people through training.
>
> Host governments in turn must treat transnational enterprises equitably, without discrimination among them and in accordance with international law. Host governments should make explicit their development priorities and the standards which transnational enterprises are expected to meet and maintain them with reasonable consistency.
>
> Governments and enterprises must both respect the contractual obligation that they freely undertake. Contracts should be negotiated openly, fairly and with full knowledge of their implications. Greater assurance that contracts will be honored will improve the international commercial environment, increase the flow of investment and expand economic transactions. Destructive and politically explosive investment disputes, which spoil the climate for large commitments and investment, will occur less frequently.

Skepticism about or hostility towards the MNE in the countries of its foreign operations is exhibited by political segments within most less developed countries and, to some extent, even by groups within the industrialized West. Let us start with the latter. Most Western European countries have powerful multinational enterprises that are organized and have their home offices within their borders: Volkswagen, Olivetti, Nestle, Lever Bros. and so on. Thus to some extent they share the point of view of management of American MNEs. Still, the European countries are conscious of the fact that the majority of the large MNEs are based within the United States, that such MNEs are actually or potentially allied with the United States in economic disputes which may bring their countries into conflict, and that these MNEs in fact represent serious competitive threats within their own borders.

These economic and political perceptions explain the careful policy of the European Economic Community (Chapter XIII) towards foreign (overwhelmingly American) MNEs. There, the dominant response may involve not restrictive policies about establishment (matters now often covered through bilateral treaties between the United States and European countries) but encouragement within the EEC countries to local companies to develop a size, economic power, market and technology which can enable them to compete with the foreign goliaths. See, for example, the discussion of encouragement of cooperation among European firms at pp. 1416–1417, infra.

In the less developed countries, the tensions are sharper. As we have noted, the attacks upon the MNEs form part of a broader antagonism towards foreign investment in general, as well as towards their sources in Western capitalism and forms of industrialization. Thus the MNE becomes, almost inevitably, the evident and stark symbol of exploitation, domination, imperialism—themes captured in the developing literature about *dependencia* that has issued from nationalistic and Marxist-oriented thinkers of Latin America. The specific bases for attack upon the MNE share the character of the general challenges to foreign investment that were described at pp. 85–90 and 449–455, supra, and that found dramatic illustrations in the expropriations examined in Chapter IV. In particular, governments or politically powerful groups in many less developed countries will stress the following arguments:

(1) Despite the initial infusion of capital, the MNEs frequently serve to "decapitalize" the foreign country, already suffering from severe balance of payments problems with respect to the accepted, hard international currencies. That is, repatriation in the form of dividends, interest or royalty payments to the parent may represent larger sums than fresh capital infusions—particularly since the successful MNE may rely upon locally generated earnings to support much of its new investment. Such repatriation may be accomplished in a furtive manner by excessive charges for imported components, knowledge or funds, and by inadequate charges for exports. Such transfer pricing may serve to subvert local tax and exchange control policies. Supposedly the MNE is peculiarly capable of concealing such activity in its multifarious and complex structure.

(2) The MNE, because of its prestige and financial stability, can unduly and harmfully absorb scarce local resources, whether in the form of credit in the local currency available from the local banking system, or in the form of sparse executive talents.

(3) Frequently (not invariably) MNEs will be accused of relegating mechanical tasks of management to personnel hired within the local countries, while retaining the higher level executive and creative functions at central headquarters. By the same token, much of the technology may be kept carefully in the hands of the MNE, so that complex

technical problems will be handled through teams of experts sent from the home country.

(4) The MNE is seen as the most articulate voice and agent of a civilization based in good part on material production and consumerism within a (qualified) framework of market organization. Such values are spread through its establishment in foreign countries. But those values may be viewed as inimical to different conceptions of national community and national growth that are held by important groups within the foreign country. That is, the very visible MNE spurs political debate and tension over the kind of development that is desired, a debate involving the form of economic organization, modes of political representation, and distribution of wealth and power.

Some criticisms are, however, distinctive to the MNE—as opposed to foreign investment in general—because of the size and power of the largest among them. We shall here note three among such arguments. First, the large MNE entering a foreign country will frequently secure a monopolistic or oligopolistic position on the local market—almost inevitably a function of the enormous financial and technological resources that it commands and of the skills which it has developed, but sometimes the result of a grant by the foreign government. Thus the MNE at once expands, structures and confines the development of the local economy. It introduces, but may by this very token permit no further introduction. Thus the normal constraints, even within traditional market theory, of competition in products and prices may not be present. Much will depend upon the size of the local market. A country such as Brazil, for example, can efficiently and profitably support several manufacturers of automobiles. A smaller country might view more than one or two plants of foreign manufacturers as inefficient—a view shared by the foreign firms themselves.

A second ground for political hostility towards the powerful MNE has been its political effect upon the local environment in which its subsidiary functions. In many less developed countries, the MNE is perceived by adherents to the tenets of western-style liberal market society as the best assurance that those tenets will prevail in their country. Natural political alliances will form between the representatives of large foreign business interests and the anti-collectivist, relatively market-oriented or state-capitalist political forces in the foreign country. Needless to say, those forces generally represent the established business or professional middle classes, rather than the blue and white collar or peasant groups.

From the perspective of the reformist or radical left, the MNE is then seen as a bulwark of conservative structures, as a force against change. The alliance over several decades, for example, between those United States copper companies with heavy Chilean investments and the conservative Chilean political parties was relatively clear—

both for immediate strategic purposes and for the larger symbolic reasons that we have sketched. But from another perspective, portions of the business and professional classes will be hostile to the MNE, regarding it as a rival force intent upon depriving them of resources and reducing them to employee status.

The political impact of the MNE becomes less subtle and more explicit as it seeks to intervene more directly in domestic affairs. Precise knowledge is hard to gain, for forms of interplay between political leaders and foreign business leaders are rarely public and explicit—except in the dramatic moments of negotiation of new concession agreements, of expropriations and so on. Such intervention in political affairs of host countries as was most recently exemplified by the activities of ITT in Chile or the efforts of ITT in this country to spur United States support of policies important to ITT (see pp. 478–481, supra) represents one of the relatively rare, now public illustrations.

The underlying sense and spirit of many of the attacks upon the MNE which we have so far described are well expressed in a recent book of two sharp critics. Consider the following passages: [5]

> . . . In the short run, the challenge of the global corporation concerns stability; in the long run, development. There has never been a time since the Great Depression when there has been more economic uncertainty around the world. But the corporate prospect of a world without borders offers something more distressing than uncertainty. It is a vision without ultimate hope for a majority of mankind. Our criterion for determining whether a social force is progressive is whether it is likely to benefit the bottom 60 percent of the population. Present and projected strategies of global corporations offer little hope for the problems of mass starvation, mass unemployment, and gross inequality. Indeed, the global corporation aggravates all these problems, because the social system it is helping to create violates three fundamental human needs: social balance, ecological balance, and psychological balance. These imbalances have always been present in our modern social system; concentration of economic power, antisocial uses of that power, and alienation have been tendencies of advanced capitalism. But the process of globalization, interacting with and reinforcing the process of accelerating concentration, has brought us to a new stage.
>
> The role of the global corporation in aggravating social imbalance is perhaps the most obvious. As owner, producer, and distributor of an ever greater share of the world's goods, the global corporation is an instrument for accelerating concentration of wealth. As a global distributor, it diverts resources from where they are most needed (poor countries and poor regions of rich countries) to where they are least needed (rich countries and rich regions).
>
> . . .
>
> The processes that lead to psychological imbalance are more difficult to analyze than the processes of social or

5. Barnet and Müller, Global Reach 364–65 (1974).

> ecological imbalance. But the World Managers have based their strategy on the principles of global mobility, division of labor, and hierarchical organization—all of which may be efficient, in the short run, for producing profits but not for satisfying human beings. The very size of the global corporation invites hierarchy. The search for economic efficiency appears to require ever more division of labor and to challenge traditional loyalties to family, town, and nation. Another name for mobility is rootlessness. There is nothing to suggest that loyalty to a global balance sheet is more satisfying for an individual than loyalty to a piece of earth, and there is a good deal of evidence that being a "footloose" and airborne executive is not the best way to achieve psychological health—for either the managers themselves or their families. By marketing the myth that the pleasures of consumption can be the basis of community, the global corporation helps to destroy the possibilities of real community—the reaching out of one human being to another.
>
> . . .

The third theme that is particular to the MNE stems from its multinational character. Its operations in any one country will generally form part of a larger maximizing strategy rather than be rooted within that country so as to take national boundaries as the relevant framework for decision making. Maximization of profits for the entire MNE enterprise with manufacturing or selling subsidiaries in, perhaps, 10 countries will involve decisions about new investment, expanding or restricting production, branching into new fields or reinforcing old ones, allocating or reallocating capital or skills or men from one country to another, and so on. Those decisions may conflict with perceptions of national welfare held by the foreign country involved. That is, tension almost inescapably arises from the different economic or political frameworks within which decisions are made, and from differences over the conceptions of welfare which the MNE or the local country may be seeking to advance. This type of problem was a cause of continuing stress between the American copper companies heavily invested in Chile and the Chilean government during the post-war years, in that the pricing policies or investment decisions of the companies (sometimes at the persuasion of the United States government) were not perceived by many within Chile to further the economic interest of that country. See p. 448, supra.

Thus the MNE is caught in a peculiar bind. The more that it is associated politically and economically with policies of an autonomous and internal character, the more suspiciously and hostilely it will be viewed by the foreign country. On the other hand, the more it is perceived as pursuing policies of a foreign or international character, the more suspiciously and hostilely it will be viewed within the United States. And indeed, precisely that phenomenon has developed in recent years.

Symptomatic of the problems within the United States have been recent hearings before the Subcommittee on Multinational Corporations of the Senate Committee on Foreign Relations.[6] The most dramatic portions of those hearings were devoted to accounts of the efforts of ITT, referred to above, to use its wealth and connections to persuade the United States government to adopt the tactics it proposed to block the entry into office in Chile of President Allende or, later, to undermine his government—at least in good part, in the interest of ITT's investments in that country.

Congressional concern was also aroused by evidence that MNEs had played a part in currency shifts during various monetary crises in the early 1970's—and, whatever had in fact occurred, that such companies had enormous latent capacities to destabilize the monetary situation through their possession of liquid assets far in excess of the reserve funds possessed by the central banks of the governments trying to keep matters under control. Investigations into the oil crises that began in October 1973 showed that the MNEs engaged in the oil business were trying to play an independent role between the oil exporting nations and the governments of importing countries, sometimes seeming to act on behalf of the OPEC governments and sometimes acting to frustrate their demands, as when they shifted oil from other sources to countries subject to Arab boycotts.

These rather specific episodes have blended with a more general concern that the national interest is being adversely affected by foreign investment, most conspicuously by MNEs. This view, held most strongly in labor union circles, is based on these supposed consequences of investment abroad: (*1*) that investment abroad exports jobs, i. e., substitutes manufacture in foreign plants by cheap foreign labor for manufacture in American plants for export abroad; (*2*) that investment abroad has an adverse impact on the balance of payments, largely because of its effect on exports; and (*3*) that the United States Treasury obtains virtually no tax revenues from overseas investments—because of the deferral and foreign tax credit provisions, pp. 1104–1105, supra. Thus, it is argued, the profitability of foreign investment to the MNEs is overbalanced by its adverse effects on the Treasury and on the American worker. All these points are vigorously challenged—both on grounds of principle and on statistical grounds —by MNE management.

These lines of argument led to the introduction of legislation known as the Hartke-Burke bill,[7] which consists in part of tax proposals discussed at p. 1118, supra; in part of provisions designed to curtail imports (among other things by removing beneficial treatment accorded products partly processed in the United States,

6. Multinational Corporations and United States Foreign Policy, Hearings before the Subcommittee on Multinational Corporations, Senate Foreign Relations Committee, 93d Cong. 1st Sess. (1973).

7. The Hartke-Burke Bill was formally entitled the Foreign Trade and Investment Act of 1971, 5.2592, 92nd Cong. 1st Sess., and H.R. 10914, 92nd Cong. 1st Sess. (1971). See Fisher, The Multinationals and the Crisis in United States Trade and Investment Policy, 53 B.U.L.Rev. 308 (1973).

shipped abroad for further work and then reentering this country); and in part of efforts to restrict the export of technology. Although there seems little likelihood that the Hartke-Burke bill or anything resembling it will come to pass, its appearance is symptomatic of growing American unease about the MNE. Particularly if the MNE becomes more "un-American" through increasing the proportion of foreign operations, foreign management and foreign stockholdings, policymakers in the United States are apt to take an increasingly skeptical view of it.

It was chiefly the anxieties of the less developed countries that led the Economic and Social Council of the United Nations to request the Secretary-General to appoint "a group of eminent persons . . . to study the role of multinational corporations and their impact on the process of development, especially that of developing countries . . ." After conducting hearings and holding several drafting sessions, the Group issued a report (E/5500/Add.1) on May 24, 1974. After analyzing the facts as it saw them, the Group developed a set of recommendations. Some are addressed to host countries, urging the improvement of negotiating skills in dealings with MNEs, including regional and world-wide organizations to provide expertise, and calling for clarity in laying down the rules for foreign investors. Some were addressed to home countries, urging them not to use MNEs as political instrumentalities, not to allow them to interfere in host country's political processes, and not to intercede for them in nationalization disputes.

Other recommendations were aimed at the establishment of an international commission on multinational corporations that would supervise the gathering of information on MNEs, serve as a forum for debates, and gradually evolve a set of recommendations that would represent a code of conduct for multinationals and governments. Dealing with specific areas of concern, the Group called for negotiation of a more standardized group of tax treaties for the protection of labor and for an agreement on antitrust problems. Some members of the Group dissented from some of the recommendations, and outside groups have regarded the report as too cautious. UNCTAD is in the process of preparing more reformist propositions. It may be some time before sufficient agreement between home and host countries can be developed, and thus before any international agreement on the topic can be put on paper.

B. INTERNATIONAL BUSINESS TRANSACTIONS: ILLUSTRATIVE PROBLEMS AND CASE STUDIES

Earlier portions of this book have developed information and conceptual frameworks that could readily be applied to the design of international business transactions. Evident examples include the materials on concessions (pp. 495–520, supra) and on the transnational reach of the tax laws (Chapter X). We here consider other characteristic types of business arrangements into which corporations whose activities extend to more than one country may enter. These transactions or problems are typical of the largest of the MNEs, as well as of very modest companies which may invest and produce in one or two foreign countries as well as the United States. The problems and case studies draw upon materials considered in other portions of the book, to which appropriate references will be made, but also introduce new topics for consideration. As we approach these problems, our framework for consideration will be that of the American corporation involved, seeking to achieve its business aims within the legal, political and economic constraints sketched in the studies which follow.

---

1. THE INTERNATIONAL ROLE OF COUNSEL

Private individuals or firms and their counsel find that pursuing business goals across national frontiers introduces them to new levels of complexity. Although in some areas there is enough traffic so that paths have become well trodden and even obvious, international transactions involve special risks. This is especially true when such transactions involve the rights of substantial numbers of parties which must endure for substantial periods if the parties are to achieve their objectives. In this section, our endeavor will be to provide a view of an international business transaction that emphasizes the different types of legal problems which impinge upon it.

While the lawyer must adjust to the novelty of a foreign transaction, the business client will encounter novelties of a different kind. Technological processes have a certain autonomy of their own; chemical reactions will be the same in a refinery in Bayonne, New Jersey, or in Bombay, India. Nonetheless, even the production manager finds differences. An American technique may not be workable or advantageous in India for various reasons. The lower cost of labor in India, or the non-availability of certain skilled specialists may make it worth while to use different production methods, substituting unskilled labor for capital intensive machinery. Still advanced technology can be, and often is, exported largely intact.

The marketing function of a foreign enterprise characteristically involves greater changes. While certain slogans such as "putting a tiger in your tank" seem to have a universal drawing power for motorists, trade-marks may be neutral or actually repulsive in other countries. Advertising must be rewritten to local tastes. Channels of distribution will be very different. A sales organization accustomed to reaching its ultimate customers through chains of supermarkets, with high volume and low mark-up, must make many readjustments if the existing distribution scheme consists of small, narrowly specialized family retail outlets relying upon few sales but a high profit margin per item. Labor relations and financial practices will obviously change from place to place.

Client and lawyer together will find the bargaining processes through which they enter a new country a strange, sometimes fascinating and sometimes frustrating experience, especially if they go beyond the boundaries of the Atlantic Community. An American brusque, "business-like" approach may put off a Japanese manager used to a more gradual, low key approach designed to enable the parties to know each other more thoroughly before a commercial agreement is reached. A representative of a United States firm accustomed to act within specific delegated authority may be puzzled by the other side's need to establish a consensus within the whole management group.

The two sides may have different conceptions of the nature of the contract that they are negotiating. Americans lean to the view that a contract should spell out with considerable detail what the parties are to do in each of the circumstances that they can presently foresee. This tendency is carried to its extreme manifestation in, for example, loan contracts where elaborate provisions state the rights and duties of the parties in event of default, insolvency and so on. Others, in Europe as well as Asia, regard a contract as an expression of an intention to collaborate in good faith towards a common goal and to seek to meet problems that may arise in a spirit of cooperation and trust. The future will take care of itself—or, as a Frenchman might say, *on verra bien.*

In the back of the American negotiators' minds may be quite different concepts about foreign businessmen or about what would happen if serious differences of interest and opinion developed. An American executive, although aware of the costs, inconvenience and uncertainty involved in litigation, is apt to contemplate it as a "natural" possibility or threat. In some countries among which Japan would generally be identified, there would be an instinctive reaction against litigation (or even formal arbitration) as unnatural, unfriendly and even slightly immoral. Their citizens would expect differences to be worked out between the parties, perhaps with the aid of friendly mediators. They might view with suspicion American counsel's insertion of elaborate provisions about matters such as choice of law, remedies if the seller fails to deliver, and so on. Thus the client-counsel team, as they negotiate a new arrangement in a foreign industrial center, may face a strange new business and legal culture even if they never stray too far from the local Hilton Hotel and its homogenized modern-international decor.

Counsel will face a special set of problems. Aware that solving problems within local law will be beyond his competence, he will look for assistance. But how does one go about locating competent counsel in Singapore or Dar-es-Salaam? Even if there is a local listing of lawyers, it will appear different from American classifications. Relatively familiar, because of its British origin, is the difference between barristers, who conduct litigation and render formal opinions, and solicitors, who draft documents, conduct negotiations and perform the functions of American "office lawyers." Other systems use different terms to draw distinctions between courtroom and office lawyers. The former may be a small, cohesive and regulated elite, while the latter may be a mixed group subject to little or no regulations. (Until recently France made no attempt to restrict access to the status of "*conseil juridique*" or legal advisor.)

In some countries the American attorney may find that he is not looking for a lawyer at all. For example, the field of tax law may have been surrendered by the legal profession to the accountants or, as in Germany, to a special profession ("*Steuerberater*"). Elsewhere one finds that one needs the services of a notary (*notario, notar, notaire*) because that functionary, rather than being a routine taker of acknowledgments and applier of seals, is the drafter and recorder of formal legal documents and possesses extensive formal training and practical experience.

Past this hurdle of choice among professionals, the U. S. attorney begins to consult with colleagues, banks, consuls and other sources of references and recommendations. He will frequently find that, aside from the local bar in country X, there are two sources of assistance. The first may be called the "expatriate bar", consisting of American-trained lawyers practicing abroad. Some are in the local offices of law firms based in the United States, staffed by lawyers rotating on a two or three-year tour of duty. They may be associated with local lawyers who have become familiar with American practices and problems. Some American-staffed firms abroad have no base in this country.

Foreign environments have varied in the cordiality of their reception of United States lawyers. In some countries, holding to sweeping concepts of the "practice of law" similar to our own, an American-trained lawyer is an unqualified layman and cannot hang out a shingle. Others have made special accommodations for foreign lawyers. Another group, including France, had regulated neither their own citizens' nor foreigners' practice of law. However, the situation in that country has changed sharply. As part of a general effort to tighten control over legal counsellors, the government put limits on foreigners. While the new arrangement sanctioned the continuation of existing foreign legal establishments, it set a deadline for the furnishing of evidence of reciprocal permission by the home government for French lawyers. This condition provoked a flurry of activity in the New York bar. In 1957, the New York courts held in In re Roel, 3 N.Y.2d 224, 165 N.Y.S.2d 31, 144 N.E.2d 24, that a Mexican lawyer who was aggressively pushing his services in obtaining swift across-the-border divorces violated the provisions of the New York Penal Law on unauthorized practice of the law.

The dissent predicted that this ruling would cause extensive difficulties to those trying to provide effective international legal services:

> When counsel who are admitted to the Bar of this State are retained in a matter involving foreign law, they are responsible to the client for the proper conduct of the matter, and may not claim that they are not required to know the law of the foreign State (Degen v. Steinbrink, 202 App. Div. 477, 195 N.Y.S. 810, affirmed 236 N.Y. 669, 142 N.E. 328). Moreover, the conduct of attorneys admitted here may be regulated by our courts . . . and dealt with when they engage in unethical practices; they may not plead in defense that since the matter involved related to the law in New Jersey or Connecticut or anywhere outside of our jurisdiction, they were not practicing law and were therefore immune from disciplinary action. A foreign law specialist, on the other hand, is not subject to discipline; he need not be a lawyer of any jurisdiction; he may be without good character; and his activities may not even be regulated under the present state of the law.
>
> The complex problem posed by the activities of foreign attorneys here is a long-standing one. It may well be that foreign attorneys should be licensed to deal with clients in matters exclusively concerning foreign law, but that is solely within the province of the Legislature. Our courts are given much control over the lawyers admitted to the Bar of our State; we have no control, however, over those professing to be foreign law experts.
>
> The serious consequences of the full reach of this injunction should not be obscured by the ill repute of Mexican divorces. Our eyes should be open to the circumstances cited by the Association of the Bar of the City of New York in support of a modification, that the principle underlying this injunction also prevents the giving of legal advice in this State on other subjects than divorce by lawyers of other countries regarding business, financial or personal transactions anywhere in the world.
>
> We are told and have no reason to doubt that many law firms in New York have offices in other cities, such as Washington, Boston, London and Paris, and that many have foreign associates who are not licensed to practice in New York. The ethical propriety of such arrangements has always been recognized, provided that it is made clear in each jurisdiction that unlicensed foreign associates are not admitted to practice in that jurisdiction. The performance of such services by American lawyers in Great Britain, France or Germany, for example, would be precluded by the application in those jurisdictions of the doctrine now announced by the majority of this court.

It required strenuous efforts on the part of the interested portion of the New York bar to obtain legislation in 1974 authorizing the Court of Appeals to make special rules for foreign practitioners operating in New York.[8] Now there will be a second source of advice

8. N.Y.Judiciary Law § 53.6; N.Y. Court of Appeals Rules §§ 521.1–521.5.

as to foreign law: practitioners qualified in the country in question but resident in New York and subject to regulation as special members of the New York bar.

When foreign counsel has been located further problems arise, such as settling his quantum of responsibility relative to American counsel. In many countries, lawyers understand their appropriate role in situations not involving litigation to be answering specific questions put by the client. It would not be thought part of the lawyer's function either to draft documents or to review them for general compliance with law. Thus American counsel will often find themselves drafting the agreements and asking foreign counsel specific questions about their legality. This procedure requires learning enough about the foreign legal system to be able to ask probing questions.

It is easy for a lawyer to go too far and slip into accepting responsibility for the proper preparation of an essentially foreign document. A warning note is struck in Degen v. Steinbrink, 202 App.Div. 477, 195 N.Y.S. 810, aff'd mem., 236 N.Y. 669, 142 N.E. 328 (1923), in which New York lawyers were held liable to their client for preparing a chattel mortgage in property in three states which turned out to be fatally defective in each. The New York court said:

> When a lawyer undertakes to prepare papers to be filed in a state foreign to his place of practice, it is his duty, if he has not knowledge of the statutes, to inform himself, for, like any artisan, by undertaking the work, he represents that he is capable of performing it in a skillful manner. Not to do so, and to prepare documents that have no legal potency, by reason of their lack of compliance with simple statutory requirements, is such a negligent discharge of his duty to his client as should render him liable for loss sustained by reason of such negligence.

In substantial cases such as a major bank loan, one party will wish to have a formal opinion of counsel to the effect that the transaction is legally valid—for example, that the contract is "lawful, valid and enforceable in accordance with its terms." With respect to a transnational agreement, a U. S. law firm would have to disclaim coverage; the opinion might, however, reach the general conclusion of validity but state that as to the law of Germany it was relying on the opinion of Messrs. Klipp und Klar of Rothenburg ob Tauber. It might tell the client that it was reasonable in relying on the opinion of Messrs. Klipp und Klar, a firm carefully chosen for the job and of good professional reputation. Particularly as to other common law jurisdictions, an American firm might state that it had investigated the law independently and saw no reason to doubt the conclusions arrived at by Messrs. Klipp and Klar. These nuances of phrasing may seem bizarre but they are important to clients and lawyers who are anxious to spell out in detail who is responsible for what.

Additional reading: Note, International Legal Practice Restrictions on the Migrant Attorney, 15 Harv.Int.L.J. 298 (1974); Note, Foreign Branches of Law Firms, 80 Harv.L.Rev. 1284 (1967); Busch, The Right of United States Lawyers to Practice Abroad, 3 Int.Law. 617 (1969). As to legal practice in particular countries, see, e. g., Hatori, The Legal Profession in Japan: Its Historical Development and Present State in Law in Japan—Legal Order in a Changing Society 111 (von Mehren ed. 1963); Perillo, The Legal Professions of Italy, 18 J.Legal Ed. 274 (1966); Kohler, The Study and Practice of Law in Germany, 54 A.B.A.J. 992 (1968); Herzog and Herzog, The Reform of the Legal Professions and of Legal Aid in France, 22 Int. & Comp.L.Q. 462 (1973).

---

2. A DISTRIBUTORSHIP AGREEMENT

We here consider the negotiation of a distributorship agreement by an American firm of modest size that manufactures a line of specialized electrical testing equipment. The firm's management is confident that the unique character of its apparatus will assure it of a market in Germany. After several trips by one of its executives to Europe, the firm located a potential distributor who seems to meet the requirements for a successful outlet in Germany. As American counsel for the firm, you are asked to pass on the legality and adequacy of the distributorship agreement before it is signed.

You should assume that the form of agreement which follows is one used by the client for other ventures. Of course you are aware of the risk in using "prepared form" contracts without an adequate grasp of what their authors had in mind or of the significance of each clause, or without the exercise of an independent judgment about its suitability for the enterprise at hand. The use of forms serves the goal of efficiency only if held within these basic constraints.

DISTRIBUTOR AGREEMENT [9]

THIS AGREEMENT, made in Junction City, Colorado, U.S.A. as of ______, 19__, between TECHNO MANUFACTURERS, INC., a corporation organized under the laws of the State of Colorado, U.S.A., (called "Manufacturer") and IMPO A. G., a ______ organized under the laws of ______ (called "Distributor"),

WITNESSETH:

WHEREAS, Manufacturer has developed and manufactures certain industrial products catalogued in Manufacturer's literature, together with certain service equipment (all called the "Techno Products"); and

WHEREAS, Distributor wishes to act as a distributor of the entire line of Techno Products with respect to the territory described in paragraph 1;

9. Taken from Moore, Agreements for the Transmission of Technology Abroad: The Distributor Relationship, 45 Denver L.J. at 60 (1968).

NOW, THEREFORE, in consideration of the undertakings and covenants set forth in this Agreement, Manufacturer and Distributor agree as follows:

1. Appointment of Distributor and Territory.

Manufacturer appoints Distributor a distributor of Techno Products with primary marketing responsibility for the following territory (called "the Territory"):

2. Distributor Relationship.

The purpose of this appointment is to provide for the development and maintenance in the Territory of a substantial volume of sales of Techno Products and adequate service of the Products in the mutual interests of Manufacturer and Distributor. Manufacturer will sell to Distributor and Distributor will purchase from Manufacturer Techno Products to be resold by Distributor. Distributor accepts its appointment and undertakes diligently to canvass for purchasers of Techno Products and in all reasonable and proper ways vigorously to promote the sale of Techno Products in the Territory. Distributor will maintain adequate sales, service and warehouse facilities in the Territory and a representative and adequate inventory of Techno Products.

3. Distributor Not Manufacturer's Agent.

This Agreement shall not constitute Distributor the agent or legal representative of Manufacturer for any purpose whatsoever, nor shall Distributor hold itself out as such. This Agreement creates no relationship of joint adventurers, partners, associates or principal and agent between the parties, and both parties are acting as principals. Distributor is granted no right or authority to assume or create any obligation or responsibility for or on behalf of Manufacturer or otherwise to bind Manufacturer or to use Manufacturer's name other than as may be expressly authorized by Manufacturer. Distributor shall bear all of its own expenses for its operation and staff, except for such items as Manufacturer shall by prior written agreement undertake to pay.

4. Manufacturer's Sales Policy.

Distributor shall carry out Manufacturer's sales policy with respect to the Territory and Techno Products as set forth in the written Sales Policy of Manufacturer as supplied to Distributor, and as may from time to time be communicated to Distributor in written additions to or revisions of such Sales Policy.

5. Shipment and Delivery.

Manufacturer shall in good faith supply requirements of Distributor for Techno Products and make shipments promptly in accordance with Distributor's orders. Whenever manufacturer shall deliver to a common carrier any Techno Products ordered by Distributor, Manufacturer shall not be responsible for any delays or damages in shipment. Distributor may specify the routing as well as consignees for shipments ordered, but in all cases billings shall be directed to Distributor by Manufacturer.

6. Failure to Ship for Reasons Beyond Manufacturer's Control.

If Manufacturer shall fail for reasons beyond its control to make shipments of any orders, such orders shall be subject to cancellation at the discretion of Distributor unless shipment is commenced within 30 days from the date called for in the order.

7. Payment.

Distributor shall purchase Techno Products from Manufacturer F.O.B. its plant at Junction City, Colorado, at such United States dollar prices as are scheduled in Manufacturer's export price list, payable in United States currency and upon terms of payment net 30 days from date of invoice with a _______% distributorship discount from list price.

8. Warranty, Servicing and Returns.

Manufacturer's warranty of Techno Products is set forth in its Sales Policy, and Distributor shall handle warranty problems, returns, obsolescence and servicing in accordance with such policy. Manufacturer shall bear once each year the out-of-pocket cost (but not salary) for one Distributor representative to attend a three week training school in Colorado for instruction in Techno Products servicing.

9. Selling Aids and Advertising.

9.1 Manufacturer shall supply to Distributor without cost reasonable quantities of Manufacturer's selling literature and displays, and other sales aids and devices as may be designed and made available by Manufacturer from time to time. Distributor shall at its own expense employ such items and participate in such trade and industry meetings and shows in the Territory as in its judgment will enhance the sale of Techno Products.

9.2 Distributor shall cause Techno Products to be advertised in suitable media in the Territory with due regard to its appeal to industry. Manufacturer shall furnish to Distributor at no expense to Distributor samples of advertising materials used in other territories, with the right to use the same, but Distributor shall not be bound by these and may in its discretion adopt such advertising methods and displays as it believes most effective for the market in the Territory. Upon advance approval of copy and media, Manufacturer will contribute up to $_______ per annum for Distributor's advertising budget for Techno Products, provided that Distributor's total annual advertising budget for Techno Products shall be at least three times the amount contributed by Manufacturer.

10. Inquiries and Information.

10.1 Manufacturer shall forward to Distributor for its handling all inquiries and orders received by Manufacturer from the Territory, both from correspondence and personal visits in the Territory, along with copies of any acknowledgments Manufacturer may have made, and Manufacturer shall make available to Distributor such sales, product and technical information as may be useful to Distributor in handling the inquiry or order.

Distributor will supply Manufacturer with information as to the disposition of all referred inquiries or orders.

10.2 On request by Distributor, Manufacturer will render such sales, product and technical information, and estimates and specifications, as shall be helpful to Distributor in promoting the sale of Techno Products. At least once each year Manufacturer shall have its representative call upon Distributor and supply any information needed concerning the use, application or development of Techno Products. Distributor shall forward reports of significant sales and technical information gained in the Territory concerning the use and development of present Techno Products and possibilities for new developments in the industry.

11. Term of Agreement; Disposition of Inventory.

11.1 The term of this Agreement shall be for three (3) years from the date hereof, but the Agreement may be terminated at any time during such period by either party without cause upon the expiration of 90 days after written notice to the other party. The term of the Agreement may be extended for successive periods by the joint written consent of both parties. If there is any such extension, the notice period for termination without cause shall be increased to six months. In the event of a breach of any term or condition of this Agreement by either party, the Agreement may be terminated by the other party upon giving 30 days written notice of such termination. In the event a petition in bankruptcy or similar proceeding shall be filed by or against either party, or if either party shall make an assignment for benefit of creditors, this Agreement may be terminated by the other party on five (5) days written notice.

11.2 In the event Manufacturer terminates this Agreement, it shall purchase or cause to be purchased from Distributor its then inventory of Techno Products which may be in unopened factory packing, and any other items that are resalable as new, provided that such items are listed on Manufacturer's then current export price list, at Distributor's cost less 15%, plus return freight cost. If Distributor shall terminate this Agreement, Manufacturer assumes no responsibility with respect to Techno Products then or thereafter in possession of Distributor, provided however, that Manufacturer will have the right within 30 days after the effective date of such termination to purchase all or any Techno Products in Distributor's possession at Distributor's cost less 15%, plus return freight cost. In the event of any termination, Distributor agrees to return all sales aids and materials in its possession at the direction of Manufacturer who shall bear the freight cost.

12. Notices.

Any notices hereunder shall be in writing and shall be deemed given when properly deposited in the normal mails, airmail postage prepaid, addressed as follows:

To Manufacturer:

Techno Manufacturers, Inc.,

____

Junction City, Colorado,
U.S.A.

To Distributor: Impo A. G.,

____

____

13. Waiver of Breach.

The failure of either party to require the performance of any term of this Agreement, or the waiver by either party of any breach of this Agreement, shall not prevent a subsequent enforcement of such term nor be deemed a waiver of any subsequent breach.

14. Amendments.

Any modification or amendment of any provision of this Agreement must be in writing and bear the signatures of the authorized representatives of both parties.

15. Disputes.

Any disputes, controversies or claims between the parties arising out of or relating to this Agreement shall be settled by arbitration in accordance with the rules of the ______ Arbitration Association. This Agreement shall be enforceable and judgment upon any award rendered by the arbitrators may be entered in any court having jurisdiction. Arbitration shall take place in ______, ______, or such other place as the parties may mutually agree.

16. Construction of Agreement; Language.

This Agreement shall be construed and the relations of the parties shall be determined, in accordance with the laws of the State of Colorado; provided, however, that if any provision of the Agreement is in violation of any applicable law, such provision shall to such extent be deemed null and void, and the remainder of the Agreement shall remain in full force and effect. The English language text of this Agreement shall be the authorized text for all purposes.

17. Assignment and Benefits.

Neither this Agreement nor any interest in it shall be assigned directly or indirectly by either party without the prior written consent of the other. Further, upon any substantial change in the ownership or management of either party, such party shall give written notice of the change and the other party may terminate this Agreement after 30 days written notice given not later than 30 days after notice of the change. Subject to the foregoing provisions of this paragraph, this Agreement shall be binding upon and inure to the benefit of the legal representatives, successors and assigns of the parties.

IN WITNESS WHEREOF, the parties have executed this Agreement as of the date first written above.

TECHNO MANUFACTURERS, INC.

By ________________________

President

IMPO A. G.

By ________________________

Title:

QUESTIONS

We pose some questions which call for the application to this problem of matters considered elsewhere in this book.

(1) Review the materials on choice of forum clauses and arbitration at pp. 809–834, supra. Then consider Art. 15 of the Distributorship Agreement. Why does it opt for an arbitration clause? If you were representing Impo, would you resist an attempt to fill in the blanks with a designation of an American organization and location? On what grounds? On what grounds might Techno resist? Does the clause, originating before the U. N. Convention on Arbitral Awards, p. 833, supra, gain the maximum enforceability obtainable under that Convention?

(2) Does this business arrangement subject Techno to the payment of German income taxes on revenues derived from sales through Impo? What portions of the German-American Convention on income taxation bear on this question (p. 1131, supra)? Could Techno arrange matters so as to minimize its exposure to United States income taxes falling on these earnings? What kinds of corporations governed by special tax law provisions might be considered as offering advantageous alternatives?

(3) Suppose that a year after the agreement is signed, the Common Market imposes either a new tariff or a quota that substantially burdens the importation into Germany of the goods covered by the Agreement. Under the Agreement (especially Arts. 5 and 7), who bears the burden of the increased cost or of the reduced number of items that can be imported? Does the matter stand differently if the cause of the problem is a new restriction on exports imposed by the United States or one on the manufacture of the item due to scarcity of materials? Is it of any consequence that the Agreement has no explicit *force majeure* clause? If you were representing a distributor who thought these possibilities were not unlikely what sort of clause would you seek to insert?

(4) The following questions about the Agreement can only be dealt with by students who have read the materials on antitrust at pp. 986–1047, supra, the section on distributorships in the European Economic Community at pp. 1349–1393, infra, and, preferably, the analyses of the law-making process in the Community at pp. 1268–1324, infra. Consider whether the Agreement in its present form attempts to confer any degree of exclusivity on the arrangement—in any of the three respects mentioned at p. 1349, infra. Consider the problems that would arise if one of the parties sought to insert a clause (a) barring the distributor from resorting to other competitive sources of supply; (b) barring Techno from selling to other distributors in Germany or (c) barring the distributor from selling outside Germany. Which law—United States or Germany or European Economic Community or all three—would have an interest in the competitive effects of such clauses? Could the parties realize any of such goals without incurring serious risks of adverse consequences?

DECISION OF 30 JANUARY 1961

German Supreme Court, 1961.
[1961] 2 Neue Juristische Wochenschrift, 1061.

Plaintiff acted, from 27.9.1954 to 6.8.1956, on behalf of defendant, a Netherlands A.G. which produces bathing suits and knit-

ted garments, as its general representative for the Federal Republic and West Berlin. After defendant had terminated the original contract from 27.9.1954 to 1.9.1955, the parties concluded on the same day a new sales representative contract, ¶ 14 of which reads:

> For all litigation in relation to this contract the appropriate court in Eindhofen is selected. All legal relations arising from the contract are determined for the present and in the future according to Netherlands law.

Later both parties terminated this contract, defendant by a letter of 31.1.1956 as of 1.9.1956, plaintiff by a letter of 6.8.1956 without delay.

Plaintiff is of the view that he is entitled to a settlement according to § 89b of the Commercial Code; he sued for a partial sum of 10,000 DM with interest in the district court at Frankfurt/Main. Defendant undisputably possesses property there. Defendant moved to dismiss. It established that the German court had no jurisdiction since the parties had agreed upon the exclusive jurisdiction of the Netherlands courts. It is of the view that a claim for a settlement by plaintiff does not exist since by the agreement of the parties Netherlands law was to be applied and no arrangement corresponding to that of Commercial Code § 89b is known to it.

The district court and court of appeals dismissed the complaint for lack of jurisdiction of the court resorted to. The appeal by plaintiff had no success.

For the reason that: 1. The lower court establishes that the will of the parties intended to agree upon the jurisdiction set forth in ¶ 14 of the contract of 1.9.1955 *as exclusive*; the effectiveness of this agreement is not negated by the fact that the parties, according to plaintiff's assertions, had not come to agreement upon several other particular points of the contract.

These declarations cause no error of law to appear . . . and are not attacked by the appeal.

2. The lower court is . . . of the view that the circumstance that mutuality is not guaranteed between Germany and the Netherlands (Civil Procedure Rules § 328 ¶ 1, no. 5) does not cause the agreement of the parties as to jurisdiction to be without effect.

It need not be decided here whether this view were also to be followed if it would in practice make execution impossible for the plaintiff . . . . For in the instant case plaintiff has no difficulties as to execution to worry about. Defendant has the greater part of its property in the Netherlands; there is no obstacle to an execution in the Netherlands against defendant on the basis of a Netherlands judgment.

3. The appeal argues that the agreement upon exclusive Netherlands jurisdiction and [substantive] law is in this case ineffective because it would lead to an evasion of the mandatory Commercial Code § 89b; the Netherlands law knows no prescription corresponding to Commercial Code § 89b.

Defendant is on the contrary of the view that the question whether the parties can effectively agree upon the exclusive competence of a Netherlands court is to be sharply separated from the question whether they were prevented from agreeing upon the application of Netherlands [substantive] law. Since the first question is to be answered in the affirmative and because thereof the complaint is to be dismissed by the German court because of its lack of jurisdiction the second question need not be further explored . . . .

It is to be conceded to the appeal that although the two questions are logically separable, still in a particular case the agreement on choice of court can serve the purpose, and can in practice bring it about, that the law of that country is to be applied whose exclusive jurisdiction is agreed upon. In case of doubt the will of the parties will point the way. Then, however, the choice of court may be ineffective if the parties could not effectively agree upon the application of the corresponding foreign law. Both questions must therefore be dealt with together.

But even with such a joint consideration [of the questions] the complaints of the appeal are not well grounded.

(a) With the help of the Introduction to the Civil Code art. 30, the agreement upon Netherlands substantive law and jurisdiction cannot be denied effect by an appeal to the binding nature of Commercial Code § 89b . . . .

That the Netherlands rules on commercial agents violate *bonos mores*, because they recognize no settlement claims, is not assumed even by the appeal. That would indeed be erroneous; for a claim to a settlement by a commercial agent was just as foreign to German law up to 1953.

The Netherlands law as to commercial agents does not conflict "with the purpose of a German law" in the sense of Introduction to the Civil Code art. 30. This provision is to be narrowly construed. It is not to be applied every time the foreign legal system departs from mandatory German legal rules. The mandatory German rule must rather be of such a fundamental and far-reaching meaning that it intends to exclude contrary foreign legal solutions. Article 30 intervenes, then, if the difference of public policy or social views between the foreign law agreed upon and the German legal system are so substantial that by the application of the foreign law the very bases of the German state or social life would be attacked.

These prerequisites are not present in the case of § 89b.

(b) The agreement as to Netherlands law and jurisdiction cannot in this case be denied effectiveness on the basis that defendant had thereby intended the evasion of the mandatory prescription of Commercial Code § 89b (a violation of Civil Code § 134).

It can be assumed that, without the agreement by the parties, their legal relations would have been judged by German courts and according to German law. It can further be assumed that defendant by the agreement as to Netherlands law and jurisdiction intended to exclude Commercial Code § 89b and, instead of it, make applicable the rules (more favorable to it) of the Netherlands law.

That does not, however, in the instant case lead to the conclusion that the agreement upon Netherlands law and jurisdiction is void according to Civil Code § 134.

The appeal refers to a case in which two Germans, with their residence and property within the country and without any contacts abroad, subject their contractual relation to a foreign legal system and an exclusive foreign judicial jurisdiction. It must be conceded to the appeal that serious objections to the effectiveness of such an agreement would arise from Civil Code § 134. Here, however, the case is otherwise. Here defendant is a stock corporation under Netherlands law with its *sitz* in the Netherlands. Its factory is in the Netherlands, just as is the important part of its property. Those are reasons which justify the defendant in wishing to subject the contract relation with plaintiff to Netherlands law and judicial jurisdiction and to bring about an agreement to that effect. Its action is therefore permissible and Civil Code § 134 not applicable.

The plaintiff's contrary conception would also lead to the result that via Civil Code § 134 the area of applicability of *ordre public*, to which the legislature consciously gave narrow limits in Introduction to the Civil Code art. 30—as has been explained under (a) above —would be substantially broadened.

(c) Whether the agreement on a foreign law and judicial jurisdiction could be denied effectiveness under the circumstances foreseen in Civil Procedure Rules § 1025(2) . . . by a corresponding application of that rule need not be decided here. The decision appealed from contains no findings that would indicate that defendant might have used its economic or social superiority to compel plaintiff to agree to the contract for Netherlands law and judicial jurisdiction. A casual reference in the opinion on appeal as to such a possibility finds no support in the substantial proofs offered by plaintiff.

(d) No advantage may be derived by plaintiff in the case to be decided here from Commercial Code § 92. That prescription provides, inter alia, that Commercial Code § 89b may be excluded by agreement with respect to a commercial agent without a branch in the country. No argument *ex contrario* may be derived from it to the effect that with respect to a commercial agent with a domestic branch the agreement for foreign law and foreign judicial jurisdiction can in no case be effective because of the mandatory nature of Commercial Code § 89b.

STATUTES RELEVANT TO THE ABOVE CASE

Commerial Code § 84 [Definition]

(1) A commercial agent is one who as an independent conducter of a business is consistently entrusted with acting as intermediary for another entrepreneur in transactions or in concluding them in the latter's name. One is "independent" who basically can freely regulate his own activity and determine his own hours of work.

. . .

Commercial Code § 89 [Cancellation]

(1) If the contractual relation is entered into for an unspecified time it can be cancelled in the first three years of the duration of the contract on six weeks' notice at the end of a calendar quarter. If a different period of notice is agreed on it must amount to a month at least; it can only be cancelled at the end of a calendar month.

(2) After a three year duration of the contract the contractual relation can only be terminated upon at least three months' notice at the end of a calendar quarter.

(3) An agreed upon period of notice must be the same for both parties. If unequal notice is agreed upon the longer period is effective for both parties.

Commercial Code § 89a [Cancellation for Important Cause]

(1) The contract relations can be cancelled by either party for important cause without observing any notice period. This right cannot be excluded or limited.

(2) If the cancellation is caused by conduct, for which the other side is responsible, the latter is obligated to make good the damage caused by the termination of the contract relation.

Commercial Code § 89b [Claim for Settlement]

(1) The commercial agent can demand of the entrepreneur, after the termination of the contractual relationship, a suitable settlement, if and insofar as

1. the entrepreneur has derived significant advantages from the business relationship with new customers, whom the commercial agent has obtained, even after the termination of the contractual relationship,

2. the commercial agent as a result of the termination of the contractual relationship loses claims to compensation which he would have had, if it had continued, from transactions already concluded with the customers obtained by him or from transactions to have arisen with them in the future, and

3. the payment of a settlement is fair considering all the circumstances.

It is equivalent to obtaining a new client if the commercial agent has extended the business relation with a customer so substantially that this economically corresponds to the obtaining of a new customer.

(2) The settlement amounts at the most to an annual compensation or other annual payment calculated on the basis of the average of the last five years of activity of the commercial agent; in case of a shorter duration of the contract the average during the term of the activity is controlling.

(3) The claim does not exist if the commercial agent has cancelled the contractual relationship without the entrepreneur's conduct having given an adequate basis therefor. The same is true if the entrepreneur cancelled the contractual relationship and there existed for the cancellation an important reason because of the delinquency of the commercial agent.

. . .

(4) The claim cannot be excluded by advance agreement . . . .

Commercial Code § 90a [Agreement not to Compete]

(1) An agreement which limits the commercial agent in his business activity after the end of the contractual relationship (agreement not to compete) must be in writing and requires the delivery to the commercial agent of a copy signed by the entrepreneur containing the agreed upon conditions. The agreement can only be made for, at the longest, two years from the end of the contractual relationship. The entrepreneur is obligated to pay the commercial agent an appropriate compensation for the term of the restraint on competition . . . .

(4) Agreements deviating from the above to the disadvantage of the commercial representative cannot be made.

Commercial Code § 92c [Commercial Agent Abroad]

(1) If the commercial agent has no branch within the country an agreement can be made contravening all of the prescriptions of this section.

. . .

Introduction to the Civil Code § 30

The application of a foreign law is not permitted if the application would be *contra bonos mores*, or contrary to the object of a German law.

Civil Code § 134

A juristic act which is contrary to a statutory prohibition is void, unless a contrary intention appears from the statute.

NOTE ON COMMERCIAL AGENT LEGISLATION

A number of other countries both in Europe (e. g., France and Belgium) and in Latin America have legislation protecting commercial agents or distributors against types of cancellation of their rights. The legislative provisions have certain family resemblances, but each presents its separate problems for the American party seeking a foothold in a foreign market. American firms have found the cancellation of distributorship agreements to be peculiarly difficult, a fact which arouses the choler of American executives accustomed to dispensing rather unceremoniously with representatives who fail to get to know their territory or to service it adequately.

These statutes seem to be motivated by a felt need to protect an "underdog" class of commercial actors, and perhaps by the sense of respect for vested rights (*situations acquises*) that characterizes some industrial societies. They are not aimed particularly at foreign interests, although their effect may be more severe on the American style of handling such arrangements.

A few points about these statutes are worth bearing in mind.

(1) What kinds of representatives are covered by the law? § 84 of the German Commercial Code seems to give a fairly clear-cut answer. Consider, however, a decision of 16 February 1961, 34 B.G.H.Z. 282. Plaintiff, although acting in his own name and thus not strictly as an agent, sought a cancellation settlement à la § 89b. The court rejected his claim, but in such terms as to make it appear that some dealers would be covered, would be regarded as "in need of protection." The court stressed the fact that the plaintiff dealer had expended 250,000 DM in the first 1½ years of his activity, largely for equipment, and had borrowed only 200,000 D.M. This, the court felt, showed that he did not present a case comparable to that of the typical agent:

> It is typical of the commercial agent that he, in contrast to the manufacturer or independent dealer, practices his activity as a rule without putting in his own capital. He generally needs for his activity no substantial funds or equipment. The chief value of his business lies in the relations—created by him—with clients, his clientele. At the end of the contract he necessarily loses the clientele to the principal. Since his business is typically conducted without equipment or capital it vanishes at the contract's end since the clientele remains with the principal and is lost to the agent although it is the chief value of his business. The

commercial agent is thus materially more strongly financially affected as a rule by the ending of a contract than an independent dealer who loses a relation to his supplier since the independent dealer keeps the capital and material assets inhering in his business.

(2) What are the formalities required of the conclusion of an agency contract?

(3) What difficulties does the law put in the way of terminating an agreement? These may include notice requirements, or specified compensation for the cancellation, or other constraints.

(4) What restrictions does the law put on the parties' freedom to contract as to compensation, non-competition, and so on? (See § 90a of the German statute.)

Note that the United States has a somewhat similar law, the Automobile Dealers Act of 1956, 15 U.S.C.A. §§ 1221–1225. It applies only to truck and car dealers (and only to those resident in the United States). One may doubt whether the typical American car dealer was "in need of protection" in terms of the German court's criteria quoted above. Is he peculiarly in need of protection under other criteria?

It seems appropriate to offer some background on the American law through a case in which a German manufacturer fell afoul of it. In Volkswagen Interamericana, S. A. v. Rohlsen, 360 F.2d 437 (1st Cir. 1966), a judgment against the regional VW organization in favor of a St. Croix, Virgin Islands distributor was reversed, but only as to damages. The court first disposed of a choice of law clause and then stated:

> Little time need be spent over defendant's reliance upon a provision of the franchise agreement restricting actions to the courts of Mexico. We need not consider whether this provision is sufficiently reasonable that it should be respected in an ordinary suit arising out of the contract. See Wm. H. Muller & Co. v. Swedish American Line Ltd., 2 Cir., 1955, 224 F.2d 806, 56 A.L.R.2d 295, cert. den. 350 U.S. 903, 76 S.Ct. 182, 100 L.Ed. 793. The Dealers' Act contains its own venue provisions which are very broad, and are designed to assure the dealer as accessible a forum as is reasonably possible. Cf. Snyder v. Eastern Auto Distributors, Inc., 4 Cir., 1966, 357 F.2d 552, cert. den. June 13, 1966, 86 S.Ct. 1889. The very purpose of the act is to give the dealer certain rights against a manufacturer independent of the terms of the agreement itself. Cf. Barney Motor Sales v. Cal. Sales, Inc., S.D.Cal.1959, 178 F.Supp. 172, 175. This protection would be of little value if a manufacturer could contractually limit jurisdiction to a forum practically inaccessible to the dealer. The act cannot so easily be thwarted.
>
> [The court then analyzed plaintiff's case on the merits and said in part:]
>
> Defendant next contends that the evidence does not support a verdict in plaintiff's favor on the merits. Before examining the record we must first inquire into the governing legal standards, which are not entirely clear from

the face of the statute. Section 1222 requires the manufacturer to "act in good faith . . . in terminating, canceling, or not renewing the franchise." Section 1221(e) defines "good faith" as

> "the duty of each party to any franchise . . . to act in a fair and equitable manner toward each other so as to guarantee the one party freedom from coercion, intimidation, or threats of coercion or intimidation from the other party: *Provided,* That recommendation, endorsement, exposition, persuasion, urging or argument shall not be deemed to constitute a lack of good faith."

For a manufacturer to condition continuation of a franchise upon certain conduct, even if characterizable as a threat, cannot constitute forbidden coercion per se. It must appear that the condition was unfair or inequitable. To hold otherwise would not only circumscribe the manufacturer's freedom to do business to an extent we cannot believe contemplated by Congress, but would lead to the absurd result that a manufacturer could not insist upon the very terms of the agreement.

Initially, we think there is an important difference between two kinds of improper conditions that a manufacturer might impose and back up by threats. Particularly suspect under the act are conditions which benefit only, or primarily, the manufacturer—for example, requirements that a dealer purchase large stocks of vehicles, spare parts, special tools or advertising matter—as distinguished from requirements that would tend to work to the mutual advantage of both parties, for example, that the dealer improve its service, or managerial efficiency. The manufacturer can easily extort demands of the first sort, increasing its own profit at the expense of the dealer's; the act's legislative history indicates that this was of particular concern to the Congress. The latter sort, even if the demands may be thought excessive under the circumstances, should not, without more, indicate that the manufacturer is taking advantage of the dealer, or using the franchise as a weapon for extortion, since the manufacturer stands to profit from his demands only if the dealer profits as well.

The jury could have found that defendant imposed several requirements upon plaintiff which, under the above analysis, if improper, would fall into the first group—conditions directly benefiting the manufacturer, but not necessarily the dealer. Plaintiff's 1956 franchise required it to stock spare parts equal in cost to ten per cent of the value of its automobile stock; the 1958 franchise required him to purchase from defendant a welding machine, a line of Vespa motor scooters, a tractor, advertising materials, and tools; plaintiff was forced to sign the 1960 renewal contract without being given time to read its terms. . . .

. . .

As we have indicated, a disfranchised dealer does not make a case under the statute merely by proving that his performance was not below minimum limits. Plaintiff makes a special showing, however, intending to establish that it was not really his performance with which defendant was dissatisfied. In particular, plaintiff alleges that starting in 1960, defendant determined to take a direct share of the retail profits in the St. Croix area. Had defendant merely wished to own a dealership itself, it might have terminated plaintiff's franchise and formed its own enterprise. But plaintiff asserts that defendant wanted a direct share of the profits without making any, or any substantial, investment; that defendant threatened plaintiff with loss of the franchise unless he agreed to admit defendant to his operation; and that when plaintiff refused, defendant made good its threat. We turn to some of the relevant evidence.

. . .

We could agree with defendant that discussions with other persons looking towards their taking over a franchise, are not only not inconsistent with a claim that the dealer's performance was inadequate, but would be only natural. The case at bar was unusual, however, in that the contemplated change-over was one in which the defendant would share. On Hinke's own testimony, this would have been "a negative situation . . . very much contrary to our doings. We feel always that we should not enter the retail field." The jury might well have found inadequately explained why, in the light of this protestation, defendant sought to establish a new dealership in which it was to participate. The jury could well find that the initially threatened termination was not in good faith. With this as a background, we believe that on the record as a whole there was a jury question whether defendant's termination of the franchise related to the conduct of plaintiff's agency, or to his rejection of the defendant as a partner upon unreasonable terms. If the latter, it was a clear violation of the Dealers' Act.

QUESTIONS

(1) Compare the German statutory provisions with the Automobile Dealers Act. Which has the advantage in terms of clarity, fairness and enforceability? Why should the courts take such apparently opposing views about the effectiveness of contractual clauses that purport to restrict the protection afforded the dealer?

(2) Examine the termination provisions in Art. 11 of the Agreement. Are there ways in which the exercise of those powers might be blocked or rendered excessively costly by the German law—if the relationship is in fact one covered by the statute? Does Art. 16 afford a way of disposing of the problem?

(3) Suppose that the parties were moved by advantages they perceived from an antitrust perspective (p. 1388, infra), to shift from an independent distributor relationship to a single sales agency. How would that affect the posture of the parties under the German statute? The German income tax situation of Techno? The exposure of Techno to litigation in Germany (p. 753, supra)?

Additional reading: The background to the American law is detailed in Kessler, Automobile Dealer Franchises: Vertical Integration by Contract, 66 Yale L.J. 1135 (1957). Macauley, Law and the Balance of Power: The Automobile Manufacturers and their Dealers (1966). The English language literature on foreign laws is growing rapidly. See Davis, Termination of a Commercial Agent in Continental Europe, 3 Texas Int.L. Forum 303 (1967); Jones, Practical Aspects of Commercial Agency and Distribution Agreements in the European Community, 6 Int.Law. 107 (1972); Flattery, Drafting and Operating Under a Foreign Distributorship Agreement, Prac. Law, Oct. 1964, p. 19; Johnson, International Distributorship and Agency Agreements, in Southwest Legal Foundation, Negotiating and Drafting International Commercial Contracts 199 (1966); Graupner, Sole Distributorship Agreements—A Comparative View, 18 Int. & Comp.L.Q. 879 (1969); Burkard, Termination Compensation to Distributors Under German Law, 7 Int'l.Law. 185 (1973).

---

3. A LICENSING AGREEMENT

An American manufacturer owning significant property rights —patents, trade-marks and unpatented trade secrets or "knowhow" —may consider licensing as an alternative path towards entering a foreign market. Tariffs and transport or manufacturing costs may make it non-competitive to produce an item in the United States and export it. Production in the foreign country may pose problems for the American entrepreneur—risk of expropriation, foreign exchange difficulties, diversion of executive talents. If a suitable local licensee can be found, a holder of patent and other rights can realize a return on its investment without running such risks.

Of course, the patentee has no great measure of control over how the operation is conducted. Will the foreign management be effective in producing or selling the item? Also, a licensee may be in a position to block the American firm from entering its market during the term of the license (see pp. 1024–1028, supra) and, at its end, may have developed its own competitive position to such a degree as to make it impractical for the American firm to compete there.

Various policies of the potential licensee's government bear on the desirability of this alternative. Its patent laws may not cover the product (if, for example, it is a medical or food product) or may not extend comprehensive protection to devices that are patentable. It must be remembered that in some less developed countries, 95% of all patents are granted to foreigners. Such countries are understandably less than enthusiastic about making the investment needed to maintain a smoothly functioning patent system. At the same time, they are concerned about the costs of importing data from abroad through licensing arrangements—but also anxious to obtain access to the store of technology built up in the developed countries.

For these reasons governments are apt to intervene in licensing arrangements to which their nationals are parties. Frequently the mechanism used is the country's exchange control system. In many countries, an international licensing agreement must be submitted to a government agency for approval, or it may later prove to be impossible to repatriate the royalties. Government surveillance may or may not be sophisticated. It is often said by licensors that the

Japanese system is the most formidable. Foreign parties who thought that they had worked out a satisfactory arrangement with their Japanese counterpart have discovered that the government will refuse to approve the transaction unless the royalty rate is reduced or other conditions are modified in favor of the Japanese party. Since the Japanese market is large and attractive and since access by direct investment has been severely limited, foreign firms are under pressure to accede to these requests and to modify their arrangements accordingly. Latin American countries are becoming increasingly aggressive in regulating licenses. Five South American countries (Bolivia, Chile, Colombia, Ecuador and Peru) formed the Andean Subregional Market (Ancom) in 1969 (see fn. 61, p. 455, supra). In 1971 those countries agreed upon common rules for treatment of foreign patents, licenses and royalties, which rules are to be applied by each member government in dealing with international licenses. The common policy is intended to prevent member nations from bidding against each other for the favors of the foreign holder of technology.

Consider now the following form of license agreement. You are counsel for an American company, Data Devices, Inc., which has developed a compact and cheap computer capable of use by small businesses. Data Devices benefits from its distinctive processes for making small transistorized components. It has a handful of patents on improvements it has made in computers and in processes for making transistors. Previously it restricted its activities to the United States, and thus has no experience abroad.

Recently an industrialist from a Latin American country visited the Data Devices plant and was impressed by its product. In turn, the company's management was convinced that the Latin American firm was capable of turning out a workmanlike product and had excellent sales connections in its region. The proposed licensee presented a proposed contract which was similar to one it had signed with a Danish firm in connection with another electronic product that it manufactures. It is willing to sign such an agreement with Data Devices.

You are counsel to Data Devices and are asked by its management whether the contract is suitable for these purposes and which if any clauses would have to be amended to make it conform to American law.

AGREEMENT [10]

An *Agreement* made this ______ day of ______ 19__ between Data Devices, Inc., a Delaware corporation having a place of business at Chicago, Illinois, hereinafter called the *Licensor*, and Companía Mercada S. A., a Guatador corporation, having a place of business at Estancia, Guatador, hereinafter called the *Licencee*.

10. The license agreement is adapted from Goldschmid, International License Contracts, A Practical Guide (1968).

WITNESSETH:

Preamble

Whereas Licensor has invented and developed a method (hereinafter called "the process") for the manufacture of a computer (hereinafter called "the product") and possesses valuable secret knowledge, formulae, information, data, and related skills useful in performing the process;

Whereas Licensor has applied for and obtained patents for both the process and the product, amongst others in the United States and in Guatador, as set forth in Annex A;

Whereas Licensor has obtained trade marks for the product amongst others in the United States and in Guatador, as set forth in Annex B, hereinafter called "the trade marks";

Whereas Licencee is an established manufacturer and trader in the electronics industry in Guatador and desires to obtain *Licensor's* know-how and the right to work *Licensor's* patents in Guatador, including the right to manufacture the product and sell it under *Licensor's* trade mark in Guatador;

Now therefore in consideration of a down payment of United States Dollars one thousand (U.S. $1,000) having been made by *Licencee* to *Licensor* and of the mutual promises, obligations and covenants set forth herein, the parties hereto agree as follows:

Definitions

As used in this agreement,

A.—The term "patent" or "patents" shall mean any letters patent or patent applications filed by or issued to *Licensor* in Guatador covering the licensed process or product, as well as any letters patent which shall thereafter issue on such applications.

B.—The term "net sales" shall mean the gross amount invoiced by *Licencee* on sales of the licensed product, less returns, rebates, trade discounts, cash discounts, sales taxes, and transportation charges allowed to purchaser on the purchase price.

C.—The term "improvement" shall mean any modification in the manufacturing process licensed hereunder which does not affect the method covered by the patents, as defined in Definition A above.

Operative Clauses

1. Licence Grant

Licensor hereby grants *Licencee* an exclusive, non-transferable, non-assignable, indivisible licence and right to manufacture, use and sell the product in Guatador under the trade mark, to practise the patent and know-how and to use any information and technical assistance respecting process and product which *Licensor* may give *Licencee* in future.

2. Disclosure of Information

Promptly after signature of this Agreement, *Licensor* shall furnish *Licencee* with all particulars, data, specifications, technological, scientific and marketing information, operational instructions relating to process and product, as far as not already in *Licencee's* possession.

3. Future Know-How

During the validity of this Agreement, *Licensor* shall, moreover, make available to *Licencee* any improvement, information and know-how related to process or product, whether acquired by *Licensor* as a result of his research and development or in any other lawful way and which he has the right to pass on to *Licencee*, and for which no additional royalty shall be payable.

4. Feed-Back

Licencee shall promptly disclose to *Licensor* any improvement or invention pertaining to process or product. At *Licensor's* request, *Licencee* shall assign to *Licensor* the entire right, title and interest to and in any such improvement or invention, as well as to file any patent applications therefor, including the right to sublicense, and without paying royalty.

5. Secrecy

Licencee shall treat as secret and confidential all know-how and information received under clauses 2 and 3 hereunder, except to the extent that they have come into the public domain. *Licencee* shall not disclose such know-how and information to any persons other than those employees requiring the know-how and information in the performance of their duties. The obligation to secrecy does not cease with expiry or termination of this Agreement.

6. Service

In accordance with the spirit of mutual goodwill and cooperation between the parties hereto, *Licensor* will normally assist *Licencee* to the best of his ability in the successful performance of the process in *Licencee's* plant. This assistance is considered adequately covered by the provisions of clauses 2 and 3 of this Agreement. Should *Licencee* nevertheless require additional assistance or technical aid from *Licensor*, *Licensor* shall try his best to comply, but shall be entitled to special remuneration at cost, at his absolute discretion, and such additional services and technical aid shall not be considered covered by royalty payment.

. . .

9. Royalty

For the benefits granted to *Licencee* under clauses 1, 2, and 3 hereunder, a royalty shall be paid by him to *Licensor*, amounting to five per cent (5%) on *Licencee's* net sales of the product, as defined in Definition B, in Guatador. Any income-tax due on *Licensor's* royalty income in Guatador shall be deducted from the royalty due and paid by *Licencee* on *Licensor's* behalf, for which official receipt shall be regularly submitted by *Licencee* to *Licensor*.

10. Minimum Royalty

Irrespective of the sales achieved in any one contract year, the following minimum royalty shall in any case be paid by *Licencee* to *Licensor:*

During the first year, counted from the date of signature of this Agreement	$2,000
During the second year	$2,500
During the third year	$3,000
During any of the remaining years	$3,500

Earnest money paid by *Licencee* to *Licensor* is to be deducted from the minimum royalty payment hereunder.

11. Reports

Royalty accrued as herein provided during each calendar quarter shall be paid not later than sixty (60) days after the end of each quarter. Each payment shall be accompanied by a statement, specifying the number of units of the product manufactured and sold during that quarter, the net sales price, the amount of royalty due thereon and the income-tax paid. Each statement should be duly verified by a responsible accounting officer in *Licencee's* firm.

12. Payment

Royalty less income-tax shall be remitted to *Licensor* in United States' currency, not later than sixty (60) days after the end of each calendar quarter, at the rate of conversion ruling on the date of remittance. Expenses of conversion and remittance shall be to *Licensor's* account.

Licencee shall use best efforts to arrange for remittance and conversion into dollars of the royalty. Should such remittance or conversion become restricted due to Government regulations, the royalty less income tax shall be deposited on *Licensor's* behalf with a Guatador bank as may be directed by *Licensor.*

Should remittance of royalty be delayed by *Licencee* beyond the sixty-days' grace period, any loss caused thereby to *Licensor* due to decline of Guatador currency shall be made good by *Licencee.*

13. Audit

Licensee shall maintain complete and accurate records of all sales on which royalty is due hereunder, which records shall once during each financial year be audited and certified by *Licencee's* own auditor on the occasion of the yearly audit and submitted to *Licensor.* Any expenses incurred due to such certification will be borne by *Licensor.*

14. Patent and Trade Mark Rights

Notwithstanding the use by *Licencee* of *Licensor's* patent and trade mark in Guatador, it is hereby expressly declared that the patent and the trade mark shall remain the exclusive property of *Licensor. Licensor* undertakes to maintain his trade mark in Guatador by renewing its registration well in time. *Licencee* agrees to use and display *Licensor's* trade mark at all times in such a manner as to exclude any doubt of *Licensor's* ownership, and so as to safeguard *Licensor's* interests particularly to prevent the trade mark from becoming generic. If so required by *Licencee, Licensor* shall issue a separate trade mark user's license to him for the lifetime of this Agreement.

15. Non-Contestation of Rights

Licencee will not contest the validity of *Licensor's* patents or trade mark under which the licence is granted herein, or *Licensor's* property rights to his know-how, information and improvements, the benefits of which are realised by *Licencee* hereunder. . . .

16. Third Parties' Patent Claims

a) *Licensor* is bona-fide owner of the patent and states to his best knowledge and belief that exercise of the methods disclosed therein does not infringe any third parties' rights. Nevertheless, *Licensor* expressly disclaims any liability in the event of any third party suing or threatening to sue *Licencee* with patent litigation due to his practising *Licensor's* patent under the licence granted hereunder.

. . .

17. Infringement of Licensor's Patents

a) Licencee shall notify *Licensor* promptly of any infringement of *Licensor's* patent in Guatador and shall provide *Licensor* with any available evidence thereof. *Licensor* may, at his discretion, take legal steps to enforce his patent rights, but is under no obligation to do so. . . .

18. Duration

This Agreement is deemed to have come into force on the date first mentioned above and shall continue up to the date of expiry of *Licensor's* latest patent in Guatador relating to the product or to the manufacturing method under which *Licencee* is licensed hereunder, unless terminated earlier as provided in clauses 20 and 21 hereunder.

19. Expiry

Upon termination or expiry of this Agreement, *Licencee* shall cease forthwith the manufacture, use and sale of the product as well as the use of the trade mark, but *Licencee* shall also thereafter be pledged to keep secret the know-how and information received hereunder, as far as they do not come into the public domain. . . .

20. Notice

a) *Licensor* may prematurely terminate this Agreement by giving three calendar months' notice by registered letter:

i) Should *Licencee* have failed to start manufacture of the product within four months after receipt of the information as per clause 2 hereunder.

ii) Should *Licencee* have failed to start sales of the product within four months from the start of production.

iii) Should *Licencee* have failed to remit royalties in terms of clause 12 hereunder except due to force majeure.

iv) In the event of a change in the controlling interest in *Licencee's* firm at the time of signature.

Provided, however, that any notice served under sub-clauses i), ii), or iii) hereunder be considered null and void if *Licencee* cures the default within expiry of the notice period.

b) Either party may terminate the Agreement with immediate effect by giving notice by registered letter:

i) In case of a suit filed or threatened in Guatador against *Licencee* for patent infringement due to *Licencee's* working *Licensor's* patent under the licence granted hereunder and *Licensor* refuses to take up the defence, or loses a suit in which he has taken up the defence, or if a court injunction is decreed against *Licencee.*

ii) In case of gross violation of the letter or spirit of the Agreement by the other party.

iii) In case of dissolution or bankruptcy of the other party.

21. Momentum Clause

In consideration of the fact that the know-how herein granted to *Licencee* also benefits his manufacturing operations concerned with articles other than the licensed product, a royalty of two per cent (2%) on his net sales of such other articles will be payable to *Licensor* for a period of two years after premature termination of this Agreement for any reason whatsoever. The provisions for reporting, calculation and remittance of royalty and audit in clauses 11, 12 and 13 apply likewise to the royalty payable under this clause.

27. Two Versions

This Agreement has been executed both in the English and Spanish languages and in case of doubt the English version shall be considered authentic.

28. Applicable Law

Notwithstanding its execution in Guatador, this contract is construed in accordance with Illinois Law.

29. Arbitration

In the event of a dispute arising out of any of the clauses hereunder, or in the case of a breach of any of these clauses, the parties shall try in the first instance to arrive at an amicable settlement. Should this fail, the dispute shall be submitted to arbitration, which shall take place at the residence of the opponent to the party seeking arbitration. Both parties shall nominate an arbitrator within a fortnight; should one party fail herein, the other party shall name the other arbitrator also. Both arbitrators shall name a third arbitrator who shall be a member of the legal profession. The decision of the board of arbitration shall be final and both parties agree to abide by the same. The board of arbitration shall also decide on each party's share of the expenses of arbitration. The arbitration shall follow the Rules of the International Chamber of Commerce in Paris.

In witness whereof, the parties thereto have caused this Agreement to be executed in duplicate by their duly authorized officers on the date and in the year first written above.

For and behalf of:	For and behalf of:
Data Devices, Inc.	Compania Mercada, S. A.
________	________
Signature:	Signature:
Designation:	Designation:
Witness:	Witness:

NOTE ON RESTRICTIVE EFFECTS OF LICENSES

As observed in connection with the antitrust materials at p. 1027, supra, there is an inherent tension between antitrust concepts and policies and those underlying the patent laws. This tension appears throughout license agreements. A number of critical issues are identified in the following directive by the Andean Commission, p. 1210, supra, setting forth conditions which its member countries should not tolerate in approving licenses by their nationals:[11]

Article 20.—The member countries shall not authorize the execution of those contracts on transfer of external techniques or patents which contain:

a. Clauses whereby the supply of techniques involves an obligation for the member country or for the recipient enterprise to acquire capital assets, intermediate assets and raw materials from a specific source or make permanent use of the personnel appointed by the enterprise supplying the techniques. In exceptional cases, the recipient country may accept this type of clauses for acquisition of capital assets, intermediate products or raw materials providing that their prices correspond to the normal levels in the international market.

b. Clauses whereby the technique selling enterprise keeps its right to the prices for sale or re-sale of the products manufactured on the basis of the respective technique.

c. Clauses whereby restrictions are established on volume and structure for production.

d. Clauses prohibiting the use of competitive techniques.

e. Clauses establishing an option for total or partial purchase in favor of the supplier of the technology.

f. Clauses which commit the purchaser of technology to disclose to the supplier the inventions or improvements accomplished through utilization of said technology.

11. Decision 24 of December 31, 1970, as translated in 10 Int. Legal Mat. 152, 159 (1971) by Messrs. Carrizosa & Vila, Bogota, Colombia. As to its implementation at the national level, see Lacey, Technology and Industrial Property Licensing in Latin America, A Legislative Revolution, 6 Int. Law. 388 (1972).

g. Clauses whereby the [licencees] [12] of patents are obligated to pay royalties on un-used patents, and

h. Other clauses with similar effects.

Except in specific cases, duly qualified as such by the corresponding organism in the recipient country, those clauses which in whatever manner prohibit or limit exportation of the products manufactured on the basis of the respective technique, shall not be accepted.

In no case shall this type of clauses be accepted with reference to subregional exchange or for exportation of similar products to third countries.

Article 21.—The intangible technical contributions shall entitle to payment of royalties upon previous authorization of the corresponding national organism, but may not be computed as a contribution of capital.

When any of such contributions be supplied to a foreign enterprise by its home office or by any of the subsidiaries of said home office, the payment of royalties shall not be approved nor any deductions accepted on such account for taxation purposes.

Compare the following analyses of hypothetical cases contained in a Memorandum of the Department of Justice Concerning Antitrust and Foreign Commerce in early 1972.[13] It is a particularly important indication of current official views because of the absence of significant litigated cases in recent years.

Transfers of Know-How and Patents

The first four cases involve transfers of patents, technology and other know-how and the question of what restriction may be attached to such transfers. In general, territorial restrictions involving patents can be achieved by licensing the foreign patent only, thus limiting the licensee to the territorial jurisdiction covered by the foreign patent. Where know-how and patents are both involved and are closely related it is usually possible to impose the same restriction on the know-how as those permitted for the accompanying patents.

Where know-how alone is involved the rule is somewhat more restrictive, but even there substantial limitations are possible if they meet the following general tests: First, the restrictions must be ancillary to carrying out the lawful primary purpose of the agreement. Second, the scope and duration of the restraints must be no broader than is necessary to support that primary purpose. And third, the restrictions must be otherwise reasonable under the circumstances. The application of these general principles may be illustrated by considering the following cases posed by critics of the antitrust laws.

12. There was an obvious translation error in this sentence, here corrected.

13. Submitted by Deputy Asst. Atty. Gen. Comegys in Export Expansion Act of 1971, Hearings before the Subcommittee on Foreign Commerce and Tourism, Senate Commerce Committee, 92d Cong. 2d Sess. 812 (1972), reprinted in 5 CCH Trade Reg. Rep. ¶ 50,129.

Case 1

An American company wishes to license technology, either patented or unpatented. The company wishes to require the licensee as a condition of the license to purchase from the American company components for the product to be made using the licensed technology. It is further posited that (1) there are competing American manufacturers of these components and (2) foreign manufacturers generally have cheaper production costs.

If it can be clearly shown that foreign manufacturers have lower production costs, the tying agreement could be upheld on the basis that, without the agreement, no American company would be likely to export the components. Under these circumstances, American foreign commerce would not be restricted. Such tying, however, is illegal under the laws of some foreign jurisdictions. See, e. g., Section 57, U. K. Patents Act.

More generally, the second assumption will often be difficult to establish. If it is not true, the fact that there are competing American manufacturers means that the restriction, while of benefit to the one firm, would inhibit exports of other American companies. Consequently the restriction would hurt rather than benefit the United States export trade. Even here, a tying agreement might be permitted when required to assure the proper functioning of the licensed technology. Cf., e. g., Dehydrating Process Co. v. A. O. Smith Corp. [1961 Trade Cases ¶ 70,069], 292 F.2d 653 (1st Cir. 1961), cert. denied 368 U.S. 931 (1961).

Case 2

Company A makes sophisticated electronic equipment in the United States and wants to license engineering know-how in England. The license agreement includes provisions for the export of machinery and components from the United States. Company A would like to deny the licensee access to the United States market because of the danger of building a competitor in its own home market, but fears that such restrictions would violate the antitrust laws.

Contrary to the example's implication, such restrictions if properly drawn may in some circumstances be legal. To the extent that the know-how could be patented under English law, the territorial restrictions could be created by transferring the English but not the United States patent rights. Restrictions on know-how ancillary to the patentable process would also be permitted to the extent that such restrictions on the patent are valid.

Although territorial restrictions on know-how prohibiting reexport to the United States pose more difficult antitrust questions, such restrictions may pass antitrust muster when reasonable under the circumstances and ancillary to the primary purpose of transferring know-how. An important factor in this regard is how readily and how quickly a foreign firm could obtain the know-how through other sources or its own efforts. Cf. United States v. Dupont [1953 Trade Cases ¶ 67,633], 118 F.Supp. 41, 219 (D.Del.

1953), aff'd [1956 Trade Cases ¶ 68,369], 351 U.S. 377 (1956). Territorial restrictions would not be permissible if unreasonable in light of the know-how involved or part of a larger illegal plan to cartelize the market. See, e. g., United States v. National Lead Co. [1944–1945 Trade Cases ¶ 57,394], 63 F.Supp. 513 (S.D.N.Y.1945), aff'd [1946–1947 Trade Cases ¶ 57,575], 332 U.S. 319 (1947); United States v. Imperial Chemical Industries [1950–1951 Trade Cases ¶ 62,923], 100 F.Supp. 504 (S.D.N.Y.1951).

Thus in Case 2 the restrictions could be upheld if the know-how being transferred is of substantial value, the territorial restrictions are limited to a reasonable period and the agreement is not part of a larger plan to divide markets between dominant firms.

Alternatively the licensor could protect itself through other means: (1) it could set the royalty rate high enough to offset any cost advantage of the foreign firm, or (2) it could integrate forward (thereby providing a greater long-run improvement in the balance of payments) to insure control of the disposition of the products.

More generally, it is important to remember that licensing of know-how in this situation may in fact have a negative impact on the balance of payments to the extent licensing is substituted for product exports or for foreign capital investment. The trade advantage of the United States is highest in products involving new technology. Early foreign licensing tends to erode this source of export strength, and it may be very difficult on the basis of self-serving statements by the licensor to determine whether export alternatives to licensing are or are not feasible. Furthermore, restricting the English company from selling in the United States could be injurious to United States buyers, an injury which may offset any export benefit.

Case 3

An American company would like to license technology, either patented or unpatented. The American company would like to include in its license agreement a provision that the licensee cannot sell the completed products in any country other than its country of domicile. The American company has determined that the licensee does not have the capability or experience to do an effective job of marketing the products in other countries, and the American company is negotiating with other similar companies to enter into similar license arrangements in other countries.

The legality of restrictions involving sales back into the domestic United States market is discussed in Case 2. Restrictions on sales in other foreign markets would not affect United States foreign commerce and, therefore, not be subject to United States antitrust jurisdiction. Consequently no problems under the United States antitrust laws would exist. It should be noted, however, that exclusive national territories would probably violate European antitrust laws. See, e. g., Grundig-Consten decision, Case Nos. 56/64 & 58/64, European Court of Justice (Common Mkt. Rptr. ¶ 8046).

If the domestic company's concern is that a foreign licensee may overextend itself and thereby dilute the quality of service, a "best efforts" clause and other contract performance criteria may solve the problem without the need for more stringent territorial limitations.

Case 4

Licensing of American-owned patents affords another example of a type of situation where our antitrust laws may hamper competition by American business with foreign competitors who are not similarly inhibited. If an Indian company, for example, is negotiating for the rights to use and develop a particular type of process for which an American and an English company hold competing patented processes, one important aspect of the negotiations may be the commitment of the patent holder to give the Indian company exclusive rights in, let us say, southeast Asia and to agree not to market the product in question in that area in competition with the Indian company.

The English or another foreign company can probably give this commitment without antitrust difficulties, but for the United States company such a commitment poses United States antitrust risks.

Contrary to the inference of the example, it is possible to give the foreign licensee an exclusive license under the foreign patent rights which excludes the American patentee, and thus create the desired guarantee of exclusiveness. A licensee, however, must rely on the strength of the patent to exclude foreign licensees, and no contractual commitments not to compete should be made. Although legal it is worth noting that an exclusive license by excluding subsequent United States sales of the product in that market may have a detrimental effect on the United States balance of payments.

QUESTIONS

(1) What does the license agreement provide about the licensee's capacity to export from Guatador (see Art. 1)? Does it permit exports *to* the United States (recall Sections 1337 and 1337a of the Tariff Act noted at p. 1026, supra)? Does it permit Data Devices to export *from* the United States to Guatador? Does it permit the licensee to export to other countries? Suppose provisions were inserted to reserve certain third-country markets to Data Devices. Would the United States Antitrust Division object (see Case 3 in its Memorandum)? What would be the position of the Andean Commission?

(2) Consider Arts. 4 and 18 of the agreement. When you combine their effect, how long might the agreement last? Why does a licensor press hard for a provision like Art. 4 if the licensee seems to have significant technological capacity? Why does the Andean Commission object as strenuously as it does in clause (f)? Would the United States have an interest in how that clause was formulated? Can you suggest a compromise solution?

(3) Arts. 15 and 21 might encounter objections from United States authorities if they were contained in a domestic agreement. Do you see what their anticompetitive effect might be? Would the same objections pertain to a foreign license?

NOTE ON ROYALTY ARRANGEMENTS

As we have seen, national governments have an acute interest in the size of royalty payments. So, naturally, do the parties. Consider the clauses, chiefly Arts. 9–13 of the agreement, which relate to royalties.

Bear in mind that under this arrangement royalties are to be paid and computed in dollars. Any contract involving a currency foreign to one of the parties exposes a party to two risks that should be apparent from pp. 1168, 1173, supra: (1) that exchange rates will change, perhaps drastically, from time to time; (2) that exchange controls will change or be newly imposed so as to render payment impossible.

Normally, private parties have several methods of safeguarding themselves against shifts in rates. It is possible to buy or sell many currencies for future delivery, paying in effect a premium over the current, or "spot", rate as the price for another party's assuming the risk of change. It may also be possible for a party, say an American exporter, to borrow from a bank in the foreign country an amount of the foreign currency equivalent at the current exchange rate to the amount of dollars it anticipates that it will ultimately receive under its contract. The party then converts that sum of foreign money at the current rate into dollars; when the payment to the party becomes due, the bank borrowings can be repaid with the same face amount of local currency regardless of its current relationship to the dollar.[14] Neither method is a complete answer to the problems of the parties to a licensing agreement, although these problems may be less acute than for parties to a sales agreement where payment for goods sold is due some years after delivery.

Another vital matter with respect to royalties is taxation. Royalties benefit from special relief under tax conventions between developed countries. See Art. VIII of the Income Tax Convention between the United States and the Federal Republic of Germany.* Less developed countries are, characteristically, unwilling to agree to such clauses limiting their right to tax the royalties as income to the recipient since they are unlikely to obtain reciprocal benefits. Whether the royalties can be fully deducted from the licensee's income as an expense under the law governing the licensee's taxes is also important.

The tax law of the licensor's home country may be crucial. At the start, the licensor may consider whether to structure the transaction in such a way that it will be considered a full disposition of property rights in the invention and, hence, a sale. As a sale, favor-

14. Thus, if the exporter expects in eight months time to be paid 6,000,000 quatadors equivalent now to $100,000, it can now borrow 6,000,000 quatadors, convert them into dollars and bring them home. In eight months time, when it duly receives the 6,000,000 quatadors, it can pay off the loan therewith even though 6,000,000 quatadors are now worth only $75,000.

able capital gains treatment might be available. Then, the licensor might seek to defer United States taxes by having the royalties received by a subsidiary incorporated abroad.

The Revenue Act of 1962, p. 1110, supra, substantially narrowed such opportunities. Under that law "foreign personal holding company income" includes royalties if not derived from the active conduct of business and if derived from related persons. FPHC income is in general taxed immediately to the American parent. FPHC income does not include royalties from licensing patents of the country where the foreign base company is itself organized. Thus the opportunities for minimizing all taxes by moving the income into a tax haven are much less favorable than they were before 1962. Still, tax-saving opportunities exist through resort to such exceptions as in Section 954(b)(3), to the effect that no foreign base income is to be attributed to a controlled foreign corporation if foreign base income amounts to less than 10% (formerly 30% before a 1975 amendment) of its total income.

QUESTIONS

(1) Assume that on January 31, 1974 the licensee received 1,000,000 pesos from a purchaser of a commodity subject to the license. At that date 10 pesos equalled one dollar. On March 31, 1974 a royalty payment was due the licensor, at which time the rate was 15 to 1. How much is due under the license agreement (Arts. 9, 12)? If you find the agreement unclear on this point, how would you rewrite it? How would you resolve the issue as an arbitrator?

(2) Why does the agreement set the royalty in terms of a percent of sales? Why not of *net* income? Why not a fixed amount? If you were somewhat suspicious of the licensee, would you find the provisions about the calculation and payment of royalties adequately protective? If a government agency were deciding on a "fair" royalty, would it conclude that this royalty was "fair"? How would it make this determination? What evidence would it seek?

Additional reading: Pollzien and Bronfen, International Licensing Agreements (2d ed. 1973); Eckstrom, Licensing in Foreign and Domestic Operations (3d ed. 1972). Many articles on international licensing and related problems are found in Idea, The Patent, Trade-mark and Copyright Journal of Research and Education.

---

4. THE MNE AND CONFLICTING ORDERS

A potential problem faced by an MNE is that its home government will issue it one set of instructions while its host government will direct to it a different set. You should review the materials on conflicting laws or orders at pp. 1014–1017, 1040–1045, and 1074–1085, supra. At its most dramatic, the conflicting-command problem strikes the MNE in wartime. In that situation the host country has plainly prevailed through seizure or regulation of all local assets. Thus while ITT factories in Germany were turning out electronic equipment for the Axis, I. G. Farben, through its plants in the United States, was lending aid and comfort to the Allies. In other circumstances the contradictory pressures are less extreme, and it is usually possible for the MNE to continue operating while more or less satisfying both countries involved.

If governments pursue more nationalistic policies, the legal-political environment will become more difficult for the MNE. Enactment of legislation such as the Hartke-Burke Bill, pp. 1118 and 1188, supra, would mean serious strains. For example, proposed limits on the use of American technology abroad would conflict sharply with the desire of other countries to use MNEs to acquire access to the newest inventions. Although not technically creating direct conflicts, proposed U. S. legislation imposing tax penalties on corporations that set up manufacturing in country X to take advantage of tax incentives which country X offers would bring the two countries onto a collision course at the MNE's expense. Taken to their extreme, nationalistic policies could cancel the competitive advantages possessed by MNEs and turn their spectacular expansion into a retreat.

We illustrate these problems with a dramatic case involving conflict between the United States Trading with the Enemy Act regulations (see pp. 110–112, supra) and French policy. The particular impetus for this conflict seems unlikly to recur, since United States policy with respect to the People's Republic of China has changed sharply; differences between it and French or other European attitudes about trade with China are now minimized. There were several such episodes in the 1950's involving principally Canada, but also Great Britain and other European countries. Similar problems developed as our policy of boycotting Cuba diverged further from that of other nations, particularly Canada and various Latin American countries.

The administration of these regulations has been affected by political considerations. Requests have been granted or denied in situations where the immediate political context obviously had significance. Thus in 1974 permission was granted to ship equipment from an Argentinean subsidiary of Ford Motor Company to Cuba, at a time when the Secretary of State was engaged in difficult political discussions with the foreign ministers of Latin American countries. Consider, by way of contrast, the report in the New York Times, December 24, 1974, p. 3, col. 7, of the cancellation, stemming from the embargo on trade with Cuba, of a contract under which the Canadian subsidiary of Litton Industries was to supply $500,000 of office equipment to Cuba:

> Officials in Ottawa predicted that this new application of the American law across the border, which Canadian nationalists see as economic imperialism, would add further strain to this country's relations with the United States, which have already suffered in recent weeks from disputes about trade in both oil and beef.

> "Canada feels that Cuba is an important market, a developing market, and we want Canadian companies who are exporting to govern their activities by Canadian law, not by the law of some other country," declared Alastair W. Gillespie, the Minister of Industry, Trade and Commerce.
>
> . . .
>
> The Canadian Government had no objection at all to the sale; in fact, it has been actively encouraging increases in trade between this country and Cuba, which have normal diplomatic relations.
>
> "The Cubans made it clear that this sale was only the beginning, and that they'd be buying a lot more office equipment, and our prospects were hopeful," said William J. Phillips, the president of the Cole Division of Litton Business Equipment Ltd., the subsidiary in Toronto.
>
> Mr. Phillips, a Canadian national, negotiated the contract in Havana a few weeks ago, and then sent it routinely to the head office of Litton in Beverly Hills, Calif., for approval.
>
> In California, a spokesman for Litton said that the company had made "an informal inquiry" to Washington about the deal and learned that if it filed an application to make the sale the application would be turned down because of the 12-year-old regulation forbidding American companies and their subsidiaries to trade with Cuba.
>
> Mr. Phillips, in Toronto, was therefore instructed to cancel the Cuban order.
>
> . . .
>
> But if Canada is trying to increase her trade with countries other than the United States, she is also trying especially hard to sell more finished goods, instead of just raw material. And since half of all the manufacturing in this country is controlled by Americans who live south of the border, some businessmen fear that the problems that came up with Litton will be coming up again.
>
> Last March a Montreal railway-equipment company got around a similar ban on selling locomotives to Cuba, by having only its Canadian directors vote for the sale while its American directors opposed it, to escape the criminal penalties of the Trading with the Enemy Act.
>
> But that is not possible in this case since all the directors of Litton's Canadian subsidiary are Americans.
>
> Today, in an editorial entitled "More U. S. Interference in Our Business," The Toronto Star, Canada's largest newspaper, outlined the nationalist view of the whole affair.
>
> "Like a haunting discordant refrain, that old bugbear the United States Trading with the Enemy Act is back, butting its nose into Canadian business. How many more legitimate business deals will be scuttled? How many more Canadian jobs will be jeopardized?"

In 1975, government policy towards trade between foreign subsidiaries of U. S. Corporations and Cuba changed. As announced in 73 Dept.State Bull. 404 (1975), it "will be U. S. policy to grant licenses."

FRUEHAUF CORPORATION v. MASSARDY

Court of Appeals, Paris, May 22, 1965.
[1965] Gazette du Palais II, Jur. 86, [1968] D.S. Jur. 147.[15]

In December 1964 Fruehauf-France, S.A., a French company in which the Fruehauf Corporation (United States) held a two-thirds stock interest, signed a contract with Automobiles Berliet, S.A., another French company, for delivery of 60 "Fruehauf" vans, valued at 1,785,310 francs, for eventual delivery to the People's Republic of China. The first deliveries were to be made in February 1965. In January 1965 the U. S. Treasury Department issued an order directing the Fruehauf Corporation to suspend execution of the contract as violating the U. S. [Foreign Assets Control] Regulations.

When Fruehauf-France approached Automobiles Berliet about rescinding the contract, Berliet refused. Fearing that failure to perform the contract would weaken the company's position to obtain future contracts from its largest customer (Berliet) and subject the company to suit for damages, the French minority directors on February 15, 1965, instituted a proceeding against the Fruehauf Corporation and the American directors before the Tribunal of Commerce of Corbeil Essonnes. On February 16 the President of the Tribunal appointed a temporary administrator to head Fruehauf-France, S.A., for three months and to execute the contract.

The Fruehauf Corporation appealed to the Court of Appeals of Paris. The Court of Appeals in a decision of May 22, 1965, affirmed the order of February 16, 1965, appointing an administrator for three months to execute the contract with Berliet. Among the considerations cited by the Court of Appeals in its decision were:

> The evidence demonstrates, without serious question, not only the clear and present interest Fruehauf-France, S.A. has in the execution of a contract made with its principal customer, Berliet, S.A., which accounts for about 40 per cent of its exports, but above all the catastrophic results which would have been produced, on the eve of delivery date, and which would be felt even today, if the contract had been breached, because the buyer would be in a position to demand of its seller all commercial damages resulting therefrom, valued at more than five million francs, following upon the break-off of its dealings with China.
>
> . . . these damages, which Fruehauf Corporation or Fruehauf-International [the United States parent companies] did not indicate any intention of assuming, would be of such an order as to ruin the financial equilibrium and the moral credit of Fruehauf-France, S.A. and provoke its disappearance and the unemployment of more than 600 workers; . . . in order to name a temporary administrator the judge-referee must take into account the interests of the company rather than the personal interests of any shareholders even if they be the majority.

15. Prepared by the editors of International Legal Materials. The editors of that publication expressed their thanks to Mrs. Rita E. Hauser for the English translation of the opinion which she provided. The English translation of the full opinion is in the library of the American Society of International Law.

COMMENT

(1) It appears that the United States Treasury ultimately ruled that Fruehauf could not control the situation because of the appointment of the French temporary administrator, and that the Foreign Assets Control Regulations could not be applied. The trailers were delivered, the regular general manager was restored to office and relations with Berliet, a major client of Fruehauf-France, were restored.[16]

(2) The jurisdictional basis for applying the Foreign Assets Control Regulations to Fruehauf-France was 31 C.F.R. § 500.329 which then, as now, reads:

> The term "person subject to the jurisdiction of the United States," includes: . . . .
>
> (3) Any corporation organized under the laws of the United States or of any State . . . of the United States; and
>
> (4) Any partnership, association, corporation, or other organization, wherever organized or doing business, which is owned or controlled by persons specified in subparagraph (1), (2), or (3) of this paragraph.

Note that the Cuban regulations contain a § 515.541 which reads in part:

> (a) Except as provided in paragraphs (b), (c), (d), and (e) of this section, all transactions incidental to the conduct of business activities abroad engaged in by any non-banking association, corporation, or other organization which is organized and doing business under the laws of any foreign country in the authorized trade territory are hereby authorized.
>
> (e) This section does not authorize any person subject to the jurisdiction of the United States other than an organization described in paragraph (a) of this section to engage in or participate in or be involved in any transaction. For the purpose of this section only, no person shall be deemed to be engaged in or participating in or involved in a transaction solely because of the fact that he has a financial interest in any organization described in paragraph (a) of this section.

QUESTIONS

(1) Is the United States claiming the right to control the conduct of the American corporation or of its French subsidiary? Is the distinction significant? Does the American claim depend on analogies to (a) the right to control the conduct of U. S. citizens (individuals) abroad, (b) the right to control activities having a substantial effect within the United States, (c) the characterization of the subsidiary as a United States national? (Compare the bases for extraterritorial legislative reach in Restatement (Second), Foreign Relations Law of the United States, p. 882,

16. Ebb, Regulation and Protection of International Business 6–7 (Suppl. 1968).

supra). What is the meaning of § 515.541 in this context? Does it make the issue depend on the presence of American directors on the subsidiary's board?

(2) What is the basis for the French claim to control the transaction? Is it superior to the American? Suppose that Fruehauf had never committed itself to a contract with regard to the trailers. How could the French government push through the transaction?

(3) If it had decided to press the matter further, how could the United States have acted? By prosecuting the parent, the subsidiaries or the officers of one or the other or both? Could effective steps be taken to perfect the assets-control regulations against a repetition of these problems?

(4) Suppose that the government of an Arabian country in which a multinational corporation based in the United States has an operating subsidiary orders the American parent to cease doing business with Israel or to cause another of its subsidiaries to cease its operations within Israel. Does the order exceed that government's regulatory competence (pp. 880–892, supra) or violate any principle of international law? If so, is there any way the United States, Israel or the MNE can react effectively?

---

5. THE INTERNATIONAL JOINT VENTURE

The high rate of foreign investment by United States firms in the post-war world—both in Western Europe and in the less developed countries of Latin America, the Middle East, Asia and Africa—has given contemporary importance to the international joint venture. For a variety of reasons, American firms may not wish to make independent investments abroad, particularly in less developed countries where the business risks or political risk of loss through expropriation may be considerable.

Political risks such as expropriation may be minimized if operators, customers and financial backers from several nations are tied together in a joint venture.[17] Apart from such risks, foreign investment may prove to be economically rewarding only at a level which exceeds the capacity or desires of any one firm. Capital from other firms in the same country or in other developed countries may be essential. This situation frequently arises in extractive enterprises, where the cost of initial investment and the volume of output in the foreign country may make attractive the notion of joint investment between the extracting enterprise and manufacturing firms in need of raw materials such as iron ore.

Often the incentive for a joint venture may stem from government policies or laws of a foreign country. For example, certain developed countries such as Japan and many less developed nations prefer or insist upon combinations of foreign and local capital, rather than 100% foreign ownership and management.[18] That local partici-

17. See, for example, the discussion of Kennecott Copper Corporation's arrangements for financing from varied sources of new investments in Chile, as discussed at p. 449, supra.

18. See the section entitled "Participation with Local Capital" in the Sri Lanka (Ceylon) Policy on Private Foreign Investment.*

pation may in turn benefit the foreign investor(s), by giving the local enterprise a more domestic flavor and thereby reducing the risk of hostile governmental policies.

Joint ventures may involve only American firms, or American and foreign firms or American firms and foreign governments. The business arrangements among the joint venturers are subject to considerable variation; division of equity interests, sales to or purchases from the jointly owned company, representation on its governing board, management duties and so on. Apart from their economic advantages to the firms involved, or possibly to the American economy as a whole if the business plans are realized, joint ventures raise larger issues of the United States' foreign economic policy: the degree to which this country encourages firms to invest abroad, perhaps in selected countries in the less developed world; the degree to which it may seek to inhibit such investment in all or certain areas for balance-of-payments or other reasons.

The joint venture raises legal problems in a number of fields. Questions familiar to the student of the close corporation in American law reappear in the international context. Can the parties each be given a right to veto significant changes of policy? What happens if the parties disagree about such issues as reinvestment of earnings, the expansion of existing plant capacity or the appointment of new managerial personnel? Can these issues be resolved by a third party or should the enterprise be dissolved?

The likelihood of the parties coming to an impasse is heightened by the enormous differences in attitudes, interests and background of, say, an American-based multinational enterprise and a small Asian or African entrepreneur. In particular a multinational enterprise that insists on tight control over all its activities is likely to find itself frustrated by the need to take account of the different views and interests of a local joint venturer who would, for example, like to expand by exporting into a market already served by another affiliate of the MNE.

Other fields raise problems. Depending perhaps on the precise amount of American stock ownership, the foreign subsidiary may be a controlled foreign corporation for American tax purposes, see p. 1110, supra, or may be subject to controls under the Trading with the Enemy Act, p. 1223, supra.

The major American law problem is apt to involve antitrust policy. As yet these issues have not been helpfully addressed by Congress or the courts. As indicated below, there is somewhat more learning as to domestic joint ventures. But even in the domestic setting, the legal status of a joint venture is less clear than would be that of a domestic equivalent of the predatory practices in American Banana or the cartel in Alcoa, pp. 1002 and 1006, supra.

Many of the decisions on international joint ventures date from the early 1950's and involved facts which largely antedated World War II. Their authority today, under changed political and economic conditions and changing attitudes towards foreign investment, is open to question. Typical of such cases were Timken Roller Bearing Co. v. United States, 341 U.S. 593, 71 S.Ct. 971, 95 L.Ed. 1199 (1951), United States v. Imperial Chemical Industries, Ltd., 100 F.Supp. 504 (S.D.N.Y.1951), and United States v. Minnesota Mining & Mfg. Co., 92 F.Supp. 947 (D.Mass.1950).

In addition to pursuing jointly formulated policies or forming jointly owned companies, the firms or individuals involved in the first two of these cases had erected a structure of related agreements on the use of patents and trade-marks which were viewed by the courts as further indication of an intention not to compete. Under the circumstances of each case and in view of the related agreements, the joint arrangements were held to be in violation of the Sherman Act. In the Timken case, the Court stated (341 U.S. at 597, 71 S.Ct. at 974, 95 L.Ed. at 1206):

> We cannot accept the "joint venture" contention. That the trade restraints were merely incidental to an otherwise legitimate "joint venture" is to say the least, doubtful. The District Court found that the dominant purpose of the restrictive agreements into which appellant, British Timken and French Timken entered was to avoid all competition among themselves or with others. Regardless of this, however, appellant's argument must be rejected. Our prior decisions plainly established that agreements providing for an aggregation of trade restraints such as those existing in this case are illegal under the Act. . . . The fact that there is common ownership or control of the contracting corporations does not liberate them from the impact of the antitrust laws. . . . Nor do we find any support in reason or authority for the proposition that agreements between legally separate persons and companies to suppress competition among themselves and others can be justified by labeling the project a "joint venture." Perhaps every agreement and combination to restrain trade could be so labeled.

In Imperial Chemical Industries, the court recognized that "[i]t is settled that joint manufacturing ventures . . . are not made unlawful *per se* by the Sherman Act . . ." But it concluded that "the very purpose with which the foreign companies here involved were concerned and the circumstances under which they were born place them under the bar." 100 F.Supp. at 557.[19]

The third case, Minnesota Mining, presented the joint-venture issue more detached from the other issues in that litigation. In the problem appearing after this Note, excerpts from the opinion of Judge Wyzanski are used to suggest some of the relevant antitrust questions. The following facts place those excerpts in context. The case involved nine (later reduced to four) American producers of coated abrasives. These producers, controlling 86% of exports of coated abrasives from

19. Patent and remedial aspects of this decision were considered at pp. 1029–1040, supra.

the United States, entered into several agreements in 1929. One agreement created an export trade corporation under Delaware law that purported to meet the definitions and requirements of the Webb-Pomerene Act, p. 994, supra. Each producer owned a stated percentage of the Export Company's stock. With minor exceptions, each agreed to export only through the Export Company, to which orders were to be referred and which was to purchase its requirements from its shareholders in proportion to their stockholdings. The Export Company established sales offices and distribution channels in foreign countries, either through contracts with independent foreign firms or through the creation of its own foreign subsidiaries. It was in competition with American producers who were not among its shareholders and whose percentage of total American exports rose to 40% in 1948. The Export Company generally sold at prices substantially higher than those of its American competitors. Sales were under the trade name "Durex," rather than the trade names of its shareholders.

Pursuant to another agreement of 1929, the same companies formed the Durex Corporation which, through its foreign subsidiaries, conducted manufacturing operation in several foreign countries. Durex and the subsidiaries were formed to bypass measures of economic nationalism—quota and tariff restrictions, import controls, foreign exchange restrictions, local preference campaigns and so on—through local production and sales. Sales by the subsidiaries, either in their home country or to other countries, displaced quantities of exports of coated abrasives from the United States. The court found that the Export Company had sought to export abrasives made in the United States when they could be sold as profitably as abrasives made by Durex's subsidiaries, but that it did not ship to areas where these subsidiaries could sell more profitably. It further found that exports of coated abrasives of the defendants had declined since 1929, in part displaced by the subsidiaries' production.

A third agreement of 1929 on patents obligated Durex's shareholders to license Durex under their foreign patents to produce coated abrasives abroad. The licensors reserved rights to fix prices and standards of manufacture for the patented products, and received royalties. These provisions were amended in various respects in 1941.

Judge Wyzanski concluded that defendants had violated Section 1 of the Sherman Act and ordered injunctive relief. The court rejected various defenses. It agreed that there could be no commerce to be "restrained or monopolized" if American enterprises could not have exported at a profit to the areas supplied by their jointly held subsidiaries because of political or economic barriers not caused by the parties. However, it viewed the evidence as insufficient to justify a finding that, absent foreign subsidiaries, "it would have been legally or economically impossible to sell at some profit a substantial volume of defendants' American-made coated abrasives." The court also held that the provisions of the Webb-Pomerene Act, although covering many activities of the Export Company, did not extend to the jointly owned manufacturing subsidiaries, the activities of Durex, and the cooperative arrangements between the Export Company and Durex. Other of the defendants' justifications are described in the excerpts in the problem below.

More recently, United States v. Pan American World Airways, Inc., 193 F.Supp. 18 (S.D.N.Y.1961), held in part that a joint venture between Pan American (an airline) and W. R. Grace & Co. (principally a shipping company), in the form of an airline called Panagra that serviced Latin America, was not of itself illegal. However, conduct by one of the parties relating to Panagra was found to violate the Sherman Act. The judgment was reversed by the Supreme Court on the ground that these matters were entrusted by statute to the Civil Aeronautics Board. 371 U.S. 296, 83 S.Ct. 476, 9 L.Ed.2d 325 (1963).

In United States v. Penn-Olin Chemical Co., 378 U.S. 158, 84 S. Ct. 1710, 12 L.Ed.2d 775 (1964), the Supreme Court handed down its most elaborate statement on joint ventures. It spoke in a domestic setting involving a company, Penn-Olin, that was organized and owned by two major chemical concerns. Penn-Olin was intended to produce sodium chlorate in the Southeastern United States. The Court found that, on the record before it, Section 1 of the Sherman Act had not been violated. However, it concluded that Section 7 of the Clayton Act, p. 992, supra, applied to the joint formation and ownership of subsidiaries as well as to mergers with or acquisition of existing companies. With respect to joint ventures generally, the Court stated:

> The joint venture, like the "merger" and the "conglomeration," often creates anticompetitive dangers. It is the chosen competitive instrument of two or more corporations previously acting independently and usually competitively with one another. The result is "a triumvirate of associated corporations." If the parent companies are in competition, or might compete absent the joint venture, it may be assumed that neither will compete with the progeny in its line of commerce. Inevitably, the operations of the joint venture will be frozen to those lines of commerce which will not bring it into competition with the parents, and the latter, by the same token will be foreclosed from the joint venture's market.
>
> This is not to say that the joint venture is controlled by the same criteria as the merger or conglomeration. The merger eliminates one of the participating corporations from the market while a joint venture creates a new competitive force therein. . . .
>
> Overall, the same considerations apply to joint ventures as to mergers, for in each instance we are but expounding a national policy enunciated by the Congress to preserve and promote a free competitive economy. . . .

The Supreme Court stated that the district court, which decided the case for defendants, had erred in relying on the ground that it was not a reasonable probability that *both* parents would have entered the market in the Southeastern United States if Penn-Olin had not been organized. Consequently, the district court had concluded, competition between the parents was not diminished by the joint venture rather than by expansion of operations of one of the parents into the area. Under the Supreme Court's opinion, "a finding should have been made as to the reasonable probability that either one of the corporations would have entered the market by building a plant, while the other would have remained a significant potential competitor." The Court vacated the judgment, remanded the case for further proceedings, including the findings to be made with respect to Section 7 of the Clayton Act, and gave the following guidance:

> We note generally the following criteria which the trial court might take into account in assessing the probability of a substantial lessening of competition: the number and power of the competitors in the relevant market; the background of their growth; the power of the joint venturers; the relationship of their lines of commerce; the competition existing between them and the power of each in dealing with the competitors of the other; the setting in which the joint venture was created; the reasons and necessities for its existence; the joint venture's line of commerce and the relationship thereof to that of its parents; the adaptability of its line of commerce to non-competitive practices; the potential power of the joint venture in the relevant market; an appraisal of what the competition in the relevant market would have been if one of the joint venturers had entered it alone instead of through Penn-Olin; the effect, in the event of this occurrence, of the other joint venturer's potential competition; and such other factors as might indicate potential risk to competition in the relevant market. In weighing these factors the court should remember that the mandate of the Congress is in terms of the probability of a lessening of substantial competition, not in terms of tangible present restraint.

On remand, the district court held that, on the record before it, there was no reasonable probability that *either* parent corporation would have entered the Southeastern sodium chlorate market if Penn-Olin had not been organized. Because of that finding, it found it unnecessary to determine whether "the other" parent would have remained a "significant potential competitor." 246 F.Supp. 917 (D. Del.1965). This decision was affirmed by an equally divided Supreme Court, 389 U.S. 308, 88 S.Ct. 502, 19 L.Ed.2d 545 (1967).

A similar stress on impairment of *potential* competition can be found in United States v. Jos. Schlitz Brewing Co., 253 F.Supp. 129 (N.D.Cal.), aff'd per curiam 385 U.S. 37, 87 S.Ct. 240, 17 L.Ed.2d 35 (1966). The case had an international flavor since the Government challenged the acquisition by Schlitz of stock control over John Labatt Ltd., a Canadian brewer which in turn controlled General Brewing Co., a United States brewer.[20] In holding the acquisition of

20. The definition of "commerce" in Section 1 of the Clayton Act refers to "trade or commerce . . . with foreign nations."

Labatt illegal under Section 7, the district court noted that "[e]ntry into American brewing markets by new American firms is highly unlikely, and the large established Canadian brewers represent the most probable sources of potential substantial competition in the United States markets." 253 F.Supp. at 148. It found that "Labatt had the desire, the intention and the resourcefulness to enter the United States markets and to make General Brewing a stronger competitor in these markets." 253 F.Supp. at 147.

Note that, in analysing the *potential* competition stressed in the Penn-Olin and Schlitz cases, it is important to distinguish between the case of a present competitive force—a firm with the capacity and existing intention to invade the given market—and the case of a future competitive force, a firm that might at some later time have considered entry. See Areeda, Antitrust Analysis 667–72 (2d ed. 1974).

In several recent cases, United States authorities have proceeded against major foreign concerns attempting to put together joint ventures with American firms. In their defence, foreign partners have argued that it is in practice unfeasible to enter the large, highly competitive and fast-moving American market by building a new organization from the ground up. Thus far, each such case has been settled by a consent decree that avoided facing the challenging legal issues. United States v. Monsanto Co., 1967 Trade Cases ¶ 72,001 (W.D.Pa.1967); United States v. Standard Oil Co., 1970 Trade Cases ¶ 72,988 (N.D.Ohio 1969).

Additional reading: Brewster, Antitrust and American Business Abroad 200–223 (1958); Donovan, Legality of Acquisitions and Mergers Involving American and Foreign Corporations under the United States Antitrust Laws, 39 So.Cal.L.Rev. 526, 40 id. 38 (1966–67); Friedmann and Kalmanoff (eds.), Joint International Business Ventures (1961) (antitrust at pp. 245–257); Weiser, Antitrust Aspects of the Joint Venture in the European Economic Community, 111 U.Pa.L.Rev. 421 (1963); Graham, Hermann & Marcus, Section 7 of the Clayton Act and Mergers Involving Foreign Interests, 23 Stan.L.Rev. 205 (1971).

PROBLEMS

Amco, a Delaware corporation, produces fertilizer. It ranks third in sales in the American market and has had the resources to expand domestically in the face of vigorous competition. Amco currently produces about 18% of the fertilizer sold in this country. It has been exporting some $7,000,000 worth of fertilizer to Guatador, an underdeveloped country, for each of the last five years. Most of the rest of Guatador's requirements, some $5,000,000 worth, have been imported from Britco, a firm in England. Other American producers have made sporadic sales to Guatador and have recently shown interest in trying to increase them.

As part of its five-term plan to expand agricultural output, Guatador proposes to commence production of fertilizers to service an anticipated demand of $25,000,000 worth annually. Costs of labor and raw material make it feasible to produce fertilizer at least as cheaply as it can be imported. The Minister of Agriculture of Guatador approached Amco and Britco with a proposal that they jointly form and finance a Guatador subsidiary to build a factory. He indicated that Guatador would be willing to offer certain incentives to such a venture. Officials in the United States Agency for International Development, which has made considerable grants and loans to Guatador, look benignly on the project, since they regard the maintenance of Guatador's political stability as hinging on its meeting domestic food requirements. Amco is interested, although plans are in a tentative state and alternatives are being explored. It is reluctant to undertake the venture alone, in view of the economic risks, even were Guatador willing to have it as sole owner. The management is sensitive to antitrust possibilities and asks the following questions of you as their counsel.

(1) Does execution of the proposal run risks under Section 1 of the Sherman Act p. 991 supra, Section 7 of the Clayton Act p. 992, supra, or both?
If the Department of Justice or Federal Trade Commission were to initiate proceedings, how do you suppose each would phrase its complaint?

(2) Suppose that Britco expressed its willingness to officials in Guatador to undertake the venture alone, in the event that Amco were unwilling or unable to participate in a joint venture. Would this fact be relevant to the defense of an antitrust charge against Amco, if Amco proceeded with the venture?

(3) Should Amco approach Guatador for governmental action on its part that would help Amco on the antitrust question? Which if any of the following would you recommend that Amco seek?

> (*a*) a tariff on fertilizer so high that no foreign fertilizer could be exported to Guatador without leading to a net loss for its producer (assuming that production is started in Guatador providing an alternative source for its customers);
>
> (*b*) a tariff on fertilizer so high that sales of fertilizer exported to Guatador would yield an exporter only 25% of its normal profit margin; or
>
> (*c*) a quota holding imports to 10% of the total demand for fertilizer in Guatador.

Consider in this connection the following excerpt from the Timken case (341 U.S. at 599, 71 S.Ct. at 975, 95 L.Ed. at 1207):

> We also reject the suggestion that the Sherman Act should not be enforced in this case because what appellant has done is reasonable in view of current foreign trade conditions. The argument in this regard seems to be that tariffs, quota restrictions and the like are now such that the export and import of antifriction bearings can no longer be expected as a practical matter; that appellant cannot successfully sell its American-made goods abroad; and that the only way it can profit from business in England, France and other countries is through the ownership of stock in companies organized and manufacturing there. This position ignores the fact that the provisions in the Sherman Act against restraints of foreign trade are based on the assumption, and reflect the policy, that export and import trade in commodities is both possible and desirable. Those provisions of the Act are wholly inconsistent with appellant's argument that American business must be left free to participate in international cartels, that free foreign commerce in goods must be sacrificed in order to foster export of

> American dollars for investment in foreign factories which sell abroad. Acceptance of appellant's view would make the Sherman Act a dead letter insofar as it prohibits contracts and conspiracies in restraint of foreign trade. If such a drastic change is to be made in the statute, Congress is the one to do it.

Note that this language comes from a case in which the court had found a long-continued practice of contractual restraints, particularly market divisions, among the defendants.

(4) If the joint venture were undertaken and then challenged, would it be helpful to argue that Amco would have larger earnings through the joint venture than by continuing to export? Evaluate the following statement from Minnesota Mining (92 F.Supp. at 962):

> It is no excuse for the violations of the Sherman Act that supplying foreign customers from foreign factories is more profitable and in that sense is, as defendants argue, "in the interest of American enterprise" . . . . Financial advantage is a legitimate consideration for an individual non-monopolistic enterprise. It is irrelevant where the action is taken by a combination and the effect, while it may redound to the advantage of American finance, restricts American commerce. For Congress in the Sherman Act has condemned whatever unreasonably restrains American commerce regardless of how it fattens profits of certain stockholders. Congress has preferred to protect American competitors, consumers and workmen.

(5) Would it be helpful to argue that, although American fertilizer exports would diminish, there would be exports of component parts of equipment for the plant, and eventually of more agricultural equipment as Guatador's farmers increased their productivity and prosperity? Evaluate the following statement from Minnesota Mining (92 F.Supp. at 962):

> Nor is it any excuse that the use of foreign factories has increased the movement of raw materials from American to foreign shores. We may disregard the point that the books are not in balance when raw materials actually transported are set off against finished products potentially transported. It is more significant that Congress has not said you may choke commerce here if you nourish it there.
>
> Nor is it any excuse that as shown by the second table referred to in finding 45 in many markets, South American, for example, defendants have been expanding their export business and that in almost all markets defendants' American competitors have been getting a constantly larger share of the available business. What defendants are charged with is restraining not eliminating export trade. If defendants had never joined to operate factories abroad, both their and possibly their competitors' export trade would have been considerably greater.

(6) Could one effectively argue that the losses to American export trade should be offset by gains to Guatador's economy? Could one bolster this argument by pointing to the United States Government's decisions to afford Guatador economic assistance? Compare the following statement (addressed to arguments of defendants that were based upon the Webb-Pomerene Act) from Minnesota Mining (92 F.Supp. at 963):

> Exculpation is also sought under the terms of the Webb-Pomerene Act . . . This is no cover for defendants' conduct. The statute is by its first section limited to that sort of "export trade" which consists of "commerce in goods . . . exported . . . from the United States . . . to any foreign nation": As the House Committee on the Judiciary stated, "The object of this bill is to aid and encourage our manufacturers and producers to extend our foreign trade." To use American capital, no matter how profitably, to extend the exclusively internal trade of a foreign country may contract but is unlikely to extend our foreign trade. Nothing in the statute, nor in its legislative history, nor in the penumbra of its policy justifies or has any bearing upon the right of defendants to join in establishing and financing factories in foreign lands. Export of capital is not export trade.

(7) Suppose that one alternative is to enter a joint venture with another American firm slightly smaller than Amco. The two firms together occupy about 35% of the American market. Would this materially increase the antitrust risks as compared with a partnership with Britco? Evaluate the following dictum from Minnesota Mining (92 F.Supp. at 963):

> . . . . The Government might formalize a charge that this same conduct of defendants constitutes a violation of that clause in section 1 of the Sherman Act governing combinations in restraint of "commerce among the several States". It may very well be that even though there is an economic or political barrier which entirely precludes American exports to a foreign country a combination of dominant American manufacturers to establish joint factories for the sole purpose of serving the internal commerce of that country is a *per se* violation of this other clause of the Sherman Act. The intimate association of the principal American producers in day-to-day manufacturing operations, their exchange of patent licenses and industrial know-how, and their common experience in marketing and fixing prices may inevitably reduce their zeal for competition *inter sese* in the American market. And unlike a combination of producers to unite in exporting to foreign countries, a combination of producers to unite in manufacturing in foreign countries has not the benefit of the statutory immunity of the Webb-Pomerene or any other Act of Congress. It may, therefore, be subject to condemnation regardless of the reasonableness of the manufacturers' conduct in the foreign countries. In this aspect the reasonableness of the foreign conduct would, like the reasonableness of domestic price-fixing, be irrelevant. . . .

(8) Suppose that Amco were to establish a plant in Guatador by itself. Would such action be subject to antitrust scrutiny? Would it be relevant that—for reasons of taxation under the Internal Revenue Code (see p. 1104, supra) or for reasons of Guatadorian law—it was advisable to form a Guatadorian subsidiary rather than a branch? Consider the following statement from Minnesota Mining (92 F.Supp. at 962):

> Nor is it any excuse that American export trade might have been equally adversely affected if there had been—or if there

should now be—established plants in Great Britain, Canada and Germany by one or more of the manufacturing defendants acting independently. Such supposititious individual action would, it is true, be a restraint upon American commerce with foreign nations. But such a restraint would not be the result of a combination or conspiracy. Hence it would not run afoul of § 1 of the Sherman Act. Nor would it, so far as now appears, have the purpose or effect of promoting one company's monopoly in violation of § 2 of the Sherman Act. Indeed the decree to be entered in this case will expressly contemplate allowing just such individual operation of foreign factories. For nothing in this opinion can properly be read as a prohibition against an American manufacturer seeking to make larger profits through the mere ownership and operation of a branch factory abroad which is not conducted as part of a combination, conspiracy or monopoly.

Additional reading: Blivens and Lovell, Joint Ventures with Foreign Partners (1966); Franko, Joint Venture Survival in Multinational Corporations (1971); Friedmann and Kalmanoff, Joint International Business Ventures (1961); Friedmann and Béguin, Joint International Business Ventures in Developing Countries (1971).

Part Six

THE DEVELOPING PROCESSES OF INTERNATIONAL ORGANIZATIONS

The political and economic chaos of the 1930's, culminating in World War II, laid bare the serious inadequacies of the existing structure of international law. Avid pursuit during that period of nationalistic policies, political and economic in character, had produced unacceptable, disastrous consequences. The traditional doctrines and processes of international law, and the fragile political foundation upon which that law rested, had proved unable to curb those policies and avert those consequences. To control or avoid the kinds of problems which had bred conflict, something more than the inherited body of customary law and the network of bilateral or multilateral treaties was essential. To be sure, something more had been attempted, but the effort to create an effective international organization in the League of Nations ended in failure.

Nonetheless, the hopes of many for world peace and greater world prosperity turned to the development of new kinds of international organizations. By far the most ambitious and significant—in its aspirations as the cardinal peacekeeping agency, in its universal membership—was the United Nations.[1] The critical work of that organization has of course been the effort to control armed conflict, although it has come to play an ever larger role in economic matters.[2]

We have briefly examined in Chapter XI two organizations which, although permeated by political considerations, are predominantly economic in character: the General Agreement on Tariffs and Trade, and the International Monetary Fund. Those organizations attempt cooperation to reduce and regulate trade barriers, and cooperation in and regulation of monetary matters. Consider why other approaches to the problems confided to them, and to the European Economic Community (EEC) explored below, have proved disappointing. Note first the deficiencies in the traditional agency for the development of international law, custom. In some areas, such as the jurisdictional immunities of diplomats, the rules of customary law have remained relatively stable over a long period of time. Custom has retained sig-

1. Selective aspects of the work of the U. N. have figured in the preceding materials. See the descriptive Note at p. 309, supra; examples of acts of the General Assembly at pp. 462–469, supra; and examples of conventions prepared within the framework of the U. N. at pp. 387–391, supra.

2. The Note at p. 313, supra, describes the economic activities of the U. N. Illustrations in these materials include the resolutions of the General Assembly on Permanent Sovereignty over Natural Resources, p. 462, supra.

nificance, although even here (see p. 314, supra) the multilateral treaty has come to play an important role through codification and resolution of some disputed points. The rules on immunities benefited more or less equally all nations, whatever their position in the world community—large or small, developed or undeveloped, democratic, Communist or fascist. There was little play for ideological controversy. Contrast a field such as expropriation. There profound ideological conflict and differences in economic interests destroyed what consensus had emerged through customary law and now obstruct the growth of a new consensus.

But more is at issue than relative harmony or diversity of ideas or interests. Recall the weaknesses in the institutions charged with the growth of customary law. The process is slow, at times chaotic, a gradual unfolding through numerous exchanges of points of view among national officials, of a rule of general acceptability. The only genuine international "institutions" participating in this process, international tribunals, have often played a marginal role—hampered by their limited jurisdiction, their precarious political foundation in the international community, and their hesitancy to strike new and creative paths.

Apply such considerations to the kinds of problems which the GATT and IMF now treat. To start with, such problems often involve sharp differences among countries in economic theory, economic interest and political ideology. There are countries that derive advantages from high or low trade barriers, from relatively free capital movements or rigorous exchange controls, from a liberal regime of foreign investment or onerous restrictions upon it. The notion of piecing out rules of conduct through the processes of customary law is hardly realistic. Moreover, the nature of these problems frustrates their resolution through such processes. The points at issue are technical and complex. They often demand not general consensus about general principles but precise agreement about precise rules. Such rules must at the same time be amenable to rapid change as circumstances may require. Exchange controls may prove advisable today, but not in several months or years; tariffs may vary in level; arguments for permitting establishment of foreign business may vary in strength among industries. A wealth of economic and political data becomes germane. The problems resist solution by the accretion of customary law or by adjudication before arbitral or judicial tribunals.

Further considerations are relevant. In its classical formulation, international law (as noted at pp. 329–332, supra) served the general function of ironing out fields of actual or potential conflict among states, particularly fields which were basic to some degree for diplomatic or commercial intercourse among states. Diplomatic immunities and the classical rule on expropriation are illustrative. Many such rules were essentially restrictive, negative in character, although sometimes attaching "affirmative" conditions to state conduct: do not arrest an ambassador; do not take alien-owned property unless you pay adequate compensation. To be sure, such rules *permitted* greater cooperation among states, but they were not conceived as instruments for cooperative schemes. Coupled with this essentially restrictive character of customary law was a jealous regard for national sovereignty and prerogatives, captured in the concept of "domestic jurisdiction." Moreover, by its nature customary law was not capable of designing the broad or the detailed framework for cooperative ventures.

To the statesmen of the postwar world, it was apparent that the traditional notions and the legal doctrines which served them were no longer valid. The inter-war years had demonstrated that matters once thought to be within exclusive national discretion, within domestic jurisdiction, could have profound and dangerous implications for the entire international community. There was a heightened awareness of interdependence within that community, an awareness partially expressed in the belief that international law must assume new functions. To be sure, avoiding or settling armed conflict became the critical goal. But new attention was paid to a law, and supporting institutions, which could achieve cooperation among nations. That "international law of cooperation" finds its most effective and forceful expression in the economic regulation and integration attempted through the EEC. It has converted many matters long thought outside the proper scope of international law into matters of international concern, either through cooperative planning, outright regulation, or regional integration.

For these reasons, custom yielded to treaties the task of solving these new problems. Bilateral treaties had indeed long performed the function of building cooperative schemes among states. Thus in treaties of friendship, commerce and navigation or in income tax treaties, countries reached agreements on mutual concessions which gave both more than they would have had through a jealous maintenance of their respective national prerogatives.

Many problems, however, do not yield to a bilateral approach. Consider, for example, the rules governing civilian air traffic or maritime rights. World-wide uniformity is here essential as a technical matter in defining the "rules of the road." Or economic rivalry may require uniformity. Thus Great Britain might be reluctant to acquiesce in the exclusion of its fishermen from certain territorial waters of Norway if rival fishermen from Holland were still allowed to fish there. Sheer pride may prevent a country from surrendering a "right" unless it feels that other powers are doing the same. At this stage we have the multilateral treaty. Its negotiation is more complex in various ways. In a sense, the negotiating process is necessarily somewhat more rigid, since ordinarily every participant in that process must make the same concessions to every other participant whereas it might prefer to grant some only to those who can offer something in return. On the other hand, the presence of many negotiators may make it possible to resolve many aspects of a polycentric problem at the same time, and to reach a solution in which each country feels that the bundle of concessions it has given to other signatories, taken as a whole, is equivalent to what it has gained. Reduction of trade barriers is a pertinent illustration.

But when nations seek international cooperation or integration in complex areas, even the multilateral treaty may prove inadequate. A forum must be established for continuing discussion, to revise policies or hammer out new rules. Particularly in economic fields of a technical and detailed character, flexibility in the rules established at the initial negotiating session will be essential. Tariff rates must be adjusted; changing circumstances may require revision of antitrust rules. Thus the need arises not only for a framework for future negotiations but for some lawmaking authority. Parallel needs may be felt for some central enforcement powers, for sanctions, and for the creation of some means for resolving disputes. In brief, the participants in a cooperative or integrative scheme may deem essential an international organization.

These were among the principal considerations which led to the creation of the EEC, to which we now turn. Our earlier discussions of the GATT and IMF were concerned principally, almost exclusively, with the substantive content and contributions of those organizations. But our examination of the EEC will emphasize as well its institutional structure and processes, the actual working of its various organs. That is, we are here interested in internal organization and life, in the developing processes of international organizations as illustrated by this novel Community.

Chapter XIII

THE EUROPEAN ECONOMIC COMMUNITY (COMMON MARKET)

Of the international organizations examined in this book, the European Economic Community (the Community, or EEC) is the most inclusive in its aspirations, the most developed in its institutional structure and the most successful in its achievements. The Community attempts nothing less than to forge a common market and a common framework for reaching basic political decisions out of the diverse economies, political structures and cultural traditions of its member nations. The continuing efforts towards an appropriate descriptive term for the Community—"supranational" or "federal" and so on—evidence the novelty of its aspirations and structures, and the difficulty of characterizing them within a traditional vocabulary for international organizations.

The Treaty of Rome* which gave birth to the Community was signed and ratified in 1957 by the six original member states: Belgium, The Federal Republic of Germany, France, Italy, Luxembourg and the Netherlands. It became effective on January 1, 1958, six years after the more limited treaty among the same six nations creating the European Coal and Steel Community, and at the same time as a third treaty creating the European Atomic Energy Community.

The Rome Treaty has been amended or supplemented in important respects by several documents. Two of those documents are of special significance for our purposes. Prior to 1967, only two EEC institutions to which we shall refer (the Court of Justice and Assembly) served the other two European communities as well. On July 1, 1967, a Treaty Establishing a Single Council and a Single Commission of the European Communities made common institutions of those two bodies. We shall refer to that treaty as the Merger Treaty, and we shall use the term "Communities" to refer to institutions or policies common to all three. The second document concerns the one expansion of membership to date, when Denmark, Ireland and the United Kingdom acceded to the European Communities on January 1, 1973 by a series of instruments. Provisions regulating the accession appear in the Act Concerning the Conditions of Accession and the Adjustments to the Treaties*, referred to below as the Act of Accession. By 1974, the Communities included nine countries with a population of about 250 million (compared to about 200 million in the United States), with a GNP about 70% of that of the United States and with per capita income about 60% of this country's.

A. CONSPECTUS OF THE EEC TREATY

In its primary goal of a common market, the Community recalls some of the motives which led to the creation of the United States out of thirteen colonies and their confederation. Its planners pointed towards this country as a cardinal illustration of what economic integration could achieve for the approximately 180 million persons then within the original six members. Some of the most pressing problems to which the EEC has given rise—conflict over the scope of the EEC's competence and powers, the relationship between Community and national laws or institutions, and so on—find close analogies in the problems which have grown out of this country's federal structure.

The type of federalism exemplified by the United States stands at one end of a spectrum of methods for integrating component parts, each with its own geographical and political identity, within a group's political, economic and legal order. Less intensively, and with careful discrimination among the fields covered, organizations such as the United Nations, GATT and the IMF impose common rules and common processes for institutional decision-making upon their member countries. Other types of cooperative arrangements between nations of a more traditional character, such as bilateral or multilateral treaties on commercial or tax matters, determine rights and duties of the parties and their nationals within important but functionally limited fields. Such treaties generally stop shy of creating institutional structures of some autonomy or independent vitality.

We have moved on a spectrum from community to contract. In its different parts, the EEC has characteristics that would appear on several points of that spectrum. Indeed, its varied participants have aspirations that look towards different points as final goals for the entire Community. Those Europeans who urge that the nine members move from a limited common market to an inclusive union see the EEC as a federation in process. Others, most effectively and eloquently represented by Charles de Gaulle when President of France, conceive of the Community in restricted terms. They stress the dominant role of the nation state in reaching basic political decisions and tend to view the Community as a structure, justified insofar as it proves to be efficient, within which nationally defined aspirations can be realized.

A study of the EEC then brings together, in the context of a young international organization, themes about international legal order which have recurred in the different settings of this book. Here again we perceive the interdependence and interrelationship of legal with political, economic and cultural processes or considerations. But a distinct theme now becomes relevant. If circumstances encourage the evolution of an international organization towards more "community", that organization will require not only the elaboration of norms, but also the construction of a complex constitutional framework of legislative, executive, administrative and judicial institutions, each distinct in character and function from corresponding domestic institutions. Problems of the allocation of power and the distribution of welfare become critical in several settings—among institutions within the Community, between the Community and its members, and among the member nations.

This brief rehearsal of fundamental considerations is meant to signal the need to view the materials below within a broader context of history, politics and culture. The materials stress the formal political-legal institutions, political-legal processes and norms of the EEC. Moreover, we treat only a few representative and illustrative problems. Both the history and fate of the Community have been and will be determined less by particular structures or norms, than by the intensity of the belief of the member countries that their own welfare and the welfare of the entire group will be advanced through progress towards more complete integration. The profound innovation has been less in structure or processes or norms than in attitudes, both governmental and popular. Such change in official and private behavior and attitudes is described in certain respects in this introductory section and, more significantly, is revealed through the new forms of legal-political consciousness which are expressed through the legal and political achievements to which we turn.

NOTE ON BACKGROUND TO AND PURPOSES OF THE COMMUNITY

The observer relating the Common Market to trends in European history would trace its political antecedents from Charlemagne through the 19th century, particularly the Concert of Europe and the national precedents of economic and political integration in such countries as Germany and Italy. Surely he would stress Europe's economic experience from the industrial revolution to World War II. The purpose of this section is more modest—to sketch the ideas and experiments of the post-war years, at first tentative and limited but increasingly bold, which culminated in the Rome Treaty.

In 1945 Western Europe—the victorious and defeated alike—lay in chaos, facing a world dominated by two superpowers. Its political and economic instability accented the threat of politically extreme movements within several countries, particularly in view of the expansion of Soviet influence in the early post-war years. Out of these conditions grew the various movements for Western European unity, movements inspired by several purposes: integration of the Western European states and thereby the creation of a degree of interdependence that would make unlikely another war among them; acceleration of the pace of economic revival by displacing national rivalries with an economic community in whose greater prosperity all could share; and achievement through this community's prosperity of an influence in world affairs that would make Western Europe a significant counterweight to the two large powers.

During the last two decades, the first of these purposes appears to have been realized—although Western European economic interdependence has become a relatively minor reason among the substantial ones that make intra-European war unlikely. The other purposes remain vital, but thus far only partly achieved and controversial as to their implementation and even redefinition. Note, for example, the possible tensions between *national* prosperity for any one member country and *European* prosperity measured by the aggregate welfare of all member countries, another way of describing the possible tension between the goal of maximization of the value of production for a united Western Europe and the distributional issue of how the increased production is to be shared among the participating nations.

In these post-war circumstances, the United States had an evident interest in assuring Europe's military security and aiding its economic revival. The military reaction to the Soviet threat took the form of the North Atlantic Treaty Organization (NATO). The response to Europe's economic crisis was massive and effective aid. Starting in 1947, the Marshall Plan, which included most Western European countries among its beneficiaries, directly contributed to European recovery and indirectly prepared a foundation for the subsequent movements towards Western European unity. It had larger aims than channeling funds into each nation to assist its independent recovery. Looking towards a European market rather than separate national markets, those administering the Plan encouraged the abolition of many restrictions on intra-European trade. As a condition to receiving aid, the United States required that the European countries consult each other and agree about their requirements and roles in the process of recovery.

The Organization for European Economic Cooperation (OEEC), formed in 1948 principally by Western European countries (with the United States and Canada as associated members), was responsive to this condition. It furthered economic cooperation, led to the reduction of many quantitative trade restrictions and fostered other measures of trade liberalization. In form, the OEEC was a traditional intergovernmental organization; its members were bound only as they voted in favor of a particular policy or measure. But the OEEC made, and induced others to make, important progress in the economic fields in which it worked. It significantly influenced the behavior of its members. In 1961 the Organization for Economic Cooperation and Development (OECD) replaced the OEEC. Its expanded membership included among other countries, the United States, Japan and Canada, and its expanded aims included the coordination of aid to underdeveloped countries as well as the economic development of its members.

In 1949, a number of Western European countries organized the Council of Europe, a partial realization of the suggestion several years earlier by Winston Churchill that there be formed a "United

States of Europe." The Council consisted of a Committee of Ministers, the foreign ministers of its member countries, and a Consultative Assembly. The Council disappointed the visionaries among its authors. It did not significantly influence later developments, and its contributions have been primarily through the conventions entered into by its members which were negotiated under its auspices—particularly the European Convention on Human Rights and Fundamental Freedoms, p. 384, supra.

The Common Market has a more direct ancestor in the important declaration in 1950 by the Foreign Minister of France, Robert Schuman. In his speech expressing principles germane to the entire "European movement," Schuman suggested that France and Germany form a pool of their coal and steel industries. He invited other nations to join. This sector integration of national economies was intended to serve a broader political purpose: the growth of a European consciousness that would ultimately displace 19th century nationalism and, in particular, the traditional hostility between France and Germany. Schuman sought to realize this European consciousness in a pragmatic fashion, through economic cooperation in limited sectors which would gradually expand to create a broader sense of solidarity. He argued that such piecemeal integration would achieve "the fusion of interest which is indispensable to the establishment of an economic community; thus will be introduced the germ of a broader and deeper community between countries long opposed to one another by bloody conflicts."

The Schuman Declaration ripened into the European Coal and Steel Community (ECSC), created in 1952 by a treaty among the six nations later to form the EEC. The treaty accomplished significant integration within this sector. It covered basic commodities such as coal, steel, iron ore, and scrap, but did not reach finished, semi-finished or related products. The institutions created by the ECSC had broad powers to build a common market in the defined field. For example, they were empowered to develop rules on competition and discrimination, to implement the treaty's requirements of abolition of import duties and quantitative restrictions among the member states, and to determine minimum and maximum tariff rates between the members and third countries. In some respects, the ECSC gave more expansive powers to community institutions than did the EEC—for example, the power to assess a tax directly upon enterprises in the member countries. But in most respects, its ambitions were narrower, for by reaching only one sector of the six economies, it did not penetrate as profoundly national economic life. Jean Monnet, a father of the European movement who became the first President of the High Authority of the ECSC, referred to that treaty as "the first expression of the Europe that is being born." Particularly in its institutional structure, the ECSC served as an important model for the EEC. It continues today as one of the three components of the European Communities.

Plans developed shortly thereafter for integration of military forces among the same six countries, through an organization to be known as the European Defense Community (EDC). That community would have created a European Army with a common uniform and unified direction, acting within the framework of NATO. The EDC looked towards the creation of a frankly political community among the six. Four of the nations had ratified this treaty when, during the 1954 Indochina crisis, the French National Assembly refused to debate ratification.

Immediately after these proposals were aborted, Jean Monnet formed the Action Committee for a United States of Europe which gave impetus to the ideas leading to the Rome Treaty. This influential committee, and a 1955 meeting of the Foreign Ministers of the six at Messina, Italy, led within the space of two years to the drafting of proposals for a Common Market through a European Economic Community and for a third Community, the European Atomic Energy Community (Euratom). Both treaties were signed in Rome in 1957 and became effective as of January 1, 1958. Even this brief résumé suggests the resilience of the European movement and the tenacity of those who, by their devotion and intellectual ingenuity, overcame defeats which might have stifled a lesser ideal.

Purposes of the Community

Articles 2 and 3 of the EEC Treaty state the broad purposes of the Community.[3] Note that the establishment of a customs union, through the elimination of internal tariffs and the creation of a common external tariff, heads the list of goals in Article 3. Most of the remaining paragraphs of that article are related to, if significant extensions of, the idea of a customs union. The central aim is one of economic integration. Progress in one direction, towards elimination of tariff and quantitative barriers, would reveal the need for progress in another. The customs union, in this sense, is less the source from which all other accomplishments of the Common Market stem than one of a series of complementary moves. Consider the following excerpt from a study of the League of Nations: [4]

> For a customs union to exist it is necessary to allow free movement of goods within the union. For a customs union to be a reality it is necessary to allow free movement of persons. For a customs union to be stable it is necessary to maintain free exchangeability of currency and stable exchange rates within the union. This implies, *inter alia,* free movement of capital within the union. When there is free movement of goods, persons, and capital in any area, diverse economic policies concerned with maintaining economic activity cannot be pursued. To assure uniformity of

3. Most of the articles from the Rome Treaty, Merger Treaty and Act of Accession which are referred to in this section appear in the Documentary Supplement. You should read them together with the text.

4. Customs Unions: A League of Nations Contribution to the Study of Customs Union Problems 74 (republished in 1947 by the United Nations).

> policy some political mechanism is required. The greater the interference of the state in economic life, the greater must be the political integration within a customs union.

To achieve the customs union and complementary goals, the member nations commit themselves in Article 5 to carry out their obligations under the Treaty—perhaps the closest analogue in the Treaty to the Supremacy Clause of Article VI of the United States Constitution. Those obligations expand as the Community develops. The Treaty does not lay down a static set of rules, as would most traditional treaties such as bilateral conventions on commercial or tax matters. Rather it establishes an institutional and constitutional framework for a process of growth. Article 8, for example, provides that the Common Market "shall be progressively established during a transitional period of twelve years," divided into three four-year stages. This period and its stages become relevant to numerous provisions of the treaty requiring certain measures to have been taken by the end of a given stage or of the entire period. Note, for example, the scheduled requirements of Articles 13, 48, 52, 67 and 116. The transitional period ended as scheduled, on December 31, 1969, despite the fact that important measures contemplated by the Treaty to have been completed were still in progress. Work towards achievement of the Community's purposes in these fields has continued since 1969, and the transitional period is perceived as but one evolutionary phase.

NOTE ON PARTICULAR GOALS OF THE COMMUNITY

The Customs Union

Articles 9 to 18 state the timetable under which the original member states were to abolish intra-Community tariffs and quantitative restrictions. In fact, the Community pursued an accelerated schedule for the reduction of the "basic" duties defined in Article 14(1), so that duties on industrial products and most agricultural products were abolished by July 1968. As of 1974, the three new members of the Community were within their transitional period as defined in the Act of Accession and its related documents. That period is to include five annual reductions, so that by 1977 the differences between the new members' tariffs and the regime among the original six will be eliminated.[5]

During the original transitional period, the original members took the required steps under Articles 19–23 to adjust their tariffs towards third countries in order to reach the common external tariff which distinguishes a "customs union" from a "free trade area." Here too an accelerated schedule was adopted, and the common external tariff was realized in July 1968. Article 19 provides that the duties under that tariff shall be at the level of the "arithmetical average" of duties applied in the four customs territories of the Community

5. The text below refers principally to the realization of Treaty goals by the original six, and does not signal at all points the different provisions applicable to the three new members, among whom there are numerous differences for periods of adjustment and exceptions.

as of January 1, 1957. Those territories refer to France, Germany, Italy and the customs union among Belgium, Luxembourg and the Netherlands which is known as Benelux. Since 1968, the Community has made continuing efforts to overcome the obstacles remaining to a genuine customs union, particularly the technical and institutional barriers represented by customs formalities, different interpretations of similar tariffs, and so on. The Community now seeks the harmonization of those customs and customs-related provisions of the member states which continue to impede the free flow of goods within, and the establishment of identical conditions of entry into, the Common Market. The significance of all such internal and external adjustments is made clear by the fact that the expanded Community of nine countries constituted in 1973 the world's largest trading bloc in volume of exports and imports.

The rules governing tariffs evidence a characteristic technique of the Treaty: the coupling of stringent requirements with guarded possibilities for their suspension or waiver. Note Articles 26 and 36. Note also the provisions of Articles 115 and 226, which affect broader areas of the Treaty.

The Treaty's cardinal goal of a customs union stems from principles of classical free-trade theory. The basic economic incentive for the Common Market—that elimination of national barriers would permit the price mechanism and market forces within the Community to allocate resources in a more efficient manner, and thus increase the value of production within the Community by moving resources to their most highly valued use—reflects the same principles which underlie the effort of the GATT to create freer world trade. By increasing competition from firms in other member states, the Treaty was to stimulate modernization. Relatively inefficient sectors of national economies would contract or perhaps disappear. Relatively efficient firms would expand through internal growth or forms of combination to serve a common rather than national market, and would thereby achieve greater economies of scale. Of course, unless all basic factors of production—labor and capital as well as goods—were assured of free movement, these goals could be thwarted; thus the complementary provisions of the Treaty described below.

It should be noted that the classical economic theory underlying customs unions and the benefits that they promise appears today more problematic. At the start, note the problems in the application of such theory to contemporary economies such as those of the Community which depart significantly from classical free-enterprise models. Through ownership of infrastructural and productive assets, through regulation, and at times through comprehensive economic planning about resource allocation within the private sector, governments play large roles in economic systems. Such roles are thought essential under contemporary ideas of governmental responsibility to secure economic growth and minimum welfare of citizens. The resulting management of the economy inevitably erodes the premises of classical theory about a self-regulating market achieving efficient resource allocation through the play of market forces, with distribution of welfare left to the market.

Thus policies of full employment, for example, may conflict internally and internationally with the goal of trade liberalization to achieve more efficient resource allocation. Moreover, within the member states there are seriously underdeveloped areas—southern Italy, to mention a prominent one—which may call for protective measures or subsidies that depart from "free trade" market principles. The Community's institutions have had to wrestle with these problems in the effort to develop a consensus over policies representing an acceptable blend of the "maximization of production" goal, and protective or welfare-redistributional measures. Such problems and policies stand as important qualifications to the theory of free trade and comparative advantage. But that theory, even as qualified, remains basic to the Community's economic goals and, indirectly, to some of its political aspirations.

When one considers the other aspect of a customs union, the creation of a common external tariff, other weaknesses in the economic rationale for the Common Market appear. Economists have questioned whether customs unions, whatever their effect upon their members, serve free-trade theory in a broader international setting. They point out that stimulation of trade and resource allocation among member countries may have the consequence of restricting or eliminating trade between the customs union and third countries which are able to produce more efficiently certain products now facing a common external tariff. They question, in brief, whether the customs union may *create* more international trade in a larger setting or simply *divert* trade from third countries to customs-union members.[6]

These last doubts are expressed if not resolved in Article XXIV of the GATT. On its face, a customs union violates Article I of the GATT. Article XXIV nonetheless permits such unions, provided that certain conditions are met. The compatibility of the Common Market with the GATT has indeed never been explicitly resolved. Committees of the GATT wrestled in 1958 with some of the complex problems in interpreting the cryptic provision of Article XXIV (5): the duties of the common external tariff "shall not on the whole be higher or more restrictive than the general incidence of the duties . . . applicable in the constituent territories" before the formation of the customs union. Paragraph (4) of that article makes explicit the concern noted above that customs unions might have a trade-diverting rather than trade-creating effect.

6. For a description of the theory of comparative advantage, see Samuelson, Economics: An Introductory Analysis 668–691 (9th ed. 1973). For an analysis of customs unions, see Meade, Problems of Economic Union (1953) and Viner, The Customs Union Issue (1950). See also the discussion of comparative advantage in relation to the GATT, at p. 1141, supra.

Working in 1958 with reports of their committees, the Contracting Parties of the GATT postponed settlement of the legal issues. Nonetheless, after the Dillon and Kennedy Rounds, conformity with Article XXIV can no longer be disputed. Various pressures exercised through the GATT have led to rounds of negotiations in which the Community has agreed to lower, upon assurance of reciprocity, the rates initially agreed upon for the common external tariff.

Other Goals of the Community

Recall the observations in the study by the League of Nations at p. 1247, supra. The progressive steps described in those excerpts did not simply follow "logically" from the starting point of the customs union. They represented ever more intense degrees of political commitment to a common enterprise. And so the Rome Treaty, in its provisions complementing those treating the customs union, raises ever greater doubts whether its signatories will reach the professed goals. We now consider the principal goals, several among which will be examined in later portions of this chapter: those treating labor mobility, establishment of economic enterprises, harmonization of legislation, and anti-competitive business practices.

Articles 48 to 51 look towards the creation of a Community-wide market for labor. Implemented in basic respects by 1968, through regulations and directives requiring national treatment for intra-Community migrant workers in such areas as jobs and housing, these articles are the essential point of departure towards further measures. For example, beyond determining the conditions under which laborers of any member country have the right to enter, work and remain in another, the Community's institutions now seek to perfect welfare benefits such as social security for migrant workers, as well as educational and training opportunities. These provisions of the Treaty are complemented by Articles 117–121, which look towards the "approximation" of national legislation governing social security and labor conditions.

A fundamental commitment of the Treaty is to assure nationals of each country that the other countries will be open to investment by them. Articles 52–58 require the elimination of national barriers to establishment of economic enterprises in the same scheduled way that characterizes the articles requiring elimination of customs duties. Some but far from all of the Community's aspirations were reached by the end of the transitional period.

Sectors of the national economies that pose distinctive economic and political problems, particularly agriculture and transport, received special attention. The agricultural issues were too complex and politically charged to be resolved by the Treaty itself with any clarity. The substantive arrangements together with the institutional structures necessary for their implementation have been developed since 1958 by a series of agreements among the member states, some reached only after the greatest tension. As in the United States, protectionist policies for the producers of most agricultural products stand as a basic derogation from the principles of market efficiency and free competition which are elsewhere espoused in the treaty.

Since special regimes govern different agricultural products, only a few principles of standard application can be stated for the entire field. In general, the Community market system—a mixture of coordinated Community and national marketing organizations—supports agreed-upon price levels through the purchase of agricultural surpluses. Support prices are established and regularly reconsidered for most agricultural products. The Community also grants export subsidies, and protects farmers against outside competition through a system of variable levies on agricultural products imported from other countries. Those levies in general raise the price of the imported products slightly above the agreed price-support levels, thereby permitting the Community authorities to realize goals such as a fair return to producers, or relative price stability insulated from world markets. The Community organizations administering the agricultural program will ultimately draw the funds necessary to support their purchase of surplus commodities from a Community budget directly financed through variable levies of imports and other sources of revenue rather than from (as has been the case) contributions from the member governments.

Articles 85–89 state the policies of the Treaty governing regulation of anticompetitive business behavior. Articles 95–99 prohibit the imposition of discriminatory taxes on imports and contemplate the "harmonization" of national laws on indirect taxation. Articles 100–102 pursue the same theme in a broader setting by providing for the "approximation" of laws of the member states which affect the functioning of the Common Market. The terms "harmonization", "approximation" and "coordination," which recur in the Treaty, appear to have no sharply defined differences. They share one characteristic which distinguishes the articles in which they appear from those parts of the Treaty creating "Community" laws, such as the common external tariff. That is, such articles treat problems which remain within the competence of national law, subject to Community controls. They look towards greater uniformity among such laws, to be achieved through lawmaking by the member states that is responsive to directives of Community institutions. Note the different technique employed by Article 220. It recognizes the need to adjust discrepancies in national laws in several areas but contemplates negotiations by the member states leading to additional treaties rather than harmonization of national laws pursuant to directives.

The members agree in Article 103 to "consider their policy relating to economic trends as a matter of common interest." Articles 104–109 require the "coordination" of economic policies and establish a Monetary Committee with consultative status. These articles clearly recognize the importance of national control over economic policy to guard, for example, the balance of payments. In this politically sensitive area, looking towards an *economic union* rather than simply a *customs union*, the Treaty is cautious. Most of its provisions are expressed in hortatory rather than imperative terms. The dilemma posed is that full economic integration implies more than the elimination of trade barriers; it may require common planning for such matters as employment policies, rates of economic expansion, and responses to inflationary pressures. The problems of international regulation of such matters become the more complicated in an organization whose members entertain different views about the role of government in planning or regulating economic life.

For such reasons, the achievements in this area of the Treaty have been relatively slight. In the early 1970's programs were formulated to achieve an economic and monetary union by December 1980. During the different stages of this program, the members would gradually coordinate credit policy, accelerate the liberalization of intra-Community capital movements (going beyond "current transactions"), coordinate short and medium term economic policy, and agree upon protective policies towards depressed regions of the Community. Close cooperation of central banks of the members was visualized. But this program has not been effectively implemented. As of 1974, the prospects for rapid progress were dim, in view of that year's severe economic problems. Even the currency agreements among members, involving interlocking parities and convertibility, were shaken by independent decisions of several member nations during 1973 and 1974 that responded to inflation and balance-of-payments problems. As noted below, the continuing proposals to strengthen an economic union, and thus the frankly political aspects of the Community, are linked in the minds of many to the status of the Assembly of the Communities.

On the other hand, there has been progress towards assuring the Community of some degree of financial autonomy from its members. In the early 1970's, the EEC budget has run about $5 billion annually to cover expenditures such as agricultural price support programs, allocations for regional development, or technical cooperation. Initially dependent upon contributions from its members for the funds to match its budgeted expenditures, the Community is moving towards a goal of achieving direct sources of revenue in 1975. Pursuant to agreements among the members and decisions of Community institutions, the members are eventually to surrender to the Community all the revenues collected through industrial and agricultural tariffs and import levies, and (as necessary) up to 1 percent of their assessments for the Community-wide value-added tax (less a 10 percent refund to the members to cover collection costs). Still, unlike the ECSC (see p. 1246, supra), the EEC has no power to tax firms or individuals within the member countries.

To assist in reallocation of labor, modernization of underdeveloped regions or industries and related matters, the Treaty establishes a European Social Fund and European Investment Bank. The purposes of these institutions are set forth in Articles 123–130. The sources of their funds are varied. The Bank, for example, has its own capital contributions by the member states, and borrows on the world capital markets. By the end of 1973, it had loaned during its 15 years over $3 billion, mostly within the member countries but to some extent in associated countries. The investments were principally of an infrastructural character, relating to matters such as energy. These loans for development of less prosperous regions within the Community have been complemented by occasional direct loan agreements between member countries.

NOTE ON THE INSTITUTIONS OF THE COMMUNITY

If ultimately dependent upon the political will of its members expressed through national elections and decision-making, the Community formally evolves through the work of its own institutions. The elaborateness of that institutional structure—with its analogues in the national separations of legislative, executive and judicial powers—distinguishes the Community from other international organizations and conveys a sense of its "presence", of its entrenchment within the European scene. The voluminous output of Community institutions may create too readily a sense of the Community's achievements and permanence. The observer may be misled into too facile an equation of elaborate structure and large bureaucracy with solid foundation, and thus ignore the fragile political base upon which the Community still builds. Nonetheless, structure and bureaucracy and output count for something, and have their own momentum and significance. The text below sketches the essentials of the institutional structure, while later materials involve closer looks at the institutions "in action" within the substantive fields examined.

Prior to 1967, two of the EEC's institutions, the Commission and the Council, served only that Community. Two other EEC institutions, the Assembly and the Court of Justice, served the other two European communities as well. In that year, the Merger Treaty became effective, replacing the Commission and the Council of the Common Market (and comparable institutions of the two other communities) with a Commission and a Council of the European communities. Note Articles 1, 2, and 9–17 of the Merger Treaty, and the parallel provisions of Article 24, converting "officials and other servants" of each of the three communities into officials and servants "of the European Communities" to form part of a single Communities-wide administration. (But note that there has been no merger of the three communities. Each treaty, for example, continues to regulate the powers of the institutions with respect to actions of the institutions within the scope of that treaty.)

At the start, you should read Articles 189–191 of the Rome Treaty. These provisions, defining the different types of action which the EEC institutions are authorized to take and the effect within a member country's legal order of each such action, are critical to an understanding of the legal-political characteristics of the Community. The materials at pp. 1324–1420, infra, examine the use and effect of regulations, directives, and decisions.

Note that in issuing regulations, the Council and Commission exercise an explicit law-making power; the regulation is "binding in its entirety and directly applicable in all Member States". Therein lies one of the most innovative aspects of the Treaty. Although requiring implementation through the appropriate decision-making organs of the member governments, directives serve indirectly this same law-making function. Indeed, as we shall see, they may have the same legal effect as regulations. Unlike regulations or directives, the decisions addressed to member states or private parties within the Community are frequently rendered after proceedings before the Commission that are adjudicatory in character.

The Commission (Article 155, and Articles 9–18 of the Merger Treaty). This body of 13 members is intended to represent the interests of the Community as such as opposed to those of the different member states. That intention is made explicit in Article 10 of the Merger Treaty. Its principal power is that of initiative, generally exercised by its putting proposals for new regulations or directives to the Council. Those proposals range from detailed and technical regulations to general programs of basic political significance. There are few exceptions to this near-exclusive power of initiative, such as the provisions for amendment of the Rome Treaty in Article 236(1).

In its role of initiator, the Commission performs a function comparable to that of the executive branch in Western democracies which formulates proposals and submits them to a legislative body. Rather like the executive in the United States, which in constitutional theory can act legislatively only pursuant to delegated or inherent powers, the Commission is given few legislative powers by the Treaty —principally with respect to the issuance of regulations treating competition and the safeguard clauses. In such situations, the Commission implements rules that are set forth in detail in the Treaty. Sometimes the Council can delegate to it the authority to issue regulations of a defined character.[7] But generally the Council has the exclusive power to issue regulations or directives, a power the Treaty qualifies in most instances by requiring the Commission to submit a proposal before the Council (unlike a domestic legislature) has the power to act. Note that under Article 149, the Council can amend proposals of the Commission only by its unanimous vote. Note also that under Article 155, the Commission need not rely upon specific authorization in the Treaty to make a recommendation, but may do so whenever it "considers it necessary".

7. See Article 48(3)(d); Regulations Nos. 19/65 and 67/67, pp. 1386 and 1389, infra.

The Commission performs its second principal function as a guardian of Community law. In supervising compliance with the Treaty by the member states or private parties, it acts in several ways. It fills the role of "policeman" in investigating suspected violations, and that of "prosecutor" in instituting proceedings against member states before the Court of Justice. Indeed it sometimes acts in a more or less adjudicative capacity. For example, the Commission has authority under Article 226 to permit member states to derogate from Treaty requirements if the state meets imposed conditions. And in fields such as antitrust, the Commission can render "decisions" permitting or condemning the conduct of private firms.

These varied functions have led to a sizeable bureaucracy. As of 1973, the Commission's staff included about 6,800 permanent posts, and 1,900 persons who were classified as "senior" officials. Inevitably this international bureaucracy poses the same problems as do national governments: rigidity, lack of creativity, and a tendency to compromise and engage in a cautious balancing of interests rather than to formulate programs which advance bolder conceptions of the Community. To some extent, such tendencies are institutionalized in the procedures through which the Commission prepares its proposals. Those procedures involve frequent contacts with national groups: professional associations, trade unions, political and parliamentary and other governmental bodies. The Commission's important power of initiative becomes imbedded in a complex political process designed to yield sufficient support for a proposal to promise well for its success when it reaches the Council.

Indeed, the consultations by the Commission during the formative stage of the legislative process extend beyond groups within or governments of member countries to the staff of the Council itself. Such developments have tended to blur the lines drawn by the Treaty between the roles of the Commission and Council. Critics have stressed the danger that this trend may inhibit the Commission's performance as a body initiating proposals from a Community perspective, and enable the member states as such to displace a Community viewpoint at the very point of formulation of legislative proposals.

The Council (Articles 145–149, and Articles 1–2 of the Merger Treaty): In its composition, the Council resembles a more traditional form of an intergovernmental body. Its nine members explicitly represent their governments as such rather than the Community. Its members, although not their number, vary. Depending upon the matter before the Council, the representatives of the member states may be ministers of foreign affairs, of agriculture, of economics and so on. No provision comparable to Article 10(2) of the Merger Treaty applies to the Council's members. Permanent delegations of the member states, headed by Permanent Representatives and including extensive staffs, have become established in Brussels, the seat of the

Commission and the Council. Now with official status (Article 4 of the Merger Treaty), the Representatives and staffs provide a continuing presence of the member governments between meetings of the Council, and have established a continuing liaison with their counterparts on the Commission's staff. Here again we observe the interpenetration of national and Community elements.

But the Council is more than a classic intergovernmental body. Through the exercise of its weighty legislative powers (e. g., Articles 48, 49 and 54) and its relationships with member states and other Community institutions, the Council plays an organic role in the life of the Community. In most respects it is the ultimate decider, particularly for the difficult political issues that are at the forefront of discussions about the future of the Community.

Note the Council's residual power to act by unanimity under Article 235. In its more characteristic role of deciding whether to approve proposals issuing from the Commission, the Council (according to the Treaty) acts unanimously or by a qualified majority involving weighted voting, as provided in different Articles of the Treaty.[8]

For a body whose functions are in large part legislative, the Council has an unusual composition. Its members are appointed directly by and indeed consist of "executive" ministers of the member states. Those members must by and large account for their acts to their own national executives or parliaments, rather than to the Community's Assembly.

The Assembly (Articles 137–144): Sometimes referred to as the Parliament, this body consists of delegates appointed by the national parliaments in accordance with Article 138(1). The Assembly sits in groupings which are defined not by the nationality of the delegates but by their political affiliations, in the traditional European fashion of ordering parties from left to right according to their political complexion. Essentially a body for debate of issues before the Community, the Assembly serves in a consultative capacity. Many draft directives or regulations must be submitted to it for comment before decision by the Council, which is free to reject or adopt suggestions in the comments. Delegates may put questions to members of the Commission and Council. Those members or representatives of the Commission often appear before committees of the Assembly to explain the Commission's work or reply to criticism by the delegates.

The weak position of the Assembly vis-a-vis the other Community institutions has stirred various proposals for amendments to the Treaty. These proposals look primarily towards a heightened power or control by the Assembly over budgetary matters and over the

8. Although Article 148 provides that the Council, absent Treaty rules to the contrary, decides by simple majority vote of its members, it should be noted that there are few Treaty provisions which do not provide for a qualified majority or unanimity.

treaty-making power of the Community. Reforms recently suggested by the Commission contemplate participation by the Assembly in the formulation of the Council's decisions about expenditures, and increased supervision over the execution of the budget. Needless to say, such budgetary matters are at the core of the Community's decisions and political prospects. The argument for a more powerful Assembly stems in part from the belief that the present decision-making structures of the Community do not comport with the democratic theories that are expressed through the governmental structures of member states. The Assembly has few effective powers over the initiator or decider of legislative matters.

Such proposals are linked by their advocates with a proposal for change in the procedures for composing the Assembly. Under the present appointive system, there are 198 members (if, as was not the case in 1973–74, all national delegations attended). In 1973 those members fell into six political groups: Christian Democrats (52), Socialists (51), Liberals and Allies (24), European Conservative Group (20), Progressive European Democrats (17), and Communists and Allies (13). There were several unattached delegates. Of course this indirect election or appointment of delegates through the national parliaments weakens the Assembly's legitimacy. Critics of the present Community argue that it never can achieve full European union of a financial and monetary character without an Assembly elected by direct suffrage—as contemplated by Article 138(3)—that would permit expanded Community powers to be exercised within a democratic structure. But the member states have been reluctant to move towards direct elections, a movement that could be accompanied by the formation of distinct political parties within them.

The proposals for direct election raise complex issues. For example, what types of electoral districts would be established within national traditions as diverse as those of France and Britain; what electoral system (single member-plurality, or the continental multiparty system) would be adopted; and would proportional representation be used? The broader political implications, as national electorates were educated to choose delegates with respect to European issues and political alignments that might not have national counterparts, are difficult to predict.

As of early 1975, the authority of the Assembly had expanded to the point where it had control over about 4% of the total Community budget, effective control over the balance remaining with the Council. In January of that year, the Assembly adopted a draft convention for direct election, the first such election to take place in May 1978. The convention is to become effective after adoption by the Council and ratification by the nine national legislatures.[9] The draft provides that the Assembly will consist of 335 members, roughly

9. The Resolution of the Assembly and the Draft Convention on the Election of Members of the European Assembly by Direct Universal Suffrage appear in CCH Common Market Reporter ¶ 9713.

double its present size, to be elected for five-year terms. Representation is to be allocated among the member countries according to population, ranging from 71 seats for Germany and 67 for the United Kingdom, to 13 for Ireland and 6 for Luxembourg. Members would continue to sit according to European party groups, not according to nationality. At the start, election rules such as voting age would be the same as those for the national parliaments in each country, although the draft looks towards eventual realization of a uniform Community procedure. But the political obstacles to ratification remained high.

Economic and Social Committee. (Articles 193–198): Several articles require that proposals for directives or regulations be submitted to this Committee for its comments before action by the Council. The function of the Committee is to give the various economic interests affected by the Treaty some direct voice in the development of Community law.

The Court of Justice (Articles 164–167): The materials at pp. 1268–1324, infra, examine the work of this distinctive international tribunal.

NOTE ON EXTERNAL RELATIONS

Unlike countries of a federal character such as the United States and Switzerland, the Community does not displace its members in all matters affecting foreign relations. Each member retains its separate representation in most international organizations, and generally pursues its own diplomatic initiatives with third countries. Indeed, as exemplified by French policy over the last decade, a member may develop strategies on basic matters such as defense that are distinct from those of the other states.

Nonetheless, the Treaty provides for a uniform Community policy on some matters towards the rest of the world. The most striking example lies in the commercial field, particularly the levels of the common external tariff. Articles 110–116, particularly Article 113 (1), define the areas in which the Community is to develop a common commercial policy towards third countries. Note the authority granted to Community institutions by Articles 114 and 116 to act towards third parties on behalf of the Community as a whole, in negotiating and concluding agreements. Moreover, in some international organizations such as the GATT, representatives of the Community negotiate directly with other countries. It is the Commission which generally represents the Community in such organizations, through negotiations and by maintaining close contacts with the United Nations and affiliated groups such as the regional economic commissions. Through the Council, the member states again retain the controlling voice, as with respect to the bargaining authority of the Commission during "rounds" of tariff negotiation within the GATT.

By 1973, 96 countries including the United States had established diplomatic relations with the Community. Note in this respect that Article 210 confers "legal personality" upon the Community. Many among these 96 nations appointed diplomatic missions headed by an ambassador, who is accredited to the Community and who submits his letters of credence to the Presidents of the Council and Commission.

The most significant of the links with other countries which the Treaty, through Article 238, authorizes the Community to enter into are the "association" agreements. Standing between full membership and limited trade and tariff accords, they are an important vehicle towards implementation of a common trade policy for the Community. Beyond reducing tariffs or quantitative restrictions and looking towards a common external tariff, they include matters such as financial aid and relaxation of barriers to the free movement of workers and to establishment. Unlike trade agreements, association can lead to the creation of new common institutions. The Community has entered into such agreements with Greece, Cyprus and Turkey. Suspension of the agreement with Greece during that country's period of military rule and problems in the Cyprus and Turkey relationships have led to a need for revision of these agreements—revisions considered in late 1974. Under the Act of Accession pursuant to which Britain entered the Community, special provisions contemplated the gradual readjustment of relationships between the Commonwealth countries, Britain and the rest of the Community. Some of those provisions look towards association agreements.

NOTE ON PROSPECTS FOR THE COMMUNITY

Revision of the Treaty

A Treaty of unlimited duration (Article 240) that confers extensive lawmaking and interpretative powers upon the institutions that it creates inevitably assumes a different character as the Community develops. As with our domestic process of constitutional interpretation, it becomes difficult other than in formal and procedural terms to distinguish this process of development of the Community's legal order from revision of the Treaty itself. Note, for example, the potential reach of Article 235, and its relationship to the provisions below treating "amendment" or "revision". Some of the most significant departures from the provisions of the Rome Treaty have occurred through political negotiations and practical compromises among the member states that have bypassed use of the formal provisions for amendment. We describe those compromises in the pages that follow, and our later examination of decisions of the Court of Justice evidence striking developments of Community law within the original constitutional framework.

When the Treaty refers to amendment or revision, it employs a variety of techniques. Note the following range of examples. Article 14 was amendable by action of the Council to accelerate the timetable for tariff reductions. Article 138(3) contemplates action both by Community institutions and the member states. Article 236 states a traditional procedure for revision. And Article 237, at issue when the three new member states applied for membership in the Community, also requires participation by the national governments according to their constitutional processes for the approval of treaties.

Crises, Status and Prospects of the Community

The alternating pattern of success and failure of the European movement prior to the Rome Treaty has continued since the Treaty's adoption. Attitudes of several members towards the Community have been no more constant than the political and economic climates since the late 1950's within which those attitudes are formed. To be sure, there are certain forces for stability. As the Community develops a network of economic relationships among its members, as it induces governments and business firms to plan and act with the Community rather than the nation as the relevant frame of reference, the likelihood of dramatic retreat from present accomplishments diminishes. The problems proliferate of returning the nine members to the status of nine distinct sovereignties.

The more realistic concern is whether the Community will continue to penetrate national life, expand its influence, and progressively displace the member governments as the critical forum in which Western Europe's future is charted and administered. Until recent years, the climate for such progressive development has been favorable. The original six Common Market countries experienced a dramatic improvement since the early 1950's in their productivity and standard of living—a phenomenon common to the industrialized nations of the world.

The concern that we noted becomes acute when that favorable environment becomes less certain. The circumstances of the mid-1970's are in this respect troubling—reduced growth rates and threats of serious recession stemming from such interrelated problems as the oil-energy crisis, inflation, unemployment and pressures upon the balance of payments of several countries. In such circumstances, the distributional questions among members of the Community become more vexing. The problem may become how to divide a static or decreasing product rather than how to distribute gains in which all, to some extent, share. In such times the vitality of the Community—its ability to withstand pressures for national protective action inconsistent with the Treaty's aims—is put to the severe test.

Basic political and economic issues produced the several crises which the Community has experienced. Serious crises arose in 1962 and 1965. The first grew out of conflict over admission of Britain into the Common Market, then strongly opposed by France; conflict between the concepts of "supranational government" and of *"l'Europe des patries"*; and conflict over issues to be resolved before achieving a common agricultural policy. A compromise agreement that left basic questions open for later resolution terminated this crisis and permitted the Community to enter into the second stage of its transitional period.

The crisis of 1965 had more ominous overtones. From July of that year until February 1966, France had no representative on the Council. In many respects the more significant work of Community organs was suspended during this period. Nonetheless, Community institutions continued to discharge those responsibilities which they already possessed. Not the Community itself but its dynamism was temporarily checked.

Agricultural problems, particularly conflicting French and German positions over the level of price supports for certain commodities, were the immediate cause. But broader issues of the ultimate role of the Community came to the fore, such as the classic tension between *"l'Europe des patries"* and the Community as a federation in process. Another problem had become significant. Was the Community to develop as a "democratic" organization, allowing some measure of initiative and control by officials directly responsible to the national populations? Or was its course to be charted by "managers," officials experienced in different fields and appointed by the member governments? Consider the following excerpts—which, to be sure, stress only one side of the story—from a news conference held by President de Gaulle in 1965: [10]

> What happened in Brussels on June 30, regarding an agricultural-financial settlement, brought to light two things: first, a persistent reluctance on the part of our partners to include agriculture in the six-member Common Market and then certain errors and ambiguities in the treaties of the European Economic Community. Sooner or later the crisis was inevitable. Indeed, the three treaties that respectively set up the Coal and Steel Community, Euratom and the Common Market were concluded before the French recovery in 1958. And that is why these treaties cover, above all, everything the other members sought. . . .
>
> Moreover the three treaties set up an executive body in the shape of a commission that was independent of the states, although its members were appointed and paid by them, and a legislative body in the shape of a European assembly composed of members of the various parliaments, none of whom had received from their voters a mandate beyond national affairs. So this embryonic body, this technocratic embryo made up largely of foreigners—which was bound to encroach upon French democracy to settle problems on which our existence depends—was not to our liking, once we had decided to take our destiny into our own hands. Everybody knows that the idea of grouping together the states of Western

10. The conference was reported in translation in the New York Times, Sept. 10, 1965, p. 2.

> Europe in the economic and, may I add, political fields has for a long time been ours. . . .
>
> We mean that nothing that is important—today in the organization of the Common Market or tomorrow in its operation—should be decided or implemented except by the Governments of the six states; that is to say, Governments controlled by their Parliaments. And we know that there is different concept of a European federation, in which the member countries, according to the dreams of those who originated it, would lose their national identities. To this plan, which really seems unrealistic, France offers the alternative of organized cooperation between states, which would probably grow toward a confederation. This is the plan that alone seems to us best suited to the nations of our continent as they are at the present time. . . .
>
> . . .
>
> We are a people who are rising—like the curve of our population, of our production, of our foreign trade, of our monetary reserves, of our standard of living, of the spread of our culture and our language, of the power of our arms, of our success in sport. That being the case, one cannot see why France should give up having a policy that is her own.
>
> . . .
>
> For us it is a matter of keeping ourselves free of all subservience. . . .

These attitudes found realization not only in France's partial withdrawal from the life of the Community, but also in its declaration that France would withdraw her military forces from NATO and terminate the "subordination that is described as integration" in that organization in 1969. The months of semi-paralysis in the Community and of intensive behind-the-scenes negotiations witnessed increasing opposition by France to one Treaty principle—that majority voting in the Council would displace unanimity requirements as the Community moved through and out of its transitional period. This issue symbolized the conflict between Community and nation. France urged a formal commitment by the six countries that any nation have the right to a veto on any matter that it considered to be of fundamental interest; the other five countries resisted such a formal step.

A meeting of the Council at Luxembourg in January 1966, with French participation, led to a compromise. The ministers agreed upon a four-point document. (1) When the Treaty provides that a majority vote is sufficient to adopt a proposal of the Commission, and when that proposal involves important national interests, the Council members will attempt to find mutually acceptable solutions. (2) In such situations, the French government expresses the view that discussion should continue until unanimity is reached. (3) The member countries acknowledge continuing divergence of viewpoints about situations where compromise cannot be achieved. (4) Nonetheless, they conclude that such divergence does not prevent the Community from resuming its full work and development.

The Luxembourg agreement, which has been characterized as one to disagree, submerged rather than resolved tensions that inevitably survived. The ministers also approved a seven-point program on improved relationships between the Council and the Commission. This program stated that, before adopting proposals of particular importance, the Commission should contact member governments through the permanent representatives at the Council, although such consultation should not affect the Commission's right of initiative.

In December 1965, then President Hallstein of the Commission stated his views about the crisis and its resolution: [11]

> . . . The central element in the Community's constitution, and its most original feature, is the relationship between the Council and the Commission. The Rome Treaty provides that a dialogue exist between these two bodies. The dialogue is intended to ensure that the particular interests of individual member states are weighed against the overall interest of the Community represented by the Commission. . . . These institutions naturally deal with politics. . . . Without actually constituting a government, they exercise functions indispensable to the modern economy and that are executed in the member states by the governments. . . .
>
> . . . How can politics be divorced from economic policy? The elimination of the political aspects of the Community would be tantamount to abandoning all idea of an European economic policy and of a large-scale economy for Europe. The merging of national economies in the continent by unifying the economic and social policies of the participating countries is part of the process of political unification of Europe. . . . It aims at a new ordering of all political power in Europe, a coalescence of the states in Europe, that will ultimately embrace foreign policy and defense. . . . [The Rome Treaty] is a compromise between the unitary concept (the "super-national") and the concept of alliance, co-operation, confederation or whatever we call the loose forms of collaboration. This Community solution is valid by virtue of law, and that is one of the most basic principles of Western civilization. . . . We doubt whether genuine progress toward full political unity can stem from any solution which does not provide for some independent institutional embodiment of the common European interest.

In explaining the Luxembourg agreement to the Assembly, the Commission stated that the voting problem may have been more imagined than real. It noted that in formulating proposals, it had always sought unanimity even where the Council could have decided by a majority vote. It stressed that the need for consultation between the Council and Commission had been understood well before 1966.

Nonetheless, this agreement has left a mark upon the Community's evolution. In the view of numerous observers, the effective injunction against majority rule has encouraged lengthy negotiation of many proposals at all levels and posed the recurrent danger of re-

11. The translation is taken from 88 European Community 8–9 (January 1966).

ducing proposals to the lowest common denominator. Even granting that the principles of the Luxembourg agreement were redundant for basic political decisions, which as a practical matter had to gain the support of all, those principles appear to have influenced decisions of lesser significance on which vote by qualified majority has become almost as improbable. An analysis in 1974 of proposals issuing from the Commission and then before the Council indicated that about 40% of the proposals were within the Treaty's rules for a qualified majority.

After the Luxembourg agreement, the major problems confronted by the Community grew out of tensions preceding the entrance into the Community of the United Kingdom (as well as Denmark and Ireland), and out of the economic setbacks of the Community's members in 1973–74. Periodic conferences among the heads of the member states have taken place, none more significant than the so-called Summit Conference in Paris in October 1972 which included the new member states.[12] The heads of state set themselves "the major objective of transforming, before the end of the present decade . . . the whole complex of the relations of the Member States into a European Union." Again they declared that they "determined to strengthen the Community by establishing an economic and monetary union", a determination that appeared more qualified two years later. The communiqué stated that economic expansion "is not an end in itself. Its first aim should be to enable disparities in living conditions to be reduced." This aspiration towards a more equal or just distribution of wealth also became the more difficult to realize in the harsher economic climate developing during 1973–74. The serious, even threatening, economic situations of Britain and Italy—the situation in Britain leading to internal political pressure for reconsideration by plebiscite of Britain's participation in the Community—raised the danger of a trend towards nationalistic and protectionist tendencies. In fact, the plebiscite of June 1975 gave strong support to Britain's participation.

But despite clouded prospects at the start of 1975, the history of the European movement counseled against too great pessimism. Periodic infusions of political will and inventiveness had overcome the earlier crises. The old issue remains: limited economic union, or more integration as to matters of basic politics. The theme common to the preceding crises—that the Community may lose its dynamism—has continuing significance. With institutions still in their infancy, life is growth and pause too long maintained may forever stifle that growth.

Dynamic movement for the Community, if it is to be regained, will not depend upon the same constellation of internal and external forces that characterized its origin and early years. The possible sources of future growth were suggestively sketched by Ralf Dahren-

12. The communiqué issued at the end of this Summit is reproduced in 10 Common Market L.Rev. 108–114 (1973).

dorf, a distinguished academic sociologist, political representative in Germany, and during four years a member of the Community's Commission. His answers to two questions in an interview in 1974, just before his departure from the Commission, are particularly relevant:[13]

> *The European Community owes its existence to pressure from outside. As this pressure has fallen off, so too integration has stagnated. Can Europe develop without pressures and threats from outside?*
>
> A certain amount of pressure from outside is not only helpful but in fact essential for the development of European union. This is particularly true nowadays, because it is no longer an easy matter to pinpoint large social groups demanding and promoting European union in furtherance of their own interests. The trade unions are split on the European question. The political parties share, as a general rule, that lukewarm feeling for Europe, vacillating between positive and and negative, which characterizes the population as a whole. Strictly speaking, this leaves only the representatives of business and industry, that is, those who can directly see the advantages of operating in a wider area.
>
> If, in the light of such social and political circumstances, one is still convinced that cooperation among the medium-sized and smaller countries of Europe is in the deep-seated interests of the majority of our people, then one must come to the conviction that a certain amount of outside pressure is necessary to make these interests once more visible.
>
> *What form would this pressure have to take?*
>
> I am very happy that we have broken free of the world of the Cold War and now live in a world geared toward the European Conference on Security and Cooperation. There can be absolutely no question today of a European Community motivated by a hostility toward the Communist countries. Outside pressure, however, can take on other forms. Europe has come to realize that subdivision into a third and fourth world, that is, a world of rich and poor developing countries, represents a challenge.
>
> The fact that joint action is required of the European countries in order to assert their self-determination in a world dominated by the superpowers should be placed in the same category as outside pressures. Neither superpower constitutes a military pressure, but then it is no longer a secret that we are progressively moving from a period of militarily oriented policy into a period of economically oriented policy. These international developments in economics and politics may provide the incentive to reactivate European integration.

Source and secondary materials: Official acts of Community organs are published in several documents, some of which are referred

13. These excerpts are taken from 182 European Community 10–11 (December 1974).

to in the following sections. Regulations, directives, decisions, recommendations, policy statements and so forth of the Commission and Council appear in the Official Journal of the European Communities. The more important of these documents from 1958–1972, preceding the entrance of the United Kingdom into the Community, have now received official English translations within the specially prepared Official Journal of the European Communities for those years (Special Eng. ed.). The Commission has published an annual General Report. From 1958–1967, these were referred to as the General Report of the Commission on the Activities of the European Economic Community. From 1967 on, these have appeared in the form of the annual General Report on the Activities of the European Communities, and the text will refer to the Seventh General Report for 1973.

The most complete and useful up-to-date collection of source materials on the Common Market (in English translations through 1972, and in the official English text thereafter) appears in the CCH Common Market Reporter. The materials include opinions of the Court of Justice and selected national-court decisions. The Community has begun publication of official English texts of decisions of the Court, in Reports of Cases before the Court. Thus far such Reports have not translated (officially) pre-1973 opinions. Opinions of the Court and a broader selection of national-court decisions relevant to the Communities also appear in the Common Market Law Reports. Two English periodicals of importance are the Common Market Law Review and the Journal of Common Market Studies. Extensive bibliographies of source and secondary materials on the Communities appear in the CCH Common Market Reporter and in annual issues of the Common Market Law Review. A monthly summary of events in the EEC appears in European Community, prepared by the European Community Information Service in Washington, D. C.

QUESTIONS

(1) Note that Articles 49, 51, 54 and 101 confer a power of final decision upon the Council. In each case, the Council acts only upon a proposal formulated by the Commission. Consider the following differences among these articles: (*a*) the different votes required of the Council (differences later influenced by the Luxembourg agreement); (*b*) whether the required vote depends upon the state of completion of the transitional period; (*c*) the kind of action which the Council is authorized to take; and (*d*) whether the Assembly or the Economic and Social Committee must be consulted. What reasons would you advance to explain the different provisions of these articles with respect to these four factors?

(2) Despite the differences in political, economic and constitutional structures in the nine member nations, the similarities are more significant. The nine member states now represent differing expressions of common themes in the Western European experience: political democracy and regulated capitalism. Moreover, the level of economic well-being within the Community, in global terms, is markedly high, although there are important differences among the members. (In 1972, in units of account equal to the 1971 dollar, the per capita income in some countries was: Germany,

3841; France, 3489; Britain, 2673; Italy, 2008. The 1972 figure for the United States was slightly over $5000.)

(*a*) Do you view the similarities in economic and political systems, and the relatively high levels of income, to be critical or even significant for the success of the first two decades?

(*b*) Would you foresee serious problems for the Community —and if so, of what character—if one of its member nations moved significantly to the left or right politically, or moved economically towards a totally planned economy?

(*c*) Would you foresee distinctively different problems emerging if the Community invited into full membership a country such as Turkey with a distinctively lower standard of living and radically different social system. If so, why?

(3) Given the composition and method of constituting the community institutions and their role in the government of the Community, can one appropriately view the Treaty as establishing a constitutional structure built on the principle of separation of legislative and executive powers? How do you evaluate President de Gaulle's description of the Community's government as a "technocratic embryo" removed from the control of the general electorate of each of the member states?

B. CONSTITUTIONAL ISSUES AND THE ROLE OF THE COURT OF JUSTICE

It is difficult to separate the two themes captured in the title to this section. The political tensions within the Community that led to its several crises were reflected in legal issues before national courts and the Community Court of Justice. The unique character of the Community and its complex relationship to national legal-political orders early brought to the fore problems of a fundamental character—problems which can properly be characterized as constitutional, since they concern allocations of competence or power and the interpretation or elucidation of basic provisions of the EEC Treaty.

Thus courts wrestled with issues of a significance reminiscent of those resolved in the constitutional decisions of our Supreme Court in the early 19th Century growing out of conflict between the state and federal legal-political orders. Some leading opinions appear below. They are accompanied by illustrative decisions of national courts which confront the same problems from a different perspective. But bear in mind that these national courts cannot be analogized to state courts within the American federalism. They are the highest courts of independent nations, the functional equivalents of our Supreme Court, and they decide within the framework of established national constitutions or traditions.

The constitutional decisions of the Court of Justice also serve to introduce the principal functions, jurisdictional bases and techniques of the Court of Justice. That the role of the Court of Justice is a critical one should be evident. Not only must the Community seek to establish uniformity in the understanding, interpretation and application of Community provisions within the member states, but it must also have some mechanism for controlling the action of the organs of the Community within the constraints of the Treaty, and for resolving disputes of a legal-political character between the member states and the Community. Read now Articles 164 to 187, and Article 192.

The Court has a broad jurisdiction. It "reviews" issues involving Community law that arose in cases before national courts and hears actions against member states, Community institutions or the Community itself that are initially brought before it. Its powers vary with the jurisdiction that it exercises. The Court may be confined to rendering an "abstract interpretation" of the Treaty; it may enter judgment against a party; it may annul an administrative act; it may award money damages. And the questions before it range from ultimate constitutional issues to minute interpretation of a regulation.

Note that—unlike other international tribunals such as the International Court of Justice—the Court's rules of procedure do not permit dissenting or separate opinions. A member and former President of the Court has stated: [14]

> The varying legal backgrounds of the judges sometimes create a problem much more difficult than . . . differences of language. As lawyers we come from six different systems of law, each with its own legal notions and legal preconceptions. Even if it is not too difficult to agree about the ruling we should hand down, it may be much harder to agree about the reasons for that ruling. . . . The ruling is given as a common sentence of the whole bench; and, even if a minority of judges should disagree, such disagreement will remain secret.
>
> In my experience, this is a good solution. If dissenting opinions were allowed, we would easily risk a splitting up of the bench into two schools, one predominantly "Latin," the other "German." It is superfluous to point out that such a trend would not contribute to the development of a common European approach. To give the Court of Justice of the European Communities its full authority as the final interpreter of Community law, it is preferable that it speak with a single voice.

The decisions and text in this section treat four topics: (1) problems of the direct applicability of Community law in disputes between private parties and national authorities; (2) the use of Article 177 by national courts; (3) conflicts between Community law and national constitutional principles; and (4) illustrations of Articles 169 and 173.

14. A. M. Donner, The Single Voice of the Court, 107 European Community 14, 15 (November 1967).

QUESTION

Compare Articles 164–167 of the Treaty with Articles 2, 3, 9, and 31 of the Statute of the International Court of Justice.* What differences does this comparison suggest between the problems in creating a judicial organ (*a*) for an organization of a dominantly economic character among countries with relatively common traditions and interests, and (*b*) for a world-wide organization of a more political character?

---

1. DIRECT APPLICABILITY OF COMMUNITY LAW

N. V. ALGEMENE TRANSPORT–EN EXPEDITIE ONDERNEMING VAN GEND & LOOS v. NETHERLANDS FISCAL ADMINISTRATION

Court of Justice of the European Communities, Case No. 26/62, February 5, 1963. Recueil Vol. IX, p. 1.[15]

An Action, the *object* of which is a request directed to the Court, pursuant to subsection (*a*) of the first paragraph and the third paragraph of Article 177 of the Treaty establishing the European Economic Community, by the Tariefcommissie, the Dutch administrative court of last resort ruling on appeals against fiscal matters, and seeking in the action pending before said court *a preliminary ruling* on the questions of:

(1) Whether EEC Treaty Article 12 has an internal effect, in other words, whether everyone to whom the law applies can, on the basis of this article, claim individual rights which the judge is bound to protect, and

(2) if so, whether the imposition of an entry duty of 8 percent on imports into the Netherlands by the plaintiff in the main issue of urea-formaldehyde from the Federal Republic of Germany constitutes an illegal increase within the meaning of EEC Treaty Article 12 or whether in this particular instance it was a reasonable modification of the entry duty applicable before March 1, 1960, a modification which, although constituting an increase in the mathematical sense, should not be considered prohibited under Article 12.

Points of Fact and of Law

I. Summary of the facts and proceedings

The facts on which this case is based and the development of the proceedings may be summarized as follows:

(1) On September 9, 1960, the N. V. Algemene Transporten Expeditie Onderneming van Gend & Loos (henceforth referred to as Van Gend & Loos), following a customs declaration made September 8 on Form D5061, imported into the Netherlands from the Federal Republic of Germany a certain amount of urea-formaldehyde,

15. The translation is taken from the CCH Common Market Reporter ¶ 8008.

designated on the import document as "*Harnstoffharz* (U. F. resin) 70, acqueous emulsion of urea-formaldehyde."

(2) On the date of importation, the product in question was classified under position 39.01–a–1 of the entry duties tariff included in the "Tariefbesluit," which came into force on March 1, 1960. The latter repeated the nomenclature of the protocol concluded between the Kingdom of Belgium, the Grand Duchy of Luxembourg and the Kingdom of the Netherlands on July 25, 1958, and ratified in the Netherlands by the law of December 16, 1959. . . .

(4) On this basis, the Netherlands Fiscal Administration applied to the import in this dispute the entry duty of 8 percent ad valorem.

(5) On September 20, 1960, Van Gend & Loos submitted to the inspector of entry duties and excises at Zaandam a protest against the application of this duty in this particular case.

In particular, it presented as arguments the following points:

On January 1, 1958, the date the EEC Treaty came into force, emulsions of amine compounds were classified under position 279–a–2 of the tariff included in the 1947 "Tariefbesluit" and burdened with an ad valorem entry duty of 3 percent.

In the "Tariefbesluit," which came into force on March 1, 1960, the 279–a–2 position was replaced by position 39.01–a.

Instead of uniformly applying for intra-Community trade an entry duty of 3 percent on all products under the former position 279–a–2, a subdivision was made: for one position, 39.01–a–1, which covered emulsions, dispersions and solutions of amine compounds exclusively, the entry duty was fixed at 8 percent; for the other products under the position 39.01–a, which also appeared under former position 279–a–2, the 3 percent entry duty in force on January 1, 1958, was retained.

In thus increasing, after the EEC Treaty came into force, the entry duty on the product involved in this dispute, the Netherlands government has violated Article 12 of the Treaty . . . .

(6) On March 6, 1961, the inspector of entry duties and excises at Zaandam rejected the Van Gend & Loos protest because it concerned not the actual application of the tariff, but the rate thereof.

(7) On April 4, 1961, Van Gend & Loos filed an appeal against this decision with the Tariefcommissie in Amsterdam.

(8) The action was given a hearing by the Tariefcommissie on May 21, 1962. . . .

In particular, the Fiscal Administration answered that at the time the EEC Treaty came into force the product in this dispute was burdened not only with a duty of 3 percent by virtue of position 279–a–2, but also with a duty of 10 percent because, due to its nature and destination, it was classified under position 332A ("synthetic and other glues, not listed or included elsewhere"), so that there was actually no increase.

(9) The Tariefcommissie, without formally pronouncing on the question of whether the product in dispute belonged under position 332A or under position 279–a–2 of the 1947 "Tariefbesluit," considered that the parties' arguments raised a question concerning the interpretation of the EEC Treaty; consequently it suspended the proceedings and, under the third paragraph of Treaty Article 177, on August 16, 1962, referred to the Court of Justice for preliminary ruling the two questions set forth above.

(10) On August 23, 1962, the parties concerned, the Member States and the EEC Commission were notified of the Tariefcommissie decision by the Registrar of the Court.

(11) Pursuant to Article 20 of the Protocol on the Statute of the Court of the EEC, written comments were filed by the parties in the main issue, by the Government of the Kingdom of Belgium, by the Government of the Federal Republic of Germany, by the EEC Commission, and by the Government of the Kingdom of the Netherlands. . . .

(13) The Advocate General gave his oral and reasoned conclusions at the hearing of December 12, 1962; he suggested that in its decision the Court answer only the first question submitted to it and declare that Article 12 of the EEC Treaty contains only an obligation incumbent upon the Member States.

II. Arguments and comments

The arguments contained in the comments submitted by the parties concerned, the Member States and the EEC Commission, in compliance with the second paragraph of Article 20 of the Protocol on the Statute of the Court of Justice of the EEC, may be summarized as follows: . . .

The *Belgian Government* holds that the first question submits to the Court a problem of a constitutional nature which is within the sole competence of a national judge in the Netherlands.

The latter is faced with two international acts, both integrated into national legislation; he must decide, on the national level—assuming that they were really contradictory—whether one Treaty takes precedence over another or, to be more exact, whether one nationally ratified law takes precedence over a subsequent nationally ratified law.

That is a typically internal question of constitutional law which is in no way subject to the interpretation of an article of the EEC Treaty and which, as it can be settled only by Dutch constitutional and case law standards, are within the sole jurisdiction of a Dutch judge.

The Belgian Government also points out that a decision on the first point submitted to the Court not only is unnecessary in order for the Tariefcommissie to render judgment, but cannot even influence the solution of the real problem which it is called upon to solve.

In fact, whatever the answer of the Court, the Tariefcommissie will have to solve the same problem; does it have the right to overlook the law of December 16, 1959, approving the Brussels Protocol, allegedly because it is in contradiction with a law—a prior law—of December 5, 1957, approving the Treaty establishing the EEC?

So the question submitted is not really a matter for preliminary ruling, since its solution cannot enable the judge in the main issue to rule definitively on the dispute pending before him.

The *EEC Commission,* on the other hand, points out that the effect of the Treaty provisions on the internal law of the Member States could never be determined by the purely national law of each of these States, but by the Treaty itself; this is therefore really a problem concerning the interpretation of the Treaty. . . .

The *Commission* stresses the importance of the answer which the Court will give to the question [whether Article 12 has an internal effect]; this answer will influence not only the interpretation, in a specific case, of the provision involved and the effect which the judiciaries of the Member States will acknowledge it to have, but also certain other Treaty provisions which are just as clear and definitive as Article 12. . . .

Community law must be effectively and uniformly applied throughout the Community.

For this reason, to begin with, the effect of Community law on the internal law of the Member States cannot be determined by such internal law, but only by Community law. Then, too, the national legal bodies are bound to apply the rules of Community law directly, and a national judge is bound to enforce the rules of Community law instead of opposite national laws, even when the latter are enacted subsequently to Community law. . . .

. . . [T]he *Netherlands Government* claims that the EEC Treaty is no different from the usual international treaty with respect to the conditions required for it to have a direct effect.

The question of whether, by virtue of Dutch constitutional law, Article 12 is directly applicable depends on the interpretation of Dutch law and is not within the competence of the Court of Justice. . . .

The *German Government* also is of the opinion that Article 12 of the EEC Treaty does not constitute a rule of law immediately applicable in all Member States; it lays down for them an international obligation (in the matter of customs policy) which must be carried out through the national bodies endowed with legislative powers. . . .

At any rate, the obligation it entails exists only vis-à-vis the other contracting States.

Under German law, a legal regulation fixing a customs duty counter to the provisions of Article 12 would be perfectly valid.

Within the framework of the EEC Treaty, legal protection of a Member State's nationals is insured only with regard to acts of the Community institutions which are of direct and individual concern to them, and this through provisions which differ from those of their national constitutional system. . . .

Opinion

I. Procedure

No objection is raised with respect to the validity of the procedure used for the request for preliminary ruling submitted, by virtue of Article 177 of the EEC Treaty, to the Court by the Tariefcommissie, a court of law within the meaning of such article. . . .

II. The first question

A. Competence of the Court

The Government of the Netherlands and the Belgian Government challenge the competence of the Court on the ground that this particular case involves a request concerning, not the interpretation, but the application, of the Treaty within the framework of the constitutional law of the Netherlands.

Specifically, they allege that the Court would not be competent to pronounce on whether the provisions of the EEC Treaty should, if necessary, be accorded preeminence either over Dutch law or over other agreements ratified by the Netherlands and incorporated into their national law; the solution to such a problem would come within the exclusive competence of the national courts, subject to the reservation that appeal may be taken according to the conditions laid down by Treaty Articles 169 and 170.

Nevertheless, in this instance the Court is not called upon to pronounce judgment regarding the application of the Treaty according to the principles of internal Netherlands law, which remains within the jurisdiction of the national courts, but it is only asked, in conformity with Article 177(a) of the Treaty, to interpret the application of Article 12 of the Treaty within the framework of Community law and in the light of its bearing on individuals. . . .

B. Merits

The Tariefcommissie first poses the question whether Treaty Article 12 has immediate effect on internal law, in the sense that nationals of the Member States could, on the basis of such article, claim rights which a national judge must safeguard.

In order to determine whether the provisions of an international treaty have such an application one must consider its spirit, its organization and its wording.

The objective of the EEC Treaty, which is to establish a common market whose operation is of direct concern to everyone within the jurisdiction of the Community, implies that this Treaty is more than an agreement creating reciprocal obligations between the contracting States. This point of view is confirmed by the preamble to the Treaty, which goes beyond governments and refers to nations, and in a more concrete manner by the establishment of bodies which institutionalize sovereign rights, the exercise of which affects the Member States as well as their citizens. It should also be noted that the nationals of the States joined in the Community are called upon to collaborate, through the European Parliament and the Economic and Social Committee, in the operation of this Community.

Furthermore, the role of the Court of Justice, within the framework of Article 177, whose purpose is to ensure uniformity of interpretation of the Treaty by the national courts, confirms the fact that the States have acknowledged that Community law has an authority which may be invoked before such courts by their nationals.

From all this it must be concluded that the Community presents a new legal order in international law for the benefit of which the Member States have, albeit to a limited extent, surrendered their sovereign rights, and whose subjects are not only the Member States but individuals as well. Thus, Community law, which is independent of the laws of the Member States, while it creates obligations for individuals, also gives rise to rights which become part of their legal heritage. These rights are created, not only when they are explicitly stated by the Treaty, but also through obligations which the Treaty lays down in a very definite manner for individuals as well as for the Member States and the Community institutions.

As for the arrangement of the Treaty in matters of customs duties and charges having an equivalent effect, it should be pointed out that the principal rule of Article 9, which bases the Community on a customs union, is the prohibition of such duties and charges. This provision appears at the beginning of the part of the Treaty which defines the "foundations of the Community"; it is applied and made more explicit by Article 12.

The text of Article 12 lays down a clear and unconditional prohibition which involves a negative rather than a positive duty. In any case, such obligation does not carry with it the reservation that the States may subordinate its functioning to a positive act of internal law.

This prohibition, by its very nature, lends itself perfectly to producing direct effects in legal relations between the Member States and persons under their jurisdiction.

There is no need for legislative intervention by the States in order for Article 12 to be carried out. The designation, in this article, of the Member States as being subject to the obligation to abstain does not imply that their nationals may not benefit thereby.

The argument drawn from Treaty Articles 169 and 170, which the three governments that submitted comments to the Court relied on in their statements, comes to naught. The fact that in the abovementioned articles the Treaty authorizes the Commission and the Member States to bring before the Court a State which has failed to carry out its obligations does not imply that it is impossible for individuals to invoke these obligations, when necessary, before a national judge; similarly, the fact that the Treaty provides the Commission with the means for ensuring regard for the obligations laid down for those subject to such obligations does not preclude the possibility of invoking infringement of these obligations in disputes between individuals brought before a national judge.

Limiting the guarantees against violation of Article 12 by the Member States to the procedures of Articles 169 and 170 would deny all direct judicial protection of individual rights to their nationals. Recourse to these articles would run the risk of being ineffective if it were to occur after the ratification of a national decision taken without regard for the Treaty provisions.

The vigilance of individuals concerned with the safeguarding of their rights entails an efficient supervision added to that which Articles 169 and 170 entrust to the care of the Commission and of the Member States. It follows from the preceding reasons that, according to the spirit, the arrangement, and the wording of the Treaty, Article 12 must be interpreted as having direct effects and giving rise to individual rights which the national courts must safeguard.

III. The second question

A. Competence of the Court

. . . [T]he question submitted by the Tariefcommissie really amounts to asking whether, by law, an actual increase of the customs duties burdening a specific product and which would be the result, not of an increase in the rate schedule, but of a new classification following the change in its tariff classification, infringes the prohibition of Treaty Article 12.

Seen from this angle, the question calls for an interpretation of this provision of the Treaty and more particularly of the bearing that may properly be given to the notion of duties applied before the coming into force of the Treaty.

The Court, then, is competent to answer the question.

B. Merits

It follows from the wording and the placement of Treaty Article 12 that in determining whether customs duties and charges having an equivalent effect have been increased in contravention of the prohibition therein contained, the duties and charges actually applied at the time the Treaty went into effect must be considered.

Furthermore, where the prohibition of Treaty Article 12 is concerned, such an illegal increase can just as well result from a tariff reorganization causing the product to be classified under a more heavily taxed position, as it can from an increase in the actual customs rate.

It is of little importance to know in what manner the increase in the customs duties occurred, seeing that in one Member State the same product was taxed at a higher rate after the coming into force of the Treaty. The application of Article 12, according to the interpretation given above, is within the competence of a national judge, who must seek to determine whether the dutiable product, in this instance urea-formaldehyde from the Federal Republic of Germany, is being taxed by customs measures put into force in the Netherlands with an import duty higher than that with which it was burdened on January 1, 1958.

On this subject the Court is not competent to rule on the merits of the contradictory assertions introduced in the course of the proceedings before it, but must leave them to be evaluated by national courts. . . .

THE COURT, ruling on the request submitted to it for preliminary judgment by the Tariefcommissie by its decision of August 16, 1962, declares:

(1) Article 12 of the Treaty establishing the European Economic Community has immediate effects and entails for persons under its jurisdiction individual rights which national courts must safeguard;

(2) In order to ascertain whether customs duties or charges having an equivalent effect have been increased, in violation of the prohibition of Treaty Article 12, the duties and taxes actually applied by the Member State involved at the time the Treaty came into force must be taken into consideration;

Such increase can arise from a tariff reorganization resulting in the product's being classified under a more heavily taxed position as well as from an increase in the customs rate applied; . . .

NOTE ON DIRECTLY APPLICABLE TREATY PROVISIONS

The question whether provisions of or acts under the Treaty are directly applicable within the member states, and produce direct effects creating rights for private parties, has figured in numerous decisions of the Court of Justice and national judiciaries. The question posed in Grad v. Finanzamt Traunstein,[16] a 1970 decision of the Court of Justice, was the effect of a decision and directive of the Council. The 1965 decision treated harmonization of national provisions affecting competition in transport by rail, road and inland waterway. It provided in part that member states should apply a "common system of added-value turnover tax" with respect to transport of goods, as soon as that system was adopted by the Council and

16. Court of Justice of the European Communities, Case No. 9/70, October 6, 1970, Recueil Vol. XVI, p. 825. The excerpts below from this opinion are taken from a translation in the CCH Common Market Reporter ¶ 8107.

put into effect by the member states. That tax system "shall, as of its effective date, replace [other specified taxes] to the extent that transports of goods by rail, road, and inland waterway are subject to [such other taxes]". The 1967 directive on harmonization of national laws on turnover taxes provided in part that member states "shall replace their present system of turnover taxes with the common added-value tax system," as defined. The laws in the member states were to be "promulgated as soon as possible," to take effect not later than January 1, 1970. As of the effective date, member states could no longer maintain or introduce other defined types of taxes upon imports or exports among member states. In an Article 177 proceeding, the Court responded in part to the questions posed to it as follows:

> In its first question, the fiscal court asks the Court of Justice whether Article 4, paragraph 2, of the Council decision in conjunction with Article 1 of the Council directive produces direct effects in the legal relations between the Member States and persons under their jurisdiction, and whether these provisions create individual rights for these persons which the national courts must safeguard.
>
> The question concerns the overall effect of provisions contained in a decision and in a directive. Under Article 189 of the EEC Treaty, a decision is binding in every respect upon those designated therein. Also under Article 189, a directive is binding upon every Member State addressed, in respect of the result to be achieved, but leaves the form and the means to the national authorities.
>
> In its statements the German Government maintains that Article 189, in distinguishing between the effects of regulations, on the one hand, and those of decisions and directives, on the other, precludes the possibility for decisions and directives to have the direct effect referred to in the question, because such effect is reserved to the regulations.
>
> If, however, under Article 189, regulations are directly applicable and thus by their nature are capable of producing direct effects, this does not mean that other types of legal acts provided for in Article 189 could never produce similar effects. Particularly the provision that decisions are binding in every respect upon the addressees permits raising the question of whether the obligation to which the decision gave rise could be invoked only by the Community institutions vis-à-vis the addressee or whether such right could also be invoked by anyone having an interest in the execution of the obligation. It would be incompatible with the binding effect attributed to a decision in Article 189 to exclude the possibility that, in principle, the obligation imposed by the decision could not be invoked by the persons concerned. Particularly in cases where the Community authorities by decision require one Member State or all the States to adopt a certain course of conduct, the useful purpose of such measure would be weakened if persons subject to the jurisdiction of such State could not invoke this effect in court and the national courts could not consider it as part of Community law. Even if the effects of a decision were not the same as those of a provision of a regulation, this difference does not preclude

> the possibility that the final result, namely, the right of a person to invoke the measure in court, might not be the same as in the case of a provision of a directly applicable regulation.
>
> Article 177, which permits the national courts to ask the Court of Justice to decide on the validity and the interpretation of all acts of the institutions, without distinction, also requires that such acts can be invoked by persons before these courts. It must therefore be determined in each case whether the provision involved is by its nature, its context, and its wording capable of producing direct effects in the legal relations between the addressee of the act and third parties.

The Court then observed that the decision and directive were clear in requiring application of the turnover tax system no later than a specific date, and prohibited introducing other specific taxes. The obligation upon member states was "mandatory and general," and "unconditional and sufficiently clear and precise to be capable of producing direct effects in the legal relations between the Member States and persons under their jurisdiction." The fact that the date for introduction of the new system "was set in a directive does not detract from the binding effect of the provision." Persons within the member states could invoke these obligations of the states before national courts.

Assuming that a Treaty provision such as Article 12 is interpreted by the Court of Justice to have direct effect, national courts confront a difficult question when a subsequently enacted national law is alleged to violate that article. From the perspective of the Court of Justice, Article 12 must prevail. But a national court decides within its own constitutional structure, and must comprehend the Treaty within that national political-legal framework.

An illustration is afforded by Belgian State v. S.A. Fromagerie Franco-Suisse "Le Ski", a 1971 decision of the Supreme Court (*Cour de Cassation*) of Belgium.[17] The Supreme Court entertained an appeal in a case involving a claim of refund by a company for duties and imports imposed by Belgium pursuant to royal and ministerial decrees promulgated subsequent to January 1, 1958. The company contended that these special duties (last ratified in a 1968 Belgian law) violated Article 12 of the Treaty. In its opinion, the Court stated in part:

> Whereas, the conflict between a rule of law established by an international treaty and a rule established by a subsequent law is not a conflict between two laws;
>
> Whereas, the rule that a law repeals an earlier law to the extent that it is in conflict with it does not apply where the conflict is between a treaty and a law;

17. Cour de Cassation of Belgium, First Section, No. 4626, May 27, 1971, [1971] 1 Pasicrisie Belge 886, reported in CCH Common Market Reporter ¶ 8141. The excerpts below from this opinion are taken from the translation in the CCH Common Market Reporter.

> Whereas, where the conflict is between a rule of internal law and a rule of international law that has direct effects in the internal legal system, the rule established by the treaty must prevail; the preeminence of the treaty results from the very nature of international treaty law;
>
> Whereas, this is so *a fortiori* where the conflict is, as in this case, between a rule of internal law and a rule of Community law;
>
> In fact, the treaties that created Community law introduced a new legal system under which the Member States limited the exercise of their sovereign powers in the areas covered by such treaties;
>
> Whereas, Article 12 of the Treaty establishing the European Economic Community produces direct effects and creates for persons individual rights, which the national courts must protect;
>
> Whereas, it follows from the foregoing considerations that the court had a duty to reject the application of the provisions of internal law that are contrary to this provision of the Treaty;
>
> Whereas, having determined that in this case the rules of Community law and the rules of internal law were incompatible, the contested decision was able to declare, without violating the legal provisions indicated in the complaints, that the effects of the Law of March 19, 1968, were "terminated to the extent that it was in conflict with a directly applicable provision of international treaty law";
>
> . . . .

In its 1973 General Report (pp. 457–58), the Commission stressed the importance of assuring that regulations are viewed as directly applicable in the member states and enter into force in all of them at the same time. By the same token, it considered essential the adherence by member states to the deadlines set in Community acts that required member states to adopt implementing measures. It commented on recent cases in which the Court of Justice opposed the practice of some members of reproducing large parts of Community regulations in the text of national laws. That practice posed the risk of divergent interpretations of those regulations by national courts, and created "doubt as to the origin and the legal nature of the clauses thus reproduced". The right of member states "to transform directly applicable rules of Community law . . . would ultimately encroach on the exclusive jurisdiction which is conferred by the EEC Treaty on the Court to rule on any question of interpretation and of validity of Community regulations."

QUESTIONS

(1) Insofar as relevant to the van Gend case, Article 177 states that the "preliminary rulings" (*à titre préjudiciel*) must concern the "interpretation" of the Treaty. Has the Court rendered a "decision" binding the Tariefcommissie and the parties and dispositive of the litigation, or an "abstract interpretation" for the benefit of the Tariefcommissie? That is, has the Court applied the Treaty to "hold" for plaintiff or defendant? If

not, what effect does the Court's opinion have upon the judgment of the Dutch tribunal?

(2) Suppose that, after the Court's decision, the Tariefcommissie imposed the larger duty for reasons that were inconsistent with the decision. Does the Treaty provide that such a decision violates a member state's duty? Would any remedies under the Treaty be open at that stage to the Dutch importer or to other parties?

---

2. THE USE OF ARTICLE 177 BY NATIONAL COURTS

NOTE ON ARTICLE 177

Article 177 is the basic technique by which the Community achieves some control over decisions of national courts. The limited character of that control reflects the political tensions faced and compromises reached by the Treaty's drafters. Recall the comparable problems before this country in its early years and landmark decisions such as Martin v. Hunter's Lessee, 14 U.S. (1 Wheat.) 304, 4 L.Ed. 97 (1816), which confirmed federal judicial review of decisions of state courts raising federal questions.

Note the description in paragraphs (10) to (13) of the van Gend opinion of the procedure to be followed before the Court renders a decision under Article 177.[18] Article 20 of the Protocol on the Statute of the Court, referred to in paragraph (11), provides that the decision of a domestic court to make a reference to the Court of Justice under Article 177 shall be communicated to the parties in the case, all member states, the Commission, and on occasion the Council. Each is entitled to submit comments to the Court.

Analogies in National Legal Systems

Although distinctive to one accustomed to Anglo-American procedures, the role of the Court under Article 177 is similar to judicial procedures in several member countries. Appellate courts in a number of civil-law countries do not "decide" a case with the same effect as, for example, our Supreme Court; they may simply state their view on the points of law relevant to the decision appealed from, and either affirm or annul the lower-court decision. That is, the court does not "reverse and remand" with instructions to enter judgment for plaintiff or defendant. Although the situation varies among countries, indeed among different tribunals within a country, the

18. Paragraph (13) refers to the "conclusions" submitted to the Court by the Advocate General. As stated in Article 166, the Advocate General serves as an independent officer of the Court. He presents his evaluation of the arguments of the parties in each case, together with his reasoned conclusions and recommendations. Unlike a characteristic *amicus curiae* submitting a brief to a court in this country, the Advocate General is to be independent of and impartial towards particular interest groups within the Community.

lower court would generally attempt to apply the principles stated by the highest court.[19]

The French dual system of civil and administrative courts affords another and closer analogy to Article 177. Civil tribunals may face questions of the legality or interpretation of administrative acts that, for example, a party might have raised as a defense to an action. In certain circumstances, the tribunal is not competent to pass upon such a defense. The issue is referred to as a *question préjudicielle*.[20] The civil judge must suspend proceedings, and the party challenging the administrative act must present the question to the competent administrative tribunal. After that tribunal has responded to the referred question, the party files the answer with the civil judge, who then continues the proceedings.[21]

Other Common Market countries have procedures comparable to Article 177. Post-war constitutions of Germany and Italy established "constitutional courts," which were given the competence to resolve constitutional issues that arose before other tribunals. Under certain conditions, a lower court before which such an issue arises must suspend proceedings and certify the question to the constitutional court, which renders its opinion. The lower court then proceeds with the litigation. Decisions of the German and Italian constitutional courts appear at pp. 1307 and 1302, supra.

Comparisons can be drawn between Article 177 and some unusual judicial procedures in the United States. For example, the highest court in several states such as Massachusetts has jurisdiction to render advisory judgments upon requests made by the legislature or other institutions. Compare with Article 177 Fla.Stat.Ann. § 25.031, intended primarily to solve the problems created by diversity jurisdiction:

> The supreme court of this state may, by rule of court, provide that, when it shall appear to the supreme court of the United States, to any circuit court of appeals of the United States, or to the court of appeals of the District of Columbia, that there are involved in any proceeding before it questions or propositions of the laws of this state, which are determinative of the said cause, and there are no clear controlling precedents in the decisions of the supreme court of this state, such federal appellate court may certify such questions or propositions of the laws of this state to the supreme court of this state for instructions concerning such questions or propositions of state law, which certificate the supreme court of this state, by written opinion, may answer.

19. Appeal from the second decision of the lower court is generally permitted. For a description of the relationship between courts of appeal and the highest French civil court, the Cour de Cassation, see Tunc, Cours de Procédure Civile 411–423 (1961).

20. The French text of Article 177 reads at the start: "*La Cour de Justice est compétente pour statuer, à titre préjudiciel* . . . ."

21. See Waline, Droit Administratif 62–66 (9th ed. 1963).

Use of Article 177 by National Courts

A recurrent problem under Article 177 has been whether national courts will act in good faith and responsibly in certifying questions within the scope of that article rather than resolving such questions themselves. The problem finds its source in the requirement that a "court or tribunal" rather than a party is to refer the matter to the Court of Justice. That Court had occasion to state in a 1965 decision: [22]

> Under Article 177 of the Treaty, it is for the national court, and not for the parties in the action pending before it, to refer to the Court of Justice. Consequently, only the national court has the right to decide what questions are to be submitted to the Court of Justice. The parties may not change their content or have them declared moot.
>
> The Court of Justice, therefore, cannot be compelled, within the special procedure of Article 177, to concern itself, on the request of one of the parties, with a question that should be submitted not by the parties but by the national court itself, or with a motion based on Article 184. Furthermore, a contrary view is based on a failure to recognize that the drafters of Article 177 intended to establish a direct cooperation between the Court of Justice and the national courts in non-adversary proceedings, in which the parties have no right of initiative and in the course of which they are merely invited to submit comments.

Note the contrast between this aspect of Article 177 and the procedures through which a case in a state court raising a federal question may be reviewed by the United States Supreme Court under 28 U.S.C. § 1257.*

A national court might refuse to refer *any* question to the Court of Justice. Or it might suspend proceedings and refer *every* question which a party alleged to raise issues within the scope of Article 177. Neither extreme is likely. Rather, the duty of the national court is to ascertain when it is sensible to make a referral, when the allegation of a right or duty under the Treaty by a party has some minimum plausibility or significance to the litigation. The duty, as so defined, leaves flexibility and discretion to the national court—a discretion whose exercise has bred controversy at the Community and national levels. The attitudes of courts have revealed differences in approach, both among nations and over time within a particular national judiciary. We here consider decisions of two judiciaries, the French (below) and English (at p. 1286, infra).

French decisions, for example, reflect variations in the understanding of Article 177 among different courts and over time. Consider two relatively early decisions, of the highest French civil and

22. Hessische Knappschaft v. Maison Singer et Fils, Case No. 44/65, December 9, 1965, Recueil, Vol. XI–11, p. 1191. The translation is taken from the CCH Common Market Reporter ¶ 8042.

administrative courts.[23] A 1963 decision of a court of appeals had fined French parties for infringing French transport coordination rules. The parties appealed, contending that Articles 77–80 of the Rome Treaty had the effect of abolishing national rules in this field and that, consequently, the fines should not have been imposed. The Cour de Cassation rejected the appeal as well as the appellants' contention that this question should be referred to the Court of Justice. It stated its views of the meaning and purpose of Article 80 of the Rome Treaty and concluded that such article "has not rendered obsolete national legislation on the coordination of transport . . . . It follows that the Court of Appeals was justified in declaring that it had jurisdiction, to the exclusion of the European Court of Justice, to rule on the alleged conflict between Community law and national law, since Article 177 of the Treaty gives jurisdiction to the Court of Justice only in matters of Community law." [24]

A 1964 decision of the Conseil d'Etat dismissed an action brought by companies engaged in the import and distribution of petroleum products in France to annul certain executive acts, on the ground that they violated the Rome Treaty. The Conseil d'Etat rejected the argument that it should refer the questions raised to the Court of Justice, for in its view such referral was possible only in a case of "doubt" over the meaning or scope of Treaty provisions relevant to a case. After analyzing the contentions of the plaintiff companies and the relevant provisions of the Treaty, the court concluded that the arguments were not substantial and that disposition of the case did not depend upon "any question of interpretation of the Treaty." [25]

These problems were the subject of a question submitted by a member of the Assembly to the Commission. Excerpts from the question and the response of the Commission appear below: [26]

> Does the Commission know that the French Conseil d'Etat . . . has, in three decisions dated January 19, 1964, January 27, 1967, and February 10, 1967, rendered an interpretation of the EEC Treaty without referring to the Court of Justice of the European Communities in accordance with Article 177 of the EEC Treaty?
>
> In the decision of January 19, 1964, the French Conseil d'Etat held that referral to the Court of Justice of the European Communities is mandatory only where there are doubts

23. Other decisions of French courts treating questions of referral under Article 177 are set forth or described at pp. 1360, 1363, 1379, infra.

24. Jean-Paul Riff et Société Grande Limonaderie Alsacienne, Cour de Cassation, Criminal Chamber, Paris, Case No. 90.549/63–B, February 19, 1964, 170 Bull. des arrêts de la cour de cass. No. 57, p. 125. The translation is taken from the CCH Common Market Reporter ¶ 8027.

25. Re Société des Pétroles Shell-Berre, Conseil d'Etat (4th Subsection), June 19, 1964. 1964 Recueil des décisions du Conseil d'état 344. An English translation of this decision appears in [1964] C.M.L.Rep. Part 12, p. 462.

26. Written question No. 100, submitted by a member of the Assembly to the Commission. [1967] J. O. No. 270, p. 2. The translation is taken from the CCH Common Market Reporter ¶ 9200.

as to the meaning or scope of a Treaty provision applicable to the action before the court, . . .

Can the decisions of the French Conseil d'Etat referred to above be reconciled with Article 177 of the EEC Treaty, or has the French Conseil d'Etat in rendering those decisions repeatedly violated Article 177 of the EEC Treaty?

Does Article 169 of the EEC Treaty apply only to violations of the Treaty by the Governments of the Member States, or is the procedure provided for in Article 169 of the EEC Treaty also applicable when the Parliament of a Member State adopts a law conflicting with the Treaty or when a court of a Member State violates Article 177 of the EEC Treaty? . . .

ANSWER

. . .

In rendering its decision, which incidentally is dated June 19, 1964, the French Conseil d'Etat followed its traditional jurisprudence, which is to refer a case for preliminary ruling only where the court is faced with a genuine difficulty of interpretation. This practice compares with similar positions taken by the courts of the other Member States.

Application of these judicial practices calls for extreme caution in the area of Community law, since that law gives rise to many difficulties of interpretation which it is not always easy for the national courts to solve. These practices do not, however, prevent the courts of last resort from submitting questions for a preliminary ruling, as is shown by the recent referrals by several supreme courts of various Member States. The French Court of Cassation, in particular, although it follows the same principles as the French Conseil d'Etat, has referred a question to the Court of Justice for a preliminary ruling under Article 177 (decision of April 27, 1967). . . .

The Commission knows of no referral by the French Conseil d'Etat to the Court of Justice pursuant to Article 177 of the Treaty.

It follows from the above that the Commission, while recognizing that a referral to the Court of Justice for a preliminary ruling in the cases mentioned would have contributed to the development of Community law, was unable to find that there had been failure to comply with the provisions of Article 177.

The Commission is of the opinion that the procedure provided for in Article 169 of the EEC Treaty is applicable in the cases referred to by the Member of Parliament. . .

QUESTIONS

(1) What principal purpose does the Court in van Gend attribute to the jurisdiction conferred upon it under Article 177? Compare the purposes underlying the certiorari or appellate jurisdiction of the United States Supreme Court under 28 U.S.C.A. § 1257.*

(2) Suppose that the Dutch tribunal had refused to request the Court to render a preliminary decision. Would any remedies under the Treaty be available to the Dutch importer? To others?

NOTE ON ENGLISH AND COMMUNITY LAW

For the American student, it is the English experience which is most striking and suggestive about the legal-political tensions created by membership in the Community. Prior to the accession of the United Kingdom to the Community on January 1, 1973, Parliament enacted The European Communities Act 1972, Ch. 68 of 1972. Section 2(1) of that Act (referred to in the Bulmer decision below) states:

> All such rights, powers, liabilities, obligations and restrictions from time to time created or arising by or under the Treaties, and all such remedies and procedures from time to time provided for by or under the Treaties, as in accordance with the Treaties are without further enactment to be given legal effect or used in the United Kingdom shall be recognized and available in law, and be enforced, allowed and followed accordingly . . . .

This subsection thus provides for the direct effect within the United Kingdom of Community law, in contrast with the characteristic practice by which Parliament would from time to time enact laws that stated all treaty-derived rules meant to have internal effect.[27] Community law was perceived as an independent legal-political order, with effect in the United Kingdom without the mediation of national laws enacting or domesticating international norms. The parliamentary debates suggest that the subsection includes the provisions of the Treaties themselves, as well as regulations, directives, and decisions.[28]

Section 2(2) complements the preceding subsection by treating those provisions of Community law which are not directly applicable. In effect, the section delegates power to proceed by executive regulations to implement such Community provisions.

The problem of the supremacy of Community law is treated in part in Section 2(4), which contemplates the supremacy of Community laws with respect to all existing acts of Parliament, including those that were not explicitly repealed by this Act. Parliamentary supremacy remained intact with respect to the fundamental principle that a later Parliament could repeal this Act or modify its terms. But the sense of the debates and Act appears to suggest that in the event of inadvertent future conflict between national and Community norms, the courts are encouraged to interpret such norms to comport with international obligation.

Section 3(1) speaks with respect to Article 177 proceedings. It provides:

> For the purposes of all legal proceedings any question as to the meaning or effect of any of the Treaties, or as to the validity, meaning or effect of any Community instrument, shall be treated as a question of law (and, if not referred to the European Court, be for

27. See the brief discussion of the English rules with respect to treaties having internal effects at pp. 623–624, supra.

28. For general discussion of the debates preceding this enactment, see Forman, The European Communities Act 1972, 10 C.M.L.Rev. 39 (1973).

determination as such in accordance with the principles laid down and by and [sic] any relevant decision of the European Court).

. . .

Again the Act recognizes that Community law is distinct from but has effect together with national law. The effect of the section is to transform provisions of Article 177 into United Kingdom law. The following decision considers the obligations imposed by the Treaty and Article 177, and provides insight into jurisprudential attitudes of the English judiciary towards this new legal-political system.

H. P. BULMER LTD. v. J. BOLLINGER S.A.

English Court of Appeal (Civil Division), May 22, 1974.
[1974] 2 All E.R. 1226, CCH Common Market Reporter ¶ 8225.

[In this litigation, the problem posed was whether producers of cider in England violated rights of French producers of the sparkling wine known as Champagne, by selling their product under labels such as "champagne cider". The litigation involved unfair competition or passing-off before England joined the Common Market in January 1973. In March of that year, the French producers amended their pleadings to claim that the use of the word "champagne" on any beverage contravened Community law, relying on several Community regulations. Each side sought declaratory relief. The French producers requested a reference by the English court to the European Court of Justice under Article 177, to seek an opinion whether the use of "champagne" in connection with other beverages contravened Community law. The court of initial jurisdiction, the High Court, refused to refer the question at that stage, stating that it would try the entire case before reaching a decision on Article 177. The French producers appealed on this question to the Court of Appeal. There appear below excerpts from the opinion in the Court of Appeal of the Master of the Rolls, LORD DENNING.]

The French producers claim that, under those regulations, the name Champagne is their own special property. It must not be applied to any *wine* which is not produced in the Champagne District of France. So much the English producers concede. But the French producers go further. The say that the name Champagne must not be applied to any *beverage* other than their Champagne. It must not, therefore, be applied to cider or perry, even though they are not wines at all. The English producers deny this. They say that the regulations apply only to *wines*—the product of grapes—and not to cider or perry—the product of apples and pears.

This is obviously a point of the first importance to the French wine trade and to the English cider trade. It depends no doubt on the true interpretation of the regulations. . . .

. . .

To make the discussion easier to understand, I will speak only of the interpretation of "the Treaty," but this must be regarded as including the regulations and directives under it. I will make reference to the English courts because I am specially concerned with them: but this must be regarded as including the national courts of any Member State.

5. The Impact of the Treaty on English Law

The first and fundamental point is that the Treaty concerns only those matters which have a European element, that is to say, matters which affect people or property in the nine countries of the Common Market besides ourselves. The Treaty does not touch any of the matters which concern solely the mainland of England and the people in it. These are still governed by English law. They are not affected by the Treaty. But when we come to matters with a European element, the Treaty is like an incoming tide. It flows into the estuaries and up the rivers. It cannot be held back. Parliament has decreed that the Treaty is henceforward to be part of our law. It is equal in force to any statute. The governing provision is Section 2(1) of the European Community Act, 1972. . . .

The statute is expressed in forthright terms which are absolute and all-embracing. Any rights or obligations created by the Treaty are to be given legal effect in England without more ado. Any remedies or procedures provided by the Treaty are to be made available here without being open to question. In future, in transactions which cross the frontiers, we must no longer speak or think of English law as something on its own. We must speak and think of Community law, of Community rights and obligations, and we must give effect to them. This means a great effort for the lawyers. We have to learn a new system. The Treaty, with the regulations and directives, covers many volumes. The case law is contained in hundreds of reported cases both in the European Court of Justice and in the national courts of the Nine. Many must be studied before the right result can be reached. We must get down to it.

6. By What Courts Is the Treaty to Be Interpreted?

It is important to distinguish between the task of interpreting the Treaty—to see what it means—and the task of *applying* it—to apply its provisions to the case in hand. Let me put on one side the task of *applying* the Treaty. On this matter in our courts, the English judges have the final word. They are the only judges who are empowered to decide the case itself. They have to find the facts, to state the issues, to give judgment for one side or the other, and to see that the judgment is enforced.

Before the English judges can apply the Treaty, they have to see what it means and what is its effect. In the task of *interpreting* the Treaty, the English judges are no longer the final authority. They no longer carry the law in their breasts. They are no longer in a position to give rulings which are of binding force. The supreme tribunal for *interpreting* the Treaty is the European Court of Justice, at Luxembourg. Our Parliament has so decreed. . . .

. . .

That article shows that, if a question of interpretation or validity is raised, the European Court is supreme. It is the ultimate authority. Even the House of Lords has to bow down to it. If a question is raised before the House of Lords on the interpretation of the Treaty—on which it is necessary to give a ruling—the House of Lords is bound to refer it to the European Court. Article 177(3) uses that emphatic word "shall." The House has no option. It must refer the matter to the European Court, and, having done so, it is bound to follow the ruling in that *particular* case in which the point arises. But the ruling in that case does not bind *other* cases. The European Court is not absolutely bound by its previous decisions; see the Da Costa en Schaake N. V. case, (1963) 2 C.M.L.R. 224. It has no doctrine of *stare decisis*. Its decisions are much influenced by considerations of policy and economics: and, as these change, so may their rulings change. It follows from this that, if the House of Lords in a *subsequent* case thinks that a previous ruling of the European Court was wrong—or should not be followed—it can refer the point again to the European Court: and the European Court can reconsider it. On reconsideration it can make a ruling which will bind that *particular* case. But not subsequent cases. And so on.

7. The Discretion to Refer or Not to Refer

But short of the House of Lords, no other English court is bound to refer a question to the European Court at Luxembourg. Not even a question on the *interpretation* of the Treaty. Article 177(2) uses the permissive word "may" in contrast to "shall" in Article 177(3). In England the trial judge has complete discretion. If a question arises on the interpretation of the Treaty, an English judge can decide it for himself. He need not refer it to the Court of Luxembourg unless he wishes. He can say: "It will be too costly," or "It will take too long to get an answer," or "I am well able to decide it myself." If he does decide it himself, the European Court cannot interfere. None of the parties can go off to the European Court and complain. The European Court would not listen to any party who went moaning to them. The European Court takes the view that the trial judge has a complete discretion to refer or not to refer: see Rheinmühlen v. Einfuhr (February 16, 1974)—with which they cannot interfere: see Heinz Wöhrmann & Sohn KG v. Commission (1963) 2 C.M.L.R. 152. If a party wishes to challenge the decision of the trial judge in England—to refer or not to refer—he must appeal to the Court of Appeal in England. . . . The judges of the Court of Appeal, in their turn, have complete discretion. They can interpret the Treaty themselves if they think fit. If the Court of Appeal does interpret it itself, the European Court will not rebuke it for doing so. If a party wishes to challenge the decision of the Court of Appeal—to refer or not to refer—he must get leave to go to the House of Lords and go there. It is only in that august place that there is no discretion. If the point of interpretation is one which is "necessary" to give a ruling, the House *must* refer it to the European Court at Luxembourg. . . .

8. The Condition Precedent to a Reference: It Must Be "Necessary"

Whenever any English court thinks it would be helpful to get the view of the European Court—on the interpretation of the Treaty—there is a *condition precedent* to be fulfilled. It is a condition which applies to the House of Lords as well as to the lower courts. It is contained in the same paragraph of Article 177(2) and applies in Article 177(3) as well. It is this: An English court can only refer the matter to the European Court *"if it considers* that a decision on the question is necessary to enable it to give judgment." Note the words "if *it* considers." That is, "if the *English court* considers." On this point again the opinion of the English courts is final, just as it is on the matter of discretion. An English judge can say either "I consider it necessary," or "I do not consider it necessary." His discretion in that respect is final. Let me take the two in order.

. . .

9. The Guide Lines

Seeing that these matters of "necessary" and "discretion" are the concern of the English courts, it will fall to the English judges to rule upon them. Likewise, the national courts of other Member

States have to rule on them. They are matters on which guidance is needed. It may not be out of place, therefore, to draw attention to the way in which other national courts have dealt with them.

The English court has to consider whether "a decision of the question is *necessary* to enable it to give *judgment.*" That means judgment in the very case which is before the court. The Judge must have got to the stage when he says to himself: "This clause of the Treaty is capable of two or more meanings. If it means *this,* I give judgment for the plaintiff. If it means *that,* I give judgment for the defendant." In short, the point must be such that, whichever way the point is decided, it is conclusive of the case. Nothing more remains but to give judgment. The Hamburg court stressed the necessity in Re Adjustment of Tax on Petrol (1966), 5 C.M.L.R. at page 416. . . .

In some cases, however, it may be found that the same point —or substantially the same point—has already been decided by the European Court in a previous case. In that event it is not necessary for the English court to decide it. It can follow the previous decision without troubling the European Court. But, as I have said, the European Court is *not* bound by its previous decisions. So if the English court thinks that a previous decision of the European Court may have been wrong—or if there are new factors which ought to be brought to the notice of the European Court—the English court may consider it *necessary* to re-submit the point to the European Court. . . .

In other cases the English court may consider the point is reasonably clear and free from doubt. In that event there is no need to interpret the Treaty but only to apply it: and that is the task of the English court. It was so submitted by the Advocate General to the European Court in the Da Costa case (1963) 2 C.M.L.R. at page 234. It has been so held by the highest courts in France: . . ..

It is to be noticed, too, that the word is "necessary." This is much stronger than "desirable" or "convenient." There are some cases where the point, if decided one way, would shorten the trial greatly. But, if decided the other way, it would mean that the trial would have to go its full length. In such a case it might be "convenient" or "desirable" to take it as a preliminary point because it might save much time and expense. But it would not be "necessary" at that stage. When the facts were investigated, it might turn out to have been quite unnecessary. The case would be determined on another ground altogether. As a rule you cannot tell whether it is necessary to decide a point until all the facts are ascertained. So in general it is best to decide the facts first.

Assuming that the condition about "necessary" is fulfilled, there remains the matter of discretion. This only applies to the trial judge or the Court of Appeal, not to the House of Lords. The English court has a discretion either to decide the point itself or to refer it to the European Court. The national courts of the various member countries have had to consider how to exercise this discretion. The cases show that they have taken into account such matters as the following:—

The length of time which may elapse before a ruling can be obtained from the European Court. This may take months and months. . . .

The importance of not overwhelming the European Court by references to it. If it were overloaded, it could not get through its work. . . .

The need to formulate the question clearly. It must be a question of *interpretation only* of the Treaty. It must not be mixed up with the facts. It is the task of the national courts to find the facts and apply the Treaty. The European Court must not take that task on itself. In fairness to it, it is desirable to find the facts and state them clearly before referring the question. . . .

The difficulty and importance of the point. Unless the point is really difficult and important, it would seem better for the English judge to decide it himself. For in so doing, much delay and expense will be saved. . . .

The expense to the parties of getting a ruling from the European Court. That influenced a Nuremberg Court in the case of the Potato Flour Tax (1964) 3 C.M.L.R. 96 at page 106. On a request for interpretation, the European Court does not as a rule award costs, and for a simple reason. It does not decide the case. It only gives advice on the meaning of the Treaty. If either party wishes to get the costs of the reference, he must get it from the English court, when it eventually decides the case: see Sociale Verzekeringsbank v. Van der Vecht (1968) 7 C.M.L.R. at page 167.

The wishes of the parties. If both parties want the point to be referred to the European Court, the English court should have regard to their wishes, but it should not give them undue weight. The English court should hesitate before making a reference against the wishes of one of the parties, seeing the expense and delay which it involves.

10. The Principles of Interpretation

In view of these considerations, it is apparent that in very many cases the English courts will interpret the Treaty themselves. They will not refer the question to the European Court at Luxembourg. What then are the principles of interpretation to be applied? Beyond doubt the English courts must follow the same principles as the European Court. Otherwise there would be differences between the countries of the Nine. That would never do. All the courts of all nine countries should interpret the Treaty in the same way. They should all apply the same principles. It is enjoined on the English courts by Section 3 of the European Community Act, 1972, which I have read.

What a task is thus set before us! The Treaty is quite unlike any of the enactments to which we have become accustomed. The draftsmen of our statutes have striven to express themselves with the utmost exactness. They have tried to foresee all possible circumstances that may arise and to provide for them. They have sacrificed style and simplicity. They have foregone brevity. They have become long and involved. In consequence, the judges have followed suit. They interpret a statute as applying only to the circumstances covered by the very words. They give them a literal interpretation. If the words of the statute do not cover a new situation—which was not foreseen—the judges hold that they have no power to fill the gap. To do so would be a "naked usurpation of the legislative power," see Magor and St. Mellons R. D. C. v. Newport Borough Council (1952) A. C. 189. The gap must remain open until Parliament finds time to fill it.

How different is this Treaty. It lays down general principles. It expresses its aims and purposes. All in sentences of moderate length and commendable style. But it lacks precision. It uses words and phrases without defining what they mean. An English lawyer would look for an interpretation clause, but he would look in vain. There is none. All the way through the Treaty there are gaps and lacunae. These have to be filled in by the judges, or by regulations or directives. It is the European way. That appears from the decision of the Hamburg Court in Re Tax on Imported Lemons (1968) 7 C.M.L.R. 1.

Likewise the regulations and directives. They are enacted by the Council sitting in Brussels for everyone to obey. They are quite unlike our statutory instruments. They have to give the reasons on which they are based (Article 190). So they start off with pages of preambles, "whereas" and "whereas" and "whereas." These show the purpose and intent of the regulations and directives. Then follow the provisions which are to be obeyed. Here again words and phrases are used without defining their import. Such as "personal conduct" in the Directive 64/221/EEC, which was considered by the Vice-Chancellor, Sir John Pennycuick in Van Duyn v. Home Office (February 14, 1974). In case of difficulty, recourse is had to the preambles. These are useful to show the purpose and intent behind it all. But much is left to the judges. The enactments give only an outline plan. The details are to be filled in by the judges.

Seeing these differences, what are the English courts to do when they are faced with a problem of interpretation? They must follow the European pattern. No longer must they examine the words in meticulous detail. No longer must they argue about the precise grammatical sense. They must look to the purpose or intent. To quote the words of the European Court in the Da Costa case (1963) 2 C.M.L.R. at page 237, "they must deduce from the wording and the spirit of the Treaty the meaning of the Community rules." They must not confine themselves to the English text. They must consider, if need be, all the authentic texts, of which there are now eight, see Sociale Verzekeringsbank (1968) 7 C.M.L.R. 151. They must divine the spirit of the Treaty and gain inspiration from it. If they find a gap, they must fill it as best they can. They must do what the framers of the instrument would have done if they had thought about it. So we must do the same. Those are the principles, as I understand it, on which the European Court acts.

11. Applied to the Present Case

To return to the three questions I asked at the beginning.

First: I think these regulations should be interpreted by the High Court and the Court of Appeal in England. But if the cases should reach the House of Lords they must be interpreted by the European Court.

Second: The task of interpretation should be done at the time of the trial or the appeal, together with the other issues in the case.

Third: The English court should apply the same principles of interpretation as the European Court would do if it had to decide the point.

I come now to the two specific questions sought to be referred. The first question raised is: "Whether . . . . the use of the word 'Champagne' in connection with any beverage other than Champagne is a contravention of the provisions of European Community law." I do not think it is *necessary* at this stage to decide that question. Take the claim for passing-off. If the French growers succeeded in this claim for passing-off in English law—for an injunction and damages—it would not be necessary to decide the point under the regulations. So the facts must be found before it can be said that a reference is "necessary."

Next take the claim of the French growers for a declaration that the use of the expression "Champagne cider" and "Champagne perry" was contrary to European Community law. Mr. Sparrow, Q. C., said that it would be necessary on this issue to decide the point on the regulations. I do not agree. It is always a matter for the discretion of the judge whether to grant a declaration or not. He could very properly say in the present case: Whatever the true interpretation of the regulations, it is not a case in which I would make any declaration on the point. Taking that view, it would not be necessary to decide the point.

Even if it could be said to be necessary to decide the point, I think that an English court (short of the House of Lords) should not, as a matter of discretion, refer it to the European Court. It should decide the point itself. It would take much time and money to get a ruling from the European Court. Meanwhile, the whole action would be held up. It is, no doubt, an important point, but not a difficult one to decide. I think it would be better to deal with it as part of the whole case, both by the trial judge and by the Court of Appeal. If it should then go to the House of Lords, it will by that time have become clear whether it is a "necessary" point or not. If it is, then the House of Lords will refer it.

The second point is: "Whether a national court should . . . refer to the Court of Justice such a question as has been raised herein." The object of this question is to get a ruling from the European Court as to the circumstances in which a national court should refer a question of interpretation to the European Court. I am quite clear that it is unnecessary to ask this question. The answer is clear. It is not the province of the European Court to give any guidance or advice to the national court as to when it should, or should not, refer a question. That is a matter for the national court itself. It is no concern of the European Court.

In my opinion Mr. Justice Whitford was right in refusing to refer either of the questions. I would dismiss the appeal.

[Concurring opinions omitted.]

QUESTIONS

The 1973 General Report of the Commission states at p. 445, with respect to the accession to the Communities of the United Kingdom: "The resulting encounter between the Anglo-Saxon legal system, the traditional feature of which is the common law and the continental systems deriving originally from Roman law and mainly expressed as written texts is a very important event in the history of law in Europe."

(1) Does the opinion in the Bulmer case illustrate for you the type of "encounter" and resulting tensions between the common law and continental systems that are suggested in the preceding quotation?

(2) Assume that the United States (with necessary constitutional amendments) were a member of a multinational organization similar in structure to the EEC. Would an American court have perceived the same tensions between domestic modes of interpretation and those described as characteristic of the Court of Justice?

3. CONFLICTS BETWEEN COMMUNITY LAW AND NATIONAL CONSTITUTIONS

FLAMINIO COSTA v. ENTE NAZIONALE ENERGIA ELETTRICA IMPRESA GIÀ DELLA EDISON VOLTA (E.N.E.L.)

Court of Justice of the European Communities, Case No. 6/64, July 15, 1964. Recueil Vol. X, p. 1141.[29]

[After the Rome Treaty was approved and ratified by Italian legislative and executive authorities, Law No. 1203 of October 14, 1957 incorporated the Treaty into Italian law, in accordance with Italian constitutional practice giving internal effect to treaties only through a law of Parliament. Two provisions of the Italian Constitution were particularly relevant to the litigation described below. Article 10 states: "The Italian juridical system conforms to the generally recognized principles of international law." Article 11 states that Italy, "on conditions of equality with the other states, agrees to the limitations of her sovereignty necessary to an organization which will assure peace and justice among nations, and promotes and encourages international organizations constituted for this purpose." [30]

Under Law No. 1643 of December 6, 1962 and implementing decrees, the Italian Government nationalized the production and distribution of electrical energy and created an organization known as E.N.E.L., to which assets of the nationalized electrical enterprises were transferred. Maître Costa, a shareholder of a utility company which had been affected by the nationalization, refused to pay an electricity bill sent to him by E.N.E.L. in the amount of 1925 lire (approximately three dollars). In proceedings before the Giudice Conciliatore of Milan, a lower court of original jurisdiction and from which no "appeal" could be taken because of the small amount of the bill, Costa argued that the Italian nationalization law violated Articles 37, 53, 93 and 102 of the Rome Treaty and consequently was invalid. Costa requested that the Giudice Conciliatore (1) refer the question of constitutionality to the Italian Constitutional Court, which under Italian law had exclusive jurisdiction to resolve constitutional issues, and (2) invoke Article 177 of the Treaty to obtain a "preliminary decision" of the Court of Justice and an interpretation of the four articles. Costa relied upon the terms of the Rome Treaty and Article 11 of the Italian Constitution.

In view of the nature of the issues raised, the Giudice Conciliatore referred the question of constitutionality to the Italian Constitutional Court. While the question was pending before the Constitutional Court but before it rendered an opinion, the Giudice Conciliatore also invoked Article 177 and put to the Court of Justice the question whether the nationalization law violated the treaty. In a decision delivered a few months before the "preliminary ruling" of the Court of Justice, the Constitutional Court held that, notwithstanding the provisions of Article 11 of the Constitution and any possible inconsistency between the nationalization law and the Treaty, an Italian court should apply the law. Any violation of the Treaty

29. The translation is taken from the CCH Common Market Reporter ¶ 8023.

30. The English translations are taken from 2 Peaslee, Constitutions of Nations 483 (2d ed. 1965).

which might result was a question that, in the Court's opinion, related only to Italy's responsibility at an international level. The Constitutional Court reasoned that Law No. 1203 of 1957, incorporating the Rome Treaty into Italian law, was simply an ordinary statute which could be modified by a later Italian statute. Thus it was unnecessary to examine whether the law and Treaty were consistent.[31] (These views of the Constitutional Court should be compared with a later opinion of that Court at p. 1302, infra.)

In the proceedings before the Court of Justice, the Italian Government claimed that the Giudice Conciliatore had erred in submitting the question. It should not have resorted to Article 177 when it was obligated under national law to apply principles of Italian law rather than the Treaty.

The Court of Justice summarized the arguments of Maître Costa, E.N.E.L., the Italian Government and the Commission about the basic constitutional issue and the articles of the Treaty. Excerpts from its opinion follow:]

Regarding the application of Article 177

Plea based on the wording of the question

There is a complaint to the effect that the question involved seeks a judgment, by virtue of Article 177, as to whether a law is in accordance with the Treaty.

Under that article, however, national courts whose decisions are, as in the instant case, unappealable, must refer to the Court of Justice for a preliminary ruling on the interpretation of the Treaty when such a question is raised before them. Under this provision, the Court of Justice may neither apply the Treaty to a specific case nor rule on the validity of an internal measure in relation to the Treaty, as it could do within the framework of Article 169.[32] It can, however, sift out from a request that has been improperly formulated by a national court those questions only that concern the application of the Treaty. Thus the Court need not rule on the validity of an Italian law in relation to the Treaty, but need only interpret the above-mentioned articles in the light of the legal data submitted by the Giudice Conciliatore. . . .

Plea based on the judge's duty to apply internal law

The *Italian Government* claims that the request of the Giudice Conciliatore is "absolutely inadmissible" because the national court cannot make use of Article 177, since it is bound to apply an internal law.

Unlike ordinary international treaties, the EEC Treaty established its own legal order, which was incorporated into the legal sys-

31. This description of the proceedings in the Italian courts is based upon the conclusions of Advocate General Lagrange which were submitted to the Court of Justice before its decision.

32. [Eds.]—In his conclusions submitted to the Court of Justice, Advocate General Lagrange had stated: "The line to be drawn between application and interpretation is certainly one of the most delicate problems presented by Article 177, particularly since this line separates the jurisdiction of the Community court and the national courts, which no judge has been given the task of settling in case of conflict. Obviously, a conflict between the Court of Justice and the highest national courts could seriously disrupt the system of judicial control established by the Treaty—a system which rests on a necessary and sometimes organic collaboration between the two jurisdictional spheres."

tems of the Member States at the time the Treaty came into force and to which the courts of the Member States are bound. In fact, by establishing a Community of unlimited duration, having its own institutions, personality and legal capacity, the ability to be represented on the international level and, particularly, real powers resulting from a limitation of the jurisdiction of the States or from a transfer of their powers to the Community, the States relinquished, albeit in limited areas, their sovereign rights and thus created a body of law applicable to their nationals and to themselves.

This incorporation into the law of each member country of provisions of a Community origin, and the letter and spirit of the Treaty in general, have as a corollary the impossibility for the States to assert as against a legal order accepted by them on a reciprocal basis a subsequent unilateral measure which could not be challenged by it. The executory power of Community law cannot, in fact, vary from one State to another because of subsequent internal laws without jeopardizing fulfillment of the Treaty objectives set forth in Article 5, paragraph 2, and without bringing about a discrimination prohibited by Article 7. The obligations agreed to in the Treaty establishing the EEC would not be unconditional, only contingent, if they could be challenged by future legislative acts of the signatories. Wherever a right to act unilaterally is given to the States it is by virtue of a specific special clause (for example, Articles 15, 93(3), and 223–225). On the other hand, requests by the States for exceptions are subject to authorization procedures (for example, Articles 8(4), 17(4), 25, 26, 73, 93(2), third subparagraph, and 226) that would be purposeless if it were possible for the States to side-step their obligations through a mere law.

The preeminence of Community law is confirmed by Article 189, under which regulations are "binding" and "directly applicable in each Member State." This provision, which contains no reservation, would be meaningless if a Member State could unilaterally nullify its effects through a legislative act that could be asserted as against the Community texts.

As a result of all these factors, it would be impossible legally to assert any internal text whatsoever against the law created by the Treaty and originating from an independent source, considering the specific original nature of that law, without robbing it of its Community nature and without jeopardizing the legal foundation of the Community itself. The transfer by the States from their internal legal systems over to the Community legal order, of rights and obligations to reflect those set forth in the Treaty, therefore entails a definitive limitation of their sovereign rights, against which a subsequent unilateral act that would be incompatible with the Community concept cannot be asserted. Thus Article 177 may be applied, notwithstanding any national law, where there is a question of Treaty interpretation.

The questions submitted by the Giudice Conciliatore regarding Articles 102, 93, 53 and 37 seek, to begin with, an answer to whether these provisions have an immediate effect or create for those subject to a State's laws rights which the domestic courts must safeguard, and if so, what these rights are.

Regarding the interpretation of Article 102

. . .

This article, which belongs to the chapter on "approximation of laws," seeks to avoid an increase in the divergencies between the national laws with regard to the Treaty objectives. Through this provision, the Member States have limited their freedom of initiative by agreeing to comply with a suitable consultation procedure. By clearly putting themselves under the obligation to consult the Commission, for preventive purposes, whenever the proposed legislation might create even a minor risk of possible distortion, the States have thus entered into an agreement with the Community that binds them as States, but does not give rise to rights for those subject to their laws which the domestic courts must safeguard.

The Commission, for its part, is bound to see to it that the provisions of this article are respected, but this duty does not give individuals a possibility to allege, within the framework of Community law and through Article 177, either a default of the State concerned, or a failure on the part of the Commission. . . .

Regarding the interpretation of Article 53

Under Article 53, the Member States agree, without prejudice to other Treaty provisions, not to introduce any new restrictions on the establishment in their territories of nationals of other Member States. The duty thus subscribed to by the States amounts legally to a simple abstention. It is not subject to any condition, and neither its execution nor its effects require the enactment of any legislation either by the States or by the Commission. It is, therefore, complete, legally perfect, and consequently capable of producing direct effects in relations between the Member States and the persons under their jurisdiction.

A prohibition so clearly expressed, which came into force with the Treaty throughout the Community and was thus incorporated into the legal systems of the Member States, is law in these States and is of direct concern to their nationals, for whose benefit it has created individual rights which the domestic courts must safeguard.

The requested interpretation of Article 53 makes it imperative that it be considered within the context of the chapter relating to the right of establishment in which it is located. After having ordered, in Article 52, the gradual abolition of "restrictions on the freedom of establishment of nationals of a Member State in the territory of another Member State," the chapter in question provides in Article 53 that these States shall not introduce any "new restrictions on the establishment, in their territories, of nationals of the other Member States." The question, therefore, is under what conditions the nationals of the other Member States enjoy freedom of establishment. Article 52, paragraph 2, is explicit on this point . . . . In order for Article 53 to be respected, it is therefore sufficient that no new measure make the establishment of nationals of other Member States subject to stricter rules than those laid down for a State's own nationals, regardless of the legal make-up of the enterprises.

Regarding the interpretation of Article 37

. . .

Article 37, paragraph 2, lays down an unconditional prohibition which constitutes, not an obligation to do, but an obligation not to do. This obligation is not accompanied by any reservation that its execution depends on a positive act of internal law. By its very nature, this prohibition can produce direct effects in the legal relationship between the Member States and the persons under their jurisdiction.

. . .

The requested interpretation of Article 37, because of the complex nature of the text and the interrelationship between paragraphs 1 and 2, makes it imperative that the latter be considered within the framework of the entire chapter of which they are a part. This chapter is devoted to the "elimination of quantitative restrictions between the Member States."

Thus the purpose of the reference in Article 37, paragraph 2, to the "principles laid down in paragraph 1" is to prevent the introduction of any new "discrimination between the nationals of Member States as regards the supply or marketing of goods." This purpose having been specified, Article 37, paragraph 1, describes and prohibits the means by which this purpose might be thwarted. Thus all new monopolies or organizations referred to in Article 37, paragraph 1, are prohibited by the reference in Article 37, paragraph 2, in so far as they tend to introduce new discriminations as to supply and marketing. The judge in the original action must therefore first investigate whether this purpose is actually thwarted, i. e., whether the measure at issue itself results in a new discrimination between the nationals of the Member States as to supply and marketing, or whether this will be a consequence of the measure.

In addition, there is reason to consider the means referred to in Article 37, paragraph 1. This article prohibits the introduction, not of all State monopolies, but of "trading" monopolies, in so far as they tend to introduce the above-mentioned discriminations. In order to come within the prohibition of this provision, the State monopolies and the organizations in question must, on the one hand, have as their purpose transactions in a commercial product that is likely to be the object of competition and of trade between the Member States and, on the other hand, play an active part in such trade. It is for the judge in the original action to decide in each case whether the economic activity concerned involves a certain product which, by its nature and because of technical or international requirements to which it is subject, can play an active part in imports or exports between the nationals of the Member States. . . .

THE COURT, ruling on the plea of inadmissibility based on Article 177, declares and decrees:

The questions submitted by the Giudice Conciliatore of Milan by virtue of Article 177 are admissible in so far as they concern, in this case, an interpretation of the provisions of the EEC Treaty, since no subsequent unilateral act can be asserted against the rules of the Community;

rules as follows:

(1) Article 102 contains no provisions capable of entailing for those subject to the law rights which the domestic courts must safeguard; . . .

(3) Article 53 constitutes a Community rule capable of entailing for those subject to the law rights which the domestic courts must safeguard.

These provisions prohibit any new measure whose object is to make the establishment of nationals of other Member States subject to stricter rules than those reserved for those subject to the law, regardless of the legal make-up of the enterprises.

(4) All of the provisions of Article 37, paragraph 2, constitute a Community rule capable of entailing for those subject to the law rights which the domestic courts must safeguard.

Within the framework of the question presented, the object of these provisions is to prohibit any new measure that is contrary to the principles of Article 37, paragraph 1, i. e., any measure, the object or effect of which is a new discrimination between the nationals of the Member States as to supply and marketing, through monopolies or organizations that must, on the one hand, have as their object transactions in a commercial product that can involve competition and trade between Member States and, on the other hand, play an active part in such trade; . . .

COMMENT

Proceedings thereafter continued before the Giudice Conciliatore of Milan. The judge held that Law No. 1643 and implementing decrees were inapplicable, and that Costa was not bound to pay E.N.E.L. Lire 1.925. 21 Foro Padano, V, 3–8 (No. 5, May 1966). The principal ground for the decision was that the Law conflicted with Article 37, as interpreted by the Court of Justice.

> . . . Electric power, both before and after Law No. 1643 became effective, was and is a commercial product capable of being the object of competition and trade among members of the E.E.C. . . . With the establishment of E.N.E.L., a monopolistic measure has been instituted which results in discrimination between Italian nationals and nationals of other member states with respect to conditions of supply and sale.

The Giudice Conciliatore quoted at length from the part of the Court of Justice's opinion declaring the supremacy of Community over national law, even if the national law was enacted after the Rome Treaty.

The Giudice Conciliatore also held that the Law could not be enforced because the Italian Government failed to consult the Commission as required by Article 102. It stated:

> . . . The Court of Justice decided that Article 102 does not create rights for individuals that may be enforced by national courts; but we think that this interpretation excludes only the right of petition by individuals before Community organs. It is not possible that the Court of Justice meant to go beyond its powers so as to prevent a citizen from bringing an action under a national legal system, in accordance with the procedural rules of that system, whenever a municipal statute has been enacted in violation of certain required procedures. The consequences under municipal law that may arise from a provision of the Treaty which has been authentically interpreted fall within the exclusive competence of national courts . . . . [Individuals can invoke this failure to comply with procedures] within the national legal system where all the laws, including those relating to procedures for the creation of law, are to be observed and their violation offends rights of every citizen to observance of rules . . . .

It should be noted that the nationalization measure had become the subject of sharp political dispute in Italy. One can question whether the views of the Giudice Conciliatore reflect principally pro-European sentiment or the domestic political controversy.

Note that, in resolving conflicts between Community and national law, the Court of Justice was not aided by an explicit "supremacy clause" comparable to Article VI of the United States Constitution.* Article 5 and the second paragraph of Article 189 are the Treaty provisions of general application which are the closest equivalents to such a clause.

The statements in the opinions in the van Gend and Costa cases that certain articles have "immediate effects" and give private parties "individual rights" which they can assert before national courts recall the problem of self-executing treaties within the United States.[33] The discussion in the Costa case of Article 102 suggests a variety of problems raised by the Treaty not only about the "self-executing" nature of an article but also about the stage at which the Court is competent to apply Treaty provisions. A number of other provisions, such as Article 226, give discretion to the Commission or other Community organs to determine whether national laws or practices are consistent with the Treaty or, if inconsistent, whether they should nonetheless be authorized as temporary derogations from Treaty requirements. If such provisions were interpreted to confer rights upon private parties to challenge national laws or practices before national courts, interpretative questions about them might come before the Court under Article 177, before the Commission or other organs had investigated a matter and reached their decisions. This consideration —comparable to the doctrine of primary jurisdiction in administrative law in this country—would surely inhibit a conclusion that treaty provisions of this character were self-executing.

QUESTIONS

(1) How does the Court support its conclusions about the relationship between the Rome Treaty and national law? Does the opinion find textual foundation in the Treaty?

(2) Suppose that Article 5 stated that the Treaty constituted "supreme law," binding upon the authorities of the member states notwithstanding any inconsistent provisions of their constitutions or laws.

(*a*) Would such a clause resolve for a national judge conflicts between the Treaty and national law posed by cases such as van Gend and Costa?

(*b*) Suppose that the United States entered into a treaty containing such a clause. One of the articles provides that nationals of the other signatory have the same right as American citizens to purchase land. Two years later, federal legislation prohibits acquisition of land containing mineral resources by aliens. An alien seeking to purchase such land from a willing vendor challenges the legality of the federal statute. What result?[34]

33. See pp. 580–588, supra.

34. Compare the decisions of the United States Supreme Court appearing at pp. 555 and 559, supra.

(*c*) What political and historical considerations would you stress in distinguishing between the effect of our Supremacy Clause upon internal federal-state relationships and the effect of a comparable clause in an international organization such as the Common Market?

(3) Does the Costa decision (a) simply restate van Gend or further develop the Community's constitutional law, (b) give the Italian court more guidance than the Tariefcommissie received as to how it *should* resolve conflicts between the Treaty and national law, (c) purport to answer this question from the perspective of an international tribunal or organization, or from the *internal* perspective of an Italian court and Italian law?

(4) Suppose that Italian officials order that a French national working in Italy be deported, pursuant to an Italian law of 1968 requiring deportation of workers in certain industries faced with an excess labor supply. The French national alleges, with good reason, that regulations of the Council, issued during the early 1960's and implementing Articles 48–51 of the Treaty, give him the right to remain and work in Italy. He challenges the deportation order before appropriate Italian authorities, who refer the constitutional issue posed by the litigation to the Italian Constitutional Court. What arguments would you stress before that court on behalf of the worker? If the decision were adverse and the worker deported, could Italy's action be challenged before the Court of Justice?

(5) In the light of the criteria noted in the van Gend and Costa opinions for determining whether provisions of the Treaty give private parties "individual rights" which national courts must safeguard, consider how the Court of Justice should decide the following cases:

(*a*) Suppose that a member state retained a duty on exports in 1963, in violation of Article 16. If an exporter had protested the tax before a national tribunal, and that tribunal had referred the question to the Court under Article 177, what decision?

(*b*) Suppose that regulations issued by the Council under Article 49 provide that workers in stated categories have the right to remain and work in another member country after one year's residence in that country. A French national, not covered by the regulations because of the nature of his employment, works in Germany and after 13 months is served with a deportation order because of an excessive labor supply in his field. He cites Article 7 of the Treaty as a defense. Assuming a reference under Article 177, what result?

(6) How faithful was the Giudice Conciliatore in its final judgment to the opinion of the Court of Justice?

NOTE ON COMMUNITY AND NATIONAL LAW

The Costa case underscores the distinction between bilateral or multilateral treaties of a traditional character and the Rome Treaty with its "supranational" or "federal" aspirations for the Community. The conflicting claims upon the judiciaries in the nine member countries recall problems faced by our own judiciary in the decisions at pp. 555, 559, supra. The Court of Justice, however, might have considered such decisions poor analogies to, remote from, the problems faced by the Italian courts in Costa. Those American decisions and such other decisions as Reid v. Covert, p. 564, supra, reflect a traditional national perspective upon international agreements—namely, the supremacy of the domestic constitutional order in instances of conflict between that order and international obligation. But the Court of Justice suggested that the Rome Treaty created a different relationship among member states. One could not meaningfully speak of "conflict" between the legal orders of the member states and the Community. Rather the opinion could be read to suggest a federal distribution of powers within a unified legal structure. But whether the Community was to be viewed as a nascent federalism, as a "supranational" organization, or simply as a unique form of international organization that resists any one characterization, the Court rejected the argument that conflicts between Community and national law were to be resolved within the differing constitutional frameworks of the member countries.

After the decision of the Italian Constitutional Court but before the Court of Justice rendered its opinion, Commission President Hallstein discussed these questions in a speech to the Assembly.[35]

> . . . The Community's legal order is . . . built into the law of the member states in many ways. Governmental bodies, administrative authorities and courts in the member states increasingly apply rules of community law. These intersections of two legal systems are not novel. Federal unions of various strengths and types provide examples. The rule that each part can only legislate validly in the area of competence allotted to it or which it has retained—a rule which, as we know, also applies to our Community—avoids a situation where different legal systems are in constant conflict. If, however, there is overlapping competence and there is a clash of equally valid rules, rules apparently requiring equal respect, it follows from the merger into a larger order that the law of the superior association prevails—but, I repeat, only in the area of its competence. . . .
>
> . . . The precedence [of the Community] which is under discussion must meet with a unified solution valid for the entire Community. Any attempt to solve this question to suit the peculiar characteristics of the member states, their constitutions and political structures, impairs the unifying character of European integration and therefore the bases of our Community. The Commission considers it particularly important to state this.

Constitutional provisions adopted after World War II in several Common Market countries either assure certain treaties of supremacy over domestic law, or are at least phrased so as to permit national courts to reach this conclusion as a matter of interpretation. See the excerpts from the Netherlands Constitution, p. 624, supra, and the

35. Débats du Parlement Européen, Session 1964–1965 (IX/64), No. 72, p. 149.

1958 French Constitution, p. 624, supra. In other countries, the picture is clouded. Costa indicates the Italian dilemma, in the context of the Italian constitutional provisions (Articles 10 and 11) set forth at p. 1293, supra. The validity of the Treaty and its implementing regulations has been challenged for over a decade in litigation in the German courts. (Relevant provisions of the German Basic Law appear at p. 623, supra.) The following litigations which involved decisions of the Italian and German Constitutional Courts illustrate these problems.

FRONTINI v. MINISTERO DELLE FINANCE

Constitutional Court of Italy, Case 183, December 27, 1973.
1974 Giurisprudenza Italiana, I, 1, 513, [1974] C.M.L.Rep. 372.

[In civil proceedings against the Minister of Finance, plaintiffs challenged the amounts of agricultural levies on certain imports that were determined by Community regulations. They raised before the lower court a number of constitutional questions which were referred by that court to the Italian Constitutional Court. The Constitutional Court deals with several of these questions in the following excerpts (taken from the English translation in [1974] C.M.L. Rep. 372) from its opinion:]

The constitutional validity of [Article 189] of the Treaty is being questioned under various aspects by means of an impugning of the implementation statute which adapted our internal law to it. It is noted in the reference orders that by Article 189 the binding effect and immediate applicability as against the state and Italian citizens of acts which have the force and power of ordinary statutes, issued from organs other than those to which the Constitution attributes the exercise of the legislative function; that thereby is introduced into our system a new source of primary legislative process, with the resultant removal of legislative power from the normal constitutionally authorised organs of the state, in matters of wide and generically characterised content; that as against Community regulations there are lacking the guarantees laid down by the Constitution for the ordinary statutes of the state (forms of promulgation and publication, possibility to promote repeal referendum, admissibility of control by this Court to protect the fundamental rights of the citizens); that, finally, via these regulations financial obligations (*prestazioni patrimoniali*) can be imposed on Italian citizens in violation of the statute monopoly (*riserva di legge*) laid down by Article 23 of the Constitution. Article 189 of the Rome Treaty would involve not only limitations on sovereignty but also "an inadmissible surrender of sovereignty, or an alteration of the fundamental constitutional structure itself of our state", and Article 11 of the Constitution would not remove the envisaged constitutional doubt "either because, apart from its value as a statement of guiding policy, it does not exclude the need of a constitutional statute for limitations of national sovereignty or because it would seem directed to ends other than the typically economic ends pursued by the setting up of the EEC".

The question must be dismissed. The EEC Treaty Ratification Act 1957, whereby the Italian Parliament gave full and complete execution to the Treaty instituting the EEC, has a sure basis of validity in Article 11 of the Constitution, whereby Italy "consents, on condition of reciprocity with other States, to limitations of sovereignty necessary for an arrangement which may ensure peace and justice between the nations" and then "promotes and favours the international organisations directed to such an aim". That provision, which not by chance is included in the "fundamental principles" of the Constitution, indicates a clear and precise political aim: the makers of the Constitution referred, in the preamble, to the adherence of Italy to the United Nations Organisation, but were inspired by policy principles of general validity, of which the Economic Community and the other European regional organisations constitute a concrete actualisation.

. . .

The makers of the Constitution, after having stated in Article 10 that the Italian legal system was in conformity with the rules of general international law, intended in Article 11 to define the opening of Italy to the most binding forms of international collaboration and organisation, and to that end formally authorised the acceptance through treaty, on conditions of equality with the other States and for the ends there set out, of the necessary "limitations of sovereignty". . . .

. . .

This grant of normative power to the organs of the EEC, with the corresponding limitation of that held by the constitutional organs of the individual member-States, was not granted unilaterally nor without Italy having acquired powers within the compass of the new institution. In signing the Rome Treaty Italy freely made a political choice of historical importance and has acquired, with its participation in the European Economic Community, the right to nominate its own representatives in the institutions of the Community—the Assembly and the Council—and to take part in the appointments to the Commission and the Court of Justice. The limitations on its sovereignty to which it has agreed have therefore their equivalent in the powers acquired in the much bigger Community of which Italy is part and with which has been actively initiated the process of integration of the States of Europe.

. . . In truth, as this Court has already stated in Costa v. Enel, Article 11 means that, when its pre-conditions are met, it is possible to sign treaties which involve limitation of sovereignty and to agree to make them executory by an ordinary statute. The provision would finish emptied of its specific normative content if it were held that for every limitation of sovereignty covered by Article 11 recourse had to be had to a constitutional statute. It is clear that it has not only a substantive but also a procedural value, in the sense that it permits such limitations of sovereignty, on the conditions and for the ends therein set out, releasing Parliament from the necessity of making use of its power of constitutional amendment.

. . . The regulations issuing from the organs of the EEC within the meaning of Article 189 of the Treaty of Rome belong to the Community's own order: its laws and the internal law of the individual member-States can be described as autonomous and distinct legal systems, albeit co-ordinated in accordance with the division of power laid down and guaranteed by the Treaty. Fundamental requirements of equality and legal certainty demand that the Community norms, which cannot be characterised as a source of international law, nor of foreign law, nor of internal law of the individual States, ought to have full compulsory efficacy and direct application in all the member-States, without the necessity of reception and implementation statutes, as acts having the force and

value of statute in every country of the Community, to the extent of entering into force everywhere simultaneously and receiving equal and uniform application to all their addressees. It is also in accordance with the logic of the Community system that EEC regulations, provided that they are complete in themselves, which as a rule characterises norms governing inter-citizen relations as the immediate source of rights and obligations both for the States and for their citizens in their capacity as subjects of the Community, should not be the subject of state-issued provisions which reproduce them, either in full or in an executory manner, and which could differ from them or subject their entry into force to conditions, even less which take their place, derogate from them or abrogate them, even in part.
. . . .

The system of relationship between Community order and internal order, as set out above, provides a sure solution for the doubts expressed in the reference order about the absence, in relation to the EEC regulations, of the guarantees which our Constitution has regarding state legislation, the enactment and publication of statutes, the admissibility of the repeal referendum and the judicial review of constitutionality. The constitutional provisions govern solely the legislative activity of the organs of the Italian State, and by their nature are not referable or applicable to the activity of the Community organs, which are governed by the Rome Treaty, which constitutes the constitution (*lo statuto fondamentale*) of the Community.

In this respect there are certain further considerations. It should first be remembered that the Treaty contains in Part V—Institutions of the Community—(Articles 137–209) a legislative organigramme of the composition, the powers, and the exercise of the functions of the various organs, and through these the Community order is shown to have a complex of statutory guarantees and its own system of judicial supervision. In so far as concerns particularly the regulations referred to in Article 189, apart from the already stated limits of sectoral competence *ratione materiae* imposed on the legislative power of the Council and the Commission by the provisions of the Treaty, it should be mentioned that the actions of those organs are subject to the supervision of the Assembly, comprising representatives delegated by the member-States, and intended, in the hoped-for later development of the process of integration, to assume a more direct political representativeness and wider powers, and that, on the other hand, the actions of the Council and Commission take place with the constant and direct participation of our Government, and so also under the indirect, but not thereby the less vigilant and attentive, supervision of the Italian Parliament.

. . .

In this same perspective too the question should be judged of the constitutional legitimacy of Article 189 of the EEC Treaty, in so far as it permits the issue of regulations involving the levy of monetary obligations. That does not involve a derogation from the statute monopoly (*riserva di legge*) laid down in Article 23 of the Constitution, since that provision is not formally applicable to the Community legislation, which comes out of an autonomous production source, part of an order which is distinct from the internal order. On the other hand, from the substantive viewpoint also, it seems obvious to observe that that historical guarantee could not be said to be violated so long as the Community regulations have statutorily to conform to the guiding principles and criteria of the Treaty instituting the Community.

Equally unfounded appear the doubts as to the lack of control by this court in protection of the fundamental rights guaranteed by our Constitution to the citizens.

It should be remembered particularly that the order of the European Economic Community contains a special system of court supervision, characterised by the fullness of jurisdiction attributed to the Court of Justice by Articles 164 et seq. of the Treaty. . . .

. . .

It should, on the other hand, be mentioned that the legislative competence of the organs of the EEC is laid down by Article 189 of the Rome Treaty as limited to matter concerning economic relations, i. e. matter with regard to which our Constitution lays down the statute monopoly (*riserva di legge*) or the reference to statute (*rinvio alla legge*), but the precise and exact provisions of the Treaty provide a safe guarantee, so that it appears difficult to form even abstractly the hypothesis that a Community regulation can have an effect in civil, ethico-social, or political relations through which provisions conflict with the Italian Constitution. It is hardly necessary to add that by Article 11 of the Constitution limitations of sovereignty are allowed solely for the purpose of the ends indicated therein, and it should therefore be excluded that such limitations of sovereignty, concretely set out in the Rome Treaty, signed by countries whose systems are based on the principle of the rule of law and guarantee the essential liberties of citizens, can nevertheless give the organs of the EEC an unacceptable power to violate the fundamental principles of our constitutional order or the inalienable rights of man. And it is obvious that if ever Article 189 had to be given such an aberrant interpretation, in such a case the guarantee would always be assured that this Court would control the continuing compatibility of the Treaty with the above-mentioned fundamental principles. . . .

. . .

INTERNATIONALE HANDELSGESELLSCHAFT mbH v. EINFUHR-UND VORRATSSTELLE FUR GETREIDE UND FUTTERMITTEL

Court of Justice of the European Communities, Case No. 11/70, December 17, 1970. Recueil Vol. XVI, p. 1125.[36]

[In this and related cases decided by the Court of Justice, the question posed was the validity of 1967 regulations of the Council and Commission. Those regulations subjected the issuance of import and export certificates for agricultural products to the deposit of a security bond guaranteeing performance of the certificate-holder's undertaking to import or export during the period of validity of the certificate. This undertaking was to be forgiven, and the deposit was to be released in event of failure to comply with the certificate's specifications, only in circumstances regarded as *force majeure*. The regulations were part of a comprehensive planning within the Community of agricultural production and trade.

An export-import firm in Germany had obtained a license to export 20,000 tons of groats. A lesser tonnage was in fact exported within the time limit, and the relevant administrative agency deduct-

36. The translation is taken from the CCH Common Market Reporter ¶ 8126.

ed a percentage of the security deposit. The exporter brought an action before a German administrative court for return of the entire deposit. That court stayed proceedings and referred to the Court of Justice, under Article 177, the question whether the provisions of the regulations (including restrictions on the power of a court to order forfeiture of a deposit only in cases of *force majeure*) were valid. The regulations were challenged before the German court, among other grounds, as violative of provisions in the German Basic Law (Constitution) guaranteeing freedom of action and economic freedom in trade. In the excerpts below from its opinion, the Court of Justice refers to the posting of a bond in connection with the issuance of export licenses as the "bond system".]

According to the reasons given in the referral decision, the administrative court has held the provisions involved to be illegal, and thus considers it essential that the existing legal insecurity be ended. The administrative court believes that the bond system is contrary to certain basic principles of national constitutional law which must be safeguarded within the framework of Community law, so that the priority of supranational law must yield to the principles of the German Basic Law. Specifically, the bond system is contrary to the principles of free development and freedom of action, economic freedom, and the principle of proportionateness, as set forth in Article 2, paragraph 1, and Article 14 of the Basic Law. The obligation to import or export resulting from the issuance of an import or export license together with the duty to post bond is an inordinate intervention in the self-determination of trade because the purpose of the regulations could have been attained through less drastic measures.

The uniform application of Community law throughout the EEC would be impaired if in deciding on the legality of acts of the Community institutions rules or principles of national law were applied. The legality of these acts can be judged only under Community law because the law created by the Treaty and hence stemming from an autonomous source cannot, because of its independent nature, be challenged in court on the basis of national law, regardless of what that may be, without losing its character as Community law and without jeopardizing the legal basis of the Community itself. Therefore, when it is claimed that the basic rights laid down in the constitution of a Member State or the basic principles of a national constitution have been impaired, this has no bearing on the legality of a Community act or its effectiveness in the territory of that State.

It must, however, be decided whether a similar guarantee under Community law was ignored, because the recognition of basic rights is one of the general principles of law which the Court of Justice must safeguard. The protection of these rights, while it was inspired by the constitutional traditions common to all Member States, must be carried over into the structure and goals of the Community. Accordingly, with regard to the doubts expressed by the administrative court, it must be decided whether the bond system violates basic rights which the Community legal order must safeguard.

[The Court found the two regulations to be valid. The issuance of import and export licenses, and the related posting of bonds guaranteeing that the transactions for which those licenses were requested were carried out, were necessary for the required knowledge and planning of the agricultural market and for the proper application of intervention mechanisms in that market. Projections would be impossible if licenses did not bind their holders to act in accordance with the license application. The bonds were the most effective means of assuring compliance—more effective, for example, than a system of fines after the fact. The exception from forfeiture of the bond for failure to comply with the license on grounds of *force majeure* was not limited to acts of impossibility but included abnormal circumstances beyond the control of the importer or exporter. Thus the exception had sufficient flexibility, and the regulations did not impose an unjustifiable or excessive burden upon the exporter.]

COMMENT

The German administrative court which stayed proceedings to seek a preliminary ruling from the Court of Justice received that ruling.[37] The German court considered relevant Community regulations to be invalid because they infringed fundamental principles of the German Basic Law. The plaintiff company's claim for a cancellation of the bond forfeiture should thus be upheld. In view of the conflict with the ruling of the Court of Justice, the administrative court determined to suspend proceedings once more and to submit the case to the German Federal Constitutional Court (*Bundesverfassungsgericht*) for a decision about the validity of the regulations, pursuant to the Constitutional Court's competence under Article 100 (1) of the Basic Law. Excerpts from that opinion of the Constitutional Court appear below.

DECISION OF THE FEDERAL CONSTITUTIONAL COURT OF THE FEDERAL REPUBLIC OF GERMANY OF 29 MAY 1974

1974 Neue Juristische Wochenschrift 1697.

[A Senate (panel) of the Constitutional Court, answering the questions submitted to it by the Administrative Court referred to above, found nothing in the guarantee of free exercise of occupations in Art. 12 of the Basic Law that was denied by the EEC rules. Portions of the opinion dealing with the competence of the Constitutional Court to accept the reference follow. On this point the panel divided 5–3.]

. . . In this case it is not enough simply to speak of the "primacy" of Community law over national constitutional law in order to justify the result that Community law must always prevail over national constitutional law, since otherwise the Community would be placed in jeopardy. Just as little as international law is put in jeopardy by Art. 25 of the Basic Law [see p. 623, supra] when it specifies that the general principles of international law have precedence only over ordinary federal legislation, and just as little as a foreign legal system is put in jeopardy when it is displaced by the *ordre public* of the Federal Republic of Germany, just so little is Community law put in question if in exceptional cases Community law cannot prevail over mandatory norms of constitutional law. The linkage of the Federal Republic of Germany (and of all member states) by the Treaty is, according to the sense and

37. Internationale Handelsgesellschaft mbH V. Einführ-Und Vorratsstelle fur Getreide und Futtermittel, Verwaltungsgericht Frankfurt am Main, Case II/2 E 228/69, November 24, 1971, reported in [1972] C.M.L.Rep. 177.

spirit of treaties, not one-sided but also binds the Community created by them to do its part to resolve the conflict here assumed—that is, to seek a solution which is compatible with a mandatory rule of the constitutional law of the Federal Republic of Germany. The appeal to such a conflict is thus not by itself in violation of the Treaty but puts in motion the Treaty mechanism within the European organs which solves the conflict politically.

. . .

5. From the relationship between the Basic Law and Community law thus presented, the following conclusions as to the competences of the European Court of Justice and the Constitutional Court:

(a) The European Court is, consistently with the rules of competence of the Treaty, responsible for deciding upon the legal effectiveness of the norms of Community law (including the unwritten elements of Community law that, in its judgment, exist) and upon their interpretation. Incidental questions from the national law of Germany (or another member state) it decides without being binding on said state. Discussions in the reasoning of its decisions that a certain content of a Community norm parallels in content or is compatible with a constitutional prescription of a national law—here with a constitutional guarantee of the Basic Law—represent *obiter dicta* that are not binding.

In the framework of this competence the Court establishes the content of Community law with binding effect for all member states. Correspondingly, the courts of the Federal Republic of Germany are obligated, within the terms of Art. 177 of the Treaty, to obtain the decision of the European Court before they take up the question of the compatibility of the norm of Community law that is important for the decision with the basic guarantees of the Basic Law.

(b) The Constitutional Court never decides, as appears from the preceding explanation, about the validity or invalidity of a prescription of Community law. It can at the most come to the result that such a prescription may not be applied by the authorities or courts of the Federal Republic of Germany insofar as it conflicts with a constitutional norm of the Basic Law. Incidental questions of Community law, it can (just as is conversely the case with the European Court) itself decide insofar as the prerequisites of Article 177 of the Treaty, which binds the Constitutional Court too, are not present or there is already a decision of the European court binding the Constitutional Court under Community law.

6. Basic rights can be legally guaranteed in several ways and correspondingly enjoy plural judicial protection. The European Court regards itself, as its case law demonstrates, as also competent to protect basic rights according to the standards of Community law, through its case law. To protect the basic rights guaranteed in the Basic Law is the task of the Constitutional Court alone in the framework of the competences allocated to it in the Basic Law. This constitutional law task can be taken from it by no other court. Insofar as citizens of the Federal Republic of Germany have a claim to the judicial protection of their rights guaranteed in the Basic Law, their status can suffer no limitations for the sole reason that they are affected directly by legal acts of authorities or courts of the Federal Republic of Germany that base themselves on Community law. Otherwise there would open up a dangerous gap in judicial protection precisely for the most elementary status rights of the citizen. Moreover, there applies to the constitution of a community of states with a libertarian-democratic constitution the same notion

that applies to a libertarian-democratic federal state. No harm is done to the Community and its libertarian (and democratic) constitution, if the members in their constitutions protect more strongly the rights of their citizens than does the Community.

. . .

The conclusion is: So long as the process of integrating the Community has not progressed so far that Community law contains a list of basic rights formulated by a parliament and a full legal force, which is an adequate match to the list of basic rights of the Basic Law, after the obtaining of a decision of the European Court as provided by Art. 177 of the Treaty, a reference by a court of the Federal Republic of Germany to the Constitutional Court in a proceeding to decide the compatibility of the norms is both permissible and necessary, if the court determines that the provision of the Community law which it regards as important to the decision is, in the interpretation given it by the Community Court, incapable of application because and insofar as it conflicts with one of the fundamental rights of the Basic Law.

. . .

COMMENT

The problem debated in the preceding decisions—the compatibility of Community and national legal-political orders with respect to guarantees to citizens in national constitutional traditions or charters—commands increasing judicial attention on the Community and national levels. Variations of the theme figure in the two following cases. In Firma J. Nold KG v. Commission [38], a 1974 decision of the Court of Justice, a wholesale trader in coal requested the Court to annul a decision of the Commission which authorized a coal sales agency to require its vendees to agree to two-year contracts, and to impose other requirements which had the effect of excluding the wholesale trader from the relevant market. The substantive issues were decided within the context of the European Coal and Steel Community Treaty. The Court concluded that the sales criteria fixed by the Commission's decision could be justified in view of the special circumstances of the coal-distribution market and of economic difficulties. It thus dismissed the application to annul the decision. Its opinion stated in part:

> The applicant finally claims a violation of certain of its fundamental rights by reason of the fact that the restrictions imposed by the new trading rules authorised by the Commission have the effect, by eliminating it from direct supply, of attacking the profitability of its undertaking and the free management of its affairs, to the point of threatening its existence. Thus, under this heading a quasi-property right is infringed, as well as the right of free exercise of its commercial activities, which are protected by the Constitution of the Federal Republic of Germany, as also by the constitutions of other member-States, and various

38. Court of Justice of the European Communities, Case No. 4/73, May 14, 1974, [1974] C.M.L.Rep. 338. The English text, taken from the source cited, differs in minor, formal respects from the later-published opinion in Reports of Cases before the Court, 1974–4, p. 491.

international instruments, particularly the European Convention for the Protection of Human Rights of 4 November 1950, including the additional Protocol of 20 March 1952.

As this Court has already held, fundamental rights form an integral part of the general principles of law which it enforces. In assuring the protection of such rights, this Court is required to base itself on the constitutional traditions common to the member-States and therefore could not allow measures which are incompatible with the fundamental rights recognised and guaranteed by the constitutions of such States. The international treaties on the protection of human rights in which the member-States have co-operated or to which they have adhered can also supply indications which may be taken into account within the framework of Community law. It is in the light of these principles that the plaints raised by the applicant should be assessed.

While protection may be ensured for the right of property by the constitutional order of all the member-States and while similar guarantees are given to the free exercise of trade, labour and other commercial activities, the rights thus guaranteed, far from appearing as absolute prerogatives, should be considered in the light of the social function of the property and activities which are protected. For that reason, rights of that type are usually guaranteed only subject to limitations relating to the public interest. In the Community legal order, it thus appears legitimate, as regards these rights, to maintain certain limits justified by the general objectives pursued by the Community, so long as the substance of the rights is not impaired. As concerns the guarantees given to undertakings in particular, they could in no case be extended to the protection of mere commercial interests or prospects, the contingent character of which is inherent in the very essence of economic activity.

The disadvantages put forward by the applicant are in reality the consequence of economic change and not of the decision in issue. It is for the applicant, confronted by the economic change caused by the recession in coal production, to face the new situation and itself to make the necessary adaptation.

QUESTIONS

(1) From the perspective of the Community, does Community Law displace and "void" inconsistent national law, whether earlier or later in time? In a case of conflict, would the Court of Justice likely state that the national law is "invalid", or simply state that it should not be applied in this instance? Compare our Supreme Court's disposition of a case in which it found a state law in violation of the federal constitution or a federal statute.

(2) From the perspective of the Community, what is the relevance after cases such as Costa of the framework of national constitutional law or practice within which national courts determine the relevance within the domestic order of Treaty obligations? What is the relevance of the traditional rule of national constitutional law that *lex posterior derogat lege priori*?

(3) What is the relevance to a national court, determining how to resolve an apparent conflict between earlier or later national law and the Treaty or acts under it that are meant to have direct effects, of the following considerations:

(*a*) In the domestic constitutional orders, a national court has (or has not) the power or competence to declare invalid a national law which violates the national constitution;

(*b*) The legal technique by which the Rome Treaty was ratified or approved—that is, by normal statute, by special statute, or by constitutional amendment;

(*c*) An argument that the Treaty or an act under the Treaty conflicts with a specific provision of the national constitution, dealing with (a) legislative procedures for tax measures or (b) protection of stated individual rights against legislative or executive interference?

(4) How effective do you consider the means in the EEC Treaty by which Community institutions can encourage or compel national judges to uphold Community norms and, in particular, to follow rulings about the interpretation of Community norms by the Court of Justice?

(5) In the 1973 General Report of the Commission, at p. 458, the Commission states: "The courts and tribunals of the Member States, even those which have so far maintained a somewhat reserved attitude, are showing a welcome tendency to acknowledge the autonomy of Community law and, in cases of conflict with national law, the primacy of Community law." Do the preceding cases in this section lead you to support or qualify this observation?

Additional reading: For a review of a number of these problems, see Bebr, How Supreme is Community Law in the National Courts, 11 C.M.L.Rev. 3 (1974).

---

4. PRACTICE UNDER ARTICLES 169 AND 173

COMMISSION OF THE EUROPEAN ECONOMIC COMMUNITY v. THE GOVERNMENT OF THE REPUBLIC OF ITALY

Court of Justice of the European Communities, Case No. 10/61, February 27, 1962. Recueil Vol. VIII, p. 1.[39]

[In accordance with decisions reached at a GATT tariff conference at Annecy in 1949, Italy applied a duty of 35% (the "old duty") to radio-electric tubes. At a conference at Geneva in 1956 among parties to the General Agreement on Tariffs and Trade, the duty on this product was reduced to 30%, with however a minimum duty of 150 lire per piece (the "new duty"). By order of the President of Italy dated July 12, 1956, the new duty became temporarily

39. The translation is taken from the CCH Common Market Reporter ¶ 8002.

effective on July 14 of that year. A circular of the Italian Ministry of Finance, dated July 13, 1956, ordered customs authorities to apply to an importer the more favorable of the new or old duty. This circular affected primarily imported pieces which had a customs value equal to or less than 428 lire, for in such situations the old duty of 35% was more favorable to an importer than the new minimum duty of 150 lire. The circular was in effect on January 1, 1957, a date relevant to the application of Article 14 of the Treaty.

The duties agreed upon at the 1956 conference were set forth in a protocol (the Sixth Protocol) which was ratified by Italy by a law of January 2, 1958, one day after the Rome Treaty became effective. A circular of the Ministry of Finance dated April 1, 1958 instructed the customs authorities to apply the new duty to *all* products, including radio-electric tubes less than 428 lire in value.

The first two reductions of 10% each of customs duties among the member states of the Common Market (see Article 14 of the Treaty) became effective in Italy in 1959 and 1960. Circulars of the Ministry of Finance directed customs authorities to apply the 10% reductions only to the new duty, rather than to the dual system more favorable to the importer which was in effect on January 1, 1957. Under these circulars, the duty on radio-electric tubes was reduced by 1960 to 24%, coupled with a minimum of 120 lire per piece.

The Commission advised the Italian Ministry of Foreign Affairs that, in its view, the circulars violated Articles 12 and 14. It contended that the Italian Government should have applied the 10% reductions to each of the two duties in effect on January 1, 1957, and should have continued to allow an importer to choose the duty which was more favorable to him. The Italian Government disagreed with this contention. The Commission, acting under Article 169, then requested the Italian Government to put an end to the alleged infringement of the Treaty within 30 days. After the Italian Government stated that it would not comply, the Commission commenced proceedings before the Court.

Excerpts from the Court's summary of the arguments of the parties and from its opinion appear below.]

The Italian Government, as *defendant*, replies that on January 1, 1957, the only lawful duty in Italy *applicable* to the products in question was the 30 percent duty with the 150 lire minimum per piece, which is therefore the only one to be considered as a basic duty within the meaning of Articles 12 and 14 of the E. E. C. Treaty. In fact, on the one hand, this duty was established by presidential Order No. 647 of July 12, 1956, which is a decree having the force of law, promulgated on the strength of a conferred legislative power . . . . On the other hand, Circular No. 3526 of the General Directory of Customs, dated July 13, 1956, authorizing the customs authorities to apply the 35 percent duty when more favorable to the importer, is not a source of law and cannot be taken into consideration by the terms of Article 14 of the E. E. C. Treaty, which refers to lawful duties. . . .

The Italian Government, *defendant*, raises an objection based on Article 234 of the E. E. C. Treaty, which provides that "The *rights* and *obligations* arising from agreements concluded between one or more Member States on the one hand, and one or more third countries on the other hand, before this Treaty came into force shall not be affected by the provisions of this Treaty".

By the GATT agreement, signed in Geneva on May 23, 1956, prior to the coming into force of the E. E. C. Treaty (January 1, 1958), Italy had consented to repeal the 35 percent duty, in force at that time, and to substitute for it a 30 percent duty, obtaining, however, as compensation the right to introduce a minimum duty of 150 lire per unit. This agreement contains obligations as well as rights for Italy, which must be maintained according to Article 234 of the E. E. C. Treaty.

It would not be possible to make the objection that the GATT agreement, signed on May 23, 1956, was ratified only after the E. E. C. Treaty came into force by the Italian Act No. 25 of January 2, 1958, because the text of Article 234 of the E. E. C. Treaty is applicable to conventions *concluded* previously, not to conventions *ratified.*

The E. E. C. Commission, *plaintiff,* replies that the term "rights and obligations" of Article 234 of the E. E. C. Treaty refers, with regard to the word "rights", to *rights of third countries* and, with respect to the word "obligations", to *obligations of Member States.* Indeed, it says, it is recognized in international law that a State, when assuming an obligation contrary to the rights it possesses by virtue of previous treaties, undertakes by the same token to renounce the use of these rights to the extent necessary for living up to its new obligation. Consequently, it is no longer customary to insert in international treaties a general reservation in favor of such rights, and the authors of the E. E. C. Treaty must have provided in Article 234 only for a procedure admitting exceptions from the provisions of the Treaty in favor of obligations assumed by Member States toward third countries at a prior time. . . .

Opinion

(A) The first thing to examine is the significance given in Articles 12 and 14, to the words "customs duties . . . or any charges having equivalent effect . . . which [the Member States] . . . levy on their trade with each other" (Article 12) and "the duty applied on January 1, 1957" (Article 14).

The plaintiff alleges that the matter deals with duties actually applied on January 1, 1958 (Article 12), and on January 1, 1957 (Article 14), thus coming to the conclusion that in the present case, one of the duties can be retained from the two tariffs, namely the one more favorable to the importer, just as it was ruled by the ministerial circular of July 13, 1956.

However, the defendant maintains that the term "applied duties" means in the sense of Articles 12 and 14 the lawfully applicable duties, and that the aforesaid circular cannot be invoked against the lawfully established tariff, viz., the 30 percent duty with 150 lire specific minimum in accordance with the order of July 12, 1956, of the President of the Italian Republic.

Plaintiff's contention is in conformity with the literal interpretation of the Treaty. In fact, the provisions in question refer to the duties which the Member States "apply" (Article 12) or to the duty "applied" (Article 14);

This contention is corroborated by the fact that the opinion held by the defendant would lead to unacceptable consequences.

In fact,—as proven also by the discussion of the parties about the circumstances under which the circular of July 13, 1956, was issued,—the defendant's contention would oblige the Commission, and eventually the Court, to inquire in each specific case into the validity of domestic administrative measures with respect to the law of the interested Member State. Such an inquiry would exceed the task assigned to these institutions by the Treaty, which task consists in watching over the orderly application of the Treaty.

Suffice it to state that by the aforesaid circular, the Ministry of Finance, in charge of the application of the decree of July 12, 1956, has given an official interpretation of the provisions therein contained, and that such provisions have been uniformly applied according to the directives of said circular. . . .

Thus, from all that precedes it must be inferred, without having to examine the other pleadings of the parties, that Articles 12 and 14 of the Treaty refer to the duties that were actually applied on January 1, 1958, and on January 1, 1957, respectively, and that therefore, in the present case, the practice of the administration of the Italian customs was in conformity with the official instructions of the authorities of competence as laid down in the circular of July 13, 1956.

(B) The defendant raises an objection based on Article 234, paragraph (1), regarding the preservation of rights and obligations resulting from previous conventions made with third countries; and it maintains that this rule authorizes, and even obliges, it to apply in all cases the 30 percent duty coupled with the specific minimum, established by the Geneva Agreements of 1956.

In fact, according to the defendant, if the Italian Republic agreed to repeal the 35 percent duty in force at that moment, and to replace it with the 30 percent duty, it did so because it obtained in return the right of introducing a minimum assessment in the amount of 150 lire per unit.

The plaintiff replies that the term "rights and obligations" of Article 234 refers, so far as "rights" are concerned, to rights of third countries, and so far as "obligations" are concerned, to obligations of Member States. Under the principles of international law, a State, assuming a new obligation contrary to the rights it possesses under a previous treaty, relinquishes by the same token these rights to the extent necessary for the fulfillment of the new obligation.

Plaintiff's interpretation is well founded and the objection raised by the defendant must be rejected.

In fact, in the matters which it regulates, the E. E. C. Treaty overrides the conventions made prior to its coming into force, including the conventions that have since been concluded under GATT.

By virtue of Article 14 of the Treaty, in order to determine the basic duty for reductions made after January 1, 1957, one must refer to the regime created by the circular of the Ministry of Finance, dated July 13, 1956.

Consequently, the defendant is wrong in assuming that, by virtue of the Geneva agreements of 1956 it had the right to apply with regard to the other Member States only one kind of duty, namely the 30 percent ad valorem duty coupled with the specific 150 lire minimum.

On the other hand, Article 14, if correctly applied, does not prejudice the rights and obligations of Member States towards third countries implied from conventions concluded prior to the coming into force of the E. E. C. Treaty.

Thus, it follows from Article 234 that the Member States and third countries, though parties to the same 1956 Geneva Agreement, are, in fact, applying different tariffs. This is the normal effect of the Treaty establishing the E. E. C. The way in which the Member

States proceed in reducing customs duties among themselves may not be criticized by third countries, provided that this customs disarmament is accomplished in accordance with the provisions of the Treaty and does not affect the rights of third countries under existing conventions. . . .

THE COURT, rejecting all further or contrary claims, declares the present action to be admissible and renders the following judgment:

(1) The Italian Government, by having applied after the date of coming into force of the Treaty, a specific 150 lire customs duty to the products in question manufactured in Member States, of a customs value of less than, or equal to, 428 lire apiece, and in taking this duty as the basis for the calculation of subsequent customs duty reductions, has failed in the obligations established by Articles 12 and 14, paragraph (1), of the Treaty; . . .

COMMENT

Note the requirements in Articles 169 and 170 of prior consultation with and a "reasoned opinion" by the Commission, before it or a member state can refer a dispute to the Court of Justice. The Commission acts under Article 169 in its "policeman" capacity, supervising compliance with the Treaty and if necessary acting as prosecutor. Thus far there have been no proceedings under Article 170. That article recalls the contentious jurisdiction of the International Court of Justice, and Articles 34 and 36 of its Statute.* It also recalls the original jurisdiction of the United States Supreme Court to resolve disputes between states.

The defense of Italy based upon Article 234 had little substance. Of course the judgment of the Court requires even greater discrimination by Italy between duties applied to products from member countries and from other contracting parties of the GATT. But such discrimination is implicit in the notion of a customs union, and thus the occasion for Article XXIV of the GATT, p. 1158, supra.

Article 234 (which refers to agreements concluded before the Rome Treaty) and Article 111 (which refers to new agreements) are closely related. To implement Article 111(1), the Council decided in 1960 that bilateral agreements signed by member countries with outsiders must contain the following clause: "Should those obligations under the Treaty establishing the European Economic Community which relate to the gradual establishment of a common commercial policy make this necessary, negotiations shall be opened as soon as feasible in order to amend this present agreement as appropriate." [40]

The Commission's power to proceed under Article 169 reaches conduct of a member state that fails to meet obligations stated not only in the Treaty but also in Community acts such as regulations or directives. Consider Commission of the European Communities v. Italian Republic,[41] a 1973 decision of the Court of Justice based upon

40. The translation is taken from the CCH Common Market Reporter ¶ 3812.33.

41. Court of Justice of the European Communities, Case No. 79/72, June 21, 1973, Reports of Cases before the

the Commission's charge that the Italian government failed to fulfill obligations under a Council directive on the marketing of forest reproductive material. The directive required member states to establish various classifications of reproductive materials and to ensure that they were not subject to marketing restrictions other than those specified in the directive. The directive also provided that member states "shall bring into force the laws, regulations or administrative provisions necessary to comply with this directive . . . not later than July 1, 1969, for [seeds and specified parts of plants]". The Commission commenced procedures under Article 169 in a letter of March 24, 1971, and instituted proceedings before the Court of Justice in December 1972 to establish that Italy had failed to fulfill its obligations within the time limit. The opinion of the Court stated in part:

> The defendant admits that it failed to observe these time limits. However, the defendant explains that under Italian laws for the trade in seeds and forest reproductive materials a law was necessary to adapt such laws to the provisions of the directive. In pursuance of this objective, a first draft law had been laid before Parliament, but the premature dissolution of the legislature did not permit its adoption within the prescribed time. Another draft law was introduced in September 1972, but it could not be enacted until May 1973. Thus the delay in implementing the obligations is due primarily to unforeseeable political circumstances occurring at the end of 1971 and the beginning of 1972.
>
> From the time Directive No. 66/404/EEC was passed, all the Member States knew that, for the first group of seeds and parts of plants, they were bound to bring into effect the necessary measures by July 1, 1967, at the latest. When certain Member States failed to comply by July 1, 1967, with the provisions of this directive, Directive No. 69/64/EEC granted them additional time, thus reminding the defaulting Member States of their obligation to institute the measures provided for. Accordingly, having failed to implement the provisions required by Directive No. 66/404/EEC before July 1, 1969, the defendant has since that date failed in the obligations arising from that directive.
>
> The defendant cannot, to justify its conduct, invoke obstacles or circumstances which arose at a time largely subsequent to that of the obligation which it is accused of not having fulfilled. The political situation thus invoked cannot, in any case, be accepted as justifying this delay. Moreover, if this draft law is passed in a short time, it does not follow that the failure to observe the provisions of the directive will cease, since the regulations and administrative provisions necessary for its application have still not been brought into force.
>
> At the hearing, the defendant again claimed that in any event it is a question of the non-observance of a directive,

Court, Vol. 1973–5, p. 667, CCH Common Market Reporter ¶ 8214. This English text, taken from CCH, differs in minor, formal respects from the later-published Reports of Cases before the Court.

and submitted that the provisions of a directive cannot be accorded the same binding force as those of a regulation.

Under Article 189 of the Treaty, a directive "shall be binding" as to the result to be achieved upon each Member State to which it is addressed, but leaves to the national authorities the choice of form and methods. The specific application of directives is all the more important since implementation is left to the discretion of Member States, and such acts would lose all effectiveness if the objectives sought were not attained within the prescribed time limits. If, in respect of Member States to which it is addressed, the provisions of a directive had no less binding an effect than that of any other rule of Community law, such an effect applies all the more to provisions containing the time limits for implementing the measures provided for.

It follows that by failing to adopt the provisions necessary to comply with Council Directive No. 66/404, as amended by Directive No. 69/64, on the marketing of forest reproductive material within the prescribed time, the Italian Republic has failed to fulfill its obligations under the Treaty.

QUESTIONS

(1) Is the Commission *required* to act under Article 169 when there is a substantial argument that a member state has failed to fulfill an obligation? An unanswerable argument?

(2) Which member state might have had an interest in instituting proceedings under Article 170 against Italy? Must the plaintiff state demonstrate any direct interest in the litigation?

(3) Note the effect accorded a judgment of the Court under Article 171. Are the circulars of the Ministry of Finance, directing customs authorities to apply the 10% reductions only to the new duty, null and void from the Community's perspective? From the perspective of an Italian court which might thereafter be faced with this question? Note the closing paragraph of the opinion.

(4) In what circumstances could the issue in this litigation have come before the Court under Article 177? In what respects would the Court's judgment under Article 177 differ from its decision under Article 169?

(5) Suppose that an Italian importer of radio-electric tubes of low value protested before an Italian court the import duties in effect in 1961, after the second 10% reduction. Do the decisions of the Court of Justice indicate that the importer has a direct and immediate "right" conferred upon him by the Treaty to pay no more than the lower duty, based upon the more favorable tariff in effect on January 1, 1957?

GOVERNMENT OF THE REPUBLIC OF ITALY v. COMMISSION OF THE EUROPEAN ECONOMIC COMMUNITY

Court of Justice of the European Communities, Case No. 13/63, July 17, 1963. Recueil Vol. IX, p. 335.[42]

An action [commenced by Italy under Article 173 of the Treaty], the *object* of which is the annulment of the January 17, 1963, decision . . . authorizing the French Republic to adopt safeguard measures, by virtue of Article 226 of the EEC Treaty, against imports of electric home refrigerators and of certain separate parts originating in Italy.

Points of Fact and of Law

I. Summary of the Facts

(1) Up until 1961 imports of refrigerators were subject in France to a license. The liberalization of intra-Community trade resulted in a considerable amount of imports from Italy into France, such imports having increased from 1961 to 1962. On December 19, 1962, the French government asked the Commission to determine safeguard measures pursuant to Article 226 of the EEC Treaty.

(2) Through its decision of January 17, 1963 . . . which is now under attack, the Commission acceded to the request and authorized the French Republic to impose a special tax on imports from Italy of electric home refrigerators and of sealed compressor units for electric home refrigerators and other parts, "unless the Italian Republic applies such tax on export." The amount of the tax was to be graduated in time and set according to product. The safeguard measures were to terminate July 31, 1963. . . .

III. Pleas and Arguments of the Parties

. . .

The *plaintiff* expresses doubts concerning the question of whether the production of refrigerators constitutes a "sector" within the meaning of Article 226, paragraph 1. Such production can be considered to be a part of the larger sector of electrical household appliances.

According to the *defendant,* the fact that a specified activity can be considered as part of a broader field does not keep it from being a "sector of the economy." At any rate, the French refrigerator industry employed more than 11,000 persons in 1961, and its gross turnover was approximately 500 million NF. . . .

The *plaintiff* contends generally that the French refrigerator industry's difficulties were not "serious" within the meaning of Article 226. If French production decreased in comparison to 1961, this was only the inevitable consequence of the liberalization of trade. To apply Article 226 to cases of such minor significance would be to "deny the Common Market."

Furthermore, Article 226 requires that the difficulties "persist" and that the safeguard measures allow for the threatened sector to be "adapted" to the Common Market. In this case, these conditions are not fulfilled. In 1962, the French producers were able actually to dispose of their entire output. As for the five factories which,

42. The translation is taken from the CCH Common Market Reporter ¶ 8014.

according to the attacked decision, were obliged to suspend production, a safeguard measure limited to a period of six months could not purely and simply bring about their reopening. All the same, it is a known fact that those were simple reconversion measures.

More specifically, the plaintiff, quoting figures, points out:

(a) French production is not sufficient to cover domestic requirements. In fact, in 1962, it was short by approximately 265,000 units.

As for the 190,000 refrigerators which, according to the attacked decision, had not been sold by the end of 1962, those were very probably surplus from the production of the years preceding 1961, and therefore obsolete models. The 1961 output was, as a matter of fact, practically absorbed by the domestic market and by exports.

. . .

The *defendant* considers that the data contained in the statement of reasons for the decision, namely:

—decrease in French production from 835,000 units to 701,600 (first ten months of 1961 and 1962, respectively);

—surplus of 193,000 units on December 31, 1962 (as against 145,000 on December 31, 1961);

—decrease in French exports from 125,000 to 96,500 (first seven months of 1961 and 1962, respectively);

—increase of Italian imports from 22,000 to 136,000, and of imports from other countries from 19,000 to 60,000 (first six months of 1961 and 1962, respectively);

—development of this situation in spite of increased consumption during 1962;

—suspension of manufacturing by five out of fifteen producers representing 95 percent of total production;

—decrease of the work force employed by these fifteen producers, as well as by two other enterprises manufacturing semi-finished products, from 10,590 (1961) to 7,370 (1962);

as well as the aggregate of the figures for 1962 subsequently obtained leave no doubt as to the "serious" nature of the situation.

. . .

[With respect to the plaintiff's charge that the decision violated Article 7 of the Treaty by adversely affecting only Italian products, the *defendant* replied that] Italian refrigerators were the only ones whose average price free-to-the-French-frontier was appreciably less than the average factory price of French refrigerators. Before the attacked decision, the Italian price was 2.245 NF (2.413 with duty) per liter, the French price 2.946 (for purposes of comparison, German refrigerators were 2.816, and those from Belgium-Luxembourg, 3.042, all including duty).

Italian refrigerators are, as in the past, competitive, their total price free-to-the-French-frontier being at present 2.682 NF, and therefore still lower than the price of German appliances or of appliances from Belgium and Luxembourg. . . .

Opinion

I. Concerning violation of basic procedural rules

. . .

The plaintiff voiced a number of complaints with a view to bringing about a ruling that the reasons given for the attacked decision do not meet the conditions required by Treaty Article 190.

The reasons given for the decision are allegedly insufficient to put the blame on Italian imports for the difficulties in question. The decision, however, took into consideration not only the volume of the various imports, but also a comparison between the price of the Italian product and the prices both of the French products and of the other imported products—prices which, according to the decision, were appreciably higher.

It has been improperly argued that the decision should also have taken into consideration the difference between the sale prices to consumers, since this is impossible to ascertain at this time because of the discounts being given and the difficulties must be evaluated from the producers' standpoint, which makes it necessary to take into consideration the prices as invoiced to wholesalers. Nor was it any more important to investigate whether or not the profit margin allowed French producers was fair, as long as there was a question of estimating the difference in price between the French product and the Italian product upon arrival in French territory, i. e., at the time both products are on the same market and at the same trading stage.

. . .

In view of the above, the claim of insufficient reasons must be rejected.

II. Concerning misuse of power

The plaintiff complains that the Commission misused the power given it under Article 226 to obtain a result subject to the anti-dumping measures of Article 91. Nothing, however, either in the attacked decision or in the defendant's attitude leads us to consider this decision as a disguised anti-dumping measure, since there was no reference to dumping. The fact that the levying of the contested tax was limited as to time and graduated is incompatible with such a measure, which would have to be taken for the duration of the practices to be fought—a period which is usually unpredictable. This plea must therefore be rejected.

III. Concerning violation of the Treaty

1. With respect to the meaning of "sector of the economy"

The plaintiff argues that the French refrigerator industry is not a "sector of the economy" within the meaning of Article 226. The manufacture of one product can constitute such a "sector" as long as this product, according to generally accepted concepts, is clearly distinguishable from other, kindred products. These conditions are, in this case, fulfilled. . . .

3. Regarding application of the notion of "serious difficulties which might persist"

Pursuant to Treaty Article 226, paragraph 1, safeguard measures may be authorized in the case of serious difficulties which might persist in one sector of the economy.

Taken by themselves, the figures furnished by the defendant showing the decrease in the French output from 1961 to 1962 and the increase of imports into France during the same period—figures which the plaintiff does not contest—imply the existence of such difficulties. One must, however, examine whether the arguments advanced by the plaintiff are likely to dispel this assumption.

The plaintiff asserts that the French output for 1962, in the amount of 265,000 units, was not enough to satisfy the needs of the internal market. This assertion is irrelevant. This circumstance does not necessarily presuppose the insufficient capacity to produce of the manufacturing plants, but could just as well be attributed to the fact that imports were actually the cause of the decrease in French production. . . .

The parties disagree as to whether the French producers' lowering of prices just before the attacked decision was taken affected all or most of the products, as the plaintiff contends, or only a very small amount of them. The plaintiff's assertion, assuming that it is correct, brings out rather the existence of "serious difficulties," since one can logically assume that a considerable price drop, spontaneously decided upon by the producers, might be symptomatic of strong competition. At any rate, if the purpose of Article 226 is to give a sector having difficulties a chance to adjust to the Common Market, it presupposes that the parties concerned are in a position to support the Commission's measures by their own efforts. Therefore, the fact that such efforts are being made does not preclude the existence of "serious difficulties."

It has therefore not been established that the defendant applied incorrectly the notion of "serious difficulties." Under these circumstances, the Court must reject this plea.

4. Concerning discrimination

The decision is alleged to have violated the principle of non-discrimination by authorizing the French government to introduce a special tax on Italian products only, and not on the same products when originating either in the other States of the Community or in third countries.

The different treatment of situations that are not comparable does not allow one to conclude automatically that discrimination exists. Thus what may seem to be a discrimination in form may actually correspond to an absence of discrimination in substance. The discrimination in substance is supposed to consist either in treating similar situations in a different manner, or in treating different situations in the same manner.

In addition, since the Commission is bound to limit its interventions to the "strictly necessary," it must be free to consider only the facts constituting the cause of the difficulties in question. It is, in any case, obliged to give "priority . . . to measures which will least disturb the operation of the Common Market." In this respect it must consider the fact that, where there is doubt, the "common" nature of the market suffers less where derogations from the rules of the Treaty occur only within the framework of relations between two Member States. . . .

It is therefore important to know whether the circumstances in this case warrant the limitation of safeguard measures to Italian imports alone.

The defendant saw in "the substantial increase of imports from the Italian Republic" the origin of the French difficulties, and consequently limited its safeguard measures to Italian products. To justify its judgment and its choice of this measure, it relied mainly on the finding that, on the one hand, the volume of imports from third countries "has not increased abnormally" and is therefore "not likely to prevent a reorganization of the French sector in question," and, on the other hand, that the price of products imported from the other Member States "does not differ appreciably from the price of similar French products and that the increase in the volume of imports, although sizeable, was not considered abnormal." The factors brought to the knowledge of the Court do not show that this estimate by the Commission is patently an erroneous one. It has not been proved that the Commission was mistaken when it stated that the price of products originating in the other Member States did not differ appreciably from the price of similar French products. It could, therefore, hold the substantial increase of Italian imports, as compared to the volume of imports from the other Member States—which it did not consider abnormal—to be a fact likely to justify the specific measure which was the object of the decision.

. . . The plea of discrimination must therefore be rejected. . . .

THE COURT, rejecting any further arguments or arguments to the contrary, declares and decrees:

(1) The suit is rejected as lacking merit. . . .

NOTE ON JUDICIAL CONTROL OF ACTS OF THE COMMUNITY'S ORGANS

Article 173 lists four grounds for review of "acts other than recommendations or opinions." Comparable grounds for review of administrative action have been developed in the legal systems of the member states. The resemblances between Article 173 and principles for review of administrative action in France are particularly striking.[43] It was dominantly the French system that inspired the draftsmen of the Treaty and that may serve as a source of interpretation of Article 173.

Compare the bases for judicial review stated in the Administrative Procedure Act, 80 Stat. 393 (1966), 5 U.S.C.A. § 706. That section provides that a reviewing court shall—

> . . . hold unlawful and set aside agency action, findings, and conclusions found to be—
>
> (A) arbitrary, capricious, an abuse of discretion, or otherwise not in accordance with law;
>
> (B) contrary to constitutional right, power, privilege, or immunity;
>
> (C) in excess of statutory jurisdiction, authority, or limitations, or short of statutory right;
>
> (D) without observance of procedure required by law;
>
> (E) unsupported by substantial evidence in a case subject to sections 556 and 557 of this title or otherwise reviewed on the record of an agency hearing provided by statute; or

43. For a description of the principal grounds developed through the case law of the Conseil d'Etat, France's highest administrative court, see Waline, Droit Administratif 448–91 (9th ed. 1963).

(F) unwarranted by the facts to the extent that the facts are subject to trial de novo by the reviewing court.

In making the foregoing determinations, the court shall review the whole record or those parts of it cited by a party, and due account shall be taken of the rule of prejudicial error.

Article 173 confers a right upon member states, the Council and the Commission to appeal *any* regulation, directive or decision of the Council or Commission. There is no requirement that any such appellant demonstrate a direct interest in the controversy. Each can become a guardian of the "public interest" in observance by Community institutions of the Treaty. Compare the role of the Commission under Article 169.

Note that Article 173 employs more guarded language in defining the conditions under which private parties can appeal acts of the Council or Commission. First, the right of appeal applies only to a "decision," although it includes a decision "in the form of a regulation" which is of "direct and individual concern" to the party. Second, note that the decision must be addressed to the party seeking review, or if addressed to another, must be of "direct and individual concern" to such party. These requirements recall the problems in the United States which are variously characterized by the courts as questions of "standing" or "ripeness" or "case and controversy." Nonetheless the important observation about this second paragraph of Article 173 is not the *limitation* of the right but the fact that the Treaty here *confers* a right upon private parties to institute litigation against organs of an international organization before an international tribunal.

QUESTIONS

(1) What is the approach of the Court in Italy v. Commission to acts of the Commission? Plenary review and de novo determinations, or considerable deference to the findings and recommendations? Which attitude would appear more appropriate in the context of Article 126?

(2) Does the Court appear to distinguish between findings of fact by the Commission and inferences drawn from these facts or the exercise of discretion in arriving at a decision? Consider particularly its statements about the "burden of proof" in these proceedings?

(3) Suppose that the Court concluded that the Commission exceeded its powers in issuing the decision. What would be the effect of such a judgment? Note Articles 174 and 176, and compare them with Article 171.

(4) Regulations will frequently be of direct concern to private parties. For example, those issued under Article 49 state the conditions under which nationals of one country can enter another to seek employment and remain there to hold it. Or regulations under the antitrust provisions may determine what categories of agreements are exempt from the Treaty's prohibitions, and thereby adversely affect persons competing with firms whose agreements have been determined to be "legal." Why do you suppose that the Treaty precludes appeals by private parties to challenge regulations?

(5) The third paragraph of Article 173 imposes a time limitation upon proceedings. Suppose that a plaintiff, in an action in a national court, seeks damages for breach of contract. The defendant argues that the contract is illegal under the antitrust provisions of the Treaty. The plaintiff relies on a regulation issued six months previously and exempting certain agreements, including the one sued upon, from the Treaty's prohibitions.

(*a*) Is the regulation immune from judicial review by the national court?

(*b*) Is it immune from judicial review by the Court of Justice, in a proceeding under Article 177? Does Article 184 appear to be relevant to this question?

(6) The Court of Justice *is* the Community's judiciary; there are no inferior courts. What comparisons and contrasts would you stress between the role of the Court of Justice in the Community and (a) the role of the federal judiciary in the United States, or (b) the role of the International Court of Justice?

COMMENT

The 1973 General Report of the Commission, pp. 69 and 480–483, provides some statistical data about the work of the Community and national courts.

As of October 1, 1973, among the original six members of the Community, there had been 448 decisions by national courts that involved Community law. Of these, 143 involved restrictive agreements, while the next largest categories were agriculture, tax provisions and customs duties.

As of December 31, 1973, 407 cases had been brought before the Court of Justice under the EEC Treaty. (Some had been dismissed on the merits or rejected as inadmissible, and 57 cases were then pending.) Of the 407 cases, 242 arose under Article 177, while 93 arose under Article 173. No actions had been brought under Article 170. The number of cases brought before the Court is evidently on the rise. In 1973, 192 cases (under the three treaties) were brought before the Court, as compared with 82 cases in 1972. There was a particularly large increase in referrals under Article 177.

C. THE STRUCTURAL FRAMEWORK AND PROCESSES FOR THE DEVELOPMENT OF COMMUNITY LAW

We have thus far considered the political and constitutional problems which the European Economic Community confronts. Now we turn to a more detailed examination of the legal institutions and processes through which the Community is administered and developed. We do so through a study of two fields of Community law.

Administration of the Common Market is a complicated business. The Treaty creates numerous institutional channels and techniques for realizing its goals. In some fields such as tariffs, Community law displaces large areas of national law; in other fields, these bodies of law coexist in a complex relationship that is reminiscent of the interplay of federal and state law within the United States. Thus Community rules may limit the discretion left to national authorities by, for example, prohibiting defined policies or conduct; the non-discrimination principle is an illustration. Or Community rules may require affirmative action of national authorities to assure that fields which remain in principle within the competence of national lawmakers nonetheless comply with a minimum Community standard. In some areas, differences among national laws are considered particularly detrimental to the Community's objectives, and thus Community norms require harmonization; Community institutions may require the enactment of uniform or similar laws in each of the member countries. Alternatively, the Treaty contemplates special conventions to be concluded among the member states that would create Community-wide law through the conventions themselves.

We have observed that Community law may be elaborated by regulations of immediate effect which require no implementation by national lawmaking authorities. We have also observed that Community organs are restricted in some fields to the use of directives that require legislative or executive acts by the member states. Whatever the path followed, the efficacy of Community law depends upon the cooperation of national legislatures, executive officials and tribunals. They are generally responsible in the first instance for the interpretation and application of that law—or in the last instance, for action properly responsive to rulings of the Commission or the Court of Justice.

Part C selects two fields of Community law as illustrations of these processes and techniques. Both fields are at the core of the Community's aspirations. Both have received extensive elaboration at the Community and national levels. Needless to say, the materials below fall short of affording a complete description of either field. Their function is to illustrate the themes described above, rather than to offer a substantive analysis of the fields themselves.

COMMENT

Prior to the accession of the United Kingdom to the Community in 1973, there were several unofficial translations into English of the Treaty, regulations or directives, decisions and opinions. Thus within the translations of the pre-1973 opinions of the Court of Justice or decisions of the Commission which appear below, there are quotations from Treaty articles or from regulations which differ from the present official texts in English that appear in the Documentary Supplement.

1. THE FREE MOVEMENT OF WORKERS AND THE RIGHT OF ESTABLISHMENT

NOTE ON FREE MOVEMENT OF WORKERS

Articles 48–51 * spell out the framework within which freedom of movement for workers is to be "secured". Those articles treat the salaried, wage-earning laborer, in contrast to the self-employed craftsman or managers or professionals who are treated in Articles 52–66.

The elimination of labor markets bounded by national frontiers is high among the priorities of the EEC Treaty. That goal inheres in the conception of a common market. It responds to basic economic aims such as efficient resource allocation that are considered vital to growth of the Community's production. And from the individual perspective, it heightens the ability of workers to maximize their income or, indeed, to find any employment whatsoever.

The core of these articles is found in the principle expressed in Article 48(2), "the abolition of any discrimination based on nationality between workers of the Member States as regards employment, remuneration and other conditions of work and employment." Thus workers can cross frontiers and claim, as a matter of legal right, equal protection with nationals—that is, national treatment. The extraordinary reach of such provisions, from both political and economic perspectives, can be grasped by the American student who contemplates the possibility of similar treaty obligations between the United States and, say, other Western Hemisphere countries. Of course, the relatively homogeneous economic and political systems of the member states, and the relatively high degree of industrialization and economic prosperity within the Common Market, mean that such a policy has milder consequences than it would among countries of radically different economic and political circumstance.

Note the specific rights described in Article 48(3), as well as the qualifications stated in the introductory clause. Article 49 describes the procedures for implementing these rights. The Council has acted under these provisions, most significantly through Regulation No. 1612/68, [1968] O.J.No.L. 257, p. 1. That regulation spells out, in general terms, the requirement of equal treatment in employment opportunities, training, membership in labor unions, claims with respect to housing, and similar matters. It confers the right to cross frontiers and reside in another country upon the family of a member, and requires national treatment with respect to education of the worker's children. It provides a framework for cooperation among member states or between the states and the Commission with respect to studies of employment opportunities, transmission of information, and coordination of national and Community institutions to match offers for jobs and employment. The task of fully implementing a number of these provisions, such as those governing vocational training and systems for manpower clearance, remains before the Community and national institutions—together with related aspects of the program for free movement of workers such as assuring continuing social security benefits for migrant workers.

By the end of 1974, there were about 1,000,000 migrant workers originating from EEC countries who were working in other EEC countries, together with about 1,750,000 of their dependents.[44] With families, there were over 10,000,000 migrant workers within the Common Market, dominantly of course with countries of origin outside the Community—principally Spain, Portugal, Yugoslavia, Greece, Turkey and countries of North Africa. This situation has posed serious economic, social and cultural problems for most of the migrant workers originating outside the Community. Such workers find assurance of minimum or national treatment not under the Treaty but only under varying and less protective national laws or, on occasion, pursuant to bilateral conventions.

In 1964, the Commission sent to the Council guidelines for an action program to provide social and political equality for all migrants, including non-EEC workers. The program would embrace vocational and language training, social services, housing, education of children, and health. Significantly, the program (if adopted and made binding by acts of Community authorities or member states) would give migrants a voice in public decisions, including full participation in local elections by 1980, provided that minimum residency requirements are met. With the exception of the United Kingdom, migrants from within or outside the Community are now excluded in the member countries from exercising political rights.

The change in national policies and laws brought about by the Treaty in this area is most vividly perceived at the frontier, when an alien seeks admission to work. Compare the provisions of the United States immigration laws, including those governing visas, at pp. 18–22, supra. Consider the following opinion involving limitations of the right to enter in the case of a Dutch national responding to an offer of employment in England.

VAN DUYN v. HOME OFFICE

Court of Justice of the European Communities, Case No. 41/74, December 4, 1974.
[1975] 1 C.M.L.Rep. 1.[45]

[Van Duyn, a Dutch national, was offered employment as a secretary in the college of The Church of Scientology in England. She was refused leave to enter the United Kingdom on grounds that the Secretary of State "considers it undesirable to give anyone leave to enter the United Kingdom on the business of or in the employment of [The Church of Scientology]". This position rested upon

44. The information in this paragraph is taken from Background Information: European Community, Background Note No. 4/1975, January 23, 1975.

45. The text, taken from the source cited, may differ in minor, formal respects from the opinion as it will be published in Reports of Cases before the Court.

views expressed by the Government that Scientology was "socially harmful", that it "alienates members of families from each other", that "its authoritarian principles and practice are a potential menace to the personality and well being" of its followers, and that its "methods can be a serious danger to the health of those who submit to them." Although under existing law there was no power to prohibit the practice of scientology, the Government concluded that it would at least prevent the entrance of aliens associated with the movement.

Van Duyn sought a declaration that she was entitled to enter and remain in England on the proposed employment by virtue of the EEC Treaty and its implementation. Her arguments relied upon Article 48 of the Treaty, upon Article 189, and upon an EEC Council Directive, 64/221, of February 25, 1964, which referred to Article 48 and which provided that "Measures taken on grounds of public policy or of public security shall be based exclusively on the personal conduct of the individual involved."

The High Court of Justice (Chancery Division), in its decision of January 14, 1974,[46] decided that Article 48 (with the 1964 directive) "raises a question of interpretation." It was indeed the first English court to refer such a question to the Court of Justice under Article 177. The questions referred are stated in the excerpts below from the opinion of the Court of Justice:]

First Question

By the first question, the Court is asked to say whether Article 48 of the EEC Treaty is directly applicable so as to confer on individuals rights enforceable by them in the courts of a Member State.

It is provided, in Article 48(1) and (2), that freedom of movement for workers shall be secured by the end of the transitional period and that such freedom shall entail "the abolition of any discrimination based on nationality between workers of Member States as regards employment, remuneration and other conditions of work and employment".

These provisions impose on Member States a precise obligation which does not require the adoption of any further measure on the part either of the Community institutions or of the Member States and which leaves them, in relation to its implementation, no discretionary power.

Paragraph 3, which defines the rights implied by the principle of freedom of movement for workers, subjects them to limitations justified on grounds of public policy, public security or public health. The application of these limitations is, however, subject to judicial control, so that a Member State's right to invoke the limitations does not prevent the provisions of Article 48, which enshrine the principle of freedom of movement for workers, from conferring on individuals rights which are enforceable by them and which the national courts must protect.

The reply to the first question must therefore be in the affirmative.

Second Question

The second question asks the Court to say whether Council Directive No 64/221 of 25 February 1964 on the co-ordination of special measures concerning the movement and residence of foreign

46. [1974] 3 All E.R. 178, [1974] 1 C.M.L.Rep. 347.

nationals which are justified on grounds of public policy, public security or public health is directly applicable so as to confer on individuals rights enforceable by them in the courts of a Member State.

It emerges from the order making the reference, that the only provision of the Directive which is relevant is that contained in Article 3(1) which provides that "measures taken on grounds of public policy or public security shall be based exclusively on the personal conduct of the individual concerned".

The United Kingdom observes that, since Article 189 of the Treaty distinguishes between the effects ascribed to regulations, directives and decisions, it must, therefore, be presumed that the Council, in issuing a directive, rather than making a regulation, must have intended that the directive should have an effect other than that of a regulation, and accordingly, that the former should not be directly applicable.

If, however, by virtue of the provisions of Article 189 regulations are directly applicable and, consequently, may, by their very nature, have direct effects, it does not follow from this that other categories of acts mentioned in that Article can never have similar effects. It would be incompatible with the binding effect attributed to a directive by Article 189, to exclude, in principle, the possibility that the obligation which it imposes may be invoked by those concerned. In particular, where the Community authorities have, by directive, imposed on Member States the obligation to pursue a particular course of conduct, the useful effect of such an act would be weakened if individuals were prevented from relying on it before their national courts and if the latter were prevented from taking it into consideration as an element of Community law. Article 177, which empowers national courts to refer to the Court questions concerning the validity and interpretation of all acts of the Community institutions, without distinction, implies furthermore that these acts may be invoked by individuals in the national courts. It is necessary to examine, in every case, whether the nature, general scheme and wording of the provision in question are capable of having direct effects on the relations between Member States and individuals.

By providing that measures taken on grounds of public policy shall be based exclusively on the personal conduct of the individual concerned, Article 3(1) of Directive No 64/221 is intended to limit the discretionary power which national laws generally confer on the authorities responsible for the entry and expulsion of foreign nationals. First, the provision lays down an obligation which is not subject to any exception or condition and which, by its very nature, does not require the intervention of any act on the part either of the institutions of the Community or of Member States. Secondly, because Member States are thereby obliged, in implementing a clause which derogates from one of the fundamental principles of the Treaty in favour of individuals, not to take account of factors extraneous to personal conduct, legal certainty for the persons concerned requires that they should be able to rely on this obligation—even though it has been laid down in a legislative act which has no automatic direct effect in its entirety.

If the meaning and exact scope of the provision raise questions of interpretation, these questions can be resolved by the courts, taking into account also the procedure under Article 177 of the Treaty.

Accordingly, in reply to the second question, Article 3(1) of Council Directive No 64/221 of 25 February 1964 confers on individuals rights which are enforceable by them in the courts of a Member State and which the national courts must protect.

. . .

[The third referred question requested the Court to rule whether Article 48 and the directive could be interpreted by a member state to entitle it to take into account, as matters of personal conduct, the fact that an individual was associated with an organization whose activities the Member State considered contrary to the public good, even though those activities were not unlawful and even though the state placed no restrictions upon its nationals who wished to take employment with the same organization. The Court here ruled that the Member State was entitled to take that association into account.]

NOTE ON PROVISIONS GOVERNING ESTABLISHMENT

Articles 52 to 58 create the framework within which rules are to be developed for the establishment of natural or legal persons in the member states to pursue economic goals, basically the production or distribution of goods and services.[47] The position of these articles in the Treaty makes explicit the relationship between establishment (without discrimination on grounds of nationality) and other goals. Titles I and II of Part Two of the Treaty deal with the free movement of goods and with agriculture. Title III, which includes Articles 48 to 58, is entitled "Free Movement of Persons, Services and Capital." Establishment is another of the complex of policies looking towards the destruction of national boundaries and the formation of one trading unit.[48]

The Treaty provisions assume significance only against the background of the national laws. The pattern of restrictions upon establishment by aliens of economic enterprises varies. In several member countries, legislation or executive decrees provide that economic activity by aliens is prohibited unless government approval is obtained. That approval might consist of a permit allowing an alien individual to engage in some commercial enterprise, or of more complex authorizations, granted under specified conditions, permitting alien corporations to extend their operations into the country.[49] Apart from such laws, a number of industrial or commercial activities, such as banking and insurance, are subject to more onerous requirements.

47. The Treaty distinguishes between restrictions on the "Right of Establishment" in Articles 52 to 58, and restrictions on the free provision of "Services" in Articles 59 to 66. The two fields are closely related; these materials consider only the first set of articles.

48. For a description of comparable problems that arise in an interstate setting in this country, see pp. 71–74, supra. The role of Friendship, Commerce and Navigation Treaties in regulating problems of establishment between the United States and foreign countries is considered at pp. 619–620, supra.

49. A summary of the principal restrictions on establishment by aliens in France appears at p. 81–84, supra. Summaries of controls on foreign investment within the EEC countries appear in the volume of the CCH Common Market Reporter entitled Doing Business in Europe.

They may affect both nationals and aliens but may be more easily satisfied by nationals. Read now Articles 52 to 58.

Article 52. The establishment provisions express the characteristic "timetable" approach of the Treaty. Liberalization of restrictions is to be progressively realized throughout the transitional period. Note that Article 52 refers to "self-employed persons." Establishment provisions are thus distinct from Articles 48 to 51. Establishment covers principally corporations and persons of an entrepreneurial, managerial or professional character.

Article 53. Recall that the Court of Justice considered this article in the Costa case, p. 1293, supra, and concluded that it was self-executing in the member states.

Article 54. Note the role of each of the Community organs in developing the General Program and issuing the directives which implement it.

Article 56. This qualification to the establishment provisions recalls the *ordre public* exceptions appearing in a large number of treaties determining rights of aliens.[50] Even as the Treaty states an exception, it attempts to define and restrict it. Acting under the second paragraph of this article, the Council issued a directive, [1964] J.O. 850, on the co-ordination of national provisions in this field. The directive curbs opportunities for arbitrary use of the "public policy" exception by defining the conditions under which it can be invoked. It states, for example, that national measures based upon it cannot be enacted to serve purely economic interests. They must refer to the personal conduct or situation (such as illness) of the aliens whom they affect. (Compare the regulation at issue in the Van Duyn case, p. 1327, supra.)

Article 57. This article treats legislative or administrative provisions which apply equally to nationals and aliens but which in practical terms discriminate between them. Requirements of national diplomas or certificates of residence as conditions to employment are characteristic illustrations.

Article 58. Compare the definitions with those in Title I of the General Program.[51]

50. See the discussion of the Hague Conventions at pp. 304–307, supra, and the discussion of *ordre public* in the Boll case, p. 293, supra.

51. Compare the discussion of the *siège social* at pp. 96–99, supra.

GENERAL PROGRAM FOR THE ABOLITION OF RESTRICTIONS ON FREEDOM OF ESTABLISHMENT [52]

The Council of the European Economic Community,

In view of the provisions of the Treaty and particularly of its Articles 54 and 132, paragraph 5,

in view of the proposal of the Commission,

in view of the opinion of the Economic and Social Committee,

in view of the opinion of the European Parliamentary Assembly,

has issued the following "general program for the abolition of restrictions on freedom of establishment within the European Economic Community."

Title I: Beneficiaries

The abolition of restrictions on freedom of establishment provided for in this general program shall be carried out . . . for the benefit of:

—nationals of the Member States . . .,

—companies set up in conformity with the laws of a Member State . . . and whose registered office, central administration or principal place of business is located within the Community . . .,

for their establishment for the purpose of pursuing a non-wage-earning activity in the territory of a Member State;

—nationals of the Member States . . . established in the territory of a Member State . . .,

—the above-mentioned companies on condition that, in case only their registered office is located within the Community . . . their activities show an effective and continuous link with the economy of a Member State . . . excluding the possibility that this link might depend on nationality, particularly the nationality of the partners or the members of the managing or supervisory bodies, or of persons holding the capital stock,

for the opening of agencies, branches or subsidiaries in the territory of a Member State.

Title II: Entry and residence

Before the expiration of the second year of the second stage of the transitional period, provision shall be made for the following:

A. The adjustment of the legislative, regulatory and administrative provisions governing, in each Member State, the entry and residence of nationals of other Member States, to the extent that such provisions are not required for reasons of public order, public security and public health, and are capable of impairing the access to and exercise of non-wage-earning activities by these nationals, in order to remove this obstruction by abolishing specifically those provisions having economic purposes; . . .

52. [1962] J.O. 36. The translation is taken from the CCH Common Market Reporter ¶ 1335.

Title III: Restrictions

Subject to the exceptions or special provisions set forth in the Treaty . . . the restrictions to be lifted according to the timetable provided for in Title IV are as follows:

A. Any prohibition on or impairment of the non-wage-earning activities of nationals of other Member States, consisting in differential treatment based on nationality as provided under a legislative, regulatory or administrative provision of a Member State or resulting from the application of such a provision or of administrative practices.

Among such restrictive provisions and practices are particularly those which, with regard to foreigners only:

(*a*) Prohibit access to or exercise of a non-wage-earning activity,

(*b*) Condition access to or exercise of a non-wage-earning activity on an authorization or on the issuance of a document, such as a foreign merchant's card or a foreign professional's card,

(*c*) Condition the granting of the authorization required for access to or exercise of the non-wage-earning activity upon additional requirements, . . .

(*h*) Bar or limit membership in companies, particularly with regard to the activities pursued by the members,

(*i*) Prohibit or restrict the right to participate in social security programs and particularly in health, accident, disability and old-age insurance and in family allotments,

(*j*) Grant less favorable treatment in the event of nationalization, expropriation or requisition.

The same applies to provisions and practices which, solely with respect to foreigners, exclude, limit or make subject to certain conditions the ability to exercise the rights normally attached to a non-wage-earning activity and, in particular, the opportunity:

(*a*) To enter into contracts and particularly manufacture and rental contracts such as the hire of services and commercial or farm leases, as well as to benefit by all the rights flowing from such contracts,

(*b*) To tender bids or to participate as co-contractor or subcontractor in public contracts or contracts with other public bodies,

(*c*) To profit by concessions or authorizations granted by the State or other bodies under public law,

(*d*) To acquire, exploit or transfer rights and property both real and personal,

(*e*) To acquire, exploit or transfer intellectual property and rights attached thereto,

(*f*) To borrow and particularly to have access to various forms of credit,

(*g*) To benefit from direct and indirect aid extended by the State,

(*h*) To sue or be sued and to exercise all rights of appeal before administrative authorities, (*i*) To be affiliated with professional organizations,

to the extent that the professional activities of the party concerned require the exercise of such opportunity.

Finally, the provisions and practices mentioned also include those which limit or impair the admission of the personnel of the principal establishment, located in one Member State, into the managing or supervisory bodies of the agencies, branches or subsidiaries opened in another Member State.

B. The conditions to which a legislative, regulatory or administrative provision, or an administrative practice, subjects the access to or exercise of a non-wage-earning activity and which, although applicable regardless of nationality, impair the access to or exercise of such activity by foreigners either exclusively or principally.

Title IV: Time-table

For the purpose of the effective elimination of restrictions on the freedom of establishment, the following time-table shall be adopted: . . .

[Title IV, by references to the different stages of the transitional period under the Treaty, states time limits within which restrictions on freedom of establishment must be eliminated. The time-table incorporates five annexes to the General Program which identify in considerable detail different industries, agricultural or commercial activities, and so on. For example, under the time-table and annexes, restrictions in such fields as textile manufacture, construction, wholesale or retail trade, banking and insurance face different deadlines.]

Title V: Mutual recognition of evidences of qualification and diplomas—Coordination

Without prejudice to Treaty Article 57, paragraph 3, or to Title IV of this general program, simultaneously with the formulation of directives intended for the putting into operation of the general program for each of the non-wage-earning activities, the question as to whether the lifting of restrictions on the freedom of establishment must be preceded, accompanied or followed by the mutual recognition of diplomas, certificates and other evidences of qualification, as well as by the coordination of legislative, regulatory or administrative provisions concerning access to and exercise of these activities, shall be examined. . . .

Title VI: Coordination of guarantees required from companies

The coordination, to the extent necessary and for the purpose of rendering them of equivalent value, of the guarantees required in the Member States from companies in order to protect the interests of the partners and shareholders as well as those of third parties, is contemplated before the expiration of the second year of the second stage of the transitional period. . . .

NOTE ON IMPLEMENTATION OF THE GENERAL PROGRAM AND ISSUANCE OF DIRECTIVES

The 1973 General Report (pp. 137–38) of the Commission states that of 123 group activities which should have been liberalized by the end of the transitional period (1970) pursuant to the General Programs for establishment and services, 76 had been completely liberalized, mostly involving industrial and craft activities. Partial liberalization had occurred in 9 other groups, while 38 group activities had yet to experience effective regulation. A total of 40 directives had been approved, and 61 proposed directives were pending. The Commission noted that the General Programs had been particularly defective with respect to the mutual recognition of diplomas and with respect to the liberal professions.

The directives vary considerably in character. Sometimes they are general and sometimes very detailed as to the measures which member states must take.[53] A directive treating real estate and business services, [1967] J.O. 140, is illustrative. It covers, with respect to business activities, such varied fields as consultant services, appraisers, advertising or employment agencies, and the organization of commercial events (fairs, exhibitions). Among the discriminatory restrictions to be removed are those requiring particular authorizations such as a foreign trader's identity card. Member states are to ensure that those benefiting from the directive can join professional or trade organizations on the same terms as nationals. The directive provides that member states have six months to implement it through legislative and administrative provisions.

Generally directives state the deadlines before which member countries must comply and require each country to inform the Commission of the measures that it has taken. Note the obligation of the Commission under Article 155 to "ensure that the provisions of the Treaty and the measures taken by the institutions pursuant thereto are applied". The 1973 General Report (p. 142) states that the Commission "is making sure that right of establishment directives . . . are correctly applied by the member states. The delays in implementing the directives in original Member States are decreasing. Seven out of the ten infraction procedures started by the Commission on the basis of Article 169 of the Treaty and still underway in 1973 were shelved when the relevant Member States implemented requisite measures."

The delays in the member states in implementing directives have varied explanations—surely in part, political resistance to some of the measures required. But perhaps in larger part, the states confronted procedural obstacles in taking the legislative or other action necessary to modify national rules. The scope of the directives is such that a single directive can require amendment of a considerable number of texts, and the competence to amend may reside in the legislature, the executive, or particular agencies. To remedy this situation, several countries enacted laws authorizing executive or administrative officials to take action to conform national laws with the directives without resort to parliamentary procedures.[54]

53. For descriptions of several present and proposed directives, see CCH Common Market Reporter ¶ 1349.

54. A survey of directives as of 1972 and of the situation under various national laws is offered in Maestripi-

Perhaps the most ambitious of the directives are those aiming at coordination of national provisions within the scope of Article 54(3)(g). There is general agreement that the differences among provisions of corporation laws within the member states act as a restraint upon free movement of persons and establishment of companies. The complexity of the problem of adequate coordination or regulation in this area stems in part from the wide variety in the forms of firms or corporate organizations within the member states. One directive in this field—treating problems of disclosure for protection of shareholders and third parties, problems of validity of acts of company officials (ultra vires contracts), and problems of nullity—has been issued. Pending proposals for directives treat matters such as the formation of limited liability companies, mergers, coordination of financial statements and the structure of corporations.[55] This effort towards harmonization finds an analogy in the movement towards uniform state laws in the United States—with the significant distinction that directives *require* compliance by member countries.

At the same time, discussion continues within the Community institutions about a proposal for a Council regulation embodying a statute for European companies, under which a so-called Societas Europaea would be formed. The Council might here proceed under Article 54(3)(g). But a more likely basis for such a directive, which goes beyond the formal meaning of harmonization, would be Article 235. Alternatively, the Community might here proceed by a special convention as contemplated by Article 220. One among the many advantages of such a Community-wide corporation law would be a facilitation of multistate activities by EEC companies that would stimulate a growth thought necessary to match the U. S. multinationals. See the Note at p. 1414, infra.

Given the delay in the issuance and implementation of directives, a delay which meant that the General Program could not be fully realized by the end of the transitional period, the question arose of the effect of the Treaty provisions themselves upon freedom of establishment and freedom to provide services. That question proved to be particularly thorny in one of the most jealously guarded areas of national regulation, that governing the practice of the liberal professions. The following case—reminiscent of the problems debated in In re Griffiths, p. 54, supra—considers this issue.

eri, Freedom of Establishment and Freedom to Supply Services, 10 C.M. L.Rev. 150 (1973).

55. Descriptions and texts of these directives appear in the CCH Common Market Reporter ¶¶ 1350–1405. A thorough analysis of these problems is provided in Stein, Harmonization of European Company Laws (1971).

REYNERS v. BELGIAN STATE

Court of Justice of the European Communities, Case No. 2/74, June 21, 1974.
Reports of Cases before the Court, 1974–5, p. 631.[56]

[Plaintiff, born of Dutch parents in Belgium and resident in that country, retained his Dutch nationality. He gained his law degree (*docteur en droit belge*) but was not able to gain admission to practice of the profession of *avocat* (a member of the profession exercising functions both of counselling and conducting litigation) in Belgium, because of a 1967 law (modifying a 1919 law) providing that no one may practice the profession of *avocat* who is not Belgian. The law provided for dispensation from the requirement of nationality to be granted by the General Council of the *Ordre des Avocats*, but plaintiff's application for dispensation was unsuccessful. On the advice of the General Council, a Royal Decree was issued in 1970 providing dispensation from the requirement of nationality for a foreigner meeting certain conditions, including proof that national law or an international agreement accorded reciprocity. Plaintiff did not meet this condition, since a 1968 Dutch law stipulated that an applicant for admission to the Dutch bar must have Dutch nationality.

Plaintiff applied in 1970 to the *Conseil d'Etat* of Belgium to annul the reciprocity condition to the Royal Decree, claiming that this provision violated Articles 52, 54, 55 and 57 of the EEC Treaty. That court stayed proceedings and referred certain questions to the Court of Justice pursuant to Article 177. In the written and oral proceedings before the Court of Justice, governments and organizations of the bar of a number of member countries submitted their interpretations and arguments about the relevant Treaty provisions. Excerpts from the opinion of the Court of Justice appear below:]

On the interpretation of Article 52 of the EEC Treaty

The Conseil d'Etat inquires whether Article 52 of the EEC Treaty is, since the end of the transitional period, a "directly applicable provision" despite the absence of directives as provided for in Articles 54(2) and 57(1) of the Treaty.

The Belgian and Irish Governments have argued, for largely the same reasons, that Article 52 does not have such an effect. Taken in the context of the chapter on the right of establishment, to which reference is expressly made by the words "within the framework of the provisions set out below," this article, because of the complexity of the subject, is said to be only the expression of a simple principle, the implementation of which is necessarily subject to a set of complementary provisions, both Community and national, provided for in Articles 54 and 57. The form chosen by the Treaty for these implementing acts—the establishment of a "general program," implemented in turn by a set of directives—confirms, it is argued, that Article 52 does not have a direct effect. It is not for the courts to exercise a discretionary power reserved to the legislative institutions of the Community and the Member States. This argument is supported in substance by the British and Luxembourg Governments, as well as by the Ordre national des avocats de Belgique, the intervening party in the main action.

56. The text, taken from CCH Common Market Reporter ¶ 8256, differs in minor, formal respects from the later-published opinion in Reports of Cases before the Court.

The plaintiff in the main action, for his part, states that all that is in question in his case is a discrimination based on nationality by reason of the fact that he is subject to conditions for admission to the profession of *avocat* which are not applicable to Belgian nationals. In this respect, he maintains that Article 52 is a clear and complete provision, capable of producing a direct effect.

The German Government, supported in substance by the Dutch Government and citing the judgment rendered by this Court on June 16, 1966, in Case No. 57/65, *Lütticke* (Recueil 1966, page 293), considers that the provisions imposing on the Member States an obligation which they must fulfill within a particular time become directly applicable when, on the expiration of this period, the obligation has not been fulfilled. At the end of the transitional period, the Member States no longer have the possibility of maintaining restrictions on the freedom of establishment since Article 52 has, as of this time, the character of a provision that is complete in itself and legally perfect. Under these conditions the "general program" and the directives provided for in Article 54 were of significance only during the transitional period, since the freedom of establishment was fully attained on its termination.

The Commission, notwithstanding any doubts it has on the subject of the direct effect of the provision to be interpreted—both in view of the reference in the Treaty to the "general program" and to the implementing directives and because of the substance of certain liberalizing directives already taken, which do not attain in every respect a perfect equality of treatment—considers, however, that Article 52 has at least a partial direct effect, in so far as it specifically prohibits discrimination on grounds of nationality.

Article 7 of the Treaty, which forms part of the "principles" of the Community, provides that within the area of application of the Treaty and without prejudice to any special provisions contained therein, "any discrimination on grounds of nationality shall be prohibited."

. . .

It appears . . . that in the system of the chapter on the right of establishment the "general program" and the directives provided for in the Treaty are intended to accomplish two functions, the first being to eliminate, during the transitional period, obstacles to attaining the freedom of establishment, and the second being to introduce into the laws of the Member States a set of provisions intended to facilitate the effective exercise of this freedom for the purpose of assisting the economic and social interpenetration within the Community in the area of activities as self-employed persons.

This second objective is the one covered, first, in certain provisions of Article 54(3), relating in particular to the cooperation between the competent authorities in the Member States and the adjustment of administrative procedures and practices, and, secondly, in the set of provisions of Article 57. The effect of the provisions of Article 52 must be decided within the framework of this system.

The rule of equal treatment with nationals is one of the fundamental legal provisions of the Community. As a reference to a set of legislative provisions effectively applied by the country of establishment to its own nationals, this rule is, in its essence, capable of being directly invoked by the nationals of all the other Member States.

In stating that the freedom of establishment shall be attained at the end of the transitional period, Article 52 thus imposes an obligation to achieve a specific result, the fulfillment of which had to be made easier by, but not made dependent on, the implementation of a program of progressive measures. The fact that this progression has not been adhered to leaves the obligation itself intact beyond the end of the period provided for its fulfillment. This interpretation is in accordance with Article 8(7) of the Treaty, which provides that the end of the transitional period shall constitute the latest date by which all the rules provided for in the Treaty must enter into force and all the measures required for establishing the Common Market must be implemented.

It is not possible to invoke against such an effect the fact that the Council failed to issue the directives provided for in Articles 54 and 57 or the fact that some of the directives actually issued have not fully attained the objective of nondiscrimination required by Article 52. After the expiration of the transitional period the directives provided for in the chapter on the right of establishment became superfluous with regard to implementing the rule of national treatment, since this is henceforth sanctioned by the Treaty itself with direct effect. These directives have, however, not lost all interest since they retain an important applicability in the field of measures intended to promote the effective exercise of the right of freedom of establishment.

Accordingly, the question presented should be answered in the sense that, since the end of the transitional period, Article 52 of the Treaty is a directly applicable provision despite the absence, in a particular area, of the directives provided for in Articles 54(2) and 57(1) of the Treaty.

On the interpretation of Article 55 of the EEC Treaty

The Conseil d'Etat further asks for a clarification of what is meant, in the first paragraph of Article 55, by "activities which in that State are connected, even occasionally, with the exercise of official authority." More precisely, the question is whether, within a profession such as that of *avocat,* only those activities inherent in this profession which are connected with the exercise of official authority are excepted from the application of the chapter on the right of establishment, or whether the whole of this profession is excepted by reason of the fact that it comprises activities connected with the exercise of this authority.

The Luxembourg Government and the Ordre national des avocats de Belgique consider that the whole profession of *avocat* is excluded from the rules in the Treaty on the right of establishment by the fact that it is connected organically with the functioning of the public service of the administration of justice. They claim that this situation results both from the legal organization of the bar, involving a set of strict conditions for admission and discipline, and from the functions performed by the *avocat* in the context of the judicial procedure where his participation is largely obligatory. These activities, which make the *avocat* an indispensable auxiliary of the administration of justice, form a coherent whole, whose elements cannot be separated.

The plaintiff in the main action, for his part, contends that at most only certain activities of the profession of *avocat* are connected with the exercise of official authority and that therefore only these activities come within the exception made in Article 55 to the principle of the freedom of establishment.

The German, Belgian, British, Irish and Dutch Governments, as well as the Commission, regard the exception contained in Article

55 as limited to those activities within the various professions concerned which are effectively connected with the exercise of official authority, subject to their being separable from the normal practice of the profession.

Differences exist, however, between the Governments referred to as regards the nature of the activities that are so excepted from the principle of the freedom of establishment, taking into account the different organization of the profession of *avocat* from one Member State to another.

The German Government in particular maintains that because of the obligatory connection of the *avocat* with certain judicial processes, especially as regards criminal or public law, there are such close ties between the profession of *avocat* and the exercise of judicial authority that large sectors of this profession, at least, should be excepted from the freedom of establishment.

Under the terms of the first paragraph of Article 55 the provisions of the chapter on the right of establishment do not apply "so far as any given Member State is concerned, to activities which in that State are connected, even occasionally, with the exercise of official authority." In view of the fundamental character of the freedom of establishment and the rule on national treatment in the system of the Treaty, the exceptions permitted in the first paragraph of Article 55 cannot be given a meaning that would exceed the objective for which this exemption clause was inserted.

The first paragraph of Article 55 must permit the Member States to exclude non-nationals from taking up functions involving the exercise of official authority which are connected with one of the activities of self-employed persons provided for in Article 52. This need is fully satisfied when the exclusion of nationals is limited to those activities which, taken on their own, constitute a direct and specific connection with the exercise of official authority.

An extension of the exception permitted in Article 55 to an entire profession would be possible only in cases where such activities were linked with that profession in such a way that the freedom of establishment would result in imposing on the Member State concerned the obligation to allow the exercise, even occasionally, by non-nationals of functions appertaining to official authority. Such an extension, is on the other hand, not possible when, within the framework of an independent profession, the activities connected with the exercise of official authority are separable from the professional activity in question taken as a whole.

In the absence of any directive issued under Article 57 for the purpose of harmonizing the national provisions relating, in particular, to the profession of *avocat*, the practice of this profession remains governed by the law of the various Member States. Any application of the restrictions on the freedom of establishment provided for in the first paragraph of Article 55 must therefore be considered separately, for each Member State, having regard to the national provisions applicable to the organization and the practice of this profession. This consideration must, however, take into account the Community character of the limits imposed by Article 55 on the permissible exceptions to the principle of the freedom of establishment in order to avoid the effectiveness of the Treaty being defeated by unilateral provisions of the Member States.

Professional activities involving contacts, even regular and organic, with the courts, including even a compulsory cooperation in their functioning, do not constitute, as such, a connection with the exercise of official authority.

In particular, the most typical activities of the profession of *avocat,* such as consultation and legal assistance and also representation and the defense of parties in court, even when the intervention or assistance of the *avocat* is compulsory or is a legal monopoly, cannot be considered as connected with the exercise of official authority. The exercise of these activities leaves the discretion of the judicial authority and the free exercise of the judicial power intact.

Accordingly, the question asked should be answered to the effect that the exception to the freedom of establishment provided for in the first paragraph of Article 55 must be restricted to those of the activities referred to in Article 52 which in themselves involve a direct and specific connection with the exercise of official authority. In any event, this description, in the context of a profession such as that of *avocat,* cannot be given to activities such as consultation and legal assistance or the representation and defense of parties in court, even if the performance of these activities is an obligation or a monopoly established by law.

. . .

QUESTIONS

(1) In many fields, the Treaty empowers the Council (and occasionally the Commission) to implement provisions through the issuance of regulations. For example, regulations under Article 49 define the conditions under which nationals of one state are entitled to seek employment and remain working in another. In the antitrust field, regulations define the cooperation required of authorities of the member states, and categories of agreements which are exempted from antitrust prohibitions. Why do you suppose that the Treaty first required issuance of a general program in the establishment field, and then authorized the Council to proceed only by directives?

(2) A directive orders member countries to abolish restrictions on establishment in the wholesale trade. Suppose that France fails to repeal or modify legislation which limits alien enterprises in this field. Could an Italian company seeking to enter the wholesale trade in France use the directive to challenge the legislation before a French court and demand the right to open a branch? If not, would it have any other avenue of relief?

(3) A Delaware corporation establishes under French law a subsidiary with its registered office in France, as permitted by Article V of the Establishment Convention between the United States and France.* The subsidiary's managing personnel are primarily American, and most decisions of importance are made in the United States. The subsidiary operates a small manufacturing plant near Paris. If it wishes to extend its operations to another Common Market country through a branch or subsidiary, can it take advantage of the General Program and the implementing directives?

(4) Compare the establishment provisions with Articles V and VII of the Franco-American Convention. Does the Rome Treaty (as fully implemented by directives and national legislation) confer more extensive rights upon a German corporation seeking to open a branch in France than the Convention does upon a Delaware corporation? If so, in what circumstances would the differences between these treaties be significant to an alien?

(5) Suppose that Article V(1) of the Franco-American Convention accorded both "national treatment" and "most-favored-nation treatment" to nationals and companies of both countries.[57] Note Article 234 of the Treaty. Would a Delaware corporation intending to purchase a French factory be able to invoke the Treaty (as implemented) if its provisions appeared more favorable than the Convention's?

(6) Consider the Treaty articles, the General Program and the implementing directives in relation to laws in the United States governing access by aliens to economic activities. What comparisons and contrasts would you draw between the methods and substance of (a) Community control of national laws and (b) federal control of state laws? What comparisons and contrasts would you draw between federal control of aliens' activities and controls within the Community of activities of non-EEC (natural or legal) persons?

---

2. COMMUNITY ANTITRUST LAW

NOTE ON GOALS OF COMMUNITY ANTITRUST POLICY

Like the tariff provisions of the Treaty, antitrust law is a prime example of a field where Community law displaces national law and creates "supreme" rules for the member nations. The national antitrust laws of the members vary widely, ranging from minimal to fairly extensive regulation of anticompetitive business conduct.[58] The materials below make occasional references to provisions of the national laws but stress the processes by which Community antitrust law develops.

Paragraphs (a) and (f) of Article 3 make evident antitrust law's importance to achievement of the Treaty's goals. Private agreements restraining competition could impede the creation of a Common Market as effectively as tariffs or laws regulating establishment. For example, an agreement between competing French and German firms requiring each to sell only within its national territory or at a common price could undermine the provisions of the Treaty

57. A number of Friendship, Commerce and Navigation Treaties do provide for most-favored-nation treatment. Article VII of the 1954 Treaty of Friendship, Commerce and Navigation between the United States of America and the Federal Republic of Germany, 7 U.S.T. & O.I.A. 1839, T.I.A.S. No. 3593, treats questions of establishment. Section 4 of that Article states: "Nations and companies of either Party, as well as enterprises controlled by such nationals or companies, shall in any event be accorded most-favored-nation treatment with reference to the matters treated in the present Article."

58. The texts of the laws of the member countries are set forth in the Guide to Legislation on Restrictive Business Practices in Europe and North America, published by the Organization for Economic Cooperation and Development. The Library of Congress made a recent compilation of these laws which appears in Hearings before the Subcommittee on Antitrust and Monopoly of the Senate Committee on the Judiciary on Foreign Trade and the Antitrust Laws, 89th Cong., 1st Sess., pt. 2, App. (1965). See also the CCH Common Market Reporter.

eliminating impediments to trade between the two countries. More generally, the Community seeks to create conditions that are conducive to economic growth; any such program must attempt to define the role of competition and the extent to which some anticompetitive practices are consistent with this general goal.

In a Report to the Assembly in 1965, Hans van der Groeben, a member of the Commission, considered competition policy's bearing upon the general economic policy of the Common Market.[59] The Report states that the antitrust provisions aim at opening domestic markets to foreign goods under rules that complement the abolition of frontier controls, at eliminating unnecessary distortions, and at developing "workable and effective" competition throughout the Common Market under appropriate regulation. It refers to competition not as an end in itself but as "a means of attaining maximum productivity, satisfaction of demands, well-being and economic freedom for everybody in the Community." [60] In recent years, officials of the Community have expressed the view (also expressed by legislators and executive officials in the United States) that control of restrictive practices may contribute to the control of inflation.

The key provisions on antitrust policy appear in Articles 85 to 89. Despite striking differences between those articles and some of our antitrust rules—for example, the contrast between the condemnation in Article 86 of *abuse* of a dominant position in the Common Market and the judicial interpretation of Section 2 of the Sherman Act, p. 991, supra—the wording of Articles 85 and 86 is often reminiscent of the Sherman Act and certain sections of the Clayton Act. American antitrust principles influenced the drafting of the Treaty. Nonetheless, the similarity in language can lead to misleading and unwarranted inferences about the directions which Community antitrust law will follow. Notwithstanding the important differences in antitrust regulation among the Common Market countries, one can state generally that these countries have a markedly different tradition from the United States with respect to the role of such regulation and the freedom given business firms to make private arrangements of substantial importance (such as cartels) that undeniably restrict competition. It is true that a basic purpose of the Treaty is to depart from that tradition. But certain historical themes will undoubtedly survive and, through provisions such as Article 85(3), continue to distinguish the European from the American scene.

More important, the proper role of competition must be determined in a significantly different political and economic environment. Antitrust policy, particularly in view of the institutional structure within which it is to be elaborated, will bear the direct imprint of economic policies formulated by Community officials. It has shown itself to be fairly particularistic in its development—that is, distin-

59. An English translation of the Report appears in the CCH Common Market Reporter ¶ 9036.

60. Compare the description of the goals of United States antitrust policy at pp. 987–996, supra.

guishing not only among kinds of agreements but also among sectors of the economy.

Article 85(1) and the first paragraph of Article 86 define the field in which Community antitrust law applies.[61] Note their references to agreements "which may affect trade between the Member States" and to abuse "of a dominant position within the common market or in a substantial part of it." Such language recalls the references to interstate commerce in Section 1 of the Sherman Act, p. 991, supra, and other of our antitrust laws. Thus national law remains in principle operative and exclusive under Article 85 for agreements or practices that affect only a national market. There is doctrinal dispute, but as yet no clear determination, whether national law prohibiting agreements consistent with Community antitrust rules can be applied to agreements that affect trade between member states or a substantial part of the Market.

The materials below treat principally Article 85, which has thus far been the subject of more extensive debate and adjudication before national and Community authorities than Article 86. During the early years of antitrust enforcement within the Community, dominant attention was paid to vertical agreements, particularly agreements for exclusive distributorships which contained restrictive clauses. The anticompetitive effects of those agreements in partitioning the Common Market into separate national territories was easy to perceive. Moreover, those agreements were relatively easy to detect. In recent years, more attention has been paid to horizontal agreements—particularly price fixing and market allocations—that violated Article 85, and to problems of abuse of dominant positions within the scope of Article 86—particularly with respect to acquisitions or mergers. The early emphasis upon specific bilateral agreements frustrating the goals of the EEC Treaty has to some extent given way to concern with broader issues of the accumulation of power. Moreover, the developing antitrust law has had to take account of firms outside the Common Market that are linked through subsidiaries or agreements to practices within it—the broad issue of the extraterritorial application of Community antitrust law to the large multinational companies based principally in the United States.

The materials start with an examination of the basic regulation in this field and describe the techniques for the elaboration and enforcement of antitrust law, together with the relationships created by the Treaty and implementing regulations between national and Community institutions. They continue with a detailed study of the problem of exclusive distributorship contracts, and conclude with a briefer consideration of the other substantive problems in Community antitrust laws that were noted above.

61. These articles do not cover certain fields which are the subject of special regulation, principally the coal and steel industries and atomic energy. Other fields, such as agriculture and transportation, have been subjected to distinct regulation by action of the Community institutions.

Additional reading: Translations of all decisions of the Court of Justice on antitrust questions appear in the CCH Common Market Reporter and in the Common Market Law Reports. Both include numerous decisions of national courts involving Community antitrust law. A bibliography on antitrust matters appears in the Common Market Reporter ¶ 9901. The Common Market Law Review and Journal of Common Market Studies contain numerous articles about this field.

NOTE ON REGULATION NO. 17

Regulation No. 17, effective March 13, 1962, is set forth in the Documentary Supplement. The comments and questions below assume familiarity with its provisions.[62]

Sanctions. Note the sanctions in the Treaty and the Regulation which can be applied to parties violating Community antitrust law:

(*a*) The basic idea is that an agreement prohibited by Article 85 (1) is "automatically void" under Article 85(2) as a matter of law, without need for a decision to that effect by a Community authority. Thus a contract between two firms which was proscribed by Article 85(1) could not provide a basis for recovery in a suit before a national court in which a party sought damages for breach of a restrictive clause. (Only those parts of the agreement that are prohibited are null and void; whether they could meaningfully be separated from the remaining clauses of the agreement would be a matter for particular decision.) Compare a defendant's contention in a contract action in a state court in this country that the clause sued upon violates federal antitrust law.

(*b*) Neither the Treaty nor Regulation provides for damages for a party injured by agreements or practices of others that violate Community law. That is, Community law offers no analogy to the treble-damage action, p. 993, supra, in the United States. Nonetheless legal principles in some member countries do permit suits for money damages against persons who have injured the plaintiff through conduct that violates certain laws. Enforcement of Community antitrust law thus depends in part upon national remedial law.

(*c*) By means of a decision, the Commission may impose fines and penalties on enterprises which violate certain provisions of the Treaty or Regulation. (Regulation Articles 15–17.) The fines are measured in units of account as used for budgetary purposes under Treaty Articles 207 and 209, one U. A. equal to .888 grams of fine gold (formerly equivalent to one dollar but varying from it since the recent dollar devaluations, and equivalent to about $1.20 in mid-1974). The fines have both punitive and deterrent functions. Compare the

62. Some problems in interpreting the Regulation are explored in a document prepared by the Commission and referred to as a Practical Guide to Articles 85 and 86 of the EEC Treaty and the Relevant Regulations: A Manual for Firms. An English translation of the Practical Guide appears in the CCH Common Market Reporter ¶ 2801. Some comments in this Note are based upon interpretative statements in the Practical Guide.

use of fines in criminal proceedings under the antitrust laws in the United States.

(*d*) The Commission can enter decisions requiring enterprises to end certain practices (Regulation Article 3). Those decisions will, on occasion, take the form of affirmative decrees, or decrees to which certain conditions are attached. The analogies in the United States are the administrative cease and desist order and the court injunction.

Article 2. Negative Clearance. The negative clearance indicates only that the Commission will not challenge an agreement or practice under Article 85. Although a request for a negative clearance does not require a notification (discussed below) by a party, the two are generally submitted together, together with a request for a declaration (Regulation Article 6) under Article 85(3). The clearance expresses the Commission's view that the Treaty's antitrust provisions are inapplicable at the outset. Thus request for a clearance is alternative to a request for a declaration under Article 85(3). (The term "declaration" when used in the text below refers to one under Article 85 (3)).

The Commission might grant a negative clearance on the ground that a particular agreement is so national (local) in character that it is not likely to "affect trade between the Member States." Although the Regulation does not indicate the effect of a negative clearance upon suits before national courts involving a contract which was the subject of the clearance, note that Article 9(3) refers to Article 2 and thus suggests that the clearance has *some* relevance to national-court proceedings.

Requests for a negative clearance are made by parties on a Form A/B drafted by the Commission (translation at CCH Common Market Reporter ¶ 2659). The form refers to the penalties under Regulation Article 15(1)(a) for providing false information. It requires a full description of the relevant agreement, and a statement of reasons why the applicant thinks that Article 85(1) is inapplicable. There are various analogies to the negative clearance in the United States, particularly "no action" letters of the SEC under the Securities Act of 1933 and informal clearances of proposed action by executive or administrative authorities responsible for enforcement of the tax or antitrust laws.

Articles 4–8. Notifications and Declarations. The procedures for notification are a critical feature of Community antitrust law. Notification is not obligatory; no fines or other sanctions can be applied *simply* because a party has failed to notify an agreement that is within the ban of Article 85(1). On the other hand, notification serves important purposes. Certain agreements, such as those covered by Articles 4(1) and 5(1), can benefit from a declaration under Article 85(3) only after their notification. Of course notification does not assure that any such declaration will issue; it is simply an indispensable condition.

Notifications are made on the same Form A/B that covers requests for negative clearance. The Form suggests that a notification seeking the benefit of a declaration does not constitute a recognition by the filing party (who can be simply one of the parties to an agreement among several firms) that the agreement is within Article 85(1). The Form refers to giving notice "if only as a precaution." The Form demands extensive economic data relevant to determining whether the four conditions to Article 85(3) have been satisfied.

Note the role of Article 4(2) in defining categories of agreements which need not be notified. It refers to agreements covering activities rooted in one nation, to certain contracts involving resale price maintenance or restrictions related to patent and trademark licenses, and to research contracts. Article 6(2) provides that a declaration by the Commission relating to such agreements can be made retroactive to any date which the Commission selects, presumably the date at which the conditions stated in Article 85(3) were first met. Contrast Article 6(1), which defines the date as of which a declaration can be made effective for agreements not within these limited categories.

As Regulation Article 1 makes clear, an agreement within Article 85(1) is "prohibited," null and void, without any official action by the Commission. Official action *is* however required under Article 6 to render valid any agreement within Article 85(1). Community antitrust law thus first brands all agreements or practices within Article 85(1) illegal, and then accords a legal validity to some among them through acts of the Commission.[63] Note that Article 8 empowers the Commission to attach conditions to declarations and, under certain circumstances, to revoke them.

Cooperative Relationships. Community and national organs form part of a complex cooperative scheme. That scheme extends from the investigation of practices or consultation before certain action is taken to the institution of proceedings and means of enforcing sanctions. Sometimes the Commission has sole competence to apply provisions of the Treaty, such as Article 85(3). (Regulation Article 9(1)). Sometimes competence is shared by authorities of the member states (Article 9(3)). The Regulation requires cooperation and aid by national authorities to enable the Commission to perform its tasks (Articles 10, 11, 13 and 14).

It is important to grasp clearly the distinction between negative clearances, relevant to Article 85(1), and declarations, relevant to Article 85(3). (Bear in mind that "declarations", as defined in this text, are also referred to as "exemptions", and are referred to as "decisions" of the Commission in Regulation Articles 6 and 8.) One further point should be noted. Individual negative clearances—that is, clearances referring to a specific agreement or practice described in

63. The group exemptions considered at pp. 1386–1393, infra, require some qualifications to these statements.

an application to the Commission—have been complemented by general "notices" of the Commission referring to described groups or agreements. The function of the notices is to advise businesses which have entered into the defined types of agreements that the Commission considers such agreements to be outside the prohibition of Article 85(1). As a general rule private parties need not obtain a negative clearance for such agreements or file a notification for purposes of a declaration.[64] The notices state that they do not prejudice other interpretations of the described agreements which may be given by competent authorities, particularly courts and very particularly the Court of Justice.

By the same token, individual notifications and requests for a declaration under Article 85(3) are not the sole method for recognition of the validity of an agreement that falls within Article 85(1). The Council has issued several regulations providing for the application of Article 85(3)—that is, providing for the grant of a group exemption—to defined categories or types of agreements and practices. The Council has based these regulations upon Article 87, and has delegated to the Commission the power to issue regulations stating that agreements or practices within the Council's regulation benefit from a declaration under Article 85(3).[65]

COMMENT

The following information describes the evolution in the business of the Commission about antitrust matters.[66]

As of March 1967, about 37,000 notifications, requests, complaints and other cases were before the Commission; over 99% involved requests by parties for negative clearances or declarations, and over 30,000 of those requests concerned exclusive distributorship contracts. Of the 30,000 agreements for exclusive dealing or distributorships that were initially notified, only about 1,500 were pending before the Commission as of April 1972. As of December of that year, there was before the Commission a backlog of 4,213 cases. Of that total, 4,052 arose through applications and notifications, 45 were based on complaints received by private parties, and 116 were based on the Commission's own investigations and initiative.

The Commission sponsored a research study in the 1960's to determine the extent to which national laws could give rise to actions

64. The CCH Common Market Reporter ¶¶ 2697–2700 contains translations of the texts of four such notices, treating contracts for exclusive representation concluded with commercial agents; some provisions of patent licensing agreements; types of cooperation between enterprises; and agreements of minor importance. All four categories are subject to stated conditions. See pp. 1388–1389, infra, for a discussion of some of these notices.

65. Such regulations of the Council and Commission appear at pp. 1386–1393, infra.

66. The statistical information in this Comment is taken from the Tenth General Report of the Commission (¶¶ 45–50), the First Report on Competition Policy (p. 57), annexed to the 1972 General Report, and the 1973 General Report (p. 154).

for money damages or injunctions brought by firms injured by practices violating Articles 85 or 86. The project indicated that, in most countries, such remedies were available.

QUESTIONS

(1) Assume that parties to an agreement within Article 85(1) and Regulation Article 4(1) intend to comply with the agreement for their mutual benefit even though it would likely be held null and void in litigation before a national court. What risks do they incur if they decide not to notify the agreement?

(2) A German firm, Bonnco, and a French competitor, Parisco, enter into a 1972 agreement with provisions for common purchases of raw materials that bring it within Article 85(1) and Regulation Article 4(1). Bonnco notifies the agreement in December 1973, and the Commission issues a declaration in 1974. Until what date could the declaration be made retroactive? Could the Commission impose fines under Article 15 for conduct by the firms consistent with the contract during 1972 and 1973? Would such action be advisable? Was the contract "null and void" until December 1973 and valid thereafter? What practical consequences would such a view have?

(3) Bonnco and Parisco (a distributor) enter into a 1974 contract giving Parisco exclusive rights to sell Bonnco's products in France but attaching various conditions to those sales. Assume that the agreement is within Article 85(1) but, given its particular provisions and general market conditions, might be able to benefit from a declaration. The agreement comes under Regulation Article 4(1) but has not been notified. You are counsel to a French distributor, competitive with Parisco, which wishes to handle Bonnco's products. Bypassing any remedies that the firm might have under French law or in the French courts, what action might it take under Community law and what results could it anticipate?

NOTE ON THE USE OF EXCLUSIVE DISTRIBUTORSHIP CONTRACTS

The decisions of the Commission, national courts and the Court of Justice on pp. 1355–1385, infra, treat different problems posed by exclusive distributorship contracts under Community antitrust law. This Note describes some characteristics of these contracts.

Contracts of exclusive distributorship between the manufacturer and the wholesaler (distributor) or retailer (dealer) of a product restrict the selling rights of either or both parties, usually territorially. The comments below treat three typical restraints.

(1) In their simplest form such contracts confer exclusive rights upon the distributor to sell the product within a defined territory. In the Common Market cases, the exclusive territory is generally a member nation. For example, Bonnco, a German manufacturer of widgets, may agree to sell to Parisco, a French distributor, and also agree not to sell widgets to any other person in France. Bonnco might enter into comparable contracts with distributors in other European countries.

Note the effect of such "sole-outlet" arrangements. Unless French dealers or consumers make the effort to purchase Bonnco widgets from suppliers in foreign countries, or unless foreign suppliers are willing to advertise or open branches in France, Parisco may have a monopoly of the French market for Bonnco widgets. There may be no "intrabrand" competition. How much freedom this gives Parisco with respect to pricing and other policies will depend upon the extent to which it faces meaningful competition from distributors of other brands of widgets—upon the extent of "interbrand" as opposed to "intraband" competition. For example, if Bonnco widgets are readily interchangeable with other brands (if, for example, we are talking about different *toothpaste* brands), competition for consumers in the widget market would remain keen.

Manufacturers and distributors offer varied justifications for the possible anticompetitive effects of these agreements. The protection given Parisco may encourage it to make the investment of funds and energy to introduce a new product or promote more intensively one already on the market. That protection may be an essential condition to various commitments by Parisco. For example, if widgets were complex products such as electronic equipment requiring servicing, the firms might contend that the agreement gave Parisco the minimum assurance against competition that would lead it to develop an expert sales staff, post-sales service operations, and so on. It further assures Parisco that other distributors will not be able to take advantage of its efforts and benefit from the developing market for Bonnco widgets without comparable investments of their own. The arrangement thus is said to spur rather than limit competition among brands. Of course, the force of this argument will depend upon the degree to which there is effective interbrand competition.

(2) A second restraint might perfect this arrangement by adding territorial restrictions upon sales by distributors. Parisco agrees not to sell widgets to any dealer or consumer outside its exclusive French territory, or indeed to any dealer or consumer in France whom Parisco knows to be a resident of a foreign country. Contracts between Bonnco and exclusive distributors in other countries may contain comparable clauses. Thus a network of truly exclusive territories has been created. The consumer loses the option available to him under the sole-outlet agreement to shop in other national markets. Intrabrand competition among Bonnco widget distributors terminates. Again, the anticompetitive effects of this arrangement will depend upon a variety of factors, including the extent to which there is meaningful interbrand competition. Justifications offered for this restriction are similar to those noted above. Either or both firms may claim that it is indispensable to the business arrangement, in the sense that Parisco would not have undertaken its selling efforts without assurance of absolute territorial protection.

(3) A third restraint might prevent Parisco from handling any products competitive with the widgets purchased from Bonnco. The

anticompetitive effects of this "full requirements" arrangement may be severe, if Bonnco's competitors were thereby foreclosed from finding satisfactory distributor outlets to reach the French market.

This simplified description of exclusive distributorship arrangements bypasses arguments of a more subtle character which may be relevant or critical to a determination of their legality. Extensive economic data may prove essential to an evaluation of the effect of a given arrangement and the sufficiency of the justifications offered for it. For example, the extent of interbrand competition may determine Parisco's freedom to set prices or other sales policies; price differentials, if any, between Bonnco widgets in France and other countries may evidence whether Parisco has a virtual monopoly of the French widget market; the size and reputation of Parisco *vis-à-vis* other distributors in the field may determine the extent to which a "full requirements" provision limits opportunities for Bonnco's competitors.

NOTE ON THE LEGALITY OF EXCLUSIVE DISTRIBUTORSHIP CONTRACTS WITHIN THE UNITED STATES

Early antitrust litigation in this country concerned primarily *horizontal* agreements between competing firms at the same stage of the production or distribution process—for example, price fixing or division of territories among competitors. Although certain kinds of *vertical* agreements (between parties at successive stages of the processes of production and distribution) had long been significant in antitrust enforcement—resale price maintenance agreements, for example—the exclusive distributorship contract had not. Thus the American experience has been unlike that of the Common Market, where exclusive distributorship contracts early became a focus of litigation and regulation.

This Note summarizes four significant American cases. Within a period of five years, the last three have defined the status under the antitrust laws of distributorship contracts with territorial restrictions on resales. The similarities between their outcomes and the acts of the Commission or decisions of the Court of Justice bear out earlier observations about the relationship between Section 1 of the Sherman Act, p. 991, supra, and Article 85 of the Rome Treaty.

Note that the "opinions" refer to "*per se* violations" of the antitrust laws and to the "rule of reason." These phrases recur in antitrust decisions but do not permit of easy or satisfactory definition. See the comments at p. 991, supra. In several respects, the "rule of reason" read into the Sherman Act bears an analogy to paragraph (3) of Article 85 of the Rome Treaty. The cases considered below illustrate this relationship.

Packard Motor Car Co. v. Webster Motor Car Co., 100 U.S.App. D.C. 161, 243 F.2d 418 (1957): In 1958, there were three dealers for Packard cars in Baltimore, including Webster. The dealer contracts were for one year, with no option of extension, although it was the custom to extend them from year to year. Zell, the largest dealer, informed Packard that it was losing money and would not continue unless given an exclusive, sole-outlet contract. Packard agreed and advised the other dealers that their contracts would not be renewed. Webster sued for treble damages, alleging violation of Article 1 and 2 of the Sherman Act.

The Court of Appeals reversed a judgment of the district court for Zell. With respect to Section 1, it stated that "it has long been clear that only unreasonable restraints of trade are unlawful." That other dealers in Packard cars were eliminated did not make the exclusive dealership illegal; nor did the fact that Zell sought the arrangement. The court stressed that Packard, a relatively small manufacturer, evidently thought it advantageous to retain its largest dealer in Baltimore and could do so only in this way. "To penalize the small manufacturer for competing in this way not only fails to promote the policy of the antitrust laws but defeats it." Note that the agreement had no territorial restrictions on resales by the dealer.

White Motor Co. v. United States, 372 U.S. 253, 83 S.Ct. 696, 9 L.Ed.2d 738 (1963): The contracts between White (a manufacturer of trucks) and its distributors and dealers contained clauses in which White granted the other party "the exclusive right" to sell its products in a defined territory. The other party agreed "to develop the [specified] territory to the satisfaction of Company" and "not to sell such trucks except to individuals, firms or corporations having a place of business and/or purchasing headquarters in said territory." The Government claimed that these provisions were *per se* violations of Section 1 of the Sherman Act. The district court entered summary judgment for the United States and issued an injunction against continuation of these practices.

On appeal, the Supreme Court reversed. It refused to lay down a rule that such territorial restrictions were *per se* illegal and ordered a trial at which White could develop economic justifications for them. It said: "We do not know enough of the economic and business stuff out of which these arrangements emerge to be certain. They may be too dangerous to sanction or they may be allowable protections against aggressive competitors or the only practical means a small company has for breaking into or staying in business . . . and within the 'rule of reason.' " [67]

Sandura Co. v. FTC, 339 F.2d 847 (6th Cir. 1964): The FTC, acting under Section 5 of the Federal Trade Commission Act, p. 992, supra, declared unlawful the territorial restrictions in contracts between distributors and Sandura, a maker of vinyl floor covering products. On review, the court noted that Sandura was a "relatively small

67. A consent decree was thereafter entered under which White agreed not to enter into or claim any rights under any understanding "to limit, allocate or restrict the territories" in which the distributor or dealer might sell. 1964 Trade Cases ¶ 71, 195 (W.D.Ohio 1964).

firm" losing ground to the industry's "giants." Sandura had met with product failures which nearly forced it into bankruptcy, and "its distribution system became badly demoralized." It sought to improve its position through a system under which each distributor was confined to sales within its own territory, in order to restore distributors' confidence and encourage initiative. There was extensive testimony that distributors would not have taken the risk of selling (and financing advertising or carrying on servicing functions) for such a risky venture without such assurance. "No dealer, however, has been subjected to the caprice of his area distributor, and no distributor is shown to have made unreasonable profits." There were also statistics as to the decline (and revival) of Sandura's sales and its small share of the market (5%) and of the industry's assets (never over 1½%).

The court, citing the White case, stated: "[S]o must we here refuse to find Sandura's arrangements illegal without examining their particular effect on competition *and* the facts offered to justify the resulting restraint." It noted the FTC's finding that Sandura's products were "in substantial competition" with other hard-surface covering materials. But it recognized "the obvious fact that closed territories do prevent the intrabrand competition that could exist if one Sandura distributor went into another's territory to compete for the custom of a dealer." Nonetheless, on the showing made, the court "felt constrained to uphold the legal sufficiency of the justification made by Sandura" and reversed the Commission.

United States v. Arnold, Schwinn & Co., 388 U.S. 365, 87 S.Ct. 1856, 18 L.Ed.2d 1249 (1967): Schwinn sold its bicycles primarily to or through 22 wholesale distributors, each of which was allocated a specific territory and could sell only to "franchised" retail dealers. Neither distributors nor dealers were restricted to handling Schwinn bicycles, and both ordinarily sold a variety of brands. There was significant interbrand competition. Schwinn sold its bicycles both by sales to distributors and by consignment or agency arrangements with distributors through which Schwinn retained ownership until the sales to dealers or the consumer public.

The Supreme Court observed that it "must look to the specifics of the challenged practices and their impact upon the marketplace in order to make a judgment as to whether the restraint is or is not 'reasonable' in the special sense in which § 1 of the Sherman Act must be read for purposes of this type of inquiry." It noted that Schwinn was not a newcomer but a leading bicycle producer, and stressed that Schwinn's ability to compete more effectively through its arrangements "is not enough to avoid the Sherman Act proscription; because, in a sense, every restrictive practice is designed to augment the profit and competitive position of its participants."

The Court affirmed the district court's holding that a *per se* violation of the Sherman Act results when a manufacturer *sells* products to his distributor subject to territorial restrictions upon resale. To allow territorial restraints "where the manufacturer has parted with dominion over the goods . . . would violate the ancient rule against restraints on alienation and open the door to exclusivity of outlets and limitation of territory further than prudence permits." The Court further ordered the decree modified so as to enjoin any requirement by Schwinn that distributors sell bicycles only to franchised dealers. However, it was "not prepared to introduce the inflexibility which a *per se* rule might bring" if applied to all vertical arrangements, including agency and consignment sales. Where the manufacturer "retains title, dominion, and risk with respect to the product," a violation of Section 1 results "only if the impact of the confinement is 'unreasonably' restrictive of competition . . . ." In view of the significant interbrand competition and the fact that distributors and dealers handled competing brands, the Court concluded that the agency arrangements survived this test. It could not brand as "clearly erroneous" the district court's findings that such arrangements did not go further than required by competitive pressures.

A vigorous dissent urged the application of the rule of reason even to outright sales to distributors. "[I]t is particularly disappointing to see the Court balk at the label 'sale', and turn from reasoned response [suggested by the White decision] to a wooden and irrelevant formula."

Lower court cases have not been entirely sympathetic to Schwinn, a commentator points out.[68] They have found reasons for not applying its *per se* approach. In most cases they have not extended it to outlaw "location clauses" that bind a dealer to sell only at stores the location of which is specified in the contract, or "primary responsibility" clauses which obligate the dealer to concentrate marketing efforts in the particular area for which he is made responsible.

It should be noted that Section 3 of the Clayton Act, 38 Stat. 731 (1914), 15 U.S.C.A. § 14 (1970) forbids contracts which bind a purchaser not to deal in goods of a competitor of the seller where their effect "may be to substantially lessen competition." It thus puts a special restraint on the kinds of clauses described in paragraph (3) at p. 1350, supra.[69] Unlike the cases in the Common Market below, none of the cases described in this Note involved such arrangements.

Additional reading: Areeda, Antitrust Analysis 526–550 (2d ed. 1974); Note, Restricted Channels of Distribution Under the Sherman Act, 75 Harv.L.Rev. 795 (1962); Note, The Supreme Court, 1966 Term, 81 Harv.L.Rev. 69, 235 (1967).

68. Robinson, Recent Antitrust Developments—1974, 30 Record N.Y.C. Bar Ass'n 142, 157–63 (1975).

69. See Tampa Electric Co. v. Nashville Coal Co., 365 U.S. 320, 81 S.Ct. 623, 5 L.Ed.2d 580 (1961).

"ELECTRIC MASSAGE INSTRUMENTS"

Landgericht, Mannheim, Germany.
Case No. 7 0 (Kart) 88/64, January 22, 1965.[70]

The plaintiff, a German import firm, imports Japanese electric massage instruments from Great Britain. It has an agreement with its British supplier making it the sole distributor in the Federal Republic of Germany and France. It markets the products under its own trademark.

On June 14, 1962, the German importer entered into an agreement with the defendant, a French firm, making the latter the sole distributor in France. The French distributor agreed, among other things, to buy a certain number of massage instruments per year from the German importer and to refrain from buying or distributing competing products. The agreement could not be terminated by either side before March 31, 1963. No notification of the agreement was filed with the EEC Commission.

When similar massage instruments, also made in Japan, appeared on the French market at considerably lower prices, the French distributor stopped buying from the German importer in September 1962. On December 20, 1962, the distributor rejected the importer's demand for fulfillment of the agreement. The German importer then sued for damages in the District Court in Mannheim.

The French distributor contends that the agreement violates Article 85, paragraph 1, of the Treaty of Rome, is null and void, and hence cannot furnish the basis for a claim for damages.

1. Requirements of Article 85(1) Examined

The sole distributorship agreement entered into between the parties on June 14, 1962, meets the conditions set forth in paragraph 1 of Article 85 of the Treaty establishing the European Economic Community. . . .

(a) The sole distributorship agreement is an agreement between two independent enterprises. There is no dispute between the parties that the agreement puts the defendant in the legal position of an independent dealer rather than in that of a commercial agent . . ..

(b) The sole distributorship agreement restricts competition in the Common Market . . . . The plaintiff, located in Germany, is prevented from supplying other distributors in France with electric massage instruments, and the defendant, located in France, is prohibited from distributing the products of competitors. In addition, the agreement limits the freedom of choice of the other market participants vis-à-vis the plaintiff and the defendant. This results from the fact that under the agreement the plaintiff is prevented from becoming a supplier of the defendant's competitors on the French market and the defendant is barred from distributing the massage instruments of the plaintiff's competitors.

This restriction of competition is perceptible . . .. The plaintiff's obligation to supply the defendant exclusively results in the defendant's having the distribution monopoly on the French market since the plaintiff, according to its pleadings, is the sole distributor in Germany and France and since it did not prove whether

70. The translation is taken from the CCH Common Market Reporter ¶ 8030.

and in what manner such massage instruments could be purchased by third parties (particularly since they are manufactured in Japan and about to be introduced on the European market). A more effective restriction of competition is practically impossible. Electric massage instruments manufactured by other firms need not be considered here since, according to the circumstances in this case, they cannot be regarded as similar goods. . . . Under these circumstances, this court, contrary to the opinion of the [German] Federal Cartel Office, considers the pleadings of the parties to be sufficient to show a perceptible restraint of competition. . . .

(c) The restriction of competition resulting from the sole distributorship agreement is liable to affect trade between the Member States of the European Economic Community. According to the preventive intent of Treaty Article 85, the term "to affect" implies an artificial deflection of the inter-State flow of goods from its normal and natural course. Whatever the harmful or beneficial effect of this deflection may be is immaterial . . ..

The fact that new products are usually introduced on markets via sole distributorship agreements, together with an exclusivity clause, does not prove that the flow of goods so channeled would take its normal, natural course and therefore would not affect trade between the Member States. Instead, the course taken by goods unhampered by such contractual regulation should be considered as normal and natural. Any restraints on competition, as in this case, imposed for reasons of technical marketing necessities probably could be taken into consideration in an exemption under Article 85, paragraph 3, of the Treaty.

2. No Exemption Due to Failure to Notify Agreement

The sole distributorship agreement is not exempt from the prohibition of Treaty Article 85, paragraph 1.

(a) There can be no exemption by the EEC Commission under Article 85, paragraph 3, of the Treaty in conjunction with Article 6, paragraph 1, of Regulation 17, since the parties failed to notify their exclusive agreement (Article 4, paragraph 1, of Regulation 17). This notification could have been given after June 14, 1962, the day the agreement was entered into, and prior to December 20, 1962, the day the defendant permanently refused to fulfill its obligations, thus cancelling the contract. . . .

3. Consequence: Agreement Null and Void

The sole distributorship agreement of June 14, 1962, is null and void in its entirety, pursuant to Article 85, paragraph 2, of the Treaty.

(a) The sole distributorship agreement is a new cartel within the meaning of Article 4, paragraph 1, of Regulation 17, because it was entered into after March 13, 1962, the date the regulation entered into force. . . .

The sole distributorship agreement cannot be exempt from the prohibition of Article 85, paragraph 1, retroactively for the period involved herein—September 1, 1962, to June 30, 1963—for which the plaintiff seeks damages for non-fulfillment. Under Article 6, paragraph 1, second sentence, of Regulation 17, the EEC Commission could at best have granted an exemption to take effect as of the date of notification, since, under Article 4, paragraph 2, of Regulation 17, the agreement was not exempt from the notification requirement. The requirements of neither subparagraph (ii)(a) nor subparagraph (ii)(b) of Article 4, paragraph 2 (on which the plaintiff expressly relied), of Regulation 17 are present in this case. . . .

The sole distributorship agreement thus cannot be considered as "provisionally valid" for the period September 1, 1962, to June 30, 1963; . . . Neither legal security nor the fact that the EEC Commission alone is competent (Article 9, paragraph 1, of Regulation 17) to grant, possibly retroactively, exemptions requires a provisional recognition of the agreement. Rather, it appears necessary to deny such a provisional recognition in order to induce parties to agreements to fulfill their notification obligations. . . .

(b) The consequences under civil law of the invalidity of the agreement are direct, according to Article 85, paragraph 2, without necessitating a constitutive or declaratory decision of the Commission, because Treaty Article 85 sets forth a genuine prohibition having direct effect, as clearly set out in Article 1 of Regulation 17 . . . .

(c) The sole distributorship agreement is null and void in its entirety (Section 139 BGB [Civil Code]), since those provisions that are void under cartel law cannot be taken out without rendering the entire agreement meaningless, in light of the parties' apparent intent. . . .

NOTE ON NATIONAL PROCEEDINGS AND COMMUNITY LAW

Although it finds that this agreement shows "a perceptible restraint of competition," the court states that Article 85(1) includes *all* agreements which are likely to affect trade between member states. It is not material whether the agreement is "likely to affect trade" in a beneficial or harmful manner; such considerations can be relevant only to a declaration under Article 85(3). When reading the decisions below of the Commission and the Court of Justice, consider in what respects, if any, their views on this critical question differ.

Note that the court assumes without discussion that Article 85 *and* Regulation 17 constitute binding rules for the German court and create rights in private parties. They are, in brief, self-executing. The status of this agreement under French or German law is not relevant, once the court concludes that it violates "supreme" Community law.

The court referred to the possibility of considering the agreement to be "provisionally valid." Other courts and a number of commentators have examined this possibility in situations where an agreement before a national court has been notified but not acted upon by the Commission or when it comes under Regulation Article 4(2).[71] But the view of the German court was vindicated in a 1973 opinion of the

71. These arguments derive in part from certain rather confusing language in the first antitrust decision of the Court of Justice. That case involved the somewhat distinct problem of the status of agreements under Article 85 between the time that the Rome Treaty entered into effect and the promulgation of Regulation No. 17, and the status of existing agreements at and after the time of promulgation of the Regulation. Kleding-Verkoopbedrijf de Geus en Uitdenbogerd v. Robert Bosch GmbH, Case No. 13/61, April 6, 1962, Recueil Vol. VIII, p. 89 (translation at CCH Common Market Reporter ¶ 8003).

Court of Justice, Brasserie de Haecht v. Wilkin-Janssen.[72] The Court confirmed in this Article 177 proceeding what had seemed apparent—namely, that for agreements entered into after Regulation No. 17 was promulgated, a notification does not have a suspensive effect upon the provision of Article 85(2) that agreements in violation of Article 85(1) are "automatically void." Thus national courts were under an obligation to "hear persons who allege nullity as a matter of law." The nullity imposed by Article 85(2) could have a bearing on all effects, past or future, of the agreement involved.

The Court paid some attention to the appropriate interaction between Community and national authorities in these situations, by stating that a national court "must examine, subject to the possible application of Article 177, whether the proceedings should be suspended so that the parties could obtain an opinion from the Commission," unless it seems clear that the agreement is outside Article 85(1) or is incompatible with it. The Court further observed, with respect to Article 9(3) of Regulation No. 17, that the Commission would not be deemed to have initiated proceedings under the articles there referred to simply by acknowledging receipt of a request for a negative clearance or for a declaration under Article 85(3).

A distinct set of problems—not further examined in these materials—arises when national-court adjudications are based upon national rather than Community antitrust law.[73] Note that Article 87(2)(e) of the Treaty is sensitive to the interaction of national and Community law; no broad "determination" of the relationship has however been made by regulation or directive. Numerous decisions of national courts have wrestled with these issues.

The principal ruling of the Court of Justice was in a 1969 proceeding under Article 177, Walt Wilhelm v. Bundeskartellamt.[74] The question posed was whether it was compatible with the Treaty, in a situation where the Commission had started a proceeding under Article 14 of Regulation No. 17, for national authorities to apply to the same facts the prohibitions of national antitrust law. The Court observed that Article 9(3) of Regulation No. 17 applied only to Community law, and had no bearing on a case where national authorities were enforcing their own internal law. It noted that the "same cartel may, in principle, be the subject of two parallel proceedings" that

72. Court of Justice of the European Communities, Case No. 48/72, February 6, 1973, Reports of Cases before the Court, 1973–2, p. 77. The excerpts below from this opinion are taken from the CCH Common Market Reporter ¶ 8170. That text differs in minor, formal respects from the later-published opinion in Reports of Cases.

73. These problems are explored in Markert, Some Legal and Administrative Problems of the Co-Existence of Community and National Competition Law in the EEC, 11 C.M.L.Rev. 92 (1974).

74. Court of Justice of the European Communities, Case No. 14/68, February 13, 1969, Recueil Vol. XV, 1969–1, p. 1. The excerpts from this opinion are taken from the translation in the CCH Common Market Reporter ¶ 8056.

would unfold at the same time before Community authorities and before national authorities under internal law. The Court viewed Article 87(2)(e) as confirming the preeminence of Community law by authorizing the Council to act. It followed that "where national decisions involving a cartel prove incompatible with a decision taken by the Commission, in a proceeding initiated by it, the national authorities must respect the effects of that decision." Specifically, where a cartel was being examined under Community rules before the Commission, national authorities could proceed under internal law provided that application of that law "does not prejudice the full and uniform application of Community law or the effect of the measures taken to implement it."

QUESTIONS

(1) Suppose that the German firm had notified the Commission of the agreement in June 1962 and had requested a declaration. At the time of the litigation, the Commission had not taken any action.

(*a*) How should the court decide? Would it be competent to render a decision on the merits?

(*b*) If the court decided this case as it did the one before it, on the ground that it was not competent to apply Article 85(3), what effect would its decision have upon the pending notification? Is there still a "contract" on which the Commission could act? If so, what problems arise for the plaintiff and defendant if, several months after the decision, the Commission declared Article 85(3) applicable to the agreement?

(2) An agreement might be challenged—perhaps in a civil proceeding similar to "Electric Massage Instruments"—under national antitrust law in situations involving different types of relationships to Community antitrust law. From the perspective of the Community's goals, which of the following adjudications in a national court under national antitrust law poses the most serious problems?

(*a*) Assume that the agreement in question (perhaps a distributorship agreement between firms in two EEC Countries with few restrictive clauses) does not violate Article 85—that is, does not come within Article 85(1). Indeed, the Commission may have issued a negative clearance under Regulation Article 2. The national court, however, finds the agreement to violate national antitrust law and thus will not enforce it.

(*b*) An exclusive distributorship agreement has benefited from a declaration under Article 85(3). A national Court determines, however, that the agreement is invalid under national antitrust law and hence cannot be enforced.

SOCIÉTÉ ARLAB IMPORT–EXPORT (S.A.R.I.E.) v. SOCIÉTÉ UNION NATIONALE DES ECONOMIES FAMILIALES (U.N.E.F.) S.A.R.L.

Tribunal de Commerce de la Seine, France, June 25, 1962.[75]

[Under a series of contracts dating back to 1934, the Arlab Import-Export Co. (S.A.R.I.E.) was the exclusive importer-distributor in France for appliances of Sunbeam Industries. The last renewal contract was entered into in 1961 with a foreign Sunbeam affiliate. It made S.A.R.I.E. exclusive representative for Sunbeam equipment in France, prohibited it from selling competitive equipment, and obligated it to organize sales services, to engage in advertising, and to set up post-sale service facilities. S.A.R.I.E. found that U.N.E.F. Co. was offering for sale in France Sunbeam electric razors that it had purchased from various foreign suppliers through rather complicated arrangements, often involving wholesaler intermediaries in more than one country. These purchases from Sunbeam's foreign vendees were apparently made without the knowledge of Sunbeam itself. S.A.R.I.E. brought this action against U.N.E.F. seeking damages and an order that U.N.E.F. stop soliciting customers in France for sales of Sunbeam appliances. The suit was based upon the French law of unfair competition allowing an action against merchants who, in contravention of rights acquired by another, purchased and sold brand products covered by an exclusive distributorship contract.

U.N.E.F. raised various defenses under French law, the antitrust provisions of the Rome Treaty and Regulation No. 17. It argued that the agreements and acts of S.A.R.I.E. constituted unfair competition under French law and the Treaty, and it brought a counterclaim for damages. Excerpts from the opinion of the court follow:]

The U.N.E.F. Co. first excepted with a request that judgment be stayed and, in addition, that the instant suit be referred to the Court of Justice for an interpretation of Articles 85 and 91 of the Treaty of Rome. It pointed out that it petitioned the Common Market Commission at Brussels for nullification of the August 28, 1961, exclusive distributorship agreement which is being enforced against it and requesting that said agreement be prohibited under a penalty to be fixed by the Commission in compliance with Regulation No. 17 implementing Articles 85 and 86 of the Treaty of Rome. Under Article 177 only the Court of Justice is competent to rule on an interpretation of Articles 85 and 86 of the Treaty of Rome. The dispute submitted to this court is, however, between two French companies, each of which considers that the actions of the other constitute acts of unfair competition in the pursuit of their respective businesses. This court is in possession of all the facts necessary for settling the dispute, and there is no reason to delve into the origin of facts that may have brought about these acts of unfair competition since the petitioning of the Brussels Commission for the purpose of having the August 28, 1961, contract declared null and void could in no case result in changing or hindering the action brought by the S.A.R.I.E. Co.

Nothing in the regulation gives the Court of Justice any special jurisdiction beyond its normal power of review of the legality of

75. The translation is taken from the CCH Common Market Reporter ¶ 8018.

the Commission's decisions. With regard to the power to find that an infringement has been committed, in order to avoid the consequences of a concurrent jurisdiction which might lead to conflicting decisions of a national court and of the Commission, and possibly of the Court of Justice when an appeal against a Commission decision is submitted to it, the regulation provides in Article 9, paragraph 3, that [quotation of paragraph (3) omitted]. The request for stay must therefore be rejected, together with the request for referral to the Court of Justice, and the merits of the case must be ruled upon.

[The court then considered the arguments of U.N.E.F. It rejected the claim that the exclusive distributorship clause violated provisions of French law relating to "refusals to deal," and it noted that most prior French decisions held that exclusive distributorship agreements did not violate French law. The court then considered defendant's arguments under the Treaty.]

(b) *Nullity under provisions of the Treaty in Rome:* The U.N.E.F. Co. cites Articles 85, 86 and 91 of the Treaty of Rome as a basis for its request for nullification of the S.A.R.I.E.-Sunbeam agreement. In fact, according to the U.N.E.F. Co., this agreement, from the standpoint of vertical distribution, is actually tantamount to a genuine monopoly having the effect of preventing and distorting competition within the Common Market, in that it would eventually restrain or even prevent the free movement of goods between Member States and would inevitably have price discrimination as its end result, since sales prices vary from country to country. [The court quoted paragraphs (1) and (2) of Article 85 of the Treaty.] At first glance, therefore, it seems that the drafters' main concern was to check any system designed to hinder competition, but that the text refers to the delicate problem of commercial agreements between enterprises which are intended to distort the rules of competition. While it is acknowledged that an agreement between producers of similar equipment in the Common Market countries or in two Member States comes directly under the prohibition of Article 85 as constituting a horizontal integration, one may question whether an agreement between a manufacturer and his exclusive distributor in one of the Common Market countries constitutes a cartel. [The court quoted paragraph (3) of Article 85.] Thus the drafters' intent was again expressed in their wish for improved production and distribution of goods. In this regard, it should be borne in mind that an exclusive distributor is committed not only to take on the responsibility for advertising in order to publicize the brand, for a guarantee service and a post-sale service, all of which may contribute to the good reputation of the brand, but also to safeguard the consumers' interests. It would be presumptuous not to make a distinction between a cartel designed to undermine the normal operation of free competition and the organization of a sales network which in the end benefits the user. Importers operating outside this network do not provide any worth-while technical and sales services, so that it can be said that without exclusive distributorship agreements foreign industries could not successfully compete with domestic industries. Actually, in the end, the real competition takes place between producers and not between distributors and it would not be desirable for competition to be carried on at that level to the detriment of the sales network organization. The sale of products other than those of prime necessity—electric razors, in spite of what the U.N.E.F. Co. maintains, cannot be classified as such—, produced by anybody, anywhere, and at the lowest price, without the security of a sound guarantee, in short, of a responsible sales organization, has nothing to do with the beneficial aspects of the principle of free competition, but would rapidly lead to a chaotic business picture that the consumer would, in the end, pay for.

Thus, even assuming that the agreement in this dispute were to be likened to a cartel, the point should be stressed that we have before us a "good" cartel to which the nullification provided for in Article 85, paragraph 1, does not apply. In fact, contracts of the S.A.R.I.E.-Sunbeam kind allow for open competition between the various Common Market brands and even make such competition easier, since the exclusive distributors vie with each other by means of advertising, improvement of sales and post-sales service—efforts which in the end find their reward or approval in the choice of the consumers. While it was the aim of the Treaty of Rome to prohibit any discriminatory practice set up by the manufacturers of one state in order to check the sale of products originating in another Member State, the S.A.R.I.E. Co., on the contrary, under its agreement, is seeking through its sales organization steadily to increase its sales of Sunbeam equipment. . . .

. . . In accordance with the order of February 24, 1961, the acts of unfair competition of which the U.N.E.F. Co. was accused are established. The U.N.E.F. Co. continued its secret imports in spite of an official clarification published in the press by the Sunbeam Industries for the benefit of French retailers and customers. These acts were repeated in spite of the S.A.R.I.E. Co.'s requests to desist and are all the more marked since the U.N.E.F. Co. enjoys the benefits of the advertising, the brand's good name and the sales services without bearing any of the costs thereof, while the sale price to the public remains the same . . .. This practice is contrary to elementary business integrity and should be stopped. . . .

[The court ordered the parties to appear before a referee who would determine the amount of damages, and ordered U.N.E.F. to stop soliciting customers for Sunbeam appliances.]

QUESTIONS

(1) The court states that the petitioning of the Commission by U.N. E.F. "could in no case result in changing or hindering the action brought by the S.A.R.I.E. Co." Do you agree?

(2) Is the court stating that the agreement is not within Article 85(1) *or* that the agreement is in any event justifiable? Under either view, is the decision sound?

(3) What was the status of the agreement with respect to the deadlines for notification under Regulation No. 17? In view of that status, could the court's holding for the plaintiff be justified on different grounds?

SOCIÉTÉ UNION NATIONALE DES ECONOMIES FAMILIALES (U.N.E.F.) v. ETABLISSEMENTS CONSTEN

Cour d'Appel de Paris, First Chamber, January 26, 1963.
1963 Dalloz Jurisp. 189.[76]

[This was an appeal by U.N.E.F. from an adverse 1962 judgment of the Tribunal de Commerce de la Seine. This case and S.A. R.I.E. v. U.N.E.F., p. 1360, supra, were apparently heard as companion cases by the Tribunal de Commerce, for its two decisions contained some identical paragraphs. The litigation raised similar problems. Consten, a French firm, entered in 1957 into a contract, renewable annually, with Grundig-Verkaufs-GmbH, a German firm, under which Consten became the exclusive importer-distributor in France for radio-electrical equipment, particularly tape recorders, manufactured by Grundig and sold under its brand name. Consten found that U.N.E.F. was offering the Grundig tape recorders for sale in France after purchasing them from various foreign suppliers without the knowledge of Grundig. Consten brought an action against U.N.E.F. seeking damages under French law for unfair competition, as well as an order that U.N.E.F. stop soliciting customers in France to buy the Grundig equipment. The Tribunal de Commerce entered judgment for Consten, ordering U.N.E.F. to pay damages and to stop soliciting customers.

U.N.E.F. based its principal arguments on appeal upon the Rome Treaty. Excerpts from the opinion of the Cour d'Appel appear below:]

Thus the question arises of determining whether such contracts could, by reason of their influence on trade between Member States, be counter to goals of the Community in view of the aims sought to be attained by the High Contracting Parties as set forth in Articles 2 and 3 of the EEC Treaty in such a way that, to the extent that their provisions could restrict competition in the Common Market, they could be subject to interdiction, perhaps nullification, and the enterprises or associations of enterprises which entered into them, subject to penalties, as set forth in Articles 85 and following of the Treaty, as well as in implementing Regulation 17.

Basing its action on Articles 85, 86, 89, and 91 of the Treaty of Rome, as well as on the regulations implementing Articles 85 and 86 . . . the manager of the U.N.E.F. Co. appealed, on March 6, 1962, to the Commission of the EEC . . . to establish the nullity of the Grundig-Consten covenant, and to prohibit it, on pain of assessment of daily fines, on the theory that the prohibition against delivery outside of the allocated territory (Article 1, § 2, of the contract), the prohibition against exports accompanied by civil sanctions (Article 8, § 4), the discriminatory pricing practice, and the exclusivity such as was agreed upon were counter to the rules against dumping, the abuse of a dominant position in the market or in a substantial part thereof (Article 5, § 4), and all constitute such violations of Articles 85, paragraph 1, 91, paragraph 2, and 86 of the EEC Treaty, since such Articles 85, paragraph 1, and 86 of said Treaty in effect prohibit cartels (i. e., agreements between enterprises, decisions of associations and concerted practices), as well as

76. The translation is taken from the CCH Common Market Reporter ¶ 8009.

the abusive exploitation of a dominant position likely to affect trade between Member States in preventing, restricting, or distorting competition within the Common Market.

The U.N.E.F. Co.'s complaint to the Commission at Brussels was registered March 13, 1962, as No. 0004, according to the letter of the Commission dated March 28, 1962, and introduced into the record below. In a letter of June 15, 1962, also introduced into the record, the Director General for Competition of the Commission at Brussels informed the complaining company that "the procedure provided under Regulation No. 17 had been set in motion," and the State Secretary for Economic Affairs notified.

In spite of the existence of this complaint and the request for arrest of judgment, the Commerce Court of the Seine felt bound to reject the interlocutory plea put before it, even though it involved a request for referral of the action to the Court of Justice of the Community for interpretation of Articles 85 and 91 of the EEC Treaty.

In disposing of the pleas presented by the U.N.E.F. Co., the judge below did not wish to go beyond the limits of internal law, confining the problem presented to a litigation between two French companies, for the solution of which he had all the necessary elements, "without having to trace the origin of circumstances which could have given rise to acts of unfair competition. The considerations of the Commission at Brussels declaring the contract of April 1, 1957, null and void could not, under any interpretation of the case, have the result of modifying or altering the nature of the acts intended by the Etabl. Consten." Thus the court refused to recognize the fact that the difficulties between the parties arose precisely out of a provision in a contract entered into between nationals who were natural or legal persons bound by the Treaty of Rome. As a result, the possible nullification of their contract by the Commission at Brussels, under Article 85 of the Treaty, must of necessity have some effect on the very basis of the request.

The court likewise rejected the request for referral to the Court of Justice solely for the reason that the regulation made no provision for specific jurisdiction of the Court beyond the normal supervision over the legality of decisions of the Commission. [The court then quoted Article 9(3) of Regulation No. 17.] . . .

In fact, after having demonstrated its uncertainty as to the nature of the contract and having debated "whether a covenant between a manufacturer and his dealer in a country of the Common Market constitutes a cartel," and after having cited the third paragraph of Article 85 . . . the judge below commented, in a somewhat ambiguous manner, that "on the theory that the agreement in issue could be construed as a cartel, one would have to emphasize that here we have a 'good' cartel not subject to the nullification provided for under Article 85, paragraph 1," thus implicitly siding in favor of non-prohibition of the Grundig-Consten contract on the basis of paragraph 3 of that article, whereas Article 9, paragraph 1, of Regulation 17 would give competence to the Commission acting under the control of the Court of Justice to make the decision declaring the prohibition of Article 85, paragraph 1, inapplicable to the contract in issue, pursuant to paragraph 3 of that article. . . .

. . . Under Article 3, paragraph 1*b*, of Regulation 17, natural or legal persons, such as the U.N.E.F. Co., who show a legitimate interest, are qualified to address to the Commission a request for establishing a violation of the Treaty. When the Commission has set its procedure in motion, it is competent to apply the provisions of Articles 85 and 86 of the EEC Treaty, according to the provisions of Article 9 of the above-mentioned regulation. It is only after this request has been made, and after the Commission's initiation of its procedure, that it must maintain a close and constant liaison with the proper authorities of the Member States, under Article 10 of the same regulation. All these conditions had been met when the letter already referred to, addressed June 15, 1962, to the complaining company by the Director General for Competition of the Commission at Brussels, requesting it, after having informed it of the institution of its procedure, to inform him, in order to assure the proper application of the rules governing competence (Article 9, paragraph 3, of Regulation 17), if proceedings were pending before the national authorities, and, if so, to indicate to him their present status. Finally, on that same June 15, 1962, this same representative of the Commission advised the French State Secretary for Internal Trade who, himself, had referred his letter to the Ministry of Justice, of the procedure now set in motion by the Commission. Thus, solely by reason of the existence of this letter of June 15, 1962, the court finds itself obliged to arrest judgment until the definitive decision of the authorities before whom now lay the complaint lodged by the U.N.E.F. Co. is reached.

Under these circumstances, the court could scarcely sustain the last plea put forth by the respondent, namely, that there is a nonseverable link between the procedure at Brussels and the procedure under national law. This assertion, in fact, compounds the error of the court which rendered its decision as though Community law did not bind national courts with the same force as internal law by reason of the express provisions of the Constitution of 1946, under the authority of which the Treaty of Rome was ratified, and the provisions of the Constitution of 1958, Article 55 of which specifically provides that

> treaties or agreements regularly ratified or approved have, from the time of their publication, an authority superior to that of the laws, without prejudice, for each agreement or treaty, to its application by the other party. . . .

FOR THESE REASONS: The court declares admissible the appeal . . . .

And, before pronouncing on the merits: It suspends judgment until a definitive decision is rendered as a result of proceedings instituted by the Commission . . . .

QUESTIONS

(1) What was the status of this agreement under Regulation Articles 4 or 5? In fact, as the Decision of the Commission below indicates, a notification was filed with the Commission on January 29, 1963, several days *after* the decision of the French court. Should an earlier notification have changed that decision?

(2) Are this and the S.A.R.I.E. cases in conflict as to the duty of national courts under Regulation Article 9 to suspend proceedings? Could you defend the decision of each court on this issue?

COMMENT

The Grundig-Consten litigation continued before the Commission and the Court of Justice. One feature of the arrangements between the parties that was critical to the decisions below was the assignment by Grundig to Consten of French rights to a trade-mark, GINT, affixed to Grundig's products. Consten alleged that under French law, its ownership of this mark enabled it to bar the importation by others of Grundig products. As background for these arguments, and for the responses of the Commission and the Court, you should read pp. 1020–1029, supra, on trade-marks and transnational antitrust problems.

DECISION OF THE COMMISSION OF THE EUROPEAN ECONOMIC COMMUNITY ON THE GRUNDIG-CONSTEN AGREEMENT

Decision of the Commission No. IV–A/00004–03344, September 23, 1964. [1964] Journal Officiel 2545.[77]

Noting the request of March 5, 1962, amended July 15, 1962, submitted by UNEF S. A. R. L., Paris (a French limited liability company) pursuant to Article 3 of Regulation No. 17, seeking a finding by the Commission that Grundig Verkaufs-GmbH, Fürth (Bavaria) (a German limited liability company), and Ets. Consten, Courbevoie (Seine) (a French limited liability company), violated the provisions of Article 85 by concluding on April 1, 1957, an "agency contract" and a supplementary agreement concerning the registration and use in France of the GINT trademark,

Noting the notification, made January 29, 1963, of the sole agency agreement of April 1, 1957, by Grundig Verkaufs-GmbH, in accordance with Article 5, paragraph 1, of Regulation No. 17,

After hearing interested enterprises and other persons, particularly the company that introduced the complaint, in accordance with Article 19 of Regulation No. 17,

After consulting the Consultative Committee on Cartels and Monopolies, in accordance with Article 10 of Regulation No. 17,

I.

The principal provisions of the contract concluded April 1, 1957, are as follows:

Grundig Verkaufs-GmbH ("Grundig") designates Ets. Consten S. A. R. L. ("Consten") as sole representative for continental France, the Saar, and Corsica for radios, tape recorders, dictating machines, and television sets manufactured by Grundig, as well as for their parts and accessories.

Consten takes over the distribution of these goods for its own account. It may neither represent other German enterprises which produce or sell similar products nor sell for its own account or for others products that compete with the products under contract or that might interfere with their sale.

In addition, Consten agrees to advertise adequately and sufficiently and at its own expense and to set up a repair shop stocking a sufficient supply of replacement parts. It must always provide faultless customer service for appliances sold by it.

77. The translation is taken from the CCH Common Market Reporter ¶ 2743.

Grundig agrees not to sell, directly or indirectly, to other persons in the territory under contract. This clause is part of a system of territorial protection applied to the entire Grundig sales organization. All Grundig purchasers, German and foreign, are prohibited from exporting or reexporting. Accordingly, Consten may make no delivery, either directly or indirectly, from its territory for or to any other country.

Consten is authorized, for the life of the contract, to use the name and emblem "GRUNDIG" to distribute Grundig products, but without being allowed to register this trademark. It is prohibited from using this trademark after expiration of the contract, regardless of the reason for such expiration.

The trademark "GINT" (Grundig International) was registered in France on October 3, 1957, in the name of Consten. This registration is based on an agreement concluded between Grundig and Consten and partially put into writing on January 13, 1959. Consten agreed that at the termination of the exclusive agreement, the GINT trademark would be assigned to Grundig or would be allowed to expire. The said trademark is affixed to all appliances manufactured by Grundig, including those sold in Germany, and also appears on business correspondence, literature, etc.

The GINT trademark was introduced by Grundig shortly after it lost a decision in the Netherlands, in December 1956, against a parallel importer, in which Grundig had attempted to ensure for the Dutch sole agent territorial protection through the GRUNDIG trademark. The GINT trademark is registered in Germany in the name of Grundig, and in several other Member States in the name of the sole representative.

[The Commission described the litigation between Consten and U. N. E. F. in the French courts, noting that one of Consten's claims alleged infringement of the GINT trademark.]

The facts may be summarized as follows:

Since April 1, 1957, Consten has been the sole importer of Grundig radios, tape recorders, dictating machines and television sets in France. After the liberalization of imports, several enterprises began to purchase Grundig equipment directly from German distributors. The most important of these parallel importers is the complainant UNEF, of Paris, which, since April 1961, has purchased Grundig appliances from German distributors, particularly from wholesalers, who have made deliveries in spite of the export prohibition imposed on them. UNEF sold this equipment to French retailers at more favorable prices than those asked by Consten. Several dealers of the Consten chain complained about this to Consten.

UNEF stated that the parallel imports made by it were prompted by the differences in prices between France and Germany. These price differences have in fact been proved. . . . In the last few years, prices for Grundig products in France showed a tendency to drop; nevertheless, Grundig and Consten admitted that at the beginning of 1964 the actual French prices of several Grundig appliances were about 20 percent higher than the actual German prices, again after subtracting customs duties and taxes. . . . Since the Grundig factory prices to Consten or to German wholesalers are essentially the same, the differences in selling prices must be explained by differences in operating margins. . . . Since the profit margin for the retailer is essentially the same in France and Germany, the reason for these differences lies at the wholesale level. . . .

II.

Article 85, paragraph 1, of the Treaty stipulates that all agreements that are liable to affect trade between Member States and that are designed to prevent, restrict, or distort competition within the Common Market or which have this effect are incompatible with the Common Market.

(1) The agreements examined here are between enterprises. They restrict and distort competition within the Common Market for the following reasons:

Grundig has agreed not to deliver, either directly or indirectly, to any other enterprise in the territory defined in the agreement. It cannot, therefore, sell, in France, the products covered by the agreement to any buyer but Consten. The obligation not to sell indirectly in the territory covered by the agreement is reinforced by the export prohibition imposed upon all buyers of Grundig products. As a result, no dealer in Grundig products established outside of France can sell these products in France.

Further, Consten in its civil suit before the Commerce Court of the Seine invoked decisions on unfair competition to enforce its sole agency agreement against third parties. Thus, all imports by third parties of Grundig products into France are intended to be prohibited.

Finally, the manner in which Grundig and Consten make use of the GINT trademark presents an additional method of protecting Consten against competition.

The GINT trademark is intended solely for Grundig products and, moreover, *all* the Grundig products in question have had the GINT trademark affixed by Grundig. The primary purpose of the GINT trademark and the sharing of the trademark rights in such a manner that the Grundig trademark is registered everywhere in the name of Grundig, whereas the GINT trademark is registered in the name of Grundig in the Federal Republic of Germany, but outside of Germany in the name of the respective sole agents, in this instance in the name of Consten, is to protect the sole agent against parallel imports. This is also demonstrated by the story of the GINT trademark.

It is not necessary to decide whether this trademark has any other purpose particularly within the scope of laws protecting industrial property. It should, however, be noted that the GINT trademark is not needed to show the origin of the goods, since the Grundig trademark already serves this purpose. . . .

It has been alleged that competition between producers is so great that distortion of competition could not possibly result from the designation of a sole representative.

Where goods pass through more than one distribution stage, it may be assumed that there is a restraint of competition within the meaning of Article 85, paragraph 1, if competition is prevented or restricted at just a single stage. . . .

In addition, with regard to branded goods such as those involved here, the products of the various manufacturers present different physical, and also, in part, different technical, characteristics. In general, therefore, a buyer can make a reliable comparison between the merchandise, and particularly between the prices, of dealers only for items bearing the same trademark. . . .

For this reason competition at the distribution stage, particularly between wholesalers distributing items bearing the same trademark, takes on special importance. This is all the more so since the costs of distribution represent a significant portion of the total cost. . . .

(2) The agreements are liable to affect trade between Member States . . . .

. . . [T]he integration of the national markets into the Common Market is impeded, if not prevented. This effect is demonstrated clearly by the differences in prices in various Member States, particularly in Germany and in France.

The supplementary agreement concerning the registration of the GINT trademark in the name of Consten also contributes to the isolation of the national markets and is therefore liable to affect trade between Member States.

The objection has been raised that the sales organization did not affect trade between Member States since trade in Grundig products between France and Germany increased substantially while it was in force.

This argument, however, cannot be accepted, since, in order for Article 85, paragraph 1, to apply, it is sufficient that a restraint of competition within the meaning of Article 85, paragraph 1, cause trade between Member States to develop under conditions other than it would have without such a restriction, and that its influence on market conditions be of some significance. . . .

III.

According to Article 85, paragraph 3, the provisions of Article 85, paragraph 1, may be declared inapplicable to an agreement . . . .

(1) The sole agency agreement of April 1, 1957, was notified on January 29, 1963, in accordance with the provisions of Article 5, paragraph 1, of Regulation No. 17.

(2) The parties, Grundig and Consten, submitted the arguments listed below, in order to justify the request made, as a precaution, by Grundig, that Article 85, paragraph 3, be applied to their sole agency agreement:

—economic facts have demonstrated that, under the present structure of the European economy, the sole agency is the only business set-up capable of solving human, financial and linguistic problems, of adapting to business customs, of coordinating a policy of expansion, and of withstanding the resulting economic risks;

—sole agents must survey the market for the manufacturer and, in particular, keep the manufacturer informed regarding technical conditions and requirements;

—the sales organization has made it possible for Grundig to increase production over the years. Consequently, the manufacturer has been able to rationalize production and to lower prices to consumers. For this reason, consumers are allowed a share of the profit resulting from these improvements in production and distribution;

—sole agents organize the general advertising for the brand, by any and all means, and maintain its good will. A parallel importer, on the other hand, normally sells a number of products of various manufacturers and therefore does not advertise just a single brand;

—sole agents must engage in "advance planning" in order that the manufacturer may adjust production to demand; . . .

—parallel importers profit unjustly by the efforts made by the sole agent with regard to service and advertising, which enables them to give their customers somewhat larger discounts; . . .

(3) The sole-agency system can lead to an improvement in the production and distribution of the products. . . .

An improvement of production and distribution is assumed in this case. A thorough examination of this question is not necessary since, as will be shown below, the other conditions of Article 85, paragraph 3, are not fulfilled.

(4) According to Article 85, paragraph 3, consumers must be allowed a fair share of the profit. In the field of trade, the word "profit" must not be understood as meaning only improvement in the distribution of the products, which, if it leads to a broader choice or to greater purchasing possibilities, also benefits the consumers . . . . [T]he consumers must also share in this, particularly with respect to prices and other conditions of sale. The determining factor in this respect is whether the share of the consumers is "fair."

With regard to prices, as mentioned in Section I, it appears that there was an appreciable gap between France and Germany . . . .

(5) The main reason that Article 85, paragraph 1, cannot be declared inapplicable, is that not all the restrictions imposed on the enterprises concerned in order to improve production and distribution of the products are indispensable . . . .

The restraint of competition contained in the sole agency agreement of April 1, 1957, that is the most significant is the agreement regarding absolute territorial protection, designed to prevent imports of the products by parallel importers into the territory covered by the agreement. . . . If, through a relaxation of territorial protection, the goal of improving production and distribution of the goods could no longer be attained, then absolute territorial protection would be indispensable. . . .

There is no apparent reason why Consten, even without absolute territorial protection, would not be in a position to concentrate on the French market as a sole agent. If Consten, as sole agent in France, sells Grundig appliances with operating margins roughly the same as those of wholesalers established in the Common Market outside of France, then no dealer established in France will find it to his advantage to obtain these products outside of France and to go through the complications involved in any import operation. . . .

If, in addition, Grundig and Consten invoke the guarantee service, in examining this argument one should start with the idea that normally a buyer can claim his right to a guarantee only from his supplier and under the conditions agreed to between them. There is consequently no reason for the sole agent to fear that possible competitors may profit from these guarantee services. . . .

Where paid post-sale service is concerned, which is far more important than the guarantee service, it is of little importance where an appliance was purchased, since repair costs must be paid by the person requesting repair. . . .

According to all the foregoing, absolute territorial protection is not indispensable and it is therefore impossible to declare that the sole agency agreement of April 1, 1957, is exempt under Article 85, paragraph 3. . . .

V.

Under Article 15, paragraph 5, of Regulation No. 17, Grundig and Consten are entitled, by virtue of the notification of their sole agency agreement, to a suspension of the fine for past actions, in spite of the incompatibility of the agreement with Article 85. . . .

VII.

The absolute territorial protection proved to be particularly damaging to the realization of the Common Market . . . . Therefore, it seems particularly appropriate to enjoin Grundig and Consten from making more difficult or from hampering parallel imports of Grundig products into France by any means whatsoever, including the use for this purpose of the GINT trademark.

This will not prevent Consten from using its rights in the GINT trademark with regard to third parties, in so far as this does not make it more difficult to engage in parallel imports of Grundig products into the territory covered by the agreement, or does not hamper such imports.

[The Commission rendered the following decision:]

Article 1. The sole agency agreement of April 1, 1957, and the supplementary agreement concerning the registration and use of the GINT trademark entered into by Grundig-Verkaufs-GmbH and Ets. Consten S. A. R. L. constitute a violation of Article 85 of the Treaty establishing the European Economic Community.

Article 2. The declaration of inapplicability provided for under Article 85, paragraph 3, of the Treaty is denied.

Article 3. The enterprises referred to in Article 1 must refrain from any and all measures designed to hinder or impede third enterprises from buying from wholesalers or retailers of their choice in the European Economic Community the products covered by the agreement for the purpose of reselling them in the territory covered by the agreement. . . .

ETABLISSEMENTS CONSTEN AND GRUNDIG–VERKAUFS–GMBH v. COMMISSION OF THE EUROPEAN ECONOMIC COMMUNITY

Court of Justice of the European Communities, Cases Nos. 56/64 and 58/64, July 13, 1966.
Recueil Vol. XII–4, p. 429.[78]

The facts on which this action is based may be summarized as follows:

[The Court stated the facts relevant to the litigation in the French courts between Consten and U. N. E. F., p. 1363, supra, and

78. The translation is taken from the CCH Common Market Reporter ¶ 8046.

summarized the decision of the Commission on the agreement between Grundig and Consten, p. 1366, supra.]

The Consten and Grundig firms, to whom the decision had been addressed, each brought an action [under Article 173 of the Treaty] to annul the decision, Consten on December 8, 1964, and Grundig on December 11, 1964.

[The Court noted that it had granted requests of the German and Italian governments to intervene in support of the plaintiffs, and of U. N. E. F. and another firm to intervene in support of the defendant. It then stated the arguments of the parties and intervenors, including the following arguments relating to the use of the GINT trademark.]

As to the demarcation between cartel law and trademark law, the *defendant* replies that the prohibition of cartels must also be applicable to the law on the protection of industrial property where agreements relating to these rights serve to create a regional division of the market, price agreements, or other restrictions of competition that have nothing to do with the protection guaranteed by these rights; if they do not, the way would be open to a circumvention of the prohibition of cartels.

Furthermore, the prohibition of the abuse of rights to the protection of industrial property is expressly recognized in the cartel law of the individual Member States. In this connection, the *intervenor Leissner* cites a decision of the French Court of Cassation to the effect that a trademark owner may not use his rights to circumvent economic legislation.

As to the influence of the agreement on the GINT trademark, the *defendant* comments that Consten's registration of the trademark in France could have been accomplished only on the basis of the agreement concluded with Grundig. The supplementary agreement thus had a decisive importance for Consten's right to the trademark.

. . .

The *plaintiff Grundig* in reply to this asserts that the agreement does not give rise to a restraint of competition, since Grundig could not, with the GINT trademark, have conferred upon Consten more rights than Grundig itself possessed.

The *defendant* replies that this argument is contradicted, as the facts lie, by decisions of Dutch and Italian courts, which hold that parallel imports are lawful so long as the foreign manufacturer also owns the domestic trademark, but that they are unlawful when the manufacturer has transferred the domestic trademark to the exclusive licensee. The argument is also irrelevant under the law, because the very purpose of the ban on cartels is to prevent a concerted action on the part of several market participants, regardless of whether the same action would be lawful if it were carried out by a single enterprise, without any agreement with others.

As to the prohibition of the exercise of the trademark right decreed in Article 3 of the decision [at p. 1371, supra], the *defendant* states that, since the supplementary agreement is subject to the cartel provisions, the actions carried out on the basis of this agreement are also subject to Article 3 of Regulation No. 17/62. The defendant considers it doubtful that the prohibition contained in Article 3 of the decision has any practical importance for the Grundig trademark.

In any case, an action against parallel imports based on this trademark should be considered as an act designed to assure Consten the absolute territorial protection which Article 3 of Regulation No. 17/62 is designed to prevent. Since the purpose of this act is unrelated to the true function of the trademark, the national law cannot in any case constitute an obstacle to the application of the competition provisions of the EEC Treaty. . . .

The *Italian Government* an intervenor, is of the opinion that the Commission does not have the power to determine whether a trademark, which has been legally registered by an enterprise, is necessary or not, and, if not, to decide that the enterprise does not have the right to use it. Because of Article 222 of the Treaty, the Commission does not have this power, and this is so even if the trademark were used for purposes of influencing competition. The contract in question cannot be declared void under Article 85, paragraph 1, since only Article 86 could be applicable if the conditions it requires are fulfilled. . . .

Opinion

. . .

Applicability of Article 85, paragraph 1, to exclusive distributorship contracts

The plaintiffs maintain that the prohibition set forth in Article 85, paragraph 1, applies only to so-called horizontal agreements. . . . With regard to these contracts, freedom of competition can be protected only by Article 86 of the Treaty.

The wording of neither Article 85 nor Article 86 can be used as a basis for a distinction between the respective fields of application of these articles according to the economic function of the parties to the contract. Article 85 applies generally to all agreements that distort competition within the Common Market, and makes no distinction between such agreements according to whether they are between competitors operating at the same economic level or between non-competitors operating at different levels. One cannot, in principle, make distinctions where the Treaty makes none.

. . . Competition can be distorted within the meaning of Article 85, paragraph 1, not only through agreements that limit it between the parties, but also through agreements that prevent or restrict competition that might take place between one of the parties and third parties. . . .

There is no point, furthermore, in comparing the situation of a producer who has entered into an exclusive distributorship agreement with the distributor of its products, and therefore is subject to Article 85, with the situation of a producer who has integrated the distribution of its products into its own enterprise in some manner, such as through a commercial representative, and therefore is not covered by Article 85. . . . The prohibition of Article 85 . . . does not apply to a situation in which a single enterprise has integrated its distribution network into its own operations. . . . In addition, while it was the intent of the Treaty, through Article 85, to respect the internal organization of an enterprise and to question it only through Article 86 where there was an abuse of a dominant position, it cannot exercise the same restraint where there is a distortion of competition resulting from an agreement between two different enterprises, which in general need only be prohibited.

An agreement between producer and distributor that is designed to restore the national partitions in trade between Member States could conflict with the basic objectives of the Community. . . .

The above pleas, therefore, are without merit. . . .

Concept of "agreements liable to affect trade between Member States"

The plaintiffs and the German Government maintain that the Commission, on the basis of an erroneous interpretation of the concept of "agreements liable to affect trade between Member States," failed to prove that trade would have been more active without the agreement objected to.

The defendant answers that that condition of Article 85, paragraph 1, is fulfilled whenever trade between Member States, because of the agreement, develops otherwise than it would have without the restriction resulting from the agreement, and when the agreement has some influence on market conditions. Such is the case in this instance, particularly because of the restrictions on the import and export of Grundig products to and from France created by the agreement in issue.

The purpose of the concept of "agreements liable to affect trade between Member States" is to separate the respective fields of application of Community law and of national law in the matter of cartel law. It is, in fact, only to the extent that an agreement may affect trade between Member States that the distortion of competition resulting from it is subject to the Community law prohibition of Article 85; otherwise, it escapes. . . .

Consequently, the pleas raised in this respect must be rejected.

Criterion of restriction of competition

. . .

The principle of freedom of competition applies to all economic levels and all aspects of competition. Competition between producers is generally more apparent than competition between distributors of the same brand. This does not, however, mean that an agreement that restricts competition between distributors should escape the prohibition of Article 85, paragraph 1, because it might strengthen competition between producers.

Furthermore, for purposes of applying Article 85, paragraph 1, it is not necessary to take into consideration the actual effects of an agreement where its purpose is to prevent, restrict, or distort competition. Consequently, the fact that the Commission's decision did not analyze the effects of the agreement on competition between similar products of different brands is not in itself a defect in the decision.

Thus the only thing remaining to be examined is whether the decision properly supported the finding that the agreement is prohibited under Article 85, paragraph 1, in that it restricted competition in the trade of Grundig products. The decision sees the infringement in the absolute territorial protection which the agreement granted to Consten on the basis of French law. . . .

In its decision, the defendant rightfully took into account the entire distribution system established by Grundig. In order to evaluate the impact of a contractual agreement, the contract must be placed in the economic and legal context within which it was concluded. This procedure cannot be considered an intrusion into legal transactions or legal relationships that were not the subject of the proceedings before the Commission.

. . . Furthermore, competition between producers generally loses its effectiveness as producers become more successful in their efforts to clearly differentiate their brands from other brands. Because distribution costs account for a substantial part of the total cost price, it appears important that competition between dealers should also be promoted. Dealers are spurred to greater efforts by competition between distributors of goods of the same brand. Because the agreement is designed to isolate the French market for Grundig products and to artificially maintain separate national markets within the Community for products of a widely distributed brand, it distorts competition within the Common Market. That is why the Commission's decision properly held that the agreement violates Article 85, paragraph 1. It does not depend upon any further economic considerations (difference between prices in France and prices in Germany, general application of the Commission's findings to a particular type of appliance, or amount of the costs borne by Consten), nor upon the correctness of the criteria used by the Commission in making its comparisons between the situation on the French market and the situation on the German market . . . .

Scope of the prohibition

Plaintiff Grundig and the German Government take exception to the fact that the Commission, in the ruling of its decision, did not exclude from the prohibition those contract terms that were found not to have the effect of restricting competition and thus narrow down the infringement. . . .

Under Article 85, paragraph 2, only the parts of an agreement that are prohibited are null and void; the entire agreement is void only if these parts cannot be separated from the rest of the agreement. The Commission should therefore, in the ruling of its decision, have limited itself to finding an infringement only for those parts of the agreement that are prohibited, or it should have specified in the statement of reasons why in its opinion those parts could not be separated from the rest of the agreement.

According to Article 1 of the decision, the finding of an infringement applies to the entire agreement. . . . Article 1 of the Commission's decision must therefore be annulled to the extent that it extends, without sufficient reasons, the nullity of Article 85, paragraph 2, to all parts of the agreement.

Finding of an infringement with respect to agreement on GINT trademark

The plaintiffs allege that the Commission violated Articles 36, 222, and 234 of the EEC Treaty and also exceeded its authority in declaring that the agreement on the registration of the GINT trademark in France serves to ensure absolute territorial protection for Consten and in thereby prohibiting, in Article 3 of the decision, Consten from invoking rights stemming from national trademark law to prevent parallel imports.

More particularly, the plaintiffs hold that the effect on competition objected to results not from the agreement but from the registration of the trademark under French law, which creates for the holder an original right in the trademark from which, under national law, the absolute territorial protection is derived. . . .

While under French law Consten, by registering the GINT trademark, became the original holder of the rights flowing from it, it could do so only because of the agreement with Grundig. Such an agreement can be subject to the prohibition of Article 85, paragraph 1. Such prohibition would have no effect if Consten could continue to use the trademark for the same purpose as that intended by the agreement that was considered to be illegal.

Articles 36, 222, and 234 of the Treaty, which were invoked by the plaintiffs, do not prevent Community law from having an influence on the exercise of industrial property rights under domestic law.

. . . The order contained in Article 3 of the ruling of the decision, to refrain from using the national trademark rights to prevent parallel imports, leaves these rights untouched, and limits their exercise in so far as necessary to enforce the prohibition of Article 85, paragraph 1. The Commission's right to issue such an order, which is provided in Article 3 of Council Regulation No. 17/62, is compatible with the Community competition system, whose rules are directly applicable and binding upon individuals. This competition system, because of its nature as described above and because of its purpose, does not permit the use of rights flowing from the trademark law of the different Member States for purposes contrary to the Community cartel law. . . .

The above arguments are therefore without merit.

Failure to hear third parties concerned

The plaintiffs and the German Government assert that Article 3 of the ruling of the decision is actually aimed at the entire system of distribution for Grundig products in the Common Market, and that the Commission thus exceeded its authority and violated the right of all persons affected by the agreement to be heard.

The prohibition resulting from Article 3 of the decision against Grundig's preventing its dealers and exclusive distributors from exporting to France is a necessary extension of the prohibition of Consten's absolute territorial protection. That prohibition therefore affects only questions that were the subject of the proceeding which resulted in the application of Article 85, paragraph 1, to the agreement between Grundig and Consten. Furthermore, the decision does not directly affect the legal validity of the agreements concluded between Grundig and its other wholesalers and distributors; it merely limits Grundig's freedom with respect to parallel imports of its products into France.

It is generally desirable for the Commission to extend its inquiries as far as possible to all persons who may be affected by its decisions. However, an interest on the part of Grundig's other dealers in the legal validity of agreements between Consten and Grundig, to which they are not parties but which actually work to their advantage, could not furnish them grounds to claim an automatic right to be invited to the proceedings which the Commission opened with respect to such agreements. This plea, therefore, is without merit.

Application of Article 85, paragraph 3: Elements necessary to qualify

. . .

. . . [T]he exercise of the Commission's powers necessarily involves complex evaluations of the economic situation. The judicial review of these evaluations must respect that character by limiting itself to an examination of the relevance of the facts and of the legal inferences drawn from them in accordance with the principles of applicable law. . . .

The Commission's decision declares that the main reason for refusing the exemption is the fact that the condition set forth in Article 85, paragraph 3, subparagraph (a), is not fulfilled. . . .

The question of whether the production or distribution of the products in question is improved as required for the exemption to be granted must be answered in light of the spirit of Article 85.

First, not every advantage derived from the agreement with regard to the production or distribution activities of the parties can be considered as such an improvement. . . . Furthermore, the very fact that the Treaty provides that the limitation of competition must be "essential" for the improvement in question clearly shows how important that improvement must be. That improvement must, in particular, offer substantial objective advantages that are capable of compensating for the detriment to competition that it engenders. . . .

In evaluating the relative importance of the various parts of the agreement, the Commission also had to evaluate their effect in relation to an objectively ascertainable improvement in the production and distribution of the products and to determine whether the resulting advantage was enough to make the restrictions on competition appear essential. This interpretation is incompatible with the theory that all arrangements of the parties must be maintained in so far as they are likely to contribute to the improvement sought. . . .

The plaintiffs complain that the Commission did not examine, on the basis of concrete facts, whether it is possible to furnish guarantee and customer service without absolute territorial protection. They particularly stress the importance to the reputation of the Grundig brand of the proper performance of such services for all Grundig equipment put on the market. . . .

With regard to the free guarantee service, the decision states that a buyer can ordinarily claim his right to such a guarantee only from his supplier and then only under the conditions agreed upon. The plaintiffs do not seriously contest this statement. . . . In fact, the UNEF company, Consten's chief competitor, which started selling Grundig products in France more recently than Consten and had to incur fairly substantial risks, nevertheless furnishes free guarantee and paid after-sale services under conditions that on the whole do not appear to have harmed the reputation of the Grundig brand. . . .

Thus the pleas raised by the plaintiffs are without merit.

The plaintiffs also complain that the Commission did not examine whether the absolute territorial protection was not essential for the recovery of the substantial costs borne by Consten to introduce Grundig products on the French market.

The defendant contends that before the decision was adopted it never had any knowledge of promotion costs that were not recovered.

The plaintiffs did not contest this statement of the defendant. The Commission was under no obligation to study this question on its own initiative. In addition, the plaintiffs' argument would in essence be tantamount to asserting that without absolute territorial protection the sole distributor would not have accepted the conditions agreed to. This circumstance, however, has no relationship to the improvements of distribution mentioned in Article 85, paragraph 3.

This plea, therefore, is rejected. . . .

The allegations against the part of the decision relating to the presence in this case of the condition set forth in Article 85, paragraph 3, subparagraph (a), considered separately and together, are without merit. Since an exemption under Article 85, paragraph 3, can be granted only if all of the requirements of this provision are fulfilled, it is not necessary to examine the arguments relating to the other conditions. . . .

THE COURT, rejecting any other conclusions or conclusions to the contrary, declares and rules:

(1) The decision of the Commission of the European Economic Community of September 23, 1964 . . . is annulled in so far as it declares in Article 1 that all of the contract of April 1, 1957, is an infringement of Article 85, including those parts of that contract that do not contribute to said infringement.

(2) For the remainder, Cases Nos. 56/64 and 58/64 are rejected as being without merit. . . .

COMMENT

In 1967, the Grundig firm modified the agreements with its distributors and informed the Commission that it would not prevent German dealers from selling its products to persons in other states. CCH Common Market Reporter ¶ 9212.

Litigation has continued both before the Commission and the Court of Justice with respect to the relationship between trade-mark law and the partitioning of the Common Market into national territories. One important example is van Zuylen Freres v. Hag A. G. [79], a 1974 decision of the Court of Justice. A Luxembourg court had referred questions under Article 177 relating to the interpretation of various Articles, including Article 85, in their bearing upon trade-mark law. The principal question posed was whether the Community rules on competition and the free movement of goods prohibited a trademark holder who enjoyed legal protection in a member state from opposing importation of products legally bearing the same trade-mark in another member state. Originally the two marks had belonged to the same holder.

The Court noted that the Treaty did not affect the status of rights in commercial property that were recognized by the legislation of a member state. Nonetheless, it observed that depending on circumstances, the exercise of those rights could be affected by prohibitions in the Treaty. It stressed that "exercise of a trademark right tends to contribute to the partitioning of the markets." Thus, a trademark holder could not be permitted to rely on the exclusiveness of his trade-mark right "with a view to prohibiting the marketing in a Member State of goods legally produced in another Member State under an identical trademark having the same origin."

QUESTIONS

(1) Note the important difference between the Court's approach to determining whether the agreement has as its "object or effect the prevention, restriction or distortion of competition," as required by Article 85(1), and determining whether the conditions of Article 85(3) have been met. Why, in the Court's view, is a detailed economic analysis required in this case only for the second determination?

79. Court of Justice of the European Communities, Case No. 192/73, July 3, 1974, CCH Common Market Reporter ¶ 8230. The excerpts from this opinion, taken from CCH, may differ in minor, formal respects from the text to be published in Reports of Cases before the Court.

(2) Have these decisions in effect created a "*per se*" rule for territorial restrictions on resale—in the sense that a declaration under Article 85(3) will *never* be granted? If you believe not, what different facts in other cases might lead the Commission to grant, and the Court to uphold, a declaration for an agreement containing these provisions?

(3) A French firm, Parisco, is a major producer of widgets. It sells under the trade-mark PINT, which it owns in both France and Germany. Parisco enters into a joint venture with a German firm to organize and finance a new German corporation, Bonnco, 50% owned by each parent. It gives Bonnco a license, for a stated royalty, to use the trade-mark on the widgets, and it exercises quality and other controls over Bonnco's production. French dealers purchase widgets from Bonnco's vendees. Assume that, under French law, Parisco has the right to bar importation of any widgets bearing the PINT trade-mark. Parisco brings an action. As counsel for a French dealer, what arguments would you make to support the dealer's right to import and sell Bonnco widgets?

SOCIÉTÉ TECHNIQUE MINIÉRE v. MASCHINENBAU ULM GMBH

Court of Justice of the European Communities, Case No. 56/65, June 30, 1966. Recueil Vol. XII–4, p. 337.[80]

[La Technique Minière (L.T.M.), a French corporation, and Maschinenbau Ulm (M.B.U.), a German company, entered into a contract in 1961 under which L.T.M. agreed to take delivery of 37 graders, to be delivered over a two-year period, for public work projects. M.B.U. granted L.T.M. the "exclusive right to sell" the graders in France. L.T.M. agreed not to sell any equipment competitive with the graders, to maintain adequate repair service, and to keep suitable replacement parts in stock. However, it retained the right to export equipment acquired from M.B.U. to other countries, and French purchasers could be supplied through parallel imports from other Common Market countries.

After six graders had been delivered, L.T.M. claimed that the machines were poorly manufactured and unsuitable for sale in France. A court-appointed expert, however, determined that the graders met the contract's requirements. M.B.U. then brought suit for breach of contract before the Tribunal de Commerce de la Seine, which entered judgment in 1964 for M.B.U. On appeal before the Cour d'Appel de Paris (First Chamber), L.T.M. pressed the argument that the contract was "null and void" since in violation of Article 85(1) of the Rome Treaty, and urged that court to refer questions of interpretation of Article 85 and implementing regulations to the Court of Justice. M.B.U. had not notified the contract to the EEC Commission pursuant to Regulations Nos. 17 and 153.

The Cour d'Appel, in its decision of July 1965, stated that it was uncertain whether every exclusive distributorship contract subject to notification must be considered within Article 85(1) as long as it had not been "cleared" under Article 85(3) pursuant to Regulation

80. The translation is taken from the CCH Common Market Reporter ¶ 8047.

No. 17. It submitted the following question to the Court of Justice for a preliminary ruling under Article 177:

> What interpretation should be given to Article 85, paragraph 1, of the Treaty of Rome and to the Community regulations issued to implement it, with respect to any contract which has not been registered and which, while granting an "exclusive selling right"
>
> —does not prohibit the licensee from re-exporting the goods it has acquired from the licensor to all other markets of the EEC,
>
> —does not contain any agreement on the part of the licensor to prohibit its licensees in other countries of the Common Market from selling its products in the territory of primary responsibility of the licensee party to the contract,
>
> —does not interfere with the right of dealers and consumers in the licensee's country to obtain supplies through parallel imports from licensees or suppliers in the other Common Market countries, and
>
> —makes the licensee's right to deliver machinery that might compete with the equipment under license subject to prior authorization by the licensor?
>
> It also submitted the following second question:
>
> Does the *ipso jure* nullity provided for in Article 85, paragraph 2, of the Treaty of Rome apply to all of a contract containing a clause prohibited by the first paragraph of that article, or can it be limited to the prohibited clause?

The Commission argued before the Court of Justice that this type contract was covered by Article 85(1), subject to possible exemption under Article 85(3). It stressed that the Commission alone had competence to apply Article 85(3), whereas Article 85(1) could be applied by the Commission or national authorities as long as the Commission had not started proceedings (citing Article 9 of Regulation No. 17). To determine if a specific contract was within Article 85(1), argued the Commission, it was necessary to interpret the phrase "liable to affect" in Article 85(1) to mean that changes in trading conditions "must be established directly by the facts or result from reasonable expectation and that the influence on trade must be fairly significant." In the Commission's view, it remained for the national court to determine whether the trade obstacles in a given case "are of some importance." If this were established, Article 85(1) applies and, in the case before the Court, the contract would "remain prohibited," since the failure to notify makes the "favorable treatment" of Regulation No. 17 unavailable.

M.B.U.'s arguments included the following views about the reach of Article 85(1):

> This exclusive representation system is currently used in international trade to open up new markets for producers and to make it possible to set up a rational sales organization. The theory that a producer can restrict its activities to production and then wait for consumers to take the initiative has absolutely no basis in economic experience. In particular, the only way small and medium-size enterprises that do not have sufficient financial resources to set up their own distribution organization outside of their own country

can engage in trade beyond its frontiers and thus adjust to the demands of an enlarged market is through the exclusive representation system.

There has been less and less opposition to the theory that exclusive representation agreements of the type in issue are perfectly compatible with the general goal of the Common Market and with the particular aims of the rules of competition. What is debated is the question of what method must be used to achieve the goal sought by common agreement. According to the Commission, exclusive representation agreements are presumed to be illegal in order for them to be given a general exemption. According to the Italian Government, they should not be included in the field of application of Article 85, paragraph 1. According to the German Federal Government, the prohibition of Article 85, paragraph 1, is applicable only under certain extremely limited conditions. Between these three concepts, a choice must be made . . . .

According to the German, Dutch, and Italian versions of the Treaty, there can be no doubt as to the question of whether, for the Commission to apply Article 85, paragraph 1, it is sufficient that an obstacle to competition have the effect that trade between Member States develops under conditions other than those that would exist without such obstacle and thus have a substantial influence on market conditions. The prohibition actually is aimed only at unfavorable effects on trade between Member States. This interpretation is substantiated by the meaning and object of the Treaty as a whole, and particularly by Article 2.

L.T.M. pressed various arguments upon the court, including the following:

The criterion to be applied in determining what agreements may be granted a negative clearance can only be an "objective and *a priori*" criterion, so as to enable the parties to decide without ambiguity on their course of conduct. Any agreement covered by Article 85, paragraph 1, should be presumed to be prohibited until the prohibition has been lifted after notification and declaration of non-applicability. This applies to all agreements that produce to any extent, regardless of how mild, one of the effects mentioned in that provision. Only agreements producing none of those effects to any extent whatsoever may be granted a negative clearance.

In spite of the inconvenience of the compulsory registration of agreements that might be granted a negative clearance, this interpretation is the only one offering an objective criterion and effective control. According to the decision in Case No. 13/61, it must therefore be assumed that it suffices that exclusive agreements may be subject to the prohibition of Article 85, paragraph 1, as a group in order for them not to be excused from notification individually. This is true even if a thorough examination were to permit such an exemption and, indeed, because this indispensable examination presupposes the application of Article 85, paragraph 3. An analysis of the effects produced by exclusive agreements shows that in most cases they come within Article 85, paragraph 1. . . . Since the Community authorities, through regulations that have the force of law in all of the Member States, decided to submit exclusive distributorship agreements to their control, it is not desirable that the national courts, via their jurisdiction with respect to the application of Article 85, paragraph 1, have the power, in their rulings and in violation of those regulations, to impair the procedures they establish and to evade the sanctions they provide.

After stating the arguments of the interested parties, the Court of Justice rendered its opinion:]

. . .

Jurisdiction of the Court of Justice

Société Technique Minière, a party in the suit brought before the Court of Appeal of Paris, complains that that court is asking, in the guise of questions of interpretation, true questions of application on which the national courts have sole jurisdiction.

. . . Although the Court does not have jurisdiction to apply the Treaty to a specific case, it may sift out from the elements of the case those questions of interpretation or of validity that are within its jurisdiction.

Furthermore, the need for arriving at a proper interpretation of the provisions in issue justifies the statement by the national court of the legal framework within which the requested interpretation must be placed. The Court of Justice thus may extract from the points of law outlined by the Court of Appeal of Paris the specific information necessary to understand the questions submitted and to prepare a suitable answer.

First Question Relating to Interpretation of Article 85, paragraph 1

The Court has been asked to interpret Article 85, paragraph 1, in relation to "any contract which, although not registered," has, under certain conditions, granted "an exclusive selling right." . . .

A contract whereby a producer grants a single distributor the right to sell its products in a specified territory does not automatically come under the prohibition of Article 85, paragraph 1. Such a contract can, however, fulfill all of the conditions set forth in that provision, because of a particular factual situation or because of the strictness of the clauses protecting the exclusive right. Since Regulations Nos. 17/62 and 153/62 have not added to the prohibitions set forth in Article 85, paragraph 1, the absence of a registration with the Commission, as provided for in those regulations, does not automatically result in the prohibition of an agreement, but it may have some bearing with respect to the exemption provided for in Article 85, paragraph 3, if it were to be established that the agreement comes within the prohibition of Article 85, paragraph 1. The prohibition of such an agreement depends solely on the question of whether, in light of the circumstances in the particular case, it objectively meets the requirements for the prohibition as set forth in paragraph 1 of Article 85. . . .

The agreement must, in addition, be "liable to affect trade between Member States." . . .

To fulfill this condition, an agreement must, on the basis of all the objective elements of law or of fact taken together, indicate that there is a sufficient degree of probability that it may have some influence, direct or indirect, actual or potential, on the flow of trade between Member States. That is why, in order to determine whether a contract containing a clause "granting an exclusive selling right" falls within the field of application of Article 85, it is necessary to know whether it is capable of partitioning the market in certain products between Member States and of thus rendering the economic interpenetration sought by the Treaty more difficult.

Finally, in order to fall under the prohibition of Article 85, paragraph 1, the agreement in issue must be "designed to prevent, restrict, or distort competition within the Common Market, or have that effect."

The alternative rather than cumulative nature of this condition —as shown by the conjunction "or"—makes it necessary first to consider the actual purpose of the agreement, taking into account the economic context within which it is to be applied. The alterations of competition referred to in Article 85, paragraph 1, must result from all or some of the clauses of the agreement itself. If, however, an analysis of these clauses does not reveal a sufficient degree of injury to competition, then the effects of the agreement must be examined. For the agreement to be prohibited, the conditions establishing that competition has actually been either prevented or perceptibly restricted or distorted must be present. The competition in question must be understood as that which would actually exist without the agreement in issue.

An alteration of competition may be suspected where the agreement appears to be necessary for an enterprise to penetrate a territory in which it was not doing business. That is why, to decide whether a contract containing a clause "granting an exclusive selling right" must be considered as prohibited because of its object or because of its effect, it is necessary to take into account, the following in particular: the nature of the products and whether or not their quantity was limited, the position and importance of the licensor and licensee on the market of the products concerned, whether the contract is isolated or is one of a group of contracts, and whether the clauses protecting the exclusiveness are rigid or possibilities are left open for other channels of trade in the same products through reexports and parallel imports.

Second Question Relating to Interpretation of Article 85, paragraph 2

Under Article 85, paragraph 2, "agreements and decisions prohibited pursuant to this article shall automatically be null and void." This provision, which is designed to ensure compliance with the Treaty, must be interpreted only in the light of its Community goal and must be limited to that framework. The *ipso jure* nullity in question applies only to the parts of the agreement that are prohibited, or to the entire agreement if it appears that those parts cannot be separated from the agreement itself. . . .

THE COURT, ruling on the questions submitted to it for preliminary ruling by the Court of Appeal of Paris in its judgment of July 7, 1965, declares:

In answer to the first question:

Contracts that include a clause "granting an exclusive selling right" do not, solely because of their nature, contain the elements constituting incompatibility with the Common Market as provided in Article 85, paragraph 1, of the Treaty.

A contract of this type, considered by itself, can, however, because of a specific factual situation or because of a particular clause, contain these elements when the following conditions are fulfilled:

(1) The agreement including a clause "granting an exclusive selling right" must have been concluded between enterprises, regardless of the position of each enterprise at any of the stages of the economic process.

(2) It must, in order to come within the field of application of Article 85, on the basis of all the objective elements of law and of fact, be such as to give rise to a reasonable expectation that it might directly or indirectly, actually or potentially, influence the flow of trade between Member States that is likely to hamper the realization of a single market between those States.

In this respect, the agreement should be examined primarily with a view to determining whether it is apt to partition the market for certain products between the Member States.

(3) It must have the object or effect of preventing, restricting, or distorting competition.

In considering the object of the exclusive licensing agreement, this finding must be based directly on the contract as a whole or on its individual clauses.

If it does not fulfill these conditions, the effects of the agreement must then be considered, and such examination must lead to a finding that it prevents or perceptibly restricts or distorts competition.

In this respect, it is necessary to examine, in particular, the strictness of the clauses granting exclusive rights, the nature and quantity of the products covered by the agreement, the position of the licensor and the licensee on the market of the products concerned, and the number of participants in the agreement or possibly in other agreements that are part of the same network.

In answer to the second question:

The nullity provided for in Article 85, paragraph 2, applies to all the provisions of a contract that are incompatible with Article 85, paragraph 1.

The consequences of this nullity for all other parts of the agreement are not governed by Community law; . . .

COMMENT

Following this decision, proceedings resumed before the Cour d'Appel de Paris (First Chamber). That court found the appeal of L.T.M. without merit and affirmed the judgment against it.[81]

After summarizing the views of the Court of Justice, the court concluded that the contract was not within Article 85(1) because it was not likely to affect trade between Member States. It so held because of L.T.M.'s right of reexport and the ability of other French firms to acquire the graders through parallel imports from other Common Market countries. To support its further conclusion that the contract could not be viewed as having the object or effect of significantly altering the competitive situation in the Common Market, the

81. Société La Technique Minière L.T.M. c. Société Maschinenbau Ulm G. m. b. H., February 22, 1967. The decision appears in [1967] Revue Trimestrielle de Droit Européen No. 1, p. 148.

court set forth economic data indicating that there was lively competition for graders within the "exclusive" territory. It stressed that M.B.U., a relatively small firm, would not have been able to penetrate the French market except through an exclusive distributorship.

QUESTIONS

(1) How effective a vehicle is Article 177 for bringing antitrust questions of this character before the Court of Justice—as compared with an appeal under Article 173 from a decision of the Commission? What problems do you see in the continued use of Article 177 as a means of elaboration of antitrust principles?

(2) How effective is the guidance which this opinion gives national courts in applying Article 85(1)? Consider the following questions from the perspective of a national court ruling on an exclusive distributorship contract between firms in different countries but without territorial restrictions on resale.[82]

(*a*) What inquiries does the court make to determine if the contract may affect trade between Member States? What is the dominant concern in resolving this question?

(*b*) What inquiries does the court make to determine if the contract has as its "object or effect the prevention, restriction or distortion of competition within the common market"? Is a detailed economic analysis necessarily required?

(3) In view of the decisions of the Commission and Court, is the appropriate analogy to the American "rule of reason" Article 85(1), as interpreted, or Article 85(3), or both? What practical consequences does your answer have?

PROBLEM

Parisco, a French firm, is the leading producer of widgets in the Common Market. Widgets are a critical component in the manufacture of certain industrial machinery. Bonnco, a German firm, is a leading producer of such machinery. In 1970, the two firms entered into a 20-year contract, under which Parisco agreed to provide Bonnco's "full requirements" of widgets before servicing orders of other firms. The parties performed the contract for two years. In view of Bonnco's expanding requirements, Parisco is unable to meet all orders of Bonnco's competitors, which offer Parisco a higher price. Parisco advises Bonnco in 1973 that it no longer intends to meet "full requirements," since it considers the contract (which has not been notified) to violate Article 85. Bonnco replies that the agreement is not within Article 85(1) and brings suit in a Tribunal de Commerce, the French court of initial jurisdiction, alleging breach of contract and seeking appropriate remedies.

The Tribunal de Commerce, citing the La Technique Minière decision, examines the markets for widgets and the industrial machinery, the relative position in these markets of the two firms, and the effect of the agreement upon trade in this field. Applying the standards defined in the Court of

82. Regulation No. 67/67, at p. 1389, infra, exempts certain contracts in this category from Article 85(1), pursuant to Article 85(3). Assume that the contract under discussion does not come within the Regulation's provisions.

Justice's opinion, it concludes that the agreement is not within Article 85(1) and grants the relief requested by Bonnco.

As counsel for Parisco, outline the alternative courses of action which it can now follow, and the problems which it would encounter in each. How does your outline lead you to evaluate the system created by the Treaty and implementing regulations for the elaboration and enforcement of Community antitrust law?

REGULATION NO. 19/65/EEC OF THE COUNCIL: APPLICATION OF ARTICLE 85(3) OF THE TREATY TO CERTAIN CATEGORIES OF AGREEMENTS AND CONCERTED PRACTICES

[1965–1966] Official Journal of the European Communities 35 (Special Eng. ed.)

The Council of the European Economic Community,

Having regard to the Treaty establishing the European Economic Community, and in particular Article 87 thereof;

. . .

Whereas in view of the large number of notifications submitted in pursuance of Regulation No. 17 it is desirable that in order to facilitate the task of the Commission it should be enabled to declare by way of regulation that the provisions of Article 85(1) do not apply to certain categories of agreements and concerted practices;

Whereas it should be laid down under what conditions the Commission, in close and constant liaison with the competent authorities of the Member States, may exercise such powers after sufficient experience has been gained in the light of individual decisions and it becomes possible to define categories of agreements and concerted practices in respect of which the conditions of Article 85(3) may be considered as being fulfilled;

. . .

Whereas under Article 6 of Regulation No. 17 the Commission may provide that a decision taken pursuant to Article 85(3) of the Treaty shall apply with retroactive effect; whereas it is desirable that the Commission be also empowered to adopt, by regulation, provisions to the like effect;

Whereas under Article 7 of Regulation No. 17 agreements, decisions and concerted practices may, by decision of the Commission, be exempted from prohibition in particular if they are modified in such manner that they satisfy the requirements of Article 85(3); whereas it is desirable that the Commission be enabled to grant like exemption by regulation to such agreements and concerted practices if they are modified in such manner as to fall within a category defined in an exempting regulation;

Whereas, since there can be no exemption if the conditions set out in Article 85(3) are not satisfied, the Commission must have power to lay down by decision the conditions that must be satisfied by an agreement or concerted practice which owing to special circumstances has certain effects incompatible with Article 85(3);

Has adopted this regulation:

Article 1

1. Without prejudice to the application of Council Regulation No. 17 and in accordance with Article 85(3) of the Treaty the Commission may by

regulation declare that Article 85(1) shall not apply to categories of agreements to which only two undertakings are party and:

(a)—whereby one party agrees with the other to supply only to that other certain goods for resale within a defined area of the common market; or

—whereby one party agrees with the other to purchase only from that other certain goods for resale; or

—whereby the two undertakings have entered into obligations, as in the two preceding subparagraphs, with each other in respect of exclusive supply and purchase for resale;

(b)—which include restrictions imposed in relation to the acquisition or use of industrial property rights—in particular of patents, utility models, designs or trade marks—or to the rights arising out of contracts for assignment of, or the right to use, a method of manufacture or knowledge relating to the use or to the application of industrial processes.

2. The regulation shall define the categories of agreements to which it applies and shall specify in particular:

(a) the restrictions or clauses which must not be contained in the agreements;

(b) the clauses which must be contained in the agreements, or the other conditions which must be satisfied.

3. Paragraphs 1 and 2 shall apply by analogy to categories of concerted practices to which only two undertakings are party.

Article 2

1. A regulation pursuant to Article 1 shall be made for a specified period.

2. It may be repealed or amended where circumstances have changed with respect to any factor which was basic to its being made; in such case, a period shall be fixed for modification of the agreements and concerted practices to which the earlier regulation applies.

Article 3

A regulation pursuant to Article 1 may stipulate that it shall apply with retroactive effect to agreements and concerted practices to which, at the date of entry into force of that regulation, a decision issued with retroactive effect in pursuance of Article 6 of Regulation No. 17 would have applied.

Article 5

Before adopting a regulation, the Commission shall publish a draft thereof and invite all persons concerned to submit their comments within such time limit, being not less than one month, as the Commission shall fix.

Article 6

1. The Commission shall consult the Advisory Committee on Restrictive Practices and Monopolies:

(a) before publishing a draft regulation;

(b) before adopting a regulation.

. . .

Article 7

Where the Commission, either on its own initiative or at the request of a Member State or of natural or legal persons claiming a legitimate interest, finds that in any particular case agreements or concerted practices to which a regulation adopted pursuant to Article 1 of this Regulation applies have nevertheless certain effects which are incompatible with the conditions laid down in Article 85(3) of the Treaty, it may withdraw the benefit of application of that regulation and issue a decision in accordance with Articles 6 and 8 of Regulation No. 17, without any notification under Article 4(1) of Regulation No. 17 being required.

COMMENT

The Court of Justice has stressed in several of its opinions the distinction between exclusive distributorship agreements between producers and independent distributors, and the producer who has integrated product distribution into its own enterprise as by use of a commercial representative.

In 1962, the Commission issued an Official Notice on Contracts for Exclusive Representation Concluded with Commercial Agents.[83] The Commission stated that contracts in which commercial agents agreed, for a specified part of the Common Market, to procure business and close transactions for another enterprise's account "are not encompassed by the prohibition laid down in Article 85, paragraph 1 . . . . The Commission considers that the determining criterion for distinguishing a commercial agent from an independent merchant is the provision made expressly or tacitly with respect to the assumption of the financial risks connected with sales or with the carrying out of the contract." Notwithstanding contrary designation by the parties, the Commission would consider any person an independent merchant if he kept on hand or was required to keep "as his own property" a considerable stock of the goods, or was entitled to or did determine the prices and terms of transactions.

Article 85(1), stated the Notice, did not embrace contracts for exclusive representation concluded with commercial agents "because neither their purpose nor their effect is to prevent, restrict or distort competition . . . . [The commercial agent] works according to the instructions and in the interest of the enterprise for which he is acting. . . . [T]he enterprise which is . . . selling is not out of the picture as a competitor; it is only using an aid, to wit, a commercial agent, to move goods in the market . . . ." The Commission noted that exclusive purchase and sale arrangements between a producer and commercial agent result in reductions in the amount of goods offered for sale in the market or in the demand from that market. "Nevertheless, the Commission sees in these restrictions a consequence of the particular mutual obligation for the commercial

83. [1962] J.O. 2921. The translated excerpts below are taken from the CCH Common Market Reporter ¶ 2697.

agent and for his employer to protect each other's interests. That is why it does not consider this to be a restriction of competition."

The Notice stated that its purpose was to give enterprises an indication of considerations which would guide the Commission in its interpretation of the Treaty. "This notice does not prejudice any interpretation which may be given by other competent authorities, particularly the courts."

REGULATION NO. 67/67/EEC OF THE COMMISSION: APPLICATION OF ARTICLE 85(3) OF THE TREATY TO CERTAIN CATEGORIES OF EXCLUSIVE DEALING AGREEMENTS

[1967] Official Journal of the European Communities 10 (Special Eng. ed.)

The Commission of the European Economic Community,

. . .

Whereas under Regulation No. 19/65/EEC the Commission has power to apply Article 85(3) of the Treaty by regulation to certain categories of bilateral exclusive dealing agreements and concerted practices coming within Article 85;

Whereas the experience gained up to now, on the basis of individual decisions, makes it possible to define a first category of agreements and concerted practices which can be accepted as normally satisfying the conditions laid down in Article 85(3);

. . .

Whereas it is not necessary expressly to exclude from the category as defined those areements which do not fulfil the conditions of Article 85(1) of the Treaty;

Whereas in the present state of trade exclusive dealing agreements relating to international trade lead in general to an improvement in distribution because the entrepreneur is able to consolidate his sales activities; whereas he is not obliged to maintain numerous business contacts with a large number of dealers, and whereas the fact of maintaining contacts with only one dealer makes it easier to overcome sales difficulties resulting from linguistic, legal, and other differences; whereas exclusive dealing agreements facilitate the promotion of the sale of a product and make it possible to carry out more intensive marketing and to ensure continuity of supplies, while at the same time rationalising distribution; whereas, moreover, the appointment of an exclusive distributor or of an exclusive purchaser who will take over, in place of the manufacturer, sales promotion, after-sales service and carrying of stocks, is often the sole means whereby small and medium-size undertakings can compete in the market; whereas it should be left to the contracting parties to decide whether and to what extent they consider it desirable to incorporate in the agreements terms designed to promote sales; whereas there can only be an improvement in distribution if dealing is not entrusted to a competitor;

Whereas as a rule such exclusive dealing agreements also help to give consumers a proper share of the resulting benefit as they gain directly from the improvement in distribution, and their economic or supply position is thereby improved as they can obtain products manufactured in other countries more quickly and more easily;

Whereas this Regulation must determine the obligations restricting competition which may be included in an exclusive dealing agreement; whereas it may be left to the contracting parties to decide which of those obligations they include in exclusive dealing agreements in order to draw the maximum advantages from exclusive dealing;

Whereas any exemption must be subject to certain conditions; whereas it is in particular advisable to ensure through the possibility of parallel imports that consumers obtain a proper share of the advantages resulting from exclusive dealing; whereas it is therefore not possible to allow industrial property rights and other rights to be exercised in an abusive manner in order to create absolute territorial protection; whereas these considerations do not prejudice the relationship between the law of competition and industrial property rights, since the sole object here is to determine the conditions for exemption of certain categories of agreements under this Regulation;

Whereas competition at the distribution stage is ensured by the possibility of parallel imports, whereas, therefore, the exclusive dealing agreements covered by this Regulation will not normally afford any possibility of preventing competition in respect of a substantial part of the products in question;

. . .

Whereas agreements and concerted practices which satisfy the conditions set out in this Regulation need no longer be notified; . . .

. . .

Has adopted this regulation:

Article 1 [84]

1. Pursuant to Article 85(3) of the Treaty and subject to the provisions of this Regulation it is hereby declared that until 31 December 1982 Article 85(1) of the Treaty shall not apply to agreements to which only two undertakings are party and whereby:

(a) one party agrees with the other to supply only to that other certain goods for resale within a defined area of the common market; or

(b) one party agrees with the other to purchase only from that other certain goods for resale; or

(c) the two undertakings have entered into obligations, as in (a) and (b) above, with each other in respect of exclusive supply and purchase for resale.

2. Paragraph 1 shall not apply to agreements to which undertakings from one Member State only are party and which concern the resale of goods within that Member State.

84. [Eds.] As amended by Commission Regulation No. 2591/72, Official Journal No. L276, December 9, 1972, p. 15.

Article 2

1. Apart from an obligation falling within Article 1, no restriction on competition shall be imposed on the exclusive dealer other than:

(a) the obligation not to manufacture or distribute, during the duration of the contract or until one year after its expiration, goods which compete with the goods to which the contract relates;

(b) the obligation to refrain, outside the territory covered by the contract, from seeking customers for the goods to which the contract relates, from establishing any branch, or from maintaining any distribution depot.

2. Article 1(1) shall apply notwithstanding that the exclusive dealer undertakes all or any of the following obligations:

(a) to purchase complete ranges of goods or minimum quantities;

(b) to sell the goods to which the contract relates under trade marks or packed and presented as specified by the manufacturer;

(c) to take measures for promotion of sales, in particular:

—to advertise;

—to maintain a sales network or stock of goods;

—to provide after-sale and guarantee services;

—to employ staff having specialised or technical training.

Article 3

Article 1(1) of this Regulation shall not apply where:

(a) manufacturers of competing goods entrust each other with exclusive dealing in those goods;

(b) the contracting parties make it difficult for intermediaries or consumers to obtain the goods to which the contract relates from other dealers within the common market, in particular where the contracting parties:

(1) exercise industrial property rights to prevent dealers or consumers from obtaining from other parts of the common market or from selling in the territory covered by the contract goods to which the contract relates which are properly marked or otherwise properly placed on the market;

(2) exercise other rights or take other measures to prevent dealers or consumers from obtaining from elsewhere goods to which the contract relates or from selling them in the territory covered by the contract.

Article 4

1. As regards agreements which were in existence on 13 March 1962 and were notified before 1 February 1963, the declaration contained in Article 1(1) of inapplicability of Article 85(1) of the Treaty shall have

retroactive effect from the time when the conditions of application of this Regulation were fulfilled.

2. As regards all other agreements notified before the entry into force of this Regulation, the declaration contained in Article 1(1) of inapplicability of Article 85(1) of the Treaty shall have retroactive effect from the time when the conditions of application of this Regulation were fulfilled, but not earlier than the day of notification.

Article 6

The Commission shall examine whether Article 7 of Regulation No. 19/65/EEC applies in individual cases, in particular when there are grounds for believing that:

(a) the goods to which the contract relates are not subject, in the territory covered by the contract, to competition from goods considered by the consumer as similar goods in view of their properties, price and intended use;

(b) it is not possible for other manufacturers to sell, in the territory covered by the contract, similar goods at the same stage of distribution as that of the exclusive dealer;

(c) the exclusive dealer has abused the exemption:

  (1) by refusing, without objectively valid reasons, to supply in the territory covered by the contract categories of purchasers who cannot obtain supplies elsewhere, on suitable terms, of the goods to which the contract relates;

  (2) by selling the goods to which the contract relates at excessive prices.

COMMENT

It appears likely that the Council and Commission will continue to make use of regulations or notices to separate the permissible from the impermissible in other areas of antitrust law, involving both vertical and horizontal agreements. Note, for example, the proposed regulation on mergers at p. 1406, infra.

Note that it is dominantly the Commission, the initiator among the Community's organs, rather than the Court of Justice or national courts which has responsibility for development of antitrust policy. Sometimes it proceeds in an *ad hoc* manner, resolving particular cases as they arise: requests for negative clearances or for declarations under Article 85(3). Sometimes, as authorized by the Council, it proceeds by regulation. Sometimes it will issue statements of policy advising the business community of its intentions *vis-à-vis* certain types of restrictive agreements or certain sectors of the economy. But whatever the technique, this body—one comprising a section on competition and a staff of economic experts—bears the primary responsibility, although subject to ultimate judicial control. Contrast the more central role played by the judiciary in the United States in development of antitrust rules, and the relative diffusion of authority in this country among the courts, the Department of Justice and such administrative agencies as the FTC. In its varied work in this field, the Commission can be thought of as a combination of legislature, expert administrative agency, and court.

QUESTIONS

(1) If you were to restate the present rules in the United States (see pp. 1351–1354, supra) and the Common Market as to the legality of exclusive distributorship contracts, *with and without* territorial restrictions on resale, what similarities and differences would emerge? To the extent that the rules coincide, are the considerations which have led the Supreme Court and the Community authorities to reach these results similar? Can you attribute differences between these rules to different notions of the role of antitrust law in the United States and the Common Market?

(2) Are you persuaded by the distinction drawn by the Supreme Court in the Schwinn case, p. 1353, supra, between outright sales to distributors and agency relationships through distributors? Are you persuaded by the distinction drawn in the Official Notice of the Commission between commercial agents and independent merchants? Is the Notice a *required* reading of Article 85(1)?

(3) In view of the decisions in the Grundig-Consten cases and Regulation No. 67/67, what similarities and differences emerge between application of Article 85(3) and application of the "rule of reason" to the American cases on exclusive distributorships?

(4) How relevant to the rules developed by the Commission (through decisions and regulations) and the Court of Justice is the assessment by these institutions of the relative importance of interbrand and intrabrand competition? Which is given priority? Is this the kind of judgment which can appropriately be made in general terms, for large categories of agreements, or should it require a more particular assessment of the facts of each case? From the point of view of spurring competition in the Common Market, what criticism can you make of the approach of these institutions?

(5) In view of the preceding material in this section, how do you evaluate the system created by the Treaty and regulations for the elaboration and enforcement of Community antitrust law? Are the processes for decision-making and the resolution of differences between national and Community authorities satisfactory? If you were drafting the Treaty and regulations *de novo,* what changes would you make from the present system? What political considerations might inhibit those changes and justify the present system?

COMMENT

The following decision in the Dyestuffs (ICI) case carries us into another area of antitrust law. It involves problems of parallel conduct with respect to prices—so-called conscious parallelism—that are strikingly reminiscent of strands of the antitrust case law within the United States.[85] Indeed, American decisions were relied upon in ar-

85. The leading American case on conscious parallelism is Theatre Enterprises, Inc. v. Paramount Film Distrib. Corp., 346 U.S. 537, 74 S.Ct. 257, 98 L.Ed. 273 (1954). See Turner, The Definition of Agreement under the Sherman Act: Conscious Parallelism and Refusals to Deal, 75 Harv.L.Rev. 655 (1962).

guments before the Commission and Court. The questions relating to the legislative (extraterritorial) reach of the Community antitrust laws are considered at p. 1417, infra.

IMPERIAL CHEMICAL INDUSTRIES LTD. v. COMMISSION

Court of Justice of the European Communities, Case No. 48/69, July 14, 1972. Recueil Vol. XVIII, 1972–5, p. 619.[86]

[In the course of an investigation stimulated by information provided by trade associations of various industries using dyestuffs, the Commission inquired whether price increases of dyestuffs in some EEC countries beginning in 1964 were the consequence of common agreement among certain enterprises. The Commission found three uniform price increases in different combinations of EEC countries: 15% in 1964; a 10% increase in 1965 for dyestuffs not covered by the first increase; and an increase ranging from 8% to 12% in 1967 for all dyestuffs. The Commission then instituted proceedings under Article 3 of Regulation No. 17, for an alleged violation of Article 85 against the enterprises allegedly taking part in concerted price fixing. Those enterprises included Imperial Chemical Industries Ltd. of London (ICI).

A letter and statement of the Commission were sent to 60 recipients, including producers of dyestuffs established in the Community and established in third countries, as well as their subsidiaries and representatives within the Community. After proceedings, the Commission in a decision of July 1969 imposed on ICI a fine of 50,000 units of account (a unit closely related in value to the dollar) for violations of Article 85(1) because of concerted practices in setting the rate of price increases in the three years noted above. Fines were also imposed upon a number of other firms organized within the Community. ICI instituted proceedings before the Court of Justice to annul the Commission's decision. Excerpts from the opinion of the Court appear below:]

Complaints Relating to Procedure and Form

(c) As to the violation of due process

Plaintiff claims that the Commission in its decision relied on facts which were not mentioned in the statement of objections so that plaintiff was unable to reply to them in the administrative proceeding.

In order to ensure the right of due process in administrative proceedings it is sufficient if the enterprises are informed of the essential elements of fact on which the objections are based. The text of the statement of objections clearly indicates the facts on which the charges against plaintiff are based. It contains all the information necessary to establish the objections raised against plaintiff, particularly the conditions under which the 1964, 1965, and 1967 price increases were announced and applied. The fact that corrections were made in the decision to reflect the exact course of these events, and these corrections were made on the basis of facts which the parties

86. The translation is taken from the CCH Common Market Reporter ¶ 8161.

were able to furnish the Commission in the administrative proceeding, cannot be used to support this complaint.

This argument is therefore unfounded.

. . .

Complaints Relating to Substance

As to existence of concerted practices

Plaintiff maintains that the Commission failed to prove the existence of concerted practices within the meaning of Article 85, paragraph 1, of the EEC Treaty for any of the three price increases referred to in the Commission's decision.

The Commission's decision considers a first element of proof of the concerted nature of the 1964, 1965, and 1967 price increases to lie in the fact that the rates of the individual price increases applied by the different producers in each country were the same, and in the fact that with but few exceptions the price increases applied to the same dyestuffs and were put into effect on almost—or even exactly—the same day. It says that these increases could not be explained simply by the oligopolistic structure of the market, and that it is hardly likely that, without a prior arrangement in concert, the major producers supplying the Common Market would, on several occasions, have raised the prices for the same of a major group of products, including special products for which the interchangeability was small or nil, and do so in several countries where the market conditions for dyestuffs are different. The Commission maintained before the Court of Justice that in order for an arrangement in concert to be present it is not necessary that the parties have a common plan for a certain market conduct. It is sufficient if they keep each other informed of their intended conduct, so that each enterprise can plan its actions in the expectation that its competitors will adopt parallel conduct.

Plaintiff maintains that the Commission's decision is based on an insufficient analysis of the market for the relevant products and on an incorrect conception of the idea of a concerted practice, since it equates a concerted practice with the consciously parallel conduct of the participants in an oligopoly, even where this conduct results from autonomous decisions of the individual enterprises determined by objective economic needs, and specifically by the need to improve the unsatisfactory profitability of dyestuffs production. The trend has been for the prices of dyestuffs to drop, because the market for these products is characterized by active competition between producers, not only in the quality of the products and in technical assistance to customers but also in the price, through substantial discounts given selectively to important customers. The uniformity of the rates of increase is due solely to the fact that one enterprise is a price leader. The large number of dyestuffs produced by each enterprise makes it impossible, in practice, to vary the price increase according to the product. Furthermore, varying price increases applied to interchangeable products are not likely to result in substantial economic advantage because of limited inventories and the time needed to adapt plant facilities to much greater demand, or because they might lead to a ruinous price war. Finally, dyestuffs that are not interchangeable account for only a small portion of producers' sales. In view of these special features of the market and the general phenomenon of steadily falling prices, any participant in the oligopoly that decided to raise its prices could reasonably expect its competitors, which are fighting the same problems of profitability, to follow suit.

Article 85, in distinguishing the term "concerted practices" from the terms "agreements between enterprises" and "decisions of associations of enterprises" attempts to show that the prohibition covers a form of coordination between enterprises that has not yet reached the point where there is a contract in the true sense of the word but which, in practice, consciously substitutes a practical cooperation for the risks of competition. A concerted practice, by its nature, does not contain all of the elements of an agreement, but it can result from a coordination that becomes manifest in the conduct of its participants. If a parallelism in conduct cannot in and of itself be considered the same as a concerted practice, it can be a decisive indication of it where it leads to competitive conditions that are not, considering the nature of the goods, the size and number of the enterprises concerned, and the extent of the market, normal market conditions. This is the case where parallel conduct makes it possible for the enterprises to achieve price stability at a level other than that which would have resulted from competition and to strengthen acquired market positions to the detriment of really free trade in the Common Market and the freedom of consumers to select their suppliers.

The question of whether there is a concerted arrangement in this case can therefore be answered correctly only if the indications given in the Commission's decision are considered not in isolation but as a whole, taking into account the special features of the dyestuffs market.

The dyestuffs market is characterized by the fact that some ten producers, which are generally large in size and often produce other chemical products or drugs in addition to dyestuffs, account for 80 percent of the market. These enterprises have very different production, and therefore also cost, structures, so that it is difficult for an individual producer to obtain knowledge of the costs of competitors. The total number of dyestuffs is very high, with each individual enterprise producing over a thousand items. The average interchangeability of these products is considered to be relatively good in the case of standard dyestuffs, but it can be very low or even nil in the case of special dyestuffs. In the case of special products, the market tends, in some cases, to form oligopolies. Because of the relatively slight role the price of dyestuffs plays in the price of the end product to the user, the elasticity of the demand for dyestuffs on the market as a whole is limited, and on a short-term basis may prompt a price rise. On the other hand, overall demand for dyestuffs is rising steadily, thus leading producers to adopt a policy that permits them to share in this growth.

The dyestuffs market in the Community is characterized by the fact that there are five isolated national markets with varying price levels, a situation that cannot be explained by differences in the costs and expenses borne by the producers in the various countries. The establishment of the Common Market thus does not appear to have had any effect on this situation, since there has been virtually no reduction in the differences in the price levels in the various States. On the contrary, it appears that each of the national markets exhibits oligopolistic features, and that on a majority of these markets the price level is formed under the influence of a price leader, which in some cases is the largest domestic producer, but in other cases may be a producer of another Member State or a third country, operating through a subsidiary. This partitioning of the markets is, in the opinion of the experts, due to the need to offer users on-the-spot technical assistance and to guarantee immediate delivery, generally in limited quantities. In this case the producers, with some exceptions, make delivery to their subsidiaries in the various Member States and, through a network of representatives and delivery points, provide whatever special assistance or supplies the customer may require. In the course of the proceeding the facts showed that even where the producer has direct contact with an important customer in another Member State prices are usually determined by the geographic location of the customer and are aligned with the price level of the national market. Although the producers have in this way adjusted to the special features of the dyestuffs market and the needs of their customers, the fact remains that the resulting partitioning of the market is capable of dividing up competition, thus isolating the users in their national markets and preventing all the producers from competing with one another throughout the territory of the Common Market. The events in dispute must be viewed against this background characterizing the functioning of the dyestuffs market.

The 1964, 1965, and 1967 price increases, which are the subject of the Commission's decision, are interrelated. The 15-percent increase in the prices of most aniline dyes that took place in Germany on January 1, 1965, merely extended to another national market the price increase applied in Italy, the Netherlands, Belgium, and Luxembourg in January 1964. The price increase for certain dyes and pigments that took place on January 1, 1965, in all the Member States except France covered all the products not covered by the first price increase. The 8 percent increase in prices made in the fall of 1967, which was raised to 12 percent in France, was intended to permit France to catch up with the 1964 and 1965 increases in which the French market had not shared because of price controls. Consequently, these three price increases cannot be separated from each other, even though they did not come about in entirely the same way.

In 1964 all the enterprises concerned announced their price increases and applied them immediately. The initiative was taken by Ciba-Italy, which, on January 7, 1964, on instructions from Ciba-Switzerland, announced and immediately put into effect a 15-percent increase. The other producers on the Italian market followed suit within two or three days. On January 9, 1964, ICI-Holland initiated a price increase in the same amount for the Netherlands, and on the same day Bayer made the same move on the Belgium-Luxembourg market. With some minor variations, namely between the price increases by the German enterprises and the increases of the Swiss and English enterprises, these increases by the various producers and for the various markets affected the same range of products, i. e., most aniline dyes other than pigments, food colorings, and cosmetic dyes.

[Discussion of the 1965 and 1967 sequences of price rises is omitted.]

These three successive price increases, viewed together, reveal a progressive cooperation between the enterprises concerned. Having learned from experience in 1964, when the increases were announced and put into effect at the same time although with slight variations in the range of products affected, the increases of 1965 and 1967 followed a different pattern, so that the enterprises taking the initiative (BASF and Geigy) announced their intention to raise prices some time before doing so. This gave them an opportunity to observe each other's reactions on the various markets and to act accordingly. Through these advance announcements, the various enterprises eliminated any uncertainty as to their future conduct and therefore also much of the normal risk connected with any autonomous change in conduct on one or more markets. This was true particularly since these announcements, resulting in overall and uniform price increases for the dyestuffs markets, made these markets transparent with respect to the rate of the increases. Therefore, the enterprises concerned, by their actions, temporarily eliminated some of the conditions of competition in the market, which prevented uniform parallel conduct.

That they did not act otherwise than in concert is corroborated by examining other market factors. In view of the number of producers involved, the European dyestuffs market cannot be considered to be an oligopoly in the strict sense of the word, since in an oligopoly price competition could no longer play an important part. These producers are powerful and numerous enough to create a substantial risk that some of them will not follow the general movement where there are price increases but will attempt to expand their share of the market by acting on their own. Furthermore, the partitioning of the Common Market into five national markets with different price levels and different structures makes it unlikely that there could be a uniform price increase taking place spontaneously and simultaneously on all the national markets. Even if a general but spontaneous price increase could conceivably take place on each individual national market, one would have to expect that the size of these increases would vary depending on the particular conditions of the various national markets. Thus, if parallel conduct with regard to prices appeared to be a desirable aim for the enterprises, attainable without risks, it is hard to imagine that such parallel conduct, because of its timing, because of the national markets, and because of the range of products involved, could come about without some prior arrangement.

. . .

The purpose of price competition is to keep prices at the lowest possible level and to promote trade between Member States, in order to permit an optimum division of activities, based on the productivity and adaptability of the enterprises. A variation in rates contributes to one of the basic objectives of the Treaty, i. e., the interpenetration of national markets, and thus also to the objective of giving consumers direct access to the sources of production in the entire Community. Because of the limited elasticity of the dyestuffs market—due to such factors as the lack of price transparency, the interdependence of the various dyes of the individual producers from the standpoint of the range of products needed by each consumer, the relatively small role that price plays in the cost to the ultimate consumer, the desirability of the customer's having a domestic supplier, and the effect of transport costs—it is particularly important to avoid any action that could artificially diminish the possibilities for interpenetration of the various national markets at the consumer level. While it is true that every producer is free to change its prices as it wishes, and in doing so to take into account the present or foreseeable conduct of its competitors, it is, on the other hand, contrary to the Treaty's rules of competition for a producer to cooperate with its competitors, in any manner whatsoever, in order to arrive at a coordinated line of action for a price increase, and to ensure the success of this increase by first eliminating any uncertainty as to their mutual conduct with respect to the essential elements of this action, such as rate, subject, time, and place of the price increases. Under these circumstances and in view of the special features of the dyestuffs market, the conduct of plaintiff together with other enterprises was designed to eliminate the risks of competition and uncertainty as to the reactions of competitors not acting in concert and to replace them with a cooperation, and this therefore constitutes a concerted practice prohibited by Article 85, paragraph 1, of the Treaty.

As to effect of concerted action on trade between Member States

Plaintiff maintains that the uniform price increases could not impair trade between Member States, since, despite the substantial differences between the prices applied in the various States, consumers have always preferred to purchase their dyestuffs on the domestic market.

It follows from the preceding, however, that the concerted practices, which were designed to maintain the partitioning of the market, could have an adverse effect on the conditions under which the trade in dyestuffs between Member States takes place. The enterprises applying these practices intended, at the time of each price increase, to reduce to a minimum the risk of a change in the conditions of competition. The uniform and simultaneous nature of the price increases served mainly to prevent customers of the various enterprises from switching suppliers and to strengthen market positions thus acquired. In this way it also helped to "cement" further the division of traditional national markets, to the detriment of truly free trade in dyestuffs within the Common Market.

The plaintiff's argument is therefore unfounded.

As to competence of the Commission

The plaintiff, which is domiciled outside of the Community, maintains that the Commission is not competent to impose fines on it for actions that it took outside the Community solely because these actions had effects within the Common Market.

Since a concerted practice is involved here, it must first be determined whether plaintiff's conduct was manifested within the Common Market. According to the above findings, the price increases took place in the Common Market and affected competition between producers operating on this market. The actions for which the fine was imposed are therefore practices carried out directly within the Common Market. What has been said with regard to the complaint relating to the existence of concerted practices indicates that the plaintiff company decided to raise the selling prices of its products for customers within the Common Market and that these increases were the same as the price increases decided on by the other producers. By availing itself of its power of direction over its subsidiaries established in the Common Market, plaintiff was able to apply its decision on that market.

Plaintiff contends that this conduct was the conduct of its subsidiaries and not its own.

The fact that the subsidiary has its own legal personality does not serve to rule out the possibility that its conduct is attributable to the parent company. This could be the case where the subsidiary, even though it has its own legal personality, does not independently determine its own market behavior but essentially follows the instructions given it by the parent company. If the subsidiary does not in fact have autonomy in determining its course of conduct on the market, the prohibition of Article 85, paragraph 1, is inapplicable to the relationship between it and the parent company, with which it forms an economic unity. Since an affiliated group so structured forms a unity, the parent company can, under certain circumstances, be held responsible for the actions of the subsidiary.

It is a matter of common knowledge that the plaintiff at the time held all or, in any event, the majority of the capital of its subsidiaries. The plaintiff could decisively influence the pricing policy of its subsidiaries in the Common Market and it did in fact make use of this power to give instructions on the occasion of the three price increases in question here. The telegrams relating to the 1964 price increase which plaintiff sent its subsidiaries in the Common Market contained binding instructions as to the prices and other conditions of sale which they were to apply to their customers. Since there is nothing to indicate the contrary, it must be assumed that the plaintiff at the time of the 1965 and 1967 price increases did not act otherwise toward its subsidiaries in the Common Market. Under these circumstances, the separation between parent firm and subsidiaries arising out of the fact that each has a distinct legal personality does not prevent their conduct on the market from being viewed as a unity for purposes of the application of the rules of competition. For this reason, it is the plaintiff that brought about the concerted practice within the Common Market.

. . .

As to the fine

In view of the number and size of the transactions through which the plaintiff took part in the illegal practices, as well as their consequences for the realization of the common market for dyestuffs, the size of the fine is in reasonable proportion to the gravity of the violation of the Community rules of competition.

. . .

The Court, rejecting any further arguments or arguments to the contrary, declares and decides:

1. The complaint is dismissed.
2. The plaintiff must bear the costs of this proceeding.

COMMENT

As the problem of exclusive distributorships and other forms of vertical arrangements becomes regulated through decisional law of the Commission and Court of Justice, and through the group exemptions under Article 85(3), horizontal practices of the type before the Court in the Dyestuffs case will command more attention. The problem is not novel in a European business scene long characterized by cartel arrangements in various sectors of the economy. Two decisions of the Commission suggest the character of the Community's response to agreements that set common prices or allocate territories among competitors.

In a 1973 decision involving the European sugar industry [87], the Commission "required [the enterprises investigated] to put an end immediately to the infringements found" and imposed fines ranging from 100,000 to 1,500,000 units of account. Major sugar producers and sellers were found to have infringed Article 85(1) "by engaging in a concerted practice having as its object and effect the control of

87. Commission Decision of January 2, 1973, Official Journal No. L140, May 26, 1973, p. 17, reproduced in CCH Common Market Reporter ¶ 9570.

deliveries of sugar on [each of a number of European national markets] and consequently the protection of that market." Particular firms were found to have exerted economic pressure on other firms to obligate them to restrict imports or exports. The broad purpose of many of the practices engaged in was to regulate sugar trade within the Community so as to protect national markets, and to structure competition within markets through agreements defining permissible channels of inter-country sales.

In a 1974 decision involving agreements between glass container manufacturers [88], the Commission found numerous provisions of agreements described as fair trading rules between manufacturers of glass containers to have violated Article 85(1). These agreements related to exchange of information about pricing and discounts, discriminatory prices and discounts, systematic undercutting of competitors, and application of a price calculation system. The general purpose of these provisions was to assure that parties to the agreement, when selling outside of a defined area, would not charge prices below those of other parties considered as the foreign national or local price leader in the territory of destination. The decision states that parties to the defined agreements "are required to bring the infringements established to an immediate end."

The following decision is the first of the Court of Justice treating Article 86 with respect to an acquisition or merger. The large question debated before this decision was whether "abuse" within Article 86 meant only action with a direct effect upon the market that was detrimental to producers, distributors or consumers, or whether it also referred to changes in the structure of enterprises resulting in a serious alteration of competition. Note the views of the Court with respect to the status of mergers or acquisitions under Article 86.

Although the American case law and writing on comparable issues of monopoly and monopolization are too extensive to summarize here, it is worthwhile to point out some statutory differences. As noted at p. 1343, supra, Article 86 differs from its counterpart, Section 2 of the Sherman Act, which makes unlawful the acquisition of a certain degree of market power without requiring a showing that the power thus obtained has been abused. One should also recall that the Community has as yet no counterpart to Section 7 of the Clayton Act, p. 992, supra, which aims directly at mergers and seeks to prevent them from creating positions of market control.[89]

88. Commission Decision of May 15, 1974, Official Journal No. L160, June 17, 1974, p. 1, reproduced at CCH Common Market Reporter ¶ 9658.

89. The American law of mergers and monopolies is summarized in Areeda, Antitrust Analysis, Chs. 2, 6 (2d ed. 1974).

EUROPEMBALLAGE CORPORATION AND CONTINENTAL CAN COMPANY INC. v. COMMISSION

Court of Justice of the European Communities, Case No. 6/72, February 21, 1973. Reports of Cases before the Court, 1973–2, p. 215.[90]

[Continental Can Company, Inc., organized in the United States and manufacturing metal containers and paper and plastic packaging materials as well as related machinery, increased its interest in 1969 to 85.5% of the capital of a German corporation, SLW, the largest producer of light metal containers in Europe. In 1970, it entered into an agreement with one of its licensees, a Dutch corporation, TDV, pursuant to which Continental agreed (1) to set up a holding company (later called the Europemballage Corporation) in Delaware to which it would transfer its interest in SLW and (2) to induce Europemballage to make a tender offer to TDV shareholders (with certain exceptions). Such TDV shareholders tendering shares would receive rights to purchase Europemballage common stock when offered to the public. Continental would supply Europemballage with the necessary funds.

Continental then formed the holding company Europemballage in Delaware. Also in 1970, TDV published the Europemballage offer to buy stock. The Commission then advised the parties that the contemplated transactions violated Article 86 of the Treaty. Europemballage nonetheless purchased the tendered shares and bonds, thus raising Continental's share interest in TDV to 91%. The Commission then instituted proceedings under Article 3 of Regulation No. 17 against Continental and Europemballage, and issued a decision in December 1971 based upon Article 86.

This decision found that Continental held through SLW "a dominant position in a substantial part of the Common Market" in the Market's types of containers noted above and in metal lids for glass jars. It also found that Continental had "abused this dominant position" through the purchase by its subsidiary, Europemballage, of about 80% of the stock of TDV. "This purchase resulted in virtually eliminating competition for the above packaging products in a substantial part of the Common Market." The decision stated that Continental "must terminate the infringement of Article 86" and "must submit proposals to the Commission before July 1, 1972" to this effect. Continental and Europemballage then appealed the decision to the Court of Justice. Excerpts from the opinion of the Court appear below:]

B. As to competence of the Commission

Plaintiffs maintain that according to the general principles of international law Continental, as an enterprise domiciled outside of the Community, is subject neither to the administrative authority of the Commission nor to the jurisdiction of the Court of Justice. Thus, they say, the Commission did not have competence to take, with regard to Continental, the decision and to direct the order contained in Article 2 of the decision to it. Furthermore, the illegal conduct charged by the Commission cannot be imputed directly to Continental but to Europemballage.

90. The translation is taken from the CCH Common Market Reporter ¶ 8171, whose text differs in minor, formal respects from the opinion in the later-published Reports of Cases before the Court.

Plaintiffs cannot deny that Europemballage, which was formed by Continental on February 20, 1970, is a subsidiary of Continental. The fact that the subsidiary has its own legal personality is not sufficient to rule out the possibility that its conduct can be imputed to the parent company. This applies particularly where the subsidiary does not determine its market conduct autonomously but in the main follows the instructions of the parent company.

It has been established that Continental caused Europemballage to make an offer, in the Netherlands, to buy stock from the TDV shareholders, and it made the necessary funds available for this purpose. On April 8, 1970, Europemballage purchased the TDV stock and bonds that were tendered at that time. Thus this operation, on the basis of which the Commission took its decision, must be imputed not only to Europemballage but also and primarily to Continental. Such an acquisition, which affects market conditions within the Community, is the type to which Community law applies. The fact that Continental does not have its seat in the territory of one of the Member States is not sufficient to remove this enterprise from the application of Community law.

The plea of lack of competence is therefore rejected.

C. As to Article 86 of the Treaty and "abuse of a dominant position"

. . .

Plaintiffs maintain that the Commission is attempting in this way, on the basis of an erroneous interpretation of Article 86 of the EEC Treaty and by exceeding its powers with the help of this provision, to introduce a control over mergers of enterprises. Such an attempt is contrary to the intent of the drafters of the Treaty, as it clearly appears not only on the basis of a literal interpretation of Article 86 but also from a comparison between the EEC Treaty and the ECSC Treaty, and from the national laws of the Member States. The examples of abuse of a dominant position listed in Article 86 confirm this conclusion, since they show that the Treaty is aimed only at practices that affect the market and harm consumers or trading partners. Furthermore, they say, Article 86 indicates that the use of the economic power which derives from a dominant position can be viewed as an abuse of a dominant position only if it is the means through which the abuse occurs. Structural measures taken by enterprises, such as the strengthening of a dominant position through a merger, do not, on the other hand, meet the test of an abuse of a dominant position within the meaning of Article 86 of the Treaty. The Commission's decision, therefore, should be reversed for lack of the necessary legal basis.

The first paragraph of Article 86 of the Treaty declares that "any abuse by one or more undertakings of a dominant position within the Common Market or in a substantial part of it shall be prohibited as incompatible with the Common Market in so far as it may affect trade between Member States." The issue is whether the word "abuse" in Article 86 refers only to actions of enterprises that can have a direct effect on the market and are detrimental to production or distribution, to purchasers or consumers, or whether it also applies to changes in the structure of an enterprise that would result in a serious alteration of competition in a substantial part of the Common Market.

This does not depend on the distinction between measures that affect the structure of an enterprise and practices that affect the market, since any structural measure can influence market conditions whenever it increases the size and economic power of the enterprise.

The decision of this question depends on the spirit, the intent, and the letter of Article 86, as well as the rules and objectives of the Treaty. Thus, the problems before us cannot be resolved by comparing Article 86 and certain provisions of the ECSC Treaty.

Article 86 is in the chapter devoted to the common rules on the policy of the Community in the area of competition. This policy is based on Article 3(f) of the Treaty, which provides that the activities of the Community shall include the establishment of a system ensuring that competition within the Common Market is not distorted. Plaintiffs' arguments that this provision contains only a general program and is not legally binding fail to take into account the fact that Article 3 considers the pursuit of the objectives it sets forth to be essential to the fulfillment of the tasks of the Community. Regarding the objectives stated under (f) more particularly, it is implemented in several provisions of the Treaty, for the interpretation of which it is decisive.

In providing for the establishment of a system ensuring that competition in the Common Market is not distorted, Article 3(f) requires, *a fortiori*, that competition not be eliminated. This requirement is so essential that without it many provisions of the Treaty would have no purpose. It also meets the requirements of Article 2 of the Treaty, which gives the Community the task of "promoting throughout the Community a harmonious development of economic activities." Thus, the restrictions of competition which the Treaty permits under certain conditions because the various Treaty objectives must be reconciled find a limit in the requirements of Articles 2 and 3 beyond which there is a danger that a weakening of competition would be contrary to the goals of the Common Market.

In order to ensure that the principles of Articles 2 and 3 of the Treaty are respected, and in order to achieve the objectives stated in those articles, Articles 85 to 90 contain general provisions for enterprises. Article 85 deals with agreements between enterprises, decisions of associations of enterprises, and concerted practices, while Article 86 concerns unilateral action taken by one or more enterprises. Articles 85 and 86 pursue the same objective at different levels, namely maintaining effective competition within the Common Market. Any alteration of competition that is prohibited when it is the result of conduct coming within Article 85 cannot become permissible if the conduct is successfully carried out under the influence of a dominant enterprise, and leads to a merger by the participating enterprises. In the absence of express provisions, it cannot be assumed that the Treaty, which in Article 85 prohibits decisions of ordinary associations of enterprises that impair competition without eliminating it, would, in Article 86, permit enterprises, through a merger into an organic unity, to attain a position of such dominance as to virtually remove any serious possibility of competition. Such a difference in legal treatment would open up in the competition law as a whole a breach that could jeopardize the proper functioning of the Common Market. If it were enough, to avoid the prohibitions of Article 85, to make the ties between the enterprises so close that they would escape the prohibition of Article 85 without falling into the field of application of Article 86, it would then be permissible to partition a substantial part of the Common Market, which would be contrary to its basic principles. The aim of the authors of the Treaty to maintain actual or potential competition in the market, even in cases where restrictions of competition are permitted, is given expression in Article 85, paragraph 3(b), of the Treaty. If Article 86 does not contain the same express provision, this is because the system it creates for dominant positions, unlike Article 85, paragraph 3, does not permit exceptions from the prohibition. In such a system, the duty to observe the basic objectives of the Treaty, particularly the objective stated in Article 3(f), follows from the imperative force of these objectives. In any case, Articles 85 and 86 cannot be construed in such a way as to contradict each other, since they are meant to achieve the same objectives.

In light of these considerations, the condition of Article 86 is to be interpreted to mean that the use of a dominant position must have been abusive in order to be prohibited. This provision lists a number of abuses, which it prohibits. The list is given only by way of examples and does not exhaust the types of abuses of a dominant position that are prohibited under the Treaty. Furthermore, as subparagraphs (c) and (d) of the second paragraph indicate, this provision relates not only to practices that are likely to cause an immediate detriment for consumers, but also to practices which, because of their effect on the structure of actual competition as referred to in Article 3(f) of the Treaty, are harmful to them. Thus, abusive conduct could be present where an enterprise in a dominant position strengthens that position to the point where the degree of domination achieved substantially hampers competition, so that only enterprises which in their market conduct are dependent on the dominant enterprise would remain on the market.

When Article 86 of the EEC Treaty is so construed, the question raised by plaintiffs as to the causal connection that should, in their opinion, exist between the dominant position and the abuse thereof is not material, since the strengthening of the position held by one enterprise can be an abuse and prohibited under Article 86 of the Treaty regardless of the methods or means used to attain it, provided it has the effects described above.

D. As to facts in the decision's statement of reasons

The Commission supported its decision by saying, among other things, that the acquisition of a majority interest in a competitor through an enterprise or group of enterprises in a dominant position could under certain circumstances represent an abuse of that position. This is the case, it says, where an enterprise in a dominant position so strengthens its position through a merger that actual or potential competition in the relevant products would be virtually eliminated in a substantial part of the Common Market.

It can, in fact, aside from any fault, be considered an abuse if one enterprise acquires a dominant position to the point that the objectives of the Treaty are circumvented through a substantial alteration of the supply situation, so that the consumer's freedom of action on the market is seriously jeopardized; this is necessarily the case where virtually all competition is eliminated. While such a limiting condition as the elimination of all competition need not be present in all cases, the Commission must, when it bases its decision on such elimination of competition, furnish grounds that are legally sufficient for this purpose, or at least prove that competition was so substantially affected that any remaining competitors can no longer provide a sufficient counterbalance.

[The Court then examined the Commission's data and findings, and found that the decision erred in its definitions of relevant markets and failed to prove, among other relevant matters, the dominant positions which it alleged for various product lines.]

It follows from all the foregoing that the decision did not sufficiently set forth the facts and evaluations on which it is based. It is therefore reversed.

NOTE ON CONTROL OF MERGERS

Although the Court reversed the Commission's decision in Continental Can, the Commission did gain judicial recognition that a merger, although not prohibited as such by Article 86, can become an abuse within the meaning of that Article through its effect upon the structure of competition. Both the immediate harm threatened to consumers and the effect of the merger upon the structure of competition were to be considered.

Nonetheless, the qualifications in the Court's opinion as well as its strict requirements for proof and analysis by the Commission led the Commission to follow another path. Rather than rely upon a gradual case-by-case elucidation of Article 86, the Commission preferred to subject mergers to systematic control through a distinct and self-contained regulatory scheme. In July 1973, it issued a draft regulation, to be submitted to the Council, on Control of Concentrations between Undertakings.[91] The regulation was prompted by the results of a study program to analyze concentrations within the EEC. The study indicated a sharp trend towards increased concentration through stock acquisitions or mergers, and a consequent large reduction in the number of manufacturers or suppliers in important fields. The draft regulation refers to this analysis of market structures which indicates that "preservation of effective competition in the Common Market . . . could be jeopardized." Thus "concentration must . . . be made subject to a systematic control arrangement."

The regulation refers to the difficulty in proceeding solely under Article 86. Thus it finds the need for "additional powers of action", afforded by Articles 87 and 235 of the Treaty. The regulation is to extend both to concentrations constituting abuses of dominant positions, and to concentrations giving the firms involved the power to prevent effective competition in the Common Market. The regulation is meant to be exclusive for the problems covered; hence Regulation No. 17 was to be inapplicable to concentrations from the date of the proposed regulation's effectiveness.

Article 1 provides that any transaction bringing about a concentration between undertakings "at least one of which is established in the common market, whereby they acquire or enhance the power to hinder effective competition" is incompatible with the Common Market insofar as concentration may affect trade between member states. The Article is meant to be immediately applicable in the member states—that is, self-executing. There are exceptions for firms whose aggregate turnover or aggregate goods and services fall below stated amounts or stated percentages within the Common Market.

91. The text of the proposed regulation appears at CCH Common Market Reporter ¶ 9586.

Article 2 defines concentration as the process whereby an undertaking "acquires control" of another or others. "Control" as defined ranges beyond a share interest, including as well a variety of contract rights. Under Article 3, if the Commission finds that the concentration is within Article 1, it may prevent its realization or, if the concentration has been put into effect, it may require separation of the undertakings or assets acquired or concentrated.

Article 4 requires that proposed concentrations between firms of defined amounts of turnover of goods and services must be notified to the Commission before being put into effect. Other concentrations may be notified. If the Commission finds a violation of Article 1, it must commence proceedings (as provided in Article 6) within a period of three months.

The regulation, in a manner comparable to Regulation No. 17, provides for acquisition of information, for investigations by authorities of the member states or by the Commission, for fines and penalties, and for review by the Court of Justice.

The Commission's Third Report on Competition Policy, annexed to its 1973 General Report, underscores that the function of this proposed regulation "is to give opportunity for the assessment of mergers prior to their consummation, regardless of whether they arise from a previously existing dominance of one of the merging enterprises." (p. 15). In its comment on Article 1 of the Regulation, the Third Report (p. 33) notes that concentrations may be viewed as incompatible with the Common Market "by virtue of the market share held or of the technical knowhow, raw materials or financial resources available to the firms concerned." Consideration is also to be given to the absolute size of the firms; their relations with buyers and sellers and non-Community firms; the competitiveness of remaining producers; barriers to market entry; the rate of technical progress; and actual or potential international competition or competition from substitute products.

COMMENT

The decision below in the Commercial Solvents case was the first victory achieved by the Commission before the Court of Justice in an Article 86 proceeding. It considers the meaning of "abuse" and of "dominant position" not with respect to a merger or acquisition, but with respect to refusal to deal with purchasers dependent upon defendant's source of supply.[92] As with the preceding decisions, we postpone discussion of the problem of legislative (extraterritorial) reach until p. 1417, infra.

92. For American case law analyzing refusals to deal as attempts to monopolize, see Areeda, Antitrust Analysis 254–257 (2d ed. 1974).

ISTITUTO CHEMIOTERAPICO ITALIANO S.p.A. AND COMMERCIAL SOLVENTS CORP. v. COMMISSION

Court of Justice of the European Communities, Cases Nos. 6 and 7/73, March 6, 1974. Reports of Cases before the Court, 1974–3, p. 223.[93]

[Commercial Solvents Corp. (CSC), a Maryland corporation with its principal office in New York, manufactures and sells products based upon nitroparaffins, including nitropropane and a derivative thereof, aminobutanol. Aminobutanol is an intermediary product for the manufacture of ethambutol and ethambutol-based specialties used as an anti-tuberculosis drug. In 1962, CSC acquired 51% of the voting stock in Istituto Chemioterapico Italiano S.p.A. (Istituto), a company incorporated in Italy with its principal office in Milan. CSC has a 50% representation on the board of directors and executive committee of Istituto; its president is chairman of the board of directors of Istituto, and has an additional casting vote.

Prior to 1970, Istituto acted as a reseller of aminobutanol produced by CSC in the United States and sold aminobutanol to, among other vendees, an Italian firm, "Zoja". Zoja in turn manufactured ethambutol-based specialties. In 1970, CSC decided that it would no longer supply aminobutanol to the EEC but would instead supply dextro-aminobutanol, an upgraded intermediate product. Istituto processes dextro-aminobutanol into bulk ethambutol and sells most of this product to other producers of specialties, using the balance for its own production of specialties. At the end of 1970, Istituto advised CSC that Zoja had placed a new order for aminobutanol, but CSC replied that none was available. Zoja was unable to obtain aminobutanol elsewhere on the world market.

In 1971, Zoja applied to the Commission to institute proceedings against CSC and Istituto under Article 3 of Regulation No. 17, for infringement of Article 86 of the Treaty. After proceedings, the Commission reached a decision in December 1972 requiring CSC and Istituto: (a) under penalty of 1000 units of account per day of delay to supply 30,000 kilograms of aminobutanol to Zoja at a price not in excess of the maximum price charged for that product; (b) under penalty of a second fine of 1000 units of account per day, to submit proposals to the Commission within a stated time period for subsequent supply to Zoja; and (c) to pay a fine of 200,000 units of account. CSC and Istituto then applied to the Court of Justice in February 1973, for the annulment of this decision of the Commission. Excerpts from the opinion of the Court of Justice appear below:]

It is necessary therefore to examine in turn the questions of (a) whether there is a dominant position within the meaning of Article 86, (b) which market must be considered to determine the dominant position, (c) whether there has been any abuse of such a position, (d) whether such abuse could affect trade between Member States, and (e) whether the applicants have in fact acted as an economic unit. The complaints of infringement of the rules of procedure and insufficient grounds for the decision will be examined in this context.

(a) Dominant position

The applicants dispute the findings in the Commission's decision that the CSC-Istituto Group has "a dominant position in the Common Market for the raw material necessary for the manufacture of etham-

93. The text of the opinion, taken from the CCH Common Market Reporter ¶ 8209, differs in minor, formal respects from the later-published Reports of Cases before the Court.

butol," on the basis that it has "a world monopoly in the production and sale of nitropropane and aminobutanol."

For this purpose they rely on documents which, they claim, establish that aminobutanol is produced by at least one other Italian company from butanone, that a third Italian company manufactures ethambutol from other raw material, that a French company produced nitropropane independently, and that another undertaking has brought on the market thiophenol, a product which is said to be used in Eastern Europe to produce ethambutol.

Finally CSC produced a statement by an expert who said that there is at least one practical method of producing nitropropane other than the method used by CSC and there are at least three other processes for producing aminobutanol without using nitropropane.

The Commission replied, without being seriously challenged, that the production of nitropropane by the French company is at present only in an experimental stage and that the researches of this company will not be developed until after the matters in issue. The information as to the possibility of manufacturing ethambutol by using thiophenol is too vague and uncertain to be seriously considered. The statement of the expert produced by CSC takes account only of well-known processes which have not proved themselves capable of adaptation to use on an industrial scale and at prices that would permit them to be marketed. The production by the two Italian companies mentioned is on a modest scale and intended for their own needs, so that the processes used do not lend themselves to substantial and competitive marketing.

The Commission produced an expert's opinion from Zoja which stated that the production of aminobutanol based on butanone on a substantial industrial scale would be possible only at considerable expense and at some risk, which is disputed by the applicants, who rely on two experts, according to whom such production would not present any difficulties or cause excessive costs.

This dispute is of no great practical importance since it relates mainly to processes of an experimental nature, which have not been tested on an industrial scale and which have resulted in only a modest production. The question is not whether Zoja, by adapting its installations and its manufacturing processes, would have been able to continue its production of ethambutol based on other raw materials, but whether CSC had a dominant position in the market in raw material for the manufacture of ethambutol. It is only the presence on the market of a raw material that could be substituted without difficulty for nitropropane or aminobutanol for the manufacture of ethambutol which could invalidate the argument that CSC has a dominant position within the meaning of Article 86. On the other hand, reference to possible alternative processes of an experimental nature or which are practiced on a small scale is not sufficient to refute the grounds of the decision.

It is not disputed that the large manufacturers of ethambutol on the world market, that is to say CSC itself, Istituto, American Cyanamid and Zoja, use raw material manufactured by CSC. Compared with the manufacture and sale of ethambutol by these undertakings, those of the few other manufacturers are of minor importance. The Commission was entitled to conclude "that in the present conditions of economic competition it is not possible to have recourse on an industrial scale to methods of manufacture of ethambutol based on the use of different raw materials."

. . .

(b) The market to be considered

The applicants rely on the sixth recital of Section II–C of the Commission's decision to conclude that the Commission considers the relevant market for determining the dominant position to be that for ethambutol. Such a market does not exist since ethambutol is only a part of a larger market for anti-tuberculosis drugs, where it is in competition with other drugs which are to a large extent interchangeable. Since a market in ethambutol does not exist, it cannot be established that there is a separate market in the raw material for the manufacture of this product.

The Commission replies that it has taken into account the dominant position in the Common Market in the raw material necessary for the production of ethambutol.

. . .

Contrary to the arguments of the applicants it is in fact possible to distinguish the market for raw material necessary for the manufacture of a product from the market on which the product is sold. An abuse of a dominant position on the market for raw materials may thus have effects restricting competition in the market on which the derivatives of the raw material are sold, and these effects must be taken into account in considering the effects of an infringement, even if the market for the derivative does not constitute a self-contained market. The arguments of the applicants in this respect and in consequence their request that an expert's report on this subject be ordered are irrelevant and must be rejected.

(c) Abuse of the dominant position

The applicants state that they should not be held responsible for ceasing to supply aminobutanol to Zoja because this was due to the fact that in the spring of 1970 Zoja itself informed Istituto that it was cancelling the purchase of large quantities of aminobutanol which had been provided for in a contract then in force between Istituto and Zoja. When at the end of 1970 Zoja again contacted Istituto to obtain this product, the latter was obliged to reply, after consulting CSC, that in the meantime CSC had changed its commercial policy and that the product was no longer available. The change of policy by CSC was, they claim, inspired by a legitimate consideration of the advantage that would accrue to it of expanding its production to include the manufacture of finished products and not limiting itself to that of raw material or intermediary products. In pursuance of this policy it decided to improve its product and no longer to supply aminobutanol except for commitments already entered into by its distributors.

It appears from the documents and from the hearing that the suppliers of raw material are limited, as regards the EEC, to Istituto, which, as stated in the claim by CSC, started in 1968 to develop its own specialties based on ethambutol, and in November 1969 obtained the approval of the Italian Government necessary for the manufacture and in 1970 started manufacturing its own specialties. When Zoja sought to obtain further supplies of aminobutanol, it received a negative reply. CSC had decided to limit, if not completely to cease, the supply of nitropropane and aminobutanol to certain parties in order to facilitate its own access to the market for the derivatives.

However, an undertaking that is in a dominant position as regards the production of raw material and therefore able to control the supply to manufacturers of derivatives cannot, just because it decides to start manufacturing these derivatives (in competition with its former customers) act in such a way as to eliminate their competition which, in the case in question, would have amounted to eliminating one of the principal manufacturers of ethambutol in the Common Market. Since such conduct is contrary to the objectives expressed in Article 3(f) of the Treaty and set out in greater detail in Articles 85 and 86, it follows that an undertaking which has a dominant position on the market for raw materials and which, with the object of reserving such raw material for manufacturing its own derivatives, refuses to supply a customer, which is itself a manufacturer of these derivatives, and therefore risks eliminating all competition from this customer, is abusing its dominant position within the meaning of Article 86. In this context it does not matter that the undertaking ceased to supply in the spring of 1970 because of the cancellation of the purchases by Zoja, because it appears from the applicants' own statement that, when the deliveries provided for in the contract had been completed, the sale of aminobutanol would have stopped in any case.

. . .

The applicants do not seriously dispute the statement in the decision to the effect that "in view of the production capacity of the CSC plant it can be confirmed that CSC can satisfy Zoja's needs, since Zoja represents a very small percentage (approximately 5–6 percent) of CSC's global production of nitropropane." . . .

(d) Effects on trade between Member States

The applicants argue that in this case it is mainly the world market that is affected, since Zoja sells 90 percent of its production outside the Common Market and in particular in the developing countries, and this is a much more important market for anti-tuberculosis drugs than the countries of the Community, where tuberculosis has largely disappeared. The sales outlets of Zoja in the Common Market are further reduced by the fact that in many Member States Zoja was blocked by the patents of other companies, in particular American Cyanamid, which prevented it from selling its specialties based on ethambutol. Therefore, abuse of the dominant position, even if it were established, would not come within the ambit of Article 86, which prohibits such an abuse only "in so far as it may affect trade between Member States."

These words are intended to define the sphere of application of Community rules in relation to national laws. It cannot therefore be interpreted as limiting the field of application of the prohibition which it contains to industrial and commercial activities supplying the Member States.

The prohibitions of Articles 85 and 86 must be interpreted and applied in the light of Article 3(f) of the Treaty, which provides that the activities of the Community shall include the institution of a system ensuring that competition in the Common Market is not distorted, and Article 2 of the Treaty, which gives the Community the task of promoting "throughout the Community harmonious development of economic activities." By prohibiting the abuse of a dominant position within the market in so far as it may affect trade between Member States Article 86 therefore covers abuses which may directly prejudice consumers as well as abuses which indirectly prejudice them by impairing the effective competitive structure as envisaged by Article 3(f) of the Treaty.

The Community authorities must therefore consider all the consequences that the conduct complained of has on the competitive structure in the Common Market without distinguishing between production intended for sale within the market and that intended for export. When an undertaking in a dominant position within the Common Market abusively exploits its position in such a way that a competitor in the Common Market is likely to be eliminated, it does not matter whether the conduct relates to the latter's exports or its trade within the Common Market, once it has been established that this elimination will have repercussions on the competitive structure within the Common Market.

Moreover, the contrary argument would in practice mean that the control of Zoja's production and outlets would be in the hands of CSC and Istituto. Finally, its cost prices would have been so affected that the ethambutol produced by it would possibly become unmarketable.

Moreover, it emerged at the hearing that Zoja is at present able to export and does in fact export the products in question to at least two Member States. These exports are endangered by the difficulties caused to this company and by reason of this trade between Member States may be affected.

(e) CSC and Istituto as one economic unit

The applicants refer to decisions of the Court and in particular to Cases Nos. 48/69, 52/69 and 53/69 of July 14, 1972 (Recueil, pages 619, 787, and 845) and dispute whether CSC effectively exercises a power of control over Istituto and whether these constitute an economic unit. The two companies have always acted independently, so that CSC cannot be deemed responsible for the acts of Istituto nor Istituto for those of CSC. Therefore, even if CSC holds a dominant position within the world market in raw materials for the manufacture of ethambutol, it has not acted within the Community, and therefore the author of the conduct complained of can only be Istituto which, however, does not have a dominant position within the market in question.

In the disputed decision, in Section II–A, CSC's holding of share capital and involvement in the administration of Istituto are set out. It is pointed out in that section that the annual reports of CSC show Istituto as one of its subsidiaries. It is inferred from the prohibition issued in 1970 by CSC to its distributors on reselling nitropropane and aminobutanol for the manufacture of ethambutol that CSC was not abstaining from exercising its power of control over Istituto. It takes note of an attempt on the part of Istituto to take over Zoja by means of a merger in which it is unlikely that CSC played no part. The conclusion is reached that "CSC holds the power of control over Istituto and exercises its control in fact at least with respect to Istituto's relations with Zoja" and it is therefore proper "to treat the companies of CSC and Istituto as constituting, in their relations with Zoja and for the purposes of the application of Article 86, a single undertaking or economic unit."

. . .

. . . It is difficult not to associate the decision by CSC no longer to sell nitropropane and aminobutanol with the fact that it made an exception in favor of Istituto, which was supplied with dextroaminobutanol for the purposes of its own production of ethambutol and specialties based on this product.

The fact, pointed out in Section III–A of the decision, that Istituto bought quantities of the nitropropane that was still available on the market for resale to paint manufacturers who were forbidden to resell for pharmaceutical purposes outside the Common Market is likewise significant.

As regards the market in nitropropane and its derivatives the conduct of CSC and Istituto has thus been characterized by an obviously united action, which, taking account of the power of control that CSC had over Istituto, confirms the conclusions in the decision that as regards their relations with Zoja the two companies must be deemed an economic unit, and that they are jointly and severally responsible for the conduct complained of. In these circumstances the argument of CSC that it did not do business within the Community and that therefore the Commission lacked competence to apply Regulation No. 17/63 to it must likewise be rejected.

II. The measures ordered and the sanctions imposed in the decision

. . .

As to the first submission, according to the wording of Article 3 of Regulation No. 17, where the Commission finds that there is an infringement of Article 86, "it may by decision require the undertakings . . . concerned to bring such infringement to an end." This provision must be applied in relation to the infringement which has been established and may include an order to do certain acts or provide certain advantages which have been wrongfully withheld as well as prohibiting the continuation of certain action, practices or situations that are contrary to the Treaty. For this purpose the Commission may, if necessary, require the undertaking concerned to submit to it proposals with a view to bringing the situation into conformity with the requirements of the Treaty.

In the present case, having established a refusal to sell which is incompatible with Article 86, the Commission was entitled to order certain quantities of raw material to be supplied to make good the refusal of supplies as well as to order that proposals be put forward to prevent a repetition of the conduct complained of. In order to ensure that its decision was effective, the Commission was entitled to determine the minimum requirements to ensure that the infringement was made good and that Zoja was protected from the consequences of it. In choosing as a guide to the needs of Zoja the quantity of previous supplies the Commission has not exceeded its discretionary power.

Therefore the first submission is unfounded.

As to the second submission, it has been established above that it cannot be inferred from the words "in so far as it may affect trade between Member States" that only the effects of a possible infringement on trade within the Community must be taken into account when it is a question of defining the infringement and its consequences. Moreover, the rather limited measure that the applicants suggested would have resulted in the production and sales outlets of Zoja being controlled by CSC–Istituto and in Zoja being in a position where its cost price would have been affected to such an extent that its production of ethambutol would have been in danger of being unmarketable. In these circumstances the Commission could well consider that maintaining an effective competitive structure necessitated the measures in question.

Although in the decision and during the course of the present proceedings the Commission has constantly avoided meeting the complaint in the way that the applicants argued it, it has on the other hand, ever since the notice of objections, maintained that since the conduct complained of was aimed at eliminating one of the principal competitors within the Common Market, it was above all necessary to prevent such an infringement of Community competition by adequate measures. Both in the decision and in the written procedure the measures taken were justified by the need to prevent the conduct of CSC and Istituto from having the effect referred to and eliminating Zoja as one of the principal manufacturers of ethambutol in the Community. This reasoning is at the root of the dispute and cannot therefore be considered as insufficient.

This submission, therefore, also fails.

III. The penalty imposed

The Commission's decision imposes jointly and severally on the companies CSC and Istituto a fine of 200,000 units of account, i. e., 125,000,000 lire. Although the seriousness of the infringement justifies a heavy fine, the duration of the infringement should also be taken into account, which in the decision was calculated as two years or more, but it might have been shorter if the Commission, which had been put on notice by the complaint of Zoja on April 8, 1971, that is, six months after the first refusal by CSC-Istituto, had intervened more quickly. Moreover, the ill effects of the conduct complained of have been limited by reason of the fact that CSC-Istituto have provided the supplies ordered in the decision.

Having regard in particular to these circumstances it is proper to reduce the fine to 100,000 units of account, namely 62,500,000 lire.

. . .

The Court hereby:

1. Orders that the application for an annulment in Cases Nos. 6 and 7/73 be rejected;

2. Orders that the fine imposed jointly and severally on the applicants by the Commission decision of December 14, 1972 (Official Journal No. L 299, pages 51 et seq.) be reduced to 100,000 units of account, namely 62,500,000 lire;

3. Orders the applicants to pay the costs.

NOTE ON DESIRABLE COOPERATION AGREEMENTS AND CONCENTRATIONS

In the development of antitrust law, one factor has proven to be increasingly significant. The member states seek not only *a* Common Market but a *powerful* Common Market, whose firms can achieve the technological advance and economies of scale necessary (1) to allow them to profit from the expanded market among the nine countries and (2) to be competitive with outside firms, particularly multinational corporations from the United States. Thus a certain ambivalence is reflected in the policies of the Community about agreements among competing firms that have clear anti-competitive effects, and about the growth of larger enterprises through stock acquisitions, mergers or contract arrangements. This Note describes some manifestations of these attitudes in decisions and other acts of Community authorities.

A good starting point is Article 85(3), which offers a framework within which such considerations may be rendered specific. Consider, for example, the Commission's decision of December 21, 1973, renewing a declaration under Article 85(3) with respect to cooperative arrangements within the marine paint industry.[94] In 1967, the Commission had exempted from the prohibition of Article 85 the Transocean Marine Paint Association, involving 20 medium-sized marine paint producers from Community and non-Community countries. That 1967 decision expired on December 31, 1972. In a 1973 decision, the Commission granted a renewal until December 31, 1978. The object of the Association, stated the decision, was to "enable its members to compete effectively in the special circumstances of the world marine paint market." This objective led members of the Association to agree to manufacture marine paints of identical composition, in the same packaging and under a common trademark. Each member was to promote sale of these paints in the country in which it was established and other territories specifically allocated to it. The members were bound to submit to quality control and to exchange licenses and benefits of experience. If they exported paints to another member's territory, they were obligated to pay a commission to the other member. Cooperation between members of the Association and other marine paint producers was prohibited unless previously authorized. The decision noted that Association members continued to be "faced with genuine competition from other marine paints producers who, owing to their large size and international links, have a worldwide sales network." The most important outside competitor had a share of 25 to 30% of the world market. The share of members of the Association amounts to 5 to 10% of the marine paint world market.

The decision noted that the agreement clearly "restricts competition between members within the Common Market and may affect trade between Member States." It decided, however, to grant an extension of its 1967 declaration since "the conditions of Article 85(3) remain fulfilled." It stated that consumers shared the benefits of these arrangements of the Association. The decision imposed conditions upon members of the Association, and required that certain of the provisions of the agreements among members be rescinded.

Some of the group exemptions established by regulations of the Council and the Commission under Article 85(3) [95] illustrate further relaxations of the ban on horizontal agreements among competing firms. Thus Council Regulation No. 2821/71 [96] notes that "creation of a Common Market requires that enterprises adapt to the conditions of this larger market. An appropriate means of adapting is through cooperation between enterprises." Article 1 authorizes the Commission to declare pursuant to Article 85(3) that Article 85(1) is not applicable to specified types of agreements between enterprises whose purpose (among other purposes) is research and development, in-

94. [1974] Official Journal No. L 19, p. 18, January 23, 1974, CCH Common Market Reporter ¶ 9628.

95. See p. 1348, supra, and see Regulations Nos. 19/65 and 67/67, pp. 1386 and 1389, supra.

96. J.O. No. L. 285, December 29, 1971, p. 46 as amended by Council Regulation No. 2743/72, J.O. No. L. 291, December 28, 1972. The excerpts from this regulation are taken from the translation in the CCH Common Market Reporter ¶ 2729.

cluding agreements relating to secret technical knowledge and to industrial specialization. The Commission exercised this power in Regulation No. 2779/72.[97] This regulation declares Article 85(1) inapplicable through 1977 to defined specialization agreements in which firms agree not to produce certain products themselves or to have them produced by other enterprises. It qualifies the principal restrictions of competition and imposes a general condition of the maximum size (share of market, turnover, and so on) of the activities to which the regulation is applicable. The Commission may withdraw the exemption "where there is reason to suspect that the rationalization does not produce substantial results or that users do not share proportionately in the resulting benefit."

A different illustration of Community attitudes towards promotion of industry through cooperation is afforded by a 1974 Council Resolution.[98] The Resolution notes the importance of data processing "for all aspects of modern society and hence for the Community and its economic and technological position in the world," and further notes the Council's awareness "that the structure of the data processing industry in the world is unbalanced and that the applications of data processing within the Community are not yet satisfactory." It observes that both competitive EEC companies and "large companies controlled from outside the Community" can "prosper in an expanding market." The Resolution expresses the view that "a more efficient and economical use of resources can be obtained through collaboration or—in suitable fields—through joint action on standards and applications." The Council then encourages the Commission to submit proposals for a limited number of joint projects in the field of data-processing, and for collaboration in standards and applications. It also notes the desirability of preparing "a systematic Community program to promote research", involving coordination of national promotional measures and, where appropriate, Community financing.

The goal of encouraging growth to assure efficient rationalization within the Common Market and to enable Common Market firms to compete with foreign multinationals also finds expression in the developing policy towards mergers. The draft Regulation on Control of Concentrations Between Undertakings, described at p. 1406, supra, states the basic prohibition upon mergers in the first paragraph of Article 1. The third subsection of that Article provides: "Paragraph 1 may, however, be declared inapplicable to concentrations which are indispensible to the attainment of an objective which is given priority treatment in the common interest of the Community." This subsection is thus the analogue to Article 85(3) of the Treaty. In its Third (1973) Report on Competition Policy, p. 1407, supra, the Com-

97. J.O. No. L. 292, December 29, 1972, p. 23. The excerpts from this regulation are taken from the translation in the CCH Common Market Reporter ¶ 2731.

98. Council Release No. R/1623 e/74, reproduced in CCH Common Market Reporter ¶ 9665.

mission noted that the causes for industrial concentration in the EEC "lie largely in the desire and need of Community firms to adapt constantly to the new scale of their markets and to improve their competitiveness on the world market." (p. 29) In commenting on Article 1 of the proposed Regulation, the Report notes that implications for industrial development cannot be ignored in the appraisal of proposed concentrations. "Certain combinations may, for instance, be the only practicable way of restoring some degree of competition in a market otherwise completely dominated by a firm with a high rate of internal growth."

NOTE ON APPLICATION OF COMMUNITY ANTITRUST LAW TO FOREIGN FIRMS AND CONDUCT

Problems of the extraterritorial reach of Community antitrust law are as complex as those posed by American antitrust law that were considered in Chapter IX. The Treaty provisions afford little help. Recall that Article 85(1) refers to agreements or practices "which may affect trade between Member States" and which have as their "effect" the prevention or distortion of "competition within the common market." Unlike the references in most United States antitrust laws to interstate *and* foreign commerce, the Treaty expresses in clear terms only the "interstate" equivalent.

Note that here, as in our earlier discussion of American antitrust law, two related but distinct issues are involved. The first question is whether the Community—normally the Commission in the first instance, and ultimately the Court of Justice—should view agreements or conduct by foreign firms taking place in whole or part outside the EEC to be within the reach of Community antitrust law if the agreements or conduct affect competition within the Community. The foreign firms may or may not have subsidiaries in the EEC which in some manner participate in their parents' conduct or implement their parents' agreements. That is, the first question is that of legislative (extraterritorial) reach. Do the Treaty and regulations apply to the foreign firm's agreements or conduct? The second issue treats difficulties in the assertion of jurisdiction over foreign firms in proceedings before the Commission or Court of Justice, and in the enforcement of any judgment (an explicit prohibition, fines, and so on) which the Commission or Court of Justice may enter.

When antitrust legislation is interpreted to include foreign firms, agreements and practices, further problems arise. To what extent can the Commission expect cooperation from home countries of the foreign firms in investigating suspected practices or agreements? Under what principles would the Commission assert jurisdiction over the foreign firms to enter orders under Article 3 or to impose fines under Article 15 of Regulation No. 17? Would those orders or fines be enforced in actions in foreign countries, and who would be the plaintiff in such actions? What relevance has the fact that the administrators and enforcers of these antitrust principles are organs of an international organization rather than of a national state?

Many of these questions remain unresolved. Several decisions of the Court of Justice in the early 1970's, as well as positions taken by the Commission before and during this period, provide some indication of the Community's position on legislative reach.

Recall that the last three decisions of the Court of Justice in these materials involve questions of legislative reach. The Dyestuffs (ICI) decision, p. 1394, supra, is the most interesting. The Commission had viewed Article 85 as applicable to ICI and had asserted jurisdiction over ICI because of the effects of ICI's practices upon prices within the Community. Indeed, the reasoning of the Commission reached almost as broadly as that in the Alcoa decision, p. 1006, supra, or as Section 18 of the Restatement (Second) of the Foreign Relations Law, p. 882, supra.

ICI argued to the Court of Justice that the Commission's decision violated international law, in that it "assumes the rules of competition of the Treaty to be applicable to all restrictions of competition that have effects within the Common Market . . . without it being necessary to establish whether the enterprises causing such restrictions have their seat inside or outside the Community". The Commission, on the other hand, argued that it was sufficient to find direct economic effects within the Community of firms and conduct outside, insofar as such conduct violated the Community's "public order" as expressed through its basic antitrust provisions. The Court, in summarizing these arguments, noted the authorities upon which litigants drew, such as the Lotus and Alcoa decisions, pp. 885 and 1006, supra.

Recall that the Court's opinion, although sustaining the Commission's decision, takes a different approach to the question of legislative reach. It stressed the relationship between ICI and its subsidiaries within the Common Market, noting that the subsidiaries lacked autonomy with respect to these pricing matters and hence should be considered, with the parent, as part of one "economic unity". But the opinion did not require that the subsidiary be wholly owned. The test in Dyestuffs and the opinions noted below is apparently more flexible, namely whether the parent had a determining influence with respect to the matter under consideration—although in all decisions of the Court of Justice thus far, subsidiaries have been at least 51% owned.

In the Continental Can decision, p. 1402, supra, the American firm argued that principles of international law required the conclusion that it was not subject to the authority of the Commission or the jurisdiction of the Court of Justice. The Court, however, stressed that the acquisition "which affects market conditions within the Community, is the type to which Community law applies". It was irrelevant that Continental Can was not organized within the EEC.

In the CSC decision, p. 1408, supra, the Court observed that CSC and Istituto "must be deemed an economic unit" with respect to their conduct toward Zoja. This conclusion undermined the argument that CSC did not "do business within the Community".

The Court has thus far stressed facts proved by the Commission which indicate close and controlling relationships between the foreign parent and the EEC subsidiary. It has therefore been able to avoid taking a strong position on a relatively pure version of the "effects" doctrine—a question that would be posed where a foreign firm had no subsidiary or branch within the Community. The problems will continue to arise in varied settings, ranging from bilateral distributorship contracts, to multilateral price or marketing arrangements, and to mergers or acquisitions. Note in this respect that Article 1 of the proposed Regulation on the Control of Concentrations between Undertakings, p. 1406, supra, refers to transactions between undertakings "at least one of which is established in the common market."

No doubt the substantive principles of the reach of the antitrust provisions and the accompanying principles of jurisdiction and enforcement will be influenced by the Community's general attitude toward foreign multinational corporations and their influence within the Community.

QUESTIONS

(1) An American exporter (Amco) and a French distributor (Parisco) enter into an agreement giving Parisco the exclusive right to distribute Amco's products in France. Parisco agrees not to carry competing products and not to purchase Amco's products from any source other than Amco. How do you think the Commission should resolve the question whether Amco is in violation of the antitrust provisions in each of the following situations:

(*a*) Amco has no branch or subsidiary within the Common Market and sells products to Parisco f. o. b. New York.

(*b*) Amco has a small office in Paris designed to assist Parisco in publicity and distribution, although no one at that office makes managerial decisions.

(*c*) Amco has no office within the Community but has entered into contracts identical with the Parisco agreement with distributors in five other EEC countries. These contracts include prohibitions of export by a distributor.

(2) A group of American exporters acting under the Webb-Pomerene Act, p. 994, supra, agree to limit or otherwise regulate exports to the EEC countries. We can treat this group as analogous to the Alliance cartel in the Alcoa decision, p. 1006, supra. Assume that the product is in high demand within the Common Market but that, for reasons of technology and patents, there is limited production within the Common Market. Should the Commission view the conduct of this group of exporters as violating Community antitrust laws? What problems would then arise?

PROBLEM

You are administrative assistant to Senator Futuro, a leader among the members of Congress urging closer economic links between this and foreign countries and more effective transnational regulation of common problems. In recent speeches, the Senator has criticized the GATT and the IMF for their shortcomings in handling certain questions within their competence, and has suggested that an organization of broader dimension, with a more developed institutional structure and greater powers, should be formed—at least among the countries of the Atlantic Community. Senator Futuro cited the EEC as an illustration of what such an organization could contribute to the economic progress of its members. He lacks, however, a precise grasp of the legal issues that would be posed if the United States considered becoming party to such a new organization. To clarify these issues, he asks you to advise him of what legal considerations, if any, might block the United States from entering into a treaty creating an organization comparable in its policies, processes and institutional structure to the European Economic Community.

In your reply, you should stress four themes as illustrative of these problems: (1) The external commercial relations of the organization (see pp. 1259–1260, supra), (2) problems comparable to the Costa case, p. 1293, supra, (3) provisions treating the right of establishment, and (4) provisions treating antitrust regulation.

INDEX

References are to pages

END OF VOLUME